◆ THE PUZZLERS™

Complete
Crossword
Puzzle
Dictionary

Compiled by
Jane Shaw Whitfield

SWEET
WATER
PRESS

THE PUZZLERS™ COMPLETE CROSSWORD PUZZLE DICTIONARY

Sweetwater Press

SWEET
WATER
PRESS

P.O. Box 531127
Birmingham, AL 35253

Library of Congress Cataloging-in-Publication Data

Whitfield, Jane Shaw
    [Webster's New World crossword puzzle dictonary]
    The puzzlers complete crossword puzzle dictionary / compiled by Jane Shaw
Whitfield.
    p. cm.
    Originally published: Webster's New World crossword puzzle
dictionary, New York: Simon and Schuster, c1975.
    ISBN 1-889372-02-1 (hardcover) – ISBN 1-889372-01-3 (pbk.)
    1. Crossword puzzles—Glossaries, vocabularies, etc. I. Title.
GV1507.C7W485 1997
793.73'2'03—dc21   97-20382
                                                       CIP

Cover design by Southern Lights Custom Publishing
Manufactured in the United States of America

FOREWORD

This reference work has been compiled especially for the millions who enjoy solving crossword puzzles and for those who construct them. But because of its comprehensive coverage of rare, arcane, technical, and dialectal terms, as well as of many proper names from geography, literature, the Bible, and the like, it is also an invaluable aid to those who enjoy solving other kinds of word puzzles or playing word games. And its listings of synonyms and of identifying facts about persons, places, and things make it as well a useful thesaurus and general reference book for the home library.

Unlike some other puzzle dictionaries on the market, this one is not merely a mechanical listing of words of six letters or fewer, offering no clue as to meanings. This list contains answers actually found in a survey of thousands of puzzles, and so you will discover here words from two to fourteen or more letters, as well as phrases and compounds of two or more words, of the kind frequently encountered in puzzles today, such as "in a trice" for "instantly" or "black eye" for "contusion."

A special feature of this book is the arrangement of the materials. All clue words are in bold-face type, alphabetically arranged, with subcategories, where these exist, in italic type, also in alphabetical order. The answer terms for each clue are arranged by the count of letters in each word (or phrase), in numerical order. Each group of answers with the same letter count are then arranged alphabetically to help you find quickly the solution to your problem fill-in.

For example: you need the six-letter name of a Greek sun god. You turn to **Greek god of**, find the subcategory *sun*, and discover after the numeral **6** the two names "Apollo" and "Helios." If you have even one letter of the answer already filled in, you know immediately which is the correct name.

In general, words are shown with their prevailing spellings, but certain rarer variants that commonly appear in puzzles are also given. Although upper-case and lower-case distinctions, and accents on foreign words, are insignificant in crossword puzzle practice, the other uses to which this book will undoubtedly be put made it desirable to observe these orthographic conventions.

So to all enthusiasts of crossword puzzles and to their creators, I hereby dedicate this WEBSTER'S NEW WORLD™ CROSSWORD PUZZLE DICTIONARY.

Jane Shaw Whitfield

ABBREVIATIONS USED IN THIS WORK

Abbr .... Abbreviation
abdom .... abdominal
aborig .... aboriginal
Acad .... Academy
adj .... adjective
adm .... admitted
Afr .... African
Agric .... Agriculture
Alex .... Alexander
Am Ind ...... American Indian
Anat .... Anatomy
anc .... ancient
Anglo-Ir .... Anglo-Irish
Anthrop .... Anthropology
Antiq .... Antiquity
Arab .... Arabian
Arch .... Architecture
Archaeol .... Archaeology
Astrol .... Astrology
Astron .... Astronomy
Austral .... Australia(n)

Babyl .... Babylonia
Belg .... Belgium
Bib .... Bible, Biblical
Biol .... Biology
Bot .... Botany
Braz .... Brazil(ian)
Brit .... Britain, British
Brit Col .... British Columbia
Buddh .... Buddhism
Bus .... Business

Can .... Canada, Canadian
Capt .... Captain
Caucas .... Caucasian
Celt .... Celtic
Cent .... Central, Century
Cent Am .... Central America
Chem .... Chemistry
Chin .... Chinese
Chr .... Christian
coll .... colloquialism
comb form .... combining form
Confed .... Confederation
Constell .... Constellation
contemp .... contemporary
Criminol .... Criminology

Dan .... Danish
Dept .... Department
derog .... derogatory
dial .... dialectal
div .... division
Du .... Dutch

E .... East
East Ch .... Eastern Church
Eccl .... Ecclesiastical
Educ .... Education
Egypt .... Egyptian
Elec .... Electricity
Eng .... England, English
Episcop .... Episcopal
equiv .... equivalent
Esk .... Eskimo
est .... established
Eur .... Europe(an)
exclam .... exclamation
ext .... extinct

FDR .... Franklin D. Roosevelt
Fem .... Feminine
Finan .... Finance, Financial
Flem .... Flemish
Fr .... France, French

Gen .... General
Geog .... Geography
Geol .... Geology
Geom .... Geometry
Ger .... German
Gov .... Governor
Govt .... Government
Gr .... Greek
Gram .... Grammar
Gr Brit .... Great Britain

Haw .... Hawaiian
Heb .... Hebrew
Hem .... Hemisphere
Her .... Heraldry
Hind .... Hinduism
Hindu .... Hindustani
Hist .... Historical
Holl .... Holland
Horol .... Horology
Hung .... Hungarian

illeg .... illegal
Ind .... India, Indian
Indo-Chin .... Indo-China
Ins .... Insurance
Internat .... International
Ir .... Irish
irreg .... irregular
Isl(s) .... Island(s)
It .... Italian

Jap .... Japanese
Jew .... Jewish

L .... Latin
Legislat .... Legislature
Lit .... Literature
Log .... Logic

Maced .... Macedonia
Malay .... Malayan
Math .... Mathematics
MD .... Doctor of Medicine
Med .... Medical
Mex .... Mexican
Mil .... Military
Mohamm .... Mohammedan
Mt(s) .... Mountain(s)
Mus .... Music
Myth .... Mythology

Nat'l .... National
Naut .... Nautical
Nav .... Naval, Navy
neg .... negative
New Test ...... New Testament
NZ .... New Zealand
No .... North
No Am .... North American

obs .... obsolete
Old Test .... Old Testament
opp .... opposite
Orient .... Oriental
Oxf Univ .... Oxford University

Penol .... Penology
Pers .... Persian
pert .... pertaining
Petrol .... Petrology
Pg .... Portuguese
Pharm .... Pharmaceutical
Philat .... Philately
Phil I .... Philippine Islands

Philol .... Philology
Philos .... Philosophy
Phonet .... Phonetics
Phys .... Physical
pl .... plural
PO .... Post Office
poet .... poetic
Polit .... Politics, Political
Polyn .... Polynesian
ppty .... property
pref .... prefix
P Rico .... Puerto Rico
Pros .... Prosody

R .... Roman
RCCh .... Roman Catholic Church
Rd .... Road
ref .... referring
Relig .... Religion
R Estate .... Real Estate
Rev War .... Revolutionary War
Rhet .... Rhetoric
Riv .... River
Rom .... Roman
rr .... railroad
Rum .... Rumania
Russ .... Russian

S .... South
Scot .... Scotland, Scottish
Scand .... Scandinavian
Shakesp .... Shakespeare
sing .... singular
sl .... slang
Slav .... Slavonic
So Afr .... South Africa
So Am .... South America
Sp .... Spanish
Surg .... Surgical
sym .... symbol

Tag .... Tagalog
Tahit .... Tahiti
Terat .... Teratology
terr .... territory
Teut .... Teutonic
Theat .... Theatrical
Theol .... Theology
Theos .... Theosophy
triang .... triangular
TID .... Ter in die
Trop .... Tropical
Turk .... Turkish
TV .... Television

U .... Union
Univ .... University
USS .... United States Ship
USSR .... Union of Soviet Socialist Republics

Vet .... Veterinary

W .... West
WAC .... Women's Army Corps
W Indies .... West Indies
WWI .... World War I

Yidd .... Yiddish
YMCA .... Young Men's Christian Association
yr .... year

Zool .... Zoology

A

A... 5. alpha, first 7. article
A 1... 5. prime 6. symbol 8. superior
10. first–class
aa (Haw)... 4. lava
aal... 8. morindin (dye), mulberry
aam (Du)... 7. measure (liquid)
11. water bucket
Aani (Egypt)... 3. ape (sacred)
6. baboon 12. cynocephalus
aardvark... 3. pig 6. farrow
8. anteater
aardwolf... 5. hyena 8. Proteles
Aaron (pert to)...
ally (Bib).. 3. Hur
brother.. 5. Moses
burial place.. 3. Hor
leader (Jew).. 9. Levitical 10. High
Priest
rod.. 4. wand (magic) 7. molding,
mullein
sister.. 6. Miriam
son.. 5. Abihu, Nadab
Aaru (Egypt Relig)... 12. fields of Aaru
14. abode of the dead
aasvogel... 7. vulture
abaca... 4. hemp 5. lupis 6. linaga
abacus... 4. slab 8. cupboard
10. calculator 11. compartment
Abaddon... 3. pit (bottomless) 4. Hell
5. Sheol 8. Apollyon (angel)
11. destruction
abaft... 3. aft 5. after 6. astern,
behind
abalone... 5. awabi, ormer, uhllo (ullo)
6. sea ear 8. ear shell
abandon... 4. quit 5. cease, leave,
remit, waive, yield 6. abjure, depart,
desert, disuse, give up, maroon,
reject, resign, vacate 7. cast off,
discard, forsake, freedom, neglect
8. abdicate, forswear, renounce
9. surrender, turpitude 10. relinquish
11. abandonment, discontinue,
unrestraint 12. carelessness,
heedlessness
abandoned... 4. left, lost 7. disused,
forlorn, given up 8. derelict,
deserted, forsaken 9. desolated,
discarded, neglected 11. surrendered
12. relinquished, unredeemable,
unrestrained
abase... 5. lower, shame 6. bemean,
depose, humble, reduce 7. degrade,
mortify 8. cast down, disgrace
9. humiliate 10. depreciate
abash... 5. shame 6. appall, dismay
7. astound, confuse, disturb, mortify
8. bewilder, confound 9. discomfit,
embarrass, humiliate 10. disconcert,
put to shame
abate... 3. ebb 4. lull, wane 5. let
up, relax, remit 6. deduct, lessen,

reduce 7. abolish, nullify, qualify,
slacken, subside 8. decrease,
diminish, discount, moderate
abatement... 5. letup 6. myosis
(miosis), rebate 8. decrease
9. lessening, reduction
10. diminution, mitigation,
moderation
abb... 4. wool, yarn 6. fleece (pert to)
Abba... 5. abbot, title 6. Father
abbe... 4. monk 6. cleric, curate,
priest
abbess... 4. amma 15. spiritual mother
abbreviate... 7. abridge, curtail,
shorten 8. compress, condense,
contract, simplify 9. epitomize
11. make briefer
abbreviation... 5. brief, lapse 6. digest
8. abstract 9. reduction
10. abridgment, compendium,
shortening 11. contraction
12. condensation
abdicate... 4. cede, quit 5. demit,
leave 6. depose, disown, resign,
retire 7. lay down 8. disclaim,
renounce, withdraw 9. surrender
10. disinherit, relinquish
Abdiel (Heb)... 5. angel 12. servant of
God
abdomen... 3. pot (sl) 4. wame
5. belly, tharm (obs) 6. paunch,
venter 7. stomach 8. potbelly
12. pelvic cavity
abdominal... 7. coeliac, gastric, ventral
11. ventricular
abdominal limb (crustacean)...
7. pleopod
Abel's brother... 4. Cain, Seth
aberration... 5. mania, wrong
6. lunacy, oddity 7. errancy,
madness 8. dementia, insanity
9. departure, deviation, variation,
wandering 10. alienation, digression,
divergence 11. abnormality,
derangement, distraction, peculiarity
12. eccentricity, irregularity
14. disorientation
abet... 3. aid, egg 4. back, help
5. egg on 6. assist, foment, incite,
second, succor, uphold 7. connive,
endorse, support, sustain 8. advocate
9. encourage, instigate
11. countenance
abeyance... 4. rest, stay 5. lapse,
pause 7. waiting 9. inertness
10. expectancy, suspension
abhor... 2. ug 4. hate, shun
6. detest, loathe 7. despise, dislike
8. execrate 9. abominate
abhorrence... 5. odium 6. hatred,
horror 7. dislike 8. aversion, loathing
9. antipathy, disliking, repulsion

10. repugnance

abide... 4. bide, live, stay, wait 5. await, dwell, pause, tarry 6. endure, remain, reside 7. sojourn 8. continue, submit to, tolerate 9. acquiesce, withstand

abide by... 3. own 4. avow, heed 5. admit, allow, yield 6. accept, follow, regard 7. concede, respect 8. adhere to 9. conform to 11. acknowledge

abiding... 7. durable, lasting 8. constant, enduring 9. permanent, steadfast 10. continuing, indwelling, persisting

Abies... 4. firs 5. pines 8. conifers 10. evergreens

abigail... 4. ayah, maid 5. bonne 7. servant 9. soubrette

Abijah's son (Bib)... 3. Asa

ability... 4. gift 5. force, might, power, skill 6. genius, talent 7. caliber, faculty, fitness, potency 8. aptitude, capacity, strength 10. capability, competence, efficiency 11. proficiency, sufficiency 13. qualification

abiosis... 11. without life

abject... 3. low 4. base, mean, meek, vile 6. humble, menial, supine 7. hangdog, ignoble, servile, slavish 8. beggarly, contrite, cringing, degraded, wretched 9. groveling, miserable 10. despicable, obsequious

abjuration... 6. denial 8. palinode (song), yielding 9. disavowal, rejection, surrender 10. abjurement, retraction, withdrawal 11. abandonment, forswearing, recantation, repudiation 12. disclamation 14. relinquishment

abjure... 4. deny, wave 6. disown, recant, reject, revoke 7. abandon, disavow 8. disclaim, forswear, renounce 9. disaffirm, repudiate

able... 3. can, fit 5. adept, smart 6. clever, fitted, suited 7. adapted, capable, learned, solvent 8. adjusted, literate, powerful, skillful (skilful), vigorous 9. competent, effective, efficient, qualified 10. omnipotent, proficient

able (pert to)... *suffix*.. 7. capable, fitness *to pay*.. 7. moneyed, solvent 8. affluent 10. prosperous *to read and write*.. 8. lettered, literate 10. book taught

ablepsia... 9. blindness

ably... 7. capably 11. competently, effectively, efficiently

abnormal... 6. albino 7. erratic, unusual 8. aberrant 9. deviative, eccentric, irregular, unnatural 11. exceptional 13. extraordinary

aboard... 4. onto 6. across 7. athwart 9. alongside

abode... 3. dar, hut 4. cell, cote, Eden, home 5. delay, house, lodge 7. habitat, Olympus, sojourn 8. dwelling, tenement 9. apartment, residence 10. habitation

abode of the dead... 3. Dar 4. Aalu, Aaru, Hell 5. Aralu, Hades, limbo, Orcus, Sheol 6. Asgard, heaven, Naraka 7. Abaddon, Elysium, Nirvana 8. paradise, Valhalla 9. perdition, purgatory 11. Pandemonium

abolish... 4. undo 5. annul, quash 6. cancel, recall, repeal, revoke, vacate 7. destroy, nullify, rescind, retract, reverse 8. abrogate, withdraw 10. annihilate, invalidate 11. countermand

abominable... 4. base, dire, foul, vile 5. awful, gross 6. odious, wicked, woeful 7. beastly, hateful 8. dreadful, grievous, infamous, shocking, terrible, wretched 9. execrable, loathsome, obnoxious 10. despicable, detestable, outrageous, unpleasant 12. disagreeable, disreputable

Abominable Snowman... 4. Yeti

abominate... 4. hate 5. abhor 6. detest, loathe 8. execrate

abomination... 3. woe 4. evil 5. odium, wrong 6. hatred, horror, plague 7. disgust, outrage 8. aversion, loathing, vexation 9. grievance 10. abhorrence, defilement, odiousness, repugnance

aboriginal... 5. first, natal 6. binghi, native 7. ancient 8. original 9. beginning, primitive 10. autochthon, indigenous

aborigines... 4. Ainu (Aino), Toda 5. lubra, Sakai, Vedda 7. cave men, Indians, natives, savages 9. indigenes, old-timers 10. Dravidians 11. preadamites

abortion... 6. arrest 7. failure 11. embryoctomy, miscarriage, miscreation 13. misconception

abound... 4. flow, teem 5. swarm 8. overflow 9. exuberate, plentiful

abounding... 4. rife 5. ample, flush 7. copious, teeming 8. abundant 9. exuberant, luxuriant, plentiful

abounding in... *blossoms*.. 7. flowery *forests*.. 6. sylvan *grass*.. 6. cressy *snow*.. 5. nival

about... 2. of, on, re 3. amb (pref) 5. anent, astir, circa 6. almost, around, nearly 8. circiter 10. concerning 13. approximately

about to happen... 8. imminent

above... 2. on, up 3. o'er, sur (pref) 4. atop, over, upon 5. aloft, super, supra (pref)

abrade... 3. rub 4. file, fret, gall 5. chafe, grate 6. scrape 9. excoriate

Abraham (pert to)... *birthplace*.. 2. Ur *concubine*.. 5. Hagar *father*.. 5. Terah *grandfather*.. 5. Nahor *grandson*.. 4. Esau *nephew*.. 3. Lot *son*.. 4. Shua (Shuah) 5. Isaac, Medan 7. Ishmael *wife*.. 5. Sarah (Sara, Sarai)

7. Keturah
abrasion... 4. flaw, gall, hurt 5. scuff
6. lesion, scrape 8. limation
9. attrition
abrasive... 4. file, sand 5. emery
6. garnet, polish, pumice 7. erodent
8. abradant, corundum 9. attritive,
sandpaper
abraxas... 3. gem 5. charm, stone
Abraxas (pert to)...
god (anc Gnostic).. 12. Supreme
Deity
source of mind.. 4. Nous
the Word.. 5. Logos
abreast... 4. even (with) 6. beside
8. opposite 9. alongside
abrege... 7. epitome 10. abridgment
abri... 4. shed 6. cavity, dugout
7. shelter
abridge... 5. brief, razee (rasee)
7. curtail, shorten 8. abstract,
condense, diminish, retrench
9. epitomize 10. abbreviate
abridgment... 6. digest 7. compend,
epitome, summary 8. abstract,
syllabus, synopsis 9. lessening,
reduction 10. compendium,
diminution 11. deprivation
abroad... 4. away 5. forth 6. astray,
widely 7. at large, broadly, distant
8. away from 9. spread out
11. widely apart
abrogate... 5. annul, quash 6. cancel,
repeal, revoke 7. abolish, rescind
8. set aside 10. put an end to
abrogation... 8. quashing 9. annulling,
cessation 10. rescinding, rescission
11. dissolution
abrupt... 4. curt, rude 5. blunt, hasty,
quick, sharp, sheer, steep, terse
6. broken, craggy, sudden
7. brusque 8. headlong, vertical
9. broken off, impetuous
10. unexpected 11. precipitous
12. disconnected 13. perpendicular,
unceremonious
abruptly... 7. briefly, in brief
8. suddenly
Absalom (pert to)...
father.. 5. David (King)
host's captain.. 5. Amasa
sister.. 5. Tamar
slayer.. 4. Joab
abscond... 3. run 4. bolt, flee, hide
5. elope 6. decamp, desert, eloine,
levant 8. steal off
absence... 4. AWOL, lack, void, want
5. exeat, leave 6. vacuum 7. silence
10. deficiency, withdrawal
13. nonappearance, nonattendance
absence of... (see also *without*)
animal, plant.. 8. lipotype
hair.. 6. acomia
pain.. 8. anodynia
pigment.. 8. alphosis
self-worth.. 7. modesty
taste.. 7. ageusia
absent... 3. off, out 4. away, gone,
lost 6. dreamy, musing, truant
7. lacking 8. absorbed 9. engrossed
10. abstracted 11. preoccupied
12. nonattendant

absinthe... 5. green (color) 6. ajenjo,
liquor
absolute... 4. alod, dead, pure, real,
true, very 5. freed, sheer, total,
utter, whole 6. empery, simple
7. certain, elative, perfect, plenary
8. absolved, complete, positive
9. arbitrary, downright, unlimited
10. autocratic, disengaged,
peremptory 11. categorical,
independent 13. unconditional
15. plenipotentiary
absolute (pert to)...
dominion.. 6. empery
property.. 4. alod 7. alodium
sovereign.. 8. autocrat
superlative.. 7. elative
time.. 9. Greenwich, universal
absolutely... 3. yea, yes 5. stark
6. wholly 7. utterly 8. entirely
10. altogether, positively, thoroughly
13. unequivocally 15. unconditionally
absolution... 6. pardon, shrive
7. penance 9. acquittal, remission
11. exculpation, forgiveness
absolve... 4. free 5. remit 6. acquit,
finish, pardon 9. discharge, exonerate
10. accomplish
absonant... 8. contrary 10. discordant
12. unreasonable
absorb... 3. eat 4. soak, suck
5. drink, eat up, learn, use up
6. corner, digest, engulf, imbibe,
soak up, sponge 7. consume,
swallow 10. assimilate, monopolize,
understand 11. incorporate
absorbed... 4. deep, lost, rapt, sunk
6. buried, intent, lost in
7. bemused, devoted, engaged
8. occupied 9. engrossed
11. monopolized, preoccupied
absorbent... 5. fomes 6. spongy
7. blotter 9. adsorbent
10. imbibitory
absorption... 10. imbibition
abstain... 4. deny, fast, hold, shun
5. avoid, cease, forgo, waive
6. eschew 7. forbear, refrain
8. restrain, teetotal, withhold
abstemious... 5. sober 7. sparing
8. moderate 9. abstinent, temperate
11. abstentious
abstinence... 6. disuse 7. encraty
8. sobriety 9. restraint, sacrifice
10. abstention, continence,
desistance, moderation, self-denial,
temperance 11. abandonment,
forbearance, self-control
13. self-restraint
14. abstemiousness, discontinuance
abstract... 4. deed, part, take 5. brief,
steal 6. deduct, noetic (purely),
remove 7. abridge, epitome, shorten,
summary 8. argument, condense,
syllabus, withdraw 9. capsulize,
statement 10. abridgment,
compendium 12. nonobjective
abstract being... 3. ens 6. entity
abstruse... 4. deep 6. hidden
7. obscure 8. esoteric, profound
9. concealed, recondite
10. acroamatic (acroatic)

16. incomprehensible
absurd... 4. wild 5. droll, inept, silly
6. stupid 7. asinine, foolish
8. fabulous 9. ludicrous
10. impossible, irrational, ridiculous
11. incongruous, nonsensical
12. inconsistent, unbelievable,
unreasonable
absurdity... 7. twaddle 8. nonsense
10. absurdness 11. foolishness
13. contradiction, impossibility
14. ridiculousness 16. inconceivability
abundance... 4. mass, much, rife
5. ample 6. galore, plenty, riches,
volume 8. fullness (fulness),
opulence, overflow, quantity
9. affluence 10. exuberance
11. copiousness, superfluity
12. extravagance, generousness
13. plenteousness
abundant... 4. lush, much, rich, rife,
teem 5. ample 6. galore, plenty
7. copious, profuse 9. abounding,
exuberant, luxuriant, plentiful
10. sufficient
abundant, not... 5. spare 6. lenten,
meager (meagre)
abuse... 4. gali, harm, hurt, maul, rail,
rape 5. crime, curse, scold, snash
6. berate, ill use, injure, insult,
malign, misuse, ravish, revile
7. calumny, deceive, obloquy,
offense, pervert, traduce, upbraid
8. dishonor, maltreat, misapply,
reproach 9. contumely, disparage,
invective, violation 10. opprobrium,
revilement, scurrility
11. debauchment, malediction,
objurgation 12. mistreatment,
vituperation
abusive... 3. mud (throw)
10. scurrilous 12. catachrestic
abut... 4. butt, join 5. touch
6. adjoin, appose, border, rest on
7. conjoin, connect 8. adjacent,
neighbor
abutment... 4. arch, pier, wall
6. alette 7. abuttal, sea wall
8. buttress, shoulder 13. fortification
abysmal... 4. deep 7. yawning
8. profound, unending 9. plumbless
10. bottomless, fathomless
abyss... 3. pit 4. Absu, gulf, hell,
hole, void, well 5. abysm, chaos,
chasm, cleft, shaft 6. cavity, vorago
15. infernal regions
Abyssinia, Ethiopia...
capital.. 10. Addis Ababa
city.. 5. Aduwa, Aksum (Axum)
6. Gondar 7. Ankober, Gambela,
Magdala
dialect.. 4. Geez
Empire (old).. 7. Axumite
Hamite.. 4. Afar
King.. 13. Haile Selassie
kingdom (former).. 4. Shoa 5. Tigre
6. Amhara
population.. 7. Hamites, Semites
8. Negroids
river (famed).. 5. Abdai (Blue Nile)
sea.. 3. Red
title (anc).. 12. Negusa Nagast

Abyssinian (pert to)...
fly.. 4. zimb
gold (artificial).. 5. talmi
lyre.. 6. kissar
tea leaves.. 3. kat
wolf.. 6. kaberu
Academe, The... 14. Academy of Plato
(Athens)
academic... 5. ideal, rigid 6. formal
7. classic, elegant 8. abstract,
pedantic, Platonic 9. scholarly
10. Ciceronian, scholastic
11. educational, impractical,
speculative, theoretical
12. conventional, hypothetical
13. institutional
academy... 5. école 6. lyceum,
manège, school, Schule 7. college,
escuela, society 8. academie,
seminary 9. accademia, institute
10. university 11. institution
Acadia... 6. Acadie 10. Nova Scotia
acarpous... 7. sterile 9. fruitless
acaudal... 7. anurous 8. tailless
accede... 5. agree, enter, grant, yield
6. assent, attain, comply, concur,
relent, submit 7. conform, consent
9. acquiesce 11. acknowledge
accelerate... 4. rush 5. speed
6. hasten, step up 7. advance,
forward, further, quicken 8. activate,
dispatch, expedite
acceleration... 5. haste 6. pickup
8. velocity 9. catalysis, hastening
10. expedition, quickening
11. advancement
accelerator... 6. muscle 7. speeder
8. throttle 9. quickener
accent... 4. beat, mark, tone 5. breve,
ictus, pitch, twang 6. brogue, stress
7. cadence, dialect 8. emphasis
9. emphasize 10. accentuate,
expression, inflection, modulation
12. accentuation
accent (pert to)...
Irish.. 4. blas 6. brogue
on last syllable.. 7. oxytone
Scot.. 4. birr
unaccented syllable.. 5. arsis
accept... 2. OK 3. buy, own 4. avow,
fang, take 5. admit, adopt, agree,
allow, grant, trust, yield 6. assent,
comply, credit, expect, ratify
7. approve, believe, certify, condone,
confess, consent, embrace, receive,
swallow (coll) 8. accredit, tolerate,
validate 9. undertake
11. countenance
accept (as one's own)...
12. nostrificate (of foreign degrees)
acceptable... 2. OK 6. worthy
7. welcome 8. eligible, passable,
pleasant, pleasing, suitable
9. agreeable, allowable, desirable,
expedient, qualified, tolerable
10. admissible 11. comfortable
12. satisfactory
accepted... 6. chosen, deemed
7. adopted, assumed, popular,
reputed, trusted 8. admitted,
approved, believed, credited,
embraced, espoused, inferred,

orthodox, received, standard,
supposed 9. customary, prevalent
10. accredited, understood,
undertaken 11. traditional
12. conventional, unquestioned
13. authoritative
access... 3. way 4. adit, door, gain
5. entry 6. avenue, entree, ingate,
tunnel 7. ingress 8. approach,
entrance, entryway, increase
9. accession, accretion, admission
10. admittance 11. entranceway
13. accessibility, attainability
15. approachability
accessible... 4. open 5. handy
6. open to, public 7. getable
8. amenable, pervious 9. admissive,
available, permeable, reachable,
receptive 10. attainable, obtainable,
open–minded, penetrable, procurable
11. persuasible 12. approachable
13. communicative
accession... 6. access, assent, attack,
growth 7. adjunct, consent, joining,
uniting 8. addition, increase
9. accretion, agreement, increment
10. acceptance, affixation,
annexation, attainment, compliance,
concession, coronation
12. acquiescence 13. reinforcement
14. aggrandizement
accessory, accessary... 5. extra, party
7. abettor 8. addition, litigant
9. adjective, appendage, assistant,
attendant, auxiliary, obbligato
10. accomplish, additional, collateral,
subsidiary 11. appurtenant,
concomitant, participant
12. accompanying, appurtenance,
contributory, nonessential, participator
13. accompaniment, supplementary
accident... 3. hap 4. luck 6. chance,
hazard, mishap 8. calamity, casualty,
disaster 9. adventure, befalling,
mischance 10. misfortune
11. catastrophe
accidental... 6. casual, chance
9. unwitting 10. contingent,
unforeseen, unintended
acclaim... 4. hail, laud 6. praise
7. applaud 8. applause
11. acclamation, approbation
acclamation... 3. cry, joy 5. shout
7. acclaim, ovation, plaudit
8. applause, approval 9. unanimity
acclimate... 5. adapt, inure 6. adjust,
season 8. accustom 9. condition,
habituate 10. naturalize
11. acclimatize, familiarize
acclivity... 4. bank, brow, hill, rise
5. climb, slope, talus 6. ascent
7. upgrade 9. ascendant (ascendent)
11. inclination
accolade... 4. fold, rite 5. award,
brace, clasp, Oscar 6. praise, reward
7. embrace, tribute 8. encomium
9. panegyric 10. enfoldment
accommodate... 3. fit 4. help, lend,
meet, suit 5. adapt, favor, lodge,
shape, yield 6. adjust, afford,
comply, invest, oblige, orient, settle,
supply 7. conform, furnish

9. reconcile 10. correspond
accommodation... 3. aid 4. loan,
room 5. limit, space, terms
6. giving, volume 7. advance,
lodging, service 8. capacity
9. advantage, provision
10. adaptation, adjustment,
attunement, conformity, settlement
11. convenience, integration,
orientation, subsistence
12. coordination 13. harmonization
14. reconciliation
accompaniment... 7. adjunct, descant,
support 8. ornament 9. attendant,
obbligato 11. concurrence
12. concomitance
accompany... 4. join 6. attend,
convoy, escort, follow, squire
7. conduct 11. synchronize
12. contemporize
accomplice... 3. pal 4. aide, ally,
chum 6. stooge 7. abettor
9. accessory, assistant, associate
11. confederate, conspirator
accomplish... 2. do 3. win 4. make,
work 5. enact, equip 6. attain, effect
7. achieve, compass, execute,
furnish, operate, perfect, produce,
realize, succeed 8. contrive, engineer
9. negotiate 10. consummate,
effectuate
accomplishment... 4. deed, feat
5. skill 8. dispatch 9. discharge,
execution 10. attainment, completion
11. achievement, acquirement,
fulfillment, performance, proficiency,
transaction 12. effectuation
accord... 5. award, grant, unity
6. accede, unison 7. comport,
concede, concert, concord, harmony,
rapport 8. diapason, symphony
9. agreement, harmonize, reconcile,
unanimity 10. accordance, conformity,
uniformity 11. concurrence
accordant... 7. attuned 8. agreeing,
suitable 9. agreeable, assenting,
consonant 10. concordant,
concurrent, consenting, consilient,
consistent 11. conformable,
homogeneous 13. corresponding
accordingly... 2. so 4. then, thus
9. therefore 12. consequently
according to... 3. a la, aux 4. alla,
fact, true 5. datal 7. a la mode
8. pursuant
accost... 4. hail, meet 5. greet, speak
6. halloo, salute 7. address
8. approach
accoucheuse... 7. midwife
account... 3. sum, tab 4. bill, cast,
sake, tale, word 5. debit, honor,
score, tally 6. assign, credit, esteem,
profit, reckon, regard, report
7. compute, memoirs, recital
9. narration, reckoning, rehearsal,
statement, summation
10. numeration, recitation
11. description, explanation,
information 13. communication
accountable... 6. liable 8. amenable,
knowable 9. divinable, traceable
10. answerable, ascribable,

assignable, calculable, explicable,
fathomable 11. explainable,
predictable, responsible
12. attributable, intelligible
13. apprehensible
14. comprehensible

accountant... 5. clerk 7. actuary,
auditor 8. reckoner 9. defendant,
registrar 10. bookkeeper, calculator

accouter, accoutre... 3. fit, rig
4. deck, gird, suit 5. array, dress,
equip, habit 6. attire, fettle, outfit
7. appoint, costume, furnish, provide

accouterment, accoutrement...
5. dress, sword 6. attire 8. trapping
9. equipment, haversack

accoy... 4. tame 5. daunt 6. soothe,
subdue

accredit... 5. trust 6. accept, affirm,
credit, depute, ratify 7. approve,
ascribe, believe, certify, confirm,
empower, endorse 8. deputize,
sanction, validate 9. authorize
10. commission

accrete... 3. add 6. attach

accretion... 4. gain 6. growth
8. addition, adhesion, increase
9. coherence, increment
10. concretion 11. coagulation,
enlargement 12. accumulation,
augmentation 13. amplification

accrue... 4. grow 5. arise, ensue,
issue 6. mature, result 7. acquire,
collect, redound 8. accresce
10. accumulate

accumulate... 4. grow, heap, mass,
save 5. amass, hoard, store
6. accrue, garner, gather, muster
7. advance, collect, store up
8. increase 9. aggregate

accumulation... 4. fund, gain, mass
5. hoard, store 7. accrual
8. gleaning, increase, treasure
9. accession, accretion, extension,
gathering 10. acervation, assemblage,
collection 11. acquisition, serendipity
12. augmentation 13. amplification
14. aggrandizement

accuracy... 6. nicety 9. exactness,
fussiness, precision, rightness
11. correctness 14. meticulousness,
scrupulousness

accurate... 4. just, nice, prim 5. close,
exact, right 6. proper, strict
7. correct, perfect, precise 8. faithful
9. syntactic 10. meticulous, particular
11. grammatical

accursed... 6. cursed, damned,
doomed 9. execrable, execrated
10. detestable 13. anathematized

accusation... 5. blame 6. attack,
charge, taxing 7. calumny
8. reproach 9. complaint
10. imputation, indictment
11. impeachment 12. denunciation

accuse... 3. tax 5. blame 6. attack,
charge, delate, indict 7. arraign,
censure, impeach 8. denounce
9. criminate 11. incriminate,
recriminate

accuser... 7. delator 8. accusant,
libelant (libellant) 9. plaintiff

10. prosecutor 11. complainant
12. incriminator

accustom... 3. use 4. wont 5. enure,
habit, inure, train 6. addict
7. educate, toughen 9. habituate
11. familiarize

accustomed... 4. used, wont 5. usual
6. enured, inured 8. familiar
9. customary, sedentary (to sit)

ace... 3. jot, one, pip, tib 4. atom,
card, dole, dram, unit, whit
5. monad, pilot, point, shark (sl)
7. aviator 8. particle, pittance,
superior 10. crackajack (sl), proficient
11. crackerjack (sl)

ace (pert to)...
ace–queen.. 6. tenace
of clubs.. 5. basto

acedia (Gr)... 5. sloth 6. torpor

acedia (Sp)... 8. flatfish

Aceldama, Akeldama (Bib)... 12. Field
of Blood, potter's field

acemila... 8. pack mule

acephalous... 8. headless
10. leaderless

acephalus... 15. headless monster

acerb... 4. sour 5. harsh, sharp
6. bitter, unripe 7. acerbic, austere,
pungent

acerbity... 7. acidity 8. acridity,
acrimony, asperity, mordancy,
pungency, severity 9. harshness
10. bitterness, causticity
11. astringency

acetic acid... 7. vinegar 8. vesicant
9. corrosive

Achaean, Achaian... 5. Greek (a)
6. Greece

ache... 4. burn, long, pain, pang
5. throb 6. grieve, sorrow, twinge
7. agonize, longing 10. suffer pain

achieve... 2. do 3. get, win 4. gain,
kill 6. arrive, attain, effect, finish
7. compass, execute, fulfill, perform,
produce, realize, succeed
8. complete, conclude, contrive
10. accomplish, consummate,
effectuate

achievement... 3. act 4. deed, feat
5. doing, stunt 6. action, record
7. arrival, exploit 8. dispatch
9. adventure 10. attainment,
escutcheon (Her) 11. fulfillment,
performance, transaction
12. effectuation 14. accomplishment,
implementation

Achilles (pert to)...
advisor.. 6. Nestor
dipped into.. 9. River Styx
father.. 6. Peleus
friend.. 9. Patroclus
horse.. 7. Xanthus
mother.. 6. Thetis
slayer.. 5. Paris
slayer of.. 6. Hector
son.. 7. Pyrrhus 11. Neoptolemus
vulnerable spot.. 4. heel

achromatic... 4. gray 8. achromic
9. achromous, colorless, uncolored
13. free from color

achropsia... 14. color blindness

acid... 4. keen, sour, tart 5. acrid,

amino, boric, malic, mucic, pyrol
6. acetic, arabic, biting, bromic,
nitric, oxalic, tannic 7. acetose,
caustic, chloric, racemic, stearic,
terebic, vinegar 9. corrosive
11. acrimonious
acid, removing ... 12. edulcoration
acidity ... 4. acor, sour 8. acrimony,
mordancy, sourness, tartness, verjuice
9. sharpness 10. bitterness
13. acidulousness
acknowledge ... 3. nod, own, pay, say
4. avow, sign 5. admit, allow, grant,
own up, reply, swear, thank, vouch,
yield 6. accede, accept, answer,
assent, attest, redeem 7. certify,
concede, confess, testify 8. disclose
9. recognize
acknowledgment ... 5. favor, reply
6. answer, avowal, avowry, shrift,
thanks 7. apology, epistle, receipt,
voucher, warrant 8. rescript
9. admission 10. acceptance,
concession, confession, disclosure,
owning up to 11. recognition
12. thanksgiving
acme ... 3. top 4. apex 5. limit
6. apogee, climax, crisis, heyday,
summit, tip–top, vertex, zenith
7. ceiling, maximum 11. culmination
12. consummation
acology, science of ... 8. remedies
acolyte ... 7. patener 8. altar boy
9. assistant
acomia ... 8. alopecia, baldness
12. hairlessness
aconite ... 8. Cammarum, Eranthis
9. monkshood
acorn ... 3. nut 4. duck 6. camata
10. meadowlark (color)
acosmic ... 11. unorganized
acquaint ... 4. tell 6. advise, impart,
inform 7. apprise 9. enlighten,
introduce 11. familiarize
acquaintance ... 3. ken 5. amigo
6. friend 7. privity 8. familiar,
intimacy, intimate 9. companion,
knowledge 10. fellowship
11. familiarity, information,
sympathizer 15. familiarization
acquainted ... 6. au fait 7. versant
8. familiar 9. cognizant
10. conversant
acquiesce ... 3. bow 5. abide, agree,
chime, yield 6. accede, assent,
comply, concur, relent, resign, submit
7. conform, consent, succumb
acquire ... 3. buy, get, win 4. earn,
gain, reap 5. adopt, catch, incur,
learn, steal 6. attain, effect, obtain,
secure 7. procure, receive
8. contract 9. cultivate
acquire (pert to) ...
　beforehand .. 7. pre–empt
　feathers .. 6. fledge
　immunity .. 14. serum injection
　knowledge .. 5. clear, study
　9. ascertain
acquit ... 4. free 5. clear 6. excuse,
pardon, pay off 7. absolve, fulfill,
release, requite 9. exculpate,
exonerate

acquittal ... 7. freeing, payment, release
8. clearing, requital 9. clearance,
discharge 10. observance
11. exculpation, fulfillment
12. satisfaction
acquittance ... 7. payment, quietus,
receipt 9. discharge, quittance
acre ... 5. field 6. arpent 7. measure
8. farmhold
acre (pert to) ...
　half .. 3. erf (S Afr)
　hundred .. 7. hectare (metric)
　quarter .. 4. rood (Brit)
acres ... 5. lands 6. estate, ground
acrid ... 4. acid, bask (dial), keen, sour,
tart 5. harsh, rough, sharp 6. acetic,
biting, bitter 7. acetose, caustic,
mordant, pungent, reeking
8. unsavory, virulent 9. acidulous,
corrosive 10. escharotic, irritating
11. acrimonious
acrimonious ... 4. acid, keen 5. acrid,
angry, gruff, harsh, irate, sharp
6. bitter 7. caustic 8. stinging
9. rancorous, resentful
acrimony ... 5. venom 6. rancor 7. ill
will, vitriol 8. acerbity, acridity,
asperity, mordancy, pungency,
rudeness, severity, sourness, tartness
9. animosity, virulence 10. bitterness,
causticity, resentment
11. astringency, crabbedness
acroamatic ... 4. oral 5. parol
6. arcane, occult, secret, verbal
8. abstract, abstruse, anagogic,
esoteric, profound 9. recondite,
unwritten 11. nuncupative
acrobat ... 7. gymnast, tumbler
8. balancer 10. ropedancer,
ropewalker 11. funambulist
13. contortionist, schoenobatist
acrochordon ... 4. wart (small)
Acrocorinth, Acrocorinthus ...
9. acropolis (Corinth) 12. Pirene
Spring (site)
acromegaly ... 7. disease
11. enlargement (head, hands, feet)
acronical, acronichal (opp of
cosmical) ... 10. rising star
11. setting star
acronyx ... 13. ingrowing nail
acrophobia ... fear of 7. heights
acropolis ... 6. refuge 7. citadel
Acropolis (pert to) ...
　Argos .. 7. Larissa
　Corinth .. 11. Acrocorinth
　Thebes .. 6. Cadmea
across ... 4. over, span 5. cross
6. thwart 7. athwart 8. crossway,
traverse 9. crossways, crosswise
10. crisscross, transverse
across (pref) ... 3. dia 4. tran 5. trans
acrostic ... 4. agla, game, poem
6. puzzle 7. erratic 8. wordplay
9. crosswise, jeu de mots, telestich
act ... 2. do 3. jus, law, lex 4. deed,
feat, play, skit, turn, work 5. actus,
emote, favor, of God, stunt
6. action, behave, demean, motion
7. comport, measure, perform,
pretend, process 8. function,
kindness, simulate 9. enactment,

represent 10. enterprise, exert power,
theatrical 11. impersonate, legislation,
performance, transaction

act (pert to) . . .
a part. . 8. simulate 9. dissemble
causing ruin. . 11. Kiss of Death
criminal. . 8. villainy
detestable. . 11. abomination
formal. . 10. instrument
game. . 7. charade
illegal. . 4. tort 5. crime 6. delict
nonsense. . 10. tomfoolery
planned. . 12. premeditated
pompously. . 11. pontificate
suffix. . 3. ure

acting . . . 5. doing 6. action, posing
7. playing, serving 8. pretense
9. dramatics, execution, operating
10. masquerade, performing,
simulating 11. make–believe
13. impersonating, impersonation

acting with force . . . 8. vehement

action . . . 2. re 3. act, res 4. deed,
feat, play, stir, suit, work 5. award,
doing, order, works 6. battle, decree,
motion, praxis, ruling 7. conduct,
contest, lawsuit, verdict, working
8. activity, behavior, demeanor,
exercise, movement, sentence
9. mechanism, operation
10. automation, enterprise
11. performance 13. pronouncement

active . . . 4. spry 5. acute, agile, alert,
brisk, quick, ready, smart, yauld
6. breezy, dapper, lively, nimble,
prompt, strong 7. dynamic, intense,
kinetic, vibrant 8. animated, forceful,
spirited, vigorous 9. assiduous,
effective, effectual, energetic,
energized, operating, pragmatic,
sprightly, vivacious 11. industrious

active, not . . . 6. static 7. dormant
11. inoperative

activity . . . 3. ado, gog, pep, vir 4. stir,
work 5. vigor 6. action, energy
7. agility, bristle 8. business,
movement 9. athletics, briskness,
operation, quickness 10. activeness,
employment, nimbleness, occupation

act of . . .
cutting. . 4. kerf 8. shearing
endearment. . 4. kiss 6. caress
God. . 8. accident
kindness. . 5. favor
leaving. . 6. congee, egress
respect. . 6. curtsy, homage
ruling. . 5. regle
self–examination. . 13. introspection
sharing. . 13. participation
witnessing. . 11. attestation
working together. . 13. collaboration
worship. . 6. prayer 8. devotion

actor . . . 3. ham 4. doer, hero, mime,
star, supe 5. agent 6. mummer,
player, worker 7. Roscius, trooper
8. aisteoir, comedian, histrion,
Thespian 9. performer, portrayer,
pretender, tragedian 10. comedienne,
dramatizer, pantomimic, personator
11. barnstormer, entertainer,
pantomimist, protagonist, tragedienne
12. impersonator

actor (personage) . . . 4. Lunt, Ward
5. Booth 7. Skinner 8. Warfield
9. Faversham

actors' group . . . 4. cast 6. troupe

actor's hint . . . 3. cue 12. teleprompter

actress (personage) . . . 5. Adams, Bates,
Hayes, Terry 6. Robson, Scheff
7. Marlowe, Russell 8. Fontanne,
Modjeska 9. Bernhardt

actual . . . 4. real, true 5. posit
7. factual, genuine, present
8. absolute, positive, tangible
9. practical, veritable 11. substantial

actual being . . . 4. esse

actuality . . . 4. fact 6. verity 7. reality
8. realness 9. existence
10. factuality 14. substantiality

actually . . . 5. quite, truly 6. indeed,
really, verily 8. actively 9. assuredly,
certainly

actuary . . . 5. clerk 9. registrar
10. accountant, bookkeeper,
calculator 13. arithmetician,
mathematician

actuate . . . 3. egg 4. move 5. force,
impel, rouse 6. arouse, induce,
prompt, propel 7. animate
8. motivate 9. stimulate

acuate . . . 7. sharpen
12. needle–shaped, sharp–pointed

acumen . . . 7. insight 8. gumption,
keenness, sagacity 9. acuteness,
sharpness 10. astuteness, perception,
shrewdness 11. discernment
12. perspicacity 14. discrimination

acute . . . 4. high, keen, tart, thin
5. canny, sharp, smart, vivid
6. accent, biting, crafty, fierce,
severe, shrewd, shrill, subtle
7. crucial, cutting, dynamic, intense,
knowing, painful, pointed, violent
8. critical, deep–felt, forceful, incisive,
piercing, poignant, rigorous, stabbing,
stinging, vigorous 9. energetic,
ingenious, sensitive 11. sharp–witted
13. perspicacious 14. discriminating

acuteness of . . .
sight. . 7. oxyopia 10. oxyblepsia
taste. . 9. oxygeusia
touch. . 8. oxyaphia

Adam (pert to) . . .
grandson. . 4. Enos
son. . 4. Abel, Cain, Seth
wife. . 3. Eve 6. Lilith (legend)

Adam's . . .
ale. . 5. water
apple. . 6. larynx 10. pomum Adami
herb. . 7. mullein
needle. . 5. yucca

adapt . . . 3. fit, set 4. suit 6. adjust,
attune, comply, modify, orient,
season 7. arrange, conform, prepare,
qualify 8. accustom, regulate
9. acclimate, condition, habituate,
harmonize, reconcile
11. accommodate

adaptable . . . 7. elastic, pliable
9. tractable, versatile 10. adjustable,
responsive 11. conformable
13. accommodative

adaptation . . . 7. fitting 10. adjustment,
attunement, conformity, regulation

11. arrangement, habituation, orientation 12. conditioning, coordination, modification 13. accommodation, harmonization, orchestration, qualification 15. familiarization

add... 3. eke, tot 4. foot, give, join, plus, tote 5. affix, annex, sum up, total, unite 6. append, attach, reckon 7. accrete, augment, compile, compute, put with, subjoin 8. increase 9. calculate 10. supplement

adda... 5. skink (scink) 6. lizard 7. reptile

addax... 6. pygarg (Bib) 8. antelope

added... 3. and 4. plus 5. extra 6. joined, united 7. affixed, annexed 8. appended, attached 9. appendant 13. supplementary

adder... 3. asp 5. Bitis, krait, snake, viper 6. nedder 7. machine, serpent 13. mathematician

addict... 4. buff 5. fiend 7. adjudge, devotee, hophead 9. habituate 15. apply habitually

addicted... 4. wont 5. prone 8. attached, disposed, inclined 9. devoted to 10. accustomed, habituated 11. given over to

addiction... 5. habit 9. surrender 10. attachment 11. enslavement

Addison's signature... 4. Clio (The Spectator) 7. Atticus (by the Pope)

addition... 3. and, ell, too 4. also, gain, plus, wing 5. farse (Relig), rider 6. addend, augend, lean–to 7. additum, adjunct, joining, uniting 8. addendum, additory, increase 9. accession, accretion, amendment, appendage, extension, reckoning 10. annexation 11. calculation, computation, enlargement 12. augmentation

additional... 3. new 4. else, more 5. added, extra, fresh, spare 7. besides, further 9. auxiliary, extrinsic 12. supervenient, supplemental 13. supplementary

additional (pert to)...
explanation.. 10. epexegesis 11. elucidation
grant.. 3. ann 5. bonus
specimen.. 6. cotype

address... 3. air, wit, woo 4. call, hail, mien, pray, tact, talk 5. abode, court, grace, greet, guise, place, skill, speak 6. accost, direct, eulogy, salute, sermon, speech 7. arrange, conduct, consign, declaim, finesse, lecture, manners, oration, prepare, prowess, request 8. behavior, demeanor, greeting, harangue, inscribe, perorate, petition, presence 9. dexterity, diplomacy, direction, discourse, ingenuity, readiness 11. comportment, destination, inscription, savoir–faire 14. sophistication, superscription

addressee... 8. occupant 10. inhabitant 12. communicator 13. correspondent

adduce... 4. cite, name 5. argue,

infer, offer, plead, quote 6. allege, assign 7. advance, mention, present, produce

Adelphi... 7. theater (Strand, London) 13. London Quarter

adeps... 4. lard 9. animal fat

adept... 3. ace, apt 4. whiz (coll) 6. adroit, artist, expert, versed 7. capable, dabster, mahatma, skilled 8. skillful (skilful) 9. alchemist (formerly), occultist 10. conversant, proficient 11. crackerjack

adequate... 3. due, fit 4. able, full 5. ample, digne, equal 6. enough 7. capable 8. all right, equalize, suitable 9. competent, effective, effectual, sufficing, tolerable 10. sufficient 12. commensurate, satisfactory 13. proportionate

adhere... 4. cleg, glue, hold 5. cling, stick 6. cleave, cohere 7. accrete, observe, persist

adherent... 4. ally 6. adnate, sticky, votary 7. dangler, sequela 8. adhesive, clinging, disciple, faithful, follower, hanger–on, partisan, sticking, upholder 9. appendage, dependent, supporter

adherent to the Crown... 4. Tory

adhesive... 3. gum, wax 4. glue 5. paste 6. cement, mastic, sticky 8. adherent, mucilage 10. tenacious

adhesiveness... 4. stay 8. tenacity 12. cohesiveness 13. tenaciousness 16. stick–to–itiveness

adhibit... 3. use 5. admit, affix, apply 6. attach, devote 7. bring in 10. administer

adieu... 4. vale 5. adios, aloha 6. good–by, so long (sl) 7. cheerio, good–bye, good day 8. au revoir, farewell 11. leave–taking

adipose... 3. fat 4. oily 5. fatty, plump, pursy, squab 9. sebaceous

adit... 3. way 4. duct 5. entry, stulm 6. access, ingate, intake, tunnel 7. channel, conduit, haulage, ingress, passage 8. approach, drainage, entrance 9. admission 11. entranceway, ventilation

adjacent... 4. abut, near, nigh 5. close, handy 6. next to 7. meeting, nearest 8. abutting, touching 9. adjoining, bordering 10. contiguous, juxtaposed 11. neighboring 12. conterminous

adject... 3. add 4. join 5. annex

adjective... 3. the 6. adnoun 7. epithet (significant) 8. modifier 9. accessory, dependent

adjective (pert to)...
demonstrative.. 4. that, this 5. these, those
suffix.. 2. ic, il 3. ent, ial, ian, ile, ish, ist, ite, ive, ous
verbal.. 9. gerundive

adjoin... 3. add 4. abut, butt, join 5. unite 6. attach, border 7. conjoin 8. neighbor

adjourn... 3. end 5. close, defer, delay 6. recess 7. suspend 8. dissolve, postpone, prorogue 11. discontinue

adjudge, adjudicate ... 3. try 4. deem, doom, find, hold, pass 5. award, judge, order 6. assign, decree, esteem, ordain, reckon, regard, settle 7. condemn 8. consider, sentence 9. determine

adjunct ... 4. ally, word 5. added 6. device 7. additum, annexed, consort 8. addition, appanage (apanage) 9. appendant, associate, auxiliary, colleague, companion, component, qualifier 11. confederate 12. appurtenance, nonessential

adjuration ... 4. oath, plea 6. appeal, avowal, charge 8. entreaty, swearing, vouching 10. deposition 11. beseechment, obsecration, obtestation

adjure ... 3. ask, beg, bid 4. bind, pray 5. plead 6. appeal, charge 7. beseech, command, entreat, implore, swear in

adjust ... 3. fit, fix, set 4. meet, size, suit, trim, true 5. adapt, align, amend, frame, group, match, right, shape 6. accord, attune, orient, remedy, settle, square 7. arrange, conform, correct, justify, mediate, rectify, redress 8. accustom, organize, regulate 9. condition, habituate, harmonize, reconcile 10. compromise, coordinate, straighten 11. accommodate, systematize

adjuster, adjustor ... 6. fitter 8. arranger 11. coordinator

adjustment ... 4. gear 5. means, terms 7. fitting, suiting 8. bearings, disposal 9. bundobust 10. adaptation, attunement, compromise, concession, conclusion, conformity, regulation, settlement 11. arrangement, disposition, habituation, orientation 12. assimilation, coordination, organization 13. harmonization, methodization, rectification 14. naturalization, reconciliation

adjutant ... 4. aide, ally 6. helper 7. officer 9. assistant, auxiliary

adjutant bird ... 5. stork 6. argala 7. hurgila, marabou

ad lib, ad libit, ad libitum ... 6. make up 7. cadenza 9. extempore, impromptu, improvise 10. at pleasure 11. play it by ear 13. accompaniment

administer ... 4. give 5. apply, issue 6. bestow, direct, govern, manage, supply, tender 7. adhibit, conduct, dispose, execute, fulfill, furnish, give out, husband, perform 8. dispatch, dispense, transact 9. discharge 10. distribute 12. administrate

administer extreme unction ... 5. anele 6. anoint

administration ... 3. use 4. rule 6. employ, giving, policy 7. conduct, regimen 8. bestowal, disposal, issuance, ministry 9. direction, execution 10. employment, government, management, regulation 11. application, directorate, disposition 12. dispensation, ministration 13. apportionment

administration of justice ... 10. judicatory, judicature

administrator ... 2. fu 5. dewan 7. alcalde, manager, provost, trustee 8. director, executor 9. dispenser, executive 12. entrepreneur

admirable ... 5. sweet 6. worthy 7. likable (likeable), winning, winsome 8. adorable, laudable 9. estimable, excellent, marvelous, wonderful 10. creditable 11. commendable, meritorious 12. praiseworthy

admiration ... 6. esteem, liking, regard, wonder 7. respect 8. surprise 9. adoration, amazement, reverence 10. wonderment 11. astoundment, idolization 12. appreciation, confoundment

admire ... 4. like, love 5. adore, honor 6. esteem, regard, revere 7. approve, idolize, respect 8. venerate

admissible ... 3. fit 4. just, sane 5. sound 6. worthy 7. apropos, germane, logical 8. apposite, eligible, rational, relevant, suitable 9. admissory, agreeable, allowable, desirable, pertinent, qualified, receptive, tolerable 10. acceptable, applicable, legitimate, reasonable 11. justifiable, permissible, warrantable 12. satisfactory

admission ... 4. adit 5. entry 6. access, assent, avowal, entree, shrift 8. entrance 9. agreement, allowance, inclusion, letting in, receiving, reception, testimony 10. accordance, admittance, allegation, avouchment, compliance, concession, confession, initiation, permission 11. affiliation, affirmation, declaration 12. acquiescence, assimilation 14. acknowledgment, naturalization 15. enfranchisement

Admission Day holiday ... 6. Nevada (Oct 31) 7. Arizona (Feb 14) 10. California (Sept 9)

admit ... 3. own 4. avow 5. adopt, allow, enter, grant, let in, own up, trust, yield 6. accept, credit, embody, permit 7. adhibit, believe, concede, confess, embrace, include, profess, receive 8. initiate 9. affiliate 10. naturalize 11. acknowledge, incorporate

admittance ... 6. access 8. entrance, sanction 9. admission, letting in 10. initiation

admitted ... 6. indeed 8. believed, conceded 12. acknowledged

admixture ... 5. alloy, blend 6. fusion 7. mixture 8. compound, infusion 10. minglement 11. combination, composition

admonish ... 4. warn 5. chide, scold 6. advise, enjoin, exhort, preach, rebuke, remind 7. caution, monitor, reprove, upbraid 8. dissuade 9. reprimand 11. expostulate,

remonstrate, give warning
admonition ... 6. advice 7. caution, censure, reproof, warning 8. reminder 10. counseling (counselling), dissuasion 11. exhortation 12. remonstrance, reprehension
ado ... 4. fuss, stir 5. doing, hurry 6. bustle, flurry, hubbub, pother, rumpus, tumult 7. trouble, turmoil 9. commotion 10. excitement 11. disturbance
adobe ... 4. clay, silt 5. brick, house (clay)
adolescent ... 3. lad 5. minor, youth 6. nonage 9. pubescent, youngster 10. developing
Adonis (pert to) ...
beloved by .. 9. Aphrodite
festival .. 6. Adonia
modern youth .. 6. a dandy
mother .. 5. Myrrh
slain by .. 8. wild boar
adopt ... 4. take 5. admit, usurp 6. accept, assume, borrow, choose, father, mother, select 7. embrace, espouse, receive, welcome 9. affiliate 10. assimilate, naturalize 11. appropriate
adoption ... 6. choice 8. espousal 9. admission, borrowing, reception 10. acceptance, assumption, conversion, redemption, usurpation 11. embracement 12. appropriation 14. naturalization
adore ... 4. love 5. enjoy, honor 6. esteem, regard, revere 7. idolize, worship 8. venerate
adorn ... 4. clad, deck 5. array, begem, drape, grace, primp, prink 6. attire, bedeck, clothe, enrich 7. bedight, bejewel, dignify, garnish 8. beautify, decorate 9. embellish
adorn (with) ...
color .. 4. gild 5. paint 7. emblaze
feathers .. 7. implume
needlework .. 9. embroider
ornaments .. 6. tinsel 7. imagery
adorned ... 4. clad 6. ornate 7. clothed, prinked 9. decorated 16. chryselephantine
adornment ... 5. decor, frill 6. frills, tinsel 10. decoration, embroidery 13. embellishment 14. beautification
ad patres ... 4. dead 12. to his Fathers
Adriatic (pert to) ...
city .. 5. Fiume 6. Venice 7. Lagosta, Trieste 8. Brandisi
island .. 7. Lagosta
peninsula .. 6. Istria
wind (cold) .. 4. bora
adrift ... 4. asea, free, lost 5. at sea, loose 6. afloat, astray, aweigh, undone 7. aimless, unfixed 8. aberrant, derelict, floating, insecure, straying, unmoored, unstable 9. erroneous 10. bewildered, unanchored, unfastened, without aim
adroit ... 4. neat 5. quick, ready, smart 6. clever, expert, habile, nimble 7. cunning 8. skillful (skilful)

9. dexterous, ingenious
adroitness ... 4. tact 5. knack, skill 7. address 9. dexterity, ingenuity, readiness, smartness
adsorbent, absorbent ... 6. spongy 7. osmotic, soaking 8. blotting 12. assimilative
adulation ... 6. praise 8. flattery 9. adoration 10. compliment
adulterate ... 3. mix 5. alter, taint 6. debase, defile 7. corrupt 8. denature 11. contaminate
adulterated ... 6. impure 7. debased 8. spurious 9. denatured 11. counterfeit 12. contaminated
adust ... 3. tan (color) 4. burn 5. burnt, dried, fiery 6. singed 7. parched 8. scorched 9. blistered
advance ... 2. go 3. aid 4. gain, inch, loan, move, near, nose, pass, push, rise (in price) 5. ahead, boost, creep, march, raise 6. better, stride 7. elevate, process, promote, propose 8. approach, heighten, increase, progress 9. aforehand, elevation, promotion, upgrading 10. accelerate, beforehand, preferment 11. advancement, development, furtherance, improvement, progression
advanced ... 3. old 4. aged 6. modern 7. elderly, forward 8. bettered, enhanced, enriched, foremost, unproved 9. venerable 10. in the front, precocious, senectuous 11. enlightened, progressive
advanced (pert to) ...
equally .. 7. abreast
study .. 7. seminar
time .. 6. modern 8. up–to–date 12. contemporary
advantage ... 3. use 4. boot, bote (bot) edge, gain, good, hold, odds 5. avail, favor, start, stead 6. behalf, behoof, profit 7. benefit, further, promote, service, vantage 8. facility, interest, purchase 9. appliance 10. expedience 11. convenience, superiority 13. accommodation, vantage ground
advantageous ... 5. handy 6. aidful, useful 7. helpful 8. edifying, salutary 9. expedient, favorable 10. auspicious, beneficial, convenient, profitable, propitious, worthwhile 11. encouraging
advent ... 6. coming 7. arrival 8. approach 11. forthcoming
Advent (Eccl) ... 14. Coming of Christ
adventitious ... 4. rale 6. casual 8. acquired 9. extrinsic 10. accidental, incidental 12. nonessential
adventure ... 3. act (heroic), hap 4. bout, dare, deed, feat, gest, risk 5. event, quest, stunt 6. action, hazard 7. episode, exploit, fortune, venture 8. escapade, incident (novel), maneuver, occasion 9. happening 10. enterprise, experience, occurrence 11. performance, undertaking 12. happenstance 13. striking event

14. accomplishment

adventurer... 4. goer 5. sport
7. bounder, gambler, Hessian, parvenu, soldier, upstart 8. gamester, hazarder, merchant, traveler
9. sportsman 10. speculator
16. soldier of fortune

adventuress... 7. demirep 10. gold digger

adventurous... 4. rash 5. risky
6. daring 8. reckless 9. dangerous, foolhardy, hazardous, venturous
11. venturesome 12. enterprising, presumptuous

adversary... 3. foe 5. enemy, Satan
6. foeman 8. opponent 9. archfiend, assailant 10. antagonist, competitor, Philistine

adverse... 3. ill 4. anti 5. loath
7. opposed 8. contrary, converse, opposing, sinister, untoward
9. reluctant, unwilling 10. afflictive, calamitous, indisposed 11. conflicting, disinclined, unfavorable
12. antagonistic, unpropitious

adversity... 6. misery 7. trouble
8. calamity, distress, hardship
9. suffering 10. affliction, misfortune, opposition 11. destitution

advert... 5. recur, refer 6. allude, return

advertent... 7. heedful 9. attentive

advertise... 4. plug, warn 5. boast, boost 6. notify 7. promote, publish
8. announce, ballyhoo, proclaim
9. publicize 10. promulgate

advertisement... 2. ad 4. bill, copy, Neon, plug, sign 6. notice, poster, spread 7. placard 10. commercial (TV)

advice... 4. rede 5. aviso 6. caveat, wisdom 7. counsel, opinion, warning
8. prudence, reminder 9. knowledge
10. admonition, suggestion
11. exhortation, information, instruction 12. consultation, deliberation, intelligence
13. consideration
14. recommendation

advice, containing... 9. mentorial

advisable... 6. proper 7. prudent
9. befitting, desirable, expedient
11. commendable
13. recommendable

advise... 4. rede, tell, warn 5. coach
6. exhort, impart, inform, remind
7. apprise, bethink, caution, counsel, suggest 8. acquaint, admonish, advocate 9. enlighten, recommend
11. communicate, familiarize, take counsel

adviser, advisor... 5. guide 6. Egeria, nestor 7. monitor 8. appriser, kibitzer (sl) 9. counselor (counsellor), informant 10. admonisher

advisers, advisors... 7. Cabinet, Council 10. councilors, counselors, informants

advocate... 3. pro 4. urge 6. advise, backer, defend, deputy, lawyer
7. endorse, espouse, pleader, support 8. attorney, champion,

defender, exponent, plead for
9. barrister, counselor, justifier, paraclete, proponent, recommend, solicitor, supporter 11. protagonist

advocate of the simple life...
14. simplicitarian

adytum... 6. shrine 7. chamber (inner), sanctum 9. sanctuary

Aeetes (pert to)...
daughter.. 5. Medea
keeper of.. 12. Golden Fleece
king of.. 7. Colchis

Aegean Island group...
10. Dodecanese (including twelve)

aegis, egis... 4. care 5. guard
6. screen, shield, symbol (anc)
7. backing, defense 8. guidance
9. fosterage, patronage
10. protection

Aello (Gr)... 5. Harpy 7. monster

Aeneid... 4. poem (Vergil)

aerage... 11. ventilation

aerate... 6. aerify 7. freshen, inflate, refresh 9. ventilate

aerial... 3. ear 4. aery, airy, mast
5. aeric, lofty 6. unreal 7. airlike, antenna 8. ethereal, fanciful, vaporous 9. pneumatic 10. chimerical
12. aeronautical 13. unsubstantial

aerie, eyrie... 4. nest 5. brood (birds)
6. family 9. penthouse

aeriform... 6. unreal 7. gaseous

aeroplane... 8. airplane

Aesir, Norse Gods... 3. Tyr (Tiu), Ull
4. Odin (Woden), Thor (Donar), Vali
5. Bragi 6. Balder, Hoenir 7. Forseti
8. Heimdall

Aeson's son... 5. Jason (Gr Myth)

affability... 6. comity 8. civility, courtesy, urbanity 9. geniality
10. amiability, cordiality, politeness
11. sociability 12. conviviality
14. gregariousness
16. companionability
17. communicativeness

affable... 4. mild 5. civil, suave
6. benign, fluent, social 7. amiable
8. gracious, sociable 9. convivial, courteous 10. accessible, gregarious
11. complaisant 13. communicative

affair... 4. duel, love 5. fight, issue, thing, topic 6. action, gadget, matter, object, soiree 7. concern, problem 8. business, interest, question, sociable 9. gathering, reception, something 10. proceeding
11. get–together, transaction
12. circumstance

affect... 4. melt, move, stir 5. feign, grate, haunt, touch 6. assume, excite, regale, relate, soften, thrill
7. concern, involve, operate, pretend, qualify 8. frequent, interest, simulate
9. influence 11. counterfeit, hypothecate

affectation... 3. air 4. pose, sham
7. display, foppery, pietism
8. elegance, pretense 9. mannerism
12. affectedness 13. artificiality
14. grandiloquence
15. pretentiousness

affected... 4. airy, sham 5. faked,

moved, posey, put–on 6. fal–lal,
formal 7. assumed, beloved, elegant,
feigned, gushing, stilted 8. disposed,
mannered 9. impressed, pretended,
unnatural 10. artificial, euphuistic
11. pretentious 12. ostentatious
13. counterfeited, grandiloquent

affected by . . .
 age . . 6. senile
 love . . 4. smit 7. smitten
 pain . . 4. pang 6. twinge
 paralysis . . 7. paretic
 wonder . . 6. marvel 9. convulsed

affectedly languid . . . 13. lackadaisical

affectedly shy . . . 3. coy, mim 4. prim
6. demure 10. coquettish

affection . . . 4. amor, love 6. animus,
defect, storge (animal) 7. disease,
emotion, feeling, illness, leaning,
passion 8. devotion, fondness,
tendency 9. attribute, infirmity,
sentiment 10. affliction, attachment,
disability, proclivity, propensity,
tenderness 11. disposition,
inclination, temperament

affectionate . . . 4. fond, soft, warm
6. ardent, loving, tender 7. adoring,
devoted, earnest, zealous
8. attached, friendly, parental,
romantic 10. headstrong
13. demonstrative

afferent . . . 6. esodic (nerves), inward
7. sensory 11. centripetal

affiance . . . 5. faith, troth, trust
6. belief, pledge, plight 7. betroth,
promise 8. credence, reliance
9. assurance, betrothal
10. confidence, engagement

affiche . . . 6. poster 7. placard

affidavit . . . 4. oath 9. statement
10. deposition 11. affirmation,
certificate, declaration

affiliation . . . 4. body, sect 5. group,
union 6. church, fusion, hookup,
league 7. faction, lineage
8. adoption, alliance, espousal,
relation 9. admission, alignment,
coalition 10. connection, federation,
fellowship, persuasion
11. association, cooperation
12. denomination, organization
13. confederation, consanguinity
14. naturalization

affinity . . . 3. kin 6. accord, family,
liking 7. kinship, rapport 8. relation,
soul mate 9. agreement
10. attraction, connection, similarity
11. propinquity, resemblance
12. congeniality, relationship
13. compatibility, rapprochement

affirm . . . 3. say 4. aver, avow 5. posit,
state, swear, vouch 6. allege, assert,
attest, avouch, ratify 7. assever,
certify, confirm, declare, endorse,
profess, testify, warrant 8. sanction,
validate 9. predicate, pronounce
10. asseverate 12. authenticate,
substantiate

affirmation . . . 3. vow 4. amen, oath,
word 5. basis 6. ground 7. premise
8. averment 9. admission, assertion,
statement, testimony 10. affirmance,

allegation, avouchment, deposition,
foundation, profession
11. declaration, proposition
12. confirmation, ratification

affirmative . . . 3. aye (ay), nod, yea,
yes 8. dogmatic, positive, thumbs up
(coll) 10. cataphatic (rare)
11. affirmation, declarative,
predicative

affirmatory . . . 9. assertive
11. affirmative, assertional

affix . . . 3. add, fix, pen, tag 4. seal
5. annex, stamp 6. anchor, append,
attach, fasten, impose 7. connect,
subjoin 9. increment
11. superimpose

afflict . . . 3. ail, try, vex 4. hurt, pain
5. upset, wound 6. grieve, harass,
sicken 7. agitate, chasten, derange,
disturb, oppress, torment, trouble
8. disorder, distress, lacerate
9. overthrow, persecute

afflicted . . . 3. sad 5. ailed 6. pained
7. smitten, wounded 8. troubled
9. depressed, suffering 10. distressed

affliction . . . 3. woe 4. airs, bane, evil,
pain, pest 5. curse, grief 6. misery,
plague 7. illness, scourge, torment,
trouble 8. calamity, distress, hardship
9. adversity 10. misfortune, visitation
12. wretchedness

afflictive . . . 6. severe 11. causing pain,
distressing

affluence . . . 4. ease, flow 6. afflux,
influx, plenty, riches, wealth
8. opulence, richness 9. abundance,
concourse, plenitude, profusion
10. prosperity

affluent . . . 4. rich 5. flush 6. fluent
7. copious, moneyed, opulent,
wealthy 8. abundant, well–to–do
9. luxuriant, pecunious, plenteous
10. prosperous

afford . . . 4. bear, cost, give, lend
5. allow, endow, grant, spare, stand,
yield 6. accord, confer, invest, supply
7. furnish, provide, support, undergo

affray . . . 3. war 4. feud, fray, riot
5. brawl, fight, melee, scrap (sl),
set–to (coll) 6. battle, combat, tumult
7. assault, contest, quarrel, scuffle
9. encounter 11. disturbance

affright . . . 5. alarm, scare 6. appall
(appal), dismay 7. confuse, startle,
terrify 8. frighten

affront . . . 4. defy, face, meet, slap
5. abuse 6. harass, insult, offend,
oppose 7. offense, outrage, provoke
8. confront, dishonor, envisage,
ill–treat, irritate 9. encounter,
humiliate, indignity 11. provocation

afghan (pert to) . . .
 fox . . 6. corsac
 language . . 11. Afghanistan
 prince . . 4. amir (ameer), emir (emeer)
 rug . . 5. Herat 6. carpet
 stitch . . 7. crochet
 wrap . . 7. blanket (woolen)

Afghanistan . . .
 capital . . 5. Kabul
 city . . 5. Herat 8. Kandahar
 language . . 6. Pushtu 7. Persian

mountain.. 9. Hindu Kush
Pass (famed).. 6. Khyber
people.. 6. Durani 7. Sistani
pony.. 4. yabu (yaboo)
religion.. 5. Islam
river.. 5. Indus
tribe.. 4. Safi, Ulus
Africa... see also *African*
desert.. 6. Libyan, Sahara 8. Kalahari
gulf.. 4. Aden 5. Gabes, Sidra
island (largest).. 10. Madagascar
lake.. 6. Nyassa 8. Victoria
   10. Tanganyika
Mt.. 5. Kenya, Natal 8. Cameroon
   9. Ruwenzori 11. Kilimanjaro
river.. 4. Nile 5. Congo, Niger
   7. Senegal, Zambezi
size (in world).. 6. second
African (pert to)...
charm, fetish.. 4. juju 6. grigri
drum.. 8. bamboula
enclosure.. 4. boma 5. kraal
garment.. 4. haik, tobe 6. kaross
grass.. 7. esparto
grassland.. 4. veld (veldt) 8. bushveld
harp (Nubian).. 5. nanga
hemp.. 3. ife
herb.. 4. ocra
instrument.. 4. gora (gorah) 5. nanga,
   rebab 6. balafo
language.. 3. Ibo 4. Zulu 5. Bantu,
   Sotho, Tonga 6. Somali, Yoruba
   7. Ashanti (Ashantee)
palm.. 6. ronier 7. palmyra
secret society.. 4. Egbo (Negro)
   8. Bachichi (cannibal)
soldier.. 5. spahi 6. askari
sorcery.. 5. obeah
spiritual power.. 4. ngai
thong (rawhide).. 4. riem
tree.. 3. oak 4. akee, baku, cola,
   etua, shea 5. artar, sassy, siris
   6. baobab
African people (pert to)...
Islamitic sect.. 9. Almohades
Natal.. 4. Zulu 6. kaffir 7. Amazulu
Negro society.. 4. Egbo 6. Ogboni
pygmy.. 4. Akka, Doko 5. Afifi, Batwa
   7. Bambute
race, tribe.. 4. Arab, Boer, Copt, Kafa
   (Kaffa), Zulu 5. Bantu, Fulah, Negro
   6. Berber, Kabyle, Kaffir, Nubian,
   Semite, Somali 7. Ashanti (Ashantee),
   Bushman, Swahili 8. Bechuana
   9. Hottentot
African wildlife (pert to)...
antelope.. 3. gnu 4. oryx 5. addax,
   eland, oribi 6. impala, rhebok
   7. blaubok (small), blesbok, gemsbok
   10. duikerbuck, hartebeest
bird.. 4. lory, taha 6. weaver
   8. umbretti 9. beefeater, hammerkop
fly.. 4. kivu 6. tsetse
goat.. 5. Capra
horse disease.. 5. surra
mammal.. 8. anteater, pangolin
monkey.. 4. mona, waag 6. baboon,
   grivet, guenon 7. guereza 8. talapoin
peacock.. 5. paauw
rhinoceros.. 6. borele 7. keitloa
rodent.. 4. jird 5. ratel
sheep.. 4. zenu 5. oudad (udad)

squirrel.. 5. xerus
stork.. 6. simbil 7. marabou
toad.. 7. Xenopus
worm.. 3. loa
aft, after... 4. anon, past, rear
   5. abaft, later, since 6. astern,
   behind 9. posterior 10. subsequent,
   succeeding
after (pert to)...
all.. 11. considering 12. nevertheless
awhile.. 4. anon 5. later
breast (Zool).. 10. metathorax
date.. 8. postdate
dinner.. 12. postprandial
dinner coffee.. 9. demitasse
prefix.. 4. meta, post
aftermath... 4. crop 5. rowen
   9. afterglow 12. consequences
aftermost... 4. last 7. aftmost
   8. hindmost, rearmost
afterpiece... 3. act 4. heel 5. epode
   exode 8. postlude 9. aftercome,
   afterpart, tailpiece
after song... 5. epode
afterthought... 6. regret, sequel
   10. reflection 13. arrière–pensée,
   second thought
afterward, afterwards... 4. next
   5. after, later, since 6. ensues 7. by
   and by 9. afterhand 10. thereafter
   11. in the future 12. subsequently
aga, agha... 5. chief, title
   9. commander
agacant, agacante... 8. exciting
   11. provocative
agacella (Her)... 8. antelope
again... 2. re (pref) 3. yet 4. anew,
   anon, back, over, then 5. ditto,
   newly, often, recur 6. afresh, de
   novo, encore, rather 7. freshly
   8. eftsoons (eftsoon), likewise,
   moreover, once more 9. twice over
   10. repeatedly, second time
   11. furthermore
against... 2. on, to, vs 3. con, non
   4. agin (dial), anti, upon 6. contra,
   versus 7. counter, opposed, towards
   8. averse to, converse, opposite
against the...
clock.. 4. race, time 7. in haste
grain.. 6. across 7. oblique
   9. backwards 10. contrarily
   11. unwillingly
law.. 7. illegal, illicit 8. wrongful
   12. illegitimate
sun.. 16. counterclockwise
agal... 4. cord (Bedouin head wrap)
agalloch... 4. agar 5. aloes 7. linalon
   8. calambac 9. eaglewood, lignaloes
agama, agamoid... 6. iguana, lizard
Agamemnon (pert to)...
brother.. 8. Menelaus
daughter.. 7. Electra 9. Iphigenia
father.. 8. Atreus
king of.. 7. Mycenae
rival.. 9. Aegisthus
son.. 7. Orestes
wife.. 12. Clytemnestra
wife's paramour.. 9. Aegisthus
agape... 4. agog, ajar 6. aghast,
   gaping 7. curious, yawning
   8. open–eyed 9. expectant, love

feast (Chr) 10. astonished,
bewildered, breathless
agate ... 3. taw 4. onyx, ruby, type
5. color 6. achate, rnarble (game),
pebble, quartz 10. birthstone,
chalcedony
agave ... 4. aloe 5. datil 6. maguey,
mescal, pulque 8. henequen
age ... 3. eon, era, old 4. aeon, date,
eral, eval, time 5. cycle, epoch,
major, minor, older, ripen 6. junior,
mature, mellow, modern, period,
remote, senior 7. century, grow old
8. eternity, lifetime, maturity
9. antiquate, senectude
10. generation
Age ... 3. Air, Ice, Jet 4. Iron, Jazz,
Yuga 5. Azoic, Kalpa, Space, Steel,
Stone 6. Atomic, Bronze, Copper,
Eocene, Gilded, Golden, Heroic, Silver
7. Glacial, Homeric, Miocene
8. Cambrian, Cenozoic, Mesozoic
10. Geological, Supersonic
11. Elizabethan
aged ... 3. eld, old 5. anile, hoary,
olden 6. feeble, infirm, senile
7. ancient, elderly, Ogygian
8. gerontic 9. Nestorian
10. senectuous
agency ... 5. means 6. action, medium,
office 8. function 9. operation
10. collection, commission, efficiency,
management 14. intermediation
15. instrumentality
Agency, News ... 2. AP, UP 3. DNB,
INS, UPI 4. Tass 5. Domei
7. Reuters 13. International
agenda ... 5. slate 7. agendum (sing),
program 9. memoranda
14. memorandum book, things to be
done
agent ... 3. spy 4. doer, test, tool
5. actor, buyer, envoy 6. author,
broker, deputy, factor, medium
7. creator, proctor, reagent, scalper
8. aumildar, emissary, operator,
salesman 9. canvasser, comprador,
consignee, go—between, operative
10. instrument, originator
11. facilitator 12. intermediary
14. representative
Ages ... 4. Dark 6. Middle
aggrandize ... 5. add to, exalt
6. extend 7. advance, enhance,
enlarge, glorify, magnify, promote
8. increase 10. exaggerate
aggravate ... 3. irk, nag, vex 4. miff,
rile, twit 5. anger, annoy, chafe,
pique, sting, taunt, tease, worry
6. nettle, pester, ruffle, worsen
7. bedevil, disturb, incense, magnify,
provoke 8. heighten, increase, irritate
9. infuriate, intensify 10. exasperate
aggravation ... 6. bother 7. anguish,
torment, trouble 8. vexation
9. annoyance, worsening
10. affliction, excitement, irritation,
resentment 11. displeasure,
provocation 12. exasperation
15. intensification
aggregate ... 3. all, sum 4. mass
5. total, whole 6. amount, volume

8. compound, ensemble 9. accretion
10. collection 11. combination
12. accumulation
aggregate (pert to) ...
definable member .. 4. unit
fruit .. 7. etaerio
in the .. 7. en masse, totally
8. together 12. collectively
of plants .. 5. flock, flora 7. cluster
aggregation ... 4. heap 5. group, union
9. congeries 10. assemblage,
collection 11. combination
12. accumulation, amalgamation
13. consolidation
aggression ... 6. attack, injury
7. assault, offense 8. invasion
9. hostility, intrusion, offensive
10. enterprise, initiative
11. provocation 12. encroachment
14. aggressiveness
aggressive ... 7. hostile, pushing
9. assertive, attacking, bellicose,
combative, offensive 10. assaulting,
pugnacious 11. belligerent,
contentious, provocative
12. enterprising
aggrieve ... 4. pain 6. grieve 7. afflict,
oppress, trouble 9. displease,
persecute, tyrannize
aggrieved ... 6. pained, woeful
7. doleful 8. mournful 9. sorrowful
10. displeased
aghast ... 4. agog 5. agape 6. afraid
8. appalled, dismayed 9. astounded,
horrified, terrified 10. astonished
agile ... 4. fast, spry 5. alert, brisk,
quick, ready, swift 6. active, lively,
nimble, prompt, supple 7. lissome,
springe 11. expeditious
aging ... 6. doting, fading 8. maturing,
ripening 9. mellowing, senescent
10. senescence
agio ... 7. premium 8. discount,
exchange 9. brokerage 13. money
changing
agitate ... 3. fan, jar, wey 4. fret,
move, plot, rile, stir 5. alarm, churn,
rouse, shake, upset 6. debate,
devise, excite, foment, incite, ruffle
7. canvass, perturb, revolve, trouble
8. disquiet, distract, distress
10. discompose
agitated ... 7. anxious, excited, ruffled
8. alarming, troubled 9. disturbed,
perturbed, turbulent 10. distressed
11. discomposed, overwrought
agitation ... 4. fury, rage, stir 5. alarm,
storm 6. debate, dither, foment,
frenzy, furore, hubbub, tumult, unrest,
uproar 7. anxiety, flutter, shaking,
turmoil 8. disorder, distress,
upheaval, vexation 9. commotion,
trepidity 10. discussion, excitement,
incitement, turbulence
11. disturbance, fomentation,
trepidation 12. deliberation,
perturbation, restlessness
agnate ... 3. sib 4. akin 6. allied
7. connate, kindred, related (father's
side) 10. equiparent 11. correlative
14. consanguineous
agnomen ... 4. name 5. alias, nomen

7. epithet, surname 8. nickname
agnus castus (Eccl)... 4. lamb
  6. chaste 14. tree of chastity
Agnus Dei, Lamb of God... 4. disk
  6. anthem, prayer 7. the Mass (part)
ago, agone... 2. by 4. erst, gone,
  over, past, yore 5. since 6. bygone,
  passed 7. extinct
agog... 4. avid, keen 5. agape, astir,
  eager 6. lively, wonder 7. all eyes,
  curious, excited, zestful
  8. open—eyed, vigilant 9. expectant,
  impatient 10. astonished, breathless
agonize... 4. pain, rack 6. grieve,
  harrow, strive 7. crucify, torture
  8. struggle 10. excruciate
agony... 4. pain, pang, rack 5. grief,
  gripe, panic, throe 7. anguish,
  torment, torture 8. distress
  9. suffering 11. crucifixion
agrarian... 5. rural 6. rustic, sylvan
  (silvan) 7. bucolic, hoosier
  8. agrestic, Arcadian, frontier,
  pastoral 10. campestral, hinterland,
  provincial 11. countrified
  12. agricultural
agree... 3. fit 4. give, jive, make,
  rime, side 5. chime, ditto, grant,
  match, rhyme, tally 6. accede,
  accord, assent, commit, comply,
  concur, engage, submit 7. bargain,
  comport, concede, conform, consent,
  promise 8. coincide, contract
  9. acquiesce, harmonize, stipulate
  10. coordinate, correspond
agreeable... 4. nice 5. amene, sapid,
  suave 6. comely, dulcet, savory
  7. amiable, likable, welcome, willing
  8. charming, friendly, obliging,
  pleasant, pleasing 9. accordant,
  compliant, desirable, indulgent
  10. acceptable, compatible,
  concordant, consenting, euphonious,
  harmonious 11. conformable,
  considerate 12. reconcilable,
  satisfactory
agreement... 4. mise, pact 5. terms
  6. accord, assent, cartel, parity,
  treaty, unison 7. bargain, compact,
  concord, consent, entente, promise,
  rapport 8. contract, covenant, identity
  9. accession, consensus
  10. accordment, comparison,
  compliance, conformity, similarity
  11. coincidence, concurrence,
  parallelism, stipulation
agrestic... 5. rural 6. rustic 7. bucolic
  8. pastoral 10. provincial
agriculture... 7. culture, farming, tillage
  8. agrology, agronomy 9. husbandry
  10. agrotechny 11. cultivation
  13. sharecropping
agriculture (pert to)...
  goddess of.. 3. Ops 4. Gaea (Gaia)
  5. Ceres, Flora 6. Pomona, Vacuna
  7. Demeter
  god of.. 4. Nabu, Nebo 6. Faunus
  8. Dionysus
  means of.. 3. hoe 4. plow (plough)
  6. harrow, header, reaper, seeder
  7. combine, planter, tractor
  8. thrasher 10. cultivator

  11. caterpillar
  ref to.. 7. georgic
  science, crop growing.. 11. arviculture
  terms.. 5. arado, grove, ranch, thorp
  6. garden, hamlet 7. cropper,
  orchard 8. haymaker, vineyard
  9. homestead
agriculturist... 6. farmer 7. planter
  10. agricolist, husbandman
Agrippina's son... 4. Nero
agrise... 5. abhor, dread 6. loathe
  7. shudder, terrify, tremble 8. affright
agronomy, study of... 11. agriculture
aground... 5. stuck 6. ashore
  7. swamped, wrecked 8. grounded,
  stranded 10. high and dry
agrypnia... 5. vigil 8. insomnia
  13. sleeplessness
agua... 4. toad 5. water
aguacate... 7. avocado
ague... 5. chill, fever 7. disease,
  malaria, shaking, shivers 9. shivering
ague tree... 9. sassafras
agueweed... 7. boneset, gentian
Ahab (pert to)...
  daughter.. 7. Athalie
  king of.. 6. Israel
  wife.. 7. Jezebel
ahead... 2. on 3. pre (pref) 4. fore
  5. afore, early 6. before, onward
  7. advance, forward, leading
  10. successful, surpassing
ahoy... 4. hail, yo—ho 5. hello 8. ship
  ahoy 9. attention
ahu... 5. mound 7. gazelle
  8. memorial
ai... 5. sloth 11. exclamation
aid... 4. abet, aide, help, pony
  5. allay, devil (printer's), favor, serve
  6. assist, helper, incite, relief,
  remedy, succor 7. benefit, service,
  stipend, subsidy, support 8. befriend,
  ministry 9. alleviate, allowance,
  assistant 10. assistance, benefactor
  11. countenance 13. accommodation
aim... 3. end, fix, way 4. bent, goal,
  plan 5. point, scope 6. aspire,
  direct, intend, intent, object, strive
  7. bearing, current, meaning,
  purpose 8. endeavor 9. direction,
  intention, objective 11. destination
aimful... 8. aspiring 10. purposeful
aimless... 4. idle 5. blind, loose
  6. chance, random 8. drifting
  9. desultory, orderless, senseless
  10. designless, unarranged,
  undirected 11. meaningless,
  purposeless, unorganized
aine... 5. elder 6. senior
air... 3. gas, oam, sky 4. aria, aura,
  mien, tune, wind 5. draft, ether,
  ozone, vapor 6. aerate, aerial,
  aspect, breath, breeze, bubble,
  manner, melody, oxygen 7. aerator,
  bearing, climate, display, hyaline,
  posture, publish, refresh 8. attitude,
  aviation, behavior, buoyance,
  demeanor, hydrogen, presence
  9. lightness, publicize, ventilate
  10. appearance, atmosphere,
  deportment, navigation
  11. haughtiness 12. stratosphere

air (pert to) . . .
  disease . . **5.** bends **7.** caisson
    12. aeroembolism
  music . . **4.** aria, lilt, solo, tune
    6. melody **7.** arietta, sortita
  passage . . **4.** duct, flue, vent
    7. pharynx **9.** ventiduct
  pressure unit . . **8.** millebar
  stone . . **8.** aerolite **9.** meteorite
  term . . **5.** aural **6.** flight, flying **9.** jet
    stream, katabatic **11.** aeronautics
  tight . . **5.** close, proof **6.** sealed
    7. compact **8.** hermetic **9.** resistant
    11. impermeable
  travel . . **6.** jet lag **7.** skyjack
aircraft . . . **3.** jet **4.** kite, link **5.** avion,
    blimp **6.** bomber, glider **7.** airship,
    aviette, balloon, biplane, chopper
    8. airplane, jetliner, triplane, turbojet,
    zeppelin **9.** amphibian, dirigible,
    fixed-wing, monoplane, orthopter,
    simulator, spaceship, transport,
    turboprop **10.** helicopter, hydroplane,
    whirlybird
aircraft (pert to) . . .
  carrier . . **7.** flattop
  designer . . **8.** Sikorsky
  formation . . **5.** fleet **7.** echelon
  inventor . . **6.** Wright (Brothers)
  motorless . . **6.** glider
  part . . **3.** fin, pod **4.** keel, tail, wing
    5. rotor **6.** cabane **7.** aileron,
    cockpit, nacelle **8.** fusilage
    9. empennage (tail)
airily . . . **5.** gaily **6.** thinly **7.** lightly,
    loftily **8.** jauntily **10.** delicately
    13. pretentiously **14.** ostentatiously
airiness . . . **6.** rarity **7.** tenuity
    8. delicacy **9.** gauziness, gustiness,
    lightness, loftiness, unreality, windiness
    10. breeziness, jauntiness
    16. lightheartedness, unsubstantiality
airing . . . **4.** walk **8.** exposure
airport (pert to) . . . **4.** beam, dock, gate,
    shed, taxi **5.** apron, pylon, tower
    6. hangar, runway, skycap **7.** airpost,
    fairway, jetport, taxiway **8.** airfield,
    airstrip, heliport **9.** aerodrome
    (airdrome), helidrome
airy . . . **3.** gay **4.** aery, cool, rare, thin
    5. foamy, light, lofty, merry, windy
    6. aerial, breezy, drafty, frothy, jaunty,
    lively **7.** gaseous, haughty, soaring
    8. animated, aspiring, delicate,
    ethereal, fanciful, feathery, flippant,
    towering, volatile **9.** gossamery,
    vivacious **10.** chimerical, phantasmal
    11. atmospheric **12.** lighthearted,
    ostentatious
aiseweed . . . **8.** goutweed
aisle . . . **4.** lane, nave **5.** alley **6.** artery,
    avenue **7.** passage **8.** corridor
    10. passageway
ait, eyot . . . **3.** oat **4.** holm, isle, reef
    5. atoll, islet **6.** island
aitu . . . **3.** god **5.** demon **6.** spirit
Aix . . . **4.** duck
aizle . . . **4.** soot **5.** ember, spark
Ajax (pert to) . . .
  called . . **11.** Ajax the Less (next
    swiftest to Achilles)

  father . . **7.** Telamen
  hero of . . **8.** The Iliad (Homer)
ajonjoli . . . **6.** sesame
akimbo . . . **4.** bent **6.** angled, hooked
    7. angular, crooked
akin . . . **3.** sib **4.** like, near **5.** close
    6. agnate, allied **7.** cognate,
    germane, kindred, related, similar
    9. connected **10.** correlated
    14. consanguineous
ala . . . **4.** wing **8.** winglike
a la . . . **2.** so **4.** thus **11.** identically
    13. in the manner of
Alabama . . .
  capital . . **10.** Montgomery
  Capitol, Confederate (2 months) . .
    10. White House (1st 1861)
  carnival . . **11.** Azalea Trail
  city . . **6.** Mobile **7.** Gadsden
    10. Birmingham
  monument . . **11.** Russell Cave
  museum . . **22.** George Washington
    Carver
  native woman (famed) . . **11.** Helen
    Keller
  President, Confederate . . **5.** Davis
    (Jefferson)
  State admission . . **12.** Twenty-second
  State bird . . **12.** yellowhammer
  State flower . . **8.** camellia
  State motto . . **21.** We Dare Defend
    Our Rights
  State nickname . . **12.** Heart of Dixie
  statue (huge) . . **6.** Vulcan
alabaster . . . **6.** gypsum, marble
    7. mineral
alacrity . . . **4.** zest **7.** avidity
    9. briskness, eagerness, immediacy,
    quickness, readiness, swiftness
    10. promptness **11.** promptitude,
    punctuality, willingness
    13. sprightliness
Aladdin (pert to) . . .
  possessor of (magic) . . **4.** lamp, ring
  spirit (of magic) . . **4.** jinn
  window . . **4.** task (impossible)
  youth (character) . . **13.** Arabian Nights
á la diable . . . **7.** deviled (devilled)
    8. seasoned
alameda . . . **4.** mall, walk **5.** prado
    9. esplanade, promenade
Alamo . . . **6.** poplar (tree) **7.** Mission
    (San Antonio, Tex)
a la mode . . . **4.** mode **5.** smart
    6. modish, spruce **7.** fashion, stylish,
    voguish **8.** up-to-date **9.** stylishly
    11. fashionably **12.** with ice cream
alan . . . **3.** dog (Her)
alar (pert to) . . . **4.** wing **6.** pteric
    8. axillary, shoulder
alarm . . . **3.** din **4.** call, fear, flap
    5. alert, broil, clock, daunt, panic,
    scare **6.** alarum, arouse, dismay,
    fright, terror, tocsin **7.** startle, terrify,
    warning **8.** affright, frighten
    11. trepidation **12.** apprehension
    13. consternation
alarmist . . . **6.** scarer **9.** pessimist,
    terrorist **10.** frightener
    11. scaremonger
alas . . . **2.** ah, ay, oh **3.** ach, heu, och

4. oime 5. alack, ohone 7. woe is me 8. lackaday

Alaska ... see also *Alaskan*
capital .. 6. Juneau
city .. 4. Nome 5. Sitka 7. Skagway 9. Anchorage, Fairbanks, Ketchikan
discoverer .. 11. Vitus Bering
fish .. 6. salmon, wachna 7. inconnu
glacier .. 4. Muir
highway .. 5. Alcan 6. Alaska
island .. 6. Kodiak, Unimak 7. Diomede (Little), Nunivak 9. Aleutians, Probilofs
mountain .. 3. Ada 5. Foraker 8. McKinley (highest in N Am), Wrangell
northernmost point .. 11. Point Barrow
peninsula .. 5. Kenai 6. Seward
rapids .. 10. Whitehorse
river .. 5. Yukon 9. Kuskokwim
State admission .. 10. Forty–ninth
State bird .. 9. (willow) ptarmigan
State flower .. 11. forget–me–not
State symbol .. 9. bald eagle
strait .. 6. Bering
volcano .. 6. Katmai 8. Wrangell

Alaskan (pert to) ...
boat .. 5. kayak, umiak 7. bidarka (bidarkee)
codfish .. 6. wachna
liquor .. 9. hoochinoo
native .. 3. Aht 5. Aleut, Haida, Tinna 6. Ahtena, Eskimo 7. Tlingit 8. Aleutian 9. Tsimpsean 10. Athapascan

albacore ... 4. tuna 5. tunny 6. bonito, germon

Albania ...
capital .. 6. Tirana
city .. 5. Berat 6. Durres, Valona 7. Scutari 8. Elbasani
dialect .. 4. Gheg, Tosk
lake .. 6. Prespa 7. Scutari
mountain .. 5. Koreb 6. Pindus
river .. 4. Drin 6. Bojana
soldier .. 7. palikar
triba .. 4. Cham

albatross ... 5. nelly (sooty) 6. burden 7. pelican 9. mallemuck

albe (anc) ... 5. album

albert (pert to) ...
jewelry .. 10. watch chain
medal .. 4. gold (for bravery)

Albion ... 7. England (Poet)

albumin ... 5. glair 7. protein 9. endosperm

alcazar ... 6. palace 8. fortress

alchemy ... 5. magic 6. change 7. sorcery 10. changeover, conversion

alcohol ... 5. drink 6. liquor 7. ethanol, spirits, talitol, terpene 8. beverage 9. aqua vitae, firewater 10. intoxicant

alcoholic beverage ... 3. gin, rum 4. beer, brew, grog, malt, mead, wine 5. booze, hooch, negus, punch, vodka 6. arrack (arrak), brandy, mao–tai, whisky (whiskey) 7. bourbon, cordial, liqueur, tequila 8. champers (Brit sl), cocktail, highball 9. applejack, champagne, moonshine

alcoholism ... 9. addiction, oenomania

10. dipsomania 11. drunkenness 12. intoxication

Alcott character ... 2. Jo 3. Amy, Meg 4. Beth

alcove ... 3. bay 4. cove, nook 5. arbor, bower, kiosk, niche, oriel 6. carrel, recess 7. cubicle, dinette, pergola 8. alhacena

alder (pert to) ...
chief .. 5. ruler 6. prince
fishing .. 3. fly (artificial)
tree .. 8. sagerose (yellow)

ale ... 3. mum 4. beer, flip 5. stout 6. alegar, liquor (malt) 8. festival

alee ... 7. leeward (opp of windward)

Aleppo (pert to) ...
city .. 5. Syria
grass .. 7. Johnson
stone .. 3. gem 5. agate 8. eye agate

alert ... 4. keen, warn, wary 5. agile, alarm, alive, aware, brisk, peart (pert), quick, ready, sharp 6. active, bright, lively, nimble, prompt 7. guarded 8. vigilant, watchful 9. attentive, observant, sprightly, wide–awake 11. circumspect

Aleut ... 4. Atka 6. Eskimo 7. Unungun 8. Unalaska

Aleutians ...
islands (chain) .. 8. volcanic
native of .. 5. Aleut
site .. 6. Alaska 9. Bering Sea

alewife ... 4. fish 7. herring, pompano, walleye 9. gaspereau

Alexander the Great (pert to) ...
birthplace .. 5. Pella (Macedonia)
conqueror of .. 6. Persia
expedition .. 10. Hellespont
horse .. 10. Bucephalus

Alexandria, Egypt ...
bishop .. 5. Arius 10. Athanasius 12. Eratosthenes
island .. 6. Pharos
obelisks .. 17. Cleopatra's Needles '(now in NY City & London)
ruler .. 7. Ptolemy
world wonder .. 10. Lighthouse (Pharos)

alfa ... 5. grass 7. esparto

alfalfa ... 3. hay 5. medic 6. clover, fodder 8. lucerne (lucern)

alforja ... 3. bag 5. pouch 6. wallet 9. saddlebag

alfresco ... 4. airy 7. open–air, outside

alga, algae ... 4. cell, moss, nori 5. Dasya, fungi 6. Alaria, diatom, fungus 7. seaweed 8. plankton 9. spirulina, stonewort

Algeria ...
capital .. 7. Algiers
Mohammedan saint .. 8. Marabout
monastery .. 5. ribat
mountain .. 5. Atlas (Range)
native .. 5. Arabs 7. Berbers, Kabyles
ruler .. 3. bey, dey
ship .. 5. xebec
soldier .. 5. spahi (spahee) 6. Zouave

algid ... 3. icy 4. cold 5. brisk, crisp, nippy 6. frigid, frosty, wintry 7. ice–cold

algodon ... 6. cotton

algology, study of ... 5. algae

8. seaweeds
Algonquian spirit... 6. manito
(manitou)
Algonquian tribe... 4. Cree, Sauk
5. Miami 6. Ottawa 7. Arapaho,
Ojibway, Shawnee 8. Cheyenne,
Delaware 9. Blackfoot
Alhambra (pert to)...
architecture.. 7. Moorish
palace, alcazar of.. 12. Moorish Kings
site.. 7. Granada (Spain)
alias... 6. anonym 7. epithet
8. cognomen, nickname 9. otherwise,
pseudonym, sobriquet
Ali Baba (pert to)...
adventurer.. 4. cave (Forty Thieves)
password to cave.. 6. Sesame
tale.. 13. Arabian Nights
alien... 3. ger 5. fremd 6. exotic,
remote 7. adverse, foreign, hostile,
opposed, strange 8. outsider,
stranger 9. foreigner, peregrine,
unrelated 10. extraneous, unfriendly
11. incongruous
alienate... 4. part, wean 6. demise,
detach, devest, divest, divide
8. disunite, estrange, separate
alienation... 4. outs 5. split 6. breach
8. disfavor 10. conveyance,
falling–out, withdrawal
12. amortization, disaffection,
estrangement
alienist... 12. psychiatrist
aliform... 8. winglike 10. wing–shaped
alight... 4. land, rest, stop 5. ditch,
lodge, perch 6. settle 7. burning,
descend, lighted 8. dismount
align, aline... 4. true 5. level, match
6. equate, line up 7. arrange,
marshal 10. collineate, straighten
11. parallelize
alike... 3. iso (comb form) 4. akin,
like, same, twin 7. similar, uniform
8. selfsame 9. duplicate, identical
10. homonymous
17. indistinguishable
aliment... 4. food, keep 5. broma,
manna 7. nurture, pabulum, support
9. nutriment, nutrition, refection
10. sustenance 11. nourishment,
refreshment
alimentary canal, part... 5. mouth
7. pharynx, stomach 9. esophagus,
intestine
alimony... 7. stipend 8. estovers
9. allotment
aline... see *align*
alipin... 5. slave (Phil)
alipod... 3. bat 10. wing–footed
aliquid... 8. somewhat 9. something
aliquot... 4. part 5. prime 7. decimal,
digital, divisor, partial 10. fractional,
reciprocal 11. submultiple (opp of
aliquant)
alive... 3. vif 4. keen 5. alert, awake,
brisk, vital 6. extant, lively, loving,
zoetic 7. animate, current, topical
8. animated, existent 9. breathing,
conscious, sensitive, sprightly
11. clear–witted, unforgotten
alkali... 3. lye 4. salt, soda
8. saltwort

alkaline... 3. reh 4. usar 6. alkali
7. antacid, nonacid
alkaline forming... 10. kaligenous
alkaloid... 6. codein, conine, eserin
7. aricine, caffein, cocaine, codeine
8. atropine, morphine 10. strychnine
13. physostigmine
alkaloid (pert to)...
bark.. 7. aricine
bean.. 13. physostigmine
beverage.. 8. caffeine (caffein)
drug.. 7. cocaine, codeine
8. morphine 10. strychnine
extract.. 6. curare (curari) 11. arrow
poison
hemlock.. 7. coniine
ipecac.. 7. emetine
lupine.. 8. lupinine
mustard seed.. 7. sinapin
all... 3. pan (pref), sum 4. omni (pref),
only, toto 5. alone, every, sum of,
total, tutti, whole 6. entire, wholly
7. perfect 8. ensemble, entirely,
totality 9. aggregate, everybody
10. altogether, completely,
everything, thoroughly 11. exclusively
all (pert to)...
absorbing.. 4. main 5. chief, prime
6. ruling 7. capital, leading, primary
8. foremost 9. paramount, principal
11. controlling
around.. 5. handy 9. versatile
devouring.. 6. greedy 9. rapacious
10. gluttonous
in all.. 9. generally 10. on the whole
inclusive.. 6. global 7. omneity
8. catholic, ecumenic, pandemic
9. universal 12. cosmopolitan
knowing.. 4. wise 6. divine
10. omniscient
powerful.. 6. divine 7. all–wise,
supreme 8. absolute, almighty
9. all–seeing 10. all–knowing,
omnipotent, omniscient, ubiquitous
the same.. 9. identical 10. equivalent
12. nevertheless
Allah... 3. God 5. deity 12. Supreme
Being
allay... 4. cool, ease 5. abate, check,
slake 6. pacify, soothe, subdue
7. appease, assuage, compose,
relieve, repress, satisfy 8. moderate
9. alleviate
allée... 4. mall, walk 5. aisle
6. avenue 7. passage
allege... 4. aver, cite 5. offer, plead,
quote, state 6. adduce, affirm,
assert, assign 7. advance, ascribe,
declare, present, pretend, profess,
propose 8. maintain 9. attribute
allegiance... 3. tie 5. bond 5. faith,
liege 6. fealty, homage 7. loyalty
8. devotion, fidelity, firmness
9. adherence, constancy
12. faithfulness 13. steadfastness
allegory... 5. fable, story 6. emblem
7. parable 8. apologue
alleviate... 4. ease 5. abate, allay,
erase, quiet, salve, slake 6. lessen,
pacify, reduce, soften, solace, soothe
7. assuage, compose, lighten, relieve
8. mitigate, moderate, palliate

9. extenuate 11. tranquilize

alley... 3. mig (marble), way 4. lane, mall, path, slum 5. aisle, byway, tewer 6. arcade, artery, byroad 8. cul–de–sac

alliance... 4. pact 5. union 6. fusion, league, treaty 7. compact, entente 8. affinity, agnation, covenant 9. coalition 10. federation 11. association, combination, confederacy 13. confederation

allied... 4. akin 6. agnate, linked, united 7. cognate, germane, kindred, leagued, related, similar 10. associated, correlated

alligator... 5. gator, niger 6. Caiman, cayman, jacare (yacare) 7. lagarto 9. crocodile

alligator pear... 7. avocado 8. aguacate

alliteration... 4. rime 5. rhyme 6. jingle 9. assonance 10. repetition

allocate... 4. deal, mete 5. allot 6. assign, locate, ordain 7. appoint, arrange, consign, reserve 9. apportion 10. distribute

allocation... 8. disposal 9. billeting 11. collocation, disposition 12. distribution

allot... 3. fix 4. cast, dole, mete 5. grant 6. assign, billet, design, intend, ordain, ration, select 7. appoint, destine, specify 9. apportion, attribute, prescribe 11. appropriate

allotment... 5. cavel, share 6. ration 7. subsidy 10. allocation, assignment, ordainment 13. apportionment

allow... 3. let 4. bear, give 5. admit, think 6. endure, permit, rebate, suffer 7. approve, concede, suppose 8. consider, discount, tolerate 9. authorize 11. acknowledge

allowance... 3. fee 4. tare, tret 5. arras, grant 6. ration 7. pension, scalage, stipend 8. appenage (prince's), discount, granting, sanction 9. admitting, allotment, conceding, tolerance 10. permission 11. scholarship 13. authorization

allowing for... 2. if 8. provided

allow to pass... 5. lapse 6. expire, revert

alloy... 3. mix 4. asem 5. blend, mokum 6. billon, fusion, oroide 7. amalgam, bullion, corrupt, mixture 8. compound 9. composite 10. adulterate, amalgamate

alloys...
copper, aluminum.. 9. duralumin
copper, sulphur.. 6. niello
copper, tin.. 6. bronze
copper, white metal.. 6. oroide
copper, zinc.. 5. brass 6. tombac
copper, zinc, iron.. 4. Aich (Chin)
copper, zinc, nickel.. 4. iron 7. paktong (packtong)
copper, zinc, nickel, iron.. 7. rheotan
German silver.. 6. albata
gold, silver.. 4. asem

iron, carbon.. 5. steel
iron, nickel.. 6. Calite (trademark)
lead, tin.. 6. pewter, solder
nickel, steel.. 5. Invar

allspice tree... 7. pimento

alltud... 5. alien, slave 9. foreigner

allude... 4. hint 5. imply, point, refer 6. relate 7. mention, suggest 8. indicate, intimate 9. insinuate

allure... 3. win 4. bait, draw, lead, lure, tice, tole 5. charm, decoy, snare, tempt 6. entice, entrap, invite, seduce 7. attract, prevail 8. inveigle, persuade 9. captivate, fascinate, influence

allurement... 4. bait, lure 5. bride 7. glamour (glamor) 8. agacerie, coquetry 10. attraction, enticement, inducement, temptation 12. inveiglement

allusion... 4. clue, hint 7. inkling 8. innuendo, instance 9. reference 11. implication

alluvial deposit... 3. mud 4. silt 5. delta, geest 6. placer

ally... 3. pal 4. aide, join 5. union 6. fellow, friend, league 7. comrade, consort, kinsman, partner 8. adherent, relative 9. associate, attendant, colleague 10. accomplice 11. confederate 12. collaborator

Alma (It)... 4. soul 6. spirit 10. cherishing, nourishing

alma... 6. fabric (silk)

almacen... 4. shop 8. magazine 9. warehouse

Alma Mater... 6. school· 7. college 9. goddesses 10. university

almanac... 5. fasti 6. record 7. calends (kalends) 8. calendar, register 9. ephemeris (obs)

almighty... 5. great 6. divine 10. omnipotent 11. all–powerful 12. irresistible

almost... 4. most, nigh 5. anear, close 6. all but, nearly 8. well–nigh 9. nearabout 13. approximately

alms... 4. dole, mite 6. aumous, bounty, corban, relief 7. charity, handout 8. donation, gratuity, pittance 12. contribution, philanthropy

alms (pert to)...
box.. 4. arca 5. chest
giver.. 5. donor 7. almoner 11. contributor 14. philanthropist
man.. 5. donee 6. pauper 7. feoffee 9. pensioner

alodium... 4. land 6. tenure 8. freehold 10. real estate

aloe, aloes... 4. drug 5. agave, plant 6. tambac 7. incense 8. agalloch

aloft... 2. up 4. high, over 5. aloof 7. skyward 8. overhead

aloha... 4. hail, love 7. good–bye 9. affection, greetings 11. salutations

Aloha State... 6. Hawaii

aloin... 4. drug 5. aloes 8. nataloin 9. barbaloin (Barbados) 12. isobarbaloin

alone... 4. solo 5. apart, solus 6. single, singly, solely, unique 8. desolate, homeless, isolated,

separate, solitary 9. exclusive,
matchless 10. unassisted
12. single–handed
13. companionless, independently,
unaccompanied
along... 2. on 3. via 4. with
6. beside, onward 7. forward
8. together
alongside... 2. by 4. near 6. beside
7. abreast 8. parallel
aloof... 6. offish, remote 7. distant,
haughty 8. reserved 10. unsociable
11. indifferent, standoffish
15. uncommunicative
aloofness... 7. reserve 10. offishness,
remoteness 11. haughtiness
12. indifference 13. unsociability
alopecia... 6. acomia 8. baldness
12. hairlessness
aloud... 4. oral 6. loudly 7. audibly,
plainly
alp... 3. tor 4. peak, pico, pike
6. summit 8. mountain 9. bullfinch
alp (Teut Folklore)... 5. demon, witch
9. nightmare
alpaca... 4. coat, paco 5. llama
7. garment
Alph... 11. sacred river (Kubla Khan)
alpha... 4. star 5. prime 6. letter
7. initial, numeral 9. beginning
alphabet... 4. ABC's 6. Sarada
(Kashmir) 9. abecedary
10. Davanagari (Sanskrit)
alphabet characters (Teut)... 4. ogam,
rune
alphabetize... 4. file 5. group, index
6. codify, letter 8. classify, tabulate
9. catalogue (catalog) 10. categorize
alpha test (Army)... 12. intelligence
alpine... 5. alpen, hilly 6. knobby
10. alpestrine 11. mountainous
Alpine (pert to)...
climber.. 10. alpestrian
dance.. 7. gavotte (gavot)
dress.. 6. dirndl
dwelling.. 6. chalet
goat.. 4. ibex
herdsman.. 4. senn
peak.. 5. Blanc 9. Monte Rosa
10. Matterhorn
plant.. 9. edelweiss
province.. 5. Tyrol
shelter.. 7. hospice
snowfield.. 4. firn, neve
tunnel.. 7. Simplon 10. St Gotthard
wind.. 4. bise 5. foehn
Alps... 5. Blanc, Tirol (Tyrol) 6. Julian
7. Dinaric 8. Jungfrau 9. Dolomites,
Monte Rosa (peak) 10. Matterhorn
already... 3. ere, yet 6. afore
6. before 7. earlier 8. hitherto
10. heretofore 11. theretofore
also... 2. as, et, so 3. and, too, yet
4. more, plus 5. besides, further
8. likewise, moreover 9. similarly
11. furthermore
altar (pert to)...
boy.. 7. acolyte
cloth.. 6. dossal (dossel) 7. haploma
9. ependytes
constellation.. 3. Ara
curtain.. 6. riddel

end of church.. 4. apse 7. chancel
Greek.. 5. bomos 6. hestia
7. eschara
Latin.. 7. scrobis
ledge.. 7. retable
platform.. 8. predella
screen.. 7. reredos
shelf, table.. 6. gradin 7. retable
8. credence
step.. 8. predella
top slab.. 5. mensa
alter... 4. geld, vary, veer 5. amend,
emend, reset, shift 6. adjust,
change, immute, modify, mutate,
revise 7. falsify 8. castrate
9. transform
alteration... 6. change 9. diversity,
variation 10. castration, correction
12. modification 13. interpolation
15. diversification
altercation... 3. row 4. feud, spat, tiff
5. fight, snarl 6. fracas, strife
7. dispute, quarrel, wrangle
8. squabble, vendetta 9. imbroglio
10. contention 11. controversy
alter ego... 4. mate, self, twin
7. oneself 10. complement
11. counterpart
alternate... 4. vary 5. proxy
6. change, deputy, rotate, seesaw
7. reverse, stand–in 8. delegate
9. oscillate 10. substitute
11. alternative, interchange,
reciprocate
alternate writing mode (anc)...
13. boustrophedon
alternative... 2. or 3. nor 5. other
6. choice, either, option, switch
7. dilemma 8. election, loophole
9. secondary 10. nip–and–tuck,
preference, substitute
11. replacement
although, altho... 4. even, when
5. while 6. albeit, though 7. despite,
whereas 15. notwithstanding
altimetry... 6. height 10. hypsometry
11. measurement
altitude... 6. height (highth) 7. heroics,
stature 8. eminence, highness,
tallness 9. elevation, loftiness
altogether... 5. fully, quite 6. bodily,
wholly 7. utterly 8. entirely, outright
9. generally 10. completely,
thoroughly 12. collectively
alto horn... 7. althorn, saxhorn
10. mellophone
altruism... 7. charity, concern
8. kindness 11. beneficence,
benevolence 12. philanthropy
alumnus (alumni)... 4. grad 5. pupil
6. alumna (alumnae) 8. graduate,
postgrad 12. postgraduate
alveary... 4. hive 6. apiary 7. beehive
alveola... 3. dip, pit 4. pore, sink
6. crater, pocket
alveolar... 6. pitted, pocked
7. notched 8. indented 9. depressed
always... 2. ay 3. aye, e'er 4. ever
6. anyway, semper 7. forever
8. evermore 9. eternally, uniformly
10. constantly, invariably
11. continually, everlasting,

perpetually, universally

ama... 4. tree 5. amula (Bib) 6. vessel

amabile... 6. gentle, tender
9. agreeable

Amadis de Gaul (Arthurian)... 4. hero
5. lover

amadou... 4. punk 6. tinder 7. styptic

amah... 5. nurse 7. servant
9. nursemaid 11. maidservant

amain... 5. apace 7. hastily, quickly,
swiftly 9. posthaste

amalgamate... 3. mix 4. fuse, join,
weld 5. blend, merge, unite
6. commix 7. combine 8. coalesce,
compound, intermix 11. consolidate

amalgamation... 6. fusion, merger
7. mixture 11. combination

Amalkite... 4. Agag (King) 5. nomad
7. Bedouin

amant... 5. lover 6. amante

amaryllis... 4. bulb, lily 5. agave, plant
6. flower 8. mistress 10. sweetheart
11. shepherdess

amass... 4. save 5. hoard, stack, store
6. gather 7. collect 8. assemble
10. accumulate

amate... 5. daunt 6. subdue
10. dishearten

amateur... 3. ham 4. tyro 6. novice
7. dabbler, fancier 8. beginner,
virtuoso 10. aficionado, apprentice,
dilettante 15. nonprofessional

amateurish... 5. inapt 9. unskilled,
untrained, untutored 10. unfinished
15. nonprofessional

Amati... 6. family, violin

amatory... 4. fond 6. ardent, erotic,
loving, tender 7. amorous, philter
9. loverlike 10. passionate

amaze... 3. awe 4. stun 7. astound,
perplex, stagger, startle, stupefy
8. astonish, bewilder, confound,
surprise 9. dumbfound, overwhelm

amazement... 3. awe 5. alarm
6. wonder 8. surprise 10. perplexity
12. bewilderment 13. consternation

Amazon... 5. Queen (Myth), river
6. virago 9. androgyne
10. warrioress 11. Penthesilea

Amazon river (pert to)...
cetacean.. 4. Inia
discoverer.. 6. Pinzon (1500)
mouth.. 4. Para
rain forest.. 5. selva
tributary.. 3. Apa 4. Napo

ambary... 2. da 4. hemp 5. fiber
6. Nolita

ambassador... 5. envoy 6. legate,
nuncio 8. diplomat, emissary,
minister 9. messenger
12. intermediary 14. representative
15. plenipotentiary

amber... 6. yellow 8. electrum

ambidextrous... 7. capable
8. two–faced 9. two–handed,
versatile 11. ambidextral, treacherous
13. double–dealing

ambiguous... 6. double 7. dubious
9. equivocal, uncertain, unsettled
10. indefinite, indistinct, mistakable
12. questionable 13. indeterminate

ambit... 5. orbit, scope 6. extent,
sphere 7. circuit 8. precinct

ambition... 4. goal, spur 6. desire
10. aspiration

amble... 4. pace, rack, trot 7. piaffer

ambrosia... 4. food 5. honey, manna
6. nectar 7. perfume 8. delicacy,
libation

ambulate... 4. hike, move, walk

ambush... 4. trap 5. snare 6. hiding,
waylay 7. mantrap 9. ambuscade
10. subterfuge 11. concealment

ameliorate... 4. ease, mend 5. emend
6. better 7. improve 8. progress
9. meliorate

amelioration... 10. betterment
11. improvement, restoration

amenable... 6. liable, pliant
7. movable 9. receptive
10. answerable, open–minded,
responsive 11. accountable,
persuadable, responsible

amend... 4. beat (dial), beet (beete)
5. alter, atone, emend 6. reform,
repeal 7. convert, correct, improve,
rectify, redress, restore

amendment... 5. rider 8. addition
10. conversion, correction
11. improvement, reformation

amends... 7. redress 8. reprisal
9. atonement 10. recompense,
reparation 11. restitution

amenities... 5. mores 7. decorum,
manners 9. etiquette 10. civilities,
courtesies 11. formalities, gentilities,
proprieties

ament... 6. catkin 7. cattail

American (pert to)...
bear.. 7. musquaw (black)
buffalo.. 5. bison
cactus.. 4. bleo 7. saguaro
carnivore.. 4. puma
cataract.. 7. Niagara (Falls)
cedar (red).. 5. savin
elk.. 6. wapiti
Japanese.. 5. Nisei 6. Kibbei
leopard.. 6. ocelot
marsupial.. 7. opossum
merganser.. 4. duck (fish–eating)
Mexican.. 6. gringo
mink.. 5. vison
moth.. 2. io
nickname.. 6. Yankee (Yank)
ostrich.. 4. rhea
palm.. 5. Sabal 8. palmetto
quail.. 5. colin
rail.. 4. sora
squirrel.. 9. chickaree (red)
vulture.. 5. urubu 6. condor

American, famed...
artist.. 5. Flagg, Peale 6. Stuart
7. Sargent 8. Rockwell, The Eight
astronomer.. 11. Rittenhouse
chemist.. 6. Carver (G Washington)
crusader (Temperance).. 12. Carrie
Nation
discoverer.. 4. Eric (The Red)
5. Cabot, Votan 8. Columbus
doctor, surgeon.. 4. Mayo 6. Schick
7. Cushing
educator.. 4. Hume, Mann 5. Eliot
10. Washington (Booker T)
explorer.. 4. Byrd 5. Boone, Clark,

Lewis, Peary 6. Carson (Kit)
9. Ellsworth
musician.. 6. Foster 8. Damrosch,
Gershwin 9. Bernstein, MacDowell,
Stokowski
naturalist.. 4. Muir 5. Beebe
7. Audubon, Burbank
patriot.. 4. Clay, Hale, Otis 5. Dawes,
Henry (Patrick), Paine (Thomas)
6. Revere
physicist.. 6. Teller (H–bomb)
pianist.. 6. Duchin, Levant
8. Horowitz, Liberace, Williams
(Roger) 10. Van Cliburn
pirate.. 4. Kidd (Capt)
poet.. 4. Nash 5. Benet, Eliot, Frost
6. Kilmer, Lowell, Millay 8. Sandburg
10. Longfellow
Red Cross organizer.. 6. Barton (Clara)
Scouts (Girl) organizer.. 3. Low
(Juliette)
sculptor.. 6. Calder 7. Borglum
singer.. 4. Pons 5. Jones, Moore
6. Farrar, Peerce 7. Kirsten, Merrill,
Tibbett 8. Anderson (Marian)
statesman.. 4. Clay, Root 6. Baruch,
Dulles 8. Harriman
suffragette.. 4. Catt (Carrie Chapman)
violinist.. 7. Menuhin
writer, novelist.. 6. Ferber 8. Faulkner
9. Hemingway
American Indian (pert to)...
chief.. 5. brave 6. sachem
child.. 7. papoose
conference.. 6. powwow
girl.. 7. Nokomis (Myth)
9. Minnehaha, Sacagawea
(Sakajawea) 10. Pocahontas
hero (Myth).. 8. Hiawatha
magician.. 6. shaman, wabeno
(Ojibway)
shelter.. 4. tent 5. hogan, tepee
(teepee) 6. wigwam 7. wickiup
(wikiup)
American Indian tribe... see also
Indian 3. Fox, Oto (Otoe), Ree, Sac,
Ute 4. Cree, Crow, Erie, Hopi, Iowa,
Pima 5. Creek, Kansa, Osage, Piute,
Sioux 6. Cayuga, Dakota, Mohawk,
Oneida, Pueblo, Seneca 7. Arapaho,
Choctaw, Mohican, Ojibway, Siksika
8. Cherokee, Chippewa, Iroquois,
Onondaga, Seminole 9. Algonquin,
Blackfoot, Chickasaw 10. Athapascan,
Muskhogean
ami... 5. lover 6. friend (law)
amiable... 6. kindly 7. lovable
8. charming, friendly, pleasant,
pleasing 9. agreeable, indulgent
10. hospitable
amicable... 4. kind 8. friendly, sociable
9. congenial, peaceable
10. harmonious
amicus curiae... 5. judge 6. deputy,
lawyer 16. friend of the court
amid, amidst... 2. in 5. among
7. amongst, between
amigo... 6. friend 8. neighbor
amiss... 3. ill 5. badly, fault, wrong
6. astray, sinful 8. faultily, improper
10. disorderly 11. erroneously

amity... 4. love 5. peace 7. harmony
10. friendship 11. sociability
12. congeniality, friendliness
amma... 6. abbess, mother (spiritual)
ammonia... 9. hartshorn 10. fertilizer
11. refrigerant
ammoniac plant... 5. oshac
ammunition (pert to)...
box.. 9. bandoleer
chest.. 7. caisson
type.. 4. arms, bomb, shot 7. bullets
8. grenades, missiles, munition,
shrapnel 10. explosives
wagon.. 7. caisson
amnesty... 6. pardon 8. oblivion
9. acquittal 13. forgetfulness
amoeba, ameba... 3. olm 4. cell
7. proteus 10. protoplasm
13. microorganism
among, amongst... 2. in 3. mid
4. amid, with 5. midst 6. amidst,
imelle 7. between
among nations... 13. international
Amor... 4. Eros 5. Cupid
AMORC... 11. Rosicrucian
amorous... 4. fond 6. ardent, erotic,
loving, tender 7. adoring, devoted
8. enamored 10. passionate
12. affectionate
amorous looks... 4. ogle 5. stare
8. coquetry 10. come–hither,
flirtation
amorphous... 8. abnormal, formless
9. deviative, shapeless, subnormal
14. uncrystallized
amorphous mineral... 4. opal
amort... 8. dejected, lifeless
9. inanimate 10. spiritless
amortize... 5. clear 6. convey, payoff,
settle 9. discharge, negotiate
amount... 3. lot, sum 4. cost, rate,
rise, unit 5. chunk, price, ratal,
store, total 6. ascend, degree
7. quantum, signify 8. quantity
amount (pert to)...
due.. 5. price 6. arrear 7. default,
deficit
mean.. 7. average
realized.. 4. take 6. intake
8. proceeds
small.. 6. morsel 7. modicum
smallest.. 5. least
to.. 3. all 4. even 5. equal, match,
total 10. correspond
amour... 6. affair 7. liaison, romance
8. intrigue, triangle 10. flirtation
ampere... 3. amp 4. unit 6. ohmage
7. current, voltage
ampersand... 3. and 4. also
Amphibia... 5. Anura, frogs, toads
7. Aglossa 8. tadpoles 9. Salientia
11. salamanders
amphibious... 5. mixed 9. adaptable
10. fifty–fifty 11. half–and–half, mixed
nature (land and water)
amphibole... 7. edenite, mineral, uralite
8. aluminum, nephrite
amphigory, amphigouri... 5. rhyme
6. jingle, poetry 8. doggerel
9. rigmarole
amphilogism, amphilogy...
9. ambiguity, duplexity (meaning)

10. equivocacy
Amphion (pert to)...
capturer of.. 6. Thebes
husband of.. 5. Niobe
son of.. 4. Zeus
twin of.. 6. Zethus
amphitheater... 4. bowl 5. arena,
cavea, scene, stage 6. circus, cirque
7. stadium 8. coliseum, platform
10. hippodrome
amphora... 3. jar, urn 4. vase
5. diota, prize 7. measure
8. ornament
ample... 4. full, rich, wide 5. broad,
large, roomy 6. enough, plenty
7. liberal 8. abundant 9. bountiful,
capacious, extensive, plenteous,
plentiful, unstinted 10. munificent
12. satisfactory
ampliation... 5. flare 9. expansion,
extension 11. enlargement
12. postponement 13. amplification
14. aggrandizement
amplify... 3. pad 5. widen 6. dilate,
extend 7. develop, enlarge
8. increase 9. aggravate, expatiate
10. exaggerate, overstress
amplitude... 4. size 6. amount
7. breadth 8. fullness 9. greatness,
plenitude 12. spaciousness
amputate... 4. trim 5. prune, sever
6. cut off 8. mutilate, retrench,
truncate
amuck, amok... 3. fit 4. rage
6. attack, frenzy, malady
12. corybantiasm
amulet... 3. gem 5. charm 6. fetish,
scarab, voodoo 7. periapt
8. ornament, talisman 10. protection
amuse... 3. wow 6. divert, please,
regale, tickle 7. beguile, gratify
8. recreate 9. entertain, titillate
10. exhilarate
amusement... 3. fun 4. play 5. farce,
mirth, sport 7. pastime 9. avocation,
diversion 10. recreation, relaxation
13. divertisement, entertainment
amusement place... 4. club, park
6. casino, midway 7. cabaret, theater
ana...: 5. books 6. events 8. analecta,
excerpts 9. Americana 10. collection
11. collectanea, compilation,
memorabilia
anachronous... 8. misdated, mistimed
10. beforehand, behindhand
anaglyph... 5. cameo, carve 6. chisel,
plaque, relief 10. embossment
Anak (Eccl)... 5. giant (Canaan)
6. Anakim
analogous... 4. like 7. similar
8. parallel 10. comparable, equivalent
11. correlative
analogue... 8. parallel 11. resemblance
13. correspondent
14. correspondence
analogy... 8. likeness, sameness
9. agreement 10. accordance,
comparison, similarity
14. correspondence
analysis... 5. assay, logic 6. biopsy,
theory 9. breakdown, diagnosis
10. compendium, discussion,

dissection 11. examination
14. classification
analyze... 5. assay, parse, study
7. discuss, dissect, examine
8. classify, describe, diagnose,
separate
Ananias (Bib)... 4. liar 8. disciple
(Damascus), Shadrack (Sidrack)
10. high priest 12. prevaricator
anarch, anarchist... 3. red 7. radical
8. nihilist 9. socialist, terrorist
13. revolutionist
anarchy... 4. riot 5. chaos 6. acracy
7. license, misrule 8. disorder
9. confusion, mobocracy, rebellion
10. ochlocracy
anathema... 3. ban 5. curse
9. damnation 11. abomination,
imprecation, malediction
Anatolian rug... 4. Kurd 5. Tuzla
anatomy... 4. body 5. build, frame
7. carcass 8. analysis, skeleton
9. formation, structure
11. arrangement
anatomy of animals... 7. zootomy
ancestor... 4. Adam, sire 5. elder,
stock 6. atavus, family, parent
8. forebear 9. patriarch, precursor
10. antecedent, forefather,
forerunner, progenitor
11. grandfather, predecessor
ancestral... 4. aval 6. avital, lineal
7. atavism 8. maternal, paternal
9. atavistic, primitive 10. hereditary
11. patrimonial
ancestral spirits... 5. lares, manes
7. lemures, penates
ancestry... 4. race, rank 5. birth,
blood 7. descent, lineage
11. antecedents 14. progenitorship
anchor... 3. fix, tie 4. hook, moor,
rest, stop 5. affix, clamp, kedge
6. attach, batten, fasten, secure
7. grapnel, killick
anchor (pert to)... 3. arm, cat, pee
4. cast, palm, tore (ring) 5. fluke
7. capstan
anchorite, anchoret... 6. hermit,
shut–in 7. ascetic, eremite, recluse,
stylite 8. homebody
anchor–shaped... 8. ankyroid
10. hook–shaped
anchovy... 4. alec 5. sauce, sprat
7. herring
ancienne noblesse... 5. elect, elite
7. royalty 8. nobility 11. aristocracy
ancient... 3. eld, old 4. aged, auld,
wise 5. adept, early, hoary, olden
7. antique 8. historic, obsolete,
outdated, primeval, pristine
9. grandeval, primitive, venerable
10. aboriginal, antiquated, preadamite
12. antediluvian
ancient (pert to)...
chariot.. 5. essed
city.. 4. Elis, Tyre 5. Argos, Sedon
6. Athens, Sparta, Thebes
drink.. 5. morat
empire.. 4. Gaul 5. Roman 6. Lydian
7. Persian 8. Assyrian, Athenian,
Chaldean, Hellenic 10. Babylonian,
Phoenician

god .. **4.** Esus (Gaulish)
isles .. **5.** Chios, Crete, Samos
  6. Aegina, Ionian, Ithaca, Lemnos,
  Lesbos, Rhodes **7.** Salamis
  8. Cyclades
language .. **4.** Pali **5.** Latin **6.** Celtic,
  Gaelic **7.** Cornish, Gaulish
mariner .. **4.** Rime (of) **5.** rover
  6. roamer, sailor, seaman
  8. seafarer, wanderer **9.** navigator
soldier .. **7.** peltast
theater .. **5.** odeum
and ... **2.** et **4.** also, plus **8.** et cetera
  9. ampersand, including
  12. additionally
andante ... **5.** largo, tempo **6.** slowly
Andean (pert to) ...
  camel .. **5.** llama
  deer .. **4.** pudu
  region, wind .. **4.** puna
  term .. **5.** grand, lofty
andiron ... **3.** dog **7.** firedog, Hessian
andrenid ... **3.** bee **10.** Andrenidae
androgyny ... **9.** sissiness
  10. effeminacy **11.** unmanliness
  15. hermaphroditism
android ... **5.** robot **9.** automaton
anecdote ... **4.** tale, yarn **5.** story
  7. account **9.** chronicle, narrative
anecdotes ... **3.** ana **7.** sayings, stories
anemone ... **7.** actinia **10.** windflower
anent ... **2.** of, on, re **4.** upon, with
  5. about **8.** opposite **10.** concerning
anesthesia, anaesthesia ...
  8. deadness, numbness
  13. insensibility
anesthetic ... **3.** gas **5.** ether
  8. freezing, Novocain, procaine
  9. pentothal **10.** chloroform
  13. refrigeration
anesthetize ... **4.** dull, numb, stun
  6. benumb, deaden, freeze **7.** stupefy
  8. etherize, paralyze **9.** narcotize
  10. chloroform **11.** desensitize
anew ... **5.** again, newly **6.** afresh, de
  novo **8.** recently
angel ... **6.** cherub, genius, seraph
  (seraf) **7.** Madonna, prophet
angel (pert to) ...
  Arab (apostate) .. **5.** Eblis
  archangel .. **5.** Uriel **7.** Gabriel,
  Michael, Raphael
  Biblical .. **6.** bishop, pastor
  Fallen .. **6.** Belial, Mammon
  financial .. **6.** backer, patron
  7. sponsor **8.** promoter
  fish .. **5.** shark **9.** spadefish
  Hebrew .. **6.** Abdiel **8.** cherubim,
  seraphim
  Jewish .. **6.** Azrael (of death)
  7. Zadkiel (of planet Jupiter)
  8. Metatron
  Mohammedan (Mus) .. **7.** Israfil
  (Israfeel)
  Moslem .. **5.** Nakir (Repudiating)
  6. Munkar (Unknown)
angelic ... **5.** godly **7.** lovable, saintly
  8. cherubic, heavenly, seraphic,
  virtuous **9.** celestial **10.** beneficent
angelica ... **4.** herb **6.** lovely **7.** liqueur
Angelus ... **4.** bell, call **6.** prayer
  8. devotion

anger ... **3.** ire, vex **4.** fume, rage, rile
  5. annoy, chafe, wrath **6.** choler,
  dander, enrage, nettle, offend,
  temper **7.** dudgeon, emotion,
  inflame, madness, passion, trouble
  8. vexation **9.** infuriate **10.** affliction,
  enragement, irritation, resentment
  11. displeasure, indignation
  12. exasperation
angered ... **3.** mad **5.** irate, wroth
  8. incensed, wrathful **9.** indignant,
  irascible
angle ... **3.** ell, tee, zig **4.** axil, coin,
  fish, fork, hade, nook **5.** acute,
  ancon, arris, right, slant, story
  6. akimbo, distal, epaule, obtuse,
  octant **7.** bastion, outlook, ravelin,
  salient **8.** attitude **9.** incidence,
  rectangle, viewpoint
angler ... **6.** fisher **7.** dibbler, trawler,
  troller **8.** piscator **9.** fisherman,
  Waltonian
angler's basket ... **5.** creel
Anglican ... **7.** English
Anglo–Celtic ... **7.** British
  10. Anglo–Saxon
Anglo–Indian (pert to) ...
  Empire founder .. **5.** Clive
  measure .. **3.** ser **4.** tola
  pageant .. **7.** tamasha
  peasant .. **4.** ryot
  princess .. **5.** begum
  wealthy .. **5.** nabob
Anglo–Saxon (pert to) ...
  armor .. **7.** hauberk
  assembly .. **4.** moot **5.** gemot
  (gemote)
  attendant .. **5.** thane
  consonant .. **3.** edh, eth
  council .. **9.** heptarchy
  councilman .. **5.** witan
  epic (heroic) .. **7.** Beowulf
  native .. **7.** English **11.** Anglo–Celtic
  prince (heir apparent) .. **8.** atheling
  slave .. **4.** esne
  tenant .. **6.** geneat
  warrior .. **5.** thane
Angora
  capital of .. **6.** Turkey
  garment .. **5.** shawl
  goat .. **6.** chamal
  wool fabric .. **6.** mohair
angry ... **3.** hot, mad **4.** sore **5.** cross,
  grame, irate, irked, vexed **6.** ireful,
  stormy **7.** enraged, painful
  8. inflamed, wrathful **9.** indignant,
  irascible, resentful, turbulent
  10. passionate
anguish ... **3.** woe **4.** bale, pain, pang
  5. agony, dolor, grief, throe
  6. misery **7.** remorse, sadness,
  torment, torture **8.** distress
  9. heartache **10.** desolation
  11. lamentation
angular ... **4.** bent, bony, edgy
  5. gaunt, sharp **6.** abrupt, akimbo,
  forked **7.** crooked, pointed, scrawny
  8. cornered, crotched
ani ... **8.** keelbill (keelbird) **9.** blackbird
animadversion ... **7.** censure, comment,
  obloquy **8.** judgment, reproach
  9. aspersion, criticism

10. imputation, reflection
12. condemnation
animadvert ... 4. note 5. watch
6. notice, regard, remark 7. censure,
comment, observe 9. criticize
(criticise)
anima humana ... 4. mind, self, soul
5. heart, human 6. psyche, spirit
animal (pert to) ...
anatomy .. 7. zootomy
back, spine .. 4. nota 5. chine
body .. 4. soma
castrated .. 3. seg (segg)
coat .. 6. pelage
cud .. 5. rumen
disease .. 8. enzootic
enclosure .. 3. pen, sty 4. cage, coop,
cote, reem, yard 5. hutch, kraal, stall
6. corral 7. pasture
fabulous .. 7. griffin
group .. 3. gam, pod 4. herd
5. drove, flock, pride 9. menagerie
hairless .. 5. pelon
hindleg part .. 4. crus
hornless .. 7. pollard
hybrid .. 4. mule 5. hinny
hypnosis .. 9. cataplexy
male .. 3. tom 4. bull, jack, stag
5. steer 8. stallion
many–egged .. 5. zooid
many–footed .. 7. polyped
molt .. 8. exuviate
mother .. 3. dam
no feet .. 4. apod
nose .. 5. snout
oar–footed .. 7. remiped
one–egged .. 4. zoon
one–footed .. 6. uniped
pet .. 4. cade
reference to .. 4. wild 6. carnal
7. bestial, fleshly, kingdom
8. domestic 12. ferae naturae
14. domitae naturae
regional .. 5. fauna
small .. 10. animalcule
symbolic .. 5. totem
track, trail .. 4. rack 5. piste, spoor
web–footed .. 8. pinniped
wing–footed .. 6. aliped
worship .. 8. zoolatry
young .. 3. cub, kid, pup 4. calf, colt,
fawn, foal, lamb 5. filly, puppy
6. kitten
animal family ...
bear .. 6. ursine
cat .. 6. feline
cow .. 6. bovine
deer .. 7. cervine
dog .. 6. canine
fox .. 7. vulpine
horse .. 6. equine
pig .. 7. porcine
sheep .. 5. ovine
wolf .. 6. lupine
animal stomach ...
1st .. 5. rumen 6. paunch
2nd .. 5. tripe 9. honeycomb,
reticulum
3rd .. 6. omasum 9. manyplies
4th .. 4. read (reed) 8. abomasum
animate ... 3. act 4. fire, live, move
5. alive, cheer, imbue, impel, liven

6. arouse, ensoul, spirit, vivify
7. enliven, inspire, organic, refresh
8. energize, vitalize 9. stimulate
10. exhilarate
animated ... 3. gay 5. alive, brisk
6. active, lively, living, minded
8. disposed (in mind), prompted
9. energetic, refreshed
animated spirit ... 6. animus
animation ... 3. pep 4. brio, dash, life
5. ardor 6. energy, gaiety, spirit
8. airiness, buoyancy, vivacity
10. excitement, liveliness, motivation
11. earnestness, inspiration
12. invigoration, vivification
13. sprightliness
animation suspended ... 6. apathy,
torpor 8. dormancy, lethargy
animé ... 6. bright 8. animated
animosity ... 5. clash, spite 6. enmity,
hatred, rancor 7. ill will 8. conflict
9. antipathy, hostility
10. antagonism, opposition,
repugnance
animoso ... 6. lively 8. animated
9. energetic
animous ... 3. hot 8. resolute,
vehement
animus ... 4. mind, will 6. desire,
spirit, temper 8. attitude, volition
9. intention 10. discretion
11. disposition, inclination
ankh (Egypt) ... 3. tau 4. life 5. cross
6. emblem, symbol
ankle ... 4. tali (pl) 5. joint, pivot, talus
6. tarsus 8. astragal 9. ginglymus
10. astragalus 11. diarthrosis
ankle cover ... 4. spat 6. gaiter
ankylostoma ... 7. lockjaw
annalist ... 6. writer 8. recorder
9. historian 10. chronicler
11. memorialist 12. chronologist
annals ... 5. diary 6. record 7. history,
journal 8. register 9. chronicle
11. publication
Annam ... 5. Hanoi 6. Tonkin
(Tongking)
Annamese ... 7. Chinese 8. Buddhist
9. Mongolian
anneal ... 4. fuse, heat 6. harden,
temper 7. inflame, toughen
8. indurate
Anne Hathaway's home ... 8. Shattery
annelid ... 3. lug 4. lurg, naid, worm
6. phylum 7. lugworm
annex ... 3. add, ell 4. join, wing
5. affix 6. append, attach, fasten
7. acquire, subjoin 8. addition
9. extension
annexation ... 7. adjunct 8. addition
9. accession 10. affixation
13. appropriation
Annie Oakley ... 4. pass 6. ticket
(free)
annihilate ... 4. undo, void 5. erase,
wreck 6. quench, reduce, stifle
7. abolish, destroy, expunge, nullify,
smother 8. decimate 9. extirpate
10. extinguish, obliterate
11. exterminate
annihilation ... 5. death 6. demise
7. passing 10. extinction

11. destruction, dissolution
13. extermination 14. extinguishment
anniversary... 5. cycle 6. course
7. jubilee, wedding 8. birthday
10. centennial, regularity
13. commemoration
annotation... 4. note 5. gloss
7. apostil, comment 8. exegesis,
notation, rescript, scholium
9. reference 10. commentary
annotator... 6. critic 7. analyst
9. expositor, expounder, publicist,
scholiast 10. glossarist
11. commentator
announce... 3. bid 4. call, tell 5. bruit
6. affirm, assert, herald, notify
7. declare, forerun, gazette, presage
8. proclaim 9. advertise, broadcast,
pronounce 10. annunciate,
promulgate
announcement... 4. fiat 5. blurb, edict
6. decree, notice 8. bulletin
9. manifesto 10. commercial
11. affirmation, declaration
12. notification, proclamation
13. advertisement
announcer... 4. page 5. crier, emcee
6. nuncio 9. harbinger, informant
10. newscaster, proclaimer
11. broadcaster
annoy... 3. irk, nag, try, vex 4. bore,
rile 5. anger, devil, harry, peeve,
spite, tease 6. bother, harass,
molest, offend, pester, ruffle
7. disturb, trouble 8. irritate
9. displease 13. inconvenience
annoyance... 4. bore, pest
8. nuisance, vexation 10. resentment
11. molestation 13. inconvenience
annoying... 4. sore 7. galling
9. vexatious 11. distressing
annual... 4. book 5. plant 6. yearly
7. etesian 10. periodical
11. publication
annuity... 5. rente, trust 6. income
(life) 7. pension, subsidy, tontine
9. allotment 10. investment, life
income
annul... 4. cass, undo, void 5. avoid,
blank, quash 6. cancel, repeal,
revoke 7. abolish, nullify, rescind
8. abrogate, derogate, overrule,
withdraw 9. disaffirm 10. invalidate,
neutralize, obliterate 11. countermand
annular... 6. banded, cyclic, ringed
8. cingular, circular
annulet... 4. ring (Her) 6. fillet
7. circlet, ringlet
annulment... 6. repeal 7. erasure,
vacatur 9. abolition 10. abrogation,
defeasance, revocation
12. invalidation 14. neutralization
annunciate... 6. affirm, assert
8. announce, proclaim
annunciation... 11. affirmation
12. announcement, proclamation
13. pronouncement
anoa... 2. ox (wild) 8. sapiutan
anode... 8. terminal (positive)
9. electrode (opp of cathode)
anodic... 12. turned toward
anodyne... 4. balm 6. opiate

7. soother 8. antalgic, narcotic,
pacifier, sedative 9. analgesic
10. depressant, palliative
anoesia... 6. idiocy
anoint... 3. oil 4. balm, cere, nard
5. anele, bribe, smear 6. chrism,
grease, spread 7. moisten
8. medicate 9. embrocate, lubricate
10. consecrate
anoli, anole... 6. lizard
anomalous... 3. odd 7. erratic,
strange, unusual 8. aberrant,
abnormal, peculiar 9. eccentric,
irregular 10. dissimilar
11. exceptional 13. unconformable
anomaly... 6. oddity, rarity
11. abnormality, nondescript
12. irregularity
anomy... 7. miracle
anon... 4. soon 5. again, later
6. mañana, thence 7. by–and–by
8. tomorrow 10. eventually
11. straightway
anonymous (opp of onomatous)...
7. unknown 8. nameless, unavowed
9. undefined
anoöpsia... 10. strabismus (upward)
Anopheles... 10. mosquitoes
anophthalmia... 13. absence of eyes
(congenital)
anopia... 15. defective vision
anorak... 12. hooded jacket (Arctic)
anorexia... 10. no appetite
anorthopia... 15. distorted vision
anosmia... 11. loss of smell
another... 3. new 4. more 5. alias,
extra, other 6. second 7. further
10. additional
another time... 5. again
10. otherwhile
ansa... 4. loop 6. handle
anserine... 6. stupid 9. gooselike
answer... 2. do 3. say 4. echo
5. avail, reply, sauce, serve
6. oracle, retort 7. defense, epistle,
respond, riposte 8. conclude,
reaction, repartee, response, solution
9. rejoinder 10. correspond,
responsory 11. acknowledge
16. counterstatement
answerable... 6. liable 8. amenable,
solvable 11. responsible
12. commensurate 13. proportionate
answer the purpose... 2. so 3. fit
4. suit 5. avail, serve 6. become
7. benefit, satisfy, suffice
ant (pert to)...
family.. 10. Formicidae, Myrmicidae
11. Formicoidea (super),
Hymenoptera
feeding on.. 13. formicivorous
genus.. 6. Eciton, Termes 7. Formica
killer.. 9. formicide
male.. 8. macraner (large), micraner
(small)
nest.. 9. formicary
ref to.. 6. formic
type.. 5. emmet 7. formica, pismire
white.. 4. anay (anai) 7. termite
wingless.. 8. ergatoid
worker.. 6. ergate 9. harvester
antacid... 6. alkali, remedy 8. medicine

9. absorbent 11. neutralizer
12. counteragent 13. counteractant
Antaeus, Antaios (Gr)... 5. giant
6. Libyan 8. wrestler
antagonism... 3. war 5. clash
8. conflict 9. antipathy, hostility
10. opposition, repugnance
11. contrariety 12. disagreement
13. counteraction
antagonist... 3. foe 5. enemy, rival
6. foeman 8. opponent 9. adversary
antagonistic... 7. hostile, opposed
8. contrary, converse, inimical,
opposite 9. repugnant 10. unfriendly
11. belligerent, disagreeing
13. counteractive
Antarctic...
Circle.. 4. Pole 6. region
continent.. 10. Antarctica
explorer.. 4. Byrd, Ross
islands.. 11. Archipelago
rel to.. 8. subpolar 9. antipodal,
South Pole
sea.. 4. Ross 7. Weddell
seal (brown) discoverer.. 7. Weddell
volcano.. 6. Erebus
ante... 3. pay, pot 4. bank, fund, pool
5. kitty, stake 7. jackpot
anteater... 5. Manis 7. echidna
8. aardvark, edentate, pangolin,
tamandua
antecede... 4. head 5. front 6. prefix
7. outrank, precede, preface
antecedent... 4. fore 5. prior, scout
6. former 7. pioneer 8. ancestor,
previous 9. foregoing, precedent,
preceding, precursor 10. forerunner,
precedence 11. voortrekker (Dutch)
12. avant–courier
antecedents... 7. fathers 9. ancestors,
forebears 10. ascendants
(ascendents) 11. forefathers
12. predecessors 13. prerequisites
antechamber... 4. hall 5. lobby
6. lounge 7. chamber 8. anteroom
9. vestibule
antedate... 7. precede, predate
8. datemark, pre–exist 10. anticipate
antelope... 3. gau, gnu, kob, nil
4. guib, koba, oryx, roan 5. addax,
bovid, eland, goral, oribi, peele,
saiga, serow 6. cabree, dzeren,
impala, nilgai, pygarg 7. blaubok,
blesbok, bubalia, chamois, gazella,
gazelle, gemsbok, sassaby
8. agacella, bontebok, steinbok
9. duikerbok, pronghorn
10. hartebeest
antenna... 4. horn, mast, palp
5. clava (Zool), tower 6. aerial, feeler
7. scanner
antepast... 6. canape, repast
8. aperitif 9. antipasto, appetizer,
foretaste 11. hors d'oeuvre,
prelibation
anteroom... 4. hall 5. lobby 6. lounge
7. chamber 9. vestibule
11. antechamber
anthem... 3. lay 4. hymn, song
5. motet, music, psalm 7. chorale
8. doxology 9. antiphony, offertory
10. responsory

anthill... 5. mound 9. formicary
anthology... 3. ana 5. album
6. corpus 7. omnibus, prayers
8. analects 9. potpourri
10. collection 11. collectanea,
compilation
Anthozoa... 6. corals, polyps
8. anemones
anthropoid... 3. ape, lar, man
6. gibbon 7. gorilla, primate,
siamang 9. orangutan (orangoutang)
10. chimpanzee, troglodyte
12. Anthropoidea (suborder)
anthropophagi... 9. cannibals,
man–eaters
anti... 6. contra 7. adverse, counter,
opposed 8. contrary, converse
13. contradictory
antiaircraft artillery... 4. guns
6. ack–ack, Archie, cannon
7. weapons 8. cannonry, ordnance
10. skysweeper
antibiotics... 5. drugs 7. vaccine
10. penicillin 12. streptomycin
antic... 4. dido 5. caper, prank, stunt
6. frolic, gambol 7. bizarre, buffoon,
gambado 9. grotesque
11. merry–andrew, monkeyshine
anticipate... 4. hope 5. await, dread
6. expect 7. foresee, obviate,
portend, prevent 8. preclude
9. forestall, foretaste, forethink
11. contemplate
anticipation... 4. hope 9. foresight,
foretaste, intuition, prolepsis
10. foreboding 11. expectation,
forethought 12. presentiment
13. preoccupation
anticlimax... 6. bathos 8. comedown,
decrease
antidote... 6. remedy 10. corrective,
preventive 11. neutralizer
12. counteragent, prophylactic
13. counteractant
Antioch... 7. capital (Syria)
antipathy... 6. hatred, nausea
7. dislike 8. aversion, loathing
9. disrelish, hostility 10. abhorrence,
antagonism, opposition, reluctance,
repugnance 11. contrariety,
detestation, inimicality
13. counteraction 14. disinclination
antipodal... 5. polar 7. counter (global)
8. contrary, opposite
14. contrapositive
antiquated... 4. aged 5. passé
6. bygone, voided 7. antique,
archaic, elderly 8. absolute, medieval
9. Victorian 10. fossilized
12. old–fashioned 13. superannuated
antique... 3. old 5. hoary, relic
7. ageless, ancient 8. dateless,
outmoded 9. venerable
12. old–fashioned
antiquities... 5. codex, ruins 6. relics
7. fossils, papyrus, remains, tablets
9. archaisms, artifacts, monuments
11. manuscripts, palimpsests
antiquity... 3. ago, eld 4. past, yore
7. oldness 9. paleology
11. ancientness, elderliness
13. aboriginality, primitiveness

antisepsis ... 7. asepsis
  11. prophylaxis 12. disinfection,
  immunization 13. sterilization
antiseptic ... 5. Salol 6. cresol, iodine
  (iodin), phenol 7. alcohol, aristol,
  aseptic 8. creosote, peroxide
  9. germicide 12. disinfectant,
  formaldehyde, prophylactic
antispasmodic ... 7. anodyne
  8. sedative 9. asadulcis (deadly
  carrot), asafetida (asafoetida)
  10. depressant 12. tranquilizer
antithesis (opp of thesis) ... 8. contrast,
  opposite 9. antipodes 10. opposition
  11. contrariety 14. contraposition
antitoxin ... 5. serum 7. vaccine
  8. antibody 9. antivenin (antivenene)
  10. antibiotic 11. antipyretic,
  immunotoxin
antler ... 3. dag 4. horn, snag, tine
  5. dague, point, prong, spike
  6. bosset, rights 8. advancer
  10. caducicorn
Antony & Cleopatra characters ...
  4. Eris, Iras 6. Caesar 7. Octavia
  9. Demetrius
antonym (opp of synonym) ...
  7. reverse 8. contrary, opposite
antrum ... 3. pit 5. sinus 6. cavern,
  cavity, hollow 10. depression
Anu ... 3. god (sky, heavens)
Anubis ... 3. god (Necropolis)
  6. Hermes
Anura ... 4. Rana 5. frogs, toads
  9. Salientia 10. amphibians
anvil ... 5. block, incus, teest 6. stithy
  7. bickern, incudes (pl) 8. beakiron
  (horned)
anxiety ... 4. care, fear 5. angst,
  dread, worry 7. concern, trouble
  8. disquiet, distress, neurosis,
  suspense 9. eagerness, misgiving
  10. foreboding, perplexity, solicitude,
  uneasiness 12. apprehension,
  restlessness
anxious ... 4. cark 5. antsy, eager
  6. uneasy 7. fearful, unquiet
  8. watchful 9. concerned, disturbed,
  expectant, impatient 10. disquieted
any ... 3. all, ary (dial), one, oni (dial)
  4. some, that, this 5. aught, every
  8. quantity 9. unlimited
  10. unmeasured 12. undetermined
anybody ... 3. any, one 5. aught
  6. anyone 7. someone, whoever
  15. no–account person
anything ... 3. any 4. some 5. at all,
  aught 7. anywise 8. no choice,
  whatever 9. something
  14. choicelessness
anything (pert to) ...
  existing .. 6. entity 8. quiddity
  of value .. 5. asset
  of value, least .. 5. plack
  puzzling .. 4. crux 11. mind–boggler
  remote .. 6. forane
  small .. 3. tot 5. minim
  spiral .. 4. gyre 5. helix
  terrifying .. 5. ghost 9. scarecrow
  true .. 4. fact 9. certitude
  worthless .. 4. mean 7. useless
  9. valueless

aoudad ... 5. sheep 7. chamois
apa ... 7. wallaba
Apache (pert to) ...
  French .. 4. thug 5. dance 8. assassin
  Indian .. 5. nomad
  Indian Chief (famed) .. 8. Geronimo
  Indian jacket (deerskin) .. 6. bietle
  State .. 7. Arizona
apart ... 3. dis (pref) 4. away 5. alone,
  aloof, aside, solus, split 6. singly
  7. asunder, distant 8. secluded,
  separate, unjoined 9. severally,
  unrelated 10. separately
apartheid ... 4. bias 5. twist 7. bigotry
  9. prejudice 11. segregation
  13. provincialism 14. discrimination
apartment ... 3. pad (sl) 4. flat
  5. condo, suite 7. chamber
  8. tenement 11. compartment,
  condominium
apathetic ... 4. dull 5. inert 6. torpid
  7. passive 8. listless, sluggish
  10. insouciant, phlegmatic
  11. indifferent, unconcerned
apathy ... 6. acedia (in a monastery),
  torpor 7. languor 8. neurosis
  9. lassitude, unconcern
  12. indifference, sluggishness
  13. insensibility, unfeelingness
ape ... 4. copy, dupe, fool, mime
  5. mimic 6. alalus, mocker, monkey,
  parrot 7. barbary, copycat, emulate,
  imitate, portray 8. imitator, mimicker,
  simulate 10. anthropoid
  11. impersonate
ape (pert to) ...
  anthropoid .. 6. pongid
  10. chimpanzee, troglodyte
  Egypt Relig .. 4. Aani
  genus .. 5. Cebus, Simia
  India .. 3. kra
  kind .. 6. simian 7. macaque
  largest .. 6. baboon 7. gorilla
  Malay .. 3. lar 5. orang 6. gibbon
  9. orangutan (orangoutang)
  nocturnal .. 5. lemur
aperitif ... 5. drink 6. canape
  8. antepast 9. antipasto, appetizer
  11. hors d'oeuvre
aperture ... 3. gap, vue 4. hole, leak,
  pore, rift, rima, slit, slot, vent
  5. chasm, chink, cleft, inlet, mouth,
  stoma 6. hiatus, window 7. fissure,
  foramen, opening, orifice, osteole
  8. fenestra 10. passageway
apex ... 3. tip, top 4. acme, cone,
  cusp, noon 5. point, spire 6. apogee,
  height, macron, summit, tittle, vertex,
  zenith 7. cacumen 8. pinnacle
  11. culmination
apex ornament ... 6. finial
aphid ... 5. Aphis, louse 6. insect
  7. puceron
aphorism ... 3. saw 5. adage, axiom,
  gnome, maxim, moral 6. dictum,
  saying 7. proverb 8. apothegm
Aphrodite (pert to) ...
  consort .. 4. Ares 10. Hephaestus
  father .. 4. Zeus
  goddess of .. 4. love 6. beauty
  Roman equivalent .. 5. Venus
  sacred birds .. 5. doves 8. sparrows

statue.. 17. Aphrodite of Cnidus (by Praxiteles)
zoology.. 9. butterfly
Apis... 4. bull (sacred)
aplomb... 5. poise 6. surety 7. balance 8. fastness, firmness, security, solidity 9. assurance, erectness, plumbness, restraint, soundness, stability 10. confidence, equanimity 11. equilibrium
apocalypse... 8. prophecy, teaching 9. discovery, scripture 10. revealment, revelation
a poco... 6. little, slowly 9. gradually
apocryphal... 4. mock, sham 5. bogus, false 6. mythic, unreal 8. doubtful, mythical, spurious 9. imitative 10. fictitious, unorthodox 11. counterfeit 15. unauthoritative
apod... 8. footless
Apodes... 4. eels 6. morays
apogee (opp of perigee)... 4. acme, apex, peak 6. climax, summit, zenith 11. culmination
apograph... 4. copy 5. tenor 7. tracing 8. transfer 9. recording 10. transcript 13. transcription
Apoidea... 4. Apis, bees 9. honeybees 11. Hymenoptera
Apollo (pert to)...
birthplace.. 5. Delos
father.. 4. Zeus
festival.. 5. Delia
god.. 3. sun (personified)
mother.. 4. Leto 6. Larona
oracle.. 6. Delphi
sage follower.. 6. Abaris
sister (twin).. 5. Diana (Rom) 7. Artemis
son.. 3. Ion 5. Hymen, Linos
apologetic... 5. sorry 7. apology 8. excusing 10. excusatory, justifying, remorseful 11. vindicative 12. propitiatory 13. justification
apologue... 4. myth 5. fable, story 6. legend 7. fantasy, parable 8. allegory
apology... 4. plea 6. excuse 7. pretext, regrets 9. makeshift 11. explanation, vindication 13. justification 14. acknowledgment
aport... 8. larboard, leftward 9. sinistrad
apostasy... 5. lapse 9. desertion, recreancy 11. backsliding
apostate... 6. bolter 7. pervert, runaway, seceder 8. deserter, recreant, renegade, turncoat, turntail 10. unfaithful
apostle... 5. saint 8. disciple, follower 10. evangelist
Apostle (Bib)... 4. John, Jude, Paul 5. James, Judas, Peter, Silas, Simon 6. Andrew, Philip, Thomas 7. Matthew 8. Barnabas, Matthias 11. Bartholomew
Apostle of...
France (Gauls).. 5. Denis
Franks.. 4. Remi
Gentiles.. 4. Paul
Germany.. 8. Boniface
Goths.. 7. Ulfilas

Indies.. 6. Xavier
Ireland.. 7. Patrick
Rome.. 4. Neri
Apostle to the Indians... 5. Eliot
apostolic... 5. faith, papal 6. gospel 8. Biblical 9. evangelic 10. pontifical, scriptural
apostrophe... 8. squiggle 9. soliloquy
apothecary... 8. druggist, gallipot 9. dispenser 10. pharmacist, posologist 13. pharmaceutist 14. pharmacologist
apothecary measure... 4. dram, pint 5. minim, ounce
apothecary weight... 4. dram 5. grain, ounce, pound 7. scruple
apothegm... 3. saw 4. dict 5. adage, axiom, gnome, maxim 6. dictum, saying 7. precept 8. aphorism
apotheosis... 5. ideal 10. exaltation 11. deification, ennoblement, idolization 12. resurrection 13. dignification, glorification, magnification 14. aggrandizement
apotheosize... 5. deify, exalt 7. ennoble, glorify, idolize 8. enshrine 11. immortalize
appall, appal... 3. awe 5. shock 6. dismay
appalling... 4. grim 5. awful 7. awesome, fearful 8. dreadful, shocking, terrible, terrific 9. frightful 10. remarkable
appalto... 8. monopoly
appanage... 7. adjunct, pendant 8. property 9. appendage, endowment 10. perquisite 11. prerogative 12. appurtenance
apparatus... 4. gear, tool 6. outfit 7. machine, rigging, trapeze 8. recorder 9. appliance, equipment, mechanism, trappings 10. instrument 13. paraphernalia
apparatus (pert to)...
distillation.. 7. alembic
dyeing.. 4. ager
heating.. 4. etna 5. stove 6. boiler 7. furnace 8. radiator
hoisting.. 3. pry 4. jack 5. davit, lever, lewis 7. capstan, derrick
planetarium.. 6. orrery
steering.. 4. helm 5. wheel 6. rudder, tiller
water.. 4. pump 5. noria 6. faucet, siphon, tremie
apparel... 3. alb 4. deck, duds, garb, gear, togs, wear 5. dress, equip, habit 6. attire 7. clothes, costume, garment, raiment, toggery, vesture 8. clothing, fatigues 10. garmenture 11. habiliments
apparent... 4. open 5. clear, overt, plain 6. patent, visual 7. certain, evident, obvious, seeable, seeming, visible 8. distinct, illusory, manifest, specious 9. notorious, plausible 10. ostensible 11. discernible, indubitable, perceivable, superficial 12. recognizable
apparently... 7. visibly 9. evidently, obviously, seemingly 10. manifestly, presumably, speciously

11. perceptibly

apparition... 4. bogy, form 5. ghost, shade, spook 6. shadow, spirit, sprite, vision, wraith 7. eidolon, fantasy, phantom, specter (spectre) 8. illusion, phantasm, revenant 9. hobgoblin 10. appearance, phenomenon, revelation

appassionato... 9. emotional 11. impassioned

appeal... 3. beg, cry 4. call, cite, plea, pray, suit 5. charm, plead 6. avouch, invoke, prayer 7. address, beseech, entreat, implore, request, solicit 8. entreaty, petition 9. importune 10. lovability, loveliness, supplicate 11. winsomeness 12. supplication

appealing... 4. nice 7. winsome 8. alluring, charming, engaging, pleasant 9. agreeable, glamorous, imploring 10. attractive, beseeching, bewitching, delightful, enchanting, entreating 11. fascinating, interesting

appear... 4. loom, seem 5. occur 6. arrive, attend, emerge 11. materialize

appearance... 3. air 4. form, look, mien 5. front, guise, looks, phase 6. aspect, format, manner, ostent 7. arrival, feature, specter (spectre) 8. illusion, presence, pretense 9. emergence, semblance 10. apparition, disclosure, revelation 11. resemblance 13. manifestation

appearance (pert to)...
book.. 6. format
false.. 8. disguise
first.. 4. dawn 5. debut 8. premiere
frontal.. 6. facade
surface.. 6. patina
truth (appearance of)..
14. verisimilitude
white.. 6. pallid

appease... 4. calm 5. allay, atone, mease, quiet, salve 6. pacify, soothe 7. content, placate, relieve, satisfy 8. mitigate 10. conciliate 11. tranquilize

appeasement... 6. relief 7. salving 8. easement 10. compromise, mitigation, palliation 12. pacification

appellation... 3. tag 4. name 5. label, style, title 7. calling, epithet 8. cognomen, nickname 9. sobriquet 11. designation 12. denomination, nomenclature 14. identification

append... 3. add 4. hang 5. affix, annex 6. adjoin, attach 7. subjoin 11. superimpose

appendage... 3. arm, awn, cue, tab, tag 4. barb, flap, lobe, tail 5. cauda, queue 6. ligule (Bot), palpus 7. adjunct, pigtail 8. addition, hanger–on, pendicle 9. accessory, tailpiece 10. dependency 12. appurtenance 13. accompaniment

appendix... 6. sequel 7. codicil, process 8. addendum, addition 9. accessory, appendage 10. dependency 12. augmentation

appertain... 4. bear 5. apply 6. affect, belong, regard, relate 7. involve, pertain

appetite... 4. zest 5. taste 6. desire, hunger, orexis, thirst 7. longing, passion 8. cupidity 9. appetency 10. hungriness, propensity

appetizer... 4. fish (sauce) 6. canape 8. antepast, aperitif 9. antipasto, foretaste 11. hors d'oeuvre

appetizing... 6. savory 7. piquant 8. tempting 9. appealing, desirable 10. attractive 11. captivating, provocative, tantalizing

applaud... 4. clap, hail, laud, root, yell 5. cheer, extol, shout 6. hurrah, praise 7. acclaim, approve, commend, endorse 10. compliment

applauders (paid)... 6. claque 8. clappers 9. claqueurs

applause... 4. clap, hand 5. bravo, éclat, huzza 6. encore, praise 7. acclaim, ovation 8. plaudits 11. acclamation 12. commendation

apple... 3. May, Spy 4. crab, pome 6. annona, pippin, rennet, russet 7. Baldwin, codling (codlin), costard, Newtown, Roxbury, winesap 8. Greening, Jonathan, Mandrake, McIntosh, queening 9. astrachan, Delicious 10. bellflower, Rome Beauty 11. Gravenstein, Northern Spy

apple (pert to)...
acid.. 5. malic
crushed.. 6. pomace
dessert.. 10. brown betty
disease.. 7. stippen
genus.. 5. Malus
juice.. 5. cider 9. applejack
love.. 6. tomato
seed.. 3. pip
shaped.. 8. pomiform

Apple of Discord (Gr Myth)... 4. Eris

apple of one's eye... 3. pet 4. idol 5. jewel, pupil 7. darling, desired 8. favorite 10. preference

applesauce... 4. bunk, pooh 5. tripe 6. phooey 7. baloney, hogwash 8. malarkey, nonsense, tommyrot 12. fiddlesticks 13. horsefeathers

appliance... 3. dam (dental) 4. tool 6. device, gadget 7. utensil 8. facility 9. commodity, implement 10. instrument 11. application, contraption, convenience

applicable... 3. apt, fit 6. usable 7. pliable 8. apposite, relative, relevant 9. compliant, pertinent 11. appropriate

application... 3. use 6. appeal, effort 7. bearing, concern, request 8. petition, recourse 9. attention, constancy, diligence, relevance, relevancy 10. connection, employment, pertinence 11. attribution, disposition, engrossment, persistence, requisition 12. perseverance 14. administration

application (body)... 4. balm 5. salve, stupe (hot) 7. plaster 8. cosmetic, poultice

apply... 3. use 4. suit 6. appose,

bestow, comply, devote, employ, relate 7. solicit, utilize 9. associate, attribute 10. administer
11. appropriate

appoggiature . . . 9. grace note
13. embellishment

appoint . . . 3. fix 4. name 5. equip
6. assign, decree, depute, detail, ordain 7. destine, prepare
8. delegate, deputize 9. designate, establish, prescribe 10. constitute

appointment . . . 4. date 5. order, tryst
7. command 8. position 9. direction, equipment, ordinance
10. engagement 11. designation
13. establishment

appointments . . . 6. things 8. fittings, fixtures 9. equipment, furniture
10. belongings, upholstery
11. acquirement, furnishings
12. accumulation, conveniences
13. accouterments, paraphernalia

apportion . . . 3. fix, lot 4. deal, dele, mete, part 5. allot, carve, share
6. assign, budget, divide 7. arrange, dispose 8. allocate 9. collocate, partition 10. distribute

appose . . . 4. abut 5. audit, liken, place
6. adjoin 7. compare, examine
9. juxtapose

apposite . . . 3. apt 4. like 5. close, match 6. timely 7. fitting, germane
8. position, relative, relevant
9. pertinent 11. appropriate

appraise . . . 4. mark, rank, rate
5. assay, gauge, judge, price, value
6. assess, evalue, praise 7. apprise, commend, measure 8. consider, estimate, evaluate 10. adjudicate, appreciate

appraiser (tax) . . . 5. rater 6. lister
8. assessor

appreciable . . . 3. any 8. tangible
9. estimable 11. perceptible

appreciate . . . 4. feel, grow, know
5. enjoy, prize, savor, value
6. admire, esteem 7. advance, amplify, approve, augment, realize, respect 8. estimate, increase, treasure

appreciation . . . 7. respect 9. appraisal, awareness, gratitude 10. estimation
11. realization, recognition, sensibility
12. gratefulness, thankfulness

apprehend . . . 3. ken, see 4. know, take 5. dread, grasp, pinch (sl) savvy, sense 6. arrest 7. capture, imagine, realize 8. conceive, perceive
10. anticipate, comprehend, understand

apprehensible . . . 8. knowable
9. scrutable 10. explicable, fathomable 11. accountable
12. discoverable, intelligible
14. comprehensible, understandable

apprehension . . . 4. fear, idea 5. alarm, doubt, dread, qualm 6. arrest
7. anxiety, capture, concern, opinion, seizure 8. distress, distrust, suspense
9. misgiving, suspicion
10. foreboding, solicitude, uneasiness
11. fearfulness, premonition

12. intelligence 13. understanding

apprehensive . . . 5. smart 6. uneasy
7. alarmed, fearful, knowing, nervous, worried 8. troubled 9. cognizant, concerned, conscious, perturbed
10. perceptive, solicitous

apprentice . . . 4. tyro 5. novice
7. amateur, trainee 8. beginner

apprize, apprise . . . 4. rate, tell
5. price, value 6. advise, assess, impart, inform, reckon 8. acquaint, appraise 9. enlighten
11. communicate

apprized . . . 5. aware 8. informed
9. cognizant

approach . . . 3. way 4. adit, come, near, road 5. stalk, verge 6. access, accost, advent, impend 7. arrival, nearing, sea gate 8. entryway, likeness, nearness, overture, resemble
11. approximate, entranceway

approachable . . . 4. open 8. gettable, passable 9. reachable 10. accessible, attainable 13. communicative

approbation . . . 5. favor, proof 6. praise
7. plaudit 8. applause, approval, sanction 10. acceptance, admiration
12. commendation, confirmation

appropriate . . . 3. apt, fit 4. akin, meet, take 5. allot, steal, usurp 6. borrow, pirate, proper, timely, worthy
7. condign, germane, related, special
8. deserved, relevant, suitable
9. befitting, expedient, favorable, opportune, pertinent 10. assimilate, monopolize, plagiarize
11. conformable

appropriately . . . 4. duly 5. aptly
6. timely

appropriation . . . 5. theft 6. corner, taking 8. monopoly 9. allotment
10. assignment, possession, usurpation

approval . . . 6. assent 7. consent, support 8. sanction 10. admiration
11. approbation, endorsement
12. ratification

approve . . . 2. OK 4. like, okay, pass, sign, test 6. attest, ratify 7. applaud, betoken, certify, confirm, endorse (indorse), signify 8. accredit, sanction, validate 9. authorize, undersign 10. appreciate
11. countenance 12. authenticate

approve of . . . 5. favor 6. accept
7. endorse (indorse) 8. sanction
11. countenance

approximate . . . 4. near 5. about, circa, match 8. approach, draw near, parallel, resemble 10. correspond

approximately . . . 5. about, circa
6. around, nearly 11. thereabouts

appui . . . 4. prop, stay 6. bridle (manège) 7. support

appulse . . . 6. syzygy 7. impinge
8. approach 9. collision
11. conjunction (Astron)

appurtenance . . . 4. gear 7. adjunct
8. addition 9. accessory, apparatus, appendage, belonging, component

appurtenant . . . 7. annexed 8. incident, relevant 9. appendant, belonging

11. appropriate
après... 5. after 10. afterwards
apricot (pert to)...
  African.. 6. meebos (dried)
  beverage.. 7. cordial, liqueur, persico
  color.. 9. red—yellow
  confection.. 6. meebos (mebos)
  Japanese.. 3. ume 4. ansu
  vine.. 6. maypop
a priori (opp of posteriori)...
  9. deductive 11. conditional,
  presumptive 12. hypothetical
  13. presumptively
apron... 3. bib 4. boot, brat, tier
  5. smock 6. barvel (barvell), runway
  7. garment, tablier 8. airstrip,
  lambskin (Masonic), pinafore
  9. appendage
apropos, a propos... 3. apt, pat
  7. germane, purpose 8. by the way,
  relevant, suitably 9. pertinent
  10. applicable, seasonable
  11. appurtenant, opportunely
  12. incidentally
apt... 3. fit, pat 4. deft 5. adept,
  prone, ready, smart 6. clever, expert,
  likely, prompt, suited 7. capable,
  elegant, subject 8. apposite,
  disposed, inclined, skillful, suitable
  9. competent, dexterous, ingenious,
  masterful, pertinent, qualified,
  teachable 10. proficient
  11. appropriate
apteral... 8. apterous, wingless
Apteryx... 3. moa (extinct) 4. kiwi
aptitude... 3. art 4. bent, gift, turn
  5. flair, skill 6. genius, talent
  7. ability, aptness, fitness, leaning
  8. penchant, tendency 9. liability
  10. likelihood, proclivity
  11. inclination 12. suitableness
  15. appropriateness
aptly... 7. exactly, readily 8. suitably
  11. pertinently
aptness... 5. skill 7. fitness
  8. tendency 9. smartness
  11. suitability 12. teachability
aqua... 3. eau 4. agua 5. water
aquatic... 6. natant, wading, watery
  8. natatory, swimming 12. grallatorial
  13. water—dwelling
Aquila... 6. eagles 13. constellation
  (Milky Way)
aquiline... 6. hanate, hooked
  7. curving 8. aduncous, unciform
  10. Roman—nosed
ara... 5. macaw 7. goddess
  (vengeance) 8. aracanga 9. screw
  pine 13. constellation
Arab... 4. waif 5. gamin, horse,
  nomad 6. Semite 7. Bedouin,
  Saracen 8. wanderer, Yemenite
  9. Caucasian
araba... 3. cab 5. coach 6. monkey
  (howling)
Arabia... see *Saudi-Arabia*
Arabian (pert to)...
  antelope.. 5. addax
  beverage.. 4. boza (bosa) 5. leban
  (lebban)
  bird.. 7. phoenix
  chief.. 5. sheik

cloth (shoulder).. 6. cabaan (caban)
demon.. 5. Eblis, jinni (jinnee)
  6. afreet
father.. 3. Abu (Ab, Abou) 4. Abba
garment.. 3. aba 4. haik 8. burnoose
gazelle.. 4. cora, oryx 5. ariel
horse.. 4. Kohl 8. kadischi, palomino
jasmine.. 4. bela
judge.. 4. cadi
juniper (Bib).. 5. retem
nomad.. 7. Saracen
peasant.. 6. fellah
physician.. 8. Avicenna
poet.. 5. Antar
prince.. 4. amir (ameer) 5. sheik
  6. sherif, sultan
romance.. 5. Antar (Antara)
ruler.. 6. caliph (calif)
Satan.. 5. Eblis 6. Azazel
scripture.. 7. Alcoran
seaport.. 4. Aden 5. Mocha
state of bliss.. 3. kef (kaif)
street urchin.. 5. gamin
tambourine.. 4. taar
tribe.. 3. Aus (anc)
vessel.. 4. dhow 6. boutre, sambuk
winds (hot).. 6. simoom (simoon)
arable land... 4. farm 5. arada, arado
  6. plowed, tilled 10. cultivated
arachnid... 4. mite, tick 6. spider
  8. scorpion 9. Arachnida
Aralu... 5. Hades
Aram (Bib)... 6. Rimmon (deity)
  7. Aramaic, Semitic 8. language
araneous... 4. thin 7. weblike
  8. delicate 10. cobweblike
arapunga... 8. bellbird 9. campanero
Arawak... 5. Guana 6. Indian
arbeit... 4. work 8. research
arbiter... 3. ump 5. judge 6. umpire
  7. arbiter, referee 8. mediator
  9. moderator 10. arbitrator
arbitrary... 6. thetic 8. absolute,
  despotic, dogmatic 9. imperious,
  unlimited 10. autocratic, capricious,
  high—handed, peremptory, tyrannical
  11. determinate, dictatorial
  13. discretionary
arbitrate... 6. decide 7. bargain,
  mediate 9. determine, intervene,
  negotiate 12. intermediate
arbitrator... 5. judge 6. umpire
  7. arbiter, referee 8. mediator
  9. moderator 11. conciliator
arbor, arbour... 5. bower, kiosk
  6. alcove, garden, pandal 7. pergola,
  retreat, trellis 11. latticework,
  summerhouse
arboreal... 6. ramous 8. branched,
  treelike 10. arboriform
arboreal mammal... 2. ai 4. unau
  5. lemur, sloth 6. aye—aye, monkey
arc... 3. bow 5. curve 6. radian
  7. azimuth, rainbow
arca... 3. box 5. chest, paten
  9. reliquary
arcade... 3. orb 4. arch, hall
  6. arches, avenue 7. gallery, portico
  8. arcature, corridor 9. colonnade,
  peristyle 10. passageway
Arcadia...
  composition.. 4. poem 5. prose

7. romance
district . . **6.** Greece
huntress . . **8.** Atalanta
pert to . . **5.** rural **8.** pastoral
poetic . . **6.** Arcady
priestess . . **4.** Auge
woodland spirit . . **3.** Pan
arcanum . . . **6.** elixir, enigma, remedy,
    secret **7.** mystery
arch . . . **3.** arc, sly **4.** ogee **5.** chief,
    hance (part), ogive, vault **6.** fornix,
    instep **7.** cunning, eminent, roguish
    8. greatest, memorial, monument
    9. principal **11.** mischievous
arch (pert to) . . .
enemy . . **5.** devil, Satan **9.** adversary
inner curve . . **8.** intrados
memorial . . **6.** pailou (pailoo)
stone . . **8.** keystone
title . . **4.** duke **6.** bishop, deacon
    7. duchess
archaic . . . **3.** old **8.** obsolete,
    old–world **10.** antiquated
    12. old–fashioned
archangel (celestial) . . . **5.** Uriel
    7. Gabriel, Michael, Raphael
archangel plant . . . **4.** mint **8.** angelica
archbishop . . . **6.** bishop (chief), exarch
    9. patriarch
arched . . . **6.** curved **7.** embowed
Archer (Astron) . . . **11.** Sagittarius
archery . . . **3.** bow **4.** vane **5.** arrow,
    clout **6.** quiver **8.** fistmele, shooting
    10. ballistics
archetype . . . **4.** idea **5.** model
    7. pattern **8.** standard **9.** prototype
Archie (sl) . . . **3.** gun **12.** antiaircraft
Archipelago (pert to) . . .
Alaska . . **9.** Alexander
Australia . . **8.** Bismarck
Indonesia (largest) . . **5.** Malay
Italy . . **6.** Aegean
architect . . . **6.** artist, author **7.** builder,
    planner **8.** designer **9.** artificer,
    draftsman **11.** constructor, enterpriser
architectural (pert to) . . .
arch . . **8.** keystone, voussoir
base . . **5.** socle **6.** plinth
construction . . **8.** tectonic
ornament (part) . . **5.** gutta **6.** bezant,
    finial, frieze **8.** acanthus, dosseret,
    fretwork **10.** chambranle
pier . . **4.** anta
space (triang) . . **8.** pediment
style . . **5.** Doric, Greek, Ionic, Tudor
    6. Gothic **7.** Baroque, Cape Cod,
    Moorish, Spanish **8.** Colonial,
    Etruscan, Georgian **9.** Byzantine,
    Palladian **10.** Corinthian, Romanesque
    11. Renaissance **13.** Mediterranean
archives . . . **6.** annals **7.** records
    8. chancery, registry **9.** documents,
    registers **10.** chronicles
arch traitor . . . **6.** Arnold (Benedict),
    Brutus **8.** Quisling **13.** Judas Iscariot
archway . . . **6.** pailou (pailoo)
arctic . . . **5.** polar **6.** boreal, frigid,
    galosh **7.** Alaskan **8.** hibernal,
    Northern, Siberian **11.** hyperborean
Arctic (pert to) . . .
base . . **4.** Etah (Greenland)
bird . . **3.** auk **4.** xema **6.** falcon

cetacean . . **7.** narwhal
current . . **8.** Labrador
dog . . **5.** Husky (Siberian) **8.** Malemute
food . . **8.** pemmican (pemican)
jacket (hooded) . . **5.** parka (parkee)
    6. anorak
native . . **5.** Aleut **6.** Eskimo, Indian
polar . . **6.** Circle
sea . . **7.** Barents **8.** Beaufort
arctoid . . . **6.** ursine **8.** bearlike
Arctoidea . . . **4.** bear **6.** weasel
    7. raccoon
ardent . . . **3.** hot **4.** avid, keen, warm
    5. eager, fiery, rethe **6.** fervid, fierce
    7. amorous, cordial, fervent, flaming,
    glowing, intense, shining, violent,
    zealous **8.** eloquent, vehement
    10. passionate **12.** affectionate,
    enthusiastic
ardilla . . . **8.** squirrel
ardor . . . **4.** élan, fire, heat, love, zeal
    5. estro, flame, gusto, verve
    6. fervor, fougue, spirit, warmth
    8. fervency **9.** affection, eagerness,
    eloquence, intensity **10.** enthusiasm
    11. impetuosity
arduous . . . **4.** hard **5.** steep **6.** trying
    7. onerous **8.** toilsome **9.** difficult,
    laborious, strenuous, wearisome
    10. burdensome, exhausting
area . . . **4.** belt, loci (pl), size, zone
    5. areal, basin, field, locus, range,
    scope, space, tract **6.** extent, locale,
    region, sector, sphere **7.** circuit,
    compass, environ, expanse
    8. province, vicinity **9.** bailiwick,
    territory **12.** neighborhood
Areca . . . **4.** palm
arena . . . **4.** bowl, oval, ring, rink
    5. court, field **6.** campus, circus
    7. cockpit, stadium, theater
    8. coliseum, platform **9.** gymnasium
    10. hippodrome **12.** amphitheater
arenose . . . **5.** sandy **6.** grainy, gritty
    8. sabulous
areola . . . **4.** halo, ring **5.** space
    6. armlet, wreath **7.** aureole, garland
    10. interstice
Ares (pert to) . . .
consort . . **9.** Aphrodite
father . . **4.** Zeus
god . . **3.** war
Roman name . . **4.** Mars
argala . . . **7.** marabou **8.** adjutant (bird)
argent . . . **5.** white **6.** silver **7.** shining,
    silvery **9.** whiteness
Argentina . . .
capital . . **11.** Buenos Aires (1535)
city . . **5.** Lanus **6.** Paraná **7.** Cordoba,
    Mendoza, Rosario
Indian . . **4.** Lule
mountain . . **5.** Andes **9.** Aconcagua
    (peak) **10.** Cordillera (Range)
native . . **7.** Mestizo
Plains . . **6.** Pampas **9.** Gran Chaco
plateau . . **9.** Patagonia
poet . . **7.** Andrade **10.** Echeverria
river . . **5.** Plata **6.** Chubut, Paraná
Argentine (pert to) . . .
color . . **7.** silvery **8.** art brown
cowboy . . **6.** gaucho
dance . . **5.** tango

Argonauts (pert to)...
destination .. **7.** Colchis (anc)
heroes (50) .. **6.** Jason's
objective .. **12.** Golden Fleece
of '49 .. **6.** miners (gold)
ship .. **5.** Argos
Argos ... **3.** dog (of Odysseus)
argosy ... **4.** ship **5.** fleet **6.** armada,
vessel **8.** flotilla
argot ... **4.** cant, jive **5.** lingo, slang
6. jargon, patois **7.** dialect
10. vernacular
argue ... **3.** rap **4.** moot, spar
5. plead, prove **6.** bicker, debate,
evince, reason **7.** contend, contest,
discuss, dispute, wrangle **8.** indicate,
maintain, persuade **10.** controvert
11. expostulate, ratiocinate,
remonstrate
argument ... **4.** case, plea, spar
5. cavil, lemma, proof, theme
6. debate, hassle **7.** defense, dispute,
fallacy, polemic, premise, sophism
8. brouhaha, squabble **9.** dialectic,
discourse, enthymeme, pro and con
10. discussion **11.** altercation,
disputation **13.** consideration,
ratiocination
argumentative ... **7.** eristic **8.** forensic
10. indicative, rhetorical
11. belligerent, contentious,
presumptive, quarrelsome
12. disputatious **13.** controversial
Argus (Gr Myth) ... **7.** monster (founder
of Argos)
Argus–eyed ... **8.** vigilant **9.** observant
11. hundred–eyed **12.** sharpsighted
argute ... **5.** acute, sharp **6.** astute,
shrewd, shrill, subtle **9.** sagacious
aria ... **3.** air, lay **4.** solo, song, tune
5. canto **6.** cantus, melody, strain
7. ariette, sortita
arid ... **3.** dry **4.** dull **6.** barren, jejune,
vacant **7.** parched, sterile, thirsty
9. anhydrous, waterless
13. unimaginative
Arid Austral zone ... **7.** Sonoran
Ariel ... **5.** angel, sylph **6.** spirit
7. lioness **9.** Jerusalem
ariel ... **7.** gazelle
Aries (Astron) ... **3.** ram **4.** sign
6. meteor **13.** constellation
aries ... **12.** battering–ram (anc)
aright ... **4.** fine, well **7.** exactly
8. directly, straight **11.** straightway
aril ... **3.** pod **7.** arillus, coating
8. arillode (false), covering
Arion ... **4.** poet (of Lesbos) **5.** horse
(talking)
arioso ... **7.** melodic, tuneful
9. melodious
arise ... **4.** lift, rise, soar, stem, zoom
5. begin, issue, mount, occur, rebel,
surge, tower, waken **6.** appear,
ascend, emerge, revolt, spring
7. emanate **9.** originate
Aristarch ... **6.** critic **10.** grammarian
Aristides ... **7.** The Just **9.** statesman
(Athens)
aristocracy ... **5.** elite **7.** peerage,
royalty **8.** nobility **10.** government,
patriciate, upper class

aristocrat ... **4.** lord, peer **5.** noble
7. aristos, Brahman, Brahmin,
grandee, parvenu **8.** cavalier, eupatrid
(Athens), nobleman **9.** blueblood,
patrician **12.** silk–stocking
aristology, science of ... **6.** dining
Aristotle (pert to) ...
birthplace .. **6.** Thrace **7.** Stagira
(Macedonia)
famed as .. **9.** scientist
11. philosopher **12.** The Stagirite
school .. **6.** Athens
teacher .. **5.** Plato
wife .. **7.** Pythias
arithmetic ... **4.** sums **7.** numbers
11. computation, enumeration,
mathematics
arithmetic terms ... **5.** prime **6.** result
7. divisor, product **8.** dividend,
multiple, quotient **9.** remainder
10. multiplier **12.** multiplicand
Arizona ...
capital .. **7.** Phoenix
city .. **4.** Yuma **5.** Tempe **6.** Bisbee,
Tucson
famed site .. **9.** Hoover Dam
11. Grand Canyon **13.** Painted
Desert **15.** Petrified Forest
Indian .. **4.** Hano, Hopi, Pima
6. Apache, Navaho (Navajo)
river .. **4.** Gila **8.** Colorado
State admission .. **11.** Forty–eighth
State bird .. **10.** cactus wren
State flower .. **6.** cactus **7.** saguaro
State motto .. **9.** Ditat Deus **11.** God
Enriches
State nickname .. **11.** Grand Canyon
ark ... **3.** vat **4.** boat, ship **5.** chest,
haven **6.** asylum, refuge, vessel
8. flatboat **9.** broadhorn, sanctuary
(Ararat)
Arkansas ...
capital .. **10.** Little Rock
city .. **8.** El Dorado **9.** Fort Smith
famed for .. **8.** diamonds (found in
Murfreesboro)
famed newspaper .. **7.** Gazette (1819)
mountain .. **6.** Ozarks **9.** Ouachitas
Park (Nat) .. **10.** Hot Springs
river .. **5.** White **11.** Mississippi
State admission .. **11.** Twenty–fifth
State bird .. **11.** mockingbird
State flower .. **12.** apple blossom
State motto .. **13.** Regnat Populus
16. Let the People Rule
State nickname .. **19.** Land of
Opportunity
arm ... **4.** limb **5.** equip, saber, sword
6. branch, member, pistol, tappet,
weapon **7.** forearm, fortify, protect,
quillon (of sword), support **8.** revolver
9. appendage **10.** projection
12. ramification
arm (pert to) ...
armpit .. **5.** oxter **6.** axilla
bone .. **4.** ulna **6.** radius **7.** humerus
hole .. **4.** scye (of sleeve)
muscle .. **6.** biceps **7.** triceps
projection .. **6.** tappet
sea .. **4.** gulf, mere **5.** bayou, firth,
inlet **7.** estuary
sundial .. **6.** gnomon

walk arm in arm.. 5. oxter
armada... 5. fleet 6. argosy
  8. armament, flotilla, squadron,
  warships 10. escadrille
Armada (famed)... 7. Spanish (1588)
  10. Invincible
armadillo... 4. apar, peba (peva)
  5. apara, poyou, tatou (tatu)
  6. mulita, peludo (giant) 7. tatouay
  10. pichiciago, Tolypeutes
  11. quirquincho (hairy)
Armageddon... 3. war 7. Megiddo
  (Bib) 8. conflict, world war
armed... 6. fitted, rigged 7. clothed,
  endowed 8. equipped, invested,
  prepared, provided, supplied
  9. furnished, outfitted 10. laquearian
  (with noose)
armed (pert to)...
  conflict.. 3. war 6. combat 7. warfare
  11. hostilities
  forces.. 4. army, host 5. ranks
  6. troops 8. military 9. besiegers
  vessel.. 3. HMS, sub, USS 5. U–boat
  9. destroyer, submarine
  10. battleship 11. battlewagon
Armenia...
  anc name.. 9. Armenenak
  capital.. 6. Erivan
  founder.. 4. Haik
  herb.. 5. cumin 7. caraway
  highlanders.. 5. Gomer
  mountain.. 6. Ararat, Taurus
  river.. 3. Kur 5. Cyrus 6. Araxes,
  Tigris 9. Euphrates
  worshiper.. 7. Yesidio (Yesdi)
  9. Gregorian
armistice... 5. peace, truce
  9. cessation 12. pacification
armoire... 5. ambry 8. cupboard,
  wardrobe 10. repository
armor... 4. arms, bard (barde), egis,
  jamb, mail, tace 5. acton, aegis,
  plate, seton, tasse 6. cuisse, gorget,
  graith, greave, helmet, lorica, sconce,
  shield, tasset, tuille 7. ailette,
  cuirass, hauberk, jambeau, panoply
  8. aventail, brassort, ordnance,
  pallette, solleret 9. cubitiere,
  epauliere, gardebras, mainferre,
  rerebrace 10. cataphract
armor–bearer... 6. squire 7. armiger,
  esquire
armored... 6. mailed 8. equipped,
  ironclad, mailclad 9. cuirassed,
  loricated, panoplied
armpit... 5. oxter 6. axilla
arms... 7. weapons 8. armament,
  ordnance 9. munitions
arms depository... 5. depot 6. armory
  7. arsenal
army... 3. mob 4. host, unit 5. array,
  crowd, horde, posse 6. forces,
  galaxy, legion, rabble, throng, troops
  9. multitude, Salvation
army (pert to)...
  brown.. 7. rosario
  commission (special).. 6. brevet
  trader.. 6. sutler
army unit... 4. ROTC 5. corps, guard
  (Nat), squad 7. brigade, cavalry,
  company, militia, platoon, Sabaoth

  (Bib) 8. division, infantry, Landwehr,
  regiment, reserves 9. artillery,
  minutemen 10. volunteers
Arnold's co–conspirator... 5. Andre
  (Maj)
aroma... 4. musk, odor, tang 5. attar,
  balmy, nidor, savor, scent, smell,
  spice 6. flavor 7. bouquet, feature,
  incense, perfume 9. fragrance,
  muskiness, redolence 11. peculiarity,
  singularity
aromatic... 5. spicy 6. savory
  7. odorous, pungent 8. fragrant,
  redolent 11. fluorescent
aromatic (pert to)...
  gum.. 5. myrrh 12. frankincense
  herb.. 4. mint 5. clary, nondo
  oil.. 4. balm 6. balsam 9. sassafras
  seed.. 4. anis 6. nutmeg 7. aniseed
  tree.. 5. aromo 6. balsam
  7. champac 8. huisache
around... 4. near, peri (pref) 5. about,
  circa 9. bordering, somewhere
  11. thereabouts 13. approximately
arouse... 4. fire, stir, wake 5. alarm,
  anger, evoke, raise, rally, roust
  6. awaken, elicit, excite, incite,
  kindle, summon 7. animate
arpa... 4. harp
arpeggio... 5. chord 7. roulade
  8. division, flourish
arraign... 4. cite 6. accuse, charge,
  indict 7. impeach 8. denounce,
  reproach 9. prosecute
arrange... 3. fix 4. cast, cite, file,
  plan, plot, sort 5. adapt, aline,
  besee, drape, ettle, frame, grade,
  preen, range, stack 6. adjust, deploy,
  design, devise 7. dispose, mediate,
  prepare, provide, seriate 8. classify,
  contract, contrive, laminate, organize,
  tabulate 9. catalogue (catalog),
  negotiate 10. distribute, paniculate
  11. alphabetize, systematize
arranged... 5. fixed, timed 6. ranked,
  sorted 7. aligned, grouped, ordered,
  orderly, planned, settled, uniform
  9. regulated 10. contracted
arranged in...
  fives.. 7. quinate
  fours.. 11. tetramerous
  hours.. 9. staggered
  rays.. 6. radial
  threes.. 7. ternate
arrangement... 3. art, rig (sails)
  4. plan, rank 5. order, setup
  6. series, syntax, system 7. echelon
  (troops), musical 8. disposal,
  neatness, trimness 9. agreement,
  condition, structure 10. adaptation,
  engagement, settlement
  11. collocation, combination,
  permutation, preparation
  12. distribution
arrant... 3. bad 6. wicked 8. rascally
  9. confirmed, shameless
  11. unmitigated 12. disreputable
array... 3. don 4. deci, robe 5. adorn,
  align, dress, order 6. clothe, muster,
  series, throng 7. arrange, dispose,
  envelop, marshal 8. clothing,
  garments 9. adornment

11. arrangement
arrears... 3. due 4. debt 5. short
7. wanting 9. arrearage, deficient
10. behindhand, defaulting
arrest... 4. halt, hold, stop 5. check,
delay, seize 6. detain, hinder,
impede, retard 7. custody, seizure
8. obstruct, restrain, stoppage
9. apprehend, hindrance, intercept,
restraint 11. retardation
arrested... 6. behind 7. checked,
delayed, impeded, stopped
8. detained, retarded 10. restrained
11. intercepted
arrested development... 6. simple
7. dwarfed, idiotic, moronic
8. backward, retarded 10. half–witted
13. unintelligent
arrival... 5. comer (anc) 6. advent,
coming 7. landing 8. approach,
reaching 10. attainment, homecoming
11. achievement
arrive... 4. come 5. debus, reach
6. alight, debark, happen 7. detrain
9. disembark
arrogance... 5. pride 7. conceit,
disdain, hauteur 8. audacity,
rudeness, snobbery 9. brashness,
insolence, loftiness 10. effrontery
11. haughtiness 12. impertinence
arrogant... 4. bold, pert 5. cocky,
lofty, proud 6. lordly, uppish
7. forward 8. impudent, insolent
9. audacious, insulting, masterful,
presuming 10. disdainful
11. domineering, high–falutin,
impertinent, overbearing
12. contemptuous, contumelious,
presumptuous, supercilious
arrogate... 5. seize, usurp, wrest
6. assume 11. appropriate
arrow... 4. barb, dart, reed, vire
(feathered) 5. guide, shaft 6. finger
7. missile, pointer 10. guideboard
arrow (pert to)...
astronomy.. 7. Sagitta
bows.. 6. bowyer (maker, seller)
case.. 6. quiver
end.. 4. nock 9. arrowhead
feather (to).. 6. fletch
handle.. 5. stele
head.. 4. dart
poison.. 4. inee, upas 5. urali
6. curare, uzarin
poisoned.. 6. sumpit 8. sumpitan
propeller.. 3. bow
shape.. 6. beloid 9. cuneiform,
sagittate
stone.. 9. belemnite
variety.. 4. self 6. footed 7. chested
9. bobtailed
arrowroot... 3. pia 5. araru 6. ararao,
starch 7. Maranta
arroyo... 5. brook, creek 6. ravine,
stream 11. watercourse
arroz... 4. rice
arse... 4. butt, rump (vulgar)
8. buttocks 9. posterior
arsenal... 4. dump 5. depot, plant
6. armory 7. factory 8. magazine
10. depository, storehouse
arsis... 5. ictus 6. accent, stress (opp

of thesis), upbeat
arson... 7. burning, cautery
9. pyromania 12. incendiarism
art... 4. wile 5. cameo, craft, knack,
skill, taste, trade 6. design
7. calling, cartoon, cunning, drawing,
science 8. aptitude, artifice, artistry,
business, ceramics, drafting, intaglio,
painting, vocation 9. dexterity,
duplicate, engraving, ingenuity,
readiness, sculpture, sketching
10. adroitness, decoration, profession
11. contrivance, photography,
portraiture 12. architecture
art (pert to)...
addict.. 8. aesthete (esthete)
decoration.. 9. sgraffito
design.. 7. graphic
fancier.. 10. dilettante
gallery.. 5. salon
grotesque.. 11. incongruous
mystic.. 6. cabala
of assaying.. 8. docimasy
of discourse.. 8. rhetoric
of embossing.. 9. toreutics
of government.. 8. politics
of horsemanship.. 6. manège
of imitation.. 7. mimicry
of manual craft.. 5. sloyd
of memory.. 10. mneumonics
of metal inlay.. 6. niello
primitive.. 9. artifacts
realistic.. 5. genre
rhyming.. 5. poesy 6. poetry
self–defense.. 6. boxing 7. fencing,
jujitsu (jiujitsu)
style.. 6. cubism, purism 7. baroque,
Dadaism, Fauvism 8. futurism
9. modernism 10. surrealism
13. impressionism
theme.. 5. motif
tooling.. 10. diesinking
transmutation.. 7. alchemy
Artemis (pert to)...
brother (twin).. 6. Apollo
epithet (Homeric).. 6. Phoebe
father.. 4. Zeus
goddess of.. 4. moon 6. nature
7. the Hunt 8. Olympian
Mother.. 4. Leto
religion.. 4. Upis
Roman equivalent.. 5. Diana
artery... 4. tube, vein 6. avenue,
street, vessel 7. channel, highway,
passage 8. ligament 10. passageway
artery (Anat)... 4. tube, vein 5. aorta
6. vessel 7. anonyma, carotid,
trachea 9. capillary, pulmonary
10. innominate
artery pulsation... 4. beat 5. ictus
artful... 3. sly 4. foxy, wily 5. cagey
6. adroit, clever, crafty, shrewd,
subtle, tricky 7. crooked, cunning,
knowing, politic 8. skillful, stealthy
9. deceitful, deceptive, designing,
dexterous, imitative 10. artificial
Artful Dodger... 3. fox 6. rascal
7. slicker 8. deceiver 11. John
Dawkins (Dickens tale) 12. crafty
person
artfulness... 5. skill 7. finesse
8. artifice, subtlety, wiliness

9. stratagem 10. cleverness, refinement, shrewdness
arthron... 5. hinge, joint, pivot 12. articulation
Arthurian abode... 6. Avalon 9. Lyonnesse (Leonnoys)
Arthurian character... 6. Arthur (King), Elaine, Merlin 7. Geraint 8. Lancelot 9. Percivale
artichoke... 6. canada, Cynara 7. chorogi, thistle 9. Jerusalem
article... 3. mat 4. item, news, term 5. scoop, story, thing 6. belief, clause, detail, gadget, object, treaty 7. camelot, feature (news), grammar, integer 8. treatise 9. commodity, editorial 10. particular 11. composition, stipulation
article (Gram)...
English.. 1. a 2. an 3. the
French.. 2. la, le, un 3. les, une
Spanish.. 2. el, un 3. las, los, una
article (of)...
agreement.. 8. contract
apparel.. 5. smock, tunic 6. duster, gaiter, mantle 8. pinafore
faith.. 5. canon, creed, dogma, tenet 6. belief 7. precept
property.. 7. chattel
virtu.. 5. curio, relic 6. rarity 7. antique
articulation... 4. tone 5. hinge, joint, sound, voice 7. voicing 8. locution, sonation 9. phonation, utterance 11. enunciation 12. vocalization 13. pronunciation
artifact... 5. curio, relic, virtu 6. fossil 7. antique, remains 8. archaism
artifice... 4. plot, ruse, wile 5. blind, chest, craft, dodge, fraud, guile, shift, trick 6. deceit 7. cunning, evasion, finesse, knavery, sleight 8. intrigue, maneuver, trickery 9. chicanery, collusion, deception, expedient, imposture, stratagem 10. connivance, imposition, subterfuge 11. contrivance, machination, skulduggery
artificer... 5. smith 6. artist, framer 7. artisan, creator, deviser, workman 8. Daedalus, inventor, mechanic 9. architect, carpenter, craftsman, goldsmith 11. coppersmith, silversmith
artificial... 4. fake, mock, sham 5. bogus, dummy, false, phony 6. ersatz, forged, unreal 7. assumed, bastard, elegant, feigned 8. affected, fabulous, spurious 9. imaginary, imitation, pretended, unnatural 11. adulterated, counterfeit, unauthentic 12. supposititious
artificial (pert to)...
butter.. 4. oleo 13. oleomargarine
channel.. 3. gat 4. leat 5. canal, flume 6. sluice
gum.. 7. dextrin
language.. 2. ro 3. Ido 5. Arulo 7. Volapuk 9. Esperanto 10. Occidental
silk.. 5. nylon, rayon
surface.. 4. rink

voice.. 8. falsetto
artillery... 4. army, guns 5. bombs 6. cannon, slings 7. cavalry, gunners, gunnery, mortars 8. ordnance 9. arbalests, catapults 10. ballistics
artillery (pert to)...
emplacement.. 7. battery
fire.. 5. salvo 6. rafale
man.. 6. gunner 8. rifleman, topechee 9. cannoneer, musketeer 11. artillarist
wagon.. 7. battery
artiodactyl... (opp of perissodactyl) 2. ox 3. pig 4. deer, goat 5. camel, sheep 6. artiad 7. giraffe 12. hippopotamus
artisan... 6. artist, limner 7. painter, workman 8. mechanic, virtuoso 9. artificer, craftsman
artist... 5. rapin (Fr pupil) 6. etcher, limner, potter 7. artisan, painter 8. designer, sculptor 9. architect, decorator 10. cartoonist, ceramacist 11. illustrator 12. photographer
artist (pert to)...
equipment.. 5. easel 7. palette 8. maquette
sleight of hand.. 4. mage 5. Magus 8. magician 9. alchemist
artiste... 5. actor, adept 6. dancer, singer 7. artisan 8. musician 9. performer
artistic... 4. pure 6. ornate 7. classic 8. graceful, skillful, tasteful 9. aesthetic (esthetic), art-minded, beautiful, exquisite
artistic (pert to)...
ardor.. 5. verve 6. spirit
dance.. 6. ballet
quality.. 6. virtue
symbol of the dead.. 5. orant
temperament.. 7. caprice, emotion
artless... 4. naif, open, rude 5. frank, naive 6. candid, simple 7. natural, sincere 8. ignorant 9. guileness, ingenuous, unskilled 10. inartistic, unaffected, uncultured 11. undesigning 15. unsophisticated
artlessness... 6. candor 7. naiveté 9. frankness, innocence 11. naturalness 13. ungenuousness
arts (pert to)...
liberal.. 7. trivium 10. quadrivium
quadrivium.. 5. music 8. geometry 9. astronomy 10. arithmetic
trivium.. 5. logic 7. grammar 8. rhetoric
aru... 6. indeed, really
arui... 5. oudad, sheep 7. chamois (Bib)
arum... 4. taro 5. calla (lily) 6. starch 9. arrowroot
arx... 7. citadel
Aryan (pert to)...
God of Fire.. 4. Agni
invader.. 4. Pict
people.. 4. Mede 5. Hindu 9. Caucasian 11. Indo-Iranian
as... 3. qua 4. como, than, thus 5. since, while 7. because, equally, similar 9. similarly

Asa... 11. King of Judah
asafetida... 8. medicine
   13. antispasmodic
Asa's son... 11. Jehoshaphat
ascend... 3. fly 4. rise, soar, upgo
   5. arise, climb, mount, scale, tower
   6. aspire, uprise 7. clamber, upsurge
ascendancy... 4. sway 7. control,
   mastery 8. dominion, prestige,
   priority 9. authority, influence,
   supremacy 10. domination
   11. sovereignty, superiority
   12. predominance 13. preponderance
ascendant, ascendent... 5. elder
   6. father 7. supreme 8. ancestor,
   forebear, superior 9. governing,
   patriarch 10. antecedent, decoration
   (Arch)
ascended... 4. rose 5. arose, risen
   6. uprose
ascending... 6. anodic, rising
   7. scaling, sloping 8. mounting,
   racemose 9. emanating
ascending signs... 5. Aries 6. Gemini,
   Pisces, Taurus 8. Aquarius
   9. Capricorn
ascenseur... 8. elevator
Ascension Day... 8. Thursday (Holy),
   (40 days after Easter)
Ascension lily... 7. Madonna
ascertain... 4. find 5. learn, prove,
   solve 6. decide 7. certify
   9. determine
ascetic... 4. yati, yoga, yogi 5. fakir,
   stoic 6. Essene, hermit, strict
   7. austere, eremite, puritan, recluse
   8. anchoret, Diogenes, solitary
   9. abstainer, anchorite, mendicant
   10. abstemious
asceticism... 4. Yoga 9. austerity,
   nephalism 10. abstention, abstinence,
   puritanism 11. anchoritism,
   teetotalism
ascribable... 3. due 9. traceable
   10. assignable 11. attributive
   12. attributable
ascribe... 5. count, refer 6. assign,
   attach, credit, impute, reckon
   7. ascribe 8. accredit 9. attribute
ascus fruit... 8. truffles
asepsis... 6. purity 7. clarity 9. sterility
   13. taintlessness
ash... 4. sorb, tree 5. rowan
   6. samara (fruit) 8. Fraxinus
ashes... 4. dust, lava, lees, slag
   5. dregs, ruins 6. embers
   7. cinders, residue
ash tree symbol (Norse Myth)...
   10. Yggdrasill (horse of Yggr)
Asia... 4. East 6. Orient, region 7. Far
   East 8. Old World 9. continent
Asia Minor...
   city (anc).. 4. Myra, Teos, Troy
   5. Ilium, Issus, Lydia 6. Nicaea,
   Sardes 7. Ephesus
   district.. 4. Aria 5. Ionia, Troad (The
   Troad) 6. Aeolis
   island.. 6. Lesbos
   language (anc).. 6. Lycian, Lydian
   8. Etruscan
   mountain.. 3. Ida
   old name.. 8. Anatolia

   sea.. 5. Black 6. Aegean 7. Marmosa
   13. Mediterranean
Asiatic (pert to)...
   barbarian (anc).. 3. Hun 6. Vandal
   desert.. 4. Gobi
   gulf.. 4. Aden, Oman, Siam 6. Tonkin
   7. Persian
   island.. 4. Java 5. Luzon, Malay
   7. Celebes, Diomede (Big), Formosa,
   Sumatra 8. Japanese, Mindanao,
   Sakhalin 11. Philippines
   mountain.. 4. Ural 5. Altai, Sayan
   7. Everest 8. Caucasus, Himalaya
   9. Hindu Kush
   native.. 4. Arab, Turk, Yuit 5. Tatar
   6. Indian, Innuit (Esk), Syrian
   7. Chinese, Malayan 8. Annamese,
   Japanese 9. Mongolian
   nomad.. 4. Arab
   river.. 2. Ob 4. Amur, Lena
   5. Hwang, Indus 6. Ganges
   7. Yangtze, Yenisei 9. Euphrates,
   Irrawaddy 11. Brahmaputra
   sea.. 4. Azov (Azof) 5. Black, China,
   Japan 6. Bering, Yellow 7. Caspian,
   Okhotsk
Asiatic animal...
   antelope.. 5. goral
   ass.. 6. onager
   camel.. 8. Bactrian 9. dromedary
   carnivore.. 5. panda, tiger
   cattle.. 4. zobo
   deer.. 4. axis 10. chevrotain
   elephant.. 7. Elephas
   fox.. 6. corsac
   gazelle.. 3. ahu
   goat.. 5. serow
   lemur.. 5. loris 6. macaco
   lynx.. 7. caracal
   mongoose.. 4. urva
   monkey.. 6. langur (long–tailed)
   ox.. 3. yak
   rodent.. 4. pika
   sheep.. 3. sha 5. uriel 6. argali
   squirrel.. 8. jelerang 10. polatouche
Asiatic bird...
   finch.. 9. brambling
   jay.. 7. sirgang
   owl.. 4. utum
   partridge.. 6. seesee
   plover.. 8. dotterel
   songless.. 5. Pitta
   talking.. 4. myna (mynah)
Asiatic snake... 3. asp 5. cobra
   8. ringhals
Asiatic storm (pert to)...
   sand.. 6. simoom (simoon) 7. tebbard
   snow.. 5. buran
   wind.. 5. buran 7. monsoon
aside... 4. away 5. apart, hence
   6. aslant, astray, beside 7. whisper
   8. sidewise 9. alongside, privately,
   sotto voce 12. interjection
asinine... 4. dumb 5. inane, inept, silly
   6. mulish, stupid 7. doltish, foolish,
   idiotic 9. obstinate
ask... 3. beg 4. quiz 5. claim, exact,
   query, speer 6. assess, demand,
   invite 7. beseech, entreat, implore,
   inquire, request, require, solicit
   8. petition, question 9. catechize,
   obsecrate (Relig) 11. interrogate

askance... 4. awry 5. askew
   7. asquint, crooked 8. sideways
   9. obliquely
askew... 4. agee, alop, awry 5. agley,
   amiss 6. faulty 7. askance, asquint,
   crooked 8. deranged 9. distorted,
   obliquely 10. catawampus, disorderly
aslant... 5. atilt 6. tilted, tipped
   7. athwart, leaning, listing, pitched,
   sloping 8. inclined 9. careening,
   obliquely
asleep... 4. dead, dull, numb
   7. dormant, unaware 8. deadened,
   sleeping, unarisen 9. oblivious,
   senseless, unruffled 10. motionless
   11. inattentive, insensitive,
   unconscious
Asoka's Empire (anc Ind)... 5. Patna
asp... 5. cobra, snake, viper 6. uraeus
   (sacred sym)
aspect... 3. air 4. look, mien, pose,
   side, view 5. angle, decil, facet,
   guise, phase, shape, sight, state
   6. decile, facies, status, visage
   7. bearing, posture, scenery
   8. attitude 9. astrology, component,
   influence, seaminess, situation
   10. appearance 11. countenance
aspen... 4. tree, wood 6. poplar
   7. quaking 9. quivering, shivering,
   trembling, tremulous, vibrating
asperge... 3. wet 4. damp 5. spray,
   water 7. baptize 8. humidify, sprinkle
asperge... 9. asparagus
Asperges... 4. rite 6. anthem
   10. sprinkling (altar)
aspergillum... 5. brush 7. sprayer
   8. baptizer 9. sprinkler
asperity... 5. rigor 7. raucity
   8. acerbity, acrimony, hardship,
   severity, tartness 9. bleakness,
   roughness 10. causticity, difficulty,
   inclemency, moroseness, resentment
asperse... 4. slur 5. abuse, decry, libel
   6. defame, malign, revile, vilify
   7. blacken, slander, traduce
   8. besmirch 9. bespatter, discredit
   10. calumniate
aspersion... 4. rite, slur 6. insult
   7. affront, baptism, calumny, outrage,
   wetting 8. innuendo 9. indignity
   10. defamation, sprinkling
   12. calumniating, calumniation
   13. disparagement
asphalt... 4. pave 5. pitch 7. bitumen,
   mineral 6. blacktop, pavement,
   uintaite 9. gilsonite 10. macadamize
asphyxia... 5. apnea (apnoea)
   7. choking 11. suffocation
   12. smotheration
aspic... 3. asp (poet) 5. jelly
   6. cannon 8. lavender 9. galantine
aspiration... 3. aim 4. hope, wish
   5. ideal 6. breath, desire
   7. pumping, sucking, suction
   8. ambition, staccato 9. breathing
   10. exhalation 11. inspiration
aspire... 4. long, plan, rise, soar
   5. tower 6. attain, desire, expect,
   intend 7. breathe, propose
ass... 3. ono (comb form) 4. dolt,
   dope, fool, jack 5. burro, jenny

assail... 4. pelt 5. beset, stone
   6. attack 7. assault 9. implicate
   11. incriminate
assailant... 3. foe 5. enemy 7. invader
   8. assailer, attacker, opponent
   9. adversary, aggressor
   10. antagonist, challenger
Assam...
   capital.. 8. Shillong
   native.. 4. Ahom 8. Assamite
   11. Indo–Chinese
   province of.. 5. India
   river.. 11. Brahmaputra
   tribe.. 2. Ao 3. Aka 4. Garo, Naga
assassin... 4. Cain, thug 5. bravo
   6. apache, cuttle, gunman, killer,
   slayer 7. gorilla, ruffian 8. murderer,
   sicarian 9. manslayer 11. slaughterer
assassination... 5. purge 6. murder
   7. killing 8. regicide 11. liquidation
   12. manslaughter
Assassin Order... 8. Ismalian
   10. Mohammedan
assault... 5. onset, storm 6. assail,
   attack, charge 7. descent, seizure
   8. invasion 9. incursion
   13. incrimination
assay... 3. try 4. test 5. prove, trial
   6. accost 7. attempt 8. analysis,
   docimasy (art), endeavor
   10. experiment 12. verification
assay cup... 5. cupel
assemblage... 3. all 4. herd 6. throng
   8. assembly, entirety 9. gathering
   12. congregation
assemblage (pert to)...
   cattle.. 5. drove, rodeo 7. roundup
   fashionable.. 5. salon
   mob.. 4. rout 6. rabble
   splendid.. 6. galaxy
   tents.. 4. camp 10. encampment
assemble... 3. pod 4. mass, meet
   5. amass, piece, rally, unite
   6. couple, gather, muster 7. cluster,
   collect, convene, convoke, recruit
   10. congregate
assembly... 4. bevy, diet, moot
   5. agora, gemot, group, synod, troop
   6. assize, sabbat 7. company,
   council, landtag, meeting 8. auditory,
   conclave (secret), folkmoot (Hist)
   9. concourse, gathering
   10. collection, convention
   11. convocation 12. congregation
assent... 3. aye, nod, yea, yes
   4. amen 5. admit, agree, grant
   6. accede, accord, concur
   7. consent 8. sanction 9. acquiesce,
   agreement 10. compliance
   12. acquiescence
assert... 3. say 4. aver, pose 5. claim,
   plead, posit, state, voice 6. affirm,
   allege, avouch, relate, uphold
   7. contend, declare, profess, protest,
   support 8. advocate 9. pronounce,
   vindicate 10. asseverate
assertion... 5. claim 6. remark, thesis
   7. premise 8. averment 9. statement
   10. assumption, hypothesis
   11. affirmation, declaration,
   maintenance, proposition, vindication
assertiveness... 10. pragmatism

14. aggressiveness

assertor... 8. affirmer, defender 9. supporter 10. vindicator

assess... 3. ask, tax 4. cess, levy, mise, rate 5. price, value 6. charge 7. measure 8. appraise, estimate

assessment... 3. fee, tax 4. levy, rate, scot 5. ratal, stock, value 6. surtax 7. pricing, scutage 8. estimate 9. appraisal, valuation 10. evaluation 11. measurement

assets... 5. funds, means 6. wealth 7. capital 8. accounts, property 9. resources

asseverate... 3. say, vow 4. aver 5. state, swear 6. affirm, allege, assert 7. contend, declare, profess, protest 8. maintain 9. pronounce

asseveration... 3. vow 4. oath (solemn) 8. averment 9. assertion 11. affirmation, declaration 13. pronouncement

assiduity... 8. industry 9. diligence 11. painstaking, persistence 12. perseverance

assiduous... 4. busy 6. active 7. intense, zealous 8. diligent, sedulous 9. energetic, laborious, unwearied 11. industrious, perseverant 13. indefatigable, unintermitted

assign... 3. fix, set 4. cast, cede, seal 5. allot, refer 6. allege, commit, detail 7. address, adjudge, appoint, ascribe, consign, empower 8. accredit, allocate, delegate, nominate, transfer 9. attribute 10. commission 11. appropriate

assignment... 3. job 4. task 5. chore, stint 6. lesson 7. mission 8. exercise, transfer 9. allotment 10. allocation, commission, commitment 11. attribution 13. specification

assimilate... 5. adapt, learn, liken 6. absorb, digest, imbibe 7. convert 10. understand 11. approximate

assimilation... 8. imbibing, learning 9. anabolism, digestion, ingestion, reduction 10. absorption, adaptation, comparison, conversion 14. naturalization

assist... 3. aid 4. abet, back, help 5. avail, boost, favor 6. attend, prompt, second, succor 7. benefit, relieve, support, sustain 8. befriend 9. accompany, subsidize

assistance... 3. aid 4. help 5. grant 6. relief, succor 7. service, subsidy, support 10. logrolling (Polit) 11. furtherance

assistant... 4. aide, ally 5. tutor 6. deputy, helper 7. abettor, famulus, servant, teacher 9. associate, attendant, auxiliary 11. subordinate 12. right–hand man

assize... 3. fix 4. rate 5. edict, trial, value 6. assess, decree 9. ordinance 10. regulation 11. instruction, measurement

associate... 3. mix, pal 4. ally, chum, mate 5. buddy, crony 6. fellow, friend, hobnob, mingle 7. combine, comrade, consort, partner 9. colleague, companion 10. accomplice 11. concomitant, confederate

associated... 6. allied, banded, joined, united 7. coupled, leagued, related 9. connected 10. affiliated, concurrent

associates... 4. crew 5. force, staff 7. retinue 9. personnel 12. constituency

association... 4. body, club 5. artel, cabal, guild, hanse (Hist), union 6. league, lyceum, symbol 7. company, society 8. alliance, relation, sodality, sorority 9. syndicate 10. fellowship, fraternity 11. affiliation, combination, comradeship, concurrence, corporation 13. communication, interrelation

assonance... 3. pun 4. rime 5. rhyme 8. paragram 9. agreement 11. paronomasia, resemblance 12. alliteration

assort... 4. sort, suit 5. adapt, class, grade, group 7. consort (with) 8. classify, separate 9. associate (with) 10. categorize, distribute

assortment... 3. mix, set 4. hash, mess, olio 5. class, group 6. jumble, medley 7. mélange, mixture, sorting 9. potpourri 10. collection, hodgepodge, miscellany 11. arrangement 14. conglomeration

assuage... 4. calm, ease 5. allay, slake 6. lessen, mellow, pacify, quench, soften, solace, soothe 7. appease, comfort, gratify, qualify, relieve, satisfy 8. mitigate, palliate 9. alleviate

assuasive... 5. balmy 6. easing 8. remedial, soothing 9. relieving, softening 10. mitigating, palliative 11. alleviative 13. tranquilizing

assume... 3. don 4. deem, sham, take 5. adopt, feign, guess, imply, infer, judge, think, usurp 6. affect, allege, betake, borrow, deduce 7. believe, imagine, premise, presume, pretend, suppose, surmise 8. arrogate, conclude, simulate 9. undertake 11. appropriate, counterfeit

assume (pert to)...
character.. 11. impersonate
different forms.. 7. protean
unduly.. 5. usurp 8. arrogate
without proof.. 11. theoretical 12. hypothetical

assumed... 6. deemed 7. alleged, implied, thought 8. affected, inferred, presumed, supposed 9. fictional, pretended 10. fictitious, understood, undertaken 11. conjectured, make–believe, presumptive, presupposed, theoretical 12. appropriated, hypothetical, suppositious

assuming... 5. lofty 8. arrogant, superior 9. presuming 10. assumptive 11. overweening, pretentious 12. presumptuous

assumption . . . 8. adoption
9. arrogance, postulate, reception
10. usurpation 11. implication,
proposition, supposition
13. appropriation, incorporation
14. presupposition
assurance . . . 4. hope, oath 5. poise,
trust 6. aplomb, belief, pledge,
surety 7. comfort, courage, promise
8. security, sureness 9. certainty,
guarantee, impudence, insurance
10. confidence, steadiness
11. assuredness, intrepidity
12. cocksureness 14. self–confidence
assure . . . 4. aver 5. vouch 6. assert,
avouch, depose, ensure, insure,
secure 7. confirm, declare, protest,
satisfy 8. convince, embolden,
persuade, reassure 9. encourage,
guarantee 10. asseverate
Assyria . . .
  capital . . 7. Nineveh
  city . . 5. Calab (Bib) 9. Khorsabad
  (ruins)
  empire (anc) . . 5. Assur (Ashur)
  language . . 6. Semite 9. cuneiform
  (written)
  people . . 6. Semite 7. Amorite (Bib)
Assyrian god . . .
  atmosphere . . 5. Hadad
  fire . . 5. Nusku
  hunt . . 7. Ninurta
  moon . . 3. Sin
  storm . . 2. Zu
  sun . . 7. Shamash
  war . . 6. Nergal 7. Ninurta
  winds . . 4. Adad 5. Hadad
Assyrian goddess . . . 5. Nanai
6. Allatu, Ishtar 9. Sarpanitu
(Zirbanit)
Assyriology, science of . . . 8. language
11. antiquities
aster . . . 4. star 9. asterwort, karyaster
10. Carduaceae
asterisk . . . 4. mark (reference), star
6. accent, figure (star) 9. highlight
10. asteriskos (Eccl)
astern . . . 3. aft 4. baft, rear 5. abaft,
after 6. behind 8. hindward,
rearward, tailward
asteroid . . . 5. Ceres (largest) 6. planet
8. starlike 9. planetoid
Asteroidea . . . 8. starfish
astir . . . 2. up 5. about, afoot, eager
6. active, moving 8. stirring
11. forthcoming
as to . . . 7. apropos, suppose
9. regarding 10. concerning,
respecting
astonish . . . 4. stun 5. amaze, appal
7. astound, stagger, startle
8. bewilder, confound, surprise
9. overwhelm
astonishing . . . 7. amazing 8. fabulous
9. appalling, marvelous, wonderful
10. incredible, remarkable
astound . . . 4. stun 5. abash, amaze,
shock 6. appall (appal), dismay
7. stagger, stupefy 8. astonish,
surprise 10. disconcert
astounding . . . 8. horrible, shocking
9. appalling, frightful 10. horrendous,

horrifying 11. astonishing
astraddle . . . 7. astride 9. horseback,
pickaback (piggyback) 10. straddling
astral . . . 6. spirit, starry 7. stellar
8. sidereal, starlike 9. celestial
11. star–studded
astray . . . 4. lost 5. amiss, wrong
6. adrift, afield, erring 8. aberrate,
mistaken 9. erroneous 10. bewildered
astray, to go . . . 3. err, sin 4. mang,
rove 5. drift, lapse, stray 6. wander
7. deviate, digress 8. miscarry
9. backslide 10. misbelieve
astriction . . . 4. bond 7. binding
8. thirlage 9. fastening 10. litigation
11. confinement, contraction
12. constipation
astride . . . 8. straddle 9. astraddle,
horseback, pickaback (piggyback)
astringent . . . 4. acid, alum, sloe, sour
5. acerb, acrid, harsh, sapan, stern
6. tannin 7. austere, bitters, caustic,
pungent, rhatany (root), styptic
9. vitriolic 10. antiseptic
11. acrimonious, argentamine
12. constrictive
astrologer . . . 8. Chaldean 9. stargazer
11. astrologian, astromancer,
Nostradamus
astrology (pert to) . . . 5. house, signs
6. aspect, zodiac 7. mansion,
mundane 8. siderism 9. horoscope,
planetary 11. horoscopist
astronaut . . . 7. Martian 8. spaceman
9. cosmonaut, rocketeer
astronomer . . . 9. stargazer
11. uranologist 12. uranographer
13. meteorologist, uranographist
astronomer, famed . . . 6. Kepler
7. Galileo 12. Eratosthenes
astronomical . . . 4. huge, vast 5. large
6. cosmic, uranic 7. immense,
mammoth, Uranian 8. colossal,
empyreal, heavenly 9. celestial
10. prodigious, stupendous,
tremendous
astronomy (pert to) . . . 4. coma (the)
5. apsis, saros (Bab) 6. syzygy
7. almanac, apsides, azimuth,
gibbous 8. sidereal 9. idiometer,
insulated 11. debilissima
astute . . . 3. sly 4. keen, wily 5. acute,
canny, smart 6. artful, clever, crafty,
shrewd 7. cunning, skilled
9. insidious, sagacious 10. discerning
14. discriminating
asunder . . . 5. apart, cleft, split
6. atwain, halved 7. divided
9. disjoined, separated
as yet . . . 8. hitherto
asylum . . . 3. ark 4. home, jail, port
5. haven 6. harbor, refuge
7. retreat, shelter 9. hospitium,
infirmary, sanctuary 10. stronghold
11. institution
asymmetrical . . . 6. uneven, warped
7. twisted, unequal 9. contorted,
distorted 11. zygomorphic
16. disproportionate
at . . . 2. by, in 4. near, nigh 5. there
8. location, position 9. direction,
situation

at (pert to)...
great length.. 7. on and on
　9. tediously
home.. 2. in 4. here 9. en famille
last.. 3. end 7. finally 9. extremely
　10. ultimately
once.. 3. now 7. readily
the same time.. 6. coeval
　10. coetaneous 12. contemporary
atabal... 4. drum 5. tabor
　10. kettledrum
atabeg... 5. title 6. vizier
Atalanta (pert to)...
defeated in romantic race by..
　10. Hippomenes 17. three golden
　apples (Gr Myth)
famed.. 8. huntress
foe.. 9. Aphrodite
husband.. 8. Milanion
legend.. 8. Arcadian, Boeotian
atalaya... 10. watchtower
atap... 4. nipa, palm
atavism... 8. heredity 9. reversion
　10. regression
ate... 5. dined, fared 6. dieted,
　gnawed, supped
Ate... 7. goddess (of infatuation)
atelier... 5. easel 6. studio
　8. workshop
a tempo... 4. time
Aten (Egypt)... 9. solar disk
ates... 8. sweetsop
athanasia... 8. athanasy
　11. immortality 13. deathlessness
　15. imperishability
athanor (Fr)... 7. furnace (alchemist's)
Athapascan Indian... 5. Tinne
　6. Apache, Navaho (Navajo)
atheist... 5. pagan 7. heathen, infidel,
　nastika 8. agnostic 10. unbeliever
　11. disbeliever, unchristian
　13. antichristian
Athena (pert to)...
attributes.. 3. owl 5. aegis 7. serpent
festival.. 11. Panathenaea
Rom equivalent.. 7. Minerva
shrine.. 9. Parthenon (Athens)
Athena, goddess of...
arts, crafts.. 6. Ergane
health.. 6. Hygeia
horses, tamer of.. 6. Hippia
light.. 4. Alea
maid of Athens.. 12. Pallas Athene
poetry.. 6. Pallas
victory.. 4. Nike
wisdom.. 8. Palladis
Athenian (pert to)...
assembly.. 4. Pnyx
Bee.. 5. Plato
general.. 8. Xenophon
lawgiver.. 5. Draco, Solon
sculptor.. 7. Phidias
statesman.. 8. Pericles 9. Aristides
　(The Just) 10. Alcibiades
temple.. 11. Nike Apteros
Athens...
capital of.. 6. Attica (anc), Greece
citadel.. 9. Acropolis
magistrate.. 5. Draco, Solon
rival.. 6. Sparta (anc)
senate.. 5. boule
temple.. 9. Parthenon

Athens of...
America.. 6. Boston 9. Nashville (The
　South)
Ireland.. 4. Cork 7. Belfast
North.. 9. Edinburgh 10. Copenhagen
Switzerland.. 6. Zurich
West.. 7. Cordoba
athlete... 7. acrobat, gymnast, tumbler
　11. funambulist, palaestrian,
　pancratiast 13. contortionist
athlete (pert to)...
foot disease.. 15. dermatophytosis
of Christendom.. 10. Scanderbeg
portico (Gr, Rom).. 6. xystus (xyst)
athletic... 5. lusty, thewy, yauld
　6. brawny, robust, sinewy, strong
　8. muscular, stalwart, vigorous
　9. acrobatic, agonistic, gymnastic
　10. palaestral (palestral)
　15. broad-shouldered
athwart... 6. across, aslant
　8. sideways, sidewise, traverse
　9. crosswise, obliquely
　10. crisscross, perversely
atimon... 9. muskmelon
Atlantean... 6. strong 7. titanic
　8. gigantic 9. Atlaslike
　10. Gargantuan
atlantes (opp of caryatids)...
　7. columns (carved men)
　9. telamones
Atlantic Sisters (Gr)... 8. Pleiades
　(stars)
Atlas (pert to)...
converted into.. 7. Mt Atlas
daughter.. 7. Calypso 8. Pleiades
famed as a.. 5. giant, Titan
king of.. 10. Mauretania
mother.. 4. Asia 7. Clymene
supporter of.. 5. earth 10. the
　heavens
Atman (Hind)... 3. ego 4. Self, Soul
　6. Brahma
atmosphere... 3. air 4. aura, mood
　5. ether, ozone 7. climate
　10. aerosphere, background
　11. environment, hydrosphere
atmosphere (pert to)...
condition.. 9. epedaphic
density.. 8. isostere, isoteric
disturbance.. 5. storm 6. static
　9. tornadoes, whirlwind
pressure.. 10. barometric
shooting star.. 6. meteor
spectrum.. 7. rainbow
atole... 5. gruel 8. porridge
atoll... 4. belt, reef (coral) 6. island
atom... 3. ace, bit, ion, jot 4. gram,
　iota, mite, whit 5. monad
　8. molecule, particle 9. corpuscle
atomic... 3. Age, ray 4. beam, bomb,
　tiny 5. power 6. energy, minute,
　number, radius, weight 7. nuclear
　9. atomistic, molecular, radiation
　10. intangible 11. microscopic
　13. infinitesimal
atomic submarine... 5. Skate 6. Triton
　8. Nautilus, Thresher 9. Sea Dragon
atomize... 4. fume 5. smash, spray
　6. aerate, gasify 7. fission, perfume,
　shatter 8. dissolve, fumigate, nucleize
　9. carbonate, decompose, evaporate,

micronize, pulverize 11. disorganize
12. disintegrate
atomy... 4. atom, mote 5. dwarf,
pygmy 6. droich, midget 8. skeleton
10. micromorph
atonement... 6. amends 7. apology,
penance, redress 8. requital
10. recompense, redemption,
reparation 11. reclamation, restitution
12. propitiation 15. indemnification
Atreus (pert to)...
brother.. 8. Thyestes
father.. 6. Pelops
king of.. 7. Mycenae
mother.. 10. Hippodamia
slayer of.. 12. Thyestes' sons
son.. 8. Menelaus 9. Agamemnon
wife.. 6. Aerope
atrium... 4. hall, room 5. court (inner)
6. cavity (Anat) 7. chamber
9. peristyle
atrocious... 4. rank, vile 5. awful,
cruel, grave 6. brutal, savage, sinful,
wicked 7. heinous, vicious, violent
8. dreadful, flagrant, horrible,
infamous, ruthless, shocking, terrible,
wretched 9. monstrous, nefarious
10. abominable, deplorable,
detestable, outrageous
atrociousness... 8. baseness, vileness
12. dreadfulness, shamefulness
13. nefariousness 15. Schrecklichkeit
atrocity... 4. evil, harm 5. abuse,
havoc, wrong 7. misdeed, outrage
8. enormity 9. indignity
12. mistreatment
atrophy... 5. tabes 7. disease
8. marasmus 10. emaciation
11. attenuation
Atropos (Gr)... 7. goddess (Fate)
attach... 3. add, fix, pin, put, tag, tie
4. bind, glue, join, vest 5. affix,
annex, hitch, paste, seize, unite
6. append, assign, fasten 7. ascribe,
connect, postfix, subjoin 9. associate,
attribute 11. superimpose
attached... 4. fond 6. adnate, welded
7. annexed, devoted, engaged,
sessile (Bot), smitten 8. cemented,
enamored
attachment... 4. bond, love 5. fancy
6. liking, regard 7. adjunct, fixture
8. addition, devotion, fidelity,
fondness 9. accession, adherence,
affection, fastening, increment
10. annexation 11. attribution
12. augmentation
attack... 3. fit 4. pang, raid 5. beset,
blitz, drive, feint, ictus, onset, sally,
siege, spasm 6. affret, assail, charge,
onrush, oppugn, sortie 7. aggress,
assault, bowling, descent, offense,
seizure 8. camisado (anc), paroxysm,
sickness 9. offensive, onslaught
10. aggression 11. enunciation
13. incrimination
attain... 2. do 3. get, win 4. earn,
gain 5. enact, reach 6. accede,
arrive, effect, obtain 7. achieve,
acquire, compass, fulfill, perform,
realize 9. discharge 10. accomplish,
consummate

attainable... 8. gettable 9. available
10. achievable
attainment... 5. skill 7. arrival
8. learning 9. accession
11. acquirement, acquisition,
cultivation, edification, realization
14. accomplishment
attar... 4. otto 5. scent 6. parfum
7. essence, perfume, rose oil
attempt... 3. aim, jab (sl), try 4. dare,
seek, stab 5. assay, ensue, essay,
fling, offer, onset, siege, trial
6. attack, effort, result 7. venture
8. endeavor 9. undertake
attend... 4. hark, heed, help, mind,
note, tend, wait 5. ensue, nurse,
serve, treat, visit 6. doctor, escort,
follow, foster, listen, result
7. conduct, hearken, nurture, observe
9. accompany
attendance... 4. draw 5. court
7. service, turnout 8. presence,
tendance 9. following
13. accompaniment
attendant... 4. maid, page 5. nurse,
staff, usher 6. caddie, escort, gillie,
porter, waiter 7. bellboy, orderly
8. follower 9. associate, attending,
companion 10. subsequent
11. concomitant, ministering
attendants, train of... 5. suite
7. cortege, retinue 9. entourage
attention... 3. ear 4. care, heed, hist,
note 6. notice, regard 7. concern,
hearing, respect, thought 8. courtesy
11. mindfulness 13. concentration,
consideration
attentive... 5. alert, awake, eared
6. intent 7. careful, heedful, mindful
8. obedient, vigilant, watchful
9. courteous, listening, observant,
wide-awake 10. meticulous,
respectful 11. circumspect,
considerate, surveillant
attenuated... 3. cut 4. fine, rare, slim,
thin 6. svelte, wasted 7. diluted,
gracile, reduced, slender, thinned,
watered 8. lessened, rarefied,
weakened 9. decreased, emaciated
attest... 4. seal 5. vouch 6. adjure,
affirm, avouch, depose 7. certify,
testify, witness 8. evidence, indicate,
manifest 9. testimony 10. deposition
12. authenticate
attestation... 4. oath (solemn) 5. proof
6. avowal 8. swearing 9. assertion
10. allegation 11. affirmation,
certificate, declaration, testimonial
13. testification 14. authentication
attic... 3. top 4. dome, head, loft,
wall 6. belfry, garret 8. cockloft
Attic... 5. salty, witty 6. simple
7. elegant, refined 8. academic,
Athenian, tasteful 9. classical
10. Ciceronian
Attic (pert to)...
Bee.. 9. Sophocles (poet)
bird.. 11. nightingale (Milton)
Muse.. 8. Xenophon
native.. 8. Athenian
school.. 9. sculpture
Attica (pert to)...

capital of.. 6. Athens
state of.. 6. Greece (anc)
famed as.. 15. world's first city
Attila... 3. Hun (leader) 5. Etzel
(fabled) 12. Scourge of God
attitude... 3. air, set 4. pose, view
5. angle, slant, stand 7. bearing,
feeling, opinion, outlook, posture,
thought 8. position, reaction
9. arabesque (dance), sentiment,
viewpoint 10. estimation, impression
attitude (reverent)... 6. salaam
8. kneeling 9. obeisance
12. genuflection (genuflexion)
attorney... 6. lawyer 7. counsel,
pleader 9. barrister, counselor
(counsellor) 11. intercessor
attract... 4. bait, draw, lure, pull
5. charm, tempt 6. appeal, beckon,
enamor, engage, entice, invite
8. interest 9. captivate, fascinate,
influence, magnetize
attraction... 4. lure, pull, star
6. appeal 7. gravity 8. affinity,
headline, interest, penchant
9. magnetism, seduction
10. allurement 11. fascination
attractive... 4. cute 6. lovely, pretty,
taking 7. winsome 8. alluring,
engaging, fetching, graceful, magnetic
9. allicient, appealing, beauteous,
beautiful, desirable 10. attracting,
delightful 11. captivating, interesting
attractive and repellent...
10. ambivalent
attrahent... 6. magnet 7. drawing
8. sinapism (Med) 10. attracting
attribute... 3. owe 5. refer, trait
6. impute, nature, symbol 7. ascribe,
feature, quality 8. property
9. adjective, qualifier, specialty
attrition... 4. wear 5. grief (Theol)
7. massage 8. abrasion, friction,
limation 9. detrition 10. contrition
attune... 4. tune 5. chime 6. accord,
adjust 7. concord, harmony, syntony
9. melodious 10. symphonize
11. concordance
atwain... 7. asunder
atweel... 5. truly 6. surely
aubade (Fr)... 3. lay 4. poem, song
6. ballad 7. concert (morning)
8. serenade
auberge... 3. inn
aubergiste... 9. innkeeper
auction... 3. bid 4. cant, roup, sale
5. block 6. vendue 7. bidding
auction (game)... 4. pool 5. pitch
6. bridge, euchre, hearts 8. pinochle
audacious... 4. bold 5. saucy
6. brazen, daring 7. defiant
8. impudent, insolent, intrepid,
spirited 9. barefaced, foolhardy,
insulting 11. adventurous,
challenging, impertinent, presumptive,
venturesome
audacity... 5. cheek, crust, nerve
6. daring 7. courage 8. defiance,
temerity 9. assurance, hardihood,
impudence, insolence, sauciness
10. effrontery, enterprise
11. presumption 12. impertinence

13. audaciousness, foolhardiness,
shamelessness
audible... 5. aloud, clear 8. distinct,
hearable 10. articulate
audible respiration... 4. sigh
audience... 3. ear 5. house, trial
6. parley, tryout 7. hearing, theater
8. audition, auditory, congress
9. interview, listeners 10. conference
12. congregation
audit... 5. check 6. reckon, verify
7. certify, collate 10. accounting
11. examination
auditor... 5. clerk 6. censor, hearer
7. actuary, apposer 8. examiner,
listener 10. accountant, bookkeeper
11. comptroller
auditorium... 4. hall, nave (anc)
5. house 7. theater 8. auditory,
building 9. Guildhall
auditory... 4. otic 5. audio, aural
6. phonic 7. hearers 8. audience
9. accoustic, auricular
12. congregation
au fait... 4. able 6. expert 7. equal to
8. informed, skillful 9. qualified
10. conversant (with)
au fond... 9. basically, primarily
11. essentially 13. fundamentally
auger... 3. bit 4. bore, tool 5. borer,
drill 6. gimlet, wimble 10. perforator
aught... 3. any 4. none, some, zero
5. ought 6. cipher 7. nothing
8. anything
augment... 3. add, eke 5. affix, annex,
exalt, swell 6. expand, extend
7. amplify, broaden, develop,
enhance, enlarge 8. increase
9. reinforce
Augsburg Church... 8. Lutheran
augur... 4. bode, omen, seer 5. sibyl,
vates (Gauls) 6. oracle 7. betoken,
presage 8. forebode, forecast,
foretell, forewarn, haruspex (Rom),
indicate, prophesy 10. anticipate,
astrologer, conjecture, soothsayer
13. prognosticate 14. prognosticator
augury... 4. omen, rite 7. auspice,
portent 8. ceremony
august... 5. awful, grand, novel, regal
6. sedate, solemn 7. courtly,
eminent, stately 8. imposing, majestic
9. dignified, honorable, important,
venerable 11. magnificent, ritualistic
12. aristocratic
August... 6. Lammas 8. Sextilis
10. First month (Rom year)
August meteor (11th of month)...
7. Perseid
auk... 4. Alca, Alle, bird (sea), falk
5. murre, noddy 6. auklet, rotche
(rotch) 7. Alcidae, dovekie
9. guillemot, razorbill
Auk... 6. Indian 7. Alaskan, Tlingit
(tribe) 9. Koluschan
aula... 4. hall, room 5. court
6. emblic (E Ind tree) 9. ventricle
aulos... 5. flute 8. woodwind
9. woodwinds (collectively)
aura... 3. air 4. halo, ring 6. astral,
circle, fringe (Psychol), nimbus
7. aureola 9. effluvium, emanation

10. atmosphere, exhalation
aureole... 4. halo 5. glory 6. circle,
nimbus
auricle... 3. ear 4. lobe 5. pinna
6. atrium (heart) 9. appendage
auricular... 4. otic 5. aural, eared
6. phonic 8. acoustic, auditory
aurifex... 9. goldsmith
aurochs... 3. tur 4. goat, urus
5. bison
aurora... 3. eos 4. dawn 5. sunup
7. sunrise 8. borealis, daybreak,
daylight 9. australis 11. polar lights
aurora borealis... 14. northern lights
auroral... 4. dawn, eoan, rosy
7. eastern, radiant, roseate
auspices... 3. aid 4. care, sign, wing
5. aegis (egis) 6. charge 7. backing,
custody 8. guidance 9. patronage
10. management, protection
11. sponsorship, supervision
auspicious... 4. good 6. timely
9. favorable, fortunate, opportune
10. convenient, propitious,
prosperous, seasonable
12. advantageous
Aussie... 6. digger 10. Australian
Auster... 9. southland, south wind
austere... 4. dour, hard 5. acrid,
harsh, rigid, rough, stern 6. bitter,
severe, strict 7. ascetic, pungent
8. exacting 10. astringent
Australasia... 7. Oceania 15. South
Sea Islands
Australasian bird... 8. lorikeet
9. pardalote
Australia... see also *Australian*
capital.. 8. Canberra
desert.. 10. Great Sandy 13. Great
Victoria
First Englishman (1688).. 14. William
Dampier
holiday.. 13. Foundation Day (Jan 26)
island.. 8. Tasmania
mountain peak.. 9. Kosciusko
ocean.. 6. Indian
river.. 5. Murray
sea.. 5. Coral 6. Tasman
Tropic (southern).. 9. Capricorn
Australian (pert to)...
bee.. 5. karbi
bedroll.. 6. bindle 7. matilda
candy.. 5. lolly
feast.. 10. corroboree
fish.. 4. mako (shark) 5. yabby
flag.. 13. Southern Cross
flower.. 7. waratah (tulip)
9. rhodanthe
hut.. 6. miamia
native.. 5. myall 6. Aussie, binghi
8. kangaroo, warragal 9. aborigine,
Dravidian
reptile.. 6. elapid, goanna, lizard
(barking, frilled)
soldier.. 5. Anzac 6. digger
Australian animal...
dog (wild).. 5. dingo
horse (wild).. 6. brumby
sheep dog.. 6. kelpie
mammal.. 7. daysure 8. duckbill,
platypus 9. blind mole
marsupial.. 4. tait 5. koala 6. wombat

7. echidna 8. anteater, kangaroo
9. phalanger, teddy bear
10. kookaburra 14. Tasmanian Devil
Australian bird... 3. emu, owl 4. lory,
titi 5. arara, ariel, galah 6. leipoa,
petrel 7. boobook, bustard, corella
(parrot), grinder, rosella (parakeet)
8. ganggang, lorikeet, lyrebird,
morepork, nightjar, paradise
9. bowerbird, cassowary, pardalote
10. flycatcher, goatsucker
11. budgereegah (parakeet)
Australian State capitals... 5. Perth
6. Darwin, Hobart, Sydney
8. Adelaide, Brisbane, Canberra
(chief) 9. Melbourne
Australian tree... 4. teak, toon
5. belah, penda 6. jarrah, mallee,
marara, she—oak, wattle 7. gunnung
(mahogany) 8. Alstonia (dogbane),
ironbark (eucalypt) 9. boobyalla
(willow)
Austria...
capital.. 6. Vienna
city.. 4. Graz, Linz 8. Salzburg
9. Innsbruck
forest belt.. 10. Wiener Wald
monarchy.. 14. Austria—Hungary
mountain.. 4. Alps 6. Otztal
9. Dolomites
mountain peak.. 10. Wildspitze
13. Gross—Glockner
Pass (famed).. 7. Brenner
river.. 3. Inn, Mur 4. Enns
6. Danube
Austrian (pert to)...
botanist.. 6. Mendel (Mendel's Law)
composer.. 6. Mozart 7. Strauss
inventor.. 8. Welsbach
pianist.. 8. Kreisler
ruler (former).. 6. Kaiser
scientist.. 5. Adler, Freud
soldier.. 5. jager
theaterman.. 9. Reinhardt (Max)
autarch... 6. despot, tyrant 8. autocrat
authentic... 4. pure, real, true 5. valid
6. native 7. certain, correct, genuine,
natural 8. bona fide, credible, official,
original, orthodox, reliable 9. firsthand
11. trustworthy 13. authoritative
authenticate... 6. affirm, attest, ratify
7. certify, confirm, warrant
8. validate 12. substantiate
authenticity... 11. genuineness,
reliability 13. dependability
15. trustworthiness
author... 4. doer, poet 5. ghost,
maker 6. parent, penman, writer
7. creator, inditer 8. annalist,
begetter, compiler, composer,
essayist, inventor, novelist, producer
9. dramatist, scribbler 10. originator
13. encyclopedist (encyclopaedist)
authoritative... 4. wise 5. valid
6. potent, ruling, strong 7. weighty
8. approved, forceful, official,
oracular, orthodox, positive, powerful
9. authentic, imperious
10. commanding, peremptory
11. dictatorial, influential
13. determinative
authoritative (pert to)...

command.. 4. fiat 5. usage
  6. decree, dictum 7. mandate
example.. 9. precedent
  10. antecedent
letter.. 4. writ 5. breve
authority... 5. judge, power, right
  6. critic, expert, oracle, regent
  7. command, warrant, witness
  8. dominion, validity 9. influence,
  testimony 10. commission,
  competency 11. connoisseur,
  prerogative 12. jurisdiction
  13. authorization
authorize... 6. accept, permit, ratify
  7. certify, charter, empower, endorse,
  entitle, justify, license, warrant
  8. accredit, delegate, sanction,
  validate 10. commission
  11. enfranchise 12. legitimatize
authorless... 8. nameless
  9. anonymous
autobiography... 7. journal, letters,
  memoirs 11. memorabilia
autochton... 6. binghi, native
  8. indigene 9. primitive
  10. aboriginal
autocracy... 8. monarchy 9. despotism
  10. absolutism 15. totalitarianism
autocrat... 4. czar (tsar) 5. mogul
  6. despot 7. arbiter, monarch
  8. dictator 9. sovereign
  10. taskmaster
autodidactic... 8. self–made
  10. self–taught 12. self–educated
autograph... 4. seal, sign 5. cross
  9. signature 11. John Hancock
automatic... 7. machine
  10. mechanical, self–acting
  11. instinctive, involuntary,
  spontaneous
automatic device... 3. gun 4. gear
  5. drill, pilot, rifle, robot 6. pistol,
  switch 8. computer, revolver
  10. six–shooter
automaton... 5. golem, robot
  6. puppet 7. android, machine
automobile... 3. cab, car 4. auto, taxi
  5. coupe 6. jalopy 7. autocar,
  flivver, machine, taxicab, vehicle
  8. motorcar
autosuggestion... 7. therapy
  8. hypnosis 9. hypnology, mesmerism
  10. psychology 14. self–suggestion
autumn... 4. fall 6. mature, old age,
  season (yearly) 7. equinox, harvest,
  October 8. maturity, November
  9. September
auxiliary... 4. ally, plus 5. extra
  6. aiding, helper 7. adjunct, helping
  9. accessory, ancillary, assistant,
  attendant, coadjutor, colleague,
  companion, secondary 10. additional,
  subsidiary, supporting
  11. confederate, cooperating,
  subordinate, subservient
  12. nonessential, supplemental
  13. supplementary
auxiliary army... 6. relief 7. support
  8. Landwehr, recruits, reserves
  11. contingents 14. reinforcements
auxiliary verb... 3. can, had, has, may
  4. hast, have, will 5. could, shall,

would 6. should
avail... 3. use 4. good, help 5. value
  6. inform, profit 7. benefit, service,
  utility 9. advantage, expedient
availability... 7. utility 9. usability
  10. usefulness 13. acquirability,
  attainability 14. serviceability
available... 4. free, open 5. handy,
  ready, valid 6. on hand, usable,
  vacant 8. unfilled 9. securable
  10. accessible, attainable, convenient,
  obtainable, unoccupied
avalanche... 5. slide 7. descent
  (sudden) 8. slippage
avant–garde... 3. van 8. vanguard
avant–propos... 7. preface
  12. introduction (remarks)
avarice... 4. lust 5. greed 7. avidity
  8. avidness, cupidity, grasping,
  rapacity, voracity 10. greediness
  12. covetousness
avarice demon... 6. Mammon
avaricious... 5. close 6. grabby,
  greedy 7. miserly 8. covetous,
  grasping 9. niggardly, penurious,
  rapacious, voracious 12. parsimonious
avatar... 8. epiphany 10. embodiment
  11. incarnation 14. transmigration
avatars of Vishnu (Hind Relig)...
  11. incarnation (deity to man)
avaunt... 4. away 5. allez, boast,
  scram, vaunt 6. begone, depart
  7. advance, vamoose
ave... 4. hail, viva, vive 8. farewell
Ave Maria... 4. bead (rosary), song
  6. prayer 10. devotional
Avena... 4. oats 7. grasses
avenge... 7. requite 9. retaliate,
  vindicate
Avenging Angels... 8. nickname (Polit
  1858) 10. Danite Band (Mormons)
Avenging Spirit... 4. Fate, Fury
  6. Erinys 7. Alastor, Atropos
avenue... 3. rue 4. land, pike, road,
  vent 5. alley 6. arcade, artery, defile,
  egress, outlet, street 7. channel,
  freeway, highway, opening
  8. corridor, turnpike 9. boulevard,
  concourse 10. passageway
  12. thoroughfare
aver... 3. say 5. state 6. affirm,
  allege, assert 7. declare, profess,
  protect 10. asseverate
average... 2. go 3. par, run 4. mean,
  rule 6. common, medial, medium,
  normal 7. balance 8. mediocre
  10. generality
averment... 6. dictum, remark
  7. witness 9. assertion, statement,
  testimony, utterance 10. allegation
  11. affirmation, attestation
  12. verification 13. pronouncement
Avernus... 4. lake (poison vapors)
  5. Hades
averse... 5. loath 7. adverse
  9. reluctant, unwilling 11. disinclined
aversion... 4. hate 5. odium
  6. hatred, horror 7. disgust, dislike
  9. antipathy, repulsion
  10. abhorrence, repugnance
  11. abomination 12. estrangement
  13. indisposition, unwillingness

aversion to ... see also *fear of*
novelty.. 9. neophobia
society.. 14. anthropopphobia
strangers.. 10. xenophobia
wine.. 10. oenophobia

avert ... 4. fend, save 5. check, deter,
evade, repel 6. forbid, retard, switch,
thwart 7. deflect, prevent 8. alienate,
prohibit 9. forestall, sidetrack

aviary ... 4. cage 5. house 7. dovecot
(dovecote) 8. ornithon 9. birdhouse,
columbary, enclosure
11. columbarium

aviation ... 6. flight, flying 7. winging
9. skyriding 10. airplaning
11. aeronautics

aviation maneuver ... 9. Immelmann
(Ger)

aviator ... 3. Ace 5. flier (flyer), pilot
6. airman, Icarus (fabled first)
7. wingman 8. aeronaut, aviatrix,
operator 9. astronaut, birdwoman,
Immelmann

avichi (Buddh) ... 4. Hell 5. Hades
9. depravity, perdition 10. underworld

avid ... 4. agog, keen 5. eager
6. grabby, greedy 7. anxious,
craving, zestful 8. grasping
9. rapacious, voracious 10. avaricious

avidity ... 4. lust 5. greed 7. avarice
8. cupidity, grasping 9. eagerness
10. greediness 12. covetousness

avion ... 5. plane 8. airplane

avisa ... 4. news 6. advice, caveat
7. tidings, warning 11. information

Avis Indica (Astron) ... 4. Apus
13. constellation

avital ... 9. ancestral

avoid ... 4. shun, snub 5. annul,
dodge, elude, evade 6. escape,
eschew, repeal, revoke, vacate
7. abstain, forbear 10. invalidate

avoidance ... 6. outlet 7. evasion,
removal 8. emptying, shunning,
vacating 9. annulment 10. withdrawal

avoirdupois ... 4. beef 6. weight
7. gravity, tonnage 8. poundage
9. heaviness

avoirdupois weight ... 3. ton 4. dram
5. grain, ounce, pound
13. hundred-weight

avow ... 3. own, vow 5. admit, swear,
vouch 6. allege, assert, pledge
7. confess, declare, profess, promise
10. avouchment 11. acknowledge

avulsion ... 7. removal 9. severance
10. extraction, separation (ppty),
withdrawal

awabi ... 7. abalone

awaft ... 6. adrift, afloat, wafted

await ... 4. bide, come, heed, loom,
pend, wait 5. abide, tarry, watch
6. ambush, attend, expect, impend,
waylay 8. approach 9. forthcome

awake ... 5. alert, alive, astir, rouse
6. arouse, excite, waking
8. open-eyed 9. attentive, conscious,
sleepless, wide-awake

awaken ... 5. awake 6. arouse, excite,
stir up 8. roust out

award ... 4. gift, give, meed, mete
5. allot, grant, medal, Oscar, prize

6. reward, trophy 7. adjudge,
present, verdict 8. accolade
9. medallion

aware ... 3. hep 4. know 5. sense
7. mindful 8. apprized, sensible
9. cognizant, conscious
11. intelligent

awareness ... 5. sense 7. feeling
9. sensation 10. impression,
perception 11. mindfulness, sensibility
13. consciousness

away ... 2. on 3. awa, far, fro, off, out
4. gone 5. aside, hence 6. abroad,
absent, begone, onward, thence
7. escaped 8. vanished 9. elsewhere

away from ...
body center.. 5. ectad 6. distal
mouth.. 6. aborad, aboral
wind.. 4. alee

awe ... 3. cow 4. fear 5. dread
6. regard, terror, wonder 7. emotion,
respect 8. astonish, frighten, surprise
9. reverence 10. admiration,
veneration, wonderment
13. consideration

aweather ... (opp of alee) 8. windward
11. weatherward

awe-inspiring ... 5. eerie (eery)
7. awesome, ghostly 8. glorious,
imposing, splendid, terrific
9. wonderful 10. impressive
11. magnificent

awe-struck ... 4. awed 9. terrified
10. astonished, fear-struck,
spellbound 12. wonder-struck
13. thunderstruck

awful ... 4. awed, ugly 5. dread, great,
gross 6. sacred, silent, solemn,
woeful 7. awesome, fearful, hideous
8. dreadful, infamous, reverent,
shocking, terrible 9. appalling,
atrocious, deathlike, ludicrous,
venerable, wonderful 10. deplorable,
impressive, outrageous, unpleasant
11. exceedingly

awkward ... 5. gawky, inapt, inept
6. clumsy, gauche 7. froward,
loutish, unhandy 8. bungling,
clownish, lubberly, perverse, ungainly,
unwieldy 9. graceless, inelegant,
lumbering, maladroit, ponderous
10. backhanded, blundering,
ungraceful 12. embarrassing,
incommodious, inconvenient

awkward age ... 4. teen 5. teens

awkward fellow ... 6. galoot
11. hobbledehoy

awless, aweless ... 4. bald 6. brazen
8. fearless, unafraid 9. bold-faced,
dauntless 10. irreverent
11. unsurprised 12. unastonished

awn ... 4. barb 5. beard (plant)
6. arista, papous 7. bristle

awning ... 6. canopy, screen, shield
7. shelter 8. velarium (anc)

AWOL ... 5. hooky 7. truancy
9. truantism 11. absenteeism

awry ... 4. agee 5. agley, amiss, askew
6. faulty 7. askance, asquint,
crooked, oblique 9. distorted
10. disorderly 11. disarranged
12. disorganized

ax, axe... 3. adz (adze), ask (dial)
   4. tool 6. hammer, poleax (poleaxe)
   7. hatchet (small) 8. axhammer
   9. discharge, dismissal
ax (pert to)...
  ancient.. 4. celt 6. chisel
  blade.. 3. bit
  execution.. 10. guillotine
  handle.. 5. helve
axial... 7. central, midmost, pivotal
axilla... 3. ala 4. axil 5. oxter
   6. armpit 8. shoulder
axiom... 3. law, saw 4. rule 5. adage,
   maxim, motto, truth 6. byword,
   dictum, saying, truism 7. dictate,
   precept, proverb, theorem
   8. aphorism, apothegm 9. principle
   11. proposition
axiomatic... 10. aphoristic, proverbial
   11. self–evident, sententious
   12. epigrammatic
axis... 3. hub 4. axle, bloc, nave,
   stem 5. pivot, stalk 6. caulis, center,
   league 7. fulcrum 8. alliance,
   vertebra 9. coalition
axle... 3. pin 4. axis 5. pivot, shaft
   6. swivel 7. spindle 8. axletree
axle tooth... 5. molar
ayal... 4. amah, maid 5. mammy
   9. governess, nursemaid
   11. maidservant
aye... 2. ay 3. pro, yea, yes 4. ever,
   vote 5. voice 6. always, assent
   8. thumbs up, viva–voce

aye–aye... 5. lemur (Madagascar)
ayes... 10. all in favor
Azazel... 5. Eblis, Satan 9. scapegoat
Azerbaijanian... 4. Turk
   14. Transcaucasian
azimuth... 3. arc 4. dial 6. circle
   7. compass, horizon 8. distance,
   magnetic 10. North point
Azores...
  capital.. 5. Angra
  city.. 5. Horta
  group (islands).. 6. St Mary 8. St
   George 9. St Michael
  locale.. 8. Atlantic (Ocean)
  owner.. 8. Portugal
Aztec (pert to)...
  calendar.. 7. Mexican
  capital (anc).. 12. Tenochtitlan
  emperor.. 9. Montezuma
  god.. 4. Xipe (sowing)
   12. Quetzalcoatl (peace)
  hero.. 4. Nata (Myth) 6. Cortez
  language.. 7. Nahuatl
  locale (anc).. 6. Aztlan
  Noah (Mex).. 6. Coxcox
  stone.. 12. chalchihuitl
  temple.. 8. teocalli
  tribe.. 9. Nahuatlan
azure... 4. blue 7. celeste, sky–blue
   8. bice blue, cerulean 9. blue vault,
   cloudless 11. lapis lazuli
azygous... 3. odd 4. only, sole
   6. single, unique 8. singular
   10. unrepeated
azymous... 10. unleavened

B

B... 4. beta 6. letter (2nd)
ba (Egypt)... 3. khu 4. soul
baa... 5. bleet
baahling... 4. lamb
Baal... 4. idol 5. deity 6. Baalim (pl)
   7. Baalath 8. false god 9. fertility
baba (pert to)...
  India.. 4. baby 5. child
  Malaya.. 4. male
  Slavic.. 5. nurse 7. midwife 8. old
   woman
  Turkey.. 5. title (of respect)
babacoote... 5. lemur (Madagascar)
Babbar... 3. Utu (Utug) 6. sun god
babbo... 5. daddy 6. father
babel... 5. clang 6. jargon, tumult
   7. discord 9. confusion
   11. pandemonium
Babel (pert to)...
  Bible.. 5. Tower 8. ziggurat
  presently.. 14. Temple of Marduk
  site (ancient).. 6. Shinar (land of)
  site (present).. 7. Babylon
babirusa, babiroussa... 9. quadruped
   (hoglike)

Babism (Persia)... 4. sect
baboon... 3. ape 5. Papio 6. chacma
   7. babuina, monster 8. mandrill
babushka... 11. grandmother
baby... 4. babe, doll 6. coward, infant,
   puppet, weanie 7. bambino, chicken
   8. juvenile, weakling 9. miniature,
   youngling, youngster 10. diminutive
baby carriage... 4. pram 5. wagon
   6. go–cart 8. stroller
   12. perambulator
babyish... 6. simple 7. dollish, puerile
   8. childish, childlike, infantile
Babylon... see also *Babylonian*
  capital of.. 9. Babylonia
  kingdom.. 4. Elam 5. Akkad (Accad)
  meaning.. 9. Gate of God
  mountain.. 6. Ararat
  river.. 6. Tigris 9. Euphrates
  World Wonder.. 14. Hanging Gardens
Babylonian (pert to)...
  abode of the dead.. 5. Aralu
  chaos.. 4. Apsu
  deity.. 5. Alalu (Alala), Siris
  earth mother.. 6. Ishtar

god.. 2. Ea, Zu 3. Anu, Bel 4. Adad,
Apsu, Irra 5. Dagan, Enlil 6. Nergal
7. Shamash
goddess.. 3. Aya 4. Nina 5. Belit
(Beltis)
hero (Myth).. 5. Adapa, Etana
9. Tilgamesh
king.. 6. Sargon 9. Habonidus,
Hammurabi 10. Nabonassar
14. Nebuchadnezzar (Nebuchadrezzar)
temple, tower.. 8. ziggurat
bacach... 6. beggar 7. cripple
bacalao... 7. codfish, grouper
bacalao bird... 3. auk 5. murre
9. guillemot
Bacardi... 3. rum
bacca... 5. berry
baccalaureate... 6. degree (college),
sermon 8. bachelor
baccate... 5. pulpy 9. berrylike
bacchanal... 7. reveler 8. carouser
Bacchanalia... 4. orgy 5. feast
7. debauch 8. festival (Bacchus)
bacchante... 6. maenad 7. bacchae
Bacchus... 4. wine 9. god of wine
baccivorous... 11. berry–eating
bachelor... 4. male 6. degree (Acad),
garçon 8. benedict, celibate
10. misogamist
bacillus... 9. bacterium
Bacis... 2. Ra 4. bull (sacred)
back... 3. aft, aid, fro 4. abet, hind,
past, rear 5. stern 6. behind,
second, uphold 7. finance, sponsor,
support, sustain 8. extrados, intrados,
resource 9. encourage, posterior
10. background
back (Anat)... 4. loin, nape 5. notum
6. dorsal, dorsum, lumbar, tergal,
tergum 7. occiput 8. backbone,
notalgia 10. opisthenar (hand)
backbone... 4. grit, guts 5. nerve,
pluck, spunk 6. mettle, spirit
7. courage, stamina, support
8. firmness, gameness, mainstay
10. dependence
backbone (Anat)... 4. axis 5. brace,
chine, spine 6. column, spinal
7. spinule, support 8. ossicles
9. vertebrae
backer... 5. angel 6. patron
7. abettor, sponsor 8. financer,
promoter, upholder 9. supporter,
sustainer 10. maintainer
background... (opp of foreground)
4. rear 5. stage 6. offing 7. horizon,
setting 8. backdrop, distance,
practice, training 9. education
10. experience 11. savoir–faire
backhanded... 6. clumsy 7. awkward,
devious 9. insincere, insulting,
sarcastic 10. circuitous
backslider... 8. apostate, deserter,
recreant 10. unfaithful
back–to–back... 7. dos–à–dos
backward... 4. back, dull, late
5. arear, loath, tardy 6. averse,
modest, stupid 7. bashful, belated,
reverse 8. arrested, dilatory, perverse,
rearward, retarded, reticent, retrorse,
reversed 9. hindwards, recessive,
reluctant, subnormal, unwilling

10. behindhand, hesitating,
regressive, retrograde 11. unfavorable
13. retrogressive, retrospective
bacon... 4. lard, pork, side 5. prize
6. flitch, gammon, rasher
8. Canadian, sowbelly
Bacon's Rebellion... 6. revolt (Va
1676)
bacteria... 5. cocci, germs 7. aerobes,
aerobia, bacilli 8. microbes, spirilla
9. organisms
bacteriologist culture... 4. agar
Bactrian camel... 9. two–humped
bad... 3. ill, mal (pref) 4. evil, fell,
foul, poor, vile 5. drole, fetid, nasty,
wrong 6. arrant, in pain, putrid,
rotten, sinful, wanton, wicked
7. corrupt, hurtful, naughty, noxious,
spoiled, tainted, unlucky, unmoral,
unsound, vicious 8. annoying,
criminal, improper, inferior, iniquity,
sinister 9. dangerous, defective,
offensive, perverted, worthless
10. iniquitous, malodorous, unsuitable
11. inexpedient, inopportune
12. disagreeable, inauspicious
bad (pert to)...
blood.. 4. feud 6. rancor 7. ill will
10. bitterness, resentment
custom.. 9. cacoethes
legislation.. 7. dysnomy
luck.. 5. deuce 7. ambsace
man's oatmeal.. 7. hemlock (poison)
11. wild chervil
badge... 3. pin 4. mark, sign, star
5. index, token 6. emblem, ensign,
plaque, shield, symbol 7. earmark
8. insignia 14. identification
badger... 3. nag, rag 4. bait 5. harry,
tease, worry 6. bother, extort,
harass, hawker, heckle, hector, pester
8. huckster
badger (animal)... 5. Meles (anc),
pahmi, ratel 6. bauson, mammal,
teledu, wombat 9. bandicoot,
mistonusk
Badger State... 9. Wisconsin
badinage... 4. fool 5. joker, sport
6. banter 8. raillery 9. badinerie,
simpleton 10. persiflage, pleasantry
badly... 3. bad, ill 4. sick 5. amiss,
wrong 6. poorly, unwell 8. faultily,
wickedly 9. viciously 11. exceedingly,
imperfectly 12. disagreeably,
unskillfully 13. unfortunately
badly off... 3. sad 7. hapless, unblest,
unhappy, unlucky 8. luckless
11. impecunious, unfortunate
12. unprosperous 14. unprovidential
baff... 4. beat, blow, thud 6. strike,
stroke (golf)
baffle... 4. balk, foil 5. cheat, elude,
evade, spike 6. defeat, delude,
muffle, puzzle, thwart 7. mystify,
nonplus 8. bewilder, confound
9. bamboozle, frustrate
10. disconcert
baffling... 7. elusive, evasive
8. puzzling 9. bothering, confusing,
dismaying 10. mystifying, perplexing,
perturbing 11. frustrating
13. disconcerting

baft . . . 3. aft 4. baff 5. abaff, cloth, shaft 6. astern

bag . . . 3. net, pac, pot, sac, sag 4. etui, grip, load, poke, sack, trap 5. ascus, belly, catch, droop, pouch, purse, seize, snare, steal 6. entrap, sachet, valise 7. bladder, capture, distend, handbag, pannier, satchel 8. reticule, suitcase 9. Gladstone, haversack, sac de nuit 10. pocketbook 11. portmanteau

bag and baggage . . . 10. completely 11. impedimenta

bagatelle . . . 3. toy 4. game 6. bauble, geegaw, trifle 7. trinket 10. knickknack, triviality 12. fiddle–faddle

Bagdad, Baghdad . . .
capital of . . 4. Iraq
character . . 6. Sinbad (The Sailor)
city . . 6. Moslem
founder (762) . . 8. Almanzor
kingdom (anc) . . 11. Mesopotamia
Oriental term . . 8. lambskin (raw)
river . . 6. Tigris
transportation (famed) . . 7. Railway

bagpipe, bagpipes . . . 5. drone, pipes 7. musette 9. Dudelsack 10. doodlesack, sordellina

bagpipe (pert to) . . .
music variations . . 7. pibroch
parts . . 4. lill, oboe 5. drone 7. chanter 9. chalumeau
player . . 5. piper
tube . . 6. drones 7. chanter
tune . . 4. port

Bahamas, Bahama Islands . . .
capital . . 6. Nassau
discoverer . . 8. Columbus
native . . 5. conch
naval base (US) . . 9. Mayaguana
San Salvador (now) . . 14. Watlings Island (Watling Island)

bahan . . . 6. poplar, willow (Bib)

bahay . . . 5. house

bahi . . . 7. fortune (gypsy)

bail . . . 3. dip 4. bond, hoop, lade, lave, ring, rynd 5. court, ladle, throw 6. bucket, dipper, handle, pledge, secure, surety 8. replevin, security 9. guarantee

bailiff . . . 5. agent, bobby, reeve, staff 6. deputy, staves (pl) 7. marshal, officer, sheriff, shrieve, steward 8. bluecoat, gendarme, overseer 9. constable 12. understeward

bailiwick . . . 6. canton, county, domain 7. commune, diocese 8. precinct, province 12. municipality

bain . . . 4. near 5. lithe, ready, short 6. direct, limber, supple 7. forward, willing

bairn . . . 3. kid, tot 4. mite 5. child 6. urchin

bait . . . 3. fly 4. feed, hook, lure, trap 5. bribe, decoy, snare 6. badger, harass, hockle 7. fulcrum, torment 8. inveigle 9. persecute 10. enticement, exasperate, temptation

bait . . . 3. dap, dib 4. fish, hook 6. dibble

bakal (Orient) . . . 9. tradesman 10. shopkeeper

bake . . . 3. dry 4. cake, cook, fire, kiln 5. roast 6. anneal, harden 8. clambake 9. dehydrate

bakehead . . . 4. rail 5. guard, shack 6. stoker 7. fireman 8. trainman

baken . . . 4. buoy 6. beacon 8. landmark

baker's dozen . . . 4. long 6. devil's 7. inbread 8. thirteen

baksheesh . . . 3. sop, tip 5. bribe 7. largess (largesse) 8. gratuity 12. compensation

bal . . . 4. ball, mine, prom

balance . . . 4. even, rest, rule 5. poise, ratio, scale, weigh 6. adjust, aplomb, normal, offset, reason, rhythm, sanity 7. average, ballast, compare, euphony, measure, remains, surplus 8. equality, equalize, leftover, residual, saneness, serenity, symmetry 9. composure, equipoise, remainder, stability 10. equanimity, neutralize, proportion, symmetrize 11. equilibrium 12. counterpoise

balanced . . . 4. even, just 6. poised 7. equable 8. measured 9. equitable 10. euphonious 11. symmetrical 13. self–possessed

balancer . . . 7. acrobat, gymnast 10. ropedancer 11. equilibrist

balcony . . . 4. dais 5. stage 6. podium 7. estrade, gallery, rostrum 8. brattice, platform

bald . . . 4. bare, dull, mere, open 5. crude, naked, plain 6. simple 7. epilose 8. depilous, hairless 9. bald–pated 11. unconcealed

baldachin, baldaquin . . . 6. canopy (St Peter's, Rome), fabric

Balder (pert to) . . .
father . . 4. Odin
god of . . 5. light, peace
mother . . 5. Frigg
slain by . . 9. mistletoe (dart)
wife . . 5. Nanna

balderdash . . . 3. rot 4. bosh 5. trash 6. bunkum, jargon 7. bombast 8. buncombe, falderal, nonsense, tommyrot 9. poppycock

baldness . . . 6. acomia 8. alopecia 11. phalacrosis 12. hairlessness

baldric . . . 4. belt (ornament) 6. zodiac 7. support (sword)

bale . . . 3. woe 4. bind, load, pack 5. truss 6. ballot, bundle, burden, misery, packet, seroon 7. anguish, package 11. encumbrance

Balearic Islands . . . 5. Iviza 7. Cabrera, Majorca, Minorca 10. Formentera

baleful . . . 3. bad, sad 4. dire 6. woeful 7. baneful, harmful, malific, noisome, noxious 8. damaging 9. ill–omened, malignant 10. pernicious 12. inauspicious

balk . . . 4. foil 5. check, ridge 6. baffle, defeat, fallow, rafter, signal (fishing), thwart 7. blunder, faux pas, stickle 9. frustrate, hindrance 10. bafflement, disappoint

14. disappointment

Balkan Peninsula...
native.. 4. Serb
river.. 3. Une 5. Saave 6. Danube
sea.. 5. Black 6. Aegean 7. Marmosa
  8. Adriatic 13. Mediterranean
State.. 6. Greece, Serbia, Turkey (Eur)
  7. Albania, Rumania 8. Bulgaria

balky... 7. restive 9. faltering,
  obstinate, shrinking, stickling

ball... 3. bal, fly, hop, lob, orb
  4. bead, clew (yarn), pill, shot
  5. dance, globe, pearl, pinda (rice)
  6. pellet, pelota, sphere 7. rissole
  8. conglobe, snowball 9. eight ball
  10. cannonball 12. medicine ball

ball (of games)... 4. golf, hand, polo,
  soft 6. basket, tennis, volley
  7. bowling, cricket, croquet, jai alai
  8. baseball, billiard, ping–pong

ballad... 3. lay 4. lied, poem, song
  5. derry, rhyme, verse 6. sonnet
  7. ballade, canzone

ballast... 5. poise 6. aplomb, steady,
  weight 7. balance 9. kentledge,
  saburrate, stabilize 10. equanimity,
  equivalent 14. counterbalance

balled up... 7. complex, mixed up,
  muddled 8. confused, fouled up
  9. befuddled, entangled, snarled up
  10. disordered 11. complicated

ballet (pert to)...
arrangement.. 12. choreography
dance.. 6. adagio 9. pantomime
dancer.. 8. coryphee, danseuse
  9. ballerina
jump.. 4. jeté 5. coupé
lover.. 11. balletomane
music.. 5. opera 6. comedy
  7. d'action 14. divertissement

balloon... 3. bag 4. ball, tire 5. barge
  (Siam), blimp, swell 6. aviate, ballon,
  dilate, expand, gasbag 7. distend,
  nacelle 8. aerostat, aircraft
  9. dirigible

balloon (type)... 4. free, kite 5. pilot
  7. captive 8. sounding
  11. montgolfier, observation

ballot... 4. bale, poll, vote 5. elect,
  slate, voice 6. select, ticket
  8. suffrage

ballyhoo... 4. plug 5. boost, noise
  6. fracas, hoopla, hubbub, ruckus,
  rumpus 7. promote 9. advertise,
  publicity 10. hullabaloo

balm... 3. oil 4. bito, calm 5. cream,
  salve 6. balsam, elixir, lotion, pacify
  7. anodyne, cushion, Melissa,
  perfume, relieve, unction, unguent
  8. liniment, mitigate, ointment
  9. calmative, fragrance, mitigator
  10. palliative

balm (pert to)... 5. Vicks 6. arnica,
  zachun 7. camphor, lanolin, menthol
  8. glycerin, ointment, vaseline
  10. petrolatum

Balm of... 6. Gilead

balmy... 4. mild 5. batty, daffy, dippy,
  drunk, goofy, moony, spicy, sweet
  6. dreamy, insane, savory 7. healing
  8. aromatic, fragrant, lenitive,
  redolent, soothing 9. ambrosial,

assuaging, emollient 10. palliative,
  refreshing 11. odoriferous
  12. sweet–scented

balsam... 3. fir 4. riga, tolu 5. resin
  6. embalm, poplar, storax
  7. benzoin, perfume 8. bdellium
  (Bib), medicine 9. oleoresin
  12. Balsam of Peru, Balsam of Tolu

Baltimore...
Belle.. 4. rose
bird.. 6. oriole
butterfly.. 7. phaeton
city of.. 8. Maryland
hemp.. 4. flax
history of.. 18. Star Spangled Banner
  (1814)

baluster... 4. post 7. support, upright
  8. banister

bam... 4. fake, hoax, mock, sham
  5. cheat, spoof, trick 6. deceit
  7. wheedle 8. flimflam 9. deception,
  imitation

bambino... 4. babe, baby, icon
  5. child, Pietà 6. infant (Christ)

bamboo (pert to)...
curtain.. 8. frontier
English.. 10. Philippine
genus.. 7. Bambuss
sacred.. 6. nandin
sprouts (pickled).. 5. achar
stems.. 4. cane
sugar.. 6. silica 9. tabasheer

bamboozle... 4. dupe, hoax 5. trick
  6. baffle, cajole, humbug 7. beguile,
  deceive, mystify, perplex 9. victimize

ban... 4. coin, tabu, veto 5. curse,
  edict, taboo, title (anc) 6. muslin,
  outlaw 7. embargo, exclude, kokumin
  8. anathema 9. interdict, ostracism,
  ostracize 10. injunction, kokumingun
  11. malediction, prohibition
  12. proscription 15. excommunication

banal... 4. flat 5. corny, stale, trite
  6. cliché, common, old hat
  11. commonplace, stereotyped
  13. platitudinous

banana... 4. Musa, saba 6. ensete
  8. Musaceae, plantain

banana (pert to)...
Bananaland.. 10. Queensland
bananalike.. 8. plantain
bird.. 4. quit 6. oriole
boa.. 5. snake
color.. 7. sunbeam
fish.. 8. ladyfish
freckle.. 7. disease
leaf.. 5. frond
oil.. 7. lacquer
Philippine.. 7. saguing
shrub.. 9. evergreen

band... 3. bar, tie 4. belt, body, crew,
  hoop, line, pack, ring, sash, zone
  5. bunch, corps, group, patte, strap,
  stria, strip, tribe, unite 6. cohort,
  collar, fascia, fillet, girdle, ligula,
  outfit, pledge, radula (Zool), tether
  7. bandage, company 8. cincture,
  encircle, ensemble, neckband, striping
  9. frequency (radio), orchestra,
  striation

bandage... 3. gag 4. bind, tape
  5. sling, spica, truss 6. ligate,

swathe 7. wrapper 8. compress,
dressing, ligature 9. accipiter,
blindfold 10. tourniquet
bandicoot . . . 3. rat 9. Perameles
bandit . . . 4. thug 5. thief 6. dacoit,
outlaw, robber 7. bandido, brigand,
footpad, ladrone 8. marauder,
picaroon 9. bandolero
10. highwayman
bandmaster . . . 5. Sousa 6. leader
7. maestro 8. choragus, director
9. conductor 13. Kapellmeister
bandolero . . . 5. thief 6. robber
10. highwayman
bandy . . . 4. beat, cart, game 5. bowed
6. curved, strive, stroke (tennis)
7. contend, embowed 8. carriage
(Ind), exchange, to and fro
9. bowlegged 11. bandy–legged,
reciprocate
bandy words . . . 5. argue 6. bicker,
parley 7. contend, wrangle
8. converse
bane . . . 3. woe 4. evil, harm, kill, pest,
ruin 5. curse, venom 6. injury,
plague, poison, slayer 7. disease
(sheep), scourge 8. murderer,
vexation 9. grievance 10. affliction,
pestilence, visitation
baneful . . . 3. ill 4. vile 7. harmful,
noxious 9. injurious 10. pernicious
11. detrimental
bang . . . 3. hit, rap 4. beat, blow,
dash, drub, kick, lift, shut, slam
5. crack, knock, pound, punch,
smack, thump, verve, whack
6. energy, report, strike, thrash, thrill
7. collide 8. coiffure
bangle . . . 5. charm 7. circlet
8. bracelet
banish . . . 3. ban 4. oust 5. exile, expel
6. deport, dispel, outlaw, punish
7. condemn, dismiss, exclude
8. relegate 9. ostracize, proscribe
10. expatriate 13. excommunicate
banister . . . 4. post, rail 8. baluster
10. balustrade
banjo . . . 7. samisen
bank . . . 3. row 4. brae, edge, heap,
quay, ripa 5. brink, flock, hurst
(sandy), marge, shoal, shore, slope,
table 6. aviate, margin, quarry,
rivage, series, stakes, strand
7. anthill, barrier, deposit, incline
8. buttress, treasury 9. acclivity,
riverside 13. fortification
bank account . . . 5. funds, means
6. assets, moneys 8. finances
9. exchequer
banker . . . 4. game 6. broker, lender
9. financier 11. moneylender
12. money–changer
bankrupt . . . 4. bust, ruin 5. broke,
smash 6. failed, quisby (sl) 7. failure
9. destitute, insolvent, moneyless,
penniless 12. impoverished
banner . . . 4. fane, flag 6. ensign,
poster 7. leading, pennant, placard
8. foremost, headline, standard,
streamer 9. exemplary 10. surpassing
banns, marriage . . . 6. notice
7. sibrede 12. proclamation

banquet . . . 4. fete 5. diffa, feast, festa
6. fiesta, junket, regale, repast,
spread 8. festival, jamboree
10. regalement
Banquo . . . 9. character (Shak)
banshee, banshie . . . 4. shee 5. fairy,
Geist, sidhe 6. spirit, sprite
bantam (pert to) . . .
cock . . 3. fop 5. dandy, sport
7. peacock 8. strutter 9. swaggerer
12. swashbuckler
Java . . 4. duck, fowl 5. breed
6. Brahma, Cochin
slang . . 4. runt 6. peewee, shrimp
sports . . 6. weight
bantamweight . . . 5. boxer (118 lbs)
7. fighter 8. pugilist 9. contender
10. contestant
banter . . . 4. jest, josh, mock, twit
5. borak, chaff, sport, tease, trick
6. delude, deride, satire 7. asteism,
wheedle 8. badinage, raillery, ridicule
10. persiflage, pleasantry
Bantu, South Africa . . .
language . . 3. Ila 8. Kongoese
people . . 5. Duala 6. Basuto
tribe . . 4. Vili, Zulu 6. Damara, Kaffir
7. Negroid, Swahili 8. Bechuana
banzai . . . 4. hail 5. hello, hullo
6. attack, charge 9. greetings
11. salutations
baobab tree (pert to) . . .
bark . . 4. rope 5. cloth, paper
fruit . . 11. monkey bread
genus . . 9. Adansonia
pulp . . 8. beverage
baptism . . . 4. rite 6. naming 7. wetting
8. ablution 9. aspersion, immersion,
sacrament 10. initiation, sprinkling
11. christening 12. consecration,
purification, regeneration (spiritual)
baptism (pert to) . . .
cloth . . 7. chrisom
dead (RCCh) . . 5. Blood 6. Desire
fire . . 9. fuertaufe
place . . 4. font 10. baptistery (anc)
receptacle . . 5. basin 7. piscina
water . . 5. laver
bar . . . 3. ban, dam, fid, pry, rod
4. bolt, deny, fess, joke, line, rack,
rail, sess, type 5. betty
(thieves'slang), block, court, deter,
easer, estop, ingot, lever, shoal,
space, staff 6. except, forbid, hinder,
ripper, saloon, stitch, stripe
7. barrier, barroom, bass–bar,
chevron, counter, crowbar, exclude,
prevent, railing, sandbar, trapeze
8. blockade, disallow, obstacle,
obstruct, preclude, prohibit
9. barricade, hindrance
10. impediment, profession,
singletree 11. obstruction,
whippletree 12. underscoring
barb . . . 3. jag 4. clip, flue, harl, herl,
seta 5. horse, point, ramus, scarf
(nun's), speed 6. setula, striga
7. bristle, feather, pinnula 8. kingfish
9. arrowhead 10. projection
Barbados Island . . .
capital . . 10. Bridgetown
drink . . 3. rum

government.. 7. British
location.. 8. Antilles (Lesser) 10. West Indies
native.. 3. Bim (nickname)
barbarian... 3. hun 4. Goth, rude 5. beast, brute 6. savage, vandal 8. cannibal, man–eater 9. untutored, vulgarian 10. extraneous, Philistine, unlettered 11. uncivilized 15. anthropophagite
barbaric... 5. cruel 6. brutal, Gothic, savage 7. foreign, inhuman, vicious 8. non–Greek, non–Latin, ruthless 9. barbarous, primitive 10. extraneous 11. uncivilized 12. non–Christian
barbarism... 6. ferity 8. rudeness, solecism 9. barbarity, crudeness, Gothicism, ignorance, vulgarism 10. coarseness, corruption, foreignism 11. impropriety
Barbarossa... 7. emperor (Rom) 8. red beard
Barbary ape... 5. magot
Barbary State (former)... 5. Tunis 7. Algiers, Morocco 12. Tripolitania
barbate... 7. bearded, stubbly 9. whiskered 11. barbigerous
barbecue... 5. feast, roast 6. animal (whole), picnic 7. brazier, hibachi 9. Dutch oven 10. shish kebab 13. entertainment (out–of–doors)
barber... 5. shave 6. figaro, shaver, tonsor 7. tonsure 10. haircutter 12. tonsorialist
Barber of Seville character... 6. Figaro, Rosina
Barcelona, Spain...
building (famed).. 6. palace (Kings of Aragon) 9. Cathedral (Gothic)
port.. 13. Mediterranean
street (famed).. 6. Rambla
bard... 4. muse, poet, scop (Hist) 5. druid, runer, vates 8. minstrel, musician (wandering) 10. Parnassian
Bard of...
Avon.. 11. Shakespeare
Ayrshire.. 5. Burns
Rydal Mount.. 10. Wordsworth
bare... 3. raw 4. bald, mere, nude, open 5. alone, empty, naked, plain, shear, sheer, stark, strip 6. barren, denude, divest, expose, reveal, simple, vacant 7. exposed, unarmed, uncover 8. desolate, disclose, stripped 9. destitute, unadorned, uncovered 10. stark–naked, threadbare 11. defenseless, unconcealed
barefaced... 4. bare, bold 6. brassy, brazen 8. impudent 9. audacious, shameless 11. undisguised
barely... 4. jimp, only 5. faint 6. hardly, merely, nudely, poorly, simply 7. nakedly 8. narrowly, scantily, scarcely 14. insufficiently
bargain... 3. buy 4. deal, pact, prig, sell 5. trade 6. barter, chisel, dicker, haggle 7. chaffer, compact, mediate 8. contract, covenant, purchase 9. agreement, Bon Marché, cheapness, negotiate 10. engagement

11. stipulation, transaction
barge... 3. ark, hoy 4. raft, scow, ship 5. ferry, float, praam, scold 6. berate, lumber, rebuke, tender 7. birlinn (birling) 9. transport
barge in... 5. enter 6. bungle, butt in, invade, push in 7. blunder, intrude
barghest... 6. goblin
bargoose... 4. duck 9. merganser, sheldrake
bark... 3. bay, yap, yip 4. bang, bast, husk, peel, rind, ross, ship, skin, tapa, yelp 5. cough, niepa, shout, strip, youff 6. bowwow, clamor, cortex, outcry, packet, scrape 7. canella 8. ballyhoo, periderm 9. sassafras
barker... 4. tout 6. pistol 7. spieler 9. solicitor 10. ballyhooer, theaterman
barking... 7. latrant 8. hylactic
Barlaam and Josaphet (Joasaph)... 11. Buddha story (Christian version)
barley... 4. bigg, food, seed 5. grain 6. ptisan, tsamba 7. Hordeum
barley (pert to)...
bird.. 6. siskin 7. wagtail (yellow), wryneck 11. nightingale
bree.. 3. ale 6. liquor
shaped.. 10. hordeiform
barlow... 9. jackknife (one–bladed)
barm... 5. froth, yeast 6. leaven 7. ferment
barn... 3. bay, mow 4. loft
barnacle... 4. bray (Her) 5. acorn, goose, leech 6. animal, sucker 8. adherent, parasite 9. sycophant 10. Cirripedia, crustacean
barnstormer... 5. actor 7. aviator 11. entertainer
baron... 4. peer 5. mogul, noble 6. daimio, tycoon 7. freeman 8. nobleman, somebody 9. financier, personage 10. capitalist 13. industrialist
baroque... 6. ornate, quaint, rococo 7. bizarre 9. irregular 11. extravagant
barracks... 4. camp, huts 6. casern, laager 9. barracoon 10. encampment
barraclade... 7. blanket (homemade)
barracuda... 4. fish, spet 5. barry (Bahamas) 6. sennet
barrage... 3. dam 4. weir 5. blitz 6. strafe 7. barrier, gunfire, milldaw 9. cannonade, roadblock 11. obstruction
barrage (military)... 3. box 5. mines 6. normal 7. balloon 8. creeping, standing 9. emergency 12. anti–aircraft
barranca... 4. bank 5. bluff 6. ravine
barratry... 6. breach, simony 8. bad faith, mala fide 10. infidelity 11. dereliction
barred... 6. cooped, fenced, grated, ribbed 7. striped 8. confined, debarred, excluded, streaked
barrel... 3. box, keg, tun 4. cade, cask, drum, knag 5. quill, speed 6. runlet, tierce 7. calamus (Zool), rundlet 8. cylinder 9. kilderkin
barrel (pert to)...

maker.. 6. cooper
miscellaneous.. 3. gun, pen 4. pipe
6. pencil
sling.. 9. parbuckle
stopper.. 4. bung
barren... 3. dry 4. arid, bare, dull
5. blank, empty, heath, inane
6. desert, effete, jejune, karroo,
meager, Sahara, stupid 7. sterile
8. desolate, impotent, unpoetic
9. infertile 10. unfruitful, unprolific
12. unproductive, unprofitable
barricade... 3. bar 4. bolt, rail, seal,
stop 5. block, close, fence 6. abatis
7. barrier, padlock 8. blockade,
obstacle, obstruct 11. obstruction
13. fortification
barrico... 3. keg 4. cask
barrier... 3. Alp, bar, dam 4. clog,
door, gate, wall, weir 5. block,
fence, hedge, panel 6. screen
7. parapet, railing 8. blockade,
boundary, fortress, obstacle, stockade,
stoppage 9. partition, restraint
10. impediment, portcullis
11. obstruction
barrikin (Eng sl)... 6. jargon
9. gibberish
barrister... 6. lawyer 7. adviser,
pleader 8. advocate, attorney
9. counselor (counsellor), solicitor
barroom... 3. bar, pub, tap 6. saloon,
tavern 7. cantina, taproom
8. alehouse 11. rathskeller
barrow... 3. hod, hog (male) 4. brae,
fell, hill, knap, moor 5. grave (anc),
mound 7. tumulus 8. mountain
11. wheelbarrow 12. Reihengräber
bartender... 5. mixer 6. barman, bistro
7. barkeep, tapster 8. publican
barter... 4. deal, sell, swap 5. trade,
truck 7. bargain, permute, traffic
8. commerce, exchange
Bartholomew (pert to)... 4. Fair, Play
(Shak) 5. Saint 6. martyr 7. Apostle
(one of 12) 8. Massacre
Bartimeus (Bib)... 6. beggar (blind)
barton... 4. farm 5. abode, manor
6. grange 7. demesne 8. farmyard,
hacienda 9. homestead
baru... 4. tree (fiber) 7. majagua
base... 3. bed, low 4. dado, evil, foot,
foul, mean, root, seat, site, sole
5. basis, basso, cause, petty, radix,
socle, voice 6. abject, bottom,
center, factor, patten, plinth, podium,
singer, sordid, vulgar, wicked
7. servile, station 8. basement,
cosmetic, degraded, infamous,
inferior, pedestal, shameful, standard
9. principle, worthless
10. despicable, foundation, villainous
12. contemptible, dishonorable,
headquarters
baseball (terms)... 3. bag, bat, box,
fan, fly, hit, lob, out, RBI, run
4. ball, base, bunt, deck, foul,
home, nine, pill, sack, save, walk,
wild 5. bench, clout, coach, count,
curve, drive, error, field, first, force,
glove, homer, liner, mound, pitch,
plate, pop–up, score, slide, sport,

swing, third 6. assist, batter, bungle,
double, dugout, fumble, ground,
putout, rubber, runner, screen,
second, series, single, sinker, stance,
strike, string, target, triple, windup
7. battery, bullpen, diamond, fielder,
floater, rhubarb (sl), squeeze, stretch
8. backstop, grounder, keystone,
knuckler, outfield, pinch–hit,
powdered, spit ball 9. sacrifice,
strikeout 10. ballplayer
baseborn... 3. low 4. mean 5. lowly,
plain 6. common, humble 7. bastard,
ignoble, lowborn 8. plebeian,
spurious 11. commonplace
12. illegitimate
based on...
evidence.. 7. damning 8. decisive
10. conclusive
experience.. 7. empiric 9. empirical
numbers.. 5. hexad 6. nonary, senary
7. tertial
baseness... 6. infamy 7. badness
9. servility, vulgarity 10. wickedness
11. inferiority 13. dastardliness,
subordination
bash... 3. bat, jab, lam 4. beat, belt,
biff, blow, conk, mash, slug, sock
5. clout, paste, punch, smack, whack
6. bruise, strike, wallop 7. clobber
Basham's King... 2. Og
bashful... 3. coy, shy 5. heloe, mousy,
timid 6. demure, modest
8. blushing, retiring, sheepish,
timorous, verecund 9. diffident
13. self–conscious
basic... 4. root 5. basal, basis
7. essence, primary 8. alkaline,
original 9. essential 10. underlying
11. fundamental
Basilian... 3. art 4. monk, rule
6. bishop 7. liturgy, St Basil (The
Great) 8. precepts 10. Cappadocia
basilica... 5. major, minor, title
6. canopy, church, shrine, temple
11. patriarchal
Basilican (pert to)...
books.. 3. sixty 6. Digest
century.. 5. Tenth
empire.. 9. Byzantine
laws.. 9. Justinian
basin... 3. bed (water), cup, pit, tub
4. bowl, cock, font, hole, sink, tank
5. laver, plain, playa, stoup 6. cavity,
chafer, coulee, ground, lavabo,
marine, valley, vessel 7. lowland,
piscina 8. curvette 9. washbasin
10. depression
basis... 4. base, fond, root 5. cause,
start 6. bottom, factor, motive,
reason, thesis 7. premise, warrant
9. assertion, principle 10. foundation,
groundwork 13. justification
bask... 3. sin, tub 4. warm 5. bathe,
revel 7. suffuse 8. apricate
9. luxuriate
basket... 3. bin, box, car (balloon),
net, ped, pod 4. caba, cage, kish,
skep, trug 5. cabas 6. dosser,
gabion, vessel, wisket 7. corbeil,
hanaper, pannier, scuttle, wattage
9. container

basket (pert to) . . .
coal mine . . 3. tub 4. corf
fig. . 5. frail 6. tapnet
fire. . 5. grate 7. cresset
fishing. . 3. pot 4. buck (eel), caul,
weel 5. crail, crate, creel 6. hamper
making. . 5. slath 6. slarth
wicker. . 3. cob 5. cesta, osier
6. hamper 7. hanaper 8. bassinet
Basque (pert to) . . .
ancestors. . 8. Iberians
cap. . 5. beret
home. . 5. Spain 8. Pyrenees
bas–relief . . . 7. carving, relievo
12. basso–relievo (basso–rilievo)
bass . . . 4. fish 5. fiber, voice (low)
6. singer 8. weakfish 13. basso
profundo
bassoon . . . 4. oboe 6. fagott 7. fagotto
bast . . . 4. bass 5. fiber
Bast (Egypt) . . . 4. Ptah 7. goddess
10. lady of life
bastard . . . 3. odd 4. heel (sl), sham
5. false, louse (sl) 7. batarde
8. abnormal, bantling, spurious
9. scoundrel 10. adulterate
12. illegitimate 13. nullius filius
baste . . . 3. hit, sew 4. cook, lard, lash,
tack, whip 6. stitch, thrash
7. trounce 8. lambaste
bastion . . . 5. redan 8. fastness
10. stronghold 13. fortification
bat . . . 3. hit, jag, lam, rap 4. belt,
blow, clip, club, slug, sock, swat,
wink 5. binge, clout, paste, smack,
spree, stick, whack 6. bender,
cudgel, racket, wallop 7. clobber
bat (mammal) . . . 6. aliped, fox bat,
kalong 7. noctule, vampire
8. serotine 9. flying fox, pipistrel
(pipistrelle), reremouse 10. Chiroptera
batch . . . 3. lot 4. heap, lump, mess,
slew 5. bunch, group, stack
6. amount, baking 7. mixture
8. quantity 10. collection
bath . . . 3. dip, tub 4. sitz 5. steam,
sweat, vapor 6. plunge, shower,
sponge 7. Finnish, mineral, sulphur
bath (pert to) . . .
Eccl. . 8. ablution
house. . 6. bagnic, cabana 8. balneary
10. natatorium
photography. . 5. toner 9. developer
Roman. . 7. balneum 11. Warm
Springs
sitz. . 5. bidet
warm. . 5. therm
bathe . . . 3. tub, wet 4. bask, lave,
swim, wash 5. flush 6. drench
7. immerse, moisten, pervade,
suffuse 8. medicate, permeate
baton . . . 3. rod 4. mace, wand
5. staff, stick 6. baston, cudgel,
fasces 7. scepter, support
9. truncheon
Batrachia . . . 5. Anura, frogs, toads
7. Surinam 8. Salienta
Battalion of Death (Russ) . . .
13. legion of women
batten . . . 5. close, gloat 6. fasten,
fatten, secure, thrive, timber
battered . . . 6. beaten, pasted

7. bruised 8. impaired 9. shattered,
weathered
battery . . . 3. set 4. guns, pack
6. cohort, series 7. assault, platoon
8. baseball (term) 9. artillery
battery (Elec) . . . 4. cell, grid, pole
5. anode, plate 6. Leyden
7. storage, voltaic 9. electrode
battle . . . 3. war 4. fray, meet, tilt
5. brush, fight, joust, scrap
6. action, affray, barney, combat,
tussle 7. contest, scuffle, warfare
8. conflict, skirmish, struggle
9. challenge, encounter
10. engagement
Battle (pert to) . . .
Bib. . 8. Aceldama 12. potter's field
Civil War. . 7. Bull Run 15. Lookout
Mountain
formation. . 4. line 5. herse, order
Great. . 10. Armageddon
Hundred Years (1346). . 5. Crecy
Revolution. . 10. Bunker Hill
slogan. . 8. aux–armes 9. battle cry
World War I. . 6. Verdun (1916)
World War II. . 11. Pearl Harbor
(1941)
battologize . . . 6. repeat 7. iterate,
recount, restate 9. reiterate
12. recapitulate
bauble . . . 3. toy 4. gaud 6. doodad,
geegaw, trifle, trivia 7. bibelot, trinket
8. falderal (folderol) 9. bagatelle,
plaything 10. knickknack
Bavaria . . .
capital. . 6. Munich
city. . 8. Augsburg, Wurzburg
9. Nuremburg 12. Ludwigshafen
freeway. . 8. autobahn
government. . 10. Third Reich
king (former). . 10. Maximilian
prince. . 6. Rupert
river. . 4. Eger, Isar
bawdry . . . 6. filthy 8. ribaldry, salacity,
unchaste 9. obscenity
11. pornography
bawl . . . 3. cry, say, sob 4. bark, howl,
roar, wail, weep, yell 5. blare, shout
6. bellow, boohoo, plaint 8. proclaim
10. vociferate
bay . . . 3. ria 4. cove, howl, roan, wail
5. bight, horse, inlet, oriel, sinus
6. recess, window 7. ululate
bay (pert to) . . .
antler. . 9. stag's tine (2nd)
bird. . 5. snipe 6. curlew, godwit,
plover
color. . 4. roan
tree. . 6. laurel
Bayard . . . 5. horse, steed (Rinaldo's)
bayonet . . . 5. lance, saber, spear,
sword 6. dagger, weapon 7. poniard
bayou . . . 5. creek, marsh 6. slough,
stream 7. channel 11. watercourse
Bayou State . . . 11. Mississippi
Bay State . . . 13. Massachusetts
bazaar . . . 4. fair, shop 6. market
7. canteen (army) 10. exposition
be . . . 2. am 3. are 4. live 5. exist
7. prevail
beach . . . 5. coast, plage, playa, praya,
sands, shore 6. shilla, strand

9. waterside
beachcomber... 4. wave 6. loafer
8. vagabond
beacon... 4. beam, flag, sign, vane
5. fanal, light, radar, radio
6. marker, pharos, signal 7. cresset,
lantern, seamark 10. lighthouse,
watchtower
bead... 4. ball, drop 5. bugle, pearl,
sight (firearm) 6. rondel 8. ornament
beads... 5. grain, sewan 6. rosary
7. chaplet, granose (antennae),
jewelry, prayers
beak... 3. neb, nib 4. bill, lora, nose,
peck, prow 5. judge, mouth, spout,
tutel 10. magistrate 11. stipendiary
beaker... 3. cup 6. vessel (Chem)
beakless... 9. erostrate
beam... 3. ray 4. emit, grin, sile, sill,
stud 5. caber, gleam, joist, shaft,
shine, smile, tonka, trave 6. girder,
mantel, rafter, timber 7. radiate,
support, trimmer 8. trabeate
bean... 4. buck, faba, gram, lima,
mung, navy, seed, soya 5. black,
coral, pinto, Sieva 6. adzuki, castor,
frijol (frijole), kidney, legume, lentil,
string 7. calabar 9. Phaseolus
bean (pert to)...
eye of.. 5. hilum
game.. 7. beanbag
licorice seed.. 9. jequirity
lima.. 4. haba
seed (string bean).. 7. haricot
shaped.. 8. fabiform
slang.. 4. buck, head 5. brain
6. dollar, noodle, trifle
bear... 3. aim, cub, lug 4. dubb, tote,
turn, ursa 5. bring, brown, bruin,
carry, clack, crank, koala, polar,
press, short, sloth, stand, ursus, yield
6. animal, endure, grouch, harbor,
Kodiak, stress, suffer, Syrian, uphold
7. Ephraim (nickname), furnish,
grizzly, incline, musquaw, produce,
support 8. cinnamon, fructify,
maintain, Melursus, sorehead, tolerate
10. speculator 11. short seller
(Finan)
bear (pert to)...
cat.. 5. panda 9. binturong
class.. 6. ursine 7. Ursidaw
color.. 6. yellow
constellation.. 9. Ursa Major, Ursa
Minor
flag.. 10. California (State)
head.. 4. hure
The.. 6. Russia
beard... 3. awn 6. arista, goatee
7. stubble, Vandyke 8. whiskers
bearded... 5. awned 7. barbate,
pappose 8. aristate 9. whiskered
beards, science of... 10. pogonology
bearer... 3. boy 5. macer, usher
6. porter, tender 7. carrier
8. cargador, conveyor, escudero
9. attendant 10. khidmatgar,
pallbearer
bearing... 3. air 4. mien, port
5. poise 6. bel air, regard
7. concern, conduct, dignity,
meaning, posture 8. behavior,

carriage, demeanor, relation, tendency
9. direction, influence, relevance
10. connection, deportment,
supporting 12. significance
bearing (Her)... 4. enté, orle 5. bevel,
pheon 6. billet
bear witness... 6. attest 7. testify
beast... 4. bête, game, lion, pard
5. brute, camel, demon, fiend, horse,
spado, tiger 6. animal, cattle,
dragon, savage 7. carrier, critter,
leopard, monster 8. behemoth,
creature 9. dromedary
beastly... 5. gross 6. animal, bloody,
carnal, odious 7. bestial, brutish,
hideous, inhuman, leonine, theroid,
ungodly 8. dreadful 9. execrable
10. abominable, disgusting
beat... 3. hit, lam, tan, taw, wap
4. bang, bash, best, cane, drub,
drum, flog, lace, lash, maul, pelt,
tund 5. baste, excel, pound, pulse,
route, scoop, throb, thump 6. bruise,
cudgel, defeat, larrup, pommel,
punish, rhythm, strike, stroke, swinge,
thrash, thresh 7. baffled, belabor,
cadence, clobber, conquer, flutter,
musical, pulsate, routine, surpass,
trounce 8. chastise, fatigued,
lambskin, overcome, vanquish
9. exhausted, pulsation
beat (pert to)...
back.. 7. repulse
black and blue.. 9. suggilate
down.. 6. haggle 7. cheapen
into plate.. 8. malleate
slang.. 4. blow 5. scoot, scram
6. beat it, skidoo 7. vamoose
traverse.. 6. patrol
beatify... 5. bless, cheer, saint
6. hallow 7. gladden, glorify
8. enshrine, sanctify
beatnik... 8. Bohemian, maverick,
sulphite 13. nonconformist
beau... 3. fop 5. blade, dandy, flame,
lover, spark, swain 6. escort, squire
7. admirer, courter 9. caballero,
inamorato 10. beau–garçon
beautiful... 4. fair, fine 5. bonny,
kalon (Gr) 6. comely, lovely, poetic,
pretty 7. elegant, Tempean
8. graceful, handsome, stunning
9. aesthetic (esthetic), exquisite
15. pulchritudinous
beautify... 4. deck, trim 5. adorn,
grace 6. bedeck, doll up, enrich
8. decorate, prettify 9. embellish,
glamorize
beauty... 5. belle, charm, glory, grace
8. elegance 10. loveliness, prettiness
11. pulchritude
beauty, famed...
Egypt.. 9. Cleopatra
Greek.. 4. Hebe 6. Graces
9. Aphrodite 11. Helen of Troy
Historical.. 4. Lais
Persian.. 4. peri 5. houri
Norse.. 5. Freya
Roman.. 5. Venus
Becken... 7. cymbals
beckon... 4. beck 5. court 6. invite,
summon 7. gesture 11. gesticulate

becloud... 5. bedim, cloud, shade, smoke 6. bemist, darken, opaque 7. conceal, encloud, obscure 8. nubilate, overcast 9. adumbrate
become... 2. go 3. fit, get, wax 4. grow, rise, suit 5. befit, grace 6. befall, beseem, mature, mellow 7. behoove, benefit 8. befuddle 9. originate
becoming... 3. fit 6. comely, decent, fitted, likely, proper, seemly, suited 7. decorum, suiting 8. decorous, pleasing, suitable, tasteful 9. befitting, expedient 11. appropriate
bec–scie... 4. duck 9. merganser
becuna... 9. barracuda
bed... 3. cot, kip, tye (feather) 4. bunk, crib, doss, lair, nest 5. basin, berth, couch 6. billet, bottom, flower, litter, pallet 7. channel, feather, stratum 8. bassinet 9. stretcher 10. foundation
bed (pert to)...
canopy.. 4. ceil 6. tester
coverlet.. 5. quilt 6. spread 7. blanket 9. comforter 11. counterpane
famed.. 15. bed of Procrustes
bedaub... 3. dab 4. blur, daub, soil 5. paint, smear, stain 6. belaud, smudge 7. bedizen, besmear 8. besmudge, ornament
bedazzle... 4. daze, stun 5. blind, shine 6. dazzle 7. astound, confuse 8. astonish, bewilder
bedeck... 3. gem 4. trim 5. adorn, array, grace, prink 6. clothe, rag out 7. bedrape 8. ornament
bedevil... 3. hex 4. foul, ride 5. abuse, tease 6. befoul, muddle, needle, pester, plague 7. bewitch, confuse, torment 8. demonize 9. diabolize, tantalize 10. complicate
bedight... 5. adorn, array, equip
bedikah... 6. ritual
bedim... 3. dim, fog 4. blur, fade 5. blear, cloud 6. bemist, darken 8. bedarken
bedlam... 3. din 6. clamor, tumult, uproar 8. madhouse 9. charivari 11. pandemonium
Bedlam (London)... 6. priory (1247) 8. Hospital (St Mary of Bethlehem)
Bedouin... 4. Arab, Moor 5. gypsy, nomad 7. Saracen, vagrant
Bedouin head cord... 4. agal
bedroll... 6. bindle 7. matilda
bee... 3. dor 4. apis 5. drone, karbi, queen 6. insect, worker 8. andrenid, angelito, honeybee 9. bumblebee 12. carpenter bee
bee (pert to)...
fear of.. 9. apiphobia
glue.. 8. propolis
hive.. 4. butt, scap, skep (straw) 6. apiary 7. alveary 8. workshop
keeper.. 8. apiarist, skeppist
sociable.. 7. husking, raising 8. quilting, spelling
study.. 10. apiculture 11. melittology
wax.. 7. beeswax, ceresin, cerotic

9. cera flava
Beebe, William... 13. ichthyologist
beef... 4. heft, kine, thew 5. brawn, sinew, steer 6. buccan (dried), cattle, muscle 8. poundage 10. brawniness 11. muscularity
Beelzebub (pert to)...
Bible.. 5. deity 6. oracle 14. prince of demons
literature.. 5. demon (Prince), devil 11. fallen angel
zoology.. 6. monkey
beer... 3. ale 4. bock, flip, hops, suds 5. lager, weiss 6. liquor, porter, swipes
beer (pert to)...
cask.. 4. butt
inventor.. 9. Gambrinus (Myth king)
mug.. 4. toby 5. stein 8. schooner
vessel.. 4. tanker 9. blackjack
beet... 4. Beta 5. chard 6. mangel 8. beet root 9. sugar beet
Beethoven, Ludwig Van (pert to)...
birthplace.. 4. Bonn (Ger)
composed.. 7. Fidelio 10. symphonies
famed as.. 7. pianist 8. composer
beetle... 3. bat, bug, dor, jut, ram 4. June, rose 5. Amara, gogga, Hispa, meloe, snout 6. chafer, elater, golach, goloch, hammer, masher, sawyer, scarab, weevil 7. ladybug, prionid 8. circulio, sharnbud, skipjack 9. cockroach, dorbeetle 10. cockchafer, Elateridae
beetlehead... 5. stupe 6. plover (bird), stupid 8. bonehead 9. blockhead 10. loggerhead
befall... 3. hap 4. come 5. occur 6. betide, chance, happen 9. eventuate, transpire
befit... 4. suit 5. serve 6. become, beseem, please
befitting... 3. fit 4. meet 6. filial, proper, seemly, timely 7. ethical, fitting, suiting 8. becoming, decorous, suitable 9. expedient 10. seasonable 11. appropriate
befog... 3. dim, fog 5. blind, cloud 6. bemist 7. becloud, conceal, confuse, mystify, obscure
before... 3. ere 5. afore, ahead, avant, early, prior 6. anteal, facing, openly, sooner 7. already, earlier, forward, yestern 8. anterior, foremost, formerly, hitherto 9. foregoing, preceding 10. beforehand, face to face, heretofore, previously 11. theretofore
before (pert to)...
birth.. 8. prenatal
long.. 4. soon
mentioned.. 4. said, same, such 5. named 6. former 10. aforenamed
others.. 5. first
this.. 3. ere 5. prior 6. erenow
before (pref)... 3. pre, pro 4. ante, prae
befoul... 4. soil 5. taint 6. bemire, defile, muddle 7. bedevil 8. entangle 10. complicate 11. contaminate
befriend... 3. aid 4. abet, help 5. favor 6. assist, foster, succor

7. benefit, support, sustain
11. countenance
befuddle... 3. fog 5. addle, besot
6. fuddle, muddle 7. becloud,
confuse 9. inebriate 10. intoxicate
beg... 3. ask, sue, woo 4. pray, sorn
5. cadge, crave, mooch, plead,
touch (sl) 6. appeal 7. beseech,
entreat, implore, solicit 8. petition
9. importune 10. supplicate
beget... 3. ean 4. sire 5. breed,
hatch, spawn 6. father 7. develop
8. engender, generate 9. procreate,
reproduce
begetter... 4. sire 5. pater 6. author,
father, mother, parent 7. creator
10. procreator, progenitor
beggar... 3. bum 4. hobo, waif
5. fakir (Moslem), gamin, lazar, rogue
6. loafer, pauper, wretch
7. almsman, dervish, vagrant, wastral
8. indigent, vagabond 9. mendicant,
suppliant 10. panhandler, ragamuffin
14. tatterdemalion
beggarly... 3. low 4. base, mean,
poor, rank 5. petty 6. abject,
meanly, paltry, vulgar 7. hangdog,
ignoble 8. bankrupt, indigent,
infamous, wretched 9. miserable,
niggardly 10. despicably, obsequious
12. contemptible
Beggars, King of (Eng)... 5. Carew
beggary... 4. want 6. penury
9. indigence, mendicity, pauperism
10. mendicancy 11. destitution,
panhandling
begin... 4. open 5. enter, start
6. attack 8. commence, initiate, take
rise 9. institute, introduce, originate
10. inaugurate
begin again... 5. renew 6. resume
10. recommence
beginner... 3. dub 4. tyro (tiro)
5. chela 6. infant, novice
7. amateur, entrant, recruit
8. begetter, freshman, neophyte
9. debutante, fledgling, initiator,
novitiate 10. catechumen, originator,
tenderfoot 11. inaugurator
beginning... 4. head, rise, root
5. alpha, birth, debut, onset, start
6. origin, outset, source 7. genesis,
infancy, opening 8. entrance,
inchoate, nascency, outstart, starting
9. inception, threshold 10. derivation,
foundation, incomplete, initiation
12. commencement, introduction
begone... 3. out 4. away, scat, shoo
5. allez, scram 6. aroint, avaunt,
depart 7. vamoose
begrudge... 4. envy 5. covey, stint
6. grudge, refuse 7. grumble
beguile... 4. dupe, lure, vamp
5. amuse, charm, cozen, elude,
spend, trick 6. delude, divert, regale
7. bewitch, deceive, ensnare, mislead
8. enthrall, intrigue 9. bamboozle,
captivate, deception, entertain,
fascinate, victimize 11. double–cross
14. disappointment
begum (Hind)... 5. queen 7. heiress
8. princess

begunk... 4. jilt 5. trick
behalf... 4. gain, good, part, sake,
side 5. avail, stead 6. affair, matter,
profit 7. benefit, defense, service,
support, welfare 8. interest
9. advantage
behalf of... 3. for 6. lieu of, rather
7. defense (of), instead
behave... 2. do 3. act 4. bear
5. carry 6. demean, deport, manage
7. conduct 8. regulate, restrain
behavior, behaviour... 3. air 4. mien
6. action, manner 7. actions,
address, bearing, conduct, decorum,
manners 8. carriage, demeanor,
maintien 10. deportment
11. comportment
behavior (pert to)...
good.. 7. decorum, P's and Q's
riotous.. 7. rampage
wicked.. 10. wrongdoing
behead... 7. execute 9. decollate
10. decapitate, guillotine
Behemoth (Bib)... 5. beast
12. hippopotamus
behest... 3. vow 5. order 7. bidding,
command, mandate, promise
10. injunction 11. commandment
behind... 3. aft 4. late, past, rear,
rump (vulgar), slow, tail 5. abaff,
abaft, after, ahind, arear, later, tardy
6. astern 7. delayed, impeded
8. arrested, backward, retarded 9. in
the past, posterior, remaining
behindhand... 4. late 5. tardy
7. arrears, belated, overdue
8. backward, dilatory, misdated,
mistimed 10. defaulting, delinquent
behind the times... 5. passé
behold... 2. lo 3. see 4. ahoy, ecce,
ecco, espy, look, scan, view 5. voilà
6. descry, regard, retain 7. discern,
observe, witness 8. maintain,
perceive
beholden... 5. bound 7. bounden,
obliged 8. grateful, indebted, thankful
9. obligated
beholder... 5. gazer 7. watcher,
witness 8. looker–on, observer,
onlooker 9. spectator
beige... 4. ecru, hopi 5. grège
6. dorado 13. reddish–yellow
being... 3. ego, ens, man, one
4. bion, body, esse, home, life, self
5. entia, gnome, human, thing, wight
6. actual, animal, entity, extant,
mortal, person 7. Adamite, essence,
present, reality 8. creature, existent,
existing, organism, presence
9. actuality, existence, personage,
something 10. individual
11. subsistence
being (pert to)...
celestial.. 4. deva 5. angel 6. cherub,
seraph
imaginary.. 4. pixy (pixie) 5. fairy,
sylph
science of.. 8. ontology
supernatural.. 6. Garuda (Hind)
Supreme.. 3. God 7. Creator
belaud... 4. laud 5. extol 6. praise
7. glorify

belay / belongings

belay... **4.** halt, quit, stop **5.** beset, cease, cover, halte **6.** fasten, invest, waylay **7.** besiege, silence **8.** encircle

belch... **4.** burp, emit, vent **5.** eject, eruct, erupt, spout, vomit **7.** gush out **8.** disgorge, eructate **9.** small beer (vulgar) **10.** eructation

beldam, beldame... **3.** cat, hag **4.** fury **5.** crone, frump, shrew, vixen, witch **6.** virago **7.** she–wolf, tigress **8.** ancestor (fem), harridan **9.** termagant **11.** grandmother

Belgian (pert to)... see also *Belgium*
anthem.. **13.** La Brabanconne
hare.. **8.** leporide
horse.. **9.** Brabancon
marble.. **5.** rance
resort.. **6.** Ostend
sheep dog.. **8.** Malinois **11.** Groenendael
violinist.. **5.** Ysaye

Belgian Congo... see *Zaire*

Belgium...
capital.. **8.** Brussels
city.. **5.** Ghent, Liege **6.** Bruges **7.** Antwerp, Louvain **9.** Charleroi
commune.. **3.** Ath
forest.. **8.** Ardennes
king.. **6.** Albert **7.** Leopold **8.** Baudouin
native.. **7.** Fleming (of Flanders), Flemish, Walloon
nickname.. **15.** cockpit of Europe
World War II Battle of.. **8.** The Bulge

Belgravia (London)... **8.** district (fashion)

Belial... **5.** devil, Satan (New Test) **10.** wickedness (Old Test) **11.** Fallen Angel

belie... **4.** deny **6.** belong, defame, oppose, oppugn **7.** besiege, falsify, gainsay, pertain, slander **8.** disclaim, disprove, surround **9.** encompass **10.** calumniate **12.** misrepresent

belief... **3.** fay (anc) ism **4.** cult, rule, sect, view **5.** credo, creed, dogma, faith, maxim, tenet **7.** opinion, precept **8.** credence, doctrine, reliance, religion, teaching **9.** assurance, certainty, principle **10.** confidence, conviction, persuasion **13.** Apostles' Creed

believe... **3.** buy **4.** deem, feel, trow, ween **5.** think, trust **6.** accept, credit, reckon **7.** suppose, swallow **8.** conceive, consider

believer (pert to)...
all religions.. **6.** omnist
facts.. **7.** realist
religion.. **5.** deist **6.** theist **9.** Adventist, Calvinist **13.** particularist

Belit (Bab)... **8.** goddess (wife of Bel)

belittle... **4.** slur **5.** decry, dwarf, scoff, scorn **6.** debase, demean, deride, impugn **7.** detract, run down **8.** minimize **9.** discredit, disparage, underrate **10.** depreciate **13.** underestimate

bell... **4.** gong **5.** codon, knell **6.** curfew, tocsin **7.** campana, cowbell **8.** carillon, doorbell **9.** ship's bell **10.** dinnerbell, schoolbell **12.** glockenspiel **13.** tintinnabulum

bell, bells (pert to)...
bird.. **9.** campanero **10.** wood thrush
botany.. **7.** corolla
evening.. **6.** curfew **7.** Angelus
flat.. **4.** gong **6.** tam–tam (Chin), tom–tom
funeral.. **5.** knell
nautical.. **8.** half hour
ringer.. **6.** toller
ringing.. **7.** peeling **14.** tintinnabulism
science of.. **11.** campanology
set of.. **6.** chimes **8.** carillon
shaped.. **11.** campaniform
specialist.. **9.** campanist **13.** campanologist
tongue.. **7.** clapper
tower.. **6.** belfry **9.** campanile
warning.. **6.** tocsin

belle... **4.** lady (fine) **5.** toast **6.** beauty **7.** charmer **8.** handsome **10.** grande dame

belles–lettres... **8.** classics **10.** humanities (The), literature

bellflower... **8.** daffodil

belligerent... **7.** hostile, scrappy, warlike **8.** choleric, militant **9.** bellicose, irascible, litigious, offensive, wrangling **10.** aggressive, pugnacious **11.** contentious, quarrelsome **12.** disputatious

belligerent's right (Internat law)... **6.** angary

bellow... **3.** cry, low, moo, say **4.** bawl, roar, wail, yawp **5.** blare, shout **6.** clamor **7.** thunder **10.** vociferate

bellows... **4.** fish **5.** gills, lungs **6.** blower, lights (Zool), rotary **8.** ctenidia (Zool)

bellwether... **5.** sheep **6.** leader, wether (with bell)

belly... **3.** bag, pot **4.** crap, wame **5.** bulge, front, tummy **6.** bottom, paunch, venter **7.** abdomen, stomach **8.** potbelly, swell out **9.** ingluvies

belong (to)... **6.** answer, inhere **7.** pertain, related **9.** appendant, ingrained, possessed (by) **10.** correspond

belonging (to)...
collector, hobbyist.. **10.** collection **11.** collectible (collectable)
dean.. **7.** decanal
era.. **7.** epochal
Fall.. **8.** autumnal
pencil (a).. **6.** desmic
people.. **7.** endemic
present (the).. **7.** current
Spring.. **6.** vernal
Summer.. **7.** estival
Winter.. **6.** hiemal

belongings... **4.** duds, gear **5.** goods, traps **6.** family, things **7.** baggage, effects, kinsmen **8.** chattels, property **9.** homefolks, relations, trappings **11.** connections, perquisites, possessions **13.** accouterments, appurtenances

beloved ... 3. pet 4. dear 6. prized
7. darling 8. precious, truelove
9. cherished, inamorata
beloved physician ... 6. St Luke
below ... 4. alow, here, less 5. Hades,
neath, sotto, under 6. aneath, in hell
7. beneath, short of 10. downstairs
11. belowstairs
Belshazzar (Bib) ... 11. crown prince
Bel's wife ... 5. Belit (Beltis)
belt ... 3. bar, bat, hit 4. area, band,
beat, blow, cest, mark, pelt, ring,
sash, sock, whip, zone 5. apron,
Libya, strap, whack, zonar 6. cestus,
cingle, cordon, fascia, fasten, fillet,
girdle, region, strait, streak, stripe
7. baldric, kurbash, sjambok,
stratum, terrain 8. cincture, encircle,
surround 9. encompass
10. cummerbund
Belteshazzar (Bib) ... 6. Daniel
belt of heaven ... 6. zodiac 7. circuit
beluga ... 5. whale (white)
Belus (pert to) ...
father of .. 4. Dido
king of .. 4. Tyre 7. Assyria
son of .. 5. Libya
sons .. 7. Cepheus, Phineus
8. Aegyptus
belvedere ... 5. cigar 7. cypress (mock)
10. watchtower 11. summerhouse
bema ... 8. platform 9. sanctuary
bemoan ... 4. pity, wail 5. mourn
6. bewail, grieve, lament, regret,
repine 7. deplore 10. sympathize
bemuse ... 4. daze 5. addle, besot
6. absorb, muddle 7. stupefy
8. befuddle, distract 10. intoxicate
ben ... 2. in 3. oil, son 4. tree
(Moringa) 6. within
bench ... 3. pew 4. banc (judge's),
seat 5. chair, court, siege, staff,
stand, stool, table 6. exedra, settee,
settle 7. terrace 8. platform,
woolsack 9. committee
bend ... 3. bow, nod, ply, sag, sny
4. bias, flex, genu, kink, knot, sway,
turn, warp 5. crimp, crook, curve,
drink, kneel, prone, squat, stoop,
twist, yield 6. buckle, crouch, curtsy,
direct, divert, humble, inflex, kowtow,
pleach, relent, salaam, strain, swerve
7. bendlet (Her), chevron (Her),
incline, refract, retract 9. genuflect,
introvert, sinuosity 10. inflection
bend (pert to) ...
an ear .. 4. hear, heed 6. listen
one's will .. 4. bias, move, sway
the elbow .. 5. drink
the knee .. 5. kneel 6. kowtow,
salaam 9. genuflect
the mind .. 5. think
bends ... 7. caisson, disease
8. blackout (aeronaut)
beneath ... 4. alow 5. below, lower
(than), 'neath, under 6. aneath,
nether 7. in Hades 11. underground
beneath one's dignity ... 8. infradig
15. infra dignitatem
benedict ... 7. husband
10. bridegroom, married man (newly)
benediction ... 4. rite 6. praise, prayer,

thanks 7. benison 8. blessing
10. invocation 12. thanksgiving
benefaction ... 4. alms, boon, gift,
good 5. favor 7. benefit, present
8. courtesy, donation, gratuity,
kindness 9. beau geste
11. beneficence, benevolence
benefactor ... 5. angel, donor
6. backer, helper, patron 8. promoter
10. befriender
beneficence ... 7. charity 8. goodness,
kindness 11. benefaction,
benevolence 12. philanthropy
beneficial ... 4. good 6. benign, useful
7. helpful 8. edifying, salutary
9. favorable, healthful, lucrative,
wholesome 10. profitable, salubrious
11. serviceable 12. advantageous,
remunerative
beneficiary ... 4. heir 5. donee
6. vassal 7. devisee, feoffee, grantee,
legatee 8. assignee 9. annuitant
benefit ... 3. aid, use 4. boon, gift,
good, help, vail 5. avail, favor, trust
6. profit, relief, succor 7. advance,
concert, improve, service, welfare
8. blessing, kindness 9. advantage
11. benefaction, convenience,
performance
benevolence ... 3. tax 4. gift, good
6. bounty, giving 7. charity
8. altruism, bestowal, blessing,
donation, kindness 10. generosity,
liberality 11. munificence
12. contribution, philanthropy
14. charitableness
benevolent ... 4. free, good, king
6. benign 7. liberal 8. generous,
princely 9. benignant, bountiful
10. altruistic, charitable, munificent
11. magnanimous 13. philanthropic
Bengal, Indian State ...
capital .. 8. Calcutta
gentleman .. 5. baboo (babu)
language .. 7. Bengali
native .. 3. Kol (Kohl) 6. banian
7. Bengali
negro .. 3. Ibo (Ebo)
river .. 6. Ganges 11. Brahmaputra
river boat .. 7. bauleah
benign ... 4. mild 5. bland 6. genial,
humane, kindly 7. benefic (Astrol),
liberal 8. gracious, salutary
9. benignant, favorable, healthful,
wholesome 10. propitious, salubrious
benignity ... 5. favor 7. benefit
8. blessing, goodness, mildness
9. salubrity 10. kindliness
11. benevolence 12. graciousness
benison ... 8. blessing 9. beatitude
10. invocation 11. benediction
benjamin ... 6. jacket 7. benzoin
8. overcoat 9. spicebush
Benjamin (Bib), (pert to) ...
father .. 5. Jacob
history .. 5. tribe
mother .. 6. Rachel
Benjamin's mess ... 6. big end
10. lion's share
benjy (Brit sl) ... 3. hat (straw)
9. waistcoat
benne ... 6. sesame

bennet... 4. herb 5. daisy 7. hemlock
bent... 3. aim, way, wry 4. bias, turn,
warp 5. drift, grass, slant, tenor,
trend, twist 6. course, curved,
desire, minded, nature, swayed
7. angular, aptness, crooked,
heather, leaning, stooped 8. aptitude,
penchant, tendency 9. obliquity,
prejudice, proneness 10. propensity
11. disposition, inclination
12. idiosyncrasy, predilection
13. prepossession 14. predisposition
Benthamism... 9. welfarism
14. utilitarianism
benthonic... 7. benthal, deep sea
benthonic plant... 6. enalid
benthos... 5. deeps 6. depths
8. ocean bed 16. Davy Jones's
locker
benumb... 3. nip 4. drug, numb, stun
5. chill 6. deaden, freeze 7. stupefy
8. paralyze 11. anesthetize,
desensitize
Beowulf... 4. poem (oldest in Teutonic
language)
bequeath... 4. give, will 5. endow,
leave 6. bestow, demise, devise,
invest, will to 7. bequest 8. transmit
bequest... 4. will 6. devise, legacy
8. heritage 9. patrimony, testament
10. birthright 11. inheritance
berate... 3. jaw, nag 4. lash, rail
5. chide, scold, slate 7. censure,
reprove, upbraid
Berber... 4. Riff 6. Hamite, Kabyle,
Taureg
berceau... 4. walk (leaf–covered)
5. arbor, bower 6. cradle
berceuse... 10. cradlesong
11. composition
bereave... 3. die, rob 5. leave, strip
6. divest, orphan, sadden 7. deprive,
despoil 10. disentitle, dispossess
bereavement... 4. loss 5. death
9. privation 10. divestment
bereft... 4. lorn 7. denuded, fleeced,
shorn of, witless 8. bereaved,
divested, orphaned, stripped
9. senseless 10. parentless,
pauperized
Bereshith (Jew)... 7. Genesis
9. Beginning
beret... 3. cap, tam 7. biretta
bergamot... 4. pear 5. snuff 6. orange
7. essence 9. fragrance
beriberi... 5. kakke 7. disease
Berkeleianism (pert to)...
founder.. 8. Berkeley (Bishop)
science.. 10. philosophy
system.. 8. idealism 13. immaterialism
Berlin, Germany...
avenue.. 14. Unter den Linden
capital.. 7. Germany
garden (Zool).. 10. Tiergarten
gate.. 11. Brandenburg
government.. 9. Reichstag
berm, berme... 4. mall, path 5. prado
6. runway 7. terrace 8. shoulder
(road)
Bermuda...
capital.. 8. Hamilton
color.. 12. geranium pink

discoverer.. 8. Bermudez
government.. 7. British
grass.. 5. decil
ocean site.. 8. Atlantic
Bernardine Order... 11. Cistercians
Berne, Bern (Switz)... 7. capital
berry... 3. haw 4. buck, seed
5. bacca, cubeb, fruit, grain, money
6. acinus, kernel
berry, fruit... 5. grape, salal
6. banana, tomato 7. currant
8. bilberry, dewberry, hagberry,
mulberry 9. bearberry, blueberry,
cranberry, raspberry 10. blackberry,
elderberry, gooseberry, loganberry,
strawberry 11. boysenberry,
huckleberry 12. checkerberry,
whortleberry
berserk... 4. amok, bunk, dock, post,
room 5. house, roost 6. billet,
marina, office, reside 8. quarters
9. situation 11. appointment
bertha... 4. cape 6. cannon, collar
7. Perchta (goddess) 9. Big Bertha
(Ger gun)
beseech... 3. beg, sue 4. pray
5. crave, plead 6. obtest 7. entreat,
implore, solicit 9. obsecrate
10. supplicate
beset... 3. dun, ply, vex 4. stud
5. harry, haunt, hem in, siege, worry
6. attack, harass, infest, invade,
obsess, plague, ravage 7. besiege
8. blockade, surround 9. beleaguer,
importune, infatuate
beset with danger... 5. risky
6. chancy 8. perilous 9. dangerous
10. jeopardous
beset with hairs... 7. barbate,
bearded
beside, besides... 2. by 3. too, yet
4. also, else, near, nigh, para (pref)
5. about, along 6. nearby
8. likewise, moreover 9. other than
11. furthermore 12. over and above
beside oneself... 3. mad 4. wild
5. crazy, rabid 6. beserk, raging,
raving 7. frantic, ranting 8. frenzied
9. desperate, overjoyed
10. distracted, distraught
11. overwrought
besiege... 5. beset 6. attack, harass,
obsess, plague 7. torment
8. blockade, surround 9. beleaguer
besmear... 3. dab 4. coat, daub,
mark, soil, spot 5. paint, smear,
stain, taint 6. bedaub 7. tarnish
8. besmudge
besmirch... 4. blot, soil 5. smear, sully
6. defile, smirch, smudge, vilify
7. besmear, blacken, tarnish
8. discolor
besom... 5. broom, hussy
besotted... 4. dull 5. drunk
7. muddled, sottish 8. obsessed
9. senseless, stupefied 10. infatuated
11. intoxicated
bespangled... 5. aglow 7. lighted,
studded, trimmed 8. spangled
9. decorated, garnished
10. glittering, ornamented
11. embellished, illuminated

bespatter... 3. wet 4. blot, spot
5. dirty, slosh, smear, stain, sully
6. splash, vilify 7. asperse, scatter,
spatter, tarnish 8. besmirch, splatter,
sprinkle 9. denigrate 10. stigmatize
bespeak... 4. mean, show 5. imply
6. ask for, attest, engage, evince
7. address, betoken, connote, exhibit,
suggest, testify 8. foretell, indicate,
manifest 11. demonstrate
best... 4. aces, beat, most, tops
5. cream, elite, queen 6. choice,
finest 7. largest 8. champion,
outstrip 9. nonpareil, overmatch
11. superlative
bestial... 3. low 4. vile 5. cruel
6. brutal, filthy, savage 7. beastly,
brutish, inhuman, sensual
8. depraved, ruthless 9. barbarous
bestow... 4. deal, give 5. allot, apply,
award, grant, spend 6. accord,
confer, convey, demise, devote,
donate, impart, render, tender
7. deposit, present 8. transmit
10. administer
bestow honor upon... 5. adorn, exalt,
grace 7. dignify, ennoble, glorify
10. aggrandize 11. distinguish
bestride... 4. pass 5. mount 7. climb
on, protect, support 8. straddle
10. bestraddle
bet... 3. bas (roulette), pot 4. play
5. stake, wager 6. gamble, hazard,
pledge
beta test (army)... 12. intelligence
bête... 5. beast, silly 6. stupid
7. foolish
betel (pert to)...
leaf.. 3. pan 4. buyo, paun (pan)
palm.. 5. areca
pepper.. 4. itmo (ikmo)
bête noir... 4. ogre 7. bugbear
10. black beast, frightener,
mumbo-jumbo, Mumbo Jumbo
bethel... 4. kirk 6. chapel, church
8. Bethesda (Jerusalem)
12. meetinghouse
bethink... 5. think 6. recall 7. reflect
8. cogitate, remember 9. cerebrate,
recollect
betide... 3. hap 4. fall 5. occur
6. befall, happen 7. betoken,
presage 9. come about, eventuate,
transpire
betimes... 4. anon, soon 5. early
7. ere long, shortly 8. directly,
speedily 9. forthwith, presently
10. beforehand, seasonably
12. occasionally
betise... 5. folly 9. asininity, silliness,
stupidity 11. foolishness
betoken... 4. mark, mean, note
5. augur 6. denote, typify
7. bespeak, connote, express,
portend, presage, purport, signify
8. evidence, indicate 9. foretoken,
symbolize
betray... 4. blab, dupe, hoax, sell
5. bluff, peach, trick 6. reveal,
seduce, tattle 7. beguile, deceive,
divulge, mislead, sell out 8. disclose,

inform on 9. bamboozle, victimize
11. double-cross
betrayal... 4. ruse 5. trick 7. sellout,
treason 8. giveaway 9. Judas kiss,
seduction, treachery 10. disclosure
betrayer... 5. Judas 6. Arnold, Brutus
7. seducer, traitor 8. derelict,
informer, Quisling, turncoat
10. treasonist 13. double-crosser,
Judas Iscariot
betroth... 4. affy, earl 5. tryst
6. engage, pledge, plight
7. espouse, promise 8. affiance,
contract, espousal 10. engagement
better... 3. top 4. more 5. amend,
emend, excel, raise (poker), safer,
wiser 6. bigger, exceed, outwit,
reform 7. advance, choicer, greater,
improve, promote, surpass, victory
8. improved, superior 9. advantage,
meliorate 10. ameliorate, preferable
11. superiority
betting term... 4. ante, odds, tout
6. parlay 7. pyramid 10. parimutuel
11. sweepstakes
between... 5. among, mesne
6. atween 7. average, betwixt
bevel... 4. edge, ream 5. angle, bezel,
slant, slope, snape, splay 6. square
7. incline, oblique 9. obliquity
beverage... 3. ade, opo (comb form),
pop, tea 4. coke, malt, maté, mead,
milk, soda 5. cider, cocoa, drink,
leban, morat (anc), punch, water
6. coffee, eggnog, frappé, nectar
7. Seltzer 8. Adam's ale, Coca-Cola,
lemonade, root beer, sourdook
9. ginger ale, orangeade, phosphate
10. buttermilk, grape juice
12. sarsaparilla
beverage (alcoholic)... 3. ale, gin, rum
4. beer, brew, grog, kava, port, raki
5. booze, cider, hooch, julep, lager,
negus, punch, smash, vodka
6. arrack, bishop, brandy, cognac,
eggnog, kumiss, kummel, likker,
porter, posset, sherry, tiswin, whisky
(whiskey), zythum (anc) 7. Bacardi,
bootleg, bourbon, cordial, liqueur,
martini, tequila 8. absinthe, aleberry,
Burgundy, cocktail, highball, muscatel,
sauterne, vermouth 9. applejack,
aqua vitae, firewater, Manhattan
10. shandygaff, Tom Collins
11. Benedictine, boilermaker,
grasshopper, mountain dew
bevy... 4. bund, gang, herd, host
5. covey, flock, group, party, troop
6. galaxy, throng 7. company
8. assembly 10. collection
bewail... 3. rue 4. keen, mean
5. mourn 6. bemoan, grieve, lament,
regret, repine, sorrow 7. deplore
bewilder... 3. fog 4. daze 5. addle,
amaze 6. baffle, dazzle, puzzle
7. buffalo, confuse, fluster, mystify,
nonplus, perplex 8. astonish,
confound, distract 9. bamboozle,
embarrass
bewilderment... 3. awe, fog 4. maze
6. wonder 9. confusion
10. perplexity 11. distraction

12. perturbation 13. disconcertion, embarrassment

bewitch ... 3. hex 5. charm, witch 6. enamor, entice, hoodoo, voodoo 7. beguile, delight, enchant 8. enthrall 9. captivate, enrapture, ensorcell, fascinate, infatuate

bewitching ... 5. siren 6. hexing, lovely 7. magical 8. alluring, charming, enticing 10. enchanting 11. captivating, fascinating

bey (Turk) ... 5. title 8. governor

beyond ... 2. by 3. too, yet 4. meta (pref), past, plus, well 5. above, extra, ultra 6. yonder 7. besides, farther, further, yonside 8. moreover 9. exceeding, Hereafter (The) 11. furthermore 12. additionally, ultraliminal

beyond hope ... 9. desperate

bezant (pert to) ...
architecture .. 4. disc 8. ornament
coin (anc) .. 7. solidus (gold)
heraldry .. 4. disc (gold)
offering (Eng king) .. 4. gold

bezel ... 4. edge 5. crown (gem), facet 6. chaton, flange 8. pavilion, template (templet) 9. obliquity

bezonian ... 6. mucker, wretch 7. budmash, caitiff, recruit 8. blighter 9. pilgarlic, scoundrel

bhikshu ... 6. gelong 7. ascetic 8. sannyasi 9. mendicant

bhut (Dravidian) ... 5. demon, ghost 6. goblin

bias ... 3. ply 4. awry, bent, turn, warp 5. amiss, slant, twist 6. desire 7. leaning, oblique 8. diagonal, slanting, tendency 9. obliquity, prejudice 10. favoritism, partiality, prepossess, transverse 11. disposition

biased ... 4. bent 6. narrow, swayed 7. bigoted, partial 8. diagonal, partisan, slanting 10. prejudiced

bib ... 3. sip, sup 4. swig 5. apron, drink, quaff 6. guzzle, imbibe, tipple, tucker 7. tablier 8. pinafore

bibacious ... 6. toping 7. drunken, sottish 8. bibulous, drinking, tippling

Bible ... 7. The Book, The Word, Vulgate 10. Scriptures, Testaments (Old, New)

Bible (pert to) ...
battle site .. 10. Armageddon
city .. 2. Ur 5. Joppa, Sidon, Sodom 6. Hebron 9. Bethlehem, Jerusalem
coin .. 6. talent
Commandments .. 9. Decalogue
Holy Land .. 9. Palestine
interpretation .. 7. anagoge
introduction .. 9. Isagogics
kingdom .. 4. Elam 6. Basham, Canaan 7. Chaldea
land of plenty .. 6. Goshen
language .. 7. Aramaic
mountain .. 4. Ebol, Zion 5. Horeb, Sinai 6. Ararat, Gilead, Moriah, Olives (Olivet), Pisgah
pause .. 5. selah
pool .. 6. Siloam
precious stone .. 6. ligure (jacinth)
Promised Land .. 6. Canaan

sea .. 3. Red 4. Dead 7. Galilee
Sermon on the Mount .. 10. Beatitudes
sheep .. 7. chamois
town .. 4. Edar 5. Babel
Wells of .. 5. Hagar, Jacob

Bible character ...
archangel .. 7. Raphael
giant .. 4. Anak 7. Goliath
High Priest .. 3. Eli
hunter .. 6. Nimrod
liar .. 7. Ananias
patriarch .. 5. Jacob 6. Israel
prophet .. 4. Amos, Joel 5. Hosea, Jonah, Micah, Nahum 6. Daniel, Haggai, Isaiah, Joseph, Joshua, Samuel 7. Ezekiel, Malachi, Obadiah 8. Habakkuk, Jeremiah 9. Zachariah, Zephaniah

Bible version ... 5. Douay, Reims 6. Geneva 7. Bishop's, Luther's, Revised, Targums, Vulgate 8. Cranmer's, Matthew's, Peshitta, Tyndale's, Wartburg, Wycliffe 9. King James, Maccabees 10. Great Bible, Septuagint 15. American Revised

bicker ... 5. argue, cavil 6. hassle, quiver, strife 7. dispute, flicker, flutter, quarrel, quibble, rhubarb (sl), wrangle 8. argument, pettifog 9. scrimmage, tremulous 10. contention 11. altercation

bicuspid ... 5. bifid, tooth, valve 6. cuspid 8. premolar 10. two–pointed 13. double–pointed

bid ... 3. beg 4. pray 5. offer, order, utter 6. charge, direct, enjoin, invite, reveal, tender 7. command, declare, entreat, offered, summons 8. overture, proclaim 9. quotation 12. presentation

biddy ... 3. hen 4. dame 5. skirt 6. female 7. chicken, Partlet 8. bedmaker 11. maidservant

bide ... 4. bear, stay, wait 5. abide, await, tarry 6. endure, remain, suffer 8. continue, tolerate 9. encounter, withstand

bield ... 3. den 4. cozy 7. comfort, courage, hearten, shelter 8. boldness, embolden 9. sheltered 10. confidence, habitation

bien ... 4. fine, good, snug

bienseance ... 7. decorum, manners 9. propriety 11. correctness, proprieties (the) 12. mannerliness 17. conventionalities

bier ... 6. coffin, litter 10. catafalque

Bier ... 4. beer

biff ... 4. bash, blow, slug, sock 5. paste, punch

bifold ... 4. dual 5. duple 6. binary, binate, double 7. twofold

bifurcate ... 3. wye (letter) 4. fork 7. forking, furcate 8. biforked, branched, forklike 9. two–forked

big ... 4. huge 5. bulky, grand, great, grown, jumbo, large 6. august, famous, mighty 7. massive, pompous, teeming 8. boastful, powerful, pregnant, swelling 9. momentous 10. tremendous

11. magnanimous, pretentious

big (pert to)...
shot.. 3. VIP
stick.. 5. power (T Roosevelt)
toe.. 6. hallux
top.. 6. circus
wig.. 3. VIP (humorous)

Big (pert to)...
Ben.. 5. clock 13. Tower of London
Bend State.. 9. Tennessee
Bertha.. 3. gun 5. Krupp (factory)
Board.. 6. Bourse 8. Exchange
  11. stock market 13. stock exchange
House.. 3. pen 6. prison (State)
  12. penitentiary
Push (WWI).. 5. Somme

bight... 3. bay 4. bend, gulf, loop
  5. angle, noose, point 6. corner,
  hollow 7. estuary

bigot... 3. bug, nut 6. zealot
  7. fanatic 9. dogmatist, hypocrite,
  illiberal 10. enthusiast, opinionist,
  positivist

bigoted... 5. petty 6. little, narrow
  10. intolerant, prejudiced
  12. narrow–minded

bijou... 5. jewel 7. trinket
bilbi, bilby... 8. kangaroo
bilbo... 5. sword 6. rapier
bilingual... 6. diglot 12. linguistical
bilious... 3. ill 8. choleric, liverish
  9. dyspeptic, jaundiced
  11. ill–tempered

bilk... 2. do 3. gyp 4. balk, hoax, sell
  5. cheat, cozen, trick 6. delude,
  fleece, illude 7. deceive, defraud,
  swindle 8. flimflam 11. hornswoggle

bill... 3. dun, neb, nib, pee, tab, Vee
  ($5) 4. beak, deed, list, menu, sign
  5. carte, money 6. docket, pickax,
  poster, ticket 7. account, invoice,
  mattock, placard, program, receipt,
  statute, voucher 8. billhook, schedule
  9. publicize, statement
  10. prospectus 11. legislative
  13. advertisement

billet... 3. bar, log 4. note, pass
  5. berth, stick, strap 6. assign,
  docket, letter, notice, ticket
  7. bearing (Her), epistle, missive,
  molding 8. dispatch, document,
  insignia, position, quarters
  11. appointment

billiard shot... 5. carom, masse
  6. cannon

Billingsgate... 4. Gate (London)
  10. fish market 12. vituperation

billow... 3. sea 4. roll, toss, wave
  5. eagre, heave, surge, swell
  6. dilate 7. distend 10. undulation

billowy... 4. wavy 5. surgy 7. surging
  8. swelling 10. undulating

bin... 3. box 4. crib, loft, vina
  5. frame, kench, pungi (Hind flute)
  6. manger 8. elevator

binary... 4. dual 6. bifold, binate,
  double, duplex 9. duplicate

bind... 3. jam, tie 4. ally, frap, gird,
  gyve, hold, lace, lash, rope, tape
  5. chain, leash, stick, truss, withe
  6. engage, fasten, fetter, pinion,
  pledge, secure 7. confine, shackle

8. obligate 10. constipate

binding... 4. tape 5. valid 6. binder,
  edging 7. girding, joining, liaison
  8. trimming, trussing, wrapping
  9. bordering, fastening, stringent
  10. astringent, compulsory, obligatory
  11. restraining, restrictive

binding (agreement)... 4. bond, pact
  7. bargain, promise 8. contract

binding (book)... 4. yapp 5. cover
  6. jacket 10. bibliopegy

binge... 4. bout 5. spree 6. bender
  8. carousal 11. celebration

bingo... 3. pop 4. bang, keno
  5. lotto, socko 6. brandy

biographer... 8. annalist 9. historian
  10. chronicler 11. biographist,
  memorialist

biography... 4. life 6. memoir
  7. history, memoire, recount
  8. memorial 11. hagiography

biological... 4. gene 5. class, genus,
  order, vital 6. biotic, family
  7. animate, organic, paracme,
  species

biology, science of... 6. botany
  7. ecology, zoology 8. eugenics,
  genetics 9. bionomics, organisms
  10. embryology, morphology,
  physiology

biopsy (Med)... 8. analysis (tissue)
  9. diagnosis 11. examination
  (microscopic)

biped... 3. man 9. two–legged
birch... 4. flog 5. stick 6. switch

birch tree (pert to)...
family.. 10. Betulaceae
genera.. 5. alder, birch, hazel
order.. 7. Fagales
product.. 16. oil of wintergreen
variety.. 5. paper, river, sweet, white
  6. cherry, yellow

bird (pert to)...
best swimmer.. 4. loon 6. gannet
cage.. 6. aviary 7. paddock
  8. dovecote
Class.. 4. Aves
crested.. 7. hoatzin 9. stinkbird
fabled, sacred.. 3. roc 4. ibis
fastest flyer.. 4. hawk 5. eagle, swift
  6. falcon
fastest runner.. 7. ostrich
feathers.. 5. remix (sing) 7. remiges
first.. 13. archaeopteryx
footless.. 4. apod
greatest traveler.. 4. tern
greatest wingspread.. 9. albatross
halcyon.. 10. kingfisher
highest flyer.. 5. goose
immortal.. 7. phoenix
killing.. 7. avicide
largest.. 6. condor 7. ostrich
  13. whooping crane
Latin.. 4. avis
life.. 5. ornis
longest–lived.. 5. macaw
lover.. 12. ornithophile
most dangerous.. 9. cassowary
naked hatched.. 11. gymnogenous
of prey (prized).. 6. falcon
oldest known.. 13. archaeopteryx
one year old.. 8. annotine

Order.. **7.** Rasores **8.** Raptores
smallest.. **14.** bee hummingbird
smartest.. **4.** crow
study.. **6.** oology
young.. **4.** eyas **8.** birdikin, nestling
9. fledgling
bird, anatomy (pert to)...
beak.. **3.** neb, nib **4.** bill, lora
5. ceral **7.** rostrum
eye process.. **6.** pecten
head.. **4.** lore **6.** pileum
jaw.. **4.** mala
leg (featherless).. **9.** cnemidium
wing part.. **5.** alula
bird, Arctic... **3.** auk **4.** gull, skua
5. brant **6.** dunlin, fulmar, jaeger
7. penguin **9.** ptarmigan
bird, colorful... **3.** kea **5.** egret,
macaw **6.** magpie, parrot, trogon
7. peacock, quetzal (quezal)
8. lyrebird **10.** kingfisher **14.** bird of
paradise
bird, common... **3.** ani, daw, owl
4. chat, dove, lark, pisk, wren
5. finch, pipit, robin, vireo **6.** dunlin,
linnet, martin, oriole, phoebe, pigeon,
shrike, siskin, thrush, towhee **7.** blue
jay, bunting, catbird, cowbird, flicker,
grackle, kinglet, sparrow, swallow,
tanager, warbler, waxwing
8. blackcap, bluebird, bobolink,
cardinal, grosbeak, kingbird, redstart,
starling, titmouse **9.** chickadee,
goldfinch, nighthawk, sandpiper
10. flycatcher, meadowlark,
turtledove, woodpecker
11. hummingbird, mockingbird,
nightingale, pyrrhuloxia
12. whippoorwill, yellowhammer
14. scarlet tanager
bird, crow family... **4.** crow, rook
5. crake, raven **6.** chough, magpie
7. corvine, jackdaw
bird, duck family... **4.** clee, coot,
lory, smew, teal, wood **5.** eider,
goose **6.** scoter **7.** gadwall, mallard,
Muscovy, pintail, pochard
8. baldpate, redshank, shoveler
9. merganser **10.** bufflehead,
canvasback
bird, flightless... **3.** emu, moa
4. dodo (ext), kiwi, rhea, weka
7. apteryx, ostrich, peacock, penguin
8. Notornis **9.** cassowary
bird, foreign...
Africa.. **4.** taha **5.** crane **6.** cuckoo
7. ostrich **8.** umbrette
10. weaverbird
Arctic.. **3.** auk **4.** gull, skua **5.** brant
6. dunlin, falcon, jaeger **7.** penguin
8. grayling **9.** gyrfalcon, ptarmigan
Asia.. **4.** myna **5.** pitta **6.** bulbul,
linnet **7.** boobook, peacock, sirgang
8. dotterel, leaf bird **9.** brambling,
muted swan
Australia.. **3.** emu **4.** kiwi, lory
5. lowan **6.** leipoa **7.** boobook,
grinder **8.** ganggang, lorikeet,
lyrebird, morepork, parakeet, platypus
9. bowerbird, cassowary, pardalote
Central America.. **6.** barbet, toucan
7. quetzal (quezal) **8.** puffbird

Cuba.. **6.** trogon **8.** tocororo **14.** bee
hummingbird
England.. **4.** kite, rook **9.** cormorant
11. carrion crow
Europe.. **4.** merl **5.** pipit, stilt
(3–toed), stork (white), swift, tarin
6. godwit, hoopoe, merlin, roller,
siskin **7.** bittern, ortolan, skylark,
starnel **8.** bee eater, dotterel,
garganey, nuthatch, redstart
9. brambling, chaffinch, gallinule,
sheldrake **10.** lammergeir, turtledove
11. nightingale, wallcreeper
12. capercaillie (grouse)
Hawaii.. **2.** io, o–o **3.** ava, iwa, poe
4. iiwi, mamo **6.** parson **7.** frigate
India.. **5.** shama **8.** amadavat,
pheasant **11.** red hornbill
Java.. **7.** sparrow **8.** rice bird **9.** fruit
dove
New Guinea.. **9.** cassowary **14.** bird
of paradise
New Zealand.. **3.** ihi, kea, moa, tui
4. kuku, weka
So America.. **4.** guan **5.** macaw
6. barbet, motmot, toucan
7. jacamar, tinamou, warrior
8. boatbill, caracara **9.** trumpeter
11. scarlet ibis
bird, game... **4.** teal **5.** brant, goose,
quail, snipe **6.** grouse, pigeon,
plover, turkey (wild) **7.** bustard,
gadwall, mallard **8.** bobwhite,
pheasant, woodcock **9.** partridge,
ptarmigan **10.** canvasback **14.** prairie
chicken
bird, group...
partridge.. **5.** covey
pheasant.. **3.** nye **4.** nide
quail.. **4.** bevy
bird, long–legged... **4.** ibis, rail, sora
5. crane, egret, heron, stilt, stork
6. avocet, curlew, jacana **7.** seriema
8. flamingo **9.** sandpiper
10. demoiselle
Bird of...
Freedom.. **9.** bald eagle
Jove.. **5.** eagle
June.. **7.** peacock
Minerva.. **3.** owl
Wonder.. **7.** phoenix
bird, pet... **4.** myna (mynah)
6. canary, parrot **8.** cockatoo,
lovebird, parakeet
bird, poultry... **4.** duck **5.** goose
6. pigeon, turkey **7.** chicken
8. pheasant
bird, shore... **4.** swan **5.** egret, heron,
stork **6.** avocet, curlew, plover, willet
7. frigate, pelican **8.** dotterel, killdeer
10. demoiselle
bird, sky... **4.** erne (ern), gier (Bib),
hawk, kite **5.** Buteo, eagle, saker
6. condor, falcon, gannet, jaeger,
merlin, osprey **7.** buzzard, harrier,
kestral, vulture **8.** caracara, ringtail
9. Accipiter **10.** lammergeir
bird, water... **3.** auk **4.** coot, gull,
ibis, loon, rail, shag, skua, swan
5. cahow, crane, grebe, heron, stork
6. curlew, cygnet, gannet, jabiru,
jacana, petrel, plover **7.** bittern,

bustard, dovekie, pelican, seriema,
skimmer 8. dabchick, flamingo,
umbrette 9. albatross, cormorant,
gallinule, guillemot, phalarope,
spoonbill 10. kingfisher, yellowlegs
biretta... 8. skullcap 9. headdress
birl... 4. spin 6. rattle 7. resolve
birth... 3. nee 4. line 5. blood, breed
6. origin 7. descent, genesis, lineage
8. heritage, nativity, nobility
9. beginning 10. derivation,
extraction, renascence
11. inheritance, Renaissance
birthday (pert to)...
astrology.. 7. casting, lineage (the
gods)
nativities.. 9. genethlic 10. genethliac
poems.. 12. genethliacon
birth flower (by months)...
Jan.. 9. carnation
Feb.. 8. primrose
Mar.. 6. violet
Apr.. 5. daisy
May.. 15. lily of the valley
June.. 4. rose
July.. 8. sweet pea
Aug.. 9. gladiolus
Sept.. 5. aster
Oct.. 6. dahlia
Nov.. 13. chrysanthemum
Dec.. 5. holly 10. poinsettia
birthmark... 4. mole 5. nevus (naevus)
birthright... 6. rights 8. heritage
9. privilege 10. possession
11. inheritance
birth seniority... 9. first–born
13. primogeniture
birthstone (by days)...
Sun.. 5. topaz 7. diamond
Mon.. 5. pearl 7. crystal
Tues.. 4. ruby 7. emerald
Wed.. 8. amethyst 9. loadstone
Thurs.. 8. sapphire 9. carnelian
Fri.. 7. cat's eye, emerald
Sat.. 7. diamond 9. turquoise
birthstone (by months)...
Jan.. 6. garnet
Feb.. 8. amethyst
Mar.. 6. jasper
Apr.. 7. diamond 8. sapphire
May.. 5. agate 7. emerald
June.. 7. emerald 11. alexandrite
July.. 4. onyx, ruby
Aug.. 8. sardonyx 9. carnelian
Sept.. 8. sapphire 10. chrysolite
Oct.. 4. opal 10. aquamarine
Nov.. 5. topaz
Dec.. 4. ruby 9. turquoise
bis... 5. again, ditto, twice 6. encore,
repeat 7. replica 8. repetend
9. duplicate 10. repetition
biscuit... 3. bun, doe 4. rusk
5. bread, cooky, scone, wafer
6. pommel 7. cracker 8. biscotin,
zwieback
bise... 4. wind (cold) 6. winter
7. Norther
bisect... 4. fork 5. cross, halve, split
6. cleave, divide
bishop... 4. Abba 7. pontiff, prelate
8. chessman, director, overseer
9. churchman, clergyman, inspector

14. superintendent
bishop (pert to)...
Bible.. 10. Great Bible
cap.. 4. hura 5. miter
revenue.. 7. annates
staff.. 7. baculus, crosier (crozier)
throne.. 3. see 4. apse
vestment.. 4. cope 5. stole 6. rochet
7. gremial, pallium 8. dalmatic
10. omophorion
bishopric... 3. see 4. seat 7. diocese
10. episcopacy, episcopate
bison... 2. ox 4. gaur, urus
7. aurochs, buffalo 9. quadruped
bisque (pert to)...
ceramics (unglazed).. 7. biscuit
color.. 9. red–yellow
food.. 4. soup 8. ice cream
term (sports).. 4. turn 5. point
6. stroke
bissext (pert to)...
calendar.. 6. Julian (Rom)
day.. 5. sixth (intercalary)
year.. 8. Leap Year
bistro... 6. tavern 7. barroom 8. wine
shop 10. restaurant
bit... 3. ace, jot, ort 4. bite, coin,
iota, mite, mote, part (acting), role,
snip, tool, tube, whit 5. check,
crumb, hitch, money, piece, scrap,
speck 6. morsel, smidge, tittle
7. portion, smidgen, traneen
8. somewhat 9. something
bit (harness)... 4. curb 6. bridle,
Pelham 7. snaffle 9. Liverpool
bit (money)...
two bits.. 7. quarter 9. ninepence
(Bahamas)
four bits.. 10. half dollar
bitch... 6. female (animal) 8. slattern,
strumpet (vulgar)
bite... 3. cut, eat, nip, zip 4. food,
gnaw, grip, hold, knap, pang, tang,
zest 5. champ, smart, snack, sting,
taste 6. morsel, nibble, pierce
8. pungency
biting... 4. acid, tart 5. acerb, acrid,
sharp 6. bitter, rodent 7. caustic,
cutting, mordant, nipping, painful,
piquant, pungent 8. piercing,
poignant, scathing, stinging
9. sarcastic, trenchant, vitriolic,
withering 10. astringent, irritating
11. acrimonious, penetrating
biting nails... 12. phaneromania
bito (pert to)...
bark.. 10. fish poison
seeds.. 6. zachun (oil)
tree.. 7. hajilij
bitter... 4. acid, cold, keen, sore, sour
5. acerb, acrid, irate, sharp
6. severe 7. cutting, hostile, pungent
8. grievous, stinging, virulent
9. rancorous, resentful
10. embittered, unpleasant
11. acrimonious, distressful,
reproachful
bitter (pert to)...
apple (herb).. 9. colocynth
chemical.. 4. alum
earth.. 8. magnesia
gentian.. 9. baldmoney

grass.. **9.** colicroot
herb.. **3.** rue **4.** aloe **5.** aloin
   8. centaury
plant.. **10.** bitterroot **11.** bittersweet
   (poisonous)
prefix.. **5.** picro
salts.. **5.** Epsom
suffix.. **6.** picrin
vetch.. **3.** ers
waters (Bib).. **5.** Marah
wintergreen.. **10.** pipsissewa
wormwood.. **8.** de Gaulle (said of)
bitterness... **3.** rue **5.** venom
   6. rancor **7.** remorse **8.** acerbity,
   acrimony, tartness, wormwood
   9. animosity, poignancy, virulence
   10. causticity, resentment
bivalve... **4.** clam, spat, Unio **5.** pinna
   6. Anomia, mussel, oyster, Teredo
   7. mollusk, pandora, scallop
   10. brachiopod (fossil form)
bivocal... **9.** diphthong (dipthong)
bivouac... **4.** camp **6.** encamp, laager
   7. camping, leaguer (Hist)
   10. encampment
biwa... **6.** loquat
bizarre... **3.** odd **5.** dedal, outré, queer
   6. absurd, exotic, quaint, rococo
   7. baroque **8.** fanciful **9.** eccentric,
   fantastic, grotesque, highflown
   11. extravagant, sensational
Bizen... **7.** pottery (unglazed)
Bizet... **8.** composer (Carmen)
bizzarro (Mus)... **7.** bizarre
   9. whimsical
blab... **6.** gossip, reveal, snitch, tattle,
   tell on **7.** blabber, chatter
   8. informer, squealer, telltale
   10. tateteller, tattletale **11.** taletelling
blabber... **4.** blab **6.** babble, gabber,
   gossip, tattle **7.** chatter, twaddle
   8. informer, nonsense
black... **3.** ink, jet **4.** ebon, evil, foul,
   inky, noir **5.** color, cruel, ebony,
   murky, negro, niger, raven, sable,
   tarry **6.** dismal, filthy, gloomy, pitchy,
   somber, sullen, wicked **7.** hateful,
   melanic, nigrine, nigrous, ominous,
   unclean **8.** atrament, menacing,
   mournful, sinister **9.** atrocious,
   lightless, nigricant **10.** calamitous,
   disastrous, forbidding
black (pert to)... see also *Black*
African.. **10.** blackamoor
alloy.. **6.** niello
and blue.. **5.** livid **7.** bruised
   10. discolored, ecchymosed,
   ecchymosis **11.** bluish–black,
   lead–colored
art.. **5.** magic **7.** alchemy **8.** wizardry
   10. black magic
ball.. **7.** exclude **9.** ostracize
bird.. **2.** Zu (Myth) **3.** ani, daw, pie
   4. crow, merl, rook **5.** amsel, ouzel,
   raven **6.** thrush **7.** jackdaw
   10. Melanesian, Polynesian
bottom.. **9.** clog dance
coffee.. **8.** café noir
diamond.. **4.** coal
duck.. **6.** Cayuga
earth.. **4.** mold **9.** Chernozem (Russ)
face.. **4.** type **5.** sheep **8.** minstrel

fish.. **6.** tautog
garnet.. **8.** melanite
gibbon.. **7.** siamang
guard.. **5.** drole, gamin, knave, rogue,
   scamp **6.** rascal **7.** vagrant, villain
   8. criminal, scalawag, scullion,
   vagabond **9.** scoundrel
   11. rapscallion
Harry.. **7.** sea bass
jack.. **4.** flag (pirate) **6.** coerce,
   cudgel, hijack **9.** strong–arm
   10. Jolly Roger
partridge.. **9.** francolin
rhinoceros.. **7.** borelle
sheep.. **10.** scapegrace
smith.. **5.** smith **6.** forger, smithy
   7. farrier
spruce.. **7.** yewpine
strap.. **8.** molasses
widow spider.. **6.** pokomo
Black (pert to)...
Bess.. **4.** mare (Dick Turpin's)
Current.. **5.** Japan
Death.. **6.** Plague (bubonic)
Foot.. **6.** Indian (Siksika)
   10. Algonquian
Friar.. **4.** monk **9.** Dominican
   (mendicant Order)
Friday.. **10.** Good Friday **14.** public
   disaster (day)
Hand.. **7.** anarchy, Camorra, Society
   (secret) **9.** blackmail
Hawk.. **3.** War (1831) **11.** Indian
   Chief
Hole.. **8.** Calcutta
Jack (General).. **5.** Logan (Civil War)
   8. Pershing (WWI)
Maria.. **7.** vehicle (prisoner's)
   14. explosive shell
Monday.. **12.** Easter Monday (1630)
Monk.. **11.** Benedictine
Plague.. **7.** bubonic
Prince.. **6.** Edward
Republic.. **5.** Haiti
Rood.. **8.** crucifix, Holy Rood (anc)
Sea (Asia).. **6.** Euxine (anc)
Sea (Russia).. **11.** Chernoe More
Shirt.. **7.** Fascist **8.** Fascisti
Watch.. **16.** Royal Highlanders
Water State (nickname).. **8.** Nebraska
blacken... **5.** sully **6.** defame
   9. denigrate
bladder... **3.** bag, sac **4.** sack
   5. pouch **6.** bubble, pocket
   7. blister, globule
blade... **3.** arm, bit, fop **4.** beau,
   dude, edge, epee, foil, leaf, vane
   5. blood, dandy, frond, knife, spark,
   spear, spire, sport, sword **6.** cutter,
   rafter (roof), runner, Toledo (sword)
   7. gallant, sabreur, scapula, traneen
   9. swordsman
blague... **6.** humbug **8.** claptrap
blah... **4.** bunk **8.** contempt, nonsense
blain... **4.** bleb, sore **5.** bulla
   7. blister, inflame, pustule
   8. swelling **9.** chilblain
Blake's symbolic figure... **3.** Zoa
blame... **5.** chide, curse, shend
   6. accuse, charge, revile **7.** accusal,
   censure, obloquy, reproof, reprove
   8. denounce, reproach **9.** criticism,

damnation, reprehend 10. accusation, imputation 11. attribution, reprobation 12. condemnation, denunciation, reprehension 14. responsibility

blameless... 7. sinless 8. innocent 9. faultless, guiltless 12. sans reproche

blameworthy... 8. culpable 10. censurable, reprovable 11. impeachable 13. reprehensible

blanch... 4. fade, pale 5. gloss, scald 6. whiten 8. etiolate 9. whitewash

blanc mange... 7. dessert, pudding

bland... 4. glib, mild, oily, smug, soft, tame 5. suave 6. gentle, smooth 7. affable 8. soothing (manner), unctuous 9. temperate 10. flattering 12. hypocritical, ingratiating, mealy–mouthed, smooth–spoken

blandishment... 7. amenity, coaxing, palaver 8. cajolery, flattery 9. wheedling 10. allurement, inducement

blank... 4. arid, bare, dash, dull, form, nude, null, void 5. empty, naked, verse 6. closed, hollow, jejune, poetry, stupid, vacant, vacuum 8. bull's–eye, document, spotless (domino) 9. fruitless, unadorned, untrimmed 10. instrument (law), tabula rasa 11. empty–headed, thoughtless 13. unembellished, unintelligent 14. expressionless

blank book... 5. album 6. tablet 8. memo book, notebook 10. memorandum, pocketbook

blanket... 3. rug 4. robe 5. bluey, cloak, cotta, cover, manta, quilt, throw 6. afghan, shroud, spread 7. lap robe 8. covering, coverlet 10. barraclade (homespun)

blankness... 7. vacancy, vacuity 8. negation 9. emptiness

blare... 4. bawl, blow, bray, honk, peal, toot 5. blast, blaze, glare 6. bellow 7. fanfare, tantara 9. tantarara

blarney... 6. bunkum 7. wheedle 8. buncombe, cajolery, flattery, soft–soap 9. adulation

Blarney Stone site... 13. Blarney Castle (Cork, Ir)

blart... 4. blab, roar 5. bleat 6. bellow

blasé... 5. bored, sated 6. casual 9. easygoing, sans souci, surfeited 10. hard–boiled, nonchalant 11. indifferent, self–assured, unconcerned, worldly–wise 12. disenchanted 13. disillusioned, disinterested, lackadaisical

blaspheme... 4. damn 5. abuse, curse, swear 6. revile, vilify 10. calumniate

blasphemy... 7. cursing, impiety 8. anathema, swearing 9. profanity, sacrilege 10. execration 11. desecration, imprecation, irreverence, malediction

blast... 3. jet, pop 4. bang, blow, gust, ruin, shot, toot 5. curse, stunt 6. blight, flurry, onrush, wither 7. blowout, explode 9. discharge,

explosion, explosive, frustrate 10. detonation, propulsion 11. fulmination

blasted... 5. blown 6. blamed, cursed, danged (sl), darned, ruined 7. wrecked 8. blighted 10. confounded

blatant... 5. crude, noisy 6. garish, puling, vulgar 7. flaring, glaring, howling, ululant, wailing 8. brawling 9. clamorous, turbulent 10. blustering, uproarious, vociferous 12. obstreperous

blate... 4. blab, dull, slow 5. bleat, blunt, prate, timid 7. bashful 8. sheepish 9. diffident 10. spiritless

blaw... 4. blow, brag 5. boast

blaze... 4. fire, gash, mark (trail), sign 5. flame, flare 6. luster 7. bonfire, flare–up 8. eruption, outburst, radiance, splendor 9. explosion, firebrand 10. effulgence 11. resplendent

blazer... 6. jacket

blazon... 4. deck, show 5. adorn, blaze, grace, paint 6. enrich, shield 7. display, étalage, exhibit, furbish 8. proclaim 9. embellish 10. coat of arms, exhibition 11. publication

blazoning arms... 8. bearings, heraldry

bleach... 3. lye, sun 4. lime 6. blanch, purify, whiten 7. decolor, lighten 8. chemical, chlorine, etiolate, peroxide 9. whiteness 10. dealbation, decolorant 11. decolorizer

bleaching vat... 4. kier 5. kieve

bleak... 3. dry, raw 4. arid, bare, cold, pale 5. gaunt, sharp 6. bitter, desert, dismal, dreary, frigid, pallid, severe 7. cutting, exposed 8. desolate, rigorous 9. cheerless, wind–blown, wind–swept 10. depressing

blear... 3. dim, fog 4. blur, dull, film 6. bleary 7. blurred 10. indistinct

bleat... 3. baa 4. blat 5. blate, whine 7. blather

bleb... 5. bulge, bulla 6. bubble 7. bladder, blister, globule, pustule, vesicle

bleed... 3. cup, tap 4. milk, soak 5. drain 6. fleece, grieve, let out, suffer 7. agonize, despoil, exploit, overtax 8. let blood, transude 9. surcharge 10. hemorrhage, overcharge

bleeding... 7. cupping 9. hemorrhea 10. hemorrhage, phlebotomy 11. venesection 12. bloodletting

blemish... 3. mar 4. blot, blue, dent, flaw, mole, mote, pock, rift, scar, spot, wart 5. crack, fault, nevus, sully, taint 6. breach, macula, macule, stigma 7. failing, fissure, freckle, lentigo 8. cicatrix, pockmark 9. birthmark, cicatrice, deformity, disfigure 10. defacement, deficiency 12. imperfection 13. disfigurement

blench... 4. duck, pale, wile 5. blink, dodge, quail, trick, wince 6. bleach, cringe, flinch, recoil, shrink, whiten 9. stratagem 10. disconcert

blend... 3. mix 4. fuse, melt
5. merge, shift, unite 6. fusion,
mingle 7. combine, mixture, scumble
8. coalesce, compound, tincture
9. commingle, composite, harmonize
10. amalgamate 11. combination,
incorporate
blended... 5. fondu, mixed 6. merged
7. mingled 9. confluent
blending... 6. crasis 11. inheritance
blessing... 4. boon, gift, good, luck,
rite 5. favor, grace 7. benefit,
benison, fortune, godsend, service,
welfare 8. good turn, kindness
9. advantage 10. benedicite, good
wishes 11. benediction, benevolence
12. felicitation 13. beatification
blight... 3. mar, nip 4. dash (hope),
ruin, rust, seer, smut 5. blast, crush,
spoil 6. freeze, mildew, wither
7. destroy, shatter 9. frustrate
10. disappoint
blighter... 4. chap 6. beggar (anc),
fellow
blimp... 6. ballon 7. airship, balloon
8. potbelly, zeppelin 9. dirigible
10. bureaucrat 12. Graf Zeppelin,
stuffed shirt
blind... 3. dim 4. ante (poker), mask,
peed, ruse, seel, slat, veil, wile
5. ciego, guise, trick 6. ambush,
scheme, screen 7. benight, conceal,
dim–eyed, eyeless, gimmick, obscure,
pretext, shutter 8. artifice, hoodwink,
jalousie, purblind, unseeing
9. dead–drunk, senseless, sightless
10. ableptical, dim–sighted,
subterfuge 11. inattentive
12. undiscerning 13. stalking–horse
blind (pert to)...
alley.. 7. impasse 8. cul–de–sac
fear.. 5. panic
girl (of Pompeii).. 5. Nydia
gut.. 6. caecum, window
10. persiennes
one eye.. 4. peed
printing for.. 7. braille
blindness... 7. anopsia, meropia (part)
8. ablepsia 9. achropsia, amaurosis
10. bleariness, nyctalopia 11. gutta
serena, hemeralopia
13. achromatopsia
blink... 4. wink 5. light, quail, wince
6. cringe, flinch 7. flicker, glimmer,
glimpse, glitter, nictate, shimmer,
twinkle 9. nictitate 10. bat the eyes
blink at... 6. accept, ignore
7. condone 8. overlook, tolerate
9. be blind to, disregard
bliss... 3. joy 4. Eden 6. heaven
7. delight, harmony, rapture
8. felicity, gladness 9. beatitude,
happiness 11. blessedness
12. spirituality 14. blithesomeness
blissful... 4. holy 5. seely 6. Edenic
7. blessed, Elysian, Utopian
8. ecstatic 9. beatified, glorified
blister... 4. bleb, blob, burn, flay
5. blain, bulge, bulla, roast 6. beat
up, bubble, oyster, scorch (with
words), thrash 7. bladder, blemish,
pustule, trounce, vesicle 9. criticize

10. vesicatory
blistered... 6. seared, singed
7. parched 8. scorched 9. vesicated
blithe... 4. airy, glad 5. merry
6. cheery, joyous 7. jocular
8. cheerful 10. blithesome
blitz... 5. shell 6. strafe 7. bombard
10. blitzkrieg
blizzard... 4. blow, wind 5. purga
7. tornado 9. snowstorm 10. snow
squall 11. white squall
Blizzard State... 11. South Dakota
bloated... 5. cured (herring), proud,
tumid 6. sodden, turgid 7. dilated,
pompous, swollen 8. inflated, puffed
up, tumefied 9. distended, flatulent,
plethoric 10. incrassate
13. emphysematous
bloated plutocrat... 9. bourgeois
10. capitalist
blob... 3. wen 4. bleb, blot, daub,
drop, lump, mark 5. bulge
6. bubble, pimple 7. blister, globule,
pustule, splotch
bloc (political)... 4. axis 5. cabal, union
6. league 7. faction 8. alliance
9. coalition 11. combination
block... 3. bar, dam, set 4. cake,
clog, cube, mass, peck, plot, stop
5. check, parry, shape, solid
6. hamper, hinder, impede, oppose,
shares, stymie 7. auction, barrier,
outline 8. blockage, obstacle,
obstruct 9. barricade 10. impediment
11. obstruction
block (pert to)...
architecture.. 5. socle 6. dentil,
mutule, plinth 7. tessera
blacksmith's.. 5. anvil
coal (Eng).. 3. jud
executioner's.. 10. guillotine
falconry.. 5. perch
finance.. 6. shares
football.. 4. clip
glacier.. 5. serac
insulating.. 6. taplet
land.. 4. city 5. tract 7. section
medicine.. 10. anesthesia
railroad.. 6. signal
sandstone (Eng).. 6. sarsen
blockade... 3. bar, dam 5. hem in,
siege 6. shut in 7. closure, exclude,
fortify 8. obstacle, obstruct
9. exclusion 11. obstruction
blockhead... 3. oaf 4. dolt, fool,
mome (anc) 5. dunce, idiot
7. half–wit, tomfool 8. bonehead,
lunkhead 11. knucklehead
blockhouse... 4. fort 7. shelter 8. log
cabin 10. stronghold
bloke... 3. man 4. bird, chap, tuff
6. fellow 9. personage
blond, blonde... 4. fair 5. color, light
6. flaxen 10. goldilocks
blood... 4. cell, clot, type, vein
5. aorta, fluid, group, grume, hemad
(haemad), hemal, hemic, ichor
(gods'), lymph, serum 6. artery,
factor, fibrin, haemal, plasma, Rhesus
(type) 8. blister, carotid 8. platelet
9. corpuscle, hemamoeba, leucocyte
10. hemachrome, hemoglobin,

hemorrhage, phlebotomy
11. erythrocyte, transfusion
12. bloodletting
blood (pert to)...
clotted.. 4. gore 5. cruor 8. thrombus
color.. 7. crimson, para red 8. blood
red, sanguine 11. sanguineous
13. sanguinaceous
disease.. 6. anemia 8. leukemia
(leukaemia, leucemia)
feud.. 8. vendetta
flower.. 5. hippo 9. blood lily
horse.. 7. blooded 12. thoroughbred
hound.. 4. lyam (lyme)
money (anc).. 3. cro 4. eric
7. galanas, wergild 9. bloodwite
particle (foreign).. 7. embolus
poisoning.. 6. pyemia (pyaemia)
pressure.. 12. hypertension
pudding.. 7. sausage
relationship.. 3. sib 6. agnate
7. cognate, kinship, kinsman, progeny,
sibship
shed.. 6. murder 7. killing, slaying
9. slaughter
stone.. 10. chalcedony
sucker.. 5. leech 8. parasite
10. sanguisuge
thirsty.. 5. cruel 8. sanguine
9. ferocious, murderous
10. sanguinary 11. ensanguined
vessel.. 3. vas 4. vein 6. artery
9. capillary
blood, kinship... 4. race, ties 5. birth,
breed, stock 6. strain 7. descent,
kinsman, lineage, royalty, sibship
8. heredity, nobility, relation 9. blue
blood, lifeblood, life force
10. extraction 13. consanguinity
bloodless... 4. pale 5. ashen, faint
6. anemic (aenemic) 7. ghastly,
inhuman 8. lifeless, peaceful
9. unfeeling 11. cold of heart
bloody... 4. gory 5. cruel, wound
6. cruent (obs), cursed 7. smeared
8. infamous 9. murderous
10. sanguinary 11. ensanguined
12. bloodstained, bloodthirsty
Bloody (pert to)...
Angle.. 11. battlefield (Spotsylvania,
1860)
Mary.. 5. Queen (Eng) 8. cocktail
bloom... 3. dew 4. glow, posy
5. blush, flush, youth 6. beauty,
flower, health, heyday, thrive
7. blossom 11. healthiness
bloomer... 5. boner, error 6. bobble,
boo–boo 7. blooper, blunder, failure,
faux pas, mistake, trouser
blossom... 4. bell, blow, grow, posy
5. bloom, ripen 6. floret, flower,
mature, thrive 7. develop, prosper
8. flourish, floweret, progress
10. effloresce 13. efflorescence
blossoming... 4. rise 6. growth
8. anthesis, blooming 9. flowerage,
flowering 10. florescent, unfoldment
11. development, florescence,
flourishing, progressing
13. efflorescence, inflorescence

blot... 3. dry, mar 4. blur, soil, spot
5. erase, error, fleck, smear, speck,
stain, sully 6. absorb, blotch, damage,
impair, smutch, soak up, sponge,
stigma 7. blacken, blemish, erasure,
expunge 9. bespatter 10. obliterate,
stigmatize 12. obliteration
blot out... 3. fix 4. dele, kill 5. purge
6. absorb, cancel, delete, efface,
excise, rub out 7. bump off, destroy,
expunge, obscure, wipe out 8. black
out 10. obliterate
blotch... 4. bleb, mark, soil, spot
5. patch, stain 6. macula, mottle,
stigma 7. blemish
blotched... 4. pied 5. pinto 6. spotty
7. mottled 8. speckled
blouse... 4. blou, sark 5. bluey, middy,
shift, shirt, smock, tunic, waist
6. basque 7. casaque 10. shirtwaist
blow... 3. dab, hit, rap, tap 4. brag,
bump, coup, gust, pant, puff, slap,
toot, waft, wind 5. bloom, devel,
feint, impel, knock, shock, sound, utter
6. expand, puff up 7. beating,
bluster, whiffle 8. calamity, disaster,
disclose, lambskin (obs)
14. disappointment
blow... 4. flee, over, rant, slog
5. boast, clout, scram 6. beat it,
betray, buffet, depart, wallop
8. squander 10. blow me down
blow (pert to)...
hard.. 6. blower 7. windbag
8. braggart 11. braggadocio
hot and cold.. 4. vary 5. shift, waver
6. seesaw 7. quibble 9. fluctuate,
vacillate 12. shilly–shally
out.. 5. douse, snuff 10. extinguish
blower... 4. blow, gale, wind 5. whale
6. puffer (fish), squall 7. bellows,
bloomer, blowgun, boaster, monsoon,
tornado 8. braggart 9. hurricane,
whirlwind, windstorm
11. braggadocio
blow up... 4. fail, rage 5. blast, bloat,
burst, fluff 6. berate, dilate, excite,
expand, forget, praise 7. blow out,
enlarge, explode, inflate 8. demolish,
detonate, disprove 9. fulminate
blowzy... 5. dowdy, ruddy, tacky
6. coarse, frowzy, sloppy, untidy
7. unkempt 8. careless, frumpish,
slovenly 10. disheveled, slatternly
blubber... 3. fat 4. weep 6. bubble
7. whimper 8. whale fat
blubbery... 3. fat 7. swollen
9. quivering 10. gelatinous
bludgeon... 3. bat, hit 4. beat, club,
mace 5. billy, bully, stick 6. coerce,
cudgel, menace 8. browbeat,
bulldoze, threaten 9. truncheon
10. intimidate, shillelagh (shillalah)
blue... 4. anil, baby, bice, bleu, navy
5. azure, beryl, Ching, email, king's,
merle, perse, royal, smalt 6. cobalt,
cyanic, French, indigo, powder
7. aniline, azarite, cesious, Dresden,
Dumont's, gobelin, lobelia, mesange,
peacock, Persian 8. caesious,

calamine, cerulean, Coventry, electric, lavender, midnight, pavonine, sapphire, wisteria 9. turquoise 10. aquamarine, cornflower

blue (pert to)... see also *Blue*
baby.. 8. cyanotic
bonnet.. 3. cap 4. Scot 6. flower (Texas State) 8. Scotsman, titmouse
china.. 7. Nanking
circle (archery).. 6. target
day.. 6. Monday
emblem of.. 6. Oxford 9. Cambridge
grass.. 3. poa
ground.. 10. kimberlite
hero.. 9. Bluebeard
melancholy.. 3. sad 6. gloomy 7. pensive, wistful 8. tristful 9. cheerless, depressed, penseroso 10. atrabiliar 11. atrabilious, melancholic 13. hypochondriac
nose.. 4. snob 5. prude 7. Puritan 10. goody–goody 11. Nova Scotian
pencil.. 4. dele, edit 6. delete, excise, revise
print.. 4, plan, plot 5. graph 6. layout 7. diagram, program 8. schedule 9. cyanotype 10. master plan, photograph, photoprint
ribbon.. 5. award, badge 10. cordon bleu, decoration
skin.. 5. livid
sky.. 5. ether, vault 6. caelum, heaven, welkin 7. the blue 8. empyrean 9. firmament 10. blue yonder, the heavens
stocking.. 4. blue 6. pedant 7. bas bleu 8. Gamaliel (Bib) 9. formalist, pedagogue 10. Parliament

Blue (pert to)...
Boy.. 8. painting (Gainsborough)
Grass State.. 8. Kentucky
Grotto site.. 5. Capri
Law State.. 11. Connecticut

Bluebeard's wife... 6. Fatima
blue–gray... 7. cesious (caesious)
blue–green... 8. calamine
bluff... 4. bank (steep), crag, curt, dupe, fool, rude, wall 5. brash, cliff, frank, gruff, krans, sheer, short 6. abrupt, crusty 7. beguile, blinder, blinker, bluffer, bluster, brusque, deceive, pretend, uncivil 8. impolite 9. bamboozle, blusterer, charlatan, falseness, four–flush, precipice 11. four–flusher 13. unceremonious
bluffer... 5. quack 9. blusterer, charlatan 10. mountebank 11. four–flusher
bluffness... 6. candor 9. bluntness 10. abruptness 11. brusqueness
blunder... 3. err, mix 4. bull, goof, slip 5. boner, botch, error, misdo 6. boo–boo, bungle, fumble 7. faux pas, mistake, stumble 8. flounder, solecism (speech) 9. mismanage
blunt... 4. curt, dull, open 5. bluff, frank, gruff, plain 6. benumb, candid, deaden, obtund, obtuse, snippy, stupid, weaken 7. artless, brusque, sincere 8. hebetate 9. ingenuous 13. unceremonious
blur... 3. bog, dim, hum 4. blob, blot,

film, mist, soil, spot 5. blear, cloud, smear, stain 6. blotch, darken, mackle 7. blemish, dimness, obscure, splotch 9. disfigure
blurb... 2. ad 4. plug 5. boost, brief 6. notice 7. write–up 8. ballyhoo 9. publicity 12. announcement, commendation 13. advertisement
blurt out... 4. blab, bolt 7. blunder 9. ejaculate
blush... 4. glow, look 5. bloom, color, flush 6. glance, mantle, redden 7. modesty, redness 9. suffusion
blushing... 4. meek 5. ruddy 6. modest 7. roseate 8. flushing, sheepish 9. reddening, rubescent 10. erubescent
bluster... 4. blow, bray, fume, rage, rant, roar 5. broil, bully, furor, noise 6. flurry, hoopla, hubbub, squall, tumult 7. roister, swagger, turmoil 8. boasting, bullying, threaten 9. agitation, confusion 10. swaggering, turbulence 11. rodomontade
blusterer... 5. bully 7. boaster 8. blowhard, braggart 9. roisterer, swaggerer 11. braggadocio 12. swashbuckler
bo... 4. hobo 5. buddy, tramp 9. sundowner 10. landlouper 11. bindle stiff
bo, boh (Burma)... 5. chief 6. leader 7. captain
boa... 5. aboma, scarf (feather), snake 8. anaconda
boar... 3. hog, sus 4. apex, hure (head) 5. swine 6. barrow, hogget (2–year) 9. hoggaster (3–year)
board... 4. deal, doll, feed, lath, side, slat, wood 5. curia (anc), enter, forum, meals, plank, table 6. border, lumber, timber 7. binding (book), council, lodging 8. approach, exchange (Finan), tribunal 9. committee, provision 11. accommodate, bed and board, directorate, refreshment 14. accommodations
boast... 4. brag, crow 5. extol, exult, glory, pride, vapor, vaunt 6. menace 7. bluster, swagger 8. braggart, flourish 9. gasconade
boastful... 4. vain 8. bragging 9. conceited, overproud, presuming 11. thrasonical 12. vainglorious 13. self–important
boat... 3. ark, bac, gig, tub, tug 4. brig, dhow, dory, junk, punt, saic, scow, ship, trow, yawl 5. aviso, balsa, barge, canoe, craft, dandy, dhoni, dingy, ferry, kayak, ketch, liner, oolak, praam, scull, skiff, U–boak, umiak, xebec, yacht 6. argosy, baidak, bateau, convoy, cutter, dinghy, dogger, launch, mistic, oomiac, packet, randan, sampan, settee, tanker, vessel, whaler 7. bidarka, caravel, coracle (anc), cruiser, gondola, masoola, piragua, pirogue, rowboat, scooter, shallop, trawler, tugboat, warship

8. dahabeah, man–of–war, palander, sailboat, seaplane 9. catamaran, destroyer, steamship, submarine 10. brigantine, windjammer 11. side–wheeler, treckschuyt
boat (pert to)...
boatswain.. 5. bosun 6. serang
captain.. 4. rais (reis) 6. master 7. skipper
deck.. 4. poop 6. flight 9. promenade
man.. 5. rower 6. bargee 7. ferrier, oarsman 9. gondolier, yachtsman
sail.. 3. jib 4. main, reef 6. lateen, mizzen
shaped.. 9. navicella, navicular
side.. 7. gunwale
song.. 7. chantey 9. barcarole
bob... 3. bow, cut, nod, rap, tap 4. bend, jeer, jerk, jest 5. cheat, filch, float, flout, plumb, shake, taunt, trick 6. bobble, curtsy, delude, hairdo, kowtow, sinker, weight 7. haircut 8. coiffure, greeting, shilling 9. obeisance, oscillate
bobac... 5. pahmi 6. marmot
bobber... 4. duck (ruddy) 5. float 6. bobfly 7. dropper 8. deadhead
bobbin... 3. pin 4. coil, cord, pirn, reel 5. braid, spool 7. spindle
bobble... 3. bob, dib (angling) 4. muff 5. shake 6. boggle, bungle, fumble 7. blunder 9. oscillate
bobby... 6. peeler 9. policeman
Boche... 6. German (a)
bodach... 5. churl, clown 7. bugaboo
bodacious... 4. bold 8. insolent, reckless 9. audacious, bumptious, insulting 12. contumelious
bode... 5. augur 6. divine 7. portend, presage 8. forebode, foreshow, foretell 13. prognosticate
bodhisattva... 8. Buddhism 13. Enlightenment
bodice... 4. belt 5. stays, waist 6. basque, girdle 7. corsage, garment
bodily... 6. carnal 7. fleshly, somatic 8. corporal, material, physical 9. corporeal 10. completely
boding... 7. ominous 10. foreboding, portentous, prediction, prognostic 12. apprehension
bodkin... 3. awl 6. dagger, needle 7. hairpin, poniard 8. stiletto 9. eyeleteer
body... 3. man 4. deha (Theos), homo, soma 5. being, human, trunk 6. corpse, entity, licham, mortal, person 7. carcass 8. creature, organism 9. substance 10. individual 13. corpus delicti 14. substantiality
body (pert to)...
armed.. 5. corps, posse
business.. 7. company 11. cooperation 12. organization
celestial.. 3. sun 4. luna, star 5. comet 6. meteor, planet
church.. 4. nave
dead.. 6. corpse 7. cadaver
division (mollusk).. 7. prosoma
injury.. 6. mayhem, trauma
petrified.. 6. fossil
political.. 4. weal 6. senate 7. cabinet 11. legislature
small.. 6. nanoid 8. dwarfish
body of...
people.. 3. mob 4. band, bevy, gang, host 5. bunch, crowd, flock, group, horde 6. rabble, throng 9. multitude
singers.. 5. choir 6. chorus
soldiers.. 4. file 5. corps, squad, troop 7. brigade, company, platoon 8. division
water.. 3. bay, sea 4. lake, pond, pool 5. fiord (fjord), inlet, ocean 6. lagoon 9. reservoir
Boeotian (pert to)...
city.. 5. Ionia (Dist) 6. Thebes
figurine.. 7. Tanagra
king (Myth).. 6. Ogyges
Boer (pert to)...
General, statesman.. 5. Botha
language.. 4. Taal 9. Afrikaans
War site.. 9. Ladysmith (S Afr)
bog... 3. bug, fen 4. blei, bold, holm, mire, moor, moss, ooze, quag, sink 5. jheel, marsh, saucy, swamp 6. morass, slough 8. quagmire 9. everglade
bogey, bogie, bogy... 3. par 5. Devil 6. goblin 7. bugaboo, bugbear
boggle... 3. shy 4. foil, quip 5. botch, cavil, demur, parry, pause, start 6. bicker, bungle, falter, object, shrink 7. dispute, quibble, scruple 8. hesitate, sidestep 9. dissemble, objection 10. difficulty, equivocate
bogglebo... 5. bogle 7. bugaboo, specter 9. hobgoblin, scarecrow
bogus... 4. fake, mock, sham 5. phony, queer 8. spurious 10. apocryphal, factitious, fictitious 11. counterfeit
bohawn... 3. hut 5. cabin 7. cottage
Bohemia...
capital.. 6. Prague
city.. 5. Praha 6. Aussig, Pilsen 7. Budweis, Teplitz 11. Reichenberg
dance.. 6. redowa
measure.. 5. stopa 6. merice
mineral.. 6. egeran
reformer.. 4. Huss
river.. 4. Elbe, Iser 6. Moldau
tribe (anc).. 4. Boii
vagabond.. 5. gypsy (gipsy)
bohunk... 6. Slovak 7. laborer 8. Bohemian, Croatian (formerly)
boil... 3. sty (styr) 4. buck, cook, fume, stew 5. churn, steam 6. bubble, pimple, seethe 7. bristle 8. furuncle
boiling... 5. angry 7. cooking, flushed, stewing 8. seething, sizzling 9. agitating, ebullient 10. smoldering
bois (Fr)... 4. wood
boisterous... 4. loud 5. noisy, rough, rowdy 6. stormy 7. blatant, excited, furious, roaring, violent 8. brawling 9. clamorous, turbulent 10. blustering, roisterous, tumultuous, unyielding 12. obstreperous
Bokhara (pert to)...
fur.. 9. astrakhan, broadtail

rug .. 8. Turkoman
sheep .. 7. karakul (caracul)
site .. 4. Asia (Russ)
bola ... 4. tree (fiber) 6. weapon
bold ... 4. deep, pert, rash, rude, snug
 5. steep, stout 6. abrupt, brazen,
 daring, heroic, raised 7. dashing,
 defiant, eminent, forward, salient,
 valiant 8. fearless, immodest,
 impudent, in relief, intrepid, powerful,
 repoussé, stalwart 9. audacious,
 confident, dauntless, shameless,
 unabashed 10. courageous
 11. lionhearted, outstanding,
 precipitous, venturesome
 12. presumptuous, stouthearted
boldness ... 5. valor 6. defial, virtue
 7. bravery, courage 8. audacity,
 defiance, salience, temerity
 9. assurance, gallantry, hardihood,
 immodesty, impudence
 10. brazenness, confidence,
 effrontery, prominence, resolution
 11. forwardness, intrepidity,
 obviousness 12. protuberance
 13. dauntlessness
 14. courageousness
bolero ... 5. dance, music, waist
 6. jacket
boliche ... 3. inn 5. bowls
Bolivia ...
capital .. 5. La Paz (Polit), Oruro (anc),
 Sucre (law)
hero .. 5. Sucre 7. Bolivar, Pizarro
Indian tribe .. 3. Uro 4. Iten, Moxo
lake .. 8. Titicaca (world's highest)
mountain .. 5. Andes 6. Sorata
 8. Illimani
product .. 3. tin 8. tungsten
river .. 4. Beni 6. Blanco
bolo ... 5. knife 7. machete 8. pacifist
 (Bolo Pasha, traitor) 9. defeatist
Bolshevik, bolshevik ... 7. Marxian,
 radical (Bolsheviki) 9. Communist
 (1918), Socialist 13. revolutionist
 14. Social Democrat 18. Third
 International
Bolshevist (Communist) leader ...
 5. Lenin 6. Stalin 7. Kosygin
 8. Bulganin 9. Krushchev
bolster ... 3. pad 4. bear, hold
 5. boost 6. pillow 7. cushion,
 support, sustain 8. maintain
bolt ... 3. bar 4. dart, flee, lock, roll,
 sift 5. arrow, rivet, scram, screw,
 shaft, speed 6. decamp, devour,
 faster, flight, pintle, secede, staple,
 toggle 7. missile, padlock 8. firebolt,
 separate 10. projectile 11. eat
 greedily, fulguration, thunderbolt
bolus ... 4. bite, clay, clod, food
 (chewed), mass, pill 6. tablet, troche
 8. mouthful
bomb ... 3. dud, egg 5. shell 6. petard
 7. grenade, missile 8. divebomb,
 fireball, surprise 9. bombshell,
 pineapple 10. projectile
bomb (type of) ... 4. time 5. stink
 6. aerial, atomic, rocket 7. nuclear,
 tear gas 8. hydrogen 10. demolition
bombard ... 3. zap 5. blitz, shell
 6. assail, attack, strafe 7. atomize,

barrage 9. cannonade
bombardier ... 5. jager 6. bomber,
 gunner 9. cannoneer, musketeer
 12. artilleryman
bombast ... 4. blow, brag, rage, rant,
 rave 5. boast 7. fustian 8. boasting,
 inflated, stuffing (hist) 9. bombastic,
 turgidity 11. rodomontade
 12. magniloquent 13. grandiloquent
bombastic ... 5. tumid 7. orotund,
 pompous, stilted 8. boastful, inflated
 12. high–sounding 13. grandiloquent
Bombay ...
capital of .. 11. Maharashtra (state)
college .. 11. Elphinstone
duck .. 10. lizard fish
hemp .. 4. sunn 6. ambary
merchant .. 4. Arab
seaport of .. 5. India
bomber ... 5. stuka 10. bombardier
Bombyx ... 4. eria, moth 8. silkworm
bona fide ... 4. real 7. genuine
 9. authentic 10. constantly, faithfully,
 legitimate
bona mano ... 3. tip 8. gratuity
bon ami ... 5. lover 6. friend
 10. good friend, sweetheart
bonanza ... 6. riches 8. El Dorado
 (Myth), gold mine (US)
Bonanza State ... 7. Montana
bond ... 3. tie, vow 4. duty, gyve, link,
 mise, pact, yoke 5. chain, nexus,
 rente 6. fetter, league 7. entente,
 manacle, shackle 8. contract,
 covenant, relation, security (Finan)
 9. agreement, captivity
 10. allegiance, connection
 11. association, certificate
bondage ... 4. yoke 6. chains
 7. serfdom, slavery 9. captivity,
 restraint, servitude, thralldom
 11. enslavement, subjugation
bondman, bondsman ... 4. esne, serf
 5. churl, helot, slave 6. thrall, vassal
 7. servant 8. bailsman 9. guarantor
bone ... 2. os 4. chip 5. boner
 6. dollar, osteon 7. blunder, counter
 (game), ossicle 8. skeleton, wishbone
 9. funny bone (humerus), pygostyle
 (bird's), whalebone
bone (Anat) ... 3. rib 4. ulna 5. femur,
 ilium, incus (ear), malar, skull, spine,
 talus, tibia 6. carpus, coccyx, fibula,
 tarsus 7. humerus, maxilla, patella,
 scapula, sternum 8. astragal, clavicle,
 mandible, phalange, vertebra
 9. calcaneus, occipital
 10. metacarpus, metatarsus
bone (pert to) ...
bonelike .. 6. osteal 7. osteoid
cell .. 10. osteoblast
china .. 7. English
curvature .. 8. lordosis
divination .. 10. osteomancy
fish .. 9. operculum
marrow .. 7. medulla
process .. 7. mastoid 8. alveolar
 9. apophysis
science .. 9. osteology
surgery .. 9. osteotomy 11. osteoclasis
 12. osteoplastic
tissue .. 6. ossein

tumor.. **7.** osteoma
bones... **4.** body, dice, form, ossa
 5. cubes, frame, money, torso, trunk
 6. end man, refuse **7.** carcass,
 ivories **8.** skeleton **11.** rattlebones
boneyard... **4.** bank (game)
 8. golgotha **9.** graveyard
 10. necropolis **11.** polyandrium
bonhomie... **8.** pleasant **9.** good
 humor **10.** affability, amiability
Bonhomme Richard... **4.** ship
 8. man–of–war (1779), (opponent of
 Serapis)
bonito, bonita... **4.** nice **6.** pretty
 8. mackerel, skipjack
bon mot... **9.** witticism **10.** jeu
 d'esprit **11.** smart saying
bonne... **5.** mammy **9.** nursemaid
 10. baby sitter **11.** maidservant
bonnet... **3.** cap, hat **4.** coif, hood,
 poke **5.** toque **7.** chapeau
 9. headdress
bonnetman... **10.** Highlander
bonny, bonnie... **3.** bon **4.** good
 5. plump **6.** comely, lively, pretty
 7. healthy, très bon **8.** handsome
 9. beautiful
Bontok... **7.** Malayan (Luzon)
 10. Indonesian
bonus... **3.** tip **4.** cash, gift **5.** batta,
 bribe, extra, share, stock (Finan)
 7. cumshaw, douceur, premium,
 rake–off, subsidy **8.** dividend, gratuity
 9. Trinkgeld **10.** honorarium
bon vivant... **7.** epicure, gourmet
 8. gourmand, hedonist, sybarite
 10. boonfellow, good fellow,
 voluptuary **12.** Heliogabalus (anc)
bony... **4.** hard, thin **6.** osteal, skinny
 7. osseous **8.** rawboned, skeletal
bonze (Far East)... **2.** bo **4.** monk
boo... **4.** hoot, jeer, razz **7.** catcall,
 feather (ostrich) **9.** raspberry
 10. Bronx cheer
boob... **4.** dupe, fool, goon, jerk
 5. chump, dunce **6.** nitwit
 7. fathead **9.** schlemiel, simpleton
boobook... **3.** owl **8.** morepork
booby hatch... **3.** can, jug **4.** jail
 6. asylum, cooler, prison
 8. hoosegow, madhouse
 11. institution (mental)
boodle... **3.** sop **4.** loot, swag
 5. booty, bribe, bunch, crowd, graft,
 money (hush) **6.** spoils **8.** caboodle
 10. pork barrel **11.** counterfeit
boohoo... **3.** rob **4.** bawl, hoot, weep
 5. shout **8.** sailfish
book... **2.** mo (abbr) **3.** day **4.** hire,
 opus, tome **5.** album, atlas, Bible,
 canto, diary, folio, liber, novel
 6. agenda, engage, ledger, manual,
 missal, primer, record, sign up,
 volume **7.** diurnal, journal, mystery
 8. brochure, libretto, register,
 schedule, songbook, whodunit
 9. paperback, storybook
 10. literature, memorandum
 11. publication
book (pert to)...
 announcement.. **5.** blurb
 back.. **5.** spine

binder.. **12.** bibliopegist
binding devise.. **7.** trindle
collector.. **10.** bibliothec
 12. bibliomaniac **14.** bibliothecaire
cover.. **5.** recto **6.** jacket
destroyer.. **11.** biblioclast
division.. **7.** chapter
lore.. **10.** bibliology
lover.. **11.** bibliophile
one versed in.. **11.** bibliognost
page.. **5.** folio
seller.. **10.** bibliopole (rare books)
sheath.. **5.** forel
size.. **6.** quarto
stealer.. **11.** biblioklept
style.. **6.** Aldine **8.** Etruscan
 9. Arabesque
treatise.. **8.** isagogue
worshiper.. **11.** bibliolater
writer.. **13.** bibliographer
book (religious)... **4.** Ordo **5.** Bible,
 Kells, Tobit **6.** Esdras, Mormon
 7. Psalter **8.** Holy Writ
 9. Apocrypha, Catechism, Testament
 10. Pentateuch, Scriptures
Book of...
 award (Harvard).. **5.** detur
 Concord.. **8.** Lutheran
 Discipline.. **12.** Presbyterian
 Hours.. **5.** Horae
 Moses (Laws).. **10.** Pentateuch
 Psalms.. **7.** Psalter
 the Dead.. **12.** Pyramid Texts
boom... **3.** hum **4.** gain, peal, raft,
 roar, spar, zoom **5.** boost, cable,
 speed, sprit, withe **6.** thrive, upturn
 7. pontoon, resound, thunder
 8. bowsprit, flourish, increase
 9. cannonade, Golden Age, outrigger
 10. navigation, prosperity
boomerang... **6.** resile **7.** rebound
 8. backfire, ricochet
Boomer State... **8.** Oklahoma
boon... **3.** gay **4.** bene, gift, good,
 nice **5.** favor, jolly **6.** jovial, kindly
 7. benefit, gleeful, godsend, present
 8. blessing **9.** convivial
 11. benefaction
boor... **3.** cad, oaf **4.** hick, lout
 5. churl, clown, yokel **6.** rustic
 7. bumpkin, cauboge, peasant, ruffian
 9. roughneck, vulgarian
 10. clodhopper, husbandman
boorish... **4.** rude **5.** gawky, surly
 6. clumsy, rustic, sullen **7.** awkward,
 crabbed, loutish, uncouth **8.** churlish,
 inurbane, lubberly, ungainly
 9. farmerish, unrefined
 11. countrified
boost... **4.** help, hike, lift, plug, push
 5. heist, raise, shove **6.** assist,
 thrust **7.** commend, hearten, inspire,
 promote, upswing **8.** advocate,
 increase **9.** promotion, publicize
 10. assistance **11.** advancement
 12. commendation
boot... **3.** pac **4.** kick, pack, sack,
 shoe **5.** armor, bonus, jemmy, kamik,
 wader **6.** buskin, fumble, rookie,
 sheath **7.** dismiss, recruit, trainee
 8. balmoral, enlistee, inductee,
 napoleon **9.** discharge

booth ... 3. hut, pew 4. crib, loge
  5. stall, stand, store 6. manger
  11. compartment
booty ... 4. gain, loot, pelf, swag
  5. graft, prize, spoil 6. spoils
  7. pillage, plunder
booze ... 4. bout 5. drink, spree
  6. liquor 8. potation
boozer ... 3. pub, sot 5. toper
  6. barfly, bibber, saloon 7. guzzler,
  reveler, tippler 8. drunkard
  9. alcoholic, inebriate
  11. dipsomaniac
Bordeaux, France ...
  capital .. 7. Gironde
  entrance gate .. 16. Porte de
  Bourgogne
  Roman name .. 9. Burdigala
  wine .. 5. Cotes, Medoc, Palus
  6. claret (best–known), Graves
border ... 3. hem, rim, tip 4. abut,
  brow, dado, edge, line, rand, rund
  5. bound, brink, flank, limit, marge,
  shore, skirt, touch, verge, wings
  6. adjoin, fringe, margin, ruffle
  7. bordure, confine, flounce, selvage,
  valance 8. boundary, frontier,
  neighbor 9. periphery 10. borderland,
  sidepieces
border (pert to) ...
  heraldry .. 4. orle 7. bordure
  lace .. 5. picot 9. hemstitch
  picture .. 3. mat 4. orle
  stamps (PO) .. 8. tressure
  wall .. 4. dado
Border Country (Russ) ... 6. Latvia,
  Poland 7. Estonia, Finland, Romania
  9. Lithuania
bordering ... 4. near 6. edging
  7. binding 8. abutting, adjacent,
  marginal, skirting, trimming
  9. adjoining, immediate
  10. contiguous
Border State (Civil War Era) ...
  8. Arkansas, Delaware, Kentucky,
  Maryland, Missouri, Virginia
  9. Tennessee 13. North Carolina
bore ... 3. irk, tap 4. drip, hole, pest,
  pill, ream 5. auger, drill, eagre (tidal
  wave), weary 6. bother, cavity, pierce
  7. caliber, carried 8. diameter,
  nuisance, ordnance (anc), puncture,
  terebate 9. penetrate, perforate, tidal
  wave, worriment 10. capability
  11. perforation
boredom ... 5. ennui 6. tedium
boring ... 3. dry 5. yawny 6. tiring
  7. irksome, tedious 8. piercing,
  tiresome, wearying 11. penetrating
boring tool ... 3. awl, bit 4. rime (Eng)
  5. auger, drill 6. gimlet, reamer,
  wimble
born ... 3. ean, nee 4. bred, foal, lamb
  5. calve, hatch, issue 7. hatched,
  quicken 9. originate
born (pert to) ...
  after father's death .. 10. posthumous
  again (Theos) .. 7. renewed
  high .. 8. imperial 11. to the purple
  14. porphyrogenite
  in the country .. 10. rurigenous
  nature .. 6. inborn

well .. 7. eugenic
borne ... 4. held 6. eolian, upheld
  7. aeolian, carried, endured
  8. produced 9. cherished, supported
  10. maintained
borné ... 6. narrow 7. limited
  12. narrow–minded
Borneo ...
  aborigine .. 4. Dyak (Dayak), Iban
  5. Dusun, Malay
  ape .. 9. orangutan (orangoutang)
  island of .. 11. Archipelago (Malay)
  mountain .. 8. Kinibalu
  pirate tribe (anc) .. 5. Bajau 9. Samal
  Laut
  protectorate .. 6. Brunei 7. Sarawak
  river .. 6. Rejang
  rubber .. 9. gutta susu
  sea .. 4. Java, Sulu 10. South China
  tree (antproof) .. 7. billian
borough ... 4. burg, town, ward
  5. burgh, manor 6. suffix
  8. precinct, township 10. municipium
  11. corporation 12. municipality
borrow ... 4. copy, take 5. adopt,
  steal, touch 8. simulate
  10. plagiarize, substitute
  11. appropriate
borsch, borscht ... 4. soup (beet juice)
  6. ragout
borzoi ... 9. wolfhound
Bos ... 2. ox 3. cow 4. beef, calf, neat
  6. cattle 8. ruminant 9. quadruped
bosh ... 4. bull, bunk 5. trash
  6. humbug, piffle 7. baloney
  8. buncombe, falderal, nonsense
  9. poppycock 10. balderdash
bosky ... 5. braky, bushy, shady, tipsy,
  woody 6. woodsy 7. fuddled,
  shadowy 11. intoxicated (Eng)
Bosnia ...
  capital .. 8. Sarajevo
  native .. 5. Croat 8. Adriatic, Croatian
  race .. 4. tall 14. Slavic–speaking
  republic (present) .. 10. Yugoslavia
  site .. 15. Balkan Peninsula
bosom ... 4. bust 5. chest 6. breast,
  dickey, spirit 7. cherish, embrace
  8. inner man, interior 9. enclosure
  (loving), innermost 10. affections
  12. heartstrings
boss ... 4. dean 6. manage, master
  7. foreman 8. director 9. supervise
  14. superintendent
boss (pert to) ...
  architecture .. 4. knob, stud
  12. protuberance
  politics .. 4. whip 6. leader 7. cacique
  (W Indies) 8. dictator
  sculpture .. 5. chase, raise 6. emboss,
  relief 7. relievo 8. ornament
  shield .. 4. umbo
bosthoon (Anglo–Ir) ... 4. boor, dolt
  5. clout
Boston ...
  building (Hist) .. 11. Faneuil Hall
  14. Old North Church
  capital of .. 13. Massachusetts
  famed names .. 6. Holmes, Lowell
  7. Emerson 8. Whittier 9. Hawthorne
  10. Longfellow
  hero .. 10. Paul Revere

history.. 8. Massacre (1770), Tea
  Party (1773)
Puritan leader.. 8. Winthrop (Gov)
river.. 7. Charles
botany (pert to)...
  development (plant).. 7. peloria
  10. craticular
  research terms.. 7. ecology
  8. cytology, taxonomy 9. pathology
  10. morphology
  science.. 7. biology 9. plant life
Botany Bay...
  colony (original).. 5. penal
  discoverer.. 4. Cook (1770)
  settlers.. 8. convicts (Eng)
  site.. 9. Australia
botch... 3. fix, mar 4. hash, mend,
  mess, mull 5. patch, spoil 6. boggle,
  bungle, fiasco, goof up, muddle
  7. blunder, failure
both... 3. two 4. duad, pair 5. twain
  6. as well 7. equally
bother... 3. ado, ail, nag 4. fuss,
  to–do 5. annoy, tease 6. badger,
  bustle, harass, molest, pester, pother
  7. concern, confuse, fluster, torment,
  trouble 8. bewilder, distress, irritate,
  nuisance 9. commotion
  10. discommode, excitement,
  perplexity 11. botheration,
  disturbance 13. inconvenience
bothersome... 6. trying 7. galling,
  irksome, onerous 8. annoying
  9. difficult, worrisome 10. disturbing
  11. troublesome
both sexes... 7. epicene, sexless
  10. effeminate
bo tree (Buddh)... 5. pipal 6. sacred
  (at Buddh Gaya)
bottle... 3. pig 4. lota, vial 5. cruet,
  flask, gourd, phial 6. carafe, carboy,
  flagon, lagena, matara, vacuum
  7. ampoule (ampule), ampulla (anc),
  costrel, enclose 8. borachio,
  calabash, decanter, preserve
  9. aryballus (anc)
bottom... 3. bed (water) 4. base, glen,
  hulk, less, root, rump, vale, vlei
  5. basin, fanny, floor, marsh, nadir
  6. coulee, hopper (RR) 7. bedrock,
  channel 9. underside 10. nethermost
bottomless... 7. abysmal, abyssal
  8. baseless 9. plumbless, soundless
  10. fathomless 12. unfathomable
boudoir... 7. bedroom, cabinet,
  chamber 10. bedchamber
bouffant... 4. full 7. bulging 9. puffed
  out
bough... 4. fork, limb, spur, twig
  5. shoot, spray, sprig 6. branch
  8. offshoot
bought... 8. boughten (dial)
  9. purchased (see also *buy*)
bouillabaisse... 7. chowder (fish)
boulevard... 4. pike 7. highway
  8. highroad, turnpike
  12. thoroughfare
bounce... 3. hop 4. bang, brag,
  bump, jump, kick, leap, snap
  5. bound, burst, carom, eject, shake,
  thump, verve 6. levity, recoil, spring
  7. bluster, bravado, rebound

  8. buoyancy, outburst, ricochet
  9. discharge, lightness 10. resilience
  11. fanfaronade, ostentation,
  springiness 16. lightheartedness
bouncer... 4. liar 5. bully 6. fibber,
  ouster 7. boaster, chucker, whopper
  8. braggart, fanfaron 9. falsehood
bound... 3. hop, run 4. jump, leap,
  skip, tied 5. ambit, limit, speed,
  taped, tiled (secrecy), vault, verge
  6. border, bounce, bourne, domain,
  hurdle, spring, sprint 7. barrier,
  certain, confine, cramped, limited,
  obliged, pledged, rebound, secured,
  trussed 8. beholden, boundary,
  confined, enclosed, frontier, precinct,
  promised, resolved, surround
  9. committed, duty–bound,
  encompass (incompass)
  10. borderland, determined,
  restrained, restricted 11. termination
  12. circumscribe
boundary... 3. end, rim 4. edge, mere
  (obs), mete, term, wall 5. ambit,
  bourn, fence, limit, march, verge
  7. barrier 8. terminus 9. perimeter
  11. conterminal, termination
  13. circumference
bounder... 3. cad 4. snob 6. rotter
  7. epicier, parvenu, upstart
bounding (Mus)... 8. saltando
boundless... 4. vast 7. endless
  8. infinite, termless 9. limitless,
  unlimited 10. unconfined
  11. illimitable 12. interminable,
  unfathomable
bounds... 4. pale 6. frames, limits,
  skirts 7. borders, margins
  8. confines, outlines 9. outskirts
  10. delineated 11. limitations
bounteous... 5. ample 6. freely, lavish
  7. liberal 8. generous, prodigal
  9. bountiful, plentiful 10. munificent
  11. extravagant
bountiful... 4. rich 7. copious, fertile,
  liberal, teeming, uberous
  8. abundant, fruitful, generous,
  prolific 9. bounteous, exuberant,
  luxuriant, plentiful
bounty... 3. fee 4. gift 5. bonus
  6. reward 7. largess, premium,
  subsidy 8. gratuity, solatium, sportula
  9. pourboire 10. generosity, liberality
  11. beneficence 12. compensation
bouquet... 4. odor, posy 5. aroma,
  cigar, spray 7. corsage, flowers,
  incense, nosegay, perfume
  9. fragrance, redolence
  10. compliment
Bourbon, bourbon...
  ancient.. 7. Reunion (Isl)
  dynasty.. 5. Spain 6. France, Naples
  famed personage.. 4. Duke
    13. French General
  famed ruins.. 7. castles (Dukes')
  liquor.. 6. whisky (whiskey)
  rose.. 9. Le Phoenix
bourd... 3. fun 4. jest 7. mockery
bourdon... 4. stop (organ) 5. baton,
  music (bagpipe), spear, staff
  6. burden (Fr), cudgel
bourgeois... 4. type (size)

8. commoner 9. common man, plutocrat 10. capitalist 11. middle—class, proletarian

bourn, bourne... 3. aim 4. goal, port 5. bound, brook, limit, realm 6. arroyo, stream 7. rivulet 8. boundary 11. destination

bourock... 3. hut 4. heap (stone) 5. crowd, mound 7. cluster

Bourse... 5. Board 8. Exchange 13. Stock Exchange

bouse... 3. cup 4. haul (Naut), swig, tope 5. booze, drink, heave 6. beaker 7. carouse

bouser... 5. toper 6. boozer, bursar 7. fuddler, swigger

bout... 2. go 3. act, war 4. coup, fray, game, spar, turn 5. cycle, fight, match, revel, round, scrap, set—to, spree, trial 6. fracas, inning, series, stroke 7. attempt, circuit, contest, exploit 8. conflict, maneuver, rotation 9. encounter 10. enterprise, prize fight 11. celebration

boutade... 4. whim 5. dance, prank 7. caprice 8. outbreak 11. composition (Mus)

boutonniere... 6. flower 7. bouquet, nosegay 8. incision 10. buttonhole

bovine... 2. ox 3. Bos, cow, yak 4. bull, dull, goat, kine, zebu 5. bison, dogie, steer, stirk, zebus 6. catalo, cattle, oxlike, stolid, stupid 7. bullock, cattalo, taurine, vaccine 8. maverick, sluggish 10. complacent 11. beef—brained

bow... 3. arc, bob, nod 4. arch, beak, bend, knot, node, prow 5. bulge, curve, debut, embow, kneel, stoop, yield 6. assent, convex, curtsy, encore, kowtow, salaam, submit, weapon 7. curtain (Theat), incline, rainbow 8. crossbow, greeting 9. obeisance 11. fiddlestick 12. bow and scrape

bow (out)... 4. exit 6. depart 7. concede, dismiss

Bow Bells (pert to)...
area.. 10. cockneydom
bells of.. 9. Bow Church (St Mary le Bow)
city.. 6. London

bowels... 3. pit 4. guts 5. abyss, chasm, depth 7. innards, insides, viscera 8. entrails, interior (earth) 10. compassion (Shak), tenderness

bower... 5. abode, arbor, cards (game), kiosk 6. alcove, pandal 7. retreat, shelter 11. summerhouse

bowfin... 4. Amia 7. mudfish

bowhead (Arctic)... 10. Right whale

Bowie, bowie (pert to)...
instrument.. 5. knife
knife inventor.. 5. Bowie (James)
Scottish.. 3. tub 4. cask 8. milk pail
State nickname.. 8. Arkansas

bowkail... 4. kale (kail) 7. cabbage

bowl... 3. cup, jug 4. ball, roll, vase 5. arena, basin, kitty (poker), mazer, rogan 6. cavity, crater, hollow, patina (anc), vessel 7. stadium 8. washbowl 9. washbasin 10. hippodrome,

receptacle 12. amphitheater

Bowl (sports)...
Abilene.. 5. Pecan
Atlanta.. 5. Peach
Dallas.. 6. Cotton
El Paso.. 3. Sun
Honolulu.. 4. Hula
Houston.. 10. Bluebonnet
Jacksonville.. 5. Gator
Memphis.. 7. Liberty
Miami.. 6. Orange
Mobile.. 6. Senior
New Orleans.. 5. Sugar
Orlando.. 9. Tangerine
Pasadena.. 4. Rose
Sacramento.. 8. Camellia

bowlegged... 6. valgus

bowler... 3. hat 5. derby 6. kegler 7. trundle

bowling... 4. ball, rink 5. alley, green, spare 6. strike 7. rolling, tenpins 8. ninepins 10. greensward, playground

Bowling Green... 4. Park (Ky, NY)

bowsprit... 3. jib 4. boom 6. steeve

box... 2. ro (Jap) 3. bin, pew, pyx 4. arca (alms), cage, case, cist, cuff, kist, kite, loge, safe, spar, tray 5. brace (faro), caddy (tea), cheat, crate, stall, vault 6. buffet, carton, casket, coffin, encase 7. confine, enclose 8. bungalow 9. fisticuff 11. compartment

box (pert to)...
alms.. 4. arca
bed.. 7. springs
cosmetic.. 4. inro
floating.. 3. car (for fish)
lifesaving.. 9. faking box
railroad.. 6. boxcar 8. box wagon
resistance.. 8. rheostat
sewing.. 5. plait, pleat
sleigh.. 4. pung
sports.. 5. score
tea.. 5. caddy 8. canister
theater.. 4. loge, seat
tree.. 8. Buxaceae

boxer... 3. dog, pug 5. champ 6. miller 7. bruiser, fighter, sparrer 8. derby hat, pugilist 11. fisticuffer 12. prizefighter 13. militia member (Chin)

boxer weight... 3. fly 5. heavy, light 6. bantam, middle, welter 7. feather 10. light heavy

boxing... 4. bout 5. match, set—to 7. contest, crating 8. pugilism, sparring 10. encasement, fisticuffs 12. shadowboxing

boy... 2. bo 3. bat, bus, lad, tad, tot 4. nino, page, puer 5. child, gamin, knave, rogue, water, youth 6. garçon, laddie, master, rascal, shaver, urchin, varlet 7. callant, gossoon 8. muchacho

boy (pert to)...
book author.. 5. Alger, Henty
errand.. 4. page 9. messenger
friend.. 4. beau 10. sweetheart
interjection.. 5. Oh boy
organization.. 6. Scouts
Scout founder.. 11. Baden—Powell

street .. 4. Arab 6. urchin
boycott ... 3. ban 6. oppose, strike
9. blackball, ostracize
brace ... 3. leg, tie, two 4. bind, cord,
gird, pair, prop, span, stay, yoke
5. spale, staff, stave, strut 6. couple
7. bandage, bracket, fulcrum, refresh,
rigging, support 8. encircle
9. reinforce, stimulate 10. invigorate,
recuperate, strengthen
bracelet ... 5. armil, armor, chain
6. sankha 7. armilla 8. handcuff,
vambrace 10. calombigas
bracer ... 4. prop 5. tonic 7. reviver,
support 8. pick–me–up, roborant
9. stimulant
bracing ... 5. crisp, tonic 10. salubrious
11. stimulating 12. invigorating
bracken ... 4. fern 5. brake, plaid
bracket ... 4. mark 5. ancon, angle,
group, strut 6. corbel, sconce
7. fixture 11. electrolier
brackish ... 4. foul 5. salty 7. saltish
8. nauseous 11. distasteful
bract ... 4. leaf 5. glume, palea, palet
6. spathe 8. bractlet 9. bracteole
brad ... 3. pin 4. nail 5. sprig
brae ... 4. bank, down, hill, moor
5. slope 6. valley 8. hillside
brag ... 4. crow 5. bluff, boast, vaunt
6. flaunt 7. blow off, bluster,
deceive, roister, swagger 8. braggart
9. gasconade 11. braggadocio
braggart ... 4. brag 6. crower
7. boaster 8. boastful, fanfaron
9. blusterer, swaggerer
11. braggadocio 12. swashbuckler
bragging ... 11. thrasonical
Brahma ... 3. God 4. fowl 5. Hindu
Brahman (pert to) ...
learned .. 6. pundit
precept .. 5. sutra 8. netineti
sacred book .. 4. Veda
Sanskrit scholar .. 6. pundit
Supreme soul .. 6. Brahma
title .. 3. Aya
Trinity .. 4. Siva 6. Brahma, Vishnu
woman created by .. 6. Alalya
Brahmin ... 4. prig, snob 7. egghead
8. highbrow 10. high–hatter
12. intellectual
braid ... 3. cue 4. cord, gimp, hair,
plat, trim 5. lacet, orris, plait, pleat,
queue, tress, twist, weave 6. oxreim,
sennit 7. entwine, outline, pigtail,
topknot 8. ornament, soutache
9. interlace 10. interweave
brain ... 4. head, mind, nous
6. psyche, reason 9. intellect,
mentality 10. encephalon, vital organ
brain (pert to) ...
canal .. 4. iter
case .. 3. pan 5. skull 7. cranium
division .. 8. cerebrum 10. cerebellum
11. pons Varolii 16. medulla
oblongata
matter .. 4. alba, dura, tela
operation .. 6. trepan 8. trephine
term .. 4. lobe, lura 6. sulcus
7. fissure 9. ventricle
11. convolution
tumor .. 6. glioma

X–ray .. 14. encephalograph
brainless ... 4. dumb 5. dizzy, giddy,
silly 6. unwise 7. asinine, foolish,
witless 9. senseless 10. unthinking
11. thoughtless 14. scatterbrained
brainy ... 5. smart 6. bright, clever
9. brilliant
brake ... 4. cage, curb, drag, fern, reef,
skid, trap 5. check, delay, snare
6. bridle, retard 7. dilemma, thicket
9. canebrake 10. decelerate
bramble ... 4. burr 5. berry, brier,
shrub (prickly), thorn 6. nettle
7. prickle, thicket 9. brierbush
10. blackberry 12. brambleberry
branch ... 3. arm, set 4. axil, fork,
limb, rame, stem, twig, wing
5. bough, class, frond, ramus, shoot,
spray, sprig, vimen, withe 6. divide,
member, ramify, sprout, stolon,
stream, switch 7. descent, diverge,
lineage 8. category, division, offshoot
9. affiliate, bloodline, filiation
10. department, descendant,
triskelion (three branches)
Branchiata (Group) ... 6. fishes
9. Crustacea 10. Amphibians
brand ... 4. burn, iron, kind, mark,
sear, smit 5. label, stamp, sword,
torch 6. smirch, stigma 7. earmark,
feature, hot iron, quality 8. gridiron
(Hist), hallmark 9. trademark
10. stigmatize
brandish ... 5. shake, swing, wield
6. flaunt 7. flutter, glitter 8. flourish
brandy ... 6. cognac 7. rosolio (cordial)
8. rossolis 11. aguardiente
brash ... 4. dash, rain, rash 5. gruff,
saucy, storm 6. scurry 7. brittle
(lumber) 8. impudent, tactless
9. impetuous
brass ... 4. cash, gall 5. alloy, braze,
cheek, money, nerve, plate 6. latten,
ormolu, platen 8. brass hat, officers,
sisterce (anc coin) 9. impudence
10. instrument (wind)
brass (wind instrument) ... 5. bugle
6. cornet, lituus (anc) 7. althorn,
brasses, clarion, saxhorn, trumpet
8. trombone 9. saxophone
10. flügelhorn, French horn
brasserie ... 6. saloon 7. brewery
8. beer shop
brassy ... 4. bold 6. aerose, brazen
8. impudent
brat ... 3. bib, elf, imp 4. film, minx,
scum 5. apron, bairn, child, cloak,
minor 6. mantle 7. garment
8. clothing 9. offspring 14. enfant
terrible, whippersnapper
brattice ... 7. support 9. partition
(mining) 10. breastwork
bravado ... 6. bounce, daring, defial
7. bluster, bombast, bravery, bravura
8. defiance 11. braggadocio
brave ... 4. bold, buck, dare, game,
hero, meet 5. boast, bravo, bully,
front, manly, showy, stout 6. daring,
endure, heroic, Indian 7. Amerind,
gallant, soldier, spartan, valiant,
warrior 8. confront, fearless, intrepid,
valorous 10. courageous, untimorous

12. stouthearted
bravery... 5. valor 7. bravado, bravura, courage
bravo... 3. mug 4. good, thug
5. rough, tough 6. bandit 7. gorilla, ruffian 8. assassin 9. blusterer, cutthroat, roisterer, roughneck, swaggerer 11. exclamation
bravura... 4. dash 5. macho 6. daring
7. bravado, bravery 10. brilliance (Mus), confidence
brawl... 3. row 4. fray, fury, rage, riot
5. broil, fight, furor, scold 6. affray, clamor, fracas, hubbub, rumpus, shindy, tumult, uproar 7. dispute, quarrel, rampage, turmoil, wrangle
10. hullabaloo, turbulence
11. altercation, embroilment
brawny... 5. beefy, burly, lusty, thewy
6. fleshy, robust, sinewy, strong, sturdy 7. callous 8. muscular, powerful, stalwart 9. corpulent
bray... 4. beat 5. blare, bleat, grind, neigh 6. heehaw, powder, thrash, whinny 9. pulverize, triturate
12. disintegrate
braze... 4. weld 5. plate (with metal)
6. solder
brazen... 4. bold, pert 5. brass, brave, harsh 6. brassy, cheeky, harden
7. aweless, callous 8. immodest, impudent, indurate, insolent, metallic
9. bold-faced, shameless, unabashed
10. unblushing 13. bronze-colored, harsh-sounding
brazier... 5. grill 6. brazer 7. hibachi
8. barbecue, gridiron 10. money chest (anc)
brazil... 3. red 4. wood (hard)
8. dyestuff
Brazil... see also *Brazilian*
capital.. 8. Brasilia 12. Rio de Janeiro (old)
city.. 5. Bahia, Belem 6. Recife, Santos 8. Sao Paulo 9. Horizonte
11. Porto Alegre, Sao Salvador
discoverer.. 6. Cabral (1500)
Falls (world wonder).. 6. Iguacu
lake.. 12. Lago dos Patos
product.. 6. coffee
river.. 5. Negro 6. Amazon, Branco, Paraná 7. Madeira, Orinoco
8. Paraguay 9. Tocantins
Brazilian (pert to)...
aborigine.. 5. Carib
ant (powerful).. 9. tucandera
bird.. 3. ani, ara 5. arara, macaw
6. cuckoo, darter, tiribo 7. maracan, sierema
crab (land).. 8. horseman
dance.. 5. samba 6. maxixe
drink.. 5. assai
flycatcher.. 6. yetapa
Indian.. 4. Anta 5. Arara, Araua, Guana 6. Tupian 8. Araquayu, Arawakan (tribe)
mammal.. 5. tapir
parrot.. 3. ara 5. macaw 6. tiriba
plant.. 4. yaje 5. caroa 7. ayapana (Med)
tree.. 3. apa 4. anda (oil), jara
5. assai (palm) 6. embuia, satiné

7. araroba, gomavel, seringa (rubber), wallaba 8. bakupari
10. barbatimao
weight.. 4. onza 5. libra 6. arroba
7. quintal
breach... 3. gap 4. rent, rift 5. break, burst, chasm, cleft, split 6. schism
7. caesura, dispute, quarrel, rupture
8. fracture, solecism 9. violation
10. disruption, falling-out, infraction, separation 12. infringement, interruption 16. misunderstanding
bread... 4. cush, food, gelt, loaf, pain (obs), pita, pone, rusk 5. azyme, miche, panis, toady, toast, tommy
6. damper, panada, sippet 7. chapati, hoecake, matzoth 8. tortilla
9. eucharist (part of), sourbread
10. livelihood
bread (pert to)...
basket.. 7. stomach
bread and butter.. 5. plate 6. letter (of thanks), pickle, staple 7. prosaic
8. juvenile
fruit.. 3. nut 4. tree 7. castana
8. chestnut
winner.. 6. earner, toiler, worker
7. workman 10. wage earner
break... 3. gap 4. dash, knap, luck, lull, rent, rift, ruin, rush, slip, snap, stop 5. blank, burst, cleft, lapse, letup, pause, smash, train 6. breach, chance, change, depose, escape, hiatus, injury, lacuna, market (Finan), recess, subdue, weaken 7. blunder, caesura (cesura), disrupt, getaway, respite, rupture, shatter, violate
8. bad break, bankrupt, breakage, breather, fracture, interval
9. interlude, jail break, violation
10. depreciate, falling-out, infraction, suspension 11. fragmentize
12. intermission, interruption
13. discontinuity
break down... 3. cry, sob 4. bawl, raze, weep 5. crush 6. boohoo, divide, master, reduce, revolt, subdue
7. analyze, crack up, dissect, resolve, unnerve 8. classify, collapse, separate
9. decompose, overwhelm, subdivide
breakdown... 7. debacle, failure
8. analysis 9. cataclysm
10. dissection, impairment, revolution
breakfast... 6. brunch (late)
8. dejeuner 10. chota hazri
break in... 4. open, tame 5. enter, force, train 6. butt in, subdue
7. barge in, intrude, prepare
9. interrupt 10. housebreak
break up... 4. cure, rift, ruin 5. decay, leave, smash, spall, split, upset
7. adjourn, atomize, crumble, disband, relieve, scatter, shatter 8. disperse, dissolve, separate, unsettle
9. decompose 10. demobilize, dispersion, disruption 11. disorganize, dissolution 12. disintegrate
breakwater... 4. dike, mole, pier
5. jetty, jutty 6. refuge, riprap 7. sea wall 8. buttress 10. embankment
11. obstruction
bream... 4. fish, scup 5. clean (Naut)

breast... **4.** bust, soul, teat **5.** bosom, cheat, gland (mammary), heart **6.** spirit, thorax **8.** inner man **9.** encounter

breast (pert to)...
absence of.. **7.** amastia
bone.. **6.** ratite **7.** sternum
breastlike.. **7.** mastoid
plate.. **4.** Urim **5.** armor, ephod **6.** gorget, lorica **7.** poitrel **12.** breastsummer
works.. **7.** defense, parapet, railing (Naut), ravelin **8.** mantelet **9.** banquette

breath... **3.** air **4.** fume, life, odor, pant, puff, wind **5.** draft, pause, prana, scent, smell, touch, vapor, whiff **6.** breeze, caress, flatus, pneuma, spirit **7.** halitus, respite, whisper **8.** breather **9.** emanation, ozostomia, utterance **10.** exhalation **11.** respiration

breathe... **3.** say, tip **4.** gulp, live, mean, pneo (comb form), rest, sigh, tell **5.** exist, imbue, imply, scent, smell, snuff **6.** evince, exhale, infuse, inhale, let out, reveal **7.** bespeak, divulge, emanate, instill (instil), pervade, respire, suspire, whisper **8.** aspirate, indicate

breathe (pert to)...
comb form.. **4.** pnea, pneo
convulsively.. **4.** sigh
hard.. **4.** pant
one's last.. **3.** die **6.** expire, perish **7.** decease, succumb
vengeance.. **9.** retaliate

breather... **4.** lull, rest **5.** break, pause, truce **6.** recess **7.** interim, respite **9.** interlude **12.** intermission

breathing... **5.** alive, vital **6.** living, zoetic **7.** animate, panting, respite **8.** animated **9.** conscious, phonation, utterance **10.** aspiration **11.** respiration, respiratory, ventilation **12.** articulation

breathing (pert to)...
apertures.. **5.** stoma **8.** spiracle
morbid.. **4.** rale **7.** stridor **8.** rhonchus
painful.. **8.** dyspnoea
pause.. **7.** caesura
smooth.. **4.** lene

breathless... **4.** awed, dead, gone, keen **5.** eager **6.** ardent, fervid, winded **7.** airless, demised, fervent **8.** deceased, lifeless, windless, wordless **9.** impatient **10.** astonished, speechless, spellbound

bred... **6.** hybrid, inbred, reared, tablet (compressed) **7.** lowbred, mongrel **8.** exogamic, purebred **9.** autogamic, crossbred, endogamic, half–caste, interbred **11.** half–blooded, impregnated, inseminated **12.** thoroughbred

bree... **4.** brow **5.** broth, scare **6.** liquor **7.** eyebrow **9.** commotion **11.** disturbance

breech... **4.** doup, rump, tall **5.** fanny, stern **6.** bottom **8.** buttocks **9.** posterior, underside

breeches... **5.** chaps, jeans, pants, trews **8.** britches, jodhpurs, trousers **10.** pantaloons **12.** galligaskins (jocular)

breed... **3.** ilk **4.** kind, race, rear, sort **5.** beget, brood, caste, class, mixed, raise, stock, train, tribe **6.** family **7.** descent, educate, lineage, mongrel, produce **8.** engender, generate, instruct **9.** originate, posterity, procreate, propagate **10.** crossbreed

breeding... **6.** polish **7.** culture, decorum, exogamy, manners, raising, rearing **8.** autogamy, endogamy, hatching, training **9.** education, fostering, gentility **10.** deportment, upbringing **11.** instruction, procreation, propagation

breeding place... **4.** nest **5.** nidus **7.** brooder **8.** hatchery **9.** incubator **10.** birthplace

breeze... **3.** air, row **4.** aura, pirr, snap, stir, wind **5.** cinch, rumor **6.** squall, zephyr **7.** ill wind, whisper **8.** duck soup, pushover **9.** commotion **11.** disturbance

breezy... **4.** airy, spry **5.** blowy, brisk, gusty, windy **6.** drafty, jaunty, lively **7.** squally **8.** animated, blustery, spirited **9.** vivaceous **12.** lighthearted

Brehon Law... **4.** eric (anc) **10.** Senchus Mor **12.** Book of Aicill

breve... **4.** note (Mus), writ **5.** brief, order **7.** compose

brevet... **4.** fiat **5.** ukase **6.** decree **7.** warrant **10.** commission **11.** certificate (teaching)

breveté... **8.** patented

breviary... **6.** manual, ritual **7.** compend, epitome

brevity... **9.** briefness, shortness, terseness **11.** conciseness, transcience **12.** succinctness

brew... **3.** ale, mix **4.** grog, plot **5.** hatch, steep **6.** cook up, foment, gather, menace, scheme **7.** concoct, distill (distil) **8.** contrive, threaten **9.** aqua vitae

brewer's grain... **4.** corn, malt **6.** barley

brewer's yeast... **4.** barm **6.** leaven

bribe... **3.** oil, sop **5.** bonus **6.** boodle, buy off, grease, suborn **9.** hush money

bric–a–brac... **6.** curios **7.** artware **8.** antiques, trinkets **9.** artifacts, objet d'art **11.** knickknacks

bric–a–brac cabinet... **7.** étagère, whatnot

brick... **3.** bat **4.** dobe, tile **5.** adobe, stone **6.** pament (pamment) **7.** clinker **8.** hardness

brick (pert to)...
color.. **3.** red **7.** Saravan
kiln.. **5.** clamp
layer.. **3.** cad (helper) **5.** mason
laying.. **8.** toothing
slang.. **3.** pip **4.** lulu **5.** dilly, peach **6.** corker, winner **8.** jim–dandy **10.** sweetheart **11.** crackerjack **12.** lollapaloosa

unburned.. 5. samel
brickbat... 4. rock 5. stone 7. affront, missile, offense 9. indignity
bridal (pert to)...
  chest.. 9. trousseau
  flower.. 13. orange blossom
  ode, song.. 9. Brautlied 11. Epithalamon (anc)
  portion.. 3. dot 5. dower, dowry (dowery)
  rite.. 7. wedding 8. marriage, nuptials
bridge... 3. tie 4. arch, bond, link, pons, pont, span 5. unite 7. connect, passage (Mus), pontoon, viaduct 9. structure 13. steppingstone
bridge (pert to)... 4. deck, game, nose 5. magas, truss 6. phoebe (bird) 7. bascule, trestle 9. dentistry 10. ponticello (Mus)
bridge, historic...
  Bridge of Boats.. 10. Hellespont
  Bridge of Sighs.. 6. Venice (Doge's Palace) 7. Al Sirat (Moslem, over infernal fire)
  Norse Myth.. 7. Bifrost (rainbow)
  Old Bridge.. 12. Ponte Vecchio (Florence It, 1345)
Bridge game... 3. bid 4. pass, ruff, slam 6. honors, points, renege, tenace 7. finesse 9. part–score
bridle... 3. bit 4. cord (kite), curb, rein 5. check, guide, smirk 6. fetter, govern, halter, master, simper, subdue 7. harness, manacle, repress, shackle, snaffle 8. cavesson, headgear, noseband, restrain, suppress 9. hackamore, headstall, restraint
brief... 4. curt, plan, writ 5. breve, charm, pithy, short, terse 6. report 7. compact, concise, laconic, summary 8. fleeting, instruct, succinct 9. condensed, ephemeral, summarize, transient 10. compendium, short–lived, transitory 11. compendious 14. inconsiderable
brier, briar... 4. burr, pipe 5. heath, shrub, spine, thorn 7. bramble, bruyère, clotbur, prickle, sticker, thistle 8. adherent 11. French brier
brig... 4. boat 6. vessel 10. guardhouse
brigade... 4. unit 6. troops 7. company 8. regiment
brigand... 5. rover, thief 6. bandit, dacoit, pirate, robber 7. bedouin, cateran, ladrone 8. picaroon 10. highwayman
bright... 3. apt, gay 4. naif, rosy 5. alert, beamy, fresh, lucid, nitid, palmy, sleek, smart, sunny, vivid, witty 6. brainy, clever, florid, garish, golden 7. halcyon, radiant, shining, unfaded 8. cheerful, colorful, flashing, gleaming, luminous, lustrous, splendid 9. brilliant, effulgent, refulgent, sparkling 10. auspicious, epiphanous, glistening, glittering, optimistic 11. intelligent, resplendent
brightness... 5. sheen 6. luster

7. sparkle 8. radiance, splendor 9. alertness, clearness, smartness 10. brilliance 12. cheerfulness, colorfulness, pleasantness
brilliance, brilliancy... 5. éclat, glory 6. luster 7. glitter, oriency, success 8. radiance, splendor 9. smartness, vividness 10. brightness, cleverness
brilliant... 5. smart, vivid, witty 6. bright 7. eminent, radiant, shining 8. gorgeous, meteoric, splendid 9. refulgent, sparkling 10. glittering 11. illustrious
brilliant group... 6. galaxy
brim... 3. hem, lip, rim 4. edge 5. brink, marge, verge 6. border, margin 7. selvage
brine... 3. sea 4. main, salt 5. brack, ocean, tears 6. pickle 7. the deep 12. preservative
bring... 3. get 4. bear, cost, haul, lead 5. carry, fetch, go get, yield 6. convey, entail, induce, obtain 7. contain, involve, require 8. comprise 9. transport
bring about... 2. do 4. make 5. cause 6. create, effect 7. achieve, produce 8. generate 9. instigate 10. accomplish, consummate, effectuate
bring around... 4. cure, heal, ween 5. renew, sober 6. revive 7. convert, restore, win over 8. persuade 10. rejuvenate
bring back... 5. fetch 6. recall, return, revive 7. restore 8. rekindle, remember, retrieve 9. recollect, resurrect
bring forth... 3. ean 4. bear, rise 5. beget, breed, cause, educe, hatch, spawn, yield 6. adduce, elicit, reveal 7. develop, produce 8. disclose, fructify, generate, manifest
bring forward... 4. cite 5. offer 6. adduce, broach, submit 7. advance, improve, promote, propose 8. manifest 9. introduce
bring into...
  bondage.. 7. enslave
  court.. 7. arraign
  harmony.. 6. attune
  position.. 5. align, aline
  union.. 9. correlate
bring together... 5. amass, group 6. gather 7. cluster, compile, reunite 8. assemble 9. harmonize, reconcile 10. accumulate
bring to light... 4. find 5. trace 6. elicit, expose, reveal 7. uncover, unearth 8. disclose, discover
bring to mind... 6. recall, remind 8. look like, remember, resemble
bring to pass... 2. do 5. cause 6. author, father 9. originate 10. accomplish, effectuate
bring up... 4. rear, spew 5. drill, raise, train, vomit 6. foster, muster 7. advance, educate, nurture, propose 9. challenge, condition, cultivate 10. discipline 11. regurgitate

bring up to date... 4. post 6. update
9. modernize 10. streamline
brink... 3. lip, rim 4. bank, brow,
edge, near 5. ditch, marge, skirt,
verge 6. border, margin
briny... 3. sea 4. salt 5. salty
6. saline 8. brackish
Brisbane, capital of... 10. Queensland
(Austral)
Brisbane tree... 3. box 8. quandong
brisk... 3. gay 4. cold, fast, keen,
racy, spry, yern 5. agile, alert, alive,
crisp, fresh, peart, quick, sharp,
tangy, zippy 6. breezy, lively, nimble,
snappy 7. caustic, pungent
8. animated, forceful, spirited,
vigorous 9. energetic, sprightly,
vivacious 11. stimulating
bristle... 4. barb, hair, seta 5. anger,
seton 6. chaeta, palpus, ruffle,
rumple, see red, setula, setule
7. acicula, prickle, stubble
bristling... 5. angry 6. horrid (anc)
7. horrent 9. offensive
bristly... 5. rough, setal 6. hispid,
setose, thorny 7. prickly, scopate,
unshorn 8. acicular, echinate
11. bristlelike
Bristol...
church (England's finest).. 15. St
Mary Redcliffe
fashion.. 6. ataunt 9. shipshape
library.. 6. oldest (British Isles)
milk.. 6. sherry
Britain...
name, ancient.. 6. Albion
name, modern.. 12. British Isles,
Commonwealth, Great Britain
13. United Kingdom
name, Roman.. 9. Brittania
native.. 5. Iceni (tribe), Jutes, Picts,
Scots 6. Angles 7. Britons, Silures
native (sl).. 5. limey (limy), tommy
7. Blighty
sea.. 5. Irish, North 8. Atlantic,
Hebrides
British (pert to)... see also *English*
battle.. 8. Hastings
boat (anc).. 7. coracle
cavalry.. 8. yeomanry
earldom (Egypt).. 7. Khartum (1898)
emblem.. 4. lion
fish.. 8. dragonet (gobylike)
oak.. 5. robur
Order of.. 9. The Garter
prison.. 4. gaol
pudding.. 4. suet 9. Yorkshire
tavern.. 3. pub 9. beerhouse, jerry
shop
thief (wharf).. 6. tosher
Z (letter).. 3. Zed
British people...
author.. 6. Austen, Barrie, Jonson
7. Dickens
buccaneer.. 4. Kidd 6. Morgan
explorer.. 4. Cook, Ross 6. Baffin
7. Stanley 9. Vancouver
11. Livingstone
hero (sea).. 6. Nelson
king (legend, Myth).. 3. Lud 4. Beli,
Bran, Brut 7. Belenus
painter.. 8. Rossetti

philosopher.. 7. Russell (Bertrand)
physicist.. 5. Boyle
poet.. 7. Chaucer 8. Browning,
Tennyson 9. Masefield
soldier.. 7. Redcoat (Hist)
Brittany... 7. Armoric 8. Bretagne
brittle... 4. weak 5. brash, candy,
crisp, frail 6. feeble, infirm, slight
7. fragile, friable 8. delicate, insecure
9. breakable, frangible
11. shatterable
broad... 4. free, girl, lake (Eng), wide
5. ample, large, roomy, thick, wench
7. breadth, diffuse, general, liberal
8. spacious, strumpet, sweeping,
tabulate, tolerant 9. expansive,
extensive 10. collective, commodious,
indefinite, voluminous
13. comprehensive
broad (pert to)...
arrow.. 5. pheon (Her) 6. stigma
8. insignia
footed.. 8. platypod
hearted.. 8. generous
11. magnanimous
minded.. 7. liberal 8. tolerant
9. receptive
broaden... 5. swell, widen 6. dilate,
expand, extend, spread 7. augment,
enlarge, ennoble 8. increase
broadly... 3. far 6. widely 10. far and
wide 11. extensively 12. indefinitely,
right and left
broadside... 4. guns, side 6. folder
7. gunfire, quarter, surface
8. enfilade, sideways 10. broadsheet,
floodlight 11. breadthwise
broadsword... 7. cutlass, Ferrara
8. claymore, scimitar
Brobdingnagian... 5. giant, titan
8. colossal, gigantic 10. gargantuan
brocade... 6. broché, fabric
8. baudekin 9. baldachin
brochan... 7. oatmeal 8. porridge
brochure... 5. tract 6. folder
7. booklet, leaflet 8. chapbook,
pamphlet
brod... 3. awl 4. goad, pike, urge
5. thorn 6. sprout 9. incentive
brode, brodee... 11. embroidered
brodyaga... 7. vagrant 8. vagabond
brogan, brogue... 4. shoe
brogue... 4. burr 5. twang 6. accent
7. dialect
broil... 4. cook, fray, fume 5. brawl,
grill, melee 6. affray, braise (braize),
scorch 7. contest, discord, dispute,
quarrel 8. conflict, grillade, scramble
10. contention, dissension, turbulence
11. altercation, embroilment
broke... 4. flat 6. busted, ruined
8. bankrupt, strapped 9. destitute,
insolvent, penniless
broken... 4. tame 5. broke, bumpy,
burst, rough, tamed 6. chined,
ruined, shaken, uneven, zigzag
7. crushed, décousu, severed,
subdued 8. bankrupt, detached,
impaired, ruptured, sporadic,
weakened 9. conquered, dispersed,
irregular, shattered, unsettled
10. incoherent, incomplete

11. fragmentary, housebroken, interrupted 12. disconnected, domesticated, intermittent 13. discontinuous

broken pottery (anc) ... 5. shard (sherd) 8. potsherd

broker ... 5. agent 6. dealer, jobber 7. cambist, scalper (ticket) 8. marriage 9. go–between, insurance, middleman, schatchen 10. pawnbroker, real estate 11. internuncio, stockbroker 12. intermediary

brokerage ... 3. fee 4. agio 6. charge 8. agiotage, business 9. exactment 10. commission

brolly ... 5. chute 8. umbrella 9. brollyhop, parachute

bromide ... 4. corn 5. trite 6. Babbit, cliché, halide, old hat 8. banality, sedative 9. conformer, criticism, platitude 10. conformist, Philistine 15. conventionalist

bronco, broncho ... 4. pony 5. horse 6. cayuse 7. mustang 10. broomstick

bronco, bucking ... 9. estrapade

broncobuster, bronchobuster ... 6. cowboy 7. trainer, vaquero

Bronx cheer ... 3. boo 4. hiss, razz 9. raspberry

bronze ... 3. aes (anc), tan 5. alloy, color 6. ormolu, patina, suntan 9. sculpture

Bronze Age ... 9. Neolithic 11. Aeneolithic

Bronze Plaques (pert to) ... *called* .. 14. Eugubine Tables (Iguvine Tables, 1444) *number* .. 5. Seven *site* .. 6. Gubbio (It)

brooch ... 3. bar, pin 4. boss, ouch 5. cameo, clasp 6. fibula (anc), shield 8. pectoral 9. breastpin

brood ... 3. fry, nye, set 4. kind, mope, mull, muse, nide, race 5. breed, covey, folks, hatch, pride (lions), young 6. clutch, family, farrow (pigs), litter, ménage, people, strain 7. lineage, progeny, reflect 8. cogitate, incubate, meditate, ruminate, soredium 9. household, offspring 11. contemplate

brood over ... 4. fret, mope 5. hover 6. grieve, ponder 7. agonize 8. remember

brook ... 3. run 4. bear, beck, burn, rill, sike 5. abide, bourn, creek, crick 6. arroyo, endure, rillet, runlet, suffer 7. freshet, rivulet 8. brooklet 9. arroyuelo, streamlet

broom ... 5. besom, shrub, spart, sweep, whisk

broth ... 4. soup 5. stock 6. brewis 8. bouillon, consommé

brother ... 3. fra 4. mate, monk 5. friar, title 6. frater, friend, member, oblate 8. alter ego, relative 9. associate 11. counterpart

brotherhood ... 5. lodge 7. kinship, society 8. sodality 10. fellowship, fraternity 11. association

12. fraternalism 13. confraternity

brotherly ... 4. kind 6. tender 8. friendly 9. fraternal 11. sympathetic 12. affectionate

Brothers ... 7. Danites (Mormon) 9. Christian (RCCh)

brothers and sisters (same family) ... 8. siblings

brow ... 3. cap, rim, tip, top 4. brae 5. brink, crest, crown 6. border, summit, tiptop, visage 7. eyebrow, feature 8. boldness, forehead 9. gangplank 10. effrontery 11. countenance

browbeat ... 3. cow 5. bully 7. buffalo, henpeck 8. bulldoze, domineer 10. intimidate

brown ... 4. dark 5. cheat, dusky 6. august, braise, tanned 9. red–yellow (class)

brown ... 3. bay, dun, nut, tan 4. ecru, faon, fawn, roan, rust, seal 5. acorn, cocoa, hazel, henna, khaki, mocha, olive, otter, sepia, snuff, sumac, tawny, tenné, toast, topaz 6. auburn, bister, bronze, burnet, coffee, copper, loutre, oriole, russet, sienna, sorrel, titian, walnut 7. asphalt (smoke), gazelle, perique, rosario (army) 8. chestnut, cinnamon, mahogany 9. buckthorn, chocolate 10. café au lait, terra cotta

brown (pert to) ... *Bess* .. 6. musket *betty* .. 5. daisy 7. pudding 10. coneflower *earth* .. 5. umber *ebony* .. 6. wamara 10. coffeewood

browned in deep fat ... 7. rissole

Brownian movement (Bot) ... 7. pedesis

brownie ... 3. elf 4. cake 5. dwarf, gnome, nisse, pixie, Scout, urisk 6. camera, goblin 9. sandpiper

Brownism (Eng) ... 17. Congregationalism

browze ... 4. brut (obs), read, scan 5. graze 6. nibble

bruckle ... 5. frail 7. brittle 9. breakable 10. changeable, inconstant

bruin ... 4. bear

bruise ... 4. bash, beat, hurt, maul 5. abuse, crush, dinge, pound, wound 6. batter, buffet, injury 7. contuse 8. abrasion, black eye 9. contusion, pulverize, triturate

bruiser ... 3. mug, pug 5. boxer, bravo, tough 7. fighter, ruffian, sparrer 8. pugilist 11. fisticuffer

bruit, bruit about ... 3. din 4. fame, hawk, tell 5. bandy, noise, rumor 6. clamor, report 9. advertise

brujo ... 8. magician, sorcerer 11. witch doctor

brumal ... 4. cold 6. hiemal, wintry 8. hibernal 10. winterlike

brune ... 6. brunet (brunette) 11. Melanochroi

Brunhild ... 5. Queen (wife of Siegfried) 8. Valkyrie (Myth)

brunt ... 3. rub 4. crux 5. pinch, shock

6. stress 7. squeeze
brush... 3. art 4. bush, comb, tail
(fox), tuft 5. besom, briar, broom,
clash, graze, groom, sweep, touch
6. artist, forest, pappus, stroke,
teazel 7. painter, scuffle, thicket
8. conflict 9. brushwood, encounter
10. paintbrush 11. undergrowth
brush aside... 5. spurn 6. reject
7. dismiss 8. shrug off 9. disregard
brush wolf... 6. coyote
brusque... 4. curt 5. bluff, blunt,
brash, brusk, frank, gruff, rough,
sharp, short 6. abrupt, candid,
snippy
brutal... 5. cruel, gross 6. animal,
carnal, coarse, savage 7. bestial,
inhuman 8. ruthless 9. barbarous
brutality... 7. cruelty 9. barbarian,
carnality 12. ruthlessness
brute... 5. beast, gross, harsh, rough
6. animal 7. beastly, bestial, sensual,
varment 8. soulless 9. barbarian,
inanimate 10. unpolished
11. uncivilized
brutish... 4. rude 5. cruel, gross
6. brutal, carnal, fierce, savage,
stupid 7. bestial, inhuman, sensual,
vicious 9. barbarous, ferocious,
insensate, unfeeling 10. insensible,
irrational
Brutus... 3. wig 6. hairdo, peruke
7. traitor (Julius Caesar)
13. chrysanthemum
Bryan's speech (1896)... 11. Cross of
Gold 13. Crown of Thorns
bryology, science of... 6. mosses
10. bryophytes, liverworts
Brython... 4. Celt 6. Briton
8. Welshman
Brythonic god... 3. Ler 4. Bran
Brythonic goddess... 9. Arianrhod
bubble... 4. bead, bleb, blob, boil,
foam 5. bulge, empty, fancy, tumor
6. burble, gurgle, murmur, ripple,
scheme, trifle 7. chimera (chimaera),
globule, trickle 8. bubbling, delusive,
illusion 9. ephemeron, intumesce,
lightness 10. effervesce
16. unsubstantiality
buccal... 4. oral 5. cheek, mouth
buccaneer... 4. Kidd (Capt) 5. rover
6. Morgan, pirate, rifler, viking
7. corsair, Lafitte, spoiler
8. marooner, picaroon 9. privateer
10. Blackbeard (Capt Teach),
freebooter
Bucephalus... 5. horse, steed
7. charger 8. war horse (Alex the
Great)
buck... 3. man, ram, rat 4. bunt, butt,
deer, goat, hare, jump, male, sore
(4-yr deer) 5. fight, sasin 6. animal,
combat, dollar, Indian, oppose
7. contest, launder, pricket
8. antelope, sawhorse 10. fallow
deer
buckaroo... 6. cowboy 7. trainer,
vaquero 8. horseman
12. broncobuster (bronchobuster)
bucket... 3. tub 4. bail, bowk, pail,
ship 5. chest, cozen, scoop, skeel

6. bailer, bushel, drench, sityla
10. bucket shop
Buckeye State... 4. Ohio
Buckingham Palace... 9. residence
11. St James Park (London)
buckle... 3. bow 4. bend, curl, kink,
warp 5. tache 6. fasten 8. marriage
9. fastening
buckthorn... 4. tree 5. brown, shrub
7. cascara, Rhamnus
buckwheat... 4. cake, coal, herb,
seed, titi 5. flour
bucolic... 4. idyl, poem, poet 5. idyll,
local, rural 6. farmer, poetic, rustic
7. eclogue, georgic 8. agrestic,
pastoral 9. bucoliast
bud... 3. deb 4. bulb, cion, germ,
grow, knop, stem 5. brier, buddy,
gemma, graft, plant, shoat, youth
6. embryo, sprout 7. blossom,
brother, burgeon, develop
8. rudiment, soredium 9. debutante,
germinate
Buddha (Gautama)... 2. Fo 4. sage
(Shakya) 5. amita, deity 7. ascetic,
teacher 8. Daibutsu 10. Blessed One
Buddhism (pert to)...
church.. 4. tera
city (sacred).. 5. Lassa (Lhasa)
evil spirit.. 4. Mara
fate.. 5. Karma
festival.. 3. Bon
friar, monk.. 2. Bo 5. arbat, bonze
6. bhikku, gelong 7. Mahatma
8. poonghia 9. Dalai Lama
goal.. 13. Enlightenment
hell.. 6. Naraka
language (sacred).. 4. Pali 5. sutra
9. Tripitaka
liberation.. 7. Nirvana
mountain (sacred).. 4. Omei (Chin)
paradise.. 4. Jodo 8. gokuraku
sect.. 3. Zen
shrine (Ind).. 4. tope 5. stupa
6. dagoba
temple.. 4. rath, Tera 6. vihara
temple column.. 3. lat
term.. 6. nidana
buddy... 3. pal 4. chum, mate
5. crony 7. brother, comrade
8. tentmate 9. bedfellow, companion
budge... 3. fur (lambskin) 4. grog,
move, stir 5. booze, brisk, stiff
6. guzzle, jocund, liquor, solemn,
tipple 7. austere, pompous
8. movement 11. nervousness
budget... 3. bag 4. bulk, plan, sack
5. funds, pouch, purse, store
6. agenda, assets, bundle, moneys,
packet, parcel, ration, wallet
7. program, stipend 8. finances,
quantity, schedule 9. allowance,
statement 12. accumulation
Buenos Aires (pert to)...
avenue (famed).. 13. Avenida de
Mayo
bourse.. 5. Bolsa
capital.. 9. Argentina
river.. 7. La Plata
buff... 3. rub 4. hide (animal) 5. color,
scour 6. polish 7. burnish, leather
buffalo (animal)...

American.. **5.** bison
Asian, African.. **2.** ox **4.** arna, Cape, gaur **8.** seladang
European.. **7.** aurochs
hybrid.. **7.** cattalo (catalo)
Indian.. **4.** arna
Philippines.. **7.** carabao, timarau
buffalo (pert to)...
grass.. **5.** grama **6.** guinea **11.** St. Augustine
pea.. **4.** plum **5.** vetch **10.** bluebonnet
slang.. **3.** cow **5.** bully **7.** perplex **8.** bulldoze, confound
Buffalo Bill... **11.** William Cody
buffer... **4.** buff **5.** guard, wheel **6.** bumper **7.** bulwark, cushion **8.** backstop, polisher
buffet... **3.** bar, box, hit **4.** beat, blow, cuff, slap, toss, whip **5.** abuse, smite, stool **6.** bruise, oppose, strike **12.** chastisement **14.** disappointment
buffet... **6.** supper **7.** counter, hassock **8.** cupboard **9.** sideboard
buffo... **7.** buffoon **10.** bass singer (comic opera), buffo–basso
buffoon... **4.** fool, mima (fem), mime, zany **5.** actor, clown, droll, mimer **6.** jester, mummer **8.** humorist, ridicule **9.** Hanswurst, harlequin **12.** Eulenspiegel (Tyll) **13.** pickel–herring (pickle–herring)
buffoonery... **6.** japery, pranks **7.** fooling **8.** clownery, drollery, trickery **9.** slapstick **10.** buffoonism **12.** harlequinade
bug (insect)... **3.** fly, sow **4.** flea, gnat, moth, pill, tick **5.** Anasa, aphid, Aphis, cimex, louse **6.** beetle, cicada, earwig, locust, mantis, needle, scarab, slater, spider, weevil **7.** firefly, hexapod, katydid, ladybug, Ranatra, termite **8.** chilipod, diplopod, mosquito, myriapod **9.** arthropod (jointed), centipede, cockroach, lightning, millipede, tarantula **10.** silverfish **11.** grasshopper
bug (slang)... **3.** nut **4.** bogy, flaw, rage **5.** craze, fault, manis **6.** defect, zealot **7.** bugaboo, bugbear, fanatic, passion **9.** energumen
bugaboo... **4.** bogy, ogre, trap (golf)
bugan... **5.** ghost **6.** spirit (evil) **9.** hobgoblin
bugger... **3.** guy, rat **4.** chap, heel **6.** booger, jasper, wretch
buggy... **3.** bus **4.** ga–ga, shay **5.** wagon **6.** cuckoo **7.** caboose, foolish, haywire, vehicle **8.** carriage, demented, infested, stanhope **9.** insectile **10.** insectlike
bug juice... **6.** liquor (strong), whisky (inferior)
bugle... **3.** iva (ragweed) **4.** bead, call (mating), honk, horn, nose, toot **7.** clarion, trumpet **9.** schnozzle **10.** instrument
bugle call... **4.** taps **6.** alerte, sennet (Hist) **7.** retreat, tantara **8.** last post, reveille

build... **4.** form, rear **5.** edify, erect, found, frame, raise, shape **6.** create, evolve, figure, nidify **7.** fashion, stature **8.** increase, physique **9.** construct, establish
building... **4.** barn, casa, crib, shed, wing **5.** annex, tower **6.** casino, castle, lean–to, making, museum **7.** edifice, factory, forming, rookery, rotunda, theater **8.** creation, dwelling, erecting, erection, tenement **9.** apartment, structure **10.** fashioning, production, skyscraper, storehouse **11.** fabrication
build–up... **5.** boost **9.** promotion **11.** advertising **12.** commendation
built... **4.** made **6.** formed, shaped **7.** crested, erected **9.** fashioned **10.** fabricated **11.** constructed
bulb... **3.** bud **4.** corm, lily, root, sego, stem **5.** onion, swell, tuber, tulip **6.** bulbil, camass, crocus, dahlia **7.** bulblet, globule, rhizome **8.** earthnut
bulbous... **5.** round **7.** bulbose, bulging **8.** swelling, tuberous
Bulgaria...
capital.. **5.** Sofia
city.. **5.** Varna **6.** Plevna, Sliven **7.** Ruschuk
native.. **6.** Bulgar
origin.. **4.** Slav **9.** Mongolian
river.. **6.** Danube, Marica (Maritsa), Struma
bulge... **3.** bow **4.** bump, edge, hump, jump, knob, odds **5.** bilge, bloat, flash, pouch, swell **6.** convex, wallet **7.** vantage **9.** advantage **10.** projection **12.** protuberance
bulk... **3.** sum **4.** loom, mass, most, size **6.** extent, staple, volume **7.** bigness, quantum **8.** majority, quantity **9.** dimension, largeness, substance, thickness **11.** massiveness **12.** accumulation **13.** preponderance
bulky... **5.** heavy, hulky, stout, thick **6.** clumsy **7.** awkward, lumpish, massive **8.** unwieldy **9.** corpulent, policemen (Eng sl), ponderous **10.** cumbersome, unwielding **11.** substantial
bull... **4.** fiat, seal **5.** edict, error, large, ukase **6.** brevet, decree, firman, humbug, letter (papal), market (Finan), rising, Taurus **7.** blunder **8.** nonsense, solecism **9.** Irish bull, policeman **10.** speculator
bull (male animal)... **2.** ox **3.** cow **4.** Apis (sacred), stot, toro, zebu **5.** moose, steer, whale **6.** walrus **7.** bullock **8.** elephant, Minotaur, terrapin
bull (slang)... **4.** blah, bosh, bunk **5.** hokum **6.** hot air **7.** baloney **8.** buncombe, flimflam
bulla... **4.** bleb, boss, case (leather), knob, seal (papal), stud **6.** button **7.** blister, globule, pendant, vesicle **8.** ornament
bulldog... **3.** ant **4.** pipe **5.** leech **7.** courage, forceps **8.** barnacle, stubborn, tenacity **9.** newspaper

(early), tenacious

bulldoze... 3. cow 5. bully, grade, level 6. coerce, harass 7. buffalo 8. browbeat 10. intimidate

bullet... 4. ball (cannon), shot, slug 6. dumdum, pellet, sinker (angling), tracer 7. missile

bulletin... 5. brief, flash 6. notice, record 7. account, message 8. newsbill 9. statement 10. newsletter, periodical 11. publication 12. announcement

bullfighter... 6. torero 7. matador, picador 8. capeador, toreador

bullfinch... 3. alp 4. nope 5. hedge 11. pyrrhuloxia 12. gray grosbeak

Bull Moose... 16. Progressive Party

bullpen (pert to)...
camp.. 8. barracks 9. enclosure
ice hockey.. 5. bench (penalty)
ring cell.. 5. toril
Western US.. 6. corral

Bull Run (battle)... 8. Manassas

bully... 4. beef 6. hector, jovial 7. gleeful, ruffian 8. browbeat, bulldoze 9. bulldozer, tormentor 10. browbeater, intimidate

bulwark... 4. bank 6. buffer, sconce 7. barrier, parapet, rampart 8. abutment, buttress 10. protection 13. fortification

bum... 3. beg 5. idler, revel, rummy, souse, spree 6. beggar, loafer, tipple, wretch 7. budmash, moocher, wastrel 8. blighter, drunkard, vagabond 9. lazzarone, schnorrer 10. panhandler

bump... 3. hit, jog 4. bang, clop, jolt, lump, meet, push, thud 5. bulge, cahot, crash, crump, knock, lower, plunk, tumor 6. demote, impact, reduce, strike 7. collide 8. demotion, dilation, swelling 9. air pocket, collision, downgrade

bumpkin... 4. boor, clod, gawk, hick, lout, rube, tike 5. yokel 6. farmer, rustic 7. cauboge, hayseed, hoosier, lumpkin 9. chawbacon 10. clodhopper

bumptious... 8. insolent 9. audacious, insulting 12. contumelious

bunch... 3. bob, lot, mop, set 4. pack, tuft, wisp 5. batch, clump, covey, crowd, flock, grist, group 6. bundle 7. cluster, company 8. assemble, quantity 9. multitude 10. congregate

bundle... 3. lot, wad 4. bale, bolt, hank, pack, send 5. bluey, bunch, fagot, sheaf, shook 6. bindle, fardel, fascis, packet, parcel, seroon 7. fascine, package, rouleau 10. collection

bung... 3. tap 4. cork, plug, stop 5. spile 6. bruise 7. contuse, stopper, stopple, tampeon, tampoon 8. bankrupt, bunghole 11. falsehood

bungle... 3. err 4. muff 5. botch, fudge 6. bobble, foozle, fumble, tailor (hunting) 7. blunder

bungling... 5. fudgy 6. clumsy 7. awkward, unhandy 8. botchery

9. unskilled 10. blundering, unskillful

bunion... 12. hallux valgus

bunk... 3. bed, kip, rot 4. blah, brag 5. abide, berth, couch, dwell, hokum, hooey, sleep 6. humbug, kibosh 7. baloney, hogwash 8. nonsense, tommyrot 9. cross–beam (logging)

Bunker Hill (Mass)... 6. battle (1775)

bunkum... see *buncombe*

Bunsen... 4. cell, disk 5. flame, valve 6. burner 9. Professor (Ger)

bunt... 3. bat, dig, jab, jog, tap 4. blow, bump, butt, pike, push, tail (Scot) 5. knock, shove 7. bunting 10. propulsion

bunting... 4. flag, hood 5. flags 6. banner, pennon 7. pennant 8. streamer

bunting (bird)... 3. red 4. cirl, corn, crow, lark, pape (Creole) 5. finch 6. indigo, towhee 7. cowbird, ortolan 8. bobolink 12. yellowhammer

buoy... 3. dan 4. bell 5. float 6. marker 7. can buoy, nunbuoy 8. bell buoy, deadhead, life buoy, spar buoy 11. mooring buoy 12. breeches buoy 13. whistling buoy

buoyance, buoyancy... 4. hope, snap 5. verve 6. bounce 7. flotage 9. lightness 10. levitation, resilience 12. floatability 16. lightheartedness

buoyant... 5. light 7. elastic 8. cheerful, floating, levitate, volatile 11. supernatant 12. lighthearted, recuperative

bur, burr... 3. nut 5. thorn 8. adherent (see also *burr*)

burble... 6. muddle 7. confuse, trouble 8. disorder

burbot... 4. ling, Lota 7. eelpout

burden... 3. key, tax 4. birn, care, cark, clog, lade, load, note, onus, task, tone 5. cargo, cross, music, tenor, voice 6. charge, cumber, hamper, saddle, weight 7. bourdon, freight, oppress, payload, refrain 8. capacity, overload, pressure 10. impediment, imposition 11. encumbrance

burdensome... 5. heavy 7. arduous, massive, onerous, weighty 8. unwieldy 9. difficult, laborious, ponderous 10. cumbersome, oppressive 11. troublesome 12. impedimental

bureau... 4. desk, shop 6. office 7. dresser 8. chambers 10. chiffonier, department

bureaucracy... 10. government 11. directorate, officialdom, officialism

burgeon... 3. bud 4. grow 5. gemma, shoot, sprit 6. sprout

burglar... 4. yegg 5. thief 9. cracksman 11. safecracker 12. housebreaker

burglary... 5. theft 6. burgle 7. larceny, robbery 8. stealage 13. housebreaking

burgle... 3. rob 8. burglary 10. burglarize

burgomaster... 5. mayor 7. alcalde
  10. magistrate 11. burghmaster
burgoo, burgout... 4. stew 5. gruel
  7. pudding (oatmeal) 8. porridge
burial... 5. inurn 7. funeral
  9. interment,. sepulture
  10. engulfment, inhumation,
  submersion 11. concealment,
  submergence
burial ground... 4. pyre 5. grave
  6. barrow 7. tumulus 8. bone yard,
  catacomb, cemetery, golgotha
  9. graveyard 10. churchyard,
  necropolis 11. polyandrium
  12. potter's field
burlesque... 3. fun 4. jest 5. farce,
  comic 6. parody, review, satire
  7. mimicry, mockery, overact,
  take–off 8. burletta, doggerel,
  ridicule, travesty 9. charivari,
  imitation, travestie 10. caricatura,
  caricature 13. entertainment
Burlingame Treaty... 11. Immigration
  (Chin 1868)
burly... 3. fat 5. bulky, large, noble,
  obese, stout 6. brawny 7. stately
  8. imposing, stalwart 9. corpulent,
  excellent
Burma, Burmese...
  alphabet.. 4. Pali
  capital (anc).. 3. Ava 4. Pegu
  capital, present.. 7. Rangoon
  city.. 8. Mandalay
  dagger.. 3. dah (dhao)
  gibbon.. 3. lar
  girl.. 4. mima
  monk.. 2. bo
  native.. 3. Lai
  relation.. 5. Thais (Tais) 6. Malays
  7. Chinese 8. Tibetans
  10. Mongolians
  religion.. 8. Buddhism
  robber.. 6. dacoit
  shed (public).. 5. zayat
  tribe.. 3. Mon, Tai 4. Laos, Shan
  7. Siamese
  viol.. 4. turr (3–stringed)
Burma Road... 6. Lashio (to China,
  1938–1942, replaced by Ledo Rd)
burn... 3. dry, tan 4. char, fire, glow,
  hurt, pain, sear, sere 5. blaze,
  brand, brook, cense, flame, scald,
  singe 6. ignite, injury, scorch
  7. cremate, encauma, flicker,
  sunburn, swelter, torrefy 9. cauterize,
  sacrifice 10. incandesce, incinerate
burner... 3. jet 4. lamp 5. torch
  6. Bunsen, candle, censer (incense)
  7. cresset 9. blowtorch
  10. lucubrator 11. incinerator
burning... 3. hot 4. fire, pain, sore
  5. afire, angry, ardor, arson, blaze,
  fiery, flame 6. ablaze, ardent, fervid
  7. blazing, cautery, excited, fervent,
  flaming, glowing, shining, zealous
  8. eloquent, feverish, inustion
  9. cremating, cremation, execution
  10. combustion, ustulation
  13. conflagration
burning place... 4. ghat 9. crematory
  10. cinerarium
burnish... 3. rub 4. buff 5. glaze,

gloss, shine 6. patina, polish
burnt... 3. red 5. dried 6. burned,
  seared, singed 7. charred
  8. hardened, scorched, sunburnt
  9. blistered, sunburned
burnt (pert to)...
  art.. 11. pyrography, pyrogravure
  color.. 4. rose 5. ocher, topaz
  6. almond, orange, russet, sienna
  8. amethyst
  sugar.. 7. caramel
burn with anger, excitement...
  4. fume 5. smoke 6. seethe,
  simmer, sizzle 7. smolder
burp... 5. belch, eruct 8. eructate
burr... 3. cut, hem 4. buzz, whir
  5. brier, drone, gnarl, knurl, thorn
  6. brogue, corona (moon), meatus
  (ear) 7. bramble, clotbur, prickle,
  silique, sticker 8. excavate, follicle
  9. cocklebur, whetstone
burro... 3. ass 4. jack 5. cuddy,
  neddy 6. dickey, donkey 7. jackass
burrow... 3. dig 4. abri, hide, hole,
  lair, mine 5. couch (otter's), lodge
  (beaver's) 6. search, tunnel 7. shelter
burrowing... 9. effodient, fossorial
  11. lithodomous (in rock)
burrowing animal... 4. mole, peba
  5. poyou 6. peludo 8. suricate
  9. armadillo
burst... 3. pop 4. bang, rend 5. blast,
  blaze, break, broke, erupt, flare,
  flash, shots, spurt 6. volley
  7. explode, flare–up, gunfire, implode
  8. outbreak, outburst, ruptured
  9. discharge, explosion, fractured
  10. detonation 11. dissiliency
burst (forth)... 4. grow 5. erupt, sally
  6. sprout
burst (pert to)...
  applause.. 5. éclat, hands 7. ovation,
  plaudit 8. clapping
  cheers.. 5. salvo
  gunfire.. 6. rafale
  laughter.. 3. fit 4. peal, roar
  10. convulsion
  temper.. 4. rage 5. scene, storm
  7. passion 9. explosion
bursting... 4. full 7. brimful, crammed,
  excited, replete 8. overfull, thrilled,
  volcanic 9. explosive, surfeited
  10. detonating 11. impassioned,
  overflowing, overwhelmed
bury... 4. hide, sink 5. cache, cover,
  inter, inurn, plant, stash 6. engulf,
  entomb, inhume 7. conceal,
  embosom, repress, secrete
  8. submerge 9. overwhelm, sepulture
bus... 6. jitney 7. omnibus 10. motor
  coach
bush... 3. tod 4. shag (hair) 5. brush,
  plain, shrub, wahoo, wilds 6. branch,
  lining 7. boscage, bushing
  8. bushveld, woodland 10. hinterland
bushed... 4. beat 5. all in 6. pooped
  7. baffled 8. dog–tired 9. exhausted,
  nonplused, perplexed, played out
  10. nonplussed
bushel... 3. foo 4. full 6. basket,
  vessel 7. measure (dry) 8. imperial,
  standard 10. Winchester

Bushido (Jap)... 11. code of honor
bushing... 4. bush 6. lining, sleeve
   (mach) 7. bearing, padding (piano)
Bushman... 3. San 4. Saan 5. nomad,
   pygmy 6. Abatua, rustic
   8. woodsman 9. aborigine
bushmaster... 5. snake
bushwhacker... 7. pioneer 8. guerilla
   10. forerunner 11. bushfighter,
   voortrekker 12. frontiersman
bushy... 5. hairy, thick, woody
   6. dumose, shaggy, woodsy
   7. hirsute, scrubby, shrubby
business... 3. job 4. firm, game, line,
   work 5. craft, house, trade 6. affair,
   career, matter, racket 7. calling,
   company, concern, pursuit
   8. commerce, industry, interest,
   practice, vocation 10. enterprise,
   occupation, proceeding, profession
   11. transaction 13. establishment
business (pert to)...
   agreement.. 6. cartel
   businesslike.. 11. pragmatical
   customer.. 6. patron
   cycle.. 9. recession 10. depression,
   prosperity 11. liquidation
   deal.. 4. turn 9. operation
   11. negotiation, transaction
   Exchange.. 4. bank 5. Bolsa
   6. Bourse 11. stock market
   man.. 6. tycoon 8. salesman
   9. solicitor
   place.. 4. mart, shop 5. store
   6. office, shoppe 8. Exchange
bust... 4. bang, fail, hand (Bridge),
   tame (bronco) 5. burst, chest, crash,
   flunk, spree 6. breast, figure
   7. degrade, explode, failure
   8. collapse, demotion, fracture
   9. sculpture 10. bankruptcy
bustard... 4. bird (Old World), kori,
   Otis 5. goose, paauw 6. curlew
   8. Otididae
busted... 4. flat 5. broke 6. broken,
   failed, ruined 7. severed 8. bankrupt,
   ruptured, strapped 9. insolvent,
   penniless 10. stone—broke
bustle... 3. ado 4. fuss, stir, to—do
   5. haste, whirl 6. flurry, hubbub,
   hustle, pother, scurry, tumult
   7. bluster, ferment, fluster, scamper,
   turmoil 8. activity 9. agitation,
   commotion 10. excitement,
   hurly—burly 11. disturbance
bustling... 6. active 7. hurried, rushing
   8. eventful, stirring
busy... 4. nosy, work 5. drive
   6. active, devote, employ, engage,
   occupy 7. engaged, on the go,
   operose 8. diligent, employed,
   meddling, occupied, on the run,
   sedulous 9. assiduous, attentive,
   laborious, officious 10. meddlesome
   11. industrious, inquisitive,
   persevering
busy... 4. dick 6. gossip 7. gumshoe,
   meddler 8. busybody, flatfoot
   9. detective
busybody... 6. gossip 8. quidnunc
   9. pragmatic
but... 2. ma 3. yet 4. even, just,

mere, save 5. hence, outer, still
   6. except 7. however, without
   10. regardless 12. nevertheless
   15. notwithstanding
butcher... 3. fly (angling), mar 4. kill,
   slay 5. botch, spoil 6. killer, vendor
   7. croaker, meatman 8. merchant,
   train—boy 9. slaughter 11. slaughterer
   12. bloodshedder
butchery... 6. murder 7. carnage
   8. business, massacre, shambles
   9. slaughter 14. slaughterhouse
butt... 3. aim, end, jut, pit, ram, tun,
   tup 4. buck, bunt, cart, cask, goat,
   rump, stub 5. cigar, hinge, joint,
   mound, piece, stump 6. target
   (archery), thrust (fencing) 7. buttock,
   parapet, project 8. flatfish
   9. cigarette 13. laughingstock
butter... 3. pat 4. coat, ghee (ghi),
   oleo 5. smear 6. bedaub, spread
   7. butyric 8. flattery 9. margarine,
   suaveness 10. semiliquid
   13. oleomargarine
butter—and—eggs... 8. flaxweed,
   ranstead, toadflax
buttercup fruit... 6. achene
   7. crowtoe
butterfingered... 6. clumsy
   7. awkward, unhandy 8. bungling,
   careless 9. all thumbs 10. blundering
butterflies (slang)... 6. nerves
   7. fidgets, jitters
butterfly (pert to)...
   American.. 7. viceroy
   family.. 10. Agapetidae
   11. Rhopalocera
   genus.. 7. Lycaena 11. Lepidoptera
   large.. 7. monarch
   larva.. 11. caterpillar
   lily.. 4. sego 8. mariposa
   peacock.. 2. io 7. buckeye
   swallowtail.. 5. black, tiger, zebra
   type.. 4. moth 5. satyr 10. fritillary,
   silverspot
buttocks... 4. butt (vulgar), hips, rear,
   rump, seat 5. fanny, podex
   6. bottom 8. haunches, maneuver
   (wrestling) 9. backsides, posterior
buttress... 4. pier, pile, prop, stay
   5. brace, tower 7. shelter, support
   8. abutment 10. projection,
   strengthen 11. counterfort
   13. fortification
buttress (Arch)... 4. pier 6. flying
   7. hanging
buxom... 3. gay 4. boon, rosy 5. jolly,
   plump 6. blithe, jocund, jovial
   7. gleeful
buy... 5. bribe 6. accept, redeem
   7. bargain, expiate 8. purchase
buy back... 6. redeem
Buyer Beware... 12. Caveat Emptor
buzz... 3. hum, saw 5. rumor, snore
   6. bustle, murmur, rumble
   7. ferment, whisper 9. fricative,
   murmuring 10. sibilation
buzzard... 4. aura (turkey), hawk, pern
   5. buteo 6. osprey, stupid 7. harrier
   9. dorbeetle, senseless
   10. cockchafer
buzz bomb... 9. doodlebug

10. bumblebomb
14. Chase–Me–Charlie

bwana (Afr)... 4. boss 6. master

by... 2. at, in, on 3. ago, bei, par,
per, via 4. away, gone, near, over,
pass (bridge), past, with 5. after,
aside 6. beside, beyond, nearby,
toward 7. abreast, close by, through
9. in reserve

by–and–by... 4. anon, soon 5. later,
sweet 6. mañana 7. betimes,
bientôt, ere long, shortly 8. directly
9. presently 11. tout à l'heure

by birth... 3. nee

bygone... 3. ago 4. lost, over, past
6. buried, bypast, gone by, passed
7. elapsed, extinct 8. departed,
preterit (preterite)

byname... 6. eponym 7. babyism,
epithet, surname 8. cognomen,
monicker, nickname 9. sobriquet
10. patronymic 11. appellation

bypass... 4. go by, miss 5. byway,
elude 6. byroad, detour, escape
7. deviate, digress 8. side path

10. circumvent, roundabout

By the Grace of God... 9. Dei Gratia

byword... 3. mot, saw 5. adage,
maxim 6. byname, phrase, saying,
slogan 7. adagium, parable, proverb
8. aphorism, nickname, reproach
9. catchword, sobriquet
10. shibboleth

by word of mouth... 4. oral 5. parol
(parole)

Byzantine Empire...
architecture.. 7. St Marks (Venice)
9. elaborate
bookbinding.. 9. unadorned (earlier)
10. bejewelled (later)
church.. 7. Eastern
city.. 14. Constantinople (Istanbul)
creator.. 11. Constantine (the Great)
historian.. 9. Procopius 11. Anna
Comnena
poetry.. 5. hymns
scepter.. 6. ferula
writer.. 6. Prazes 7. Priscus, Romanus

Byzantium... 14. Constantinople
(Istanbul)

C

C... 4. clef 7. cedilla, century,
hundred, keynote

caama... 3. fox 4. asse 10. hartebeest

cab... 4. pony, taxi 7. measure,
purloin, shelter, taxicab, vehicle
8. carriage (anc) 9. cabriolet
10. locomotive (part) 11. translation

cabal... 4. clan, plot 5. group, junta,
party 7. chatter, complot, coterie,
dispute, faction 8. intrigue
9. camarilla, collusion, Committee
10. complicity, conspiracy

cabala... 7. mystery 9. mystic art,
occultism

cabalessou... 9. armadillo (giant)

cabalistic... 6. occult 7. cabalic
8. abstract, anagogic, esoteric,
mystical 10. mysterious

caballeria... 7. measure (land)
8. chivalry 10. knighthood

caballero... 5. lover, rider 6. knight
8. cavalier, horseman 9. chevalier,
gentleman 10. equestrian

caballo... 5. horse

cabaret... 3. inn 4. cafe 6. hostel,
posado, tavern 7. barroom 9. night
club, roadhouse 11. café dansant
13. entertainment

cabbage... 3. kos (cos) 4. cole, kale,
palm 5. colza, savoy 7. collard
8. colewort, kohlrabi 11. cauliflower
15. Brussels sprouts

cabbage (pert to)...
curly leaf.. 5. savoy
daisy.. 11. globeflower

fermented.. 5. kraut
headless.. 4. kale
salad.. 4. slaw
seed.. 5. colza
slang.. 4. crib, fool 6. pilfer
7. fathead, purloin 9. numbskull
11. cabbagehead, knucklehead
species.. 8. Brassica
tree.. 4. palm 7. angelin 8. palmetto
white.. 9. butterfly
yellows.. 7. disease (destructive)

caber... 4. apar, beam, pole 6. rafter,
timber

cabin... 3. hut 4. shed 5. booth,
coach (Naut), house, hovel, lodge,
shack 6. cabana, saloon 7. caboose
10. blockhouse

cabinet... 3. box, den 4. Body, buhl,
case 6. bureau, closet, office
7. almirah, boudoir, council, étagère,
whatnot 8. cellaret, cupboard,
ministry 9. committee

cable... 4. boom, cord, rope, wire
5. chain, twine 6. fasten, hawser
7. coaxial, measure, molding,
ropeway 8. telegram 9. cablegram

cable (pert to)...
car.. 7. telpher
holder (Naut).. 7. wildcat 10. cable
wheel
post.. 4. bitt

cabling... 9. rudenture

cabochon... 5. jewel, stone (uncut),
style (convex cut) 8. ornament

caboodle... 3. all, kit, lot 5. bunch,

whole 10. collection 14. kit and
caboodle
caboose... 3. car (RR) 5. buggy
6. galley 7. kitchen 9. deckhouse
cabotin... 5. actor (strolling)
9. charlatan
cachaca... 3. rum (white)
cache... 4. hide, hole 5. stash, store
7. conceal, hide–out, retreat
8. hideaway 10. storehouse
cachet... 4. seal 5. sigil, stamp, wafer
6. signet 7. capsule
cachilla... 8. white man
cachot... 7. dungeon
cackle... 3. gab 4. cank, chat, crow,
talk 5. clack, laugh, prate 6. babble,
gabble, giggle, gossip, jabber
7. chatter, prattle 8. laughter
cacodemon... 4. deva 5. devil, fiend,
Indra 10. evil spirit
cacology... 10. bad diction, corruption
(speech) 16. mispronunciation
cacophonous... 7. raucous 8. jangling,
strident 9. diaphonic, dissonant
10. discordant 11. unmelodious
cacophony... 5. clash 6. jangle
7. discord 8. diaphony (Mus)
9. harshness 10. dissodence
cactus... 4. bleo 5. agave 6. chaute,
cholla, mescal 7. Opuntia, saguaro
8. fishhook 9. Turk's–head
11. prickly pear 12. Echinocactus
cad... 4. boor, chum, heel, hick
5. yokel 6. mucker 7. bounder,
servant 8. townsman 9. scoundrel,
vulgarian
cadaver... 4. body (dead) 5. stiff
6. corpse 7. carcass 8. skeleton
cadaverous... 4. pale 5. gaunt, lurid
6. sickly, wasted 7. ghastly, haggard
9. emaciated 10. attenuated,
corpselike
caddis (pert to)...
bait.. 3. fly 4. worm 5. cadew
material.. 4. yarn 5. twill 6. crewel
7. worsted
worm.. 5. larva (aquatic)
caddle... 4. fuss 5. annoy, worry
6. gossip 7. confuse, trouble
8. disarray 9. confusion
cade... 3. keg, oil (Med), pet 4. cask,
lamb (orphan) 6. barrel, coddle,
petted
cadeau... 4. gift
cadence... 4. beat, lilt, tone 5. meter
6. rhythm 7. balance 9. free verse,
vers libre 10. modulation
cadence... 4. half 5. trill 6. plagal
7. perfect 9. authentic, deceptive,
imperfect, suspended 11. interrupted
cadency (Her)... 4. rose 5. label
6. mullet 7. annulet, martlet
8. crescent 10. fleur–de–lis
11. cross moline
cadenza... 7. cadence 8. flourish
cadet... 3. son 4. pleb 5. color (blue),
youth 6. junior 10. midshipman
cadge... 3. beg 4. hawk 5. fakir,
mooch 6. beggar, hawker, mumper,
peddle, sponge, vendor 7. carrier,
moocher, sponger 8. huckster,
sannyasi

cadgy... 6. wanton 7. lustful
8. cheerful, mirthful
Cadmus (pert to)...
daughter.. 3. Ino 6. Semele
father.. 6. Agenor
founder of.. 6. Thebes (Boetia)
sister.. 6. Europa
wife.. 8. Harmonia
cadre... 4. list, unit 5. frame, panel
6. line–up, roster, scheme
8. cadastre, register, schedule,
skeleton 9. framework
caduceus (Gr Antiq)... 4. wand
(Hermes') 5. staff 6. symbol
8. insignia (Med Corps)
Caesar (pert to)...
betrayer.. 6. Brutus
colleague.. 7. Bibulus
death site.. 4. Nola
Emperor, Dictator of.. 4. Rome
fatal day.. 4. Ides (of March)
11. Ides of March
language.. 5. Latin
rival.. 6. Pompey
river.. 7. Rubicon
sister.. 4. Atia
uncle.. 11. Caius Marius
wife.. 8. Cornelia
caesura, cesura... 4. rest 5. break,
colon, comma, pause 8. interval
12. interruption
cafard... 5. bigot, blues 6. humbug
9. hypocrite 10. depression
café... 5. coffe 6. coffee
10. restaurant 11. coffeehouse
café (pert to)...
au lait.. 5. brown 6. alesan
10. French nude
creme.. 5. suede (color)
noir.. 4. musk (color) 11. black coffee
parfait.. 8. beverage
cafetière... 9. coffeepot 10. percolator
caffeine... 6. coffee, theine (in tea)
8. alkaloid 9. stimulant
cafila... 7. caravan (camel)
cage... 3. mew, pen 4. coop 6. corral
7. confine, goal net, impound
8. goal post
cagey... 3. sly 4. foxy, wary, wily
5. canny, leery 6. artful, crafty,
shifty, shrews 7. cunning, evasive.
knowing
Cain (pert to)...
brother.. 4. Abel
founder of.. 5. Enoch (1st city)
Land of.. 3. Nod
slayer of.. 4. Abel
son.. 5. Enoch
cairn... 4. heap (stones) 6. menhir
8. catstone (catstane), landmark,
memorial, monument
Cairo...
capital.. 5. Egypt
city gate (famed).. 9. Bab–el–Nasr
mosque.. 12. Sultan Hassan·
resident.. 7. Cairene
river.. 4. Nile
seaport.. 10. Alexandria
tomb.. 10. Mehemet Ali
warrior.. 9. Rameses II
caisson... 3. box 4. case 5. chest,
wagon 7. chamber

caitiff... 4. base, mean, vile
  6. coward, wicked, wretch
  7. budmash, captive 10. despicable
cajole... 4. coax, urge 5. cheat, jolly
  6. delude 7. flatter, palaver,
  sweeten, wheedle 8. blandish
  9. importune 10. honeyfogle
Cajun (pert to)...
  descent.. 6. French (Canadian)
  dialect.. 5. Cajun
  home (present).. 9. Louisiana
  native of.. 6. Acadia (Nova Scotia)
cake... 3. bun, wig 4. bake, food,
  lump, mass, wigg 5. batty, block,
  crust, solid, torte, wafer 6. gateau,
  harden 7. bannock, congeal, oatcake,
  pancake 8. corn pone, solidify
  9. charlotte, simpleton
  11. griddle–cake
cake (pert to)...
  almond paste.. 7. ratafia
  corn.. 4. pone
  flat.. 7. placent
  fried.. 7. cruller 8. doughnut
  Lenten.. 6. cimbal, simnel
  Scotch.. 4. farl (farle) 5. scone
  unleavened.. 8. tortilla
Cake Day (Scot)... 8. hogmanay (New
  Year's)
calabar bean... 6. myotic, ordeal
  7. eserine 8. alkaloid
  13. physostigmine
calabash... 5. gourd 6. baobab, bronze
  (color)
calaboose... 4. gaol, jail 5. choky,
  clink 6. bagnio, lockup, prison
  8. bastille, calabozo 9. Bridewell
calamitous... 3. sad 4. dire, evil
  5. black 6. tragic, woeful 7. adverse,
  baleful, ruinous, unhappy 8. grievous,
  tragical, wretched 10. afflictive,
  deplorable, disastrous
  11. cataclysmic, destructive,
  distressful, unfortunate
  12. catastrophic
calamity... 4. blow, evil, ruin 5. wrack
  6. mishap 7. tragedy 8. casualty,
  disaster, distress, fatality 9. adversity
  10. affliction, misfortune
  11. catastrophe, direfulness,
  unhappiness 12. wretchedness
calathiform... 9. cup–shaped
calcarea... 5. coral 7. sponges
calceiform... 10. orchidlike
  13. clipper–shaped
calcitrant... 8. stubborn
  12. recalcitrant
calcitrate... 4. boot, kick 6. oppose
calculate... 3. aim 4. deem, rate, tell
  5. allow, count, frame, judge, score,
  tally, think 6. cipher, deduce, figure,
  gather, number, reckon 7. average,
  compute, suppose 8. conclude,
  estimate 9. determine, enumerate
calculated... 7. advised, studied,
  weighed 8. measured
  10. considered, deliberate
  11. intentional 12. contemplated
calculating... 8. plotting, scheming
  9. computing, designing, judicious
  10. estimating, numerative, reflecting,
  thoughtful 11. circumspect,

considerate 14. discriminative
calculator... 5. table 6. abacus
  7. suan pan (swan pan, Chin)
  8. computer 9. estimator, tabulator
  10. parimutuel 11. Comptometer,
  totalizator
caldron, cauldron... 3. pot, red
  (color), vat 6. boiler, kettle, mortar,
  retort 7. alembic 8. crucible
Caleb (pert to)...
  daughter.. 7. Achsaph
  literally.. 3. dog
  son.. 3. Hur, Iru
  spy of.. 6. Canaan
calèche... 7. vehicle (Quebec)
Caledonia (anc)... 8. Scotland
Caledonia bird... 4. kagu
Caledonian... 5. brown 6. Scotch
  8. Scotsman, Scottish
calefacient... 4. warm 6. remedy
  7. heating 11. calefactory
calendar... 4. list, Ordo 5. index, slate
  6. docket, line–up, record
  7. almanac, calends (kalends),
  program 8. register, schedule
  9. catalogue, ephemeris
  10. chronology, prospectus
calendar (type)... 5. Roman, Swiss
  6. Jewish, Julian 7. Chinese
  9. Cotsworth, Gregorian, perpetual
  13. International (fixed)
calenture... 4. glow 5. ardor, fever
  7. passion, pyrexia 9. febrility,
  sunstroke
calepin... 4. book (ref) 7. lexicon
  10. dictionary
calf... 3. leg (part) 4. dolt, fool, skin
  6. bovine, island, weaner 7. iceberg,
  leather 9. youngling
calf (pert to)...
  flesh.. 4. veal
  hide.. 3. kip
  leg (part).. 5. sural
  motherless.. 5. dogie 8. maverick
  sweetbread.. 9. ris de veau
  time.. 5. youth
Caliban (pert to)...
  character.. 5. brute, slave (The
  Tempest)
  deity.. 7. Setebos
  mother.. 7. Sycorax (witch)
caliber, calibre... 4. bore 7. ability
calico... 4. dame 5. cloth 6. salloo
  8. goldfish 12. multicolored
calico (pert to)...
  bird.. 9. turnstone
  bush.. 6. laurel
  horse, pony.. 5. pinto 7. piebald
  printing.. 4. teer 7. topical
calid... 3. hot 4. mild, warm 6. genial
  7. burning, thermal
California...
  bay.. 7. Monterey
  capital.. 10. Sacramento
  city.. 6. Fresno 7. Oakland 8. San
  Diego, Stockton 9. Long Beach
  10. Los Angeles 12. San Francisco,
  Santa Barbara
  desert.. 6. Mojave 8. Colorado
  discoverer.. 6. Cortez (1535)
  flower.. 5. poppy
  history.. 8. Gold Rush (1848),

Missions 11. Sutter's Mill
lake.. 5. Tahoe 8. Elsinore 9. Salton
Sea
lowest point.. 11. Death Valley
mountain.. 6. Lassen, Shasta
7. Whitney
oldest living thing.. 8. redwoods
14. General Sherman (tree)
15. bristlecone pine
river.. 4. Kern 7. Feather, Russian
10. Sacramento
pageant.. 10. Rose Parade
17. Tournament of Roses
State admission.. 11. thirty–first
State motto.. 6. Eureka
State nickname.. 6. Golden
caliph, calif... 3. Ali (4th) 4. Imam
(Imaum), Omar 6. Othman 7. Abu
Bekr 8. Islamite
Caliph Ali's descendants... 5. Alids
(Alides)
caliphate... 7. Omniads, Shiites
(Sectaries) 8. Idrisids 9. Fatimites
calk, caulk... 4. copy, plug, stop
5. close, sleep (Naut sl) 6. calque,
catnap, chinse, plug up, stop up
7. occlude
call... 3. bid, cry, dub, hip, nod
4. ahoy, beck, dial, name, plea, ring,
soho, sook (hog), taps, term, yell
5. alarm, basis, cause, clepe, rally,
rouse, shout, style, visit, waken
6. appeal, demand, ground, invoke,
motive, muster, option, reason,
sennet, signal, slogan, summon
7. appoint, bidding, collect, convoke,
fanfare, summons, trumpet
8. assemble, nominate, occasion,
reveille 9. battle cry, challenge,
designate, induction, telephone,
watchword 10. denominate, invitation
11. recruitment, requisition
12. conscription 13. justification
call (pert to)...
attention.. 6. direct, remind 8. point
out
back.. 6. recall, recant, repeal, revive,
revoke 7. retract 8. remember
9. recollect
down.. 6. invoke 7. bawl out,
reprove, tell off
evil upon.. 8. execrate
forth.. 5. evoke, rouse 6. elicit,
excite, induce, prompt, summon
names.. 4. cite 5. abuse, curse
6. insult, revile, vilify 8. besmirch
10. vituperate
together.. 6. muster, summon
7. convoke
to mind.. 4. cite 8. remember
9. visualize
callant, callan... 3. boy, lad 4. chap
5. youth 6. fellow, garçon, laddie
8. customer, muchacho
11. hobbledehoy
calle... 6. street
called... 5. named 6. dubbed, y–clept,
yermed 7. y–cleped
calling... 3. art, nod 4. beck, lure,
name, work 5. trade 6. career,
metier, naming, outcry 7. bidding,
mission, pursuit, styling, summons

8. biddance, business, labeling
(labelling), practice, vocation
9. condition, evocation
10. employment, invitation,
occupation, profession
13. circumstances
calling crab... 7. fiddler
calling hare... 4. pika
Calliope... 4. Muse (poet) 5. organ
8. asteroid
Calliope's son... 7. Orpheus
callous, calloused... 4. horn, sear
5. horny, inure 6. harden, seared
8. hardened 9. heartless, indurated,
unfeeling 10. impervious
11. hardhearted 12. thick–skinned
14. pachydermatous
callow... 5. crude, green 6. tender,
unripe, vernal 7. budding
8. immature, unformed 9. unfledged
10. unseasoned 11. undeveloped
15. unsophisticated
callus... 6. tyloma
calm... 3. lay 4. cool, dill, fair, lull,
mild 5. allay, balmy, peace, quiet,
sober, still 6. becalm, hushed, pacify,
placid, sedate, serene, smooth,
soothe, steady 7. appease, compose,
halcyon, orderly, pacific, placate,
restful, unmoved 8. peaceful, tranquil
9. quiescent, unruffled
10. phlegmatic 11. tranquilize,
undisturbed 13. dispassionate,
imperturbable
calmant, calmative... 7. anodyne,
soother 8. lenitive, pacifier, sedative,
soothing 10. depressant, palliative
11. alleviative 12. tranquilizer
calmato (Mus)... 4. calm 8. tranquil
calmness... 4. calm, lull 5. peace,
poise, quiet 6. repose 8. quietude,
serenity 9. composure, placidity
10. equanimity, quiescence
11. restfulness, self–control
calor... 4. heat 5. therm 7. thermal
calorifics... 4. heat 7. heating
calumniate... 4. slur 5. belie, libel
6. accuse, revile 7. asperse, slander,
traduce 9. blaspheme
calumnious... 7. abusive 8. derisive,
insolent, libelous 9. insulting
10. defamatory, derogatory,
slanderous 11. maledictory,
opprobrious
calumny... 5. abuse 7. lampoon,
slander 9. contumely 10. detraction,
scurrility 11. malediction
12. vilification
calvary... 8. crucifix
Calvary (Bib)... 8. Damascus, Golgotha
9. Jerusalem
Calvinism (pert to)...
author.. 6. Calvin
doctrine.. 5. Grace 9. Atonement,
Depravity (total) 12. Perseverance (of
Saints) 14. Predestination
site.. 6. Geneva
Calvinistic Methodist... 5. Welsh
10. Whitefield 14. Lady Huntingdon
Calypso... 6. Ogygia (home)
8. Cytherea, sea nymph (The
Odyssey)

calyx... 3. cup 4. husk 5. galea, sepal 6. corona 7. corolla 8. epicalyx, perianth
camarada... 7. comrade, partner 9. companion
camaraderie... 8. good will 11. familiarity 14. good–fellowship
camarilla... 5. cabal 6. clique 7. council
camata... 6. acorns 8. oak fruit
cambist... 6. banker, broker 9. financier 11. moneylender 12. money–changer
Cambodia...
  capital.. 6. Angkor 8. Pnom–Penh
  language.. 5. Khmer 9. Cambodian
  religion.. 8. Buddhism
  seaport.. 6. Kampot
Cambria... 5. Wales
Cambridge University (pert to)...
  English examination.. 6. tripos
  English student.. 5. sizar 6. optime (honor)
  Massachusetts.. 3. MIT 7. Harvard
camel... 4. oont 5. llama 6. deloul, mammal, vicuna 7. Camelus 8. Bactrian (2–humped) 9. Camelidae, dromedary
camel hair shawl... 8. cashmere
camelopard... 7. giraffe 13. constellation
Camelot... 6. legend 10. King Arthur, palace site, Round Table
cameo... 4. onyx 7. relievo 8. anaglyph
camera type... 5. Kodak 7. Brownie 10. Rollieflex
Cameroon...
  capital.. 7. Yaounde (Afr)
  native.. 4. Sara
  river.. 5. Shari
  seaport.. 6. Douala
  tribe.. 3. Abo 5. Bantu
Camino Real (Calif)... 9. Royal Road 12. El Camino Real, King's Highway
Camorra (It)... 12. organization (secret)
camouflage... 7. falsify 8. disguise 9. dissemble 10. false front 12. misrepresent
camp... 4. clan, tent 5. abode, etape, junto, tabor 6. campoo, clique, laager 7. bivouac, faction 10. encampment
campaign... 5. serve 7. crusade 9. operation
camphorated tincture of opium... 9. paregoric
campus... 4. quad 5. field (academic)
can... 3. jar, may, tin 6. hopper, vessel 7. capable 8. canister, conserve 9. competent 10. receptacle
can... 5. skill 7. ability 9. competent 10. receptacle
can (sl)... 3. jug, tin 4. boot, bump, fire, jail, john, kick 6. bounce, cooler, toilet 7. dismiss 9. discharge 11. give the gate
Canaan... 9. Palestine 12. Promised Land
Canada... see also *Canadian*
  capital (Federal).. 6. Ottawa

  city.. 7. Toronto 8. Hamilton, Montreal, Winnipeg 9. Vancouver
  discoverer.. 9. John Cabot (1497)
  Hudson's Bay Co.. 8. fur trade
  native.. 6. French 7. English
  nickname.. 6. Canuck
  park.. 6. Jasper
  peninsula.. 5. Gaspé
  police.. 8. Mounties 12. Royal Mounted (7,000)
  river.. 5. Peace, Slave 6. Fraser, Nelson, Ottawa 8. Gatineau 9. Athabasca, Churchill, Mackenzie 10. St Lawrence
Canadian (pert to)...
  flour.. 6. Shorts (milling) 8. canaille
  jay.. 9. moose bird 10. whisky jack
  lynx.. 5. pishu
  plum.. 6. cheney
  porcupine.. 5. urson 7. cawquaw
  squaw.. 6. mahala
canaille... 3. mob 4. ruck 6. rabble, ragtag, Shorts 8. riffraff 10. roughscuff
canal... 4. duct, iter (brain), pipe, tube 5. drain 6. meatus 7. acequia, channel 10. waterspout 11. watercourse
Canal... 4. Erie, Kiel, Suez 6. Panama 13. Sault Ste Marie (Soo)
Canal Zone Lock... 5. Gatun 10. Miraflores
canard... 4. duck, hoax 5. rumor 6. humbug 9. falsehood
canary... 6. yellow 8. song–bird, songster, weakling
Canary Islands...
  capital.. 9. Santa Cruz (Teneriffe)
  city.. 9. Las Palmas (Grand Canary)
  commune.. 4. Icod
  owner.. 5. Spain
cancel... 4. blot, dele, kill, omit, undo 5. annul, erase 6. delete, excise, recall, repeal, revoke 7. abolish, destroy, nullify, rescind, retract 8. write off 10. invalidate, neutralize, obliterate 11. countermand
cancellation... 6. repeal 7. erasure 8. deletion, write–off 10. moratorium 12. obliteration
cancer... 4. evil 5. tumor 6. canker, growth 7. sarcoma 8. neoplasm 9. carcinoma
Cancer... 4. crab 7. mansion (moon) 10. zodiac sign 13. constellation
cancion... 4. song 5. lyric
Candia... 5. Crete (Isl)
candid... 4. fair, just, open, pure 5. frank 6. direct, honest 7. sincere 9. guileless, impartial, ingenuous 10. impersonal 13. dispassionate 15. straightforward
candidate... 6. seeker 7. aspirer, electee, nominee 8. aspirant, selectee 9. applicant, appointee, postulant 10. solicitant
candidate list... 4. leet 5. slate 6. roster
Candide (pert to)...
  hero, title.. 5. novel
  novel, author.. 8. Voltaire
  philosophy.. 8. optimism

candied... 5. sweet 7. honeyed
  9. congealed, incrusted, preserved
  10. flattering, granulated
  12. crystallized
candied sea holly... 6. eryngo (eringo)
candle... 3. dip, wax 5. light, power,
  taper 6. bougie, cierge, tallow, votive
  7. paschal 8. bayberry 9. chandelle
candlestick (pert to)...
  Bib.. 6. lampad
  branched.. 9. girandole
  ornamental.. 10. candelabra
  Scot.. 6. crusie
  spike.. 7. pricket
  three–branched.. 9. tricerion
  torch type.. 8. flambeau
  wall.. 6. sconce
candlewood... 6. flower 8. ocotillo
candor... 8. fairness, openness
  9. frankness, sincerity, unreserve
  10. directness 11. artlessness,
  unrestraint 13. outspokenness
candy... 5. sweet 6. penide (pulled),
  sweets 7. sweeten 8. crystals
  9. granulate, sweetmeat
  10. confection 11. crystallize
  13. confectionary
candy (type)... 4. mint 5. fudge, taffy
  6. bonbon, nougat, toffee 7. brittle,
  caramel, fondant, panocha, penuche,
  praline 8. licorice, lollipop
  9. chocolate 11. marshmallow
candytuft... 6. iberis
cane... 3. rod 4. beat, club, reed,
  stem, whip 5. crook, sorgo, staff,
  stick, sugar 6. bamboo, rattan
  7. bagasse, bourdon, sorghum,
  sucrose 9. handstaff, truncheon
  12. swagger stick
canescent... 5. hoary, white 7. grizzly,
  silvery, whitish 9. snow–white
Canfield... 9. solitaire
canine... 3. cur, dog, fox, pug, pup
  4. lobo, mutt, tike 5. dingo, pooch,
  puppy, whelp 6. animal, coyote
  7. Canidae, doggish, laniary, mastiff,
  mongrel, reynard 8. dogtooth,
  eyetooth
canis... 3. dog
Canis Majoris... 13. Constellation (with
  Dog Star, Sirius)
cannibalism... 9. barbarity, endophagy
  10. perversion 11. blood thirst
  13. anthropophagy
cannon... 3. gun 5. crash 6. mortar
  7. firearm, robinet 8. dog of war,
  howitzer, ordnance 9. artillery,
  collision
cannon (pert to)...
  ball.. 6. pellet 7. missile
  bore.. 6. breech
  fire.. 7. barrage
  handle.. 4. anse
  nautical.. 5. chase
  part.. 8. cascabel
  pivot.. 8. trunnion
  platform.. 10. terreplein
  plug.. 7. tampion
  shot.. 5. grape
  shoulder part.. 7. rimbase
cannonade... 4. boom, peal, roar
  5. blitz, shell 6. rumble, strafe

11. bombardment
canny... 3. sly 4. foxy, wary, wily
  6. artful, frugal, shrewd, subtle
  7. cunning, knowing, prudent, thrifty
  8. cautious 9. sagacious
canoe... 4. kiak, pahi, proa, waka
  5. bongo, bungo, kayak, umiak,
  waapa 6. corial, dugout, oomiak,
  pitpan 7. almadia, buckeye (bugeye),
  coracle, piragua, pirogue
  12. pambanmanche
canon... 3. law 4. code, list, rule,
  type 5. model, nodus (Mus)
  6. belief, clergy, decree, ritual
  7. measure, precept 8. decision
  9. catalogue, criterion 10. regulation
  11. composition 12. constitution
canonical... 4. None (hour), Sext
  (hour) 5. Lauds, Prime 6. Matins
  7. creedal 8. dogmatic, orthodox
  9. doctrinal 10. scriptural
  11. theological 14. ecclesiastical
canonization... 8. sainting
  10. ordainment, ordination
  12. consecration, enshrinement
canopy... 3. sky 4. ceil, cope, dais,
  tent 5. cover, shade, vault
  6. awning, tester 7. blanket,
  marquee, shelter 8. caponier
  (caponiere), ciborium, pavilion
  9. baldachin, firmament
canorous... 5. clear 8. sonorous
  9. melodious 10. euphonious
cant... 3. tip 4. lean, list, sing, song,
  sway, tack, tilt 5. angle, argot,
  chant, lingo, pitch, slang, slope,
  whine 6. careen, intone, jargon,
  patois, snivel 7. auction, incline,
  mummery 8. pretense 9. hypocrisy
  10. intonation, sanctimony
  17. sanctimoniousness
cantabank... 6. singer (ballad)
cantador... 6. singer (folk songs)
cantankerous... 8. perverse
  9. malicious 10. contention,
  ill–natured 12. cross–grained
cantata... 5. motet 8. serenata
  9. pastorale
canter... 4. gait, lope 6. gallop
  (Canterbury) 8. vagabond
Canterbury...
  archbishop.. 7. Cranmer, Primate
    13. Thomas à Becket (murdered)
  capital (Eng).. 14. ecclesiastical
  famed building.. 8. Cathedral
  gallop.. 5. aubin 6. canter
  Tales, author.. 7. Chaucer
canticle... 3. lay, ode 4. hymn, lied,
  song 5. carol, ditty 6. Te Deum
Canticle of Canticles (Bib)...
  11. Song of Songs 13. Song of
  Solomon
cantilena... 6. legato, melody
  8. graceful
cantina... 3. bag 6. pocket, saloon
  7. canteen
cantle... 4. nook, part 5. crown, slice
  6. corner, saddle (part) 7. segment
  11. cornerpiece
canto... 4. book, song 5. poems (div
  of), tenor, verse 6. cantus, melody,
  poetry 7. descort

canton... 3. Uri (Switz) 6. county
7. commune, quarter 8. district,
insignia (Her), mofussil (Ind)
9. bailiwick, partition
cantor... 6. leader, singer 7. soloist
8. melodist, vocalist 9. precentor
cantoria... 7. balcony, gallery (choir)
cantrip... 5. charm, magic, spell, trick
canty... 6. lively 7. chipper 8. cheerful
9. sprightly
Canuck... 8. Canadian
canvas... 4. sail, tent, tuke (tewke)
5. cloth 6. circus 7. picture, tentage
8. covering, likeness, pavilion
9. tarpaulin 14. representation
canvasback... 4. duck
canvass... 4. poll 5. study 6. survey
7. examine, inquiry, solicit
8. campaign, consider 10. scrutinize
11. electioneer 12. solicitation
13. questionnaire
canyon, cañon... 4. abra (mouth)
5. chasm, dalle (wall), gorge, gulch
6. arroyo, coulee, ravine, violet
7. couloir
canzone, canzonetta... 4. poem, song
6. ballad, melody 8. canzonet,
madrigal
caoba... 8. mahogany, muskwood
caoutchouc... 3. ule 6. caucho, rubber
cap... 3. fez, hat, lid, taj, tam 4. atef,
coif, hood, kepi 5. beret, boina,
busby, shako, toque 6. barret,
biggin, bonnet, calpac, cloche, pileus,
turban 7. biretta (beretta), calotte,
calpack, chapeau 8. Balmoral,
havelock 9. headdress, headpiece,
shtreimal, sou'wester, zucchetto
10. cervelière 11. mortarboard,
tam-o'-shanter
cap (outer part)... 3. lid, tip, top
4. dome, fuze, peak, type 5. cover,
crown, excel, match, spire, trump
6. summit, top off 7. capital (Arch),
overlie, patella 8. complete
9. copestone, detonator
capa... 5. cloak 6. mantle 7. tobacco
capability... 5. power, skill 6. genius
7. ability, caliber, faculty, potency
8. ableness, adequacy, capacity
10. competence 13. qualification
capable... 3. apt, can, fit 4. able
5. adept 6. expert 7. equal to,
skilled 8. adequate 9. competent,
effective, efficient, qualified
10. proficient 12. accomplished
capable of...
boring.. 10. zylotomous
carrying.. 9. portative
flying.. 6. volant
growing.. 6. viable
living in harmony.. 10. compatible
penetration.. 8. pervious
suffering.. 8. passible 9. sensitive
capable of being...
ascertained.. 12. determinable
cultivated.. 6. arable
cut.. 7. sectile
defended.. 7. tenable
done.. 10. effectible
heard.. 7. audible
prevented.. 9. avertible

proved.. 8. testable 12. demonstrable
regulated.. 12. controllable
separated.. 9. divisible
spread.. 10. infectious
12. communicable
thrown.. 7. missile
uttered.. 7. effable
capacious... 4. full, much, wide
5. ample, broad, large, roomy
8. generous, spacious 9. expansive,
extensive 10. commodious,
voluminous 12. considerable
13. comprehensive
capacity... 4. role, room, size 5. limit,
power, skill, space 6. extent, spread,
status, talent, volume 7. caliber,
content, faculty, fitness, measure
8. adequacy, aptitude, function,
position, relation, strength
9. character 10. capability, efficiency
11. capacitance (Elec)
12. intelligence 13. accommodation
capacity for knowing... 9. intellect
cap and bells... 6. bauble, comedy
(symbol), motley 7. costume, marotti
9. headdress
caparison... 3. rig 4. tack 5. armor,
dress, get–up 6. livery 7. harness,
housing, panoply 10. horsecloth
12. horse blanket
cape... 3. ras 4. hood, mino, naze,
ness, spur 5. amice, cappa, cloak,
fichu, orale, point, sagum, talma
6. mantle, sontag, tippet 8. pelerine
(fur) 9. Inverness
cape (pert to)...
gooseberry.. 4. poha
hen.. 4. skua 6. petrel
pigeon.. 7. pintado
polecat.. 5. zoril
ruby.. 6. garnet, pyrope
sheep.. 9. albatross (Naut term)
Cape Cod turkey... 7. codfish (humor)
Cape Dutch... 9. Afrikaans (language)
Cape of Good Hope discoverer...
4. Diaz (1488)
caper... 3. tea 4. dido, leap, romp,
skip 5. antic, berry, dance, frisk,
prank 6. cavort, frolic, gambol,
prance 8. capriole, marigold
9. privateer (Hist)
capercaille... 6. grouse 13. cock of
the wood
caper herb family... 6. Cleome
8. Capparis 9. Polanisia
10. clammyweed 13. Capparidaceae
Cape Town... 7. capital (U of S Afr)
Cape Verde Island (Afr)... 3. Sal
Cape Verde negro... 5. Serer
capias... 4. writ 6. caveat 7. process,
warrant 8. mandamus 9. nisi prius
capillary... 4. fine, tube 6. minute,
vessel 7. slender 8. hairlike, trichoid
capilliform... 7. thready 8. hairlike
capillus... 4. hair
capistrate... 6. cowled, hooded
capital... 3. top 4. city, main, rare,
seat, type 5. chief, crest, crown,
funds, major, means, prime, vital
6. assets, letter, ruling, supply
7. leading, primary, serious, weighty
8. cardinal, dominant, foremost,

splendid **9.** excellent, financial, important, paramount, principal, prominent **10.** commanding, preeminent, shoestring
capitalism ... **8.** politics **10.** government **11.** bourgeoisie **14.** free enterprise
capitalist ... **5.** baron **6.** tycoon **7.** rich man **8.** investor **9.** bourgeois, financier, plutocrat
capital letter ... **6.** uncial **9.** majuscule
capital punishment ... **5.** noose **7.** gallows, hanging **8.** shooting, the chair **9.** beheading, execution, fusillade **10.** guillotine **12.** decapitation **13.** electrocution
capitano ... **3.** don **4.** capo **5.** chief **7.** captain, headman
capitate ... **7.** globose **8.** enlarged, headlike
Capitol (pert to) ...
Federal .. **10.** Washington (DC)
State .. **10.** Statehouse
capitulate ... **4.** cede, fall **9.** surrender
capitulation ... **6.** resumé, review, treaty **7.** recount, summary **9.** agreement, reckoning, rehearsal, statement, summation, surrender **10.** compendium **11.** enumeration, stipulation **14.** relinquishment
capon ... **3.** hen **4.** cock, fowl **6.** pullet, rabbit (castrated) **7.** chicken, poulard, poultry, rooster
caporal ... **4.** boss **7.** foreman, tobacco **8.** overseer
capote ... **4.** hood **5.** cloak **6.** bonnet, mantle, piquet **8.** overcoat
capped ... **7.** crested, pileata, pileate
Capri ...
beverage .. **4.** wine (white)
color .. **4.** blue **9.** blue–green
island site .. **11.** Bay of Naples
ruins (famed) .. **7.** palaces (Tiberius) **8.** grottoes **10.** Blue Grotto
caprice ... **3.** fad, toy **4.** kink, mood, whim **5.** fancy, freak, humor, prank, quirk **6.** vagary **7.** whimsey (whimsy) **8.** crotchet, escapade, flimflam
capricious ... **5.** moody **6.** fickle, fitful **7.** erratic, wayward **8.** fanciful, freakish, humorous, notional, sporadic, unsteady **9.** arbitrary, crotchety, eccentric, fantastic, whimsical **10.** inconstant **12.** inconsistent **13.** temperamental
Capricorn ... **4.** goat **7.** mansion (of Saturn) **10.** zodiac sign **13.** constellation
capriole ... **4.** leap **5.** caper **6.** cavort, curvet, gambol
capsicum ... **4.** herb **5.** chili **6.** pepper
capsize ... **5.** spill, upset **7.** subvert, tip over **8.** overturn **9.** overthrow **10.** turn turtle
capsule ... **3.** sac **4.** pill **5.** ascus, brief, theca, wafer **6.** précis, sheath **7.** enclose, epitome **8.** abstract, envelope, pericarp, seedcase, synopsis **10.** compendium
capsulize ... **5.** brief **7.** abridge, outline **8.** abstract, condense **9.** epitomize, summarize

captain ... **4.** skip **5.** chief, ruler **6.** leader, master, patron, police **7.** headman, officer, skipper **8.** overlord **9.** commander **10.** shipmaster
Captain Kidd ... **6.** pirate
Captains Courageous (pert to) ...
author .. **7.** Kipling
setting .. **9.** Grand Bank (Newfoundland)
tale of .. **7.** romance
caption ... **5.** title **6.** legend, rubric **7.** capture, seizure **8.** headline, subtitle
captious ... **6.** severe **7.** carping, cynical, peevish **8.** caviling, critical **9.** bickering, paltering, quibbling **12.** equivocatory, faultfinding **13.** hypercritical
captivate ... **4.** lure, vamp **5.** charm, snare **6.** allure, enamor, ravish, seduce **7.** attract, becharm, beguile, bewitch, capture, delight, enchant **8.** enthrall **9.** enrapture, fascinate, infatuate, transport
captive ... **4.** bond, serf **5.** helot **6.** détenu, thrall, unfree, vassal **7.** hostage **8.** conquest, enslaved, prisoner **10.** subjugated
captivity ... **6.** duress **7.** bondage, durance, serfdom, slavery **9.** detention, servitude, thralldom **10.** internment, subjection **11.** confinement, impoundment **12.** imprisonment **13.** incarceration
captor ... **5.** taker **7.** catcher **8.** capturer
capture ... **3.** beg, nab, net, win **4.** gain, haul, take **5.** catch, pinch, raven, snare **6.** arrest, collar **7.** caption, seizure **9.** apprehend, detention **12.** apprehension
capuche (Eccl) ... **4.** cowl, hood
capuchin ... **3.** sai **5.** Cebus **6.** monkey, pigeon
caput ... **3.** cap, top **4.** head **5.** crest, crown **7.** chapter, section **9.** paragraph
car ... **4.** auto, cart, jeep, tram **5.** coupe, motor, sedan, truck, wagon **6.** hot rod, jalopy, wheels (sl) **7.** caboose, chariot, clunker (sl), compact, flivver, machine, Pullman, vehicle **8.** carriage **9.** dune buggy, hatchback **10.** automobile, subcompact
carabao ... **5.** mango **7.** buffalo
carabinieri ... **9.** policeman **10.** carabineer
caracal ... **3.** fur **4.** lynx, pelt
caracara ... **4.** hawk **8.** carancha
caracole ... **5.** caper (manège) **9.** staircase
caract ... **5.** charm **6.** symbol (magic)
carafe ... **6.** bottle
carafon ... **8.** decanter
carapace ... **5.** plate, shell (turtle) **6.** chitin, lorica, shield **7.** carapax
caravan ... **3.** van **5.** wagon **6.** cafila (camel) **9.** cavalcade, motorcade **10.** expedition, procession
caravansary ... **3.** inn **4.** khan (chan)

5. hotel, serai 6. hostel, imaret,
posado 8. hostelry 9. resthouse,
roadhouse
carbine... 5. rifle 6. musket 7. escopet
carbohydrate... 5. sugar 6. starch
7. dextrin, glucose, lactose, maltose,
sucrose 8. dextrose, glycogen,
nutrient 9. cellulose 10. saccharide,
saccharose
carbon... 4. coke, copy, fuel, lead,
soot 7. diamond, residue 8. graphite
carbonate... 3. ore 5. trona 6. aerate,
natron 9. carbonize 11. chemicalize
carbon dioxide... 3. gas 6. dry ice
7. seeding (cloud) 11. refrigerant
Carborundum... 5. emery 8. abrasive
14. silicon carbide
carcass... 4. body 5. bones, kreng
(whale) 6. corpse 7. cadaver,
remains 8. skeleton
carcer... 5. stall (Rom circus) 6. prison
card... 3. map, tum 4. comb, menu,
post, rove 6. docket, domino, oddity,
postal, record, ticket 7. calling,
program 8. calendar, schedule
9. character 13. communication
card game... 3. gin, hoc, loo, pan
4. bank, faro, keno, skat 5. cinch,
comet, monte, pitch, poker, rummy,
stuss, tarot, whist 6. bridge, casino,
écarté, hearts, piquet, rounce
7. auction, bezique, canasta, cassino,
cayenne 8. baccarat, contract,
cribbage, pinochle 9. solitaire
10. panguingui
card game term... 3. ace 4. meld,
pass, pone, slam, trey, vole 5. joker,
pedro, tarot 6. cathop, misère,
tenace, tricon 7. declare 9. mistigris
cardinal... 3. red 4. bird, fish, main
5. chief 6. bishop, deacon, number,
priest, ruling 8. crowning, dominant,
foremost 9. paramount, principal
10. preeminent
cardinal (pert to)...
astrology.. 5. nadir 6. zenith
astronomy.. 10. solstitial
11. equinoctial
biology.. 7. maximum, minimum,
optimum
compass point.. 4. east, west
5. north, south
number.. 7. primary (one, two, three)
office.. 6. datary 7. dataria
virtues.. 7. justice 8. prudence
9. fortitude 10. temperance
virtues (Theol).. 4. hope 5. faith
7. charity
cardinal's hat... 3. red 4. rank
6. office
care... 4. duty, fret, heed, reck, task,
tend, wish 5. aegis, worry 6. desire,
regard 7. anxiety, caution, cherish,
concern, custody, keeping
9. attention, patronage 10. affliction,
protection, solicitude 11. carefulness,
heedfulness, supervision, thriftiness
12. jurisdiction 13. consideration
careen... 3. tip 4. cant, heel, keel,
lean, list, tilt 5. slant, slope
career... 3. set 4. flow, flux, line, work
6. course, stream 7. calling, mission,

passage, pursuit 8. business,
practice, progress, vocation
10. occupation, profession
care for... 4. help, like, love, mind,
reck, tend 5. fancy, guard, nurse,
prize, watch 6. attend, dote on,
foster, mother, relish, wait on
7. nurture 10. appreciate
carefree... 5. happy 6. jaunty
8. debonair 10. insouciant
12. lighthearted
careful... 4. wary 5. canny, chary,
exact 7. anxious, guarded, heedful,
mindful, prudent, thrifty 8. cautious,
discreet, gingerly, vigilant
9. advertent, attentive
10. meticulous, scrupulous,
solicitous, thoughtful 11. circumspect,
considerate, painstaking, punctilious
careless... 3. lax 5. loose 6. rakish,
remiss, sloppy 8. heedless, mindless,
reckless, slipshod, slovenly
9. impulsive, negligent, unheeding,
unmindful 10. nonchalant, regardless,
unthinking 11. inadvertent,
thoughtless, unconcerned
13. inconsiderate
carelessness... 8. bungling, disorder
9. disregard, unconcern
10. blundering, negligence
11. nonchalance 12. heedlessness,
indifference, recklessness
13. impulsiveness
15. inconsideration, thoughtlessness
caress... 3. pat, pet 4. bill, kiss
5. touch 6. coddle, cosset, dandle,
fondle, pamper, stroke
10. endearment
caressing... 7. hugging, kissing
8. fondling 9. endearing
cargo... 4. load 5. goods 6. burden,
charge, lading 7. carload, freight
8. boatload, shipload 9. truckload
cargo (pert to)...
afloat.. 7. flotsam
cast overboard.. 6. jetsam
loader, unloader.. 9. stevedore
Carib... 6. Indian
caribou... 4. deer 8. reindeer
caricature... 5. comic 6. overdo,
parody 7. cartoon, picture 8. satirize,
travesty 9. burlesque 10. caricatura,
distortion 12. exaggeration
caricaturist... 6. artist 8. humorist,
parodist 10. burlesquer
caries... 5. decay (Dent) 10. ulceration
carillon... 4. lyra 5. bells (fixed)
6. chimes 12. glockenspiel
cark... 3. vex 4. care, heed, load
5. pains, worry 6. burden, charge,
harass 7. trouble 8. distress
carl, carlot... 4. boor 5. churl
6. rustic 7. peasant, villein
8. bondsman 10. husbandman,
pinchpenny
Carmelite... 3. nun 4. monk 5. friar
8. White Nun 10. White Friar
carmen... 4. poem, song
11. incantation
Carmen... 5. gypsy, opera (1875)
7. heroine, romance
carmine... 3. red 5. color, stain

7. crimson, scarlet
carnage... 8. butchery, massacre
9. bloodshed, slaughter
10. decimation
carnal... 4. lewd 6. bodily, fleshy
7. earthly, mundane, sensual, worldly
9. corporeal 11. unspiritual
12. bloodthirsty
carnation... 3. red 4. pink, self
7. bizarre, picotee 8. Dianthus
carnelian... 4. sard 9. copper red
10. chalcedony
carnival... 4. fair, show 6. circus
7. revelry 8. feasting, festival
9. amusement, Mardi Gras
11. merrymaking 12. masquerading
carnivore... 3. cat, dog 4. bear, lion,
puma, seal 5. civet, coati, genet,
hyena, otter, panda, ratel, sable,
tiger, ursus 6. badger, mammal,
marten, weasel 7. meerkat, raccoon
8. mongoose 9. ichneumon
10. cacomistle
carnivorous... 10. meat–eating,
predaceous 11. omophageous
carol... 3. lay 4. lied, lilt, noel, sing,
song 5. dance (anc) 6. ballad,
warble 7. rejoice
Caroline Islands (coral)... 3. Yap
5. Parao 6. Ponape
carom... 4. bump 6. bounce, cannon,
strike 8. ricochet
carousal... 4. lark, orgy, romp
5. binge, feast, fling, revel, spree
6. frolic 7. banquet, carouse, revelry,
wassail
carouse... 4. birl 5. bouse, drink,
spree, toast 9. dissipate
carpet... 3. mat, rug 4. Agra, Kali,
Kuba 5. Herat (Herati), namda, tapis
6. nammad, Wilton 7. drugget
8. Brussels, flooring, moquette
9. Axminster, broadloom
11. Baluchistan
carpetbagger... 8. swindler
10. politician
carriage... 3. air 4. mien, pose
7. bearing, posture 8. attitude,
demeanor, presence 10. deportment
carriage (pert to)...
English.. 6. waggon 7. growler
8. dormeuse, stanhope
French.. 6. fiacre 7. caliche, voiture
general.. 3. bus, cab, car, gig, rig,
van 4. baby, hack, pram, shay, trap
5. buggy, coach, wagon 6. calssh,
chaise, cisium, dennet, go–cart,
hansom, landau, surrey, tandem
7. cariole, chariot, omnibus, phaeton,
tallyho, vehicle 8. carryall, clarence,
dearborn, rockaway, victoria
9. kittereen, landaulet
10. conveyance, shandrydan
12. perambulator
history.. 7. tumbrel, vis–à–vis, whiskey
8. curricle
Indian.. 4. okka 5. tonga 6. gharry
7. hackery
Italian.. 7. vettura
one–horse.. 3. gig 4. shay 5. sulky
Orient.. 4. sado 10. jinrikisha

Philippines.. 9. carromata
Russia.. 5. araba 6. troika 7. droshky
9. tarantass
carried... 5. borne, giddy, toted
6. carted, lugged 8. conveyed,
ravished 11. transported
carrier... 3. boy 4. mail, mule, rail,
ship, wave 5. crate 6. bearer, coolie,
pigeon, porter, redcap, runner, vessel
7. courier, drayman, express
8. cargador, conveyor, teamster
9. messenger, stevedore
carrier (pert to)...
disease.. 3. fly, rat 7. typhoid
8. mosquito
Indian.. 5. Tinne (Brit)
staff.. 5. macer
carrion... 4. vile 6. corpse, rotten
7. carcass, corrupt 9. loathsome
carrion (pert to)...
bug.. 6. beetle
buzzard.. 4. hawk 7. vulture
8. caracara
flower.. 5. morel
fungus.. 9. stinkhorn
carrot... 5. drias (deadly) 6. Daucus
(Old World) 9. Ammiaceae
10. nivernaise (glazed), umbellifer
carrousel... 9. whirligig
10. roundabout, tournament
12. merry–go–round
carry... 3. lug 4. bear, cart, hold,
take, tote, wart 5. ferry 6. convey
7. conduct, publish 8. transfer,
transmit 9. transport
carry away, off... 3. win 6. abduct,
eloign, enamor, remove 7. succeed
9. fascinate 10. accomplish
carry on... 4. rage, wage 6. endure,
frolic, manage 7. conduct, operate
8. continue 9. misbehave, persevere
carry out, through... 2. do 5. apply
6. ravish 7. execute, perform, sustain
8. complete, continue, transact
10. accomplish
cart... 4. dray, wain 5. carry, sulky,
wagon 6. convey, reckla, telega
7. morfrey (morphrey), tumbrel (anc),
vehicle (2–wheeled)
carta, Charta... 4. deed 5. Magna
(Eng) 7. charter 9. parchment
cartage... 7. drayage, portage
8. carriage, teamster, truckage
10. expressage 14. transportation
carte... 3. map 4. card, list, menu
5. chart 7. diagram 10. bill of fare
cartel... 4. bloc (Polit), defy, pact, pool
5. paper, truce, trust 6. letter
7. compact, entente 8. covenant
9. agreement, challenge, syndicate
10. convention 11. arrangement
Carthage... see also *Carthaginian*
capital.. 13. Vandal Kingdom
destroyer.. 6. Romans
queen.. 4. Dido
rebuilt by.. 8. Augustus
Carthaginian (pert to)...
apple.. 11. pomegranate
foe.. 4. Cato
general.. 6. Xerxes 8. Hannibal
god.. 6. Moloch 8. Melkarth
language.. 5. Punic

Lion.. **8**. Hannibal
magistrate.. **7**. suffete
name (later).. **15**. Justinianopolis
wars (three).. **5**. Punic
Carthusian Order (pert to)...
founder.. **7**. St Bruno
monastery.. **7**. Certosa (It, 1396)
site.. **8**. Grenoble (Fr)
cartilage... **4**. bone (ossified) **6**. tissue
  7. gristle
cartload... **6**. fother
cartograph... **3**. map **4**. plat **5**. chart
cartoon... **6**. design, sketch **7**. pattern,
  picture **10**. caricature
cartoonist... **4**. Arno, Capp, Ding, Nast
  6. Disney
cartouche... **5**. shell **6**. corbel, design,
  shield (Her), tablet **7**. console
  9. cartridge **10**. cantilever (Arch)
cartwheel... **4**. coin **5**. dollar
  8. somerset **10**. handspring,
  somersault
carve... **3**. cut, hew **4**. form, make
  5. chase, grave, sever, shape
  6. chisel, cleave, furrow, incise
  7. engrave, fashion **9**. apportion,
  fabricate, sculpture
carving... **5**. cameo **8**. diaglyph,
  intaglio **9**. anaglyphy, embossing,
  sculpture **11**. anaglyptics
caryatid... **6**. column, figure (fem)
  8. pilaster **11**. priestesses (temple)
casa... **5**. adobe, cabin, house
  8. building
cascade... **4**. fall, linn **5**. Falls, Sault
  7. Niagara **8**. cataract **9**. waterfall
case... **3**. box **4**. etui, file **5**. cover,
  crate, crush (sl), event, folio
  6. carton, coffer, pillow, sheath,
  victim **7**. attaché, cabinet, example,
  holster, lawsuit **8**. argument,
  covering, cupboard, instance
  9. condition, portfolio **10**. receptacle
  12. circumstance
case (in any)... **3**. yet **4**. even
  6. anyhow, anyway **7**. anywise,
  however **8**. possibly, provided
  10. regardless **15**. notwithstanding
case (pert to)...
arrow.. **6**. quiver
book.. **5**. forel
bottle (liquor).. **8**. cellaret
cigar.. **7**. humidor
conscience (Sci).. **9**. casuistry
grammar.. **6**. dative **8**. ablative,
  genitive, vocative **10**. nominative
history (disease).. **6**. record
  9. anamnesis
image (Bib).. **5**. ephod
jewel, relics.. **3**. tye **4**. apse
spore.. **5**. ascus
surgeon's.. **7**. trousse
cash... **4**. coin, dust (gold) **5**. darby,
  funds, money **6**. silver, specie
  7. capital, coinage, mintage
  8. currency **9**. spondulix
cashmere... **4**. goat, wool **5**. shawl
  6. fabric
casino... **6**. tavern **7**. cabaret, cassino
  (game) **8**. ballroom, gambling
  9. roadhouse **11**. summerhouse
cask... **4**. butt, case, drum, pipe

5. terce **6**. bareca, barrel, casket,
  firkin, tierce **8**. puncheon **9**. kilderkin
cask (pert to)...
amt when not filled.. **6**. ullage
bulge.. **5**. bilge
oil.. **4**. rier
part.. **3**. lag **4**. hoop **5**. stave
rim.. **5**. chime (chimb)
support.. **8**. stillage
casket... **3**. box, pyx, tye (jewel)
  4. cist, kist, tomb **5**. chest
  8. cassette **11**. sarcophagus
casserole... **4**. dish, mold **5**. brown
  (color) **6**. vessel **8**. saucepan
cassine... **4**. game (card)
cast... **3**. hue **4**. form, hurl, kind, look,
  mold, role, shed, tone, toss, type
  5. eject, fling, heave, model, pitch,
  sling, throw **6**. glance, matrix, squint,
  troupe **7**. pattern **8**. template
  9. facsimile **10**. impression,
  strabismus **16**. dramatis personae
cast (pert to)...
aside.. **4**. jilt, junk, shed **5**. scrap
  6. reject **7**. discard
away.. **5**. eject, wreck **6**. unmoor
  9. shipwreck
blame.. **6**. accuse **7**. censure
  8. reproach **9**. reprehend
off.. **4**. doff, knit, molt, shed **5**. untie
  6. unmoor **7**. discard **9**. eliminate
castaway... **6**. pariah **7**. outcast
  8. derelict **9**. reprobate
caste... **4**. race, rank **5**. breed, class,
  stock **6**. status **7**. lineage, society
  8. standing
caste (Ind)... **3**. Dom, Meo **4**. Ahir,
  Jati, Koli, Magi, Mali, Pasi, Teli
  5. Gaddi, Sudra, Varna **6**. banian,
  pariah, Vaisya **7**. Brahman
  9. Kshatriya
caster, castor... **4**. vial **5**. cruet, horse
  (old), wheel **6**. roller, vessel
  (condiment)
castigate... **5**. emend **6**. punish,
  revise, strafe **7**. chasten, correct,
  reprove **8**. chastise, penalize
  9. criticize **10**. discipline
Castile... **4**. soap **7**. kingdom
Castilian... **7**. Iberian, Spanish
castle... **4**. fort, keep **5**. house, tower,
  villa **6**. donjon **7**. chateau, citadel
  8. fortress **10**. stronghold
  13. fortification
Castor (pert to)...
brother (twin).. **6**. Pollux
constellation.. **6**. Gemini
mother.. **4**. Leda
stars.. **6**. Castor, Pollux
castrate... **4**. geld, spay **5**. alter,
  prune **10**. emasculate
castrated (pert to)...
bull.. **5**. steer
cat.. **3**. gib
horse.. **7**. gelding
man.. **6**. eunoch
rooster.. **5**. capon
casual... **5**. stray **6**. chance, random
  9. offhanded **10**. contingent,
  fortuitous, incidental, occasional,
  unforeseen **11**. indifferent
  14. unpremeditated

casual observation... 6. remark
casualty... 6. chance, hazard, injury,
mishap 7. payment, tragedy
8. accident, calamity, disaster, fatality
9. mischance 10. misfortune
11. contingency, contretemps
12. misadventure
casus (pert to)...
act of God.. 14. casus fortuitus
common law.. 12. casus omissus
conscience.. 17. casus conscientiae
Latin.. 4. case 5. event 8. occasion
treaty.. 13. casus foederis
war.. 10. casus belli
cat... 3. gib 4. balu, eyra, lynx, pard,
puma 5. alley, civet, Felid, Felis,
genet, hyena, manul, ounce, tabby,
tiger 6. caffre, cougar, feline, jaguar,
margay, ocelot, pajero, rasset, serval
7. cheetah, dasyure, leopard,
panther, wildcat 9. catamount,
grimalkin
cat (pert to)...
fear of.. 12. ailurophobia, aleurophobia
fish.. 4. pout, raad 6. hassar, tandan
7. eelpout
game.. 6. tipcat
gut.. 5. tharm 6. string (violin)
slang.. 6. hepcat
term.. 5. kitty, shrew, tabby, vixen
6. kitten 8. ailuroid 9. chessycat,
Mehitabel (Mehetabel)
cat (species)... 4. Manx 5. Manul,
Tibet 6. Angora, Caffre, Margay
7. Burmese, Maltese, Persian,
Siamese, Turkish 8. Cheshire,
Egyptian 9. Abyssinian, Chinchilla
13. tortoise–shell (black and yellow)
cataclysm... 4. ruin 6. deluge
7. debacle 8. calamity, disaster, The
Flood, upheaval 10. convulsion,
inundation, revolution 11. catastrophe
catacomb... 4. tomb 5. crypt, vault
6. grotto, locule 8. cemetery
(underground) 9. Appian Way
catalepsy... 6. trance 8. hypnosis
9. cataplexy 10. thanatosis
catalogue... 4. book, file, list 5. index,
tally 6. codify, digest, record
8. calendar, classify, pamphlet,
register, schedule, tabulate
11. enumeration
catamaran... 4. boat, raft 5. balsa,
float 6. vessel 7. jangada
catamount... 3. cat 6. cougar
12. catamountain
catapult... 4. hurl 5. shoot, sling
6. engine, onager 7. robinet
8. arbalest, ballista, scorpion
9. slingshot
cataract... 4. fall, linn 5. Falls, flood,
sault (soo) 6. deluge 7. cascade,
disease, Niagara, opacity (eye),
torrent 8. downpour, Victoria
9. cachoeira, waterfall
cataria... 6. catnip
catasta... 5. stage (slave traffic)
6. stocks 8. scaffold
catastrophe... 4. doom, ruin 6. finale,
mishap, payoff 7. tragedy
8. calamity, disaster 9. cataclysm

10. denouement, misfortune,
revolution 11. termination
catastrophic... 4. dire 5. black
7. ruinous 10. calamitous,
deplorable, disastrous
catawba... 4. wine 5. color (red),
grape 6. Indian
catch... 3. get, nab 4. draw, hear,
hold, hook, take, trap 5. fault, ketch,
prize, reach, rondo, seize, snare,
trick, troll 6. detent (clock), engage,
entrap, ignite 7. attract, capture,
seizure 8. overtake 9. intercept
catch (pert to)...
a likeness.. 4. draw 6. depict
7. portray
a ride.. 4. hook 5. hitch, thumb
9. hitchhike
sight of.. 3. see 4. espy 6. behold,
descry 7. discern, glimpse
catchword... 3. cry, cue 6. byword,
phrase, slogan 7. formula
10. shibboleth
cate... 4. food 6. viands 8. dainties
10. delicacies, provisions (bought)
catechism... 5. guide 6. belief, manual
9. questions (set of) 11. instruction
(oral)
catechumen... 5. chela, pupil
6. layman, novice 7. convert
8. disciple, neophyte
categoric, categorical... 6. direct
7. crucial, logical 8. absolute,
explicit, positive 9. arbitrary,
pragmatic 10. convincing
11. dictatorial, unequivocal,
unqualified
category... 4. head 5. class, genre,
genus, group, order, state 6. branch,
family, specie 7. bracket, species
8. division 12. denomination
14. classification
catena... 5. chain 6. series
8. sequence 10. continuity
catenary... 5. curve (Math) 9. chainlike
cater, cater to... 4. feed 5. favor,
humor, serve, toady 6. oblige,
pander, please, purvey 7. indulge,
procure, provide, satisfy 10. minister
to 11. diagonalize 13. cater–cornered
caterpillar... 4. grub, weri 5. aweto,
eruca, larva 7. tractor
caterwaul... 3. woo (derog) 4. meow,
wail 5. court, miaow 7. screech
cathedral... 3. dom 4. fane (anc)
5. duomo 6. church 8. official
10. ex cathedra 13. authoritative
Cathedral...
England.. 6. Durham 9. Salisbury
France.. 5. Reims (Rheims) 6. Amiens
9. Notre Dame
Istanbul (Constantinople).. 8. St
Sophia
Italy.. 7. Lateran, St Mark's
Rome.. 8. St Peter's
Scotland.. 7. St Giles
cathedral (pert to)...
chair (Bishop's).. 8. cathedra
chapter member.. 10. capitulary
church.. 3. dom 7. Lateran (Rome)
city.. 3. Ely (Eng)
passage.. 5. slype

catholic... 4. wide 5. broad 6. church, global 7. general, liberal 8. orthodox, pandemic 9. Christian, universal 10. ecumenical 12. cosmopolitan
Catholic publication... 4. Ordo
catkin... 5. ament, spike 7. cattail
catlike... 5. catty 6. feline 8. stealthy 9. noiseless
catling... 3. cat (little) 6. kitten, string (violin)
Cato (pert to)...
author of.. 13. De Agri Cultura
famed as.. 7. General 9. statesman 10. ambassador (to Carthage)
nickname.. 8. The Elder 11. Cato of Utica
Catoism... 9. austerity, harshness
cats... 8. Kilkenny
cat's cradle... 3. hei 4. game 7. ribwort
cat's-paw... 4. dupe, gull, loof, pawn, tool 5. cully, hitch (knot) 6. breeze (Naut), puppet, stooge 10. instrument
cattail... 4. musk, reed, tule 5. ament, raupo, teree 6. catkin, totora 7. matreed 9. Typhaceae
cattle... 3. Bos 4. cows, kine, neat, oxen, stot, yaks 5. asses, goats, mules, sheep, stock, swine 6. bovine, camels, horses, llamas, niatas, rabble, Taurus 7. banteng, chattel 8. bullocks, property 9. livestock
cattle (breed)... 4. Zebu 5. Angus, Devon, Kerry, Niata, Welsh 6. Brahma, Durham, Jersey, Sussex 7. Dishley 8. Guernsey, Hereford, Holstein, Longhorn 9. Charolais, Leicester, Shorthorn 14. Santa Gertrudis
cattle (pert to)...
collection.. 4. herd 5. drove
disease.. 7. murrain 10. rinderpest
driver.. 6. drover
food.. 5. agist 6. forage
herder.. 6. cowboy, drover
hybrid.. 4. Zobo 7. cattalo 9. cattleyak
motherless.. 6. dogies
pen.. 4. crew 5. barth, reeve
shed.. 6. hemmel
stealer.. 7. abactor, abigeus, rustler
unbranded.. 9. mavericks
catty... 6. feline, weight 7. catlike, cattish 8. spiteful, stealthy 11. treacherous
cauboge... 4. boor 7. bumpkin
Caucasian... 4. race, Slav, Turk 5. gypsy, Latin, Norse, Osset, Pshav, white 6. Hebrew, Semite, Teuton, Viking 8. Armenian, Bohemian, Georgian, White Man 10. Anglo–Saxon 11. Xanthochroi
Caucasian (pert to)...
blond.. 6. Teuton 8. Estonian 11. Xanthochroi
brunette.. 7. Iberian 8. Armenian 11. Melanochroi
Chinese.. 4. Lolo, Nosu
dialect.. 4. Andi, Avar, Svan
European.. 8. Japhetic

goat (wild).. 3. tur
liquor.. 5. kefir
Moslem.. 3. Laz (Laze, Lazi) 7. Sunnite
mountain.. 8. Caucasus
peak.. 6. Elbrus (Elbruz), Kazbek
cauchemar... 9. nightmare
caucus... 7. meeting (Polit), primary 8. assembly
cauda... 4. scut, tail 9. appendage
caudata... 5. newts 8. Amphibia 11. salamanders
caught... see also *catch* 5. treed 7. latched 8. cornered
caught (pert to)...
napping.. 7. unready 8. unprimed 10. unprepared
sight of.. 3. saw 6. espied 8. descried
up in.. 4. tied 7. engaged, tangled 8. absorbed, intent on, involved 10. implicated
caul... 3. net 6. basket 7. netting, network, omentum 8. membrane
cause... 5. aetio (comb form), agent, basis, drive, greed 6. create, factor, ground, induce, motive, reason, source 7. crusade, produce, provoke 8. campaign, etiology, movement, occasion 9. originate 10. mainspring 13. justification
cause (pert to)...
approach.. 7. attract
be done.. 4. writ 11. fieri facias
bring about.. 6. effect
buy and sell.. 7. whipsaw
coagulate.. 4. curd 6. curdle 7. congeal, thicken
contract unevenly.. 6. pucker
face East.. 6. orient
harm.. 4. bane
irritate.. 6. rankle
raise in relief.. 6. emboss
remember.. 6. remind
roll.. 7. trundle
speed up.. 10. accelerate
take root.. 8. radicate
causerie... 4. chat, talk 6. parley 7. article 8. converse, treatise 9. paragraph 10. discussion 12. conversation
causes, science of... 8. etiology
causeuse... 4. sofa 9. tête-à-tête
causeway... 4. dike 7. highway 10. embankment
causing...
destiny.. 5. fatal
emotion.. 7. emotive
forgetfulness.. 8. nepenthe
laughter.. 8. risorial
motion.. 6. motile
caustic... 4. acid, tart 5. acrid, curve (optic), sharp 6. biting, bitter, severe 7. burning, cutting, erodent, mordant, pungent, pyrotic 8. snappish, stinging, virulent 9. corrosive, satirical, vitriolic 10. astringent, escharotic 11. acrimonious, penetrating
caustic agent... 3. lye 4. alum, lime 7. erodent 9. quicklime
causticity... 7. acidity 8. acerbity,

acrimony, asperity, pungency, tartness
9. mordacity 10. bitterness
11. astringency 13. corrosiveness
cautel... 5. trick 7. caution
8. prudence 9. direction (Eccl)
10. precaution
cauterize... 4. burn, char, sear
5. brand, singe 7. torrefy
cautery... 7. burning, searing
8. inustion 10. instrument
13. cauterization
caution... 4. card (coll), care, heed,
warn 5. aviso 6. advice, caveat,
notice, oddity 7. anxiety, counsel,
precept, proviso, warning 8. forecast,
prudence, wariness 9. chariness,
vigilance 10. admonition, providence,
solicitude 11. exhortation,
forethought, mindfulness
12. cautiousness, notification,
watchfulness 14. circumspection
cautious... 4. wary 5. canny, chary
6. Fabian 7. careful, guarded,
heedful, mindful, prudent
11. circumspect
cautiously... 6. cagily, warily
7. cannily, charily 8. gingerly
9. carefully, guardedly, heedfully,
mindfully, prudently 10. discreetly
13. circumspectly
cavalcade... 4. raid, ride 5. march
6. parade, review 7. caravan,
pageant 9. motorcade 10. procession
cavalier... 3. gay 4. coin (Fr), curt
5. brave, frank, lover, rider 6. escort,
knight, squire 7. admirer, brusque,
esquire, gallant, haughty, soldier
8. horseman, Royalist 9. caballero,
cavaliere, chevalier, Roundhead
10. disdainful, equestrian
12. high–spirited, supercilious
cavalry... 4. army 6. horses, yellow
(color) 8. horsemen 10. knighthood
cavalry (pert to)...
horse.. 6. lancer
man.. 5. spahy, uhlan 6. Hussar,
lancer 7. dragoon, trooper
unit.. 5. troop
weapon.. 5. lance, saber 9. demilance
cave... 3. den, mew 4. abri, cove,
grot, hole, lair 5. antre, cover, lodge
(beaver), speos 6. antrum, cavern,
cellar, covert, dugout, grotto,
subway, tunnel 7. chamber, shelter,
spelunk 10. subterrane
cave (pert to)...
fish.. 9. blindfish
man.. 11. Paleolithic
nature of.. 9. speluncar
study of.. 10. speleology
cave canem... 11. Beware of Dog
cave dweller... 10. troglodyte
Cave of Adullam... 9. Seceeders
(1866)
caviar, caviare... 3. roe 5. garum
6. relish 8. delicacy, fish eggs
cavil... 4. cark, carp, marl, quip
5. dodge, evade, parry, shift
6. bicker, boggle, haggle, palter
7. quibble, shuffle 9. criticize,
pussyfoot 10. equivocate
caviler... 5. momus 6. critic, hedger

8. frondeur, quibbler 10. criticizer
11. equivocator, faultfinder
cavity... 3. dip, pit, sac, vug (voog)
4. aula, bore (gun), cava, hole, sink,
well 5. abyss, antra, atria, bursa,
chasm, fossa, fosse, geode, lumen,
shaft, sinus 6. antrum, areole,
atrium, caries, coelom, crater, hollow
7. cochlea, loculus 10. depression
11. compartment
cavort... 4. dido, romp, skip 5. antic,
caper, cut up, frisk, prank 6. curvet,
gambol, prance 7. flounce, gambade,
gambado
cavy... 3. pig 4. paca 5. stray
6. agouti, rodent 8. capybara
(capibara) 9. guinea pig
caw... 3. cry 5. croak, quark, quawk
11. exclamation
cay... 3. kay 5. islet
cease... 3. end 4. quit, rest (law),
stop 5. avast, pause, stint 6. desist,
perish 7. abandon, fade out, refrain
8. intermit, leave off, shutdown
9. disappear, pretermit
11. discontinue
ceaseless... 7. endless, nonstop
8. constant, unbroken, unending
9. continued, incessant, perennial,
perpetual, unceasing 10. continuous
12. interminable 13. round the
clock, uninterrupted
ceaselessness... 9. constancy
10. continuity, incessancy, perpetuity
11. endlessness 14. successiveness
cease to be... 3. die 6. expire, perish
8. dissolve 9. disappear
cease to please... 4. pall
Cebus... 3. sai 6. monkey 8. capuchin
cecils... 10. croquettes
cecity... 9. blindness
Cecrops (pert to)...
daughter.. 5. Herse 8. Aglauros
founder of (tradition).. 6. Athens
king of.. 6. Attica
symbol.. 7. half man 10. half dragon
cedar (pert to)...
bird.. 7. waxwing
class.. 7. conifer
fruit.. 6. cedron
genus.. 5. Thuja, Toona 6. Cedrus
9. Juniperus
green.. 5. cedre
moss.. 8. hornwort
type.. 5. savin 6. deodar, sabine
7. incense, juniper, Lebanon (Bib),
Spanish 10. arborvitae
11. cryptomeria
cede... 5. grant, waive, yield 6. assign,
confer 7. abandon 8. renounce
9. surrender 10. capitulate, relinquish
cedula... 3. tax 6. permit 8. schedule,
security (Finan) 10. obligation
11. certificate
ceil... 4. line 5. cover 7. overlay
8. wainscot
ceiling... 4. acme, roof 5. astel, limit,
price, trave 6. apogee, lining, screen,
utmost 7. curtain, lacunar, maximum,
plafond 8. covering 9. lacunaria
10. planchment, visibility
12. consummation

celebrant... 6. priest (Eucharist)
9. worshiper (worshipper)
11. communicant
celebrate... 4. keep, laud, sing
5. extol, honor, revel 6. herald,
praise 7. glorify, maffick, observe,
roister 8. emblazon, proclaim
9. solemnize 11. commemorate,
memorialize
celebrated... 5. famed, noted
6. famous 7. feasted, honored,
popular 8. far–famed, observed,
renowned 9. distingué, well–known
11. illustrious 13. distinguished
celebration... 4. bout, fete, rite
5. fling, revel, spree 6. bender
7. fanfare, jubilee 8. ceremony,
function 9. epinicion, festivity,
rejoicing 10. observance
13. commemoration
celebrity... 3. VIP 4. fame 5. éclat,
glory 6. notary 7. notable
8. luminary, somebody
10. famousness, popularity
11. recognition
celerity... 5. haste, speed 8. dispatch,
rapidity, velocity 9. swiftness
10. speediness
celery... 4. ache 8. smallage (wild)
9. Ammiacaea
celestial... 6. astral, divine, uranic
7. angelic, sky blue 8. ethereal,
heavenly 12. paradisaical
Celestial (pert to)...
being.. 5. angel 6. cherub, seraph
body.. 4. star 5. comet 6. nebula
city.. 6. heaven, utopia 9. Jerusalem
empire.. 7. Chinese, Tien Chu
equator.. 8. meridian
mind elevation.. 7. anagoge
teacher.. 6. Taoist
celibate... 4. monk 6. single
8. bachelor, monastic, Platonic,
spinster 9. abstinent, continent,
unmarried
cell... 3. egg, kil 4. cyst, germ, ovum
5. cnida, crypt 6. cytode, prison
7. alveola, cellule, dungeon
11. compartment
cell (pert to)...
animal.. 6. amoeba (ameba) 7. rotifer
8. protozoa
biology.. 7. energid, meiosis, mitosis,
nucleus, spireme
cell–like.. 9. celliform
division.. 5. linin 7. spireme
8. amitosis
eating.. 9. cytophagy
Egyptian (tomb).. 6. serdab
honeycomb.. 8. alveolus
Irish.. 3. kil (kill)
locomotive.. 5. sperm, zooid
Roman.. 4. alla, naos
study.. 8. cytology
substance.. 5. linin
walls.. 9. cellulose
cellaret... 4. case 8. tantalus
9. sideboard
Celt... 4. Erse, Gael, Manx, Scot
5. Welsh 6. Breton 7. Cornish
Celtic (pert to)...
abbot.. 5. coarb

bard.. 6. Ossian
cattle.. 2. ox
church.. 9. Christian
deity.. 7. Taranis
foot soldier.. 4. kern
horse.. 4. pony (Shetland)
Island.. 4. Manx
language.. 4. Erse
minstrel.. 4. bard
Mother of Gods.. 3. Ana (Anu)
mountain.. 3. ben
Neptune.. 3. Ler
nickname.. 10. Turtleback
Order.. 5. Druid
people.. 5. Gauls, Irish, Scots, Welsh
7. Bretons, Britons
perfume.. 4. nard 9. spikenard
sun god.. 3. Lug (Lugh)
cembalo... 8. dulcimer 11. harpsichord
12. clavicembalo
cement... 4. bind, fuse, glue, join,
paar, pave 5. putty, stick, unite
6. cohere, fasten, mastic, mortar,
solder 8. adhesive, concrete,
pavement, solidify
cemetery... 6. litten 7. Calvary
8. boneyard, catacomb, Golgotha,
lich gate (entrance), mortuary
9. graveyard, mausoleum
10. churchyard, necropolis
11. polyandrium 12. potter's field
cenobite... 4. Monk 5. Order (anc)
6. Essene 7. recluse
cenotaph... 4. tomb (empty)
7. memento 8. memorial, monument
censer bearer... 7. acolyte 8. altar
boy, thurifer
censor... 5. judge 6. critic 7. monitor
8. censurer, reviewer, superego
11. faultfinder
censure... 4. flay 5. blame, chide,
slate, targe 6. accuse 7. chasten,
condemn, impeach, inveigh, reprove,
slating 8. reproach 9. damnation,
expurgate, reprimand 11. reprobation
12. condemnation, denunciation,
reprehension
cent... 4. coin, game (old) 5. penny
6. copper, trifle 7. hundred, red cent
centaur (Myth)... 4. race (Thessaly)
6. Nessus 8. Lapithae, man–horse
(half man) 9. bucentaur, Centaurus
(Astron)
centennial... 4. game (dice)
9. hundredth, red–yellow
11. anniversary
Centennial State... 8. Colorado
center... 3. cor, hub 4. base, core,
nave 5. axial, focus, heart, midst
6. kernel, marrow, middle
7. midmost, nucleus, pivotal, seaport
8. emporium
center (pert to)...
away from.. 6. distal
bull's–eye.. 5. clout 6. target
line.. 6. axiate, cesura
center of...
attention.. 8. cynosure
earth.. 9. epicenter
gravity.. 6. kernel 7. centrum
nervous system.. 5. brain
sail.. 4. bunt

target .. 3. eye 8. bull's—eye
centerpiece ... 4. bowl 7. epergne
centipede ... 4. rope (Naut) 6. earwig,
insect 8. chilipod, myriapod
central ... 3. mid 4. arch, main
5. axial, basic, chief, focal, prime
6. master, middle 7. capital, centric,
leading, midmost, pivotal, primary
8. cardinal, dominant, foremost
9. principal 11. equidistant
Central America ...
bird .. 7. jacamar 8. puffbird
boat .. 6. cayuco, pitpan
country .. 6. Panama 8. Honduras
9. Costa Rica, Guatemala, Nicaragua
10. El Salvador
Indian .. 4. Maya 5. Carib
monkey .. 4. mono
rodent .. 4. paca
snake .. 10. bushmaster
tree .. 3. ebo, ule 5. amate
9. sapodilla
Central Asia (pert to) ...
gazelle .. 3. ahu
wild horse .. 6. tarpan
wind storm .. 5. buran
Central State ... 6. Kansas
centuries (ten) ... 7. chiliad
century ... 3. Age 4. aeon (eon)
7. centred (anc), hundred 8. eternity
9. centenary 10. centennial
century plant ... 4. aloe 5. agave
6. maguey
ceorl (Eng Hist) ... 5. churl, thane
7. freeman, villein
cepa ... 5. onion
cephalon ... 4. head (Zool)
cephalopod ... 3. ink (secretion)
5. sepia 6. cuttle 7. octopus
10. cuttlefish
ceramics ... 4. tile 5. china, delft,
spode 6. mosaic 7. pottery, Satsuma
8. crockery, majolica, Wedgwood
9. porcelain
ceramics term ... 4. clay, kiln, laun
5. adobe, stove, wheel 6. sleeve (silk)
7. furnace 8. ceramist 10. ceramicist
12. ceramography
ceratoid ... 5. horny 8. hornlike
10. horn—shaped
cere ... 3. wax 4. wrap (dead body)
6. anoint 12. protuberance (bird's)
cereal ... 4. bran, mush, rice 5. grits,
gruel, maize, wheat 6. farina, hominy
7. granola, oatmeal 8. porridge
10. corn flakes
cereal grass ... 3. oat, rye 4. ragi
5. grain, maize, wheat 6. barley,
raggee
cereal spike ... 3. ear
cerebellum ... 5. brain (part)
cerebral (pert to) ... 4. lobe 5. brain
6. speech 8. arteries, peduncle
9. consonant (Phonet) 11. crus
cerebri, hemispheres
cerebrum ... 5. brain 10. encephalon
cere cloth ... 7. wrapper (corpse)
8. cerement, chrismal 12. grave
clothes
ceremonial ... 4. prim 5. stiff
6. custom, formal, ritual 7. precise,
service, studied 8. ceremony,

function, liturgic 9. formality
11. punctilious 12. conventional
ceremonial (pert to) ...
chamber .. 4. kiva
departure .. 6. congee
splendor .. 9. pageantry
ceremonious ... 6. formal, polite
7. precise 8. gracious 9. attentive,
courteous 10. ceremonial, respectful
11. deferential, ritualistic
ceremony ... 4. form, pomp, rite, show
6. parade, review, ritual 8. function
9. formality, solemnity
10. observance 11. performance
ceremony, without ... 6. humbly,
meekly, simply 7. quietly 8. casually,
modestly 9. sans façon
10. informally 15. unceremoniously
Ceres, Rom (pert to) ...
astronomy .. 8. asteroid (lst found)
father .. 6. Saturn
Feast .. 8. Cerialia (Apr 19)
Goddess of .. 4. Corn 5. Grain
9. Fertility 11. Agriculture
Greek name .. 7. Demeter
mother .. 3. Ops
Cereus ... 6. cactus 7. saguaro
13. night—blooming
cerise ... 5. color 7. blue—red, fuchsia
10. cherrylike
ceroplastics ... 8. modeling, waxworks
certain ... 3. one 4. sure 5. clear,
exact, fixed, plain 7. assured,
decided, insured, precise 8. absolute,
definite, positive 9. certified,
confident, exclusive, indubious,
undoubted, warranted
10. guaranteed, inevitable,
undeniable, undoubting
11. determinate, trustworthy
14. unquestionable
16. incontrovertible
certainly ... 3. yea, yes 4. amen
5. truly 6. indeed, really, surely, verily
7. clearly, in truth, utterly 8. actually,
of course 9. assuredly, precisely
10. absolutely, by all means,
definitely, inevitably, positively
certainty ... 6. pledge, shoo—in, surety
8. sureness 9. assurance, certitude
13. inevitability, infallibility
certificate ... 5. check, money
6. ticket 7. diploma, voucher
10. credential 11. testimonial
certificate (pert to) ...
financial .. 3. IOU 5. draft, scrip
9. debenture
India .. 5. hundi
medical (Eng college) .. 8. aegrotat
certification ... 2. OK 3. fix 5. proof
8. sanction 10. validation
11. affirmation, attestation, certificate,
endorsement 12. confirmation,
ratification 13. ascertainment,
authorization 14. substantiation
certify ... 5. prove, swear, vouch
6. assure, attest, avouch, ratify, verify
7. approve, confirm, endorse, witness
8. accredit, validate 9. ascertain,
determine, establish, guarantee
11. acknowledge, corroborate
cerulean ... 4. blue 5. azure

7. sky–blue
cerumen... 6. earwax
cervine... 8. deerlike
cess... 3. bag, tax 4. cede, duty, levy,
toll 5. yield 6. assess, impost, tariff
7. revenue 9. surrender
10. assessment
cessation... 3. end 4. lull, stay
5. letup, truce 7. respite
8. abeyance, desition 9. interlude
10. suspension 12. intermission,
interruption 14. discontinuance
cetacea, cetacean... 3. orc 4. apod,
orca, susu (blind) 5. whale 6. whales
7. cowfish, finback, grampus, narwhal
(narwal), rorqual
Cete... 5. whale 10. The Cetacea
Cetus... 8. The Whale 13. constellation
(Equator)
Ceylon...
capital.. 7. Colombo
city.. 5. Galle, Kandy (famed Buddhist
Temple) 6. Jaffna
mountain peak.. 14. Pidurutalagala
ocean.. 6. Indian
old name.. 9. Taprobane
people.. 5. Tamil 6. Malays, Veddas
8. Malabars 10. Singhalese
Ceylon (pert to)...
boat.. 5. dhoni (doni)
canoe.. 5. balsa
Festival.. 8. Perahera
garment.. 6. sarong
hill dweller.. 4. Toda
monkey.. 4. maha 6. langur, rillow
moss.. 4. alga 6. Jaffna 7. gulaman
8. agar–agar
palm.. 7. talipot
rat.. 9. bandicoot
sand (sea bottom).. 4. paar
tree.. 4. doon
chabouk, chabuk (Ind)... 4. whip
9. horsewhip
chacma... 6. baboon
chafe... 3. cut, irk, rub, vex 4. fret,
fume, fuss, gall, heat, rage, skin,
warm 5. anger, annoy, grate, grind,
pique, scuff, worry, wound
6. abrade, banter, excite, harass,
injure, nettle, rankle 7. inflame
8. irritate
chaff... 3. hay 4. bran, husk, quiz,
twit 5. dregs, fluff, husks, palea,
straw, trash, waste 6. banter,
cobweb, glumes, refuse, scraps
7. remains, residue, tailing 8. raillery,
ridicule, riffraff
chaffer... 5. trade, wares 6. buying,
dicker, haggle, higgle, market
7. bargain, chaffer, chatter, selling
9. negotiate 11. merchandise
chafing dish... 7. cresset
chagrin... 7. anxiety, mortify
8. distress, troubles, vexation
13. mortification
chain... 4. bind, bond, boom, gyve,
reef, torc 5. cable, range 6. catena,
fasten, fetter, secure, series, tether,
torque 7. creeper, sorites
15. contravallation (fort series)
chair... 4. seat, sill 5. bench, sedan
6. rocker, throne 7. enchair, speaker

chair (pert to)...
back.. 5. splat 7. upright
collegiate.. 10. fellowship
13. professorship
cover.. 4. tidy 12. antimacassar
India.. 6. musnud
Japan.. 4. kago
maker.. 5. caner 6. reeder
chair (type of)... 4. camp, deck, easy,
high, lawn, wing 6. lounge, Morris,
swivel 7. contour, folding, steamer,
Windsor 8. armchair, captain's,
electric, fauteuil, straight
10. ladder–back 11. overstuffed
chairman... 7. officer, speaker
8. director 9. moderator
chalcedony... 4. onyx, opal, sard
5. agate 6. jasper, quartz 7. opaline
9. carnelian 11. chrysoprase
Chaldean (pert to)... 2. Ur 4. seer
6. Semite 10. astrologer, soothsayer
13. Neo–Babylonian (language)
chalice... 3. ama, cup 5. amula (anc),
calix, grail 6. goblet 8. daffodil
chalice pall... 4. veil 8. animetta
chalk... 4. draw, mark, pale, tick
5. score 6. blanch, bleach, crayon,
credit, pastel, whiten 7. account,
drawing 9. limestone, reckoning
chalker... 7. milkman (Eng sl)
chalklike... 10. calcareous
chalky... 5. white 7. crumbly, friable,
powdery 10. cretaceous
challenge... 4. dare, defy, gage
5. claim, doubt, query 6. accost,
cartel, defial, demand, impugn
7. dispute, protest 8. quesion,
reproach 10. accusation, controvert
11. questioning
chamal... 4. goat (Angora)
chamber... 4. cave, hall, kiva, room
5. court 6. camera, cavity
7. bedroom, boudoir, cabinet,
chambre, cubicle 10. bedchamber
11. compartment
chamber (pert to)...
harem.. 3. oda
heart.. 7. auricle 9. ventricle
King's.. 9. camarilla
music.. 14. sonata da camera
chambers... 4. flat 5. suite 6. office
9. apartment, bicameral (Legis)
14. Inns of Chancery (Eng)
chameleon... 6. lizard 10. vacillator
13. changeability, constellation
chamfer (to)... 5. bevel, carve, flute,
score 6. chisel, groove
chamois... 5. Gemse, izard 8. antelope
champ... 4. bite, chew, mash
5. gnash 6. victor 7. trample
11. battlefield
champagne... 4. wine 9. red–yellow
13. chrysanthemum
champaign... 5. field, plain 7. expanse
11. battlefield
champion... 3. Ace 4. best, hero
5. champ 6. defend, expert, victor,
winner 7. espouse, fighter, titlist
8. advocate, defender 9. combatant,
conqueror 10. unexcelled
champion (pert to)...
Christian (anc).. 3. Cid

constellation.. 7. Perseus
knight (legend).. 7. Paladin
Spanish.. 12. conquistador
chance... 3. die, hap, lot 4. fate, luck,
odds, risk, turn 6. casual, gamble,
happen, mishap, tossup 7. fortune,
lottery, tychism 8. fortuity, Lady
Luck, occasion 9. happening,
mischance 10. likelihood
11. opportunity, possibility, probability
12. happenstance
chancel (pert to)...
part.. 4. bema
screen.. 4. jube
seats.. 7. sedilia
change... 4. flux, move, turn, vary,
veer 5. alter, amend, break, coins,
money, shift 6. modify, mutate,
switch 7. caprice, convert, deviate,
variety 8. transfer 9. diversity,
transform, transmute, variation
10. alteration, fickleness, modulation
11. inconstancy, vicissitude
12. substitution 13. metamorphosis
14. transformation 15. diversification
change (pert to)...
color.. 3. dye, wan 4. fade, pale
5. blush 6. blanch, redden
medicine.. 11. heterotopia
mind.. 6. repent 12. tergiversate
music.. 4. muta
order of.. 9. metabolic, rearrange,
transpose
changeable... 6. fickle, fitful, mobile
7. erratic, flighty, mutable, protean
8. freakish, notional, unstable,
variable, volatile, weathery
9. alterable, chameleon, metabolic,
uncertain, unsettled, whimsical
10. capricious, inconstant
15. interchangeable
changeling... 3. oaf 4. dolt 5. idiot
7. waverer 8. imbecile, renegade,
turncoat 9. simpleton 10. substitute
(child)
channel... 3. bed, cut, gat, way
4. dike, duct, gate, gurt, lane, leat,
pass, vein 5. basin, canal, ditch,
drain, flume, flute, fosse, radio, river,
sinus, stria 6. alveus, avenue, coulee,
groove, gutter, outlet, sluice, trench,
trough 7. conduit, tideway
8. aqueduct, tailrace 9. broadcast
10. passageway
Channel Islands... 4. Sark (Sercq)
6. Jersey 8. Alderney
chanson... 4. song 5. lyric 6. ballad
chant... 3. say 4. sing 6. intone,
melody, warble 7. introit, singing
8. canticle 10. intonation
11. composition
chanter... 6. cantor, singer 7. bagpipe
(part), intoner, sparrow (hedge)
8. songster, vocalist 9. chanteuse,
chorister
chanticleer... 4. cock 7. rooster
11. cock–a–doodle
14. cock–a–doodle–doo
chaos... 2. Nu (Egypt) 3. pie (type)
4. gulf, mess 5. abyss, babel, chasm
7. anarchy 8. disorder 9. confusion,
imbroglio 10. unruliness

13. orderlessness
Chaos (pert to)...
daughter.. 3. Nox, Nyx
parent of.. 5. earth 6. heaven
8. Creation
son.. 6. Erebus
chaotic... 6. muddle 8. confused,
formless 12. disorganized
chap... 3. boy, buy, guy, lad, man
4. kibe (sore) 5. buyer, chink, cleft,
crack, scout, split, youth 6. barter,
choose (Scot), fellow, galoot
7. chapman 8. customer
chapeau... 3. cap, hat, lid 5. beret
chapel... 4. cape, cope, cowl, hood
5. altar, choir 6. bethel 7. chantry,
galilee, oratory, service, Sistine
8. sacellum (anc) 9. reliquary
chaperon... 4. hood 6. attend,
duenna, escort 8. guardian
9. attendant 10. gooseberry
chaplet... 4. band 5. beads
6. anadem, wreath 7. garland,
prayers 8. beadroll, insignia, necklace
chappaul... 9. squawfish
chaps... 8. overalls 10. chaparajos
chapter... 4. Sura 5. topic 6. clause
7. council, meeting, passage,
section, Society 8. division
9. capitular 10. fraternity
12. organization
chaptrel... 6. impost
char... 4. burn 5. trout 6. scorch
8. charcoal, sandbank
character... 4. hero, kind, mark, role,
sign, star 5. trait 6. cipher, letter,
nature, repute, status, symbol
7. quality 8. function 9. reference
10. reputation 11. temperament
14. characteristic
character (pert to)...
giver.. 5. toner
Hebrew.. 3. Tav, Taw
Irish.. 5. Ogham
musical.. 3. bar 4. clef, rest
5. neume
of people.. 5. ethos
real.. 7. essence
science of.. 8. ethology
Teutonic.. 4. rune
characteristic... 4. mark 5. habit, trait
7. feature, impress, quality, typical
8. peculiar, symbolic 9. attribute,
character, idiopathy, lineament,
specialty 11. distinctive, peculiarity,
singularity, symptomatic
13. individualism
characteristic (pert to)...
descent.. 6. racial
peculiar.. 9. idiopathy
spirit.. 5. ethos
tone (Mus).. 7. seventh
characterization... 4. role 5. drama
9. depiction, portrayal
11. description, distinction
13. impersonation 14. identification,
representation
characterize... 4. mark, name 5. enact
7. engrave, imprint, portray
8. describe, inscribe 9. delineate,
designate, epitomize, represent
11. distinguish

characterized by...
abstinence.. 7. ascetic
bacteria exclusion.. 7. asepsis
cruelty.. 7. Neronic
exact thinking.. 13. ratiocinative
melody.. 6. ariose
poison (bloodstream).. 6. sepsis
pomposity.. 13. grandiloquent
characterless... 5. inane 9. colorless,
  pointless
charcoal... 4. coke, fuel, lave, peat
  5. black, chark 6. carbon, fusain
  7. drawing, residue 9. boneblack,
  briquette
charge... 4. bill, cost, dues, fill, load,
  onus, rate, task, toll, ward 5. blame,
  chore, debit, onset, order, price,
  trust 6. accuse, advice, advise,
  allege, amount, attack, client,
  commit, credit, demand, dictum,
  impute, indict 7. assault, command,
  concern, custody, expense, impeach,
  keeping, mandate, precept, primage,
  protégé 8. guidance, insignia,
  instruct, tutelage 9. dependent,
  electrify, exactment 10. accusation,
  commission, imposition, impregnate,
  injunction, management
  11. arrangement, attribution,
  instruction, supervision
  13. incrimination 14. responsibility
charge of affairs... 8. diplomat
  15. chargé d'affaires
charge off... 5. debit 6. forget
  7. dismiss, forgive 8. discount
charges (law)... 4. dues, fees 5. costs
  9. retainers
charge with...
crime.. 6. indict 7. impeach
  11. incriminate
debt.. 5. debit
gas.. 6. aerate
offense.. 6. accuse
to.. 5. blame 7. ascribe 9. attribute
charily... 6. cagily, warily 8. frugally
  9. carefully, thriftily 10. cautiously
  12. economically, suspiciously
chariness... 7. caution 8. caginess,
  distrust, wariness 9. frugality
  11. heedfulness, thriftiness
chariot... 3. car 4. biga, cart, rath
  (ratha), wain 5. essed (anc), wagon
  7. vehicle 8. quadriga
charioteer... 6. Auriga (Astron), Ben
  Hur
charitable... 3. big 4. kind 6. kindly
  7. lenient, liberal 8. generous,
  tolerant 9. forgiving, indulgent
  10. altruistic, benevolent, bighearted
  11. beneficent 12. eleemosynary,
  humanitarian 13. compassionate,
  philanthropic
charity... 4. alms, dole 6. bounty,
  virtue 7. handout, largess
  8. lenience, pittance 9. tolerance
  10. almsgiving, liberality
  11. benevolence 12. philanthropy
charity dispenser... 7. almoner
charivari... 5. babel 6. medley, uproar
  8. serenade (mock) 10. callithump
charlatan... 5. faker, fraud, phony,
  quack 6. humbug 7. empiric

  8. impostor 9. pretender
  10. medicaster, mountebank
Charlemagne, Emperor (pert to)...
brother.. 8. Carloman
emperor of.. 7. The West
father.. 5. Pepin (the Short)
name also.. 15. Charles The Great
nephew.. 7. Orlando
charm... 3. obi 4. lure, mojo, play,
  song 5. grace, magic, oomph, spell
  6. allure, amulet, appeal, beauty,
  enamor, entice, fetish, glamor, scarab
  7. beguile, bewitch, cantrip, delight,
  enchant, glamour, periapt
  8. breloque, elegance, entrance,
  ornament, talisman 9. captivate,
  fascinate, sex appeal, sweetness
  10. allurement, attraction, brimborion
  (brimborium), lovability
  11. captivation, conjuration,
  incantation, pulchritude, winsomeness
  12. antinganting 14. attractiveness,
  delightfulness
charmer... 5. siren 6. beauty
  7. enticer 8. exorcist, magician,
  sorcerer 9. bewitcher
charming... 7. winsome 8. alluring,
  pleasing 10. bewitching, delightful
  11. captivating, fascinating
chart... 3. map 4. list, plat, plot
  7. diagram
charter... 4. hire 5. carta, grant
  6. charta, firman, treaty 7. license
  9. privilege (special), purwannah
chartreuse... 4. mold (cookery)
  5. color 7. liqueur
Chartreuse... 9. monastery 18. La
  Grande Chartreuse (Grenoble)
chary... 4. wary 5. cagey 6. frugal,
  skimpy 7. thrifty 8. cautious
  10. suspicious 12. parsimonious
Charybdis... 6. Scylla 8. Galofaro
  9. whirlpool (Messina)
chase... 3. gun (Naut), set (gem)
  4. hunt, park, race 5. chevy (chivy),
  raise, sport, track 6. emboss, follow,
  furrow, groove, hasten, pursue,
  shikar, stroke (tennis) 7. engrave,
  pursuit, repulse 8. ornament
  12. steeplechase
Chase (The), goddess of... 5. Diana
chasm... 3. gap, pit 4. gulf, hole, rift,
  well 5. abyss, cleft, shaft 6. breach,
  canyon, cavity, hiatus 7. fissure,
  opening 8. crevasse
chasma... 7. yawning
chasse... 4. step (dance) 6. shrine
  9. reliquary
chaste... 4. pure 6. modest, simple
  8. innocent, virtuous 9. continent,
  uncorrupt, undefiled, unmarried
  10. immaculate
chasten... 4. rate 5. smote 6. punish,
  refine 7. correct 8. chastise,
  penalize, restrain 9. castigate
  10. discipline
chastened... 4. meek 5. smote
  7. subdued 8. punished, purified,
  tempered 10. restrained
chastise... 4. beat, slap, whip
  5. amend, blame, scold, spank, taunt
  6. punish, rebate, rebuke, swinge

7. correct, reprove 9. castigate
10. discipline
chastity ... 6. purity, virtue
9. cleanness 10. chasteness
12. virtuousness
chat ... 3. gab, rap, yak 4. chin, coze,
jist, talk, tove 5. prate 6. babble,
confab, gabble, gibber, gossip, jabber
7. chatter, prattle 8. causerie,
chitchat, converse 12. conversation
14. chitter–chatter
chatelaine ... 3. pin 4. etui, hook
5. clasp, purse, watch 6. brooch,
torque
chattels ... 4. naam 5. goods, money,
wares 6. estate 7. effects
8. holdings, property 9. livestock,
principal 11. possessions
chatter ... 3. gab, yap 5. clack, prate
7. clatter, prattle
chatterer ... 3. jay, mag 4. bird, piet
6. magpie 10. chatterbox
chatty ... 3. pot (earthen) 4. glib
5. gabby 7. affable 8. sociable
9. garrulous, prattling, talkative
14. conversational
Chaucer (pert to) ...
author of .. 15. Canterbury Tales
Inn .. 9. (The) Tabard
pilgrimage city .. 10. Canterbury
style of work .. 7. novella
chauvinist ... 5. jingo 6. Rajput
7. chauvin, patriot 8. jingoist
9. warmonger 10. militarist
cheap ... 5. small, tacky, tinny, trade,
value 6. cheesy, paltry, plenty, sleazy
7. abashed, bargain, chintzy, cut–rate,
reduced, schlock 9. niggardly
11. inexpensive
cheat ... 2. do 3. ban, con, fob, gyp
4. bilk, fake, flam, hoax, liar, rook,
scam, sell, sham 5. cozen, elude,
guile, phony, scalp 6. deceit, fleece,
humbug, hustle, illude, rip–off
7. deceive, finesse, sharpen, swindle
8. artifice, impostor 9. bamboozle,
overreach, stratagem, victimize
10. thimblerig 12. bait–and–switch
check ... 3. nip, tab 4. balk, curb,
damp, mark, rein, stem, stop, test
5. agree, brake, count, delay, limit,
money, plaid, repel, stunt, tally
6. bridle, cheque, detain, detent,
impede, oppose, rebuff, retard, ticket,
verify 7. counter, examine, inhibit,
measure, monitor, pattern, repress
9. hindrance, restraint 12. verification
check (pert to) ...
in .. 3. die 6. arrive 8. register
out .. 3. die 5. croak, leave 6. assess
8. withdraw
pattern .. 11. houndstooth
game, term .. 5. chess 8. gambling
checkered ... 4. vair 5. diced, plaid
6. mosaic, tartan, varied 7. checked
10. changeable, tesserated,
variegated 11. diversified
checkers, chequers ... 4. game
8. draughts (Brit)
cheek ... 4. gall, gena, jowl 5. brass,
bucca, crust, malar, nerve 8. audacity,
chutzpah 9. impudence

10. buccinator
cheer ... 3. rah 4. yell 5. bravo, elate,
huzza, liven, mirth, salvo 6. gaiety,
hurrah, regale, repast, salute, solace
7. animate, applaud, console, gladden,
hearten, jollity, refresh, rejoice
8. applause, inspirit, pleasure, vivacity
9. encourage, merriment
10. exhilarate 12. conviviality
cheerful ... 3. gay 4. gleg (Scot), rosy
5. happy, peart, sunny 6. blithe,
cheery, genial, hearty, jocund, joyful
8. gladsome, homelike 9. contented,
lightsome 12. lighthearted
cheerfulness ... 3. joy 4. glee
5. cheer, mirth 6. gaiety 7. jollity
8. gladness, hilarity 9. happiness,
merriment 12. exhilaration
cheerio ... 5. adios, aloha, skoal, toast
6. hurrah, prosit 8. au revoir,
farewell, Godspeed 9. greetings
cheerless ... 3. sad 4. cold, drab
5. drear 6. dismal, dreary, gloomy
7. forlorn, joyless, unhappy
8. dejected 9. unsmiling
10. depressing, melancholy
11. dispiriting 12. disconsolate
cheese ... 3. pot 4. bleu, brie, edam,
feta, jack 5. cream, Gouda, Swiss
6. barrie, Dunlop, mysost, Romano,
zieger 7. Cheddar, cottage, fromage,
Munster, sapsago 8. American,
Monterey (jack), Parmesan
9. Camembert, Limburger, Roquefort
10. Gorgonsola, Neufchatel
cheese dish ... 6. fondue, omelet,
quiche, strata 7. rarebit, soufflé
cheesy ... 3. bad 6. paltry 8. inferior
9. worthless 12. disreputable
cheetah ... 3. cat 5. youse (youze)
7. guepard (gueparde)
cheilos ... 3. lip
chela ... 4. claw 6. novice 8. disciple
Chelonia ... 7. reptile, turtles
9. tortoises
chemical (pert to) ...
analysis .. 5. assay
cleanser .. 6. kryton
etching .. 11. chemigraphy
strength .. 5. titer (titre)
term .. 3. gas 4. acid, atom, base, salt
5. imine 6. alkali, eluate 7. hormone,
nonacid, organic, radical, valence
8. catalyst, compound 10. bathoflore
11. bathochrome
vessel .. 4. etna 6. aludel, retort
7. alembic 8. crucible, reductor
chemical suffix ... 2. ac, el, yl 3. ane,
ene, ile, ine, ole, ose 4. enol, olic,
osan
chemin de fer ... 7. railway
8. baccarat, railroad
chemist ... 7. analyst 8. druggist
9. alchemist 10. apothecary,
biochemist 12. iatrochemist (anc)
cherish ... 3. aid, hug, pet, woo
4. love 5. adore, cheer, nurse, prize
6. caress, faddle, fondle, foster
7. care for, comfort, nourish, nurture,
protect, support 8. enshrine,
remember, treasure 9. cultivate,
encourage, entertain

cherry... 3. pin 4. Bing, bird, gean, ming 5. black 6. egriot, Prunus 7. capulin, marasca, mazzard, Morello, oxheart 8. Napoleon 9. amarelles, bigarreau, Queen Anne 11. chokecherry, Montmorency

cherub... 5. angel, child, saint 6. seraph, spirit 7. darling, eudemon 8. cherubim, seraphim

chess (pert to)...
chessman.. 4. king, pawn, rook 5. piece, queen 6. bishop, castle, knight
Italian.. 7. scacchi
term.. 4. dual, move 5. debut 6. chassé, fidate, gambit 7. end game, opening, problem 9. checkmate, en passant, rook's tour, stalemate 10. fianchetto

chesslike... 8. scacchic

chest... 3. ark, box 4. arca, cist, kist 5. bahut 6. breast, cajeta, coffer, coffin, locker 7. highboy, wanigan (wangan) 10. chiffonier 11. gardeviance

chest (pert to)...
ammunition.. 7. caisson
animal.. 7. brisket
human.. 6. thorax 7. midriff
sound.. 4. rale
sepulchral.. 6. larnax

Chester (Eng), inhabitant... 8. Cestrian

chesterfield... 4. sofa 5. divan 8. overcoat 9. cigarette, davenport

chestnut... 4. ling, rata 5. horse, water 6. marron 7. buckeye 8. Aesculus, Castanea 10. breadfruit, chinquapin

chestnut... 4. joke 6. cliché 7. bromide 8. banality

chestnut color... 4. roan 5. brown 6. sorrel 12. reddish—brown

chevalier... 5. cadet (nobility), noble 6. knight 7. gallant 8. cavalier, horseman 10. greenshank (bird)

chevron... 4. beam 5. glove 6. rafter, stripe, zigzag 8. insignia

chevrotain... 4. napu 7. deerlet, kenchil, meminna 9. Tragulina

chevy... 3. cry (hunting) 4. game, hunt 5. chase 6. flight, harass, pursue 7. torment

chew... 3. cud 4. bite, chaw, gnaw, quid 5. champ, chomp, grind, munch 6. chavel, ponder 8. meditate, ruminate 9. masticate

chiasma... 11. decussation 12. intersection

chiasmus... 9. inversion (of words)

chib (Gypsy)... 6. tongue 8. language

chic... 4. trig, trim 5. natty, smart 6. modish, spruce 7. stylish

Chicago's nickname... 9. Windy City

chicanery... 4. ruse, wile 5. feint, trick 6. deceit 7. knavery 8. artifice, trickery 9. stratagem 11. skulduggery

chickadee... 8. titmouse 10. Pebthestes

chicken... 3. hen 4. cock, fowl, girl 5. biddy, capon, chick, deedy, fryer, poult, young 6. coward, pullet 7. broiler, rooster 8. cockerel, weakling 9. youngling 11. chanticleer, milquetoast

chickenhearted... 5. timid 8. cowardly 12. fainthearted

chicory... 6. endive 7. succory 12. Cichoriaceae

chide... 4. rate 5. blame, scold 6. berate, rebuke 7. censure, reprove, wrangle 8. admonish, reproach 9. reprimand

chief... 3. dux, top 4. arch, head, main, rais (reis) 5. first, forte, major, mogul 6. leader, primal, staple, syndic 7. kingpin, supreme 9. directing, governing, paramount, potentate, principal, prominent 11. predominant

chief (pert to)...
African.. 3. dey 4. kaid 5. negus 6. induna
Am Indian.. 6. sachem 7. Osceola 8. sagamore
Arab.. 5. sheik
Chinook.. 4. tyee
Cossack.. 6. ataman, hetman
Egypt.. 3. Min (Panopolis)
Europe.. 6. syndic
Germany.. 6. Führer (Fuehrer), Kaiser
Iran.. 9. ayatollah
Italy.. 4. doge, duce
Japan.. 6. mikado, shogun
Mexico.. 7. cacique
Nepal.. 4. Rais
Oriental.. 4. kahn 6. sirdar
Persia.. 4. shah
Russia.. 4. czar (tsar)
Spain.. 7. alcalde
Tibet.. 9. Dalai Lama
Turkey.. 3. aga (agha) 6. vizier

chilblain... 6. pernio

child... 3. imp, tad, tot 4. babe, baby, bata, brat, teen, tike 5. bairn, cupid, elfin, fetus 6. cherub, childe (anc), infant, urchin 7. adoptee, nestler, preteen, progeny 9. offspring 10. descendant

childish... 4. weak 5. naive, petty, young 6. senile, simple 7. babyish, kiddish, puerile, unmanly 8. immature 9. infantile, kittenish

children (pert to)...
doctor.. 12. pediatrician
mythology.. 6. Titans
Patron Saint.. 5. Santa
slain by Herod.. 12. The Innocents
study of.. 8. pedology 10. pediatrics

Chile... see also *Chilean*
cape.. 4. Horn
capital.. 8. Santiago (1541)
city.. 4. Lota 5. Arica 8. Valdivia 10. Concepcion, Valparaiso (1543)
conqueror.. 7. Pizarro 8. Valdivia
desert.. 7. Atacama
explorer.. 8. Magellan (1520)
mountain.. 5. Andes
river.. 3. Loa 6. Biobio
settlement (southernmost).. 8. Navarino (Isl) 14. Puerto Williams

Chilean (pert to)...
coconut.. 7. coquito
evergreen.. 6. pepino 10. arborvitae

shrub (poison).. 5. lithi
wind.. 5. sures 11. sures pardos
workman.. 4. rote
chiliad... 8. thousand 9. millenium
　　13. thousand years
chill... 3. ice, raw 4. ague, cold,
　　damp 5. algor, frost, rigor
　　6. damper, formal, shiver 7. malaria
　　8. coldness, coolness, dispirit
　　10. depressing 11. refrigerate
chilly... 3. raw 4. ague, cold 5. gelid
　　6. aguish, freeze, frosty
　　12. refrigerated
chiloplasty... 10. lip surgery
　　12. mouth surgery
chime... 4. bell, peal, ring, suit
　　5. agreé, bells, prate, rhyme
　　6. accord, concur, cymbal, jingle
　　7. harmony
chimera... 5. dream, fancy, vapor
　　6. bubble, utopia 7. monster
　　8. illusion, paradise (fool's)
chimerical... 4. vain 7. utopian
　　8. delusive, fanciful, romantic
　　9. fantastic, imaginary, unfounded
chimney... 3. lum 4. flue 5. cleft,
　　stack, tewel 10. smokestack
chimpanzee... 6. gibbon, nchega
　　7. gorilla
chin... 4. talk 5. genio (comb form)
　　6. mentum, weight (Chin)
　　8. converse 10. chew the rag
　　11. genioplasty (Surg), mentoplasty
　　(Surg)
china... 7. Dresden, pottery
　　8. crockery 9. porcelain
　　11. earthenware
China... see also *Chinese*
　Buddha.. 2. Fo
　capital.. 7. Nanking
　capital, former.. 7. Peiping (Peking)
　city.. 4. Amoy, Tsin, Wuhu 6. Canton,
　　Hankow, Ningpo 7. Foochow,
　　Nanking, Soochow 8. Hangchow,
　　Shanghai, Tientsin
　dynasty.. 3. Han, Kin, Sui 4. Chou,
　　Hsia (BC), Ming, Tsin, Yuan 5. Ching
　　6. Mongol (Kublai Khan's)
　island.. 5. Matsu 6. Quemoy, Taiwan
　　(Formosa)
　magistrate.. 5. tupan 6. tuchun
　　8. mandarin
　Mainland.. 15. People's Republic
　Military Academy.. 7. Whompoa
　Mongol.. 3. Hun
　mountain.. 7. Kuen–lun 9. Himalayas
　nickname.. 14. Flowery Kingdom
　philosopher.. 6. Laotse 9. Confucius
　poet.. 4. Li Po 7. Li Tai Po
　race.. 9. Mongoloid
　religion.. 6. Taoism 8. Buddhism
　　9. Confucian 12. Confucianism
　river.. 5. Peibo 7. Hwanglo, Yangtze
　sea.. 5. China 6. Yellow
　treaty port.. 4. Amoy
　Chinese (pert to)...
　antelope.. 6. dzeren
　boat.. 4. junk 5. tanka 6. sampan
　cabbage.. 7. pakchoi
　card game.. 6. fantan
　carpet.. 6. Khotan 7. Kashgar,
　　Yarkand 9. Samarkand, Turkestan

Catholic Church.. 11. Tien Chu T'ang
　　12. Tien Chu Chiao
chestnut.. 4. ling
confection.. 8. chowchow
deer.. 8. elaphure
defense.. 4. Wall (2,000 mi long)
desert.. 4. Gobi 5. Shamo
dragon.. 6. chi–lin
fabric.. 3. sha 7. nankeen
festival (Spring).. 9. Ch'ing Ming
flute.. 4. tche (che)
fruit.. 6. litchi (nut)
ginger.. 9. galingale
God.. 4. Shen (Chr) 7. Shangti, Tien
　　Chu (RCCh)
gong.. 6. tam–tam, tom–tom
grass.. 5. ramee
idol.. 4. joss 6. pagoda (pagod)
instrument.. 3. che, kin 4. tche
　　5. sheng (cheng)
jade.. 2. yu
jute.. 7. chingma
laborer.. 6. coolie
lily.. 9. narcissus
liquor.. 6. samshu (rice)
literary degree.. 8. hsiu tsai
monkey.. 4. douc
nurse.. 4. amah
officer.. 4. kwan
oil.. 4. tung
ox.. 4. zebu
pagoda.. 3. taa
paradise (Buddh).. 4. Jodo
　　7. Ching–tu 8. Gekuraku
philosophy.. 10. Yang and Yin
religion.. 6. Taoism 8. Buddhism
　　12. Confucianism
residence (official).. 5. yamen
screen (folding).. 10. Coromandel
silkworm.. 4. sina 9. ailanthus
sky.. 4. tien
society (secret).. 3. hui (hoey) 4. tong
vessel.. 4. junk 6. lorcha
Chinese Wall, Great (pert to)...
builder.. 15. Ch'in Shih Huang Ti
composition.. 7. granite (blocks)
length in miles.. 11. two thousand
time.. 2. BC
chink... 4. rent, rift, rima, rime, ring
　　5. cleft, crack 6. cranny, furrow
　　7. bunting (bird), fissure
　　10. interstice
chinook... 4. herb, wind 6. salmon
　　7. quinnat
Chinook (pert to)...
chief.. 4. tyee
tribe.. 8. Flathead
State (nickname of).. 10. Washington
chinquapin... 3. oak 6. bonnet (water)
　　8. chestnut
chip... 3. cut, hew 4. coin 5. break,
　　carve, flake, piece, scrap, token
　　6. chisel, gallet (stone) 7. counter
chipmunk... 6. hackee
chipped stone (instrument)...
　　9. paleolith
chipper... 5. chirp 6. babble, chisel,
　　hammer, lively 7. chirrup, twitter
　　8. cheerful
chirognomy... 9. palmistry
　　10. chiromancy
chironomy... 7. gesture (hands)

9. pantomime

chiropter... 3. bat 6. aliped

chirp... 3. pew (pue) 4. peep
5. cheep, chirl, tweet 7. chirrup,
twitter

chisel... 3. cut, gad, hew 4. celt
(anc), form, pare 5. bruzz, burin,
carve, cheat, drove, gouge, grave
6. furrow, jagger, mallet, peeker,
pommel 7. engrave, swindle
9. sculpture

chit... 4. note, runt, wisp 5. child,
shoot 6. sprout 10. memorandum
14. recommendation

chitarra, chitarrine... 6. guitar

chiton... 7. garment (anc), mollusk

chivalrous... 5. brave 6. gentle, heroic
7. gallant, valiant 8. knightly
9. courteous 11. magnanimous

chive... 4. stab 5. onion, plant
6. garlic

chloride... 3. ore 4. salt 5. ester
7. calomel

chlorine... 2. Cl 7. bromine, halogen,
radical 8. cyanogen, fluorine

chloroform... 4. dope, kill 6. poison
7. stupefy 9. narcotize
11. anesthetize

chlorophyll... 5. ester, green 7. etiolin
9. deodorant

chocolate... 5. brown, cacao, candy,
cocoa, color 6. pinole 8. beverage
13. Sterculiaceae

choice... 4. beat, rare, will 5. prime
6. dainty, option, select, tidbit
8. election, free will, uncommon
9. recherché, selection
10. preference, well–chosen
11. alternative

choir... 6. chorus 7. singers

choir leader... 6. cantor 9. precentor

choke... 3. gag, jam, ram 4. clog
5. burke, check 6. hinder, impede,
muffle, stifle 7. garrote, repress,
smother 8. obstruct, strangle, throttle
9. constrict, suffocate

choler... 3. ire 4. bile, foam, gall,
rage 5. anger, wrath 6. spleen
10. resentment 11. biliousness
12. irascibility

choleric... 5. angry, testy 7. bilious,
enraged, iracund 8. wrathful
9. dyspeptic, irascible 10. passionate

chololith... 9. gallstone

choose... 3. opt 4. cull, like, list, pick,
want 5. elect 6. desire, optate,
prefer, select

choosing... 6. optant 8. eclectic,
elective 9. selecting

chop... 3. axe, cut, hew, jaw, lop
4. dice, fell, hack, jowl, meat, raze,
seal 5. cheek, mince, prune, sever,
stamp 7. griskin 8. noisette (eye of)

choppy... 5. bumpy, rough 6. uneven
7. jolting 8. unstable, variable
9. irregular 10. changeable,
incoherent 13. discontinuous

chord... 4. rope 6. radius, secant,
string, tendon 7. concord, harmony
8. arpeggio, concento, filament

chord (terms)... 5. major, minor, tonic,
triad 6. broken, common, tetrad

7. seventh 8. dominant, unbroken
10. enharmonic

chords... 4. tune 7. cadence, cantata

chore... 3. job (odd) 4. task, work
5. stint 10. assignment

chorography... 5. chart 7. diagram
10. topography 11. cartography,
description (region), ichnography

chortle... 5. laugh, snort 7. chuckle,
snortle

chorus... 4. echo 5. choir 6. accord,
outcry, unison 7. refrain, singers
8. chanters 9. unanimity

chorus (pert to)...
girl.. 7. chorine, chorist
leader.. 8. choragus 9. conductor
small.. 7. octette

Chosen (anc)... 5. Korea

Chosen People... 10. Israelites

chrism... 7. unction, unguent
10. anointment 12. confirmation

christen... 4. name 6. launch
7. baptize 10. denominate,
inaugurate 12. Christianize

Christian (pert to)...
Eastern.. 5. Uniat
feast.. 5. agape (anc) 8. Epiphany
9. Christmas
martyr (first).. 7. Stephen
philosopher (anc).. 6. Jesuit
9. Schoolman 10. Scholastic
sect.. 7. Docetae
symbol.. 5. orant (fem)

Christmas (pert to)...
bag.. 6. piñata
carol.. 4. Noel
decoration.. 6. crèche
feast.. 4. Yule
mummer.. 6. guiser
plant.. 5. holly 9. evergreen, mistletoe
term.. 4. Noel, Xmas 8. Nativity,
Yuletide 11. Weihnachten

Christ's–thorn... 4. nabk

chromosome... 2. id 5. idant
8. biophore, germ cell

chronic... 7. abiding 8. constant,
enduring, habitual 9. confirmed
10. continuous, inveterate, persistent
14. valetudinarian

chronicle... 4. sard 5. annal, diary
6. record 7. account, archive, history
8. register 9. narrative
10. chronology

chronicler... 6. writer 8. annalist,
compiler, recorder 9. historian
12. chronologist

chronology error... 9. prolepsis

chronometer... 5. clock, timer, watch
6. ghurry 7. sundial 9. hourglass,
metronome, timepiece

chrysolite... 5. green (color) 7. olivine,
peridot

chthonian... 4. gods (underworld)
7. hellish, worship 9. diabolist
11. demonolater

chub... 4. bass, dace, dolt, fool, lout
6. shiner, tautog 8. fallfish
9. hornyhead, squawfish

chubby... 3. fat 5. plump, pudgy,
round 6. stocky, stubby 9. corpulent

chuck... 4. beef, cast, food, hurl, jerk,
toss 5. fling, heave, pitch, throw

9. eliminate
chuckle... 5. cluck, laugh 6. cackle,
wabble 7. chortle
chuff... 3. fat 4. boor 5. churl, clown,
cross, proud, sulky, surly 6. chubby,
elated, rustic 9. conceited
11. ill–tempered
chum... 3. pal 4. bait, pard 5. buddy,
crony 6. fellow, hobnob 7. company,
comrade, consort, partner
8. playmate, roommate 9. associate,
classmate, colleague, companion
chump... 3. ass 4. dolt, dupe, fool,
head 5. block, booby 8. endpiece
chunk... 3. dab, gob, pat, wad
4. hunk, junt, lump, slug (metal)
5. stick, stump, throw 8. fragment
chunky... 3. fat 4. game (Am Ind),
junt 5. lumpy, stout, tubby
6. chubby, portly, stocky, stodgy,
stubby 8. thickset
church... 3. dom 4. fane (anc), kirk,
sect 5. abbey 6. bethel, temple
7. Lateran, minster, templet
8. basilica, conclave 9. cathedral
10. House of God, worshipers
11. Christendom 12. denomination
church (pert to)...
assistant.. 5. Elder
attendant.. 6. sexton, verger
calendar.. 4. Ordo
Court.. 10. Consistory
dignitary.. 4. dean 6. bishop, priest
7. prelate, primate 8. benefice,
minister
dissenter.. 7. sectary 10. anti–Nicean,
anti–Nicene
doctrine (State, church).. 8. Erastian
dominion.. 10. sacerdotum
doorkeeper.. 7. ostiary
Elder.. 9. Presbyter
feast.. 4. utas (octave of) 6. Easter
governing body.. 7. classis
law.. 5. canon, synod 7. council
part.. 4. apse, bema, nave 5. altar,
canon 7. narthex 8. transept
10. clerestory
peace device.. 8. irenicon
property.. 5. glebe
Roman.. 7. Lateran 8. basilica
seats.. 4. pews 7. sedilla
service (part).. 3. pax 4. Mass
5. crede 7. epistle, introit, sanctus
8. Agnus Dei, blessing
9. communion
stipend.. 7. prebend
traffic (preferments).. 6. simony
vessel.. 3. ama, pyx (pix) 6. lavabo
8. ciborium
vestry.. 8. sacristy
churl... 3. cad, oaf 4. boor, carl, hind,
lout, serf 5. ceorl, knave 6. rustic
7. bondman, freeman, peasant, villain
9. vulgarian 10. countryman
churlish... 4. mean 5. gruff, rough,
surly 6. rustic, sordid, sullen, vulgar
7. boorish, crabbed, knavish
9. gruffness, niggardly
10. ill–humored 11. countrified
churn... 4. beat, kirn, stir, whip
5. mixer, shake 6. beater, seethe,
vessel 7. agitate 8. agitator, emulsify

chute... 4. tube 5. flume, scarp, slide
6. trough 7. channel, incline,
passage 9. parachute
cibel... 5. chive, onion 7. shallot
ciborium... 3. pyx 6. canopy, coffer,
vessel
cicada... 6. dog–day, locust
9. Cicadidae
cicatrix... 4. mark, scar 7. blemish
Cid... 3. Ruy 4. hero, poem 5. Chief
6. leader (Christian) 7. Rodrigo
cider (weak)... 6. perkin
Cid's sword... 6. colada
cienaga... 5. marsh, swamp
cigar... 4. rope, toby 5. claro
6. concha, corona, Havana, stogie
7. cheroot, culebra, londres
8. cigarite, colorado, panatela
9. belvedere, cigarillo
cigarette... 3. fag 4. pill 5. cubeb
6. gasper, reefer 9. cigarillo
cilium... 4. hair, lash 7. eyelash
8. barbicel, ciliolum, filament
9. eyewinker
cimarron... 6. maroon 7. bighorn, wild
dog 8. district (Okla)
cimex... 6. bedbug
Cimmerian, Homer Myth... 4. dark
5. Nomad (anc) 6. gloomy (abode)
8. Cimmeria
cinch... 4. game (cards), grip, sure
5. girth 6. fasten 7. harness (part)
9. certainty, sure thing
cinders... 3. ash 4. lava, slag
5. ashes, dross 6. embers
7. residue 8. clinkers
cinerarium... 8. mortuary
cinerator... 7. furnace 9. crematory
11. crematorium, incinerator
cingular... 7. annular 8. circular
cinnamon... 5. brown, spice 6. cassia
8. ishpingo (S Am)
10. Cinnamomum
cinque... 4. dice, five
cipher... 3. nil 4. code, zero 5. aught
6. figure, nobody, number, symbol
7. compute 9. calculate, character,
nonentity
circa... 5. about 6. around
13. approximately
Circe (pert to)...
brother.. 6. Aeetes
father.. 6. Helios
Island abode.. 5. Aeaea
role, Odyssey.. 5. siren 7. charmer
9. sorceress, temptress
sister.. 5. Medea
circle... 3. orb 4. halo, hoop, loop,
ring 5. ambit, orbit, rhomb, rigol,
round, wheel 6. clique, cordon,
girdle, rotate, sphere 7. annulus,
aureole, circuit, compass, enclose,
revolve 9. circulate, encompass
13. circumference
circle (pert to)...
astronomy.. 6. tropic
celestial.. 6. colure 10. almucantar
Japan.. 4. maru
luminous.. 6. corona
of hell (8th).. 9. Malebolge
of monoliths.. 8. cromlech 9. cyclolith
part.. 3. arc 6. areola, octant, radius,

sector 7. sextant 8. diameter
circuit... 3. lap, orb 4. bout, gyre,
loop, tour, zone 5. ambit, cycle,
orbit, relay, round, route 6. circle,
detour 7. compass 9. round trip
10. revolution
circuit court... 4. eyre
circuitous... 4. mazy 6. curved
7. crooked, devious, sinuous, twisted,
vagrant, winding 8. circular, flexuous,
indirect, tortuous 9. deceitful,
deviating, underhand, wandering
10. roundabout, serpentine
12. disingenuous, labyrinthine
14. circumlocutory
circular... 5. round 6. ringed
7. annular, discoid, program
8. cingular, coronary, ringlike
9. crownlike, orbicular 10. circuitous,
roundabout 13. advertisement
circular (pert to)...
enclosure.. 3. lis (liss)
indicator.. 4. dial
letter.. 10. encyclical
ornament.. 6. patera
circulate... 4. pass 5. issue 6. circle,
rotate, spread 7. diffuse, publish
8. monetize 9. propagate
11. disseminate
circumference... 4. girt 5. ambit,
bound, girth 6. bounds 7. circuit,
compass 8. encircle, surround
9. outskirts, perimeter, periphery
circumscribe... 5. bound, fence, limit
6. define 7. enclose, environ
8. encircle, restrict 9. encompass
circumscribed... 6. finite, narrow
9. definable 10. restricted
circumspect... 4. wary 5. chary
7. careful, politic, prudent
8. cautious, discreet 9. judicious
10. thoughtful 11. considerate
circumstance... 4. fact, item, pomp
5. event, state 7. proviso
8. incident, occasion, position
9. condition, provision, situation
10. occurrence, particular
11. arrangement, opportunity,
stipulation
circumstantial... 5. exact 6. minute
7. precise 8. detailed 10. evidential,
incidental, particular 11. conditional
12. nonessential
circumvent... 5. cheat, evade
6. delude, entrap, outwit, thwart
7. capture, circuit, deceive
8. surround 9. encompass, frustrate
circus... 4. hawk, ring, show 5. arena
6. big top, circle, cirque 7. harrier,
theater 8. carnival, side show
12. amphitheater
circus (pert to)...
concessionaire.. 7. grifter
hawk.. 15. circus assimilis
rider.. 8. desultor
Roman.. 13. Circus Maximus
sideshow.. 6. freaks
superintendent.. 10. ringmaster
cirque... 6. circle, corrie 7. circlet
cis (pref)... 8. this side
cist... 3. box, pit 5. chest 7. chamber
8. cistvaen (kistvaen)

Cistercian... 4. monk, Rule
(Benedictine) 5. Order 8. Trappist
cistern... 3. bac, sac, tub, vat
4. back, tank, well 7. cuvette,
raintub 9. impluvium, reservoir
citadel... 3. arx 4. fort 5. Alamo,
tower 6. castle 7. bastion, bulwark
8. fastness, fortress 9. acropolis
10. stronghold 13. fortification
14. propungnaculum
citation... 5. honor 6. eulogy, notice
7. mention, summons 8. subpoena
9. quotation 11. enumeration
12. verification
cite... 5. quote 6. adduce, allege,
repeat, summon 7. extract
8. indicate
citizen... 3. cit 6. native 7. citoyen,
denizen (of beasts), dweller
8. civilian, townsman 10. inhabitant
citizenship... 10. citizenism
15. enfranchisement
citron... 5. melon 6. cedrat (cedrate),
citrus, yellow
citrus fruit... 4. lime 5. lemon
6. orange 7. kumquat 8. citrange,
shaddock 10. grapefruit
cittern, cithern... 4. lute (anc)
6. zither 7. cithara, gittern
city... 4. town 8. township
10. metropolis 12. municipality
city (parts)... 4. ward 5. civic, urban
8. district, precinct
City of...
Bells.. 10. Strasbourg
Bridges.. 6. Bruges
Brotherly Love.. 12. Philadelphia
Churches.. 8. Brooklyn
David.. 9. Jerusalem
Dead (The).. 8. cemetery
10. Necropolis
Elms.. 8. New Haven
Gods.. 6. Asgard (Asgarth)
Golden Gate (The).. 12. San Francisco
Great King.. 9. Jerusalem
Hundred Towers.. 5. Pavia
Kings.. 4. Lira
Lilies.. 8. Florence
Magnificent Distances..
10. Washington (DC)
Masts.. 6. London
Palms (Bib).. 7. Jericho
Prophet (The).. 6. Medina
Rams.. 6. Canton
Saints.. 8. Montreal
Seven Hills.. 4. Rome
Straits.. 7. Detroit
Sun (the).. 7. Baalbek 10. Heliopolis
Victory.. 5. Cairo
Violated Treaty.. 8. Limerick
Violet Crown.. 6. Athens
civet... 5. fossa, genet, rasse
6. foussa, musang 7. nandine
10. paradoxure
civic... 5. civil, urban 6. public
7. burghal, oppidan 9. municipal
12. metropolitan
civil... 4. hend (hende) 5. suave
6. decent, polite, public, urbane
7. affable, courtly, elegant, secular
8. discreet, gracious, obliging,
polished, well-bred 9. courteous,

political 10. respectful
11. complaisant 13. condescending
civil (pert to)...
  dress.. 5. mufti 7. civvies
  fraud (Rom).. 11. stellionate
  process.. 4. writ
  strife.. 6. stasis
  wrong.. 4. tort
civility... 6. comity 7. amenity
  8. courtesy, urbanity 9. attention,
  etiquette, gentility 10. affability,
  politeness
civilization... 6. kultur, polish
  7. culture 10. refinement
  11. cultivation
civilize... 4. tame 6. polish
  8. humanize, urbanize 9. cultivate
  11. domesticate
clad... 5. robed 6. decked, garbed
  7. arrayed, attired, clothed, dressed
  9. appareled, garmented
claim... 3. hak (hakh) 4. case, lien,
  name 5. right, title 6. assert,
  demand 7. preempt, profess, require
  8. arrogate, maintain, pretense
  (pretence), proclaim 9. postulate
  10. pretension
claimant... 7. claimer 9. applicant,
  plaintiff, pretender 10. solicitant
clairvoyance... 3. ESP 7. insight
  8. lucidity, sagacity 9. intuition
  10. divination 11. penetration
clairvoyant... 4. seer 7. prophet,
  seeress 9. sagacious 12. clearsighted
clam... 3. Mya 5. Chama, razor, Solen
  6. gweduc, Mactra, quahog
  7. mollusk 10. veneriform (shape)
clam destroyer... 6. winkle
  10. periwinkle
clammy... 4. cool, damp, dank, soft
  5. moist, mucid 6. sticky, sweaty
clamor... 3. cry, din, hue 4. roar, wail
  5. decry, noise, vocal 6. hubbub,
  outcry, racket, uproar 10. hullabaloo
clamorous... 4. loud 5. noisy
  7. blatant, clamant, excited
  8. brawling 9. demanding, insistent,
  turbulent 10. blustering, uproarious,
  vociferous
clamp... 4. vise 6. fasten 9. appliance
clan... 3. set 4. camp, club, cult,
  gens, race, sept 5. group, party,
  tribe 6. circle, clique, family
  7. coterie, society
clan (quarrel)... 4. feud 8. vendetta
clandestine... 3. sly 5. privy 6. covert,
  secret 7. furtive, illicit 8. stealthy
  9. concealed, underhand
  10. frandulent, undercover
  11. unobtrusive 13. surreptitious
clang... 4. ding, ring 5. clank, sound
  6. jangle 7. ringing
clang color... 6. timbre 8. tonality
clangor... 3. din 4. ring 5. clang,
  noise 6. fracas, hubbub, jangle,
  racket, ruckus, rumpus, tumult,
  uproar 7. discord, ringing
clank... 4. ring 5. clang 7. ringing
clapper... 4. bell, clap 5. bones
  (minstrel)
claque... 8. chaqueur, opera hat

9. applauder
clarify... 5. clear 6. filter, purify,
  refine, render, strain 7. cleanse,
  explain, rectify
clash... 3. jar 4. bang, bump 5. crash
  6. impact, jangle, tussle 7. collide,
  scuffle 8. conflict, disagree, skirmish
  9. collision, encounter, hostility
  10. dissonance
clasp... 3. hug 4. belt, grip, hasp,
  hold, ouch (anc), tach 5. grasp,
  morse (priest's), seize, stick, tache
  (anc) 6. buckle, enwrap, fasten,
  secure 7. agraffe (agrafe), embrace,
  tendril 8. fastener 10. chatelaine
class... 3. ilk 4. rank, sect 5. caste,
  genus, grade, order, tribe 6. brevet
  (mil), status 7. station 8. category,
  classify, division 9. catalogue
  14. classification
class (learned)... 8. literate, literati
  14. intelligentsia
classical... 4. pure 5. Attic 6. chaste
  7. classis, elegant 8. academic,
  literary, tasteful 10. Ciceronian
classification... 4. rank, sort 5. genus,
  grade 6. rating, system 7. species
  8. analysis, category, grouping
  12. distribution
classify... 4. list, rank, rate, sort, type
  5. grade, label, range 6. assort,
  digest, ticket 7. aggroup, arrange
  8. register 9. catalogue
clatter... 3. din, jar 5. noise, rumor
  6. babble, gabble, hubbub, racket,
  rattle, rumpus, tattle, uproar
  7. chatter, prattle 9. commotion
  11. disturbance
clause... 5. rider 6. phrase
  7. passage, proviso, section
claustral... 9. cloistral 10. cloistered
claw... 4. hand, nail, unce 5. chela,
  cloof, clufe, talon 6. nipper, unguis
claw... 3. dig 4. grab, grip, pull, tear
  5. grasp, seize 6. clutch, scrape,
  snatch 7. grapple, scratch
clay... 3. mud 4. marl, mire, soil
  5. argil, earth 6. corpse, kaolin
clay (pert to)...
  baked.. 4. tile 5. brick
  box.. 6. sagger
  covered.. 6. lutose
  mix.. 3. pug
  mold.. 3. dod
  molded.. 7. fictile
  nodule.. 10. eaglestone
  pipe.. 2. TD 10. meerschaum
  plug.. 4. bott
  polish.. 5. rabat
  softening.. 8. malaxage
  variety.. 4. bole, loam, marl 5. gault,
  ocher, tasco 8. petuntse
clayey... 4. soft 5. adobe, bolar
  6. earthy 12. argillaceous
clean, cleanse... 4. dust, swab, wash,
  wipe 5. brush, purge, rinse, scrub
  6. kosher, purify, refine 7. cleanse,
  deterge, launder 8. absterge,
  depurate, renovate 9. disinfect,
  elutriate, expurgate
cleanness... 6. purity (of life) 7. clarity
  8. chastity, elegance, neatness,

pureness, tidiness 10. immaculacy
13. impeccability

clear... 3. net, rid 4. free, gain, over,
pure 5. clean, lucid, plain 6. acquit,
excuse, exempt, hurdle, limpid,
pardon, purify 7. absolve, concise,
crystal, evident, explain, graphic,
lighten, release 8. apparent, distinct,
incisive, luculent 9. cloudless,
exonerate, extricate, vindicate

clear land... 7. thwaite (Eng)

clearsighted... 4. keen 10. discerning
13. perspicacious

cleat... 4. bitt 5. level, strip, wedge
7. joinery

cleave... 3. cut 4. part, rend, rive,
tear 5. clave, cling, clove, crack,
sever, shear, split 6. adhere, bisect,
cohere, divide, pierce 7. dispart
8. separate

cleek... 5. marry, pluck, seize
6. clutch, snatch

clef... 1. C, F, G 4. alto, bass
6. treble 7. descant, soprano
9. character

cleft... 3. gap 4. reft, rent, rift, rima
5. chasm, chink, crack, notch, riven,
split 6. chappy, cranny, gaping,
recess 7. crevice, fissure 8. scissure

cleft palate operation...
13. staphyloraphy (staphylorrhaphy)

clemency... 5. favor, grace, mercy
6. lenity 7. quarter 8. kindness,
leniency, mildness 10. compassion,
indulgence 11. forbearance

Clemens (Samuel) pen name...
9. Mark Twain

clench... 4. fist, grip, grit, hold
5. grasp 6. clinch, clutch
8. purchase 9. interlock

Cleopatra (pert to)...
attendant.. 4. Iras
downfall.. 3. asp
lover.. 6. Antony (Marc), Caesar
obelisk (two).. 6. Needle
queen of.. 5. Egypt
river.. 4. Nile

clepe... 3. bid 4. call, name 6. invite,
invoke 7. address 8. christen

clergy... 5. cloth 6. pulpit
9. clergymen, clericals 10. priesthood

clergyman... 4. abbé, dean 5. canon,
vicar 6. cleric, curate, divine, parson,
pastor, priest, rector 7. dominie,
prelate 8. minister, preacher, sky
pilot 9. presbyter 12. ecclesiastic

clergywoman... 3. nun 8. minister
9. parsoness, priestess 10. religieuse

cleric, non... 4. laic

clerical... 7. scribal 11. ministerial

clerical (pert to)...
attire.. 3. alb 5. amice, cloth, fanon,
orale, stole
collar.. 5. rabat
hat.. 7. biretta

clerk... 3. nun 4. monk 5. write
6. cleric, hermit, layman, scribe
7. scholar (anc) 8. salesman
9. assistant, clergyman
12. ecclesiastic

cleronomy... 8. heritage
11. inheritancy

clever... 3. apt 4. able, cute, deft
5. handy, slick, smart, witty
6. adroit, astute, brainy, bright,
expert, habile, nimble 7. amiable,
cunning, parlous 8. pleasing, skillful,
talented 9. brilliant, dexterous,
ingenious 11. good–natured

cleverness... 4. tact, wits 5. skill
6. esprit 7. cunning 9. ingenuity,
smartness, wittiness 10. adroitness,
astuteness, shrewdness

clew, clue... 3. key 4. ball, loop
(Naut) rope 5. globe 6. cocoon,
tackle (see also *clue*)

cliché... 4. joke 5. banal, trite 6. old
saw 7. bromide 8. banality, chestnut
9. Joe Miller, platitude

click... 3. rap 4. snap 5. clack 6. go
over 7. prosper, succeed

click beetle... 3. dor (dorr) 6. elater

cliff... 3. gat 4. crag, klip, rock, wall
5. bluff, cleve, crest, scarp, slope
6. rocher 7. clogwyn 8. palisade
9. precipice 10. escarpment

climax... 3. cap, epi (Arch) 4. acme,
near, peak, shut 5. tight 6. apogee,
result, summit 7. heights
11. culmination 12. consummation

climb... 3. fly, gad 4. shin 5. grimp,
scale, speel 6. ascend, ascent
7. clamber, upgrade 9. acclivity

climbing... 7. scaling 8. scandent
10. scansorial

climbing plant... 3. hop, ivy 4. bine,
nito, vine 5. betel, liana 6. bryony

clime... 4. zone 5. realm, tract
6. region 7. climate

clinch... 4. bind, grip, hold, seal
5. grasp, prove, seize 6. clutch,
fasten, secure 7. confirm, grapple
8. conclude, purchase 9. establish

cling... 4. hold 5. stick 6. adhere,
cohere

clingfish... 6. testar

clink... 4. rime, slap 5. rhyme
6. jingle, lockup, prison, strike
9. assonance

clinquant... 4. gold, sham 6. tinsel
8. frippery, tinseled 10. glittering

clip... 3. bob, lop, mow 4. barb,
blow, dock, gaff, snip, trim 5. clasp,
prune, shear 6. clutch, fasten
7. curtail, scissor, shorten
8. ornament 10. instrument

clique... 3. set 4. cell, clan, club, ring
5. group, Junta, junto 6. circle
(people) 7. coterie

Cloaca Maxima (anc Rome)...
5. sewer 10. repository

cloak... 3. aba 4. cape, mask, pall,
wrap 5. cover, grego, jelab, manta,
sagum 6. abolla, capote, dolman,
mantle, mantua, screen, serape,
shield 7. chlamys (anc), conceal,
galabia, manteau, paenula (anc),
paletot, pelisse, pretext, protect
8. disguise 9. dissemble, new–market
10. witzchoura

clobber... 3. hit 4. beat, conk, poke,
swat 5. clout, punch, whack
6. defeat, strike, wallop

clock... 3. nef (ship's) 4. dial, time

5. knock 6. record 7. digital
8. recorder, sidereal 9. clepsydra,
metronome, timepiece 10. isochronon
11. chronometer
clockwise... 6. deasil (dessil)
11. withershins 14. dextrorotation,
dextrorotatory
clog... 4. stop 5. choke, dance
6. daggle, hamper, impede
8. encumber, obstruct, restrain
clog shoe... 4. geta 5. sabot
6. chopin, cobcab (Orient), patten
7. chopine
cloister... 4. stoa 5. abbey 6. arcade,
friary, immure, priory 7. confine,
convent, nunnery, retreat
9. anchorage, hermitage, monastery,
peristyle 10. passageway
cloistered... 7. recluse 8. enclosed,
monastic 11. sequestered
close... 2. at, by 3. end 4. near, nigh,
seal, shut, slam 5. dense, finis, stivy
6. finale, finish, period, secret, stingy,
sultry 7. airless, extreme, occlude,
related 8. complete, conclude,
familiar, imminent, intimate, stifling
9. extremity, secretive, terminate
11. approximate, termination
13. juxtaposition
close (pert to)...
eyes (the).. 4. seel 5. blink
fasten.. 6. batten
of day.. 8. eventide 9. nightfall
poetic.. 4. nigh 5. anear
tightly.. 3. bar 4. bung, seal
6. clench, enseal 8. obturate
closely... 4. just 6. almost, barely,
nearly 8. narrowly
closely allied... 6. chummy
7. germane 8. intimate
closeness... 7. density, secrecy
8. fidelity, intimacy, likeness,
nearness, sameness 9. tightness
10. chumminess, narrowness,
similarity, stinginess, strictness,
sultriness 11. airlessness,
compactness, conciseness, familiarity,
resemblance 14. oppressiveness
closet... 5. ambry, cuddy, emery
6. locker, pantry 7. cabinet
8. cupboard, wardrobe 9. cloakroom,
storeroom
closing device... 3. key 4. lock, snap
5. clasp, hinge, latch 6. Velcro (tm),
zipper
closing measure (Mus)... 4. coda
clot... 4. lump, mass 5. grume
7. thicken 8. coagulum, concrete
9. coagulate 12. crassamentum
cloth... 3. net, tat 4. brin, crea, drap,
felt, lamé, silk, tapa, wool 5. adati,
baize, bezan, bluet, carda, crash,
crepe, denim, khaki, linen, manta,
nylon, orlon, rayon, satin, scrim,
surat, tamis, terry, tulle, twill, voile
6. alpaca, burlap, calico, canvas,
chintz, cotton, damask, dimity,
dowlas, duffel, faille, jersey, madras,
mohair, muslin, nankin, pongee,
poplin, samite (gold), sateen, velour
7. acetate, baracan, brocade,
bunting, cambric, challis, chiffon,

drap d'or, flannel, foulard, gingham,
nankeen, organdy, organza, percale,
sacking, spandex, taffeta, ticking,
worsted 8. cashmere, chambray,
corduroy, cretonne, drilling,
nainsook, Shantung 9. crinoline,
gabardine, polyester, sailcloth,
tarpaulin, tricotine 10. broadcloth,
seersucker 11. cheesecloth, drap
d'argent (silver), marquisette
cloth (pert to)...
checkered.. 5. plaid
finisher.. 7. beetler
piece.. 4. bolt 5. scrap
ridge.. 4. wale
selvage.. 4. roon 6. border 7. listing
twilled.. 5. denim, serge
weaving.. 4. warp, weft, woof
clothe... 3. tog 4. deck, garb, gird,
robe, vest 5. array, drape, dress,
endue, indue 6. afford, enrobe, invest
7. empower, provide, sheathe
8. accouter
clothes... 3. rig 4. duds, garb, togs
5. guise, habit, jeans, Levis 6. attire,
bikini, briefs 7. apparel, costume,
raiment, regalia, threads (sl)
8. clothing, garments, leotards,
swimsuit 9. dungarees
10. bedclothes, garmenture
11. habiliments, investiture
cloud... 3. fog, low 4. dust, film, haze,
mist, rack, scud 5. nepho (comb
form), nubia, stain, sully, taint, vapor
6. cirrus, damage, darken, defame,
defect, nebule, nimbus, shadow,
stigma 7. blacken, blemish, cumulus,
nubilus, obscure, pea–soup, stratus,
tarnish, tornado 8. cat's–tail, cocktail,
overcast 10. horizontal
clouds (pert to)...
astronomy.. 4. coma 9. nubeculae
kind.. 6. cirrus, nimbus 7. cumulus,
fractus, stratus 9. mare's–tail
luminous.. 5. nimbi
Magellanic.. 5. Major, Minor
photography.. 9. nephogram
science of.. 9. nephology
seeding.. 10. nucleation
vapory.. 4. rack
cloudy... 4. dark, hazy 5. filmy, foggy,
misty, murky, shady, vague 6. gloomy,
lowery, opaque 7. nebular, obscure
8. confused, overcast, vaporous
9. cloudlike 10. indistinct, lackluster
clout... 3. hit, jab, rag 4. blow, bump,
clod, mend, nail, swat 5. patch,
power, shred, smack 9. influence
12. handkerchief
clove... see also *cleave* 5. spice
clover... 3. red 4. bush 5. lotus, snail,
white 6. alsike 7. crimson, melilot,
prairie, spotted 9. Melilotus
clown... 3. oaf 4. boor, fool, lout,
mime, mome, zany 5. comic, Kelly
(Emmet), mimer, yahoo 6. jester,
rustic 7. buffoon 9. harlequin
10. countryman 11. merry–andrew
clownish... 4. rude 5. gawky, rough
6. clumsy, coarse, rustic 7. awkward,
boorish, ill–bred, loutish, uncivil
8. churlish, ungainly

9. untutored 10. buffoonish
11. countrified
cloy... 4. clog, glut, pall, sate
5. gorge, stuff 6. accloy 7. satiate,
satisfy, surfeit
club... 3. bat, hit 4. beat, join, mace
5. billy, clout, staff, unite, yokel
6. cudgel, league, weapon 7. society
8. bludgeon, spontoon
9. boomerang, espantoon
10. nulla–nulla, pogamoggan
11. association
club (pert to)...
actors.. 6. Friars
historic.. 5. Whigs 8. Jacobins
10. Cordeliers
Service.. 7. Kiwanis
Women's (first).. 7. Sorosis
clubfoot... 7. talipes 9. deformity, pes
valgus 13. talipes valgus
club–shaped... 7. clavate
clue, clew... 3. key, tip 4. data, hint
5. scent 6. thread 7. inkling
8. evidence 9. suspicion
11. fingerprint
clump... 3. tod 4. heap, lump, thud,
tuft 5. bunch, chunk, group, motte
(mott), patch, stamp 6. growth,
trudge 7. cluster, thicket
clumsy... 4. ugly 5. bulky, gawky,
inapt, inept, unfit 6. gauche, oafish
7. awkward, uncouth, unhandy
8. slipshod, ungainly, unwieldy
9. inelegant, lumbering, maladroit,
misshapen 10. blundering,
cumbersome, left–handed
13. inappropriate
clumsy person... 4. gawk 5. jumbo,
staup 7. bungler
clupeoid fish... 7. herring
cluster... 4. crop, cyme, gang, tuft
5. bunch, clump, group 6. huddle
8. fascicle 9. glomerule
cluster (pert to)...
bean.. 4. guar 6. legume
fibers.. 3. nep
flowers.. 6. raceme 7. rosette
8. anthemia, panticle
fruit.. 6. grapes
spores.. 5. sorus
stars.. 8. Globular, Pleiades (The)
clustery... 8. racemose
clutch... 3. nab 4. claw, grip, hold,
nest 5. brood, catch, clasp, grasp,
seize 6. clench, cletch, crisis
clyster... 5. enema 6. lavage
9. injection
Clytemnestra's mother... 4. Leda
cnemis... 4. shin 5. tibia
coach... 3. car, rig 5. prime, stage,
train, tutor 6. direct, fiacre, jarvey
7. adviser, prepare, tallyho, teacher
8. carriage, equipage, instruct,
preparer 9. charabanc 10. instructor
coach dog... 9. Dalmatian
coachman... 3. fly (angling) 4. fish,
jehu, whip 6. driver
coagulate... 3. gel, jel, set 4. cake,
clot, curd, lump 6. curdle, posset
7. congeal 8. solidify
coagulator... 6. enzyme, rennet
coagulum... 4. clot, curd 5. grume

7. clabber
coal... 4. fuel 5. black, ember
6. carbon, cinder 7. lignite, residue
coal (pert to)...
bin.. 6. bunker
car.. 3. dan 4. corf, tram 6. hopper
dust.. 4. coom (coomb), culm, smut
gas.. 7. Pintsch 9. acetylene
miner.. 7. collier
miner's disease.. 11. anthracosis
oil.. 8. kerosene
tar.. 5. lysol, pitch 6. cresol, decane,
phenol 7. toluene
tunnel.. 4. adit
type.. 3. egg, nut, pea 4. dant, hard,
peat, soft 6. broken, cannel
8. charcoal, chestnut 9. buckwheat
10. anthracite, bituminous
coalition... 5. trust, union 6. fusion,
hookup, league, merger 7. society
8. alliance 10. federation
11. affiliation, combination,
confederacy, conjunction
coalition advocate... 9. fusionist
coals... 5. gleed 6. embers 7. cinders
coarse... 3. fat, low 4. dank, lewd,
rude, vile 5. broad, crass, gross,
thick 6. carnal, earthy, impure,
ribald, rustic, vulgar 7. goatish,
obscene, sensual 8. granular,
immodest, indecent, inferior, unchaste
9. inelegant, offensive, unrefined
10. unfinished, unpolished
coarse (pert to)...
grain.. 4. meal
grass.. 4. reed 5. sedge 6. quitch
hominy.. 4. corn, samp
coast... 4. sail 5. beach, glide, shore,
slide 6. rivage 7. seaside
8. seaboard, seashore
coast (pert to)...
dweller.. 7. orarian
live oak.. 6. encina
projection.. 4. cape, ness
coat... 4. jupe 5. cloak, frock, parka,
tunic 6. blazer, capote, duster,
jacket, raglan, reefer, trench, tuxedo,
ulster 7. cassock, cutaway, paletot,
slicker 8. gossamer, Mackinaw,
tegument 9. newmarket, redingote
coat (pert to)...
fastener.. 4. frog 6. zipper
of animal.. 3. fur 4. pelt, wool
6. pelage 8. feathers
of arms.. 5. crest 8. blazonry
10. escutcheon
of mail.. 6. byrnia 7. hauberk
of the eye (inner).. 6. retina
coati... 5. Nasua 6. narica 7. raccoon
coating (pert to)...
cake.. 5. glacé, icing 8. frosting
copper, bronze.. 6. patina
grain.. 4. bran
medical.. 9. collodion
metal.. 5. plate
seed.. 5. testa 6. tegmen
10. endopleura
tin, lead.. 5. terne
vitreous.. 6. enamel
coax... 3. beg, ply 4. lure, urge
5. press, tease 6. cajole, entice,
exhort 7. beguile, flatter, implore,

wheedle 8. blandish, inveigle,
persuade 9. importune
10. manipulate

cob ... 4. axis, blow, gull, loaf, mole,
pier, swan 5. block, chief, horse
6. basket, leader, muffin, spider
7. beating, corncob 8. dumpling
10. breakwater

cobbler ... 3. pie 5. coler, sutor
6. bungle, repair, souter 7. botcher,
crispin 9. fortescue (fortesque),
shoemaker

cobbra ... 4. head 5. skull

cobby ... 5. stout 6. hearty, lively,
stocky 10. headstrong

cobra ... 3. asp 4. Naga (Myth), Naja
5. mamba, snake, viper 8. ringhals

cobweb ... 3. net 4. trap 5. snare,
wevet 7. fiction, network 8. filament,
gossamer 9. intricacy

cobweblike ... 8. araneous 9. arachnoid

cocaine ... 4. coca, snow (sl)
8. narcotic 9. mydriatic
10. anesthetic

coccus ... 4. cell 5. spore
9. bacterium, cochineal

cochleate ... 6. spiral 11. shell–shaped

cock ... 3. nab, tap 4. bird, heap,
kora, pile, vane (weather) 5. strut,
valve 6. faucet, grouse, leader,
muckna 7. rooster, swagger

cockade ... 4. knot 7. rosette

Cockade State ... 8. Maryland

cockatoo ... 3. ara 5. arara (palm),
galah 6. parrot 8. ganggang

cockle ... 4. boat, gith, kiln, oast
5. shell, stove 6. pucker 7. mollusk,
wrinkle

cockpit ... 3. pit 4. well 5. arena,
cabin (airplane) 7. gallera

cockscomb (coxcomb) ... 5. crest, plant

cocktail ... 5. cloud, drink, horse
6. beetle 9. appetizer

cocky ... 4. pert 5. saucy 6. jaunty
7. stuck–up 9. conceited

cocoa ... 5. broma, cacao 8. beverage
9. chocolate 11. theobromine

coconut (pert to) ...
fiber .. 4. coir, kyar
India .. 6. nargil (narghile)
meat .. 5. copra

cocoon ... 3. pod 4. bave (silk), clew,
kell, pupa 9. chrysalis

cod ... 3. bib, cor 4. fish, ling
5. scrod, sprag 6. burbot, cultus,
gadoid 7. bacalao

coddle ... 3. pet 4. baby, cook
5. humor, spoil 6. caress, fondle,
pamper 11. mollycoddle

code ... 3. law 5. canon, codex, Morse,
salic 6. digest, equity, signal, symbol
7. pandect, precept
12. Commandments

codfish (pert to) ...
Alaska .. 6. wachna
genus .. 5. Gadus
ready for cooking .. 5. scrod
type .. 3. cod, red 4. cusk, rock
6. Murray, tomcod 7. buffalo

codger ... 5. crank, miser 6. oddity

codicil ... 4. will 5. rider 6. sequel
8. addition, appendix 10. instrument

Cody (William) ... 11. Buffalo Bill

coerce ... 4. curb 5. force 6. compel
7. dragoon, enforce, repress
9. blackjack, strong–arm, terrorize
10. intimidate

coercion ... 5. force 6. duress
8. violence 10. compulsion,
constraint

coffee (pert to) ...
bean .. 3. nib
container .. 8. canister
cup holder .. 4. zarf
extract .. 8. caffeine
kind .. 3. Rio 4. Java 5. Milds,
Mocha 6. Bogota, Brazil, Santos
7. Sumatra, Turkish 8. Medellin
9. Maracaibo
mix .. 7. chicory
pot .. 6. biggin 10. percolator

coffin ... 3. box, urn 4. bier, case, kist,
mold 5. chest, crust 6. basket,
casing, casket 11. sarcophagus

coffin (pert to) ...
cloth .. 4. pall 5. cloak
litter .. 4. bier
nail .. 9. cigarette
prehistoric .. 4. cist 5. chest

cog ... 3. cam 4. boat (fishing), gear
5. catch, cheat, cozen, tenon, tooth
7. ratchet, wheedle 8. sprocket
9. deception

cogent ... 5. valid 6. potent, strong
7. telling 8. powerful 9. effective
10. compelling, conclusive,
convincing, persuasive

cogitate ... 4. mull, muse, plan
5. think 6. ponder 8. meditate
9. cerebrate

cognizance ... 3. ken 4. heed, plea
5. badge (knight's) 9. knowledge
11. recognition 12. apprehension

cognizant ... 5. aware 7. knowing
8. sensible 9. conscious
10. perceptive 11. intelligent

cognomen ... 4. name 5. title
6. y–clept 7. surname 8. nickname
10. patronymic 11. appellation

coheir ... 5. joint 8. parcener

cohere ... 5. agree, cling, serry, stick,
unite 6. adhere, cleave 9. glutinate

coherence ... 5. cling 8. adhesion,
cohesion, sticking 9. adherence,
connected 11. consistency

coil ... 4. ansa, clew, curl, loop, mesh,
wind 5. querl, twine, twist 6. spiral
7. haycock 8. encircle
11. convolution

coiled ... 7. tortile, twirled

coin ... 3. rin, sou, yen 4. cash, cent
5. money, penny, stamp 6. specie

coin (pert to) ...
Bib .. 6. talent
brass .. 13. Rosa Americana (1722)
gold .. 3. lev 4. ryal (rial) 5. daric,
eagle 6. guinea
minor .. 4. doit
parts of .. 4. flan 5. field, tails, verso
6. legend 7. exergue, obverse (front),
reverse
silver .. 4. batz, obol, ryal (rial)
5. crown, ducat, sceat 6. tester
tester .. 6. shroff (saraf)

coincide... 5. agree, check, chime,
match, tally 6. concur 7. consent
10. correspond 11. synchronize
coincident... 9. consonant
10. concurrent 12. contemporary
coiner... 8. inventor 9. neologist
(words) 10. fabricator
13. counterfeiter
coins (pert to)...
roll of .. 7. rouleau
science of .. 11. numismatics
specialist .. 11. numismatist
colander... 5. sieve 6. filter, sorter
8. strainer
Colchis King... 6. Aeetes
cold... 3. icy, nip, raw 4. dank, dead,
drow, dull, frio, sure 5. algid, bland,
bleak, frore (anc), gelid 6. chilly,
frigid, frosty 7. chilled, cinched
8. chilling, reserved, unheated
9. heartless 10. lackluster
11. indifferent, passionless,
unconscious
cold (pert to)...
blooded .. 9. heartless, unfeeling
13. dispassionate, heterothermal
14. poikilothermal
feet .. 9. cowardice
infection .. 4. post 5. rheum 6. coryza
7. catarrh
sore .. 6. herpes 7. simplex, vesicle
14. herpes labialis
steel .. 5. sword 7. bayonet, weapons
term .. 8. frigoric
wind .. 4. bise
Coleoptera... 7. beetles, insects
Coleridge's sacred river... 4. Alph
(Kubla Khan)
colewort... 4. kale 7. cabbage
colic... 4. pain 5. gripe, spasm
7. tormina 10. enteralgia
11. stomachache
coliseum... 4. bowl 5. arena 6. circus
7. stadium, theater 9. Colosseum
10. hippodrome 12. amphitheater
collaborate... 3. aid 6. co–work
8. coauthor 9. cooperate
10. fraternize
collage... 6. gluing 7. montage
8. abstract, adhesive 9. cyclorama
collapse... 4. cave, fail, fall 5. crash,
slump 6. cave–in, defeat
7. crack–up, debacle, deflate, failure
8. downfall 9. breakdown, shrinking
10. bankruptcy, exhaustion
11. prostration
collar... 4. band, grab, ruff 5. chain,
rabat, ruche 6. arrest, bertha, rabato,
tackle, torque 7. barghan, capture,
harness (part), shackle 8. carcanet,
neckband 10. pickadilly
collate... 5. audit, check 6. verify
7. certify, compare, examine
collateral... 5. extra 6. margin
7. related 8. indirect, relation (folks),
security 9. accessory, secondary
10. contingent, obligation, subsidiary
11. subordinate 12. nonessential
collation... 3. tea 4. meal 5. lunch
6. repast, sermon 7. address,
reading 8. luncheon, treatise
10. collection, comparison,

conference 12. consultation,
contribution
colleague... 6. fellow 7. compeer,
comrade, consort, partner
8. camarada, confrere 9. associate,
companion 11. confederate
collect... 3. bag, tax 4. levy, mass
5. amass, glean, raise, rally
6. deduce, forage, garner, gather,
muster, prayer, sheave 7. compile,
procure 8. assemble, mobilize
9. aggregate 10. accumulate,
congregate
collection... 3. ana, bag, set 4. book,
olio 5. group, hoard, store 6. rosary,
sorite 8. assembly, donation, offering
9. aggregate, congeries, gathering,
repertory 10. assemblage, repertoire
11. acquisition
collection (pert to)...
anecdotes .. 3. ana 4. data
8. analecta
animals (wild) .. 3. zoo 9. menagerie
bubbles .. 4. foam
curiosities .. 6. museum
documents .. 4. Veda 6. corpus
7. dossier
fruit .. 7. syncarp
implements (Surg) .. 7. trousse
of four .. 6. tetrad
of twenty–four .. 5. quire
poems .. 5. sylva 9. anthology
proper names .. 11. onomasticon
type .. 4. font
writing .. 10. literature
collector (pert to)...
bird eggs .. 8. oologist
books .. 10. bibliothec 11. bibliophile
12. bibliomaniac
coins .. 11. numismatist
rent .. 8. landlord
stamps .. 11. philatelist
colleen... 4. girl, lass, maid 6. damsel,
maiden 7. girleen
college... 6. school 7. academy,
society 9. Alma Mater, institute
10. université, university
11. corporation, institution
college (pert to)...
campus .. 4. lawn, quad 7. grounds
graduate .. 6. alumna 7. alumnus
license for absence .. 5. exeat
official .. 4. dean 5. prexy 6. beadle,
bursar, regent 7. proctor
collegiate... 8. academic 9. collegian,
scholarly 11. college–bred
collide with... 3. hit, ram 5. clash,
crash 6. hurtle, strike 7. contend
8. conflict, disagree
collier... 5. miner 6. plover
collieshangie... 3. row 7. quarrel
8. squabble 11. disturbance (noisy)
collision... 4. bump 5. clash, crash
6. impact 7. smashup 8. accident
9. hostility 11. composition,
impingement 12. interference
colloquial... 6. common 8. everyday,
familiar, informal 9. unstudied
10. vernacular 11. undignified
14. conversational
colloquy... 4. chat, talk 6. parley
9. discourse 10. conference

12. conversation
Cologne Kings (legend) . . . 4. Magi
  6. Gaspar 8. Melchior 9. Balthasar
Colombia . . .
 capital . . 6. Bogota (1538)
 city . . 4. Cali 5. Pasto 8. Medellin
  9. Cartagena 10. Santa Marta
 Falls . . 10. Tequendama
 Liberator . . 7. Bolivar (Simon)
 mountain . . 5. Andes 11. Cordilleras
 river . . 9. Magdalena
colonize . . . 6. gather, people, settle
  8. populate 9. establish
colonizer . . . 3. ant 6. oecist
  7. planter, settler
colonnade . . . 3. row (columns) 4. stoa
  6. arcade 7. columns, pillars, portico
  8. cloister 9. peristyle
colony . . . 4. body 5. group, swarm
  8. dominion 9. community
  10. dependency, settlement
colophon . . . 4. logo 6. emblem
  9. bookplate 11. inscription (book)
color . . . 3. dun, dye, hue 4. tint, tone
  5. blush, paint, shade, stain, terne,
  tinge 6. flaxen, nuance, pastel, sallow,
  timbre 7. piebald, pigment 8. tincture
  (Her) 10. complexion
color (pert to) . . .
 application (paste) . . 7. impasto
 blending . . 4. teer 5. fondu
  9. scumbling
 blind . . 13. achromatopsia
 clouded . . 9. nebulated
 colorful . . 9. chromatic
 colorless . . 4. drab, dull, pale 6. pallid
  7. whitish 8. blanched
  10. achromatic
 irregularity . . 5. fleck 6. streak
  10. rivulation
 material . . 5. eosin, morin, smalt
  7. pigment 11. chlorophyll
 off color . . 6. risqué 8. improper
 organ . . 8. clavilux
 paint, rouge . . 6. ruddle 7. blusher
 science of . . 10. chromatics
  11. spectrology
 variegated . . 7. rainbow, The Flag,
  vibgyor 8. spectrum 11. iridescence
Colorado . . .
 canyon . . 5. Black 10. Royal Gorge
 capital . . 6. Denver
 city . . 5. Aspen, Lamar 6. Pueblo
  7. Boulder, Manassa, Manitou
 Indian . . 7. Arapaho
 lake (highest) . . 10. Frozen Lake
 Mt peak . . 6. Elbert 9. Pike's Peak
 park . . 5. Estes 15. Garden of the
  Gods
 river . . 4. Gila 6. Platte 8. Arkansas
 State admission . . 12. Thirty–eighth
 State bird . . 11. lark bunting
 State flower . . 9. columbine
 State motto . . 13. Nil Sine Numine
  (Nothing Without God)
 State nickname . . 10. Centennial
colossal . . . 4. huge 5. great, large
  6. absurd, superb 7. mammoth
  8. gigantic 9. monstrous
colossal beast . . . 8. behemoth (Bib)
colt . . . 3. gun 4. foal 5. filly, horse
  8. yearling

Columbus (pert to) . . .
 birthplace . . 5. Genoa (It)
 companion . . 5. Ojeda
 discoverer . . 7. America (1492)
 landing site . . 11. San Salvador
 sailing site . . 5. Palos (Sp)
 vessel . . 4. Nina 5. Pinta 10. Santa
  Maria
column . . . 3. lat (Buddh) 4. anta
  5. pylon, shaft, stele (stela) 6. pillar
  7. telamon 8. baluster, caryatid,
  pilaster
column (pert to) . . .
 base . . 5. socle 6. plinth 9. stylobate
 military . . 4. unit 9. formation
 Order (Arch) . . 5. Doric, Ionic
  6. Tuscan 9. Composite
  10. Corinthian
 ref to . . 5. train 7. cortege
  8. cylinder, memorial, monument
  10. procession
 shaft . . 4. fust 5. scape 8. apophyge
 term . . 5. bague, galbe, shank
  7. capital, entasis
coma . . . 4. daze, tuft 5. carus, sleep,
  sopor 6. stupor, trance 9. catalepsy
  12. sluggishness 13. insensibility
  15. unconsciousness
comatose . . . 6. drowsy, torpid
  9. apathetic, lethargic 10. cataleptic,
  insensible 11. unconscious
comb . . . 4. card, wave 5. cock's, crest,
  curry, groom, scour, tease 6. search
  7. rummage 8. caruncle
combat . . . 3. war 4. cope, duel, fray,
  tilt 5. fight, joust (anc), repel
  6. action, battle, karate, kung fu,
  oppose, strife 7. contest, jujitsu,
  scuffle 8. argument, conflict
  9. withstand 10. antagonize,
  contention, engagement
combat (pert to) . . .
 challenge . . 6. cartel 8. gauntlet
 code . . 6. duello
 scene . . 5. arena 8. coliseum
combatant . . . 6. dueler 7. battler,
  fighter 8. disputer 9. contender
  10. competitor, contestant
combative . . . 8. militant 9. agonistic,
  bellicose 10. aggressive, pugnacious
  11. belligerent, contentious
combination . . . 4. gang, pact, pool
  5. blend, combo, party, trust, union
  6. clique, fusion, hookup, league,
  merger 7. amalgam, combine, faction,
  mixture 8. alliance, coalesce,
  ensemble, junction 9. camarilla,
  coalition, synthesis 10. embodiment
  11. aggregation, association,
  confederacy, unification
  12. undergarment 13. incorporation
combine . . . 3. add, mix 4. join, pool
  5. merge, unite 6. concur, mingle
  7. machine 10. synthesize
combining form . . .
 above, beyond . . 3. sur 5. ultra
 across . . 4. tran 5. trans
 bad . . 3. dys, mal
 black . . 4. mela
 earth . . 3. geo 5. terra
 equal . . 3. iso 4. homo, pari
 far . . 3. tel 4. tele

good.. **2.** eu
hundred.. **4.** cent
inner, within.. **4.** ento (ent)
kidney.. **4.** reni
middle.. **4.** medi **5.** medio
mountain.. **3.** oro
needle.. **3.** acu
new.. **3.** neo
not.. **2.** un **3.** non
old, ancient.. **5.** paleo
one.. **3.** uni **4.** mono
outside, without.. **3.** ect, ext **4.** ecto
personal.. **4.** idio
soft.. **4.** leni
stone.. **4.** lith
thought.. **4.** ideo
thrice.. **3.** ter
tooth.. **6.** odonto
touch.. **3.** tac
up, upward.. **3.** ano
watery.. **4.** sero
comblike... **7.** ctenoid **8.** pectinal
combustible... **5.** fiery, quick
  7. piceous **8.** volcanic **9.** irascible
  10. accendible **11.** hot–tempered,
  inflammable
combustion... **4.** fire **6.** tumult
  7. blazing, flaming **8.** ignition
  9. agitation, confusion, cremation
  12. inflammation **13.** conflagration
come... **3.** hop **4.** near **5.** issue, occur
  6. appear, arrive, happen
  8. approach **9.** transpire
come (pert to)...
across.. **3.** pay **4.** meet **7.** confess
  10. contribute
back.. **6.** answer, retort, return
  7. rebound, recover **8.** remember,
  repartee
before.. **4.** lead **7.** precede, prevene
  8. antecede
between.. **8.** estrange, interlie
  9. interpose, intervene
by.. **3.** get **4.** gain **6.** obtain
  7. acquire, inherit, receive
forth.. **3.** jet **4.** gush, spew **5.** hatch,
  issue, occur **6.** appear, emerge,
  spring **7.** emanate **9.** originate
together.. **4.** join, knit, meet **5.** clash
  7. collide, convene **8.** assemble,
  converge
come (to)...
light.. **7.** develop
maturity.. **5.** ripen
pass.. **5.** occur **6.** befall, betide,
  happen **9.** eventuate
rest.. **3.** sit **5.** light **6.** settle
comedian, comedienne... **4.** buff
  5. actor, comic **6.** player **7.** farcist
  8. funnyman **9.** dramatist
comedy... **5.** drama, farce, revue
  7. comedie **8.** travesty **9.** burlesque,
  slapstick
comestibles... **4.** food **5.** manna
  8. eatables, victuals
comfort... **4.** ease **5.** cheer, quilt
  6. relief, solace, soothe, succor
  7. confirm, console, enliven, fortify,
  refresh, relieve, support, sustain
  8. inspirit, nepenthe (drug)
  9. enjoyment **10.** invigorate,

strengthen **11.** consolation
12. satisfaction
comfortable... **4.** cozy, easy, snug
  5. scarf **8.** adequate, cheerful,
  homelike, wristlet **9.** contented,
  endemonic **10.** complacent,
  prosperous **11.** consolatory,
  encouraging
comforter... **5.** quilt **6.** tippet
  7. solacer **8.** pacifier **9.** Paraclete
comfortless... **7.** forlorn **8.** desolate
  9. cheerless, heartsick **10.** despairing
  11. distressing **12.** disconsolate,
  inconsolable
comic, comical... **3.** odd **5.** cutup,
  droll, funny, queer, witty **6.** absurd,
  quaint **7.** cartoon, risible
  8. comedian, farcical, humorous
  9. burlesque, laughable, ludicrous,
  quizzical, whimsical **10.** capricious,
  outlandish
coming... **3.** due **6.** access, advent,
  future **7.** arrival, forward, looming
  8. eventual, expected, imminent
  9. imminence **11.** approaching,
  forthcoming
coming into being... **7.** genesis,
  nascent
comity... **7.** amenity, suavity **8.** civility,
  courtesy, urbanity **10.** affability
command... **3.** bid, gee, haw, hup
  4. bade, beck, fiat, hest, rule, sway
  5. avast, check, edict, exact, grasp,
  order, power, ukase **6.** behest,
  charge, compel, decree, direct,
  enjoin, govern **7.** control, dictate,
  mandate, mastery **8.** dominion,
  restrain **9.** authority, prescribe
  10. domination **11.** commandment
  12. jurisdiction
commander... **3.** cid **5.** chief, ruler
  6. leader **7.** admiral, captain, skipper
  8. dictator, governor, myriarch,
  overlord
commander, Eastern... **3.** ras **4.** amir,
  emir, Imam, khan, rani **5.** ameer,
  begum, dewan, emeer, nawab, Nizam
  6. caliph, regent, Sultan
commanding... **8.** dominant
  9. imperious **10.** imperative
  13. authoritative
commandments... **4.** laws **6.** orders,
  tables **8.** mandates, precepts
  9. Decalogue (Ten)
comme il faut... **8.** properly
  9. correctly **10.** decorously **12.** as it
  should be
commemoration... **7.** service
  8. Encaenia (Oxford Univ)
  10. observance **11.** anniversary,
  celebration, remembrance
  13. solemnization
commence... **4.** open **5.** arise, begin,
  start **6.** spring **8.** initiate **9.** originate
commencement... **4.** rite **6.** source
  8. ceremony, nascency **9.** beginning,
  formality, inception, novitiate
  10. initiation
commend... **4.** plug **5.** boost, extol,
  offer **6.** assign, commit, praise,
  remand, resign **7.** approve, deliver,
  entrust **8.** advocate, delegate

9. recommend 10. compliment
commendation... 4. hype, plug, puff
5. boost, kudos 8. approval
10. assignment, commitment,
compliment, delegation
11. approbation, consignment,
entrustment
comment... 4. note, talk 6. gossip,
postil, remark, report 7. descant,
discuss, explain, mention 8. annotate,
critique 9. criticism, discourse
commentary... 5. gloss 6. memoir
7. remarks 8. treatise 9. memoranda
10. annotation 11. explanation
commerce... 5. trade 7. traffic
8. dealings 9. communion
11. interchange 13. communication
commis... 5. agent, clerk 6. deputy
commiserate... 4. pity 7. condole,
console 10. sympathize
commiseration... 4. pity, ruth
5. mercy 6. sorrow 7. empathy,
feeling 8. sympathy 10. compassion,
condolence
commission... 4. duty, task 5. allot,
board, share, trust 6. brevet, depute,
office, ordain 7. empower, mandate,
mission, payment, rake–off, warrant
8. delegate 9. authority
10. assignment, constitute,
delegation, deputation
11. performance 12. perpetration
commissioned... 8. allotted, assigned,
breveted 9. delegated
10. accredited, authorized
commissioner... 5. envoy 6. dubash,
legate 7. steward 8. delegate,
emissary, official 9. commissar
commissure... 4. seam 5. cleft, joint,
mitre, raphe 6. stitch, suture
7. closure 8. juncture 10. interstice
commit... 2. do 3. con 4. game
(cards) 5. refer 6. remand 7. confide,
consign, entrust, promise
8. memorize, relegate
10. commission, perpetrate
commode... 3. cap 5. chest
8. fontange 9. washstand
10. chiffonier
commodious... 3. fit 5. ample, roomy
6. proper 8. suitable 9. capacious,
expansive, opportune 10. convenient
11. comfortable, serviceable
13. accommodating
commodity, commodities... 5. goods,
wares 6. profit 7. staples
common... 4. park 5. cheap, plain,
stale, trite, usual 6. mutual, paltry,
vulgar 7. average 8. familiar,
frequent, mediocre, ordinary, plebeian
9. customary, household, universal
11. commonplace
common (pert to)...
ancestor.. 4. Adam 10. progenitor
funds.. 4. pool 7. tontine
gender.. 6. unisex 7. epicene
informer.. 7. delator
people.. 3. mob 5. demos, gente
6. vulgus 7. demotic 8. populace
commonly accepted... 7. vulgate
commonly thought... 8. putative
commonplace... 5. banal, daily, stale,

theme, trite, usual 6. truism
7. humdrum, prosaic 8. ordinary,
workaday 9. platitude
commonwealth... 5. group, State
7. society 8. Kentucky, Virginia
9. Australia, community
12. Pennsylvania 13. Massachusetts
commotion... 3. ado 4. fray, riot,
to–do, whir 5. flare, tizzy 6. flurry,
fracas, hubbub, rumpus, tumult, unrest
7. turmoil 8. foofaraw, uprising
9. agitation, confusion
10. concussion (med), excitement,
turbulence 12. perturbation
commune... 4. area, soil 5. realm,
share 6. confer, impart 7. kibbutz
8. converse 9. communion
10. commonalty 11. intercourse
(spiritual) 12. conversation
Commune of Paris (1871)...
10. government
communicate... 3. say 4. give, join
5. share 6. bestow, impart, inform
7. apprize 8. converse, transmit
9. communion
communication... 4. word 5. radio
6. letter, report 7. account, contact,
epistle, message 8. buzzword,
feedback 9. statement
10. communique, connection
11. computerese, impartation,
information, intercourse 12. body
language 14. word processing
communion... 5. share 6. church
7. concord, rapport 8. converse
9. agreement 11. intercourse
12. denomination 13. participation
Communion... 9. Eucharist, Sacrament
10. intinction, Last Supper
communion (pert to)...
bread (blessed).. 4. host 5. wafer
7. eulogia 9. antidoron
cloth.. 8. corporal, corporas
plate.. 5. paten 12. processional
table.. 5. altar
vessel.. 3. ama, pyx
communique... 4. word 7. message
8. dispatch 13. communication
comose... 5. hairy 6. tufted
compact... 4. etui, firm, pact, plot,
snug, trim 5. brief, close, dense,
pithy, press, solid, terse, tight
6. treaty, united, vanity 7. concise,
crowded, entente, leagued, serried
8. alliance, compress, contract,
covenant, succinct 9. agreement,
condensed 10. compressed,
conspiracy 11. compendious,
sententious, stipulation
companion... 3. pal 4. ally, fare, mate,
twin 5. amigo, crony 6. fellow,
shadow 7. Achates, compeer,
comrade, consort 8. alter ego,
co–worker 9. associate
11. confederate, counterpart
companionship... 5. amity 7. society
10. fellowship, fraternity
11. comradeship, sociability
13. accompaniment
company... 3. set 4. band, bevy,
body, crew, gang, ging, host
5. crowd, flock, group, party, troop

6. circle, cohort, throng, troupe
9. concourse, gathering
company (pert to)...
detachment.. 5. posse
people, players.. 4. bevy, crew, gang,
team 5. troop 6. galaxy, guests,
troupe 9. cavalcade
ships.. 5. fleet 6. armada
8. squadron
soldiers.. 5. corps, squad 7. brigade,
phalanx, platoon 9. battalion
travelers.. 7. caravan 8. pilgrims,
tourists 9. merchants
comparative... 5. equal, rival
8. relative 10. comparable, relational
compare... 4. even 5. liken 6. confer,
semble 7. collate, examine
8. contrast
comparison... 6. simile 7. parable
8. likening, metaphor
10. accordance, similarity
11. parallelism
compartment... 3. bin 4. cell, part
5. stall 6. alcove 7. cellule,
chamber, quarter 8. district, division
10. department
compass... 3. arc 4. area, plot, ring
5. guide, range (Mus), reach, solar,
sweep 6. attain, bounds, circle,
curved, degree, extent 7. circuit,
divider, enclose, imagine 8. circular,
distance, surround
compass (pert to)...
housing.. 8. binnacle
part.. 3. pen 6. needle
point.. 4. airt 5. rhumb 7. azimuth
sight.. 4. vane
suspender.. 6. gimbal
compassion... 4. pity, ruth (anc)
5. mercy 8. humanity, sympathy
10. condolence 13. commiseration
compassionate... 6. gentle, humane
7. clement, pitiful 8. merciful
11. sympathetic, warmhearted
12. sympathizing
compatible... 8. affinity, suitable
9. accordant, agreeable, congruous
10. consistent, harmonious
12. congeniality
compeer... 4. mate, peer 5. equal,
match, rival 7. comrade
9. companion
compel... 4. urge 5. drive, force,
impel, press 6. coerce, incite, oblige,
obsess 7. actuate, dragoon, require
9. constrain, influence, instigate
compelling... 6. urgent 7. driving
8. pressing 9. insistent, necessary,
obsessing 10. compulsory,
motivating, obligatory, persuasive
compelling assent... 6. cogent
compelling attention... 9. insistent
compendious... 5. brief, short, terse
7. compact, concise 8. abridged,
succinct 9. condensed
10. summarized
compendium... 5. brief 6. abrégé,
digest 7. capsule, epitome, medulla,
pandect, summary 8. abstract,
syllabus, synopsis 9. comprisal
10. abridgment 11. compilation,
contraction 12. abbreviation

compensate... 3. pay 5. atone, repay
6. reward 7. redress, requite
9. indemnify 10. recompense,
remunerate 14. counterbalance
compensation... 3. pay 4. hire
5. bonus, wages 6. manbot
(manbote), reward, salary 7. penalty,
stipend 8. gratuity, pittance, requital,
solatium 9. atonement, indemnity
10. reparation 12. remuneration,
satisfaction 15. indemnification
compete... 3. vie 4. cope 5. match
6. outvie, strive 7. contend, contest,
emulate
competence... 5. means, skill
7. ability, fitness 8. adequacy,
capacity, property 10. capability,
efficiency 11. proficiency, sufficiency,
suitability 13. effectiveness,
qualification
competent... 3. apt, can, fit 4. able
5. capax, smart 7. capable
8. adequate, suitable 9. effective,
effectual, efficient, qualified
10. catechumen, sufficient
12. appertaining (to)
competition... 5. match, trial 6. strife
7. contest, rivalry 8. ambition,
concours 9. emulation 10. corrivalry
compilation... 5. cento 6. digest
9. Americana 10. collection
compile... 3. add 4. edit 5. amass
6. gather 8. assemble
complacent... 4. smug 6. bovine
7. fatuous 9. contented, satisfied
11. considerate 13. self-satisfied
complain... 4. beef, carp, fret, kick,
pule, wail 5. gripe, growl, whine
6. accuse, bewail, grieve, grouse,
lament, murmur, mutter, repine,
squawk, yammer 7. deplore, grumble,
protest 9. bellyache
complaint... 6. charge, lament, malady
7. ailment, disease, illness, protest
8. disorder, repining, reproach
9. grievance, murmuring
10. accusation, imputation
11. declaration, lamentation
complaisance... 6. regard 7. amenity,
concern, suavity 8. civility, courtesy,
urbanity 10. indulgence, solicitude,
submission, toleration
13. consideration
complaisant... 4. easy, kind 5. civil
6. polite 7. lenient 8. gracious,
obliging 9. compliant, courteous
complement... 4. crew 7. adjunct
8. addition, complete
10. correspond, supplement
11. counterpart
complete... 3. all, end 4. dead, fill,
full, sole 5. stark, total, utter, whole
6. effect, entire, finish, intact, mature
7. achieve, execute, germane,
perfect, plenary, realize 8. absolute,
conclude, detailed, outright
9. terminate 10. accomplish,
complement, consummate
11. unqualified
completely... 3. all 5. fully, quite,
stark 7. solidly, totally, utterly
8. entirely

completeness... 9. entelechy, integrity
complex... 4. mazy 5. mixed
  6. knotty 7. twisted 8. involute,
  involved 9. entangled, intricate,
  perplexed 10. interlaced
  11. complicated
complexion... 4. blee, mode, tone
  5. color, guise, tinge 10. appearance
compliance... 6. assent 7. consent
  9. accession, obedience
  10. concession, conformity,
  observance, submission
  11. willingness 12. acquiescence
compliant... 6. docile 7. duteous,
  dutiful, willing 8. obedient
  10. submissive 11. acquiescent,
  complaisant, conformable
complicated... 6. daedal 7. complex,
  Gordian, snarled, tangled 8. involved
  9. difficult, embroiled, intricate
  11. embarrassed 12. labyrinthine
complication... 4. node (drama)
  5. nodus 7. illness 9. complexus
  10. complexity 11. combination
compliment... 6. praise 7. adulate,
  commend, flatter 8. encomium,
  flattery 12. blandishment,
  commendation 14. congratulation
comply... 4. obey 5. agree, yield
  6. accede, accord, assent, submit
  7. conform, observe 9. acquiesce
compone... 6. settle 7. arrange,
  compose 8. compound
component... 3. ion 4. part 5. basis
  6. factor 7. element 8. integral
  10. ingredient 11. constituent
comport... 3. act 6. accord, behave
  7. conduct 10. correspond
comportable... 8. suitable
  10. consistent
compose... 3. pen 4. calm, form,
  make 5. order, score, write
  7. arrange, fashion, prepare
  8. compound, melodize 9. reconcile
  10. constitute 11. orchestrate,
  tranquilize
composed... 4. calm, cool 5. quiet,
  sober, wrote 6. sedate, serene
  7. consist 8. arranged, tranquil
  9. collected 11. unflappable
composed of...
  flat plates.. 9. lamellate
  lobes.. 6. lobate
composer... 6. author 7. idylist
  (idyllist) 10. compositor, typesetter
composer of...
  Aida.. 5. Verdi
  Carmen.. 5. Bizet
  Faust.. 6. Gounod
  La Boheme.. 7. Puccini
  Merry Widow.. 5. Lehar
  Mikado.. 8. Sullivan
  Naughty Marietta.. 7. Herbert
  Stars and Stripes Forever.. 5. Sousa
composition... 4. opus 5. piece,
  theme 6. make–up 7. melange
  9. formation, synthesis
  12. constitution, construction
composition (pert to)...
  literature.. 5. cento, essay, poesy,
  prose 6. poetry, satire, thesis
  8. treatise 10. brainchild

music.. 2. op 4. aria, glee, hymn,
  opus 5. drama, étude, motet, nonet,
  opera, rondo, suite 6. anthem,
  septet (septuor), sextet (sestet),
  sonata 7. duetino, quartet
  8. concerto, oratorio, postlude,
  symphony
composure... 6. repose 8. calmness,
  coolness, serenity 9. placidity
  10. equanimity, quiescence,
  sedateness 11. tranquility
compound... 3. mix 4. olio 5. agree,
  amide, ester, oxide, pyran, unite
  6. anisil, elixir, iodide, ketone
  7. ammonia, combine, farrago,
  metamer 8. tincture 9. composite
comprehend... 3. see 4. know
  5. grasp, sense 6. embody, fathom
  7. enclose, imagine, include, involve,
  realize 8. comprise, conceive
  10. understand
comprehensible... 8. exoteric,
  included, knowable 9. comprised
  11. conceivable, discernible,
  perceptible 12. intelligible
comprehensive... 4. full, wide
  5. large 7. generic, knowing
  8. thorough 9. extensive, inclusive,
  universal 11. compendious
compress... 4. firm 5. cling, crowd,
  pinch, press, stupe 7. compact,
  densify, embrace, squeeze 8. astringe,
  condense, contract, decrease
comprise, comprize... 5. imply
  6. number 7. contain, embrace,
  enclose, include, involve 8. perceive
  10. comprehend, constitute
compromise... 4. bind 6. adjust
  8. compound, trade–off 9. agreement
  10. adjustment, concession,
  settlement 11. appeasement,
  arbitration
compulsion... 5. drive, force
  6. duress, urging 7. impulse
  8. coaction, coercion 9. necessity,
  obsession 10. compelling
compulsory... 7. driving 9. mandatory,
  necessary 10. compelling, imperative,
  obligatory 11. involuntary
compunction... 3. rue 5. guilt, pangs,
  qualm 6. regret 7. remorse
  8. pricking 9. penitence
  11. impenitence 13. regretfulness
compute... 5. count, score, tally
  6. cipher, figure, number, reckon
  8. estimate 9. calculate, enumerate
computer terms... 3. bit 4. byte,
  GIGO 5. BASIC, COBOL, coder, input,
  modem 6. access, analog, glitch
  7. digital, FORTRAN 8. data base
  (bank), hard copy, printout, software,
  terminal 9. mainframe, videodisc
  10. floppy disc 11. computerese
  12. minicomputer
  13. microcomputer, word processor
  14. cathode–ray tube
comrade... 3. pal 4. ally, chum, mate,
  peer 5. buddy, crony 6. fellow, frater
  7. compeer 8. camarada, sidekick
  9. associate, colleague, companion
con... 2. no 3. nay 4. know, read
  5. cheat, learn, steer, study

6. peruse 7. convict, deceive,
swindle 8. memorize, negative
10. understand 13. confidence man
conceal... 4. dern, hide, mask, palm,
veil 5. cloak, cover, derne, eloin,
feign 6. eloign, pocket, screen
7. secrete 8. bescreen, disguise,
enshield
concealed... 5. doggo 6. covert,
hidden, latent, perdue, secret, veiled,
velate 7. covered, larvate, obscure,
unknown, velated 9. disguised,
incognito, insidious 11. clandestine
concede... 3. own 5. admit, agree,
allow, grant, yield 6. accord
7. confess, consent 8. consider
9. surrender 11. acknowledge
conceit... 3. ego 4. idea 5. fancy,
pride 6. vagary, vanity 7. caprice,
egotism, foppery, tympany 8. priggery
12. boastfulness
conceited... 4. smug, vain 5. proud
7. foppish 8. arrogant, boastful,
priggish 9. egotistic, pragmatic
11. egotistical, opinionated
12. stuffed shirt
conceivable... 7. tenable 8. credible
9. plausible 10. believable,
imaginable 12. intelligible
conceive... 5. dream, fancy, think
6. create, devise, ideate 7. imagine,
produce, realize, suppose, suspect
9. originate 10. understand
concentrate... 4. mass 5. focus
6. center 7. compact, densify,
extract 8. condense, converge
9. intensify 10. centralize
11. consolidate
concept... 4. idea 5. image
7. opinion, thought 8. category
conception... 4. idea 5. image, savvy
6. notion 7. conceit, opinion
9. pregnancy 12. apprehension
13. comprehension, understanding
concern... 4. care, firm, sake 5. event,
grief 6. affair, affect, import, matter
7. anxiety, pertain 8. business,
interest, salience 9. relevance
10. importance 11. consequence
12. significance 13. consideration
concerning... 2. of, on, re 3. for
4. over, upon 5. about, anent
9. regarding 10. respecting
concert... 6. aubade 7. recital
9. agreement, unanimity
11. co–operation, performance
concert hall... 5. odeum (odeon)
6. lyceum 7. theater 9. music hall,
playhouse
concession... 5. grant 6. market
7. consent 8. discount
10. compromise, confession
13. qualification
concierge... 6. porter, warden
7. ostiary 8. chokidar 10. doorkeeper
conciliate... 4. ease 6. pacify
7. appease, mollify, placate
9. reconcile 10. propitiate
conciliatory... 6. assent, irenic
8. irenical 9. appeasing, forgiving
10. mollifying
concise... 4. curt, neat 5. brief, crisp,

pithy, terse 6. précis 7. laconic,
pointed, serried, summary 8. succinct
11. compendious, sententious
13. comprehensive
conclude... 3. end 4. rest 5. close,
infer 6. deduce, endeth, finish, settle
7. arrange, presume, resolve,
suppose 8. complete 9. determine,
terminate
conclusion... 3. end 4. last 5. close,
finis 6. finale, finish, result
8. decision, epilogue 9. deduction,
diagnosis, inference 10. completion
13. determination
conclusive... 5. final, valid 8. decisive,
ultimate 9. mandatory
10. convincing, evidential
11. irrefutable, sockdologer (answer)
12. unanswerable
concoct... 3. mix 4. brew, cook, make
6. devise, digest, invent, scheme
7. perfect, prepare 9. fabricate
concoction... 4. dish, plan, plot
6. device 7. mixture 8. compound
9. falsehood, invention
11. combination, fabrication,
preparation
concomitant... 9. accessory, attendant,
co–operant 10. coincident, concurrent
11. synchronous 12. accompanying,
simultaneous
concord... 4. tune 5. chord, peace
6. accord, treaty, unison 7. concert,
harmony, rapport 8. symphony
9. agreement, unanimity
concordant... 8. agreeing, harmonic,
unisonal 9. consonant, unanimous
10. harmonious 11. conformable
13. correspondent
concrete... 4. hard, pave 5. béton,
solid 6. cement 7. congeal, plaster
8. hardness, pavement, solidify
11. substantial
concur... 5. agree, chime, unite
6. accede, assent 7. approve,
combine, consent 9. acquiesce,
co–operate 11. synchronize
concurrence... 6. united 7. joining
9. adherence, concourse, unanimity
11. coincidence, conjunction
convergence, co–operation, parallelism
concurrent... 5. joint 6. united
7. meeting, uniting 8. parallel,
syndrome 9. unanimous
10. associated, coincident, synergetic
11. co–operative, synchronous
12. accompanying, simultaneous
concussion... 5. clash, shock, smash,
wound 6. injury, trauma 9. collision
condemn... 3. ban 4. doom 5. blame,
decry 6. adjudge, censure, convict
8. penalize, sentence
condense... 3. mix 5. unite 6. absorb,
decoct, deepen, harden, lessen,
narrow, reduce 7. abridge, combine,
compact, densify, enhance, shorten,
squeeze, thicken 8. compress,
contract, diminish, heighten, solidify
9. constrict, intensify
11. concentrate, consolidate
condensed... 7. compact, concise,
cramped, tabloid 9. shortened

10. compressed, contracted
12. concentrated
condenser (anc)... 9. Leyden jar
condescend... 5. deign, stoop
6. submit, unbend 7. concede,
descend 9. patronize, vouchsafe
condign... 3. fit 4. just 6. severe,
worthy 7. fitting 8. adequate,
deserved, suitable
condiment... 3. soy 4. dill, mace,
mint, sage, salt 5. chili, clove, curry,
sauce, spice 6. catsup, garlic,
ginger, nutmeg, pepper, relish
7. cayenne, ketchup, mustard,
paprika, vinegar 9. seasoning
10. peppermint
condition... 2. if 4. case, haze, rank,
term 5. covin, limit, stage, state
6. estate, fettle, health, plight, status
7. posture, proviso, quality, station
8. capacity, position, standing
9. requisite, situation 10. limitation
11. predicament 12. circumstance
condition (pert to)...
favorable.. 4. odds
flushed.. 4. rosy
habitual.. 5. tenor
hypnotic.. 4. daze 6. stupor, trance
7. narcose
made.. 7. premise
murk.. 3. fog 4. haze, mist 5. gloom
proper.. 6. kilter
stipulation.. 7. proviso
conditionally... 2. if 8. provided
11. tentatively 13. provisionally
condone... 5. remit 6. accept, excuse,
pardon 7. absolve, forgive 8. tolerate
11. countenance
condor... 6. falcon 7. vulture
conduce... 4. lend, tend 5. serve
6. effect 7. advance, dispose,
incline, redound 10. contribute
conducive... 6. useful 7. helpful
11. implemental, serviceable
12. instrumental
conduct... 3. act, run 4. lead, mien,
rule 5. guide, usage, usher
6. action, convey, convoy, direct,
escort, govern, manage 7. bearing,
comport, control, manners
8. behavior, demeanor, regulate
9. operation, supervise
10. deportment, management
11. comportment, superintend
conduct (pert to)...
a cause.. 5. plead
breach.. 6. guilty
doctrine of.. 6. morals
one's self.. 6. behave, demean
7. comport
conducting inward... 9. afference
conductor... 5. guide 6. escort, leader
7. cathode, maestro, manager
8. cicerone, director, operator,
trainman
conduit... 3. way 4. adit, duct, pain,
pipe, tube 5. canal, sewer 6. course
7. channel 8. aqueduct
cone (pert to)...
conelike.. 5. conic 6. pineal
7. conical
pine.. 8. strobile

silver.. 4. pina
tree.. 5. larch 7. conifer
confab, confabulation... 4. chat, talk
7. palaver, prattle 8. chinfest, talkfest
12. conversation
confection... 3. jam 5. candy, dulce,
icing, jelly 6. cimbal, comfit, nougat,
sweets 7. caramel, fondant, praline,
succade 8. preserve 9. sweetmeat
11. bittersweet, marshmallow
confederacy... 5. cabal, hanse, union
6. fusion, league 8. alliance,
covenant 9. coalition 10. complicity,
conspiracy, federation 11. affiliation,
association, combination
13. consolidation
confederate... 3. pal, reb 4. ally
5. stall 7. abettor 9. accessory,
assistant, associate, auxiliary
10. accomplice
confer... 4. give 6. advise, bestow,
invest, parley 7. collate, commune,
consign, consult, counsel 8. ordinate
(knighthood) 10. deliberate
conference... 5. trust 6. huddle,
parley, powwow 7. council, palaver
9. interview 10. discussion
12. consultation
conferring respect... 9. honorific
conferring title... 9. ennobling
confess... 3. own, rue 4. avow
5. admit, own up 6. regret, repent,
reveal, shrive 7. concede
11. acknowledge
confession... 5. credo (of faith), creed
6. avowal, shrift 9. admission,
communion 10. profession
14. acknowledgment
(acknowledgement)
confetti... 5. paper 6. ribbon
7. bonbons 9. cascarons (in
eggshells) 10. sweetmeats
11. confections
confidant... 6. friend 8. intimate
confide... 4. hope, rely 5. trust
6. commit, depend, repose
confidence... 5. faith, poise 6. belief,
morals, secret 7. courage
8. credence, sureness 9. assurance,
impudence 10. effrontery
12. impertinence
confident... 4. smug, sure 6. secure
7. assured, certain, hopeful, reliant
8. cocksure, positive, sanguine,
unafraid 9. convinced 10. determined
confidential... 5. privy 6. secret
7. private 8. esoteric, intimate
9. auricular 10. unquotable
11. trustworthy
confidentially... 7. sub rosa
configuration... 4. form 5. shape
6. figure 7. contour, Gestalt, pattern
8. asterism 13. constellation
confine... 3. dam, hem, mew, pen,
sty, tie 4. bind, cage, coop, jail,
lock 5. bound, limit, stint 6. border,
immure, intern, secure, strain
7. compass 8. imprison, restrain
9. enclosure 11. incarcerate,
restriction 12. circumscribe
confined... 4. pent 5. bound, caged
6. shut–in 7. cribbed, endemic,

limited 8. esoteric, impended,
interned 9. bedridden, impounded,
invalided, parochial
confinement... 5. limbo 7. durance,
lying–in 9. detention, isolation,
restraint 10. cabin fever, childbirth
12. accouchement, imprisonment
13. incommunicado
15. circumscription
confirm... 4. seal 5. prove 6. assure,
attest, ratify, settle, verify 7. approve,
fortify, sustain 8. convince, sanction,
validate 9. establish 11. corroborate
12. substantiate
confirmed... 6. proved 7. chronic
8. habitual, ratified 10. encouraged,
inveterate 11. established
confiscate... 5. seize, usurp
7. impound 11. appropriate
conflagrant... 5. afire 6. ablaze,
aflame 7. blazing, burning
conflagration... 4. fire 5. blaze, fever
8. wildfire 9. holocaust
12. inflammation
conflict... 3. war 4. bout, duel, fray
5. clash, fight, run–in 6. action,
battle, combat, oppose, strife, tussle
7. contend, contest, discord
8. clashing, struggle 9. antipathy,
collision, encounter, hostility
10. contention, donnybrook,
opposition 11. competition
confluence... 4. flow 5. crowd
6. stream 7. flowing (together),
meeting 8. junction 10. assemblage
11. concurrence, convergence
12. assimilation
conform... 2. go 3. fit 4. lean, obey,
suit 5. adapt, agree 6. adjust,
concur, settle 7. compose, consent,
observe 8. coincide, fine–tune
9. reconcile 11. accommodate
conformity... 6. dharma 7. harmony
8. legality, symmetry 9. agreement,
congruity 10. compliance
15. conventionality
confound... 3. mix 5. abash, amaze
6. baffle, dismay, puzzle, thwart
7. astound, buffalo, mystify, nonplus,
perplex 8. astonish, bewilder
9. dumbfound, embarrass, frustrate
10. complicate, contradict, disconcert
11. intermingle
confront... 4. face, meet 5. front
6. oppose 7. compare 9. encounter
confrontation... 6. crisis 7. face–off
8. showdown 9. encounter
10. opposition
confuse... 3. mix 4. maze 5. abash,
addle, upset 6. baffle, flurry, jumble,
muddle 7. derange, fluster
8. befuddle, bewilder, disorder,
distract, entangle 9. embrangle
10. complicate, disarrange,
discompose, disconcert
confused... 7. chaotic, jumbled, rattled
8. deranged 9. chagrined, flustered,
perplexed, uncertain 10. indistinct
confusion... 3. ado, din 4. mess, moil
5. babel, chaos 6. jumble, pother,
welter 7. anarchy, clutter, turmoil
8. disarray, disorder 9. abashment,

agitation 10. perplexity
11. derangement 12. bewilderment
13. embarrassment
confute... 4. deny 5. rebut 6. answer,
expose, refute 7. dismiss
8. confound, overcome, redargue
9. overwhelm (by argument)
congeal... 3. gel, ice, set 4. rime
6. freeze 7. pectize, thicken
congenial... 4. boon 7. kindred
8. friendly 9. accordant, agreeable
10. affinitive, compatible
11. sympathetic
congenital... 6. inborn, innate
7. connate, genetic, natural
14. constitutional
conger... 3. eel 8. cucumber
13. Leptocephalus
congeries... 4. heap 9. amassment
10. collection 11. aggregation
congestion... 3. jam 4. heap
8. fullness, stoppage 9. gathering
11. obstruction 12. accumulation
Congo...
  capital .. 11. Brazzaville
  city .. 6. Makoua 7. Louboma
  port .. 11. Pointe Noire
  river .. 5. Congo (Zaire) 6. Sangha
congratulate... 4. laud 5. bless
6. salute 7. rejoice 8. macarize
10. compliment, felicitate
congregate... 4. herd, mass, meet
5. group, troop 6. gather, muster
7. collect 8. assemble 9. forgather
congregation... 4. mass 5. house,
laity 7. council 8. assembly, audience
9. gathering 10. collection
11. churchgoers
congress... 4. diet 5. synod
6. durbar, indaba, soviet 7. council,
meeting 8. assembly, conclave
9. Sanhedrin 10. convention,
parliament 11. convergence,
convocation, legislature
12. congregation
congruous... 3. fit 4. meet 6. proper
7. fitting 8. agreeing, becoming,
suitable 9. consonant
conic, conical... 8. parabola
9. pyramidal 10. cone–shaped,
funnellike
conifers... 4. yews 5. pines 6. cedars
7. larches, Pinales, Sabines, spruces,
Torreys 8. hemlocks, Soledads
9. Coniferae, Corsicans
10. evergreens
conjecture... 3. aim 5. ettle, guess,
opine, think 6. divine 7. conjoin,
imagine, presume, suppose, surmise,
suspect 8. supposal 9. inference
10. assumption, hypothesis
11. supposition
conjoin... 4. join, link, yoke 5. hitch,
unite 6. adjoin, concur 7. combine,
connect 8. corelate 9. correlate
conjoined parts... 6. adnexa
conjointly... 10. hand–in–hand
conjugal... 7. marital, nuptial
9. connubial 11. matrimonial
conjugate... 4. join 5. yoked
6. couple, united 7. coupled, related
8. bijugate, combined

10. paronymous 12. etymological
conjugation... 5. union 6. fusion
7. duality, joining, uniting
10. assemblage 11. combination
13. juxtaposition
conjunct... 6. united 8. combined
9. conjoined, corporate
conjunction... 2. as, et, if, or 3. and,
but, nor 4. than, that 5. since,
union 6. casual, though 7. whether
10. connection 11. adversative,
association, combination, concurrence,
correlative
conjure... 4. pray 5. charm 6. adjure,
enjoin, invoke, juggle, summon
(magic) 7. beseech, enchant, entreat,
implore 10. supplicate
conjure (up)... 5. raise 6. call up
8. exorcise (exorcize), remember
9. visualize
conjurer, conjuror... 4. mage
6. voodoo, wizard 7. juggler
8. exorcist, magician
conk... 4. head, nose 5. decay (tree)
conk out... 4. fade, fail 5. stall
6. fizzle, perish, weaken
connate... 4. akin 6. allied 7. cognate,
related, similar 9. congenial
10. congenital
connect... 3. tie 4. ally, join, link,
meet 5. unite 6. adjoin, attach,
couple, enlink, fasten, relate
7. bracket, succeed 9. associate,
hyphenate
connected... 3. met 5. telic
6. adnate, joined 7. serried, similar
8. coherent, inlinked, syndetic
10. continuous, correlated
Connecticut...
capital.. 8. Hartford
city.. 6. Darien, Mystic 7. Meriden
8. Hartford, New Haven 9. Waterbury
10. Bridgeport
college (famed).. 4. Yale (1701)
historic site.. 10. Charter Oak (1687,
Hartford)
museum.. 6. Barnum (P T)
river.. 6. Thames 9. Naugatuck
10. Hoosatonic 11. Connecticut
State admission.. 5. Fifth
State Motto.. 21. Qui Transtulit
Sustinet (He Who Transplants
Sustains)
State nickname.. 6. Nutmeg
12. Constitution
connecting link... 3. tie 4. bond
6. connex 7. kiaison 8. ligament,
vinculum 11. intermedium
12. intermediary
connection... 4. bond 5. nexus, union
6. clevis, family, series 7. kinship,
passage 8. alliance, commerce,
junction, relation 9. coherence,
go–between, relevance 10. continuity
11. association, intercourse
12. intermediary, relationship
13. communication, juxtaposition
conner... 5. pilot 6. balker, tester
7. peruser 8. examiner 9. inspector
connive... 4. plot, wink 5. blink
6. scheme 7. collude, complot,
finagle 8. conspire, contrive,

maneuver, overlook
conniving... 8. scheming 9. collusive,
deceitful 10. conspiring
11. calculating
connoisseur... 5. judge 6. expert
7. epicure, gourmet 8. gourmand
11. cognoscente, connaisseur
connotation... 5. sense 6. import,
intent 7. meaning, purport
10. denotation 11. implication
12. significance 13. comprehension
connubial... 7. martial, nuptial
8. conjugal 11. matrimonial
12. epithalamium (song)
conquer... 3. win 4. beat, best
5. crush 6. defeat, humble, master,
reduce, subdue 7. subject
8. overcome, overturn, surmount,
vanquish 9. discomfit, overpower,
overthrow, subjugate
conqueror... 4. hero 6. captor, Cortez,
victor, winner 7. subduer
10. subjugator 12. conquistador
conquest... 6. Norman (1066)
7. mastery, triumph, victory
consanguinity... 5. nabob 7. kinship,
sibship 8. affinity, relation (blood)
12. relationship
conscience... 4. mind, self 6. psyche
8. superego 9. casuistry
conscientious... 7. dutiful, servile
8. faithful 10. fastidious, meticulous,
scrupulous 11. punctilious
conscientious objection... 7. scruple
conscious... 4. keen 5. alive, awake,
aware, vital 7. animate, feeling
8. sensible, sentient 9. breathing,
cognizant 13. self–conscious
consecrate... 4. sain 5. bless, exalt
6. anoint, devote, hallow, ordain
7. glorify 8. dedicate, sanctify
consecrated (pert to)...
bread.. 4. host 5. wafer
oil.. 6. chrism
thing.. 6. sacrum
consent... 4. give 5. agree, grant,
yield 6. accede, accord, assent,
concur, permit 8. approval
9. acquiesce 10. compliance,
permission 11. concurrence
13. understanding
consequence... 3. end 5. event
6. course, effect, result, weight
7. dignity, outcome 8. pursuant (in),
sequence 9. aftermath, inference,
influence, loftiness, outgrowth
10. importance, notability
11. distinction
consequential... 7. pompous
8. eventual 9. important
13. self–important
consequently... 2. do 4. ergo, then
5. hence 9. as a result, therefore,
wherefore 12. subsequently
13. consecutively
conservative... 4. Tory 5. staid
7. die–hard, fogyish, old–line
8. moderate 10. long–haired
11. reactionary 12. preservative
13. unprogressive
conserve... 3. jam 4. save 5. guard,
uvate 6. defend, secure, shield,

uphold 7. protect, sustain
8. maintain 9. preserves, sweetmeat
consider... 3. ain, see 4. care, deem,
heed, muse, rate 5. judge, think,
treat, weigh 6. esteem, intend,
ponder, regard 7. discuss, examine,
reflect, revolve 8. cogitate, meditate,
ruminate 10. deliberate
11. contemplate
considerable... 5. great, large
7. notable, several 8. numerous
9. important 10. noteworthy,
remarkable 13. authoritative
considerate... 4. kind 6. gentle
7. careful, heedful, prudent, serious
8. obliging 9. attentive, judicious
10. deliberate, reflective, solicitous,
thoughtful
consideration... 4. self 5. study
6. esteem, regard 7. respect,
thought 9. attention, deference,
incentive, influence 10. cogitation,
importance, meditation, reflection,
reputation, rumination
11. examination 12. compensation,
deliberation
considering... 2. if 5. since 8. after
all, inasmuch, in view of
consign... 5. allot 6. assign, commit,
devote, remand, resign 7. deliver,
entrust 8. transfer 11. subscribe to
consignee... 6. factor 7. awardee
8. assignee 9. committee
consign to...
a place.. 8. allocate
prison.. 6. commit, send up
ruin.. 4. doom
unimportance.. 8. relegate
consistent... 5. equal, solid, stiff
7. equable, logical, uniform
8. coherent 9. agreement,
consonant, steadfast 10. persisting
consisting of...
cavities.. 9. cellulose
layers (thin).. 8. laminate
names.. 8. onomatic
one word.. 7. monepic
pages.. 7. paginal
three measures.. 8. trimeter
three spots.. 4. trey
three styles (Bot).. 10. tristylous
two parts.. 6. binary
consist of... 5. imply 6. embody
7. contain, embrace, enclose, involve
8. comprise (comprize)
consolation... 6. solace 7. comfort
10. condolence
console... 4. desk 5. cheer, organ,
table 6. solace, soothe 7. bracket,
cabinet, comfort, support, sustain
9. alleviate, encourage
consolidate... 4. knit, mass 5. merge,
unify, unite 7. combine, densify
8. coalesce, compress, organize,
solidify 9. intensify 10. strengthen
consonant... 4. lene, surd 5. lenis,
nasal, velar 6. dental, labial
7. lingual, palatal, spirate 8. gutteral
9. accordant, congruous
10. compatible, concordant,
consistent
consonant (pert to)...

hissing.. 8. sibilant
rustling.. 9. fricative
voiceless (breathed).. 6. atonic
7. spirate
consort... 4. Devi (of Siva), mate, wife
5. group, Sakti 6. mingle, spouse
7. husband, partner 9. associate,
colleague, companion, harmonize
11. combination, confederate,
conjunction
conspicuous... 6. famous, signal
7. eminent, glaring, obvious, salient,
visible 8. distinct, lionized, manifest,
striking 9. important, prominent
10. celebrated, noticeable, remarkable
11. illustrious, outstanding
13. distinguished
conspiracy... 4. plot 5. cabal, unite
6. scheme 8. intrigue 9. collusion
10. connivance 11. confederacy,
machination
conspire... 4. plot 5. unite 6. concur,
scheme 7. collude, complot, finagle
9. fainaigue 11. confederate
constable... 3. cop 5. staff 6. beadle,
keeper, warden 7. bailiff 8. tipstaff
9. policeman
constabulary... 6. bureau (police)
10. constables
constancy... 4. zeal 5. ardor, faith,
truth 6. fealty, garnet (symbol)
7. honesty, loyalty 8. devotion,
fidelity 9. adherence, continual,
eagerness, integrity, stability
10. allegiance, attachment,
permanence, perpetuity, uniformity
11. devotedness, earnestness
12. faithfulness
constant... 4. firm, true 5. fixed
7. regular, uniform 8. faithful,
resolute 9. continual, invariant,
parameter (Math), perpetual, steadfast
10. continuous, invariable, persistent
12. unchangeable
constant desire... 4. itch 9. hankering
Constantine (pert to)...
birthplace.. 4. Nish (Nis) 7. Naissus
(now Yugoslavia)
known as.. 8. The Great
title.. 7. Emperor (Rome)
Constantinople...
official name.. 8. Istanbul
patriarch.. 9. Nestorius
site.. 6. Turkey (Eur)
constellation... 5. stars 6. galaxy
8. asterism 10. luminaries
13. configuration (stars)
Constellations (partial list)...
arrow.. 7. Sagitta
bears (Dipper).. 9. Ursa Major, Ursa
Minor
Bird of Paradise (S Pole).. 4. Apus
bull.. 6. Taurus
crab.. 6. Cancer
crane.. 4. Grus
dog.. 5. Canis
dragon.. 5. Draco
eagle.. 6. Aquila
fishes.. 6. Pisces
goat.. 9. Capricorn
goldfish.. 6. Dorado
hunter.. 5. Orion (most conspicuous)

lion.. 3. Leo
Noah's Ark.. 4. Argo
Northern Crown.. 14. Corona Borealis,
  Northern Lights
peacock.. 4. Pava
scorpion.. 7. Scorpio
serpent (sea).. 5. Hydra
Southern Cross.. 4. Crux
swan.. 6. Cygnus
Twins.. 6. Gemini
virgin.. 5. Virgo
water bearer.. 8. Aquarius
whale.. 6. Cestus
winged horse.. 7. Pegasus
wolf.. 5. Lupus
Constellations' brightest star...
  3. Cor
Constellations of the Zodiac...
  3. Leo 5. Aries, Libra, Virgo
  6. Cancer, Gemini, Pisces, Taurus
  7. Scorpio 8. Aquarius
  11. Capricornus, Sagittarius
constituent... 5. voter 6. factor,
  matter 7. elector, element, essence
  8. elective 9. component
  10. ingredient 11. determinant
  (Math)
constituent of...
  blood serum.. 7. opsonin
  coal.. 6. carbon
  coffee, tea.. 8. caffeine
  hair, nails.. 7. keratin
  oil of cloves.. 7. eugenol
constitute... 4. form 5. enact, found
  6. create, depute 7. appoint,
  compose 8. legalize 9. determine,
  establish
constitution... 3. law 6. crasis,
  custom 7. passage 8. creation
  9. enactment, essential, ordinance,
  structure 11. composition, institution
  12. organization
Constitution (ship)... 12. Old Ironsides
constitutional... 5. legal, valid
  6. innate 9. essential, healthful
  12. governmental 13. dispositional
constitutional (pert to)...
  health.. 4. walk 8. exercise
  right.. 9. franchise
  temperament.. 6. crasis
  vigor.. 5. nerve
Constitution State... 11. Connecticut
constrain... 4. curb, urge 5. chain,
  check, drive, force, impel, press
  6. compel, oblige 7. confine, repress
  8. restrain 11. necessitate
constrained... 6. forced, modest
  7. cramped 8. moderate, reserved
  9. obligated
constraint... 4. bond, urge 5. force
  6. duress, stress 7. modesty, reserve
  8. coercion, pressure 9. restraint,
  stiffness 10. compulsion, moderation
  11. confinement
constrict... 3. tie 4. bind 5. cramp
  6. narrow, shrink 7. squeeze, tighten
  8. astringe, condense, contract
  10. constringe
constriction... 9. narrowing, stricture,
  tightness 11. contraction
  13. strangulation
constrictor... 3. boa 5. snake

7. serpent, styptic 9. sphincter
10. compressor
construct... 4. make, rear 5. build,
  erect, frame 6. create 7. compose
  9. establish, fabricate, originate
constructive... 7. virtual 8. creative,
  implicit 9. anabolism 10. suggestive
  14. interpretation, interpretative
construe... 5. parse 6. deduce, render
  7. explain 9. interpret, translate
consuetude... 5. habit, usage
  6. custom
consuetudinary... 6. manual (customs),
  ritual 9. customary
consult (with)... 6. advise, confer, take
  up 7. discuss 10. deliberate
consultation... 7. counsel 8. audition,
  congress 9. interview 10. conference,
  discussion 12. deliberation
consume... 3. eat, use 4. burn
  5. spend, waste 6. absorb, devour,
  expend 7. destroy (fire) 8. squander
  9. dissipate 12. disintegrate
consumed... 3. pau
consummate... 3. end, top 4. ripe
  5. ideal 6. finish, utmost 7. achieve,
  perfect 8. complete 10. accomplish
consumption... 3. use 4. loss
  5. decay, waste 6. eating
  7. disease, using up 8. phthisis
  9. decrement 11. destruction
  12. tuberculosis 13. deterioration
contact... 4. meet 5. touch, union
  6. impact, syzygy (Astron)
  7. meeting, oscnode (Math)
  8. junction, tangency, touching
  10. contiguity 13. communication
contain... 4. have, hold, keep 5. cover
  6. embody, number, retain
  7. embrace, enclose, include, involve,
  subsume 8. comprise, restrain
  9. divisible (by) 10. comprehend
container... 3. bag, bin, box, can,
  cup, jug, lug, pan, pod, pot, tin,
  tub, urn, vat 4. case, crib, ewer,
  pail, sack, vase 5. crate, cruet,
  pouch 6. basket, bottle, carboy,
  carton, hamper, hatbox 7. capsule,
  hanaper 8. canister, decanter
containing...
  air.. 9. pneumatic
  antimony.. 8. stibiate
  boron.. 5. boric 7. boracic
  carbon.. 7. organic 13. carboniferous
  copper.. 6. cupric
  fire.. 7. igneous
  gold.. 4. doré 5. auric
  iron.. 6. ferric
  silver.. 5. lunar
  slag.. 6. drossy
  ten.. 6. denary
  tin.. 7. stannic
containing maxims... 6. gnomic
contaminate... 4. slur, soil 5. stain,
  sully, taint 6. befoul, defile, infect,
  poison 7. corrupt, debauch, degrade,
  pollute, vitiate 8. dishonor
  9. desecrate 10. adulterate
contemn... 4. defy, hate 5. scorn,
  spurn 6. reject 7. despise, disdain
contemplate... 4. muse, plan, scan,
  view 5. study 6. design, expect,

intend, ponder 7. examine, foresee,
propose 8. consider, envision,
meditate
contemplation... 5. study 6. musing
7. theoria, thought 8. scrutiny
9. foresight, intuition 10. expectancy,
reflection 11. examination,
expectation, speculation
contemplative... 6. sedate 7. pensive
10. meditative, reflective, ruminative,
thoughtful 11. speculative
13. retrospective
contemporary... 6. coeval 7. present
10. coetaneous, coexistent,
coincident 11. concomitant,
synchronous 12. simultaneous
15. contemporaneous
contempt... 4. fico, geck 5. scorn,
shame, sneer 7. despect, disdain
8. defiance, derision, ridicule
9. arrogance, contumely
10. disrespect 12. disobedience
contemptible... 3. low 4. base
5. cheap, petty, sorry 6. abject,
paltry, sordid 7. pitiful 8. beggarly,
inferior, unworthy 9. groveling,
worthless 10. despicable
13. insignificant
contemptuous... 6. sneery 7. haughty
8. insolent, scornful 10. disdainful
12. contumelious, supercilious
contemptuous action... 9. indignity
10. incivility
contend... 3. vie, war 4. cope, deal,
race 5. argue, fight 6. assert, bicker,
insist, strive 7. compete, contest,
grapple, quarrel, wrangle 8. contrive,
maintain, militate
content, contents... 4. list, room
5. index, space 6. amount, please,
volume 7. filling, gratify, makings,
satisfy, suffice 8. capacity
9. contented, happiness, satisfied
10. components, dimensions
11. ingredients
contention... 3. war 4. feud
6. combat, debate, strife 7. quarrel,
rivalry 8. argument, conflict, struggle,
variance 9. emulation 10. dissension,
litigation 11. altercation, competition,
controversy 12. disagreement
contentious... 7. peevish 8. perverse
9. combative, litigious, wrangling
10. pugnacious 11. belligerent,
dissentious, quarrelsome
13. argumentative
contentment... 4. ease 5. bliss
8. pleasure 11. peace of mind
12. satisfaction 13. contentedness,
gratification
conterminous... 4. next 8. abutting,
adjacent, proximal 9. adjoining
contest... 3. sue, vie 4. agon, bout,
cope, deny, game, race, tilt
5. argue, set–to, trial 6. debate,
oppose, strife, strive, tryout
7. contend, dispute, tourney, wrangle
8. argument, disclaim, litigate,
skirmish, struggle 9. emulation
10. engagement 11. altercation,
competition
contest (pert to)...

art of.. 10. agonistics
draw.. 9. stalemate
log hurling.. 5. roleo
prize.. 5. stake
undecided.. 4. draw
contestant... 5. rival 6. player
7. athlete, entrant 8. opponent
9. candidate, combatant, contender
10. competitor
contiguous... 4. near, next
8. adjacent, touching 9. adjoining,
immediate, proximate 11. neighboring
Continent... 4. Asia 6. Africa, Europe
7. Eurasia, Lemuria 8. Atlantis (lost),
Cascadia 9. Australia, Greenland
10. Antarctica 12. North America,
South America
contingency... 4. case 5. event
6. chance 8. accident, casualty,
exigency, juncture 9. emergency,
liability 11. eventuality, possibility,
uncertainty
contingent... 6. casual 8. eventual
9. dependent (law), provisory
10. accidental, fortuitous, incidental
11. conditional, provisional
continual... 7. endless, eternal, regular,
undying, uniform 8. constant,
enduring, frequent, unbroken
9. ceaseless, connected, continued,
incessant, perennial, permanent,
perpetual, unceasing 10. continuous,
invariable 11. everlasting, intermitted,
unremitting 12. imperishable
13. uninterrupted
continually... 3. aye 4. ever 5. often
7. eternal 9. eternally 10. constantly
11. perpetually, unceasingly
12. continuously
continuation... 6. sequel 8. addition,
sequence 10. continuity
11. continuance, propagation,
protraction 12. postponement,
prolongation
continue... 3. run 4. go on, last, stay
5. abide 6. endure, extend, remain,
resume 7. perdure, persist, proceed,
sustain 8. protract 9. persevere,
steadfast (be)
continuing... 5. still 7. chronic,
durable, lasting 9. permanent
10. continuous 11. persevering
continuous... 7. chronic, endless,
uniform 8. unbroken 9. continued,
perpetual 13. uninterrupted
contorted... 3. wry 4. bent 6. coiled,
warped 7. garbled, gnarled, twisted,
wristed 8. deformed 9. perverted
contour... 4. form, line 5. curve,
graph 6. figure 7. isobase, outline,
profile 9. lineament, periphery
13. configuration
contra... 6. offset 7. against, counter,
reverse 8. contrary, opposite 9. vice
versa 10. conversely 12. contrariwise
contraband... 7. bootleg, illegal, illicit
8. unlawful 9. moonshine
10. prohibited
contract... 4. hale, knit, pact 5. incur,
lease 6. cartel, engage, pledge,
reduce, shrink 7. bargain, compact,
promise, shorten, shrivel 8. covenant

9. agreement, constrict, indenture
10. convention, obligation, straighten
11. arrangement 13. understanding
contraction... 3. tic 4. coup, fist
5. spasm 7. elision, systole
8. decrease 9. reduction, short–hand,
stricture 11. compression
contrada... 3. way 4. ward 6. street
7. quarter
contradict... 4. deny 5. belie, rebut
6. impugn, negate, oppose, refute
7. gainsay 10. counteract
contradiction... 6. denial 7. paradox
10. opposition, refutation
11. contrariety 13. counteraction
contradictory... 7. denying 8. contrary,
opposite 10. refutatory
12. inconsistent
contrary... 7. adverse, counter,
froward, opposed, reverse
8. captious, inimical, opposite,
perverse, refutive 9. different,
repugnant 10. discordant, unorthodox
12. antagonistic
contrast... 7. compare 8. opposite
11. contrariety
contravene... 4. defy 6. hinder,
oppose, refute, thwart 7. violate
8. infringe 9. disregard
contravention... 6. denial 9. violation
10. opposition, refutation
contribute... 3. aid 4. give 6. donate
7. benefit, conduce, provide
9. subscribe
contribution... 3. tax, tip 4. boon,
gift, scot 6. tariff 7. payment, tribute
8. donation 12. subscription
13. participation
contrite... 6. abject, humble
8. penitent 9. repentant, sorrowful
10. remorseful 11. penitential
contrition... 7. remorse 9. attrition,
penitence 11. compunction
contrivance... 3. art 5. means, shift
6. design, devise 7. coinage,
machine, measure, project 8. artifice,
intrigue 9. expedient, invention,
makeshift 11. contraption
contrive... 4. plan, plot 5. frame,
hatch, weave 6. design, devise,
invent, manage, scheme 7. fashion,
project 9. fabricate
control... 4. hold, rein, rule, sway, test
5. check, gripe, guide, leash, power,
wield 6. direct, govern, manage,
subdue 7. conduct, mastery, preside,
regimen 8. dominate, dominion,
ironhand, regulate, restrain
9. direction, influence, regulator,
restraint 10. management, regulation
11. self–control, superintend
controller, comptroller... 7. auditor
8. governor 9. dominator, regulator
controversial... 7. eristic, polemic
9. eristical, polemical, pro and con
11. contentious 12. disputatious,
questionable 13. argumentative
controversy... 6. debate 7. dispute,
quarrel, wrangle 8. argument
10. contention 11. altercation
12. disagreement, disputatious
controvert... 4. deny, moot 5. argue

6. debate, oppose, refute 7. discuss,
dispute 10. contradict
contumacious... 6. unruly 7. riotous
8. mutinous, perverse 9. seditious
10. headstrong, rebellious, refractory,
unyielding 11. disobedient, intractable
12. ungovernable 13. insubordinate
contumelious... 7. haughty 8. insolent
9. insulting 10. derogatory,
despiteful, disdainful
12. contemptuous
contumely... 5. scorn 8. contempt
9. indignity, insolence 10. revilement
11. humiliation, malediction
contusion... 4. blow 6. bruise, injury
8. black eye 13. discoloration
conundrum... 5. rebus 6. enigma,
puzzle, riddle 7. charade
convalesce... 5. rally 7. recover,
recruit 10. recuperate
convene... 3. sit 4. come, meet
5. unite 6. summon 8. assemble
10. congregate, foregather
convenient... 5. handy, ready 6. fitted,
nearby, suited, timely 7. adapted
8. suitable 9. agreeable, available,
opportune 10. accessible,
commodious, seasonable
11. comfortable
convent... 4. meet 6. concur, friary,
priory 7. convene, nunnery
8. cloister, lamasery 9. monastery,
sanctuary
convention... 4. rule 5. usage
6. accord, custom 7. meeting
8. assembly 9. gathering, tradition
10. assemblage, compliance,
conformity
conventional... 5. fixed, nomic, usual
6. formal, modish 7. correct
8. accepted, orthodox 9. customary
10. ceremonial 11. established,
traditional
converge... 4. meet 5. focus, unite
conversant (with)... 5. adept 6. expert,
versed (in) 7. skilled 8. familiar
9. practiced 10. acquainted,
proficient
conversation... 4. chat, talk 7. trialog
8. causerie, converse, dialogue
9. communion, discourse
10. conference 11. association
13. conversazione, interlocution
conversationalist... 6. talker
9. converser 10. discourser
12. confabulator
convey... 4. cede, deed, pass, send
5. bring, carry, eloin, grant
6. assign, convoy, demise, devise,
impart, import 7. dispone 8. transfer,
transmit 9. transport 10. commission
11. communicate
conveyance... 3. bus, car, van
4. auto, sled, taxi, tram 5. plane,
train 6. demise, litter 7. cession,
norimon, trailer, vehicle 8. airplane,
carriage 10. automobile
conveyer, conveyor... 6. bearer,
coolie, pigeon (homing), porter
7. bheesty, carrier 8. cargador
9. stevedore
convict... 4. damn 5. felon, lifer

6. refute, termer, trusty 7. condemn, culprit 6. refute 8. criminal, prisoner 10. malefactor
conviction... 4. hope 6. belief 7. opinion 9. certainty 10. persuasion 12. condemnation
convince... 6. assure, subdue 7. confute, jawbone 8. overcome, persuade 9. overpower
convincing... 5. proof 6. cogent, potent 7. telling 8. assuring 10. conclusive, persuasive, satisfying
convivial... 3. gay 4. gala 5. jolly, merry 6. festal, jovial, joyful, joyous, social 7. festive, jocular 9. hilarious
convocation... 4. diet 5. synod 7. bidding, council, meeting, summons 8. assembly, congress 10. convention 12. congregation
convoke... 4. call 6. summon 7. convene 8. assemble
convoy... 5. guard, guide 6. attend, escort 7. conduct 8. navigate 9. accompany, conductor
convulse... 5. amuse, shake 6. regale 7. agitate, disturb, torture 9. entertain 10. discompose
convulsion... 5. cramp, spasm, throe 6. tumult, uproar 8. laughter, paroxysm 9. agitation, commotion 10. revolution 11. disturbance
cony, coney... 3. das, fur 4. dupe, hare, pika 5. daman, hyrax 6. burbot, rabbit
cony catcher... 5. cheat 7. sharper 8. swindler
coo... 4. bill (and), curr 5. chirr 6. murmur, mutter
cook... 4. bake, boil, chef, stew 5. broil, roast, sauté, spoil (chess), steam, trill 6. braise, seethe 7. parboil, stir–fry 8. barbecue, magirist 9. charbroil, cuisinier
cookie... 5. scone 7. biscuit, brownie 8. macaroon 10. gingersnap, ladyfinger, shortbread
cooking (pert to)...
art.. 8. magirics
device.. 3. wok 4. etna, olla 5. grill, plate, stove 6. spider 7. griddle 9. autoclave, microwave (oven)
room.. 6. galley 7. cuisine, kitchen 8. scullery 11. kitchenette
scent.. 4. reek 5. nidor
cool... 3. fan, ice 4. calm 5. chill, fresh, nervy, sober, tepid 6. chilly, freeze, sedate, temper 7. unmoved 8. careless, composed, impudent, mitigate, reserved, tranquil 9. apathetic, collected, unruffled 10. nonchalant, unfriendly, unsociable 11. indifferent, levelheaded, unconcerned 13. dispassionate, imperturbable, self–possessed
cooler... 4. icer, jail 6. icebox, lockup, prison 7. chiller 10. ventilator 11. refrigerant 12. refrigerator
coolness... 4. cold 5. nerve 6. aplomb 7. reserve 12. indifference 14. unfriendliness
coop... 3. mew, pen 4. cage, cote, yard 5. court, hutch 7. confine

9. enclosure
cooper... 5. drink 6. vessel 8. grogshop (floating) 11. barrel maker 12. wine retailer
cooperate... 4. join, tend 5. agree, coact 6. concur 7. combine, conduce, connive 8. conspire 9. interface, synergize 10. contribute 11. collaborate
coordinate... 5. talky 6. adjust 7. syntony (radio) 8. classify, equalize, organize, regulate 9. harmonize, integrate 10. proportion 11. systematize
copious... 4. full, rich 5. ample 7. diffuse, profuse 8. abundant, numerous 9. exuberant, plenteous, plentiful 11. overflowing
copper... 2. Cu 3. aes 4. cent, coin 5. metal, penny 6. cuprum 9. policeman 12. reddish–brown
copper (pert to)...
alloy.. 5. brass 6. bronze, oroide
brass.. 6. chalco
cup.. 3. dop
engraving.. 9. mezzotint
film.. 6. patina
kettle (anc).. 5. lebes
pewter.. 7. rheotan
Copperfield characters... 4. Dora 6. Dartle 8. Micawber 9. Uriah Heep 11. Little Emily
coppice... 4. bosk, holt 5. copse, grove 6. growth 7. boscage, thicket 9. brushwood, underwood
Coptic (pert to)...
church.. 8. Egyptian
color.. 7. oxblood
title.. 4. anba
copy... 3. ape 4. news 5. model, Xerox (tm) 6. ectype, follow 7. edition, estreat, imitate, pattern, replica, reprint, tracing 8. protocol, revision 9. duplicate, imitation 10. transcribe, transcript 11. counterfeit 12. reproduction
coquet, coquette... 4. vamp 5. flirt 7. amorous 11. hummingbird
coquille... 5. shell 7. ruching
Coquille... 6. Indian 10. Athapascan
coquin... 5. knave, rogue 6. rascal
coral... 3. red 6. polyps, porite 8. Anthozoa 9. madrepore, millepore
coral (pert to)...
branch.. 7. ramicle
division.. 7. Aporosa
formation.. 5. palus
island.. 3. key 5. atoll
ridge.. 4. reef 5. shoal
snake.. 5. Elaps 6. garter 7. Micurus
worm.. 6. palolo
cord... 3. guy, rib 4. lace, line, rope, welt, wood 5. sinew, twine 6. lariat, sennet, spinal, string, tendon 7. measure (cubic), skirreh 8. corduroy, shoelace 9. hamstring 11. clothesline
cordage... 5. ropes 7. rigging 8. ropework
cordelle... 6. hauler 7. towline, towrope
cordial... 4. real, warm 6. ardent,

elixir, genial, hearty, liquor **7.** fervent, liqueur, sincere, zealous **8.** friendly, vigorous **9.** unfeigned **10.** hospitable
cordial (liqueur)... **5.** shrub **6.** kummel **8.** anisette, periscot **9.** Cointreau **11.** Benedictine, crème de moka **13.** crème de menthe
cordiality... **4.** zeal **5.** ardor **6.** fervor **7.** ardency **8.** kindness, warmness **9.** geniality **11.** hospitality **12.** empressement, friendliness
core... **3.** ame, hub, nub, nut **4.** gist, nave, pith **5.** heart, nowel **6.** center, kernel, matrix **7.** nucleus **9.** substance
Corinthian (pert to)...
Age.. **5.** plush **11.** extravagant
color.. **3.** red **4.** pink **6.** purple
Epistles (Bib).. **12.** New Testament
General (Rom).. **9.** Flaminius
King.. **8.** Polybius
Spring.. **14.** Pirene Fountain
Temple.. **5.** Doric **7.** Minerva
cork... **3.** ork **4.** bark, bung, plug **5.** float, shive, suber (oak) **7.** blacken, stopgap, stopper, stopple
corm... **4.** bulb (flower)
cormorant... **4.** bird, shag **5.** norie, scart, urile **8.** ravenous **9.** snakebird, voracious **13.** Phalacrocorax
corn... **4.** joke **5.** grain, grist **6.** cliché, kaffir, kernel, liquor
corn (pert to)...
bread.. **4.** pone **8.** dumpling **10.** corndodger
goddess.. **5.** Ceres
hulled.. **4.** samp **6.** hominy
Indian.. **3.** Zea **5.** maize
lily.. **4.** Ixia **8.** bindweed **10.** wandflower
liquor.. **6.** whisky (whiskey)
meal.. **4.** masa **7.** hoecake
porridge.. **5.** atole
salad.. **8.** fetticus
Corn Belt... **4.** Iowa, Ohio **6.** Dakota, Kansas **7.** Indiana **8.** Illinois, Missouri, Nebraska **9.** Minnesota
Corncracker State... **8.** Kentucky
corner... **2.** in **4.** nook, pose, trap, tree **5.** angle, coign (coigne), herne, ingle, niche, quoin
cornered... **5.** cater (diagonal), sharp **7.** angular, up a tree **10.** cornerwise
cornerstone... **4.** coin **5.** quoin **8.** keystone **10.** foundation
Cornhusker State... **8.** Nebraska
cornice... **4.** drip, eave **7.** antefix **8.** astragal
Cornish... **3.** elm **4.** fowl **5.** heath **7.** dialect, diamond (Cornwall)
Cornwallis surrender site... **4.** York (Va)
corolla... **5.** galea (Her), petal **8.** perianth
corollary... **6.** effect, porism, result **7.** adjunct **8.** addition **9.** deduction **11.** proposition
corona... **4.** coin, halo **5.** cigar, crown **6.** circle **7.** aureole, circlet, garland, scyphus **8.** Borealis **11.** corona lucis
Corona Australis... **13.** Southern Crown

Corona Borealis... **13.** Northern Crown
coronet... **5.** crown, tiara **6.** anadem, circle, diadem, wreath **8.** insignia, ornament
corporate... **5.** joint **6.** united **7.** leagued **8.** conjoint **10.** associated
corporeal... **5.** hylic, somal **6.** bodily **7.** fleshly, somatic **8.** corporal, material, physical, tangible
corpse... **4.** body **7.** cadaver, carcass **9.** endowment (Eccl)
corpulent... **3.** fat **5.** bulky, obese, stout **6.** fleshy
corpuscle... **11.** poikilocyte, schistocyte **12.** erythroblast
corral... **3.** mew, pen, sty **4.** coop, herd **5.** atajo, pound, tambo **7.** impound **8.** stockade **9.** enclosure, inclosure
correct... **2.** OK **4.** edit, okay, true **5.** amend, emend, right **6.** better, proper, punish, reform, remedy, revise, strict **7.** chasten, improve, perfect, rectify, regular, retouch **8.** accurate, definite, orthodox, rigorous **9.** faultless **10.** particular, scrupulous **11.** grammatical, punctilious **12.** conventional
correlative... **2.** or **3.** nor **6.** mutual **7.** similar **8.** conjoint **10.** reciprocal **11.** conjunction, counterpart **13.** corresponding
correspond... **3.** fit **4.** suit **5.** agree, equal, match, tally **6.** accord **7.** comport **8.** assonate (sound), coincide, parallel **9.** analogous, harmonize **11.** parallelize
correspondence... **4.** mail **8.** homology (Biol), identity, symmetry **10.** conformity, epistolary, similarity **11.** equivalence, intercourse
corresponding... **8.** balanced **9.** analogous, homologic, isometric **10.** coinciding **11.** paralleling
corridor... **4.** hall **5.** aisle **6.** airway, arcade **7.** gallery **10.** passageway
corrige (obs)... **6.** punish **7.** correct
corrigible... **8.** amenable **10.** submissive **11.** rectifiable
corroborate... **5.** prove **7.** certify, confirm, support **8.** calidate, roborate **9.** establish **12.** adminiculate, substantiate
corroborative... **11.** adminicular
corrode... **3.** eat **4.** bite, etch, gnaw, rust **5.** erode, waste **11.** deteriorate **12.** disintegrate
corrosive... **4.** acid **7.** caustic, erodent, erodine, mordant **9.** corroding **10.** escharotic **14.** disintegrative
corrugate... **5.** crimp **6.** rugate **7.** crumble, wrinkle **8.** crumpled, furrowed, wrinkled
corrupt... **3.** rot **5.** bribe, taint, venal **6.** Augean, debase, putrid, rotten **7.** attaint, crooked, defiled, deprave, putrefy, vitiate **8.** polluted **9.** dishonest **11.** adulterated **12.** contaminated
corruption... **5.** taint **6.** pidgin

(language) 8. impurity 9. chicanery,
pollution 10. debasement, defilement,
distortion 11. depravation,
putrescence 12. adulteration
13. contamination

corsage ... 5. waist 6. bodice
7. bouquet (boquet), flowers

corsair ... 5. rover 6. pirate
7. Saracen 8. picaroon, rockfish
9. buccaneer, privateer
10. freebooter

Corsica ...
capital .. 7. Ajaccio
birthplace of .. 8. Napoleon
feud (blood) .. 8. vendetta
seaport .. 6. Bastia

cortege ... 5. train 6. parade
7. funeral, retinue 10. procession

Cortes palace site ... 8. Coyoacan
(Mexico)

cortex ... 4. bark, peel, rind

corundum ... 3. gem 5. emery
7. mineral 8. abrasive

corundum colors ...
blue .. 5. white 8. sapphire
brown .. 14. adamantine spar
green .. 7. emerald
purple .. 8. amethyst
red .. 4. ruby
topaz .. 6. yellow

coruscate ... 5. gleam, shine 7. glitter,
radiate, sparkle 11. scintillate

cosmetic ... 5. cream, henna, paint,
rouge 6. enamel, lotion, make-up
7. blusher, mascara 8. lipstick,
toiletry 11. beautifying

cosmic ... 4. vast 5. great 7. orderly
8. catholic, infinite 9. grandiose,
universal 10. harmonious

Cosmic Order ... 4. Rita (Vedic law)

Cossack (pert to) ...
chief .. 6. ataman, hetman
district .. 6. Voisko
native .. 5. Tatar 7. Russian
squadron .. 6. sotnia
village .. 8. stanitsa (stanitza)
whip (knotted) .. 5. knout

cosset ... 3. pet 4. lamb 6. caress,
coddle, cuddle, fondle, pamper

cost ... 4. loss, rate 5. price
6. amount, charge, figure, outlay,
rental 7. expense 9. detriment,
suffering 11. deprivation, expenditure

costa ... 3. rib 4. vein (Bot) 5. ridge
6. border, midrib

Costa Rica ...
capital .. 7. San José
crater (world's greatest) .. 4. Poas
discovered .. 8. Columbus (4th visit)
export .. 6. coffee 7. bananas
port .. 5. Limon 10. Puntarenas

costate ... 6. ribbed (Bot)

costermonger ... 6. coster, hawker
7. peddler 9. costerman 11. apple
seller

costly ... 4. dear, rich 8. gorgeous,
splendid 9. expensive, sumptuous
10. high-priced 11. extravagant

costume ... 3. rig 4. garb, suit
5. dress, habit 6. attire, tights
7. apparel, raiment 8. clothing

cot ... 3. bed, hut, pen, set 4. boat (Ir),

coop, cote 5. cabin, cover, house
6. cabana 7. charpoy, cottage,
shelter 8. bedstead

cote ... 3. hut, pen 4. coop 5. house
7. cottage, shelter 9. sheepfold

coterie ... 3. set 4. clan, club, ring
5. cabal, group, junto 6. circle, clique
9. camarilla (secret)

cottage ... 3. cot, hut 4. shed
5. cabin, house, villa 6. cabana
7. shelter 8. bungalow

cottager ... 6. cottar (cotter) 7. cottier,
laborer, peasant

cotton (pert to) ...
cloth .. 4. jean, lawn 5. denim, khaki,
scrim, surat, terry 6. calico, dimity,
madras, nettle 7. batiste, percale
fiber .. 4. lint 6. staple 7. viscose
gin inventor .. 7. Whitney (Eli)
knot .. 3. nep
layer .. 7. batting
medical .. 5. gauze 6. sponge
raw .. 5. bayal
roll .. 4. slub
seed .. 4. bole, boll
seed sugar .. 9. raffinose
staple .. 6. upland (short) 8. Egyptian
(long) 14. Sea Island (long)
twisted .. 5. lisle 6. thread

Cotton State ... 7. Alabama

couch ... 3. bed, cot 4. lair, sofa
5. divan 6. canapé, canopy, litter,
lounge, pallet, phrase 8. loveseat
9. embroider (with gold), stretcher

cougar ... 3. cat 4. lion, puma
7. panther 9. catamount

cough ... 4. bark (sl), hack 6. tussis

council ... 4. diet, rede 5. cabal, synod
6. senate 7. cabinet 8. assembly,
conclave, tribunal 10. conference,
parliament 12. consultation
15. League of Nations

council table cover ... 5. tapis

counsel ... 4. rede 6. advice, advise,
confer, lawyer 8. guidance
9. recommend 10. suggestion
11. instruction 12. deliberation

counselor, counsellor ... 4. sage
6. lawyer, mentor, nestor 7. adviser,
advisor, counsel 8. attorney
9. barrister, solicitor

count ... 3. sum, tot 4. tale, tell
5. check, judge, relay, tally
6. number, reckon, rely on
7. compute, summary 8. nobleman,
quantify 9. calculate, enumerate,
reckoning, summation 12. capitulation

Count (pert to) ...
Mayence .. 3. Gan 7. Ganelon
Monte Cristo .. 6. Dantes
Rousillon .. 7. Bertram

countenance ... 3. aid 4. abet, brow,
face, mien 6. aspect, permit, visage
7. approve, endorse, support
8. approval, sanction, tolerate
9. composure, encourage
10. appearance, permission

counter ... 4. chip 5. table, token
7. adverse 8. computer, contrary,
opposite 9. retaliate 10. calculator

counteract ... 6. offset, oppose, thwart
7. nullify 8. antidote 10. neutralize

11. countermand

counter current... 4. eddy 5. swirl
6. vortex 9. whirlpool
12. counterforce

counterfeit... 4. base, fake, mock,
sham 5. bogus, false, feign, forge,
phony, queer 6. assume, forged,
unreal 7. falsify, forgery, imitate
8. simulant, spurious 10. artificial,
fictitious 11. unauthentic

counterirritant... 4. moxa 5. seton
6. arnica, iodine, pepper 7. mustard

countermand... 5. annul 6. cancel,
forbid, recall, revoke 7. abolish,
reverse 8. prohibit 9. frustrate
10. counteract 12. counterorder

counterpane... 5. quilt 8. bedcover,
coverlet 9. comforter 10. counterpin
11. comfortable

counterpart... 4. copy, like, twin
5. image 6. double, eponym (name)
8. parallel 9. duplicate
10. complement, equivalent

counterpoise... 6. offset 8. equalize
10. compensate, counteract
12. counterforce 14. counterbalance

countersign... 4. sign 6. signal
7. tessera 8. password 9. signature,
watchword 10. mot de passé, open
sesame 12. counterstamp

countersink... 4. ream 5. bevel
6. deepen 7. chamfer

countertenor... 4. alto (male)
8. falsetto

counterthrust (fencing)... 7. riposte
(ripost) 12. return thrust

countless... 8. infinite 10. numberless,
unnumbered 11. innumerable
12. incalculable

countrified... 5. rural 7. boorish,
hickish, uncouth 8. inurbane
10. unpolished

country... 4. land, pais (law), vale
5. rural, state, weald 6. nation,
region 9. territory 10. fatherland
12. commonwealth

country (pert to)...
alien.. 7. enclave, exclave
ancient.. 4. Aram, Elis, Gaul
bumpkin.. 4. clod, jake, rube
5. churl, yokel 9. greenhorn
gallant.. 5. swain
mythical.. 2. Oz
native (earliest).. 9. aborigine
Roman.. 8. campagna
term.. 5. rural, urban 6. rustic
8. agrestic, pastoral, praedial (predial)

countryman... 4. rube 5. yokel
6. rustic 7. hayseed, patriot, peasant
10. compatriot, home towner

county... 4. seat 5. shire 6. domain,
parish 8. district

coup... 3. buy 4. blow, move (games)
5. scoop, upset 6. barter, strike,
stroke (master) 8. overturn, strategy
9. trump card

coup de grâce... 9. deathblow

coup de main... 6. attack (sudden)
8. strategy 9. stratagem

coup d'état... 6. stroke (political)
8. strategy

couple... 3. duo, tie, two 4. bond,

dyad, join, link, mate, pair, span,
team, twin, yoke 5. brace, marry,
twain, unite 6. Gemini 7. bracket

coupled... 5. gemel, mated 6. braced,
joined, linked, paired, teamed, united
7. leagued, married

couplet... 3. two 4. pair 5. brace,
verse 7. distich, doublet

coupon... 5. scrip, stock, token
6. ticket 11. certificate (Finan)

courage... 4. grit, sand, will 5. heart,
metal, nerve, pluck, valor 7. bravery,
heroism, prowess 8. audacity,
boldness, firmness 9. fortitude,
gallantry, hardihood 11. intrepidity
12. fearlessness 13. dauntlessness

courageous... 4. bold, game 5. brave,
hardy, manly, stout 6. daring, heroic,
spunky 7. gallant, spartan, valiant
8. fearless, intrepid, knightly,
resolute, stalwart, valorous
11. adventurous 12. enterprising,
stouthearted

courant... 4. romp 5. caper 6. letter
7. gazette, running (Her)
9. messenger, newspaper

courier... 5. guide 8. dragoman,
horseman 9. attendant, messenger

course... 3. run 4. flow, line, mode,
path, road, rote, tack 5. route,
study, trend 6. career, manner,
method, policy, series, stream
8. progress 9. direction, procedure
10. succession

course (pert to)...
college.. 7. seminar
direct.. 7. beeline
regular.. 4. rote 6. regime 7. routine
roundabout.. 6. detour 11. indirection

course of...
action.. 5. habit 7. routine
9. procedure
eating.. 4. diet
instruction.. 6. lesson
procedure.. 4. rule
thought.. 5. tenor

courser... 5. horse, steed 6. hunter,
plover 7. charger 8. war horse

court... 3. see (papal), woo 4. area,
eyre, fawn (upon), rota 5. atria,
curia, dairi, gemot, patio, spark
6. palace, parvis, street 7. council,
tribune 8. tribunal 10. attendance,
curry favor, quadrangle

court (Eng)... 3. soc 4. eyre, leet
8. woodmate 10. court–baron

court (pert to)...
assistant.. 5. staff 6. elisor
crier, cry.. 4. hear, oyez (oyes)
6. beadle
criminal.. 6. assize
exemption, excuse.. 6. essoin
game.. 6. tennis 9. badminton
hearing.. 4. oyer
minutes.. 4. acta
order.. 4. writ 5. arret 6. capias
7. summons 8. subpoena
public.. 5. forum 8. forensic
sitting.. 7. session

courteous... 5. civil 6. gentle, polite,
urbane 7. affable, gallant
8. debonair, gracious 9. attentive

10. respectful
courtly... 4. hend (hende) 5. aulic, civil 7. elegant, gallant, stately 9. dignified 10. obsequious 11. ceremonious
courtship... 4. suit 6. plight, wooing 7. romance 8. courting
covenant... 4. bond, pact 6. engage 7. bargain, compact, entente, promise 8. contract 9. agreement, stipulate, testament 11. undertaking
Covenant of God to Noah... 7. rainbow
cover... 3. cap, lap, lid 4. coat, cozy, hide, mask, pale, pave, roof, span, veil 5. blind, crust, drape, tapis 6. canopy, mantle, purdah, screen, shield, thatch 7. elytron, overlay, shelter 8. chrismal, coverlet 9. tarpaulin 10. overspread
cover (pert to)...
alloy.. 5. terne
cork.. 9. corticate
crumbs.. 5. bread
dots.. 7. stipple
figures (Her).. 4. seme
straw.. 6. thatch
turf.. 3. sod
up.. 4. bury 5. inter 7. conceal 8. submerge 10. camouflage
with wax.. 4. cere
covering... 3. mat, rug 4. caul, film, hull, tile 5. apron, armor, shell, testa 6. awning, carpet, cestus, lorica, pelage, screen, shroud 7. epeiric, shelter, tegumen, wrapper 8. lineolum, pericarp 9. caparison 10. integument, protection 11. smoke screen
covering (head)... 3. cap, hat, wig 4. hood 5. beret, scarf, snood 6. bonnet, peruke, toupee 7. chapeau 10. fascinator
coverlet... 5. quilt 6. afghan, spread 7. blanket, lap robe 11. counterpane
covert... 3. den, lie 4. abri, lair 6. hidden, refuge, secret 7. covered, private, thicket 9. concealed, disguised, insidious, sheltered
covet... 4. envy 5. crave, yisse (obs) 6. aspire, desire, grudge, hanker 7. long for 8. begrudge
covetousness... 5. greed 7. avarice
covey... 4. bevy, pack 5. brood, flock, hatch 6. flight 7. company 9. multitude
cow... 3. awe 5. abash, daunt 7. overawe, terrify 8. browbeat, frighten 10. intimidate
cow (animal)... 3. Bos 4. calf, kine, moil 5. Angus, bossy, brock (obs), Kerry, vache 6. bovine, heifer 7. pollard 8. Ayrshire, maverick, moulleen
cow (pert to)...
barn.. 4. byre, shed 5. reeve, stall 6. stable 7. vaccary, vachery
food (chewed).. 3. cud 5. rumen
hornless.. 6. mulley 7. pollard 8. moulleen
sea.. 6. dugong, walrus 7. manatee, Sirenia 12. hippopotamus

tether.. 4. rope 6. baikie
unbranded.. 8. maverick
young.. 4. calf 6. heifer
coward, cowardly... 3. shy 5. sneak 6. afraid, craven, scared 7. caitiff, chicken, dastard, milksop 8. poltroon, recreant, weakling 9. dastardly, fraidy-cat, jellyfish 12. uncourageous 13. pusillanimous
cowboy... 5. roper 6. herder 7. llamero, puncher, vaquero 8. jackaroo, neatherd 12. broncobuster (sl)
cowboy breeches... 5. chaps 8. jodhpurs
cower... 4. fawn 5. crawl, quail, stoop 6. cringe, crouch, grovel
cowfish... 3. ray 4. toto 7. dolphin, grampus, manatee 8. porpoise
cowled... 9. cucullate
coxcomb... 3. fop 4. dude, fool 5. cleat (Naut), dandy 8. popinjay
coy... 3. shy 4. arch 5. timid 6. demure, modest 7. bashful 10. coquettish 13. self-conscious
coyote... 4. wolf (prairie)
Coyote State... 11. South Dakota
coypu... 6. nutria, rodent
cozen... 5. cheat, trick 7. beguile, deceive, defraud
cozy... 4. easy, snug 6. chatty 8. cheerful, familiar, homelike, sociable 9. contented, talkative 11. comfortable
crab... 3. Uca 4. king, Maia (genus) 5. ayuyu (Guam) 6. partan, spider 7. fiddler, limulus, mollusk, Ocypode 8. Lithodes 9. horseshoe 10. crustacean
crabbed... 5. cross 6. bitter, crusty, morose, trying 7. bilious, peevish 8. abstruse, liverish 9. difficult, fractious, irascible, irregular 10. perplexing
crab claw... 5. chela 6. metope, nipper
crab eater... 4. seal 5. heron 7. opossum, raccoon
crachoir... 8. cuspidor, spittoon
crack... 4. blow, chap, clap, flaw, kibe, leak, quip, rift, rime, snap 5. brack, break, chink, craze, spang, split 6. breach, cleave, cranny 7. crackle, crevice, fissure, rupture 8. fracture
Cracker State... 7. Georgia
crackle... 4. snap 5. craze (art), crink 9. crepitate
crackman... 4. yegg 7. burglar
cradle... 4. slee (ship's) 7. infancy, nursery 8. bassinet, cunabula 10. beginnings, incunabula
cradle book... 11. incunabulum
Cradle of Liberty... 11. Faneuil Hall (Boston)
cradle song... 7. lullaby 8. berceuse 13. Schlummerleid
craft... 3. art 4. boat 5. skill, trade 6. device, tender 7. cunning, finesse, know-how, prowess 8. aptitude, vocation 9. dexterity 10. employment, handicraft,

occupation, watercraft **12.** skillfulness
craftsman . . . **6.** artist, writer
　7. artisan, workman **9.** artificer
crafty . . . **3.** sly **4.** foxy, slim, wily, wise
　6. artful, astute, shifty, shrewd, subtle,
　tricky **7.** cunning **8.** skillful (skilful)
　9. deceitful, ingenious, underhand
　10. fraudulent **13.** Machiavellian
　15. Mephistophelean
crag . . . **3.** tor **4.** spur **5.** arête, cliff
　7. nunatak **9.** precipice
craggy . . . **5.** rough **6.** cliffy, clifty,
　jagged, knotty, rugged
cram . . . **4.** fill **5.** choke, crowd, drive,
　force, gorge, press, study, stuff
　9. overstuff **10.** gluttonize
cramp . . . **4.** pain **5.** stunt **6.** hamper
　7. confine, seizure **8.** compress,
　restrict **9.** hindrance, paralysis
　(muscle) **11.** restriction
cranberry . . . **3.** red **9.** sourberry
cranberry center of trade . . .
　10. Barnstable (Mass)
crane . . . **3.** gib, jib **5.** davit, jenny,
　titan **7.** derrick, machine
crane . . . **4.** Grus **5.** heron, sarus
　7. Gruidae **9.** cormorant
　10. Gruiformes **13.** constellation
cranial nerve . . . **5.** radix, vagus
cranium . . . **5.** skull **8.** cerebrum
crank . . . **3.** wit **4.** bear, crab **5.** crook,
　winch **6.** griper, grouch, handle
　7. fanatic, growler, hothead
　8. frondeur, grumbler, sorehead
　9. eccentric **10.** bellyacher,
　crosspatch, monomaniac
cranny . . . **4.** hole, nook **5.** chink, cleft,
　crack **6.** corner, furrow **7.** crevice,
　fissure **8.** crevasse
crash . . . **4.** bank, fail **5.** smash
　7. debacle, failure, intrude, shatter
　8. accident **9.** collision
　10. bankruptcy
crate . . . **3.** box **4.** case **6.** basket,
　cradle, encase, hamper **8.** airplane
　9. container **10.** automobile
crater . . . **3.** pit **6.** cavity **7.** caldera
　13. constellation (The Cup)
cravat . . . **3.** tie **4.** teck **5.** ascot, stock
　7. bandage, bolo tie, necktie
　9. neckcloth **10.** four–in–hand
crave . . . **3.** ask, beg **4.** long, seek
　5. covet, yearn **6.** desire, hanker
　7. beseech, entreat, implore, request,
　solicit **10.** supplicate
craven . . . **6.** afraid, coward **7.** caitiff,
　dastard **8.** cowardly, poltroon,
　recreant **12.** fainthearted
　13. pusillanimous
craving . . . **4.** pica **6.** desire, thirst
　7. longing **8.** appetite, yearning
craw . . . **3.** maw **4.** crop **6.** gebbie
　7. gizzard, stomach **9.** ingluvies
crawfish . . . **5.** yabby (yabbie) **7.** back
　out, crawdad, lobster, retreat
　8. crayfish
crawl . . . **4.** fawn, inch, shug **5.** creep
　6. cringe, grovel, recant
crayon . . . **5.** chalk **6.** pastel, pencil
　8. charcoal
craze . . . **3.** fad **4.** flaw, maze **5.** crack
　(ceramics), crush, furor, mania, vogue

6. defect, whimsy **7.** crackle, fashion
　9. infirmity **11.** infatuation
craze (for) . . . see also *madness, mania*
　foreign customs . . **9.** xenomania
　freedom . . **14.** eleutheromania
　love (erotic) . . **10.** erotomania
　music . . **9.** melomania
　setting fires . . **9.** pyromania
　shopping . . **9.** oniomania
　single subject . . **9.** monomania
　stamps (postage) . . **11.** timbromania
　stealing . . **11.** kleptomania
　wandering . . **10.** dromomania
　wealth . . **10.** plutomania
crazed . . . **4.** amok **6.** insane, marked
　(with crazes) **7.** severed **8.** deranged
　10. distraught
crazy . . . **3.** mad **4.** amok, loco, luny
　6. dottle, insane **7.** damaged, foolish,
　unsound **9.** deficient
cream . . . **4.** best, ream **5.** elite
　6. lotion **8.** sillabub (with wine)
cream of tartar . . . **5.** argol
crease . . . **4.** fold, ruck **5.** crimp, pleat
　7. wrinkle **9.** plication
create . . . **4.** make **5.** build, cause,
　clone, hatch **6.** invent **7.** fashion,
　produce **8.** generate **9.** originate
creation . . . **3.** art **5.** virtu, world
　6. cosmos, making **7.** classic, fantasy,
　forming, product **8.** artifact, universe
　9. objet d'art **10.** providence
　11. composition, fabrication,
　manufacture, masterpiece
creator . . . **5.** maker **6.** author
　8. designer, inventor, producer
　10. originator
Creator . . . **3.** God **5.** Maker
　7. Jehovah **8.** Almighty, Demiurge
　11. King of Kings
creature (pert to) . . .
　civetlike . . **3.** cat
　duplicate . . **5.** clone
　elflike . . **4.** peri **6.** hobbit
　evil . . **7.** hellcat **8.** hellicat
　fire . . **10.** salamander
　folklore . . **3.** elf **4.** Yeti **5.** dwarf, fairy,
　pixie **9.** sasquatch
　ghost . . **11.** poltergeist
　minute . . **10.** animalcule
　outer space . . **5.** alien
　sentient . . **6.** animal
　timid . . **4.** deer **5.** sheep
　underground . . **5.** gnome
　water . . **5.** sylph **6.** undine
　winged (Myth) . . **6.** wivern
　10. cockatrice
credence . . . **5.** trust **6.** belief, credit
　8. affiance, reliance **10.** acceptance,
　confidence, dependence
　15. trustworthiness
credential . . . **7.** voucher
　11. certificate, testimonial
　14. recommendation
credible . . . **6.** likely **7.** tenable
　8. probable **9.** plausible
　10. believable **11.** well–founded
credit . . . **5.** faith, honor, trust **6.** belief,
　esteem, impute **7.** account, believe
　8. accredit, credence **10.** estimation,
　regulation **15.** trustworthiness
creditor . . . **5.** agent (collection)

6. debtee, dunner, usurer 7. Shylock (greedy)

creed ... 5. credo, dogma, tenet
6. belief, Nicene 8. Apostles'
9. Catechism 10. Athanasian, confession

creek ... 3. rio 4. burn, slue, wick
6. arroyo, estero, slough, spruit, stream

creel ... 4. rack, trap 6. basket (fish)

creep ... 5. crawl, prowl, skulk, slink, sneak, steal (away) 6. grovel
8. scramble 9. pussyfoot

creeping ... 4. slow 7. reptant
8. crawling 10. slithering
11. reptatorial

Cremona, famed names ... 5. Amati
6. violin 10. Guarnerius
12. Stradivarius

crena ... 4. gash, kerf, nick 5. cleft, notch 7. scallop 10. depression
11. indentation

creole ... 6. French 7. mestizo
9. half–breed, janissary

Creole State ... 9. Louisiana

crepitate ... 4. snap 7. crackly

crescent ... 4. cusp, horn, lune
5. curve 8. meniscus

crescent–shaped ... 4. horn, lune
6. bicorn, lunate 7. lunular
8. lunulate 10. horseshoe, meniscate, semilunar

crest ... 3. top 4. comb, peak, tuft
5. arête, crown, ridge 6. copple, crista, height, summit 7. panache, topknot, wave top 8. feathers, insignia, pinnacle 9. cockscomb
11. mountaintop

crested ... 6. capped, topped, tufted
7. coppled, cristed, crowned, pileate

creta ... 5. chalk

Crete ...
  capital .. 5. Canea
  city .. 6. Candia, Khanis
  civilization (anc) .. 6. Aegean, Minoan
  king (anc) .. 5. Minos (Gr)
  monster .. 8. Minotaur (man, bull)
  mountain .. 3. Ida 9. Theodoros
  priests .. 7. Curetes

cretin ... 5. idiot 8. imbecile

crevice ... 3. gap 4. rift 5. chink, cleft
6. cranny 7. fissure, opening
8. peephole 10. interstice

crew ... 3. men 4. band, body, gang, pack 6. force, staff 7. company
9. employees, personnel

crib ... 3. bed, bin, den (gambling)
5. cheat, stall, steal 6. Cratch
(stars), manger, pilfer 7. brothel
8. Praesepe

cricket ... 4. game, grig 6. acheta, cicada, locust 7. katydid 9. footstool
10. Orthoptera 11. grasshopper

cricket (pert to) ...
  game term .. 3. bye, run 6. yorker
  noise .. 5. chirp 7. stridor
  symbol (Myth) .. 4. tice 5. ashes

cried ... 4. wept 6. bawled, called, wailed, yelled 7. shouted, uttered
8. lamented, screamed, shrieked
9. exclaimed 10. proclaimed

crime ... 3. sin 4. evil 5. guilt, wrong

6. delict, felony, mayhem 7. offense
8. delictum, iniquity 9. violation
10. illegality, wickedness, wrongdoing
11. malfeasance

crime (pert to) ...
  benefice (Eccl) .. 6. simony
  goddess (Myth) .. 3. Ate
  of 1873 .. 12. Silver Dollar
  scene .. 5. venue

Crimea ...
  city .. 5. Kerch, Yalta 10. Sevastopol
  isthmus site .. 8. Black Sea
  Russian .. 4. Krim
  sea (Russ) .. 4. Azof

criminal ... 4. thug, yegg 5. crook, felon, thief 6. nocent 7. convict, yeggman 8. swindler 9. desperado, dishonest, felonious 10. malefactor, recidivist 11. blameworthy, disgraceful
13. reprehensible

criminal refuge ... 7. Alsatia
11. Whitefriars (London)

criminology ... 8. penology

crimp ... 4. curl, fold 5. frizz, notch, plait 6. ruffle, thwart 7. crinkle, wrinkle 8. Shanghai

cringe ... 4. fawn 5. cower, quail, sneak, wince 6. flinch, grovel, shrink, submit 7. truckle

crinkle ... 4. curl, kink, turn, wind
5. twist 6. rustle 7. wrinkle

crinose ... 5. hairy 7. hirsute
11. barbigerous

cripple ... 4. halt, hock, lame, maim
6. injure, weaken 7. amputee, disable 8. handicap 9. hamstring
12. incapacitate

crisis ... 5. cycle, peril 8. exigency, juncture 9. criterion, emergency
11. climacteric

crisp ... 4. cold 5. curly, flaky, sharp, short, spalt 7. brittle, concise, crackle, crinkle, friable 8. clear–cut
9. frangible

criterion ... 4. norm, rule, test, type
5. canon, model 7. measure
8. standard 9. yardstick

critic ... 5. judge, Momus (Myth)
6. censor, slater, Zoilus 8. collator, reviewer 9. literator 11. connoisseur, criticaster, faultfinder

critical ... 4. edgy 7. carping, crucial, cynical, Zoilean 8. captious, caviling, exacting 10. censorious, particular
12. faultfinding 13. hairsplitting
14. discriminating

Critical system of philosophy ...
10. Kantianism

criticism ... 3. rap 5. cavil, roast
6. report, review 7. censure, Zoilism
8. critique, judgment 9. aspersion
10. commentary

criticize, criticise ... 3. pan 4. carp, flay 5. cavil, judge, knock, slate
6. review 7. censure, comment
8. castigate 10. animadvert

Croatian ... 4. Slav 5. Croat
11. Yugoslavian

Croatian capital ... 6. Zagreb

crock ... 3. ewe (old), jug, pot, urn
4. smut, soil, soot 5. horse (old)
7. ceramic 8. potsherd

11. earthenware
crocodile . . . 3. goa 5. nakoo 6. gavial, mugger 7. reptile, sophism 9. Niloticus 10. Crocodilia, Crocodilus
crocus . . . 4. bulb, herb, iris 6. flower, yellow 7. saffron
croft . . . 5. crypt, field, vault 6. carafe, cavern 7. hillock
crone . . . 3. ewe (old), hag 5. witch 6. beldam (beldame)
Cronus (pert to) . . .
  god of . . 8. Harvests
  father . . 6. Uranus
  son . . 4. Zeus
  wife . . 4. Rhea
crony . . . 3. pal 4. chum 5. buddy 6. friend 9. companion 10. playfellow
crook . . . 4. bend, warp 5. angle, curve, staff, thief 6. akimbo 7. crosier 8. criminal, insignia 10. camshachle
crooked . . . 3. wry, zag 4. agee, awry, bent 5. agley, askew, false 6. aslant, curved, hooked, zigzag 7. angular, askance, asquint, oblique 8. deformed 9. dishonest, distorted 10. circuitous, fraudulent 12. dishonorable
crooked legs . . . 8. rhebosis (rhaebosis) 10. tortuosity
croon . . . 3. hum 4. boom, sing, wail 5. whine 6. bellow, lament, murmur 8. complain
crop . . . 3. lop, maw 4. clip, craw, dick, reap, whip 5. belly, shear, yield 6. gebbie, growth, sheave 7. harvest, produce, soilage, stomach 11. cultivation
cross . . . 2. go 3. tau 4. crux, ford, rood 5. bless, corse, irate, staff 6. oppose, thwart, touchy 7. athwart, fretful, oblique, peevish, pettish 8. crucifix, insignia, monument, obstruct, petulant, snappish, swastika (swastica), traverse 9. hybridize, intersect, irritable 10. disappoint, transverse 11. crucifixion
cross (pert to) . . .
  archaeology . . 4. ankh
  astronomy . . 13. Southern Cross
  barred . . 11. trabeculate
  beam . . 5. spale, trave 6. girder
  bow . . 8. arbalest
  breed . . 5. Husky (dog) 6. hybrid
  British . . 6. Celtic
  Egypt . . 10. life symbol
  eye . . 9. esotropia 10. strabismus
  heraldry . . 6. pattée 7. erminee, patonce
  Latin . . 12. crux commissa
  palm . . 5. bribe (gypsy)
  St Anthony's . . 3. tau
  stroke . . 5. serif
  tau–shaped . . 10. crux ansata
crossing . . . 6. voyage 7. chiasma, fording, passage 8. cheating, opposing 9. hybridism 10. traversing 13. crossbreeding
crossing (famed) . . .
  Alps . . 8. Hannibal, Napoleon
  Hellespont . . 6. Xerxes

  Pyrenees . . 8. Hannibal
  Rubicon . . 6. Caesar
crouch . . . 4. bend, fawn 5. cower, squat, stoop 6. cringe, grovel, hunker
crow . . . 3. daw 4. brag, rook 5. aylet, boast, crake, raven, vaunt 6. chough, Corvus, Indian (Sioux) 7. corvine, jackdaw 8. laughter 13. constellation
crowbar . . . 5. jimmy, lever 7. gablock
crowberry . . . 5. shrub 8. bilberry 9. cranberry
crowd . . . 3. jam, mob 4. bike (Scot), cram, host, pack, push, ruck, urge 5. crush, drive, drove, horde, press, serry, swarm, three, wedge 6. galaxy, hasten, legion, masses, throng 7. squeeze 8. compress 9. multitude 10. assemblage
crowded . . . 6. packed 7. compact, crammed, serried, teeming 8. numerous, populous 9. congested, jampacked
crown . . . 3. cap, top 4. atef, coin, pate, peak, poll, tiar 5. crest, miter (mitre), tiara 6. anadem, circle, corona, diadem, fillet, reward, summit, trophy, wreath 7. chaplet, coronet, garland, glorify, install 8. coronate, enthrone, ornament, pinnacle, surmount
crowning glory . . . 8. last word
crucial . . . 5. final 6. severe, trying, urgent 7. crossed 8. critical, decisive 9. cruciform 13. demonstrative
crucible . . . 3. pot 4. etna, test 6. retort, vessel 10. conversion
crucifix . . . 3. pax 4. rood 5. cross 6. emblem
crucifixion . . . 5. death (on a cross) 7. torture 9. execution, suffering 11. persecution
crude . . . 3. raw 4. rude 5. crass, green, rough 6. callow, coarse, common, garish, savage, vulgar 8. unseemly 9. inelegant, rough–hewn, tasteless, uncourtly, unrefined 10. outlandish, unpolished 13. inexperienced
crudity . . . 7. rawness 9. crassness, harshness, roughness, vulgarity 10. immaturity
cruel . . . 4. fell, hard 5. harsh 6. brutal, savage, severe, unkind 7. inhuman, painful, unhuman 8. dreadful, fiendish, pitiless, ruthless, tyrannic 9. ferocious, heartless, merciless, murderous, truculent 11. remorseless
cruelty . . . 9. brutality 10. inclemency, inhumanity 12. ruthlessness 13. heartlessness 15. remorselessness
cruelty, lover of . . . 6. sadist 9. masochist
cruet . . . 3. ama 4. vial 6. bottle, caster (castor), vessel 7. ampulla, urceole
cruller . . . 7. olycook (olykoek) 8. doughnut 9. friedcake
crumb . . . 3. bit 5. break, piece 6. little 8. fragment
crumble . . . 5. decay 6. molder, powder

7. friable 9. pulverize
12. disintegrate
crumple... 4. ruck 6. crease, raffle,
rumple 7. wrinkle 9. corrugate
cruor... 4. gore 5. blood, ichor
crusade... 5. cause, drive, issue, jihad
(jehad) 7. crusado 8. campaign
10. expedition
Crusades... 8. Holy Land 9. Children's
(1212)
crush... 3. jam 4. bray, mash, sink
5. crash, crowd, grind, press, smash
6. bruise, crunch 7. conquer,
mortify, oppress, shatter, squeeze
8. compress, suppress 9. humiliate,
pulverize 11. infatuation
crushed sugar cane... 7. bagasse
crust... 4. rind 5. shell 8. dumpling,
exterior 9. impudence 11. lithosphere
14. aggressiveness
crustacean... 4. crab 5. prawn
6. huitre, isopod, limpet, mussel,
oyster, shrimp 7. limulus, lobster,
scallop 8. barnacle, crawfish, starfish
9. shellfish, trunkfish 10. coquillage,
periwinkle
crustacean (pert to)...
extinct.. 5. Eryon
footless.. 4. apod, apus
fossil.. 9. trilobite
genus.. 5. Hippa 6. Triops 7. Caridea
(Carida) 8. Copepoda, Decapoda
10. Notostraca
larva.. 5. alima
limb.. 6. endite, podite
crutch... 5. brace, staff, stave
6. crotch 7. support
cry... 3. baa, caw, cri, hue, mew, olé,
sob 4. alas, barr, call, evoe, home,
hoot, mewl, pish, pule, wail, weep,
yell, yelp 5. alack, avast, bleat,
crook, miaou, yoick 6. bellow,
boohoo, clamor, outcry, scream,
shriek, slogan, snivel, squawk
7. tantivy (hunting), trumpet, weeping
8. entreaty, jeremiad, lackaday,
proclaim 10. shibboleth
11. lamentation
cry (out)... 5. crake, decry, shout
6. accuse, clamor, object, scream,
suffer 7. censure, exclaim
8. complain, denounce 10. vociferate
crying... 6. puling, urgent 7. clamant,
heinous, howling, sobbing, weeping
9. insistent, notorious
crying bird... 6. Aramus 7. courlan,
limpkin 8. raillike
cryptic... 4. Rite (Freemasonry)
6. hidden, occult, secret 8. puzzling
9. concealed, enigmatic
10. mysterious 11. problematic
12. hieroglyphic
cryptogram... 4. code 5. agama
7. writing (secret) 8. symbolic
crystal... 4. dial 5. clear, glass, lucid
6. argent (Her), quartz 7. diamond
8. pellucid 9. glassware, snowflake
11. crystalline, transparent
crystal (pert to)...
diamond.. 7. glassie
gazer.. 4. seer 7. diviner 8. presager
10. soothsayer 13. fortuneteller

gazing.. 4. scry
twin.. 5. macle
crystalline... 4. pure 8. pellucid
11. transparent 12. crystal–clear
crystalline (pert to)...
colorless.. 7. orcinol
compound.. 5. oscin 6. anisil, dulcin
mineral.. 4. spar 7. apatite
8. elaterin, feldspar
rock.. 7. diorite, greisen
salt.. 5. borax 8. analgene (analgen)
cub... 3. bin, boy, fox, pen, pup
4. bear, coop, crib, lion, shed
5. shark, stall, tiger, whale, whelp
8. boy scout, cupboard 9. youngling
Cuba...
capital.. 6. Havana
castle.. 5. Morro
city.. 8. Santiago 10. Bahia Honda,
Guantánamo
discoverer.. 8. Columbus (1492)
island.. 11. Isle of Pines (Isla de
Pinos)
mountain.. 8. Camaguey 9. Las Villas
12. Pico Turquino
nickname.. 18. Pearl of the Antilles
province.. 7. Oriente
Cuban (pert to)...
asphalt.. 9. chapapote
bird.. 6. trogan 8. tocororo
dance.. 5. rumba
fish.. 4. bobo
rodent.. 5. hutia (jutia) 6. pilori
rum.. 7. Bacardi
cube... 3. die 4. dice 5. solid 6. triple
7. tessera (marble) 10. third power
cubic (pert to)...
body.. 3. die 4. dice
decimeter.. 5. litre
math.. 9. isometric
measure.. 4. cord
meter.. 5. stere
shape.. 6. cuboid 8. cubiform
cubicle... 4. cell, room, tomb
7. bedroom, chamber, roomlet
9. cubiculum
cuckoo... 5. mimic 8. imitator,
songbird
cuckoo (pert to)...
ally.. 3. ani
American.. 8. Coccyzus
bees.. 9. Nomadidae
bird (Orient).. 4. coel (koel)
cap.. 9. monkshood
family.. 9. Cuculidae
fool.. 7. wryneck
pint.. 4. arum 10. cuckoo spit
cucumber... 4. cuke, pepo 6. pedata
(sea), pepino
cucurbit... 5. flask, gourd 7. matrass
cud... 4. bite, quid 5. rumen
8. merycism
cuddle... 3. hug, pet 6. fondle, nestle
7. snuggle
cudgel... 3. bat, hit 4. beat, club,
drub 5. baste, staff, stave, stick
6. alpeen 7. belabor 9. fustigate,
shillalah (shillelagh)
cue... 3. nod, rod, tip 4. ball, clue,
hint, role, tail 5. braid, queue, twist
6. prompt 8. billiard (term), function
9. catchword 10. intimation

cuerpo... 4. body, hulk 5. naked, torso 10. dishabille (in)

cuff... 3. hit 4. band, blow, slap 5. clout 6. strike 8. chastise, gauntlet, handcuff 12. chastisement

cuirass... 4. mail 5. armor 6. lorica 11. breastplate

cul–de–sac... 5. alley (blind) 7. impasse 14. pouch of Douglas

cull... 4. pick 6. assort, choose, select 8. separate

culmination... 3. end 4. acme, apex, auge, noon 6. ascent, climax, result, vertex, zenith 10. perfection 12. consummation

culpability... 5. blame, fault, guilt 11. criminality 15. blameworthiness

culpable... 6. faulty, guilty 7. immoral 8. criminal 9. accusable, imputable 10. censurable, indictable 11. blameworthy 12. reproachable 13. reprehensible

cultivate... 3. ear (dial), hoe 4. farm, grow, plow, teel, till 5. court, train 6. excite, foster, harrow, plough, refine 7. educate, improve 8. approach, civilize

cultivated... 4. grew, hoed 6. seeded, tilled, urbane 7. genteel, refined 8. cultured, polished, well–bred

cultivation... 5. tilth 7. culture, farming, tillage 9. husbandry 10. refinement 12. civilization

culver... 4. dove 6. pigeon 10. wood pigeon

cumbersome... 5. bulky 6. clumsy 8. cumbrous, unwieldy 10. burdensome

cummer... 4. lass 5. witch 6. friend (girl) 7. midwife 9. companion, godmother

cummerbund... 4. band, belt, sash 6. cestus, girdle

cumshaw... 3. tip 5. bonus 6. thanks 7. present 8. gratuity

cunning... 3. sly 4. cute, foxy, wile, wily 5. sharp, skill 6. artful, clever, crafty, dainty, shrewd, subtle, tricky 7. politic, shyness 8. dextrous, foxiness, skillful, stealthy, trickery 9. designing, dexterity, ingenious, ingenuity, insidious 13. Machiavellian

cunningly formed... 6. daedal (dedal)

cup... 3. ama, can, dop, mug, tyg 4. tass, teet, Toby 5. calyx, chark, cruse, cupel, cylix, grail, jorum, ladle, stein 6. beaker, goblet, noggin, trophy 7. chalice, tumbler

cupbearer... 4. Hebe, saki 8. Ganymede

cupboard... 3. kas 5. ambry (anc) 6. buffet, closet, larder, pantry 7. armoire, dresser 8. aparador 9. sideboard

Cupid... 3. boy, Dan 4. amor, Eros, Kama, love 5. Freya 7. Amorino, cupidon

Cupid (pert to)...
mother.. 5. Venus
sweetheart.. 6. Psyche
title.. 3. Dan

cupidity... 4. lust 5. greed 6. desire 7. avarice, avidity, longing 8. appetite, avidness, rapacity

cuplike (pert to)...
calyx.. 9. calicular
stone.. 5. geode
vessel.. 4. zarf

cupola... 4. dome, kiln 5. tower 6. concha (Arch) 7. ceiling, furnace (foundry)

cur... 3. dog 4. mutt 7. gurnard (fish), mongrel 9. goldeneye

curare, curari... 5. urali 7. extract 9. Strychnos 11. arrow poison

curate... 4. abbé 6. cleric, parson, pastor, priest 7. dominie 9. clergyman

curator... 6. keeper 7. manager, steward 8. guardian 9. custodian, librarian, treasurer

curb... 3. bit 4. rein 5. check, limit 6. arrest, border, bridle, market (Finan) 7. control, inhibit, repress 8. restrict 9. hindrance, restraint

curd... 4. crud 6. casein

curds and whey... 7. clabber

cure... 4. balm, heal, salt 5. smoke 6. elixir, remedy, rizzor 7. nostrum, panacea, restore, therapy 8. preserve 10. corrective

curio... 8. artifact 9. bric–a–brac, curiosity

curiosity... 5. curio 6. gabion (rare), oddity, prying, wonder 8. interest 9. exception, spectacle 14. meddlesomeness 15. inquisitiveness

curious... 3. odd 4. rare 5. nosey (nosy), outre, queer 6. prying, quaint 7. careful, strange, unusual 8. cautious, meddling, singular 9. inquiring, intrusive 10. meticulous 11. inquisitive

curl... 4. coil, kink, lock, roll 5. crimp, crisp, frizz, tress, twirl, twist 6. marcel, spiral 7. crinkle, frizzle, ringlet 8. curlicue 9. corkscrew 11. convolution

curled... 5. curly, spiry 6. coiled 7. crimped, savoyed, twisted 8. wrinkled (Bot)

curlew... 4. bird, fute 5. kioea, snipe, whaup 6. marlin 7. bustard 8. whimbrel

curlewlike... 6. godwit 9. sandpiper

curly... 4. wavy 5. kinky, oundy (obs) 6. crispy, frizzy, kinked 8. crinkled

curmudgeon... 4. crab 5. churl, miser 7. niggard 8. tightwad 9. skinflint

currant... 3. red 5. berry, Ribes 6. raisin, rizzar (rizzart)

currency... 5. money, scrip 6. dinero 9. publicity 10. greenbacks, popularity, prevalence 15. fashionableness

current... 4. eddy, flow, race (water), rife, tide 5. draft, going, rapid, trend, usual 6. course, stream 7. present, topical 8. existent 9. direction, prevalent 11. fashionable

current regulator...
electric.. 9. rheometer

12. galvanometer
physiology.. 11. hematometer
curriculum... 7. courses, studies, Three R's 8. curricle
curry... 4. comb, cook, drub 5. dress, groom 6. cajole 9. condiment
curry favor... 6. cajole 7. flatter, smoodge (smooge), wheedle
curse... 3. ban 4. bane, damn, oath 5. swear 7. bewitch, malison 8. anathema, execrate 9. blaspheme 10. affliction 11. imprecation, malediction 13. excommunicate
cursed... 6. damned, odious, wicked 7. hateful 8. damnable, shrewish 9. execrable 12. cantankerous
Cursores... 5. birds (long–legged) 7. spiders (wolf)
Cursoria... 6. mantes (mantis) 10. Orthoptera 11. cockroaches
cursory... 5. hasty 6. fitful, roving, slight 7. passing 8. careless, rambling 9. desultory, irregular 10. evanescent 12. disconnected, unmethodical
curt... 4. buff 5. bluff, brief, brusk, gruff, short, terse 6. abrupt 7. brusque, concise, curtate, laconic 9. condensed
curtail... 3. lop 4. crop, dock, pare, slip 5. short 6. lessen, reduce 7. abridge, shorten 8. compress, decrease, diminish, retrench
curtain... 4. mask, veil 5. drape, shade 6. coster (altar), encore, purdah, riddel, screen, shadow, shield 7. drapery, secrecy, shelter, vitrage 8. portiere
curtsy, curtsey... 3. bow, nod 4. bend 6. kowtow, salaam 12. genuflection
curvature... 3. arc, bow 4. arch, bend 5. plane, sinus 6. camber 7. arching, curving, evolute 8. aduncity, cyrtosis, lordosis, vaulting 9. curvation 11. convolution
curve... 3. arc, bow, ess 4. arch, bend, ogee, turn 5. crook, polar 6. spiral, toroid 7. cissoid, evolute, flexure 8. extrados, parabola, sinusoid 9. curvature, sinuosity
curved (pert to)...
arch.. 8. arciform, arcuated
glass.. 4. lens
inward.. 5. adunc 8. aduncous
molding.. 4. ogee
planking (ship's).. 3. sny
process.. 5. hamus (Zool)
roundabout.. 10. circuitous
staircase.. 8. caracole
wedge.. 3. cam
curvet... 4. leap 5. bound, caper, frisk, prank 6. frolic, gambol
cush... 3. cow 5. money 7. cookery, sorghum
Cush (pert to)...
father.. 3. Ham
land of.. 8. Ethiopia 10. land of Cush
son.. 4. Seba 6. Nimrod
cushion... 3. pad 4. mute, seat 6. ignore, pillow, sachet 7. brioche, conceal, dashpot, muffler 8. plantula,

pulvinus, suppress, swelling (Queen Mary's) 9. pulvillus 10. pincushion
cusk... 4. fish (codlike), tusk 5. torsk 6. burbot
cusp... 3. end, tip 4. apex, peak 5. crown, point 6. cantle, corner 8. paracone
custard... 4. flan 7. charlet, pudding
custard apple... 4. tree 5. papaw 8. sweetsop
custodian... 5. guard 6. bailee, jailer, keeper, warden, warder 7. curator, janitor 8. curatrix, guardian
custody... 4. care, keep 5. trust 6. charge 8. guidance 10. protection 12. guardianship, jurisdiction
custom... 3. fad, law, mos, use 4. mode, wont 5. habit, mores, usage, vogue 7. fashion 8. practice 9. patronage, tradition 10. consuetude, consuetudo
customary... 5. usual 6. wonted 7. general, usitate 8. habitual, orthodox 11. traditional 12. conventional
customs... 4. duty 5. mores, taxes
cut... 3. bob, lob, lop, mow, nip, rip 4. blow, chop, crop, dock, edit, fell, gash, hack, make, mode, nick, open, pain, pare, reap, slit, snee, snip, snub, trim 5. canal, carve, cleft, lance, notch, piece, plate, scarp, sever, share, shear, shorn, slash, slice, slish (Shak), snick, split, vogue 6. dilute, furrow, injury, mangle, reduce, trench 7. affront, curtail, engrave, offense, sectile, serrate, truancy, whittle 8. discount, excision, incision 9. engraving, indignity, reduction 10. adulterate
cut (pert to)...
and furrow.. 7. chamfer
and polish.. 8. lapidate
and weave.. 5. plash
back.. 6. polled 7. shorten
capable of being.. 7. sectile
down.. 5. razee
fine.. 5. mince
in.. 7. intrude 9. interpose, interrupt, introduce
in half.. 9. dimidiate
in squares.. 6. dice
into.. 6. incise
jaggedly.. 4. snag
out.. 6. excide, excise
up.. 6. frolic, grieve 9. apportion, misbehave
vertically.. 5. scarp, slice
with shears.. 4. snip 5. shirl
cutaneous... 4. skin 6. dermal, dermic
cute... 4. keen 5. peart, sharp 6. brainy, clever, dainty, pretty, shrewd 7. cunning 10. attractive 11. picturesque
cuticle... 4. skin 5. cutin, cutis 8. membrane, pellicle 9. epidermis, scarfskin 10. integument
cut of beef... 4. loin, ribs, rump 5. chine, roast, steak 6. corned, cutlet, rosbif, saddle 7. brisket, icebone 8. shoulder 9. aitchbone, roundbone

cut off ... 3. bob 4. crop, dock, drib, snip 5. elide, pared, roach (Naut) 6. bereft, bobbed, divest, lopped, screen 7. abscind, abscise, clipped, deprive, severed 8. amputate 9. amputated, apocopate, intercept 10. disinherit

cut off (pert to) ...
by bits .. 4. drib
edges (coins) .. 3. nig
on slant .. 4. bias 5. bevel, miter
short .. 3. bob 4. crop
syllable .. 5. elide
with die .. 4. dink
wool .. 3. dod (dodd)

cut short ... 3. bob, lop 4. crop, dock, halt, stop 5. check 6. arrest 7. clipped, cropped, curtail, shorten 9. terminate

cutter ... 4. boat 5. knife, sloop, tooth 6. sleigh, vessel 7. incisor

cutting ... 4. cold, slip, tart 5. piece, scion, sharp 6. biting, secant, severe 7. caustic, incisal, satiric, sectile 8. chilling, piercing 9. sarcastic, severance, trenchant 10. separating 11. penetrating 12. adulteration

cutting (pert to) ...
diamonds (imperfect) .. 4. bort
edge .. 5. blade
in two .. 6. secant
last letter of word .. 7. apocope
off .. 7. apocope 10. abscission, amputation
tool .. 3. axe (ax), bit 4. adze 5. razor 6. chisel
wit .. 6. satire

cuttle ... 4. thug 5. knife 7. ruffian 8. assassin 9. swaggerer

cuttlebone ... 7. osselet

cuttlefish ... 5. Sepia, squid 7. mollusk, octopus

cuttlefish secretion ... 3. ink (black)

cuttyhunk ... 11. fishing line

Cyclades Islands (Gr) ... (200 in all) 3. Ios 5. Delos (smallest), Melos, Naros, Paros, Tenos, Thera 6. Andros 7. Amorgos, Myconus

cycle ... 3. Age, eon, era 4. aeon 5. orbit, recur, saros (Astron), wheel 6. course, period, series 7. bicycle, circuit 8. electric, tricycle 9. Arthurian 10. revolution 12. Carlovingian (Charlemagne)

cyclone ... 5. storm 6. baguio 7. tornado, twister, typhoon 9. hurricane

cyclopean ... 4. huge, vast 7. massive, one–eyed 8. gigantic

Cyclops (pert to) ...
assistant to .. 6. Vulcan (Fire God)
father .. 6. Uranus
forger of .. 12. thunderbolts
home .. 6. Sicily (Mt Etna)
oddity .. 7. one–eyed
race (Myth) .. 6. giants

cygneous ... 8. swanlike

cygnet ... 4. swan

cylinder ... 4. drum, pipe, roll, tube 5. inker, stele 6. barrel, gabion, platen, record, roller, rounce, terete 10. cylindroid

cylindrical ... 5. conic 6. terete 7. tubular

cymbal, cymbals ... 3. tal, zel 6. Becken, piatti 7. potlids 8. doughnut

Cymric ... 5. Welsh 9. Brythonic

Cymric (pert to) ...
bard .. 6. Merlin 7. Aneurin
god of the dead .. 5. Pwyll
god of the sky .. 7. Gwydion
god of the sun .. 4. Lleu
god of the waves .. 5. Dylan

cynic ... 5. Timon 7. ascetic, doglike, egotist, snarler 9. pessimist 11. misanthrope

Cynic (pert to) ...
pupil .. 8. Socrates
school .. 10. Philosophy
teacher .. 8. Diogenes
teaching .. 6. virtue

cynical ... 7. currish 8. captious, snarling 9. sarcastic 11. pessimistic 12. misanthropic

cynosure ... 5. guide 8. lodestar (loadstar), polestar 9. celebrity, North Star 13. constellation

cyprinoid (fish) ... 2. id 3. ide, orf (orfe) 4. bass (black), carp, chub, dace 6. chevin, shiner 7. herring (lake) 8. fallfish 9. hornyhead, squawfish

Cyprus ...
capital .. 7. Nicosia (Sicily)
colonizer (anc) .. 11. Phoenicians
history .. 11. New Stone Age
mountain .. 7. Troodos
port .. 7. Lornaca 8. Limassol 9. Famagusto

Cyrenaic (pert to) ...
city .. 6. Cyrene
country .. 9. Cyrenaica (Afr)
division of .. 5. Libya
harbor .. 6. Tobruk 7. Bengazi
philosophy .. 8. hedonism, pleasure

Cyrene ... 4. city (anc) 5. nymph 7. goddess

cyrus ... 5. crane, sarus

Cyrus the Elder (pert to) ...
conqueror of .. 7. Babylon
founder of .. 6. Persia (Empire)
king of .. 5. Lydia, Media
subduer of .. 9. Palestine

cyst ... 3. box, sac, wen 5. chest, pouch 7. vesicle

Czar ... 4. Ivan, tsar, tzar 5. Peter 8. Nicholas

Czechoslovakia ...
capital .. 6. Prague (Praha)
city .. 5. Praha 6. Pilsen 7. Ostrava 10. Bratislava
empire (anc) .. 7. Bohemia, Moravia 8. Slovakia
forest .. 12. Great Bohemia
mountain, peak .. 3. Ore 6. Tatras 11. Carpathians
people .. 6. Czechs 7. Slovaks
river .. 4. Elbe (Labe), Iser, Oder 6. Vltava

cziganny ... 5. gypsy

D

D... 3. 500 6. letter (4th)
dab... 3. hit, tap 4. blow 5. paint,
smear 6. expert, lizard, smooth
7. dabster 8. flatfish
dabble... 4. mass 5. dally 6. befoul,
meddle, paddle, potter, splash,
tamper, trifle 7. spatter 8. sprinkle
dabbler... 7. trifler 8. sciolist
10. dilettante
dabchick... 5. grebe 9. gallinule
dacha (Russ)... 5. villa 12. country
house
dacoit... 6. bandit, robber
dacry, dacryo (comb form)... 5. tears
dactyl... 3. toe 4. foot 6. finger
8. dactylus
dactyliomancy... 17. divination by
rings (finger)
dactylogram... 11. fingerprint
dactylology... 12. sign language
Dadaism... 4. cult 8. negation
daddy-longlegs... 5. stilt 6. curlew,
spider, Tipula 7. spinner
daedal, dedal... 4. rich 6. varied
8. artistic, skillful (skilful)
9. ingenious, intricate 10. variegated
Daedalus (Gr Myth)... 9. artificer
daffodil... 6. yellow 9. narcissus
10. bellflower
daffy, daft... 3. gay, mad 4. wild
5. batty, crazy, giddy, goofy, loony
6. insane 7. foolish, idiotic
Dagda (pert to)...
  children.. 6. Aengus (Angus), Brigit
  famed as.. 7. harpist
  Gaelic name.. 7. Jupiter
  god of.. 10. pagan Irish
dagger... 4. dirk, kris, snee 5. kalar
6. anlace, bodkin, creese 7. bayonet,
poniard 10. misericord
Daibutsu (pert to)...
  famed image.. 6. Buddha
  Japanese Bronze.. 11. Great Buddha
  site.. 8. Kamakura (near Tokyo)
daily... 4. a day 7. diurnal, journal
9. hodiurnal, newspaper, quotidian
11. day in day out
daily food... 4. fare 5. bread
10. livelihood 11. subsistence,
substenance
dainties... 5. cates, estes 7. titbits
(tidbits)
dainty... 4. fair, fine, rare 5. frail,
small 6. choice, pretty, select
8. elegance 9. exquisite, toothsome
10. fastidious
dairy... 4. farm 8. creamery
9. lactarium
dairymen caste (Ind)... 4. Ahir

dais... 5. stage, table 7. estrade
8. platform
daisy... 5. gowan, oxeye 6. morgan,
Shasta 7. Gerbera 9. Whiteweed
dale... 4. dell, dene, vale 5. spout
6. dingle, ravine, trough, valley
dalles... 5. dells 11. canyon walls
dalliance... 4. chat 5. delay 6. gossip,
trifle 8. fondling, trifling 10. flirtation
dally... 3. toy 5. tarry 6. dawdle,
linger 13. procrastinate
Dalmatia...
  capital.. 7. Spalato (Yugoslavia)
  cherry.. 7. marasca
  coast.. 8. Adriatic
  dog.. 5. coach 8. carriage
  home of.. 10. Diocletian
  people.. 5. Serbs 8. Adriatic
    9. Yugoslavs
  product.. 4. lace
dam... 4. stay, stem, stop, weir
5. Aswan, block, check, choke,
Gatun (CZ) 6. Hoover (Boulder),
mother, Norris, parent 7. barrier
8. millpond, obstruct, Oroville,
restrain 9. Roosevelt 10. Bull Shoals,
Glen Canyon 11. Grand Coulee
damage... 3. mar 4. harm, hurt, loss,
noxa 6. impair, injury, mayhem,
scathe, strafe 8. disserve, sabotage
9. detriment, vandalism
10. impairment
daman... 4. cony (Bib) 5. Hyrax
6. mammal 8. Procavia
Damascus, Syria (pert to)...
  Bib scene.. 20. Street Called Straight
  division.. 6. Jewish, Moslem
    9. Christian
  history.. 16. world's oldest city
    (inhabited)
  mosque (renowned).. 7. Ommiade
  river.. 5. Abana 6. Barada
damask... 3. red (color) 5. cloth, steel
(Damascus) 8. to deface (the Great
Seal, Eng)
dame... 4. lady, Miss 5. Madam, title
6. matron, Nature, parent
damn... 4. cuss, ruin 5. abuse, curse
6. shucks 7. accurse, condemn,
swear at
damsel... 4. girl, lass 5. Rhoda (Bib),
wench 7. colleen 10. damoiselle
dance... 4. jazz, prom, skip, trip
5. frisk, glide 6. cavort, frolic,
gambol 7. flicker, flutter, rejoice,
saltate 10. tripudiate
dance (pert to)...
  art.. 12. choreography
  clumsily.. 6. balter
  mimetic (Rom).. 5. Salii 7. Luperci

146

8. Curetics
movement.. **6**. chassé, gestic
7. saltant **9**. pirouette
step.. **3**. pas **5**. coupe **6**. chassé
7. gambado (gambade), shuffle
8. glissade **9**. arabesque, grapevine
10. pigeonwing
dance (type)... **3**. bal, hop, jig, toe
4. ball, clog, haka, kolo, polo, reel,
shag **5**. gavot (gavotte), pavan,
polka, tango, waltz **6**. althea, apache,
ballet, bolero, cancan, corant, maxixe,
minuet, morris, redowa, rhumba
(rumba), shimmy, square, watusi
7. beguine, coranto (old), courant,
foxtrot, gavotte, hoedown, mazurka,
one–step, ridotto, tempete, two–step
8. bunny hug, cakewalk, courante,
fandango, halliard (anc), hornpipe,
lanciers, rigadoon **9**. allemande (anc),
butterfly, farandole, polonaise,
quadrille **10**. Charleston, tarantella
11. schottische (schottish)
dancer... **6**. hoofer **7**. danseur
8. coryphee, danseuse, stripper
9. ballerina, ecdysiast, jitterbug
11. terpsichore **13**. choreographer
dancer (pert to)...
Bib.. **6**. Salome
Egyptian.. **4**. alme (almeh) **7**. ghawazi
8. Baramika
Japanese.. **6**. geisha (girl)
Oriental.. **4**. hula **6**. nautch
8. bayadere
dancing (pert to)...
arrangement.. **12**. choreography
Muse of.. **11**. Terpsichore
term.. **6**. ballet, chassé, gestic
7. hoofing, saltant
dandelion... **4**. herb **5**. plant **6**. yellow
9. Taraxacum
dandified... **7**. foppish
dandify... **6**. spruce **7**. adonize,
smarten **8**. titivate (tittivate)
dandy... **3**. fop **4**. beau, dude, good,
toff **5**. daisy **6**. Adonis **7**. coxcomb
9. exquisite **11**. Beau Brummel
dangerous... **3**. bad **4**. dire **5**. feral,
risky **6**. chancy **7**. ominous, parlous
8. alarming, critical, insecure,
perilous **9**. hazardous **10**. jeopardous,
precarious
dangle... **3**. lop **4**. hang, loll, yawl
5. droop, swing **6**. flaunt, mizzen
Daniel (pert to)...
Bib.. **4**. Book (Old Test) **7**. prophet
(Heb)
form of verse.. **7**. lyrical, sestina
verse adopted by.. **5**. Dante
8. Petrarch
Danish... see also *Denmark*
capital.. **10**. Copenhagen
council (anc).. **8**. Rigsraad
country.. **7**. Denmark
doctor.. **6**. Finsen
export.. **8**. cryolite
fiord.. **3**. Ise
flag.. **9**. Dannebrog
island.. **3**. Als (Alsen) **5**. Faroe
9. Greenland
King (anc).. **6**. Canute
native.. **4**. Dane **12**. Scandinavian

parliament.. **7**. Rigsdag
prince (legend).. **6**. Hamlet
settlers in Ireland.. **6**. Ostmen
dank... **3**. wet **4**. damp **5**. humid,
moist, muggy
Dan McGrew... **11**. Hound of Hell
danseuse... **7**. danseur **8**. coryphee
9. ballerina
Dante (pert to)...
birthplace.. **8**. Florence
famed as.. **4**. poet **6**. lyrist
famed poem.. **12**. Divine Comedy
poem's companion.. **6**. Vergil (Virgil)
poem's division.. **4**. Hell **6**. Heaven
9. Purgatory
poem's love.. **8**. Beatrice
Danube River (pert to)...
end.. **8**. Black Sea
source.. **11**. Black Forest
tributary.. **4**. Isar, Raab **5**. Drava
6. Morava
Danubian (pert to)...
color.. **5**. green
fish.. **6**. huchen (huch)
goose.. **10**. Sevastopol
Danzig...
Polish name.. **6**. Gdansk
river site.. **7**. Vistula
Sea.. **6**. Baltic
territory of (now).. **6**. Poland
dap... **3**. bob, dab, dib, dip
6. bounce, dibble, guddle **7**. rebound
Daphne (pert to)...
Bib.. **4**. Park (Antioch, Syria)
father.. **5**. Ladon **6**. Peneus
lover.. **6**. Apollo
transformation.. **10**. laurel tree
dapper... **4**. braw, neat, pert, trim
5. natty, sleek **6**. jaunty, little, lively,
spruce **7**. dashing, finical
dappled... **6**. dotted **7**. flecked,
piebald, spotted
dare... **4**. daze, defy, face, osse, risk
5. brave **6**. assume, dazzle
7. venture **8**. confront, defiance,
paralyze **9**. challenge, undertake
daring... **4**. bold, rash **5**. brave, manly
8. boldness, defiance **9**. audacious,
foolhardy **11**. adventurous,
venturesome **12**. enterprising
dark... **3**. dim, mum, sad **4**. ebon
5. black, blind, dense, faint, mirky,
murky, night, unlit, vague **6**. closed,
gloomy, occult, opaque, secret,
wicked **7**. joyless, melanic, obscure,
stygian **8**. abstruse, ignorant,
moonless **9**. ambiguous, atrocious,
Cimmerian (realm), lightless, nightfall,
tenebrous, uncertain **10**. foreboding,
indistinct
dark (pert to)...
Ages.. **6**. Middle **8**. Medieval
9. Neolithic
Continent.. **6**. Africa (formerly)
10. unexplored
horse.. **7**. unknown **9**. candidate
hue.. **5**. dusky, swart **6**. somber
7. swarthy
moon area.. **4**. mare
darken... **3**. dim **4**. dull **5**. blind,
umber **6**. darkle, sadden, shadow
7. becloud, blacken, confuse, eclipse,

enshade 8. bewilder 9. obfuscate

darkness... 4. dark, dusk, mirk, murk
5. shade 6. Erebus, shadow
7. dimness, tenebra 9. blackness,
blindness, ignorance, obscurity
10. opaqueness

darling... 2. jo 3. pet 4. dear, idol,
lief 5. cheri, sweet 6. minion
7. acushla, beloved 8. favorite
9. mavournin 10. mavourneen,
sweetheart 13. cushlamochree
(cushlamachree)

darnel... 4. tare, weed 5. grass
6. Lolium

dart... 4. barb, bolt, flit, leap, vire
5. arrow, bound, lance, scoot, shoot,
start, throw 6. dartle, elance, glance,
spring, weapon 7. javelin, missile,
stinger 8. jaculate

Darwinism... 9. Evolution (theory,
1858) 12. Evolutionism

das, dasse... 6. badger

dash... 4. code, élan, gift, race, ruin,
rush, slam 5. ardor, crash, haste,
onset, plash, smash, speed, swash
6. energy, obelus (anc), spirit, sprint,
strike, stroke 7. bravura, spatter,
splurge 8. confound, gratuity
9. animation 11. punctuation

dashing... 3. gay 4. fast 5. showy
6. dapper, jaunty, sporty 7. stylish

dastardly... 4. base, foul 6. craven
8. cowardly

data... 5. facts, logic 7. grounds (for
facts) 11. information

date... 3. age 4. line (newspaper),
time 5. fruit, tryst 6. person
10. engagement 11. appointment

date (pert to)...
birth.. 5. natal
coin line.. 7. exergue
error.. 11. anachronism
fruit of.. 4. palm
plum.. 6. sapote

daub... 3. dab 4. blob, gaum, soil,
teer 5. paint, smear, stain, sully
6. bedaub 7. besmear, picture (art),
plaster 8. scribble

daughter... 5. child 7. cadette
9. offspring 10. descendant

daughter of...
Inachus (river god).. 2. Io
Night.. 7. Nemesis
the moon.. 7. Nokomis
the Spanish king.. 7. infanta

daunt... 3. awe, cow 4. faze 5. amate
(anc) 6. dismay, subdue 7. overawe,
repress 10. discourage, dishearten,
intimidate

dauntless... 4. bold 7. aweless
(awless) 8. fearless, intrepid, resolute
9. dreadless 11. unfaltering

davenport... 3. bed 4. desk, sofa
5. divan 12. Chesterfield

David (Bib)...
daughter.. 5. Tamar
father.. 5. Jesse
helpers.. 4. Igal 5. Abner
7. Shammah
king of.. 6. Israel (40 years)
slayer of.. 7. Goliath
son.. 7. Solomon

wife.. 7. Abigail

davit... 4. spar 5. crane

dawdle... 3. lag 4. idle, poke, toit
5. dally 6. linger, loiter, potter, trifle
9. vacillate 10. dillydally
13. procrastinate

dawn... 2. eo (comb form) 3. Eos
(goddess), red 4. morn 5. sunup
6. appear, aurora, sink in 7. sunrise
8. daybreak 9. beginning, penetrate

day (pert to)...
Athenians, Jews.. 6. sunset
Babylonians.. 7. sunrise
blindness.. 10. nyctalopia
11. hemeralopia
divisions.. 5. lunar, solar 8. sidereal
dream.. 4. muse 5. fancy 7. fantasy,
reverie 8. phantasy
Egyptians, Romans.. 8. midnight
god.. 5. Horus
nursery.. 6. crèche
scholar.. 7. externe

Day of...
Atonement.. 9. Yom Kippur
Brahma.. 9. Maha Yugas
doom.. 8. Judgment

day's march... 5. étape

day's work... 4. darg (dargue)

daze... 3. fog 4. asea, maze, stun
5. sopor, swoon 6. benumb, dazzle,
stupid, trance 7. confuse, stupefy
8. bewilder 9. dumbfound
12. razzle–dazzle

dazzling... 6. bright, garish 7. glaring
8. blinding, gorgeous 9. beautiful,
brilliant 11. bewildering

dead... 3. fey 4. flat, numb, obit
5. amort, blind, inert, napoo, passé
6. active, barren, lapsed 7. defunct,
expired, insipid, tedious 8. ad patres,
complete, deceased, inactive, lifeless,
obsolete 9. apathetic, inanimate
10. lusterless, motionless, spiritless,
unexciting 11. nonexistent

dead (pert to)...
Dead Sea apple.. 12. Apple of
Sodom
Dead Sea country.. 4. Moab
5. Sodom 8. Gomorrah
language.. 5. Latin
rise from the.. 7. resurge
9. reanimate, resurrect
set (slang).. 8. full tilt, hell–bent
tree.. 7. rampike (rampick)

deaden... 4. damp, dull, mute, numb
6. muffle, obtund, opiate, weaken
7. relieve, repress 8. enfeeble
10. devitalize

deadly... 4. dire, mort 5. fatal
6. lethal, mortal 7. deathly
8. venomous 10. implacable,
lifelessly 11. destructive, internecine

deaf... 4. surd 7. earless
10. intolerant 11. inattentive,
preoccupied

deaf alphabet... 11. dactylology
12. sign language

deaf and dumb... 9. surdomute
10. deaf–mutism 11. surdimutism

deafness... 6. amusia (tone) 7. surdity
13. insensibility

deafness operation... 8. fenestra

deal... 3. lot 4. dole, give, mede,
mete, sale, sell 5. allot, share, trade,
treat 6. parcel 7. dispose, portion,
wrestle 8. business, dispense,
quantity 9. apportion, entertain
10. administer, distribute
dealer (pert to)...
cattle.. 6. drover, herder
cloth.. 6. draper, mercer
drug.. 8. druggist 10. apothecary,
pharmacist 14. pharmacopolist
retail.. 6. grocer, monger 8. merchant
9. tradesman
stock exchange.. 6. broker, jobber,
trader 11. stockbroker
dean, dene... 4. dell 6. valley
dean... 4. head, Inge 5. decan, doyen
6. fellow (Educ), master, senior,
verger 7. officer 9. churchman,
principal
dear... 5. chere, cheri, deary, lover,
sugar, sweet 7. beloved, darling
8. precious 9. expensive
10. sweetheart
dearth... 4. want 6. famine, rarity
7. paucity, poverty 8. rareness,
scarcity, sparsity
death... 4. doom, mort, obit 5. sleep
(eternal) 6. demise 7. decease,
passing, quietus, release
10. euthanasia (mercy), expiration
11. evanishment
death (pert to)...
after.. 10. posthumous
eternal.. 9. perdition
foreboding.. 6. funest 7. doleful
lawless.. 8. lynching
notice.. 4. obit 5. orbit 8. obituary
of a deity.. 4. Mors
rattle.. 4. rale
stoning (by).. 8. lapidate
deathlessness... 9. athanasis
11. immortality 15. everlastingness
debacle... 4. rout 5. crash, flood
7. washout 8. collapse, stampede
9. breakdown, cataclysm
11. catastrophe, destruction
debar... 3. bar 4. deny 5. estop
6. forbid, hinder, refuse 7. exclude
8. obstruct, preclude, prohibit
debark... 4. land 8. go ashore
9. disembark
debase... 5. abase, alloy, lower
6. demean, demote, reduce
7. corrupt, degrade, deprave
8. disgrace 10. adulterate, depreciate
11. deteriorate
debasement... 8. demotion
9. abasement, abjection, reduction,
vitiation 11. degradation
13. deterioration
debatable... 4. moot 9. refutable
10. disputable 11. contestable
13. controversial
debate... 4. agon (anc), moot
5. argue, forum, plead, weigh
6. reason 7. analyze, closure,
cloture, dispute, wrangle
8. argument, consider, forensic,
militate 9. quodlibet 10. deliberate,
discussion 11. controversy
12. deliberation, dissertation
13. argumentation
debauch... 4. bout, orgy 5. broil,
spree, taint 6. defile, seduce, splore
7. mislead 8. carousal, escapade
9. disaffect, dissipate
11. contaminate
debauchee... 4. rake, roué 5. satyr
7. rounder 9. libertine 10. profligate
debenture (Finan)... 4. bond 5. claim
6. pledge 7. voucher 10. instrument
11. certificate
debilitated... 4. weak 5. seedy
6. feeble, infirm, sapped, sickly
7. languid 8. asthenic, impaired,
weakened 9. enfeebled, langorous
11. devitalized
debility... 5. atony 7. languor
8. adynamia, asthenia, cachexia,
weakness 9. infirmity, lassitude
10. feebleness, sickliness
debit... 4. debt 5. entry 6. charge
debonair, debonaire... 4. airy
5. suave 6. breezy, jaunty, urbane
7. affable, buoyant 8. carefree
debris... 4. junk 5. attle, ruins, scrap,
talus, trash 6. litter, refuse, rubble
7. deposit, remains, rubbish
8. detritus 10. clamjamfry
debt... 3. due, IOU, sin (Bib)
7. arrears, default 8. trespass
9. arrearage, liability 10. obligation
debut... 3. bow 8. entrance (formal)
9. coming out 12. introduction,
presentation
debutante... 3. bud, deb 6. subdeb
9. socialite
decade... 3. ten 9. decennium
decadence... 5. decay 7. decline
13. deterioration, retrogression
decamp... 4. flee 6. depart
7. abscond, vamoose
12. absquatulate
decanter... 4. ewer 5. croft 6. bottle,
carafe, vessel (liquors)
decapod... 4. crab 5. prawn 6. shrimp
7. Homarus, lobster 8. Decapoda
10. crustacean
decay... 3. rot 4. blet, doty 5. spoil,
waste 6. caries, wither 7. crumble,
mortify, putrefy 8. spoilage
9. decadence, decompose
11. deteriorate, dissolution
13. decomposition, deterioration
deceased... 4. dead, gone, late 6. at
rest 7. defunct, demised
8. decedent, departed
deceit... 5. covin, craft, fraud, guile,
guise 7. cunning 8. artifice,
cozenage, intrigue, subtlety, trickery,
wiliness 9. chicanery, deception,
duplicity, imposture, mendacity,
sophistry, treachery 10. craftiness,
sneakiness 13. deceitfulness,
dissimulation 14. tergiversation
15. treacherousness
deceitful... 4. wily 5. false 6. artful,
crafty, sneaky, tricky 8. guileful,
scheming, trickish 9. deceptive,
gnathonic, insincere 10. fraudulent
11. treacherous 13. Machiavellian
deceive... 3. cog, lie 4. bilk, dupe,
flam, fool, gull, hoax, sile 5. cheat,

cozen, elude, hocus, trick, troil
6. baffle, delude, illude, seduce
7. beguile, mislead 8. hoodwink
deceiver... 3. gay 5. cheat 6. hoaxer,
trepan (trapan) 8. betrayer, impostor
9. trickster
decency... 7. decorum, fitness,
modesty 8. chastity, niceness
9. propriety 10. seemliness
12. tastefulness
decent... 4. kind 6. comely, kindly,
proper, seemly 7. clothed
8. adequate, gracious, suitable,
tasteful 9. tolerable
deception... 3. lie 4. hoax, wile
5. cheat, fraud, guile 6. deceit,
misled 7. fallacy 8. artifice, deceived,
flimflam, illusion 9. duplicity,
imposture
deceptive... 5. vague 8. illusive,
illusory 9. deceiving, sirenical (sirenic)
10. fallacious
decide (upon)... 3. opt 4. vote
5. adapt, elect, judge 6. choose,
settle 7. referee, resolve 9. arbitrate,
ascertain, determine, influence
decima... 4. stop (organ) 5. tenth,
tithe 8. interval
decimal... 3. ten 5. tenth 7. tenfold
8. repetend
decimate... 3. few 4. kill, slay
5. burke, tenth 6. divide 7. destroy
8. subtract 9. devastate, slaughter
decipher... 4. read 5. crack
6. decode, detect 7. unravel
8. discover 9. translate
decision... 4. grit 5. arret, nerve,
pluck 6. mettle, report 7. verdict
8. firmness 10. conclusion,
resolution, settlement
12. announcement 13. determination
decisive... 3. end 5. final 7. certain,
crucial 8. critical, resolute
9. mandatory 10. conclusive,
convincing
decisive moment... 6. crisis
deck (ship's)... 3. gun 4. main, poop
5. orlop, upper 6. bridge 7. scupper
(gutter) 8. hatchway, platform
9. promenade 10. forecastle
deck... 4. gild 5. adorn, array, cards
(playing), equip 6. blazon, clothe,
enrich 7. bedizen, dress up
8. emblazon
declaim... 4. rant, rave 5. orate, spiel,
spout 6. herald, recite 8. denounce,
harangue, perorate 9. discourse
11. declamation
declamation... 7. lecture 9. elocution
10. recitation
declaration... 3. vow 4. oath
6. avowal, decree, oracle 8. pleading
(law) 9. assertion, manifesto,
testimony 10. confession (of faith)
11. affirmation 12. proclamation
13. pronouncement
declare... 3. say 4. aver, avow, meld
5. bruit, state 6. affirm, allege,
assert, blazon, herald, spread
7. publish 8. announce, indicate,
maintain 9. advertise
declare (pert to)...

against.. 6. indict
as fact.. 5. posit
innocent.. 6. acquit
declension... 4. drop, fall 5. slope
7. decline, descent, refusal
10. inflection 13. deterioration
decline... 3. dip, ebb, set 4. fade, fail,
fall, flag, sink, wane 5. droop, repel,
slope, slump, stoop 6. refuse, reject,
weaken 7. dwindle 8. decrease,
downhill 9. decadence, declivity,
repudiate 10. retrograde
12. depreciation
declivity... 3. dip 4. drop, hill
5. scarp, slope 7. descent
8. downgate 9. downgrade
decoction... 4. sapa (sape) 6. apozem,
cremor, tisane 7. boiling
10. extraction 11. preparation
decompose... 3. rot 4. frit 5. decay
7. resolve 10. photolysis
12. disintegrate
decorate... 4. deck, trim 5. adorn,
honor 6. emboss 7. bedizen,
brocade, miniate 8. beautify,
ornament 9. scrimshaw
decorated... 5. fancy 6. ornate
7. adorned 8. nielloed 9. sigillate
(pottery) 11. embellished
decoration... 4. buhl 5. gutta (anc),
medal 6. plaque, purfle, ribbon
7. epergne, festoon, garnish 8. gold
star, ornament, trimming
9. adornment, garniture, sgraffito
10. cordon bleu, emblazonry,
embroidery
decorous... 4. calm, prim 5. grave,
quiet, staid 6. decent, demure,
modest, proper, sedate, seemly,
serene 7. fitting, regular, settled
8. becoming, composed, suitable,
tasteful 9. unruffled 12. conventional
decorticate... 4. bark, flay, husk, pare,
peel, skin 5. strip 9. excoriate
decoy... 4. bait, lure, tole 6. capper,
entrap 8. by–bidder 9. come–on man
11. stool pigeon
decrease... 3. ebb 4. drop, sink, wane
5. abate, waste 6. decess, lessen,
reduce, shrink 7. decline, dwindle,
shorten, slacken, subside
8. compress, diminish, moderate
9. abatement, deduction, deflation,
lessening 10. diminution
11. contraction 12. depreciation
decree... 3. act, law 4. bull, fiat, rede
(anc), will 5. arret, canon, edict,
enact, irade, order, ukase 6. dictum,
ordain 7. command, mandate, verdict
8. decision, rescript 9. ordinance
decree beforehand... 7. destine
decree nisi... 7. divorce
decrepit... 3. old 4. aged, lame, weak
6. infirm, senile, wasted (with age)
7. worn out 8. unstable, unsturdy
decry... 3. boo 4. slur 5. lower
7. condemn, degrade, detract
8. belittle, denounce, derogate
9. discredit, disparage, underrate
10. depreciate, undervalue
dedal... see *daedal*
dedicate... 6. devote, hallow

7. address 8. inscribe
10. consecrate
deduce... 5. infer 6. deduct, derive,
elicit, evolve 7. suppose
deduct... 4. bate, faik, take 6. remove
8. discount, retrench, separate,
subtract
deduction... 6. rebate 7. reprise
8. discount, illation 9. allowance,
corollary, induction, inference,
reasoning, syllogism
deed... 3. act, ado 4. feat, fiat, gest
(geste) 5. actum, actus, stunt, title
6. action, doings 7. exploit
8. contract, tenendum
11. achievement, malefaction,
performance
deem... 5. judge, opine, think
6. esteem, regard 7. believe,
presume, suppose 8. conclude,
consider 10. adjudicate
deemed... 7. assumed, reputed
8. adjudged, inferred, presumed,
supposed 10. considered
deep... 3. low, pit 4. rich, wide, wise
5. great 6. hidden, remote, solemn
7. learned, obscure, serious
8. immersed, involved, powerful,
profound 9. engrossed, entangled,
sagacious 10. deep–seated,
mysterious
deep (pert to)...
dish pie.. 7. cobbler
sea.. 6. depths
seated.. 8. habitual 9. ingrained
11. established
sleep.. 5. sopor
sound.. 4. bell, gong
deepen... 5. lower 6. dredge
7. broaden, enhance 9. aggravate,
intensify 10. strengthen
deer... 3. elk, red, roe 4. buck, fawn,
hart, hind, maha, stag 5. eland,
moose, ratwa 6. fallow, sambar,
wapiti 7. caribou, deerlet, roebuck
8. reindeer, ruminant
deer (pert to)...
antler.. 3. dag 4. snag 8. tres–tine
(royal)
Asiatic.. 6. sambar
barking.. 7. muntjac (muntjak)
deerlike.. 10. chevrotain
female.. 3. doe, roe 4. hind
genus.. 4. Dama 6. Cervus
8. Cervidae
Japanese.. 4. sika
Java.. 4. napu 7. muntjac (muntjak)
Lapland.. 8. reindeer
male.. 4. buck, hart, stag 6. havier
7. brocket (brok), pricket
meat.. 7. venison
mouse.. 7. plandok
Oriental.. 4. axis, Rusa 5. kakar
6. chital, rativa, sambar 7. kanchil,
muntjac (muntjak)
Russian.. 4. olen
S American.. 4. pita 6. guemal
(guemul) 7. brocket, spitter
Tibet.. 4. shou
tiger.. 6. cougar
tracks.. 3. run 4. slot
type.. 3. red, roe 4. mule 6. fallow

11. black–tailed, white–tailed
deface... 3. mar 4. ruin, scar 5. spoil
6. damage, injure 7. blemish, distort
9. discredit, disfigure
defamation... 5. libel 7. calumny,
slander, spatter 8. disgrace, dishonor
9. aspersion 10. defilement,
detraction
defame... 5. libel 6. accuse, charge,
infamy, malign, vilify 7. asperse,
blacken, detract, slander, traduce
8. dishonor 10. calumniate
default... 4. fail, lack, loss, mora
7. deficit, failure, neglect
9. deficient, denigrate, oversight
10. nonpayment 11. delinquency
14. nonfulfillment
defeat... 4. beat, best, lose, rout
5. worst 6. baffle, derout, master,
refute 7. beating, clobber, confute,
conquer, failure, mastery, repulse,
triumph (over), undoing 8. Waterloo
9. frustrate, overthrow 10. disappoint
11. subjugation 12. discomfiture
14. disappointment
defeating... 7. beating, routing
10. anatreptic, conquering
11. vanquishing
defeatism... 6. malism 7. Boloism
10. retreatism
defect... 4. flaw, lisp, lock, quit, want
5. fault 7. blemish, forsake
8. withdraw 9. discredit
10. deficiency, inadequacy
12. imperfection, irregularity
defection... 4. loss 7. failing, failure
9. desertion 10. abjurement
11. abandonment
defective... 3. bad 4. lame 5. idiot
6. cretin, faulty 7. half–wit, lacking
8. crippled 9. deficient, imperfect,
subnormal 10. incomplete
defective vision... 6. anopia, myopia
defend... 4. save, ward 5. guard,
plead, shend, watch 6. screen,
secure, shield, uphold 7. contest,
justify, protect, shelter, support,
sustain 8. enshield, preserve
10. controvert
defendant... 4. reus 7. accused,
libelee, suspect 8. appellee
10. respondent
defender... 8. advocate, champion
9. justifier, protector 10. vindicator
defense... 4. boma, fort, plea 5. alibi,
guard 6. abatis (abattis), glacis
(slope) 7. bulwark, rampart, ravelin
8. estacade (dike), sepiment,
stockade 10. protection
12. counterscarp 13. justification,
machicolation
defenseless... 7. aidless, forlorn,
unarmed 8. helpless 9. unarmored,
unguarded 10. undefended,
unshielded 11. unfortified,
unprotected
defer... 3. bow 4. wait 5. delay
6. retard 7. adjourn, suspend
8. postpone, protract, stave off
13. procrastinate
defer (to)... 5. yield 6. admire, regard,
submit 7. concede, respect

9. recognize 11. acknowledge

deference... 5. honor 6. esteem, fealty, homage, regard 7. respect 8. courtesy 9. reverence 10. politeness, submission 12. complaisance 13. consideration

deferential... 8. obeisant 9. attentive, courteous 10. respectful, submissive 11. ceremonious

defiance... 6. defial 8. audacity, boldness 9. challenge, disregard, insolence

deficiency... 4. lack, want 6. dearth, ullage 7. aneuria, deficit 8. scarcity, shortage 10. inadequacy 13. insufficiency 14. incompleteness

deficient... 5. minus, short 6. faulty, meager (meagre), scarce 7. lacking, missing, wanting 8. inferior 9. defective, imperfect 10. inadequate, incomplete 12. insufficient

defile... 4. file, pass (Mt), soil 5. dirty, gorge, notch, sully, taint 6. befoul, debase, ravine, vilify 7. corrupt, debauch, deprave, pollute, tarnish 8. dishonor 10. passageway

define... 3. fix 4. name 5. bound, limit 6. decide 7. delimit, explain, outline 8. boundary 9. delineate, determine, stipulate 11. distinguish 12. characterize, circumscribe

defined (sharply)... 8. clear-cut 9. trenchant

defined track... 3. rut 4. slot

definite... 4. sure 7. certain, limited, precise 8. absolute, distinct, explicit, manifest, positive 10. undeniable 11. determining, unqualified 12. unmistakable 14. unquestionable

definitely... 10. explicitly, positively 12. conclusively, unmistakably

definition... 6. naming 7. clarity, meaning 9. sharpness 11. description, explanation 12. delimitation, distinctness 14. interpretation

deflation... 7. decline 8. collapse 9. reduction 10. cheapening 11. devaluation, humiliation 12. depreciation

deflect... 4. bend, warp 5. avert 6. divert 7. deviate

deformed... 5. varus 7. taliped 8. formless 9. amorphous, distorted, grotesque, loathsome, malformed, misshapen, monstrous 10. clubfooted

defraud... 3. gyp, rob 4. bilk, gull 5. cheat, cozen 6. fleece 7. swindle

deft... 3. apt, fit, pat 4. meet, trim 5. adept, handy, quick 6. adroit, clever, expert 8. skillful (skilful) 9. dexterous, masterful

defunct... 3. die 4. dead, gone 6. depart, finish 7. extinct 8. deceased 11. nonexistent

defy... 4. dare 5. beard, brave, stump 6. cartel 7. disdain, disobey 9. challenge

degenerate... 6. debase, wicked, worsen 7. atrophy, corrupt, degrade, deprave 8. decadent 10. retrogress

11. deteriorate

degeneration... 7. decline 9. decadence, turpitude 10. degeneracy 11. degradation 13. deterioration, retrogression

degradation... 5. shame 7. censure, decline 8. demotion, disgrace, ignominy 9. reduction, turpitude 10. debasement, punishment 11. humiliation 13. deterioration

degrade... 5. abase, lower 6. debase, demean, demote, depose, humble 7. corrupt 8. disgrace, dishonor 9. humiliate 10. depreciate

degrade (socially)... 8. declassé

degree... 4. rank, step, tate 5. class, grade, order, point, scope, shade, stage, stair 6. extent 7. station 8. capacity, relation 9. intensity

degree (pert to)...
academic.. 8. bachelor 9. doctorate, masterate 11. engineering 13. baccalaureate
highest.. 13. summa cum laude
slight.. 5. shade 9. gradation
to what.. 9. howsoever 10. howsomever

dehydrate... 3. dry 5. dry up 6. wither 8. preserve 9. anhydrate, dessicate, evaporate, exsiccate

deify... 5. exalt 7. ennoble, glorify, idolize 8. enshrine 11. apotheosize, immortalize

deign (pert to)... 7. consent 9. vouchsafe 10. condescend

deity... 2. El 3. Dea, God 4. Deus, deva 5. numen 6. Elohim 7. goddess, godhead, godhood 8. Almighty, Divinity, Immortal 12. Supreme Being

deity (aboriginal)... 4. mana, Zemi 5. huaca, wakan 6. manito (manitou), nagual, orenda, pokunt 8. tamanoas

deity (pert to)...
avenging.. 6. Erinys 7. Alastor, Anteros
destroying.. 4. Siva (Shiva)
evil.. 5. Sebek (crocodile-headed)
hearth.. 5. Vesta
household.. 3. Lar 7. Penates
human sacrifice.. 6. Moloch
judge of the dead.. 4. Yama
love.. 4. Amor, Eros 5. Cupid
mockery.. 5. Momus
music.. 6. Apollo
solar.. 5. Mentu (Ment, falcon-headed)
sun.. 2. Ra
supreme.. 6. Ormazd
two-faced.. 5. Janus
underworld.. 3. Dis 4. Gwyn 5. Pluto 6. Osiris
war.. 4. Ares
woodland.. 3. Pan 4. faun 5. satyr 7. silenus

dejected... 3. sad 5. amort 6. abased, droopy 7. à la mort, lowered 8. downcast 9. depressed, prostrate 10. despondent 11. downhearted, low-spirited

dejection... 7. lowness, sadness

10. depression, melancholy
11. despondency
Delaware...
beach.. 8. Rehoboth
capital.. 5. Dover
church (oldest Prot).. 9. Old Swedes
city.. 5. Lewes 9. New Castle
10. Wilmington (Fort Christina,
1638)
corporation.. 6. DuPont
product.. 9. chemicals 13. Blue Hen
chicks
river.. 8. Delaware 10. Brandywine
State admission.. 5. first
State motto.. 22. Liberty and
Independence
State nickname.. 5. First 7. Diamond
delay... 3. lag 4. halt, mora, stay,
wait 5. block, check, dally, defer,
demur, pause, tarry 6. arrest, detain,
hinder, impede, loiter, retard
7. confine, setback 8. lateness,
obstruct, postpone, reprieve,
slow–down 9. detention, hindrance
10. cunctation, moratorium
13. procrastinate 15. procrastination
delayed... 4. late, slow 5. tardy
7. belayed, overdue 10. behindhand
delectable... 6. savory 8. luscious
pleasing 9. ambrosial, delicious
10. delightful 11. scrumptious
delegate... 4. name, send 6. assign,
commit, depute, deputy, legate
7. appoint, consign, entrust
8. deputize 9. authorize
10. commission 12. commissioner
14. representative
delete... 4. dele 5. erase 6. cut out,
excise, remove 7. edit out, expunge
9. eradicate 10. obliterate
deleterious... 7. harmful, hurtful,
noxious 9. injurious 10. pernicious,
prejudiced 11. destructive,
detrimental, prejudicial
deletion... 4. stet 7. apocope
8. excision 9. expunging
delf, delft... 3. pit 4. mine 6. quarry
Delhi... 7. capital (Ind)
deliberate... 4. cool, muse, pore, slow
5. study, think, weigh 6. ponder
7. discuss, reflect, studied
8. consider, measured, prepense
9. calculate, leisurely, speculate,
unhurried, voluntary 11. contemplate,
intentional, premeditate
12. premeditated 13. dispassionate
deliberately... 6. slowly 7. tardily
8. by design 9. expressly, purposely,
willfully 13. intentionally
delicacy... 4. cate, tact 5. snack, taste
6. caviar, luxury, nicety, tidbit
7. finesse, frailty, tenuity 8. fineness,
niceness, softness, subtlety
9. exactness, fragility, precision
10. daintiness, refinement, slightness
11. sensitivity·
delicate... 3. sly 4. fine, lacy, nice,
soft 5. frail, light 6. dainty, mignon,
petite, pretty, queasy, subtle, tender
7. elegant, fragile, minikin, refined,
tenuous 8. araneous, graceful,
luscious, tasteful 9. exquisite,

sensitive 10. fastidious, meticulous,
scrupulous 11. considerate
delicious... 5. tasty 8. luscious
9. ambrosial, nectarean
10. delightful, nectareous
delight... 3. joy 4. glee 5. amuse,
bliss, charm, exult, mirth 6. divert,
please, ravish, regale, relish
7. enchant, gratify, overjoy
8. pleasure 9. delectate, enrapture,
happiness 13. gratification
delightful... 6. lovely, savory
7. amusing, winsome 8. charming,
engaging, pleasant 9. appealing,
delicious, enjoyable 10. enchanting
11. fascinating
delineate... 3. map 4. draw, limn, line
5. trace 6. define, depict 7. outline,
picture, portray 8. describe
9. represent
delinquency... 7. default, failure
8. omission 9. violation
10. nonpayment 11. malfeasance,
misdemeanor, misfeasance
13. nonobservance
deliquesce... 4. give, melt 6. ramify
7. liquefy 8. diminish, dissolve
delirious... 6. insane, raving 8. frenzied
9. wandering (mental)
14. disorientation
delirium... 4. fury, rage 6. frenzy,
lunacy 7. madness, passion
8. insanity 9. phrenitis
10. aberration, excitement,
unsaneness 11. derangement
13. hallucination
deliver... 4. free, give, save 5. speak
6. commit, impart, ransom, redeem,
render, resign 7. consign, release,
relieve 8. transfer 9. discharge,
enunciate, extradite, surrender
deliver of evil spirits... 8. exorcise
deliver oration... 7. declaim
dell... 4. dale, dene, vale 5. slade
6. dalles (pl), dingle, ravine, valley
Delos...
famed for.. 5. ruins 10. Stone Lions
island group.. 8. Cyclades
sea.. 6. Aegean
Delphi, Delphoi (Gr)...
modern name.. 6. Kastri
oracle.. 7. Delphic 8. Delphian
priestess.. 6. Pythia
delude... 3. jig 4. dupe, flam, fool,
hoax 5. elude, trick 6. befool
7. beguile, deceive, mislead
9. bamboozle, frustrate, victimize
11. double–cross
deluge... 5. flood 6. drench 7. freshet,
Niagara, torrent 8. cataract, flooding,
inundate, overflow, submerge, The
Flood 9. cataclysm, overwhelm
10. oversupply 14. superabundance
delusion... 4. ruse 6. mirage
7. fallacy, fantasm 8. illusion,
phantasm 9. deception
10. misleading 13. hallucination
delve... 3. dig 4. mine, till 5. gouge,
scoop, spade 6. exhume 8. excavate
demand... 3. ask, COD, cry, dun, fee
4. call, need 5. claim, query 6. elicit
7. require 8. exaction, question

9. requisite, ultimatum
11. requirement, requisition
demeanor, demeanour... 4. mien
7. bearing, conduct, posture
8. behavior, carriage
11. comportment
demented... 3. mad 4. daft, loco, luny
5. crazy, loony 6. crazed, insane
7. cracked 8. deranged
10. unbalanced 11. disoriented
Demeter... 7. goddess (Agric)
demigod... 4. hero 5. satyr (sylvan)
6. Triton 7. godling, half–god
10. semidivine
demise... 5. death, lease 6. convey
7. decease 8. bequeath
10. alienation, conveyance
demit... 4. quit 5. leave 6. resign,
vacate 8. abdicate 10. relinquish
11. resignation
demiurgic... 8. creative 9. formative
demivolt... 4. jump 5. vault (half)
6. curvet 8. capriole
Democrat (Polit slang)... 6. Hunker
demoded... 5. passé 6. passed
10. out of style
demolish... 4. rase, raze, ruin, undo
5. wreck 7. destroy, shatter
9. devastate, dismantle, overthrow
11. disassemble
demon, daemon... 3. hag, imp, nat
4. atua, jinn, Mara, ogre, Rahu
5. asura, devil, Eolis, fiend, genie,
jinni (jinnee), lamia, Satan 6. afreet
7. Amaimon, villain 8. Asmodeus
9. cacodemon (cacodaemon)
demoniac... 8. devilish, fiendish
demons (pert to)...
adjurers.. 9. exorcists
assembly of.. 6. sabbat
charm against.. 10. demonifuge
possessed of.. 8. demoniac
theory of.. 10. demonology
worship of.. 11. demonolatry
demonstrate... 4. show 5. prove
6. evince, typify 7. display, explain,
portray 8. manifest 9. exemplify
demonstrative... 7. gushing 8. effusive
9. emotional 10. indicative
11. explanatory 12. affectionate,
illustrative
Demosthenes (Gr)... 6. orator
(greatest)
demur... 4. stay 5. delay, pause, tarry
6. linger, object (to) 7. scruple
8. demurrer, hesitate 9. objection
12. irresolution
demure... 3. coy, mim, shy 4. prim,
smug 5. grave, staid, timid
6. sedate, solemn, stuffy 7. bashful,
prudish, serious 8. decorous
den... 4. cave, dell, lair, nest, room
5. cavea (anc), group (scouts), haunt,
study 6. cavern, grotto, hollow,
ravine 7. retreat 8. hideaway
denial... 5. cross 7. refusal
8. demurrer, negation 9. disavowal,
disowning, rejection 10. refutation
11. deprivation 12. disallowance
13. disaffirmance
denizen... 3. cit 6. native 7. citizen,
dweller, hellion (of hell) 9. indweller

10. inhabitant 11. cosmopolite
Denmark... see also *Danish*
anc name.. 5. Thule
capital.. 10. Copenhagen
city.. 6. Nyborg (Fyn Isl), Odense
7. Aalborg 8. Elsinore
founder.. 7. Absalon (Axel)
Hamlet's grave.. 8. Elsinore
island possession.. 6. Faroes
9. Greenland
peninsula.. 7. Jutland
river.. 5. Guden
ruler (anc).. 6. Canute (Kanute)
denomination... 3. ism 4. cult, name,
sect 5. class, party, value 6. church,
number, school 7. society
8. category 10. persuasion
11. appellation, designation,
stipulation
denote... 4. mark, mean, note, show
5. imply 6. convey 7. bespeak,
betoken, connote, express, purport,
signify 8. indicate 10. denominate
denoting (pert to)...
equal pressure.. 8. isobaric
final end (Gram).. 5. telic
usual action.. 9. usitative
denouement... 3. end 5. issue
6. result 7. outcome (plot)
8. solution 10. revelation
denounce... 4. damn 6. accuse, assail,
scathe 7. arraign, censure, condemn,
upbraid 9. reprobate 10. denunciate,
stigmatize
de novo... 3. new 4. anew 5. fresh,
newly 6. afresh
dense... 4. dewy, firm 5. close, crass,
gross, heavy, solid, thick 6. opaque,
stupid 7. compact, crowded
8. populous, thickset 11. thickheaded
density... 4. dord (Chem) 8. dumbness
9. stupidity 11. compactness
dent... 3. pit 4. dint 5. dinge, notch,
tooth 6. batter, hollow, indent
7. imprint 10. depression, impression
11. indentation
dentagra... 7. forceps 9. dentalgia,
toothache
dental (pert to)...
appliance.. 3. dam 6. scaler
7. forceps
drill.. 8. cavitron
filling.. 5. inlay
measure.. 10. dentimeter
toothache.. 8. dentagra 9. dentalgia
dentate... 7. serried, toothed
dentine... 5. ivory
dentist... 10. exodontist
12. orthodontist 14. prosthodontist
denude... 4. bate 5. scalp, strip
6. divest, expose, unrobe 7. uncover
denunciation... 6. menace, threat
7. inveigh 8. reproach
10. accusation 11. arraignment
deny... 4. nego 5. debar 6. abjure,
impugn, negate, recant, refuse,
renege 7. confute, disavow, dispute,
gainsay 8. disclaim, forswear,
traverse 9. repudiate 10. contradict,
contravene, controvert
deodar (species)... 5. cedar
depart... 2. go 3. die 4. exit, quit

5. leave, mosey 6. decamp, demise, egress, perish 7. abscond, vamoose 8. separate (Chem), withdraw

depraved... 4. evil, vile 6. shrewd, wicked 7. corrupt, immoral, vicious 8. vitiated 9. debauched, dissolute, perverted 10. degenerate

depravity... 8. depraved 9. turpitude 10. corruption, wickedness 15. incorrigibility

depreciate... 4. fall 5. lower, slump 6. debase, lessen, reduce, shrink 7. cheapen, deflate 8. belittle, discount, pejorate, vilipend 9. disparage 10. undervalue

depreciation... 8. decrease, discount 9. deflation 10. cheapening, pejoration 12. belittlement 13. disparagement 14. undervaluation

depredator... 5. thief 6. looter, robber 7. spoiler 8. marauder, ravisher 9. despoiler, plunderer

depress... 4. dent, sink 5. lower 6. dampen, deepen, deject, indent, reduce, sadden 7. flatten, imprint, oppress 8. dispirit, enfeeble 10. discourage

depressed... 3. low, sad 4. dire, sunk 6. dismal, oblate 8. dejected, downcast 9. debruised (Her), flattened (vertically) 10. dispirited 11. downhearted 12. disheartened

depressing... 5. chill 6. dismal, dreary, gloomy, somber 7. joyless 9. saddening 10. melancholy

depression... 3. col, dip, pit 4. dent, fall 5. blues, fossa (Anat), gloom, gully 6. cavity, crater, ravine, trough, vapors 10. melancholy 11. despondency, humiliation

deprivation... 4. loss, want 7. deposal, ousting, removal 9. privation, unseating 10. divestment 11. bereavement

deprive... 3. rob 4. take 5. debar, mulct, strip 6. divest, remove 7. bereave, despoil 10. dispossess

deprived of...
authority.. 9. dethroned
life.. 5. slain 6. killed 12. exterminated
limb.. 6. maimed
natural qualities.. 9. denatured
possessions.. 12. expropriated
professional standing.. 8. laicized
rank.. 7. deposed
reason.. 8. demented
vigor.. 6. sapped 8. deadened, unnerved 9. enervated, enfeebled

depth... 5. abyss, midst 6. extent 9. intensity 10. profundity

depths... 3. sea 5. adyta (spiritual), ocean 16. Davy Jones's locker

depute... 6. assign, devote 7. appoint 8. delegate, deputize

deputy... 5. agent, envoy, proxy, vicar 6. legate 8. alter ego 9. alternate 10. substitute

deracinate... 6. evulse, unroot, uproot 7. extract (forcibly)

deride... 3. pan 4. dupe, geck, gibe, jeer, mock, razz 5. cheat, fleer, flout,

scoff, scorn, trick 6. insult 8. ridicule

derision... 5. fleer, scorn 7. asteism, mockery 8. contempt, ridicule

derivation... 6. effect, origin, source 7. descent, lineage 9. deduction, education, evolution 10. derivative 12. transmission

derivation of...
descent.. 7. lineage 8. pedigree 9. genealogy
name (race, tribe).. 7. eponymy
word.. 9. etymology

derivative of...
bauxite.. 8. aluminum
benzine.. 6. phenol
coal tar.. 8. creosote
flax.. 5. linen
mercury.. 11. quicksilver
milk.. 6. lactic
morphine.. 6. heroin
pitchblende.. 6. radium 7. uranium
sorrel.. 10. oxalic acid

derogate... 5. annul, decry 6. repeal 7. detract 8. restrict, withdraw 9. disparage

derogatory... 10. detracting, detractory, pejorative 11. deprecatory, disparaging 12. depreciatory

derrick... 3. rig 4. spar 5. crave, hoist, tower 6. lifter, steeve, tackle 7. hangman, staging

dervish... 4. monk 5. fakir, friar 6. beggar, fakeer 7. ascetic 11. religionist

dervish cap... 3. taj 4. atef

dervishes...
howling.. 8. Rufaiyah
wandering.. 12. Kalandariyah
whirling, dancing.. 10. Maulawiyah

descend... 4. fall, sink 5. deign, stoop 6. alight, unbend 7. decline 9. gravitate 10. condescend

descendant... 3. son 5. child, scion 8. daughter, offshoot 9. offspring

descendants... 5. breed 7. progeny 9. posterity

descent... 4. drop, fall, root 5. birth, issue, scarp, slope, stock 7. assault, decline, lineage 8. ancestry, downfall, invasion (sea), pedigree 9. declivity, incursion, posterity 10. extraction 11. degradation

describe... 4. name 5. paint, parse, state 6. define, depict, relate 7. explain, express, narrate, outline 9. delineate, designate, represent 12. characterize

description... 4. idyl, kind, sort 5. idyll 7. account, version 8. features, relation 9. discourse, narration, narrative, portrayal 10. definition 11. delineation, explanation 14. representation 18. descriptio personae

descry... 3. see 4. espy, view 6. behold, detect, reveal 7. discern, observe, witness 8. discover 9. determine 11. distinguish

Desdemona's husband... 7. Othello

desecrate... 5. abuse 6. misuse 7. profane, violate 8. misapply

Deseret... 4. Utah (1849)

desert... 3. due 4. bolt, fail 5. merit,
oasis 6. defect, renege, reward
7. abandon, forsake 8. desolate
10. apostatize, relinquish, wilderness
desert (pert to)...
Africa.. 5. El Erg 6. Karroo
Algeria.. 3. Erg
Australia.. 10. Great Sandy 13. Great
Victoria
beast.. 5. camel
dweller.. 4. Arab
Mongolia (Asia).. 4. Gobi
phenomenon.. 6. mirage
prospector.. 3. rat
ship.. 5. camel
shrub.. 5. ratem 6. Alhagi 7. juniper
(Bib)
train, travelers.. 7. caravan
wind (hot).. 6. simoom (simoon)
7. sirocco
deserter... 3. rat 6. bolter 8. apostate,
recreant, renegade, turncoat, turntail
deserved... 3. due 4. fair, just
5. rated 6. earned, worthy
7. condign, merited 8. rightful
9. justified, warranted
11. appropriate
deserving... 6. worthy 8. laudable
10. creditable, entitled to
11. commendable, meritorious
12. praiseworthy
desiccated... 3. dry 4. arid, sere
5. dried 6. seared 7. parched
9. preserved 10. dehydrated,
exsiccated
design... 3. aim, art, end 4. draw,
form, idea, mean, plan, plot 5. ettle
6. intent, layout, motive, object,
scheme, sketch 7. destine, drawing,
meaning, outline, pattern, propose
8. artifice, artistry, contrive
11. arrangement
design (pert to)...
carved.. 4. seme 5. cameo 8. intaglio
metal, glass.. 4. etch 6. niello
ornamental.. 9. medallion
10. needlework
pattern.. 5. batik 6. mosaic
skin.. 6. tattoo
designate... 3. fix, set 4. call, mark,
name, show 5. state, style, title
6. select 7. appoint, entitle, specify
8. describe, indicate, nominate
9. determine, stipulate
10. denominate 11. distinguish
12. characterize
designation... 4. name 7. meaning
9. selection 10. indication
12. denomination 13. signification
desire... 3. yen 4. care, urge, want,
wish 5. covet, crave, yearn 6. aspire,
hunger, prefer, thirst 7. craving,
longing, passion, request 8. appetite
9. appetency, eagerness
10. desiderium 11. inclination
desire (pert to)...
expectant.. 4. hope
greatly.. 6. aspire
liquid.. 6. thirst
ungovernable.. 5. mania
desirous... 4. avid 5. eager 6. ardent
7. envious, lustful, willing

8. covetous, spirited 9. ambitious
10. solicitous
desist... 2. ho 3. end 4. don't, halt,
quit, stay, stop 5. cease 6. lay off
7. forbear, refrain 8. cut it out
11. discontinue
desk... 4. ambo, dais 5. board, table
6. pulpit 7. lectern, rostrum
8. kneehole 9. monocleid
(monocleide), secretary 10. escritoire
desolate... 3. sad 4. arid, lorn, ruin
5. alone, bleak, drear, gaunt
6. barren, dismal, gloomy, lonely,
ravage 7. forlorn 8. deserted,
forsaken, solitary, wretched
9. destitute 10. depopulate
11. comfortless, uninhabited
desolation... 3. woe 4. ruin 5. gloom,
grief, havoc, waste 6. ravage
7. sadness 10. gloominess,
loneliness, melancholy 11. destitution,
destruction, devastation, forlornness
12. depopulation, solitariness,
wretchedness
despair... 11. desperation,
despondency, forlornness
12. hopelessness
desperado... 5. brave 6. outlaw
7. ruffian 8. criminal 10. lawbreaker
desperate... 3. mad 4. rash, wild
7. frantic, furious 8. headlong,
heedless, hopeless, reckless
10. despairing, desponding,
distraught, infuriated 11. extravagant,
precipitate 13. irretrievable
despicable... 4. base, vile 6. odious,
shabby 8. terrible, unworthy,
wretched 9. miserable
12. contemptible, contemptuous,
disreputable, vilipendious
despise... 4. defy, hate 5. scorn,
scout, spurn 6. detest, slight
7. contemn, disdain 8. vilipend
9. disregard
despised being... 6. pariah 7. outcast
despoil... 3. rip, rob 4. riot 5. reave,
rifle, strip 6. divest, fleece, injure,
ravage, ravish 7. bereave, debauch,
deprive, disrobe, pillage, plunder
9. depredate
despondency... 7. despair
10. depression 11. desperation
13. heartlessness
despot... 4. czar (tsar), lord 6. master,
satrap, tyrant 8. autocrat, dictator
9. patriarch
despotic... 8. arrogant 9. arbitrary,
tyrannous 10. autocratic, tyrannical
11. dictatorial, patriarchal
12. governmental
dessert... 3. ice, pie 4. cake 5. fruit,
glacé, sweet 6. mousse, pastry,
sweets 7. parfait, pudding, sherbet,
strudel 8. ice cream 10. shoofly pie
destination... 3. end 4. goal, port
5. bourn (bourne) 7. address, destiny
9. objective
destine... 4. doom, fate 5. allot
6. design, devote, intend, ordain
7. appoint 8. set apart 9. designate
10. foreordain, predestine
12. predetermine

destiny... 3. end, lot, ure (anc)
4. bahi, doom, eure, fate, goal
5. karma, stars 6. Kismet 7. fortune
11. destination
destitute... 4. void 5. needy 6. bereft,
devoid 7. forlorn, lacking
8. bankrupt, forsaken, homeless
9. abandoned, penniless
10. down–and–out
destitution... 6. penury 7. poverty
11. deprivation 12. helplessness
destroy... 3. end 4. kill, rase, raze,
root, ruin, sack, slay, undo 5. abash,
annul, erase 6. ravage 7. abolish,
consume, nullify, unbuild
8. decimate, demolish, overturn
9. dismantle, eradicate
10. annihilate, neutralize
11. exterminate
destroyer... 3. hun 6. ruiner, vandal
7. marplot, wrecker 8. nihilist,
saboteur 9. iconclast (of images)
11. torpedo boat
destroying angel... 6. Danite
7. Abaddon, Amanita (fungus)
8. Apollyon
destruction... 4. loss, ruin 5. havoc,
waste 7. killing 8. downfall,
genocide, ravaging, sabotage,
shambles 9. holocaust, overthrow,
perdition, ruination 10. decimation,
demolition, desolation, extinction,
subversion 11. devastation,
dissolution, extirpation
13. extermination
destructive... 5. fatal 6. deadly, mortal
7. baleful, fateful, ruinous 8. aneretic
(anaeretic), ravaging 10. calamitous,
catawampus, pernicious, subversive
desuetude... 6. disuse, nonuse
9. cessation 12. obsolescence
13. nonemployment
14. discontinuance
desultory... 4. idle 5. hasty 6. roving,
wanton 7. aimless, cursory, wayward
8. rambling, unsteady, wavering
9. deviative, orderless, unsettled
10. discursive, inconstant
detach... 4. part, wean 5. sever
7. disjoin, isolate 8. disunite,
separate, withdraw 9. disengage
detached... 4. free 5. alone, aloof,
scarp 7. detaché, retired, severed
8. isolated, secluded, separate,
solitary 9. unrelated, withdrawn
11. unconnected 12. disconnected
detachment... 8. disunion
9. aloneness, aloofness, isolation,
seclusion, unconcern 10. separation
11. disjunction 14. demobilization
detail... 4. item, unit 6. assign
7. appoint, itemize, minutia, narrate,
specify 9. enumerate, narrative
10. particular 12. technicality
details... 6. trivia 8. minutiae
11. particulars
detain... 4. hold, keep, stop 5. check,
delay 6. arrest, hinder, intern, retard
8. imprison, restrain, withhold
detect... 3. see, spy 4. show, spot,
tail 6. accuse, descry, reveal
7. discern, find out, uncover

8. discover, perceive 9. recognize
detective... 4. dick 6. beagle, sleuth,
tailer, tracer 7. gumshoe, spotter
8. exposing, flatfoot, Hawkshaw,
mouchard 9. operative
12. investigator
detent... 3. dog 4. pawl 5. catch,
click, fence 6. tongue 7. ratchet
detention... 5. delay 6. duress
7. detinue 9. captivity, hindrance
10. detainment, internment
11. restraining, retardation,
withholding 12. imprisonment
deter... 5. daunt, delay, repel
6. divert, hinder 7. prevent
8. restrain 10. discourage, disincline
deterge... 5. purge 6. purify
7. cleanse 8. depurate 9. elutriate
detergent... 4. soap 7. cleaner,
purging, saponin (saponine), smectic,
solvent 8. cleanser, medicine, purifier
9. cleansing 10. abstergent, lixiviator
deteriorate... 4. wear 6. impair,
weaken, worsen 10. degenerate,
retrogress
deterioration... 5. decay 7. decline
9. decadence 10. debasement,
declension, impairment, perversion
11. degradation 12. degeneration
13. retrogression
determinate... 5. fixed 6. cymose
7. certain, special 8. definite,
resolute, resolved, specific 9. arbitrary
10. definitive, invariable
11. established, unqualified
determination... 4. will 5. limit, proof
6. choice 7. purpose, resolve, verdict
8. decision, firmness, judgment
9. impulsion 10. conclusion,
definition, discussion, resolution,
settlement 11. disputation,
measurement, termination
12. decisiveness, dijudication,
resoluteness 13. specification
determine... 3. end 5. impel, learn,
prove, state 6. assess, choose,
decide, define, direct, ordain, settle
7. delimit, resolve, specify
8. conclude, discover 9. arbitrate,
ascertain, stipulate, terminate,
variously 10. dijudicate, foreordain
determined... 3. set 4. sure 5. fixed
6. mulish 7. assured, cinched,
decided, settled 8. foregone,
perverse, resolute, stubborn
9. obstinate, pigheaded
detest... 4. hate 5. abhor 8. execrate
9. abominate
detestable... 6. odious 7. hateful
8. accursed, terrible 9. abhorrent,
execrable, loathsome, obnoxious
10. abominable 12. contemptible
dethrone... 6. depose, disbar, divest
7. uncrown 8. disbench
detonation... 4. bang, boom 5. blast
7. blowout 8. backfire 9. discharge,
explosion 10. combustion
detract... 6. deduce, deduct, vilify
7. asperse, traduce 8. belittle,
derogate, distract, subtract, withdraw
9. disparage 10. depreciate
detraction... 5. delay 7. calumny,

slander 9. aspersion 10. belittling
11. distraction, subtraction
detriment... 4. hurt, loss 6. damage,
injury 8. mischief, weakness
10. impairment, impediment
12. disadvantage
detrimental... 7. baleful, baneful,
harmful, hurtful, noxious 9. injurious
10. pernicious 11. deleterious,
mischievous, prejudicial
15. disadvantageous
Deus Fidius... 7. Jupiter
Deus vobiscum... 12. God be with
you
Deus vult... 8. God wills (anc cry)
deuterogamy... 6. digamy
Deuteronomy (pert to)...
comprising.. 10. law of Moses
Fifth Book of.. 10. Pentateuch
meaning.. 11. repeated law (of
Moses)
devastate... 4. rape, ruin, sack
5. havoc, strip, waste 6. ravage
7. destroy, pillage, plunder, scourge
8. demolish, desolate 10. depopulate
devastation... 4. ruin 5. havoc, waste
6. ravage 7. scourge
develop... 4. grow 5. arise, ripen,
train 6. appear, detect, evolve,
expand, mature, reveal 7. advance,
convert, enlarge, expound, further,
improve, perfect, promote
8. discover, generate 9. elaborate
(details)
developed... 4. ripe, zoon 5. adult
6. mature, mellow 7. grownup
8. improved 9. perfected
10. precocious
development... 6. growth 7. changes,
endysis 8. increase, maturity
9. evolution, expansion, formation,
unfolding 10. maturation
11. elaboration, improvement,
ontogenesis 12. phylogenesis
devest... 5. strip 6. denude, divest
7. deprive, undress 8. alienate
Devi (Hind)... 3. Uma 4. Kali
5. Durga, Gauri 6. Chandi, Shakti
7. heroine, Parvati 8. divinity
9. Haimavati
deviate... 3. err, yaw 4. hade, miss,
slew, vary, veer 5. sheer, stray
6. change, depart, swerve, wander
7. deflect, digress, diverge
deviation... 3. yaw 5. lapse 6. change
7. circuit, synesis 8. aberrant
9. aberrance, deformity, departure,
diverging, obliquity, variation
10. deflection, difference, digressing,
digression, distortion, divergence
11. abnormality 12. eccentricity
device... 4. plan, tool 5. motto, shift,
trick 6. design, desire, gadget,
scheme 7. adjunct, compass, project,
purpose 8. artifice, insignia
9. appliance, expedient, implement,
invention, stratagem 10. instrument
11. contrivance
device (pert to)...
bark peeling.. 8. stripper
clamping.. 4. vise 7. pincers
distilling.. 7. alembic

fabric stretching.. 7. stenter
heating.. 4. etna 5. stove
hoisting.. 5. crane, davit, lewis
6. garnet 7. derrick 8. elevator
9. parbuckle
leveling.. 6. gimbal
measuring.. 4. gage, tape 5. chain,
gauge, meter, ruler 9. ergometer,
yardstick 10. micrometer
nautical.. 4. bitt 5. cleat, otter
6. becket 8. paravane
regulating.. 5. valve 9. remontoir
spraying.. 8. atomizer 9. sprinkler
steering.. 4. helm 5. wheel 6. rudder,
tiller
stopping.. 5. brake, sprag
devil... 3. imp 4. deil, deva, evil, haze
5. annoy, demon, error, fiend, grill,
ruler (of Hell), Satan, tease
7. hellion, serpent, tempter, torment
8. printer's 9. archenemy, daredevil,
dust devil
devil (pert to)...
dog.. 6. marine
bird.. 3. owl 5. swift 10. goatsucker
fish.. 3. ray 5. manta, whale (gray)
7. octopus
grass.. 7. Bermuda
lore.. 10. demonology
tree.. 4. dita
Devil, the... 5. Deuce, Eblis, Satan
6. Azazel, Belial, Diablo, Teufel
7. Ahriman, Amaimon (Amammion),
diavolo, Evil One, Lucifer, Old Nick,
Sammael, Shaitan (Sheitan)
8. Apollyon, Asmodeus, Diabolos
9. Archenemy, Archfiend, Beelzebub
11. Auld Clootie 14. Mephistopheles
devilish... 5. cruel 6. daring, rakish,
wicked 7. extreme, hellish, satanic
8. fiendish, infernal 9. chthonian
10. demoniacal 11. mischievous
deviltry... 6. malice 7. cruelty, devilry
8. mischief 9. diablerie, diabolism
10. black magic, wickedness
12. fiendishness
devious... 6. errant, erring, roving,
sinful 7. oblique, vagrant, winding
8. rambling, tortuous 9. deviative,
eccentric 10. circuitous
11. out-of-the-way
14. unconventional
devise... 3. aim 4. form, plan
5. array, build, frame 6. create,
divide, evolve, invent, scheme, will to
7. appoint, arrange, bequest,
concoct, fashion 8. bequeath,
contrive 9. fabricate 10. distribute,
excogitate 11. distinguish
deviser of IQ test... 5. Binet
devoid... 4. free, void 5. empty
6. faulty, vacant 7. without
9. destitute 11. nonexistent
devoid of...
feeling.. 9. apathetic, insensate
interest.. 6. jejune
devote... 3. use, vow 5. apply
6. employ, hallow, resign 7. address
consign, destine 8. dedicate, set
apart 10. consecrate 11. appropriate
devoted... 5. loyal, pious, vowed
6. doomed, loving 7. zealous

8. addicted, constant, faithful, friendly, obedient 9. dedicated, engrossed, patriotic

devotee ... 3. fan, ist, nun 4. monk 6. votary 7. epicure, fanatic, Pietist 8. aesthete (esthete), partisan

devotion ... 4. love, zeal 5. ardor, piety 6. novena, prayer 7. pietism, worship 9. addiction, adoration, constancy 10. attachment, dedication, devoutness, friendship 11. devotedness, earnestness, engrossment 12. consecration 13. appropriation, religiousness

devour ... 3. eat 4. bolt, gulp, wolf 5. gorge, use up, waste 6. absorb, engulf 7. consume, engorge, swallow (up) 8. prey upon 9. devastate 10. annihilate

devout ... 4. holy, warm 5. godly, pious 6. hearty, solemn 7. cordial, devoted, saintly, sincere, zealous 8. reverent 9. religious, righteous 10. worshipful

dew ... 4. rime 5. bedew, bloom, roris

dewy ... 5. roral, roric

dexterity ... 3. art 5. knack, magic, skill 7. ability, address, aptness, finesse, sleight 8. aptitude, deftness, facility 9. smartness 10. adroitness 15. right–handedness

dexterous ... 3. apt 4. deft, yare 5. adept, handy, quick, ready 6. adroit, artful, clever 7. skilful 8. skillful 11. right–handed

dextral ... 5. right (to the) 9. favorable

diabolical ... 5. cruel 6. wicked 7. beastly, demonic, hellish, satanic, ungodly 8. damnable, demoniac, devilish, fiendish, infernal

diacritic ... 4. mark 5. point 7. symptom 10. diagnostic 14. distinguishing

diacritical mark ... 5. breve, tilde 6. tittle 9. diaeresis (dieresis)

diadem ... 5. crown, tiara 6. anadem, circle, emblem, empire, fillet 7. coronet 8. headband, insignia, ornament 11. sovereignty

diaeresis, dieresis ... 4. mark 5. break 8. division 10. resolution

diagnose ... 7. analyze 8. construe 9. interpret

diagnosis ... 8. analysis, decision, nosology 9. prognosis 14. interpretation

diagonal ... 4. bias 7. oblique 8. bendwise (Her) 10. transverse 11. cater–corner 13. cater–cornered

diagram ... 4. draw, icon, plan, plot, tree 5. chart, epure, gamut, graph 6. design 7. drawing 9. blueprint

dial ... 4. disk 5. plate 8. horologe 9. indicator, timepiece 11. chronometer

dialect ... 5. idiom, lingo 6. patois, speech 7. diction 8. language, locution, parlance 10. vernacular

dialect (pert to) ...
Afrikaans .. 4. Taal
Aramaic .. 6. Syriac
Aryan .. 4. Pali
provincial .. 6. patois
Semitic .. 4. Geez

diameter ... 2. pi (3.1416) 4. bore 5. width 6. module, radius 7. breadth, caliber (calibre) 9. thickness

diametric, diametrical ... 6. averse 7. adverse 8. antipode, opposite 9. antipodal, diametral

diamond ... 3. gem, ice 5. cards, field (baseball), jager, jewel, plane 6. carbon 7. adamant, infield, lozenge, rhombus 8. treasure

diamond (pert to) ...
crystal .. 7. glassie
cutting .. 4. bort
cutting cups .. 3. dop
famed .. 4. Pitt 5. Sancy 6. Orloff 7. Lesotho (601 carat) 8. Cullinan, Koh–i–noor 9. Excelsior 10. Great Mogul 14. Star of the South
surface .. 5. facet
weight .. 5. carat (karat)

Diamond State ... 8. Delaware

diaphanous ... 4. fine, thin 5. filmy, gauzy, lucid, sheer 6. flimsy 9. gossamery 11. translucent, transparent

diaphragm ... 4. wall 6. middle, septum 7. midriff 9. partition

diary ... 3. log 6. record 7. journal 8. register 9. chronicle 13. autobiography

diaskeuast ... 6. editor 7. reviser

diatribe ... 6. screed, tirade 7. lecture 8. berating, harangue 9. invective, philippic 10. discussion (prolonged)

dice ... 3. cog, die (sing) 4. cube, game, sice (6's) 5. bones, craps, cubes 7. ivories, tessera

Dickens characters ... 3. Tim 4. Dora, Nell 5. Fagin, Miggs, Sikes 6. Cuttle 7. Barnaby 9. Pecksniff 10. Chuzzlewit 11. Oliver Twist

Dickens pseudonym ... 3. Boz

dictate ... 3. law 4. rule 5. maxim, order, utter 6. advise, dictum, enjoin, impose 7. command, deliver, require, suggest 9. prescribe 10. injunction

dictatorial ... 5. bossy 6. lordly 7. pompous 8. absolute, arrogant, despotic, dogmatic, oracular, positive 9. imperious, masterful, pragmatic 10. autocratic, dogmatical, imperative, peremptory 11. categorical, domineering, magisterial, opinionated, overbearing 13. authoritative

diction ... 5. style 8. language, parlance, phrasing 9. elocution 10. vocabulary 11. enunciation, phraseology 14. expressiveness

dictionary ... 5. words 7. calepin, lexicon 8. wordbook 9. reference 10. vocabulary 11. terminology

dictionary compiler ... 7. Webster (Noah) 13. lexicographer

dictum ... 3. saw 5. adage, maxim 6. saying 7. opinion, precept, proverb 8. aphorism, apothegm 11. declaration

didactic... 8. teaching 9. mentorial 10. preceptive 11. instructive
dido... 5. antic, caper, prank, trick 6. frolic
Dido (also Elissa)... 5. Queen (of Carthage) 8. Princess (Tyrian)
die... see also *dice* 4. fade, mold, pass, seal, wane 5. stamp 6. expire, perish, recede, vanish, wither 7. decease, succumb 8. languish 12. extinguished (to be)
die–hard... 4. Tory 11. British Army 12. Conservative
dies... 3. day
dies atri... 9. black days
dies faustus... 13. favorable omen (day of)
diet... 4. fare 5. board 6. Hoftag, ration, viands 7. Council, Landtag, regimen 8. assembly, Kreistag 9. allowance, nutrition, Reichstag 10. Parliament
Diet (of)... 5. Worms (1521) 6. Speyer (1529), Spires 8. Augsburg (1530)
dietetics... 8. sitology 9. nutrition 12. biochemistry, dietotherapy
differ... 4. vary 5. clash 7. dispute, dissent, quarrel 8. disagree
difference... 3. sum 5. shade 6. nuance 8. variance 10. inequality, unlikeness 11. contrariety, distinction, distinguish 12. disagreement, discriminate 13. differentiate, dissimilarity
different... 4. many 5. novel, other 6. divers, sundry, unlike 7. diverse, several, unequal, unusual, variant 8. assorted, contrary, distinct, manifold, opposite, separate, variform 9. divergent, otherwise 10. dissimilar, variegated 11. diversified 13. heterogeneous
different place... 9. elsewhere 10. otherwhere
difficulty... 3. bar, rub 4. clog, crux, knot, snag 5. cavil, check, demur, nodus 6. plight, scrape, strait 7. barrier, problem, trouble 8. obstacle 9. hindrance 10. impediment, ruggedness 11. obstruction 12. disagreement
difficulty in swallowing... 9. dysphagia
diffidence... 5. doubt, qualm 7. anxiety, modesty 8. distrust, humility, timidity 10. hesitation 11. bashfulness 12. apprehension
diffident... 3. coy, shy 5. timid 6. modest 7. anxious 8. doubtful, reserved, retiring 9. shrinking, unwilling 11. distrustful 12. apprehensive
diffuse... 4. full, shed 5. strew 6. expand, extend, prolix 7. copious, perplex, pervade, publish, radiate, refract, verbose 8. disperse 9. redundant 10. widespread
diffused... 5. loose 6. sparse 7. flowing 9. dispersed
diffusion... 7. osmosis 9. pervasion, radiation 10. dispersion, refraction

dig... 3. jab 4. find, grub, mine, open, pion, prod, root 5. delve, dwell, spade 6. exhume, loosen, pierce, plunge, search, thrust 7. extract, unearth 8. excavate 10. understand
digamy... 11. deuterogamy 12. twice married (legally)
digest... 4. code 5. brief 6. abrégé, codify 7. epitome, Pandect 8. abstract, classify, synopsis 10. assimilate, compendium
digestion... 6. pepsis 8. eupepsia 9. dyspepsia, ingestion 10. absorption 12. alimentation, assimilation
digestive secretions... 4. bile, gall 6. pepsin, rennin 7. chalone, gastric, glucase, hormone, maltase 8. salivary, thyroxin 9. endocrine 10. intestinal, pancreatic
digestive tract... 7. enteron 15. alimentary canal
digger... 3. loy, pal 4. plow, wasp 5. spade 6. Indian, sapper 7. comrade, soldier 8. Levelers 9. excavator 12. New Zealander
digit... 3. toe 4. unit 5. thumb 6. finger, number (under 10) 7. dewclaw, integer, measure
digits repeated... 8. repetend
digitus... 6. finger, tarsus 8. dactylus
dignified... 5. grand, lofty, manly, sober, staid 6. august, graced, sedate 7. courtly, pompous, togated 8. decorous, ennobled, imposing, majestic 9. venerable 11. ceremonious 12. aristocratic
dignify... 5. exalt, grace, honor 7. elevate, ennoble 9. solemnize 11. distinguish
dignitary... 3. don 4. rank 5. mogul 6. priest, sachem 7. magnate, notable, prelate 9. clergyman
dignity... 4. rank 5. grace, honor 6. status 7. decorum, majesty 8. nobility, prestige, standing 9. loftiness, nobleness 10. excellence, sedateness
digraph... 8. ligature 9. diphthong
digress... 4. veer 5. shift 6. swerve, wander 7. deviate, diverge 8. divagate 9. turn aside 10. transgress
digression... 4. loop 6. ecbole 7. circuit, episode 8. excursus 9. deviation, excursion, obliquity 10. discussion
digressive... 8. rambling 9. deviative, excursive, wandering 10. circuitous, discursive
dike, dyke... 3. bar, dig, gap 4. bank, gulf, ha–ha, mole, pond, pool 5. ditch, levee, mound 7. barrier, channel 8. causeway, estacade 9. earthwork 10. embankment 11. watercourse 13. fortification
diked land... 6. polder
dike rock... 7. odinite
dilapidation... 4. ruin 5. decay, waste 7. breakup 9. disrepair 10. impairment 11. dissolution 13. decomposition 14. disintegration

dilate... 5. bulge, swell, widen
6. expand 7. distend, enlarge, inflate
9. expatiate
dilation... 7. ectasia, ectasis
8. swelling 9. expansion
10. dilatation, distension
dilatory... 3. lax 4. slow 5. slack,
tardy 6. fabian, remiss 8. backward,
delaying, inactive, sluggish
10. behindhand 13. lackadaisical
15. procrastinating
dilemma... 4. trap 5. brike (obs),
snare 8. argument, quandary
10. perplexity 11. alternative,
predicament
dilettante... 7. amateur, dabbler,
devotee, esthete (aesthete)
diligence... 4. care, heed 6. effort
7. caution 8. industry, sedulity
9. assiduity, attention, constancy
10. stagecoach 11. application,
earnestness, painstaking
12. heedlessness, perseverance,
sedulousness 15. industriousness
diligent... 4. busy 6. active 7. operose
8. sedulous 9. assiduous, attentive,
laborious 11. industrious, persevering
dill, dill seed... 4. anet, herb 5. anise
(Bib) 6. fennel
dillydally... 3. lag 6. linger, loiter,
trifle 9. vacillate 12. shilly–shally
13. procrastinate
dilute... 3. cut 4. thin 6. debase,
rarefy, reduce, weaken 8. lengthen
9. attenuate 10. adulterate
12. denaturalize
diluted... 4. thin, weak 7. reduced,
thinned, watered 10. attenuated
dim... 3. dull, fade, pale 5. bleak,
blear, faint 6. darken 7. darkish,
dimness, eclipse, obscure 8. overcast
10. caliginous, indistinct, mysterious
dimension... 4. size 6. extent, height,
length 7. breadth 9. magnitude,
thickness 11. measurement
13. circumference
diminish... 3. ebb 4. bate, fade, pare,
ploy, wane 5. abase, abate, lower,
peter, taper 6. lessen, recede,
reduce, weaken 7. curtail, dwindle
8. decrease, subtract 9. disparage
diminution... 5. abate, taper 7. litotes
8. decrease, lowering 9. decrement,
lessening, reduction 10. moderation
diminutive... 3. wee 4. runt, slip
5. minny, small 6. bantam, little,
peewee, petite 7. bendlet
diminutive suffix... 2. el, ie 3. ole,
ule 4. ette
dimmer... 8. rheostat
din... 4. ding 5. clang, noise
6. clamor, hubbub, racket, rattle,
tumult, uproar 7. clatter, turmoil
9. commotion
dingle... 4. dale, dell, glen, ring, vale
6. jingle, tingle, tinkle, valley
7. tremble 9. storm door
dining room... 4. hall 5. salon
6. spence 7. cenacle 8. mess hall
9. refectory 12. salle à manger
dining science... 10. aristology
dinosaur... 7. reptile 8. sauropod

9. Sauropoda 10. Diplodocus,
Morosaurus 11. Ornithopoda,
Stegosaurus 12. Brontosaurus,
Ceratosaurus, Megalosaurus,
Palaeosaurus 13. Atlantosaurus,
Tyrannosaurus
diocese... 3. see 6. parish 8. district,
province 9. bishopric 12. jurisdiction
Diocletian martyr (Rome)... 5. Agnes
Dionysus (pert to)...
birthplace.. 6. Thebes
father.. 4. Zeus
festival.. 8. Dionysia
god of (Gr).. 4. wine (Bacchus, later)
10. vegetation
lover.. 6. Selene
mother.. 6. Semele
Dioscuri, The (Gr Myth)... 4. cult
5. twins (Castor and Pollux)
8. Castores 10. Polydeuces
dip... 3. dap, dib, sop 4. bail, dunk,
lade 5. merge, merse, pitch, rinse,
scoop, slope, souse 6. candle,
plunge 7. baptize, immerse
9. declivity 10. pickpocket 11. hors
d'oeuvre
diphthong, dipthong... 5. sound
7. digraph 8. ligature
diploma... 8. testamur 9. sheepskin
10. credential 11. certificate,
testimonial
diplomacy... 4. tact 7. address,
cunning 9. dexterity 10. artfulness,
discretion 11. arbitration,
diplomatism, negotiation, savoir–faire
diplomat... 5. doyen (head), envoy
6. consul 7. attaché 8. emissary,
minister 10. ambassador, politician
15. chargé d'affaires, plenipotentiary
diplomatic... 6. crafty 7. cunning
8. consular 11. mediatorial
diplomatic corps, staff... 7. embassy
8. legation 17. corps diplomatique
dipsomania... 9. addiction, oenomania,
potomania 10. alcoholism
15. delirium tremens
dipthong... see *diphthong*
dire... 3. bad 4. base, evil, rank, want
5. awful, fatal, needy 6. deadly,
dismal, funest, odious 7. baneful,
doleful, fearful, ghastly 8. dreadful,
horrible, terrible, ultimate
10. oppressive 12. inauspicious,
overpowering
direct... 3. ain, bid, con 4. bend,
boss, head, lead, turn 5. order,
pilot, refer, steer, teach 6. govern,
manage 7. avigate, command,
conduct, marshal 8. instruct, straight
9. influence
direction... 3. way 4. airt, bent, care,
east, west 5. avast, belay, north,
route, south, trend 6. advice, course
7. address, command, pointer
8. guidance 10. management
11. instruction 15. superintendence
directly... 4. soon 6. pronto 7. shortly
8. as soon as, promptly 9. forthwith,
instantly, presently 11. immediately
directly opposite... 9. antipodal,
diametric 10. intipodean
director... 4. boss 5. aimer (gunner)

6. conner, leader 7. manager,
teacher 8. governor, producer
14. superintendent

direful... 4. dire 6. woeful 8. dreadful,
terrible 10. calamitous

dirge... 4. keen, Mass, song 5. psalm,
rites 6. lament 7. requiem
8. coronach

dirigible... 4. Roma 5. blimp
7. balloon 10. Shenandoah 12. Graf
Zeppelin

Dirigo... 5. I Lead 7. I Direct (Maine
motto)

dirk... 4. snee, stab 5. knife, sword
6. dagger

dirt... 3. mud 4. dust, foul, land,
muck, soil 5. earth, filth, grime, stain
6. gossip, refuse 7. scandal, slander
9. obscenity

dirty... 4. foul, mean 5. dingy, foggy,
gusty, mucky, nasty 6. bemire, filthy,
soiled, stormy, untidy 7. clouded,
muddied, squalid, sullied

dis (pert to)...
Greek.. 5. Pluto
Norse.. 5. Freya 7. spirits 9. Valkyries
11. superhumans
prefix.. 5. twice 6. double
Roman.. 3. Dis 8. Dis pater
12. realm of Pluto

disable... 4. main 5. unfit 6. impair,
weaken 7. cripple 9. disparage,
hamstring 10. disqualify
12. incapacitate

disadvantage... 3. out 4. harm, hurt
6. damage, injury 7. penalty, trouble
8. drawback, handicap 9. detriment,
liability, prejudice 12. inexpedience
13. inconvenience

disagreeable... 4. edgy 5. cross, nasty
7. fulsome 8. unsavory 9. dissonant,
invidious, irritable, offensive,
repugnant 10. ill–humored,
unpleasant 11. displeasing,
ill–tempered, incongruous
13. uncomfortable

disagreement... 5. clash 7. detente,
discord, dispute, dissent, wrangle
8. variance 9. diversity
10. contention, difference, dissension,
unlikeness 11. contrariety,
controversy, discrepancy, incongruity
13. nonconformity
16. misunderstanding

disappear... 2. die 4. face, pass
5. cease 6. be lost, perish, vanish
7. dwindle 8. evanesce 9. evaporate

disappoint... 4. balk, bilk, fail, fall, foil
6. baffle, thwart 7. let down
9. frustrate 10. disenchant, dissatisfy
11. disillusion

disappointment... 3. rue 6. defeat
7. failure 10. bafflement
11. frustration 15. dissatisfaction

disapprobation... 5. odium
11. disapproval 12. condemnation
13. disparagement

disapproval... 3. boo 4. hiss, veto
7. censure, protest 9. objection,
rejection 12. condemnation
14. disapprobation

disarrange... 4. muss 5. upset 6. foul

up, jumble 7. disturb 8. disorder,
unsettle 10. discompose
11. disorganize

disarray... 5. strip 6. unrobe
7. despoil, undress, unkempt
8. disorder 9. confusion, ungarment
10. disarrange, dishabille
12. discomposure, dishevelment

disaster... 4. evil, ruin 6. mishap
8. accident, calamity, casualty, fatality
9. cataclysm, mischance
10. misfortune 11. catastrophe
12. misadventure

disastrous... 4. dire 7. unlucky
8. ill–fated 9. ill–boding
10. calamitous 11. destructive,
unfortunate 12. unpropitious

disavow... 4. deny 6. abjure, disown,
recant, refuse 7. decline, retract
8. disclaim, renounce 9. disaffirm,
repudiate

disbeliever... 5. pagan 7. atheist,
heathen, heretic, infidel 9. agnostic

disburse... 5. spend 6. defray, expend,
pay out

disbursement... 5. outgo 6. outlay
7. payment 8. spending
11. expenditure

disc... see also _disk_ 3. man 4. dial,
puck 5. medal, plate, quoit, wheel
6. circle, record 7. discoid 8. artifact
9. gyroscope, medallion

discard... 4. drip, shed 5. scrap, sluff
6. disuse, reject, remove
7. abandon, cast off, dismiss, forsake
9. eliminate, eradicate, throw away

discern... 3. see, spy 4. espy, know,
read, view 5. sight 6. behold,
descry, detect 7. witness 8. discover,
perceive 10. understand
11. distinguish 12. discriminate
13. differentiate

discernible... 7. evident, obvious,
visible 8. apparent, distinct,
knowable, manifest 11. conspicuous,
perceptible 15. distinguishable

discerning... 4. sage 5. acute, sharp
6. astute, shrewd 9. sagacious
14. discriminating, discriminative

discernment... 4. tact 6. acumen
7. insight 8. sagacity 9. sharpness
10. astuteness, perception,
shrewdness 12. perspicacity
14. discrimination

discharge... 2. do 4. bang, cass, fire,
sack, shot 5. blast, egest, eject,
erupt, expel, exude, flash, salvo,
shoot, speed 6. acquit, bounce,
defray, exempt, pay off, report,
unload, volley 7. dismiss, execute,
explode, payment, quietus, release
8. emission, eruption 9. acquittal,
dismissal, excretion, execution,
explosion, fusillade 10. accomplish,
detonation, observance
11. performance

disciple... 5. chela, Judas, pupil
7. apostle, convert, learner, scholar,
student 8. adherent, believer, follower

disciples (Bib)... 6. twelve (72,
Vulgate) 10. Christians

disciplinarian... 7. Puritan, teacher,

trainer 8. martinet
discipline... 4. rule, whip 6. govern,
punish 7. chasten, control, culture,
educate, penance, scourge 8. training
9. education, restraint 10. correction,
punishment 11. castigation,
instruction, self–control
12. chastisement 13. regimentation
disclaim... 4. deny 6. abjure, cry out,
disown, recant, refuse, reject
7. disavow 8. abnegate, disallow,
renounce 9. repudiate
disclose... 4. bare, open, show, tell
5. utter 6. expose, impart, reveal,
unmask, unveil 7. divulge, uncloak,
unclose 8. discover, indicate
disclosure... 6. exposé 8. exposure
9. discovery, revealing, unmasking,
unveiling 10. appearance, revealment,
revelation
discolor... 4. spot 5. stain 6. bruise
7. distain (anc), tarnish
9. ecchymose (by blood)
discolored... 4. doty (by decay)
5. faded 7. altered 8. ustulate
10. variegated
discomfit... 4. balk, rout 5. upset
6. baffle, defeat, dismay 7. confuse
9. embarrass, frustrate, overthrow
10. disconcert
discomfiture... 4. rout 6. defeat, flurry
7. letdown 9. confusion, overthrow
10. bafflement 11. frustration
13. embarrassment, inconvenience
14. disappointment
discomfort... 4. pain 6. sorrow
7. misease 8. distress 9. annoyance
10. uneasiness 11. displeasure
13. embarrassment, inconvenience
discommode... 6. bother, molest, put
out 7. trouble 9. incommode
13. inconvenience
discompose... 4. fret 5. upset
6. excite, flurry, rubble 7. agitate,
confuse, derange, disturb, fluster
8. unsettle 9. embarrass
10. disarrange, disconcert
disconcert... 5. abash, alarm 6. rattle,
thwart 7. confuse, disturb, fluster,
nonplus 8. bewilder 9. discomfit,
embarrass 10. disarrange
disconnect... 5. sever 6. detach,
unyoke 7. disjoin 8. disunite,
separate, uncouple
disconnected... 6. broken 8. detached,
rambling 9. desultory, scattered
10. disjointed, incoherent
11. unconnected
disconsolate... 3. sad 6. gloomy,
woeful 7. forlorn 8. desolate,
hopeless 9. sorrowful 10. despairing,
despondent, melancholy
12. inconsolable
discontent... 6. misery, unrest
8. disquiet 10. inquietude,
uneasiness 11. displeasure,
unhappiness 14. discontentment
15. dissatisfaction
discontinue... 3. end 4. drop, quit,
stop 5. cease 6. desist, give up
7. abandon, refrain 8. intermit
9. terminate

discord... 3. din 5. noise 6. strife
7. dissent 8. disunity, variance
9. cacophony, Discordia, harshness
10. antagonism, contention,
difference, discordant, disharmony,
dissension, dissonance 11. altercation
12. disagreement
discord (goddess of)... 3. Ate 4. Eris
discordant... 5. harsh 7. grating,
jarring 8. contrary, jangling
11. cacophonous, disagreeing,
incongruous, quarrelsome,
unmelodious 12. inconsistent,
inharmonious 14. irreconcilable
discordant (pert to)...
music.. 8. scordato
serenade.. 9. charivari 10. callithump
sound.. 6. jangle
discount... 3. cut 4. agio 6. rebate
9. abatement, allowance, reduction
10. concession, percentage
discourage... 4. damp 5. check,
daunt, deter 6. deject, dismay,
oppose 7. depress 8. dispirit,
dissuade 10. dishearten
discourse... 4. talk, tell 5. essay,
paper (written), prose, speak, spiel
6. homily, lesson, screed, sermon
7. account, address, article, declaim,
discant, dissert, expound, lecture,
narrate, oration 8. converse, treatise
9. expatiate, narrative 10. exposition,
recitation 12. conversation,
dissertation
discourteous... 4. rude 7. uncivil
8. impolite, insolent 9. ungallant
10. ungracious 13. disrespectful
discover... 3. see 4. espy, find
5. learn 6. descry, detect, expose
7. exhibit, find out, uncover, unearth
9. apprehend, ascertain
discoverer... 3. spy 5. scout
discoverer of...
America.. 4. Eric (the Red) 7. Vikings
8. Columbus (1492)
blood circulation.. 6. Harvey
electric light.. 6. Edison
North Pole.. 5. Peary (1909)
radium.. 5. Curie (Madame)
South Pole.. 8. Amundsen (1911)
telegraph.. 5. Morse (Samuel)
telephone.. 4. Bell (Alexander)
vaccination.. 6. Jenner
discovery, logic of... 8. heuretic
discredit... 5. doubt 7. asperse, falsify,
scandal 8. disgrace, dishonor,
disprove, distrust 9. disbelief,
disparage, disrepute, misgiving,
suspicion 10. invalidate
11. discredence
discreet... 4. wary 5. civil 6. polite
7. careful, mindful, politic, prudent
8. cautious 9. judicious, selective
11. circumspect 12. noncommittal
13. discretionary
discrepancy... 8. variance 9. disaccord,
disparity, diversity 10. difference
11. contrariety 12. disagreement
13. inconsistency 15. incompatibility
discretion... 4. tact, will 6. option
7. caution, reserve 8. judgment,
prudence, wariness 11. disjunction

12. cautiousness, discreetness
13. discontinuity, judiciousness,
secretiveness 14. circumspection,
discrimination
discretionary ... 7. politic, prudent
8. discreet 9. arbitrary, judicious,
voluntary 10. prudential
11. considerate 14. discriminating
discriminate ... 6. divide, screen,
secern 8. separate, set apart
11. distinguish 13. differentiate
discrimination ... 5. taste 6. acumen,
option 9. prejudice 10. discretion
11. discernment, distinction,
penetration, segregation
discursive ... 6. roving 7. cursory
9. desultory, diffusive, wandering
10. circuitous, digressive
discus ... 4. disk 5. plate, quoit
discuss ... 3. air, rap 4. moot
5. argue, treat 6. confer, debate,
parley 7. bargain, canvass, dispute,
dissert, mention 9. discourse
discus thrower ... 10. discobolus
disdain ... 5. pride, scorn 7. askance,
contemn, despise 8. contempt
9. arrogance 11. haughtiness
16. contemptuousness
disease ... 6. malady 7. ailment, illness,
trouble 8. disorder, sickness
9. affection, infirmity 10. affliction,
disability 11. derangement
disease (of) ...
animals (Afr) .. 5. nenta
apoplexy .. 4. esca
apples .. 7. stippen 9. bitter pit
blood .. 6. anemia 8. leukemia
(leukaemia, leucemia)
cattle .. 5. hoose (hooze) 6. nagana,
wheeze 7. anthrax
chickens .. 3. pip 4. roup
diet .. 7. rickets 8. pellagra, rachitis
divers .. 5. bends 7. caisson
dog .. 5. lyssa 6. rabies
11. hydrophobia
eye .. 6. caligo 7. pinkeye 8. cataract,
glaucoma, trachoma 9. amaurosis
14. conjunctivitis
fungus .. 6. mildew 9. elm blight
Oriental .. 8. beriberi
painful .. 7. lumbago 9. arthritis
plant .. 4. rust, smut 5. ergot, scald
6. Panama (banana) 7. erinose (grape)
potato, tomato .. 8. dartrose
skin .. 5. hives, psora 6. eczema,
herpes, tetter 7. scabies 8. impetigo,
shingles 9. psoriasis, urticaria
10. erysipelas
stonecutter's .. 9. silicosis
sugar cane .. 5. sereh
disease (pert to) ...
classification .. 8. nosology
10. nosography
decline .. 9. catabasis
determination of .. 9. diagnosis
germ transfer .. 7. vection
native to .. 7. endemic
outlook .. 9. prognosis
science of .. 8. etiology, medicine
spread of .. 8. epidemic
suffix .. 4. itis, osis
treatment .. 7. therapy 12. kinesiatrics

disembark ... 4. land 6. alight, debark
7. deplane, detrain, pile out (sl)
disembowel ... 3. gut 10. eviscerate
disengage ... 5. clear 6. detach,
loosen 7. release 8. liberate, unfasten
9. extricate 11. disencumber,
disentangle 12. disembarrass
disentangle ... 4. card, comb 5. clear,
loose, ravel, solve 6. evolve, sleave,
sleeve 7. unravel, unsnare, untwine,
untwist 8. simplify 9. disengage,
extricate 10. disinvolve, unscramble
disfavor ... 7. dislike 8. distaste
9. detriment, disrepute 10. alienation
11. disapproval, displeasure
14. discountenance
disfigure ... 3. mar 4. scar 6. deface,
deform, injure, mangle, uglify
7. blemish 8. mutilate
disgorge ... 4. barf (sl), spew, vent
5. eject, eruct, erupt, expel, heave,
vomit 7. exhaust 9. discharge
10. relinquish 11. regurgitate
disgrace ... 5. abase, odium, shame,
shend, sully 7. attaint, degrade,
distain, obloquy, upbraid 8. dishonor,
ignominy, reproach 9. discredit,
disesteem, disrepute, humiliate
10. opprobrium 11. abomination,
humiliation 13. disparagement
disguise ... 3. mum (mumm) 4. mask,
veil 5. cloak, feign 6. covert, masque
7. conceal, costume, falsify, pretend
9. dissemble, incognito, inebriate
10. camouflage, masquerade
11. dissimulate 12. misrepresent
disgust ... 6. nausea 7. offense,
quarrel 8. aversion, loathing, nauseate
9. animosity, annoyance, antipathy,
revulsion 10. abhorrence, repugnance
11. abomination
disgusting ... 5. nasty 6. filthy, odious
9. loathsome, obnoxious, offensive,
repellent, repulsive, revolting,
sickening
dish ... 3. jar, pot 4. boat (gravy)
5. cruse, nappy, paten, plate
6. patera, saucer, tureen 7. charger
(anc), platter, ramekin 9. casserole
dish (food) ... 5. kibbe (kibbeh), pilaf,
pilau, salmi 6. hachis, haslet, omelet,
potage, ragout 7. bok choy, chowder,
falafel (felafel), pudding, soufflé
10. egg foo yong, shish kabob
11. ratatouille
dishabille ... 6. kimono 7. neglige,
undress 8. bathrobe, negligee,
peignoir 9. housecoat, nightgown
dishearten ... 5. amate (anc), appal,
daunt, deter, unman 6. deject, dismay
7. depress, unnerve 8. dispirit
10. disconcert, discourage
disheveled ... 5. tousy 6. frowzy,
mussed, shaggy, untidy 7. ruffled,
tousled, tumbled, unkempt
8. deranged, uncombed
10. disarrayed, disordered
11. disarranged
dishonest ... 4. base 5. false 6. crafty,
unjust 7. corrupt, crooked, knavish
8. rascally, scheming 9. deceitful,
truthless 10. fraudulent, perfidious

untruthful 12. dishonorable
dishonor... 5. shame 6. defame,
infamy 7. debauch, degrade, obloquy
8. disgrace, ignominy, reproach
9. desecrate, disrepute, improbity
10. disrespect, opprobrium
13. disparagement
dishonorable... 7. ignoble 8. infamous,
shameful 9. dishonest 10. inglorious
11. disesteemed, disgraceful
12. disreputable
disillusion... 10. disquixote
disillusioned... 8. thwarted
12. disappointed, disenchanted
disinclination... 7. dislike 8. aversion,
distaste 10. reluctance, repugnance
12. disaffection 13. indisposition
disinclined... 6. averse 8. indolent
9. reluctant, unwilling 10. indisposed
disinfectant... 5. Lysol 6. cresol,
iodine, phenol 7. alcohol
9. germicide 10. antiseptic
12. formaldehyde
disintegrate... 5. decay, erode
7. break up, corrode, crumble,
disband, resolve 8. dissolve
9. decompose 11. disorganize
disjoin... 4. part, undo 5. sever, untie
6. detach, sunder, unhook 7. unhitch
8. disunite, separate, unbutton
9. disengage 10. disconnect,
dissociate
disk, disc... 4. puck 5. medal, paten,
plate, quoit, wafer, wheel 6. harrow,
record, sequin 7. discoid, medalet
9. faceplate, gyroscope, medallion
dislike... 4. mind 5. odium 6. detest
8. aversion, distaste 9. antipathy,
disrelish 12. disaffection
dislike of children... 9. misopedia
dislike of home... 9. ecophobia
disloyal... 5. false 6. fickle, untrue
9. faithless 10. inconstant,
perfidious, unfaithful 11. treacherous
dismal... 3. sad, wan 4. dark
5. black, bleak, drear, lurid
6. dreary, gloomy, somber 7. doleful,
joyless, Stygian, unhappy, unlucky
8. dolorous, dreadful, funereal,
lonesome, mournful, overcast, sinister
9. ill–omened, sorrowful
10. calamitous, depressing,
lugubrious 11. pessimistic,
unfortunate
dismantle... 4. raze, undo 5. strip
6. divest 7. deprive, destroy, disrobe,
uncloak 8. demolish 11. disassemble
dismay... 4. fear 5. alarm, daunt
6. appall, fright, terror 8. affright,
bewilder 9. dejection 10. depression,
disconcert 12. apprehension
13. consternation
14. discouragement
dismiss... 4. drip, fire 5. amand,
amove, eject, exile, remue 6. acquit,
bounce, depose, recall, refute, shelve
7. forgive, release 8. relegate
9. discharge, disregard 10. relinquish
dismount... 6. alight 7. descend,
unhorse, unmount 11. disassemble
disobedient... 7. forward, froward,
wayward 8. mutinous 10. rebellious,

refractory 11. intractable
12. contumacious
disorder... 3. tic 4. mess, riot
5. chaos, deray, snarl 6. malady,
tumult 7. ailment, anarchy, derange,
illness, misdeed 8. disarray, paranoia,
sickness 9. confusion, craziness,
distemper, paranomia
10. discompose, revolution
11. lawlessness, misdemeanor
12. irregularity 13. indisposition
14. disarrangement
15. disorganization
disorderly... 3. bad 5. mussy, rowdy
6. unruly 7. chaotic, naughty, violent
8. confused, rowdyish, slipshod
9. irregular, offensive, turbulent
12. ungovernable, unmanageable
disorganization... 5. decay 7. anarchy,
breakup, split–up 8. disorder
10. separation 11. destruction,
dissolution 13. disbandonment
14. disarrangement, disintegration
disown... 4. deny 5. expel 6. recant,
reject 7. disavow 8. disclaim,
renounce 9. disaffirm, repudiate
10. disinherit
disparage... 4. slur 5. decry, lower (in
rank) 6. slight 7. degrade, detract
8. dishonor, minimize 10. depreciate,
disapprove, discourage, undervalue
11. incongruity
disparagement... 7. diasyrm
8. disgrace 9. indignity
10. detraction 12. depreciation
disparaging... 8. decaying
10. defamatory, pejorative
11. unfavorable
dispart... 4. open, rend, rive 5. break,
sever, split 6. cleave, divide
dispassionate... 4. cool, fair 6. serene
8. composed, moderate 9. collected,
impartial, temperate, unruffled
11. unemotional 12. unprejudiced
dispatch... 4. kill, mail, post, send,
slay 5. haste, speed 6. hasten
7. message 8. celerity, conclude,
expedite 9. diligence 10. accelerate,
accomplish, promptness
dispatch boat... 5. aviso 6. packet
Dis pater (Rom)... 3. god (underworld)
5. Pluto (Gr) 12. realm of Pluto
dispel... 6. vanish 7. scatter
8. disperse 9. dissipate
dispensation... 6. scheme 7. economy
9. exemption, remission
10. dispersion, management,
misericord (misericorde)
11. arrangement 12. distribution
13. apportionment 14. administration
dispense... 4. deal, dole, give, vend
6. effuse, excuse, exempt 7. absolve
8. disperse 9. apportion
10. administer
dispenser of alms... 7. almoner
disperse... 3. sow 4. rout 5. strew
6. branch, spread, vanish 7. diffuse,
refract, scatter 9. apportion, dissipate
10. distribute 11. disseminate
dispirit... 3. cow 4. damp 5. daunt
6. deject 7. depress 10. discourage,
dishearten, intimidate

displace... 6. depose, mislay, remove 8. misplace 9. discharge, dislocate, supersede 10. substitute

display... 3. air 4. pomp, show, wear 5. array 6. evince, flaunt, parade, set out 7. exhibit, pageant, splurge 8. emblazon 9. advertise 10. appearance 11. demonstrate, ostentation 13. manifestation

display (pert to)...
case.. 10. show window
in public.. 5. stage
of emotion.. 10. enthusiasm
of force (distant).. 9. telenergy
of temper.. 5. scene 9. spectacle

displease... 3. vex 4. miff 5. anger, annoy, pique 6. offend 7. provoke 8. irritate 10. dissatisfy

displeasure... 5. anger 7. disgust, dislike, offense, trouble 8. disfavor, distaste 10. resentment, uneasiness 11. indignation, unhappiness 14. disapprobation 15. dissatisfaction

dispose (of)... 3. set 4. give, mind, sell, tend 5. order, place 6. adjust, assign, bestow, settle 7. arrange, destroy, discard, testate 8. give away, regulate 9. eliminate 10. distribute, relinquish

disposed... 5. prone 7. settled, willing 8. arranged, assigned, inclined 11. distributed

disposed (pert to)...
favorably.. 7. propend
to cling together.. 8. clannish
to doubt.. 9. skeptical
to please.. 11. complaisant

disposition... 3. use 4. bent, bias, mood, turn 6. animus, giving, morale, nature, temper 7. control 8. tendency 9. character 10. management, settlement 11. arrangement, elimination, temperament 12. organization 13. apportionment

dispossess... 5. eject, evict 6. divest, refute 8. disseize

dispossessed... 6. bereft, ousted 7. ejected, evicted 8. deprived, divested

disproof... 6. answer, denial 8. negation, rebuttal 10. refutation 11. confutation 12. invalidation

disprove... 5. belie, rebut 6. refute 7. confute 9. discredit 10. invalidate

disputation... 6. debate 7. polemic 8. argument 10. contention 11. controversy 12. conversation

disputatious... 7. eristic, polemic 11. contentious, quarrelsome 13. argumentative, controversial

dispute... 4. deny, feud, moot, spar 5. brawl, broil 6. bicker, debate, haggle, higgle, naggle 7. contest, dissent, protest, quarrel, wrangle 8. argument, squabble 11. altercation, controversy

disqualify... 5. debar 9. indispose 10. invalidate 12. incapacitate

disquiet... 3. vix 4. fret 5. alarm 6. excite 7. agitate, concern, disturb 8. distress, frighten 12. apprehension

disquisition... 5. essay 10. discussion 12. dissertation

disregard... 4. snub 6. ignore, slight 7. neglect 8. defiance 9. unconcern 11. inattention

disreputable... 3. low 4. base 5. seamy 7. raffish 8. shameful, unworthy 13. discreditable 15. persona non grata

disrespect... 7. affront 9. disesteem, insolence 10. incivility 11. discourtesy

disrespectful... 7. uncivil 8. impudent, insolent 10. irreverent 12. discourteous

disrupt... 4. part (forcibly), rend, tear 5. upset 6. thwart 11. disorganize

dissatisfaction... 8. vexation 10. discontent 11. displeasure, unsatisfied

dissect... 3. cut 6. divide 7. analyze 8. separate 9. anatomize

disseize (law)... 4. oust 5. evict 6. depose 10. dispossess 11. expropriate

dissemble... 4. hide 5. cloak, feign 7. conceal 8. disguise 9. disregard 11. counterfeit

disseminate... 3. sow 6. effuse, spread 7. publish, scatter 8. disperse 9. circulate, propagate

dissension... 7. discord 8. brouille, friction 10. dissidence 12. disagreement

dissent... 3. nay 8. apostasy, disagree 10. separation 12. disagreement, nonagreement 13. nonconformity 14. nonconcurrence

dissenter... 7. heretic, Sectary 8. apostate, recusant 9. protester 10. Protestant 13. nonconformist

dissertation... 5. essay, tract 6. debate, thesis 7. article, lecture 8. treatise 9. discourse 10. discussion, exposition 12. disquisition

dissidence... 7. dissent 8. variance 9. cacophony 10. difference, dissension 12. disagreement

dissimilarity... 7. variety 9. disparity, diversity 10. difference, unlikeness, unsameness 13. dissimilation, heterogeneity 17. heterogeneousness

dissipate... 5. spend, waste 6. dispel, expend 7. consume, scatter, shatter 8. dispense, dissolve, squander 9. disappear

dissipation... 4. loss 9. decrement, diffusion 10. dispersion, profligacy 11. consumption, prodigality 12. intemperance 13. disappearance, dissoluteness 14. disintegration

dissolute... 3. lax 4. lewd, wild 5. loose 6. loosed, rakish, wanton, wicked 7. lawless, vicious 8. reckless, uncurbed 9. abandoned, debauched, unbridled 10. dissipated, licentious, profligate 11. demoralized 12. unrestrained

dissolve... 4. fuse, melt 5. solve 7. adjourn, liquefy 9. decompose, disappear 11. disorganize

12. disintegrate
dissolved ... 6. solute 7. soluble
dissonant ... 5. harsh 7. grating, jarring
8. jangling 9. deviative, different,
differing 10. discordant, discrepant
11. disagreeing, unmelodious
12. inconsistent, inharmonious
13. contradictory
dissuade ... 5. deter 6. advise, dehort,
divert 8. admonish 10. discourage,
disincline 11. expostulate
distaff side ... 5. women 6. female
distain ... 5. stain, tinge 6. define
7. tarnish 8. discolor
distance ... 4. step, yond 5. depth,
range, space 6. offing 7. mileage,
reserve, yardage 8. coldness, outstrip
9. aloofness, antiquity, dimension
10. remoteness
distant ... 3. far, tel, yon 4. afar, cold,
tele (pref) 5. aloof 6. remote,
utmost, yonder 7. foreign 8. ulterior
distaste ... 7. disgust 8. aversion
9. disrelish 10. repugnance
11. displeasure 14. disinclination
15. dissatisfaction
distasteful ... 7. hateful 8. nauseous,
unsavory 9. loathsome, offensive
10. disgusting, unpleasant
11. displeasing, unpalatable
12. disagreeable
distemper ... 3. vex 4. soak 5. anger,
color, steep 6. dilute, malady, ruffle
7. ailment, disease, disturb
8. painting (process), sickness
13. indisposition
distend ... 4. grow 5. bulge, swell
6. dilate, expand, spread 7. enlarge,
inflate, stretch 8. lengthen
distended ... 5. tumid 7. bloated,
swollen 8. inflated, patulous, puffed
up
distich ... 7. couplet 8. two lines
distill, distil ... 4. leak 6. decoct,
infuse 7. extract, squeeze, trickle
8. vaporize
distilling device ... 5. flask 6. retort
7. alembic 10. distillery
distinct ... 4. fair 5. clear 7. audible,
obvious, precise, several 8. explicit,
manifest 9. different 10. individual
13. distinguished
distinction ... 4. rank 5. honor
6. repute 8. nobility 9. clearness,
greatness, variation 10. difference
14. discrimination 15. differentiation
distinctive ... 7. typical 8. peculiar
9. prominent 14. characteristic,
discriminative
distinctive mark ... 4. sign 5. badge
6. cachet, emblem, symbol
distinctive quality ... 6. genius, talent
9. specialty
distinguish ... 6. secern 7. discern
8. perceive, separate 9. recognize
12. discriminate 13. differentiate
distinguished ... 5. great, noted
6. famous, marked 7. defined,
eminent, honored, special 8. laureate,
renowned, superior 9. different,
egregious, prominent 10. celebrated
11. conspicuous, illustrious

13. extraordinary 14. characteristic
distort ... 4. warp 5. screw, twist,
wrest 6. deform 7. contort, falsify,
pervert 10. camshackle
12. misrepresent
distorted ... 4. awry 6. rubato
7. twisted
distortion ... 5. loxia 10. perversion
12. malformation
distract ... 5. craze 6. divert, harass,
madden, puzzle 7. confuse, perplex
10. distraught
distracted ... 3. mad 7. frantic
8. distrait, diverted, rambling
9. disturbed 10. distraught
11. overwrought
distraction ... 6. frenzy, tumult
7. despair, madness 8. disorder
9. agitation, confusion, diversion
10. dissension, perplexity
11. derangement, disturbance,
inattention 12. perturbation
distress ... 3. ail 4. pain 5. agony,
annoy, grief, worry 6. danger, grieve,
harrow, misery 7. anguish, anxiety,
perplex, poverty, trouble 8. distrain,
vexation 9. necessity 10. affliction,
discomfort
distress call ... 3. SOS
distribute ... 3. dot, sow 4. deal, dole,
mete 5. allot, share 6. assign,
assort, divide, spread 7. deal out,
prorate, scatter 8. allocate, classify,
dispense, disperse 9. apportion,
broadcast 10. administer
distribution ... 8. disposal 9. allotment
10. dispersion 11. arrangement,
disposition 12. dispensation
13. apportionment 14. classification
distribution of favors ... 9. patronage
11. benefaction
distributor ... 5. agent 6. agency
8. merchant 11. broadcaster
district ... 4. pale, slum, ward 5. realm
6. canton, domain, ghetto, region
7. circuit, demesne, quarter
8. province 9. bailiwick, territory
District of Columbia ... see
Washington, DC
distrust ... 5. doubt, qualm 8. jealousy,
mistrust, wariness 9. misgiving,
suspicion, treachery
disturb ... 3. vex 4. riot, roil 5. alarm,
annoy, rouse, roust, upset 6. excite,
molest, ruffle 7. agitate, derange,
fluster, perturb, trouble 8. disorder,
distract 9. interrupt 10. discompose,
disconcert
disturbance ... 5. alarm, brawl
6. hubbub, rumpus, static, tumult,
uproar 7. anxiety, clatter 8. stramash
9. agitation, annoyance, commotion,
confusion 10. excitement, turbulence
11. derangement 12. perturbation
disturbed ... 6. uneasy 7. annoyed,
excited, inquiet, unquiet 8. agitated
10. bewildered 12. disconcerted
disunion ... 9. severance 10. alienation,
detachment, dissension, separation
11. disjunction 13. disconnection
disunite ... 3. rip 4. part 5. sever,
untie 6. divide, sunder, unteam,

unyoke 7. discerp, disjoin, unravel
8. alienate, separate 9. dismember

disuse . . . 6. misuse, nonuse
7. abandon, discard 8. disusage
9. desuetude 11. antiquation,
discontinue 12. obsolescence

ditch . . . 3. sap 4. dike, hole, moat,
rine 5. canal, evade, fossa, fosse,
rhine 6. escarp, furrow, relais, trench
7. abandon, acequia, channel

dithyramb . . . 3. ode 4. hymn 6. poetry
7. epithet (of Dionysus)

ditty . . . 3. lay 4. poem, sing, song
5. carol 6. saying 7. canzone
8. canticle

diurnal . . . 5. daily 8. everyday
9. quotidian

divan . . . 4. sofa 5. couch 6. leewan,
settee 9. davenport 12. Chesterfield

dive . . . 4. swim 6. plunge, resort,
saloon 7. brothel, descend, descent,
explore 8. submerge

divergence . . . 7. theorem 9. deviation,
obliquity 10. difference, separation
12. disagreement, divarication

divers . . . 5. cruel 6. sundry 7. several,
various 8. perverse 9. different

diver's disease . . . 5. bends 7. caisson

diverse . . . 6. sundry, unlike 7. several,
various 8. distinct, separate
9. different, multiform

diver's gear . . . 8. flippers
12. respirometer

diversify . . . 4. vary 6. change
7. variate 9. variegate 10. distribute
13. differentiate

diversion . . . 4. game, play 5. hobby,
sport 6. change 7. pastime
8. apostasy 9. amusement
10. deflection, recreation
11. distraction 13. entertainment

diversity . . . 7. variety 10. difference
11. variegation 12. multiformity

divert . . . 5. amuse, avert, parry
7. deflect, delight 8. dissuade,
distract, recreate 9. entertain
10. disincline

divest . . . 4. doff, reft, tirl 5. strip
6. debunk, depose 8. unclothe
10. dispossess

divide . . . 3. lot 4. fork, part 5. cleft,
halve, sever, share, slice, space, split
6. bisect, cleave, septum, sunder
7. prorate 8. alienate, classify,
separate 9. apportion, bifurcate,
calculate, dismember, partition,
segregate, watershed 11. distinguish

divide (pert to) . . .
areas (small) . . 8. areolate
feet . . 4. scan
four parts . . 4. paly (Her) 7. quarter
many parts . . 8. fraction 9. multisect
seven parts . . 9. septimole
steps . . 8. graduate
transversely . . 12. cross–section
two parts . . 6. bisect

divided . . . 4. enté (Her), reft 5. bifid,
split, zoned 6. halved, parted
7. partial, partite, septate
8. aerolate, bifidate, unjoined
9. alienated, disunited 11. distributed

dividend . . . 5. bonus, share 6. number

7. payment

divination . . . 3. art (magic) 4. omen,
sors 6. augury, sortes 7. presage
9. intuition

divination by . . .
ashes (sacrificial) . . 11. tephromancy
cards . . 10. cartomancy
dead spirits . . 10. necromancy
dreams . . 11. oneiromancy
eggs . . 7. oomancy
fig leaf . . 9. sycomancy
figures . . 8. geomancy
fire . . 9. pyromancy
footprints . . 10. ichnomancy
forehead . . 11. metapomancy
fountains . . 9. pegomancy
letters of a name . . 7. nomancy
  8. onomancy
mice . . 8. myomancy
moon . . 10. seleomancy
neighing horse . . 10. hippomancy
oracles . . 9. theomancy
palmistry . . 10. chiromancy
pebbles . . 9. thrioboly
romantic medium . . 5. daisy
salt . . 9. halomancy
serpents . . 10. ophiomancy
smoke (sacrificial) . . 10. capromancy
stars . . 11. sideromancy
straws (burning) . . 11. sideromancy
sword . . 13. machairomancy
verses . . 13. rhapsodomancy
wands, rods . . 11. rhabdomancy
water . . 10. hydromancy
weather . . 9. aeromancy
wild animals . . 11. theriomancy
wine . . 9. oenomancy

divine . . . 5. divus, guess, pious
6. priest, sacred, superb 7. foresee,
godlike, predict 8. forebode, foretell,
heavenly, minister, prophecy
9. beautiful, celestial, clergyman,
religious 10. anticipate, superhuman,
theologian 12. supernatural

divine (pert to) . . .
being . . 4. deva
breath . . 4. soul
force . . 5. deity, numen 6. spirit
gift . . 8. blessing
inspiration . . 8. afflatus
messenger . . 7. apostle
opinion . . 14. theologoumenon
power . . 7. entheos (obs)
utterance . . 8. prophecy
wisdom . . 8. theogamy
word . . 5. grace, logos
work . . 7. theurgy

divining rod . . . 4. wand 6. dowser
9. doodlebug

divinity . . . 3. God, Ler 4. Deus, Lord
5. Allah, deity, Khuda, Mazda
6. Brahma, Christ 7. Jehovah,
Saviour, Taranis, Trinity 8. Almighty

division . . . 4. part, sect, unit 5. share
6. schism, sector 7. faction, section
8. cleavage, disunion, variance
9. allotment, bisection, partition
10. alienation, department, separation
11. compartment, disjunction
12. distribution 13. apportionment,
disconnection, dismemberment
14. classification

14. classification
division (pert to)...
center (Biol).. **9.** centriole
city.. **4.** ward **5.** block **8.** precinct
French.. **6.** canton **7.** Commune
  10. department **14.** arrondissement
mankind.. **4.** race
poem.. **5.** canto, verse **6.** stanza
time.. **3.** Age, Eon (Aeon), Era
  6. Eogaea (Zool)
zone (earth).. **6.** frigid, torrid, tropic
  9. temperate
divorce, Mohammedan law... **5.** talak
divot... **3.** sod **4.** clod, turf
divulge... **4.** tell **6.** expose, impart,
  reveal **7.** confide, publish, uncover
  8. disclose, discover, proclaim
  11. communicate
Dixie, Dixieland... **4.** song **6.** utopia
  7. Sunbelt **8.** The South (US)
dizziness... **5.** whirl **7.** vertigo
  9. giddiness **10.** fickleness
dizzy... **5.** crazy, giddy, tipsy **6.** fickle,
  stupid **7.** foolish **8.** confused,
  swimming, unsteady **9.** delirious
  10. capricious **11.** vertiginous
Djibouti, east Africa...
city.. **5.** Obock **6.** Dikkil
gulf.. Aden
do... **2.** ut (Mus) **3.** act, pay **4.** dost,
  fare, make, suit, work **5.** avoid, cause,
  cheat, exert, serve, solve **6.** answer,
  effect, finish **7.** achieve, deceive,
  execute, perform, produce, prosper,
  suffice **8.** transact **9.** discharge
  10. administer
docile... **4.** calm, tame **6.** gentle
  7. duteous **9.** compliant, teachable,
  tractable
dock... **4.** clip, pier, slip **5.** basin, jetty,
  plant, wharf **6.** cut off, deduct,
  hangar **7.** curtail, shorten
  8. waterway **9.** anchorage
  12. witness stand
docket... **4.** list, mark **6.** record, ticket
  8. calendar, schedule **11.** certificate
docking post... **7.** bollard
dock worker... **6.** loader **7.** laborer
  9. stevedore **12.** longshoreman
doctor... **3.** cut, fly (angling) **4.** dose
  5. spike, title, treat **6.** degree, dilute,
  healer, intern (interne) **7.** surgeon,
  teacher **9.** physician **10.** adulterate,
  veterinary **12.** psychiatrist
doctrine... **3.** ism, ist **4.** rule **5.** credo,
  creed, dogma, logic, maxim, tenet
  6. gospel **7.** article, opinion, precept
  8. position **9.** principle
doctrine (pert to)...
existence (Philos).. **6.** henism
finality (Theol).. **11.** eschatology
good.. **8.** agathism
inevitability.. **8.** fatalism
philosophy.. **10.** pragmatism
secrecy.. **6.** cabala **8.** esoteric
selfishness.. **6.** egoism
doctus... **7.** learned
document... **4.** deed, writ **5.** paper,
  proof, scrip **6.** escrow **7.** archive
  11. corroborate
document (pert to)...
copy (true).. **5.** Xerox **7.** estreat

8. syngraph **9.** duplicate, photostat
depository.. **8.** archives
file, report.. **7.** dossier
hamper.. **7.** hanaper
dodecade... **5.** dozen **6.** twelve (series)
dodge... **4.** duck, jouk, snub **5.** avoid,
  cheat, elude, evade, parry, trick
  6. escape, palter **7.** deceive
  8. artifice **9.** expedient
dodger... **7.** biscuit, shirker
  8. deceiver, handbill
dodo... **3.** moa **4.** bird (extinct)
doe... **3.** tag, teg **4.** deer, hind
doer... **5.** actor, agent, maker
  6. author, factor, worker **7.** manager
  8. attorney, executor, producer
  9. performer
doff... **4.** vail **5.** strip **6.** divest,
  remove **7.** take off, undress
dog... **3.** cur, pug **4.** foot, lyam (lyme)
  5. canis, hound, pooch, whelp
  6. canine, fallow, shadow, wretch,
  yelper **7.** mongrel **9.** carnivore
  13. constellation
dog (breed)... **3.** pom **4.** chow, Dane
  5. boxer, husky **6.** basset, beagle,
  collie, lucern, nootka, poodle, Saluki,
  setter, Sussex **7.** bulldog, griffon,
  mastiff, pointer, Samoyed, Shih Tzu,
  spaniel, terrier, whippet **8.** Airedale,
  Doberman, Keeshong, Labrador,
  Malemute, Pekinese, Sealyham,
  shepherd **9.** Chihuahua, dachshund,
  Dalmatian, greyhound, Pekingese,
  retriever, schnauzer, St Bernard,
  wolfhound **10.** bloodhound,
  Pomeranian, schipperke **11.** Skye
  terrier **12.** gazelle hound **13.** Boston
  terrier
dog (pert to)...
Buster Brown.. **4.** Tige
Cape (hunting).. **8.** cynhyena
days.. **8.** canicule
F D R's.. **4.** Fala (Falla)
ferocious.. **7.** agouara
fictional.. **4.** Asta, Toby
house.. **6.** kennel
howl.. **9.** ululation
like.. **6.** cynoid
mythical.. **7.** Cerebus
part.. **5.** flews **7.** dewclaw
short-eared (Her).. **4.** alan (aland)
star.. **6.** Sirius **8.** Canicula
Victor records.. **6.** Nipper (His
  Master's Voice)
wild.. **5.** dhole, dingo **6.** bandog,
  kolsun **8.** cimarron
Doge's barge... **9.** Bucentaur
dogfish... **5.** shark **6.** burbot
  9. blackfish **10.** nursehound
dogma... **4.** code **5.** tenet **6.** belief,
  dictum, ritual **7.** precept **8.** doctrine
  9. Levitical, principle
dogmatic... **7.** certain **8.** absolute,
  positive **9.** assertive, canonical,
  doctrinal, pragmatic **11.** dictatorial,
  doctrinaire, magisterial, opinionated
dogmatism... **10.** pragmatism
  11. intolerance
dogwood... **5.** osier **6.** cornel
  7. boxwood
do it again... **5.** itero

dole... 4. alms, mete 5. grief
6. sorrow 8. pittance 9. allotment
10. distribute, misfortune
12. distribution
doleful... 3. sad 4. dree 5. drear
6. dismal, dreary, rueful, woeful
8. doloroso, dolorous, grievous,
jeremiad, mournful 10. lugubrious,
melancholy
doll... 3. toy 4. baby (toy), girl
6. moppet, puppet 9. miniature,
plaything
dolphin... 4. fish, inia 5. bouto
6. dorado, dugong, sea pig
8. Cetacean, porpoise 9. goosebeak
10. bottlenose
dolt... 3. ass, oaf 4. clod, dope, loon,
lout, moke 5. dunce, idiot 7. dullard
8. clodpate, dumbbell, numskull
9. blockhead, dumb bunny
10. ignoramus
domain... 5. realm 6. empery, empire,
sphere 7. country, demesne
8. dominion
dome... 4. arch, head, roof (Astron)
5. spire, tower 6. cupola, turret
Domesday, doomsday... 4. Book (Eng
Hist) 11. Judgment Day 13. Great
Domesday 14. Little Domesday
17. Domesday of St Paul's
domestic... 4. tame 5. domal
7. servant 9. enchorial, home–grown,
intestine (not foreign)
domestic establishment... 6. ménage
9. household
domicile... 5. abode, house 7. habitat
8. dwelling 9. residence
10. habitation
dominant... 5. chief, chord 6. ruling
7. regnant, supreme 8. superior
9. ascendant, governing, imperious,
paramount, principal
10. pre–eminent, prevailing
11. influential, outweighing,
overtopping 12. preponderant
13. authoritative, overbalancing
dominate... 4. boss, rule, sway
5. reign 6. govern 7. command,
control, overtop, possess
11. predominate
domineering... 6. lordly 7. haughty
8. arrogant, blustery 9. imperious,
masterful 10. oppressive
11. overbearing
Dominican Republic...
capital.. 12. Santo Domingo
city.. 14. Ciudad Trujillo
discoverer.. 8. Columbus
island site.. 10. Hispaniola
oldest city (W Hem).. 12. Santo
Domingo (1496)
dominion... 4. rule, sway 5. realm
6. empery, empire, sphere 7. control
9. authority, hierarchy (celestial)
12. jurisdiction
domino... 3. pip (spot) 4. game (in
pl), hood, mask 5. amice, cloak,
ivory 7. costume
dominoes, galloping... 7. ivories
donate... 3. tip 4. give 6. bestow
7. present
done... 4. fini 5. baked, ended, finis

6. agreed, cooked 7. through
8. finished, tired out 9. completed,
concluded, exhausted
done (pert to)...
by stealth.. 13. surreptitious
by word of mouth.. 5. parol
for pay.. 9. mercenary
with effort.. 5. labor
Don Juan's girl (novel)... 6. Haidee
donkey... 3. ass 4. moke 5. burro,
neddy 6. onager
donna... 4. Dona, lady, wife
5. madam, woman 8. mistress
Don Quixote's steed... 9. Rosinante
doom... 3. fey, lot 4. fate, ruin
5. death 7. condemn, destine,
destiny 8. sentence 11. destruction
doomed... 3. fey 5. death, fated,
goner 9. sentenced
doomsday... 8. Ragnarok
11. Judgment Day (see *Domesday*)
door... 4. gate 6. portal 7. doorway,
opening, passage, postern
11. entranceway 12. porte–cochere
doorframe... 3. dar 4. jamb, rail,
sash, sill 5. janua, panel, stile
6. lintel 9. threshold
doorkeeper... 4. hasp 5. tiler 6. porter
7. durwaum, ostiary 8. chokidar
9. concierge
dope... 3. hop, LSD 4. hemp
6. mescal, opiate, peyoti (peyote)
7. fathead 8. narcotic 9. marijuana
Dorian Festival (Sparta)... 6. carnea
(carneia)
Dorian magistrates... 6. ephors
Doric Order (Gr Arch)...
capital.. 6. abacus
frieze fillet.. 6. taenia
frieze space.. 6. metope
history.. 6. oldest 8. simplest
dormant... 5. inert 6. asleep, latent,
torpid 7. resting 8. inactive, sleeping
9. quiescent
dormer window... 5. oriel 6. gablet
7. dormant (obs), lucarne
dormeuse... 5. couch 8. carriage
(sleeping), nightcap
dormouse... 4. Glis, loir 5. lerot
6. rodent
dorsal (pert to)...
back.. 5. notal, notum 6. dorsum,
lumbar, neural, tergal, tergum
column.. 6. spinal
dose... 5. bolus, draft, treat 6. potion
7. portion
dot... 3. jot 4. clot, code, lump
5. dowry, fleck, point, speck, telia
(fungus) 6. period 7. stipple
dote... 3. rot 5. decay, dowry
6. babble, dotage, dotard, drivel,
stupor 7. portion (marriage)
8. imbecile
dotted... 5. pinto 7. piebald, specked,
studded 8. stippled 9. sprinkled
11. diversified
Douay Bible... 4. Aree
double... 2. di (pref) 4. dual, fold,
twin 5. duple, plait, twice 6. binary,
binate, duplex, folded 7. twofold
8. artifice, two–faced 9. deceitful,
duplicate, insincere, intensify

11. counterpart
double (pert to)...
bars (Her).. 5. gemel
cross.. 7. deceive, two–time
dagger.. 6. diesis
edged.. 9. ancipital
ghost (live person).. 11. counterpart
12. Doppelgänger, doubleganger
meaning.. 9. equivocal
doubt... 5. demur, waver 8. hesitate,
mistrust, question 9. misgiving,
suspicion 10. Pyrrhonism, skepticism
11. uncertainty
doubter... 5. cynic 6. Humist
7. skeptic 10. Pyrrhonist
doubtful... 7. dubious 8. wavering
9. ambiguous, equivocal, uncertain,
undecided 10. hesitating, improbable,
precarious 11. distrustful, vacillating
12. questionable, unbelievable,
undetermined 13. problematical
doubtful authority... 6. mythic, unreal
10. apocryphal
dough... 4. cash, mash 5. money,
paste 6. leaven, noodle
doughnut... 6. sinker 7. cruller, simball
9. friedcake
dour... 5. harsh, stern 6. gloomy,
severe 9. obstinate 10. inflexible
dove... 3. nun 4. blue (color), Inca
5. color 6. culver, pigeon
7. Columba, tumbler
Dove, the... 6. symbol (Relig)
10. Holy Spirit
dovefoot... 8. geranium (wild)
dovekey, dovekie... 3. auk 4. Alle
6. rotche 9. guillemot
dowdy... 3. pie (deep–dish) 6. pastry,
shabby, untidy 7. pudding 8. slovenly
10. slatternly
dowel... 3. pin 4. coak 5. tenon
6. fasten, pintle
dower... 3. dos 5. dowry, endow,
grant 6. dotate 7. bequest
8. dotation, jointure
down... 2. de (pref) 3. nap 4. fuzz,
hair 5. adown, below, floor
7. descent 8. softness
downcast... 3. low, sad 7. lowered
8. dejected 9. bowed down,
depressed 10. despondent, dispirited
11. discouraged, downhearted
downright... 4. flat 5. blunt, plain,
sheer, stark, utter 6. arrant, candid
8. positive, thorough 10. absolutely,
forthright 11. unqualified
13. unceremonious
downy... 4. soft, wary 5. nappy, pilar,
quiet 6. placid 7. villous 8. feathery
10. flocculent, lanuginose, lanuginous
dowry... 3. dos, dot 4. gift 5. dower,
sulka 6. talent 9. endowment
dowser's tool... 4. wand 6. willow
Doxology... 4. hymn 6. praise
7. Kaddish
doze... 3. nap, nod 5. sleep
6. catnap, drowse, snooze 7. stupefy
(obs)
draft, draught... 3. map, nip 4. dose,
dram, draw, plan, pull, swig
5. drink, epure 7. current, diagram,
drawing, outline 8. protocol, recruits,

traction 9. conscript 10. money
order
drag... 3. lag, lug, tow, tug 4. clog,
draw, hale, haul, pull, sing, tump
5. drawl, scent (hunt), smoke, trail
6. drogue, harrow 7. grapnel
8. dragrope, linger on, obstacle
10. conveyance
dragoman... 11. interpreter (official)
dragon... 4. lung 5. drake, Rahab (Bib)
6. animal, duenna, lizard, musket
(anc), pigeon 7. dragoon, monster
(Her), serpent 10. earthdrake
14. Dragon of Komodo
drain... 3. gaw, sap 4. lade, loss,
sink, sump 5. ditch, dreen, empty,
rhine, sewer, siver 6. filter, trench
7. acequia, alberca, channel,
consume, exhaust, outflow
11. watercourse
dram... 3. nip 4. mite, slug 5. draft,
drink 6. drachm 8. potation
11. indifferent
drama (pert to)...
beginning.. 8. Dyonysia (anc)
form.. 4. play 5. opera 6. comedy
7. tragedy 10. peripeteia
11. composition
parts.. 8. epitasis, protasis
12. introduction
scenery.. 7. diorama
dramatic... 4. wild 5. stagy, vivid,
vocal 6. poetic, scenic 8. thespian
10. histrionic, theatrical
11. pretentious, spectacular
12. melodramatic
dramatic piece... 4. skit
drastic... 5. stern 6. fierce, severe
7. intense, radical 8. rigorous
draught... see *draft*
Dravidian (pert to)...
country (anc).. 5. India
ghost.. 4. bhut
language.. 5. Tamil 8. Kanarese
12. Dravido–Munda
native.. 5. Croat 8. Croatian
people.. 4. Nair 6. Slavic
soldier.. 8. Croatian
draw... 3. lug, tie, tow, tug 4. drag,
etch, haul, limn, lure, plot, pull, tole
5. draft, smoke 6. allure, arroyo,
convey, entice 7. attract, conduct,
extract, lottery 8. delineate
10. attraction
draw (pert to)...
away.. 6. abduce, divert 7. detract
close.. 4. loom, near 5. hover
8. approach
forth.. 5. educe 6. elicit, ferret
7. extract
off.. 6. siphon 7. extract 8. abstract,
withdraw
through an eye.. 4. rove
together.. 4. coul, frap, lace, rake
8. assemble
drawback... 5. fault, wince 6. defect,
resile, retire 8. obstacle 9. objection
12. disadvantage
drawing... 3. art 5. draft 7. diagram,
hauling, picture, pulling 8. doodling
9. animation 10. attracting,
extracting

drawing back... 9. retrahent
drayage... 6. charge 7. cartage, haulage 8. truckage 14. transportation
dread... 3. awe 4. fear 5. timor 6. dismay, horror, terror 7. anxiety 8. affright, disquiet 9. reverence 12. apprehension
dreadful... 4. dire 6. horrid 7. awesome, fearful, hideous 8. horrible, terrible, terrific 9. frightful 10. formidable, outrageous
dreadnaught, dreadnought... 5. cloth 7. garment 8. fearless 10. battleship, fearnought
dream... 4. muse, rêve 5. fancy 6. bubble, vision 7. imagine, reverie, romance, suppose 8. illusion, stargaze 11. contemplate
dream (pert to)...
interpretation.. 10. oneirology
interpreter.. 12. oneirocritic
tranquility.. 3. kef (keef) 7. reverie
dreamer... 4. seer 7. fantast 8. idealist, puffbird 9. visionary 11. romanticist 13. castle–builder
dreamy... 3. kef (keef) 6. poetic 7. languid 8. soothing 9. visionary 11. imaginative
dreary... 3. sad 4. dull, gray 5. bleak, ourie 6. dismal, elenge, gloomy, remote 7. doleful, tedious 9. cheerless 10. depressing, foreboding, melancholy, monotonous 11. comfortless
dredge... 4. tong (for oysters) 5. scoop 6. burrow, deepen, grains, tunnel 8. excavate
dregs... 4. faex, lees, marc, silt 5. draff, dross, magma 6. refuse, scoria, sludge 7. grounds, hogwash, residue 8. riffraff, sediment 9. settlings 10. faex populi
drench... 4. hose, soak 5. douse, draft, imbue, purge, scour, souse 6. potion 7. immerse 8. inundate, permeate, saturate, submerge
drenched... 4. asop 5. asoak 6. doused, soaked 9. saturated
dress... 3. rig, tog 4. deck, garb, gown, suit, trim 5. getup, mufti, preen 6. attire, clothe, enrobe, livery, toilet 7. apparel, threads (sl) 8. clothing, decorate, negligee 10. habiliment 13. mother hubbard
dress (pert to)...
flax.. 3. ted
gaudily.. 5. prank 7. bedizen, spangle
leather.. 3. taw, tew 5. curry
of Mecca pilgrims.. 5. ihram
riding.. 5. chaps, habit 7. hacking (jacket) 8. jodhpurs 10. chaparajos
stone.. 3. dab, nig 5. nidge
surgically.. 5. dight, panse 7. bandage 8. ligature
up.. 4. dude 5. preen, primp 6. spruce 8. titivate
dressed loosely... 8. discinct, ungirded
dressing... 4. lint 5. sauce 7. bandage, pledget, raiment, reproof

8. attiring, scolding 9. condiment, neatsfoot (leather) 11. castigation
drew... see *draw*
dried... 4. sere 5. wiped 6. seared, wasted 7. drained, parched, wizened 9. shriveled 10. dehydrated, desiccated, exsiccated
dried meat... 7. biltong (biltongue), charqui 8. pemmican 10. jerked beef
dried tubers (orchids)... 5. salep
drift... 3. aim, sag 4. idle, pile, sail, soar, tide, tool 5. float, stray, tenor, trend 6. course, intent 7. deposit, impetus, meaning 8. crescent (sidewise), movement, seaweeds, tendency 9. deviation
drill... 3. gad, row (seeds), tap 4. bore 5. auger, borer, train 6. baboon, pierce 7. machine 8. excavate, exercise, practice, rehearse 9. perforate
drilling... 5. denim 7. nurture 8. training 11. inculcation
drink... 3. ade, ale, bib, lap, nip, pop, rum, sip, tea, tot 4. flip, fram, grog, shot, slug, soda, soma, swig, tope 5. bouse, draft, julep, negus, posca, punch, quaff, skink, toast, toddy, water 6. caudle, coffee, imbibe, liquor, mai tai, mao–tai, posset, potion, ptisan, tipple 8. beverage, cocktail, highball, sillabub 9. decoction 10. intoxicant, mixed drink
drink (pert to)...
ancient.. 5. morat
Arabian.. 4. boza
English.. 7. wassail 8. champers
fond of.. 8. bibulous
frozen.. 6. frappé
gods (of the).. 6. nectar
honey.. 4. mead 5. morat
hot.. 5. salep, toddy 6. posset, saloop
Irish.. 10. shandygaff
Japanese.. 4. sake
mix.. 5. setup 8. vermouth 9. grenadine
rum.. 5. bumbo
Russian.. 5. vodka 6. kumiss (koumiss)
Spanish.. 7. tequila
together.. 9. symposium
tropical.. 7. sangria 8. sangaree
Turkish.. 4. raki 5. airan, arrak
drinking salutation... 5. skoal, toast 6. prosit 7. propine, slainte
drinking vessel... 3. mug 4. bowl, tass 5. cylix (anc), glass, gourd, jorum, mazer, stein 6. goblet, rhyton 7. tankard 8. schooner 10. Vaphio cups (gold)
drip... 4. bore, drop, leak 5. droop 7. dribble, falling, trickle
drive... 3. caa 4. herd, ride, slog, urge 5. force, guide, impel, pilot, press, rouse 6. attack, compel, energy, propel, thrust 7. crusade, operate 8. campaign 10. compulsion
drive (pert to)...
away.. 4. rout 5. chase, exile, expel, repel 6. banish, dispel, rebuff 7. repulse 8. disperse
down.. 4. tamp
frantic.. 4. loco 6. madden 7. bedevil

obliquely.. 3. toe 5. slice
stakes.. 4. camp, park 6. locate, settle
drivel... 4. dote 5. drool 6. slaver 7. slobber, twaddle 8. nonsense
driveler... 4. fool 5. doter, idiot 6. dotard, prater 8. jabberer 9. blatherer, chatterer
driver... 4. club (golf), jehu 6. drover, hammer, mahout, sarwan 7. speeder 8. coachman, engineer, motorist, operator, overseer, reinsman 9. propeller 10. charioteer, taskmaster
drizzle... 4. mist, rain, smur 6. mizzle (misle)
droll... 3. odd 4. zany 5. comic, merry, queer, witty 6. jester 7. amusing, buffoon, waggish 8. farcical, humorous 9. diverting, laughable, whimsical 10. ridiculous 11. merry–andrew
drollery... 3. wit 4. jest 5. farce, humor 6. puppet 9. absurdity 10. buffoonery
dromedary... 4. oont 5. camel (one–hump) 6. hageen 7. Camelus 8. Bactrian (two–hump)
drone... 3. bee, dor, hum 4. male (bee) 5. idler, snail 7. bagpipe, humming 8. sluggard 9. non–worker, slow mover
drool... 6. drivel, slaver 7. dribble, slabber, slobber
droop... 3. lop, sag 4. flag, hang, loll, pine, sink, tire, wilt 6. nutate, slouch 7. decline 8. languish
drooping... 4. alop, weak 5. loose 7. hanging, nodding, sinking 8. dejected, fatigued 11. languishing
drooping eyelids... 6. ptosis
drop... 4. bead, blob, dose, dram, drib, drip, fall, omit, shed, sink, slot, stop, tear 5. candy, dreep, droop, gutta, lower, minim, remit 6. letter, plunge 7. abandon, descent, distill (distil), earring, globule, pendant, trickle 8. ornament, trapdoor 9. declivity 10. relinquish
drop (pert to)...
anchor.. 4. moor
by drop.. 7. guttate 9. guttation
measure.. 7. pipette 11. stactometer
nautical.. 5. hance
serene.. 9. amaurosis (Med)
vowel.. 5. elide
dropsy... 5. edema 8. hydropsy, swelling
dross... 4. lees, scum, slag 5. chaff, dregs, scobs, sprue, waste 6. refuse, scoria, sinter (iron)
drove... 4. herd 5. crowd, drive, flock
drover... 4. boat 6. dealer (cattle), driver 8. herdsman
drowse... 3. nid, nod 4. doze 5. dover (Eng), sleep 6. snooze
drowsiness... 7. languor 8. dullness, lethargy 9. lassitude, oscitance 10. narcolepsy, sleepiness 12. listlessness, sluggishness
drowsy... 4. logy 6. sleepy 8. oscitant, soothing 9. somnolent, soporific

drudge... 3. fag 4. grub, hack, mail, plod, toil 5. labor, slave 6. toiler 7. plodder
drug... 4. alum, dope, dull, numb 6. opiate 7. stupefy 8. narcotic, sedative 10. medication 11. anesthetize
drug (pert to)...
action.. 7. synergy
addict.. 6. junkie
analgesic.. 6. Anacin 7. aspirin 10. acetanilid, phenacetin
anesthesia.. 3. gas 5. ether 8. Novocain 10. chloroform
dangerous.. 11. thalidomide
emetic.. 6. ipecac 11. ipecacuanha
eye.. 8. atropine 10. belladonna
forgetfulness.. 8. nepenthe
narcotic.. 3. hop, kif 4. hemp 5. bhang, daggo, opium 6. codein 7. cocaine 9. marijuana
sedative.. 7. bromide, Seconal, Veronal 8. barbital, Nembutal 11. scopolamine 13. phenobarbital
drugget... 3. mat, rug 5. cloth
druggist... 8. gallipot 10. apothecary, pharmacist
Druids (anc)... 5. Order (Relig) 9. conjurers 12. philosophers
drum... 4. beat 5. naker, snare, tabor, tombe 6. atabal, barrel, tambor (tambour), tom–tom, tympan 7. taboret, timbrel, timpany 8. cylinder, tympanum (ear)
drum (pert to)...
call.. 4. dian (diana) 6. rappel, tattoo 8. rataplan
Indian.. 6. nagara
nautical term.. 7. capstan
Oriental.. 6. tom–tom 7. anacara
drunkard... 3. sot 4. soak 5. souse, toper 6. addict, barfly, boozer 7. guzzler, tippler 9. alcoholic, inebriate 11. dipsomaniac
dry... 3. sec, ted 4. arid, blot, brut, dull, keen, seco, sere, wipe 5. drain, parch, vapid 6. aerify, barren, jejune, shrewd 7. insipid, sterile, thirsty, xerotic 8. solidify, tiresome 9. dehydrate, fruitless, pointless 12. unprofitable 13. uninteresting
dryad... 5. deity, Napea, nymph, oread
duck... 3. dip 4. flee, fowl 5. dodge, douse 6. plunge 7. bob down
duck (breed)... 4. Anas, coot, pato, skua, smee, smew, teal 5. Anser, eider, scaup 6. Aythya, Nyroca, Peking, scoter 7. mallard, Muscovy, pintail, pochard, Spatula, widgeon 8. Anatinae, bluebill, shoveler (shoveller) 9. harlequin, merganser, sheldrake 10. bufflehead, canvasback, ring–necked
duck (pert to)...
baby.. 8. duckling
class.. 3. sea 5. river 7. Muscovy
disabled.. 4. lame
ducklike.. 5. decoy 8. duckbill
fabric.. 5. cloth
flock (mallards).. 4. sord
flower.. 12. lady's slipper
game.. 6. tenter

hawk.. **6.** falcon **7.** harrier
litter.. **4.** team
male.. **5.** drake
ruddy.. **5.** noddy
duct... **3.** vas **4.** main, pipe, race, tube **5.** canal **7.** channel, passage, trachea **8.** aqueduct
ductile... **6.** docile, facile, pliant **7.** elastic, plastic, tensile **8.** flexible, tractile, yielding **9.** compliant, complying, malleable, tractable **10.** manageable
dude... **3.** fop **5.** dandy **7.** coxcomb, Johnnie **10.** tenderfoot
dudeen... **4.** pipe (tobacco)
due... **4.** debt, duty, just, meed, owed **5.** owing **6.** charge, lawful **7.** exactly **8.** adequate, directly, expected, rightful **9.** appointed **10.** ascribable, sufficient
duel... **4.** tilt **5.** fence **6.** combat **7.** contest **8.** conflict **9.** monomachy **12.** satisfaction
duelist's aide... **6.** second
duet... **3.** duo **8.** duettino
dug... see *dig*
dugong... **7.** manatee, Sirenia **8.** Halicore
dugout... **4.** abri, cave, shed **5.** canoe **6.** cavity **7.** pirogue, shelter
dulcet... **5.** sweet **6.** ariose **7.** tuneful **8.** pleasant, soothing **9.** agreeable, melodious **10.** harmonious
dulcimer... **6.** citole **7.** bagpipe, cembalo **8.** psaltery **10.** instrument
dull... **3.** dim, dry, dun **4.** dead, drab, gray, logy, poky **6.** barren, cloudy, deaden, dismal, dreary, drowsy, jejune, leaden, muffle, obtund, obtuse, sleepy, somber, stupid **7.** doltish, irksome, prosaic, tedious **8.** lifeless, listless, overcast, sluggish, stagnant, tiresome **9.** apathetic, inanimate, saturnine, unfeeling **10.** insensible, lackluster, melancholy, slow–witted **13.** unimaginative
dull (pert to)...
finish.. **3.** mat (matte)
heavy.. **4.** logy **5.** leady **6.** stodgy
of cloth.. **6.** starry (Eng)
statement.. **9.** platitude
dullard... **3.** oaf **4.** dope, mope **5.** dunce **8.** dumbbell, numskull **9.** dumb bunny
dumb... **4.** mute **6.** aphony, silent, stupid **7.** aphonia **8.** ignorant, taciturn **9.** inanimate, irregular **10.** speechless **12.** inarticulate
dumbfounded... **6.** amazed **7.** crabbed **9.** staggered, surprised **10.** astonished, bewildered **11.** overwhelmed **13.** flabbergasted
dummy... **3.** pel **4.** copy, dolt, mort (cards), sham **5.** model **6.** pontic, silent **9.** imitation, mannequin, nonentity **10.** figurehead, substitute **11.** counterfeit
dump... **3.** tip **4.** bump, game (Eng), jail, sell, thud, tune **5.** empty, hovel **6.** plunge, unload **7.** discard **10.** rendezvous

dumpling... **7.** biscuit, gnocchi **10.** appleberry
dupe... **3.** fox **4.** bilk, cull, tool **5.** cheat, fraud, trick **6.** delude, sucker **7.** cat's–paw, deceive, mislead
duplicate... **4.** copy, game (cards), twin **6.** double, duplex **7.** estreat, mislead, replica, twofold **8.** likeness **9.** analogous, facsimile, identical, replicate **10.** transcript **11.** counterpart **12.** reproduction
duplicated... **7.** dittoed **8.** repeated **10.** repetitive
duplicity... **5.** fraud, guile **6.** deceit **7.** duality **9.** deception, duplexity, falsehood, treachery **13.** dissimulation, double–dealing
durable... **4.** firm **5.** stout, tough **6.** staple **7.** lasting **8.** constant, enduring **9.** permanent **10.** continuing, persistent **11.** everlasting, substantial
duration... **3.** age **4.** date, span, term, time **6.** period **8.** eternity, lifetime **10.** durability, permanence **11.** continuance
during... **4.** time **5.** while **6.** whilst **7.** pending, through **10.** throughout
dusk... **4.** dark **5.** dusky, gloom, slate (color) **8.** gloaming, twilight
dusky... **3.** dim, sad **4.** dark, dusk **5.** murky, tawny, umbra **6.** gloomy, somber **7.** swarthy **8.** blackish **10.** melancholy
dust... **4.** cash, coom (coomb), dirt, gold, pilm, soil **5.** briss, brush, chaff, clean, color, earth, money, stive, stour (dial), trash **6.** corpse, pollen, powder **7.** dryness, turmoil **9.** commotion, confusion, sweepings
dust (pert to)...
flax.. **5.** pouce
flour.. **5.** stive
glacier.. **10.** kryokonite
reduce to.. **4.** mull
speck.. **4.** mote
Dutch (pert to)... see also *Netherlands*
cheese.. **4.** Edam **7.** cottage
country.. **7.** Germany, Holland **11.** Netherlands
man.. **10.** Hogen–Mogen
news agency.. **5.** Aneta
painter.. **4.** Hals
poet.. **7.** Da Costa
pottery.. **4.** delf (delft) **9.** delftware
river.. **3.** Eem **4.** Maas **5.** Meuse
scholar.. **7.** Erasmus (Humanist)
woman, wife.. **4.** frow
uncle.. **3.** eme (dial), oom
Dutch East Indies (Indonesia)...
capital.. **7.** Batavia (former), Jakarta (Djakarta)
islands (3,000), largest.. **4.** Bali, Java **6.** Borneo (part) **7.** Celebes, Sumatra **8.** Malaysia (part) **9.** New Guinea (part)
renamed.. **9.** Indonesia
Dutch Guiana (Netherlands Antilles)...
capital.. **10.** Paramaribo
mountain.. **10.** Tumuc Humac
renamed.. **7.** Surinam
dutiful... **6.** devout, docile **7.** duteous

8. obedient, reverent 9. compliant
10. respectful, submissive
11. deferential, reverential
duty... 3. job, tax 4. care, onus, rite,
task, toll 5. chore, stint, trick
6. devoir, dharma, excise, heriot
(anc), impost, tariff 7. payment,
respect 9. reverence 10. imposition,
obligation
dwale... 5. sable (Her) 6. opiate,
potion 9. soporific 10. belladonna,
nightshade
dwarf... 3. elf, urf 4. grig, puny, runt
5. crile, gnome, midge, pygmy
(pigmy), small, stunt, troll 6. droich,
durgan, midget 7. manikin, Pacolet,
stunted 9. dandiprat, micrander
10. diminished, homunculus
dwarfish... 6. nanoid
dwarfishness... 6. nanism
Dwarfs, The Seven... 3. Doc
5. Dopey, Happy 6. Grumpy, Sleepy,
Sneezy 7. Bashful
dwell... 4. bide, harp, live, stay
5. abide, delay, lodge, pause, tarry
6. linger, remain, reside
dwelling... 3. hut 4. flat 5. abode,
hotel, house, hovel 6. duplex, shanty
7. trailer 8. abidance, domicile,
tenement 9. apartment, residence
10. habitation
dwelling (pert to)...
house (law).. 8. messuage
in field.. 10. arvicoline
in groves.. 10. nemoricole
of dead (Bab).. 5. Aralu
of souls (Polyn).. 2. Po
Oriental.. 3. dar
dwindle... 4. melt, wane 5. taper,
waste 6. lessen, shrink, sicken

8. decrease, diminish 10. degenerate
dyad... 3. two 4. duad, pair
6. couple, dyadic
Dyak, Dayak... 5. tribe (Borneo)
7. blowgun 8. sumpiter 9. aborigine
dye... 4. anil 5. color, imbue, stain,
tinge 7. pigment 8. colorant
dye stuff (pert to)...
blue.. 4. woad (wad, wade)
brown.. 5. erika, sumac
indigo.. 4. anil
mulberry.. 3. aal
red.. 4. chay 5. aurin, eosin, henna
6. isatin, madder, relbun 7. annatto,
magenta 8. morindin 9. rhodamine
10. orseilline
violet.. 5. murex 6. archil
yellow.. 7. xanthic 8. luteolin,
orpiment 10. quercitron
dyke... see *dike*
dynamic... 4. keen 5. acute, vivid
6. potent 7. intense, kinetic
8. forceful, forcible 9. energetic,
strenuous
dynamite inventor... 5. Nobel (1866)
dynamo (pert to)...
attachment.. 10. commutator
inventor.. 7. Faraday
machine.. 9. generator
part.. 5. rotor 8. armature
dynast... 5. ruler 6. prince 8. governor
dynasty... 4. race 8. dominion,
lordship 10. succession
11. sovereignty
dynasty (pert to)...
Chinese.. 2. Fo 3. Han, Yin 4. Isin,
Ming, Sung, Tang
Spanish.. 6. Ommiad
dysphoria... 7. illness 8. debility
dyvour... 6. beggar 8. bankrupt
dzeren... 8. antelope

E

E... 7. Epsilon (Gr)
Ea (Bab)... 3. God 5. deity
each... 3. all, per 5. alike, every
6. apiece, singly 10. separately
12. individually 14. distributively
eager... 3. apt 4. agog, avid, keen,
yare 5. agasp, sharp 6. ardent,
greedy, intent 7. anxious, burning,
excited, thirsty, willing, zealous
8. desirous, spirited 9. strenuous
eager beaver... 7. hustler 8. go—getter
10. enthusiast
eagerness... 4. élan, zeal 5. ardor
6. fervor 7. avidity 8. alacrity,
cupidity, fervency 9. alertness,
readiness 10. enthusiasm, impatience
13. impetuousness
eagle... 4. erne (ern), gier (Bib), seal
6. bergut, eaglet, emblem

8. standard (Rom) 13. constellation
(Milky Way)
eagle (pert to)...
American.. 4. bald
brood.. 5. aerie, eyrie
coin.. 4. gold
European.. 3. sea 5. harpy 6. golden
8. imperial
genus.. 6. Aquila
heraldry.. 8. allerion
male.. 6. tercil
sacred to Jupiter.. 9. Jove's bird
S America.. 9. eagle hawk
scout badge.. 5. merit
Eagles... 14. Fraternal Order
eagre (acker)... 4. bore, flow, wave
5. flood (tidal)
ear... 4. head 5. auris 7. auricle,
hearing 8. orillion 9. appendage,

attention, orecchion (obs)
ear (pert to)...
anvil.. 5. incus
bone.. 6. stapes, tegman 7. stirrup
canal.. 7. cochlea 9. labyrinth
    10. Eustachian, scala media
external.. 6. concha
grain.. 3. epi 5. spica 6. mealie,
    rizzom (ressum)
hammer.. 7. malleus
inflammation.. 6. otitis
middle.. 8. tympanum
part.. 5. helix, pinna 6. tragus
science.. 7. otology
shell.. 5. ormer 7. abalone
specialist.. 6. aurist 9. otologist
stone.. 7. otolith
term.. 4. otic 5. aural
wax.. 7. cerumen
earache... 6. otalgy 7. otalgia
early... 4. soon 7. ancient, betimes,
    matinal 9. premature, primitive
    10. beforehand, beforetime
earn... 3. get, win 4. gain 5. ettle,
    merit 7. acquire, deserve
earnest... 5. arles (pledge), grave,
    sober, staid 6. ardent, hearty, pledge,
    sedate, solemn 7. handsel (money),
    serious, sincere, zealous 8. resolute
    9. heartfelt, important 10. thoughtful
    12. wholehearted
earnestly... 8. solemnly 9. intensely,
    zealously 10. resolutely
earphone... 7. trumpet (double)
    8. otoscope 9. auriphone, topophone
    (double) 11. stethescope
earring... 4. hoop 6. earbob, pendle
    7. earstud, pendant 9. girandole
    (girandola)
earth... 3. erd 4. clay, clod, dirt, land,
    marl, muck, sand, soil, vale 5. geest,
    loess, sloam, terra 6. ground, planet,
    rideau 7. topsoil 8. alluvium
earth (pert to)...
center.. 10. geocentric
    12. centrosphere
comb form.. 3. geo
deformation.. 10. epeirogeny
formed beneath.. 8. hypogene,
    plutonic
formed by ores.. 9. supergene
formed on surface.. 7. epigene
god (Egypt).. 3. Geb (Keb)
goddess.. 4. Erda, Gaea (Gaia), Tari
    6. Semele 7. Demeter
produced by.. 6. mortal
    11. terrigenous
satellite.. see *satellite*
volcanic.. 5. trass
earthdrake... 6. dragon
earthly... 7. mundane, secular, terrene,
    worldly 8. temporal 11. terrestrial,
    universally, unspiritual
    13. materialistic
earthmover... 6. digger 7. backhoe,
    leveler 9. bulldozer, excavator
    10. steam shovel
earth pig... 8. aardvark
earthquake... 5. quake, seism
    7. temblor 12. diastrophism

earthstar... 6. fungus 7. Geaster
earthworm... 7. annalid, dew worm,
    ipokoea 9. Lumbricus
earthy... 3. low 5. gross 6. coarse
    7. worldly 8. material 9. unrefined
ease... 4. calm, rest 5. abate, allay,
    peace, quiet, relax 6. pacify, relief,
    repose, soothe 7. assuage, comfort,
    content, leisure, relieve, slacken
    8. facility, mitigate 9. alleviate,
    disburden, enjoyment 10. prosperity,
    relaxation, solicitude 11. informality,
    tranquilize 12. tranquillity (tranquility)
easily... 4. eath (eith) 6. gently, slowly,
    softly 7. readily 8. smoothly
    11. comfortably, dexterously
    12. effortlessly
easily (pert to)...
broken.. 6. shelly 7. fragile, friable
frightened.. 8. skittish
managed.. 6. docile
moved.. 6. mobile
offended.. 9. sensitive
split.. 8. schistic
understood.. 5. lucid
east... 4. Asia, dawn 6. Levant, Orient
    7. sunrise 8. eastward
East Africa...
hartebeest.. 4. tora
house (mud).. 5. tembe
republic.. 5. Kenya 7. Somalia
island.. 8. Zanzibar
tribes.. 3. Luo 4. Embu, Teso
    5. Bantu, Masai 6. Kikuyu, Mau Mau
    7. Nilotes
vessel.. 4. dhow
East India... see also *East Indian*
drink.. 4. nipa
fan.. 6. punkah (punka)
gateway (temple).. 5. toran (torana)
hat, helmet.. 5. topee (topi)
money of account.. 4. anna
mountain pass.. 4. ghat (ghaut)
musical instrument.. 4. vina 5. ruana,
    saron
police station.. 5. thana (tanna)
sailing vessel.. 5. dhoni (doni)
    7. patamar
sugar, molasses.. 3. gur
    10. massecuite
water vessel (brass).. 4. lota (lotah)
East Indian animal...
antelope.. 5. bongo, takin 6. impala,
    nilgai 8. axis deer
cattle.. 4. gaur, zebu 5. gayal, tsine
    7. banteng
civet.. 6. musang 10. paradoxure
goat (wild).. 4. tahr 7. markhor
lemurlike.. 7. tarsier
raccoonlike.. 3. wah 5. panda
rat.. 9. bandicoot
swine.. 8. babirusa (babiroussa)
East Indian bird...
broadbill.. 4. raya
bulbul.. 4. kala
falcon.. 5. besra
fruit pigeon.. 6. treron
thrush.. 5. shama
weaverbird.. 4. baya
East Indian people...

boatswain .. **6.** serang
chief .. **6.** sirdar
groom .. **4.** syce
harem .. **6.** zenana
native sailor, soldier .. **5.** sepoy
  6. lascar
nurse .. **4.** amah, ayah
peasant .. **4.** ryot
poet .. **6.** Tagore
princess .. **4.** rani (ranee)
robber .. **6.** dacoit
title .. **4.** raja **5.** rajah, sahib
warrior .. **5.** singh
East Indian tree, plant ...
bark .. **4.** lodh **5.** niepa
cedar .. **6.** deodar
cotton .. **5.** simal
fiber .. **4.** jute
fruit .. **3.** bel **6.** lanseh (lansa)
gum .. **4.** kino
herb .. **5.** tikor **6.** sesame **7.** roselle
mahogany .. **4.** toon
mulberry .. **4.** tapa
palm .. **3.** tal (fiber) **4.** nipa (thatch)
  5. sural (juice), toddy **7.** palmyra
pea .. **4.** dhak **5.** Butea
rubber .. **3.** saj
shade .. **6.** banyan
timber .. **3.** saj, sal (saul) **4.** poon, teak
  5. siris **6.** sissoo
walnut .. **6.** lebbek
east wind ... **5.** Eurus
easy ... **4.** calm, slow **5.** loose, suave
  6. cinchy, facile, gentle, simple
  7. natural **8.** gullible, informal,
  moderate, tranquil, unforced
  9. leisurely, unhurried
  10. manageable, nonchalant,
  unaffected **11.** comfortable,
  complaisant, unconcerned
easy–going ... **4.** calm **11.** unflappable
easy job ... **8.** sinecure
easy mark ... **4.** dupe, gull **6.** sucker,
  victim **7.** cat's–paw
eat ... **3.** sup **4.** dine, etch, feed, gnaw
  5. board, erode **6.** devour, ravage
  7. consume, corrode, destroy
eat (pert to) ...
between meals .. **4.** nosh **5.** bever,
  snack
by rule .. **4.** diet
earth, clay .. **8.** geophagy
  12. chthonophagy
greedily .. **3.** lab **4.** glut **5.** gorge,
  scarf (down) **6.** gobble, pig out (sl)
  7. edacity **8.** voracity
eatable ... **6.** edible **8.** esculent,
  gustable **10.** comestible
eater ... **5.** diner **7.** epicure, glutton,
  gourmet **8.** gourmand
eating (pert to) ...
alone .. **9.** monophagy
comb form .. **7.** phagous
decay .. **12.** saprophagous
fish .. **11.** piscivorous
  13. icthyophagous
flesh, raw .. **9.** omophagia
flesh–eating .. **9.** creophagy
  10. zoophagous **11.** carnivorous
man–eating .. **12.** androphagous
  13. anthropophagy
nuts .. **10.** nucivorous

  11. nuciphagous
plants, herbs .. **11.** herbivorous
  12. phytophagous
roots .. **12.** rhizophagous
eavesdrop ... **3.** bug **4.** drip **6.** harken,
  listen **7.** wiretap **10.** stillicide
  14. listen secretly
ebb ... **3.** low **4.** neap, sink, tide, wane
  5. abate, decay **6.** recede, reflux,
  retire **7.** decline, dwindle, shallow,
  subside **8.** decrease
ebb and flow ... **5.** surge **6.** aestus
  (estus) **11.** alternation
ebb tide ... **8.** low water
ebullition ... **7.** boiling, ferment
  8. bubbling **9.** agitation, commotion
  12. fermentation **13.** effervescence
eccentric ... **3.** cam (shaft), odd
  5. flaky, kinky **6.** weirdo **7.** erratic,
  strange **8.** abnormal **9.** erratical,
  irregular **11.** nonconformist
  15. idiosyncratical
eccentricity ... **6.** oddity **9.** queerness
  10. aberration, erraticism
  11. abnormality, peculiarity,
  strangeness **12.** idiosyncrasy,
  irregularity **13.** nonconformity
  17. unconventionality
Ecclesiastes ... **8.** Koheleth (Gr)
echidna ... **7.** monster (Gr Myth)
  8. anteater
echinoderm ... **8.** starfish **9.** sea urchin
echo ... **4.** mute, stop (organ) **5.** nymph
  (Myth), reply **6.** repeat **7.** imitate,
  resound, respond **8.** resemble,
  response **9.** duplicate **10.** repetition
  13. reverberation
echoism ... **12.** onomatopoeia
Eciton ... **4.** ants (legionary)
eclipse ... **5.** cloud, sully **6.** darken
  7. obscure, surpass **10.** extinguish
ecliptic term ... **5.** lagna, orbit
  6. circle **9.** penumbral
ecology, oecology ... **4.** sere **6.** botany
  7. biology **9.** bionomics, sociology
  10. bioecology
economical ... **5.** canny, chary
  6. frugal, saving **7.** careful, thrifty
  8. domestic **9.** provident
  12. parsimonious
economics terms ... **5.** T–bill
  7. bailout **8.** bankable, cash flow,
  rollover **9.** plutology **10.** monetarism,
  production (wealth)
economize ... **4.** save **5.** skimp, stint
  6. scrimp **7.** husband, utilize
  8. retrench
economy ... **4.** care **6.** saving, thrift
  7. cutback **8.** prudence **9.** canniness,
  husbandry **10.** providence
ecstasy ... **5.** bliss **6.** trance
  7. emotion, rapture **9.** enrapture
ecstatic ... **4.** rapt **7.** rapture
  9. rapturous, rhapsodic
ectad ... **7.** outward
ecto (comb form) ... **7.** outside, without
  8. external
Ecuador (pert to) ...
capital .. **5.** Quito
export .. **7.** bananas
hat .. **6.** Panama **8.** 'Jipijapa'
island .. **9.** Galapagos

mountain . . 5. Andes
reptile . . 6. iguana 8. tortoise
volcano . . 10. Chimborazo
ecumenical . . . 7. general, liberal
8. catholic, tolerant lip. universal,
world–wide 12. cosmopolitan
eczema . . . 6. herpes, tetter 8. eruption
9. salt rheum
edacity . . . 5. greed 7. avarice
8. appetite, gulosity, voracity
10. greediness
eddy . . . 4. bore, gulf 5. gurge, surge,
swirl, whirl 6. vortex 7. current,
wreathe 9. whirlpool
Edentate (Zool) . . . 6. sloths
7. mammals 9. aardvarks, anteaters
10. armadillos
edge . . . 3. hem, jag, lip, rim 4. brim,
brow, side 5. arris, brink, crest,
marge, sharp, sidle (to), splay, verge
6. border, flange, labrum, margin
7. ambitus, selvage 8. acrimony,
pungency, selvedge 9. advantage,
sharpness 10. escarpment
edged . . . 5. erose 6. crenate
8. bordered, invected (Her)
edging . . . 3. hem 4. lace, welt 5. frill,
ruche 6. border, fringe, ruffle
7. binding, bordure (Her), flounce,
tatting
edgy . . . 5. sharp 7. angular, nervous
8. critical, snappish 9. excitable,
impatient 13. sharp–cornered
edict . . . 3. act, ban 4. Bull (Pope's),
fiat 5. arret, dicta (pl), irade, order,
ukase 6. assize, decree, dictum,
firman 7. command, mandate
8. decretal 9. ordinance
12. proclamation
edification . . . 8. learning 9. knowledge
11. improvement, instruction
edifice . . . 5. house 6. church, palace,
temple 7. Capitol 8. building
9. structure 10. tabernacle
edify . . . 5. build, teach 7. educate,
improve 8. instruct, organize
9. construct, enlighten, establish
Edinburgh . . .
burgh . . 5. Leith
capital of . . 8. Scotland
county . . 10. Midlothian
famed street . . 9. Royal Mile
Gaelic name . . 7. Dun Edin (Dunedin)
nickname . . 16. Athens of the North
site . . 12. Firth of Forth
edit . . . 5. emend 6. direct, excise,
redact, revise, reword 7. arrange,
correct, prepare
edition . . . 4. copy 5. issue 6. number
7. version
editions (Bib) . . .
eight texts . . 7. octapla
four texts . . 8. tetrapla
six texts . . 7. hexapla
style and type . . 7. Elzevir (1583)
editor . . . 7. analyst, newsman, reviser
8. arranger, redactor 9. annotator,
gazetteer 10. journalist, supervisor
11. commentator 12. newspaperman
Edom . . . 5. Teman (Bib) 7. Idumaea
Edomite . . . 4. Esau 5. Isaac, Jacob
8. Idumaean

educate . . . 4. rear 5. teach, train
6. inform 7. develop 8. instruct
9. cultivate, enlighten 10. discipline
12. indoctrinate
educated . . . 6. taught 7. erudite,
learned, trained 8. cultured,
informed, lettered, literate
11. enlightened
education . . . 8. breeding, literacy,
training 9. opsimathy (late in life),
schooling 10. discipline
educe . . . 4. draw 6. deduce, elicit,
evolve, obtain, secure
eel (pert to) . . .
colorful . . 5. moray 7. Muraena
genus . . 8. Anguilla 13. Leptocephalus
marine . . 5. elver 6. conger
mud . . 5. siren
sand . . 4. grig
young . . 5. elver
eellike . . . 4. lant, ling 7. eelpout,
lamprey 8. Ophidion 10. anguilloid
11. Lepidosiren
eels, fishing for . . . 7. sniggle
eels, migration of . . . 7. eelfare
eelworm . . . 4. nema 8. Nematoda
9. roundworm 10. vinegar eel
eerie, eery . . . 5. scary, timid, weird
6. gloomy, spooky 7. awesome,
fearful, uncanny 9. deathlike,
unearthly 10. frightened
efface . . . 5. erase 6. cancel, delete
7. blot out, expunge 10. obliterate
effect . . . 4. does 5. close, éclat, force,
mneme 6. mirage, obtain, result
7. achieve, compass, conjure,
execute, fulfill, meaning, operate,
outcome, perform, reality, realize
8. complete 9. discharge, execution,
influence 10. accomplish,
appearance, consummate, impression
11. consequence, performance
effective . . . 4. able 6. active, actual,
cogent 7. capable, telling
8. adequate, eloquent, equipped,
striking 9. brilliant, competent,
effectual, efficient, operative,
trenchant 11. efficacious, influential
effects . . . 5. goods, wares 8. movables,
property
effeminate . . . 3. sop 5. sissy
6. female, tender 7. cockney,
epicene, womanly 8. feminine,
womanish 9. Sybaritic
11. mollycoddle 12. overdelicate
13. overemotional
effervescent . . . 5. fizzy 6. bubbly, lively
7. boiling, hissing 8. bubbling,
mousseux 9. ebullient, sparkling
10. boisterous
effete . . . 4. aged, idle 5. spent
6. barren 7. worn out 9. exhausted,
fruitless 11. ineffectual
efficacious . . . 4. able 5. valid
6. potent 9. effective, effectual,
operative 11. influential
efficacy . . . 4. dint 5. force, power
6. virtue 7. ability, potency
10. efficiency
efficiency . . . 5. power, skill 7. ability,
utility 8. efficacy 10. capability,
competence 11. proficiency

12. productivity 13. effectiveness
15. efficaciousness
efficient... 4. able 7. capable, operant
9. competent, effective, effectual,
operative 10. productive
12. businesslike
effigy... 4. copy, icon 5. image
8. likeness 9. facsimile, jackstraw,
semblance 11. resemblance
effluvium... 4. aura, fume, odor
9. ectoplasm, emanation
efflux... 3. end 6. expiry, runoff
7. outflow 8. effusion 9. effluence,
emanation
effodient... 9. burrowing, fossorial
effort... 3. try, tug 4. dint, jump, toil,
will, work 5. assay, burst, labor,
nisus, pains, trial 6. strain
7. attempt, conatus, trouble
8. endeavor, exertion, struggle
11. application
effrontery... 5. brass 8. audacity,
boldness 9. arrogance, impudence,
sauciness 11. presumption
effulgence... 5. aglow, glory 6. luster
8. radiance, rutilant, splendor
10. brightness, brilliance
effusive... 7. gushing 9. exuberant,
rhapsodic 13. demonstrative
eft... 4. evet, newt 6. lizard, triton
7. urodele 10. salamander
egest... 4. emit, void 7. excrete
9. discharge, ejaculate, eliminate
egg... 3. nit, ova (pl), ove 4. goad,
ovum, prod, urge 5. ovule 6. incite
9. instigate
egg (pert to)...
bird's.. 7. chalaza (white of), treadle
(embryo)
case.. 6. ovisac
comb form.. 2. oo 3. ovi
part.. 7. latebra
shaped.. 4. ooid, oval 5. ovate, ovoid
6. ooidal 9. ovaliform
shell.. 5. shard 6. ovisac
undeveloped.. 5. addle
white.. 5. glair 7. albumen
yolk, yelk.. 7. liaison 8. lecithin
eggplant... 9. melongena
eggs (pert to)...
feeding on.. 9. ovivorous
fish.. 3. roe 5. berry, spawn
preserved.. 5. pidan
tester of.. 7. candler
two at a time.. 8. ditokous
egis, aegis... 4. care 5. guard
6. shield, symbol (anc) 7. backing,
defense 8. advocacy, auspices,
guidance, tutelage 9. fosterage,
patronage 10. protection
11. sponsorship
ego... 3. man 4. self 5. atman (Hind)
6. psyche, spirit 7. conceit, jivatma
(Hind) 11. selfishness
egress... 4. exit 5. issue 6. outlet
8. issuance 9. departure
egret... 5. heron, plume 8. aigrette
Egypt, UAR... see also *Egyptian*
capital.. 5. Cairo
Christian.. 4. Copt
city (ruined).. 5. Luxor, Tanis
6. Karnak, Thebes

dam.. 5. Aswan
desert.. 5. Dakla
gulf.. 4. Suez 5. Aqaba
language (anc).. 6. Coptic
lighthouse (anc).. 6. Pharos
mother.. 3. Mut
peninsula.. 5. Sinai
philosopher.. 8. Plotinus
port.. 4. Said, Suez 10. Alexandria
queen.. 9. Cleopatra
river.. 4. Nile
ruler.. 5. pasha 6. caliph 7. khedive
ruler.. 6. Farouk 7. Busiris (Myth),
Pharaoh, Ptolemy, Rameses
sea.. 3. Red 13. Mediterranean
Egyptian (pert to)...
abode of dead.. 4. Aaru (fields of)
6. Amenti
antelope.. 7. bubalis
ape (sacred).. 4. Aani
beetle.. 6. scarab
bird (crocodile).. 6. sicsac
bird (sacred).. 4. Benu, ibis
7. phoenix
bull.. 4. apis
cobra.. 4. haje
cross.. 3. tau 4. ankh (emblem of
life) 10. crux ansata
crown.. 4. atef
dancing girl.. 4. alma (alme, Almeh)
7. ghawazi 8. Baramika
dog.. 6. saluki (gazelle hound)
headdress of ruler.. 6. Uraeus
heaven.. 4. Aaru
lizard.. 4. adda 5. skink
lute.. 5. nable
paper.. 7. papyrus
solar disk.. 4. aten
soul.. 2. Ba 4. khet, sahu
stone (famed).. 7. Rosetta
symbol.. 3. asp 6. scarab (beetle)
tomb.. 6. serdab (cell) 7. mastaba
watchman.. 6. ghafir (ghaffir)
writing.. 13. hieroglyphics
Egyptian god of...
day.. 5. Horus
earth.. 3. Geb, Keb
life.. 4. Ptah
pleasure.. 3. Bes
primeval fluid.. 2. Nu
sea.. 5. Aegir
sun.. 2. Ra 3. Tem (Tum) 4. Atmu
5. Mentu (Ment) 7. Khepera
11. Harpocrates
supreme.. 4. Amen (Amon)
underworld.. 6. Osiris 7. Hershef
unknown.. 2. Ka
wisdom.. 5. Thoth 6. Dhouti
Egyptian goddess of...
arms.. 4. Anta
fertility.. 4. Isis
gods.. 4. Sati
motherhood.. 4. Apet
sea.. 3. Ran
truth.. 4. Maat
eidolon... 5. image 7. phantom
8. illusion 10. apparition
eight, eighth (pert to)...
day (every).. 5. octan
feast day.. 4. utas
group.. 5. octad, octet 6. octave
7. octette

heaven.. 5. stars (fixed)
number.. 4. ocho 6. ogdoad
philosophy.. 8. Diagrams
sided.. 9. octagonal
tone, note.. 4. unca 6. quaver (8th)
  8. diatonic
eighteen inches... 5. cubit
Eire... 4. Erin 7. Ireland
ejaculate... 4. emit, oust, void
  5. blurt, eject, evict, expel
  7. exclaim 8. dislodge
eject... 4. emit, oust, spew, void
  5. evict, expel, spout, spurt
  6. banish 7. extrude 9. discharge,
  eliminate
ejection... 6. ouster 8. eviction
  9. expulsion 11. elimination
eke (out)... 3. add, imp, tab 4. also,
  etch 8. addition, appendix (dial),
  increase, piece out 10. postscript
El... 3. God 5. deity
elaborate... 6. ornate, refine
  7. develop, improve, perfect, studied
  9. embellish, perfected, superfine
  11. complicated, high–wrought
Elam capital... 4. Susa (anc)
élan... 4. dash 5. ardor 6. spirit
  9. eagerness 10. enthusiasm
elapse... 2. go 3. die, fly, run 4. flit,
  pass, slip 5. lapse 6. expire
elastic... 6. pliant, rubber 7. buoyant,
  ductile, springy 8. flexible, stretchy
  9. expansive, resilient
  12. recuperative
elasticity... 4. give 6. elater, spring
  7. pliancy, rebound 9. ductility
  10. resilience
elated... 6. jovial 7. gleeful
  8. exultant, jubilant 9. overjoyed
Elbe tributary... 4. Eger, Iser
elbow... 5. ancon, joint, nudge
  6. jostle 8. chelidon (hollow of)
El Camino Real... 9. Royal Road
  12. King's Highway (Pac Hwy)
elder... 3. iva 4. ainé, blue (color)
  5. berry, judge, ruler 6. Mormon,
  senior 7. ancient 8. ancestor
  10. forefather
eldest... 5. eigne 6. oldest 8. earliest
  9. firstborn
eldritch... 4. wild 5. eerie (eery), weird
  9. frightful
elect... 3. ort 4. name 5. elite
  6. choose, select 9. designate
election... 6. choice 11. alternative
  13. determination 14. discrimination
electric (pert to)...
atom.. 8. electron
condenser (anc).. 9. Leyden jar
conductor.. 6. ohmage
current.. 2. AC, DC 7. circuit
force.. 4. elod
generator.. 6. dynamo
light.. 3. arc 4. neon
  12. incandescent
meter.. 7. ammeter 9. voltmeter,
  wattmeter
particle.. 3. ion 6. cation (kation)
power.. 7. wattage
safety device.. 4. fuse
unit.. 3. ohm, rel 4. volt, watt
  5. farad, henry, joule 6. ampere,

proton 7. coulomb, oersted
  8. kilowatt
electrical wonders... 6. Venus V
  9. Surveyor V 11. Oroville Dam
  12. nuclear plant
electricity... 5. juice, power
  10. illuminant
eleemosynary... 4. alms, free
  7. charity 10. almsgiving
elegance... 5. charm, grace, taste
  6. beauty, polish 9. propriety
  10. ornateness, politeness, refinement
  13. sumptuousness
elegant... 4. rich 6. dressy, ornate,
  soigné, urbane 7. courtly, genteel,
  refined 8. graceful, handsome,
  polished, tasteful 9. admirable,
  beautiful, excellent 10. fastidious
  11. fashionable 13. grandiloquent
element... 3. air 4. fire 5. earth,
  water
elementary... 5. basic 6. simple
  7. primary 8. inchoate, original
  9. beginning 11. fundamental
elephant... 3. cow 4. bull, calf
  5. hathi, rogue 6. tusker
  8. behemoth 9. pachyderm
elephant (pert to)...
apple.. 7. Feronia
boy.. 4. Sabu
call, cry.. 4. barr 7. trumpet
enclosure, trap.. 6. keddah
goad.. 5. ankus
keeper.. 6. mahout
seat.. 6. howdah
tusk.. 5. ivory 9. scrivello
young.. 4. calf
elevate... 4. lift, rear 5. elate, exalt,
  raise 6. refine, uplift 7. advance,
  dignify, ennoble, glorify, inspire,
  promote 10. exhilarate
elevated... 2. el 5. lofty, risen
  6. elated 7. exalted, sublime
  8. eminence
elevation... 4. hill 6. height (highth)
  9. promotion 10. exaltation
  11. composition (Eccl), distinction
  13. glorification
elevation of the mind... 7. anagoge
elevator... 3. bin 4. cage, lift, silo
  9. ascenseur
eleven... 7. hendeca (comb form)
elf... 3. fay, hob, imp, nix 4. peri
  5. fairy, gnome, ouphe, pixie
  6. goblin, sprite 7. brownie
elfish... 5. elfin 6. elvish, impish
  7. elflike, tricksy 8. eldritch
  11. mischievous
Elgin Marbles... 10. sculptures (by
  Phidias)
elicit... 3. get 4. draw, pump
  5. claim, educe, evoke, exact, wrest,
  wring 6. deduce, demand, entice,
  extort, induce, obtain 7. extract
elide... 4. dele, omit 5. annul
  6. ignore 7. destroy, nullify, shorten
  8. demolish, suppress 9. eliminate
eligible... 3. apt, fit 4. meet
  6. worthy 8. entitled, suitable
  9. competent, desirable, qualified
  10. acceptable, admissible
Elijah... 7. prophet 8. oratorio

14. John the Baptist (Bib)
eliminate... 3. rid 4. kill 5. erase,
expel 6. detach, remove 7. discard,
divulge, exclude, excrete, release
8. evacuate, separate 9. segregate
11. exterminate
Elisha... 7. prophet 8. disciple (of
Elijah)
elision... 7. syncope 9. severance
10. abridgment, shortening
11. suppression (vowel)
elite... 5. stars 6. flower, galaxy
7. fashion, society 9. beau monde
10. upper crust
elixir... 6. remedy 7. cure–all, essence,
extract, heal–all, panacea
8. medicine, tincture 10. catholicon
12. quintessence
elixir of life... 11. elixir vitae
Elixir of Love... 13. L'Elisir d'Amore
elk... 4. deer 5. Alces, eland, moose
6. sambar, wapiti
ellipse, elliptical... 5. curve, ovoid,
ovule
elm (pert to)...
 borer.. 6. beetle, lamiid
 fruit.. 6. samara
 genus.. 5. Ulmus
 rock, wing (kinds).. 5. wahoo
Elm City... 8. New Haven
Elmo... 11. patron saint (sailors)
elocution... 7. oratory 8. rhetoric
9. eloquence 10. expression
elocutionist... 6. reader 7. reciter
11. elocutioner 13. recitationist
eloge... 6. eulogy 7. address, oration
8. encomium, eulogium
eloign... 6. convey, remove 7. conceal
elongate... 6. extend, remove
7. stretch 8. continue, lengthen,
protract
elongated... 4. lank, long 6. linear,
oblong 7. prolate, slender
8. extended 9. stretched
10. attenuated
elope... 6. decamp 7. abscond, skip
out 8. slip away
eloquence... 7. fluency, oratory
9. discourse, elocution
14. expressiveness
eloquence, teacher of... 6. rhetor
eloquent... 5. vivid 10. Ciceronian,
expressive, meaningful, oratorical
11. significant
else... 2. or 4. ense (ens) 5. if not,
other 9. otherwise 10. additional
12. accompanying
elsewhere... 4. away 5. alibi (law)
elucidate... 5. clear, lucid 7. clarify,
clear up 8. simplify 9. interpret
10. illustrate
elude... 4. flee, foil, mock, shun
5. avoid, dodge, evade 6. baffle,
befool, escape 10. circumvent
elusive... 4. eely 6. subtle 7. elusory,
evasive 8. baffling 9. equivocal
10. impalpable
elves... see *elf*
Elysium (Myth)... 8. paradise
em... 2. en (half) 4. unit (Elec)
emaciated... 4. lean 5. gaunt
6. peaked, wasted 7. pinched

10. attenuated, cadaverous
emanation... 4. aura, odor 5. light,
niton (radium), vapor 7. outcome
8. creation, effluvia 9. ectoplasm,
radiation 10. exhalation, generation
11. consequence
emancipation... 6. rescue 7. freedom,
release 10. liberation
11. manumission
15. enfranchisement
emasculate... 4. geld, spay 5. unman
6. soften 8. castrate 9. expurgate,
sterilize 10. effeminize
embalmer... 5. cerer 9. mortician,
preserver 10. undertaker
embankment... 3. dam 4. bund, dike
5. levee, revet, shore 7. barrier,
pilapil (rice field) 8. buttress
10. breakwater 13. fortification
embargo... 5. edict, order 7. exclude
8. blockade, prohibit, stoppage
9. exclusion 10. impediment
11. prohibition, requisition
embark... 4. sail, ship 6. depart,
invest, unmoor 7. cast off, entrain
embarrass... 5. abash, shame
6. hamper, hinder, impede
7. confuse, fluster, involve, mortify,
nonplus 8. bewilder, confound,
encumber, handicap 9. discomfit,
dumbfound 10. complicate,
disconcert
embarrassment... 5. shame
9. abashment, confusion
11. involvement, predicament
12. discomfiture, entanglement
13. inconvenience, mortification
embellish... 3. gem 4. deck, gild
5. adorn, array, dress, gouge, grace
6. bedeck, enrich 7. bedrape,
enhance, garnish 8. beautify,
emblazon, furbelow, ornament
9. embroider 10. exaggerate
embellishment... 9. garniture
10. decoration, furbishing
12. exaggeration 13. ornamentation
ember... 3. ash 4. coal (live), izle
5. gleed 6. cinder 7. residue
embers... 5. ashes 8. emotions (past),
memories
embezzle... 5. steal, swipe 6. lessen,
thieve, weaken (obs) 7. purloin
8. peculate, squander 9. dissipate
11. appropriate
embitter... 4. sour 5. anger
7. envenom 8. acerbate
10. antagonize, exacerbate
emblazon... 4. laud 5. color, extol
6. praise 7. display, exhibit, glorify
9. celebrate, embellish
emblem... 3. rue 4. mace, sign, type
5. badge, crown, image, token,
totem 6. device, figure, symbol
7. balance (justice), coronet, sceptor
9. prototype
emblematic... 5. typal 7. typical
8. symbolic 10. figurative
14. characteristic
embodiment... 4. Apis 6. avatar,
matter 7. epitome 9. inclusion
10. enfoldment 11. combination,
composition, incarnation

12. organization 13. incorporation
14. representative 15. personification
embolden... 5. nerve 6. assure
7. hearten 8. reassure 9. encourage
embosom... 6. foster 7. cherish,
embrace, enclose 8. surround
embrace... 3. hug 4. fold, gain, hold,
love, wrap 5. adopt, clasp, cling,
grasp, inarm, seize 6. accoll (obs),
caress, enfold 7. cherish, contain,
enclose, espouse, include, involve,
welcome 8. comprise, encircle,
greeting, surround 9. encompass
embroider... 7. falsify 8. decorate,
ornament 9. embellish
10. exaggerate
embroidery... 8. appliqué 9. hardanger
embroidery frame... 7. taboret
(tabouret)
embroil... 5. upset 6. jumble
7. agitate, disturb, perplex, trouble
8. convulse, disorder, distract
9. commingle, implicate
10. complicate, discompose
eme... 5. uncle 6. friend, gossip
emend... 4. edit, mend 5. amend,
right 6. better, remedy, revise
7. correct, improve, rectify
emerald... 5. beryl, color, green
7. smaragd
Emerald Isle... 4. Erin 7. Ireland
emerge... 3. dip 4. pend, rise
5. hatch, issue 6. appear
7. debouch, emanate
10. disembogue
emergency... 5. pinch 6. clutch, crisis,
strait 8. exigency, juncture
9. extremity, necessity 10. substitute
emery... 6. pumice 8. abradant,
abrasive, corundum 9. sandpaper
emesis... 6. puking 7. spewing
8. vomiting 12. disgorgement
13. regurgitation
emeute... 4. riot 6. Putsch
8. outbreak 10. insurgence
12. insurrection
emigrant... 6. emigré 7. migrant,
outgoer, settler 8. colonist, stranger
9. immigrant, migratory (of birds)
eminence... 4. hill 5. title 6. height,
rideau 7. dignity 9. authority,
elevation, greatness, loftiness
10. famousness, importance,
projection 11. superiority
13. transcendency
eminent... 4. arch, high 5. great,
lofty, noted 6. famous, marked,
signal 8. renowned, superior,
towering 9. important 10. celebrated,
protruding 11. illustrious
13. distinguished
emissary... 3. spy 5. agent, scout
8. delegate, diplomat
emit... 4. glow, reek, shed 5. eject,
eruct, exude, issue, pluff, voice
6. exhale 7. distill (distil), emanate,
publish, radiate 8. opalesce (colors),
transmit 9. discharge, irradiate
emmet... 3. ant 7. pismire 8. formicid
emollient... 4. balm 8. ointment,
soothing 9. lubricant, softening
emolument... 4. fees, gain 5. wages

6. profit, salary 7. stipend, tribute
9. allowance 12. compensation
emotion... 5. agony, stoic 6. pathos
7. feeling, passion 9. agitation,
gratitude, sensation, sentiment
10. excitement 11. disturbance,
sensibility
emotionless... 9. apathetic, impassive,
unfeeling 10. spiritless
11. unemotional 12. unresponsive
emperor... 4. czar, tsar 5. Mogul
7. monarch 9. commander,
imperator, sovereign
emphasis... 6. accent, stress
7. cadence 8. salience
10. insistence 14. impressiveness
emphasize... 6. accent, insist, stress
7. point up 9. punctuate
10. accentuate
emphatic... 7. earnest 8. forcible,
positive, striking 9. energetic,
insistent 10. expressive
11. significant
empire... 4. rule, sway 5. green
(color), reign, state 6. domain
7. control, country
Empire (pert to)...
of the Rising Sun.. 5. Japan
State.. 7. New York
State of the South.. 7. Georgia
empiric... 4. fake 5. cheat, quack
8. impostor 9. charlatan
10. mountebank
employ... 3. use 4. busy, coax, hire
5. apply, exert 6. devote, occupy
7. concern, entrust, service
10. occupation
employees... 4. crew, gang, help
5. force, hands, staff 9. personnel
10. associates
employer... 4. user 5. hirer 6. master
8. consumer 12. entrepreneur
employment... 3. use 4. work
5. trade 7. calling, purpose, service
8. business, vocation 10. occupation,
profession
emporium... 4. fair, mart 5. store
6. bazaar, market 10. exposition
empower... 6. enable 7. entitle
8. delegate, deputize 9. authorize
10. commission
empty... 4. idle, toom, vain, void
5. blank, clear, drain, inane
6. hollow, hungry, jejune, vacant,
vacate 7. deplete, foolish, vacuous
8. evacuate, unfilled 9. insincere
.10. unburdened, unoccupied
empusa (Gr Myth)... 5. fungi
7. specter 9. hobgoblin
empyrean... 3. sky 5. ether 6. Caelus,
welkin 7. heavens, the blue
emulate... 5. equal, outdo, rival
7. compete, imitate, vie with
11. competition
emulsion... 9. demulcent
10. semiliquid, suspension
enable... 5. equip 6. clothe
7. empower, qualify 9. authorize
10. capacitate
enact... 4. pass, play 6. decree,
enjoin, ordain, record 7. actuate,
appoint, perform 9. legislate,

represent 10. constitute
11. impersonate
enactment... 3. law 4. veto 5. canon, edict, usage 6. decree 7. statute
9. ordinance 11. legislation
encamp, encampment... 4. camp, tent
5. siege 7. bivouac, camping
enchant... 5. charm 6. delude
7. bewitch, delight 8. ensorcel
9. captivate, enrapture, fascinate
enchantment... 5. charm, magic, spell
7. sorcery 8. witchery
10. allurement, necromancy, witchcraft 11. bewitchment, fascination, incantation
enchantress... 5. Circe, Medea
7. charmer 9. bewitcher, sorceress, temptress
encina... 7. live oak
encircle... 3. orb 4. gird, ring, zone
5. belay, inorb, twist 6. enfold
7. besiege, circuit, enclose, environ, include, wreathe 8. surround
12. circumscribe
encircled... 4. girt 5. orbed, paled, zoned 6. belted, forded, hooped, ringed 7. enlaced 8. enclosed, enfolded, wreathed 10. surrounded
enclose... 3. hem, mew 5. bound, fence 6. corral, encase, engulf
7. enclave, envelop, harness, include
8. imprison, surround 9. encompass
12. circumscribe
enclosed... 4. pent, sept (area)
7. encased 8. confined
10. surrounded
enclosure... 3. pen 4. bawn, cage, yair (yare), yard 5. carol (cloister), kraal (craal), sekos 6. corral
8. contents, poundage, stockade
encomium... 4. hymn 5. eloge
6. eulogy, praise 7. tribute
8. accolade 9. panegyric
encompass... 4. ring 5. hem in
6. begird, effect 7. besiege, circuit, compass, contain, enclose, environ, include 8. encircle, surround
10. accomplish 12. circumscribe
encompassing... 7. ambient
13. circumambient
encore... 3. bis 4. echo, over 5. again
8. applause, once more
encounter... 4. bout, meet 5. brave, brush, fight, incur, onset 6. attack, breast, oppose 7. collide, meeting
8. conflict 10. engagement, experience
encourage... 4. abet, urge 5. boost, cheer, impel, nerve, rally 6. assure, exhort, foster, incite 7. advance, comfort, console, hearten, inspire, promote 8. embolden, inspirit
9. instigate, stimulate
11. countenance
encouragement... 3. aid 7. comfort
9. fosterage, incentive
10. inducement 11. emboldening
encroach upon... 5. poach 6. invade, trench 7. impinge, intrude
8. infringe, overstep, trespass
encumber... 4. clog, load 5. check
6. burden, hamper, hinder, retard,

saddle 7. involve, oppress
8. entangle, handicap, obstruct, overload 9. embarrass
10. overburden
encumbrance... 5. alien (law), claim
6. burden 9. dependent
10. impediment
encyclic... 6. letter 7. pandect
8. circular, treatise 10. encircling
13. comprehensive
encyclopedic learning, person of...
10. polyhistor 13. encyclopedist
end... 3. aim, neb, tip, toe 4. fate, kill, ruin, tail 5. amend, close, death, finis, limit, omega, point, telos, upend 6. expire, finale, finish, result, thirty 7. destroy, purpose
8. complete, conclude, dissolve
9. cessation, determine, extremity, intention, objective, terminate
10. completion 11. termination
end (pert to)...
arrow.. 4. nock
boundary.. 5. bourn 7. abuttal
cloth.. 7. remnant
game.. 4. goal
man.. 8. minstrel
news.. 6. thirty
timber.. 5. tenon
endanger... 4. risk 6. expose, hazard
7. imperil 10. compromise, jeopardize
endeavor... 3. aim, try, vie 4. seek
5. essay, ettle, nisus, tempt
6. effort, strive 7. attempt
8. struggle
endemic... 6. native 10. indigenous
14. characteristic
ending... 5. death 6. result
9. cessation, desinence
10. completion, conclusion
11. destruction, termination
endless... 4. many 6. eterne
7. eternal, undying 8. eternity, infinite, numerous, unending
9. boundless, continual, incessant, perpetual, unceasing, unstinted
10. continuous 11. everlasting
12. interminable 13. uninterrupted
endorse, indorse... 4. sign 6. attest, second 7. approve, support
8. sanction 9. authorize, guarantee
endorsement... 4. fiat, visa (vise)
8. approval, sanction 9. provision, signature 10. acceptance, validation
12. ratification 14. authentication
endow... 3. dow, due 4. dote, vest
5. dower, endue, indue 6. bestow, clothe, enrich, give to, invest
7. empower, furnish, provide
endowment... 4. gift 5. dower, grant
7. talents 8. appanage (apanage)
9. insurance, provision
11. empowerment, instruction (Mormon)
endue... 5. endow, teach 6. clothe, digest, invest, supply 7. empower
endurable... 8. bearable 9. tolerable
10. sufferable 11. supportable
endurance... 7. stamina 8. patience, strength 9. fortitude, suffering
10. durability, permanence, sufferance

11. continuance, resignation
12. perseverance
endure ... 4. bear, bide, dree, last, live, tide, wear 5. abide, allow, brook, stand 6. afford, remain, suffer 7. condone, persist, sustain, undergo 8. continue, tolerate 9. persevere, withstand
enduring ... 7. durable, lasting, patient 9. permanent 11. persevering, substantial, unforgotten 13. long–suffering
enemy ... 3. foe 5. devil, force, fremd (frenne), hater, rival, Satan 6. foeman 8. opponent 9. adversary 10. antagonist
energetic ... 5. fresh 6. active 8. forceful, forcible, vigorous 9. strenuous 11. industrious
energy ... 2. go 3. erg, pep, vim 4. bent 5. force, nerve, power, vigor 6. spirit 7. potency, sthenia 8. strength 9. animation
energy (pert to) ...
lack of .. 5. atony 6. anergy 7. aneuria, inertia 8. asthenia
mental .. 9. psychurgy
personified .. 6. Shakti
potential .. 5. ergal
unit .. 3. erg 5. ergon
enervate ... 3. sap 5. drain, unman 6. weaken 7. exhaust, unnerve 8. enfeeble 10. debilitate
enfeeble ... 4. numb 6. sicken, soften, weaken 7. depress 8. enervate 9. attenuate 10. debilitate
enfilade ... 4. rake 5. vista 7. barrage 9. broadside 11. arrangement (in rows)
enfold, infold ... 4. fold, wrap 5. clasp, cover 6. infold 7. embrace, envelop 8. surround
enforce ... 5. drive 6. assail, compel 7. execute, inspire 9. constrain, encourage, intensify, reinforce 10. invigorate
enfranchise ... 4. free 5. admit 7. deliver, set free 8. liberate 10. emancipate
engage ... 4. bind, draw, hire, rent 5. lease 6. absorb, embark, employ, enlist, induce, occupy, pledge 7. attract, betroth, engross, involve, promise 8. contract, entangle 9. interlock, intermesh
engaged ... 4. busy 5. hired 6. bonded, meshed 7. earnest, entered, pledged, versant 8. embedded, employed, involved, occupied, promised 9. affianced, betrothed, engrossed 10. contracted
engaged in controversy ... 9. disputant
engagement ... 4. date 6. battle 7. promise 9. betrothal, encounter 10. attachment 11. appointment, involvement
engaging ... 5. sapid 6. taking 8. alluring, duelling 10. attractive, delightful 11. interesting
engender ... 3. sow (seeds) 5. beget, breed, cause 6. excite 7. develop, produce 8. generate, occasion 9. call

forth, procreate, propagate
engine ... 3. gin, ram 5. mogul, motor 6. onager 7. machine, robinet, turbine 10. locomotive
engine (type) ... 3. gas 5. motor, solar, steam 6. Diesel, rocket 8. gasoline 10. combustion
engineer ... 4. plan 7. manager 8. computer, contrive, designer, inventor, maneuver, operator, therblig 9. construct 11. constructor, superintend
engineer (type) ... 5. civil, corps, sales 6. driver, mining 7. planner 8. chemical, geodetic, military, railroad, research, sanitary 9. hydraulic 10. electrical, industrial, mechanical, structural 11. electronics 12. aeronautical, construction 14. administrative
engird ... 6. begird, circle, girdle 7. envelop 8. encircle, ensphere
England ... see also *English*
called .. 6. Albion (anc) 7. Britain 9. Britannia
capital .. 6. London
city .. 3. Ely 4. Hull, York 5. Derby, Leeds 6. Exeter 7. Bristol, Croydon 8. Brighton, Coventry, Hastings, Plymouth 9. Liverpool, Sheffield 10. Birmingham, Epsom Downs, Manchester, Nottingham, Portsmouth 11. Southampton
college (famed) .. 4. Eton 6. Harrow, Oxford 9. Cambridge, Sandhurst (military)
conqueror .. 5. Danes 6. Angles, Saxons 7. Normans
constitution .. 10. Magna Carta (1215) 12. Bill of Rights (1688)
county .. 4. Kent 5. Devon, Essex 6. Dorset, Sussex 9. Yorkshire
emblem .. 4. lion, rose
House of .. 4. York 5. Blois, Tudor 6. Stuart 7. Hanover, Windsor 8. Normandy 9. Lancaster 11. Plantagenet
island .. 5. Wight 6. Scilly, Virgin 7. Bahamas, Bermuda, Channel, Solomon 8. Falkland, Windward 9. Isle of Man
king (anc) .. 6. Arthur (legend), Egbert 8. Ethelred 9. Ethelwulf
native (anc) .. 4. Celt, Dane, Jute 5. Saxon 8. Anglican 9. Sassenach 10. Anglo–Saxon
river .. 3. Exe 4. Avon, Ouse 5. Trent 6. Thames
royal residence .. 7. Windsor
street (London) .. 10. Piccadilly 12. Threadneedle
English (pert to) ...
bride's gift .. 3. dos
court .. 4. eyre (circuit), leet (anc)
dislike of .. 11. Anglophobia
district .. 4. Soho
estate (feudal) .. 4. fief
excuse (legal) .. 6. essoin
festival (country) .. 3. ale
field .. 5. croft
forest .. 5. Arden 8. Sherwood
freeman .. 5. ceorl, thane, thegn

hamlet.. **4.** dorp
heather.. **4.** ling
lawyer.. **9.** barrister, solicitor
leave of absence (school).. **5.** exeat
lover of.. **10.** Anglophile
Marbles.. **6.** Oxford **7.** Arundel
money of account.. **3.** ora
news agency.. **6.** Reuter
Parliament process.. **7.** Hansard
political party.. **4.** Tory, Whig
  8. Laborite **12.** Conservative
porcelain.. **5.** Spode **8.** Wedgwood
prehistoric site.. **8.** Piltdown
race course.. **5.** Ascot **9.** Newmarket
  10. Epsom Downs
races (famed).. **5.** Derby **7.** The Oaks
sheep (blackface).. **4.** Lonk
song (mock).. **12.** lillibullero
stolen article (on thief).. **7.** mainour
symbol.. **4.** bull, lion, rose
thicket.. **5.** copse **7.** spinney
tract (sandy).. **4.** dean (dene)
trolley.. **4.** tram
uplands.. **5.** downs
wren.. **6.** tomtit
English Channel... **8.** La Manche
English, famed...
composer.. **6.** Handel **7.** Stainer
diarist.. **5.** Pepys
engraver.. **3.** Pye **7.** Hogarth
essayist.. **4.** Elia (Charles Lamb), Lang
  6. Steele **7.** Addison
explorer.. **4.** Ross **5.** Cabot **6.** Baffin,
  Beatty, Hudson **7.** Raleigh
  10. Shackleton
financier.. **7.** Gresham
historian.. **4.** Bede **7.** Spelman,
  Toynbee **8.** Macaulay
humorist.. **4.** Lear (Edward)
mathematician.. **5.** Hooke **6.** Gunter
murderer (famed).. **4.** Aram
navigator.. **4.** Cook **5.** Drake
  6. Nelson
painter.. **4.** Lear **6.** Turner
  7. Hogarth, Lutyens, Millais
philosopher.. **7.** Spencer
physicist.. **7.** Faraday
poet.. **5.** Noyes **8.** Browning,
  Tennyson **9.** Masefield, Swinburne
printer.. **6.** Caxton
reformer.. **4.** Owen **6.** Spence
saint.. **6.** George (patron saint)
  7. Alphege, Swithin
scientist.. **6.** Newton
spy (in Am Rev).. **5.** André
statesman.. **4.** Peel, Pitt **7.** Baldwin,
  Balfour, Walpole **8.** Cromwell,
  Disraeli, Thatcher **9.** Churchill
  11. Chamberlain, Lloyd George
surgeon.. **5.** Haden, Paget **6.** Lister
theologian.. **5.** Booth **6.** Becket
  7. Tyndall **8.** Wycliffe **10.** Whitefield
thesaurus compiler.. **5.** Roget
engrave... **3.** cut **4.** etch, rist
  5. carve, chase, hatch, infix **6.** chisel,
  incise **7.** enchase, impress, imprint,
  stipple **9.** sculpture
engraver's tool... **5.** burin
engraving... **3.** cut **5.** print
  7. etching, chasing, tooling
  8. celature, incising, intaglio
  9. stippling **10.** xylography (wood)

  11. lithography **12.** glyptography
engross... **6.** absorb, engage
  10. monopolize **11.** concentrate
engrossed... **4.** busy, rapt **6.** intent
  8. absorbed, employed **10.** interested
engulf... **4.** gulf, gulp **5.** swamp
  6. absorb **7.** swallow **8.** inundate,
  submerge **9.** overwhelm
enhance... **4.** lift **5.** exalt, extol, raise
  7. advance, augment, elevate, enlarge,
  magnify **8.** increase **9.** aggravate
  10. exaggerate
enigma... **3.** why **5.** rebus **6.** puzzle,
  riddle **7.** charade, mystery
  9. conundrum **11.** mind-boggler
enigmatic... **6.** arcane, mystic
  8. puzzling **12.** inexplicable
enjoin... **3.** bid **5.** order **6.** advise,
  charge, decree, direct, forbid
  7. command **8.** admonish, prohibit
enjoy... **4.** bask, have **5.** savor
  6. relish **10.** appreciate
enjoyment... **4.** ease, zest **6.** relish
  7. delight **8.** felicity, fruition, pleasure
  9. amusement, happiness
enlarge... **3.** eke **4.** ream **5.** swell
  6. dilate, expand, extend, spread
  7. amplify, augment, develop, distend
  8. increase **9.** expatiate
  10. exaggerate
enlargement... **8.** increase
  9. expansion, extension
  12. augmentation **13.** amplification
enlighten... **5.** teach **6.** inform
  7. educate, explain **8.** enkindle,
  instruct **10.** illuminate **11.** disillusion
enlightened person... **10.** illuminate
enlist... **4.** join, list **6.** engage, enroll,
  induce, muster
enliven... **5.** amuse, cheer, rouse
  7. animate, comfort, inspire, refresh
  8. brighten, energize, inspirit
  9. encourage, stimulate
  10. exhilarate, invigorate
enmity... **3.** war **4.** feud **6.** hatred,
  malice, rancor **7.** discord **8.** aversion
  9. antipathy, disaccord, hostility
  10. antagonism, repugnance
  11. malevolence **14.** unfriendliness
ennead... **4.** gods (nine), nine
  18. Ennead of Heliopolis (famed)
ennoble... **5.** exalt, honor, raise
  6. uplift **7.** elevate, glorify, promote
ennui... **4.** bore **5.** bored **6.** tedium
  7. boredom, fatigue, languor
  9. weariness **15.** dissatisfaction
enormous... **4.** huge, vast **5.** great
  6. wicked **7.** immense, massive,
  titanic **8.** abnormal, colossal, gigantic,
  infamous **9.** atrocious, excessive,
  monstrous **10.** inordinate, prodigious,
  stupendous
Enos' father... **4.** Seth
enough... **4.** enow **5.** ample, basta,
  fully, quite **6.** plenty **8.** adequate
  9. amplitude **10.** sufficient
  12. satisfactory
enounce... **5.** state, utter **8.** proclaim
  9. enunciate, pronounce
enow... **9.** presently
enrage... **5.** anger **6.** madden
  7. incense, inflame **9.** infuriate

enraged . . . 5. irate 7. angered
8. maddened 10. infuriated

enraptured . . . 6. enrapt 8. ecstatic
9. delighted, entranced
10. enravished

enravished . . . 4. rapt 9. enchanted,
entranced, rapturous 10. enraptured

enrich . . . 4. lard 5. adorn, endow
6. fatten 7. improve 8. increase,
ornament 9. embellish, fertilize

enroll . . . 4. coil, join, list, roll 5. enter
6. enlist, induct, unfurl, wrap up
7. engross, impanel 8. initiate,
register 11. matriculate

ens . . . 5. being 6. entity 7. essence

ensconce . . . 4. hide 5. cover 6. settle
7. conceal, protect, shelter
9. establish

ensemble . . . 3. all 5. decor, group,
whole 7. costume

enshroud . . . 4. wrap 6. clothe, swathe
7. conceal, enclose 8. enshrine

ensiform . . . 12. xiphisternum

ensign . . . 4. flag 6. banner 7. officer
8. gonfalon, standard 9. oriflamme
(oriflamb, anc)

ensign of Othello . . . 4. Iago

enslave . . . 8. enthrall

ensnare . . . 3. web 4. trap 5. benet,
catch, innet, noose 6. allure,
enmesh, entrap, seduce 7. involve

ensorcell, ensorcel . . . 7. bewitch,
enchant

ensue . . . 6. follow, pursue, result
7. imitate, succeed 8. come next

ensuing . . . 4. next 9. resultant
10. subsequent, succeeding

ensure . . . 6. assure, insure, secure
7. protect, warrant 9. guarantee

entad . . . 6. inward (opp of ectad)

ental . . . 5. inner (opp of ectal)

entangle . . . 3. mat, web 4. mesh, mire
5. afoul, ravel, snarl, twist 6. enlace,
enmesh, puzzle, raffle 7. confuse,
ensnare, involve, perplex 8. bewilder
9. embarrass 10. interweave

entanglement . . . 4. knot 5. snare, snarl
6. abatis 8. obstacle 9. barricade,
imbroglio 10. barbed wire, complexity
11. involvement

enter . . . 4. join, list 5. begin, start,
train 6. engage, enlist, enroll, insert,
record 8. initiate, inscribe, register
9. introduce, penetrate
11. participate

enter (pert to) . . .
career . . 6. incept
legal objection . . 5. demur
with hostility . . 6. invade
without permission . . 7. intrude
8. encroach, infringe

enterprise . . . 4. firm 5. essay 6. daring
7. attempt, crusade, exploit, venture
10. initiative 11. undertaking

enterprising . . . 4. bold 6. daring
9. energetic 11. up–and–coming

entertain . . . 4. fete 5. amuse, treat
6. divert, regale 7. beguile, cherish
8. interest

entertainer . . . 5. actor 6. dancer,
singer 7. actress, speaker
8. magician 9. performer

11. pantomimist 12. impersonator

entertainment . . . 4. play 5. party,
revue, sport 6. kermis (kermess),
repast 7. pastime, ridotto, theater
8. entr'acte, musicale 9. amusement,
diversion, reception, wayzgoose
10. recreation 12. Roman holiday

enthusiasm . . . 4. élan, fire, zeal, zest
5. ardor, craze, estro, furor (furore),
mania, verve 6. fervor 7. ecstasy
8. interest 9. animation, eagerness,
transport 10. exaltation

enthusiast . . . 3. fan 5. bigot 6. rooter,
zealot 7. devotee, fanatic

enthusiastic . . . 5. eager, nutty, rabid
6. active, ardent 7. zealous
10. interested

entice . . . 4. bait, coax, lure, tole
5. decoy, tempt 6. allure, cajole,
incite, seduce 7. attract, wheedle
8. inveigle, persuade

enticement . . . 9. seduction
10. allurement, attraction, incitement,
inducement, persuasion, temptation
12. inveiglement

entire . . . 3. all 5. cover (Philat), sound,
total, utter, whole 6. intact
7. perfect, sincere, upright
8. complete, faithful, stallion
9. integrate, undivided
10. unimpaired 11. unqualified
12. undiminished

entirely . . . 3. all 5. clean, fully, stark
6. solely, wholly 7. totally 9. every
inch, perfectly, sincerely
10. completely

entitle . . . 3. dub 4. call, name, term
5. style 6. assign, enable, impute
7. empower, qualify 9. authorize,
designate 10. denominate

entity . . . 3. ens 4. soul, unit 5. being,
entia, thing 7. integer 8. infinity
(Math) 9. existence

entomb . . . 4. bury 5. inter, inurn
6. hearse, inhume 7. confine
9. sepulture

entourage . . . 5. suite, train 7. retinue
10. associates, attendants
12. surroundings

entr'acte . . . 3. act 5. dance, music
7. interim 9. interlude

entrails . . . 4. guts 6. bowels
7. insides, viscera 8. interior
10. intestines

entrance . . . 3. way 4. adit, door, gate
5. entry, inlet 6. access, portal
7. gateway, ingress, postern
9. admission, insertion, threshold,
vestibule 10. admittance

entrance (pert to) . . .
church (Eastern) . . 5. Great 6. Little
formal . . 5. debut 12. introduction
hostile . . 9. incursion
temple (Buddh) . . 5. toran (torana)

entranced . . . 4. rapt 8. dreaming
9. delighted, overjoyed
10. fascinated, hypnotized, spellbound
11. overpowered

entrap . . . 3. net 4. trap 5. catch,
decoy, noose, snare 6. tangle
7. beguile, ensnare 8. entangle,
inveigle

entreat... 3. ask, beg, woo 4. pray
5. crave, halse (obs), plead
6. adjure, appeal 7. beseech,
implore, solicit 8. petition
9. importune 10. supplicate

entreaty... 4. plea, suit 6. appeal,
prayer 7. request 8. petition
10. invitation 11. importunity
12. solicitation, supplication

entree, entrée... 4. dish 6. access
7. ingress, opening 9. admission
10. permission (to enter)

entrench... 6. invade 7. enter on,
fortify, intrude 8. encroach, trespass
establish

entrenchment... 7. defense, parapet
9. intrusion 10. protection
12. encroachment, infringement
13. establishment

entrepot... 5. depot, store
9. warehouse 10. depository

entrepreneur... 7. provost 9. executive
10. impresario 13. administrator

entrust... 6. commit 7. confide,
consign 8. delegate 10. commission

entry... 4. hall, item, lane, post
7. ingress 8. entrance, register
9. admission, vestibule
10. contestant, memorandum
12. introduction

entwine... 4. lace 5. clasp, twine,
twist, weave 6. enlace 7. wreathe
9. interknit

enumerate... 4. list, tell 5. count
6. detail, number, reckon, relate
7. compute 8. estimate, name over,
rehearse 9. calculate, catalogue
(catalog) 12. recapitulate
13. particularize

enumeration... 4. list 5. count
6. census 10. numeration
14. recapitulation

enunciate... 3. say 5. utter 6. affirm
7. declare 8. announce, proclaim
9. postulate, pronounce
10. articulate

enunciation... 9. statement, utterance
11. affirmation, attestation,
declaration 12. announcement
13. pronouncement, pronunciation

envelop... 4. case, wrap 5. cover
6. clothe, encase, enwrap, infold,
invest, sheath, shroud 7. conceal,
enclose, sheathe 8. encircle,
surround 9. encompass, enwreathe
10. integument

envelope... 3. bur (burr) 5. cover,
curve 6. jacket 7. conceal, rampart,
vesicle, wrapper 8. membrane
10. integument

enveloped... 6. amidst 7. covered
10. surrounded

envenom... 5. taint 6. poison
8. embitter

envious... 7. jealous 8. covetous,
grudging, spiteful 9. green-eyed
10. begrudging

environ... 3. hem 6. suburb
7. compass, envelop, hedge in,
involve, purlieu 8. encircle, outskirt,
surround 9. encompass

environment... 4. area 6. medium,

milieu 7. setting, suburbs, terrain
8. environs 10. background
12. neighborhood, surroundings
13. encompassment

envisage... 4. face 8. confront
9. visualize 11. contemplate
12. meet squarely

envision... 5. dream 7. picture
9. visualize 11. contemplate
12. meet squarely

envoy... 5. agent 6. legate, l'envoi,
stanza 7. refrain 8. ablegate,
delegate, diplomat 9. messenger
10. ambassador, postscript
12. commissioner

envy... 5. covet 6. grudge 8. jealousy
12. covetousness

enwrap, inwrap... 4. roll, wrap
6. clothe, enfold, infold 7. engross
8. surround

enzyme... 3. ase (suff) 5. bread (Eccl)
6. lotase, olease, pepsin, rennin,
urease 7. amylase, ferment, laccase,
ptyalin, trypsin 8. diastase, protease
9. digestant

enzyme activator... 11. biocatalyst

eoan... 7. auroral 8. daybreak, easterly

eon, aeon... 3. age, era 4. time
5. cycle 8. eternity 10. generation

ephemeral... 7. diurnal 9. chickweed,
deciduous, transient 10. short-lived

ephemeris... 5. diary 7. almanac,
journal 8. calendar 10. periodical
11. publication

Ephesus (pert to)...
city of.. 6. Greece (anc)
famed for.. 5. ruins 12. Christianity
site.. 9. Aegean Sea
temple.. 7. Artemis
visitor (early).. 6. St Paul

Ephraim... 4. bear (grizzly) 5. tribe
8. fruitful

epi... 6. finial

epic... 3. cid 4. epos, poem, saga
5. epode 6. Aeneid (by Vergil),
epopee, heroic 9. narrative

epicene... 7. neutral, sexless
10. effeminate

epicure... 6. friand (obs) 7. glutton,
gourmet 8. gourmand, Sybarite
10. voluptuary 11. connoisseur

epidemic... 4. pest 6. plague
8. pandemic 9. prevalent, spreading
10. contagious, pestilence

epidermis... 4. skin 7. cuticle
8. ectoderm 9. scarfskin

epigram... 3. mot, saw 4. poem, quip
5. adage, maxim 6. dictum, saying
7. distich 11. inscription (obs)

epigraph... 5. motto, title 9. quotation
11. inscription

Epiphany (Eccl)... 5. Feast (Jan 6)

Epirus, oracle of... 6. Dodona (Mt
Tomarus, Gr)

episode... 5. event, story 8. incident
10. digression (Mus), occurrence

epistle... 4. note, post 6. billet,
lesson, letter 7. message, missive,
writing 8. dispatch, rescript
13. communication

epitaph... 7. writing (monument) 8. hic
jacet 11. inscription

epithet... 4. name, term 5. label
6. byname 7. agnomen 9. sobriquet
11. appellation (significant)
epitome... 6. digest 7. summary
8. abstract 9. comprisal
10. abridgment, compendium
epitomize... 7. abridge, curtail
8. abstract, compress, condense,
contract, diminish 9. capsulize
epoch... 3. age, day, eon, era 4. date,
time 5. event 6. period
epopee... 4. epic, epos, poem
5. genre (epic) 6. poetry (epic)
epoptic... 6. mystic, secret
equable... 4. even 6. steady
7. uniform
equal... 3. iso (pref), par, tie 4. both,
even, fere (obs), just, pari (pref),
peer, same 5. match, rival
7. compeer, emulate, equable,
uniform 8. adequate, parallel
9. equitable, identical 10. coordinate,
equivalent, substitute 11. counterpart
12. commensurate 13. proportionate
equal day and night...
11. equidiurnal, equinoctial
equal density (atmospheric)...
8. isoteric
equality... 3. par, tie 6. equity, owelty
(payment), parity 7. egalite, isonomy
(law) 8. adequacy, evenness, fairness,
identity, sameness 10. uniformity
12. impartiality
Equality State... 7. Wyoming (first
with Woman Suffrage)
equalize... 4. even 5. equal, level,
match 6. equate, smooth 7. balance
10. symmetrize
equally... 2. as 4. equi (pref) 5. alike
6. evenly, justly 11. identically
15. correspondingly
equanimity... 5. poise 6. aplomb
7. balance 8. calmness, evenness,
serenity 9. assurance, composure
10. confidence, equability
11. tranquility 12. tranquillity
equilibrium... 5. poise 7. balance
8. equality 9. stability 10. equanimity
equine... 3. ass 4. colt, foal, mare
5. filly, horse, steed, zebra 6. donkey
equine cry... 5. neigh 6. whinny
equip... 3. arm, fit, imp, rig 4. deck,
gear, gird 5. dress, endow
7. costume, furnish, qualify
8. accouter
equipment... 4. gear 5. armor
6. outfit, tackle, traits (personal)
7. ability, panoply (warriors)
8. equipage 9. apparatus
11. preparation 12. accouterment,
accoutrement
equitable... 4. fair, just 5. right
6. honest 7. upright 9. impartial
10. bonitarian (Rom law), reasonable
equity... 4. laws 6. rights 7. honesty,
justice 8. fairness 9. rectitude
11. uprightness
equivalence... 3. par 7. valence
8. equality, sameness 10. relativity
11. correlation
equivalent... 5. alike, equal
9. identical 10. tantamount

equivocal... 7. dubious, obscure
8. doubtful, puzzling 9. ambiguous,
enigmatic, uncertain 10. amphibolic,
mysterious, perplexing
13. indeterminate, problematical
equivocate... 3. lie 5. dodge, evade,
fence, shift 6. palter, trifle
7. quibble, shuffle 11. prevaricate
12. tergiversate
era... 2. AD, BC 3. age, eon 4. date,
time 5. cycle, epoch 6. period
10. Anno Domini 12. Before Christ
eradicate... 4. dele, root, weed
5. annul, erase 6. remove, uproot
7. abolish, destroy, epilate, extract,
root out 9. eliminate, extirpate
10. annihilate 11. exterminate
erase... 4. dele, kill 5. arase (obs)
6. cancel, delete, efface, excise
7. expunge, relieve 10. obliterate
Erasmus (Dutch)... 6. lovely 7. scholar
Erastus (Swiss)... 9. physician
10. theologian
ere... 4. also, soon 5. early, prior
6. before, erenow, sooner 7. earlier,
ere long 8. erewhile, formerly
10. before long, previously, sooner
than
Erebus (pert to)...
brother.. 3. Nox
father of.. 3. Day 6. Aether
Greek myth.. 8. darkness (nether)
native of.. 5. Hades
son.. 5. Chaos
erect... 4. lift, rear, stay 5. build,
found, raise, stand, upend 6. raised
7. elevate, upright 8. uplifted,
vertical 9. construct, establish,
institute 13. perpendicular
eremite... 6. hermit 7. recluse
8. anchoret, solitary 9. anchorite
erenow... 5. prior 8. erewhile, formerly
10. heretofore
ergo... 5. hence 9. therefore
Erin... 4. Eire 7. Ireland
Eritrea, Africa...
capital.. 6. Asmara
coastline of.. 8. Ethiopia
ruler.. 7. England (formerly It)
site.. 6. Red Sea
ermine... 3. fur 4. robe (emblem)
5. stoat (stot) 6. clothe, lasset,
weasel 7. ermelin
erode... 3. eat 4. gnaw, wear
7. corrode, decline, destroy
11. deteriorate 12. disintegrate
erotic... 6. loving, sexual 7. amative,
amatory, amorous 8. doctrine (of
love)
err... 3. sin 4. miss, slip 5. stray
6. bungle 7. blunder, deviate
10. transgress 12. miscalculate,
misinterpret
Er Rai... 5. stars 8. shepherd
errand... 4. task, trip 7. journey,
mission 8. business (special)
10. commission
errand boy... 4. page 7. bellboy,
bellhop, courier 9. messenger
errant... 6. erring, roving 7. peccant
8. fallible 9. deviating, erroneous,
itinerant, wandering 10. journeying

erratic... 5. queer, rogue 6. whacky
   7. nomadic, strange 8. abnormal
   9. eccentric, irregular, planetary,
   wandering 10. capricious, changeable
erroneous... 5. false, wrong 6. untrue
   7. peccant 8. illusory, mistaken
   9. wandering
error... 3. sin 4. flub, muff, slip
   5. boner, lapse 6. errata (pl), miscue
   7. blunder, falsity, misstep, mistake
   8. iniquity 11. anachronism,
   misjudgment 14. miscalculation
ersatz... 5. proxy, token 9. vicarious
   10. equivalent, substitute
   11. alternative, replacement
   12. substitution
Erse... 5. Irish 6. Celtic, Gaelic
erst, erstwhile... 4. also, once 5. first
   6. former, sooner 8. earliest, formerly
   10. heretofore, previously
erudite... 4. wise 7. learned
   8. cultured, educated, literate
   9. scholarly
erudition... 4. lore 6. finish, wisdom
   7. letters 8. learning, pedantry
   9. knowledge
eruption... 4. rash 6. geyser
   7. volcano 8. ejection, outbreak,
   outburst 9. commotion, exanthema
   10. nettlerash 13. efflorescence
Esau (pert to)...
   Bible ref.. 7. Genesis
   brother.. 5. Jacob
   father.. 5. Isaac
   home.. 4. Seir
   mother.. 7. Rebekah
   name (later).. 4. Edom
escape... 4. flee 5. dodge, elope,
   elude, evade, spill 7. evasion
   9. avolation 13. circumvention
escargot... 5. snail
escarpment... 5. cliff, slope
   9. precipice 13. fortification
eschar... 4. scab, sore 5. crust
   6. slough
escharotic... 7. caustic, mordant
   8. stinging 9. corrosive
escheat... 4. fall 5. lapse 6. revert
   (land) 7. forfeit 9. reversion
   10. forfeiture
eschew... 4. shun 5. avoid 7. abstain,
   refrain
escolar... 4. fish 8. mackerel (like)
escort... 3. see 4. beau 5. guard
   (honor), usher 6. attend, convoy,
   gigolo, squire 7. conduct, retinue
   8. chaperon 9. accompany
   13. accompaniment
escritoire... 4. desk 6. bureau
   7. dresser 9. secretary 10. secretaire
escrow... 4. bond, deed (deposit)
   9. muniments
esculent... 6. edible 7. eatable
   8. gustable 10. comestible
escutcheon... 4. fess (band), orle
   (voided) 5. crest 6. shield
esker, eskar... 2. os 4. osar (pl)
   5. drift, hills, mound, ridge
Eskimo... 3. Ita 4. Yuit 5. Aleut
   6. Innuit 10. skraelling 11. Yikirgaulit
   (Diomede Isles)
Eskimo (pert to)...

   boat, canoe.. 5. kayak, umiak
   (oomiac)
   boot (sealskin).. 5. kamik
   coat (bird skin).. 5. parka 6. temiak
   color.. 5. brown (rustic)
   dog.. 5. Husky 8. Malemute
   family.. 9. Eskimauan
   fish.. 4. Atka 8. mackerel
   hut, house.. 5. igloo, tupek (tupik)
   jacket.. 6. temiak
   knife (woman's).. 3. ulu
   memorial post.. 3. xat
   settlement.. 4. Etah
   totem.. 4. pole, post 6. symbol
esne... 4. serf 5. slave 8. hireling
esophagus, oesophagus... 4. crop,
   gula 6. gullet, throat 7. pharynx
esoteric... 5. inner 6. occult, secret
   7. private 8. abstruse, initiate,
   personal 9. recondite 12. confidential
esoteric doctrine... 6. cabala
esoteric wisdom... 6. gnosis
espalier... 7. epaulet, railing, trellis
Español... 7. Spanish
especial... 5. chief 7. special
   8. peculiar, uncommon
Esperanto... 3. Ido 8. language
   (Internat)
espionage... 4. espy 6. spying
   11. observation (secret)
   14. reconnaissance
esplanade... 4. walk 5. drive, level,
   Prado, praya 6. strand 7. walkway
espousal... 7. wedding 8. adoption,
   ceremony 10. acceptance
   11. embracement
espouse... 3. wed 4. bind, mate
   5. adopt, marry 6. defend, pledge
   7. betroth, embrace, support
   8. maintain, plead for
esprit de corps... 3. wit 6. spirit
   8. devotion 10. enthusiasm,
   fellowship 11. partisanism
esprit fort (Relig)... 11. freethinker
espy... 3. see 5. watch 6. behold,
   descry, detect 7. discern 8. discover
   9. look about
esquire... 5. title 6. escort, gentry
   7. armiger 8. escudero, nobleman
   11. armor–bearer 12. shield–bearer
essay... 3. try 4. test 5. assay, chris
   (Rhet), paper, theme, tract, trial
   6. effort, thesis 7. attempt
   8. endeavor, treatise 11. composition
   12. disquisition, dissertation
esse... 5. being (real) 9. existence
essence... 3. ens 4. gist, odor, pith
   5. attar, being, scent 6. nature
   7. element, extract, perfume
   9. principle, substance
   12. quintessence
essential... 5. vital 6. mortal
   7. needful 8. existent, inherent
   9. necessary, necessity
   13. indispensable
essential oil... 8. volatile 12. attar of
   roses
essential part... 4. core, crux, gist,
   pith 7. element 8. inherent
   10. inwardness
establish... 3. fix 4. base, seat
   5. build, enact, erect, found, plant,

prove, set up 6. create, ground,
locate, ordain, settle 7. confirm,
pre—empt 8. ensconce, legalize,
radicate (rare) 9. ascertain, originate
established... 5. fixed 6. proved,
rested, stable 11. naturalized,
traditional 12. conventional
established (pert to)...
  church.. 9. Episcopal (Eng)
  rule.. 8. standard
  thing.. 4. fact
  truth.. 8. verified
establishment... 4. mill 5. plant
  6. custom, menage 7. factory
  9. structure 12. organization
establishment of cordial relations...
  13. rapprochement
establishment of new plant home...
  6. ecesis
estate... 4. alod, fief (feudal), rank
  (social) 5. manor, title 6. assets,
  equity 7. alodium, demesne, fortune
  8. interest, property 9. situation
esteem... 4. dear 5. adore, honor,
  judge, pride, value 6. admire, regard,
  repute, revere 7. respect 8. appraise,
  venerate 10. appreciate
  13. consideration
ester of...
  silicic acid.. 8. silicate
  stearic acid.. 7. stearin 8. stearate
  tropic acid.. 7. tropate
  vinegar.. 7. acetate
esthetic, aesthetic... 6. essene
  8. artistic, tasteful 9. beautiful
estimable... 6. worthy 8. valuable
  9. admirable, honorable, reputable,
  venerable 10. measurable
  12. praiseworthy
estimate... 3. aim, set 4. gage, rank,
  rate 5. audit, gauge, guess, prize,
  think 6. assess, repute 7. adjudge,
  compute, measure, opinion
  8. appraise, judgment 9. calculate,
  statement, valuation
Estonia...
  capital.. 5. Revel 7. Tallinn
  industry.. 3. oil
  island.. 5. Oesel
  peasant (rich).. 5. kulak
  ruler.. 4. USSR
estop... 3. bar 4. fill, halt, plug, stay
  6. impede, stop up 7. prevent
  8. prohibit
estrange... 4. part, wean 6. divert,
  divide 8. alienate, disunite, separate
estreat... 4. copy 6. amerce, sconce
  7. extract 9. duplicate, penalties
  (law)
estuary... 3. bay 4. Pará 5. firth, frith,
  Plata
etch... 3. cut 4. bite 5. infix
  7. corrode, engrave, impress (upon)
eternal... 6. eonian 7. aeonian,
  ageless, endless, lasting 8. enduring,
  immortal, timeless 9. boundless,
  ceaseless, immutable, incessant,
  unceasing 10. unchanging
  11. everlasting 12. imperishable,
  interminable, unchangeable
Eternal City... 4. Rome
eternal death... 9. perdition

eternal home... 6. heaven 12. The
  Hereafter
eternity... 3. eon 4. aeon, ages, olam
  8. Olam haba
etesian... 4. wind (Aegean Sea)
  6. annual 8. seasonal 10. periodical
ether... 3. air, sky 5. ester, space
  6. anisol, heaven (anc) 8. empyrean
  10. anesthetic
ethereal... 4. rare 5. aerie (aery), light
  7. fragile, slender, tenuous
  8. delicate, heavenly, vaporous
  9. celestial 10. atmosphere (earth's),
  spiritlike 11. phantomlike
  13. unsubstantial
ethereal (pert to)...
  being.. 5. sylph
  color.. 7. sky blue
  fluid.. 5. ichor (icor)
  poetic.. 4. aery
  salt.. 5. ester
ethical... 5. moral, right 7. upright
  8. virtuous
ethics... 6. morals 8. hedonics
  10. principles (moral) 11. highest
  good, summum bonum 12. Magna
  Moralia (Aristotle)
Ethiopia (Abyssinia)...
  capital.. 10. Addis Ababa
  city.. 5. Adowa
  colony.. 7. Eritrea
  empress.. 7. Zauditu
  king (Myth).. 5. Negus 6. Memnon
  native.. 5. Negro 6. Hamite
  10. Abyssinian, black–a–moor
  river.. 3. Omo 4. Juba 5. Abbai (Blue
  Nile)
  ruler.. 7. Menelik 13. Haile Selassie
  tribes (anc).. 5. Bejas, Galla
  7. Hamites, Semites
Ethiopian (pert to)...
  ape.. 6. gelada
  banana.. 6. ensete
  dialect.. 4. Geez
  lily.. 5. calla
  Torah.. 5. tetel
ethnic... 5. pagan 6. racial 7. gentile,
  heathen
ethnology... 5. races (Man)
ethology... 7. manners 9. bionomics,
  character
ethos (opp of pathos)... 9. attitudes
  (moral), esthetics
etiquette... 4. form 5. label, mores
  6. ticket 7. decorum, manners
  9. amenities, propriety 10. civilities
etiquette, breach of... 8. solecism
Etruria, Italy... see *Etruscan*
Etruscan (pert to)...
  bookbinding (anc).. 9. classical
  deity.. 3. Lar, Uni
  pottery.. 8. bucchero (black)
  race.. 7. Rasenna 8. Tursenoi,
  Tyrrheni
  soothsayer.. 8. haruspex (a)
  soothsayer's function.. 8. extispex
ettle... 3. try 4. plan 6. aspire,
  design, intent 8. consider, endeavor
etui, etwee... 4. case 7. trousse
etymology... 10. word origin
eucalyptus... 4. lerp (laap, juice)
  7. gum tree 8. eucalypt

Eucharist (pert to)...
administer to.. 6. housel 8. viaticum (dying)
plate.. 5. paten
rite.. 9. Communion (Holy) 11. Lord's Supper
wafer.. 4. host
wafer vessel.. 8. ciborium
wine.. 5. krama
wine vessel.. 3. ama 5. amula
Euclid (Gr)... 8. geometer (BC)
eulogist... 9. encomiast 10. panegyrist
eulogize... 4. laud 5. boost, extol 6. praise 7. commend, glorify 9. celebrate 10. panegyrize
eulogy... 5. eloge 6. hesped (Heb), praise 7. oration 8. citation, encomium 9. laudation, panegyric
euphony... 5. meter 6. melody, rhythm, speech (ease of) 7. harmony
Eurafrica... 5. Egypt 6. Europe 7. Algeria 9. Abyssinia (anc)
Eurasia... 4. Asia 6. Europe 7. Scythia (anc)
Eurasian (pert to)...
herb.. 6. yarrow 7. gosmore
mint.. 6. Nepeta
people.. 5. Finns 7. Ugrians 9. Armenians, Turanians
eureka... 11. exclamation 12. I Have Found It (Calif motto)
Euripedes (Gr)... 4. poet (BC)
Europe... see also *European*
basin (coal).. 4. Saar
battlefield.. 5. Marne 6. Verdun 8. Normandy, Waterloo 11. Belleau Wood
capitals.. 4. Bonn, Oslo, Riga, Rome 5. Berne, Paris, Sofia 6. Athens, Berlin, Lisbon, Madrid, Moscow, Prague, Warsaw 8. Belgrade, Budapest, Helsinki 9. Amsterdam, Bucharest, Stockholm 10. Copenhagen, Monte Carlo
country (anc).. 4. Elis (Gr) 7. Etruria (It)
country (modern).. 5. Italy, Spain 6. France, Greece, Latvia, Monaco, Norway, Poland, Russia, Sweden 7. Denmark, Finland, Germany, Hungary, Rumania 8. Bulgaria, Portugal 10. Yugoslavia 11. Netherlands, Switzerland 14. Czechoslovakia
gulf.. 4. Riga 7. Bothnia
health resort.. 5. Baden 10. Baden Baden (Ger)
invaders.. 4. Huns 5. Arabs, Turks 7. Mongols
kingdom (anc).. 5. Arles 6. Aragon 8. Burgundy
lake.. 9. Zuider Zee (Holland)
lancer.. 5. uhlan 6. hussar
mountain region.. 4. Alps 5. Tyrol
race (anc).. 5. Goths 7. Teutons 9. Visigoths 10. Ostrogoths
river.. 4. Elbe, Isar 5. Loire, Meuse, Rhine, Rhone, Seine, Volga 6. Danube 7. Dneiper, Moselle
sea.. 4. Aral, Azov 5. North 6. Baltic
strait.. 8. Bosporus
valley.. 4. Ruhr

European (pert to)...
antelope.. 7. chamois
bat.. 8. serotine
bird.. 3. ani, mew (gull) 4. kite, stag 5. glede, mavis, ousel, serin 6. godwit, linnet, marten, merlin (falcon) 7. bittern, ortolan, starnel 8. dotterel, garganey 9. brambling, gallinule 10. turtledove 11. lammergeier 12. capercaillie
bison.. 7. aurochs
clover.. 6. alsike
dog.. 7. griffin
fish.. 3. gar 4. dace, rudd, spet, tope (shark) 5. sprat 6. allice, barbel, brasse, morgay, turbot
grape.. 6. muscat
linden.. 4. teil
mint.. 6. hyssop 9. horehound
mouse.. 4. loir, vole 5. lerot
polecat.. 7. fitchew
rodent.. 3. erd 4. loir 5. stoat (ermine) 6. leriot 7. hamster
sandpiper.. 4. ruff 5. terek
squirrel.. 5. sisel 10. polatouche
tree.. 4. cade (juniper), sorb (apple) 5. carob 9. terebinth
wheat.. 5. emmer (speltz) 7. einkorn
evacuant... 6. emetic 8. diuretic 9. cathartic, purgative
evacuate... 4. void 5. empty, expel 6. depart, vacate 7. deprive, exhaust 8. withdraw 9. discharge
evade... 3. gee 4. foil, shun 5. avoid, dodge, elude, parry, shirk, shunt 6. baffle, escape, illude 7. beguile, quibble 8. slip away 10. circumvent
evanescent... 8. fleeting 9. ephemeral, transient, vanishing 11. impermanent 12. disappearing 13. infinitesimal
evangelical... 7. Gospels 8. orthodox 10. Protestant, scriptural
Evangeline (pert to)...
home.. 6. Acadia
lover.. 7. Gabriel
poem by.. 10. Longfellow (1847)
evangelist... 6. Graham, Sunday (Billy) 7. apostle, Roberts 9. McPherson
evaporate... 3. dry 5. steam 6. escape, exhale 7. avolate 8. vaporize 9. cease to be, dehydrate, disappear
evasion... 5. dodge, shift 6. escape 8. avoiding 9. avoidance, quibbling, shuffling 12. equivocation 13. circumvention, secretiveness
evasive... 3. sly 4. eely 6. shifty 7. elusive, elusory 9. deceitful, quibbling, secretive
eve... 3. iva (herb), wet 4. dusk, thaw 6. sunset 12. on the brink of, on the verge of
even... 3. e'en, tie 4. just, tied 5. equal, exact, level, match, plane 6. placid, smooth, square, steady 7. abreast, balance, equable, neutral, regular, uniform 8. directly, parallel 9. impartial, precisely 11. symmetrical
even (if)... 8. although 12. nevertheless 15. notwithstanding
even (so)... 3. yes 12. nevertheless

evener... 9. equalizer 10. doubletree
evenglow... 3. red (color) 8. twilight
evening... 5. Abend 6. sunset
evening dress... 4. gown 6. jewels,
   tuxedo 8. slippers (high heel) 9. full
   dress, headdress 10. dinner coat
   11. tie and tails 17. swallow–tailed
   coat
event... 4. fate (obs), game 5. drama,
   issue 6. result 7. contest, episode,
   scandal 8. incident 9. adventure,
   happening, milestone 10. conclusion,
   occurrence 11. consequence,
   termination 12. circumstance
event (pert to)...
   extraordinary.. 10. phenomenon
   supernatural.. 7. miracle
   theater.. 6. opener 8. premiere
   turning point.. 6. crisis 8. decision,
   landmark
eventide... 4. dusk 6. sunset, vesper
   7. evening, sundown 8. twilight
   9. nightfall
eventually... 3. yet 6. lastly 7. finally
   10. ultimately
ever... 3. e'er 4. anon 5. at all
   6. always 7. forever 10. constantly
   11. perpetually
Everest peak... 6. Lhotse (28,100 ft)
evergreen shrub... 4. Ilex, moss, Olax,
   titi 5. heath, holly, savin, toyon
   6. laurel 7. baretta, jasmine
   9. perennial 12. rhododendron
evergreen tree... 3. fir, yew 4. pine
   5. carob, cedar, larch, olive, Taxus
   6. balsam, deodar, spruce, tarata
   7. conifer, hemlock, madrona,
   redwood
everlasting... 6. eterne 7. aeonian,
   agelong, durable, endless, eternal,
   forever, lasting, tedious 8. enduring,
   evermore, immortal, infinite
   9. continual, incessant, perpetual,
   unceasing, wearisome 10. immortelle,
   indefinite 11. never–ending,
   strawflower 12. Eternal Being,
   imperishable 13. unintermitted,
   uninterrupted
every... 3. all, any, ilk 4. each, ilka
   6. entire 8. complete
every one, everyone... 3. all 4. each
   9. everybody 10. individual
everything... 3. all, sum 5. total
evict... 4. oust 5. eject, expel, prove
   6. remove 7. confute 8. force out
eviction... 6. ouster 9. ejectment
   11. dislodgment 13. dispossession
evidence... 4. clue, sign 5. proof,
   token 6. attest, evince 7. constat
   (law), probate, support 8. argument,
   manifest, rebuttal 9. testimony
   10. indication 15. circumstantiate
evident... 5. clear, plain 6. patent
   7. obvious, visible 8. apparent,
   manifest, palpable 9. notorious
   11. indubitable
evil... 3. bad, ill, mal (pref) 4. bane,
   vile 6. injury, sinful, wicked
   7. adverse, baleful, corrupt, hurtful,
   immoral, malefic, misdeed, satanic,
   unsound, vicious 8. depraved,
   iniquity, sinister 9. injurious,

malignant, offensive 10. calamitous,
   malevolent, pernicious, wrongdoing
   12. unpropitious
evil (pert to)...
   child.. 3. imp
   deed.. 3. sin 4. harm
   devil (little).. 9. deevilick (Scot)
   doer.. 5. cheat 9. miscreant,
   wrongdoer 10. malefactor
   omen.. 5. knell
   spirit.. 5. bugan, demon, devil, ghoul,
   Satan 6. Belial 7. Ahriman, Amaimon
   8. Asmodeus 9. cacodemon,
   demonkind, lost souls
evils... 4. ills, mala
evince... 4. show 7. display, exhibit,
   express, provoke 8. convince,
   evidence, indicate, manifest
evoke... 4. call (out) 5. educe, voice
   6. elicit, prompt, summon 7. conjure
evolution... 7. biogeny, cosmism
   8. heredity, maneuver, movement
   9. Darwinism, phylogeny, unfolding,
   unrolling 10. evolvement
   11. development 13. manifestation,
   Spencerianism
evolve... 4. emit 5. educe 6. create,
   deduce, derive, unfold, unroll
   7. develop, grow out 9. disengage,
   expatiate, extricate 11. disentangle
ewe... 3. keb 4. lamb 5. crone (old),
   sheep 6. theave
ewer... 3. jug 5. crock 7. pitcher
exacerbate... 5. anger 6. incite
   8. embitter, irritate 9. aggravate
exact... 4. just, levy, nice 6. assess,
   demand, elicit, extort, formal, minute,
   oblige, strict 7. careful, correct,
   literal, precise, regular, require
   8. accurate 10. methodical,
   meticulous
exact (pert to)...
   opposite of.. 8. antipode 9. antipodal
   penalty.. 4. fine 7. estreat
   thinking.. 13. ratiocination
   vengeance.. 6. avenge
exacting... 6. severe, strict 7. arduous
   8. critical 9. demanding, elicitory
   10. fastidious 12. extortionate
exacting devotion (exclusive)...
   7. jealous
exactly... 3. due 5. spand 6. nicely
   7. quite so 8. as you say
   9. precisely 10. accurately
exaggerated... 5. outré 8. enhanced,
   enlarged, overdone, romanced
   9. excessive, increased, magnified
   10. overstated 11. exceptional
   13. overestimated 14. misrepresented
exaggerated comedy... 5. farce
exalt... 5. elate, extol, raise 6. praise
   7. elevate, ennoble, glorify, inspire,
   promote, worship 8. enthrone,
   increase, sanctify 10. aggrandize
exalted... 5. grand, noble, sheen
   6. elated 7. refined, sublime
   8. elevated, extolled 9. dignified
   11. illustrious
examination... 4. test 5. audit, trial
   7. inquiry 8. research, scrutiny,
   specimen 10. discussion, inspection
   11. inquisition 13. investigation

examine... **3.** pry, spy, try (law)
4. pore, scan, sift, test **5.** audit,
probe, quest **6.** censor, debate,
ponder **7.** analyze, collate, discuss,
explore, inspect **8.** consider
10. scrutinize **11.** interrogate
examiner... **6.** censor, conner, tester
7. auditor, officer (court) **9.** inspector
example... **4.** case, norm, type
5. bysen (obs), model **6.** sample
7. pattern, warning **8.** instance,
paradigm, specimen **9.** exemplify,
precedent **12.** illustration
15. exemplification
ex animo... **9.** sincerely **12.** from the
heart
excavate... **3.** dig **4.** cave, mine
5. dig up, scoop, stope **6.** dredge,
exhume, quarry **9.** hollow out
excavation... **3.** pit **4.** hole, mine
5. stope **6.** cavity, dugout **7.** digging
8. opencast
exceed... **3.** top **4.** pass **5.** excel,
outdo **6.** outvie, overdo **7.** eclipse,
outrank, surpass **8.** outstrip, overstep
9. overshoot, transcend
11. predominate
exceedingly... **4.** many, very
9. extremely **13.** extraordinary
excel... **3.** cap, top **4.** beat, best
5. outdo, outgo, rival **6.** better,
exceed, precel **7.** surpass
8. dominate, outshine **9.** transcend
excellence... **4.** meed **5.** merit
6. desert, virtue **7.** classic, probity
9. supremacy **13.** inimitability
excellent... **4.** A–one, best, fine, good
5. bravo, prime, super **6.** choice,
select, tiptop, worthy **7.** capital,
corking **8.** skillful (skilful), stunning,
valuable **9.** admirable, exquisite,
first–rate **12.** transcendent
except... **3.** bar, but **4.** omit, save
6. exempt, reject, unless **7.** besides
9. eliminate, other than
exception... **4.** plea **5.** cavil, doubt
6. oddity **7.** dissent **8.** demurrer
9. condition, exclusion, exemption,
objection, rejection **11.** restriction
exceptional... **4.** rare **7.** notable,
unusual **8.** superior, uncommon
9. exclusive, wonderful
10. remarkable **11.** outstanding
13. extraordinary
excerpt... **4.** cite **5.** quote, scrap
6. choice **7.** extract, passage
(selected) **9.** selection
excess... **3.** too **4.** over, plus **5.** luxus
7. nimiety, overage, profuse, surplus
10. indulgence (undue), redundancy
11. superfluity **12.** intemperance
14. immoderateness, superabundance
excess (solar over lunar month)...
5. epact
excessive... **3.** too **5.** undue **6.** overly
7. extreme, profuse **8.** overmuch
9. fanatical, plethoric **10.** exorbitant,
immoderate, inordinate, redundancy
11. exaggerated, extravagant
12. unreasonable
excessive (pert to)...
development.. **11.** hypertrophy

fear.. **5.** panic **6.** phobia
gushing.. **8.** effusion
waste.. **12.** extravagance
excessively... **3.** too **5.** enorm
6. unduly **12.** exorbitantly,
inordinately **13.** intemperately
exchange... **4.** swap **5.** bandy, trade
6. barter, resale, rialto **7.** dealing,
traffic **9.** transpose **10.** substitute
11. interchange, reciprocate
exchange (pert to)...
discount.. **4.** agio
for money.. **4.** cash, sell
letters.. **10.** correspond
place.. **4.** mart **5.** store **6.** bourse,
market, shoppe
premium.. **4.** agio
visits.. **3.** gam
exchequer... **4.** fisc (fisk) **5.** funds,
purse **8.** finances, treasury
11. possessions (money)
excise... **3.** tax **4.** toll **6.** impost
exciseman... **5.** gager **7.** officer
8. revenuer
excision... **7.** erasure, removal
10. cutting off, cutting out, mutilation
11. destruction, extirpation
excite... **4.** fire, roil, spur, stir, urge
5. elate, impel, rouse **6.** arouse,
awaken, bestir, incite, kindle, prompt,
stir up **7.** agitate, animate, inflame,
provoke, psych up **8.** energize,
interest **9.** electrify, impassion,
instigate, stimulate
excited... **4.** agog **6.** hoopla
7. aroused, fevered, keyed up
8. agitated, startled **10.** interested
11. impassioned
excited, not easily... **6.** stolid
7. stoical **9.** impassive
excitement... **3.** ado **4.** stir **5.** fever
6. furore **7.** emotion, ferment
9. agitation, commotion
10. incitement, irritation
11. disturbance, stimulation
exciting... **5.** kicky **6.** gung–ho, hectic
7. parlous **8.** alluring **9.** desirable,
thrilling **10.** delightful **11.** interesting,
provocative
exciting compassion... **7.** piteous
exclamation... **2.** ah, lo, oh, so
3. aha, bah, boo, fic, hep, oho, tut,
ugh, yah **4.** ahem, alas, drat, egad,
evoe, phew, pish, rats, yech **5.** bravo,
humph, pshaw **6.** indeed, shezam
7. kerwham **9.** alackaday
11. ejaculation **12.** interjection
exclude... **3.** bar **4.** omit **5.** debar,
eject, expel **6.** banish **7.** shut out
8. disallow, preclude, prohibit
9. eliminate **13.** excommunicate
exclusive... **5.** aloof, ritzy **6.** select
7. special **8.** limiting, snobbish
9. seclusive **10.** definitive, unsociable
11. prohibitive, restrictive
exclusive right... **6.** patent
10. concession **11.** restriction
excoriate... **4.** flay, gall, peel **5.** strip
6. abrade **9.** criticize
excrescence... **4.** boss (Arch), lump
6. growth, nodule **9.** appendage,
outgrowth **10.** protrusion

excrete ... 5. egest 9. discharge, eliminate

excruciating ... 7. painful, racking 9. agonizing, torturing 11. distressing

excursion ... 3. row 4. ride, sail, tour, trek, trip 5. jaunt, sally 6. junket, outing, ramble 7. circuit, journey, outlope 8. circuity 10. expedition

excusable ... 6. venial 9. allowable, justified 10. defensible, exemptible, pardonable, remissible 11. justifiable

excuse ... 4. plea 5. alibi, remit 6. acquit, essoin, pardon 7. absolve, apology, condone, forgive, pretext 8. overlook 9. exonerate, extenuate

execrable ... 7. impious 9. nefandous

execute ... 2. do 3. act 4. hang, kill, vest 6. direct, effect, finish, manage 7. conduct, enforce, perform 8. carry out, complete, transact 10. accomplish, administer

execution ... 4. writ 7. hanging 10. production, punishment 11. achievement, performance, transaction 14. accomplishment

exegate ... 6. leader 7. adviser 8. dragoman 11. interpreter

exegesis ... 7. explain 9. interpret 10. exposition, expounding

exemplar ... 5. ideal, model 7. example, paragon, pattern 8. specimen 9. archetype

exemplary ... 8. laudable, monitory 11. commendable 12. exemplifying, praiseworthy 14. representative

exemplify ... 4. copy 6. typify 7. explain 10. illustrate, transcribe

exempt ... 4. exon 5. clear 6. immune 7. absolve, release 8. dispense, excepted, excluded, released, set apart 10. privileged

exemption ... 6. essoin 7. freedom 8. immunity, impunity, navicert 12. dispensation

exercise ... 3. ply, ure (anc), use 4. task, yoga 5. drill, étude, exert, train 6. action, employ, lesson, praxis, school, tai chi 7. display, jogging, problem, workout 8. activity, aerobics, ceremony, practice, training 9. athletics 10. exhibition, gymnastics, isometrics

exertion ... 5. essay, trial 6. effort 7. attempt 8. endeavor

exhalation ... 4. aura, fume 5. steam 6. breath 7. halitus 9. effluvium, emanation 10. expiration 11. evaporation 12. vaporization

exhale ... 4. emit 6. vanish 7. exhaust, respite 9. transpire 10. breathe out

exhaust ... 3. fag, sap 4. emit, jade, tire 5. drain, empty, spend, waste, weary 6. exhale, overdo, weaken 7. consume, deplete, fatigue 9. discharge 10. impoverish

exhausted ... 4. done, worn 5. spent, tired 6. used up 7. emptied, petered (out) 8. dog-tired, forspent

exhaustion ... 6. effete 7. burnout, fatigue 9. depletion, lassitude 11. prostration 14. impoverishment

exhibit ... 3. air 4. fair, shew (anc), show, wear 5. stage, state 6. evince, expose, flaunt, parade, reveal 7. display 8. disclose, evidence, manifest 9. spectacle 11. demonstrate 15. circumstantiate

exhibit (pert to) ...
colors (change of) .. 8. iridesce, opalesce
pleasure .. 5. gloat, revel (in)
taste (refined) .. 6. ostent 7. elegant

exhibition ... 4. fair, show 9. spectacle 10. exposition 11. ostentation 13. manifestation

exhibition room ... 10. panopticon

exhilaration ... 6. gaiety 7. jollity 8. gladness, hilarity 9. animation, merriment 10. excitement, joyousness 11. gleefulness, refreshment 12. cheerfulness, invigoration

exhort ... 4. urge, warn 6. advise, dehort, incite, preach 7. caution 9. encourage, stimulate

exhume ... 3. dig 5. delve 7. unearth 8. disinter, exhumate

exigeant ... 8. exacting 11. importunate

exigency ... 4. need, urge 6. crisis 7. demands, urgency 8. juncture, pressure 9. emergency, extremity, necessity 12. requirements

exigent ... 4. writ 6. strict, urgent 8. critical, exacting, pressing 9. demanding, necessary 10. compelling 13. indispensable

exile ... 6. banish, deport 7. outcast 8. outlawry, relegate 9. expulsion 10. banishment, expatriate 12. expatriation, proscription

exist ... 2. am, be, is 3. are 4. live 5. alive 6. abound 9. be present

existence ... 3. ens 4. esse, life 5. actus, being, entia 6. extant 7. essence, reality 8. presence 9. actuality 13. manifestation

existing (pert to) ...
fancifully .. 9. imaginary 10. transitory
name only (in) .. 7. nominal, titular
now .. 6. extant 7. current, present 9. immediate
same time .. 15. contemporaneous
way of .. 9. lifestyle

exit ... 3. die 4. door, gate, vent 5. going, go out, issue 6. egress, outlet 7. leaving, passage (out), walkout 9. departure

exitus ... 5. death, issue 6. exodus, outlet 7. outcome

exlex ... 6. outlaw

ex libris ... 8. colophon 9. bookplate

exodus ... 4. Book (Bib), exit 5. going 6. flight, hegira 9. departure

exonerate ... 4. free 5. clear 6. acquit 7. absolve, release, relieve 9. disburden (obs), exculpate

exorbitant ... 5. undue 9. excessive 10. high-priced

exorbitant interest ... 5. usury

exorcism ... 5. spell 7. formula 9. expulsion (of evil spirits) 11. conjuration, incantation

exordium ... 5. proem 7. preface,

prelude 8. overture 9. beginning
12. introduction
exoteric... 8. exterior, external, outsider
14. comprehensible
exotic... 5. alien 7. foreign, strange
8. colorful, ulterior 9. not native,
peregrine, unrelated 10. extraneous,
outlandish
expand... 4. grow, open 5. sheet,
splay, tract 6. dilate, spread
7. broaden, develop, distend, enlarge
9. expatiate, intumesce
expanse... 3. sea 4. main (broad)
5. ocean, plain, reach, tract
6. desert, extent, spread 7. stretch
8. eternity (time) 9. expansion
expansion... 4. size 6. extent, growth,
spread 8. dilation, increase
10. distention 11. development,
enlargement, expatiation
expansive... 4. wide 5. broad, large
7. elastic, liberal 8. effusive,
spacious 9. bombastic, grandiose
11. extensional, sympathetic
12. unrestrained 13. comprehensive
expatiate... 5. dwell 6. dilate
7. descant, enlarge 10. widespread
expatriate... 5. exile, expel 6. banish,
outlaw 7. exclude, outcast
9. ostracize 13. excommunicate
expect... 4. deem, hope, wait
5. await, think 6. intend 7. suppose
10. anticipate
expectation... 4. hope 9. imminence,
intention 12. anticipation
expedience... 6. wisdom 7. fitness
10. adaptation, timeliness
11. suitability
expedient... 4. wise 5. shift 6. timely
7. fitting, politic, ressort, stopgap
8. artifice, resource 9. advisable
10. profitable 12. advantageous
expedite... 3. hie 4. easy, free
5. hurry, light, speed 6. hasten
7. further, quicken 8. dispatch
10. accelerate, facilitate
expedition... 5. drave, foray, haste,
speed 6. safari 7. Crusade, entrada,
journey 8. Crusades 9. excursion,
hastening
expel... 4. oust, void 5. eject, evict,
exile 6. banish, exhale 7. extrude
9. discharge, eliminate
10. dispossess
expend... 3. pay, use 5. spend, waste
7. consume 8. disburse
10. distribute
expenditure... 5. outgo, price 6. outlay
7. expense, payment
11. consumption 12. disbursement
expense... 4. cost 5. price 6. outlay
9. allowance 11. consumption
12. disbursement
expensive... 4. dear, high 5. fancy,
steep 6. costly, lavish 7. liberal
10. high-priced 11. extravagant
experience... 3. see, try 4. feel, have,
know, test 5. maxim, sense, skill
6. ordeal, suffer, wisdom 7. emotion,
undergo 8. facility 9. knowledge,
sensation 10. occurrence

experience (pert to)...
  pleasure.. 5. enjoy
  regret.. 6. repent
  suffering.. 7. calvary
  worldly.. 14. sophistication
experiment... 3. try 4. test 5. essay,
proof, prove, trial 6. verify
11. observation
expert... 3. ace 4. deft 5. adept
6. adroit, clever, habile, master
7. casuist (in conscience) 8. artistic,
skillful 10. proficient 11. connoisseur,
experienced 12. professional
expiate... 5. atone, purge 6. purify,
shrive (anc)
expiation... 4. rite 6. amends
7. redress 8. piacular 9. atonement
10. redemption 12. compensation,
propitiation
expire... 3. die, end 4. pass 5. cease,
lapse 6. elapse, perish 7. breathe
(out) 9. terminate
explain... 5. clear, solve 6. define
7. expound, premise 8. describe
9. elucidate, interpret
11. demonstrate
explanation... 6. theory 7. meaning
8. exegesis, scholium, solution
10. exposition 11. description,
explication 13. clarification
14. interpretation 15. exemplification
explanatory description... 5. title
7. titulus
expletive... 3. gee 4. egad, gosh,
oath 5. curse, there, voilà 6. behold
8. addition 9. added word
11. exclamation
explicit... 4. open 5. exact, fixed
6. candid 7. express, precise
8. absolute, distinct, implicit,
manifest, positive 9. outspoken
11. unambiguous, unequivocal,
unqualified 13. unconditional
14. discriminating
explode... 3. pop 4. fail 5. blast,
burst 6. blow up 7. implode
8. backfire, detonate
exploit... 3. act (heroic) 4. dare, deed,
feat, gest, milk 5. bleed 7. heroism
9. advantage 10. overcharge
11. achievement
exploration, modern... 10. space
probe
explore... 4. look, view 5. probe
6. search 7. examine 8. discover
9. penetrate 11. investigate
explorer... 5. diver 7. pioneer
10. discoverer
explorer... 4. Byrd, Eric, Gama
7. Johnson (Osa), Wilkins (Hubert)
8. Amundsen, Magellan 9. Ellsworth
explosion... 3. pop 4. bank 5. blast,
noise 6. report 7. failure 8. outburst
10. detonation
explosive... 3. cap, TNT 4. mine
5. niter, shell 6. amatol, petard,
powder, tittle, tonite 7. cordite,
grenade, lyddite 8. dynamite
9. cartridge, cellulose, fulgurite,
guncotton, pyroxylin 11. firecracker
13. nitroglycerin 15. trinitrotoluene
exponent... 4. note 5. index

7. symptom 9. explainer, expounder
10. explaining 11. interpreter
expose... 3. air 4. bare, open
6. divest, reveal, unmask 7. exhibit,
unearth 8. disclose, discover,
endanger 9. ventilate 10. exposition
expose to danger... 11. periclitate
expose to scorn... 6. satire 7. pillory
exposition... 4. fair 6. bazaar, expose,
lesson 7. display 8. exposure,
treatise 9. discourse, spectacle
10. disclosure, exhibition
11. abandonment, explanation
12. dissertation 14. interpretation
expostulate... 5. orate 6. advise,
demand 7. call for, discuss, protest
8. complain, dissuade
11. remonstrate
exposure... 8. disproof, jeopardy,
openness, snapshot 9. liability
10. appearance, disclosure,
exposition, visibility
express... 3. say 4. mean, show
5. exude, speak, state, train, utter,
voice 6. depict, evince, extort,
phrase 7. betoken, carrier, declare,
exhibit, expound, extract, signify,
testify 8. describe, dispatch, indicate,
intimate, manifest 9. delineate,
messenger, posthaste, utterance
11. declaration
express (pert to)...
censure.. 10. animadvert
disapproval.. 9. deprecate
fervor.. 7. enthuse
gratitude.. 5. thank
indirectly.. 5. imply
in words.. 6. phrase
numerically.. 8. evaluate
regard.. 6. praise 10. compliment
regret.. 9. apologize
sympathy.. 7. condole, console
10. grieve with 11. commiserate
expressing...
doubt.. 10. dubitative
extra phrase (Gram).. 12. periphrastic
feeling.. 7. emotive
past tense.. 11. preteritive
pique.. 5. pouty
praise.. 9. laudatory
expression... 4. grin, show, term
5. scowl, smile 6. aspect, oracle,
phrase 7. diction, meaning
8. locution 9. statement, utterance
10. extraction, indication
11. delineation 13. manifestation
14. representation
expression (pert to)...
mathematics.. 8. equation
of approval.. 4. clap 7. ovation
8. applause
of contempt.. 3. fie 5. pshaw, sneer
of disapproval.. 6. rebuke
of ideas.. 4. mode 5. style 7. fashion
of politics.. 4. vote
of weariness.. 4. sigh
peculiar.. 5. idiom
without.. 7. deadpan
expressive motion... 7. gesture
13. gesticulation
expulsion... 5. exile 10. banishment,
expiration 11. elimination

expunction... 4. blot 7. erasure
10. effacement 12. obliteration
expunge... 4. dele 5. erase 6. cancel,
delete, efface, excise, rub out 7. blot
out, destroy 9. strike out
10. annihilate, obliterate
expurgate... 5. bathe, purge
6. censor, excise, purify 7. cleanse
exquisite... 4. fine, rare 6. dainty,
superb 7. perfect, refined 8. delicate
9. beautiful, delicious, matchless
10. delightful, fastidious
exsanguine... 6. anemic 9. bloodless
exsiccate... 3. dry 4. arid, sear 5. dry
up, parch 7. exhaust 9. evaporate
extant... 5. being 7. in vogue,
present, visible 8. existent, existing
extempore... 5. ad lib 7. offhand
9. impromptu 13. improvisation
14. unpremeditated
extend... 2. go 3. eke, jut, lie, run
4. give, span 5. bulge, reach,
renew, steal, widen 6. deepen,
deploy, expand, spread 7. amplify,
broaden, draw out, proffer, prolong,
radiate, stretch 8. continue, increase,
lengthen, postpone, protract, protrude
10. exaggerate, straighten
extended... 4. open 5. broad
6. valued 7. assured, diffuse
8. expanded, spacious
10. lengthened 12. outstretched
extended view... 8. panorama
extension... 4. area 5. range, scope
6. extent 8. addition, duration,
increase, sequence 9. expansion
10. denotation 11. continuance,
enlargement, lengthening
12. augmentation 13. extensiveness
extension of time... 4. stay 7. respite
extensive... 4. vast, wide 5. broad,
large 7. immense, titanic
8. expanded, spacious 9. expansive,
wholesale 10. widespread
11. far–reaching
extent... 4. area, bulk, room, side, writ
5. areal, range, reach, scope
6. amount, degree, length
7. breadth, compass, expanse,
measure 8. distance, frontage
9. dimension 10. assessment (Hist),
denotation, proportion
extenuate... 4. thin 6. excuse, lessen,
reduce, sicken, weaken 7. justify
8. diminish, palliate 9. attenuate
extenuating... 10. justifying, qualifying
exterior... 5. ectad (toward), ectal,
outer 7. outside 8. external
10. extraneous
exterminate... 4. kill 5. expel
7. abolish, destroy 8. get rid of
9. eradicate, extirpate 10. annihilate
extermination... 9. expulsion
11. destruction, eradication
extern... 7. outward 8. exterior,
external 9. extrinsic
external... 4. ecto 5. outer, outre
6. nonego 7. outside 8. cortical
10. extraneous
external appearance... 5. guise,
image, looks 6. aspect 8. features
9. semblance

extinct... 4. dead, past 5. passé
7. defunct, died out, expired
8. quenched 11. nonexistent
12. extinguished
extinct bird... 3. moa 4. dodo
extinction... 5. death 9. quenching
11. destruction 12. annihilation
extinct reptile... 11. pterodactyl
extinguish... 5. annul, choke, douse,
quell 6. quench, stifle 7. destroy
8. suppress
extirpate... 4. dele, root, stub
5. erase, expel 6. excise, uproot
7. destroy 9. eradicate
11. exterminate
extol... 4. laud 5. exalt, kudos
6. praise 7. applaud, commend,
elevate, glorify 8. emblazon
9. celebrate
extort... 5. bleed, exact, steal, wrest,
wring 6. compel, elicit, wrench
7. extract 10. overcharge
extortion... 7. robbery, seizure
8. exaction, rapacity 10. extraction,
oppression, overcharge
extortionist... 5. harpy 7. vampire,
vulture 9. profiteer 11. blackmailer
extra... 3. bye 4. over 5. added,
spare, super 7. surplus 8. superior
9. accessory 10. additional
extra cache... 5. stock, store
7. reserve 9. reservoir
extract... 4. cite, pull 6. deduce, elicit,
select 7. essence, estreat, excerpt
8. withdraw
extract (pert to)...
balsam.. 7. toluene
Bible.. 7. passage 8. pericope
forcibly.. 6. evulse
newspaper.. 8. clipping
orchid (climbing).. 7. vanilla
extraction... 5. birth, stock 6. origin
7. essence, excerpt 8. tincture
9. parentage 10. withdrawal
extraneous... 5. outer 6. exotic
7. foreign 9. extrinsic, separated,
unrelated 11. unessential
extraordinary... 3. odd 4. rare, unco
5. great 7. notable, special, unusual
8. singular 9. irregular, marvelous,
wonderful 10. noteworthy, remarkable
11. exceptional 13. distinguished
extravagance... 5. waste 6. excess
8. wildness 9. abundance
10. fanaticism, lavishness
11. exorbitance, prodigality
12. exaggeration, intemperance,
recklessness
extravagant... 3. E la 4. ee la (Mus),
high (priced) 5. outré 6. absurd
7. baroque, bizarre, diffuse, fanatic
8. boastful, prodigal, wasteful
9. excessive, fanatical, fantastic,
luxurious, plentiful 10. digressive
11. intemperate 12. unrestrained
extreme... 3. end 4. last, sore
5. final, great, ultra 6. excess,
severe, utmost 7. drastic, intense,
outward, radical 8. farthest, greatest,
ultimate 9. excessive, extremity,
fanatical, outermost 10. conclusive,
immoderate

extreme fear... 5. panic 6. horror
extreme unction... 5. anele 9. last
rites, sacrament
extremist... 7. radical 8. ultraist
extremity... 3. end, tip 4. foot, limb
(body), pole 5. verge 6. border,
crisis, summit 8. terminal
9. necessity 11. termination
extricate... 4. free 5. loose 6. evolve,
rescue, wangle 7. extract 8. liberate
9. disengage 10. disembroil
11. disentangle 12. disembarrass
extrinsic... 7. foreign, outward
8. external 9. objective
10. accidental (Log), contingent,
extraneous, incidental
12. adventitious, nonessential
extrovert... 11. personality (opp of
introvert)
exuberance... 6. excess, plenty
8. overflow, rankness, vivacity
9. abundance, animation, profusion
10. friskiness, liveliness, luxuriance
11. copiousness 14. superabundance
exuberant... 6. frisky, lavish 7. fertile,
profuse 8. effusive, fruitful, thriving
9. luxuriant, plentiful 11. overflowing
13. superabundant
exudation... 3. gum, lac, tar 5. pitch,
resin 6. oozing 8. emission, sweating
9. discharge, excretion
exude... 4. emit, ooze, reek 5. sweat
7. excrete, give out 9. discharge
exult... 3. joy 4. crow, leap (obs), rave
5. boast, elate, ovare, pride
7. rejoice 8. jubilate
exultant... 5. ovant 6. elated
exultation... 3. joy 7. delight
8. boasting 9. jubilance, rejoicing
10. jubilation
exults... 5. leaps 7. glories, springs
9. jubilates
eye... 2. ee 3. orb, see 4. auge, glim,
hole, ogle 5. optic, organ (human),
sight, watch 6. look at, peeper
7. observe, witness 10. scrutinize
eye (pert to)...
absence of pupil.. 6. acorea
black.. 5. mouse 6. shiner
brow.. 4. arch 6. eebree
11. supercilium
cavity.. 5. orbit 6. hippus, socket
disease.. 8. cataract, glaucoma,
hypopyon, trachoma 9. amblyopia
14. conjunctivitis
disorder.. 6. squint 7. walleye
9. exotropia 10. strabismus
dropper.. 7. pipette
glass.. 4. lens 7. lorgnon, monocle
8. pince-nez 10. spectacles
inflammation.. 6. ititis 7. uveitis
lash, lashes.. 5. cilia (pl) 6. cilium
lid.. 8. palpebra
part.. 4. iris, uvea 5. pupil 6. cornea,
retina
to blind (falconry).. 4. seel
eyelet... 7. cringle, grommet, ocellus
8. loophole, peephole
eyetooth... 6. cuspid 8. dogtooth
eyot... 3. ait 4. holm 5. islet
eyra... 7. wildcat
eyrie, eyry... 4. nest 5. aerie, nidus

F

F... **6.** letter (6th)
fabes... **10.** gooseberry
fabian... **7.** caution **8.** dilatory, inaction **15.** procrastination
Fabian... **7.** General (Rom), Society
fable... **3.** lie **4.** myth **5.** story **6.** legend **7.** fabliau, fantasy, fiction, Marchen, parable **8.** allegory, apologue, folk tale **9.** falsehood
fable (pert to)...
being.. **5.** troll
king.. **3.** Log
monster.. **4.** ogre **7.** centaur
narrator.. **10.** parabolist
writer.. **5.** Aesop
fabric... **5.** build, cloth **6.** tissue **7.** texture **8.** erection, material **9.** framework **11.** workmanship **12.** construction
fabric (types of)... **3.** rep **4.** alma, duck, felt, gros, jean, lawn, leno, silk **5.** baize, batik, beige, crash, crepe, denim, linen, nylon, pekin, rumal, satin, scrim, serge, suede, tulle, tweed, twill, voile, wigan **6.** agaric, alpaca, burlap, calico, canvas, chintz, cotton, dimity, étoile, madras, mohair, moreen, muslin, penang, pongee, poplin, ratiné, sateen, tricot **7.** batiste, brocade, bunting, challis, chiffon, delaine, elastic, etamine, flannel, galatea, gingham, hernani, paisley, percale, satinet, ticking, worsted **8.** cashmere, chambray, chenille, corduroy, cretonne, drilling, prunella, sarcenet, Shantung, sheeting, whipcord **9.** crinoline, gabardine, grenadine, lansdowne, matelassé, paramatta **10.** broadcloth, seersucker, terry cloth
fabric (pert to)...
dealer.. **6.** mercer
ornamental.. **4.** lace **8.** fagoting
silk, watered.. **5.** moiré
silk and gold.. **4.** acca (anc) **7.** brocade
twill.. **6.** caddis (cadis)
velvet.. **5.** panne, terry **6.** velure **7.** velours
waste.. **5.** mungo
window shade.. **7.** Holland
woven.. **6.** tricot
fabricate... **4.** coin, form, make, mint **5.** build, frame, weave **6.** create, devise, invent, scheme **7.** falsify, fashion, produce, trump up **9.** construct **11.** manufacture
fabrication... **3.** lie, web **5.** guile **6.** cogger, deceit, making **7.** fiction, forging, untruth **9.** falsehood,

invention **12.** construction
fabulist... **4.** liar **5.** Aesop **11.** storyteller
fabulous... **6.** absurd **7.** feigned **8.** mythical **9.** fictional, imaginary, legendary **10.** fictitious, remarkable **11.** astonishing **12.** mythological
fabulous (pert to)...
animal.. **7.** unicorn **9.** rosmarine (walrus)
beast.. **4.** lung **6.** dragon, wivern **7.** griffon, serpent **10.** earthdrake
being.. **6.** Lapith, Nessus **7.** centaur
bird.. **3.** moa, roc **4.** rukh
facade... **4.** face **5.** facia, front **7.** frontal
face... **3.** mug **4.** dare, defy, dial, line, meet, moue, phiz **5.** brave, cover, front **6.** answer, obvert, oppose, phizog, visage **7.** grimace **8.** boldness, confront, envisage, exterior, features, pretense **9.** encounter, impudence **10.** effrontery **11.** countenance, physiognomy, self–respect
face (pert to)...
bone.. **6.** zygoma (cheek) **7.** maxilla (jaw)
east.. **9.** orientate
gem.. **5.** facet
lifting.. **13.** rhytidoplasty
masonry.. **5.** revet
nose.. **11.** rhinoplasty
pains.. **4.** ague **13.** tic douloureux
surgery.. **14.** blepharoplasty (eyelid)
to face.. **6.** afront **7.** vis–à–vis
value.. **3.** par
faces (twelve)... **12.** dodecahedron
facet... **4.** face **5.** bezel, culet **6.** aspect, collet **8.** exterior
facetious... **5.** droll, funny, witty **6.** facete, jocose **7.** comical, jesting **8.** laughter **9.** whimsical
facia... **5.** plate **6.** tablet
facial pain... **3.** tic **4.** ague **9.** neuralgia **13.** tic douloureux
facient... **4.** doer **5.** agent **10.** multiplier
facile... **4.** easy **5.** quick, ready **6.** expert, fluent, gentle, pliant **7.** affable, lenient, pliable **9.** compliant, teachable
facilitate... **3.** aid **4.** ease, help **6.** assist
facility... **3.** art **4.** ease, help **5.** éclat, means, skill **7.** address, pliancy **8.** easiness **9.** readiness **10.** adroitness, expertness, pliability **11.** convenience, furtherance **13.** accommodation

facing... 6. lining, veneer 7. coating,
surface 8. opposite
facing (pert to)...
  glacier direction.. 5. stoss
  inward.. 8. introrse
  outward.. 8. extrorse
facsimile... 4. copy 5. match
  7. replica 9. duplicate
  11. counterpart
fact, facts... 4. data, deed, feat, fiat
  5. datum, event, posit, truth
  6. really 7. keynote, lowdown,
  paradox 9. actuality
fact collector... 7. statist
  12. statistician
faction... 4. bloc, camp, sect, side
  5. cabal, junto, party 6. clique
  7. machine (Polit) 11. combination,
  partisanism
factious... 9. demagogic, seditious,
  turbulent
factitious... 4. made (by art), mock,
  sham 5. phony 9. unnatural
  10. artificial 11. make–believe
factor... 4. ager, gene 5. agent, cause
  6. detail 9. component
  11. constituent
factotum... 4. maid 5. do–all
  7. servant 8. busybody
faculties... 4. wits 6. senses
  7. talents 9. abilities, aptitudes
  12. capabilities
faculty... 3. art 4. body, ease, gift
  6. talent 7. ability, know–how
  8. aptitude, teachers 9. endowment
  (mental) 12. professorate
fad... 4. rage, whim 5. craze, fancy,
  hobby 6. custom 7. caprice, fashion
faddist... 10. monomaniac
fade, fade out... 3. age, dim, dow,
  wan 4. flat, pale, wilt 5. daver,
  decay, peter 6. perish, vanish,
  weaken, wither 7. decline, insipid
  8. discolor, dissolve, languish
  9. disappear 11. deteriorate
faded... 3. dim 4. dull, pale 5. faint,
  passé 8. impaired
Faerie Queene (pert to)...
  author.. 7. Spenser
  character.. 3. Ate, Una 5. Guyon,
  Truth 7. Acrasia 8. Gloriana
  theme.. 8. chivalry 10. knighthood
  type work.. 4. poem 8. allegory
fag... 4. flag, hack, jade, tire, toil,
  work 5. droop, slave, weary
  6. drudge, menial 7. exhaust,
  fatigue, untwist (rope end)
  8. drudgery 9. cigarette
fag end... 3. end 4. tail 6. scraps,
  tag end 7. remnant 8. last part,
  leavings
Fagin... 3. Jew (Oliver Twist)
Fagin's pupil... 12. Artful Dodger
  (John Dawkins)
fagot, faggot... 4. bind 5. bunch
  6. bundle, emblem (Her) 8. firewood,
  slattern
fail... 3. ebb, err 4. flop, lack, miss,
  sink 5. decay, flunk, lapse 6. defect,
  desert, weaken 7. decline, exhaust
  8. unbetide 9. fall short
  10. disappoint, go bankrupt

11. deteriorate
failed admission... 11. blackballed
failed to follow suit... 7. reneged
failure... 3. dud 4. flop, foil, lack,
  lose, miss 5. decay, fault, lapse
  6. defeat, fiasco 7. default
  10. bankruptcy, deficiency, insolvency,
  nonsuccess, suspension
  11. delinquency
faint... 3. din, ill 4. pale, soft, weak
  5. swelt, swoon, timid 6. feeble,
  sickly 7. languid 8. cowardly,
  fatigued, listless, timorous
  10. indistinct, oppressive
faintness... 5. qualm (sudden)
  7. dimness, syncope 8. paleness,
  weakness 10. feebleness
fair... 4. just, mart 6. bazaar, blonde,
  comely, honest, kermis 8. festival,
  mediocre, rainless, unbiased
  9. impartial 10. auspicious,
  reasonable 12. unprejudiced
  13. dispassionate
fairy, faery... 3. elf, fay 4. peri, pixy
  5. genie, magic, nymph, ouphe, pixie
  6. elfkin, sprite 7. brownie, gremlin
  8. illusion
fairy (pert to)...
  abode (Scot).. 4. shee (sidhe)
  death spirit.. 7. banshee
  evil.. 4. ogre, puck 9. hobgoblin
  fort.. 3. lis (liss)
  German.. 6. kobold
  Irish.. 10. cluricaune, leprechaun
  king.. 6. Oberon
  Persian.. 4. peri
  queen.. 3. Mab, Una 7. Titania
  Scandinavian.. 5. nisse
  tale.. 3. fib 7. Marchen 8. allegory
  9. narrative
faith... 4. hope 5. creed, piety, troth,
  trust 6. belief, credit, verily, virtue
  7. loyalty 8. credence, fidelity
  9. assurance, authority, orthodoxy
  10. confidence 11. credibility
faithful... 4. fast, feal, leal, true
  5. liege, loyal, pious 6. devout,
  steady, trusty 7. devoted, sincere,
  staunch 8. constant, obedient,
  reliable 9. believers, steadfast,
  veracious
faithful friend... 7. Achates (Vergil's
  Aeneid)
faithless... 5. false, punic 6. fickle,
  untrue 8. apostate, disloyal, shifting
  9. deceptive, mercurial, skeptical
  10. perfidious, unfaithful
  11. incredulous, irreligious,
  treacherous, unbelieving
  12. falsehearted
fake... 3. rob 4. sham 5. cheat, fraud,
  trick 7. trump up 8. doctor up
  9. deception, fabricate, imitation
  11. counterfeit
faker... 5. cheat, fraud 7. bluffer
  8. impostor 9. hypocrite, pretender
fakir... 4. sect (Moslem, Islam), yogi
  7. dervish 9. mendicant
falcon... 4. hawk 5. besra, saker
  6. laggar, lanner, luggar, merlin,
  shahin (shaheen), sorage, tercel
  7. kestrel, sakeret 8. lanneret,

F
I

Raptores 9. gyrfalcon (gerfalcon),
peregrine
falcon, military... 8. ordnance
falconry term... 4. hood, jess, lure,
seel 6. rebate 7. hawking
fall... 3. ebb 4. bang, drop, plop,
ruin, sink, slip 5. crash, spill
6. autumn, defeat, perish, plunge,
tumble 7. descend, descent, devolve,
failure, plummet, relapse 8. collapse,
commence, downfall, rainfall
9. abatement, overthrow, surrender,
waterfall 10. depreciate, subversion
11. degradation, precipitate
fall (pert to)...
back.. 6. recede, recoil 7. relapse,
retreat 10. retrogress
behind.. 3. lag 4. lose 7. regress
guy.. 5. patsy
in.. 4. cave 5. agree, lapse
6. concur, line up 8. collapse
9. terminate
rhythmical.. 6. cadent
short.. 4. lack, want 10. disappoint
fallacious... 4. wily 5. false 6. crafty,
untrue 8. delusive, guileful
9. deceitful, deceptive, erroneous,
illogical, insidious 10. fraudulent,
misleading 13. disappointing
fallacy... 5. error 6. idolum
7. sophism 9. deception, falseness,
sophistry 13. deceitfulness
false... 4. sham, tale 5. bogus, paste
6. betray, impugn, pseudo, untrue
7. mislead 8. apostate, spurious
9. deceitful, deceptive, erroneous,
faithless, incorrect, insincere,
pretended, unfounded 10. fictitious,
mendacious, traitorous, unfaithful,
unreliable, untruthful 11. counterfeit
12. illegitimate
false (pert to)...
friend.. 5. Judas 7. traitor
front.. 8. disguise 11. affectation
fruit.. 10. pseudocarp
god.. 4. idol
hearted.. 9. deceitful 10. perfidious
11. treacherous
items.. 6. spuria
jewelry.. 5. paste 6. strass
reasoning.. 10. paralogism
report.. 5. rumor 6. canard 7. slander
show.. 6. tinsel
wing (bird's).. 5. alula
falsehood... 3. lie 4. tale 7. falsity,
fiction, perjury, untruth 9. imposture,
mendacity 11. counterfeit, fabrication
12. exaggeration
falseness... 5. error 8. illusion
9. deception, falsehood 10. infidelity
falsetto... 5. voice (false) 10. artificial
11. high–pitched
falsify... 3. lie 5. belie, forge
7. distort, pervert 8. disprove
10. adulterate 11. counterfeit
12. misrepresent
Falstaff... 5. opera (Verdi) 9. character
(Shak)
falter... 3. lag 4. fail 5. demur, pause,
waver 6. flinch, quaver, totter
7. stagger, stammer, stumble,
tremble 8. hesitate, lose hope

fame... 4. note 5. éclat, glory, kudos
6. renown, repute
famed... 7. eminent, honored, popular
8. renowned 9. notorious
10. celebrated
familiar... 4. easy 5. usual
6. common, versed 7. affable
8. domestic, frequent, friendly,
habitual, informal 9. companion,
customary, well–known
10. accustomed, colloquial,
conversant 12. domesticated,
presumptuous 13. unconstrained
familiarity... 8. intimacy 9. awareness,
knowledge, liberties 10. affability
12. acquaintance (close), friendliness
familiarize... 6. inform 8. accustom
9. habituate
family... 3. ilk, kin 4. clan, line, race
5. class, group, house, tribe
6. stirps 7. kindred, lineage
9. community, household, posterity
10. kith and kin
family (pert to)...
bees.. 5. apina 7. Apoidea
favoritism.. 8. nepotism
herbs.. 7. Ranales
Italians (famed).. 4. Este
kings.. 7. dynasty
name.. 7. surname
famous... 5. named, noted 7. eminent,
namable, notable 8. renowned
9. excellent, notorious
10. celebrated, remarkable
13. distinguished
famous murderer... 4. Aram, Cain
9. Bluebeard
famous pirate... 4. Kidd (Capt)
fan... 4. blow, cool, vane, whip
5. punka (punkah) 6. blower, foment,
incite, rooter, spread, thresh, winnow
7. admirer, devotee, refresh
9. stimulate, strike out (baseball),
ventilate 10. enthusiast
fanatic, fanatical... 3. mad 5. bigot,
crank, crazy, rabid 6. maniac, zealot
7. devotee, frantic, lunatic 8. frenzied
9. energumen, phrenetic
10. enthusiast, unbalanced
11. extravagant, overzealous
12. enthusiastic 13. nonconformist,
overreligious
fanatical partisan... 6. zealot
fancied... 6. unreal 7. dreamed,
ideated 8. favorite, imagined
9. well–liked 10. ornamental
fanciful... 3. odd 5. queer 7. bizarre,
strange 9. fantastic, grotesque,
visionary, whimsical 10. capricious,
chimerical 11. imaginative
13. grandiloquent
fancy... 3. fad 4. idea, like, love,
ween, whim 5. dream, freak
6. design, desire, devise, humour,
ideate, megrim, notion, ornate,
vagary 7. caprice, conceit, fantasy,
imagine, impulse, suppose, thought
8. illusion, phantasy, superior
9. expensive 10. conception,
impression 11. extravagant,
imagination, inclination
12. ostentatious

fandango... 3. hop 4. ball, prom
5. dance 7. cantico
fandango bird... 7. manakin
Faneuil Hall (1742)... 4. hall
6. market (Boston) 15. Cradle of
Liberty
fanion... 4. flag 6. guidon, marker
fanon... 4. cape (Pope's) 5. orale
6. banner 7. maniple
fan–shaped... 10. flabellate
fan sticks (radiating)... 4. brin
7. panache
fantastic... 3. odd 5. outré, queer
6. absurd, rococo, unreal
7. baroque, bizarre, caprice, foppish,
unusual 8. fanciful, freakish, illusory
9. eccentric, grotesque, visionary
10. capricious, chimerical, irrational
11. extravagant, imaginative
12. phantastical
fantastic imitation... 6. parody
8. travesty
fantasy... 5. dream, fancy, story
6. vision 7. caprice, phantom,
romance 8. illusion 10. apparition
13. hallucination
far... 3. tel (pref) 4. afar, long, tele
(pref) 6. marked, remote
9. separated 10. abstracted
farce... 4. mime, play 5. drama
(humorous), exode, humor, stuff
6. comedy 7. mockery 8. stuffing
9. burlesque, forcemeat
farceur... 5. joker 8. comedian
9. dramatist
fare... 3. eat 4. diet, food, rate
5. crowd, going, swarm, table
7. conduct, journey, passage,
prosper, succeed 9. passenger
10. expedition
farewell... 3. ave 4. vale 5. adieu,
adios, aloha, congé (formal)
7. good–bye, leaving, parting 8. au
revoir, Godspeed 9. bon voyage
11. leave–taking
farinaceous drink... 6. ptisan
farinaceous food... 4. sago 5. flour,
grain, salep, wheat 7. cereals
farm... 4. plot, till, torp 5. croft, ranch
6. grange, rancho 7. acreage,
cotland 9. cultivate
farm (pert to)...
English.. 6. barton
laborer.. 4. hind 6. farmer, tiller
prefix.. 4. agro
repairer.. 10. plowwright
Spanish.. 8. hacienda
steward.. 7. granger
tenant.. 6. cotter
farmer... 4. ryot 5. kulak 6. grower,
tiller 7. cropper, metaver, peasant,
planter, rancher 10. agronomist,
cultivator 13. agriculturist
faro term... 4. bank 5. monte, stuss
6. cathop, layout
Faroe (Faeroe) Islands...
called also.. 12. Sheep Islands
capital.. 9. Thorshavn
magistrate.. 4. foud
rule.. 5. Norse (anc) 7. Denmark
whirlwind.. 2. oe
far–reaching... 4. deep, long 5. scope

7. intense 9. extensive
farrow... 3. pig 6. litter
farsighted... 6. shrewd 9. provident,
sagacious 10. presbyopic
11. foresighted 12. clearsighted
farther, further... 4. also 7. thither
8. moreover 10. additional
farthest... 5. final 6. inmost, utmost
7. endmost, extreme, longest
fascia... 4. band, sash 6. fillet, ribbon
7. bandage
fascinate... 5. charm 6. allure,
enamor, thrill 7. bewitch, delight,
enchant 8. entrance, interest
9. captivate, enrapture
fascinating... 5. siren 8. alluring,
charming 10. attractive, bewitching,
delightful 11. interesting
Fascist (1919)... 6. Pareto
9. Mussolini 10. Black Shirt
fashion... 3. fad, fit, ton, way
4. make, mode, mold, rage
5. adapt, carve, craze, feign, forge,
frame, guise, model, shape, style,
vogue 6. create, custom, invent
7. compose 8. contrive 9. construct,
fabricate, smartness 10. appearance
fashionable... 5. smart 6. formal,
modish 7. a la mode, in vogue,
stylish 8. up–to–date 10. conforming
13. well–appearing
fast... 5. agile, fixed, fleet, hasty,
quick, rapid, sound, space, stuck,
swift 6. lively, speedy, staple
7. abiding, soundly 8. enduring,
securely 10. profligate, stationary,
unyielding 11. expeditious
fasten... 3. bar, pin, tie 4. bind, clip,
lace, lash, moor, nail, rope, seal,
tack, wire 5. affix, belay, chain,
clamp, clasp, latch, paste, rivet
6. attach, secure, solder, staple,
tether, toggle 7. padlock
fastening... 5. desmo (comb form)
fastest (pert to)...
animals.. 6. coyote 7. cheetah
8. antelope
birds.. 5. eagle, goose 7. ostrich
fast horse... 6. pelter
fastidious... 4. nice 6. dainty
7. elegant, finical, precise 8. critical,
delicate, exacting, overnice
9. squeamish 10. meticulous,
particular, scrupulous
fastness... 4. fort 6. fixity 7. citadel
8. celerity, firmness, velocity
9. stability 10. profligacy, stronghold
fat... 4. lard, oily, suet 5. adeps, fatty,
lipin, obese, olein, stout 6. axunge
(goose), grease, portly, steato (pref),
stocky, tallow 7. adipose, lanolin,
opulent, paunchy, stearin, wealthy
9. corpulent, plentiful 10. profitable
fatal... 5. fated, deadly, doomed,
lethal, mortal 7. fateful, ominous
8. destined 9. condemned, prophetic
10. calamitous, disastrous
11. destructive
fatality... 4. fate 5. death 8. disaster
10. deadliness
fatally... 8. mortally 9. ruinously
fate... 3. end, lot 4. doom, luck, ruin

5. karma 6. chance, kismet
7. destiny, fortune 8. disaster,
downfall 13. inevitability
fateful... 5. fated 6. deadly
9. momentous 10. inevitable,
portentous 11. destructive,
predestined
Fates (Gr)... 6. Clotho, Moirae (group
of Three) 7. Atropos 8. Lachesis
Fates (Norse)... 4. Urth 5. Norns
(group of three), Skuld 9. Verthandi
Fates (Rom)... 4. Fata, Mona 5. Morta
6. Decuma, Parcae (group of three)
father... 2. pa 3. Abu, dad 4. abba,
papa, père, sire 5. adopt, friar,
padre, pater, vater 6. priest, senior
7. creator 8. generate 9. confessor,
procreate 11. acknowledge
Father (of)...
Ajax.. 7. Telamon
Christmas.. 10. Santa Claus
English learning.. 4. Bede
engraving.. 3. Pye
Evil.. 5. Satan
his country.. 6. Cicero (Rom), Medici
(It) 10. Washington (US)
history.. 9. Herodotus
Mankind (Myth).. 7. Iapetus
New York.. 13. Knickerbocker
Ocean.. 7. Neptune
the Gods.. 6. Amen–Ra
Time.. 10. Methuselah
Waters.. 11. Mississippi
father (pert to)...
land.. 6. native
land, love of.. 10. philopater
term.. 6. agnate 8. paternal
wise.. 6. mentor
fatherless... 6. orbate 7. forlorn
8. helpless, orphaned
fathom... 3. try 4. test 5. delve,
plumb, solve, sound 7. measure,
plummet 8. encircle 9. penetrate
10. understand 13. take soundings
fatigued... 5. bored, faint, jaded,
spent, tired, weary 6. fagged
7. languid, wearied 9. exhausted
Fatima (pert to)...
character in.. 14. Arabian Nights
father.. 8. Mohammed
husband.. 9. Bluebeard
fatten... 4. feed 6. batten, enrich
7. improve, prosper 8. pinguefy
fatty... 5. suety 6. greasy 7. adipose
9. aliphatic
fatty (pert to)...
acid.. 6. adipic 7. valeric
degeneration.. 8. adiposis
substance, sheep.. 5. suint
tumor.. 6. lipoma
fatuous... 4. vain 5. inane, silly
6. vacant 7. foolish, idiotic, witless
8. demented, illusory, imbecile
9. insensate 11. thoughtless
faucet... 3. peg, tap 4. cock 6. spigot
7. fixture, hydrant, petcock
fault... 4. hade, lode, slip, vice
5. cavil, cleft, culpa (law), error,
lapse, tache (anc) 6. defect, foible
7. blemish, blunder, demerit, failing,
frailty, misdeed, offense 8. fracture
10. peccadillo 11. delinquency

12. imperfection
faultfinder... 6. carper, nagger
7. caviler 10. complainer, criticizer
faultfinding... 7. carping, nagging
8. captious, caviling, critical
9. censorial
faultless... 4. pure 5. right 7. correct,
paragon, perfect 8. flawless, innocent
9. blameless 10. impeccable
13. unimpeachable 14. irreproachable
faultlessness... 8. accuracy
9. innocence 10. perfection
11. preciseness
faulty... 3. ill 5. amiss, unfit 6. guilty
8. culpable 9. blemished, defective,
deficient, erroneous, imperfect
11. blameworthy
faun... 3. Pan 5. deity, satyr
6. Faunus 10. Praxiteles
Faust... 4. hero 5. drama (Goethe),
opera
faux pas... 5. error, gaffe 6. booboo
7. blunder, misstep, mistake
favor, favour... 3. aid 4. boon, gift,
help 5. bless, grace, token
6. esteem, letter, regard 8. good
will, kindness, leniency, resemble
9. patronage, patronize, privilege
10. assistance, concession,
favoritism, partiality, permission
11. approbation
favorable... 4. good, kind, rosy
6. benign, timely 7. helpful, hopeful,
popular 8. friendly, gracious, pleasing
9. approving, opportune
10. auspicious, beneficial, propitious
11. complaisant 12. advantageous
favorite... 3. pet 4. lamb (pet)
6. minion 7. darling 10. preference
favoritism... 4. bias 7. leaning
8. nepotism 10. partiality
12. predilection
fawn... 3. doe 4. buck, coax, deer,
faon (color) 5. color, cower, crawl,
creep, toady 6. cringe, grovel, shrink
7. truckle 10. ingratiate
fawning... 7. servile 8. toadyish
9. truckling 10. obsequious
11. bootlicking, sycophantic
fawnskin (classic art)... 6. nebris
fay... 3. elf 5. fairy 6. sprite
fealty... 4. duty 6. homage 7. loyalty,
respect 8. fidelity 9. constancy
10. allegiance, obligation
fear... 3. awe 5. alarm, dread, panic
6. dismay, fright, horror, phobia,
terror 7. anxiety 8. venerate
9. apprehend, cowardice, reverence
11. nervousness 13. consternation
fear (of)...
animals.. 9. zoophobia
bees.. 9. apiphobia
being alone.. 10. autophobia,
monophobia
blood.. 10. hemophobia
cats.. 12. aelurophobia
crossing streets.. 11. dromophobia
crowds.. 11. ochlophobia
darkness.. 11. nyctophobia,
scotophobia
death.. 11. necrophobia
disease.. 10. nosophobia

enclosures.. 14. claustrophobia
fire.. 10. pyrophobia
food.. 10. cibophobia
heights.. 10. acrophobia
  11. hypsophobia
holy things.. 11. hagiophobia
men.. 11. androphobia
new things.. 9. neophobia
open spaces.. 11. agoraphobia
pain.. 10. algophobia
places (certain).. 10. topophobia
poison.. 10. toxiphobia
reptiles.. 13. herpetophobia
sea.. 14. thalassophobia
strangers.. 10. xenophobia
sunlight.. 11. heliophobia
thirteen.. 13. tridecaphobia
weeds.. 11. runcophobia
fearful... 4. dino (pref), dire 5. awful,
  pavid, timid 6. afraid, craven
  7. anxious, nervous 8. dreadful,
  horrible, timorous 9. appealing,
  frightful 11. distressing, frightening
  12. apprehensive
fearless... 4. bold 5. brave 6. daring
  7. impavid 8. harmless, intrepid
  9. audacious, confident, dauntless,
  undaunted 10. courageous
feast... 4. fete, meal 5. agape, epulo,
  revel 6. junket, picnic, regale, repast
  7. banquet, gratify 8. carousal,
  festival 9. carrousel
Feast (of)...
  Lanterns (Jap).. 3. Bon
  Lots.. 5. Purim
  Nativity.. 9. Christmas
  Pentecost (weeks).. 8. Shabuoth
  Tabernacles.. 7. Succoth
feasting... 6. dining 9. epulation
feat... 3. act 4. deed 5. stunt
  7. exploit 11. achievement,
  performance 14. accomplishment
feather... 4. deck, flaw (jewel), tuft
  5. adorn, penna, plume, quill
  6. clothe, fletch, hackle, trifle
  7. plumage 9. lightness
feather (pert to)...
  an arrow.. 6. fledge, fletch
  barb.. 7. pinnula 8. barbicel
  bird (area).. 7. pteryle
  featherlike.. 7. pinnate
  filament.. 4. dowl
  key (machine).. 6. spline
  molt.. 3. mew
  repair (falconry).. 3. imp
  shaft.. 5. scape
feathered... 5. swift 6. plumed,
  winged 7. fledged 8. pennated,
  plumaged 10. ornamented
feature... 4. face 5. motif, trait
  6. aspect 7. special 8. headline,
  resemble 9. component, lineament
  10. appearance, comeliness
  11. countenance 14. characteristic
features... 3. mug 4. face 5. looks
  6. visage 7. outline 9. geography
February birthstone... 8. amethyst
federation... 5. union 6. league
  8. alliance 10. government
  11. affiliation 13. confederation
fed up... 5. bored, jaded 7. wearied
  8. satiated 9. surfeited

fee... 3. feu, tip 4. fief, rate, wage
  5. bribe 6. charge, estate (law)
  8. gratuity, retainer 9. emolument
  10. honorarium
feeble... 4. aged, lame, puny, weak
  5. dotty 6. infirm 10. indistinct
  11. debilitated
feeble–minded... 5. anile 9. infirmity
  10. irresolute, weak–willed
  11. vacillating
feed... 4. dine, meal, sate 5. stoke
  6. fodder, gavage 7. engorge,
  foldage, furnish, indulge, nourish,
  nurture, pannage (swine)
  9. encourage, provision
feel... 3. ail, air 4. palp 5. grope,
  sense, touch 6. handle, suffer
  7. examine, explore, quality, texture
  8. perceive 10. atmosphere,
  experience
feel (pert to)...
  compunction.. 6. repent
  dejection.. 6. repine
  fear.. 2. ug
  melancholy.. 6. grieve
  worth of.. 10. appreciate
feeler... 4. palp, test 6. barbal, palpus
  7. antenna 8. question, tentacle
feeling... 4. feel, tact, view 5. hunch,
  touch 7. emotion, opinion, passion
  8. attitude 9. sensation, sentiment
  10. atmosphere, experience,
  perception 11. sensibility
  13. consciousness
feeling (pert to)...
  capable of.. 5. emote 8. sentient
  9. sensitive
  displeasure.. 9. resentful
  hostility.. 6. animus 9. animosity
  ill.. 7. malaise 10. discomfort
  impassive.. 8. stoicism
  joyful.. 6. jocund
  offense.. 5. pique
  superiority.. 9. arrogance
  without.. 6. apathy, steely 7. callous
  8. numbness 9. unfeeling
  13. insensibility
feet... see also *foot*
  designating.. 5. podal
  having.. 6. pedate
  number.. 7. footage
  two (Pros).. 6. dipody 7. dimeter
  9. ditrochee
  without.. 4. apod 6. apodal
  8. footless
feign... 3. act 4. sham 5. fable
  6. affect, assume, gammon, garble,
  invent 7. connive, imagine, pretend
  8. malinger (illness), simulate
  9. dissemble 11. counterfeit,
  make–believe
feint... 5. appel (fencing), blind, shift,
  trick 6. attack (mock), thrust
  7. mislead, pretext 8. artifice,
  pretense
Felicia... 7. thistle 9. happiness
felicitate... 4. laud 5. bless
  8. macarize 10. compliment
  12. congratulate
felicity... 5. bliss, grace 7. aptness,
  success 8. aptitude 9. happiness,
  well–being 11. achievement (happy),

blessedness 12. blissfulness

Felidae... 4. cats, lion, lynx, pard, puma 5. tiger 6. jaguar 7. cheetah, leopard, wildcat

feline... 3. sly 5. Felis 6. animal 7. catlike, furtive 8. stealthy 11. treacherous

Felis... 3. cat

fell... 3. cut, hem, hew 4. beat, hill, kill, pelt, ruin, skin 5. cruel, level 6. fierce, fleece, lay low, mighty, savage 7. brutish, tumbled 9. barbarous, ferocious, overthrow, prostrate

fellow... 3. lad, man 4. beau, chap, peer 5. equal 6. member, person 7. comrade 8. neighbor 9. associate, companion 10. sweetheart 11. confederate

fellow (pert to)...
accomplice.. 7. abettor 9. accessory 11. confederate
awkward.. 4. boor, gawk
clumsy.. 3. oaf 4. lout, pleb 5. yahoo 7. bumpkin
coward.. 3. cad, fop 4. drip 7. bounder 8. spalpeen
droll.. 3. wag 4. card
old.. 6. geezer 7. callant
small.. 6. shaver
smart.. 5. aleck
young.. 4. chap 5. blade, youth 7. younker 9. stripling

fellowman... 7. brother 11. fellow being

fellowship... 4. sect 5. guild, union 7. company 8. alliance, sodality 9. communion 10. membership 11. affiliation, comradeship, partnership, scholarship 12. friendliness 13. companionship

felon... 3. bum 4. wild 5. cruel 6. wicked 7. convict, culprit, outcast, villain, whitlow 8. criminal, disloyal 9. infection, malignant, murderous 10. malefactor, paronychia, traitorous

felony... 3. sin 5. crime, wrath 6. daring, deceit 8. baseness, burglary, outlawry 9. treachery 10. illegality, wickedness 11. misdemeanor

female... 4. bibi, dame, doña, girl, gyne, lady, miss 5. donna, femme, rhyme, squaw, woman 6. maiden, matron 7. distaff, dowager, fair sex, Sahibah 8. mistress 9. weaker sex

female (pert to)...
architecture.. 8. Caryatid
comb form.. 5. gyneo, thely
erudite.. 10. pedantress
fox.. 5. vixen
government.. 8. gynarchy
hormone.. 8. estrogen
monster.. 6. gorgon
prayerful.. 5. orant
spirit.. 7. banshee
suffix.. 4. ette
term.. 8. gynecoid
warrior.. 6. Amazon

feminine... 4. soft, weak 6. female, gender, tender 7. womanly 8. maidenly 10. effeminate

femme fatale... 4. vamp 5. siren 7. Lorelei, vampire

femur... 3. hip (bone) 4. bone (thigh), coxa

fen... 3. bog 4. moor, pool 5. marsh, swale 7. The Fens

fence... 3. aha 4. bank, duel, ha–ha, pale, rail, wall 5. close, ditch, fight, hedge, stile 6. paling, picket, secure 7. barrier, confine, enclose, fortify, protect, railing 8. palisade, prohibit 9. enclosure, swordplay 11. self–defense

fencing (pert to)...
breastplate.. 8. plastron
defense.. 5. carte, parry, prime, sixte 6. octave, quinte, tierce 7. seconds, septime
master.. 7. lanista
position.. 9. pronation 10. supination
sword.. 4. epee, foil, tuck 5. extoc 6. rapier
term.. 4. volt 7. corrida 8. estocado
thrust.. 6. remise 7. riposte

fend... 4. ward 5. avert, parry, shift 6. defend, resist 7. prevent, repulse, ward off

fender... 5. guard 6. buffer, bumper, shield, sluice 7. cushion 9. fireguard 10. firescreen 11. splashboard

fenestra... 6. window 7. foramen, opening, orifice

Fenian... 5. Irish 11. Brotherhood

fennel... 4. herb 6. Seseli 7. Azorian, Nigella

feral... 4. wild 6. deadly, ferine, savage 7. bestial, untamed 8. funereal, unbroken 9. malignant 12. uncultivated

feretory... 4. bier 6. chapel, shrine (saint's) 8. feretrum

ferment... 4. barm, brew, fret, sour, stum, zyme 5. anger, fever, yeast 6. enzyme, foment, leaven, rennin, seethe, uproar 7. glucase, maltase 8. diastase, disorder 9. agitation 10. effervesce, turbulence

fermentation... 6. unrest 9. agitation, chemistry, leavening 10. ebullition 13. effervescence

fermenting vat... 4. gyle

fern... 4. tara 5. brake, heath, holly 6. osmund, spider 7. bracken 8. polypody 10. maidenhair 11. elephant–ear

fern (pert to)...
family.. 12. pteridophyte
genus.. 6. Anemia
leaf.. 5. frond
scale.. 8. ramentum

ferocious... 4. grim, wild 5. cruel, feral 6. bloody, brutal, fierce, savage 7. acharne, inhuman 8. pitiless, ravenous, ruthless 9. barbarous, malignant, merciless, murderous, rapacious, truculent 10. implacable, malevolent, relentless, sanguinary 11. remorseless 12. bloodthirsty

ferret... 3. hob 4. hunt, jill, tape 5. worry 6. badger, harass, search, weasel 7. polecat

ferrotype... 7. tintype 10. photograph

ferrum... 2. Fe (sym) 4. iron
ferry... 7. traject 9. transport 10. sail across
ferryboat... 3. bac 4. pont 6. wherry
ferryman... 6. Charon (River Styx) 7. ferrier
fertile... 4. rank, rich 7. teeming 8. abundant, fruitful, prolific 9. exuberant, inventive, plenteous, plentiful 10. productive
fertilizer... 4. marl 5. guano 6. pollen 7. compost, nitrate 8. dressing 9. phosphate
ferule... 3. rod 5. ruler 6. fennel 10. punishment
fervency... 4. heat, keen, zeal 5. ardor, eager, fiery, gusto, verve 6. fervor, warmth 7. ardency, passion 9. eloquence, vehemence 12. empressement 15. impassionedness
fervent... 3. hot 4. keen, warm 5. eager, fiery 6. ardent, fervid 7. excited, intense, zealous 8. eloquent, vehement 10. passionate 11. impassioned
fervid... 3. hot 5. fiery 6. ardent, tropic 7. boiling, fervent, zealous 8. vehement 11. impassioned
fervor... 4. rage, zeal, zest 5. ardor 7. ecstasy, passion 11. earnestness
fester... 6. rankle 7. abscess, pustule, putrefy 9. suppurate
festival... 3. ale, bal 4. fete, gala 5. Delia (Apollo), feast, revel, Seder 6. Easter, Kermis 7. holiday, uphelya 8. apodosis (Church) 9. Christmas, Mardi gras 10. Parentalia, Saturnalia
festive... 3. gay 4. gala 5. merry 6. joyous 8. mirthful, sportive 9. convivial
festivity... 3. joy 4. fete, gala 5. mirth, revel 6. gaiety 7. jollity, whoopee 8. festival, jamboree 10. joyfulness 11. celebration, merrymaking 12. conviviality
fetch... 3. get 5. bring, reach 6. attain, deduce, revive 7. achieve 8. go and get, retrieve
fetching... 8. alluring, charming, pleasing 10. attractive, delightful 11. fascinating
fete... 4. gala 5. feast, party 6. fiesta 8. carnival, festival 10. Saturnalia 13. entertainment
fetid... 4. olid, rank 5. fusty 7. noisome 10. malodorous 11. ill—smelling
fetish... 3. obi 4. idol, joss, juju 5. charm, image, totem 6. amulet, avatar, mascot 7. Dahoman 8. talisman
fetter... 4. band, bond, gyve, iron 5. chain 6. hamper, hobble, hopple, thrall 7. enchain, manacle, shackle
feud... 4. fief, fray 5. broil 6. affray, estate, strife 7. contest, dispute, quarrel 8. vendetta 9. hostility
feudal (pert to)...
  estate.. 3. fee 4. fief, soke
  French.. 4. feod

lord.. 6. tenure 8. overlaid, suzerain
payment.. 6. socage
service.. 5. banal
tenant.. 4. leud 6. vassal
tribute.. 6. heriot
fever... 4. ague 5. ardor 6. frenzy 8. delirium, sickness 9. calenture 10. excitement
fever (pert to)...
  heat.. 9. sunstroke
  intermittent.. 5. octan 7. quartan
  malarial.. 4. ague
  marsh.. 6. elodes 7. helodes
  subsidence.. 12. defervescent
  term.. 7. febrile, pyretic
  tropical.. 6. dengue 9. calenture
feverish... 5. hasty 7. excited, febrile, fervent, fevered 8. restless 9. delirious, overeager 10. disordered
fey... 4. dead 5. dying, elfin, fatal, spell 9. enfeebled, visionary 12. otherworldly
fez... 3. cap 5. busby, shako 8. tarboosh 9. headdress
fiat... 3. act 5. edict, order 6. decree 7. command 8. decision, sanction
fiber... 3. nap, nep, tal 4. bast, eruc, imbe, lint, pile, pita, silk, yarn 5. datil, istle, kapok, linen, nerve, rayon, sisal 6. fibril, raffia, staple, thread 7. filasse, texture 8. fibrilla, filament
fiber plant... 4. hemp, imbe, palm 5. abaca, agave 6. ambary, cotton, linaga
fibers... 5. hairs 7. strands 9. filaments
fibula... 4. bone (arm) 5. class 6. brooch (anc), buckle 9. safety pin
fickle... 5. false 6. mobile 7. mutable 8. unstable, unsteady, variable, wavering 9. changeful, deceitful, faithless, unsettled 10. capricious, changeable, inconstant, irresolute, unfaithful 11. vacillating
fiction... 4. tale 5. false, fancy, novel, story 6. legend 7. coinage, figment, forgery, romance 9. falsehood, invention 11. fabrication
fictitious... 5. false 6. poetic, pseudo (pref) 7. assumed, feigned 8. chimeric 9. imaginary, imitative, pretended 10. artificial
fictitious name... 5. alias 6. anonym 7. pen name 8. nickname 9. pseudonym, stage name 10. nom de plume 11. nom de guerre
fidelity... 5. topaz, troth, truth 6. fealty 7. honesty 8. accuracy, devotion, veracity 9. adherence, constancy, exactness 10. allegiance 12. faithfulness
fidget... 4. fuss 5. worry 6. twitch 9. dysphoria 10. uneasiness 12. restlessness
fidgety... 5. jerky 6. uneasy 7. nervous, restive, twitchy 8. bustling, restless 9. excitable, impatient
fiducial... 4. firm 5. solid, sound 6. secure, stable 7. trusted 8. trustful 9. confident

11. trustworthy

fiduciary... 4. held (in trust) 5. trust 7. founded, holding, in trust, trustee 12. confidential

fief... 3. fee 4. feud 6. estate

field... 3. lea, lot 4. acre, ager, land, mead, rand 5. croft, glebe, range, tract 6. campus, ground, meadow, sphere 7. compass, diamond, expanse, pasture, savanna (savannah), terrain 8. clearing, gridiron 11. battlefield

field (pert to)...
athletic.. 4. oval 5. arena, court, track 6. course, sphere 7. diamond, stadium 8. gridiron
bloodshed.. 8. Aceldama (Akeldama) 13. Ager Sanguinis
duck.. 7. bustard
god of.. 4. Faun
mouse.. 4. vole
snow.. 4. neve
stubble.. 5. rowen
term.. 5. agral 8. agrarian 10. campestral

fiend... 3. foe 5. demon, devil, enemy, Satan 6. addict, wizard 7. Amaimon (Amamon) 9. archfiend 10. evil spirit

fiendish... 5. cruel 6. wicked 7. Avernal, demonic 8. demoniac, devilish, diabolic

fierce... 4. grim 5. cruel, eager 6. raging, savage 7. furious, racking, violent 9. ferocious, impetuous, truculent 10. catawampus, forbidding, passionate 11. belligerent, overwrought 12. overpowering

fierceness... 7. cruelty 8. violence 10. truculence

fiery... 3. hot, red 4. sore 5. angry 6. ardent 7. burning, excited, fervent, flaming, glowing, igneous, parched, violent 8. choleric, feverish, inflamed, spirited, vehement 9. impetuous, irascible 10. mettlesome, passionate 11. hot-tempered, inflammable

fiery cross... 5. alarm 6. emblem, signal, symbol 8. crantara 10. call to arms

fiesta... 5. color 7. holiday 8. festival 9. festivity

fifish... 6. cranky 9. half crazy

Fifteenth Amendment... 16. Negro Citizenship (1870)

fig... 4. fico 5. eleme, gruit 6. Carica, Fiscus, Smyrna, trifle

fig basket... 5. cabas, seron

fight... 3. row, war 4. bout, duel, fray, mell, tilt 5. brawl, melee, scrap 6. affray, attack, barney, battle, combat, oppose, strife, strike, strive 7. contest, quarrel, warfare 8. conflict, struggle 9. pugnacity 13. combativeness

fighter... 7. battler, duelist, soldier, warrior 8. champion, pugilist, scrapper 9. combatant

fighting... 3. war 4. game 6. plucky 7. warlike 8. militant 10. contention, pugnacious 11. belligerent

fig leaf... 6. symbol (modesty)

8. clothing (Bib), covering

figment... 5. fancy 7. fiction 9. falsehood, invention

figurative... 6. florid 7. flowery, typical 8. allusive 9. numerical 12. emblematical, metaphorical

figure... 4. body, dash, dope, form, nude, rank, type 5. digit, image, judge, price, shape, solve 6. aspect, emblem, entail, number, symbol 7. diagram, numeral, outline, pattern 8. ornament, phantasm 9. calculate, celebrity, character, personage 10. appearance, impression, similitude 11. distinction

figure (pert to)...
column.. 6. elamon 7. telamon 8. Atlantes, Caryatid, pilaster
geometric.. 4. cone, lune 5. prism, rhomb 6. isagon, isogen, isogon (rare) 7. ellipse, rhombus 8. pentagon, triangle 13. parallelogram, quadrilateral 16. parallelepipedon
praying.. 6. orant
repeated digits.. 8. repetend
speech.. 5. trope 6. aporia, simile 8. metaphor
star-shaped.. 8. pentacle

figured... 4. rich 6. ornate 7. façonné 10. ornamented

figurine... 4. doll 7. carving, tanagra 9. sculpture, statuette

Fiji Island, Viti Levu...
capital.. 4. Suva
export.. 5. sugar
mountain.. 8. Victoria
natives.. 9. cannibals (anc) 11. Melanesians
ruler.. 7. British

filament... 4. barb, dowl (dowle), hair 5. fiber (fibre), harle 6. strand, thread

filament lamp... 12. incandescent

filbert... 3. nut 5. brown, hazel 7. Corylus 8. hazelnut

filch... 3. nim, rob 4. beat 5. steal, theft 6. pilfer 7. purloin

file... 3. row 4. list, rasp, rate 5. enter, march, store 6. abrade, smooth 7. sharpen 8. classify 9. catalogue 10. pickpocket 11. triggerfish (filefish)

file (combmaking)... 5. grail (graille) 6. carlet 7. quannet

filibeg... 4. kilt 5. skirt

filibuster... 6. pirate 7. impeder 8. thwarter 9. legislate 10. freebooter, obstructer 14. obstructionist

filicide... 6. murder (child by parent)

filigree... 4. lace 5. adorn (with) 7. pattern 8. fanciful 10. decorative 13. unsubstantial

Filipino, Filipina (pert to)...
homeland (mostly).. 5. Luzon
native of.. 11. Philippines
tribe.. 5. Bikol (Bicol) 7. Malayan (Christian), Tagalog (Tagal), Visayan (see also *Philippine*)

fill... 3. pad 4. calk, feed, glut, hold, plug 5. block, close, gorge, stuff

6. occupy, stop up 7. execute, fulfill, pervade, satiate, satisfy, suffuse 8. complete, compound, permeate 10. accomplish 11. superabound

fille... 4. girl 8. daughter

filled... 5. dated 7. replete 8. suffused 9. saturated

filled with crevices... 7. areolar

fillet... 4. band, orle, ring, tape 5. snood, tiara 6. anadem, border, ribbon, taenia 7. bandage 8. headband, insignia 9. lemniscus, scantling 10. tenderloin

fillet (Arch)... 5. stria 6. cimbia, listel, reglet, regula, taenia 7. chaplet, molding (part)

filly... 4. colt, foal, girl, mare

film... 4. brat, haze, scum, skin, veil 5. cover, layer 6. lamina, patina 7. coating 8. pellicle 10. photograph

filmy... 3. dim 4. fine 5. gauzy, misty 6. cloudy, opaque 7. clouded 9. laminated 10. indistinct

fils... 3. son

filter... 4. ooze 5. clean, drain 6. purify, strain 7. trickle 8. colature 9. percolate

filth... 4. dirt, muck, slut 5. lucre 6. vermin 7. squalor 9. excrement, obscenity, scoundrel

filthiness... 8. cenosity 9. fetidness, obscenity 10. odiousness

filthy... 3. low 4. foul, vile 5. dirty, fetid, gross 6. impure, odious, putrid 7. obscene, squalid, unclean 9. polluting 10. licentious

filthy lucre... 4. gain (shameful) 5. money

fimbriated... 5. edged 7. fringed 8. bordered (Her), margined

fin... 3. arm 4. five, keel

fin (pert to fish)...
median.. 4. anal 6. caudal, dorsal
paired.. 6. pelvic 7. ventral 8. pectoral

final... 3. end 4. last 5. be—all, telic 7. dernier 8. decisive, definite, eventual, ultimate 9. mandatory, ultimatum 10. conclusive, definitive 11. unqualified 13. determinating

final argument... 11. ultima ratio

finale... 3. end 4. coda 5. close 6. result 8. swan song 10. completion, conclusion 11. termination

finality... 5. finis 6. finale, finish, windup 10. conclusion 11. termination 12. decisiveness 14. conclusiveness

finally... 10. eventually, ultimately 12. conclusively

final outcome... 5. issue 6. upshot 10. denouement

financial... 6. fiscal 8. monetary 9. pecuniary

finch... 4. moro 5. Junco, serin, spink, tarin 6. burion, linnet, siskin, towhee 7. chewink, redpoll 9. brambling, chaffinch, Fringilla

find... 3. get 4. gain 5. learn 6. detect, locate, summon, supply

7. procure, provide 8. discover, meet with, perceive 9. determine, discovery, good thing 10. experience 11. acquisition

find fault... 4. beef, carp 5. cavil 8. complain 9. criticize

finding... 7. verdict 8. solution 9. discovery 11. serendipity

find out... 5. learn, solve 6. detect 8. discover 9. ascertain

fine... 3. fit 4. good, lacy, pure, rare, thin 5. dandy, filmy, frail, gaudy, noble, sharp, sheer 6. ornate, slight, smooth 7. elegant, fragile, healthy, perfect, powdery, precise, slender 8. absolute, ethereal, handsome, polished, skillful, superior 9. beautiful, excellent, sensitive 10. fastidious, pulverized, surpassing

finery... 6. beauty 7. clothes, gaudery, gewgaws 8. elegance, fineness, frippery, ornament 10. decoration, lavishness 11. refinements

finesse... 5. skill 6. purity, serene 7. cunning 8. artifice, card play, subtlety, thinness 9. clearness, good taste, stratagem 10. refinement 14. discrimination (subtle)

finger... 3. toy (with) 4. hook 5. digit, touch 6. dactyl, handle, pilfer 7. measure, purloin

finger (pert to)...
alphabet.. 11. dactylology
cymbal.. 8. castanet
fish.. 8. starfish
flower.. 8. foxglove
fore.. 5. index 7. pointer
little.. 6. pinkie 7. minimus 9. auricular
middle.. 6. medius
ring.. 7. annular
stall.. 3. cot
term.. 7. digital

fingernail moon... 6. lunule

fingernail overgrowth...
10. onychauxis

fingerprint (term)... 4. arch, loop 5. whorl 9. composite 11. dactylogram 12. dactyloscopy

finial... 3. epi, tee

finical... 4. nice 5. fussy 6. dainty, dapper, jaunty, spruce 7. finicky, foppish, mincing, prudish 8. delicate 9. finicking, squeamish 10. fastidious, meticulous 11. overprecise 14. overscrupulous

finis... 3. end 4. goal 6. finale 8. finality 10. conclusion 11. culmination

finish... 3. end 4. kill 5. chare, close, matte (mat), style 6. enamel, polish 7. destroy, perfect, surface, texture 8. complete, conclude 9. terminate 10. completion, consummate, perfection

finished... 3. o'er 4. done, fine, over, ripe 5. ended 6. closed 7. refined, stopped 8. climaxed, complete, lustered, polished 9. completed, concluded, perfected 10. terminated

finite... 7. fleshly, limited 9. definable 10. restricted, terminable

11. conditional
fink... 3. spy 4. scab 5. finch
8. informer 13. strikebreaker
Finland... see also *Finnish*
capital.. 8. Helsinki (Helsingfors)
Finnish for Finland.. 5. Suomi
government.. 8. republic
island.. 5. Aland
language.. 6. Magyar 7. Swedish
8. Estonian
legislature.. 9. Eduskunta
port.. 3. Abo 5. Turku 9. Mariehamn
Finnish (pert to)...
bath.. 5. sauna
dramatist.. 4. Kivi 7. Waltari
people.. 5. Finns, Suomi 9. Karelians
10. Tavastians
fire... 4. heat, zeal 5. blaze, fever,
flame 6. excite, fervor, igneus, ignite,
incite, kindle 7. barrage, explode,
inspire 8. detonate, illumine
9. discharge, eloquence
11. inspiration 12. inflammation
13. conflagration
fire (pert to)...
basket.. 5. grate 7. cresset
comb form.. 4. igni
cracker.. 6. petard
dog.. 7. andiron
fear of.. 10. pyrophobia
god.. 6. Vulcan
opal.. 7. girasol (girasole)
power over.. 10. ignipotent
worshiper.. 5. Parsi 9. pyrolater
10. ignicolist
firearm... 3. gat, gun 5. piece, rifle
6. musket 7. demihag, rimbase (part)
8. ordnance, revolver 9. harquebus
(arquebus)
firearms discharge... 9. fusillade
fired... 3. lit 4. shot 5. baked 6. on
fire (Her) 7. excited 8. inspired
10. discharged
fireman... 4. vamp 6. fueler, stoker
8. trainman 9. fire–eater
11. firefighter
fireplace... 5. fogon, forge, ingle
6. hearth 9. inglenook 13. Franklin
stove
fireside (home)... 11. hearthstone
firewood... 6. billet
fireworks... 4. caps, gerb 6. flares
7. fizgigs, gunfire, rip–raps, rockets
8. serpents 9. pinwheels, sparklers,
torpedoes 10. girandoles
12. firecrackers, Roman candles
firm... 4. fast, hard, safe, sure, trig
5. dense, fixed, rigid, solid, sound,
stout, tight 6. secure, stable, stanch,
steady, strict, strong 7. compact,
company, decided, devoted, staunch
8. faithful 9. immovable, steadfast
10. determined, unslipping, unyielding
11. substantial
firmament... 3. sky 5. vault 6. Caelus,
welkin 7. heavens 8. empyrean
firmly set... 5. fixed, solid 6. rooted
10. inveterate
firmness... 8. fidelity, rigidity, solidity,
strength, tenacity 9. constancy,
stability 10. immobility, steadiness
11. reliability 15. indissolubility

firmness, want of... 5. loose 6. laxity
8. weakness 11. instability, vacillation
firn... 3. ice 4. neve, snow
firs... 5. Abies, pines
first... 5. chief, front, prime 6. maiden,
primal, primus 7. highest, initial,
leading, primary 8. earliest, foremost,
original 9. beginning, elemental,
principal 10. primordial
first (pert to)...
appearance.. 5. debut 8. premiere
born.. 5. eigne 6. eldest
Christian martyr.. 7. Stephen
coin (silver).. 8. sesterce
days of Rom month.. 7. calends
(kalends)
fruits (Eccl).. 7. annates
letter.. 4. Alif 5. Aleph
stages.. 8. inchoate 9. rudiments
world navigator.. 8. Magellan
fish... 3. dib 4. food 5. angle, drail,
seine, troll 6. Pisces
13. constellation
fish (types of)... 2. id 3. cat, cod, gar,
ray 4. bass, carp, char, chub, cusk,
dace, goby, hake, ling, opah, parr,
peto, pike, ruff, scup, shad, sisi,
sole, tuna, ulua 5. bream, cisco,
fluke, guppy, perch, porgy, shark,
skate, smelt, snook, sprat, trout,
tunny, wahoo 6. barbel, bonito,
bowfin, burbot, conger, darter,
marlin, minnow, puffer, redfin,
salmon, shiner, sucker, tarpon,
tautog, turbot 7. alewife, anchovy,
catfish, crappie, croaker, dogfish,
garfish, grouper, haddock, halibut,
herring, hogfish, jewfish, lamprey,
mudfish, oquassa, pollack, pompano,
redfish, sardine, sawfish, sunfish,
torpedo, walleye 8. albacore, blue
fish, bluegill, bonefish, bullhead,
chimaera, filefish, flatfish, flounder,
goldfish, grayling, kingfish, lumpfish,
mackerel, menhaden, pickerel,
pilchard, sailfish, sergeant, sting ray,
sturgeon, toadfish, weakfish
9. barracuda, cigarfish, devilfish,
jellyfish, namaycush, sheatfish,
whitefish 10. barramunda, butterfish,
candlefish, hammerhead, yellowtail
11. muskellunge (see also *mammal*)
fish (pert to)...
adhering.. 4. pega 6. remora
ascending rivers.. 7. anadrom
10. anadromous
bait.. 3. chum 5. chack 6. minnow
9. killifish (killy)
basket.. 4. caul 5. creel, slath (slarth)
bivalve, mollusk.. 4. clam, slug
5. snail, whelk 6. limpet, mussel,
oyster 7. abalone, Ocypode (crab),
scallop
caviar–yielding.. 7. sterlet
climbing, jumping.. 5. saury
6. anabas 7. skipper
club.. 6. muckle
codfish.. 4. cusk 5. torsk 7. bacalao,
buffalo
comb form.. 7. ichthyo
crustacean.. 3. Uca 4. crab 6. shrimp
7. lobster 8. Decapoda

devil.. 3. ray 5. manta
eaters.. 12. ichthyophagi
eating.. 11. piscivorous
    14. ichthyophagous
fabled (Pers).. 4. Mahi (Mah)
gaff (through ice).. 5. ching
game.. 4. tuna 5. chiro, sword, trout
    6. marlin, salmon, tarpon 8. grayling
    11. muskellunge
genus.. 4. Amia (bowfin), Mola
    (sunfish) 5. Elops (tarpon), Perca
    (perch) 8. Haliotis (abalone),
    Octopoda (octopus)
hook.. 5. Kirby, snell (part)
    8. Aberdeen, barbless, Carlisle,
    Limerick
largest (freshwater).. 8. arapaima
like.. 8. ichthyic
line.. 6. nossel (norsel) 7. spillet
living by.. 9. piscatory
living on.. 12. ichthyophagy
man–eating.. 6. caribe 7. piranha
mollusk.. see bivalve
nest building.. 5. acara
net.. 4. fyke 5. seine, snell, trawl
    7. boulter, spiller
pond.. 7. piscina 8. aquarium
roe.. 6. caviar
salmon.. 3. fog 4. masu, parr
    5. sprod 6. alevin 7. gilling
sauce.. 4. alec
spear.. 3. gig
taboo.. 13. ichthyophobia
treatise.. 11. ichthyology
worship.. 12. ichthyolatry
young brood.. 3. fry
fisherman... 6. angler 8. piscator
fishery... 7. piscary
fishing... 4. chug (through ice)
    8. snelling 9. halieutic, piscation
fishing vessel... 5. smack 6. seiner
    7. trawler
fishy... 4. dull 6. vacant 8. fishlike
    9. deceptive, dishonest
    10. improbable, lusterless, suspicious,
    unreliable 11. extravagant
    14. expressionless
fissure... 3. gap 4. leak, lode, open,
    rent, rift, rima, seam, slit, vein
    5. break, chasm, chine, chink, cleft,
    crack, sever, split 7. crevice
fissured... 5. cleft 6. rimate, rimose
fist... 4. duke, hand (closed) 5. nieve
    6. clench 8. tightwad
    11. handwriting
fit... 3. due, fay, pat 4. able, gear,
    meet, mesh, ripe, suit, whim
    5. adapt, equip, fancy, ready, spasm,
    train 6. attack, enmesh, frenzy,
    proper, stroke, suited 7. adapted,
    caprice, conform, healthy, prepare,
    tantrum 8. disposed, dovetail,
    eligible, outbreak, suitable
    9. competent, qualified
    11. accommodate, appropriate
fit (pert to)...
    an arrow (archery).. 4. nock
    fury.. 4. rage
    groove (Arch).. 4. dado
    resentment.. 4. huff, mood 5. pique
        7. tantrum
    to eat.. 6. edible

to till.. 6. arable
fitchew... 5. skink, zoril 7. foumart,
    polecat
fitful... 8. restless, unstable, variable
    9. impulsive, irregular, orderless,
    spasmodic 10. capricious, convulsive
    12. intermittent
fitly... 4. duly 5. right 6. timely
    8. properly, suitably 10. decorously
fitness... 7. decorum 9. congruity
    10. expedience, timeliness
    11. eligibility, suitability
    12. preparedness
fitting... 3. apt, pat 4. just, meet
    6. proper, seemly, timely
    8. adapting, suitable 9. expedient
    11. appropriate
five (pert to)...
    Books of Moses.. 10. Pentateuch
    children (born at once)..
        11. quintuplets
    Civilized Tribes (Ind).. 5. Creek
        7. Choctaw 8. Cherokee, Seminole
        9. Chickasaw
    comb form.. 5. penta
    cornered.. 11. pentagonous
    divided by.. 11. quinquesect
    dollar bill.. 1. V 3. fin 5. fiver
    feet.. 10. pentameter
    five–year period.. 6. pentad 7. lustrum
        (census) 12. quinquennial
    fold.. 9. quintuple
    group.. 6. pentad 8. fivesome
    lines (nonsense).. 8. limerick
    Nations (Ind Confed).. 7. Cayugas,
        Mohawks, Oneidas, Senecas
        9. Onondagas
    trump card (auction pitch).. 5. pedro
fix... 3. peg, pin, set 4. mend, moor,
    nail 5. amend, brace, bribe, imbed,
    limit, stamp 6. adjust, anchor,
    cement, define, fasten, ossify, punish,
    repair, settle 7. arrange, confirm,
    delimit, dilemma, prepare, rectify
    8. organize, solidify 9. condition,
    establish, stabilize, stipulate
    10. prearrange
fixed... 3. set 4. firm 5. rigid
    6. formal, intent, nailed, static
    7. assured, limited, settled, special
    8. arranged, habitual 9. immovable,
    permanent, unwinking
    11. established, prearranged,
    traditional
fixed (pert to)...
    allowance.. 4. diet 6. ration
        7. stipend 10. remittance
    beforehand.. 13. predetermined
    by choice.. 8. elective
    manner.. 9. immovably
    star.. 4. Veda
    time.. 3. era 4. date, fast
fizgig... 9. fireworks, whirligig
flabellate... 9. fan–shaped
flabrum... 3. fan 9. flabellum
flaccid... 4. limp, weak 6. flabby
    8. yielding
flag... 3. sag 4. fail, fane, iris, pave,
    pine, sign, weak, wilt 5. Roger
    (pirate) 6. banner, burgee, colors,
    cornet, ensign, fanion, flower, guidon,
    pennon, signal 7. bunting, calamus,

decline, pennant 8. gonfalon,
masthead, standard, streamer,
vexillum 9. banderole 16. Quincunx
of Heaven
flagging ... 4. weak 7. languid
8. pavement 10. flagstones, spiritless
11. languishing
flagging in energy ... 9. lassitude
flagitious ... 6. wicked 7. corrupt,
heinous 8. criminal, flagrant
10. scandalous, villainous
flagon ... 3. jug 4. ewer 5. stoup
6. bottle, carafe 7. canteen
8. demijohn
flagpole standard ... 7. bracket
9. bracciale
flagrant ... 4. rank 5. great 6. absurd,
wanton, wicked 7. glaring, hateful,
heinous, obvious, scarlet, violent
8. infamous, terrible 9. abandoned,
atrocious, monstrous, nefarious
10. profligate, villainous
flail ... 4. beat, flag, whip 6. thrash,
weapon (anc) 7. swingle
flam ... 4. hoax 5. cheat, spoof, trick
6. cajole 7. pretext 8. drumbeat,
flimflam 9. deception, falsehood
flambeau ... 5. torch (flaming)
7. cresset 11. candlestick
flamboyant ... 4. wavy (Arch) 6. florid,
ornate 9. brilliant, flamelike
11. resplendent
flame ... 3. arc 4. beam, burn, fire,
glow, leye (obs), love, zeal 5. ardor,
blaze, flare, flash, glare, ingle, light,
lover 6. redden 7. scarlet
8. flammule (small) 10. brightness,
sweetheart
flamen ... 6. priest (anc)
flamenco ... 5. dance (gypsy)
Flaminian Way ... 4. Rome
Flanders, Belgium ...
brick .. 4. Bath
capital .. 5. Ghent (East) 6. Bruges
(West)
city .. 5. Alost 6. Ostend 7. Dixmude
(Dixmuide)
people (anc) .. 5. Celts 6. Franks
11. Burgundians
poppy .. 9. corn poppy
flap ... 3. tab 4. blow, slap, sway,
wave 5. skirt 6. dangle, lappet,
stroke 7. flapper, flutter
9. appendage
flare ... 5. blaze, flame, flash, fusee,
glare, light 6. signal, spread
7. display, flicker 8. outburst
10. illuminate
flaring ... 5. gaudy 6. spread
7. burning, glaring 8. dazzling,
flashing
flash ... 4. show 5. blaze, burst, gleam,
glint, shine, spark 6. glance, signal
7. display, glimmer, glisten, glitter,
instant, shimmer, sparkle 8. dispatch
9. telegraph
flashing ... 5. showy 6. flashy
8. meteoric, snapping 9. transient
flashy ... 3. gay 5. fiery, gaudy, showy
6. frothy, garish, sporty 7. raffish
8. vehement 9. flaunting, impetuous
13. grandiloquent

flask ... 4. ewer, olpe 5. betty
6. flagon 7. ampulla, canteen
9. aryballus (aryballas, anc)
flask–shaped ... 10. lageniform
flat ... 3. low 4. palm 5. banal, blunt,
level, molle, plain, plane, prone,
stale, suite, tract, vapid 6. boring,
dreary, wholly 7. insipid, uniform
8. tenement, unbroken 10. horizontal
flat (pert to) ...
boat .. 3. ark 4. punt, scow 5. barge
breastbone .. 6. ratite
canopy .. 6. tester
flatfoot .. 9. pes planus 13. talipes
planus
iron .. 7. sadiron
nosed .. 6. simous
piece .. 4. slab
surface .. 4. area 6. pagina 7. tabular
worm .. 9. planarian, trematode
flatfish ... 3. dab 4. sole 5. brill, fluke
6. acedia, turbot 7. halibut
8. flounder
flatten ... 4. even 5. level 6. deject,
smooth 7. depress 8. dispirit
9. prostrate 10. discourage,
dishearten
flattened ... 6. evened, oblate
7. leveled 8. smoothed 9. applanate
flatter ... 3. oil 4. coax, palp 5. charm,
float 6. cajole, caress, please, praise,
smooge, soothe 7. adulate, beguile,
blarney, flutter 8. blandish
9. encourage 10. compliment,
ingratiate
flatterer ... 6. flunky, glozer 7. Jenkins
8. adulator, courtier, parasite
9. sycophant
flattering ... 9. adulatory, gnathonic,
insincere 10. obsequious
13. complimentary
flattery ... 5. gloze, taffy 6. praise
7. blarney, eyewash, fawning, palaver
8. cajolery 9. adulation
10. compliment, sycophancy
14. obsequiousness
flaunt ... 4. wave 5. boast, vaunt
6. parade 7. display, flutter
8. brandish
Flavian, House of Flavius,
Emperors ... 5. Titus 8. Domitian
9. Vespasian
Flavian Amphitheater ... 9. Colosseum
(Rome)
flavor ... 4. gust, odor, tang, zest
5. aroma, imbue, sapid, sapor,
sauce, savor, scent, taste 6. season
7. perfume 8. piquancy 9. flavoring
14. characteristic
flaw ... 3. gap, mar 4. rase, rift
5. cleft, fault 6. breach, defect
7. blemish, fissure, sophism
8. fracture 12. imperfection
flax ... 3. lin, tow 5. linen
flax (pert to) ...
capsule .. 4. boll
dust .. 5. pouce
filaments .. 4. harl
process plant .. 7. rettery
refuse .. 3. pob, tow 5. hurds
seed .. 7. linseed
soak .. 3. ret

weed.. 8. toadflax
flaxweed... 8. toadflax
flay... 4. peel, skin 6. fleece
　7. censure, reprove, scarify
　9. criticize, excoriate
flea... 4. puce 5. pulex 6. beetle,
　chigoe 7. chigger, cyclops
　8. reminder 13. Ctenocephalus
fleam... 6. lancet, stream
　10. millstream
fleck... 4. flea, mark, spot 5. flake
　6. blotch, dapple, streak, stripe
　7. freckle, speckle, stipple 8. particle
　9. variegate
flection, flexion... 7. bending, turning
flee... 3. fly, run 4. shun 5. avoid,
　elope, evade, speed 6. vanish
　7. abandon, forsake 9. disappear
fleece... 3. abb, nap 4. flay, pile, skin,
　wool 5. fleck, mulct, sheer, strip
　6. divest 7. despoil, swindle
　10. overcharge
fleer... 4. gibe, jeer, mock 5. flout,
　scoff, sheer, taunt
fleet... 4. fast, flit, flow, navy, sail,
　swim 5. drift, group, quick, rapid,
　swift 6. armada, hasten, nimble,
　speedy 9. transient 10. evanescent,
　transitory
fleeting... 7. passing 9. transient
　10. evanescent, transitory
Fleet Street... 5. Fleta (book written
　in prison) 6. prison (London)
　11. London press
Flemish painter... 5. David 6. Rubens
　7. Van Dyke
flesh... 3. kin 4. body, meat, pink,
　pulp, race (human) 6. family, fatten,
　muscle 7. kindred, kinsmen, mankind
　8. humanity 10. mortality
flesh (pert to)...
　eating.. 8. omophagy (raw)
　9. omophagia 10. omophagous,
　zoophagous 11. carnivorous,
　creophagous
　fond of.. 12. sarcophilous
　like.. 7. carnose
　lust for.. 9. carnality
　resembling.. 7. sarcoid
　slain animals.. 7. carnage
fleshpots... 6. plenty, wealth 10. high
　living, prosperity 12. fat of the land
fleshy... 3. fat 5. beefy, human,
　obese, plump, pulpy, stout 6. carnal
　7. adipose, carnose 9. corpulent
fleshy fruit... 4. pear, pome 5. bacca,
　berry, drupe
fleur–de–lis... 3. lis (Her) 4. iris, lily,
　luce 6. emblem
flew... see *fly*
flexible... 4. limp 5. lithe 6. limber,
　pliant, supple 7. elastic, lissome
flexion, flection... 9. anaclasis
flexure... 4. genu 5. crook 7. bending
flicker... 4. burn, flit 5. blaze, glare,
　waver 7. flutter, high–hoe
　10. woodpecker
flickering... 7. burning, lambent
　8. flickery 9. irregular
flier, flyer... 3. ace 4. bird 5. pilot,

train 6. airman, gamble, insect
　7. aviator, speeder, sunfish, venture
　11. speculation
flight... 3. hop 4. rout 5. arrow
　(volley), flock, skein (wild fowl), speed
　6. exodus, fletch (arrows), flying,
　hegira, perron, stairs, throng
　7. soaring 8. escapism, mounting,
　stampede, swarming 9. excursion,
　formation, migration 10. volitation
flighty... 5. barmy, swift 6. fickle, fitful
　7. foolish 8. fanciful, freakish, volatile
　9. frivolous 10. capricious
flimflam... 5. freak, hocus, trick
　6. humbug 7. caprice, swindle
　8. nonsense, trifling 9. deception,
　deceptive 11. nonsensical
flimmer... 7. flicker, glimmer
flimsy... 4. limp, rare, thin, vain, weak
　5. frail 6. feeble, paltry, sleazy,
　slimsy 7. flaccid, shallow, trivial
　9. illogical 11. superficial
　13. unsubstantial
flinch... 4. game 5. quail, start, wince,
　wonde 6. blench, cringe, falter,
　flense, recoil, shrink, swerve
fling... 3. shy 4. dart, dash, gibe,
　hurl, toss 5. cheat, dance, flock
　(sandpipers), revel, sling, sneer, throw
　6. baffle, spirit 7. cast off, sarcasm
　9. prostrate
flint... 5. chert, clint, silex 6. quartz
　7. lighter 8. hardness 9. firestone,
　skinflint
flip... 3. hop, tap 4. flap, glib, snap,
　toss 5. drink (spiced), flick, flirt,
　throw 6. fillip 8. flippant, turn over
　10. somersault 11. impertinent
flippant... 4. flip, glib, pert 5. cocky
　6. chatty, fluent 8. impudent
　10. persiflate 11. impertinent
flipper... 3. arm, fin, paw 4. hand
　5. panel 8. flapjack
flirt... 3. toy 4. dart, fike, flip, jerk,
　jilt, mash, play, toss 5. dally
　6. coquet, fillip, masher, trifle
　7. trifler 8. coquette 11. philanderer
flirtation... 5. dance 8. coquetry,
　trifling 9. love affair
flit... 3. fly 4. dart 5. glide, hover
　6. nimble 7. flicker, flutter, migrate
flitter... 3. rag 5. hover, piece
　6. tatter 7. flicker, flutter, fritter
　8. fragment
flittermouse... 3. bat
float... 4. buoy, cork, hove, lure, raft,
　ride, sail, soar, swim, waft 5. balsa,
　drift, hover, ladle 6. launch
　7. support 8. navigate, undulate
　9. transport 10. inaugurate
floating... 4. free 5. awash, loose
　6. adrift, natant 7. buoyant,
　movable, rumored 8. changing,
　drifting, shifting 9. launching,
　wandering
floating herb... 7. frogbit
　16. Hydrocharitaceae
flock... 4. bevy, fold, herd, pack, raft
　6. flight, hirsel 7. company
　9. multitude 10. assemblage,
　collection 11. aggregation
flock (pert to)...

bees .. 4. hive 5. swarm 6. colony
cattle .. 4. herd
fish .. 5. shoal
geese .. 5. skein 6. gaggle
herons .. 5. sedge
insects .. 5. swarm
like .. 6. gregal
lions .. 5. pride
partridge .. 5. covey
pheasants .. 4. nide (nid)
sandpipers .. 5. fling
walrus .. 3. pod
flocks, god of ... 3. Pan
floe ... 3. ice 4. berg
flog ... 3. cat, tan 4. beat, cane, goad,
    lash, wale, welt, whip 6. larrup,
    punish, strike, thrash 8. chastise
flogging ... 4. toco (toko) 7. beating
    8. whipping 9. thrashing
    10. punishment 12. chastisement
flood ... 3. sea 5. eagre, spate
    6. deluge, drench, excess 7. freshet,
    torrent 8. cataract, inundate, overflow
    9. cataclysm 10. oversupply
    14. superabundance
flood (pert to) ...
disaster .. 9. Galveston (1900),
    Johnstown (1889)
gate .. 4. gool, lock, slow 6. sluice
    8. penstock
lights .. 5. klieg
tidal .. 5. eagre
floor ... 4. base, pave, sill 5. chess
    (pontoon), story 6. baffle, bottom,
    defeat 7. coaming, silence
    9. overthrow 10. substratum
floor leader ... 4. whip
flora ... 6. plants 11. florilegium
flora and fauna ... 5. biota
Florence gallery ... 5. Pitti 6. Uffizi
Florentine (pert to) ...
color .. 7. scarlet
family (famed) .. 6. Medici
lily .. 6. giglio
school .. 6. Tuscan
sculptor .. 8. Ammanati, Ghiberti
florid ... 3. red 5. ruddy 6. ornate,
    rococo 7. flowery, flushed
    8. enriched, rubicund 10. figurative,
    melismatic, rhetorical 11. embellished
    13. grandiloquent
Florida ...
capital .. 11. Tallahassee
city .. 5. Miami, Tampa 7. Key West
    8. Sarasota 9. Pensacola 11. St
    Augustine (1565) 12. St Petersburg
discoverer .. 11. Ponce de Leon
    (1513)
fish .. 6. mullet, shrimp, tarpon, testar,
    tetard 8. blue crab
flower .. 13. orange blossom
Indian .. 8. Seminole
lake .. 10. Okeechobee
museum .. 10. Circus Hall (Ringling)
plant .. 7. coontie
river .. 8. Suwannee
State admission .. 13. twenty–seventh
State motto .. 22. Liberty and
    Independence
State nickname .. 8. Sunshine
swamp, park .. 10. Everglades
trail .. 7. Tamiami

flounce ... 4. flap, fold, jerk, trim
    5. caper, frill, twist 6. edging, frolic
    8. flounder, struggle
flounder ... 4. roll 6. bungle, muddle,
    welter 7. stumble 8. struggle
    9. fluctuate
flounder (fish) ... 3. dab 5. fluke
    6. plaice, turbot 8. flatfish
flour ... 4. bran, meal 6. farina, pinole,
    powder 9. middlings, pulverize
flour (pert to) ...
diabetic .. 9. aleuronat
gravy .. 4. roux
maker .. 6. miller
pudding .. 4. duff
flourish ... 4. grow, show, wave
    5. vaunt 6. flaunt, paraph (signature),
    thrive 7. display, fanfare, prosper,
    roulade 8. arpeggio, brandish,
    ornament 9. embellish, luxuriate
    11. ostentation
flout ... 4. defy, gibe, jeer, mock
    5. fleer, scoff, scout, sneer, taunt
    6. insult 8. ridicule
flow ... 3. jet, run 4. bore, flow, flux,
    gush, ooze, pour, roll, teem 5. glide,
    issue, river, spout 6. abound, afflux,
    course, stream 7. current, fluency,
    flutter 9. streaming 10. outpouring
flow (pert to) ...
along .. 4. lave
back .. 7. redound
jet .. 4. gush 5. spurt
out .. 5. exude, issue, spill
over .. 5. slosh, spill 6. deluge, engulf
    8. inundate 9. overwhelm
tide .. 3. ebb 4. flow, neap
flower ... 3. bud 4. best, blow
    5. bloom 6. unfold 7. blossom,
    develop, essence, produce
    8. choicest, ornament 11. Four
    Hundred (Society)
flower (types of) ... 3. gul (rose) 4. iris,
    ixia, lily, pink, rose 5. aster, calla,
    canna, daisy, pansy, peony, phlox,
    poppy, stock, tulip 6. azalea,
    cosmos, crocus, dahlia, lupine,
    maypop, orchid, oxalis, violet, zinnia
    7. arbutus, begonia, fuchsia, gentian,
    passion, petunia, rhodora, verbena
    8. amaranth, arethusa, camomile,
    cyclamen, daffodil, geranium,
    hepatica, hyacinth, larkspur, magnolia,
    marigold, Mariposa (lily), primrose,
    sweet pea 9. amaryllis, calendula,
    carnation, edelweiss, gladiolus,
    hollyhock, mayflower, narcissus, water
    lily 10. cornflower, delphinium,
    fleur–de–lis, marguerite, mignonette,
    nasturtium, periwinkle, poinsettia,
    snapdragon 11. forget–me–not,
    strawflower 13. chrysanthemum
    15. lily of the valley
flower (pert to) ...
arranging .. 7. ikebana
bed, garden .. 8. floretum, parterre
bloom (full) .. 8. anthesis
bud (sauce) .. 5. caper
bunch .. 4. posy 7. bouquet, corsage,
    nosegay
bursting into .. 12. efflorescent
cluster, clustered .. 4. cyme 5. umbel

8. racemose 9. glomerule
10. paniculate
largest.. 9. rafflesia (3–ft diameter)
like.. 7. anthoid
meadow–grown.. 6. pratal
part.. 4. stem 5. bract, calyx, petal,
sepal, torus 6. carpel, pistil
7. corolla, petiole 8. epicalyx,
peduncle, perianth
poet's.. 8. asphodel 9. narcissus
sacred.. 5. lotus
seed.. 5. ovule
shaped.. 7. fleuron
small.. 7. fleuret
stand.. 7. epergne
flower, shrub... 5. lilac 6. azalea,
laurel 7. dogwood, heather, jasmine,
spiraea, syringa 8. bayberry,
hawthorn 9. jessamine, mistletoe,
sagebrush 10. bitterroot
12. rhododendron
flower, vine... 8. clematis, wisteria
11. honeysuckle 12. morning glory
flower, wild... 5. bluet, daisy
6. cactus, clover, myrtle, pasque
7. anemone, cowslip 8. bluebell,
camellia 9. buttercup, goldenrod,
mayflower, sunflower 10. bluebonnet
12. lady's–slipper
flowering again... 9. remontant
flowers... 9. flowerage
flowers, goddess of... 5. Flora (Rom)
Flowery Kingdom... 5. China
flowing... 5. fluid 6. afflux, fluent
7. copious, cursive, emanant, fluxing
8. coursing, eloquent 9. streaming
10. transitive
flowing (pert to)...
from source.. 6. rising 9. emanating
together.. 9. confluent
veil.. 5. colet (anc)
well.. 6. gusher
fluctuate... 4. roll, vary, veer 5. waver
7. vibrate 8. intermit, undulate,
unsteady 9. oscillate, vacillate
10. irresolute 12. undetermined
flue... 4. barb 5. fluke 6. funnel,
tunnel 7. chimney
fluent... 4. glib 5. fluid, ready
6. facile, smooth, solute 7. copious,
elegant, flowing, gliding, verbose,
voluble 8. eloquent 9. talkative
10. loquacious
fluff... 4. down, girl, lint, yarn 5. floss
6. bungle 8. softness 9. lightness
fluffy... 4. soft 5. downy, drunk, fuzzy,
linty 8. feathery 9. forgetful
12. undependable
fluid... 3. gas, ink, oil 4. bile, milk
5. ichor, serum, water 6. fluent,
liquid, plasma, watery 7. flowing
8. floating, nonsolid
fluke... 4. fish, worm 5. blade (whale)
8. accident, flatfish, flounder
flume... 5. shoot 6. raving, sluice
7. channel, conduit
flunk... 4. fail, miss, slip 5. shirk
6. flinch 7. back out
flunky, flunkey... 4. snob 5. toady
6. cookee, lackey 7. footman,
servant 8. henchman 9. stagehand
flurry... 3. ado 4. fret, gust 5. haste,

hurry 6. bustle, squall 7. bluster,
fluster, flutter 8. snowfall
9. agitation, commotion, confusion
10. excitement
flush... 3. hot, jet 4. full, glow, gush,
rush 5. blush, cards, color, drunk,
fever, rinse, ruddy 6. drench, lavish,
redden, thrill 7. healthy, wealthy
8. abundant, affluent, prodigal,
rosiness, squarely, unbroken
10. prosperous
flushed... 3. hot, red 4. ruby
5. aglow, drunk 6. elated, florid
7. excited, fervent 8. blushing,
exultant, feverish, reddened
fluster... 4. move 5. shake 6. bustle,
excite, flurry, pother 8. distract
10. excitement 11. distraction
flute... 5. crimp, twill 6. furrow,
groove 7. magadis 9. organ stop,
wineglass 10. instrument
flute (pert to)...
bagpipe part.. 7. chanter
nose.. 3. bin 5. pungi
player.. 6. aulete 7. tooter
shrill.. 7. piccolo
stop.. 7. ventage
transverse.. 4. fife
fluting... 5. strix 7. gadroon, shading
10. decoration
flutter... 4. flap, flit, wave 5. float,
haste, hover, waver 6. bustle, ruffle
7. agitate, pitapat 8. disorder
9. agitation, confusion, palpitate
flux... 4. flow, fuse, melt 5. flood,
purge, resin, rosin, smalt, smear
6. course 7. flowing, liquefy, outflow,
solvent
fly... 3. hop 4. flee, flit, leap, melt,
soar, wave, whir, wing 5. alate,
float, glide, speed 6. aviate, elapse,
escape, insect, spring, vanish
7. avigate, avolate 8. fishhook
9. cease to be, disappear
fly (types of)... 3. bot 4. gnat
5. cadew, horse, house, midge
6. Asilus, caddis, gadfly, punkie,
tsetse 7. Diptera, nosee–um
8. dipteron, lacewing, mosquito
11. caterpillar
fly (pert to)...
African.. 4. zimb (zebub) 6. tsetse
agaric.. 8. mushroom (poisonous)
artificial.. 4. harl 5. alder, sedge
6. Cahill, claret 7. grannom
blow.. 4. eggs 5. larva
catcher.. 4. tody 6. peewee (pewit),
phoebe 8. kingbird
flying... 5. a–wing, brief, hasty, yarak
(falcon) 6. volant, waving 7. fleeing
8. fleeting, floating 9. temporary,
transient 12. aeronautical
flying (pert to)...
adder.. 9. dragonfly
boat.. 8. airplane, seaplane
9. amphibian
cat.. 5. lemur 6. marmot
Dutchman.. 5. opera 7. mariner
(fabled) 8. wanderer
fox.. 3. bat 6. kalong
island.. 6. Laputa (Gulliver's Travels)
machine.. 9. gyroplane, orthopter

foal ... 4. colt 5. filly 8. Equuleus (Astron) 9. youngling
foam ... 4. barm, boil, fume, rage, scum, suds 5. froth, spume, yeast 6. trivia 7. bubbles
foaming ... 7. spumous 8. bubbling 10. fermenting, infuriated 11. overwrought
fob ... 4. sham 5. cheat, trick 6. impose, pocket 7. palm off 8. ornament
focal point ... 8. omphalos
focus ... 6. center 8. converge, omphalos 10. adjustment 11. concentrate
fodder ... 3. hay 4. corn, feed 5. straw, vetch 6. forage, silage, stover 7. stubble 8. ensilage 9. pasturage, provender
fodder (pert to) ...
  pit .. 4. silo
  storage .. 6. haymow
  store .. 6. ensile
  stored .. 6. silage
foe ... 4. army 5. enemy, rival 8. opponent 9. ill–wisher
fog ... 4. blur, daze, haar, haze, mist, roke, smog 5. brume, cloud, vapor 6. nebula, opaque, stupor 7. aerosol, confuse, pogonip (Sierras) 9. confusion
fogdog ... 5. stubb 8. fogeater
foggy ... 3. dim 4. dull, hazy, roky 5. dense, misty, vague 6. cloudy, opaque 7. muddled, obscure 8. confused, nubilous 9. beclouded, uncertain 10. indistinct 12. muddleheaded
foghorn ... 5. siren, voice (hoarse) 6. signal
fogle ... 12. handkerchief (thieves')
fogy ... 4. dull, slow 6. dotard, fogram, Hunker 8. mossback 10. Barnburner 12. conservative, old–fashioned 16. overconservative
foible ... 5. blade (part), fault 7. failing, frailty 8. weakness 9. infirmity 12. imperfection
foil ... 4. balk 5. actor, metal, sheet, stump, sword 6. defeat, offset, outwit, stooge, thwart, weapon 7. failure, repulse 9. frustrate 10. disappoint 11. frustration
Foism ... 8. Buddhism
foist ... 4. palm 5. cheat 7. intrude 9. interpose 11. interpolate
fold ... 3. end, lap, pen, ply 4. coil (serpent), fail, furl, loop, pile, reef, ruga, sile, tuck, wrap 5. clasp, close, crimp, drape, laity, plait, pleat, plica 6. crease, dewlap, double, infold, lamina, lappet, rimple, suffix 7. entwine, envelop, plicate (fanlike) 8. collapse 9. plicature 10. go bankrupt
folded, not ... 8. eplicate
folder ... 7. booklet, leaflet 8. pamphlet 13. advertisement
foliage ... 5. spray 6. leaves, ramage 7. bouquet, leafage, umbrage 8. ornament (Arch)
folio ... 4. case, leaf 5. paper (folded)

6. folder, number (serial)
folk ... 4. race 5. tribe 6. nation, people 8. servants 9. followers, relatives, retainers 11. aggregation
folk (pert to) ...
  learned .. 7. pedants
  lore .. 6. legend 9. mythology, tradition 12. superstition
  song .. 4. fado, lied 7. art song, lullaby 9. Kunstlied, Volkslied
  tale .. 4. myth, saga 5. fable, Nancy 6. legend, mythos, mythus 7. fantasy, parable
follow ... 3. dog, tag 4. heed, heel, next, nose, obey, seek, tail 5. after, ensue, trace, trail 6. pursue, result, shadow 7. conform, draggle, emulate, imitate, observe, replace, succeed 8. come next, practice, supplant 9. persevere, supervene 10. understand
follower ... 3. fan, ist (suff), ite (suff), son 4. aper 5. lover (of) 6. copier, ensuer, votary, zealot 7. devotee, pursuer, sequent 8. adherent, believer, disciple, henchman, partisan 9. Christian, dependent, satellite 10. enthusiast 11. cuadrillero
follower of ...
  Arius .. 5. Arian
  Buddha .. 8. Buddhist
  Confucius .. 9. Confucian
  Falstaff .. 3. Nym
  Mohammed .. 6. Moslem 8. Islamite
following ... 4. next, sect 5. suant 7. ensuing, pursuit, sequent 8. trailing 9. resultant 10. subsequent, succeeding, successive 13. accompaniment
following (pert to) ...
  exact words .. 7. literal
  one's death .. 10. posthumous
  stories .. 6. sequel, series
folly ... 3. sin 5. crime 6. levity, lunacy 7. blunder, foolery, madness 8. lewdness, unwisdom 9. silliness 10. desipience, imprudence, wantonness 11. foolishness 12. indiscretion
foment ... 3. egg 4. abet, brew, spur 5. bathe, rouse 6. arouse, excite, incite 7. agitate, cherish 9. encourage, instigate
fomentation ... 6. lotion, stupes 10. excitement 11. instigation 13. encouragement
Fomoriana (Celt Myth) ... 10. sea robbers (race of)
fonda ... 3. inn 5. hotel 6. fonduk
fondle ... 3. pet 4. neck 5. ingle 6. caress, coddle, cosset, foster, pamper 7. cherish 8. blandish
fondling ... 3. pet 4. fool 5. ninny 9. caressing, simpleton 10. love–making
fondly ... 6. dearly 8. tenderly 14. affectionately
fondness ... 3. gra 4. love 6. desire, doting, liking, relish 8. appetite 9. affection 10. attachment, propensity
fond of ...

hunting .. **7.** venatic
sea .. **15.** thalassophilous
wife (overly) .. **8.** uxorious
font ... **3.** jet **4.** fons, lava **5.** stoup
  6. source, spring **7.** piscina
  8. fountain **9.** reservoir
food ... **3.** cud, pap **4.** cate, chow,
  diet, eats, fare, grub, junk (food), meat,
  tofu **5.** bread, manna, scran **6.** bulgur
  (wheat), cereal, gluten, quiche, snacks,
  Tex–Mex, viands **7.** aliment, cuisine,
  edibles, tapioca **8.** chili dog,
  fast–food, kreplach, munchies, victuals
  9. nutriment, nutrition, provender
  10. sustenance **11.** charcuterie,
  comestibles, nourishment
food (pert to) ...
animal .. **6.** forage **9.** provender
bit .. **4.** bite **6.** morsel **7.** munchie
devotee .. **7.** epicure, gourmet
digestant .. **5.** chyle
digested (partly) .. **5.** chyme
dislike of .. **9.** sitomania
  10. cibophobia
element .. **7.** protein, vitamin
fasting (Lenten) .. **9.** xerophagy
gods, the .. **6.** amrita **8.** ambrosia
heavenly .. **5.** manna
impure .. **4.** tref
provide .. **5.** cater, scaff **6.** tucker
room .. **5.** ambry **6.** pantry, spence
  7. butlery, pantler
fool ... **3.** ass, toy **4.** butt, dolt, dupe,
  jerk, nerd, nizy, raca (Bib), simp
  5. clown, idiot, moron, ninny
  6. dotard, jester, noodle, trifle, turkey
  7. buffoon, deceive, dingbat, fathead
  9. ignoramus, simpleton
foolhardy ... **4.** rash **7.** Icarian
  8. reckless **11.** adventurous
fool hen ... **6.** grouse
foolish ... **3.** mad **4.** daft, raca, rash,
  zany **5.** inane, inept, silly **6.** absurd,
  harish **5.** palty **6.** simple, stupid,
  unwise **7.** asinine, fatuous, idiotic,
  puerile, witless **9.** brainless, desipient,
  imprudent, ludicrous, senseless
  10. illadvised, irrational, ridiculous
  12. preposterous **13.** insignificant
foolish fancy ... **7.** chimera (chimaera)
foolishness ... **5.** folly **6.** levity
  9. absurdity, stupidity **10.** triviality
fool's bauble ... **7.** marotte
fool's gold ... **6.** pyrite
foot ... **3.** pad **6.** paw pes (pref)
  4. base, hoof, inch (part), sole, step,
  walk **5.** sum up, tread **6.** reckon
  7. residue **9.** calculate, extremity
foot (pert to) ...
bone .. **6.** tarsus **10.** metatarsus
care of .. **8.** pedicure, podiatry
  9. chiropody **11.** chiropodist
lever .. **5.** pedal **7.** treadle
like .. **8.** pediform
measure .. **4.** inch
part .. **3.** toe **4.** arch, heel, sole
prefix .. **4.** pedi
race course (anc) .. **7.** diaulos
reference to .. **5.** pedal, podal
rest .. **4.** rail **7.** cricket, hassock,

ottoman, support **8.** footrail
  9. footstool
sole .. **7.** plantar
unstressed part (Pros) .. **5.** arsis
foot, feet (metric) ... **4.** iamb, mora,
  unit **6.** dactyl, dipody, iambus
  7. anapest, dimeter, pyrrhic, spondee,
  tripody **8.** trimeter **9.** hexameter
  10. heptameter, pentameter
football terms ... **3.** end **4.** trap
  5. guard, slant **6.** center, safety,
  tackle **7.** flanker, lineman **8.** goalpost,
  receiver **9.** touchdown
  10. linebacker, yard marker
  11. quarterback
footed ... **5.** biped **7.** bipedal,
  megapod (large), metered
footing ... **4.** lace, rank **5.** basis,
  dance, tread **6.** status **7.** support
  8. foothold, progress, standing
  9. condition **11.** calculation
footman ... **6.** varlet, walker **7.** servant
  9. attendant **10.** pedestrian
footprint mold ... **7.** moulage
footway ... **7.** catwalk (Naut)
fop ... **3.** nob **4.** Adon, buck, dude
  5. dandy, puppy, sport, swell
  6. Adonis, masher **7.** coxcomb,
  gallant **9.** exquisite, pretender
  12. boulevardier
foppish ... **6.** dapper, spruce **7.** finical,
  foplike **8.** dandyish **9.** conceited,
  dandified
for ... **2.** to **3.** pro **5.** spite
  7. because, instead **8.** behalf of
  9. intending **10.** indicating
  11. preparation
for (pert to) ...
each .. **3.** per
example .. **2.** as, eg **4.** vide
  13. exempli gratia
fear .. **4.** lest
most part .. **6.** mostly **7.** chiefly,
  usually **9.** generally
nothing .. **6.** gratis, naught
  9. lagniappe (lagnappe)
this reason .. **4.** ergo **5.** hence
forage ... **4.** food, mast, raid **5.** spoil
  6. browse, ravage **7.** plunder
  9. pasturage
foramen ... **4.** pore **7.** opening, orifice,
  passage **8.** fenestra
foray ... **4.** raid **6.** ravage, sortie
  7. pillage **9.** incursion
forbear ... **4.** lose, shun **5.** avoid
  6. desist, endure **7.** abstain, decline,
  refrain **8.** part with **9.** be patient
forbearance ... **5.** mercy **6.** disuse,
  lenity **8.** leniency, mildness, patience
  9. tolerance **10.** abstinence,
  temperance **11.** forgiveness,
  placability
forbid ... **3.** ban **4.** deny, tabu, veto
  5. debar, taboo **6.** disbar, hinder,
  impede, oppose **7.** exclude, inhibit,
  prevent **8.** disallow, preclude, prohibit
  9. interdict, proscribe
  11. countermand
forbiddance ... **3.** ban **4.** veto
  11. unallowable **12.** illiberality,

interdiction, proscription
forbidden city ... 5. Lhasa (Tibet),
Pekin (walled, now Peiping)
forbidden food (Bib) ... 4. tref
8. terephah
forbidding ... 4. grim, ugly 5. plain,
stern 6. fierce, odious 9. offensive,
revolting 10. prevention, unpleasant
11. displeasing, prohibitive
force ... 3. vim, vis 4. dint, make, urge
5. drive, impel, power, press, repel,
staff, vigor 6. coerce, compel, effect,
energy, extort, hasten, strain
7. impetus, meaning 8. eloquent,
momentum, pressure, validity,
violence 9. constrain, influence,
puissance 10. compulsion, constraint
11. necessitate
force (pert to) ...
alleged .. 2. od
armed .. 4. army 5. posse
by seizure .. 5. usurp
down .. 7. detrude
full .. 5. amain
substance .. 8. catalyst
unit .. 4. dyne 5. staff, tonal
7. poundal
forced ... 7. labored 9. reluctant,
unwilling 10. artificial, compulsory,
farfetched 11. constrained
forced feeding ... 6. gavage
forceful ... 5. valid 6. mighty, potent,
strong 7. dynamic 8. eloquent,
emphatic, vigorous 9. effective,
energetic 10. compulsory
forces ... 4. army 5. armed 6. troops
forcible ... 6. cogent, mighty, potent
7. violent, weighty 8. eloquent,
emphatic, positive, puissant
9. energetic 10. compulsory,
impressive 11. influential
forcible entry ... 10. effraction
forciform ... 6. forked 7. furcate
11. forficulate 14. scissors–shaped
ford ... 4. wade 5. cross 6. stream
fore ... 3. way 5. front, prior, track
6. former 7. journey
forebear ... 4. sire 5. elder 6. parent
8. ancestor 10. antecedent,
forefather, progenitor
forebode ... 5. augur 7. betoken,
portend, predict, presage 8. foretell
15. prognostication
foreboding ... 6. augury 8. croaking,
sinister 11. pessimistic, presagement
12. apprehension, presentiment
forecast ... 4. bode, plan 6. scheme
7. foresee, fortune, predict
8. foretell, prophecy 9. calculate,
foresight, foretoken 10. foreordain,
prediction 12. predetermine
forecaster ... 4. seer 5. vates 6. oracle
7. diviner, palmist, prophet
8. dopester, presager 10. astrologer,
soothsayer 11. Nostradamus
13. meteorologist 14. prognosticator
foreclose ... 5. debar 6. hinder
7. prevent, shut out 8. preclude
10. dispossess
foredoom ... 4. doom 7. predict
12. predestinate

foredoomed ... 3. fey 5. fatal
8. accursed
forefather ... 4. sire 5. elder 6. parent
8. ancestor, forebear 10. progenitor
forefinger ... 5. index
foregather ... 4. meet 7. convene
8. assemble 9. encounter
forego, forgo ... 6. pass by 7. neglect,
precede 8. renounce
foregoing ... 4. past 5. above
6. former, prefix 7. leading
10. antecedent
foregone ... 4. past 8. previous
11. predestined, preordained,
preresolved 13. predetermined
foregone conclusion ... 9. certainty
forehead ... 4. brow 8. calvaria,
glabella, sinciput 9. assurance
10. effrontery
forehead, divination by ...
11. metopomancy
forehead, frontal ... 7. metopic
foreign ... 4. xeno (comb form)
5. alien, fremd 6. exotic, remote
7. distant, outside (of country),
strange 8. excluded 9. extrinsic,
peregrine, unrelated 10. extraneous,
outlandish 11. incongruous
12. adventitious
foreign (pert to) ...
accent .. 4. burr 6. brogue, patois
7. dialect
crystals (Geol) .. 7. epigene
disease .. 7. ecdemic
insertion .. 13. interpolation
place .. 6. forane
quarter .. 4. Para 5. Latin 6. French
7. enclave
service residence .. 9. consulate
foreigner ... 5. alien 6. gringo
8. outsider, stranger 9. outlander,
uitlander 10. tramontane
12. ultramontane
foreland ... 8. headland 10. promontory
forelock ... 4. bang 7. cowlick, fetlock
8. linchpin 9. cotter pin, fastening
(armor)
foreman ... 4. boss 5. chief 6. leader
7. juryman, overman 10. supervisor
14. superintendent
foremost ... 5. chief, first, front
7. leading, supreme 8. headmost
13. most important
forensic ... 10. rhetorical
13. argumentative
foreordain ... 7. destine 9. predicate,
preordain 12. foreordinate,
predestinate, predetermine
forerun ... 6. herald 7. advance,
prelude, presage 8. announce,
antecede 9. forestall, introduce,
prefigure 10. anticipate, foreshadow
forerunner ... 4. omen, sign 6. augury,
herald 8. ancestor 9. harbinger,
messenger, precursor 10. forefather,
foreganger, progenitor, prognostic
11. predecessor
foreshadow ... 6. shadow (beforehand)
7. presage 9. adumbrate, prefigure
foresight ... 8. sagacity 9. prevision
10. precaution, prediction,
prescience, prevoyance, providence

11. omniscience 13. foreknowledge

forest... 4. wold, wood 5. grove, woods 6. jungle, timber 8. woodland 9. greenwood 10. timberland, wilderness

forest (pert to)...
deity.. 3. Pan 7. Aegipan
fire.. 5. crown, stand 6. ground 7. surface
fire—finding instrument.. 7. alidade
glade.. 6. camass (camas, cammas)
love of, lover of.. 9. nemophile, nemophily
regarding.. 6. sylvan 7. nemoral
tilled.. 7. thwaite
warden.. 6. ranger

forestall... 6. hinder 7. exclude, head off, prevent 9. intercept 10. anticipate, monopolize

foretell... 4. bode, spae 5. augur, insee 7. portend, predict, presage 8. forebode, forecast, prophesy 10. vaticinate 13. prognosticate

foretelling... 6. augury 7. fatidic 9. fatidical, prophetic 10. vaticinant

forethought... 8. prepense, prudence 9. foresight, provident 10. deliberate, precaution 12. aforethought, anticipation 13. premeditation

foretoken... 4. omen 7. presage 8. foreshow, indicant 10. presignify 13. preindication, prognosticate

foretooth... 5. biter 6. cutter 7. incisor 9. milk tooth

forever... 3. ake (Maori), aye (ay) 4. olam, ever 6. always, eterne 7. endless 8. infinity 9. continual, perpetual 10. constantly, invariably 11. ceaselessly, continually, incessantly, perpetually, unceasingly 12. interminably, unchangeably 13. everlastingly

forewarning... 4. omen 7. caution, portent 9. informing 10. admonition, foreboding

foreword... 5. proem 7. preface, prelude 8. exordium, preamble, prologue 12. introduction

forfeit... 4. fine, lose, loss 5. forgo, mulct 6. forego, pledge 7. deodand, penalty

forfeiture... 4. fine, loss 5. dédit, mulct 7. penalty 10. amercement

forfend... 5. avert 6. forbid 7. prevent, protect 8. preserve, prohibit

forfex... 6. shears

forgather... 4. meet 7. consort, convene 8. assemble 9. encounter 10. fraternize

forge... 4. coin, form, mint 5. feign 6. create, smithy, stithy, swinge 7. falsify, imitate 8. bloomery, smithery 11. counterfeit

forgery... 4. sham 7. fiction 9. falsehood, invention 11. counterfeit, fabrication 13. falsification

forget... 4. omit 5. lapse, remit 6. slight 7. neglect 9. disregard 11. disremember

forgetfulness... 5. Lethe (Myth), lotus (legend) 7. amnesia, amnesty

8. Manassah, oblivion 12. carelessness, heedlessness 13. obliviousness

forgive... 5. remit, spare 6. acquit, excuse, pardon 7. condone

forgiveness... 6. pardon 9. remission 10. absolution 11. condonation, exoneration, magnanimity

forgiving... 6. humane 8. merciful, placable 9. remissive 11. magnanimous

forgo... 4. quit 5. leave, waive 6. give up, resign 7. abstain, forbear, forfeit, forsake, neglect, refrain 8. overlook, renounce 9. do without 10. relinquish

forhoo... 7. abandon, despise

fork... 4. tine 5. prong 6. expend, pay out 7. dilemma, diverge 10. divaricate, divergence, headstream 11. bifurcation

fork (pert to)...
garden.. 5. graip
pickle.. 13. runcible spoon
table.. 5. salad 6. dinner, oyster 7. dessert 8. ice—cream

forked... 5. bifid 6. horned, ramous 7. divided, furcate 8. branched, crotched 9. ambiguous, equivocal 10. bifurcated, branchlike

forlorn... 4. reft 5. alone 6. abject, bereft 8. deserted, desolate, forsaken, helpless, pitiable 9. abandoned, destitute, miserable 10. friendless 12. disconsolate

form... 4. body, cast, idea, mold, rite 5. build, guise, model, shape 6. beauty, create, figure, invent, ritual 7. compose, contour, formula, outline, pattern, profile, species, variety 8. ceremony, conceive, document 9. establish, formality 10. appearance 11. arrangement 12. conformation 13. configuration, questionnaire 15. conventionality

form (pert to)...
bust.. 6. taille
chainlike.. 8. catenate
deceptive.. 5. ghost 7. specter 8. phantasm
display.. 4. rack
good.. 4. chic 6. fettle
government.. 6. polity
hollow.. 5. shell
into fabric.. 4. knit, spin 5. weave
primitive.. 9. prototype
spiral.. 5. helix
suffix.. 5. shape 10. resembling

formal... 4. prim 5. exact, stiff 6. solemn 7. orderly, outward, precise, regular, stilted 8. affected, apparent, starched 9. formative 10. ceremonial, methodical 11. pharisaical, ritualistic, superficial 12. conventional

formal introduction... 5. debut 12. presentation

formalities... 5. rites 9. etiquette 10. ceremonies

formal warning... 5. alarm 6. caveat 12. caveat emptor

format... 4. size 5. shape, style

formation... 4. form 5. order
  9. structure 11. arrangement,
  composition 12. construction
formation (pert to)...
  chain (twisted).. 9. torquated
  geologic.. 7. terrain, terrane
  military.. 4. line 5. herse 7. echelon
  sand.. 4. dene, dune
formed... 4. made 5. built 7. created,
  decided, matured, settled 8. arranged
  9. fashioned, organized
  11. constructed
formed (pert to)...
  by law.. 9. corporate
  by lips.. 6. labial
  mountain foot.. 8. piedmont
  on earth's surface.. 7. epigene
  plates (two).. 11. bilamellate
formed into...
  chain.. 8. catenate 9. torquated
  fabric.. 4. spun 5. woven 7. knitted
  mass (hard).. 4. iced 5. caked
  6. frozen 9. congealed
  mosaic.. 9. tessellar 11. tessellated
former... 2. ex 3. old 4. erst, late,
  once, past 5. front, prior 6. passed,
  whilom 7. ancient, earlier 8. previous
  9. foregoing, preceding
  10. antecedent
former days... 3. eld, old 4. yore
formerly... 3. nee 4. erst, once, then
  6. before, whilom 7. one-time
  8. sometime 9. aforetime, erstwhile
  10. heretofore, previously
formicary... 7. anthill 8. ant's nest
formicid... 3. ant 5. emmet
  7. Formica
formidable... 7. fearful 8. alarming,
  dreadful, menacing, terrible
  9. difficult 11. redoubtable,
  threatening
formless... 5. arupa 7. anidian, chaotic
  9. amorphous, shapeless
  13. indeterminate
Formosa, Taiwan...
  capital.. 6. Taipei
  city.. 6. Tainan 7. Hualien, Keelung
  9. Kaohsiung
  group.. 6. Penghu (64 Isls)
  island.. 5. Matsu 6. Quemoy
formula... 3. law 4. form, rule
  5. axiom, creed, lurry, maxim, model
  6. method, recipe, ritual
  12. prescription
forsake... 4. deny, quit, shun 5. avoid,
  leave 6. depart, desert, refuse, reject
  7. abandon 8. renounce, withdraw
  9. surrender
forsaken... 4. lorn 6. vacant 7. forlorn
  8. deserted, lovelorn, rejected
  9. abandoned
forspeak... 5. curse 6. forbid
  7. asperse, bewitch 8. renounce
  10. relinquish
fort... 5. redan, tower 6. abatis,
  castle, escarp, glacis (bank of)
  7. bastion, bulwark, castlet
  8. bastille, fastness, fortress
  10. stronghold 13. fortification,
  propugnaculum
Fort (Fr Ind War)... 9. Necessity
forth... 3. out 4. away 6. abroad,

onward 7. forward, outward
forthright... 5. ahead 7. frankly
  8. forwards 9. downright
  11. immediately, straightway
  13. straightforth
forthwith... 3. now 6. pronto
  8. promptly 9. summarily
  11. immediately, straightway
fortification... 4. wall 5. redan
  6. abatis 7. bastion, citadel, defense,
  parados, ravelin, redoubt 8. barbette
  (part), fortress 10. stronghold
  13. corroboration, strengthening
fortify... 3. arm, man 4. gird 5. add
  to, spike, stank 6. defend, secure
  7. confirm, refresh 8. embattle
  10. adulterate (drink), invigorate,
  strengthen, vitaminize 11. corroborate
fortitude... 6. virtue 7. bravery,
  courage 8. strength 9. endurance
  10. resolution 12. resoluteness
  14. impregnability
fortress... see *fort*
fortuitous... 3. hap 6. chance
  10. accidental 12. unexpectedly
fortunate... 5. happy, lucky 6. timely
  7. favored 10. auspicious,
  prosperous, successful
  12. providential
fortune... 3. hap, lot 4. doom, fate,
  luck 6. chance, estate, riches, wealth
  7. destiny, success 8. accident
  10. prosperity 13. circumstances
fortune (pert to)...
  gypsy.. 4. bahi
  ill.. 9. mischance
  planet (Astrol).. 5. Venus 7. Jupiter
  teller.. 4. seer 5. sibyl, Tyche
  6. oracle 7. spaeman
forward... 2. on, to 3. aid 4. abet,
  bold, fore, help, pert, send, ship,
  vain 5. ahead, along, eager, front,
  impel, ready, relay, saucy, ultra
  6. active, bright, hasten, onward
  7. deliver, earnest, extreme, further,
  radical, willing 8. advanced,
  immodest, impudent, transmit
  9. audacious, encourage
  10. precocious 11. progressive
  12. presumptuous
forward moving (Zool)... 5. proal
  (digestion) 11. mastication
fosse, foss... 3. pit 4. moat 5. canal,
  ditch, fossa, grave 6. cavity, trench
  10. depression
fossil, fossils... 5. relic, stone
  7. antique, remains
fossil (pert to)...
  egg.. 7. ovulite
  footprint.. 7. ichnite
  resin.. 5. amber
  shell.. 6. dolite 8. ammonite
  site.. 8. Badlands (Dakota, Nebraska)
  study of.. 12. paleontology
  toothlike.. 8. conodont
  worm track.. 7. nereite
foster... 4. rear 5. breed, nurse
  7. cherish, gratify, indulge, promote
  9. cultivate
fosterage... 7. nurture
  11. development
foster child... 4. dalt 5. norry (nurry)

7. stepson 8. nursling
12. stepdaughter
fought... see *fight*
foul... 3. bad 4. olid, ugly 5. dirty,
fetid, grimy, nasty, reeky, spoil, sully
6. defame, filthy, malign, odious,
putrid, rotten, thwart, unfair
7. abusive, confuse, noisome,
obscene, profane, unclean
8. entangle, indecent, infamous,
shameful, stagnant, stinking
9. dishonest, obnoxious
10. complicate, malodorous,
scurrilous 11. contaminate,
ill–smelling, unfavorable
12. inauspicious, unpropitious
foul play... 6. murder, unfair (play)
7. perfidy 8. violence 9. deception,
treachery 10. unfairness
found... 3. fix 4. base, cast 5. endow,
set up 6. attach, create 9. establish,
institute, originate
foundation... 3. bed 4. base, plot, sill
5. basal, basis 6. legacy, riprap
7. bedding, charity, premise, support
8. cosmetic, creation, donation,
pedestal 9. placement
11. corporation 13. justification
found by chance (thing)...
11. serendipity
founded on...
base.. 10. predicated
evidence.. 10. evidential
experience.. 7. empiric 9. empirical
imagination.. 7. Utopian
founder... 4. fail, fall, sink 6. author
7. capsize, creator, stumble
8. miscarry 9. break down, organizer
10. originator
foundling... 3. oaf 4. waif 5. child
(unclaimed) 6. orphan 8. derelict,
nursling
fountain... 3. jet, spa 4. font, head,
well 6. spring 9. reservoir
11. scuttlebutt (ship's)
12. fountainhead
fountain (pert to)...
god of.. 4. Fons
Muse (Gr).. 8. Aganippe
nymph.. 5. naiad 6. Egeria
of Lions.. 8. Alhambra (Granada, Sp)
four (pert to)...
bits.. 7. quarter (silver)
Books.. 8. Classics (Chin)
footed.. 8. tetrapod
genii, of Amenti.. 13. Horus' children
group.. 6. tetrad
Hundred.. 5. elect, elite 7. society
letters, word of.. 9. tetragram
seas.. 13. Great Britain's
senses (Bib).. 15. interpretations
four–flusher... 5. cheat, fraud
7. bluffer 8. impostor 9. pretender
fourth (pert to)...
Caliph.. 3. Ali
century martyr.. 8. St Blaise
estate.. 5. press 10. newspapers
part.. 6. fardel 7. quarter
stomach (cow).. 8. abomasum
fowl... 3. hen 6. bantam, Gallus
7. Blue Hen, broiler, chicken,
Dorking, leghorn, Minorca, poultry,

rooster, seafowl 8. pheasant
9. guinea hen, waterfowl
11. chanticleer
fox... 3. cub, tod 4. stag 5. vixen
fox (pert to)...
African.. 4. asse
Asian.. 5. adive 6. corsac
female.. 5. vixen
genus.. 6. Vulpes
hedge (hunter's).. 4. oxer
foot.. 3. pad
Indian.. 10. Algonquian
Russian.. 6. corsac 7. karagan
foxglove... 9. digitalis
foxy... 3. sly 6. artful, crafty
7. cunning
foyer... 5. lobby 8. anteroom, entrance
9. greenroom
fracas... 3. row 5. brawl, melee,
set–to 6. uproar 7. quarrel
9. commotion 11. disturbance
fraction... 3. bit 4. part 5. piece,
scrap 6. sector 7. element, ruction
8. division, fragment 9. commotion
fractious... 4. ugly 5. cross 6. unruly
7. peevish, waspish 8. perverse,
snappish 9. irritable 10. ill–humored
11. disobedient
fracture... 4. rend 5. break, cleft,
crack 6. breach, injury 7. rupture
fragile... 4. weak 5. brash, frail
6. frough (obs), infirm, slight
7. brittle 8. delicate, slattery
9. frangible
fragment... 3. bit, ort 4. chip, grot,
part, snip 5. groat, piece, relic,
scrap, shard, sherd, shred, torso (art)
6. morsel, sippet 7. flinder
8. fraction
fragments... 3. ana 6. fardel, groats,
rubble 8. buttings, excerpts, flinders
10. miscellany 11. smithereens
fragrance... 4. odor 5. aroma, elemi,
smell 7. incense, perfume
9. redolence
fragrant... 4. nard 5. balmy, olent,
spicy, sweet 7. odorous 8. aromatic,
redolent 9. ambrosial 11. odoriferous
12. sweet–scented
13. sweet–smelling
frail... 3. thin, weak 5. woman
6. basket (fig), feeble, sickly, slimsy
7. brittle, fragile 8. strumpet,
unchaste 10. weak–willed
12. destructible
frailty... 5. fault 6. defect 7. failing
8. thinness, weakness 9. fragility,
infirmity 12. imperfection
frame... 4. body, make, plan, rack,
sess, sill 5. build, easel, grate,
herse, knape 6. abacus, border,
charge (falsely), direct, tenter
7. carcass, chassis, cresset (torch),
fashion, prepare, setting, taboret
8. conceive, skeleton 9. construct
10. prearrange
framework... 4. rack, sill 5. cadre,
shell 6. cradle 7. trestle 8. skeleton
11. scaffolding
France... see also *French*
anc name.. 4. Gaul 6. Gallia
Bay.. 6. Biscay

Botanical Gardens.. 16. Jardin des Plantes
capital.. 5. Paris
city.. 4. Nice 5. Lyons 7. LeHavre 8. Bordeaux, Toulouse 9. Marseille 10. Strasbourg
dread of.. 11. Gallophobia
island.. 6. Comoro (Afr), Tahiti 7. Corsica, Réunion 10. Guadeloupe (Leeward), Martinique (Windward) 12. New Caledonia
lover of.. 10. Gallophile
mountain.. 4. Alps, Jura 5. Pelat 8. Pyrenees 9. Mont Blanc 11. Pic Montcalm
port.. 4. Caen 5. Brest, Havre 6. Calais, Toulon 8. Bordeaux 9. Dunkerque (Dunkirk)
resort.. 3. Pau 5. Vichy 6. Cannes, Menton (Mentone) 7. Riviera 11. Aix–les–Bains (anc)
river.. 3. Lys 4. Yser 5. Aisne, Eiser, Loire, Meuse, Rhône, Seine
Southern.. 4. Midi
Verdun battle site.. 4. Vaux
franchise... 4. vote 5. right 6. patent 7. freedom, license 8. immunity, suffrage 9. exemption
frank... 4. free, mail, open 5. blunt, naive, plain 6. candid, direct, honest 7. artless, liberal, sincere 8. generous 9. ingenuous, outspoken 10. unreserved 11. frankfurter 15. straightforward, unsophisticated
frankincense... 4. thus 8. gum resin, olibanum 9. fragrance
Frankish (pert to)...
dynasty.. 11. Carolingian, Merovingian
king.. 5. Pepin 6. Clovis
law.. 5. Salic
site.. 4. Gaul
tribe (anc).. 6. Salian
Franklin, Benjamin... 11. Poor Richard
frantic... 3. mad 4. mang 5. moved, rabid 7. furious 8. frenetic, frenzied 9. delirious, desperate, turbulent 10. distracted, distraught 11. overwrought
frappé... 3. ice 5. chill 6. freeze 7. dessert, mixture (sweet) 8. beverage
fraternal... 4. kind 5. order, twins 7. society 8. friendly 9. brotherly
fraud... 4. fake, sham, wile 5. cheat, covin, craft, guile 6. deceit, ringer 7. defraud, roguery 8. artifice, cozenage, impostor, subtlety, swindler, trickery 9. deception, imposture, stratagem 10. imposition 13. circumvention
fraudulence... 9. improbity 10. subreption
fraudulent... 4. fake, wily 5. snide 6. crafty, quacky 7. cunning, knavish 8. cheating, guileful, spurious 9. deceitful, deceiving, deceptive, designing, dishonest, insidious 10. fallacious 11. counterfeit, treacherous
fraught... 4. lade, load 5. cargo, equip, laden 6. burden, filled

7. freight 9. freighted, transport
fray... 4. fret (cloth), wear 5. broil, dread, melee, panic, ravel 6. affray, combat, fright, hassle, terror, tumult 7. contest, frazzle, ruction 9. commotion 12. apprehension
freak... 4. flam, lune, whim 5. fancy, prank, sport 6. streak, vagary 7. caprice, checker, crochet, monster 9. eccentric, variegate 11. monstrosity 12. whimsicality
freakish... 7. curious 9. eccentric, fantastic, whimsical 10. capricious, changeable
freck... 4. bold, hale 5. eager, frack, lusty, ready, stout 6. strong 7. forward 8. desirous
freckle... 4. mark, spot 7. blemish, ephelis, lentigo, speckle 10. ferntickle
free... 3. rid 4. easy, open 5. clear, frank, loose 6. acquit, candid, exempt, gratis, immune, vacant 7. absolve, inexact, manumit, not busy, release, relieve, unbound 8. liberate 9. extricate, footloose, voluntary 10. autonomous, gratuitous, unconfined, unhampered 11. emancipated 12. uncontrolled, unrestrained, unrestricted
free (pert to)...
bacteria.. 7. aseptic, sterile
difficulty.. 9. extricate
doubt.. 7. resolve
flesh (dietary).. 6. maigre
knots.. 7. enodate, unravel
reproach.. 9. blameless
slavery.. 7. manumit 10. emancipate
suspicion.. 5. clear, purge 6. acquit 7. absolve 9. exculpate, exonerate
sweetness.. 3. sec
freebooter... 5. rover 6. pirate 8. pillager 9. plunderer 10. filibuster
freed... 3. rid 6. loosed, spared, untied 8. released 9. delivered, liberated 10. manumitted 11. emancipated
freedom... 6. candor 7. leisure, liberty, license 8. latitude 9. exemption, privilege 11. manumission 12. emancipation, independence
freedom (pert to)...
abused.. 7. liberty (excess), license
from doubt.. 9. assurance, certitude
from sepsis.. 7. asepsis
Freedom Our Rock (motto)... 7. Tammany (1789)
free enterprise... 6. policy 8. commerce 10. capitalism 15. noninterference
freely... 6. gratis 7. largely, readily 9. bountiful, copiously, liberally, willingly 10. abundantly, generously 11. bounteously, plenteously, plentifully, voluntarily 12. gratuitously
freeze... 3. ice 5. be–ice, chill 6. steeve 7. congeal, terrify 8. preserve, solidify 9. stabilize 11. anesthetize, refrigerate
freezing, science of... 10. cyrogenics
freight... 4. load, ship 5. cargo, laden, train 6. burden, charge, lading 7. fraught, rattler 8. shipment

9. transport 14. transportation
freight boat... 5. barge 9. freighter
freit, freet... 4. omen 5. charm
fremd (obs)... 5. alien 7. foreign,
   hostile 9. unrelated
French (people)...
   artist, painter.. 4. Doré 5. Corot,
     David, Monet 6. Gervex, Greuze,
     Renoir 7. Gauguin, Lemoine, Matisse
     8. Daubigny, Rousseau
   author.. 4. Hugo, Loti, Zola
     5. Dumas, Renan, Verne (Jules)
     6. Balzac, Proust
   caricaturist.. 7. Gavarni
   chemist.. 7. Gautier, Holbach, Pasteur
   composer.. 4. Lalo 5. Bizet, Ravel
     6. Gounod 7. Debussy
   conqueror (anc).. 6. Clovis
   crusader.. 7. Godfrey (of Bouillon)
   dramatist.. 6. Favart 8. Quinault
   dynasty.. 5. Caput 6. Valois
   Foreign Legion creator, 1831..
     8. Philippe (Louis)
   impressionist.. 5. Monet 8. Pissarro
   marshal.. 3. Ney 4. Foch, Niel, Saxe
     5. Murat
   naturalist.. 8. Audebert
   navigator.. 9. Freycinet
   pantomimist.. 7. Pierrot
   patron saint.. 5. Denis 6. Martin
   philosopher.. 5. Bayle, Camus
     6. Pascal 7. Abelard 8. Rousseau
     9. Descartes
   physician.. 7. Laveran
   physicist.. 5. Binet 6. Ampere
   poet.. 6. Villon 7. Gilbert, Mistral
     8. Rousseau 9. Deschamps
   radical.. 7. Jacobin
   scientist.. 5. Curie 7. Pasteur
   sculptor.. 4. Etex 5. Barye, Rodin
     6. Gerome, Millet
   statesman.. 4. Coty 5. Laine, Laval,
     Morny 6. Carnot 7. Briande, Herriot
     8. DeGaulle
   therapist.. 4. Coué
French (pert to)...
   academic rank.. 6. agrégé
   Academy.. 12. The Institute
   and.. 2. et
   annuity.. 5. rente
   anthem.. 12. Marseillaise
   article.. 2. la, le, un 3. les, une
   beast.. 4. bête
   calender (Rev).. 6. Nivose 7. Ventose
   champagne.. 2. Ay
   cheese.. 4. Brie 6. Chevre
     9. Camembert
   chorus (male).. 7. orpheon
   coach.. 6. fiacre
   coat–of–arms.. 10. fleur–de–lis
   coffee (black).. 8. café noir
   company (Bus).. 3. cie
   crown (gold coin).. 3. ecu
   cult (art).. 7. Dadaism
   daisy.. 10. marguerite
   dance.. 3. bal 5. gavot 6. cancan
   decree, edict.. 5. arrêt
   dialect.. 6. patois
   dugout.. 4. abri
   father.. 4. père
   fortification.. 7. parados
   fugitive.. 6. émigré

   God.. 4. Dieu
   hairdresser.. 7. friseur
   hat.. 5. beret 7. chapeau
   here.. 3. ici
   inn.. 6. hostel
   lace.. 5. Cluny
   language (Provence).. 9. Provençal
   laugh.. 3. ris
   liquor.. 8. absinthe (banned 1915)
   mask.. 4. loup
   morning.. 5. matin
   mountain peak.. 3. pic
   narcissus.. 10. polyanthus
   native.. 8. Gallican
   nursemaid.. 5. bonne
   ornaments (set of).. 6. parure
   outcast.. 5. Agote, Cagot 6. pariah
   pancake.. 5. crepe
   parliament.. 5. Sénat
   pastry.. 7. dariole, galette
   plane.. 5. avion
   poem, poetry.. 3. dit 6. aubade,
     rondel
   police.. 6. Sûreté 8. gendarme
   political club.. 7. Jacobin
   porcelain.. 6. Sèvres 7. Limoges
   priest.. 4. abbe, père
   racecourse.. 7. Auteuil
   restaurant.. 4. café 6. bistro
   sauce.. 8. ravigote 9. allemande
   school.. 5. école, lycée
   school of painting.. 8. Barbizon
   securities.. 6. rentes
   smoking room.. 9. estaminet
   soldier.. 5. poilu 6. Zouave
   stable.. 6. écurie
   stock exchange.. 6. Bourse
   storm.. 5. orage
   street.. 3. rue
   summer.. 3. été
   theater.. 16. Comédie Française
   verse.. 3. lai 4. alba 6. rondel
     7. ballade, virelay
   wall.. 3. mur
   water.. 3. eau
   wind.. 7. mistral
   wine.. 5. Medoc 6. Barsac, brandy,
     claret, Cognac, masdeu 8. Bordeaux,
     Burgundy, sauterne 10. Beaujolais
   world.. 5. monde
Frenchman... 4. frog, Gaul 6. froggy,
   Picard (of Picardy) 8. Parisian
   9. frogeater
Frenchy... 6. Gallic
frenzied... 4. amok 5. rabid
   7. enraged, frantic, madding
   8. maddened 9. turbulent
   11. overwrought
frenzy... 3. mad 5. furor, mania
   7. frantic, madness 8. delirium
   9. agitation 10. excitement,
   turbulence
frequent... 3. oft 5. haunt, often,
   usual 6. common 7. current
   8. familiar, habitual, intimate (with)
   9. recurrent 10. persistent
frequenter... 7. habitué, visitor
   8. attender
frère... 5. friar 7. brother
fresh... 3. new 4. good, lush 5. relay,
   ruddy, sound, sweet 6. florid, lively,
   strong, unused 7. healthy, unfaded,

untried 8. impudent, original
10. additional, refreshing, unimpaired
13. inexperienced
freshen . . . 4. cool 5. renew 6. revive
7. refresh, sweeten
freshet . . . 4. gush 5. flood, spate
6. stream 7. outflow, torrent
10. inundation (sudden)
freshman . . . 5. frosh 6. novice
7. student
freshness . . . 7. newness, novelty
8. verdancy 9. impudence
11. originality
freshwater fish . . . 2. id (ide) 4. chub,
dace, inid (porpoise) 6. anabas
7. herring 8. drumfish
fret . . . 3. eat, nag, orp, rub, vex
4. fray, fume, gall, gnaw, stew
5. adorn, annoy, chafe, grate, tease,
worry 6. abrade, grieve, harass,
plague, strait 7. agitate, consume,
disturb, network, roughen
8. diminish, irritate, ornament
fretful . . . 5. angry 6. repine 7. peevish,
pettish 8. captious, petulant
9. impatient, irascible, irritable,
plaintive, querulous 10. ill–humored,
ill–natured
friable . . . 5. crisp, frail, mealy, short
7. brittle 8. fragible
friar . . . 3. fra 4. fish (small), monk
5. abbot, Minor 6. lister (obs)
7. brother 8. cenobite, Minorite,
Teresian (anc) 9. Carmelite,
Dominican 10. Franciscan
11. Augustinian
friction . . . 7. erasure, rubbing
8. clashing 9. attrition, disaccord
10. resistance 12. disagreement
13. counteraction
friend . . . 3. ami, pal 4. ally, amie,
chum, kith, sect 5. amigo, crony
7. comrade 8. promoter
9. associate, attendant, companion,
supporter 10. benefactor, sweetheart,
well–wisher
Friend . . . 6. Quaker
friendless . . . 5. alone 7. forlorn
8. helpless 9. destitute (friends)
friendly . . . 3. sib 4. kind 7. affable
8. amicable, homelike, sociable
9. favorable 10. harmonious,
hospitable 11. comfortable
Friendly Islands . . . 5. Tonga
friendship . . . 4. kelt 5. amity
7. harmony 8. good will, relation
9. affection, right hand
10. attachment 12. friendliness
frieze . . . 4. band (sculptured) 5. adorn,
chase 6. taenia (Doric) 8. ornament,
trimming 10. decoration, embroidery
Frigga, Norse Myth (pert to) . . .
goddess . . 3. sky
maid . . 5. Fulla
named for . . 6. Friday
wife of . . 4. Odin
fright . . . 3. awe 4. fear, ogre 5. alarm,
panic, scare, shock 6. terror
7. eyesore 13. consternation
frighten . . . 3. cow 5. alarm, appal,
scare 7. startle, terrify 10. intimidate
frightened . . . 3. rad 5. eerie, timid

6. afraid 8. skittish
frightful . . . 5. awful, great 6. horrid
7. hideous 8. alarming, dreadful,
horrible, shocking, terrible, terrific
11. frightening
frightfulness . . . 13. atrociousness
15. Schrecklichkeit
frigid . . . 3. icy 4. cold 5. stiff
6. formal 8. freezing, impotent,
reserved
frijol, frijole . . . 4. bean
frill . . . 4. purl 5. jabot, ruche (rouche)
6. border, edging, ruffle 8. furbelow
9. frillback (pigeon) 11. superfluity
fringe . . . 4. lace, loma, tuft 5. thrum
6. border, edging, margin 8. ciliella,
trimming
frisk . . . 4. skip 5. brisk, caper 6. frolic,
gambol, lively, search 7. disport,
rejoice
frisky . . . 3. gay 6. lively 7. playful
8. sportive 10. frolicsome
frisson . . . 5. chill 6. quiver, shiver, thrill
7. shudder 10. excitement
frivolous . . . 5. giddy, petty 6. fickle,
slight 7. fatuous, trivial 9. worthless
13. shallow–witted
frock . . . 4. gown, wrap 5. dress, tunic
6. jersey, kirtle (anc), mantle
7. garment, soutane
frog . . . 3. pad (horse's) 4. Rana, toad
5. Anura 6. peeper 7. croaker,
paddock, tadpole 8. Amphibia,
pollywog 9. Batrachia, Frenchman,
Salientia 10. hoarseness
froglike . . . 6. ranine
frogman . . . 5. diver 6. seaman
7. swimmer 9. Frenchman
frog pond . . . 8. ranarium
frolic . . . 3. fun 4. lark, ogle, play,
ramp, romp 5. binge, caper, frisk,
prank, spree, trick 6. gambol, shindy
7. disport, marlock, shindig, wassail
8. carousal
frolicsome . . . 3. gay 5. merry 6. frisky
7. playful, waggish 8. sportive
from . . . 2. at, de (pref), of 3. apo
(pref) 4. away 5. above, out of
6. source 8. away from, downward
from (pert to) . . .
beginning to end . . 4. over 7. through
egg to apple . . 16. ab ovo usque ad
mala
head to foot . . 7. cap–a–pie
slang . . 10. soup to nuts 11. stem to
stern
front . . . 3. bow, van 4. face, fore
5. aface, afore, blind (false), fore
(obs) 6. before, façade 7. obverse
8. confront, mediator 9. forefront
10. appearance, figurehead
11. affectation 12. intermediary
frontier defense . . . 11. arcifinious
frontiersman . . . 5. Boone 6. Carson
(Kit)
frost . . . 3. ice, mat 4. cold, foam, rime
5. chill 6. freeze, whiten 7. failure
8. severity (manner)
14. unfriendliness
frosty . . . 3. icy 4. cold, gray, rimy
5. chill, hoary, white 6. frigid
8. freezing, inimical 10. unfriendly

froth ... 4. foam, scum, suds 5. spume, yeast 6. lather 7. bubbles
frothy ... 5. foamy, light, sudsy 7. spumous 8. sillabub
frow ... 4. froe (tool), wife 5. woman 6. maenad 8. slattern
froward ... 5. cross 7. peevish, wayward 8. perverse, petulant, scolding, shrewish, untoward 9. obstinate 10. refractory, unyielding 11. disobedient 12. ungovernable
frowl ... 9. guillemot
frown ... 5. gloom, lower, scowl 6. glower
frowsey, frowzy ... 5. musty 7. unkempt 8. slovenly 9. offensive 10. discordant, disordered
frozen ... 4. cold 5. frore (anc), froze, gelid, glacé 6. chilly, mousse 7. chilled 9. congealed, terrified, unfeeling, unmovable 10. unyielding 11. coldhearted 12. refrigerated
frugal ... 5. chary 6. meager, saving 7. careful, sparing, thrifty 9. provident 10. economical, unwasteful 11. inexpensive 12. parsimonious
frugality ... 6. thrift 7. economy 9. parsimony
fruit (types of) ... 3. fig 4. lime, pear, plum, pome 5. apple, berry, drupe, grape, guava, lemon, mango, melon, olive, peach, pomum 6. banana, cherry, orange, papaya, pawpaw, pomelo 7. apricot, azarole, genipap, tangelo 8. shaddock 9. persimmon, tangerine 10. grapefruit, watermelon 11. pomegranate
fruit ... 4. diet, food 5. yield, young 7. benefit, product 9. offspring, outgrowth, posterity 11. consequence
fruit (pert to) ...
aggregate .. 7. etaerio
astringent .. 4. sloe
basket .. 6. pottle
buttercup .. 6. achene 8. achenium
class .. 6. simple 9. aggregate 10. collective
cordial .. 7. ratafia (ratafee)
decay .. 4. blet
dried .. 6. raisin 7. apricot
drink .. 3. ade 6. nectar
Goddess .. 6. Pomona
gourd .. 4. pepo 7. chayote
grapefruit .. 6. pomelo
imperfect .. 6. nubbin
jelly substance .. 6. pectin
Jove's .. 9. persimmon
part .. 7. epicarp 8. mesocarp, pericarp 9. sarcocarp
preserve .. 7. compote 9. marmalade
pulpy .. 3. uva
rose .. 3. hip
study of .. 9. carpology
tree .. 4. date, nuts 5. regma 6. camato, samara (winged)
tropical .. 3. fig 4. date 5. guava, mango, papaw (pawpaw) 6. papaya
fruitful ... 7. fertile, uberous 8. abundant, prolific 9. plenteous
fruitfulness, goddess of ... 7. Demeter

fruitless ... 4. vain 6. barren 7. sterile, useless 10. profitless 11. ineffectual 12. unprofitable, unsuccessful
frump ... 3. vex 4. mock, snub 5. crone, flout, shrew 6. gossip, insult 7. provoke 8. irritate
frustrate ... 4. balk, bilk, foil 5. block, cross, elude 6. baffle, blight, defeat, outwit, thwart 7. nullify 8. confound 9. checkmate 10. circumvent, disappoint, disconcert
frustrater ... 7. marplot 8. thwarter
frustration ... 4. balk 6. defeat, fiasco 13. circumvention 14. disappointment 15. disillusionment
fry ... 4. cook 5. brood (fish), group, saute, young 7. stir-fry 9. offspring
frying pan ... 6. spider 7. skillet
fubsy ... 5. plump, short 6. chubby
fuddle ... 4. bout (drinking) 5. drink (strong), spree 6. muddle, tipple 7. confuse 9. confusion, inebriate
fudge ... 4. fake 5. candy, cheat 6. bungle, humbug 7. trump up 8. nonsense 9. makeshift 10. substitute 11. counterfeit
Fuegian ... 3. Ona 5. tribe 6. Indian, Yakgan 8. Alikuluf 14. Tierra del Fuego (pert to)
fuel ... 3. gas, log, oil 4. coal, coke, peat 6. diesel, elding 7. gasohol, nuclear, synfuel 8. gasoline 9. petroleum 11. combustible
fugie ... 4. cock (nonfighter) 6. coward
fugient ... 7. fleeing 8. retiring
fugitive ... 5. exile 6. outlaw, roving 7. fleeing, refugee, roaming, runaway 8. fleeting, unstable, vagabond, volatile 9. fugacious, strolling, uncertain 10. evanescent
fugue ... 5. theme, tonal 7. amnesia, stretto (stretta) 9. psychosis, ricercare
fulcrum ... 4. axis, bait, prop 5. pivot, scale (fish), thole 7. support
fulfill ... 4. meet 6. finish, redeem 7. execute, satisfy 8. complete 10. accomplish, effectuate
fulfillment ... 8. fruition 9. execution, flowering 10. completion 11. performance 14. accomplishment
full ... 3. fat 4. fill 5. drunk, sated 6. entire, filled, rotund 7. perfect, plenary, replete, satiety 8. abundant, adequate, complete, occupied, resonant, satiated, thorough 9. satisfied
full (pert to) ...
blooded .. 6. virile 8. rubicund 12. thoroughbred
bloom .. 8. anthesis, blooming, maturity
control .. 7. mastery 10. domination
force .. 5. amain
house .. 3. SRO
full of ...
cracks .. 6. rimose
hollows .. 8. lacunose
love .. 7. amative, amatory
meaning .. 5. pithy 10. meaningful
openings (tiny) .. 6. porous
sand .. 7. arenose 8. sabulous
substance .. 5. meaty

suffix.. 3. ose
thorns.. 6. briary
vigor.. 5. lusty
fulness, fullness... 4. much
  7. orotund, pleroma, satiety, surfeit
  9. abundance, greatness, plenitude,
  repletion, resonance 10. perfection
  12. completeness
fulsome... 3. bad, fat 4. base, foul,
  full 5. nasty, plump, suave
  7. copious, overfed 8. abundant
  9. offensive, overgrown, repulsive
  10. disgusting
Fulton's Folly... 8. Clermont
fumble... 5. grope 6. bungle, huddle,
  mumble 7. confuse
fume... 4. odor, rage, rant, reek
  5. anger, smoke, steam, vapor
  8. outburst 10. excitement,
  exhalation
fun... 4. gell, jest, joke, play 5. chaff,
  sport 9. amusement, merriment
function... 3. act, use 4. duty, rite,
  role, work 5. party 6. office
  7. calling, operate, purpose, service
  8. ceremony, province
  10. providence
function (pert to)...
  math.. 4. sine 6. cosine
  mind.. 8. ideation
  social.. 3. tea
functional... 8. official 9. operative
  11. ceremonious, utilitarian
fund... 5. basis, money 6. bottom,
  supply 7. capital, provide, revenue
  10. foundation, groundwork
fundamental... 4. tone 5. basal, basic,
  vital 7. basilar, organic, primary,
  radical 8. original, rudiment
  9. elemental, essential, principle
  10. elementary
Fundamental Orders (US Hist)...
  8. document (1639) 12. Constitution
  (first, 1639 Conn)
funds... 5. means 6. assets, moneys
  8. finances
funeral... 5. rites 6. burial 8. exequies
  9. obsequies 10. procession
funeral (pert to)...
  bell.. 5. knell
  ceremony.. 6. exequy
  hymn, song.. 5. dirge, éloge, elogy
  7. requiem 8. threnody
  oration, poem.. 5. elegy
  pile.. 4. pyre
  procession.. 6. exequy 7. cortege
  vase.. 3. urn
funereal... 3. sad 4. dark 6. dismal,
  solemn 8. exequial, mournful
  9. dirgelike
fungi... 5. rusts, Uredo 6. mildew
  7. Boletus
fungoid... 6. fungal, fungus
fungus... 4. bunt, mold, rust, smut
  5. ergot, morel, uredo 6. agaric,
  mildew 7. aminita, blewits, boletus,
  geaster, truffle 8. mushroom, puffball
  9. toadstool
fungus, edible... 5. morel 7. truffle
  8. mushroom
funguslike... 6. agaric
funk... 4. kick, odor, rage 5. panic,

smell (bad), smoke, spark 6. flinch,
  fright, shrink, terror 8. frighten
  9. cowardice, touchwood
funnel... 4. cone, flue, pipe, tube
  6. hopper 7. channel
funnel–shaped... 8. choanoid
funny... 3. odd 5. comic, droll, queer,
  witty 7. comical, rowboat (Eng),
  strange 8. humorous 9. eccentric,
  laughable
fur... 3. fox 4. mink, pelt, seal, vair
  5. coypu, fitch, genet, otter, sable,
  skunk 6. badger, ermine, martin,
  nutria 7. miniver (anc) 8. squirrel
  10. chinchilla
fur (pert to)...
  collective.. 6. peltry
  cover.. 4. pelt 6. pelage
  garment.. 4. robe 5. stole 6. tippet
  7. pelisse
  tippet.. 8. palatine
furbish... 3. rub 4. vamp 5. clean,
  scour 6. polish 7. burnish, touch up
  8. renovate 9. embellish
Furies... 5. Dirae 6. Alecto, ghosts,
  Semnae 7. Erinyes (Erinys), Magaera,
  spirits (avenging) 9. Eumenides,
  Tisiphone
Furies, The Three... 6. Alecto
  7. Magaera 9. Tisiphone
furious... 5. angry, hasty 6. fierce
  7. frantic, violent 8. frenzied,
  vehement 9. impetuous, turbulent
  10. boisterous, passionate,
  tumultuous 11. overwrought
furl... 4. roll, wrap 6. bundle, inroll
furlough... 5. leave 14. leave of
  absence
furnace... 4. etna, kiln, oven 5. forge,
  stove 7. caldron, reactor, rotator,
  smelter
furnish... 3. fit 4. bear, give, lend
  5. adorn, cater, endow, equip, indue
  6. afford, fit out, render, supply
  7. appoint, provide
furnishing... 7. fitting 8. fixtures,
  ornament 9. adornment, apparatus,
  furniture, provision 10. enrichment
furnish with...
  funds.. 5. endow
  meals.. 5. board, cater
  Mil equipment.. 8. accoutre
  tapestry.. 5. arras
  wings.. 3. imp
furniture... 5. goods 6. Empire, graith,
  outfit 7. Regency (Regence)
  8. hardware, Sheraton, supplies
  9. equipment 10. decoration,
  housewares 11. Chippendale,
  Renaissance
furor... 4. fury, rage 5. anger, craze
  6. fervor, flurry, frenzy, furore, tumult
  7. madness 10. excitement,
  turbulence
furrow... 3. rut 4. plow 6. groove,
  gutter, trench 7. channel, wrinkle
furrowed... 5. rutty 6. rivose
  7. grooved
further... 3. aid, and, new, yet
  4. abet, more 7. advance, develop,
  improve, promote, remoter, thither
  10. additional

furtherance ... 3. aid 4. help 6. relief, succor 8. progress 9. promotion 11. advancement, development

furtherer ... 7. abettor 8. promoter

furthermore ... 3. and, yet 4. then 5. again 7. au reste, besides 8. moreover 10. in addition 12. additionally

furtive ... 3. sly 4. wary 6. covert, secret, sneaky, stolen 8. skulking, stealthy 9. deceitful 11. clandestine

fury ... 3. ire 4. rage 5. anger, wrath 6. frenzy 7. madness 8. violence 10. excitement, turbulence 13. desperateness

Fury ... 6. Erinys, Spirit (avenging) 7. Atropos

furze ... 4. Ulex, whin 5. gorse, shrub

fuse ... 4. flux, frit (partly), melt 5. blend, smelt, unite 6. anneal, mingle, solder 7. combine, liquefy 8. dissolve 9. detonator

fusee ... 5. flair, torch 6. signal

fusion ... 5. alloy, blend, union 7. melting, mixture, nuclear 8. fluidity

9. coalition

fuss ... 3. ado 4. spat, to–do 5. busle 6. bother, bustle, pother, tumult 7. bombast, dispute, quarrel, trouble 8. brouhaha 9. confusion

fussy ... 7. finical 8. overnice 10. fastidious, meticulous

fustian ... 4. rant 5. cloth, tumid 7. bombast, pompous 8. claptrap, inflated 9. bombastic, worthless

fustic ... 3. dye 5. amber, morin 7. dyewood

futile ... 4. idle, vain 6. otiose 7. trivial 8. hopeless 11. ineffectual

futility ... 8. nugacity 10. invalidity 11. uselessness 12. bootlessness

future ... 3. yet 4. to be 5. later, still, tense 6. fiancé 8. expected, intended 9. hereafter 11. prospective

fuzzy ... 5. downy, hairy 6. fluffy 7. blurred, frizzly 9. imperfect 10. indistinct

fyke ... 3. net 6. bag net

fylfot ... 8. swastika 9. gammadion

G

G ... 4. tone (scale) 6. letter (7th)

gab ... 3. lie 4. mock, talk 5. boast, mouth, prate, scoff, taste 6. tongue 7. chatter, deceive 9. utterance

gabardine ... 6. cotton, woolen

gabble ... 4. chat 6. babble, jabber, mumble 7. chatter 8. nonsense

gabelle ... 3. tax 5. likin (imports) 6. excise, impost

gaberdine ... 4. gown 5. frock 6. mantle 7. garment (loose) 8. covering, pinafore 9. gabardine

gable ... 4. roof (part) 7. aileron (half) 8. pediment

gablock ... 4. gaff, spur 5. spear 6. gaffle 7. crowbar 8. gavelock

Gabon, Africa ...
capital .. 10. Libreville

Gabriel (pert to) ...
astrology .. 10. moon spirit
New Test .. 6. herald 11. good tidings
Old Test .. 5. angel
tradition .. 9. archangel (one of seven), messenger

gaby ... 4. fool 9. simpleton

gad ... 3. bar, God (oath), rod 4. goad, roam, rove, whip 5. ingot, spear, staff 6. billet, chisel, wander 7. on the go, run wild, traipse (trapes) 8. gadabout 9. gallivant

Gad (pert to) ...
Bib .. 7. prophet
deity (Bib) .. 7. Fortune
father .. 5. Jacob
tribe .. 6. Gadite, Israel (one of seven)

gadabout ... 3. gad 6. roving 7. dogcart, gadding, on the go

Gaddang, Gaddan ... 7. Malayan 8. language (Indonesia)

gadfly ... 6. botfly, insect 8. horsefly

gadget ... 6. device, jigger 7. gimmick 8. gimcrack 11. contrivance, thingumajig

Gadsden Purchase (1853) ... 5. tract 7. Arizona 9. New Mexico

gadwall ... 4. duck

Gaea, Gaia ... 12. Earth Goddess

Gael ... 4. Celt, Kelt, Manx, Scot 10. Highlander

Gaelic (pert to) ...
for John .. 3. Ian
hero .. 6. Ossian
language .. 4. Erse
native .. 4. Erse 5. Irish 6. Celtic, Keltic, Scotch
pagan god .. 5. Dagda (harpist)
sea god .. 3. Ler
spirit .. 7. banshee
warriors .. 7. Fenians

gaff ... 4. hoax, hook, scam, spar, spur, talk 5. fraud, spear, trick 6. deceit, fleece, gamble 7. chatter, prating 8. trickery 9. spearhead

gaffer ... 4. hick, rube 6. old man 11. electrician (TV)

gag ... 4. hoax, joke 5. choke, retch 7. closure, prevent, shackle 8. obstruct, one–liner, restrain, silencer 9. imposture 10. instrument 13. interpolation

gage, gauge... 4. rule, test 5. scale
6. device, pledge 7. measure
8. capacity, defiance, diameter
(firearm), mortgage, security
9. challenge 11. measurement

gaggle... 5. flock (geese), group
(women) 6. cackle

gaiety, gayety... 4. gala, glee, show
5. mirth 6. finery 7. jollity
8. vivacity 9. festivity, merriment,
showiness 10. liveliness
12. colorfulness, conviviality

gain... 3. get, net, win 4. earn, pelf,
reap 5. booty, clear, lucre, reach
6. attain, come by, obtain, profit,
secure, trover 7. acquire, benefit,
procure, realize 8. addition, arrive at,
increase 9. advantage 11. acquisition
12. accumulation 13. amplification

gainsay... 4. deny 6. forbid, impugn,
oppose, refute 7. dispute
10. contradict, controvert

gait... 3. run, way 4. lope, pace, trip,
trot, walk 5. amble, order, strut, tread
6. canter, gallop 8. slowness, velocity

gaiter... 4. boot, spat 5. strad
6. puttee 7. legging 8. overshoe
11. galligaskin

gala... 4. fete, pomp 6. festal, fiesta,
gaiety 8. festival 9. festivity
11. celebration

Galago... 5. lemur

Galatea... 7. heroine 8. sea nymph
9. sculpture (Pygmalion)
11. shepherdess

galaxy... 6. throng 8. Milky Way
10. assemblage 11. celebrities

gale... 4. gust, wind 5. storm
8. outburst 9. hurricane

galea... 6. helmet

galeate... 12. helmet-shaped

Galen (Gr)... 9. physician

Galilean (pert to)...
 astronomer.. 7. Galileo
 province.. 9. Palestine
 religion.. 9. Christian
 town.. 4. Cana 8. Tiberias

gall... 3. vex 4. bile, fret 5. annoy,
chafe, grate, spite 6. bitter, harass,
rancor 8. irritate 9. impudence,
secretion, virulence

gallant... 4. hero 5. dandy, lover,
noble, spark, swain 6. escort, suitor
7. stately 8. cavalier, cicisbeo
9. attentive, courteous
10. chivalrous, courageous

gallantry... 7. bravery, courage,
display 8. courtesy 9. courtship
11. intrepidity

galleon... 6. vessel (sailing)

gallery... 3. poy 4. hall 5. salon
6. dedans, loggia, museum
7. passage, veranda 8. audience,
corridor, platform 9. promenade
10. ambulatory 11. observatory

galley... 4. boat, tray 6. vessel
7. caboose, caravel (caravelle),
dromond, kitchen 8. cookroom

galley, Roman...
 one-bank oared.. 7. unireme
 two-bank oared.. 6. bireme
 three-bank oared.. 7. trireme

 six-bank oared.. 7. hexeris
 slave.. 5. rower 6. drudge

Gallic... 4. Gaul 6. French 7. Frenchy

Gallic chariot... 5. essed

gallimaufry... 4. hash, olio, stew
6. medley, ragout 9. potpourri
10. hodgepodge

gallipot... 6. vessel (Medit) 8. druggist

gallo... 7. rooster 12. fighting cock

gallop... 3. run 4. lope, ride 6. canter
7. tantivy

gallopade... 5. dance, galop 6. curvet

gam... 3. leg 4. herd 5. visit
6. school

Gambia, Africa...
 capital.. 6. Banjul

gambit... 4. move 7. comment,
opening (chess) 8. maneuver
9. launching 10. concession

gamble... 3. bet 4. dice, game, risk
5. stake, wager 6. chance, exacta,
hazard, plunge 8. perfecta
9. speculate, totalizer 10. parimutuel,
superfecta 11. daily double,
uncertainty

gambler... 5. shill 7. sharper

gambol... 3. hop 5. bound, caper,
prank 6. cavort, curvet, frolic

Gambrinus (King)... 6. brewer (1st)

game... 4. lark, play, prey 5. brave,
dodge, prank, sport 6. frolic, gamble,
gritty, plucky, quarry 7. contest,
pastime 8. resolute 9. amusement,
diversion 10. courageous

game, ball... 4. golf, polo, pool
5. rugby 6. hockey, pelota, soccer,
squash, tennis 7. cricket, croquet
8. baseball, football 11. racquetball

game, beans... 6. fan-tan
8. beanbags

game, board... 4. keno 5. bingo,
chess, lotto 7. pachisi (parchesi)
8. checkers, cribbage, Monopoly
10. backgammon

game, card... 3. gin, pam 4. bank,
faro, skat 5. pitch, poker, rummy,
whist 6. bridge, écarté, flinch, hearts
7. bezique, canasta, cassino, old
maid, seven-up

game, club... 4. golf 6. hockey
7. cricket

game, court... 6. pelota, squash,
tennis 7. jai alai 9. badminton

game, parlor... 5. jacks 7. marbles
8. charades, dominoes
11. tiddlywinks

game plan... 6. scheme 8. strategy

game, ring... 6. quoits

gamin... 3. tad 4. serf 6. urchin
7. mudlark 10. street Arab

gamut... 5. orbit, range 6. extent
7. compass

gamy... 4. game 7. lustful 8. sporting
12. high-flavored

gander... 5. goose 6. stroll
9. simpleton

Gandhi (Hind)... 6. Indira, leader
7. Mahatma (Mohandus)

gang... 3. mob, set 4. band, crew,
pack, team, walk (cattle) 5. group,
horde, sheet (Print), shift 6. clique
7. company 9. pasturage

gangling ... 5. lanky 9. spindling
gangrene ... 5. decay 6. slough
8. necrosis 9. sphacelus
13. mortification
gangster ... 4. thug 5. thief 6. bandit
7. mobster 8. criminal, hireling
9. racketeer
gannet ... 4. ibis, Sula 5. booby,
goose, solan 6. gander
gap ... 3. col 4. hole, pass 5. break,
chasm, cleft, fault, meuse, shard,
space, split 6. breach, hiatus,
lacuna, lacune, ravine 7. opening
gaping ... 5. agape 6. chappy
7. ringent, yawning 9. expectant
garb ... 5. array, dress, habit, style
6. clothe 7. apparel, costume,
fashion, raiment, uniform 8. clothing
10. appearance, habiliment
garbed ... 4. clad 7. attired, dressed,
habited
garble ... 5. alloy 6. mangle 7. distort,
falsify, pervert 8. mutilate
12. misinterpret, misrepresent,
sophisticate
garden ... 3. bed 4. yard 5. hardy,
patch 6. jardin, verger 7. topiary
8. outfield 9. arboretum, cultivate,
enclosure, herbarium
garden (pert to) ...
Berlin .. 10. Tiergarten
Bible .. 4. Eden
city .. 4. Kent 6. Sicily 7. Chicago
8. Touraine
colony .. 5. Natal
Colorado .. 9. of the Gods
Kansas .. 9. of the West
kind of .. 5. truck 8. kaleyard
9. botanical 10. zoological
State .. 9. New Jersey
garden implement ... 3. hoe 4. fork,
rake 5. graip, mower 6. scythe,
sickle, trowel, weeder
Garfield's death site ... 7. Elberon
(NJ)
Gargantua (pert to) ...
character .. 4. King (Rabelais romance)
son .. 10. Pantagruel (giant)
gargantuan ... 4. huge 7. titanic
garish ... 5. gaudy, showy 7. flighty,
glaring 8. dazzling
garland ... 3. lei 6. anadem, circle,
corona, fillet, rosary, trophy, wreath
7. chaplet, coronal, festoon
8. headband 9. anthology
11. compilation
garlic ... 4. herb, moly 5. clove
6. ramson
garment ... 4. cape, coat, gown, robe,
suit, vest, wrap 5. cloak, dress,
frock, shift, simar, smock, stole, tunic
6. coatee, duster 7. pelisse, raiment,
surcoat, topcoat 8. overcoat,
vestment
garment (pert to) ...
African .. 6. kaross
ancient .. 5. burel
Arab .. 3. aba
clerical .. 3. alb 5. amice 6. chimer
7. cassock, zimarra 8. surplice
cover .. 5. apron 8. overalls, pinafore
9. coveralls

Eskimo .. 5. parka
Jewish .. 5. ephod
knight's .. 6. tabard
patchwork .. 5. cento
thin .. 8. gossamer
garner ... 4. reap 5. amass, store
6. gather 7. collect 10. accumulate
garnet ... 3. gem, red 5. color
6. aplome, pyrope 7. olivine (green)
8. cinnamon (stone), essonite
(yellow), melanite (black)
9. almandine (almandite, dark red),
uvarovite (green)
garnish ... 4. trim 5. adorn 6. attach,
bedeck 7. fetters 8. decorate,
ornament
garnishment ... 4. lien 7. summons
8. ornament 10. attachment,
decoration
garret ... 4. loft 5. attic 6. turret
8. cockloft 10. watchtower
garrot ... 9. goldeneye (duck)
10. tourniquet
garrote, garrotte ... 8. strangle
9. execution 10. throttling
13. strangulation
garrulous ... 5. gabby, wordy 6. chatty
7. diffuse 9. talkative 10. loquacious
gas ... 4. brag, talk 5. vapor 6. poison
7. chatter 8. gasoline, nonsense
10. anesthesia, asphyxiate, illuminant
11. anesthetize
gas ... 3. air 4. neon 5. argon, ether,
ozone, radon, xenon 6. arsine,
butane, ethane, helium, ketene,
nebula (luminous), oxygen 7. methane
8. chlorine, cyanogen, etherion,
hydrogen, nitrogen 9. butadiene
gascon ... 7. boaster 8. braggart
11. braggadocio 12. swashbuckler
gasconade ... 4. brag 5. boast
7. bluster, bravado 11. fanfaronade,
rodomontade
gaseous ... 4. smog, thin 5. smoke
7. tenuous 8. vaporous
13. unsubstantial
gash ... 3. cut 5. cleft, notch, sever,
slash 6. furrow, gossip, injury, tattle
8. incision
gasp ... 3. say 4. pant, yawn 5. utter
7. breathe
gasping ... 5. agasp 7. panting
gastropod ... 4. slug 5. Harpa, Murex,
Oliva, snail, whelk 6. Nerita, volute
7. abalone, mollusk 8. sea snail
gat ... 3. gun, rod 7. channel, passage
8. revolver
gate ... 3. dar 4. door, hole, pass
5. start (racing), toran, valve
6. defile, portal 7. barrier, opening,
postern 8. Lion–Gate 9. floodgate,
turnstile 10. Needle's Eye
(Jerusalem), portcullis
gateau ... 4. cake
gather ... 4. bale, brew, fold, meet,
reap 5. amass, glean, pleat, rally,
shirr 6. bundle, deduce, garner,
muster, pucker 7. acquire, collect,
compile, convene, convoke, harvest,
procure, suppose 8. assemble
10. accumulate
gatherer, collector of ...

coins.. 11. numismatist
money.. 5. miser
news.. 8. reporter 10. journalist
stamps.. 11. philatelist
gathering... 3. sum 4. stag 5. crowd,
party, troop 6. galaxy, smoker
7. abscess, meeting 8. swelling
10. assemblage, harvesting
11. contraction 12. accumulation,
congregation 14. conglomeration
gaucho... 6. cowboy (pampas)
8. herdsman, horseman
gaucho weapon... 4. bola
gaud... 4. jest, joke 5. adorn, fraud,
paint, sport, trick 6. finery, flashy,
gewgaw 7. trinket 8. artifice,
ornament
gaudy... 4. fine, loud 5. cheap, feast,
showy 6. flashy, flimsy, garish,
tawdry, tinsel 7. glaring, trinket
9. flaunting 11. pretentious
12. meretricious, ostentatious
13. overdeveloped
gaufre... 4. iron (waffle) 6. waffle
gauge, gage... 4. norm, rate, rule, size
5. judge, scale, value 6. assess
7. measure 8. estimate
gauge (pert to)...
airplane.. 10. tachometer
distance.. 10. micrometer
miles.. 8. odometer
pointer.. 3. arm
rain.. 8. udometer
velocity.. 11. speedometer
wind.. 10. anemometer
Gaul... 5. Aedui 6. France, Gallia
9. Frenchman
Gauls... 4. Remi 5. Celts, Cymry
gaunt... 4. bony, lank, lean, thin, ugly
5. spare 7. haggard 8. desolate
gauntlet... 4. cuff 5. armor (part),
glove 7. bandage
gaur... 5. gayal 7. buffalo
gauss... 4. unit (Elec)
Gauss... 13. mathematician
gauze... 4. haze, leno 5. crape, lisse,
marli (marly) 6. barege, filter, tissue
8. dressing
gauze film on wine... 8. beeswing
gavage... 7. feeding
gave... see *give*
Gavia... 4. loon
gavial... 11. crocodilian
gaw... 4. gape 5. drain 6. trench
gawk... 4. dolt, gowk, left, lout
5. booby, stare 9. simpleton
gawky... 6. clumsy, cuckoo, stupid
7. awkward, foolish 8. clownish
gay... 4. airy, glad 5. drunk, gaudy,
jolly, merry, riant, showy 6. blithe,
cheery, jovial, joyful, joyous, lively
7. dashing, festive, gleeful
8. cheerful, colorful, rory–tory,
sportive 9. convivial, sprightly,
vivacious 10. frolicsome, profligate
12. lighthearted
gay time... 4. lark 5. spree
8. jamboree
gazabo, gazebo... 4. cony 6. rabbit,
turret 7. balcony, blunder, whopper
11. summerhouse
gaze... 3. con, eye 4. gape, look,

moon, peer, pore, scan 5. glare,
gloat, stare 6. glower, regard
gazelle... 3. ahu, goa 4. admi, cora,
dama, kudu, mohr, oryx 5. ariel,
brown, korin 7. chikara (4–horn),
corinne, dibatag 8. antelope
9. springbok
gazette... 7. journal, publish
8. announce 9. newspaper
15. Arkansas Gazette (1819)
gazetteer... 7. newsman 9. newspaper
10. dictionary
gear... 3. cam, rig 5. equip, goods,
tools, wheel 6. things 7. baggage,
conform, harness, rigging 8. adjust
to, clothing, cogwheel, garments
9. equipment, mechanism, trappings,
vestments 10. appliances, implements
gecko... 6. lizard 7. tarente
geese... 5. brant, quink, solan
geese (pert to)...
fat.. 6. axunge
flock.. 4. raft 6. gaggle
genus.. 4. Chen 5. Anser 6. Branta
Gekko... 6. lizard
gelatin, gelatine... 4. agar, food, jell
5. jelly 6. collin 7. protein
8. agar–agar
gelid... 3. icy 4. cold 6. frozen
gem... 4. jade, onyx, opal, ruby, sard,
type 5. agate, beryl, jewel, pearl,
stone, topaz 6. garnet, ligure, spinel,
zircon 7. cat's–eye, diamond,
emerald, jacinth 8. amethyst,
hawk's–eye, sapphire 9. carnelian,
moonstone 10. aquamarine
11. alexandrite, lapis lazuli 12. star
sapphire
gem (pert to)...
artificial.. 5. paste
carver.. 8. lapidary
Egyptian.. 6. scarab
flaw.. 8. gendarme
food.. 6. muffin
imperfect.. 5. loupe
semiprecious.. 5. cameo 8. intaglio
six rays.. 7. asteria
surface.. 5. bezel, facet
weight.. 5. carat
gemel... 4. bars (Her), twin 6. paired
7. coupled, doubled
gemsbok... 4. goat, oryx 7. chamois
Gem State... 5. Idaho
gendarme... 4. blue, flaw (gem)
5. guard 6. police 7. soldier, trooper
9. policeman 10. cavalryman
gender... 3. sex 5. breed, genus
7. grammar (term) 8. engender
genealogy... 4. tree 5. order (of
descent) 6. family 7. account,
history, lineage, peerage, progeny
8. pedigree, register 9. offspring
genealogy of the gods... 8. theogony
gener... 8. son–in–law
general... 5. gross, usual, vague,
whole 6. common, public 7. officer
8. catholic, communal 9. extensive,
prevalent, universal, well–known
10. encyclical, indefinite
11. approximate
general (pert to)...
agreement.. 5. chief, court

aspect .. 6. facies
chief .. 6. Führer, Il Duce 9. president
    10. Grand Mogul 13. Generalissimo
court .. 5. Synod
direction .. 5. tenor, trend 6. course
favor .. 7. popular 10. popularity
feature .. 5. motif
group .. 8. ensemble
orders .. 7. routine
rule .. 5. canon
summary .. 8. synopsis
type .. 7. average
generalize ... 5. widen 6. extend,
    reason, spread 7. broaden
    12. universalize
General Sherman (pert to) ...
    Civil War march .. 15. Atlanta to the
    Sea
    giant trees .. 8. sequoias
    tree .. 10. eucalyptus
generate ... 5. beget, breed, cause
    6. create 7. develop, produce
    8. engender 9. originate, procreate,
    propagate
generation ... 3. age 7. descent
    8. lifetime 9. epigonous (later),
    formation, genealogy 10. production
    11. abiogenesis, procreation
generosity ... 10. liberality
    11. hospitality, magnanimity,
    munificence
generous ... 4. free 5. large 7. liberal
    8. tolerant 9. indulgent, plentiful,
    unstinted 10. hospitable
    11. magnanimous
genesis ... 4. Book 5. birth 6. origin
    (of races) 8. nascency 9. beginning,
    ethnology, etymology, inception
    10. generation
genet ... 3. fur 5. civet
genethliac ... 5. stars (influence)
    9. birthdays
Geneva Cross ... 8. Red Cross
genial ... 4. warm 5. bland 6. jovial,
    kindly 7. amiable, festive, nuptial
    8. cheerful, friendly, pleasant
    9. expansive 10. enlivening
geniculate ... 5. kneel
genie ... 4. jinn 6. genius
genius ... 5. deity, jinni 6. talent
    7. ability, prodigy 9. endowment
    (supreme) 11. inspiration
    12. intelligence
Genoa lace ... 4. tape 6. bobbin
    7. macramé 13. gold and silver
genos ... 4. clan, gens, race
genre ... 3. art (style) 4. kind, sort
    5. genus 6. gender 7. species
    8. category
genteel ... 6. polite 7. refined
    8. wellborn, well–bred
Gentiles ... 6. goyims 10. Christians,
    non–Moslems
    14. non–Mohammedans
gentle ... 4. calm, easy, meek, mild,
    soft, tame 5. bland, quiet 6. docile,
    humane, kindly, tender 7. amabile
    (Mus), clement, genteel, refined,
    subdued 8. moderate, peaceful,
    soothing, tranquil, wellborn
    9. courteous, honorable, temperate,
    tractable 10. chivalrous

    11. considerate 13. compassionate
gentleman ... 3. sir 6. knight
    7. esquire, shoneen (would–be),
    younker 8. nobleman
gentleness ... 6. lenity 8. elegance,
    leniency, meekness, softness
    9. lightness 10. kindliness,
    moderation 11. genteelness
genuflect ... 5. kneel 6. curtsy
genuine ... 4. pure, real, true 5. frank,
    pucka (pukka) 7. germane, sincere
    8. existent 9. authentic, simon–pure,
    unalloyed, veritable 10. unaffected
    13. unadulterated
genus ... 4. kind, sort 5. class, order
genus, animal life ...
    animals (one–celled) .. 6. Amoeba
        8. Protozoa 9. Rhizopoda
    ants .. 6. Eciton
    apes .. 5. Simia
    armadillos .. 9. Glyptodon
    auks .. 4. Alle
    bears .. 5. Ursus
    bees (honey) .. 4. Apis
    beetles .. 10. Coleoptera
    birds .. 7. Ratitae
    bivalve mollusks .. 6. Anomia
        8. Estheria
    bugs (long–legged) .. 5. Emesa
    cats .. 5. Felis
    cattle .. 3. Bos
    crabs .. 4. Maia
    dogs .. 5. Canis
    ducks .. 3. Aix 4. Anas 7. Harelda
        8. Clangula
    elks .. 5. Alces
    fish .. 6. Cybium, Remora 7. Girella,
    Muraena
    flies .. 6. Asilus 8. Glossina (tsetse)
    frogs .. 4. Rana 5. Anura 8. Amphibia
        9. Batrachia
    geese .. 4. Chen 5. Anser
    goats .. 5. Capra
    gulls .. 4. Xema
    herons .. 7. Egretta
    hogs .. 3. Sus
    horses .. 5. Equus
    insects .. 10. Coleoptera
    lemurs .. 6. Galago
    lizards .. 3. Uta 5. Agama
    mammals .. 4. Homo
    Man .. 11. Homo sapiens
    marten .. 7. Mustela
    mice .. 3. Mus
    monkeys (spider) .. 6. Ateles
    moose .. 5. Alces
    moths .. 5. Tinea
    oysters .. 6. Ostrea
    peacocks .. 4. Pavo
    pigeons (crowned) .. 5. Goura
    porcupines .. 7. Hystrix
    porpoise .. 4. Inia
    rats .. 6. Spalax
    roadrunners .. 9. Geococcyx
    scorpions .. 4. Nepa
    seabirds .. 4. Sula
    sloths .. 11. Megatherium
    slugs .. 5. Arion
    snails .. 5. Mitra 6. Nerita, Triton
        8. Geophila
    snakes .. 4. Eryx (sand) 7. Ophidia
    spiders .. 7. Agalena

squirrels.. 7. Sciurus
swans.. 4. Olar 6. Cygnus
ticks.. 6. Ixodes
tortoises.. 4. Emys
turkeys.. 9. Meleagris
wasps.. 5. Vespa
whales.. 4. Orca 5. Areta
  9. Sibbaldus (blue)
genus, plant life...
  algae (blue–green).. 10. Gloeocapsa
  apple trees.. 5. Malus
  cabbage.. 3. Cos
  currant.. 5. Ribes
  elms.. 5. Ulmus
  evergreen, heaths.. 5. Erica
  fern.. 6. Anemia
  fungi.. 7. Boletus 10. geoglossum
  grasses.. 3. Poa (blue) 5. Avena
   6. Elymus 7. Setaria
  herbs.. 4. Arum 6. Asarum, Asitis
   (mustard), Cassia, Seseli
   7. Hedeoma, Linaria 8. Solidago
  holly.. 4. Ilex
  ipecac.. 4. Evea
  ivy.. 11. Hedera helix
  lily.. 7. Bessera
  maples.. 4. Acer
  olives.. 4. Olea
  orchids.. 5. Vanda 7. Listera
  palms.. 5. Areca, Assai 6. Bacaba
  poplar.. 5. Alamo
  rhubarb.. 5. Rheum
  vines (woody).. 6. Hedera
geode... 3. vug (vugg, vugh, voog)
  5. druse 6. nodule
geological (pert to)...
  division.. 3. eon, era
  era.. 6. Eocene 7. Miocene
   8. Cenozoic, Mesozoic 9. Paleozoic
   11. Archaeozoic
  period.. 4. Dyas, Lias 5. Trias
  prelife.. 5. Azoic
  zone (fossil).. 6. assise
geologist... 6. Strabo (anc Gr)
  8. geognost 12. mineralogist
geometric (pert to)...
  angle.. 9. incidence
  axis.. 8. abscissa
  contact.. 10. osculation
  curve.. 6. spiral 7. evolute
  pottery.. 7. Dipylon (anc)
geometric figure... 4. cone, cube,
  lune 5. prism 6. gnomon, oblong,
  square 7. hexagon, octagon, polygon,
  rhombus 8. heptagon, pentagon,
  triangle 9. rectangle, trapezoid
  10. quadrangle 13. parallelogram
geometric proposition (pert to)...
  ratio.. 2. pi (3.1416)
  surface.. 4. tore 5. nappe
  term.. 4. sine 5. locus 6. secant
   7. tangent 11. asses' bridge
geometry (pert to)...
  figure.. 6. conoid 9. ellipsoid
   10. paraboloid
  mathematician.. 6. Euclid, Pascal
  proposition.. 6. porism
geoponic... 5. rural 6. rustic
Georgia...
  capital.. 7. Atlanta
  city.. 5. Macon 7. Augusta

   8. Columbus, Marietta, Savannah
   9. Brunswick
  holiday.. 10. Georgia Day (Feb 12)
  memorial.. 11. Warm Springs
   16. Little White House (FDR)
  mountain.. 7. Lookout 9. Blue Ridge
   11. Alleghenies
  peak.. 9. High Point 13. Brasstown
   Bald
  river.. 8. Savannah, Suwannee
  settler (1st).. 10. Oglethorpe
  State admission.. 6. Fourth
  State nickname.. 5. Peach 7. Cracker
   16. Empire of the South
  swamp.. 10. Okefenokee
Georgian of the Caucasus... 4. Svan
georgic... 4. poem (rural)
geosphere... 5. earth
Geraint, Sir... 6. Knight (Round Table)
germ... 3. bud 4. ovum, seed
  5. spore 6. embryo, origin
  7. microbe 8. bacteria (pl)
  9. bacterium 13. microorganism
germ (free)... 7. aseptic 10. antiseptic
German... 3. Hun 5. Boche, jerry
  6. Almain (Alman), Teuton
  9. Deutscher
German (pert to)... see also Germany
  air force.. 9. Luftwaffe
  airplane.. 5. Gotha, Stuka 7. Dornier,
   Heinkel, Junkers 13. Messerschmitt
  article.. 3. das, der, ein
  battleship.. 8. Graf Spee (1939)
  beverage.. 5. lager
  cake.. 5. torte
  castle.. 7. schloss
  Christmas.. 11. Weihnachten
  dance.. 9. allemande
  drinking salute.. 6. prosit
  folklore.. 5. gnome 6. kobold
  gun.. 6. Bertha (Big)
  hail.. 4. heil
  highway.. 8. autobahn
  knight.. 6. Ritter (title)
  language.. 7. Deutsch
  law.. 5. Salic
  league.. 4. Bund 6. Verein
   9. Hanseatic 10. Turnverein
  letter.. 4. rune
  lyric poems.. 6. lieder
  mister.. 4. Herr
  ox (wild).. 4. urus
  parliament.. 9. Bundestag, Reichstag
  people.. 5. Quadi 6. Franks, Saxons
   7. Teutons, Vandals 8. Lombards
   9. Prussians 10. Herminones
  police.. 7. Gestapo
  prison.. 6. stalag
  society.. see league (above)
  song.. 4. lied
  student set.. 7. Kommers
  teacher.. 6. docent 12. privatdocent
  title.. 3. Von 4. Graf, Herr 6. Ritter
  tribal group.. 3. gau
  union.. 9. Auschluss
  vowel change.. 6. umlaut
  wheat.. 5. spelt
  wine.. 4. wein 5. Rhine 7. Moselle
  woman.. 4. frau 8. fraulein
  yes.. 2. ja
germane... 4. akin 6. allied 7. kindred
  8. relevant 11. appropriate

German people (famed)...
actor.. 8. Jannings (Emil)
astrologer.. 5. Faust
astronomer.. 5. Galle 6. Kepler
author.. 4. Dahn 5. Ebers
    8. Brentano
bacteriologist.. 4. Koch (Nobel Prize,
    1905)
biographer.. 6. Ludwig
chemist.. 6. Bunsen
composer.. 3. Abt 4. Bach 5. Hasse
    6. Handel, Wagner
deity.. 5. Donar (thunder)
educator.. 5. Grimm 6. Beneke
    7. Francke
Egyptologist.. 5. Ebers
general.. 6. Rommel
geographer.. 6. Ritter
Gestapo chief.. 7. Himmler
goldsmith (anc).. 5. Faust
historian.. 4. Dahn 5. Moser
    7. Neander (Eccl)
inventor.. 6. Diesel
metaphysician.. 4. Kant 5. Lange
mystic.. 7. Eckhart
naturalist.. 9. Ehrenberg
neurologist.. 5. Ebing 6. Krafft
painter.. 5. Durer 7. Lessing
pathologist.. 6. Eberth
philologist.. 5. Grimm, Heyne
philosopher.. 4. Elze 5. Groos, Hegel,
    Weber 6. Ritter 8. Spengler
    9. Feuerbach
physician.. 8. Hufeland
physicist.. 3. Ohm 5. Weber
    6. Franck 7. Doppler 10. Fahrenheit
pianist.. 5. Bauer
poet.. 4. Elze 5. Heine 6. Goethe,
    Uhland 7. Lessing 8. Schiller
president (first).. 5. Ebert
sculptor.. 5. Begas
Socialist.. 10. Liebknecht
theologian.. 5. Bauer 6. Spener
    (Pietist) 7. Francke
Germany...
capital.. 4. Bonn 6. Berlin
cathedral town.. 5. Essen
city.. 3. Ulm 4. Bonn, Gera
    5. Baden, Emden, Essen, Gotha
    6. Munich
coal region.. 4. Ruhr, Saar 6. Aachen
East.. 10. Third Reich
empire.. 14. Deutsches Reich
kingdom.. 6. Saxony 7. Bavaria,
    Hanover
lake.. 9. Constance
leader.. 6. Hitler (Fuehrer), Kaiser
    13. von Hindenburg
mountain.. 4. Harz
port.. 5. Emden
river.. 3. Aar 4. Elbe, Iser, Oder,
    Ruhr 5. Rhine, Saale
steel region.. 5. Essen
West.. 15. Federal Republic
wine (white).. 4. hock
germicide... 6. iodine (iodin), phenol
    10. antiseptic 12. disinfectant
germinate... 3. bud 4. grow 5. beget
    6. sprout 7. develop 8. vegetate
    10. effloresce
Geronimo... 6. Apache (Chief)
gerrymander (Polit)... 6. divide (unfairly)

    10. manipulate
gesticulation... 6. motion 7. gesture
gesture... 3. act 4. gest (geste), sign
    5. sanna 6. beckon, behave, motion
    7. perform, pretext 8. carriage (body)
    11. gesticulate 13. gesticulation
get... 3. pen, win 4. earn, hear, pain,
    take, trap 5. beget, fetch, incur,
    learn 6. attain, become, derive,
    induce, obtain, profit, secure
    7. achieve, acquire, capture, prepare,
    procure, receive 8. contract, contrive,
    discover 9. ascertain, determine
    10. understand
get along... 3. age 5. hurry
    6. begone, depart, manage, move on
    7. advance, prosper
get around... 5. evade 6. cajole,
    outwit, spread 7. deceive 9. circulate
    10. circumvent
get off... 5. start, utter 6. alight,
    depart, escape, go free 8. dismount
get out... 4. exit 5. scram 6. elicit,
    escape, reveal 7. draw out, leak out,
    publish 8. evacuate 9. extricate
get over... 4. move 5. cover
    6. bridge, finish 7. recover
    8. surmount 9. make clear
Ghana, capital of... 5. Accra (Gold
    Coast)
ghastly... 3. wan 4. grim, pale
    5. lurid 6. dismal, grisly, pallid
    7. deathly, hideous 8. gruesome,
    horrible, shocking, terrible
    9. deathlike, frightful 10. cadaverous
ghost... 3. Ker 5. larva (Rom Relig)
    lemur, shade, spook 6. daemon,
    spirit, wraith 7. banshee (banshie),
    eidolon, phantom, specter
    8. phantasm, revenant
    10. apparition, glimmering, substitute
    11. ghostwriter, poltergeist
ghostly... 5. eerie (eery) 8. spectral
    9. spiritual
giant... 4. huge, ogre 5. Titan
    6. afreet, nozzle, thurse 7. monster
    8. colossus 9. monstrous
    10. gargantuan, prodigious,
    tremendous
giant (pert to)...
Biblical.. 7. Goliath, Rephaim
classic.. 5. Atlas
crafty.. 5. Cacus
Greek.. 5. Mimas
hundred–armed.. 9. Enceladus
land, country.. 9. Utgarthar
    10. Jotunnheim 11. Brobdingnag
Norse.. 4. Ymir (Ymer) 5. Mimir
    6. Jotunn (Jotun) 12. Utgartha–Loki
one–eyed.. 5. Arges 7. Brontes,
    Cyclops 10. Polyphemus
primeval.. 4. Ymir 5. Titan
    12. Utgartha–Loki
rock.. 9. Gibraltar 13. Stone Mountain
    (Atlanta)
sea god.. 5. Aegir
seer.. 5. Mimir
strong.. 6. Samson, Targan
    7. Antaeus 8. Hercules
Teutonic.. 4. Wade 5. Aegir
thousand–armed.. 4. Bana
three–hundred handed, many–handed..

8. Briareus
giantess (Teut Myth)... 4. Norn
gibbed... 9. castrated (cat)
gibber... 4. chat, hump, talk (rapid)
  5. stone (loose) 6. mumble
  7. boulder, chatter 8. swelling
gibberish... 4. talk 5. lingo 6. jargon,
  patois, patter 8. nonsense
gibbet... 3. jib 4. hang 7. gallows
  9. execution
gibbon... 3. ape, lar 6. wou–wou
  7. hoolock, siamang 10. anthropoid
gibe... 4. jape, jeer, jibe, quip 5. fleer,
  flirt, flout, scoff, sneer, taunt
  6. heckle
Gibraltar...
  named for (legend).. 5. Gobir
  ruled by.. 12. Great Britain
  site.. 5. Spain (coast)
giddy... 4. reel 5. dizzy, tipsy, whirl
  6. fickle 7. flighty 8. gyratory,
  heedless 9. delirious
  14. scatterbrained
gift... 4. alms, bent, boon, dole, free
  5. bribe, grant, knack, token
  6. legacy, talent 7. aptness, faculty,
  largess (largesse), present
  8. aptitude, blessing, donation,
  gratuity 9. endowment, lagniappe
  (lagnappe), readiness 11. serendipity
  12. contribution
gifted... 7. endowed 8. talented
gigantic... 4. huge 5. giant, large,
  titan 7. immense, mammoth
  8. colossal, enormous 9. colossean,
  monstrous 10. prodigious
giggle... 5. laugh (silly), te–hee
  6. tee–hee, titter 7. chuckle, snicker,
  snigger
Gila monster... 4. Gila 6. lizard
gild... 4. coat, lure 5. adorn, paint,
  tempt 7. aureate, falsify 8. brighten
  9. embellish
gilding... 4. gilt, gold 6. ormolu
  7. coating 8. ornament, painting
gill... 5. brook, leach, organ, penny
  6. tipple, valley, wattle 7. measure
  10. sweetheart
gimcrackle... 3. fob, toy 5. showy
  6. bauble, gewgaw, paltry, trifle
  7. trinket 8. trumpery, whimwham
  15. Jack–of–all–trades
gimlet... 3. awl 4. tool 5. drink
  (mixed) 6. wimble
gimp... 5. orris (upholstery) 6. fabric,
  thread 7. galloon 8. fishline,
  trimming
gin... 4. game, sloe, tool, trap, whim
  5. snare, trick 6. device, liquor,
  scheme, thresh 7. machine
  8. artifice, schnapps 11. contrivance
ginger... 3. pep 5. color 6. Asarum,
  energy, lively, mettle, spirit
  8. pungency, Zingiber 9. rootstalk
gingerbread... 4. cake 5. money
  6. flimsy, frills, wealth 8. ornament
  (tawdry) 11. superfluity
gingerly... 6. warily 7. charily
  9. carefully, finically, guardedly
  10. cautiously 12. fastidiously
gingham... 5. cloth 8. umbrella
  (cheap)

gipsy... see *gypsy*
giraffe... 5. okapi 6. mammal, spinet
  10. camelopard 13. constellation
girasol, girasole... 4. opal
  9. artichoke, sunflower
gird... 4. belt, bind, gibe, girt, sill
  5. brace, equip, scoff, sneer
  6. fasten, girdle, secure 7. enclose,
  environ 8. surround 10. strengthen
girder... 4. beam 5. truss 6. timber
  7. support
girdle... 3. obi 4. band, belt, cest,
  ring, sash 6. cestus, cingle, circle,
  corset 8. cincture, encircle
  10. cummerbund
girdle bone... 12. sphenethmoid
Girdle of Venus (pert to)...
  bridal.. 11. power of love
  palmistry line.. 8. hysteria
  11. nervousness
girl... 3. sis 4. bint, chit, dame, lass,
  minx, miss 5. filly, sissy, skirt
  6. damsel, female, giglet, hoyden
  (hoiden), lassie, maiden, shiver, thrill,
  tomboy 7. colleen, damosel, fillock,
  ingénue, roebuck 10. sweetheart
  11. maidservant
girlish... 4. pert 5. sissy 7. artless
  8. immature, maidenly 10. flapperish
girt... 4. band 6. fasten, saddle
  7. besiege 9. encircled
girth... 4. band, hoop, size 5. brace,
  strap 6. girdle, saddle 7. measure
  8. encircle 13. circumference
gist... 3. nub 4. core, crux, meat, pith
  5. point (main) 7. essence, meaning
give... 3. gie 4. hand 5. endow,
  grant, yield 6. accord, afford,
  bestow, confer, devote, donate,
  impart, remise, render, supply
  7. present, proffer, provide
  9. attribute, vouchsafe
  10. administer, elasticity
give (pert to)...
  and take.. 11. reciprocity
  authority.. 7. empower
  away.. 5. break, grant, marry, yield
  6. bestow, betray 7. discard, divulge,
  succumb 8. disclose 9. sacrifice
  10. relinquish
  back.. 4. echo 5. remit 6. recede,
  remand, remise, retire, return
  7. replace, restore, retreat
  birth to.. 4. foal 5. calve 6. farrow,
  mother 9. originate
  expectation.. 7. promise
  forth.. 4. emit 5. blaze 6. afford,
  exhale 7. publish
  information.. 4. tell 6. inform, report
  7. divulge, publish 8. disclose
  9. advertise
  out.. 4. deal, emit 5. exude, issue,
  print, utter (publicly) 6. report,
  weaken 7. declare, publish, release
  8. announce 9. apportion, circulate
  prominence.. 4. star 7. feature
  8. headline
  up.. 4. cede, emit, fail, quit 5. demit,
  waive, yield 6. betray, disuse, resign,
  vacate 7. abandon, despair, succumb
  8. abdicate, part with, renounce,
  swear off 9. sacrifice, surrender

10. relinquish
given ... 5. dated, datum, fixed
    6. stated 7. assumed, granted
    8. accorded, addicted, bestowed,
    inclined, set forth 10. determined,
    disposed to
given (pert to) ...
    by word of mouth .. 4. oral 5. parol
    name .. 7. surname
    particularly .. 9. specified
given (to) ...
    experiment .. 7. empiric
    expression .. 13. demonstrative
    meditation .. 13. contemplative
    suspicion .. 9. querulent
giving ... 6. ceding 7. largess (largesse)
    9. bestowing 10. conferring, liberality
    12. philanthropy, presentation
    13. administering
giving name to a country ...
    8. eponymic
giving up ... 8. yielding
    10. abandoning, despairing
    11. sacrificing 12. surrendering
    13. relinquishing
glacial (pert to) ...
    deposit .. 6. placer 7. moraine
    direction .. 5. stoss (opp to lee)
    drift .. 8. diluvium
    dust .. 10. kryokonite
    erosion wall .. 6. cirque
    mill .. 6. moulin
    ridge .. 4. kame (Scot) 5. esker (eskar)
    snow .. 4. neve
glaciarium ... 4. rink (skating)
glacis ... 5. slope 7. incline
    13. fortification
glack ... 4. fork (road) 6. defile, ravine,
    valley
glad ... 3. gay 4. fain 5. merry
    6. elated, joyful, joyous 8. animated,
    cheering, pleasing 9. animating,
    beautiful, delighted, gratified
    11. exhilarated, well–pleased
    12. exhilarating
gladden ... 5. cheer, elate 6. please
    7. gratify
gladdy ... 12. yellowhammer
glade ... 4. dell, nemo (comb form),
    vale 5. laund 6. valley 8. clearing
    9. everglade, open space
gladiator ... 6. fencer 7. lanista
gladiator's arena ... 4. ludi
gladly ... 4. fain, lief 5. fitly 6. freely
    7. eagerly, readily 8. joyfully, properly
    9. willingly 10. cheerfully, preferably
gladsome ... 4. glad 6. blithe, joyful
    7. festive, jocular, pleased
    8. cheerful
Gladstone ... 3. bag (travel) 4. wine
    7. Liberal (Party) 8. carriage,
    Irishman 11. portmanteau
glad tidings ... 3. joy 6. gospel
    7. evangel
glamorous ... 8. alluring, charming
    10. bewitching 11. fascinating
glance ... 3. eye 4. hint, leer, look,
    ogle, scry, skew 5. flash, gleam,
    glint, touch 6. allude, signal
    7. glimpse
gland ... 5. gonad, liver, lymph, ovary
    6. spleen, thymus 7. adrenal,

carotid, parotid, thyroid 8. pancreas,
    salivary 9. pituitary 10. suprarenal
gland (pert to) ...
    enlargement .. 6. ademia
    full of .. 7. adenose
    glandlike .. 7. adenoid 9. glandular
    inflammation .. 8. adenitis
    secretion .. 7. hormone
    tumor .. 7. adenoma
glaring ... 5. clear, plain 6. bright,
    garish 7. evident, flaring, obvious,
    staring, visible, vividly 8. apparent,
    distinct, flagrant, manifest
    9. barefaced 11. conspicuous
glass ... 4. lens, pony 5. glaze, purex
    6. goblet, liquor, mirror, seidel
    7. binocle, crystal, reflect, tumbler
    9. barometer, binocular, hourglass,
    telescope 10. microscope, opera
    glass 11. stactometer, thermometer
glass (pert to) ...
    blue .. 5. smalt
    device .. 7. ironman
    flask .. 7. matrass (mattrass)
    French for .. 5. verre
    furnace, oven .. 4. lehr (leer) 5. bocca,
    siege, tisar 7. drosser (part)
    like .. 6. vitric 8. vitreous
    material .. 4. frit (fritt)
    mineral .. 7. hyalite 8. feldspar
    molten .. 7. parison
    mosaic .. 7. tessera
    paste (jewelry) .. 6. strass
    red .. 7. schmelz (schmelze)
    refuse .. 4. calx
    rod .. 5. punty (pontil)
    sheet .. 4. pane 5. slide 7. platten
    showcase .. 7. vitrine
    volcanic .. 6. pumice 8. obsidian
    worker .. 7. glazier
glass (type of) ... 3. cut 4. milk
    6. safety 7. hobnail, Lalique, plastic,
    stained, Swedish 8. Fostoria,
    Sandwich, Venetian 9. Fiberglas,
    Plexiglas, Vitalglass
glass blowing (pert to) ...
    annealing term .. 4. fuse, heat
    glass content .. 4. sand, zinc
    6. potash, temper 7. soda ash
    oven .. 4. lehr (leer)
    rod .. 5. punty (pontil)
glazier's diamond ... 5. emery (emeril)
glazing machine ... 8. calender
gleam ... 3. ray 4. glow 5. flash, glint,
    gloze, light 7. glimmer, shimmer
    8. radiance 9. coruscate
    10. brightness
glean ... 4. reap 5. sheaf (of hemp)
    6. bundle, deduce, gather 7. collect,
    harvest, procure
glee ... 3. joy 4. club, song 5. mirth
    7. delight 8. pleasure 9. merriment
    12. cheerfulness
glen ... 4. dale, dell, vale 6. dingle,
    ravine, valley 10. depression
glib ... 4. easy, oily 5. suave 6. facile,
    fluent, smooth 8. castrate, flippant,
    slippery 9. talkative 10. loquacious
glide ... 4. sail, skid, slip, soar
    5. coast, slide
gliding over ... 7. lambent
    10. slithering

glimmer... 3. bit 4. hint, leam
  5. blink, flash, gleam, glint
  7. glimpse, glitter 10. perception
  (slight)
glimpse... 4. view (quick) 5. flash,
  tinge, trace 6. glance, luster
  7. glimmer, inkling
glisten... 5. flash, shine 7. glister,
  sparkle 9. coruscate
glitter... 5. glare, gleam, shine
  7. glimmer, glisten, sparkle
  9. coruscate, showiness
  14. attractiveness
gloaming... 4. dusk 8. twilight
  9. darkening 11. candlelight
globe... 3. map, orb 4. ball, moon
  5. earth 6. sphere 10. hemisphere
  (half)
Globe, The... 7. Theater (London, first
  to play Shakespeare)
globular... 5. beady 7. globose
  9. orbicular, spherical 10. orbiculate
  11. globe–shaped
globule... 4. bead, blob, drop, pill,
  tear 5. minim 6. bubble 8. spherule
glochis... 4. hair (barbed) 7. bristle
glockenspiel... 4. lyra, stop (organ)
  8. carillon 10. instrument
gloom... 5. cloud, frown, scowl
  7. dimness, sadness 8. darkness
  9. dejection, heaviness, obscurity
  10. cloudiness, depression,
  melancholy, sullen look
gloomy... 3. dim, sad, wan 4. dark,
  dour, glum 5. drear, eerie, lurid,
  moody, murky 6. cloudy, droopy,
  lowery, morose 7. obscure
  8. darkling, dejected, dolesome,
  downcast 9. darkening, depressed,
  tenebrous 10. depressing, foreboding,
  tenebrific 11. pessimistic
  12. disheartened
Gloomy Dean... 4. Inge
gloomy person... 7. killjoy
Gloria... 4. rite 8. doxology
glorification... 6. praise 7. worship
  8. doxology, honoring 9. festivity
  10. apotheosis 13. jollification
  14. sanctification
glorify... 4. laud 5. adore, bless, exalt,
  extol, honor 6. praise 7. elevate,
  worship 8. beautify, sanctify
  9. celebrate
glorious... 3. sri 5. grand, noble
  6. elated, superb 7. eminent, radiant
  8. ecstatic, renowned, splendid
  9. beautiful, hilarious 10. celebrated,
  delightful 11. illustrious, magnificent,
  resplendent 12. praiseworthy
glory... 4. fame, halo 5. bliss
  (celestial), boast, éclat, honor
  6. heaven, nimbus (cloud of), praise,
  renown 8. grandeur 10. admiration,
  brilliancy, effulgence 11. distinction
  13. glorification
gloss... 4. glow 5. color, sheen, shine
  6. enamel, luster, polish, remark
  7. burnish, pretext 8. glossary,
  palliate 9. extenuate 10. brightness,
  commentary 14. interpretation
gloss over... 4. fard (obs), wink
  5. blink, color 6. excuse 8. palliate

glossy... 5. glacé, nitid, shiny, sleek
  6. luster, sheeny, smooth 7. radiant,
  shining 8. lustrous, polished
  10. reflecting
glove... 3. mit 4. mitt 5. trank
  (shaped) 6. boxing, ceatus, mitten
  7. gantlet 8. gauntlet
  12. mousquetaire
glow... 4. burn 5. ardor, flame, flush,
  glean, shine 6. beauty, redden
  7. redness 9. eloquence
  10. luminosity 13. incandescence
glower... 4. gaze 5. glare, scowl, stare
glowing... 3. red 4. warm 5. drunk
  6. ardent, cadent 7. burning,
  excited, fervent, flushed 8. eloquent,
  luminous 9. beautiful 12. enthusiastic
glucose... 5. rutin, sugar 8. dextrose
glue... 3. fix 4. join 5. paste, stick
  6. adhere, cement, fasten, sizing
  7. gelatin 8. adhesive, fastener
  9. viscosity
glum... 3. sad 5. moody 6. dismal,
  gloomy, sullen 8. frowning
glut... 4. cloy, fill, sate 5. gorge, stuff
  6. pamper 7. engorge, satiate,
  satisfy, surfeit 8. overfill, overload,
  plethora, saturate
gluten... 3. gum 4. glue 6. fibrin
  7. gliadin 8. adhesive
glutinous... 4. sizy 5. gluey 6. viscid
  8. adhesive
glutton... 6. rascal, wretch 7. epicure
  8. gourmand 9. cormorant,
  scoundrel, wolverine 11. gormandizer,
  greedy eater
gluttony... 5. greed 7. edacity
  8. voracity 12. intemperance
  13. voraciousness
glycerine machine man... 8. effetman
gnar, gnarr (of dogs)... 5. growl, snarl
gnarl... 4. knot 5. growl, snarl, twist
  6. tangle 7. contort, distort, roughen
  10. contortion 12. protuberance
  (tree)
gnarled... 5. rough 6. knotty, rugged
  7. complex, knotted, twisted
  12. cross–grained
gnash... 4. bite 5. grate, grind (teeth)
gnat... 3. fly 5. nidge 6. insect
  8. mosquito
gnaw... 3. eat 4. bite, chew 5. grind,
  waste 6. rankle 7. corrode 8. wear
  away
gnede... 6. scanty 7. lacking, miserly,
  sparing
gnib... 5. ready, sharp 6. clever
gnome... 3. elf, imp, saw 5. bodie,
  bogey, dwarf, maxim, nisse
  6. goblin, kobold, sprite 8. aphorism
gnomic... 8. didactic 10. aphoristic
gnomic poets (Gr)... 5. Solon
  8. Theognis (of Megara)
  10. Phocylides (of Miletus)
gnostic... 4. wise 6. shrewd
  7. knowing 9. sagacious
Gnostic... 6. Ophite 7. Abraxas
  (Abrasax), Sethite
gnu... 6. kokoon 8. antelope
go... 3. act, die, gae, run 4. fail, fare,
  game, move, pass, turn, walk, wane,
  wend, work 5. leave, sally 6. betake,

decamp, depart, elapse, embark,
energy, extend, result, retire, travel,
weaken 7. advance, entrain, journey,
proceed 8. continue, diminish,
withdraw 9. eventuate, harmonize
go (pert to)...
around.. 6. detour 7. circuit
8. surround
ashore.. 4. land 9. disembark
astray.. 3. err
at.. 6. attack 9. undertake
away.. 4. exit, scat, shoo 5. scoot,
scram 6. begone, depart
9. disappear
back.. 3. ebb 6. recede, repass,
retire, return, revert 7. regress,
retrace
before.. 7. precede 8. antecede
11. participate
down, under.. 4. fail, sink 7. capsize,
descend, founder, succumb, undergo
8. submerge 11. deteriorate
easily.. 4. lope 5. amble
furtively.. 5. steal 6. tiptoe
over.. 5. renew 6. revise 7. retrace
8. rehearse, traverse 9. backtrack,
re—examine
through.. 4. pass 5. spend 6. suffer
7. exhaust (fortune), persist, undergo
9. persevere 10. experience
up.. 4. fail, rise 5. arise, raise
6. ascend
with.. 4. suit 5. agree, court
6. accord 8. coincide 9. accompany
10. understand
goa.. 5. Tribe (Queensland) 6. mugger
7. gazelle
goad... 3. egg 4. poke, prod, prog,
spur, urge 5. ankus (elephant),
decoy, impel, prick, sting, thorn,
valet (manège) 6. incite 7. inflame
8. irritate, stimulus 9. incentive
goal... 3. aim, end 4. base, fate,
home, mark 5. bourn (bourne),
Mecca, reach, score, Thule (Myth)
6. object 7. purpose 9. objective
11. destination
goanna.. 6. iguana, lizard 7. monitor
goat... 4. buck, dupe 5. brown
6. engine, lecher 9. scapegoat
13. laughingstock
goat (pert to)...
astronomy.. 9. Capricorn
fig.. 8. caprifig
fish.. 6. mullet
get one's.. 3. irk, vex 4. rile 5. pique
6. nettle
god.. 3. Pan
haircloth.. 5. Tibet (Thibet) 6. camlet
hair cord (Bedouin).. 4. agal
goat (type of)... 3. kid, ram, tur, zac
4. ibex, tahr, urus 5. Capra, goral,
pasan (pasang), serow, takin
6. Alpine, Angora, chamal, Jemlah,
mammal 7. aurochs, markhor
8. Cashmere, ruminant
goatsucker... 4. bird 7. dorhawk,
grinder 9. nighthawk
12. whippoorwill
gob... 4. lump, mass 5. choke, mouth
6. sailor 8. mouthful, quantity
goby... 4. fish, mapo

go—by... 4. snub 7. evasion, passing
13. circumvention
god (Myth, Relig)...
Babylonian.. 2. Zu 3. Anu, Sin
4. Adad, Enzu, Nama, Nebo (Nebu)
5. Aruru, Cirru, Dagan, Nintu
8. Ningirsu 10. Ninkhursag
11. Ningishzida
Celtic.. 6. Aengus
Cymric.. 4. Lleu (Llew)
Egyptian.. 2. Ra 3. Bes, Dis, Geb
(Keb), Min, Seb 4. Amen, Amon,
Ptah 5. Horus, Thoth 6. Dhouti,
Osiris
false.. 4. Baal, idol 6. Mammon
Greek.. 4. Ares, Zeus 5. Comus,
Hymen, Momus, Pluto 6. Hermes,
Somnus 7. Bacchus 8. Dionysus
Hebrew.. 3. Jah 7. Jehovah
Hindu.. 4. Agni, Deva, Kama, Siva
(Shiva) 6. Varuna
household.. 3. Lar 5. Lares 6. Penate
Irish.. 5. Dagda (pagan)
love of, for.. 5. piety 6. bhakti
9. theophile
Norse.. 2. Er, Ve 3. Tyr, Ull, Van
4. Loki, Odin, Thor, Ymir 5. Aesir,
Donar, Vanir, Wodin
Roman.. 4. Jove 5. Comus, Janus,
Orcus 7. Bacchus, Mercury 8. Dis
pater
Semitic.. 5. Hadad 6. Nergal
Supreme.. 3. Dei, Deo, Dio 4. Deus,
Soul, Zeus 6. Elohim, Spirit
12. Infinite Mind, Supreme Being
Teutonic.. 3. Tiu 4. Hoth
god (of)...
agriculture.. 4. Nebo 6. Faunus
beauty.. 6. Aengus (Oengus)
beginnings, creation.. 4. Ptah, Zeus
5. Janus 6. Varuna
commerce.. 5. Vanir 7. Mercury
darkness, evil.. 3. Set, Sin 6. Nergal
day.. 5. Horus
dead.. 5. Orcus 6. Osiris
discord.. 4. Loki
earth.. 3. Geb (Keb), Seb 5. Dagan
east wind.. 5. Eurus
evil.. 2. Zu 3. Set, Sin 6. Nergal
fate.. 5. Moira (Moera)
fire.. 4. Agni 5. Girru 6. Vulcan
flocks.. 3. Pan
January.. 5. Janus
joy.. 5. Comus
justice.. 7. Forseti (Forsete)
law.. 4. Zeus
lightning.. 4. Agni
love.. 4. Amor, Ares, Eros, Kama
5. Bhaga, Cupid 6. Aengus (Oengus)
March.. 4. Mars
marriage.. 5. Hymen
medicine.. 11. Ningishzida
mountains.. 5. Atlas 7. Olympus
music.. 6. Apollo
Northmen.. 5. Aesir
oceans.. 7. Oceanus
poetry.. 5. Bragi
ridicule.. 5. Momus
sea.. 7. Neptune, Proteus
sky.. 3. Anu
sleep, dreams.. 6. Somnus
8. Morpheus

storm.. 2. Zu 6. Teshup
sun.. 2. Ra (Re) 6. Apollo, Nergal
thunder.. 4. Thor 7. Jupiter
Thursday.. 4. Thor
Tuesday.. 3. Tiu, Tyr
underworld.. 3. Dis 5. Pluto 6. Osiris
   7. Serapis 8. Dis pater
   11. Ningishzida
war.. 3. Ira, Tyr 4. Mars 5. Woden
   8. Ningirau
wealth.. 5. Bhaga 6. Plutus
Wednesday.. 5. Woden
wind.. 4. Adad 5. Eolus, Eurus,
   Hadad 6. Aeolus, zephyr 8. Favonius
wine.. 7. Bacchus 8. Dionysus
wisdom.. 4. Nebo 5. Thoth 6. Dhouti
woods.. 7. Silenus
youth.. 6. Apollo
goddess... 3. Ate, Dea, Eir, Eos, Nox,
   Nyx, Ops, Pax, Uni 4. Apet, Eris,
   Fury, Gaea, Hera, Isis, Leda, Maat,
   Nike, Nina, Sati 5. Aruru, Damia,
   Diana, Doris, Epona, Freya, Hygea,
   Irene, Pakht, Salus, Venus, Vesta
   6. Allatu, Athena, Aurora, Cybele,
   Hecate, Hestia, Ningal, Pietho,
   Selene, Semele, Tellus, Vacuna
   7. Artemis, Demeter, Minerva, Parvati
   9. Aphrodite, Eumenides, Mnemosyne
   10. Persephone, Proserpina
goddess of...
agriculture.. 3. Ops 7. Demeter
arts.. 6. Athena, Pallas
beauty.. 3. Sri 5. Freya, Venus
   7. Lakshmi
dawn.. 3. Eos 5. Ushas 6. Aurora,
   Matuta
destiny.. 4. Fate 5. Moira, Parca
discord.. 3. Ate 4. Eris
earth.. 4. Gaea 5. Aruru 6. Ishtar,
   Tellus
Eskimos.. 5. Sedna
fertility.. 7. Demeter
fire.. 6. Hestia
fortune.. 5. Tyche
freedom.. 7. Feronia
fruit.. 6. Pomona
grain, harvest.. 3. Ops 5. Ceres
Hawaiians.. 4. Pele
healing.. 3. Eir 4. Gula
health.. 5. Damia, Hygea, Salus
hearth.. 5. Vesta
history.. 4. Saga
horses.. 5. Epona
hunt.. 5. Diana 6. Vacuna
infatuation.. 3. Ate
justice.. 7. Nemesis
light.. 6. Lucina
love.. 5. Venus 6. Ishtar 9. Aphrodite
magic, witchcraft.. 6. Hecate
marriage.. 4. Hera
maternity.. 4. Apet
mischief.. 3. Ate 4. Eris
moon.. 4. Luna 5. Diana 6. Phoebe,
   Selene (Selena)
mother of the gods.. 4. Rhea
nature.. 4. Rhea 5. Nymph 6. Cybele
night.. 3. Nox, Nyx
peace.. 3. Pax 5. Irene 6. Athena
poetry.. 5. Erato
rainbows.. 4. Iris

sea.. 5. Doris
seasons.. 5. Horae
summer.. 6. Aestus
sun.. 5. Pakht (Pacht)
trees.. 6. Pomona
truth.. 4. Maat
underworld.. 4. Fury 6. Allatu
   10. Persephone, Proserpina
vengeance.. 3. Ara, Ate 7. Nemesis
victory.. 4. Nike
virtue.. 5. Fides
war.. 5. Anath, Bella
wealth.. 3. Sri 7. Lakshmi
wisdom.. 6. Athena 7. Minerva
youth.. 4. Hebe
Godforsaken... 6. vacant 7. forlorn
   8. desolate, wretched 9. neglected
godly... 5. pious 6. devout, divine
   7. saintly 9. religious, righteous
godmother... 6. cummer (kimmer)
   7. sponsor
God's...
abode.. 7. Olympus
acre.. 10. churchyard
board.. 14. communion table
country.. 4. home 8. homeland
   9. Vaterland 10. fatherland
cupbearer.. 8. Ganymede
fluid (vein).. 5. ichor (icor)
food.. 8. ambrosia
gods, The (pert to)...
death of.. 9. theoktony
marriage of.. 8. theogamy
messenger of.. 6. Hermes
mother of.. 4. Rhea
Twilight of.. 8. Ragnarok
worship of.. 9. theolatry
Goetae... 7. wizards (anc) 9. sorcerers
   14. thaumaturgists
Goethe (pert to)...
home.. 6. Weimer (Ger)
masterpiece.. 5. Faust
talent.. 4. poet 8. novelist
   9. dramatist
goffer, gauffer... 5. crimp, flute, plait
   (lace, paper)
gog... 3. bog 4. stir 9. agitation
Gog (Bib)... 5. Ruler (of Magog), tribe
goggle... 3. eye 4. roll 5. state
   6. squint 11. roll the eyes
goggler... 4. fish (oceanic)
goggles... 6. screen 7. glasses
   8. blinkers, eyeshade 10. spectacles
going... 6. moving, travel 7. current,
   working 9. departure 10. obtainable
   11. in operation
gola... 7. granary 9. storeroom
   11. Indian caste
golach, goloch... 6. beetle, earwig
   9. centipede
Golconda... 6. wealth 8. rich mine
gold... 2. Au 3. oro 4. gelt, gilt
   5. aurum, color, lucre, metal, money
   6. riches, wealth 7. bullion
gold (pert to)...
alloy.. 4. asem 6. oroide
artificial.. 8. Mannheim
assayer cup.. 5. cupel
bar.. 5. ingot
braid, lace.. 5. orris
brick.. 7. swindle
coin (US).. 5. eagle

compound.. **6.** auride
containing.. **4.** doré
discoverer (US).. **6.** Sutter (1849)
field (Bib).. **5.** Ophir
fish.. **9.** shubunkin
fool's.. **6.** pyrite
gilding.. **6.** ormolu **9.** imitation
Heraldry.. **2.** or
King (Myth).. **5.** Midas
land of (Bib).. **5.** Ophir
like.. **5.** auric **7.** aureate
measure.. **5.** carat
Rush.. **8.** Klondike (1897)
  10. California (1849)
seekers (Calif).. **9.** Argonauts (1849)
  11. Forty–Niners
symbol.. **2.** Au
vein.. **4.** lode
washing pan.. **5.** cupel
gold and silver... **11.** noble metals
golden... **4.** gilt **5.** auric, blest
  6. blonde, yellow **7.** aureate,
  aureous, halcyon **8.** metallic,
  precious, valuable **9.** Pactolian
  10. auspicious **11.** flourishing
golden (pert to)...
Age.. **9.** Saturnian, siècle d'or
apple.. **3.** bel **4.** Eris (goddess)
  5. Paris (giver) **6.** tomato
bird.. **6.** oriole
bough.. **9.** mistletoe
Fleece seeker.. **5.** Jason **8.** Argonaut
Fleece ship.. **5.** Argos
rod.. **8.** solidago
goldenrod (pert to)...
genus.. **8.** Solidago
State Flower of.. **7.** Alabama
  8. Kentucky, Nebraska
goldfish... **4.** carp **9.** shubunkin
Goldfish (Astron)... **6.** Dorado
golf (pert to)...
club.. **4.** iron **5.** baffy, spoon
  6. driver, mashie, putter **7.** brassie,
  midiron, niblick
hazard.. **4.** trap **5.** stymy **6.** bunker
  11. restriction
score.. **3.** par **4.** bogy (bogie)
  5. eagle **6.** birdie
stroke.. **4.** baff, chip, hook, loft, putt
  5. drive, slice
term.. **3.** ace, par, tee **4.** baff, fore
  5. bogey, divot, eagle, green, slice
  6. birdie, dormie, sclaff, stymie
  (stimy) **7.** gallery
Golgotha... **7.** Calvary **8.** cemetery
goliath... **4.** frog **5.** crane, giant,
  heron
Goliath (pert to)...
Bib.. **5.** giant (Philistine)
death site.. **4.** Elah
home.. **4.** Gath
slayer.. **5.** David
Gomorrah (Bib)... **5.** Sodom
  13. wicked country
Gomuti palm... **5.** areng
gondola race (Venice)... **7.** regatta
gone... **3.** ago, off **4.** dead, left, lost,
  past, yore **5.** since **6.** absent,
  passed, ruined **8.** departed, past
  hope, vanished **9.** forgotten
  10. infatuated
goober... **6.** peanut

good... **2.** eu (pref) **3.** bon, fit **4.** able,
  full, gain, just, kind **5.** ample, godly,
  moral, nifty, pious, sound, valid
  6. benign, devout, expert, profit,
  savory **7.** genuine, helpful, liberal,
  trained, upright **8.** decorous, interest,
  pleasing, salutary, suitable, virtuous
  9. admirable, competent, enjoyable,
  estimable, excellent, favorable,
  honorable, indulgent, reputable
  10. auspicious, beneficial,
  courageous, gratifying, profitable,
  sufficient **11.** commendable,
  well–behaved **12.** considerable,
  satisfactory, stouthearted
good (pert to)...
bye.. **4.** ta–ta **5.** adieu, adios, ciaou
  6. so long **7.** cheerio **8.** farewell
for nothing.. **4.** mean **5.** idler
  6. wretch **7.** useless **8.** indolent
  9. worthless **11.** rapscallion
health.. **5.** skoal **6.** prosit
management.. **6.** eutaxy
mighty.. **7.** skookum
ordinarily.. **8.** mediocre
spirit.. **6.** daemon **8.** Eudaemon
  12. agathodaemon
tidings.. **6.** gospel **7.** evangel
will.. **5.** favor **9.** affection, readiness
  11. benevolence **12.** friendliness
goodness.. **5.** piety **6.** virtue
  8. kindness, validity **9.** godliness,
  propriety **10.** excellence, generosity,
  savoriness
goods... **5.** wares **7.** ability **8.** chattels,
  property **11.** information, merchandise
goods cast overboard, sunk...
  5. lagan (lagend) **6.** jetsam
  7. flotsam **10.** contraband
goose... **4.** bean, dupe, fool, gull, iron,
  snow, tule **5.** Anser, brant, solan
  6. Canada, gander, gannet, goslet
  7. gosling, graylag (greylag)
  8. barnacle **12.** white–fringed
goose (pert to)...
grease.. **6.** axunge
pygmy.. **6.** goslet
relating to.. **8.** anserine
story character.. **5.** ganza
gooseberry... **5.** fabes (color)
  6. escort, groser (groset), thapes
  8. chaperon, feaberry
gopher... **5.** snake **6.** rodent **7.** burglar
  8. squirrel, tortoise **10.** salamander
Gopher State... **9.** Minnesota
gore... **3.** mud **4.** dirt, dung, stab
  5. blood, cloth (triang), filth, slime
  6. pierce **8.** heraldry **9.** bloodshed,
  penetrate
gorge... **3.** eat **4.** bolt, glut, sate
  5. chasm, gully **6.** canyon, coulee,
  defile, nullah, ravine, valley **7.** choke
  up, overeat, pitcher, satiate **8.** overfill
gorgeous... **5.** grand, showy
  8. colorful, dazzling **9.** beautiful
  10. delightful **11.** magnificent,
  resplendent
gorgon... **4.** ogre, ugly **7.** Jezebel
  (Bib), monster
Gorgons (Gr Myth)... **6.** Medusa,
  Stheno **7.** Euryale **9.** sentinels
gorilla... **3.** ape **4.** thug **5.** brute

6. monkey 8. assassin
gorilla man . . . 9. Du Chaillu (brought ape from Africa)
gormandizer . . . 9. chowhound
   11. . trencherman
gorse . . . 5. furze 7. juniper
goshawk . . . 5. Astur 6. tercel
gospel . . . 5. faith, truth 6. belief
   7. epistle, evangel 8. doctrine
   9. orthodoxy, selection (Bib)
   10. revelation 11. glad tidings
   12. proclamation
Gospels (Four) . . . 11. diatessaron
gossip . . . 3. cat, eme, gup 4. chat,
   news, talk 5. on–dit 6. claver,
   gabble, norate, report, tattle
   7. clatter 8. idle talk, quidnunc
   9. chatterer 10. newsmonger,
   talebearer
gossoon . . . 3. boy, lad (serving)
   5. youth 6. garçon
got . . . see *get*
Gotham . . . 9. Newcastle (Eng) 11. New
   York City
Gothamite . . . 9. New Yorker
Gothic (pert to) . . .
   alphabet . . 11. Moeso–Gothic
   architecture . . 6. French
   design . . 7. writing 12. architecture
   era . . 10. Middle Ages
   people . . 4. rude 5. Goths 6. fierce
   7. Teutons
   printing type . . 5. Doric 9. square–cut
gouge . . . 4. tool 5. cheat 6. chisel,
   groove 7. defraud, swindle
   8. impostor 10. imposition
Gounod's opera . . . 5. Faust
gourd . . . 4. pepo 5. color, flask, melon
   6. squash 8. calabash, cucurbit
   9. Cucurbita 11. calabazella
gourmand . . . 5. eater (luxurious)
   6. taster 7. epicure, glutton, gourmet
   10. fastidious, gluttonous, voluptuary
   11. connoisseur
gourmet . . . 7. epicure 8. gourmand
   11. connoisseur
gout . . . 4. clot, drop 6. blotch
   7. disease 9. arthritis
govern . . . 3. run 4. curb, lead, rein,
   rule 5. reign 6. bridle, direct,
   manage 7. conduct, control, preside
   8. dominate, regulate, restrain
   9. influence, supervise
governess . . . 4. ayah 5. nurse
   6. abbess, duenna 8. guardian
   12. instructress
government . . . 4. rule, sway 6. polity
   7. control, regimen 10. management
   12. jurisdiction 14. administration
government (pert to) . . .
   agent . . see *representative* below
   centralized . . 12. totalitarian
   church . . 9. hierarchy 10. hierocracy
   foe . . 3. Red 9. anarchist, mercenary,
   terrorist
   form . . 6. polity
   grant . . 6. patent
   in exile . . 7. de facto
   lands . . 5. amani
   levy . . 3. tax 6. impost
   official . . 10. bureaucrat
   representative . . 6. consul 8. diplomat,

minister 10. ambassador
   science of . . 8. politics
   strong . . 5. power
   system . . 6. regime
   vicarious . . 7. regency
   without . . 6. acracy
government by . . .
   church . . 9. hierarchy 10. hierocracy
   few . . 9. oligarchy
   God . . 8. theonomy
   holy body . . 9. hagiarchy
   10. hagiocracy
   inner control . . 8. endarchy
   law . . 9. nomocracy
   men . . 9. andocracy
   mob . . 10. ochlocracy
   no one . . 6. acracy
   rich . . 10. plutocracy
   seven . . 9. heptarchy
   six . . 12. sextumvirate
   slaves . . 10. doulocracy
   ten . . 8. decarchy (dekarchy)
   three . . 8. triarchy 11. triumvirate
   women . . 11. gynecocracy
   worst men . . 12. kakistocracy
governor . . . 4. woon 5. chief, nabob,
   ruler 6. dynast, regent 7. alcalde,
   decarch (of 10 men), viceroy
   8. decurion, director 9. mechanism
   10. magistrate
gown . . . 4. robe, toga 5. cloak, dress,
   frock 6. chiton, clothe, cyclas, invest,
   kimono, mantle 7. cassock, college,
   garment, matinee, soutane (Eccl)
   sultane 8. negligee, peignoir
   9. nightgown
gozell, gozill . . . 10. gooseberry
gozzard . . . 9. gooseherd
gra . . . 4. love 5. agrah 6. liking
   8. fondness 10. sweetheart
grab . . . 3. nab 4. game (cards), take
   5. grasp, seize 6. arrest, clutch,
   snatch, vessel
grabble . . . 4. feel 5. grope 6. grovel,
   sprawl 7. harvest 11. appropriate
grace . . . 4. fate, luck, note, tact
   5. adorn, charm, favor, honor,
   mercy, title 6. beauty, become,
   bedeck, polish, prayer, virtue
   7. dignify, enhance 8. clemency,
   easiness, elegance, kindness, reprieve
   10. comeliness, refinement,
   seemliness 12. graciousness,
   thanksgiving
graceful . . . 4. airy, easy, feat
   6. comely, seemly 7. elegant, fitting,
   tactful 8. charming, debonair
   9. beautiful, courteous, sylphlike
   11. appropriate
Graces, The Three (Gr Myth) . . .
   5. Aegle (Mother) 6. Aglaia
   (Brilliance), Thalia (Bloom)
   10. Euphrosyne (Joy)
gracile . . . 4. slim, thin 6. slight
   7. slender
gracious . . . 4. kind 5. suave 6. benign,
   urbane 7. affable 8. generous
   9. courteous, favorable
grackle . . . 3. daw 4. bird, myna
   7. jackdaw 9. blackbird
gradation . . . 4. step 5. scale, steps
   6. ablaut, nuance, series, stages

7. degrees 10. graduation, succession

grade ... 4. even, rank, rate, size, sort, step 5. level, order 6. assort, degree, school, smooth 7. arrange, incline 8. classify, gradient, graduate

gradual ... 4. easy, slow 6. gentle 9. leisurely

graduate ... 4. pass, size 5. grade, taper 6. alumna 7. alumnus, promote, student 8. shade off

graffito (scratched crudely) ... 7. drawing 10. scratching 11. inscription

Graf Spee blown up ... 7. Uruguay (1939)

graft ... 3. dig 4. cion (scion), join, toil, work 5. ditch, fraud, labor, spade, unite 6. boodle, fasten, inarch, trench 7. bribery, implant, joining

grafted (Her) ... 4. enté

Grail ... see *Holy Grail*

grain ... 3. jot, rye 4. atom, bran, corn, dram, food, grit, iota, malt, meal, mite, oats, rice, whit 5. fiber, maize, scrap, spark, trace, wheat 6. barley, millet, sesame 8. particle

grain (pert to) ...
Bible .. 4. ador
bundle .. 5. sheaf 7. sheaves
chaff .. 4. bran, grit
cracked .. 6. groats
ear of .. 5. spike 6. ressum (rizzom)
exchange (Finan) .. 3. pit
feeding on .. 11. granivorous
fungus, disease .. 4. rust, smut 5. ergot 6. mildew
goddess of .. 5. Ceres
ground .. 4. meal 5. flour, grist
husks .. 4. bran 5. straw
measure .. 6. thrave
mill .. 5. quern
mixture .. 6. fodder 7. farrage 9. bullimong
small .. 7. granule
spike .. 3. ear 6. rizzom
stack .. 4. rick
storage, warehouse .. 3. mow 4. silo 5. hutch 8. elevator

grammar (pert to) ... 5. parse 6. gender, simile, syntax 7. diction, parsing, prosody, synesis, wordage 8. enallage, language, metaphor, paradigm 9. accidence, etymology, phonology 10. conformity, declension, inflection 11. conjugation

grammatical case ... 6. dative 8. ablative, genitive, vocative 9. objective 10. accusative, nominative

grampus ... 3. arc 4. orca 5. whale 6. killer 7. dolphin 8. cetacean

granada ... 11. pomegranate

Granada Moorish Castle site ... 8. Alhambra (Sp)

granary ... 3. bin 6. grange 8. cornloft 10. repository, storehouse (grain)

grand ... 4. epic 5. great, large, lofty, money, noble, piano 6. august, epical, famous, superb, swanky 7. eminent, sublime 8. gorgeous,

majestic, splendid, thousand 9. dignified, grandiose, important, sumptuous 11. illustrious, magnificent

Grand Canyon State ... 7. Arizona

grandchild ... 2. oe, oy

grandchild, great ... 5. ieroe

grandee ... 7. magnate 8. nobleman 10. clarissimo

grandeur ... 5. glory 7. dignity, majesty 8. elegance, eminence, vastness 9. greatness, immensity, sublimity 10. augustness 11. stateliness

grandeval ... 4. aged 7. ancient

grandfather ... 4. aiel (obs), avus 6. atavus 8. gudesire

grandiloquent ... 5. grand, lofty 6. turgid 7. pompous 9. bombastic 12. magniloquent

grandiose ... 4. epic 5. grand 6. turgid 8. imposing 9. bombastic, flaunting 12. ostentatious

Grandma Moses ... 17. Anna Mary Robertson

grandmother ... 6. beldam (beldame), granny, gudame 7. grandam (grandame), grandma 8. babushka

grandparent (pert to) ... 4. aval

grandson ... 6. nepote

Grand Teton peak ... 7. Wyoming

grange ... 4. farm 7. granary 9. farmhouse 11. association (1867) 18. Patrons of Husbandry

granite ... 4. rock 5. stone 6. aplite, marble, quartz 8. feldspar 9. pegmatite

Gran Quivira ... 5. ruins (mission) 16. National Monument (N M)

grant ... 4. cede, deed, enam, gift, give, lend, loan, mise 5. admit, allow, bonus, jagir (jaghar), spare 6. accord, bestow, confer, demise, permit, remise 7. appease, concede, confess, subsidy 8. appanage, sanction, transfer 10. conveyance 11. acknowledge

granulated ... 5. rough 6. coarse 7. grained 8. granular, hardened 12. crystallized

grape ... 3. fox, uva 5. Tokay 6. Malaga, Muscat 7. Catawba, Concord, Hamburg, Mission, Niagara 8. Delaware, grenache, Isabella, Thompson 9. Chasselas, muscadine 10. sweetwater 11. scuppernong

grape (pert to) ...
cluster .. 6. raceme
color .. 7. blue–red 9. cathedral
conserve .. 5. uvate
cultivation .. 11. viticulture
dried .. 4. pasa 6. raisin
family, genus .. 5. Vitus 8. Vitaceae
juice .. 4. dibs, must, sapa, stum
military .. 4. shot
pomace .. 4. marc, rape
preserve .. 7. raisine
residue .. 4. marc, rape 6. pomace
seed .. 4. acinus
sugar .. 7. maltose 8. dextrose

grapefruit ... 6. pomelo 8. shaddock 12. Citrus Maxima

grapevine ... 4. caro 5. rumor 6. canard, report 8. maneuver

(wrestling), pipeline 9. dance step
11. information, underground

graph ... 5. chart 7. contour, diagram,
drawing

graphic ... 5. clear, drawn, vivid
7. written 8. engraved 9. pictorial
11. descriptive, picturesque,
significant 12. diagrammatic

grasp ... 4. grip, hent (obs), hold, take
5. catch, clasp, gripe, seize
6. clinch, clutch, gowpen (gowpin)
7. control 8. handgrip 9. apprehend
10. comprehend, understand

grasping ... 4. avid 5. close 6. greedy
7. holding, miserly 8. covetous
9. rapacious 10. avaricious,
prehensive 11. acquisitive
13. comprehending, understanding

grass ... 3. eel, hay, Poa, rye 4. cane,
Coix, crab, gama, herb, oats, reed,
rice, rush, tare, wire 5. ankee,
Avena, Briza, brome, chess, goose,
grain, grama, hedge, otate, spart,
spear 6. bamboo, barley, darnel,
fescue, marram, millet, redtop,
sesame, switch 7. alfalfa, Bermuda,
buffalo, esparto, Hordeum, Poeceae,
timothy 8. mesquite 9. blue–grass,
Boutelous

grasshopper ... 4. grig 6. cicada, locust
7. katydid

grassland ... 3. lea, sod 4. mead, veld
(veldt) 5. llano, range, sward
7. pasture, prairie, savanna
(savannah)

grate ... 3. rub 4. fret, grid, grit, rasp
5. annoy, chafe, grind 6. abrade,
scrape 7. network 8. irritate

grateful ... 7. cumshaw (beggar's
phrase), welcome 8. pleasing,
thankful 10. gratifying
12. appreciative

gratification ... 6. relish, reward
8. gratuity, pleasure 10. indulgence,
recompense

gratified ... 4. glad 7. pleased

gratify ... 5. favor, grace, humor
6. arride, foster, pamper, please
7. appease, delight, flatter, indulge,
requite, satisfy 10. remunerate

grating ... 4. grid 5. grate, grill, harsh,
raspy 6. grille 7. lattice, network
8. strident 9. partition 10. irritating
11. latticework 12. nerve–racking

gratis ... 4. free 6. freely 9. on the
cuff 10. for nothing, gratuitous, on
the house 12. gratuitously

gratitude ... 5. grace 6. praise, thanks
12. appreciation, gratefulness,
thankfulness

gratuitous ... 4. free 5. given 6. gratis,
wanton 7. assumed 8. baseless,
needless 9. voluntary 10. groundless
11. superfluous, unwarranted

gratuity ... 3. fee, tip 4. dole, gift,
give, vail 5. bonus, bribe 6. bounty
7. cumshaw, pension, present
9. baksheesh (bakshish), buonamano,
lagniappe (lagnappe), pourboire

grave ... 3. pit, urn 4. bier, tomb
5. fosse (foss), sober, staid
6. sedate, solemn, trench 7. earnest,

engrave, serious 8. sermonic
9. important, momentous, ponderous,
sculpture, sepulcher

grave (pert to) ...
cloth .. 6. shroud 8. cerement
9. cerecloth
coffin .. 4. pall
comb form .. 5. serio
mound (anc) .. 6. barrow 7. hillock,
tumulus
person .. 10. sobersides
robber .. 5. ghoul

gravel ... 5. geest, grain, stone
6. baffle, defeat, refute 7. calculi,
erratic (boulder), pebbles
10. meerschaum (color)

graven ... 6. etched 7. infixed
8. engraved 10. sculptured

gravestone ... 5. stele (stela) 6. cippus,
marker, pillar 8. monument
9. tombstone 11. sarcophagus

gravitation ... 7. descent, gravity
10. attraction

gravity ... 6. weight 7. dignity, sadness
8. enormity, grimness, sobriety
9. formality, solemnity 10. attraction,
importance 11. earnestness,
seriousness, weightiness
12. significance 13. momentousness

gravity law, discoverer ... 6. Newton

gray, grey ... 3. dim, old, sad 4. aged,
dark, dull, gris, obex 5. dingy, hoary,
polio (comb form), sober 6. animal
(gray), dismal, somber 7. hueless,
neutral, silvery 9. cheerless
10. achromatic

gray, grey (color) ... 3. ash, bat, dun
4. ashy, dove, iron, lead, mole, zinc
5. acier, ashen, dusty, mouse, pearl,
slate, smoke, steel, taupe 6. French,
Oxford, Quaker, reseda, silver
7. cesious, dappled, grizzle
8. charcoal, cinereal, gunmetal
10. battleship, dapple–gray
13. pepper–and–salt

graze ... 3. eat, rub 4. drab, rase, skim
5. brush, shave 6. browse, feed on,
scrape 7. scratch

grease ... 3. fat, oil, tip 4. daub, lard,
mort, saim, soil 5. bribe, smear,
suint 6. axunge 7. fatness, fawning,
lanolin 8. flattery 9. lubricate

greasy ... 4. oily 5. dirty, gross, thick
6. smooth 8. slippery, unctuous
10. indelicate

great ... 3. big 4. good, huge, vast
5. ample, chief, large, major, stout,
whole 6. famous, grande 7. drastic,
eminent, extreme 8. intimate,
numerous 9. elaborate, important
11. magnanimous 12. considerable
13. distinguished

great (comb form) ... 5. macro, megal

Great (pert to) ...
Barrier (NZ) .. 4. Otea (Isl) 9. coral
reef
Beyond .. 5. grave 9. afterlife,
hereafter 10. after world, The
Unknown 11. eternal home
14. beyond the grave
Cham of Literature .. 13. Samuel
Johnson (Dr)

Circle sailing .. **10.** orthodromy
Commoner .. **4.** Clay, Pitt **7.** Stevens
(Thaddeus) **9.** Gladstone
Divide .. **7.** Rockies **8.** Rocky Mts
9. watershed (US) **14.** Rocky
Mountains **17.** Continental Divide
Fire .. **6.** London (1666) **7.** Chicago
(1871)
Lakes .. **4.** Erie **5.** Huron **7.** Ontario
8. Michigan, Superior
Mogul .. **5.** Akbar (Hind) **7.** diamond
Names .. **6.** Hector **8.** Hercules,
Lysander **9.** Alexander
Pyramid .. **6.** Cheops
Spirit (Ind) .. **4.** Mana, Zemi **5.** Wakan
6. Manito (orenda), Pokunt
White Way .. **8.** Broadway (NY)
Great Britain ... **5.** Wales **7.** England
8. Scotland **12.** Commonwealth
13. United Kingdom **15.** Northern
Ireland
greatest ... **6.** utmost **7.** extreme,
noblest
greatness ... **9.** largeness
10. importance **11.** magnanimity
Greco, Graeco (comb form) ... **5.** Greek
7. Grecian
Greece ... see also *Greek*
ancient .. **4.** Elis **5.** Argos, Doris, Ionia
6. Attica, Epirus, Hellas **7.** Argolis,
Boeotia
cape .. **5.** Melea **7.** Matapan
capital .. **4.** Elis (anc) **6.** Athens
citadel .. **9.** Acropolis
city .. **6.** Patras, Sparta **7.** Corinth,
Piraeus **8.** Salonika, Thessaly
island .. **5.** Chios, Corfu, Crete, Samos
6. Lesbos **10.** Dodecanese,
Samothrace
mountain .. **3.** Ida **5.** Athos **6.** Peleon,
Pindus **7.** Olympus **9.** Parnassus
peninsula .. **6.** Balkan
river .. **4.** Arta **7.** Hellada **9.** Archelous
sea .. **6.** Aegean, Ionian
seaport .. **4.** Enor, Volo **5.** Corpu,
Pylos **8.** Salonika **9.** Gallipoli
Greek, Grecian (pert to) ...
abbess .. **4.** amma
alphabet .. see *Greek alphabet*
altar .. **7.** eschara
architecture .. **5.** Doric, Ionic **6.** xystus
(part) **10.** Corinthian
assembly .. **4.** pynx **5.** agora
avenging spirit .. **3.** Ate, Ker **6.** Erinys
boat .. **6.** caique
bowl (golden) .. **5.** depas
breath .. **6.** pneuma
chariot .. **4.** biga
church section .. **6.** andron, bemata
citadel .. **9.** Acropolis
city (Greek for) .. **5.** polis
commander (anc) .. **7.** navarch
commune .. **4.** deme, nome
contest .. **4.** agon (anc) **6.** Delian
7. Pythian, Olympic **8.** marathon
courtesan (Athen) .. **5.** Thais
culture, literature .. **7.** classic
9. classical
cup, bowl .. **5.** depas **6.** cotula
cupid .. **4.** Eros
dance (anc) .. **6.** hormos **7.** pyrrhic,
strophe **9.** dithyramb

department .. **8.** nomarchy
dish .. **5.** gyros **9.** souvlakia
early .. **5.** Arius **6.** oecist
epic .. **5.** Iliad **7.** Odyssey
female worshipper .. **5.** orant
garment .. **5.** tunic **6.** chiton, peplos
gravestone .. **5.** stele
horse (talking) .. **5.** Arion
hospitality .. **5.** zenia
judge .. **6.** dicast
language .. **6.** Romaic
lawgiver .. **5.** Minos, Solon
magistrate .. **6.** archon, eparch
7. nomarch
mistress .. **7.** hetaera (hetaira)
monster .. **8.** Typhoeus (100–headed)
note .. **4.** nete **5.** neume **6.** pneuma
9. hexachord **10.** tetrachord
Old Testament .. **10.** Septuagint
platform .. **4.** bema **7.** logeion
poem .. **5.** Iliad **7.** Odyssey
portico .. **4.** stoa, xyst
sacred enclosure .. **5.** sekos
sacred object .. **6.** sacrum
sacrificial offering .. **5.** hiera
8. sphagion
school .. **7.** Eleatic
serpent .. **4.** seps **6.** Python
slave .. **5.** Baubo, helot, iambe
6. penest
soldier .. **7.** hoplite
song .. **5.** melos
sorceress .. **5.** Circe
spirit .. **5.** Momus (evil)
temple .. **4.** naos **5.** cella (part)
theater .. **5.** odeon
war cry .. **5.** alala
youth (would–be citizen) .. **7.** ephebus
Greek alphabet ... **2.** Mu, Nu, Pi, Xi
3. Chi, Eta, Phi, Psi, Rho, Tau
4. Beta, Iota, Zeta **5.** Alpha, Delta,
Gamma, Kappa, Omega, Sigma, Theta
6. Lambda **7.** Digamma (obs), Epsilon,
Omicron, Upsilon
Greek Furies ... **6.** Alecto, Erinys
7. Magaero **9.** Tisiphone
Greek god of ...
atmosphere .. **5.** Hadad
chief .. **4.** Zeus
dreams .. **8.** Morpheus
fire .. **6.** Vulcan
flocks .. **3.** Pan
heavens .. **6.** Uranus
love .. **4.** Eros
lower world .. **5.** Hades
ridicule .. **5.** Momus
river .. **8.** Eridanus
sea .. **6.** Nereus
storm .. **6.** Teshup **7.** Hittite
sun .. **6.** Apollo, Helios **7.** Phoebus
vegetation .. **8.** Dionysus
war .. **4.** Ares **8.** Enyalius
winds .. **5.** Eurus **6.** Aeolus
youth .. **6.** Apollo, Pothos (winged)
Greek goddess of ...
agriculture .. **7.** Artemis, Demeter
beauty .. **9.** Aphrodite
chase .. **7.** Artemis
clouds .. **5.** Niobe
dawn .. **3.** Eos **7.** Alcmene, Ariadne
discord .. **4.** Eris
earth .. **2.** Ge **4.** Gaea

fate.. **5.** Moira
fortune.. **5.** Tyche
heaven.. **4.** Hera
infatuation.. **3.** Ate
magic.. **6.** Hecate (3–headed)
memory.. **9.** Mnemosyne
moon.. **2.** Io **5.** Diana **6.** Selene
nature.. **7.** Artemis
night.. **3.** Nyx **4.** Leto **6.** Hecate
peace.. **5.** Irene
phallus.. **5.** Baubo
retribution.. **7.** Nemesis
underworld.. **6.** Hecate (Hekate)
vengeance.. **3.** Ara **7.** Nemesis
victory.. **4.** Nike
wisdom.. **6.** Pallas **7.** Minerva
youth.. **4.** Hebe
Greek Myth...
   character.. **5.** Niobe, Sinon **6.** Adonis,
      Gorgon, Rhesus **7.** Calchus, Icarius,
      Pandora, Phrixos **8.** Atalanta,
      Endymion, Meleager, Tantalus
      12. Erichthonius
   deity.. **5.** Satyr, Titan **6.** Cronus
   enchantress.. **5.** Circe, Medea
   giant.. **7.** Antaeus **9.** Enceladus
      (100–armed)
   huntress.. **8.** Atalanta
   monster.. **8.** Typhoeus (100–headed)
   nymph.. **5.** Oread **6.** Nereid
   serpent.. **6.** Python
   spirit (evil).. **5.** Momus
Greek personalities...
   astronomer.. **12.** Eratosthenes
   author.. **6.** Lucian
   biographer.. **8.** Plutarch
   counselor.. **6.** Nestor
   dramatist.. **9.** Aeschylus (Poet),
      Euripedes, Sophocles
      12. Aristophanes
   fabulist.. **5.** Aesop
   geographer.. **6.** Strabo
   hero.. **4.** Ajax **5.** Talos **6.** Nestor,
      Thesus **7.** Cecrops **10.** Hippolytus
   historian.. **8.** Xenophon **9.** Dionysius,
      Herodotus **10.** Thucydides
   mathematician.. **6.** Euclid
      10. Archimedes
   painter.. **7.** Apelles, El Greco
   patriarch.. **5.** Arius
   philosopher.. **5.** Galen, Plato, Timon
      6. Nestor **8.** Diogenes **9.** Aristotle
      10. Heraclitus, Parmenides,
      Pythagorus, Xenophanes
      11. Anaximander
   physician.. **5.** Galen
   poet.. **5.** Arion, Homer **6.** Pindar
      7. Thespis **8.** Anacreon **9.** Aeschylus
   poetess.. **6.** Erinna, Sappho
      7. Corinna
   sage.. **6.** Thales
   sculptor.. **5.** Myron **7.** Phidias
   statesman.. **8.** Pericles **9.** Aristides
green... **3.** raw **4.** vert **5.** fresh, mossy
   6. callow, praseo (comb form),
   unripe **7.** emerald, verdant
   9. malachite, unskilled, untrained
   11. flourishing **13.** inexperienced
   15. unsophisticated
green (pert to)...
   back.. **4.** frog **11.** legal tender (US)
   blue.. **4.** cyan, saxe **7.** sistine

   comb form.. **6.** praseo
   eyed.. **7.** jealous
   famous.. **6.** Gretna (Scot)
   film.. **6.** patina
   gray.. **5.** olive **6.** reseda
   pale.. **7.** celadon
   pigment.. **10.** terre–verte
   quartz.. **5.** prase
   sickness.. **9.** chlorosis
   tea.. **5.** Hyson
green–back herring... **5.** cisco
Greenland...
   Bay.. **6.** Baffin
   capital.. **8.** Godthaab
   Danish word.. **8.** Crönland
   explorer.. **9.** Frobisher (1576)
      10. Eric the Red
   natives.. **6.** Eskimo (mostly)
   settlement.. **4.** Etah
   strait.. **5.** Davis
   whale.. **5.** right
Green Mt Boys' leader... **10.** Ethan
   Allen (1775)
Green Mt State... **7.** Vermont
greenness... **5.** color **8.** sourness
   9. ignorance **10.** immaturity
   11. gullibility **12.** inexperience
Greenwich time (London)...
   8. absolute, standard **16.** Royal
   Observatory
Greenwich Village... **9.** Manhattan
   11. New York City
greeting... **3.** ave, how **4.** hail **5.** hallo
   6. accoil, halloa, salute **7.** address,
   welcome **8.** saluting **9.** reception
   10. compliment, salutation
   14. correspondence
gregarious... **6.** common, social
   7. affable **8.** sociable
   12. social–minded **13.** communicative
grego... **5.** cloak **6.** jacket **9.** greatcoat
Gregory... **4.** Code (Rom law), Pope,
   year **5.** chant, staff (Mus) **6.** church
   8. calendar
grenier... **5.** attic
grey... see *gray*
grid... **5.** grill **7.** grating, griddle,
   network **8.** gridiron **13.** football field
grief... **3.** rue, woe **4.** care, pain, ruth
   5. abuse, dolor, trial **6.** mishap,
   sorrow **7.** anguish, offense, remorse,
   sadness **8.** disaster, distress,
   document **9.** grievance, suffering
   10. affliction **11.** bereavement,
   lamentation
grieve... **3.** cry, rue **4.** erme, pain
   5. mourn, wound **6.** lament, sorrow
   7. afflict **8.** complain, distress
   10. discomfort
grievous... **4.** sore **6.** bitter, severe
   7. doleful, heinous, intense
   8. terrible **9.** sorrowful
   10. disastrous, oppressive
   11. distressing, gravaminous
griff... **4.** claw, glen **6.** griffe, ravine
griffe... **4.** spur (Arch) **7.** mulatto
griffin, griffon... **6.** charge (Her)
   7. monster **10.** decoration
grig... **3.** eel **5.** annoy, dwarf
   7. cricket, heather **8.** irritate
   9. tantalize **11.** grasshopper
grill... **4.** cook **5.** broil **7.** griddle,

network, torture 8. gridiron
10. restaurant 11. interrogate
12. cross–examine

grille . . . 6. window (ticket) 7. grating,
network

grilse . . . 6. salmon 7. botcher

grim . . . 4. dour, sour 5. gaunt, harsh,
stern 6. grisly, horrid, savage, sullen
7. ghastly, hideous 8. horrible,
pitiless, ruthless, sinister 9. ferocious,
frightful, merciless, repellent
10. forbidding, inexorable, relentless,
unyielding

grimace . . . 3. mop, mow, mug 4. face,
mock, moue, pout, sham 8. pretense
10. distortion 11. affectation

grimalkin . . . 3. cat 5. vixen 6. feline
8. old woman

grime . . . 4. dirt, smut, soot 5. sully
9. blackness

grin . . . 5. fleer, smile, smirk

grind . . . 3. dig, rub, vex 4. bray, grit,
mull, whet 5. crush, gnash, grate,
study 6. abrade, drudge, harass,
polish, powder, satire, school, squash
7. operate, routine, sharpen
8. drudgery 9. comminute, masticate,
pulverize, triturate

grinder . . . 5. molar, tooth, tutor
8. sideshow 9. announcer
10. flycatcher, goatsucker

grinding . . . 6. boning 7. grating
9. attrition 10. burdensome,
irritating, tyrannical 12. excruciating

grinding (pert to) . . .
mental . . 6. boning 8. cramming,
studying
stone . . 4. mano 6. metate, muller
9. millstone
substance . . 5. emery 8. abrasive

gringo . . . 5. alien 8. American
9. foreigner 10. Englishman

grip . . . 3. bag 4. hold 5. clasp, cleat,
ditch, drain, grasp, seize, spasm
6. clench, clutch, furrow, grippe,
handle, obsess, trench, valise
7. control, illness 8. gripsack,
handfast

gripe . . . 4. grip, hold, pain 5. annoy,
brake, colic, grasp, pinch, spasm
6. clutch, harass 7. afflict, control,
mastery, vulture 8. complain, distress
9. complaint 10. affliction,
oppression

griskin . . . 4. chop, loin 5. steak

grisly . . . 4. grim 5. harsh 7. ghastly,
hideous 8. gruesome, terrible
9. deathlike 10. forbidding

grist . . . 3. lot 4. malt 5. grain, grind
8. quantity (bees)

grit . . . 4. sand 5. nerve, pluck
6. gravel 7. bravery, courage, Liberal
9. sandstone 11. persistence
12. perseverance

grivet . . . 4. tota, waag 6. monkey

grizzly bear . . . 7. Ephraim (hunter's)
15. Ursus horribilis

groats . . . 5. grain, wheat (cracked)
6. cereal

grog . . . 3. rum 5. rumbo 8. beverage
9. firewater

groggy . . . 5. dazed, drunk, shaky, tipsy

8. unsteady, wavering 9. tottering

groin . . . 4. lisk 6. inguen

groom . . . 4. syce, tidy 5. brush, curry,
dress, preen, train 7. hostler,
servant, shopboy 9. assistant,
stableman 10. bridegroom,
manservant

groove . . . 3. rut 4. dado 5. chase,
croze, flute, scarf, stria, track
6. furrow, rabbet, raggle, scrobe,
sulcus 7. channel, rifling, routine
8. philtrum 10. excavation
11. canaliculus

grooved . . . 6. fluted 7. striate, sulcate
11. canalicular 12. canaliculate

grope . . . 4. feel 6. fumble, search
7. grabble, grubble

groper . . . 4. fish 7. grouper

grosbeak . . . 5. finch 8. hawfinch

gros point . . . 4. lace (Venetian)
6. stitch (Aubusson) 8. tapestry
(Gobelin) 11. cross–stitch

gross . . . 3. fat 5. obese 6. brutal,
coarse, earthy, greasy, impure, vulgar
7. brutish, massive, obscene,
sensual, witless 8. flagrant, indecent,
receipts 9. aggregate, unrefined
10. indefinite, indelicate, scurrilous

grotesque . . . 3. odd 5. antic, clown,
freak 6. unique 7. awkward, baroque,
bizarre 8. deformed, fanciful
9. fantastic 11. incongruous

grotesque figure (Chin) . . . 5. magot

grotto . . . 3. den 4. blue, cave, grot
5. crypt, speos, vault 6. cavern,
recess 8. catacomb

ground . . . 3. bog 4. acre, area, base,
clay, clod, farm, land, moor, park,
plot, root, soil 5. basis, cause, earth,
field, hurst, marsh, ridge, solum,
swale, train 6. belief, bottom, milled,
region 7. country, gritted, opinion,
premise, terrain (terrane) 8. initiate,
instruct 9. establish, territory,
viewpoint 10. background,
foundation, substratum

ground (pert to) . . .
beetles . . 5. Amara
berry . . 9. cranberry 12. checkerberry
grain . . 4. bran, meal 5. flour, grist
nut . . 5. chufa, gobbe 6. goober,
peanut
squirrel . . 5. Xerus 6. gopher, hackee,
rodent 8. chipmunk 11. spermophile

groundhog (pert to) . . .
American . . 6. marmot
day . . 9. Candlemas (Feb 2)
home . . 8. Puxatori
termed . . 6. marmot, rodent
8. aardvark, whistler 9. woodchuck
10. whistlepig

groundless . . . 4. idle 5. false
8. baseless 9. unfounded
11. unwarranted 13. unsubstantial

grounds . . . 4. lees, park 5. basis,
dregs 7. residue 8. scruples

group . . . 3. set 4. band, bevy, clan,
crew, gang, herd, pack, sect, sept,
team, unit 5. batch, bunch, class,
clump, corps, flock, genus, order,
panel, shift, tribe 6. legion, troupe
7. arrange, bracket, cluster,

company, species 8. assemble,
category, classify, division
10. assemblage 11. aggregation

group (pert to)...
actors.. 6. troupe
animals.. 3. gam, nid, nye, pod
4. herd, nide 5. covey, drove, pride
(lions)
birds.. 4. Pici (woodpeckers)
brilliant.. 6. galaxy
far out.. 6. hippie 7. hipster
laymen.. 5. laity
political.. 4. bloc, ring 5. party
7. machine
singer.. 4. duet 5. choir, octet
6. chorus 7. chanter, quartet
(quartette)
students (graduate).. 7. seminar
trees.. 4. tope 5. copse, grove,
woods 7. alameda, orchard, pinetum
(pines)

group (quota of)...
eight.. 5. octad, octet (octette)
five.. 6. pentad
four.. 6. tetrad 7. quartet (quartette)
nine.. 6. ennead
seven.. 6. heptad, septet (septette)
six.. 6. sextet (sextette)
ten.. 5. decad 6. decade
three.. 4. trio 5. triad, trine 7. Trinity
two vowels.. 6. digram 7. digraph
9. diphthong

grouped... 7. classed 8. agminate,
arranged, gathered 9. assembled,
collected, organized 10. classified

grouper... 4. fish 5. guasa 6. groper
8. rock hind

grouse... 4. bird 6. repine 7. grumble
8. complain 9. ptarmigan
12. capercaillie

grouse (pert to)...
courtship.. 3. lak
red.. 7. Lagopus
ruffed.. 6. Bonasa

grouty... 5. cross, sulky 6. crabby,
grumpy 7. grouchy

grove (pert to)...
living in.. 7. nemoral
mango.. 4. tope
pine.. 7. pinetum
poplar.. 7. alameda
sacred.. 5. Altis (Gr), Nemus (to
Diana)
small trees.. 5. copse

grovel... 4. fawn, roll 5. crawl, creep
6. cringe, crouch, shrink, tumble,
wallow, welter 7. debauch, truckle
8. flounder

groveling, grovelling... 6. abject
7. fawning 9. prostrate, truckling
11. bootlicking

grow... 3. bud, wax 4. come 5. raise
6. accrue, expand, mature, thrive
7. augment, develop, enlarge,
improve, produce 8. increase,
vegetate 9. cultivate

grow (pert to)...
dark.. 6. darkle
dim.. 5. blear
intense, profound.. 6. deepen
thin.. 8. emaciate
tiresome.. 4. bore, pall

together.. 7. accrete
worse.. 11. deteriorate

growing (pert to)...
angry.. 8. irascent
from without.. 9. ectogenic
10. ectogenous
in.. 6. linose
on trees.. 10. epidendral, epidendric
11. xylophilous (fungus)
out from.. 3. bud 4. stem 5. enate
6. sprout
spontaneously.. 9. adventive
together.. 7. accrete, joining
8. adhering

growing in...
clusters.. 8. racemose
fields.. 8. agrestal 9. agrestial
10. campestral
ground.. 9. geogenous
mud.. 9. uliginose
pairs.. 6. binate
rubbish.. 7. ruderal
snow.. 5. nival
water.. 7. aquatic

growl... 4. girn, gnar, rome 5. snarl
6. mutter 7. grumble 8. complain

growler... 3. cab, can 4. bass (black)
7. iceberg, pitcher 8. clarence

growth... 3. bud, wen 4. rise 5. felon,
shoot, tumor 6. effect, result
8. increase, swelling 9. expansion
10. vegetation 11. consequence,
development, enlargement
12. augmentation

growth (pert to)...
from within.. 8. endogeny
from without.. 9. ectogenic
10. ectogenous
fungus.. 4. mold, moss 6. mildew
marine.. 7. seaweed
of wood.. 5. copse 7. coppice
9. brushwood
premature.. 9. precocity
process of.. 8. nascency
retarding.. 9. paratonic

grub... 3. dig 4. food, plod, root,
spud 5. larva, mathe, slave, stump
6. assart, drudge, maggot, search
7. plodder 8. victuals

grubby... 5. dirty, grimy, small
8. dwarfish, infested, slovenly,
toadfish

grudge... 4. envy 5. covet, spite
6. hatred 7. grumble 8. begrudge
10. resentment

grudging spender... 8. tightwad

gruel... 4. diet 6. cereal, liquid
7. disable 8. porridge

grueling, gruelling... 6. trying
9. demanding, punishing, weakening
10. exhausting

gruesome... 4. ugly 6. grisly, horrid,
sordid 7. ghastly, hideous, macabre
9. deathlike

gruff... 4. deep, rude, sour 5. bluff,
harsh, surly 6. clumsy, hoarse,
morose, severe 7. austere, bearish,
brusque

grum... 4. glum, sour 6. sullen
8. gutteral 13. harsh-sounding

grumble... 4. fret, hone, kick 5. growl,
snarl 6. grouse, mumble, mutter,

repine, rumble 7. maunder
8. complain
guacharo... 6. owlish 7. oilbird
10. goatsucker
Guam...
capital.. 5. Agana
discoverer.. 8. Magellan (1521)
idol, fetish.. 5. anito
island.. 7. Mariana
mountain peak.. 6. Lamlam
port.. 4. Apra
guanaco... 5. llama (like) 6. alpaca
guarantee... 6. avouch, ensure, insure,
surety 7. endorse, promise, warrant
8. guaranty, security, warranty
9. agreement
guaranty... 4. bond 6. pledge
8. security, warranty 9. agreement,
assurance, guarantee
guarapucu... 5. wahoo
guard... 3. van 4. care, curb, keep,
tend, tile 5. tiler, watch 6. bantay,
bridle, convoy, defend, escort, fender,
gaoler, jailer, keeper, patrol, picket,
police, shield, warden 7. defense,
protect 8. restrain, sentinel,
watchman 9. attention, protector
10. cowcatcher, precaution,
protection
guarded... 4. wary 7. careful
8. cautious, defended, discreet,
vigilant, watchful 9. protected
10. restrained 11. circumspect,
sentinelled
guardhouse... 4. brig
guardian... 5. angel, tutor 6. helper,
keeper, patron, warden 7. trustee
8. defender, tutelary 9. custodian,
protector 10. mystagogue (Church
relics)
guardian (Gr)... 5. Argus (100–eyed)
8. Cerberus (3–headed)
guardianship... 4. care 6. charge
7. custody, tuition 8. guidance,
tutelage 13. protectorship
Guatemala...
ant.. 5. kelep
bird (sacred).. 7. quetzal (quezal)
capital.. 13. Guatemala City
coin (gold).. 7. quetzal
fruit (avocadolike).. 4. anay
Indian tribe.. 4. Inca
port.. 7. San José 10. Champerico
13. Puerto Barrios
ruins.. 5. Mayan
volcano.. 4. Agua 5. Fuego
gudgeon... 4. bait, dupe, goby
9. killifish 10. allurement
gue... 5. rogue 7. sharper
guenon... 6. monkey (long–tailed)
guerdon... 5. crown, prize 6. reward
8. requital 10. recompense
guereza... 6. monkey
Guernsey... 6. brandy, cattle, Island
(Channel) 7. garment
guess... 5. fancy, think 6. divine
7. imagine, presume, surmise,
suspect 8. estimate 10. conjecture
guest... 6. caller, inmate, lodger,
patron 7. visitor 9. inquiline (insect)
Guiana...
British capital.. 10. Georgetown

Dutch (Surinam) capital..
10. Paramaribo
French capital.. 7. Cayenne
guide... 3. con, key 4. clew, clue,
lead, rein, sign, sley 5. order, pilot,
steer, teach, tutor, usher 6. advise,
direct, dirigo, govern, guidon
7. adviser, conduct, courier, marshal
8. Baedeker (book), cicerone,
director, polestar, regulate
9. regulator
Guido (scale)... 2. ut 3. alt, A re, B
mi, E la (highest) 5. E la mi, gamut
7. alamire
guild... 5. hanse 7. society
10. fellowship 11. association,
brotherhood
Guildhall statue (London)... 3. Gog
5. Magog (1708)
guile... 5. craft 6. deceit 9. duplicity,
falseness, treachery 11. furtiveness
guileless... 5. naive 6. simple
7. artless, natural, sincere
8. innocent
guillemot... 3. auk 4. coot 5. murre
guilt... 3. sin 4. sake 5. culpa
8. iniquity, peccancy 10. guiltiness,
wickedness 11. criminality, culpability
14. impeachability
guilty... 6. nocent 8. culpable
Guinea, W Afr...
capital.. 7. Conakry (Konakri)
city.. 4. Boke, Labe
export.. 7. bananas 10. pineapples
government.. 8. republic
mineral.. 4. gold 7. bauxite
8. diamonds
tree.. 4. akee
tribe.. 6. Fullah 7. Malinke, Soussou
guinea fowl... 3. hen 4. keet
6. turkey 7. pintado 8. pheasant
guinea pig... 4. boar, cavy 5. Cavia
8. capybara
guise... 3. way 4. form, garb, mask,
mien, mode 5. cloak, cover
6. aspect, custom 7. fashion, pretext
8. behavior 9. semblance
10. appearance
guitar (pert to)...
Hindu.. 4. vina
like.. 4. lute 7. bandore
octaves.. 5. three
Oriental.. 5. sitar
pitch (term).. 5. dital
ridge.. 7. samisen
small.. 7. ukulele
strings, number.. 3. six
gula... 4. cyma, neck, ogee 6. gullet
7. cavetto, molding
gulch... 5. cleft, gorge 6. arroyo,
coulee, ravine
gulf... 3. bay, pit, sea (landlocked)
4. eddy 5. abyss, basin, chasm,
cleft, inlet 6. vorago 7. opening
9. whirlpool 10. separation (wide)
gull... 4. dupe, fool, gray 5. brick,
cheat, cully, fraud 7. cheater,
deceive, defraud, mislead 8. impostor
gull (bird)... 3. cob (cobb), mew
4. Lari, pirr, skua, tern, Xema
5. pewit (laughing) 7. Larinae
8. seedbird 9. kittiwake

gullet... 3. maw 4. tube 5. gully
  6. throat 7. channel, harness (part)
  9. esophagus
Gulliver, Lemuel (pert to)...
  brutes.. 6. Yahoos (race of)
  character, story by.. 5. Swift
  romance.. 16. Gulliver's Travels
  voyage.. 6. Laputa 8. Lilliput
  9. Houyhnhnm 11. Brobdingnag
gully... 3. gut 4. wadi (wady) 5. drain,
  gorge, gulch 6. arroyo, gutter, ravine
  7. couloir 11. watercourse
gum... 3. ase 4. chew, lerp (larp,
  laarp) 5. elemi, myrrh, xylan
  6. acacia, arabic, chicle, conima,
  thwart, tupelo 7. camphor, deceive,
  elastic, gingiva 8. bdellium (Bib),
  mucilage 12. frankincense
gum (pert to)...
  Africa.. 4. kino 7. catechy
  Asia.. 6. Storax 8. galbabum
  Australia.. 5. tuart
  Central America.. 6. chicle
  Egypt.. 5. kikar
  India.. 5. amrad
  Philippines.. 8. galagala
  United States.. 5. Nyssa 6. tupelo
gumbo... 3. mud 4. okra (ocra), sail,
  soup 6. patois
gumboil... 7. abscess, parulia
gummy... 5. lumpy 6. viscid
  7. viscous 8. adhesive, resinous
gumption... 8. sagacity 10. enterprise,
  initiative, shrewdness
gums... 3. ula 6. resins 8. gingivae
gun... 3. gat, rod 4. iron, pump, roer
  5. Maxim, rifle, thief, tommy
  6. ack–ack, Archie, barker, Bertha,
  cannon, mortar, pistol, Rodman
  7. bazooka, carbine, firearm, Gatling,
  machine, shotgun 8. amusette,
  ordnance, revolver
gun (pert to)...
  blow.. 8. sumpitan
  caliber.. 4. bore
  case (leather).. 7. holster
  chamber.. 5. gomer
  cleaner.. 6. ramrod
  cotton.. 5. nitro 9. explosive, pyroxylin
  mount.. 6. turret
  platform.. 11. emplacement
gunfire... 5. salvo 6. strafe 8. enfilade
gunner... 10. bombardier
  12. artilleryman
guppy... 6. minnow 8. Lebistes
  9. killifish
gurnard... 4. fish 6. rochet, Trigla
  8. dragonet, sea robin
guru (Ind)... 7. teacher
gush... 3. jet 4. flow, pour 5. emote,
  spurt 7. chatter 10. outpouring
  14. sentimentalize
gushing... 7. flowing 8. diffused,

effusive, spurting 9. exuberant
  11. sentimental 13. demonstrative
gusset... 4. gore 7. bracket
  9. abatement (Her)
gust... 4. blow, gale, scud, wind
  5. berry, blast, storm 6. flurry, squall
  8. outburst 10. excitement
gusto... 4. élan, zest 5. savor, taste
  6. fervor, liking, relish 9. eagerness
  12. appreciation
gut... 3. sac (silkworm) 5. gully
  6. bowels, catgut, defile, strait
  7. destroy, plunder 8. entrails
  9. intestine 10. disembowel,
  eviscerate
guts... 5. belly, force, pluck 6. vitals
  7. courage, insides, stamina,
  stomach 8. backbone, gluttony
  10. intestines
gutta... 4. drop, spot 5. latex
  7. campana, marking 8. ornament
guttate... 7. spotted 8. droplike
gutter... 4. rone 5. brook, ditch, drain,
  eaves, gully, siver 6. cullis, groove
  7. channel, conduit, scupper
  11. watercourse
gutteral... 3. dry 4. burr 5. husky,
  velar 6. hoarse 7. rasping, throaty
guttersnipe... 4. Arab 5. gamin
  6. poster 9. ragpicker, sandpiper,
  vulgarian
guy... 3. rod 4. flee, rope, stay, vang
  5. chaff, chain, guide 6. banter,
  decamp, effigy (Guy Fawkes), fellow,
  person
Guy Fawkes Day... 13. Gunpowder
  Plot (Eng, Nov 5,1605)
guzzle... 3. tun 4. tope 5. drain,
  drink, spree 6. gutter, liquor, throat,
  tipple 7. debauch, swallow
gymnast... 7. acrobat, athlete, teacher
gymnastics... 9. exercises
  10. acrobatics 12. calisthenics
gypsy (pert to)...
  book.. 3. lil
  devil.. 5. theng
  Dutch.. 8. Heidenen
  horse.. 3. gri (gry)
  Hungarian.. 7. Czigany
  husband.. 3. rom
  India.. 7. Bazigar
  language.. 6. Romany
  man.. 4. chal
  sea.. 6. Selung
  Spanish.. 6. gitano 7. Zincalo
  Syrian.. 5. Aptal
  term.. 4. calo 5. nomad
  woman.. 4. chai (chi)
gyrate... 4. spin 5. twirl, whirl
  6. rotate 7. revolve
gyre... 5. demon, whirl 10. revolution
gyves... 5. irons 6. chains 7. fetters
  8. shackles

H

H... 5. aitch, zygal (shaped) 6. letter (8th), symbol 8. aspirate
haab... 8. calendar (Mayan)
haar... 3. fog
haba... 4. bean 8. lima bean
Habakkuk... 4. Book (Old Test) 7. prophet
habble... 5. brawl 6. gabble, hobble, uproar 9. confusion 10. difficulty
habeas corpus... 4. writ 7. summons (you have the body)
habile... 3. apt, fit 4. able 6. adroit, clever, expert 8. skillful (skilful), suitable 9. dexterous
habiliment... 4. garb 5. dress, habit 6. attire 7. apparel, costume, raiment 8. clothing, vestment 11. furnishings
habilitate... 5. dress, equip 6. clothe, fit out 7. entitle, qualify (for teaching)
habit... 3. rut, use 4. garb, suit, vice, wont 5. array, dress, haunt, usage 6. attire, clothe, custom, joseph (riding), nature 7. costume 8. clothing, habitude, practice 9. mannerism 10. deportment, habiliment
habitat... 4. home 5. abode, house, hovel 6. harbor, reside 7. exhibit (museum), lodging, station
habitation... 4. ecad, home 5. hovel 6. ghetto, warren (rabbit) 7. lodging 8. domicile, dwelling, tenement 9. occupancy, residence
habitual... 5. usual 6. common, wonted 7. orderly, regular 9. customary 10. accustomed, inveterate
habituate... 5. enure, inure 6. addict, inborn, season, settle 8. accustom, frequent, inherent 9. acclimate 11. acclimatize, familiarize
habitué... 8. attender 10. frequenter
hacendero... 6. farmer 10. proprietor
hache... 2. ax 7. hatchet
hacienda... 4. farm 5. abode, croft 6. estate 7. revenue 13. establishment
hack... 3. cut, hew 4. chop, jade, rent 5. coach, cough, devil, horse (rented), sever 6. drudge, mangle, writer 8. carriage, mutilate 9. mercenary 11. chronometer
hackberry... 6. Celtis 8. hapberry, oneberry 10. sugarberry
hackee... 8. chipmunk
hackle... 3. fly (angling) 4. comb, hack 6. shiner, temper 7. feather, hatchel, plumage 11. stickleback
hackneyed... 3. saw 5. banal, corny,

trite 6. cliché 8. timeworn 10. threadbare 11. commonplace, stereotyped 13. platitudinous
Hades... 3. pit 4. hell 5. abyss, limbo 7. inferno 9. perdition 10. lower world, underworld 11. netherworld
Hades (pert to)...
Babylonian.. 5. Aralu
capital.. 11. Pandemonium
god.. 5. Pluto
Greek.. 8. Tartarus
Hebrew.. 5. Sheol 7. Abaddon, Gehenna 8. Apollyon
Hindu.. 6. Naraka
mother.. 4. Rhea
river.. 4. Styx 5. Lethe 7. Acheron
Roman.. 3. Dis 5. Orcus
hadj... 10. pilgrimage
haft... 4. ansa, grip, hold 6. handle 8. dwelling
hag... 4. Fury, goad 5. crone, ghost, Harpy, vixen, witch 6. beldam (beldame), goblin 8. harridan, old woman 9. hobgoblin
hageen, hagein... 9. dromedary
hagfish... 5. borer 6. Mysine 7. lamprey (lowest existing craniate vertebrate)
haggard... 4. bony, lank, lean, pale, thin, wild 5. gaunt, spare 6. wanton 7. anxious, untamed 8. harrowed, unchaste, wild–eyed 9. deathlike, suffering, untrained 10. cadaverous 11. intractable, overwrought
haggle... 3. cut, hew 4. hack, prig 5. cavil 6. chisel, dicker, higgle, palter 7. bargain, chaffer, stickle, wrangle
Hague, The... 7. capital (Neth)
Haida (pert to)...
famed for.. 6. totems 7. carving 10. seamanship
Indian.. 15. British Columbia
tribe.. 11. Skittagetan
hail... 3. ave, ice 4. ahoy, call 5. avast, greet, skoal 6. accost, health, signal 7. acclaim, address, graupel, pellets
hair... 3. cue, fur, mop 4. lock, mane, seta, shag 5. pilus, plume, tress 6. thread 7. bristle 8. filament 10. narrowness
hair (pert to)...
accessory.. 3. net, pin 8. barrette
Angora.. 6. mohair
band.. 5. snood 6. fillet
braid.. 3. cue 4. fall 5. queue 7. pigtail
cell.. 12. Organ of Corti
cloth.. 3. aba 5. shirt 6. cilice

comb form .. **4.** pilo
curly .. **10.** cymotrichy
disease .. **8.** dandruff, psilosis
dresser .. **7.** friseur (Fr), stylist
dryness .. **7.** xerasia
excessive growth .. **7.** pilosis
flaxen .. **5.** linus
horse's foot .. **7.** fetlock
intestinal .. **6.** villus
liquid for .. **3.** set **5.** spray **6.** lotion
   7. relaxer
lock .. **5.** tress **7.** earlock, ringlet
   8. lovelock **9.** dreadlock
loss of .. **8.** alopecia, baldness
of the .. **6.** crinal
remover .. **9.** decalvant, epilatory
   10. depilatory
straight .. **10.** leiotrichy
style .. **3.** set **4.** Afro, tete, updo
   6. hairdo **7.** chignon, cornrow
   8. coiffure
tuft .. **4.** coma **5.** beard **6.** goatee
   7. cirrose, Galways, Vandyke
   8. whiskers **9.** sideburns
wave .. **4.** perm **6.** marcel
wig .. **6.** peruke **7.** periwig
wooly .. **9.** ulotrichy
hairiness ... **7.** villous **9.** villosity
hairless ... **4.** bald **5.** acoma
   7. acomous, epilose **8.** depilous,
   glabrous
hairpin ... **6.** bodkin **8.** bobby pin
hairsplitting ... **9.** quibbling
   11. distinction **13.** hypercritical
   14. hypercriticism, overparticular
hairy ... **4.** noil **5.** pilar **6.** comate,
   comoid, comose, crinal, pilose, shaggy
   7. bristly, crinose, hirsute **8.** trichoid
Haiti, Haitian ...
bandit .. **4.** caco
capital .. **12.** Port–au–Prince
dance .. **5.** mambo
discoverer .. **8.** Columbus (1492)
evil spirit .. **4.** baka (boko)
island .. **10.** Hispaniola **15.** Greater
   Antilles
language .. **6.** Creole, French, patois
liberator .. **9.** Toussaint
product .. **6.** coffee
sweet potato .. **6.** batata
hake ... **4.** fish **5.** idler, tramp **6.** loiter
   7. handgun **8.** kingfish
halberd ... **4.** bill **5.** frame (flogging)
   6. glaive, weapon (Mil)
halcyon ... **4.** bird, calm **8.** peaceful,
   tranquil **10.** auspicious, kingfisher
Halcyone (pert to) ...
changed to .. **10.** kingfisher
daughter of .. **6.** Aeolus
wife of .. **4.** Ceyx (Gr)
hale ... **3.** tug **4.** drag, draw, haul, pull,
   well **6.** hearty, robust, strong
   7. healthy **8.** vigorous **9.** strapping
half ... **4.** demi, hemi, part, semi, term
   5. share **6.** moiety **7.** divided, partial
   8. division, semester **9.** equal part,
   bisection **11.** imperfectly
half (pert to) ...
and half .. **5.** equal, mixed **6.** halved
   7. neutral
boot .. **3.** pac (pack) **6.** buskin
man, half bull .. **8.** minotaur

man, half horse .. **7.** centaur
mask .. **6.** domino
moon–shaped .. **9.** semilunar
nelson (wrestling) .. **4.** hold
stem to stern .. **8.** midships
turn (manège) .. **8.** caracole (caracol)
wit .. **4.** dolt **5.** dunce **9.** blockhead
Half Moon ship (pert to) ...
captain .. **11.** Henry Hudson
country .. **11.** Netherlands
first to sail .. **11.** Hudson River (1609)
Halicarnassus, famed for ...
Historians (Gr) .. **9.** Dionysius,
   Herodotus
monument .. **9.** Mausoleum (Tomb of
   Mausolus, 325 BC)
hall ... **4.** aula, room, sala **5.** entry,
   foyer, odeum (odeon) **6.** atrium,
   lyceum **7.** hallway, passage, theater
   8. corridor **9.** vestibule
   10. auditorium, passageway
hallow ... **5.** bless **8.** dedicate,
   sanctify, venerate **9.** celebrate
   10. consecrate
hallowed place ... **4.** fane, holy
   5. altar **6.** bethel, church, shrine,
   temple **9.** cathedral, synagogue
hallucination ... **6.** mirage **7.** chimera,
   fantasy **8.** delusion **9.** nightmare
hallux ... **3.** toe **5.** digit
halo ... **3.** arc **4.** aura, glow, nimb, ring
   5. glory, light **6.** areola, brough,
   circle, corona, nimbus **7.** aureole
   (aureola) **8.** encircle, halation
halt ... **3.** end **4.** camp, lame, limp,
   stop **5.** cease, check, pause, stand
   6. arrest, hold up, maimed **7.** limping
   8. blockage, crippled, lameness
   9. mutilated **10.** standstill
halter ... **4.** hang, rope **5.** noose, strap
   6. hamper **7.** shackle **8.** cavesson,
   restrain **9.** hackamore
halting ... **4.** lame **6.** maimed
   7. limping **8.** spavined
   10. hesitating, stammering
halting place ... **4.** camp **5.** étape
   7. bivouac **10.** encampment
halved ... **9.** dimidiate
Hamburg, Germany ...
color .. **5.** white **6.** yellow **7.** carmine
   11. carmine lake
fowl .. **11.** Leghornlike
fruit .. **5.** grape
lace .. **6.** edging
root (edible) .. **7.** parsley
steak .. **4.** beef
hamiform ... **6.** curved, hooked
   7. hamulus **8.** aquiline
   10. hook–shaped
Hamilton (pert to) ...
dynamics .. **8.** equation
famed as .. **9.** statesman
   11. philosopher **13.** mathematician
math .. **10.** quaternion
Hamite (N Afr) ... **5.** Fulah **6.** Berber,
   Somali (Somal)
hamlet ... **4.** dorp, vill **5.** aldea (aldee),
   casal (casale), thorp (thorpe)
   7. grouper (fish), village
Hamlet (pert to) ...
character .. **11.** Shakespeare
country .. **7.** Denmark

friend.. **7.** Horatio
site.. **8.** Elsinore
hammer... **4.** beat, claw, jack, maul, peen, tack, tamp **5.** gavel, kevel, madge, pound **6.** beetle, martel, oliver, sledge, strike, swinge **7.** belabor **8.** malleate
hammer (pert to)...
bird.. **8.** umbrette
blacksmith's.. **6.** fuller, oliver
bricklayer's.. **6.** scutch
end.. **4.** poll
face.. **4.** trip
head.. **4.** peen **5.** shark
medical.. **6.** plexor **7.** plessor
out.. **5.** anvil, forge
smite.. **5.** skite
stone.. **5.** kevel, spall
hamper... **3.** ped **4.** clog, curb, load, slow **5.** cramp, crate, maund **6.** basket, burden, fetter, hinder, hopple, impede, seroon **7.** confine, hanaper, manacle, shackle, trammel **8.** encumber, restrain, restrict **9.** container, embarrass **10.** impediment
Ham's son... **4.** Cush
hamster... **6.** rodent **8.** Cricetus
hamus... **4.** hook **7.** process (Zool)
hanaper... **6.** basket, hamper
hand... **3.** paw **4.** fist, give, mano, palm, part, pass, side, till **5.** claut, grasp, index, manus, power, share, skill **6.** agency, worker **7.** ability, pointer, workman **8.** applause, tendency, transmit **9.** craftsman, handiwork, signature **10.** metacarpus **11.** handwriting, performance **15.** instrumentality
hand (pert to)...
back of.. **10.** opisthenar
bag.. **4.** etui, grip **5.** cabas, purse **8.** reticule
book.. **4.** tome **5.** codex **6.** manual **9.** vade mecum
cuffs.. **7.** darbies **8.** manacles **9.** bracelets
handful.. **4.** kirn **6.** gowpen **7.** maniple **8.** quantity
measure.. **8.** fistmele
me–down.. **4.** used, worn **5.** cheap **9.** ready–made **10.** secondhand
of the.. **6.** chiral, manual
palm.. **4.** loof **6.** thenar
picked.. **5.** eleme **6.** choice **8.** selected
script.. **6.** Neskhi (Neski)
stone (grinding).. **4.** mano
without.. **7.** amanous
writing.. **11.** chirography
writing on walls.. **4.** doom, mene (Bib), omen **8.** graffito
handicap... **4.** lisp, race **6.** burden, hamper, hinder, impede **8.** encumber, equalize, penalize **9.** advantage **10.** impediment, stuttering **11.** encumbrance **12.** disadvantage
handicraftsman... **7.** artisan
handkerchief... **7.** malabar **8.** mouchoir **9.** neckcloth **11.** neckerchief

handle... **3.** ear, paw, ply, use **4.** ansa, bail, deal, feel, haft, hilt, knob, maul, name, toat, tote **5.** helve, pilot, snath, swipe, title, touch, treat, wield **6.** deal in, direct, manage, rounce, second, sneath, tiller **7.** control, operate
handle (pert to)...
awkwardly.. **6.** fumble, mumble
carelessly.. **6.** cajole **7.** tweedle
roughly.. **4.** maul **6.** bruise, injure, mangle
shaped.. **6.** ansate
skillfully.. **6.** manage **7.** control **10.** manipulate
hands (pert to)...
nautical.. **4.** crew, gang
off.. **4.** don't, quit, stop **5.** taboo **6.** desist **9.** interdict
on hips.. **6.** akimbo
without.. **7.** amanous
handsome... **5.** ample **6.** comely, heppen (dial) **7.** elegant, gallant, liberal **8.** generous, gracious, pleasing, suitable **9.** agreeable, beautiful **10.** jimpricute **11.** appropriate, magnanimous **12.** considerable
handwriting on the wall... **4.** mene (Bib) **8.** graffito, upharsin
handy... **4.** deft **5.** adept, ready **6.** adroit, heppen, nearby, wieldy **8.** skillful (skilful) **9.** dexterous, versatile **10.** accessible, convenient
hang... **3.** sag **4.** pend, rest, sway **5.** cling, drape, droop, hover, knack **6.** cleave, dangle, depend **7.** execute, meaning, suspend
hang (pert to)...
around.. **4.** loaf, wait **6.** loiter **8.** frequent
back.. **3.** lag **5.** demur, loath **6.** falter **9.** reluctant
down.. **3.** lop **4.** lave **5.** droop **6.** depend
loosely.. **3.** lop **4.** flag, loll **6.** bangle, dangle
on, onto.. **5.** cling **6.** adhere, depend **9.** persevere
over.. **6.** impend
together.. **4.** loin **6.** cohere **9.** co–operate
hanger–on... **3.** bur **5.** toady **6.** heeler **8.** follower, loiterer, parasite **9.** appendage, dependent, sycophant, toadeater (menial) **10.** blackguard
hanging... **5.** arras, drape, loose **7.** curtain, pendant (pendent), pensile, valance **8.** downcast, pendency **9.** execution, suspended
hanging (pert to)...
Eccl.. **6.** dorsal, dossal (dossel)
Gardens of Babylon, builder.. **14.** Nebuchadnezzar (Nebuchadrezzar)
ornament.. **6.** bangle **7.** pendant
stage.. **7.** scenery
hangman... **8.** carnifex **9.** Jack Ketch **11.** executioner
hangman's noose... **4.** rope **6.** hempen
hangnail... **6.** agnail **7.** whitlow
hangout... **5.** joint **10.** rendezvous

hank... 3. ran (twine) 4. coil 5. skein
hanker after... 5. crave, yearn
  6. aspire, desire, hunger 7. long for
Hannibal (pert to)...
  accomplishment.. 8. Punic War (2nd)
  father.. 13. Hamilcar Barca
  native of.. 8. Carthage
  rank.. 7. General (genius)
  victory at.. 6. Cannae
Hanover, House of... 8. Victoria
Hanukkah, Hanukka... 7. holiday
  (Jew) 16. Festival of Lights (Bib)
  17. Feast of Dedication (Jew)
haphazard... 6. chance, random
  8. accident, careless 9. orderless
haply... 9. perchance
happen... 4. come, fall, fare 5. evene
  (obs), occur 6. arrive, befall, betide,
  chance, mayhap 9. eventuate,
  transpire
happening... 4. fact 5. event (chance)
  6. tiding 7. episode 8. incident,
  periodic, sporadic 10. occurrence
happily... 5. fitly, haply 6. gladly
  9. tactfully, willingly 10. blissfully,
  cheerfully, gracefully 11. contentedly,
  opportunely 12. auspiciously,
  felicitously, prosperously, successfully
  13. appropriately
happiness, science of...
  11. eudaemonics
happy... 3. apt 4. cosh, glad 5. blest,
  faust, lucky, ready, seely, sunny
  6. joyful, timely 7. blessed, content,
  fitting 8. cheerful 9. contented,
  fortunate, pertinent 10. auspicious,
  felicitous, propitious, prosperous
Happy Valley... 8. paradise (of
  Rasselas, Andrew Jackson)
hara–kiri (Jap)... 7. seppuku, suicide
harangue... 3. nag 4. rant 5. orate,
  spiel, spout 6. screed, speech, tirade
  7. address, declaim, expound,
  lecture, oration
harass... 3. din, fag, nag, try, vex
  4. bait, fret, gall, haze, jade, raid,
  tire 5. annoy, beset, bully, chafe,
  grind, harry, tease, weary, worry
  6. badger, bother, heckle, hector,
  molest, pester, plague 7. agitate,
  disturb, hagride, perplex, provoke,
  torment, trouble 8. distress, irritate
  9. persecute, tantalize
harbinger... 4. host, omen 5. usher
  6. herald 7. presage, shelter
  8. fourrier, harborer 9. informant,
  messenger, precursor 10. forerunner
harbinger of Spring... 5. robin
  6. crocus
harbor, harbour... 3. bay 4. cave,
  port 5. haven 6. covert, foster,
  refuge 7. lodging, outport, retreat,
  shelter
hard... 3. fit 4. cold, dour, firm, iron,
  mean 5. close, harsh, rigid, stern,
  stony 6. knotty, robust, steely, stingy,
  strict, strong 7. callous, onerous
  8. diligent, rigorous, toilsome
  9. difficult, heartless, intricate,
  strenuous, stringent, wearisome
  10. inflexible, relentless, unyielding
  12. impenetrable, incorrigible

  13. unsympathetic
hard (pert to)...
  boiled.. 4. hard 5. tough 6. strict
  7. callous 8. hardened 10. solidified
  13. sophisticated
  coal.. 10. anthracite
  money.. 6. silver 8. metallic
  prefix.. 3. dys
  question.. 5. poser
  rubber.. 7. ebonite 9. vulcanite
  shell.. 6. lorica
  stone.. 7. adamant (diamond)
  wood.. 4. mabi, teak 5. maple
  6. walnut 8. mahogany
harden... 3. gel, set 4. cake, kern
  5. enure, inure, steel 6. freeze,
  ossify, temper 7. toughen
  8. indurate, solidify 9. habituate
  10. strengthen
hardened... 4. hard 5. caked
  6. frozen, wicked 7. callous, steeled
  8. indurate, obdurate, ossified
  9. heartless, reprobate, unfeeling
  10. impenitent, impervious,
  inveterate, solidified 12. impenetrable
hardening of the arteries...
  16. arteriosclerosis
hardening of the eyeball...
  8. glaucoma
hardheaded... 5. boche (Boche)
  6. German, shrewd, strict
  9. obstinate, sagacious
hardhearted... 4. mean 5. cruel
  7. callous 8. pitiless 9. unfeeling
  13. unsympathetic
hardship... 5. rigor 6. injury 7. trouble
  8. hardness 9. adversity, privation
hardtack... 5. bread 7. galette
  10. sea biscuit
hardwood... 3. ash, oak 4. ipil, mabi,
  teak 5. maple 6. walnut
  8. mahogany
hardy... 4. bold, hale, rash 5. brave,
  lusty, stout 6. daring, strong
  7. healthy, spartan 8. intrepid,
  resolute 9. audacious, confident
  10. courageous
hare... 3. doe, wat (watt) 4. buck,
  cony, pika (tailless) 5. lapin, Lepus
  6. rabbit, rodent, tapeti 7. leveret
hare (pert to)...
  constellation.. 5. Lepus
  harelike.. 6. agouti 8. leporine
  tail.. 4. scut
  track.. 4. slot
  type.. 10. cottontail, jack rabbit
harem... 5. serai 6. purdah, zenana
  8. seraglio 9. gynaeceum
harem room... 3. oda (odah)
harem slave... 9. odalisque (odalisk)
hark... 4. heed, hist 6. listen
  7. hearken, whisper 9. attention
harkened... 5. heard 6. heeded
  8. listened 9. hearkened
harlequin... 4. duck (sea) 5. clown,
  color 7. buffoon 9. fantastic, trickster
  11. masquerader 12. multi–colored,
  parti–colored
Harlequin (comedy)... 11. pantomimist
harm... 3. mar 4. bane, dere, evil,
  hurt, pain 5. grief, wrong
  6. damage, impair, injure, injury,

scathe (scath), sorrow
10. misfortune, wickedness
12. disadvantage
harmful ... **3.** bad **4.** evil, upas
6. nocent **7.** baneful, hurtful, malefic,
noisome, noxious **8.** damaging,
sinister **9.** injurious **10.** pernicious
11. deleterious, detrimental
12. insalubrious
harmless ... **5.** seely **6.** unhurt
8. dehorned, unharmed
9. innocuous, undamaged, uninjured
11. unoffending
harmonious ... **6.** syntax **7.** harmony,
musical, orderly, spheral, tuneful
9. accordant, agreeable, congruous,
consonant, eurythmic (eurhythmic),
melodious **10.** compatible,
concordant, euphonious
11. conformable, symmetrical
harmonize ... **2.** go **3.** gee **4.** tone
5. agree, blend, chime **6.** attune
7. conform, consist **9.** reconcile
10. correspond, symmetrize,
sympathize
harmony ... **4.** tone, tune **5.** music,
order, triad, unity **6.** accord, cosmos,
melody, unison **7.** concord, euphony
8. symmetry **9.** agreement,
harmonics **10.** conformity,
consonance
harness ... **4.** gear **5.** armor, equip
6. graith, tackle **7.** uniform
8. accouter, ornament **9.** caparison,
parachute
harness part ... **3.** tug **4.** hame, rein
5. trace **6.** collar, halter, terret
7. apparel **9.** hackamore
10. breastband, martingale
harp ... **4.** arpa, koto, lyre, Lyra (Astron)
5. nanga **8.** Irishman **11.** clairschach
harp (pert to) ...
　key .. **5.** C Flat
　octaves (number) .. **11.** six and a half
　pedals .. **5.** seven
　star .. **12.** Harp of Arthur
　strings .. **8.** forty–six
harping ... **7.** humdrum, tedious
9. iterating, repeating **11.** repetitious
harpoon ... **5.** spear **7.** javelin **8.** lily
iron
harpsichord ... **6.** spinet **8.** clavecin
9. lyrichord **12.** clavicembalo
harpy ... **3.** bat **5.** eagle, fiend
9. plunderer **12.** extortionist
Harpy (Myth) ... **5.** Aello, ghoul
7. Celaeno, monster (part bird,
woman), Ocypete, Podarge (The Iliad)
harridan ... **3.** hag **5.** vixen, witch
6. virago **7.** Jezebel **8.** strumpet
9. termagant
harrier ... **3.** dog **4.** hawk **5.** bully,
hound **7.** heckler **8.** badgerer
9. tormentor
harrow ... **4.** dish, pain **5.** harry, herse
(Hist), wound **7.** oppress, torment,
torture **8.** distress, lacerate
9. cultivate, formation (geese),
implement
harrowing ... **7.** painful, racking, tilling
9. agonizing, torturous

11. cultivating, distressing
12. heart–rending
harry ... **3.** vex **4.** sack **5.** annoy,
hound, worry **6.** harass, hector,
plague, ravage, ravish **7.** agitate,
besiege, pillage, plunder, violate
8. lay waste **9.** persecute
Harry ... **5.** Devil (Shak)
harsh ... **3.** raw **4.** dure, grim
5. acerb, acrid, asper, crude, gruff,
raspy, stern, stiff **6.** bitter, coarse,
severe, unkind **7.** drastic, painful,
pungent, rasping **8.** clashing,
gutteral, jangling, rigorous, strident
9. inclement, offensive, repellent
10. discordant, relentless
11. acrimonious, disagreeing
harshness ... **5.** rigor **7.** raucity
8. acrimony, pungency, severity
9. gruffness **11.** raucousness
hart ... **4.** deer, stag **5.** spade
hartebeest ... **4.** asse, tora **5.** caama
(kaama) **6.** lecama **7.** bubalis
8. antelope **10.** Alcelaphus
Harvard College honor ... **4.** book
5. detur **12.** let it be given
harvest ... **4.** crop, gain, rabi, reap
5. fruit, yield **6.** autumn, gather,
reward **7.** acquire, produce
harvest (pert to) ...
　god .. **6.** Cronus, Saturn
　goddess .. **3.** Ops **5.** Ceres
　home .. **4.** kirn, mell **6.** hockey
　moon .. **4.** full **15.** autumnal equinox
　second .. **9.** aftermath
　tick .. **6.** acarid
hash ... **4.** food **5.** mince **6.** jumble,
medley, ragout **7.** mixture
10. hodgepodge **11.** gallimaufry, olla
podrida
hashish ... **4.** hemp **5.** bhang (bang)
8. cannabis, narcotic
hassle ... **4.** fray **5.** brawl, melee
hasten ... **3.** hie **4.** scud, urge
5. amain, apace, hurry, scamp,
speed **7.** further **8.** expedite
10. accelerate **11.** precipitate
hastened ... **3.** ran **4.** hied, sped
5. raced **6.** rushed **7.** hurried,
scooted **8.** galloped **9.** expedited
11. accelerated **12.** precipitated
hasty ... **4.** fast, rash **5.** brash, eager,
fleet, quick, swift **6.** speedy, sudden,
urgent **7.** cursory, hurried **8.** reckless
9. impetuous, impulsive, premature
11. expeditious, precipitate
hasty pudding ... **4.** mush **9.** stirabout
hat ... **3.** fez, tam, top **4.** felt, hood,
silk **5.** beret, derby, gibus, opera,
straw, terai, toque **6.** bonnet, cloche,
cocked, fedora, Panama, sailor,
topper, turban **7.** chapeau, picture,
pillbox, porkpie, tricorn **8.** sombrero
9. headdress, sou'wester, stovepipe,
ten–gallon **11.** mortarboard
13. three–cornered
hat (pert to) ...
　antique .. **7.** bycoket (bycocket),
　petasos (petasus)
　covering .. **8.** havelock
　crown .. **4.** poll
　defensive .. **4.** coif

Eccl.. 7. biretta 9. Cardinal's
military.. 5. shako
opera.. 4. tile 5. gibus 6. topper
pass (the hat).. 10. collection
slang.. 4. plug 5. dicer
stovepipe.. 8. caroline
under one's.. 6. secret 9. to oneself
hatch ... 4. door, gate, line (art), plot
  5. breed 6. invent 7. concoct,
  produce 8. contrive, hatchway,
  incubate 9. floodgate, originate
  10. bring forth, sluice gate
hatchet ... 2. ax (axe) 3. adz (adze)
  4. mogo 8. tomahawk
hate ... 4. miso (comb form) 5. abhor,
  odium 6. detest, hatred, loathe,
  rancor 7. despise, dislike
  9. abominate, antipathy
hateful ... 6. odious 7. heinous
  8. terrible 9. abhorrent, execrable,
  invidious, loathsome, malicious,
  obnoxious, offensive, revolting
  10. abominable, detestable,
  disgusting 11. distasteful
  12. disagreeable
hater of ...
  children.. 10. misopedist
  mankind.. 11. misanthrope
  marriage.. 10. misogynist
  mathematics.. 8. misomath
  newness.. 9. misoneist
  sights.. 11. misoscopist
  strangers.. 8. misoxene
  work.. 11. ergophobiac
hatred ... 5. odium 6. enmity, rancor
  8. aversion 9. animosity, malignity
  10. abhorrence, repugnance
  11. detestation, malevolence
hatred of ...
  argument.. 8. misology
  change.. 9. misoneism
  children.. 9. misopedia
  God, gods.. 10. misotheism
  mankind.. 11. misanthropy
  marriage.. 8. misogamy
  strangers.. 8. misoxeny
  10. xenophobia
  war.. 9. polemical 11. misopolemic
  wisdom.. 9. misosophy
  women.. 8. misogyny
hauberk ... 5. armor 9. habergeon
haughty ... 4. airy, bold, high 5. lofty,
  noble, proud 6. snooty 7. fatuous,
  stately 8. arrogant, cavalier, orgulous,
  scornful 10. disdainful, hoity–toity
  11. domineering, highfalutin
  12. contemptuous, supercilious
haul ... 3. lug, tow, tug 4. cart, drag,
  draw, pull 5. booty, bouse, catch,
  check, shift 9. reprimand, transport
haul down a flag ... 6. strike
haunch ... 3. hip 4. huck 10. leg and
  loin 12. hindquarters
haunch bone ... 10. innominate
haunt ... 3. den 4. dive, nest 5. ghost,
  habit 6. infect, obsess, resort
  7. torment 8. frequent, practice
hautboy ... 4. oboe
have ... 3. get, hae, own 4. hold,
  keep, know 5. beget, trick 6. accept,
  effect, retain 7. cherish, perform,
  possess, swindle 10. experience,

understand, suffer from
have (pert to) ...
  ambition.. 6. aspire
  charge.. 4. tend
  on.. 4. wear
  thoughts of.. 6. ideate
  to do with.. 4. deal
  weight.. 8. militate
haven ... 3. bay 4. port 5. hithe
  (small), inlet 6. asylum, harbor,
  recess, refuge 7. shelter 9. sanctuary
havier ... 4. deer
having (pert to) ...
  blind end.. 6. caecal
  branches.. 6. ramose
  clamp, pincers.. 7. chelate
  dignity.. 8. majestic
  equal sides.. 9. isosceles
  eyes.. 7. oculate
  faith.. 8. trusting
  featherlike petals.. 7. pinnate
  feelers.. 9. antennate
  fingers.. 8. digitate
  foreknowledge.. 9. prescient
  four feet.. 11. quadrupedal
  harmful quality.. 9. innocuous
  leaves.. 6. foliar 7. foliate
  limits.. 6. finite
  local designation.. 7. topical
  lumps.. 7. noduled
  more than one mate.. 9. polyandry
  no angles.. 6. agonic
  no interest.. 6. supine
  no teeth.. 7. edental 8. edentate
  nothing to do.. 6. otiose
  one foot.. 6. uniped
  pits, depressions.. 7. foveate
    9. foveolate
  plane surfaces.. 7. faceted
  pointed end.. 6. peaked 7. cuspate
    8. aristate
  power over fire.. 10. ignipotent
  power to believe.. 9. creditive
  reflecting surface.. 8. specular
  same ending.. 11. conterminal
  same parents.. 7. germane
  sawlike edge.. 7. serrate
  scales.. 8. perulate
  scalloped edge.. 7. crenate
  taste.. 5. sapid
  thorns.. 7. spinate
  three broods yearly.. 11. trigoneutic
  two feet.. 5. biped 7. bipedal
  two horns.. 6. bicorn
  two meanings.. 9. ambiguous
  unequal sides.. 7. scalene
  web feet.. 8. pinniped
  wings.. 4. alar
having a ...
  backbone.. 10. vertebrate
  beak.. 8. rostrate
  beard.. 8. aristate
  handle.. 6. ansate
  large nose.. 6. nasute
  shield.. 9. clypeated
  stem.. 9. petiolate
  tail.. 7. caudate
  tuft.. 6. comose
  veil.. 6. velate
  will.. 7. testate
havoc ... 4. harm 5. botch, waste
  7. destroy 11. destruction,

devastation 12. annihilation
haw... 4. sloe 5. fence, hedge
   6. eyelid (3rd) 7. stammer
   8. hawthorn, messuage, turn left
   9. enclosure 11. exclamation
Hawaii... see also *Hawaiian*
capital.. 8. Honolulu
city.. 4. Hilo 7. Wailuku
district.. 7. Lahaina
explorer.. 4. Cook (Capt)
harbor.. 5. Pearl (bombed 12/7/41)
islands (major).. 4. Maui, Oahu
   5. Kauai, Lanai 6. Hawaii, Niihau
   7. Molokai 9. Kahoolawe
lake.. 5. Waiau
native.. 10. Polynesian
old name.. 15. Sandwich Islands
peak.. 8. Mauna Kea, Mauna Loa
   9. Waialeale
resort.. 7. Waikiki
Southernmost point (US).. 5. Ka Lae
State admission.. 8. Fiftieth
State bird.. 13. Hawaiian goose
State flower.. 8. hibiscus
State nickname.. 5. Aloha
   20. Paradise of the Pacific
volcano.. 7. Kilauea 8. Mauna Loa
   (largest active)
Hawaiian... 6. Kanaka
   10. Melanesian, Polynesian
   16. South Sea islander
Hawaiian (pert to)...
banquet, feast.. 7. ahaaina
basket.. 2. ie
beverage.. 4. kava 8. kavakava
bird.. 2. io, o–o 3. iwa 4. iiwi, mamo
   (ext), noio, o–o–a–a 6. olomao (thrush)
   8. drepanis
canoe.. 5. waapa
chant.. 4. mele
cloth, clothes.. 4. kapa, tapa
coffee.. 4. kona
dance.. 4. hula
fern.. 4. pulu
fibre (pine).. 2. ie
fish.. 3. awa 4. ulua 5. akule, lania
flower wreath, garland.. 3. lei
food.. 3. poi 4. kalo, taro
garment.. 6. holoku, muumuu
god.. 5. Wakea 7. Kanaloa (Pantheon)
goddess.. 4. Pele (volcanoes, fire)
gooseberry.. 4. poha
grass.. 6. emoloa
greeting.. 5. aloha
herb.. 3. pia (starch root)
king (first).. 10. Kamehameha
lava.. 2. aa 8. pahoehoe
loincloth, girdle.. 4. malo
musical instrument.. 7. ukulele
pepper.. 3. ava 4. kava 8. kavakava
precipice.. 4. pali
Queen.. 8. Kamamalu
royalty.. 4. alii
seaweed (edible).. 4. limu
shampoo, massage.. 8. lomi–lomi
shrub.. 3. pia 4. akia, pulu 5. olona
temple.. 5. heiau
tern.. 4. noio
veranda.. 5. lanai
windstorm.. 4. kona
woman.. 5. haole 6. wahine
yam.. 3. hoi

hawfinch... 8. grosbeak
hawk... 3. cry 4. hunt, sell, vend
   6. peddle 7. canvass 9. plunderer,
   warmonger
hawk (bird)... 2. io 3. hen 4. eyas,
   kahu, kite, nyas, seel (blind) 5. Astur,
   Buteo 6. falcon, osprey, tercel (tiercel)
   7. buzzard, Cooper's, goshawk,
   harrier, kestrel, puttock, sparrow,
   vulture 8. caracara 9. Accipiter,
   red–tailed
hawker of fruit (Eng)... 6. coster
   12. costermonger
hawk–eyed deity... 2. Ra
Hawkeye State... 4. Iowa
hawking... 7. hunting, vending
   8. falconry
hawk moth... 6. sphinx 8. sphingid
hawksbill... 4. pawl 6. turtle
   8. tortoise
hawkshaw... 6. sleuth 9. detective
   11. sleuthhound
hawk's nest... 5. aerie (aery)
hawser... 4. line, rope
hawser post... 4. bitt 7. bollard
hawthorn... 3. may 5. hazel (fruit)
   6. red haw 7. haw tree 9. mayflower
Hawthorne, Nathaniel... 6. author
   8. novelist
hay... 6. fodder 7. timothy
hay (pert to)...
bird.. 7. hay jack 8. black cap
   9. sandpiper (pectoral)
bundle.. 3. mow 4. bale, cock, rick
   5. stack
fork.. 5. pikel (pikle), pitch
herb.. 8. sainfoin
mown.. 5. swath
second cutting.. 5. rowen
spreader.. 6. tedder
stack.. 4. rick 7. hayrick
storage site.. 3. mow 4. barn, loft,
   silo
hazard... 3. fog 4. dare, game, jump,
   risk 5. peril 6. gamble, sanger, stroke
   7. imperil, jeopard, presume, venture
   8. cabstand, casualty, endanger,
   jeopardy 11. restriction
hazardous... 5. hairy (sl), jumpy, risky
   6. chancy, queasy, unsafe 7. unsound
   8. perilous 9. uncertain, venturous
   10. fortuitous 11. speculative,
   venturesome
haze... 3. fog 4. beat, film, glin (at
   sea), mist, smog 5. scold, smoke,
   vapor 7. dimness, drizzle 8. frighten
hazy... 3. dim 5. filmy, foggy, misty,
   smoky, thick, vague 6. cloudy,
   opaque, stupid 7. muddled, nebular,
   obscure 8. overcast 9. invisible,
   uncertain 10. indistinct
he... 2. il 3. man 4. ipsi, male 6. any
   one, letter 7. pronoun
head... 3. aim, nob 4. lead, pate, poll,
   tete 5. caput, chief, skull 6. noggin,
   noodle (sl), source 7. cranium
head (pert to)...
abbey.. 5. abbot 6. abbess
back of.. 7. occiput
bald.. 6. acomia 9. pilgarlic
bone.. 8. parietal 9. occipital
Gorgon.. 6. Medusa (Myth)

hard.. 5. boche
of hair.. 5. crine
pert to.. 8. cephalic
proportion.. 14. mesitacephalic
shaven.. 7. tonsure
shrunken.. 7. tsentsa
headache... 6. megrim 8. migraine
  11. cephalalgia
head covering... 3. cap, hat, tam, wig
  4. hair, hood, veil 5. beret, miter,
  scalp 6. bonnet, peruke, toupee,
  wimple 7. biretta 8. sombrero
  10. fascinator
headdress... 3. wig 4. pouf, tête
  5. busby, miter, shako, tiara
  6. coiffe, diadem, hennin, peruke,
  pinner 7. bandore, buzz wig, coronet,
  periwig 8. coiffure, headtire
headdress (Egypt)... 6. uraeus (with
  sacred asp)
headhunters (Luzon)... 7. Igorots
heading... 3. top 5. front, title, topic
  6. pillow 7. bolster, caption
  8. headline 9. direction
  12. decapitation
headland... 4. cape, mull, ness
  5. morro, ridge 10. promontory
headless... 6. stupid 7. acephal,
  topless 9. acephalus (monster)
  10. acephalous
headline... 6. banner 7. caption,
  display, heading
headliner... 4. star 7. feature
  8. composer
headlong... 4. rash 5. hasty, steep
  6. head–on, sudden 8. reckless
  9. headfirst, impetuous, impulsive
  10. recklessly 11. impulsively,
  precipitate, precipitous
headpiece... 3. cap, hat, top 4. atef
  5. crown 6. halter, helmet, lintel
  7. fitting 8. covering, ornament, skull
  cap 9. headboard, headdress,
  headstall
head–shaped... 8. capitate
headstrong... 4. rash 6. entêté, unruly
  7. violent, wayward 9. obstinate
  11. intractable, opinionated
  12. contumacious, ungovernable
heal... 4. cure, knit, mend 6. doctor,
  pacify, remedy, repair 7. correct,
  restore 9. cicatrize
healing (pert to)...
agent.. 6. balsam
compound.. 4. balm
goddess.. 3. Eir
magic.. 6. powwow
process.. 4. scar 8. cicatrix
remedy.. 8. curative, sanative
science.. 9. iatrology
suffix.. 7. iatrics
health (pert to)...
care.. 7. welfare
comb form.. 4. sani
conditions.. 8. sanitary
goddess.. 5. Salus 6. Hygeia
  7. Minerva
Latin.. 5. salus
neurotic.. 13. hypochondriac
resort.. 3. spa 7. springs
symbol.. 5. pansy

healthful... 7. healthy 8. curative,
  salutary, sanatory 9. medicinal
  10. salubrious
healthy... 4. hale, sane, well
  6. hearty, robust 8. salutary,
  vigorous 9. healthful, wholesome
  10. salubrious
heap... 3. cop 4. dess, load, lump,
  pile, pyre, raff, raft 5. amass, cairn,
  crowd, stack 6. plenty, sorite, throng
  7. cumulus 9. multitude
  10. accumulate
heaped... 5. piled 7. stacked
  8. acervate 9. collected
hear... 3. see 4. feel, heed, oyez
  (oyes) 5. favor, judge, learn
  6. attend, listen 7. hearken (harken)
  8. listen to, perceive 9. attention
  10. adjudicate
hearer... 7. audient, auditor
  8. disciple, listener 9. hearkener
  (harkener) 12. eavesdropper
hearing (pert to)... 3. act, aid, ear
  4. otic, oyer 5. aural, sense
  (special), sound, trial 6. otosis, tryout
  7. earshot 8. audience, audition,
  auditory 9. attention, auricular,
  interview, knowledge
hearken, harken... 4. hear, heed
  6. attend, listen 7. give ear, inquire
hearsay... 4. talk 5. bruit, rumor
  6. gossip, report 8. evidence
heart... 3. cor 4. card, core, gist, life,
  love, mood, soul 5. cheer, organ
  6. center, depths, kardia, middle,
  spirit, vitals 7. courage, emotion,
  essence, feeling 9. affection,
  substance 10. conscience
  11. temperament
heart (pert to)...
ache.. 5. grief 6. sorrow 7. anguish
active.. 7. sthenic
beat.. 5. pulse, throb 7. systole
  8. diastole 9. pulsation
  10. palmoscopy
bleeding (flower).. 8. dicentra
burn.. 4. envy 6. enmity 7. burning,
  pyrosia 8. jealousy 10. cardialgia,
  discontent, heartscald (heart–scaud)
cavity.. 6. atrium
chamber.. 6. atrium 7. auricle
  9. ventricle 11. ventriculum
contraction.. 7. systole
disease.. 14. angina pectoris
Egypt.. 2. Ab 4. hati
expansion.. 8. diastole
felt.. 4. dear, deep, real, true
  7. genuine, sincere
shaped.. 7. cordate
valve.. 6. mitral 8. bicuspid
  9. tricuspid
hearten... 5. cheer 7. comfort
  8. embolden, inspirit, reassure
  9. encourage
hearth... 4. home 5. ingle 6. astrer
  (pert to) 8. fireside 9. fireplace
hearth goddess... 5. Vesta 6. Hestia
hearty... 4. hale, real, rich, warm
  5. heavy, lusty 6. active, robust,
  stanch 7. cordial, earnest, fervent
  8. friendly, vigorous 9. convivial,
  energetic, unfeigned 10. nourishing

11. substantial
heat . . . 4. fire, race, warm, zeal
5. ardor, calor, cauma, fever, tepor
6. degree, warmth 7. inflame,
passion 10. excitement
11. temperature
heat (pert to) . . .
heating . . 9. calorific
measure . . 5. therm (therme) 7. calorie
(calory) 10. centigrade, Fahrenheit
pert to . . 7. thermic
plaster . . 4. mull 7. steatin
principle . . 7. caloric
white . . 13. incandescence
heater . . . 4. etna, kiln, oven 5. forge,
stove, tisar 6. boiler, retort
7. brazier, furnace 8. annealer,
register 12. electron tube
heath . . . 4. moor 5. Erica, plain, savin,
waste 8. tamarisk 10. underbrush
heathen . . . 5. pagan 6. ethnic, paynim
7. gentile, godless, infidel
10. unbeliever 11. irreligious
13. unenlightened
heathen deity . . . 4. idol 5. image
6. symbol
heather . . . 5. color, Erica, plant
9. crowberry plant
heaume . . . 6. helmet (armor)
heave . . . 4. cast, draw, hurl, lift, toss
5. fling, hoist, pitch, raise, retch,
scena, throw 11. rise and fall
heaven . . . 3. sky 4. ciel, Eden 5. ether
6. utopia, welkin 7. arcadia, Elysium,
Nirvana 8. empyrean, Paradise,
Valhalla (Valhall) 9. firmament
heavenly . . . 5. godly 6. divine, sacred
7. angelic, blessed, uranian
8. supernal 9. beautiful, celestial
10. delightful
heavenly (pert to) . . .
being . . 5. angel, saint 6. cherub,
seraph 7. Madonna 8. cherubim, Dei
Mater, seraphim
belt . . 6. galaxy, zodiac
body . . 3. sun 4. luna, moon, star
5. comet 6. planet 8. luminary
city . . 4. Zion 12. New Jerusalem
path . . 5. orbit
solar apparatus . . 6. orrery
sphere . . 8. empyrean
twins (Gemini) . . 6. Castor, Pollux
heavens . . . see *heaven*
heaves . . . 9. emphysema
heavy . . . 3. sad 4. deep, dull, hard,
role 5. actor, dense, grave, great,
inert, massy 6. coarse, gloomy,
leaden, sleepy, strong, viscid
7. doleful, onerous, serious, villain,
violent, weighty 8. burdened,
grievous, overcast, pregnant, profound
9. difficult, ponderous 10. afflictive,
burdensome, encumbered, oppressive
11. substantial 13. consequential
heavy (pert to) . . .
handed . . 6. clumsy 7. awkward,
unhandy 8. bungling 9. maladroit
10. oppressive
headed . . 4. dull, logy 6. drowsy,
stupid
hearted . . 3. sad 10. despondent,

melancholy
laden . . 6. loaded 8. careworn
9. oppressed 12. weighted down
with moisture . . 6. sodden
Hebrew . . . 3. Jew 4. Zion 6. Habiri,
Habiru, Semite 7. Semitic
Hebrew (pert to) . . .
abode of the dead . . 5. Sheol
acrostic . . 4. agla
amulet . . 4. agla
demon . . 8. Asmodeus
eternity . . 4. Olam 8. Olam haba
excommunication form . . 5. herem
festival . . 5. Purim, Seder 8. Passover
flute (Bib) . . 8. nehiloth
forbidden . . 4. tref
God . . 2. El 5. Eloah 6. Adonai,
Elohim 7. Jehovah
grammar . . 7. stative
greeting . . 6. Shalom
instrument (lyrelike) . . 4. asor
kinsman . . 4. goel
law book . . 5. Torah (Tora) 6. Talmud
7. Mishnah (Mishna) 8. Tosephta
10. Pentateuch
lesson (Nebiim) . . 9. haphtarah
marriage custom . . 8. levirate
month (Spring) . . 4. Abib 5. Nisan
Order (Cenobite) . . 6. Essene
plural ending . . 2. im
prayer shawl . . 7. tallith
proselyte . . 3. ger
psalm of praise . . 6. hallel
quarters . . 6. ghetto
rabbis, teachers . . 6. sabora
7. amoraim, tannaim 8. saboraim
sacred objects . . 4. Urim 7. Thummin
school . . 5. heder (cheder)
spice (anc) . . 6. stacte
town . . 6. Mizpah (Mizpeh)
trumpet . . 7. shophar (shofar)
underworld . . 5. Sheol
Hebrew alphabet . . . 2. he, pe
3. mem, nun, sin, tav, vau 4. ayin,
beth, caph, koph, resh, shin, yodh
5. aleph, cheth, gimel, sadhe, zayin
6. daleth, lamedh, samekh
Hebrides, New . . .
administrators . . 6. French 7. British
church . . 6. Celtic (early)
islands . . 4. Iona, Skye 5. Banks
6. Torres
people . . 10. Melanesian
type rule . . 11. Condominium
hecatomb . . . 9. sacrifice 11. hundred
oxen
hecco . . . 8. hickwall 10. woodpecker
heckle . . . 4. gibe 6. badger, hackle,
harass
hectic . . . 5. fever, flush 7. excited
8. feverish, restless 9. reddening
11. consumptive
hector . . . 5. bully, worry 6. harass
7. bluster, swagger 8. browbeat
9. roisterer 10. intimidate
Hector (pert to) . . .
character in . . 5. (The) Iliad
companion . . 8. Diomedes
father . . 5. Priam
mother . . 6. Hecuba
slain by . . 8. Achilles
wife . . 10. Andromache

heddle . . . 4. loom 5. blade (with eyelet) 7. weaving
hedge . . . 3. bar, haw, hem, pen 4. boma 5. fence 6. hinder, raddle 7. barrier, enclose, quibble 8. boundary, obstruct, sidestep, surround
hedgehog . . . 6. animal, tenrec, urchin 7. dredger, echidna, echinus, pudding (fruit) 8. herisson, hurcheon 9. porcupine 11. transformer
hedge trimmer . . . 7. plasher, topiary
hedonism (pert to) . . .
advocate . . 8. Cyrenaic 9. Epicurean
doctrine of . . 8. pleasure
heed . . . 3. ear 4. care, hear, mind, note, obey 6. attend, listen, notice, regard 7. caution, observe 8. consider 9. attention, be careful, diligence 10. cognizance, solicitude 11. observation
heedful . . . 4. wary 5. alert 6. attent 7. careful, mindful 8. cautious, vigilant 9. advertent, attentive 11. considerate
heedless . . . 6. remiss 8. careless 9. desperate, impulsive, negligent 10. insouciant, regardless 11. improvident, inadvertent, inattentive, thoughtless, unobservant, without heed 13. inconsiderate
heel . . . 3. cad, tip 4. cant, foot (part), knob, tilt 5. stern 6. careen, follow 7. bounder, deviate, incline 9. scoundrel 12. protuberance
Heidi author . . . 12. Johanna Spyri
heifer . . . 3. cow 4. quey 5. stirk, woman 6. bovine 8. terrapin (fem) 10. colpindach
height . . . 3. alt, top 4. apex 5. crest, pitch 6. summit 7. stature 8. altitude, eminence, highness 9. elevation 10. The Heavens
heighten . . . 5. raise 7. augment, elevate 8. increase 9. aggravate, intensify 10. exaggerate
height of action, drama . . . 10. catastasis
heimlich . . . 10. reticently 12. mysteriously
Heimweh . . . 9. nostalgia 12. homesickness
heinous . . . 3. bad 6. odious, wicked 7. beastly (Brit), hateful 8. flagrant, infamous, terrible 9. atrocious, malicious 10. outrageous
heir . . . 5. scion 7. heritor, legatee 8. atheling (apparent), parcener (joint) 9. firstborn, inheritor, successor 11. beneficiary
Hejaz . . .
city . . 5. Islam, Mecca 6. Medina
monument . . 14. Tomb of Mohammed (Mosque of the Prophet)
district of . . 11. Saudi Arabia
shrine . . 5. Kaaba
helcos . . . 5. ulcer
helcos (pert to) . . .
repair . . 11. helcoplasty
science . . 9. helcology
ulceration . . 8. helcosis

held . . . see *hold*
Helen of Troy (pert to) . . .
abductor, lover . . 5. Paris
brother–in–law . . 9. Agamemnon
famed for . . 6. beauty
husband . . 8. Menelaus (King)
mother . . 4. Leda
sister of . . 11. The Dioscuri
helical . . . 5. helix (formed) 6. spiral
helical year . . . 6. Sothic
helicoid . . . 6. curved, ear rim (like) 10. snail shell (like)
helicon . . . 4. tuba
helicopter (pert to) . . . 5. rotor 7. chopper 8. autogiro (autogyro), heliport 9. eggbeater 10. whirlybird
helicopter developer . . . 8. Sikorsky
heliophobia . . . 14. fear of sunlight 16. sensitivity to sun
Heliopolis . . . 12. City of the Sun (Egypt)
Helios . . . 3. Sol 6. sun god 16. Colossus of Rhodes
helix . . . 4. coil 5. snail 6. spiral
hell . . . 5. grave, Hades, limbo 7. dungeon, inferno 9. perdition, purgatory 10. underworld
hell (pert to) . . .
bottomless pit . . 9. barathrum
capital of . . 11. Pandemonium
Hebrew . . 5. Sheol
Hindu . . 6. Naraka
Iliad . . 8. Tartarus
Jewish . . 6. Tophet 7. Gehenna
Norse . . 7. Niflhel (Neflheim)
Queen . . 3. Hel
Roman . . 3. Dis 5. Orcus
hellbent . . . 7. dead set, like mad 8. full tilt, reckless 10. determined, recklessly 12. determinedly
Hellene . . . 5. Greek
Hellenistic school (Sculp) . . . 9. Pergamene
Hellespont, Turkey . . .
ancient name . . 9. Gallipoli (Strait of)
city . . 6. Abydos (legend), Sestos
legend . . 4. Hero 7. Leander (swimmer)
modern name . . 11. Dardanelles (The)
helm . . . 5. wheel 6. helmet, rudder, summit, tiller 7. control 10. management 12. steering gear
helmet . . . 5. armet, armor, galea, topee (topi) 6. casque, heaume, morion, sallet, sconce 7. basinet, hard hat
helmet (pert to) . . .
flap . . 8. aventail
lower part . . 6. beaver
nose guard . . 5. nasal
opening . . 3. vue
part . . 4. bell 5. crest, visor (vizor) 7. ventail 8. aventail
shaped . . 7. galeate
helmet of Hades . . . 5. magic 8. Tarnhelm 9. invisible, Tärnkappe
helminth . . . 4. worm
helmsman . . . 5. pilot 6. conner, guider 8. coxswain 9. steersman
helot . . . 4. esne, serf 5. slave 6. thrall, vassal 7. servant
help . . . 3. aid 4. abet, back, cure

5. avail, boost, serve, stead 6. assist,
relief, remedy, succor 7. benefit,
forward, further, improve, prevent,
relieve, servant, serving, subsidy,
support, sustain
helper . . . 3. aid (aide) 8. teammate
9. assistant, paramedic
10. apprentice, benefactor
helpful . . . 6. useful 7. helping
8. salutary 10. beneficial, tiding over
12. contributory, instrumental
helpless . . . 4. limp, weak 7. forlorn
8. impotent, unaiding 9. destitute,
powerless, spineless 10. bewildered,
unsupplied 11. defenseless,
unprotected 12. irremediable
helpmate . . . 4. wife 5. spouse
6. helper 7. husband 8. helpmeet
9. assistant, companion
Helsinki, Finland . . . 7. capital
helter-skelter . . . 5. haste, hurry
7. hastily 8. disorder 9. confusion
10. carelessly, recklessly
helve . . . 5. lever 6. handle
hem, hem in . . . 3. pen 4. edge
5. beset 6. border, margin
7. environ, stammer 8. hesitate,
surround 9. hem and haw
11. circumscribe, exclamation
hemal, haemal (pert to) . . . 5. blood
12. blood vessels
hemeralopia . . . 12. day blindness (opp
of nyctalopia)
hemi . . . 4. half, semi (pref)
hemiplegia . . . 9. paralysis (body half)
hemlock . . . 3. kex 5. Tsuga 6. conium
(fruit) 9. evergreen, poisoning
hemophilia . . . 8. bleeding
10. hemorrhage (uncontrollable)
hemp . . . 3. ife, kef 4. flax, keef, kief,
rine, sunn 5. abaca, bhang, istle, sisal
(sizal) 6. fennel, Manila 7. hashish,
lhiamba (liamba) 8. cannabis
hemp (pert to) . . .
bagasse . . 6. linaga
cannabis . . 5. ganja (smoking)
fabric . . 6. burlap
filament . . 4. harl
leaves . . 5. sabzi
like . . 9. cannabine
loose . . 5. oakum
resin (narcotic) . . 6. charas
seed . . 5. rogue, scamp
short . . 3. tow
hen . . . 4. fowl, wife 6. pullet
hen (pert to) . . .
Chaucer character . . 7. Partlet
clam . . 4. surf 5. pismo
hawk . . 7. buzzard, harrier
heath . . 4. gray 6. grouse (black)
poison . . 7. hebenon, henbane
water . . 9. gallinule
hence . . . 2. so 4. away, ergo, thus
8. away from 9. therefore
henchman . . . 4. page 5. groom
6. gillie, squire 7. mafioso
8. follower, hanger-on 9. attendant,
supporter 12. right-hand man
hend, hende . . . 4. fair, kind, near
5. civil 6. clever, comely, gentle,
kindly 8. gracious, pleasant, skillful
(skilful) 9. dexterous 10. convenient

heortology, science of . . . 14. liturgical
year
hepar . . . 5. liver 8. compound (Chem)
hepatitis . . . 12. liver disease
Hephaestus (Gr Relig) . . . 9. god of Fire
Hepplewhite . . . 9. furniture
heptad . . . 5. seven (group of)
Hera (pert to) . . .
husband . . 4. Zeus
mother of . . 4. Ares, Rhea
rival . . 2. Io 4. Leto
herald . . . 5. crier 6. tabard
7. presage, usher in 8. announce,
point man, proclaim 9. harbinger,
messenger 10. forerunner
heraldic (pert to) . . .
balls . . 5. palle (6 balls of Medici)
band . . 3. bar 4. fess, fill
barnacle . . 4. brey
bearing . . 4. ente, gore, orle 5. pheon
6. charge 8. tressure
boss . . 5. rumbo
charge . . 5. fusil, gyron 7. bearing,
humetty (humettee)
circle (gold) . . 6. bezant
cross . . 4. nowy, paty, urde 6. cleche,
pattée (patté), raguly 7. patonce,
saltier (saltire)
decoration . . 4. seme 5. crest
design (fur) . . 4. pean, vair
division . . 4. ente, paly 5. barry
6. canton 7. compone
11. counterpaly
embattled . . 8. bretessé
end (metal) . . 7. boterol (boteroll)
large . . 5. pavis
lozenge (voided) . . 6. mascle
opening . . 6. rustre
panel . . 9. hatchment (death)
sardonyx . . 8. sanguine
scalloped, edged . . 8. invected
segment . . 6. flanch
ship . . 7. lymphad
star . . 6. mullet 7. estoile
stripe . . 4. pale
swallow . . 10. hirondelle
winged . . 4. aile
wreath . . 5. torse 7. chaplet, garland
heraldic (pert to animals) . . .
head . . 8. caboshed (caboched)
bear . . 5. grise
beast, running . . 7. courant
beast, sitting . . 5. assis 6. sejant
beasts . . 6. enurny
beast's leg . . 4. gamb (gambe)
bird . . 7. issuant (half visible), martlet
9. half eagle
duck (footless) . . 6. cannet (cannette)
fish, swimming . . 6. naiant
headless . . 5. etète
heraldic (pert to color) . . .
black . . 5. sable
blue . . 5. azure
brown . . 5. tenne
gold, yellow . . 2. or
green . . 4. vert
purple . . 7. purpure
red . . 5. gules
heraldic shield (pert to) . . .
back . . 8. aversant
back to back . . 8. addorsed
bent . . 9. debruised

broken.. 5. rompu
Danes.. 5. raven
England.. 14. lilies of France
facing each other.. 8. affronté
savages.. 6. tattoo
toward spectator.. 4. gaze 7. gardant
tribe of Judah.. 4. lion
herb... 3. pia, rue 4. aloe, anet, balm,
dill, hemp, mint, moly, sage, woad,
yamp 5. anise, basil, nondo, sedge,
senna, tansy, thyme 6. arnica,
borage, catnip, cicely, clover, endive,
fennel, hyssop, jacoby, madder,
yarrow 7. boneset, caraway, chervil,
chicory, figwort, gentian, ginseng,
henbane, parsley, ragwort
8. abelmosk, licorice, marjoram,
rosemary, samphire, tarragon
9. coriander, digitalis, spikenard
10. elecampane, pennyroyal,
turtlehead
herb (pert to)...
bitter.. 4. rue 4. aloe 5. tansy
7. boneset 8. centaury 9. snakehead
10. turtlehead
dill.. 4. anet
genus.. 3. Iva 4. Arum, Ruta
5. Galax, Inula, Lemna, Rubia
6. Cassia, Mentha, Oxalis, Sagina
7. Alpenia, Anemone, Freesia,
Hedeoma, Tellima, Tovaria
8. Hepatica, Psorales 9. Grundelia
living on.. 11. herbivorous
12. phytophagous
mythical.. 4. moly
narcotic.. 4. hemp
onionlike.. 5. chive
poisonous.. 4. loco 6. conium
7. hemlock, henbane 9. hellebore
salad.. 6. endive 7. chicory
10. watercress
Hercules (pert to)...
father.. 4. Zeus
hero of.. 8. strength 12. twelve
labors
mother.. 7. Alcmene
statue.. 7. Farnese
stone.. 9. loadstone
sweetheart.. 4. Iole
wife.. 4. Hebe
herd... 3. mob 5. crowd, drive, drove,
flock, guard 6. gregis, rabble
7. shelter 11. aggregation
herd's grass... 7. timothy
herdsman... 4. senn 6. drover
7. vaquero (vaciero) 8. Damoetas,
ranchero, wrangler
herdsman's god... 5. Pales
here... 3. ici, now 5. hereat, hither
7. present 8. vicinity 9. this place
11. in this place
here and now... 8. thisness
9. haecceity 11. specificity
here and there... 5. about 6. passim
10. everywhere
hereditary... 6. inborn, innate, lineal
8. heirship 9. ancestral, descended,
lineality 11. inheritable, inheritance,
patrimonial
heredity... 4. gene 5. birth 7. atavism
8. heritage 10. Mendel's law
11. inheritance

heretic... 9. dissenter, sectarian
10. schismatic 13. nonconformist
heretofore... 6. erenow 7. prior to
8. formerly, hitherto, previous
heritage... 3. lot 9. cleronomy
10. birthright 11. inheritance
heritrix, heretrix... 7. heiress
herl, harl... 3. fly (angling) 4. barb
hermeneutics... 14. interpretation
(Scriptures)
Hermes (pert to)...
birthplace.. 7. Cyllene
character.. 6. herald 9. messenger
father.. 4. Zeus
god of.. 5. youth 7. science
9. eloquence, invention
mother.. 4. Maia
Roman equivalent.. 7. Mercury
shoes (winged).. 7. talaria
hermetic... 6. closed, sealed
7. magical 8. airtight 10. alchemical
hermetic art... 7. alchemy
hermit... 4. monk 5. cooky 7. ascetic,
eremite, recluse, stylite (Hist)
8. headsman 9. anchorite, pillarist
11. hummingbird
hermitary... 3. hut 4. cell
hern, herne... 4. hers, hook 5. heron
6. corner
hero... 4. idol, star 5. model
7. demigod, warrior 8. champion
9. celebrity, conqueror
11. protagonist
hero (pert to)...
American.. 5. Allen (Ethan), Bowie
6. Bonham, Travis 8. Crockett
Babylonian.. 5. Etana
deified.. 7. demigod
genealogy.. 9. heroogony
Greek.. 3. Ion 4. Ajax
legendary.. 6. Amadis, Roland
7. Paladin, Tancred
lore.. 9. heroology
Persian.. 6. Rustam (Rustum)
romantic.. 4. Erec 6. Amadis
7. Leander
Russian.. 4. Igor
heroic... 4. bold, epic, huge 5. brave,
great, noble 6. epical, poetic, viking
7. extreme, gallant, valiant
8. fearless, intrepid, powerful
10. courageous 11. magnanimous,
venturesome
heroic poem, story... 4. epic, epos
6. epopee
heroine... 4. Tess 5. actor 6. Esther,
Europa 8. Atalanta 9. celebrity
11. demigoddess
heroism... 5. valor 7. bravery, courage
9. fortitude 11. magnanimity
13. unselfishness
heron... 5. Ardea, crane, egret, herle
7. Bittern 8. Ardeidae, heronsew
9. Great Blue 10. Great White, Little
Blue
heron flock... 5. sedge
herpes... 6. eczema 8. cold sore,
shingles
herring... 3. cob 4. alec, brit, raun
(fem), sile 5. cisco, matie, sprat
7. alewife, anchovy, shadine
8. scuddawn

herring (pert to)...
 barrel.. 4. cade, cran
 bone.. 7. pattern 11. arrangement
 fry.. 4. sile
 herringlike.. 5. cisco 7. anchovy
 young.. 4. brit 5. sprat (sprot)
Herse (Gr)... 7. goddess (dew)
Hershef (Egypt)... 5. deity (tutelary)
hesitate... 3. haw, hem 4. wait
 5. delay, demur, pause, stall
 6. falter, loiter 7. stammer
 13. procrastinate
hesitation... 5. doubt, pause, waltz
 9. faltering, hesitancy 10. reluctance,
 stammering 11. uncertainty,
 vacillation 15. procrastination
hesped (Heb)... 6. eulogy 7. funeral
Hesperides (pert to)...
 group name.. 10. Atlantides
 guards of.. 12. golden apples (Hera)
 nymph.. 5. Aegle 6. Hestia
 7. Hespera 8. Arethusa, Erytheia
Hesperus... 4. poem (Wreck of the
 Hesperus) 5. Venus 6. Hesper
 11. evening star
Hessian... 3. fly 5. boots, Hesse
 6. German 9. mercenary
 10. adventurer
hest... 6. behest 7. command,
 precept, promise 10. injunction
Hestia (pert to)...
 goddess of.. 6. hearth
 guard of.. 12. golden apples
 mother.. 4. Rhea
hetaera, hetaira (Gr)... 4. Lais
 6. Phryne 8. mistress, paramour
hetaerocracy, governed by...
 8. hetaerae 10. college men
Heterodontus... 5. shark
heterodox... 9. heretical
 10. unorthodox 11. nonorthodox
heterogeneous... (opposed to
 homogeneous) 5. mixed 6. unlike
 7. diverse 9. different 10. dissimilar
 11. diversified 13. miscellaneous
hew... 3. cut 4. chop, fell, hack
 5. carve, sever
hex... 3. hag, six 4. jinx 5. lamia,
 spell 7. bewitch 9. sorceress,
 witchwife
hexad... 3. six 6. sestet
hexameter verse...
 meter.. 7. six feet
 terms.. 4. iams 8. dipodies, trochees
 9. anapaests
hexapod... 7. six feet 9. six–footed
hexarchy... 9. six States (group)
hexastich, poem or stanza... 8. six
 lines 9. six verses
heyday... 3. joy 4. acme 8. wildness
 11. high spirits 12. highest vigor
 14. frolicsomeness
heyrat... 8. kinkajou (obs)
Hezekiah (pert to)...
 Biblical.. 4. King (12th)
 kingdom.. 5. Judah
 mother.. 3. Abi
hiatus... 3. col, gap 5. break, chasm,
 pause, space 6. lacuna 7. fissure,
 opening 8. interval 12. interruption
Hiawatha (pert to)...
 character, poem by.. 10. Longfellow

 grandmother.. 7. Nokomis
 mother.. 7. Wenonah
 tribe (Ind).. 8. Iroquois
hibernate... 6. hole up (summer in
 torpor), winter 8. estivate
 10. latibulize
Hibernia... 4. Erin 7. Ireland
Hibernian (pert to)...
 color.. 5. green
 native.. 8. Irishman
 secret society (US 1832)..
 24. Ancient Order of Hibernians
hickory... 4. cane 5. Carya, pecan
 6. switch 8. kiskatom 9. shellbark
hidalgo... 5. title 8. nobleman (lower
 class)
hidden... 4. dern, lurk 5. inner, perdu
 6. arcane, buried, cached, closed,
 covert, latent, masked, occult, secret
 7. covered, cryptic, obscure,
 unknown 8. abstruse, screened,
 secluded, secreted 9. concealed,
 latescent 10. mysterious
 11. clandestine
hide... 3. kip 4. bury, cyst, dern
 (derne), lurk, mask, pelt, skin, veil
 5. cache, cloak, cover, skulk
 6. screen, shroud 7. conceal,
 eelskin, rawhide, secrete 8. carucate,
 disguise, ensconce, suppress
 9. dissemble 10. camouflage
hidebound... 5. bound, petty 6. little,
 narrow 7. bigoted 9. barkbound
 10. restrained (opinion)
 11. strait–laced 12. conventional,
 narrow–minded 13. hyperorthodox
hideous... 4. grim, ugly 6. grisly,
 horrid, odious 7. ghastly 8. scabrous,
 terrible 9. frightful, revolting
 10. detestable, terrifying
hiding place... 3. mew 4. lair
 5. cache 9. latibulum
hi–fi devotee... 10. audiophile
high... 3. alt, dry, ela (note) 4. tall
 5. aloft, drunk, great, noble, steep
 6. costly, shrill 7. eminent, haughty
 8. elevated, foremost, stranded,
 towering 9. excessive, expensive
high (pert to)...
 and mighty.. 8. arrogant 9. imperious
 brow.. 4. snob 7. Brahmin, egghead,
 high–hat, learned 12. intellectual
 14. intelligentsia
 flown diction.. 8. euphuism
 flying.. 7. Icarian 9. visionary
 11. extravagant, pretentious
 12. ostentatious 13. grandiloquent
 handed.. 9. arbitrary 10. autocratic,
 imperative 11. domineering,
 overbearing
 hat.. 8. snobbish 12. aristocratic
 priest.. 3. Eli (Israel) 11. Melchezedek
 (Mormon)
 sounding.. 4. loud 7. fustian
 9. high–toned 13. grandiloquent
 spirited.. 4. edgy 5. fiery 6. lively
 9. excitable 10. mettlesome
 11. high–mettled
 strung.. 4. taut 5. tense 7. nervous
 9. excitable
 time.. 3. fun 5. binge, spree
 8. carousal 11. opportunity

toned .. 5. tense 7. stylish 8. elevated
9. dignified 11. fashionable
highest ... 3. top 4. best 6. utmost
7. maximum, supreme, topmost
8. bunemost, dominant 9. nth
degree, uppermost
highest (pert to) ...
comb form .. 4. acro
dice number .. 3. six 4. sise (sice)
point .. 3. top 4. acme, apex 5. crest
6. apogee, climax, summit, vertex,
zenith 7. ceiling, noonday
8. meridian, noontide, pinnacle
11. ne plus ultra
highway ... 3. via, way 4. bahn, iter,
path, pike, road, toby 6. artery,
course, street 7. beltway, freeway,
parkway, thruway, (throughway)
8. arterial, autobahn, turnpike
9. boulevard, concourse
10. expressway 12. thoroughfare
highwayman ... 5. thief 6. bandit,
robber 7. brigand, footpad, ladrone
8. hijacker 9. bandolero
10. bushranger, highjacker
hike ... 4. jerk, toss, walk 5. hitch,
march, raise, throw, tramp
8. backpack, increase
hilarious ... 3. mad 5. merry, noisy
7. festive 8. mirthful 9. ludicrous
hilarity ... 4. glee 5. mirth 6. gaiety,
levity 7. jollity, whoopee 8. laughter
9. joviality 10. jocularity, joyousness
12. cheerfulness, exhilaration
hill ... 3. kop, tor 4. dene, dune, heap,
holt, kame, knob, loma, mesa, paha,
rath 5. bargh, butte, esker, morra,
mound 6. barrow, summit
9. acclivity, elevation, monadnock
hill myna ... 8. starling
hillside ... 4. bank, brae, hill, knop,
ramp 5. cleve (cleeve), cliff, knoll,
scarp, slope 6. glacia
hilt ... 4. haft 6. handle
hilum ... 3. eye (bean) 5. hilar, notch
7. opening (kidney)
Himalaya (pert to) ...
antelope .. 5. goral, serow
bear .. 5. bhalu
bearcat .. 5. panda
bird .. 5. monal (pheasant) 6. chough
(crow)
cat .. 5. ounce
dweller .. 8. Nepalese
formations .. 7. Siwalik
goat .. 4. ibex, kail, tahe
kingdom .. 5. Hunza
mountain peak .. 3. Api 7. Everest,
The Hump
pass .. 7. Nathula
plant .. 4. nard (Med)
sheep (wild) .. 6. bharal, nahoor
swamp .. 5. Terai
tree .. 3. fir (silver) 5. Neoza (pine)
6. Bhutan, deodar (cedar)
himself ... 4. ipse
hind ... 3. doe 4. back, deer, rear, stag
6. caudal, haunch, rustic 7. peasant,
servant 9. domestic 9. posterior
11. hindquarter
hind (red fish) ... 7. grouper 8. cabrilla
hinder ... 3. bar 5. block, check,

cramp, debar, delay, deter, embar
6. cumber, hamper, impede, retard
7. prevent 8. restrain 9. posterior
hindrance ... 3. bar, rub 4. clog, snag,
stop 5. check, delay 8. obstacle
9. deterrent, restraint, stricture
10. impediment 11. obstruction
12. interruption
Hindu, Hindoo ... 4. Koli, Sikh
5. Tamil 6. Indian 9. Hindustan
Hindu (pert to) ...
alphabet .. 6. Sarada
apartment .. 5. mahal
ascetic .. 4. yati, yogi 5. sadhu
atheist .. 7. nastika
author of law .. 4. Manu (Code)
bird .. 5. Munia 6. garuda
Buddha's mother .. 4. Maya
caravansary .. 8. choultry
carriage .. 6. gharry (gharri)
caste .. 4. Bhil 5. Palli, Sudra, Tamil
7. Brahman
ceremony .. 7. sraddha
city (sacred) .. 5. Mecca 7. Benares
9. Allahabad
coin .. 4. anna
cymbals .. 3. tal
dancing girl .. 8. bayadere
darkness (spiritual) .. 5. tamas
deity .. 4. Deva, Rama, Siva (Shiva),
Yama 5. Ahura, Asura 6. Brahma,
Vishnu 7. Krishna 8. Trimurti
deity consort .. 5. sakti
dialect .. 5. Tamil
division .. 5. Patti, Taraf 6. zillah
7. Pargana
Dravidian .. 5. Tamil
drink (sacrificial) .. 4. soma
evil spirit .. 4. Mara 5. asura
6. yaksha
festival .. 4. Holi, tali 6. Dewali, Pongal
9. Dashahara
first mortal to die .. 4. Yama
flute .. 3. bin 5. pungi
garment .. 4. sari (saree)
Gautama's wife .. 6. Ahalya
gentleman (Mr) .. 5. baboo (babu), sahib
giant .. 4. Bana (thousand–armed)
government .. 6. sircar
guitar .. 4. vina 5. sitar
hero .. 4. Nala
incarnation .. 4. Rama 5. asura
6. yaksha
jackal .. 4. kola
king .. 5. Rajah
language (oldest) .. 5. Tamil
language (sacred) .. 4. Pali
loincloth .. 5. dhoti
magic .. 4. jadu (jadoo), maya
magician .. 4. yogi 5. fakir
meal (wheat) .. 4. atta (ata)
mendicant .. 4. naga 8. sannyasi
merchant .. 6. banian (banya)
7. goladar
mind .. 5. manas
monkey god .. 7. Hanuman
mountain .. 4. Meru
mystic .. 4. yogi
nursemaid .. 4. ayah
paradise .. 7. Nirvana
patriarch .. 5. Pitri
peasant .. 4. ryot

philosophy.. 4. yoga, Yuga 5. tamas
physicist.. 5. Raman (Nobel 1930)
pillar.. 3. lat
poet.. 5. rishi 6. Tagore (Nobel
  1913)
reign.. 3. raj
sage.. 5. rishi 6. Dharma
  7. Gautama, Mahatma
savant.. 5. swami
scarf.. 4. sari (saree)
serpent (semi–human).. 4. Naga
servant.. 5. hamal
slave.. 4. dasi (fem)
soldier.. 4. sikh 5. sepoy
supernatural being.. 6. Garuda
swan.. 5. hansa
syllable of assent.. 2. om
Taraf ruler.. 8. tarafdar
title.. 3. Sri 4. Raja, Rana, Rani
  5. Rajah, Ranee 6. sirdar
  8. maharaja (maharajah)
tree (sacred).. 5. pipal 6. bo tree
tribesman.. 4. Naga
tunic.. 4. jama (jamah)
underworld (series).. 6. Patala
village.. 5. abadi
virtue.. 6. sharma
widow (cremation).. 6. suttee
woman (first).. 6. Ahalya
Hindu Ages, Yoga...
1st.. 5. Krita
2nd.. 5. Treta
3rd.. 7. Dvapara
4th.. 4. Kali
end.. 7. Pralaya
total.. 4. Maha 10. Manvantara
Hindu goddess... 3. Sri, Uma 4. Devi,
  Kali 5. Durga, Gauri 6. Chandi,
  Shakti 7. Lakshmi, Parvati
  9. Haimavati (Durga)
Hindu god of...
ancestors.. 5. Pitri
dead.. 4. Yama
fire.. 4. Agni
love.. 4. Kama
spirit.. 5. Asura
unknown.. 2. Ka
wisdom (elephant–headed).. 6. Ganesa
  (Ganesha)
Hindu religion...
abode of gods.. 4. Meru
call to prayer.. 4. azan (adan)
ceremony, rite.. 7. araddha
congregation.. 5. samaj
convert (to Islam).. 6. shaikh
creator.. 6. Brahma
cremation.. 4. sati 6. suttee
doctrine, destiny.. 5. karma
first human to die (deified).. 4. Yama
hell.. 6. Naraka
Hinduism.. 5. Agama 6. Tantra
  7. Jainism 8. Buddhism
  10. Brahmanism
holy man.. 5. Sadhu (Sadh)
image worship.. 5. arati
incarnation.. 4. Rama 6. avatar
  11. Ramachandra
literature (sacred).. 4. Veda 7. Shastra
lord of the world.. 9. Jagannath
  (Jagannatha)
monastery.. 4. math
philosophy (life).. 5. artha, atman,

prana 6. tattva
prayer, call to.. 4. azan (adan)
prayer rug.. 5. asana, Melas
religion.. 5. Agama 6. Tantra
  7. Jainism 8. Buddhism
  10. Brahmanism
scripture.. 4. Veda 5. Agama
  6. Tantra 7. Shastra
sect.. 4. Jain (Jaina), Sikh 6. tantra
Shastra (4 parts).. 5. aruti 6. purana,
  smriti, tantra
Siva worshiper.. 5. Saiva
Supreme Spirit.. 5. atman 7. jivatma
teacher.. 4. guru 5. swami
Trimurti (Triad).. 4. Siva 6. Brahma,
  Vishnu
trinity, triad.. 8. Trimurti (Siva,
  Brahma, Vishnu)
unorthodox.. 7. Jainism
widow (cremation).. 6. suttee
Hindustan (pert to)...
dialect.. 4. Urdu 10. Hindustani
people.. 9. Dravidian
poet.. 5. Siraj (Beng)
rice.. 7. aghanee
tribesman.. 4. toda
hinge... 3. pan (part) 4. axis, axle,
  hang, knee, turn 5. joint, pivot,
  stand 6. depend, fasten, lamina,
  pintle
hint... 3. cue 5. imply, refer, tinge,
  trace 6. allude, glance 7. eyewink,
  inkling, suggest 8. allusion, innuendo,
  intimate, reminder 9. insinuate
  10. intimation, suggestion
  11. insinuation, supposition
hip... 3. hop, pod 4. coxa, limp, miss,
  skip 6. haunch 8. greeting
hip, hips (pert to)...
bone.. 4. coxa 5. ilium 7. os coxae
  10. innominate
muscle.. 9. iliopsoas
nerve.. 7. sciatic (largest)
rose fruit.. 10. pseudocarp
Hippocrates (pert to)...
drug.. 5. mecon (possibly opium)
famed as.. 9. physician (Gr)
oath.. 11. Hippocratic
hippopotamus... 5. hippo 6. seacow,
  zeekoe 8. behemoth (Bib)
hippopotamus, thong of hide...
  7. chicote
Hiram... 9. most noble 10. King of
  Tyre (Bib)
hire... 3. let, use 4. hack, rent
  5. bribe, lease, price, wages
  6. employ, engage, reward, salary
  7. charter, stipend 9. allowance
  12. compensation
hireling... 4. esne, serf 5. slave, venal
  8. employee 9. mercenary
hirmos... 4. hymn 8. canticle
  9. troparion
hirondelle (Her)... 7. swallow
hirsel... 4. herd 5. flock 7. pasture
hirsute... 5. hairy, rough 6. coarse,
  shaggy 7. boorish, bristly, uncouth
Hispania (anc)... 16. Spain and
  Portugal
hispid... 5. rough 7. grooved
  8. strigose
hiss... 3. boo, tst 4. fizz 7. condemn

8. derision, sibilate 10. effervesce, sibilation

historian ... 5. actor 6. writer
8. annalist 10. chronicler

history ... 5. drama 6. events, memoir
7. account 8. relation, treatise
9. chronicle, narrative

history (pert to) ...
development .. 8. ontogeny
Father of .. 9. Herodotus
muse of (Gr Myth) .. 4. Clio
period .. 3. era
personal .. 7. memoirs 9. biography, genealogy 13. autobiography
study, knowledge of .. 10. historical 12. historiology

histrio ... 5. actor

histrion ... 5. actor

histrionics ... 6. acting, actors
9. theatrics 11. theatricals

hit ... 3. bop, lob, rap, tap 4. blow, bunt, slam, slap, slog, suit, swat
5. flick, knock, shoot, smite
6. buffet, larrup, please, strike
7. succeed, success 9. collision

hitch ... 3. hop, tie, tug 4. halt, jerk, knot, limp, pull, yoke 5. catch, cling, crick, marry, unite 6. enlist, fasten, hobble 8. obstacle 9. hindrance
10. enlistment

hitherto ... 3. ago, yet 5. as yet
7. prior to 8. formerly, until now

hit or miss ... 6. casual 8. at random, by chance, careless 9. haphazard

Hittite (pert to) ...
ancestor (Bib) .. 4. Heth
city .. 6. Hamath, Pteria (ruins)
country .. 6. Khatti (Asia Minor)
people (anc) .. 8. Hittites
10. aborigines
storm god .. 6. Teshup (Teshub)

hoar ... 4. aged, gray, rime 5. hoary, white 7. ancient 9. hoarfrost, venerable

hoard ... 5. amass, lay up, store
6. garner, supply 7. husband
8. treasure, treasury 10. accumulate, collection

hoarder ... 5. miser 6. storer
9. treasurer

hoarfrost ... 3. rag 4. hoar, rime
7. needles (ice) 9. Jack Frost

hoarse ... 3. old 4. aged, gray
6. remote (in time) 7. ancient
9. canescent

hoatzin, hoactzin ... 4. anna 5. hanna
8. pheasant 9. stinkbird
11. Opisthocomi (group)

hoax ... 3. bam 4. bilk, ruse, sham
5. bluff, cheat, trick 6. canard
7. deceive 8. artifice 9. deception

hob ... 3. elf, hub, peg, pin 4. game, mark 5. clown, fairy, havoc 6. ferret, rustic, sprite 7. hobnail 8. mischief
9. fireplace, hobgoblin

hobble ... 4. clog, gait (unequal), halt, limp 5. dance 6. fetter, tether, wabble 7. dilemma, pastern, shackle
11. predicament

hobbledehoy ... 4. gawk 5. youth

hobbler ... 5. pilot 7. boatman, hoveler, laborer, soldier 8. retainer

hobby ... 3. fad, nag 5. dolly, horse
6. falcon 7. bicycle, pastime
9. avocation, plaything
10. hobbyhorse 12. rocking horse

hobgoblin ... 3. elf, imp 4. bogy, pixy, Puck 5. scrat 6. sprite 7. bugaboo
9. coltpixie 10. apparition 15. Robin Goodfellow

hobnob ... 9. associate (with), drink with, hit or miss

hobo ... 3. bum 5. tramp 6. beggar
7. vagrant 8. vagabond

hock ... 3. ham 4. pawn 5. ankle, joint, thigh (man) 6. pledge
7. disable 9. hamstring

hockey (pert to) ...
ball, disk .. 3. nur 4. knur, puck
cup .. 7. Stanley (prize)
goal .. 4. cage
stick .. 6. shinny 7. cammock
team number .. 5. seven

hocus ... 4. drug 5. cheat 6. liquor (drugged) 7. deceive, falsify
8. cheating, trickery 10. adulterate

hocus–pocus ... 5. cheat, trick
6. bunkum, humbug 7. juggler
8. flimflam, nonsense, quackery
9. deception, trickster 11. incantation
12. charlatanism 13. sleight of hand
15. juggler's formula

hod ... 3. tub 4. hide 6. barrow, trough 7. scuttle

hodgepodge ... 4. mess, olio, stew
5. cento 6. medley 7. mélange, mixture 10. miscellany
11. gallimaufry, olla–podrida

hog ... 3. pig, sow, Sus 4. bene, boar, galt, gilt 5. sheep (unshorn), shoat, swine 6. barrow 8. babirusa (babiroussa), javelina 9. boschvark, razorback

hog ... 6. corner (the market) 7. glutton
8. slattern 9. take it all
10. locomotive, monopolist

hog (pert to) ...
breed .. 5. Essex 9. Hampshire
food .. 4. mast
ground .. 6. marmot
hoglike .. 7. porcine
salted side .. 5. bacon 6. flitch
shears (snout) .. 7. snouter
thigh (cured) .. 3. ham

hogfish ... 7. capitan, pigfish
8. scorpene

hoggerel ... 5. sheep 6. hogger

hoggery ... 4. hogs 5. greed
11. beastliness 14. hoggish manners

hoggish ... 6. filthy, greedy 7. porcine, selfish, swinish 10. gluttonous

hogshead ... 4. cask 6. barrel
7. measure

hogwash ... 5. swill, waste

hoi polloi ... 3. mob 5. herde
6. masses, rabble 7. the many
8. populace 9. multitude

hoist ... 4. lift, sail 5. boost, heave, hoise, raise 7. elevate 8. elevator

hoisting device ... 3. gin 4. jack
5. crane, davit, lewis 7. capstan, derrick 8. elevator, windlass
9. parbuckle

hoity–toity ... 5. giddy, proud 6. snooty

7. flighty, haughty 8. arrogant
11. exclamation, harum–scarum,
patronizing, thoughtless
13. irresponsible
hold... 3. own 4. bind, have, keep,
lien, seat, stow 5. avast, cling,
delay, grasp, judge 6. adhere, arrest,
cleave, clench, defend, detain,
endure, harbor, regard, retain
7. contain, control, custody
8. consider, foothold, maintain,
thurrock (ship's), treasury
9. anchorage, constrain, entertain,
prosecute 11. compartment
hold (pert to)...
  back.. 3. dam 4. last, stem 5. delay,
  deter, stint 6. detain, hinder, refuse,
  retard 7. abstain, inhibit, repress
  8. restrain
  belief.. 7. suppose
  dear.. 7. cherish
  fast.. 5. cling 6. adhere 9. persevere
  forth.. 5. offer, speak 7. declaim,
  descant, exhibit, expound
  8. continue, maintain, propound
  off.. 5. avert, delay 7. repulse, ward
  off 9. stay aloof, temporize
  on.. 4. stop, wait 6. endure, retain
  7. forbear 8. continue
  opinion.. 4. deem
  out.. 4. last 6. endure, refuse, resist
  7. exclude 8. continue
  session.. 3. sit 7. convene
  8. assemble
  together.. 6. adhere, cohere 8. be
  joined 9. co–operate
  up.. 3. rob 4. buoy, halt, lift, rein
  5. check, delay, raise 6. hinder,
  resist, retard 7. display, exhibit,
  pillory (to scorn), robbery, support,
  sustain
  water.. 5. sound 10. consistent
holder... 3. cop (yarn) 4. file
5. owner, payee 6. bearer, binder,
lienor, tenant 7. trustee 8. endorsee
9. mortgagor, possessor, recipient
10. receptacle
hold in...
  check.. 4. curb, rein 6. arrest, bridle
  7. control 8. restrain
  custody.. 4. jail 6. detain, intern
  hand.. 6. assure 7. control, promise,
  toy with
  mind.. 6. harbor 7. cherish
  9. entertain
holding... 5. asset, claim, stake, tenet,
title, trust 6. belief, equity, estate,
tenure 8. interest, property
9. retention 10. possessing,
possession, supporting
holding fast... 9. tenacious
10. persistent
holding sway... 7. regnant
8. dominant, reigning
hole... 3. den, pit 4. bore, cave, cove,
dive, flaw, gulf, lair, nook, slot, vent
5. abyss, chasm, fault, hovel, place,
shaft 6. burrow, cavern, cavity,
cellar, hollow, prison 7. impasse,
opening, orifice, ostiole
10. excavation 11. predicament
hole (pert to)...

bowling ball.. 4. grip
cable (ship's).. 5. hawse
enlarger.. 6. reamer
implement.. 3. awl, eye 4. bore
  5. drill 8. stiletto
metal mold.. 5. sprue
mud.. 6. wallow
wall.. 5. niche
water.. 5. oasis
whirlpool.. 5. gourd (obs)
Holi (or Hoolee)... 8. festival (Hind)
holia... 6. salmon (humpback)
holiday... 4. fete 5. feria, merry
  6. fiesta, jovial, outing 7. festive,
  playday 8. festival, vacation
  9. convivial, festivity 10. recreation
holiness... 5. piety, title (Pope)
  8. sanctity 9. godliness
  10. sacredness 11. saintliness
  13. righteousness
Holland... 11. Netherlands (which see)
Holland...
  capital.. 8. The Hague (Court)
    9. Amsterdam
  city.. 3. Ede 5. Doorn 6. Leyden
    9. Amsterdam, Rotterdam
  government.. 8. monarchy
  liquor.. 3. gin 8. schnapps
  oddity.. 5. dikes 6. canals, tulips
  painter.. 6. Rubens 7. Van Eyck
  people.. 5. Dutch
  port.. 4. Edam
  pottery.. 5. delft (delf)
  province.. 4. Edam 7. Drenthe,
  Zeeland
  river.. 3. Ems, Lek 5. Meuse, Rhine
    7. Scheldt (Schelde)
  sea.. 5. North
  village.. 3. Ede
hollow... 3. den, pit 4. thin, void
  5. bight, empty, false, gaunt, sinus
  6. cavern, cavity, cirque, corrie,
  groove, hungry, socket, sunken,
  vacant 7. concave, unsound
  8. capsular, specious 9. cavernous,
  depressed, faithless, insincere,
  worthless 10. sepulchral
  12. unsatisfying
hollowed... 6. cavate 7. concave,
glenoid
holly... 4. holm, hull, Ilex 5. yapon
  6. hulver, laurel 8. Eryngium
  9. blackjack, Ilicaceae 10. Sapindales
hollyhock... 5. color 7. Althaea,
blue–red 9. perennial
holm... 3. oak 5. holly, islet, marsh
  7. bottoms, low land
holobaptist... 12. immersionist
holocaust... 9. sacrifice (by fire)
  11. destruction 13. burnt offering
holy... 5. godly, pious 6. chaste,
devout, sacred 7. epithet (Relig),
sainted 8. hallowed 9. venerated
Holy, holy (pert to)...
  carpet.. 5. kiswa (kiswah)
  comb form.. 5. hagio
  Joe.. 6. sky pilot 9. clergyman
  oil.. 6. chrism 7. unction
  Ones.. 9. Innocents (slain by Herod)
  pilgrim.. 6. palmer
  receptacle.. 5. cruet, stoup
  Rood.. 5. cross 8. crucifix

water sprinkler.. 11. aspergillum
Holy Grail (pert to)...
castle.. 9. Monsalvat (Mt)
guardian.. 8. Amfortas
knight.. 7. Galahad
legend.. 8. Sangraal (Sangreal)
quest by.. 4. Bors 7. Galahad
9. Percivale
terms.. 7. platter, wine cup
homage... 5. dulia, honor, liege
6. fealty, latria 7. loyalty, ovation,
respect, worship 9. deference,
obeisance, reverence 10. allegiance
12. commendation
homard... 7. Homarus, lobster
hombre... 3. man 4. homo, male
6. fellow
home... 4. care, goal (games), kern
(kirn), nest 5. abode, astre, grave,
heart 6. asylum, estate, hearth
7. habitat, village 8. domicile,
dwelling 9. residence 10. fatherland,
habitation
home (pert to)...
base.. 3. den 5. plate
dislike.. 9. ecophobia
Home Sweet Home author.. 5. Payne
(John Howard 1823)
Irish King's.. 4. Tara
of the gods.. 7. Olympus
of the Golden Fleece.. 7. Colchis
homely... 4. ugly 5. plain 6. humble,
kindly, simple 7. plainly 8. domestic,
homelike, informal, plebeian,
uncomely 9. unsightly 10. intimately
11. comfortable 13. unpretentious
homemade... 5. plain 6. simple
8. domestic, handmade, homespun
Homer (pert to)...
birthplace.. 5. Chios (claimed)
book.. 5. Iliad 7. Odyssey
burial place.. 3. Ios (Isl)
hero.. 6. Aeneas
Homer's poems (pert to)...
rhapsodists.. 9. Homeridae
student, reciter of.. 7. Homerid
8. Homerist
study of.. 10. Homerology
style.. 7. Homeric
homesickness... 7. Heimweh 9. mal
du pays, nostalgia
homespun... 5. cloth, plain, rough
6. coarse, russet 8. domestic,
homemade 10. not elegant,
unpolished (person)
homicide... 5. morth 6. murder
7. killing 12. manslaughter
homily... 5. adage 6. sermon
8. assembly, converse
9. communion, discourse
homing pigeon... 13. carrier pigeon
hominy... 4. samp 5. maize 10. hulled
corn
Homo sapiens... 3. man 4. homo
9. anthropos
Honduras...
capital.. 11. Tegucigalpa
city.. 4. Tela 6. Roatan 8. Trujillo
12. Puerto Cortes
discoverer.. 8. Columbus
gulf.. 7. Fonseca
Indian tribe.. 5. Lenca

language.. 7. Spanish
people.. 6. Indian 7. Spanish
river.. 4. Ulua 5. Negro 6. Patuca
hone... 4. long, pine 5. delay, dress,
stone (sharpening), strop, yearn
6. lament 7. grumble, sharpen
8. oilstone 9. whetstone
honest... 4. open 5. frank 6. candid,
chaste 7. genuine, up and up,
upright 8. faithful, suitable, virtuous
9. guileless, honorable, ingenuous,
integrity 10. creditable
13. unadulterated 15. straightforward
honesty... 5. honor 6. equity
7. justice 8. fairness 9. integrity,
rectitude 11. genuineness,
uprightness 12. truthfulness
15. trustworthiness
honey... 3. mel 5. melli (comb form),
sweet 6. nectar 7. sweeten
10. endearment
honey (pert to)...
bear (sloth).. 8. Melursus
bearing.. 11. melliferous
bee.. 4. Apis 6. dingar 7. deseret
9. mellifera
bird.. 3. iao 6. manuao 10. honey
eater
buzzard.. 4. kite, pern
comb.. 4. raat 5. favus 8. alveolus
drink.. 4. mead 5. morat
flowing.. 11. mellifluent, mellifluous
pert to.. 8. melissic
sucking.. 11. mellisugent, mellivorous
yellow.. 6. dorado 10. melichrous
Hong Kong...
capital.. 8. Victoria
government.. 11. Crown Colony
island.. 12. Stonecutters
peninsula.. 7. Kowloon
Honolulu...
capital of.. 6. Hawaii
island site.. 4. Oahu
port.. 11. Pearl Harbor
suburb.. 3. Ewa
honorable, honourable... 5. moral,
title 7. upright 8. honorary
9. estimable, reputable, venerable
10. creditable 11. commendable,
illustrious, meritorious, respectable
honorably... 5. nobly 6. fairly, justly
8. worthily 9. equitably, reputably,
uprightly
honorarium... 7. douceur
honored... 5. famed, feted 6. graced
7. awarded, revered 8. knighted
9. accoladed
hood... 4. corf, cowl, hide, mail
(armor) 5. amice, blind, cloak
6. bonnet, camail, capote
7. capuche (capouch) 8. babushka,
burnoose (burnous), capsheaf,
covering, liripipe, mozzetta, tapadera
12. strong-arm man
hood (suff)... 9. condition
hooded... 9. cucullate
hooded seal... 11. bladdernose
hoodwink... 4. dupe, fool, hide, wile
5. blear, blind, cheat, cover, cozen
6. befool, delude 7. deceive, mislead
9. blindfold
hooey... 4. blah, bunk 5. tripe

7. baloney, hogwash 8. buncombe, malarkey, nonsense 13. horsefeathers

hoof... 4. clee, frog, walk 5. cloof (clufe, cluve) 6. ungula 7. pastern (part) 8. periople (part), pododerm

hoof–paring tool... 8. butteris

hoof–shaped... 8. ungulate

hoof track... 5. piste

hook... 4. gaff, lure 5. catch, chape, cleek, crome, curve, hamus, snare, steal 6. anchor, clevis, fasten, hangle, tenter 7. hamulus

hookah, hooka... 4. pipe 8. narghile

hooked... 6. curved, hamate 7. angular, cleeked 8. aduncous (adunc), anchoral, aquiline, uncinate

Hooker (Thomas)... 9. clergyman 18. Luther of New England

hooks (group)... 5. Party (Neth) 9. pulldevil, scrodgill 10. Kabbeljaws (Nobles)

hookworm... 7. Necator 9. Uncinaria

hooligan... 6. loafer 7. gorilla, hoodlum, ruffian 8. larrikin

hoop... 4. bail, band, ring 5. clasp 6. circle, wicket 7. circlet 8. surround

hoop skirt... 9. crinoline 11. farthingale

Hoosier poet... 5. Riley (J Whitcomb)

Hoosier State... 7. Indiana

hop... 3. fly 4. drug, halt, jump, leap, limp, trip, vine 5. bound, caper, dance, frisk, opium 6. flight, gambol, spring 8. narcotic

hope... 3. bay 4. opal, spes, Spes (Goddess) 5. haven, inlet, trust 6. aspire, desire, expect 7. cherish, promise 8. optimism, reliance 11. expectation 12. anticipation

hoped for... 7. sperate

hopeful... 8. probable, sanguine 9. confident, expectant 10. propitious

hopeless... 4. vain 6. futile 7. forlorn, useless 8. downcast 9. desperate, incurable 10. despairing, despondent 11. ineffectual 12. disconsolate, irremediable 13. irrecoverable, irretrievable

hopelessness... 7. despair 8. futility 13. impossibility

hop kiln... 4. oast (ost)

hoplite... 7. soldier

hopper... 3. box 5. chute 6. dancer, jumper, leaper 7. penguin (rock) 10. receptacle 11. grasshopper

hopscotch... 6. pebble, peever 7. pallall

Horace... 4. poet 10. Ars Poetica

Horae (Gr Relig)... 4. dike (justice) 6. Eirene (peace) 7. Eunomia (wisdom) 9. goddesses 11. Book of Hours

horal... 6. hourly

horde... 4. army, camp, clan, pack 5. crowd, swarm, tribe, troop

Horde, Golden... 6. Tatars (Mongol)

Horde, Great (Anthrop)... 5. Kazak 7. Kirghiz

horizon... 4. blue 5. limit, range 6. circle, sea rim 7. azimuth, sea line, sky line 8. junction (earth and sky), boundary

horizon glass... 7. sextant

horizontal... 4. flat 5. level 8. parallel (to horizon)

hormone... 8. estrogen 9. cortisone

horn... 4. Cape, cusp, gore, peak, tuba 5. alarm, bugle, cornu, keras, siren 6. antler, beaker, cornet, vessel 7. buccina, process (animal), trumpet 8. tentacle 9. appendage

horn (pert to)...
blare.. 4. toot 7. fanfare, tantara 9. tantarara
comb form.. 5. kerat 6. kerato
crescent moon.. 4. cusp
drinking (anc).. 6. rhyton
insect's.. 7. antenna
Jewish.. 7. shophar (shofar)
player.. 6. bugler 9. cornetist, trumpeter
producing.. 11. keratogenic
trumpet.. 6. kerana (kerrana)
unbranched (antler).. 3. dag 7. pricket

hornbill... 4. bird, tock 6. homrai, toucan 8. Buceros

horned animal (Myth)... 7. Unicorn 9. Monoceros

horned rattlesnake... 3. asp 5. viper 8. cerastes 10. sidewinder

horned toad... 6. lizard 9. Iguanidae

hornet... 4. wasp 5. Vespa 6. crabro

horny tissue... 7. keratin 8. keratoid (ceratoid), keratose (ceratose)

horologe... 4. dial 5. clock, watch

horoscope... 3. map 5. chart 6. scheme 7. diagram

horrendous... 7. fearful 8. horrible

horrible... 4. dire, grim 6. grisly, horrid, odious 7. ghastly, hideous 8. dreadful, shocking, terrible 9. atrocious, frightful, revolting 10. detestable, horrendous

horror... 3. awe 4. fear 5. dread 6. aghast, terror 8. aversion, distress 10. abhorrence 11. abomination, detestation 13. consternation

hors d'oeuvre... 6. canapé, relish 8. aperitif 9. antipasto, appetizer

horse... 3. cob, nag 4. colt, foal, mare, mule, plug, pony, prad, race, stud 5. beast, burro, draft, filly, genet (jennet), hobby, mount, pacer, steed 6. bronco (broncho), cheval, dobbin, donkey, equine, garran, hippos, maiden, pelter, rouncy 7. caballo, cavalry, charger, courser, Equidae, gelding, hackney, harness, mustang, prancer, quarter, stepper, trotter 8. roadster, stallion, trotting 9. broomtail

horse (pert to)...
ankle.. 4. hock
arena.. 10. hippodrome
Australian.. 5. dingo, myall 8. warragal, yarraman
breastplate.. 7. poitrel (peytrel)
broken–down.. 6. garran, gleyde
buyer (of nags).. 5. coper 7. knacker
calico.. 5. pinto
collar.. 7. bargham
comb form.. 4. hipp 5. hippo 6. hippus

command.. 3. gee, haw, hup
4. whoa 6. giddap
covering.. 9. caparison
cry.. 5. neigh 6. whinny
dealer.. 7. chanter, scorser
disease.. 5. surra (surrah) 6. heaves,
lampas, spavin 7. founder, lampers
draft.. 9. Percheron
family.. 7. Equidae 9. Miohippus,
Orohippus
fast.. 6. pelter
feed box.. 6. manger
female.. 4. mare, yaud 5. filly
fly.. 4. cleg (clegg) 6. botfly
foot.. 4. frog, hoof 7. fetlock, pastern
forehead.. 8. chanfrin
gait.. 3. run 4. lope, pace, trot, walk
6. canter, gallop
genus.. 5. Equus
giant (Norse).. 7. Goldfax
goddess.. 5. Epona
gray.. 8. schimmel
hide.. 8. cordovan
hired.. 4. hack
hoof (part).. 7. caltrop 8. periople
laugh.. 5. snort 6. guffaw, heehaw
leap.. 6. curvet, hurdle 9. ballotade
lover.. 10. hippophile
mackerel.. 5. atule, tunny 6. bonita
male.. 4. stud 7. gelding 8. stallion
manège term.. 5. longe, mount
6. pesade 7. piaffer, saccade
8. caracole 9. estrapage
measure.. 4. hand
miracle (Myth).. 5. Arion
monster (fabled).. 11. Hippocampus
old.. 4. jade, yaud 5. skate
8. harridan, old paint
opera.. 7. Western
pace.. 4. lope, trot 5. amble
6. canter
pack.. 7. sumpter
pair.. 4. span, team
pasturage right.. 9. horsegate
piebald.. 5. pinto
pole.. 5. poler, wheel
prehistoric.. 8. Eohippus
10. Mesohippus, Pliohippus
13. Protorohippus
racer.. 4. pony 6. mudder, plater,
staker
ref to.. 6. equine, equoid, hippic
9. caballine
relay (remounts).. 6. remuda
riding.. 3. cob
rope.. 5. longe 6. halter
roundup.. 5. rodeo
saddle.. 3. cob 5. mount 7. palfrey
shoer.. 7. farrier 10. blacksmith
slang.. 3. nag 4. hack, plug
6. dobbin 8. bangtail
small.. 3. cob, tit 4. pony 5. bidet,
genet (jennet) 8. Galloway, Shetland
sorrel.. 4. roan 8. chestnut
spirited.. 4. Arab 5. steed 6. rearer
7. courser
stable of.. 6. string
study of.. 9. hippology
swift.. 6. pelter 7. Pacolet
talking (Myth).. 5. Arion
three (harnessed).. 6. tandem

7. unicorn
track, arena.. 10. hippodrome
trappings.. 5. manta 6. tackle
7. harness 9. caparison
trotting.. 6. Morgan
turn.. 7. passade
war.. 5. steed 7. charger 8. destrier
(anc)
white–streaked face.. 4. shim
wild.. 6. bronco, tarpan 7. mustang
8. warragal (warrigal)
winged.. 7. Pegasus
horse, breed... 4. Arab, Barb 5. Shire,
Waler 6. Cayuse, Morgan 7. Arabian,
Belgian, Hackney, Mustang, Suffolk
8. Galloway, Normandy, Palomino,
Shetland 9. Appaloosa, Miohippus,
Percheron 10. Clydesdale
horse, color... 3. bay, tan 4. pied,
roan 5. cream, pinto 6. calico, sorrel
7. brindle, dappled, piebald
8. chestnut, palomino, schimmel,
skewbald 10. flea–bitten
horse, famed (and rider)... 4. Tony
(Tom Mix) 5. Grani (Sigurd)
6. Bayard (Rinaldo), Rienzi (Gen
Sherman), Silver (Lone Ranger),
Trojan (legend), Whitey (Zachary
Taylor) 7. Alborak (Mohammed),
Morengo (Napoleon), Pegasus (Gr
Myth), Trigger (Roy Rogers), Xanthus
(Achilles) 8. Comanche (Gen Custer),
Sleipnir 8–legged (Odin), Soapsuds
(Will Rogers) 9. Black Bess (Dick
Turpin), Houyhnhnm (Gulliver's
Travels), Incitatus (Caligula), Rosinante
(Don Quixote), Traveller (Gen Robt E
Lee) 10. Bootlegger (Will Rogers),
Bucephalus (Alexander the Great),
Cincinnati (Gen Grant), Copenhagen
(Wellington at Waterloo), King Philip
(Gen Forrest) 11. Black Beauty
(legend), Vegliantino (Orlando)
12. Little Sorrel (Stonewall Jackson)
horseman... 5. rider 6. cowboy
7. centaur, vaquero 8. buckaroo
10. cavalryman, equestrian
12. broncobuster
horsemanship... 6. manège
horseradish tree... 3. ben (oil)
5. behen (behn) 7. Moringa
Horus (pert to)...
bird.. 6. falcon
father.. 6. Osiris
hawk–headed god of.. 3. day
mother.. 4. Isis
slayer of.. 4. Seth
hospice... 3. inn 6. asylum, imaret
9. hospitium, infirmary
hospitable... 6. kindly 7. cordial
8. friendly, gracious 9. receptive,
welcoming 10. neighborly
hospital... 6. crèche, refuge
9. ambulance (mobile), infirmary
10. nosocomium, sanatorium,
sanitarium 11. institution,
xenodochium 12. ambulatorium
hospitality... 7. accueil, welcome
8. open door 9. open house,
xenodochy 10. cordiality
13. receptiveness
host... 3. sum (obs) 4. army 5. swarm

6. legion, throng 8. assemble,
landlord 9. multitude, sacrifice
11. entertainer
hostel . . . 3. inn 5. hotel, motel
6. tavern 8. lodgings 9. residence
(student)
hostelry . . . 3. inn 5. hotel 6. hostel,
tavern 11. caravansary
hostile . . . 5. enemy 7. adverse (law),
opposed 8. contrary, inimical
10. malevolent, unfriendly
11. belligerent 12. antagonistic
13. unsympathetic
hostilities . . . 3. war 5. feuds, raids
hostility . . . 5. anger 6. animus, enmity,
hatred, rancor 7. ill will, warfare
8. opponent 9. animosity, antipathy
10. antagonism, bitterness,
opposition, resentment 11. contrariety
13. antisocialism 14. unfriendliness,
vindictiveness
hostler . . . 5. groom 7. equerry
9. innkeeper, stableboy, stableman
Host vessel . . . 3. Pyx 5. paten
hot . . . 3. red 5. calid, eager, fiery
6. fervid, raging, recent, torrid,
urgent 7. burning, calidus, excited,
fervent, glowing, peppery, violent
8. feverish, sizzling, vehement
10. hot–blooded, passionate
hot cakes . . . 8. kneepads (army sl)
hotel . . . 3. inn 5. lodge 6. hostel,
tavern 7. albergo 11. caravansary
hot–tempered . . . 5. angry, breth, fiery
7. enraged, iracund 8. choleric,
wrathful 10. hot–blooded
Hottentot, S Africa (pert to) . . .
cloak . . 6. kaross
hut . . 5. kraal
mixed native . . 6. Griqua
musical instrument . . 4. gora (gorah)
nickname . . 9. Khoi–Khoin (Koi–Koin)
(men of men)
purest tribe . . 5. Namas 7. Namaqua
race . . 6. Bantus 7. Bushmen
tribe . . 6. Damara, Herero
9. Ovahehero
hound . . . 4. hunt 5. chase, track
6. follow, pursue 7. devotee
9. scoundrel
hound (animal) . . . 4. alan 6. Afghan,
basset, beagle, setter 7. harrier,
skirter 8. Cerberus (Myth), elkhound,
foxhound 9. boarhound, dachshund,
deerhound, greyhound, staghound,
wolfhound 10. bloodhound,
otterhound
hounds, relay of . . . 8. avantlay
hour (pert to) . . .
astrology . . 7. inequal 9. planetary
by the . . 5. horal 6. horary
Eccl . . 4. sext 9. canonical
Latin . . 4. hora 5. Horae (Book of
Hours)
measure . . 9. hourglass
term . . 4. time 6. period 7. measure
8. interval
houri . . . 5. nymph (Moham)
Hours, Book of . . . 5. Horae
house . . . 3. eco (comb form) 4. casa,
firm, home 5. abode, cover, lodge,
tribe 6. billet, family 7. cottage,

enclose, lineage, mansion, quarter,
shelter, theater 8. audience,
bungalow, Congress, domicile,
dwelling 9. playhouse, residence,
workhouse 10. habitation, Parliament
house (pert to) . . .
astrology . . 7. mansion, mundane
9. planetary
boarding . . 3. inn 5. hotel 6. tavern
9. dormitory
comb form . . 3. eco 4. oeco, oiko
correction . . 9. Bridewell (Eng)
11. reformatory
dog . . 6. kennel
government . . 5. Lords 7. Commons
15. Representatives
ranch . . 4. casa 6. casita 8. hacienda
roof . . 9. penthouse
small . . 3. hut 4. nest 5. cabin, shack
stately . . 5. villa 6. palace 7. mansion
summer . . 6. casino, gazebo
9. belvedere
warming . . 6. infare
household (pert to) . . .
deity . . 5. Lares 7. Penates
domestic . . 6. family, menage
fairy . . 4. Puck
linen . . 6. napery
housekeeping . . . 8. oikology
10. management 11. hospitality
House of . . . 4. Keys (Isle of Man)
5. David, Lords, Peers 7. Bishops,
Commons, Windsor 11. Seven
Gables
housewarming . . . 6. infare
11. merrymaking
Houston, Texas . . .
capital . . 8. Republic (Texas, 1837)
college . . 4. Rice
named for . . 10. Sam Houston (Gen)
nickname . . 12. Space City USA
site . . 11. Ship Channel
site of . . 4. NASA
hovel . . . 3. den, hut 4. shed 5. cabin,
hutch, shack 6. dugout 7. shelter
hover . . . 4. flit, soar 5. brood, drift,
float 6. linger 7. shelter 9. hang
about 12. be irresolute
however . . . 3. but, how, tho, yet
6. anyhow, though 7. at least
8. although 11. at all events
12. nevertheless 15. notwithstanding
howl . . . 3. bay, cry 4. wail, yell, yowl
6. lament 7. ululate
howling monkey . . . 5. araba
hoyden, hoiden . . . 4. rude 5. a romp
6. tomboy 7. ill–bred
Hoyle (Edmond) . . . 6. writer
12. encyclopedia (of games)
hub . . . 3. hut 4. axle, nave 6. center
(centre) 7. hummock
12. protuberance (rough)
Hub (The) . . . 6. Boston
hubbub . . . 3. ado, din 4. game (US
Ind), stir 6. bustle, clamor, outcry,
racket, rumpus, tumult, uproar
8. rowdy–dow 9. agitation,
commotion, confusion 10. turbulence
hubristic . . . 8. arrogant, insolent
12. contemptuous
hubshi . . . 5. Negro
huck . . . 3. hip 4. hook, howk

huckleberry / Hundred Days 268

6. haunch, higgle, hollow 7. bargain
huckleberry ... 5. bacca 9. blueberry
  12. Vacciniaceae
huckleberry endocarp ... 6. pyrene
huckster ... 6. broker, hawker, vendor
  7. peddler 8. pitchman, retailer
  9. middleman
huddle ... 3. hug 5. crowd 6. bustle,
  confer, jumble, mingle 7. confuse
  8. assemble, disorder, grouping
  (football) 9. confusion, skinflint
  10. conference 14. conglomeration
Hudson (pert to) ...
  boat .. 8. Half Moon (Henry Hudson's)
  explorer .. 11. Henry Hudson
  River School .. 8. Painters (19th Cent)
  River seal .. 7. muskrat
hue ... 4. form, tint, tone 5. color,
  guise, shade, shout, swart, tinge
  6. outcry 7. swarthy 8. shouting
  10. complexion
huff ... 4. puff 5. anger, bully, swell
  6. offend 7. inflate
hug ... 4. hold 5. clasp, seize
  6. adhere 7. embrace, welcome
  8. greeting
huge ... 3. big 4. vast 5. giant, great,
  large 7. immense, mammoth,
  massive, monster, titanic 8. colossal,
  enormous, gigantic 9. monstrous
  10. gargantuan
Huguenot ... 10. Protestant
Huguenot leader ... 6. Adrets (Baron)
hui (Chin) ... 4. firm 5. guild 7. society
  (secret) 11. partnership
huisache ... 4. wabe (wabi) 5. shrub
  7. popinac
huissier ... 5. usher 7. bailiff, sheriff
  10. doorkeeper
huitre ... 6. oyster
hulky ... 5. bulky, large 6. clumsy
  7. hulking, loutish
hull ... 3. pod 4. free, husk 5. calyx,
  frame (ship), shell, shoot, strip
  8. covering
hullabaloo ... 3. din 6. clamor
  (clamour), hubbub, outcry, racket,
  tumult, uproar 9. confusion
hulled corn ... 4. samp 5. maize
  6. hominy
hulver ... 5. holly
hum ... 4. buzz, sing (with closed lips)
  5. croon, drone 6. murmur
  7. deceive
human ... 3. man 4. homo, kind
  6. humane, mortal 7. Adamite
  8. merciful
human (pert to) ...
  being .. 3. man 6. mortal, person
  7. Adamite 8. creature
  bondage .. 7. slavery
  race .. 3. man 7. mankind
  skull .. 10. death's—head
  structure .. 7. anatomy
  trunk .. 5. torso
humble ... 3. low 4. mean, meek, mild,
  poor 5. abase, abash, demit, lower,
  lowly, plain 6. modest, simple,
  subdue 7. degrade, mortify
  8. chastise, deferent, disgrace,
  plebeian, reverent 9. humiliate
  10. unassuming 12. unpretending

humbug ... 4. bosh, fake, flam, guff,
  hoax, sham 5. cheat, fraud, guile,
  trick 7. deceive, mislead 8. pretense
  9. deception, imposture, stratagem
humid ... 4. damp, dank 5. moist
  6. sultry 8. vaporous
humiliate ... 5. abase, abash, shame
  6. humble, nither 7. affront, degrade,
  mortify 8. disgrace
humiliation ... 7. subdual 9. abasement
  11. disgraceful 13. mortification
humility ... 6. humble (spirit)
  7. modesty 8. meekness, mildness
  9. lowliness (mind) 10. humbleness
hummingbird ... 3. ava 4. star
  5. sylph, topaz 6. rufous, Sappho
  7. colibri, Lucifer 8. calliope
  9. sheartail, thornbill, thorntail
  10. rackettail 11. Trochilidae
humor, humour ... 3. fun, wit 4. baby,
  mood, whim 5. blood, cater, fancy,
  fluid, freak, quirk 6. comedy, levity,
  nature, please 7. caprice, gratify,
  indulge 8. drollery 10. comicality
  11. inclination, temperament
humorist ... 3. wag 5. comic, droll
  8. comedian 11. entertainer
humorous ... 5. funny, humid, moist,
  witty 6. jocose 7. amusing, jocular
  9. facetious, laughable, whimsical
  10. capricious
hump ... 4. arch, hunk, lump 5. bulge,
  exert, hurry, mound, sulks
  7. hummock 8. shoulder
  12. protuberance
humpbacked ... 6. humped, kyphos
  8. deformed, kyphosis 9. camel back
  11. hunchbacked
humpbacked fish ... 5. whale
  6. salmon, sucker 9. whitefish
humus ... 4. mold, soil 5. humin,
  mulch
Hun ... 6. Attila, vandal 7. soldier
  9. barbarian 10. Ephthalite
hunch ... 4. bend, hump, lump
  5. crook, fudge, shove 6. chilly,
  crouch, frosty, thrust 9. intuition
  12. protuberance
Hunchback of Notre Dame (pert to) ...
  character .. 9. Esmeralda (gypsy),
  Quasimodo (The Hunchback)
  French name .. 16. Notre Dame de
  Paris
  literature (famed) .. 5. novel
hunched ... 7. gibbous
hundred (pert to) ...
  comb form .. 5. centi, hecto
  7. hecaton
  eyed being .. 5. Argus
  fold .. 8. centuple 12. centuplicate
  historian (of centuries) ..
  11. centuriator
  Latin .. 6. centum
  men, soldiers .. 7. century
  12. centumvirate
  number .. 7. ten tens 9. five score
  symbol .. 1. C
  victim sacrifice .. 8. hecatomb
  weight .. 6. cental 7. centner
  years .. 7. century 9. centenary,
  centurial
Hundred Days (pert to) ... 8. Napoleon,

Waterloo (Battle 1815)
hundred percent... 5. quite 8. entirely
   10. altogether 14. unquestionable
hundredth of a right angle... 4. grad
Hundred Years War... 5. Crecy
   (Cressy)
hung... see *hang*
Hungarian (pert to)... see also *Hungary*
   army.. 6. Honvéd 9. Honvédség
   cavalryman.. 6. Hussar
   dance.. 7. czardas
   gypsy.. 7. tzigane
   hash.. 7. goulash
   legislature.. 8. Felsohaz
   measure.. 5. antal, itcze
   partridge.. 6. Perdix
   physicist.. 6. Teller
   poet.. 5. Arany
   Pretender to the throne.. 4. Otto
   racial unit.. 3. Hun 6. Magyar
   surgeon.. 6. Schick
   turnip.. 8. kohlrabi
   wine.. 5. Tokay
Hungary (People's Republic of)...
   capital.. 8. Budapest (Budapesth)
   city.. 6. Szeged (Szegedin)
      8. Debrecen 9. Kecskemet
   government.. 9. Communism
   lake.. 7. Balaton 10. Neusiedler
   mountain.. 5. Tatra 11. Carpathians
   Plain (fertile).. 6. Alfold
   port.. 5. Fiume
   river.. 4. Raab 5. Drava (Drave)
      6. Danube, Theiss 7. Vistula
hunger... 4. long, want 6. acoria,
   desire, famine, thirst 7. craving
   8. appetite, coveting, voracity
   9. esurience
hungry... 4. avid, poor 5. eager
   6. barren, hollow, jejune 7. starved
   8. esurient, famished, indigent
   10. avaricious
Hung Society (secret)... 5. Triad (Man,
   Earth, Heaven) 6. Deluge
hunt... 3. dig 4. seek 5. chase, delve,
   hound, probe, quest, track, trail
   6. ferret, follow, pursue, search,
   shikar
hunter... 3. dog 5. green, horse,
   jager, Jason, Orion 6. cuckoo,
   Nimrod 7. shikari (shikaree), stalker,
   trapper, venerer 8. huntsman
hunting (pert to)...
   act of.. 3. venery 7. pursuit
      10. cynegetics
   coyotes.. 7. wolfing
   dog.. 5. dhole 6. basset, beagle,
      setter 7. pointer
   Dogs (Astron).. 13. Canes Venatici
   expedition.. 6. safari
   fond of.. 7. venatic
   horn.. 5. bugle
   leopard.. 7. cheetah
hurdy–gurdy... 4. lire, rota 5. organ
   (street) 7. sambuke 10. instrument
   (lutelike), waterwheel
hurl... 4. cast, pelt, rush, toss
   5. fling, pitch, sling, throw 6. elance
   (dart), hurtle 9. overthrow
hurlbarrow... 11. wheelbarrow
hurled... 4. cast, sent 5. flung, slung,

threw 6. pelted, tossed 7. hurtled,
   twisted 8. betossed
hurly–burly... 5. storm 6. tumult,
   uproar 9. agitation, confusion
   10. excitement
huron... 6. grison (animal) 9. black
   bass
Huron... 4. lake 6. Indian 9. Iroquoian
hurrah... 3. joy 4. viva 5. cheer,
   huzza, shout 7. triumph 8. applause
   10. hallelujah 11. exclamation
   13. encouragement
hurricane... 5. storm 6. baguio
   7. cyclone, Hurakan (god), tornado,
   typhoon (in China Sea)
hurry... 3. hie 4. rush, scud 5. chase,
   haste, impel, sessa, speed 6. hasten,
   scurry, tumult, urge on 7. quicken
   8. dispatch, expedite 9. agitation,
   commotion 10. expedition
   11. disturbance, precipitate
hurst... 4. hill, wood 5. copse, grove,
   knoll 6. hillock (wooded)
hurt... 4. harm, maim, pain 5. lesed,
   parry 6. damage, grieve, impair,
   injure, injury, offend 8. distress,
   mischief 9. detriment 10. impairment
hurtful... 6. malign, nocent 7. baneful,
   harmful, malefic, nocuous, noisome,
   noxious, painful 9. injurious
   10. pernicious 11. destructive,
   detrimental, prejudicial
   15. disadvantageous
hurtle... 4. dash, push 5. clash, fling
   6. assail, jostle 7. collide, resound
   8. brandish
husband... 3. eke 4. mate, save
   5. marry, store 6. direct (frugally),
   farmer, spouse, tiller 7. espouse,
   granger, manager, steward
   8. conserve 9. cultivate, economize
   10. husbandman
husbandry... 6. thrift 7. economy,
   farming, tillage 10. management
   (domestic) 11. agriculture, cultivation
husband's brother... 5. levir
hush... 3. tut 4. calm, hist, lull
   5. allay, quiet, still 6. soothe
   7. appease, silence 10. keep secret
husk... 4. bran, leam, rind 5. shood,
   shuck, straw
husky... 3. dry 5. burly, harsh
   6. hoarse, strong 7. raucous
   8. powerful
Husky... 3. dog 6. Eskimo
   8. Malemute
huss... 7. dogfish
hussar... 4. fish (banded) 6. dolman
   (jacket) 10. cavalryman, skirmisher
hussy... 4. girl, jade 8. strumpet
   9. housewife
hustings... 5. court 8. platform
   (Guildhall)
hut... 3. cot 4. cote, isba, shed, skeo
   (fisherman's) 5. cabin, hogan, hovel,
   igloo, jacal, scale 6. lean–to, shanty,
   wigwam
hutch... 3. bin, box, car, hut, pen
   4. coop 5. chest, hoard, hovel
   6. coffer, humped, shanty, warren
hyacinth (pert to)...
   color.. 5. tenne 7. blue–red

genus.. 10. Hyacinthus
mineral.. 6. zircon
myth.. 4. iris, lily (Turk's cap)
of Peru.. 9. Cuban lily
precious stone.. 8. sapphire (legend)
wild.. 6. camass
hybrid... 7. mongrel 9. half–breed
hybrid (pert to)...
buffalo.. 7. cattalo
dog.. 5. Husky 7. mongrel
fruit.. 7. plumcot, tangelo 8. citrange
horse.. 4. mule 5. hinny, jenny
vegetable.. 6. pomato
zebra.. 7. zebrass, zebrula 8. zebrinny
hydra... 4. evil 6. polyps
11. thermometer
Hydra (Gr)... 6. island 7. serpent
13. constellation
hydraulic (pert to)...
brake.. 8. cataract
element.. 5. water
engine.. 3. ram 6. tremie
product.. 5. power
hydria... 3. jar 6. kalpis
hydrocarbon... 5. tolan (tolane)
6. ethane, octane, pinene, pyrene,
tolane, toluol 7. benzene, methane,
terpene 9. acetylene
hydrocarbon radical... 4. amyl
6. pentyl
hydrocyanic acid... 7. cyanide, prussic
8. fumigant
hydrogen... 1. H 3. gas 7. element
(univalent)
hydroid... 9. polyplike
hydrophobia... 5. lyssa 6. rabies
Hydrus... 12. water serpent (fabled)
13. constellation
hyena... 6. mammal 8. aardwolf
9. earthwolf 13. Tasmanian wolf
hygienic... 7. sterile 8. sanitary
9. healthful 10. uninfected
12. prophylactic
hylophagous... 10. wood–eating
hymenopter, hymenopteron... 3. ant,
bee, fly 4. wasp 9. ichneumon
hymn... 3. ode 4. song (of praise)
5. dirge, music, paean (pean)
6. anthem, hirmos, Te Deum
7. chorale 8. doxology 9. Trisagion
11. recessional

hymn (pert to)...
book.. 6. hymnal
composer.. 7. hymnist
12. hymnographer
science of.. 9. hymnology
singing of.. 7. hymnody
victory.. 9. epinicion
hypnotic... 6. opiate, sleepy
8. mesmeric, narcotic, sedative
9. soporific 12. somnifacient
13. sleep–inducing
hypnotist... 6. Mesmer 9. mesmerist
10. hypnotizer
hypnotize... 5. charm 6. dazzle
8. entrance 9. fascinate, mesmerize,
spellbind
hypochondriac... 4. hypo 6. insane
7. invalid (imaginary) 8. dejected,
neurotic 9. depressed, psychotic
10. nosomaniac
hypocrisy... 4. cant 6. deceit
8. feigning 9. falseness
10. sanctimony, simulation
11. outward show
hypocrite... 4. fake 5. cheat 7. tartufe
(tartuffe) 8. deceiver 10. dissembler
hypocritical... 5. false 8. specious
9. insincere 11. pharisaical
13. sanctimonious, self–righteous
hypodermic glass vessel...
7. ampoule (ampule)
hypodermic injection... 4. shot
11. inoculation
hypothesis... 3. ism 6. theory
7. premise, theorem 8. proposal
9. condition, postulate
10. assumption 11. proposition,
supposition
hypothetical... 8. academic
11. conditional, conjectural,
speculative, theoretical
hypothetical (pert to)...
being.. 3. ens 5. entia (pl) 6. entity
biological unit.. 2. id
force.. 2. od
medium.. 5. ether
hyrax... 8. procavia
hyssop... 4. mint 11. aspergillum
hysteria... 7. anxiety 12. emotionalism
hysterical... 7. frantic 8. frenzied,
wild–eyed 9. emotional
12. uncontrolled

I

I... 2. me 3. eye 4. iota (Gr), self 6. letter (9th), myself 7. pronoun
I (pert to)...
big .. 3. ego
excessive .. 8. iotacism
love .. 3. amo
Iago... 7. villain (Othello)
iambus... 4. foot, iamb
iatrics (comb form)... 11. treatment of
iatrology... 7. healing 8. treatise
Iberia... 5. Spain 7. Georgia (anc)
ibex... 3. sac, tur, zac 4. kail (kyl) 6. sakeen 8. antelope
ibid... 6. lizard 7. monitor
ibidem... 4. ibid 9. same place
ibis... 5. guara, stork 9. gourdhead
Ibsen (pert to)...
famed as .. 4. poet 9. dramatist
native of .. 6. Norway
story character .. 3. Ase 4. Gynt, Nora
ice... 4. rime 5. frost, glacé, glaze 6. freeze 7. congeal, diamond, jewelry 11. refrigerant, refrigerate
ice (pert to)...
bartender's .. 5. rocks (sl)
cream dish .. 4. cone, soda 6. frappé, mousse, sundae 7. parfait
dessert .. 5. glacé 6. frappé 7. sherbet
fine, slushy .. 4. grue, hail, sish, snow 5. flake, frost, sleet
fishing .. 4. chug
glacier .. 4. neve 5. serac
mass .. 4. berg, calf, floe 5. serac 6. icecap 7. glacier, growler
pendent .. 6. icicle
sea .. 6. sludge
Iceland...
airport .. 9. Kopavogur
assembly .. 7. Althing
bird .. 4. gull 6. falcon 10. gyrofalcon
capital .. 9. Reykjavik
city .. 3. Hof 8. Akureyri
dramatist .. 12. Siguryonsson
epic .. 4. Edda
first discoverer .. 8. Norseman (about 870)
giant .. 4. Atli
glacier .. 6. Jökull 11. Orafajökull
god .. see *Norse god(s), goddess*
government .. 8. republic (1944)
legends .. 5. Eddas, Sagas 12. Volsunga Saga
Parliament .. 7. Althing (world's oldest)
product .. 7. herring
sculptor .. 9. Sveinsson
volcano .. 5. Askja, Hekla, Katla
ichneumon... 3. fly 8. mongoose 9. Herpestes 12. hymenopteron
ichor... 5. fluid (of the gods)

ichthus... 4. fish 6. amulet, symbol 8. talisman
ichthyophagy... 10. fish eating
icicle... 7. shoggle 10. stalactite, stalagmite
icing... 8. frosting, meringue
icterus... 6. oriole 7. disease 8. jaundice 10. yellowness
ictus... 4. beat (rhythm), blow 6. accent, stress, stroke
icy... 4. cold 5. algid, gelid 6. frigid, frosty, frozen 7. glacial 8. chilling
id... 4. idem, unit 5. idant 6. libido, psyche, suffix 7. the same
Idaean (pert to)...
dweller of .. 5. Mt Ida
goddess .. 4. Rhea (Crete) 6. Cybele (Asia Minor)
nature goddess .. 6. Cybele 11. Great Mother
Idaho...
capital .. 5. Boise
city .. 7. Orofino 9. Pocatello
crop (famed) .. 8. potatoes
dam .. 5. Oxbow 8. Brownlee
famed citizen .. 5. Borah (Sen)
monument .. 16. Craters of the Moon
mountain .. 8. Sawtooth 11. Bitterroots
river .. 5. Snake
salmon (landlocked) .. 7. kokanee
State admission .. 10. Forty–third
State bird .. 8. bluebird
State flower .. 7. syringa
State motto .. 11. Live Forever 12. Esto Perpetua
State nickname .. 8. Gem State
ide (id)... 3. orf (orfe) 4. fish 7. the same
idea... 4. clue, idée, ideo (comb form) 5. ethic, motif 6. belief, notion 7. concept, meaning, opinion, wrinkle 10. impression 11. supposition
ideal... 4. type 5. dream, model, Thule (Myth) 6. unreal 7. paragon, pattern, perfect, typical, Utopian 8. complete, exemplar, fanciful 9. faultless, imaginary, visionary 10. conceptual, consummate, idealistic 11. mental image, theoretical 12. intellectual
idealist... 7. dreamer 8. romancer 9. visionary 11. illusionist
idealistic... 9. fictional, visionary 10. starry–eyed 13. philosophical
ideate... 5. think 6. invent 7. imagine 8. conceive 9. prefigure
identical... 4. same, self, twin 5. alike, equal 10. equivalent, tantamount
identification... 3. tag 4. disk, sign

5. badge, brand 6. naming
7. earmark 11. recognition,
unification
identify... 4. name 5. place, prove
8. coalesce 9. designate, establish
13. associate with
identity... 5. unity 7. oneness
8. equality, sameness 9. exactness
11. homogeneity 13. individuality
ideologist... 7. dreamer 8. theorist
9. visionary
idiocy... 7. amentia, anoesia, fatuity,
idiotry 10. deficiency (mental)
11. foolishness
idiograph... 9. trademark
idiom... 6. phrase 7. diction
8. language 11. peculiarity
idiosyncrasy... 9. mannerism
11. peculiarity 12. eccentricity
14. characteristic
idiot... 3. oaf 4. dolt, fool 5. booby,
dunce, moron 6. cretin, nitwit
7. dullard, half–wit 8. imbecile
9. blockhead, simpleton
idiotic... 4. daft 5. crazy 7. foolish
9. senseless 12. feeble–minded
idle... 4. laze, lazy, loaf, sorn, vain
5. drone, empty, inert 6. loiter,
otiose, tiffle, truant, unused, vacant
7. leisure, loafing, trivial, useless
8. baseless, inactive, indolent,
slothful, trifling 9. unfounded,
worthless 10. groundless,
unemployed, unoccupied
11. ineffectual, unwarranted
idleness... 5. folly, sloth 6. vanity
7. inertia 8. delirium, faniente,
laziness 9. silliness 10. inactivity,
triviality 15. lightheadedness
idler... 4. hobo 5. drone 6. loafer
7. dawdler, lounger 8. loiterer
idol... 3. god (sacred) 4. Baal, icon,
zemi 5. afgod, deity (heathen), eikon,
satyr 6. effigy, fetish, idolum, statue
7. darling, fallacy, phantom, picture
8. impostor 9. pretender
idolater... 5. pagan 6. adorer
7. admirer, Baalist, Baalite, heathen
8. idolizer 9. worshiper
idolize... 5. adore 6. esteem, revere
7. worship 10. idolatrize
idyl, idyll... 4. poem 5. image
7. bucolic, eclogue, picture
8. pastoral
i. e... 5. id est 6. that is
if... 2. si 3. gif 8. granting, provided
9. supposing
if ever... 4. once
if not... 4. else, nisi (law) 6. unless
igneous rock... 4. boss, dike, trap
5. magma 6. basalt 7. peridot
10. granophyre 11. molten magma
ignis... 4. fire
ignite... 4. burn, fire, heat 5. light
6. kindle 7. blaze up, flare up 9. set
fire to
ignoble... 3. low 4. base, mean, vile
6. menial 8. plebeian, shameful
11. disgraceful 12. dishonorable,
disreputable
ignoramus... 4. dolt, fool 5. dunce
6. nitwit, no bill (law)

11. know–nothing
ignorance... 5. tamas (Hind)
9. nescience 12. inexperience
ignorant... 7. unaware 8. nescient
9. unknowing, untutored
10. illiterate, unlettered
13. inexperienced, unintelligent
ignore... 3. cut 4. omit, snub
7. condone, disobey, neglect
8. overlook 9. disregard, eliminate
Igorot... 6. Bontok 7. Nabaloi
8. Kankanai 10. Indonesian
iguana... 6. goanna (goana), lizard
7. monitor, tuatara 9. Iguanidae
10. lace lizard
I Have Found It... 6. Eureka (Calif
motto)
ihi (Maori)... 7. skipper 8. halfbeak
10. stitchbird
IHS... 5. Jesus 6. symbol 10. In hoc
signo
iiwi... 4. bird
ikbal... 7. arrival 8. prestige
10. prosperity
Iknaton... 9. Amenhotep, Amenophis
(IV)
ikona... 9. greenhorn, simpleton
ileum... 9. intestine (small)
ilex... 5. holly 7. holm oak
11. Paraguay tea
Iliad (pert to)...
founder (anc).. 4. Troy 5. Ilium
poem author.. 5. Homer
poem character.. 4. Ajax 6. Hector
7. Stentor 8. Achilles, Brisseis
9. Agamemnon, Cassandra
ilium... 4. bone (pelvic)
Ilium... 4. Troy (anc)
ill... 3. bad, mal (comb form) 4. evil,
hard, poor, rude, sick 5. badly,
wrong 6. ailing, malice, poorly,
savage, unkind 7. noxious, painful,
unlucky 9. dangerous, difficult
10. disastrous, indisposed, iniquitous,
malevolent, unpolished, unskillful
11. unfavorable, unfortunate,
unwholesome 12. disagreeable,
inauspicious
ill (pert to)...
at ease.. 7. awkward 9. graceless,
maladroit
bred.. 4. rude 7. uncivil 8. impolite
9. bourgeois
hap.. 10. misfortune
humored.. 5. cross, moody
natured.. 4. dour 5. cross, moody,
surly 6. morose, sullen 7. crabbed
10. crosspatch
tempered.. 7. bilious 8. choleric
timed.. 5. inapt 8. untimely
9. premature 10. malapropos
11. inexpedient, inopportune
will.. 6. enmity, malice
11. malevolence
illegal... 4. foul 7. illicit 8. outlawry,
unlawful, wrongful 10. contraband,
unofficial 12. illegitimate,
unauthorized
illegal entry... 6. ringer
illimitable... 4. vast 8. infinite
9. boundless 11. measureless
12. immeasurable, unrestricted

Illinois...
airport.. 5. O'Hare
capital.. 8. Vandalia (first)
11. Springfield
city.. 5. Elgin 6. Peoria 7. Chicago,
Decatur 8. Evanston, Waukegan
9. Centralia
lake.. 8. Michigan
slogan.. 13. Land of Lincoln
State admission.. 11. Twenty–first
State nickname.. 7. Prairie
illiterate... 6. unread 8. ignorant,
untaught 9. inerudite, unlearned,
unrefined, untutored, unwritten
illness... 6. malady 8. cachexia,
sickness 9. complaint, distemper
10. affliction 13. indisposition
illuminant... 3. gas 4. lamp
9. petroleum 10. Kleig light
illuminate... 5. adorn, color, light
6. illume 7. explain, lighten, miniate
8. emblazen, illumine 9. elucidate,
enlighten, irradiate, rubricate
10. illustrate
illumination, unit of... 3. lux 4. phot
illusion... 5. fancy 6. mirage
7. chimera, fallacy, mockery,
phantom 8. delusion, phantasy
9. deception, false show
10. apparition 13. hallucination,
misconception
illusive... 5. false 6. unreal 8. spectral
9. deceitful, deceptive, imaginary
10. phantasmal, transitory
illusory... 5. false 8. delusory, illusive
9. deceptive, erroneous, imaginary,
unfounded 10. fallacious
illustrate... 4. cite, draw 5. adorn
7. explain, picture 8. beautify
9. elucidate, exemplify, represent
10. illuminate
illustrious... 5. noble, noted
6. famous, heroic 7. eminent,
exalted, radiant 8. glorious, luminous,
renowned, splendid 9. brilliant,
honorable 10. celebrated
image... 3. god 4. copy, icon, idea,
idol, ikon, type 6. alraun, aspect,
effigy, idolon, mirror, recept, sphinx,
statue, typify 7. eidolon, phantom,
picture, portray 8. illusion, likeness,
phantasm 9. semblance
10. apparition, conception,
simulacrum 11. counterpart
12. reproduction
imaginary... 5. ideal 7. fancied
8. fanciful, illusory, mythical
10. fictitious
imaginary disease... 9. nosomania
imagination... 5. dream, fancy
8. phantasy, poetical
imagine... 5. dream, fancy, opine,
think 6. ideate 7. suppose
8. conceive 10. conjecture
imam... 6. caliph, priest (Moham)
imbecile... 4. dolt, weak 5. anile,
idiot, inane, moron 6. cretin, dotard,
feeble, stupid, witlet 7. fatuous,
idiotic, witling 9. driveling
10. half–witted 12. feeble–minded
imbed... 5. embed, inset 6. cement
9. establish

imberbe... 9. beardless
imbibe... 4. soak 5. drink, imbue,
learn 6. absorb, inhale 8. saturate
10. assimilate
imbroglio... 5. brawl 11. embroilment,
predicament 16. misunderstanding
imbrue... 3. fig, wet 4. soak 5. color,
stain (with blood), steep 6. defile,
drench 7. moisten 8. saturate
imbue... 3. dye 5. steep, teach, tinge
6. infuse, leaven 7. ingrain, inspire
8. permeate, saturate, tincture
9. inculcate 10. impregnate
imitant... 9. imitation 11. counterfeit
imitate... 3. ape 4. copy, mime, mock
5. mimic 6. borrow 7. emulate
8. pastiche, resemble, simulate
9. dissemble, reproduce
imitation... 4. copy, echo, sham
5. apery, apism, paste 6. ectype,
olivet (pearl), parody 7. mimesis,
mimicry 8. travesty 9. burlesque
10. caricature, simulation
12. onomatopoeia
imitative... 5. apish 8. apatetic
9. emulative, imitation 10. simulative
11. counterfeit
immaculate... 4. pure 5. clean
6. chaste 8. spotless, unsoiled
9. faultless, undefiled, unstained,
unsullied
immanence... 7. inbeing 9. inherence
10. indwelling, innateness
immanent... 5. inner 6. inward
8. internal 9. intrinsic 10. indwelling
immaterial... 6. slight 8. trifling
9. spiritual 10. impalpable, intangible
11. disembodied, incorporeal,
unimportant 12. supernatural
13. insignificant, unsubstantial
immature... 5. crude, green 6. callow,
unripe 7. untried 8. untimely,
youthful 9. premature 10. unfinished
11. undeveloped
immeasurable... 7. endless 8. infinite
9. boundless, unlimited 10. indefinite
11. illimitable, innumerable
12. immensurable, incalculable,
unfathomable 13. indeterminate
16. incomprehensible
immediacy... 9. awareness, closeness
10. directness 11. punctuality
immediate... 4. next 6. direct, prompt
7. instant, nearest, present
10. continuous, succeeding
immediately... 3. now 4. anon
7. closely 8. directly, promptly
9. instantly, therewith 11. straightway
12. without delay
immemorial... 3. old 7. ageless,
ancient 8. dateless 9. out of mind
11. prehistoric, traditional
immense... 4. huge, vast 5. grand,
great 6. superb 7. mammoth, titanic
8. enormous, infinite 9. monstrous
10. prodigious, unmeasured
immerge... 3. dip 4. sink 5. merge
6. engulf, plunge 7. immerse
8. inundate, submerge
immerse... 3. dip 4. bury, dunk, sink
5. douse, souse 6. absorb, plunge
7. baptize, engross 9. overwhelm

imminent... 7. nearing 8. menacing, upcoming 9. impending 10. near at hand 11. approaching, forthcoming, overhanging, threatening

immobile... 3. set 5. fixed, inert 6. stable 8. moveless 9. immovable, obstinate, unfeeling 10. inflexible, motionless, stationary

immoderate... 5. ultra, undue 7. extreme 9. excessive 10. exorbitant, inordinate 11. extravagant, intemperate 12. unreasonable

immolation... 8. oblation, offering 9. sacrifice

immoral... 3. bad 6. wicked 7. corrupt, vicious 8. depraved, indecent 9. dissolute 10. licentious, misconduct

immortal... 6. divine 7. abiding, endless, eternal, godlike, undying 8. enduring 9. ambrosial, ceaseless, celebrity, perpetual 10. superhuman 11. amaranthine, everlasting 12. imperishable 13. incorruptible

Immortal (Taoism)... 8. Chang Kuo

immortality... 4. fame 6. amrita (conferring) 9. anathasia 11. lasting fame 13. deathlessness 15. everlastingness

immovable... 3. pat 4. fast, firm 5. fixed, rigid 6. stable 7. adamant 8. immobile, obdurate 9. obstinate, unfeeling 10. inflexible, stationary

immunity... 7. freedom 8. impunity 9. exemption 10. resistance (power of) 11. unrestraint

immure... 4. wall 6. entomb 7. confine 8. imprison, surround 9. encompass 11. incarcerate

immutable... 4. firm 6. stable 7. eternal 8. constant 9. obstinate 10. inflexible, invariable 12. unchangeable 13. unadulterated

imp... 3. bud, elf, fay 4. brat, cion, pixy, slip 5. child, demon, devil, fairy, graft, rogue, scion, shoot, youth 6. repair (falconry), spirit, sprite 7. progeny 9. offspring

impact... 4. pack, slam 5. brunt, force, shock, wedge 6. effect, stroke 7. contact, impulse, meaning 8. striking 9. collision, fix firmly, impinging

impair... 3. mar 4. harm, hurt, ruin, rust, wear 5. break, spoil 6. damage, debase, injure, lessen, reduce, weaken 7. vitiate 8. decrease, enfeeble 11. deteriorate

impairment of...
    capital.. 4. loss 7. deficit
    character.. 6. injury 10. defamation 11. degradation 13. deterioration
    nerve (a).. 11. anerethisia

impale... 4. edge, gore, join (Her), spit, stab 5. hem in, spike 6. border, pierce, punish 7. confine, torture 8. encircle, surround

impalement... 5. calyx 8. stabbing 10. punishment 11. coats of arms (united)

impalpable... 4. fine 10. immaterial, intangible 13. infinitesimal

impart... 3. say 4. give, lend, tell 5. grant, share, yield 6. confer, convey, inform, reveal 7. divulge 8. disclose, discover 9. partake of 10. distribute 11. communicate

impartial... 4. even, fair, just 7. neutral 8. unbiased 9. equitable 12. unprejudiced 13. disinterested, dispassionate

impartiality... 7. justice 8. fairness 10. neutrality 11. unprejudice 17. disinterestedness

impassable... 6. stolid 9. impassive 10. impervious, unpassable 11. impermeable, unnavigable 12. impenetrable

impasse... 8. cul–de–sac 9. stalemate 10. blind alley

impassible... 9. impassive, unfeeling

impassioned... 6. ardent 7. amorous, zealous 8. eloquent, vehement 10. passionate

impassive... 4. calm 6. serene 7. passive 9. apathetic 10. impassable 12. invulnerable 13. insusceptible

impatient... 5. eager, testy 6. uneasy 7. anxious, fretful, itching, peevish, restive 8. choleric, petulant, restless 9. impetuous, irascible, irritable 10. intolerant

impavid... 8. fearless

impeach... 4. harm 6. accuse, charge, hinder, impair, impede, indict 7. arraign, censure, prevent 9. challenge, criminate, discredit, disparage

impeccable... 8. flawless, innocent 9. faultless 10. immaculate

impede... 3. bar, let 4. clog 5. block, debar, estop 6. hamper, hinder, retard, stymie (stimy) 8. encumber, obstruct, restrict

impediment... 3. bar, rub 4. snag 5. hitch 6. defect, malady 7. baggage, barrier 8. obstacle 9. hindrance 10. difficulty 11. encumbrance, obstruction

impel... 3. put 4. move, urge 5. drive, force, forge 6. compel, incite, induce, obsess, prompt, propel 7. actuate 9. constrain, influence

impel a boat... 3. oar, row 4. pole 5. scull

impelling force... 7. impetus 8. momentum

impending... 7. nearing 8. awaiting, imminent, menacing 9. hindering 11. overhanging, threatening

impenetrable... 5. dense 10. impervious 11. impregnable, inscrutable 12. inaccessible, unfathomable 13. unimpressible 14. unintelligible

impenitent... 8. obdurate 10. uncontrite 11. unrepentant, unrepenting

imperative... 4. mood (Gram) 6. needed, urgent 7. binding 8. pressing 9. directive, imperious, mandatory, necessary

10. compulsory, obligatory,
peremptory 13. authoritative
imperceptible... 6. subtle 9. invisible
10. insensible 13. inappreciable,
indiscernible, infinitesimal
14. unintelligible
imperfect... 3. mal (pref) 4. cull
5. frail 6. faulty, second 7. errable
8. fallible, immature, impaired
9. blemished, defective
10. inadequate, incomplete
imperfection... 4. flaw, vice 5. fault
6. defect 7. blemish, failing
8. fraility, weakness 10. deficiency
11. shortcoming 14. incompleteness
imperfectly... 8. slightly
12. inadequately
imperial... 5. regal, royal 6. kingly,
lordly, purple 8. majestic
9. imperious, masterful, monarchal,
sovereign
imperial (pert to)...
Academy.. 6. Han—lin (Chin)
blue.. 5. smalt
cap.. 5. crown
city (anc).. 4. Rome
domain.. 6. empire
legislature.. 4. Diet (Jap)
officer.. 8. palatine
imperil... 4. risk 6. expose
8. endanger 10. jeopardize
imperious... 6. lordly 7. haughty
8. arrogant, despotic, dominant,
pressing 10. commanding,
compelling, tyrannical 11. dictatorial,
domineering, overbearing
imperishable... 7. eternal, undying
8. enduring, immortal 11. everlasting
14. indestructible
impermanent... 8. fleeting, temporal,
unstable 9. ephemeral, momentary,
temporary, transient 10. evanescent,
short—lived
impersonate... 3. ape 4. pose 6. pose
as, typify 7. portray 9. exemplify,
personate (law), personify, represent,
symbolize
impertinence... 4. sass 9. impudence,
insolence, unfitness 10. incivility
11. impropriety, irrelevance
impertinent... 4. rude 5. saucy
7. ill—bred 8. impudent, insolent
9. frivolous, officious 10. inapposite,
irrelevant 12. inapplicable,
inconsequent 13. disrespectful
imperturbability... 8. ataraxia (ataraxy),
serenity
imperturbable... 4. calm, cool
6. placid, serene, steady 8. tranquil
9. impassive 10. phlegmatic
13. dispassionate
impervious... 5. tight 6. opaque
7. callous 10. impassable
12. impenetrable, inaccessible
impetuosity... 5. ardor 6. fougue
8. rashness
impetuous... 3. hot 4. rash 5. eager,
hasty, heady, sharp 6. ardent, bensel
(motion), fervid, sudden 7. furious,
violent 8. forcible, headlong, reckless,
vehement 9. impulsive
10. passionate 11. precipitate

impetus... 4. birr 7. impulse
8. momentum, stimulus 9. incentive
impi (Zulu)... 8. armed men, warriors
impignorate... 4. pawn 6. pledge
8. mortgage
impious... 7. godless, profane
9. nefandous, undutiful 10. irreverent
11. irreligious
impish... 5. elvan 6. elfish 7. puckish
9. malignant 11. mischievous
implacable... 6. enmity
11. immitigable 12. unappeasable
14. uncompromising
implant... 4. root 5. infix, inset, plant
6. enroot, infuse, insert 7. enforce,
engraft, impress, inspire, instill
9. establish, inculcate, inoculate,
insinuate, introduce
implement... 3. kit 4. peel, tool
5. dolly, knife, means, scoop, tongs
6. pestle, petard 7. fulfill, utensil
8. carry out, complete, material,
scissors 9. equipment
10. accomplish, instrument
implement (pert to)...
ancient.. 4. celt 6. eolith 9. paleolith
(stone)
cleaning.. 3. mop 5. broom, brush
6. vacuum 7. sweeper
hide flesher.. 6. slater
holding.. 5. tongs 6. pliers
8. tweezers
lifting.. 3. pry 5. crane, lever, tongs
lumbering.. 4. tode 6. peavey (peavy)
nap.. 6. teasel
printing.. 5. biron, press 6. brayer
reaping.. 5. mower 6. reaper, scythe,
shears, sickle
surgical.. 7. scalpel 9. tenaculum
threshing.. 5. flail
implicate... 5. imply 7. embroil,
entwine, involve 8. entangle
10. interweave 11. incriminate
implicit... 5. tacit 7. implied, virtual
8. complete, inherent 9. entangled,
potential 11. unqualified
12. constructive 13. unquestioning
implied... 5. tacit 11. inferential
12. not expressed
implore... 3. ask, beg 4. pray 5. crave
7. beseech, entreat, solicit
8. petition 10. supplicate
imply... 4. hint, mean 5. argue
6. infold 7. connote, involve,
suggest, suppose 9. predicate
impolite... 4. rude 5. crude, rough
7. uncivil 10. ill—behaved,
mannerless, ungracious, unmannerly,
unpolished 12. discourteous
13. disrespectful
impolitic... 6. unwise 9. untactful
10. indiscreet 11. inexpedient
12. undiplomatic
import... 5. drift, sense, value
6. denote, weight 7. betoken,
meaning, signify 8. commerce,
indicate 9. introduce, of concern
10. importance 11. consequence,
implication, importation, merchandise
importance... 6. moment, stress,
weight 8. prestige 9. influence
10. famousness 11. consequence,

importunity 12. solicitation

important... 5. grave 6. famous, urgent 7. pompous, weighty 8. material 9. momentous 11. considerate, influential, significant, substantial 12. considerable, ostentatious 13. consequential

import tax... 4. duty 6. tariff

importune... 3. beg, ply, tax, woo 4. coax, push, urge 5. beset, impel, plead, press 6. appeal, cajole 7. entreat, press on

importunity... 11. importunate, pertinacity 12. solicitation

impose... 3. tax 4. duty, levy 6. burden, entail 7. command, confirm (Eccl), exploit, inflict, intrude, obtrude, penalty, presume 10. discommode

imposing... 5. noble, regal 6. august 7. stately 9. dignified, grandiose 10. commanding, impressive 11. ceremonious 13. grandiloquent

impossible... 6. absurd 8. hopeless, terrible 9. insoluble 10. outlandish 11. unthinkable 12. unimaginable 13. contradictory, impracticable

impost... 3. tax 4. levy, task, toll 5. abwab 6. custom, excise, surtax, tariff, weight 7. tribute 8. handicap

impostor... 4. fake 5. fraud, phony, quack 6. humbug 7. empiric 9. charlatan, pretender 10. mountebank

imposture... 5. fraud, trick 8. delusion, quackery 9. deception 10. imposition

impotent... 4. weak 6. barren 7. cripple, sterile 9. deficient, incapable, powerless 13. uninfluential

impound... 5. pen in, seize, store 6. freeze 7. collect 8. imprison 9. reservoir 10. confiscate 11. appropriate

impoverish... 4. ruin 6. beggar 7. despoil, exhaust 8. bankrupt, make poor 11. make sterile

imprecation... 4. oath 8. anathema 10. execration 11. malediction

impregnable... 4. hard 10. inviolable 12. inexpugnable, invulnerable 13. unconquerable

impregnate... 5. imbue 6. infuse 8. fructify 9. fertilize, inculcate

impresa... 5. maxim, motto 6. device, emblem

impresario... 7. manager 9. conductor, projector (opera) 12. entrepreneur

impress... 3. awe, fix 4. bite, dent, levy, mark, seal 5. press, print, stamp 6. affect, effect, enlist, indent 7. engrave, imprint 8. printing, shanghai 9. conscript, engraving, inculcate 10. commandeer, impression 11. indentation 14. characteristic

impressed... 4. awed 7. infixed, stamped 8. affected, engraved 9. imprinted

impression... 4. form, idea, mark 5. hunch, print, stamp 6. macule, signet 7. emotion, opinion 8. printing

9. engraving, sensation 10. appearance 11. inculcation, indentation, supposition

impressionable... 6. pliant 7. plastic 9. sensitive, teachable 10. responsive 11. suggestible, susceptible

impressive... 6. solemn 8. dramatic, eloquent 9. arresting, grandiose 10. convincing

imprint... 3. fix 4. dint 5. infix, press, stamp 6. indent 7. edition, engrave 8. printing 9. engraving

imprison... 4. bond, cage, gaol, jail 5. limit 6. arrest, detain, immure, intern, lock up 7. confine, impound 8. restrain 11. incarcerate

imprisonment... 4. band 6. duress 8. coercion 9. restraint 10. constraint, immurement, internment 11. confinement, impoundment 13. incarceration

impromptu... 6. extemp 7. offhand 11. extemporary 13. improvisation 14. extemporaneous 15. autoschediastic

improper... 3. ill, pah 4. evil 5. amiss, wrong 6. vulgar 7. illegal, naughty 8. indecent, unseemly, unsuited, untoward 9. incorrect, inelegant 10. inaccurate, indecorous, indelicate, unbecoming, unsuitable

impropriety... 5. wrong 8. solecism 9. indecency, vulgarity 11. malapropism, misbehavior

improve... 4. mend 5. amend, edify, emend, moise, train 6. better, employ, uplift 7. advance, augment, correct, enhance, perfect, promote, recover, rectify, upgrade 9. cultivate, get better, intensify, meliorate 10. ameliorate, recuperate

improvident... 4. rash 8. prodigal, wasteful 9. negligent 10. thriftless 11. thoughtless

improvise... 5. ad lib 6. invent 7. ad libit 9. ad libitum 11. extemporize 13. autoschediaze

imprudence... 5. brass 8. rashness 9. hardihood 12. indiscretion, recklessness

impudence... 5. cheek 8. rudeness 9. flippancy, indecency, insolence 10. brazenness, disrespect 12. impertinence 13. shamelessness

impudent... 4. bold, pert, rude 5. brash, saucy 6. brazen 8. flippant, insolent, malapert 9. audacious, shameless 11. impertinent 13. disrespectful

impugn... 4. deny 5. blame 6. assail (by words), oppose, refute 7. asperse, censure, gainsay

impulse... 3. ate 4. rush, urge 5. force 6. motive 7. impetus 8. instinct 9. incentive 11. instigation

impulsive... 5. hasty, quick 6. moving 9. impellent, impetuous 10. motivating 11. instinctive 13. ill—considered

impure... 4. foul, lewd 5. dirty, mixed 6. filthy, unholy 7. bastard, defiled,

obscene, unclean 8. unchaste
10. inaccurate, unhallowed
11. adulterated, unwholesome
impure metal . . . 5. alloy, matte
6. speiss
impure rock . . . 5. chert 9. flintlike
imputation . . . 7. censure 8. charging
9. aspersion, criticism
10. accusation, ascription
11. attribution, insinuation
impute . . . 6. accuse, charge, credit,
impart, reckon, regard 7. arraign,
ascribe 8. consider 9. attribute
impy . . . 11. mischievous
in . . . 2. at 4. amid, into 5. among
6. at home, inside, within
in (pert to) . . .
abundance . . 5. store 6. galore
accordance . . 8. pursuant
addition . . 3. too, yet 4. also, more,
plus 11. furthermore
all directions . . 8. everyway
12. everywhither
an undertone . . 9. sotto voce
as much as . . 3. for 5. since
6. seeing 7. because, insofar
back . . 3. aft 5. arear 6. astern
7. postern
behalf of . . 3. for, pro 7. favor of
camera . . 9. in private 10. in
chambers
common . . 4. same 5. alike
concert . . 8. together
contact . . 8. touching 9. attingent
current style . . 3. a la 7. alamode,
popular
existence . . 6. extant
fact . . 5. truly 6. indeed 7. de facto
favor of . . 3. aye, pro, yea
good health . . 3. fit 4. hale 7. healthy
love . . 7. smitten 9. enamoured
need . . 7. straits 8. distress
open air . . 7. outdoor 8. al fresco
passing . . 9. en passant
place of . . 3. for 5. stead 7. instead
possession . . 5. title 6. seizin
private . . 8. in camera
regard to . . 5. anent
rows . . 4. arow 6. serial 7. aligned
(alined)
so far as . . 3. qua
spite of . . 6. mauger 7. despite,
however 11. nonetheless
standing position . . 7. statant
store . . 5. ready 7. waiting 8. awaiting
straight lines . . 8. e regione
succession . . 6. series 8. serially,
seriatim
the future . . 5. hence, later 6. mañana
12. subsequently
the know . . 3. hep
the same place . . 4. ibid 6. ibidem
the year of . . 4. anno
truth . . 6. certes, indeed, verily
8. forsooth
what way . . 3. how 7. quo modo
inability . . . 9. impotence
10. inadequacy, incapacity
12. incapability, incompetence
inability to . . .
articulate . . 7. inaudia
chew . . 8. amasesis

comprehend . . 11. acatalepsia
move . . 7. apraxia
name objects . . 9. paranomia
read . . 6. alexia
stand erect . . 7. astasia
swallow . . 7. aphagia
inaccessible . . . 8. reserved
10. unsociable 11. out–of–the–way
12. unattainable 14. unapproachable
inaccurate . . . 5. loose 6. faulty
7. inexact 9. defective, erroneous,
imperfect, incorrect
13. ungrammatical
inaction . . . 6. torpor 7. inertia
8. abeyance, idleness 9. inertness
10. suspension
inactive . . . 4. idle 5. inert 7. abeyant,
neutral, not busy 8. sluggish
9. sedentary 10. indisposed
inadequacy . . . 9. inability
10. deficiency, inequality
11. inferiority 12. incompetence
13. insufficiency 14. incompleteness
inadvertence . . . 5. error 7. neglect
11. inattention 12. carelessness,
heedlessness 15. thoughtlessness
inadvertent . . . 9. negligent, unwitting
11. inattentive
inadvertently . . . 10. heedlessly
11. unwittingly 12. neglectfully
inane . . . 4. vain, void 5. empty, inept,
silly 6. famous 7. fatuous, foolish,
puerile, trivial 8. trifling 9. frivolous
11. ineffectual, thoughtless
13. characterless
inappropriate . . . 5. inept, undue
8. untimely 10. irrelevant, unsuitable
11. inexpedient
inapt . . . 5. inept 10. unsuitable
inattentive . . . 3. lax 6. absent, remiss
8. careless, heedless 9. negligent,
unheeding, unmindful 10. distracted,
regardless 11. inadvertent
inaugurate . . . 5. admit, begin, start
6. induct 7. install, instate, usher in
8. initiate 9. auspicate, institute,
introduce 10. consecrate
inauspicious . . . 7. adverse, ominous,
unlucky 8. sinister, untimely
9. ill–omened 12. unpropitious
inborn . . . 6. allied, inbred, innate,
native 7. cognate, natural 8. inherent
10. connatural
inbred . . . 6. inborn, innate
9. endogamic 10. bred within 15. to
the manner born
Inca (pert to) . . .
descent . . 6. the sun
empire . . 4. Peru (11th cent)
government . . 11. communistic
king . . 9. Atahualpa (15th cent)
prince . . 7. Huascar (16th cent)
incalculable . . . 8. infinite 9. boundless,
uncertain, very great 11. illimitable
12. immeasurable 13. unforeseeable
incandescent . . . 5. clear, light, white
7. glowing, shining
incantation . . . 5. magic, spell
6. powwow 7. sorcery 8. exorcism
10. hocus–pocus, mumbo jumbo
incapable . . . 6. unable 8. impotent
11. incompetent, inefficient,

unqualified 12. disqualified
incapacitate... 7. cripple, disable,
invalid 10. disqualify 11. render unfit
incapacitated... 8. crippled, disabled
9. hamstrung, paralyzed
11. invalidated 12. disqualified
13. superannuated (retired)
incarcerate... 5. hem in 6. immure,
intern, lock up, retire 7. confine,
impound 8. imprison 10. disqualify
incarnate... 4. rosy 6. embody
9. enshrined 11. incorporate,
personified 12. impersonated
incarnation... 6. avatar, Christ
10. embodiment
Incarnation of Vishnu (eight)...
4. Apis, Rama 7. Krishna (8th)
incase... 3. box, can 4. pack 5. box
up, cover, crate 6. carton
7. enclose, package 8. surround
incaution... 4. rash 6. unwary
8. careless, heedless, reckless
9. impolitic, imprudent 10. indiscreet
incendiarism... 5. arson 9. pyromania
incendiary... 5. firer 7. exciter
8. agitator, arsonist, incitive
9. seditious 10. instigator
12. inflammatory
incense... 3. ire 5. anger 6. arouse,
enrage, incite 7. inflame, provoke
8. irritate 9. instigate
incense (pert to)...
burner.. 6. censer 8. thurible
9. incensory
carrier.. 8. thurifer
Hebrew for.. 7. keturah
pert to.. 5. aroma, spice 7. perfume
9. fragrance, redolence
product.. 5. matti, myrrh 6. storax
7. linaloa 8. gum resin, olibanum,
pastille, thurible 9. lignaloes,
tacamahac 12. frankincense
sacrifice.. 8. oblation
spice.. 6. balsam, stacte
tree bearing.. 7. linaloa 8. agalloch,
calambac 9. Boswellia
vessel.. 6. censer 7. navette
incensed... 3. mad 5. angry, irate,
vexed, wroth 6. peeved, piqued
7. angered, enraged, nettled
8. wrathful 11. exasperated
incentive... 4. brod, call, goad, spur,
urge, whet 5. spark 6. motive
7. impulse, rousing 8. inciting,
stimulus 9. influence 10. incitement,
inducement 11. provocation,
stimulative 13. encouragement
inception... 6. origin, source
9. reception 10. inchoation, initiation
12. commencement
15. intussusception
inceptive... 9. beginning 10. inchoative
incessant... 7. endless 8. constant
9. ceaseless, continual, perpetual
10. continuous 11. unremitting
13. unintermitted
inch (pert to)...
barometric.. 6. degree
forward.. 4. edge 7. crowhop
inch by inch.. 9. gradually, piecemeal
meal.. 9. gradually
three parts.. 11. barleycorns (anc)

twelve parts.. 5. lines
twelve seconds.. 6. a prime (anc)
verb.. 5. creep 7. measure
inches... 4. hand (4), nail (2 1/4),
span (9)
inchoate... 6. partly 8. initiate, recently
9. beginning, incipient
10. incomplete
inchpin... 10. sweetbread
incident... 5. event 7. episode, subject
8. accident, casualty 9. befalling,
happening 10. incidental, occurrence
11. contingency 12. circumstance,
slight matter
incidental... 3. bye 6. casual, chance,
liable 8. episodic 9. accessory,
extrinsic 10. accidental, contingent,
fortuitous, occasional 11. subordinate
12. nonessential 13. parenthetical
incidentally... 6. obiter 8. by chance,
by the way 9. en passant, in passing
incinerate... 4. burn 7. consume,
cremate
incipient... 4. seat 6. induct 7. initial
8. inchoate 9. beginning, embryonic
10. commencing, inaugurate
11. rudimentary
incise... 3. cut 4. open 5. carve,
lance, sever 6. furrow 7. engrave
incised... 6. carved 7. notched
8. engraved, furrowed 9. laciniate
10. laciniated
incision... 3. cut 4. gash, slit 5. cleft
6. furrow, injury 7. cutting
9. engraving 10. laceration,
separation 11. penetration
incite... 3. egg, tew 4. abet, fire,
goad, prod, spur, urge 5. impel,
sting 6. arouse, foment, stir up,
suborn 7. agitate, animate, inflame,
provoke 9. encourage, stimulate
inclemency... 4. cold 5. rigor
8. coldness, severity, violence
9. bleakness, frigidity, harshness
13. mercilessness
inclination... 3. dip, nod 4. bent,
bias, love, urge 5. fancy, grade,
slant, slope, taste, trend 6. animus,
bowing, desire, liking, nature
8. aptitude, penchant, tendency
9. affection, attention, deviation,
direction, intention, obeisance,
proneness 10. attachment, proclivity,
propensity 11. disposition
12. predilection 13. prepossession
incline... 3. dip, tip 4. bend, cant,
heel, lean, tend, tilt 5. alist, bevel,
grade, slant, slide, slope, trend 9. be
willing, gravitate
inclined... 3. apt, dip 4. wont
5. prone 6. sloped 7. leaning,
pronate, willing 8. disposed
11. predisposed
inclined (pert to)...
plane.. 4. ramp 7. oblique
to believe.. 9. credulous
to droop.. 3. sag
to sin.. 13. transgressive
inclose... see also *enclose* 3. hem,
pen, pin 4. case, mure 5. embar
6. encase, encave, incase
7. enclose, environ

inclosure ... 3. pen, ree, sty 4. cage, cote, sept 5. hutch, kraal 6. corral 8. sepiment 9. enclosure 10. impalement

include ... 6. shut up 7. confine, contain, embrace, enclose, inclose, involve 8. comprise 9. encompass

including ... 8. covering 10. comprising, containing 12. encompassing 13. comprehensive

incognito ... 6. veiled 7. feigned 8. disguise, not known 10. camouflage

incoherent ... 5. loose 6. broken 8. detached, inchoate 9. delirious, illogical 11. incongruous 12. disconnected, inconsequent, inconsistent

income ... 4. gain 5. rente, wages 6. profit, return, usance 7. annuity, pension, produce, revenue, tontine 8. interest, proceeds, receipts 9. emolument

incommensurate ... 7. unequal 12. insufficient 14. unsatisfactory 16. disproportionate

incommode ... 3. vex 5. annoy 6. molest, plague, put out 7. disturb, trouble 8. disquiet 13. inconvenience

incomparable ... 7. eminent, unalike 8. peerless 9. matchless, unrivaled 10. surpassing 11. superlative 12. transcendent, without equal

incompatible ... 9. differing 10. intolerant 11. disagreeing 12. inconsistent, inharmonious 13. contradictory, unsympathetic 14. irreconcilable

incompetence ... 9. inability, unfitness 10. disability, inadequacy 13. insufficiency 15. unqualification

incompetent ... 5. inept, unfit 7. wanting 8. impotent 9. incapable 10. unskillful 11. inefficient 12. disqualified, insufficient 14. incommensurate

incomplete ... 5. crude 6. undone 7. lacking 8. immature, inchoate 9. defective, deficient, imperfect, partially 10. unfinished

incomprehensible ... 8. infinite 9. wonderful 10. miraculous, mysterious, unreadable 11. unthinkable 12. unfathomable, unimaginable 13. inconceivable, unconceivable 14. unintelligible

incongruity ... 9. inharmony 10. dissonance 11. incoherence 12. disagreement, inexpedience 13. inconsistency 14. unsuitableness

incongruous ... 5. alien 6. absurd, motley 8. off–color 9. differing, illogical 10. solecistic, unsuitable 12. disagreeable, inconsistent, inharmonious 13. inappropriate

inconsequent ... 7. invalid 8. unproved 9. illogical 10. irrelevant 11. impertinent, unimportant 12. inconsistent 13. inconsecutive

inconsiderate ... 4. rash 5. hasty 6. unkind 8. careless, heedless

9. imprudent, impulsive 10. ill–advised, incautious, indiscreet, neglectful 11. improvident, injudicious, thoughtless

inconsistent ... 9. differing, dissonant, fanatical, illogical 10. discordant, discrepant, incoherent, inconstant 11. incongruous 12. incompatible, inharmonious 13. contradictory 14. irreconcilable

inconspicuous ... 9. unseeable 10. out of sight, unapparent 12. not prominent 13. imperceptible, indiscernible

incontestable ... 7. certain 10. undeniable 11. indubitable, irrefutable 13. unimpeachable 14. unquestionable

inconvenience ... 6. bother 8. disquiet 9. incommode 10. uneasiness 11. awkwardness, disturbance 12. disadvantage, untimeliness, unwieldiness

inconvenient ... 5. unfit 7. unhandy 8. annoying, improper, unwieldy 10. unsuitable 11. inexpedient, inopportune, troublesome 12. unreasonable 15. disadvantageous

incorporate ... 3. mix 4. fuse 5. blend, merge, unite 6. embody 7. combine, include 8. embodied 10. assimilate

incorporation ... 5. union 9. inclusion 10. embodiment 11. affiliation, association, combination, composition, incarnation 12. assimilation

incorporeal ... 7. phantom 8. bodiless 9. spiritual 10. immaterial 13. unsubstantial

incorrect ... 5. wrong 6. faulty 8. improper 9. erroneous, inelegant 10. inaccurate, solecistic, unbecoming 13. ungrammatical

incorrect naming of objects ... 9. paranomia

incorruptible ... 4. just 7. upright 8. immortal 11. trustworthy 14. indestructible

increase ... 3. add, eke, wax 4. gain, grow, rise 5. add to, amass, raise, swell 6. accrue, dilate, enrich, expand, extend 7. accrete, advance, augment, enhance (inhance), inflate, promote, upswing 8. heighten, multiply 9. accession, aggravate, crescendo, expansion, extension, increment, intensify 10. accelerate 11. aggravation, enlargement 13. amplification 15. intensification

incredible ... 8. fabulous, unlikely 9. fantastic, marvelous, wonderful 10. improbable, remarkable 12. unbelievable

increment ... 6. growth 8. addition, increase 11. enlargement 12. augmentation

incriminate ... 6. accuse 7. involve 9. implicate, inculpate

incubator ... 8. couveuse, isolette

incubus ... 4. ogre 5. demon, dream 6. burden 9. nightmare 10. evil spirit 13. hallucination

inculcate... 5. imbue, infix 7. implant, impress, instill (instil) 12. indoctrinate
incumbent... 5. vicar 6. rector
8. resident 9. clergyman, impending, overlying 10. burdensome, obligatory (upon) 11. threatening
12. superimposed
incumbents... 3. ins
incunabula... 7. infancy 10. beginnings
incur... 5. bring 6. accrue, entail
7. bring on 8. be liable, contract, fall into 10. be involved
incurable... 8. hopeless 9. apathetic
11. inattentive, indifferent, unconcerned, uninquiring
12. uninterested 13. uninquisitive
incur hostility... 10. antagonize
11. contend with
incursion... 4. raid 5. foray 6. attack, influx, inroad 8. invasion 9. intrusion
incus... 4. bone (ear) 5. anvil
6. hammer
indecency... 8. impurity 9. immodesty, indecorum, obscenity, vulgarity
10. indelicacy, unchastity
indecent... 5. gross 6. impure, vulgar
7. obscene 8. immodest, improper, uncomely 9. offensive 10. ill-looking, indecorous, indelicate 11. inexpedient
indecision... 5. doubt 10. hesitation
11. uncertainty, vacillation
12. irresolution
indecisive... 7. dubious 8. formless
9. uncertain 10. hesitating, indefinite, indistinct, irresolute 11. unsupported, vacillating 12. inconclusive
indecorous... 4. rude 5. wrong
6. coarse, vulgar 7. uncivil
8. impolite, improper, indecent, unseemly 9. inelegant 10. out of place, unbecoming 11. inexpedient
indefatigable... 6. active 8. sedulous, tireless, untiring 9. unwearied, weariless 10. unwearying
11. persevering
indefinite... 5. loose, vague
7. general, inexact, neutral
8. formless 9. ambiguous, equivocal, uncertain 10. inexplicit, unmeasured
12. undetermined 13. indeterminate
indefinite amount... 3. any 4. some
5. about 10. more or less
indehiscent (pert to)...
fruit.. 3. uva 4. pepo (gourd)
5. apple, grape 6. orange, samara
9. sunflower
legume.. 3. pea 4. bean 6. loment
vegetable.. 5. melon 6. squash, tomato 7. pumpkin 8. cucumber
indelible... 4. fast 5. fixed 8. deepfelt
9. permanent 10. inerasable
12. ineffaceable, ineradicable, inexpungible 13. unforgettable
indelicate... 5. gross 6. coarse, vulgar
7. fulsome 8. impolite, improper, indecent, unseemly 9. offensive, unrefined 10. indecorous, unbecoming
indemnification... 9. atonement
10. recompense 11. restitution
12. compensation 13. reimbursement

indemnify... 3. pay 6. recoup, secure
8. make good 9. reimburse
10. compensate, recompense
indent... 3. cut, jag 4. dent 5. inlay, notch, press, stamp, tooth
6. emboss, furrow, recess, zigzag
7. impress, imprint, press in
8. contract, covenant, draw upon
9. indenture 11. requisition
indentation... 3. jab 4. dint, nick
5. choil, notch 6. crenel, furrow, hollow, recess 7. imprint 8. crenelet
10. depression, impression
indented... 6. dented, jagged, milled
7. notched, sinuous 8. serrated (Her)
9. impressed 10. undulating
indenture... 4. dent 5. notch
8. contract, document 9. agreement
10. depression 11. indentation
independence... 7. freedom
9. exemption 10. competency, neutralism, Urania blue
13. unrelatedness 14. nonpartisanism
15. self-subsistence
independent... 4. free 5. Party (Polit)
7. neutral, wealthy 8. separate
9. competent, exclusive, free-lance, isolative, sovereign, uncoerced, unrelated 12. irrespective, uncontrolled, unrestricted
13. self-governing
independent land... 7. alodium (law)
indescribably... 9. ineffably
11. wonderfully
indeterminate... 5. vague 7. apeiron, general, neutral, obscure 8. formless, infinite
index... 4. face, file, fist, list 5. guide, ratio, table 6. gnomon 7. pointer
8. exponent 9. indicator
10. forefinger, indication
India... see also *Indian*
anc.. 9. Hindustan
Bay.. 6. Bengal
Cape.. 7. Comorin
capital.. 4. Agra (anc) 5. Simla (summer) 8. New Delhi
city.. 4. Agra, Gaya 5. Dacca, Delhi, Poona, Surat 6. Bombay, Jaipur, Lahore, Madras, Madura, Nagpur, Nysore 8. Calcutta, Kolhapur, Mandalay, Mirzapur, Shahpura
10. Darjeeling
city, sacred.. 5. Nasik 7. Benares
kingdom.. 5. Asoka, Nepal
mountain.. 5. Ghats 8. Sulaiman (Throne of Solomon) 9. Himalayas, Hindu Kush 12. Vindhya Hills
Persian name (anc).. 9. Hindustan
region.. 3. Goa 5. Assam, Surat
6. Baroda 7. Benares, Kashmir
relics (famed).. 8. Taj Mahal (Agra)
10. Kutab Minar 11. Ajanta Caves
river.. 6. Kistna
State.. 4. Rewa 5. Delhi 6. Baroda, Indore, Jaipur, Madras, Marwar, Punjab, Rampur, Sakkim 7. Manipur
Indian (pert to)...
aeon.. 5. kalpa
animal.. 4. zebu 5. sasin 6. nilgai
apartment.. 6. zenana
army officer.. 4. naik (naig)

7. jemadar
attorney.. 6. muktar
bandit.. 6. dacoit
bard.. 4. bhat
bird.. 4. baya, kala, koel, kyak
    5. sarus, shama 6. seesee, shahin
    8. amadavat
boat.. 5. dhoni (doni)
book (sacred).. 6. Avesta
bracelet.. 6. sankha
bread (unleavened).. 8. chapatty
breakfast.. 5. hazri
buffalo.. 4. arna (arnee)
carpet.. 4. Agra
carriage.. 4. ekka 5. tonga 6. gharry
    (gharri)
caste.. 3. Jat, Meo 4. Ahir 5. Sudra,
    Varna 6. Lohana, Rajput, Vaisya
    7. Brahman (Brahmin) 9. Kahatriya
cavalryman.. 5. sowar 7. ressala
charm.. 6. mantra
chief.. 4. Raja 5. Rajah 6. sirdar
    7. Gaekwar
cigarette (cheap).. 4. biri
claim (legal).. 3. hak (hakh)
college (Sanskrit).. 3. tol
Court, Supreme.. 6. Sudder
crocodile.. 6. gavial, mugger (muggar,
    muggur)
cymbal.. 3. tal
dagger.. 5. katar
dam.. 6. anicut (annicut)
dancer (fem).. 8. bayadere
dancing girls.. 6. nautch
deer.. 4. axis 5. kakar 6. sambur
deity.. 4. Deva
demon.. 4. bhut 5. asura 6. daitya
devil's tree.. 4. dita
dialect.. 4. Urdu 5. Hindi, Tamil
    7. Prakrit
disciple.. 5. chela
dog.. 5. dhole 6. pariah
drama.. 6. nataka
drink.. 4. soma 5. bhang (bang)
    6. arrack
dust storm.. 7. peesash, shaitan
    (sheitan)
elephant.. 5. hathi
elephant driver.. 6. mahout
elephant trappings.. 5. jhool
epic.. 8. Ramayana 11. Mahabharata
falcon.. 6. shahin (shaheen)
father.. 4. babu
festival.. 4. Holi, Mela 6. Dewali
    10. Rathayatra
fig tree (sacred).. 5. pipal 6. banian,
    banyan
garment.. 4. sari 7. luhinga
gateway.. 5. toran
ghost.. 4. bhut
god.. 4. Deva, Yama 5. Shiva
goddess.. 4. Amma
governor.. 5. nazim
grove.. 5. Sarna
guard.. 7. daloyet
hall.. 6. durbar
handkerchief.. 7. malabar
harem.. 5. serai 6. zenana 8. seraglio
heiress.. 5. Begum
herb.. 6. sesame 7. curcuma,
    tumeric, zeodary

holy.. 3. sri (shri)
holy powder.. 4. abir (perfumed)
hunt.. 6. shikar
intoxicant.. 4. soma
jungle.. 5. shola
king.. 4. Shah
king of serpents (Myth).. 6. Shesha
    (Sesha)
king's son.. 8. shahzada
knife.. 3. dah 5. kukri
lady.. 7. sahibah
language.. 4. Urdu 5. Hindu, Tamil
    8. Sanskrit (anc)
leader.. 13. Mahatma Gandhi
legal claim.. 3. hak (hakh)
leopard.. 7. cheetah
licorice.. 9. jequirity (bean)
loincloth.. 5. dhoti
lover of.. 9. Indophile
mahogany.. 4. toon
mail.. 3. dak (dawk)
medicine man.. 6. Shaman
mendicant.. 5. fakir
merchant.. 8. soudagar
midwife.. 4. dhai
Minister of Finance.. 5. Dewan
mountain pass.. 4. ghat
musical instrument.. 5. ruana
narcotic.. 4. bang 5. bhang
    7. hashish
native.. 5. Hindu, Sepoy, Tamil
    8. Assamese 10. Hindustani
Negro.. 6. hubshi
palanquin (conveyance).. 6. palkee
    (palhi)
palm.. 7. Calamus, malacca
peasant.. 4. ryot
pheasant.. 5. monal (monaul)
philosopher.. 4. Yogi
pillar.. 3. lat
pipe.. 6. hookah
police.. 4. peon 5. sepoy
police station.. 5. thana
priest.. 5. mobed 6. shaman
prince.. 4. rana
princess.. 4. rani (ranee) 5. Begum
queen.. 4. rani (ranee) 8. maharani
religious body.. 5. samaj 7. ajivika
    (anc)
resort.. 3. Abu 5. Mt Abu
rope dancer.. 3. nat
rubber.. 10. caoutchouc
ruler.. 4. rana 5. nabob, nawab,
    nizam
sage.. 6. pundit
sailor.. 5. lascar
sarsaparilla root.. 7. nunnari
servant.. 3. par 4. amah, maty
sheep.. 5. urial 6. nahoor
shrine.. 6. dagoba
silkworm.. 3. eri
snake.. 5. krait 6. bongar, katuka
soldier.. 4. peon 5. sepoy, singh
split pea.. 3. dal
study of.. 8. Indology
sugar (crude).. 3. gur 9. tabasheer
    (bamboo)
Supreme Court.. 6. Sudder
sword (short).. 5. kukri
syllable of assent.. 2. om
tapir.. 8. saladang

tariff . . **6.** zabeta
teacher . . **6.** mullah (mulla)
temple . . **4.** rath **12.** Seven Pagodas
 (of Madras)
title of respect . . **3.** sri (shri) **4.** mian
tower . . **5.** minar, sikar **7.** sikhara
tree . . **3.** saj **4.** dita, teak **5.** dhava
 6. banyan, sissoo
umbrella . . **6.** chatta
water carrier . . **7.** bheesty (bheestie)
wheat . . **4.** suji
wine . . **5.** shrab
yellow (color) . . **5.** piuri **7.** majagua
Indian, American (pert to) . . .
chief . . **5.** Logan **6.** Joseph, Philip,
 sachem **7.** Cochise, Pontiac
 8. Geronimo, Red Cloud, Tecumseh
 9. Massasoit **10.** Crazy Horse
 11. Sitting Bull, Spotted Tail
dance . . **7.** cantico
festival . . **8.** potlatch
hatchet . . **8.** tomahawk
hero . . **4.** Rama (S Am)
largest tribe . . **6.** Navaho (Navajo)
lodge . . **5.** hogan, igloo, tepee
 6. wigwam **7.** wickiup
married . . **5.** squaw (fem) **6.** sannup
 (male)
Mexico . . **4.** Maya **5.** Aztec
 7. Tehueco
money . . **5.** sewan (beads) **6.** wampum
Newfoundland . . **6.** Micmac
pipe (peace) . . **7.** calumet
pony . . **6.** cayuse
richest tribe . . **5.** Osage
S America . . **3.** Ona **4.** Cara (anc),
 Inca, Peru, Tupi **5.** Carib **6.** Arawak,
 Aymara **7.** Quechua
Spirit, Great . . **6.** Manito **7.** Manitou
 12. Gitchi Manito
squaw . . **6.** mahala
symbol . . **5.** totem
tax, impost . . **5.** abwab
village . . **6.** pueblo
water lily . . **5.** wokas (wocas)
Indiana . . .
capital . . **12.** Indianapolis
city . . **4.** Gary **6.** Muncie **7.** Hammond
 9. Vincennes **10.** Terre Haute
industrial region . . **7.** Calumet
monument (Hist) . . **7.** Lincoln
 12. Indian Mounds **13.** Wyandotte
 Cave
post office (famed) . . **10.** Santa Claus
river . . **6.** Maumee, Wabash
 10. Tippecanoe
State admission . . **10.** Nineteenth
State bird . . **8.** cardinal
State flower . . **5.** peony
State motto . . **19.** Crossroads of
 America
State nickname . . **7.** Hoosier
Indian tribes . . . **3.** Aht, Fox, Oto
 (Otoe), Ree, Sac, Ute **4.** Cree, Crow,
 Erie, Hano, Hopi, Iowa, Maya, Mono,
 Sauk, Yuma, Zuni **5.** Aleut, Cadoo,
 Carib, Coree, Creek, Haida, Huron,
 Miami, Moqui, Omaha, Osage, Piute,
 Ponca, Sioux, Sooke, Teton, Yazoo
 6. Ahtena (Alaska), Apache, Biloxi,
 Cayuga, Dakota, Eskimo, Isleta,
 Lenape, Mohawk, Mojave, Navaho,

 Nootka, Oneida, Paiute (Piute),
 Pawnee, Santee, Seneca, Siwash
 7. Amerind, Bannock, Catawba,
 Chinook, Ojibway, Tlingit, Yavanai
 8. Arapahoe, Cherokee, Chippewa,
 Comanche, Iroquois, Kickapoo, Nez
 Percé, Onondaga, Sagamore,
 Seminole, Shoshone **9.** Algonquin,
 Athabasca, Blackfoot, Chickasaw,
 Winnebago **10.** Muskhogean
 12. Narragansett
indicate . . . **4.** cite, hint, mark, mean,
 show **5.** point **6.** denote, evince,
 reveal, sketch **7.** bespeak, betoken,
 connote, declare, display, signify,
 specify **8.** disclose, evidence,
 intimate, manifest, point out, register
 9. designate, foretoken
indicated . . . **6.** marked, signed
 7. denoted, implied **8.** presumed
 9. betokened, portended, suggested
indicating succession . . . **7.** ordinal
indication . . . **4.** clue, hint, mark, note,
 omen, sign **5.** proof, token, trace
 6. signal **7.** reading (a) **8.** evidence
 10. suggestion **13.** manifestation
indicative . . . **7.** ominous
 10. evidential, indication, meaningful,
 suggestive **11.** connotative
 13. significative
indicator . . . **4.** dial, hand, sign, vane
 5. arrow, gauge, index, level
 6. gnomon **7.** indices (pl), pointer
 9. grape fern (belief) **10.** instrument
 11. annunciator, thermometer
 15. telethermometer
indicia (sing **indicium**) . . . **5.** marks,
 signs **6.** tokens **8.** markings (PO)
 11. appearances, indications, metered
 mail
indict . . . **6.** accuse, charge, decree
 7. arraign, impeach **8.** proclaim
indictive . . . **8.** declared **9.** appointed
 10. proclaimed
indictment . . . **6.** charge
 10. accusation, imputation
 11. arraignment
indifference . . . **5.** shrug **6.** apathy
 7. inertia **8.** coldness **9.** unconcern
 10. mediocrity, negligence, neutrality
 12. carelessness, heedlessness,
 unimportance **13.** insensibility
 14. insignificance
indifferent . . . **3.** ill **4.** cold, cool, sick
 5. blasé **6.** casual, poorly
 7. neutral, stoical, uneager
 8. careless, heedless, listless,
 mediocre **9.** apathetic
 10. nonchalant, regardless
 11. adiaphorous, unimportant
 12. nonessential, uninterested
indigence . . . **4.** lack, need, want
 6. penury **7.** poverty **10.** deficiency
indigene . . . **6.** native **8.** habitant
 9. primitive **10.** autochthon
indigenous . . . **6.** inborn, innate, native,
 rooted **7.** edaphic, endemic, natural
 8. endemism, inherent
 13. autochthonous
indigent . . . **4.** free, poor, void
 5. needy **6.** bereft **7.** lacking,
 wanting

8. beggarly 9. destitute, penniless
10. pauperized 11. impecunious,
necessitous 15. poverty–stricken
indigestion... 8. disorder, phthisis
9. dyspepsia 10. immaturity
indignant... 3. hot 5. angry, irate,
wroth 7. annoyed 8. incensed,
wrathful 9. resentful 11. exasperated
indignation... 3. ire 4. base, fury
5. .anger, wrath 7. disdain
8. contempt
indignity... 7. affront, dudgeon
10. uncivility
indigo... 3. dye 4. anil, blue
indigo (pert to)...
bale of.. 6. seroon
compound.. 6. isatin
plant.. 4. anil
source.. 7. indican 9. indigotin
wild.. 8. Baptisia
indirect... 7. devious, oblique
9. deceitful, dishonest 10. circuitous,
contingent, misleading, roundabout
indirect expense... 8. overhead
indiscreet... 4. rash 5. hasty, silly
6. unwise 7. foolish, witless
8. careless, heedless 9. imprudent
10. incautious 11. injudicious
12. undiscerning 13. inconsiderate
indiscriminate... 5. mixed 7. mingled
9. extensive, haphazard, orderless,
wholesale 13. heterogeneous
indispensable... 5. basic, vital
6. needed 7. exigent 8. integral
9. essential, requisite, right–hand
10. imperative 13. irreplaceable
indisposed... 3. ill 4. sick 6. averse
9. unwilling 10. disordered, unfriendly
11. disinclined
indisposition... 7. ailment, illness,
malaise 10. averseness, reluctance
13. unwillingness
indisputable... 4. sure 7. certain,
evident 8. positive 10. undeniable
11. indubitable 12. irrefragable
13. incontestable
indistinct... 3. dim 4. hazy 5. vague
7. blurred, obscure, unclear
8. confused 9. ambiguous, undefined
10. indefinite 16. undiscriminating
17. indistinguishable
indite... 3. pen 5. write 6. phrase
7. compose 8. describe, inscribe
individual... 3. man, one 4. bion, idio
(comb form), self, sole, unit, zoon
6. egoist, person, single 7. special
8. organism, selfsame 9. identical
11. inseparable, personality
individuality... 5. being, seity
6. nature 7. oneness 8. ethology,
identity, selfness
individually... 9. severally
10. personally 12. each by itself
14. distributively
Indo–Aryan (pert to)...
deity.. 5. Indra
native of.. 5. India
speech.. 5. Aryan
type.. 4. Jats 7. khatris, Rajputs
Indo–Chinese (pert to)...
language.. 3. Tai (Thai)
mammal.. 4. zebu

river.. 6. Mekong
State (former French).. 4. Laos
7. Vietnam 8. Cambodia
indoctrinate... 5. coach, edify, imbue,
teach 8. instruct 12. rehabilitate
indolence... 5. scorn, sloth 7. inertia,
languor 8. inaction, laziness
10. ergophobia 11. lotus–eating,
spring fever 13. indisposition
indolent... 4. idle, lazy 5. inert
6. otiose 8. inactive, slothful,
sluggish 10. unemployed
indomitable... 10. invincible
11. intractable, "never say die"
13. unconquerable
Indonesia...
capital.. 7. Jakarta (Djakarta)
formation.. 11. archipelago (once
world's largest)
former name.. 7. Batavia 15. Dutch
East Indies
government.. 8. Republic (1950)
islands (3,000 in all).. 4. Bali, Java
7. Sumatra 8. Sulawesi (Celebes)
9. New Guinea (W half)
10. Kalimantan (W Borneo)
president.. 7. Sukarno
race.. 5. Dyaks (Dayaks) 7. Battaks
(Bataks), Igorots 8. Balinese,
Javanese
religion.. 6. Moslem
shrine.. 6. dagoba
indorse, endorse... see *endorse*
indorsement, endorsement... 4. visa,
visé (passport)
Indra (Hindu)... 3. God 5. Deity, Sakra
(Sakka)
indubitable... 4. fact, sure 7. evident
10. infallible, undeniable
11. irrefutable 12. irrefragable,
unanswerable 13. incontestable
14. unquestionable
16. incontrovertible
induce... 4. lead, move, urge
5. cause, impel, infer 6. allure, elicit,
entice, incite 8. persuade
9. influence, instigate, prevail on
inducement... 6. motive, reason
8. stimulus 9. incentive, influence
10. persuasion 13. consideration
induct... 6. enroll 7. bring in, install
8. initiate 9. conscript, introduce
inductance unit... 5. henry
inductile... 10. inflexible, unyielding
induction... 5. logic 7. causing
8. entrance 9. accession, beginning,
deduction 10. conclusion, initiation,
production 12. commencement,
conscription, installation, introduction
indue... 5. endow 6. assume, clothe,
draw on, invest, supply (spiritual)
7. furnish
indulge... 3. pet 5. grant, humor, yield
6. pamper 7. cherish, gratify
indulgences... 8. excesses
10. tolerances
indulgent... 4. easy 7. lenient, patient
8. tolerant, yielding 9. compliant
10. permissive 11. considerate,
intemperate
indurate... 6. harden 7. callous
10. solidified

indurated... 3. set 5. fixed
9. calloused 10. solidified
industrial magnate... 6. shogun,
tycoon
industrious... 4. busy 6. active
7. zealous 8. diligent, sedulous
9. assiduous 11. intentional,
painstaking 13. indefatigable
industry... 4. toil, work 5. labor, trade
7. concern 8. commerce 9. diligence
12. perseverance, sedulousness
indweller... 6. native 7. denizen
8. indigene
indwelling... 7. inbeing 8. immanent,
inherent 9. immanence, inherence
10. inhabiting
inearth... 5. inter 6. inhume
inebriacy... 11. drunkenness
12. intemperance
inebriate... 3. sot 5. addle, drunk,
toper 7. stupefy, tippler 8. drunkard
10. exhilarate (by liquor), intoxicate
ineffable... 4. surd 6. sacred
9. wonderful 11. unspeakable,
unutterable 13. indescribable,
inexpressible 15. unpronounceable
ineffaceable... 9. indelible
10. inerasable 12. ineradicable
ineffectual... 4. vain, weak 6. futile
7. useless 9. fruitless 10. unavailing
11. inefficient 12. unsuccessful
13. inefficacious, uninfluential
inefficient... 6. unable 10. indisposed
11. incompetent 12. unproficient
inelegant... 6. clumsy, vulgar
8. indecent 9. deficient (in beauty)
11. unbeautiful
inept... 4. null, void 5. silly, unfit
6. absurd 7. foolish 8. unsuited
10. out of place, unbecoming,
unskillful, unsuitable 11. inexpedient
inequality... 9. disparity, diversity
10. inadequacy, unevenness
12. disagreement, variableness
13. disproportion
ineradicable... 7. lasting 9. indelible,
permanent 12. ineffaceable
inerrant... 8. unerring 10. infallible
inert... 4. dead, lazy 6. latent, stupid,
supine, torpid 7. passive 8. inactive,
lifeless, listless, slothful, sluggish
9. apathetic, inanimate, lethargic
10. motionless, phlegmatic
inertia... 9. indolence, inertness
10. immobility
inesculant (rare)... 9. indelible
inestimable... 9. priceless
10. invaluable 12. incalculable
inevitable... 3. due 5. fated
7. nemesis 9. necessary
11. unavoidable
inexorability... 5. rigor 9. obstinacy
10. strictness
inexorable... 6. strict 9. obstinate
10. inflexible, relentless, unyielding
inexpedience, inexpedient... 6. unwise
8. untimely 9. ignorance, impolitic,
imprudent, unfitting 10. indiscreet,
unwiseness 11. inadvisable
15. disadvantageous
inexperience... 6. unwise 9. ignorance,
imprudent 10. immaturity, indiscreet

11. inadvisable 12. unprofitable
14. unskillfulness
15. disadvantageous
inexperienced... 3. raw 4. naif
5. green, naive 6. callow
8. ignorant, immature, prentice
9. unskilled 10. amateurish
11. unpracticed
inexplicable... 11. undefinable
12. supernatural 13. preternatural,
unaccountable, unexplainable
inextricable... 4. mazy 5. stuck
8. involved 9. intricate 10. insolvable
infallible... 4. sure, true 6. gospel
7. certain 8. inerrant, unerring
9. inerrable 11. indubitable
infamous... 4. base 6. odious, wicked
8. shameful, terrible 9. negarious
10. detestable 11. ignominious
12. contemptible, disreputable
infamy... 5. shame 8. disgrace,
dishonor, ignominy, reproach
9. disrepute 10. opprobrium
11. abomination
infancy... 8. babyhood, minority
9. beginning
infant... 4. babe, baby 5. child, minor
6. novice 8. bantling 9. foundling
infantryman... 6. Zouave 7. dog-face
8. chasseur 9. musketeer
11. footslogger, foot soldier
14. gravel agitator
infatuated... 7. foolish, smitten
8. enamored, obsessed 9. bewitched
10. captivated, enraptured
12. enthusiastic
infatuation... 3. ate, mad 4. love
5. craze, folly 10. enthusiasm
11. foolishness
infeasible... 8. unlikely 10. improbable,
unsuitable 13. impracticable
infect... 5. taint 6. defile, excite,
poison 7. corrupt, deprave, pollute
11. contaminate
infection... 7. disease 8. epidemic
9. pollution 11. implication (law),
inspiration 13. contamination
infelicity... 6. misery 9. inaptness
10. misfortune 11. unhappiness
12. inexpedience, untimeliness,
wretchedness
infer... 4. hint 5. drive, guess, imply
6. deduce 7. presume, suppose,
surmise 8. conclude, construe
inference... 5. truth 8. illation
9. corollary, deduction
10. assumption, conclusion
11. implication, proposition
inferential... 8. illative 9. deductive,
inducible 10. deductible, suggestive
15. inconsequential
inferior... 3. bad 4. less, poor
5. baser, lower, minor, petit, petty
6. lesser, menial, nether 7. humbler,
unequal 8. anterior, mediocre
10. inadequate, low-blooded
11. subordinate
inferior lawyer... 9. leguleian
11. pettifogger
infernal... 6. cursed, plaguy, wicked
7. hellish, satanic 8. damnable,
devilish 9. chthonian, execrable,

malignant, Tartarean 10. demoniacal, detestable, outrageous

inferno (pert to)...
Bib.. 4. Hell 5. abyss, limbo
Buddah.. 6. Naraka
Egypt.. 6. Amenti
ferry to.. 4. Styx
Hebrew.. 5. Sheol 7. Abaddon, Gehenna
myth.. 5. Aralu, Hades, Orcus 7. Acheron, Niflhel 8. Tartarus

infest... 3. vex 5. annoy, beset 6. assail, molest, plague 7. overrun, torment 8. frequent

infidel... 5. deist, pagan 6. Kaffir 7. atheist, Saracen, skeptic 8. agnostic 10. unbeliever 11. freethinker 12. non–Christian 13. non–Mohammedan

infidelity... 6. deceit 7. perfidy 8. unbelief 9. misbelief, treachery 10. disloyalty 11. incredulity 13. faithlessness

infinite... 4. vast 5. vague 6. divine 7. endless, eternal, immense, perfect 9. boundless, limitless, unlimited 10. indefinite 11. illimitable, interminate, omnipresent, The Absolute 12. all–embracing, interminable, undetermined 13. inexhaustible, The Omnipotent 16. all–comprehensive

Infinite Being... 3. God
Infinite knowledge... 11. omniscience

infinitesimal... 5. small 7. minimum 9. invisible, molecular 10. evanescent 11. microscopic

infirm... 4. weak 5. anile, frail 6. senile 7. fragile 8. decrepit 9. doddering 10. irresolute 11. vacillating

infirmity... 6. defect, foible, malady, old age 7. disease, failing, frailty, illness 8. debility, weakness 10. feebleness

inflame... 4. burn, fire 5. anger 6. arouse, enrage, excite, ignite, kindle, madden, rankle, redden 7. incense 8. irritate 10. exasperate

inflammable... 5. fiery 6. tinder 7. piceous 8. burnable 9. excitable, irascible, irritable 10. accendible 11. combustible

inflammable substance... 6. ethane, tinder 7. acetone, bitumen

inflammation... 8. ignition, soreness 10. congestion, excitement, incitement

inflammation (pert to)...
bladder.. 8. cystitis
bone.. 7. rickets 8. osteitis 13. osteomyelitis
ear.. 6. otitis
eye.. 6. iritis 7. uveitis
joints.. 4. gout 9. arthritis 10. rheumatism
spinal cord.. 13. poliomyelitis
stomach.. 9. gastritis
suffix.. 4. itis
vein.. 9. phlebitis

inflect... 3. bow 4. bend 5. curve 7. decline, deflect 8. modulate

inflection, inflexion... 4. tone 5. angle, curve 7. bending 8. paradigm 9. accidence 10. modulation

inflexible... 4. iron 5. rigid, stiff 6. strict 8. obdurate, rigorous 9. immovable, immutable, obstinate, unbending 10. implacable, inexorable, relentless, unyielding 11. unalterable 14. uncompromising

inflict... 3. add 4. deal 5. wreak 6. impose, punish

inflorescence... 4. cyme 5. whorl 6. cymose 7. budding, flowers 8. racemose 9. flowerage, flowering 10. unfoldment 13. efflorescence

inflow... 6. influx 9. inpouring 11. inspiration

influence... 3. win 4. lead, move, pull, sway 5. aegis (egis), bribe, force, impel, lobby 6. affect, effect, induce, influx, leaven, obsess 7. control, inspire, mastery 8. dominate, effusion, persuade, prestige 9. authority, determine

influence (world–wide)... 8. ecumenic

influenced... 6. biased 7. induced, pliable (easily) 8. affected 10. prejudiced

influential... 6. potent, strong 7. weighty 8. momentus, powerful 9. effective 13. authoritative

influx... 4. tide 5. firth, mouth (river) 6. import, inflow 7. estuary, illapse 9. influence, inpouring 11. debouchment

infold... see *enfold*

inform... 4. tell 5. teach, train 6. advise, notify, report 7. animate, apprise, inspire 8. instruct 9. enlighten

informal... 7. offhand 9. irregular

information... 3. air, tip 4. data, lore, news 5. aviso, datum, facts 6. digest 7. advices, tidings 9. knowledge 10. annotation 11. instruction 12. intelligence

informed... 2. up 3. hep 4. up on, wise 6. posted 8. apprised, educated, versed in 10. instructed 11. enlightened

informer... 3. spy 4. tout 6. gossip, snitch, teller 7. delator 8. affirmer, betrayer, mouchard, reporter, telltale 9. informant, spokesman 10. talebearer, tattletale

informer (sl)... 4. fink, nark 6. canary, snitch 7. stoolie 8. snitcher, squealer 9. blabberer 11. stool pigeon 12. blabbermouth

infraction... 6. breach 8. fracture, trespass 9. intrusion, violation 12. encroachment, infringement, overstepping 13. transgression

infrequency... 6. rarity 7. fewness 8. rareness, solitude 9. isolation 12. uncommonness

infrequent... 4. rare 6. scarce, seldom, sparse 8. uncommon 9. spasmodic 10. occasional

infrequently... 6. rarely, seldom 8. not often, sparsely

infringe... 6. defeat, refute 7. confute, destroy, violate 8. encroach, overstep, trespass 9. frustrate
infringement... 6. breach, piracy (copyright) 9. intrusion, violation 10. infraction 12. overstepping 14. nonfulfillment
infundibulum... 4. cone, lura 10. gray matter (brain)
infuriate... 5. anger 6. enrage, incite, madden 8. irritate 10. antagonize
infuscate... 6. darken 7. obscure
infuse... 4. fill, shed 5. steep 6. drench 7. implant, instill 9. insinuate, introduce
infusion... 3. tea 4. wort 8. affusion, tincture 9. admixture, decoction, inpouring 12. instillation
ingang... 5. porch 8. entrance 10. intestines
ingenious... 5. sharp, smart, witty 6. adroit, clever, daedal, gifted, shrewd, subtle 8. skillful, talented 9. Daedalian, deviceful 11. intelligent, resourceful
ingenuity... 5. skill 6. candor, genius 10. adroitness 11. originality 13. inventiveness
ingenuous... 4. naif, open 5. frank, naive, noble, plain 6. candid, innate 7. artless, sincere 8. freeborn, innocent 9. guileless 10. unreserved 15. unsophisticated
ingest... 3. eat 5. learn 6. take in 7. consume, swallow
ingot... 3. gad, pig 4. mold 5. metal 7. bullion
ingratiate... 4. fawn 7. commend, flatter 9. insinuate, introduce
ingredient... 6. factor 7. element 9. component 11. constituent
ingress... 4. go in 5. entry 6. access, portal 8. entrance 9. reception 11. entranceway
ingrowing nail... 7. acronyx
inhabitant... 3. cit 6. inmate, people, tenant 7. citizen, denizen 8. resident
inhabitant (pert to)...
  Alaska.. 9. sourdough
  desert.. 4. Arab 5. nomad
  earliest.. 9. aborigine
  foreign.. 5. alien
  Maine.. 10. down–easter
  moon.. 8. selenite
  northern.. 6. Yankee 11. Septentrion (Lowell)
inhabitants, equator's other side... 8. antiscii 10. antiscians
inhabited... 5. lived 7. dwelled, peopled 8. occupied, tenanted 9. populated
inhabiting (pert to)...
  caves.. 8. spelaean (spelean) 10. troglodyte
  ground.. 9. terricole 11. terricolous
  groves.. 7. nemoral 10. nemoricole
  islands.. 7. nesiote
  lakes.. 9. lacustral
  sea.. 7. pelagic 15. thalassophilous
  seashore.. 8. littoral
inhale... 4. suck 5. smell, smoke, sniff 7. breathe, inspire, respire

inharmonious... 7. jarring 9. differing, dissonant, unmusical 10. discordant 11. conflicting, disagreeing
inherent... 6. inborn, innate 7. infixed 8. immanent 9. immanence, intrinsic 10. indwelling, subsistent 11. instinctive 13. indispensable
inheritance... 6. legacy 7. bequest, legitim 8. heirship, heredity, heritage, Salic law 9. cleronomy 10. birthright
inheritance diminisher... 6. abator
inheritor... 4. heir 6. coheir 7. heiress, legatee 10. coparcener 11. beneficiary
inhibit... 5. check 6. forbid, hinder 8. prohibit, restrain 9. interdict
inhibition... 3. ban, bar 4. writ 7. embargo 8. checking 9. hindrance, restraint 10. impediment 11. prohibition 12. interdiction
inhuman... 4. fell 5. cruel 6. brutal, savage 7. bestial, brutish 8. devilish, nonhuman 9. barbarous, ferocious 10. demoniacal, diabolical
inhumation... 6. burial 9. arenation, interment
inhume... 4. bury 5. inter, inurn 7. deposit, inearth
inimical... 7. adverse, hostile, opposed 8. contrary 10. unfriendly 11. belligerent, unfavorable
iniquity... 3. sin 4. evil, vice 5. crime 7. misdeed 9. injustice 10. immorality, wickedness
initial... 6. paraph 9. incipient 11. large letter 12. commencement
initiate... 4. open 5. admit, begin, epopt (anc) 6. induct 7. install, instate 8. inchoate 10. inaugurate 11. preinstruct
initiation... 8. ceremony 9. admission 10. admittance 12. inauguration, introduction
injection... 4. hypo 5. enema 7. clyster 9. immission
injudicious... 4. rash 6. unwise 9. impolitic, imprudent 11. inexpedient
injunction... 3. ado 4. writ 5. order, union 6. behest 7. mandate, precept 9. direction 11. prohibition
injure... 3. mar 4. harm, hurt, lame, maim 5. wound, wrong 6. assail, damage, grieve, impair, scathe 7. affront, slander, tarnish
injurious... 3. bad 4. evil 7. abusive, harmful, hurtful, noxious 10. defamatory, slanderous 11. detrimental, mischievous
injury... 3. ill, mar 4. dere (obs), evil, harm, hurt, loss, pain, tort 5. wound, wrong 6. damage, lesion, mayhem, trauma 7. slander 9. detriment, indignity, injustice 10. impairment
injustice... 5. wrong 6. injury 7. umbrage 8. hardship, inequity, iniquity 10. imposition, unfairness
ink... 3. jet 5. black 7. blacken 8. atrament, blacking
ink (pert to)...

bag.. 3. sac (fish)
berry.. 5. holly 6. indigo
black.. 10. atramental
  11. atramentous
cap.. 8. mushroom
fish.. 5. squid 6. cuttle
pad.. 7. tompion (tampion)
ref to.. 10. atramental
source.. 7. inkweed, oak gall
  8. inkstone, pokeweed 9. gallberry
spreader.. 6. brayer
inkle... 4. hint, tape, yarn 5. braid,
  twist 6. thread 8. intimate
inkling... 4. hint 5. rumor 6. desire,
  report 10. intimation 11. supposition
inlaid... 6. mosaic 7. adorned, set into
  9. champleve, decorated
inlay... 4. buhl, line 5. inset 6. insert,
  mosaic, niello, tarsia 7. filling,
  implant 8. buhlwork, intarsia
  9. champleve
inlet... 3. bay, ria, voe 4. cove, slew,
  sump 5. admit, bayou, bight, creek,
  fiord (fjord), firth, inlay 6. estero,
  recess, strait 7. estuary, orifice
  8. entrance, waterway
inn... 3. pub 4. khan 5. abode, fonda,
  hotel, motel, serai 6. hostel, imaret,
  posada, tavern 7. albergo, cabaret,
  hospice, locanda, osteria, pension,
  shelter 8. alehouse, hostelry
  9. roadhouse 11. caravansary
innate... 4. born 6. inborn, inbred,
  native 7. natural 9. ingrained,
  inherited, intrinsic 10. congenital,
  hereditary, inveterate 11. instinctive
  14. constitutional
innate ability... 6. genius, talent
innate idea (Philos)... 11. immortality
inn courts... 11. Inner Temple
inner... 4. ento (comb form) 5. ental
  6. inside, inward, secret 7. obscure
  8. esoteric, interior, internal
  9. intestine 10. indistinct
  14. intramolecular
inner circle... 3. set 4. clan, club,
  ring 5. group, junta, junto 6. clique
inner man... 4. mind, self, soul
  6. psyche 7. stomach
innermost coating... 6. intima
Inner Temple... 11. Inns of Court
Innisfail... 4. Eire, Erin 7. Ireland
  15. Island of Destiny
innocence... 6. purity 7. diamond
  11. sinlessness 12. harmlessness
  13. guiltlessness, innocuousness
innocent... 4. Holy, pure 5. idiot,
  naive, seely 6. benign, lawful
  7. artless, sinless, upright 8. spotless
  9. destitute, guiltless, ingenuous,
  permitted, simpleton, stainless,
  unsullied 10. unblamable
  12. simple–minded 13. free from
  guilt
innocuous... 8. harmless, hurtless,
  innocent 9. innoxious 11. inoffensive,
  unoffending
innovation... 3. new 6. change
  7. novelty 13. prolification
innuendo... 4. hint, slur 6. change
  7. meaning 9. aspersion
  10. intimation 11. implication

indirection, insinuation
Innuit... 4. Yuit (Eskimo)
innumerable... 6. legion, myriad
  8. infinite, numerous 9. countless
  10. numberless
inodorous... 8. odorless 9. scentless
inopportune... 8. ill–timed, untimely
  10. malapropos, unsuitable
  11. contretemps, inexpedient
  12. embarrassing, unseasonable
inordinate... 5. undue 9. excessive,
  fanatical 10. disordered, disorderly,
  exorbitant, immoderate
  11. unregulated 12. unrestrained
inorganic... 7. mineral 9. inanimate
  13. nonbiological
inquest... 4. jury 5. quest, trial
  6. assize, search 7. inquiry
  11. examination 13. investigation
inquire... 3. ask 4. seek 5. query
  7. examine 8. question
  11. interrogate, investigate
inquirer... 6. seeker 7. querier,
  student, zetetic 8. searcher
inquiry... 5. query 6. examen, tracer
  7. examine, seeking 8. question,
  research 11. examination
  13. investigation
inquisition... 5. trial 6. search
  7. inquiry 8. tribunal 11. examination
  13. investigation
Inquisition... 6. French (1772)
  7. Spanish (1480–1834)
inquisitive... 4. nosy 5. peery
  6. prying 7. curious 8. meddling
  10. meddlesome
inquisitor... 6. tracer 7. coroner,
  sheriff 8. examiner
in re... 10. concerning 13. in the
  matter of
inroad... 4. raid 5. foray 8. invasion,
  trespass 9. incursion, intrusion,
  irruption 12. overstepping
  13. transgression
insane... 3. mad 4. daft, loco, luny
  5. batty, crazy, loony 6. crazed
  7. cracked, foolish, frantic, rammish,
  touched, witless 8. demented,
  deranged 9. non compos 15. non
  compos mentis
insane urge to steal...
  11. kleptomania
insanity... 5. mania 6. frenzy, lunacy,
  trance 7. madness 8. delirium,
  dementia 10. alienation
  11. derangement 16. mental
  deficiency
inscribe... 4. draw, etch 5. infix,
  stamp, write 6. blazon, enroll
  7. address, engrave, impress
  8. dedicate, depencil
inscribed... 5. runed 7. written
  8. engraved, recorded 10. registered,
  rupestrian (on rocks)
inscription... 4. text 5. motto, title
  6. legend 7. epitaph, writing
  8. colophon, epigraph, graffito
  9. lettering, sgraffito 10. dedication
  14. superscription
inscrutable... 6. secret 8. abstruse
  10. mysterious 12. impenetrable,
  inexplorable, unfathomable

16. incomprehensible
insect... 3. ant, bee, bug, dor, fly
4. flea, gnat, lerp, lice, mite, moth,
tick, wasp 5. aphid, borer, cadew,
emmet, leech, louse, roach, Vespa
6. acarid, beetle, cicada, earwig,
hornet, locust, mantis, sawfly, scarab,
spider 7. ant lion, chigger, firefly,
gallfly, katydid, ladybug, pismire,
termite 8. bullhead, glowworm,
mosquito, stinkbug, turicata
9. bumblebee, butterfly, caddis fly,
centipede, cockroach, dragonfly,
ichneumon, tsetse fly, tumblebug
10. silverfish 11. caterpillar,
grasshopper 12. yellow jacket
insect (pert to)...
adult.. 5. imago
aquatic.. 7. Ranatra
arboreal.. 7. katydid
back.. 5. notum
Bible.. 7. ant lion
butterfly.. 11. Lepidoptera
egg.. 3. nit
eyes.. 6. ocelli 7. stemmas
feelers.. 5. palps 8. antennas
9. tentacles
fly.. 4. zimb 7. Diptera
hymenopterous.. 3. ant, bee 4. wasp
6. sawfly 7. gallfly
immature.. 4. grub, pupa 5. larva
6. maggot 9. chrysalis
immature covering.. 6. cocoon
leg.. 6. proleg
like.. 8. entomoid
long-legged.. 5. emesa
10. harvestman 13. daddy-longlegs
mature.. 5. imago
molting.. 6. instar 7. ecdysis
parasitic.. 4. lice 5. louse
plant.. 5. aphid, aphis, borer, thrip
plate.. 6. scutum
praying.. 6. mantis
reference to.. 11. entomologic
relationship to host.. 7. metochy
10. parasitism
science.. 10. entomology
sound.. 5. chirr 7. stridor
stage.. 4. pupa 5. imago, larva
6. instar 9. chrysalis
stinging.. 3. ant, bee 4. wasp
6. hornet 7. sciniph (Bib) 12. yellow
jacket
wingless.. 4. flea 6. aptera
wing vein.. 5. media
Insectivora (mammals)... 5. moles
6. shrews 7. desmans, tenrecs
9. hedgehogs
insecure... 5. risky, shaky 6. infirm,
unsafe, unsure 7. dubious, rickety,
unsound 8. unstable 9. dangerous,
hazardous 10. precarious
insensate... 5. blind, harsh 6. brutal,
unwise 7. fatuous, foolish 8. lifeless
9. inanimate, unfeeling, untouched
10. insensible, insentient
11. insensitive 13. unintelligent
insensibility... 4. coma 8. neurosis
9. analgesia 13. lack of feeling
insensible... 4. slow 7. gradual,
unaware 9. apathetic, inanimate,
insensate, senseless 11. indifferent,

unconscious 13. inappreciable
insert... 4. gore 5. foist, graft, immit,
inset, panel, wedge 7. ingraft
8. interact, ornament 9. interface,
interpose, introduce 11. intercalate,
interpolate
insertion... 5. inset 9. injection
10. embroidery, needlework
insertion (pert to)...
cords in cloth.. 5. shirr
day in calendar.. 13. intercalation
newspaper.. 2. ad 13. advertisement
phrases, words.. 11. parenthesis
sound in a word.. 9. anaptyxis
10. epenthesis
inset... 5. panel 6. inflow, influx
10. phenocryst
inside out, turning... 5. evert
8. aversion 9. evertible
insidious... 4. deep, wily 7. cunning
8. guileful 9. deceitful, dishonest
11. full of plots, treacherous
insight... 3. ken 6. acumen
9. intuition 11. discernment,
penetration 12. clairvoyance
13. understanding
insignia... 3. bar 4. ankh, flag
5. badge, cross, crown 6. banner,
emblem, symbol 7. chevron, regalia,
scepter 8. caduceus, swastika
15. hammer and sickle
insignificance... 6. trifle 9. smallness
10. slightness 12. unimportance
insignificant... 4. puny 5. minor,
petit, petty, small, zilch 6. paltry
7. trivial 8. inferior 9. senseless
11. meaningless, unimportant
12. contemptible 13. inconsiderate
insignificant object... 8. molehill
insincere... 5. false 8. affected
9. deceptive 12. hypocritical
insinuate... 4. hint 5. enter, imply
6. allude, infuse 8. intimate
9. penetrate 10. ingratiate
insinuation... 4. hint 5. sneer
8. innuendo 9. aspersion, insertion,
intrusion 10. intimation
12. ingratiation, interjection
insipid... 3. dry 4. dead, dull, flat,
tame 5. heavy, prosy, stale, vapid,
wimpy (sl) 6. jejune 7. prosaic
8. lifeless, mediocre 9. tasteless
10. monotonous, namby-pamby,
spiritless, unanimated, wishy-washy
11. indifferent 13. uninteresting
insisted... 5. urged 6. held to
7. pressed 8. demanded 9. persisted
10. maintained, stipulated
insnare... see *ensare*
insolence... 5. serve 6. insult
8. defiance 9. arrogance, contumely,
impudence 11. haughtiness
insolent... 4. pert, rude 7. abusive,
defiant 8. arrogant, impudent
9. insulting 10. disdainful
11. extravagant, impertinent,
overbearing 12. contemptuous,
contumelious 13. disrespectful
insouciant... 8. carefree
11. indifferent, unconcerned
inspect... 3. pry, spy 4. view
5. grade 7. examine 10. scrutinize

inspector... 4. ager 6. conner, grader, police, sealer, tester 8. examiner, overseer

inspiration... 6. sprite 8. afflatus, hiccough 9. influence, intuition 10. exhalation, inhalation, motivation

inspire... 4. fire 5. cheer, exalt 6. infuse, inhale 7. animate, breathe, enliven 8. motivate 9. encourage, infatuate 11. communicate (to the spirit)

inspired power... 7. entheos

inspiring... 8. cheering, eloquent 11. provocative

inspiring (pert to)...
awe.. 4. fear 5. awful, eerie
confidence.. 11. encouraging
favor.. 13. prepossessing
horror.. 6. grisly

inspirit... 5. cheer, elate, rouse 7. animate, enliven, hearten, inspire, quicken 9. encourage 10. ingratiate, invigorate

instability... 8. weakness 10. changeable, insecurity, mutability, unsafeness 11. inconstancy 12. irresolution, unsteadiness 13. changeability, unreliability

install... 4. seat 6. induct, ordain 7. instate 8. initiate 9. establish 10. inaugurate

instance... 4. case, suit 6. motive 7. example, request, urgency 8. occasion 10. suggestion 11. instigation

instant... 3. pop 4. time, urge 5. flash, trice 6. direct, minute, moment, second, urgent 7. current, solicit 8. pressing 9. immediate, importune 11. importunate

instantly... 3. now 8. directly, in a flash, in a trice

instate... 5. admit, endow 6. invest 7. install 9. establish

instead of... 4. else 5. stead 6. in lieu, rather 10. equivalent, substitute

instigate... 3. egg 4. abet, goad, move, prod, spur, urge 5. impel 6. foment, incite, suborn 7. provoke 8. motivate 9. stimulate

instigator... 5. urger 7. abettor, exciter, inciter 8. agitator, fomenter, inflamer, provoker 10. ringleader

instill, instil... 5. imbue 6. impart, infuse, pour in 7. pervade 9. inculcate, insinuate

instinct... 5. knack 6. libido, talent 7. impulse 8. aptitude 11. instigation, orientation

instinctive... 6. innate 7. natural 8. inherent, original 9. automatic, intuitive 11. involuntary, spontaneous

institute... 5. erect, found 6. create, ordain, school 7. academy, college, precept, society 8. initiate, organize, seminary 9. originate, principle 10. inaugurate 12. organization

Institute (The)... 5. Gaius 6. France 8. Politics 10. Technology

institute a suit... 3. sue 7. go to law 8. litigate 9. prosecute

Institution, International (maritime)...

7. Veritas 13. Bureau Veritas

instruct... 4. show 5. coach, edify, order, teach, train 6. advise, direct, inform 7. command, confirm, educate, nurture 9. enlighten 10. discipline 12. indoctrinate

instruction... 3. act 4. lore, news 6. lesson, report 7. precept, tuition 8. pedagogy, teaching, tutorage 9. paideutic 11. information 13. propaedeutics

instructive... 8. didactic, sermonic 10. commanding, preceptive 11. educational, informative 12. propaedeutic

instructor... 5. tutor 6. mentor 7. adviser, teacher, trainer 8. lecturer 9. preceptor, professor

instrument... 4. barb, bill, deed, tool, writ 5. agent, means 6. medium 7. utensil, writing 8. document 9. implement 11. contrivance

instrument, musical (pert to)...
ancient.. 4. asor, lyre 5. rebab, rocta, shawn 7. cithern, theorbo 8. penorcon, psaltery
brass.. 4. horn 6. cornet 7. helicon
keyboard.. 5. organ, piano 6. spinet 10. clavichord 11. harpsichord
percussion.. 4. drum, gong 5. bells 6. chimes 7. cymbals, marimba 8. carillon 9. castanets, xylophone 10. vibraphone 12. glockenspiel
sacred (Mormon).. 4. Urim 7. Thummim
stringed.. 4. asor, harp, lute, lyre, rota 5. banjo, cello, ribec (ribeck), viola 6. fiddle, guitar, violin 7. ukulele 8. dulcimer, mandolin 10. hurdy–gurdy
stringed (anc).. 7. bandora
supplementary.. 7. ripieno
wind.. 3. sax 4. horn, oboe, reed, tuba 5. flute, organ 6. cornet 7. althorn, bassoon, ocarina, piccolo, trumpet 8. clarinet, trombone 9. accordion, flageolet, harmonica, saxophone

instrument, others (pert to)...
astronomical.. 5. armil
Biblical.. 4. Urim
butcher's.. 5. steel 7. cleaver
communication.. 9. telegraph, telephone 10. hydrophone
cooking (eggs).. 7. oometer
cutting.. 5. knife, razor 6. scythe, shears, sickle 7. cutlery 8. scissors, strickle
drawing.. 10. pantograph
gripping.. 4. vise 5. clamp, tongs 7. pincers 8. tweezers
legal.. 4. deed, writ 6. escrow
mathematics.. 6. abacus 8. mesolabe
measure.. 7. ammeter 8. odometer, otoscope, rheostat 9. barometer, koniscope, rheometer 11. pyronometer
medical.. 6. trocar (trochar) 7. dilator, levator, ligator, scalpel 8. trephine
mining.. 6. jumper
music.. 4. bell 9. ergograph, metronome

navigating.. 7. pelorus, sextant
optical.. 7. alidade (alidad)
  9. periscope, telescope
pointed.. 3. awl 6. stylet, stylus
  8. stiletto
time.. 11. chronometer, chronoscope
two–pronged.. 6. bident
instrumental... 6. useful 7. helpful
  9. conducive, promoting, symphonic
  10. orchestral 11. implemental,
  serviceable
instrumental (pert to)...
composition.. 5. fugue, rondo
  6. sonata 7. cantata 8. symphony
grammar.. 4. case
introduction.. 7. intrada
instrumentality... 5. means 6. agency,
  medium 7. organon 9. mechanism
insubordinate... 8. mutinous
  10. unresigned 11. disobedient
  12. contumacious, unsubmissive
insubstantial... 5. frail 6. flimsy
  9. illogical 10. unreliable
  12. apparitional
insufficient... 5. short 6. scanty,
  scarce 7. unequal, wanting
  9. deficient 10. inadequate
  14. incommensurate, unsatisfactory
insular... 5. alone 6. narrow
  7. nesiote 8. detached, islander,
  isolated, secluded 9. illiberal,
  insulated, sclerosis, separated,
  unrelated 10. contracted 12. Island
  of Reil (Anat)
insulated... 5. isled, taped 8. isolated
  9. separated 10. segregated
insulating material... 4. tape 5. kapok
  6. balata, Kerite 7. okonite 10. fiber
  glass 12. friction tape
insult... 3. cag 4. mock, slur 5. flout
  6. offend, revile 7. affront, assault,
  offense, outrage 8. contempt
  9. contumely, indignity
insulting... 8. arrogant, insolent
  9. offensive 10. affrontive
  13. disrespectful
insurance... 4. risk 7. annuity, promise
  8. guaranty, security, warranty
  9. assurance 10. protection
insurance group... 7. tontine
insurance personnel... 5. agent
  6. broker 7. actuary 8. adjuster
insurgent... 5. rebel 8. agitator,
  mutineer, revolter 10. rebellious
  13. insubordinate
insurmountable... 10. impassable,
  invincible 11. insuperable 13. beyond
  control
insurrection... 4. riot 6. mutiny, revolt
  8. sedition, uprising 9. rebellion
  10. insurgence, revolution
intact... 5. sound, whole
  9. unchanged, undefiled, undivided,
  uninjured, untouched 10. unimpaired
intaglio... 3. die, gem 6. relief
  7. carving 9. engraving
intangible... 5. vague 7. phantom
  10. immaterial, impalpable
  13. imperceptible, insubstantial,
  unsubstantial
integer... 3. one 5. whole 6. entity,
  number 8. integral

integral... 3. all 5. inner, whole
  8. totality 9. component, essential
integration... 5. whole 10. adjustment
  11. unification 12. coordination,
  equalization 13. accommodation
integrity... 5. unity 6. purity, virtue
  7. honesty, probity 9. innocence,
  soundness 12. completeness
integument... 4. aril, coat, derm, skin
  5. testa 8. covering, envelope
  10. investment
intellect... 3. wit 4. mind, nous
  5. inwit, mahat 6. genius, noesis,
  reason 7. noetics, wise man
  9. mentality 12. intelligence
  13. understanding
intellectual... 6. brainy, mental, noetic,
  sophic 7. egghead, learned
  8. highbrow 11. intelligent
intelligence... 4. mind, news 5. sense,
  spies 6. acumen, spirit 8. capacity
  9. intellect, knowledge
  11. information 13. understanding
intelligent... 3. apt 4. sane 5. acute,
  aware, smart 6. astute, bright,
  versed 7. knowing, skilled 8. rational,
  sensible 9. cognizant
  13. understanding
intelligentsia... 8. literati 10. illuminati
  11. the educated 13. intellectuals
intelligible... 5. clear, plain
  8. knowable 10. cognizable,
  conceptual, explicable, fathomable
  11. perspicuous 13. suprasensuous
  14. comprehensible, understandable
intelligibly... 6. simply 7. clearly,
  lucidly, plainly 13. unequivocally
  14. comprehensibly, understandably
intemerate... 4. pure 9. inviolate,
  undefiled
intemperance... 6. excess 8. bibacity,
  gluttony, severity, tippling
  10. debauchery, inclemency
  11. drunkenness 12. inabstinence,
  incontinence
intemperate... 6. Frigid (Zone), severe,
  Torrid (Zone) 7. extreme 8. addicted,
  bibulous 9. excessive, inclement,
  indulgent 10. gluttonous,
  immoderate, inordinate
  12. ungovernable, unrestrained
intend... 3. aim 4. mean, plan
  5. serve 6. design, direct, expect,
  regard, set out, strive 7. proceed,
  propose 8. aspire to, attend to,
  consider
intended... 5. meant 8. designed,
  purposed, remedial 9. affianced,
  betrothed, meditated 10. calculated,
  considered 11. deliberated, intentional
  12. contemplated
intense... 4. deep 5. great, vivid
  6. strong 7. violent 8. powerful
  9. energetic 10. high degree
intensely... 4. very 5. quite 7. acutely
intensify... 6. deepen 7. enhance
  8. condense, heighten, increase
  9. aggravate
intensity... 5. depth 6. deepen,
  degree, energy 7. density
  8. loudness, softness, strength
  9. greatness, vehemence

12. colorfulness

intent ... 4. rapt 5. eager, tense
6. design 7. earnest, meaning,
purpose 9. intention

intention ... 3. aim, end 4. will
6. animus, design, motive, object
7. concept, healing, meaning,
purpose 8. intentio 13. determination

intentional ... 5. aimed, meant
7. knowing 8. designed, intended
9. voluntary 10. calculated, deliberate
12. contemplated

intently ... 7. eagerly, fixedly
9. earnestly, zealously 10. diligently,
sedulously 11. attentively, steadfastly

inter (pref) ... 5. among, intra
6. mutual, within 7. between
10. reciprocal

inter (verb) ... 4. bury 5. inurn
6. entomb, inhume 7. inearth

intercalary month ... 6. Veadar 8. leap
year 10. bissextile

intercalate ... 6. insert 11. interpolate

intercede ... 6. umpire 7. bargain,
mediate, referee 9. arbitrate, go
between, interpose, intervene

intercessor ... 5. agent, front
6. bishop, Christ 8. mediator
9. middleman 10. interceder
11. internuncio

interchange ... 5. trade 6. barter
7. permute 8. commerce, exchange
9. alternate 10. transposal
11. alternation, reciprocate, retaliation

intercourse ... 7. dealing 8. commerce
10. connection, fellowship
12. conversation 13. communication

interdependence ... 9. mutuality
13. interrelation 16. interaffiliation

interdict ... 3. ban 4. veto 5. debar,
taboo (tabu) 6. forbid 7. inhibit
8. prohibit 9. proscribe

interest ... 4. hold, weal 5. savor,
share, usury 6. behalf, engage
7. attract, concern 9. entertain

interested ... 4. rapt 7. partial 8. a
party to, involved, partisan
9. attentive 10. prejudiced

interesting ... 8. exciting 10. attractive
11. provocative

interfere ... 5. clash 6. hinder, meddle,
molest, tamper 7. intrude
9. interpose, intervene
11. intermeddle

interim ... 7. respite 8. interval,
meantime 9. interlude, meanwhile
12. intermission

interior ... 5. inner 6. center, inland,
inside, secret 8. internal 9. enclosure

interjection ... 2. eh, lo 3. bah
4. ahem, alas, egad, haha, whew
7. heavens 11. ejaculation,
exclamation

interlace ... 3. mix 5. braid, unite
9. alternate, interlink 10. intertwine,
interweave 11. interpolate, intersperse

interlock ... 4. knit, mesh 5. unite,
weave 6. device, engage 7. connect
9. interjoin, interlace 11. interrelate

interlope ... 6. insert 7. intrude,
obtrude 9. interfere, intervene
11. intermeddle, interpolate

interloper ... 8. intruder 10. trespasser
11. gate crasher

interlude ... 5. farce, pause, truce
6. verset 7. interim, respite
8. entr'acte, overture, versicle
10. intermezzo 11. performance
13. entertainment

intermediary ... 5. agent 6. medium,
middle 8. mediator 9. go–between
10. interagent 11. intervening,
mediatorial

intermediate ... 5. mesne 6. grades,
medial, medium, middle 7. aniline
(dye), mediate 8. mediator
9. naphthols 11. interjacent,
intervening 12. intermediary

interminable ... 4. aeon, long
7. endless, eternal 8. infinite,
unending 9. boundless, limitless,
perpetual, unlimited 10. continuous,
protracted

intermission ... 4. rest 5. pause
6. recess 7. respite 8. entr'acte,
interval 9. cessation 10. suspension
12. interruption

intermit ... 4. stop 5. cease, recur
7. suspend 9. interpose, interrupt
11. discontinue

intermittent ... 6. broken, fitful
8. periodic 9. irregular, recurrent,
spasmodic 11. alternating

internal ... 5. inner 6. inside, inward,
mental, within 7. revenue
8. domestic, esoteric, interior
9. intrinsic, spiritual

internal organs ... 6. vitals 7. viscera

international (pert to) ...
agreement .. 4. pact 6. accord, treaty
7. entente 8. suzerain
business combine .. 6. cartel
fixed calendar .. 9. Cotsworth
language .. 2. Ro 3. Ido 5. Arulo
7. Volapük 9. Esperanto
10. Occidental 11. Interlingua

interpolate ... 5. alter 6. insert
7. corrupt, implant 11. intercalate

interpose ... 7. intrude, mediate
9. intercede, interfere, interject,
intervene, introduce

interpret ... 4. read, rede, scan
6. define 7. explain, expound
8. construe, diagnose, exegesis
9. elucidate, translate

interpretation ... 5. sense 8. solution
9. rendering 10. definition
11. explanation, translation

interpretation, science of ...
7. anagoge (Bib) 8. exegesis
9. dittology 12. hermeneutics

interpreter ... 5. ulema 6. gnomon
7. exegete, latiner 8. dragoman,
exponent 9. catechist, exegetist,
explainer, go–between, hermeneut
12. oneirocritic (dreams)

interrogate ... 3. ask 4. pump, quiz,
test 5. query 7. examine, inquire
8. question 9. catechize

interrogation ... 7. eroteme (question
mark) 8. erotisis, question, quizzing
11. examination, questioning

interrupt ... 4. stop 5. break, check
6. arrest, hinder, thwart 7. break in,

intrude 8. obstruct 9. intercept
11. interpolate
interrupter (electric)... 8. rheotome
interruption... 3. gap 5. pause
6. hiatus 7. interim 8. interval
9. cessation, hindrance
10. suspension 11. obstruction
12. intermission, intervention
13. interposition
intersect... 3. cut 4. meet 5. cross
6. divide, pierce 9. decussate
10. intercross
intersperse... 6. insert, thread
7. scatter 9. diversify
interstice... 4. mesh, pore 5. chink,
crack, space 6. areola 7. crevice
8. interval 10. interspace
intertwine... 5. unite, weave
8. entangle 9. interknit, interlace
10. intertwist
interval... 3. gap 4. rest 5. break,
lapse, pitch, space 6. degree, period,
recess 7. diastem, interim, respite
8. diastema, distance, half step
10. interspace 12. intermission,
interruption
intervals, at... 8. brokenly, fitfully
11. haphazardly, irregularly
12. occasionally 14. intermittently
15. longo intervallo
intervene... 7. intrude, mediate
9. interlude, interpose 10. lie
between 11. come between
intervening (pert to)...
between, among.. 11. interjacent
law.. 5. mesne
space.. 8. distance
time.. 7. interim 9. interlude
interweave... 3. mat 4. plat 5. braid,
plait, plash 6. enlace, raddle, splice,
wattle 8. intermix 9. interlace
13. twist together
intestinal... 7. enteric 8. visceral
intestine (pert to)...
coating.. 4. caul
comb form.. 6. entero
part.. 5. colon, ilium, large, small
6. caecum, rectum 7. jejunum
8. appendix, duodenum
15. alimentary canal
intestines... 4. guts 6. bowels
8. entrails
intimacy... 9. closeness
10. connection, friendship
11. association, familiarity, sociability
intimate... 3. sib 4. hint, near
6. friend, united 8. familiar, friendly,
informal, personal, sociable
9. confidant, innermost
12. confidential
intimation... 3. cue 4. clue, hint
5. trace 7. inkling 9. reference
10. foreboding, indication, suggestion
11. supposition 12. announcement,
notification
intimidate... 3. awe, cow 5. abash,
bully, daunt, deter 7. overawe, terrify
8. browbeat, frighten, threaten
intolerance... 7. bigotry 9. dogmatism,
prejudice 10. impatience, narrowness
12. illiberality
intolerant... 6. narrow 7. bigoted

8. dogmatic 9. impatient
10. prejudiced 11. not enduring
intolerant person... 5. bigot 7. fanatic
intone... 4. sing 5. chant, croon,
sound 7. introit
intoxicated... 3. lit, sot 4. tosy
5. drunk, heady, tipsy 6. boiled
7. fervent, fuddled, maudlin
8. besotted, temulent 9. befuddled
10. inebriated
intractable... 5. tough 6. sullen, unruly
7. restive, willful (wilful) 8. indocile,
perverse, stubborn 9. obstinate,
unbending, unpliable 10. headstrong,
inflexible, refractory 11. unteachable
12. ungovernable
intransitive... 6. neuter, verbal
8. confined 10. in transitu
intrenchment... 2. pa (pah) 4. fort
7. defense, parapet 8. stockade
12. encroachment, infringement
intrepid... 4. bold 5. brave 6. heroic
7. doughty, valiant 8. fearless,
resolute 9. dauntless, undaunted
10. courageous
intrepidity... 5. nerve, valor
7. courage, prowess 8. boldness,
valiancy 9. gallantry
intricacy... 9. sinuosity 10. complexity,
involution, perplexity 11. complexness
12. complication, entanglement
intrigue... 4. plot 5. amour, cabal
6. brigue, scheme 8. artifice,
cheating 9. fascinate 10. conspiracy
11. machination
intrinsic... 4. real, true 5. inner
6. inborn, inbred, inward, native
7. genuine, natural 8. immanent,
implicit, inherent 9. essential,
necessary 11. inseparable
13. indispensable
intrinsically... 5. truly 6. really
10. internally 11. essentially
intrinsic being... 7. essence
introduce... 5. immit, start, usher
6. broach, herald, infuse, insert,
submit 7. bring in, preface, present,
sponsor 8. acquaint, approach,
initiate, innovate 10. inaugurate
11. preinstruct
introduced from foreign country...
6. exotic 10. extraneous
introduced serum... 10. inoculated
introduction... 5. debut, guide, proem
7. introit, isagoge, preface
8. exordium, foreword, preamble
9. insertion 10. innovation
11. instruction, preparation
12. inauguration, presentation
introduction (pert to)...
Biblical.. 9. isagogics
drama (anc).. 8. protasis
new words.. 7. neology
spurious matter.. 13. interpolation
introductory... 9. prefatory, prelusive
11. preliminary
introit... 4. hymn, rite 5. psalm
8. entrance 12. introduction
introrse... (opp of extrorse) 12. facing
inward
introversion... (opp of extroversion)
9. inversion, reticence

intrude... 5. enter 6. invade, meddle
8. encroach, infringe, overstep,
trespass 9. interfere, interlope
intruder... 7. invader 8. outsider
9. buttinsky 10. interloper, trespasser
intrust, entrust... 6. commit
7. confide, consign 8. delegate
10. commission
intuition... 5. hunch 6. noesis, regard
7. insight 9. knowledge, reference
13. contemplation
intuitive... 6. noetic, seeing 7. sensing
10. perceiving 11. instinctive
inulase... 6. enzyme
inunction... 7. unguent 8. inunctum,
ointment
inundate... 3. dip 4. dunk 5. douse,
drunk, flood 6. deluge, engulf
7. baptize, immerse 8. overflow,
submerge 9. overwhelm
10. oversupply
inure... 6. harden, season 7. benefit,
callous, toughen 8. accustom
9. habituate
inurn... 4. bury 5. inter 6. entomb
invade... 4. raid 5. enter (foeman),
usurp 6. attack, infest 7. intrude,
overrun, violate 8. encroach, trespass
invader... 4. Pict 8. attacker, intruder
9. aggressor, assailant 10. trespasser
invalid... 4. null, sick, void, weak
5. frail 6. feeble, infirm, sickly
8. nugatory 11. ineffectual
14. valetudinarian
invalidate... 4. undo 5. annul, quash
7. abolish, nullify, vitiate 8. disprove
10. disqualify, neutralize
invalidism... 13. indisposition
17. valetudinarianism
invaluable... 6. useful 8. precious
9. priceless, worthless
11. inestimable
invariable... 7. uniform 8. constant
10. unchanging 12. unchangeable
invasion... 4. raid 5. foray 6. attack,
breach, inroad 8. entrance (hostile)
9. incursion, intrusion, irruption
10. infraction 11. infestation
invective... 5. abuse, curse 6. tirade
7. inveigh, railing 8. diatribe
10. revilement 11. malediction
12. vituperation
inveigle... 4. lure, rope 5. snare
6. allure, entice, entrap, seduce
7. deceive, wheedle 10. lead astray
invent... 4. coin 5. frame 6. create,
design, devise 7. concoct 8. discover
9. fabricate (mentally), originate
inventive... 6. adroit 7. fertile
8. creative, original 9. ingenious
inventor... 7. creator 8. imaginer
10. discoverer, originator
inventor, discoverer of...
airplane.. 6. Fokker, Wright (Bros)
baseball.. 9. Doubleday
brake (safety).. 4. Otis
cotton gin.. 7. Whitney
dynamite.. 5. Nobel
electric light.. 6. Edison
elevator.. 4. Otis
gun.. 4. Colt 5. Maxim 9. Remington
harp (Bib),. 5. Jubal

lamp (safety).. 4. Davy
phonograph.. 6. Edison
printing.. 9. Gutenberg
radio.. 8. De Forest
sewing machine.. 4. Howe
steamboat.. 5. Fitch 6. Fulton
steam engine.. 4. Watt
telegraph.. 5. Morse
wireless.. 7. Marconi
X–ray.. 8. Roentgen
inventory... 4. list 5. index 7. account
8. register 9. catalogue (catalog)
10. tally sheet
inverse... 8. inverted, opposite,
reversed
inversely club–shaped... 9. obclavate
inversely oval... 7. obovate
inversion... 8. overturn, reversal
9. overthrow, reversion
10. conversion 12. introversion
invert... 7. capsize, convert, pervert
(obs), reverse, tip over 8. overturn
9. transpose 10. turn turtle
invertebrate... 5. polyp 6. insect,
sponge 7. mollusk 9. spineless
10. weak–willed
invest... 3. don 4. vest, wrap
5. array, dress, endow, indue, spend
6. clothe 7. empower, envelop,
instate 8. surround
invest (pert to)...
authority.. 8. accredit, sanction
ministry.. 6. ordain
sovereignty.. 8. enthrone
investigate... 3. pry 4. sift 5. probe,
study, track 6. excuse, search
7. discuss, explore 8. indagate
10. scrutinize
investigation... 6. examen 7. inquiry,
zetetic 8. research 9. discovery,
heuristic 10. discussion
11. examination
investiture... 7. clothes, vesture
8. clothing, covering 9. induction
10. holy orders, investment (money),
ordination 11. instatement
12. installation 15. enfranchisement
investment... 5. siege 7. finance,
garment 8. blockade, clothing,
covering, purchase, vestment
9. endowment 11. empowerment
investment list... 9. portfolio
inveterate... 3. old 6. rooted
7. chronic 8. habitual, hardened
9. confirmed, ingrained
10. deep–rooted 11. established,
traditional 15. long–established
invidious... 6. odious, ornery
7. envious, hateful 9. malignant
14. discriminating (unjustly)
invigorate... 3. pep 5. brace, cheer,
nerve, renew 6. vivify 7. animate,
enliven, fortify, refresh 8. energize
9. stimulate 10. exhilarate,
strengthen
invigorating... 4. cool 5. tonic
8. cheering 10. energizing,
life–giving, refreshing 11. stimulating
invincible... 10. unbeatable
11. indomitable 13. unconquerable
inviolate... 6. sacred, secret
8. faithful, unbroken 9. unchanged,

undefiled, unstained **10.** inviolable, unimpaired, unprofound
13. incorruptible

invisible ... **3.** hid **6.** hidden
10. indistinct, unapparent
13. infinitesimal, undiscernible, unperceivable

Invisible, The ... **3.** God
11. Rosicrucian **16.** German Protestant

invisible emanation ... **4.** aura

invitation ... **3.** bid **4.** call **7.** bidding, summons **10.** allurement, inducement
12. solicitation

invite ... **3.** ask, beg, bid, try **4.** bade
5. court, order, tempt **6.** allure, entice, induce **7.** request, solicit
9. encourage

invocation ... **4.** call, plea, rite
6. appeal, prayer, sermon
7. summons **8.** entreaty
11. conjuration, incantation
12. supplication

invoice ... **4.** bill **7.** account (written)
8. manifest **9.** reckoning **12.** bill of lading

invoke ... **3.** beg **4.** pray **6.** appeal
7. address, conjure, entreat, implore, solicit **8.** draw down **10.** supplicate

involuntary ... **9.** not willed, reluctant, unwilling, unwitting **11.** instinctive, spontaneous **13.** unintentional

involve ... **3.** lap **4.** coil, wind, wrap
5. imply **6.** employ, entail, evince, infold **7.** concern, ensnare, entwine, envelop, include **8.** interest
9. embarrass, implicate
10. complicate **11.** incriminate

involved ... **7.** complex, implied
8. involute, tortuous **9.** engrossed
10. implicated

involving punishment ... **8.** punitive

invulnerable ... **10.** invincible
11. impregnable, insuperable
12. impenetrable, unassailable

inward ... **4.** into **5.** entad, inner
6. inside **7.** ingoing, muffled
8. interior, internal **9.** spiritual
10. internally

inwards ... **8.** entrails **10.** intestines

Io ... **7.** goddess (Gr) **9.** butterfly, satellite (of Jupiter)

iodine, iodin (pert to) ...
comb form .. **3.** iod **4.** iodo
compound .. **6.** iodide
containing .. **5.** iodic **6.** iodous
poisoning .. **6.** iodism **9.** iododerma
source .. **4.** kelp **8.** sea water **9.** salt peter **12.** thryoid gland
standard .. **9.** idiometry
substitute .. **7.** Aristol

ion ... **5.** anion **6.** cation (kation)
8. electron, particle (Elec)

Ionian (pert to) ...
city .. **4.** Teos (birthplace of Anacreon)
islands .. **5.** Greek **9.** Asia Minor
mode (Mus) .. **6.** Lydian

Ionic (pert to) ...
architecture .. **5.** Order
dialect .. **5.** Greek
poetry .. **4.** foot **5.** meter
printing .. **4.** type

iota ... **3.** ace, jot **4.** atom, mite, star (9th brightest), whit **6.** letter (Gr), tittle **8.** particle

Iowa ...
capital .. **9.** Des Moines
city .. **4.** Ames **8.** Waterloo
9. Davenport, Fort Dodge, Marquette, Sioux City **10.** West Branch **11.** Cedar Rapids
famed attractions .. **10.** Hoover home **12.** Effigy Mounds **17.** Little Brown Church
famed first .. **12.** apple orchard (1799)
famed names .. **6.** Joliet **7.** Dubuque
9. Marquette
flower .. **8.** wild rose
locale .. **8.** farm belt (Midwest)
river .. **8.** Missouri **11.** Mississippi
State admission .. **11.** twenty–ninth (1846)
State nickname .. **7.** Hawkeye

ipecac ... **4.** evea **6.** emetic **7.** emetive
9. purgative

irade ... **6.** decree (Turk)

Iran ... see also *Iranian*
capital .. **7.** Teheran (Tehran)
city .. **6.** Abadan, Shiraz **7.** Isfahan
conqueror .. **6.** Darius **9.** Alexander
founder .. **5.** Cyrus (the Great)
lake .. **7.** Rezaieh
mountain .. **6.** Elburz, Zagros
8. Damavand (peak)
parliament .. **6.** Majlis (Mejlis)
people .. **3.** Tat **7.** Indians
ruins .. **10.** Persepolis (Shiraz)

Iranian (pert to) ...
almond .. **5.** badam
books .. **5.** Koran, Yasma **6.** Avesta
country .. **4.** Elam **5.** Media
demigod .. **4.** Yima
demon .. **7.** Ahriman
diadem .. **3.** taj
dynasty .. **6.** Safavi, Seljuk
10. Sassanidae
fire worshiper .. **5.** Parsi (Parsee)
god .. **6.** Ormazd (Supreme) **7.** Mithras
Koran student .. **5.** hafiz
poet .. **4.** Omar **5.** Saadi
Relig founder .. **9.** Zoroaster
tapestry .. **7.** susanee
tentmaker .. **4.** Omar

Iraq, Mesopotamia ...
capital .. **6.** Bagdad (Baghdad)
culture (anc) .. **8.** Sumerian
historic city .. **2.** Ur **5.** Eridu
7. Babylon, Nineveh
historic Valley .. **15.** Tigris–Euphrates
port .. **5.** Basra (Busrah)
product .. **3.** oil **4.** date **5.** sheep
river .. **6.** Tigris **9.** Euphrates

irascibility ... **3.** ire **6.** choler
9. crossness, testiness **10.** perversity
11. waspishness **12.** churlishness, irritability

irate ... **3.** hot **5.** angry, wroth
7. enraged **8.** incensed **9.** irascible

ire ... **5.** anger, wrath **7.** madness
8. vexation **9.** vehemence
10. enragement, resentment
12. exasperation

ireful ... **5.** angry, wroth **7.** iracund
9. irascible **10.** passionate

Ireland ... 4. Eire, Erin 5. Irena 6. Old
    Sod, Ulster 8. Hibernia 9. Innisfail
    11. Emerald Isle, Erin go brath
    14. Ireland Forever
Ireland (pert to) ... see also *Irish*
Bay .. 6. Bantry, Dingle, Galway
    7. Donegal
capital .. 4. Tara (old) 6. Dublin
channel .. 5. North 9. St George's
city .. 4. Cobh (Queenstown), Cork,
    Tara 6. Galway, Tralee, Ulster
    7. Belfast, Donegal, Kildare, Wexford
    8. Kilkenny, Limerick 9. Tipperary
island .. 4. Aran
legislature .. 4. Dail
mountain .. 7. Errigal 13. Carrantuohill
river .. 3. Lee 4. Erne, Suir 6. Liffey
    7. Shannon
sea .. 5. Irish
seaport .. 4. Cobh 6. Tralee
seat of archbishops .. 6. Armagh
irenic ... 7. henotic 8. peaceful
    11. harmonizing 12. conciliatory
iridescent ... 7. opaline 9. prismatic
    10. opalescent
iris ... 4. flag 6. flower 7. rainbow
iris (pert to) ...
astronomy .. 8. asteroid (7th)
color .. 11. reddish–blue
eye part .. 4. uvea 5. irian
Florentine .. 5. orris (orrice)
inflammation .. 6. iritis
mineral .. 6. quartz (iridescent)
Iris, goddess ... 7. rainbow
Irish (pert to) ...
alphabet (early) .. 4. ogam (ogham)
battle cry .. 3. abu (aboo) 9. To
    Victory 11. Erin go brath
cattle .. 5. Kerry
churchman .. 7. erenach (herenach)
club, cudgel .. 10. shillalagh (shillalah)
convention (anc) .. 4. Feis 10. Feis of
    Tara
cordial .. 10. usquebaugh
dagger (anc) .. 5. skean
dance .. 3. jig 4. rink 10. rinkafadda
emblem .. 8. shamrock
exclamation .. 3. aru 5. arrah
fairy, spirit .. 4. shee (sidhe)
    7. banshee (banshie) 10. leprechaun
festival .. 4. feis
goblin .. 5. pooka
god .. 3. Ler (sea)
goddess .. 4. Dana
king's home .. 4. Tara
landholding .. 7. rundale
legislature .. 10. Oireachtas (House)
    11. Dail Eireann (Chamber)
    13. Seanad Eireann (Senate)
liquor house (illegal) .. 7. shebeen
love, sweetheart .. 3. gra
moss .. 9. carrageen
peasant .. 4. kern (lerne)
pig .. 5. bonav
policeman .. 8. spalpeen
potato city .. 7. Youghal
queen (folklore) .. 4. Medb
Society (secret) .. 6. Fenian
soldier .. 4. kern (kerne) 10. galloglass
tenant .. 4. saer
tribal lord .. 6. tanist
verse .. 4. rann

whisky, whiskey (illegal) .. 6. poteen
    (potheen)
Irish (people) ...
ancestor (fabled) .. 3. Mil 6. Miledh
author .. 4. Shaw 5. Wilde
chemist .. 5. Boyle
composer .. 7. Herbert
Irishman .. 4. Aire, Celt, Gael
    6. Teague 8. Milesian 9. Hibernian,
    Orangeman 10. Eireannach
lawyer .. 6. brehon
Nuns (Order) .. 15. Ladies of Loretto
patriot .. 5. Emmet, Tandy 6. Oakboy
poet .. 5. Colum, Moore, Wilde, Yeats
    7. Russell (George)
refugee .. 7. fuidhir
saint (patron) .. 7. Patrick
Saxon .. 8. Sasanach
sea robbers (Myth) .. 9. Fomorians
surgeon .. 6. Colles
tribe (family) .. 4. sept 5. cinel
irk ... 3. vex 4. bore, tire 5. annoy,
    weary 6. nettle 7. disgust, trouble
    10. exasperate
irksome ... 5. vexed, weary 7. operose,
    painful, tedious 8. annoying
    9. fatiguing, vexatious, wearisome
    10. burdensome, exhausting,
    monotonous 12. disagreeable
iron ... 2. Fe (symbol) 5. harsh, metal,
    power, press 6. ferrum, fetter,
    mangle, pistol, severe 7. firearm,
    manacle, shackle, sideros
    8. firmness, handcuff, hardness,
    strength 10. inflexible, unyielding
    11. unrelenting
iron (pert to) ...
casting .. 5. mitis
comb form .. 5. ferro 6. sidero
compound .. 5. steel
containing .. 6. ferric
dog .. 7. firedog
dross .. 6. sinter
herb .. 8. Vernonia 9. ironweeds
lump .. 3. pig
magnet .. 8. armature
meteoric .. 8. siderite
ore .. 7. turgite 8. hematite, siderite
    11. sesquioxide
ref to .. 6. ferric 7. ferrous
    8. siderous
rod .. 5. punty (puntee)
salts of .. 10. chalybeate
sand .. 7. iserine
science of .. 10. siderology
symbol .. 2. Fe
tailor's .. 5. goose
tool .. 6. lifter
vessel, basket .. 7. cresset
ironclad ... 6. severe 7. armored,
    Monitor (ship) 8. exacting, rigorous
    9. stringent
ironic, ironical ... 3. dry 7. cynical,
    satiric 9. sarcastic 10. figurative
    11. Rabelaisian
irons ... 5. gyves 6. chains 7. fetters
    8. manacles, shackles 9. handcuffs
Ironsides ... 7. cavalry (Cromwell's)
    8. Cromwell
ironwood ... 4. acle 5. olive 6. colima
    7. breakax 8. hornbeam
    9. stavewood

irony ... 6. banter, satire 7. lampoon, sarcasm 8. ridicule

Iroquoian Indian ... 4. Erie 5. Huron 6. Cayuga, Mohawk, Oneida, Seneca 7. Wyandot 8. Cherokee, Onondaga 9. Conestoga, Tuscarora

Iroquois (pert to) ...
famed .. 11. Five Nations
native of .. 7. New York 9. Wisconsin
tribes (Five) .. 6. Cayuga, Mohawk, Oneida, Seneca 8. Onondaga

irrational ... 6. stupid 9. fanatical, illogical, senseless 10. ridiculous 11. impractical 12. preposterous, unreasonable 13. unintelligent

irregular ... 4. wild 5. erose, rough 6. fitful, rugged, uneven 7. atactic, crooked, devious, erratic, mutable, styptic, unequal 8. aberrent, abnormal, atypical, informal, variable 9. anomalous, desultory, distorted, eccentric, haphazard, orderless, unsettled 10. changeable, immoderate, inconstant 11. intemperate 12. unsystematic

irregularity ... 6. ataxia (muscular) 7. anomaly 8. disorder 9. deviation 10. distortion 11. abnormality, informality 12. eccentricity

irrelevant ... 7. foreign 9. unrelated 10. extraneous 11. impertinent, unessential 12. inconsequent 13. insignificant

irreligious ... 5. pagan 7. godless, impious, profane 11. unreligious

irreparable ... 4. gone, lost 6. ruined 11. irrevocable 12. incorrigible, irremediable 13. irrecoverable, irretrievable

irrepressible ... 7. Homeric (laughter) 12. ungovernable, unrestrained

irrepressible conflict ... 8. civil war

irreproachable ... 7. perfect 9. blameless 10. impeccable, inculpable

irresolute ... 6. fickle, unsure 8. doubtful, unstable 9. uncertain, undecided 10. capricious, changeable, inconstant 12. undetermined

irresolution ... 10. fickleness, indecision 11. fluctuation, uncertainty, vacillation 14. capriciousness

irresponsible ... 6. fickle 7. lawless 8. carefree 9. insolvent 12. independable 13. unaccountable, untrustworthy

irretrievable ... 8. hopeless 9. incurable 11. irreparable 12. irremediable, unchangeable 13. irrecoverable

irreverence ... 7. impiety 8. dishonor 9. profanity 10. disrespect

irrevocable ... 3. end 4. past 5. final 10. inevitable, past recall 11. unalterable 12. beyond recall, unchangeable

irrigate ... 3. wet 5. water 6. dilute, sluice 7. moisten, refresh

irritable ... 4. edgy 5. cross, techy, testy 6. cranky, ornery, touchy 7. fretful, iracund, peevish, tempery,

twitchy 8. snappish

irritate ... 3. irk, nag, vex 4. fret, gall, rasp, rile 5. anger, annoy, chafe, cross, grate, peeve, pique, rouse, sting, tease 6. excite, incite, madden, needle, nettle, rankle 7. incense, provoke 10. exacerbate, exasperate 14. rub the wrong way

irritated ... 4. sore 5. afret, testy 6. peeved 7. annoyed, nettled, rankled 8. provoked

irritation ... 4. itch 5. pique 6. temper 9. annoyance 10. resentment 12. exasperation

irruption ... 5. foray 6. inroad 8. invasion 9. incursion

Irving pseudonym ... 13. Knickerbocker (Diedrich)

is ... 6. exists 10. represents 11. personifies

Isaac (pert to) ...
Bib .. 9. patriarch (Heb)
father of .. 4. Esau 5. Jacob
grandfather of .. 4. Edom
husband of .. 7. Rebekah
son of .. 5. Sarah 7. Abraham

Ishmael (pert to) ...
ancestor .. 11. Ishmaelites
Bib .. 6. pariah 7. outcast
father of .. 8. Nebaioth
son of .. 5. Hagar 7. Abraham

isinglass ... 4. huso, mica 7. gelatin 8. agar–agar

Isis (pert to) ...
daughter of .. 3. Geb, Nut
goddess of .. 9. fertility 10. motherhood
identified with .. 7. Dog Star
mother of .. 4. Sept (Horus)
represented (at times) ..
9. cow–headed
shrine of .. 5. Iseum (Iseium)
wife of .. 6. Osiris

Islam, religion (pert to) ...
founder .. 7. Mahomet
God .. 5. Allah
people .. 7. Moslems
prophet .. 8. Mohammed

Islamic (pert to) ...
convert .. 5. ansar
holy city .. 5. Mecca 6. Medina
mosque .. 6. masjid
pilgrimage .. 5. Kaaba (Caaba) 10. Black Stone
Supreme Being .. 5. Allah
teacher .. 4. alim 5. ulema 6. mullah (mulla)

island ... 3. ait, cay, ile, key 4. calf, cayo, eyot, holm, isle, reef 5. atoll, islet 7. isolate 8. insulate

island (pert to) ...
city .. 8. Montreal
coral .. 5. atoll 8. Zanzibar
enchanted .. 4. Bali
fabled .. 4. Meru 6. Avalon, Bimini 8. Atlantis
fabulous .. 7. Zangbar
group .. 8. Antilles, Marshall 11. archipelago
inhabitant, native .. 7. nesiote 8. islander
universe (Astron) .. 6. galaxy

Island of ...
 Langerhans .. 8. pancreas
 Odysseus .. 6. Ithaca
 Reil .. 5. brain
 Saints .. 4. Erin
Isle of Man ...
 Celtic name .. 4. Manx
 city .. 4. Peel 6. Ramsey 7. Douglas
 division .. 5. Treen
 judge .. 8. deemster (dempster)
 legislature .. 7. Tynwald
 mountain peak .. 8. Snaefell
 Northern point .. 4. Ayre
 site .. 8. Irish sea
Isle of Wight ...
 Queen's summer home .. 12. Osborne
  House
 site .. 10. English Sea
 sport (famed) .. 9. yacht race
 town .. 7. Newport
 watering place .. 4. Ryde
Isles of Galway Bay ... 4. Aran
ism ... 4. cult 5. dogma, ideal, tenet
  6. belief, school, system 8. doctrine,
  practice 11. abnormality
isochromatic ... 9. same color
isochronal ... 9. equal time
  11. uniform time
isocracy ... 9. equal rule 10. equal
  power
isodont (Zool) ... 10. alike teeth
isogonal ... 11. equal angles
isolate ... 4. isle 6. enisle 7. seclude
  8. insulate, separate 9. segregate,
  sequester 10. quarantine
isolation ... 8. escapism, solitude
  9. seclusion 10. insulation, loneliness,
  separation 11. segregation
isomer ... 7. metamer 8. compound
  (Chem)
isonomy ... 11. equal rights
isonym ... 7. paronym 8. same name
isosceles ... 10. equal sides (triangle)
Israel (Bib) ... 4. Jews 5. Jacob, Zions
  13. Hebrew Kingdom
Israel (pert to) ... see also *Israelite*
 appellation .. 8. Jeshurun
 capital .. 9. Jerusalem
 city .. 4. Acre 5. Elath, Haifa, Jaffa
  7. Galilee, Jericho, Tel Aviv
 desert .. 5. Negev
 dust storm .. 7. khamsin
 lawgiver .. 5. Moses
 Plain of .. 6. Sharon
 priest .. 3. Eli
 river .. 6. Jordan
 sea .. Dead 7. Galilee
 song (Zionist) .. 8. Hatikvah
 statesman .. 4. Meir 5. Begin
Israelite (pert to) ...
 hero .. 6. Gideon
 judge .. 4. Elon 8. Jephthah
 king .. 4. Ahab, Jehu, Saul (1st)
  5. David (2nd) 7. Solomon
 lawgiver .. 5. Moses
 priest .. 3. Eli
 tribe .. 3. Dan 5. Asher 6. Reuben
 tribe, priestly .. 4. Levi
issue ... 3. son 4. come, emit, flow,
  gush 5. arise, child, sally, spout,
  stock, topic, utter 6. effect, emerge,
  escape, sortie, source, upshot

7. edition, emanate, proceed, product,
  progeny 8. question 9. emergence,
  offspring, posterity 11. consequence,
  publication
Istanbul (Constantinople) ...
 ancient name .. 9. Byzantium
 capital of .. 6. Turkey (to 1923)
 foreign quarter .. 4. Pera
 Greek quarter .. 5. Fanar
 site .. 8. Bosporus 10. Golden Horn
isthmus (pert to) ...
 American .. 6. Panama
 anatomy .. 6. fauces
 Greek (anc) .. 7. Corinth
 Siam .. 3. Kra
it ... 5. charm, thing 6. itself, person
  7. egotist, pronoun
Ita ... 4. Acta 7. Negrito
Italian (pert to) ... see also *Italy*
 card game .. 5. tarot
 carriage .. 7. vettura
 cathedral .. 5. duomo
 cheese .. 6. Romano 8. Parmesan
  10. mozzarella
 condiment .. 6. tamara (tamarind)
 deity .. 4. faun
 dish .. 5. pizza 7. calzone 8. braciola
  11. saltimbocca
 dome, peak .. 4. cima
 entertainment .. 5. festa 7. ridotto
 food .. see *pasta*
 grape .. 6. verdea
 hamlet .. 5. casal
 house .. 4. casa 6. casino (summer)
 inlay .. 6. tarsia
 inn .. 7. locanda
 innkeeper .. 7. padrone
 lady .. 5. donna 7. signora
 lake .. 4. lago
 law .. 6. Latium 8. Jus Latii
 lover .. 7. amoroso
 magistrate (anc) .. 8. podestra
 marble .. 4. Neri 7. carrara, cipolin
 marsh .. 7. maremma
 opera house .. 7. La Scala (1778)
 peasant .. 7. paesano 9. contadino
 photographers .. 9. paparazzi (press)
 pottery .. 8. majolica
 secret society .. 6. Maffia (Mafia)
  7. Camorra
 sheep .. 6. merino
 vessel .. 9. trabacolo
 wind (hot) .. 7. sirocco
 wine .. 4. Asti 5. Capri 7. Chianti,
  Orvieto 12. Asti Spumante
Italian (pert to people) ...
 anti-Fascist .. 6. Sforza
 architect .. 8. Bramante
 astronomer .. 6. Secchi 7. Galileo
 author .. 5. Dante
 deity .. 6. Faunus
 dictator .. 9. Mussolini
 educator .. 10. Montessori
 explorer .. 8. Columbus, Vespucci
  9. Marco Polo
 family (princely) .. 4. Este 5. Doria
  6. Medici
 family (violin) .. 5. Amati
 friend (outside) .. 10. Italophile
 geographer .. 5. Amoretti
 goddess .. 3. Ops 4. Juno 5. Diana
 hero .. 7. Orlando

historian.. 4. Dion 5. Cantu
king.. 7. Umberto
musician.. 5. Guido, Verdi 7. Puccini,
Rossini 9. Scarlatti
naturalist.. 4. Poli
noblewoman.. 8. Marchesa
11. Marchioness
painter.. 5. Lippi 6. Giotti 7. da
Vinci, Raphael 10. Botticelli
11. Della Robbia 12. Michelangelo
patriot.. 7. Foscolo 9. Garibaldi
people.. 7. Italici 8. Umbrians
9. Etruscans, Ligurians
philosopher.. 7. Rosmini
physician.. 5. Abano 9. Eustachio
physicist.. 5. Volta 7. Galvani,
Marconi
poet.. 4. Redi 5. Dante, Tasso
7. Manzoni 8. Annunzio, Casanova,
Petrarch 9. Boccaccio
saint.. 4. Neri 7. Aquinas (Thomas)
sculptor.. 5. Dupre, Leoni
8. Ammanati 12. Michelangelo
singer.. 5. Patti 6. Caruso
statesman.. 5. Rossi 8. Gioberti
11. Machiavelli
theologian.. 7. Peronne
tribe (anc).. 5. Aequi
Italy...
Alps.. 5. Cozie 6. Carnac, Julian
7. Atesine, Letiche, Pennine
8. Maritime 9. Lepontine
capital.. 4. Rome
city.. 4. Lodi, Pisa 5. Anona, Fiume,
Genoa, Milan, Padua, Pavia, Trent,
Turin 6. Mantua, Modena, Naples,
Spezia, Venice, Verona 7. Messina,
Palermo, Pompeii, Ravenna, Trieste
8. Brandisi, Florence, Sorrento
commune.. 6. Rivoli (Hist) 7. Trieste
country (anc).. 7. Etruria, Lucania,
Tuscany
gulf.. 7. Salerno
historical site.. 10. Blue Grotto
18. Leaning Tower of Pisa
island.. 4. Elba 5. Capri, Leros
6. Eschia, Sicily 8. Sardinia
lake.. 4. Como 6. Albano, Lugano
8. Maggiore
mountain.. 4. Alps, Rosa 5. Blanc
12. Gran Paradiso
port (fishing).. 6. Amalfi
resort.. 4. Lido 5. Capri 6. Agnone
7. Riviera
river.. 2. Po 4. Arno 5. Tiber
sea.. 6. Ionian 8. Apennine

10. Tyrrhenian
strait.. 7. Messina, Obranto
volcano.. 4. Etna 8. Vesuvius
9. Stromboli
itch... 4. reef, riff 5. mange, psora
6. desire, eczema 7. scabies, sycosis
9. cacoethes, hankering, psoriasis,
sensation 10. irritation
ite... 8. adherent, disciple, follower
item... 3. bit 4. news 5. asset, entry,
scrap, topic 6. detail 7. article,
integer 9. commodity
10. memorandum 11. information
iter... 4. eyre, road (Rom) 7. circuit
iterate... 6. recite, repeat, retell,
review 7. recount 8. rehearse
iteration... 5. recap 10. repetition
11. restatement
ithand... 8. constant, diligent
14. unintermittent
itinerant... 5. mover, nomad 6. roamer
7. nomadic 8. gadabout 9. traveling,
unsettled, wandering, wayfaring
itinerary... 4. gest (royal), plan
5. route 6. prayer, record
8. register, roadbook 9. directory,
guidebook
Ivanhoe (pert to)...
author.. 5. Scott
character.. 5. Boeuf 6. Cedric,
Rowena, Ulrica
hero.. 7. Ivanhoe
ivories (pert to)...
anatomy.. 5. teeth
game.. 4. dice
piano.. 4. keys
ivory (pert to)...
anatomy.. 5. tooth 7. dentine
block.. 4. dice 7. tessera
carving.. 9. toreutics
color.. 5. white (off)
Latin.. 4. ebur
mixture (dust, cement).. 7. eburine
plum.. 11. wintergreen
tower.. 7. retreat
ivy... 5. Rheus, sumac 11. Hedera
helix
iwa... 11. frigate bird
IWW... 6. sab–cat (emblem), wabbly
(Chin), wobbly
Izaac Walton... 9. fisherman
izar (Hind)... 4. star 7. garment 9. loin
.cloth
izle... 4. root 5. ember, spark
Izmir... 6. Smyrna
izzat... 5. honor 6. credit 8. prestige
10. reputation

J

J... 3. Jay 6. letter (10th)
ja (Ger)... 3. yes
jaal goat... 4. ibex 5. beden
jab... 3. dig, hit, jag 4. poke, prod,
   stab 5. punch 6. strike, thrust
jabber... 4. chat 5. prate 6. babble,
   gabble, jargon 7. chatter, twaddle
   8. nonsense 9. gibberish
Jabberwock... 6. Jubjub 7. monster
   (Through the Looking Glass)
Jabberwocky... 4. poem 6. prolix
   8. nonsense 10. double talk
jabble... 6. splash 7. dashing
   8. rippling 9. agitation, confusion,
   splashing
jabiru... 5. stork
jack... 3. can, jug, man 4. card, coat,
   flag, male, pump 5. hoist, knave,
   money 6. lifter, sailor 7. mariner
   8. nickname
jackal... 3. dog (wild) 4. dieb, kola,
   Thos 7. cat's-paw 8. henchman
jackass... 3. ass 4. deer (mule), dolt,
   fool, hare, nerd 6. clover, donkey,
   rabbit 7. morwong, penguin, witling
   9. blockhead
jackdaw... 3. daw, kae 4. crow
   7. grackle
jacket... 4. coat, Eton, pelt 5. cover
   (book) 6. blazer, blouse, bolero,
   casing, jerkin, jumper, reefer
   7. garment, Mae West, wrapper
jacket (pert to)...
   Arctic.. 6. anorak
   armor.. 5. acton
   Eskimo...6. temiak
   horseback riding.. 7. hacking (jacket)
   knitted.. 6. jersey, sontag 7. sweater
   8. cardigan
   Levant.. 5. grego
   Scottish.. 4. jupe
   Spanish.. 8. chaqueta
Jack Ketch... 7. hangman (Eng)
   11. executioner (public)
jackknife... 6. barlow 8. penknife
   11. toadstabber, toadsticker
jackstones... 4. dibs, game
   7. pebbles
Jacob... 6. Israel 9. patriarch
Jacob (pert to)...
   brother.. 4. Edom, Esau
   daughter.. 5. Dinah
   father-in-law.. 5. Laban
   parents.. 5. Isaac 7. Rebekah
   retreat.. 5. Haran
   son.. 3. Gad, Dan 4. Levi 5. Asher,
   Judah 6. Reuben (oldest)
   wife.. 4. Leah 6. Rachel
Jacobin... 4. Club 5. Friar (Dominican)
   7. plotter, radical, Society

   8. Democrat (Fr 1789)
Jacob's ladder... 4. herb 8. hyacinth
   10. belladonna 11. bittersweet
   12. Solomon's seal
jade... 4. bore, tire 5. green, horse,
   stone, wench 7. fatigue 8. strumpet
jaded... 8. fatigued, shopworn
   9. dissolute 10. bedraggled
jaeger (jager)... 4. gull (like), skua
   6. teaser
jager... 6. hunter 7. diamond
   8. huntsman, rifleman
jagged... 5. erose, rough, sharp
   6. barbed, pinked, ragged, rugged
   7. cutting, notched, pointed, slashed
   8. serrated 10. saw-toothed
jagua... 4. palm 7. genipap
jaguar... 3. cat 4. puma 5. ounce
   6. cougar 7. panther 11. snow
   leopard
Jah (Heb)... 3. God 7. Jehovah
jai alai... 4. game 5. cesta 6. pelota
   7. fronton
jail... 3. jug 4. brig, gaol 5. clink
   6. cooler, lockup 7. slammer (sl)
   8. hoosegow 9. Bridewell (London),
   calaboose 11. incarcerate
jailer, jailor... 5. guard 6. gaoler,
   keeper, warden 7. alcaide, turnkey
jail sentence... 3. rap
jalousie... 5. blind 7. shutter
Jamaica...
   beverage.. 3. rum 4. jake
   capital.. 8. Kingston
   cucumber.. 7. gherkin
   ebony.. 10. crocuswood
   island.. 10. West Indies
   pepper.. 8. allspice
   tree (drug).. 7. quassia
jangle... 5. brawl, chide, noise, prate
   6. babble, gossip 7. chatter, grate on,
   quarrel, ringing, whimper
Janizary (anc)... 5. slave 7. soldier
Janus (Rom)... 3. god (two-faced)
Japan... 5. Jipun (Chin), Nihon, Nisei
   6. Nippon 7. Cipango (of Marco
   Polo)
Japan... see also *Japanese*
   capital.. 4. Nara (anc) 5. Kyoto (anc),
   Tokyo
   city.. 4. Kobe 7. Sapporo
   8. Kawasaki, Kumamoto, Nagasaki,
   Yokohama, Yokosuka 9. Hiroshima
   10. Kitakyushu
   current.. 8. Kuroshio
   islands.. 6. Honshu, Kyushu
   7. Shikoku 9. Haikkaido (Yezo)
   mountain.. 8. Fujiyama
   naval base.. 8. Yokosuka
   port.. 4. Kobe 5. Osaka 6. Nagoya

8. Yokohama
protectorate.. 9. Manchukuo
river.. 4. Yalu (Annock)
shrine.. 7. Toshogu (at Nikko)
spring (hot).. 6. Hakone
volcano.. 9. Asamayama
Japanese (pert to)...
airplane.. 4. Zero
annals, chronicles.. 7. Nihongi
apricot.. 3. ume
army (conscription).. 6. geneki
army officer.. 7. samurai
art of self–defense.. 4. judo 7. jujitsu
(jujutsu, jiujutsu)
badge (family).. 3. mon
banjo.. 7. samisen
battle cry.. 6. banzai
brazier.. 7. hibachi
button (carved).. 7. netsuke
cape.. 4. mino
cedar.. 4. sugi
chess.. 5. shogi
church (Buddhist).. 4. tera
circle, ship (suffix).. 4. maru
deer.. 4. sika
dog.. 6. tanate
drama.. 2. no 6. no–gaku
drink.. 4. sake
entertainer.. 6. geisha
festival.. 3. Bon 15. Feast of Lanterns
fish.. 3. ayu, tai 4. fugu
flower arranging.. 7. ikebano
flower design.. 10. Shin, Soe, Tai
(Heaven, Man, Earth)
game (forfeits).. 3. ken
gateway.. 5. torii
girdle.. 3. obi
girdle box.. 4. inro
greeting.. 6. banzai
herb (edible).. 3. udo
legislature.. 4. Diet
litter (covered).. 7. norimon
news agency.. 5. domei
newspaper (Tokyo).. 12. Asahi
Shimbun
outlaw.. 5. ronin
pagoda.. 3. taa
painting school.. 4. Kano
palanquin, litter.. 4. pago 7. norimon
persimmon.. 4. kaki
plant.. 3. udo (edible) 6. sugamo
porgy.. 3. tai (fish)
pottery.. 7. Satsuma
prefecture.. 2. fu
radish.. 6. daikon
religion.. 6. Shinto 8. Buddhism
9. Shintoism
robe.. 6. kimono
salmon.. 4. masu
screen (partition).. 5. shoji
seaweed.. 4. nori
self–defense, art of.. 4. judo 7. jujitsu
(jujutsu, jiujutsu)
ship suffix.. 4. maru
shout (greeting).. 6. banzai
shrine.. 7. Toshogu (at Nikko)
silk.. 7. habutai 8. chirimen (crepe)
silkworm.. 4. eria 7. yamamai
sock (separate big toe).. 4. tabi
song.. 3. uta
suicide.. 7. seppuku 8. hara–kiri
(hari–kari)

tree.. 5. akeki, kiaki 7. camphor,
hinooki
verse.. 5. hokku, tanka 6. haikai
wrestling.. 4. sumo
Japanese people...
aborigine.. 4. Ainu (Aino)
admiral.. 3. Ito 4. Togo
admirer.. 11. Japanophile
American–born.. 5. Issei, Nisei
army officer.. 7. samurai
baron.. 6. daimio
Buddha, Great.. 8. Daibutsu
caste (nobility).. 7. kwazoku
clan.. 7. Satsuma 8. Fujiwara,
Minamoto
deity.. 5. Amita (Amida) 8. Amitabba
Emperor.. 8. Hirohito
Emperor, founder.. 5. Jimmu (660
BC)
Emperor, title.. 5. Tenno 6. Mikado
God of Happiness.. 7. Jurojin
10. Fuku–roku ju
nobility (caste).. 7. kwazoku
outlaw.. 5. ronin
paradise (of Amita).. 4. Jodo
race.. 4. Ainu
jape... 4. fool, jeer, jest, jipe, mock
5. fraud, trick 6. banter, deride
japery... 4. jest, joke 7. jesting
8. trickery 10. buffoonery
jar... 4. jolt 5. grate, shake 6. incase,
rattle 7. startle, vibrate 8. preserve
9. vibration
jar... 3. jug, urn 4. ewer, lute
(rubber), olla 5. cadus (anc), crock,
cruse 6. dolium, goglet, hydria
7. amphora, terrine 10. jardiniere
jararaca... 7. serpent 10. fer–de–lance
11. jararacussu
jardiniere... 3. jar, jug, urn 4. vase
5. stand (plant) 9. flowerpot
jargon... 4. cant 5. argot, idiom, lingo,
slang 6. drivel, patois, patter, zircon
7. Chinook, Yiddish 8. nonsense
9. gibberish 10. vocabulary (secret)
jasmine, jasmin... 4. bela 5. color,
papaw 7. jessamy 9. jessamine
Jason (pert to)...
friend, sweetheart.. 5. Medea
heroes.. 9. Argonauts
quest.. 12. Golden Fleece
ship.. 4. Argo
son.. 5. Aeson
uncle.. 6. Pelias
jaundice... 7. disease, icterus
8. jealousy 9. prejudice
10. yellowness
jaunt... 4. ride, trip 6. ramble
7. journey 9. excursion
jaunty... 4. airy 5. perky, showy, smart
6. dapper, rakish 7. finical, stylish
12. lighthearted
Java... see also *Javanese*
city.. 7. Batavia, Jakarta (Djakarta)
8. Samarang, Surabaya 9. Surakarta
island group.. 10. East Indies
Java Man (anc).. 15. Pithecanthropus
(erectus)
location.. 7. equator 16. Malay
Archipelago
Javanese (pert to)...
arrow poison.. 4. upas

badger.. 5. ratel 6. teledu
carriage.. 4. sado (sadoo)
cotton.. 5. kapok
dancers.. 6. bedoyo
dog (wild).. 5. adjag
ox (wild).. 7. banteng
pantomime.. 6. topeng
plum.. 5. jambo (jambul) 6. lomboy
puppet show.. 6. wajang (wayang)
rice field.. 5. sawah
squirrel.. 8. jelerang
temple.. 6. chandi (candi)
tree.. 4. upas 5. ligas 7. gondang
javelin... 3. bat 4. dart, pike 5. lance,
  spear 6. jereed (jirid) 7. assagai
  (assegai)
javelina... 4. boar 7. peccary
jaw.. 3. maw 4. chop 5. scold
  6. berate, splash 7. chatter, orifice
  8. scolding
jaw (pert to)...
angle of.. 6. gonion
bone.. 7. maxilla 8. mandible
comb form.. 6. gnatho
disease.. 7. lump jaw
  13. actinomycosis
formation.. 8. gnathism
Greek for.. 7. gnathos
muscle.. 8. masseter
ref to.. 5. malar 7. gnathic
without.. 8. agnathic
jawab... 5. reply 6. answer, mosque
  (false Arch)
jay... 3. gae 4. bird, blue, dupe
  9. chatterer
jayhawker... 6. Kansan, spider
  7. soldier 8. guerilla
Jayhawker State... 6. Kansas
jazz... 4. jive 5. dance, music, swing
  9. syncopate 11. syncopation
jealous... 7. envious, zealous
  8. doubtful, grudging, vigilant,
  watchful 9. jaundiced 10. solicitous
  11. distrustful 12. apprehensive
jealousy... 4. envy 5. doubt 7. rivalry
  8. distrust, jaundice, mistrust
  12. covetousness
jeans... 8. overalls, trousers
jeer... 4. gibe, hoot, jape, mock
  5. flout, scoff, sneer, taunt 6. deride
  8. ridicule
Jehovah... 3. God, Jah 4. Lord
  6. Yahweh (Yahwe) 8. Almighty (The)
  12. Supreme Being
Jehovah's comfort... 8. Nehemiah
jehu (humorous)... 8. coachman
  10. fast driver
Jehu's father (Bib)... 11. Jehoshaphat
jejune... 3. dry 4. arid 5. banal,
  empty, stale, trite 6. barren, hungry,
  meager 7. insipid 8. foodless
  12. unproductive
jelly... 3. jam, rob (rhob) 4. food,
  sapa 5. aspic 6. pectin 7. gelatin
  8. gelatine, Kei Apple 10. semiliquid
jellyfish... 5. quarl 6. coward, medusa
  7. acaleph 8. weakling 9. Acalephae
jellyfish (pert to)...
class.. 9. Acalephae
group.. 10. discophora
part.. 6. pileus 8. umbrella
  10. exumbrella

stinging.. 9. sea nettle
swim organ.. 5. stene
jemmy... 4. boot (riding) 5. jimmy,
  lever 7. crowbar 9. greatcoat
Jena (Ger)... 5. glass 6. battle (1806)
jenna... 8. Paradise (Moham)
jennet... 3. ass 5. horse 6. donkey
jenny... 3. ass 5. crane (moving)
  6. female 8. airplane 13. spinning
  wheel
jenny (pert to)...
billiards.. 6. hazard
folklore.. 4. wren
howlet.. 3. owl 5. owlet
machine.. 13. spinning wheel
spinner.. 3. fly (angling)
jeopardize... 4. risk 6. expose, hazard
  7. imperil 8. endanger
jeopardy... 4. risk 5. peril 6. hazard,
  menace
jeremiad... 3. woe 6. lament, plaint,
  tirade 9. complaint
jerk... 3. tic 4. flip, jolt, push, yank
  5. shake, tweak 6. chorea, thrust,
  twitch 7. charqui
jerkin... 4. coat 6. jacket, salmon
  9. gyrfalcon, waistcoat
jeroboam... 4. bowl 6. battle, goblet
Jeroboam... 4. King (of Israel)
jerry... 5. aware 6. flimsy, Geremy,
  German 7. knowing 9. beer house,
  conscious
jersey... 5. cloth 6. cattle, jacket
Jersey Red... 5. swine
  11. Duroc–Jersey
Jersey tea... 11. wintergreen
  12. checkerberry
Jerusalem... 5. Ariel, Salem 8. Holy
  City 11. City of David
Jerusalem (pert to)...
artichoke.. 7. girasol 10. topinambou
capital of.. 6. Israel
corn.. 5. durra
Garden.. 10. Gethsemane
haddock.. 4. opah
hill.. 6. Olivet 13. Mount of Olives
historic site.. 11. Wailing Wall
  12. Mosque of Omar 13. Mount of
  Olives (Olivet) 18. Garden of
  Gethsemane
mosque.. 4. Omar
pool.. 6. Siloam 8. Bethesda
region.. 5. Perea 6. Gilead
Relig.. 7. Judaism 12. Christianity
  13. Mohammedanism
spring.. 5. Gihon 6. Siloam
star.. 7. salsify
Sunday.. 11. Refreshment
thorn.. 7. catechu 12. Christ's–thorn
willow.. 8. oleaster
jess... 5. strap (hawk's leg) 6. ribbon
jessamy... 3. fop 5. dandy 7. jasmine
jessant (Her)... 7. issuing 9. lying over
jessur... 5. viper (Russell's)
jest... 3. fun, mot, wit 4. fool, jape,
  jeer, joke, quip 5. droll, prank, sport,
  taunt, trick 6. banter, rail at, trifle
  8. ridicule
jester... 4. fool, mime 5. clown
  7. buffoon, goliard 8. humorist
  11. merry–andrew
jester's cap... 7. coxcomb

Jesuit... 5. Order 7. casuist, sectary 8. explorer 9. intriguer 10. missionary 14. Society of Jesus (S J)

jet... 3. jut 4. gush, spew 5. black, ebony, ladle, raven, spout, spray, spurt 6. burner, nozzle, stream 7. mineral, outpour 8. spouting 9. black onyx

jet coal... 6. cannel

jetty... 4. mole, pier 5. wharf 8. buttress

Jew... 6. Essene, Hebrew, Semite 9. Israelite

jewel... 3. gem 4. naif, opal, ruby 5. beryl, stone 6. garnet 7. bearing, diamond, emerald 8. ornament 9. bespangle, brilliant 10. rhinestone 13. precious stone, precious thing

jewel cutter... 10. lapidarist

jeweler's glass... 5. loupe

jeweler's weight... 4. tola 5. carat (karat, kerat)

jewelry... 3. ice 4. ring 5. paste 6. parure, strass 7. costume 10. bijouterie

Jewish... 6. Hebrew 7. Yiddish 9. Israelite

Jewish (pert to)...
  academy (Talmudic).. 8. Yeshinah
  adherent.. 7. Zionist
  benediction.. 5. Shema
  Bible.. 5. Torah (Tora) 6. Gemara, Talmud 7. Haggada, Halakah 10. Pentateuch
  calendar.. 4. Adar, Ahab, Elul, Iyar 5. Nisan, Sivan, Tebet 6. Kislev, Shebat, Tammuz, Tishri, Veadar (leap year) 7. Heshvan
  Day of Atonement.. 9. Yom Kippur
  Dispersion.. 8. Diaspora
  divorce.. 3. get (gett)
  doctrine.. 7. Mishnah (Mishna)
  enemy (Bib).. 5. Haman
  faction.. 7. Zealots
  father, patriarch.. 7. Abraham
  festival.. 5. Purim, Seder (Sedar) 7. Sukkoth
  greeting, peace.. 6. Shalom
  high priest.. 3. Eli 4. Ezra 5. Aaron, Annas 8. Caiaphas
  high priest costume.. 4. urim 5. abnet 7. petalon, tallith, yamilke
  historian.. 8. Josephus
  holiday.. 7. Sukkoth 8. Hanukkah (Hannukka), Tishabov 11. Rosh Hashana (Rosh Hashonoh)
  horn.. 7. shophar (shofar)
  lawgiver.. 5. Moses
  leader.. 8. Nehemiah
  liturgy.. 6. minhah (PM) 9. shaharith (AM)
  loaves (unleavened).. 9. shewbread (showbread)
  mystical writing.. 6. atbash
  patriots.. 9. Maccabees
  prayer book.. 6. siddur
  prophet.. 6. Elijah
  psalms of praise.. 6. hallel
  quarter (living).. 6. ghetto
  ram's horn.. 7. shophar (shofar)
  slaughter (Relig).. 8. shehitah

  song (Zionist anthem).. 8. Hatikvah (Hattikvah)

jew's harp... 8. guimbard 9. crembalum

Jezebel (pert to)...
  epithet.. 5. vixen 6. virago 8. strumpet
  father.. 7. Ethbaal
  husband.. 4. Ahab (King)
  murdered (caused to be).. 6. Naboth

jib... 3. gib, jaw 4. balk, boom, sail, spar, tack 5. crane, shift 6. fleece 8. underlip

jibe... 3. fit 4. gibe 5. agree, shift 9. harmonize

jiff, jiffy... 5. trice 6. moment 7. instant, quickly 9. instantly, twinkling

jig... 4. jerk, jolt 5. dance 6. ballad, twitch 8. fishhook

jigger... 4. club, dram

jiggle... 5. sauce, shake

jimmy... 3. pry 5. handy, smart 6. spruce 7. coal car, crowbar, pry open 10. sheep's head

jimson weed... 6. dature 10. stramonium, thorn apple 11. apple of Peru

jingle... 4. poem, rime 5. clink, rhyme 6. tinkle 13. two–wheeled car

jinn, jinnee... 5. demon, Eblis, genie 6. afreet 8. jenniyeh

jinx... 3. hex 5. Jonah 6. hoodoo, whammy

jitters... 6. nerves 7. dithers, fidgets 8. trembles

jittery... 4. edgy 5. jumpy 7. nervous

jivatma (Hind)... 4. soul 9. life force 10. life energy 11. human spirit

Joan of Arc's appellation... 7. pucelle 13. Maid of Orleans

job... 3. act 4. hire, task 5. chare, chore, stint 8. position, sinecure

Job (pert to)...
  Book.. 9. patriarch 12. Old Testament
  friend.. 6. Zophar
  home.. 2. Uz
  literally.. 9. afflicted 10. persecuted

jockey... 3. pad 5. cheat, racer, rider 6. outwit 7. cushion 8. cavalier, horseman, minstrel, vagabond 9. Earl Sande (famed)

jocose... 3. dry 5. droll, lepid, merry 7. jocular 8. humorous 9. facetious

jocular... 3. gay 4. airy, loco 5. droll, funny, merry, witty 6. elated, jocund, lively, ribald 7. comical, festive, gleeful, jesting, playful, waggish 8. animated, mirthful 9. convivial, facetious, hilarious, laughable, vivacious 10. frolicsome

jocund... 3. gay 4. airy 5. merry 6. lively 7. jocular 8. cheerful, sportive

jog... 4. gait, jolt, lope, plod, push, trot, walk 6. canter, notify, remind, trudge 8. slow pace 9. suggest to

John... 3. Ian 4. Ivan, Jack, Juan 8. Chinaman, Johannes 9. policeman

John (pert to)...
  Bull.. 10. Englishman
  Company.. 9. East India

Crow .. **7**. buzzard (turkey)
Doe (law) .. **7**. a nobody **9**. false name
Hancock .. **9**. autograph, signature
Q Public .. **6**. people **8**. populace
johnnycake ... **4**. pone **7**. hoecake
   9. corn bread
join ... **3**. add, mix, pin, tie, wed
   4. ally, fuse, link, lock, meet, pair,
   seam, team, weld, yoke **5**. annex,
   blend, enter, graft, group, hitch, marry,
   merge, unite **6**. adjoin, attach,
   cement, concur, couple, engage,
   enlist, fasten, mingle, solder, splice,
   suture, syzygy **7**. combine, conjoin,
   connect **8**. assemble, coalesce,
   compound **9**. associate
   11. incorporate
joint ... **3**. ell, hip **4**. dive (sl), knee,
   node, seam **5**. alula, elbow, hinge,
   miter, nexus, tenon, wrist **6**. rabbet,
   resort **7**. hangout, pastern
   8. coupling, dovetail **12**. articulation
joint (pert to) ...
   cavity .. **5**. bursa
   firs .. **7**. ephedra
   fluid .. **7**. synovia **8**. synovial
   grass stem .. **4**. culm
   pert to .. **5**. nodal **9**. articular
   put out of .. **6**. lucate **9**. dislocate
   without .. **10**. acondylous
joke ... **3**. fun, gag, pun **4**. fool, hoax,
   jape, jest, quip **5**. prank, rally, sport
   6. banter, humbug **7**. bromide
   8. chestnut, one–liner
joker ... **3**. dor, wag, wit **4**. card
   7. buffoon, farceur, gagster
   8. humorist **9**. mistigris
jollity ... **4**. jest **5**. mirth **6**. gaiety
   8. hilarity **9**. enjoyment, festivity,
   joviality, merriment **12**. conviviality
jolly ... **6**. banter, jovial, mellow
   7. flatter, jocular **9**. make merry
Jolly Roger ... **5**. Roger **10**. pirate flag
jolt ... **3**. jar, jig, jut **4**. blow, butt, stun
   5. shake, shock **6**. jostle, jounce
   7. startle **8**. astonish, jail term
   (thieves')
Jonah (pert to) ...
   Bib .. **7**. prophet (Heb)
   Book .. **12**. Old Testament
   slang .. **4**. jinx
   swallowed by .. **5**. whale
Jordan ...
   capital .. **5**. Amman
   city .. **7**. Jericho, Samaria
   9. Bethlehem
   historic trove .. **14**. Dead Sea Scrolls
   official name .. **9**. Hashemite (The)
   people (anc) .. **7**. Essenes
   region .. **5**. Perea **6**. Basham
   river .. **6**. Jordan
Jorth (pert to) ...
   goddess .. **5**. Earth
   husband .. **4**. Odin
   named also .. **6**. Forgyn
   son .. **4**. Thor
Joseph (pert to) ...
   Bib .. **9**. patriarch
   buyer of .. **8**. Potiphar
   called also .. **17**. Joseph of Arimathea
   coat of .. **10**. many colors
   father .. **5**. Jacob

   mother .. **6**. Rachel
   son .. **5**. Jesus **7**. Ephraim
josh ... **3**. guy, kid **5**. chaff, spoof,
   tease **6**. banter
Joshi (Ind) ... **10**. astrologer,
   astronomer
Joshua (pert to) ...
   associate .. **5**. Caleb
   Book .. **12**. Old Testament
   burial place .. **5**. Gaash
   successor to .. **5**. Moses
   tree .. **5**. yucca
jostle ... **4**. jolt, push, rush **5**. crowd,
   elbow, joust, shake, shove **6**. hustle,
   joggle, jounce, thrust
jot ... **3**. ace, bit **4**. atom, iota, item,
   mite, whit **5**. minim, point, speck
   6. tittle **7**. smidgen **8**. particle
jouk ... **4**. dart, duck, fawn, hide
   5. cheat, dodge, evade, perch, roost,
   skulk **6**. cringe **9**. obeisance
Joule, James P ... **9**. physicist
journal ... **3**. log **5**. diary, paper
   6. record **7**. daybook, diurnal,
   logbook, support **8**. magazine, register
   9. chronicle **10**. periodical
   11. account book
journalist ... **6**. editor, legman
   7. newsman **8**. reporter **9**. columnist,
   gazetteer **11**. interviewer
   13. correspondent
journey ... **3**. run **4**. fare, iter, ride,
   tour, trek, trip, wend **5**. jaunt
   6. travel, voyage **7**. odyssey
   8. traverse **9**. excursion
   10. expedition, pilgrimage
   13. peregrination
journey (pert to) ... **4**. eyre (circuit)
   6. viatic **8**. anabasis (upward)
   9. itineracy, itinerary, traveling
   10. travelling
joust ... **4**. bout, spar, tilt **6**. combat
   10. tournament
Jove ... **7**. Jupiter
jovial ... **5**. jolly, merry **6**. elated,
   joyous **7**. festive, jocular **8**. Jovelike
   9. convivial, hilarious
   14. mirth–inspiring
jowl ... **3**. jaw **4**. chop **5**. cheek
   6. dewlap, wattle **7**. jawbone
joy ... **4**. glee **5**. bliss, exult, gelid
   6. gaiety **7**. delight, ecstasy, rapture,
   rejoice **8**. felicity, gladness, hilarity,
   pleasure **9**. beatitude, happiness,
   merriment, transport **10**. exultation
   12. exhilaration
joyous ... **3**. gay **4**. glad **5**. happy,
   merry **6**. blithe, elated, festal, joyful
   7. festive, gleeful, jocular **8**. cheerful,
   mirthful
jubilant ... **6**. elated **8**. exultant,
   exulting **9**. overjoyed, rejoicing
   10. triumphant
Judah (pert to) ...
   ancestry .. **12**. tribe of Judah
   brother .. **4**. Levi **6**. Reuben, Simeon
   father .. **5**. Jacob
   kingdom .. **9**. Palestine
   son .. **2**. Er **6**. Shelah
   translation (Heb) .. **10**. celebrated
Judas (pert to) ...
   Bible .. **7**. apostle, traitor **8**. betrayer,

deceiver, disciple
called.. 8. Iscariot
historic.. 13. Paschal candle
kiss.. 8. betrayal 11. double–cross,
  treacherous
priest.. 4. oath
suicide site.. 8. Aceldama
Judea (pert to)...
governor.. 6. Pilate
king.. 3. Asa 5. Herod 7. Jehoram
  11. Jehoshaphat
location.. 5. Berea
people.. 4. Jews
province of.. 9. Palestine
judge... 3. try 4. deem, rate 5. opine,
  think 6. critic, puisne 7. arbiter,
  referee, suppose 8. deemster,
  estimate, mediator, sentence
  9. arbitrate, criticize 10. adjudicate,
  magistrate 11. connoisseur
judge (pert to)...
bench.. 4. banc (bancus)
chamber.. 6. camera
circuit.. 4. iter
gavel.. 4. mace
group.. 5. bench 9. judiciary
of the dead.. 6. Osiris
opinion.. 12. obiter dictum
sittings.. 7. assizes
summary.. 6. postea
judgment... 4. doom 5. arrêt, award,
  sense, taste 7. censure, opinion
  8. decision, judicium, sentence
  9. criticism 10. conclusion,
  discretion, persuasion (Relig),
  punishment 11. arbitration, sensibility
judgment (pert to)...
creditor.. 13. quasi contract
day.. 7. last day 8. Dies Irae,
  doomsday
left to one's.. 13. discretionary
note.. 10. promissory
seat.. 3. bar 5. mercy 8. tribunal,
  woolsack
judicial... 5. legal 8. critical
  9. judicious 10. judicatory
judicial (pert to)...
council.. 5. cabal, junta, junto
  7. coterie
hearing.. 5. trial
order.. 4. writ 6. elegit, venire
  7. precept
security.. 7. custody
judicious... 4. wise 7. politic, prudent
  8. cautious, discreet 9. sagacious
  10. discerning 11. circumspect,
  well–advised
jug... 4. ewer, jail, olpe, toby
  5. askos, buire, cruse, gotch
  6. flagon, gomlah, lockup, prison,
  tinaja, urceus 7. pitcher
  13. Schnabelkanne
Juggernaut... 6. Vishnu (Hind)
juggler... 5. cheat, trick 7. buffoon
  8. deceiver 13. sleight of hand
  14. legerdemainist
Jugoslavia, Yugoslavia...
area.. 6. Kosovo 8. Dalmatia
brandy.. 5. rakia 9. slivovitz
capital.. 8. Belgrade
language.. 7. Slovene
  10. Macedonian, Serbo–Croat

leader.. 4. Tito
monarch.. 5. Peter
money.. 5. dinar
organization.. 9. Comitadji
people.. 4. Cerb 5. Croat 7. Slovene
juice... 3. rob, sap 4. milk (plant),
  must, stum 5. fluid, latex, syrup
  (sirup) 7. essence, hebenon, moisten
  10. succulence 11. electricity
jujitsu, jiujitsu... 11. self–defense
juju... 5. charm, magic 6. amulet,
  belief, fetish, voodoo
jujube... 3. ber 5. fruit, jelly
  7. lozenge 8. Zizyphus
Jules Verne's captain... 4. Nemo (the
  Nautilus)
Julian Emperors (first Five)... 4. Nero
  8. Augustus, Caligula, Claudius,
  Tiberius
jumble... 2. pi 3. mix 4. cake, hash,
  heap, mess, raff, stir 5. blend,
  botch, chaos, shake 6. medley,
  muddle 7. agitate, confuse, mixture
  8. disorder, riffraff
jumble type... 3. pie (pi)
jump... 3. hop, lep 4. leap, move
  (checkers) 5. bound, caper, halma,
  salto, scold, start, vault 6. chorea,
  escape, hurdle, spring, twitch
  7. saltary, saltate 8. increase
  9. advantage 10. transition
jumping (pert to)...
adjective.. 7. saltant
Frog, tale by.. 9. Mark Twain
music.. 7. saltato
rodent.. 5. mouse 6. jerboa
  11. kangaroo rat
stick.. 4. pogo, pole
junction... 4. axil, seam 5. union
  6. suture 7. joining, meeting
  11. combination, concurrence
juncture... 4. pass 5. joint, pinch
  6. crisis, strait 8. exigency, quandary
  9. emergency 10. connection
  11. conjuncture, predicament
  12. articulation
June bug... 3. dor 6. beetle, May bug
  8. figeater
jungle... 4. camp 7. thicket
  8. woodland 11. dense growth
  12. complication
jungle (pert to)...
dweller.. 5. beast 6. savage
fever.. 7. malaria
grass.. 3. poa
ox.. 4. gaur 5. gayal 7. timarau
sheep.. 7. muntjac
junior... 5. cadet, petty 6. puisne,
  recent 7. student, younger 8. inferior
  9. unskilled
juniper... 4. cade, puny 5. cedar,
  gorse, retem (raetem), savin
junket... 4. dish (milk), food, meal
  5. feast 7. banquet 8. festival
  9. excursion, sweetmeat
Juno (pert to)...
consort.. 7. Jupiter
goddess (Rom).. 3. sky 5. light
identified with.. 4. Hera
messenger.. 4. Iris
junta, junto... 5. cabal 6. circle,
  clique 7. coterie, council, faction

8. intrigue 11. combination
jupe ... 4. coat 5. jupon, shirt, skirt, tunic 6. bodice, jacket
Jupiter (pert to) ...
angel .. 7. Zadkiel
astronomy .. 6. planet (largest)
daughter .. 4. Bura
deity .. 4. Jove 9. Father Sky
festival .. 14. Vinalis sustica
god of .. 7. Heavens
heraldry .. 5. azure
lover .. 2. Io
son .. 6. Castor, Pollux
triad .. 4. Juno 7. Minerva
wife .. 4. Juno
Jupiter, god of ...
law .. 6. Fidius 10. Dius Fidius
lightning .. 6. Fulgur
rain .. 7. Pluvius
thunder .. 6. Tonans
jurat ... 5. juror 8. recorder
10. magistrate (Channel Isls)
jure ... 3. jus (ius), law 5. right
13. jurisprudence
jurisprudence ... 3. law, soc 4. soke
5. power (legal) 6. charge, sphere
7. control, custody, emirate
9. authority, consulate
10. government, judicature, patriarchy
juror ... 6. dicast 7. assizer, juryman
9. venireman
jury ... 5. panel, tales (additions)
6. venire
jus ... 3. law 5. gravy, juice 10. legal power, legal right
just ... 4. fair, tilt 5. equal, exact, valid
7. logical, upright 8. provided, unbiased 9. equitable, righteous
10. legitimate

just begun ... 8. inchoate
justice ... 4. doom 5. right 6. equity, virtue 8. fairness, fair play, justness
9. rectitude 10. judicature 11. give and take 12. rightfulness
justice of the peace ... 6. squire
10. magistrate
justification ... 7. apology, defense
11. vindication
justify ... 5. clear 6. defend, excuse
7. absolve, support, warrant
8. maintain, sanction, underpin
9. authorize, exculpate, vindicate
12. substantiate
justly ... 5. truly 6. fairly 7. equally
8. honestly 9. equitably
10. deservedly
justness ... 7. fitness, justice
8. accuracy, validity 9. exactness
11. correctness
Justus ... 4. just
jute ... 5. fiber, gunny 6. burlap
7. sacking
Jute ... 4. Dane 9. Jutlander
jutty ... 4. mole, pier 5. jetty
7. project 8. buttress, protrude
juvenile ... 5. actor, young, youth
8. immature, youthful 9. youngling, youthlike 11. undeveloped
juvia ... 9. Brazil nut
juxta ... 4. near 6. nearby
juxtaposition ... 5. touch 7. contact
8. nearness 9. proximity
10. contiguity, side by side
jynx ... 5. charm, spell 7. wryneck
10. woodpecker
Jynx ... 11. woodpeckers
J'y suis, j'y reste ... 18. I am here; here I remain

K

K ... 5. kappa (Gr) 6. letter (11th)
Ka ... 3. God (Hind)
Kaaba, Caaba (pert to) ...
content .. 10. Black Stone (of Mecca)
location .. 11. Great Mosque (Mecca)
pilgrimage .. 7. Islamic
praying direction .. 6. Kiblah
shape .. 7. cubical
kaama ... 10. hartebeest
Kaddish ... 8. Doxology
Kadiak, Kodiak, bear ... 5. brown
7. Alaskan
Kaffir (pert to) ...
club weapon .. 10. knobkerrie
country .. 11. South Africa
creed .. 10. unbeliever
13. non–Mohammedan
race .. 5. Bantu
servant .. 6. umfaan
tribes (world's tallest) .. 4. Xosa, Zulu
5. Pondo, Temby

warriors .. 4. impi
weapon .. 4. keri 10. knobkerrie
Kaiser brown ... 6. ginger
Kaiser's residence ... 5. Doorn
kaka ... 6. parrot
kakapo ... 6. parrot 9. owl parrot
kakar ... 7. muntjac
kakariki ... 6. lizard
kaki ... 5. stilt (bird) 9. persimmon
kakkak ... 5. heron 7. bittern
kakke ... 8. beriberi
kala ... 6. bulbul (bird)
kale ... 4. cole 5. money 7. cabbage, collard 8. colewort, corecole
kaleidoscopic ... 7. varying
10. changeable, variegated
Kali (pert to) ...
Hindu .. 10. evil genius
Persian .. 6. carpet
Vedic Myth .. 12. tongue of Agni (fire–god)

kallah... 5. bride (Jew)
kamavachara... 6. heaven (Buddh)
Kamchatka...
  capital.. 13. Petropavlovsk
  peninsula.. 7. Siberia
  people.. 7. Russian 9. Mongolian
  sea.. 6. Bering 7. Okhotsk
Kamehameha Day... 7. holiday (Haw)
Kamerad... 7. comrade 9. surrender
kamik... 12. sealskin boot
Kammerspiel... 5. drama 7. theater
Kanaka... 3. man 8. Hawaiian
  10. Melanesian, Polynesian
  16. South Sea islander
Kanaloa... 3. God (Pantheon)
kangaroo (pert to)...
  class.. 9. marsupial
  family.. 12. Macropodidae
  female.. 3. doe, gin, 'roo
  giant.. 8. forester
  leaping.. 6. jeroba 7. bettong
  (bettonga)
  male.. 5. bilby (bilbi)
  rat.. 7. pototoo
  reference to.. 7. wallaby
  11. macropodine
  small.. 7. wallaby
  young.. 4. joey
kangaroo court... 9. mock court, moot
  court 14. irregular court
Kansas...
  capital.. 6. Topeka
  city.. 5. Dodge 7. Abilene, Wichita
  10. Hutchinson, Kansas City
  11. Leavenworth
  Eisenhower home.. 7. Abilene
  military post.. 9. Fort Riley
  penitentiary.. 11. Leavenworth
  State admission.. 12. Thirty–fourth
  State motto.. 16. Ad Astra per
  Aspera (To the Stars Through
  Difficulties)
  State nickname.. 9. Sunflower
kapok tree... 7. God tree 9. Ceiba
  tree 10. silk–cotton
kappa... 1. K (Gr) 4. star 6. letter
  (10th)
karakul, karakule... 5. sheep
  9. astrakhan, broadtail
karma... 4. fate 7. destiny 8. casualty
Kartvelian people... 4. Svan (Svane)
  9. Georgians 10. Imeritians,
  Svanetians
kasha... 4. mush (Russ)
Kashmir, India...
  alphabet.. 6. Sarada
  capital.. 8. Srinagar
  deer.. 6. hangul
  official.. 6. pundit
Kashyapa (Vedic Myth)... 8. tortoise
Kaskaskia... 5. epoch 6. Indian
  10. Algonquian
kat... 5. shrub 8. narcotic
katar... 6. dagger
katchung... 6. peanut
katogle... 8. eagle owl
kava, kavakava... 6. Kawaka, pepper
kayak... 5. canoe
kea... 6. parrot
Keat's poem... 8. Endymion, Hyperion
keek... 3. spy (of rival fashions)
  6. peeper

keel... 4. cool, seel, ship, skeg, tilt
  6. careen, ruddle, timber (ship's)
  7. capsize 8. overturn, red ocher,
  turn over 10. guinea fowl
keelbill, keelbird... 3. ani
keeling... 7. codfish
keel–shaped... 6. carina 7. carinal
keen... 4. avid, cute, gare, good, nice,
  tart 5. acute, alert, eager, sharp,
  smart, snell, vivid, witty 6. astute,
  bitter, clever, shrewd, shrill
  7. caustic, fervent 9. sensitive,
  trenchant 11. acrimonious,
  penetrating
keenness... 4. edge 5. acies (of sight),
  nifty 6. acumen 8. acrimony,
  pungency 9. acuteness, eagerness,
  sharpness, smartness, wittiness
keep... 4. save 6. detain, retain
  7. confine, custody, fulfill, husband,
  reserve 8. conserve, maintain,
  preserve, restrain, withhold
  14. accommodations
keep (pert to)...
  account.. 5. score
  afloat.. 4. buoy
  apart.. 7. seclude 8. separate
  back, out.. 3. bar, dam 4. save
  5. debar, delay 6. detain, except,
  hinder, retard 7. exclude, reserve
  8. restrain, withhold
  from.. 5. avoid, delay 7. abstain,
  boycott, prevent
  hidden.. 7. secrete
  in.. 6. retain
  off.. 4. fend 7. prevent, repulse, ward
  off
  on.. 6. endure 9. persevere
keeper... 5. guard 6. warden
  9. constable, custodian, possessor
  10. maintainer
keeper of...
  birds.. 8. aviarist
  borders.. 8. margrave
  door.. 5. tiler
  elephant.. 6. mahout
  golden apples (Myth).. 6. Ithunn
  (Ithun)
  parks.. 6. ranger
  prison.. 6. gaoler, jailer, jailor, warden
  7. turnkey
keeping... 4. care 5. board, guard,
  trust 7. custody 8. tutelage
  9. retention 10. caretaking,
  conformity, possession, preserving,
  protection 11. maintenance
  12. guardianship
keeve... 3. tub 4. tuft 5. knoll, plume
  8. haystack
kef... 6. dreamy 7. languor
  12. tranquillity (tranquility)
keg... 3. tun, vat 4. cade, cask
  6. firkin
kelly... 5. derby, killy (fish)
kelp... 4. game 5. sight, wrack
  7. insight, seaweed 9. water lily
ken... 4. lore 9. recognize
  10. cognizance, prescience
  13. understanding
Kentish freedman... 4. laet
Kentucky...
  bluegrass.. 3. poa

capital .. **9.** Frankfort
city .. **7.** Paducah **9.** Lexington
   10. Louisville **12.** Bowling Green
famed road .. **15.** Wilderness Trail
famed sights .. **7.** Obelisk (J Davis)
   8. Fort Knox, Log Cabin (Lincoln)
   11. Federal Hill (My Old Ky Home),
   Mammoth Cave
famed sport .. **13.** Kentucky Derby
   (Churchill Downs)
mountain .. **4.** Pine **10.** Cumberland
pioneer .. **11.** Daniel Boone
river .. **4.** Ohio **10.** Cumberland
State admission .. **9.** Fifteenth
State name meaning (Indian) ..
   8. tomorrow
State nickname .. **9.** Bluegrass
Kenya, E Africa ...
   capital .. **7.** Nairobi
   product .. **3.** tea
   tribe .. **4.** Embu
kept ... see *keep*
Ker (Gr) ... **4.** doom, fate **5.** ghost
   6. spirit
kermis, kermess ... **4.** fair **8.** festival
kernel ... **3.** nut **4.** core, gist, meat,
   pith, seed **5.** grain, heart **6.** acinus,
   nutmeg **7.** nucleus
ketch ... **4.** Jack, saic, ship **6.** vessel
ketone ... **5.** irone **6.** carone
   7. acetone, camphor **8.** deguelin
kettle ... **3.** pot **4.** drum, pail **6.** kibble
   7. caldron **8.** cauldron **9.** teakettle
   10. kettledrum
kettledrum ... **4.** drum **5.** naker, tabor
   6. atabal **7.** anacara **8.** tympanon
key ... **4.** clue, crib, isle, quay, reef,
   tone **5.** islet, pitch, tasto **6.** clavis,
   cotter, fasten, island, opener, switch,
   tapper **7.** digital **8.** mainstay, solution
   11. explanation, fundamental,
   translation
keyed up ... **4.** agog **5.** eager, fired
   7. aroused, stirred **8.** hopped up,
   worked up **10.** stimulated
Keys, House of ... **9.** Isle of Man,
   officials
Keystone State ... **12.** Pennsylvania
khan ... **3.** inn **4.** lord **6.** prince
   9. resthouse **11.** caravansary
kiang ... **5.** diver **6.** onager **7.** wild ass
kick ... **4.** blow, boot, funk, punt
   6. energy, object, thrill **7.** grumble,
   protest **8.** complain, pungency,
   sixpence **9.** complaint **10.** calcitrate,
   enthusiasm
Kickapoo ... **6.** Indian **10.** Algonquian
kickshaw ... **3.** toy **6.** trifle **7.** trinket
   8. delicacy
kid ... **3.** guy **4.** fool, goat, hoax, joke,
   josh, twit **5.** child, jolly, suede
   6. banter, humbug **8.** antelope
   (young), yeanling **9.** youngling
kidang ... **4.** deer **7.** muntjac
kidney ... **4.** neer **5.** gland, reins
   7. nephros
kidney (pert to) ...
   comb form .. **6.** nephro
   disease .. **7.** nephria **9.** nephritis
   pyramid .. **9.** reniculus
   reference to .. **4.** reni **5.** renal
   6. vitals **7.** nephric

shaped .. **8.** reniform
stone .. **6.** pebble **8.** nephrite
kiki ... **14.** castor oil plant
kill ... **4.** slay, veto **5.** blast, creek
   6. defeat, murder **7.** channel,
   destroy, execute, silence **8.** dispatch,
   immolate, lapidate, massacre,
   overbeat **9.** slaughter
   11. assassinate, exterminate
killer ... **4.** Cain **6.** gunman, slayer
   7. butcher **8.** cannibal, man–eater,
   mongoose, murderer **9.** cutthroat
   12. assassinator
killer whale ... **3.** orc **4.** orca
   7. grampus
killing ... **5.** fatal **6.** deadly, murder
   7. amusing, carnage, cleanup
   (speculation), garrote **8.** homicide
   9. execution **10.** euthanasia
   11. captivating **12.** overpowering
killing of ...
   brother .. **10.** fratricide
   cats .. **8.** felicide
   father .. **9.** patricide
   man .. **8.** homicide
   mother .. **9.** matricide
   old men (tribal) .. **8.** senicide
   self .. **7.** suicide **9.** martyrdom
   sister .. **10.** sororicide
   wolf .. **8.** lupicide
kiln ... **4.** oast, oven **5.** clamp, stove,
   tiler **7.** furnace
kilo (pref) ... **8.** thousand
kind ... **3.** ilk **4.** good, race, sort, type
   5. class, genre, genus, order, seely,
   style **6.** benign, gender, humane,
   loving, strain **7.** kindred, lenient,
   species **8.** gracious **9.** benignant
   10. benevolent **11.** sympathetic
   12. well–disposed
kindle ... **4.** burn, fire **5.** brood, light,
   rouse, young **6.** excite, ignite, incite,
   litter **7.** animate, inflame, provoke
kindly ... **4.** mild **6.** benign, blithe,
   genial, humane **7.** natural
   8. benignly, heartily **9.** agreeably,
   benignant, indulgent **10.** beneficent,
   legitimate, pleasantly **11.** sympathetic
kindness ... **5.** favor **8.** clemency,
   goodness, humanity, mildness
   9. benignity **10.** compassion,
   generosity, gentleness, indulgency,
   tenderness
kindred ... **3.** sib, tie **4.** akin, clan, kith
   5. blood **6.** allied, family **7.** cognate,
   descent, kinship, kinsmen, related
   8. kinsfolk **9.** relations
   12. relationship **14.** consanguineous
kine ... **4.** cows **6.** cattle
kinetic ... **6.** active, moving
king ... **3.** rex, rey, roi **4.** rank **5.** chief,
   ruler **6.** master **7.** regulus
   8. chessman **9.** potentate, sovereign
king (pert to) ...
   beasts .. **4.** lion
   birds .. **5.** eagle
   chamber .. **9.** camarilla
   cheeses .. **4.** Brie
   child .. **6.** prince **8.** princess
   dwarfs .. **8.** Alberich (Ger)
   fairies .. **6.** Oberon
   family .. **7.** dynasty

gods.. 7. Jupiter
heaven.. 3. God 6. Christ
herrings.. 4. opah 7. oarfish
    8. chimaera
mackerel.. 4. cero
March (The).. 5. Sousa
metals.. 4. gold
monkeys.. 7. guereza
murder of.. 8. regicide
myth.. 4. Atli 5. Midas
myth (classical).. 4. Zeus 7. Jupiter
rivers.. 6. Amazon
serpents (race of).. 6. Shesha (Sesha)
symbol.. 7. scepter (sceptre)
vultures.. 4. papa
waters.. 7. Neptune, Pacific
Woods (The).. 13. Rex Nemorensis
King Arthur (pert to)...
abode.. 6. Avalon 7. Camelot
battleground (fatal).. 6. Camlan
home.. 8. Caerleon (on the Usk)
Knights of the Round Table..
    6. Gawain 7. Galahad 8. Lancelot,
    Tristran 9. Percivale
Queen.. 9. Guinevere
quest of.. 9. Holy Grail (The)
shield.. 7. Pridwin
sword.. 9. Excalibur
kingdom... 5. realm 6. empire, estate
    8. dominion, kingship, monarchy
kingdom (pert to)...
ancient.. 4. Elam, Moab
Asia.. 5. Nepal
between Spain, France.. 7. Navarra
    (Navarre)
confusion.. 5. Babel
divisions.. 6. animal 7. mineral
    9. vegetable
Indo–China.. 5. Annam (Anam)
kingfish... 4. cero, haku, opah
    7. kingpin, pintado 8. big wheel
    9. threadfin
kingly... 5. grand, noble, regal, royal
    6. august 7. leonine 8. imperial,
    majestic, princely 9. dignified,
    sovereign 11. monarchical
King of...
Albania.. 3. Zog
Bashan.. 2. Og
Bulgaria.. 5. Boris
Greece (anc).. 9. Agamemnon
Israel.. 4. Ahab, Jehy, Saul 5. David
    7. Solomon 8. Jeroboam
Judea.. 3. Asa
Kings.. 3. God 6. Christ
Men.. 4. Odin, Zeus 7. Jupiter
Oriental.. 11. King of Kings
Persia (Iran).. 5. Cyrus 6. Xerxes
Troy.. 5. Priam
Tyre.. 5. Hiram
Visigoths.. 6. Alaric
Kipling, Rudyard (pert to)...
award.. 10. Nobel Prize (1907)
birthplace.. 6. Bombay
poem (for Queen Victoria)..
    11. Recessional
kissing, science... 13. philematology
knee (pert to)...
bend.. 9. genuflect
bent.. 10. geniculate
bone.. 6. rotula 7. kneepan, patella
britches.. 6. smalls 8. knickers

on bended.. 7. humbled 8. obeisant
    10. submissive, worshipful
    12. supplicatory
kneeling desk... 8. prie–dieu
knew... see *know*
Knickerbocker, Father... 9. New
    Yorker (Hist)
knickknack... 3. toy 6. bauble,
    gewgaw, trifle 7. trinket 8. gimcrack
knife... 4. bolo, snee, stab 5. corer,
    prune 6. cutter, weapon
knife (pert to)...
Burmese.. 3. dah
Hindu.. 5. kukri
Irish.. 5. skean 8. skean dhu
Malay.. 4. kris 6. barong, creese
New Zealand.. 4. patu
one–bladed.. 6. barlow
Scottish.. 4. dirk
Spanish.. 7. machete
surgical.. 7. scalpel 10. greffotome
Turkish.. 8. yataghan (yatagan)
US Navy.. 7. cutlass
knife maker... 6. cutler
knife–throwing game...
    11. mumbletypeg
    12. mumble–the–peg
knight (pert to)...
adventure.. 8. errantry
adventurer.. 8. cavalier 9. caballero,
    chevalier
cloak.. 6. tabard
combat.. 5. joust
ensign.. 8. gonfalon, gonfanon
errant.. 7. Paladin
hero.. 7. Paladin
servant.. 4. page 6. varlet
title.. 3. Sir 8. banneret
wife.. 4. Dame, Lady
wreath (with crest).. 4. orle
Knight of the Round Table... 3. Kay
    6. Gawain 7. Galahad, Paladin
    8. Lancelot, Tristram 9. Percivale
Knight of the Rueful Countenance...
    10. Don Quixote
knit... 4. bind, heal, join, seam
    5. plait, unite, woven 6. cement,
    couple, fasten 7. conjoin, connect,
    wrinkle 8. contract 9. interlace
    11. consolidate
knitting machine guide... 4. sley
knitting stitch... 4. knit, purl
knob... 3. nub 4. boss, head, hill,
    lump, node, stud, umbo 5. bulge,
    knurl 6. croche (antler), pommel
    8. tubercle 12. protuberance
knobkerrie... 4. club, kiri 5. stick
knock... 3. hit, rap, tap 4. bang,
    bash, beat, bump, dash, glow, hill,
    pass, slay, snop 5. pound, thump
    6. hammer, jostle, strike 7. collide
    9. criticism, criticize, disparage
    12. faultfinding
knock (pert to)...
about.. 6. travel, wander
down.. 4. fell, raze 6. deject, strike
    8. vanquish
off.. 3. die 6. deduct, recess
    9. improvise
out.. 2. KO 4. kayo
knocking... 6. rat-tat 7. rapping,
    tapping 9. rat-tat-tat

9. freighted
lading... 4. load 5. cargo 6. burden 7. freight
ladle... 3. dip 4. bowl 5. scoop, spoon 6. dipper
lady... 4. burd (anc), dame 5. donna 6. domina, female, senora 7. signora 8. ladylove 13. harlequin duck
lady (pert to)...
bird.. 6. beetle 7. Vedalia
fish.. 6. wrasse
killer.. 4. wolf 5. shiek 7. Don Juan 8. Casanova
like.. 6. female, polite 7. genteel 8. feminine
Lady Godiva's town... 8. Coventry
Lady of the Lake character (legend)... 6. Merlin, Vivian
Lady's Book author... 5. Godey
lady's–slipper... 6. balsam, orchid 8. Noah's ark 9. nerveroot
lady's–thumb... 9. peachwort, persicary
lag... 4. slow 5. delay, tardy 6. dawdle, linger, loiter 7. belated 10. dillydally, fall behind
lagarto... 9. alligator 10. lizard fish
laggard... 4. slow 5. idler 7. lagging 8. backward, dilatory, indolent, loiterer, sluggish 9. loitering, straggler
La Gioconda... 8. Mona Lisa
lagniappe, lagnappe... 5. pilon 7. largess (largesse), present (trifling) 8. gratuity
lagoon... 4. lake, pond, pool 5. atoll
laic... 3. lay 5. civil 6. layman 7. secular 8. temporal
lair... 3. bed, den, pen 4. cave, shed, trap 5. abode, couch 6. cavern 7. retreat
Lais (Gr)... 7. hetaera (of Corinth) 8. mistress 14. beautiful woman
laissez faire, laisser faire... 5. let go 7. let pass 8. inaction, inactive 9. do–nothing, passivism, unconcern 12. indifference 15. noninterference
Laius' son... 7. Oedipus (of Thebes)
lake... 4. loch, mere, pond, pool, tarn 5. lacus 6. lagoon 7. carmine (color)
lake (pert to)...
bass.. 4. rock 6. calico
deposit.. 5. trona
duck.. 5. scaup 7. mallard
dweller.. 10. lacustrian
dwelling.. 7. crannog
growing in.. 10. lacustrine
Hades (of).. 7. Avernus
highest.. 8. Titicaca
pert to.. 9. lacustral
poet (Eng).. 6. lakist 7. Southey 9. Coleridge 10. Wordsworth
State.. 8. Michigan
lama... 4. monk 5. Dalai
Lamaism... 8. Buddhism
Lamaism, Buddhism (pert to)...
convent.. 8. lamasery
dignitary.. 8. hutukhtu
palace site.. 5. Lhasa
priest, monk.. 4. lama 6. Getsul 9. Dalai Lama, Grand Lama
reliquary, stupa.. 7. chorten
lamb... 3. ean, ewe 4. cade, yean 5. gigot, sheep 6. cosset 7. eanling,

lambkin 8. yearling 9. youngling 10. endearment
Lamb, Charles... 4. Elia (pen name)
lambaste... 4. beat, whip 6. thrash 7. reprove
lambent... 7. glowing, radiant 8. wavering 10. flickering 11. gliding over
Lambeth (London)... 6. palace (of Archbishops) 15. religious center
Lamb of God... 7. paschal 8. Agnus Dei
lame... 4. halt 7. halting, limping 8. crippled, disabled, hobbling 9. defective 11. inefficient
lame (pert to)...
brains.. 9. balminess, daffiness, goofiness, wackiness
duck.. 7. session 9. insolvent 10. politician, speculator
Lamech (pert to)...
descendant of.. 4. Cain
father of.. 5. Jabal, Jubal 9. Tubal–cain
lament... 3. rue 4. keen, moan, sigh, wail, weep 5. mourn 6. bemoan, bewail, grieve, plaint, regret, repine, yammer 7. condole, deplore, elegize, weeping 8. jeremiad
lamentation... 3. cry, woe 5. dolor, grief, tears 6. sorrow 7. anguish, wailing
Lamentations... 4. Book (Old Test)
lamia... 5. witch 7. monster, vampire (Myth) 8. cub shark 9. sorceress
lamina... 4. obex (brain) 5. blade, flake, hinge, layer
lamp... 4. davy, etna 5. light, torch 6. crusie 7. lantern, lucigen 9. veilleuse
lamp (pert to)...
black.. 4. soot
holder.. 11. candelabrum
lighter.. 5. spill
safety.. 4. davy 7. Geordie
slang.. 6. look at
waving of.. 5. arati
lampadedromy (Gr)... 8. foot race (with torch)
lampoon... 4. skit 5. squib 6. iambic 8. ridicule, satirize 10. pasquinade
lampoon writer... 8. satirist
lamprey... 3. eel 6. ramper
Lamps of the Lord... 5. yucca (blooms)
Lancashire (Eng)... 6. Eccles
lance... 3. cut 4. dart, hurl, stab 5. blade, spear 6. incise, launch, pierce, weapon 7. javelin
lance (pert to)...
battle.. 5. joust
head.. 5. morne
knight.. 10. lansquenet (Hist)
officer.. 4. Jack
surgical.. 6. lancet
Lancelot... 6. Knight 13. Lancelot du Lac
Lancelot's beloved... 6. Elaine
lancer... 5. uhlan 6. Hussar 7. cossack, soldier, spearer
land... 3. lot 4. acre, farm 5. arada, downs, field, range, tilth 6. alight,

debark, ground, region 7. country,
  pasture 9. disembark
land (pert to)...
absolute ppty.. 4. alod 7. alodium
alluvial.. 5. delta
ancestral.. 5. ethel
assessor.. 8. cadastre (cadaster)
church.. 5. glebe
heritable.. 4. odal, udal
holding.. 6. tenure 9. leasehold
leasehold.. 5. feoff
locked in.. 13. mediterranean
mythical.. 4. Eden 6. Utopia
  9. Shangri–La
northernmost.. 5. Thule (Greenland)
open.. 4. moor, wold 5. heath
pile.. 5. cairn
prefix.. 4. agro
reversion.. 7. escheat
sandy.. 4. dene
surveyor.. 9. arpenteur
Sussex tract (Eng).. 5. laine
treeless.. 5. llano 6. steppe 7. prairie
verb.. 3. win 4. gain 5. catch
  6. secure 7. capture
waste.. 5. heath
landed estate... 5. manor 7. demesne
landing place... 4. deck, dock, pier,
  quay 5. field, levee, strip, wharf
  7. airport 8. platform 9. staircase
landmark... 4. copa, tree 5. senal
Land of (the)...
bondage.. 5. Egypt
Cush.. 8. Ethiopia
Eden (East of).. 3. Nod
Enchantment.. 9. New Mexico
Leal.. 6. Heaven
Little Sticks (Canada).. 19. Barren
  Islands border
Midnight Sun.. 6. Alaska, Norway
O'Cakes.. 8. Scotland
Opportunity.. 8. Arkansas
Plenty.. 6. Goshen
Promise.. 6. Canaan
Regrets.. 5. India
Rising Sun.. 5. Japan
Rose.. 7. England
Shamrock.. 4. Eire 7. Ireland
sleep.. 3. Nod
Steady Habits.. 11. Connecticut
Thistle.. 8. Scotland
Thousand Lakes.. 7. Finland
White Elephant.. 4. Siam
landscape... 7. paysage, scenery,
  topiary
landslide... 9. avalanche
  10. éboulement
Landsmaal, Landsmal... 8. language
  (Norway)
Landstag... 4. Diet 8. assembly
  11. legislature
lane... 4. path, road 5. alley, route,
  track 6. airway, course, gullet, throat
  7. channel, red land 8. footpath
  10. passageway
language... 6. langue, speech, tongue
  7. dialect, diction 11. parlance
  9. utterance 11. linguistics
language (pert to)...
acquiring.. 12. chrestomathy
ancient.. 4. Pali 5. Aryan, Greek,
  Latin 6. Hebrew 7. Chinese

  8. Sanskrit
artificial.. 2. Od, Ro 3. Ido
  7. Volapük 9. Esperanto
classical.. 5. Greek, Latin
conversant in.. 9. pantoglot
dead.. 4. Pali
deaf–mute.. 11. dactylology
expression, peculiar.. 5. idiom, lingo
  6. jargon 7. dialect 13. colloquialism
international.. 2. Od, Ro 3. Ido
  7. Volapük 9. Esperanto
pert to.. 8. semantic
pretentious.. 7. bombast
  11. highfalutin'
Romance.. 5. Latin 6. French
  7. Catalan, Italian, Spanish
  9. Provençal 10. Portuguese
sacred.. 4. Pali
sign.. 11. dactylology
thieves'.. 5. argot
languid... 4. slow, weak 5. faint, inert,
  weary 6. dreamy, feeble, sickly,
  supine, torpid 7. passive 8. careless,
  drooping, flagging, heedless, indolent,
  sluggish 9. apathetic 10. spiritless
languish... 3. die 4. fade, fail, flag,
  pine, wilt 5. droop, faint 6. repine,
  sicken, weaken, wither 7. decline
languor... 3. kef (kief) 7. fatigue
  8. dullness, weakness 9. indolence,
  lassitude 10. dreaminess, drowsiness,
  stagnation 12. listlessness,
  sluggishness
lanky... 4. lean, tall, thin 5. gaunt,
  spare 12. loose–jointed
lanner... 6. falcon
Lanterns, Feast of (Jap)... 3. Bon
Laodicean... 8. lukewarm 9. apathetic
  11. indifferent
Laos...
aborigine.. 3. Kah
capital.. 9. Vientiane 12. Luang
  Prabang
native.. 7. Chinese
  14. Thai–Indonesian
religion.. 8. Buddhism
river.. 6. Mekong
tribesman.. 3. Yun
lap... 3. sip 4. fold, lick, wrap 5. drink
  6. ripple, tipple 7. circuit
lapel... 4. fold 5. rever 6. facing,
  lappet
lapicide... 11. stonecutter
lapidate... 4. kill (by stoning), pelt
  5. stone
lapin... 6. rabbit
lapis lazuli... 4. blue 5. stone
  8. lazurite, sapphire 10. azure stone
Lapland...
people.. 5. Lapps 10. Laplanders
  11. Ural–Altaics 12. tent–dwellers
sledge (traveling).. 5. pulka (pukk)
sledge puller.. 8. reindeer
town.. 6. Kiruna
waterfalls.. 11. Harspranget
lappet... 4. flap, fold, lobe 5. lapel
  6. wattle 9. appendage
lapse... 3. err 4. fall, slip 5. error,
  fault, pause 6. expiry 7. decline,
  misstep, relapse 8. apostasy
  9. reversion
lapsus... 4. slip 5. error

12. inadvertence
lapsus calami... 10. lipography
12. slip of the pen
lapsus linguae... 15. slip of the tongue
lapwing... 4. gull 5. pewee, pewit 6. plover
larceny... 5. theft 7. robbery 8. burglary, stealage 10. scrounging
larch... 5. Larix 8. tamarack
lard... 3. fat 4. line, pork 5. adeps, bacon, baste, enarm 6. axunge, cerate, enrich, fatten, grease 7. garnish 8. saindoux 9. lubricate
larder... 6. pantry 7. buttery 8. cupboard 12. commissariat
lares (Rom)... 4. gods (household) 7. spirits
large... 3. big, nth 4. bold, huge, much, vast 5. ample, bulky, burly, giant, great, loose, scads 7. copious, immense, leonine, liberal, massive, titanic, weighty 8. colossal, enormous, gigantic, spacious 9. excessive, extensive, plentiful 11. exaggerated 12. considerable 13. comprehensive
large (pert to)...
artery.. 5. aorta
comb form.. 5. macro
fish.. 4. opah, tuna 9. swordfish
intestine.. 5. colon 6. caecum, rectum
knife.. 4. bolo, snee
lettered.. 6. uncial
number.. 4. slew 6. myriad
pulpit.. 4. ambo
volume.. 4. tome
largess, largesse... 4. gift 6. bounty 7. charity, present 10. generosity, liberality 11. beneficence
largest bird... 6. condor 7. ostrich 13. whooping crane
largest fish (freshwater)... 8. arapaima
larghetto... 9. slow tempo
larghissimo... 8. very slow
lariat... 4. rope 5. honda (part), lasso, noose, reata, riata
lark... 5. ghost (anc), prank, revel 6. frolic 7. skylark, titlark 8. songbird 9. adventure, Alaudidae, parchment (color)
larrigan... 8. moccasin
larrikin... 5. rough, rowdy 6. loafer 10. street Arab
larrup... 3. hit 4. beat, blow, flog, whip
larva... 3. bot (bott) 4. grub, pupa 5. redia 6. embryo, maggot 7. atrocha 8. cercaria 9. chrysalis, doodlebug 11. caterpillar
lascivious... 4. lewd 5. bawdy 6. erotic, wanton 7. lustful, sensual 9. lecherous, salacious 10. libidinous, licentious
laser... 9. light beam
lash... 3. tie 4. beat, bind, flag, whip 5. scold, smite 6. splice, strike 7. scourge
lass... 4. girl 6. lassie, maiden 7. colleen 11. maidservant
lassitude... 7. languor 8. debility,

lethargy, weakness 9. weariness
lasso... 4. lash, rope 5. noose, reata (riata), snare 6. lariat 8. cabestro
last... 3. end 5. final, omega 6. endure, latest, lowest, newest, penult, ultima, utmost 7. extreme, supreme 8. eventual, rearmost, terminal, ultimate 9. penultima 10. antepenult, conclusive, most recent
last (pert to)...
at last.. 6. Eureka
but one.. 6. penult
cry.. 10. dernier cri
evening.. 9. yesterday
long.. 7. outwear, perdure 9. perendure
month.. 3. ult 6. ultimo
offer.. 9. ultimatum
person in contest.. 4. mell
shoe.. 5. block
syllable but one.. 6. penult
syllable but two.. 10. antepenult
Last (pert to)...
Assize.. 11. Last Inquest 12. Last Judgment
Days of Pompeii character.. 4. Ione 5. Nydia 7. Glaucus
Gospel.. 4. Mass
of the Gothic Kings.. 8. Roderick
of the Mohicans.. 5. Uncas (Chief)
Supper.. 6. Christ 9. disciples
lasting... 4. long 6. stable 7. abiding, durable, eternal 8. constant 9. continual, lingering, permanent, steadfast 11. substantial, unforgotten
lasting briefly... 9. ephemeral, temporary
lat... 6. column, pillar
latchet... 3. tap 4. lace (leather) 5. strap, thong 9. fastening
late... 3. neo (comb form), new 4. sero 5. tardy 6. former, recent 7. belated, overdue 8. neoteric 10. behindhand
latent... 5. inert 6. hidden 7. dormant 9. disguised, potential, quiescent, suspended 10. underlying
later... 4. anon, soon 5. after 6. future, mañana, puisne 9. posterior, presently 12. subsequently
lateral... 5. flank, raphe 8. indirect, sideward
lath... 4. slat 9. wood strip
lathe... 4. tool 7. mandrel
lather... 4. foam, suds 5. froth
Latin (pert to)...
alphabet letters.. 9. twenty–one
and.. 2. et
bath.. 7. balneum
behold.. 4. ecce
booth.. 7. taberna
bowl.. 6. patina
bronze.. 3. aes
church.. 8. Catholic
couch.. 9. accibutum
country.. 6. French 7. Italian, Spanish
dish.. 4. lanx 6. patina
foot.. 3. pes
God.. 3. Dei, Deo 4. Deus 7. Mercury

goddess.. 3. Dea
grammar (case).. 6. dative 8. ablative, genitive, vocative 10. accusative, nominative
historian.. 6. Justin
holidays.. 5. feria
hymn.. 13. Adesti Fideles
javelin.. 5. aclys, pilum
land.. 4. ager
law.. 6. Latium
life.. 4. vita
people.. 6. Romans
poet.. 4. Ovid 6. Horace
pronoun.. 2. tu 3. ego, hic 4. ille, ipse, iste
quarter (section).. 5. Paris 10. New Orleans
ram.. 5. aries
rite.. 4. orgy 5. sacra
seat.. 5. sella
trumpet.. 4. tuba 7. buccina
Way.. 9. Via Latina
latite... 4. lava
latitude... 4. zone 5. scope, width 6. extent 7. breadth, freedom 8. distance 10. liberality
latrant... 7. barking
latter... 4. last 5. final 6. latest 9. foregoing 10. more recent
Latter–day Saint... 6. Mormon
lattice... 6. grille 7. trellis 8. cancelli 9. crossbars, framework 12. crossed slats
latticelike... 7. grating 8. espalier 9. clathrate 10. cancellate
Latvia...
capital.. 4. Riga
city.. 6. Dvinsk, Libava (Libau)
money unit.. 3. lat (gold)
people.. 5. Letts
river.. 2. Aa
laud... 4. sing 5. extol 6. praise 7. applaud, commend, glorify, magnify 8. eulogize
laudable... 9. admirable, estimable 11. commendable, meritorious 12. praiseworthy
laudatory... 9. panegyric 10. flattering 11. approbatory, encomiastic 12. commendatory
laugh... 4. roar 5. fleer, smile, snort 6. cackle, deride, giggle, guffaw, hawhaw, tee–hee 7. chortle, chuckle 8. ridicule 10. cachinnate
laughable... 3. odd 5. droll, funny, merry, queer, witty 7. amusing, comical, jocular, risible, strange, waggish 8. humorous, sportive 9. burlesque, diverting, facetious, ludicrous 10. ridiculous
laughing... 3. gay 5. merry, riant 6. rident
laughing (pert to)...
bird.. 4. loon 10. woodpecker
falcon.. 4. hawk
gas.. 12. nitrous oxide
jackass.. 10. kingfisher, kookaburra
pert to.. 8. gelastic
laughter... 4. gelo (comb form) 5. gelos, mirth, risus 6. guffaw 12. cachinnation
launch... 4. hurl 5. begin, float, lance,

shove, start, throw 6. plunge 7. descant 9. undertake 10. inaugurate
laureate... 4. poet 6. decked (with laurel) 7. drowned, honored 13. distinguished
laurel... 3. bay, ivy, oak, oil 6. daphne, Kalmia, salmon 8. magnolia 9. sassafras, spoonwood
laurel wreath... 7. Iresine
lava... 2. aa, oo 3. ash 5. ashes 6. coulee, latite, scoria 8. lapillus, pahoehoe
lava field... 8. pedregal
lavaliere, lavalier... 7. pendant 8. ornament
lavatory... 5. basin 7. piscina 8. washroom 9. washbasin
lave... 4. lade, pour, wash 5. bathe, rinse 6. drench 8. absterge
lavender... 4. mint 6. purple 7. blue–red, perfume 9. fragrance
laver... 4. bowl 5. basin 6. trough, vessel 7. cistern, seaweed
Lavinia (pert to)...
father.. 7. Latinus
husband.. 6. Aeneas
mother.. 5. Amata
myth.. 5. Roman
lavish... 4. free, lush, rank, wild 5. spend 7. profuse 8. abundant, generous, prodigal, reckless, squander 9. bountiful, exuberant, impetuous, luxuriant, plentiful, unstinted 10. immoderate 11. extravagant 12. unrestrained 13. superabundant
law... 3. act, jus, lex 4. bill, code, jure, nisi, rule 5. axiom, canon, droit, edict, mercy, mesne 6. decree, equity, Latium, police 7. justice, precept, statute 9. enactment 12. constitution 13. jurisprudence
law (pert to)...
action.. 3. res 4. suit 5. actus 6. trover 7. impeach, implead 8. gravamen, replevin 9. ademption
Bible.. 6. Mosaic 12. Old Testament
claim.. 4. lien
code.. 9. Hammurabi 10. codex juris 16. Codex Justinianus
decree.. 4. nisi 5. edict
degree.. 3. LLD
divine.. 11. commandment
document.. 4. deed, writ 6. capias, elegit
drafting.. 10. nomography
evidence.. 7. constat
expert (US).. 5. Moore (John B)
for fourth offender (NY).. 6. Baumes
German Franks.. 5. Salic
goddess.. 4. Maat (Egypt)
heredity.. 8. Gresham's
Manu.. 5. sutra
mathematics.. 7. formula
morals.. 7. conduct
Moses.. 5. Torah (Tora) 10. Pentateuch
offender.. 5. felon 6. sinner 8. criminal 9. wrongdoer
offense.. 4. tort 5. crime, malum 6. delict
pert to.. 3. res 9. judiciary

philology.. 6. Grimm's
science.. 8. nomology
  13. jurisprudence
student.. 8. stagiary
thought.. 7. noetics
warning.. 6. caveat
within the.. 5. licit 8. judicial
wrong.. 4. tort
lawful... 3. due 5. legal, licit, valid
  9. permitted 10. legitimate
  11. permissible
lawgiver... 5. Moses
lawless... 4. lewd 6. unruly 7. illegal
  10. anarchical, disorderly
lawlessness... 4. riot 6. mutiny
  7. anarchy, license 12. disobedience
lawmaker... 5. solon 7. senator
  10. legislator 11. congressman
lawn... 5. green 7. batiste 9. grassplot
  12. village green
lawyer... 5. agent 6. jurist, legist
  7. abogado, shyster 8. advocate,
  attorney, lawgiver 9. barrister,
  counselor (counsellor), leguleian,
  solicitor 11. intercessor, pettifogger
lax... 4. dull, free, limp, open, slow
  5. loose, slack, tardy 6. remiss
  7. lenient 8. backward, dilatory,
  inactive, indolent, not tense
  9. dissolute, scattered 10. licentious,
  unconfined 12. unrestrained
lay... 3. bet, put 4. lair, pave, poem,
  song 5. allay, ditty, place, quiet,
  stake, still 6. ballad, hazard, impose,
  impute, pacify 7. appease, ascribe,
  deposit, relieve, store up 9. direction
  10. profession
lay (pert to)...
aside.. 5. table 6. remove, shelve
  7. dismiss, reserve 8. postpone
  9. segregate
away.. 4. heap, hive 5. amass,
  cache, hoard, store 7. husband
  8. treasure 10. accumulate
bare.. 5. strip 6. denude, expose,
  reveal 7. uncover
down.. 3. bet, set 5. level 6. give up
  7. declare, deposit 9. postulate,
  prescribe, stipulate, surrender
off.. 4. don't, stop 5. cease
  6. recess 7. dismiss, measure
out.. 4. plan 5. set up 6. design
  7. pattern
waste.. 6. ravage 7. destroy
  8. desolate 9. depredate, devastate
layer... 3. bed 4. coat, derm, tier,
  uvea 5. sloam (earth) 6. lamina
  7. stratum (strata, pl)
  10. substratum
lazar... 5. leper 9. loathsome
lazaretto, lazaret... 8. hospital 9. pest
  house 10. lazar house
laziness... 7. inertia 8. oisivity,
  vagrancy 9. indolence
  10. ergophobia, remissness
  12. slothfulness 13. shiftlessness
lazy... 3. lax 4. idle, slow 5. slack
  6. otiose, remiss 7. dronish, laggard
  8. dilatory, inactive, indolent, slothful,
  sluggish 9. shiftless 13. lackadaisical
lazy man... 3. bum 4. lusk 5. drone,
  idler 6. rotter 9. lazybones

  11. Weary Willie
lea... 4. mead 5. haugh 6. meadow
  7. pasture 9. grassland
leach... 3. wet 7. moisten 9. lixiviate,
  percolate
lead... 3. cue, key, van 4. cart, clue,
  head, lode 5. begin, guide, pilot,
  plumb, usher 6. direct, entice,
  escort, govern, induce 7. conduct,
  pioneer, precede 8. antecede,
  guidance 9. direction, influence,
  precedent 10. precedence
lead (mineral)... 4. came (rod), gray,
  shot 6. ceruse, fother, galena,
  leaden, strass (glass) 7. bullets,
  plummet 8. graphite, litharge,
  plumbago
lead astray... 4. lure, mang 6. allure,
  delude, entice, induce 7. deceive,
  pervert 8. inveigle
leader... 4. head 5. chief, guide,
  sinew 6. cantor, tendon 7. special
  8. choragus, director 9. chieftain,
  conductor 10. forerunner
leader (Eccl)... 3. fra 4. pope 5. rabbi
  6. bishop, priest 8. cardinal,
  minister, preacher 10. evangelist
leading... 5. chief, first 6. ruling
  7. guiding 8. foremost, in the van
  9. directing, governing
  11. controlling
leaf... 3. ola 4. gear, page 5. blade,
  frond, petal, sepal 6. areola, ligula,
  spathe 7. tendril
leaf (pert to)...
book.. 5. folio
bud.. 5. gemma
curvature.. 8. epinasty (down)
  9. hyponasty (upward)
floating.. 3. pad
green.. 11. chlorophyll
heart-shaped.. 9. obcordate
mold.. 5. humus
network.. 6. areola
part.. 5. bract, costa, stoma
  6. pagina, stipel 7. petiole
  9. petiolule
point, pointed.. 5. mucro
  9. mucronate 13. mucroniferous
pore.. 8. lenticel
secretion.. 4. lerp
stalk.. 7. petiole 8. petiolus
vein.. 3. rib 5. costa
leafless... 9. aphyllous
leaflet... 5. pinna, tract 6. folder
  7. booklet 8. pamphlet
  13. advertisement
league... 4. band, Bund 5. Hanse,
  union 7. combine 8. alliance
  9. coalition 10. federation
  11. affiliation, combination
  13. confederation
League of Nations site... 5. Paris
  (1920) 6. Geneva (Secretariat)
League of the Iroquois... 11. Five
  Nations
Leah's sister... 6. Rachel
leak... 3. drip, hole, seep 5. crack
  6. escape, run out 7. crevice, fissure
  10. be revealed
leal... 4. just, real, true 5. legal, loyal
  6. lawful 7. correct, genuine

8. accurate, faithful

lean . . . 4. bare, cant, lank, poor, rely,
slim, tend 5. gaunt, slope, spare
6. barren, meager 7. scraggy,
slender 8. not plump 9. deficient,
gravitate

lean (pert to) . . .
animal, person . . 4. ribe (Scot)
emaciated . . 6. marcid
make . . 8. macerate
towards . . 6. prefer

Leander's love . . . 4. Hero

leaning . . . 5. slope 6. desire
7. pronate, tending 8. aptitude,
enclitic, penchant, tendency
9. prejudice 10. partiality

Leaning Tower . . . 4. Pisa 6. Venice
7. Bologna 8. Zaragoza

lean–to . . . 4. roof, shed, wing 5. shack
9. extension (bldg)

leap . . . 4. dive, jump, ramp, skip
5. bound, caper, lunge, salto, spang,
vault 6. spring 7. saltary 8. capriole

leaping . . . 7. jumping, salient, saltant
8. bounding, salience 9. saltation

learn . . . 4. lere (anc) 6. master
8. memorize 9. ascertain, determine

learned . . . 3. wot 4. read, sage
6. legist 7. erudite 8. lettered,
literate, schooled 9. scholarly
12. well–informed

learned man . . . 6. pundit 7. scholar,
teacher 8. mastered 9. professor

learning . . . 3. art, ken, wit 4. lore
7. culture 8. pedantry 9. education,
erudition, knowledge, philology (love
of), philomath 11. scholarship

lease . . . 3. let 4. hire, rent 5. weave
6. demise, remise, tenure 8. contract

leasehold . . . 6. rental, tenure

leash . . . 4. bind, cord, lash, lune
(hawking) 5. reins, three 6. fasten,
string, tierce 9. restraint
11. subjugation

leash hound . . . 5. limer

least . . . 5. grain 6. little, lowest,
merest 7. minimum 8. minority,
shortest, simplest, smallest
9. slightest

leather . . . 4. hide, skin 5. aluta, leder
(old spelling) 6. vellum 7. canepin
8. cheveril (cheverel) 9. toughness

leather (kinds) . . . 3. kid, kip 4. calf,
napa, vici 5. Mocha, suede
6. patent, saddle, skiver 7. chamois,
Morocco 8. cordovan 9. sheepskin

leather (pert to) . . .
artificial . . 7. keratol
bookbinding . . 4. roan 6. levant
bottle . . 4. olpe 6. matara
cuirass . . 6. lorica
glove . . 5. suede, trank 8. capeskin
pare . . 5. skive
patch . . 5. clout
piece of . . 5. strap, thong 6. latigo
pouch (Highlander's) . . 7. sporran
process . . 3. tan, taw
strap . . 5. thong 6. latigo
term . . 8. efflower
tool . . 6. skiver
worker . . 6. chamar, tanner 8. chuckler

leatherneck . . . 6. marine

leave . . . 2. go 4. quit 6. depart, retire,
vacate 7. liberty 9. allowance
10. permission

leave (pert to) . . .
desolate . . 7. bereave
empty . . 6. vacate
isolated . . 6. desert, maroon
of absence . . 5. exeat 8. furlough
off . . 4. don't, stay 5. cease 6. desist
out . . 4. omit, skip 8. pass over
taking . . 5. adieu 6. congee
7. vamoose 9. departure

leaven . . . 4. barm 5. imbue, yeast
6. enzyme 7. corrupt (implied),
ferment, pervade 10. impregnate

leaves . . . 5. pages, shaws 6. sepals
7. foliage

leaves, feeding on . . .
13. phyllophagous

leavings . . . 4. left, orts, rest 5. culls,
dregs, dross, waste 6. refuse
7. remains, residue 8. remnants

leban, lebban . . . 5. drink 8. beverage,
sour milk

Lebanon capital . . . 6. Beirut

Lebanon city . . . 7. Tripoli

lech (anc) . . . 4. slab 8. capstone,
monument

lecher . . . 7. glutton 8. gourmand,
parasite 9. debauchee, libertine

lectern . . . 4. ambo, desk 6. pulpit
10. escritoire

lecture . . . 4. jobe, rate 5. scold
6. lesson 7. declaim, expound,
lection, reproof, reprove 8. instruct,
scolding 9. discourse 10. admonition

lecturer . . . 6. docent, reader 7. teacher
9. prelector

Leda (pert to) . . .
geology . . 4. clay (marine)
husband . . 4. Zeus
mother of . . 6. Castor, Pollux
11. Helen of Troy
zoology . . 7. mollusk

ledge . . . 4. berm, edge, lode, reef, sill
5. shelf 7. retable, stratum

leechlike . . . 8. bdelloid

lees . . . 5. draff, dregs 8. sediment

leeward . . . (opp of windward)
9. protected, sheltered

Leeward Islands . . . 5. Nevis
7. Antigua, Barbuda, Redonda
8. Anguilla, Sombrero 10. Montserrat
13. St Christopher

Leeward Islands group . . . 6. Virgin
7. Society

leeway . . . 10. enough rope

left . . . see also *leave* 3. haw, kay
8. departed, larboard 9. abandoned,
remaining

left (pert to) . . .
aground . . 6. neaped 8. beneaped
animal (motherless) . . 4. cade 5. dogie
comb form . . 8. sinistro
hand (Mus) . . 8. sinistra
hand page . . 5. verso
hand pitcher . . 8. southpaw
out . . 7. omitted 8. excluded
10. eliminated
spirally . . 11. sinistrally
to one's judgment . . 13. discretionary
toward the . . 5. aport 9. sinistrad,

sinistral 12. levorotatory (Chem)
left–handed ... 6. clumsy, gauche
7. oblique 8. southpaw 9. insincere,
insulting 14. sinistromanual
16. counterclockwise
left–handed marriage ...
10. morganatic
leftist ... 7. liberal, radical
10. left–winger, liberalist
11. progressive
leg (pert to) ...
armor .. 4. jamb 6. greave 7. jambeau
bone .. 4. shin 5. tibia 6. fibula
calf .. 5. sural
insect .. 4. coxa
joint .. 4. hock, knee 5. thigh
longest bone .. 5. femur
of lamb (cooked) .. 5. gigot
term .. 4. crus 5. jambe 6. crural
legacy ... 4. gift, will 6. devise
7. bequest, codicil 9. testament
10. bequeathal
legal ... 4. leal 5. licit, valid 6. lawful
10. authorized, legitimate
legal (pert to) ...
abstract .. 6. précis
act, thing .. 5. actus
action .. 3. res 4. case 7. detinet,
lawsuit, summons
case, postponed .. 7. remanet
claim .. 4. lien
confirmation .. 10. validation
contestant .. 6. suitor 8. litigant
9. plaintiff
critic .. 6. censor
decree, divorce .. 10. decree nisi
defense .. 5. alibi
delay .. 4. mora
denial, stoppage .. 8. estoppel
extract .. 7. estreat
order .. 4. writ
paper .. 4. deed, writ 5. lease
6. escrow
possession .. 6. seizin (seisin)
power (to take) .. 7. prender (prendre)
process .. 6. caveat 7. detinet
right, by .. 6. ex jure
security .. 4. bond
surrender .. 6. remise
legally competent ... 5. capax
legate ... 5. envoy 8. bequeath,
delegate 10. ambassador, diplomatic
legend ... 4. Edda, myth, saga, tale
5. fable 7. history 9. narrative,
tradition 11. inscription
legendary ... 8. fabulous 9. imaginary,
narrative 11. traditional
12. mythological
legendary (pert to) ...
goddess (slave) .. 5. Baube, lambe
primate .. 6. Dubric
water sprite .. 6. undine
legendry ... 7. legends (collectively)
leggings ... 5. chaps, spats 6. strads
7. gaiters, greaves, puttees
8. gamashes, gambados
12. galligaskins
legislate ... 3. act 5. elect, enact
8. pass laws 10. put through
legislative (pert to) ...
agent .. 8. lobbyist
assembly .. 4. diet 6. assize, senate

8. congress 10. parliament
group .. 4. bloc
legislator ... 5. solon 7. senator
8. lawgiver, lawmaker 9. statesman
11. congressman 14. representative
legislature ... 4. Diet 5. House
6. Senate 8. Congress 9. bicameral
(2 branches)
legitimate ... 4. real, true 5. legal, licit,
valid 6. cogent, lawful 7. genuine
9. permitted 11. efficacious,
justifiable
legman ... 8. newshawk
legume ... 3. pea, pod, uva 4. bean,
soya 6. clover, lentil, loment
7. alfalfa
leisure ... 4. ease, time, toom 5. otium
6. otiose 7. freedom 9. spare time
11. convenience, opportunity
lemming ... 4. maki, vari 5. mouse
6. rodent
lemur ... 5. indri, loris, makis, potto
6. anguid, aye–aye, colugo, galago,
macaco, monkey 7. tarsier
8. Anguidae, mongoose
10. angwantibo
Lenape ... 6. Indian (Del)
lend ... 4. loan 5. grant 6. devote (to)
7. advance
length (pert to) ...
measure .. 4. area 5. gauge 6. linear,
volume
ten meters .. 9. decameter
three–quarters inch .. 5. digit
time .. 3. age, eon, era 6. moment,
period
two and 1/4 inches .. 4. nail
unit .. 6. micron, parsec (Astron)
lengthen out ... 7. prolong, stretch
8. continue, elongate, protract
lengthwise ... 5. along 12. horizontally
14. longitudinally
lenient ... 3. lax 4. easy, mild
7. clement, patient 8. merciful,
relaxing, tolerant 9. assuasive,
emollient, softening
Lenin (pert to) ...
birthplace .. 9. Ulyanovsk
famed as .. 8. Dictator (Russ)
real name .. 7. Ulianov
Leningrad (Russ) ... 9. Petrograd
12. St Petersburg 15. Window on
the West
lenis ... 4. soft 6. gentle, smooth
lenitive ... 4. mild 6. gentle
8. mitigant, ointment, remedial
9. assuasive, emollient, mitigator,
relieving, softening 10. palliative,
qualifying
lens ... 5. toric 7. bifocal, lentoid
8. meniscus, sunglass 9. lenticula
10. anastigmat 13. apochromatism
Lent ... 6. carême 9. Forty days, Great
Fast 12. Quadragesima
lentamento ... 6. slowly
lentando ... 9. retarding 14. becoming
slower
lenticula ... 7. freckle, lentigo (freckly)
lento ... 4. slow
Leo constellation star ... 7. Regulus,
the Lion
leopard ... 4. pard 5. ounce 6. jaguar,

ocelot 7. cheetah, panther
leper... 5. lazar, mesel 6. Naaman
(Bib)
Lepontine Alps... 10. Monte Leone
(peak)
lepra... 7. leprosy 14. Hansen's
disease
Lesbos... 5. Assos (Aristotle's)
6. Island (Sappho's) 8. Mytilene
Les Miserables author... 4. Hugo
(Victor)
lessen... 4. bate, wane 5. abate,
lower, peter, relax 6. impair, minify,
narrow, reduce, shrink, weaken
7. cut down, relieve 8. decrease,
diminish, mitigate, moderate, palliate
11. deteriorate
lesser... 4. less 5. minor (Mus)
7. smaller 8. inferior
Lesser Bear (Astron)... 9. Ursa Minor
Lesser Dog (Astron)... 10. Canis Minor
Lesser Lion (Astron)... 8. Leo Minor
let... 4. hire, rent 5. allow, lease,
leave 6. hinder, impede, permit
7. prevent
let (pert to)...
down.. 5. lower 8. comedown,
drawback, relaxing 10. slackening
14. disappointment
fall.. 4. drop, slip 5. spill 7. mention
in.. 5. admit, enter 6. insert
it be given.. 5. detur
it stand.. 3. sta (Mus) 4. stet
up.. 4. rest 5. cease, pause, relax
6. slow up 7. slacken 8. decrease
lethal... 5. fatal, feral 6. deadly, mortal
7. deathly, killing 11. destructive
12. death–dealing
lethargic... 4. dull 5. heavy, inert
6. drowsy, sleepy, torpid
8. comatose, listless 9. apathetic
lethargy... 4. coma 5. sleep, sopor
6. apathy, stupor, torpor 7. languor
8. hebetude, neurosis 9. lassitude
10. drowsiness (morbid)
Lethe... 5. abyss, Hades, river
8. oblivion 13. forgetfulness
lethiferous... 6. deadly 11. destructive
Leto (pert to)...
mother of.. 6. Apollo 7. Artemis
Roman name.. 6. Latona
wife of.. 4. Zeus
letter... 4. note, type 7. epistle,
message 9. character
13. communication
letter (pert to)...
bright star.. 4. Beta
carrier.. 6. correo 7. mailman,
postman
cross stroke.. 5. serif
first.. 7. initial
letter for letter.. 9. literatim
marks.. 5. breve
of advice.. 11. lettre d'avis
of challenge.. 6. cartel
representation.. 10. literation
short.. 4. line, note 6. billet
sloping.. 6. italic
sound loss (last).. 7. apocope
two letters (one sound).. 7. digraph
9. diphthong

writer.. 13. correspondent
letters (pert to)...
decorate with.. 7. miniate
10. illuminate
man of.. 9. literatus
ref to.. 8. literary
lettuce... 3. cos 4. head 7. Lactuca,
romaine
leukocyte... 9. corpuscle (white)
Levant... 4. East 6. Orient 7. leather
(Morocco) 8. East wind
Levantine (pert to)...
country.. 13. Mediterranean
garment.. 6. caftan
herb.. 6. madder
ketch.. 3. bum 4. jerm, saic 5. xebec
6. settee 8. levanter
valley.. 4. wadi (wady)
wind.. 7. Morocco
levee... 4. bank, dike, pier, quay
5. ridge 6. durbar, trench
8. assembly 9. reception
10. embankment
level... 4. even, fell, flat, just, raze
5. equal, grade, plane, plani (comb
form), point 6. peavey (peavy),
smooth, steady, topple 7. flatten,
terrace, uniform 8. demolish,
equalize, parterre 12. well–balanced
lever... 3. bar, lam, pry 5. crank,
jimmy, pedal, prise 6. peavey
(peavy), tappet, tiller 7. crowbar,
treadle
leviathan (pert to)...
animal (Bib).. 5. whale 6. dragon
9. crocodile
embroidery.. 6. canvas
11. cross–stitch
political.. 12. (the) commonwealth
size.. 4. huge 7. titanic
10. formidable
Levi's father (Bib)... 5. Jacob
Levite... 5. tribe 10. descendant
Levitical... 7. Aaronic 9. Aaronical
10. priesthood (Mormon)
Leviticus... 10. Pentateuch
levity... 6. gaiety 8. buoyancy
9. frivolity, lightness 10. triviality,
volatility
levy... 3. tax 4. fine, wage (war)
5. rally, stent 6. assess, impose
7. collect, estreat 9. recruital
lex... 3. law 7. statute
lexicon... 4. book (of words)
10. dictionary, vocabulary
lex loci... 13. law of the place
lex non scripta... 12. unwritten law
liability... 4. debt 5. debit 8. cessavit
9. proneness 10. likelihood,
obligation 11. possibility
14. responsibility
liable... 3. apt 5. bound 6. likely
7. exposed, subject 10. answerable,
chargeable 11. responsible
liable (pert to)...
likely to.. 3. apt 5. prone
11. predisposed
not liable.. 6. exempt
to objection.. 13. exceptionable
to penalty.. 6. guilty
Lia Fail... 12. Stone of Scone
15. Coronation Stone (Ir)

liaison... 4. link 7. joining 8. intimacy, intrigue 11. co–operation 18. intercommunication

liana... 4. cipo 5. vines (woody) 9. wild grape

liar... 5. cheat 6. fibber 7. Ananias, wernard (obs) 8. deceiver, fabulist, perjurer 12. prevaricator

Lias system... 8. Jurassic

libation... 5. drink 8. oblation, offering, potation

libel... 4. bill 6. defame 7. lampoon, request, slander 8. circular (obs), handbill, roorback 10. defamation 11. certificate, declaration 12. supplication

liberal... 4. free, Whig 5. ample, frank 7. copious, profuse 8. eclectic, generous 9. bountiful, extensive, plentiful 10. hospitable, munificent 11. broad–minded, magnanimous 12. uncontrolled

liberate... 4. flee, free 5. loose 6. redeem 7. deliver, manumit, release 8. separate, unfetter 9. disengage 10. emancipate

Liberia...
capital.. 8. Monrovia
city.. 8. Buchanan 10. Greenville
gulf.. 5. Sidra
language.. 3. Kru 7. English
people.. 3. Vai (Vei) 5. Negro

liberty... 4. ease, free 5. leave 7. freedom, license 9. exemption, privilege 10. permission 11. opportunity

librarian... 7. bookman 10. bibliosoph, bibliothec 13. bibliothecary

Libya, Africa...
astronomy.. 4. Mars (portion)
capital.. 7. Tripoli 8. Benghazi
district.. 6. Fezzan 9. Cyrenaica 12. Tripolitania
language.. 7. Hamitic
oasis (saline).. 6. Sebkha (Sebka)
people.. 5. Arabs
sea.. 13. Mediterranean

Libya, Gr (pert to)...
children.. 5. Belus 6. Agenor
heroine of.. 5. Libya
husband.. 8. Poseidon

license... 5. right 6. bandon, permit 7. dismiss, freedom, liberty 8. sanction 9. approbate, authority, authorize, privilege 10. permission 11. lawlessness 13. authorization

licentious... 3. lax 4. lewd 5. loose 7. immoral, lawless 9. debauched, dissolute 10. lascivious, profligate 12. uncontrolled, unrestrained

licet... 6. lawful 7. granted 12. it is conceded

lichens (pert to)...
abounding in.. 9. lichenose
derivative.. 4. moss 5. usnic 6. litmus
genus.. 5. Usnea 7. Evernia
study of.. 11. lichenology

licit... 3. sue 4. just 5. legal 6. lawful 9. permitted

lick... 3. lap, win 4. flog, whip 5. lap up, taste 6. baffle, defeat, thrash

7. conquer 8. overcome, vanquish

licorice... 5. abrin 9. jequirity

lid... 3. cap, hat 4. bred, case, roof 5. cover 6. eyelid 7. stopper 9. operculum

lid, put on the... 3. end 6. hush up 7. license 8. complete, suppress

lie... 3. fib 4. rest 7. falsify, falsity, recline, untruth 9. deception, falsehood, mendacity 10. equivocate 13. prevarication

lie (pert to)...
at ease.. 4. loll 5. droop 6. dangle
face down.. 7. pronate
hidden, in ambush.. 4. lurk, plot 6. in wait 9. insidiate 11. concealment
in warmth.. 4. bask 9. luxuriate
low.. 6. abased 9. prostrate
prostrate.. 4. flat 5. creep 6. grovel

Liebestraum composer... 5. Liszt

Liechtenstein, Europe...
capital.. 5. Vaduz
government.. 12. principality
language.. 6. German
religion.. 8. Catholic

lief (anc)... 4. dear, fain, glad 7. willing 8. disposed 9. agreeably, favorably

lieutenant... 6. deputy 10. substitute 11. locum tenens

life... 3. vie, bios 5. being 6. always, energy, spirit 8. vitality, vivacity 9. animation, existence

life (pert to)...
after death.. 8. Olam–haba
animal.. 4. bios 5. biota (flora, fauna)
biology.. 4. bios
comb form.. 3. bio
giving.. 9. animative 11. procreative
god of.. 6. Faunus
insurance.. 7. tontine
jacket (sl).. 7. Mae West
later, older.. 8. autumnal
lifelike.. 5. alike, vital 6. biotic 9. realistic
plant.. 4. bios 5. biota
principle.. 5. atman, prana, tenet 6. spirit
prolonger.. 6. elixir
science of.. 7. anatomy, biology, zoology 12. paleontology
sea.. 5. coral 8. plankton
staff of.. 5. bread
without.. 4. dead 5. azoic 8. lifeless 9. inanimate

lifeless... 4. abio (comb form), dead, dull, flat 5. amort, azoic, heavy, inert, vapid 6. jejune, torpid 8. inactive, listless 9. bloodless, exanimate, inanimate, powerless, tasteless 10. lackluster, spiritless, unanimated

lifetime... 3. age, day, eon (aeon) 6. always 8. duration 10. generation

lift... 3. aid, pry 4. jack, perk 5. boost, exalt, heave, hoist, raise, steal, theft 6. puff up, thrill 7. derrick, elevate, improve, inspire 8. elevator 11. inspiration

lifting device... 4. jack, pump

5. crane, davit, lever, tongs
7. capstan, derrick, erector
8. elevator, heighten, windlass
lifting muscle ... 7. erector, levator
ligament ... 4. bond, cord 6. tendon
7. bandage
ligan, lagan ... 6. debris, jetsam
7. flotsam
ligature ... 3. tie 4. band, bond, cord,
note 6. amulet, binder, taenia
7. bandage
light ... 3. arc, gay, sun 4. dawn, easy,
glim, lamp, lume, mild, pale, soft
5. flare, flood, klieg, laser, taper
6. alight, aspect, blonde, bright,
candle, gentle, ignite, illume, medium,
window 7. cresset, fragile, glimmer,
glowing, trivial 8. buoyancy, daylight,
delicate, illumine, lambency, radiance,
trifling 9. effulgent 10. brightness,
luminosity, weightless 11. information
12. incandescent
light (pert to) ...
apparatus .. 9. holophote
circle .. 4. halo, nimb 6. corona,
nimbus 7. aureola, aureole
cloud .. 6. nimbus
coating .. 4. film
footed .. 4. fast 5. agile
globe .. 4. bulb
god .. 6. Balder (Baldr)
handed .. 4. deft
headed .. 5. dizzy 6. fickle
9. beeheaded
image .. 8. spectrum
leading .. 8. luminary
reflector .. 4. lens 6. mirror
refractor .. 5. prism
science .. 6. optics
source .. 3. sun
touch .. 3. dab
unit .. 3. lux, pyr 4. phot, watt
5. lumen 6. carcel, Hefner
without .. 4. dark 7. aphotic, obscure
8. starless 9. pitch–dark
10. caliginous
yellow .. 5. amber
light and airy ... 7. tenuous
8. delicate, ethereal
light and quick ... 6. nimble, volent
light dress fabric ... 6. merino
8. cashmere 9. bombazine, paramatta
(parramatta)
lighten ... 4. ease 5. allay, cheer, clear
6. reduce 7. gladden, relieve
8. brighten, illumine, jettison
9. alleviate, disburden 10. illuminate
lighter ... see also *light* 4. scow
5. barge 7. gabbard, igniter, pontoon
8. chopboat (Chin)
lighthearted ... 3. gay 6. upbeat
7. buoyant 8. carefree, cheerful,
jubilant 9. vivacious
Light Horse Harry ... 3. Lee (Gen
Henry Lee)
lighthouse ... 5. tower 6. beacon,
pharos 7. seamark 10. watchtower
lightness ... 6. gaiety, levity
8. airiness, buoyancy, sobriety
9. flippancy, frivolity, giddiness
10. fickleness, triviality, volatility,
wantonness 11. flightiness,

inconstancy, instability
12. unsteadiness 14. weightlessness
15. thoughtlessness
lightning ... 4. lait 5. flash, levin
6. stroke 8. flashing 9. discharge
lightning (pert to) ...
bug .. 6. beetle 7. firefly
discharge .. 4. bolt 11. thunderbolt
form .. 4. fork 5. chain, sheet
reference to .. 8. fulgural
rod .. 8. arrester
stone .. 9. fulgurite
war .. 10. blitzkrieg
lightsome ... 3. gay 4. airy 5. agile,
clear, light, lucid, merry 6. fickle,
nimble 7. lighted 8. cheerful,
cheering, graceful, luminous, unsteady
9. frivolous 12. lighthearted
lights out ... 4. taps
ligneous ... 5. woody 6. wooden,
xyloid 8. firewood
lignite ... 4. coal
like ... 2. as 4. copy, love 5. enjoy,
equal, liken, savor 6. admire, desire
7. similar 10. comparable
11. counterpart, homogeneous
like (pert to) ...
bone .. 6. osteal
fern .. 7. frondose, frondous
gland .. 7. adenose
gold .. 7. aureate
house, dome .. 5. domal
kneecap .. 7. rotular 10. rotuliform
sea lion .. 7. otarian, otarine
suffix .. 2. ar, ic 3. ine, oid, ose
likeable, likable ... 6. genial
8. charming, pleasant
likelihood ... 8. prospect 10. good
chance 11. possibility, probability
14. apparently true
likely ... 3. apt, fit 5. prone 6. comely
8. credible, feasible, probable, suitable
9. promising 11. verisimilar
likeness ... 4. copy, icon, twin
5. clone, guise, image 6. effigy,
statue 7. parable, picture, replica
8. parallel, portrait 9. imitation,
semblance 10. comparison,
photograph, similarity 11. counterfeit
12. reproduction 14. representation
likewise ... 3. too 4. also 5. ditto
8. moreover 11. furthermore
liking ... 4. like, love, lust 5. fancy
6. comely 7. delight 8. pleasing
10. preference 12. predilection
lilac ... 5. lilas, mauve 6. purple
7. syringa
lilac throat ... 11. hummingbird
Lilliputian ... 4. tiny 5. dwarf, minim
6. midget 7. dwarfed 10. diminutive
lilt ... 3. air 4. song, tune 5. swing
6. poetic, rhythm 7. rejoice
lily ... 2. ti 3. lis 4. aloe, ixia, sego
5. calla, lotus, onion, water, wokas
(wocas), yucca 6. Allium, Nuphar
8. daffodil, mariposa, martagon,
soaproot 9. narcissus
lily (pert to) ...
family, genus .. 4. aloe 6. Tulipa
7. Bessera 9. Liliaceae
10. Hyacinthus
grass .. 10. cuckoopint

iron.. **7.** harpoon
of France.. **10.** fleur–de–lis
shaped.. **7.** crinoid **9.** crinoidal
water.. **8.** Castalia, Nymphaea
lily of the valley (pert to)...
bud.. **3.** pip
Cape Cod.. **13.** barney–clapper
English.. **6.** mugget
family.. **15.** Convallariaceae
liliaceous plant.. **5.** yucca
shrub.. **10.** fetterbush
tree.. **6.** sorrel
lima bean disease... **6.** mildew
9. yeast spot
liman... **5.** marsh **6.** lagoon
limb... **3.** arm, fin, imp, leg **4.** wing
5. bough, scamp **6.** branch, member
7. flipper **9.** anaclasis
limber... **4.** limp, weak **5.** agile, lithe,
loose **6.** flabby, pliant, supple
7. flaccid, lissome **8.** flexible, yielding
limbo... **4.** hell, jail **6.** prison
9. purgatory
limbs, absence of... **6.** amelia
7. acolous
lime... **4.** calx **5.** color, fruit
8. chlorine, fumigant **9.** deodorant,
quicklime **11.** green–yellow
12. linden yellow
limen... **9.** threshold
limestone... **4.** calp, malm **5.** chalk
6. marble, oolite **8.** pisolite
lime tree... **6.** linden, tupelo
limey... **6.** sailor **7.** soldier
limit... **3.** end, fix, ori (comb form)
4. term **5.** allot, bourn **6.** summit
7. confine **8.** boundary, capacity,
restrain, restrict, terminal
11. restriction, termination
12. consummation
limited... **3.** few **5.** local, scant
6. finite, narrow, scanty **7.** bounded,
topical **8.** confined, reserved
9. astricted, parochial **10.** restricted
11. conditional, topopolitan
13. circumscribed
limiting... **7.** hedging **10.** qualifying,
relational **11.** restraining, restricting,
restrictive
limn... **4.** draw **5.** paint **6.** depict
7. portray **8.** decorate **9.** delineate
10. illuminate
limp... **3.** hop, lax **4.** halt, soft, thin,
weak **5.** loose **6.** flabby, limber
7. flaccid **8.** drooping, flexible
9. inelastic **13.** unsubstantial
limpid... **4.** pure **5.** lucid **6.** bright
7. crystal **8.** pellucid **11.** translucent,
transparent **12.** intelligible
Lincoln, Abraham (pert to)...
assassin.. **15.** John Wilkes Booth
birthplace.. **8.** Kentucky (1809)
debater.. **7.** Douglas (Stephen A)
dog.. **4.** Fido
mother.. **10.** Nancy Hanks
Secy of State.. **6.** Seward
Secy of War.. **7.** Stanton
son.. **10.** Robert Todd
wife.. **8.** Mary Todd
Lincoln (pert to)...
color.. **9.** Carthamus **11.** yellow–green
sheep (breed).. **7.** English

Lindbergh, Charles A (pert to)...
birthplace.. **7.** Detroit (1902)
flight field.. **9.** Roosevelt (LI)
flight to (1927).. **5.** Paris (1st)
retreat.. **10.** Illiec Isle (Fr)
wife.. **10.** Anne Morrow
linden... **3.** lin **4.** lime, teil **5.** Tilia
line... **3.** row **4.** arow, axis, cant, ceil,
clew, cord, face, mark, race, rail,
rein, rule, seam, side **5.** agone,
align, raphe, ridge, route, stria, track
6. crease, isobar, policy, series,
streak, stripe **7.** engrave, outline
8. boundary, vocation, wainscot
9. delineate
line (pert to)...
adjusting.. **9.** alinement
central.. **4.** axis
comb form.. **4.** lino
conceptual, geological.. **6.** agonic,
isotac, tropic **7.** equator **8.** isothere,
isotherm, latitude, meridian
9. longitude
equidistant.. **8.** parallel
fine (type).. **5.** leger, serif
fishing.. **5.** snell **7.** ratline (ratlin)
imaginary.. **7.** equator, Maginot
mathematics.. **4.** sine **5.** agone
6. secant **7.** tangent
measure.. **3.** gry **4.** rule
meteoric.. **6.** isobar
nautical.. **6.** earing **7.** halyard,
hawsing
poetic.. **5.** stich, verse
racing.. **4.** wire
raised.. **4.** weal, welt **5.** ridge
selling.. **11.** merchandise
soldiers.. **4.** file, rank **6.** cordon
transport.. **5.** stage **7.** carrier
8. carriage
type.. **5.** agate, serif
up, lineup.. **4.** plan **5.** align
6. muster **7.** arrange **8.** schedule
9. formation **11.** arrangement,
parallelize
lineage... **3.** kin **4.** race **5.** birth,
blood, stock, tribe **6.** family, strain
7. descent **8.** pedigree **9.** offspring
10. extraction, progenitor
lineal... **6.** racial **10.** continuous,
delineated **12.** genealogical
lineman... **3.** end **5.** guard **6.** center,
tackle **7.** wireman **11.** electrician
linen... **4.** crea, duck, lawn, lint
5. crash, gulix, inkle (tape), toile
6. barras, damask, dowlas, napery,
sheets **7.** cambric, Holland, lockram
ling... **4.** fish, hake **5.** heath **6.** burbot
7. eelpout, Gidadae, heather
8. chestnut
linger... **3.** lag **4.** drag, idle, wait
5. dally, defer, delay, dwell, hover,
tarry **6.** dawdle, go slow, loiter,
remain **8.** continue, hesitate
13. procrastinate
lingerie... **9.** underwear **10.** underlinen
11. underthings **14.** unmentionables
lingering... **5.** delay **7.** chronic
8. dilatory, slowness **10.** protracted
lingo... **4.** cant **6.** jargon, lingua,
patois, patter, tongue **8.** language
lingua... **5.** lingo **6.** jargon, tongue

11. hypopharynx
lingual... 7. glossal 9. lingulate
   10. linguiform, tonguelike
linguistics... 6. syntax 7. grammar
   8. language 9. phonology, semantics
   10. lexicology
link... 3. tie 4. bond, join, loop, yoke
   5. annex, nexus, torch, unite
   6. couple, member, relate
   7. connect, liaison, passage
   8. catenate 12. intermediary
linkage... 5. tie–up, union 6. hookup
   7. joinder, joining 8. junction
   11. conjunction
linking... 7. liaison 9. annectent
links in a chain... 7. hundred
lion... 3. cat, cub, leo 4. puma
   5. simba 6. cougar, Lionel, lionet
   8. Felis leo 9. celebrity 12. King of
   Beasts
Lion (pert to)...
   England.. 8. heraldry
   God.. 3. Ali
   Lucerne.. 11. Switzerland (Sculpture)
   St Mark.. 6. Venice (winged)
   the North.. 6. Sweden (King
   Adolphus)
lionlike... 6. feline 7. catlike, leonine
lip... 3. jib, rim 4. edge, kiss, talk
   5. cheil, words 6. flange, labium,
   labrum, speech 7. cheilos
   8. labellum 10. mouthpiece
   12. impertinence
lip (pert to)...
   comb form.. 5. chilo, labio
   formed.. 6. labial
   inflammation.. 9. cheilitis
   ornament.. 6. labret
   service.. 9. hypocrisy 10. sanctimony
   12. unctuousness
   surgery.. 9. chilotomy 11. chiloplasty
   tumor.. 7. chiloma
lipped... 6. labial 7. labiate
liquefy... 4. fuse, melt, thaw
   6. reduce 8. dissolve, fluidify
   10. deliquesce
liqueur... 5. crème, noyau, sirup
   6. cognac, genepi, kummel
   7. cordial, curaçao, ratafia
   8. absinthe, anisette 9. Cointreau
   11. Benedictine
liquid... 5. clear, fluid 6. watery
   7. flowing 8. beverage, manifest, not
   solid
liquid (pert to)...
   assets.. 4. cash 5. money
   9. resources
   chemical.. 7. acetone 8. furfural
   inflammable.. 3. gas 5. ether
   7. alcohol 8. gasoline
   oily.. 5. olein 7. aniline, picamar
   soap.. 6. napalm
   thick.. 3. tar 4. dope 5. syrup (sirup)
   weak.. 5. blash
liquidate... 4. kill 6. depose, pay off,
   settle 8. amortize 9. discharge
   11. exterminate
liquor... 3. ale, dew, gin, rum, rye
   4. beer, brew, grog, lush, sake, wine
   5. hooch, kefir, punch, stout, vodka
   6. arrack (arak), arrope, elixir, whisky
   (whiskey) 8. cocktail, highball

9. applejack, moonshine
   10. chasse–café
liquor container... 3. keg 5. flask
   6. barrel, bottle 8. cellaret, decanter
liquor maker... 6. abkari (Ind), brewer
   7. vintner 9. distiller
liquor server... 6. barman 7. barmaid,
   skinker (anc), tapster
liquor shop... 3. bar 6. saloon, tavern
   7. barroom, cabaret, shebeen (Scot),
   taproom 8. alehouse 9. groghouse,
   honky–tonk 11. rathskeller (ratskeller)
liripipe, liripoop (Hist)... 4. hood
   5. scarf 6. dotard, tippet
lissom... 5. layer 7. stratum
   8. platform 12. strand of rope
lissome... 5. agile, lithe 6. limber,
   nimble, supple 7. willowy 8. flexible
list... 3. tip 4. edge, file, roll, rota,
   rote 5. index, limit, panel, table
   6. careen, edging, enlist, record,
   roster, stripe 7. catalog, incline
   8. calendar, classify, manifest,
   register, schedule, tabulate
   9. catalogue, enclosure, inventory,
   repertory 10. repertoire
   11. enumeration
list (pert to)...
   actors.. 4. cast
   competitors.. 5. entry, slate
   foods.. 4. menu 5. carte
   investments.. 9. portfolio
   memoranda.. 5. scrip
   officers.. 6. roster
   references.. 5. index
listen... 3. ear 4. hear, heed 6. attend
   7. give ear, hearken (harken)
   8. overhear 9. eavesdrop
listening... 7. audient 9. attentive
listing... 4. list 6. strips 7. selvage
   10. enlistment, enrollment
listless... 4. dull 6. abject, drowsy,
   moping, supine 7. languid
   8. careless, heedless, sluggish
   9. apathetic 10. spiritless
   11. unconcerned 13. uninteresting
litchi nut... 8. rambutan
literary... 6. versed 8. lettered
   9. classical 11. book–learned
literary (pert to)...
   composition.. 5. cento, essay, opera
   8. rhetoric
   criticism.. 9. epicrisis
   drudge.. 4. grub, hack
   extracts.. 9. anthology
   fragments.. 3. ana 5. notes
   8. analecta, analects
   laws.. 9. copyright
   piracy.. 10. plagiarism
   selection.. 7. excerpt
   style.. 5. prose 6. purism 8. pedantic
literature... 4. book, epic, Veda
   5. drama, lyric, novel 6. ballad,
   poetry 7. fiction, writing
   10. nonfiction 13. belles–lettres
lithe... 4. slim 6. limber, supple, svelte
   7. lissome, slender 8. flexible
Lithuania...
   capital.. 5. Vilna (Vilnius) 6. Kaunas
   (Kovno)
   Jew.. 6. Litvak
   people.. 5. Balts, Letts 6. Aestii

port.. 8. Klaipeda (Memel)
river.. 6. Niemen
litigant... 6. suitor 9. defendant,
disputant, litigator, plaintiff
litigation... 4. suit 7. contest, dispute,
lawsuit 10. contention, discussion
litigious... 10. disputable
11. belligerent, contentious
litten... 7. lighted 8. cemetery
10. churchyard
litter... 3. bed, hay 4. bier, mess
5. couch, dooly (doolie), mulch,
straw, young 6. coffin, jumble
7. clutter, rubbish 9. palanquin,
stretcher
litter of pigs... 6. farrow
little... 3. sma, wee 4. puny, tiny,
weak 5. brief, petit, petty, scant,
short, small 6. dapper, petite, slight
7. not much 8. trifling 9. niggardly
11. unimportant 12. narrow–minded
14. inconsiderable
little (pert to)...
bethel.. 6. chapel (seaman's), church
by little.. 6. slowly 7. peu à peu
9. piecemeal, poco a poco
comb form.. 5. steno
devil.. 3. imp 4. minx 5. rogue
7. ruffian 13. mischief–maker
fellow.. 6. shaver
finger, toe.. 7. minimus
flag.. 9. banderole
music term.. 4. poco
ring.. 7. annulet
Little Rhody... 11. Rhode Island
Little Women, author... 6. Alcott
(Louisa)
littoral... 4. zone (marine) 5. shore
7. coastal 9. bordering
liturgical... 10. ceremonial
11. ritualistic
liturgy... 4. rite 6. ritual 8. ceremony
14. consuetudinary
live... 5. dwell, exist 6. reside
7. breathe 8. continue, have life
live (pert to)...
by sponging.. 5. cadge
by stratagems.. 5. shark
by wits.. 5. cheat 7. deceive, falsify
13. Machiavellize
earlier.. 8. pre–exist
in.. 7. inhabit
in tents.. 5. nomad 7. scenite
in the country.. 9. rusticate
live... 5. alert, alive, vital, vivid
6. bright, lively, living, virgin (mineral)
7. charged, not dead 8. vigorous
9. energetic 11. electrified
lively... 3. gay, vif 4. airy, grig, keen,
pert, spry, yare 6. active, blithe,
bright, snappy 7. animate, buoyant,
pungent, tittupy (tittuppy) 8. spirited
9. energetic, sprightly, vivacious
10. enlivening, rebounding
11. interesting 12. effervescent
liver (pert to)...
comb form.. 6. hepato
disease.. 9. cirrhosis, hepatitis
duct.. 4. bile
pert to.. 5. hepar 7. hepatic
resembling.. 8. hepatoid
Liverpool native... 12. Liverpudlian

liverwort... 6. Riccia 8. agrimony,
hepatica 9. bryophyte
living... 4. life 5. alive, being, quick
6. extant 7. animate, organic, topical
8. benefice, existent, lifelike
10. livelihood 11. subsistence
living (in, on, near)...
currents.. 5. lotic
ground.. 7. epigeal
holes.. 11. latebricole
leaves.. 13. phyllophagous
oxygen.. 7. aerobic
plane (same).. 8. coplanar
poverty.. 11. necessitous
river bank.. 9. riparious
rivers, streams.. 9. rheophile
seas (deep).. 8. bathybic
shores.. 8. littoral
solitude, seclusion.. 10. eremitical
11. eremiticism
tents.. 7. scenite
together.. 11. contubernal
living (pert to)...
again.. 6. Buddha 7. revived
8. Hutukhtu 9. redivivus
being.. 5. wight 6. animal
8. organism
capable of.. 6. viable
dull.. 10. vegetation
individual.. 4. bion
near the ground.. 7. epigeal
together.. 8. intimate 11. contubernal
(contubernial)
lixivium... 3. lye 6. bleach 8. cleanser
lizard... 3. dab, eft 4. adda, gila,
newt, seps, uran 5. agama, anoli,
gecko, skink, varan 6. dragon,
hardim, iguana, moloch 7. monitor,
saurian, tuatera 8. basilisk
9. chameleon 10. chuckwalla,
salamander
llama... 6. alpaca, vicuna 7. guanaco
load... 3. jag 4. fill, lade, onus
5. cargo 6. burden, charge, weight
7. fraught, freight, oppress, prepare
8. contents, encumber 10. imposition
11. encumbrance
loaded... 5. drunk, flush, laden, ready
7. charged, fraught 8. burdened,
weighted 10. in the chips
loader of vessels... 9. stevedore
loadstone, lodestone... 6. magnet
8. terrella 9. magnetite
loaf... 4. idle, lump 5. bread 6. loiter,
lounge 9. Eucharist
loafer... 5. idler 6. beggar 7. lounger
8. vagabond
loam... 3. rab 4. clay, lime, silt, soil
5. chalk, loess, regur
loan... 4. lend 6. borrow 7. advance
10. provisions 13. accommodation
loath... 6. averse 7. hostile
9. disliking, reluctant, unwilling
loathe... 4. hate 5. abhor 6. detest
7. despise, dislike 9. abominate
loathsome... 4. foul, vile 5. nasty
6. odious 7. cloying, hateful
9. abhorrent, offensive, repellant
10. abominable, disgusting
lob... 3. box, cop 4. step, till, toss,
vein 5. stair, throw 7. lugworm,
pollack 9. chandelle

lobby... 4. hall, room 5. foyer
  8. anteroom, corridor, coulisse
  9. enclosure, vestibule 10. wirepuller
  13. pressure group
lobe... 5. alula 6. earlap, lappet, lobule
  7. pendant
lobster (pert to)...
  claw.. 5. chela 6. nipper, pincer
  eggs.. 3. roe 5. coral
  French.. 6. homard
  genus.. 7. Homarus, Macrura
  8. Nephrops
  part.. 6. thorax
  tail.. 6. telson
  trap.. 3. pot 4. corf 5. creel 6. bow net
local... 7. edaphic, topical 8. regional
  9. parochial 10. epichorial (epichoric)
  13. autochthonous
local court... 5. gemot (gemote)
locale... 4. site 5. place, scene, venue
locality... 4. area, spot 5. place, situs
  7. endemic, habitat 8. position
locate... 4. find, spot 6. settle
  7. situate 9. establish
locatio... 7. leasing, letting
location... 4. seat, site, spot 5. locus,
  place, situs 6. ubiety 7. habitat
  8. district 9. situation
  12. neighborhood
locator of forest fires... 7. alidade
loch... 3. bay 4. lake, pond 5. inlet, lough
lock... 4. bolt, hasp, hold 5. Gatun,
  latch 6. cotter, detent, fasten, fetter
  8. fastener 9. floodgate
lockjaw... 7. tetanus, trismus
  11. ankylostoma
lockman... 8. summoner (Isle of Man)
  11. executioner
lock of hair... 4. curl 5. tress
  6. berger 7. daglock, ringlet
  8. lovelock, spit curl
lockup... 3. jug 4. jail 5. clink
  6. cooler 8. hoosegow (hoosgow)
  9. calaboose
loco... 3. mad 4. daft 5. craze, crazy
  6. crazed 7. disease 10. moonstruck
  15. non compos mentis
locomotion... 6. lation (Astrol), moving,
  travel 7. transit 8. progress
locomotive... 3. hog 5. dolly, mogul
  6. diesel, dinkey, engine, mikado
  9. iron horse
locomotive cowcatcher... 5. pilot
locus... 4. area, drug, site 5. place
  8. locality
locus (pert to)...
  in quo.. 5. where 12. place in which
  sigilli.. 14. place of the seal
locust... 4. weta 6. beetle, cicada,
  cicala, kowhai 7. Locusta
  9. wetapunga 11. grasshopper
locust (pert to)...
  berry.. 5. drupe 9. glamberry
  bird.. 4. dial 7. grackle 8. starling
  10. white stork
  like.. 6. mantis
  plant.. 5. senna
  sound.. 7. stridor 10. stridulate
  tree.. 5. carob, honey 6. acacia
lode... 3. vug (vugg) 4. path, road,

vein 5. canal, drain, ledge 6. course
  7. deposit 8. waterway
lodestar... 8. cynosure, polestar
  11. guiding star
lodestone, loadstone... 6. magnet
  8. terrella 9. magnetite
lodge... 3. hut, lie 4. camp, tent
  5. cabin, hovel 6. billet, encamp,
  reside 7. deposit, quarter
  11. brotherhood
lodge doorkeeper... 5. tiler
lodging... 3. inn 4. gite, room
  5. abode, hotel, roost 6. billet,
  harbor (harbour), tavern 8. barracks,
  dwelling, hostelry, quarters
  9. dormitory, harborage (harbourage)
  10. habitation
loess... 4. loam, silt, soil
lof... 6. praise 7. measure
loft... 3. bin 4. balk 5. attic
loftiness... 6. height 7. dignity
  8. eminence 9. eloquence
  11. distinction, magnanimity
lofty... 4. high, tall 5. proud 6. aerial,
  Alpine, Andean 7. eminent, exalted,
  haughty, stately, sublime 8. arrogant,
  elevated, eloquent, majestic, towering
  9. dignified 11. magisterial,
  magnanimous 13. distinguished
lofty place... 4. peak 5. aerie, eyrie
  (eyry) 6. summit 8. eminence,
  pinnacle
log... 4. birl, slab 5. diary 6. record
  8. firewood, mountain, puncheon,
  register 11. speedometer
log (pert to)...
  cock.. 10. woodpecker
  gin.. 6. jammer
  hauler (sled).. 4. tode
  implement.. 6. nigger, peavey (peavy), rosser
  measure.. 7. scalage
  noser.. 6. sniper
  rolling.. 7. birling
  section.. 5. spalt
  support.. 3. nog
logarithmic terms... 3. bel 5. curve
  6. spiral 7. ellipse, tangent
  9. decrement
logarithm inventor... 6. Napier
loge... 3. box 5. booth, stall
loggerhead... 4. tool 6. turtle
  7. fathead 8. bonehead, numskull
  9. blockhead 10. thickskull
loggia... 7. gallery
logging (pert to)...
  boots.. 4. pacs
  rock.. 6. loggan
  sled.. 4. tode 7. travois (travoise)
  wheels.. 7. katydid
logic... 9. reasoning 13. argumentation
logic (pert to)...
  fallacy.. 6. idolum
  induction.. 7. epagoge
  proposition.. 5. lemma 7. ferison
  9. enthymeme, obvertend
  specious.. 7. sophism
  term.. 5. Darii, Ferio 8. Celarent
logical... 4. sane 5. sound, valid
  8. coherent, credible, rational
  9. plausible 10. consistent, reasonable

logician... 8. reasoner
logogriph... 5. rebus 6. riddle
  7. anagram 8. logogram
logy... 4. dull 6. drowsy 8. sluggish
Lohengrin (pert to)...
  character.. 4. Elsa 8. Parsifal
  composer.. 6. Wagner (1850)
  Knight.. 15. Knight of the Swan
loin (pert to)...
  beef.. 10. tenderloin
  mutton.. 4. rack 5. chump
  pork.. 7. griskin
loincloth... 5. dhoti, pagne 7. G–string
  11. breechcloth
loir... 8. dormouse
Loire, France...
  Dept capital.. 12. Saint Etienne
  river's old name.. 5. Liger
  town.. 6. Nantes
  tributary.. 5. Indre
loiter... 3. lag 5. dally, delay, tarry
  6. dawdle, linger 7. saunter
loiterer... 4. slug 5. drone, idler
  6. lagger 7. dawdler, laggard
  8. sluggard
Loki (pert to)...
  god.. 7. Discord 8. Mischief
  wife.. 5. Sigyn
loll... 4. hang 5. droop 6. dangle,
  frowst (froust), lounge, repose, sprawl
  7. recline
loma, lomita... 4. hill
Lombard (pert to)...
  ancient.. 6. cannon
  historic.. 4. bank, loan
  Italy.. 5. tribe
  King.. 6. Alboin (legend)
  school.. 11. Renaissance
  street.. 6. London
Lombardy province... 4. Como
lomboy... 8. Java plum
lomilomi (Haw)... 3. rub 7. massage,
  shampoo
London, England...
  art gallery.. 4. Tate
  bank.. 27. Old Lady of Threadneedle
  Street
  borough.. 6. Ealing
  bridge.. 6. Thames
  bridle path.. 9. Rotten Row
  brown.. 9. carbuncle
  clock.. 6. Big Ben
  club (Whigs).. 6. Kit–Kat
  district.. 4. Soho 7. Alsatia, Lambeth,
  Mayfair (fashion) 9. Wimbledon
  10. Marylebone
  hawker.. 6. coster
  monument (Guildhall).. 3. Gog
  5. Magog
  Opera Company.. 12. Sadler's Wells
  porter.. 6. George
  prison.. 7. Newgate 9. Bridewell
  quarter.. 8. Vauxhall
  roisterer (Hist).. 3. mum
  Roman name.. 6. Agusta
  stables.. 4. mews
  stock exchange.. 17. Throgmorton
  Street
  street.. 9. Cheapside, Whitehall
  10. Piccadilly 11. Throgmorton
  12. Threadneedle
Londoner... 7. Cockney

Londres... 5. cigar
lone... 3. one 5. alone 6. lonely,
  single 7. forlorn 8. solitary
  9. unmarried 12. unfrequented
loneliness... 8. loneness, solitude
  9. aloneness, dejection, isolation
  10. depression, desolation
  12. lonesomeness
lonely... 4. lorn 6. dreary 8. desolate,
  lonesome, secluded, solitary
  10. friendless 11. sequestered
  12. unfrequented
Lone Star State... 5. Texas
long... 3. yen 4. pine 5. crave, wordy,
  yearn 6. aspire, prolix, thirst
  7. lengthy, tedious 8. tiresome
  9. prolonged, wearisome
  10. protracted
long (pert to)...
  ago, since.. 3. eld 4. yore
  beard.. 9. graybeard 10. bellarmine
  (jug)
  discourse, speech.. 6. screed, tirade
  7. descant 9. philippic, rigmarole
  dog.. 9. dachshund, greyhound
  dozen.. 8. thirteen
  established.. 8. habitual 10. inveterate
  11. traditional
  for.. 4. hope, pine 5. covet, crave
  horn.. 6. cattle (Tex)
  inlet.. 3. ria
  journey.. 4. trek 7. odyssey
  jump.. 5. halmo
  letters.. 7. screeds
  life.. 9. longevity
  limbed.. 5. rangy
  lived.. 9. macrobian
  periods.. 4. ages, eons
  scarf.. 4. sari
  suffering.. 7. patient 10. forbearing
  Tom.. 3. gun 8. titmouse
  windedness.. 9. garrulity, prolixity
  13. longiloquence
longing... 3. yen 6. desire, pining
  7. craving, wistful 8. yearning
  9. hankering, nostalgia
longitudinal... 10. euthytatic (stress),
  lengthwise
longshoreman... 6. docker, loader,
  lumper, stower 9. stevedore
  10. roustabout
loo... 3. pam 4. game
look... 3. con, ken, pry, see 4. haze,
  heed, leer, peep, scry, seek, seem
  5. point, stare, watch 6. appear,
  expect 7. examine, inspect, observe
  8. indicate, perceive 9. search for
look (pert to)...
  after.. 4. tend 5. serve 6. follow
  7. care for 9. keep vigil, supervise
  at.. 3. eye 4. face, scan, upon
  6. regard 7. examine
  back.. 6. recall 7. retrace
  8. remember 9. recollect 10. call to
  mind
  down upon.. 4. leer, snub 5. fleer,
  gloat 7. askance, despise
  forward to.. 5. await 6. expect
  7. foresee 10. anticipate
  like.. 8. resemble
  obliquely.. 4. skew
  slyly.. 4. leer, ogle, peer

sullen.. 5. frown, lower 6. glower
toward.. 4. face
upon.. 2. at 4. deem 6. behold
  11. contemplate
lookout... 4. view 5. guard, watch
  6. conner 7. outlook 9. vigilance
looks... 4. cons, face, kens, sees
  5. peers, pores, pries, seeks, seems
  6. visage 8. features 9. resembles
  10. appearance 11. countenance
loom... 3. auk 4. loon, tool 6. appear,
  puffin, vessel, weaver 7. machine
  9. guillemot, implement
  10. receptacle
loom part... 3. lam 4. caam, leaf, sley
  5. easer, lathe, lever 6. heddle
loon... 5. diver (great Northern), Gavia,
  grebe, wabby 10. Gavia immer
loon... 4. dolt 6. menial (anc), rascal
  7. lunatic
loop... 3. eye, tab 4. ansa, clew, kink
  5. bight, bride, honda, noose, picot,
  sling, wootz (iron) 6. becket
  7. folding 8. doubling
loophole... 4. hole, plea 5. mense,
  oilet 6. escape, eyelet, outlet
  7. opening, pretext 8. aperture
loop–shaped... 9. fundiform
  11. sling–shaped
loose... 3. lax 4. free, limp 5. slack
  6. detach, remiss, unlash, wanton,
  wobbly 7. escaped, immoral,
  movable, relaxed, slacken, unbound,
  unleash 8. insecure, unstable
  9. discharge (gun, arrow)
  10. unconfined 11. improvident
  12. loose–moraled
  14. unconventional
loose (pert to)...
ends.. 4. dags 5. slack 7. tagrags
  8. restless
garment.. 5. simar 6. banion, chimar,
  kimono 7. zimarra 8. peignoir
jointed.. 5. lanky, rangy 6. wobbly
  7. rickety 10. ramshackle
loosely dressed... 8. discinct
loosen... 4. ease, free, undo 5. pried,
  relax 6. soften 7. slacken
looseness... 7. laxness 8. limpness
  9. slackness, vagueness
  10. remissness, wantonness
loot... 3. rob 4. gelt, haul, sack, swag
  5. booty 6. spoils 7. pillage,
  plunder, seizure 10. contraband
looter... 6. rifler, sacker 7. ravager,
  spoiler 8. marauder, pillager
lop (off)... 3. bob, cut 4. oche, sned,
  trim 5. droop, prune 6. cut off,
  snathe 8. truncate
lopsided... 4. alop 7. leaning
  8. top–heavy 10. unbalanced
  13. unsymmetrical
loquacious... 4. glib 6. chatty
  7. voluble 9. garrulous, talkative
  10. chattering
loquacity... 7. fluency, leresis
  8. glibness 9. gabbiness, garrulity
  12. effusiveness
lord... 3. aga (agha), bey, God 4. earl,
  peer, rule, tsar 5. liege, ruler, title
  6. master, prince 7. Jehovah,
  marquis, Saviour 8. governor,

nobleman, seignior, suzerain, viscount
  10. proprietor 11. Jesus Christ
Lord (pert to)...
Buddhism.. 6. Buddha
Jacobite.. 3. Mar
of Heaven.. 7. Tien Chu (Chin)
of Lords.. 8. Demiurge (Plato)
  11. King of Kings 13. Prince of
  Peace
of Wisdom.. 5. Mazda 6. Ormazd
Lord have mercy upon us...
  12. Kyrie eleison 14. Christe eleison
lordly... 6. uppish 8. arrogant,
  despotic 9. dignified, masterful
  10. tyrannical 11. domineering,
  overbearing
Lord's Prayer... 11. Pater Noster
lore... 4. lear 6. advice, wisdom
  7. counsel 8. learning 9. erudition,
  mythology, tradition 12. superstition
lorgnette... 7. lorgnon 8. eyeglass
  10. opera glass
lorica... 5. shell 7. cuirass
  11. Breastplate (St Patrick's)
lorikeet... 6. lories, parrot
loris... 5. lemur
lorn... 6. bereft 7. forlorn 8. deserted,
  desolate, forsaken 9. abandoned
  11. Godforsaken
loro... 10. monk parrot, parrot fish
lose... 4. fail, miss, omit 5. leese
  (obs), spill, waste 6. forget, mislay,
  perish 7. forfeit, let slip 8. estrange,
  squander 9. incur loss 10. wander
  from
lose (pert to)...
balance.. 4. trip 7. stumble
courage.. 7. despair, despond
flesh.. 8. emaciate
freshness.. 4. fade, wilt 6. wither
ground.. 7. regress 8. slow down
  9. fall short 10. fall behind
luster.. 7. tarnish
vigor.. 3. fag, sag 4. fail, flag, pine
  6. weaken 7. decline
loser... 6. victim 7. also ran
  8. defeatee, underdog
loss... 4. ruin, weak 6. damage, injury
  9. decrement, detriment, privation
  10. forfeiture 11. bereavement,
  destruction
loss of...
commodities.. 6. ullage
eyebrows, lashes.. 9. madarosis
feeling.. 7. agnosia 10. anesthesia
  (anaesthesia)
hair.. 8. alopecia
loved one.. 11. bereavement
memory.. 7. amnesia
reason.. 7. amentia
smell.. 7. anosmia
speech.. 4. mute 6. alalia 7. aphasia
  10. laloplegia
voice.. 7. aphonia
willpower.. 6. abulia
lost... 4. asea, gone, lorn 5. unwon
  6. hidden, ruined, sinful, wasted
  7. mislaid 8. absorbed, confused,
  defeated, obscured, vanished
  9. abandoned, forfeited, forgotten,
  perplexed, reprobate, subverted
  10. abstracted, bewildered,

dissipated, overthrown, parted with
11. preoccupied 13. irreclaimable,
irretrievable

lost (pert to)...
cause.. 8. Civil War
color.. 5. faded, paled
consciousness.. 7. fainted, swooned
life fluid.. 4. bled
to view.. 5. perdu
tribes (ten).. 10. Israelites

lot... 3. tax 4. doom, fate, luck,
much, plat 5. share 6. chance,
hazard, studio 7. destiny, fortune,
portion 9. allotment, great deal
13. apportionment

Lot (pert to)...
father.. 5. Haran
penalty.. 12. pillar of salt
sister.. 6. Milcah
son.. 4. Moab
uncle.. 7. Abraham

lots, divination by... 9. sortilege

lottery... 4. game 5. bingo, lotto
6. chance, raffle 7. Genoese, grab
bag 11. sweepstakes

lottery prize... 4. tern (from three
numbers)

lotus... 7. nelumbo 10. chinquapin

lotus (pert to)...
bird.. 6. jacana
eaters.. 9. indolents, Lotophagi
11. daydreamers
tree.. 4. sadr 6. jujube, nettle
9. persimmon

loud... 5. crass, gaudy, noisy, showy
6. coarse, flashy, garish, vulgar
7. blatant, booming 8. vehement
9. clamorous, turbulent, unrefined
10. blustering, boisterous,
tumultuous, vociferous
11. stentorious 12. obstreperous

loudmouthed... 10. scurrilous,
stentorian 11. thersitical

Louise de la Ramée (novelist)...
5. Ouida (pen name)

Louisiana...
bird.. 7. pelican
capital.. 10. Baton Rouge
city.. 10. New Orleans, Shreveport
county.. 6. parish
dialect.. 6. Creole
dish (cooked).. 9. jumbalaya
flower.. 8. magnolia
hero.. 6. De Soto, de Vaca, Pineda
7. La Salle
native.. 5. Cajun 6. Creole, French
7. Acadian, Spanish
purchased from.. 8. Napoleon (1803)
river.. 5. Pearl 6. Sabine
11. Mississippi
State admission.. 10. Eighteenth
State motto.. 22. Union, Justice,
Confidence
State nickname.. 7. Pelican
tradition.. 10. pirate lore

Louis Viaud (author)... 10. Pierre Loti
(pen name)

lounge... 4. loaf, loll, sofa 5. divan
6. frowst, repose 7. recline

louse... 5. aphis 6. cootie, insect,
slater 8. Anoplura, arachnid
9. Hemiptera, scoundrel

lout... 3. oaf 4. boor, clod, dolt
6. lubber, rustic 7. bumpkin

loutish... 4. rude 7. awkward, boorish,
ill–bred 8. clownish 11. countrified

lovable... 7. amiable 8. adorable,
charming 9. desirable, endearing

love... 3. amo, gra, woo 4. like
5. adore, amore, fancy 6. liking
7. charity 8. fondness, good will
9. affection 10. endearment,
sweetheart

love (pert to)...
affair.. 7. liaison, romance
10. flirtation
apple.. 6. tomato
bird.. 6. parrot
call.. 3. coo
feast.. 5. agape
flower.. 4. lily
full of.. 4. dote 6. doting, erotic
7. amative 9. idolizing
god of.. 4. Amor, Ares, Eros, Kama
5. Bhaga, Cupid
goddess of.. 5. Athor, Freya (Freyja),
Venus 6. Ishtar 9. Aphrodite
intrigue.. 5. amour
knot, token of.. 6. amoret
meeting.. 5. tryst 10. rendezvous
of.. 5. phile (comb form)
parental.. 6. storge
potion.. 7. philter
science.. 9. erotology
song.. 6. serena (evening) 8. madrigal

lover... 4. beau 5. amant, Romeo
6. minion 7. amorist, Don Juan
8. paramour 9. enamorato
10. sweetheart

lover of... see also *craze for*
animals.. 10. zoophilist
beauty.. 8. aesthete (esthete)
wealth.. 9. plutocrat
work.. 9. ergophile

Lover's Leap... 10. Cape Ducato

Lovers' Quarrels... 12. amantium Irae

loving... 4. fond 5. phile (comb form)
6. ardent, erotic 7. adoring, amative,
amatory, amorous, devoted
8. charming, enamored, romantic
11. sentimental 12. affectionate

loving cup... 3. tyg (tig)

low... 3. bas, moo 4. base, deep,
neap, orra 5. faint 6. humble,
menial, sneaky, vulgar, wicked
8. dejected, indecent, infamous,
inferior, plebeian 9. inelegant
11. unfavorable

low (pert to)...
born.. 4. rude 5. lowly 6. common
7. lowbred 8. plebeian
bred.. 5. crude 6. coarse, vulgar
brow.. 9. ignoramus
church.. 11. evangelical
comedy.. 8. travesty
country.. 7. Belgium, Holland
9. Luxemburg 11. Netherlands
German.. 5. Saxon 8. Frankish
12. Plattdeutsch
in spirits.. 4. blue 6. megrim
8. dejected, downcast 10. dispirited,
melancholy 11. crestfallen
Roman wall.. 5. spina
shrubs, plants.. 4. moss 5. Erica

syllable (Mus).. 2. ut
tide.. 3. ebb 4. neap 8. low water
lower... 3. dip 4. vail, vase 5. abase,
demit, frown, neath 6. bemean,
debase, deepen, demean, demote,
humble, lessen, meaner, nether,
reduce 7. cheapen, degrade, depress,
descent 8. diminish, inferior
10. depreciate
lower (pert to)...
case letter.. 5. small
Empire.. 9. Byzantine
geology.. 5. Chalk (Eng) 6. strata
7. stratum
most.. 6. bottom, lowest 7. bedrock
10. nethermost
world.. 4. hell 5. earth, Hades, limbo,
orcus, Sheol 7. Abaddon, Gehenna
8. Cerberus 9. perdition, purgatory
lowering... 4. dark 6. gloomy, sullen
7. ominous 8. frowning 9. deepening
10. cheapening 11. threatening
lowery... 6. cloudy, gloomy 8. lowering
lowest (pert to)...
animal life.. 6. amoeba (ameba)
deck.. 5. orlop
least.. 5. minim 6. bottom
7. minimum
pedestal member (Arch).. 6. plinth,
quadra
peer (ranking).. 5. baron
point.. 5. depth, nadir 6. bottom
10. nethermost
point, planet.. 7. perigee
lowing... 6. mooing 7. mugient
9. bellowing
lowland... 4. flat, holm, spit 5. plain,
terai 6. bottom 8. molehill
lowly... 4. mean, meek 6. humble,
humbly, meekly, menial, modest
8. inferior, modestly, plebeian
12. unpretending
loxia... 7. wryneck 9. crossbill
loy... 5. slick (tool), spade
loyal... 4. feal, leal, true 5. liege
6. stanch 7. staunch 8. constant,
faithful, obedient
loyalty... 5. faith 6. fealty, homage
8. devotion, fidelity 9. constancy
10. allegiance, stanchness
(staunchness) 12. faithfulness
13. steadfastness
Loyolite... 6. Jesuit
lozenge... 5. candy, facet 6. jujube,
tablet, troche 7. diamond, molding
8. pastille (pastil, pastile)
11. perforation
lubber... 4. boor, dolt, gawk, lout
5. churl, drone, idler, thick 6. sailor
8. landsman 11. grasshopper
lubricity... 8. lewdness
10. smoothness 12. slipperiness
lubricous... 4. lewd 6. tricky, wanton
7. elusive 8. unstable 10. lascivious
lucban... 8. shaddock
luce... 4. pike 10. fleur–de–lis
lucent... 5. clear 6. bright 7. shining
11. translucent, transparent
lucern... 3. dog 4. lynx
lucerne... 4. herb 6. fodder 7. alfalfa
11. purple medic
lucet, luce... 4. pike (fish)

Lucia's home... 10. Lammermoor
lucid... 4. sane 5. clear, vivid
6. bright, lucent 7. shining
8. luminous, pellucid 11. translucent
12. intelligible
luck... 3. hap 4. cess 5. deuce
6. chance 7. ambsace 8. fortuity
11. good fortune
lucky... 5. canny, happy 6. timely
9. fortunate 10. auspicious 11. good
fortune
lucky animal... 6. mascot
lucky token... 4. mojo 5. charm
6. amulet 7. periapt 8. talisman
9. alectoria 10. rabbit foot
12. antinganting
lucrative... 3. fat 6. paying 7. gainful
10. productive, profitable, worthwhile
12. remunerative
lucre... 4. gain, pelf 6. profit, riches
9. emolument 11. acquisition
lucubrate... 18. burn the midnight oil
ludicrous... 5. antic, comic, droll,
funny 6. absurd 7. amusing, comical,
jesting, risible 9. burlesque, laughable
10. ridiculous
Ludolphian... 2. pi (3.14159)
14. Ludolph's number
Luftpost... 7. airmail, air post
lug... 3. box, ear, hug 4. drag, hale,
haul, loop, pull, tote 5. carry
6. basket 9. container
lugs... 4. airs 7. clothes (showy),
tobacco 10. affections
lugubrious... 3. sad 6. woeful
7. doleful 8. grievous, mournful
9. plaintive 10. lamentable
lugworm... 3. lob 7. annelid
9. Arenicola
luhinga... 9. petticoat
lukewarm... 4. cool 5. tepid 6. tepefy
8. tepidity 9. not ardent
10. irresolute 11. indifferent
lumber... 4. wood 6. bungle, litter,
refuse, rumble, timber, trudge
7. lombard 9. rough wood
10. pawnbroker 11. impedimenta
lumberman... 6. logger, sawyer, scorer
9. timberman 10. lumberjack,
woodcutter
lumberman's half boot... 3. pac
lumberman's sled... 4. tode
7. go–devil, travois (travoise)
luminary... 3. sun 4. fire, star 5. light
7. wise man 9. celebrity
12. illumination, leading light
luminescence... 7. foxfire
12. fluorescence
15. phosphorescence
luminous... 5. clear, lucid 6. bright
7. shining 9. brilliant
11. enlightened, illuminated,
intelligent, transparent
14. phosphorescent
luminous circle... 4. halo
luminous impression... 9. phosphene
10. afterimage
lummox... 4. boor, dolt, lout 5. yahoo
7. bumpkin, bungler 12. clumsy
fellow
lump... 3. gob, lob, wad 4. beat,
blob, clot, hunk, loaf, mass 5. bulge

6. nodule, nubble, nugget, thresh
7. cluster 8. swelling
12. protuberance
lump (pert to)...
butter .. 3. pat
clay .. 4. clag, clod
metal .. 3. pig 5. ingot
lumpish... 4. dull 5. bulky, inert
6. clumsy, stolid, stupid 7. boorish
8. sluggish 9. heaviness, inertness,
ponderous 11. countrified
13. shapelessness
lumpy... 5. drunk, rough 6. choppy
7. gnarled, nodular
lumpy jaw... 6. big jaw
13. actinomycosis
luna... 6. silver 11. moon goddess
lunacy... 4. moon 5. mania
7. madness 8. insanity 9. craziness
11. derangement, foolishness
lunar... 5. orbed 6. lunate
8. crescent, moonlike 9. celestial,
satellite 10. moon–shaped
lunar (pert to)...
appulse .. 7. eclipse
bone .. 7. lunatum
cycle .. 7. Metonic 9. Callippic
deity .. 6. Selene (Selena)
halo .. 6. corona, nimbus 7. aureola
lunatic... 3. mad 5. crazy, idiot, loony
6. insane, madman 8. demoniac
9. moonstruck
lunatic asylum... 9. Bethlehem
(London)
lunch... 5. snack 6. brunch, repast,
tiffin 8. brown–bag, luncheon,
nuncheon 10. collation
11. refreshment
lunchroom... 6. eatery 10. coffee
shop, restaurant 12. luncheonette
lundyfoot... 5. snuff (by Lundy Foot)
lunge... 3. cut, jab 4. grab, pass, stab
5. feint, swing 6. thrust
lungs (pert to)...
ailment .. 9. emphysema 10. chalicosis
12. tuberculosis
having .. 9. pulmonate
part .. 5. lobes 6. lights 7. bronchi,
trachea
sound .. 4. rale 6. rattle
lurch... 4. joll, roll, sway 5. lunge
6. careen, topple 7. deceive
8. flounder 10. disappoint
lure... 4. bait, trap 5. decoy, snare,
tempt 6. allure, entice, invite
7. attract, beguile, trumpet, tweedle
10. enticement
lurid... 3. wan 4. dark, pale 5. color,
vivid 6. dismal, gloomy 7. ghastly,
obscene 9. deathlike 11. sensational
lurk... 4. hide, lote (obs) 5. creep,
prowl, skulk, slink, sneak 9. lie in
wait, pussyfoot
luscious... 4. rich 5. sweet
6. creamy, wanton 7. cloying,
honeyed 8. sensuous 9. delicious
10. lasciviousness, voluptuous
lush... 4. soft 5. drink, drunk, juicy
6. lavish, limber, liquor, mellow
7. verdant 8. flexible 9. luxuriant,
succulent 11. intoxicated
lusory... 7. playful 8. sportive

lust... 5. greed 6. desire, libido
7. craving, longing, passion 8. virility
14. lasciviousness
luster, lustre... 4. naif 5. glory, gloss,
sheen, shine 6. beauty, polish
7. glitter, lustrum 8. radiance,
schiller, splendor 10. brightness
11. distinction, iridescence
lusterless... 3. dim, mat 4. dead, dull,
flat 14. expressionless
lustful... 4. lewd 5. randy
9. lecherous 10. lascivious
lustrous... 4. naif 5. nitid 6. agleam,
bright 7. radiant, shining
11. illustrious, transparent
lustrous mineral... 4. spar
lustrum (Roman)... 6. census, luster
12. purification (5 yrs), quinquennium
lusty... 6. active, robust, strong, sturdy
7. healthy 8. vigorous 9. corpulent
lute... 4. clay, ring (rubber), seal
6. cement
lute, lutelike... 4. asor 6. guitar
7. bandore, pandore, theorbo, ukulele
8. archlute (archiluta)
lute tablature... 7. lyraway
lutjanoid fish... 4. sesi 7. snapper
Luxembourg...
capital .. 10. Luxembourg
government .. 10. Grand Duchy
language .. 6. French, German
13. Letzeburgesch
river .. 7. Moselle
luxuriant... 4. lush, rank, rich
6. ornate, uberty 7. fertile, opulent,
profuse, teeming 8. abundant, prolific
9. bounteous, Sybaritic
luxuriate... 4. bask 5. revel
8. flourish
luxurious... 5. plush, ritzy 6. ornate,
superb 8. imposing 9. expensive,
grandiose, sumptuous 10. impressive
11. extravagant
luxury... 4. lust 7. lechery
8. elegance, pleasure, richness
10. prosperity, sensuality
11. superfluity 12. extravagance
13. gratification, sumptuousness
14. voluptuousness
luxury lover... 7. reveler 8. Sybarite
Luzon...
dialect .. 6. Itaves
mountain .. 3. Iba 6. Pagsan (Sicapoo)
people .. 5. Malay 7. Tagalog
8. Tinggian (Tinguian)
savage .. 6. Igorot (Igorrote)
seaport .. 5. Vigan 6. Aparri, Cavite
volcano .. 5. Mayon
lyam... 5. leash (Her) 10. bloodhound
lycanthrope... 8. werewolf
9. loup–garou
Lycia (pert to)...
citizen .. 6. Lycian
city .. 4. Myra
district of .. 9. Asia Minor
language .. 5. Greek 6. Lycian
Lydia...
capital .. 6. Sardis
dynasty of .. 5. Gyges 7. Croesus
13. Cyrus the Great
name, later .. 6. Persia
name, old .. 5. Ionia

queen.. 7. Omphale
river.. 8. Pactolus
ruins.. 6. temple
lye... 4. buck 6. bleach, potash
8. lixivium
lying... 5. false 6. deceit 7. fudging
9. decumbent, mendacity, reclining,
recumbent 10. untruthful
lying (pert to)...
across.. 10. transverse
at mountain base.. 8. piedmont
hidden.. 6. latent 11. delitescent
in.. 12. accouchement
near earth's axis.. 5. polar
on the back.. 5. prone 6. supine
7. passive
lymph... 3. sap 5. chyle, fluid, serum,
water 6. plasma 7. cassein
lynch... 4. hang 6. murder, punish
(lawlessly) 7. execute
lynx... 6. bobcat, lucern 7. caracal,
wildcat 8. carcajou 13. constellation

lynx–eyed... 7. oxyopia
lyre... 4. asor, harp 6. kissar, sabeca,
trigon, zither 7. cithara, cittern,
testudo 8. phorminx
lyre (pert to)...
bird.. 6. Menura 8. lyretail, pheasant
shaped.. 6. lyrate
tree.. 5. tulip
turtle.. 11. leatherback
lyric (pert to)...
Arabic.. 5. gazel
Muse.. 5. Erato 10. Polyhymnia
music, poetry.. 3. lay, ode 4. epic,
poem 5. epode, melic, rhyme (rime),
verse, vocal 6. epopee, poetic
7. canzone, musical, rondeau
8. operatic, palinode 9. dithyramb
poet.. 5. odist
lyrical... 6. epodic
lyrichord... 11. harpsichord
lyssa... 6. rabies 11. hydrophobia
lyssophobia... 17. fear of hydrophobia

M

M... 2. Mu (Gr) 6. letter (13th)
8. thousand
Ma (Ma Bellona)... 7. goddess
(fertility)
maarib (Jew)... 7. liturgy
Maat (Egypt)... 7. goddess (justice)
Mab (Queen Mab)... 4. poem 10. fairy
queen
mabolo... 4. plum 7. camagon
macabre... 4. grim 5. lurid, weird
6. grisly 7. ghastly 8. gruesome
12. Dance of Death
macaco... 5. lemur 6. Macaca
7. macaque 10. Barbary ape
macan... 4. rice
macao... 4. game (gambling)
Macao... 6. Island 7. seaport
macaque... 6. machin, monkey
Macassar... 7. seaport (Celebes)
macaw... 3. ara 5. arara 6. parrot
7. maracan 8. aracanga (blue and
red), ararauna (blue and yellow)
Macbeth (pert to)...
author.. 11. Shakespeare (1605)
character.. 4. Duff, Ross 5. Angus
6. Hecate, Lennox 7. Macduff
murder victim.. 6. Duncan
play type.. 7. tragedy
rival.. 7. Macduff
McBurney's Point (Med)...
13. abdominal wall
Maccabees... 11. Hasmonaeans
14. fraternal order, Jewish patriots
maccaboy... 5. snuff
mace... 4. maul 5. baton, gavel, spice
(nutmeg), staff 6. ensign, mallet
7. scepter (sceptre)
mace bearer... 5. macer 6. beadle

Macedonia, Balkans...
capital (anc).. 5. Pella
city.. 5. Berea 6. Edessa 8. Salonika
people.. 6. Greeks 8. Serbians
9. Albanians 10. Bulgarians
ruler.. 6. Philip 9. Alexander (the
Great)
site.. 15. Balkan Peninsula
macerate... 3. ret, vex 4. soak
5. steep 6. soften 7. mortify,
oppress, torture 8. emaciate
9. waste away
machete... 4. bolo, fish 5. knife
6. guitar 11. cutlass fish
Machiavellian, Machiavelian... 4. wily
6. crafty 7. cunning 8. guileful,
scheming 9. deceitful
12. falsehearted
machila... 7. hammock
machin... 6. monkey 7. macaque
machinate... 4. plan, plot 6. scheme
8. contrive, maneuver
machination... 6. design, device,
scheme 7. machine 8. intrigue
9. stratagem 10. conspiracy
machine... 3. car 4. auto 6. device,
engine 7. vehicle 9. apparatus,
automaton 10. automobile
11. association, standardize
machine (pert to)...
cloth maturing.. 4. ager
cloth stretching.. 6. tenter
cotton.. 3. gin 4. mule 5. baler
glazing.. 8. calender
hay.. 5. baler 6. tedder
hoisting.. 3. gin, pry 4. pump
5. crane, davit, lever, tongs
7. derrick
hummeling.. 5. awner

hydraulic .. 9. telemotor
imitating .. 9. automaton
military .. 3. ram 6. onager
mixing .. 9. malaxator
ore .. 6. vanner
planing .. 8. surfacer
planting .. 6. seeder
political .. 5. party 6. system
　7. faction
reckoning .. 6. abacus 9. tabulator
　10. calculator
rubber shaping .. 8. extruder
stage effect .. 13. deus ex machina
tool .. 5. drill, lathe
machine gun ... 4. nest (hidden place)
　5. Maxim 6. cannon 7. Gatling
　9. Hotchkiss 10. chatterbox
machine–made ... 11. stereotyped
machine power, energy ... 5. input
　6. output
machinist ... 7. artisan 8. mechanic
mackerel ... 5. atule, spike, tunny
　6. sierra, tinker
mackerel (pert to) ...
bait .. 9. jellyfish
bird .. 7. wryneck 9. kittiwake
genus .. 7. Scomber
goose .. 9. phalarope
like .. 4. cero 6. bonito 7. escolar
net .. 7. spiller
shark .. 9. porbeagle
sky .. 6. clouds 9. striation
small (allowable size) .. 5. spike
　6. tinker 7. blinker
mackle ... 4. blur, spot 6. blotch,
　macule
macrobiotic ... 9. long–lived
mad ... 4. vain, wild 5. angry, crazy,
　irate, rabid, vexed 6. insane, maniac
　7: enraged, foolish, frantic, furious
　8. demented, frenetic, maniacal,
　reckless 9. hilarious, turbulent
　10. distraught, infatuated, infuriated
　12. arreptitious
Madagascar, Malagasy ...
animal .. 5. indri, lemur 6. aye–aye,
　tenrec (tendrac) 9. babacoote
capital .. 10. Tananarive
cattle .. 4. zebu (humped)
city .. 7. Majanga 8. Tamatave
civet .. 7. fossane
govenment .. 8. Republic (1960)
language .. 16. Malayo–Polynesian
native .. 4. Hova 8. Sakalava
palm .. 6. raffia
religion .. 7. Animist 9. Christian
Madam ... 3. Mrs 4. Frau, lady,
　Ma'am 5. donna, hussy 6. Madame,
　Señora 8. goodwife, mistress
　9. courtesan
madcap ... 3. wag 4. rash, wild
　5. blood 6. madman 7. hotspur,
　violent 8. reckless 9. daredevil,
　foolhardy
madden ... 3. vex 5. craze 6. enrage,
　incite 7. incense 9. infuriate
　10. antagonize
madder ... 2. al 3. aal, red 4. herb,
　rose (color) 5. brown, Rubia
　6. orange, violet, yellow 7. crimson,
　xanthin 9. turkey–red
made ... 5. built 7. created, trained

　8. invented, prepared, produced,
　rendered 10. artificial, successful
　11. constructed 12. enfranchised,
　manufactured
made (pert to) ...
accurate .. 5. trued
believe .. 7. feigned 9. pretended,
　simulated
blind .. 6. seeled
clear .. 9. explained 10. elucidated
destitute .. 6. bereft
fun of .. 6. jeered, mocked 7. derided
　9. ridiculed
hard, obdurate .. 7. steeled
light of .. 7. dwarfed 9. belittled
　10. disparaged
over .. 8. reformed, revamped
　9. remodeled
plain .. 9. evidenced, exhibited
　10. manifested
public .. 5. aired 7. accused, delated
　8. reported
scalloped edges .. 6. pinked
sound .. 7. bleated, rumbled, swished
tart .. 7. euchred
up .. 9. composite 10. artificial,
　fabricated 12. manufactured
up mind .. 7. decided
valid .. 6. proved 9. confirmed
　13. authenticated
whole again .. 7. renewed
　10. reconciled 13. redintegrated,
　re–established
Madeira Islands ...
capital .. 7. Funchal
embroidery .. 6. eyelet
nut .. 6. walnut
owner of Islands .. 8. Portugal
wind .. 5. leste
wine .. 4. bual 5. tinta (red)
　7. malmsey, sercial 8. verdelho
wood .. 8. ironwood (white), mahogany
madhouse ... 5. chaos 6. asylum,
　bedlam 8. nuthouse
madman ... 3. nut 4. coot, loon
　6. maniac 7. lunatic 9. phrenetic
madness ... 3. ire 4. fury, rage
　5. anger, mania 6. frenzy, lunacy
　8. insanity 9. agitation, theomania
　(Relig) 11. foolishness, inspiration
Mad Parliament (1258) ...
　18. Provisions of Oxford
Madras, India ...
capital .. 6. Madras
city .. 5. Adoni, Arcot 7. Calicut
export .. 4. lace 7. fabrics 9. kerchiefs
　(for turbans)
government .. 10. presidency
madrepore ... 5. coral 6. fossil, marble
　8. Acropora 12. Madreporaria
Madrid, Spain ...
architecture .. 7. Moorish
boulevard .. 5. Prado 12. Salon de
　Prado
noted buildings .. 7. Armeria
　11. Prado Museum, Royal Palace
madrigal ... 3. ode 4. glee, poem
　5. lyric, music 6. verses
maduro ... 5. cigar 6. mature
　11. dark–colored
maelstrom ... 5. churn 6. foment
　7. turmoil 9. whirlpool (Norway)

maestro... 6. master 7. teacher
8. composer, musician 9. conductor
13. Kapellmeister
maestro-di-cappela... 11. choirmaster
Mae West... 8. life belt
Maffia... 9. syndicate 10. underworld
12. organization (Sicilian)
maffle... 6. muddle, mumble
7. confuse, stammer 8. squander
mafoo, mafu (Chin)... 5. groom
9. stable boy
mag... 6. magpie 7. chatter
8. titmouse 9. halfpenny
magadis... 5. flute 9. monochord
magazine... 4. shop 5. depot, store
6. review 7. arsenal, chamber (gun),
tabloid 9. ephemeris, reservoir,
warehouse 10. periodical, repository,
storehouse
magazine rifle... 6. Mauser
8. repeater
mage... 5. Magus 6. Merlin 7. Houdini
8. conjurer, magician
magenta... 3. dye 7. fuchsia
maggot... 4. grub, mawk 5. larva,
mathe 6. notion 7. caprice, Diptera
12. eccentricity
Magi (Three Wise Men)... 6. Gaspar
8. Melchior 9. Balthasar
magic... 3. art 4. juju, mana, maya,
rune, show 5. charm, fairy, spell
6. voodoo 10. necromancy
11. conjuration, enchantment,
legerdemain
magic (pert to)...
art (black).. 7. demonry 9. diablerie,
diabolism
art (white).. 5. turgy 7. theurgy
ejaculation.. 2. om (um) 6. sesame
goddess.. 5. Circe 6. Hecate
image.. 5. sigil 8. sigillum
lantern.. 11. epidiascope
12. stereopticon
lantern slide.. 6. tinter
staff, wand.. 6. rhabdo 8. caduceus
symbol.. 5. charm 6. caract, fetish
8. pentacle 9. pentalpha
word.. 2. om (um) 6. presto, sesame
10. abacadabra
magical... 6. goetic (goety)
8. charming
magician... 4. mage 5. magus
6. Merlin, wizard 7. Houdini, juggler
8. conjurer, mandrake, sorcerer
9. archimage, charlatan, enchanter
11. entertainer, necromancer,
thaumaturge 13. thaumaturgist
15. prestidigitator
magician (pert to)...
attendant.. 7. famulus
command.. 6. presto 11. abracadabra
manual.. 8. grimoire
magirics... 7. cookery
magirist... 4. cook
magisterial... 5. lofty, proud
6. august, lordly 7. haughty, stately
8. arrogant, dogmatic, judicial, official
9. dignified, imperious, masterful
10. commanding 11. dictatorial,
domineering, overbearing
13. authoritative
magistrate... 4. doge 5. ephor, judge

6. aedile (edile), archon, bailli,
puisne, syndic 7. alcaide (alcaid),
alcalde, bailiff
magistrate's orders... 4. acta
magma... 5. dregs 8. sediment
10. molten rock, suspension (Pharm)
magna cum laude... 14. with great
honor
magnanimous... 4. free 5. lofty, noble
7. exalted, liberal 8. generous
9. honorable, unselfish, unstinted
10. high-minded 11. great of mind
13. disinterested
magnate... 4. lord 5. baron, mogul,
noble 6. bashaw, bigwig, tycoon
7. grandee, richman 9. personage
11. millionaire
magnesium (pert to)...
limestone.. 8. dolomite
nitrate.. 9. saltpeter
silicate.. 4. talc
sulphate.. 10. Epsom salts
magnet... 7. terella 8. solenoid
9. loadstone, lodestone
magnet (type)... 3. bar 9. horseshoe
10. artificial
magnetic... 10. attractive, electrical
14. attractiveness
magnetism... 5. oomph 8. polarity
magnificence... 5. glory 8. grandeur,
splendor 15. superexcellence
magnificent... 5. grand, regal
6. lavish, superb 7. exalted,
pompous, sublime 8. imposing,
palatial, splendid, striking 9. brilliant,
grandiose, sumptuous 10. munificent
magnify... 4. laud 5. exalt, extol
6. expand, praise 7. enlarge, glorify,
worship 8. increase 9. intensify,
overstate 10. exaggerate
magnitude... 4. size 6. extent
7. bigness 8. grandeur, nobility
9. extension, greatness
Magnolia State... 11. Mississippi
magnum... 4. bone (wrist) 6. bottle
9. capitatum
magnum opus... 9. great work
11. achievement
magpie... 3. daw, mag, pie 4. Pica,
piet (pyet) 5. madge, scold
6. pigeon, talker 9. chatterer
10. chattermag
magpie type...
diver.. 4. smew
shrike.. 7. tanager
maguari... 5. stork
magus... 8. magician 9. one of Magi
Magyar... 3. Hun 9. Hungarian
Mah (Persian)... 9. moon angel
maha... 10. sambar deer
Mahabharata (blind king, Hind)...
13. Dhritarashtra
mahajan, mahajun (Ind)... 8. great
man 11. moneylender
mahal... 8. Taj Mahal 9. residence
(summer) 10. apartments, Natal
brown
mahala... 5. squaw
maharaja, maharajah... 5. ruler
6. prince
maharani, maharanee... 5. queen
mahatma... 4. sage 7. wise man

9. great soul, occultist 21. Great
White Brotherhood (member)
mahogany . . . 3. roe (burl) 4. toon,
wood 5. brown 6. totara 7. ratteen
maholi . . . 5. lemur
Mahomet . . . see *Mohammedan*
Mahound . . . 5. Devil 8. Mohammed
mahout . . . 6. driver (elephant), keeper
Mah to Mahi . . . 10. Fish to Moon
Maia (pert to) . . .
mountain nymph . . 7. Arcadia
son . . 6. Hermes
star . . 8. Pleiades
maid . . . 4. girl, lass 5. bonne, woman
6. damsel, maiden, virgin 7. abigail,
servant 8. spinster 9. tirewoman
Maid (of) . . .
Astolat . . 6. Elaine
Athens . . 12. Theresa Macri
Lydia . . 7. Arachne (changed to a
spider)
Orléans . . 9. Joan of Arc
Zeus . . 2. Io (changed to heifer)
maidenhair . . . 4. fern 8. Adiantum
10. Venus's hair
maidenhair tree . . . 6. gingko
maidenly . . . 6. gentle, modest 7. girlish
9. unmarried
maigre . . . 4. diet, fish
mail . . . 3. dak (dawk) 4. post 5. armor
7. consign, letters, plumage
8. dispatch
mail, coat of . . . 5. armor 6. byrnie
(brinie) 7. broigne, cuirass (part),
hauberk, panoply
mail boat . . . 6. packet
maim . . . 6. injure, mangle, mayhem
7. disable 8. mutilate 9. tear apart
main . . . 3. sea 4. duct 5. chief, first,
great, prime, sheer, utter 6. mighty,
potent 7. chiefly, conduit, leading
8. foremost 9. conductor, essential,
principal 10. on the whole
11. essentially 13. most important
main (pert to) . . .
act (drama) . . 8. epitasis
beam . . 6. girder 7. walking
part . . 4. body
point . . 3. jet, nub 4. crux, gist, pith
post . . 9. sternpost
sea (poet) . . 11. Spanish Main
(Caribbean Sea)
Maine . . .
bay . . 5. Casco 13. Passamaquoddy
capital . . 7. Augusta
city . . 4. Saco 5. Hiram, Orono
6. Bangor 8. Lewiston, Portland
11. Millinocket
college . . 5. Bates, Colby 7. Bowdoin
Easternmost city . . 8. Eastport
Easternmost point . . 19. West Quoddy
Head Light
Easternmost town . . 5. Lubec
lake . . 6. Sebago 9. Moosehead
mountain . . 5. Kineo 8. Cadillac,
Katahdin
resort . . 9. Bar Harbor
resort island . . 8. Mt Desert
river . . 8. Kennebec 9. Penobscot
State admission . . 11. Twenty–third
State motto . . 6. Dirigo 7. I Direct
State nickname . . 8. Pine Tree

trout . . 7. oquassa
Maine, The . . . 10. battleship (Sp–Am
War)
maintain . . . 4. aver, hold, keep
5. claim 6. affirm, allege, assert,
avouch, defend, endure, insist, retain
7. justify, support, sustain
8. continue, preserve
maintainable . . . 7. tenable
maintenance . . . 3. aid 6. upkeep
7. alimony, defense, support
9. retention 10. livelihood,
sustenance 11. continuance
12. conservation, preservation,
sustentation
maison . . . 5. house
Maison Carrée . . . 12. Norman Temple
(Nimes)
maison de santé . . . 6. asylum
8. hospital 10. sanatorium
maître d'hôtel (famed) . . . 5. Oscar
maize . . . 3. Zea 4. corn 7. mealies
maja, majo . . . 5. belle, dandy
majestic . . . 5. grand, great, lofty,
noble, regal, royal 6. august, kingly
7. stately, sublime 8. elevated,
eloquent, imperial, splendid
9. dignified, grandiose
11. ceremonious, magnificent
majesty . . . 5. title 7. crowned (Her),
dignity 8. grandeur 9. eloquence,
greatness, loftiness, sceptered (Her)
major . . . 3. dur (Mus) 6. course
(study), ditone 7. greater, officer
8. legal age, majority
major–domo . . . 6. butler 7. bailiff,
steward 9. seneschal
majority . . . 3. age 4. most 6. quorum
7. greater 8. maturity 9. majorship,
plurality, seniority 12. more than half
make . . . 2. do 4. earn, form, gain,
kind 5. shape 6. compel, create,
induce, render 7. compose, execute,
produce 8. contrive, generate
9. structure 10. accomplish
11. composition, manufacture
make (pert to) . . .
affidavit . . 4. affy
allowance . . 5. abate, admit
7. concede
allusion to . . 7. mention
amends . . 5. atone 7. redress
as if . . 7. pretend 8. as though
bare . . 5. strip 6. balden, denude
believe . . 4. sham 5. feign 7. pretend
8. pretense
better . . 5. widen 6. soften
7. broaden, improve 9. meliorate
10. ameliorate
book . . 10. record bets
buoyant . . 8. levitate
calm . . 5. allay, quiet 6. serene
7. appease, compose
certain . . 6. assure, ensure
cheerful . . 6. solace 7. comfort,
console
choice . . 3. opt 4. cull 6. choose,
select 7. pick out
clean breast of . . 7. confess
8. disclose
clear . . 7. explain 9. elucidate
coins . . 4. mint

countercharge.. 11. recriminate
crisp.. 9. embrittle
deduction.. 6. rebate
desolate.. 5. strip 7. bereave
diminutive.. 9. bantamize
do.. 3. eke 5. get by 8. piece out
 9. improvise
eccentric.. 8. decenter
edging.. 3. tat 7. crochet
effective.. 6. compel 7. enforce
enduring.. 6. anneal, temper
equal.. 6. equate
evident.. 6. evince
familiar.. 8. accustom
famous.. 8. eternize 11. immortalize
fast.. 4. snub 5. belay 6. batten,
 secure
faulty.. 6. impair 7. vitiate
 11. contaminate
firm.. 3. fix 5. brace 6. cement
fit.. 4. suit 5. adapt 6. adjust
 7. conform
foolish, stupid.. 4. daff 8. stultify
 10. ridiculous
fun of.. 3. rib 5. scoff 8. ridicule
glass.. 7. platten
good.. 7. absolve, justify, succeed
 9. indemnify, vindicate
happy.. 5. elate 7. beatify 8. felicify
 (obs)
hard, harsh.. 5. steel 6. freeze
 7. roughen
harmonious.. 6. attune
headway.. 4. gain 7. advance
 8. progress
holy.. 5. bless 6. hallow
 10. consecrate
honorable.. 5. exalt 6. uplift
 7. ennoble
ineffective.. 4. void 5. annul
insensible to pain.. 11. anesthetize
 (anaesthetize)
into law.. 5. enact 9. legislate
known.. 6. impart, reveal 7. divulge,
 publish, uncover 8. disclose,
 discover, proclaim
lace.. 3. tat 7. crochet
less dense.. 4. thin 6. rarefy
less smooth.. 7. roughen
level.. 4. true
light.. 6. jetsam 8. illumine, jettison
lively.. 8. energize
love.. 3. coo, woo 5. court
merry.. 5. laugh 6. banter 7. disport
mild.. 8. mitigate, modulate
moral.. 8. ethicize
much of.. 6. praise 7. enthuse, lionize
 10. exaggerate
muddy.. 4. roil
notes.. 8. annotate
out.. 4. know 5. solve 6. decode,
 draw up 7. analyze, discern
 8. contrive, decipher 10. understand
over.. 4. redo 6. revamp 7. convert
 9. refashion, reproduce
pale, sickly.. 8. etiolate
possible.. 6. enable
pottery.. 7. spattle
precious.. 6. endear
pretentious.. 7. buckram
public.. 3. air 5. bruit, noise
 6. delate 7. publish 9. divulgate

 11. acknowledge
ready.. 4. gear 5. coach, prime
 7. prepare
reparation.. 5. atone
resistance.. 5. rebel 6. mutiny, revolt
secure.. 3. fix, pin 4. nail, snub
 5. belay 6. batten, fasten
shift.. 9. temporary
short work of.. 6. hasten 7. destroy
 10. accomplish
shrill noise.. 10. stridulate
smooth.. 4. buff, iron 5. sleek, slick
 6. scrape
spruce.. 4. perk 7. smarten
strong.. 7. stouten
thin.. 9. attenuate
three–cornered.. 11. triangulate
unhappy.. 8. embitter 10. exacerbate
up.. 5. atone, build 6. invent, settle
 7. compose, concoct, prepare
 8. assemble, cosmetic 9. construct,
 improvise, reconcile 10. compensate
use of.. 5. apply 6. borrow, employ
 7. utilize 11. appropriate
waste (law).. 7. estrepe
watertight.. 4. calk, seal
white.. 6. blanch, bleach
worse.. 9. aggravate
zealous.. 7. enthuse
maker of...
arrows.. 8. fletcher
barrels.. 6. cooper
bundles.. 5. baler
infusion.. 7. steeper
knives.. 6. cutler
pottery.. 6. potter 8. ceramist
makeshift... 7. stopgap
maki... 5. lemur
mal (comb form)... 3. bad, ill 5. badly
 7. disease 8. sickness
Malabar (pert to)...
bark.. 5. ochna
nutmeg.. 10. Bombay mace
palm.. 7. talipot
rat.. 9. bandicoot
Malacca... 7. seaport (Malaya)
Malachi... 4. Book (Old Test)
 7. prophet
malachite... 4. bice 5. green
 6. copper 7. pigment
maladroit... 6. clumsy 7. awkward,
 unhandy 8. bungling 9. all thumbs,
 graceless 10. blundering, left–handed,
 ungraceful
maladventure... 6. mishap
 8. escapade 12. ill adventure
malady... 4. amok 7. ailment, disease,
 illness 8. disorder, sickness
 9. complaint, distemper
 13. indisposition
mala fide... 10. in bad faith
Malaga... 4. city (Sp), wine
 10. oxblood red
Malagasy lemur... 6. aye–aye
Malagasy region... 10. Madagascar
malaise... 4. pain 10. discomfort,
 uneasiness
malapert... 4. bold, pert 5. saucy
 8. impudent
malaria... 5. miasm 6. miasma
 10. strophulus
malaxation... 7. massage 9. softening

Malay Archipelago...
animal.. 4. mias 5. tapir, tsine
  6. gibbon, taguan 7. banteng
apparel.. 4. baju 5. banju 6. sarong
buffalo.. 4. gaur 7. carabao, seldang
canoe.. 4. proa 5. prahu
chief (tribal).. 4. dato (datto)
crane.. 5. sarus
dagger, knife.. 6. creese (kris), parong
disease (jumping).. 4. Lata (Latah)
gentleman.. 3. sir 4. tuan
island.. 4. Bali, Java 5. Timor
  7. Celebes, Sumatra 9. New Guinea
  11. Philippines
isthmus.. 3. Kra
language.. 7. Tagalog
native.. 5. Bajau 6. Ifugao 8. Filipino
  9. Samal Laut 10. sea gypsies
palm.. 6. Arenga, gomuti (gomuto)
  8. Saguerus
pygmy.. 4. Aeta
rice field.. 5. sawah
seaport.. 7. Malacca
state.. 5. Kedah, Perak 6. Jahore
tree.. 4. upas 5. kapur, niepa, terap
  6. durian (fruit)
vessel.. 4. toup 6. lugger
Malaysia...
capital.. 11. Kuala Lumpur
malcontent... 5. rebel 6. Fenian,
  uneasy 7. repiner 8. agitator,
  grumbler 10. rebellious
  12. discontented
male... 2. he 3. cob, him, tom 4. bull,
  dude, galt, jack, stud 5. andro (comb
  form), macho, manly 6. tercel, virile
  7. rooster 8. stallion 9. masculine
male (pert to)...
column (Arch).. 7. Telamon
  8. Atlantes
One Hundred eyes.. 5. Argus
malediction... 5. curse 6. threat
  7. malison, slander 8. anathema
  11. imprecation 12. denunciation
malefaction... 5. crime 7. offense
  9. malum in se
malefactor... 5. felon 7. culprit
  8. criminal, evildoer 9. wrongdoer
malevolence... 4. hate 5. pique, spite
  6. grudge, malice, rancor 7. ill will
  8. inimical 9. animosity, malignity
  10. bitterness
malevolent... 4. evil 6. hating
  7. envious, hateful 8. spiteful
  9. malicious, rancorous
  11. ill–disposed
malfeasance... 7. misrule 8. impolicy
  10. wrongdoing 11. evil conduct,
  illegal deed
malfeasant... 8. criminal, evildoer
malgré... 9. in spite of
  15. notwithstanding
malheur... 10. misfortune
Mali, Africa...
capital.. 6. Bamako
malice... 4. envy, evil 5. malum,
  pique, spite, wrong 6. rancor 7. ill
  will 9. animosity, malignity, malintent
  10. bitterness 11. malevolence
malicious... 4. evil, mean 6. bitter,
  malign, ornery 7. hateful 8. sinister,
  spiteful 9. rancorous, resentful,

  vitriolic 11. ill–disposed
  12. cantankerous, unpropitious
malicious (pert to)...
destruction.. 5. arson 8. sabotage
  9. vandalism
gossip.. 4. dirt 7. scandal, slander
intention.. 6. animus
maliform... 11. apple–shaped
malign... 4. evil 5. abuse, libel
  6. deadly, defame, revile, vilify
  7. asperse, baleful, harmful, slander,
  traduce 8. badmouth, virulent
  10. calumniate 12. unpropitious
malignancy... 6. malice 9. virulence
  10. deadliness 11. harmfulness,
  noxiousness
malignant... 3. ill 4. evil 5. felon
  6. deadly, wicked 7. harmful,
  heinous, vicious 8. spiteful, virulent
  9. felonious, invidious, malicious,
  poisonous, rancorous 10. rebellious
  11. deleterious
maligner... 8. libelist 9. slanderer
malignity... 4. evil, hate 5. spite,
  venom 11. harmfulness, heinousness
maline(s)... 3. net 11. Mechlin lace
malingerer... 6. truant 7. quitter,
  shirker, slacker, welsher
malison... 5. curse 11. malediction
malkin... 3. cat, mop 4. drab, hare
  6. sponge 8. slattern 9. scarecrow
mall... 4. gull, walk 5. alley, plaza,
  prado 6. arcade, mallet 7. alameda
  8. assembly 9. esplanade, promenade
  14. shopping center
mallangong... 8. duckbill
mallard... 4. Anas, duck 5. drake
malleable... 4. soft 6. pliant
  7. ductile, plastic 9. teachable
mallemuck... 6. fulmar, petrel
  9. albatross
mallet... 3. tup 4. club, mace, maul
  5. gavel, madge 6. beater, beetle,
  driver, hammer
malm... 4. marl 5. chalk
malmsey... 4. wine
malodorous... 4. rank 5. fetid
  6. rotten 7. noisome, odorous
  11. ill–smelling, odoriferous
malt (pert to)...
froth.. 4. barm
ground.. 5. grist
infusion.. 4. wort 9. sweetwort
liquor.. 4. beer, suds 6. swipes
material.. 5. grain 6. barley
mixture.. 6. zythum 7. maltate
vinegar.. 4. wort 6. alegar
Malta, Mediterranean Isle...
capital.. 8. Valletta
fever.. 8. undulent
group island.. 4. Gozo 6. Comino
Maltese... 3. cat 5. cross 6. Knight,
  native (of Malta)
maltreat... 5. abuse 6. misuse 8. ill
  treat 9. do wrong by
malty... 5. drunk
malum... 4. evil 5. wrong 7. offense
malversation... 9. extortion (in office)
  10. corruption 11. evil conduct,
  fraudulence, misbehavior
mammal... 3. ape, man 4. homo
  5. whale 10. vertebrate

mammal... 2. ai, ox 3. ape, bat, cat, cow, dog, hog, orc, pig, rat, yak 4. bear, bull, deer, lion, mink, mole, paca, seal, tait, zebu 5. camel, coati, daman, koala, lemur, llama, moose, mouse, okapi, otter, ounce, panda, ratel, rhino, sable, shark, sheep, swine, tapir, tayra, whale 6. alpaca, badger, desman, dugong, marten, monkey, ocelot, rytina (ext), tenrec (tendrac), walrus, weasel 7. dolphin, manatee, opossum, peccary, raccoon 8. aardvark, anteater, antelope, elephant, kangaroo, mongoose, reindeer 10. chevrotain, rhinoceros 12. hippopotamus

mammal (pert to)...
coat.. 4. hide, skin 6. pelage
cud–chewing.. 8. ruminant
edentate.. 8. anteater, pangolin, tamandua (anteater)
extinct.. 6. rytina 8. mastodon 9. Glyptodon
flying.. 3. bat
largest.. 5. whale
man.. 6. Bimana (group)
meat–eating.. 9. carnivore
nipple.. 4. teat 8. mammilla
omnivorous.. 3. hog, pig 5. swine
Order.. 7. Cetacea 8. Edentata, Rodentia
Order, highest.. 7. Primata 8. Mammalia
Order, lowest.. 9. Marsupial
plantigrade.. 7. raccoon
primate (except Man).. 10. Quadrumana
scaled.. 8. pangolin
shelled.. 9. armadillo
smallest.. 5. shrew
snake–eating.. 8. mongoose
toothless.. 8. edentate
web–footed.. 6. aliped
wing–footed.. 6. aliped
zebralike.. 6. quagga

mammock... 4. tear 5. break, scrap 8. fragment

mammon... 5. money 6. riches, wealth 11. fallen angel (Bib) 15. demon of cupidity

mammoth... 5. giant, large (very) 7. titanic 8. behemoth, elephant, gigantic, mastodon 9. pachyderm 11. Dinotherium 12. hippopotamus

man... 3. arm, fit, rig 4. homo, male 5. adult, equip, fit up, human, staff 6. outfit, person 7. fortify, furnish, mankind, prepare, someone 9. human race 10. human being

man (of)...
all work.. 4. mozo 6. Friday 8. factotum 9. assistant
Blood and Iron.. 8. Bismarck
Destiny.. 9. Bonaparte (Napoleon)
Galilee.. 11. Jesus Christ
God.. 5. saint 6. priest 9. clergyman 12. ecclesiastic
law.. 6. lawyer 7. counsel 8. attorney 9. counselor (counsellor)
learning.. 6. pundit, savant 7. scholar 9. literatus 11. litterateur
quackery.. 7. buffoon 9. trickster

10. mountebank
the sea.. 3. tar 6. merman, sailor
the signs.. 12. homo signorum
the woods.. 6. rustic 8. silvanus, woodsman 9. orangutan
the world.. 6. layman 11. cosmopolite 12. sophisticate
war.. 7. frigate, soldier, warrior

man (pert to)...
aged.. 3. vet 9. patriarch 12. octogenarian
bachelor.. 4. stag 8. celibate
bald.. 9. pilgarlic
conceited.. 7. coxcomb
cunning.. 5. rogue 6. rascal 7. shyster 10. mountebank
dissolute.. 4. roué
eccentric, elderly.. 4. sire 5. uncle 6. codger, gaffer 11. grandfather
effeminate.. 9. androgyne
entire (soul and body).. 3. ego
fashionable.. 3. fop 4. dude 5. dandy 11. Beau Brummel 12. boulevardier
fungus.. 9. earthstar (the)
handsome.. 6. Adonis
hardheaded.. 5. Boche
hard–pressed.. 3. Job
important.. 4. hero, lion 5. chief, nabob 6. tycoon 7. mugwump
Isle of, capital.. 7. Douglas
lady's.. 4. beau 6. fiancé
lawless.. 7. ruffian
learned.. 6. pundit, savant 7. erudite, scholar 9. literatus 11. philologist
like.. 7. android 10. anthropoid
little.. 6. mankin, shrimp, squirt 10. homunculus
loud–voiced.. 7. stentor
lowbred.. 4. serf 5. churl 6. rustic 7. peasant 8. plebeian
medicine, magic.. 6. shaman
millionaire.. 7. Croesus 10. capitalist, Corinthian
newspaper.. 6. editor 8. reporter 10. journalist
old.. 5. elder 7. veteran 12. octogenarian
prehistoric.. 4. cave 6. Ice Age 8. eolithic, Grimaldi, Piltdown 9. neolithic 11. paleolithic
red.. 6. Indian
strong.. 6. Samson 8. ironside
wise.. 4. sage, seer 5. solon 6. nestor 7. Solomon
without a country.. 5. Nolan (Philip)

manacle... 4. gyve, iron 5. chain 6. fetter 7. shackle 8. handcuff 9. restraint

manada... 4. herd 5. drove, flock

manage... 3. man, run 4. boss, head, lead, tend 5. cater, dight, guide, pilot, wield 6. direct, govern 7. control, husband, operate 8. contrive, engineer 10. administer, manipulate

manageable... 4. easy, tame, yare 6. docile, wieldy 7. ductile 9. compliant, tractable 10. governable 12. controllable

management... 4. care 6. charge, menage 7. conduct, control, gestion 9. direction 10. government

11. negotiation
manager... 4. boss 6. gerent
　　7. steward 8. director, governor,
　　operator, overseer 9. economist
　　12. entrepreneur 13. administrator
managery... 7. cunning 8. artifice
　　9. frugality, husbandry
　　10. management 12. manipulation
　　14. administration
mañana... 8. tomorrow 10. before
long
manas (Hind)... 3. ego 4. mind
Manasseh... 5. tribe (Israel) 11. King
of Judah
Manchuria...
　　capital.. 6. Mukden (old)
　　9. Changchun
　　government.. 9. Communist (Chin)
　　Japanese name.. 9. Manchukuo
　　native.. 9. Mongolian
　　river.. 4. Amur, Liao, Yalu
manciple... 5. slave 7. servant,
　　steward 8. purveyor
mandarin (pert to)...
　　bird.. 4. duck
　　city.. 9. Chungking
　　color.. 3. red
　　dialect.. 7. Chinese
　　figure in Chiness dress, seated..
　　9. grotesque
　　fruit.. 6. orange 9. tangerine
　　official.. 8. governor 10. bureaucrat
　　residence.. 5. yamen
　　ware.. 9. porcelain
mandate... 5. edict, order 6. behest,
　　charge, decree, mandat 7. bidding,
　　command, precept 9. direction
　　10. injunction, referendum
mandatory... 10. imperative, obligatory,
　　preceptive
mandible... 3. jaw 4. beak 5. chops,
　　molar (part) 9. chelicera
mandrel, mandril... 3. hob 4. axle,
　　pick (miner's) 5. arbor 7. spindle
mandriarch... 9. monk ruler
mandrill... 6. baboon
mane... 4. hair, juba, shag 6. thatch
manege... 6. school (riding)
　　7. academy (riding) 8. cavesson
　　(halter)
manes (Rom)... 4. gods (lower world)
　　7. spirits
maneuver, manoeuvre... 4. ruse
　　5. trick 6. device, jockey, scheme,
　　tactic 7. operate 8. artifice, intrigue,
　　strategy 9. stratagem 10. manipulate
　　13. Immelmann turn
mangabey... 6. monkey
manger... 3. bin 4. crib, meal, rack
　　6. bunker, trough 7. banquet
mangle... 3. cut, mar 4. hack
　　5. press 6. bruise, injure, ironer
　　8. calender, demolish, lacerate,
　　mutilate 9. dismember
mango (pert to)...
　　bird.. 6. oriole 11. hummingbird
　　fish.. 9. threadfin
　　fruit.. 5. amini, bauno, drupe, melon
　　9. muskmelon
　　grove.. 4. tope
mangy... 4. mean 5. itchy, seedy

6. ronyon, scurvy, shabby 7. squalid
　　12. contemptible
manhandle... 4. maul 5. abuse
　　7. rough up 8. maltreat, mistreat
mania... 4. rage 5. craze, furor
　　6. frenzy, furore, lunacy 7. madness,
　　passion 8. delirium 10. alienation
　　11. fascination, infatuation
mania (for)...
　　buying.. 9. oniomania
　　drink.. 9. potomania 10. dipsomania
　　foreign customs.. 9. xenomania
　　narcotics.. 10. narcomania
　　religion.. 9. theomania
　　stealing.. 10. erotomania
　　11. kleptomania
　　wandering.. 10. dromomania
　　work.. 9. ergomania
manifest... 4. list, open, show
　　5. clear, index, overt 6. evince,
　　liquet, patent 7. declare, evident,
　　express, obvious, visible 8. apparent,
　　disclose 11. indubitable
　　12. indisputable, unmistakable
manifestation... 4. aura 5. phase
　　7. display 8. evidence
　　10. appearance, disclosure,
　　exhibition, indication, revelation
　　13. demonstration
manifestation of...
　　deity.. 4. Apis 7. serapis
　　divinity.. 6. Christ 8. Epiphany
　　Vishnu.. 6. avatar
manifesto... 5. edict 6. decree
　　8. evidence, rescript 11. declaration
　　(public) 12. announcement
　　13. demonstration
manikin... 5. dwarf, model, pygmy
　　6. figure 7. phantom 9. mannequin
Manila...
　　boat.. 6. bilalo
　　capital of.. 11. Philippines
　　hemp.. 5. abaca
　　hero.. 5. Dewey (Adm)
　　island site.. 5. Luzon
　　native.. 7. Chinese, Tagalog
　　9. Filipinos
maniple... 5. fanon, orale 7. handful,
　　phalanx, platoon
manipulate... 3. rig, use 4. work
　　5. pilot, treat, wield 6. handle,
　　manage 7. operate
manipulation... 5. using 8. handling,
　　intrigue 9. operation, stratagem
　　10. management, use of hands
Manitoba, Canada...
　　capital.. 8. Winnipeg
　　Indian.. 4. Cree
　　lake.. 8. Manitoba
　　river.. 3. Red
mankind... 3. man 4. Adam, folk
　　7. menfolk 8. humanity 9. human
　　race
mankind (pert to)...
　　division.. 4. race 5. tribe
　　group (kindred).. 6. ethnos, socius
　　hater.. 11. misanthrope
　　science.. 9. ethnogeny, ethnology
　　12. anthropology
manly... 4. bold 5. adult, brave, hardy,
　　noble 6. daring 8. resolute
　　9. honorable, masculine, undaunted

10. courageous
manna... 4. food (miracle), lerp (laap, laarp) 7. godsend 10. gazangabin
manner... 3. air, way 4. kind, mien, mode, sort 5. guise, style 6. aspect, custom, method 7. fashion 8. behavior 10. appearance, deportment
manner (pert to)...
frenzied.. 4. amok 5. amuck, huffy 7. haughty
law.. 5. modus
like.. 4. thus 6. in kind 8. parallel
meddlesome.. 9. officious
meditative.. 13. contemplative
rough.. 7. brusque 10. irreverent
mannerism... 4. mode 8. elegance 11. affectation
mannerly... 4. nice 5. moral, suave 6. seemly 8. decorous, politely 9. courteous 10. well-spoken 12. ingratiating
manner of...
making something.. 7. facture
pronouncing.. 6. accent, brogue
speaking.. 7. grammar
manners... 5. mores 8. behavior 9. amenities, etiquette
Mannheim gold... 5. brass
mano (comb form)... 4. hand
manoc... 4. fowl (jungle) 7. chicken, rooster
manor... 4. hall 5. abode 6. estate 7. demesne, mansion
manred... 6. homage 9. vassalage 10. leadership (in war)
mansion... 4. seat 5. house, manor, manse 8. dwelling 9. astrology
manta... 3. ray (fish) 4. wrap 5. cloak, cloth 7. blanket 8. mantelet (mantlet) 9. devilfish
mantilla... 4. cape, veil 5. cloak
mantis... 4. Cagn (deity) 6. insect 7. mantoid 9. rearhorse
mantis crab... 7. squilla
mantle... 4. cape, cope, robe 5. cloak, cover 6. capote, kittel 7. garment 8. filament, insignia, mantelet, mantling (Her), vestment 10. witzchoura 11. mantelletta
manto... 3. ore 4. gown 5. cloak 6. mantle, mantua
mantoid... 6. mantis
Mantua (pert to)...
birthplace of.. 6. Vergil (Virgil)
capital.. 7. Mantova
walled by.. 11. Charlemagne
Manu (Myth)...
laws.. 8. creation, religion
progenitors of.. 3. Man
Seventh Age, author of.. 10. Code of Manu (Hind laws)
manual... 4. book 7. clavier (Mus), didache 8. exercise, handbook 14. consuetudinary
manual (pert to)...
alphabet (deaf).. 11. dactylology
arts.. 6. crafts
crafts.. 5. sloyd (sloid, slojd) 10. handicraft
digit.. 3. toe 5. thumb 6. finger 8. dactylar

ritual.. 7. rituale 8. breviary 9. formulary
manufacture... 4. make 6. invent 7. produce, trump up 9. fabricate
manufacturer of drugs, liquors... 6. abkari (abkary)
manumission... 7. freeing 10. liberation (slave) 12. emancipation
manumit... 4. free 5. let go 6. unhand 7. dismiss, release 8. liberate
manuscript (Ms, Mss)... 4. copy (author's), opus 5. codex, folio 7. writing 8. document 11. composition, handwriting 13. written by hand
manuscript (pert to)...
back.. 5. dorso
blank space.. 6. lacuna
copier.. 6. scribe
mark (old).. 6. obelus
many... 6. divers 7. diverse, several, various 8. frequent, manifold, numerous 9. different, multitude 10. multiplied
many (pert to)...
footed.. 8. multiped
prefix.. 4. poly, vari 5. multi
sided.. 9. versatile 12. multilateral
times.. 5. often 10. frequently
manyplies... 12. third stomach (ruminant)
mao... 7. peacock
Maori (pert to)...
Adam, ancestor.. 4. Tiki
bird.. 3. tui 4. weka (flightless)
canoe, raft.. 4. moki, waka
charm (grotesque).. 7. heitiki
compensation.. 3. utu
fish.. 4. hiku 7. rainbow 9. trumpeter
hero.. 4. Maui
people.. 9. cannibals (anc) 10. aborigines
priest.. 7. tuhunga
sect.. 7. Ringatu
tatooing.. 4. moko
tree.. 5. mapau
tribe.. 3. Ati 4. Hapu
village.. 4. kaik (kaika)
weapon.. 4. mere, patu, rata 6. marree
Maoriland... 10. New Zealand
map... 4. plat 5. chart, image 6. charte, design, isobar (weather line), sketch, survey 7. diagram, epitome, explore, picture 9. delineate 10. embodiment 14. representation
maple (pert to)...
bowl.. 5. mazer, rogan (sap)
flowering.. 8. abutilon
genus.. 4. Acer 9. Aceraceae
insect scale.. 10. pulvinaria
seed.. 6. samara
sugar tube.. 5. stile
tree.. 8. box elder 9. moosewood
map maker... 4. Eric (Father) 7. charter 8. Mercator 12. cartographer
mapo... 4. goby (fish)
mar... 4. ruin, scar 5. botch, spoil 6. damage, deface, impair, mangle

7. blemish 8. mutilate 9. disfigure
Mar... 4. Lord (Jacobite)
marabou, marabout... 5. stork
  6. argala, covert 8. adjutant
maracan... 5. macaw
maranon... 6. cashew
marasca, maraschino... 6. cherry
marasma... 5. waste 7. disease
  10. emaciation 12. malnutrition
maraud... 3. rob 4. loot, raid, rove,
  sack 6. forage 7. brigand, cateran,
  pillage, plunder 10. plundering
marble... 3. mib, mig, taw 4. cold,
  hard 5. agate, white 6. basalt,
  marmor 7. pattern (mottled)
  8. dolomite 9. limestone, sculpture,
  unfeeling
marble (pert to)...
  Belgian.. 5. rance
  Catalonia.. 8. brocatel (brocatelle)
  cork (tree).. 9. tambookie
  famous.. 6. Parian 7. Carrara
    8. Pentelec
  game.. 3. taw 5. alley
  group (famed).. 5. Elgin (Marbles)
  made of.. 9. marmoreal
  mosaic.. 7. tessera
  Roman.. 7. cipolin
  slab.. 5. dalle
marbled... 9. marmorate
Marbles... 5. Elgin 7. Arundel
marc... 6. refuse, spirit 7. residue
  14. eau de vie de marc
marcato (Mus)... 6. marked
  8. accented, emphatic
march... 4. fill, hike, step, trek
  5. troop 6. border, parade
  7. advance, proceed 8. boundary,
  drumbeat, frontier, lockstep,
  movement, progress, smallage
  9. cavalcade, quickstep
March King... 5. Sousa (John Philip)
marcid... 4. weak 7. decayed, tabetic
  8. withered 9. exhausted
  10. emaciating
Marcobrunner... 4. wine (White Rhine)
Mardi Gras... 8. carnival 10. fat
  Tuesday (literal) 13. Shrove Tuesday
Mardi Gras King... 3. Rex
mare... 4. yaud 5. filly, horse
  6. goblin, grasni (gypsy) 7. incubus,
  specter, trestle 8. the blues
  9. nightmare 10. blue devils,
  melancholy
marge, margent... 3. rim 4. brim,
  edge, side 5. brink, shore 6. border,
  fringe, margin 8. marginal
margin... 3. rim 4. brim, edge, rand,
  room, side 5. brink, limit 6. amount,
  border, reward 10. collateral
margin (pert to)...
  business.. 5. gross
  notched.. 5. erose
  note.. 7. apostil 8. scholium
    10. annotation
  scalloped.. 7. crenate
  set in.. 6. indent
  straighten (to).. 5. align
marginal note... 4. kere (kri, keri)
  7. apostil 8. scholium 10. annotation
marigold... 5. aster, boots, caper,
  finch 6. orange (cadmium)

7. cowslip, Tagetes
marijuana... 3. hay 4. hemp 6. reefer
  7. tobacco (wild) 8. locoweed
  9. cigarette
marikina... 7. tamarin 8. marmoset
marimba... 9. xylophone
marina... 4. dock 5. basin
  9. esplanade, promenade (seaside)
marinal... 6. marine, sailor, saline
marine... 3. tar 5. jolly, naval
  7. mariner, oceanic, pelagic
  8. maritime, nautical 11. leatherneck
marine (pert to)...
  animal.. 3. orc 4. brit, seal 5. coral,
    polyp 6. dugong, Otaria, teredo,
    walrus 7. manatee, mollusk, octopus
  clam.. 8. shipworm
  crustacean.. 4. brit 8. barnacle
  fauna, flora.. 7. benthos
  fish.. 5. shark 8. menhaden
  gastropod.. 5. conus (snail), murex
    7. terebra
  growth.. 4. kelp 5. algae 6. enalid
    7. seaweed 10. ditch grass
  individual.. 6. merman 7. mermaid
  skeleton.. 5. coral
  slogan.. 6. gung–ho
mariner... 3. gob, tar 4. salt 5. Jacky
  6. sailor, seaman 8. waterman
mariner's card... 5. chart
mariner's compass points...
  6. rhumba
marionette... 4. doll, duck 6. figure,
  puppet
maritime... 5. naval 6. marine
  7. oceanic 8. nautical
marjoram... 3. dot 4. mint 6. origin
  8. origanum 9. flavoring
mark... 3. aim, tee 4. heed, line,
  note, rist, seal, sign 5. brand, label,
  notch, score, stain, stamp, trait
  6. denote, symbol, target
  7. betoken, blemish, earmark,
  engrave, impress, imprint, insigne
  8. evidence, identify, insignia,
  landmark 9. emphasize, objective,
  punctuate, signature, trademark
  10. indication 11. distinction,
  distinguish 14. characteristic
mark (pert to)...
  bad.. 7. demerit
  bounds.. 7. delimit 9. demarcate
  contest (in a).. 5. bogey (bogie)
  critical.. 6. obelus
  diacritical.. 5. tilde 6. tittle 7. cedilla
  disgrace.. 6. stigma
  fingerprint.. 5. whorl
  logic.. 11. differentia
  misconduct.. 7. demerit
  off.. 4. plot 6. assign 7. measure
    12. characterize, circumscribe
  of homage.. 7. ovation
  of whip.. 4. wale, welt
  out.. 6. cancel 10. obliterate
  possessive.. 10. apostrophe
  printing.. 4. dele, stet 5. caret
    6. dagger, diesis, obelus 7. obelisk
    10. apostrophe
  pronunciation.. 5. breve 6. macron
  proofreading.. 4. dele 5. caret
  prosody.. 7. caesura, triseme
    9. diaeresis, tetraseme

punctuation.. 4. dash 5. colon,
comma 6. period 9. diaeresis
(dieresis), semicolon 10. apostrophe
question.. 7. eroteme (erotema)
reference.. 4. star 6. dagger, diesis
8. asterisk
with bars.. 5. grill
with dots, spots.. 6. dapple 7. stipple
with pointed instrument.. 6. scrive
with ridges.. 3. rib
marked by...
dispute.. 13. controversial
maneuvering.. 8. tactical
nicety.. 7. elegant
small areas.. 9. areolated
time.. 5. dated
marked with...
colors.. 7. mottled 10. variegated
11. psychedelic
depressions.. 7. dimpled
furrows.. 6. rivose
grooves.. 6. lirate
lines.. 5. ruled 6. linear, notate
sables (Her).. 8. pelleted
spots.. 6. notate 7. mottled
stripes.. 7. lineate
zones.. 6. zonate
marker... 4. buoy 5. pylon 6. scorer,
signal 7. brander, counter, monitor
8. bookmark, marksman, monument,
recorder 9. indicator
market... 4. mart, sale, sell, shop
5. forum, trade 6. rialto, square
9. clientele
market (pert to)...
bonds.. 5. float
day (Rom).. 7. nundine
French.. 8. débouché
place.. 4. sook 5. agora, plaza, store
6. bazaar, rialto 8. emporium,
exchange
marketable... 6. staple 7. salable
8. in demand, vendible
12. merchantable
markhor... 4. goat
marking (crescent)... 6. lunula, lunule
7. lunulet 9. engraving
markings... 7. rasceta
marksman... 4. shot 6. gunner, sniper
7. shooter 9. Orangeman
Mark Twain (pert to)...
category.. 8. humorist
character.. 9. Tom Sawyer
15. Huckleberry Finn
name.. 13. Samuel Clemens
tale.. 9. Gilded Age 10. Roughing It
15. Innocents Abroad
marl... 4. malm 5. earth, fiber
6. manure 7. deposit (earthy), marlite
9. greensand 10. fertilizer,
overspread
marli... 4. lace 5. gauze, tulle
6. border (raised on dish)
marlin... 6. curlew, godwit 8. sailfish
9. spearfish
marlinspike... 3. fid 4. bird, tool
6. jaeger 8. skua gull
marmalade... 3. jam 6. Achras, sapote
8. plum tree, preserve 12. mammee
sapota
marmit... 6. kettle 7. soup pot
marmite (Mil)... 4. bomb (soup kettle)

5. shell
marmor... 6. marble
marmoset... 4. mico (black–tailed)
6. monkey, sagoin 7. tamarin
marmot... 5. bobac 6. rodent
7. Marmota 8. Arctomys, whistler
9. ground hog, woodchuck
maroon... 5. slave 7. abandon, cast
off, forsake, isolate 8. chestnut
13. leave helpless
marquee... 4. tent 6. canopy
marriage... 5. union 7. wedding,
wedlock 9. matrimony 10. nuptiality
11. espousement
marriage (pert to)...
absence of.. 5. agamy
age.. 6. mature, nubile
broker.. 9. schatchen 10. matchmaker
forswearer.. 8. celibate
god.. 5. Hymen
goddess.. 4. Hera
hater.. 10. misogamist
intermarriage.. 13. miscegenation
late in life.. 8. opsigamy
more than one.. 6. bigamy, digamy
8. polygamy 9. polyandry, tetragamy
(4th) 11. deuterogamy
notice.. 5. banns
of the gods.. 8. theogamy
outside the tribe.. 7. exogamy
pert to.. 7. marital, spousal
8. hymeneal 9. connubial, endogamic
portion.. 3. dot 5. dotal, dowry
promise.. 7. betroth 8. affiance
secret.. 9. elopement
married... 5. wived 6. wedded
8. espoused 9. connubial
married (pert to)...
more than once at a time..
9. polyandry (woman)
once at a time.. 8. monandry
person.. 4. wife 6. spouse
7. husband 8. benedict
twice.. 6. bigamy, digamy
11. deuterogamy
marrow... 4. pith 6. center
7. essence, medulla 9. substance
Mars... 3. god (of War) 4. Ares
6. planet, war–god
Mars (pert to)...
altar.. 13. Campus Martius (field of
Mars)
constellation.. 3. Ara
festival.. 5. March 7. October
pert to.. 5. Arean 7. Martian
priests.. 5. Salii
red.. 5. totem
satellites.. 6. Deimos, Phobos
ship.. 8. moon ship 9. spaceship
sons (twin).. 5. Remus 7. Romulus
spot.. 5. oasis
Marseillaise... 4. song (1792)
Marseille, France...
capital of Dept.. 14. Bouches du
Rhone
church.. 9. Notre Dame
fort.. 11. Rue Noailles 13. Rue
Cannebière
old name.. 8. Massilia
seaport site.. 13. Mediterranean
marsh... 3. bog, fen 4. meer, mire,
moor, slue 5. liman, swale, swamp

6. morass, saline, slough
7. maremma
marsh (pert to)...
bird.. 4. sora 5. snipe, stilt
crocodile.. 3. goa
elder.. 3. Iva
fever.. 7. helodes
gas.. 7. methane 8. firedamp
grass.. 5. sedge, spart
hawk.. 5. harpy 7. harrier
hen.. 4. rail
inhabiting.. 12. limnophilous
mallow.. 5. altea
marigold.. 5. boots, calla 7. cowslip
pert to.. 8. paludine
shrub.. 4. reed 5. sedge 7. bulrush,
cattail 8. moorwort 12. pickerelweed
marshal... 3. Ney (Fr) 4. lead 5. align,
aline, array, groom, guide, range,
usher 6. direct, parade 7. farrier,
officer 8. official
Marshall Islands...
chains (two).. 6. Ralick (eleven isls)
7. Rattach (13 isls)
government.. 11. trusteeship
WWII scene.. 6. Bikini 8. Eniwetok
9. Kwajalein
marshberry, marshwort... 9. cranberry
marshy... 3. wet 5. boggy, fenny,
liman 7. moorish 8. morassey,
paludine
marsupial... 4. frog, tait 5. kaola
6. wombat 7. opossum, wallaby
8. kangaroo 9. bandicoot, phalanger,
tapoatafa 10. Diprotodon
11. Marsupialia
marsupium... 5. pouch
martel (Hist)... 6. hammer
martel–de–fer... 6. weapon
12. hammer of iron
marten... 3. fur 4. pelt 5. sable
6. mammal 7. Mustela
martial... 4. Mars (pert to) 5. brave
7. warlike 8. fighting, militant,
military
Martinique...
capital.. 8. St Pierre (former) 12. Fort
de France
formation.. 8. volcanic
mountain peak.. 9. Mont Pelée
martyr... 4. kill 5. title 7. Stephen
(Christian), torture 8. sufferer
marvel... 4. gape 6. wonder
7. miracle, portent, prodigy
8. astonish
marvelous... 6. superb 7. strange
9. wonderful 10. improbable,
incredible, remarkable 11. astonishing
13. extraordinary
Maryland...
bay.. 10. Chesapeake
capital.. 9. Annapolis
city.. 9. Baltimore
Hist site.. 8. Antietam 10. State
House (nation's oldest) 11. Fort Mc
Henry
mountain.. 8. Backbone, Piedmont
11. Appalachian
race (famed).. 9. Preakness
12. Steeplechase
race track.. 5. Bowie 6. Butler, Laurel
7. Pimlico

school.. 9. Annapolis (Acad)
12. Johns Hopkins
settler.. 7. Calvert (Leonard)
State admission.. 7. Seventh
State motto.. 22. Manly Deeds,
Womanly Words
State nickname.. 4. Free 7. Old Line
mash... 4. feed, ogle, pulp 5. crush,
flirt, press, smash, steep 6. jumble,
soften 7. mixture 9. pulverize
11. infatuation
mashal... 7. parable, proverb
masher... 5. dandy, flirt, ricer
7. utensil 10. pulverizer
11. philanderer
masjid... 6. mosque
mask... 4. ball, loup, veil 5. cloak,
cover, dance, drama, onkos
6. domino, screen 7. conceal,
pretext 8. disguise 10. subterfuge
masked... 6. comedy, cowled, hidden,
veiled 7. larvate, obscure
8. shrouded 9. concealed, disguised
masker... 5. mimer 6. mummer
11. masquerader
maslin... 5. brass 6. kettle 7. mixture
(grain) 9. potpourri
Masonic doorkeeper... 5. tiler
masonry... 6. ashlar 9. revetment
mass... 3. cob, dab, gob, mop, pat,
wad 4. blob, body, bulk, load, loaf,
lump, roll, size 5. solid 8. quantity
9. large part, magnitude 11. large
amount 12. accumulation,
congregation
mass (pert to)...
book.. 6. missal
collection.. 9. aggregate
directory (RCCh).. 4. ordo
for dead.. 7. requiem
matter.. 5. molar
molten glass.. 7. parison
nerve tissue.. 8. ganglion
tangled.. 3. mop 4. shag
vestment (Eccl).. 5. amice
Massachusetts...
capital.. 6. Boston (1630)
city.. 5. Salem 7. Concord
8. Plymouth 9. Cambridge, Lexington
10. Gloucester, New Bedford
12. Provincetown
college (oldest, US).. 7. Harvard
explorer.. 5. Cabot 7. Gosnold
9. Capt Smith (John)
hero.. 10. Paul Revere
island.. 9. Nantucket 15. Martha's
Vineyard
mountain.. 3. Tom 8. Greylock
10. Berkshires
river.. 10. Housatonic 11. Connecticut
school (first free).. 6. Dedham (1649)
settlers.. 8. Pilgrims, Puritans
State admission.. 5. Sixth
State nickname.. 8. Bay State 9. Old
Colony
massacre... 5. havoc 6. pogrom
7. carnage 8. butchery, decimate,
genocide 9. slaughter
massage... 3. rub 5. knead 6. stroke
7. therapy
massive... 3. big 4. bold 5. bulky,
large, massy 7. weighty 8. imposing

9. ponderous 10. impressive
11. substantial
mast... 3. cue, fid 4. pole, spar
5. stick, stuff (oneself)
master... 3. man, rab 4. lord, mian,
rule 5. chief, judge, rabbi, tutor
6. expert, humble, subdue
7. captain, conquer, maestro,
padrone, subject, teacher
8. dominate, overcome, regulate,
surmount, vanquish 9. commander,
conqueror, craftsman, preceptor,
subjugate
master (pert to)...
African.. 5. bwana
Eton.. 4. beak
fencing.. 7. lanista
hard.. 6. despot
Indian.. 5. sahib
music.. 7. maestro
of a house.. 13. paterfamilias
of ceremonies.. 2. M C 5. emcee
of Heaven.. 16. Celestial Teacher
of the horse.. 7. equerry
stroke.. 4. coup
masterful... 6. lordly 7. haughty
8. arrogant, skillful 9. arbitrary,
imperious 10. commanding
11. dictatorial, domineering,
magisterial, overbearing
13. authoritative
mastery... 4. gree 5. power, skill
7. control, victory 8. dominion
10. ascendancy 11. proficiency
12. vanquishment
mastic... 3. asa, gum 5. resin
6. liquor 8. adhesive 9. red–yellow
masticate... 4. chew 5. crush, grind
8. macerate
mastiff... 3. dog 5. burly, matin
7. massive
mastodon... 5. giant 6. animal,
Mammut 7. mammoth 8. behemoth
9. dinothere 10. Dinotheres,
Mammutidae 11. Dinotherium
mat... 3. rug 4. dull (finish) 5. doily,
platt, twist 7. webbing 8. entangle,
material 10. interweave, lusterless
matador (pert to)...
garment.. 4. cape
staff.. 6. muleta (with red flag)
sword.. 7. estoque
matagasse... 11. butcherbird
match... 3. pit 4. copy, game, mate,
pair, peer, sort 5. equal, fusee,
marry, tally, vesta 7. compare,
contest, lighter, lucifer 8. coincide,
marriage, parallel 10. correspond
11. counterpart
matched... 5. mated 6. paired, pitted,
teamed 7. equaled (equalled)
matchless... 5. alone 6. unlike
7. unequal 8. peerless 9. unequaled
10. inimitable 12. incomparable
matchlock... 3. gun 7. gunlock
mate... 4. pair, wife 5. equal, marry,
match 6. seaman, spouse
7. comrade, husband, mariner,
partner 9. companion
11. confederate, counterpart
matelassé... 6. fabric 8. quilting
(imitation) 13. ornamentation

material, materiel... 4. data 5. goods,
stuff 6. fabric, matter, plasma,
staple, swatch 7. weighty
8. relevant, supplies, tangible
9. apparatus, corporeal, equipment,
essential 11. substantial
12. nonspiritual 13. materialistic
material (pert to)...
building.. 4. frit, lime, tile, wood
5. adobe, brick, rabat, tapia
6. cement, thatch 7. plywood
8. asbestos, Masonite 9. wallboard
discard.. 4. slag 5. scrap 6. refuse
7. rubbish
dress.. 4. silk, wool 5. crepe, linen,
satin, surah, tulle, tweed 6. baleen,
faille, sennit, tricot, velvet
8. corduroy
household.. 5. scrim 6. carpet,
damask, lampas, mohair, napery
7. drapery 8. tapestry
needlework.. 4. lace, yarn 6. thread
8. arrasene, chenille
paper.. 3. wax 4. bond, news, note,
rice 6. letter, tissue, vellum
7. drawing, writing 8. wrapping
9. cardboard, onionskin, parchment
11. papier–mâché
polishing.. 11. rottenstone
materia medica... 7. acology
10. leechcraft
maternal... 7. enation 8. motherly
10. motherlike
math... 6. mowing 9. aftermath,
monastery
mathematician... 6. Euclid 7. actuary
9. physicist, Whitehead
mathematics (pert to)...
abbreviation.. 3. QED
arbitrary.. 5. radix 9. parameter
deduction.. 8. analysis
diagram.. 5. graph
element.. 4. cube, root 6. factor
7. decimal, divisor, formula, minuend
8. dividend, fraction, quotient,
repetend 10. multiplier, subtrahend
12. multiplicand
equation.. 2. pi 4. cosh, sine, surd
6. cosine
factor.. 10. quaternion
instrument.. 6. sector 7. compass
8. arbalest
number.. 5. digit
operation, operator.. 5. nabla
6. scalar 7. operand 10. quaternion
proposition.. 7. theorem
quantity.. 6. addend, augend, scalar
sheets of.. 4. cone 5. nappe
symbol.. 5. digit 7. facient, operand
12. multiplicand
type.. 4. pure 6. higher 7. algebra,
physics 8. abstract, calculus,
geometry 10. arithmetic, elementary,
quadratics 12. trigonometry
mathemeg... 7. catfish
matie... 7. herring
matin... 6. aubade (song) 7. morning,
service 8. watchdog 11. morning
song 13. morning prayer
matinee... 5. levee, party, salon
6. soiree 8. negligee 9. reception
13. conversazione, entertainment

matipo... 4. wood (fuel) 5. napau
matka, matkab... 4. seal
matlow... 6. sailor
matrass... 4. tube 5. flask 6. bottle,
carafe 8. bolthead
matriculate... 4. list 5. admit, adopt,
enter 6. enroll 8. register
10. naturalize
matrimonial... 7. marital, nuptial,
spousal 8. conjugal, hymeneal
9. connubial
matrimony... 7. wedlock 8. marriage
matrix... 3. bed 4. cast, form, mold,
womb 5. cutis 6. gangue
10. foundation, impression
matron... 4. dame, wife 5. widow
11. housekeeper
matter... 3. gas, pus 4. body, gear,
malm, pith 5. atoms, fluid, vapor
6. affair, amount, solids 7. problem,
trouble 8. business, elements,
material 10. importance
11. constituent 12. circumstance
matter (pert to)...
alluvial.. 5. geest
celestial.. 6. nebula
coloring.. 5. eosin 10. endochrome
fatty.. 5. sebum
noxious.. 6. miasma
of doubt.. 7. dubiety
of fact.. 7. literal, prosaic 9. practical,
pragmatic
of law.. 3. res
of note.. 8. notandum
particle.. 4. atom
perfume.. 7. essence
spinal cord.. 4. alba
uniform (physics).. 7. inertia
volcanic.. 2. aa, oo 4. lava
mature... 3. age, due, old 4. ripe
5. adult, grown, ripen 6. digest,
mellow, season 7. develop, fall due,
grow old, perfect 8. complete
9. full-grown, perfected, ratheripe
maturity... 8. ripeness 9. adulthood,
readiness 10. falling due
11. development
matutinal... 5. early, matin 7. morning
12. antemeridian
maty... 7. servant
maud... 3. rug 5. plaid, shawl
maudlin... 5. beery, drunk, silly, tipsy
7. tearful, weeping 10. lachrymose
11. sentimental (overly)
maul, mall... 4. beat, bung, club,
mace, mall, moth 5. abuse, gavel,
staff 6. beetle, bruise, mallet
maumet... 3. god (false), guy 4. doll,
idol 5. image 6. puppet
9. scarecrow
maund, maun... 3. beg 6. basket,
hamper 7. begging, measure
Maundy... 4. alms 8. ceremony
10. Last Supper
Maundy Thursday (Bib)... 8. Holy
Week 13. washing of feet
Mauritius, Ile de France...
capital.. 9. Port Louis
government.. 7. British
product.. 5. coral, sugar
site.. 11. Indian Ocean
Mauser... 5. rifle 7. firearm

mauve... 5. lilac 6. mallow, purple,
violet 10. atmosphere (color)
maverick... 4. calf (orphan) 5. dogie
6. animal 8. newcomer
13. nonconformist
mavis, mavie... 6. thrush
maw... 4. craw, crop 6. gullet, mallow
7. gizzard, stomach
mawk... 6. maggot
mawkish... 5. vapid 6. sickly
8. nauseous 9. squeamish
10. disgusting 11. sentimental
maxilla... 7. jawbone
maxim... 3. saw 4. dict, rule
5. adage, axiom, gnome, motto,
tenet, truth 6. saying 7. precept,
proverb 8. aphorism, apothegm
10. apophthegm
maxims... 5. logia 9. moralisms
maximum... 4. most 5. limit
7. highest, supreme 8. greatest
12. consummation
maximus... 7. largest
may... 3. can 6. be able 9. be
allowed 11. in one's power,
opportunity
May (pert to)...
apple.. 8. mandrake
bird.. 6. thrush
cock.. 5. melon 6. plover
curlew.. 8. whimbrel
Duke.. 6. cherry
festival.. 7. Beltane (anc)
First.. 7. Beltane 14. May-day festival
fish.. 9. killifish
flower.. 7. arbutus 8. hawthorn,
marigold 9. calla lily 10. stitchwort
12. cuckooflower
fly.. 3. dun 7. shad fly 9. ephemerid
goddess.. 4. Maia
gowan.. 5. daisy
Maya... 3. Mam (tribe) 6. Indian
8. Pokonchi
Mayan calendar...
five added days.. 5. uayeb
no leap year.. 5. solar
twenty-day month.. 5. uinal
year.. 4. haab
Mayan underworld... 7. xibalba
maybe... 2. if 7. perhaps 8. possibly
9. perchance 11. conceivably,
possibility, uncertainty
Mayfair... 6. London (fashionable)
Mayflower (pert to)...
boat of.. 8. Pilgrims (1620)
Compact.. 9. agreement (1620)
sister ship.. 9. Speedwell
mayhap... 7. perhaps 12. peradventure
mayor... 5. maire 7. alcalde
10. magistrate 11. burgomaster
mazarine... 4. blue (color from Cardinal
Mazarin)
maze... 5. fancy 7. stupefy
8. confound, delirium, delusion
9. confusion, deception, labyrinth
12. bewilderment, complication
mazed... 4. lost 7. in a maze
9. stupefied 10. bewildered
mazuma... 5. money
mead... 5. drink 6. meadow
8. hydromel 9. metheglin
meadow... 3. lea 4. mead 5. field,

haugh, pampa, swale 7. pasture,
savanna (savannah) 9. grassland
10. agostadero
meadow (pert to)...
chicken.. 8. sora rail
crocus.. 7. saffron
crowfoot.. 9. buttercup
hen.. 4. coot, rail 7. bittern
mouse.. 4. vole 8. arvicole
part.. 5. swale
sage.. 6. salvia
saxifrage.. 6. seseli
sweet.. 7. Spiraea
meager, meagre... 4. arid, bare, lank,
poor, slim 5. gaunt, scant, spare
6. barren, jejune, lenten, narrow,
sparse 7. starved, sterile, trivial
9. emaciated 10. inadequate
meal... 3. tub 4. bran, dune, mess
5. feast, grout, salep, snack
6. bucket, fodder, powder, ration,
repast, tiffin 7. banquet 8. sandbank
9. collation, pulverize
mealy... 4. pale 7. friable, powdery
10. soft–spoken 11. farinaceous
12. mealymouthed
mealy (pert to)...
Amazon.. 6. parrot
back.. 6. cicada
bird, duck.. 5. squaw
bug.. 4. pest 5. scale 10. pear blight
mouth.. 7. warbler
tree.. 9. arrowwood, wayfaring
mealy–mouthed... 5. suave
10. flattering 12. hypocritical
13. sanctimonious
mean... 3. low 4. base 5. petty,
small, snide, solar (time), sorry
6. common, denote, design, humble,
intend, medium, menial, middle,
midway, paltry, shabby, sordid, stingy
7. average, ignoble, purport, purpose,
servile, squalid 8. beggarly, ordinary,
plebeian, shameful, wretched
9. difficult, malicious, niggardly,
penurious 10. despicable,
ill–humored, spiritless 11. closefisted,
disgraceful 12. contemptible,
dishonorable, narrow–minded,
parsimonious
mean clef (Mus)... 5. C clef
meaning... 4. null (without) 5. sense
6. import, intent, spirit 7. purport
8. semantic 9. intending, intention,
knowledge 10. understand
12. significance 13. signification
14. interpretation
meaningless... 4. rote 5. banal, derry
7. aimless 9. senseless
10. designless 11. purposeless
13. insignificant
meanness... 6. infamy, malice
8. baseness, ill–humor 9. servility
10. humbleness, paltriness,
sordidness, stinginess 11. inferiority
means... 5. funds 7. capital
8. averages 9. resources
11. wherewithal
means of...
access.. 4. adit 5. inlet 7. ingress
8. aperture
communication.. 4. note 5. flags,

phone, radio, smoke 6. letter, postal,
tom–tom 8. telegram 9. telegraph,
telephone
livelihood.. 4. work 5. labor, trade
8. vocation 10. profession
outlet.. 4. door, exit 6. egress
8. aperture
support.. 5. funds 6. assets
7. aliment 11. maintenance
meantime... 5. while 7. interim
8. interval, same time 9. meanwhile
measles... 7. rubella, rubeola
8. morbilli
measure (pert to)...
area.. 2. ar 3. are, rod 4. acre, area,
mile, rood 6. square 7. geodesy,
hectare, section 8. township
Bible.. 3. cab (kab), kor, log 4. epha
5. cubit, homer
gauge.. 3. erg, lea (yarn) 5. ergon,
level, plumb, scale, stone 6. denier,
square 7. calorie (calory), compass,
sextant 8. calipers, quadrant
length.. 3. ell, mil, rod 4. foot, hand,
inch, knot, mile, nail, pace, rule,
tape, yard 5. chain, cubit, meter
6. league 7. furlong 9. kilometer,
yardstick 10. centimeter, micrometer,
millimeter
nautical.. 4. knot 6. fathom, league
paper.. 4. page, ream 5. quire, sheet
poetry.. 6. dipody, iambic, rhythm,
sestet 7. anapest, couplet, distich,
tripody 8. quatrain 9. hexameter
10. ottava rima, pentastich,
tetrameter, tetrastich 11. Alexandrine
printer.. 2. em, en 4. pica 5. agate
volume, weight.. 3. ton, tun (wine)
4. bale, butt, cord 5. carat, liter,
minim, ounce, pound, quart
6. barrel, bushel, finger, gallon,
magnum, pottle 8. hogshead,
teaspoon 9. kiloliter 10. tablespoon
measurement... 4. size 6. amount,
alnage, extent, metage 7. azimuth
8. abscissa, capacity, quantity
9. substance 11. calculation,
mensuration
measuring instrument... 6. stadia
7. alidade, caliper 8. odometer
12. perambulator (surveyor)
meat... 4. beef, fish, food, lamb, pork
5. flesh 6. fillet, kernel, mutton,
quarry 7. brisket 9. aitchbone
(icebone), spareribs
meat (pert to)...
ball.. 7. rissole 9. croquette,
hamburger
cured, dried.. 3. ham 5. bacon
6. flitch, jerked 7. biltong (biltongue)
8. pemmican
jellied.. 5. aspic
minced, roll.. 7. rissole
roasted.. 5. cabob (kabob)
9. barbecued
slaughterhouse.. 8. abattoir
smoking place.. 6. buccan (bucan)
stew.. 8. mulligan 9. lobscouse
meatus... 4. burr (ear) 5. canal
7. opening, passage
meaty... 5. pithy, solid 11. substantial
Mecca, Arabia... 8. Holy City 16. City

of the Prophet
Mecca (pert to) . . .
  birthplace of . . 8. Mohammed
  capital . . 5. Hejaz
  color . . 11. Tuscan brown
  famed for . . 5. Kaaba (Caaba, Kaabeth)
    10. Black Stone 11. Great Mosque
  governor . . 6. sherif (shereef)
  pilgrimage . . 4. hadj
  pilgrim's dress . . 5. ihram
  rug . . 6. Shiraz
mechanic . . 7. artisan, workman
  8. operator 9. artificer, craftsman,
  machinist, operative
mechanical . . . 8. machinal
  9. automatic, practical, technical
  11. involuntary, stereotyped
mechanical (pert to) . . .
  adjustment . . 9. tentation
  drawing . . 8. drafting
  law, motion . . 8. dynamics, kinetics
  lever . . 6. tappet
  part . . 5. rotor 6. stator
mechanics . . . 9. technique
  11. mechanology
mechanism . . . 4. gear, tool 5. means
  6. tackle 7. control, rigging
  9. apparatus, machinery, technique
medal . . . 4. coin, disk (disc) 5. badge
  6. plaque 9. medallion
  10. decoration
medallion . . . 4. coin 5. cameo, medal,
  panel 6. tablet 8. ornament
meddle . . . 3. pry 4. nose 6. dabble,
  tamper 7. obtrude 9. interfere
meddler . . . 8. busybody 9. pragmatic
meddlesome . . . 7. Paul Fry 8. meddling
  9. officious 11. inquisitive,
  pragmatical
Mede . . . 6. Median 7. Persian
medial, median . . . 4. mean 5. mesne,
  raphe (valve) 6. medium, middle
  7. average 11. intervening
  12. intermediate
Median . . . 4. Magi, Mede 5. Medic
mediate . . . 5. opine 9. intercede,
  interpose, reconcile
mediator . . . 5. muser 7. arbiter
  9. go–between 10. interagent
  11. intercessor
medic . . . 3. doc 6. clover, doctor,
  median, medico 9. physician
medical (pert to) . . .
  comb form . . 3. oma 4. itis 6. iatric
  7. iatrics
  compound . . 5. hepar
  fluid . . 5. blood, lymph, serum
  man . . 5. medic 6. shaman, voodoo
  monster . . 5. teras
  officer . . 7. coroner
  practitioner . . 2. MD 6. doctor, intern
  (interne) 7. surgeon 8. sawbones
  system . . 7. therapy 9. allopathy
  10. homeopathy, psychiatry
  term . . 8. curative 9. medicinal
medical terms . . .
  chicken pox . . 9. varicella
  flat feet . . 9. pes planus
  headache . . 11. cephalalgia
  heartburn . . 7. pyrosis
  hives . . 9. urticaria
  measles . . 7. rubella, rubeola

  mumps . . 9. parotitis
  whooping cough . . 9. pertussis
medicinal (pert to) . . .
  agent . . 3. tea 6. tisane 9. decoction
  bark . . 6. cartex
  dropper . . 7. pipette
  equal parts . . 3. ana
  herb, plant . . 3. rue 4. aloe 5. ergot,
  jalap, orris, senna, tansy 6. arnica,
  cohosh, ipecac 7. boneset, chirata,
  comfrey 8. licorice, valerian
  pain allaying . . 7. anodyne 8. sedative
  9. goofballs, paregoric
  11. barbiturate
  patent . . 7. nostrum
  remedy . . 5. drops, salve 6. elixir,
  iodine 7. panacea 8. antidote,
  ointment
  science . . 7. biology 10. physiology,
  psychology
  tablet . . 4. pill 6. troche 7. lozenge
  term . . 4. drug 11. therapeutic
mediety . . . 6. loiety 10. moderation,
  temperance
medieval, mediaeval . . . 7. archaic
  10. Middle Ages
medieval (pert to) . . .
  galley (ship's) . . 3. nef 5. xebec
  6. bireme, galiot (galliot) 7. dromone
  (dromon), trireme, unireme
  garment . . 6. tabard
  headdress . . 6. abacot
  helmet . . 5. armet
  instrument (stringed) . . 5. rebec
  (rebeck)
  money of account . . 3. ora
  monster . . 5. golem 9. automaton
  12. Frankenstein
  shield . . 3. ecu 6. scutum
  title, teacher . . 8. magister
  weapon, club . . 4. mace 5. oncin
Medina, Saudi Arabia (pert to) . . .
  anc name . . 9. Lathrippa
  Mohammed supporters . . 6. ansars
  sacred city of . . 5. Islam
  tombs . . 4. Omar 6. Fatima
  8. Mohammed
mediocre . . . 4. mean, so–so 6. medium
  7. average 8. middling, ordinary,
  passable 9. tolerable 11. indifferent
meditate . . . 4. muse, plan, pore
  5. brood, study, watch, weigh
  6. ponder 7. purpose, reflect, revolve
  8. cogitate, consider 11. contemplate
meditation . . . 4. yoga 7. thought
  8. devotion 10. rumination
  11. thanatopsis 13. contemplation
  14. omphaloskepsis
mediterranean . . . 6. inland 7. midland
  10. landlocked
Mediterranean (pert to) . . .
  boat . . 3. nef 4. saic 5. xebec (zebec)
  6. galiot (galliot), mistic (mistico),
  settee (setee) 7. felucca, hexeris
  cat . . 5. genet
  coast . . 7. Riviera
  falcon . . 6. lanner
  fish . . 6. remora
  fowl . . 7. leghorn
  fruit . . 5. olive 7. azarole
  gulf . . 5. Tunis
  herb . . 4. Ammi

inland.. 3. sea
island.. 4. Elba, Gozo 5. Crete, Malta
 6. Candia, Cyprus, Ebusis, Sicily
 7. Majorca 8. Belearic (group),
 Sardinia
island, volcanic.. 6. Lipari, Salina
 7. Vulcano 9. Stromboli
port.. 5. Tunis 7. Tunisia
storm.. 7. borasca (borasco, borasque)
tree.. 5. carob 7. azarole
wind.. 6. solano 7. etesian, gregale,
 mistral, sirocco 8. levanter
 10. euroclyden
medium... 4. agar (cultured), doer,
 mean 5. color, organ 6. degree,
 medial, oracle 7. average, psychic
 8. mediator, mediocre
 10. instrument, interagent
 11. environment 12. intermediary,
 spiritualist
medley... 4. olio 5. relay 6. jumble
 7. ferrago, mélange, mixture
 8. fantasia, mingling 9. potpourri
 10. hodgepodge, salmagundi
medrick... 4. gull (Bonaparte's), tern
 (Wilson's)
medulla... 4. pith 6. marrow
 7. summary 9. oblongata
 10. compendium
Medusa (Myth)... 6. Gorgon, Stheno
 (sister) 9. gorgoneum
Medusa's head (pert to)...
constellation (cluster).. 7. Perseus
star.. 5. Algol
vegetable.. 8. mushroom
Zool.. 10. basket fish
meed... 5. bribe, merit, repay, share
 6. desert, reward 7. bribery
 10. recompense
meek... 4. mild 6. docile, gentle,
 humble, modest 7. pacific, patient
 8. moderate, yielding 10. spiritless,
 submissive
meerkat... 6. monkey
meerschaum... 4. pipe 6. gravel
 (color) 7. seafoam 9. sepiolite
meet... 3. fit 4. face, game, join
 5. equal, match, touch 6. battle,
 combat, concur 7. collide, conform,
 contact, contest, convene, fulfill,
 satisfy 8. assemble, confront
 9. encounter 10. congregate,
 experience, rendezvous
meet halfway... 7. mediate
 10. compromise
meeting... 4. mall, race 5. court,
 gemot (gemote), joint, synod, tryst,
 union 6. caucus, powwow, séance
 7. contact, joining 8. assembly,
 conclave, junction 9. encounter,
 gathering, in contact 10. conference,
 convention, converging, rendezvous
 11. convergence 12. congregation,
 intersection
mega, meg (comb form)... 5. great
 6. mighty
megalith... 5. stone (huge) 6. dolman
 7. boulder 8. monument (Prehist)
megapode, megapod... 6. leipoa
 9. mound bird 10. jungle fowl
 11. brush turkey
megascope... 12. magic lantern

megaseism... 10. earthquake
megrim, megrims... 4. whim 5. fancy,
 freak, humor 8. headache
 9. dizziness 12. hypochondria
Mehitabel, Mehetabel... 3. cat
Mekong River tribe... 3. Moi (Asian)
mel... 5. honey
melancholia... 7. sadness 8. neurosis
 9. nostalgia, psychosis
 10. depression
melancholy... 3. sad 4. blue, dark,
 glum 5. drear, gloom 6. sombre,
 sorrow 7. doleful, sadness
 8. atrabile, liverish, tristful
 9. dejection 10. depressing,
 depression, dispirited, lamentable
 11. despondency, downhearted,
 pensiveness 12. hypochondria,
 mournfulness
Melanesia... 14. Pacific Islands
Melanesian (pert to)...
island.. 4. Fiji 7. Solomon 11. New
 Hebrides
native.. 4. Fiji 6. Papuan
 10. Polynesian
superbeing.. 5. adaro
mélange... 4. olio 6. jumble, medley
 7. mixture 9. pasticcio
 10. miscellany 14. conglomeration
melee... 3. row 4. fray 5. fight
 6. affray 7. contest, diamond (small
 cut) 8. skirmish 9. commotion
melicocca... 5. genip 9. soapberry
melicratum... 4. mead 8. beverage,
 hydromel
melilotus... 6. clover
meliorate... 6. soften 7. improve
 10. ameliorate
melisma... 6. melody 7. cadenza
Melissa... 4. balm 12. Old World mint
mell... 3. mix 4. maul 5. grain (last
 cut), honey 6. beetle, hammer,
 mallet, meddle, mingle
mellow... 4. rich, ripe, soft 5. drunk
 6. genial, jovial, mature, tender
 7. amiable, matured 9. melodious
melodic... 6. ariose 7. cadenza,
 melisma 9. melodious
melodious... 6. ariose, arioso, dulcet
 7. musical, tunable, tuneful
 10. harmonious
melodist... 6. singer 8. composer,
 musician 9. harmonist
melodramatic... 8. dramatic, romantic
 11. sensational
melody... 3. air 4. aria, tune 5. canto,
 charm, dirge, melos, music
 6. rhythm, strain 7. harmony,
 melisma, rosalia 9. cantilena,
 cantilene 11. tunefulness
melon... 4. musk, pepo 6. casaba
 7. Persian 8. honeydew
 9. muskmelon, red–yellow
 10. cantaloupe, paddymelon,
 watermelon
melon (pert to)...
financial.. 4. plum 8. dividend
like.. 5. gourd
pear.. 6. pepino
political.. 5. graft 6. spoils
melongena... 7. brinjal (brinjaul)
 8. eggplant

melos... **4.** song **6.** melody
melt... **3.** run **4.** frit, fuse, thaw
   5. smelt, swale **6.** render, soften
   7. liquefy **8.** diminish, dissolve
   9. disappear **12.** disintegrate
member... **4.** limb, part **5.** organ
   6. branch, fellow, joiner **7.** section
   8. belonger, district, enlistee, enroller
   9. associate
member (pert to)...
   boy's club.. **3.** cub **5.** scout
   Caliph dynasty.. **6.** Omniad
   chapter (Eccl).. **9.** capitular
   crew.. **4.** hand
   diplomatic staff.. **6.** consul **7.** attaché
   8. minister **10.** ambassador
   Jewish brotherhood.. **6.** Essene
   laity.. **6.** layman
   literary club.. **9.** academist
   11. academician
   oldest.. **4.** dean
   regiment.. **8.** legioner **9.** grenadier,
   legionary **11.** legionnaire
   religious sect.. **5.** Amish **6.** Quaker,
   Shaker
   Roman Catholic society.. **6.** Jesuit
   State.. **7.** citizen
   swing band.. **6.** hepcat **7.** swinger
membrane... **4.** caul, skin, tela
   5. lemma **6.** lamina **8.** ectoderm,
   striffin
membrane (pert to)...
   brain.. **13.** meninges mater
   diffusion.. **7.** osmosis
   ear.. **7.** eardrum
   fold.. **5.** plica
   optical.. **6.** retina
   weblike.. **4.** tela
memento... **5.** relic, token **6.** trophy
   8. keepsake, memorial, souvenir
   11. remembrance
Memnon (pert to)...
   famed statue.. **11.** vocal Memnon
   father.. **8.** Tithonus
   Greek name.. **9.** Amenhotep
   king of.. **8.** Ethiopia
   mother.. **3.** Eos (Aurora)
   war hero.. **6.** Trojan
memoir... **4.** hint, note **5.** éloge, essay
   6. record, report **7.** account, history
   9. biography, narrative, reminding
   10. memorandum **12.** dissertation
   13. autobiography
memorabilia... **3.** ana **5.** notes
   6. record **7.** memoirs **8.** memories
memorable... **7.** namable, notable
   9. reminding **11.** reminiscent
memorandum... **4.** chit, note **5.** diary
   6. minute, record **7.** tickler
   8. protocol, reminder
memoria... **4.** tomb **6.** chapel, church,
   shrine **8.** monument **9.** reliquary
memorial... **6.** memoir, memory,
   record, trophy **8.** mnemonic,
   monument **10.** memorandum
   11. celebrative, remembrance
   12. recollection **13.** commemorative
memorial mound... **5.** cairn (stone),
   totem (carved)
memory... **4.** mind **6.** recall
   9. retention **11.** remembrance
   12. recollection, reminiscence

   13. commemoration
memory (pert to)...
   aid.. **10.** anamnestic
   book.. **5.** diary **9.** scrapbook
   jog.. **6.** remind
   loss of.. **5.** lethe **7.** amnesia, aphasia
   (partial) **13.** forgetfulness
   term.. **6.** mnesic **8.** mnemonic
Memphis, Egypt (pert to)...
   deity.. **2.** Ra (Re) **3.** Shu, Tem
   dynasty.. **8.** Memphite
   god, chief.. **4.** Ptah
men (pert to)...
   armed body.. **5.** posse
   gymnasts.. **8.** acrobats
   learned.. **8.** erudites, literati
   mechanical.. **6.** robots
   of same tongue.. **6.** langue
   old.. **7.** gaffers **10.** patriarchs
   party of.. **4.** stag **6.** smoker
   section, Gr Church.. **6.** andron
   single.. **5.** stags **9.** bachelors,
   celibates
   slang.. **6.** blokes
   Three Wise.. **4.** Magi (Gaspar,
   Melchior, Balthazar)
   wild.. **7.** savages **9.** cannibals
menace... **6.** threat **8.** forebode,
   threaten **10.** intimidate
   11. fulmination
menacing... **7.** ominous **8.** imminent
   11. threatening
menage... **4.** club **7.** society
   9. homestead, household, husbandry
   10. management **12.** housekeeping
menagerie... **3.** zoo **10.** collection,
   Tiergarten
menald (said of horses)... **8.** speckled
   10. variegated
Menaspis... **5.** shark (crescent–shaped)
mend... **3.** fix, sew **4.** cure, darn,
   heal, knit **5.** alter, amend, botch,
   emend, moise, patch **6.** better,
   cobble, reform, repair **7.** correct,
   improve **9.** reconcile **10.** ameliorate
mendacious... **5.** false, lying **6.** untrue
   7. in error **9.** truthless **10.** fallacious
mendacity... **3.** lie **5.** lying **6.** deceit
   7. falsity, fibbery, untruth
mendicant... **5.** fakir **6.** beggar
   7. begging
mendicant order... **10.** Carmelites,
   Dominicans **11.** Franciscans
   12. Augustinians
mendole... **4.** fish **8.** cackerel
Menelaus' wife... **11.** Helen of Troy
menhaden... **4.** pogy **7.** sardine
   8. bonyfish **10.** mossbunker
menhir... **5.** stone (standing)
   8. monolith
menial... **6.** flunky, varlet **7.** servant,
   servile, serving, slavish
meninges membrane... **8.** pia mater
   9. arachnoid, dura mater
meniscus... **4.** lens **8.** crescent
   12. crescent moon
Mennonite leader... **11.** Menno
   Simons
Mennonite sect... **5.** Amish
meno... **4.** less **5.** month (comb form)
menology (Eccl)... **8.** calendar, register
Menominee, Menomini... **5.** Falls

(Wis), river 6. Indian 9. whitefish
Menorah... 11. candelabrum (Jew)
12. organization
mensk... 5. adorn, favor, grace, honor
6. credit 8. ornament 9. reverence
12. graciousness
mental... 7. phrenic 9. of the mind,
psychotic 11. intelligent
12. intellectual
mental (pert to)...
alienation.. 8. insanity
deficiency, deficient.. 5. ament, idiot,
moron 6. idiocy 8. imbecile
discipline.. 8. mathesis
disorder.. 7. aphasia 8. insanity,
neurosis, paranoia 9. psychosis
11. megalomania 12. hypochondria
13. forgetfulness, schizophrenia
faculties.. 4. mind, wits
feeling.. 7. emotion
image, picture.. 4. idea 6. idolus
8. phantasm 10. conception
peculiarity.. 12. idiosyncracy
science, study.. 10. New Thought,
psychiatry
state.. 6. morale 7. doldrum
(doldrums) 8. euphoria
strain.. 7. tension
mentality... 4. mind 5. sense
6. acumen, sanity 9. endowment,
intellect 11. mental power
12. intelligence
mention... 4. cite, mind, name
5. refer, speak, trace 6. denote,
notice, record, remark 7. specify,
vestige 8. citation, indicate 9. make
known, statement 10. indication
mentor... 7. adviser, teacher, wise
man 10. instructor
mentum... 4. chin
menu... 4. card, list 5. carte
8. schedule 10. bill of fare
Mephistopheles... 5. devil, Faust,
Satan
mephitis... 4. odor 5. skunk, smell
6. stench 7. polecat 10. exhilation
(earth)
mercantile... 5. trade 7. trading
10. commercial, industrial
mercenary... 4. hack 5. hired, venal
6. sordid 7. Hessian 8. hireling,
salaried, vendible
merchandise... 4. ware 5. goods,
wares 7. effects 9. vendibles
10. emporeutic (pert to)
11. commodities 12. stock in trade
merchant... 5. buyer 6. trader
7. vintner 10. shopkeeper, trafficker
11. storekeeper
merchant (pert to)...
group.. 5. guild, hanse 6. cartel
Indian.. 4. seth
League.. 9. Hanseatic
ship.. 6. argosy 8. Indiaman
wine.. 7. vintner
Merchant of Bagdad... 7. Sindbad
Merchant of Venice character...
6. Portia 7. Antonio, Shylock
merci... 6. thanks
merciful... 4. kind, mild 6. humane,
tender 7. clement, lenient
9. benignant 10. charitable

13. compassionate
merciless... 5. cruel 8. pitiless
9. unsparing 10. relentless
13. unsympathetic
mercurial (pert to God Mercury)...
4. fast 5. swift 6. active, clever,
fickle 8. metallic 9. saturnine
11. money–making
mercurous chloride... 7. calomel
mercury... 5. azoth, guide, metal
7. chibrit, element 9. barometer
11. quicksilver, temperature,
thermometer
Mercury (pert to)...
astronomy.. 6. planet (smallest)
god of.. 8. commerce
Greek name.. 6. Hermes
staff.. 8. caduceus
statue, image.. 5. herma
winged cap.. 7. petasos (petasus)
winged shoes.. 7. talaria
mercy... 4. pity, ruth 5. grace
6. blithe, lenity 7. charity
8. clemency, lenience, leniency
9. tolerance 10. compassion,
indulgence 11. forbearance
mercy killing... 10. euthanasia
mercy seat... 5. bench 11. golden
plate (on the Ark), Throne of God
12. judgment seat 13. seat of
justice
mere... 3. sea 4. bare, lake, only,
pool, sole, such, wisp 5. bound,
limit, sheer, small 6. divide, simple
8. absolute, boundary, landmark, only
this
mère... 6. mother
merely... 4. also, just, only 5. quite
6. barely, purely, simply, singly,
solely 7. utterly 8. entirely, scarcely
9. unmixedly 10. absolutely
mere show... 4. airs 5. front
8. pretense 9. formality
10. pretension 11. affectation
mere taste... 3. nip, sip 4. gulp
7. draught
merganser... 3. nun 4. duck, smee,
smew 6. Mergus 7. bec–scie
8. Merginae 9. goosander
merge... 4. sink 5. blend, unite
6. mingle 7. combine, immerse
8. coalesce 11. consolidate
merger... 4. pool 5. union 6. cartel,
fusion 8. monopoly 10. absorption
12. amalgamation
meridian... 3. top 4. apex, noon
5. plane 6. midday, summit, zenith
8. latitude, southern 9. celestial
11. culmination 12. highest point
meringue... 5. icing 8. egg white,
frosting
Merino... 4. wool, yarn 5. sheep
merit... 4. earn, meed 5. worth
6. desert, reward 7. deserve
10. excellence
merited... 3. fit 4. just 6. worthy
8. adequate, deserved, suitable
9. warranted
meritorious... 5. valid 6. worthy
7. merited 9. deserving, honorable
12. praiseworthy
merlin... 6. falcon

Merlin... 7. prophet, romance
  8. magician
mermaid... 5. siren 6. merrow
  7. Oceanid, swimmer 8. sea nymph
  9. sea spirit 14. marine creature
mermaid's hair... 4. alga
mero... 4. fish 5. guasa 7. grouper
  8. rock hind
merogenesis... 12. segmentation
meropia... 9. blindness (partial)
meros... 5. thigh 10. meropodite
merriment... 3. fun 4. glee 5. mirth
  6. gaiety (gayety) 8. laughter
  9. amusement, diversion
  11. merrymaking
merrow... 7. mermaid
merry... 3. gai, gay 4. glad 5. funny,
  happy 6. blithe, bonnie, jocose,
  jovial, joyous 7. comical, festive,
  gleeful, jocular 8. cheerful, mirthful,
  sportive 9. favorable, hilarious,
  sprightly 13. sweet–sounding
merry–andrew... 4. mime, zany
  5. antic, clown, joker 6. jester
  7. buffoon 8. merryman
merry–go–round... 9. carrousel
  (carousal) 17. revolving platform
merrymaking... 4. reel 5. momus,
  revel 7. festive, wassail 9. festivity,
  merriment 12. conviviality
merrythought... 8. wishbone
merrytrotter... 5. swing 6. seesaw
merrywing... 4. duck 9. goldeneye
  10. bufflehead
merse... 3. dip 5. marsh 6. plunge
  7. immerse
merycism... 7. chewing 10. rumination
mesa... 7. mesilla, oakwood (color),
  terrace 14. flat–topped hill
mesel... 5. leper
mesh... 3. net, web 5. catch 6. areola
  7. complex, ensnare, netting, network
  10. crisscross 11. interaction
mesial plane... 5. meson (Zool)
  6. median, middle
mesmeric... 11. fascinating, hypnotizing
  12. irresistible, spellbinding
mesmeric force... 2. od
Mesopotamia...
  ancient city.. 2. Ur 5. Eridu
  7. Babylon, Ninevah
  city.. 5. Basra, Mosul 6. Edessa
  colloquialism.. 6. Mespot
  culture.. 8. Sumerian
  export.. 3. oil
  language.. 6. Arabic
  people (anc).. 8. Aramaean (Aramean)
  river.. 6. Tigris 9. Euphrates
  wind.. 6. shamal
Mesopotamian... 5. Iraqi
Mesozoic era... 7. reptile 8. dinosaur
  10. evergreens, ganoid fish
mesquin... 4. mean 6. shabby, sordid
mesquita... 6. mosque
mesquite... 5. pacay 7. thicket
  8. Prosopis 9. algarroba
mesquite bean flour... 6. pinole
mess... 4. meal 5. batch, share, spoil
  6. bungle, jumble, litter 7. eyesore,
  failure, mixture 8. disorder
  9. confusion 11. predicament
  12. kettle of fish

mess (up)... 5. botch, spoil 6. muss
  up 7. clutter, derange, shuffle
  10. disarrange
message... 4. news, note, wire, word
  5. cable 6. brevet, letter, notice
  7. epistle, evangel, tidings
  8. dispatch, telegram
  10. communiqué 13. communication
message medium... 5. Ouija
messenger... 4. Iris, page, sand, toty
  5. angel, envoy 6. herald, nuncio,
  Revere (Paul) 7. apostle, carrier,
  courier, prophet, totyman
  8. delegate, minister 9. estafette
  (estafet) 10. forerunner
messenger bird... 9. secretary
Messenger of the Gods... 6. Hermes
  (Gr) 7. Mercury (Rom)
Messiah... 6. Christ 7. Saviour (Savior)
  8. Oratorio (Handel) 9. deliverer
Messina Rock... 6. Scylla
messy... 5. dirty 6. untidy 7. jumbled
  8. slovenly 10. disordered
mestive... 8. mournful
mesto... 3. sad 7. pensive
met... 3. sat 7. equaled, measure
  11. measurement (see also *meet*)
metabolism... 9. anabolism
  10. catabolism 12. assimilation
  13. dissimilation, metamorphosis
  14. transformation
metacarpus... 4. bone
metad... 3. rat
metagnomy... 10. divination
metagnostic... 10. unknowable
metal... 3. tin 4. gold, iron, lead, zinc
  5. steel 6. cobalt, copper, erbium,
  nickel, radium, silver, sodium
  7. cadmium, calcium, element,
  gallium, iridium, lithium, mercury,
  terbium 8. cast iron 9. potassium
  11. quicksilver
metal... 6. mettle, spirit 8. material
  9. substance
metal (pert to)...
  bar.. 3. gad 5. ingot
  cake.. 4. slag
  casting.. 3. pig
  cement.. 6. solder
  clippings.. 7. scissil
  coarse.. 5. matte
  coat.. 6. patina
  color.. 9. pearl blue
  content.. 3. ory
  crude.. 5. matte
  deposit.. 4. lode
  disc.. 5. paten
  dross.. 4. slag
  electric.. 6. magnet
  filings.. 5. lemel
  forging term.. 5. sprue
  goldlike.. 6. oroide
  impurity.. 7. regulus
  layer.. 4. seam, vein 5. stope
  lightest.. 7. lithium
  lump.. 3. pig 4. slug 6. nugget
  patch.. 6. solder
  plate.. 4. foil, shim
  rare.. 6. erbium 7. iridium, terbium,
  yttrium 8. platinum
  refuse.. 4. slag 5. dross 6. scoria
  rock.. 3. ore

science of.. 10. metallurgy
tag.. 5. aglet (aiglet)
test.. 5. assay
tool.. 5. swage 7. stemmer
ware.. 4. tole 6. Revere
worker.. 6. welder 7. riveter
   9. goldsmith 11. silversmith
metamerism... 12. segmentation (Zool)
metamorphosis... 6. change
   9. oxidation 10. hydrolysis
   12. degeneration, ossification
   14. transformation
metaphor... 5. trope 6. simile
   10. comparison 11. tralalition
metaphysics... 5. being 6. nature
   8. ontology, theology 9. cosmology
   10. psychology
mete... 4. give, goal 5. award
   7. measure 8. boundary 9. apportion
   10. distribute
meteor... 5. bolis 6. Bielid, bolide,
   Leonid, Lyraid 7. Arietid, Perseid
   8. fireball 9. Andromede
meteorite (pert to)...
   iron.. 10. siderolite
   shower.. 6. Leonid 9. Andromede
   (Andromedid)
   stony.. 8. aerolite
meteor mark... 6. crater
meteorology... 9. astronomy
   10. atmosphere 11. climatology
meter, metre... 5. gauge 6. rhythm
   7. cadence, measure 8. measurer
meter (pert to)...
   cubic.. 5. stere
   measure.. 5. litre
   millionth.. 6. micron
   prosody.. 4. mora
   square.. 7. centare
   ton.. 5. tonne
   unit term.. 3. are 6. decare
   9. decameter, decastere
   weight.. 4. gram
methane... 8. paraffin
metheglin... 4. mead 8. beverage
mether... 3. cup
method... 3. way 4. mode, plan, rule
   5. means, order, usage 6. course,
   manner, system 7. fashion, process
   9. procedure 11. arrangement
   14. classification
methodic, methodical... 6. formal
   7. orderly, regular 10. systematic
Methuselah (pert to)...
   Bib.. 7. aged man 9. Patriarch
   father.. 5. Enoch
metic... 5. alien 7. settler
   9. immigrant
meticulous... 4. nice, prim 5. fussy
   7. careful, fearful, precise 8. exacting
   9. selective 10. fastidious, scrupulous
   14. discriminating
métier... 4. line 7. calling 8. business
   10. occupation, profession
metis, metisse... 7. mulatto
   8. octoroon 9. half-breed
Metis... 8. asteroid 9. Zeus's wife
metrical... 8. measured, poetical,
   rhythmic
metrical composition... 4. poem
   5. poesy 6. poetry

metrical foot... 4. iamb 6. iambus
   7. anapest, spondee, trochee
   8. choriamb
metrical stress... 4. scan 5. arsis,
   ictus 6. thesis
metronome (Maelzel's)... 5. timer
metropolis... 4. city, seat, town
   6. center 8. district 9. metropole
metropolitan... 5. chief, urban
   6. bishop, center 7. leading
   9. principal
mettle... 5. ardor, honor, nerve, pluck,
   spunk 6. spirit 7. courage
   9. fortitude 11. temperament
meuse, muse... 3. gap 4. hole
   7. opening 8. loophole
Meuse River... 4. Maas
mew... 3. cob, den 4. cage, cast,
   coop, gull, molt, shed 5. miaow,
   miaul 6. change 7. seagull, stables
   8. spicknel 11. concealment,
   confinement
mewl... 3. cry, mew 6. squall
   7. whimper
Mexican (pert to)... see also *Mexico*
   agave.. 5. datil 6. zapupe
   8. henequen
   almond.. 7. Malabar
   American.. 6. gringo
   ancient.. 4. Maya 5. Aztec, Nahua
   6. Mixtec, Toltec 7. Zapotec
   antelope.. 9. pronghorn
   asphalt.. 9. chapapote
   bean.. 6. frijol 7. frijole
   bedbug.. 8. conenose
   beverage (alcoholic).. 6. mescal,
   pulque 7. tepache
   bird.. 6. jacana, towhee 7. jacamar,
   tinamou 8. zopilote
   blanket.. 6. serape
   brigand.. 7. ladrone
   bull.. 4. toro
   cactus.. 6. chaute, mescal
   cape.. 6. serape
   cat.. 6. margay
   cherry tree.. 7. capulin
   chief.. 4. jefe 12. jefe politico
   cloak.. 5. manta
   cockroach.. 9. cucaracha
   common land (law).. 6. ejidos
   coral drops (lily).. 7. Bessera
   cottonwood.. 5. alamo
   dance (solo).. 8. guaracha
   dish.. 5. atole, chili (chile), tacos
   6. tamale 8. frijoles, tortilla
   9. enchilada 13. chili con carne
   dog.. 9. Chihuahua
   dollar.. 4. peso 5. adobe
   dove.. 4. Inca
   drug.. 7. damiana
   elm.. 6. mezcal 8. Ulmaceae
   estate, farm.. 8. hacienda
   fever.. 10. tabardillo
   fish (food).. 6. salema 7. totuava
   game (card).. 4. frog
   grass.. 3. mat 5. otate 6. petate
   8. henequen
   herdsman.. 8. ranchero
   hog.. 7. peccary
   hut, house.. 5. jacal
   insect.. 8. turicata
   labor system.. 7. peonage

landmark.. **5.** senal
masonry.. **5.** adobe
moon god (Aztec).. **6.** Meztli
mullet.. **4.** bobo
musical instrument.. **6.** clarin (anc)
   7. maracas
Noah.. **6.** Coxcox
onyx.. **6.** tecali
orange.. **7.** Choisya
peasant.. **4.** peon
persimmon.. **7.** chapote
phlox.. **6.** cobaea
plant, shrub.. **4.** pita **5.** agave,
   amole, datil, istle, sisal, sotol, yucca
   6. maguey **8.** ocotillo
   10. candlewood, Dasylirion
rose.. **9.** portulaca
saloon.. **7.** cantina
sandal.. **8.** huaracho (huarache)
sauce.. **7.** Tabasco
scarf.. **6.** tapalo
shawl.. **6.** serape
stirrup.. **7.** estribo
stirrup hood.. **8.** tapadera (tapadero)
sugar.. **7.** panocha
tea.. **6.** basote **7.** apasote
thong.. **5.** romal
throwing stick.. **6.** atlatl
tree.. **3.** ule **5.** alamo, ocote
   6. colima, poplar **7.** capulin
   10. cottonwood
war god.. **7.** Mexitli
yucca.. **5.** izote (isote)
Mexican people...
   composer.. **6.** Chavez
   conqueror.. **6.** Cortez
   Dictator.. **4.** Diaz
   historian.. **6.** Orozco
   painter.. **6.** Rivera
Mexico...
   battleground.. **6.** Puebla
   capital.. **10.** Mexico City
   city.. **6.** Merida, Puebla **7.** Durango,
   Tampico **8.** Mazatlan, Monterey, Vera
   Cruz **11.** Guadalajara
   conqueror.. **6.** Cortes (Cortez)
   hero.. **6.** Juarez **11.** Poncho Villa
   lake.. **7.** Chapala
   mountain.. **12.** Popocatepetl
   peninsula.. **4.** Baja **7.** Yucatan
   people.. **5.** Mayas **6.** Aztecs
   7. Toltecs **10.** Cuitlateco
   river.. **9.** Rio Grande
   volcano.. **6.** Colima **7.** Jorullo, Orizaba
   12. Ixtaccihuatl, Popocatepetl
mezzanine... **8.** entresol, low story
miaow, miaou... **3.** mew
mias... **9.** orangutan
miasma... **4.** fume **6.** poison
   7. malaria, malodor **9.** contagion
mib... **7.** a marble
mica... **4.** talc **5.** glist **7.** biotite
   8. chlorite, silicate **9.** damourite,
   hydromica, isinglass, muscovite
   10. lepidolite
Micah... **4.** Book (Old Test) **7.** prophet
mice... **3.** Mus **5.** voles **7.** rodents
miche... **5.** skulk, sneak **6.** lie hid
   7. conceal
micher... **5.** sneak, thief **6.** truant
Michigan...
   capital.. **7.** Lansing

city.. **5.** Flint **7.** Detroit, Lansing
   8. Ann Arbor **9.** Marquette
explorer.. **7.** Jolliet, Nicolet
   9. Marquette **13.** Sault Ste Marie
river.. **4.** Cass **5.** Huron
State admission.. **11.** Twenty–sixth
State motto.. **6.** Tuebor **11.** I Will
   Defend
State nickname.. **9.** Wolverine
mickey finn... **5.** drink **8.** narcotic
Micky... **8.** Irishman
mico... **6.** monkey **8.** marmoset
micraner... **3.** ant (small)
micro (comb form)... **4.** moth **5.** petty,
   small
microbe... **4.** germ **5.** virus
   8. organism **9.** bacterium
   13. microorganism
microcosm... **4.** body (humerous)
   5. world (small) **8.** universe
microscopic (pert to)...
   algae.. **6.** amoeba, diatom
   anatomy.. **9.** histology
   size.. **5.** small **6.** minute **9.** very
   small **13.** infinitesimal
microspores... **6.** pollen
Midas (Gr)... **13.** King of Phrygia
midday... **4.** noon **7.** noonday
   8. meridian, noontide
midday nap... **6.** siesta
middle... **5.** mesne, midst **6.** center,
   centry, median, medium, mesial
   7. central **8.** interior **11.** intervening
   13. intermediator
middle (pert to)...
   Age.. **8.** Medieval
   class.. **9.** bourgeois **11.** proletarian
   comb form.. **3.** mes **4.** medi, meso
   finger.. **6.** medius **10.** third digit
   ground.. **4.** mean **7.** average
   9. mid–course
   man.. **5.** agent **6.** broker, medium
   8. mediator **9.** go–between
   11. intercessor **12.** intermediary
middling... **4.** fair **6.** medium, middle
   7. average, between, midland
   8. mediocre, moderate, ordinary
   10. middle–aged
midge... **3.** fly **4.** gnat **6.** midget,
   punkie **7.** minutia
Midi... **8.** The South (France)
Midian king... **3.** Evi **4.** Reba
Midian priest... **6.** Jethro
midriff... **9.** diaphragm
midshipman... **5.** cadet **6.** reefer
   8. toadfish
Midsummer Night's Dream (play)...
   4. Puck, Snug **6.** Bottom, Oberon
   7. Titania
midwife... **4.** baba, dhai **6.** cummer
   (kimmer) **11.** accoucheuse
mien... **3.** air, eye **4.** look **5.** guise
   6. aspect, manner, ostent
   7. bearing, posture **8.** behavior,
   carriage, demeanor **10.** appearance,
   deportment
miff... **3.** vix **4.** tiff **5.** anger **6.** offend
   7. dudgeon, quarrel **9.** displease,
   sulkiness **10.** sullenness
mig... **4.** duck **7.** a marble
might... **3.** arm **5.** force, power
   7. ability **8.** efficacy, strength

9. greatness
mighty... 4. huge, vast, very
6. potent, strong 7. eminent, violent
8. enormous, forcible, powerful,
puissant 9. extremely 10. omnipotent
11. efficacious 13. authoritative
migniard... 6. dainty, minion
7. mincing 8. delicate, mistress
mignon... 5. small 6. dainty, petite
7. blue–red 8. delicate, graceful
mignonette (pert to)...
color.. 5. green 6. reseda
emblem of.. 6. Saxony
herb.. 6. reseda
tree.. 5. henna
vine.. 7. Madeira, tarweed
migraine... 6. megrim 8. headache
10. hemicrania
migrate... 4. move, trek 8. resettle,
transfer 12. transmigrate
migration... 4. trek 5. exode
6. exodus 7. passage 8. shifting
(Chem) 10. relocation
migratory... 6. moving, roving
7. nomadic 9. peregrine, wandering
migratory (pert to)...
ant.. 6. driver
cell.. 9. leucocyte
thrush.. 5. robin
mihrab... 4. slab 5. niche 7. chamber
(mosque)
Mikado... 5. dairi, opera, title
9. red–yellow, sovereign
Mikado character... 4. Ko–Ko
6. Yum–Yum 7. Pooh–Bah
Mikania... 7. dogbane, thistle
11. Willugbaeya (Willugheia)
12. Ancylocladus
mike... 4. loaf 6. loiter
10. microphone
mil... 5. mille 8. thousand
milady... 5. woman 6. madame
10. noblewoman 11. gentlewoman
Milan (pert to)...
hat.. 5. straw
opera house.. 5. Scala
point.. 10. bobbin lace 12. point de
Milan
mild... 4. calm, kind, meek, soft, warm
5. bland 6. benign, gentle
7. clement, insipid, lenient
8. benedict, gracious, lenitive,
moderate, soothing, tranquil
9. assuasive, indulgent, temperate
10. mollifying 11. considerate
mildew... 4. mold, must, rust, smut
6. blight, fungus 8. honeydew
mild expression... 9. euphemism
mild offense... 6. delict
mile (term)... 3. sea 7. statute
8. nautical 9. Admiralty
12. geographical
Miledh... 8. ancestor (fabled)
Milesian... 4. Celt 8. Irishman
10. Miledh's son
milestone... 5. stele 7. waymark
8. landmark, milepost
milfoil... 4. herb 6. yarrow
milieu... 7. ecology 8. ambience
11. environment 12. surroundings
militant... 7. hawkish, warlike
8. battling, fighting 9. combating,

combative 11. contentious
military... 7. martial 8. soldiers
military (pert to)...
advance.. 8. anabasis
aide.. 7. attaché
base.. 4. camp 5. depot, field
7. billets 8. barracks, firebase,
quarters 10. encampment
call.. 6. tattoo 8. reveille
cap.. 4. kepi 5. busby, shako
cap, hat cover.. 8. havelock
cloak.. 5. sagum (anc)
commission.. 6. brevet
defense.. 4. fort 6. abatis
depot.. 4. base
division.. 4. unit 5. corps, squad
7. company, platoon 8. regiment
engine.. 6. onager 7. robinet
expedition to Holy Land.. 7. Crusade
force.. 4. army 5. ranks, troop
6. legion 7. reserve 8. soldiery
guard.. 6. patrol
horsemen.. 7. cavalry, hussars
infraction.. 4. AWOL
inspection.. 5. drill 6. parade, review
instrument.. 5. bugle 7. althorn
landing point.. 9. beachhead
maneuver.. 6. tactic
messenger.. 7. estafet
night attack.. 8. camisade
obstruction.. 6. abatis
officer.. 5. major 7. captain, colonel,
general 8. corporal, sergeant
9. brigadier, subaltern 10. lieutenant
operations.. 8. campaign, strategy
order.. 7. command
organization.. 5. cadre
pit.. 10. trou–de–loup
police.. 2. MP 9. gendarmes
12. constabulary
punishment.. 4. brig 9. strappado
quarters.. 4. camp 7. billets
8. barracks 10. cantonment
salute (artillery).. 5. salvo
science.. 3. war 7. war game
8. warcraft 9. logistics
service stripes.. 9. hashmarks
signal.. 7. chamade (anc)
staff.. 5. cadre
storehouse.. 5. étape 7. arsenal
supplies.. 8. materiel, ordnance
survey.. 11. reconnoiter
testament, will.. 11. nuncupative
tool (hook–shaped).. 4. croc (anc)
truck (cannon).. 6. camion
vehicle.. 4. jeep, tank 6. camion
7. caisson
militate... 5. fight 6. debate, rebuff
7. contend 8. conflict
milk... 3. lac 5. cream, drain, fluid
6. elicit, suckle 7. despoil, draw out,
exploit, extract 8. beverage
milk (pert to)...
beverage.. 4. whig 10. buttermilk
coagulator.. 4. ruen 6. rennet
curd.. 5. zeiga 6. casein
curdled.. 6. yogurt 7. clabber
fermented.. 5. kefir 6. kumiss
(koumiss) 7. matzoon
fish.. 3. awa 6. Chanos, sabalo
food (fasting).. 10. lacticinia
glass.. 7. opaline 8. cryolite

mouse . . 6. spurge
pail . . 5. bowie, eshin
pert to . . 6. lactic 7. lactary, lacteal
product . . 6. cheese, yogurt
sap . . 5. latex
sop . . 5. sissy 11. mollycoddle
sour . . 4. curd, whey, whig 6. blinky
store . . 5. dairy 9. lactarium
strainer . . 6. milsey (milsie)
sugar . . 7. lactose
watery part . . 4. whey
with (milk) . . 6. au lait
milkweed . . . 6. spurge 7. dogbane
    10. sow thistle 14. Asclepiadaceae
milkwood . . . 8. Moraceae 9. paperbark
milky . . . 4. mild, tame, weak 5. timid,
    white 6. gentle, liquid 7. lacteal
    8. emulsion, emulsive, lactesce (to
    become), timorous 10. effeminate
Milky Way . . . 6. Galaxy 9. Via Lactea
    14. galactic circle
Milky Way black spaces . . .
    9. Coalsacks
mill . . . 3. box 4. beat, coin (to)
    5. crush, dress, fight, grind, knurl,
    quern, shape 6. finish, powder,
    thrash 7. factory, machine, serrate
    8. arrastra, snuffbox, vanquish,
    workshop 9. comminute, pulverize,
    transform 10. move around
    12. housebreaker
mill (pert to) . . .
beetle . . 9. cockroach
bill . . 3. adz
clapper . . 10. chatterbox
course . . 4. lade 8. millrace, tailrace
end . . 7. remnant
run of . . 7. average 8. millrace,
    ordinary
millefleurs . . . 7. perfume
millenarian . . . 8. chiliast
millennium . . . 6. period, utopia
    9. millenary 13. thousand years
millepede . . . 6. insect 8. myriapod
millepore . . . 5. coral 9. madrepore
miller . . . 3. ray 4. moth 5. boxer
    7. harrier 8. pugilist 10. flycatcher
miller's thumb . . . 4. bird, fish
    7. warbler 8. titmouse (long–tailed)
    9. goldcrest
millesimal . . . 10. thousandth
millet . . . 4. moha 5. bajra, grass,
    hirse, milly 8. cenchrus
    9. broomcorn 10. hirse grass
    14. non–Moslem group
millimeter . . . 6. micron 14. thousandth
    part
millions, one thousand . . . 7. billion
millions of millions . . . 9. trillions
Mills grenade . . . 4. bomb
milo . . . 5. durra 12. grain sorghum
Milvus . . . 4. kite
Milwaukee . . . 21. German Athens of
    America
mime . . . 3. ape 4. aper, copy 5. actor,
    clown, mimic 6. jester, mummer
    7. buffoon, imitate
mimesis . . . 7. mimicry 9. imitation
mimic . . . 3. ape 4. aper, copy, mime,
    mimo, mock 5. actor 6. mummer,
    parrot 7. buffoon, copying, imitate,
    mimetic 8. imitator 9. imitative

    11. counterfeit
mimicry . . . 5. apery, apism 7. mimesis,
    mockery 8. parrotry
mimic thrush . . . 11. mockingbird
Mimidae, Miminae . . . 7. catbird
    8. thrasher 11. mockingbird
Mimir . . . 5. giant
mimsey . . . 4. prim 7. prudish
min . . . 5. ruler 6. memory, prince,
    remind 8. remember
    11. remembrance
Min (Egypt) . . . 3. god (procreation)
    5. deity
Minar . . . 4. myna 5. Kutab (Delhi),
    tower
minaret . . . 4. lamp 5. tower
    10. lighthouse
minaway . . . 6. minuet
mince . . . 3. cut 4. chop, dice, hash
    5. slash 8. diminish, prim step
    9. subdivide 10. short steps
minced meat . . . 7. rissole
minced oath . . . 4. drat, egad
minchen . . . 3. nun
minchery . . . 7. nunnery
minchiate . . . 5. tarot
mind . . . 4. care, heed, mens, obey,
    reck, tend, will 6. desire, memory,
    psyche 7. opinion 9. intellect,
    intention 11. remembrance
    12. intelligence
mind (pert to) . . .
development . . 13. psychogenesis
jubilant . . 7. elation
peace of . . 8. ataraxia, calmness
    16. imperturbability
pert to . . 6. mental 7. phrenic
picture . . 4. idea 5. image
split . . 13. schizophrenic
Mindanao . . .
language . . 3. Ata
site . . 11. Philippines
town . . 4. Dapa 5. Davao
    9. Zamboanga
tribe . . 3. Ata 4. Moro 5. Lutao
    6. Bagobo, Illano
volcano . . 3. Apo 9. Malindany
mindful . . . 8. disposed 9. observant,
    regardful 11. remembering
mine . . . 2. my 3. bal, dig, mio, pit,
    sap 4. meum 5. stope 6. cavity,
    quarry 7. gallery, passage
    10. excavation 12. entrenchment
mine (pert to) . . .
basket, tub . . 4. corf
ceiling . . 5. astel
coal . . 3. rob
deviation (lode) . . 4. hade
device (sweeper) . . 3. gad 8. paravane
entrance, passage . . 4. adit 5. stulm
excavation . . 5. stope
floor . . 4. sill
guardian (Myth) . . 5. gnome
holes . . 7. gophers
prop . . 5. sprag, stull
reservoir . . 4. sump 8. standage
shack . . 3. doe
shaft . . 4. sump 6. upcast
signalman . . 5. cager 7. cageman
step . . 7. stemple (stempel)
surface . . 6. placer
thrower . . 6. minnie 11. minenwerfer

tunnel.. **5.** stulm
vein.. **4.** lode
waste.. **3.** gob **4.** goaf
worker.. **5.** cager, miner **8.** onsetter
miner (pert to)...
disease.. **8.** phthisis
instrument.. **4.** dial
lamp.. **4.** davy
pick.. **3.** gad **7.** mandrel
sieve.. **6.** dillue
worm.. **8.** hookworm
mineral... **3.** ore, tin **4.** alum, iron
 5. pitch **6.** barite, egeran, gangue,
 iolite, pinite, quartz **7.** apatite,
 asphalt, ataxite, bullion, epidote,
 felsite, felspar **8.** danalite, edentite,
 misenite **9.** uraninite
mineral (ore)...
black.. **3.** jet **6.** cerine, yenite (Elba)
 7. niobite **8.** graphite **10.** minguetite
blue–green.. **5.** beryl
brittle.. **7.** euclase
brown.. **6.** cerine, egeran, rutile
 9. elaterite
calcium, plus.. **7.** calcite **8.** calespar,
 diopside
crosslike.. **10.** staurolite
dark.. **7.** minette
fibrous.. **8.** asbestos (abeston)
flaky.. **4.** mica
gray white.. **5.** trona
green.. **7.** alalite, erinite **9.** malachite
gunpowder.. **5.** niter **7.** thorite
hard.. **4.** ruby **6.** spinel (spinelle)
 7. adamant
jelly.. **8.** vaseline
jewelry.. **8.** diopside
lustrous.. **4.** spar **7.** blendes
magnetic.. **9.** lodestone (loadstone)
nonmetallic.. **5.** boron **6.** iodine
plaster of Paris.. **6.** gypsum
rare, brittle.. **7.** euclase, thorite
red.. **4.** ruby **6.** garnet
soft.. **4.** talc
waxlike.. **9.** ozocerite **11.** hatchettine
white, colorless.. **6.** barite, gypsum
yellow.. **5.** topaz **6.** pyrite **7.** epidote
mineral (pert to)...
cavity.. **3.** vug (vugg, vugh, voog)
dark spot.. **5.** macle
deposit.. **4.** lode **6.** placer
greasy.. **7.** atopite
oil.. **5.** colza
pitch.. **7.** asphalt
pocket.. **4.** nest
salt.. **4.** alum
spring.. **3.** spa **4.** well
tallow, wax.. **9.** ozocerite
 11. hatchettine
tar.. **6.** maltha
water.. **6.** lithia **7.** Seltzer **8.** alkaline
Minerva (pert to)...
feast.. **11.** Quinquatrus
flower, plant.. **6.** azalea
goddess of.. **5.** civic **6.** health
 11. handicrafts
shield.. **5.** aegis (egis)
temple site.. **8.** Aventine (Rome)
ming... **6.** remind **7.** mention, recount
 8. remember
Ming (Chin)... **7.** dynasty
mingle... **3.** mix **4.** fuse, meld

 5. admix, blend, merge, unite
 7. combine, concoct **8.** coalesce,
 intermix **9.** associate **10.** amalgamate
 11. consolidate
mingle–mangle... **6.** jumble, medley
 7. mixture **9.** potpourri
 10. hodgepodge, miscellany
minhag (Jew)... **6.** custom, manner
 7. liturgy
miniate... **5.** paint **8.** decorate,
 luminate **9.** rubricate
minikin... **4.** type **5.** baize **6.** dainty
 7. elegant, mincing **8.** affected,
 delicate **10.** diminutive
minim... **3.** jot **4.** drop **5.** Order
 (RCCh) **6.** minute **8.** smallest
 11. small amount
minimize... **6.** reduce **7.** detract
 8. belittle **9.** disparage
 10. depreciate **13.** underestimate
minimum... **3.** jot **5.** least **6.** lowest
minion, minionette... **4.** idol, neat
 5. lover **6.** dainty, pretty **7.** darling,
 elegant **8.** delicate, favorite, ladylove,
 mistress, paramour
minister... **4.** tend **5.** angel, cater,
 serve **6.** afford, attend, curate,
 parson, pastor, priest, supply
 7. furnish **8.** diplomat, executor,
 preacher **9.** clergyman, officiate
ministerial... **7.** serving **9.** executive
 12. instrumental **14.** administrative,
 ecclesiastical
minister's home... **5.** manse
 9. parsonage
Minnesota...
capital.. **6.** St Paul
city.. **6.** Duluth **11.** Minneapolis
hero.. **14.** Father Hennepin
lake.. **3.** Red **10.** Minnewaska
land of.. **16.** Ten Thousand Lakes
mountain.. **6.** Cayuna, Mesabe
 9. Vermilion
river.. **3.** Red **10.** St Lawrence
 11. Mississippi
State admission.. **12.** Thirty–second
State motto.. **13.** L'Etoile du Nord
 14. Star of the North
State nickname.. **6.** Gopher **9.** North
 Star
Minoan... **6.** Cretan **7.** culture (Prehist)
 8. language
minor... **3.** key **4.** less, mode **5.** friar
 (Franciscan), petit, petty, scale, youth
 6. course, infant, league, lesser
 7. smaller **8.** inferior, interval,
 underage **9.** youngling
minority... **3.** few **6.** nonage
 7. smaller **8.** underage
 10. immaturity **11.** inferiority
Minos (pert to)...
daughter.. **7.** Ariadne
father.. **4.** Zeus
king of.. **5.** Crete
mother.. **6.** Europa
Minotaur (Gr)... **7.** monster (half man,
 half bull)
minster... **6.** church **9.** monastery
minstrel... **3.** lay **4.** bard, poet, show
 6. end man, troupe **7.** gleeman,
 goliard **8.** jongleur, musician
 9. troubador **11.** entertainer

minstrel show (pert to)...
end man.. 5. bones
middleman.. 12. interlocutor
part.. 4. olio
mint... 3. aim 4. blow, coin, sage
  5. basil, feint, money 6. hyssop,
  intend, invent, mentha, ramona
  7. attempt, purpose, venture
  8. endeavor 9. fabricate
mint (pert to)...
charge, levy.. 8. brassage
  11. seigniorage
drink.. 5. julep
family.. 5. basil 6. catnip 8. calamint
  9. Lamiaceae
genus.. 6. Ramona 7. Melissa
geranium.. 8. costmary
hog.. 8. shilling
sauce.. 5. money
minuet... 5. dance 7. scherzo
minus... 4. lack, less 6. absent, bereft,
  defect 7. short of, without
  8. subtract 10. deficiency
minuscule... 4. type 5. petty, small
  6. letter (lower case) 10. diminutive
minute... 3. jot, wee 4. mite, note,
  tiny 5. draft, petty, small 6. atomic,
  little, moment, period, record, slight,
  tittle 7. instant 8. atomical, trifling
  10. memorandum 11. unimportant
  12. sixty seconds 14. circumstantial
minute (pert to)...
animal.. 10. animalcule
details.. 11. particulars
difference.. 5. shade
glass.. 9. hourglass
Jack.. 10. timeserver
opening.. 4. pore 5. stoma
organism.. 5. monad, spore
  8. zoospore
part.. 6. tittle
particle.. 4. atom, iota, mote
record.. 8. protocol
minutely... 9. continual, unceasing
  11. every minute
minutes... 4. acta 6. record
minutia... 6. detail, minute 11. minor
  detail, petty matter
minx... 4. brat, doll, miss 6. pet dog
  7. colleen 8. pert girl 9. saucy girl,
  saucy jade 13. mischief–maker
minyan... 6. quorum 7. pottery
Miohippus... 5. horse
miqra... 9. Bible text (Heb)
mir (Pers)... 4. head 5. chief, title
  9. president
miracle... 4. feat, play 5. anomy
  6. marvel, wonder 10. occurrence,
  phenomenon 17. supernatural event
miracle scene... 4. Cana
miracle wheat... 7. poulard
miracle worker... 8. magician
  11. thermaturge
miraculous... 9. marvelous, wonderful
  12. supernatural 13. wonder–working
mirador... 5. brown, oriel 6. loggia,
  turret 7. balcony 9. bay window
  10. watchtower
mirage... 5. serab 7. chimera, reflect
  8. illusion 10. phenomenon
mire... 3. bog, mud, wet 4. glar, moil,
  ooze, slud 5. addle, dirty, marsh,

slush, stall 7. sludder
mirror... 5. glass 7. crystal, paragon,
  pattern, reflect 8. exemplar,
  speculum 9. reflector 11. image
  worker 12. looking glass
mirror iron... 12. spiegeleisen
mirth... 3. fun, joy 4. glee 6. gaiety
  (gayety), levity, spleen 7. delight,
  jollity 8. gladness, hilarity
  9. happiness, merriment, rejoicing
  10. joyousness 12. cheerfulness
mirthful... 3. gay 5. happy, jolly
miry... 4. oozy 5. boggy, muddy, slimy
  6. filthy, lutose
mis (comb form)... 5. amiss, wrong
misadventure... 6. mishap 8. accident,
  calamity, casualty, disaster
  9. mischance 10. misfortune
misandry (opp of misogyny)...
  12. dislike of man (by woman)
misanthrope... 5. cynic, Timon (Shak)
  8. man hater 9. pessimist
  12. mankind hater
misapply... 5. misdo 6. misuse
  12. misinterpret
misapprehend... 7. mistake
  8. misapply 11. misconceive
  13. misunderstand
misbegotten... 8. deformed
  12. illegitimate
miscalculate... 3. err 8. misjudge
  9. misreckon, overshoot
miscall... 5. abuse 6. revile
  7. misname 9. read amiss
  12. mispronounce
miscarriage... 5. lapse 6. mishap
  7. failure, misdeed, mistake
  8. abortion 9. mischance
  11. misdemeanor
  13. mismanagement 14. premature
birth
miscegenation... 8. marriage
  13. interbreeding, intermarriage
miscellaneous... 5. mixed 6. medley,
  varied 7. blended, diverse, mingled
  8. combined 12. conglomerate
  13. heterogeneous 14. indiscriminate
miscellany... 6. medley 7. mixture
  8. excerpts 9. anthology
  10. collection 11. odds and ends
mischance... 6. mishap 8. calamity,
  disaster 10. misfortune
  12. misadventure
mischief... 3. ill 4. evil, harm
  5. wrack 6. damage 7. trouble
mischief (pert to)...
god.. 4. Loki
goddess.. 3. Ate 4. Eris
maker.. 8. agitator 12. troublemaker
mischievous... 4. arch 6. elfish
  (elvish), impish 7. harmful, mocking,
  naughty, parlous, roguish, waggish
  8. sportive
misconduct... 7. offense
  10. wrongdoing 11. delinquency,
  misbehavior, misdemeanor
  13. mismanagement
miscreant... 6. rascal, wretch
  7. heretic, villain 8. polisson
  9. reprobate 10. unbeliever, villainous
  11. fallen angel, misbeliever
  12. unscrupulous

miscue ... 3. err 4. miss, slip 5. error
6. bungle 7. mistake
misdeed ... 5. crime, wrong 7. offense
8. wrongful 11. misdemeanor
misdemeanor ... 3. sin 4. tort
5. crime 7. misdeed, offense
10. illegality, wrongdoing
11. misbehavior
mise ... 4. levy 5. grant 6. layout,
treaty 8. expenses (law), immunity
9. privilege
miser ... 5. hunks, Nabal (Bib)
6. nipper, wretch 7. boarder, niggard
miserable ... 3. sad 6. abject, paltry
7. forlorn, pitiful, unhappy
12. disconsolate, disreputable
misericord, misericorde ... 4. hall, pity
5. mercy 6. dagger 9. refectory
10. compassion 12. dispensation
miserly ... 4. mean 5. close, tight
6. stingy 7. chintzy (sl) 8. churlish,
covetous 9. niggardly, penurious
10. avaricious 12. parsimonious
misery ... 3. woe 5. grief 7. anguish,
avarice, poverty, sadness 8. calamity,
distress 9. heartache, privation
10. affliction, misfortune
11. despondency, Pandora's box,
unhappiness 12. covetousness,
wretchedness 13. niggardliness
misfeasance ... 5. wrong 8. trespass
10. wrongdoing
misfortune ... 3. ill 4. evil, harm
6. mishap 7. bad luck, reverse,
setback 8. calamity, disaster
9. adversity, holocaust, mischance
11. catastrophe 12. misadventure
misgiving ... 5. doubt, qualm
7. anxiety 10. foreboding
12. apprehension
mishap ... 4. slip 8. accident, casualty
10. misfortune 11. contretemps,
miscarriage 12. misadventure
Mishnah, Mishna ... 4. Moed 5. tenet
6. Nashim 7. Nezikim 8. doctrine,
Halakoth, Kodashim, Tohoroth
9. tradition
misinterpret ... 3. err 4. warp
7. distort, misread 8. misjudge
misjudge ... 3. err 11. misconstrue
12. miscalculate
misky ... 5. foggy, misty
mislay ... 4. lose 8. displace, misplace
misle ... 4. mist, rain 6. mizzle
7. drizzle
mislead ... 4. fool 5. blear 6. delude,
seduce 7. deceive 8. misguide
9. deception, misbehave, misinform
misleading ... 5. false 7. crooked
8. illusory 9. deceptive
10. fallacious, fraudulent
12. misinforming 14. misinformation
mislippen ... 6. delude 7. neglect,
suspect 10. disappoint
mismanage ... 5. blunk, misdo
6. bungle, misuse 9. mishandle
misogynist ... 8. celibate 10. woman
hater
misplace ... 4. lose 6. mislay, misset
8. displace 9. dislocate, mislocate
11. anachronism

misplay ... 3. err 5. error 6. renege
7. mismove 9. wrong play
misprise, misprize ... 5. scorn
6. slight 7. despise, disdain, mistake
8. contempt 9. underrate
10. misprision, undervalue
13. underestimate
misprision ... 5. scorn 7. mistake
8. contempt, misprize
10. misconduct 11. misdemeanor
12. depreciation
16. misunderstanding
mispronunciation ... 8. cacology
10. bad diction
misrepresent ... 5. belie 7. deceive,
distort, falsify 8. disserve
miss ... 2. Ms. 3. err 4. chit, fail, girl,
lack, lose, omit, skip 5. evade, lapse,
title 7. failure, mistake 8. mistress
9. fall short 10. prostitute
12. mademoiselle
missal ... 4. book (Eccl) 8. breviary
missel ... 9. mistletoe
misshapen ... 4. ugly 8. deformed
9. distorted, monstrous, unshapely
missile ... 2. MX 4. ICBM, Nike, Thor
5. Atlas, Snark, Titan 6. rocket
7. grenade, matador 8. Redstone
9. Minuteman
missing ... 3. out 4. gone, lost
6. absent 7. lacking, wanting
8. vanished 11. nonexistent
mission ... 3. job 4. body, duty, task
5. Alamo 6. charge, church, errand
7. calling, embassy 8. legation,
outreach 10. assignment, commission,
delegation, deputation, missionary
missionary ... 7. apostle 8. emissary,
preacher 10. evangelist
Missionary Ridge ... 11. Chattanooga
(Tenn)
Mississippi ...
capital .. 7. Jackson
city .. 6. Biloxi 7. Natchez 8. Gulfport
9. Vicksburg 13. Pass Christian
explorer, colonizer .. 6. De Soto
9. Iberville
festival .. 9. Mardi gras (Biloxi)
king crop .. 6. cotton
kite (bird) .. 9. everglade
mountain .. 6. Woodal
river .. 5. Yazoo 11. Mississippi
State admission .. 9. Twentieth
State bird .. 11. mockingbird
State flower .. 8. magnolia
State motto .. 14. Virtute et Armis (By
Valor and Arms)
State nickname .. 5. Bayou
Mississippian (Geol) ...
15. Eocarboniferous (system)
Mississippi River head ... 10. Lake
Itasca (Minn)
Mississippi River nickname ...
10. Great River 14. Father of Waters
missive ... 4. note 6. billet, letter
7. message, missile 8. document
Missouri ...
capital .. 13. Jefferson City
city .. 7. Sedalia, St Louis 8. Hannibal,
St Joseph
famed native .. 6. Carver (G W),

Truman (Pres) 9. Mark Twain
  10. Jesse James
gourd .. 11. calabazilla
mountains .. 6. Ozarks
river .. 8. Big Muddy, Missouri
  11. Mississippi
skylark .. 13. Sprague's pipit
State admission .. 12. Twenty–fourth
State bird .. 8. bluebird
State flower .. 8. hawthorn
State nickname .. 6. Show Me
sucker (fish) .. 10. black horse
misspelling ... 10. cacography
misspend ... 4. lose 5. waste
  8. squander 10. spend amiss
misstep ... 4. slip, trip 7. faux pas
mist ... 3. dim, fog 4. blur, film, gray,
  haze, rain, smur 5. bedim, brume,
  cloud 7. droplet 9. obscurity
  11. uncertainty
mistake ... 3. err 4. bull, goof, slip
  5. boner, botch, error, fault, folly
  7. blooper, blunder, erratum, violate
  8. miscount, solecism
  11. anachronism 12. inadvertence
  13. misconception
  15. misapprehension
mistaken ... 5. wrong 9. erroneous
  12. misconceived 13. misunderstood
  14. judging wrongly
mistletoe ... 6. emblem (Okla), missel,
  Viscum 9. Loranthus
mistonusk ... 6. badger
mistress ... 4. bibi (beebee) 5. title,
  woman 6. matron 7. control, teacher
  8. Dulcinia, ladylove 9. concubine,
  governess, patroness 10. proprietor,
  sweetheart
Mistress of ...
Adriatic .. 6. Venice
Charles II .. 4. Nell
Seas .. 12. Great Britain
World .. 4. Rome (anc)
misty ... 3. dim 4. hazy, roky 5. foggy,
  rouky, vague 6. blurry, cloudy, hoarse
  7. obscure, shadowy 10. indistinct
  13. unenlightened, unilluminated
misuse ... 5. abuse 6. revile 7. pervert
  8. maltreat, misapply, wrong use
  9. misemploy 12. misrepresent
misuse of words in speech ...
  11. heterophemy, malapropism
mite ... 3. bit, jot 4. atom, coin, mote
  5. child, speck 6. acarus, insect
  7. bdellid, chigger, smidgen (smidge)
  8. acaridan, particle
miter, mitre ... 4. belt 5. frank, joint,
  tiara 6. fillet, girdle, gusset, tavern
  7. petalon (Eccl) 8. dovetail,
  headband, insignia 9. headdress
mithridate ... 8. antidote 9. electuary
  12. alexipharmic
mitigate ... 4. ease, tone 5. abate,
  allay, mease, relax, remit, slake
  6. lessen, reduce, soften, temper
  7. appease, mollify, qualify, relieve
  8. diminish, lenitive, moderate, palliate
  9. alleviate, extenuate, meliorate
mitigation ... 6. relief 9. abatement
  10. diminution, moderation
  11. extenuation 13. mollification
mix ... 3. pug (clay) 4. ease, join,

meng, stir 5. addle, blend, cross,
  knead, unite 6. jumble, mingle,
  muddle 7. combine, fluster
  8. coalesce 9. associate
  10. complicate
mixable ... 8. miscible
mixed (pert to) ...
breed .. 7. mongrel
type .. 2. pi
with water .. 6. slaked
with yeast .. 6. barmed, frothy
mixer ... 5. whisk 6. beater 7. mingler
  9. eggbeater, (food) processor
mixture ... 4. hash, mash, olio
  5. blend, chaos, mixed 6. batter,
  medley, miscue 7. amalgam, mélange
  8. compound, solution
  9. admixture, potpourri
  10. hodgepodge 11. combination,
  preparation
mixture (pert to) ...
beverage .. 5. clary 10. shandygaff
cement .. 5. putty
medicinal .. 5. hepar 6. potion
  12. prescription
metallic .. 6. speiss
sand and clay .. 4. loam
mix–up ... 5. melee, snafu 6. muddle,
  tangle 8. conflict 9. confusion
Mizar ... 4. Zeta (Great Dipper)
mizmaze ... 9. confusion
  12. bewilderment
mizzenmast ... 9. aftermast, third mast
mizzle ... 4. mist, rain 5. misle
  6. decamp 9. slink away
mizzy ... 3. bog 8. quagmire
Mnenosyne (pert to) ...
ancestor .. 5. Titan
goddess .. 6. memory
mother of .. 8. The Muses
moa ... 6. ratite (flightless) 8. Dinornis
moab ... 3. hat (anc)
Moabite (pert to) ...
dwelling (Bib) .. 7. Dead Sea
language .. 7. Semitic
mountain .. 4. Nebo
people .. 4. Emim
stone (Bib) .. 11. black basalt
moan ... 3. cry 4. suum, wail
  5. groan, sough 6. bemoan, bewail,
  grieve, lament, suffer 9. complaint
  11. lamentation
moat ... 4. foss (fosse) 5. ditch
  6. trench 13. fortification
mob ... 3. set 4. gang, herd, mass
  5. crowd, drove, flock, group, Mafia,
  taunt 6. clique, rabble, throng
  7. company 8. canaille, populace
mobile ... 7. movable 8. not fixed
  9. versatile 10. changeable
Mobile Bay hero ... 8. Farragut (Adm)
mobile home ... 3. van 6. camper
  7. caravan (Brit), trailer
mob member ... 6. rioter 7. Mafioso
  8. criminal, mobocrat 9. roisterer
mobocracy ... 7. mob rule
Moby Dick (pert to) ...
author .. 8. Melville (Herman)
character .. 4. Ahab 5. Peleg
theme .. 7. whaling 10. White Whale
moccasin ... 3. pac 4. shoe 5. snake
  6. Flower (Minn State), orchid

8. larrigan 10. argus brown
11. cottonmouth
moch... 4. moth
mocha... 4. bark, town (Arab)
6. coffee, dollar 7. leather 9. moss
agate
mock... 3. ape 4. defy, gibe, jape,
jibe, sham 5. feign, fleer, flout,
mimic, scoff, sneer, taunt 6. delude,
deride 7. imitate, mockery, pretend
8. ridicule 10. disappoint
11. counterfeit
mock (pert to)...
brawn.. 10. headcheese
cucumber.. 11. balsam apple
duck.. 4. meat 8. pork chop
hero.. 5. comic
jewelry.. 5. logie, paste 9. imitation
lead, ore.. 10. sphalerite
moon.. 10. paraselene
nightingale.. 7. warbler 8. blackcap
olive.. 9. axbreaker 12. cherry laurel
orange.. 7. syringa (seringa)
plane.. 8. sycamore
sun.. 9. parhelion
turtle.. 9. calf's head
mockage... 7. mimicry, mockery
9. imitation
mocker... 5. mimic 7. scoffer
8. deceiver 11. mockingbird
mockernut... 7. hickory
mockery... 5. farce 6. satire
7. mimicry, sarcasm 8. derision
9. imitation 11. counterfeit
mockingbird... 5. Mimus
mode... 3. fad, way 4. form 5. flair,
style, vogue 6. manner, method
7. fashion, variety
mode (pert to)...
expression.. 10. vernacular
government.. 6. regime, system
logic.. 7. Ferison (3rd figure)
procedure.. 5. order 6. system
speech.. 8. parlance 11. phraseology
standing.. 4. pose 6. stance
7. posture 8. position
model... 3. act 4. form, idea, mold,
norm, plan, plat, pose 5. ideal,
image, shape 7. example, manikin,
measure, paragon, pattern, templet
8. ensample, paradigm, standard,
template 9. archetype, mannequin,
precedent 11. meritorious
12. reproduction
model (of)...
a word.. 8. paradigm
a work.. 9. archetype
excellence.. 7. paragon 8. exemplar
solar system.. 6. orrery
11. planetarium
moderate... 4. bate, ease, slow, some
5. abate, lower, slake 6. frugal,
lessen, soften, temper 7. control,
lenient, mediate, modesto
8. mediocre, modulate, slow down
9. temperate 10. reasonable
11. inexpensive 12. conservative
14. inconsiderable
moderation... 7. control 9. abatement,
restraint 10. diminution, governance,
limitation, mitigation 11. restriction
13. temperateness

moderator... 5. judge 6. umpire
7. arbiter 8. mediator 10. arbitrator,
controller
modern... 3. neo (pref), new 4. late
6. latter 7. present 8. neoteric
modernize... 6. update 10. streamline
Modern School of Art... 4. Dada
7. Dadaism (1920)
modern Syriac script... 5. serta
8. peshitta
modest... 3. coy, mim, shy 6. chaste,
demure, humble, seemly 8. reserved,
retiring, virtuous 9. diffident
11. well–behaved 13. unpretentious
14. inconsiderable
modesty... 7. decency, reserve,
shyness 8. chastity, humility, pudicity
10. diffidence, humbleness
11. self–control
modicum... 3. bit 4. drop 5. minim,
share 6. little 11. small amount
12. small portion
modification... 4. tone 6. change,
umlaut 9. variation 10. adaptation,
alteration, limitation 13. qualification
15. differentiation
modify... 4. vary 5. alter, limit
6. change, master, temper
7. assuage, qualify 8. attemper,
mitigate, moderate, quantify
9. influence 13. differentiate
modish... 4. chic, trim 5. smart 7. in
vogue, stylish 8. vogueish (voguish)
11. fashionable
modiste... 8. milliner 9. couturier
10. couturière, dressmaker
modulated... 5. toned 6. merged
7. adapted, attuned, changed,
intoned 8. softened, tempered
9. inflected, regulated
modulation... 4. tone 6. change
8. shifting 9. tempering
10. alteration, inflection, moderation
moggan... 8. stocking 10. knit sleeve
moggy... 3. cat, cow 4. calf 7. pet
name 8. slattern 9. scarecrow
mogo... 7. hatchet
mogul... 4. lord 5. nabob 6. tycoon
7. magnate 8. autocrat 9. dignitary
10. locomotive, panjandrum
14. great personage
Mogul... 6. Empire, Mongol 7. dynasty
9. Mongolian
Mohammed (pert to)...
birthplace.. 5. Mecca
daughter.. 6. Fatima
flight to Mecca.. 6. hegira
horse.. 5. Fadda (white mule)
7. Alborak
names.. 7. Mahomet, Mahound
son–in–law.. 3. Ali
Mohammedan (pert to)...
angel of death.. 6. Azrael
ascetic.. 4. Sufi 5. fakir (fakeer)
8. Marabout
caliph.. 3. Ali 4. Omar 6. Othman
7. Abu Bekr
chief.. 3. aga (agha) 4. dato (datto)
5. sayid 6. Caliph
crier (for prayer).. 7. muezzin
crusader's enemy (Moslem)..
7. Saracen

deity.. **5.** Allah **9.** Termagant
demon.. **5.** afrit, eblis, jinni (jinnee)
  7. Shaitan (Sheitan)
Malay (Javanese).. **6.** Sassak
Moslem.. **5.** hanif **9.** Mussulman
noble.. **4.** amir (ameer), emir
nymph.. **5.** houri
officer.. **3.** aga **5.** diwan **6.** vizier
  (vizir)
princess, queen.. **5.** begum
saint.. **3.** pir **6.** santon
scholars, body of.. **5.** ulema
sect.. **6.** Wahabi (Wahabee, Wahhabi)
student (Theol).. **5.** softa
successor.. **6.** Caliph (Calif)
teacher.. **5.** mufti **6.** mullah (mollah)
unbeliever.. **6.** Kaffir (Kafir)
Mohammedanism (pert to)...
Bible, book.. **5.** Koran **7.** Alcoran
bier, tomb.. **5.** tabut
cap.. **3.** taj
caravansary.. **6.** imaret
crusade.. **5.** jihad (jehad)
custom, tradition.. **6.** sunnah
divorce.. **5.** talak **7.** mubarat
dome, over tomb.. **6.** turbeh
Easter.. **3.** Eed
Fast (annual).. **7.** Ramadan
festival.. **6.** Bairam
garment.. **4.** izar **6.** jubbah
house (men's part).. **8.** selamlik
instrument.. **5.** rebab
marriage custom.. **5.** iddat
marriage settlement.. **4.** mahr
Messiah, priest.. **4.** Imam (Imaum)
  5. Mahdi
monastery.. **5.** ribat
platform, porch.. **7.** mastaba
prayer.. **4.** azan (adan) **5.** namaz
property (law).. **6.** mushaa
religion.. **6.** Moslem **8.** Islamism
saber.. **8.** yataghan (yatagan)
salutation.. **6.** salaam (salam)
shrine (Mecca).. **5.** Kaaba (Caaba,
  Kaabeh) **10.** Black Stone
veil.. **7.** yashmak (yashmac)
war (Relig).. **5.** jihad (jehad)
moho... **4.** rail **9.** gallinule **10.** honey
  eater
mohr... **7.** gazelle
moider... **4.** toil **5.** crowd, worry
  6. wander **7.** smother **8.** bewilder,
  encumber
moiety... **4.** half, part (small)
  7. portion
moil... **4.** spot, tire, toil **5.** labor, taint
  6. seethe **7.** torment, trouble,
  turmoil **8.** drudgery **9.** confusion
  10. defilement
moiré... **7.** clouded, watered
moist... **3.** wet **4.** damp, dank, dewy,
  uvid **5.** humid, rainy **7.** tearful
moisten... **3.** wet **4.** hose, moil
  5. bedew, spray **6.** anoint, dampen,
  sparge **8.** humidify, sprinkle
moisture... **3.** dew, fog **5.** vapor,
  water **6.** liquid **8.** dampness,
  dankness, dewdrops, humidity
moisture (pert to)...
body.. **6.** humors **9.** exudation
condensed.. **4.** drip, drop
excess, swelling.. **5.** edema

expose to.. **3.** ret
remove.. **4.** wipe **5.** wring
mojo... **4.** Moxo **5.** charm (voodoo)
  6. amulet **7.** majagua
moke... **4.** dolt, mesh **5.** horse
  6. donkey **7.** network **8.** minstrel
  9. performer
moki... **4.** raft
moko... **9.** tattooing
moky... **5.** foggy, misty
molar... **5.** tooth **6.** molary
  7. chopper, grinder **8.** grinding
molarimeter... **11.** thermometer
molasses... **5.** sirup **7.** treacle
  8. theriaca
mold, mould... **3.** die **4.** cast, form,
  must **5.** humus, knead, nowel,
  plasm, sprue **6.** blight, growth
  (fungus), matrix, mildew **7.** moulage
  9. sculpture **12.** reproduction
Moldavia, Rumania...
balm.. **4.** mint
capital.. **5.** Balta **8.** Tiraspol
govt.. **9.** Socialist
molding... **3.** ess **4.** bead, beak,
  cyma, ogee, reed, tori **5.** conge,
  gulla, ovolo, splay, torus **6.** fascia,
  fillet, listel, reglet, scotia **7.** cavetto,
  cornice, reeding, shaping **8.** astragal,
  bezantee **12.** reproduction
molding (pert to)...
convex.. **5.** torus
decoration.. **4.** dado
egg and dart.. **9.** arrowhead
series.. **7.** surbase
suit of.. **8.** ledgment (ledgement)
moldy, mouldy... **5.** fusty, mucid,
  musty, stale **8.** mildewed
mole (rat)... **4.** gray **5.** fault, nevus
  (naevus), shrew, snake, Talpa, taupe
  6. rodent **7.** blemish, Nesokia
  9. birthmark **12.** imperfection
molecule... **3.** ion **4.** atom, unit
  6. steric **8.** particle
molest... **4.** harm **5.** annoy, tease
  6. bother, harass, pester **7.** disturb
  8. mistreat **9.** incommode
  13. interfere with
Molière (pert to)...
author of.. **5.** drama, plays
  6. comedy, L'Avare, satire **8.** Tartuffe
character (story).. **5.** Damis **6.** Eraste,
  Scapin **7.** Dorante
mollify... **4.** calm **5.** allay, relax, sleek
  6. pacify, relent, soften, temper
  7. appease, lighten, qualify, relieve
  9. alleviate **10.** conciliate
mollitious... **8.** sensuous **9.** luxurious,
  softening
mollusk... **3.** asi **4.** clam, pipi, slug,
  spat **5.** chama, snail, squid, whelk
  6. cockle, limpet, mussel, oyster
  7. abalone, bivalve, octopus, scallop,
  veliger **8.** univalve **10.** cuttlefish
mollusk... **5.** Anoma, Chama, Murex
  6. Chiton **7.** Astarte, Etheria
  8. Buccinum, Mollusca, Nautilus
mollusk (pert to)...
bait.. **6.** limpet
eight-armed.. **7.** octopus
freshwater.. **7.** etheria
marine.. **7.** abalone, scallop

8. nautilus
shell.. 4. test 5. testa 6. cockle,
  cowrie (cowry)
shell, without.. 4. slug
shell concretion.. 5. pearl
teeth.. 6. radula
ten–armed.. 5. squid
young.. 4. spat
mollycoddle... 6. coddle, pamper
  8. weakling 12. spoiled child
  13. effeminate boy
Moloch (pert to)...
Bible.. 5. deity
doctrine.. 4. evil
zoology.. 6. agamid, lizard
Molotov cocktail... 4. bomb
molt, moult... 3. mew 4. cast, mute,
  shed 7. ecdysis 8. exuviate
molten rock... 2. aa
Moluccas, Spice Islands...
capital.. 7. Amboina
island.. 5. Banda
product.. 5. spice
site.. 9. Indonesia
moly... 4. herb (fabled) 6. garlic
momble... 6. jumble, tangle
mome (anc)... 4. fool 7. buffoon
  9. blockhead
moment... 4. time 5. avail, flash,
  nonce, point, trice, value 6. crisis,
  minute, second, weight 7. impetus,
  instant 9. influence, twinkling
  10. importance 11. consequence
  13. consideration, signification
momentary... 9. ephemeral, transient
  10. transitory 13. instantaneous
momentous... 7. weighty 8. eventful
  9. important 11. influential
  13. authoritative
momo... 3. owl
Momus (Gr)... 3. god (of ridicule)
  6. critic 11. faultfinder
mon... 5. badge (imperial) 7. kikumon
  13. chrysanthemum
monachal... 8. celibate, monastic
  9. claustral
monad... 3. one 4. atom, unit
  5. deity, monas 8. particle
  10. individual 12. Supreme Being
monadnock... 4. hill 8. mountain (NH)
Mona Lisa (pert to)...
famed for.. 5. smile (subtle)
named also.. 10. La Gioconda
painter.. 7. da Vinci
site (of picture).. 6. Louvre (The)
monandry... 10. one husband (at a
  time)
monarch... 4. czar, king, shah
  5. chief, queen, ruler 6. dynast,
  kaiser, sultan 7. czarina, emperor
  9. potentate, sovereign 13. royal
  highness
monarch... 9. butterfly
  13. constellation
monastery... 5. abbey 6. friary, priory
  7. convent, hospice, nunnery
  8. cloister
monastery (pert to)...
head.. 3. dom 5. abbot
Pavia.. 10. Carthusian
room... 4. cell
Tibet.. 8. lamasery

monastic... 4. monk 5. friar
  7. monkish 8. celibate 9. claustral
monde... 5. globe, world (fashion)
  6. circle (fashion) 7. coterie, société,
  society 9. beau monde
monetary... 7. coinage 8. currency
  9. financial, pecuniary
money... 3. wad 4. cash, coin, grig,
  mina, pelf 5. frank, funds, lucre,
  maneh, uhllo (ullo) 6. mazuma,
  talent, wampum, wealth 8. currency
  10. spondulics (spondulix) 11. legal
  tender
money (pert to)...
ancient.. 3. aes
bank (Eur).. 5. banco
box, chest.. 4. arca, safe, till, tray
  5. chest 6. drawer 7. brazier
  8. register
changer.. 6. banker, broker, shroff
  (saraf), usurer 7. cambist
coinage.. 4. mint
English slang.. 7. ooftish (oof)
found.. 5. trove
gamblers'.. 6. barato
gift.. 4. alms 7. bequest
  9. endowment
lender.. 6. banker, usurer 7. Shylock
  10. pawnbroker
luck.. 6. barato 7. handsel
maker.. 6. coiner, minter
  13. counterfeiter
manual.. 7. cambist
matters.. 6. fiscal 9. economics
of account.. 3. ora
paper.. 4. bill, kale 7. lettuce
pledge.. 5. arles
premium.. 4. agio
roll (coins).. 7. rouleau
shell.. 5. uhllo (ullo) 6. cowrie (cowry)
slang.. 4. gilt, jack, lour 5. rhino
  6. boodle, wampum
spinner.. 5. usurer 10. speculator
to coin.. 4. mint
wildcat.. 9. yellow dog
worthless.. 4. pelf
moneyed... 4. rich 5. flush 7. opulent,
  wealthy 8. affluent, well–to–do
  10. prosperous, well–heeled
monger... 6. dealer, mercer, trader,
  vendor 7. peddler 8. merchant
  9. tradesman
mongler... 9. sandpiper
Mongol... see also *Mongolian*
  5. Asian, Tatar 9. yellow man
Mongolian (pert to)...
ass (wild).. 8. chigetai
capital.. 4. Urga
conjurer.. 6. shaman
conqueror.. 9. Tamerlane
desert.. 4. Gobi
dynasty.. 4. Yuan
monk, priest.. 4. lama
religion.. 9. Shamanism, Shintoism
  12. Confucianism
river.. 3. Pei 4. Onon
tribe.. 3. Lai 4. Lapp 5. Ordos
  7. Khalkas, Tsaktar 9. Ouryantai
mongoose... 4. urva 5. lemur
  9. ichneumon
mongrel... 3. cur 5. mixed 6. hybrid
  10. crossbreed 14. stilt sandpiper

mongrel fish... 5. skate (angelfish)
  8. tullibee (whitefish)
monial... 3. nun
moniker... 4. name 8. nickname
monition... 6. advice, notice
  7. summons, warning
  10. admonition, dissuasion, intimation
  11. forewarning
monitor... 4. ship (Civil War), uran
  5. varan 6. lizard, manual, mentor,
  nozzle 7. adviser, student, warning
  8. conenose (bug), director, recorder,
  reminder 9. informant
monk... 3. fra 4. bede, lama, saki
  5. fakir, friar, padre 6. ferret,
  monkey 7. ascetic, caloyer, dervish
  8. anchoret, capuchin, celibate,
  cenobite 9. anchorite, bullfinch,
  touchwood
monkey (pert to)...
  African.. 4. waag 5. potto 6. grivet,
  vernet
  American.. 4. saki 5. acari 7. ouakari
  8. marmoset 9. beelzebub
  bearded.. 8. entellus
  bonnet.. 4. zati 5. toque
  bread.. 6. baobab
  chimpanzee.. 6. nchega
  crying.. 4. kaha
  cups.. 9. nepenthes 12. pitcher plant
  family.. 10. Catarrhina
  flower.. 7. mimulus (herb)
  genus.. 5. Cebus 6. Ateles
  7. Colobus, Saimiri, Tarsius
  8. Alouatta
  handsome.. 4. mona
  house.. 5. apery
  howling.. 4. mono 5. araba 7. stentor
  8. alouatte
  large.. 5. sajou
  Madagascar.. 8. mangabey (mangaby)
  organ grinder.. 5. Cebus 8. capuchin
  Oriental.. 7. macaque
  puzzle.. 5. piñon
  small.. 8. marmoset
  South American.. 4. titi 6. grison
  9. beelzebub
  spider.. 7. sapajou
  squirrel.. 7. saimiri
  tailless.. 3. ape
  wrench.. 7. spanner
monk's hood... 4. cowl
monkshood... 4. atis 7. aconite
  9. dandelion
monoceros... 4. fish (one–horned)
  7. sawfish, Unicorn 9. swordfish
  13. Constellation
monochord... 7. concord, harmony
  9. sonometer 10. clavichord,
  instrument
monocle... 8. eyeglass
monocleid, monocleide... 4. desk (one
  key) 7. cabinet
monocracy... 9. autocracy
  13. undivided rule
Monodelphia... 7. mammals
  8. Eutheria
monody... 3. ode 4. poem (lament),
  song 5. dirge 6. melody
  9. homophony
monogamy... 11. one marriage
monogram... 6. cipher, sketch

  7. outline 8. initials 9. character
monolith... 5. stone 6. menhir, pillar,
  statue 8. monument
monologue... 6. speech 9. soliloquy
monomachy... 4. duel 6. combat
monopoly... 5. grant, right, trust
  6. corner 7. charter, control
  9. privilege, syndicate 10. possession
  (exclusive)
monotonous... 4. dead, drab, dull
  5. drone, thrum 6. dreary, samely
  7. humdrum, tedious 8. singsong
  9. wearisome 11. repetitious
monotony... 6. tedium 8. sameness
  9. wearisome 10. sameliness,
  uniformity 15. repetitiousness
monoxylon, monoxyle... 4. boat
  5. canoe
monseigneur... 5. title 6. My Lord
monster... 4. ogre 5. fiend, harpy,
  teras 6. dragon, ellops, geryon,
  gorgon, sphinx 8. behemoth,
  Cerberus 11. monstrosity
monster (pert to)...
  classic.. 8. minotaur
  comb form.. 6. terato
  eight–headed.. 6. Scylla
  fabled.. 5. harpy 6. kraken, sphinx
  7. centaur 9. bucentaur
  flame–breathing.. 7. chimera
  (chimaera)
  half man, half bull.. 8. minotaur
  headless.. 9. acephalus
  like.. 8. teratoid
  man–eating.. 4. ogre 5. lamia
  medical.. 5. teras
  three–bodied.. 6. Geryon (slain by
  Hercules)
  twin.. 10. xiphopagus
  two–bodied.. 7. disomus
  two–headed.. 10. dicephalus,
  opodidymus
  winged.. 5. harpy
monstrous... 4. huge, ugly, vast
  5. enorm (anc) 6. absurd, wicked
  7. strange, titanic 8. deformed,
  gigantic, infamous 9. fantastic,
  monstrous, unnatural 10. prodigious,
  stupendous 12. overpowering,
  overwhelming 13. extraordinary
Montana
  capital.. 6. Helena
  city.. 5. Butte 8. Anaconda, Billings
  10. Great Falls
  Historic site.. 14. Custer Cemetery
  lake.. 8. Flathead
  mountain.. 7. Rockies 17. Continental
  Divide
  park.. 7. Glacier 11. Yellowstone
  peak.. 7. Granite
  reservation (Ind).. 4. Cree, Crow
  5. Sioux 8. Cheyenne, Chippewa
  9. Blackfeet
  State admission.. 10. Forty–first
  State motto.. 13. Gold and Silver
  State nickname.. 8. Treasure
montanto... 6. rising 10. broadsword
Monte Cristo, Count of (pert to)...
  author.. 5. Dumas (Alexandre)
  hero.. 6. Dantès
Montenegro... 10. Yugoslavia
montero... 3. cap (hunter's) 6. ranger

8. forester, huntsman, mountain
Montezuma (pert to)...
  Chief of.. 6. Aztecs
  cypress.. 9. ahuehuete
  hero of.. 6. Mexico
  prisoner of.. 6. Cortez
  ruins, site of.. 6. Pueblo
month (pert to)...
  astronomy.. 5. lunar, solar
  half.. 9. fortnight
  revolution.. 8. sidereal 9. synodical
  term.. 5. epact 6. ultimo 7. proximo
  twelfth part.. 8. calendar
monticule... 4. cone (volcano)
  5. mount 7. hillock 10. prominence
  (small)
montilla... 6. sherry
Montmorency... 6. cherry
monture... 5. frame, horse (saddle),
  mount
monument... 4. tomb 5. cairn, stele
  (stela), tower, vault 6. bilith, dolmen
  7. obelisk 8. cenotaph, cromlech,
  monolith 9. sepulcher 10. gravestone
  11. commemorate, remembrance
monumental... 4. high 5. great
  7. mammoth, massive, notable
  8. colossal 10. impressive, sculptural,
  stupendous
Monumental City... 9. Baltimore
moo... 3. low (of a cow) 6. lowing
mooch... 4. loaf 5. skulk, sneak, steal
  6. loiter, pilfer 7. vagrant
moocha... 6. girdle 9. loincloth
mood... 3. tid 4. tone, vein, whim
  5. freak, humor 6. nature 7. caprice
  11. disposition
moody... 3. sad 4. glum 5. sulky
  6. gloomy, sullen 7. pensive
  9. whimsical 10. capricious
mool... 4. bury, mold, soil 5. earth,
  grave 6. mingle 7. crumble
mools... 10. chilblains
moon... 4. idle, Luna 5. Diana
  6. Phoebe, wander 7. Cynthia
  8. crescent 9. satellite 13. celestial
  body
moon (pert to)...
  age (first of year).. 5. epact
  area.. 4. mare
  Astrol.. 6. Cancer (mansion), planet
  autumn.. 7. harvest
  beam.. 3. ray 9. pearl blue
  bird.. 11. goldencrest
  blindness.. 10. nyctalopia
  calf.. 4. dolt 7. monster 8. born fool,
    imbecile
  comb form.. 5. selen
  fern.. 8. moonwort
  festival.. 8. neomenia
  fish.. 4. opah 6. minnow 7. sunfish
    9. spadefish
  flower.. 10. oxeye daisy
  gazing.. 16. absent–mindedness
  geographer.. 13. selenographer
  god.. 3. Sin 6. Nannar
  heraldry.. 6. argent
  inhabitant.. 8. Selenite
  instrument.. 11. selenoscope
  lighter.. 9. serenader 10. moonshiner
    11. night worker
  lily.. 10. moonflower
  mad.. 7. lunatic
  mock.. 10. paraselene
  month.. 5. lunar
  new.. 6. phasis
  phase.. 7. gibbous, horning
  picture of.. 11. selenograph
  point.. 4. cusp, horn 5. apsis
    6. apogee 7. perigee
  position.. 6. octant
  raker.. 10. stupid lout
    12. woolgatherer
  stone.. 3. gem 8. feldspar
    10. hecatolite
  struck.. 7. lunatic 8. obsessed
  Uranus's.. 5. Ariel
  valley.. 4. rill (rille) 5. cleft
moon goddess...
  Greek.. 6. Hecate, Phoebe 7. Artemis,
    Cynthia
  Italian.. 5. Diana
  Phoenician.. 6. Tanith (Tanit)
    7. Astarte
  Roman.. 3. Dea 5. Virgo 9. Caelestis
moonish... 7. flighty 10. capricious
moonshine... 5. empty 6. liquor,
  poteen, whisky (whiskey) 7. bootleg
  8. egg sauce, nonsense
  10. balsamweed
moony... 5. round 6. dreamy
  9. moonlight 10. abstracted
  14. crescent–shaped
moor... 3. bog, fen 4. hill, root
  5. heath, marsh, swale 6. anchor,
  fasten, secure 9. fix firmly
Moor... 6. Berber, Moslem
  7. Moorman, Saracen 8. goldfish
  (black), Moroccan
moor (pert to)...
  berry.. 9. cranberry
  bird.. 6. grouse
  blackbird.. 5. ouzel
  buzzard.. 5. harpy 7. harrier
  cock.. 9. blackcock
  dance.. 7. morisco
  grass.. 5. heath 6. sundew
  hen.. 4. coot 9. gallinule
  monkey.. 7. macaque
  stone.. 7. granite
Moorish... 6. Moslem 8. Moresque
Moorish (pert to)...
  garment.. 5. jupon
  horse.. 4. barb (Barbary)
  judge.. 4. cadi
  kettledrum.. 5. tabor 6. atabal
  Order.. 7. Alcazar 8. Alhambra
    9. horseshoe, Saracenic
  palace.. 7. Alcazar
moose... 3. elk 4. alce 5. eland
  7. society (Loyal Order)
moose bird... 9. Canada jay
moot... 4. pose 5. argue, plead, speak
  6. debate 7. discuss, propose
mop... 4. swab, wipe 5. scrub
  6. merkin 7. drink up, grimace
  9. blindfold, implement
mope... 4. sulk 5. dumps, idler
  6. grieve
moppet... 3. tot 4. baby, doll, tike
  7. darling, toddler 9. youngster
mora... 4. tree (Trinidad) 5. delay,
  stool 7. default 8. syllable
  9. footstool 11. Spartan army

12. postponement

moral ... 4. good, pure 5. maxim
6. lesson 7. epimyth, ethical,
upright, virtual 8. likeness, virtuous
9. righteous

moral (pert to) ...
excellence .. 6. virtue
fault .. 4. vice
law .. 9. Decalogue
obligation .. 4. duty
poem .. 3. dit
principle .. 7. precept
story .. 5. fable 7. parable
8. apologue

morale ... 4. hope, zeal 6. morals,
spirit 8. morality 10. confidence

moralist ... 4. prig 7. teacher
9. moralizer 10. sermonizer

morality ... 6. amoral, ethics, virtue
13. righteousness

morals ... 8. morality 10. ethography

morass ... 3. bog, fen 4. moor
5. marsh, swamp 6. slough
8. quagmire 9. everglade

moratorium ... 5. delay 10. suspension

Moravia, capital ... 5. Brünn (Brno)

Moravian ... 9. Christian 10. Herrnhuter
13. Unitas Fratrum 19. Church of
the Brethren

moray ... 3. eel 6. hamlet 7. Muraena
8. food fish 10. Muraenidae

morbid ... 4. sick 6. gloomy 7. ghastly,
unsound 8. diseased 9. unhealthy
11. unwholesome

morbid (pert to) ...
appetite .. 10. adephagous
complex .. 11. inferiority
condition .. 8. ochlesis
desire for music .. 9. melomania
displacement .. 7. ectopia

morbus ... 7. disease, illness

morceau ... 3. bit (Mus) 6. morsel

mordant ... 4. acid, keen 6. biting
7. burning, caustic, pungent
8. scathing 9. corrosive, sarcastic
11. acrimonious

more ... 3. yea 4. also, mair, plus,
some 5. again, extra 6. plural
7. greater 10. additional
13. approximately

more (pert to) ...
cunning .. 5. slyer 6. tricky
difficult .. 6. harder
distant .. 8. ulterior
mature .. 5. older, riper
miserly .. 6. closer, meaner, nearer
not any .. 4. dead, past 8. vanished
11. nonexistent
or less .. 4. some 8. somewhat
13. approximately
over .. 3. and 4. also, else
7. besides, further, thereto
precious .. 6. dearer
relative .. 11. comparative
severe .. 7. sterner
so .. 3. yea
than .. 4. over 5. above 6. beyond
9. exceeding 10. in excess of
than enough .. 3. too
than one .. 4. many 6. plural
7. several
than this .. 3. yes

unusual .. 5. rarer
vapid .. 6. staler

morel ... 6. fungus 8. mushroom

morello ... 4. ruru 6. cherry
7. boobook 8. morepork, mulberry
(color)

morena ... 8. brunette

mores ... 7. customs, manners
9. etiquette 11. conventions

Moreton Bay ... 9. Australia

Morgan ... 5. horse 10. sea dweller

morganatic marriage ...
10. left–handed (royal)

morgay ... 7. dogfish

morglay ... 5. sword

morgue ... 8. mortuary 9. deadhouse,
stolidity 11. haughtiness, impassivity

Morgue (The) ... 17. Library of
Congress

moribund ... 4. sick 5. dying 9. near
death

moriform ... 14. mulberry–shaped

morindin dye ... 2. al

morion ... 6. helmet, quartz 8. cabasset

Mormon Church (pert to) ...
Band (Polit) .. 6. Danite (1837)
cricket .. 11. grasshopper
emblem .. 3. bee
Indian .. 8. Lamanite
instrument .. 4. Urim 7. Thummin
officer .. 5. Elder
official name .. 36. Church of Jesus
Christ of Latter Day Saints
patriarch .. 11. Joseph Smith
12. Brigham Young
prophet .. 6. Moroni
State .. 4. Utah
tea plant .. 7. Brigham
tree .. 11. black poplar

morning (pert to) ...
clouds .. 4. velo
coat .. 7. cutaway
concert .. 6. aubade
glory .. 3. nil 7. ipomoea
14. Convolvulaceae
goddess .. 3. Eos
performance .. 7. matinee
prayer .. 5. matin
reception .. 5. levee
star .. 4. Mars 5. Venus 6. Saturn
7. Daystar, Jupiter, Lucifer, Mercury
8. Phosphor
term .. 4. dawn 5. matin, wight
6. Aurora 7. sunrise 9. matutinal

moro ... 5. finch

moro (comb form) ... 6. stupid

Moro ... 6. Moslem

Morocco ...
capital .. 5. Rabat
city .. 7. Tangier 10. Casablanca
color .. 3. red
enclave .. 4. Ifni
famed site .. 5. Casba
hat .. 3. fez
island .. 7. Madeira
Jewish quarter .. 8. El Millah
language .. 6. Arabic
leather imitation .. 4. roan
military expedition .. 5. harka
millet .. 12. Johnson grass
people .. 4. Arab, Moor 6. Berber
plateau .. 6. mesata

ruler.. 4. king 5. malek 6. sultan
soldier.. 5. askar
morology... 5. folly 8. nonsense
moron... 4. dull 5. ament, idiot, zombi
  6. nitwit, stupid 8. imbecile, sluggish
  12. stupid person
morose... 4. blue, dour, glum, grum,
  sour 5. moody, surly 6. crusty,
  gloomy, sullen 7. crabbed, unhappy
  9. splenetic 10. embittered
Morpheus (Gr)... 10. god of Sleep
  11. god of Dreams
morphine... 6. heroin 8. hypnotic
  9. analgesic, calmative
morphology... 7. anatomy 8. cytology
  9. histology 10. embryology
  12. organography
morris... 4. game 5. chair, dance
morro... 4. hill 6. Castle (Havana)
  7. hillock 11. point of land
Mors (Rom)... 5. Death, deity
Morse... 4. code, lamp 8. alphabet
morsel... 3. ort 4. bite, chip 5. piece,
  scran (sl), scrap, snack 6. tidbit,
  titbit 7. morceau 8. delicacy,
  fragment 11. small amount
mort... 4. dead, lard 5. death, fatal
  6. deadly, grease, salmon
  9. abundance
mortacious... 4. very 9. extremely
mortal... 5. fatal, human 6. deadly,
  lethal 10. perishable
mortally... 5. amort 6. deadly 7. à la
  mort, deathly, fatally 9. extremely
  10. grievously
mortar... 3. rab 4. bowl 5. putty
  6. cannon 7. mortier 10. night light
  (Hist)
mortarboard... 3. cap (Acad)
mortgage... 4. bond, pawn 6. pledge
mortician... 8. embalmer
  10. undertaker 15. funeral director
mortification... 5. decay, shame
  7. chagrin 8. gangrene, vexation
  11. humiliation
mortify... 5. abase, abash, abuse,
  shame, spite 6. ashame, deaden,
  humble 7. chagrin 9. embarrass,
  humiliate
mortis causa... 15. by reason of
  death
mortise, mortice... 6. cavity, insert
  8. amortize 10. foundation
mortuary... 4. gift (burial) 6. morgue
  7. funeral 8. funereal 9. deadhouse,
  sepulcher 10. cinerarium
  12. corsepresent (offering, Hist)
mosaic... 5. virus 6. design
  7. ceramic, picture 10. decoration,
  variegated 11. tessellated
mosaic (pert to)...
  apply.. 7. incrust
  gold.. 6. ormolu
  law.. 5. Torah (Moses)
  piece.. 7. tessera
Moscow...
  capital of.. 6. Russia
  citadel.. 7. Kremlin
  river.. 6. Moskva
  shrine.. 9. Lenin Tomb, Red Square
  Third Internat.. 9. Comintern
Moselle... 4. Saar, wine 5. river,

Ruwer 9. Rhine wine
Moses (pert to)...
  Bible.. 7. prophet 8. lawgiver
  brother.. 5. Aaron
  emissary.. 5. Caleb
  father.. 5. Amram
  father–in–law.. 6. Jethro
  law.. 5. Torah (Tora) 10. Pentateuch
  mother.. 8. Jochebed
  mountain.. 4. Nebo
  sister.. 6. Miriam
  successor.. 6. Joshua
  wife.. 8. Zipporah
mosey... 6. depart, stroll 7. shuffle
Moslem... 5. Hanif, Islam, Salar
  7. Saracen 9. Mussulman
  10. Mohammedan
Moslem (pert to)...
  ablution.. 4. wudu (widu, wuzu)
  cap.. 3. fez, taj
  capturer of Jerusalem.. 4. Omar
  caste.. 5. mopla (moplah)
  chief.. 4. dato (datto), rais
  city (holy).. 5. Mecca
  college, school.. 8. madrasah
    (madrasa, madrasseh)
  dagger.. 7. khanjar
  deity.. 5. Allah, Eblis
  devil.. 5. Eblis
  devotee.. 6. santon 7. dervish
  Easter.. 3. Eed
  guide (spiritual).. 3. pir
  interpreter.. 5. ulema
  invocation.. 9. bismillah
  javelin.. 6. jereed
  judge.. 4. cadi
  lawyer.. 5. mufti
  market, booth.. 4. sook
  monastery.. 5. ribat 7. khankah
  mosque.. 6. masjid
  noble.. 4. amir (ameer), emir
  officer.. 5. dewan (diwan)
  pilgrimage to Mecca.. 4. hadj
  prayer.. 4. azan (adan)
  priest.. 4. imam (imaum)
  saint.. 3. pir 6. santon 8. Marabout
  sect.. 6. Senusi (Senousi, Senussite)
  shrine, Mecca.. 5. Kaaba (Caaba,
    Kaabeh)
  teacher.. 4. Alim 8. mujtahid
  title.. 3. Sid 5. Sayid (Said)
  tradition.. 7. Al Sirat (Bridge to
    Paradise)
  tribesman.. 4. Moro
  Turkish.. 5. Salar
  university.. 8. madrasah (madrasa)
  viceroy.. 7. Saracen
mosque... 4. Omar 5. Kaaba (Caaba)
  6. masjid 11. Great Mosque
mosque tower... 7. minaret
mosque warden... 5. nazir
mosquito (pert to)...
  bite preventive.. 10. culicifuge
  coast.. 8. Honduras 9. Nicaragua
  comb form.. 6. culici
  destroyer.. 8. culicide
  disease.. 7. malaria 11. yellow fever
  family.. 9. Culicidae
  fish.. 8. gambusia
  genus.. 5. Aedes, Culex 7. Diptera
    8. Mansonia 9. Anopheles, Culicidae
    10. Psorophora

hawk .. **9.** dragonfly, nighthawk
Indian drink .. **6.** mushla
larvae .. **8.** wigglers
plant .. **4.** mint **10.** pennyroyal
shaped .. **10.** culiciform
term .. **7.** culicid **11.** gallinipper
moss ... **3.** bog, rag **4.** agar **5.** Maium,
money, Musci, swamp **6.** lichen,
morass **7.** skeeter **8.** agar–agar
9. treebeard
moss (pert to) ...
back .. **4.** dodo, fogy (fogey) **9.** old
turtle **10.** fuddy–duddy, Southerner
(1861) **12.** conservative
berry .. **9.** cranberry
capsule .. **9.** operculum
color .. **5.** green
coral .. **8.** bryozoan
duck .. **7.** mallard **8.** moss–head
9. merganser
fish .. **8.** menhaden **10.** mossbunker
grown .. **10.** antiquated
kind .. **4.** peat **7.** Spanish
like .. **6.** mnioid
mossy ... **4.** dull **5.** boggy, downy
6. marshy, stupid **9.** crumbling
most ... **7.** highest, maximum
8. greatest, main part, majority
9. nearly all
most favorable ... **7.** optimum
Most High ... **3.** God **12.** Supreme
Being
most northerly land ... **5.** Thule
mot ... **5.** adage, maxim, motto
7. opinion **9.** witticism
mote ... **4.** atom, hill, iota **5.** match,
speck, squib **6.** barrow, height, trifle
7. tumulus **8.** eminence, particle
mote nut ... **5.** carap
motet ... **4.** hymn **6.** anthem, choral
moth ... **2.** io **5.** egger, tinea
6. lappet, miller **7.** noctuid, Tineina
8. forester (8–spotted), Tineidae
9. Tineoidea **11.** Lepidoptera
moth (pert to) ...
hawk .. **10.** goatsucker
kind .. **5.** gypsy **6.** carpet **9.** browntail
spot (Med) .. **8.** chloasma
spot (wing) .. **8.** fenestra
mother ... **2.** ma **3.** dam **4.** amma
5. adopt, mamma, mater **6.** abbess,
parent **7.** care for, creator
8. ancestor, begetter, genetrix,
producer **10.** procreator
mother (pert to) ...
church .. **9.** cathedral **16.** Christian
Science
goddess .. **6.** matris **7.** Shaktis
10. sapta–matri (7 mothers)
goddess of motherhood (Egypt) ..
4. Isis
godmother .. **4.** Rhea **6.** cummer
(kimmer) **9.** Brigantia
Goose character .. **5.** Simon, Sprat
6. Bo–peep
Govt .. **10.** matriarchy, metrocracy
house .. **7.** convent **9.** monastery
Hubbard .. **4.** gown **5.** dress
Maid .. **10.** Virgin Mary
Mother Carey's chickens .. **7.** petrels
(stormy)
Myth (Gr) .. **5.** Niobe

related .. **6.** enatic
spiritual .. **4.** amma
Tagalog .. **3.** Ina
motherly ... **8.** maternal
mother of ...
Castor .. **4.** Leda
gods .. **4.** Rhea **9.** Brigantia
Graces .. **5.** Aegle
Nature .. **6.** Cybele
Night .. **3.** Nox, Nyx
pearl .. **5.** nacre **7.** abalone
presidents .. **8.** Virginia
States .. **8.** Virginia
the month .. **4.** Moon
motif ... **5.** theme, topic **6.** edging
7. subject
motion ... **3.** bob **4.** lipe, move
5. impel, trend **6.** seesaw, travel,
tremor, unrest **7.** gesture, propose,
request, suggest **8.** kinetics, mobility,
movement, petition
motionless ... **5.** inert, rigid, still
6. static **8.** immobile, stagnant
10. stationary, stock–still
motion picture terms ... **4.** film, show
5. flick, klieg (light), movie, rerun
6. cinema **7.** cartoon, feature
9. filmstrip, videotape **11.** golden
oldie **12.** silver screen
motivate ... **4.** move **5.** force, impel
6. compel, incite, induce, propel
7. actuate, animate, promote, trigger
9. stimulate
motive ... **4.** sake, spur **5.** cause,
motif, topic **6.** reason **7.** pretext
8. stimulus **9.** incentive, influence,
intention **10.** incitement, inducement
11. instigation **13.** consideration
motley ... **5.** mixed **6.** fabric
7. diverse, mixture, mottled
9. checkered, diversity **10.** variegated
12. parti–colored **13.** heterogeneous
motor ... **5.** mover, rotor **6.** Diesel,
dynamo, engine **7.** turbine **8.** motor
car **9.** locomotor **10.** automobile
motor speed control ... **8.** governor,
rheocrat
mottled ... **3.** roe **4.** pied **5.** pinto
6. calico **7.** dappled, marbled,
piebald, spotted **13.** pepper–and–salt
mottled soap ... **7.** castile
motto ... **3.** mot **5.** adage, axiom,
gnome, maxim **6.** advice **7.** empresa
(impresa), precept **8.** aphorism
9. principle **11.** inscription
motto of ...
Boy Scouts .. **10.** Be Prepared
Coast Guard .. **11.** Always Ready
13. Semper paratus
Order of the Garter .. **20.** Honi soit qui
mal y pense
Queen Elizabeth .. **11.** Semper Eadem
13. Always the Same
mouche ... **5.** patch (black)
mouchoir ... **12.** handkerchief
mouflon, moufflon ... **5.** sheep
mould, mold ... **5.** knead **6.** matrix
moulrush ... **7.** pollack (food fish)
mound ... **3.** dam, dun, tee **4.** bank,
dene, doon, dune, heap, hill, terp,
tomb, tump **5.** knoll **6.** bounds
7. barrier, bulwark, rampart, tumulus

8. boundary 9. elevation
10. embankment 13. fortification
mound (pert to) . . .
 bird . . **8.** megapode
 City . . **7.** St Louis
 lily . . **5.** yucca
 memorial . . **5.** cairn
 of light . . **8.** Kohinoor (diamond)
 Polynesian . . **3.** ahu
 prehistoric . . **5.** matte
 Scottish . . **5.** toman
mount . . . **3.** fly, set (jewel) **4.** glue,
 hill, lift, pony (polo), rise **5.** arise,
 climb, horse, paste **6.** ascent
 7. elevate **8.** increase, mountain
 10. promontory
Mount (pert to) . . .
 Etna city . . **7.** Catania
 Everest peak . . **6.** Lhotse
 Parnassus fountain, spring . . **8.** Castalia
mountain . . .
 Africa . . **11.** Kilimanjaro
 Alaska . . **8.** McKinley
 Asia . . **7.** Everest
 Babylonia . . **6.** Ararat
 California . . **6.** Shasta **7.** Whitney
 Crete . . **3.** Ida
 Europe . . **4.** Ural **8.** Pyrenees
 fabled . . **4.** Meru
 Greek (Myth) . . **7.** Helicon
 Japan . . **8.** Fujiyama
 legendary . . **3.** Kaf, Qaf (Moslem)
 4. Meru
 Mexico . . **12.** Popocatepetl
 Montana . . **6.** Tetons
 Switzerland . . **4.** Alps **10.** Matterhorn
 Thessaly . . **4.** Ossa **6.** Pelion
 U S Chain . . **5.** Rocky **7.** Sawback,
 Sierras **9.** Blue Ridge
 11. Appalachian
 Yukon . . **5.** Logan
mountain (pert to) . . .
 ash . . **5.** rowan
 badger . . **6.** marmot
 balsam . . **3.** fit
 banana . . **3.** fei
 barometer . . **8.** orometer
 beaver . . **8.** sewellel
 blackbird . . **5.** ouzel
 cat . . **4.** lynx **6.** bobcat, cougar
 10. cacomistle
 comb form . . **3.** oro
 cowslip . . **8.** auricula
 crest, spur . . **5.** arête
 curassow (pheasant) . . **10.** oreophasis
 defile . . **3.** gap **4.** gate, ghat (ghaut),
 pass **5.** gorge
 depression . . **3.** col
 dew . . **6.** whisky
 eagle . . **6.** golden
 goat . . **4.** ibex
 highest . . **7.** Everest
 ice . . **4.** berg **7.** glacier
 ivy . . **6.** laurel
 lake . . **4.** tarn
 lion . . **4.** puma **6.** cougar
 lodge . . **4.** gite
 low . . **5.** butte
 nymph . . **5.** oread
 oak . . **8.** chestnut
 peak . . **3.** tor
 raspberry . . **10.** cloudberry

 rose . . **6.** laurel
 sheep . . **7.** bighorn **13.** Rocky
 Mountain
 shrub . . **10.** fetterbush
 sickness . . **7.** soroche
 State . . **7.** Montana
 sunset . . **9.** alpenglow
 Tatars . . **5.** Tauli
 witch . . **9.** quail dove
mountaineer . . . **7.** climber
 11. backsettler
mountains, science of . . . **7.** orology
 9. orography
mountant . . . **6.** raised, rising
 8. mounting **9.** ascendant
mountebank . . . **4.** gull **5.** cheat, quack
 7. buffoon, empiric **8.** impostor
 9. charlatan, pretender **11.** quack
 doctor
mounted men . . . **7.** knights
mounting . . . **6.** ascent **7.** rimbase,
 seating, setting **9.** adjusting,
 equipment **13.** embellishment
mourn . . . **3.** rue **4.** erme, long, sigh,
 wail, weep **6.** bemoan, bewail,
 grieve, lament, murmur, repine,
 sorrow **7.** deplore
mourner . . . **6.** keener, wailer **7.** griever
 8. lamenter
mournful . . . **3.** sad **6.** repine **7.** elegiac
 8. grievous **9.** elegiacal, plaintive,
 saddening, sorrowful, threnodic,
 woebegone
mournful poem . . . **5.** elegy
mourning . . . **3.** sad **4.** garb **5.** crape,
 weeds (dress) **6.** lament, sorrow
 7. drapery **9.** sorrowing **10.** black
 badge **11.** lamentation
mourning dress . . . **5.** weeds **6.** sables
mouse . . . **3.** erd, Mus **4.** buck, vole
 5. prowl, shrew **6.** jerboa, migale
 7. harvest, toy with
mouse (pert to) . . .
 bird . . **4.** coly **6.** shrike
 color . . **4.** gray
 deer . . **7.** plandok **10.** chevrotain
 ear . . **8.** hawkweed **9.** bloodwort,
 chickweed **11.** forget-me-not
 fish . . **9.** sargassum
 hare . . **4.** pika
 hound . . **6.** weasel
 kind . . **6.** pocket **7.** harvest, jumping
 leaping . . **6.** jerboa
 milk . . **6.** spurge
 mouselike . . **6.** murine
 web . . **6.** cobweb, phlegm
 8. gossamer
mousse . . . **7.** dessert **9.** moss green
 12. gelatine dish
moutan . . . **5.** peony
mouth . . . **2.** os **3.** mow, mun **4.** boca,
 dupe, lade, lick **5.** inlet, stoma
 6. cavity, rictus **7.** declaim, opening,
 orifice **8.** aperture, lorriker
 9. impudence
mouth (pert to) . . .
 away from . . **6.** aboral
 deformity . . **7.** harelip
 disease . . **6.** canker **10.** stomatitis
 furnace . . **5.** bocca
 glands . . **8.** salivary
 muscle . . **7.** caninus

organ.. **4**. harp **7**. Pandean
    8. jew's–harp **9**. crembalum,
    harmonica
part.. **3**. lip **5**. uvula **6**. palate
    7. pharynx
pert to.. **4**. oral **6**. rictal, stomal
    8. stomatic
piece (Mus).. **10**. embouchure
through the.. **7**. peroral
tissue.. **3**. gum
toward.. **4**. orad
wide, gaping.. **6**. rictus
mouthed, loud... **11**. thersitical
mouton... **5**. sheep **9**. prison spy
movable... **6**. mobile **10**. changeable
    12. transferable
movable property... **8**. chattels
move... **3**. act, gee, mog, say
    4. goad, sell, spur, stir **5**. budge,
    cause, impel, rouse, shift **6**. excite,
    incite, induce, kindle, motion,
    prompt, travel **7**. actuate, advance,
    animate, propose, provoke
    9. instigate, recommend, stimulate
move (pert to)...
    about.. **8**. locomote
    along.. **5**. mosey, scram **7**. maunder
    back.. **3**. ebb **6**. recede, retire, revert
        7. retreat **10**. retrogress
    back and forth.. **6**. teeter, wigwag
        7. shuttle **9**. oscillate
    clumsily.. **4**. joll
    false.. **4**. balk **5**. feint
    forward.. **4**. edge, scud **5**. drive
        7. advance **8**. progress
    furtively.. **5**. slink, sneak
    heavily.. **3**. lug **6**. fidget, lumber,
        trudge
    in circles.. **4**. purl
    place to place.. **7**. migrate
        8. emigrate
    quickly.. **3**. ply **4**. dart, dash, scud,
        shot **5**. scoot, spank **6**. bustle,
        gallop, hurtle
    restlessly.. **6**. kelter
    rhythmically.. **5**. dance
    sideways, sidewise.. **4**. slue **5**. sidle
    slowly.. **3**. jog, lag **4**. edge, inch,
        pant
    smoothly.. **4**. slip **5**. glide, skate,
        slide
    spasmodically.. **6**. twitch
    to and fro.. **3**. wag **4**. flap, sway
    together.. **5**. unite **8**. converge
    towards each other.. **8**. converge
    towards the east.. **9**. orientate
    unsteadily.. **4**. reel **6**. wabble
        7. stagger
    up and down.. **3**. bob **6**. teeter
    with exertion.. **5**. heave
    with measured tread.. **5**. march
moved by entreaty... **8**. exorable
moved easily... **5**. loped **6**. mobile
    8. affected **9**. emotional
movement... **5**. cause, trend **6**. action,
    motion, rhythm, travel **7**. emotion,
    gesture, impulse **8**. activity,
    maneuver, progress
movement (pert to)...
    backwards.. **13**. retrogression
    dance step.. **4**. lilt **6**. chassé
        9. pirouette

music.. **4**. moto **7**. con moto
of ships.. **5**. heave, pitch, scend
of waves.. **4**. roll, toss **5**. surge
    6. tumble, welter
vibratory.. **6**. tremor
moving... **6**. active, motile **7**. nomadic
    8. eloquent, exciting, pathetic
    9. affecting, impelling, traveling
    10. motivating
moving stairway... **9**. escalator
mow... **3**. cut, lay, mew **4**. dess, fell,
    heap, mass, math, mock, raze, stow
    5. mouth, stack **6**. garner, smooth
    7. cut down, grimace, harvest,
    shorten **9**. cornfield
mowana... **6**. baobab
mowing... **7**. cutting, mockery
    8. derision **9**. grimacing
    10. harvesting, meadowland
mowing machine... **5**. mower
    6. scythe, sickle
moxieberry... **9**. snowberry
moy... **4**. mild **6**. demure, gentle
    8. affected
moyen... **3**. way **5**. means **6**. agency,
    course **8**. property **9**. influence
Mozambique...
    Bay.. **8**. Mossuril
    capital.. **15**. Lourenco Marques
    native.. **3**. Yao
    port.. **10**. Mozambique
mozo... **10**. manservant
Mrs... **5**. madam **8**. goodwife, Mistress
mucaro... **3**. owl
much... **3**. lot **4**. high, many **5**. great
    7. greatly **8**. abundant, uncommon
    9. great deal **10**. indefinite
    12. considerable
muchacha... **4**. girl, lass
muchacho... **3**. boy, lad **7**. servant
mucid... **5**. musty, slimy **6**. clammy,
    mucous **8**. muculent
mucilage... **3**. gum **5**. paste
    6. mucago **8**. adhesive **9**. lubricant
mucilaginous... **5**. moist **6**. sticky,
    viscid
muckender... **12**. handkerchief
mucker... **4**. fall (from a horse), mess
    6. muddle, wretch **8**. disorder
    9. confusion, vulgarian
muckle... **4**. club, fret **6**. bother,
    putter
muckraker... **7**. defamer **8**. vilifier
    9. slanderer
mud... **4**. mire, muck, silt, slop
    5. abuse, gumbo, limus, shine
    6. gobbet, sludge **12**. offscourings
    14. abusive charges
mud (pert to)...
    bath.. **10**. illutation
    dab.. **8**. flounder
    dauber.. **4**. wasp
    devil.. **10**. hellbender
    eel.. **5**. siren
    hole.. **6**. puddle **8**. quagmire
    lark.. **5**. gamin, horse **6**. magpie,
        urchin
    like.. **7**. luteous
    living in.. **10**. limicolous
    peep.. **9**. sandpiper **11**. meadow pipit
    pike.. **5**. saury
    puppy.. **10**. hellbender, salamander

rake .. **5.** claut
shoveler .. **13.** spoonbill duck
snipe .. **8.** woodcock
sunfish .. **4.** bass **8.** warmouth
teal .. **9.** greenwing
volcano .. **5.** salse
Mudcat State ... **11.** Mississippi
muddle ... **3.** mix **4.** daze, mess, soss,
stir **5.** addle, botch, snafu **6.** bemuse,
bollix, jumble **7.** confuse, perplex,
stupefy **8.** befuddle, bewilder,
confound, disorder, squander
10. intoxicate **11.** predicament
muddled ... **3.** ree **5.** drunk, muzzy,
tipsy **7.** burbled, fuddled **8.** confused
9. befuddled, entangled
muddlehead ... **4.** dolt **9.** blockhead
muddy ... **4.** base, miry **5.** dingy, dirty,
roily, slaky **6.** lutose, opaque, slushy,
turbid **7.** clouded, obscure
8. confused **9.** besmeared
muddy places ... **7.** wallows
muezzin ... **4.** azan (adan) **5.** crier
(Moham)
muff ... **5.** beard, cover **6.** bungle
7. bungler, failure **8.** feathers
11. mollycoddle, whitethroat
muffed ... **5.** vexed **7.** crested
9. irritated
muffet ... **11.** whitethroat
muffetee ... **7.** muffler **8.** wristlet
muffin ... **3.** cob, gem **5.** bread, hazel,
plate, scone **7.** biscuit, crumpet,
English, popover
muffle ... **3.** gag **4.** damp, dull, mute,
wrap **6.** deaden, mumble, shroud,
stifle **7.** conceal **8.** decorate,
envelope **9.** blindfold, soft-pedal
muffler ... **3.** gag **4.** mute **5.** scarf
6. muzzle, tippet **8.** silencer
10. suppressor
mufflin ... **8.** titmouse
mufti ... **5.** dress (civilian)
mufti (Moham) ... **4.** alim **5.** judge
6. priest **8.** assessor, official
mug ... **3.** cup **4.** cram, dupe, face,
fool, Toby **5.** mungo, pulse, sheep,
study **6.** noggin **7.** drizzle, grimace
8. quantity **10.** photograph
muga ... **4.** moth, silk **11.** caterpillar
mugger ... **3.** goa **6.** robber, tinker
7. peddler **9.** crocodile
mugget ... **8.** woodruff **15.** lily of the
valley
muggins (game) ... **5.** cards **7.** penalty
8. dominoes
muggy ... **4.** damp, warm **5.** humid,
moist, moldy **6.** sticky, stuffy, sultry
10. sweltering **11.** whitethroat
mug house ... **6.** tavern **7.** barroom
8. alehouse, pothouse
mugient ... **6.** lowing **9.** bellowing
mugwump ... **5.** chief **8.** apostate,
objector **11.** independent, nonpartisan
16. Republican bolter
Muhammed ... see *Mohammed*
muir ... **4.** wall
muirfowl ... **9.** red grouse
muishond ... **5.** zoril **6.** weasel
mujer ... **4.** wife **5.** woman
mulberry ... **2.** al **5.** Morus **6.** murrey
10. blackberry **12.** thimbleberry

mulberry (pert to) ...
bark (paper) .. **4.** tapa (tappa)
beverage .. **5.** morat
bird .. **8.** starling
dye .. **3.** aal **8.** morindin
fig .. **8.** sycamore
purple .. **7.** blue-red **8.** camerier
tree .. **5.** Morus
wild .. **7.** yawweed
mulch ... **5.** straw **6.** ground, leaves
7. sawdust
mulct ... **4.** fine, scot **6.** amerce,
defect, punish **7.** blemish, deceive,
penalty, swindle **10.** amercement
mulcter ... **7.** amercer
mule ... **4.** mewl, mool, mute **5.** coble,
hinny, jenny **6.** acemia, hybrid
7. slipper, tractor **9.** chilblain
10. crossbreed, locomotive
15. obstinate person
mule (pert to) ...
chair .. **7.** cacolet
driver .. **7.** skinner **8.** muleteer
drove .. **5.** atajo
killer .. **6.** mantis
leading .. **8.** cencerro
skinner .. **6.** driver
untrained .. **9.** shavetail
muleteer ... **4.** peon **6.** driver
mulga ... **6.** acacia, shield
muliebria ... **8.** feminine
muliebriety ... **9.** womanhood
10. femininity **11.** womanliness
mulier ... **4.** wife **5.** woman **6.** mother
mulish ... **6.** hybrid, sullen **7.** asinine,
sterile **8.** stubborn **9.** obstinate
mull ... **3.** cow **4.** crag, dust, heat,
mess, mold **5.** crush, grind, snout,
spice **6.** fumble, muddle, muslin,
muzzle, ponder **7.** failure, rubbish,
squeeze, steatin, sweeten **8.** cogitate,
consider, ointment, ruminate, snuffbox
9. pulverize **10.** promontory
11. contemplate
mullah ... **6.** priest **7.** teacher (Moham)
mullet ... **4.** bobo, fish, star **6.** puffin
mullet hawk ... **6.** osprey
mulligan ... **4.** stew
mulligatawny ... **4.** soup
mulligrubs ... **5.** blues, colic, sulks
mullock ... **5.** spoil, waste **6.** refuse
(mine) **7.** rubbish
mulloway ... **7.** jewfish
multi (comb form) ... **4.** many
multifarious ... **8.** manifold
9. multifold, multiplex **10.** multiphase
multifold ... **7.** diverse **8.** manifold,
multiple, numerous
multilingual ... **8.** polyglot
multiped ... **10.** many-footed
multiplier ... **6.** bulbil **7.** facient
8. operator
multiply ... **5.** breed **6.** spread
7. amplify, magnify **8.** increase
9. calculate, pluralize, procreate
multitude ... **3.** mob **4.** host, many,
mass, much **5.** crowd, horde, shoal,
swarm **6.** legion, throng **7.** myriads
8. populace **9.** profusion
11. bourgeoisie **12.** numerousness
multitudinous ... **6.** myriad
mum ... **3.** ale **4.** mute **6.** silent

8. taciturn 11. not speaking

mumble... 4. chew, mump 6. chavel, fumble, mutter, patter

mumbo jumbo... 6. genius 7. bugaboo 12. superstition 13. awesome person

mummer... 5. actor 6. guiser 7. buffoon 9. performer

mummy... 5. brown, Congo (color), relic 6. corpse, mother 7. cadaver, carcass

mummy apple... 6. papaya

mump... 3. beg 5. cheat, sulks 6. mumble, sponge 7. deceive, grimace 6. impose upon

mumpish... 4. dull, glum 5. sulky 6. sullen

mumruffin... 8. titmouse

mundane... 6. cosmic 7. earthly, horizon, secular, terrene, worldly 8. temporal 11. unspiritual

mundatory... 9. cleansing 11. purificator

mundil... 6. turban (embroidered)

mungo... 4. herb, wool (reclaimed) 8. mongoose, mung bean 13. mongoose plant

municipal... 5. civic, urban 7. oppidan 9. political 10. municipium

munificence... 6. bounty 7. largess (largesse) 10. generosity, liberality 13. bounteousness, unselfishness

muniment... 6. record 7. defense 8. evidence, writings 9. valuables 10. furnishing 13. fortification

munity... see *immunity* 9. privilege

munshi (Hind)... 6. writer 7. teacher 9. secretary 11. interpreter

muntjac, muntjak... 5. kakar, ratwa 6. kidang

mura (Jap)... 7. village 9. community

Mura... 6. Indian

mural... 4. wall (pert to) 5. crown 8. painting

murder... 4. kill, slay 7. carnage 8. homicide 9. slaughter 11. assassinate 12. manslaughter

murder of...
brother.. 10. fratricide
father.. 9. patricide
king.. 8. regicide
mother.. 9. matricide
own child.. 9. prolicide
parent.. 9. parricide
prophet.. 8. vaticide
sister.. 10. sororicide
spouse (by the other).. 10. mariticide
wife.. 9. uxoricide
woman.. 8. femicide

murderous... 4. gory 5. cruel 6. bloody, deadly, savage 7. killing 10. sanguinary 12. bloodthirsty

mure... 4. meek, soft, wall 6. gentle, immure, modest 8. imprison

murk, mirk... 3. fog 4. dark, mist 5. gloom 6. opaque 7. blacken 8. darkness 9. dark color 11. dark–colored

murky, mirky... 4. dark 5. dense, foggy, thick 6. gloomy, opaque 7. obscure, stained 11. dark–colored 12. impenetrable

murmur... 3. coo, hum 4. blow, curr, fret, purl 6. babble, mutter, repine 7. trickle, whisper 8. complain

muscle... 4. beef, thew 5. brawn, sinew, teres 6. flexor, lacert, tensor 8. lacertus, retentor

muscle (pert to)...
affection.. 5. crick 6. ataxia
bending.. 6. flexor
chemistry.. 6. inosic 8. inosinic
column.. 10. sarcostyle
contracting.. 7. agonist
expander.. 7. dilator
extending.. 8. extensor
eyeball.. 6. rectus
lifting.. 7. levator
loin, tenderloin.. 5. psoas
lower.. 9. depressor
raising.. 7. deltoid, erector, levator
recording.. 8. ergogram 9. ergograph
round.. 5. teres
segment.. 8. myocomma
sense.. 11. kinesthesia
separating.. 11. divaricator
spasm.. 5. tonus
stretching.. 6. tensor
sugar.. 8. inositol
trapezius.. 10. cucullaris
triangular.. 7. deltoid
turning.. 7. evertor, rotator
two–headed.. 6. biceps

muscovite... 4. mica 11. yellow–green

Muscovite... 7. Russian

muscular... 4. wiry 5. beefy, thewy 6. brawny, mighty, sinewy, strong, torose 8. athletic, stalwart, vigorous

muscular (pert to)...
contraction (involuntary).. 3. tic 5. spasm
co–ordination.. 7. synergy
in–co–ordination.. 6. ataxia 15. locomotor ataxia
non–co–ordination in walking.. 6. abasia
spasm.. 5. tonus
stomach.. 7. gizzard

muse... 4. mull, poet, rune 5. dream 6. ponder 7. bagpipe, reverie 8. cogitate, consider, meditate, ruminate

Muse of...
astronomy.. 6. Urania
choral song.. 11. Terpsichore
comedy.. 6. Thalia
dancing.. 11. Terpsichore
eloquence.. 8. Calliope
history.. 4. Clio
joy.. 4. Tara
music.. 7. Euterpe
poetry.. 5. Erato (lyric) 6. Thalia (bucolic) 8. Calliope (heroic)
tragedy.. 9. Melpomene

Muses... 4. Clio 5. Erato 6. Thalia, Urania 7. Euterpe 8. Calliope, Polymnia (Polyhymnia) 9. Melpomene 11. Terpsichore

Muses (pert to)...
epithet.. 7. Pierian
fountain.. 8. Aganippe (near Thebes)
mother of.. 9. Mnemosyne
mountain.. 6. Pierus 7. Helicon 9. Parnassus

number.. 4. nine
sacred place.. 5. Aonia (Boeotia)
spring.. 7. Pierian
The Muses (Gr).. 8. Pierides
musette... 3. air, bag 4. oboe
   7. bagpipe, gavotte
museum... 6. Louvre 7. gallery
   8. Ptolemy I 10. Pinakothek
   11. glyptotheca, pinakotheke
   14. Madame Tussaud's
museum keeper... 7. curator
   9. custodian
mush... 3. cut 4. call, face, pulp
   5. atole, march (over snow), notch
   6. cereal, indent, sepawn 8. flattery,
   umbrella 12. hasty pudding
   14. sentimentality
mushroom... 5. morel, plant 6. agaric,
   anchor, fungus 7. parvenu, upstart
   8. umbrella 11. beaver brown
mushroom (pert to)...
   disease.. 5. flock
   edible.. 5. morel 11. chanterelle
   poisoning.. 8. mycetism
   poisonous.. 7. amanita 9. toadstool
   stem.. 5. stipe
   umbrella top.. 6. pileus
music (pert to)...
   abridgment.. 7. ridotto
   accompaniment.. 9. obbligato
   aftersong.. 5. epode
   all voices.. 5. tutti
   as written.. 3. sta
   chapel.. 9. a cappella
   character.. 3. bar, key 4. clef, rest,
      slur 5. cleft, neume, segno
   chord.. 8. arpeggio
   clear–cut.. 8. staccato
   closing measure.. 4. coda
   comic.. 6. bouffe
   do.. 2. ut
   drama.. 5. opera
   duet.. 3. duo
   encore.. 3. bis
   flourish.. 7. cadenza
   half note.. 5. minim
   half tone.. 8. semitone
   impassioned, emotional..
      12. appassionato
   interlude.. 6. verset
   interval.. 6. octave 7. tritone
   introduction.. 7. prelude
   it proceeds.. 2. va
   knowledge.. 10. musicology
   lead cue.. 5. presa
   left–handed.. 8. sinistra
   light notes.. 6. ottava
   low pitch.. 5. grave
   lutelike.. 10. hurdy–gurdy
   major.. 3. dur
   major third.. 6. ditone
   melodious.. 6. arioso
   melody.. 5. melos
   nine–piece composition.. 5. nonet
   one performer (choral).. 4. soli
   opera (comic).. 6. bouffe
   organization.. 4. band 5. Ascap, choir
      6. chorus 8. symphony 9. orchestra
   organ stop.. 6. dulcet, tromba
      7. celesta
   performance.. 7. recital
   phrase.. 9. leitmotiv (leitmotif)

pick.. 8. plectrum
pitch C.. 2. du
pompous.. 7. orotund
refrain.. 5. epode 8. repetend
repetition.. 5. rondo
scale.. 5. gamut
sestet.. 7. sestuor
sextuplet.. 7. sestole (sestolet)
soprano part.. 5. canto
speaking part.. 8. parlando
study.. 5. étude
tenor part.. 5. canto (original)
theme.. 4. tema
third.. 6. tierce
three–chord note.. 5. triad
thrice.. 3. ter
time.. 4. temp 6. giusto
timing device.. 9. metronome
twice.. 3. bis
variations, set of.. 7. partita
whimsical.. 8. bizzarro 9. capriccio
musical direction (pert to)...
   accented.. 8. sforzato 9. sforzando
   bold.. 6. audace
   brisk.. 5. tanto 7. animato
   detached.. 8. spiccato, staccato
   dying away.. 7. calendo
   emphatic.. 7. marcato
   evenly.. 10. egualmente
   fantastic.. 11. carpiccioso
   fast.. 4. vivo 5. tosto 6. presto,
      vivace 10. tostamente
   faster.. 7. stretto
   fluctuating.. 6. rubato
   gay.. 7. giocoso 10. brilliante
   gentle.. 5. dolce
   half.. 5. mezzo
   held firmly.. 6. tenuto
   high.. 3. alt
   hurried.. 7. agitato
   less.. 4. meno
   let it stand.. 3. sta
   lightly.. 10. con agilita
   little by little.. 9. poco a poco
   lively.. 6. vivace 7. allegro, animato
   loud.. 5. forte 10. fortissimo
   louder.. 9. crescendo
   lutelike.. 10. hurdy–gurdy
   more rapid.. 7. stretto (stretta)
   movement (with).. 7. con moto
   muted.. 5. sorda, sordo
   narrating.. 8. narrante
   one by one.. 7. uno a uno
   quick.. 6. presto
   quickening.. 11. affrettando
   quicker than.. 7. andante 9. andantino
   repeat.. 3. bis 6. da capo 7. ripresa
   sadly.. 7. dolente 8. doloroso
   shake.. 5. trill
   silent.. 5. tacet
   sliding.. 9. glissando
   slow.. 5. largo, lento, molto, tardo
      6. adagio 7. andante
   slow (very).. 5. molto
   slowing.. 9. allentato 10. ritardando
      11. rallentando
   smooth.. 6. legato
   soft.. 5. dolce, piano
   softer.. 10. diminuendo
   spirited.. 7. con moto
   strict tempo.. 6. giusto
   sustained.. 6. tenuto 9. sustenuto

tenderly .. **10.** affettuoso, con affetto
turn .. **5.** verte **9.** gruppetto
vivacious .. **7.** con brio
musical form ... **3.** jig, ode **4.** aria,
jazz, jive, olio, opus, punk (rock), scat,
song, soul **5.** derry, dirge, disco,
elegy, fugue, melos, motet, opera,
salsa **6.** arioso, ballad, medley,
melody, minuet, reggae, sonata
7. ragtime, toccata **8.** carillon (bells),
hornpipe, operetta, oratorio, serenade,
symphony **9.** barcarole, bluegrass,
interlude, polonaise **11.** rock and roll
12. boogie woogie
musical instruments ... **3.** sax
4. asor, drum, fife, harp, horn, lute,
lyre, oboe, pipe, reed, tuba, viol
5. banjo, bugle, cello, Dobro, flute,
organ, piano, rebec (rebeck), rocta,
tabor, viola **6.** atabal, cither, citole,
cornet, fiddle, guitar, spinet, tabret,
violin, zither **7.** althorn, bagpipe,
bandore, bassoon, celesta, clarion,
clavier, gittern, helicon, marimba,
musette, ocarina, pandora, theorbo,
trumpet, ukulele **8.** castanet, clarinet,
dulcimer, keyboard, mandolin,
trombone **9.** flageolet, saxophone
10. concertina, sousaphone (tuba),
tambourine **11.** harpsichord,
synthesizer, violoncello
musical instruments (foreign) ...
Africa .. **5.** nanga **7.** kalimba (thumb
piano), sistrum
China .. **3.** kin
E Indies .. **4.** bina
Egypt .. **7.** sistrum
Greece .. **7.** cithara (anc)
Hindu .. **4.** vina (anc)
India .. **5.** ruana
Italy .. **6.** tromba
Japan .. **7.** samisen (shamisen)
10. shakuhachi
Java .. **8.** gamelang (gamelan)
Mexico .. **6.** clarin **7.** maracas
Spain .. **6.** atabal **8.** castanets
musician ... **4.** bard **5.** piper
6. hepcat, lyrist, singer **7.** chorist,
crooner, drummer, fiddler, flutist,
pianist, yodeler **8.** bandsman,
composer, minstrel, organist
9. conductor, serenader, troubador,
violinist **10.** prima donna, trombonist
11. clarinetist, keyboardist,
minnesinger, saxophonist
12. interlocutor **13.** Kapellmeister
musicians' group ... **4.** band, duet, trio
5. nonet **6.** septet, sextet **7.** nonetto,
quartet **8.** ensemble, septette,
sextette, symphony **9.** orchestra,
quartette
musicians' patron saint ... **7.** Cecilia
musk ... **4.** deer **7.** perfume
musk (pert to) ...
beaver .. **7.** muskrat
cat .. **5.** civet
cattle .. **4.** oxen
cucumber .. **11.** cassabanana
deer .. **10.** chevrotain
duck .. **7.** Muscovy
hog .. **7.** peccary
melon .. **10.** cantaloupe

okra .. **8.** abelmosk
shrew .. **6.** desman
weasel .. **5.** civet
muskellunge ... **4.** fish, pike
musket ... **4.** hawk **5.** rifle **7.** firearm
9. flintlock
Musketeers, Three ... **5.** Athos
6. Aramis **7.** Porthos **9.** D'Artagnon
muskmelon ... **6.** atimon, casaba
10. cantaloupe
muskrat ... **5.** shrew **6.** desman
7. ondatra
Muslim ... see *Moslem*
muslin ... **3.** ban, cap **4.** mull **5.** doria,
shela **6.** canvas, gurrah **7.** organdy
8. nainsook, sheeting, tarlatan
muss ... **4.** mess, soil **5.** chaos, dirty
6. bitter, muddle, rumple, tousle
7. confuse, wrinkle **8.** dishevel,
scramble, squabble **10.** disarrange
mussel ... **4.** food, naid, unio **5.** horse,
moule, naiad **6.** byssus, mucket, nerita
7. mollusk, Mytilus
Musselman ... **6.** Moslem **7.** Saracen
10. Mohammedan
must ... **4.** mold, musk, sapa, stum
5. juice, ought, shall **6.** blight,
mildew, refuse **7.** malodor
9. necessity **10.** obligation
mustang ... **5.** horse, pinto **6.** bronco,
sphinx
mustard ... **5.** nigra, senvy **7.** sinapis
8. charlock
mustard (pert to) ...
chemistry .. **8.** sinapine
gas .. **7.** yperite
genus .. **7.** Sinapis **8.** Brassica
plaster .. **8.** sinapism
Mustelidae ... **5.** minks **7.** badgers,
martens, weasels
muster ... **4.** levy **5.** erect **6.** gather,
summon **7.** collect, marshal
8. assemble, comprise
10. assemblage
muster out ... **7.** disband
musty ... **3.** bad, old **4.** damp, hoar,
rank **5.** fetid, fusty, moist, moldy,
rafty, stale, trite **6.** rancid **7.** pungent
mutable ... **6.** fickle **7.** erratic
8. variable **9.** alterable, changeful
mute ... **3.** mum **4.** dumb, lene, surd
6. muffle, silent **8.** deadener, silencer,
taciturn **9.** voiceless **10.** speechless
mutilate ... **3.** mar **4.** geld, hack, maim
6. deface, deform, garble, injure,
mangle **7.** cripple, destroy **8.** castrate
9. dismember, tear apart
mutinous ... **6.** unruly **9.** seditious,
turbulent **10.** rebellious, refractory
11. intractable
mutiny ... **6.** Putsch (Swiss), revolt,
strife, tumult **9.** commotion, rebellion
12. insurrection **15.** insubordination
mutter ... **5.** growl **6.** murmur, patter,
plaint **7.** grumble, maunder
8. complain **9.** mussitate
mutton ... **4.** meat **5.** cabob (kabob),
gigot, sheep **6.** candle
muttonfish ... **4.** sama **5.** pargo
7. abalone, eelpout, mojarra, snapper
mutual ... **4.** plan **5.** joint **6.** common

8. intimate 9. symbiotic
10. reciprocal, responsive
15. interchangeable
mutual understanding... 9. agreement,
unanimity 12. consentience,
co–ordination 13. interrelation
17. interrelationship
mux... 4. mess 5. batch
muy... 4. very 7. greatly
muzhik, muzjik... 7. peasant
muzzle... 3. gag 4. cope, maul, nose
5. mouth, snout 6. clevis, thrash
7. shackle, sheathe, silence
8. restrain 10. respirator
my... 3. mes, mon 4. mine 7. due to
me 11. exclamation
myall... 4. wild, wood (fragrant)
6. acacia 11. uncivilized
mycoderma... 5. fungi 6. mother
(formed on wine) 8. membrane
(ferment)
mycophagy... 11. eating fungi
15. eating mushrooms
myna, mynah... 4. bird 7. grackle
8. starling
Mynheer... 8. Dutchman
myo (comb form)... 6. muscle
myomancy, divination by...
14. muscle movement
myopic... 11. nearsighted
myriad... 11. innumerable, ten
thousand 13. multitudinous
myriapod... 9. centipede
myrmicid... 3. ant
myrtle... 8. ramarama 10. periwinkle
11. candleberry
mysterious... 4. dark 6. arcane,
mystic, occult, secret 7. cryptic
8. abstruse, esoteric 9. recondite,
sphinxian 10. cabalistic
12. inexplicable, unfathomable
mystery... 4. cult, rune 6. arcane,
cabala, enigma, puzzle, secret
7. arcanum, esotery, miracle
8. whodunit 9. sacrament
13. inexplainable
19. incomprehensibility
mystic... 4. seer, yogi 5. magic, runic
6. occult, orphic, secret 7. cryptic,

Mahatma 8. cabalist, esoteric,
symbolic 9. enigmatic, recondite
10. cabalistic, mysterious
mystic (pert to)...
cry.. 4. evoe
doctrine.. 5. cabal 7. esotery
8. esoteric
initiate.. 5. epopt (Gr Antiq)
ocean isle.. 6. Avalon
theosophy.. 6. cabala
word.. 2. om 7. abraxas
11. abracadabra
mystical... 6. muddle, puzzle
7. confuse, cryptic, furtive, obscure
9. enigmatic, obfuscate
mystical (pert to)...
character (Teut Myth).. 8. Eckehart
meaning.. 7. anagoge
word.. 11. abracadabra
mystify... 5. befog 6. muddle, puzzle
7. becloud, confuse, perplex
8. befuddle, bewilder 9. bamboozle,
obfuscate
myth... 4. tale 5. fable, fancy, story
6. legend 7. figment, parable
9. apocrypha, falsehood
mythical... 7. fancied 8. fabulous
9. fictional, imaginary, legendary
10. fictitious 12. mythological
mythical (pert to)...
being.. 6. Garuda, Icarus 7. centaur,
griffin
bird.. 3. roc
deity.. 6. Moloch (tyrant)
demon.. 4. Rahu (tail called Kehu)
hero.. 4. Ajax 8. Achilles
heroine.. 4. Leda 6. Europa
8. Atalanta
hunter.. 5. Orion
island.. 8. Atlantis
king (Hind).. 4. Nala
monster.. 4. ogre 7. chimera
mother.. 5. Niobe
river.. 4. Styx
serpent.. 5. Apepi
winged creature.. 7. Alborak
woman.. 6. Gorgon, Medusa, Stheno
7. Euryale
mythogony, science of... 5. myths
mythologist... 9. mythmaker

N

N... 2. en, Nu 8. nitrogen (symbol)
nab... 4. grab 5. catch, seize
6. arrest, nibble, snatch 7. capture
9. apprehend
Nabal's wife (Bib)... 7. Abigail
nabob... 5. nawab 6. bigwig, tycoon
7. viceroy 8. governor 9. plutocrat
10. viceregent
nacelle... 4. boat 7. shelter
nacket... 3. boy 4. cake 5. lunch

6. caddie 8. saucy boy
nacre... 9. shellfish 10. conchiolin
13. mother–of–pearl
Nadab (Bib)... 12. King of Israel
nadir... 4. pole 11. lowest point (opp
zenith)
nag... 4. pony, twit 5. annoy, cobra,
horse, scold, snake, tease 6. heckle,
hector, peck on, pester, plague
7. henpeck 8. harangue

nagor ... 8. antelope, reedbuck
nahoor ... 5. sheep 6. bharal
naiad ... 5. nymph 6. mussel, Nereid
7. limniad, Oceanid
nail ... 3. cut, hob 4. brad, claw, spad,
stud, tack, wire 5. clout, spike,
sprig, talon 6. fasten, secure, unguis,
ungula 7. capture, measure
8. sparable 9. finishing, intercept
12. upholstering
nail (pert to) ...
headless .. 5. sprig
ingrowing .. 7. acronyx
marking, fingernail .. 6. lunule
size .. 8. tenpenny
slanted .. 4. toed
naissance ... 5. birth 6. origin
naive ... 5. frank 6. simple 7. artless,
ingenue 8. childish, gullible, untaught
9. guileless, ingenuous, unworldly
10. simplicity 13. unphilosophic
15. unsophisticated
naked ... 4. bald, bare, mere, nude,
open 5. clear, plain 6. barren,
meager 7. exposed, literal, obvious
8. manifest, stripped 9. unadorned,
uncovered 11. defenseless,
unprotected, unsupported
nakoo ... 6. gavial 9. crocodile
namaycush ... 5. togue, trout
namby–pamby ... 5. inane, silly, vapid
7. insipid 10. wishy–washy
11. sentimental
name ... 3. dub, nom 4. call, cite,
term 5. clepe, nomen, style, title
6. y–clepe 7. appoint, entitle,
mention 8. cognomen, identify
9. celebrity, enumerate, personage
10. denominate, reputation
11. appellation, designation
12. denomination
name (pert to) ...
added .. 7. agnomen
assumed .. 3. pen 5. alias 7. John
Doe 9. incognito, pseudonym,
sobriquet 10. nom de plume
bad .. 7. caconym
binomial .. 8. teutonym
by location .. 7. toponym
derivation .. 7. eponymy
family (father's) .. 7. eponymy
9. patronymy
fictitious .. 9. pseudonym
first .. 9. baptismal, Christian,
praenomen
Japanese .. 4. maru
known .. 9. onomatous
nickname .. 7. moniker (monicker)
8. cognomen
nominate .. 9. designate
secret .. 9. cryptonym
spelled backwards (real name) ..
6. ananym
surname .. 7. eponymy
technical .. 4. onym
unknown .. 9. anonymous
wrong .. 8. misnomer
name as agent ... 6. depute
named ... 5. cited 6. called, y–clept
(y–cleped)
named for a god ... 10. theophorous

nameless ... 7. bastard, obscure 8. not
known 9. aforesaid, anonymous,
unnamable 10. unrenowned
12. illegitimate 13. indescribable,
inexpressible 15. undistinguished
namelessness ... 9. anonymity
namely ... 5. to wit 9. expressly,
nominally, videlicet (viz)
names, divination by ... 8. onomancy
names, science of ... 11. onomatology
namesake ... 6. eponym 7. homonym
nanga ... 4. harp
nanism ... 12. dwarfishness (opp of
gigantism)
Nanking ...
capital .. 5. China (1932–1937)
color .. 12. Naples yellow
province .. 7. Kiangsu
river site .. 7. Yangtze
nanoid ... 8. dwarfish
nanpie ... 6. magpie
naos ... 5. cella 6. shrine, temple
Naos ... 4. star
nap ... 3. nod 4. doze, pile, shag, wink
5. fluff, grasp, seize, sleep, steal
6. duffel, siesta, snooze
nape ... 5. nucha, nuque, scrag
6. scruff, turnip 7. niddick
9. auchenium
napellus ... 9. monkshood
napery ... 5. linen (table)
napiform ... 12. turnip–shaped
napkin ... 5. doily, towel 6. diaper
8. kerchief 9. serviette
11. neckerchief
Naples ...
biscuit .. 10. ladyfinger
famed building .. 9. Cathedral (Gothic,
1272)
red .. 5. ochre 6. Indian
site .. 11. Bay of Naples
napoleon ... 4. game 6. pastry 7. top
boot 11. reddish–blue, sweet cherry
13. crimson clover
Napoleon I (pert to) ...
birthplace .. 7. Ajaccio (Corsica)
brother–in–law .. 5. Murat
death site .. 8. St Helena
exiled to .. 4. Elba
father .. 7. Charles
island .. 5. Capri
marshal .. 3. Ney (executed)
title .. 7. Emperor (of France)
warfare site .. 5. Ligny, Malta
7. Marengo 8. Waterloo
10. Alexandria
napped (short) ... 3. ras
nappy ... 3. ale 4. dish 5. downy,
heady, wooly 6. liquor, shaggy,
sleepy 7. foaming 10. inebriated
napu ... 10. chevrotain
Naraka (Hind) ... 4. hell
Narcissus (Gr) ... 6. egoist 14. beautiful
youth
narcosis ... 5. sleep 10. drowsiness
narcotic ... 4. dope, drug, hemp, junk
5. bhang (bang), ether, opium
6. heroin 7. anodyne, cocaine,
hashish 8. hypnotic, mandrake,
morphine 9. soporific 10. belladonna,
hyoscyamus, stramonium
narcotic (pert to) ...

dose .. 3. fix 5. locus
package .. 6. bindle
seller .. 6. pusher 7. peddler
user (group) .. 6. love–in 9. snow
party
nard ... 6. anoint 8. matgrass,
ointment, rhizomes
nardoo, nardu ... 6. clover
nares ... 8. nostrils
narghile, nargile, nargileh ... 4. pipe
6. hookah
nargil ... 7. coconut
nark ... 3. spy 5. annoy 8. informer
11. stool pigeon
Narragansett ... 3. Bay 5. horse
6. Indian, turkey
narrate ... 4. tell 6. detail, recite, relate
7. recount 8. describe
narration ... 4. tale 5. drama (acted),
story 6. detail 7. account, recital
8. relation 9. discourse, narrative,
rehearsal
narrative ... 4. epic, epos, myth, poem,
saga, tale 5. conte, drama, fable,
story 6. legend 7. account, episode,
history, parable 8. allegory, anecdote
9. narration, statement
narrator ... 9. raconteur 11. storyteller
narrow ... 4. mean, poor 5. inlet,
scant, taper 6. linear, strait
7. closely, slender 8. strictly
9. confining, illiberal, niggardly
10. restricted, straighten
11. reactionary 12. parsimonious
13. circumscribed
narrow (pert to) ...
comb form .. 4. sten 5. steno
leather strip .. 5. thong
minded .. 5. petty 6. biased
7. bigoted 10. intolerant, prejudiced
opening .. 4. rima, slot 9. stenopaic
souled .. 10. ungenerous
narrowly incised ... 9. laciniate
narrows ... 5. sound 6. strait
narthex ... 7. portico 9. asafetida
(asafoetida)
narwhal, narwal ... 5. whale
8. cetacean
nasab (Moham Law) ... 7. kinship
13. consanguinity
nasal ... 4. nose 5. sound 6. narine,
rhinal, twangy 11. inspiratory
nascency ... 5. birth 6. origin
7. genesis 9. beginning
naseberry ... 9. sapodilla
Nasi ... 6. prince 8. Gamaliel
9. patriarch
Nasicornia ... 10. rhinoceros
nasology ... 9. nose study
Nassau ...
capital .. 7. Bahamas
hamlet .. 7. grouper
sports .. 7. golf
nastika ... 7. atheist
nasty ... 4. foul, mean 5. dirty 6. filthy,
odious 7. obscene 8. indecent,
unsavory 9. offensive
12. disagreeable, dishonorable
Nasua ... 5. coati 6. coatis
nasute ... 10. large–nosed
nasutiform ... 8. noselike
natal ... 6. inborn, native 7. gluteal,

nascent 9. from birth
Natal ... 7. seaport (Braz) 8. Province
(S Afr)
natator ... 7. swimmer
natatorium ... 4. pool 6. plunge
12. swimming hole
natchbone ... 9. aitchbone
Natchez ... 4. city (La) 6. Indian
nation ... 4. host, race 5. caste, class,
state 6. people, polity 7. country
9. community, multitude
national ... 4. blue 6. racial 7. citizen,
federal
nationality ... 4. race 6. nation
8. nativity 9. statehood
11. nationalism
national salute ... 13. Twenty–one
guns
native ... 3. ite, son 5. natal 6. innate,
normal, simple 7. genuine, natural,
primary 8. inherent, original, primeval
9. unbranded 10. aboriginal,
indigenous, unaffected 11. not
acquired
native (pert to) ...
agent .. 9. comprador (compradore)
bear .. 5. koala
cat .. 7. dasyure
dog .. 5. dingo
Indian .. 4. Arab
juniper .. 9. blueberry
Madagascan .. 4. Hova
naturalized person .. 7. denizen
plant, animal .. 8. indigene
salt .. 6. halite
nativity ... 5. birth 9. beginning,
horoscope, sculpture
Nativity, The ... 8. festival
9. Christmas 13. birth of Christ
natterjack ... 4. toad
natty ... 4. chic, neat, tidy, trim
6. spruce 10. fastidious
Natty Bumppo's alias ... 7. Hawkeye
15. Leatherstocking
natural ... 3. raw 4. born 5. flesh,
usual 6. common, cretin, expert,
inborn, inbred, innate, normal
7. genuine, regular, typical
8. informal, inherent, lifelike, ordinary
9. character (Mus), dice throw,
unassumed, unfeigned 10. unaffected
natural (pert to) ...
capacity .. 9. endowment
condition .. 4. norm
group .. 4. race 6. ethnic, family
location, position .. 4. site 5. situs
not (natural) .. 5. alien 8. acquired
10. artificial
philosophy .. 7. physics
science .. 10. physiology
voice (Mus) .. 7. dipetto
naturalist ... 4. Muir (John) 7. animist,
Burbank (Luther) 9. biologist, scientist
11. taxidermist
naturalize ... 5. adapt 8. accustom
9. acclimate 11. domesticate,
familiarize
nature ... 4. kind, self, sort, soul, type
6. cosmos 7. essence 8. tendency,
universe 11. naturalness,
temperament 14. characteristic
nature (pert to) ...

concealed .. **7**. latency
divinity of .. **5**. dryad, naiad, nymph
god .. **3**. Pan
goddess .. **6**. Cybele **7**. Artemis
in the raw .. **6**. nudity
of the case .. **9**. ipso facto
worship .. **11**. physiolatry
natus ... **4**. born
nausea ... **4**. pall **5**. qualm **8**. loathing,
  mal de mer **10**. queasiness
  11. seasickness
nauseous ... **7**. fulsome, mawkish
  9. loathsome, offensive, sickening,
  squeamish **10**. disgusting
nautical ... **5**. naval **6**. marine
  7. oceanic **8**. maritime
nautical (pert to) ...
  almanac .. **9**. ephemeris
  direction .. **5**. avast, belay
  hail .. **4**. ahoy
  instrument .. **3**. aba **7**. compass,
    pelorus, sextant
  measure .. **3**. ton **4**. knot **6**. fathom
    7. sea mile
nautilus ... **7**. mollusk **8**. argonaut
  9. submarine **10**. diving bell
Navaho, Navajo ... **5**. hogan **6**. Indian
  7. blanket **9**. red–yellow
naval ... **6**. marine **8**. nautical
naval (pert to) ...
  brigade .. **7**. militia
  commander .. **7**. navarch
  depot .. **4**. base
  device .. **6**. dolter
  officer .. **5**. bosun **6**. ensign, yeoman
    7. admiral, captain **9**. boatswain
    (bosun), commander **10**. lieutenant
nave ... **3**. hob, hub, nef **4**. apse, fist
  5. nieve **7**. apsidal
navel ... **6**. middle, orange **8**. omphalos
  9. umbilicus **10**. depression
navigate ... **4**. keel, sail **7**. avigate
  11. ship science
navigator ... **5**. navvy **12**. third
  command (or 4th)
navy (fleet) ... **7**. tankers **8**. cruisers,
  flattops, gunboats **10**. destroyers,
  submarines **11**. battleships **12**. mine
  sweepers **13**. hospital ships
  16. aircraft carriers
navy (pert to) ...
  bean .. **6**. kidney
  coffee .. **3**. mud
  color .. **4**. blue **10**. marine blue
  drinking fountain .. **11**. scuttlebutt
  fleet .. **6**. armada **13**. combat vessels
  plug .. **7**. tobacco
  ships, collectively .. **5**. fleet **6**. armada
  song .. **13**. Anchors Aweigh
  training camp .. **8**. boot camp
  underwear .. **8**. skivvies
nawab, nabob ... **5**. ruler, title
  7. viceroy
nay ... **2**. no **4**. deny **5**. flute, never
  6. denial, naysay, refuse **7**. refusal
  8. negative **11**. prohibition
nayaur ... **5**. sheep
nayword ... **6**. byword **7**. proverb (of
  reproach) **9**. watchword
Nazarene (pert to) ...
  artist .. **8**. Overbeck (of Rome)
  disciple .. **9**. Christian

native .. **11**. Jesus Christ
native of .. **8**. Nazareth
Nazi ... **9**. Hitlerite
Nazi emblem ... **6**. fylfot **8**. swastika
nchega ... **6**. monkey **10**. chimpanzee
neanic ... **8**. immature, youthful
neap ... **4**. tide **6**. tongue (vehicle)
  7. low tide **8**. low water
Neapolitan (pert to) ...
  dance .. **10**. tarantella
  fever .. **8**. undulent
  Italian .. **6**. Naples
  medlar .. **5**. fruit **7**. azarole
  music .. **5**. chord (6th)
  ointment .. **9**. mercurial
  yellow .. **6**. Naples
near ... **2**. at **4**. nigh **5**. about, close,
  handy **6**. around, within **7**. closely,
  related **8**. adjacent, approach,
  imminent, intimate **11**. approximate
  13. propinquitous
nearby, near–by ... **3**. gin **4**. nigh
  5. anent, handy **6**. beside, nearly
  7. close by, close to, vicinal
  8. adjacent **9**. adjoining
  10. convenient
Nearctic ... **9**. Greenland, Holarctic
  11. Palaearctic **13**. Arctic America
Near East ... **7**. Balkans **12**. Balkan
  States
Near East valley ... **4**. wadi (wady)
  5. oasis **6**. ravine
nearest ... **4**. next **7**. closest
  9. proximate
nearly ... **5**. about **6**. almost **7**. closely
  8. narrowly **10**. similarity
  13. approximately
nearness ... **8**. affinity, intimacy,
  likeness, relation **9**. closeness
  11. propinquity
near of kin ... **7**. germane
nearsighted ... **6**. myopic **8**. purblind
  12. narrow–minded, shortsighted,
  undiscerning
neat ... **3**. pat **4**. prim, smug, snod,
  tidy, trig, trim **5**. natty **6**. adroit,
  dapper, spruce **7**. orderly, perjink,
  precise **9**. shipshape **10**. meticulous,
  perjinkety **12**. spick–and–span
neatherd ... **7**. cowherd **8**. herdsman
neathmost ... **6**. lowest
neb ... **3**. tip **4**. beak, bill, face, kiss,
  nose **5**. point, snout
Nebo, Nebu ... **8**. mountain (Bib)
  11. god of wisdom
Nebraska ...
  capital .. **7**. Lincoln
  city .. **5**. Omaha **8**. Hastings
    11. Scottsbluff
  Indian .. **4**. Otoe **5**. Omaha **6**. Pawnee
  meaning .. **11**. water valley
  railroad (1865) .. **12**. Union Pacific
  river .. **6**. Nemaha, Platte **8**. Missouri
  State admission .. **13**. Thirty–seventh
  State motto .. **20**. Equality Before the
    Law
  State nickname .. **4**. Beef
    10. Cornhusker
nebula ... **3**. sky **4**. mist **5**. cloud,
  vapor **10**. atmosphere
Nebula of ... **4**. Lyra **5**. Orion
  9. Andromeda

nebulous / neighborhood

nebulous... 4. hazy 5. misty, vague
6. cloudy 7. clouded, nebular
8. nebulose
nebulous envelope... 4. coma
9. chevelure
necessarily... 8. perforce
11. unavoidably 12. consequently
13. indispensably
necessary... 5. vital 7. needful
9. essential, mandatory, requisite
11. requirement, unavoidable
13. indispensable
necessitate... 5. force, impel
6. compel, entail, oblige 7. require
9. constrain
necessity... 4. food, need, want
5. drink 7. aliment, poverty, urgency
9. neediness 10. constraint
14. inevitableness
neck... 4. hals (halse) 5. crane, scrag,
swire 6. cervix, fondle, strait
7. channel, embrace, isthmus
neck (pert to)...
armor.. 6. gorget 8. gorgerin
artery.. 7. carotid
back of.. 4. nape 5. nucha, nuque
6. scruff
frill.. 5. jabot, ruche 6. wimple
land.. 6. strake 9. peninsula
muscle.. 8. scalenus
pendant.. 6. locket 9. lavaliere
piece.. 3. boa 5. amice, rabat, scarf,
stole 6. collar
water.. 6. strait
zoology.. 4. gula 6. wattle 7. withers
neckcloth... 6. cravat 7. muffler
9. barcelona 11. neckerchief
neckerchief... 7. belcher 8. kerchief
12. handkerchief
necklace... 5. beads 6. torque
7. baldric, chaplet, rivière
11. shark's-teeth
neckpiece... 3. boa 5. ascot, rabat,
scarf, stole 6. collar 8. kerchief
necktie... 3. tie 4. band 5. ascot,
scarf 6. cravat 10. four-in-hand
necrology... 9. death roll 13. death
register 14. obituary notice
necromancy... 5. goety, magic
7. sorcery 9. sortilege
11. conjuration, enchantment
necropolis... 8. cemetery
necropsy... 7. autopsy
10. post-mortem
nectar... 3. red 5. drink, honey
8. beverage
nectar of the gods... 8. ambrosia
neddy... 6. donkey 13. life preserver
need... 4. lack, poor, thar, want
7. poverty, require, urgency
8. exigency 9. extremity, necessity
10. compulsion, deficiency
11. requirement
needle... 3. sew 4. acus, goad, sail
5. tease, thorn 6. bodkin, pierce
7. darning, obelisk 9. astatizer
10. upholstery
needle (pert to)...
bath.. 3. jet 9. sprinkler
bird.. 9. phalarope 10. needlebill
bug.. 4. Nepa 7. Ranatra
case.. 4. etui (etwee)

fish.. 3. gar 8. pipefish
gun.. 11. Dreyse rifle
kind.. 5. blunt, sharp 7. between,
crochet, darning 8. knitting
long-eyed.. 10. embroidery
medical.. 10. hypodermic
needlelike body.. 7. spicule
needlework.. 7. crochet, sampler
8. knitting 10. embroidery
record.. 10. phonograph
shaped.. 6. acuate 7. acerose
8. acicular
under the skin.. 5. seton
needy... 4. poor 7. almoner
8. indigent 9. necessary, penniless,
requisite 10. distressed
neel-bhunder... 8. wanderoo 10. blue
monkey
neep... 6. turnip
ne'er-do-well... 5. idler 6. wretch
8. poltroon 9. schlemiel
14. good-for-nothing
nef... 4. nave 5. clock (ship-shaped)
nefarious... 6. wicked 7. heinous,
impious 8. horrible, infamous, terrible
9. atrocious 10. detestable,
iniquitous, villainous
nefas... 6. sinful
negate... 4. deny 6. refuse, refute
7. nullify 8. disprove 10. counteract
negative... 2. ir, ne, no 3. nay, non,
nor, not 4. deny, film, veto 5. minus
6. refuse 7. neutral 8. disprove,
negation 9. privative
13. contradiction
negative (pert to)...
electrode, pole.. 7. cathode (kathode)
eyepiece.. 8. Campani's 9. Huygenian
ion.. 5. anion
sign.. 5. minus
neglect... 4. fail, omit, slip, snub
5. shirk 6. slight 7. failure
8. omission 9. disregard, negligent,
pretermit 11. inattention
negligee... 4. gown, robe 6. attire
8. peignoir
negligence... 7. laxness 9. oversight,
unconcern 10. remissness
11. inattention 12. carelessness,
inadvertence
negligent... 3. lax 4. lash 6. remiss,
supine 8. careless, heedless
10. neglectful 11. unconcerned
negotiate... 4. deal, pass 5. treat
6. manage, treaty 7. bargain,
mediate 8. transact
Negrito (pert to)...
African.. 4. Akka 5. Batwa, Pygmy
7. Bambute, Bushman
Dutch New Guinea.. 6. Tapiro
Indonesian.. 3. Ata 4. Aeta (Ita)
Malay.. 6. Semang
Negro (pert to)...
dance.. 4. juba
dish.. 9. jambalaya
Egyptian.. 6. Nubian
friend of.. 10. negrophile
magic (anc).. 6. voodoo
spiritual.. 8. Swing Low
neigh... 4. akin 6. whinny 7. whicker
neighborhood... 7. purlieu 8. environs,
vicinity 9. proximity 10. thereabout

neighborhood law... 5. venue
neither masculine nor feminine...
   6. neuter 7. sexless
neither right nor wrong...
   11. adiaphorous, indifferent
Nemesis... 7. avenger, goddess,
   penalty
nemoral... 6. sylvan 14. living in a
   grove
neology... 8. new words 9. neologism
   11. new doctrine 14. new
   expressions
neonatus... 7. new baby, newborn
neophobia *(fear of)*... 6. the new
neophyte... 4. tyro 6. novice
   7. convert 8. beginner 9. proselyte
   10. catechumen
neosology *(study of)*... 10. young birds
neoteric... 3. new 4. late 6. modern,
   recent
nep... 6. catnip
Nepal...
   aborigines.. 10. Mongolians
   capital.. 8. Katmandu
   district.. 7. Mustang
   mountain.. 7. Everest 9. Himalayas
   ruler.. 9. Maharajah
nepesh... 4. soul 10. animal soul
   12. divine breath
nephew... 4. neve 6. nepote
nephrite... 4. jade 7. mineral
   11. kidney stone
nephroid... 8. reniform
   12. kidney–shaped
nephros... 6. kidney
nepote... 6. nephew 8. grandson
nepotism... 9. patronage
   10. favoritism, preference
Neptune... 3. sea 5. ocean 6. sea
   god
Neptune *(pert to)*...
   Astron.. 6. planet (3rd largest)
   Celtic.. 3. Ler
   consort.. 7. Salacia
   emblem.. 7. trident
   Greek.. 8. Poseidon
   Roman.. 6. sea god
   son.. 6. Triton
   wife.. 6. Medusa
Nereid (Gr)... 8. sea nymph
Nero *(pert to)*...
   excesses.. 7. cruelty 13. burning of
   Rome (64 AD)
   mother.. 9. Agrippina
   Roman title.. 7. Emperor
   wife.. 6. Sabina 7. Octavia
nerve... 4. pulp 5. cheek, fiber, pluck,
   sinew 6. aplomb, energy, tendon,
   tissue 7. courage, nervure
   8. audacity, coolness, strength
   10. resolution
nerve *(pert to)*...
   action.. 9. neurergic
   cell.. 4. axon 6. neuron
   center.. 8. ganglion
   comb form.. 5. neuro
   fiber.. 5. motor 7. sensory
   8. afferent, efferent
   force.. 7. neurism
   gray matter.. 7. cinerea
   inflammation, medical.. 8. neuritis,

neurosis 9. neurotomy
   10. neurectasy, neurolysis, neuropathy
   11. neurologist 13. tic douloureux
network.. 4. rete 6. plexus
of Wrisberg.. 6. facial
operation.. 10. neurolysis
passage.. 4. rete 5. hilum 8. ganglion
ref to.. 6. neural, neuric 7. neuroid
   8. neurotic
root.. 5. radix
science.. 9. neurology
sheath.. 9. medullary
tissue.. 7. cinerea, neurine
   9. neuroglia
tumor.. 6. glioma 7. neuroma
nerveless... 4. dead 5. inert
   9. foolhardy, powerless
   10. courageous
nervous... 5. tense, timid 6. neural,
   touchy 7. fearful, jittery 8. eloquent,
   neurotic, timorous 9. excitable,
   sensitive 10. high–strung
   12. apprehensive
nervous *(pert to)*...
   affliction.. 3. tic 6. ataxia, chorea
   7. aphasia 8. neurosis
   energy deficiency.. 7. aneuria
   seizure.. 4. amok (amuck)
   system, center.. 5. brain, spine
   system, description.. 11. neurography
   system, name.. 9. neuronymy
   system, science.. 9. neurology
   system, specialist.. 12. neuropathist,
   psychiatrist
   tissue tumor.. 11. neurocytoma
ness... 4. cape 8. headland
   10. promontory
nest... 3. bed, den, nye, web 4. inro
   5. abode, aerie, eyrie, group, haunt,
   nidus 6. cuddle, series (graduated)
   7. lodging, retreat 9. residence
   10. nidificate 13. breeding place
nest *(pert to)*...
   boxes.. 4. inro
   eagle's.. 5. aerie, eyrie (eyry)
   pheasant's.. 4. nide
   spider's.. 3. web
   squirrel's.. 4. dray (drey)
   swallow's.. 9. nidus avis
   to build.. 6. nidify
nestle... 3. pet 4. nest 6. cuddle,
   pettle, settle 7. protect, shelter,
   snuggle
nestling... 4. bird 5. child 9. fledgling,
   youngling
Nestor *(pert to)*...
   famed for.. 6. wisdom
   King of.. 5. Pylos
   known as.. 4. sage 7. adviser 8. The
   Elder 9. Patriarch
net... 3. gin, web 4. mesh, toil, trap,
   weir 5. clear, lacis, score, seine,
   snare, weave 6. profit 7. enclose,
   network, trammel 8. receipts
   9. reticulum
net *(pert to)*...
   fishing.. 4. fyke 5. seine, trawl
   7. trammel
   hair.. 5. snood
   lacemaking.. 5. lacis
   silk.. 5. tulle 6. maline
   winged (lacy).. 12. neuropteroid

Netherlands... see also *Dutch, Holland*
  capital.. 9. Amsterdam
  cheese.. 4. Edam
  city.. 5. Delft 7. Utrecht
    9. Eindhoven, Rotterdam
  gin.. 8. schnapps
  government.. 8. monarchy
  government seat.. 8. The Hague
  inhabitant.. 5. Dutch 7. Flemish
  lake.. 7. Haarlem
  legislative body.. 4. Raad
  low land.. 6. polder
  port.. 9. Rotterdam
  possession.. 7. Surinam (Dutch
    Guiana) 8. Antilles (W Ind)
  river.. 3. Eem 5. Meuse, Rhine
    6. Ijssel (Yssel), Kromme
  sea (inland).. 9. Wadden Sea, Zuider
    Zee 10. Ijssel Lake, Ijsselmeer
nettle... 3. vex 4. fret, herb, line,
  whip 5. anger, annoy, pique, rouse
  6. incite, Urtica 7. provoke 8. irritate
  10. Parietaria, Urticaceae
nettle (pert to)...
  bird.. 11. whitethroat
  geranium.. 6. coleus
  rash.. 5. hives, uredo 9. urticaria
  sea.. 5. cnida
network... 3. web 4. caul, fret, kell,
  lace, mesh, moke, rete 5. chain
  6. cobweb, plexus, reseau, sagene
  7. webwork
neume... 5. neuma 6. pneuma
neurad... 12. to neural side
neural... 6. dorsal, nerval 7. ventral
  9. posterial
neuralgia... 3. tic 4. pain 8. face
  ague 13. tic douloureux
neuter... 6. gender 7. neither, neutral,
  sexless 9. impartial
neutral... 7. antacid 8. mediocre,
  middling, negative, unbiased
  10. achromatic 11. indifferent,
  nonpartisan 12. noncombatant,
  noncommittal
neutral equilibrium... 7. astatic
neutralize... 5. annul 6. offset
  7. nullify, vitiate 9. frustrate
  10. counteract 11. countervail
  14. counterbalance
Nevada...
  capital.. 10. Carson City
  city.. 3. Ely 4. Elko 6. Sparks
    7. Boulder 8. Las Vegas
  lake.. 4. Mead 6. Mohave
    7. Pyramid
  mine (famed).. 12. Comstock Lode
    (1859)
  mountain.. 7. Rockies, Wasatch
    13. Sierra Nevadas
  native Indian.. 6. Digger
  resort.. 4. Reno 8. Las Vegas (The
    Meadows) 9. Lake Tahoe
  State admission.. 11. Thirty–sixth
  State motto.. 16. All For Our Country
  State nickname.. 6. Silver
    9. Sagebrush
neve... 4. firn, snow 6. nephew
  7. glacier
nevel, nevell... 9. fisticuff
never... 4. nary 6. nowise 7. not ever
  8. at no time, not at all 9. by no

means, nevermore
nevertheless... 3. but, yet 5. still
  6. anyhow 7. however
  15. notwithstanding
nevus... 4. mark, mole 5. tumor
  7. blemish 9. birthmark
new... 3. neo (pref) 4. anew, late,
  nova (star) 5. fresh, novel 6. growth,
  modern, recent 8. neoteric, original,
  untested 9. recreated, renovated
  12. unaccustomed 13. inexperienced
New Brunswick...
  capital.. 11. Fredericton
  city.. 6. St John
  gulf.. 10. St Lawrence
new but yet old... 10. novantique
New England (pert to)...
  book.. 6. Primer
  explorer.. 13. Capt John Smith
  native.. 6. Yankee
  theology.. 9. Calvinism
Newfoundland...
  city.. 7. St John's 9. Grand Bank
  discoverer.. 9. John Cabot (1497)
  gulf.. 10. St Lawrence
New Guinea, Papua Island...
  capital.. 6. Rabaul
  hog (wild).. 4. bene
  island size (world).. 5. third
  native.. 6. Papuan
  parrot.. 4. lory
  port.. 4. Daru 7. Moresby
  region.. 10. Melanesian
  river.. 3. Fly
New Hampshire...
  capital.. 7. Concord
  city.. 6. Durham 7. Hanover
    8. Merrimac 10. Manchester,
    Portsmouth
  cog rail (first).. 12. Mt Washington
  lake.. 13. Winnipesaukee
  mountains.. 5. White
  Our Town.. 13. Grover's Corner
  park.. 13. Crawford Notch, Dixville
    Notch
  range.. 12. Presidential
  river.. 8. Merrimac 11. Connecticut
  sculpture.. 14. Great Stone Face
    (Profile Peak)
  State admission.. 5. Ninth
  State motto.. 13. Live Free or Die
  State nickname.. 7. Granite
New Jersey...
  capital.. 7. Trenton
  city.. 6. Camden, Newark 7. Raritan
    9. Montclair 12. Fort Monmouth,
    New Brunswick
  college.. 9. Princeton (1746)
  inventor.. 6. Edison
  naval air station.. 9. Lakehurst
  poet.. 11. Walt Whitman
  resort.. 7. Cape May 8. Wildwood
    9. Ocean City 10. Asbury Park
    12. Atlantic City
  river.. 7. Raritan
  State admission.. 5. Third
  State motto.. 20. Liberty and
    Prosperity
  State nickname.. 6. Garden
New Mexico...
  capital.. 7. Santa Fe
  city.. 4. Taos 7. Roswell
    11. Albuquerque

Fort.. **5.** Tejon
Indian Reservation.. **5.** Acoma (Sky
  City) **11.** Chaco Canyon
peak.. **7.** Wheeler
river.. **4.** Gila **5.** Pecos **8.** Canadian
space center.. **6.** Sandia **8.** Holloman,
  Kirtland **9.** Los Alamos **10.** White
  Sands
State admission.. **12.** Forty–seventh
State bird.. **10.** road runner
State flower.. **5.** yucca
State motto.. **12.** Crescit Eundo
  15. It Grows as It Goes
State nickname.. **17.** Land of
  Enchantment
State wonder.. **15.** Carlsbad Caverns
new moon festival... **8.** neomenia
news... **5.** flash, scoop **6.** report
  7. courier, evangel, tidings
news agency... **2.** AP **3.** DNB, UPI
  4. Tass **5.** Aneta, Domei **7.** Reuters
  9. syndicate
newspaper (pert to)...
editor.. **7.** reviser **8.** redactor
file.. **6.** morgue
popular name.. **7.** gazette
writer.. **8.** reporter **9.** columnist
  10. newscaster **13.** correspondent
newsstand... **5.** booth, kiosk, stall
new star... **4.** nova
newt... **3.** eft **6.** lizard, triton
  10. salamander
New Testament... **6.** Gospel
  8. Epistles **15.** Pauline Epistles
new wine... **4.** must
new word, usage... **7.** neology
  9. neologism, neoterism
New York...
borough.. **5.** Bronx **6.** Queens
  8. Brooklyn, Richmond **9.** Manhattan
buyer (for $24).. **11.** Peter Minuit
capital.. **6.** Albany
city.. **5.** Utica **7.** Buffalo, New York
  8. Saratoga **9.** Rochester
  11. Schenectady **12.** Poughkeepsie
college.. **7.** Colgate, Cornell
  8. Columbia **9.** West Point
Falls.. **7.** Niagara
Indian.. **6.** Oneida, Seneca **8.** Iroquois
  9. Tarrytown
Irving's home.. **9.** Tarrytown
island.. **6.** Staten **9.** Manhattan
monument.. **7.** Obelisk **10.** Grant's
  Tomb **15.** Statue of Liberty
mountains.. **9.** Catskills
name, old.. **12.** New Amsterdam
nickname.. **6.** Gotham **8.** Big Apple
river.. **4.** East **6.** Harlem, Hudson
river channel.. **8.** Hell Gate
section (famed).. **4.** SoHo
  16. Greenwich Village
State admission.. **8.** Eleventh
State bird.. **8.** bluebird
State flower.. **4.** rose
State motto.. **9.** Excelsior **10.** Ever
  Upward
State nickname.. **6.** Empire
New Yorker... **8.** Dutchman
  9. Gothamite **13.** Knickerbocker
New Zealand...
capital.. **10.** Wellington
city.. **7.** Dunedin **8.** Auckland,
  Hamilton **12.** Christchurch

discoverer.. **6.** Tasman
explorer.. **4.** Cook (Captain James)
location.. **12.** South Pacific
native.. **5.** Maori **10.** Polynesian
peak.. **6.** Mt Cook
sect.. **7.** Ringatu
soldier.. **5.** Anzac
tribe.. **3.** Ati **5.** Maori
volcano.. **7.** Ruapehu
New Zealand (pert to)...
bird... **3.** kea, moa, poe **4.** titi, weka,
  kiwi **7.** apteryx, boobook, wrybill,
  Xenicus
caterpillar.. **5.** aweto
club, weapon.. **4.** mere
mahogany.. **6.** totara
mollusk.. **4.** pipi
myrtle.. **8.** ramarama
morepork.. **4.** peho, ruru
palm.. **5.** nikau
parrot.. **6.** kakapo **9.** owl parrot
pigeon.. **4.** kuku
reptile.. **7.** tuatara
white pine.. **5.** kauri (kaury)
next... **4.** then **5.** aware, neist
  7. closest, nearest, proximo
  9. adjoining, immediate
  10. contiguous, succeeding
next to... **6.** almost, beside, nearly
  8. adjacent
next to last syllable... **6.** penult
  11. penultimate
nexus... **3.** tie **4.** bond, link **5.** group
  6. series **10.** connection
  15. interconnection
Nez Percé... **6.** Indian **11.** pierced
  nose
Niagara... **5.** flood, grape (green)
Niagara Falls (pert to)...
cataract.. **8.** American, Canadian
  9. Horseshoe
division between.. **10.** Bridal Veil,
  Goat Island
point of interest.. **14.** Cave of the
  Winds
nib... **3.** end **4.** beak, bill **5.** point
  (pen), prong **6.** tongue
nibble... **3.** eat, nab, nip **4.** gnaw,
  peck **5.** champ, munch **6.** browse
Nicaragua...
capital.. **7.** Managua
city.. **7.** Granada
lake.. **7.** Managua
mountain range.. **10.** Cordillera
river.. **4.** Coco, Tuma **7.** San Juan
nice... **4.** fine, good, kind, neat
  6. dainty, proper, queasy, subtle,
  tickle **7.** elegant, finical, genteel,
  prudish, refined **8.** exacting, pleasant,
  pleasing, suitable **9.** agreeable,
  squeamish **10.** appetizing, delightful,
  fastidious, particular, scrupulous
  11. considerate, punctilious,
  well–behaved **13.** hypercritical
  14. discriminating, discriminative
Nicene Creed... **10.** Confession
nicety... **7.** finesse, modesty
  8. accuracy, delicacy **9.** precision
  11. preciseness **13.** squeamishness
niche... **4.** apse, nook **5.** space
  (recessed) **6.** alcove, covert, recess
  7. retreat, secrete **10.** tabernacle

nick... 3. gap 4. dent, dint, slit
5. notch, steal 7. swindle
nickel (pert to)...
alloy .. 5. Invar
bronze .. 11. cupranickel
coin .. 13. five–cent piece
color .. 4. gray 6. nimbus
compound .. 8. argenton
11. maillechort
silver .. 6. German
symbol .. 2. Ni
nickelodeon... 4. juke 7. jukebox,
theater (5–cent)
nickname... 3. pun 6. monica
7. agnomen, epithet, misname,
moniker (monicker), pet name
8. cognomen, misapply
10. soubriquet
nicknaming pun... 12. prosonomasia
nictate... 4. wink 5. blink 7. twinkle
9. nictitate
nid... 3. nod 10. bend and bob
nide... 4. nest 5. brood
nidge... 3. nig 5. shake 6. quiver
nidificant... 12. nestbuilding
nidology, science... 10. birds' nests
nidor... 5. aroma, scent
nidus... 4. nest 5. abode 7. nucleus
13. breeding place
Nietzsche... 11. philosopher
nieve... 4. fist, hand
niffer... 7. bargain 8. exchange
niffy–naffy... 7. finical 8. trifling
Niflheim, Nifelheim (Norse Myth)...
8. Universe (division of) 10. Nine
Worlds
nifty... 5. smart 7. stylish 8. very
good
Nigeria...
capital .. 5. Lagos
city .. 3. Ede 6. Ibadan
export .. 5. cocoa
plains .. 5. Bornu
tribe .. 4. Eboe 5. Benin
niggardly... 5. scant 6. paltry, sordid,
stingy 9. penurious, scrimping
10. avaricious 12. parsimonious
nigh... 2. at 3. nei 4. left, near
5. about, anear, close 6. almost,
direct, nearly 8. adjacent
10. contiguous 11. neighboring
night... 4. nuit 5. death 7. evening
8. darkness, wee hours 9. adversity,
nightfall 11. concealment
night (pert to)...
bird .. 5. potoo 8. nightjar
9. nighthawk 10. goatsucker,
nightchurr, owl swallow, shearwater
11. nightingale
blindness .. 10. nyctalopia
cap .. 6. biggin
club .. 4. café 5. disco 6. bistro
7. cabaret 11. discotheque
goddess .. 3. Nox, Nyx
jasmine .. 10. hursinghar
Norse .. 4. Nott
sight (only) .. 11. hemeralopia
wandering .. 11. noctivagant
nightfall, at... 6. sunset 9. acronical
(achronical) (opp of cosmical)
nightingale... 6. thrush 8. philomel
9. bed jacket

night jar... 5. potoo 10. goatsucker
nightmare... 3. alp 4. Mara, ogre
5. dream 7. incubus 9. cauchemar
13. hallucination
nightshade... 5. morel (moril)
7. henbane 10. belladonna
11. bittersweet
nigrescent... 8. blackish
nihil... 7. nothing, no value
nihil debet... 13. he owes nothing
nihil ex nihilo... 7. nothing (comes)
11. from nothing
Nihilist... 9. anarchist, Socialist
Nile (pert to)...
bird .. 4. ibis 7. wryneck
boat .. 5. baris 6. nuggar 8. dahabeah
city .. 7. Rosetta
color .. 3. boa 5. green
dam .. 5. Aswan
Falls .. 5. Ripon
fish .. 5. bagre 8. mormyrid (sacred)
god .. 4. Hapi
headstream .. 6. Kagera
houseboat .. 8. dahabeah
island .. 4. Roda (Rhoda)
waste .. 4. sudd
nilgai... 8. antelope
nimble... 4. deft, fast, flit, gleg, lish,
spry 5. agile, alert, brisk, fleet, quick,
smart, swift 6. active, adroit, clever,
lively, prompt, volant
nimbose... 6. cloudy, stormy
7. clouded 8. nebulous, nubilous,
overcast
nimbus... 4. disk, halo 5. cloud, vapor
6. fabric, gloria, nickel 7. aureole
10. atmosphere
nimiety... 6. excess 10. redundancy
niminy–piminy... 7. mincing, refined
10. effeminate
nimmer... 5. thief
Nimrod (Bib)... 5. ruler 6. hunter
8. Cush's son
nimshi... 4. fool 7. half–wit 11. silly
person
Nimshi's son (Bib)... 11. Jehoshaphat
nine (pert to)...
angles .. 7. nonagon
banded armadillo .. 4. peba
based on .. 8. novenary
Books of nine chapters .. 7. Enneads
comb form .. 6. ennead
composition for nine .. 5. nonet
days' devotion .. 6. novena
eyes .. 7. lamprey
gems .. 7. Vikrama
gods .. 9. Etruscans
group .. 6. ennead, nonary 18. Ennead
of Heliopolis
headed monster .. 5. Hydra
inches .. 5. span
number .. 5. ennea, nueve
pert to .. 8. enneadic
players .. 8. baseball
poetic .. 8. ninefold
Nineteenth amendment...
14. Woman's Suffrage
Nineveh (Bib)...
capital .. 7. Assyria
famed for .. 11. excavations (1814)
Nine Worlds (Norse)... 3. Hel
6. Asgard 7. Alfheim, Midgard

8. Niflheim, Vanaheim
10. Jotunnheim 12. Muspellsheim
13. Svartalfaheim
Nine Worthies ... 5. David, Judas
6. Arthur, Caesar, Hector, Joshua
7. Godfrey 9. Alexander
11. Charlemagne
ninny ... 4. clod, dolt, fool, nerd
9. blockhead, simpleton
ninth ... 5. nones (day before Ides)
8. enneatic, ninefold
11. ennea–eteric (year)
Ninth of Ab (Jew) ... 7. fast day
ninut ... 6. magpie
Niobe (pert to) ...
changed by Zeus to .. 5. stone
father .. 8. Tantalus
husband .. 12. King of Thebes
nip ... 3. bit, cut, sip 4. bite, clip,
dram, peck 5. blast, cheat, check,
chill, clamp, draft, drink, hurry, pinch,
seize, sever, steal, thief 6. benumb,
blight, catnip, cut off, freeze, snatch,
tipple 7. shorten, squeeze
8. compress 10. pickpocket
nipa (pert to) ...
drink .. 9. alcoholic
mat .. 6. thatch
palm .. 4. atap
palm sap .. 5. sugar 7. alcohol
nipcheese ... 5. miser 6. purser
nipper ... 3. boy, lad 4. claw, grab
5. biter, drink, miser, thief 6. cunner,
mitten, urchin 7. gripper, incisor,
pincers 12. costermonger
nippers ... 6. pliers 7. pincers 8. leg
irons, pince–nez 9. handcuffs
nipple ... 3. pap 4. teat 7. mamelon,
papilla 8. mammilla 10. projection
12. protuberance
nippy ... 4. cold 5. brisk 6. active,
biting 7. nipping, pungent
8. grasping, vigorous
Nirvana ... 4. rags 6. heaven
8. oblivion 12. emancipation
Nisan (Jew calendar) ... 10. first month
(Mar–Apr)
nisi ... 5. if not 6. unless
nissen ... 6. goblin, kobold 7. brownie
nisus ... 7. impulse 8. endeavor,
striving
nit ... 3. egg 4. mite 8. parasite
nitency ... 6. luster 10. brightness
niter, nitre ... 6. natron 9. saltpeter
13. sodium nitrate 16. potassium
nitrate
nither ... 5. blast 6. debase, shiver
7. oppress, tremble 9. humiliate
nithing (anc) ... 6. coward 7. niggard
nitid ... 3. gay 6. bright 8. lustrous
nitric acid ... 10. aqua fortis
nitrogen ... 3. azo (comb form), gas
5. azote 7. element 10. atmosphere
nitrogen compound ... 7. ammonia
nitroglycerin, nitroglycerine ...
8. dynamite (1846) 9. explosive,
guncotton
nitrous oxide ... 3. gas 10. anesthetic
11. laughing gas
nitty–gritty ... 4. base, crux, gist
7. essence
Niue, Pacific island ...

territory of .. 10. New Zealand
niveau ... 5. level
niveous ... 5. snowy, white (shining)
nix ... 2. no 5. no one 6. forbid,
nobody, sprite 7. nothing
Njorth, Njord (Norse) ... 3. god
(fertility) 5. Vanir
Njorth's daughter ... 5. Freya (Freyja)
7. goddess (love and beauty)
Njorth's son ... 3. god 4. Frey
no ... 3. naw, nay, nit 4. baal, dead,
gone, none 5. not so 6. denial,
no–gaki, not any 8. not at all
Noah, Bib (pert to) ...
boat .. 3. Ark
dove .. 7. Columba
father .. 6. Lamech
flood .. 6. Deluge
Genesis .. 9. patriarch
grandson .. 4. Aram
landing, the Ark .. 6. Ararat
raven .. 6. Corvus
son .. 3. Ham 4. Shem 7. Japheth
nob ... 4. head, nave 6. hobnob
8. nobleman 9. personage
nobby ... 4. boat 5. smart 7. stylish
Nobel powder ... 10. Ballistite
noble ... 4. epic, fine, peer 5. ducal,
grand, lofty, manly 6. epical
7. eminent, grandee, liberal, stately,
sublime 8. elevated, generous,
imposing, renowned, splendid
9. dignified, high birth, honorable
10. impressive 11. illustrious,
magnanimous, magnificent
12. aristocratic
nobleman ... 3. sir 4. duke, earl, lord,
peer 5. baron 6. barony, flaith, thakur
7. baronet, grandee, marquis
8. margrave, optimate, viscount
9. blueblood, patrician 10. aristocrat,
chess piece
nobleness of birth ... 6. eugeny
noblewoman ... 4. lady 5. begum
7. duchess, peeress 8. baroness,
contessa, countess, marquise
11. marchioness
nobody ... 4. none 5. no one
7. nebbish 8. no person
9. jackstraw, nonentity 10. not
anybody
nocent ... 6. guilty 7. harmful, hurtful
8. criminal (opp of innocent)
nocturnal ... 5. night 7. nightly
8. darkness, nocturne
nocturnal (pert to) ...
animal .. 3. bat 4. coon 5. lemur, ratel
6. possum 7. opossum
astronomy .. 9. astrolabe
bird .. 3. owl
signs .. 8. zodiacal
nocturne ... 7. lullaby 8. serenade
10. night scene (art)
nocuous ... 7. hurtful, noxious
nod ... 3. bow 4. bend, bock, doze,
tend, wink 6. beckon, signal
7. bidding 8. greeting
Nod (Bib) ... 9. Land of Nod 10. East
of Eden
nodding ... 6. nutant 7. annuent,
weeping (as a willow) 8. cernuous,
drooping

noddy... 3. auk 4. fool 6. drowsy, fulmar, noodle, sleepy 7. foolish, hackney 9. simpleton

node... 4. knob, knot, knur, plot 5. joint, nodus 7. dilemma 8. swelling 10. difficulty 12. complication, protuberance

nodule... 4. auge, bump, knot, lump, mass 5. geode 7. granule, nablock 8. tubercle 12. complication

nodus... 4. knot, node 10. difficulty 12. complication

noel... 5. carol (Xmas), shout 9. sign of joy

Noel... 6. Natale 9. Christmas

noeud... 3. bow 4. knot

nog... 3. peg, pin 5. block 6. eggnog, noggin 8. treenail 9. brickwork

nogada... 10. pecan candy

nogal... 5. pecan

noggin... 3. cup, mug 4. head, pate

noise... 3. din, pop, rap 4. bang, boom, klop, roar, rout 5. blare, blast, bruit, chang, clang, click, rumor, sound 6. clamor, outcry, racket, report, strife, uproar 7. brattle, chortle, discord, quarrel, rapping 9. shoutings

noise (pert to)...
ghost.. 11. poltergeist
harsh.. 4. bray 7. stridor 9. caterwaul
respiration.. 4. rale
rustling.. 5. swish
Scotch.. 5. chang
water.. 5. plash 6. ripple, splash
whirring.. 4. burr

noised... 6. dinned 7. rumored 8. reported

noisemaker... 4. horn 5. siren 6. rattle 7. clacker, whistle 8. whiz–bang

noisome... 3. bad 4. foul 5. fetid, nasty 7. harmful, noxious 8. stinking 9. offensive 10. malodorous, pernicious 11. destructive, unwholesome 12. insalubrious

noisy... 4. loud 7. blatant 8. brawling, clattery 9. clamorous, turbulent 10. blustering, boisterous, vociferous 12. obstreperous, rattley–bang

nom... 4. name

nomad... 4. arab 5. gypsy 6. roamer, Romany 7. Bedouin, Saracen, scenite, zingaro 8. wanderer

nomadic... 9. itinerant

nomarchy (Gr)... 4. nome 8. province 10. department

nom de plume... 7. pen name 9. pseudonym

nomen... 4. gens, name 7. agnomen 8. cognomen 9. praenomen

nomenclature... 4. name 5. onymy 8. glossary, onymatic, register 10. dictionary, Latin names, vocabulary 11. designation, terminology

nominal... 3. par 6. unreal 7. not real, titular, topical 8. so–called

nominal recognizance (law)... 3. Doe

nonage... 6. neanic 8. immature, minority, pupilage, youthful

nonary... 9. nine group 10. base of

nine 11. group of nine

nonbeliever... 5. pagan 7. atheist, heathen, infidel 8. agnostic 11. disbeliever 12. non–Christian

nonce... 3. now 8. meantime 11. temporarily

nonchalant... 4. cool 6. casual 8. careless 10. insouciant 11. indifferent, unconcerned 13. imperturbable

noncompliance... 7. refusal 12. disobedience 13. recalcitrance

non compos mentis... 7. unsound 8. demented, deranged 11. disoriented

nonconformist... 7. heretic, sectary 8. objector, recusant 9. dissenter, protester

nondescript... 11. exceptional 13. indescribable 14. indeterminable

none... 2. no 4. nary 5. nones, no one 6. nobody, not any, not one 10. nobody else

nonentity... 7. a nobody, nullity 8. nihility, nonbeing 9. res nihili 11. nothingness 12. nonexistence

nonessential... 8. needless 9. extrinsic 10. adiaphoron, incidental, irrelevant 11. superfluous 12. adventitious

non licit... 8. unlawful

non–Mahometan... 5. Kafir 6. giaour 9. non–Moslem

nonmetallic... 4. spar 5. argon, boron 6. carbon, helium, iodine, oxygen 7. bromine 8. chlorine, nitrogen

nonpareil... 4. type 7. paragon 8. nonesuch, peerless 9. unrivaled 11. unsurpassed 14. painted bunting

nonplus... 4. stop 5. blank, stump 6. baffle, puzzle, thwart 7. mystify, perplex 8. quandary

nonproductive... 6. barren 7. sterile 9. fruitless

nonprofessional... 3. ham, lay 4. laic 5. laity 7. amateur 10. apprentice

nonsense... 3. bah 4. bosh, bunk, tosh 5. folly, stite 6. drivel, humbug, jargon 7. blarney, foolery, trifles, twaddle 8. falderal, flimflam, trumpery 9. absurdity, frivolity, poppycock, senseless, silliness 10. balderdash, tomfoolery, triviality 11. monkeyshine 12. fiddle–dee–dee

nonsense verse... 9. amphigory (amphigouri), rigmarole

non tanto (Mus)... 9. non troppo, not as much

noodle... 4. fool, head 5. brain, ninny 9. blockhead, simpleton 12. stupid person

nook... 4. cant, cove 5. angle, herne, niche 6. corner, cranny, recess 7. crevice 10. promontory

noon... 6. midday, summit 8. meridian, noontide 9. ninth hour 11. noon of night (poet)

noonday rest... 6. siesta

noose... 3. tie 4. bond, hang, loop 5. snare 6. circle, halter 7. laniard (lanyard) 12. hangman's rope

Nootka... 3. Aht, dog 6. Indian

norati... 5. noise 6. gossip

Norbertine... 12. Premonstrant
Nordic... 8. Germanic
　　12. Scandinavian
norie... 9. cormorant
norm... 4. rule, type 5. model, norma
　　7. average, measure, pattern
　　8. standard, template
norma... 4. rule 5. gauge, model
　　6. square 7. pattern 8. standard,
　　template 13. constellation
normal... 3. par 4. just, mean, sane
　　5. usual 6. common 7. average,
　　logical, natural, orderly, regular, typical
　　8. everyday, ordinary 9. customary
Norman... 6. French 7. crimson
　　8. Northman 10. Romanesque
　　17. conquest of England (1066)
Normandy...
　　beach.. 5. Omaha
　　capital.. 4. Caen 5. Rouen (old)
　　city.. 5. Havre 6. Dieppe 7. Alençon
　　9. Cherbourg
　　conqueror.. 5. Rollo 8. William I
　　governed by.. 6. France (1940)
　　Viking duke (anc).. 5. Rollo
Norn (Teut Myth)... 4. Urth, Wyrd
　　5. Skuld 9. Verthandi
Norse... 9. Norwegian
　　12. Scandinavian
Norse (pert to)...
　　abode of gods.. 6. Asgard 8. Valhalla
　　alphabet.. 6. runics
　　ash tree, universe.. 10. Yddgrasill
　　bard.. 5. scald (skald) 7. sagaman
　　collected songs, myths.. 4. Edda
　　demon (Fire).. 4. Surt (Surtr)
　　earth.. 7. Midgard
　　epic.. 4. saga
　　explorer.. 11. Leif Ericson
　　first man.. 4. Askr
　　giant.. 4. Loki, Ymir (Ymer) 5. Jotun
　　6. Fafnir
　　horse.. 8. Brimfaxi 9. Skinfaksi
　　horse (Odin's).. 10. Yggdrasill
　　king.. 4. Atli
　　language (old).. 9. Icelandic
　　maidens (Odin's).. 8. Valkyrie
　　man.. 8. Northman
　　monster.. 6. kraken 7. Midgard
　　patron saint.. 4. Olaf
　　poem.. 4. rune
　　toast.. 5. skoal
　　warrior.. 8. berserker
　　watchdog (Hel's).. 4. Garm (Garmr)
　　wolf.. 6. Fenrir
Norse goddess of...
　　death, underworld.. 3. Hel, Ran
　　fate.. 4. Norn, Urth, Wyrd
　　flowers.. 5. Nanna
　　giantess.. 4. Nott
　　love, beauty.. 5. Freya
　　peace, healing.. 3. Eir
　　sky.. 5. Frigg (Frigga)
Norse God of...
　　day.. 3. Dag
　　evil.. 4. Loki
　　fertility.. 4. Frey (Freyr) 6. Njorth
　　(Njord)
　　giants.. 4. Ymir
　　justice.. 4. Frey 7. Forseti
　　light.. 6. Balder
　　night.. 4. Nott

　　poetry.. 4. Odin 5. Bragi
　　primeval (the world).. 4. Ymir (Ymer)
　　sea.. 5. Aegir
　　thunder.. 4. Thor
　　war, wisdom.. 4. Odin (Wodin)
　　watchfulness.. 8. Heimdall
Norse gods, chief... 3. Tyr (Tiu)
　　4. Frey, Jarl, Loki, Odin (Othin,
　　Wodin), Thor (Donar), Vali, Ymir
　　5. Aesir (group) 6. Balder, Njorth
　　7. Asynjur (group), Forseti
　　8. Heimdall
North (far)... 6. Arctic
North Africa... see also *Africa*
　　country.. 7. Algeria, Tunisia
　　fruit.. 3. fig 4. date
　　people.. 4. Moor 6. Berber, Hamite,
　　Libyan
　　port.. 4. Sfax
North America... see also *America*
　　Indian blanket.. 6. stroud
　　mountain, highest.. 8. McKinley
　　orchid.. 8. arethusa
　　owl.. 7. wapacut
　　rail.. 4. sora
　　reindeer.. 7. caribou
　　river, longest.. 5. Yukon 8. Missouri
　　11. Mississippi
　　snake.. 5. adder
North Atlantic (pert to)...
　　cape.. 5. Sable
　　island.. 7. Britain, Iceland, Ireland
　　9. Greenland, Manhattan
　　sea gull.. 4. skua
North Carolina...
　　cape.. 4. Fear 7. Lookout 8. Hatteras
　　capital.. 7. Raleigh
　　city.. 6. Durham 9. Asheville
　　explorer.. 6. De Soto 9. Verrazano
　　famed person.. 12. Virginia Dare
　　16. Sir Walter Raleigh
　　first flight.. 9. Kitty Hawk
　　mountain.. 10. Mt Mitchell
　　pine.. 8. loblolly
　　river.. 3. Tar 5. Neuse 6. Peedee
　　(Yadkin)
　　State admission.. 7. Twelfth
　　State bird.. 8. cardinal
　　State flower.. 7. dogwood
　　State motto.. 14. Esse Quam Videri
　　20. To Be Rather Than To Seem
　　State nickname.. 7. Tarheel 8. Old
　　North
North Dakota...
　　capital.. 8. Bismarck
　　city.. 5. Fargo, Minot
　　fort.. 6. Mandan 7. Lincoln
　　11. Abercrombie
　　historic site.. 24. International Peace
　　Garden
　　mountain.. 10. White Butte
　　reservoir.. 8. Garrison
　　State admission.. 8. Fortieth (or
　　Thirty–ninth)
　　State bird.. 10. meadowlark
　　State flower.. 11. prairie rose
　　State nickname.. 5. Sioux
　　11. Flickertail
northeaster... 4. gale, wind 5. storm
Northern... 6. boreal 11. hyperborean
　　13. septentrional
Northern constellation... 3. Cor

9. Andromeda
northernmost world (inhabitable)...
   5. Thule 9. Trondheim
North Pole... 10. boreal pole
North Sea... 6. Baltic, German
North Sea arm... 8. Kattegat
   9. Skagerrak (Skager–Rak)
North Sea canal... 4. Kiel
North Star... 7. Polaris 8. Cynosure,
   lodestar (loadstar), polestar
north wind... 6. Boreas
   10. tramontane
Norway... see also *Norwegian*
  capital.. 4. Oslo 11. Christiania (old)
  city.. 6. Bergen 7. Drammen
    9. Trondheim
  county.. 5. fylke
  inlet.. 5. fiord (fjord)
  mountain.. 6. Kjolen
  parliament.. 8. Storting (Storthing)
  patron saint.. 4. Olaf (Olaus)
  phenomenon.. 11. midnight sun
    14. Northern Lights
  plateau.. 5. fjeld
  river.. 2. Oi 4. Tana 7. Glommen
Norwegian (pert to)...
  bird.. 4. rype 9. ptarmigan
  cart.. 11. stolkjaerre
  dance.. 7. halling
  duck.. 7. widgeon
  embroidery.. 9. hardanger
  goblin.. 5. Nisse 6. kobold
  guardian spirit.. 6. fylgja 8. hamingja
  haddock.. 8. rosefish
  language.. 5. Norse 8. Rigsmaal
    9. Landsmaal
  liquor.. 7. akevitt
  sea monster.. 6. kraken
  tales.. 4. Edda
Norwegian people...
  author, explorer.. 8. Sverdrup
  composer.. 5. Grieg
  dramatist.. 5. Ibsen
  explorer.. 6. Nansen (Nobel Prize)
  king.. 6. Harold (The Fairhaired)
    15. Harold Hardraade
  philologist.. 5. Assen
  raiders.. 7. Vikings
  saint.. 4. Olaf (Olaus)
  violinist.. 7. Ole Bull
  zoologist.. 4. Sars
nose... 3. neb, pry 4. conk, prow
   5. nasus, scent, smell, snout
   6. meddle, muzzle, nuzzle 8. olfactor
   9. detective, proboscis
   11. investigate
nose (pert to)...
  ailment.. 6. coryza 8. rhinitis
  bees, birds.. 4. lore 5. lorum
  bleeding.. 9. epistaxis
  cartilage.. 6. septum
  glasses.. 8. pince–nez
  large.. 6. nasute
  muscle.. 7. nasalis
  opening.. 5. naris (nares, pl) 7. nostril
  partition.. 5. vomer
  plug.. 12. rhineurynter
  relating to.. 5. nasal 6. narial, rhinal
  snub.. 6. simous
  surgery.. 11. rhinoplasty
noseband (bridle)... 6. misrol
nosegay... 4. posy 7. bouquet,

perfume 9. fragrance 10. frangipani
(tree)
nosocomium... 8. hospital
nosography, nosology *(science of)*...
   7. disease
nostalgia... 8. yearning 11. wistfulness
   12. homesickness 14. sentimentality
nostology *(study of)*... 8. senility
   10. geriatrics 11. gerontology
Nostradamus... 4. seer 7. prophet
   10. astrologer
nostril... 5. naris (nares, pl) 6. narial
   9. olfactory
nostril–shaped... 8. nariform
nosy... 5. nasal 6. prying 7. curious
   8. fragrant 10. malodorous
   11. inquisitive
Nosy, Old (nickname)... 16. Duke of
  Wellington
not (pert to)...
  any.. 2. no 4. nane, nary, none
    7. no trace
  at all.. 5. nohow 6. nowise
  easy.. 7. labored
  either.. 7. neither
  feral.. 4. tame
  harmed.. 9. unscathed
  having a will.. 9. intestate
  hollow.. 5. solid
  in motion.. 5. fixed 6. stable, static
    7. stabile 10. stationary
  in the least.. 6. nowhit
  moral.. 6. amoral 7. immoral
  open (fruit).. 11. indehiscent
  prefix.. 2. il, im, in, ir, un 3. non
  professional.. 4. laic 7. amateur
  qualified.. 5. unfit
  running (stream).. 8. stagnant
  separable.. 11. indivisible
  settled.. 4. moot
  subjugated.. 7. unbowed
  suitable.. 5. inept
  the same.. 5. other 9. different
  to know.. 5. unken 10. unfamiliar
notable... 6. famous 8. historic
   9. celebrity, important, memorable,
   notorious 10. noteworthy, remarkable
   13. distinguished, extraordinary
notandum... 4. note 5. entry
   10. memorandum
notary... 5. notar 8. attestor,
  notebook, official 9. scrivener
   12. notary public, stenographer
notation... 4. memo, note 5. entry
   7. comment, marking 9. etymology
   10. annotation
notator... 5. noter 8. recorder
   9. annotator
notch... 3. gap, jap 4. dent, dint,
  kerf, nick, nock 5. cleft, crena, score
   6. defile, dentil (Her), indent
   7. passage 8. undercut 9. indenture
   11. indentation
notched bar (door)... 4. risp
notched opening (Anat)... 5. hilum
note... 2. ut 3. jot 4. chit, heed,
  mark, memo, sign, sole, song, tone,
  tune 5. breve, gloss, sound, token
   6. billet, notice, postil, record,
  remark, report 7. apostil (apostille),
  comment, epistle 8. dispatch,
  eminence, indicate, marginal,

scholium 9. character 10. annotation, importance, indication, memorandum, reputation 11. certificate, observation
note (pert to)...
death sound.. 4. mort
explanatory.. 5. gloss 8. scholium
half.. 5. minim
high.. 3. alt, E la
marginal.. 6. postil 7. apostil (apostille)
musical.. 5. breve 6. ecbole 7. punctus
stem of.. 5. filum
notebook... 6. street 7. estreat 8. ratebook 10. adversaria, memorandum
noted... 4. seen 5. famed 6. famous, marked 7. eminent, notable 8. far–famed, renowned 9. distingué, prominent, well–known 10. celebrated
notes... 5. duole 6. strain 7. tiralee 11. solmization
nothing... 3. nil, nox 4. luke, rien, void, zero 5. nihil 6. naught, nichil, nought, trifle 7. a nobody 9. nonentity 11. empty–handed 12. nonexistence
nothing doing... 4. calm 6. hushed, no dice, no soap, placid 7. I refuse 9. by no means, God forbid, quiescent
notice... 2. ad 3. see 4. heed, idea, mark, mind, news, note, sign 5. blurb, edict, quote 6. advice, espial, notion, regard, remark 7. affiche, mention, observe, warning 8. bulletin, citation 9. attention 10. commentary 11. information, observation 12. announcement, intelligence 13. advertisement
notice (pert to)...
advance.. 8. ballyhoo
death.. 4. obit 8. obituary
marriage.. 4. bans 5. banns
notify... 4. cite, page, tell, warn 6. inform, remind 7. apprise, declare, publish 8. announce
notion... 4. idea, view, whim 5. freit 6. belief, theory, vagary 7. caprice, impulse, opinion 9. intention 10. conception, denotation, knickknack 11. supposition
notionable... 8. fanciful 9. whimsical
notional... 6. unreal 9. imaginary, visionary, whimsical
notions... 5. goods, wares 11. commodities, merchandise
notoriety... 4. fame, plug 5. éclat 8. ballyhoo 9. limelight, publicity, spotlight
notorious... 5. known, noted 6. arrant, famous, notour 8. flagrant, infamous, talked of 10. recognized 11. conspicuous
notorious character... 5. James (Jesse) 7. Cochise, Younger 8. Geronimo, Jennings, Murietta 9. Jack Ketch, Wyatt Earp 11. Billy the Kid, Poncho Villa, Sitting Bull 12. Calamity Jane 13. John Dillinger 14. Wild Bill Hickok
notum... 4. back

notus... 4. back (comb form)
notwithstanding... 3. but, yet 5. still 6. mauger (maugre), though 7. despite, however 8. although 9. in spite of 12. nevertheless
nought, naught... 3. bad, nil 4. zero 5. wrong 7. nothing, useless 9. worthless
noughty... 3. bad 9. worthless
noumenal... 4. real 5. ontal (opp of phenomenal)
noun... 7. subject
noun (pert to)...
gender, common.. 7. epicene
indeclinable.. 6. aptote
irregular.. 5. pecus 11. heteroclite
suffix.. 2. et, ia 3. ent, ery, ier, ion, ior, ist, ite 4. ence
verbal.. 6. gerund
nourish... 4. feed, grow 5. nurse 6. foster, suckle, supply 7. support, sustain 9. cultivate 13. promote growth
nourishing... 6. alible 8. nutrient 9. nutritive 10. alimentary
nourishment... 3. aid 4. food 5. manna, meats 7. aliment, pabulum 9. nutriment, nutrition 10. sustenance 13. nutritiveness 14. nutritiousness
nous... 4. mind 8. ready wit 9. intellect 11. world spirit
Nova... 4. star
Nova Scotia...
bay.. 5. Fundy 10. Chedabucto
cape.. 5. Canso
capital.. 7. Halifax
greens.. 11. sea plantain
island.. 10. Cape Breton
lake, salt.. 7. Bras d'Or
native.. 7. Acadian 8. Bluenose
poetic name.. 6. Acadia (Acadie)
settlement, first.. 9. Port Royal
novel... 3. new 4. book, rare 5. fresh, story 7. fiction, romance, strange, unusual 8. original
novelty... 3. fad 7. newness 9. freshness 10. innovation, recentness 11. originality
novice... 3. nun 4. puny, tyro (tiro) 5. chela, rooky 6. tyrone 7. amateur, convert, learner 8. beginner, freshman, initiate, neophyte, newcomer 9. fledgling, greenhorn, postulant 10. apprentice, catechumen 11. abecedarian 13. alphabetarian
novitiate... 6. novice 9. probation 14. apprenticeship
now... 3. noo 4. here 6. at once 7. present 8. at present, forthwith, instantly 10. very lately 12. at this moment
nowhere... 5. limbo 6. absent 7. no place 8. oblivion 9. nowhither 11. nonexistent, not anywhere, nullibicity
nowhere else... 5. there
nowise... 8. not at all
Nox (pert to)...
brother.. 6. Erebus
daughter.. 10. Hesperides
goddess (Rom).. 5. Night

husband .. **5.** Chaos
noxious ... **4.** evil **5.** nasty, yucky (sl)
6. nocent, odious **7.** baneful, harmful,
hurtful, noisome **9.** injurious,
miasmatic **10.** corruptive, pernicious
11. destructive, unwholesome
12. insalubrious
nozzle ... **3.** tew **4.** nose, vent
5. giant, snout **6.** nuzzle, outlet,
tuyère **7.** conduit **9.** sprinkler
nuance ... **5.** shade **9.** gradation,
variation **10.** refinement
nub ... **4.** gist, knob, knot, knub, lump,
neck, snag **9.** main point
12. protuberance
Nubia (pert to) ...
afterglow .. **14.** second twilight
animal .. **4.** goat **5.** horse
autonym .. **6.** Berber **7.** Barabra
harp .. **5.** nanga
tribe .. **4.** Nuba
nubia ... **4.** wrap **5.** cloud
nucha ... **4.** nape, neck
nuclear complex ... **7.** Oedipus
nuclear energy (terms) ... **4.** mass
6. fusion, ionize **7.** fission, neutron,
reactor, tokamak **8.** hydrogen,
meltdown
nuclear network fiber ... **5.** linin
nucleus ... **4.** core **5.** cadre, focus,
umbra **6.** center, kernel **8.** rudiment
nude ... **4.** bare **5.** color, naked
6. Season (color) **7.** denuded
8. stripped, undraped **9.** unadorned,
unclothed, undressed
nudge ... **3.** jog, nog **4.** knub, lump,
poke, prod, push **5.** block, elbow
6. jostle, remind, signal
nudibranch ... **7.** mollusk
nugatory ... **4.** vain **7.** invalid, trivial
8. trifling **9.** worthless
11. ineffectual
nuisance ... **4.** bane, bore, harm, hurt,
pest **6.** injury **9.** annoyance
nuit ... **5.** night
null ... **4.** void **6.** vacant **7.** invalid
8. nugatory **11.** nonexistent
13. inefficacious, insignificant
nullifidian ... **7.** skeptic **9.** nullibist,
skeptical **10.** unbeliever
11. disbeliever
nullify ... **4.** undo, void **5.** annul
6. cancel, negate **7.** abolish, destroy
8. abrogate **10.** counteract, neutralize
numb ... **6.** clumsy, freeze, stupid,
torpid **8.** benumbed, deadened,
helpless **9.** apathetic, incapable,
rigescent **10.** insensible
12. anesthetized
number ... **3.** sum **5.** count, digit, limit
7. integer, numeral **8.** quantity
9. aggregate, enumerate
10. complement **11.** information
number (pert to) ...
added .. **6.** encore
again .. **10.** renumerate
by tens .. **7.** decimal
cardinal .. **7.** primary (one, two)
consecutively .. **5.** folio
copies (printed) .. **7.** edition
describable .. **6.** scalar
irrational .. **4.** surd

least whole .. **4.** unit
lucky .. **5.** seven
many .. **4.** herd **6.** myriad **7.** several
9. multitude **12.** considerable
ordinal .. **5.** first **6.** second (etc)
third power .. **4.** cube
votes .. **4.** poll
whole .. **7.** integer
numbles, nombles ... **6.** umbles
7. inwards **8.** entrails
numbness ... **6.** torpor **10.** rigescence
numeral ... **5.** Roman **6.** Arabic, figure
9. character
numerous ... **4.** lots, many **7.** copious,
crowded **8.** abundant, measured,
thronged **9.** plentiful
Numidia (pert to) ...
city .. **5.** Hippo
crane .. **10.** demoiselle
language (written) .. **5.** Punic **6.** Tuareg
7. Hamitic
modern kingdom .. **7.** Algeria
numskull ... **4.** dolt, nerd **5.** dunce
nun ... **4.** moth, smew **5.** Clare
(Franciscan), Vesta **6.** monial, pigeon,
sister **8.** titmouse, votaress
9. priestess **13.** Lady of Loretto
nun bird ... **6.** Monasa **8.** puffbird
nunciate ... **9.** announcer, messenger
nuncio ... **6.** legate **8.** delegate
9. messenger **11.** internuncio
nuncupate ... **7.** declare **8.** dedicate,
inscribe, proclaim **9.** designate
nuncupative ... **4.** oral **9.** unwritten
(will) **11.** designative
nun headdress ... **6.** wimple
nunnari root ... **12.** sarsaparilla
nunnery ... **5.** abbey **7.** convent
8. cloister
nunnery head ... **6.** abbess
nunni ... **7.** blesbok (blesbuck)
8. antelope
Nuphar ... **12.** spatterdocks **16.** yellow
pond lilies
nuptial ... **6.** bridal **7.** marital
9. connubial **11.** matrimonial
nurse ... **4.** amah, ayah, feed, rear, tend
5. bonne, mammy **6.** caress, suckle
7. care for, cherish, nourish, nurture,
nutrice **9.** nursemaid
nursed ... **3.** fed **6.** tended **7.** cradled,
suckled **8.** nurtured **9.** nourished
nursery ... **6.** crèche, school **7.** day
care (center)
nurse shark ... **4.** gata
nurture ... **3.** aid **4.** feed, rear
5. nurse **6.** foster **7.** care for,
cherish **8.** breeding, training
9. education, encourage, nutriment
nut ... **4.** anta, kola (cola) **5.** acorn,
betel, pecan, piñon **6.** almond, Brazil,
cashew, litchi, peanut, walnut
7. filbert, hickory, maranon
8. beechnut, chestnut **9.** butternut
nut (pert to) ...
bearing .. **10.** nuciferous
brown .. **5.** hazel **6.** walnut
8. chestnut
coal .. **10.** anthracite
collectively .. **4.** food **5.** shack
9. beechnuts
confection .. **8.** marzipan

cracker . . **4.** crow
eating . . **10.** nucivorous
  11. nuciphagous
edible part . . **6.** kernel
grass . . **5.** sedge
Med . . **4.** kola **5.** bichy **9.** gourounut
odd . . **9.** eccentric
palm . . **5.** betel, lichi **7.** coconut
ref to . . **5.** nucal
shell . . **4.** case, hull **6.** trifle
Nut (pert to) . . .
consort of . . **3.** Geb
daughter . . **4.** Isis **8.** Nephthys
goddess of . . **5.** earth
son . . **2.** Ra
nutation . . . **3.** nod **7.** nodding
nuthatch . . . **4.** bird **5.** sitta **6.** xenops
  8. titmouse **9.** nutpecker
nutmeg . . . **4.** mace **5.** drupe **6.** beaver
  (color)
nutmeg (pert to) . . .
bird, finch . . **5.** cowry **10.** weaverbird
family . . **13.** Myristicaceae
tree . . **6.** camara
Nutmeg State . . . **11.** Connecticut
nutpecker . . . **8.** nuthatch
nut quad . . . **6.** en quad
nutria . . . **3.** fur **5.** grège **10.** beaverlike
nutria fur bearer . . . **5.** coypu
nutrice . . . **5.** nurse
nutriment . . . **4.** food **7.** aliment,
  pabulum **9.** nutrition **11.** nourishment
nutritious . . . **9.** alimental
  10. alimentary, nourishing
nuts . . . **4.** food, mast **5.** shack
  9. beechnuts
nutty . . . **4.** gaga, zest **5.** queer, smart,
  spicy **7.** amorous, piquant
  10. unbalanced **11.** fascinating
  14. cracker–brained
nuzzle . . . **5.** nurse **6.** burrow, cuddle,
  foster, nestle **7.** cherish **8.** make
  snug
nyctalopia . . . **14.** night blindness

nye . . . **4.** eyas, nest, nide **5.** brood
nymph . . . **4.** nais **5.** deity, dryad,
  naiad, oread, siren, sylph **6.** Nereid
  7. Oceanid **9.** hamadryad
nymph (pert to) . . .
Arcadian . . **4.** Syrinx
beloved of Narcissus . . **4.** Echo
color . . **4.** pink
Cretan . . **8.** Cynosura
fountain, river . . **4.** nais **5.** naiad
  6. Egeria
German legend . . **7.** Lorelei
Greek . . **4.** Echo **6.** Daphne
  8. Arethusa
Hesperides (one of) . . **5.** Aegle
  7. Hespera
hills, mountain . . **5.** oread
laurel tree . . **6.** Daphne
Messina Strait . . **6.** Scylla
Mohamm paradise . . **5.** houri
monster . . **6.** Scylla
Mt Ida . . **6.** Oenone
ocean . . **5.** siren **6.** Nereid **7.** Galatea,
  Oceanid **10.** Callirrhoe
pursued by Apollo . . **6.** Daphne, Syrinx
  8. Arethusa
Queen . . **3.** Mab
sea bird . . **6.** Scylla
tree . . **5.** Dryad **9.** Hamadryad
water . . **5.** Naiad **6.** Undine **7.** Hydriad
woods . . **5.** Dryad **8.** Arethusa
  9. Hamadryad
young . . **7.** nymphet
Nymphaea . . . **8.** Castalia **11.** water
  lilies
nymphs . . . **10.** Atlantides, Hesperides
nystagmus . . . **14.** eyeball disease
Nyx, Nox (pert to) . . .
daughter . . **4.** Eris
father . . **5.** Chaos
goddess of . . **5.** Night
mother of . . **11.** Day and Night
Nzambi . . . **7.** goddess (Afr) **11.** earth
  mother

O
Q

O

O (pert to) . . .
interjection . . **11.** exclamation
letter . . **5.** tenth
mathematics . . **4.** zero **6.** cipher
pref (family) . . **5.** Irish
oaf . . . **4.** boor, dolt, lout **5.** idiot,
  ouphe, yokel **9.** blockhead, simpleton
  10. changeling
oafish . . . **6.** simple, stupid
oak . . . **4.** club **5.** brave, color, oaken,
  stout **6.** strong **7.** Quercus
  8. hardness, strength **13.** artificial fly
oak (pert to) . . .
apple . . **4.** gall **10.** she–oak cone
beauty . . **4.** moth
California . . **5.** roble **6.** encina

comb form . . **6.** querci
evergreen . . **4.** holm, ilex **5.** holly
family . . **8.** Fagaceae
fern . . **8.** polypody
fruit . . **5.** acorn **6.** camata
fungus . . **10.** armillaria
gall . . **8.** oak apple
Jerusalem . . **7.** ambrose
kinds . . **3.** bur, red **5.** black, white
  6. ground, poison, willow
  8. chestnut **10.** canyon live
plantation . . **9.** quercetum
resembling . . **9.** roboreous
tannin . . **7.** quercic **9.** quercinic
thicket . . **9.** chaparral
Turkey . . **6.** cerris

web.. 10. cockchafer
young.. 8. flittern
oam... 5. steam 7. warm air
Oannes (Bab)... 5. deity (part man, part fish)
oar... 3. row 5. blade, remus, rower, scull 6. paddle, propel 7. oarsman
oar (pert to)...
  blade.. 4. palm, peel
  feather.. 5. remex
  fulcrum, lock.. 5. pivot, thole
  lop.. 6. rabbit
  shaft.. 4. loom
  shaped.. 7. remiped 8. remiform
oars (pert to)...
  collective.. 6. oarage, sculls
  one bank.. 7. unireme
  reverse.. 6. sheave
  three banks.. 7. trireme
  two banks.. 6. bireme
oasis... 3. ojo 4. wadi (wady) 5. Gafsa 6. Dakhla 11. fertile spot
oast... 4. kiln, oven
oat (pert to)...
  cake.. 5. caper
  ear (Old World).. 4. bird 7. wagtail
  fowl.. 11. snow bunting
  genus.. 5. Avena 6. oathay
  grass.. 4. ulla 9. chaparral
  husks.. 5. shood (shude)
  like.. 10. avenaceous
  rent (paid as).. 7. avenage
oath... 3. God 4. aith, drat, egad 5. bedad, curse 6. pledge 7. serment 9. affidavit, holy smoke, profanity 10. deposition 11. affirmation
Obadiah (Bib)... 6. Quaker 7. prophet
obbligato... 8. required 13. accompaniment, indispensable
obduction... 7. autopsy 8. covering
obdurate... 4. firm, hard 5. rough, stony 6. mulish, rugged 7. adamant, callous 8. stubborn 9. heartless, obstinate, unbending, unfeeling 10. impenitent, inflexible, insensible, unyielding 11. hardhearted, intractable
obedient... 6. docile 7. duteous, dutiful, orderly 8. amenable, yielding 9. attentive, compliant 10. submissive 11. conformable
obeisance... 3. bow 5. binge, congé 6. curtsy, fealty, homage 9. deference 10. respectful 14. obsequiousness
obeisance, to make... 3. bow 6. congee, curtsy, salaam
obelisk... 5. pylon 6. guglia (guglio), needle, obelus, pillar 16. Cleopatra's Needle
Oberon (pert to)...
  Astron... 9. satellite
  character of.. 11. Shakespeare
  classic.. 4. poem 5. opera
  husband of.. 7. Titania
  Myth.. 13. King of Fairies
obese... 3. fat 5. puffy, pursy, squab, stout 6. fleshy, turgid 8. liparous 9. corpulent
obey... 3. ear 4. hear, mind 5. yield 6. comply, submit

obfuscate... 3. dim 6. darken, opaque 7. confuse, perplex 8. bewilder
obi... 4. sash 6. girdle
obit... 4. rest 5. death 6. notice 7. decease, release 8. obituary 9. obsequies 10. necrologue 11. Requiem Mass 12. mortuary roll
obiter... 9. in passing 12. incidentally
obiter dictum... 7. opinion (of judge)
object... 3. aim, end 4. goal, hulk 5. cavil, demur, scoff, thing 6. appose, expose, motive, oppose 7. article, grammar, protest, purpose 9. intention
object (pert to)...
  bulky.. 4. hulk
  circular.. 7. trundle
  cloudlike.. 6. nebula
  illustrative.. 6. realia (pl)
  rare.. 5. curio 7. antique
  rational.. 8. noumenon
  sacred.. 4. Urim 7. Thummim
  small.. 4. mite
object for...
  devotion, worship.. 4. icon, idol 5. totem 6. fetish
  dread.. 5. bogey (bogie) 6. goblin 8. the Devil
  going and coming.. 6. errand
  greed.. 5. lucre, money 6. wealth
  knowledge.. 7. scibile
objection... 3. bar 5. cavil 7. protest, quarrel 8. demurrer, obstacle 9. exception 11. disapproval
objectionable... 9. offensive 11. exceptional, inexpedient 13. uncommendable
objective... 3. aim, end 4. goal 6. motive, target 7. purpose
objector, conscientious... 6. conchy
objects (Bib)... 4. Urim 7. Thummim
objects (floating)... 7. flotsam
objurgate... 5. abuse, chide, scold 6. rebuke 7. reprove, upbraid 9. reprimand
oblate... 5. oblat 7. devoted 9. dedicated, flattened (opp of prolate)
obligated... 5. bound 6. in debt 7. obliged 8. beholden 9. obstringe
obligation... 3. tie, vow 4. bond, debt, duty, oath, onus 7. promise 8. civility, contract 9. agreement, necessity 10. compulsion 11. obstriction
obligatory... 7. binding 8. imposing, required 9. mandatory, necessary 10. compulsory
oblige... 4. bind, pawn 5. favor 6. compel, engage 7. gratify 8. obligate 9. constrain, obstringe 11. accommodate
obliged... 7. favored 8. beholden, grateful 9. duty bound
obliging... 4. kind 7. helpful 9. agreeable, courteous, indulgent 11. complaisant, considerate 13. accommodating
oblique... 4. cant, skew 5. bevel, slant, slope 7. obscure, scalene 8. inclined, perverse, sidelong, sidewise, sinister, slanting

9. underhand 10. circuitous,
collateral, transverse 12. disingenuous
oblique angle... 5. acute 6. obtuse
obliquely... 4. skew 6. aslant
7. askance 8. sideways, sidewise
9. on the bias 10. slantingly
obliterate... 4. blot, dele 5. erase
6. cancel, delete, efface, sponge
7. expunge
obliteration... 6. rasure 7. erasure
8. deletion 10. extinction
oblivion... 7. nirvana, silence
9. unfeeling 13. forgetfulness
15. unconsciousness
oblivion, producing... 8. nepenthe
oblivion, river of... 5. Lethe
oblivious... 6. asleep 8. heedless
9. forgetful, unfeeling 10. abstracted
11. unconscious
oblong... 8. elliptic 9. elongated
11. rectangular 12. quadrangular
obloquy... 5. abuse 6. infamy
7. calumny 9. criticism
11. malediction 12. reprehension
obnoxious... 4. vile 5. nasty
6. odious, rancid 7. hateful
8. amenable, infamous, terrible
9. offensive 13. objectionable
oboe... 4. reed 5. shawm (anc)
7. hautboy, musette 8. schalmei
(schalmey) 9. chalumeau
obscuration... 7. eclipse 9. darkening,
vagueness
obscure... 3. dim, fog 4. dark, hazy,
slur 5. bedim, blind, mirky, misty,
murky 6. cloudy, darken, delude,
mystic, opaque, remote 7. becloud,
conceal, eclipse, shadowy, unknown
8. darkling, formless, nameless,
nubilous, obstruse, oversile (obs)
9. enigmatic, undefined
10. indistinct, unrenowned
obscurity... 3. fog 5. gloom
7. dimness, opacity, unknown
8. darkness 9. nonentity, vagueness
12. formlessness 13. imperspicuous
14. insignificancy, uncomprehended
obsecrate... 7. beseech, entreat
10. supplicate
obsequies... 5. wakes 8. funerals
9. last rites
obsequious... 5. slick 6. abject
7. devoted, dutiful, fawning, servile,
slavish 8. cringing, funereal,
obedient, toadying 9. attentive,
compliant 11. subservient
observance... 3. act 4. form, rite
6. custom 8. behavior, ceremony,
practice 9. attention, deference,
sacrament, vigilance 10. conformity
11. celebration
observant... 7. careful, heedful, mindful
8. faithful, vigilant, watchful
9. attentive, regardant, regardful
observation... 4. idea 6. espial, remark
7. opinion 9. attention
observatory... 4. Lick 6. Yerkes
7. lookout, Palomar 8. Mt Wilson
11. planetarium
observe... 2. lo! 3. eye, see, spy
4. espy, heed, keep, nark, note,
obey, tout 6. behold, notice, remark

7. conform, examine, witness
8. preserve 9. celebrate, solemnize
observed, to be... 8. notandum
10. memorandum
observer... 4. eyer, nark 7. aviator,
student, witness 8. beholder,
informer, looker–on, onlooker
9. spectator 11. stool pigeon
obsess... 5. beset, haunt 6. harass
7. bewitch, possess 8. demonize
9. influence, preoccupy
obsession... 5. mania 8. impelled
11. bewitchment 13. spirit control
obsignate... 4. seal 5. stamp 6. ratify
obsolete... 3. old 5. passé 6. effete
7. archaic, disused, effaced, outworn,
worn out 9. out of date
10. antiquated 12. old–fashioned
obstacle... 3. dam 4. snag 6. hurdle
9. hindrance 10. difficulty,
impediment 11. obstruction
obstetrician... 6. doctor
10. accoucheur
obstetrix... 7. midwife
obstinate... 3. set 5. balky, tough
6. dogged, mulish, sullen 7. willful
8. perverse, stubborn 9. pigheaded
10. determined, headstrong,
self–willed 11. opinionated
obstreperous... 5. noisy 6. unruly
7. blatant 9. clamorous, turbulent
10. vociferous 11. disobedient
12. ungovernable
obstruct... 3. bar, dam, dit 4. clog,
ditt, stop 5. beset, block, check,
choke, delay 6. arrest, hamper,
oppose, stop up 7. occlude
9. barricade, embarrass, interfere,
interrupt
obstruction... 3. ban, dam 4. clog,
reef, snag 7. barrier 8. obstacle
9. hindrance 10. difficulty, filibuster,
impediment 11. retardation
obtain... 3. buy, eke, get, win
4. earn, fang, gain 5. fetch, reach
6. attain, derive, elicit, secure
7. achieve, acquire, capture, prevail,
procure, receive
obtain (pert to)...
by intimidation.. 9. blackmail
by threats.. 6. extort
control of.. 6. corner 8. overcome
equivalent.. 6. recoup
obtest... 6. beg for 7. beseech
10. supplicate
obtrude... 5. eject, expel 6. impose
7. intrude
obtrusive... 7. forward, pushing
9. intrusive, officious
obtund... 4. dull 5. blunt, quell
6. deaden 8. moderate
obtuse... 4. dull 5. blunt, crass, dense
6. stupid 9. unfeeling 11. insensitive
obvelation... 7. veiling 10. concealing
obverse... 5. front 8. converse
10. complement 11. counterpart
obviate... 7. head off, rule out
8. preclude 9. forestall 10. anticipate
obvious... 5. clear, gross, plain
7. evident, patient 8. apparent,
distinct, manifest, palpable
11. conspicuous, open and shut

obvolute ... 7. twisted 9. contorted, convolute 11. overlapping
occasion ... 4. sele, time 5. cause, event, nonce 6. excuse, motive 7. pretext 8. ceremony, exigency, function, incident 9. condition, happening 11. opportunity 12. circumstance
occasional ... 3. odd 4. orra 5. stray 6. casual 10. incidental, infrequent
occasionally ... 7. at times 9. sometimes 10. now and then 11. at intervals 12. sporadically
occasive ... 8. westward 10. setting sun
Occident ... 4. West 6. sunset 17. Western Hemisphere (opp of Orient)
Occidental ... 6. ponent 7. The West, Western 9. Hesperian
occiput ... 10. back of head 11. back of skull
occlude ... 3. dam 4. shut 5. close 6. shut up 8. obstruct
occult ... 5. magic 6. hidden, mystic 7. alchemy, cryptic 8. esoteric 9. concealed, recondite 10. mysterious, necromancy 11. supernormal 12. supernatural
occultation ... 4. gone, lost 7. eclipse 11. concealment
occultism ... 6. cabala 7. mystery
occult science ... 9. esoterics
occupant ... 6. inmate, tenant 10. inhabitant
occupation ... 3. job 4. call, note, work 5. hobby, trade 6. career, tenure 7. calling, pursuit 8. business, vocation 9. avocation 10. employment, habitation, possession, profession 11. engrossment
occupied ... 3. sat 4. busy, held 6. filled 7. engaged 8. employed, pervaded 9. engrossed, inhabited
occupy ... 3. use 4. fill, hold 6. employ, engage, expend, invest 7. engross, inhabit, oversit, pervade, possess 8. interest
occur ... 4. come, fall, meet 5. clash 6. appear, befall, betide, happen
occurrence ... 3. hap 5. event 8. incident, presence, scenario 9. existence, happening 10. appearance 11. eventuality 12. circumstance
occurring (pert to) ...
after death .. 10. posthumous
at nightfall .. 9. acronical
often .. 8. frequent 10. frequently
ocean ... 3. sea 4. brim, deep, main 5. brine 6. depths, pelago 8. great sea
ocean (pert to) ...
approach .. 7. sea gate
bottom .. 3. bed
crop cultivation .. 11. mariculture
deep .. 7. bathyal
deepest, lowest .. 5. hadal 8. bathybic 12. bathypelagic
division .. 6. Arctic, Indian 7. Pacific 8. Atlantic 9. Antarctic

floating matter .. 5. algae 7. flotsam
geography .. 12. oceanography
mammal .. 4. seal 5. whale
on (the ocean) .. 4. asea
periodic motion .. 4. tide
person .. 8. aquanaut, oceanaut 9. skin diver 10. scuba diver
ref to .. 7. pelagic 9. Neptunian
route .. 4. lane
sealing .. 7. pelagic
vessel .. 6. Sealab 9. submarine 10. bathyscaph 11. bathysphere
Oceania, Oceanica ... 9. Melanesia, Polynesia 10. Micronesia 12. Pacific lands
Oceanids (Gr Myth, pert to) ...
father .. 7. Oceanus
mother .. 6. Tethys
nymphs .. 13. three thousand
Oceanus (Gr Myth, per to) ...
children .. 5. Doris 8. Eurynome (goddess), Oceanids
god of .. 6. rivers
wife .. 6. Tethys
ocellus ... 3. eye 6. stemma 7. eyespot
ocelot ... 3. cat 7. leopard
ocher, ochre (pert to) ...
red .. 5. tiver 7. almagra 8. hematite 9. faded rose
yellow .. 3. sil 7. Chinese 8. limonite 9. ochrolite
ochlocracy ... 7. mob rule
ochlophobia (fear of) ... 6. crowds
ocotillo ... 5. shrub 10. candlewood
ocracy ... 9. group rule
octad ... 5. eight (group)
octaemeron ... 12. eight–day fast
octagon ... 8. octangle 11. eight angles
octahedron ... 10. eight faces
octameter ... 8. octapody 9. eight feet
octarchy ... 11. rule by eight
octastich ... 6. octave 10. eight lines 11. eight verses
Octateuch (Old Test) ... 10. Eight Books (1st)
octave ... 4. utas 5. eight 6. eighth 8. wine cask 10. eight notes
Octavia (pert to) ...
sister of .. 8. Augustus
wife of .. 10. Mark Antony
Octavian ... 7. Library (Rome's 1st) 16. committee of eight (one of)
octet, octette ... 7. huitain 12. group of eight
October (pert to) ...
bird .. 8. bobolink
birthstone .. 4. opal 5. beryl
Club .. 9. political
drink .. 3. ale
month .. 5. tenth
octogenarian ... 13. eighty–year–old
octopod ... 9. eight arms, eight legs
Octopoda (Roder) ... 8. mollusks (8–armed) 9. argonauts, octopuses
octopus ... 5. poulp (poulpe)
octroi, octroy ... 3. tax 9. privilege 10. concession
ocular ... 3. eye (pert to) 5. optic, sight 6. visual 10. ophthalmic
oculus ... 3. eye 14. Corona Borealis

odd... 4. orra, rare 5. droll, extra, outré, queer 6. uneven, unique 7. azygous, bizarre, strange, unequal, unusual 8. unpaired 9. eccentric, remaining, unmatched 10. occasional

oddity... 9. queerness 11. peculiarity, singularity 12. eccentricity, idiosyncrasy

odds... 6. gamble 7. dispute, quarrel 8. gambling, variance 9. advantage 10. difference, dissension, inequality 11. probability 12. disagreement 13. probabilities

odds and ends... 4. orts 6. refuse, scraps 7. mixture, remains 8. remnants 10. miscellany

ode... 4. like (suff), poem 5. psalm 8. canticle, serenata

ode (type)... 7. Lesbian, regular 8. Horatian, Pindaric 9. irregular

odeon... 4. hall 7. gallery, theater

Odin (pert to)...
attendants.. 9. Valkyries
god of.. 3. war 6. poetry, wisdom
hall.. 8. Valhalla
horse.. 8. Sleipner
son.. 4. Tyre, Vali 6. Balder
Teutonic name.. 5. Woden
wife.. 5. Frigg

odious... 4. foul, vile 5. nasty 7. hateful 8. infamous, terrible

odium... 6. hatred, infamy 9. antipathy 10. abhorrence, opprobrium 11. detestation

odontist... 7. dentist

odontology *(science of)*... 5. teeth 9. dentistry

odor, odour... 4. fume, funk, nose 5. aroma, fetor, nidor, scent, smell 6. flavor 7. essence, malodor, perfume 9. fragrance, redolence

odor, meat cooking... 5. fumet (fumette)

odorous... 8. aromatic, fragrant, redolent, smelling

Odysseus (pert to)...
chieftain.. 9. Trojan War
dog.. 5. Argos
father.. 7. Laertes
hero of.. 10. The Odyssey (Homer)
king of.. 6. Ithaca (Gr)
magic herb.. 4. moly
modern name.. 7. Ulysses
wife.. 8. Penelope

oecist... 9. colonizer

oecodomic... 13. architectural

Oedipus (pert to)...
daughter.. 8. Antigone
father.. 5. Laius (King of Thebes)
mother.. 7. Jocasta

oeno (comb form)... 4. wine

oenomancy... 12. wine prophecy

oenophilist... 9. wine lover

oenopoetic... 10. wine making

oestrus... 4. fury 5. sting 6. desire, frenzy 7. impulse 8. stimulus

of... 2. in, on 4. over, upon, with 5. about, avent 10. indication

of (pert to)...
a chamber.. 7. cameral
a class (related).. 7. generic
a father.. 6. agnate

a flock.. 6. gregal
a forefather.. 9. ancestral
a grandfather.. 4. aval
all.. 3. ava
a mother.. 7. cognate
an epoch.. 4. eral
an order.. 7. ordinal
a wife.. 7. uxorial
common gender.. 7. epicene
each.. 3. ana
earth.. 4. geal
equal value.. 10. comparable
French.. 2. du 3. des
great importance.. 7. capital 9. momentous
high standing.. 8. sterling
little importance.. 5. petty 7. trivial
morning.. 5. matin 7. matinal
New Stone Age.. 9. Neolithic
no avail.. 6. futile
nostrils.. 6. narine
old age.. 8. gerontal
planet's path.. 7. orbital
recent times.. 6. lately 9. latter–day
reign.. 6. regnal
river banks.. 8. riparian
same family.. 7. cognate, germane
sound.. 5. tonal
summer.. 7. estival
tears.. 8. lacrimal
the country.. 5. rural
the mouth.. 4. oral
the third degree.. 7. cubical
the throat.. 5. gular
the tongue.. 7. glossal
the wrist.. 6. carpal
this day.. 9. hodiernal
thread color.. 7. ficelle
winter.. 6. hiemal
yore.. 5. olden

off... 3. ill 4. agee, away, doff 5. aside 6. begone, insane, remote 7. distant, tainted 9. dissonant, erroneous, imperfect, right–hand 10. unemployed

offal... 5. filth 6. ordure, refuse 7. carrion, garbage, rubbish

offbeat... 14. unconventional

off–color... 6. risqué 7. dubious 8. inferior

offend... 3. cag, sin, vex 4. miff 5. anger, annoy, pique, wound 6. assail, insult, revolt 7. affront, do wrong, mortify 9. displease

offender... 6. sinner 8. criminal 9. wrongdoer 10. malefactor 12. transgressor

offense... 3. sin 5. crime, delit, fault, grief, malum 6. delict, felony, insult 7. outrage, umbrage 8. trespass 9. indignity 10. resentment 11. delinquency, misdemeanor, stellionate

offensive... 4. foul, ugly 6. attack, odious, ribald, vulgar 7. abusive, eyesore, fulsome, harmful, obscene 8. invading, shocking 9. assailant, attacking, insulting, obnoxious, repugnant, revolting 10. aggressive, malodorous, scurrilous 11. approbrious, displeasing, distasteful 12. disagreeable

13. transgressive

offer . . . 3. bid 6. adduce, tender
7. proffer, propine, propose
8. immolate, overture 9. ultimatum
offered for sale . . . 6. vended
9. auctioned
offering . . . 4. gift 6. corban
7. deodate, present 8. oblation
9. sacrifice
offering resistance . . . 8. renitent
offhand . . . 8. careless, informal,
slapdash 9. extempore, impromptu
10. carelessly, nonchalant
11. extemporary 12. nonchalantly
15. autoschediastic
office . . . 4. duty, post, rite, wike (obs)
5. place, trust 7. station
8. ceremony, function, position
9. situation 11. appointment
office (pert to) . . .
chief . . 7. manager
divine . . 9. akolouthia
for the dead . . 7. trental
holder . . 8. placeman
of a datary (Roman Curia) . . 7. dataria
of a ruler . . 7. regency
relinquish (to) . . 5. demit
third hour . . 6. tierce
officer . . . 6. tindal 7. bailiff, command,
conduct, general, manager, marshal,
sheriff 8. adjutant, avigator, director
9. constable, policeman, president
officer (pert to) . . .
assistant . . 4. aide
Brit Royal Guard . . 4. exon
chief executive . . 3. dey 4. czar
5. mayor 7. emperor, monarch,
premier 8. governor 9. president
10. chancellor
church . . 5. elder 6. sexton
civil law . . 6. notary, police 7. bailiff,
marshal, sheriff 9. constable,
policeman 10. magistrate
club . . 7. steward
corrupt . . 7. grafter
despotic . . 6. satrap
diplomatic . . 7. attaché
Jewish Relig . . 6. parnas
King's stables . . 6. avener
monastic . . 5. prior
naval . . 6. ensign, yeoman
parish . . 6. beadle, bedral
ship's . . 9. boatswain (boson)
weights, measures . . 6. sealer
official . . . 6. formal 9. authentic
10. functional 13. authoritative
official (pert to) . . .
command . . 5. edict
despotic . . 6. satrap
game . . 5. judge 6. umpire 7. referee
government . . 10. bureaucrat
insurance . . 7. actuary 8. adjuster
itinerant (Hist) . . 6. missus
mark . . 5. stamp
order (RCCh) . . 8. rescript
proclamation . . 5. ukase 6. decree
record . . 5. actum
state . . 8. governor 9. secretary
officious . . . 4. cool, pert 5. saucy
6. formal 8. arrogant, impudent,
official 9. pragmatic 10. meddlesome
11. efficacious, impertinent,

pragmatical 12. contemptuous
officiousness . . . 10. pragmatism
offing . . . 10. background
offshoot . . . 3. rod 5. scion 6. branch,
member 8. addition 9. by–product
10. descendant 12. organization
offspring . . . 3. son 4. brat, seed
5. child, fruit, issue, sprig 6. origin,
result 7. produce, product, progeny
8. fountain 9. posterity
10. descendant
oficina . . . 5. works 6. office 7. factory
10. laboratory
often . . . 3. oft 9. many times
10. frequently, repeatedly 11. over
and over 13. time after time
ogdoad . . . 5. eight 10. eight group
ogee . . . 4. gula 5. talon 7. molding
9. cyma recta 11. cyma reversa
ogle . . . 3. eye 4. gaze, leer 5. stare
7. examine
Ogpu . . . 8. Gay–Pay–Oo (Russ secret
service)
O Henry . . . 6. Porter (Wm Sydney)
Ohio . . .
capital . . 8. Columbus
city . . 5. Akron 6. Dayton, Toledo
9. Cleveland 10. Cincinnati
first settlement . . 8. Marietta
hero . . 12. Anthony Wayne (Gen)
lake . . 4. Erie
name meaning (Indian) . . 14. Beautiful
River
State admission . . 11. Seventeenth
State motto . . 27. With God All Things
are Possible
State nickname . . 7. Buckeye
oil . . . 3. ben, fat 4. balm, ghee
5. bribe, oleum 6. aceite, anoint,
asarum, grease, olanin 8. flattery,
medicate, painting 9. lubricant,
lubricate, petroleum 10. illuminant
oil (pert to) . . .
beetle . . 5. meloe
berry . . 5. olive
bird . . 8. guachare
cask . . 4. rier
class . . 5. fatty, fixed 6. animal
7. mineral 8. volatile 9. essential,
vegetable
cloth . . 8. linoleum
coal . . 8. photogen
comb form . . 2. ol 3. ole
fish . . 7. escolar
flask . . 4. olpe
gauge . . 9. oleometer
glands (birds) . . 9. uropygial
11. elaeodochon
lamp . . 7. lucigen
mineral . . 7. naphtha
plant . . 6. sesame 9. castor–oil
prefix . . 2. ol
rock . . 5. shale 9. limestone
seed . . 3. til (teel) 6. sesame
7. linseed 8. rapeseed 10. castor
bean, cottonseed
skin . . 5. sebum
stone . . 4. hone 9. whetstone
term . . 5. oleic
tree . . 4. eboe (ebo), tung 5. mahua
6. illupi 7. oil palm 9. candlenut,
castor–oil

tube .. **5.** vitta
whale .. **5.** sperm
oil of ...
  cloves .. **7.** eugenol
  myrcia .. **6.** bay oil
  orange blossoms .. **6.** neroil
  roses .. **4.** otto **5.** attar (atar)
  salt .. **7.** bittern
oils ... **10.** elaeoptene (elaeopten) (opp
  of stearoptene)
oily ... **3.** fat **4.** glib **5.** bland, oleic,
  suave **6.** olease, supple **7.** pinguid
  8. unctuous **9.** compliant, plausible
  10. flattering, oleaginous
  11. insinuating, subservient
  12. hypocritical
oily liquids ... **3.** tar **6.** cresol, octane
  7. aniline, picamar **8.** creosote
oily tissue ... **3.** fat
ointment ... **4.** balm, cere, lard, nard
  5. salve **6.** balsam, carron, cerate,
  ceroma, grease **7.** pomatum, unguent
  8. liniment **9.** spikenard, xeromyron
  10. petrolatum **11.** embrocation
Oise (France) ... **5.** Aisne (tributary),
  river **10.** department
Ojibway secret order ... **4.** mide
  (meda) **9.** midewiwin
ojo ... **5.** oasis
OK ... **6.** righto **7.** correct
Okinawa ...
  capital .. **4.** Naha
  island group (64) .. **6.** Ryukyu
  prefecture of .. **5.** Japan
Oklahoma ...
  capital .. **12.** Oklahoma City
  city .. **3.** Ada **4.** Enid **5.** Tulsa
  6. Lawton **8.** Muskogee
  9. Claremore **12.** Bartlesville
  Five Civilized Tribes .. **5.** Creek
  7. Choctaw **8.** Cherokee, Seminole
  9. Chickasaw
  lake .. **6.** Texoma
  migrant from .. **4.** Okie
  mountain .. **5.** Ozark **8.** Ouachita
  museum .. **6.** Indian **8.** Woolaroc
  native son (famed) .. **10.** Will Rogers
  old name .. **15.** Indian Territory
  State admission .. **11.** Thirty–third
  State bird .. **10.** flycatcher
  State flower .. **9.** mistletoe
  State motto .. **16.** Labor Omnia Vincit
  (Labor Conquers All)
  State nickname .. **6.** Sooner
okra ... **5.** bendy, gumbo **6.** mallow
old ... **3.** ald, eld **4.** aged **5.** anile
  6. infirm, senile **7.** ancient, antique,
  archaic **8.** obsolete **9.** doddering,
  senescent, venerable **10.** antiquated
old (pert to) ...
  age .. **6.** senile **7.** geratic **8.** gerontic,
  senility **10.** geriatrics (Med),
  senescence **11.** gerontology
  ancient (very) .. **7.** Ogygian
  billy, granny .. **5.** squaw
  fashioned .. **4.** fogy **7.** antique
  9. primitive **12.** conservative
  hat .. **5.** trite **9.** out–of–date
  maid .. **5.** prude **10.** fussbudget
  man .. **5.** elder, timer **6.** codger,
  gaffer, geezer, Nestor **8.** kangaroo
  10. fuddy–duddy

sailor .. **3.** tar **4.** salt
saying .. **3.** saw **5.** adage, maxim
time .. **3.** eld **4.** syne
woman .. **3.** hag **4.** fogy **5.** crone
  6. dotard, gammar
womanish .. **5.** anile **6.** senile
  10. effeminate
Old (pert to) ...
  Bailey .. **12.** English court
  Bay State .. **13.** Massachusetts
  Dominion .. **8.** Virginia
  Empire .. **4.** Maya
  English alphabet .. **10.** Anglo–Saxon
  Faithful .. **6.** geyser
  Franklin State .. **9.** Tennessee
  Gentleman Harry .. **5.** Devil
  Gooseberry .. **5.** Devil, Satan
  Glory .. **15.** Stars and Stripes
  Guard (Waterloo) .. **9.** Napoleon's
  Hickory .. **13.** Andrew Jackson
  Ironsides .. **15.** USS Constitution
  Kingdom .. **7.** Memphis (Egypt)
  Lady of Threadneedle Street ..
    13. Bank of England
  Line State .. **8.** Maryland
  Man of the Mountain .. **7.** Profile (The)
  Noll .. **14.** Oliver Cromwell
  North Church .. **12.** Christ Church
  North State .. **13.** North Carolina
  Rough and Ready .. **16.** (Gen) Zachary
    Taylor
  Serpent .. **5.** Satan
  Sod .. **4.** Erin **7.** Ireland
  Sol .. **3.** sun
  Stone Age .. **11.** Paleolithic
  Three Stars .. **8.** (Gen) Grant
  World .. **7.** Eastern
olden ... **6.** bygone
older ... **5.** elder **6.** senior **8.** ancestor
oldest ... **4.** dean **6.** eldest **7.** stalest
Old Testament (pert to) ...
  Books (number) .. **10.** Thirty–nine
  Elohim .. **3.** God (The Hexateuch)
  Hexateuch .. **13.** first Six Books
  Land of riches .. **5.** Ophir
  objects (sacred) .. **4.** Urim
    7. Thummim
  Pentateuch .. **10.** Law of Moses
    14. first Five Books
  writer .. **7.** Elohist (The Hexateuch)
Old World (pert to) ...
  ape .. **7.** Primate **10.** Catarrhina
  carnivore .. **5.** genet
  falcon .. **5.** saker
  herb .. **5.** tansy
  lizard .. **5.** Agama
  shrub .. **4.** Olax
oleaginous ... **4.** oily **5.** oleic
  8. unctuous
oleander ... **6.** Nerium
  11. rhododaphne **12.** rhododendron
oleoresin ... **5.** anime, elemi **6.** balsam
  7. copaiba
oleum ... **3.** oil
olfaction ... **7.** osmesis **8.** smelling
  12. sense of smell
olfactory organ ... **4.** nose **8.** olfactor
olid ... **4.** foul **5.** fetid **6.** rancid, smelly
  . malodorous **11.** strong smell
oligarchy ... **10.** rule by a few
olinda bug ... **6.** weevil
olio ... **4.** olla, stem **6.** medley

7. mixture 8. chowchow
9. burlesque, potpourri
10. collection, hodgepodge
11. olla–podrida
oliphant... 8. elephant 9. ivory horn
oliprance... 4. romp, show 7. jollity
11. merrymaking, ostentation
olive (pert to)...
branch.. 5. child, peace 6. symbol
(peace)
color.. 11. yellow–green
dun.. 3. fly (fishing)
enzyme.. 6. olease
family.. 8. Oleaceae
fly.. 3. dun 4. gnat 5. quill
gray.. 10. Scotch gray
gum.. 6. olivil
overripe.. 5. drupe
stuffed.. 6. pimola
true.. 4. Olea
wild.. 8. oleaster
yard.. 6. olivet
yellow.. 9. moss green 10. chartreuse
olla... 3. jug, pot 4. olio 8. palm leaf
(palmyra) 11. olla–podrida
olla–podrida... 4. hash, olio 6. medley
10. hodgepodge
oloroso... 6. sherry
olpe... 5. flask 8. oenochoë 11. wine
pitcher
olycook, olykoek... 7. cruller
8. doughnut
Olympia... 4. ship 7. capital (Wash)
8. heavenly 9. sanctuary (anc)
Olympiad... 14. four–year period
Olympian god... 4. Ares, Zeus
6. Apollo, Hermes 8. Dionysus,
Hercules, Poseidon 10. Hephaestus
Olympian goddess... 4. Hera
6. Athena, Hestia 7. Artemis,
Demeter 9. Aphrodite
Olympic cupbearer... 8. Ganymede
Olympic Games (pert to)...
honor of.. 4. Zeus
period.. 14. four years apart
revival site.. 6. Athens (1896)
site (first).. 4. Elis 7. Olympia
time of games.. 8. four days
Olympieion, Olympium... 6. temple
(Athens)
Olympus (Gr)... 3. sky 5. Mount
6. heaven 8. mountain
Olympus (Hind)... 4. Meru
Omaha... 4. city (Neb) 5. Sioux
6. Indian
Omar Khayyam (pert to)...
country.. 4. Iran 6. Persia
fish (fabled).. 3. mah
poem.. 8. Rubaiyat
omasum... 6. manyplies 10. psalterium
12. third stomach
ombro (comb form)... 4. rain
ombrometer... 9. rain gauge
omega... 3. end 4. last 5. final
6. letter (Gr)
omen... 4. bode, sign 5. abode, knell,
token 6. augury 7. auspice, portent,
presage 8. forebode, foreshow
9. abodement 10. divination
15. prognostication
omer... 5. ephah, sheaf 9. fifty days
(Passover to Pentecost)

ominous... 4. dour, trim 8. sinister
9. ferocious 10. inexorable,
portentous 12. inauspicious
omission... 4. want 5. caret, error
7. neglect 9. oversight
10. deficiency, leaving out
13. nonobservance
omission of end syllables...
7. apocope
omission of words... 8. ellipsis
omit... 4. dele, pass, skip 5. elide
6. delete, ignore 7. exclude
11. leave undone
omitting... 7. elision 9. excepting,
excluding 10. precluding
omneity... 7. allness
16. all–comprehensive
omnipotent... 6. divine 8. almighty
9. unequaled, unlimited
11. all–powerful
omniscient... 4. wise 6. divine
7. learned 10. all–knowing
omnitude... 7. allness 8. totality
12. universality
omnivorous... 6. greedy 9. all–eating
10. gluttonous
omoplate... 7. scapula
omphalos... 3. hut 4. knob 5. altar,
navel 6. center 9. umbilicus
on... 2. at 4. atop, upon 5. above,
ahead, along 6. toward 7. against,
forward 10. concerning
13. juxtaposition
On (Bib)... 7. Baalbek 8. holy city
10. Heliopolis (Egypt) 12. City of the
Sun
on (pert to)...
account of.. 3. for
all sides.. 5. about 6. around
and on.. 7. forever, tedious
9. tediously
behalf of.. 3. for
dit.. 5. rumor 6. report
going.. 7. forward 10. proceeding
grand scale.. 4. epic
hand.. 4. here 7. present 9. available
high.. 5. aloft
other side.. 4. over 6. across
sheltered side.. 4. alee
this side.. 3. cis (pref) 9. cisalpine
10. cismontane, cispontine
windward side.. 8. aweather
onager... 3. ass 5. kiang 8. catapult
once in a while... 9. erstwhile
10. now and then 12. occasionally
once upon a time... 6. one day
7. the past, time was 8. formerly
10. the long ago
Oncorhynchus... 6. salmon
ondoyant... 4. wavy (art)
one... 2. an, un 3. ace, ain, ein
4. unit 5. alone, unity, whole
6. person, single 9. unmarried
10. individual
one (pert to)...
after the other.. 8. serially, seriatim
12. successively
bearing heraldic arms.. 7. armiger
behind the other.. 6. tandem
born in serfdom.. 4. neif
bringing good luck.. 6. mascot
by one.. 6. apiece, singly 10. one at

a time 12. individually
comb form.. 3. uni 4. mono
curious.. 6. gossip 8. quidnunc
despondent in views.. 9. pessimist
fond of women.. 11. philogynist
footed.. 6. uniped
frantic for freedom..
    15. eleutheromaniac
gigantic in size.. 5. giant, titan
happy in views.. 8. optimist
horse.. 5. petty 6. little 8. inferior
    10. second–rate 13. insignificant
in a thousand.. 6. oddity 7. paragon,
    prodigy
in second childhood.. 6. dotard
instructed in secret system.. 5. epopt
    8. initiate
living on another.. 8. parasite
moving stealthily.. 7. prowler
sided.. 5. askew 7. partial
    10. prejudiced, unilateral
thousand.. 3. mil
time.. 7. quondam 8. formerly
undergoing change.. 6. mutant
oneberry... 9. hackberry
    14. partridgeberry
one devoted to...
deviltry.. 7. hellion
fast driving.. 4. jehu 7. speeder
indolence.. 10. daydreamer,
    lotus–eater
own opinion.. 5. bigot
physical feats.. 7. athlete
pursuit.. 3. ist (suff)
table delicacies.. 7. epicure
onefold... 6. simple, single 7. sincere
    9. guileless
onegite... 8. amethyst
Oneida... 6. Indian 8. Iroquois
    9. Community (NY)
oneiros... 5. dream
oneirotic... 6. dreams (pert to)
oneism... 6. egoism, monism
oneness... 5. union, unity 7. concord
    8. identity, sameness 9. agreement,
    aloneness, constancy 10. loneliness,
    singleness, uniformity, uniqueness
    11. singularity 13. undividedness
one of...
ancient race.. 4. Mede 7. Iberian
Buddhist precepts.. 6. nidana
Persian dynasty.. 8. Sassanid
religious sect.. 10. Anabaptist
the Bears.. 4. Ursa
the Greek Wise Men.. 6. Thales
the initiated.. 5. epopt
twins.. 5. gemel (Her)
onerous... 4. load 5. heavy 6. burden
    7. onerose 9. difficult, laborious,
    ponderous 10. burdensome,
    oppressive 12. impedimental
one versed in...
children's diseases.. 12. pediatrician
law.. 6. legist
literature.. 6. savant 9. literatus
memory.. 9. mnemonist
politics.. 9. statesman
religious law.. 8. canonist
resources, wealth.. 9. economist
one who...
absconds.. 6. eloper 8. decamper,

deserter
appropriates.. 9. pre–emptor
attacks.. 9. aggressor
believes in all religions.. 6. omnist
believes in personal God.. 5. deist
believes in self.. 9. solipsist
beseeches.. 7. pleader
brings meat to royal table.. 7. dapifer,
    steward
cherishes.. 8. fosterer
collects voluntary taxes.. 6. tither
conveys property.. 7. alienor
dies for a cause.. 6. martyr
differs.. 4. anti 9. dissenter, dissident
disowns.. 10. repudiator
displays learning.. 6. pedant
disposes by will.. 7. devisor
edits.. 7. reviser
feigns illness.. 10. malingerer
fights for cause.. 8. crusader
forsakes faith principles.. 8. apostate
frustrates a plan.. 7. marplot
gives up.. 9. abnegator
grants by deed.. 7. remiser
hates argument.. 10. misologist
hates people.. 11. misanthrope
holds office.. 2. in 9. incumbent
inculcates.. 7. infuser 9. instiller
inflicts retribution.. 7. nemesis
misuses authority.. 6. satrap
plunders.. 6. sacker 8. pillager
practises palmistry.. 11. chiromancer
prevents entrance.. 5. hajib
quarrels.. 5. rowdy
removes nuisance.. 6. abator
rules, manages.. 6. gerent
sells provisions to troops.. 6. sutler
shoots from ambush.. 6. sniper
sponges.. 6. cadger 8. parasite
stays.. 5. bider
summons spirits.. 8. evocator
testifies.. 8. deponent
transfers property.. 7. alienor
ongall... 5. onset 6. attack
onion... 3. set (bulbs) 4. boll, bulb,
    cepa, leek 5. chive, cibol, pearl,
    reeve 6. Allium 7. Bermuda, onionet,
    shallot 8. eschalot, rareripe, scallion
onkos (Gr)... 7. topknot
only... 4. just, lone, mere, sole
    5. chief 6. lonely, merely, simple,
    simply, single, singly, solely
    8. uniquely 11. exclusively
    13. companionless 14. above all
    others
onocentaur... 3. ape 5. demon
    (fabled)
onomasticon... 7. lexicon
    10. dictionary, vocabulary (Gr)
onomatology *(science of)*... 5. names
    11. terminology
onomatopoeic... 6. echoic 9. imitative
    (of natural sound)
onset, onslaught... 6. attack
    7. assault 11. rushing upon, setting
    upon
Ontario...
Bay.. 6. Hudson
capital.. 7. Toronto
city.. 6. Ottawa 7. Timmins
    8. Hamilton
lake.. 9. Great Lake (one of five)

province.. 6. Canada
river.. 6. Ottawa, Thames 7. Niagara
  10. St Lawrence
ontogeny... 9. evolution
ontology *(science of)*... 5. being
  7. reality
onus... 4. duty, load 6. burden, charge
  10. impediment, imposition,
  obligation
onus probandi... 13. burden of proof
onward, onwards... 5. ahead, forth
  6. future, moving 7. forward
  8. forwards, progress 9. in advance
onychauxis... 14. nail overgrowth
onyx... 6. nicolo (niccolo), tecali
ooid... 9. egg–shaped
oology *(science of)*... 8. bird eggs
oomancy *(divination by)*... 4. eggs
oont... 5. camel 13. beast of burden
oop... 4. join 5. unite
oopak, oopack... 3. tea (black)
oorial... 3. sha 5. sheep, urial
ooze... 3. bog 4. drip, leak, seep,
  sipe, soak 5. exude, marsh 6. be
  damp 7. leather 8. transude
  9. percolate
oozy... 4. miry 5. muddy, slimy
opah... 4. fish, soko 8. kingfish
  9. Lampridae
opal... 3. gem 4. blue 5. stone
  7. hyalite 10. pearliness
opal, variety of... 4. wood 5. black,
  noble, pitch, resin 6. common
  7. girasol, hyalite 8. menilite,
  precious 9. cacholong, geyserite,
  harlequin 10. chalcedony
opalescent... 6. pearly 7. opaline
  8. irisated 10. iridescent
opaque... 4. dark 6. obtuse, stupid
  7. obscure 8. eyeshade 10. not
  shining 13. unilluminated 14. not
  transparent
open... 3. ope 4. ajar, bare, free,
  undo 5. agape, begin, clear, frank,
  overt, plain, start, untie 6. candid,
  honest, patent, public, reveal, unbolt,
  unfold, unfurl, unlock, unseal, unstop,
  vacant 7. artless, evident, exposed,
  natural, obvious, sincere, unbosom,
  unclose 8. apparent, commence,
  disclose, expanded, initiate, patulous,
  revealed, unclosed, unfasten
  9. spreading, uncertain, uncovered,
  unfeigned 10. accessible, unreserved
  11. unprotected 12. questionable
open (pert to)...
acknowledgment.. 6. avowal
air.. 8. alfresco
and shut.. 7. assured, obvious
  11. prearranged
bursting.. 10. dehiscence
cabinet.. 7. étagère
country.. 5. veldt, weald
court.. 4. area 5. patio
door.. 6. policy 11. hospitality
eyed.. 7. curious 8. vigilant
  9. attentive, expectant
for discussion.. 4. moot
fully.. 4. wide 9. dehiscent, full–blown
land.. 4. moor 5. heath 6. desert,
  plains
out.. 6. deploy (Mil)

partly.. 3. mid 4. ajar
passage in forests.. 5. glade
to scorn.. 9. derisible
to view.. 5. overt
opening... 2. os 3. bay, gap 4. door,
  gate, hole, loop, pore, rift, slot, vent
  5. cleft, mouth, sinus, start
  6. breach, eyelet, hiatus, outlet,
  portal 7. display, foramen, initial,
  orifice, vacancy 8. aperture, fenestra,
  position 9. admission, beginning
  10. passageway, unfoldment
  11. entranceway, opportunity
opening (pert to)...
chess.. 6. gambit
ear.. 4. burr
enlarge.. 4. ream
from 3rd ventricle (Anat).. 4. pila
having.. 10. fenestrate
in a mold.. 6. ingate
minute.. 5. stoma
narrow.. 4. rima, slot 7. crevice
  9. stenopaic
nasal.. 4. nare
small.. 4. pore 5. chink 6. cranny,
  eyelet, lacuna 7. foramen, orifice,
  pinhole
wide (Bot).. 9. dehiscent
openings... 3. ora 7. stomata
openwork... 6. eyelet 7. Madeira,
  tracery 10. decoration
opera (pert to)...
comic (singer).. 5. buffa, buffo
  7. buffoon
glass.. 7. binocle 9. binocular,
  lorgnette
hat.. 5. crush, gibus 6. topper
kind.. 4. soap 5. horse 8. burletta
singer.. 4. bass, diva 5. buffa, buffo,
  tenor 7. buffoon, soprano 10. basso
  buffo, coloratura
solo.. 4. aria 5. scena
star.. 4. diva 10. prima donna
text.. 8. libretto
opera, composer... 5. Bizet, Gluck,
  Verdi 6. Glinka, Gounod, Handel,
  Hayden, Mozart, Wagner 7. Puccini,
  Rossini 9. Donizetti 11. Deems
  Taylor 14. Rimski–Korsakov (Korsakoff)
opera, drama... 4. Aida 5. Boris,
  Faust, Orfeo, Thais, Tosca
  6. Bohême, Carmen, Coq d'or,
  Daphne, Isolde 7. Alceste
  9. Lohengrin, Pagliacci, Rigoletto
  10. Magic Flute, Prince Igor,
  Tannhäuser 11. Don Giovanni, Il
  Travatore 13. Peter Ibbetson
  14. Tales of Hoffman 15. Hansel
  and Gretel, Madame Butterfly
  16. Marriage of Figaro
operation... 6. action, agency
  7. surgery 8. creation 9. influence
  11. functioning, transaction
operation, surgical... 5. major, minor
  6. trepan 8. excision 9. resection
  10. amputation, castration
  11. exploratory 12. appendectomy,
  hysterectomy 13. tonsillectomy
operative... 6. worker 7. artisan,
  working 8. mechanic 9. detective
operative, become... 5. inure (enure)
operator... 5. agent, quack 6. dealer,

worker 7. creator, handler, surgeon
10. mountebank, speculator
operculum (Bot)... 3. cap, lid
7. stopper 8. covering
operose... 4. busy 8. diligent
9. difficult, laborious 11. painstaking
Ophidia... 6. snakes 8. reptiles,
serpents 9. Serpentes
ophidian... 5. snake, viper 7. serpent
ophiolatry... 12. snake worship
ophthalmic... 6. ocular 7. optical
9. eye region
ophthalmology, science... 6. the eye
opiate... 4. drug, hemp, snow
5. opium 6. heroin 7. anodyne,
cocaine, hashish (hasheesh), soother
8. narcotic 9. analgesic, paregoric
11. somniferous 12. somnifacient
opine... 4. deem 5. judge, think
6. remark 7. opinion, suppose
10. conjecture
opinion... 4. idea, view 6. belief,
esteem, notion, report 7. feeling
8. judgment 9. sentiment
10. estimation, impression, ober
dictum, reputation
opinion (pert to)...
expert.. 9. expertise
expression, common.. 5. theme
expression, formal.. 4. vote
religious, unorthodox.. 6. heresy
opinions (pert to)...
collection.. 9. anthology, symposium
professed.. 5. credo
opium... 4. drug 8. narcotic
10. intoxicant
opium (pert to)...
concentrate.. 6. heroin
derivative (Chem).. 7. meconic
Egyptian.. 8. thebaine
extract.. 7. chandoo (chandu), codeine
8. morphine 9. narcotine
10. papaverine
overuse.. 8. opiumism
poppy seed.. 3. maw
source.. 5. poppy
tincture.. 9. paregoric
variety.. 6. Indian, Smyrna, Turkey
7. Chinese, Persian
opodeldoc... 7. plaster 8. liniment
opodidymus... 7. monster (two–headed)
opossum... 7. Marmosa 9. didelphid,
marsupial, phalanger
opossum (pert to)...
S America.. 5. quica 7. sarigue
variety.. 5. mouse, water, wooly
water.. 5. yapok (yapock)
wood.. 10. silver bell
opponent... 3. foe 4. anti 5. enemy,
rival 7. adverse 8. opposite
9. adversary, combatant
10. antagonist
opportune... 3. fit, pat 5. ready
6. timely 7. apropos 8. suitable
9. expedient, well–timed
10. convenient 11. appropriate
opportunist... 10. politician, vacillator
opportunity... 4. turn 6. chance
7. opening 8. occasion
12. circumstance 16. suitable
occasion
oppose... 3. pit 4. deny, face 5. fight,

rebel 6. expose, oppugn, refute,
resist 7. contest, exhibit, gainsay
8. confront 10. antagonize,
contradict, contravene, counteract
opposed... 3. met 4. anti, vied
5. coped 6. averse, pitted
7. adverse, fronted 8. contrary,
renitent, resisted 9. contested,
withstood 12. oppositional
opposed (pert to)...
against.. 6. pitted
lee.. 5. stoss
to change.. 7. die–hard
11. reactionary 12. conservative
to entad (inward).. 5. ectad
zenith.. 5. nadir
opposite... 5. polar 6. facing
7. adverse, antonym, hostile,
opposed, reverse 8. contrary,
converse 9. different, repugnant
10. opposition 12. antagonistic
13. contradictory 14. contrapositive
opposite (pert to)...
directly.. 10. antipodean
exact.. 8. antipode
in action, in nature.. 5. polar
7. inverse
prefix.. 6. contra
science.. 3. art
to spring tide.. 4. neap
opposition... 9. hostility, opponency
10. antagonism, antithesis, refutation,
resistance 11. contrariety, disapproval
13. contradiction
oppress... 4. rape 5. crush 6. burden,
harass, nither (Scot), ravish
7. depress, swelter 8. distress,
macerate, suppress 9. overpower,
overwhelm, persecute, tyrannize
10. extinguish
oppressive... 5. harsh 6. severe,
stuffy, sultry 7. onerous 8. rigorous
9. ponderous 10. burdensome,
depressing, tyrannical
oppressor... 4. czar (tsar), Nero
6. despot, tyrant 8. autocrat,
burdener 11. Simon Legree
opprobrious... 7. abusive 8. despised,
infamous 9. insulting, offensive
10. scurrilous 11. disgraceful
12. contumelious
opprobrium... 5. odium 6. infamy
8. disgrace 11. malediction
oppugn... 6. assail, oppose
10. controvert, counteract
oppugnant... 7. hostile, opposed
8. contrary 12. antagonistic
13. counteractive
Ops (pert to)...
called also.. 10. Ops Consiva
consort of.. 6. Consus, Saturn
Festival.. 6. Opalia
Greek counterpart.. 4. Rhea
Roman goddess of.. 7. Harvest
opsigamy... 14. old–age marriage
opt... 4. pick 5. elect 6. choose
11. make a choice
optic... 6. ocular, visual 11. optological
optical (pert to)...
device.. 9. stenopaic
glass.. 4. lens
illusion.. 6. mirage

instrument.. 5. prism 7. alidade,
reticle 9. eriometer, optometer
10. microscope
membrane.. 6. retina
organ.. 3. eye
optic defect... 6. myopia
optimistic... 4. rosy 7. hopeful,
roseate 8. cheerful, sanguine
9. expectant 10. auspicious
optimum... 4. best 7. maximum
13. most favorable
option... 6. choice, future (Finan)
7. refusal 8. free will 11. alternative
13. right to choose
optional... 8. elective 9. voluntary
10. permissive 13. not compulsory
opulence... 6. plenty, riches, wealth
9. abundance, affluence, amplitude,
profusion
opulent... 4. rich 6. lavish 7. profuse,
wealthy 8. abundant, affluent
9. luxuriant
opulus... 11. guelder–rose
13. cranberry tree
opus... 4. work 5. étude
10. embroidery, needlework
11. composition
oquassa... 5. trout
oracle... 4. seer 5. sibyl 6. Dodona,
medium, mentor 7. prophet, wise
man 8. Delphian (Delphic)
10. revelation
oracular... 4. wise 5. vatic (vatical)
9. prophetic 10. predictive
11. forecasting
orage... 5. storm 7. tempest
oral... 5. parol, vocal 6. spoken, verbal
10. not written 11. nuncupative
orang... 9. orangutan (orangutang)
orange (pert to)...
Bowl site.. 5. Miami
bird.. 7. tanager
color.. 5. ocher, peach 6. carrot
7. apricot 8. mandarin
flower oil.. 6. meroli
genus.. 6. Citrus
heraldry.. 5. tenné
kind.. 4. mock 5. hedge, navel,
Osage 8. bergamot, mandarin,
Valencia 9. tangerine
leaf.. 6. karamu
marigold.. 9. tangerine
membrane.. 4. zest
mock.. 7. seringa
seed.. 3. pip
Orangeman... 14. North Irelander
orangutan... 4. mias 5. orang, Pongo,
satyr, Simia
orate... 5. plead, speak, spiel
8. harangue
oration... 5. éloge 6. eulogy, prayer,
sermon, speech 7. lecture
8. encomium, petition 9. discourse
orator... 6. rhetor 7. speaker
9. perorator 10. petitioner
11. rhetorician, spellbinder
orator, famed... 5. Bryan (Wm
Jennings) 6. Cicero 9. Churchill
11. Demosthenes
oratory... 6. chapel 7. chantry
9. elocution, eloquence
orb... 3. eye, sun 4. ball, moon, star

5. earth, globe, world 6. bereft,
circle, planet, sphere 7. enclose
8. encircle, insignia, surround
orbed... 5. lunar, round
orbit... 4. path 5. globe, route
6. sphere 7. circuit 10. trajectory
orbit (pert to)...
cavity.. 9. eye socket
curve.. 10. trajectory
of a planet.. 7. ellipse
point.. 5. apsis
point, farthest.. 6. apogee
orc, Orca... 5. whale 7. grampus
orchestra (pert to)...
bells.. 12. glockenspiel
circle.. 7. parquet 8. parterre
small.. 11. symphonette
orchestra instrument group...
brass.. 4. horn, tuba 6. cornet
7. trumpet 8. trombone
percussion.. 4. drum 7. cymbals,
timpani (tympani) 8. triangle
strings.. 5. cello, viola 6. violin
10. contrabass 11. violoncello
wind.. 4. oboe 5. flute 7. bassoon
8. clarinet
orchid... 4. Disa 5. vanda 6. Ophrys
7. Listera, lycaste, pogonia
8. arethusa, Cattleya, Oncidium
9. cymbidium, puttyroot 10. letterleaf
orchid (pert to)...
appendage.. 8. caudicle
handsomest.. 4. Disa
largest.. 10. letterleaf
meal.. 5. salep
petal.. 8. labellum
tuber, root.. 5. salep 7. cullion
Orcus... 3. God (Rom) 5. Hades, Pluto
(Gr) 10. lower world
ordain... 4. plan 5. allot, enact, equip
6. decree 7. appoint, arrange,
command, destine, install 8. canonize
9. institute 10. predestine
ordeal... 4. gaff, test 5. trial
7. sorcery 8. judgment
10. experience (painful)
order... 3. bid 4. fiat, ordo, rank, rule,
sect, will 5. array, class, edict,
genus, money 6. cosmos, decree,
direct, enjoin, genera (pl), manage,
system 7. arrange, command,
dispose, mandate, prepare, verdict
8. regulate, sequence 9. condition,
procedure 10. injunction
11. arrangement
order (pert to)...
back.. 6. remand
connecting.. 6. in turn 8. seriatim
cosmic.. 3. tao 4. rita
for writ.. 7. precipe
good.. 6. eutaxy
grammar.. 5. taxis
judicial.. 4. fiat, writ 7. summons
proper.. 6. kilter
written.. 6. billet
Order, architecture... 5. Doric, Ionic
6. Tuscan 8. Etruscan 10. Corinthian
Order, association... 4. Club 5. Guild
7. DeMolay, Society, St Clare
8. Sodality, Sorority 9. The Garter,
Trappists 10. Fellowship, Fraternity,
Sisterhood 11. Brotherhood, Eastern

Star, Purple Heart 12. The Rising
Sun
ordered ... 4. bade, trim 7. regular
8. arranged, measured, ordained
9. regulated
orderly ... 4. neat, tidy, trim 7. regular,
uniform 8. obedient, peaceful
9. attendant, regularly, shipshape
10. methodical, systematic
order of ...
amphibians .. 5. Anura
aquatic animals .. 7. Cetacea
holy beings .. 9. hierarchy
insects .. 7. Diptera
mammals .. 8. Edentata, Primates
mites .. 6. acarid
the day .. 8. schedule 12. instructions
whales .. 4. Cete
ordinal ... 6. number, ritual, serial
10. succession 11. Book of Rules
(Eccl), categorical
ordinance ... 3. law 4. rite 5. bylaw,
edict 6. assize, decree 7. control,
statute 8. decretum 9. allotment,
direction, enactment, sacrament
10. management, regulation
ordinarily ... 7. plainly, usually
8. commonly 9. generally, naturally
11. customarily
ordinary ... 4. ruck, so–so 5. judge,
nomic, plain, prosy, usual
6. common, normal, tavern
7. average, natural, prosaic, vulgate
8. everyday, habitual, mediocre,
plebeian, workaday 9. of the Mass
10. table d'hôte
ordinate ... 6. ordain 7. appoint,
orderly, regular 8. moderate
9. harmonize 10. co–ordinate
ordination ... 5. order 11. appointment,
arrangement, disposition
12. organization
ordnance ... 4. guns 5. armor, orgue
7. petards, rabinet, weapons
8. armament, firearms, supplies
9. artillery, torpedoes
10. ammunition 14. apparatus belli
ordo ... 5. order 11. publication
ore ... 3. tin 4. gold, iron, lead, paco
5. brass, metal, ochre 6. copper,
silver, speiss 7. mercury, mineral,
seaweed, uranium 8. cinnabar,
tungsten 9. loadstone (lodestone)
11. quicksilver
ore (pert to) ...
box .. 6. sluice
deposit .. 4. lode, mine 7. bonanza
fuser .. 7. smelter
horizontal layer .. 5. stope
impure .. 6. speiss
iron .. 5. ocher 8. hematite
9. magnetite
lead .. 6. galena
loading platform .. 4. plat
machine separator .. 6. vanner
refuse .. 6. scoria 8. tailings
roller .. 9. edgestone
silver .. 5. noble (metal)
sluice .. 5. trunk
stirrer .. 5. dolly
tin .. 5. scove
trough .. 6. strake

vein .. 4. lode 5. scrin, stope
worthless .. 5. matte
oread ... 5. nymph 7. seamaid
Oregon ...
capital .. 5. Salem
caves .. 11. Marble Halls
city .. 6. Eugene 7. Astoria, Medford
8. Portland 12. Klamath Falls
crab apple .. 7. powitch
emigrant route .. 11. Oregon Trail
famed persons .. 4. Gray (Capt)
5. Astor, Clark, Lewis
Indian .. 5. Modoc 7. Chinook,
Klamath 8. Nez Percé
mountain .. 4. Hood 5. Coast
8. Cascades
native nickname .. 7. webfoot
river .. 5. Rogue 7. Klamath
8. Columbia 10. Willamette
State admission .. 11. Thirty–third
State motto .. 8. The Union
State nickname .. 6. Beaver
13. Sawdust Empire
wind .. 7. chinook
oremus ... 9. let us pray
Oreortyx ... 5. quail
Orestes (pert to) ...
father .. 9. Agamemnon
friend .. 7. Pylades
mother .. 12. Clytemnestra
sister .. 7. Electra
wife .. 8. Hermione
orf, orfe ... 3. ide 4. fish
orfevrerie ... 7. jewelry 9. gold plate
organ (pert to) ...
anatomy .. 3. ear, eye 4. lung, nose
5. brain, heart, liver 6. kidney,
syrinx, tongue, tonsil 7. viscera (pl)
bristlelike .. 4. seta
desk .. 7. console
fish .. 8. drumfish
honey–secreting .. 7. nectary
plant .. 5. stoma 7. tendril
motion .. 6. muscle
respiratory .. 4. lung
secretion .. 5. gland
spider's spinner .. 9. spinneret
stop (music) .. 8. register
tactile .. 6. feeler 8. tentacle
organic ... 5. state, vital 6. innate
8. inherent 9. organized
10. structural 11. fundamental
14. constitutional
organic (pert to) ...
compound .. 5. amine 6. enzyme,
ketone
disease .. 11. organopathy
memory .. 5. mneme
radical .. 5. ethyl
remains .. 5. azoic
soil .. 5. humus
organism (pert to) ...
bacterial .. 4. germ 7. microbe
body of .. 4. soma
elementary .. 5. monad
minute .. 5. spore 6. amoeba
pelagic .. 6. nekton
plant .. 5. spore
potential .. 7. idorgan
sea .. 6. nekton 7. benthos
8. plankton
type .. 5. plant 6. animal 9. vegetable

vegetable.. 4. tree 5. plant
organization... 4. bloc, sect, unit
  5. cadre, guild, party, setup
  6. empire 11. association,
  corporation 12. constitution
  13. establishment 14. classification
organized body... 5. corps, posse
organized matter... 5. fauna, flora
  6. living, nekton 7. animate, benthos
  8. plankton
organology, science... 10. phrenology
  13. splanchnology
organoscopy... 10. phrenology
orgueil... 5. pride 11. haughtiness
orgy... 4. lark, romp 5. binge, revel,
  rites (anc), spree 6. frolic, ritual,
  shindy 7. debauch, revelry, shindig,
  wassail 8. carousal 11. celebration,
  merrymaking
oribi... 7. bleebok, Ourebia 8. antelope
oriel... 3. bay 6. recess, window
  7. balcony, gallery, portion
  8. corridor 10. moucharaby
  11. meshrabiyeh (Moham)
orient... 4. dawn 7. eastern, shining,
  sunrise 8. oriental, pellucid
  11. resplendent
Orient... 4. Asia, East 6. Levant
oriental (pert to)...
  abode, gateway.. 3. dar
  animal.. 4. zebu
  archangel.. 5. Uriel
  beverage.. 6. arrack
  building.. 6. pagoda
  burden bearer.. 5. hamal
  cap (sheepskin).. 6. calpac (calpack)
  caravansary.. 4. khan 5. serai
  6. imaret
  carpet.. 4. kali
  carriage.. 10. jinrikisha (jinricksha)
  cart, wagon.. 5. araba
  chief.. 4. Khan 6. Mikado
  Christian.. 5. Uniat
  corn.. 4. para
  cosmetic.. 4. kohl
  council.. 5. Divan
  cymbals.. 4. zels
  deity.. 3. Bel
  destiny.. 6. Kismet
  disease.. 8. beriberi
  dish.. 4. rice 5. pilau (pilaw) 6. pilaff
  8. chop suey, chow mein
  drug.. 5. opium 6. heroin 7. hashish
  (hasheesh)
  drum.. 6. tom–tom
  dulcimer.. 6. santir
  fan.. 3. ogi
  food.. 4. rice 5. salep
  garment.. 3. aba 6. sarong
  guitar.. 5. sitar
  head cover.. 6. turban
  hospice.. 6. imaret
  inn.. 5. serai
  instrument (Mus).. 7. samisen
  laborer.. 6. coolie (cooly)
  leader.. 4. amir (ameer)
  liquor.. 4. sake, saki
  litter.. 5. dooly (doolie) 9. palanquin
  lute.. 3. tar
  maid.. 4. amah, ayah, eyah
  manservant.. 5. hamal 6. coolie
  marketplace.. 6. bazaar

monkey.. 7. macaque
nurse.. 4. amah, ayah (governess)
obeisance.. 6. salaam (salam)
pagoda.. 3. taa
people.. 4. Sere (anc) 5. Asian, Malay
  6. Indian 7. Chinese, Eastern, Tartars
  (Tatars) 8. Japanese
  10. Mohammedan
pipe.. 8. narghile
rice paste.. 3. ame
rug.. 8. sedjadeh 11. Baluchistan
ruler.. 4. Khan, Shah 5. sahib (saheb)
  6. caliph (calif), sultan
sabre.. 8. scimitar
sailor.. 6. lascar
sash.. 3. obi
tambourine.. 5. daira
taxi.. 7. ricksha (rickshaw)
  10. jinrikisha
trousers (women).. 9. shaksheer
vessel (sailing).. 4. dhow, saic
wagon.. 5. araba
warehouse.. 6. godown
wind.. 7. monsoon
worker.. 6. coolie (cooly)
orifice... 4. hole, lura, pore, vent
  5. inlet, mouth, porus, stoma
  6. outlet, porule 7. chimney,
  opening, ostiole 8. aperture,
  bunghole, spiracle
origin... 3. nee 4. rise, root, seed
  5. alpha, birth, cause, start
  6. nature, parent, source 7. genesis
  9. beginning, etymology, inception,
  parentage 10. inconabula, provenance
  11. provenience 12. commencement,
  fountainhead
original... 3. new 5. basic, first, novel
  6. fontal, native, primal, primer,
  unused 7. genuine, pattern, primary
  8. pristine 9. aborigine, beginning,
  inventive, primitive 10. inimitable
  11. fundamental, origination
  12. commencement
original copy... 6. ectype
originate... 4. coin, open, rise, stem
  5. arise, begin, breed, start
  6. author, create, derive, invent
  7. emanate, produce 8. generate,
  initiate 11. etymologize
originator... 5. cause, maker
  7. creator 8. inventor, producer
  9. contriver 10. discoverer
oriole... 5. pirol 6. golden, hooded,
  loriot, Mimeta 7. orchard
  8. Bullock's 9. Baltimore, Icteridae
Orion (pert to)...
  Astron.. 7. Dog Star 10. Canis Major
  11. Orion's Hound 13. constellation
  color.. 11. Holland blue
  Gr Myth.. 6. hunter
  Jacob's Staff.. 10. Yard and Ell
  13. Golden Yardarm
  slain by.. 7. Artemis
  star.. 5. Rigel
orison... 6. prayer
Orkney Islands, Scotland...
  capital.. 8. Kirkwall
  Firth.. 8. Pentland
  fishing grounds.. 4. haaf
  island, largest.. 6. Pomona
  President, Supreme Court.. 4. foud

stone tower (Prehist).. 5. broch
orle (Her)... 6. border, fillet, wreath
   7. bearing, chaplet 10. escutcheon
   (voided)
Orloff... 5. horse 7. diamond (Russ,
   194 3/4 carats)
orlop... 4. deck (lowest)
Ormazd (Pers)... 5. deity (supreme)
ormer... 7. abalone 8. ear shell
ornament... 4. ouch, semé 5. adorn,
   decor, gutta, honor 6. amulet,
   brooch, emboss, finery, sequin
   7. antefix 8. appliqué, decorate
   9. embellish 10. decoration
   13. embellishment
ornament (pert to)...
  apex.. 6. finial
  ball.. 6. pompon
  bell–shaped.. 9. clochette
  Bible.. 4. Urim
  boat–shaped.. 3. nef
  brilliant.. 4. gaud 5. spang 6. sequin,
   tinsel 7. spangle
  circular.. 7. rosette
  delicate.. 7. tracery
  diamond–shaped.. 11. epigonation
  dress.. 5. jabot 9. stomacher
   10. embroidery
  egg–shaped.. 3. ove
  hair, head.. 4. comb 5. tiara
   8. barrette
  indented.. 5. chase
  Japanese girdle.. 4. inro
  leaves and grapes.. 6. pampre
  magical.. 6. amulet
  mantel.. 7. bibelot, trinket
  pendant.. 6. bangle, tassel 7. earring
   9. lavaliere (lavalier)
  pretentious.. 6. rococo
  protuberant.. 4. boss
  raised design.. 7. brocade
  scroll–like.. 6. volute
  set of.. 6. parure
  setting in.. 5. inlay 7. emblema
  silverware.. 7. gadroon
  spiral.. 5. helix
  terminal.. 6. finial
  wall.. 6. plaque, sconce
ornamental (pert to)...
  bottle.. 8. decanter
  button.. 4. stud
  description.. 5. fancy 10. decorative
  lace edge.. 5. picot 7. tatting
  metal.. 6. niello
  raised.. 7. brocade
  stand.. 7. étagère
  vase.. 3. urn
ornamented... 6. chased, etched,
   tooled 8. engraved
ornate... 3. gay 5. fancy 6. florid,
   tawdry 7. adorned 9. decorated
ornery... 8. perverse, stubborn
   9. malicious 11. ill–tempered
ornithoid... 8. birdlike
ornithology *(study of)*... 5. birds
ornithon... 6. aviary
oro... 4. gold 5. money
Oro... 3. God (Tahiti)
oro (comb form)... 5. month, serum
   8. mountain
orology *(science of)*... 9. mountains
orotund... 7. pompous 9. bombastic

orp... 4. fret, weep
Orpheus (pert to)...
  astronomy.. 6. Cygnus
  eighteenth century.. 6. Handel
  father.. 6. Apollo
  mother.. 8. Calliope
  poet.. 8. Thracian
  reference.. 6. Orphic
  river.. 6. Hebrus
  wife.. 8. Eurydice
Orphic... 3. egg (Creation's) 5. hymns
   7. tablets (gold) 13. Book of the
   Dead (rites)
orphrey... 10. embroidery (gold)
orpit (Scot)... 7. fretful
orra... 3. odd 5. oddly 10. not
   matched, occasional, unemployed
   13. miscellaneous
ort... 3. end 4. bits 5. scrap
   6. refuse, scraps 7. remnant
   8. leavings, leftover
orthodox... 7. Trinity 8. accepted,
   approved, believer, standard
   9. canonical, customary
   12. conventional
Orthodox Moslem... 5. hanif
orthography... 8. spelling
ortolan... 7. bunting 8. bobolink, sora
   rail, wheatear
Oryx... 5. beisa 7. gazelle, gemsbok
   8. antelope, leucoryx
os... 4. bone 5. mouth, osker (Geol)
   7. opening
Osage... 5. river 6. Indian (Sioux)
   10. orange tree
Osaka, Japan... 7. capital
   10. prefecture
oscillate... 3. wag 4. rock, sway, vary
   5. swing, waver, weave 7. vibrate
   9. fluctuate
Oscines... 12. singing birds
oscitancy... 6. gaping 7. yawning
   8. dullness, lethargy 10. drowsiness
oscitant... 4. dull 6. drowsy, gaping,
   sleepy 7. yawning 8. careless,
   sluggish 9. apathetic
osculate... 4. buss, kiss
osculation... 4. kiss 7. contact, kissing
osier... 3. rod 4. wand 6. sallow,
   willow 7. dogwood
Osiris, Egypt (pert to)...
  brother.. 3. Set (Seth)
  crown.. 4. atef
  enemy.. 3. Set 7. brother
  father.. 3. Geb
  god.. 9. fertility 10. underworld
  god (Gr).. 8. Dionysus
  husband of.. 4. Isis
  king of.. 5. Egypt
  mother.. 3. Nut
  seat.. 6. Abydos
  son.. 5. Horus 6. Anubis
Osmanli... 4. Turk 8. language
osmesis... 8. smelling 9. olfaction
osmosis... 10. absorption
   12. infiltration
osprey... 4. hawk 7. feather (hat)
   8. fish hawk 9. ossifrage
   10. breakbones
ossature... 8. skeleton 9. framework
   (Arch)
osse... 4. dare 7. attempt, presage,

promise 8. prophecy
osseous... 4. bony, hard 10. ossiferous
ossifrage... 5. eagle 6. osprey
  11. lammergeier
ossuary... 3. urn 4. tomb
  10. depository 12. charnel house
  13. burial chamber
ostend... 6. reveal 7. exhibit
  8. manifest 11. demonstrate
ostensible... 5. shown 6. avowed
  7. alleged, seeming 8. apparent,
  declared, specious 9. exhibited,
  plausible, professed
ostent... 3. air 4. mien 5. token
  7. portent 10. appearance
ostentatious... 4. arty, vain 5. dashy
  6. sporty 7. pompous
  11. conspicuous, pretentious
ostiole... 4. pore 5. stoma 7. orifice
  8. aperture
ostler... 7. hostler 9. stableman
ostracize... 5. exile, expel 6. banish,
  deport 7. cast out, exclude
  9. extradite 10. expatriate
ostrich... 3. emu 4. Rhea 5. nandu
  8. Struthio 9. cassowary
ostrichlike... 11. struthiform
ostrich tail feather... 3. boo
Otaheite... 6. Tahiti
otalgia... 7. earache
Othello (pert to)...
  opera by.. 5. Verdi
  tragedy by.. 11. Shakespeare
  villain.. 4. Iago
  wife.. 9. Desdemona
other... 2. or 5. alter, ither 6. either,
  second 8. one of two 9. different
  10. additional
others... 7. the rest 9. remaining
otherwise... 2. or 5. alias, ossia, other
  6. or else 9. different 10. contrarily
  11. differently
Othman... 4. Turk 5. Osman 6. sultan
  7. Osmanli, Ottoman, Turkish
Othman's successor... 3. Ali
otiant... 4. idle 8. in repose
  10. unemployed
otiose... 4. idle 6. at ease, futile
  7. sterile, useless 8. indolent
  12. functionless
otium... 7. leisure
otkon... 4. okee (oki) 5. demon
  (Iroquois)
otologist... 6. aurist 9. ear doctor
ottava... 6. eighth, octave
ottava rima... 15. eight–line stanza
ottavino... 7. piccolo
ottoman... 4. seat 5. couch, stool
  7. cricket 9. footstool
Ottoman (pert to)... see also *Othman*
  color.. 9. vermilion
  court.. 5. Porte 12. Sublime Porte
  Empire.. 7. Turkish
  fabric.. 6. ribbed 10. corded silk
  governor.. 3. bey, dey 5. pasha
  leader.. 5. Osman
  native.. 4. Turk
  poetry (couplet).. 4. beyt
  province.. 6. eyalet (former) 7. vilayet
  Turkish.. 7. Osmanli
oubliette... 7. dungeon (top opening)

ouch... 5. bezel, clasp, jewel
  6. brooch 8. ornament
  11. exclamation
ought... 4. duty, must, zero 5. at all,
  aught, owned 6. cipher, should
  7. behoove, nothing 8. anything, in
  need of 9. possessed 10. obligation
Ouija board... 10. planchette
ouk... 4. week
ouphe... 3. elf 6. goblin
Our (pert to)...
  Father.. 11. Lord's Prayer
  French.. 5. notre
  Lady.. 10. Virgin Mary
  Lady's–mint.. 9. spearmint
  Lady's Wand (Astron).. 10. Orion's
  Belt
  Lady's Way.. 6. Zodiac
ourie... 4. cold 5. dingy 6. dreary
ousia... 6. nature 7. essence
  9. substance, true being
oust... 3. bar 5. eject, evict
  6. depose, remove 7. turn out
out... 3. odd 4. away 5. drunk
  6. absent, beyond, excuse, issued,
  outlet 9. published 10. dislocated,
  extinguish 11. unconscious
  12. extinguished, not available
out and out... 8. absolute, complete,
  outright, thorough 9. downright
  13. thoroughgoing
outbreak... 4. rash, riot 5. burst, spurt
  6. emeute, tumult 7. outcrop,
  ruction 8. eruption, hysteria, outburst
  12. insurrection 13. recrudescence
outburst... 4. gale 5. blast, flare, flash
  8. ejection, eruption 9. explosion
  10. ebullition
outcast... 5. exile, leper, ronin
  6. pariah 7. quarrel 8. castaway,
  derelict, vagabond 10. expatriate
outclass... 5. excel, outdo 6. outvie
  7. outrank, surpass 8. outshine
  10. outperform
outcome... 5. issue 6. effect, outlet,
  result, sequel, upshot 7. emanate,
  product 8. solution 10. denouement
  11. consequence
outcry... 4. wail, yell 5. alarm, shout
  6. clamor, plaint 7. suction
  8. proclaim 11. exclamation
outdo... 5. excel 6. defeat, exceed,
  outwit
outdoor game... 4. polo 6. hockey,
  tennis 7. cricket, croquet
outer... 5. ectad, ectal 7. outside,
  outward 8. exterior, external
  9. objective 10. extraneous
outer (pert to)...
  boundary.. 9. perimeter
  coat.. 4. coat, hull 5. testa 6. extine,
  jacket 8. tegument
  garment.. 4. suit, wrap 5. cloak,
  dress 7. paletot, sweater
  8. mackinaw, mantilla, overcoat,
  raincoat
  layer of roots.. 7. exoderm
  opposed to.. 5. ental
  shell.. 4. test
  skin.. 9. epidermis
Outer Mongolia...
  capital.. 4. Urga 14. Ulan Bator

Khoto
desert . . 4. Gobi
outermost . . . 6. utmost 7. extreme,
outmost 8. far–flung, farthest
outfit . . . 3. kit, rig 4. gear, suit, unit
5. equip, group 7. company, costume
8. wardrobe 12. organization
13. paraphernalia
outflow . . . 4. gush, teem 6. deluge,
efflux 7. freshet, outflux, outpour
8. effusion 10. ebullience
outgate . . . 4. exit, vent 6. egress,
outlet 7. outcome
outknee . . . 6. bowleg
outlander . . . see *outsider*
outlandish . . . 3. odd 6. remote
7. bizarre, foreign, strange, uncouth
8. freakish 9. barbarous, inelegant,
unrelated 10. extraneous, impossible,
tramontane
outlaw . . . 5. horse, ronin 6. bandit,
banish 7. brigand, outcast
8. criminal, fugitive 9. ostracize,
proscribe
outlet . . . 4. exit, vent 5. bayou
6. stream 7. culvert, opening,
outcast, passage
outline . . . 3. map 5. chart, draft,
frame, shape 6. sketch 7. contour,
drawing, summary 8. scenario
9. adumbrate, delineate, lineament,
perimeter, summarize
10. compendium 11. delineation
13. configuration
outlook . . . 5. scope, vista, watch
7. purview 8. frontage, prospect
9. viewpoint 10. perception
11. probability 12. watchfulness
outmoded . . . 5. passé 7. offbeat
8. outdated 10. superseded
outmost . . . 5. final, utter 6. remote,
utmost 8. farthest 9. extremest,
outermost, uttermost 15. farthest
outward
out of . . .
agreement . . 6. dehors
danger . . 4. safe
date, style . . 3. old 5. passé
10. antiquated
place . . 5. inept
sorts . . 5. nohow 7. peevish
the ordinary . . 7. unusual
the question . . 10. impossible
the way . . 5. aside 6. afield
outpeer . . . 5. excel 7. surpass
output . . . 3. cut 5. expel, power, yield
6. amount, energy 7. turnout
10. production
outraged . . . 6. abused, harmed
8. insulted, offended 9. affronted
10. infuriated, mistreated
outrageous . . . 6. absurd 7. furious,
heinous, obscene 8. flagrant
9. atrocious, excessive, monstrous
10. exorbitant, scandalous
11. disgraceful, unwarranted
outré . . . 3. odd 6. absurd 7. bizarre
10. immoderate 11. extravagant
Outre–Mer . . . 13. Book of Travels
(Longfellow, 1835)
outremer . . . 12. beyond the sea,

foreign parts
outrigger . . . 4. proa, spar 5. canoe
outright . . . 8. thorough 10. completely
11. unqualified 12. unreservedly
outrival . . . 5. excel 6. outvie
7. eclipse, outrank 8. outclass,
outshine, outsmart, outstrip
outside . . . 3. exo (pref) 4. ecto (comb
form) 8. exterior, external, outdoors
10. extraneous 11. superficial
outsider . . . 5. alien 8. stranger
9. auslander, foreigner, Uitlander
outspoken . . . 4. free 5. blunt, frank
6. candid, direct 10. unreserved
13. communicative
outstanding . . . 3. due 5. famed, noted
6. famous, unpaid 7. eminent,
obvious 8. exterior 9. important,
principal, prominent 10. projecting
11. conspicuous, uncollected
outstrip . . . 4. best, lead 5. excel,
outdo 7. surpass 8. outrival
outward . . . 5. ectad, evert, outer, overt
6. formal, spiral 8. apparent, exterior,
external, manifest 9. extrinsic
11. superficial
outwit . . . 4. balk, best, foil 5. block,
check, cross 6. baffle, thwart
9. checkmate, frustrate
10. circumvent, disappoint
outwork (Fort) . . . 7. ravelin 8. tenaille
(tenail)
ouvrage . . . 4. work
ouzel, ousel . . . 4. piet 6. thrush
8. whistler 9. blackbird
oval . . . 5. ovate, ovoid 6. circle
7. ellipse 10. elliptical 11. ellipsoidal
ovale . . . 3. egg
ovate . . . 4. bard, oval 7. obovate
(inversely)
oven . . . 3. umu 4. kiln, oast (oste)
7. furnace 8. hot place
9. microwave 12. brick chamber
oven (pert to) . . .
glass annealing . . 4. lehr (leer)
hop drying . . 4. oast
mop . . 6. scovel
over . . . 3. o'er, too 4. also, anew, atop
5. above, again, ended, super, supra
8. finished
overact . . . 3. haw 5. emote, spout
overalls . . . 5. chaps 8. trousers
10. chaparajos
overbearing . . . 7. haughty 8. arrogant,
cavalier, snobbish, subduing
9. imperious 10. highhanded
11. domineering 12. overpowering
overcast . . . 3. dim 4. dark 5. cloudy,
darken, gloomy 10. overturned (Geol)
overcoat . . . 5. benny, parka 6. capote,
raglan, slip–on, ulster 7. paletot,
surtout, topcoat 9. greatcoat,
inverness (sleeveless)
overcome . . . 3. awe, win 4. beat
5. crush 6. beaten, defeat, exceed
7. conquer 8. outstrip, overbear,
overturn, persuade, surmount,
unnerved, vanquish 9. overpower,
overthrow, overwhelm, prostrate
overcrowded . . . 9. congested
overdue . . . 4. late 5. tardy 7. belated

8. mistimed

overfeed... 4. glut 6. agrote, pamper
7. satiate, surfeit 8. overfill
9. crapulate, overstuff

overflow... 4. teem 5. spate
6. abound, deluge, outlet 7. copious,
overrun 8. inundate, opulence,
overload, plethora, teem with
9. abundance, pour forth
10. ebullience

overfond of... 4. dote 5. silly

overfull... 8. inflated, satiated
9. plethoric 10. overloaded

overhang... 3. jut 6. beetle 7. project,
suspend 9. advantage 11. over and
over

overlapping... 8. obvolute 9. imbricate,
syphering

overloaded... 6. turgic 8. inflated,
overfill 9. bombastic, plethoric

overlook... 4. face, miss, scan, skip,
snub 6. acquit, excuse, ignore,
slight, survey 7. absolve, condone,
forgive, neglect, overtop 9. disregard,
oversight, rise above, supervise

overlord... 6. master 8. domineer,
governor 9. tyrannize

overly... 3. too 8. careless
9. negligent 11. overbearing,
superficial 12. supercilious

overmodest... 7. prudish 8. priggish
11. puritanical, strait–laced

overnice... 5. fussy 6. purist
7. elegant, finicky 8. affected
10. fastidious

overpower... 3. awe 4. rout, stun
5. crush 6. dazzle, defeat, master,
subdue 7. conquer 8. overbear,
overcome, vanquish 9. overthrow,
overwhelm

overpowering... 6. fierce 8. exciting
12. overwhelming

overreach... 4. dupe 5. cheat
6. exceed, nobble, outwit, overgo,
strain 7. deceive 10. circumvent

overrun... 5. crush, swarm 6. abound,
desert, exceed, infest, outrun, ravage,
spread 7. destroy, pervade, run over,
trample 8. overflow 9. overwhelm
11. superabound

overscrupulous... 7. prudish
9. overexact 10. overstrict
14. overfastidious

overshadow... 5. excel 6. darken
7. eclipse, obscure, shelter
8. dominate 9. overcloud

overshoe... 3. gum 6. arctic, galosh
(galoshe)

oversight... 4. care 5. error, lapse,
watch 6. charge 7. control, neglect
8. omission 9. direction
10. inspection 11. supervision
12. guardianship, surveillance
13. nonobservance

overskirt... 7. pannier (anc) 10. upper
skirt

oversleeve... 6. armlet

overspread... 5. cover 6. infest
7. overrun, pervade 8. disperse,
suffused

overt... 4. open 6. patent, public
7. obvious 8. apparent, manifest

10. open to view

overtake... 5. catch, reach, seize
6. detect, rejoin 7. ensnare
9. apprehend, captivate

overthrow... 4. down, rout, ruin
5. worst 6. defeat, depose, refute,
unseat 7. conquer, deposal, destroy,
ruinate, unhorse 8. demolish,
disprove, overcome, overturn,
vanquish 9. prostrate 10. revolution

overthrown... 6. fallen, ruined
8. defeated 9. disproved

overtones... 5. tones 8. partials
9. harmonics

overtop... 5. dwarf, excel 7. obscure,
surpass 8. go beyond, overhead,
override 9. transcend 10. tower
above

overture... 5. offer, proem 7. opening,
prelude 8. aperture, proposal
11. composition, proposition
13. peace offering

overturn... 3. tip 4. tilt 5. throw,
upset 6. topple 7. capsize, conquer,
destroy, overset, reverse, subvert
9. overthrow, overwhelm

overweight... 7. obesity
11. overbalance 13. preponderance

overwhelm... 4. bury, rout 5. crush
6. defeat, deluge, engulf 7. confute,
conquer, engross, immerse, oppress
8. overturn, submerge 9. overpower,
overthrow

Ovidae, Ovinae... 5. goats, sheep

oviparous... 11. ovoviparous 12. egg
producing (opp of viviparous)

ovoid, ovoidal... 7. egglike
9. egg–shaped

ovule... 3. egg 4. seed 6. embryo,
ovulum

ovum... 3. egg 4. seed 5. spore
6. gamete 8. germ cell

owe... 3. due, own 7. possess 9. be
obliged 10. be indebted

ower... 6. debtor

owl (pert to)...
barn.. 4. lulu 5. padge
breed.. 6. pigeon
eagle.. 7. katogle 14. Tiger of the
Wood
eye.. 4. disc
family.. 9. Strigidae
female.. 3. hen
genus.. 4. Bubo 5. Ninox, Strix
7. Syrnium
horned.. 4. Bubo 6. aziola (small)
8. Hush–wing
light.. 4. dusk
like.. 4. owly 8. strigine
parrot.. 4. kakapo
Puerto Rican.. 6. mucaro
short–eared.. 8. marsh owl
tawny.. 8. billywix
term.. 4. hoot 11. bird of night
13. bird of Minerva
white.. 7. wapacut
young.. 4. utum 5. owlet

own... 4. have 5. admit 7. confess,
possess 11. acknowledge

owner... 6. master 7. planter
(plantation) 8. landlady, landlord
10. proprietor

ownership... **4.** oadl (anc law)
　5. claim **7.** tenancy **8.** dominium,
　interest, property **10.** possession
　11. seigniorage **12.** seignioralty
　14. proprietorship
ox... **5.** beeve, steer **6.** bovine
　8. strength **13.** beast of burden
ox (pert to)...
　Celebes.. **4.** anoa
　genus.. **3.** Bos
　harness.. **4.** yoke
　horned.. **4.** reem
　India.. **4.** gaur
　like.. **5.** bison **6.** bovine **7.** taurine
　stall.. **5.** boose
　Tibetan.. **3.** yak
　type.. **4.** zebu
　wild.. **4.** urus **7.** banteng
　working.. **4.** aver
　yoke.. **4.** span
oxeye... **4.** boce (fish) **5.** daisy
　6. dunlin, plover
oxford... **4.** gray, shoe **5.** cloth
Oxford (pert to)...
　college accts.. **6.** battel
　color.. **4.** blue, gray

　Marbles.. **7.** Arundel
　Museum.. **9.** Ashmolean (1683)
　officer.. **6.** beadle (bedel at Oxford)
　　(bedell at Cambridge)
　scholarship.. **6.** Rhodes
　school.. **10.** University (1570)
　sheep (hornless).. **4.** Down
oxide of iron... **4.** rust
oxide of sodium... **4.** soda
oxidize... **4.** rust **5.** erode **9.** sulphuret
　(Philat)
oxter... **3.** arm **6.** armpit **7.** embrace
oxtongue... **5.** plant **7.** biltong,
　bugloss
oxwort... **9.** butterbur
oxygen... **3.** gas **5.** oxide, ozone
　7. element
oxyopia... **10.** extra sight
oyster... **6.** huitre **7.** bivalve, mollusk
oyster (pert to)...
　gatherer.. **7.** tongman
　rake.. **5.** tongs
　shell.. **4.** husk, test **5.** shuck
　spawn.. **6.** cultch
　young.. **4.** spat
Ozark State... **8.** Missouri
ozone... **3.** air **6.** oxygen

P

P... **2.** Pi **6.** letter (16th)
pa... **4.** Papa **6.** father
pa, pah... **4.** fort **7.** village
　10. settlement (fortified)
paauw... **7.** bustard
pabulum... **4.** food, fuel **7.** aliment,
　support **9.** nutriment **10.** sustenance
　11. nourishment
pac, pack... **8.** half boot, moccasin
paca... **6.** rodent **9.** Cuniculus
pace... **3.** run **4.** gait, lope, rate, step,
　trot, walk **5.** speed **7.** measure
　8. movement, velocity
pace (L)... **5.** peace
Pace... **5.** Pasch **6.** Easter
pachyderm... **8.** elephant
　10. rhinoceros **12.** hippopotamus,
　Pachydermata
pachydermous... **11.** thick–walled
　12. thick–skinned
pacific... **4.** calm **6.** irenic, serene
　8. irenical, peaceful, tranquil
　9. peaceable, quiescent
　12. conciliatory
Pacific (pert to)...
　Coast tree.. **7.** madrona **8.** knob pine
　Highway.. **10.** Camino Real
　island bird.. **4.** kagu
　island shark.. **4.** mako **11.** blue
　　pointer
　island tree.. **4.** ipil
　islands.. **4.** Guam, Wake **5.** Samos
　　7. Oceania **8.** Caroline, Tasmania

　　9. Melanesia, Polynesia
　　10. Micronesia
　shrub.. **5.** salal
　States.. **6.** Oregon **10.** California,
　　Washington
　stepping stones.. **9.** Aleutians (Russia
　　to America)
Pacific Ocean discoverer... **6.** Balboa
pacifier... **3.** sop **4.** ring (baby's)
　6. nipple **7.** soother **8.** sedative
　10. peacemaker
pacify... **4.** calm, ease, lull **5.** abate,
　allay **6.** soften, soothe **7.** appease,
　assuage, mollify, placate **8.** mitigate,
　palliate **9.** alleviate **10.** conciliate,
　propitiate **11.** tranquilize (tranquillize)
pack... **3.** ram, set, wad **4.** cram, fill,
　load, stow, tamp **5.** carry, flock,
　horde, steve, truss **6.** bundle, embale
　8. assemble, encumber, quantity,
　send away
pack (pert to)...
　animal.. **3.** ass **5.** burro, camel, llama
　　6. donkey
　back.. **8.** knapsack
　horse.. **7.** sumpter
　horse bag.. **5.** kyack **7.** pannier
　of hounds.. **6.** kennel
package... **3.** pad **4.** bale **5.** fadge
　6. bundle, packet, parcel, robbin
　(peppers), seroon **11.** combination
packing... **4.** lute, seal **7.** stowage
　9. packaging **10.** rubber ring

paco... 3. ore 6. alpaca
Pacolet... 10. swift horse
pact... 6. pactum 7. bargain
8. contract 9. agreement
Pactolian... 6. golden
Pactolus, Myth (pert to)...
famed for.. 5. Midas 11. gold–bearing
river (Asia Minor).. 5. Lydia
pad... 3. mat, paw 4. fill, foot, frog,
line, path, walk 5. quilt, stuff, track,
tramp 6. tablet, trudge 7. bedding,
bolster, cushion, footpad
8. notebook, protract, saturate
9. footprint, pulvillus 10. highwayman
pad (pert to)...
cloth.. 7. housing 11. saddlecloth
hair.. 3. rat
harness, part.. 5. panel 6. terret
7. housing 10. horsecloth
perfume.. 6. sachet
padding... 6. lining 7. wadding
8. softness, stuffing 11. superfluity
paddle... 3. oar, row 4. beat, stir,
wade, whip 5. blade, board, scull,
spank, spoon 6. dabble, propel
7. flipper 8. lumpfish
paddle (pert to)...
English.. 7. trample 8. lumpfish
9. tread upon 10. paddlecock
Scotch.. 3. hoe 4. spud
paddock (pert to)...
paddockstool.. 9. toadstool
piper.. 9. horsetail
stone.. 10. greenstone
paddy... 4. rice, soft 7. padlike
8. cushiony 9. rice field 10. hod
carrier
Paddy... 7. Patrick 8. Irishman
paddymelon... 7. wallaby
Paddy's hurricane (Naut)... 4. calm
paddywhack... 4. beat, blow
6. temper 9. ruddy duck, thrashing
padge... 7. barn owl
padmasana... 11. cross–legged
(Buddha style), lotus–shaped
padre... 4. monk 6. Father, priest
8. chaplain, minister
padrona... 8. landlady, mistress
padrone... 6. master, patron
8. landlord 9. innkeeper
paedarchy... 14. rule by children
pagan... 6. ethnic, paynim 7. heathen
10. heathenism, idolatrous, unbeliever
11. irreligious
Paganalia... 8. festival (Rom)
pagan god... 4. idol
page... 3. boy 4. leaf 5. child, folio
6. summon 9. attendant, messenger
page (pert to)...
beginning.. 7. flyleaf
book.. 5. folio 6. cahier, sheets
lady's.. 7. esquire 8. escudero
left–hand.. 5. verso
number.. 5. folio
right–hand.. 5. recto
title.. 5. unwan 6. rubric
12. frontispiece
pageant... 4. pomp, show 5. drama
6. parade 7. tableau 8. aquacade
9. spectacle 10. exhibition
11. ostentation
pages... 7. paginal 8. paginate

Pagliacci... 5. opera 9. character
pagne... 9. loincloth, petticoat
pagoda... 2. ta 3. taa 4. idol
5. booth 6. temple
11. summerhouse
pagoda (pert to)...
finial.. 3. tee
sleeve.. 12. funnel–shaped
stone.. 12. Agalmatolite
tree.. 6. banyan 10. frangipani
paha... 4. hill 5. ridge (glacial)
pahi... 4. ship 5. canoe (seagoing)
pahmi... 5. bobac 6. marmot
paho... 7. pahutan 11. prayer stick
pahutan... 5. mango
paid... 5. hired 6. cashed 7. content,
settled, yielded 9. satisfied
10. discharged
paideutics... 8. pedagogy, teaching
paid office (without work)...
8. sinecure
paid out... 5. spent 8. expended
9. disbursed
paigle... 7. cowslip 8. crowfoot
10. stitchwort 12. cuckooflower
pail... 3. can, pan 4. beat 6. bucket,
harass, situla, thrash, vessel
8. cannikin
paillasse, palliasse... 3. bed (masonry)
8. mattress (straw)
pailles... 6. straws (cookery)
paillou, pailoo... 7. archway
(memorial)
pain... 3. ail 4. ache, agra, pang
5. agony, labor, thraw, throb, wound
6. grieve, stitch 7. afflict, ailment,
gnawing, torture, trouble 8. disquiet,
distress 9. suffering 10. affliction,
punishment
painful... 4. sore 7. careful 8. diligent
9. difficult, laborious 10. afflictive,
unpleasant 11. industrious,
painstaking
painkiller... 7. anodyne 8. medicine,
sedative 9. analgesic, calmative
10. depressant
painstaking... 5. fussy 7. careful,
labored 8. diligent, thorough
9. assiduity, assiduous, laborious
paint... 4. coat, draw, limn 5. adorn,
color, rouge, stain 6. depict, parget,
sketch 7. picture, pigment, portray
8. cosmetic, describe 9. delineate,
embellish 11. application (Med)
paint (pert to)...
blue, green.. 4. bice
comb form.. 5. picto
face.. 4. fard
glossy.. 6. enamel
Latin.. 6. pinxit
spreader.. 7. spatula
through pattern.. 7. stencil
with vermilion.. 7. miniate
paintbrush... 8. hawkweed 10. painted
cup 11. St John's wort
painted... 6. coated 7. colored,
feigned 9. disguised, portrayed
10. artificial, variegated
painted (pert to)...
bat.. 11. Vespertilio
beauty.. 9. butterfly
bunting.. 5. finch

duck.. 8. mandarin 9. harlequin
enamel.. 7. Limoges
hyena.. 14. Cape hunting dog
lady.. 7. thistle 8. sweet pea
   9. butterfly
process.. 7. scumble
trillium.. 9. wake–robin
turtle.. 8. carapace
painter... 4. puma 6. cougar
   7. panther
painter... 4. Dali 5. Monet 6. Millet,
   Rubens 7. da Vinci, El Greco,
   Picasso, van Gogh 8. Reynolds,
   Whistler 9. Rembrandt
   12. Gainsborough, Grandma Moses,
   Michelangelo
Painter's Easel... 6. Pictor
   (constellation)
painting... 3. oil 5. genre, mural, Pietà
   (sacred), secco 6. fresco, marine
   7. impasto, tempera 9. encaustic,
   grisaille, landscape 10. cerography
   11. portraiture 12. illustration
pair... 3. duo, two 4. dyad, mate,
   span, team, yoke 5. brace, unite
   6. couple
paired... 5. gemel (Her) 7. coupled,
   leagued
pairs, growing in... 6. binate, double
paisano... 7. peasant 10. countryman,
   road runner
pal... 4. chum, pard 5. buddy, crony
   6. cobber 7. partner 9. companion
   10. accomplice
palace... 5. court, Doges, house
   (Astrol) 6. palais 7. palazzo
   10. praetorium (pretorium)
paladin... 4. hero 6. knight (Round
   Table)
Paladins of France... 9. The Twelve
palais... 6. palace 10. courthouse
Palamedes... 4. hero (Trojan War)
palampore... 7. hanging (cotton)
   8. bedcover
palanquin, palankeen... 4. kago
   5. dooly (doolie), palki 6. litter,
   palkee 10. conveyance
palanquin bearer... 5. hamal 6. sirdar
palas... 4. dhak, tree (yellow dye)
palatable... 5. sapid, tasty 6. savory
   8. pleading, seasoned 10. acceptable
palate... 4. cion 5. taste, uvula, velum
   6. relish 10. epipharynx
palatine... 4. bone 6. artery, county
   8. palatial
Palatine Confession... 10. Heidelberg
palaver... 4. talk 6. confer 7. chatter
   8. converse, flattery 10. conference
   12. conversation
pale... 3. dim, wan 4. ashy, fade, lily
   5. ashen, fence–lurid, pasty, stake,
   white 6. blanch, bounds, paling,
   pallid, pallor, sallow, sickly, sphere
   7. haggard, obscure, whitish
   8. palisade 9. deathlike 10. indistinct
palea, palet... 4. fold 5. bract, scale
   6. dewlap 8. ramentum
paleo (comb form)... 3. old 7. ancient
paleolithic culture... 8. Stone Age
Paleozoic... 10. Appalachia
Palestine (pert to)...
ancient name.. 6. Canaan

animal.. 4. cony (Bib) 5. daman
conqueror.. 5. David, Turks
   11. Constantine
country (anc).. 4. Edom 5. Endor
   (Indur) 8. Nazareth 9. Philistia
lake.. 7. Dead Sea, Galilee
language.. 7. Aramaic
mountain (Bib).. 4. Zion 6. Carmel,
   Gilead, Hermon 13. Mount of Olives
plain, steppe.. 5. Negeb 6. Sharon
river.. 6. Jordan
town, district.. 4. Gaza 5. Haifa
   7. Samaria 9. Jerusalem
paletot... 4. coat 8. overcoat
pali... 9. precipice 10. steep slope
pali (comb form)... 5. again
   8. backward
Pali... 7. dialect (anc) 12. dead
   language
palimpsest... 9. parchment, rewritten
   10. re–engraved 15. codex rescriptus
palindrome (same backward, forward)...
   8. wordplay 9. inversion
paling... 5. fence, limit, palis, stake
   6. fading, picket 7. fencing
   9. enclosure
palisade... 5. cliff, fence, stake
   6. picket 7. defense, enclose, fortify
   8. espalier, palisado, surround
   9. precipice 10. impalement
   13. fortification
pall... 4. pale 5. cloak, cover, faint,
   qualm 6. coffin, mantle, nausea
   7. secrecy 12. graveclothes
pallall... 9. hopscotch
palle... 5. balls 8. six balls (Medici)
pallet... 3. bed 4. pate 5. quilt
   7. blanket 8. mattress 9. headpiece,
   paillasse
palliard... 6. beggar, lecher, rascal
   8. vagabond
palliate... 4. hide 5. abate, cloak,
   cover, gloss 6. excuse, lessen, soften
   7. conceal, qualify, relieve, shelter
   8. disguise, mitigate, moderate
   9. alleviate, extenuate
pallid... 3. wan 4. gray, pale 5. pasty,
   white 6. anemic, sallow
Pallu... 10. Reuben's son (Bib)
palm... 4. hand (part) 5. areca, bribe,
   steal 6. bacaba, handle, rattan,
   stroke, trophy
palm (pert to)...
civet.. 6. musang
cockatoo.. 5. arara
down.. 7. pronate
drink.. 5. assai
drink (alcoholic).. 4. beno, nipa
hand.. 6. palmus, thenar
handlike.. 7. palmate
house.. 8. palmetum
lily.. 2. ti
mat.. 6. petate
off.. 5. foist
ref to.. 10. palmaceous
sap (fermented).. 5. toddy
starch.. 4. sago
sugar.. 7. jaggery
thatch.. 4. nipa
palm (tree)...
African.. 7. palmyra (sugar, wine)
Arab.. 4. doum (doom)

Asiatic .. 4. atap, nipa
betel .. 5. areca, bonga 6. pinang
book .. 4. tara 7. taliera
Brazil .. 7. urucuri (urucury)
bussu, thatching .. 7. troolie (trooly)
cabbage .. 5. Sabal 8. palmetto
Ceylon .. 4. tala 7. talipot (fanleaf)
climbing, flexible .. 6. rattan
dwarf .. 5. Sabal
E Indies .. 4. atap, nipa 7. jaggery
  (sugar), tokopat (hat)
fan .. 7. talipot 8. palmetto
fiber .. 3. tal 6. raffia 8. piassava
  (piassaba)
Florida .. 5. royal
gingerbread tasting .. 4. doum (doom)
leaf .. 3. tal 4. olla (ola)
  12. chiquichiqui
Malayan, feather .. 4. irok 6. gomuti
palmyra .. 4. brab, olla 6. ronier
Philippine (coconut) .. 4. niog
pinnate .. 5. assai, nikau 7. calamus,
  feather
S America .. 5. bussu, datil 6. tooroo
  12. chiquichiqui
spiny .. 6. grugru
palmate ... 6. antler, webbed
  10. hand–shaped
palmer ... 6. ferule 7. pilgrim (Holy
  Land) 8. date palm
  15. prestidigitator
Palmetto State ... 13. South Carolina
palmistry ... 10. chirognomy,
  chiromancy
palmodic (Med) ... 5. jerky
palp ... 6. feeler, palpus 8. tentacle
palpable ... 5. plain 6. patent
  8. manifest, tangible 9. touchable
  10. noticeable, ponderable
palpebra ... 6. eyelid
palpebrate ... 4. wink
palpitate ... 4. beat, drum 5. throb
  7. flutter, pulsate
palpitation ... 7. flutter, tremble
  9. pulsation, quivering, throbbing
  10. excitement
palsied ... 5. shaky 9. paralyzed,
  tottering
palter ... 5. shift 6. babble, haggle,
  mumble, parley 7. bargain, chatter,
  quibble 9. vacillate 10. equivocate
  11. prevaricate
paltry ... 4. mean, vile 5. petty, trash
  6. trashy 7. pitiful, rubbish
  8. picayune, trifling 9. worthless
  10. despicable 12. contemptible
pampas ... 5. Pampa 6. plains (treeless)
pamper ... 3. pet 4. cram, glut
  5. humor, spoil 6. caress, coddle,
  cosset, cuddle, dandle, posset
  7. gratify, indulge 11. mollycoddle
pamphagous ... 10. omnivorous
pamphlet ... 5. tract 6. folder
  7. booklet, leaflet 8. brochure
pan ... 3. tab 4. part, tina (mining),
  wash 5. basin, roast, title (nobility)
  6. frying, lappet, spider, vessel
  7. cranium, hardpan, portion, skillet,
  subsoil 8. ridicule, saucepan
  9. criticize 10. acetabulum
pan (comb form) ... 3. all 5. every

Pan (pert to) ...
animal .. 3. ape 10. chimpanzee
god (Gr) .. 6. flocks
instrument .. 4. pipe, reed
music .. 9. Pan's pipes
Pipes of .. 6. syrinx 8. Panpipes
Roman identity .. 6. Faunus
seat of worship .. 7. Arcadia
son .. 7. Silenus
panacea ... 4. cure 6. elixir, remedy
  7. allheal (plant), cure–all
  8. nepenthe 10. catholicon
  11. panchreston
panache ... 4. tuft (feathered) 5. plume
  7. swagger
Panama ...
bay .. 5. Limon
capital .. 10. Panama City
city .. 5. Colon 6. Balboa 9. Cristobal
engineer .. 8. Goethals
gulf .. 6. Darien
Indian .. 4. Cuna
isthmus of .. 6. Darien (old name),
  Panama 7. San Blas
redwood .. 5. quira
river .. 7. Chagres
Panama Canal Lock ... 5. Gatun
  10. Miraflores
panarchy ... 13. universal rule
panaris ... 5. felon 7. whitlow
  10. paronychia
panary ... 5. bread 11. breadmaking
panatela ... 5. cigar
pancake ... 6. froise (fraise) 7. fritter
  11. griddlecake
Pancake Day ... 13. Shrove Tuesday
pancreas ... 5. gland 10. sweetbread
  16. Isle of Langerhans
panda ... 7. bearcat
pandemonium ... 4. hell 5. noise
  6. tumult, uproar
Pandemonium (pert to) ...
abode of .. 6. demons
capital of .. 4. Hell
palace of .. 5. Satan
pert to .. 15. infernal regions
pander ... 4. bawd, pimp 5. cater,
  serve 7. toady to 12. administer to
pandle ... 7. a shrimp
Pandora's Box ... 6. plague 9. human
  ills
Pandora's husband ... 10. Epimetheus
panegyric ... 5. éloge, elogy 6. eulogy
  7. oration, writing 8. encomium
  9. discourse, laudation
pang ... 3. fit 4. pain 5. throe
  6. twinge 8. paroxysm
pangolin ... 5. Manis 8. anteater
  9. Pholidota
panhandle ... 3. beg
Panhellenic ... 5. games (Isthmian)
  6. Greece 10. fraternity (Greek–letter)
panic ... 4. fear, fray 5. alarm, chaos,
  scare 6. fright 8. stampede
pannier ... 6. basket, dosser (dorser)
  7. corbeit 9. overskirt
panoply ... 7. defense 11. suit of
  armor
panorama ... 4. view 5. scene
  7. picture, scenery 9. cyclorama
pant ... 4. beat, gasp 5. heave, throb
  7. breathe, pulsate 11. palpitation

Pantagruel (pert to)...
character (romantic).. 5. giant
companion.. 7. Panurge
father.. 9. Gargantua
pantaloon, pantaloons... 5. pants
6. dotard, old man 8. breeches,
trousers 11. Patron Saint (Venice)
Pantheon (pert to)...
aggregate.. 4. gods 7. deities
builder.. 7. Hadrian (120 AD)
building.. 6. shrine, temple 10. le
Pantheon (Paris) 16. Westminster
Abbey
Rome.. 15. Temple of the Gods
panther, painter... 4. pard, puma
6. cougar, jaguar, ocelot 7. leopard
pantler... 6. butler 7. servant
pantry... 5. ambry 6. larder 7. buttery,
pannier, pantler 8. cupboard
pants... 5. chaps 7. drawers
8. trousers 10. chaparajos
(chaparejos), pantaloons
panuelo... 6. collar 8. kerchief
9. neckcloth
pap... 4. teat 6. nipple 8. mammilla,
soft diet
papa... 3. dad 4. clay, Pope
6. baboon, father, potato, priest
7. vulture
papal... 9. apostolic 10. pontifical
papal (pert to)...
book of decrees.. 8. decretal
chancery.. 6. datary
Court.. 3. See 5. Curia
envoy.. 8. ablegate
letter.. 4. bull
reformer.. 7. Gregory
seal.. 5. bulla
vestment.. 5. fanon, orale
paper (pert to)...
absorbent.. 7. blotter
broken.. 5. casse
brown.. 6. manila
coated.. 6. charta
collection.. 7. dossier
copy.. 6. carbon
crinkled.. 5. crepe
crisp.. 6. pelure
currency.. 5. scrip
cutlet wrap.. 8. papilote
damaged.. 5. casse, salle 6. retree
design.. 9. watermark
fine.. 5. linen 6. vellum 9. parchment
flower.. 11. strawflower
folded.. 5. folio
for pounding gold sheets.. 7. cutches
gummed.. 5. label, stamp 7. plaster,
sticker
legal.. 4. writ 5. title
measure.. 4. page, ream 5. quire,
sheet
nautilus.. 8. argonaut
official.. 5. targe 8. document
pad.. 6. tablet
postage stamp.. 6. pelure
size.. 3. cap 4. copy, demy, pott,
quad 5. atlas, crown, folio, legal
6. octavo 8. foolscap, imperial
9. colombier
small piece.. 5. scrip
thin.. 4. rice 6. pelure, tissue
9. onionskin

transfer.. 12. decalcomania
untrimmed.. 6. deckle (deckel)
10. deckle edge 11. deckle–edged
writing size.. 3. cap
paper chase... 13. hare and hounds
papilla... 6. nipple 10. projection
papule... 6. papula, pimple
papyra (comb form)... 5. paper
papyrus... 4. pith, reed 5. paper,
sedge 6. scroll
par... 2. by 5. value 7. average, by
way of, strokes, through 8. equality,
superior
parable... 4. myth, tale 5. fable, story
8. allegory, apologue
10. comparison, similitude
parabola... 5. curve
parade... 4. pomp, show 5. march
6. flaunt 8. flourish, grandeur,
splendor 9. pageantry, promenade,
spectacle 10. pretension, procession
11. ostentation 12. magnificence
13. formal display
paradigm... 5. model 7. example,
pattern
paradisaic... 6. Edenic
Paradise... 4. Eden 5. Jenna
6. Aidenn, heaven, Utopia 7. Elysium
Paradise (pert to)...
apple.. 5. dwarf
Arabic form.. 6. Aidenn
Buddhist, Western.. 4. Jodo
fool's.. 5. limbo
grosbeak.. 9. cutthroat (bird)
Mohammedan.. 5. Jenna
plumage.. 14. bird of paradise
poem (Milton).. 12. Paradise Lost
16. Paradise Regained
river.. 5. Gihon (Bib)
tree.. 9. China tree
paragon... 4. type 5. ideal, match,
model 7. diamond (100 carats),
paladin, pattern 8. parallel
9. nonpareil
paragram... 3. pun
Paraguay...
capital.. 8. Asunción
city.. 9. Paraguari 10. Concepcion,
Villarrica
language.. 7. Guarani, Spanish
river.. 6. Paraná 8. Paraguay
tea.. 4. maté 5. yerba 11. yerba de
maté
parakeet... 5. green 6. parrot, puffin
11. budgereegah (budgerygah)
paralysis... 5. palsy 6. paresis
10. hemiplegia, paraplegia 11. loss
of power
paralyze... 5. scram 6. benumb,
deaden 7. astound, terrify, unnerve
paramount... 3. top 5. chief, liege
6. ruling 7. supreme 8. dominant,
superior 9. principal 10. preeminent
13. most important
paramour... 5. amour, leman, lover,
wooer 8. mistress 9. gallantry
10. sweetheart
paranoia... 9. catatonia, monomania,
nosomania
parapet... 5. redan 7. barrier, bulwark,
rampart
parasite... 3. bur, sug 5. drone, toady

6. Gnatho, insect, sponge 7. entozoa
8. hanger–on 9. entophyte,
sycophant
parasite (pert to)...
animal.. 6. cuckoo 7. cowbird,
entozoa
external.. 12. ectoparasite
internal.. 7. entozoa
marine.. 6. remora, sponge
plant.. 9. entophyte
slang.. 6. flunky
trout.. 3. sug
parasitic (pert to)...
fish.. 6. remora
fungus.. 4. rust 6. lichen
worm.. 8. trichina (larva)
parcel... 3. lot 4. mete, part 5. piece,
solum (law) 6. bundle, packet
7. package, portion 8. fragment
parch... 3. dry 4. burn 5. dry up,
roast, toast 6. scorch 7. shrivel,
torrefy
parched... 4. sere 5. burnt, dried
7. thirsty 8. withered
parchment (pert to)...
bookcover.. 5. forel (forrel)
fine.. 6. vellum
manuscript.. 10. palimpsest
roll.. 4. pell 6. scroll
school.. 7. diploma
pard... 4. chum 5. tiger 7. comrade,
leopard, panther, partner
10. camelopard 11. confederate
pardesi (Hind)... 9. foreigner, outlander
pardie, parde, pardi (anc)... 4. oath
6. indeed, surely, verily 9. certainly
pardon... 5. mercy, remit, spare
6. acquit, excuse 7. absolve,
amnesty, condone, forgive 8. tolerate
9. acquittal, remission
10. absolution, indulgence (Eccl)
11. forgiveness
pardonable... 6. venial 8. expiable
9. excusable 10. forgivable
pardon chair, stall... 12. confessional
pare... 3. cut 4. peel, skin 5. shave
6. cut off, remove, resect
parent... 3. dad 4. sire 5. pater
6. father, mother, source 7. genitor
8. begetter 10. progenitor
parental affection (animal)... 6. storge
parget... 4. coat 5. paint 7. plaster
8. decorate, ornament 9. whitewash
parhelion... 3. sun (mock)
pariah... 3. dog (half–wild) 7. outcast
8. commoner, low caste
parian... 6. marble, market
Parian... 5. Paros 6. marble
(sculptural) 9. porcelain
parimutuel machine... 9. totalizer
11. totalizator
Paris (pert to)...
blue.. 6. cobalt 8. Prussian
daisy.. 10. marguerite
Garden (London).. 10. bear garden
green.. 11. insecticide
Paris, France...
anc name.. 7. Lutetia (Lutice)
capital of.. 6. France
criminal.. 6. apache
famed sites.. 6. Louvre 8. Pantheon
9. Notre Dame 10. Montmartre

11. Eiffel Tower 13. Champs Elysées,
Napoleon's Tomb
native.. 8. Parisian
patron saint.. 5. Denis (Denys)
racecourse.. 7. Auteuil
river.. 5. Seine
subway.. 5. Metro
Paris, Gr legend...
brought about.. 9. Trojan War
10. Fall of Troy
father.. 5. Priam (King of Troy)
killer of.. 8. Achilles
mother.. 6. Hecuba
wife.. 6. Oenone
parish... 5. laity 7. diocese 8. district
9. parochial
paristhmion... 6. tonsil
park... 4. area (enclosed) 5. place,
tract 6. claire, common, settle
7. pasture (Eng) 8. woodland
9. grassland, pleasance
10. playground 11. reservation, set
and leave
Park, Highway...
Avenue.. 9. Manhattan
Lane.. 6. London
Row.. 9. Manhattan
Park, Historical... 6. Shiloh 8. Pea
Ridge, Saratoga 9. Minute Man
10. Gettysburg, Morristown
12. Harper's Ferry, Independence
Park, US... 4. Zion 7. Glacier,
Olympic (rain forests) 8. Sequoyah
(Sequoja), Yosemite 9. Haleakala,
Mesa Verde 10. Everglades, Mt
McKinley, Shenandoah 11. Grand
Canyon, Kings Canyon, Yellowstone
12. Harper's Ferry 15. Petrified
Forest
parlay, parley... 4. chat 5. parle, treat
6. confer 7. discuss 8. converse
10. conference, discussion
11. arbitration
parliament... 4. Diet 8. Congress
11. legislature
parlous... 4. keen 5. risky 6. shrewd
7. cunning 8. shocking 9. dangerous
Parnassian... 4. muse, poet
9. butterfly 10. Parnassius
Parnassus, Greece...
mountain.. 6. Phocis
site of.. 6. Delphi 8. Castalia
(fountain) 13. Delphic Apollo
symbol of.. 6. poetry
parody... 5. farce 6. satire 7. mockery,
take–off 9. burlesque, imitation
10. caricature
paroemia... 7. proverb
parol, parole... 4. oral, word
6. speech 7. freedom, promise,
release 8. pleading 11. word of
mouth
paronomasia... 3. pun 7. punning
8. wordplay 9. assonance
12. agnomination
paroxysm... 3. fit 4. pang 5. throe
6. access, attack, frenzy 7. illness
9. agitation 10. fit of anger
12. exacerbation
paroxysm of grief... 5. agony
parricide (murder of)... 7. kinsman
parrot... 3. ara, hia, kea 4. jako, kaka,

loro, lory 5. arara, cagit, macaw, polly
6. kakapo, tiriba 7. corella, lorilet
8. cockatoo, lorikeet, lovebird,
parakeet 9. Psittacus (Old World)
14. Psittaciformes

parrot (pert to) . . .
disease . . 11. psittacosis
genus . . 6. Nestor 9. Psittacus
gray . . 4. jako
green . . 5. cagit
hawk . . 3. hia
long–tailed . . 5. macaw
monk . . 4. loro
New Zealand . . 4. kaka
owl . . 6. kakapo
parrot fish . . 4. loro, scar 5. lauia
6. scarid 7. labroid 8. Labridae,
Scaridae
parrotlike (tongued) . . 12. anthropoglot
sheep–killing . . 3. kea
short–tailed . . 7. lorilet
parry . . . 4. fend, ward 5. avert, avoid,
elude, evade, shift 6. refute, thwart
pars . . . 4. part
Parsee Bible . . . 10. Zend Avesta
Parsei, Parsi . . . 6. Gheber (Ghebre)
11. Zoroastrian 13. fire worshiper
Parsifal (pert to) . . .
character . . 6. Knight
healer of . . 8. Amfortas
son . . 9. Lohengrin
parsimonious . . . 4. near 5. close
6. frugal, meager, skimpy, sordid,
stingy 7. miserly, sparing
8. covetous, grasping 9. illiberal,
mercenary, penurious 10. avaricious
parsley . . . 4. herb 5. cumin 7. garnish
9. Ammiaceae, flavoring
parsley camphor . . . 6. apiole
parson . . . 6. rector 8. minister,
preacher, reverend 9. clergyman
parsonage . . . 5. gleve, manse, tithe
7. rectory 8. benefice, vicarage
9. pastorate 10. presbytery
parson bird . . . 3. tui
part . . . 3. cut, die 4. open, role, twin
5. allot, break, piece, sever, share
6. depart, divide, member, sunder
7. analyze, disband, disjoin, divorce,
portion, section, segment 8. dissever,
disunite, division, fragment, function,
separate 9. component
part (pert to) . . .
basic . . 4. core, pith 7. essence,
nucleus
choice . . 5. cream, elite 6. marrow
coarse . . 5. dregs
composite . . 7. section
corresponding . . 7. isomere
essential . . 4. core, gist, pith 5. heart
extra . . 5. spare
greater . . 4. bulk
hardest . . 5. brunt
infinitesimal . . 4. atom, mite
insignificant . . 3. bit 4. iota 6. trifle
kept . . 6. retent
main . . 4. body 5. trunk
narrow . . 4. neck
proportional . . 5. quota
rootlike . . 7. radicle
sawlike . . 5. serra
segment . . 5. tmema

small . . 3. bit, jot 4. iota 6. detail
7. snippet
smallest . . 4. whit 5. minim
solo accompaniment . . 8. obbligato
tenth . . 5. tithe
unpaid . . 6. arrear 9. arrearage
uppermost . . 3. top 4. peak 6. upside
7. topside
winglike . . 3. ala
with . . 7. discard 10. relinquish
partage . . . 4. part 5. share 7. portion
8. division
partake . . . 3. eat 5. share 7. receive
11. participate
partan . . . 4. crab
parted . . . 5. cleft 6. cloven 7. divided,
severed 9. separated
11. apportioned
parterre . . . 10. level space 12. theater
boxes, theater space 17. ornamental
gardens
parthogenesis . . . 7. apogamy
10. thelyotoky 12. reproduction
partial . . . 6. biased, unfair, unjust
7. limited 8. not total, one–sided,
partisan 9. imperfect 10. fractional,
incomplete, prejudiced
11. predisposed 13. foolishly fond
partiality . . . 4. bias 6. desire
9. injustice, prejudice 10. preference
11. inclination, partisanism
12. partisanship, predilection
participant . . . 6. sharer 7. entrant
8. partaker 9. accessory, colleague
12. participator
particle . . . 3. ace, bit, ion, jot 4. atom,
drop, iota, mite, mote, whit 5. grain,
piece, shred, spark 6. tittle
7. globule, granule, smidgen
particle (pert to) . . .
electric . . 3. ion 5. anion 6. proton
least possible . . 5. minim
minute . . 3. jot, ray 4. atom, iota
5. grain, speck 7. granule
negative . . 3. nor, not
nuclear . . 5. gluon, meson, quark
6. baryon, hadron
parti–colored . . . 4. pied, roan 5. pinto
6. motley 8. piebald 9. harlequin
10. variegated 11. polychromic
particular . . . 4. item, nice, part, sole
5. event, fussy 6. detail 7. precise,
special, topical 8. detailed, especial,
peculiar, separate, specific
9. attentive 10. fastidious, individual,
overminute 11. persnickety
12. circumstance, technicality
partisan, partizan . . . 4. pike 5. staff
6. zealot 7. partial 8. adherent,
advocate, follower 9. supporter
10. fractional, prejudiced
partition . . . 4. wall 5. allot 6. divide,
screen, septum 7. scantle 8. set
apart 9. apportion, severance
10. distribute, separation
13. apportionment
partitioned . . . 7. septate
partly . . . 6. in part 9. partially
partly illuminated . . . 6. shaded
8. adumbral 9. penumbral
partly open . . . 4. ajar
partner . . . 3. pal 4. ally, mate, wife

6. sharer, spouse 7. comrade,
husband 9. associate, coadjutor,
colleague 10. accomplice
11. confederate, participant
partnership... 4. firm 7. cahoots,
co–mated 8. business, contract
10. fellowship 11. affiliation
13. participation
part of...
anchor.. 4. palm
bird wing.. 5. alula
cannon.. 5. chase
church.. 4. apse, nave 5. altar
7. chancel 8. transept
circle.. 3. arc 6. degree 7. segment
compass.. 6. needle
ear.. 4. lobe 5. pinna 6. tragus
8. tympanum 9. labyrinth
eye.. 4. iris, uvea 5. pupil 6. cornea,
retina
flower.. 4. stem 5. calyx, petal, sepal
foot lever.. 5. pedal 7. treadle
fort.. 5. redan 7. bastion
head.. 4. pate 5. scalp, skull
7. cranium
minstrel show.. 4. olio 5. bones
6. end man 12. interlocutor
newspaper.. 3. ear 4. item, page
6. by–line 9. editorial
optical measure.. 7. alidade
printing press.. 6. platen
rifle (anc).. 4. tige
ship.. 3. bow 4. brig, deck, helm,
keel, mast 5. stern, wheel 6. anchor,
bridge, rudder 8. steerage
step.. 5. riser, tread 6. nosing
theater.. 3. box 4. loge 5. foyer,
stage 7. balcony, curtain, gallery,
parquet 8. parterre 9. orchestra
turtle.. 7. calipee 8. calipash
partridge... 4. hill, snow, yutu
5. covey (flock) 6. bamboo, chukar
(chukor), Perdix, seesee 7. cinerea,
tinamou 8. raw umber 9. francolin
11. Francolinus 12. ruffed grouse
party... 3. tea 4. ball, drum, sect,
side 6. clique, fiesta, person
7. company, faction 8. sociable
9. reception 10. detachment
11. association, combination
12. participator
party (pert to)...
deserter.. 6. bolter
evening.. 6. soiree
lawn.. 4. fete
man.. 8. partisan
member.. 8. Democrat, Federate
9. Communist, Dixiecrat, Greenback
(Hist), Socialist 10. Republican
11. Independent
men's.. 4. stag 6. smoker
Parvati (pert to)...
consort.. 4. Siva
father.. 7. Himavat
goddess.. 8. mountain
parvenu... 4. snob 7. upstart
12. nouveau riche
Pasch, pasch... 4. lamb, moon
6. candle, Easter, supper 8. Passover
10. Good Friday 11. candlestick,
celebration
pascual... 8. pascuage, pastures

pasear... 4. walk 6. parade, stroll
9. promenade 11. perambulate
pasha, pacha... 3. dey 4. emir 5. title
6. bashaw (early) 8. nobleman
10. magistrate
pashalik (pashalic)... 9. territory
(pasha's) 12. jurisdiction
pashm... 6. fleece (Tibetan goat)
pasigraphy... 6. system (Universal)
7. symbols 8. language
Pasiphae (pert to)...
mother of.. 7. Ariadne
son.. 8. minotaur (monster)
wife of.. 5. Minos
pasquinade... 5. squib 6. satire
7. lampoon, pasquil
pass... 2. go 3. die, end, gap
4. ghat, hand, lane, pace, step
5. canto, enact, gorge, lapse, occur,
relay, spend, throw 6. convey, crisis,
defile, elapse, exceed, happen,
passus, perish, permit, ratify, ticket
7. excrete, passage 8. hand over,
passport, surmount, transfer
10. permission 11. Annie Oakley
13. complimentary
pass (pert to)...
Alpine.. 3. col
around.. 5. skirt 6. detour
as genuine.. 5. cheat, foist
11. interpolate
away.. 3. die, end 6. perish, vanish
9. cease to be, disappear, obsolesce
by.. 4. cote, omit, skip, snub
6. elapse, forego, ignore 7. proceed
8. overlook 9. disregard
hurriedly.. 7. scamper, skitter 9. skim
along
into.. 5. glide, merge 6. become
7. get to be 9. penetrate
judgment.. 4. rule 6. decree, ordain
8. sentence
on.. 3. die 6. confer, ratify
7. advance 8. bequeath, continue
out.. 3. die 4. exit 5. faint 7. be
dazed 9. disappear 11. be dead
drunk 13. be unconscious
over.. 4. omit, skip 5. cross
6. elapse, excuse, exempt, ignore,
slight 7. condone, exclude, neglect
8. overlook, transfer, traverse
sudden.. 5. lunge
through.. 5. cross, reeve (cringle)
6. pierce 7. pervade, undergo
8. traverse 9. penetrate
10. comprehend, experience
up.. 4. snub 5. evade 6. reject
7. decline 9. disregard
without touching.. 5. clear
passable... 4. so–so 7. current
8. mediocre, moderate, traveled
9. navigable, tolerable, traversed
10. acceptable, accessible, admissible
12. satisfactory
passado (fencing)... 6. thrust
passage... 4. adit, exit, flue, ford,
gang, hall, iter 5. aisle, allay, allée,
canal, death 6. atrium, avenue,
egress, travel, voyage 7. channel,
excerpt, journey, transit 8. corridor,
incident, progress, sanction
9. enactment, migration

10. transition 11. altercation, negotiation, preterition
12. thoroughfare

passage (pert to)...
book.. 7. excerpt
brain.. 4. iter
closed end.. 7. impasse 8. cul–de–sac
covered.. 4. pawn
history.. 5. alure
mine.. 4. sill 5. stope
narrow.. 3. gut 5. aisle, alley, gully, slype 6. defile, strait
river.. 7. estuary

passageway... 4. hall, lane, ramp, slip 5. aisle, alley, lumen 6. access, arcade, avenue, defile, outlet, strait, tunnel 7. gangway 8. corridor

passant... 7. cursory, walking (Her) 8. passer–by 9. ephemeral, excelling 10. surpassing, transitory

passé... 4. aged, past, worn 5. faded 6. gone by 8. obsolète 10. antiquated 13. superannuated

passed (pert to)...
by.. 6. bygone, former 8. preterit (preterite)
over.. 7. fleeted 11. preterition
through pores.. 7. osmosed 8. dialyzed 9. permeated, transuded

passenger... 4. fare 6. pigeon, trekku 7. pilgrim, tourist 8. commuter, traveler, wayfarer 9. sightseer, transient

passerine bird... 5. finch 7. sparrow 8. songbird

passing... 7. cursory 8. elapsing, fleeting 9. departing, enactment, ephemeral, exceeding, happening, transient, vanishing 10. surpassing, transitory 11. preterition

passion... 3. ire, yen 4. love, lust, rage, zeal 5. anger, craze, wrath 6. desire 7. emotion, feeling 9. eloquence, martyrdom 10. enthusiasm, excitement

passion (pert to)...
flower.. 6. maypop 11. passionwort
flower family.. 10. Passiflora
for doing great things.. 11. megalomania
music.. 8. oratorio
Play.. 14. Christ's Passion (Oberammergau)
Week.. 8. Holy Week

passionate... 3. sad 5. angry 6. ardent 7. amorous, excited, fervent, pitiful, violent 8. agitated, eloquent, vehement 9. emotional, irascible 10. passionato 11. hot–tempered, impassioned

passionless... 4. calm 8. painless 9. heartless, unfeeling 10. spiritless 11. unemotional 13. dispassionate

passive... 5. inert, quiet, stoic 6. stolid 7. languid, patient 8. inactive 9. apathetic 10. submissive 11. acquiescent, indifferent, unresisting

Passover (pert to)...
festival.. 5. Seder 6. Jewish
lamb.. 7. paschal
psalm.. 6. hallel 14. Egyptian Hallel

sacrifice.. 11. paschal lamb
The (Passover).. 5. Pasch

passport... 4. pass, visa (vise) 5. congé 6. congee, permit 8. document 11. safe conduct

passus... 5. canto

password... 9. watchword 10. mot de passé, open sesame 11. countersign

past... 2. by 3. ago 4. date, dead, gone, over, yore 5. after, since 6. beyond, ultimo 7. elapsed, outworn 8. foregoing, yesterday

pasta... 7. gnocchi, lasagna, ravioli 8. linguini, macaroni 9. fettucini, manicotti, spaghetti 10. vermicelli

paste... 3. pap, poi 4. glue, sham 5. dough, stick 6. mastic, strass 8. adhesive, frippery, mucilage 10. confection 13. stick together

pastel... 6. light 6. crayon, sketch 9. pale color

pastille... 6. troche 7. lozenge

pastime... 4. game 5. hobby, sport 9. amusement, diversion 10. recreation 13. entertainment

pastor... 5. rabbi 6. curate, divine, keeper, parson, priest, rector 8. chaplain, guardian, minister, Reverend, shepherd

pastoral... 4. poem 5. drama, rural 6. poetic 7. romance 14. ecclesiastical

pastoral (pert to)...
cantata.. 8. serenata
crook, staff.. 5. pedum 7. crosier
god.. 3. Pan
oboe.. 7. musette
pert to.. 6. rustic 8. agrestic, herdsman, shepherd
pipe.. 3. oat 4. reed
poem.. 4. idyl 7. bucolic, eclogue

pastry... 3. pie 4. tart 6. Danish, éclair 7. dariole, strudel 8. napoleon, pandowdy, turnover 9. cream puff, shortcake 10. pâtisserie

past tense... 8. preterit (preterite)

pasturage, right of... 9. horsegate

pasture... 3. ham, lea 4. feed, food 5. agist, grama, grass, graze 6. meadow 9. grassland 10. agostadero

pasture bird... 6. plover 7. sparrow

pat... 3. dab, fit, paw, tap 4. blow, lump 5. fixed, impel, known, throw 6. caress, smooth, stroke 7. flatten 9. immovable 10. seasonable

Patagonia (S Am)...
city.. 11. Punta Arenas
deity.. 7. Setebos
Indian tribe.. 9. Tehuelche
nearby island.. 14. Tierra del Fuego
race (said of).. 6. giants 7. Big Feet, tallest 9. Patagones
rodent.. 4. cavy 8. capybara, Caviidae
strait.. 8. Magellan (Magallanes)

patamar (pattamar)... 6. vessel (Naut) 7. courier 9. messenger

patata... 6. potato 11. sweet potato

patch... 4. mend, vamp 5. bodge, botch, clump, cover, field 6. blotch 8. appliqué

cobble, parcel 8. addition
9. reconcile
patch (pert to)...
cloth .. 5. clout
imprinting .. 5. friar
metal .. 6. solder
of trees .. 4. mott
patcher (humorous)... 6. sartor
patchwork... 5. quilt 6. jumble, pillow,
scraps 7. mixture 9. checkered,
fancywork, fragments
10. hodgepodge
pate... 3. pie, top 4. head 5. brain,
crown, pasty, patty 6. badger
pâté de foie gras... 5. patty (goose
liver and truffles)
patella... 3. pan 4. bone, dish, vase
7. kneecap, kneepan
paten... 4. disc, dish, disk 5. plate
7. patener (bearer of)
patent... 4. open 5. berat (Turk), right
7. license, warrant 8. document,
manifest 9. available, copyright,
privilege, trademark 10. accessible,
protection, university
12. unobstructed
pater... 6. father, priest
Pater Noster... 11. Lord's Prayer
Paternoster Row... 6. street (London)
Pater Patriae... 18. Father of his
country (Cicero, Marius, Trajan,
Washington, etc)
path... 3. way 4. lane, line 5. piste,
route, swath, track, trail 6. course
7. footway
path (pert to)...
along a slope .. 4. berm (berme)
animal .. 5. piste, spoor 6. roddin
7. rodding
of energy .. 7. ergodic
of moving parts .. 5. locus
of planets .. 5. orbit
Spanish .. 6. camino, comino
pathetic... 3. sad 5. teary 8. dolorous,
grievous, stirring 9. affecting
10. lamentable
pathological... 6. morbid 9. unhealthy
pathological reaction... 7. allergy
patience... 9. endurance, fortitude,
solitaire, tolerance 10. submission,
sufferance 11. forbearance,
resignation 12. acquiescence,
perseverance
patient... 4. calm, meek 6. client
8. tolerant 9. unsettled
11. persevering 13. long–suffering
patio... 5. court 9. courtyard
patriarch... 4. Noah, sire 5. elder,
pater 6. bishop, father 7. aged man,
veteran 9. churchman
10. Methuselah 13. paterfamilias
patrimonial... 9. inherited
10. hereditary
patrimony... 8. heritage 10. birthright
11. ancient rite, inheritance
patriot... 4. Cato (Rom), Otis (Am)
5. jingo 7. chauvin 9. flag–waver
10. chauvinist, countryman
patriotism... 10. chauvinism
11. nationalism 13. love of country
patrol... 5. guard 7. protect
8. traverse 9. keep guard

13. perambulation
patron... 5. buyer, guest 6. backer,
seller, trader 8. customer, guardian
9. financier, protector, supporter
10. benefactor
patronage... 5. aegis (egis), favor
6. defend 7. support 8. auspices
9. clientele, fosterage 10. assistance
13. condescension, encouragement
patronizing... 8. deigning 9. financing,
revealing 10. sponsoring
13. condescending
patrons (group)... 7. backers, masters
9. clientele, customers
Patron Saint of...
beggars .. 5. Giles
boys .. 8. Nicholas
England .. 4. Anne 6. George
fishermen .. 5. Peter
France .. 5. Denis
Ireland .. 7. Patrick
lawyers .. 4. Ives
motherhood .. 6. Gerard
musicians .. 7. Cecilia
Pueblo Indians .. 7. Stephen
sailors .. 4. Elmo
Scotland .. 6. Andrew
shoemakers .. 7. Crispin
swineherds .. 7. Anthony
Venice .. 4. Mark 9. Pantalone
Wales .. 5. David
patten... 4. clog 5. skate 8. footgear,
overshoe, snowshoe
pattern... 4. norm, seme 5. habit,
model 6. design, format 7. diagram,
paragon 8. paradigm, parterre,
template
pavilion... 4. tent 5. cover, kiosk
6. canopy 8. covering 9. gloriette
10. tabernacle
pavis... 5. cover 6. screen, shield
7. protect
paw... 3. pad, pud 4. foot, hand
5. patté, pedal 6. handle, stroke
7. foreleg (Her) 8. forefoot
10. manipulate
pawl... 4. bolt, sear, trip 5. click
6. detent, pallet, tongue 7. ratchet
9. mechanism
pawn... 4. gage, hock, tool 6. pledge
7. counter, peacock 8. chessman,
guaranty, hockshop 9. put in pawn
10. pawnbroker
Pawnee... 6. Indian
pawnie... 7. peacock
pay... 3. aby (abye), fee, tip 4. ante,
meet, wage 5. remit, repay
6. defray, reward, salary, suffer
7. requite, satisfy 9. indemnify,
reimburse, retaliate 10. compensate,
punishment, recompense, remunerate
11. retribution 12. compensation
pay (pert to)...
attention .. 4. heed 6. listen
back .. 6. rebate, refund 9. reimburse,
retaliate
dirt .. 3. ore
envelope .. 5. wages 6. salary
7. stipend
extra .. 5. bonus 8. kickback
for .. 3. aby (abye) 5. atone 6. suffer
off .. 6. punish 7. requite 9. pay in

full, retribute 10. compensate
out.. 5. spend 6. expend, settle
  7. hand out 8. disburse
  10. distribute 12. exorbitantly
  14. through the nose
up.. 4. ante 6. settle 9. liquidate
paymaster... 6. burser, purser
  7. cashier
payment... 3. cro, fee 4. dues, mail
  6. return 8. defrayal, requital
  10. punishment, recompense
  12. chastisement, compensation
payment (pert to)...
  for homicide, murder.. 3. cro 4. eric
  (Brehon Law) 7. galanas (Welsh),
  wergild (weregild)
  immediate.. 4. cash
  upon delivery.. 3. COD 14. cash on
  delivery
paynim... 5. pagan 7. heathen, infidel
  8. Pagandom 10. Mohammedan
payong... 8. umbrella (golden)
paysage... 7. picture (landscape)
  9. landscape
pea (pert to)...
  bird.. 6. oriole
  chick.. 4. gram 5. Cicer
  everlasting (Bib).. 9. vetchling
  family.. 8. Fabaceae
  flour (seasoned).. 9. Erbswurst
  heath.. 7. carmele
  pigeon.. 3. dal 5. arhar
  sausage.. 9. Erbswurst
  shaped.. 8. pisiform
  soup.. 3. fog (dull yellow)
  split.. 3. dal
  tree.. 8. laburnum
  tropical.. 4. dove 7. Zenaida
  12. mourning dove
  vine.. 8. earthpea
peace... 3. pax 5. amity, quiet, truce
  6. accord, repose 7. harmony,
  Nirvana, silence 8. ataraxia (ataraxy),
  serenity 9. stillness 10. quiescence
  11. tranquility
peaceable... 5. quiet, still 6. irenic,
  silent 7. henotic, pacific 8. amicable,
  tranquil 9. quiescent 10. concordant,
  harmonious 11. undisturbed
peaceful... 4. calm 5. irene 6. irenic,
  placid, serene 7. halcyon, pacific
  8. tranquil 11. comfortable
peace pipe... 7. calumet
peach... 5. fruit 6. accuse, betray,
  brandy, indict, inform 7. impeach
  8. quandong 9. red–yellow
peach (pert to)...
  cordial.. 7. persico 8. persicot
  family.. 12. Amygdalaceae
  French.. 8. persicot
  grafted (quince).. 9. melocoton
  like.. 6. almond
  origin.. 3. China
  stone.. 7. putamen
  variety.. 7. Elberta 8. Crawford
  9. freestone, nectarine 10. clingstone
peacock... 3. mao 4. Pavo (Astron),
  pawn, pose 5. strut 9. swaggerer
peacock (pert to)...
  blue (color).. 4. paon
  butterfly.. 2. io
  fan.. 9. flabellum

feather part.. 4. marl
female.. 6. peahen
fish.. 6. wrasse
flower.. 9. poinciana
heron.. 7. bittern
ref to.. 7. peafowl 8. pavonine
tail spot.. 3. eye
peak... 3. alp, epi, pic, top, tor
  4. acme, apex, cone, crag, cusp,
  dent, dolt 5. crown, piton, slink,
  sneak, steal 6. finial, shrink, summit
  8. headland, mountain 9. simpleton
  10. promontory
Peak... 5. Borah, Logan 7. Everest, St
  Elias 8. McKinley 9. Mont Blanc
  10. Matterhorn 11. Kilimanjaro
  12. Popocatepetl
peal... 4. boom, clap, echo, ring, toll
  6. appeal, shovel 7. resound,
  summons, thunder 8. carillon
peanut... 5. pinda (pindal, pindar)
  6. goober, trifle 8. earthnut,
  earthpea, katchung
pear (pert to)...
  alligator.. 7. avocado
  cider.. 5. perry
  Latin.. 5. pirum
  prickly.. 4. tuna 5. nopal 7. Opuntia
  shaped.. 8. pyriform
  shaped vessel.. 6. aludel
  squash.. 7. chayote
  type.. 4. Bosc 8. Bartlett
pearl... 3. gem 4. drop 5. nacre,
  tooth, white 9. margarite
pearl (pert to)...
  bird.. 10. guinea fowl
  color.. 4. blue 13. mother–of–pearl
  eye.. 8. cataract
  imitation.. 6. olivet
  of great luster.. 6. orient
  opal.. 9. cacholong (opaque)
  oyster.. 7. Avicula
  seed.. 7. aliofar (obs)
  vegetable.. 5. onion
pearly... 5. milky, quick, smart
  7. opaline, whitish 8. pellucid
  10. opalescent 11. flourishing
Pearly Gates (Bib)... 6. heaven, twelve
peasant... 4. boor, hind, peon, serf
  5. clown, knave, swain 6. carlot,
  cotman, cottar, rascal, rustic
  10. countryman
peasant (pert to)...
  Arab, Syria.. 6. fellah
  cropsharer.. 7. metayer
  English.. 4. hind 5. churl
  Indian.. 4. ryot
  Irish.. 4. kern (kerne) 7. cottier
  like.. 4. base, rude 8. clownish
  Russian.. 5. kulak (rich)
  Scottish.. 4. tyke (tike) 6. cotter
  (cottar)
pease... 5. quiet 6. pacify 7. appease
  9. reconcile
peasecrow... 4. tern
peat... 3. bog, pet 4. coal, fuel, moor,
  moss, turf 6. minion 7. darling
  8. favorite 11. combustible
peat (pert to)...
  cutter.. 5. piner
  moss.. 8. sphagnum
  turf spade.. 5. slave

wood.. 11. loosestrife
peau... 4. skin (silks) 6. fabric
peba... 9. armadillo
pebble... 5. scree, stone, talus
6. quartz 7. chuckie (chucky), crystal,
psephos 11. gravelstone, pebblestone
peccadillo... 4. slip 5. error, fault,
lapse 12. indiscretion
peccant... 3. bad 5. wrong 6. guilty,
morbid, wicked 7. corrupt, sinning,
spoiled 9. incorrect, unhealthy
12. insalubrious
peccary... 6. mammal (piglike)
7. Tagassu, Tayassu 8. javelina
pech... 4. pant 11. breathe hard
pecht (Scot)... 5. fairy, gnome, pygmy
peck... 3. dab, dot, eat, nag 4. food,
hole, jerk, kiss 5. pitch, prick, throw
6. peggle, stroke 7. measure
8. quantity 11. large amount
peck at... 3. nag 4. carp, twit
5. tease 6. attack, harass
pectase... 6. enzyme
peculiar... 3. odd 4. idio (comb form)
5. queer 6. oddish, unique
7. curious, special, strange, typical
8. distinct, separate, singular
9. different, eccentric 10. particular
14. characteristic
peculiar expression... 5. idiom
peculiarity... 4. kink 5. quirk, trait
6. oddity 7. oddness 9. mannerism
10. partiality 11. singularity
12. eccentricity 14. characteristic
peculiar to a district... 7. endemic
pecuniary... 6. fiscal 8. monetary
9. financial
pedagogue... 5. tutor 6. pedant
7. teacher 12. schoolmaster
pedal... 4. foot 5. lever 6. driver
7. treadle 9. propeller
pedant... 4. prig 5. tutor 6. dorbel,
purist 9. formalist, pedagogue
10. conformist 12. bluestocking,
precisionist, schoolmaster
peddle... 4. hawk, sell, vend 6. piddle,
retail 11. disseminate
peddler, pedlar... 6. cadger, coster,
hawker, mugger, sutler 7. chapman
8. huckster 9. vivandier
12. costermonger
peddler's French... 6. jargon (thieves')
9. gibberish
pedestal... 7. support 10. foundation
pedestal part... 3. die 4. base, dado
5. socle 6. plinth, quadra
pedestrian... 3. ped 4. dull, slow
5. hiker 6. hoofer, walker
11. commonplace 12. foot traveler
13. unimaginative
pedicel... 3. ray (of an umbel) 4. stem
5. stalk 8. peduncle
pediculosis... 9. lousiness
Pediculus... 4. lice
pedigree... 6. stemma 7. descent,
lineage 8. ancestry, register
9. genealogy 10. family tree
pedio (comb form)... 4. sole 6. instep
pedology... 9. soil study 10. child
study
pedometer... 5. watch 8. odograph
10. instrument, passometer

pedregal... 9. lava field
pedum... 5. crook, staff (pastoral)
peduncle... 4. stem 5. scape, stalk
7. pedicel, pedicle, sessile
peek... 3. pry 4. peep 5. chirp, flash
6. glance 7. glimpse 9. look slyly
peekaboo... 4. game 6. bopeep
peel... 4. bark, pare, rind, skin
5. slipe, stake, strip 6. cut off,
lamina, shovel 8. car blade, palisade,
stockade
peel (off)... 4. harl, pare, tear 7. come
off 8. get loose 11. decorticate
peeler... 4. crab (shedding), yarn
5. corer 7. hustler 8. pillager
9. policeman
peep... 3. pry 4. peek, peer, pule,
skeg 5. cheep, chirp, pipit, sight
(firearms) 6. glance, squeak
7. crevice 8. peephole 9. sandpiper
peephole... 4. hole 6. eyelet
8. aperture 9. sighthole
peer... 4. duke, earl, fere, gaze, mate
5. baron, equal, match, noble, stare,
stime (styme) 7. marquis
8. nobleman, superior, viscount
Peer Gynt (pert to)...
drama, poem by.. 5. Ibsen
mother.. 3. Ase
music suite by.. 5. Grieg
peerless... 9. matchless, nonpareil,
paper size, unequaled, unmatched
10. unexcelled 11. ne plus ultra,
superlative
peesweep, peeseweep... 7. lapwing
10. greenfinch
peetweep... 9. sandpiper (spotted)
peeved... 4. sore 7. annoyed, nettled
9. irritated
peevish... 3. coy 4. sour 5. cross,
sulky, techy, testy 6. crusty, morose,
touchy 7. fretful, pettish, spleeny,
waspish 8. captious, choleric,
contrary, perverse, petulant, snappish
9. irascible, irritable, querulous,
splenetic
peg... 3. hob, leg, nob, nog, pin
4. dram, skeg 5. drink, stake, tooth
6. drudge, fasten, reason 7. pretext,
support 9. persevere, recognize
peg (pert to)...
cribbage.. 4. game
iron.. 5. piton
out.. 7. croquet
shoe.. 5. cleat
wood.. 5. spill, thole 8. treenail
pega... 5. shark 6. remora
Pegasus... 5. horse (winged), steed
13. constellation
Pegasus's rider... 11. Bellerophon
pegomancy, divination by...
7. springs 9. fountains
peho... 8. morepork
peignoir... 8. negligee 12. dressing
gown, dressing sack
pejorative... 11. disparaging
12. depreciatory
Peking, Pekin... 4. blue, city, duck
7. spaniel
pelagic... 6. marine 7. oceanic
9. underseas
pelagic organism... 6. nekton

7. benthos 8. plankton
Pele... 7. goddess (volcanoes)
pêle–mêle... 8. pellmell
Peleus (pert to)...
  father.. 6. Aeacus
  King of.. 9. Myrmidons
  son.. 8. Achilles
  wife.. 6. Thetis
pelf... 3. fur, rob 4. gain 5. booty,
  lucre, money, spoil, trash 6. pilfer,
  profit, refuse, riches, wealth
  7. rubbish 10. ne´er–do–well
Pelias (pert to)...
  daughter.. 5. Medes
  King of.. 6. Iolcus
  nephew.. 5. Jason
  son.. 7. Acastus
pelican (pert to)...
  heraldry.. 10. in her piety
  symbolic of.. 6. Christ 7. charity
Pelican State... 9. Louisiana
pell... 3. fur 4. hide, pelt, skin
  5. hurry 6. hasten 13. parchment
  roll
pellagra... 5. zeism
pellar, peller... 6. wizard 8. conjurer
pellet... 4. ball, pill 6. bullet
  7. granule, missile, pallion
pellicle... 4. film, scum 6. lamina
  7. coating 8. membrane
pell–mell, pellmell... 10. vehemently
  12. furious haste 13. helter–skelter
pellock... 8. porpoise
pellucid... 5. clear 6. bright, limpid
  8. luminous 11. translucent,
  transparent 12. intelligible
pelmet... 7. valance (short)
Peloponnesus...
  capital.. 7. Corinth
  city.. 7. Argolis
  League.. 11. Confederacy
  peninsula (Gr).. 5. Morea
  12. Peloponnesos (old), Peloponnesus
  (modern)
  race (anc).. 6. Dorian 7. Spartan
  School.. 6. Dorian 9. Sculpture
  War.. 12. Athens–Sparta (BC)
Pelops (pert to)...
  father.. 8. Tantalus
  son.. 6. Atreus 8. Thyestes
  wife.. 10. Hippodamia
pelota... 4. ball, game 5. cesta
  7. fronton, jai alai
pelt... 3. fur 4. blow, fell, hide, push,
  skin 5. stone 6. hurl at, pelage,
  refuse, strike, thrust 7. apparel (of
  skins), rubbish 8. woolfell
peltry... 4. furs, pelt 5. skins
peludo... 9. armadillo (six–banded)
pelvic bone... 5. ilium 7. ischium
  8. seat bone
pelvic–shaped... 11. basin–shaped
pemmican... 4. meat (dried) 7. buffalo,
  venison
pen... 3. cot, sty 4. bolt, coop, gaol
  5. abode, hutch, quill, write
  6. fasten, indite 7. confine
  9. enclosure 12. penitentiary
pen (pert to)...
  like.. 7. styloid
  name.. 6. anonym 9. pseudonym
  10. nom de plume

point.. 3. neb, nib 4. stub
text.. 5. ronde
penalize... 4. fine 5. mulct 6. punish
  8. handicap
penalty... 4. fine, loss 7. forfeit
  8. handicap, hardship
  10. punishment, repentance
Penang Islands capital...
  10. Georgetown
penchant... 4. bent 6. desire, liking
  7. leaning 8. tendency 10. attraction
  11. inclination 12. decided taste
pendant... 3. bob, tag 4. tail 5. aglet
  (aiglet), queue 6. tassel 7. eardrop,
  earring, hanging 8. appendix,
  pendulum 9. lavaliere 10. chandelier
pendent... 3. lop 4. pend 7. hanging
  8. appended 9. impending,
  pendulous 11. jutting over,
  overhanging
pendent cone (limestone)...
  10. stalactite
pendulous fold, skin... 6. dewlap
Penelope (pert to)...
  father.. 7. Icarius
  husband.. 7. Ulysses 8. Odysseus
  island.. 6. Ithaca
  suitor.. 7. Agelaus
penetrate... 4. bore, gore, stab
  5. delve, elbow, enter 6. pierce
  7. pervade 8. permeate 9. perforate
  10. move deeply
penetrating... 4. cold, deep 5. acute,
  sharp 6. shrill, subtle 7. caustic,
  odorous 8. incisive 9. pervading,
  sagacious, searching
penetration... 6. acumen 7. ingress,
  insight 9. acuteness, sharpness
  11. discernment, perforation
  14. discrimination
Peneus (pert to)...
  father of.. 6. Daphne
  genus of.. 6. prawns
  god of.. 11. Peneus River (Thessalia)
penguin... 3. auk 6. Johnny 10. rock
  hopper
penguin (pert to)...
  aviation.. 13. training plane
  duck.. 12. Indian Runner (duck)
  genus.. 8. Eudyptes
  nest.. 7. rookery 10. penguinery
  type.. 4. king 6. Adelie 7. emperor,
  jackass
peninsula... 4. neck 6. penile
  10. chersonese
Peninsula...
  Asia.. 5. Malay
  Cimbrian, Cimbric.. 7. Jutland
  Iberia.. 5. Spain
  Seward.. 6. Alaska
  Tauric.. 6. Crimea
  Thracian.. 9. Gallipoli
penitent... 5. sorry 8. contrite
  9. repentant
penitential discipline... 7. penance
penitential period... 4. Lent
pennant... 4. fane, flag, whip
  6. banner, burgee (yacht), ensign,
  pennon, pinion 9. banderole
pennant fish... 11. cobblerfish
pennate... 6. winged 7. pinnate
  9. feathered, penniform

pennon... 4. flag, wing 6. banner, pinion 8. streamer
Pennsylvania...
capital.. 10. Harrisburg
city.. 4. Erie 7. Reading 8. Scranton 10. Pittsburgh 12. Philadelphia
famed site.. 10. Gettysburg 11. Liberty Bell, Valley Forge 16. Independence Hall
founder.. 11. William Penn
mountain.. 5. Davis 11. Alleghenies
named, first.. 10. Penn's Woods
river.. 4. Ohio 8. Delaware 10. Schuylkill 11. Susquehanna
State admission.. 6. second
State motto.. 28. Virtue, Liberty and Independence
State nickname.. 8. Keystone
penny... 4. cent, coin 5. pence 6. copper, stiver 8. denarius (Bib)
penologist, famed... 5. Lawes
penology, study of... 11. criminology 18. punishment for crime
pensive... 3. sad 5. mesto, sober 6. dreamy, musing 7. wistful 10. meditative, melancholy, reflective, thoughtful 13. contemplative
pentastich... 4. poem 6. stanza 7. strophe 10. five verses
Pentateuch... 5. Torah (Tora) 10. Law of Moses 14. First Five Books (Old Test) 16. Five Books of Moses
Pentecost... 8. festival 10. Whitsunday
Pentheus (pert to)...
grandson of.. 6. Cadmus
King of.. 6. Thebes
mother.. 5. Agave
penthouse... 6. lean-to 7. leaning, pentice 9. apartment (roof) 11. overhanging
penury... 4. want 7. poverty 9. indigence, privation 10. scantiness 11. destitution, miserliness
peon... 4. pawn (chess), serf 7. laborer, peasant, soldier 9. attendant, constable, messenger, policeman
peony... 4. piny 6. moutan 7. Paeonia 11. Burmese ruby
people... 3. kin, men 4. folk, ones, race, Rais 5. demos, laity 6. family, nation, public 7. kinsmen, persons 8. populace, subjects 9. citizenry 10. population
people (pert to)...
Am Indian, Eskimo.. 7. Amerind
ancient.. 5. Medes 6. Greeks, Romans 7. Sabines 9. Egyptians, Etruscans
class, lowest.. 8. canaille
common.. 6. vulgar 7. tilikum (tilicum)
headless (Myth).. 8. Acephali
old-fashioned.. 6. prudes 7. squares 13. antediluvians
ref to.. 4. laic 6. ethnic 7. demotic
Spanish.. 5. gente
wild young.. 10. rantipoles
people (of)...
culture (earliest).. 8. Grecians
gentle birth.. 6. gentry
one government.. 6. nation
rank.. 11. aristocracy, aristocrats

the people.. 6. ethnic
peopled... 5. abadi (Ind village) 8. occupied, populous 9. populated
pep... 2. go 3. vim 4. dash 6. energy 7. quicken 9. stimulate 10. initiative, liveliness
pepper... 4. pelt 5. shoot 6. energy 7. bombard 8. sprinkle 9. condiment
pepper (pert to)...
betel.. 4. siri (sirih)
black.. 11. Piper nigrum
box.. 5. tower 8. spitfire
Capsicum, source of.. 7. cayenne, chilies (chili), paprika
climbing.. 5. betel 6. nigrum
condiment.. 7. cayenne, paprika
dulse.. 7. seaweed (red)
genus.. 8. Capsicum
grass.. 5. crass 8. pillwort
sauce.. 7. Tabasco
turnip.. 15. jack-in-the-pulpit
pepper (pert to country)...
Australia.. 4. kava (cava) 8. kavakava
Borneo.. 4. kava (cava)
Guinea.. 5. chili 8. Capsicum
Malay.. 4. siri (sirih)
Spain.. 7. paprika, pimento 8. allspice, pimiento
pepper-and-salt... 4. gray 17. harbinger-of-spring
peppermint... 3. oil 4. herb 6. spirit 7. essence, gum tree, lozenge, menthol (camphor)
peppery... 5. fiery 7. piquant, pungent 8. choleric, spirited, stinging 10. passionate 11. hot-tempered
per... 2. by 7. for each, through 9. by means of 11. according to
peradventure... 3. hap 5. doubt 7. it may be 8. possibly 11. uncertainty
perambulate... 4. walk 6. ramble, stroll 8. traverse 9. promenade, walk about
perceive... 3. see 4. hear, know, note 5. sense 6. behold, descry, detect, divine, notice, remark 7. discern, observe, sensate 9. apprehend 10. comprehend, understand 11. distinguish 12. discriminate
perceptible... 5. faint 7. tactile, visible 8. knowable, manifest, tangible 10. cognizable 11. appreciable, discernible, perceivable
perception... 3. ear 4. tact 5. sense, taste 6. acumen, seeing 8. sagacity 9. awareness, sensation 10. cognizance 11. discernment 13. consciousness 14. discrimination
perceptive... 7. knowing 8. sensible 9. sagacious 14. discriminative
perch... 3. bar, peg, rod, sit 4. fish, pole 5. aerie, barse, roost, sit on, staff 6. alight, aviary, sauger, settle, weapon 7. measure 9. trumpeter
Percheron... 5. horse 15. Percheron Norman
perchers... 5. birds 7. candles 8. Passeres 10. Insessores
percolate... 4. ooze, seep, sift, silt, sipe 5. exude, leach, steep 6. filter, strain 7. trickle 8. permeate, transude

percussion... 9. collision
10. concussion, detonation
percussion instrument... 4. drum,
gong 5. bells, bones, traps
6. Becken, chimes, tom–tom
7. celesta, cymbals, marimba, potlids
8. carillon, clappers, triangle
9. castanets, xylophone
10. tambourine, vibraphone
12. glockenspiel
perdition... 4. hell, loss (soul), ruin
5. wreck 9. damnation
11. destruction
peregrinate... 6. travel, wander 7. go
about, sojourn
peregrine... 5. alien 6. exotic, falcon
7. foreign, pilgrim, strange
9. foreigner
perempt... 5. quash 6. defeat
7. destroy
peremptory... 5. final 7. express
8. absolute, arrogant, decisive,
dogmatic, positive, resolute
9. arbitrary, mandatory
10. compulsory, conclusive,
imperative, obligatory 11. dictatorial
13. authoritative 16. incontrovertible
perennial... 7. lasting 8. constant,
enduring 9. continual, evergreen,
permanent, perpetual, unceasing
10. continuous 12. never–failing
perennial (pert to)...
climbing.. 5. liana (liane)
grass.. 4. lyme 6. Elymus (genus)
7. wild rye
herb.. 4. Geum 5. avens
weed.. 8. toadflax
perfect... 4. holy, pure, sole 5. ideal,
model, teleo (comb form), whole
6. entire 7. correct, develop, improve
8. finished 9. blameless, faultless,
inviolate, righteous 10. consummate,
satisfying 11. unqualified
perfection... 4. acme 5. ideal
7. paragon 8. accuracy, maturity
10. completion, excellence
13. faultlessness
perfectly... 5. quite 7. ideally, rightly,
utterly 9. correctly 10. absolutely,
accurately, altogether, completely,
flawlessly, thoroughly
perfecto... 5. cigar (tapering)
perficient... 6. actual 9. effective,
effectual
perfidious... 6. shifty 8. disloyal
9. faithless 11. disaffected,
treacherous 12. falsehearted
perfidy... 7. treason 8. apostasy
9. duplicity, treachery 10. disloyalty
13. faithlessness
perforate... 4. bore, dock 5. drill,
punch 6. pierce, pounce, riddle
9. penetrate 10. umbilicate
perforated...
block.. 3. nut
initials (Philat).. 10. stamp marks
nozzle.. 4. rose
space.. 5. brain
sphere.. 4. bead
perforation... 4. bore, hole 6. eyelet
8. aperture, piercing, punching
perform... 2. do 3. act 4. play

5. enact, exert 6. effect 7. execute,
fulfill, produce 8. complete, transact
9. officiate 10. accomplish, bring
about, perpetrate
performance... 3. act 4. test, work
6. action 7. exploit 8. ceremony
9. operation 10. completion,
exhibition, observance, production
12. consummation
14. accomplishment
performance (pert to)...
clumsy.. 6. bungle
daytime.. 7. matinee
for one.. 4. solo
notable.. 4. feat
of duty.. 8. feasance
performer... 4. doer 5. actor
6. dancer, worker 8. magician,
musician, thespian 9. pretender
15. prestidigitator
perfume... 4. balm, odor 5. aroma,
attar, orris, savor, scent, smell
7. bouquet, cologne, essence, rose
oil 9. fragrance, redolence
10. frangipani
perfume (pert to)...
base.. 4. musk 9. ambergris
cherry.. 7. mahaleb
essence.. 8. bergamot
medicated.. 8. pastille (pastil)
musky.. 5. civet
oriental.. 5. myrrh 7. incense
12. frankincense
scent.. 7. jasmine 8. lavender
10. heliotrope
toilet.. 6. bay rum 12. eau de
Cologne
unguent.. 6. pomade
violet.. 5. irone
pergola... 5. arbor, bower, kiosk
6. pandal 7. balcony, trellis
9. colonnade 11. summerhouse
perhaps... 5. maybe 6. ablins (Scot),
belike, mayhap 8. doubtful, possibly,
probably 9. perchance 10. contingent
peri... 3. elf 5. about (pref), fairy
6. beauty
periapt... 5. charm 6. amulet
pericarp... 3. pod 5. berry, shell
8. seedcase
Pericles (Gr)... 9. statesman
periculum (Rom law)... 4. risk 5. peril
6. danger
perigee (Astron)... 12. nearest earth
(opp of apogee)
peril... 4. risk 6. danger, hazard,
menace 8. jeopardy
perilously high... 7. Icarian (flying)
perimeter... 5. ambit 6. border
7. outline 8. boundary 9. periphery
period... 3. age, day, dot, end, eon,
era, eve 4. stop, term, time, year
5. cycle, epoch, limit, spell
6. degree, moment, season
8. duration, sentence 10. conclusion
11. termination
period (pert to)...
historical.. 4. eral 6. Eocene
7. Neocene
penitential.. 4. Lent
statutory.. 10. limitation
Tertiary.. 6. Eocene 7. Miocene,

Neocene 8. Pliocene
periodic... 4. eral 6. annual 7. etesian
8. seasonal 9. recurrent
10. rhythmical 12. intermittent
periodic (pert to)...
sea motion.. 4. tide
wind.. 2. oe 7. chinook, etesian,
monsoon
windstorm.. 2. oe 7. tornado
9. whirlwind
periodical... 5. paper 6. review
7. etesian, journal 8. magazine
9. recurring 11. publication
periodical cicada... 6. locust (17 yrs)
period of...
delay.. 10. moratorium
dryness.. 7. drought
evolution.. 6. hemera
fifty days.. 13. quinquagesima
five years.. 6. pentad
holding.. 6. tenure
instruction.. 7. session
possession.. 5. lease
probation.. 6. parole
prosperity.. 4. boom 6. golden
recovery.. 13. convalescence
14. reconstruction
sleep.. 11. hibernation
ten years.. 6. decade
time.. 3. age, day, eon 4. span
work.. 4. turn 5. shift, spell, watch
youth.. 6. nonage
peripatetic... 7. walking 8. rambling
Peripatetic (pert to Aristotle)...
6. school 8. disciple 10. Philosophy
peripheral... 6. distal 7. outmost
8. external 9. outlinear 10. round
about
periphery... 3. lip, rim 4. brim
5. ambit 6. areola, border
8. confines 9. perimeter
10. borderland 13. circumference
perique... 7. tobacco (strong) 10. otter
brown
perish... 3. die, rot 4. fade 5. decay,
waste 8. pass away, squander
9. cease to be, disappear 11. be
destroyed
perissodactyl... 15. odd–numbered
toes
peristyle... 7. columns (range of)
8. corridor 9. colonnade
10. peripteral
peritoneum fold... 7. omentum
periwig... 3. wig 6. frizzy, peruke
9. shellfish 10. periwinkle
periwinkle... 4. blue 5. snail
6. mussel, myrtle 9. evergreen
perjink... 4. neat, nice 7. precise
perjure... 7. violate 8. forswear
perjury... 9. violation 12. breech of
oath 13. false swearing
perk... 5. preen, prink 7. smarten
9. percolate 10. perquisite
perkin... 5. cider
perk up... 7. cheer up, improve, raise
up, refresh 10. recuperate
permanent... 5. fixed 6. innate, stable
7. abiding, durable, lasting
8. constant, enduring, inherent
9. perpetual 10. changeless,
continuing 12. unchangeable

permeate... 5. imbue 7. pervade
8. saturate
permission... 5. grace, leave
7. consent, license 9. allowance
10. sufferance 13. authorization
permissive... 8. optional 9. allowable,
permitted, tolerated 10. consenting,
permitting 13. power of choice
permit... 3. let 4. leve 5. allow, grant,
leave 6. suffer 7. consent, license,
warrant 8. tolerate 9. authorize
10. permission
permit to live... 5. spare 8. reprieve
permutate... 6. change 9. rearrange
11. interchange
permutation... 6. barter
11. interchange 13. transmutation
14. transformation
pern... 6. Pernis 7. buzzard (honey)
pernicious... 4. bane 5. fatal
6. anemia, deadly, malign, wicked
7. baleful, baneful, harmful, hurtful,
noisome, noxious, ruinous, vicious
10. villainous 11. deleterious
pernio... 9. chilblain
perorate... 5. speak (at length)
7. declaim 8. harangue 9. expatiate
perpendicular... 4. sine 5. erect,
plumb, sheer, steep 7. apothem,
upright 8. binormal, vertical
9. rectitude 10. standing up
11. precipitous
perpetrate... 6. commit 7. perform
12. carry through
perpetual... 7. endless, eternal
8. constant, unending 9. continual,
perennial, permanent, unceasing
10. continuous 11. everlasting
perpetually... 9. endlessly, eternally
11. ceaselessly 12. interminably
perpetuity... 7. annuity 8. eternity
11. endless time
perplex... 3. vex 4. cark 5. amaze
6. puzzle, riddle 7. confuse
8. bewilder, entangle 9. obfuscate
10. complicate
perplexity... 3. fog 6. tangle
7. anxiety, dilemma, problem
8. question 9. confusion, situation
10. complexity 11. distraction
12. bewilderment, complication
perquisite... 3. tip 4. gain 6. boodle
8. appanage, gratuity
perquod... 7. whereby
per se... 6. itself 8. directly
11. essentially 13. intrinsically
perse... 4. blue
persecute... 5. annoy, harry, hound
6. harass 7. afflict, oppress, torment
8. hunt down 9. martyrize
persecution... 9. treatment
10. harassment, oppression
12. mistreatment
Persephone (pert to)...
abductor.. 5. Hades
Attica, name.. 4. Kore (Cora)
deity of.. 11. agriculture
father.. 4. Zeus
Greek name.. 11. Persephassa
mother.. 7. Demeter
Orphic literary name.. 8. Despoina
queen of.. 15. infernal regions

Roman name .. 10. Proserpine
(Proserpina)
Perseus (pert to) . . .
Astron .. 13. Constellation
father .. 4. Zeus
mother .. 5. Danae
slayer of .. 6. Medusa
perseverance . . . 8. patience
9. constancy 10. resolution,
steadiness 11. persistence, pertinacity
13. steadfastness
persevere . . . 5. abide 6. endure, insist,
keep on 7. carry on, persist
8. continue
Persia (Iran, Irani) . . . see also *Persian*
capital .. 7. Teheran (Tehran)
city .. 5. Niriz 6. Abadan, Shiraz,
Tabriz 7. Hamadan, Ispahan
country (anc) .. 4. Elam 7. Chaldea
gulf .. 4. Oman 7. Persian
gulf port .. 7. Bushire 9. Mohamerah
gulf province .. 6. Kuwait
gulf wind .. 6. shamal
lake .. 7. Rezaieh, Urumidh (Salt)
mountain .. 6. Ararat, Elburz, Zagros
9. Hindu Kush
pert to .. 6. Persic
river .. 5. Safid 9. Euphrates
ruins .. 10. Persepolis (Shiraz)
Persian (pert to) . . . see also *Iranian*
blue .. 10. regimental
calendar reformer .. 9. Jalalaean
(Jalalian)
carpet, rug .. 4. kali 5. Herat (Herati),
Senna 6. Kerman, Tabriz
11. Baluchistan
cushion .. 6. musnud
diadem .. 3. taj
door .. 3. dar
evergreen .. 4. olax
grass .. 6. millet
gum .. 10. tragacanth
hat .. 3. fez 6. turban
idiom .. 7. persism
javelin .. 6. jereed (jerid)
rose .. 3. gul
rug .. see *carpet* (above)
screen .. 6. purdah
Persian animals, birds, fruit . . .
apple .. 6. citron
bird .. 6. bulbul
cat .. 6. Angora
deer .. 5. maral 6. fallow
gazelle .. 4. cora
lamb .. 9. astrakhan, broadtail
lynx .. 7. caracul
tick (venomous) .. 8. Miana bug
Persian Myth, Religion . . .
angel .. 3. Mah
deity .. 6. Ormazd (Supreme)
demigod, hero .. 4. Yima
demon .. 7. Apaosha
fairy .. 3. elf, fay 4. peri
fire worshiper .. 5. Parsi (Parsee)
god of light .. 7. Mithras
mystic .. 4. sufi
nymph .. 5. houri
religion founder .. 9. Zoroaster
religious doctrine .. 6. Babism
(Babiism)
sacred books (Zoroastrian) .. 6. Avesta

scriptures (Moham) .. 5. Koran
spirit .. 7. Ahriman
Persian people, government . . .
assembly (1906) .. 6. Majlis (Mejlis)
caste (priestly) .. 4. Magi 7. Wise Men
chief .. 3. mir 4. Shah
chief's wife, lady .. 4. bibi
civil officer .. 4. khan
dynasty .. 5. Kajar 7. Arsacid
8. Selencid 10. Sassanidae
(Sassanid)
governor (anc) .. 6. satrap
King .. 4. Shah 5. Cyrus 6. Darius,
Xerxes
language (anc) .. 4. Zend 7. Pahlavi
(Pahlevi)
natives .. 5. Kurds, Medes, Mukri,
Perse 6. Aryans
New Year's Day .. 7. Nowroze
people .. 7. Hadjemi, Iranics
8. Iranians
poet .. 4. Omar 5. Hafiz, Saadi
ruler .. 4. Shah 6. atabeg (atabek),
Sultan
student (Koran) .. 5. hafiz
trader .. 4. Sart
tribe .. 4. Leks, Lurs 5. Arabs, Kurds,
Turks 7. Gypsies 8. Baluchis
Wise Men .. 4. Magi
persiflage . . . 6. banter 8. raillery
persimmon . . . 4. kaki 7. chapote
persist . . . 4. last, urge 6. endure
7. prevail 9. persevere
persistent . . . 7. durable 8. constant,
habitual 10. determined, inveterate
11. persevering 13. indefatigable
persistently opposed . . . 8. renitent
9. obstinate 12. recalcitrant
person . . . 3. one 4. body, soul
5. being, wight 6. figure 8. creature
9. character 10. individual
person (pert to) . . .
accuser, challenger .. 9. appellant
acting for another .. 5. proxy
9. alternate
baptized (anc) .. 11. illuminatus
base .. 7. caitiff, hangdog
bringing bad luck .. 4. jinx 5. Jonah
bringing good luck .. 6. mascot
canonized .. 5. saint
careless .. 7. trifler 11. pococurante
charged with high mission .. 7. apostle
charitable .. 9. samaritan
cheerful .. 8. optimist
clumsy .. 3. oaf 5. staup 6. lummox
7. bungler
common .. 3. lay 8. roturier
conceited .. 4. prig
contemptible .. 3. cad 4. heel, toad
7. bauchle (Scot)
crazed .. 6. maniac 10. monomaniac,
psychopath
credulous .. 5. Simon
cruel .. 5. fiend
dishonorable .. 6. rotter
dissolute .. 4. roué
drunken .. 4. lush
dull .. 4. dolt 5. dunce, moron, stock
6. dorbel 9. blockhead
dwarf .. 5. shurf
educated .. 6. pedant, pundit, savant
7. erudite, learned, student

8. cultured, highbrow 9. literatus
12. intellectual
emitting smoke .. 7. whiffer
enterprising .. 8. go–getter
fabulously rich .. 5. Midas
foolish .. 3. sop 4. zany 5. clown,
idiot, nutty 6. dotard 7. bonkers,
buffoon 9. simpleton
gigantic .. 5. giant, titan 7. monster
gloomy .. 7. killjoy 10. crosspatch
good luck .. 6. mascot
grotesque .. 9. golliwogg
guilty .. 7. culprit, transgressor
held as pledge .. 7. hostage
image of .. 4. doll, idol 5. clone
6. poppet, puppet
impatient .. 6. fidget 7. hotspur
important .. 3. VIP 5. mogul
7. magnate, notable 9. personage
indifferent .. 5. stoic
inexperienced .. 9. greenhorn
insignificant .. 5. sprat 6. little, nobody
lazy .. 5. drone 8. sluggard
learned .. see *educated* (above)
left–handed .. 6. clumsy 8. sinister
9. portsider
loud–voiced .. 7. stentor 8. blowhard
low–bred .. 3. cad 6. vulgar
miserly .. 9. skinflint 10. curmudgeon
non–Jewish .. 5. Aryan 7. Gentile
overmodest .. 5. prude 8. bluenose
perfidious .. 5. snake 7. traitor
9. faithless
rapacious .. 4. wolf 5. harpy
relaxed .. 4. calm 8. laid–back
representing another .. 5. proxy
7. stand–in 9. alternate
respondent to appeal .. 8. appellee
rich .. 7. wealthy 9. plutocrat
10. capitalist 11. millionaire
rude, ill–mannered .. 4. boor 5. yahoo
scatterbrained .. 6. madcap
self–centered .. 6. egoist 7. egotist
9. extrovert, introvert
self–righteous .. 8. pharisee
sharp–eyed .. 5. alert, Argus
sick .. 9. aegrotant, bedridden
skilled .. 6. artist, master 7. artisan
8. mechanic
staff (Mil) .. 10. aide–de–camp
stupid .. 3. ass 4. dolt, gump, nerd
5. moron, stock
supercilious .. 4. snob 9. conceited
thankless .. 7. ingrate
unclassified .. 11. nondescript
unique .. 4. oner
unknown .. 7. inconnu 8. inconnue
unmarried .. 6. maiden, single
8. bachelor, celibate, spinster
untidy .. 5. messy 6. grungy
8. slipshod, slovenly 9. litterbug
valorous .. 4. hero 5. champion
violent–tempered .. 6. tartar
wealthy .. 5. nabob, pluto (comb form)
10. capitalist 11. millionaire
who reads, writes .. 8. literate
witty .. 3. wag 7. punster
8. comedian 10. comedienne
worthless .. 5. lorel, losel
writ serving .. 6. elisor
young .. 9. stripling
14. whippersnapper

personage ... 5. image, mogul
7. bearing, stature 8. great man,
one's body, portrait
13. impersonation
persona grata ... 13. welcome person
16. acceptable person
personal (pert to) ...
appearance .. 8. presence
comb form .. 4. idio
history .. 6. memoir
ornament .. 6. parure
ownership, land .. 6. estate
7. demesne 8. chattels, property
personality ... 3. ego 5. being
6. person 8. identity 13. individuality
15. distinctiveness
persona non grata ...
18. unacceptable person
personate ... 5. enact 7. feigned
9. represent 10. personated
11. counterfeit
personification ... 3. Una (truth)
10. embodiment 11. attribution
14. representation
person of ...
age .. 5. major
courage .. 7. Spartan
eighty years .. 12. octogenarian
encyclopedic learning .. 10. polyhistor
fifty years .. 15. quinquagenarian
forty years .. 14. quadragenarian
great intellect .. 6. genius
nervous disorders .. 8. neurotic
ninety years .. 12. nonagenarian
one hundred years .. 11. centenarian
seventy years .. 14. septuagenarian
sixty years .. 12. sexagenarian
skill .. 6. master, talent 7. magnate
persons of ...
a familiar set .. 7. coterie
a family tree .. 6. stirps
groups .. 4. army, band, team
6. chorus, troupe 7. company
8. assembly 9. orchestra
organized bodies .. 5. corps, posse
perspicacity ... 6. acumen, vision
8. sagacity 9. acuteness
11. discernment, penetration
perspicuity ... 8. lucidity, sagacity
12. translucency, transparency
perspiration ... 5. sudor, sweat
7. sudoric 8. hard work
11. evaporation, saline fluid
13. transpiration
persuade ... 4. coax, sway, urge
6. entice, induce, reason 7. convert,
suasion 8. convince, inveigle
9. influence, plead with, stonewall
persuasible ... 6. pliant
11. persuadable
14. open–mindedness
persuasive ... 8. eloquent 9. impelling
10. convincing, persuading
pert ... 3. gay 4. bold, keen 5. brash,
sassy, saucy 6. clever, comely,
dapper, daring, lively, nimble
7. forward 8. handsome, skillful
9. exquisite, officious, sprightly
11. impertinent 12. presumptuous
pert (girl) ... 4. chit, minx
pertain ... 5. belie 6. belong, relate
7. adjunct 8. function, peculiar

9. accessory, appendage, appertain, attribute

pertaining to . . .

act of rising . . **6.** ortive **7.** eastern
agriculture . . **7.** georgic
ancestral type . . **9.** atavistic
ancient Nile city . . **4.** Sais (Saite)
ancient Troy . . **5.** Iliac
anything remote . . **6.** forane
apostles . . **7.** Petrine
Asiatic (old) . . **8.** Chaldean
Asiatic mountain . . **6.** Altaic
Athens . . **5.** Attic
authorized doctrine . . **8.** dogmatic **10.** dogmatical
birthmark . . **6.** nevoid (naevoid)
body . . **5.** somal
body of land . . **11.** continental
book description . . **13.** bibliographic
both ears . . **8.** binaural
both sexes . . **6.** unisex **7.** epicene
breadmaking . . **6.** panary
breastbone . . **7.** sternal
bristles . . **5.** setal
bunch . . **5.** comal
canonical hours . . **7.** matinal
carving . . **6.** glypic **7.** glyptic
cheek . . **5.** malar
church, part . . **7.** apsidal
city . . **5.** civic, urban
cod family . . **6.** gadoid
coins . . **12.** numismatical
colors . . **9.** chromatic
construction . . **8.** geodesic, tectonic
cork . . **7.** suberic
cough . . **7.** tussine
court . . **5.** aulic **9.** judiciary
crown . . **7.** coronal
dance . . **6.** gestic **13.** terpsichorean
daughter . . **6.** filial
dawn . . **4.** eoan
day (ordinary) . . **6.** ferial
desert wastes . . **6.** eremic
diaphragm . . **7.** phrenic
dogma . . **9.** levitical
doves . . **9.** columbine
downward air . . **9.** katabatic
downy . . **5.** dotal
dreams . . **7.** oneiric **9.** oneirotic
ducks . . **7.** anatine
early church . . **9.** patristic
early culture . . **8.** eolithic
earth . . **4.** geal **5.** terra **7.** teluric **9.** planetary
earthquake . . **7.** seismic
east . . **4.** dawn, eoan **7.** auroral
elms . . **9.** ulmaceous
engraving . . **7.** glyptic
equal rights . . **3.** ERA **6.** libber
essence . . **5.** basic
exhaustion . . **7.** burnout **9.** tiredness
fallow deer . . **6.** damine
fashion . . **5.** modal **6.** preppy, trendy
fasting . . **8.** anorexic **9.** abstinent
fats . . **6.** adipic, sebaic **9.** cellulite
feet . . **5.** pedal
fields . . **8.** agrarian
fine arts . . **9.** aesthetic (esthetic)
fingers . . **7.** digital
first principles . . **9.** elemental
fissure . . **5.** rimal
flood . . **7.** diluvian

flowers . . **9.** floscular **10.** florescent
forehead . . **7.** metopic
frogs . . **6.** anuran, ranine
funeral music . . **10.** threnodial
funerals . . **8.** exequial
gospel . . **9.** evangelic
gulls . . **6.** larine
gums (Anat) . . **8.** gingival
hair . . **5.** pilar **7.** blow–dry
hands . . **6.** chiral, manual
head . . **8.** cephalic
heaths . . **8.** ericetal
holiday . . **6.** ferial (Eccl), festal
honey . . **10.** melaginous
horse . . **6.** equine
house . . **5.** domal (Astrol)
hypothetical force . . **4.** odic
infernal regions . . **7.** avernal
ink . . **10.** atramental
insects . . **11.** entomologic
intellect . . **6.** noetic
iron . . **6.** ferric
islands . . **7.** insular
jaw . . **10.** mandibular
kidney . . **5.** renal
knots . . **5.** nodal
land . . **8.** praedial (predial)
language meaning . . **8.** semantic
laughter . . **8.** risorial
leg . . **6.** crural **7.** fibular
lips . . **6.** labial
liver . . **7.** hepatic
living organism . . **13.** parasitologic
lockjaw . . **7.** tetanic
love . . **6.** erotic **7.** amatory **8.** erotical
male . . **5.** macho, manly **7.** agnatic
marriage . . **7.** marital **8.** hymeneal
marsh . . **8.** paludine
meaning, in language . . **8.** semantic
medicine . . **6.** iatric **8.** iatrical
medulla oblongata (brain) . . **6.** bulbar
memory . . **6.** mnesic **7.** mnestic **8.** mnemonic **13.** retrospective
midday . . **8.** meridian
milk . . **7.** lactary, lacteal
mind . . **6.** mental **7.** phrenic
money matters . . **5.** T–bill **7.** bailout **8.** economic
morning . . **5.** matin, sunup **7.** matinal **9.** matutinal
motion . . **7.** kinetic
mouth . . **4.** oral **7.** oscular, palatal **8.** stomatic
mustard family . . **11.** cruciferous
nephew . . **7.** nepotal
north wind . . **6.** boreal
nose . . **5.** nasal **6.** narial, rhinal
nut . . **5.** nucal
ocean . . **7.** pelagic
old age . . **6.** senile **7.** geratic **8.** gerontic **9.** geriatric
Old World . . **13.** gerontogenous
peacock . . **8.** pavonine
people . . **4.** laic **7.** demotic
pigs . . **7.** porcine
pleasure . . **7.** hedonic
priests . . **10.** sacerdotal
prophecy . . **9.** vaticinal
public . . **7.** cameral
public prayer . . **8.** liturgic **10.** liturgical
punishment . . **5.** penal **8.** punitive
queen . . **7.** reginal

rainbow.. 6. iridal
reason.. 6. noetic
region without earthquakes..
    11. peneseismic
rhubarb.. 7. rheumic
river.. 5. amnic
river bank.. 8. riparian
rock.. 7. petrean
royal court.. 5. aulic
salvation.. 8. soterial 9. soterical
sarcasm.. 8. ironical
school of philosophy.. 7. Eleatic
sea.. 6. marine 7. oceanic, pelagic
    9. thelassic
seacoast.. 8. littoral
sense of taste.. 9. gustatory
sepulchral mound.. 7. tumular
shin, shinbone.. 7. cnemial
ship's sails.. 5. velic
singing birds.. 6. oscine
skull.. 5. inial
sole of foot.. 7. plantar
spring.. 6. vernal
stars.. 6. astral 7. stellar 8. sidereal
state affairs.. 9. pragmatic
stepmothers.. 8. novercal
storks.. 7. pelagic
summer.. 7. estival (aestival)
    8. festival
sun.. 5. solar 6. heliac
tail.. 6. caudal
teaching.. 9. pedagogic
tears.. 8. lacrimal
tempo.. 6. agogic
the plague.. 6. loimic
the skin.. 5. deric 6. dermic
thread.. 5. filar
tile.. 7. tegular
time.. 7. chronic
tin.. 7. stranic
tissue.. 5. telar
tongue.. 7. glossal, lingual
tortoises.. 9. chelonian
touch.. 7. tactile
travel.. 6. viatic
trees.. 8. arboreal
verse stress.. 5. ictic
walls.. 5. mural 8. parietal
wax.. 5. ceral
weight.. 5. baric 8. ponderal
whales.. 5. rotal
wife.. 7. uxorial
wine.. 5. vinic
wine making.. 10. oenopoetic
wings.. 5. alary
winter.. 6. hiemal
womanhood.. 9. muliebral
woods.. 6. sylvan
wrist.. 6. carpal
pertaining to country...
Asiatic.. 8. Chaldean
Asiatic mountain.. 6. Altaic
Athens.. 5. Attic
Carthage.. 5. Punic
Celts.. 4. Erse
Cretan language.. 6. Minoan
Dissenters' meeting house.. 7. pantile
    (from the roofing)
England.. 8. Anglican
Ethiopian religion.. 6. Coptic
France.. 6. Gallic
Franks.. 5. Salic

Gentiles.. 6. ethnic
German State.. 8. Bavarian
Greek epic.. 9. Homerical
Greek philosophy.. 7. Eleatic
    8. Platonic
Greek race (anc).. 6. Aeolic
Greek valley.. 6. Nemean 8. Argolian
Hindu books, writing.. 5. Vedic
    7. Tantric
Hindu philosophy, inertia.. 5. tamas
Irish.. 6. Celtic, Gaelic
Isle of Man.. 4. Manx
Mars.. 5. Arean
Mediterranean.. 6. Levant
Moses.. 6. Mosaic
Nile city (anc).. 4. Sais (Saite)
Norse poem.. 5. runic
Passover.. 7. Paschal
Red Sea colony.. 8. Eritrean
Rhine.. 7. Rhenish
Scotch Highlander.. 6. Gaelic
Spice Islands.. 7. Molucca
Troy (anc).. 5. Iliac 6. Trojan
Vulcan.. 11. Mulcibirian
West Indies.. 9. Antillean
pertenencia... 10. concession
    11. mining claim
Perth.. 6. Atholl (Athole) 7. Ontario
    9. Australia
pertinacious... 4. firm 8. adhering,
    resolute 9. tenacious 10. determined,
    inflexible, persistent, unyielding
    11. persevering
pertinacity... 9. obstinacy
    11. persistency
pertinence... 7. fitness 9. relevancy
    10. timeliness 12. appositeness
perturb... 5. alarm 6. excite
    7. agitate, derange, disturb, fluster,
    trouble 8. bewilder, disorder, distress
    9. confusion
perturbation... 5. alarm 7. anxiety,
    fluster 9. agitation, confusion
    10. excitement 11. fearfulness
    12. bewilderment, irregularity
pertusion... 8. piercing, punching
    11. perforation, punched hole
pertussis... 5. cough 13. whooping
    cough
Peru... see also Peruvian
    capital.. 4. Lima 5. Cuzco (Inca)
    14. City of the Kings
    hero.. 7. Bolivar, Pizarro
    lake.. 8. Titicaca
    mountain.. 5. Andes 10. Cordillera
    port.. 6. Callao 7. Iquitos
    8. Mollendo
    river.. 4. Sama 5. Santa 6. Amazon
    7. Maranon, Ucayali 8. Urubamba
    ruins.. 4. Inca 5. huaco (relics)
Peruvian (pert to)...
    animal.. 4. paco 5. llama 6. alpaca
    bark.. 8. cinchona
    goddess of fertility.. 4. Mama
    inn, tavern.. 5. tambo
    king (petty).. 7. cacique
    plant.. 3. oca
    rodent.. 10. chinchilla
    tinamou.. 4. yutu
    tree.. 8. cinchona
    university.. 9. San Marcos
    volcano.. 7. El Misti

wind (cold) .. 4. puna
pervade ... 4. fill 5. imbue 6. extend
8. permeate, traverse 9. penetrate
pervading ... 9. prevalent, universal
perverse ... 3. awk 4. awry, wogh
5. wrong 6. cranky, erring
7. corrupt, forward, froward,
wayward, willful (wilful) 8. contrary,
petulant 9. obstinate 10. ill–humored
perversion ... 5. error 6. misuse
8. apostasy 9. sophistry
10. corruption, distortion
13. falsification 17. misinterpretation,
misrepresentation
perversion of taste ... 7. malacia
pervert ... 4. ruin 5. upset 6. divert,
misuse 7. corrupt, distort, falsify,
heretic 8. apostate, overturn,
renegade 9. turn aside
10. degenerate, lead astray
12. misinterpret, misrepresent
pervulgate ... 7. publish
Pesach, Pesah ... 8. Passover (Feast)
pesante ... 5. heavy 10. impressive
peshkash ... 3. tax 7. present, tribute
8. offering
peskar ... 5. agent 7. steward
8. minister 10. accountant
pesky ... 6. plaguy 7. teasing
9. harassing 10. tormenting
pes planus ... 8. flatfoot 13. talipes
planus
pess ... 7. hassock (church)
pessimist ... 5. cynic 6. malist
9. defeatist, worrywart
pessimistic ... 6. gloomy 7. cynical
8. cowardly, hopeless 10. despairing,
foreboding, uncheerful
pest ... 3. nag 4. bane 6. plague
7. ragweed 8. epidemic, nuisance
9. annoyance 10. pestilence
pester ... 3. nag, rib 5. annoy, tease,
worry 6. badger, harass, impede,
infest 7. torment 8. entangle
9. importune 10. overburden
pestilence ... 4. bane 7. disease,
scourge 8. epidemic 13. bubonic
plague
pestilent ... 6. deadly 7. noxious
8. annoying 9. pestering, poisonous
10. contagious, infectious, pernicious
11. mischievous, troublesome
pestle ... 4. club 6. muller 7. crusher,
pounder
pes valgus ... 9. bowlegged 13. talipes
valgus
pet ... 4. dear, tiff 5. humor 6. caress,
coddle, cosset, dandle, fondle,
pamper 7. darling, dudgeon, indulge
8. cade lamb, favorite
10. endearment
petals (pert to) ...
flower .. 7. corolla
having .. 8. petalous
orchid .. 8. labellum
ref to .. 5. whorl 8. petaline, petaloid
without .. 9. apetalous
petard ... 9. explosive 11. firecracker
peteman (thieves' sl) ... 5. thief
7. burglar 8. peterman
9. cracksman, fisherman (Hist)
10. safeblower

Peter (pert to) ...
Bell .. 4. poem
Bible .. 5. Simon (also called)
7. epistle (New Test)
Ibbetson .. 5. novel
Pan .. 3. boy 4. play
Pan dog .. 4. Nana
the Great .. 4. Czar
the Great's father .. 6. Alexis
the Hermit .. 8. Crusader (1st)
peter out ... 4. fade, fail, tire, wane
6. weaken 7. dwindle 9. cease to
be
petiole ... 4. stem 5. stalk 8. peduncle
9. leafstalk 10. mesopodium
petit ... 4. mean 5. petty, small
6. little 13. insignificant
petite ... 5. small 6. demure, little
petite (pert to) ...
bourse .. 6. Market (Finan)
marmite .. 4. soup
noblesse .. 8. nobility (lesser)
petition ... 3. ask, beg, sue 4. plea,
pray 5. apply, plead 6. prayer
7. entreat, relator, request, solicit
8. entreaty 10. supplicate
peto ... 5. wahoo
petrified ... 8. hardened 9. terrified
15. carved from stone
petrified body ... 6. fossil
petrify ... 4. numb 6. deaden, harden
7. astound, stupefy 8. paralyze
11. become stone
petroglyph ... 11. rock carving 15. rock
inscription
Petrograd ... 9. Leningrad
petroleum product ... 6. butane, diesel
7. naphtha, propane 8. gasoline
petrology (science of) ... 5. rocks
petrosal ... 4. bone 5. sinus, stony
7. petrous 8. ganglion
petticoat ... 4. girl, kilt 5. jupon,
pagne, woman 6. kirtle 8. basquine
9. undercoat, waistcoat
10. fustanella, underskirt
petticoat tails ... 7. teacake
9. shortcake
pettifogger ... 4. tyro 5. quack
6. lawyer 7. shyster 8. attorney
pettish ... 7. fretful, peevish 9. irritable
pettle ... 6. cuddle, nestle, potter
7. cherish
petto ... 12. in one's breast 15. in
contemplation
petty ... 4. mean, orra 5. minor, small
6. paltry 7. trivial 8. childish,
inferior, nugatory, trifling 9. miniscule
10. diminutive 11. small–minded,
subordinate, unimportant
12. narrow–minded 13. insignificant
14. inconsiderable
petty (pert to) ...
captain .. 9. centurion
fault .. 10. peccadillo
larceny .. 10. scrounging
mullein .. 7. cowslip
objection .. 5. cavil
prince .. 6. satrap
petulance ... 8. ill humor, pertness
9. insolence, sauciness
10. wantonness 11. peevishness,
pettishness

petulant... 4. pert 5. cross, huffy,
saucy, testy 6. wanton 7. forward,
fretful, peevish, wayward, willful
8. contrary, immodest, insolent
9. querulous

peu à peu... 9. by degrees 14. little
by little

pewee... 5. pewit 6. phoebe
8. woodcock 10. flycatcher

pewit... 5. pewee 7. lapwing
12. laughing gull

Pfefferkuchen... 11. gingerbread

Phaëthon, Class Myth (pert to)...
bird.. 4. swan
car.. 3. sun
father.. 6. Helios
sun god.. 6. Helios

phagomania... 8. insanity
16. insatiable hunger

Phalacrocorax... 5. coots
10. cormorants

phalacrosis... 8. alopecia, baldness

phalanger... 5. tapoa 9. marsupial

phalanx... 4. bone 5. pawns 6. troops
7. company (Mil) 8. infantry

phalera... 4. boss 5. cameo

phantasm... 5. dream, fancy, ghost
6. idolum, spirit 7. eidolon, fantasy,
phantom, specter (spectre)
8. delusion, illusion 10. apparition

phantasy, fantasy... 5. fancy, image
6. autism 8. daydream
11. imagination

phantom... 5. fairy, ghost 7. eidolon,
specter (spectre) 10. simulacrum

Pharaoh (Bib)... 4. faro, king

Pharaoh (pert to)...
ancestor.. 2. Ra
chicken, hen.. 7. vulture (Egypt)
fig.. 8. sycamore
mouse.. 9. ichneumon

phare... 6. beacon, pharos
10. lighthouse

pharisee... 7. pietist 9. hypocrite

pharmacology... 5. drugs 13. materia
medica

pharos... 5. cloak 6. beacon
10. chandelier (Eccl), lighthouse,
watchtower

phase... 5. facet, stage 6. aspect
7. caprice, chapter, horning (moon)

phases, having many...
11. Hydra–headed

phasm... 6. meteor 7. phantom

pheasant... 5. cheer, monal 6. pukras
7. kallege 8. tragopan 12. ruffed
grouse

pheasant (pert to)...
brood.. 3. nye 4. nide (nid) 5. flock
cuckoo.. 6. coucal
duck.. 7. pintail 9. merganser
finch.. 7. waxbill
genus.. 10. Oreophasis
wren.. 7. emu wren

pheasant species... 5. argus, blood
6. golden, silver 7. kallege
8. curassow 9. Mongolian
10. ring–necked 12. Lady Amherst's

phenomenal... 7. unusual 8. eventful,
sensible 9. objective, wonderful
13. extraordinary

phenomenon... 4. fact 5. event

(unusual) 7. prodigy

phial... 3. cup 4. bowl, vial 6. bottle,
vessel

phiale... 5. laver 6. vessel 8. fountain
(Eccl)

Phi Beta Kappa (pert to)...
badge.. 8. watch key
founding.. 21. William and Mary
College (1776)
meaning.. 24. Philosophy the guide of
life
society.. 11. Greek–letter (oldest)

philabeg (filibeg)... 4. kilt

Philadelphia...
city.. 12. Pennsylvania
fleabane.. 7. skevish
lawyer.. 6. shrewd
meaning.. 13. brother–loving
ref to.. 12. Philadelphus (Ptolemy II)

philander... 5. flirt, lover 7. opossum
10. flirtation, love–making, lover of
men

philanthropic... 6. humane
10. benevolent 12. eleemosynary

philanthropist... 5. donor 8. altruist,
do–gooder 9. Robin Hood
10. benefactor, benevolist,
Montefiore, Rothschild
12. humanitarian

philanthropy... 7. charity 8. good will
10. almsgiving 11. beneficence,
benevolence (opp of misanthropy)

Philippic... 6. screed, tirade 7. oration
8. diatribe 9. Philippus

Philippine, Philippines...
archipelago.. 4. Sulu 5. Malay
bay.. 6. Manila
capital.. 6. Baguio (summer), Manila
10. Quezon City
city.. 5. Albay, Davao 6. Cavite
7. Dagupan
district.. 7. Lepanto
fort.. 4. Gota 10. Corregidor
island.. 4. Cebu 5. Leyte, Luzon,
Panay, Samar, Ticao 6. Negros
7. Palawan, Paragua 8. Mindanao
mountain.. 3. Apo, Iba 5. Mayon
river.. 4. Abra, Agno 5. Pasig
8. Mindanao, Pampanga
university.. 10. Santo Tomas (1611)
volcano.. 3. Apo 5. Mayon

Philippine (pert to)...
animal.. 5. civet, lemur
ant, termite.. 4. anay (anai)
barracks.. 7. cuartel
boat, canoe, raft.. 5. balsa, banca
breadfruit.. 7. camansi
buffalo.. 7. carabao, timarau (timerau)
chair (on poles).. 7. talabon
dagger.. 4. itac
drink.. 4. beno 5. bubud
fabric.. 4. pina 9. pineapple
fetish, idol.. 5. anito
food.. 3. poi 4. Musa, saba, taro
hemp.. 5. abaca 6. Manila
house.. 5. bahay
knife.. 4. bolo
litter, pole chair.. 7. talabon
lizard.. 4. ibid (monitor)
mango.. 5. bauno 7. pahutan
market day.. 7. tiangue
melon.. 6. atimon

mudfish .. **5.** dalag
palm .. **4.** nipa **6.** anahau (anahao)
parrot (green) .. **5.** cagit
reptile .. **6.** python
rice .. **4.** paga **5.** macan
rice field bank .. **7.** pilapil
river .. **4.** ilog
shrub .. **4.** alem
sweetsop .. **4.** ates
town .. **4.** agoa
tree .. **3.** tui **4.** ipil (ypil) **5.** asana,
   ligas, narra, yacal **6.** molave
   7. Eugenia, tindalo **8.** macaasim
turnip .. **7.** cincoma
vehicle (public) .. **9.** carromata
water jar .. **5.** banga
wood .. **4.** teak **5.** ebony **6.** sandal
   8. mahogany
Philippine people (pert to) ...
discoverer .. **8.** Magellan (1521)
farmer .. **3.** tao
headman .. **4.** datu
language .. **4.** Moro **7.** Tagalog (Tagal)
   8. Pilipino
Luzon savage .. **4.** Aeta **6.** Igorot
   (Igorote)
Muslim, Moslem .. **4.** Moro
native .. **3.** tao **4.** Moro, Sulu
native race .. **3.** Lao **4.** Aeta (dwarf)
   7. Tagalog, Visayan
native worker .. **7.** polista
Negrito .. **3.** Ati **4.** Aeta
patriot .. **5.** rizal
peasant .. **3.** tao
priest (Moro) .. **7.** pandita
servant .. **4.** bata **5.** alila
tribe (Chr) .. **5.** Bikol (Bico, Vicol)
tribe (pagan) .. **6.** Italon
Philistine ... **5.** enemy **7.** prosaic
   9. philister **10.** conformist,
   uncultured **12.** antagonistic
   13. prosaic person, unenlightened
Philistine (pert to) ...
anc name .. **9.** Palestine, Philistia
assimilated by .. **7.** Semites
city .. **4.** Gaza **5.** Ekron (Bib)
god .. **4.** Baal **5.** Dagon
philo (comb form) ... **6.** fond of, loving
philogeant ... **12.** lover of earth
philogyny ... **11.** love of women
philology ... **11.** linguistics **14.** love of
   learning
Philomela (pert to) ...
father .. **7.** Pandion (King of Athens)
sister .. **6.** Procne
turned into .. **7.** swallow
   11. nightingale
philosopher ...
American .. **7.** Emerson **9.** Santayana
Chinese .. **9.** Confucius
Dutch .. **7.** Spinoza
English .. **5.** Bacon
French .. **5.** Renan **8.** Rousseau,
   Voltaire
German .. **4.** Kant **9.** Nietzsche
   12. Schopenhauer
Greek .. **4.** Zeno **8.** Socrates
Scottish .. **4.** Hume
Seven Sages (7 Wise Men of Greece) ..
   4. Bias **5.** Solon **6.** Chilon, Thales
   8. Pittacus **9.** Cleobulus
   10. Epimenides (or Periander)

Philosopher of ...
Farney .. **8.** Voltaire
Malmesbury .. **6.** Hobbes
Sans Souci .. **17.** Frederick the Great
Syracuse .. **4.** Dion
Wimbledon .. **14.** John Horne Tooke
philosopher's school ... **7.** Eleatic
philosophical ... **4.** wise **7.** erudite,
   logical, sapient **8.** rational
   9. temperate, unruffled
philosophical being ... **6.** entity
philosophy (pert to) ...
choice of .. **11.** eclecticism
of law .. **13.** jurisprudence
of pantheists .. **5.** Stoic
sublimated .. **17.** Transcendentalism
theory .. **4.** yoga **9.** pantheism,
   Platonism, solipsism **12.** epistemology
phlegmatic ... **4.** calm, dull, slow
   5. inert **6.** mucous, watery
   7. viscous **8.** sluggish **9.** apathetic
phlogistic ... **5.** fiery **6.** heated
   7. burning **11.** impassioned
   12. inflammatory
Phoebad ... **7.** seeress **9.** priestess
   (Delphian) **10.** prophetess
Phoebe (pert to) ...
daughter .. **4.** Leto
epithet of .. **7.** Artemis
mother .. **4.** Gaea (earth goddess)
poetic .. **4.** moon
phoebe ... **4.** fish **5.** craps, pewit
   6. peewee **9.** satellite (Saturn)
   10. flycatcher
Phoebus ... **3.** Sol **6.** sun god
Phoenicia ...
capital city .. **4.** Tyre **5.** Sidon
Colony .. **5.** Hippo **8.** Carthage
deity .. **4.** Baal
famed for .. **9.** purple dye
   10. navigation
goddess of fertility .. **6.** Baltis
   7. Astarte
god of healing .. **6.** Eshmun (Eshmoun)
king .. **6.** Agenor
region .. **5.** Syria
Phoenix ... **4.** bird (fabled), palm
   7. capital (Ariz)
phonetic (pert to) ...
science .. **9.** phonology
sound .. **7.** phoneme
stop .. **9.** occlusive
system .. **5.** romic
phonic ... **6.** spoken, voiced
   7. sounded **8.** auditory **9.** accoustic,
   vibration
phony (comb form) ... **5.** sound, voice
phony ... **4.** fake **9.** contrived,
   simulated **11.** counterfeit
photograph ... **4.** film **5.** image, photo
   7. picture **8.** likeness, portrait
   9. ferrotype, pictorial, portrayal
   10. centerfold, heliograph
   12. photogravure
photographic bath ... **5.** toner
   7. reducer **9.** developer
photography, science of ... **5.** light
   6. optics **7.** photics
photography inventors ... **4.** Land
   6. Niepce, Talbot **8.** Daguerre
photometric unit ... **3.** pyr, rad
phrase ... **5.** idiom **6.** remark, saying,

slogan 7. diction, epigram, epithet, passage 8. flattery 9. catchword 10. expression 11. phraseology
phraseology . . . 5. style 6. jargon 7. diction, wording 8. parlance
phratry (Hist) . . . 4. clan 5. group
phrenetic . . . 3. mad 5. crazy 6. madman 7. fanatic, frantic, violent 9. delirious 10. passionate
phrenology, science of . . . 5. skull 10. craniology
Phrygia, Asia Minor . . .
  cap (comical) . . 10. liberty cap
  deity . . 5. Attis
  Eccl Hist . . 9. Montanist
  founder . . 7. Gordius (800 BC)
  King . . 5. Midas
  marble (anc) . . 9. pavonazzo (pavonazzetto)
  music . . 4. mode
  river . . 7. Meander
phylactery (Eccl) . . . 4. case 5. charm, chest, miter 6. amulet, infula, record, scroll
phylarchy . . . 12. rule by tribes
phyletic . . . 6. racial 7. descent, species 12. phylogenetic
phyllophagous . . . 15. feeding on leaves
physical . . . 6. bodily 7. natural, somatic 8. material 9. corporeal
physical force . . . 10. attraction
physical unit . . . 3. erg
physician . . . 5. medic 6. doctor, healer, intern 7. coroner 8. restorer
physician (pert to) . . .
  ancient . . 5. Galen
  comb form . . 5. iatro
  French Nobel Prize . . 7. Laveran
  Greek (anc) . . 5. Galen 11. Asclepiades
  quack . . 10. medicaster
  symbol . . 8. caduceus
physicist . . . 7. Faraday, Galvani, Marconi 10. naturalist
physiognomy . . . 3. mug 4. face 11. countenance 14. external aspect, interpretation
physique . . . 4. body 6. figure
physis (Gr) . . . 6. nature
phytology, science of . . . 6. botany, plants
piacle . . . 3. sin 5. crime, guilt 7. offense 15. sacrificial rite 17. expiatory offering
pian . . . 5. tumor 9. frambesia
piano (pert to) . . .
  direction . . 10. pianissimo (softly)
  duet, upper part . . 5. primo
  dumb keyboard . . 10. digitorium
  early . . 6. spinet
  Italian . . 10. Cristofori
  keyboard . . 7. clavier 8. pedalier
  pedal . . 7. celeste
  pianolike . . 7. celesta
  player . . 7. pianola
  slang . . 11. eighty–eight
  small . . 8. pianette
piatti . . . 7. cymbals
piazza . . . 5. campo, porch 6. square 7. gallery, portico, veranda
pic . . . 4. peak 8. picayune
picacho . . . 4. hill 5. butte

picador . . . 3. wit 6. jester 7. debater 8. horseman (with lance), toreador 11. bullfighter
picaro . . . 5. knave, rogue 7. sharper 8. vagabond 10. picaresque
picaroon . . . 5. rogue, thief 6. pirate, rascal 7. brigand, corsair 8. prey upon
pick . . . 4. cull, gaff, peck, sort 5. elect, pluck, strum 6. assort, choose, indent, pickax, pierce, select 7. diamond (card), harvest, the best 8. plectrum, the elite 9. toothpick
pick (pert to) . . .
  flaws . . 5. cavil
  out . . 6. pilfer, select 7. acquire, procure, specify 9. eliminate, segregate 11. distinguish
  pick–me–up . . 5. tonic 6. bracer 9. kittiwake, stimulate 11. restorative
  up . . 4. tidy 6. arrest 7. improve 9. stimulant 10. recuperate
picked . . . 4. trim 5. piked, spiny 6. choice, chosen, culled, dainty, peaked, spruce 7. adorned, plucked, pointed 8. stripped 10. fastidious
pickerel . . . 4. fish, pike 9. Esox niger 12. walleyed pike
picket . . . 3. peg 4. pale, post, tern 5. fence, guard, stake 6. bullet, fasten, paling, sentry, tether 7. enclose, fortify, shackle 8. sentinel 10. go on strike
pickle . . . 4. alec, peck 5. achar, brine 6. dawdle, nibble, piddle, pilfer, trifle 7. chutney, vitrial
pickled . . . 5. drunk 6. soused 9. marinated
pickled pig's feet . . . 5. souse
pickle fork . . . 8. runcible
pickle–herring . . . 7. buffoon 11. merry–andrew 12. Pickelhering
pickpocket . . . 4. wire 5. thief 6. bulker
picnic . . . 3. fun 4. camp, play 6. junket, outing 9. festivity
Pict (anc) . . . 4. Scot 5. Aryan 9. aborigine
Pictland . . . 8. Scotland
pictorial . . . 8. painting 11. illustrated, picturesque
Pict's house (Archaeol) . . . 8. dwelling (subterranean)
picture . . . 3. oil 4. copy, draw, icon 5. image, print, scene 6. chromo, depict, pastel 7. diorama, etching, portray, porture, tableau 8. describe, likeness, painting, portrait 9. engraving, paintings, represent, visualize 10. photograph 11. description 14. representation
picture (pert to) . . .
  mounting, border . . 3. mat 5. frame 8. kakemono, makimono (scroll)
  moving . . 4. film 5. movie 6. cinema
  positive . . 5. print
  puzzle . . 5. rebus
  small . . 5. cameo 9. miniature
  stand . . 5. easel
  viewer . . 11. alethoscope, stereoscope 12. magic lantern, stereopticon
picturesque . . . 5. vivid 6. scenic 7. graphic 9. pictorial

picuda... 9. barracuda (great), picudilla (small)
picudo... 6. weevil 10. boll weevil
piddle... 3. toy 4. pick, play 6. putter, trifle 9. waste time
pie... 4. food, mess 5. chaos, patty 6. jumble, magpie, pastry 7. cobbler, dessert, measure 9. confusion
piebald... 4. pied 5. mixed, pinto 6. motley 7. mongrel, mottled, pintado 10. variegated 13. heterogeneous
piece... 3. bit 4. join, part, role 5. crumb, drama, piece, scrap, shred 6. sample 7. measure, portion, writing 8. chessman, fragment, specimen, treatise
piece (pert to)...
  armor.. 5. tasse (tace) 8. corselet
  de résistance.. 6. entrée 8. main dish
  door, jamb.. 6. lintel
  eccentric.. 3. cam
  fastening.. 3. gib
  fitted.. 4. shim 5. tenon
  flat.. 4. slab, slat 5. flake, strip
  meal.. 9. by degrees, fragments 12. piece by piece 14. little by little
  metal.. 3. sow
  neck.. 3. boa 5. rabat, scarf, stole 8. kerchief
  of one's mind.. 6. rebuke 7. reproof 13. candid opinion
  out.. 3. eke 6. cantle
  preventing slippage.. 5. cleat
  short.. 4. skit
  side.. 3. rib 5. stave
  split off.. 6. sliver, splint 8. splinter
  tapering.. 4. gore 6. gusset
  work (art).. 4. pavé 6. mosaic, niello
pieces of...
  eight.. 6. dollar, escudo
  meat.. 5. cabob
  silk waste.. 4. noil
pied... 4. foot 5. pinto 7. colored (2 or more colors), dappled, piebald 10. variegated 12. parti-colored
pied (pert to)...
  blackbird.. 6. thrush
  brant.. 5. goose
  diver.. 4. smew
  duck.. 8. Labrador
  Friar (Eccl Hist).. 9. mendicant
  monk.. 10. Bernardine, Cistercian
  Piper of Hamelin.. 8. musician 10. rat charmer
  widgeon.. 8. garganey 9. goldeneye
Piedmont, Italy... 7. capital (Turin)
pieplant... 7. rhubarb
pier... 4. anta, dock, mole, quay 5. groin, wharf 6. pillar 7. landing 8. buttress, gatepost 9. promenade 10. breakwater
pierce... 4. bore, cold, gore, pain, tart 5. enter, gride, lance, probe, spear, spike, sting, wound 6. riddle, tunnel 7. discern 8. puncture 9. penetrate, perforate 10. comprehend
piercing... 4. keen, loud 5. acute 6. shrill 7. caustic, clearly, painful, piteous, pungent, sharply, shrilly, spiking, violent 8. deep-felt, poignant, spearing, stabbing

9. searching
Pieria, Macedonia (pert to)...
  epithet of.. 5. Muses
  native.. 7. Pierian
  reference to.. 6. poetry 9. knowledge
  seat of.. 5. Muses
piet... 5. ouzel 6. magpie 7. piebald 10. chatterbox, chattering 11. saucy person
Pietà (It)... 9. sculpture 10. Virgin Mary
pietose (Mus)... 11. sympathetic 13. compassionate
piety... 4. pity, zeal (worship) 6. filial 8. devotion, holiness, religion 9. reverence 10. compassion, devoutness, sanctimony 11. dutifulness
pig... 3. car (RR), ham, hog, sow 4. boar, pork 5. bacon, crosk, flask, swine 6. farrow 7. casting, dogboat, glutton 8. pressman, sixpence, slattern 9. policeman 11. stoolpigeon
pig (pert to)...
  bed.. 3. pen, sty 5. reeve 6. pigsty
  female.. 3. sow 4. gilt
  guinea.. 4. cavy
  headed.. 6. stupid 9. obstinate
  iron.. 5. ingot
  iron, ballast (Naut).. 9. kentledge
  iron, cast.. 9. kentledge (Mil)
  last of litter.. 4. runt
  lead, weight.. 6. fother
  litter.. 6. farrow
  piglike.. 7. hoglike, porcine, suiform
  piglike animal.. 7. peccary 8. babirusa
  potato.. 7. cowbane
  rat.. 9. bandicoot
  skin.. 6. saddle 8. football
  yoke.. 7. sextant 8. quadrant
  young.. 5. grice, shoat 6. farrow, piglet 9. gruntling
pigdan... 8. spittoon
pigeon... 3. nun 4. barb, dove, dupe, fowl, girl, gull, ruff 5. heart, piper, pluck, sweet 6. coward, fleece, pouter, roller, turbit 7. fantail, jacobin, pintail, tumbler 9. trumpeter
pigeon, pidgin (pert to)...
  Australia.. 5. wonga 10. wonga-wonga
  berry.. 7. dogwood 9. Juneberry, wild elder
  blood.. 6. garnet
  carrier.. 5. homer 6. homing 10. scandaroon
  extinct.. 4. dodo
  food.. 7. saltcat
  genus.. 5. Goura 7. Columba
  hawk.. 6. falcon, merlin
  house.. 7. dovecot 9. columbary
  ref to.. 12. peristeronic
  short-beaked.. 4. barb
  wood.. 6. cushat 8. ringdove
  young.. 5. piper
pigment... 3. red 4. blue, gray, pink 5. black, brown, color, green, ocher (ochre), paint, white 6. orange, purple, yellow 8. colorant
pigment (pert to)...
  arsenic, yellow.. 8. orpiment
  black.. 3. tar 5. sepia 7. melanin

blue.. 5. smalt
blue–green.. 4. bice
brown.. 5. sepia, umber 6. bister
  (bistre), sienna (burnt) 7. cypress
brownish yellow.. 6. sienna
calico yellow.. 7. canarin (canarine)
coal tar.. 7. aniline
cuttlefish.. 5. sepia
madder root.. 7. rubiate
orange red.. 7. realgar
oxide of lead.. 8. massicot
red.. 7. turacin
yellow.. 5. ocher (ochre) 7. etiolin
pigmy... see *pygmy*
pignus... 4. pawn 6. pledge
pig's feet... 9. pettitoes
pigtail... 5. braid, queue 7. tobacco
  (rolled) 8. rope's end (Naut)
pika... 6. rodent
pike... 3. ged (gedd) 4. fish, luce, pick
  6. beacon, pickax
pike (pert to)...
North American.. 11. muskellunge
perch.. 6. sauger
pikelike.. 3. gar 4. luce 5. lucet
  6. robalo 8. robalito 9. barracuda
walleyed.. 4. doré
pikel, pikle... 7. hayfork 9. pitchfork
pikelet... 7. crumpet
piker... 5. thief, tramp 6. coward
  7. gambler, quitter, shirker, vagrant
  8. tightwad
pilar... 5. downy, hairy
pilaster... 4. anta 6. alette (part),
  column
Pilate (Bib)... 10. procurator (Judean)
pilchard... 7. sardine
pile... 3. awn, mow, nap 4. heap,
  load, mole, pier, rick, shag
  5. amass, slack, spile, stake 6. heap
  up, pillar, wealth 7. fortune, store
  up, texture
pile (pert to)...
burning.. 4. pyre
defense.. 8. estacade
driver.. 7. fistuca
of hay.. 3. mow 4. dess, rick
  5. stack
up.. 4. heap 7. smashup, store up
  9. shipwreck 10. exaggerate
pilfer... 3. rob 4. lift, loot 5. filch,
  steal, swipe 6. rustle (cattle), snitch
  7. purloin
pilgrim... 5. exile (Relig) 6. palmer
  8. crusader, newcomer, traveler,
  wanderer, wayfarer 9. immigrant,
  sojourner 10. tenderfoot
  12. peregrinator
Pilgrim (pert to)...
father.. 9. John Alden
Fathers.. 11. Separatists (1620)
garment.. 5. ihram (Mecca)
landing.. 12. Plymouth Rock (1620)
Scotch.. 6. palmer
ship.. 9. Mayflower, Speedwell
pilgrimage to Mecca... 4. hadj
Pilgrim's bottle... 7. ampulla, costrel
Pilgrim's Progress... 8. allegory
  (Bunyan)
pill... 3. rob 4. ball, bore, pare, pell,
  pool 5. bolus, creek 6. bullet, pellet,
  pilule 8. medicine 9. cigarette

11. decorticate
pillage... 4. flay, loot, prey, sack
  5. booty, harry, spoil, strip 6. rapine,
  ravage 7. despoil, plunder, robbery
  9. depredate, extortion 10. spoliation
pillar... 4. post, slab 5. shaft, stele
  (stela), tower 6. column 7. support
  8. mainstay, monument, pedestal
pillar (pert to)...
airfield.. 5. pylon
Buddhist.. 3. lat
carved.. 9. totem pole
little.. 8. pillaret
of society.. 9. personage
pillarlike.. 6. stelar
saint.. 7. recluse, stylite
tall, slender.. 7. obelisk
with front figure.. 7. osiride
Pillars of Hercules site... 5. Abila,
  Calpe 17. Strait of Gibralter
pillbox... 3. cap, hat 8. brougham,
  fortress 13. fortification
pillory... 4. yoke 5. stock, trone
  6. cangue, punish
pillow... 3. pad 5. block 7. cushion,
  support
pillow (pert to)...
case, cover.. 4. sham, slip
long.. 7. bolster
stuffing.. 5. kapok 8. feathers
pilose... 5. hairy 6. pilous
pilot... 4. lead 5. flyer, guide, steer
  6. aviate, direct, leader 8. director,
  helmsman, preacher 9. clergyman,
  navigator 10. cowcatcher
pilot (pert to)...
bird.. 6. plover
expert.. 3. ace
fish.. 6. remora 9. amberfish,
  whitefish
house.. 10. wheelhouse
jacket.. 9. pea jacket
sky.. 8. preacher 9. clergyman
snake.. 10. copperhead
weed.. 9. rosinweed
whale.. 9. blackfish
Piltdown, England (pert to)...
Hist yield.. 7. Dawn Man, fossils
Prehist station.. 6. Sussex
piltock... 8. coalfish
pilum... 6. pestle 7. javelin
pilus... 4. hair
Pima... 5. Opata 11. Indian tribe
pimento... 6. pepper 7. paprika
  8. allspice, pimiento
pin... 3. hob, peg, pen 4. axle, bolt,
  coak (coag), join 5. affix, badge,
  dowel, rivet, thole 6. brooch, cotter,
  fasten, secure, trifle 7. confine,
  enclose, gudgeon, jewelry, spindle,
  stopper, trenail 8. linchpin, ornament,
  transfix 10. chatelaine
pin (pert to)...
axle.. 8. linchpin
dial.. 5. style
fish.. 11. stickleback
game.. 7. skittle
grass.. 9. alfilaria (forage)
jackstraw (game).. 8. spilikin (spillikin)
meat fastener.. 6. skewer
quoits.. 3. hob
sailmaker's.. 3. fid

small.. 3. peg 4. lill
with looped head.. 7. eyebolt
pinafore... 5. apron, smock 7. tablier
  8. sun dress
Pinafore... 5. opera (Gilbert & Sullivan)
pinag... 4. lake (rain season)
piñata... 5. globe (swinging, with gifts)
pinax... 4. dish 5. table 6. plaque,
  scheme, tablet 7. picture
  9. catalogue
pinbone... 7. hipbone
pince–nez... 7. glasses, nippers
  10. eyeglasses
pincers... 3. tew 5. chela, tongs
  6. pliers 7. forceps, pinette
pinch... 3. nip, rob 4. pain, raid
  5. cramp, gripe, pugil (anc), steal,
  stint, tweak 6. arrest, crisis, extort,
  scrimp, snatch, snitch, strait, twinge
  7. afflict, confine, squeeze, urgency
  8. compress, contract, exigency,
  straiten
pinchbeck... 4. sham 5. alloy (cheap
  jewelry) 8. frippery, spurious
  11. counterfeit
pinched... 4. poor, thin 8. squeezed
  10. compressed, contracted,
  distressed, straitened
pinchem... 8. titmouse
pinda... 6. peanut
Pindar... 4. poet (lyric)
pindaric... 3. ode 9. irregular
  12. unrestrained
pine... 4. flag 5. waste, yearn
  6. grieve, lament, needle, repine,
  sicken, weaken, wither 8. languish
  11. deteriorate
pine (pert to)...
Brazil.. 6. paraná
chemical.. 5. pinic
exudation.. 5. resin, rosin
family.. 3. fir 5. larch, piñon
  6. spruce
finch.. 6. siskin
fir.. 6. balsam 12. Balm of Gilead
fruit.. 4. cone
genus.. 5. Pinus
gum.. 8. sandarac
knot.. 7. dovekie
leaf.. 6. needle
low–growing.. 5. piñon
mahogany.. 6. totara
New Zealand.. 5. kauri (kaury)
Pacific coast.. 8. knobpine
Philippine.. 7. Amboina 8. galagala
screw.. 3. ara 6. pandan
tar extract.. 6. retene
tulip.. 10. pipsissewa
pineal... 5. brain, gland 8. pine cone
pineapple... 4. bomb, pina 5. fiber,
  fruit 6. ananas 8. pine cone
  12. Bromeliaceae
pineapple (pert to)...
cheese.. 7. Cheddar
cloth.. 4. pina
segment.. 3. pip
weed.. 8. marigold
Pine Tree State... 5. Maine
pinguescent... 9. fattening
pinguid... 3. fat 4. oily, rich 5. fatty
  8. unctuous
pinguitude... 7. fatness, obesity

  8. oiliness 10. greasiness
pink... 3. cut, Red 4. deck, rose, stab
  5. adorn, blink, color, coral, smart,
  wound 6. flower, indent, minnow,
  pierce, salmon, vessel 7. radical,
  serrate 8. decorate, grayling
  9. carnation 11. fashionable
pink (pert to)...
coat.. 10. foxhunter's
eye.. 4. duck 14. conjunctivitis
family.. 7. Campion 9. Carnation
  15. Caryophyllaceae
fish.. 8. gobylike
genus.. 6. Silene
lady.. 3. fly (fishing) 8. cocktail
needle.. 9. alfilaria
Pearl.. 6. azalea
pill.. 7. cure–all
root.. 8. wormroot
pinkeen... 6. minnow 19. insignificant
  person
pinna... 3. fin 4. wing 7. auricle,
  feather, leaflet
pinnace... 4. boat 5. woman 6. tender
  (Naut) 9. procuress 10. prostitute
pinnacle... 3. epi, tee, tor 4. acme,
  apex, peak 5. crest, crown, serac,
  spire 6. finial, needle, summit
pinnate... 11. featherlike
pinniped... 4. seal 6. walrus
pinochle term... 3. dix 4. meld
piñon... 4. pine, seed 8. pignolia
  12. monkey puzzle
pintado... 4. cero, fish, sier (fish)
  5. pinto 6. chintz, pigeon, sierra
pintail (pert to)...
duck.. 4. smee 5. river, ruddy
grouse.. 4. sand 11. sharp–tailed
pinto (horse)... 4. pied 6. calico
  7. mottled, painted, piebald, spotted
Pinto... 6. Indian (Pakawa tribe)
pinwing... 7. penguin
pioneer... 4. lead 5. guide, miner
  6. digger, open up 7. settler
  8. colonist, explorer 9. excavator
  10. forerunner
Pioneer's Day... 4. Utah (July 24)
  5. Idaho (June 15)
pious... 5. godly, loyal 6. devout,
  worthy 9. excellent, religious
  11. reverential 13. sanctimonious
pip... 3. ace 4. paip, peep, roup,
  seed, spot, trey 7. disease
  12. officer's star
pipe... 2. TD 3. see, tee 4. blow,
  clay, duct, reed, tube 5. spout, voice
  6. convey, dudeen, hookah (hooka),
  outlet 7. channel 9. brierwood
pipe (pert to)...
connection.. 3. ell, tee 5. cross,
  elbow
dream.. 8. illusion 10. bemusement
end.. 4. taft 6. nozzle
line.. 9. grapevine
Oriental.. 8. narghile (nargile)
pastoral, shepherd's.. 3. oat 4. reed
  7. larigot 9. flageolet
peace.. 7. calumet
player.. 5. fifer 8. shepherd
short.. 6. dudeen
smoke.. 5. tewel
steam.. 5. riser

tobacco.. **10**. meerschaum
wood.. **5**. brier (briar) **9**. brierwood
wrench.. **8**. Stillson
pipette... **6**. taster, tubule **7**. dripper
pipit... **7**. titlark
piquancy... **4**. zest **5**. spice
  8. pungency, raciness, tartness
  11. conciseness
piquant... **4**. racy, tart **5**. salty, sharp,
  spicy, zesty **7**. concise, cutting,
  pungent **11**. interesting, provocative
pique... **4**. dive, fret, goad **5**. anger,
  annoy, sting, tempt **6**. grudge, incite,
  nettle, offend **7**. dudgeon, offense,
  provoke, umbrage **8**. irritate
  9. displease **10**. irritation, resentment
  11. displeasure
pir (Moham)... **4**. tomb **5**. guide, saint
pirate... **6**. robber **7**. corsair, mariner
  8. marauder, picaroon **9**. buccaneer
  10. freebooter **11**. appropriate
pirate (famed)... **4**. Kidd **6**. Morgan
  7. Lafitte **10**. Blackbeard (Capt
  Teach)
pirate (pert to)...
  bird.. **10**. jaeger gull
  flag.. **5**. Roger
  gallows.. **7**. yardarm
  perch.. **8**. Xenarchi
  weapon.. **4**. snee
piraya... **6**. caribe (fish) **7**. piranha
pirogue... **5**. canoe **7**. piragua
pirol... **6**. oriole
Pisa, Italy...
  capital of.. **7**. Tuscany
  famed for.. **9**. campanile **12**. Leaning
  Tower
  river.. **4**. Arno
pis aller... **10**. last resort
piscary... **7**. fishery **12**. fishing place
  13. fishing rights
piscatology (*science of*)... **7**. angling,
  fishing **10**. halieutics
Pisces... **4**. fish **6**. fishes
  13. constellation
piscina... **4**. tank **5**. basin (Eccl)
  8. fishpond **9**. reservoir
Piscis Volans... **10**. flying fish
  13. constellation
Pisgah (pert to)...
  site.. **4**. Nebo **8**. mountain (top)
  view.. **12**. Land of Canaan **13**. Land
  of Promise
  viewer.. **5**. Moses
pismire... **3**. ant **5**. emmet
pistachio... **3**. nut **5**. green
piste... **4**. path **5**. spoor, track, trail
  10. racecourse
pisteology, pistiology... **5**. faith
  6. belief
pistil... **5**. ovary **6**. carpel
  9. gynoecium
pistol... **3**. dag **7**. firearm **9**. derringer
pistol (pert to)...
  case.. **7**. holster
  lock.. **5**. rowet
  slang.. **3**. gat, rod **6**. barker, cannon,
  heater
pistology (Theol)... **5**. faith
piston... **7**. plunger
pit... **4**. cave, hole, mine, pool, sump,
  tomb, trap, well **5**. abyss, arena,

grave, sluig, snare **6**. cavity, slough
  7. alveola, cockpit, dungeon
  8. audience **9**. waterhole
  10. excavation **13**. Stock Exchange
pit (pert to)...
  anatomy.. **5**. fossa, fovea
  botany.. **7**. alveola, pitamen
    8. endocarp
  bottomless.. **7**. Abaddon
  fodder.. **4**. silo
  Hades.. **4**. hell
  Hawaiian.. **3**. imu
  theater.. **7**. parquet
  viper.. **9**. Viperidae **11**. rattlesnake
pitch... **3**. key, tar **4**. camp, hurl, tilt,
  tone, toss **5**. black, color, erect,
  fling, heave, lurch, resin, sense,
  slope, throw **6**. degree, encamp,
  plunge, settle, topple **7**. incline
  8. flounder **9**. sales talk
pitch (pert to)...
  high.. **6**. shrill
  identity.. **6**. unison
  inflammable.. **7**. piceous
  mineral.. **7**. asphalt, bitumen
  music.. **4**. flat **6**. accent, stress
    8. paranete **9**. tonometer
  pitchlike.. **7**. piceous
pitchblende... **6**. radium **7**. uranium
pitched ball, curving away...
  8. outshoot
pitcher... **3**. jug **4**. ewer, olla, olpe,
  toby **5**. gorge **8**. cruisken (cruiskeen),
  oenochoe (wine), southpaw
  (left–handed)
pitcher (pert to)...
  plant, genus.. **9**. Nepenthes
    10. Cephalotus, Sarracenia
  plus catcher.. **7**. battery
  shaped.. **9**. urceolate
  shaped vessel.. **8**. aiguière
piteous... **5**. pious **6**. devout, paltry,
  tender **7**. pitiful, pitying **8**. pitiable
  13. compassionate
pitfall... **3**. pit **4**. lure, trap **5**. decoy,
  snare **6**. danger **10**. difficulty
pith... **3**. jet, nub **4**. gist, meat, pulp
  6. center, kernel, marrow
  7. essence, meaning, nucleus
  9. substance
pith helmet... **3**. cap, hat **5**. topee
  (topi)
pith tree (Nile)... **7**. ambatch (ambash)
pithy... **4**. soft **5**. crisp, meaty, pulpy,
  terse **7**. laconic **10**. meaningful
  12. epigrammatic
pithy (pert to)...
  expression.. **7**. epigram
  saying.. **3**. mot
  sentence.. **5**. motto
pitiable... **3**. sad **6**. woeful **7**. piteous
  8. grievous, terrible **9**. miserable,
  sorrowful **10**. lamentable
pitiful... **4**. mean **6**. paltry **7**. piteous
  8. pathetic, shameful **10**. despicable
  12. contemptible **13**. compassionate,
  tenderhearted
pitiless... **5**. cruel **8**. ruthless
  9. merciless **10**. relentless
  13. unsympathetic
pitpit... **8**. guitguit **12**. honey creeper
Pitri, Hindu (pert to)...

ancestor of.. 4. gods 6. demons
  10. four castes
  Prajapatis, one of.. 10. progenitor
  (human race)
  semidivine.. 6. father 9. patriarch
  10. forefather
pittance... 4. alms, dole, gift, scat
  7. bequest 8. donation 9. allowance
  11. small amount
pity... 4. ruth 5. mercy, yearn
  7. remorse 8. clemency, sympathy
  10. compassion, condolence,
  repentance 13. commiseration
pivot... 3. toe 4. slew, slue, turn
  5. hinge 6. pintle, swivel
pivotal... 4. crux 5. polar 7. turning
pixy, pixie... 3. elf, imp 5. fairy
  6. goblin, sprite 13. mischief–maker
Pizarro (pert to)...
  adventurer.. 7. Spanish
  conqueror of.. 4. Peru
  founder of.. 4. Lima (capital)
placable... 8. peaceful 9. agreeable,
  forgiving, peaceable 10. appeasable
placard... 4. bill, post 5. edict
  6. notice, poster 7. affiché
  9. manifesto, stomacher
  12. proclamation
placate... 4. calm 6. pacify, soothe
  7. appease 10. conciliate
  11. tranquilize
place... 3. put 4. lieu, site, spot
  5. abode, locus, posit, situs, stead
  6. locale, locate, region, street
  7. arrange, demesne, deposit
  8. classify, location, position
  9. recognize, situation
place (of)...
  amusement.. 4. park 6. casino,
  midway
  bliss.. 4. Eden 8. paradise
  confinement.. 3. pen 4. brig, cage,
  coop, gaol, jail, stir 6. asylum,
  corral, prison 7. dungeon
  9. calaboose 12. penitentiary
  confusion.. 5. Babel
  content.. 7. Arcadia
  darkness.. 6. Erebus
  exit.. 6. egress
  honor.. 9. right hand
  origin.. 6. cradle, source
  refuge.. 3. ark 4. port 5. haven
  resort.. 7. purlieu
  rest.. 3. bed, den 4. lair, nook
  5. chair, couch, grave, niche
  sleep.. 3. bed 4. doss 5. berth,
  couch 6. pallet 7. hammock
  suffering.. 10. Armageddon,
  Gethsemane
  trial.. 5. venue
place (pert to)...
  apart.. 6. enisle 7. isolate
  9. sequester
  beneath.. 9. infrapose
  between.. 9. interpose
  burial.. 5. grave 8. catacomb,
  cemetery 9. graveyard 10. necropolis
  by itself.. 7. isolate
  camping.. 5. étape
  confidence in.. 7. entrust
  different.. 10. otherwhere
  for boats.. 7. portage

for candles.. 9. chandlery
forest (open).. 5. glade
for keeping animals.. 3. zoo 4. barn
  7. pasture 9. menagerie
frequented.. 4. dive 5. haunt
  6. resort
from which jury is taken.. 5. venue
hallowed.. see *sacred* below
hiding.. 3. mew 4. lair 5. niche
high.. 7. eminent 8. eminence
horse training.. 4. ring 5. longe
in a row.. 5. align, aline
in bondage.. 7. enslave
in order.. 7. arrange 11. systematize
in statu quo.. 7. put back, replace,
  restore
interpretation on.. 8. construe
landing.. 4. dock, pier 5. wharf
  7. airport
market.. 4. mart 5. agora 6. rialto
meeting.. 5. tryst
of.. 4. lieu 5. stead
on mound.. 3. tee
opposite.. 6. appose
over.. 11. superimpose
sacred.. 4. fane 5. altar 6. chapel,
  church, shrine, temple 9. synagogue
  10. tabernacle
side–by–side.. 9. collocate, juxtapose
sleeping.. 3. bed 4. bunk 5. berth,
  couch 6. pallet 7. hammock
under.. 9. infrapose
under restraint.. 6. arrest, intern
value upon.. 5. price 6. assess
  8. appraise, estimate
wet.. 4. slew 5. marsh 6. slough
wrestling.. 5. arena 9. palaestra
(palestra)
placed... 3. put 7. located
  8. arranged, situated 10. classified
placed in lodgings... 6. roomed
  8. billeted
placid... 4. calm 5. quiet, suant
  6. demure, gentle, serene
  8. composed, peaceful 9. agreeable,
  quiescent, unruffled 11. undisturbed
pladaroma... 5. tumor (eyelid)
plafond... 7. ceiling 14. contract
  bridge
plage... 5. beach
plagiarism... 6. piracy 8. cribbing,
  stealing 10. purloining
  13. appropriation
plague... 3. dun, vex 4. bane, pest,
  twit 5. harry, tease, worry 6. harass,
  hector, infest 7. scourge, torment
  8. epidemic, nuisance 10. Black
  Death, pestilence 11. infestation
plaguy... 6. vexing 8. annoying
  9. difficult, harassing 10. tormenting
  11. troublesome
plaice... 8. flatfish, flounder
plaid... 4. maud 6. tartan
plain... 3. lea 4. chol, mesa, moor,
  wold 5. blunt, camas, clear, frank,
  heath 6. lenten 7. artless, evident,
  genuine, legible, obvious, prairie
  8. apparent, distinct, explicit, ordinary
  9. downright, primitive, unadorned
  10. unaffected
plain (pert to)...
  clothes.. 10. unofficial

dealing.. 4. open 5. frank
knitting.. 12. garter stitch
of Mars.. 9. palmistry
spoken.. 15. straightforward
Plains (pert to)...
Arctic.. 6. tundra
Europe.. 6. steppe
Florida.. 7. savanna (savannah)
Italy.. 8. campagna
Russia.. 6. steppe, tundra
S African.. 6. pampas
Sp American.. 4. vega 5. llano
6. salada (salt–covered)
Plains Indians... 6. Kiowan, Siouan
7. Caddoan 10. Algonquian,
Athapascan, Uto–Aztecan
plainsman... 6. cowboy 7. llanero
8. herdsman
Plains of Abraham... 10. Quebec City
plaint... 6. bewail, lament 9. complaint
11. lamentation
plaintiff... 4. suer 6. orator 7. accuser
8. claimant, libelant (libellant)
10. complainer 11. complainant
plaintive... 3. sad 5. cross 7. elegiac,
fretful, peevish, pettish, wailful,
wistful 8. mournful, petulant, repining
9. lamenting, sorrowful
10. melancholy 11. complaining
12. discontented
plait... 4. fold, hair, knit, lace, plat
5. braid, pleat, weave 6. pleach,
wimple 9. corrugate, interlace
10. interweave
plaited... 5. Milan (straw) 6. folded,
kilted, sennit (palm leaves)
8. pleached 10. interlaced
11. intertwined
plan... 3. map, way 4. form, idea,
line, plat, plot 5. chart, draft, ettle,
frame, setup 6. design, devise,
intend, layout, method, scheme
7. arrange, diagram, outline, pattern,
project 8. engineer, strategy
9. calculate, procedure
11. arrangement, contemplate,
preconceive, premeditate
plan (pert to)...
architecture.. 5. draft, épure
frustrator of.. 7. marplot
preliminary.. 4. idea 6. map out
8. proposal
secretly.. 4. plot 7. connive
8. conspire
planate... 5. plane 9. flattened
plancher... 3. bed 5. board (occult),
floor, plank 6. pallet 8. planking,
platform
plancier... 6. soffit 7. cornice
plandok... 9. mouse deer
plane... 3. fly 4. even, flat, ramp,
scar, tool 5. level 6. degree, smooth
7. jointer, surface 8. airplane
10. smoothness
plane (pert to)...
block.. 5. stock
boundary.. 9. perimeter
four–angled.. 6. square 7. rhombus
8. tetragon 10. quadrangle
handle.. 4. tote (bench plane)
inclined.. 4. ramp 5. chute
iron.. 5. blade

kind.. 3. mig 5. stuka 6. router
measure.. 10. planimeter
smoothing, chamfering.. 5. howel
tree.. 6. chinar (Orient) 8. Platanus
type.. 5. bench, block, stock
6. trowel 7. jointer, routing
planet... 4. Mars, star 5. Earth, Pluto,
Venus 6. Saturn, Uranus 7. Jupiter,
Mercury, Neptune 8. wanderer
planet (pert to)...
astrology.. 9. alfridary
brightest.. 5. Venus
cone.. 8. strobile
course.. 5. orbit
minor.. 9. satellite
nearest sun.. 7. Mercury
orbit.. 7. ellipse
red.. 4. Mars
remotest.. 5. Pluto (1930)
resembling.. 8. asteroid
ringed.. 6. Saturn
satellite.. 4. moon
shadow.. 5. umbra
small.. 8. asteroid
sphere.. 6. oblate
planet (solar system) by size...
7. Jupiter 6. Saturn 7. Neptune
6. Uranus 5. Earth, Venus, Pluto
4. Mars 7. Mercury
planetarium... 5. Zeiss 6. orrery
planetary... 7. earthly, erratic
9. celestial, wandering, worldwide
planetology (study of)... 7. planets
10. satellites
plangor... 4. wail 11. lamentation
planisphere... 7. sextant 9. astrolabe
plank... 3. sny 4. deal, slab 5. board,
shole, stone 6. timber 7. pay down
8. planking 10. gravestone
plank down... 3. pay 7. advance,
deposit
planner... 8. designer, engineer,
gardener 9. architect, projector
plant... 3. fix, sow, spy 4. ache, bury,
herb, seed, trap 5. cache, decoy,
shrub 6. clover 7. falsify 8. colonize,
workshop 9. deception, detective,
equipment, vegetable
plant (pert to)...
abnormal environs.. 4. ecad
adjustment.. 6. ecesis
air.. 8. epiphyte
appendage.. 7. stipula
biggest.. 10. Aspidistra
body.. 6. cormus 7. thallus
bud.. 4. cion 5. scion
climbing.. 4. vine 6. liana
coloring matter.. 11. chlorophyll
crossbred.. 6. hybrid
cross–fertilization.. 9. phytogamy
disease.. 4. gall, rust, smut 5. ergot
7. blister 8. ramentum
embryo.. 8. plantule
enchantment–proof.. 7. haemony
(Milton's Comus)
flowerless.. 4. fern 6. lichen
9. cryptogam 11. Cryptogamia (opp
of phanerogam)
growing on rock.. 6. lichen
growing on sea bottom.. 6. enalid
growing wild.. 9. agrestial
history.. 12. phytogenesis

legendary, forgetfulness.. **5.** lotus
male.. **3.** mas
mosslike.. **6.** orpine
mushroom type.. **6.** fungus
native.. **8.** indigene
orifice.. **5.** stoma
pigment lacking.. **6.** albino
poisonous.. **4.** atis **6.** datura
   7. amanita **8.** oleander
poisonous to cattle.. **4.** loco
   8. locoweed
pore.. **8.** lenticel
round–leaved.. **9.** pennywort
science of.. **6.** botany
seedless.. **6.** agamic
stem, stalk.. **4.** bine **5.** haulm
   6. caulis
tequila–yielding.. **5.** agave
tissue.. **7.** tapetum
without chlorophyll.. **6.** albino
without petals.. **9.** apetulous
woody.. **6.** xyloid
plant (type of)...
aconite.. **4.** bikh
agave, century plant.. **4.** aloe, pita
   9. amaryllis
ammoniac.. **5.** oshac
anise.. **4.** dill
aquatic.. **6.** sugamo **7.** frogbit
   8. plankton
aromatic.. **4.** mint, nard **5.** basil,
   tansy, thyme **8.** tarragon
arum.. **4.** sago **6.** starch **9.** arrowroot
aster family.. **5.** daisy **8.** fleabane
bitter.. **3.** rue
bitter vetch.. **3.** ers
box.. **5.** Buxus **7.** boxwood
broom.. **5.** spart **6.** Canary **7.** genista
bryophytic.. **4.** moss
burdock.. **5.** elite **8.** Xanthium
burning bush.. **5.** wahoo
butter–and–eggs.. **8.** ranstead
cactus.. **5.** dildo **6.** cereus, chaute,
   mescal **8.** saguaro **9.** xerophyte
century.. **4.** aloe **5.** agave **6.** maguey
dill.. **4.** anet
evergreen.. **3.** ivy **5.** holly **6.** laurel
   8. conifers **9.** mistletoe
everlasting.. **6.** orpine **11.** live–forever
furze.. **4.** ulex **5.** gorse
garlic (wild).. **4.** moly
leguminous.. **3.** pea **4.** bean
   6. Cassia, clover, lentil
lilaceous.. **4.** aloe, iris, leek **5.** lotus,
   onion, tulip, yucca
linen.. **4.** flax
medicinal.. **4.** alem, aloe **5.** anise,
   wahoo **6.** arnica, cacoon, catnip,
   ipecac **7.** aconite, boneset, gentian,
   lobelia, rhatany **8.** camomile
pea family.. **7.** Cytisus
perennial.. **4.** Geum **5.** avens
   10. sneezewort
poisonous.. **6.** datura **8.** oleander
poisonous to cattle.. **8.** locoweed
poisonous to fowl.. **7.** henbane
prickly, thorny.. **5.** brier **6.** cactus,
   nettle, teasel **8.** thistle
satinpod (transparent).. **7.** honesty
soap.. **5.** amole
tapioca.. **7.** cassava
thorny.. see *prickly* **6.** fatsia

trifoliate.. **6.** clover **8.** shamrock
plant, typical of...
Africa.. **5.** argel (arghel)
Alps.. **9.** edelweiss
Arabia.. **3.** kat (stimulant)
Australia.. **5.** Hakes, lilac **6.** Correa
   7. columba, fuchsia **8.** Rutaceae
China.. **5.** ramie
Egypt.. **5.** anise, cumin **7.** aniseed
   8. nepenthe
Hawaii.. **5.** olona
Japan.. **3.** tea **5.** acuba **6.** quince
   7. cydonia **8.** japonica
Japan (vine).. **8.** Bignonia **14.** trumpet
   creeper
Mexico.. **4.** chia **5.** datil **6.** salvia
   9. sabadilla
Peru.. **3.** oca **7.** rhatany
Philippines.. **4.** alem (Med) **6.** agamid
Spain.. **3.** aji **6.** pepper **8.** Capsicum
Syria.. **5.** cumin
tropical vine.. **8.** redwithe
   10. tillandsia
tropics.. **4.** arum, palm, taro
   5. agave, zamia **7.** dasheen, hamelia
   8. mangrove
plantain... **6.** banana
plantation pines... **7.** pinetum
plantation trees... **4.** holt **6.** forest
   7. nopalry (cactus), orchard
planters, Govt of... **11.** plantocracy
plantigrade mammal... **5.** panda
plaque... **5.** medal, patch **6.** brooch,
   tablet **8.** ornament, platelet (Anat)
plash... **4.** plop, pool **5.** swash
   6. puddle, ripple, splash
plasm... **4.** mold **6.** matrix
plasma... **4.** cell, whey **5.** blood (fluid)
   10. protoplasm
plaster... **4.** teer **5.** gesso, grout, salve
   6. gypsum, parget, stucco
   8. adhesive, poultice **9.** inebriate
plastered... **5.** drunk **7.** crocked,
   smeared **8.** mortared
plasterer... **5.** mason
plaster of Paris... **5.** gesso
   6. gypsum **15.** calcium sulphate
plastic... **3.** pug **5.** gesso, vinyl
   6. slurry **7.** ductile, fictile, pliable,
   viscose **8.** creative **9.** compliant,
   formative, teachable
   14. impressionable
plastic, commercial... **6.** Lucite
   7. Formica **8.** Bakelite, Vinylite
   9. Plexiglas
plasty (pert to)...
comb form.. **7.** molding
eyelid.. **14.** blepharoplasty
face lift.. **13.** rhytidoplasty
nose.. **11.** rhinoplasty
plat... **3.** map **4.** flat, plan, plot
   5. braid, chart, field, level, plain,
   plait, pleat **6.** flatly, scheme
   7. outline, plateau **8.** absolute,
   directly, straight **9.** tableland
   10. interweave **15.** straightforward
platanist... **4.** fish, susu
plate... **3.** gib **4.** disc, dish, shoe
   (horse) **5.** paten **6.** lamina, patera
   7. coating, denture, overlay
   9. bookplate, engraving
   10. receptacle

plate (pert to)...
  armor.. **6.** cuisse (cuish)
  battery.. **4.** grid
  bone (Anat).. **7.** scapula
  cooking.. **4.** grid
  culture.. **8.** bacteria
  Eccl.. **5.** paten **6.** patina
  graduated.. **4.** dial
  holder.. **8.** cassette
  horny.. **5.** scute
  horse.. **6.** plater
  insect (bony).. **6.** scutum
  mark.. **8.** hallmark **9.** engraving
  numbered.. **4.** disc
  of glass.. **5.** slide
  perforated metal.. **3.** dod
  ship–shaped.. **3.** nef
plateau... **4.** dish, mesa, puna **5.** plain
  6. plaque, salver **9.** tableland
platform... **3.** map **4.** dais, deck,
  k'ang, plan **5.** arena, chart, plank,
  stage **6.** lissom, lyceum, podium,
  policy, pulpit, scheme **7.** estrade,
  outline, rostrum, soapbox, tribune
  8. hustings **9.** bandstand **14.** public
  speaking
platform (pert to)...
  fort.. **8.** barbette
  gun.. **11.** emplacement
  mining.. **6.** sollar (soller)
  nautical.. **7.** foretop, maintop
  9. gangplank
  scaffold (funeral).. **10.** catafalque
  wheeled.. **5.** float
platic (Astrol)... **8.** not exact
  9. imperfect
plating... **5.** armor **6.** lamina
  7. shoeing
platinum wire... **4.** oese
platitude... **6.** cliché, old hat, truism
  7. bromide **8.** banality **9.** staleness,
  triteness **11.** commonplace
  15. commonplaceness
Plato (pert to)...
  famed for.. **9.** Dialogues
  10. philosophy
  founder of.. **7.** Academe, academy
  name, real.. **10.** Aristocles
  pupil of.. **8.** Socrates
platoid... **4.** flat **5.** broad
Platonic (pert to)...
  idea.. **5.** eidos
  love.. **4.** pure **5.** ideal **6.** chaste
  8. virtuous **10.** idealistic
  11. comradeship
  philosophy.. **8.** idealism **9.** Platonism
  11. theoretical
  solids.. **10.** hexahedron, octahedron
  11. icosahedron, tetrahedron
  12. dodecahedron
platoon... **3.** set **4.** unit **5.** squad
  7. company, coterie **11.** subdivision
platoon school... **4.** Gary (Ind)
platter... **4.** dish, lanx **5.** grail, plate
  6. record **9.** scutellum
platter–shaped... **10.** scutellate
platyfish... **8.** moonfish
platypus... **8.** duckbill
plaudit... **5.** cheer, éclat **6.** encore
  8. applause, approval, clapping,
  encomium **10.** plaudation
  11. acclamation, approbation

plausible... **8.** credible, probable,
  specious **10.** applausive, believable,
  ostensible, plauditory, reasonable
  11. conceivable
plausible excuse... **5.** alibi
play... **3.** act, fun, toy **4.** game, jest,
  romp **5.** dally, drama, enact, feign,
  sport, wager **6.** affect, frolic
  7. disport, operate, pretend
  9. amusement, diversion, melodrama,
  pantomime **10.** recreation
  11. impersonate **13.** entertainment
play (pert to)...
  exhibit a.. **5.** stage
  for time.. **5.** stall
  house.. **5.** movie **6.** cinema
  7. theater **9.** dollhouse
  musical.. **5.** opera **8.** burletta,
  operetta
  outline.. **8.** scenario
  part.. **4.** role **7.** prelude **8.** epilogue,
  epitasis, prologue
  pranks.. **4.** haze
  silent.. **9.** pantomime
  story.. **8.** scenario
  stupid.. **5.** boner
  the bagpipe.. **5.** skirl **6.** doodle
  the buffoon.. **5.** droll
  the coquette.. **5.** flirt
  tricks.. **4.** hoax, shab
  truant.. **5.** miche
  unskillfully.. **5.** strum
  upon words.. **3.** pun **11.** paronomasia
playa... **5.** beach, shore **7.** salt pan
playboy... **4.** fool **5.** clown, cutup
  7. buffoon, reveler **8.** carouser
  10. merrymaker **12.** Jack of Trumps
  (Spoilfive)
player... **3.** dub **4.** star **5.** actor, idler,
  piper **7.** gambler, trifler **8.** gamester,
  musician, stroller, thespian
  9. frolicker, performer
  11. barnstormer
player on words... **7.** punster
playful... **3.** gay **6.** lusory **7.** jocular
  8. humorous, playsome, sportive
  9. facetious, kittenish
  11. mischievous
playing cards... **4.** deck, pack
  6. tarots
playlet... **4.** skit **9.** short play
plaything... **3.** die, toy **4.** dupe
  6. bauble **7.** cat's–paw
plea... **4.** suit **5.** claim **6.** abater,
  appeal, excuse, prayer **7.** apology,
  defense, pretext **8.** argument,
  entreaty, pretense **10.** advocation,
  allegation **13.** nolo contendere
plead... **3.** beg, sue **5.** argue
  6. adduce, allege **7.** entreat, implore
plead (for)... **7.** entreat, justify, solicit
  10. supplicate
pleader... **4.** suer **6.** lawyer
  8. advocate **9.** entreater, justifier
  11. intercessor
pleading... **4.** oyer **8.** advocacy,
  demurrer, entreaty **9.** imploring,
  objection **10.** litigation
  12. intercession, supplication
pleasant... **3.** fun, gay **4.** nice
  5. merry, sweet **6.** genial **7.** affable,
  amusing, leesome, winsome

8. cheerful, friendly, humorous, pleasing, sportive 9. agreeable, diverting, laughable, sprightly
pleasant (pert to) . . .
manners . . 9. amenities
sound . . 6. dulcet 8. euphonic 9. melodious 10. harmonious
to peruse . . 8. readable
weather . . 4. fair, fine 6. bright 8. rainless 9. cloudless
please . . . 4. like, suit 5. fancy 6. arride 7. appease, content, delight, gratify, indulge, placate, satisfy 9. vouchsafe
pleased . . . 4. fain, game, glad 5. happy 9. contented, gratified
pleasing . . . 4. cool, lief, nice 5. sooth 6. comely, eesome, savory 7. amiable, roseate, welcome 8. pleasant 9. agreeable, desirable 10. delectable 11. pleasureful
pleasurable . . . 7. hedonic 8. pleasant 10. gratifying
pleasure . . . 3. joy 4. gree, will, wish 5. mirth, sport 6. choice, gaiety 7. delight, purpose 8. gladness, hedonism, hilarity 9. amusement, diversion, enjoyment, happiness, merriment 11. delectation 12. satisfaction 13. gratification
pleasure (pert to) . . .
god . . 3. Bes
ground . . 4. park 9. pleasance
pert to . . 7. hedonic
philosophy . . 8. Hedonism
seeker . . 5. sport 7. epicure, playboy 8. hedonist
pleat . . . 4. fold 5. braid, plait
pleater . . . 8. plicator
plebeian . . . 4. pleb (Rom) 6. common, vulgar 7. ignoble, ill–bred, lowborn 8. ordinary
plebiscite . . . 4. vote 6. decree 10. referendum
pleck . . . 4. plot (ground), spot 5. speck, stain 9. enclosure
plectrum . . . 4. pick 5. uvula 6. tongue 7. malleus 8. plectron
pledge . . . 3. bet, vas, vow 4. bond, gage, gate, oath, pawn, seal, wage 5. swear, toast, troth 6. engage, parole, plight 7. chattel, earnest, promise 8. guaranty, mortgage, obligate, security 9. assurance 10. collateral 11. impignorate
pledget . . . 4. swab 8. compress
Pleiad (pert to) . . .
Alexandria . . 10. Seven Poets
French . . 10. The Pléiade
lost Pleiad . . 6. Merope 7. Electra
philosophical (Gr) . . 12. Seven Wise Men
Pleiades (pert to) . . .
Seven Daughters of Atlas . . 10. Atlantides
star . . 4. Maia 7. Sterope 8. Asterope
star cluster . . 8. in Taurus (Constellation)
plenary . . . 4. full 5. great 6. entire 7. perfect 8. absolute, complete 9. unlimited 11. unqualified
plenipotentiary . . . 5. envoy 8. diplomat, minister 10. ambassador

plenteous . . . 6. plenty 7. copious, fertile, liberal 8. abundant, fruitful, generous 9. bounteous, bountiful, plentiful 10. productive
plentiful . . . 4. full, rich, rife 5. ample 6. lavish 7. copious, fertile, liberal, opulent, profuse 9. abounding, bounteous, bountiful 13. superabundant
plentifully . . . 6. galore 9. abounding, abundance
plenty . . . 4. enow 6. enough, galore, uberty 8. fullness 9. abundance, plenitude 10. perfection 11. copiousness 12. completeness, considerable 14. superabundance
plenum . . . 5. space 8. assembly, fullness (of space) (opp of vacuum)
pleon . . . 6. telson 7. abdomen
pleonasm . . . 8. fullness 10. redundancy 11. diffuseness, reiteration
plethora . . . 4. glut 6. excess 9. repletion 14. superabundance
plethoric . . . 6. turgid 8. inflated, overfull 9. bombastic 10. overloaded
plexiform . . . 4. rete 7. network 11. complicated
plexus . . . 4. rete 5. solar 7. network
pliable . . . 4. limp 6. limber, pliant, supple 7. plastic 8. flexible, suitable 9. compliant, teachable
pliant . . . 7. bending, pliable, tensile, willowy 8. flexible, workable, yielding 9. adaptable, compliant
plicate . . . 4. fold 5. pleat 6. folded 7. plaited
plight . . . 4. fold 5. braid, plait 6. status 7. embrace, promise 8. position 9. condition, situation (bad) 11. predicament
plinth . . . 4. orlo 7. subbase
Pliosaurus (extinct) . . . 7. reptile
plod . . . 3. dig, mog 4. slog, toil, tore 6. drudge, trudge
plodder . . . 3. fag 4. grub, hack 5. slave 6. drudge
plot . . . 3. lot, map 4. acre, area, brew, burn, pack, plan, plat 5. cabal, frame, tract, trick 6. design, scheme, scorch, secret 7. diagram, project 8. conspire, intrigue 10. conspiracy, prearrange 11. machination
plot (of ground) . . . 3. lot 4. acre, area, plat 5. grave, tract 7. terrain
Plotinus . . . 11. philosopher (Alexandrian School)
plotted . . . 7. charted, hatched 8. lineated 9. conspired 10. delineated 11. prearranged
plotter . . . 5. Haman 7. Jacobin, planner, schemer 8. agitator 9. contriver 11. conspirator
ploughshare (plowshare) part . . . 6. colter (coulter)
plover . . . 4. dupe 5. piper, sandy 7. lapwing 9. courtesan, sandpiper, shorebird
plover (pert to) . . .
crab . . 5. drome
crested . . 7. lapwing
egg . . 11. darning ball
genus . . 12. Charadriidae

Old World.. 8. dotterel, killdeer
page.. 6. dunlin 9. sandpiper
quail.. 13. plain wanderer
ring.. 5. pandy
plow... 4. rove, till 5. break, miner, scaut 6. furrow, turn up 7. break up 8. reinvest 9. cultivate
plow (pert to)...
fish.. 3. ray
gang.. 6. oxgang 7. measure
light.. 10. Plow Monday 13. hoggler's light
man.. 6. rustic 10. countryman, husbandman
part.. 4. buck, chip, hale 5. share, slade, stilt 6. clevis, colter
type.. 5. sulky 8. mole plow
plowed land... 5. arada, arado
pluck... 3. pug, rob, tug 4. grab, jerk, pick, pull 5. nerve, spunk, steal, strip, strum 6. avulse, divest, fleece, gather, twitch 7. courage, harvest, pick off, plunder, strip of, swindle 10. resolution, straighten (wool)
plucky... 4. game 5. brave, nervy 6. spunky, sticky 8. adhesive, resolute, spirited 10. courageous
plug... 3. peg, tap, top 4. blow, bung 5. horse, knock, punch, shoot, spile, wedge 7. commend, hydrant, stopper, stopple, tobacco 9. persevere, publicity, publicize 12. commendation
plug (pert to)...
board.. 11. switchboard
cannon muzzle.. 7. tampion (tampeon, tampoon)
dentristy.. 7. filling
hat.. 4. tile 5. gibus 6. topper
medical.. 4. clot 6. fibrin, tampon 7. embolus
slender.. 5. spill
up.. 4. calk (caulk)
plum... 5. drupe, money, prune 6. Prunus 8. dividend 9. good thing, sugarplum
plum (pert to)...
beetle.. 8. curculio
bitter.. 4. sloe
California (wild).. 5. islay
coco.. 5. icaco
England.. 6. damson
Europe.. 7. bullace
hybrid.. 7. plumcot
India.. 7. hog plum
Java.. 7. jambool (jambul) 8. jambolan
type.. 4. gage 6. damson 9. greengage, wild–goose 11. Reine Claude
plumage... 4. down 6. hackle 7. floccus (first down) 8. feathers, ornament
plumb... 4. seal, true 5. delve, gauge, sound, utter 6. adjust, fathom, sinker, weight (lead) 7. examine, measure, plummet 8. absolute, complete, vertical 9. downright 13. perpendicular
plumbage... 8. leadwork
plumbog... 9. raspberry (dwarf)
plumcot... 6. hybrid 11. plum apricot

plume... 5. crest, egret, preen, pride 6. plumet 7. feather, panache 8. decorate, plumelet
plummet... 4. dive, drop, fall, lead, plop, test 5. pitch, sound, swoop 6. fathom, plunge, weight 9. criterion
plump... 3. fat 4. drop, dull, fall, plop, rude, sink, tidy 5. blunt, buxom, flock, fubsy, obese 6. chubby, dilate, fatten, flatly 7. distend 8. blurt out, straight 9. corpulent, filled out 10. vertically 11. well–rounded
plumpness of person... 9. stoutness 10. embonpoint
plunder... 3. rob 4. boot, loot, pelf, prey, raid, rape, sack 5. booty, poach, raven, reave, rifle, strip 6. boodle, fleece, maraud, profit, rapine, ravage, spoils 7. despoil, pillage 8. spoliate 9. depredate
plundered... 4. reft 6. looted, robbed
plunderer... 5. thief 6. looter, pirate, preyer, raider, robber 7. spoiler, stealer 8. pillager 10. freebooter
plunge... 3. bet, dip 4. dash, dive, fall, pool, risk, sink 5. douse, drive, lunge, plumb, souse 6. gamble, thrust 7. baptize, immerse 8. flounder 9. gravitate, overwhelm, speculate
plunge (into)... 4. clap, dive 5. begin 7. immerge, immerse 9. set to work, undertake
plunger... 5. diver 6. risker 7. gambler 10. speculator
plunk... 4. blow, drop, pull, push, sink, thud 5. drive, plump, strum, throw 7. a dollar 10. play truant
plurality... 8. majority 9. multitude 11. greater part, large number
plural marriage... 8. polygamy
Plutarch (Gr)... 10. biographer
Pluto (pert to)...
Astron.. 6. planet (most remote)
god of.. 10. lower world
Greek name.. 5. Hades
kingdom.. 5. Hades
Roman name.. 3. Dis 5. Orcus
wife.. 10. Proserpina
plutocracy... 13. rule by wealthy 17. dominion of the rich
Plutus (pert to)...
god of.. 6. wealth
son of.. 6. lasion 7. Demeter
pluvia... 4. rain 9. pluviosus
pluviometer, pluvioscope... 9. rain gauge
pluvious... 5. rainy 7. pluvial
ply... 4. bend, fold, mold, sail, urge 5. exert, plait, wield 6. employ, handle, lamina 8. navigate 9. importune, thickness
pneuma... 4. soul 5. neume 6. breath, spirit 9. breathing, life force, vital soul
pneumology *(science of)*... 5. lungs 17. respiratory organs
poach... 3. mix, ram 4. poke, push, sock, stir 5. drive, force, shirr (egg), steal 6. thrust 7. trample 8. encroach, trespass

poacher... 7. lurcher, stalker, widgeon
Poblacht... 8. Republic
Pocahontas (pert to)...
  father.. 8. Powhatan (Chief)
  husband.. 9. John Rolfe
  Indian title.. 8. Princess
  name.. 12. Rebecca Rolfe
  rescuer of.. 9. John Smith (Capt)
pocket... 3. bag, bin, cly, fob, sac
  4. poke, sack, take 5. money,
  pouch, purse 6. cavity, hollow
  7. conceal, confine, enclose
  8. envelope
pocketbook... 3. bag, lil 5. pouch,
  purse 6. income, wallet 8. notebook
  9. resources
pod... 3. bag, kid, sac. 4. aril, boll
  5. belly, carob, chili, pouch, shuck
  6. legume
poem... 3. dit, lay, ode 4. Edda, epic,
  epos, hymn, rune, saga 5. elegy,
  epode, idyll, psalm, verse 6. ballad
  (ballade), jingle, rondel (roundelle),
  sonnet 7. eclogue, erotics, rondeau
  8. limerick, rondelet 9. dithyramb
  10. villanelle 11. acatalectic
poem (pert to)...
  division.. 5. canto, epode, verse
  6. stanza 7. refrain
  eight lines.. 7. triolet
  famed.. 5. Iliad 7. Odyssey
  foot.. 6. iambic 7. anapest, pyrrhic
  imitation.. 6. parody
  line.. 5. stich 6. octave, septet,
  sestet, tercet 7. couplet, triplet
  8. cinquain, quatrain
  meter.. 6. iambic 8. spondaic,
  trochaic 9. dactyllic, hexameter
  10. anaepestic (anapestic),
  pentameter
  ref to.. 5. meter, rhyme, verse
  7. cadence, helicon 8. feminine,
  scansion 9. masculine
  religious.. 4. hymn 5. psalm
  rhythmic break.. 7. caesura
  satirical.. 3. dit 6. parody
poem, famed...
  Homer.. 5. Iliad 7. Odyssey
  Khayyám.. 8. Rubáiyát
  Milton.. 12. Paradise Lost
  Ovid.. 13. Metamorphoses
  Poe.. 8. The Raven
  Poem in Marble.. 8. Taj Mahal
  poem of declaration.. 8. Invictus
  Shakespeare.. 7. Macbeth
  Spenser.. 12. Faerie Queene
poems... 5. poesy, sylva 6. poetry
poet... 4. bard 5. odist, rimer 6. lyrist
  7. dreamer 8. laureate 9. poetaster,
  rhymester, versifier
poet (famed)...
  German.. 5. Heine
  mythology.. 6. Ossian
  Negro.. 11. Braithwaite
  Persian.. 7. Khayyám
  Sierra.. 13. Joaquin Miller
Poet Laureate (a few)... 6. Dryden
  7. Spenser 8. Tennyson 9. Ben
  Jonson, Masefield 10. Wordsworth
poetry (pert to)...
  Muse of.. 5. Erato 6. Thalia
  8. Calliope

  Norse god of.. 5. Bragi
  School of (anc).. 9. Parnassus
  type.. 4. epic 5. lyric 6. ballad
  8. didactic 9. free verse, narrative
  10. blank verse
pogoniate... 7. bearded
pogonip... 3. fog (Sierras)
pogonology *(study of)*... 6. beards
pogrom... 8. massacre
poi... 4. food, taro, then (Mus)
poignant... 4. keen 5. acute 6. biting,
  bitter 7. cutting, pungent
point... 3. aim, dot, jab, jot, neb, nib,
  pin 4. apex, barb, cape, gaff, gist,
  node, peak, stop, tack 5. focus,
  prong, quill, spike 6. bodkin, direct,
  needle, period, summit, zenith
  7. apicula, punctum 10. breakwater,
  promontory
point (pert to)...
  antler, branch.. 4. snag
  astronomy.. 5. apsis 6. syzygy
  central, pivotal.. 4. crux
  farthest from earth.. 6. apogee
  focal.. 9. epicenter
  geometry.. 6. acnode 7. crunode
  highest.. 4. acme, apex, peak
  6. summit, zenith 8. meridian
  pinnacle
  lace.. 10. petit point 11. needlepoint
  law.. 3. res 5. locus
  lowest.. 5. nadir 6. bottom
  mathematics.. 5. unode
  nearest earth.. 7. perigee
  of contact.. 5. focus
  of debate.. 8. issue, topic
  of honor.. 7. scruple
  of view.. 5. angle, slant 8. attitude
  opposite zenith.. 5. nadir
  reference to.. 6. apical
  salient.. 7. feature
  starting, golf.. 3. tee
  strong.. 5. forte
  utmost.. 7. extreme
  weak.. 4. flaw 5. fault 6. foible
pointed... 5. aimed, noded, piked,
  sharp, terse 6. acuate, marked,
  peaked 7. angular, concise, conical
  8. aculeate, piercing, poignant
  spicated, stinging 9. acuminate,
  pertinate, spiculate 10. emphasized
  11. conspicuous, significant
  12. epigrammatic
pointed (pert to)...
  architecture.. 5. ogive 6. Gothic
  end.. 4. cusp
  fox.. 3. red
  instrument.. 3. awl, gad 4. prod
  6. gimlet, stylet
  rod.. 4. goad
pointer... 3. arm, dog, tip 4. sign
  5. index 6. fescue, gnomon
pointless... 4. dull 5. blunt, inane,
  silly, vapid 6. stupid 7. insipid,
  witless
poise... 6. aplomb 7. balance, ballast
  8. carriage 9. composure, equipoise,
  stability
poison (pert to)...
  arrow.. 4. inee, upas 5. urari
  6. curare (curari)
  deadly.. 4. bane, upas 5. arrow

7. arsenic, cyanide, hemlock
10. strychnine
study of.. 10. toxicology
poissarde... 8. fishwife, low woman
poisson... 4. fish
poisson bleu... 7. catfish 8. bluefish, grayling
poitrel... 5. armor, plate 9. stomacher
11. breastplate
poke... 3. bag, jab, jog, pry 4. bore, goad, prod, root, sack 5. grope, nudge, probe, purse 6. dawdle, potter, search, thrust, wallet
7. project, tobacco
poker... 3. rod 6. beadle 7. bugbear, pochard 9. hobgoblin
poker (pert to)...
face.. 8. immobile
form of.. 4. draw, stud
painting.. 10. pyrography
picture.. 11. pyrogravure
stake.. 3. pot 4. ante 6. roodle
poky, pokey... 4. dull, mean, slow
5. dowdy, small 6. bonnet, narrow, shabby 7. cramped, tedious
Poland... see also *Polish*
ancestors.. 5. Lakha, Slavs
ancient name.. 7. Polonia
capital.. 6. Warsaw
city.. 4. Lodz 6. Gdynia, Krakow, Lublin
river.. 7. Dnieper, Vistula
Poland China... 5. swine
polar... 5. curve 6. Arctic 7. guiding
8. opposite 9. Antarctic, magnetism
Polar base (exploration)... 4. Etah
Polaris... 5. Alpha 9. North Star
11. guiding star
pole... 3. bar, oar, pew, poy, rod, xat
4. axle, beam, mast, prop, spar
5. shaft, sprit, staff, stool, totem
pole (pert to)...
bad end.. 7. raw deal
burn.. 7. disease (tobacco)
cat.. 5. skunk, zoril 6. ferret, musang
7. fitchew 8. Putorius 9. scoundrel
cat weed.. 12. skunk cabbage
electric.. 5. anode, pitch 7. cathode
8. magnetic 9. electrode
Gaelic.. 5. caber
head.. 7. tadpole
Spanish.. 4. pale, palo
star.. 5. guide 7. polaris 8. lodestar
9. North Star 13. l'Etoile du Nord
vehicle.. 4. cope, crab 5. thill
well.. 5. sweep
polemic... 9. disputant 11. contentious
13. argumentative, controversial
polenta... 8. porridge
poles of cold... 7. Siberia
(Verkhoyansk) 12. Grinnell Land (Fort Conger)
police (pert to)...
badge.. 6. buzzer, shield
club.. 8. spontoon
man.. 3. cop 5. guard 6. bobbie, copper, peeler, Ranger 7. officer, sheriff, trooper 9. constable, detective, N W Mounted
11. carabinière (carabineer)
station.. 5. thana 6. lockup
8. bargello

policy... 3. wit 4. plan 6. wisdom
8. regulate, sagacity 9. insurance
10. government, management, shrewdness 11. contrivance
13. judiciousness 14. administration
policy of segregation... 9. apartheid
polish... 3. rub 4. buff 5. glaze, gloss, rabat, scour, shine 6. finish, luster, smooth 7. burnish, culture, furbish
8. brighten, civilize, elegance, lapidate, levigate, urbanity
10. refinement
Polish (pert to)...
Bull.. 13. Constellation
cake.. 4. baba
carriage.. 7. britska
composer, pianist.. 6. Chopin
10. Paderewski
dance.. 7. mazurka 9. polonaise
11. cracovienne (krakowiak)
nobleman.. 7. starost
premier.. 10. Paderewski (pianist)
president (1st).. 10. Philsudski
scientist.. 5. Curie (Madame)
polishing material... 5. emery, rabat, rouge 6. pumice 11. rottenstone
polite... 4. neat, tidy 5. civil, suave, urban 6. gentle, smooth, urbane
7. gallant, genteel, refined
8. polished 9. courteous, debonaire (debonair, debonnaire) 10. cultivated
11. complaisant
politesse... 10. politeness (formal)
11. cleanliness, courtliness
12. decorousness
politic... 4. wary 7. cunning, tactful
8. cautious, discreet 9. judicious, political, politique, provident
10. diplomatic
political (pert to)...
boss.. 7. cacique
district.. 4. city, ward 5. State
6. canton, county, parish 7. borough
10. palatinate
economy.. 9. economics
faction.. 4. bloc, ring 5. junta, party
7. machine
hanger–on.. 6. heeler 10. ward heeler
influence.. 5. lobby, rally 6. caucus
party (old).. 4. Tory, Whig 9. Politique
politician... 7. schemer 9. intriguer, statesman 11. gerrymander
12. politicaster
politics... 7. cunning 8. scheming
10. government, profession
15. partisan rivalry 16. political affairs
Polizei... 9. the police
poll... 3. cut, tax 4. clip, head, roll, vote 5. shear, skull 6. fleece, survey
7. despoil 8. election, schedule
pollan... 9. whitefish
polled... 5. shorn 6. shaved
8. hornless
pollen... 4. seed 6. anther 8. fine dust 11. microspores 13. fertilization
pollen brush (bee's)... 5. scopa
pollenization... 5. xenia 13. fertilization
pollent... 6. strong 8. powerful
poller... 5. voter 6. barber
9. plunderer 11. extortioner, taxgatherer

pollex... 5. thumb 11. bastard wing (bird) 13. dactylopodite
pollex impression... 10. thumbprint
polliwog... 7. tadpole
pollute... 4. soil 5. taint 6. befoul, defile, ravish 7. corrupt, debauch, profane 9. desecrate, inebriate 11. contaminate
pollution... 8. impurity 9. infection 10. corruption, defilement 13. contamination
Pollux (pert to)...
brother (twin).. 6. Castor
father.. 4. Zeus
mother.. 4. Leda
protector of.. 7. sailors
star.. 13. Beta Geminorum
Polonius... 8. courtier (Shak)
polony... 7. sausage
poltergeist (folklore)... 5. ghost 6. spirit
poltfoot... 8. clubfoot
poltroon... 4. idle, lazy 6. coward, craven, wretch 7. buffoon, dastard 8. cowardly 9. dastardly 10. ne'er–do–well, scaramouch
polverine... 6. potash (of Levant) 8. pearlash
polyandrium (Gr)... 8. cemetery
polyandry... 8. polygamy 14. plural husbands (Tibet)
polychromatic... 10. variegated
polyglot... 6. jargon 9. languages (confusion of) 10. dictionary 11. philologist 21. Complutensian Polyglot (Bib)
polygon... 6. isagon 7. decagon, hexagon, nonagon, octagon 8. heptagon 9. dodecagon
polygyny... 8. polygamy 11. plural wives
polyhedron... 5. solid 6. figure 14. trisoctahedron 17. triakisoctahedron
polymny... 10. sacred song
Polynesia...
native.. 5. Maori 6. Kanaka 8. Hawaiian 10. Melanesian
ocean.. 7. Pacific
origin (probable).. 7. Savaiki (Isl)
South Sea Island group.. 5. Samoa 6. Hawaii, Tahiti 7. Savaiki 10. New Zealand
Polynesian (pert to)...
butterfly.. 2. io
chestnut.. 4. rata
cloth.. 4. tapa
demon.. 4. atua
dragon.. 3. ati
goddess of volcanoes.. 4. Pele
god of forests.. 4. Tane
hero.. 4. Maui
homeland (fabled).. 7. Havaiki
loincloth.. 5. pareu
memorial.. 3. ahu
oven.. 3. umu
social tradition.. 6. tattoo
tribe.. 3. Ati
wages, reward.. 3. utu
polyp... 5. coral, Hydra, tumor 10. sea anemone 12. invertebrate
polyphone... 4. lute

polytropic... 9. versatile
pomade... 6. anoint 7. pomatum, unguent 8. ointment
pome... 4. pear 5. apple, fruit 6. quince 11. pomegranate
pomelo... 8. shaddock 10. grapefruit
Pomerania (pert to)...
animal.. 3. dog
capital.. 7. Stettin
formerly.. 5. duchy (Prussia)
river.. 4. Oder
pomme de terre... 6. potato
Pomona... 4. city (Calif) 7. college, goddess (of fruit)
pomp... 5. pride, state 6. parade 7. cortege, display, pageant 8. grandeur 9. pageantry, spectacle 10. ceremonial 11. ostentation 12. magnificence
pompano... 7. alewife
Pompeii, Italy (pert to)...
10. earthquake, excavation, Mt Vesuvius (site)
pompous... 5. budge 6. august, stilty 7. Podsnap (Dickens), stilted 9. bombastic, grandiose 11. ceremonious 12. high–sounding, ostentatious, stuffed shirt
Ponce de Leon (pert to)...
discoverer of.. 7. Florida 15. Fountain of Youth
famed as.. 8. explorer
landing site, America.. 11. St Augustine
pond... 4. pool 5. ocean (humorous) 6. lagoon 7. lakelet
pond (pert to)...
apple.. 9. evergreen
crow, hen.. 4. coot
dogwood.. 10. buttonbush
duck.. 7. mallard
fish.. 7. sunfish
frog.. 8. ranarium
glass.. 8. aquarium
ponder... 4. mull, muse, pore 5. brood, opine, weigh 7. perpend, reflect 8. appraise, cogitate, consider, evaluate, meditate, ruminate
ponderous... 4. dull, huge 5. bulky, heavy 7. weighty 8. ungainly 9. important, momentous 11. elephantine
pongee... 4. silk 6. tussah 8. shantung
poniard... 4. dirk, kill 5. sword 6. dagger, pierce
ponica... 8. gardener
pont... 5. ferry, float 6. bridge 7. caisson, pontoon 9. ferryboat
Pontiac... 4. city (Mich) 5. Chief (Ottawa Indian) 6. Indian
pontiff... 4. pope 6. bishop 8. pontifex
pony... 3. cab, nag 4. crib 5. glass, horse, pinto 6. bronco 7. Express (mail, 1860), piebald 8. Shetland 11. translation
pooch... 3. dog 5. pouch
pooka... 6. goblin 7. specter
pool... 3. lin, pot 4. carr, fund, game, linn, mere, pond, tank, tarn 5. kitty, stake 6. cartel, lagoon, league, puddle

7. alberca, plashet 9. billiards,
reservoir, resources 10. natatorium
11. aggregation
pool ball... 3. cue 4. spot 6. ringer
poon tree... 5. domba, keena
poor... 3. bad 4. mean, thin 5. needy
6. feeble, humble, meager, paltry,
shabby, sickly 7. hapless, unlucky
8. indigent, inferior 9. destitute,
illogical, imperfect, infertile
10. unskillful (unskilful)
11. impecunious, unfavorable,
unfortunate 12. impoverished,
inauspicious, insufficient
14. unsatisfactory
poor (pert to)...
creature.. 9. pilgarlic
joe.. 5. heron
John.. 3. cod 4. hake 8. mean fare
man's remedy.. 8. valerian
Richard.. 8. Saunders (Richard)
section of city.. 4. slum 6. ghetto
7. skid row 10. shantytown
soldier.. 9. friarbird
poorly... 3. ill 5. badly 8. abjectly,
meagerly, shabbily 10. indisposed
11. defectively 13. disparagingly
pop... 4. bang, snap, soda 5. bulge,
burst, crack 6. bubble 7. concert
8. beverage
popadam... 5. wafer (fried) 10. popper
cake
popdock... 8. foxglove
pope... 3. fin 4. ruff 6. bishop, puffin,
shrike, weevil 8. beverage
9. bullfinch 14. painted bunting
Pope (pert to)...
cathedral.. 7. Lateran
collar.. 5. orale
court officer.. 6. datary
crown.. 5. tiara 6. triple
first.. 5. Peter
headdress.. 5. miter (mitre)
name.. 4. Pius 5. Ratti 7. Gregory
palace.. 7. Vatican
poetry.. 10. Essay on Man
scarf.. 5. fanon
popeler... 7. sea gull 9. spoonbill
popinac... 8. huisache
popinjay... 6. parrot
poplar... 5. abele, alamo, aspen,
bahan, white 10. cottonwood
12. balm of Gilead
poplar (pert to)...
Arabic.. 5. bahan, garab
balsam.. 9. tacamahac
Fr black.. 4. liar 10. cottonwood
N American.. 7. Populus 8. Lombardy
white.. 5. abele, bolle
poppy... 3. maw 4. Papaver (opium),
ponceau 8. foxglove
poppycock... 3. rot 4. bosh
8. nonsense
populace... 3. mob 4. mass
5. demos, plebs 6. people
11. inhabitants 12. common people
popular... 3. lay, pop 5. cheap, liked,
usual 6. famous, simple, vulgar
7. crowded, demotic, secular
8. accepted, epidemic, favorite,
populous 9. prevalent, well-known,
well-liked 11. fashionable, proletarian
12. nontechnical
popular belief... 4. lore 7. opinion
9. tradition 12. old wives' tale,
superstition
popularity... 4. fame 5. vogue
10. reputation 15. fashionableness
popular success... 3. hit
population study... 10. larithmics
porcelain... 4. frit 5. china 6. kaolin
7. ramekin (mold)
porcelain (kind)... 5. Spode 6. Sèvres
7. celadon, Dresden, Limoges
8. Haviland
porch... 4. door, stoa 5. stoop
6. harbor, loggia 7. galilee, gallery,
portico, veranda 8. entrance
9. colonnade
porcine animal... 3. hog, pig, sow
5. shoat, swine 6. porker 7. peccary
8. babirusa (babiroussa) 9. razorback
porcupine (pert to)...
anteater.. 7. echidna
Canada.. 5. urson 7. cawquaw
disease.. 10. ichthyosis
grass.. 5. stipa
species.. 6. rodent, tenrec (tendrac)
8. hedgehog, quill pig
pore... 3. con 4. duct, gaze, vent
5. stare, stoma, study 6. ponder
7. eporose (without), opening, orifice,
ostiole 8. lenticel
porgy... 4. fish, scup 5. bream, pargo
6. pagrus, red tai
pork (pert to)...
barrel.. 4. fund (Polit) 6. boodle
chop.. 7. griskin
fish.. 5. sisi
porker... 3. hog, pig 5. swine, sword
(obs)
porpoise... 4. Inia 6. seahog
7. dolphin, pellock 8. cetacean,
Phocaena
porr... 4. cram, kick, poke, push, stir
5. poker 6. thrust
porrect... 6. tender 7. present
porridge... 3. pob 4. pobs, samp
5. atole, brose, grout, gruel
6. cereal 7. oatmeal, polenta,
pottage 9. stirabout
port... 4. gate, left, mien, wine
5. armor, haven 6. harbor, portal
7. airport, bearing, opening, posture
8. carriage, demeanor, larboard,
porthole, portside 10. deportment
11. destruction
portable... 6. mobile 7. movable
portable altar... 10. altar stone,
superaltar (Hist)
portal... 4. door, gate 5. porch
7. gateway 8. entrance 9. vestibule
12. porte-cochere
portcullis... 3. bar 4. shut 5. herse
7. barrier, grating, lattice (Her)
13. fortification
Porte... 12. Ottoman court (anc),
Sublime Porte
porte-bonheur... 5. charm 6. amulet
porte-cochere... 5. porch (carriage)
7. gateway
portefeuille... 9. portfolio
portend... 4. bode 5. augur
7. betoken, predict, presage

8. forebode, foreshow, foretell, prophecy 9. foretoken

portent... 4. omen, sign 6. marvel, ostent 7. prodigy 11. forewarning

portentous... 4. dire 5. fatal, grave 6. solemn 7. fateful, ominous 8. sinister 9. monstrous, wonderful 10. impressive 13. extraordinary

porter... 3. ale 4. beer 5. hamal (hammal), stout (drink) 6. bearer 7. carrier, janitor 9. attendant 10. doorkeeper

Porter's pseudonym... 6. O Henry

Portia (pert to)...
character (Merchant of Venice).. 7. heiress
husband.. 8. Bassanio
husband's friend.. 7. Antonio
maid.. 7. Nerissa

portico... 4. stoa 6. atrium, xystus (xyst) 7. pteroma, veranda 9. colonnade, peristyle, vestibule

portion... 3. bit, cut, dab, lot 4. dole, dose, dunt, fate, half, mete, part, some 5. piece, share, whack 6. moiety, parcel 7. section, segment 8. quantity 9. allotment, apportion, partition

portion (pert to)...
curve.. 3. arc 7. segment
detached.. 6. coupon
inheritance.. 7. legitim 9. dead's part
marriage.. 5. dowry
sectional.. 5. curve
widow's.. 5. dower

Portland (pert to)...
arrowroot, sago.. 4. arum
beds (Eng).. 11. Upper Oolite 13. Upper Jurassic
city of.. 5. Maine 6. Oregon
stone.. 6. cement 8. concrete
vase.. 9. Barberini (Rom palace) 10. cameo glass

portmanteau... 3. bag 4. word (blended) 5. cloak 6. mantle, valise

portoise... 7. gunwale 8. portlast

Porto Rico... see Puerto Rico

portrait... 4. copy 5. image 7. picture 8. likeness, painting 10. similitude 11. description, portraiture 12. lifelikeness 14. representation

portrait on dollars...
fifty.. 5. Grant
five.. 7. Lincoln
five hundred.. 8. McKinley
five thousand.. 7. Madison
one.. 10. Washington
one hundred.. 8. Franklin
one hundred thousand.. 6. Wilson
one thousand.. 9. Cleveland
ten.. 8. Hamilton
ten thousand.. 5. Chase
twenty.. 7. Jackson
two.. 9. Jefferson

portray... 3. act 4. draw, form, limn 5. enact, frame, image, paint 6. depict 7. fashion, picture 8. describe 9. delineate, represent

portrayal... 3. act 5. drama 7. process 8. portrait 9. depiction 11. delineation, description

portreeve... 5. mayor 7. bailiff

Port Royal... 15. Cistercian abbey (Versailles)

Portugal... see also Portuguese
bridge.. 7. Salazar
capital.. 6. Lisbon
city.. 5. Braga 6. Aveiro, Guarda, Oporto 7. Granada
island.. 6. Azores 7. Madeira 8. Principe
mountain.. 15. Serra da Estrella
peninsula.. 7. Iberian
port.. 6. Aveiro
province.. 3. Goa 5. Macao, Timor 9. Cape Verde 10. Mozambique
resort.. 7. Estoril
river.. 5. Tagus (Tajo)

Portuguese (pert to)...
author.. 9. de Lobeira
bird, fish.. 8. man–of–war
ceremonial (Inquisition).. 8. auto de fe
coin (gold).. 6. escudo 7. milreis (old)
lady.. 4. dona
legislature.. 6. Cortes 12. Cortes Geraes
money of account.. 4. reis
navigator.. 6. da Gama 8. Magellan
wine.. 5. porto

Portunus (Rom Relig)... 10. god of gates

posada... 3. inn 5. hotel

Posaune... 8. trombone 9. organ stop

posca... 5. drink (Hist)

pose... 3. put, sit 5. model 6. baffle, puzzle, stance 7. nonplus, posture, pretend, propose 8. attitude, position, pretense, propound 9. postulate 11. affectation, impersonate

Poseidon (pert to)...
attributes.. 5. horse 7. dolphin, trident
cult site.. 7. Corinth
father.. 6. Cronus
god of.. 3. sea 6. waters
mother.. 4. Rhea
wife.. 10. Amphitrite

poser... 5. facer 6. puzzle 7. problem, sticker 14. attitudinarian

posh... 5. smart 6. spruce 7. elegant 9. luxurious

position... 3. job, lie 4. pose, rank, seat, site 5. coign (coigne), place, situs, stand, state 6. manner, stance, ubiety 7. opinion, posture, premise 8. attitude, location, prestige, proposal 9. viewpoint 11. affirmation, supposition

position (pert to)...
anchorlike.. 5. apeak
fencing.. 7. septime
finder (gun).. 13. triangulation
golf.. 6. stance
inescapable.. 7. impasse
of affairs.. 6. status
relative.. 8. standing
secure.. 7. footing
with no responsibility.. 8. sinecure

positive... 4. plus, sure 5. exact 6. actual, thetic 7. certain 8. dogmatic, emphatic 9. assertive, convinced, downright 11. dictatorial

positive (pert to)...

charge (Elec).. 8. positron
evidence.. 7. constat
pole.. 5. anode
saying.. 6. dictum
school, criminology.. 10. Lombrosian
  (by Lombroso)
positivism... 7. Comtism 9. certainty,
  dogmatism 10. confidence
  11. materialism
positure... 7. posture 11. arrangement,
  disposition 13. configuration
posnet... 3. pot (3–footed)
  8. saucepan
poss... 4. beat, dash, push 5. drive,
  knock, pound, stamp 6. thrust
posse... 5. crowd 6. throng
  7. company 9. armed band
  10. detachment (police)
possess... 3. own 4. have, know, take
  5. haunt 6. inform, occupy
  7. bewitch, inhabit 8. convince,
  demonize, persuade
possessed... 5. hadst, owned
  6. insane 7. haunted 8. demoniac,
  obsessed 9. bewitched
possessing (pert to)...
feeling.. 6. souled
flavor.. 5. sapid, tasty
land.. 5. acred
pincer claws.. 8. chelated
power.. 11. plenipotent
sensation.. 8. sentient
special ability.. 6. gifted 8. talented
possession... 4. hold 5. asset
  6. taking, wealth 7. control, country,
  mastery 8. dominion, property
  9. obsession, ownership
  10. equanimity 11. bewitchment
possession (pert to)...
again.. 6. revest
law.. 6. seizin (seisin)
not in (possession).. 6. devoid
suffix.. 3. ose
possessions... 6. assets, estate, wealth
  7. effects 8. property
posset... 4. turn 6. curdle, pamper
  8. beverage, infusion 9. coagulate
possibility... 4. bare 7. latency
  9. liability, potential 10. good
  chance, likelihood 11. contingency
  13. improbability 16. prospective
  value
possible... 6. latent, liable, likely
  8. feasible 9. plausible, potential
  11. practicable
possibly... 5. maybe 7. perhaps
  9. perchance 11. conceivably
post... 3. bet, dak (dawk), xat 4. bitt,
  fort, list, mail, trot 5. enter, newel,
  opium, place, stake, totem 6. alette,
  assign, hasten, inform, marker, office,
  pillar, pledge 7. bollard, placard,
  station, upright 8. dispatch, position
  9. messenger, sternpost 12. enter
  account
post (pert to)...
adverb.. 5. after, later 9. afterward
boat.. 4. mail 5. stage 6. packet
boy.. 7. courier 9. postilion (postillion)
dance (army sl).. 8. struggle
goal (anc).. 4. meta
Indian memorial.. 3. xat 5. totem

meridian.. 9. afternoon
mortem.. 7. autopsy 8. necropsy
  10. after death
office.. 6. correo
prefix.. 5. after 6. behind
  10. subsequent
stair.. 5. newel
postage stamp paper (pert to)...
design.. 8. spandrel
paper.. 6. pelure
pattern.. 6. burele 8. burelage
poster... 4. bill, card 7. placard,
  sticker 8. bulletin 9. messenger
  10. billposter
posthumous... 5. after 10. after death,
  post–mortem
postiche... 9. false hair 10. artificial
  11. counterfeit
postilion... 5. guide 7. postboy
  9. postrider
postimpressionist... 6. cubist, Derain
  7. Cezanne, Matisse
postpone... 4. wait 5. defer, delay,
  remit, table 6. put off, shelve
  7. adjourn, reserve, suspend 8. hold
  over, prorogue 10. pigeonhole
  11. subordinate 13. procrastinate
postponement... 7. remanet, respite
  8. deferral, reprieve 9. deferment
  11. prorogation
postprandial... 11. after dinner
postulate... 6. assume 7. prelude,
  premise 9. condition, predicate,
  stipulate 10. hypothesis
  11. stipulation, supposition
posture... 4. pose 6. stance
  8. attitude, position, pretense
  9. viewpoint 11. frame of mind
pot... 3. jug, pan 4. olla 5. belly,
  crock, cruse 6. aludel, kettle, liquor,
  teapot 7. amphora (anc), caldron
  9. flowerpot 10. jardiniere
potash... 6. potass, saline 7. potassa
  8. pearlash 18. potassium carbonate
potassium (pert to)...
bitartrate.. 13. cream of tartar
bromide.. 8. sedative
carbonate.. 6. potash
compound.. 4. alum
dichromatic.. 6. chrome
iodide.. 8. medicine
nitrate.. 5. niter 9. saltpeter
permanganate.. 8. oxidizer
  12. disinfectant
sulphate.. 4. alum
potate... 9. liquefied
potation... 5. draft, drink 6. liquor
  8. beverage, tippling 12. drinking
  bout
potato... 3. oca, yam 4. papa, spud
  5. tuber
potato (pert to)...
beetle.. 8. hardback
bogle.. 9. scarecrow
French.. 12. pomme de terre
French style.. 9. lyonnaise
genus.. 10. Solanaceae
Indian.. 4. yamp
moss.. 9. pondgrass
S Am.. 7. Uruguay
sweet.. 6. patata
potator... 5. poter 7. tippler

potboiler... 4. book 6. writer
   8. painting (for quick money)
   9. potwaller
potdar... 7. assayer, cashier, weigher
potence, potency... 3. vis 4. élan
   5. cross, power 6. energy, gibbet
   7. gallows 8. virility 9. authority,
   influence
potent... 4. able 6. cogent, mighty,
   strong, virile 7. dynamic, warrant
   (Mil) 8. forcible, heraldry, powerful,
   puissant, virulent 9. effective, efficient
   11. efficacious, influential
   13. authoritative
potentate... 4. amir (ameer), emir
   (emeer) 5. mogul, ruler 6. dynast,
   prince 7. emperor, monarch
   8. syzerain 9. sovereign
potential... 4. mood (Gram) 5. ergal
   6. latent, mighty 8. possible
   11. influential, in the making,
   possibility, undeveloped
potentiality... 5. power 7. latency
   11. possibility
poter... 5. toper 7. drinker
potgun... 5. rumor 6. cannon, mortar,
   pistol 8. braggart
pothead... 7. dullard 8. terminal (Elec)
   9. blackfish
pother... 3. ado, row 4. fuss, stir
   5. worry 6. bother, bustle, harass
   7. fluster, perplex, trouble
   9. commotion 10. excitement,
   perplexity 11. disturbance
   12. perturbation
potherb... 4. mint 6. greens
   7. spinach
pothook... 3. rod 4. hook (S–shaped)
   5. crook 6. scrawl, stroke (S–like)
   9. pot lifter 10. iron collar (penalty)
pothouse... 3. bar, low 6. saloon,
   tavern, vulgar 7. barroom
   8. alehouse, grogshop, mughouse
   11. public house
potiche... 4. vase 7. ceramic
potion... 4. dose, dram, drug 5. draft,
   drink 7. draught, philter 8. nepenthe
potlatch... 4. gift 5. feast 8. Festival
potomania... 10. dipsomania
   15. delirium tremens
potong... 5. crown 6. wreath 9. head
   cloth
potoroo... 11. rat kangaroo
potpourri... 4. olio, stew 6. medley
   7. mixture, perfume 9. anthology
   11. olla–podrida, salamagundi
potrero... 4. farm 7. pasture
   10. cattle farm
pottage... 4. soup 6. brewis
   8. porridge
pottah... 5. lease 6. tenure 9. title
   deed
potter... 3. pry 4. mess, poke, push
   6. dawdle, doodle, meddle, putter,
   tamper, trifle 7. saunter 8. ceramist
potter's clay, earth... 4. slip 5. argil
   6. galena, kaolin 8. alquifou
   10. terra cotta
potter's wheel... 4. disk 5. lathe,
   throw 6. jigger, pallet (palet)
pottery... 5. Delft 6. Samian
   7. celadon (Chin), keramos (Gr)

   8. Arretine (It), ceramics, Majolica (It)
   9. delftware (Holland), keramikos (Gr)
   11. earthenware 14. terra sigillata
   (anc)
pottery (pert to)...
   black.. 6. basalt
   broken.. 5. shard (sherd)
   decorate.. 6. stamps 9. sigillate
   decoration.. 11. sigillation
   firing box.. 6. sagger
   glasslike.. 8. vitreous
   glaze.. 6. enamel
   mineral.. 8. feldspar
   paste.. 9. barbotine
   red.. 7. aretine
pottle... 3. pot 6. basket, vessel
   7. tankard
potty... 3. pot 5. crazy 7. foolish,
   haughty 8. trifling 12. supercilious
   13. insignificant
pot–valiant... 10. courageous (when
   drunk)
pouch... 3. bag, pod, sac 4. cyst,
   poke, sack 5. bulge, bursa, purse
   6. gipser (Hist), pocket 7. bladder,
   mailbag, silicle, sporran (sporan)
   10. pocketbook
pouch bone... 9. marsupial
pouched (pert to)...
   dog.. 9. thylacine 13. Tasmanian wolf
   frog.. 9. marsupial
   gopher.. 6. pocket
   mouse.. 9. marsupial
   rat.. 8. kangaroo
   rodent (cheek–pouched)..
      11. spermophile
   stork.. 8. adjutant
poultry... 4. fowl, hens 5. cocks,
   ducks, geese 6. capons 7. Bantams,
   peahens, pigeons, turkeys
   8. chickens, peacocks, roosters,
   volaille 9. cockerels, pheasants
   10. guinea fowl
poultry (breeds)... 6. Ancona, Bantam,
   Brahma 7. Cornish, Dorking,
   Hamburg, Leghorn, Minorca
   9. Wyandotte 12. Plymouth Rock
   14. Rhode Island Red
poultry (pert to)...
   disease.. 3. pip 4. roup, tick
   dish.. 9. galantine
   farm.. 7. hennery
pounamu... 4. jade 6. weapon
   8. nephrite 10. greenstone
pound... 3. hit, ram 4. beat, ding,
   drum, maul, pond, tamp 5. money,
   pen up, thump 6. bruise, hammer,
   kennel, prison 7. impound
   9. enclosure, pulverize
pounding instrument... 6. hammer,
   pestle
pounds (100)... 6. cental
   13. hundredweight
pour... 3. flow, gush, rain, teem, vent,
   well 5. flood 6. abound, effuse,
   stream 7. niagara, radiate, torrent
   8. downpour 9. discharge
   11. extravasate
pour (pert to)...
   molten glass.. 7. dagrade
   molten steel.. 4. teem
   off.. 5. drain 6. decant

oil upon.. **6.** anoint, pacify
out.. **11.** extravasate
sacrificial liquid.. **6.** libate
pouring hole (mold)... **5.** sprue
pout... **3.** bib, mop **4.** fish, moue, sulk
5. pique **7.** catfish, eelpout, grimace
9. sulkiness
poverty... **4.** lack, need, want **5.** illth
(opp of wealth) **6.** dearth, penury
8. leanness, poorness, scarcity
9. indigence, pearlweed
11. destitution
powder... **4.** dust, talc **5.** boral
6. pollen, yttria **7.** crumble
8. cosmetic, sprinkle **9.** explosive,
pulverize
powder (pert to)...
antiseptic.. **6.** formin **7.** aristol
bag.. **6.** sachet
festival (Ind).. **4.** abir (perfumed)
goa.. **7.** araroba
heater, melter.. **6.** sinter
insecticide.. **9.** hellebore
medical.. **8.** tannigen
perfumed.. **6.** empasm
polishing.. **5.** emery **7.** tripoli
smokeless.. **6.** poudre **8.** amberite
stamping.. **6.** pounce
powdered (Her)... **4.** semé
power... **3.** arm, art, can, jet, vis
4. dint, gift, iron, sway, will
5. force, magic, might, steam, vigor
6. degree, energy **7.** control, faculty,
magnate, potency **8.** capacity,
efficacy, strength **9.** authority,
eloquence, influence, magnetism,
puissance **10.** efficiency, government
11. mathematics (term)
power (pert to)...
creative.. **6.** Shakti
device.. **9.** telemotor
hammer.. **4.** trip
inherent.. **6.** energy
of attorney.. **5.** agent **10.** procurator
of feeling.. **7.** sensate
of mind.. **4.** wits
of resistance.. **7.** stamina
persuasive.. **8.** rhetoric **9.** political
sovereign.. **6.** throne
spiritual.. **8.** divinity
superior.. **10.** prepotency
under one's.. **10.** subjugated
unit.. **3.** erg **4.** dyne **8.** kilowatt
powerful... **4.** loud **5.** great **6.** cogent,
mighty, potent, strong **7.** drastic,
intense, leonine, skookum
8. eloquent, forcible, puissant
9. effective, effectual, efficient
10. armipotent, convincing
11. efficacious, influential
13. authoritative
powerful force... **6.** libido
powerful man, businessman...
5. titan **6.** tycoon **7.** magnate
powerless... **4.** weak **8.** impotent
pownie... **7.** peacock
powwow... **6.** frolic, priest **7.** meeting
8. assembly, ceremony, congress,
conjurer **9.** gathering **10.** conference,
convention
poyou... **9.** armadillo
prabble... **7.** chatter, quarrel

8. squabble
practic... **6.** artful, shrews **7.** cunning,
skilled **9.** difficult, practical, practiced
11. experienced
practicable, practical... **5.** utile
6. usable, useful **7.** virtual, working
8. feasible, possible, workable
9. available, expedient, operative,
pragmatic, realistic **11.** pragmatical,
utilitarian
practical (pert to)...
Christianity.. **10.** New Thought
example.. **6.** praxis
joke.. **4.** hoax **5.** trick **6.** humbug
judgment.. **7.** ethical (Kant)
practically... **9.** virtually **11.** essentially
13. approximately
practice, practise... **2.** do **3.** ply, ure,
use **4.** plot, rite **5.** drill, habit, train,
usage **6.** action, addict, custom,
scheme, tryout **7.** perform
8. ceremony, exercise, intrigue,
rehearse, training, vocation
9. procedure **10.** experience,
experiment, observance
practice (pert to)...
corrupt.. **5.** abuse
established.. **5.** canon **6.** custom
fraud.. **5.** cheat, shark **8.** trickery
specific.. **6.** praxis
voice.. **8.** intonate
witchcraft.. **3.** hex
practicer of evasions...
13. tergiversator
practicer of palmistry...
11. chiromancer
prad... **5.** horse
pragmatic... **7.** meddler, skilled
8. busybody, dogmatic, meddling
9. conceited, officious, practical
10. systematic **11.** opinionated
pragmatical... **8.** dogmatic **9.** officious,
practical **10.** meddlesome
11. commonplace
Prague, Praha...
capital of.. **14.** Czechoslovakia
famed bldg.. **10.** University (1st in
Cent Eur, 1348)
famed teachers (anc).. **4.** Huss
6. Jerome
founder.. **14.** Duchess Libussa (722)
prairie... **3.** bay **5.** llano, plain
6. camass (camas, cammas),
meadow, steppe **7.** quamash
(camass) **9.** grassland **10.** prairillon
prairie (pert to)...
anemone, crocus.. **12.** pasque flower
antelope.. **9.** pronghorn
apple.. **9.** breadroot
artichoke.. **9.** sunflower
berry.. **9.** trompillo
chicken.. **6.** grouse
dog.. **6.** marmot
mud.. **5.** gumbo
pigeon.. **6.** plover **9.** sandpiper
rose.. **14.** Baltimore belle
schooner.. **12.** covered wagon
squirrel.. **11.** spermophile
tree (clump).. **5.** motte
weed.. **10.** cinquefoil
wolf.. **6.** coyote
Prairie State... **8.** Illinois

praise... 4. laud 5. bless, extol, honor, kudos 6. eulogy 7. acclaim, applaud, commend, glorify, magnify, plaudit 8. applause, encomium, eulogize, macarize 9. adulation, celebrate, panegyric 11. approbation 12. commendation
praise (pert to)...
continual.. 5. chant
high.. 5. extol 8. encomium
hymn of.. 8. doxology
insincere.. 4. bull 7. flatter 8. flattery
of another's blessing.. 8. macarism 9. Beatitude
to God.. 7. Laus Deo
Ye The Lord.. 8. Alleluia (Alleluiah) 10. Hallelujah (Halleluiah)
praiseworthy... 8. laudable 11. commendable, meritorious
prana (Hind)... 6. spirit 9. life force 10. life breath
prance... 4. gait 5. caper, dance 6. cavort, spring 7. swagger
prank... 3. jig 4. fold, joke, prat 5. antic, caper, pleat, shine, trick 6. frolic, prance 7. caprice, dress up 8. escapade 11. monkeyshine
prankish... 9. facetious 10. frolicsome 11. mischievous
prate... 3. gab 4. chat, talk 6. gossip 7. chatter, twaddle 8. nonsense
prattle... 3. gab 4. chat, talk 5. clack, prate 6. babble 7. blather 12. impudent talk, trifling talk
prawn... 6. shrimp 10. crustacean, shrimp pink
pray... 3. ask, beg, sue 7. entreat, implore, request, worship 8. devotion 10. supplicate
praya... 4. bund, road 5. beach 6. strand
prayer... 3. ave 4. bead, bene, plea, suit 5. credo, grace, matin 6. litany, orison, vesper 7. request, worship 8. petition 12. intercession, supplication
prayer (pert to)...
book.. 4. ordo 6. missal 7. portass (portas) 8. breviary
call (Moham).. 4. azan (adan)
call tower.. 7. minaret
cloak.. 6. zizith (fringed) 7. tallith
evening.. 7. complin (compline) 9. night song
figure.. 5. orant
Incarnation.. 7. Angelus 11. Angelus Bell
liturgical.. 6. litany 7. complin
Lord's (prayer).. 11. Paternoster
morning.. 7. matin
nine days' devotional.. 6. novena
response.. 8. antiphon
short.. 5. grace
stick.. 4. paho
praying... 8. entreaty 9. precation 12. supplication
praying cricket... 6. mantis
praying figure... 5. orant
preach... 6. exhort 7. expound, lecture 8. advocate, homilize 9. discourse, sermonize
preacher... 6. parson, rector

7. evangel, teacher 8. homilist, lecturer, minister 9. clergyman, pulpiteer
preaching... 6. sermon 7. kerygma (kerugma) 10. preachment 11. exhortation
preaching friar... 9. Dominican
Preaching of Peter... 9. Apocrypha
preamble... 5. proem 7. preface, prelude 11. preliminary 12. introduction
prebellum... 7. antewar 12. before the war
prebend... 7. stipend 8. benefice 9. allowance
precarious... 7. assumed, dubious 8. insecure, unstable 9. hazardous, uncertain, unsettled 10. unreliable
preceded... 3. led 8. prefaced, was prior 9. anteceded, antedated 10. introduced, went before 13. had precedence, occurred first
precedence... 3. pas 4. lead, rank 8. priority 12. anteposition
precedent... 4. sign 5. model, usage 7. example, leading 8. anterior, decision, standard 10. antecedent, forerunner 11. going before
preceding others... 5. first 7. leading, ternary (by threes) 10. antecedent
precept... 4. rule, writ 5. adage, axiom, maxim, order, sutra (sutta), torah (tora) 6. belief 7. command 8. doctrine 9. direction 11. commandment, instruction
preceptor... 4. guru 5. guide, tutor 6. master, mentor, mullah, pundit 7. teacher 8. educator 10. instructor
precinct... 5. ambit, space 6. region 8. boundary, district, environs
precious... 4. dear, rare 5. great 6. costly, valued 7. beloved, elegant, perfect 8. complete, esteemed, overnice, valuable 9. downright 10. beloved one, fastidious, particular
precious (pert to)...
Blood (RCCh).. 5. Feast (July 1)
garnet.. 6. pyrope
stone.. 3. gem 4. opal, ruby 5. pearl, topaz 6. garnet, ligure 7. diamond, emerald, jacinth (Bib) 8. hyacinth, sapphire
stone, sometimes.. 7. cat's-eye 11. alexandrite
precipice... 4. crag, linn, pali 5. bluff, cliff 9. declivity
precipitancy... 5. haste 8. rashness
precipitation... 3. gel 4. fall, hail, mist, rain, snow 5. haste, sleet 8. downpour 9. hastening 11. prematurity 12. acceleration, condensation, recklessness
precipitous... 4. rash 5. hasty, steep 6. abrupt, sudden 7. rushing (headlong) 9. very rapid 11. precipitate
précis... 6. sketch 7. epitome, pandect, summary 8. abstract, synopsis 9. summarize
precise... 4. prim 5. exact 7. correct, literal, special 8. accurate, definite, detailed, overnice 10. meticulous,

overminute, particular, scrupulous
11. ceremonious, punctilious
preciseness... 9. exactness
10. strictness 12. definiteness
14. fastidiousness
precision... 6. nicety 8. accuracy
9. exactness, formality
11. preciseness 12. definiteness
preclude... 3. bar 4. omit, stop
5. avert, debar, estop 6. hinder,
impede 7. head off, prevent, shut
out 8. prohibit
precocious... 7. forward 8. advanced
9. premature
preconceive... 6. ideate, precox
7. presume 8. foreknow, prejudge
9. predecide 10. presuppose
predatory... 7. looting 9. marauding,
pillaging, piratical 10. plundering,
predaceous (predacious)
11. destructive
predatory bird... 3. owl 4. hawk, kite
6. falcon
predatory raid... 5. foray
predestine... 4. doom, fate 6. decree,
ordain 7. appoint 9. determine,
foretoken 10. foreordain
predetermine... 4. bias 7. destine
8. prejudge 9. prejudice, preordain
10. prepossess 11. premeditate
predicament... 3. fix 4. pass 5. state
6. plight, scrape 7. dilemma,
impasse 8. quandary 9. condition,
situation
predicator... 4. seer 5. friar
7. prophet 8. preacher 9. predicter
predict... 4. bode, dope, omen
7. foresee, portend, presage
8. forecast, foretell, prophecy
13. prognosticate
prediction... 6. augury 8. prophecy
9. foresight 10. foreboding
11. foretelling 15. prognostication
predilection... 4. bias 6. desire
8. tendency 9. prejudice
10. favoritism, partiality, preference,
propensity 11. disposition
13. preconception 14. predisposition
predominant... 5. chief 6. ruling
8. reigning, superior 9. hegemonic
11. controlling, influential,
outstanding
predominate... 5. excel 7. prevail
8. dominate 10. be superior
12. preponderate
pre—eminent... 3. top 4. only, star
5. chief 7. palmary, ranking
8. superior 9. excellent, principal
11. outstanding
pre—emption... 8. monopoly, purchase
10. prior right 13. appropriation
preen... 3. pin, sew 4. perk 5. clasp,
dress, groom, plume, primp
6. bodkin, brooch, stitch 9. make
sleek
preface... 5. front, proem 6. herald,
prayer 7. prelude, problem
8. exordium, foreword, preamble,
prologue 10. paraphrase
12. introduction
prefect, praefect... 4. dean (Jesuit)
6. chih fu 7. monitor, officer

8. director, minister, official
9. president 10. magistrate
prefecture... 7. eparchy
prefer... 5. elect, offer 6. choose,
select 7. outrank, present, proffer,
promote 9. be partial 12. give
priority
preference... 6. choice 8. favorite,
priority 9. advantage 10. favoritism
11. alternative, prior choice
12. predilection
prefiguration... 4. omen 9. foretoken,
prototype 12. typification
13. preindication
prefigure... 7. imagine, suggest
8. foretell 10. foreshadow
prefix for...
about.. 3. amb 4. peri
above.. 3. epi, sur 5. hyper, super,
supra
across.. 3. dia 4. tran 5. trans
again.. 2. re
against.. 4. anti
ahead.. 3. pre
all.. 4. omni
alongside.. 3. par 4. para
an.. 2. al
apart.. 2. se 3. dia, dis
appearing to.. 5. quasi
around.. 4. peri
away.. 3. aph, apo
back.. 2. re 3. ana
backward.. 5. retro
bad.. 3. dys, mal
badly.. 3. mis
beauty.. 5. calli (kalli)
before.. 2. ob 3. pre, pro 4. ante,
prae
beside.. 3. par 4. para
between.. 3. dia 4. meta 5. inter
black.. 4. atra
blood.. 4. haem, hemo
bone.. 4. oste 5. osteo
both.. 4. ambi
Chinese.. 4. sino 5. chino
clear.. 4. delo
dawn.. 2. eo
difficult.. 3. dys
distant.. 3. tel 4. tele
double.. 2. di
down.. 2. de 4. cata
earnest.. 5. serio
earth.. 3. geo
eight.. 3. oct 4. octa, octo
equal.. 3. iso
equally.. 4. equi
evil.. 3. mal
far.. 3. tel 4. tele
faulty.. 3. mis
fictitious.. 6. pseudo
fire.. 3. pyr
for.. 3. pro
former.. 2. ex
four.. 5. tetra
from.. 2. ab, de, ec
from away.. 3. apo
gas.. 4. aero
good.. 2. eu
half.. 4. demi, hemi, semi
hard.. 3. dys 6. stereo
ill.. 3. mal, mis
in, into.. 2. en

lizard.. **5**. saura, sauro
many.. **4**. mult, poly **5**. multi
modern.. **3**. neo
mountain.. **3**. oro
nail.. **4**. helo
negative.. **2**. il, ir, un **3**. mon
new.. **3**. neo
not.. **2**. il, im, ir, un **3**. non
numerical.. **3**. uni
one.. **3**. uni **4**. mono
out of, outer.. **2**. ec, ex **3**. ect, exo
   4. ecto
over.. **3**. epi, sur **5**. super, supra
possession.. **3**. ose
pray.. **3**. ora
priority.. **3**. pre
recent.. **3**. neo
release.. **2**. un
reversed.. **2**. di
same, equal.. **3**. iso **4**. equi, homo
separation.. **2**. di **3**. dis
shoulder.. **6**. humero
single.. **4**. mono
son of.. **3**. Mac
ten.. **3**. dec **4**. deca
this side of.. **3**. cis
three, thrice.. **3**. ter, tri **4**. tris
through.. **3**. dia, per
to.. **2**. ap
together.. **3**. com, con, cor, syn
toward.. **2**. ob, oc
turning.. **4**. roto
twice.. **2**. bi, di
twofold.. **2**. bi, di **3**. dua
under.. **3**. sub
upon.. **2**. ep **3**. epi
upward.. **3**. ana, ano
very much.. **3**. eri
well.. **2**. eu
with.. **3**. col, com, pro, syl, syn
within.. **3**. eso **4**. endo **5**. intra
without.. **2**. se **3**. ect **4**. ecto
wood.. **4**. xylo
wrong.. **3**. mis
pregnancy... **6**. cyesis **10**. cyesiology
prehistoric (pert to)...
   animal.. **7**. reptile **8**. dinosaur,
      mastodon **9**. phytosaur
   continent.. **8**. Atlantis (Atalantis)
   man.. **4**. cave, Dawn **11**. lake dweller
   ref to.. **9**. primitive
   tool.. **6**. eolith
prejudiced... **6**. biased **7**. partial
   8. partisan **11**. opinionated
   12. prepossessed
prejudicial... **9**. injurious
   11. detrimental **15**. disadvantageous
prelate... **4**. head, pope **5**. abbot,
   chief **6**. bishop, priest **7**. primate,
   red—blue **8**. minister, superior
   9. Monsignor (Monsignore)
prelector, praelector... **6**. reader
   7. teacher **8**. lecturer **9**. professor
preliminary... **5**. prior **7**. preface,
   prelude **8**. entrance, previous,
   proemial **9**. precedent, prefatory,
   threshold **10**. antecedent
   11. preparatory **12**. introduction,
   introductory
preliminary memo... **8**. protocol
preliminary plan... **4**. idea
prelude... **5**. proem **6**. verset

   7. preface **8**. overture, ritornel
   (ritornelle)
premature... **6**. infant **8**. too early,
   untimely **10**. precocious
premier... **3**. bet (gambling) **5**. chief
   7. leading **8**. earliest **9**. principal
   13. prime minister
premiere... **4**. show **10**. first night
   12. presentation **16**. first
   performance
premium... **4**. agio **5**. bonus, prize,
   stake **6**. reward **8**. gratuity, interest
   10. recompense
premonition... **5**. hunch **6**. notice
   7. warning **8**. forecast
   10. foreboding **11**. forewarning,
   information **12**. presentiment
preoccupied... **4**. lost **6**. absent, filled
   8. absorbed, observed **9**. engrossed
   10. abstracted, pre—engaged **13**. lost
   in thought
preparation... **8**. training **9**. equipment,
   study hour **10**. groundwork
   11. making ready **12**. introduction
preparation (pert to)...
   of a dress.. **7**. fitting
   place.. **10**. laboratory, paratorium
   sugar, for candy.. **7**. fondant
   without.. **5**. ad lib **9**. impromptu
prepare... **3**. fit, fix, get **4**. cook, gird,
   make, pave, yark **5**. adapt, equip,
   ready, train **6**. adjust **7**. arrange
prepare (pert to)...
   by boiling.. **6**. decoct
   for golf game.. **3**. tee
   for melting glass.. **4**. frit
   for publication.. **4**. edit
   for seasoning.. **8**. marinate
   skins.. **3**. taw
prepared... **5**. armed, ready
   7. adapted, groomed, skilled, trained
   8. equipped, provided
prepared instruction...
   13. propaedeutics
preponderance... **6**. weight
   8. dominion, majority **9**. influence
   11. outweighing, superiority
prepose... **6**. prefix **7**. preface
   11. place before
preposition... **2**. at, by, ex, in, of, on,
   to, up **3**. off, out, tae **4**. into, onto,
   over, unto, upon, with
prepossession... **4**. bent, bias
   9. obsession, prejudice
   10. preference **11**. inclination
   12. predilection **13**. appropriation,
   preconception **14**. predisposition
presage... **4**. bode, omen, osse, sign
   5. token **6**. augury, betide, divine
   7. portend, predict **8**. forebode,
   foretell **10**. prediction, prognostic
   11. preindicate **13**. foreknowledge
presager... **7**. prophet **9**. foreboder
presbytery... **6**. church, clergy
   7. council **8**. ministry **9**. parsonage
   10. presbyters
prescribe... **3**. set **5**. allot, guide,
   limit, order **6**. advise, bestow, direct,
   ordain **7**. control, dictate
   9. designate
presence... **4**. mien, port **7**. bearing,
   posture, specter **8**. phantasm

9. existence, proximity
10. apparition, appearance,
attendance 11. personality
present... **3.** now **4.** boon, gift, give
5. grant, nonce, offer **6.** bestow,
bounty, donate **7.** largess (largesse)
8. donation, gratuity **9.** introduce
10. contribute **11.** benefaction
present (pert to)...
for acceptance.. **6.** tender
pupil to teacher.. **8.** minerval
time.. **3.** now **5.** nonce, today
7. current **8.** juncture
to customers.. **7.** freebie, premium
8. giveaway **9.** lagniappe (lagnappe)
to foreign ambassador.. **6.** xenium
presentation... **4.** gift, plan **5.** debut,
offer **7.** present **8.** bestowal,
donation, offering **10.** appearance,
exhibition **12.** introduction
presently... **4.** anon, soon **6.** at once
7. shortly **8.** nowadays **9.** forthwith
10. before long **11.** immediately
preservation... **6.** saving **9.** retention,
safeguard **10.** protection
11. maintenance, safekeeping
12. conservation, perpetuation
preservative... **4.** salt **5.** spice
7. alcohol, vinegar **10.** protective
14. sodium benzoate
preserve... **3.** can, jam, tin **4.** corn,
cure, keep, salt, save **5.** guard, jelly,
spare, store **6.** defend, pickle, retain,
secure, shield, uphold **7.** compote,
protect, sustain **8.** conserve, maintain
9. freeze–dry, safeguard
preserve (pert to)...
by drying.. **9.** desiccate
fruit.. **7.** compote **9.** marmalade
grape.. **5.** uvate (conserve)
in brine.. **4.** corn, cure, salt
in oil.. **8.** marinate
president... **4.** head **5.** ruler
8. governor **14.** chief executive
President (US)... **4.** Ford, Polk, Taft
5. Adams (John), Adams (John Q),
Grant, Hayes, Nixon, Tyler **6.** Arthur
(Chester), Carter, Hoover, Monroe,
Pierce, Reagan, Taylor, Truman,
Wilson **7.** Harding, Jackson, Johnson
(Andrew), Johnson (L B), Kennedy,
Lincoln, Madison **8.** Buchanan,
Coolidge, Fillmore, Garfield, Harrison
(Benj), Harrison (Wm Henry), McKinley,
Van Buren **9.** Cleveland, Jefferson,
Roosevelt (Theo), Roosevelt (F D)
10. Eisenhower, Washington
President (pert to)...
place.. **10.** Oval Office, White House
power.. **4.** veto
press... **3.** dun **4.** cram, iron, urge
5. crowd, force, wedge **6.** compel,
hasten, smooth, throng, thrust
7. impress, squeeze **8.** compress,
condense, insist on **9.** extractor,
importune **10.** compulsion, journalism,
newspapers **12.** conscription
press (pert to)...
ancient.. **6.** Aldine
bookbinder.. **7.** smasher
corrector.. **11.** proofreader

critic.. **6.** censor **8.** reviewer
ranks.. **5.** serry
pressed (pert to)...
amber.. **8.** amberoid
cheese.. **7.** cheddar
grapes, residue.. **4.** marc (mark)
into a mass.. **7.** kneaded
together.. **5.** dense **6.** mashed
7. compact, crowded, serried
pressing... **6.** urgent, urging
7. exigent **9.** insistent
10. compelling, extraction, motivating
11. importunity
pressure... **4.** urge **5.** force
6. compel, stress, weight **7.** squeeze,
urgency **8.** exigency, instancy
9. authority, influence
10. compulsion, constraint,
harassment **11.** compression
pressure (pert to)...
barometer.. **7.** mesobar
boiler, cooker.. **9.** autoclave
instrument (for liquids).. **9.** manometer
10. piezometer **11.** Bourdon tube
of necessity.. **7.** urgency
resisting.. **8.** renitent
unit.. **5.** barad
prestidigitation... **8.** juggling
11. legerdemain **13.** sleight of hand
prestige... **4.** bias, face, sway **5.** clout,
éclat **6.** renown, repute **7.** sorcery
8. illusion **9.** authority, deception,
influence **10.** importance
11. superiority
presto... **5.** magic **7.** command,
passing, quickly **8.** suddenly
9. instantly **10.** rapid tempo
11. immediately **13.** instantaneous
presumably... **7.** no doubt **8.** probably
10. ostensibly, supposedly
presume... **4.** dare, hope **5.** imply,
judge, think **6.** assure, impose
7. suppose, venture **10.** presuppose
11. preconceive **14.** take for granted
presumption... **4.** hope **6.** daring
7. opinion **8.** audacity **9.** arrogance,
impudence, insolence **10.** effrontery
11. implication, probability,
supposition
presumptive... **5.** brash **7.** assumed,
Icarian **8.** arrogant, inferred, probable
10. evidential
presumptuous... **5.** undue **7.** forward,
haughty **8.** arrogant, insolent
9. foolhardy **11.** venturesome
pretend... **3.** act, aim **4.** fake, sham
5. claim, feign, feint **6.** affect, allege,
assume, pose as **7.** presume, pretext,
profess **8.** disguise, simulate
11. impersonate, make believe
pretended... **4.** sham **7.** alleged
8. affected, intended, proposed,
so–called **10.** ostensible
pretended omission (Rhet)...
9. apophasis **11.** paraleipsis
(paralepsis)
pretender... **4.** idol, snob **5.** cowan,
quack **6.** seemer **7.** Aeolist (Eolist)
8. claimant, impostor **9.** charlatan
10. mountebank **11.** fourflusher
pretense, pretence... **3.** act **4.** flam,

ruse, sham, show 5. claim, cloak,
cover, feint, horse, study 6. excuse,
tinsel 7. pretext 8. artifice, stalking
10. appearance, masquerade,
subterfuge 11. affectation, fabrication,
ostentation
pretentious... 4. arty 5. showy
6. rococo 7. elegant, pompous
8. affected, boastful 9. high–flown
12. ostentatious 13. grandiloquent
pretentious words, use of...
9. bombastic 10. lexiphanic
pretermit... 4. omit 6. pass by
7. neglect, suspend 8. intermit, pass
over 9. interrupt
pretext... 4. flam, plea 5. cloak, cover,
trick 6. excuse 8. pretense (pretence)
9. deception, semblance
pretty... 3. toy 4. cute, fair, joli, very
5. bonny (bonnie) 6. clever, comely,
lovely, rather 7. dollish, finical,
foppish 8. handsome 9. ingenious,
tolerably 10. attractive, knickknack
11. good–looking, interesting
15. pulchritudinous
prevail... 3. win 5. exist 6. induce,
subdue 7. succeed, triumph
8. dominate, frequent 9. prevalent
11. predominate
prevailed... 3. got, won 5. urged
9. succeeded, triumphed
prevailing... 4. rife 5. chief, usual
6. common 7. current, general
8. abundant, dominant 9. prevalent
10. widespread 11. predominant
prevail upon... 4. urge 6. induce
8. persuade
prevalent... 4. rife 6. potent
7. current 8. dominant, powerful
9. extensive 10. prevailing,
successful, victorious, widespread
11. efficacious, influential
prevaricate... 3. lie 5. evade
7. deviate, quibble, shuffle
prevene... 7. prevent 9. forestall
10. anticipate
prevent... 4. warn 5. avert, debar,
deter, estop 7. ward off 8. preclude
9. forestall, frustrate 10. circumvent
preventative, preventive... 8. antidote
9. deterrant 12. prophylactic
previous... 4. past 5. prior 6. before,
former 7. earlier 8. untimely
9. foregoing, preceding, premature
11. unwarranted
previously... 4. erst 6. before
7. earlier 8. formerly 9. aforesaid
10. heretofore
prey... 3. rob 5. booty, spoil
6. quarry, victim 7. plunder
prey (to seize)... 9. raptorial
prey upon... 3. eat 4. feed 5. ravin
(raven) 7. plunder, torment
8. predacity
Priam (pert to)...
daughter.. 8. Polyxena 9. Cassandra
grandfather.. 4. Ilus
King of.. 4. Troy
servant.. 7. Agelaus
son.. 5. Paris 6. Hector 7. Troilus
wife.. 6. Hecuba
price... 3. sum 4. cost, fare, odds,

rate 5. offer, value, worth 6. charge
7. expense 10. estimation,
excellence, recompense
12. preciousness
priceless... 7. amusing 8. precious
10. high–priced, invaluable, not
salable
prick... 4. goad, pain, pang 5. sting,
wound 6. pierce 7. prickle, remorse
8. distress
pricked... 6. dotted, pinked 7. pointed
9. punctured
prickle... 4. burr, prod, seta 5. spike,
thorn 6. pierce, tingle 7. acantha
8. stinging
prickly... 6. tingly 7. pointed
8. echinate
prickly (pert to)...
flower.. 4. burr
pear.. 4. tuna 5. nopal 6. cactus
7. Opuntia
plant.. 3. ash 5. briar, elder 6. teasel
7. juniper, lettuce, thistle
12. Hercules'–club
pride... 6. vanity 7. conceit, egotism
9. arrogance, proudness
11. self–respect
priest... 3. Eli, fra 4. abbé, curé,
lama, père 5. clerk, druid, padre
6. cleric, father 7. prester
9. oratorian
priest (pert to)...
assistant.. 7. acolyte
Brit order (anc).. 5. Druid
cap.. 5. miter (mitre) 7. biretta
collar.. 5. amice, stole
fish.. 8. rockfish
mantle.. 4. cope
newly ordained.. 9. priesteen
priest–in–the–pulpit.. 10. cuckoopint
relating to.. 10. sacerdotal
tribe (Israel).. 4. Levi
vestment.. 3. alb 5. ephod
8. scapular
priestly caste... 4. Magi 7. wise men
prig... 3. beg, fog, pan 4. buck, snob
5. dandy, filch, plead, prink, prude,
steal, thief 6. haggle, pilfer, purist,
tinker 7. bargain, entreat, pitcher
8. pilferer
priggish, prim... 7. prudish
8. snobbish, thievish
prim... 4. fish, neat, smug 5. primp,
smelt 6. demure, formal 7. precise,
prudish 8. decorous
prima donna... 4. diva 6. singer
prima facie... 7. at sight 9. first view
10. apparently
primal... 5. basic, chief, first
7. primary 8. original 9. elemental,
primitive
primary... 5. basic, color, first
6. primal 7. initial 8. election,
primeval, pristine 9. elemental,
essential, firsthand, primitive, principal
10. elementary 11. fundamental
primary (pert to)...
armament.. 6. cannon
circles.. 7. equator, horizon
8. ecliptic, galactic
colors.. 3. red 4. blue 6. yellow
primate, bishop... 10. Archbishop

Primates (Order of)... 3. ape, man
  5. lemur 6. mammal, monkey
  8. marmoset 9. orangutan
  (orangoutang)
prime... 4. best, dawn 5. first, paint
  7. primary, the best 8. original,
  primeval 9. primitive
prime minister... 7. premier
primer... 5. paint 8. hornbook,
  textbook, type size 9. detonator
  10. battledore
primeval... 6. primal 7. primary
  8. original, pristine
primeval deity... 5. Titan
primitive... 5. basic, first 6. embryo,
  native, quaint 7. ancient, priscan
  8. pristine 10. aboriginal, antiquated
  11. fundamental
primitive (pert to)...
  area.. 5. Idaho 8. Colorado
  art objects.. 9. artifacts
  group.. 6. ethnos
  self.. 2. id 8. instinct
primness... 8. neatness, niceness
  9. stiffness 11. preciseness
primo... 5. chief, first 12. leading
  tenor
primordial... 7. primary 8. original
  9. elemental, primitive 10. prototypal
  11. rudimentary 12. first created
primrose (pert to)...
  called.. 10. an innocent 13. flower of
  youth
  color.. 6. yellow 10. snapdragon
  genus.. 7. Primula 11. Primulaceae
  green.. 5. color
  League.. 13. Conservatives (Eng)
  path.. 7. sensual
prince... 4. knez 5. prinz 7. dynasty,
  monarch 8. archduke 9. potentate,
  princekin, sovereign 10. princeling
prince (pert to)...
  Albert.. 9. frock coat
  allowance.. 8. appenage
  petty.. 6. satrap
princely... 5. noble, regal, royal
  6. kingly 10. munificent
  11. magnificent
princely Italian family... 4. Este
Prince of...
  Afghanistan.. 4. amir
  apostate angels.. 5. Eblis
  Apostles.. 6. St Paul 7. St Peter
  darkness.. 5. devil, Satan 7. Ahriman
  demons.. 5. devil 9. Beelzebub
  destruction.. 9. Tamerlane
  evil spirits.. 7. Sammael
  liars.. 5. Pinto
  Peace.. 7. Messiah 11. Jesus Christ
  Spanish poetry.. 4. Vega
  the Church.. 8. cardinal
  the ode.. 7. Ronsard
  the sonnet.. 6. Bellay 15. Joachim du
  Bellay
  this world (Bib).. 5. Satan
  Tunis.. 3. bey
princess (pert to)...
  literally.. 5. Sarah
  loved by Cupid.. 6. Psyche
  loved by Zeus.. 6. Europa
  Mohammed.. 5. begum
  mythical.. 5. Danae 8. Atalanta

royal.. 14. eldest daughter
Tyrian.. 4. Dido (Elissa)
principal... 3. top 4. arch, head, main
  5. chief, major, prime 6. Führer,
  leader, master, origin, source
  7. captain, leading, palmary, primary
  8. foremost 9. important, organ
  stop, preceptor 10. capital sum
  11. outstanding
principality... 6. Monaco
principal meal (Rom)... 4. cena
principle... 4. rule 5. axiom, canon,
  prana, tenet 6. dictum 7. precept,
  theorem 9. essential 10. foundation
principle (pert to)...
  active in tobacco.. 8. nicotine
  distance.. 11. perspective
  Hindu.. 5. Sakti
  life, theosophy.. 5. prana, tenet
  musical.. 8. tonality
  vital.. 4. soul 5. anima
principles... 5. creed 9. generalia
  10. essentials 12. generalities
princox, princock... 7. coxcomb
  9. pert youth
prink... 4. deck, wink 5. adorn, preen,
  primp 6. bedeck, glance 7. dress up
print... 5. stamp 7. edition, engrave,
  impress, picture, publish
  11. indentation
printed (pert to)...
  defamation.. 5. libel
  fabric.. 4. silk 6. calico 7. percale
  sheets.. 8. pamphlet
printer... 8. pressman 9. publisher
  11. typographer 12. lithographer
printer (pert to)...
  aid.. 5. devil 10. apprentice
  dauber.. 5. biron
  direction.. 4. stet
  hand ink roller.. 6. brayer
  ink pad.. 6. dabber
  manuscript.. 4. copy
  mark.. 4. dash, stet 5. caret, serif,
  tilde 8. asterisk
  measure.. 2. em, en 4. pica
  type, mixed.. 3. pie (pi)
printing (pert to)...
  blur.. 6. mackle, macule
  cylinder.. 6. rounce
  error.. 7. erratum
  form.. 3. die
  for the blind.. 7. braille
  mark.. 4. dele 6. diesis 8. ellipsis
  measure.. 2. em, en 5. agate
  metal block.. 4. quad
  press part.. 6. platen, rounce
  7. frisket
prion... 6. petrel 7. sea bird
prior... 3. ere 4. fore, past 6. before,
  former 8. previous, priorate
  9. preceding 10. antecedent
priority... 10. precedence 11. order of
  time
priory... 5. abbey 8. cloister
priscan... 9. primitive
Priscian... 7. grammar 10. grammarian
Priscilla (pert to)...
  Bib.. 16. Christian convert
  color.. 7. fog blue
  Hist.. 7. Puritan
  husband.. 9. John Alden

tale . . 24. Courtship of Myles Standish
prism (optical device) . . . 5. Porro
prismatic . . . 10. iridescent, variegated
prison . . . 3. jug 4. brig, gaol, jail, keep,
   quod 5. clink 6. carcer
   10. guardhouse 12. penitentiary
prison (pert to) . . .
   courtyard . . 4. quad
   English (old) . . 7. Newgate 9. Bridewell
   French . . 8. Bastille
   guarded . . 10. panopticon
   keeper . . 5. guard 6. gaoler, jailer,
   keeper, warden 7. turnkey
   Russian . . 5. gulag
   slang . . 3. jug 4. quod, rock 5. clink,
   limbo 6. cooler 7. slammer 8. big
   house, hoosegow
   spy . . 6. canary, mouton
Prisoner of . . .
   Chillon . . 16. Francois Bonivard
   Vatican . . 4. Pope
prisoner's release . . . 6. parole
pristine . . . 7. primary 8. original
   9. primitive
prittle–prattle . . . 7. chatter, prattle
   8. chitchat 9. chatterer, empty talk
privacy . . . 7. privity, retreat, secrecy
   8. solitude 9. seclusion
private . . . 5. privy 6. covert, secret
   7. one's own 8. esoteric, eyes–only,
   hush–hush, personal, secluded,
   separate, solitary 11. sequestered
   12. confidential
   15. uncommunicative
privateer . . . 4. Kidd (Capt) 5. caper
   6. pirate 7. corsair, soldier (not
   enlisted) 9. freelance
privately . . . 5. aside 6. secret 8. in
   secret 10. personally, unofficial
   12. unofficially
privation . . . 4. loss, want 6. misery
   7. poverty 8. hardship
   10. divestment 11. destitution
privilege . . . 3. soc, use 5. favor, right
   7. charter 8. easement 9. advantage
   10. concession 12. carte blanche
privileged . . . 6. exempt 8. licensed
prix . . . 5. prize
prize . . . 3. cup 5. award, booty, Detur
   (Harvard), medal, plate, price, purse,
   stake, value 6. assess, esteem, ribbon,
   trophy 7. premium, respect
   8. treasure
prize fight . . . 2. go, KO 3. TKO
   4. bout, spar 6. boxing 7. contest
   8. knockout, pugilism 10. fisticuffs
pro . . . 3. aye, for 6. before 8. behalf
   of 9. in front of 12. professional
probability . . . 4. odds 6. chance,
   shoo–in (sl) 7. vantage 9. liability
   10. conclusion, good chance,
   likelihood, likeliness 11. credibility
probe . . . 3. dig 4. prod, tent 5. sound
   6. feeler, pierce, search, stylet
   7. examine, explore, feel out, inquiry
   10. instrument, scrutinize
probity . . . 6. virtue 7. honesty
   9. integrity, rectitude 11. uprightness
problem . . . 3. nut 4. crux, knot
   6. enigma, riddle 7. theorem
   8. question 9. situation

pro bono publico . . . 16. for the public
   good
proboscis . . . 4. nose 5. snout, trunk
procaccia . . . 4. cart (carrier's)
   7. carrier
procacious . . . 4. pert 8. insolent,
   petulant
procacity . . . 8. pertness 9. insolence,
   petulance
Procavis . . . 4. cony 5. hyrax 6. rabbit
procedure . . . 4. step 5. order
   6. custom, method, policy, system
   7. process 8. behavior
   11. continuance
proceed . . . 2. go 4. fare, move, pass,
   wend 5. arise, issue 6. derive
   7. emanate 8. continue, progress
   9. originate
proceed (pert to) . . .
   hastily . . 5. speed
   leisurely . . 5. amble, mosey (mosy)
   on one's way . . 4. wend
   rapidly . . 4. zoom 6. gallop
proceeding . . . 4. step 5. actum
   6. course 7. conduct, measure,
   process 8. activity, behavior
   9. procedure 11. transaction
proceeding (pert to) . . .
   by threes . . 7. ternary
   from earth . . 8. telluric
   from the sun . . 5. polar
proceedings . . . 4. acta 5. trial
   6. doings 7. affairs, lawsuit, minutes
   8. activity
proceeds . . . 4. gain, goes 6. income
   7. marches, profits, returns
procerity . . . 6. height 8. tallness
process . . . 4. cook, writ 5. lapse (of
   time), order 6. course, notice
   7. advance, mandate, summons
   8. progress 9. emanation, operation,
   outgrowth, procedure, sterilize
process (pert to) . . .
   beak (small) . . 9. rostrulum
   electroplating, steeling . . 8. acierage
   fabric coloring . . 5. batik
   fish (winglike) . . 3. fin
   in organisms . . 6. moisis
   of development . . 7. nascent
   pointed . . 3. awn
   steel making . . 8. Bessemer
   11. cementation
   surveying . . 13. triangulation
   transferring pictures . . 5. decal
   12. decalcomania
procession . . . 4. file 5. train 6. parade
   7. cortege 8. sequence 9. formation
prochein, prochain . . . 4. next
   7. nearest
proclaim . . . 4. hype (sl), tout 5. blaze,
   voice 6. herald 7. declare, enounce,
   presage, publish 8. announce
   10. promulgate
proclamation . . . 4. fiat 5. bando,
   banns (bans), blaze, edict, ukase
   6. decree, notice 9. manifesto
   12. announcement, promulgation
proclivity . . . 4. bent 6. desire
   7. leaning 8. tendency
   10. propensity 11. disposition,
   inclination

procrastinate... 5. defer, delay, stall
7. soldier 8. postpone
procrastination... 5. delay, stall
7. laxness 10. hesitation
11. vacillation 12. dilatoriness
procrastinator... 7. delayer, trifler
8. deferrer
procreant... 8. fruitful 9. producing
10. generating 11. propagative
Procrustes (Gr legend)...
10. highwayman (Attica)
14. Procrustean bed
procurator... 5. agent 6. lawyer
7. proctor, steward
procure... 3. get 4. gain 5. bring,
fetch 6. effect, elicit, induce, obtain
7. acquire 8. contrive, purchase
prod... 3. egg, jab 4. goad, poke,
urge 6. thrust
prodigal... 4. cloy 6. lavish 7. spender
9. plentiful 10. squanderer
11. extravagant, intemperate,
spendthrift, squandering
prodigality... 5. waste 9. abundance
12. extravagance, intemperance
13. superabundant
prodigious... 4. huge 5. great
7. amazing, immense 8. enormous
9. marvelous, monstrous, wonderful
10. miraculous, portentous,
tremendous 11. astonishing
13. extraordinary
prodigy... 4. omen, sign 6. genius,
marvel, oddity, wonder 7. miracle
prodition... 7. treason 8. betrayal
produce... 2. do 4. bear, make, show,
wage 5. carry, cause, stage, yield
6. author, create, effect 7. exhibit,
product 8. engender, generate,
receipts 9. originate 10. accomplish
11. merchandise
produce (pert to)...
copy of.. 4. type
effect.. 3. act
ideas.. 6. ideate
noise.. 5. sound
produced... 8. extended 9. elongated,
prolonged
produced (pert to)...
by heat.. 7. igneous 8. volcanic
by kitchen gardens.. 7. olitory
8. potherbs
by wind.. 7. aeolian
regularly.. 6. staple
producer... 4. doer 6. farmer, parent
7. creator 10. theaterman
12. manufacturer
producing (pert to)...
cold.. 7. algific
fire.. 8. sparking
illusions.. 15. phantasmagorial
poison.. 6. septic
product... 3. sum 4. crop 5. fruit
6. result 7. hormone 8. artifact,
creation 9. commodity, outgrowth
production... 3. hit 4. book, work
5. fruit 7. produce 8. creation
9. execution, extension
14. accomplishment
productive... 4. rich 7. fertile, gainful
8. creative, fruitful 9. inventive
10. generative

proem... 7. preface, prelude
8. foreword, preamble
12. introduction
profane... 6. misuse, unholy, wicked
7. godless, impious, ungodly, worldly
8. temporal 9. desecrate
10. unhallowed 11. blasphemous,
unspiritual 12. unsanctified
profess... 4. avow 5. claim, feign
6. affirm, allege 7. declare
11. acknowledge
profession... 5. claim, faith, trade
6. avowal, career, metier 7. calling,
pretext 8. vocation 9. testimony
10. occupation 11. affirmation
14. acknowledgment
professional... 4. paid 5. hired
6. expert 7. skilled, trained
8. finished
professional, non... 3. lay 4. laic
7. amateur 9. unskilled
proffer... 3. bid 4. give 5. offer
6. tender
proficient... 3. apt 5. adept 6. expert,
versed 7. skilled 12. accomplished
profile... 4. draw, form 7. contour,
diagram, outline, picture 9. biography
14. representation
profit... 3. net 4. boot, gain, good,
mend 5. avail 6. return 7. benefit,
rake–off, results 8. interest
9. advantage 11. share of gain
12. remuneration
profitable... 6. paying, useful
7. helpful 8. repaying 9. expedient,
lucrative 10. beneficial
12. remunerative
profligate... 6. wicked 7. corrupt,
spender, vicious 8. depraved,
prodigal, wasteful 9. abandoned,
dissolute, reprobate 10. overthrown
11. extravagant
profound... 4. deep, wise 5. heavy
7. abysmal, intense, learned
8. abstruse, complete, deep–felt,
poignant 9. downright, recondite,
sagacious 11. far–reaching
12. encompassing, unfathomable
13. thoroughgoing
profundity... 5. depth 6. wisdom
8. deepness 12. abstruseness
profuse... 6. galore, lavish 7. diffuse,
liberal, palaver 8. abundant,
generous, numerous, prodigal,
wasteful 9. bountiful 10. munificent
11. extravagant, overflowing
profusion... 6. plenty 9. abundance
11. diffuseness, prodigality
12. extravagance, lavish supply
progenitor... 4. sire 6. parent
8. ancestor 9. precursor
10. forefather
progenitor of giants (Norse Myth)...
4. Ymir 8. rime–cold
progeny... 3. son 4. race 5. issue
6. family 7. outcome 8. children,
daughter, outbirth 9. offspring,
parentage, resultant 11. descendants
prognosis... 7. outlook 8. forecast
9. diagnosis 10. prediction
14. interpretation
prognosticate... 4. bode, omen

7. betoken, predict, presage
8. forebode, foreshow, foretell, prophecy 9. foretoken

program, programme... 4. bill (printed), card, plan 5. edict 6. notice, policy 7. outline 8. bulletin, platform, schedule, syllabus 9. broadcast, catalogue, programma 10. prospectus 12. proclamation, prolegomenon 13. advertisement

programma... 5. edict 6. decree, notice 7. preface 12. prolegomenon

progress... 4. fare, tour, wend 5. march 6. course, travel 7. advance, journey 10. expedition 11. progression

progress (pert to)...
chart.. 5. Gantt
clumsily.. 8. scramble
intelligently.. 6. egress 7. telesis (telesia)
laborious.. 4. plod, wade
outward.. 6. egress
weakly.. 6. feebly

progressive... 6. modern, onward 7. forward, gradual, liberal 9. advancing, improving 11. consecutive 12. enterprising

prohibit... 3. ban, bar, bid 5. debar, estop, taboo (tabu) 6. enjoin, forbid, hinder 7. prevent 9. interdict

prohibited... 7. illegal, illicit 8. unlawful

prohibition... 3. ban 7. embargo 8. estoppel 9. exclusion 10. prevention, temperance 11. forbiddance 12. interdicting

project... 3. jet, jut 4. abut, cast, idea, plan 5. shoot 6. beetle, design, device, scheme 7. pattern, problem 8. contrive, proposal, protrude 9. intention 10. conception 11. undertaking

projectile... 4. bomb 5. shell 6. bullet, rocket 7. missile, torpedo 8. parabola 9. cartridge

projection... 3. arm, ear, fin, jag, toe 4. barb, cape, lobe, ness, prop, snag 5. apsis, bulge, ledge, prong, redan, socle, tenon 6. lobule, tappet 8. headland

projet... 4. plan 6. design

prolific... 6. fecund 7. fertile, teeming 8. fruitful 9. inventive 10. generative 11. propagative 12. reproductive

prolix... 5. wordy 7. diffuse, verbose 8. tiresome 9. prolonged, rigmarole, wearisome 10. long-winded, pleonastic, protracted

prolocutor... 6. orator 7. speaker, teacher 8. chairman 9. spokesman 10. mouthpiece 11. Lord Speaker (Eng)

prolong... 4. spin 7. draw out 8. continue, lengthen, postpone, protract

prolonged... 7. chronic, delayed 8. extended 9. continued, postponed 10. lengthened, protracted

promenade... 4. mall, walk 6. airing, marina, pasear 7. alameda, gallery

Prometheus (pert to)...
famed as.. 5. Titan (a)
poem (Shelley).. 17. Prometheus Unbound
tale, tragedy.. 15. Prometheus Bound 16. Prometheus Loosed 24. Prometheus the Fire Bringer

prominence... 4. cusp 6. height 8. eminence, prestige, salience 9. greatness 10. famousness, importance 11. distinction, obviousness, prosiliency 12. distinctness, protuberance

prominent... 4. high, star 5. great 6. famous, marked 7. obvious, salient 8. distinct, manifest 9. important 10. celebrated, noticeable, prosilient, protruding 11. conspicuous, distinctive, outstanding 13. distinguished

promiscuous... 5. mixed 8. careless 9. haphazard, orderless 14. indiscriminate

promise... 3. vow 4. hope, oath 5. swear 6. engage, parole, pledge, plight, votive (by vow) 7. betroth, predict 8. affiance, contract, give hope 9. assurance, ray of hope 11. declaration

Promised Land... 6. heaven, utopia 8. Paradise 9. millenium, Shangri-La 11. Happy Valley 13. Celestial City

promontory... 3. tor 4. cape, naze (nase), ness, scaw 5. mount, point 8. headland 10. projection

promote... 4. help 5. exalt, nurse 6. extend, prefer 7. actuate, advance, dignify, elevate, finance, further, improve 8. increase 9. advertise, encourage, patronize

promoter... 5. agent 6. backer 7. planner 8. lobbyist 9. financier, publicist

promotion... 6. brevet 7. advance 10. preferment 11. advertising, furtherance, improvement

prompt... 3. cue 4. easy, hint, soon, tell, yare (anc) 5. alert, early, quick, ready 6. advise, remind 7. animate, suggest 8. punctual 11. expeditious

prompter... 3. aid 4. cuer 6. pit man, reader 7. inducer, reciter 8. reminder

promptly... 4. tite (anc) 6. at once 7. quickly 9. willingly

promulgate... 7. declare, publish 8. proclaim 9. make known

prone... 3. apt 4. bent, flat 5. apish 6. supine 7. willing 8. downward 9. prostrate, recumbent 13. ventricumbent

prone to sin... 8. peccable

prong... 3. nib, peg 4. fang, fork, tine 5. spike, tooth 6. branch

pronghorn... 6. cabree (cabrie) 9. prong buck, springbok

prong key... 7. spanner

pronoun... 2. he, it, me, my, us, we, ye 3. her, him, one, she, thy, who, you 4. that, thee, them, they, thou, what, your 5. these, those 6. itself, myself 7. herself, himself, oneself, ourself 8. one's self, yourself

9. ourselves 10. themselves

pronoun (possessive)... 2. my 3. her,
his, its, our 4. hers, mine, one's,
ours, your 5. their, yours 6. theirs

pronounce... 3. say 5. bless (holy),
speak, utter 6. affirm, assert
7. adjudge, declare, deliver
8. announce 9. enunciate
10. adjudicate, articulate, assibilate

pronouncement... 6. decree
8. judgment 9. manifesto
11. affirmation, declaration
12. announcement

pronto... 5. quick 7. quickly
8. promptly 11. immediately

pronunciation... 4. burr 8. orthoepy
9. utterance (clear) 11. enunciation

pronunciation mark... 5. tilde
7. cedilla 8. dieresis

proof... 4. test 5. trial 6. result
7. outcome 8. evidence 9. testimony
11. galley proof 12. confirmation,
verification 13. certification

proofreader's mark... 4. dele, stet
5. caret, space

prop... 3. beg, gib, nog 5. brace,
shore, sprag, staff, stell 6. shorer
7. fulcrum, support 9. stanchion

propagate... 5. breed 6. extend,
spread 7. diffuse, publish
8. disperse, engender, generate,
increase, multiply, transmit

propel... 3. row 4. pole, push, urge
5. drive, impel 7. project

propeller... 3. fan, gun, oar 4. vane
5. screw 6. driver 9. plane part

propensity... 4. bent 6. desire
7. leaning 8. aptitude, tendency
9. proneness 10. proclivity
11. disposition, inclination

proper... 3. fit 4. fine, just, meet,
prim, smug 5. exact, right 6. chaste,
decent, goodly, honest, kilter
7. correct 8. decorous, inherent,
orthodox, suitable 9. excellent,
expedient 11. appropriate,
grammatical, respectable
12. conventional

properly... 5. fitly 7. rightly, utterly
8. decently, strictly, suitably
9. correctly 11. expediently
14. conventionally

proper sense of worth... 5. pride

property... 3. res 4. bona, gear
5. asset, goods, trait 6. estate,
nature, realty, wealth 8. holdings
9. attribute, copyright, ownership
10. real estate 11. peculiarity,
possessions 14. characteristic

property (pert to)...
act to regain.. 8. replevin (repleven)
destruction of.. 8. sabotage
9. vandalism
landed property.. 9. cadastral
light without heat..
15. phosphorescence
movable.. 4. gear 8. chattels
no private ownership..
11. aspheterism
of matter.. 7. inertia
one's own.. 7. alodium
right.. 4. lien

stolen.. 4. loot, pelf 5. lucre, spoil
suit for recovery.. 6. trover
transferrer.. 7. alienor, grantor
wife to husband.. 3. dos
woman's (Hindu).. 9. stridhana
(stridhan)

prophecy... 6. oracle 9. utterance
10. prediction 11. foretelling

prophesy... 4. osse 5. augur
7. predict, presage 8. forecast,
foreshow, foretell 10. vaticinate
11. preindicate 13. prognosticate

prophet... 4. seer 6. medium, oracle
7. psychic 8. Mohammed, preacher,
presager 9. John Smith, predictor
10. soothsayer 11. Joseph Smith
(Mormon)

prophet (Bib)... 4. Amos 5. Cyrus,
Hosea 6. Elijah (Elias) 7. Malachi,
Obadiah

prophet, murder of... 8. vaticide

prophetess... 5. sibyl 7. seeress
9. Cassandra (of evil)

prophetic, prophetical... 5. vatic
6. mantic 7. fateful, vatical
8. oracular 9. vaticinal
10. divinatory, presageful
11. predicative

propinquity... 7. kinship 8. nearness
9. proximity 12. neighborhood,
relationship 13. consanguinity

propitiate... 5. atone 6. pacify
8. atone for 10. conciliate

propitiation... 9. atonement, expiation
12. pacification, satisfaction
14. reconciliation

propitious... 4. rosy 5. happy, lucky
6. benign, timely 7. helpful
9. favorable, opportune, promising
10. auspicious, benevolent,
prosperous 12. advantageous,
well–disposed

proponent... 8. advocate
10. propounder

proportion... 4. part, rate 5. quota,
ratio, share 6. adjust, extent
7. analogy, compare, euphony,
prorate 8. equalize, symmetry
9. apportion

proportional... 4. rate 8. relative
10. comparable, respective
11. dimensional

proportionate... 5. equal 8. adequate,
relative 9. analogous 10. respective
11. comparative 13. corresponding

proposal... 3. bid 4. plan 5. offer
6. feeler, motion 8. marriage
9. intention 10. nomination,
suggestion 11. proposition,
supposition

propose... 5. image, offer, state, toast
6. intend, submit 7. purpose
8. nominate, propound 9. postulate

proposed (pert to)...
for consideration.. 9. suggested
for debate.. 6. mooted
international language.. 2. Ro 3. Ido
9. Esperanto

proposition... 4. plan 5. axiom, lemma
6. porism, thesis 7. project
8. empirema, proposal 9. corollary
11. supposition, undertaking

proposition, proof of... 18. reductio
ad absurdum
propound... 6. submit 7. propose
8. set forth 9. postulate
proprietary... 5. owner, title
8. interest, medicine (secret)
9. ownership 10. proprietor
12. landed estate
propriety... 7. decency, decorum,
fitness 8. standard 9. ownership
10. convention, expedience,
properness 11. correctness, suitability
12. tastefulness 13. possessorship
propugnaculum... 7. bulwark, defense
8. fortress
prorogue... 5. defer 6. extend
7. adjourn, prolong 8. postpone,
protract
prosaic... 4. drab, dull, flat 5. plain,
prosy 6. prolix, stupid 7. humdrum,
insipid, tedious 8. ordinary, tiresome
10. unexciting 11. commonplace
12. matter–of–fact 13. unimaginative
proscribe... 3. ban 6. forbid, outlaw
7. condemn (to death) 8. prohibit,
restrain 9. interdict, ostracize
proscription... 5. exile 8. outlawry
11. prohibition 12. interdiction
prosecute... 3. sue 4. urge 5. chase
6. intend (law), pursue 7. carry on,
enforce, execute
prosecutor... 6. lawyer 7. accuser,
relator 8. attorney
proselyte... 3. ger (to Judaism)
7. convert
proseuche, proseucha... 7. oratory
9. synagogue 13. place of prayer
prosody... 13. versification
prospect... 4. view 5. buyer, scene,
vista 6. survey 7. explore, foresee,
outlook 8. customer 9. applicant,
candidate, foresight, intention
10. contestant 11. probability
12. anticipation
prosper... 4. fare 5. cheve, speed
6. thrive 7. succeed 8. flourish
prosperity... 3. hap, ups 4. boom,
weal 6. thrift 7. success, welfare
9. well–being 11. good fortune
Prospero (pert to)...
character.. 9. Ferdinand
daughter.. 7. Miranda
servant.. 5. Ariel
slave.. 7. Caliban
The Tempest.. 11. Duke of Milan
prosperous... 4. weal 5. lucky, palmy,
sonsy (sonsie) 7. wealthy 8. thriving
9. favorable, fortunate
10. auspicious, successful
11. flourishing
prostitute... 4. drab 5. venal 6. harlot
7. corrupt 8. infamous 12. street
walker
prostrate... 4. flat, raze 5. abase,
prone 6. fallen, grieve, supine
7. exhaust 8. helpless, supinate
9. flattened, recumbent
10. obsequious, submissive
prosy... 3. dry 4. dull 6. jejune
7. prosaic, tedious 11. commonplace
13. plain–speaking
protagonist... 4. hero, lead (theater)

5. actor 6. leader 8. advocate,
champion, defender 9. contender,
principal, spokesman 11. participant
Protagorus (Gr)... 7. Sophist, teacher
11. philosopher
protasis... 5. maxim 9. drama part
11. proposition 12. introduction
protect... 3. arm 4. save 5. guard
6. defend, insure, police, screen,
sheath, shield 7. cherish, shelter
8. enshield, preserve 9. safeguard
protected... 5. armed 6. shaded
7. aproned, guarded 8. shielded
12. invulnerable
protection... 3. bib, lee 4. coat, fort,
moat 5. aegis (egis), apron, armor,
guard, shade, shell, smock 6. glacis,
refuge, safety 7. defense, parapet,
shelter 8. havelock, passport, security
11. safekeeping 12. preservation
protector... 6. patron, regent
8. defender, guardian 10. safekeeper
protector of vineyards (Gr)...
7. Priapus
protégé... 4. ward 6. charge
9. dependent
Proteida... 7. Proteus 10. amphibians
11. salamanders
protein... 6. casein 7. albumin,
mucedin, peptone 8. globulin,
lecithin, nutrient 9. protamine
11. chlorophyll
protein (pert to)...
blood.. 6. fibrin 8. globulin
castor oil bean.. 5. ricin (poison)
egg.. 7. albumin
milk.. 6. casein
muscles.. 8. creatine
seeds.. 7. edestin 8. aleurone,
prolamin
Proteles... 8. aardwolf
protest... 4. aver, beef, deny 6. assert
7. declare 9. objection, stipulate
10. asseverate 11. expostulate
13. expostulation
protestation... 6. avowal (public)
7. protest 11. affirmation, obtestation
12. asseveration, supplication
Proteus (pert to)...
biology.. 3. olm 6. amoeba
8. bacteria 10. salamander
Gr Myth.. 6. sea god
Shakespeare.. 17. Gentleman of
Verona
protocol... 5. rules (official) 7. compact
8. schedule 9. agreement, etiquette
10. memorandum (diplomatic)
12. original copy
protograph... 9. holograph
12. illustration (of species)
protoplasm... 5. spore 7. nucleus
9. archetype, cytoplasm
10. primordium 11. basis of life
protoplasmic (pert to)...
body.. 8. ectosark 9. ectoplasm,
endoplasm
cell.. 6. amoeba (ameba)
cell contents.. 9. metaplasm
substance.. 3. gel
Protozoa... 6. amoeba (ameba),
Lobosa, phylum 11. unicellular
protract... 4. spin 5. defer, delay

6. extend 7. prolong, stretch
8. continue, elongate, lengthen,
postpone, protrude 9. expatiate
protrude... 3. jut 5. bulge 6. exsert
7. project 9. thrust out
protuberance... 3. jag, nub, wen
4. boss, bump, cere, hump, knob,
knot, lobe, lump, node, snag, wart
5. bulge, caput, inion, knurl, torus
8. eminence, swelling 9. extrusion
10. projection
proud... 4. vain 5. grand, lofty, noble
6. elated, lordly 7. haughty, pleased,
stately, valiant 8. arrogant, boastful,
imposing, splendid 9. conceited,
gratified 10. impressive
11. independent, magisterial,
magnificent 12. presumptuous,
supercilious
prove... 3. try 4. test 5. check, nurse
6. evince, try out, verify 7. confirm,
justify, probate 8. identify, manifest
9. ascertain, establish
11. corroborate, demonstrate
prove false... 6. refute
Provençal dialect... 9. langue d'oc
provender... 3. hay 4. food 5. grain
6. fodder 8. ensilage
proverb... 3. saw 5. adage, axiom
6. byword, enigma, saying
8. aphorism, link verb, paroemia
proverbial... 10. aphoristic
11. sententious 12. epigrammatic
provide... 4. give 5. cater, endow,
endue, equip, stock, treat, yield
6. afford, ration, supply 7. care for,
finance 9. make ready 10. contribute
provided... 2. if, so 5. boden
6. sobeit 8. afforded, equipped,
prepared, supplied 11. on condition
13. conditionally
Providence founder... 13. Roger
Williams (1636)
provident... 4. wise 6. frugal, saving
7. prudent, thrifty 9. judicious
10. economical 11. precautious,
preparatory
providential... 5. lucky 7. prudent
9. opportune, provident
10. miraculous 11. foresighted
province... 4. area, beat, nome
5. arena, range, shire, tract
6. colony, domain, empire, eparch,
region, sphere 7. circuit, diocese,
kingdom 8. district 9. territory
10. palatinate (royal) 12. jurisdiction
provincial... 4. rude 5. crude, local,
rural 6. narrow 7. insular, limited
8. suburban 10. restricted,
uncultured 11. countrified
12. narrow–minded
15. unsophisticated
provincialism (diction)... 6. patois
10. patavinity
provision... 4. fare, food 5. board,
stock, store 6. vivres 7. proviso
9. condition 11. preparation
provisional... 9. makeshift, temporary,
tentative 10. promissory, substitute
11. conditional, preparatory
12. experimental 14. circumstantial
provision seller (Mil)... 6. sutler

proviso... 5. salvo 6. clause
provocative... 9. desirable, provoking
10. appetizing, stirring up, suggestive
11. interesting
provoke... 3. ire, vex 4. bate, goad,
move, rile, spur, stir 5. anger,
annoy, start 6. arouse, incite, induce,
invite, invoke, nettle, offend, stir up,
summon 7. incense 8. irritate
9. challenge 10. antagonize,
exasperate
provoking... 8. annoying, exciting
10. suggestive 11. interesting
12. antagonizing
provoking laughter... 7. risible
prow... 3. bow 4. beak, duty, good,
proa, stem 5. brave, honor, prore
6. steven 7. courage, gallant, gun
deck
prowess... 5. valor 9. gallantry
proximal... 9. immediate (opp of distal)
proximate... 4. next 6. direct
7. closest, nearest 9. immediate
10. succeeding
proximity... 8. nearness, nighness,
relation, vicinity 9. adjacence,
closeness 11. propinquity
proxy... 5. agent, power 6. agency,
ballot, deputy 7. proctor 9. authority
10. procurator, substitute
prudence... 6. virtue, wisdom
7. caution, economy 8. sagacity
9. foresight 11. calculation,
forethought 13. judiciousness
14. circumspection
prudent... 4. wary, wise 5. canny
6. frugal 8. cautious, discreet
9. judicious, penny–wise, provident
10. economical 11. circumspect,
considerate
prudish... 4. prim 8. priggish
prune... 3. cut, lop 4. clip, food, frog,
plum, trim, weed 5. dress, plume,
preen, purge, shape 6. anoint 7. cut
down, tonsure 9. simpleton
prunelike fruit... 9. myrobalan
pruning knife... 8. serpette
prurient... 7. itching, longing, lustful
10. lascivious
Prussia...
bay.. 4. Kiel 6. Danzig
10. Pomeranian
cathedral city.. 5. Essen 7. Cologne
10. Düsseldorf
city.. 6. Aachen
color.. 4. blue 12. gold pheasant
Knight.. 8. Noachite
lagoon.. 4. haff 12. Frisches Haff
lancer.. 5. Uhlan
land aristocracy.. 6. Junker
legislature.. 7. Landtag
mountain.. 4. Harz
resort.. 3. Ems
river.. 3. Ems 4. Elbe, Oder, Saar
seaport.. 4. Kiel 5. Emden 7. Stettin
State.. 6. German
pry... 4. nose, peek 5. lever, mouse,
snoop 6. meddle, search
prying... 7. curious, peeking, peeping,
peering 8. snooping 9. searching
10. meddlesome 11. inquisitive
psalm (pert to)...

book.. 7. Psalter
Fiftieth, Vulgate.. 8. Miserere
Mass opening.. 7. introit
Ninety–fourth, Vulgate.. 6. Venite
Psalms (Old Test)... 7. Psalter
psalterium... 4. lyra 6. omasum
  7. stomach 9. manyplies
psammite... 4. rock 9. sandstone
psephology... 7. pebbles (study of)
psephomancy... 19. divination by
  pebbles
pseudatoll... 9. coral reef
pseudo... 4. sham 5. bogus, false
  6. untrue 7. feigned 8. spurious
  9. deceptive, imitation, pretender
pseudologist... 4. liar (humorous)
pseudology... 5. lying 9. falsehood
pseudonym... 5. alias 6. anonym
  7. pen name 10. nom de plume
pseudonym (famed)...
  C L Dodgson.. 12. Lewis Carroll
  Mary Ann Evans.. 11. George Eliot
  Samuel Clemens.. 9. Mark Twain
  W S Porter.. 6. O Henry
psychagogic... 9. inspiring
  10. attractive, persuasive
psyche... 4. mind, self, soul 6. spirit
psychic... 6. mental 9. spiritual
  10. Gnosticism 11. incorporeal
  12. spiritualist, supernatural
  13. psychological
psychic (pert to)...
  emanation.. 4. aura
  devotion.. 6. autism
  monism.. 10. one reality
psychotic... 3. mad 6. insane
  8. neurotic 12. psychopathic
Ptah (pert to)...
  Egypt Relig.. 8. chief god (of
  Memphis)
  father of.. 3. men 4. gods
  representation.. 5. mummy
  symbolic of.. 4. life 8. strength
ptarmigan... 4. rype 6. grouse
pterodactyl... 7. reptile (extinct)
  9. pterosaur 11. ornithosaur
pterography *(description of)*...
  8. feathers
pteroid... 8. fernlike, winglike
pteropod... 6. Clione (Arctic)
  7. mollusk
ptilosis... 7. plumage 9. madarosis
  10. loss of hair 15. loss of
  eyelashes
ptisan... 3. tea 5. drink 6. coddle
  9. decoction
Ptolemy (pert to)...
  author of.. 8. Almagest
  birthplace.. 5. Egypt (130 AD)
  famed as.. 10. astronomer,
  geographer
public... 3. inn 4. open 5. state
  6. people, vulgar 8. communal
  9. clientele, community
public (pert to)...
  assembly.. 4. Diet
  conveyance.. 3. bus, cab, car 4. taxi,
  tram 5. train 10. jinrikisha (jinricksha)
  display.. 10. exhibition
  13. exhibitionism
  edict.. 3. ban 12. proclamation

entertainment.. 7. ridotto
hangman (Eng).. 9. Jack Ketch
lands.. 4. ager (Hist) 6. domain
official.. 6. notary
position.. 8. official
storehouse.. 5. étape
walk.. 4. mall 7. alameda
  9. esplanade, promenade
publication... 4. book 8. pamphlet,
  printing 12. notification, proclamation,
  promulgation
publication (pert to)...
  article.. 7. feature
  condensed.. 7. tabloid
  make–up.. 6. format
  prelim.. 9. prodromus
publicist... 5. solon 6. Gallup, lawyer,
  writer 10. journalist, publicizer
  11. commentator
publish... 4. edit, vent 5. issue, print
  6. blazon, delate 7. divulge
  8. proclaim 10. promulgate
  11. disseminate
publish (pert to)...
  abroad.. 8. promulge
  after death.. 10. posthumous
  banns.. 7. betroth 8. marriage
  far and wide.. 6. blazon
  without authority.. 6. pirate
  10. plagiarize
publisher's description (book)...
  5. blurb 13. advertisement
publisher's inscription (book)...
  5. facts 8. colophon
Puccini heroine... 4. Mimi
pucker... 4. fold 5. bulge, purse
  6. crease 7. anxiety, fluster, wrinkle
  8. contract
puckered... 7. bullate 8. wrinkled
  10. contracted
puckish... 6. impish 8. Pucklike
  10. mysterious 11. mischievous
pud... 3. paw 4. hand 8. forefoot
pudding... 4. duff, mush, plum, sago
  6. junket 7. custard, dessert, tapioca
  8. roly–poly, softness, stuffing (game)
  9. Yorkshire
puddle... 3. mud 4. mess, pond, pool
  5. plash, swamp 6. muddle
  7. plashet, pollute
puddle duck... 7. mallard
puddock... 4. kite, toad 7. buzzard
  9. enclosure (paddock)
pueblo... 4. town 7. village
Pueblo (pert to)...
  ceremonial chamber.. 4. kiva
  Indian (American).. 4. Hopi, Piro,
  Tano, Zuni 5. Acoma 7. Keresan
  12. cliff dweller
  water jar.. 4. olla
puerile... 4. weak 5. young
  7. babyish, trivial 8. childish,
  juvenile, youthful 12. simple–minded
Puerto Rican (pert to)...
  bark, beverage.. 4. mabi
  dove.. 4. rola
  fish.. 4. sama, sisi 8. porkfish
Puerto Rico... see also *Puerto Rican*
  capital.. 7. San Juan
  city.. 5. Ponce 7. Arecibo
  discoverer.. 8. Columbus
  first settlement.. 7. Caparra

government.. 12. Commonwealth
Indian name.. 9. Borinquen
island (off shore).. 4. Mona
  7. Culebra
island group.. 15. Greater Antilles
politically.. 12. Commonwealth
program (Polit).. 18. Operation
  Bootstrap
sea.. 9. Caribbean
puff... 4. blow, blub, chug, flam, pant,
  pegh (Scot), pouf, waff 5. elate
  7. efflate
puffbird... 6. barbet 8. barbacou
pug... 3. dog, elf 4. moth, puck, snub
  5. chaff, dwarf 6. harlot, refuse
  (grain), sprite 8. bargeman, mistress,
  pugilist 9. footprint, hobgoblin
pugging... 8. grasping, thieving
pugilistic... 6. fistic 10. pugnacious
pugnacious... 9. combative
  11. belligerent, quarrelsome
pugnacious man... 12. fighting cock
pug–nosed... 5. camus (camuse)
puisne... 4. puny 5. judge, later, petty
  6. feeble, junior 9. associate,
  unskilled 10. law student, subsequent
  11. subordinate
puissance... 5. force, might, power
  8. strength 9. authority
puissant... 6. mighty, potent
  7. mastery 8. forcible, powerful
  13. authoritative
pulchritude... 5. grace 6. beauty
  10. comeliness, loveliness
pule... 4. peep 5. cheep, whine
  7. ululate, whimper
pulicat... 8. bandanna (bandana)
puling... 6. sickly 7. babyish, howling,
  whining 8. childish, delicate
Pulitzer prizes... 6. awards
  10. journalism, literature
pull... 2. pu 3. lug, tow, tug 4. drag,
  draw, haul, yank 5. bouse, drink,
  tweak 6. effort, strain 7. attract,
  extract 9. influence 10. attraction
pull (pert to)...
apart.. 4. rend, tear 7. destroy
  8. demolish, enfeeble, separate
back.. 5. demur 6. recoil 7. retract
  8. withdraw
down.. 4. fell, raze 9. dismantle
off.. 3. pug 6. avulse, commit
  8. carry out 10. accomplish
one's leg.. 4. hoax, joke 7. deceive,
  flatter 8. hoodwink 9. make fun of
out.. 5. leave 6. secede 7. extract
  9. eradicate
up.. 4. stop 5. elate 6. aviate
  7. arraign, extract
pullet... 4. fowl 5. child 7. bivalve
  8. poullard
pulley (pert to)...
groove.. 5. gorge
grooved.. 5. fusee (fuzee)
part.. 4. arse
wheel.. 6. sheave (grooved)
pulp... 3. pap 4. marc, mash, mass
  5. chyme 8. magazine 10. fleshy
  part
pulpit... 4. ambo, bema, dais, desk
  5. stage 6. clergy 7. rostrum
  8. platform, scaffold

pulpy... 5. mushy 7. squashy
pulpy (pert to)...
dregs.. 5. magma
fruit.. 3. uva 4. pome 6. sidder
  (siddow)
state.. 4. mash, soft 6. fleshy
pulsate... 4. beat, drum 5. throb
  7. vibrate
pulsation... 5. ictus 6. moving, rhythm
  7. impulse, systole 8. acrotism
  (failure), vitality 9. throbbing, vibrating
pulsatory... 8. rhythmic, systolic
  9. throbbing
pulse... 3. dal (split) 5. seeds (edible),
  throb 6. rhythm 7. beating
  8. resonate 9. pulsation, throbbing
pulse family... 3. pea 8. Fabaceae
pulverize... 4. bray, mull 5. crush,
  grind 6. abrade, powder 7. atomize
  8. levigate 9. triturate
  12. disintegrate
pulverulent... 5. dusty 7. crumbly
  8. powdered
puma... 6. cougar 7. Quechua
  (Kochua)
pummel... 4. beat, maul 5. thump
  6. batter, buffet, hammer, pommel,
  strike
pump... 3. gin, ram 4. draw, emit,
  quiz 5. eject 6. elicit, propel
  7. extract 10. pulsometer
  11. interrogate
pumpernickel... 5. bread (Westphalian)
pump handle... 5. sweep, swipe
pumpkin (pert to)...
head.. 4. dolt 7. Puritan
  9. blockhead, Roundhead
seed.. 7. sunfish 8. sailboat
yam.. 11. sweet potato
pun... 4. yoke 8. paragram
  9. assonance, equivoque (equivoke),
  witticism 11. paronomasia
punch... 3. die 4. blow, poke, prod,
  tool 5. douse, drink, negus, paste
  6. liquor, pierce 7. mattoir (etcher's)
  8. beverage, puncture 9. perforate
  11. punch cattle
Punch and Judy dog... 4. Toby
Punch Bowl... 6. crater 9. graveyard
  (Honolulu), hot spring (Yellowstone)
puncheon... 3. die 4. cask 5. punch,
  stamp 6. dagger
puncher... 6. cowboy 10. cowpuncher,
  perforator
punching... 8. piercing 9. pertusion
punctilious... 4. nice 5. exact
  6. formal, strict 7. correct, precise
  8. exacting 9. observant
  10. meticulous, scrupulous
punctuation mark... 3. dot 4. dash,
  star 5. brace, breve, colon, comma,
  tilde 6. dagger, hyphen, period, tittle,
  umlaut 8. brackets, ellipsis
  9. ampersand, semicolon
  10. apostrophe, circumflex
  11. exclamation 12. question mark
pundit... 6. nestor, savant 7. Brahmin,
  scholar, teacher 10. learned man
pung... 4. sled 6. sleigh
pungent... 4. keen, racy, sour, tart
  5. acrid, acute, sharp, smart, snell
  6. biting, bitter 7. caustic, odorous,

painful, peppery, piquant 8. piercing, poignant, stabbing 11. stimulating

pungent herb... 6. Asarum

punish... 4. fine 5. mulct, spank, wreak 6. amerce 7. chasten, correct 8. chastise, penalize 9. castigate 10. discipline

punishment (pert to)...
Brehon law.. 4. eric
by torture.. 9. strappado
church.. 15. excommunication
condign.. 11. retributive
law.. 5. peine
term.. 5. penal 7. penalty, revenge 8. punitive
Turk, Chin.. 9. bastinade
Welsh law (anc).. 3. cro 7. galanas

punitive... 5. penal 10. revengeful, vindictive 11. castigatory

Punjab, India...
capital.. 6. Lahore (West) 8. Amritsar (East)
language.. 7. Panjabi
name meaning.. 10. Five Rivers
soldier.. 4. Sikh
summer capital.. 5. Simla

punk... 3. bad 5. child 6. amadou 7. lighter 8. inferior 9. touchwood

punto... 3. hit 5. joint (fencing) 6. stitch (needle)

puny... 4. weak 5. frail, petty 6. little, meager, puisne, sickly 8. delicate 14. inconsiderable

pupa... 5. shell 9. chrysalis

pupil... 3. eye, son 4. tyro 5. élève, youth 7. écolier, learner, scholar 8. disciple, neophyte

puppet... 3. guy 4. doll 5. image 6. maumet 9. miniature, nonentity 10. figurehead, marionette

puppeteer, famed... 4. Sarg

puppy... 3. dog, fop 5. shark, whelp

purblind... 10. dim-sighted 11. partly blind 12. narrow-minded, undiscerning

purchasable... 5. venal 8. bribable, hireling 9. mercenary 11. corruptible

purchase... 3. buy, win 4. earn, hold 5. bribe 6. buying, obtain 7. acquire, bribery, procure 8. barratry, foothold, leverage

purchaser... 5. buyer 6. patron, vendee 8. customer 9. acquéreur 13. adjudicataire

purdah (Ind)... 4. veil 6. screen 7. curtain

pure... 4. neat, real 5. clean, fresh, godly, sheer, utter 6. candid, chaste, simple, vestal 7. genuine, perfect, refined, unmixed 8. absolute, filtered, innocent 9. downright, faultless, inviolate, stainless, undefiled, unsullied 11. pure-blooded, uncorrupted, unqualified 13. unadulterated

purga (Russ)... 8. blizzard 9. snowstorm

purgative... 5. jalap 6. physic 8. absterge 9. catharsis, cathartic, cleansing

purgatory... 4. hell 5. limbo 6. erebus 7. torment

purified... 10. elutriated

purified wool fat... 7. lanolin (lanoline)

purify... 5. clean, purge 6. filter, refine, spurge 7. cleanse, epurate 8. lustrate, renovate, sanctify 9. elutriate

purifying... 7. smectic 8. depurant 9. cathartic, cleansing 10. distilling

Purim... 7. holiday 8. festival (Jew) 11. Feast of Lots

puritan... 5. prude 7. ascetic 9. precisian 10. Separatist

puritan clergyman... 10. Cartwright

puritanical... 6. strict 7. ascetic 11. strait-laced 13. hyperorthodox

purity... 8. chastity 9. innocence

purl... 4. eddy 5. frill 6. murmur, ripple 7. trickle

purloin... 5. filch, steal, swipe 6. finger 11. appropriate

purple... 4. bice, lake, plum, puce 5. lilac, mauve, pansy, regal, showy 6. damson, orchid, ornate, Tyrian, violet 7. Cassius, magenta, mollusk, pigment 8. amaranth, Burgundy, imperial, mulberry 9. brilliant, cathedral 11. sovereignty

purple (pert to)...
bottle.. 4. moss
cactus.. 8. Missouri
death adder.. 10. black snake
emperor.. 9. butterfly
Forbidden City.. 5. Lhasa
granadilla.. 13. passion flower
haw.. 7. capulin (Mex) 8. bluewood
Heart, Order of.. 5. medal (Mil) (est by Washington, re-est.1932)
laurel.. 12. rhododendron
lily.. 8. Turk's cap
martin.. 7. swallow
navy.. 10. marine blue
nightshade.. 9. trompillo

purport... 4. feck, gist, mean 5. sense, tenor 6. allege, import, intent 7. meaning 9. substance

purpose... 3. aim, end 4. goal, idly, main, plan, sake 5. avail 6. design, intend, intent, motive 7. meaning, resolve 8. function 9. determine, discourse, intention, objective, predesign

purposive... 5. telic

purse... 3. bag, cly 5. pouch 6. pucker, wallet 7. wrinkle 8. crumenal (obs) 10. pocketbook 12. porte-monnaie

purser... 5. clerk (ship's) 6. bursar 7. boucher, cashier 9. paymaster

purse rat... 12. pocket gopher

pursue... 3. run 4. hunt, seek, tack 5. chase, court 6. follow 7. carry on, proceed 9. persecute 10. specialize

pursuit... 5. chase, quest, scent 9. objective 10. occupation

purvey... 5. cater 6. supply 7. foresee, provide

purveyor of untruth (Bib)... 7. Ananias

purview... 4. body (statute) 5. field (law), range, scope 7. compass 8. province

push... 2. go 4. bunt, butt, gang,

ping, pole, prod, urge 5. crowd, elbow, impel, nudge, press, shove 6. attack, energy, propel, thrust 9. importune, offensive (Mil) 10. forge ahead, propulsion 12. press forward

pusillanimous... 4. base, weak 5. timid 6. craven 8. cowardly 12. fainthearted, mean–spirited

put... 3. set 4. butt, dupe, fool, sail 5. place, throw 6. impose, option, phrase, repose, rustic 7. deposit 8. invest in 9. attribute

put (pert to)...
an end to.. 5. quash (law)
away.. 4. kill 5. store 6. murder
back.. 6. demote 7. replace, restore
before.. 6. appose
down.. 6. humble 7. degrade,
   deposit, depress 8. suppress
forth.. 5. exert 7. propose 9. circulate
off.. 4. doff, haft, sail 5. defer, delay,
   evade 8. postpone
on alert.. 5. alarm 6. alarum
out.. 3. vex 4. oust 5. eject
   9. ostracize 10. expatriate
over.. 4. bilk 5. cheat, trick
   7. deceive

put in, into...
action.. 6. excite
holy place.. 8. enshrine
motion.. 6. arouse
opposition.. 3. pit
order.. 4. trim 5. mense 6. settle
   7. arrange 8. organize
   11. systematize
rapture.. 8. entrance
relation to.. 9. correlate
   10. coordinate, co–ordinate
rhythm.. 5. meter
scabbard.. 7. sheathe

putrefaction... 3. rot 5. decay
   13. decomposition 14. disintegration

puttee... 6. gaiter 7. legging

put to...
flight.. 4. rout
strain.. 3. tax
trouble.. 10. discommode
use.. 5. apply
wrong use.. 8. misapply

put up... 3. pay 4. ante, hang
   5. build, offer 6. pledge 7. install
   8. nominate 9. construct

put up with... 4. bear 5. stand
   6. endure, permit 7. stomach
   8. tolerate

puzzle... 3. cap 4. crux, pose 5. griph
   (griphus), poser, rebus 6. enigma,
   riddle 7. anagram, confuse, mystify,
   nonplus, paradox, perplex, problem
   8. entangle 9. conundrum
   10. complicate, disconcert

puzzle (pert to)...
monkey.. 5. piñon
picture.. 5. rebus
word.. 7. charade 9. crossword
   10. anacrostic

puzzling... 6. knotty 10. perplexing
   11. enigmatical, paradoxical

pygarg, pygargus... 5. addax 8. sea
   eagle 9. quadruped (Bib)

Pygmalion (pert to)...

color.. 5. brown
endowed with life.. 7. Galatea (statue)
king of.. 6. Cyprus
sister.. 4. Dido
talented as.. 8. sculptor

pygmy, pigmy... 3. elf 4. Akka, Doko,
   pixy 5. atomy, Batwa, dwarf, gnome,
   minim, short 6. Abongo, Achuas
   7. manikin 9. dandiprat

pygmy (pert to)...
hog.. 7. Porcula
musk deer.. 10. chevrotain
owl.. 8. gnome owl
rattlesnake.. 10. massasauga
squirrel (smallest known).. 9. Sciuridae

pyic... 8. purulent, virulent

pyknic... 3. fat 5. round, stout

pylon... 4. post 5. tower 6. marker
   7. gateway 14. monumental mass

pyosis... 3. pus 4. boil
   11. suppuration

pyramid... 4. cone, heap, pile, tomb
   5. tower 8. monument 9. speculate

pyramid (pert to)...
builder, largest.. 6. Cheops (khufu)
Egypt.. 9. The Sphinx 12. Great
   Pyramid, Tomb of Cheops
group.. 5. Gizeh 7. Menkare
   8. Chephren 9. Mycerinus
kidney (Anat).. 7. Perrein
   10. Malpighian
Mexico.. 7. Benares
site of Cheops.. 4. Giza (Gizeh)
texts.. 12. inscriptions 13. Book of
   the Dead
world wonder.. 12. Great Pyramid,
   Tomb of Cheops

pyramidal... 4. huge 7. angular,
   conical 8. enormous, imposing

pyre... 4. bier, heap, pile
   9. cremation, death fire

Pyrenees (pert to)...
bandit.. 8. Miquelet
mountain chain.. 11. France–Spain
peak.. 9. Pic d'Aneto 11. Pic de
   Méthou
resort.. 3. Pau
State.. 7. Andorra (Fr)

pyriform... 10. pear–shaped

pyrology (study of)... 4. heat

pyromaniac... 7. firebug 8. arsonist
   10. incendiary

pyrope... 3. red 6. garnet 7. mineral

pyrophobia... 11. dread of fire

pyrotechnics... 7. oratory, science
   9. fireworks

pyrrhic... 4. foot (Pros) 5. dance

Pyrrhic victory... 11. at great cost

pyrrho (comb form)... 3. red 5. tawny

Pyrrho (Gr)... 7. teacher (Pyrrhonism)

pyrrhotist... 7. redhead

Pyrrhulexia... 5. finch 8. grosbeak

Pythagorus (Gr)...
birthplace.. 5. Samos
daughter.. 4. Camo
famed as.. 11. philosopher
friend.. 5. Damon
teacher of.. 8. theorems 18. influence
   of numbers

Pythian (pert to)...
contests.. 6. Delphi
Festival.. 11. Panhellenic

patron.. 6. Apollo
term.. 8. ecstatic 9. phrenetic
python... 3. boa 8. anaconda
Python (pert to)...
  home.. 11. Mt Parnassus
  myth.. 14. monster serpent
  slaver.. 6. Apollo
  survivor of.. 10. muddy earth (anc)
pythonic... 4. huge 6. Pythia (Delphi),

python 8. oracular 9. monstrous
pythonism, art of... 8. prophecy
  10. divination
pyx, pix... 3. box 4. test, veil
  5. chest 6. coffer, vessel (Eccl)
  8. binnacle, ciborium 10. tabernacle
pyxie... 5. shrub 9. evergreen
pyxis... 3. box 4. Argo (Astron), vase
  9. jewel case

Q

Q... 5. queue 6. letter (17th)
QED... 21. Quod Erat Demonstrandum
Q–ship (Eng)... 11. mystery ship
qua, quabird... 10. night heron
quachil... 12. pocket gopher
quack... 3. cry (duck) 5. faker
  7. empiric 8. impostor 9. charlatan,
  pretender 10. medicaster,
  mountebank
quack medicine... 6. patent
  7. nostrum
quad (pert to)...
  printing.. 5. crown 7. quadrat
  school.. 4. yard 6. campus
  10. quadrangle
  slang (Brit).. 5. horse
quadra... 6. fillet, listel, plinth
quadragenarian... 12. forty–year–old
  (person)
Quadragesima... 4. Fast, Lent
  6. Sunday (1st in Lent) 7. Holy Day
  9. Forty Days
quadrangle... 5. plane (four–angles)
  6. square 7. rhombus 8. tetragon
quadrant... 4. gill 6. fourth
  7. measure, quarter 8. farthing, six
  hours 10. instrument, semicircle
quadrate... 4. suit 5. adapt, agree,
  ideal 6. square 7. conform, perfect,
  squared 8. balanced 10. correspond
  13. correspondent
quadriga... 3. car 7. chariot (4–horse)
  10. four horses
quadrumane... 3. ape 6. mammal
  7. gorilla, Primate (except Man)
  10. chimpanzee 13. feetlike hands
quadruped... 3. ass, cat, cow, dog
  4. bull, calf, colt, foal, lion, mule
  5. burro, horse, jenny, panda, tiger
  6. badger, donkey, mammal
  7. bullock 10. four–footed
quaff... 5. draft, drink 6. tipple
quag... 5. quake 6. quiver 8. quagmire
quagga... 5. zebra 7. wild ass
quaggy... 5. boggy, fenny 6. spongy
  7. queachy 8. yielding
quagmire... 3. bay, fen 4. lair
  5. marsh, swamp 6. morass
  11. predicament
quahog... 4. clam
quail... 3. cow 4. bird 5. colin, cower,

quake, shake 6. blench, curdle,
flinch, shrink, tremor, Turnix
7. massena, tremble 8. bobwhite,
Coturnix 9. coagulate, courtesan,
eddish hen
quail (pert to)...
  button.. 6. Turnix
  call.. 4. pipe
  color.. 9. hair brown
  flock.. 4. bevy
  French.. 6. caille
  hawk.. 6. falcon
  quailhead.. 11. lark sparrow
  snipe.. 9. dowitcher
quaint... 3. odd 4. wise 5. proud
  6. expert, pretty, proper 7. curious,
  prudent, refined, strange, uncouth
  8. fanciful, peculiar
quake... 5. shake 6. quiver, shiver,
  tremor 7. shudder, tremble, vibrate
  10. earthquake
Quaker (pert to)...
  bird.. 9. albatross (sooty)
  city.. 12. Philadelphia
  colonizer.. 4. Penn (Wm)
  color.. 4. drab, gray 5. acier
  poet.. 6. Barton 8. Whittier
  sect.. 16. Society of Friends
  sect founder.. 9. George Fox
  State.. 12. Pennsylvania
qualified... 3. fit 4. able 6. fitted
  7. adapted, capable, enabled, limited
  8. eligible, entitled, equipped,
  modified, prepared, tempered
  9. competent 10. restrained,
  restricted 11. conditional
qualify... 3. fit 4. name 5. abate,
  adapt, be fit, equip, limit, train
  6. enable, modify, soften, temper
  7. assuage, prepare 8. diminish,
  mitigate, modulate, quantify, regulate,
  restrain, restrict
quality... 5. prime, trait, value
  6. nature, pathos, strain 7. caliber,
  texture 8. accident, capacity, inferior,
  nobility, property 9. attribute,
  character, specialty 10. difference,
  excellence 14. characteristic
quality of heredity... 9. lineality
qualm... 4. pall 5. demur, doubt,
  spasm 6. nausea, regret 7. scruple

9. faintness, misgiving
11. compunction **12.** apprehension
quandary... **3.** fix **5.** pickle, plight,
strait **7.** dilemma **10.** perplexity
11. predicament
quandy... **9.** squaw duck
quant... **11.** punting pole
quantity... **3.** ace, any, gob, lot, sea,
sum **4.** bulk, dose, drop, mass, much,
raff, raft, scad, size, some **5.** batch,
scads, store **6.** amount, cupful,
degree, extent, hatful, number, oceans
7. handful
quantity (pert to)...
fixed.. **5.** quota **8.** constant
mathematics.. **4.** surd **5.** graph
6. scalar, vector
minute.. **4.** atom, dram, iota, mill
standard.. **4.** unit **9.** allotment
time unit.. **4.** rate
quantum... **4.** body **5.** share
6. amount, energy, theory **7.** atomics,
portion **8.** quantity
quap... **5.** heave, throb **6.** quaver
9. palpitate
Quapaw... **5.** Sioux **8.** Arkansas
11. Indian tribe
quarantine... **7.** confine, isolate
8. pratique (marine) **9.** forty days
(law), isolation, segregate
11. confinement
quarantine flag... **6.** yellow
7. warning **10.** yellow jack
quarenden... **5.** apple (deep red)
quarentene... **4.** rood **7.** furlong
quark... **3.** caw **5.** croak, quawk
quarl, quarle... **4.** sour, tile **5.** brick
6. cundle, medusa **9.** jellyfish
quarred... **6.** soured **7.** curdled (beer)
quarrel... **3.** row **4.** spat, tiff, tile
5. arrow, brawl, broil, cavil, flite
(flyte), gnarr, scene, scrap **6.** affray,
bicker, chisel, dustup, hassle
7. diamond, wrangle **8.** argument,
squabble **9.** complaint
10. accusation, Donnybrook,
free-for-all **11.** altercation
12. disagreement
16. misunderstanding
quarrel (pert to)...
hereditary.. **4.** feud **8.** vendetta
noisy.. **6.** fracas, jangle, uproar
over.. **6.** bicker **7.** contend, dispute
petty.. **4.** miff, spat, tiff
quarrelsome... **8.** choleric, petulant
9. irascible, irritable, litigious
10. discordant, pugnacious
11. belliferent, contentious
13. argumentative
quarry... **4.** delf, game, heap, mine,
prey **6.** victim **8.** entrails, excavate
12. object hunted
quart... **5.** gills (eight) **6.** fourth
7. measure **8.** schooner
quarter... **4.** coin, side **5.** house
6. fourth, region **7.** measure, two bits
8. insignia, semester **9.** direction,
dismember **10.** quadrature (Astron),
quadrisect
quarter (pert to)...
acre.. **4.** rood
animal.. **5.** horse

astronomy.. **10.** quadrature
fathom.. **6.** fourth
military.. **8.** clemency (to enemy)
music.. **4.** note **8.** crotchet
nautical.. **4.** deck, lift **6.** galley
pint.. **4.** gill
sports.. **4.** back **11.** quarterback
quartered... **8.** billeted
12. quartersawed (wood)
quarters (living)... **4.** camp, room
5. abode **7.** housing, lodging, shelter
8. barracks, diggings, lodgings,
lodgment **9.** dormitory
Quartodeciman... **10.** paschalist
quartz... **4.** onyx, sard **5.** flint **6.** silica
7. mineral
quartz (pert to)...
banded, spotted.. **4.** onyx **5.** agate
6. jasper **8.** sardonyx
blue-red.. **10.** bloodstone, heliotrope
brown.. **5.** smoky **9.** cairngorm
brownish-red.. **7.** sinople
chalcedony.. **4.** sard **9.** carnelian
11. chrysoprase
flint.. **9.** hornstone **10.** touchstone
glass.. **6.** silica
green.. **5.** prase (dull) **6.** plasma
(bright) **11.** chrysoprase
hard.. **5.** flint
opaque.. **6.** jasper
purple.. **8.** amethyst
red.. **4.** sard **9.** carnelian
ruby-red.. **7.** rubasse
silica.. **5.** silex
transparent.. **11.** rock crystal
violet.. **8.** amethyst
yellow.. **5.** topaz (false) **7.** citrine
quash... **4.** cass, void **5.** abate, annul,
crush, quell, shake **6.** hush up,
subdue **7.** shatter **8.** suppress
9. overthrow **10.** extinguish
quasi... **4.** as if **6.** pseudo **8.** as it
were, as though **9.** seemingly
Quasimodo... **9.** Low Sunday (1st
after Easter)
quatern... **8.** fourfold **10.** quadrangle
12. four quarters (having)
quaver... **5.** shake, trill **6.** quiver
7. tremble, tremolo, vibrate
11. trepidation **13.** tremulousness
quawk... **3.** caw **5.** heron (night)
7. screech **8.** quagmire
quay, key... **4.** pier **5.** levee, wharf
7. landing
queachy... **5.** boggy, bushy, fenny
6. marshy, swampy
quean... **4.** girl, jade, slut **5.** vixen,
wench **6.** harlot
queasy... **4.** sick **8.** delicate, qualmish,
ticklish, troubled **9.** hazardous, ill at
ease, nauseated, squeamish, uncertain,
unsettled
Quebec...
battle site.. **15.** Plains of Abraham
capital.. **6.** Quebec (province)
city.. **6.** Verdun **8.** Montreal
11. Three Rivers
founder.. **9.** Champlain (1608)
river.. **10.** St Lawrence
vehicle.. **7.** calèche (2-wheeled)
quebrada... **3.** gap **5.** brook, gorge
7. fissure

qued, quede ... 3. bad 4. evil 8. The Devil

queen ... 3. ant, bee, cat 7. empress, goddess, monarch 8. chessman, honeybee 9. sovereign 10. chess piece 11. playing card

queen (pert to) ...
bee .. 8. honeybee
cactus .. 7. Mexican 10. ornamental
conch .. 5. shell
fern .. 5. royal
pigeon .. 7. crowned

Queen (pert to) ...
Bernice's Hair (Astron) .. 13. Coma Berenices
City of the Lakes .. 7. Buffalo
City of the West .. 10. Cincinnati
Mab .. 11. Fairie Queen (Rom/Juliet)
Victoria .. 14. Widow of Windsor (nickname by Kipling)

Queen Anne's ...
lace .. 6. carrot (wild)
melon .. 6. dudaim
War .. 17. Spanish Succession
War treaty .. 14. Peace of Utrecht

queen of ...
chess .. 4. fers
fairies .. 3. Mab 7. Titania 8. Gloriana
gods .. 4. Hera (Gr), Juno (Rom)
Hearts .. 9. Elizabeth
heaven .. 10. Virgin Mary
Isles (Brit) .. 6. Albion
night .. 4. moon
Sheba .. 6. Balkis (Koran)
Spades (solo) .. 5. basta
the Adriatic .. 6. Venice
the Antilles .. 4. Cuba
the East .. 7. Antioch (Syria), Batavia (Java), Zenobia
the tides .. 7. the moon
the underworld .. 3. Hel

queen's (pert to) ...
arm .. 6. musket
flower .. 9. bloodwood
hub .. 7. tobacco
July flower .. 8. damewort
ware .. 9. Wedgewood

Queensland (Austral) ...
animal .. 8. kangaroo 9. koala bear (teddy bear)
bean .. 8. snuffbox
capital .. 8. Brisbane
fire tree .. 5. tulip
fish .. 9. trumpeter
hemp .. 4. sida 6. lucern 9. jellyleaf 11. paddy lucern
plum .. 8. Burdekin
tree (timber) .. 3. box 4. pine 5. beech, ebony 10. sandalwood 12. Dundathu pine

queer ... 3. odd, rum 4. sham 5. false, funny 6. insane, thwart 7. strange 8. peculiar, singular, spurious 9. eccentric, fantastic, interfere 10. disconcert, suspicious 11. counterfeit 12. questionable

queer fellow ... 4. coot, goop 6. galoot, geezer 9. character

queersome ... 3. odd 7. strange 8. abnormal

Queer Street ... 9. imaginary

queest ... 8. ringdove

queet ... 4. coot 5. ankle

quell ... 3. end 4. calm 5. allay, crush, quash, quiet 6. pacify, reduce, soothe, stifle, subdue 7. destroy, repress 8. suppress 9. overpower 10. extinguish

quench ... 4. cool, damp, sate 5. allay, check, slake, still 6. stifle, subdue 7. assuage, gratify 8. suppress 10. discourage, extinguish 11. clamp down on

quenelle ... 8. meatball

Quercus ... 4. oaks

queriman ... 4. fish 6. mullet

quern ... 4. mill (grain)

quernal ... 5. crown (oak leaves)

querulous ... 7. fretful, peevish 9. plaintive 11. complaining 12. faultfinding

query ... 5. doubt 6. murmur 7. inquire, inquiry, whining 8. question

quest ... 3. bay (dog's) 4. hunt, seek 6. desire, pursue, search 7. inquest, request 8. seek alms 9. adventure 12. solicitation

question ... 3. ask 4. quiz 5. cavil, doubt, grill, poser, query, scout, topic 6. riddle 7. dispute, inquire, inquiry, problem 8. erotesis 9. catechize (catechise) 11. interrogate, uncertainty 12. interpellate (formally) 13. interrogation

question, out of the ... 6. absurd 7. refused 8. hopeless, rejected 10. impossible, prohibited 11. unthinkable

questionable ... 4. moot 7. dubious 8. doubtful 9. debatable, dishonest, uncertain 10. disputable, improbable 12. unbelievable 13. problematical

questioning (prolonged) ... 11. inquisition

question mark ... 7. erotema, eroteme

quet ... 3. auk 5. murre 9. guillemot

quethe ... 3. say 4. call, tell, will 5. quoth, speak 6. clamor 8. bequeath 9. testament

quetzal, quezal ... 6. trogon 14. national emblem (Guatemala)

Quetzalcoatl ... 10. god of winds (Aztec)

queue ... 3. cue 4. hair, line (waiting), tail 7. pigtail 9. lance rest

quey ... 6. heifer

quia–quia ... 9. cigarfish

quib, quibble ... 3. pun 4. carp, quip 5. argue, cavil, cheta, evade 7. shuffle

Quiche, Indian ... 5. Mayan

quick ... 3. apt 4. deft, fast, yare 5. agile, alert, brisk, fiery, fleet, hasty, rapid, ready, smart, swift 6. lively, nimble, presto, prompt, pronto, speedy, sudden 7. animate 9. dexterous, impatient, impulsive, sprightly, vital part 10. passionate 11. expeditious, hot–tempered

quicken ... 5. hurry, rouse, speed 6. excite, hasten, incite, revive, vivify 7. animate, further, refresh, sharpen

8. energize, expedite 9. stimulate
10. accelerate 11. resuscitate
12. reinvigorate
quickly... 4. cito, fast, soon 5. apace
6. presto, pronto 7. briefly, hastily,
rapidly 8. promptly, speedily, vigorous
quickness... 4. nous (humor) 5. haste
6. acumen 7. acidity, agility
8. alacrity, celerity, dispatch,
pungency, rapidity 9. acuteness,
briskness, fleetness, sharpness,
smartness 10. expedition, promptness
13. impulsiveness
quicksand... 3. bog 4. syrt 6. Syrtis
quickset... 5. hedge 7. thicket
8. hawthorn
quicksilver... 5. metal 7. mercury
quid... 3. cud, fid 6. guinea
7. essence, tobacco 9. sovereign
quidam... 8. somebody 10. one
unknown
quidnunc... 6. gossip 7. what now
11. inquisitive
quid pro quo... 9. tit for tat
10. equivalent, substitute
11. interchange
quiescent... 5. quiet, still 6. at rest,
latent, silent, static 8. sleeping
10. motionless
quiet... 2. sh 3. pet 4. calm, ease,
hush, lull, mild 5. peace, sober, still
6. gentle, hushed, modest, placid,
smooth, soothe 7. halcyon, restful,
silence 8. peaceful, tranquil
9. contented, peaceable, quiescent,
reposeful, unruffled 10. unmolested
11. undisturbed
quietist... 6. mystic (Quietism)
quietive... 8. sedative
quietly... 6. calmly, gently, simply
8. modestly, silently 9. patiently,
peaceably, privately 10. composedly
11. noiselessly 16. unostentatiously
quietude... 4. rest 5. peace 6. repose
7. silence 10. quiescence
12. tranquillity (tranquility)
quietus... 4. mort, obit 5. death
6. defeat 7. release 9. acquittal,
deathblow, discharge (of debt)
quiff... 4. coif, puff 5. whiff
quilkin... 4. frog, toad
quill... 3. cop, pen 5. remex
6. bobbin 7. spindle
quilt... 3. pad 4. flog, gulp 5. duvet
6. caddow 7. swallow 8. coverlet
9. patchwork 11. comfortable,
counterpane
quin... 7. scallop
quincentenary... 11. anniversary
13. commemoration 16. five hundred
years
quindecemvir (Rom)... 10. custodians
(Sibylline Books), fifteen men
quink... 5. brant, goose
quinoa... 6. cereal 7. pigweed
Quinquagesima Sunday... 10. before
Lent 12. Shrove Sunday
quinque (comb form)... 4. five
quinsy... 10. sore throat 11. tonsillitis
quint... 3. tax (one 5th) 7. E string
8. interval, schooner (5-masted)
9. organ stop

quintal... 13. hundredweight
quintessence... 3. col 5. elite 6. elixir
7. essence, the best 10. perfection
quip... 3. mot 4. gibe, jest 5. sally,
taunt 6. oddity 7. caprice, quibble
8. gimcrack 9. witticism
12. equivocation
quires, twenty... 4. ream 6. sheets
(20)
quirk... 4. quip, turn 5. clock, shift,
twist 7. caprice, evasion, quibble
8. flourish 9. deviation, mannerism,
witticism 12. eccentricity
quirt... 4. whip 5. romal
quis... 8. woodcock
quisby... 5. idler, queer 8. bankrupt
10. down and out
quit... 3. rid 4. free, stop 5. cease,
clear, leave, pay up, repay, yield
6. depart, resign 7. abandon,
discard, forsake, release, relieve,
requite 8. abdicate, liberate,
renounce 9. surrender 10. relinquish
11. discontinue
quitclaim... 6. acquit 7. release
12. convey a claim 13. deed of
release 14. relinquishment
quite... 3. all, yes 4. very 5. stark,
truly 6. really, wholly 7. totally
8. entirely, somewhat 10. absolutely,
completely, positively
quite so... 8. that is so, very true,
very well
quite some... 12. considerable
quittance... 5. repay 6. return
7. requite 8. reprisal, requital
9. atonement, departure, repayment
10. recompense 11. acquittance
quitter... 5. piker 6. coward, truant
7. shirker, welsher
quiver... 4. case 5. quake, shake
6. quaver, sheath, shiver, tremor
7. flicker, tremble, tremolo, vibrate
11. trepidation
quiver leaf... 5. aspen
Quivira (pert to)...
famous for.. 6. wealth
sought by.. 8. Coronado (1541)
town site.. 6. Kansas
Quivira, Gran... 12. mission ruins
16. National Monument (N Mex)
qui vive... 5. alert 7. excited
9. challenge 12. who goes there
quixotic... 7. utopian 9. visionary
10. Don Quixote (like)
11. impractical
quiz... 4. hoax, jest, joke, mock
5. coach 6. banter 8. ridicule
11. examination, inquisitive,
interrogate, questioning
quizzical... 3. odd 7. amusing, teasing
9. bantering, eccentric, inquiring,
perplexed
quizzing... 6. banter 11. questioning
quizzing glass... 7. monocle
8. eyeglass
quod... 3. jug 6. prison 8. imprison
quoddies... 7. herring
quod erat demonstrandum... 3. QED
24. which was to be demonstrated
quodlibet... 6. medley 8. fantasia,
subtlety 13. what you please

quoit... 4. disc 6. discus
quoit pin... 3. hob
quoits... 4. game 8. cromlech
    10. stone cover
quo modo... 5. means 6. manner,
    method
quondam... 6. former 8. formerly,
    sometime
quorum... 7. council 8. majority
    10. select body
quota... 4. part 5. share 6. ration
    10. proportion
quotable... 7. citable
quotation... 5. chria, cital, motto,
    price, stock 7. passage 8. citation

    10. memorandum, repetition
quotation mark... 9. guillemet
quote... 4. cite, name 5. price
    6. adduce, repeat 7. extract
    9. quotation, reference
quoth... 4. said 5. spoke
quotha... 6. indeed 8. forsooth
quotidian... 5. daily 8. day by day,
    every day, ordinary 9. recurring
    11. commonplace
quotient... 6. number, result
quotity... 5. group, quota 7. integer
    10. collection
quotum... 5. quota, ratio
quo vadis... 16. whither goest thou
Quo Vadis tyrant... 4. Nero

R

R... 3. rho (Gr) 6. letter (18th)
Ra, Egypt Relig (pert to)...
    atmosphere.. 3. Shu
    god of.. 3. sun
    morning sun.. 7. Chepera, Khepera
    night sun.. 7. Sokaris
    representation.. 3. cat 4. lion
        5. Bacis (bull) 6. falcon 9. solar disk
    rising sun.. 5. Horus 9. Marmachis
    setting sun.. 3. Tem
    solar disk.. 4. Aten
    son.. 6. Khonsu
    son of.. 3. Nut (the sky)
    wife.. 3. Mut
raad... 15. electric catfish
raad... 7. council (S Afr) 9. volksraad
raadzaal... 11. council hall (S Afr)
rab... 5. mixer (mortar) 6. beater
Rab... 5. title 6. master, rabban
    7. teacher 8. Gamaliel
rabato, rebato... 4. ruff 6. collar
    9. piccadill
rabbet... 4. weld 5. miter 6. groove,
    recess 7. channel 8. dovetail
rabbi... 4. lord 5. rabat, title
    6. master 7. teacher 9. clergyman
    11. breastpiece
rabbi (pert to)...
    examiners.. 8. sabaraim (saboraim)
    interpreters.. 7. amoraim
    teachers.. 7. tannaim
rabbit... 4. cony (coney), hare, tyro
    5. bunny, lapin 6. animal, novice,
    rodent 10. cottontail 11. Belgian
    hare
rabbit (pert to)...
    breeding ground.. 6. warren
        8. rabbitry
    ear.. 7. antenna 8. toadflax
    female.. 3. doe
    fever.. 9. tularemia
    fiction.. 6. Harvey
    fish.. 8. chimaera 9. globefish,
        porcupine

    foot.. 5. charm 8. talisman
    fur.. 4. cony (coney) 5. lapin
    genus.. 5. Lepus
    male.. 4. buck
    mouthed.. 10. harelipped
    rat.. 9. bandicoot
    S America.. 6. tapeti
    shelter.. 5. hutch
    stew.. 12. hasenpfeffer
    tail.. 3. fud 4. scut
rabbitry... 5. hutch 6. warren
rabble... 3. mob 4. herd, raff, rout,
    skim, stir 5. crowd 6. ragtag, tumult
    7. bobtail 8. canaille, riffraff
    9. confusion, rigmarole, the masses
    12. accumulation (chaotic)
rabble rouser... 6. ragtag
Rabelais (Fr)... 6. author 8. satirist
    9. Gargantua (1st work)
rabid... 3. mad 6. raging 7. frantic,
    furious, rampant, violent 8. frenzied
    9. fanatical 10. infuriated
rabies... 5. lyssa 11. hydrophobia
raccoon, ally of... 5. coati, panda
race... 3. cut, hie, run 4. flow, lane,
    line, rush, slit, sort, stem 5. breed,
    caste, flume, relay, speed 6. course,
    family, nation, people, strain
    7. contest, regatta, running, scratch
    10. passageway 11. competition,
    watercourse
race (pert to ethnos)...
    ancient.. 4. Mede 6. Belgae, Sabine
        7. Hittite, Iberian, Walloon
    comb form.. 4. geno
    family.. 3. ilk 6. stirpo
    human.. 3. Man
    mythical.. 7. centaur
    prehistoric.. 5. Aryan, Brunn
    rule by.. 10. ethnocracy
    science of.. 9. ethnology
    undivided.. 9. holethnos
    wandering.. 5. gypsy (gipsy)
race (pert to horses)...

R
S

chariot .. **13.** Circus Maximus
gait .. **4.** lope, pace, trot
horse .. **4.** pony **5.** racer **6.** maiden,
mantis, plater **8.** bangtail
handicap .. **6.** impost
open .. **10.** Donnybrook, free–for–all
racecourse, racetrack (pert to) ...
3. lap **4.** heat, oval, tout, turf
5. track **6.** circus (anc), colors
7. raceway, tipster **8.** dopester
Rachel (pert to) ...
daughter of .. **5.** Laban
mother of .. **6.** Joseph **8.** Benjamin
sister of .. **4.** Leah
wife of .. **5.** Jacob
racing colors ... **5.** silks
rack ... **3.** gin **4.** gait, gear, pain, ruin
5. agony, frame **6.** punish, strain,
wrench **7.** agonize, support, torment,
torture **9.** framework **10.** excruciate
rack (pert to) ...
barrel .. **3.** job
comb .. **9.** toothcomb
corn .. **4.** crib
floating .. **5.** vapor
plate .. **5.** creel
skin of .. **6.** rabbit
racket ... **3.** bat, din **5.** fraud, noise,
revel **6.** bustle, clamor, crosse, outcry,
scheme **8.** vocation **9.** commotion
15. illicit business
rackety ... **5.** noisy **8.** clattery, exciting
9. turbulent **10.** boisterous
racy ... **5.** brisk, fresh, naive, smart,
spicy **6.** lively, risqué **7.** piquant,
pungent, zestful **8.** eloquent,
spirited, stirring **11.** interesting
12. exhilarating, full–flavored
rad ... **4.** unit **5.** eager, quick, ready
6. afraid, elated **11.** exhilarated
radar (pert to) ...
beacon .. **4.** buoy **5.** racon **6.** ramark
navigation .. **5.** navar
range (Navig) .. **5.** loran **6.** shoran
sight .. **5.** scope **6.** radome, screen
7. display
signal .. **3.** pip **4.** beam, blip **5.** pulse
11. transceiver, transponder
sounding .. **5.** rawin **9.** ionosonde
television .. **7.** teleran
raddle ... **3.** rod **4.** beat, twig
5. cheat, color, fence, hedge
6. branch, hurdle, ruddle, thrash
7. wheedle **10.** interweave
radeau ... **4.** raft **5.** gloat
radial ... **3.** ray **8.** quadrant
9. diverging
radiance ... **5.** beamy, glare, light, nitor,
sheen **6.** beauty, luster **7.** beaming,
glitter, glowing, lambent, shining
8. splendor **9.** brilliant, radiation
10. brilliancy, effulgence
12. cheerfulness
radiant ... **5.** aglow, beamy, sheen
7. beaming, glowing, lambent, shining
8. glorious **9.** beautiful, diverging,
effulgent **11.** resplendent
radiate ... **4.** beam, emit, shed
5. gleam, shine **7.** diffuse, diverge,
emanate **9.** irradiate **10.** illuminate
radiation ... **5.** alpha (particle), light,

polar (point) **10.** divergence
12. illumination **13.** radiant energy
radiation unit ... **3.** rad, rem
8. roentgen
radical ... **3.** red **4.** atom, left, root,
surd **5.** basic, radix, ultra, vital
7. capital, drastic, extreme
8. cardinal, reformer **9.** extremist
10. foundation **11.** fundamental
radicated ... **6.** rooted **11.** established
radicle ... **4.** root **5.** radix **6.** etymon
7. rootlet
radio (pert to) ...
activity .. **7.** fallout **9.** radiation
antenna .. **6.** aerial
detector .. **5.** radar **11.** transceiver
frequency .. **5.** audio
interference .. **6.** static
operator .. **2.** CB **3.** ham (amateur)
11. dit–da–artist **12.** citizens' band
rays .. **5.** beams
receiver, interfering .. **7.** blooper
tube .. **4.** grid **5.** diode
radium (pert to) ...
discoverer .. **5.** Curie (1898)
emanation .. **5.** niton, radon
paint .. **8.** luminous
source of .. **7.** uranite **9.** carnotite
radius ... **4.** area, bone **5.** spoke
6. circle, extent **8.** diameter
radix ... **4.** root **6.** etymon, source
7. radical, radicle
raff ... **4.** heap, rake, scum **5.** sweep,
trash **6.** jumble, litter **7.** rubbish
8. leavings, riffraff
raffia ... **4.** palm **5.** fiber **6.** jupati
raffish ... **3.** low **6.** common, flashy,
frowsy **7.** unkempt **9.** worthless
12. disreputable
raffle ... **6.** chance, rabble, tangle
7. confuse, crumple, lottery, perplex,
serrate **8.** entangle, plucking, riffraff
9. stripping **10.** plundering
raft ... **3.** lot **4.** spar **5.** balsa, float
6. rafter **7.** to flock **10.** collection
(large)
raft–breasted (Ornith) ... **6.** ratite
raft duck ... **5.** scoup **7.** redhead
8. bluebill
rag ... **3.** fog **4.** mist, sail **5.** cloth,
scold, shred **6.** berate, catkin, lichen,
tatter **7.** ragtime, remnant **8.** farthing
9. hoarfrost **11.** syncopation
rag (pert to) ...
bag .. **10.** depository
doll .. **3.** toy **6.** moppet, puppet
10. marionette
fish .. **10.** Icosteidae
rag picker .. **5.** tramp
weed .. **3.** Iva
wool .. **5.** mungo **6.** shoddy
ragamuffin ... **8.** titmouse **9.** ragged
boy **14.** tatterdemalion
rage ... **3.** fad **4.** fume, fury, gret,
ramp, rant, tear **5.** anger, chafe,
craze, furor (furore), storm, wrath
6. fervor, frenzy **7.** bluster, passion
8. violence **9.** vehemence
10. excitement
ragged ... **5.** harsh, rough **6.** jagged,
raguly (Her), scoury, shabby, uneven

7. shreddy 9. defective, dissonant,
irregular 10. straggling
11. dilapidated
raging... 4. grim 5. rabid 7. acharne
8. storming 9. ferocious, turbulent
10. blustering, infuriated
11. overwrought
raglan... 8. overcoat 11. sleeve style
Ragnarok, Norse (pert to)...
leader.. 4. Loki
meaning.. 16. world destruction
repeopler of the world.. 3. Lif
10. Lifthrasir
ragout... 4. beef 5. civet, salmi
6. mutton 7. goulash, haricot
rahdar... 14. tollroad keeper
raid... 4. tata 5. foray, seize 6. inroad
8. invasion 9. incursion
rail... 3. bar, jaw 4. coot, jest, rant,
sora 5. cloak, crake, dress, scoff,
scold 6. banter, revile, septum (altar)
7. courlan, garment, inveigh, limpkin,
ortolan 8. reproach
railbird... 4. bird, weka 5. crake
7. clocker, wood hen 9. spectator
12. horse watcher
railing... 5. fence, rails 7. barrier,
parapet 10. balustrade
raillery... 5. chaff, sport 6. banter
7. asteism (Rhet) 8. badinage,
ridicule 10. persiflage
railroad (pert to)...
flare.. 5. fusee
signal.. 9. semaphore
sleeper.. 3. tie 7. pullman
switch.. 4. frog
torpedo.. 9. detonator
worker.. 6. dinger 8. strapper
11. gandy dancer
Rail Splitter... 14. Abraham Lincoln
raiment... 4. garb 5. amice, dress
7. apparel, clothes, vesture
8. clothing, garments
rain (pert to)...
cloud.. 6. nimbus
coat.. 4. mino 6. poncho 7. slicker
comb form.. 5. hyeto, ombro
6. pluvio
fine.. 4. mist 6. serein
fowl.. 6. cuckoo 10. woodpecker
11. channelbill
gauge.. 8. udometer 10. hyetometer
glass.. 9. barometer
icy.. 4. hail 5. sleet
protection.. 9. ombrifuge
short.. 6. shower
storm.. 5. spate 13. precipitation
study.. 9. hyetology, ombrology
sudden.. 5. plash, spate 6. deluge
7. torrent 8. downpour
rainbow... 3. arc 4. arch, iris, omen
rainbow (pert to)...
bridge (Norse Myth).. 7. Bifrost (to
Asgarth)
chaser.. 9. visionary 11. doctrinaire
flower.. 4. iris
goddess.. 4. Iris
term.. 6. iridal
tree.. 5. saman 8. genisaro
unit.. 4. inch
worm.. 8. nematode 9. earthworm
rainy... 3. wet 7. showery

rais, reis (Moslem)... 5. chief, title
7. captain (ship's)
Rais... 10. Mongoloids
raise... 3. end 4. grow, levy, lift, rear,
stir 5. boost, breed, erect, exalt,
heave, hoist, rouse 6. awaken,
excite, gather, leaven, muster,
remove, uplift 7. collect, elevate,
enhance, lighten, present, produce,
provoke, recruit 8. heighten, increase
9. construct, cultivate, promotion,
propagate 10. aggrandize
raise (pert to)...
a nap.. 5. tease 6. teasel
Cain.. 3. Ned 4. hell 5. cut up 7. be
noisy 10. vociferate
the dead.. 13. lift the anchor
vegetables.. 12. olericulture
raised... 4. bred, hove 6. buoyed,
enlève, hefted, lifted, reared
7. hoisted 8. elevated, leavened,
produced, promoted
raised (pert to)...
spirits.. 6. elated
to 3rd power.. 5. cubed
troops.. 6. levied 7. drafted
11. conscripted
type.. 7. braille
uproar.. 6. rioted
with a bar.. 7. levered
raisin... 4. pasa 5. grape, lexia
raja, rajah... 4. king, rana 5. title
6. prince 9. dignitary
raja's consort... 4. rani (ranee)
8. princess
Rajmahal hemp... 5. fiber 9. jiti fiber
Rajput... 5. caste 9. Kshatriya
rake... 3. rut 4. comb, path, raff, roué
5. slope, teeth, track 6. lecher
7. debauch, seducer 8. enfilade,
Lothario 9. cultivate, implement,
libertine
rakehell... 4. free, rake 9. debauched,
debauchee, dissolute 10. dissipated,
licentious, profligate
rakh... 3. hay 8. hayfield 9. grassland
raki, rakee... 7. spirits (distilled)
rale... 6. rattle 8. rhonchus
11. morbid sound
rallentando... 9. direction (Mus)
10. ritardando, slackening
Rallidae... 5. birds, coots, rails, wekas
6. crakes 10. gallinules
rally... 6. banter 7. recover, reunite
8. assemble, recovery, ridicule
10. assemblage, call to arms
rallying cry... 4. call 6. slogan
9. battle cry, bugle call
ralph... 5. raven
ram... 3. hit, pun, tup 4. buck, butt,
tamp 5. Aries, crash, sheep
6. rancid, wether 7. collide
Rama... 11. Ramachandra (7th of
fame) 19. incarnation of Vishnu
ramada... 5. arbor 7. pergola
Ramadan (Moham)... 7. fasting
10. ninth month (for fasting)
ramage... 4. wild 5. rough 6. branch
(tree), unruly 7. untamed 8. frenzied
ramage hawk... 8. brancher
ramass... 6. gather 7. collect
ramberge... 6. galley (swift)

ramble... 3. gad 4. roam, rove, walk
5. jaunt, prowl, range 6. stroll,
wander 7. deviate, digress, saunter
8. straggle
rambling... 7. devious 9. desultory,
deviation, deviative, wandering
10. circuitous, discursive, distracted
14. discursiveness
rambunctious... 4. wild 6. unruly
10. rampageous 12. obstreperous
14. uncontrollable
ramentum... 5. palea (palet) 6. scales
8. a shaving, particle (minute)
Rameses Dynasties (pert to)...
famed for.. 5. ruins 7. papyrus
kings.. 6. twelve
site.. 5. Egypt
ramex... 6. hernia 10. varicocele
ram–headed goat... 5. Ammon
ramie... 4. hemp, rhea 5. plant (fiber)
7. garment 9. Boehmeria 10. China
grass
ramification... 3. arm 5. ramus
6. branch 8. offshoot 9. branching
10. divergence 12. embranchment
rammack... 4. gawk, romp 5. scamp
rammel... 4. hard 6. coarse 7. new
milk, raw milk 9. brushwood
11. undergrowth
Ramona (pert to)...
heroine.. 9. half–breed (Ind)
novel by.. 7. Jackson (Helen Hunt)
shrub.. 4. mint
ramp... 3. rob 4. rage, romp, walk
5. bound, climb, crawl, creep, storm
6. dupery, unruly 7. incline,
rampage, swindle 8. gradient,
platform 9. helicline, impetuous
10. cuckoopint
rampant... 6. fierce, unruly, vallum
(anc) 7. ramping 8. abundant, reared
up (Her) 9. exuberant, prevalent,
unchecked 10. rampageous
12. high–spirited, unrestrained
13. perpendicular
rampart... 4. wall 5. agger, mound,
redan 6. escarp 7. barrier, bulwark,
defense, parapet, ravelin 8. buttress
9. earthwork 10. embankment
13. fortification
ram's horn (Heb)... 7. shophar (shofar)
ran... 4. fled, sped 6. flowed
7. coursed, managed, trotted
8. operated
ran (pert to)...
aground.. 8. decamped, levanted,
stranded
away.. 4. fled 6. eloped
9. absconded
out.. 5. spilt 7. petered, spilled
rana (Ind)... 5. title 6. prince
Rana.. 5. frogs 10. amphibians
(tailless)
ranarium... 8. frog pond
rance... 4. prop 6. marble 7. support
ranch... 4. casa, farm 6. estate
8. estancia, hacienda
ranchero... 6. cowman 7. vaquero
8. herdsman 9. cattleman
rancid... 4. rank 5. musty, stale
6. reechy 9. obnoxious, offensive

10. unpleasant
rancor, rancour... 3. ire 4. gall
5. spite 6. enmity, hatred, malice,
rankle 7. ill will 9. animosity
10. resentment
rand... 4. edge, rant 5. ridge, storm
6. border, margin
random... 5. stray 6. casual, chance
7. aimless 8. casually 9. at liberty,
haphazard, orderless 10. accidental,
fortuitous 11. haphazardly
randy... 4. wild 5. revel, spree
6. beggar, coarse, frolic, virago
7. canvass 8. carousal 9. festivity
10. disorderly 11. ill–mannered
12. unmanageable
rang (pert to)... see also *ring*
loudly.. 7. clanged
mournfully.. 6. tolled 7. knelled
slowly.. 6. tolled
range... 3. row 4. ally, area, line,
rank, roam, size 5. align, gamut,
orbit, scope 6. limits, ramble, region,
series, wander 7. arrange, compass,
earshot, habitat, pasture 8. classify,
mountain 9. cookstove
range (pert to)...
finder.. 9. mekometer, telemeter
10. trekometer
man.. 5. rider 6. warden
of hills.. 5. ridge
of knowledge.. 3. ken
of stables.. 4. mews
rangle... 5. stray 6. wander
8. entangle, straggle
rani, ranee (Hind)... 4. wife 5. queen
7. empress 8. princess
rani (Romany)... 4. lady, wife
Ranier, Mt... 10. Washington (State)
ranine... 5. frogs 7. Raninae 8. mink
frog
rank... 3. bad, row 4. file, foul, line,
rate, size, tier 5. caste, class, grade,
gross, order, range 6. degree,
estate, rancid, status, wicked
7. arrange, glaring, tainted
8. absolute, abundant, classify,
eminence, flagrant, indecent,
infamous, nobility, palpable, position,
prestige, unsavory 9. downright,
formation, luxuriant, plentiful
10. malodorous 11. distinction
rank (pert to)...
and file.. 4. army 8. regulars
10. commonalty 11. third estate
celestial.. 9. hierarchy
exalted.. 8. eminence
military (old).. 8. banneret
noble.. 10. patriciate
rider.. 8. reckless 10. highwayman
social.. 5. caste
rankle... 5. chafe 6. fester 7. putrefy
8. make sore 9. suppurate 10. be
inflamed
rann... 5. verse 6. stanza, strain
ransack... 4. rake, sack 5. rifle
6. search 7. plunder, rummage
ransom... 4. fine 6. redeem, rescue
7. expiate 8. recovery
ranstead... 8. toadflax (yellow)
13. butter–and–eggs
rant... 4. rage, rail, rave 5. boast

6. steven 7. bluster, bombast, declaim 9. gay frolic 10. get excited
rantipole ... 4. wild 6. rakish, unruly 9. termagant
ranula ... 4. cyst
Ranunculaceae ... 7. anemone 8. aconitum, clematis, crowfoot 10. delphinium, ranunculus
rap ... 3. bop, hit 4. bang, blow, gibe, grab, knap, tirl 5. knock, steal 6. rascal, snatch, trifle 8. betrayal, sentence (prison) 9. criticism, reprimand 10. punishment 11. skein of yarn
rapacious ... 6. greedy, rapine 8. grasping, ravenous 9. devouring, voracious 10. avaricious, predacious
rapacity ... 5. greed, ravin (raven) 6. rapine 8. appetite 9. predacity
rapid ... 4. fast 5. fleet, quick, swift 7. stretto (stretta)
rapidity ... 5. haste, speed 8. celerity, velocity 9. fleetness, quickness
rapidly ... 5. amain, apace 7. quickly, swiftly 8. snappily
rapids ... 5. rifts 6. dalles
rapier ... 5. bilbo, sword 6. verdun 7. ricasso (part)
rapine ... 7. pillage, plunder 8. spoiling 10. ravishment, spoliation
rapport ... 6. accord 7. empathy, harmony 8. relation 9. agreement 11. co-operation (hypnotism)
rapt ... 8. absorbed, ecstatic 10. enraptured, interested 11. preoccupied, transported
rapture ... 3. joy 4. love 5. bliss 6. trance 7. delight, ecstasy 8. rhapsody 9. transport 10. exultation
rapturous ... 8. ecstatic
rare ... 3. odd, raw 4. thin 6. scarce, seldom, sparse 7. notable, unusual 8. rarefied, uncommon 10. infrequent 11. undercooked
rare (pert to) ...
 bird .. 8. rara avis
 earth .. 6. cerium 7. terbium, yttrium
 metallic element .. 7. yttrium
 object .. 5. curio 6. oddity 7. antique
Rare Ben, inscription ... 15. tomb of Ben Jonson (Westminster Abbey)
rarebit ... 10. cheese dish 11. Welsh rabbit
rarefy ... 4. thin 6. dilute, expand 9. attenuate
rarely ... 6. finely, seldom 8. not often, scarcely 9. extremely, unusually 11. beautifully 12. infrequently
rarity ... 6. oddity 7. fewness, tenuity 8. scarcity, thinness 11. infrequency
ras ... 4. cape 6. prince 11. short-napped 13. Fascist leader
rasa ... 3. sap (tree) 5. fluid, taste 6. amrita, flavor 7. essence 11. living water
rascal ... 3. cad, imp 5. knave, rogue, scamp 6. varlet 9. miscreant
rascally ... 4. mean 6. impish 7. knavish, roguish 8. scampish 11. mischievous
rase ... 3. cut, rub 4. tear 5. graze,

level 6. scrape 7. scratch
rash ... 3. mad 4. wild 5. giddy, hasty, heady, hives, scamp 6. unwary, wanton 7. Icarian 8. careless, eruption, heedless 9. desperate, exanthema, impetuous 10. headstrong, incautious, indiscreet 11. temerarious, thoughtless
rasher ... 5. piece, slice 7. portion 9. thin slice
rashness ... 6. acrisy 7. acrisia 8. temerity 9. hastiness
rasion ... 6. filing 7. erasing, rasping, shaving 8. scraping
Rasores ... 4. fowl 5. birds 6. quails 7. turkeys 8. Columbae, Gallinae 9. pheasants 10. partridges
rasp ... 3. rub 4. file 5. belch, chafe, erupt, grate 6. abrade, offend, scrape 8. irritate 9. raspberry
raspberry ... 3. red 5. apple, Rubus 6. raspis 7. plumbog 8. blackcap
rasping ... 5. harsh 7. chafing, grating, raucous 8. grinding, scraping, very fast 9. offensive 10. irritating
raspings ... 6. refuse 7. filings, remains
rasse ... 5. civet
rasure ... 3. cut 5. shave 7. erasure, polling, scratch, tonsure 8. scraping 12. obliteration
rat ... 3. rut 4. scab, snob, wart 5. track 6. desert, ratton, rodent 7. scratch, traitor 8. deserter 9. hairpiece, scoundrel
rat (pert to) ...
 fish .. 8. chimaera
 goose .. 11. common brant
 hare .. 4. pika
 kangaroo .. 7. Potorus 9. marsupial
 pineapple .. 7. pinguin
 poison .. 8. ratsbane
 ratlike .. 4. vole
 rhyme .. 6. jargon 13. doggerel verse
ratafia ... 7. biscuit (almond), curacao, liqueur (Danzig)
ratchet ... 4. pawl 5. click 6. bobbin, detent
rate ... 4. fare, pace 5. price, ratio, style, tempo, value 6. assess, berate, charge, reckon, regard 7. account, deserve, premium, reprove 8. appraise, classify, estimate, evaluate, interest
rate (of exchange) ... 4. agio 5. batta
rath (anc) ... 4. hill, home (walled)
rath, ratha ... 3. car 6. temple (Seven Pagodas, Madras) 7. chariot
Rathaus ... 8. town hall
rathe, rath ... 4. soon 5. eager, quick, speed 7. betimes, quickly 8. speedily
rather ... 3. ere, yes 6. before 7. earlier, however, instead 8. somewhat 9. more truly, tolerably 10. especially, preferably 11. immediately 14. on the other hand
ratification ... 4. amen 5. logic 8. sanction 9. reasoning 11. endorsement 12. confirmation
ratify ... 4. amen, pass, seal 6. enseal, verify 7. approve, confirm, consent, endorse 8. roborate, sanction

9. authorize

ratio... 2. pi 4. rate, sine 5. share
6. cosine, ration 7. portion
10. proportion

ratiocination... 5. logic 7. thought
9. reasoning

ration... 5. share 6. budget 8. relation
9. allotment, allowance, provision
11. calculation

rational... 4. sane, wise 5. sober
7. logical 8. sensible 9. reasoning
10. reasonable 11. philosophic

rationale... 6. reason 11. explanation
12. the how and why

ratio scripta... 13. written reason

ratite... (opp of carinate) 7. Ratitae
8. unkeeled 14. flat breastbone

ratite bird... 3. emu (emeu), moa
7. ostrich 9. cassowary

ratoon... 5. shoot, stalk 6. spring,
sprout

rattan, ratan... 4. cane, palm, sega,
whip 6. switch 7. calamus

ratteen... 8. mahogany

rattle... 3. toy 4. herb, rale, rick, tirl
5. annoy, clack 6. assail, prison
(Nav), racket, uproar 7. agitate,
chatter, clapper, clatter, confuse,
fluster, maracas, prattle 8. nonsense
9. chatterer, rapid talk
10. disconcert, noisemaker

rattle (pert to)...
bones.. 8. clappers, snappers
9. castanets
headed.. 8. confused
11. empty–headed 13. rattlebrained
mouse.. 3. bat
nut.. 10. chinquapin
pate.. 3. ass
root.. 7. bugbane

rattlesnake... 7. rattler 8. belltail,
Crotalus, pit viper 9. Sistrurus

rattlesnake (pert to)...
bean.. 6. cedron
bite.. 9. meadow rue
fern.. 9. chain fern, sporangia
flag (Maine).. 13. Don't Tread on Me
(Hist)
herb.. 9. baneberry
leaf.. 8. plantain
pilot.. 10. copperhead
plantain.. 6. orchid
variety.. 3. red 6. banded, timber
7. prairie 11. diamondback
venom.. 8. crotalus

rattletrap... 6. gewgaw 7. rickety
8. claptrap, the mouth
10. knickknack, ramshackle

ratton... 3. rat

ratwa... 7. muntjac

raucous... 3. dry 4. bray, loud
5. harsh, noisy 6. hoarse, raucid,
rauque 8. strident 11. cacophonous

rauk, roke... 4. poke, stir 5. vapor
7. scratch

raun... 3. roe 4. fish 5. spawn

ravage... 4. loot, ruin, sack 5. havoc,
spoil, waste 6. damage, infest
7. debauch, destroy, overrun, pillage,
plunder 9. devastate 10. desolation
11. despoilment, devastation,
infestation

ravages of time... 13. deterioration
14. disintegration

rave... 4. rage, rant 5. crush, storm
7. bluster, declaim, enthuse 8. be
insane, harangue

ravel... 4. fray 6. runner, slough,
unwind, 7. involve, unravel, untwist,
unweave 8. entangle, separate
11. disentangle, loose thread

ravelin... 7. railing 8. demilune,
half–moon 13. fortification

raven... 4. bird, crow 6. Corvus
8. standard (vikings) 10. raven–black
11. Corvus corax

Raven (The)... 4. poem (Edgar Allen
Poe)

ravening... 3. mad 5. rabid 6. greedy,
prying 8. desirous 9. rapacious,
turbulent

ravenous... 6. greedy 8. edacious
9. rapacious, voracious
10. gluttonous 11. catawampous

ravine... 3. gap 4. dell, linn (lin), wadi
(wady) 5. chine, gorge, gulch, slade,
strid 6. arroyo, clough, gulley, nullah
8. barranca

ravish... 3. rob 4. rape 5. seize
7. corrupt, debauch, delight, despoil,
plunder, violate 8. deflower, entrance
9. enrapture, transport

raw... 4. cold, sore 5. bleak, crude,
naked 6. chilly, unripe, vulgar
7. natural, not spun, untried
8. immature, indecent, uncooked
9. inclement, unskilled, wind–swept
10. unprepared 11. undeveloped,
unprocessed 13. inexperienced

rawboned... 4. lank 5. gaunt
7. angular 8. skeletal

rawbones... 5. Death 8. skeleton

raw–flesh–eating... 9. omophagia

rawhide... 4. skin (untanned), whip

rawhide whip... 5. knout, quirt, thong
7. sjambok

raw sugar... 9. cassonade

rax... 5. reach 6. become, strain
7. stretch

ray... 4. beam, dorn, soil, X–ray
5. array, dress, gamma, order, skate
(fish) 6. defile, radius, stripe, vision
7. besmear, raiment 8. particle,
radiance, stingray 11. arrangement,
irradiation

raya... 9. broadbill

rayless... 4. dark 5. blind

rayon... 3. ray 5. fiber 6. radius
14. postal district (Switz)

raze, rase... 3. cut 4. fell, ruin
5. erase, graze, level, shave
6. efface, scrape 7. destroy
8. demolish 9. dismantle, prostrate
10. obliterate

razee... 3. cut (Naut) 5. prune
7. abridge

razor (pert to)...
back.. 3. hog 4. boar 5. ridge
10. roustabout (circus)
bill.. 3. auk 7. skimmer
billed auk.. 4. falk 5. murre, noddy
clam.. 5. Solen 11. chopa blanca
grinder.. 10. goatsucker
sharpen.. 4. hone 5. strop

stone.. 9. whetstone 10. novaculite
strap.. 5. strop
type.. 6. safety 7. rattler
razz... 5. chaff, tease 6. banter, deride
  8. ridicule 9. raspberry
razzle–dazzle... 5. cinch (game), spree
  6. dazzle 7. confuse 8. bewilder
  9. commotion 10. noisemaker
re... 4. back (pref) 5. about, again,
  anent, tone D (Mus) 8. syllable
  (Mus) 10. concerning
Re... 2. Ra (Egypt) see also *Ra*
reach... 4. come, gain, hawk, ryke,
  spar, spit 5. equal, retch 6. advene,
  arrive, attain, extend, length
  7. achieve, compass, earshot,
  expanse, possess, stretch
  8. distance, overtake 9. influence
  10. understand
reach (pert to)...
across.. 4. span
for applause.. 9. captation
high point.. 9. culminate
out.. 6. extend 7. stretch
under.. 7. subtend
up.. 6. aspire
reaction... 4. kick 6. change (Chem)
  7. tropism 8. response 9. influence
  10. opposition
reactionary... 4. Tory 10. malcontent
  12. conservative, recalcitrant
read... 3. con 4. pore, scan, skim, tell
  5. guess, solve 6. advise, browse,
  peruse, recite, relate 7. counsel,
  declare, discern, foresee, prelect
  (praelect), stomach 8. decipher,
  describe, foretell 9. interpret
  10. understand
readable... 7. legible 12. decipherable
reader... 6. lector, lister, primer
  (McGuffey) 7. browser, license,
  reciter, speaker, teacher 8. anagnost
  (anagnostes), literate, textbook
  9. churchman, prelector (praelector)
  10. pocketbook 11. proofreader
  12. elocutionist
readily... 6. at once, easily 7. quickly
  8. probably 9. willingly 10. very
  likely
readjust... 7. readapt, restore
  9. rearrange 11. reconstruct
  12. rehabilitate
ready... 3. apt, fit, fix 4. bain, free,
  here, ripe, yare 5. alert, apert,
  eager, handy, point, quick 6. facile,
  fitted, prompt 7. willing 8. cheerful,
  disposed, inclined, prepared, skillful
  9. dexterous 12. unhesitating
ready acceptance... 11. embracement
ready for... 6. awaits 8. liable to
  10. in store for 11. prepared for
ready–to–wear... 12. haute couture
real... 4. true, very 5. pucka (pukka)
  6. actual 7. factual, genuine, sincere
  8. absolute, existent, handmade,
  tangible 9. authentic, veritable
  10. unaffected 11. substantial
real (pert to)...
being.. 6. entity
estate.. 5. lands 6. domain, houses,
  realty 7. demesne 8. easement,

freehold, property 9. tenements
  13. hereditaments
map.. 4. plot
name (backwards).. 6. ananym
school.. 10. Realschule
realistic... 5. vivid 8. lifelike
  9. practical 11. descriptive
reality... 5. truth 7. realism
  11. genuineness
reality, non–existent... 8. nihilism
realize... 3. get, win 4. gain, know
  5. sense 7. convert 8. conceive
  10. accomplish
realm... 6. domain, empire, region,
  sphere 7. country, demesne, kingdom
  8. division, province 10. department
  12. jurisdiction
realm (of)...
darkness (Myth).. 2. po
Jamshid.. 6. Persia
perfection.. 6. Utopia
ream... 4. bore, foam, scum 5. widen
  6. bundle 7. enlarge 8. bevel out
  11. countersink 14. enormous
  amount
reanimate... 5. rally 6. revive
  7. refresh 11. resuscitate
  12. reinvigorate
rear... 3. aft 4. back, grow, lift, loom,
  rise, rump 5. breed, build, erect,
  raise, stern, train 6. behind, foster
  7. arriere, educate, elevate, produce
  8. instruct 9. construct, establish,
  posterior 10. background
rear (pert to)...
admiral.. 7. two bars (silver)
commodore, yacht club.. 7. officer
end.. 6. breech 7. hind end
  9. afterpart, posterior
horse (insect).. 6. mantis
most.. 4. last
toward.. 3. aft 5. abaft 6. astern
  8. backward, rearward
rearing up (horse)... 5. stend
  6. pesade
rearrange... 4. sort 8. readjust
  10. reordinate, reorganize
reason... 5. argue, cause, logic, sense,
  think 6. deduce, ground, motive,
  sanity 7. discuss 8. argument,
  conclude, judgment, question,
  solution 9. discourse, intellect
  11. explanation, ratiocinate, rationalize
  13. justification, understanding
reason (pert to)...
discursively.. 11. ratiocinate
doctrine of, author.. 10. Anaxagoras
higher.. 4. mind, nous 5. logic
Latin.. 5. causa
ostensible.. 7. pretext
pert to.. 6. noetic
proof of.. 8. argument
want of.. 7. amentia
why.. 5. cause 6. motive
reasonable... 4. fair, just, sane
  6. proper 7. logical 8. rational
  9. equitable, plausible, practical
  10. fair–minded 11. inexpensive,
  intelligent, justifiable
reasoning (pert to)...
basis of.. 7. premise
delusive.. 7. fallacy

exact.. 5. logic
harmonize.. 11. rationalize
plausible.. 8. specious
reassure... 6. assure, solace
  7. comfort, console, hearten
  8. embolden, give hope
reata... 4. rope 5. lasso, riata 6. lariat
reave... 3. rob 4. rend, tear 5. break,
  burst, seize, split 7. plunder
reb... 5. rebel
rebate... 5. check 6. reduce, weaken
  8. diminish, discount 9. abatement,
  deduction, remission
rebato (Hist)... 4. ruff 6. collar, rabato
  9. piccadill
Rebekah (pert to)...
  husband.. 5. Isaac
  sister.. 5. Laban
  son.. 4. Esau 5. Jacob
rebel... 3. reb 4. rise 6. resist, revolt
  8. renounce, turncoat 9. insurgent
  13. revolutionist
rebellion... 5. Great (Eng 1642–49)
  6. mutiny, revolt 8. American (Civil
  War 1861–65) 10. resistance,
  revolution 12. insurrection,
  renunciation
rebellious... 8. mutinous 9. insurgent
  10. refractory 12. contumacious
  13. insubordinate, revolutionary
rebirth... 7. revival 9. salvation
  10. conversion 11. renaissance
  13. reincarnation
rebound... 4. stot 5. carom
  6. bounce, recoil, re–echo, spring
  7. resound 8. rebounce, ricochet
  11. reverberate
rebuff... 4. slap, snub 5. chide, scold
  6. defeat, lesson, recoil, refuse,
  reject, resist 7. censure, refusal
  (brusque), reprove, repulse
  9. reprimand
rebuke... 3. nip 4. slap 5. check,
  chide 6. rebuff 7. repress, reproof,
  reprove 8. admonish, reproach,
  restrain 9. criticize, reprehend,
  reprimand 11. comeuppance
recalcitrant... 5. rebel 8. renitent
  9. obstinate, recoiling, resistant
  10. rebellious, refractory
  11. disobedient 12. ungovernable
recall... 5. annul 6. encore, recant,
  remind, repeal, revoke, summon
  7. retract 8. remember, withdraw
  9. recollect, reminisce
  11. recantation 12. recollection
recant... 6. abjure, revoke 7. disavow,
  retract 8. renounce, withdraw
  9. repudiate 10. contradict
recapitulate... 5. essay, sum up
  6. repeat, review 7. restate
  8. argument 9. reiterate, summarize
recapture... 6. recall, regain, retake
  7. recover
recede... 3. ebb 4. wane 6. depart,
  retire 7. deviate, regress, retreat
  8. withdraw 10. retrograde
receipt... 5. axiom 6. acquit, answer,
  recipe 7. formula 12. prescription
  14. acknowledgment
receipts... 7. the take

receive... 3. get 4. hold, take
  5. admit, greet, learn, reset
  6. accept, assent, derive, obtain,
  take in 7. acquire, contain, procure
  9. apprehend
receive (pert to)...
  a confession.. 6. shrive
  a reward.. 4. reap
  stolen property.. 5. reset
receiver... 5. donee, fence 7. catcher
  8. believer 9. recipient, treasurer
  10. receptacle
receiver (pert to)...
  fixed income.. 7. rentier
  profits (law).. 6. pernor
  property in trust.. 6. bailee
  stolen property.. 5. fence
recension... 6. review 8. revising,
  revision 9. reviewing
  11. enumeration, examination
recent... 3. new 4. late, past 5. fresh
  6. former, modern 7. current,
  newborn 8. neonatal, neoteric
receptacle... 3. bag, bin, box, can,
  cup, pan 4. case, cask, cyst (anc),
  etui, pail, tank, tray, vase 5. basin,
  crock 6. basket, bottle, bucket,
  carton, holder, hopper 7. compote,
  hanaper, platter 8. canister, catchall
  9. container 10. repository
receptacle (pert to)...
  assayer's, stonecutter's.. 7. sebilla
  botany.. 5. torus
  coal.. 3. bin
  corporal (RCCh).. 5. burse
  grain.. 3. bin 8. elevator
  holy water.. 5. stoup
  vote.. 6. situla
reception... 3. tea 5. levee, salon
  6. infare, soiree 7. accueil, ovation,
  receipt, welcome 8. ceremony,
  sociable 9. admission, interview,
  intuition 12. housewarming
  13. entertainment
reception hall, room... 5. salon
  6. atrium, parlor 9. vestibule
receptionist... 4. host 7. hostess
  8. landlord
receptive... 6. pliant 8. sensible
  9. acceptant, admissive, teachable
  10. hospitable, open–minded
  11. persuasible
receptor... 5. basin 8. receiver
  10. dispositor (Astron), sense organ
recess... 3. ala, bay, pan (leaf)
  4. apse, nook, rest 5. crypt, niche,
  pause, sinus, space 7. adjourn,
  respite, retreat 9. recession, seclusion
  11. indentation 12. intermission
recipe... 5. axiom 7. formula, receipt
  12. prescription
recipient... 4. heir 5. donee 7. legatee
  8. receiver
reciprocal... 5. joint 6. mutual, shared
  8. exchange 9. alternate
  11. convertible, correlative, retaliatory
  15. interchangeable
reciprocate... 5. bandy 6. accord,
  concur 8. exchange 9. alternate,
  retaliate 10. correspond
  11. interchange
recision... 6. repeal 7. pruning

9. canceling (cancelling)
10. rescinding

recital... 4. tale 5. story 6. lesson,
speech 7. account, concert
(exhibition) 8. musicale 9. narration,
narrative, rehearsal 10. recitation,
repetition 11. enumeration, reiteration

recitation... 6. lesson, speech
7. reading 10. exhibition

recite... 4. tell 5. quote, speak, state
6. relate, repeat 7. declaim, narrate,
recount 8. rehearse, tell over
9. enumerate, pronounce
12. recapitulate

recite (pert to)...
in monotone.. 6. intone
metrically.. 4. scan
rhetorically.. 7. declaim
to music.. 5. chant 10. cantillate

reciter... 4. book (of extracts) 5. roter
7. relator, speaker 8. narrator

reck... 4. care, deem, heed, mind
6. regard 7. concern 8. estimate

reckless... 4. rash 5. perdu (perdue)
6. madcap 7. hotspur 8. careless,
heedless 9. desperate, hotheaded,
imprudent 10. neglectful, regardless
11. indifferent, thoughtless,
unconcerned 13. inconsiderate

reckon... 4. aret (arette), date, deem,
tell 5. class, count, judge, tally, think
6. impute, number, regard, repute
7. account, compute, include,
suppose 8. consider, estimate,
evaluate 9. calculate, enumerate

reckoning... 3. sum 4. bill, shot
5. score, tally 6. esteem 7. account,
verdict 8. counting 9. summation
10. estimation 11. calculation

reckoning instrument... 6. abacus
7. tabulator 10. calculator

reclaim... 4. tame 5. renew, train
6. ransom, recall, redeem, revoke
7. convert, recover, restore 8. civilize
10. regenerate 12. rehabilitate

recline... 3. lay, lie, sit 4. lean, loll,
rest 6. repose 7. incline, lie down

reclining... 4. flat 5. prone 6. supine
7. lolling 8. couchant, reposing
9. prostrate, recumbent

recluse... 3. fra, nun 4. monk
6. hermit, hidden, secret, shut up
7. ascetic, eremite, retired (from
world) 8. anchoret, isolated, solitary
9. anchorite 10. cloistered
11. sequestered

recognition... 4. fame 6. recall
9. detection 10. cognizance
11. discernment
14. acknowledgment

recognize... 3. see 4. know 5. admit
6. detect 7. consent 8. identify,
perceive 10. appreciate, recognosce
11. acknowledge

recoil... 3. shy 4. funk 5. quail
6. flinch, resile, shrink 7. rebound,
retreat 8. reaction, withdraw

recollect... 6. recall, revive 7. think of
8. remember 10. call to mind

recollection... 4. mind 6. memory
9. anamnesis 11. remembrance
12. reminiscence

recommence... 5. renew 6. resume
8. return to 9. begin anew

recommend... 4. tout, urge 6. advise,
commit, denote, praise 7. commend,
consign, entrust 8. advocate

recompense... 3. fee, pay 4. meed
5. repay 6. reward 8. requital
9. indemnify, reimburse
10. compensate, remunerate
11. reciprocate

recompense (pert to)...
Brehon Law.. 4. eric
Germanic law.. 7. wergild
Scot law.. 3. cro
Welsh law.. 7. galanas

reconcile... 4. suit, wean 5. atone
6. adjust, pacify, settle 7. cleanse
(Eccl), conform, reunite 9. harmonize
10. conciliate, propitiate

reconciliation... 7. harmony, reunion
10. adjustment, conformity
12. pacification 13. reconcilement

reconciliator... 10. arbitrator,
reconciler 13. intermediator

recondite... 4. dark, deep 6. hidden,
mystic, occult 7. cryptic 8. abstract,
abstruse, esoteric 9. concealed

reconnaissance... 6. survey
8. scouting 11. examination

reconnoiter... 5. scout 6. survey

reconstruct... 6. recast, remake
7. rebuild, remodel 9. reproduce
11. reestablish

record... 3. log, tab 4. disc, file, list,
memo 5. annal, diary, enter, entry,
score 6. agenda, legend, memoir,
postea 7. archive, estreat, history
8. memorial, register 9. chronicle
10. chronology, transcribe, transcript

record (pert to)...
criminal investigation.. 7. dossier
document.. 8. protocol
earth tremor.. 11. seismograph
formal.. 4. vita 8. register
historic.. 6. annals 7. rotulet
keeper.. 9. registrar 10. chartulary
of events.. 5. annal, fasti 7. history
official.. 5. actum
pictorial.. 5. graph
ship's voyage.. 3. log
year's.. 5. diary 8. calendar

recording terms... 2. LP 4. reel, tape
5. album, Dolby 6. needle, stereo,
stylus 7. capstan 8. cassette
9. cartridge, videotape

recount... 3. min 4. tell 5. sum up
6. reckon, relate, repeat, retail
7. narrate 8. rehearse 9. enumerate,
reiterate 12. recapitulate

recoup... 4. gain 7. recover
8. retrieve 9. indemnity, reimburse
10. compensate

recourse... 3. use 5. recur 6. access,
betake, refuge, resort, return, revert
7. retreat

recover... 3. get 4. cure, gain, heal
5. rally, reach, upset 6. obtain,
recoup, redeem, regain, rescue,
resume 7. get well, reclaim, recruit
8. overcome, retrieve 9. repossess
10. convalesce, recuperate

recovery... 6. return 7. salvage

9. retrieval 11. reclamation,
reformation, restoration
recreant... 6. coward, wretch
7. dastard, knavish 8. apostate,
betrayer, cowardly, deserter
9. reprobate 10. unfaithful
recreation... 4. food, game, meal, play
5. sport 7. holiday, renewal
8. vacation 9. amusement, diversion
11. refreshment 12. reproduction
14. reconstruction
recrement... 5. dross 6. refuse, scoria
recruit... 5. raise 6. enlist, gather,
muster, novice, revive, rookie
7. recover, refresh, restore
8. assemble, inductee, newcomer
9. conscript, reinforce, replenish
12. reinvigorate
rectangle... 10. quadrangle
13. parallelogram
rectangular... 6. oblong
12. quadrangular
rectify... 5. amend, emend, right
6. adjust, better, reform, remedy
7. correct, justify 8. emendate,
regulate, set right 10. straighten
rector... 5. chief 6. leader, master
(Oxford), pastor 8. director, governor
9. churchman, clergyman
10. headmaster
rectory... 8. benefice 9. personage
recumbent... 4. idle 5. lying, prone
7. leaning, resting 8. inactive,
reposing 9. reclining
recuperate... 4. rest 6. recoup, regain
7. improve, recover, restore 9. get
better, reimburse
recur... 5. again 6. repeat, return
7. persist, reoccur 8. reappear
recurrent... 10. repetitive
recurring (pert to)...
continually.. 8. constant
10. habitually, repeatedly
ninth day.. 5. nonan
seventh day.. 6. septan
third day.. 7. tertian
red... 4. rosy 5. color, ruddy 7. radical
8. blushing, inflamed, rutilant,
sanguine 9. bloodshot
12. bloodstained 13. revolutionary
red (color)... 4. fire, lake, pink, puce,
rose, ruby, tile, wine 5. blood, brick,
canna, coral, flame, flesh, henna,
poppy 6. auburn, cerise, cherry,
claret, damask, maroon, minium,
raddle, salmon, titian, Turkey
7. anemone, annatto, carmine,
Chinese, crimson, lobster, magenta,
nacarat, scarlet, stammel 8. cardinal,
cinnabar 9. carnation, carnelian,
vermilion
red (pert to)...
cap (Turk).. 8. tarboosh
cell.. 11. erythrocite
corpuscle.. 10. hemoglobin (source of)
dog.. 4. game 8. banknote
dye.. 3. aal, lac 4. chay (choy)
5. aurin (aurine), eosin (eosine)
8. morindin
gum.. 10. strophulus
hair.. 6. titian
herring.. 4. ruse 9. diversion

minded.. 7. radical
planet.. 4. Mars
race.. 7. Indians
robbin.. 14. scarlet tanager
truffle.. 12. melanogaster
viper.. 10. copperhead
Red (pert to)...
Book.. 7. Austria 13. Royal Kalendar
Crescent.. 8. Red Cross (Turk)
Cross.. 9. St George's (Eng)
Friar.. 13. Knight Templar
Guard.. 4. Army 7. Russian
Hand.. 13. Badge of Ulster
Horse.. 10. Kentuckian
Planet.. 4. Mars
Polled.. 6. cattle (hornless)
Prince.. 7. Russian (Frederick Charles)
Ribbon.. 14. Order of the Bath
Rose.. 16. House of Lancaster
Russian.. 9. Bolshevik
Sea.. 14. Erythraean main
Sea city.. 9. Leningrad
Sea colony.. 7. Eritrea
Sea gulf.. 5. Aqaba
Square.. 6. Moscow
The Red.. 4. Eric (Scand)
Triangle.. 4. YMCA (symbol)
redact... 4. edit 5. draft, frame
6. revise
redactor... 6. editor 7. reviser
9. redacteur
reddish (pert to)...
blue.. 5. smalt 9. damascene
brown.. 3. bay 4. roan 5. henna
6. auburn, russet, sorrel 8. chestnut
dye.. 7. annatto
yellow.. 5. amber 6. orange
rede... 6. advice, relate 7. counsel,
explain, predict 9. interpret
redeem... 3. pay 6. ransom, regain,
rescue 7. convert, fulfill, reclaim,
recover 8. liberate 10. repurchase,
substitute
redeemer... 4. goel (Heb) 7. saviour
(savior) 9. deliverer, liberator
11. emancipator
Redeemer, The... 8. Son of God
10. The Messiah, The Saviour
11. Jesus Christ
redintegrate... 5. renew, unite
7. restore 9. reconcile
11. re—establish
redness... 4. glow 8. blushing
10. erubescent, rubescence
redolence... 4. odor 5. aroma, scent
9. fragrance, sweetness
redolent... 5. balmy 7. odorous,
scented 8. aromatic, fragrant
11. impregnated, reminiscent
redouble... 6. re—echo, repeat
7. reflect, reprise (fencing)
9. intensify 10. ingeminate, repetition
11. reduplicate
redoubt... 4. fear 5. doubt 6. reduit
7. defense, ravelin
redound... 5. surge 6. abound, return
7. conduce, resound 8. flow back,
overflow 10. contribute (to)
11. reverberate
redpoll... 5. finch 6. linnet 7. warbler
Red Polled cattle... 8. hornless
redress... 4. help 5. amend, emend

6. reform, remedy 7. correct, relieve
8. atone for, reprisal 9. atonement
10. correction, recompense,
reparation 11. reformation, restitution
reduce ... 3. cut 4. bant, bate, pare,
thin 5. abase, abate, lower, razee
6. demote, derate, humble, lessen,
subdue, weaken 7. abridge, analyze,
cheapen, conquer, curtail, deplete,
qualify, relieve, shorten 8. decrease,
diminish, discount, minimize,
moderate 9. subjugate
10. impoverish, slenderize
reduce in flesh ... 8. emaciate
reduce in rank ... 6. demote
reduce to ...
ashes .. 7. cremate
average .. 4. mean 6. equate
bondage .. 7. enslave
common measure .. 12. commensurate
half .. 9. dimidiate
lower grade .. 6. demote 7. degrade
mean time .. 6. equate
spray .. 7. atomize
reduction ... 6. rebate 7. subdual
8. decrease, demotion, discount,
lowering 9. weakening
10. abridgment, cheapening,
conversion, moderation
reduction (pert to) ...
in value .. 12. depreciation
to absurdity .. 18. reductio ad
absurdum
to common level .. 15. standardization
to compactness .. 12. condensation
to standard .. 15. standardization
redundancy ... 6. excess 7. profuse
8. pleonasm, verbiage 9. prolixity,
talkative, tautology, verbosity
10. repetition 11. periphrasis
13. diffusiveness 14. circumlocution
redundant ... 6. lavish 7. copious,
diffuse, verbose 9. excessive,
exuberant, plethoric 10. pleonastic
11. overflowing, repetitious,
superfluous 13. superabundant
ree ... 3. dam 4. sift, wild 5. crazy,
drunk, river 6. harbor, riddle
7. channel, fuddled 8. coalyard
9. enclosure, sheepfold
re-echo ... 7. resound 11. reverberate
reechy ... 5. fetid 6. rancid
reed ... 4. stem, tube 5. arrow, straw
6. thatch 10. instrument
reed (pert to) ...
bird .. 4. wren 7. babbler, warbler
8. bobolink
buck .. 5. bohor, nagar 8. antelope
bunting .. 7. sparrow 8. reedling
loom .. 4. sley
mace .. 7. cattail, matreed
measure (Jew) .. 9. six cubits
pipe .. 5. kazoo 8. mirliton
reef ... 3. bar, cay (cayo), key (quay)
4. itch, lode, sail, vein 5. islet,
mange, shoal 6. island 7. shorten
8. eruption
reef (pert to) ...
coral .. 3. key
knot .. 6. square
mining .. 4. lode, vein
nautical .. 5. sails

sand .. 3. bar
reefer ... 5. miner 6. jacket, oyster
9. cigarette 10. midshipman
reek ... 3. fug, rig 4. fume 5. equip,
exude, smell, smoke, steam
7. malodor, seaweed 8. fetid air,
smell bad, vaporize 10. exhalation
reel ... 4. eddy, pirn, rock, sail, sway,
wind 5. dance, lurch, spool, swift
(yarn), swing, waver, wince 6. tatter
7. scrieve, stagger 8. flounder,
titubate, windlass 12. Virginia reel
reeling ... 5. drunk 7. swaying, winding
8. rotating
reem (Bib) ... 6. animal (horned), wild
ox 7. unicorn
re-embody ... 7. combine, reshape
10. reorganize 11. reincarnate
13. reincorporate
reeve ... 3. pen 4. ruff 5. strip
6. thread 8. official (Eng Hist)
9. enclosure, sheepfold
refect ... 7. refresh, restore
refectory ... 6. frater (monastery)
8. mess hall 10. dining hall
refer ... 4. cite 5. apply, recur
6. allude, appeal, charge, impute,
relate, return 7. ascribe 9. appertain,
attribute
refer (to) ... 4. harp 6. advert
7. consult, mention
referee ... 5. judge 6. umpire 7. arbiter
8. attorney 9. moderator
10. arbitrator
reference ... 6. regard 7. respect
8. allusion, relation 9. character,
relevance 10. connection, pertinence
14. recommendation
reference (pert to) ...
book .. 5. atlas 8. handbook, syllabus
9. thesaurus 10. dictionary
12. encyclopedia
referendum ... 4. vote 7. mandate
8. politics 10. plebiscite
refine ... 5. smelt 6. rarefy 7. clarify,
elevate, improve, sublime
9. elaborate, sensitize, sublimate
refined ... 4. fine, nice, pure, rare
5. urban 6. chaste 7. elegant,
smelted 8. cleansed, highbred,
purified, well-bred 9. clarified,
courteous, perfected 10. cultivated,
fastidious, meticulous
refined spirit ... 5. grace 6. elixir
refinement ... 5. taste 6. polish
7. finesse 8. delicacy, elegance,
fineness 9. gentility 11. cultivation,
rarefaction 13. clarification
refinery (ore) ... 7. smelter
refining cup ... 5. cupel
reflect ... 3. say 4. muse, pore
5. radar, think 6. divert, mirror,
ponder 7. deflect 8. cogitate,
consider, meditate, ruminate, turn
back 9. reproduce 11. reverberate
reflecting ... 6. musing 9. judicious
10. reflective, ruminating, thoughtful
11. insinuating 13. reverberatory
15. casting reproach
reflection ... 4. idea 5. image, light
6. musing 7. bending, thought
8. reaction, thinking 10. cogitation,

meditation, rumination
12. afterthought, recollection
13. consideration, contemplation
reflex... 4. bent 6. turned 8. allusion,
reaction, reversed 9. duplicate,
reflected 13. introspection
reflux... 3. ebb 6. ebbing, reflow
8. backflow, reaction 9. refluence,
returning
reform... 4. mend 5. amend, emend,
renew 6. better, remake, remass,
repair 7. convert, rebuild, reclaim,
rectify, restore 9. amendment
10. regenerate 11. reformation
reformation... 7. rebirth
10. conversion, emendation
12. regeneration, reproduction
15. re—establishment
Reformation leaders (Hist)... 4. Knox
6. Calvin, Luther, Ridley 7. Cranmer,
Latimer, Zwingli 8. Campbell
11. Melanchthon
reformer... 7. amender, reviser
9. reformado, reformist 10. politician
refraction... 7. rebound 9. dioptrics
10. deflection, dispersion
11. anaclastics
refractor... 5. prism 9. telescope
refractory... 7. restive 8. indocile,
stubborn 11. disobedient
12. ungovernable
refrain... 4. curb, shun 5. avoid,
cease, derry, epode 6. chorus,
govern 7. abstain, forbear
8. response, restrain
refrain from using... 5. spare
7. boycott
refresco... 4. food 5. drink
11. refreshment
refresh... 3. air, dew 4. cool 5. cheer,
renew, slake 6. repose, revive
7. freshen, relieve 8. recreate,
renovate 9. reanimate, replenish
10. invigorate, strengthen
11. refreshment 12. reinvigorate
refreshing... 5. balmy 7. bracing
8. regaling 10. heartening
11. stimulating 12. exhilarating
refrigerant... 3. ice 6. cooler
7. ammonia, coolant, cryogen
refrigeration... 7. cooling 8. cryogeny
10. anesthetic, cryogenics
12. preservation
refuge... 3. ark 4. plea 5. haven
6. asylum, covert, excuse 7. retreat,
shelter 8. hospital, recourse, resource
9. sanctuary 10. protection, safety
zone
refugee... 5. exile, fleer 6. émigré
7. escapee, evacuee 8. fugitive,
renegade
refulgence... 6. luster 8. radiance,
splendor 10. brilliancy
refund... 5. repay 6. rebate
9. reimburse
refurbish... 4. vamp 5. renew
8. brighten, renovate 11. recondition
refusal... 3. nay 6. denial 9. rejection
11. declination
refuse... 3. cot (wool), ort 4. balk,
coom (coomb), culm, deny, junk,
marc, scum 5. attle, chaff, dregs,

dross, repel, scrap, trash, waste,
weeds 6. debris, give up, litter,
midden, naysay, reject, renege,
scoria, scraps 7. abandon, bagasse,
cast off, decline, garbage, hogwash,
repulse 8. disclaim, leavings,
oddments, renounce, withhold
9. excrement, repudiate 11. odds
and ends
refuse to...
accept.. 6. reject
acknowledge.. 7. disavow 9. repudiate
comply.. 12. recalcitrant
proceed.. 4. balk
refutation... 6. answer 8. disproof,
elenchus, rebuttal 11. confutation
refute... 4. deny, meet 5. rebut, refel
6. assoil 8. disprove, elenctic,
redargue 9. overthrow 10. contradict
regain... 6. recoup 7. get back,
recover 8. retrieve 9. get back to
10. reach again
regal... 5. royal 6. groove, kingly
7. channel, stately 8. imperial,
majestic, splendid 9. dignified,
sovereign
regale... 4. dine, fete 5. amuse, feast,
treat 7. gratify, refresh 9. entertain
11. refreshment
regalia... 6. finery 7. costume,
emblems, symbols 8. insignia
11. decorations 12. special dress
13. paraphernalia
regard... 3. air, awe 4. care, deem,
gaze, heed, hold, look, love, mind,
obey (law), rate, sake, view 5. honor,
judge, think, treat 6. aspect, behold,
esteem, remark, repute 8. attitude,
consider, estimate, hold dear, listen
to 9. attention, relevance, viewpoint
10. appearance, estimation
11. contemplate, observation
13. consideration
regard (pert to)...
for others.. 8. altruism
for other's wish.. 9. deference
highly.. 6. admire 7. lionize
with approval.. 6. admire
with deference.. 5. honor 7. respect
with veneration.. 6. revere
regardful... 7. careful, mindful
8. cautious 9. attentive, observant
10. altruistic, respectful, thoughtful
11. considerate
regarding... 2. re 5. anent
10. concerning, respecting
regardless... 6. anyhow 8. careless,
heedless, slighted 9. negligent
10. neglectful 11. inattentive,
indifferent, unconcerned, unobservant
15. notwithstanding
regards... 8. respects 9. greetings
11. compliments
regatta cup... 5. Platt 8. Carnegie,
Grimoldi
regency... 4. rule 8. dominion
10. government
regenerate... 5. shape 6. redeem,
reform, revive 7. convert, restore
8. re—create 9. reproduce
11. fashion anew
regeneration... 7. renewal, revival

9. reversion 10. re–creation
11. reformation 12. reproduction
14. divine function
regent ... 5. ruler 6. deputy, ruling
7. regnant 8. governor
Regent diamond, 137 carats (pert
to) ...
included in .. 11. State jewels (France)
named for .. 14. Regent of France
placed in .. 6. Louvre
sold (1717) to .. 4. Pitt (Gov of
Madras, Ind)
regime, regimen ... 4. diet, rule
6. system 7. therapy
10. government, regulation
14. administration
regiment ... 4. unit, wing 6. outfit
8. organize 11. systematize
regiment, framework of ... 5. cadre
regina ... 5. queen
region ... 4. area, belt, zone 5. clime,
place, realm, space, tract 6. sphere
7. climate, cockpit, country,
demesne, kingdom, section
8. district, province
region (pert to) ...
beyond Jordan .. 5. Perea 6. Basham
blissful .. 4. Eden
comb form .. 5. nesia
desert .. 3. erg 5. waste
indefinite .. 5. tract
infernal .. 7. Avernal 8. Tartarus
meteorological .. 6. pleion
wooded .. 4. wold
woodless .. 5. weald
region of ...
contentment .. 6. Arcady
dead (Egypt Myth) .. 6. Amenti
fabled wealth .. 8. Eldorado
nether darkness .. 6. Erebus
opposite side earth .. 9. Antipodes
Solomon's gold (Bib) .. 5. Ophir
register ... 3. act 4. list, roll 5. annal,
entry, index 6. docket, enlist, enroll,
record 7. rotulet 8. archives,
recorder, schedule 9. catalogue,
chronicle, necrology, registrar
11. account book, matriculate
registrar ... 8. recorder 9. accounter
regius ... 5. royal 13. professorship
regret ... 3. rue 4. ruth 5. grief, sorry
6. repent, repine, sorrow 7. deplore,
remorse 9. penitence 10. repentance
11. compunction 12. self–reproach
regretful ... 5. sorry 8. repining
9. repentant
regular ... 4. even 5. usual 6. formal,
normal, smooth, stated 7. correct,
orderly, typical, uniform 8. constant,
habitual, ordinary, ordinate, rhythmic,
standard 9. isometric 10. systematic
regularity ... 5. order 8. symmetry
9. constancy 10. smoothness,
uniformity
regularly ... 6. always 7. usually
8. properly, smoothly 9. correctly
10. constantly, habitually
12. methodically, periodically
13. symmetrically
regulate ... 3. set 4. rule 6. adjust,
direct, govern, manage, ordain,
remedy 7. arrange, control, dispose

8. organize 9. influence, methodize
11. standardize
regulation ... 3. law 4. rule 5. bylaw,
order 6. system 7. control, precept
9. direction, principle
regulator ... 7. control 8. governor,
rheostat 9. rheometer
Regulus ... 4. king, star 5. Alpha
8. warblers 9. Cor Leonis (star)
rehabilitate ... 7. restore 9. reeducate,
reinstall
rehash ... 7. restate 9. réchauffé
rehearse ... 3. say 4. tell 5. speak,
sum up, train 6. detail, recite, relate,
repeat, try out 7. mention, narrate,
recount 8. describe 9. enumerate,
reiterate 12. recapitulate
rehoboam ... 3. hat 4. bowl 6. flagon
8. jeroboam
Rehoboam (Bib) ... 11. King of Judah
(1st) 12. King of Israel (last)
reif ... 7. plunder, robbery
reign ... 3. raj 4. rule, sway 5. guide,
realm 6. empire 7. kingdom, prevail
8. dominion, flourish 11. sovereignty
12. supreme power
Reign of Terror (Fr Hist) ... 7. anarchy
9. bloodshed, despotism
12. confiscation
reimburse ... 3. pay 5. repay 6. refund
7. pay back, replace 9. indemnify
10. recompense
Reims, Rheims (pert to) ...
capital (anc) .. 4. Remi
famed building .. 9. Cathedral (Gothic)
famed site .. 15. crowning of kings
(Fr)
rein ... 4. curb, stop 5. check, leash
6. direct, retard 7. control
8. reindeer, restrain 9. hindrance
10. bridle part
reina ... 8. rockfish
reindeer ... 6. tarand 7. caribou
13. constellation
reindeer (pert to) ...
age, epoch .. 11. Paleolithic
flower .. 9. buttercup (white)
genus .. 8. Rangifer
reinforce ... 4. back 5. add to, brace,
reman 7. restore, support
9. intensify, replenish 10. strengthen
reinforcement ... 7. adjunct, support
8. addition 13. replenishment,
strengthening
reins ... 5. loins 7. harness, kidneys
9. restraint
reis ... 6. escudo 7. milreis 14. money
of account
reit ... 5. sedge 7. seaweed
reiterate ... 4. drum, harp 6. repeat
8. rehearse 12. recapitulate
reject ... 5. repel, spurn 6. disown,
recuse (law), refuse 7. decline,
discard, dismiss 8. athetize, disallow
9. repudiate
rejectamenta ... 5. wrack 6. refuse,
reject 7. rubbish 9. excrement
rejection ... 6. heresy 7. discard,
refusal 8. ejection 9. exclusion,
objection 11. disapproval, repudiation
rejoice ... 5. cheer, elate 7. delight,
gladden 8. jubilate

rejoinder . . . **5.** reply (law) **6.** answer, retort, return **8.** comeback

rejuvenate . . . **6.** revive **7.** restore **9.** stimulate **12.** reinvigorate

relâche . . . **10.** relaxation **12.** intermission **13.** no performance (Theat)

relapse . . . **4.** sink **5.** lapse **7.** subside **8.** slip back **9.** backslide, reversion **10.** recurrence, regression **11.** falling back **12.** recidivation

relate . . . **4.** tell **5.** state **6.** assert, detail, recite, report **7.** narrate, pertain, recount **8.** describe, rehearse **9.** appertain, associate

related (pert to) . . .
by blood . . **3.** sib **4.** akin **7.** cognate
on father's side . . **6.** agnate **7.** cognate **8.** agnation
on mother's side . . **5.** enate **6.** enatic **7.** cognate, enation **9.** umbilical
to land . . **8.** praedial (predial)

relating to . . .
bread . . **6.** panary
Chinese . . **7.** Sinitic
dancing . . **6.** gestic **13.** choreographic
fruit jelly . . **7.** pectous
grandparents . . **4.** aval
Hindu literature . . **5.** Vedic
life . . **5.** vital
morn . . **7.** matinal **8.** forenoon
motion . . **7.** kinetic **9.** kinematic
realities . . **7.** factual **9.** entelechy
soft palate . . **5.** velar
vascular fluid . . **5.** hemic

relation . . . **3.** kin **4.** mode, tale **6.** status, ubiety **7.** account, analogy, kinship, kinsman, recital, telling **8.** relative **9.** character, narration, reference, rehearsal, rishtadar (Hind law) **10.** connection **13.** consanguinity

relationship . . . **4.** outs **7.** kinship, kinsman, metochy **8.** affinity, relative **13.** consanguinity

relative . . . **3.** eme, kin, sib, son **4.** aunt **5.** niece, uncle **6.** allied, cousin, father, mother, nephew, sister **7.** brother, kindred **8.** apposite, daughter, kinsfolk **9.** pertinent **11.** comparative, correlative **13.** corresponding, proportionate

relative (pert to) . . .
favor to . . **8.** nepotism
rank . . **6.** degree
to . . **7.** apropos **12.** in proportion

relax . . . **4.** ease, open, rest **5.** abate, loose, remit **6.** divert, loosen, soften, unbend **7.** detente, slacken **8.** mitigate, slow down

relaxed . . . **4.** calm, cool **5.** casual **8.** laid–back **9.** easygoing

relay . . . **3.** dak (dawk) **4.** race **5.** shift **6.** remuda **7.** relieve **8.** avantlay **10.** television (station)

release . . . **4.** drop, free, trip, undo **5.** death, let go, loose, undam, unpen, untie **6.** acquit, escape, exempt, loosen, parole, remise **7.** deliver, freedom, manumit, receipt, relieve, unleash, unloose **8.** liberate **9.** discharge **10.** liberation, relinquish **11.** acquittance, deliverance

relegate . . . **5.** exile, refer **6.** assign, banish, commit, deport, depute, remove **7.** ascribe, consign, discard, dismiss, exclude **8.** delegate

relent . . . **5.** abate, yield **6.** regret, soften, submit **7.** slacken

relentless . . . **6.** strict **9.** merciless **10.** inflexible, unyielding **11.** persevering, unremitting

relevant . . . **7.** germane **9.** pertinent **10.** sufficient **11.** referential

reliable . . . **4.** safe, sure **5.** tried **6.** stable, trusty **7.** solvent **8.** true–blue **11.** trustworthy

reliance . . . **4.** hope **5.** trust **6.** belief **8.** mainstay **10.** confidence, conviction, dependence

relic . . . **5.** curio, huaca, huaco, ruins **7.** antique, memento, remains **8.** artifact, fragment, memorial, souvenir, survival **9.** antiquity

relic cabinet . . . **7.** étagère, whatnot

relict . . . **5.** widow **7.** widower **8.** survivor

relied . . . **6.** banked **7.** counted, reposed, trusted **8.** confided, depended, reckoned

relief . . . **3.** aid **4.** bote (bot), dole, ease, fret (Arch), help **5.** spell **6.** remedy, succor **7.** comfort, outline, redress, relieve, welfare **8.** easement **10.** assistance, embossment, mitigation, substitute, sustenance **11.** alleviation, deliverance **15.** indemnification

relieve . . . **3.** aid **4.** cure, ease, free, help **5.** abate, allay, clear, raise, spell **6.** assist, remedy, remove, succor **7.** assuage, lighten, redress, refresh, support, sustain, unloose **8.** diminish **10.** substitute

religion (pert to) . . . **4.** sect **5.** creed, deism, faith, piety, trust **6.** belief, hermit, schism, theism, voodoo **8.** monastic, theology **9.** solipsism **10.** conformity, persuasion

religion, type . . . **5.** Islam **6.** Taoism **7.** Jainism, Judaism **8.** Buddhism, Hinduism **9.** Mormonism, Moslemism, Muslimism, Shintoism **11.** Anglicanism, Catholicism **12.** Christianity, Confucianism **13.** Mohammedanism, Protestantism

religious . . . **4.** holy **5.** exact, godly, pious, rigid **6.** devout, sacred **7.** devoted, fervent, zealous **9.** born–again, pharasaic, spiritual **10.** devotional, meticulous, scrupulous **11.** theological **13.** conscientious

religious (pert to) . . .
assembly . . **12.** congregation
belief . . **5.** deism **6.** omnist **10.** monotheism
brotherhood . . **8.** sodality **9.** ecumenism **10.** fellowship **11.** ecumenicism
center . . **7.** Lambeth (Eng)
composition . . **5.** motet
cult, sect . . **5.** fakir **6.** Shaker, Shinto **7.** Pietism, Sikhism **8.** cenobite **9.** anchorite **11.** Hare Krishna

devotee .. **5.** fakir
devotion .. **6.** novena
division .. **6.** schism
expedition (Mil) .. **7.** crusade
fasting .. **4.** Lent **9.** Ember Days
  10. Ember Weeks
festival .. **4.** mela (Ind) **5.** Purim (Jew)
madness, mania .. **9.** theomania
metaphysics .. **7.** gnostic
musical .. **6.** anthem
offering .. **7.** deodate **8.** oblation
Order member .. **6.** Marist **7.** Templar
poem .. **5.** psalm
primitive .. **6.** voodoo
psalm .. **4.** hymn, poem, song
publication (RCCh) .. **4.** ordo
relinquish ... **3.** let **4.** cede, quit
  5. forgo, leave, waive, yield
  6. desert, desist, forego, give up,
  remise, resign **7.** abandon, forsake,
  release **8.** abdicate, renounce
  9. surrender **11.** leave behind
  12. withdraw from
relinquishment ... **9.** surrender
  11. abandonment **12.** renunciation
reliquary, reliquiae (pl) ... **3.** box
  4. arca, tomb **5.** chest **6.** casket,
  chasse, shrine **8.** monument
relish ... **4.** gust, tang, zest **5.** achar,
  enjoy, gusto, sauce, taste **6.** canape,
  caviar, degust, flavor, liking
  8. pleasure **9.** condiment, degustate,
  enjoyment, flavoring, seasoning
  11. hors d'oeuvre **13.** gratification
relucent ... **5.** lucid **6.** lucent
  7. radiant, shining **8.** lightish
  9. refulgent
reluctance ... **8.** aversion
  10. repugnance **13.** indisposition,
  unwillingness **14.** disinclination
reluctance unit (Elec) ... **3.** rel
reluctant ... **5.** chary, loath **6.** averse
  8. hesitant, not ready **9.** resisting,
  unwilling **11.** disinclined
reluctate ... **5.** repel **6.** oppose
  9. repudiate
rely ... **4.** hold, lean, rest **5.** count,
  trust **6.** cleave, depend, reckon,
  repose **7.** confide
rely on, upon ... **4.** hope **5.** trust
  6. depend, lippen **7.** believe
remain ... **3.** lie **4.** bide, last, rest, stay
  5. abide, tarry **6.** endure, reside
  8. continue
remainder ... **4.** rest, stub **5.** relic,
  stump **6.** estate **7.** balance, remnant,
  residue, surplus **8.** fragment,
  leavings, residual, residuum
remaining ... **4.** left, over **6.** ledger
  (leger) **7.** durable, remnant, staying,
  surplus **8.** residual **9.** permanent
remaining stationary ... **6.** static
  7. waiting **8.** awaiting
remains ... **5.** ashes, ruins, stays
  6. corpse, relics **7.** cadaver, fossils
  9. remainder
remanent ... **4.** left **7.** further, lasting,
  remains, remnant, residue
  8. enduring, leftover, residual
  9. permanent, remainder
  10. additional **13.** supplementary
remark ... **3.** say, see **4.** heed, note

5. gloss, state **6.** notice, regard
  7. comment, observe **8.** perceive,
  point out **9.** statement
  10. annotation, commentary,
  indication **11.** observation
  12. interjection
remark (pert to) ...
amusing, witty .. **3.** gag **4.** quip
clever .. **3.** mot
commonplace .. **9.** platitude
smarting .. **7.** sarcasm, stinger
upon .. **7.** explain
witless .. **5.** boner
remarkable ... **5.** great **7.** notable,
  strange, unusual **8.** uncommon
  9. wonderful **10.** noteworthy,
  noticeable, observable
  11. conspicuous **13.** extraordinary
Rembrandt (pert to) ...
birthplace .. **6.** Leyden (Neth)
color .. **5.** brown
famed as .. **6.** etcher (Dutch)
  7. painter
style .. **14.** Rembrandtesque
remedial ... **6.** remedy (pert to)
  7. healing **8.** curative, panacean
  10. corrective **11.** therapeutic
remedy ... **3.** aid, fix **4.** bote (bot),
  cure, gain, help **5.** amend **6.** doctor,
  relief **8.** antidote, medicine
  10. assistance, reparation
remedy (pert to) ...
cure–all .. **6.** elixir
mysterious (of Paracelsus) ..
  7. arcanum
quack .. **7.** nostrum
soothing .. **4.** balm **6.** balsam
universal .. **7.** panacea
remember ... **3.** min **9.** recollect,
  reminisce **10.** keep in mind
remembrance ... **4.** fame **5.** token
  6. memory, Minnie, trophy
  7. memento **8.** allusion, memorial,
  reminder, souvenir **12.** recollection
  13. commemoration
remex ... **12.** quill feather
remind ... **6.** prompt, recall
  8. remember **13.** call attention
reminder ... **4.** memo, twit **7.** memento
  8. souvenir **10.** memorandum
  11. remembrance
reminiscence ... **3.** act **4.** fact
  5. power **6.** memory **8.** anecdote
  10. experience **11.** memorabilia
  12. recollection
remise ... **6.** giving, return **7.** release,
  replace, respite **8.** granting
  9. remission, surrender
remiss ... **3.** lax **5.** slack **7.** lenient
  8. careless, dilatory, heedless
  9. negligent **10.** neglectful
  11. inattentive, thoughtless
remissness ... **7.** neglect **9.** indolence
  10. negligence **12.** improvidence
remit ... **3.** pay **5.** relax **6.** acquit,
  assign, cancel, excuse, pardon,
  reduce, resign **7.** absolve, forgive,
  release, restore, suspend **8.** abrogate,
  liberate, mitigate, recommit
  9. surrender
remnant ... **3.** ash, end, ort, rag
  4. dreg, left, rest, stub **5.** piece,

relic, scrap, shred, trace 7. oddment, remains, yet left 8. fragment 9. remainder, remaining 10. suggestion

remolade... 5. sauce 8. dressing, ointment

remonstrate... 5. plead 7. protest 8. point out 11. expostulate

remontant... 14. flowering again

remora... 4. fish, pega (pegora)

remord... 5. taint 6. ponder, rebuke 7. afflict, censure, remorse

remorse... 4. pity 6. regret, sorrow 8. distress 9. penitence, repentent 10. compassion 11. compunction

remorseful... 5. sorry 7. pitiful 8. contrite, merciful, penitent, pitiable 9. regretful 13. compassionate

remorseless... 8. pitiless 9. merciless, unpitying 10. implacable, inflexible, relentless, unmerciful 11. unregretful

remote... 3. far, off 5. alien, vague 6. elenge, forane, ultima 7. distant, foreign 8. abstruse, reserved, secluded, ulterior 10. farfetched, unsociable 11. out-of-the-way

remote control... 10. pushbutton, tele–action

remote region... 5. Thule (Greenland)

remotest... 7. endmost, very end 8. farthest 14. ghost of a chance

removal... 8. ejection 9. deduction 10. divestment, evacuation, extraction 11. elimination 12. transference

remove... 3. rid 4. dele, doff, move, void, weed 5. erase, evict, expel, strip 6. change, debunk, delete, depose, divest, eloign (law) 7. dismiss, extract, relieve 8. abstract, displace, evacuate, put aside, transfer 9. eliminate, eradicate, translate 11. assassinate

remove (pert to)...
cover.. 5. uncap
from office.. 4. oust 6. depose, recall
moisture.. 3. dry 5. wring 9. dehydrate
point of origin.. 6. distal
seed from flax.. 6. ribble
seeds.. 3. gin, pit
stalk.. 5. strig
to another place.. 8. transfer 9. translate
whole blubber.. 6. flense

removed... 4. took 5. apart 6. betook, remote 7. distant, far away 8. reserved, secluded 9. separated, unrelated 10. unsociable

remover... 6. porter 7. carrier, drayman, solvent 9. scavenger 10. contractor, eradicator

remunerate... 3. pay 5. repay 6. reward 7. requite, satisfy 9. reimburse 10. compensate, recompense

remuneration... 3. pay 6. reward 7. payment 8. pittance, requital 9. emolument 10. recompense 12. compensation, satisfaction 13. reimbursement

Remus (pert to)...
brother.. 7. Romulus

father.. 4. Mars
legendary founder of.. 4. Rome (with brother)
slayer.. 7. Romulus

renable... 4. glib 5. ready 6. fluent 8. eloquent

renaissance... 7. rebirth, revival

Renaissance (pert to)...
Archit.. 12. Roman classic
art.. 10. neoclassic
associated with.. 8. Petrarch
furniture.. 6. carved 7. English, Flemish
Italian reference.. 12. Resorgimento (new arising)
lace.. 10. Battenburg

renal... 6. kidney 7. nephric

renascence... 7. rebirth, revival 14. The Renaissance

rencounter... 4. duel 5. clash 6. action, combat, flight 7. contest, meeting 8. conflict 9. collision

rend... 3. rip 4. rive, tear 5. break, burst, sever, split, wrest 7. extract, rupture 8. fracture

render... 3. pay, put 4. give, make, melt 6. return 7. clarify, convert, deliver, execute, extract, narrate, present, requite 8. transmit 9. translate 10. understand 11. communicate

render (pert to)...
accessible.. 4. open
agreeable.. 7. dulcify
angry, choleric.. 6. enrage
conformable to Eng.. 7. Anglify 9. Anglicize
divine.. 5. deify
dull.. 8. hebetate
enduring.. 6. anneal
fat.. 3. try 6. try out
fertile.. 6. enrich
free from bacteria.. 9. sterilize
ineffective.. 4. void 5. annul 10. invalidate
intelligible.. 9. elucidate
less pliant.. 7. stiffen
muddy, turgid.. 4. roil
oblique.. 5. splay
obscure.. 6. darkle 9. obfuscate
sharp.. 9. acuminate
unconscious.. 4. stun

rendezvous... 5. tryst 6. refuge 7. meeting, retreat 11. appointment

rendition... 7. account 8. delivery 9. surrender 10. extraction 11. performance, translation 14. interpretation

renegade... 3. rat 5. rebel 7. pervert, traitor 8. apostate, deserter, fugitive, turncoat

renege... 4. deny 6. desert, revoke 7. decline 8. renounce

renew... 6. resume, revamp, revive 7. convert, refresh, restore 8. renovate 10. invigorate, regenerate 12. redintegrate

renewal... 10. conversion, renovation, resumption 11. restoration

renitent... 7. opposed 9. reluctant, resistant 12. recalcitrant

rennet... 3. lab 5. apple 6. curdle,

rennin 7. extract 9. coagulate
rennin... 6. enzyme
renommé... 8. renowned
10. celebrated
Renommist... 8. braggart, renowner
9. swaggerer
renounce... 4. cede, deny 5. forgo
(forego), waive 6. abjure, desert,
disown, recant, reject, renege, resign
7. abandon, forsake, retract
8. abnegate, forswear, swear off
9. repudiate, surrender 10. relinquish
12. abrenunciate
renouncement... 9. rejection
10. temperance 11. abandonment,
recantation
renovate... 5. renew 6. repair, resume,
revive 7. restore 10. regenerate
renown... 4. fame, note 5. éclat, glory
10. reputation
renowned... 5. famed, noted
6. famous 10. celebrated
11. illustrious 13. distinguished
rent... 3. let, pay 4. dues, hire, hole,
slit, tear, toll, tore, torn 5. break,
cleft, lease, share, split 6. reward
7. revenue, rupture, slitted, tribute
8. tattered
rent (pert to)...
asunder.. 5. rived
harvest.. 7. onstand
in oats.. 7. avenage
paid.. 3. tac
renter... 6. lessee, lodger, tenant
renunciation... 6. denial 9. disavowal,
rejection, surrender 10. abjuration,
disclaimer, temperance
11. abandonment, recantation
14. relinquishment
repaid in kind... 10. retaliated
repair... 3. fix 4. darn, heal, mend
5. amend, patch, renew 6. doctor,
remedy, resort 7. correct, rebuild,
restore 8. atone for 9. condition
13. betake oneself
reparation... 6. amende, amends,
remedy, repair, reward 7. damages,
redress 8. reprisal, requital
9. atonement, indemnity
10. recompense 11. restitution
12. compensation, satisfaction
repartee... 3. wit 4. reply 6. retort
7. riposte
repast... 3. tea 4. feed, meal 5. feast,
lunch, treat 6. tiffin 8. mealtime,
prandial 9. collation
repatriate... 5. exile 6. banish
10. expatriate
repay... 4. meed 6. answer, avenge,
refund, return 7. requite, restore
9. reimburse, retaliate
10. compensate, recompense,
remunerate
repeal... 5. annul, emend, forgo
(forego) 6. appeal, cancel, recall
7. abandon, abolish, rescind, retract,
reverse 8. abrogate, renounce,
withdraw
repeat... 4. copy, echo, rame 5. recur
7. iterate, restate 8. remember
9. duplicate, reiterate
repeat (pert to)...

mathematics.. 8. repetend
mechanically.. 6. parrot
noisily.. 3. din
performance.. 6. encore
twice (pref).. 3. bis
repeating... 4. rote 10. repetitive
11. repetitious
repel... 5. avert, check 6. offend,
oppose, rebuff, refuse, reject, resist,
revolt 7. disgust, repulse 9. drive
back, force back
repellent... 5. harsh 6. odious
9. repulsive, resistant, revolting
repent... 3. rue 6. reform, regret
9. do penance
repentance... 4. ruth 5. shame
6. regret 9. penitence 10. contrition
11. compunction
repercussion... 4. blow 6. impact
9. afterclap, aftermath 10. reflection
repertory... 4. list 5. index, store
8. calendar, magazine, treasure
9. catalogue 10. collection,
repertoire, storehouse
repetition... 4. rote 5. troll 6. encore
8. iterance 9. iteration 11. reiteration
14. recapitulation
repetition (pert to)...
biology.. 6. merism
music.. 5. rondo 7. tremolo
rhetoric.. 8. anaphora 9. tautology
sound.. 4. echo
sounds (slight).. 6. patter
repetitive... 8. habitual 9. redundant
11. repetitious
repine... 4. fret 6. lament, regret
7. grumble 8. complain
replace... 4. stet 5. reset, stead
6. repone 7. restore 8. supplant
9. discharge, supersede
10. substitute
replaceable... 10. expendable
replenish... 4. feed, fill 5. store
6. refill 7. perfect, provide
8. complete
replete... 3. fat 4. full 5. sated
6. filled, gorged 7. bloated
8. abundant 9. surfeited
replevin... 4. bail, writ 8. recovery
replica... 3. bis 4. copy 6. repeat
9. duplicate, facsimile
reply... 4. echo 5. rebut 6. answer,
oracle, rejoin, retort 7. defense,
epistle, respond 8. reaction, repartee,
response 9. rejoinder 11. retaliation
report... 3. cry, pop 4. bang, note
5. bruit, rumor, sound, state, story
6. delate, recite, relate, repute
7. account, hearsay, recital, verdict
8. describe 9. narration, narrative,
statement 10. accounting,
commentary, responsory
11. information, publication
report (pert to)...
common.. 6. gossip
false, absurd.. 5. rumor 6. canard
7. slander
following lightning.. 7. thunder
for duty.. 14. present oneself
official.. 7. hansard
of proceedings.. 6. cahier
reporter... 3. cub 6. legman, pistol

7. newsman 8. newshawk
9. informant 12. newspaperman
reporter's rounds... 8. newsbeat
reporter's sign off... 6. thirty
repose... 3. lie, sit 4. ease, rely, rest
  5. peace, place, sleep 7. deposit,
  recline 9. quiescent, quietness
  10. quiescence, relaxation
repository... 3. ark 4. file 5. vault
  6. chapel (RCCh), museum
  8. treasury 9. confidant, sepulcher
  10. depository, storehouse
  11. auction room
reposoir... 5. altar
repoussé... 7. art work
reprehensible... 8. blamable, culpable
  9. accusable, obnoxious
  10. censurable, reprovable
  11. blameworthy
reprehension... 5. blame 7. censure,
  reproof 9. reprimand 11. reprobation
  12. condemnation, denunciation
represent... 5. enact 6. denote,
  depict, typify 7. betoken, exhibit,
  portray, produce 8. describe
  9. delineate
representation... 3. art 4. copy, icon,
  idea, idol, show 5. drama 6. avowal,
  symbol 7. picture 9. depiction,
  enactment, portrayal, spectacle
  10. exhibition, profession
  11. delineation, description,
  portraiture 12. reproduction
representation (pert to)...
  by characters (Mus).. 8. notation
  graphic.. 5. chart
  Medusa's head.. 9. gorgoneum
  mental.. 5. image 7. eidolon,
  phantom
  of scene.. 7. tableau
  of solar system.. 6. orrery
  of star.. 7. estoile
  small.. 5. model 9. miniature
representative... 4. heir, type
  5. agent, envoy 6. deputy, legate
  7. example, tribune, typical
  8. delegate, exponent, symbolic
  9. successor 10. ambassador,
  legislator, lieutenant, substitute
  12. illustrative
repress... 4. curb, rein, stop 5. check,
  crush, quell 6. hush up, muffle, stifle
  7. put down 8. restrain, suppress
  9. overpower
reprieve... 5. delay 6. pardon, relief
  7. relieve, respite 8. postpone
reprimand... 5. chide, scold, slate
  6. rebuke 7. censure, reprove
reprisal... 7. revenge, revenue
  8. requital 11. retaliation
reproach... 4. taca, twit 5. abuse,
  blame, chide, shend, taunt
  6. accuse, revile, vilify 7. censure,
  condemn, reproof, sarcasm, upbraid
  8. disgrace, dishonor 9. disrepute,
  invective 10. accusation, opprobrium
  12. vilification
reproach, free of... 9. blameless
reprobate... 6. disown, reject, wicked
  7. abandon, corrupt, knavish, vicious
  8. depraved, hardened, recreant
  9. condemned, miscreant, reprehend,

scoundrel 10. black sheep
  12. unprincipled 13. reprehensible
reproduce... 4. copy 6. recite, remake,
  repeat 8. multiply 9. duplicate,
  propagate
reproduction... 4. copy 6. ectype,
  recall 7. picture, replica 8. likeness
  10. repetition 11. counterpart,
  duplication 14. representation
reproductive... 5. gamic, spore
  10. recreative 12. regenerative
reproof... 5. roast 6. rebuke
  7. chiding 8. disgrace, reproach
  9. reprimand 10. admonition,
  censurable, refutation
  11. blameworthy, confutation
  12. reprehension 13. reprehensible
reprove... 4. rate 5. blame, chide,
  scold 6. berate, rebuke 7. censure,
  correct, upbraid 8. admonish,
  reproach 9. objurgate, reprehend,
  reprimand
reproving... 10. admonitive
reptile... 4. toad, worm 5. snake,
  viper 6. dragon, iguana, lizard, turtle
  7. monitor, serpent 8. creeping,
  Reptilia 9. scoundrel
reptile (pert to)...
  class.. 8. Reptilia
  crocodile.. 6. mugger
  extinct.. 9. pterosaur 10. diplodocus
  11. pterodactyl, Pterosauria
  group.. 6. Sauria
  hard–shelled.. 6. iguana, turtle
  8. terrapin, tortoise
  iguanalike.. 7. tuatara
  large.. 3. boa 9. alligator, crocodile
  10. salamander
  lizard.. 3. eft 4. adda, newt, seps
  5. skink (scink) 6. Anolis, iguana,
  moloch 7. monitor 9. chameleon
  10. chuckwalla 11. Gila monster
  Mesozoic.. 8. dinosaur
  myth.. 6. dragon 8. basilisk
  10. cockatrice, salamander
  oldest.. 9. sea turtle
  salamander.. 3. eft 4. newt
  scale.. 5. scute
  snake.. 3. asp 5. adder, cobra, krait
  6. garter, python 8. anaconda,
  Squamata 10. copperhead
reptilian... 7. saurian
Reptilian Age... 8. Mesozoic
Republic... 5. State 6. France
  7. Andorra (Andorre) 9. San Marino
  10. commonweal, government
  12. United States
Republican Party... 3. GOP
  7. mugwump (bolter 1884)
Republic of Plato... 4. Book (famed)
  8. dialogue 10. ideal State
repudiate... 4. deny 6. abjure, disown,
  recant, reject 7. disavow, discard,
  exclude 8. renounce
repugnance... 4. hate 5. odium
  6. nausea 7. disgust, opposed
  8. aversion, loathing 9. antipathy,
  hostility 10. abhorrence, antagonism,
  opposition, reluctance
  12. disagreement
repugnant... 6. odious 7. adverse,
  hostile, opposed 8. inimical

9. offensive, repellent, repulsive
10. refractory 11. distasteful
12. incompatible 14. irreconcilable
repulse... 5. repel 6. denial, rebuff
7. refusal 9. rejection
repulsive... 4. ugly, vile 5. nasty
6. odious 7. fulsome 9. offensive,
repellent, resistant, revolting
10. disgusting, forbidding,
malodorous
repurchase... 6. redeem
reputable... 6. worthy 9. estimable,
honorable 10. creditable
11. respectable
reputation... 4. fame, name, note
5. glory, honor 9. celebrity, notoriety
11. distinction 13. consideration
repute... 4. hold, word 5. éclat, honor
6. credit, esteem, regard, report,
revere 8. prestige 9. reputable
10. popularity, reputation
reputed... 6. deemed 7. assumed
8. accepted, presumed, putative,
supposed 10. understood
request... 3. ask, beg 4. plea, pray,
suit 6. appeal, behest, demand
7. entreat, solicit 8. entreaty,
petition, rogation 12. supplication
requiescat in pace... 11. rest in
peace
requiescence... 6. repose
requin... 5. shark 8. man–eater
require... 3. ask 4. need 5. claim,
exact, force 6. charge, compel,
demand, enjoin, entail, oblige
8. obligate 11. necessitate
requisition... 5. order 6. demand
11. application, requirement
requital... 7. payment, revenge
8. reprisal 10. recompense
11. retaliation, retribution
12. compensation
requite... 3. pay 5. atone, repay
6. avenge, return, reward
7. revenge, satisfy 9. retaliate
10. compensate, recompense
11. interchange
reredos... 4. wall 6. screen
9. back–plate (armor), partition
reremouse... 3. bat
res... 5. point, thing 6. matter
rescind... 5. annul 6. cancel, recall,
recant, repeal, revoke 7. abolish
8. abrogate
rescue... 3. aid 4. free, save
6. ransom, redeem, regain 7. deliver,
reclaim, recover, release 8. delivery,
liberate 9. extricate 11. deliverance
rese... 4. rage, rush 5. hurry, onset,
quake, shake 7. impulse, tremble
8. rashness
resemblance... 6. ringer 7. analogy
8. affinity, likeness 9. agreement,
semblance 10. similarity, similitude
resembling (pert to)...
bark.. 11. corticiform
comb.. 8. pectinal
goose.. 8. anserine
gypsum.. 11. alabastrine
horse.. 6. equoid
man.. 7. android
minute animals.. 11. animalcular

rind.. 8. cortical
salt.. 6. haloid
seed.. 6. ovular
snakes.. 7. elapine 8. viperine
star.. 7. stellar 8. stellate 9. stellated
turf.. 5. soddy
wall.. 5. mural
resentment... 3. ire 5. pique, spite
6. choler, enmity, hatred, malice,
rancor 7. dudgeon, umbrage
9. animosity, malignity
11. displeasure, indignation
reservation... 5. tract 8. preserve
9. reticence 10. engagement,
limitation 11. withholding
13. qualification
reserve... 4. bank, fund, keep, save
5. allot, spare, stock, store
6. engage, refuge 7. backlog,
modesty, shyness 8. coldness,
distance, postpone, withhold
9. exception, restraint, retention,
reticence, sanctuary 10. constraint,
diffidence, limitation, substitute
11. self–control, taciturnity
reserved... 3. coy 4. cool, kept, unco
5. aloof, saved, staid, taken
6. modest, sedate 7. distant
8. reticent 15. uncommunicative
reservoir... 4. font, pool, sump
5. store 6. cavity, cenote, supply
7. piscina, reserve 8. fountain
reservoir of Pecquet (Anat)...
12. lymph channel 13. cisterna chyli
res gestae... 5. deeds, facts
8. exploits 10. things done
resiant... 7. present 8. resident
reside... 4. bide, live, room, stay
5. abide, dwell, lodge 6. remain
7. sojourn 8. habitate
residence... 4. home, seat, stay
5. abode 6. palace 7. deanery
8. domicile, dwelling 9. consulate,
residency 10. habitation
residencia... 5. court, trial
resident... 3. cit 6. intern, tenant
7. burgess, citizen 8. diplomat,
occupant 10. inhabitant
residual... 7. remnant 8. residuum
9. remainder
residue... 3. ash, ort 4. coke, dreg,
marc, rest, silt, slag 5. ashes
6. pomace, relics 7. balance,
remains, remnant 8. leavings,
sediment 9. remainder
residuum... 7. residue 8. hangover,
leavings 9. remainder
resign... 4. cede, quit 5. demit, waive,
yield 6. give up, submit 7. abandon,
consign 8. abdicate, renounce
9. surrender 10. relinquish
resignation... 5. demit 8. patience
9. demission, endurance
10. abdication, submission
12. renunciation 14. relinquishment
resigned... 9. contented
10. submissive 11. acquiescent
13. uncomplaining
resilient... 7. buoyant, elastic
8. cheerful 9. recoiling
10. rebounding 11. returning to
12. recuperative

resin... 3. gum, lac 4. aloe, tolu
    5. amber, anime, copal, jalap, rosin
    6. dammar, mastic
resin (pert to)...
    aromatic.. 4. balm 5. elemi, myrrh
      6. balsam 7. acouchi, camphor,
      copaiba 8. sandarac 12. frankincense
    Bib.. 8. bdellium
    bitter.. 8. labdanum (ladanum)
    brown (mineral).. 9. elaterite
    Chian turpentine.. 3. alk
    fossil.. 5. amber, retinite
    gum.. 5. gugal (googul)
    hard.. 5. rosin
    medicinal.. 7. aroeira 9. asafetida
      (asafoetida)
    narcotic.. 6. charas
    pine.. 7. galipot
    soft.. 5. animé, copal, elemi
    translucent.. 8. sandarac
    tropical.. 5. copal
    varnish ingredient.. 6. dammar
    yellowish.. 5. amber 7. gamboge
resinous substance... 3. gum, lac
    5. copal 7. shellac
resist... 4. fend, stem 5. rebel, repel
    6. defeat, oppose 7. prevent, ward
    off 8. outstand 9. withstand
    10. counteract
resistance... 6. rebuff 7. defense
    8. rheostat 9. hostility 10. opposition
resistant... 5. tough 8. obdurate
    9. resisting 10. unyielding
    13. counteractive
resisting... 7. hostile 8. opposing
    9. oppugnant, tenacious
    12. antagonistic
resisting (pert to)...
    description.. 11. indefinable
    power.. 4. wiry
    pressure.. 8. renitent
    pressure bar.. 5. strut
resolute... 4. bold, firm 5. fixed, stern
    6. gritty, steady 7. decided
    8. constant, positive, resolved,
    unshaken 9. desperado, obstinate,
    steadfast 10. determined, inflexible,
    unyielding 11. perseverant,
    persevering
resolution... 4. firm 5. nerve
    6. motion, steady 7. courage,
    purpose, resolve, verdict 8. analysis,
    decision, resolved, strength
    9. assurance, constancy, fortitude
    10. conversion, conviction, relaxation,
    separation 11. persevering
    12. perseverance 13. determination,
    steadfastness 15. disentanglement
resolve... 4. melt 5. lapse (law),
    parse, relax, solve 6. assure, decide,
    dispel, inform, reduce, settle
    7. analyze, explain, purpose, unravel
    8. convince, dissolve, separate
    9. determine, transform
    11. disentangle
resonance... 8. sonority, vibrance
    10. resounding
resonant... 7. echoing, ringing, vibrant
    8. sonorous, sounding
    10. resounding 11. reverberant
resort... 3. spa 4. dive 5. haunt
    6. betake, casino, refuge 7. finagle,

purlieu 8. frequent, recourse,
resource 9. expedient, fainaigue,
honky–tonk
resound... 4. echo, peal, ring 6. be
    loud, re–echo 8. proclaim
    11. reverberate
resounding... 4. loud 13. reverberating
resource... 5. means, skill 6. refuge,
    resort, supply 9. expedient
    10. capability 11. contrivance
resourceful... 5. sharp 9. Daedalian,
    ingenious
resources... 5. funds, means, money
    6. assets, supply 7. resorts
    10. expedients 12. contrivances
respect... 3. awe 4. heed 5. defer,
    favor, honor 6. aspect, detail,
    esteem, homage, regard, repute,
    revere 7. concern, observe, regards
    8. attitude, venerate 9. attention,
    deference, relevance, reverence,
    viewpoint 10. politeness
    13. consideration
respectable... 6. decent 9. estimable,
    honorable, reputable, tolerable
    11. presentable
respectful... 5. civil 6. polite
    7. careful, duteous, heedful
    8. reverent 11. deferential
respective... 6. mutual 7. careful,
    heedful, several, special 9. attentive,
    regardful 10. particular
    12. distributive
respiration... 4. rale, sigh 7. eupnoea
    9. breathing
respire... 7. breathe
respite... 4. rest 5. delay, frist, pause
    6. breath 7. leisure 8. postpone,
    reprieve 9. extension (time)
    10. suspension 11. opportunity,
    short shrift 12. intermission
resplendent... 5. grand 7. aureate,
    radiant, shining 8. lustrous, splendid
    9. beautiful, brilliant, refulgent
    10. epiphanous 11. illustrious
respond... 4. echo 5. react, reply
    6. accord, answer, retort 8. response
    10. correspond 11. reciprocate
response... 4. echo 5. reply
    6. answer, anthem, chorus
    7. rapport, refrain 8. antiphon (Mus),
    reaction
responsibility... 4. care, duty, onus
    6. charge 8. solvency 11. reliability
    14. accountability 15. trustworthiness
responsible... 6. liable 7. solvent
    8. amenable, reliable 10. answerable
    11. accountable, respectable,
    trustworthy
responsive... 6. pliant 7. elastic
    8. reactive 9. answering, sensitive,
    teachable 10. open–minded
    11. persuasible, sympathetic
res publica... 5. state 8. republic
    10. commonweal 12. commonwealth
rest... 3. lay, set, sit 4. base, calm,
    ease, lair, lean, prop, seat, slip, stay,
    stop 5. cease, death, found, pause,
    peace, quiet, relax, renew 6. depend,
    desist, ground, repose, settle
    7. balance, leisure, recline, refresh,
    remains, remnant, reposal, respite,

silence, support, surplus 8. at anchor, interval, lodgment, residuum
9. cessation, quietness, remainder, stillness 10. quiescence, remain idle
12. intermission, peacefulness, tranquillity
rest (pert to)...
assured .. 9. be certain, believe me
at rest .. 4. abed, dead 6. otiose
11. comfortable
day .. 7. Sabbath
foot .. 4. rail 7. hassock, ottoman
house (Orient) .. 5. serai
reading .. 7. caesura (cesura)
restaurant ... 4. café, deli (sl) 5. diner
6. eatery 7. automat, beanery, tearoom 8. fast-food, pizzeria, snack bar 9. cafeteria 10. coffee shop
11. rathskeller 12. luncheonette
resting ... 4. abed 7. dormant
8. drowsing 9. quiescent
resting place ... 4. tomb 5. étape, roost 6. hearth 7. lairage, landing, support 8. quarters
restitution ... 6. return 9. atonement, repayment 10. recompense, reparation 12. compensation
13. reinstatement
restless ... 5. antsy, hyper, itchy
6. roving, uneasy 7. agitato, fidgety, fretful, unquiet, restive, wakeful
8. agitated 9. impatient, sleepless, unceasing, unrestful, unsettled, wandering 10. changeable, reposeless
12. discontented
restoration ... 6. repair, return
7. renewal, revival 8. recovery
10. renovation, reparation
11. improvement, restitution
14. redintegration
15. reestablishment
restorative ... 6. acopon 7. anodyne
8. remedial 10. reparative
restore ... 4. cure, heal 5. renew, repay 6. redeem, refund, repone, revive 7. rebuild, recover, replace
8. renovate 9. reinstate
11. reconstruct, reestablish
12. redintegrate, rehabilitate
restore (pert to)...
after cancelling .. 4. stet
certainty, confidence .. 8. reassure
to former position .. 9. reinstate
to original condition .. 9. refurbish
to proper position .. 5. right
restrain ... 3. dam 4. bate, bind, curb, rein, stay 5. check, cramp, deter, limit, stint 6. arrest, bridle, fetter, halter, hinder, tether 7. abridge, confine, control, inhibit, overawe, qualify, repress 8. restrict, suppress, withhold 9. constrain, detention
restraint ... 3. bit 4. curb, stop
5. check, force 7. durance, modesty, reserve 9. condition, hindrance, reticence 10. abridgment, constraint, inhibition, limitation, moderation, repression, temperance
11. confinement, deprivation, self-control 12. tastefulness
restraint, lack of ... 9. looseness
restrict ... 3. tie 4. bind, curb

5. bound, cramp, limit, scant, stint
6. censor, coerce, modify 7. confine, qualify, repress 10. specialize
12. circumscribe
restricted ... 5. local 6. narrow
7. limited, topical 9. exclusive
10. restrained 11. specialized
restriction ... 5. stint 9. restraint
10. limitation, narrowness, regulation, tightening 11. reservation
12. constriction 13. qualification
resty ... 5. quiet 7. restive 8. sluggish
result ... 3. end, sum 4. rise 5. arise, ensue, event, fruit, issue, total
6. accrue, answer, effect, follow, sequel, spring, upshot 7. proceed, product 8. solution 9. aftermath, deduction, eventuate, terminate
10. conclusion 11. achievement, consequence, termination
resume ... 5. recur, renew 6. reopen
7. recover 8. reoccupy 9. epitomize, reiterate, summarize 10. recommence
résumé ... 8. abstract
10. compendium 11. work history
resurrection ... 6. rising 7. revival
10. apotheosis 11. restoration
resuscitate ... 6. revive 7. restore
8. revivify
ret ... 3. rot 4. soak 5. steep
6. expose, impute 7. ascribe
retable ... 5. ledge, shelf 6. gradin (gradine) 8. predella
retail ... 4. sale, sell 6. repeat
8. dispense, disperse
retain ... 4. hold, keep, save, stet
6. employ 8. maintain, preserve, remember 9. recollect
retainer ... 3. fee 4. cage 6. menial, minion, vassal, yeoman 7. servant
9. attendant, bodyguard
retaining wall ... 9. revetment
retaliate ... 5. repay 6. avenge
7. requite 12. make requital
retaliation ... 6. talion (Mosaic law, eye for eye, tooth for tooth) 7. revenge
8. reprisal, requital 10. punishment
11. comeuppance, retribution
retard ... 4. clog, drag, slow 5. defer, delay, laten 6. belate, deaden, detain, hinder, impede 8. keep back, obstruct, postpone, slow down
retardant ... 4. clog, drag 6. remora
8. obstacle
retardate ... 6. impede 8. retarded
retch ... 3. gag 4. barf (sl), hawk, spit
5. reach, vomit 6. expand, extend, strain 7. stretch, upchuck
rete ... 3. net 6. plexus 7. network
retention ... 6. memory 7. custody, holding, keeping 8. tenacity
11. maintenance, self-control
retentive ... 6. memory 7. keeping
9. tenacious 12. recollective
retenue ... 7. reserve 10. discretion
11. self-control 13. self-restraint
rethe ... 5. cruel 6. ardent, fierce, severe
retiary ... 6. spider 7. netlike
9. gladiator, retiarius
reticence ... 7. reserve, silence
9. restraint 13. secretiveness

reticulated... 3. web 6. meshed, netted 7. network 12. intercrossed
reticule... 3. bag 4. etui 5. cabas (caba) 7. handbag, reticle, workbag
reticulum... 7. network, stomach (2nd) 9. neuroglia
retinue... 4. crew 5. harem, suite, train 6. escort 7. cortege, service 8. equipage 9. entourage, retainers 10. attendants
retire... 6. depart, depose, pay off, recede, vanish 7. go to bed, retreat 8. withdraw 9. disappear, discharge
retired... 4. abed, left, lone, paid 7. receded 8. departed, emeritus, recessed, resigned, secluded, solitary, vanished, withdrew 9. pensioned 10. disengaged 11. disappeared, sequestered
retirement... 7. deposal, payment, privacy, retreat 8. solitude 9. departure, recession, reticence 10. withdrawal 11. resignation 13. disemployment
retiring... 3. shy 6. modest 8. reserved, reticent 9. diffident 10. not forward, retreating 11. unobtrusive
retort... 3. mot 4. quip 5. reply 6. answer 7. riposte (ripost) 8. repartee 9. retaliate 11. retaliation
retract... 6. abjure, disown, draw in, recent, repeal 7. disavow, rescind, swallow 8. take back 9. repudiate
retraction... 6. repeal 8. palinode 10. revocation, withdrawal 11. recantation
retrad... 8. backward 11. posteriorly
retral... 8. backward 9. posterior 10. retrograde
retreat... 3. den 4. abri, lair, nest, nook, rout 6. asylum, recede, recoil, refuge, retire 7. privacy, retiral, sanctum, shelter 8. fallback, solitude 9. departure, katabasis, seclusion 10. retirement, withdrawal
retrench... 6. cut off, excise, lessen, reduce 7. abridge, curtail, cut down 8. decrease, diminish 9. economize, intercept
retrenchment... 3. cut 8. excision 9. lessening, reduction 10. abridgment 11. curtailment, economizing
retribution... 3. pay 6. return, reward 7. nemesis 8. reprisal, requital 9. vengeance 10. punishment 11. restitution 12. Last Judgment
retrieve... 5. fetch 6. redeem, regain, rescue, revive 8. make good
retrograde... 4. slow 6. recede, retral, revert 7. regress 8. backward, decadent, rearward 10. regressive 11. deteriorate 12. reversionary
retroussé... 6. pugged (nose) 8. turned up
retund... 4. beat, dull 5. blunt 6. refute, subdue 9. attenuate, drive back 10. render weak
return... 5. recur, repay, reply 6. answer, render, repeat, report, revert 7. regress, relapse, requiet,

respond, restore 9. repayment 11. restitution, retaliation
return (pert to)...
 day.. 12. answer to writ
 evil for evil.. 7. revenge 9. retaliate
 tennis term.. 3. lob
 thrust (fencing).. 7. riposte (ripost)
 to.. 6. resume 7. relapse, revisit
 to 1st theme (Mus).. 7. reprise
returns... 5. gains, polls 8. receipts
reune... 4. join 7. reunite 10. reassemble
reunion... 7. joining 8. sociable 14. reconciliation
re–up... 8. re–enlist
reus... 9. defendant
Reuter's News Agency... 6. London
reveal... 3. bid 4. bare, jamb, open, tell, wray 6. impart, unveil 7. divulge, exhibit, uncover 8. disclose, discover, evidence, indicate, manifest 11. communicate
reveal (in trust)... 7. confide
reveal intentionally... 4. tell 6. betray, expose 7. divulge, mislead
reveille... 4. call 5. levet 6. signal (sunrise)
revel... 3. joy 4. orgy, riot, wake 5. feast, spree, watch 6. frolic 7. carouse, delight, rejoice, revelry, wassail 8. carousal, festival 11. celebration, merrymaking 12. conviviality
revelant... 5. clear 8. manifest 12. intelligible
revelation... 6. oracle, vision 8. The Bible 9. discovery 10. appearance, disclosure 13. communication, manifestation
Revelation (Bib)... 10. Apocalypse
revelry... 3. joy 4. evoe, orgy, riot 6. revels 8. carnival, carousal 9. revelment, revelrout 11. merrymaking
revenant... 5. ghost 7. eidolon, specter (spectre) 9. recurring 10. apparition
revendicate... 7. reclaim, recover 10. real action
revenge... 6. avenge 7. requite 8. reprisal, requital 9. retaliate, vengeance 10. punishment 11. retribution
revenue... 3. tax 5. yield 6. income, profit 7. annates
reverberate... 4. echo, ring 5. repel, reply 6. return 7. rebound, reflect, resound
reverberation... 4. echo 9. reboation 10. reflection, resounding
revere... 4. love 5. adore, honor 6. esteem, regard, repute 7. respect, worship 8. venerate
reverence... 3. awe 5. dread, honor, piety 7. respect, worship 8. venerate 9. adoration, deference 10. veneration
reverent... 5. pious 6. devout 7. dutiful 10. respectful, worshipful
reverie... 4. muse 5. dream 6. notion, trance, vision 7. fantasy
reversal... 6. defeat, repeal

9. inversion, reversion
14. tergiversation
reverse... 4. back 5. upset 6. back
up, defeat, invert, repeal, revert,
revoke 7. relapse 8. contrary,
converse, opposite, overturn
9. transpose 10. misfortune
reversion... 6. estate 7. revival
8. transfer 9. inversion
10. regression 11. inheritance
reversion (pert to)...
ancestral.. 7. atavism 9. atavistic
insurance.. 7. annuity
land.. 7. escheat
revert... 5. react, recur 6. advert,
return 7. regress, relapse
11. antistrophe
revest... 4. robe 5. dress 6. attire,
clothe 8. reinvest 9. reinstate
review... 4. edit 6. parade, relate,
survey 8. critique, remember
9. criticism, criticize, re–examine
10. certiorati, commentary,
compendium, discussion, inspection,
periodical, reconsider
11. examination, reiteration
12. recollection 15. reconsideration
reviewer... 6. critic, writer
11. commentator
revile... 4. rail 5. abuse, curse
6. berate, debase, vilify 7. asperse
8. reproach, ridicule
revise... 4. edit 5. amend, emend
6. redact 7. correct, rewrite
8. readjust
revision... 7. revisal 10. correction,
emendation 11. rebeholding
13. re–examination
revival... 7. rebirth, renewal
10. quickening 11. reanimation,
renaissance, restoration
12. resurrection
revive... 4. stum (wine) 5. rally,
renew, rouse 6. come to 7. enliven,
recover, refresh, respire, restore
8. rekindle, remember 11. resuscitate
revocate... 6. recall, revoke 7. repress
revocation... 6. repeal 8. reversal
10. retraction, withdrawal
11. recantation
revoke... 5. adeem, annul 6. abjure,
cancel, recall, recant, renege, repeal,
revive 7. abolish, retract 8. abrogate
9. fainaigue 11. countermand
revolt... 5. rebel 6. mutiny, offend,
strike 8. nauseate, sedition, uprising
9. rebellion 10. revolution
12. insurrection
revolting... 4. ugly 7. hideous
8. shocking 9. offensive, repellent
10. disgusting, nauseating
revolution... 4. gyre, turn 5. cycle,
epoch, round 6. revolt 7. circuit
8. disorder, rotation 9. rebellion
revolutionary... 3. new 7. radical
12. catastrophic 15. insurrectionary
Revolutionary hero... 5. Allen (Ethan),
Gates 6. Revere 8. Burgoyne
10. Cornwallis, Washington
15. Lighthorse Harry (Gen Lee)
revolve... 4. pirl, roll, spin, turn
5. recur, wheel, whirl 6. circle,

gyrate, ponder, rotate 7. trundle
8. meditate 9. circulate
10. deliberate
revolver... 3. gat, gun, rod 6. pistol
7. firearm 10. six–shooter
revolving... 3. orb 4. cowl (metal cap)
6. rotary
revolving (pert to)...
in thought.. 8. perusing
light.. 10. lighthouse
part.. 3. cam 5. rotor
storm.. 7. cyclone
revue... 6. medley, review 9. burlesque
13. musical comedy
reward... 3. pay, utu 4. meed
5. award, bonus, merit, Oscar, yield
6. hallow (to hounds) 7. guerdon
8. reprisal 10. recompense,
remunerate 11. retribution
12. compensation, remuneration
reword... 5. alter 7. restate
8. rephrase 9. reiterate
10. paraphrase
rex... 4. king
rey... 4. king
Reynard... 3. fox (epic character)
rezai... 8. coverlet (quilted)
rhamn... 7. Rhamnus 9. buckthorn
rhapontic... 7. rhubarb 8. knapweed,
pieplant
rhapsodic... 6. poetic 8. ecstatic
rhapsodist... 4. poet 8. minstrel
9. visionary 10. enthusiast
rhapsody... 6. jumble, medley
9. utterance (ecstatic) 10. recitation
11. composition
rhea... 3. emu (emeu) 5. nandu
7. ostrich
Rhea (pert to)...
called.. 15. Mother of the Gods
father.. 6. Uranus
home.. 5. Mt Ida (Crete)
mother.. 4. Gaea
mother of.. 4. Hera, Zeus 5. Hades
8. Poseidon
wife of.. 6. Cronus
rhebok... 5. peele 8. antelope
Rheims... see *Reims*
rhema... 4. term, verb, word
rheophile... 15. living in streams
rhetoric... 7. diction, oratory
9. eloquence 11. composition
rhetorical term... 6. aporia, simile
10. antithesis, oratorical
11. catachresis
rhetoric digression... 6. ecbole
rheumatism root... 7. wild yam
rheumatism weed... 10. Indian hemp,
pepsissewa
rhexis... 7. rupture
rhinal... 5. nasal 6. narial
rhine... 5. ditch, drain 6. runnel
Rhine (pert to)...
breed.. 7. rabbits
native.. 11. Rhinelander
nymph.. 7. Lorelei
ref to.. 7. Rhenish
tributary.. 4. Ruhr 6. Neckar
wine.. 7. Moselle
rhino... 4. cash, nose (comb form)
5. money 10. rhinoceros
rhinoceros (pert to)...

Bib .. 4. reem
bird .. 8. hornbill 9. beefeater
black .. 6. borele 7. keitlos
Malay .. 5. abada
viper .. 5. snake (poisonous)
rhizopod ... 6. amoeba 8. Protozoa
Rhoda ... 4. rose
Rhode Island ...
bay .. 12. Narragansett
capital .. 10. Providence
city .. 7. Newport 9. Pawtucket
   10. Woonsocket
famed cotton mill .. 6. Slater
first U.S. synagogue .. 5. Touro
founder .. 13. Roger Williams (1636)
Rebellion .. 5. Dorr's (1842)
resort .. 7. Newport 11. Block Island
river .. 9. Pawtucket 10. Blackstone
settlers .. 8. Puritans
State admission .. 10. Thirteenth
State motto .. 4. Hope
State nickname .. 11. Little Rhody
Rhode Island Red ... 4. fowl
Rhodesia ... see *Zimbabwe*
rhododaphne ... 8. oleander
Rhoeadales ... 5. poppy
   11. Papaverales
rhomb ... 7. rhombus 10. magic wheel
   11. spinning top
rhomboid ... 13. parallelogram
rhombus ... 5. rhomb
   13. parallelogram (equilateral)
Rhone tributary ... 5. Isere
rhubarb ... 5. clash, Rheum 6. hassle
   7. citrine, dispute, yawweed
   8. argument, pieplant 9. rhapontic
   10. discussion
Rhus ... 5. sumac 7. wax tree
rhyme, rime ... 4. poem 6. poetry,
   rhythm 7. measure 9. assonance
rhythm ... 4. beat, lilt 5. meter, pulse,
   swing, tempo 6. poetry 7. cadence,
   euphony, measure, pattern
   8. movement, rhythmus, symmetry
rhythmical break ... 7. caesura
ria ... 5. creek, inlet
rial ... 4. coin, king 5. great, noble,
   royal 6. prince 8. splendid
   9. excellent, stag's horn
   11. magnificent
rialto ... 4. mart 6. Bridge (Venice),
   market 7. theater 8. exchange
riant ... 3. gay 6. blithe, bright
   7. smiling 8. laughing
riata ... 4. rope 5. lasso 6. lariat
rib ... 4. bone, meat, vein 5. costa,
   ridge 6. lierne
ribald ... 3. low 4. lewd. 6. coarse,
   erotic, harlot, risqué, vulgar
   7. obscene 10. scurrilous
   11. blasphemous 12. ribble–rabble
riband ... 6. ribbon
ribbed ... 3. rep 5. piqué 6. corded,
   ridged 7. costate
ribble–rabble ... 6. gabble, rabble,
   ribald 7. chatter 10. incoherent
ribbon ... 3. bow 4. band, sash
   5. strip 6. cestus, fillet, riband
   10. decoration
ribbon (pert to) ...
badge .. 6. cordon
band .. 5. corse 9. banderole

fish .. 7. oarfish 8. dealfish
inked .. 10. typewriter
knot .. 7. rosette
ribbonlike .. 8. taenioid
snake .. 6. garter
Society .. 7. Ireland
worm .. 8. tapeworm 9. nemertine
ribwort ... 8. plantain
rice (pert to) ...
bird .. 4. rail, sora 8. bobolink
dish .. 5. pilaf (pilau, pilaw) 7. risotto
   8. kedgeree 9. jambalaya, ricetable
drink .. 5. bubud
feeding on .. 11. oryzivorous
field .. 5. paddy
hen .. 9. gallinule
inferior .. 4. chit, pago
paste .. 3. ame
rat .. 8. Oryzomys
refuse .. 5. shood (shud)
Spanish .. 5. arroz
wild .. 4. reed
wine .. 4. sake
rich ... 3. fat 5. opime 6. creamy,
   fecund, fruity, mighty, ornate, potent
   7. copious, fertile, moneyed, opulent,
   wealthy 8. abundant, affluent,
   colorful, powerful, resonant, valuable
   9. bountiful, expensive, luxuriant,
   sumptuous 10. in the chips
   13. grandiloquent
rich (pert to) ...
English slang .. 4. oofy 6. oofier
man .. 5. Dives (Bib), Midas, nabob
   7. Croesus 9. plutocrat 10. capitalist
   11. millionaire
richard ... 9. plutocrat
riches ... 5. lucre, means 6. mammon
   (Bib), wealth 7. bonanza, big bucks (sl)
   8. opulence 9. affluence, megabucks
   (sl) 10. prosperity
riches, demon of ... 6. Mammon
rick ... 4. heap, pile 5. noise, scold,
   stack, twist 6. pile up, rattle, sprain,
   wrench 7. chatter
rickets ... 7. disease 8. rachitis
rickety ... 4. weak 5. crazy, shaky
   6. senile 7. unsound 8. unstable,
   unsteady 9. tottering 10. ramshackle
rickle ... 4. heap, pile, rick 5. stack
   6. jingle, rattle
rickrack ... 5. braid 6. edging
   9. insertion
ricksha, rickshaw ... 10. jinrikisha
ricochet ... 5. carom 7. rebound
   10. bounce back
rid ... 4. doff, free, kill 5. clear, empty
   6. remove, rescue 7. deliver, destroy,
   discard 9. dispose of, drive away,
   eliminate 11. disencumber
riddance ... 6. escape 7. discard
   11. elimination 14. relinquishment
riddle ... 3. ree 4. crux, sift 5. rebus,
   sieve 6. enigma, pierce 7. perplex
   8. separate 9. conundrum, perforate
ride ... 4. twit 5. drive, float 6. pester,
   travel 7. be borne, journey, overlap
   8. domineer, ridicule 9. carrousel
   (carousel), cavalcade, excursion
   10. forest road 12. merry–go–round
   13. roller coaster
ride (pert to) ...

herd .. 9. guard over
off .. 4. polo (term)
roughshod over .. 9. tyrannize
shank's mare .. 4. walk
to hog, pig .. 11. boar hunting
to line .. 4. herd
rident ... 5. riant 7. smiling 8. laughing
rider ... 5. ryder 6. clause, knight
  7. allonge, codicil 8. addition,
  horseman 9. performer
  10. freebooter, highwayman
  11. endorsement, mosstrooper
Rider Haggard's novel ... 3. She
ridge ... 3. aas, rib 4. hill, rand, wale,
  weal, welt 5. arête, bulge, chine,
  crest 7. wrinkle
ridge (pert to) ...
  anatomy .. 4. ruga 6. carina
  barrier .. 5. parma
  between furrows .. 7. porcate
  8. porcated
  coral .. 4. reef
  glacial .. 2. os 5. esker (eskar)
  military .. 6. rideau
  mountain .. 4. loma 5. arête 6. sierra
  narrow, raised .. 4. wale
  oak .. 9. blackjack
  raised by stroke .. 5. wheal, whelk
  short .. 4. kame
  sloping .. 6. cuesta
  steep .. 7. hogback
  stony .. 4. rand
  zoology term .. 5. varix
ridicule ... 3. guy, pan 4. butt, gibe,
  jeer, mock, quiz, twit 5. chaff, irony,
  sneer, taunt 6. banter, deride, satire
  7. asteism, mockery, sarcasm
  8. derision, raillery 9. burlesque
ridiculous ... 5. funny 6. absurd
  7. amusing 8. farcical 9. grotesque,
  laughable, ludicrous 10. impossible,
  outrageous 12. preposterous,
  unbelievable
ridiculous failure ... 6. fiasco
riding (pert to) ...
  bitts .. 11. anchor cable
  breeches .. 8. jodhpurs
  dress, costume .. 5. habit
  knot .. 8. slipknot
  rhyme .. 7. couplet
  school .. 6. manège
  whip .. 4. crop 5. quirt
rife ... 7. replete, rumored 8. abundant
  9. abounding, plentiful, prevalent
  10. prevailing, widespread
riff ... 6. rapids, riffle, ripple 7. midriff
  9. diaphragm 13. improvisation
riffle ... 7. shallow, shuffle, wavelet
riffraff ... 3. mob 4. mean 5. offal
  6. rabble, refuse, trashy 7. rubbish
  9. sweepings
rifle ... 3. rob 5. reeve, steal, strip
  6. Mauser, search, snider 7. carbine,
  despoil, firearm, pillage, plunder,
  ransack
rifle (pert to) ...
  accessory .. 6. ramrod
  ball .. 5. Minié 6. bullet
  bird .. 14. bird of paradise
  bomb .. 7. grenade
  French .. 9. chassepot
  old form .. 4. tige

rifler ... 4. hawk 6. robber
rift ... 3. gap, lag 4. rima, rive
  5. break, cleft, split 6. cleave, divide
  10. falling out
rig ... 3. fit 4. gear, suit 5. dress,
  equip 6. lateen 7. bedizen, costume,
  rigging, vehicle 9. Bermudian (Naut)
Riga (pert to) ...
  balsam .. 5. resin (Swiss pine)
  capital of .. 6. Latvia
  native .. 4. Lett 7. Latvian
  rine .. 4. hemp
rigging (ship) ... 4. gear, rope, spar
  6. tackle 9. equipment
right ... 3. fit, pat 4. fair, true
  6. adjust, dexter, proper, remedy
  7. correct, justice, upright
  8. becoming, suitable 9. equitable,
  faultless, franchise, privilege, propriety
  10. put in order 11. appropriate,
  prerogative 13. justification
right (pert to) ...
  angled .. 10. orthogonal
  comb form .. 6. dextro
  exclusive .. 6. patent 10. concession
  hand .. 6. dexter
  hand page .. 5. recto
  law .. 5. droit
  neither right nor wrong ..
  11. adiaphorous
  of belligerent (Naut) .. 6. angary
  of ownership .. 5. title
  of procedure .. 3. pas
  real estate .. 8. easement
  royal .. 7. regalia
  time .. 3. tid
  to choice .. 6. option
  to pasture .. 6. eatage
  turn .. 3. gee
righteous ... 4. holy, just 5. godly,
  moral, pious 6. worthy 7. upright
  8. virtuous 9. believers, blameless,
  equitable, guiltless
righteousness ... 6. equity, virtue
  8. holiness 9. godliness, rectitude
  11. uprightness
rightful ... 4. just, true 5. legal, right
  6. honest, lawful, proper 7. fitting,
  genuine 9. equitable 11. appropriate
rigid ... 3. set 4. firm, hard 5. exact,
  stern, stiff, tense 6. formal, narrow,
  not lax, severe, strict 7. ascetic,
  austere 8. rigorous 9. obstinate,
  stringent, unbending 10. inflexible,
  meticulous, unyielding
rigidity ... 7. tensity 8. hardness,
  severity 9. exactness, obstinacy,
  stiffness
rigol ... 4. ring 6. circle, groove
  7. channel
Rigoletto ... 5. dance, opera (Verdi)
rigor, rigour ... 4. cold, fury 7. cruelty
  8. asperity, rigidity, severity, violence
  9. exactness, harshness, rigidness
  10. shuddering, strictness
  13. inflexibility
rigor mortis ... 10. stiffening (death)
  12. rigor of death
rigorous ... 4. cold 5. exact, harsh,
  rigid, stern, stiff 6. severe, strict
  7. austere, drastic, violent
  8. accurate 9. inclement, obstinate,

puritanic 10. inexorable, inflexible,
relentless
rikk... 10. tambourine
rile... 3. vex 4. roil 5. anger, muddy
6. offend 7. agitate 8. irritate
9. turbidity
rill... 5. brook 6. course, runnel
7. rillock, rivulet 9. streamlet
rim... 3. lip, web 4. band, brim, edge,
orle, tire 5. bezel, brink, felly (felloe),
verge 6. border, flange, margin,
shield 7. enclose, horizon, rimrock
8. boundary 9. perimeter
rima... 5. cleft 7. fissure 8. aperture
10. breadfruit
rima oris... 16. space between lips
rim ash... 9. hackberry
rimate... 8. fissured
rime... 4. hoar, poem, rent 5. chink,
cleft, crack, frost, rhyme 6. poetry
7. fissure 8. aperture 9. assonance,
hoarfrost 10. ladder step
rime—cold giant (Norse)... 4. Ymir
(Ymer)
rimple... 4. fold 6. ripple, rumple
7. wrinkle
rimption... 3. lot 9. abundance
Rinaldo's steed... 6. Bayard
rind... 4. bark, husk, peel, skin
5. crust 6. cortex 7. epicarp
9. hoarfrost
rindle... 5. brook 6. runnel 7. rivulet
ring... 3. rim, set 4. band, halo, hoop,
peal, toll 5. arena, bague, chime,
group, knell 6. circle, clique, collar
7. annulus, circlet, coterie, resound
8. encircle, insignia, ornament,
surround 9. encompass
11. association
ring (pert to)...
  around.. 7. environ
  around the sun.. 6. corona
  barrel.. 4. hoop
  bill.. 4. duck
  bird.. 11. reed bunting
  comb form.. 4. gyro
  dove.. 6. cushat
  finger.. 5. third
  fruit jar.. 4. lute
  gem crown.. 5. bezel
  gem setting.. 6. chaton
  gun carriage.. 7. lunette (lunet)
  harness part.. 6. terret
  horse training.. 5. longe
  Latin.. 7. annulus
  leader.. 6. rouser 9. demagogue
    12. rabble—rouser
  little.. 7. annulet, circlet
  ornament (metal).. 3. bee (angling)
  ouzel.. 6. thrush
  rope.. 7. grommet
  sail.. 4. hank 8. ringtail
  tail.. 3. cat 4. coon 5. lemur
    6. godwit, marlin 10. cacomistle
    11. golden eagle (young)
ringed boa... 5. aboma
ringed worm... 7. annelid
ringhals... 5. snake (spitting)
ringing... 7. clangor, orotund, pealing,
tolling 8. clanging, resonant
10. resounding
ringle—eye... 7. walleye

ringlet... 4. curl, lock 5. tress
6. circle 7. circlet 9. fairy ring
ringworm... 5. tinea 6. tetter
7. disease, serpigo 9. millepede
rink... 4. hero, race, ring 6. circle,
course 7. warrior 8. encircle, ice
sheet (skating) 9. encounter
rinse... 4. lave, sind, wash 5. flush
6. sluice 7. cleanse 8. absterge
rinthereout, rintherout (Scot)...
5. tramp 7. vagrant 8. vagabond
rio... 5. river 6. coffee, stream
Rio de Janeiro... 7. capital (old, Braz)
Rio Grande... 5. river 7. disease
(lettuce)
riot... 3. din 5. brawl, melee
6. clamor, excess, pogrom, revolt,
tumult, uproar 7. dispute, quarrel,
revelry 8. carousal, disorder, violence
9. commotion
riotous... 4. raid 5. aroar 6. wanton
7. violent 9. dissolute, luxuriant,
seditious 10. profligate, tumultuous
12. unrestrained
riotous jollity... 9. dissolute
11. saturnalian
rip... 3. cut 4. rend, rent, tear
5. break, horse (old) 7. riptide
9. debauchee, libertine, reprobate
10. fish basket, laceration
ripe... 3. fit 5. ready, rife 6. mature,
mellow 7. plunder 8. finished,
prepared, rareripe 9. developed,
full—grown, perfected
10. consummate
ripen... 3. age 5. addle 6. digest,
mellow, nature 7. develop, perfect,
prepare 8. complete, grow ripe
riposte, ripost... 5. reply 6. answer,
retort, thrust 8. repartee
ripping... 5. bully, grand, swell
9. admirable, hunky—dory 12. fine
and dandy
rippit... 9. fist fight
ripple... 3. cut, lap 4. fret, purl, riff,
tear, wave 5. acker, eagre, graze
6. dimple, murmur 7. crinkle,
disturb, scratch, trickle, wavelet
11. corrugation
ripple grass plantain... 7. ribwort
ris de veau... 10. sweetbread
rise... 4. grow, soar, well 5. arise,
begin, climb, get up, mount, raise,
reach, rebel, start, surge, tower
6. ascend, ascent, attain, be high,
emerge, growth, height, revolt,
spring, thrive 7. succeed
8. eminence, flourish, increase,
levitate, reaction 9. acclivity,
ascension, beginning, elevation,
originate 11. development
rise (pert to)...
  above.. 4. loom 8. surmount
    11. triumph over
  again.. 7. resurge 11. resurrected
  and fall of the sea.. 5. scend, tidal
    6. welter
  by buoyancy.. 8. levitate
  gradually.. 4. loom
  hawk's.. 6. mounty
  high.. 5. tower
risible... 5. funny 6. absurd

9. laughable

rising... 6. ascent, ortive, revolt
7. growing, montant, sloping, surgent
8. elevated, emergent, gradient (by
degrees), swelling 9. acclivity,
advancing, ascending, ascension
rising and falling... 5. tidal 7. surging
8. undulant
risk... 4. dare 5. peril 6. chance,
danger, expose, gamble, hazard,
injury, plight 7. venture 8. endanger
10. investment 12. disadvantage
risky... 6. risqué 9. hazardous
11. venturesome
risp... 3. rub 4. file, rasp, tirl 5. stalk
7. bulrush, scratch
risper... 11. caterpillar
risqué... 4. racy 5. risky, salty
8. off–color 9. hazardous
10. suggestive
rissle... 4. pole 5. staff, stick
risus... 5. laugh 8. laughter
rit (rare)... 3. cut, rip 4. slit, tear
5. split 6. pierce 7. scratch
ritardando... 9. direction, retarding
10. slackening 11. rallentando
rite... 4. cult, form 6. ritual, sacrum
7. formula, liturgy, tonsure
8. ceremony 9. solemnity
10. ceremonial, initiation, observance
12. patriarchate
ritratto... 7. picture 8. portrait
Ritter... 6. knight
ritual... 4. book, code, cult, form, rite
5. feast, salat 6. novena, prayer
7. liturgy 8. ceremony
10. ceremonial
ritus... 5. usage 6. custom
ritzy... 5. smart (vulgarly), swank
6. swanky 11. pretentious
16. ultra–fashionable
rivage... 4. bank, duty 5. coast, green,
shore
rival... 3. foe, vie 4. even, peer
5. excel, match 7. compete, emulate
8. emulator, opponent
10. antagonist, competitor
11. compete with
rivalry... 4. feud 9. emulation
11. competition
rive... 3. rip 4. bank, open, rent, rift,
tear 5. cleft, sever, shore, split
6. cleave 8. lacerate
rive droite... 9. Right Bank (Seine)
rive gauche... 8. Left Bank (Seine,
Paris, including Latin Qtr)
rivel... 6. shrink 7. shrivel, wrinkle
river... 2. ea 3. ria, rio, run 4. ilog
5. amnis, brook, creek 6. stream
7. rivulet, torrent 8. riverlet
9. streamlet
river (pert to)...
arm (of sea).. 7. estuary
bank.. 4. ripa 5. levee
bank, pert to.. 8. riparian
bed.. 4. holm 6. alveus, bottom
7. channel
bend.. 5. oxbow
boat.. 3. ark
delta branch.. 5. bayou
dog.. 10. hellbender
dragon.. 9. crocodile

duck.. 4. teal
fish (spawning, from sea)..
10. anadromous
horse.. 5. hippo 12. hippopotamus
inlet.. 4. slew 5. fiord (fjord)
6. slough
islet.. 3. ait 4. holm
mouth.. 4. lade 5. delta 7. estuary
mussel.. 4. unio
Near East.. 4. wadi (wady)
Nile measure.. 9. Nilometer
nymph.. 4. nais 5. naiad
rat.. 5. thief
ref to.. 5. amnic
region (near).. 8. riverine
siren.. 7. Lorelei
thief.. 3. rat 6. ackman
winding.. 3. ess
river in...
Africa.. 4. Nile, Tana 5. Niger
Austria.. 4. Iser 5. Drava
Bavaria.. 4. Eger, Isar
Belgium.. 4. Yser
Bohemia.. 4. Elbe, Iser
Brazil.. 3. Rio
Bulgaria.. 5. Mesta
China.. 3. Wei 6. Yellow 7. Hwang
Ho
England.. 4. Isis 6. Thames
France.. 5. Seine
Germany.. 6. Danube
Italy.. 4. Arno 5. Tiber
Netherlands.. 3. Eem 4. Maas
(Meuse)
S America.. 6. Amazon
Siberia.. 2. Ob 4. Lena
Switzerland.. 3. Aar 5. Reuss
river of...
Annie Laurie.. 4. Nith
Caesar.. 7. Rubicon
lower regions.. 4. Styx 5. Lethe
7. Acheron
woe.. 7. Acheron
rixy... 4. tern
road... 3. via, way 4. iter, path, raid
5. agger 7. estrada, highway,
journey, passage 8. pavement
9. incursion, roadstead
10. expedition
road (pert to)...
block.. 3. dam 4. weir
goose.. 5. brant
hog.. 8. motorist 10. monopolist
horse.. 6. saddle (horse)
impassable.. 7. impasse
man.. 7. drummer, peddler
8. salesman 9. canvasser
map.. 5. chart, globe 9. directory
master.. 10. supervisor
11. trackmaster
nautical.. 9. roadstead
no outlet.. 8. cul–de–sac
paving.. 6. Tarmac 7. ballast,
macadam
runner.. 6. cuckoo
scraper.. 4. harl
weed.. 8. plantain
roam... 2. go 3. err, gad 4. rove
5. prowl, range 6. ramble, stroll,
wander 7. meander 9. gallivant
roan... 3. horse (bay, gray, chestnut)
8. antelope 9. sheepskin, yellow–red

roanoke... 6. wampum
Roanoke...
city.. 8. Virginia
famed as.. 11. First Colony (1584)
famed for.. 12. Virginia Dare (1st white child, 1587)
settler.. 16. Sir Walter Raleigh 19. Sir Richard Grenville
roar... 4. bell, blow, boom, rote (surf) 5. brool, laugh, shout 6. bellow, steven 7. ululate 8. cry aloud 9. loud sound
roaring... 5. aroar, great 7. booming, riotous 10. disorderly
Roaring (pert to)...
Forties.. 8. Broadway (NYC)
game.. 7. curling (Scot)
Twenties.. 14. Golden Twenties 16. Age of Red Hot Mamas
roast... 4. beef, cook 5. cabob, parch 6. assate, banter 7. torrefy 8. ridicule 9. criticize
roasting (pert to)...
ear.. 4. corn
jack.. 9. smokejack
stick.. 4. spit
rob... 4. loot, pelf 5. pinch (sl), reave, rifle, steal, touch 6. pilfer, ravish, snatch, snitch 7. despoil, pillage, plunder 10. plagiarize
robbed... 5. stole 6. rubato (Mus) 8. snatched, snitched
robber... 4. yegg 5. crook (sl), thief 6. bandit, reaver, rifler 7. brigand, burglar, yeggman 8. pillager 9. despoiler, embezzler, larcenist, peculator 10. depredator, highwayman, shoplifter
robber (pert to)...
grave.. 5. ghoul
high seas.. 6. pirate 7. corsair 9. privateer
highway.. 7. footpad, ladrone
Indian.. 6. dacoit
robbery... 4. reif 5. theft 6. burgle, piracy 7. larceny, pillage, plunder 8. burglary 10. spoliation 11. depredation
robe... 5. array, cover, dress, tunic 6. invest, mantle 7. costume, garment 8. clerical, vestment
robe (pert to)...
bishop's.. 6. chimer
camel's hair.. 3. aba
long.. 5. talar
loose.. 5. cymar (symar)
royal.. 6. ermine, purple
robin... 4. bird, lout, tody 6. thrush 7. bumpkin 8. trimming 9. redbreast 10. toxalbumin
robin (pert to)...
dipper.. 14. bufflehead duck
runaway.. 7. dewdrop
sandpiper.. 4. knot 5. snipe 9. dowitcher
songbird.. 8. accentor
Robin Bluestring... 13. Robert Walpole
robinet... 6. cannon 9. chaffinch
Robin Goodfellow... 4. Puck 6. sprite 9. hobgoblin
Robin Hood (pert to)...

famed as.. 6. archer, outlaw, yeoman
followers.. 9. Friar Tuck 10. Little John, Maid Marian
forest.. 8. Sherwood (Eng)
habit.. 11. robbing rich (for the poor)
Robinson Crusoe's man... 6. Friday
roborant... 4. drug 5. tonic 6. bracer 8. pick—me—up 9. stimulant
roborean... 5. oaken, stout 6. strong
robot... 9. automaton
Rob Roy... 5. canoe 6. outlaw (Scot) 15. Robert MacGregor
robust... 4. hale 5. hardy, lusty, rough, sound, stout, wally 6. hearty, sinewy, strong, sturdy 7. healthy 8. muscular, vigorous
roc... 4. bird (Arabian Nights) 7. simurgh (simurg)
rocca... 4. hold 6. donjon 8. fortress
rock... 3. orc 4. lull, peak, sway, trap, tufa, tuff 5. agate, chert, cliff, quiet, shake, slate, stone 6. basalt, egeran, gneiss, refuge, schist, teeter 7. diamond, missile 8. dolomite, porphyry, strength 9. whinstone 10. promontory
rock (pert to)...
black.. 6. basalt
brittle.. 5. shale
broken.. 4. sand 5. attle
cavity.. 5. druse
chain.. 4. reef
coarse.. 8. psammite, psephite
crystal.. 6. silica
crystalline.. 6. gneiss, schist
decomposed.. 6. gossan
fluid.. 4. lava
fragments.. 5. scree 8. detritus, xenolith
geyser deposit.. 6. sinter
glacial.. 7. moraine
granitelike.. 6. gneiss
granular.. 6. oolite, quartz 7. diorite 10. rockallite
gray.. 5. slate 8. andesite
igneous.. 4. boss, trap 6. basalt 7. peridot
jutting.. 3. tor 4. crag
nodule.. 5. geode
pinnacle.. 4. scar 6. needle
porous.. 4. tufa, tuff
rounded.. 6. rognon
science.. 9. petrology
Sicilian.. 6. Scylla (opp Charybdis)
stratified.. 5. shale
suffix.. 3. ite, yte
volcanic.. 4. tufa 6. basalt, domite, latite
rock, animal...
badger.. 4. cony
cavy.. 6. rodent
dassie.. 6. rabbit
goat.. 4. ibex
kangaroo.. 7. wallaby
squirrel.. 11. spermophile
rock, bird...
blackbird.. 9. ring ouzel
dove.. 9. guillemot 10. rockpigeon
duck.. 9. harlequin
goose.. 9. kelp goose
grouse.. 9. ptarmigan
hawk.. 6. falcon, merlin

hopper.. **7.** penguin
lark.. **5.** pipit
pigeon.. **10.** sand grouse
sandpiper.. **5.** pipit, snipe
shrike.. **10.** rock thrush
starling.. **5.** ouzel
swallow.. **10.** rock martin
rock, fish...
  bass.. **5.** black **7.** striped
  clam.. **5.** borer
  cod.. **7.** grouper
  cook.. **6.** wrasse **7.** whiting
  eel.. **6.** gunnel
  gurnet.. **9.** fortescue
  hind.. **7.** grouper (spotted)
  lobster.. **8.** crayfish
  salmon.. **7.** codfish **9.** amberfish
  sucker.. **7.** lamprey
  trout.. **9.** greenling
rock, flora...
  bell.. **9.** columbine
  brake.. **8.** polypody
  candytuft.. **8.** gold–dust
  cedar.. **7.** juniper
  cranberry.. **8.** mountain
  elm.. **11.** slippery elm
  garden.. **6.** alpine
  geranium.. **8.** alumroot
  hair.. **6.** lichen
  lily.. **9.** columbine **12.** pasqueflower
  maple.. **5.** sugar
  melon.. **10.** cantaloupe
  shrub.. **9.** buckthorn
rocket... **5.** lance **6.** ascend, ascent,
  fire at **8.** aircraft, firework
  9. skyrocket, spaceship
rocket (famed)... **5.** Titan **6.** Apollo,
  Gemini, Saturn **7.** Jupiter, Mercury
  8. Redstone
Rock of Chickamauga... **6.** Thomas
  (Gen), (Civil War)
rocks... **5.** money
rocks, on the... **7.** aground
  8. bankrupt, stranded **10.** saxicoline
rocky... **4.** hard **5.** stony **6.** rugged
  7. sickish **8.** obdurate, unsteady
  9. unfeeling
Rocky Ford... **9.** muskmelon
Rocky Mountain...
  group.. **5.** Coast **8.** Cascades
  12. Sierra Nevada
  park.. **5.** Estes
  peak.. **6.** Elbert **8.** McKinley
  popular name.. **7.** Rockies
  range.. **5.** Teton, Uinta
rococo... **6.** florid **7.** baroque, bizarre
  9. fantastic, grotesque
  13. ornamentation
rod... **3.** gat, gun **4.** pole, wand, whip
  5. baton, perch, power, scion, staff
  7. measure, scepter
rod (pert to)...
  comb form.. **5.** rhabd **6.** rhabdo
  fibrous.. **5.** lytta
  flat.. **6.** ferula, ferule
  grooved.. came (stained glass)
  knitting.. **6.** needle
  meat–holding.. **4.** spit
  mechanical.. **6.** piston
  metal.. **7.** stemmer
  mixing.. **3.** rab
  pointed.. **4.** goat, spit

rodlike.. **9.** vergiform
rotating.. **7.** spindle
short.. **6.** toggle
spinning.. **7.** spindle
rodd... **8.** crossbow, stonebow
rodent... **4.** cony, hare, paca **5.** hutia
  (jutia), mouse, stoat **6.** agouti
  (agouty), beaver, gerbil, gopher,
  marmot, murine **7.** lemming, leveret
  8. chipmunk, hedgehog, mongoose,
  squirrel **9.** guinea pig, porcupine
rodent (pert to)...
  Andes.. **8.** abrocome
  aquatic.. **6.** beaver **7.** muskrat
  Belgian.. **8.** leporide
  burrowing.. **6.** marmot **8.** sewellel
  disease.. **9.** tularemia
  European.. **4.** cony **5.** lerot
  fur–bearing.. **6.** beaver
  genus.. **3.** Mus **5.** Lepus
  gnawing.. **3.** rat **4.** mole
  hare.. **6.** rabbit
  jumping.. **6.** jerboa
  largest.. **8.** capybara (capibara)
  migrating.. **7.** lemming
  Mongoloid.. **3.** rat **6.** gopher
  12. pocket gopher
  mouselike.. **4.** vole
  rabbitlike.. **4.** pika
  reference to.. **7.** gnawing **8.** rosorial
  S American.. **4.** degu **5.** coypu
  6. agouti **8.** capybara **10.** chinchilla
  spiny.. **9.** porcupine
rodeo... **4.** show **7.** roundup
  9. spectacle **11.** performance (public)
rodomontade... **4.** brag, rant **5.** boast
  7. bluster **8.** boastful, boasting,
  braggart, bragging
roe... **2.** ra **3.** doe **4.** deer, hind, raun
  5. coral (lobster) **8.** fish eggs
Roentgen, Röntgen (Wilhelm)...
  famed as.. **9.** physicist
  famed for.. **5.** X–rays **10.** Nobel Prize
  (1901) **12.** Roentgen rays
rogan... **4.** bowl (wooden)
  10. receptacle (maple sap)
Roger's plane (Will)... **9.** Winnie May
rogue... **3.** imp, wag **4.** kite **5.** cheat,
  knave, scamp, shark, tramp
  6. beggar, pirate, rascal **7.** corsair,
  vagrant, villain **8.** elephant, picaroon,
  vagabond **13.** mischief–maker
roguish... **3.** sly **4.** arch **5.** pawky
  7. knavish **8.** espiegle, rascally
  10. frolicsome, picaresque
  11. mischievous
roguishly... **5.** slyly **8.** impishly, trickily
  10. prankishly
roid... **5.** rough **6.** severe **7.** riotous
  10. frolicsome **12.** unmanageable
roil... **3.** vex **4.** foul, roam, romp
  5. anger, annoy, horse (Flemish),
  muddy **6.** fidget, ruffle, wander
  7. agitate, disturb **8.** irritate
roister... **4.** brag, rude **5.** bully
  7. bluster, boorish, swagger, violent
  9. gilravage
roisterer (Hist)... **3.** mun
rojo... **3.** Red **6.** Indian (Mex)
  7. Redskin
roke... **3.** fog **4.** stir **5.** moist, smoke,
  steam, vapor **8.** moisture

roker... 3. ray 8. rockling 9. thornback
roky... 4. damp 5. foggy, misty, smoky
   6. hoarse
role... 4. duty, part 6. office
   8. capacity, function 9. character
   13. impersonation
roll... 3. bun, rob 4. coil, film, food,
   furl, list, pell, rota, sway, wind, wrap
   5. trill, troll 6. billow, bundle, rotate,
   rumble, scroll 8. bankroll, cylinder,
   rotation
roll (pert to)...
  along.. 7. trundle
  back.. 6. reduce 8. retrench
  bread.. 3. bap
  butter.. 3. pat
  cloth.. 4. bolt
  coins.. 7. rouleau
  fish.. 7. rissole
  hair.. 3. rat 7. chignon
  military.. 5. cadre 6. roster
  the bones.. 4. dice 10. shoot craps
  tobacco.. 5. cigar
  to one side.. 5. lurch
  up.. 4. furl 6. bundle 10. accumulate
roller... 4. wave 5. inker, skate, towel
   6. canary, caster, fillet, pigeon,
   platen 7. bandage, rotator, sirgang
   8. cylinder 10. Holy Roller, pulverizer
rolling (pert to)...
  movement.. 6. welter
  pin.. 6. roller 8. cylinder
  stock.. 7. coaches, engines
   8. cabooses, Pullmans 9. motor cars
   11. locomotives
  stone.. 8. wanderer
  weed.. 10. tumbleweed
rollix... 4. play 6. frolic 7. rollick
romaine... 10. cos lettuce
romal... 5. quirt, thong
Roman... 5. brave, Latin 6. frugal,
   honest, simple 7. Italian
Roman (pert to)... see also *Rome*
  afterpiece (theater).. 5. exode, farce
   8. travesty
  alcove.. 8. tablinum
  apostle (Bib).. 4. Neri
  assembly.. 5. forum 7. comitia
  augur.. 6. auspex
  awning.. 8. velarium
  barrack, hut.. 6. canaba (cannaba)
  basilica.. 7. Lateran
  booth, shelter.. 7. taberna
  bowl.. 6. patina
  boxing glove.. 6. cestus
  breastplate.. 6. lorica
  bronze.. 3. aes
  building.. 5. aedes (worship)
  case.. 5. bulla (for amulets)
  cathedral.. 7. Lateran
  chariot.. 5. essed (esseda)
  chest.. 4. cist
  circus post.. 4. meta
  circus wall.. 5. spina
  cistern.. 9. impluvium
  citadel.. 3. arx
  citizen (nonvoting).. 8. aerarian
  clan.. 4. gens
  cloak.. 5. sagum (Mil) 6. abolla
   7. planeta
  concert hall.. 5. odeum
  court (Pope's).. 5. Curia

  cuirass.. 6. lorica
Curia office.. 6. datary 7. dataria
date.. 4. ides 5. nones 7. calends
dish.. 6. patera
division (Polit).. 5. curia
earthwork (Mil).. 5. agger
Empire district.. 5. Pagus
era.. 5. Varro
farce.. 5. exode
festival days.. 5. feria 10. feriae Jovi
   (festivals of Jupiter)
fish sauce.. 4. alec 5. garum
foot coverage, sock.. 3. udo
galley.. 6. bireme 7. trireme
garment.. 4. toga 5. palla, stole,
   tunic
general's cloak.. 12. paludamentum
   (paludament)
Govt of two men.. 10. duumvirate
Hades.. 5. Orcus 10. lower world
hairpin.. 4. acus
hall (concert).. 5. odeum
helmet.. 5. galea
highway.. 3. via 4. iter
highway, famed.. 9. Appian Way
hills.. 7. Viminal 8. Aventine, Palatine,
   Quirinal 9. Esquiline 10. Capitoline
javelin.. 5. pilum
land (public).. 4. ager
language.. 5. Latin
law.. 3. jus 4. cern
law, divine.. 3. fas
market day.. 7. nundine
marriage.. 13. confarreation
matron's garment.. 5. stola, stole
meal (chief).. 4. cena (coena)
military cloak.. 5. sagum
military machine.. 7. terebra
military unit.. 6. legion 7. maniple
money.. 3. aes
ornament (neck).. 5. bulla
palace.. 7. Lateran
peace.. 3. pax
provisions (free).. 6. annona
ram (battery).. 5. aries
religious law.. 3. fas
religious rite.. 5. sacra
road.. 4. iter 6. Appian (paved)
robe.. 4. toga
room.. 3. ala 6. atrium 8. tablinum
seat.. 5. sella
shelter, shop.. 7. taberna
shield.. 6. scutum
soldier's protection.. 7. testudo
spirits (group).. 5. manes 7. lemures
tablet (writing).. 7. diptych
temple.. 4. naos 5. cella
tent.. 7. taberna
theater.. 5. odeum
travesty.. 5. exode
vase.. 7. amphora (wine) 8. murrhine
warship.. 6. bireme 7. trireme
Way (famed).. 6. Appian
wine shop.. 7. taberna
romance... 5. fancy, novel, story
   7. fantasy, fiction, romanza, romaunt
   8. idealize 9. falsehood, sentiment
   11. imagination
romance (pert to)...
  language.. 6. French 7. Catalan,
   Italian, Spanish 9. Provençal
   10. Portuguese

ref to.. **8**. knightly **10**. chivalrous
verse.. **7**. sestina
Roman god (of)...
chief.. **4**. Jove **7**. Jupiter
dead.. **5**. Orcus
fire.. **6**. Vulcan
Hades.. **3**. Dis **5**. Pluto **8**. Dispater
households.. **5**. Lares **7**. Penates
husbandry, animals.. **6**. Faunus
love.. **4**. Amor **5**. Cupid
mirth.. **5**. Comus
sun.. **3**. Sol
Supreme.. **4**. Jove **7**. Jupiter
two–faced.. **5**. Janus
underworld.. **3**. Dis **5**. Pluto
   8. Dispater
war.. **4**. Mars **8**. Quirinus
Roman goddess (of)...
agriculture.. **3**. Ops **5**. Ceres
beauty.. **5**. Venus
burials.. **8**. Libitina
childbirth.. **6**. Lucina
crops.. **6**. Annona
dawn.. **6**. Aurora
earth.. **6**. Tellus
fertility.. **6**. Annona
handicrafts.. **7**. Minerva
harvests.. **3**. Ops
health.. **7**. Minerva
hearth.. **5**. Vesta
horses.. **5**. Epona
love.. **5**. Venus
moon.. **4**. Luna **7**. Phoebus
mothers, nursing.. **6**. Rumina
night.. **3**. Nox
peace.. **3**. Pax **5**. Irene
religion.. **4**. Maia
strife.. **9**. Discordia
victory (war).. **6**. Vacuna
womanhood.. **4**. Juno
Roman people...
author.. **5**. Pliny, Varro
biographer.. **5**. Nepos
Bishop.. **4**. Pope
boy (free birth).. **8**. camillus
Catholic priest.. **8**. sacerdos
Catholic Society.. **6**. Jesuit
consul.. **6**. Scipio
Cupid.. **4**. Eros
deity.. **4**. faun
Diana.. **7**. Artemis
dictator.. **5**. Sulla **11**. Cincinnatus
diviner.. **5**. augur **6**. auspex
divinity (chief).. **4**. Jove
Emperor.. **4**. Nero, Otto **5**. Titus
   7. Maximus **8**. Tiberius
   11. Constantine **12**. Heliogabalus
Eros.. **5**. Cupid
farmer.. **7**. colonus
Fates.. **4**. Nona **5**. Morta **6**. Decuma
General.. **5**. Sulla, Titus **6**. Antony,
   Marius, Scipio
ghosts.. **7**. lemures
gladiator.. **7**. Samnite **9**. retiarius
gladiator trainer.. **7**. lanista
governor.. **9**. proconsul
guard.. **6**. lictor
historian.. **4**. Livy **5**. Nepos **7**. Sallust
   8. Appianus (Appian)
judge.. **6**. aedile (edile)
king (1st).. **7**. Romulus
king's adviser (Myth).. **6**. Egeria

magistrate, official.. **5**. augur **6**. aedile
   (edile), censor, consul **7**. praetor
   (pretor), tribune
maiden, betrayer to Sabrines..
   7. Tarpeia
military officer.. **9**. proconsul
Naturalist.. **5**. Pliny
nun.. **6**. vestal
nymph (fountain).. **6**. Egeria
officer.. **6**. lictor **8**. triumvir (one of
   three)
official of public games.. **7**. Asiarch
orator.. **5**. Pliny **6**. Cicero
palace officer.. **8**. palatine
patriot.. **4**. Cato
people (anc).. **7**. Sabines **8**. Samnites
   9. plebeians **10**. patricians
philosopher.. **4**. Cato **6**. Seneca
   7. Rosmini
physician.. **11**. Aesculapius
poet.. **4**. Ovid **5**. Lucan **6**. Horace,
   Vergil **7**. Juvenal (satirical)
politician, courtier.. **7**. Sejanus
priest.. **5**. epulo **8**. tresviri (10 in all)
   9. decemviri **10**. septemviri
priest, serving a god.. **6**. flamen
priestess.. **6**. vestal
priests of Faunus.. **7**. Luperci
race (conquered).. **6**. Sabine
saint.. **4**. Neri
scholar.. **5**. Varro
serf.. **6**. colona (fem) **7**. colonus
   (male)
slave (befriended lion).. **9**. Androcles
soldiers (body of).. **6**. cohort
statesman.. **4**. Cato **6**. Caesar, Cicero,
   Seneca
Tarquin rulers.. **9**. Etruscans
tenant farmer.. **7**. colonus
triumvirate, first.. **6**. Caesar, Pompey
   7. Crassus
triumvirate, second.. **6**. Antony
   7. Lepidus **8**. Octavius
troops.. **6**. alares
tyrant.. **4**. Nero
virgin.. **6**. vestal
writer (comic).. **7**. Terence
Romany, Rommany... **5**. gypsy
   10. mascot blue
Rome...
cathedral (world's largest).. **8**. St
   Peter's
churches.. **7**. Lateran **8**. Castello,
   Gandolfo
conqueror.. **6**. Alaric
founder (legendary).. **7**. Romulus
hills.. **5**. Seven **6**. Sabine **7**. Viminal
   8. Aventine, Palatine, Quirinal
lake.. **4**. Nemi
original city.. **12**. Roma Quadrata
palace (world's largest).. **7**. Vatican
peak (Capitoline).. **8**. Tarpeian
port (anc).. **5**. Ostia
prairie.. **8**. Campagna
river.. **5**. Tiber
seat of.. **7**. Holy See **11**. Vatican City
site, ancient.. **13**. Campus Martius
site, founding.. **12**. Palatine Hill
street (famed).. **5**. Corso
Romulus (pert to)...
brother.. **5**. Remus
city site.. **12**. Palatine Hill

father.. 4. Mars
founder (Myth).. 4. Rome
king (1st).. 4. Rome
mother.. 6. Sylvia
rescued from.. 5. Tiber
suckled by.. 7. she–wolf
ronde... 6. script (heavy) 9. round
hand
rondeau... 4. game, poem 5. rondo
6. rondel
rondel, rondelle... 4. poem 5. tower
(Fort) 8. round gem
rondure... 9. plumpness, roundness
ronier... 7. palmyra
ronin... 6. outlaw 7. outcast, samurai
rood... 5. cross (holy), goose
7. measure 8. crucifix
roodebok... 6. impala 9. duikerbok
roof... 3. hip 4. dome, eave, flat,
nave, tile 5. cover, gable, slate, spire
6. cupola, lean–to 7. chopper,
gambrel, mansard, pitched, shingle
8. housetop, thatched 9. penthouse
10. jerkinhead
roof (pert to)...
boards (thin).. 4. sark
brain cover.. 4. tela 14. telachorioidea
frame (raised).. 7. coaming
material.. 3. tin 4. tile 5. paper, slate
6. copper, shakes 7. roofage
8. shingles
mouth.. 6. palate
ornament.. 3. epi
tile.. 7. pantile
timber.. 6. rafter
tin (coating).. 5. terne
tool.. 3. zax
Roof of the World, Asia... 6. Pamirs
(The) 9. Bam i Dunya
rook... 4. bird, crow, dupe 5. cheat
6. castle 7. defraud, sharper
8. chessman 9. ruddy duck
rookery... 4. slum 9. confusion
13. breeding place (rooks, herons,
penguins) 14. breeding ground (seals)
rookie, rooky... 6. novice 7. recruit
8. beginner, newcomer
rooky... 4. roky 5. foggy
room... 3. ala (anc), den 4. aula, cell,
hall, sala, seat, shed 5. attic, lodge,
place, salon, scope, space 6. cellar,
leeway, pantry, parlor, reside
7. chamber, drawing, laundry,
nursery, quarter 8. capacity
9. apartment, storeroom
11. opportunity
room (pert to)...
church (bishop's).. 4. apse
convent.. 9. parlatory
dining.. 7. cenacle, dinette
9. refectory
harem.. 3. oda
household.. 5. ewery
inner.. 3. ben
large.. 4. aula, hall 7. rotunda,
theater 10. auditorium
monastery.. 4. cell
outer.. 3. but
pantry.. 6. larder 8. cupboard
prayer.. 7. oratory
Pueblo Ind ceremonial.. 4. kiva
Roman.. 6. atrium

ship's.. 4. brig 5. cabin, salon
sleeping.. 5. lodge 6. dormer
7. barrack, bedroom, chamber
9. dormitory
tower (bell).. 6. belfry
roomy... 4. airy 5. ample 8. spacious
9. capacious, expansive
10. commodious 11. large–framed
roon... 5. shred 6. border 7. darling
8. treasure
roorback, roorbach... 3. lie 6. canard
7. lampoon 9. falsehood
roose... 5. boast, vaunt 6. praise
Roosevelt...
president, 26th.. 8. Theodore
president, 32nd.. 8. Franklin
roost... 3. bed, sit 4. jouk, pole, rest
5. perch 6. settle 7. lodging,
support
rooster... 4. cock, male (animal)
5. gallo 7. percher 11. chanticleer
12. fighting cock
root... 4. bulb, word 5. cheer, plant,
radix, tuber 6. source 7. radical
8. take root 9. establish
root (pert to)...
aromatic.. 9. sassafras
edible.. 3. oca, yam 4. beet, eddo,
taro 6. carrot, potato, radish, turnip
7. parsnip 8. rutabaga
food (Maori).. 3. roi
medicinal.. 4. atis 5. jalep 6. ipecac,
senega 7. Senegal
out.. 4. seek 7. extract 9. eliminate,
eradicate
perfume.. 5. orris
pungent.. 6. ginger
starch.. 7. cassava
stock.. 7. rhizome
stringy.. 5. watap (watape)
taro.. 4. eddo
word.. 4. etym 6. etymon
rooted... 8. habitual 9. implanted
10. deep–seated 11. established,
traditional
rootlet... 7. radicel, rhizoid, taproot
rope... 3. tew, tie, tye 4. bind, cord,
line, rood 5. cable, cigar, lasso,
longe, noose, reata, wanty 6. fasten,
halter, hawser, lariat, string, tether
7. cordage, lanyard, measure
8. hangman's, inveigle
rope (pert to)...
boat's.. 4. rode 6. hawser 7. painter
chain.. 3. tye 9. stern fast
dancer, walker.. 8. balancer
11. equilibrist, funambulist
flag raising.. 7. halyard
gun carriage.. 8. prolonge
guy.. 4. stay, vang
nautical.. 3. tye 4. vang, wapp
6. parrel (parral) 7. snotter
of onions.. 5. reeve
security device.. 4. butt 5. cleat
ship's.. 3. tye 4. stay, vang
6. hawser, shroud 7. painter, ratline,
snotter
splicer's tool.. 3. fid
straw, twisted.. 5. sugan (soogan)
two strand.. 7. marline
walker.. 11. funambulist
ropery... 6. banter 7. roguery

roral ... 4. dewy, rory 5. roric
rorqual ... 5. whale 7. finback
Ros ... 10. Slav rulers (Russ),
Varangians
rosary ... 4. aves 5. beads (prayer)
7. chaplet (of roses), garland
8. devotion
rose ... 3. cut (jewelry) 5. color, flush,
Rhoda 6. emblem, flower, nozzle,
symbol, window 7. fixture
rose (pert to) ...
apple .. 4. plum 6. cherry 7. jambool
8. poma rosa
beetle .. 6. chafer, weevil
City .. 8. Portland (Oreg)
colored .. 8. alluring 10. auspicious,
optimistic
cross .. 6. symbol 11. Rosicrucian
14. cross in a circle
genus .. 4. Rosa 6. Acaena
8. Rosaceae
hiller .. 7. rosella 8. parakeet
moss .. 9. portulaca
of Sharon .. 6. Althea
petal oil .. 4. otto 5. attar
rash .. 7. roseola
under the rose .. 6. secret 7. sub
rosa
wild .. 9. eglantine
Rosetta Stone (pert to) ...
decipherer .. 11. Champollion
famed for .. 11. inscription
13. hieroglyphics
site found .. 4. Nile (1799)
type .. 11. black basalt
roster ... 4. list, roll, rota 5. slate
8. schedule
rostrum ... 4. beak, dais, prow
5. snout, stage 6. pulpit 8. platform
9. proboscis
rosy ... 3. red 4. pink 7. flushed,
roseate 8. blooming, blushing
9. rosaceous 10. auspicious,
optimistic
rot ... 3. die 5. decay, spoil 6. blight
7. corrupt, disease, putrefy
8. nonsense 9. decompose
10. degenerate 12. putrefaction
13. decomposition
rota ... 4. Club (Eng), list, roll 5. court,
round (Mus) 6. roster 15. Sacra
Romana Rota
rotate ... 4. roll, spin, turn, whiz
5. recur, wheel 6. gyrate 7. rabatte,
revolve, trundle 8. rotiform
rotation ... 4. spin, turn 5. round
7. turning 8. sequence
10. revolution, succession
rotator ... 5. rotor 6. muscle 7. whirler
9. carrousel 12. merry–go–round
rotche, rotch ... 5. goose, rotge
7. dovekie
rote ... 6. course, custom, system
7. by heart, routine 8. par coeur,
practice 9. condition
roti ... 5. roast 7. roasted
rotor ... 5. wheel 6. roller, stator
7. rotator, turbine 8. impeller
rotten ... 3. bad 4. foul, punk
5. doted, fetid 6. putrid, wicked
7. decayed, tainted, unsound
8. depraved, unstable 9. dishonest,

offensive, putrefied 10. putrescent,
undermined 13. disintegrated
Rotten Row (Hyde Park, London) ...
12. thoroughfare (equestrian)
rottenstone ... 6. polish 7. tripoli
rotter ... 3. cad 7. bounder, shirker,
slacker 10. blackguard
rottgoose ... 5. brant
rotund ... 5. plump, round, stout
6. chubby 7. rounded 8. roly–poly
9. corpulent, spherical
Rotwelsch ... 5. argot, slang 6. jargon
14. secret language
roué ... 4. rake, wolf 7. rounder
9. debauchee, libertine
rouge ... 5. blush, flush 6. polish,
redden 7. radical 8. cosmetic
rough ... 4. hard, rude 5. crude, draft,
harsh, raspy, rowdy, seamy, stern
6. broken, choppy, coarse, hoarse,
rugged, severe, shaggy 7. boorish,
inexact, jarring, jolting, ruffled
8. scabrous, unsmooth 9. imperfect,
turbulent 10. incomplete, tumultuous,
unfinished 11. approximate
rough (pert to) ...
avens .. 6. bennet (herb)
cloth .. 5. terry
footed (bird) .. 9. feathered
hair .. 4. shag
hewn .. 6. brutal 10. unpolished
12. uncultivated
house .. 5. cut up 9. rowdiness
10. disorderly, noisy sport
jest (Mus) .. 9. charivari
neck .. 4. boor 5. rowdy, tough
rider .. 9. Roosevelt (Teddy)
10. cavalryman
rock .. 4. crag
shod (to ride) .. 7. trample
8. dominate 9. tyrannize
rough and ...
hoarse .. 7. raucous
lean .. 6. craggy
ready .. 4. rude 10. unpolished
Ready .. 6. Taylor (Gen Zachary)
roughen ... 4. chap, shag 8. asperate
roughly ... 6. rudely 7. harshly
8. coarsely, severely, unevenly,
vulgarly 9. brusquely 10. unsmoothly
13. approximately
roughness ... 6. lipper (of the sea)
8. acrimony, asperity, pungency,
unfinish 9. gruffness, harshness,
vulgarity 10. hoarseness
roughsome ... 5. rough 6. rustic
7. uncouth
roulade ... 3. run 8. arpeggio, division,
flourish 13. vocal flourish
roulette ... 3. bas (bet) 4. disk, game
5. wheel 6. roller 8. wagering
rounceval ... 5. giant, large 6. strong,
virago 9. termagant
round ... 4. beat, bout, rota, rung, turn
5. cycle, orbed, rondo 6. circle,
curved, rotate, rotund, series, sphere
7. circuit, routine 8. circular, globular
9. in a circle, spherical
11. cylindrical
round (pert to) ...
bone .. 3. hip
building .. 7. rotunda

clam.. 6. quahog
fish.. 9. whitefish
head.. 5. Swede 7. Puritan
house.. 5. cabin, coach 6. lockup,
   prison 10. watch house
of applause.. 7. plaudit
regular.. 4. beat
robin.. 6. angler, letter 7. pancake,
   request 9. cigarfish
worm.. 4. nema 7. ascarid, Ascaris,
   eelworm
roundabout... 5. about, dance
   6. detour, jacket 7. ambient, devious
   8. indirect 10. circuitous
   13. approximately 14. circumlocution
rounded (pert to)...
heap of stone.. 5. cairn
irregularly.. 7. gibbous
leaf.. 6. retuse
molding.. 5. ovolo
projection.. 4. lobe 5. tooth
scalloped.. 7. crenate
Round Table (pert to)...
knight.. 7. Galahad 8. Lancelot
seating.. 7. knights (King Arthur's)
site.. 7. Camelot
type.. 6. marble
roundup... 5. rodeo
roup... 4. cold 6. clamor 7. auction
   8. shouting 10. hoarseness
rouse... 3. hie 4. stir, wake 5. alarm,
   raise, start, upset, waken 6. awaken,
   bestir, elicit, excite, kindle 7. disturb
   9. stimulate
rouser... 7. stirrer 8. surprise
   9. demagogue (demagog)
   10. instigator
roussette... 5. shark 7. dogfish 8. fruit
   bat
roust... 4. roar, stir 5. rouse
   6. bellow, tumult 7. current (tidal),
   roaring 9. bellowing
roustabout... 6. lumper 7. laborer
   8. handy man 12. longshoreman
rout... 3. low, mob 4. bray, roar
   5. crowd, snort 6. bellow, defeat,
   rabble 7. debacle, scatter
   8. disperse, stampede, vanquish
   9. agitation, discomfit, overpower,
   overthrow 11. put to flight
route... 3. way 4. line, path 5. march
   6. detour 7. circuit
routh... 6. plenty 8. abundant
   9. abundance, plentiful
routier... 6. robber 7. brigand 9. free
   lance, plunderer
routine... 3. rut 5. grind, habit, order,
   round, troll 6. course, system
   7. regular 8. everyday 9. treadmill
rove... 3. gad 4. flit, part, roam
   5. range, stray 6. maraud, ramble,
   stroll, swerve, wander, washer
   7. deviate 8. straggle
rover... 5. nomad 6. bandit, pirate,
   viking 7. corsair, pilgrim, vagrant
   8. marauder, wanderer
roving... 8. errantry 9. desultory,
   deviative 10. discursive
row... 3. air, oar 4. file, fuss, live,
   spat, tier 5. align, brawl, broil
   6. lineup, paddle, propel, series
   7. quarrel, ruction 9. commotion

rowboat... 3. cog, gig 4. dory
   5. canoe, coble, skiff 6. randan
rowdy... 5. cutup, rough, tough
   7. boorish, ruffian 8. larrikin,
   plug–ugly 10. boisterous, disorderly
rowdy contention... 10. donnybrook
rowel... 4. spur 5. wheel
rowen... 4. crop (secondary) 5. field
   7. stubble 9. aftermath
rowing... 5. sport 6. randan 7. regatta
   8. sculling
rox... 3. rot 5. decay
royal... 4. real, rial, stag, true 5. basil,
   noble, regal 6. august, kingly
   7. stately 8. imperial, majestic,
   princely, splendid 9. dignified,
   sovereign 11. magnificent
royal (pert to)...
agaric.. 8. mushroom
bay.. 6. laurel
color.. 4. blue 5. smalt
court.. 5. aulic 6. ermine
crest.. 10. fleur–de–lis (Fr)
deer's antler.. 8. tres–tine
fur.. 6. ermine
mace.. 7. scepter (sceptre)
martyr.. 8. Charles I (Eng, 1649)
maundy.. 4. alms
officer.. 7. naperer
rights.. 7. regalia
rock snake.. 6. python
stables.. 4. mews
stars (Astrol).. 7. Antares, Regulus
   9. Aldebaran, Fomalhaut
Royal (pert to)...
Academy.. 4. Arts (1768)
Arcanum.. 7. Society (1877)
Canadian Mounted Police..
   8. Mounties 16. Northwest Mounted
Castle.. 8. Balmoral
Crown.. 5. tiara
Highlanders.. 10. Black Watch
Highness.. 5. title 6. prince
   8. princess
House.. 5. Tudor 6. Stuart, Valois
   7. Bourbon, Hanover, Windsor
Oak (Eng Hist).. 7. lottery
   10. Shropshire
Psalmist.. 9. King David
Scot.. 16. Lothian Regiments
royet... 4. wild 6. unruly 7. romping
   11. mischievous
rub... 4. crux, fret, wipe 6. abrade,
   polish, scrape, smooth, stroke
   7. burnish, massage 8. friction,
   irritate 9. hindrance, triturate
rub (pert to)...
away.. 6. abrade
down.. 4. comb 5. curry, groom
   7. massage
elbows.. 9. associate 10. fraternize
off.. 5. erase 6. abrade, remove
   10. obliterate
out.. 4. kill 5. erase 6. cancel,
   efface, excise 7. expunge, wipe out
   10. obliterate
wrong way.. 6. ruffle 8. irritate
   9. displease 10. antagonize
rub–a–dub... 6. clamor 7. clatter,
   pit–a–pat, rat–a–tat 8. rattatoo
   9. drumbeats
Rubáiyát (pert to)...

author.. 11. Omar Khayyám
stanza form.. 8. quatrain
translator.. 10. Fitzgerald (1859)
rubber... 4. para 5. stare 6. eraser
7. ebonite, elastic 8. massager,
sight–see 10. caoutchouc
rubber (pert to)...
city.. 5. Akron
hard.. 7. ebonite
India (pure).. 10. caoutchouc
plant.. 5. Ficus
ring.. 4. lute 6. gasket
sap.. 5. latex
shoe.. 6. galosh (galoshe)
tree.. 3. ule 7. guayule
wild.. 5. Ceara 6. caucho
rubbish... 4. junk, ross 5. attle, dross,
stent, trash, waste 6. debris, refuse,
rubble, trashy 8. nonsense, riffraff,
trumpery 9. worthless
rubble... 5. brash, chalk, stone, trash
7. rubbish 8. nonsense
11. foolishness
rube... 4. dolt 6. rustic 7. hayseed
rubedity... 7. redness 9. ruddiness
rubella... 7. measles, rubeola
rubescent... 3. red 8. flushing
9. reddening 10. erubescent
rubiator... 4. rake 5. bully 6. rascal
Rubicon... 5. river (Caesar's)
9. Fiumicino (modern)
rubicund... 3. red 4. ruby 5. ruddy
6. florid 7. redness
rubric... 3. rod 6. paraph, ritual
8. category, red chalk 14. title page
in red
rubrics (book of)... 4. ordo
ruby (pert to)...
bird.. 11. hummingbird
heraldry.. 5. gules
stained quartz (red).. 6. Ancona
7. rubasse 9. Mont Blanc
stone.. 3. gem 5. balas 6. spinel
type.. 4. size
ruck... 3. rut, sit (on eggs) 4. heap,
pile, rick 5. cower, crowd, squat,
stack 6. crease, crouch, furrow,
horses (race), pucker 7. wrinkle
9. multitude 10. generality
ruckus... 3. ado, row 5. fight
6. rumpus, uproar 7. quarrel, ruction
8. outbreak 9. commotion
rudd... 3. hue 4. carp, fish 6. redden
7. azurine, redness 10. complexion
rudder... 4. helm 5. guide
rudder part... 8. bearding 9. whipstaff
rude... 3. raw 4. curt 5. rough, rowdy
6. clumsy, coarse, rugged, simple,
vulgar 7. boorish, uncouth
8. ignorant, insolent 9. barbarous,
inclement, makeshift, turbulent,
unlearned, unskilled, untrained
10. boisterous, unpolished
11. impertinent, uncivilized
12. discourteous
rudeness... 6. ferity 8. curtness
9. impudence, insolence, vulgarity
11. raucousness 12. impertinence
rudiment... 5. first 6. anlage, embryo,
origin 7. element 9. first step
rudimentary... 5. basic 7. initial

8. original 9. beginning, elemental,
embryonic, vestigial 11. undeveloped
rudimentary digit... 7. dewclaw
rue... 4. rake, Ruta 6. grieve, regret,
repent, sorrow 7. afflict, deplore
10. bitterness, compassion,
repentance 14. disappointment
ruff... 3. ree 5. pride, reeve, ruche,
trump 6. collar, fringe, rebato
7. sunfish 8. drumbeat 9. sandpiper,
vainglory
ruffian... 4. fish, pimp, thug 5. rowdy,
tough 6. brutal, cuttle, pander
8. assassin, paramour, the Devil
9. cutthroat, desperado, murderous,
vulgarian
ruffle... 3. vex 4. fret, roil 5. anger,
annoy, frill, jabot 6. edging, muddle,
nettle, rumple, tousle 7. agitate,
disturb, flounce, fluster, shuffle
8. dishevel, disorder, drumbeat,
irritate 9. balayeuse 10. disarrange,
discompose
ruffler... 5. bully 7. boaster, ruffian
8. braggart 9. swaggerer
10. attachment (sewing)
rug... 3. mat 4. maud, shag
5. Senna, throw 6. carpet, hooked,
petate 7. Chinese, drugget, steamer
8. coverlet, Oriental 9. Samarkand
ruga... 4. fold 7. wrinkle 8. membrane
Rugby... 5. Fives 6. Rugger, school
(Eng) 8. football
Rugby term... 9. scrum half,
scrummage
rugged... 4. rude 5. asper, hardy,
harsh, rough, surly 6. craggy, fierce,
robust, seamed, shaggy, strong,
sturdy 7. austere, crabbed, healthy,
uncivil 8. vigorous, wrinkled
9. irregular, not smooth, turbulent
11. substantial
rugged mountain crest... 5. arête
ruin... 4. bane, doom, fate, loss
5. blast, havoc, spoil, wrack, wreck
6. defeat 7. debauch, destroy,
subvert 8. bankrupt, demolish,
downfall 9. perdition 10. desolation,
subversion 11. destruction,
devastation
ruined... 4. gone 7. spoiled, wrecked
8. bankrupt, defeated 9. destroyed
11. dilapidated 12. irremediable
ruinous... 6. deadly 7. baneful,
decayed 10. demolished, disastrous,
pernicious, submersive, tumbledown
11. destructive
ruins... 5. relic, wreck 7. remains
rukh... 6. forest, jungle
rule... 3. law 4. norm, sway 5. axiom,
guide, habit, order, regle, reign
6. decree, govern, manage, method,
regime, screed 7. counsel, measure,
precept, prevail, regency, regimen
8. dominate, persuade, standard
9. criterion, direction, influence,
principle 12. jurisdiction
15. totalitarianism
rule by...
children.. 9. paedarchy
ecclesiasts.. 9. hierarchy
one.. 8. monarchy

race.. 10. ethnocracy
ten.. 8. decarchy
the mob.. 9. mobocracy
the people.. 9. democracy
tribes.. 9. phylarchy
rule out... 6. cancel, excise 7. obviate
ruler... 3. min 4. amir (ameer), czar,
emir, lord 5. queen 6. despot,
dynast, ferule, gerent, prince, regent,
satrap, sultan, tyrant 7. emperor,
monarch 8. autocrat, governor,
hierarch, measurer 9. potentate
ruling... 3. law 6. decree 7. average,
regnant, statute, verdict 8. decision,
reigning 9. governing, prevalent
11. predominant 12. drawing lines
rullion... 4. shoe 6. sandal
rum... 3. dye (blue), odd 4. good
5. queer, tafia (taffia) 6. liquor
8. Demon rum
rumal... 6. fabric 8. kerchief (man's)
Rumania...
capital.. 9. Bucharest
city.. 4. Cluj, Iasi 7. Ploesti
king.. 5. Carol (former)
mountains.. 10. Carpathian
port.. 6. Galati (Galatz)
privileged class.. 5. boyar (boyard)
river.. 6. Danube
rumble... 4. boom, seat (back)
5. rumor 6. murmur, ripple, stir up
9. complaint 11. rolling tone
rumen... 3. cud 5. tripe 6. gullet,
paunch 7. stomach (1st)
ruminant... 2. ox 3. cow, yak 4. bull,
deer, gaur, goat, oryx, zebu
5. bison, camel, eland, gayal, llama,
moose, okapi, sheep, steer
6. alpaca, nilgai, vicuna, wapiti
7. banteng, buffalo, caribou,
chamois, gemsbok, giraffe
8. antelope, elephant, reindeer,
seladang 9. dromedary, nannygoat,
pronghorn 10. cud–chewing,
hartebeest, meditative, rhinoceros,
thoughtful
ruminant (pert to)...
division.. 8. Ungulata 10. Ruminantia
first stomach.. 5. rumen 6. paunch
fourth stomach.. 8. abomasum
9. rennet bag
second stomach.. 9. reticulum
third stomach.. 6. omasum
9. manyplies 10. psalterium
ruminate... 4. chew, muse 6. ponder
7. reflect 8. consider, meditate
rummage... 4. junk 6. litter, search
7. collect (by search), ransack
rumor, rumour... 4. Fama, talk
5. bruit, noise, story 6. norate,
report 7. hearsay, tidings
11. scuttlebutt
rump... 4. bone 6. breech, sacrum
7. meat cut 8. bankrupt, buttocks
9. remainder
rumpade... 3. rob 6. hold up
rumple... 4. muss 5. touse 6. crease,
ruffle, tousle 7. crinkle, crumple,
wrinkle 8. dishevel 10. disarrange
rumpus... 3. row 6. fracas, hubbub,
uproar 9. commotion, confusion
11. disturbance

rumtytoo... 8. ordinary
11. commonplace
run... 2. go 3. fly, gad, hie 4. dart,
flee, flow, lope, melt, race, scud,
tend, trot 5. blend, hurry, speed,
trend 6. charge, course, elapse,
endure, extend, manage, pursue,
sprint, stream 7. average, liquefy,
operate, proceed, roulade, routine,
smuggle, stretch, trickle 8. continue
9. discharge, suppurate
run (pert to)...
about.. 5. wagon 6. gadder
8. roadster, runagate, vagabond
after.. 5. chase, fetch, toady
6. pursue 7. lionize
aground.. 6. strand 7. founder
along the edge.. 5. skirt
away.. 4. bolt, flee 5. elope
6. decamp, escape 8. stampede
before the wind.. 4. scud
between ports.. 3. ply
down.. 3. hit 4. find 5. trace 7. run
over 9. exhausted 11. dilapidated
12. deteriorated
out.. 3. end 5. lapse, waste
6. elapse, emerge, escape
7. exhaust 8. squander
over.. 6. browse, exceed, ponder
7. trample 8. overflow 9. reiterate
quickly, swiftly.. 4. dart, race, scud
5. scoot 6. gallop, sprint 7. scuttle
stocking.. 6. ladder
through.. 4. stab 6. pierce 7. inspect,
pervade 8. rehearse, squander,
transfix 11. superabound
up against.. 4. find 9. encounter,
stumble on 10. experience
runagate... 7. runaway 8. apostate,
fugitive, renegade, vagabond,
wanderer
rundle... 4. ball, coil, rung, step
5. round 6. circle, roller, sphere,
stream
rune... 5. magic 6. secret, symbol
7. mystery 9. character (anc)
rung... 4. step 5. round, spoke, stair,
tread 6. degree, rundle 7. girdled,
ratline
runic... 5. verse 6. poetic 7. writing
8. alphabet (anc), Norsemen
runner... 3. ski (skee) 4. sled 5. miler,
racer, stolo 6. stolon 7. tendril
8. operator, procurer, salesman,
smuggler, sprinter 9. messenger,
solicitor
running... 7. current, cursive, fleeing,
flowing, melting 9. advancing,
prevalent, smuggling 10. continuous
running knot... 5. noose
running race... 5. relay 6. sprint
running toad... 10. natterjack
runt... 3. elf 4. chit (letter), wrig
5. dwarf, pygmy 6. pigeon
10. diminutive
runway... 4. file, ramp 8. airstrip
rupa... 4. body, form (visual)
rupee... 4. anna, coin 14. money of
account
rupestrian... 14. composed of rock
15. inscribed on rock
ruption... 7. ruction, rupture

8. bursting

rupture... 4. rent 5. break, burst
6. hernia, injury, rhexis 7. quarrel
9. hostility 10. disruption, falling out,
separating

rural... 6. rustic 7. bucolic 8. agrestic,
pastoral 12. agricultural

rural (pert to)...
deity.. 3. Pan 6. Faunus
genus.. 6. potato
life.. 8. pastoral
poem.. 7. eclogue, georgic
Spanish.. 9. policeman
term.. 8. agrestic

Rusa... 4. deer 6. sambar

ruse... 4. fall, slip, wile 5. fraud, trick
6. deceit 8. artifice 9. stratagem
10. subterfuge

rush... 3. jet 4. dart, dash, flow, scud
5. brook, haste, hurry, plant, press,
scoot, spate, speed, surge 6. charge,
course, defeat, demand, hasten,
runlet, sortie 7. cattail, repulse
8. outburst, reed mace, stampede
9. attention, thronging

rush (pert to)...
forth.. 5. sally
hour.. 4. peak
light.. 6. candle, feeble
nut.. 5. chufa
Scot.. 5. sprat (herb) 6. Juncus
toad.. 10. natterjack
wheat.. 10. couch grass

rusk... 5. bread 7. biscuit

rusma... 9. quicklime 10. depilatory

Russia... see also *Russian*
capital.. 6. Moscow 9. Petrograd (old)
citadel.. 7. Kremlin
city.. 4. Baku, Kiev, Omsk 5. Minsk
6. Rostov 7. Kharkov 8. Smolensk
9. Leningrad (St Petersburg),
Petrograd 10. Sevastopol (Sebastopol)
11. Vladivostok
coal fields.. 6. Donets (Ukraine)
fleet base.. 10. Sevastopol, Stalingrad
former name.. 7. Muscovy
founder.. 4. Ivan 15. Ivan the Terrible
gulf.. 4. Azov
isthmus.. 7. Karelia
lake.. 5. Onega 6. Baykal 7. Aral Sea
10. Caspian Sea
mountains.. 4. Ural 8. Caucasus
peninsula.. 4. Kola 6. Crimea
resort.. 5. Yalta 6. Crimea
river.. 2. Ob 4. Amur, Lena, Neva,
Ural 5. Volga 6. Donets 7. Dneiper,
Yenisei
sea.. 4. Azov 5. Black, White
6. Baltic 7. Caspian
strait.. 6. Bering

Russian (pert to)...
antelope.. 5. saiga
aristocratic order.. 4. knez 5. Boyar
assembly.. 4. duma, rada 7. zemstoo
association, guild.. 5. artel
bank.. 4. game
beer, beverage.. 5. kvass, vodka
boat.. 6. baidak (baydak)
braid (trim).. 8. soutache
calendar (to 1918).. 6. Julian
cap (peasant).. 4. aska
carriage.. 6. drosky, troika

9. tarantass (tarantas)
cart, wagon.. 6. telega
cathedral.. 5. sober
cloak (fur).. 5. shuba
council.. 4. duma, rada 6. soviet
dance (rustic).. 7. ziganka
decree.. 5. ukase
dog (wolfhound).. 6. borzoi
7. owtchah
dress (peasant).. 7. sarafan
duke, prince.. 4. knez (kniaz)
edict.. 5. ukase
fur (lamb).. 7. karakul (karakule)
9. astrakhan
guild.. 5. artel
hemp.. 4. rine
hut.. 4. isba
leather.. 5. jufti (jufts) 6. Bulgar
8. shagreen
marsh, lagoon.. 5. liman
massacre.. 6. pogrom
musical instrument.. 5. gudok, gusla
9. balalaika
naval academy.. 6. Frunze
news agency.. 4. Tass
parliament.. 4. duma
peasant.. 4. Slav 5. kulak 6. muzhik
(muzjik)
plain (treeless).. 6. steppe, tundra
police (secret).. 5. Cheka
pound.. 4. pood
prince, duke.. 4. knez (kniaz)
satellite.. 7. sputnik
soup (cabbage).. 5. stchi (shchi)
6. borsch
stockade.. 5. etape
synod.. 5. sobor
tea urn.. 7. samovar
turnip.. 8. rutabaga
villa.. 5. dacha
wagon (springless).. 6. telega
wheat.. 5. emmer
whip.. 4. plet (plete) 5. knout
wolfhound.. 6. borzoi
yes.. 2. da

Russian people...
chess champ (1892).. 8. Alekhine
composer.. 3. Cui 10. Rubenstein,
Stravinsky 12. Tschaikovsky
14. Rimsky–Korsakov
conqueror.. 6. Tatars 7. Mongols
Cossack.. 5. Tatar
czar.. 4. Ivan 13. Peter the Great
duke.. 5. kniaz (knez, knyoz)
empress.. 7. Czarina, Tsarina
General.. 10. Timoshenko
grand duke.. 8. Nicholas
language deviser.. 8. Zamenhof
9. Esperanto (pseudonym)
leader.. 5. Lenin 6. Stalin 7. Molotov
8. Brezhnev
little Russian.. 7. Russene (Ruthene)
monk.. 8. Rasputin
novelist.. 7. Tolstoy
people.. 4. Lett, Slav 7. Cossack
8. Russniak 9. Muscovite, Ruthenian
poet.. 7. Pushkin, Yesenin
9. Pasternak
premier.. 5. Lenin 7. Kosygin,
Molotov 8. Bulganin 10. Kruschchev
saint.. 4. Olga
teacher, monk.. 7. starets

Youth Union.. 8. Comsomol
rust... 3. eat 5. erode 6. aerugo,
patina 7. erosion, oxidize
9. corrosion
rustic... 4. boor, carl, rube, rude
5. churl, clown, Damon, rough, rural,
swain, yokel 6. coarse, simple,
sturdy, sylvan 7. artless, awkward,
boorish, bucolic, Corydon, plowboy
8. agrestic, pastoral 9. agrestian
10. clodhopper, countryman,
unpolished
rustic (pert to)...
lover.. 5. swain
maiden.. 9. Thestylis
peasant.. 4. boor
pipe.. 4. reed
poetic.. 4. carl
verse.. 4. idyl (idyll)

rustle... 4. flow 5. steal, swish, whisk
7. crinkle 11. sound softly
rut... 5. ditch, track 6. furrow, groove,
strake 7. routine, wrinkle
Ruth (pert to)...
Book.. 12. Old Testament
country.. 4. Moab
husband.. 4. Boaz
mother–in–law.. 5. Naomi
ruthless... 5. cruel 8. pitiless
9. merciless 10. ironfisted
rye... 5. bread, grain, grass 6. cereal,
whisky 9. gentleman (gypsy)
rye bread... 5. black 10. knackebrod
12. pumpernickel
ryot... 6. farmer, tenant 7. peasant
Rytina... 6. dugong, sea cow
7. manatee 12. Hydrodamalis
14. Steller's sea cow
Ryukyu Islands... 7. Okinawa

S

S (pert to)...
curve.. 4. ogee
letter.. 10. nineteenth
shaped.. 7. sigmate, sigmoid
suffix.. 6. plural
Saal... 4. hall, room (large)
sabalo... 6. tarpon 8. milkfish
sabana... 5. plain 7. plateau, savanna
(savannah)
sabbat... 8. assembly (demons), festival
(orgies)
Sabbatarian... 9. ritualist 11. Russian
sect
Sabbath... 6. Sunday 7. holy day
sabbatical year... 7. seventh
8. vacation 14. leave of absence
sabbatism... 4. rest 9. ritualism
12. intermission (labor)
Sabbatist (pert to)...
devotee of.. 4. cult (Oriental)
member.. 6. Semite
named for.. 5. Sabbe (goddess)
8. Sambathe
saber, sabre (pert to)...
bean.. 4. jack
bill.. 6. curlew
fish.. 7. cutlass
knot.. 8. military
legged (horse).. 12. sickle–hocked
Mohammedan.. 8. yataghan (yatagan)
oriental.. 8. scimiter
toothed.. 3. cat 5. tiger
12. machairodont
wing.. 11. hummingbird
sabino... 9. ahuehuete, rock cedar
sabio... 4. sage 6. priest 7. wise man
sable... 4. ebon, pelt 5. black, brush
6. mammal, marten 8. antelope
10. mysterious, Russia iron
sabotage... 6. damage, mayhem

9. undermine 11. destruction
(malicious)
Sabrina... 10. river nymph 11. River
Severn
sabuline, sabulous... 5. sandy
6. gritty 8. psammous
10. arenaceous
sabutan... 5. fibre, straw
sac... 3. bag 4. cyst, sack 5. ascus,
bursa, pouch, purse, theca 6. cavity,
pocket, saccus 7. saccule, vesicle
8. sacculus
Sac, Sauk... 11. Indian tribe
sacalait... 7. crappie 8. warmouth
9. killifish
saccadic... 5. jerky 9. twitching
11. eye movement
saccharine... 5. sweet 7. honeyed
10. sweetening
saccos... 7. tunicle 8. vestment
sacerdocy... 10. priesthood 13. priestly
order
sacerdos... 6. priest
sachem... 5. chief (Indian) 8. governor
(Tammany)
sachet... 3. bag 5. pouch 6. powder
7. perfume 8. reticule 11. perfumed
pad
sack... 3. bag 4. loot, poke, wine
5. ascus, bursa, catch, pouch, purse
6. defeat, ravage, secure 7. pillage,
plunder 8. desolate 9. discharge,
dismissal
sack (pert to)...
baseball.. 3. bag 4. base
Bible.. 8. mourning
but.. 4. butt, cask 8. trombone (anc)
cloth.. 7. penance, sacking 15. garb
of penitence
dress.. 4. robe 6. jacket, sacque

sacrament... 3. act 4. oath 5. token
6. pledge, symbol 7. mystery
8. ceremony, covenant, practice
9. communion, Eucharist
10. intinction (to administer)
Sacramento (pert to)...
capital, river.. 10. California
cat.. 10. horned pout
pike.. 9. squawfish
salmon.. 7. quinnat
sacrarium (anc)... 6. chapel, shrine
7. oratory 8. sacristy 9. sanctuary,
synsacrum
sacred... 4. holy 6. divine 7. blessed
8. hallowed, reverend 9. dedicated,
inviolate, religious, venerable
10. inviolable, sacrosanct
11. consecrated 13. sanctimonious
sacred (pert to)...
bark.. 7. cascara 14. cascara sagrada
bean.. 11. Indian lotus
beetle.. 10. scarabaeus
bird.. 4. ibis
book.. 5. Bible, Koran
bo tree.. 3. fig 5. pipal
bull.. 4. apis, zebu
chest.. 4. arca 9. reliquary
comb form.. 5. hagio, hiero
dialect (Buddh writings).. 4. Pali
grove.. 5. Altis (Olympia)
image.. 4. icon (ikon) 5. Pietà
instrument.. 4. Urim 7. Thummim
malady.. 8. epilepsy
monkey.. 6. baboon, rhesus
8. entellus
most.. 10. sacrosanct
music.. 4. hymn 5. chant, motet
8. oratorio
river (Ind).. 6. Ganges (Ganga)
room.. 8. sacristy
traffic (in sacred things).. 6. simony
weed.. 7. vervain
wine vessel.. 3. ama
writ.. 10. Scriptures
sacrifice... 4. lose, loss 5. offer
6. give up, victim 8. chiliomb
(1,000 oxen), hecatomb (100 oxen),
immolate, libation, oblation, offering
9. atonement, holocaust, martyrdom,
privation, surrender 11. crucifixion,
destruction
sacrificer... 6. martyr
sacrificial fire... 5. ignis
sacrilege... 7. robbery (church)
9. blasphemy 11. desecration,
profanation
sacrilegious... 7. impious
10. irreverent 11. blasphemous,
irreligious
sacrosanct... 4. holy 6. sacred
8. ironical, most holy
sad... 3. bad 4. blue, dark, dire, dull
5. dusky, sorry 6. solemn, somber,
triste, wicked 7. doleful, pensive,
unhappy 8. dejected, downcast,
grievous, pathetic, shameful, terrible
9. cheerless, depressed, sorrowful
10. calamitous, deplorable,
depressing, melancholy
11. distressing, unfortunate
saddle... 4. meat (cut of), ride, seat
5. ridge 6. burden 7. harness (part)

8. encumber, straddle
saddle (pert to)...
back.. 4. hill 5. ridge
bag.. 7. alforja, pannier
blanket.. 6. corona, tilpah
boot.. 7. gambado
cloth.. 5. cover 7. housing
8. shabrack 9. appendage
10. horsecloth
elephant.. 6. howdah
girth.. 5. cinch
horse.. 5. mount 6. remuda 7. palfrey
light.. 5. pilch 7. pillion
pack.. 7. aparejo
part.. 6. cantle, crutch, pommel
8. tapadera (tapadero) 9. saddlebow
place behind.. 5. croup
rock.. 6. oyster
strap.. 5. girth 6. latigo
saddler... 4. seal 5. horse 6. cozier
7. cobbler, lorimer 8. merchant
9. shoemaker
sadness... 5. dolor 6. pathos, sorrow
9. dejection 10. gloominess,
melancholy 11. unhappiness
13. sorrowfulness
sad tree... 10. hursinghar (dye yield)
safari... 4. tour, trip 6. junket
7. caravan, journey 10. expedition,
pilgrimage
safe... 4. pete (thieves' sl), sane, sure
5. chest, vault 6. closet, secure,
unhurt 8. cautious, cupboard,
unharmed 9. protected, strongbox
11. trustworthy
safeblower... 7. burglar, peteman
8. peterman
safe conduct... 4. pass 5. cowle,
guard 6. convoy, escort 8. passport
10. precaution, protection
safekeeping... 4. care 7. custody,
storage 10. protection
12. preservation
safety lamp (miner's)... 4. Davy
safety rail... 9. guardrail
saffron... 6. crocus, yellow
10. colchicine
sag... 4. bend, hang, reed, rush, sink,
wilt 5. drift, droop, sedge, slump
6. weaken 10. depreciate
saga... 4. Edda, epic, tale 5. story,
witch 6. legend 7. recital, sagaman
9. narrative
Saga... 7. goddess, seeress
sagacious... 4. sage, wise 5. aware,
witty 6. argute, astute, shrewd
7. politic, sapient 9. judicious
10. discerning, farsighted
11. penetrative 13. perspicacious
sagacity... 3. ken 6. acumen, wisdom
9. acuteness, quickness
10. shrewdness 11. discernment,
penetration 13. judiciousness
sage... 4. mint, wise 5. solon
6. astute, Salvia, shrewd 7. sapient
9. counselor, judicious, sagebrush
10. discerning 11. philosopher
Sage (of)...
Chelsea.. 7. Carlyle (Thomas)
Concord.. 7. Emerson (Ralph W)
Emporia.. 5. White (Wm Allen)
Ferney.. 8. Voltaire

Monticello .. **9.** Jefferson (Thomas)
Pylos .. **6.** Nestor
sage (pert to) ...
  Bethlehem .. **9.** spearmint
  cheese .. **7.** Cheddar
  chippy .. **14.** Brewer's sparrow
  cock, hen .. **6.** grouse
  family .. **4.** mint
  rose .. **5.** alder (yellow)
  tea .. **5.** tonic
Sagebrush State ... **6.** Nevada
sagene ... **5.** seine **7.** measure,
  network
sagitta ... **7.** otolith **8.** keystone (Arch),
  The Arrow
Sagittarius ... **6.** bowman **9.** The
  Archer **13.** constellation
sago (pert to) ...
  palm .. **6.** gebang, gomuti
  plant .. **10.** cuckoopint
  product .. **6.** starch
  tree .. **7.** coontie
sagoin ... **8.** marmoset
saguaro ... **6.** cactus, flower
saguing ... **6.** banana
Sahara ... **5.** cocoa (color), leste (wind)
  6. desert
sahib ... **5.** title **6.** master
  9. gentleman
sai ... **6.** monkey **8.** capuchin
said ... **6.** stated **7.** uttered
  9. aforesaid **15.** before–mentioned
said to be ... **7.** reputed, rumored
  8. reported
saiga ... **8.** antelope
Saigon nickname ... **14.** Paris of the
  East
sail ... **3.** jib, lug **4.** luff, tack **5.** craft,
  float **6.** vessel, voyage **8.** navigate
sail (pert to) ...
  around .. **14.** circumnavigate
  close to wind .. **4.** luff
  end .. **7.** yardarm
  fish .. **12.** basking shark **15.** quillback
  sucker
  fore and aft .. **7.** spanker
  foresail .. **9.** spinnaker
  part .. **4.** clew, yard **5.** leech
  rope .. **5.** sheet **6.** earing
  secure, lash .. **7.** trice up
  strings .. **10.** reef points
  type .. **3.** jib, lug, top, try **4.** main,
  reef, stay **6.** lateen, mizzen, square
  7. topsail **8.** mainsail, save–alls
  12. mutton–legger
sailboat ... **4.** yawl **5.** ketch, skiff,
  sloop, yacht **7.** caravel (caravelle)
sailing term ... **3.** leg, run **4.** asea,
  beat, jibe, scud, tack **5.** hoist (sail),
  point, reach **7.** gliding
sailing vessel ... **4.** bark (barque), brig,
  saic, yawl **5.** sloop **7.** frigate
  8. schooner **10.** barkentine
  (barquentine), windjammer
sailor ... **3.** gob, tar **4.** salt, wave
  5. middy **6.** lascar, matlow
  7. mariner, voyager **8.** seafarer
  10. bluejacket, lobscouser (sl)
sailor (pert to) ...
  associate at meals .. **8.** messmate
  clothes .. **11.** bell–bottoms
  kit .. **8.** ditty bag **9.** housewife

knot .. **8.** geranium
mess tub .. **3.** kid
patron saint .. **4.** Elmo
song .. **7.** chantey **9.** barcarole
Saimiri ... **4.** titi **6.** monkey **8.** squirrel
sain doux ... **4.** lard **6.** grease
saint ... **3.** Ste **5.** angel **7.** apostle,
  pietist **8.** canonize, enshrine, sanctify
  10. holy person **11.** godly person
Saint (pert to) ...
  Anthony's fire .. **10.** erysipelas
  Buddhist .. **5.** arhat
  Elmo's fire (or light) .. **6.** corona,
  Helena **9.** corposant
  Esprit .. **9.** holy ghost
  Francis of Assisi .. **11.** il Poverello
  13. little poor man
  Gaudens .. **8.** sculptor
  George's flag .. **14.** national emblem
  Helena's hemlock .. **7.** jellica
  John Lateran .. **12.** Mother Church
  John's bread .. **5.** carob **9.** algarroba
  Leger (Eng) .. **9.** horse race
  Luke's summer .. **12.** Indian summer
  Martin .. **13.** Bishop of Tours
  Martin's feast .. **9.** Martinmas
  Mary–le–Bow .. **15.** Cheapside Church
  (Cockney area)
  Mohammedan .. **3.** pir
  Patrick's breastplate .. **6.** lorica
  Paul .. **12.** Saul of Tarsus
  Paul's Church (London), designer ..
  18. Sir Christopher Wren
  Peter's dome architect ..
  12. Michelangelo
  Vitus' dance .. **6.** chorea
Saint, patron ...
  children's .. **8.** Nicholas (Santa Claus)
  English .. **6.** George
  French .. **5.** Denis
  hospitals .. **9.** John of God **10.** Juan
  Ciudad
  Irish .. **7.** Patrick
  Italian .. **7.** Anthony
  lawyer's .. **4.** Ives
  lover's .. **9.** Valentine
  sailor's .. **4.** Elmo
  Scottish .. **6.** Andrew
  Spanish .. **5.** James
  Welsh .. **5.** David
saints (pert to) ...
  biography .. **9.** hagiology
  11. hagiography
  tomb .. **6.** shrine
  worship of .. **10.** hagiolatry
sajou ... **6.** monkey **7.** sapajou
sake ... **4.** beer **6.** motive, reason
  7. purpose **8.** beverage (rice)
salacious ... **4.** lewd **5.** horny (sl)
  7. lustful, obscene **8.** unchaste
  9. lecherous
salad plant, vegetable ... **4.** bibb
  5. cress **6.** celery, endive
  7. cabbage, lettuce, romaine
  10. watercress
salamander ... **3.** eft **4.** newt **5.** poker
  6. triton **7.** axolotl, Caudata, urodela
  9. fire–eater **10.** hellbender
  12. pocket gopher
salary ... **3.** fee, pay **4.** hire, wage
  5. wages **6.** reward **7.** stipend
  8. pittance **9.** allowance, emolument,

salt money (anc) 10. honorarium
  12. compensation, remuneration
salat... 6. prayer (facing Mecca)
sale... 4. deal, vend 6. barter,
  demand, market 7. auction, handsel
  (1st in morning) 8. contract
  11. black market
salesman... 5. agent 6. vendor
  7. drummer 9. solicitor
  14. representative 18. commercial
  traveler
salient... 4. bold 6. trench 7. eminent,
  jetting, jumping, leaping, obvious
  8. bounding, extended 9. prominent
  10. noticeable, protruding
  11. conspicuous
salient angle... 5. arris, Doric
Salientia... 5. Anura, frogs, toads
  8. Amphibia (tailless)
salient point... 7. feature (detail)
saline... 5. salty 6. salina 8. solution
  10. saliferous
saliva... 7. spittle 8. digester, ptyalism
salivary gland... 8. racemose
sallow... 3. wan 4. gray, pale
  5. muddy, pasty 6. pallid
  9. yellowish
sally... 4. jest, leap, trip 5. issue,
  jaunt, start 6. sortie 7. journey
  8. escapade, outburst 9. witticism
salmagundi... 4. hash, olio, stew
  6. medley 7. mixture 9. potpourri
  10. periodical (old)
salmon... 4. fish 5. color 6. orlean,
  sauqui 7. annatto, saumont
salmon (pert to)...
  adult.. 7. gilling
  after spawning.. 4. kelt
  cured.. 6. kipper
  dog.. 4. keta
  family.. 10. Salmonidae
  female.. 4. raun 6. baggit
  genus.. 12. Oncorhynchus
  herring.. 8. milkfish
  humpbacked.. 5. haddo, holia
  kind.. 7. quinnat
  landlocked.. 7. kokanee
  male.. 3. gib 6. kipper
  newly hatched.. 4. pink
  second year.. 6. hepper
  silver.. 4. coho
  small.. 4. peal 6. grilse
  third year.. 4. mort
  trout.. 5. sewen
  young.. 3. fog 4. parr 5. smolt
  6. grilse, samlet 7. essling
Salome (pert to)...
  Bib.. 6. dancer
  father.. 8. Herodias
  grandfather.. 5. Herod
  opera, by.. 7. Strauss
salon... 7. gallery 8. New Salon
  (Paris), Old Salon 9. reception
  10. assemblage, exhibition
  11. drawing room
Salon del Prado (Madrid)...
  9. promenade
saloon... 3. bar 4. deck 6. tavern
  7. barroom, cantina, gallery
  8. dramshop, groggery 11. drawing
  room
saloop... 8. hot drink 9. sassafras

salt... 3. sal 4. cure 5. brine, taste
  6. flavor, halite, sailor, saline
  8. piquancy 9. seasoning
  10. antiseptic, corrective 14. sodium
  chloride
salt (pert to)...
  acetic acid.. 7. acetate
  alkaline.. 5. borax
  astringent.. 4. alum
  block, rock.. 3. pig
  boric acid.. 6. borate
  cat.. 4. lump 10. pigeon food
  comb form.. 4. sali
  cracker.. 7. saltine
  dish for.. 10. saltcellar
  ethereal.. 5. ester
  flat.. 5. playa
  lake.. 5. shott (chott)
  marsh, pond.. 6. salina
  native.. 6. halite
  nature of, like.. 6. haloid
  of the earth.. 7. the best
  10. commonalty
  peter, petre.. 5. niter
  rock, block.. 3. pig
  spring.. 4. lick
  tax.. 7. gabelle
  tree.. 4. atle (atlee) 5. cedar
  7. tamarix 8. tamarisk
  working.. 7. halurgy
  works.. 7. saltern, saltery 9. salthouse
saltant... 7. dancing, jumping, leaping
  8. bouncing, bounding
salted... 5. briny, cured 6. corned
  7. treated 8. brackish, hardened,
  seasoned 11. experienced
salty... 3. reh 5. briny, salic, witty
  6. risqué, saline
salubrious... 4. good 8. salutary
  9. healthful, wholesome
  10. beneficial
salutary... 7. healthy 8. curative
  9. medicinal 10. salubrious
  11. restorative
salutation... 2. hi 3. ave 4. hail
  5. aloha, hello, howdy, skoal
  6. curtsy, homage, kowtow, Mizpah
  (Mizpeh), prosit, salaam (salam)
  7. Dear Sir 8. greeting, serenade
salute... 4. hail, kiss 5. greet
  6. homage, signal 7. address
salvage... 4. save 6. redeem, rescue
  10. redemption 11. reclamation
salvation... 8. soterial 10. liberation,
  redemption 11. deliverance,
  soteriology 12. preservation
salve... 3. tip 4. balm, cure 5. allay,
  quiet 6. anoint, cerate 7. assuage,
  relieve 8. flattery, medicate, ointment
  9. gloss over, lubricate, mitigator
  10. medication
salver... 4. tray 9. flatterer 11. serving
  dish
salvo... 6. excuse 7. gunfire, pretext,
  proviso, quibble, rockets 8. applause
  9. discharge, exception
  11. projectiles, reservation
Samaria (pert to)...
  capital (anc).. 6. Israel
  deity.. 6. Nibhaz
  destroyer.. 6. Romans
  founder.. 4. Omri (925 BC)

people.. 9. Assyrians
province of.. 9. Palestine
rebuilder.. 5. Herod (the Great)
Samaritan, good... 5. aider 6. helper
   10. befriender, benefactor
   11. helping hand
Sambal (Zambal) language... 4. Tino
sambar (sambur)... 4. deer, maha,
   rusa
same... 2. id 3. ilk, one 4. ibid, idem,
   self 5. alike, ditto 7. cognate, identic
   8. selfsame 9. identical
   10. equivalent
sameness... 6. parity, tedium
   7. analogy, oneness 8. identity,
   monotony 9. alikeness 10. similarity,
   uniformity 11. equivalence
   14. correspondence
Samian (pert to)...
   island.. 5. Samos
   Sage.. 10. Pythagoras
   sea.. 6. Aegean
   ware.. 8. Arretine
samlet... 4. parr 6. salmon (young)
Samoa...
   capital.. 4. Apia
   councilor.. 7. faipule
   islands.. 8. American
   islands, main.. 5. Manua, Upolu
   6. Savaii 7. Tutuila
   natives.. 10. Polynesian
   owl (barn).. 4. lulu
   political council.. 4. fono
   town.. 8. Pago Pago
   warrior.. 3. toa
samovar... 3. urn 6. teapot
Samoyed, Samoyede... 3. dog (Arctic)
   8. Siberian
sample... 4. test 5. model, taste
   6. swatch 7. example, pattern
   8. specimen
sampler... 8. original 9. archetype
   10. needlework
Samson (pert to)...
   Bib.. 5. judge (Israelite)
   death site.. 4. Gaza (Syria)
   famed as.. 9. strong man
   opera.. 16. Samson and Delilah
   tribe.. 3. Dan
   wife.. 7. Delilah (betrayer)
Samuel... 4. Book (Old Test) 5. judge
   7. prophet
samurai... 6. vassal 7. officer
Sana native... 8. Yemenite
San Andreas rift... 15. earthquake
   fault (Calif)
San Antonio mission... 5. Alamo
sanative... 7. healing 8. curative,
   sanatory
Sancta Sanctis... 20. Holy things for
   the holy
sanctify... 5. honor 6. hallow
   10. consecrate 11. free from sin
sanctimonious... 4. holy 6. sacred
   7. saintly 8. affected 12. hypocritical
sanction... 4. abet, amen, fiat
   6. assent, permit, ratify 7. approve,
   endorse, support 8. approval
   9. approbate, authority, authorize
   11. countenance, endorsement
   12. ratification 13. authorization
sanctity... 8. holiness 9. godliness,

solemnity 10. sacredness
   11. saintliness 13. inviolability
sanctuary... 4. bema, fane, holy, naos
   5. abbey, bamah, cella, haven
   6. priory, refuge, temple 7. Alsatia,
   convent, retreat, shelter 8. cloister
   9. monastery 10. penetralia
sanctum... 3. den 5. study 6. adytum,
   office 7. retreat
sand... 4. grit 5. arena, nerve, pluck,
   stone
sand (pert to)...
   applied to body.. 9. arenation
   bog.. 4. syrt 9. quicksand
   eel.. 4. grig 6. launce
   flea.. 6. chigoe, red bug 7. chigger,
   sandboy
   fluke.. 7. sand dab 8. flounder
   hill, mound.. 4. dene, dune
   hog.. 7. laborer (in compressed air)
   8. tunneler (tunneller)
   inhabiting.. 11. arenicolous
   like (sand).. 9. arenulous
   10. arenaceous
   man.. 5. genie
   mixture (clay).. 4. loam 9. sandstone
   pear.. 5. Pyrus
   submerged bank.. 3. bar 5. hurst,
   shoal
   sugar.. 5. niter
   widgeon.. 7. gadwall
sandal... 4. boat, shoe, sock 7. talaria
sandpiper... 3. ree 4. knot, pume,
   ruff, stib 5. stint (long–toed)
   6. dunlin 8. pectoral, triddler
sandstone... 7. sarsens 8. ganister
Sandwich Islands... 6. Hawaii
   8. Hawaiian
sandy... 6. desert, gritty 7. arenose
   8. granular, sabulous, Scotsman
   9. sandpiper 10. arenaceous, ring
   plover
sane... 5. lucid, sound 7. logical
   8. rational, sensible 9. practical
   10. reasonable
San Francisco Mil Post... 8. Presidio
sang... 5. blood, sheng 7. chanted,
   ginseng, Society
sang–froid... 8. coolness 9. cold
   blood, composure 11. insouciance
sanguinary... 3. ant (slave) 4. gory
   5. cruel 6. bloody, yarrow
   8. sanguine 9. bloodroot, murderous
   12. bloodthirsty
sanguine... 4. warm 5. ruddy
   6. ardent 7. hopeful 8. blood–red
   9. confident 10. optimistic
   12. bloodthirsty
sanity... 6. reason 8. lucidity, saneness
   9. soundness 13. wholesomeness
San Juan Hill... 4. Cuba (Battle,
   1898)
San Juan Indian... 4. Tewa
San Kuo... 13. Three Kingdoms (Shu,
   Wei, Wu)
San Marino, Europe (pert to)...
   famed as.. 11. oldest State (Eur)
   government.. 8. Republic (smallest)
   mountains.. 8. Appenine
   site.. 8. Mt Titano
sannup... 6. Indian (married male) (opp
   of squaw)

Sanskrit (pert to)...
college .. **3.** tol
dialect .. **4.** Pali
drama .. **9.** Sakuntala (Shakuntala)
epic .. **8.** Ramayana
god .. **4.** Kama (Cupid), Vayu (wind)
   5. Indra (Great) **6.** Aditya
goddess .. **3.** Uma (Splendor) **4.** Devi
   (Mother) **5.** Aditi, Gauri
human spirit .. **7.** jivatma
literature .. **5.** sruti (shruti)
period .. **5.** Vedic
Phonet (sounds) .. **6.** sandhi
poem (epic) .. **11.** Race of Raghu,
   Raghuvamsha
poet .. **8.** Kalidasa
sacred books .. **4.** Veda
soul .. **5.** atman
treatise .. **9.** Upanishad
Santo Domingo ... **7.** capital
   (Dominican Republic)
sap ... **3.** gum **4.** boob, dupe, fool,
   mine, seve, upas **5.** drain, fluid,
   lymph, sapor **6.** juices, trench,
   weaken **7.** essence, schnook
   8. unsettle **9.** simpleton, undermine
sapid ... **5.** tasty **7.** zestful **8.** flavored
   9. palatable, toothsome
sapient ... **4.** sage, wise **6.** shrewd
   7. knowing **8.** profound **9.** sagacious
   10. discerning
sapiutan ... **4.** anoa **6.** wild ox
sapodilla ... **5.** chico **6.** chicle, zapote
   7. nispero **9.** naseberry
sapor ... **5.** savor, taste **6.** flavor, relish
sapper ... **5.** miner **6.** digger
   9. excavator
Saracen ... **4.** Arab **5.** nomad, pagan
   6. Muslim (Moslem) **7.** heathen,
   infidel, ragwort **9.** Moor's head (Her)
Saracen Knight ... **8.** Ruggiero
Sarah (pert to)...
bird .. **9.** wake–robin
husband .. **7.** Abraham
mother of .. **5.** Isaac
slave of .. **5.** Hagar
sarcasin ... **4.** gibe **5.** irony, taunt
   6. satire **8.** ironical, ridicule
sarcastic ... **3.** dry **6.** biting, ironic
   7. caustic, cutting, satiric **8.** ironical,
   sardonic **9.** malicious **10.** mordacious
sarcophagic ... **10.** sarcophagy
   11. flesh–eating **13.** sarcophageous
sarcophagus ... **5.** chest **6.** coffin
   9. limestone **11.** Assian stone, lapis
   Assius
sardine ... **4.** bang **7.** alewife, anchovy,
   herring (young) **8.** pilchard
Sardinia, Italy ...
capital .. **8.** Cagliari
island .. **13.** Mediterranean
sheep .. **7.** mouflon (moufflon)
tower (Prehist) .. **6.** nuragh
sardonic ... **3.** dry **6.** ironic, morose
   7. cynical, satiric **8.** derisive
   9. sarcastic **11.** Rabelaisian
sartor ... **6.** tailor
sash ... **3.** obi **4.** band, belt, benn, tobe
   6. girdle **8.** casement
   10. cummerbund
sash pulley weight ... **5.** mouse

Saskatchewan, Canada ...
capital .. **6.** Regina
city .. **8.** Moose Jaw **9.** Saskatoon
sassaby ... **8.** antelope
sassafras (pert to)...
nut .. **8.** pichurim
oil of (part) .. **6.** safrol
tea .. **6.** saloop
tree .. **4.** ague
Satan ... **5.** Demon, Devil, Eblis, fiend
   6. Belial **7.** Lucifer, Tempter
   9. archfiend **14.** Mephistopheles
   16. Prince of Darkness
Satan (pert to)...
angel (bottomless pit) .. **8.** Apollyon
associate .. **6.** Azazel **9.** Beelzebub
before his fall .. **7.** Lucifer
Jewish .. **8.** Asmodeus
Scottish .. **4.** deil
son .. **3.** Imp (jocular)
satanic ... **5.** cruel **6.** wicked
   8. devilish, infernal **10.** diabolical
satchel ... **3.** bag **4.** case, etui, grip,
   sack **5.** cabas **6.** valise
sate ... **4.** cloy, glut **5.** gorge
   7. gratify, satiate, satisfy, surfeit
   8. saturate
sated ... **4.** full **5.** blasé **6.** gorged
satellite ... **4.** Echo, luna, moon
   5. Atlas **6.** comsat, planet
   7. aerosat, Landsat, Sputnik, Telstar
   8. Explorer, follower, Vanguard
   9. companion, dependent
satellite of Jupiter ... **2.** Io (1st)
   6. Europa (2nd) **8.** Callisto,
   Ganymede
satellite of Saturn ... **4.** Rhea
   5. Dione, Mimas, Titan **6.** Phoebe,
   Tethys **8.** Hyperion **9.** Enceladus
satellite of Uranus ... **5.** Ariel
   6. Oberon **7.** Titania, Umbriel
satellite's orbit ... **4.** path
   14. geosynchronous
Sati (Egypt) ... **5.** Queen
satiate ... **4.** cloy, glut, pall, sate
   5. gorge **7.** gratify, satisfy, surfeit
satin ... **4.** silk **6.** étoile, fabric,
   sateen, satiny **9.** satinette
   10. smoothness
satire ... **3.** wit **5.** irony, spoof
   6. parody **7.** lampoon
satiric, satirical ... **3.** dry **6.** bitter,
   ironic **7.** abusive, caustic, cutting
   8. ironical, poignant **9.** burlesque,
   sarcastic **11.** reproachful
satisfaction ... **3.** cro **4.** duel
   6. amends **7.** comfort, content,
   payment, satiety **8.** adequacy,
   pleasure, reprisal **9.** atonement
   10. recompense, reparation
   11. contentment, fulfillment
   12. compensation, propitiation,
   remuneration **15.** indemnification
satisfied ... **5.** proud, sated **7.** content,
   pleased **8.** satiated **9.** contented,
   convinced, gratified **10.** paid in full
satisfy ... **2.** do **3.** pay **4.** fill, sate,
   suit **5.** atone, solve **6.** pay off,
   please, supply **7.** assuage, content,
   fulfill, gratify, indulge, requite, satiate
   8. atone for, convince

satrap (anc)... **5.** ruler **6.** despot,
   prince **8.** governor, overlord
saturate... **3.** ret, sop, wet **4.** fill, soak
   5. imbue, souse, steep **6.** drench,
   seethe **7.** satiate **8.** overfill, permeate
   10. impregnate
saturated... **4.** full **6.** soaked, sodden
Saturday... **6.** Samedi **9.** sabbatine
   13. Jewish Sabbath
Saturn (pert to)...
   Astron.. **6.** planet
   consort.. **3.** Ops
   god of.. **4.** seed
   Latin.. **8.** Saturnus
   rings.. **7.** moonlet **9.** particles
   rings, part.. **4.** ansa
   satellite.. **4.** Rhea **5.** Dione, Titan
      7. Iapetus **8.** Hyperion
   Temple treasury (State).. **8.** aerarium
saturnalia... **4.** orgy **7.** debauch
   8. Festival (of Saturn)
   11. pandemonium
saturnine... **6.** dismal, gloomy, somber
   8. funereal
satyr... **4.** faun **5.** deity **7.** demigod,
   silenus **9.** butterfly, capripede,
   orangutan
sauce... **3.** soy **4.** alec, pulp **5.** caper,
   curry, garum, gravy, pesto **6.** gansel,
   tahini **7.** catchup (catsup), soubise,
   Tabasco, veloute **8.** amandine,
   dressing, marinara **9.** espagnole,
   insolence, seasoning **11.** beurre blanc
   12. impertinence
saucy... **4.** bold, pert, vain **5.** brash,
   cocky, sassy, smart **7.** forward
   8. impudent, malapert **9.** officious
   11. impertinent **13.** disrespectful
Saudi Arabia...
   city.. **5.** Islam
   founder.. **7.** Ibn Saud (1913)
   gulf.. **7.** Persian
   Mohammed's tomb.. **6.** Medina
   mosque.. **5.** Kaaba
   peninsula.. **7.** Arabian
   provinces.. **4.** Asir, Nejd **5.** Hejaz
      6. El Hasa
   sea.. **3.** Red
   sect.. **6.** Wahabi (Wahabee, Wahhabi)
sauerbraten... **8.** pot roast
sauger... **9.** pike perch
Saul (pert to)...
   concubine.. **6.** Rizpah
   daughter.. **6.** Michal
   father.. **4.** Kish
   herdsman.. **4.** Doeg
   of Tarsus.. **4.** Paul
   uncle.. **3.** Ner
   wife.. **7.** Ahinoam
   witch of.. **5.** Endor
Sault Ste Marie... **3.** Soo **6.** rapids
   9. ship canal
saumont... **6.** salmon
sauna... **4.** bath (Finnish)
saunter... **3.** jog, lag, mog **4.** roam,
   rove, walk **5.** range, stray **6.** dawdle,
   loiter, lounge, potter, ramble, stroll,
   wander **8.** ruminate
sauqui... **6.** salmon
saurian... **6.** lizard, Sauria **7.** reptile,
   crocodile

sausage... **6.** banger, salami
   7. bologna, chorizo, saveloy
   8. kielbasa (kolbasi), rolliche
   9. bratwurst, pepperoni
   10. knackwurst
sausage-shaped... **9.** allantoid
   10. botuliform
savage... **3.** att **4.** rude, wild **5.** brute,
   cruel, feral, yahoo **6.** ferine, fierce,
   Indian **7.** brutish, howling **8.** cannibal,
   pitiless **9.** atrocious, barbarian,
   ferocious, merciless, primitive
   11. uncivilized **12.** uncultivated
savanna, savannah... **5.** plain
   9. grassland **11.** level region
savant... **4.** sage **6.** pundit **7.** scholar
   9. scientist **10.** classicist
   12. intellectual, man of letters
save... **3.** but **4.** keep **5.** catch,
   hoard, lay by **6.** except, redeem,
   rescue, scrimp **7.** prevent, protect,
   reserve, salvage **8.** conserve
   9. economize, excepting, safeguard
   10. accumulate
savin, savine... **5.** cedar **7.** juniper
   9. evergreen
savior, Saviour... **8.** Redeemer
   9. deliverer, liberator
   11. emancipator, Jesus Christ
savoir-faire... **4.** tact **5.** poise, savvy
   (sl) **7.** culture **9.** gentility **12.** ease of
   manner, mannerliness
savor, savour... **4.** odor, zest **5.** nidor,
   sapor, scent, smack, smell, taste
   6. flavor, relish **9.** degustate
savory, savoury... **5.** sapid, tasty
   7. piquant **8.** gustable **9.** agreeable
   10. appetizing, delightful
saw... **3.** cut **4.** dict **5.** adage, maxim
   6. cliché, saying, truism **7.** noticed,
   proverb **9.** platitude, serration
saw (kind)... **3.** jig, rip **4.** band, buzz,
   hack, whip **5.** crown, power
   7. keyhole **8.** crosscut
saw (pert to)...
   back.. **6.** sierra
   bill.. **6.** motmot **9.** merganser
   buck.. **8.** sawhorse **13.** ten-dollar bill
   crosscut.. **5.** briar
   fish.. **3.** ray
   grass.. **5.** sedge
   horse.. **4.** buck, rack **7.** sawbuck
   log.. **5.** edger
   of sawfish.. **5.** serra
   surgeon's.. **6.** trepan (trephine)
   teeth.. **5.** tines
   two-bladed.. **6.** stadda
sawmill gate... **4.** sash
saw-whet... **10.** Acadian owl
saxhorn... **4.** tuba **7.** althorn **8.** bass
   tuba **9.** saxcornet
saxifrage... **6.** Seseli
Saxon (pert to)...
   color.. **5.** smalt **8.** Saxe blue
      10. Bremen blue **13.** indigo carmine
   king.. **6.** Egbert **8.** Ethelred
      14. Alfred the Great
   language.. **10.** Anglo-Saxon
      12. Plattdeutsch
   people.. **7.** English **9.** Sassenach
      10. Anglo-Saxon **11.** Lowland Scot

serf.. **4.** esne
swineherd.. **5.** Gurth (Ivanhoe)
warrior.. **5.** thane
Saxony capital... **7.** Dresden
　10. Wittenburg (anc)
say... **4.** aver, cite, tell **5.** gnome,
　speak, state, utter **6.** affirm, answer,
　assert, assume, recite, remark,
　speech **9.** authority **11.** declaration
　12. conversation
say (pert to)...
a blessing.. **5.** bensh
again.. **6.** repeat **7.** restate
　9. reiterate
further.. **3.** add
no (to).. **6.** negate, refuse **8.** prohibit
　10. disapprove
one thing, mean another.. **6.** palter
　7. falsify **9.** fluctuate **10.** equivocate
　12. be capricious
uncle.. **4.** cede **9.** surrender
　10. capitulate **15.** throw in the
　towel
saying... **3.** dit, mot, saw **4.** quip
　5. adage, axiom, maxim **6.** byword,
　enigma, phrase, remark **7.** proverb
　8. aphorism, apothegm
　11. declaration
saying, sayings (pert to)...
collection of.. **9.** gnomology
criterion, party cry.. **10.** shibboleth
dogmatic.. **6.** dictum
religious.. **5.** logia
scab... **3.** rat **4.** sore **5.** crust, mange
　6. rotter **7.** blemish **8.** deserter
　9. scoundrel **12.** incrustation
　13. strikebreaker
scabbard... **6.** sheath **7.** holster,
　pilcher **13.** emblem of peace
scabbard fish... **7.** cutlass **9.** frostfish
scaddle... **5.** cruel, timid **6.** fierce
　7. nervous **8.** skittish, thievish
　11. mischievous
scads... **4.** gobs, wads **5.** heaps,
　money, piles **6.** oodles **11.** great
　number **12.** considerable
scaffold, scaffolding... **5.** easel, stage
　7. staging, support **8.** platform
　9. grain loft
scalawag, scallawag... **5.** scamp
　6. rascal **7.** sculpin **10.** scapegrace
scale... **3.** hut **4.** husk, peel, rate,
　shed, size **5.** climb, crust, flake,
　gamut **6.** ascend, degree, ladder,
　lamina, rustre (anc armor), series,
　weight **7.** compare, measure
　12. incrustation
scale (pert to)...
botany.. **5.** palea
color.. **10.** tintometer
comb form.. **4.** cten **5.** cteno, lepis
duck.. **9.** merganser, sheldrake
fish.. **6.** ganoid **8.** scabbard
grand.. **4.** epic
music.. **3.** E la (highest note)
　5. gamut, minor **9.** chromatic,
　hexachord **10.** tetrachord
slide.. **7.** vernier
tail.. **6.** rodent
Zool.. **6.** scutum
scallop... **4.** quin **5.** crena, notch
　7. mollusk **9.** serration, shellfish

12. summer squash
scalloped... **6.** cooked **7.** notched
　8. invected (Her) **9.** crenulate
scalpel... **5.** knife **6.** lancet **7.** dissect
　8. bistoury
scaly... **5.** flaky **6.** crusty, scabby,
　scurfy **7.** leprose **8.** squamous
scamp... **3.** imp **5.** cheat, knave,
　rogue **6.** rascal, slight **7.** bacalao,
　codfish **8.** scalawag, spalpeen
　9. scoundrel **15.** worthless fellow
scamper... **3.** hie, run **4.** dash, race,
　scud **5.** haste **6.** hasten **7.** brattle
　9. hasten off, skedaddle **11.** hasty
　flight
scan... **3.** eye **6.** browse, peruse
　7. examine **10.** scrutinize
　11. contemplate **16.** recite metrically
scance... **5.** blame, shine **6.** glance
　7. comment, glitter
scandal... **5.** odium, shame **6.** gossip
　7. calumny, offense, slander
　8. disgrace, ignominy
　10. defamation, detraction,
　opprobrium **11.** abomination
scandalous... **6.** wicked **8.** libelous,
　terrible **10.** defamatory, slanderous
　11. disgraceful, opprobrious
Scandinavia, countries... see also
　Scandinavian **6.** Norway, Sweden
　7. Denmark, Iceland
Scandinavian (pert to)...
alphabetical character.. **4.** rune
ash tree.. **10.** Yggdrasill
author.. **8.** Andersen (Hans C)
bay.. **5.** fjord
explorer.. **4.** Eric
goblin, brownie.. **5.** nisse **6.** kobold
god.. **4.** Lake, Thor
goose.. **5.** nisse
hall of Odin (heroes' souls)..
　8. Valhalla
legend.. **4.** Edda, saga
maiden of Odin.. **8.** Valkyrie
navigator.. **4.** Eric
people.. **4.** Dane, Lapp **5.** Swede
　8. Norseman **9.** Norwegian
people, type.. **8.** Teutonic
pert to.. **5.** runic
plateau.. **5.** fjeld
rulers.. **10.** Varangians
saga narrator.. **7.** sagaman
sea monster (fabled).. **6.** kraken
supernatural being (dwarf or giant)..
　5. troll
scant... **3.** few **5.** chary **6.** meager,
　narrow, scarce, slight, sparse
　7. slender, sparing **12.** parsimonious
scanty... **4.** rare **6.** meager (meagre),
　narrow, scarce, sparse **7.** scrimpy
　12. insufficient **14.** inconsiderable
scapegoat... **4.** goat (Bib) **9.** sacrifice
　10. substitute
scapegrace... **5.** scamp **8.** scalawag
　(scallawag) **9.** reprobate
　10. profligate **12.** incorrigible
scar... **3.** arr, shy **4.** seam, sear
　5. cliff, mound **7.** blemish **8.** cicatrix
scarce... **4.** rare **5.** short **6.** scanty
　7. sparing **8.** uncommon **9.** deficient
　10. infrequent
scarcely... **6.** barely, hardly **7.** but just

12. infrequently

scarcity... 4. lack, want 6. dearth, famine, rarity 7. paucity 8. rareness 11. infrequency 13. insufficiency

scare... 3. cow 5. alarm, panic 7. startle, terrify 8. affright, frighten

scarecrow... 4. ogre 5. bogle 6. effigy, goblin, malkin, shewel (sewel) 9. jackstraw 10. frightener 11. hide–and–seek

scarf... 3. boa, tie 4. sash 5. ascot, cloud, nubia 6. tippet 7. muffler 9. rigolette 10. fascinator

scarf (pert to)...
bird.. 9. cormorant
broad.. 5. shawl
clerical.. 5. fanon, orale, rabat, stole
feather.. 3. boa
head.. 10. fascinator
Hindu.. 4. sari
India.. 7. dopatta
Mexico.. 6. tapalo
skin.. 7. cuticle 9. epidermis

Scarlet Letter... 5. novel (Hawthorne)

Scarlet O'Hara's home... 4. Tara

scarp... 5. cliff, pitch 7. descent, incline 9. declivity

scary... 5. eerie, timid, weird 7. ghostly, uncanny 8. alarming 12. easily scared

scat... 4. hiss 5. burst, smash 6. buffet 7. scatter

scat, scatt (Orkney Isls)... 3. tax 7. tribute

scathe... 4. flay, harm, hurt 6. assail, damage, injury, scorch 7. scarify 9. excoriate 10. misfortune

scatter... 3. sow, ted 4. deal, rout 5. spray, strew 6. dispel, litter, shower, splash, spread 7. bestrew, diffuse, radiate 8. disperse, separate, squander 9. circulate, dissipate 10. disarrange, strew about

scattered... 4. semé 5. dealt 6. sparse, strewn 8. confused, sparsile, sporadic 9. broadcast, dispersed, separated, sprinkled 10. widespread 11. distributed

scattering... 3. few 8. Diaspora 10. dispersion, separating 13. dissemination

scatty... 7. showery

scaup... 4. duck 8. bluebill 9. blackhead, broadbill

scavenger... 4. bird 8. organism 10. saprophyte 16. garbage collector

scaw... 8. headland 10. promontory

scene... 4. site, view 5. anger, sight, vista 6. locale 7. diorama, picture, tableau

scene (pert to)...
behind the.. 8. secretly 9. backstage, invisible
inside.. 7. neorama
last.. 6. finale
of action.. 5. arena, stage 6. sphere
of confusion.. 5. babel
of miracle (Bib).. 4. Cana
opera.. 5. scena
wright.. 6. artist 8. designer (scenery), stageman

scenic... 8. dramatic 9. panoramic

11. picturesque

scenic (pert to)...
enigma.. 7. charade
pert to.. 5. stage 7. episode, scenery
representation.. 7. diorama 13. motion picture

scent... 4. aura, clue, nose, odor 5. aroma, flair, nairn, nidar, smell, spoor 6. detect 7. perfume 9. fragrance

scented... 5. olent 6. odored 8. perfumed, smelling 11. odoriferous

scepter, sceptre... 3. rod 4. mace 5. baton, staff 6. emblem (royal) 8. insignia 11. sovereignty

schedule... 4. card, list 5. slate 7. program 8. calendar, document 9. catalogue, inventory

scheme... 3. aim 4. lark, plan, plot 5. cabal 6. device, devise, racket, system 7. complot, concoct, diagram, epitome, outline, project, purpose 8. artifice, contrive 9. boomerang 10. conspiracy, enterprise 11. machination

schemer... 7. plotter 8. conniver, finagler 9. intriguer

schism... 4. rent, sect 5. split 6. breach 7. dissent, faction 8. division 10. falling–out, separation

schismatic... 7. heretic, sectary 8. apostate 9. dissenter, sectarian 10. factionist

schist... 4. mica, rock 5. slate 10. hornblende

scholar... 6. pedant, savant 7. learner, student 8. disciple 11. philologist

scholarly... 7. erudite, learned 8. academic, studious 9. philomath 10. scholastic

scholarship... 5. burse 8. learning 9. education, erudition, knowledge 10. foundation 11. instruction

school... 4. cult, sect 5. class, drill, flock, order, teach, train 7. convent, educate, seminar 8. instruct, seminary 9. institute

school (pert to)...
book.. 6. primer, reader 7. speller
English.. 4. Eton 6. Oxford 9. Cambridge
French.. 5. école, lycée
German.. 6. schule
head, inspector.. 9. scholarch
master.. 7. dominie 9. pedagogue (pedagog)
ref to.. 10. scholastic
riding.. 6. manège
teacher.. 4. marm
term.. 8. semester
wrestling.. 9. gymnasium, palaestra (palestra)

school of...
art.. 4. Dada
Fine Arts.. 9. Wagnerian
fishes.. 5. shoal
philosophers.. 7. Eleatic
philosophy.. 7. Gnostic
seals.. 3. pod
thieves.. 4. gang
whales.. 3. gam, pod

schooner... 4. boat, brig, tern 5. glass

6. vessel 7. measure, prairie (Hist)
schuit, schuyt ... 5. sloop 6. vessel
7. eelboat
science ... 3. art 5. ology, skill
9. knowledge 11. proficiency
science of ...
agriculture .. 8. agronomy
better living .. 9. euthenics
breeding .. 8. eugenics
character .. 8. ethology
children's diseases .. 10. pediatrics
(paediatrics)
controversy .. 8. polemics
creatures .. 10. entomology
dining .. 10. aristology
doctrines .. 9. esoterics
ears .. 7. otology
family symbols .. 8. heraldry
forest trees .. 7. silvics (sylvics)
good .. 6. ethics 9. euthenics
10. agathology
government .. 8. politics
happiness .. 11. eudaemonics
healing .. 9. iatrology
health .. 7. hygiene
kissing .. 13. philematology
language .. 9. philology, semantics
11. linguistics
life .. 7. biology 10. entomology
light .. 6. optics
mind .. 10. psychology
moral conduct .. 6. ethics
organism behavior .. 7. ecology
(oecology) 9. bionomics
philosophy .. 6. noesia
reality .. 10. philosophy
reasoning .. 5. logic
rocks .. 9. petrology
sea (the) .. 12. oceanography
self–defense .. 4. judo 7. jujitsu
sound .. 9. acoustics
theology interpretation .. 8. exegesis
12. hermeneutics
verse .. 7. prosody
virtue .. 8. aretaics
words .. 9. semantics
scientific ... 5. exact 9. realistic,
technical 16. precise knowledge
scimitar, scimiter ... 4. snee 5. saber
8. billhook
scintilla ... 4. atom, iota, whit
5. spark, trace 7. modicum
scintillate ... 5. flash, gleam, spark
7. be witty, glitter, twinkle
9. coruscate 10. be eloquent
scion, cion ... 3. son 4. slip 5. graft,
shoot 10. descendant
scold ... 3. jaw, nag 4. carp, rail, rate
5. chide, shrew 6. berate, chider,
rebuke 7. reprove, upbraid
8. admonish 9. reprimand
scolding ... 7. froward 8. reproach,
shrewish 10. upbraiding
12. admonishment, reprimanding
sconce ... 3. top 4. head 5. brain,
mulct, skull 6. screen 7. bulwark,
lantern, redoubt, skelter
11. candlestick, counterfort
scoop ... 4. bail, beat, lade, news
5. empty, ladle, spoon 6. bucket,
hollow, shovel 8. excavate, gather in

scoop out ... 3. dig 5. gouge
6. chisel, hollow 7. fashion
scope ... 4. area, room 5. ambit,
arena, range, reach 6. degree,
domain 7. compass, freedom, liberty
8. latitude 9. gyroscope, intention,
periscope, telescope 10. microscope
11. stethoscope 12. kaleidoscope,
spectroscope
scorch ... 4. burn, char, sear, sere
5. parch, singe, speed 7. shrivel
9. criticize
scordato ... 9. out of tune 14. made
discordant
score ... 3. peg, run, sum, tab 4. debt,
gain, goal, rate 5. corge, judge,
notch, scold, slash, tally 6. berate,
furrow, groove, points, reason, twenty
7. account, arrange, scratch
8. incision 9. calculate, tally mark
10. obligation 11. arrangement,
composition, orchestrate
12. indebtedness
scoria (volcano) ... 4. lava, slag
5. dross 6. refuse 7. residue
scorn ... 4. defy, geck, mock 5. spurn
6. deride, reject 7. contemn,
despise, disdain 8. contempt,
derision, disgrace 9. contumely
scornful ... 8. derisive, insolent
10. disdainful 12. contemptuous,
contumelious
Scorpio (pert to) ...
constellation in .. 8. Milky Way
genus .. 8. Scorpius
night mansion of .. 4. Mars
pictured as .. 8. scorpion
star (brightest) .. 7. Antares
zodiac sign .. 6. eighth
scorpion ... 4. nepa 7. alacran, scourge
(Bib) 8. arachnid, catapult 10. pine
lizard, vinaigrier 11. vinegarroon
(vinagron) 15. blue–tailed skink
Scot ... 3. Mac 4. Celt, Gael 5. Saxon
6. Sawney 7. bluecap 8. Scotsman
10. Caledonian, Highlander
Scotland ... see also *Scottish*
capital .. 9. Edinburgh
city .. 3. Ayr 5. Perth 6. Atholl
(Athole), Dundee 7. Glasgow
(largest), Renfrew 8. Aberdeen
9. Inverness
congress (musical) .. 3. Mod
district .. 6. Argyll, Atholl
10. Midlothian
famed site .. 9. Trossachs (Lady of the
Lake) 10. Loch Lomond 11. Loch
Katrine
firth .. 3. Tay 4. Loch 5. Clyde, Forth,
Moray, Tweed
islands .. 6. Orkney 8. Hebrides,
Shetland
Latin name (anc) .. 9. Caledonia
moors .. 10. Lochar Moss
mountain .. 9. Grampians
poetic name .. 6. Scotia 9. Caledonia
resort .. 4. Oban
river .. 3. Ayr, Dee, Tay 5. Afton,
Clyde, North, Tweed 6. Teviot
7. Deveron
seaport .. 4. Leth 6. Dundee
Scotland Yard headquarters ...

6. London 18. Metropolitan Police
Scott, Sir Walter (pert to)...
estate.. 10. Abbotsford (Scot)
famed as.. 4. poet 8. novelist
novel.. 7. Ivanhoe
poem.. 13. Lady of the Lake
Scottish (pert to)...
accent.. 4. birr
alder.. 3. arn
attendant (hunter's).. 6. gillie (gilly)
bagpipe music.. 7. pibroch
beret.. 3. tam 11. tam–o'–shanter
bird.. 3. gae (blue) 6. grouse
7. snabbie (snabby) 9. swinepipe
blessing.. 6. rebuke 8. scolding
blood money.. 3. cro 7. galanas
blue.. 6. homage 8. infernal
11. reddish–blue
bluebell.. 8. harebell
boat.. 4. zulu 7. coracle, skaffie
bonnets.. 8. mushroom
brandy.. 6. Athole
breeches.. 5. trews
brier, briar.. 4. rose
broth.. 5. brose
bull, ox.. 4. stot
cake (tea).. 5. scone
cap.. 3. tam 8. Balmoral 9. Glengarry
11. tam–o'–shanter
carpet.. 13. Kidderminster
cattle.. 8. Aberdeen 9. Ayrshire
celebration.. 4. kirn (harvest)
child.. 5. bairn 6. scuddy (naked)
church.. 4. kirk
cloth.. 4. kelt 6. tartan
coalfish.. 7. glashan, sillock
court officer.. 5. macer
cup.. 4. tass
dagger (anc).. 4. dirk
dagger, knife.. 8. skean dhu
dance.. 4. reel 5. fling 9. ecossaise
10. strathspey 13. Highland fling
devil.. 4. deil 6. Hornie
dirge.. 8. coronach (as on bagpipes)
duck.. 4. coot 6. scoter
earth.. 4. eard
elder.. 7. tobacco
elm.. 7. wych–elm
excuse.. 6. sunyie
eye.. 2. ee
family (same).. 3. ilk
festival.. 3. Mod 7. uphelya (Epiphany)
fish.. 4. sile 7. sillock 8. spalding
fog.. 4. haar
Gaelic.. 4. Erse
ghost.. 6. taisch
girl.. 4. lass 6. lassie, towdie
7. winklot
goblin.. 8. barghest
godmother.. 6. cummer (kimmer)
grandchild.. 2. oy (oye)
grandfather.. 8. gudesire
hill, hillside.. 4. brae 6. strone
icicle.. 7. shoggle
kilt.. 7. filibeg
kiss (stolen).. 8. smoorich
lake.. 4. loch
language.. 4. Erse 6. Lallan (Lalland)
liquor.. 5. scour 6. Athole 7. whitter
lovage.. 10. sea parsley
money, silver.. 6. siller
nephew.. 6. nepote

New Year's Day.. 7. Cake Day
8. hogmanay
nightingale.. 7. warbler
ox, bullock.. 4. nowt
plaid.. 4. maud 6. tartan
porridge.. 5. brose
pouch, purse (kilt front).. 7. sporran
pudding.. 6. haggis
reel (fishing).. 4. pirn
rod, over the door.. 10. willow wand
sausage.. 9. whitehass (whitehawse)
schoolmaster.. 3. dux
shawl (plaid).. 4. maud
stream, brook.. 4. sike
sweetheart.. 2. jo
sword.. 8. claymore
toad.. 3. ted 4. taed
tobacco.. 5. elder
topaz.. 9. cairngorm
townhall.. 8. tolbooth (tollbooth)
uncle.. 3. eme
village.. 3. rew
waistcoat (under).. 6. fecket
whirlpool.. 7. swilkie
whisky.. 9. Glenlivet (Glenlivat)
10. usquebaugh
window.. 7. winnock
youth.. 6. chield (chiel) 7. callant
(callan)
scoundrel... 3. cad 5. cheat, knave,
scamp 6. varlet 7. villain
8. scalawag 9. miscreant
10. blackguard 11. rapscallion
scoup... 3. run 4. leap, skip
7. scamper
scourge... 4. bane, flog, lash, whip
6. punish, swinge, switch 8. chastise
10. affliction, infliction, punishment
Scourge of God... 6. Attila (King of
Huns)
Scourge of Princes... 7. Aretino (It
satirist)
scout... 3. spy 5. flout, scoff
7. lookout, servant 8. emissary,
watchman 9. guillemot
11. reconnoiter 14. razor–billed auk
scow... 4. acon 6. garvey 7. lighter
scowl... 5. frown, lower 6. aspect
(gloomy), glower 7. wrinkle (brow)
10. sullen look
scraggly... 5. rough 6. ragged
7. unkempt 9. irregular
scraggy... 4. bony 5. rough
6. meager, rugged, skinny
7. knotted, scrawny, stunted
scram... 6. begone, benumb, decamp
7. vamoose
scramble... 4. push 5. climb, crowd,
crush 6. jostle, strive 7. clamber,
scatter 8. struggle
scrap... 3. bit, end, ort, rag 4. chip,
junk 5. fight, melee, piece, waste
6. morsel, refuse 7. cutting, discard,
excerpt, extract, quarrel, remnant
8. fragment, ramentum
scrape... 3. row, rub 4. rake, rasp
5. grate, graze, shave 6. abrade, eke
out, injure, sclaff 7. collect, scratch
9. economize, obeisance 10. difficulty
11. predicament
scraper... 4. harl (wool), tool
6. barber, rasper 7. abrader, fiddler,

strigil **8.** grattoir

scrappy... **9.** irregular **10.** pugnacious **11.** contentious, fragmentary, quarrelsome

scratch... **3.** mar, rit, rub **4.** claw, draw, itch, mark, rake, rist, tear **5.** erase **6.** cancel, injury, scrape **7.** blemish, roughen, scarify **8.** scribble, withdraw

scrawl... **6.** doodle **7.** scratch **8.** scribble

scrawny... **4.** lean, poor, thin **5.** spare **6.** skinny **7.** scranny **8.** rawboned

scream... **3.** cry **4.** wail, yell **6.** shriek, squeal **7.** screech

screamer... **5.** swift (bird) **7.** blunder **8.** headline

scree... **5.** stone, talus **6.** debris, pebble

screech... **3.** cry, say **6.** outcry, scream, shriek, squeal **7.** ululate

screech (pert to)...
hawk.. **10.** goatsucker
martin.. **5.** swift
owl.. **4.** barn **5.** Scops

screed... **4.** list, rend, tear **5.** shred **6.** tirade **7.** lecture **8.** fragment **12.** dissertation

screen... **3.** net **4.** hide, laun, mask, sift, sort, veil **5.** arras, blind, cloak, pavis, shade, sieve, spier **6.** defend, grille, riddle, sifter, sorter **7.** conceal, curtain, protect, reredos, shelter **8.** parclose **9.** partition, safeguard **10.** protection **12.** discriminate

screw... **3.** key **4.** coil, turn **5.** horse, twist **6.** fasten, gimlet, rotate, spiral **7.** contort, distort, tighten, turnkey **9.** bargainer, propeller, skinflint **10.** contortion, thumbscrew

screwlike... **6.** spiral **7.** spiroid

scribble... **6.** doodle, scrawl **7.** scratch **8.** scrabble

scribe... **5.** clerk **6.** author, jurist, lawyer, penman, writer **8.** recorder **10.** amanuensis, cuttlefish, journalist **13.** bibliographer

scriggle... **5.** twist **6.** squirm **7.** wriggle **8.** curlicue

scrimmage... **3.** row **5.** fight **6.** tussle **8.** football (term), practice, skirmish, struggle

scrimp... **4.** save **5.** scant, stint **6.** scanty, scrape, sparse **7.** sparing **9.** economize

scrip... **3.** bag **4.** list **5.** money **6.** wallet **7.** writing **8.** document, schedule

script... **5.** ronde **6.** letter **7.** writing **8.** scenario **10.** manuscript, typescript **11.** handwriting

scriptural... **7.** written **8.** Biblical, orthodox

scriptural interpreter... **7.** exegete

scripture... **4.** writ **5.** motto, truth **7.** passage, writing **8.** document **10.** manuscript **11.** inscription **13.** sacred writing

Scripture, Scriptures... **4.** text **5.** Bible **6.** lesson **7.** Oracles, passage, Vulgate

Scripture interpretation... **8.** exegesis

12. hermeneutics

scrivello... **4.** tusk (elephant's)

scrivener... **6.** notary, scribe, writer **8.** recorder **10.** amanuensis

scroll... **4.** list, roll **5.** draft **6.** record, spiral, volute **7.** engross, writing **8.** document, inscribe, schedule, streamer **9.** parchment

scroll roll... **8.** makimono

scrub... **3.** mop, rub **4.** mean, runt, tree, wash **5.** clean, dwarf, scour **6.** drudge, paltry **7.** cleanse **8.** inferior **10.** undersized

scrubby... **4.** base **6.** paltry, shabby, stubby **7.** bristly, shrubby, stunted **10.** underbrush **13.** insignificant

scruff... **4.** nape, scum, slur **5.** crust, dross, scuff **6.** refuse **7.** surface **8.** dandruff

scruple... **4.** coin **5.** demur, qualm **6.** object, weight **9.** small part **10.** hesitation **13.** unwillingness

scrupulous... **4.** nice **5.** exact **6.** formal, proper, strict **8.** qualmish **10.** fastidious, meticulous **11.** punctilious **13.** conscientious

scrutinize... **3.** eye, pry **4.** scan **5.** probe **7.** examine, inspect, observe

scud... **4.** dash, foam, gust, rain, sail, skim **5.** speed **6.** clouds, shower

scuffle... **4.** fray **5.** melee **6.** strive, tussle **7.** contend, contest, shamble, shuffle **8.** struggle

sculduddery... **9.** grossness, obscenity

scull... **3.** oar **4.** gull **5.** shoal, skate **6.** basket, paddle, propel **7.** rowboat

scullion... **4.** base **6.** menial **7.** servant **10.** dishwasher, kitchenman

scullog, scullogue... **6.** farmer, rustic **7.** laborer

sculp... **5.** carve **7.** engrave **8.** seal skin **9.** engraving, sculpture

sculptor... **6.** artist, carver, imager, molder **8.** chiseler **13.** constellation **19.** Apparatus Sculptoris (constellation)

sculptor (famed)... **5.** Rodin **7.** Cellini, Phidias **10.** Praxiteles **12.** Michelangelo, Saint Gaudens

sculptor's tool... **6.** chisel, graver **9.** ébauchoir

sculpture... **4.** form **5.** carve, model **6.** figure, statue **9.** engraving **11.** alto–relievo

scum... **4.** film, foam **5.** cover, dross, froth, scurf, spume **6.** refuse, scoria **7.** coating **8.** riffraff **10.** impurities

scup... **5.** bream, porgy

scurrility... **5.** abuse **9.** indignity, obscenity

scurrilous... **3.** low **4.** vile **5.** gross **6.** vulgar **7.** abusive **8.** indecent, scurrile **9.** insulting **11.** foulmouthed, opprobrious

scurry... **3.** hie **4.** dash **5.** scoot, speed **6.** flurry, hasten **7.** scamper, scuttle **9.** skedaddle

scurvy... **4.** base, mean **7.** disease **12.** contemptible, discourteous

scuttle... **3.** hod, run **4.** dish, sink

5. haste, scoot 6. basket, hasten, scurry, shovel 7. octopus, platter 8. hatchway 10. cuttlefish
scutum... 5. scute 6. shield 13. constellation (Milky Way) 15. Scutum Sobieskii
Scylla (pert to)...
father.. 5. Nisus
home.. 4. rock (coast of Italy)
lover.. 5. Minos
menace to.. 9. seafarers
Myth.. 7. monster
transformed to.. 7. sea bird
scythe... 2. sy (sye) 5. swath
scythe handle... 5. snath, snead
sea... 3. Red 4. Aral, Azov, Ross, wave 5. Black, brine, China, ocean, swell, water 6. aequor 7. Caspian 8. seashore 9. Caribbean
sea (pert to)...
adder.. 8. pipefish 11. stickleback
anemone.. 5. polyp
Antarctic.. 4. Ross
arm.. 4. gulf, meer, mere 5. bayou, firth 7. estuary
bird.. 3. auk 4. erne (ern), gull, smew, tern 5. booby, cahow, solan 6. gannet, petrel, puffin 9. albatross 10. shearwater
comb form.. 3. mer
cow.. 6. dugong, rytina (Steller's), walrus 7. manatee 8. sirenian 12. hippopotamus
cucumber.. 7. trepang
devil.. 9. angelfish, devilfish
dog.. 4. seal (Her) 6. fogdog, sailor
dragon.. 8. dragonet, sea horse
dread of.. 14. thalassophobia
duck.. 5. eider, scaup 6. scoter
eagle.. 4. erne (ern) 6. osprey
ear.. 7. abalone
eel.. 6. conger
farer.. 3. tar 6. sailor, seaman 7. mariner
foam.. 5. froth 9. sepiolite 10. meerschaum
fowl.. 3. auk 4. gull, tern 6. gannet, petrel
fox.. 5. shark
god, deity.. 3. Lar 5. Aegir 6. Triton 7. Neptune, Phorcus, Proteus 8. Poseidon
goddess.. 4. Nina 5. Doris 10. Amphitrite
gull.. 3. cob, mew 9. kittiwake
hare.. 7. mollusk
hen.. 4. skua 9. guillemot
hog.. 8. porpoise
holly root.. 6. eryngo (eringo)
ladder.. 6. Jacob's
lion.. 4. seal
mammal.. 4. seal 5. whale 6. dugong 7. manatee 11. bladdernose
mouse.. 4. duck (harlequin) 6. dunlin 7. annelid
nymph.. 5. naiad, siren 6. nereid 7. oceanid
onion.. 6. squill
otter.. 5. kalan
owl.. 6. puffin 8. lumpfish
pig.. 6. dugong 7. dolphin

8. porpoise
pumpkin.. 8. cucumber
quail.. 6. auklet 9. turnstone
raven.. 7. sculpin 9. cormorant 10. squaretail
reference to.. 5. naval 6. marine 7. oceanic, pelagic 8. maritime 9. Neptunian, thalassic
robber.. 6. jaeger, pirate 7. corsair 9. buccaneer, privateer
serpent.. 5. Hydra 8. snake eel
shell.. 5. conch
sickness.. 8. mal de mer 9. naupathia
spider.. 10. spider crab
turtle.. 5. green 9. hawksbill 10. loggerhead, thalassian 11. leatherback
unicorn.. 7. narwhal
urchin.. 5. heart 10. echinoderm, Spatangina 13. cushionflower
wolf.. 4. seal 6. pirate 9. privateer, submarine
sea king... 3. Ler 5. chief 6. pirate, Viking 7. Neptune
seal (pert to)...
bearded.. 5. ursuk 6. makluk
breeding ground.. 7. rookery
eared.. 5. otary
flock.. 3. pod
fur (fem).. 5. matka (matkah)
harp (male).. 7. saddler
leather.. 3. pin
limb.. 7. flipper
skin.. 5. sculp
type.. 3. fur 7. sea lion 8. elephant, pinniped
young.. 3. pup
sealed instrument... 6. escrow
seam... 4. line, load, scar 5. joint, ridge, strip 6. burden, groove, stitch, streak, suture 7. crevice, stratum 9. horseload 10. interstice, packsaddle
seaman... 3. gob, tar 6. sailor, Seabee 7. mariner
seaman's chapel... 6. bethel, church
seamark... 6. beacon 10. lighthouse
seamy... 5. rough 8. wrinkled 12. disreputable
séance... 7. session, sitting 9. treatment
séance holder... 6. medium
sear, sere... 3. dry 4. burn, cook 5. parch 6. braise, scorch, wither 7. dried up, shrivel 8. deadened, withered 9. cauterize 10. threadbare 11. deteriorate
search... 4. comb, fish, hunt, look, seek 5. frisk, ghoom, grope, probe, quest 6. ferret, forage, survey 7. inquire, ransack, rummage, zetetic 9. expiscate 10. scrutinize 11. investigate
searchlight... 4. beam 10. flashlight
seashell... 4. clam 5. conch, snail 7. scallop
season... 3. age 4. fall, salt, tide, time 5. devil, inure, spice 6. flavor, mature 7. qualify 8. accustom, preserve 11. acclimatize
season (pert to)...

Astron.. 5. Aries, Libra 6. Cancer
11. Capricornus
Eccl.. 4. Lent 6. Advent, Easter
7. Trinity 8. Epiphany 9. Christmas
11. Whitsuntide
Lent.. 6. carême
Scot.. 4. sele
yearly.. 6. Autumn, Spring, Summer,
Winter
seasonable... 6. timely 7. apropos
seasoning... 4. sage, salt 5. spice,
thyme 6. cloves, garlic, pepper
7. mustard, paprika 8. allspice,
estragon, marjoram, rosemary,
turmeric 9. condiment
Seasons, goddesses of...
justice.. 4. Dike
order (Universe).. 5. Horae
peace.. 6. Eirene
wise laws.. 7. Eunomia
seat... 3. pew 4. root, site 5. bench,
chair, embed, sella, stool 6. settee,
settle 7. install 9. establish
seat (pert to)...
church.. 3. pew 6. sedile
of justice.. 4. banc
of self.. 3. ego
on elephant.. 6. howdah
outdoor.. 6. exedra
privileged.. 6. curule
series (one of).. 6. gradin (gradine)
seaweed... 4. kelp 5. algae, dulse,
laver, varec, wrack 6. Alaria
8. agar–agar
secco... 3. dry
secern... 7. secrete 8. separate
11. distinguish 12. discriminate
Secessionist (S Carolina)... 5. Rhett
secluded... 5. aloof, apart 6. hidden,
lonely, remote, secret 7. private,
retired 8. debarred, expelled, isolated,
recessed, retiring, screened, solitary
9. cloistral, concealed
seclusion... 7. privacy, retreat
8. solitude 9. aloofness, exclusion
10. quarantine, retirement, separation
second... 3. aid 4. abet, back, echo,
time 5. jiffy, trice 6. assist, attend,
backer, double, moment 7. instant,
support, sustain 8. inferior
9. assistant, encourage, imperfect,
prototype, reinforce 11. corroborate,
subordinate
second (pert to)...
childhood.. 6. dotage, dotard
8. senility
crop.. 5. rowen
lieutenant.. 9. shavetail
number.. 6. addend
rate.. 8. inferior, mediocre
Republic.. 6. French (1848–52)
sight.. 6. myopia 7. psychic
9. intuition 12. clairvoyance
team.. 5. scrub 9. Yannigans
thought.. 6. sequel 12. afterthought
15. reconsideration
secondary... 4. less 5. minor
6. deputy 8. inferior, offshoot
9. auxiliary, dependent, satellite
10. contingent, derivative,
second–rate, subsequent, substitute
11. subordinate, unessential

12. nonessential, quill feather
secondary color... 5. green 6. orange,
purple
secondary school... 4. prep 5. lycée
7. academy 10. Realschule
secrecy... 4. tile 6. hiding 7. mystery,
privacy, privity 8. velation
9. reticence, seclusion
10. confidence 11. concealment
secret... 3. key 4. dern 5. close,
inner, privy 6. arcane, covert, hidden,
mystic, occult 7. arcanum, cryptic,
mystery, private, unknown 8. esoteric,
intimate (armor), reticent, secluded,
skullcap 9. concealed, recondite,
secretive, underhand 10. confidence,
mysterious 11. clandestine
12. confidential 13. surreptitious
secret (pert to)...
agent.. 3. spy 5. scout 6. espier
7. spotter 8. emissary
13. undercover man
council.. 5. by–end, junto 7. purpose
language.. 5. argot 7. dialect
meeting.. 5. tryst
movement.. 7. stealth
name.. 9. cryptonym
place.. 5. cache 6. adytum
7. sanctum 9. sanctuary
society.. 3. hui (Chin) 4. tong
7. Camorra (It)
secretary... 4. bird, desk 5. agent
6. scribe 7. officer 8. recorder
9. confidant 10. amanuensis,
escritoire
secrete... 4. bury, hide, stow 5. exude
7. conceal
secretion (pert to)...
gland.. 7. hormone
inflammation.. 3. pus
liver.. 4. bile
mammal gland.. 9. lactation
mouth.. 6. saliva
nasal.. 10. secernment
scale, insect.. 3. lac
shrubs.. 4. lerp
whale.. 9. ambergris
secretly... 5. aside, slyly 7. sub rosa
8. covertly 9. not openly
13. clandestinely
sect... 4. clan, cult, part 5. Alogi
(Hist), class, group, order, party
6. essene, school, Yezidi (Kurdish)
9. following, Mennonite
10. shibboleth (Bib)
12. denomination
sectarian... 7. heretic 8. partisan
9. dissenter, heterodox
13. nonconformist
14. denominational
section... 4. area, part, plot 5. panel,
piece, slice, tmema, torso 6. region
7. portion, segment, ternion
8. parabola, surgical 9. paragraph,
signature 11. subdivision
secular... 3. lay 4. laic 5. civil
6. laical 7. earthly, profane, worldly
8. temporal 9. centuried, temporary
secure... 3. fix, get, pin 4. bind, easy,
fast, firm, moor, nail, safe, tape
5. fetch, spike, trice (sail) 6. elicit,
ensure, fasten, obtain, stable

7. acquire, assured, certain, procure, receive 8. make fast 9. confident, guarantee 10. dependable 11. undisturbed

security... 4. bail, gage 5. guard 6. pledge, safety, vadium 7. defense, shelter 8. guaranty 9. guarantee, insurance, stability 10. protection

sedate... 4. calm 5. douce, quiet, sober, staid 6. demure, proper, serene, solemn 7. serious, settled 8. composed, decorous 9. dignified, unruffled 11. unobtrusive 13. contemplative, dispassionate

sedative... 6. remedy 7. anodyne, bromide, chloral, veronal 8. atropine, barbital, lenitive, soothing 9. calmative, mitigator, paregoric 10. palliative, phenacetin 12. tranquilizer (tranquillizer) 13. phenobarbital

sedent... 7. sitting (statue)

sediment... 4. lees, silt 5. dregs 7. deposit, grounds, siltage 9. settlings

sedition... 6. revolt, strife, tumult 7. treason 9. commotion 10. dissension, turbulence

seditious... 7. riotous 8. factious 9. turbulent 11. treasonable 15. insurrectionary

seduce... 4. lure 5. decoy, tempt 6. allure, enamor, entice 7. corrupt, mislead 8. inveigle

seducer... 7. enticer, tempter 8. Lothario 9. debaucher

seduction... 5. charm 10. allurement, corruption, temptation 11. debauchment

sedulous... 4. busy 6. steady 8. diligent, untiring 9. assiduous, laborious, unwearied 10. persistent 11. persevering, unremitting

see... 3. spy 4. espy, heed, know, look, scry, seat, view 5. visit 6. behold, descry, detect 7. diocese, discern, witness 8. discover, perceive 9. apprehend, interview, visualize 10. comprehend, understand 11. contemplate

seed... 3. egg, pip, pit, sow 4. germ 5. grain, ovule, plant, sperm, spore 6. kernel, origin 7. lineage, progeny 8. rudiment 9. beginning 11. descendants

seed (pert to)...
apple.. 3. pip
aromatic.. 5. anise 7. aniseed, caraway
coat.. 3. pod 4. aril, burr, husk 5. testa 6. carpel 8. pericarp
container, envelope.. 3. bur (burr), pod 6. loment, vessel 7. capsule
edible.. 3. pea 4. bean 5. grain 6. lentil
enclosing soft fruit.. 5. drupe
flower.. 6. pistil
immature.. 5. ovule
lemon, orange, apple.. 3. pip
licorice.. 9. jequerity
medicinal.. 8. flaxseed
Moringa, tropical.. 3. ben

naked (one–seeded fruit).. 6. achene (akene)
oak.. 5. acorn
one–celled.. 6. carpel
part.. 6. tunica
poppy, opium.. 3. maw
underground.. 6. peanut
winged.. 6. samara

seeds (pert to)...
cocoa.. 5. cacao
feeding on.. 11. granivorous
perfume.. 8. abelmosk
rudiments.. 3. ova 4. eggs, pips, pits 6. ovules, sperms

seedy... 5. dingy, lousy, tacky 6. shabby 7. worn out 8. slovenly 10. spiritless 11. spawn–filled 12. bearing seeds

seek... 3. beg 4. hunt 5. essay 6. pursue, search 7. explore, solicit 8. endeavor 9. neologize (new words) 11. investigate

seeker... 6. prober, tracer 7. pursuer, zetetic 8. aspirant, searcher 9. applicant 10. petitioner

seeker of...
knowledge.. 10. philonoist
new words.. 9. neologist
pleasure.. 7. epicure 8. hedonist

seem... 4. look 6. appear 7. pretend 8. resemble

seeming... 5. guise, quasi 8. apparent, illusion, illusory, pretense, specious 9. befitting

seeming contradiction... 7. paradox

seeming truth... 14. verisimilitude

seemly... 3. fit 4. meet 6. comely, decent, proper, suited 7. elegant, fitting 8. decorous, tasteful 9. expedient

seep... 4. leak, ooze 5. exude 6. filter 8. transude 9. percolate

seer, seeress... 5. sibyl 6. oracle, scryer 7. Phoebad, prophet 9. predictor, visionary 10. forecaster, prophetess, soothsayer 11. Nostradamus 14. prognosticator

seesaw... 6. teeter, tilter 7. pastime 9. alternate, crossruff, fluctuate, vacillate 11. oscillation 12. teeter–totter

seethe... 4. boil, stew, teem 5. be hot, steep 6. bubble 7. be angry

segment... 3. pip 4. part 5. tmema 6. cantle 7. portion, section 8. fragment 12. cross section

segment (pert to)...
botany.. 5. tmema 7. lacinia
corresponding part.. 7. isomere
curve.. 3. arc
shaped.. 5. toric
Zool.. 6. somite, telson 8. metamere, somatome

seine... 3. net 5. trawl 6. sagene 7. dragnet, network

seism... 10. earthquake

seize... 3. bag, cly, cop, nab, net 4. bind, bite, grab, grip, take, trap 5. annex, catch, grasp, ravin, reave, usurp, wrest 6. arrest, clutch, collar, fasten, ravish, snatch 7. capture, embargo, grapple 8. distrain

9. apprehend, lay hold of
10. confiscate, understand
11. appropriate
seizin ... 9. occupancy 10. possession
seizing ... 4. cord 7. lashing
9. arresting, raptorial
seizure ... 3. fit 4. grip, hold 5. spasm
6. arrest, attack, frenzy, seizin
9. ownership 10. convulsion,
occupation 11. manucapture
seladang ... 4. gaur 7. buffalo
selah (Bib) ... 4. sign 5. pause
select ... 4. cull, name, pick, take
5. elect, elite 6. choice, choose,
picked 7. appoint, pick out, specify
9. exclusive, segregate 10. registrate
11. distinguish, outstanding
selection ... 5. piece 6. choice
7. analect, excerpt, passage
10. collection 11. appointment
selective ... 5. draft 8. eclectic
9. exclusive 10. particular
14. discriminative
self ... 3. ego, own 4. same 5. being
6. person, psyche 7. oneself
10. individual 11. personality
self (pert to) ...
acting .. 9. automatic, voluntary
assertion .. 6. egoism, vanity
centered .. 7. selfish 9. egotistic
10. egocentric 11. independent
12. self–absorbed
comb form .. 4. auto
complacent .. 13. self–satisfied
confidence .. 5. poise 6. aplomb
9. assurance 11. self–reliant
contained .. 8. reserved 10. controlled,
sufficient (in itself) 11. independent
15. uncommunicative
control .. 8. stoicism 9. restraint
10. automation, discipline,
equanimity, temperance
defense .. 6. karate, jung fu 7. jujitsu
determination .. 8. autonomy
12. independence
enjoyment .. 13. gratification
esteem .. 5. pride 6. vanity
7. concept, ego–trip
evident .. 5. clear 9. axiomatic
examination .. 13. introspection,
introspective
French .. 3. soi
love of .. 6. egoism
ref to .. 8. personal
reproach .. 7. remorse
righteous .. 5. pious 9. Pharisaic
13. sanctimonious
14. holier–than–thou
same .. 9. identical
satisfied .. 4. smug 6. jaunty
Scottish .. 3. sel (sell)
worship .. 8. idolatry 9. autolatry
selfish ... 5. grabby (sl) 11. egotistical,
self–seeking 12. self–centered
sell ... 4. vend 5. scalp, trade
6. barter, market, retail 7. auction,
bargain 8. convince, exchange,
persuade 9. negotiate
sell (out) ... 6. betray, desert 8. inform
on 9. victimize
seller ... 6. dealer, vender, vendor

7. peddler 8. merchant, salesman
9. tradesman 10. saleswoman
semantics ... 8. meanings
11. semasiology
semblable ... 4. like 5. alike
7. seeming, similar 8. apparent,
suitable 10. ostensible, resembling
11. conformable
semblance ... 4. copy, face, form
5. guise, image 6. aspect, figure
7. pretext, umbrage 8. illusion
10. appearance, similarity
11. countenance, presumption,
resemblance
semeiology, semeiotics ... 5. signs
(signaling) 11. diagnostics
14. interpretation, symptomatology
semester ... 4. term 6. course, period
Seminole chief ... 7. Osceola
(1804–38)
Semitic (pert to) ...
deity .. 4. Baal
dialect .. 4. Geez
god (evil) .. 6. Moloch
language .. 5. Iraqi 6. Syrian
7. Arabian, Aramaic 8. Egyptian
11. Palestinian
people .. 6. Harari 8. Moabites
tribe (nomadic) .. 6. Shagia (Shaikiyeh)
semper eadem ... 13. always the same
(motto of Queen Elizabeth)
semper fidelis ... 13. always faithful
semper idem ... 13. always the same
semper paratus ... 11. always ready
senate ... 5. boule 7. council (Rom)
8. assembly 11. legislature
18. administrative body
send ... 4. mail, ship 5. drive, grant,
issue, speed 6. bestow, convey,
export, launch, propel 7. forward
8. dispatch, transmit 10. commission
send (pert to) ...
back .. 5. remit 6. remand, return
11. reverberate
by different person .. 5. relay
off .. 5. start 6. launch 7. impulse
8. dispatch 11. consignment
13. demonstration
out .. 4. emit, spew 5. shoot
out rays .. 7. radiate
payment .. 5. remit
to an address .. 7. deliver
Seneca ... 6. Indian 9. Iroquoian
Senegal, Africa ...
capital .. 5. Dakar
ebony .. 9. blackwood
gazell .. 5. korin
gum .. 9. gum arabic
mahogany .. 9. cailcedra
native .. 10. Senegalese
senescence ... 5. aging 10. growing
old
senicide ... 13. killing old men (tribal)
senility ... 6. dotage, old age
8. caducity, dementia 10. feebleness
senior ... 4. aine, dean 5. chief, elder
7. ancient, student 8. superior
sensation ... 5. sense 6. thrill, uproar,
wonder 7. emotion 8. rhigosis (cold)
10. perception 12. great success
sensational ... 5. lurid 6. superb

8. dramatic, exciting 9. emotional
12. melodramatic

sense... 4. feel, mind, sane 5. flair,
sight, smell 7. feeling, meaning
8. sapience 9. awareness, intuition,
sensation, sentience 10. perception,
understand 11. discernment,
recognition 12. intelligence

senseless... 5. inept 6. insane, stupid,
unwise 7. fatuous, foolish, idiotic,
inanity 9. illogical, inanimate,
insensate, unfeeling 10. irrational
11. meaningless, purposeless,
unconscious 12. unreasonable
13. unintelligent

sense of...
 beauty.. 8. aesthete (esthete), tasteful
 9. aesthetic
 dignity.. 5. pride
 distance.. 11. telesthetic
 hearing.. 8. audition 12. auscultation
 humor.. 10. risibility
 sight.. 6. vision
 smell.. 7. osmatic 9. olfaction
 taste.. 6. palate

sense organ... 3. ear, eye 4. nose,
skin 6. tongue 8. receptor, sensilla

senses... 4. wits 6. sanity 7. sensory
9. sensation

sensible... 4. sane 5. aware, privy,
sound 7. logical, prudent 8. rational
9. cognizant, practical, sensitive
10. reasonable, responsive
11. intelligent, susceptible

sensitive... 4. nice, sore 5. acute
6. pliant, tender, touchy 7. sensory
8. sensible 9. receptive
10. responsive 11. susceptible
14. discriminating, impressionable

sensitivity... 9. emotional, hebetated
(blunted) 11. sensibility 12. irritability
14. discrimination

sentence... 4. doom 5. maxim, motto
6. phrase, remark, saying
7. condemn, passage, thought,
verdict 8. decision, judgment,
proposal 9. statement
12. condemnation

sentence (pert to)...
 balance.. 7. parison
 clause (concluding).. 8. apodosis
 concluding.. 8. epilogue (epilog)
 construction.. 6. syntax
 difficult articulation.. 13. tongue
 twister
 introductory.. 8. protasis
 judicial.. 5. futwa
 pithy.. 5. motto 8. aphorism
 punishment.. 11. year and a day
 subordinate part.. 6. clause, phrase

sententious... 5. pithy, terse
7. concise, laconic 10. aphoristic
13. grandiloquent

sentient... 4. mind 5. aware 7. feeling
8. sensible 9. conscious, sensitive
10. perceptive 13. consciousness

sentiment... 5. toast 7. emotion,
feeling, opinion 8. attitude
10. perception, sentimento
11. sensibility 14. sentimentality

sentimental... 6. loving 7. maudlin,
mawkish 8. romantic 9. emotional

13. lackadaisical

sentimental song... 11. strephonade

sentinel... 5. guard 6. picket, sentry
7. vedette (mounted) 8. watchman
10. lookout man, watchtower

sepad... 5. think 7. believe, suppose

sepal... 4. leaf 5. petal

separate... 4. open, part, shed, sift,
sort 5. alone, apart, sever, space
6. cleave, detach, divide, secern,
single, sleave, sunder, winnow
7. disband, diverge, diverse, divided,
divorce, isolate 8. alienate, discrete,
distinct, peculiar, secluded
9. disjoined, partition, segregate,
sequester, unrelated 10. dissociate,
particular, respective
11. disembodied, unconnected

separate (pert to)...
 Chem.. 11. fractionate
 from others.. 5. aloof 8. isolated
 metal from ore.. 5. smelt
 thread.. 6. sleave

separation... 6. tmesis 7. divorce
8. autotomy 9. partition, secession,
seclusion 10. alienation
11. disjunction, segregation
13. sequestration 14. discontinuance,
discrimination

separatist... 7. heretic, seceder
8. apostate 9. dissenter
12. secessionist 13. nonconformist

sepia... 3. dun, ink 5. color
7. pigment 10. cuttlebone, cuttlefish

sepiment... 5. hedge 7. defense
9. enclosure

Sepiola... 10. cuttlefish

sepiolite... 10. meerschaum

sepoy... 7. soldier 9. policeman

seps... 6. lizard 7. serpent

sept... 4. clan 5. class, seven, tribe
7. lineage

septic... 6. morbid, pyemia (pyaemia)
8. diseased, infected, poisoned
9. gangrened, mortified, poisonous
10. septicemia (blood poison)

sepulcher, sepulchre... 4. bury, tomb
5. crypt, grave, vault 6. entomb
9. sepulture 10. repository

sepulchral... 5. urnal 6. gloomy,
hollow 7. charnel 8. funereal
9. deep–toned

sepulchral (pert to)...
 chest.. 4. cist
 mound.. 7. tumulus
 vault.. 6. burial 8. catacomb,
 monument 9. interview

sequel... 5. issue 6. effect, series,
upshot 7. outcome 8. follow up,
sequence, sequitur 9. posterity
10. succession

sequela... 7. disease (resulting)
8. adherent 9. inference
10. conclusion 11. concomitant,
consequence 15. morbid condition

sequence... 5. gamut 6. course
(usual), series, tierce (three cards)
8. straight 10. succession

sequential... 9. deducible, resultant
10. continuous, succeeding
11. consecutive

sequestered... 6. lonely, secret

7. private, recluse, retired
8. isolated, secluded, solitary,
withdraw 9. concealed, separated
12. unfrequented
sequitur... 9. inference, influence, it
follows 14. natural sequent
sequoia, Sequoia... 4. Park (Calif)
6. Indian (famed for alphabet) 7. big
tree, conifer, redwood
seraglio... 5. harem, serai 6. zenana
9. enclosure
serape... 5. shawl 7. blanket
seraph... 5. angel 6. cherub
seraphic... 7. angelic, sublime
8. cherubic 9. unworldly
Serb... 4. Slav 7. Serbian (Servian)
Serbia, Yugoslavia...
church.. 8. Orthodox
conqueror.. 5. Turks
hero.. 6. Dushan, Nemaya (1159)
queen.. 7. Natalie
Revolutionary.. 7. Chetnik
sere... 4. claw, sear, worn 5. talon
6. effete, yellow 8. withered
10. desiccated
serenade... 4. sing 5. music
8. serenata 9. charivari, entertain
10. callithump 11. celebration
serene... 4. calm, cool 5. clear, quiet
6. placid 8. peaceful, serenity,
tranquil 9. collected, unruffled
11. undisturbed 12. tranquillity
(tranquility)
serenity... 5. peace 6. repose
8. calmness, coolness 9. composure
10. quiescence
serf... 4. esne, neif (fem), peon
5. helot, slave 6. thrall, vassal
7. captive, villein
series... 3. set 4. nest 5. class,
gamut, group 8. sequence
9. seriation 10. succession
series, connected... 5. chain, suite
6. catena
series of...
discussions.. 9. symposium
heroic events.. 4. epos
meetings.. 7. session
pictures.. 8. panorama
races.. 7. regatta
rings.. 4. coil
six.. 5. hexad
steps.. 5. scale
syllogisms.. 7. sorites
travels.. 7. odyssey
serious... 4. keen 5. grave, serio
(comb form), sober, staid 6. demure,
sedate, solemn 7. capital, earnest,
weighty, zealous 8. resolute
9. important 10. thoughtful
seriousness... 4. zeal 7. gravity
10. importance 11. earnestness
sermon... 4. talk, text 5. psalm
6. homily, lesson, preach 7. address,
lecture, reproof 8. harangue
9. discourse, preaching
10. admonition
seron... 5. crate 6. hamper
7. boxwood, spanner
serotine... 3. bat 4. adda 9. late
bloom
serpent... 3. asp 4. seps (anc)

5. cobra, krait, racer, snake
serpent (pert to)...
deity, of good.. 12. agathodaemon
13. agathos daemon
fabulous.. 5. Hydra 6. dragon
8. basilisk 11. amphisbaena
large.. 3. boa 5. aboma 6. python
8. jararaca
monster.. 6. ellops
Old.. 5. Satan
semihuman (Hind Myth).. 4. Naga
sky (Vedic Myth).. 3. Ahi
worshipers (Gnostic).. 7. Ophites
serpentine... 4. wily 5. snaky
6. subtle, zigzag 7. sinuous, winding
8. diabolic, tempting 9. snakelike
10. circuitous, meandering
serpigo... 8. ringworm 11. skin disease
serrano... 12. squirrelfish
serrate... 7. notched, toothed
8. indented 10. saw–toothed
serried... 5. dense 7. compact,
concise, crowded
serum... 4. whey 5. blood, fluid
6. serous 9. antitoxin
servant... 3. gyp 4. bata, cook, maid,
maty, mozo, serf, syce 5. agent,
boots, chela, nurse, slave, valet
6. bildar, butler, flunky, garçon, gillie
(gilly), menial, servus, vassal, wallah
(walla) 7. equerry (nobleman's)
8. coistrel, domestic, handmaid
9. assistant 11. chamberlain
servant of God... 6. bishop
serve... 2. do 3. act, aid 4. deal,
help, wait 5. avail, cater 6. assist,
succor 7. advance, bestead, forward,
further, suffice, work for 8. bear
arms, fight for 9. officiate
10. administer, distribute
serve (pert to)...
as accomplice.. 4. abet
as escort.. 6. squire
food.. 4. wait 5. cater 7. dish out
religion.. 4. obey 7. worship
tennis.. 7. deliver
server... 4. tray 6. player, salver
7. acolyte
Servia... see Serbia
service... 3. aid, use 4. help, mail,
Mass, rite 5. favor, matin 6. employ,
ritual 7. benefit, nocturn, utility
8. ceremony, evensong, kindness,
ministry 9. servitude 10. attendance,
employment 12. ministration
service tree... 4. sorb 5. rowan
servile... 4. mean 6. abject, menial,
minion 7. fawning, slavish
8. cringing, faithful 9. dependent,
parasitic, truckling 10. obsequious,
submissive 11. subservient,
sycophantic
Servite... 9. mendicant 13. Order of
Friars (1233)
servitude... 7. bondage, serfdom,
service, slavery 8. servitus
9. vassalage 14. apprenticeship
sesame... 3. oil 4. herb 5. benne
7. gingili (seed), teel oil 8. ajonjoli,
sesamine
Sesame, Open... 10. magical key
12. magic command (Arab Nights)

sess... 4. heap, pile 9. soap frame
session... 5. court 6. séance
  8. assembly 11. legislature
set... 3. lay 4. form, heal, laid, pose,
  post 5. brood, class, fixed, group,
  place, posit, ready, staid, stand
  6. adjust, clique, define, fasten,
  formal, ossify, series, settle
  7. confirm, congeal, coterie, station,
  stiffen 8. regulate, solidify
  9. coagulate, designate, direction,
  obstinate, stabilize 10. collection,
  determined, solidified 11. established,
  prepared for
set (pert to)...
afloat.. 6. launch
against.. 6. oppose 10. antagonize
apart.. 5. allot, elect, taboo
  6. exempt 7. isolate, reserve,
  seclude 8. allocate, separate
  9. segregate, sequester
  11. distinguish 13. differentiate
aside.. 4. void 5. annul 6. except,
  reject 7. abolish, discard, dismiss,
  earmark, exclude 8. overrule,
  postpone
at an angle.. 4. cant
back.. 4. loss 5. check 6. demote,
  hinder, recess 7. relapse 8. restrain,
  slow down
exclusive.. 5. elect, taboo 6. clique
fire to.. 6. ignite, kindle 7. emblaze,
  inflame 8. irritate
firmly.. 5. embed, plant, posit
  6. cement, ossify
forth.. 5. adorn 6. depart, expose, lay
  out 7. arrange, commend, display,
  enounce, exhibit, explain, expound,
  present, promote, propone, publish
  8. announce, decorate, indicate,
  manifest 9. translate 10. promulgate
  11. demonstrate
free.. 6. acquit 7. absolve, release,
  unloose 8. liberate 10. emancipate
  11. disillusion
off.. 6. incite, offset 7. measure
  8. beautify, detonate 9. demarcate,
  embellish 11. distinguish
on firm basis.. 9. establish
out.. 4. plot 5. allot, begin
  7. arrange
right.. 5. teach 6. adjust, direct,
  remedy 11. disillusion
up.. 3. rig 4. plan 5. build, cause,
  erect, exalt, hoist, print, raise
  7. elevate, finance, install
  9. construct, establish
  10. inaugurate, prearrange
set (pert to in)...
a groove.. 5. dadoe
a row.. 4. tier 5. align, aline, range
columns.. 7. tabular 8. tabulate
from margin.. 6. indent
operation.. 4. move 5. start 6. launch
opposition.. 3. pit
order.. 5. align 6. adjust 7. arrange
set (pert to of)...
eight.. 6. ogdoad
friends.. 7. coterie
jeweled ornaments.. 6. parure
laws.. 4. code 8. statutes
on end.. 5. upend 10. topsy–turvy

opinions.. 5. credo
organ pipes.. 5. stops
rules.. 4. code
sheets (paper).. 5. quire
seta... 4. hair 5. spine 7. bristle,
  feather
Seth (pert to)...
brother.. 4. Abel, Cain
father.. 4. Adam
son.. 4. Enos
wife.. 8. Nephthys
setting... 5. scene 6. locale
  8. mounting, planting
  10. background
settle... 3. fix, pay 4. nest, root, seat,
  sink 5. agree, clear, lodge, order,
  prove, quiet, solve 6. assign, assure,
  decide, locate, pay off, purify, secure,
  soothe 7. arrange, clarify, confirm,
  mediate, resolve 8. colonize,
  ensconce, regulate 9. designate,
  determine, establish, reconcile
  10. strengthen 11. tranquilize
settled... 4. paid 5. ended, fixed
  6. proved, sedate 7. assured,
  decided, located 9. steadfast
  10. unchanging 11. established
settled in advance...
  13. predetermined
settled in mind... 10. equanimity
settlement... 3. dos 4. camp
  6. colony, hamlet 7. payment
  8. fixation, sediment, showdown
  9. community, endowment
  10. adjustment 12. colonization,
  conciliation, satisfaction
  13. determination, establishment
Settlement House... 9. Hull House
  (Chicago) 10. University (NY)
  11. Toynbee Hall (London)
settler... 6. Sooner (Okla) 7. pioneer,
  planter, Puritan 8. colonist
  9. immigrant
settlings... 4. lees 5. dregs
  8. sediment 10. settlement
  12. precipitates
seven (pert to)...
angles.. 8. heptagon 9. septangle
arts.. 5. logic, music 7. grammar
  8. geometry, rhetoric 9. astronomy
  10. arithmetic
comb form.. 5. hepta, septi
days and nights.. 8. sennight
fold.. 8. septuple
gods of happiness.. 5. Ebisu, Hotei
  6. Benten 7. Daikoku, Jurojin
  8. Bishamon 10. Fuku–roku–ju
group.. 6. heptad, septet 8. septuple
  12. septemvirate
Hills.. 4. Rome
languages.. 9. heptaglot
Latin.. 6. septum
number.. 8. hebdomad 9. septenary
Old Test Books (1st seven)..
  10. Heptateuch
Seas.. 11. world oceans
Stars.. 8. Pleiades
tones.. 10. heptachord, heptatonic
seventy... 12. septuagenary
seventy–day period...
  12. septuagesima
seventy–year–old... 14. septuagenarian

sever... 3. cut, lop 4. part, rend
5. break 6. behead, cleave, detach,
divide, except, exempt 7. disjoin
8. accurate, disunite, separate
9. interpose, segregate
10. decapitate, disconnect, dissociate
12. disassociate

several... 4. many 6. divers, sundry
7. diverse, various 8. distinct
9. different 10. respective

severe... 3. bad 4. dure, hard, keen,
sore, tart 5. acute, cruel, exact, grave,
harsh, rigid, snell, sober, stern
6. biting, bitter, chaste, sedate,
simple, solemn, strict, taxing, trying
7. arduous, austere, condign, drastic,
extreme, intense, painful, serious,
violent 8. accurate, rigorous
9. draconian, strenuous, stringent
10. censorious, restrained

severe critic (of Alexandria)...
9. Aristarch

severity... 5. rigor 7. cruelty
8. hardness, pungency, violence
9. austerity, exactness, gruffness,
harshness, solemnity, sternness,
stiffness 10. bitterness, difficulty,
inclemency, simplicity, strictness
12. rigorousness

Seville cathedral tower... 7. Giralda

Seville orange... 9. red–yellow
12. bitter orange

Sèvres blue... 5. color 9. bleu de
roi, porcelain 11. bleu céleste

sew... 4. mend 5. baste, unite
6. fasten, needle, secure, stitch

sewan... 5. beads, money 6. wampum

sewing... 6. sutile 8. suturing
9. stitching 10. needlework

sewing case... 4. etui

sewing machine inventor... 9. Elias
Howe

sexagenarian... 13. a sixty–year–old

sexagesimal... 5. sixty

sexes, common to both... 6. unisex
7. epicene

sexless... 6. neuter 7. epicene

sextet, sextette... 6. sestet 8. six
parts 10. group of six 13. six–line
stanza

sexton... 6. beetle 7. sacrist
9. sacristan 12. underofficer

sextuplet... 7. sestole (sestolet) 8. six
notes

sha... 5. sheep, urial (ooriel)

shabbash... 5. bravo 8. well done

Shabbath... 7. Sabbath (Jew)

shabbiness... 8. baseness, slovenry
9. seediness

shabby... 4. base, mean, worn
5. dowdy, faded, ratty, seedy, tacky,
yucky 6. grungy, paltry, ragged,
scurvy, scuzzy, sleazy 7. outworn,
shagrag, squalid 10. despicable,
ragamuffin, threadbare
12. contemptible

shack... 3. coe, hut 4. husk, plug
5. chase, hutch, tramp 6. shanty
7. stubble 8. vagabond 9. hibernate

shackle... 3. tie 4. band, bind, bond,
gyve, iron, ring 5. chain 6. fetter,
hobble, hogtie, impede, pinion
7. manacle, trammel 8. restrain

shackled... 4. tied 5. bound, gyved
6. curbed, ironed 7. hobbled
8. fettered, hampered, hindered,
manacled 10. restrained

shad... 4. fish 5. Alosa 7. crappie,
mojarra

shade... 3. hue 4. dull, roof, tint, tone,
veil 5. ghost, tinge, visor 6. awning,
canopy, darken, degree, follow,
nuance, screen, shadow, shield, sprite
7. eclipse, foliage, parasol, protect,
shelter, umbrage 10. overshadow,
protection 11. adumbration

shade, affording... 9. umbratile

shadow... 3. dim, dog, spy 4. hide,
tail 5. cloud, image, umbra 6. attend,
screen 7. blacken, conceal, protect,
remains 8. follower, hanger–on,
illusion, penumbra 9. adumbrate,
detective 10. protection

shadow fighting... 9. sciamachy

shadowless... 6. ascian

Shadrach (pert to)...
enemy.. 14. Nebuchadnezzar
name once.. 7. Ananias 9. Hannaniah
one of three Hebrew youths..
7. Meshach 8. Abednago, Shadrach

shady... 4. dark 5. faint, fishy
6. umbral 7. shadowy 9. deceitful,
dishonest, underhand 10. indistinct,
unreliable 12. questionable

shaft... 3. pit, rod 4. axle, fust, mine,
orlo (part), stem, tige, tole 5. arrow,
scape, shank, spire, stalk, thill, tower,
trunk 6. column, tongue 7. feather,
missile, obelisk 8. monument
9. flagstaff

shag... 3. nap 4. hair, mane, pile
5. chase, dance 6. follow, rascal
7. tobacco 9. cormorant, make rough
10. blackguard

shaggy... 5. bushy, furry, nappy, rough
6. ragged 7. hirsute, unkempt, villous
8. confused (of thought), uncombed
10. unpolished

shagrag... 6. ragged, tagrag
7. unkempt 8. rascally

shake... 3. jar, jog, wag 4. jolt, rock,
stir, sway, toze 5. swing, trill
6. dither, dodder, quiver, shimmy,
shiner, weaken 7. agitate, flutter,
shingle, shudder, tremble, tremolo
8. enfeeble 10. earthquake

Shakespeare (pert to)...
actor.. 4. Ward 7. Gielgud, Olivier,
Sothern 8. Modjeska
called.. 10. Bard of Avon
character, female.. 6. Juliet, Portia
7. Ophelia 9. Cleopatra
character, male.. 5. Romeo, Timon
6. Antony, Hamlet 7. Macbeth,
Othello 8. Falstaff
forest.. 5. Arden
river.. 4. Avon
site.. 6. Verona 8. Elsinore
villain.. 4. Iago
wife.. 11. Anne Hathaway

shaky... 6. infirm, wabbly, wobbly
7. fearful, nervous, unsound

8. agitated, unsecure 9. tottering, trembling, uncertain, unsettled 10. precarious, unreliable 12. questionable

shale... 4. rock 5. flake, scale 8. dandruff

Shalimar Gardens... 6. Lahore

shallow... 5. shoal 6. lagoon (lagune) 7. cursory, trivial 9. depthless, frivolous, insincere 11. superficial

sham... 3. ape 4. fake, hoax, mock 5. dummy, false, fraud, trick 6. deceit, humbug 7. feigned 8. pretense 9. imitation, imposture, pretended

Shamash (pert to)...
centers of worship.. 5. Larsa 6. Sippar
consort.. 3. Aya (Ai)
deity (Babylon).. 6. sun god
messenger.. 6. Bunene
Sumerian equivalent.. 3. Utu (Utug) 6. Babbar

shame... 5. abash 7. mortify 8. disgrace, dishonor 9. humiliate 11. abomination, humiliation, impropriety

shameful... 4. mean, vile 5. gross 6. wicked 8. flagrant, improper, indecent, infamous, terrible 9. degrading 10. outrageous, scandalous 11. disgraceful, ignominious 12. dishonorable, disreputable, vituperative

shameless... 6. arrant, brazen 8. immodest, impudent 9. audacious 10. unblushing 11. brazenfaced

shammer... 8. impostor

shanghai... 6. abduct, to drug 9. slingshot

shank... 3. leg 4. crus, gamb (gambe) 7. meat cut 12. travel on foot

shape... 4. bend, form, mold (mould), plan 5. frame, model 6. adjust, create, cut out, design, devise, figure 7. arrange, conform, contour, develop, fashion, incline 8. phantasm 10. appearance, figuration 11. arrangement

shaped like a...
comb.. 9. pectinate
shield.. 7. peltate, scutate
strap, thong.. 6. lorate
urn.. 9. urceolate

shapeless... 7. lumpish 8. deformed, formless 9. amorphous, contorted, distorted, unshapely

shapely... 3. fit 4. neat, trim 6. comely, gainly 10. well-formed 11. symmetrical 16. well-proportioned

shapes (ornamental, garden)... 5. topia 7. topiary

share... 3. cut, lot 4. dole, part 5. enter, quota 6. ration 7. partake, portion 8. take part 9. allowance, apportion 11. co-operative, participate

sharecropper... 7. metayer

shark... 5. fraud 6. lawyer 8. parasite, swindler 9. trickster

shark (fish)... 4. gata, mako, tope 5. lamia (cub), Rhina 6. Galeos, Galeus, requin 7. dogfish, tiburon 8. man-eater, Mustelus, Selachii, sharklet, Squatina 9. porbeagle 10. Carcharias, hammerhead 11. Carcharodon, Galeorhinus

shark-clinger... 4. pega 6. remora

sharp... 4. acid, curt, edgy, keen, tart 5. acerb, acrid, acute, alert, brisk, crisp, edged, harsh, quick, smart, steep, witty 6. abrupt, astute, bitter, crafty, shrill 7. angular, caustic, cutting, nipping, painful, pointed, pungent, sharper 8. incisive, poignant 9. penetrant, sagacious, sarcastic, trenchant 10. discerning, proficient 11. acrimonious, penetrating, well-dressed

sharp (pert to)...
answer.. 6. retort
blow.. 4. slap
cornered.. 7. angular
edged.. 5. arris
flavor.. 4. tang
make.. 10. cacuminate
pointed.. 5. acute
saw.. 8. titmouse
Scot.. 5. snell 6. snelly
sighted.. 4. keen 6. astute 7. lyncean
sound.. 4. ping
Tuesday.. 13. Shrove Tuesday
witted.. 6. shrewd 10. discerning 11. intelligent

sharpen... 3. nib, ted 4. edge, hone, whet 5. grind, point, strop 6. acuate 7. enhance, quicken 9. intensify 10. cacuminate

sharper... 5. cheat, knave, rogue 6. keener 8. deceiver, swindler 9. trickster

shatter... 5. blast, break, crash, smash, split 8. splinter

shave... 3. cut 4. pare 5. cheat, strip 6. cut off 7. swindle, tonsure 9. cut prices, thin slice

shaver... 3. boy, lad 4. tool 5. cheat 6. barber 8. swindler 9. youngster 11. extortioner

shavetail... 4. mule 6. ensign 10. lieutenant

shawl... 5. manta 6. serape 7. paisley 8. cashmere

Shawnee (pert to)...
chief.. 8. Tecumseh
Indian tribe.. 9. Algonquin
location (present).. 8. Oklahoma

sheaf... 4. kern, omer 6. bundle 7. cluster 11. hyperpencil

shear... 3. cut 4. clip, snip, trim 5. sever 6. fleece, remove 7. scissor, whittle

shears... 5. lewis 6. forfex 8. secateur

sheatfish... 4. wels 7. catfish

sheath... 4. case 5. forel (book), glove, ocrea, theca 6. sleeve, spathe 7. stipule 8. scabbard

sheathe... 4. wrap 5. cover, drape 6. encase 7. envelop 8. enshroud

sheave... 5. wheel 6. pulley 9. back water, eccentric

shebang... 6. affair, boodle, outfit 7. concern 11. contrivance

13. establishment 14. kit and caboodle

she–cat . . . **4.** elle **9.** grimalkin

shed . . . **3.** hut **4.** abri, cote, lair, molt **5.** hovel, scale, spill **6.** effuse, hangar, lean–to, slough **7.** cottage, diffuse, radiate, shelter

shed (light) . . . **4.** glow **7.** explain, radiate **10.** illuminate

shedding . . . **7.** ecdysis (Zool), molting

sheen . . . **5.** glint, gloss, shine **6.** luster **7.** glitter, shimmer **8.** splendor **9.** shininess **10.** brightness

sheep . . . **3.** ewe, ram, sha, teg, tup **4.** buck, lamb, Ovis, zenu **5.** bidet, dumba, oudad **6.** argali, cosset, gimmer, hogget, mutton, sheder, wether **8.** ruminant, shearhog, yeanling **9.** blackface

sheep (pert to) . . .
cry . . **3.** baa **5.** bleat
disease . . **3.** coe, gid, rot **4.** bane **5.** braxy **7.** anthrax
faced . . **3.** shy **7.** bashful **8.** sheepish
female . . **3.** ewe, teg **6.** sheder
flock leader . . **10.** bellwether
fold . . **3.** ree **4.** cote **5.** kraal, reeve, stell **6.** church
head . . **5.** jimmy **8.** powsowdy
headed . . **5.** silly **6.** stupid **12.** simple–minded
kidney extract . . **5.** renes
laurel . . **6.** Kalmia
leg wool . . **4.** gare
male . . **3.** ram, tup **4.** buck **5.** heder **6.** wether
owner's mark . . **4.** smit **6.** ruddle
pet . . **6.** cosset
sheeplike . . **5.** ovine **9.** tractable
skin, leather . . **4.** pelt, roan **5.** basil **7.** chamois, diploma **8.** woolfell
stealing . . **7.** abigest
tick . . **3.** ked
wild . . **3.** sha **4.** Ovis **5.** urial **6.** aoudad, argali, bharal, nayaur **7.** mouflon (moufflon) **9.** Thian Shan (Marco Polo's)

sheep, breeds . . . **6.** Merino, Romney **7.** Cheviot, Delaine, Dishley, Karakul, Suffolk, Targhee **8.** Cotswold, Dartmoor **9.** Kerry Hill, Leicester, Southdown, Teeswater **10.** Corriedale, Dorset Horn, Oxford Down, Shropshire **13.** Hampshire Down

sheer . . . **4.** mere, pure, thin, turn **5.** brant, steep, utter **6.** abrupt, swerve **7.** deviate, unmixed **8.** absolute **9.** deviation, downright, undiluted **10.** completely, diaphonous **11.** transparent **13.** perpendicular

sheet . . . **4.** leaf, rope, sail **5.** paper **6.** shroud **9.** cover with, duodecimo (12–fold), newspaper, sheathing

sheik, sheikh . . . **4.** Arab **5.** chief **6.** prince

shelf . . . **4.** berm (berme), reef, sell **5.** ledge, shoal **6.** mantel **7.** stratum **8.** postpone, put aside

shell . . . **3.** pod **4.** boat, bomb, husk **5.** conch, crust, shard, shuck **6.** cowrie (cowry) **7.** bombard,

capsule, grenade, missile **8.** carapace, exterior, shrapnel **9.** cartridge **10.** projectile

shell (pert to) . . .
button source . . **5.** troca **6.** lorica, mucket
cone . . **7.** admiral
ear . . **7.** abalone
explosive . . **3.** dud **4.** bomb **7.** grenade
fish . . **4.** clam, pipi **6.** cockle, limpet, mussel, oyster **7.** abalone, lobster, mollusk, scallop **8.** barnacle **9.** trunkfish
fossil . . **8.** ammonite
game . . **10.** thimblerig **13.** sleight of hand
marine . . **6.** cowrie (cowry)
money . . **6.** hawok, sewan, uhllo (ulo) **6.** cowrie, wampum
out . . **4.** give **6.** expend, pay out
protective . . **6.** lorica
ridge . . **4.** lira **5.** varix
seaweed . . **8.** frustule
spiral . . **5.** chank, whelk **8.** caracole
trumpet (Triton's) . . **5.** conch

shelter . . . **3.** lee, pad **4.** abri, camp, cote, digs, port, roof, shed, skug, tent **5.** condo, cover, haven, house, hutch, shack, shade **6.** asylum, burrow, dugout, hangar, harbor, refuge, screen, shield **7.** defense, hospice, pillbox, protect, retreat **8.** mantelet (mantlet), quarters, security **9.** coverture, sanctuary **10.** protection

sheltered side . . . **3.** lee **4.** alee **7.** leeward

shelve . . . **5.** slope, table, waive **6.** retire **7.** dismiss, incline **8.** postpone, put aside **10.** pigeonhole

Shem (pert to) . . .
brother . . **3.** Ham
descendant . . **6.** Semite
father . . **4.** Noah
son . . **3.** Lud **4.** Aram, Elam

shenanigan . . . **7.** foolery **8.** trickery, zaniness **9.** horseplay **10.** hanky–panky **11.** monkeyshine

shend . . . **3.** mar **4.** harm, ruin **5.** spoil **6.** injure, revile **7.** destroy, stupefy **8.** confound, disgrace, reproach

Sheol . . . **4.** Hell **5.** Aralu, grave, Hades **6.** the pit, Toppet **7.** Abaddon, Gehenna **10.** underworld **11.** nether world **14.** abode of the dead

shepherd . . . **5.** guide **6.** direct, escort, feeder, herder, pastor, shadow **8.** guardian, herdsman **9.** clergyman

shepherd, shepherds (pert to) . .
band of . . **10.** pastoureau
dog . . **5.** sheep **6.** collie
flute . . **7.** musette **9.** flageolet
god . . **3.** Pan
pipe . . **3.** oat **4.** reed **7.** larigot
spider . . **13.** daddy longlegs
staff . . **4.** Kent **5.** crook

sheriff (pert to) . . .
aide . . **5.** posse
deputy . . **6.** elisor **7.** bailiff
jurisdiction . . **9.** bailiwick
sheriffdom . . **10.** shrievalty

sherry . . . **5.** jerez, Xeres **7.** oloroso
8. montilla
Shetland Islands (pert to) . . .
fishing grounds (deep–sea) . . **4.** haaf
kingdom of . . **8.** Scotland
land, fee simple . . **4.** udal
promontory . . **4.** noup
Supreme Court Pres . . **4.** foud
viol . . **3.** gue
shewbread, showbread (Bib) . . .
6. ritual **10.** unleavened
shibboleth (Bib) . . . **4.** mode **5.** habit
6. saying, slogan **9.** criterion,
watchword **11.** peculiarity (speech)
shield . . . **3.** écu **4.** boss, umbo
5. aegis (egis), armor, cover, pavis,
pelta, scute, shade, shell, targe (anc)
6. defend, scutum, target
7. defense, protect, shelter
8. insignia **9.** protector
10. escutcheon, protection
shield (pert to) . . .
Athena's . . **5.** aegis (egis)
bearer . . **8.** escudero
border . . **4.** orle **7.** bordure
emblem . . **7.** impresa
French (anc) . . **8.** rondache
heraldry . . **4.** enté **6.** points
part . . **4.** enté, orle, umbo
Roman . . **6.** scutum
sacred . . **6.** ancile (Rom)
shaped . . **7.** peltate, scutate
8. aspidate
shift . . . **4.** eddy, fend, jibe, move, ruse,
stir, tack, veer **5.** shunt, smock, trick
6. baffle, change, device, rustle
7. deviate, pretext, quibble **8.** artifice,
mutation, transfer **9.** deviation,
expedient, fluctuate, vacillate
10. conversion, subterfuge
12. redistribute **13.** transposition
shifty . . . **6.** crafty, tricky **7.** devious,
evasive, furtive **9.** deceitful, makeshift
10. changeable **11.** treacherous
shill, shillaber (circus term) . . . **5.** decoy
8. employer, hanger–on
10. accomplice
shillalagh, shillalah . . . **4.** club
6. cudgel **7.** sapling
shilly–shally . . . **8.** hesitate **9.** vacillate
10. hestation, indecision
11. vacillation
Shiloh . . . **4.** town (anc) **6.** Seilun
(modern) **9.** sanctuary (the ark)
10. battle site (Tenn)
shimmy . . . **5.** quake **6.** quiver
7. chemise, tremble, vibrate **9.** jazz
dance, vibration
shin . . . **5.** climb, tibia **6.** cnemis
7. foreleg
shindy . . . **3.** row **4.** lark, orgy, riot,
romp **5.** dance, party, revel, spree,
wince **6.** frolic, uproar **7.** wassail
8. carousal **9.** commotion, festivity
11. merrymaking
shine . . . **3.** ray **4.** beam, beek, star
5. excel, gloss, prank **6.** polish
7. furbish, glisten, glister, glitter,
radiate, splurge **8.** rutilate **9.** irradiate
shiner . . . **6.** bruise **8.** black eye
9. bootblack **10.** dollarfish
shingle . . . **4.** sign, wood **6.** hairdo

7. haircut, overlap **8.** chastise,
coiffure, detritus **9.** signboard
shining . . . **5.** aglow, lucid, nitid, shiny
6. glossy, lucent **7.** beaming,
glowing, radiant **8.** luminous, lustrous,
nitidous, rutilant, splendid **9.** refulgent
10. glistening, glittering
11. illustrious, irradiating, resplendent
Shinto (pert to) . . .
adherent . . **9.** Shintoist
cult . . **8.** Japanese
deity . . **8.** Hachiman
temple . . **3.** sha **5.** jinja (jinsha)
7. yashiro
temple gateway . . **5.** torii
temple deity . . **5.** Jinja (Jinsha)
shiny . . . **5.** nitid, sleek **6.** bright
7. radiant, shining **8.** luminous,
nitidous **9.** unclouded
ship . . . **3.** ark **4.** lade, load, send
5. liner, tramp **6.** argosy, vessel
7. freight, steamer **9.** freighter,
transport **10.** watercraft
ship (pert to) . . .
abandoned . . **8.** derelict
apparatus . . **5.** crane, davit, winch
7. bollard, capstan **8.** windlass
Argonaut's . . **4.** Argo
armored . . **7.** carrack, cruiser
9. destroyer, submarine
attendant . . **7.** steward
auxiliary . . **4.** dory, life **6.** dinghy
(dingy), tender
biscuit . . **8.** hardtack **10.** pilot bread
cabin . . **6.** saloon **9.** stateroom
cargo . . **5.** oiler **6.** tanker **7.** oreboat
11. supertanker
deck . . **4.** main, poop **5.** orlop, upper
deck, cut down . . **5.** razee
deserter . . **3.** rat
duck shooting . . **4.** skag
flat bottom . . **4.** keel **5.** barge
fleet . . **6.** armada
invoice . . **8.** manifest
jail . . **4.** brig
kitchen . . **6.** galley **7.** caboose
Levantine . . **4.** saic
loader . . **9.** stevedore
12. longshoreman
Mediterranean . . **5.** xebec **6.** galiot
(galliot) **7.** polacre
officer . . **4.** mate **6.** purser **7.** steward
9. boatswain (bosun)
one–masted . . **5.** sloop
part . . **4.** brig, keel, skeg **5.** stern,
waist **6.** bridge, rudder **8.** binnacle,
taffrail
permit to enter . . **8.** pratique
platform (boarding) . . **9.** gangplank
privateer . . **10.** brigantine
prow . . **5.** prore (Poet)
quarters . . **5.** berth **8.** steerage
10. forecastle (fo'c's'le)
record . . **3.** log
rope . . **4.** line **6.** hawser **7.** halyard,
lanyard, painter, ratline
sailing . . **4.** bark (barque), dhow, proa,
saic **5.** ketch, sloop, xebec **6.** caique,
cutter, galley, lugger **7.** Geordie,
pinnace, polacre
side . . **3.** lee **4.** port **9.** starboard
three–oar bank . . **7.** trireme

twin–hulled .. 9. catamaran
two–oar bank .. 6. bireme
Venetian .. 9. frigatoon
voyage record .. 3. log
war .. 3. sub 7. cruiser, flattop
  9. destroyer, submarine
  11. dreadnaught
window .. 4. port 8. porthole
worm .. 5. borer 6. teredo
ship, famed ... 4. Nina 5. Maine, Pinta
  6. Bounty 7. Monitor, Titanic
  8. Clermont, Half Moon, Merrimac
  9. Mayflower 10. Golden Hind, Santa
  Maria 12. Constitution (Old Ironsides)
  15. Bonhomme Richard
shipment ... 5. cargo 7. carload
shippage ... 3. fee 4. levy 8. shipping
shipshape ... 3. nef (clock) 4. neat,
  tidy, trim 7. orderly
shipwreck, cargo overboard ...
  6. jetsam 7. flotsam
shire ... 5. horse 6. county 8. district,
  province 11. subdivision
shirk ... 4. duck, pike 5. avoid, dodge,
  evade, slink 7. goof off 9. fainaigue
  (finagle)
shirker ... 5. piker 6. truant 7. quitter,
  slacker 8. embusqué 10. malingerer
shirt ... 4. polo, sark 6. blouse,
  camisa, cilice, skivvy, T–shirt
  8. pullover
shiver ... 5. quake, shake 6. be cold
  7. shatter, shudder, tremble, vibrate
  8. fragment 11. trepidation
shivering ... 4. cold 6. creepy
  7. nervous, shaking 8. fragment
  9. agitation, twitching 10. chilliness
shoal ... 3. bar 4. bank, reef, spit
  5. crowd, flock 6. throng 8. sand
  bank (shallow) 9. multitude
shock ... 3. jar 4. blow, heap (grain),
  jolt, stun 5. appal, brunt, bushy
  (hair), shake, stack, start 6. appall,
  impact, offend, stroke, trauma
  7. disgust, horrify, startle, terrify
  8. calamity, frighten, paralyze
  9. collision, electrify 10. concussion
shock absorber ... 7. cushion, snubber
shocking ... 3. bad 5. awful, lurid
  6. horrid 7. ghastly, hideous
  8. horrible, terrible 9. appalling,
  frightful, offensive, revolting, startling
  10. abominable
shoe (pert to) ... 4. boot, clog, geta,
  mule, pump 5. horse, moyle, sabot,
  scuff 6. ballet, bootee, brogan,
  buskin, gillie, loafer, Oxford, patten,
  planch (planche), sandal, secque
  7. chopine, rullion, slipper, sneaker,
  talaria 8. moccasin, sabotine, solleret
  10. clodhopper
shoe (pert to) ...
form .. 4. last, tree
grip .. 5. cleat
lace .. 3. tie 5. aglet (aiglet), lacet
  6. lacing 7. latchet 8. bootlace
  10. shoestring
maker .. 5. sutor 7. cobbler, Crispin
  (patron saint) 8. zapatero
part .. 3. cap 4. rand, vamp, welt
  6. insole 7. counter 9. inner sole
shoebill, shoebird ... 5. stork

shoemaker's patron saint ... 7. Crispin
shogun ... 5. chief, title (Jap) 6. tycoon
  7. shikken
shoneen ... 4. snob 5. toady
shoot ... 3. rod 4. bine, dart, film, fine,
  hunt, kill, plug, twig, weft 5. bough,
  craps, eject, gemma, plant, scion,
  snipe, spear, sprig, throw, tuber,
  vimen 6. branch, sprout, stolon
  7. execute, project 9. discharge
  10. descendant, photograph
shooting (pert to) ...
fish .. 10. archer fish
iron .. 6. pistol 7. firearm 8. revolver
match .. 3. tir 5. skeet
objective .. 6. target
star .. 5. comet 6. meteor 7. cowslip
shop ... 4. mart 5. burse, store
  6. market, saloon 7. atelier
  8. boutique, emporium
shopping mania ... 9. oniomania
shore ... 4. bank, prop 5. beach, coast,
  marge, playa 6. rivage, strand
  7. support 9. foreshore, waterside
  10. run aground, waterfront
shore (pert to) ...
bird .. 3. ree 5. snipe 6. avocet,
  curlew, plover, wading 9. Limicolae
inhabiting .. 8. littoral
pine .. 4. sand 8. tamarack
  9. lodgepole 10. hack–me–tack
recess .. 3. bay 4. cove 5. bayou,
  inlet
short ... 4. curt, rude 5. brief, brusk,
  scant, terse 6. abrupt, scanty
  7. curtate, friable, summary
  8. abridged, succinct 12. insufficient
short (pert to) ...
and pointed .. 5. terse
and stout .. 5. dumpy 6. stocky,
  stodgy 8. roly–poly, thickset
essay .. 5. tract
legged .. 8. breviped
letter .. 4. chit
lived .. 9. ephemeral
stop .. 5. delay, pause 7. respite
  8. interval 9. cessation
shortage ... 4. want 6. ullage
  10. deficiency 13. insufficiency
shorten ... 3. bob, cut, lop 4. clip,
  dele, dock 5. elide 6. lessen,
  reduce, reef in 7. abridge, curtail
  8. condense, contract, decrease, hold
  back 9. decurtate 10. abbreviate
shortening a syllable ... 7. systole
shorthand ... 5. Gregg 6. Pitman
  8. Tironian (Rom) 11. stenography
  12. brachygraphy, speed writing
shortly ... 4. soon 6. curtly, not far
  7. harshly, quickly 8. abruptly
  9. presently
shortsighted ... 4. dull 6. myopic,
  obtuse 8. purblind 11. nearsighted
Shoshone Indian ... 3. Ute 4. Hopi
  5. Piute 7. Bannock 8. Comanche
shot ... 4. dram 5. carom, speed
  6. birdie, bullet, gamble, pellet,
  ruined 7. gunfire, missile, worn out
  8. marksman, unnerved 9. discharge
  10. detonation, photograph, projectile
  11. dilapidated, vaccination
shoulder ... 5. carry, shelf 6. épaule

7. meat cut, scapula, support
8. buttress, omoplate
shoulder (pert to)...
armor.. 9. épaulière
badge, ornament.. 7. epaulet
blade.. 7. scapula 8. omoplate
comb form.. 3. omo 6. humero
inflammation.. 6. omitis 7. omalgia
of a road.. 4. berm (berme)
reference.. 7. humeral 8. scapular
shout... 3. cry 4. call, hoop, hoot,
root, yell 5. cheer 7. acclaim
8. applause, laughter
shouting... 6. clamor, crying 7. calling,
hooting, yelling 9. bellowing
shove... 4. push 5. drive, eject, elbow
6. propel, thrust
shovel... 4. peel, spud 5. scoop,
skeet, spade 7. scooper 8. strockle
10. antler part
show... 4. lead 5. movie, prove, revue,
teach 6. cinema, escort, evince,
reveal 7. betoken, display, divulge,
exhibit 8. evidence, indicate, instruct,
manifest 11. demonstrate
13. demonstration
show (pert to)...
case (glass).. 7. vitrine
deference.. 3. bow 6. salaam
disapproval.. 3. boo 4. hiss, pout
house.. 4. hall 5. odeum, opera
6. circus 8. coliseum, showboat
musical.. 5. revue
off.. 6. flaunt 10. grandstand
of learning.. 6. pedant
pompous.. 6. parade 7. display,
pageant 9. cavalcade 10. exhibition
to a seat.. 5. guide, usher 6. escort
7. conduct
up.. 6. appear, arrive, attend, expose
shower... 4. bath, give, rain 6. abound
8. sprinkle
shower of meteorites... 6. Leonid
(from Leo) 9. Andromede
showing...
animal remains.. 6. zootic
care.. 9. attentive, regardful
11. considerate
display.. 10. exhibition
12. presentation
envy.. 9. invidious
first.. 8. premiere
good judgment.. 6. astute 8. sensible
showy... 3. gay 4. arty, loud 5. gaudy
6. flashy, garish, sporty, tinsel
7. pompous 8. gorgeous, splendid,
striking 9. sumptuous
12. ostentatious 13. grandiloquent
shred... 3. rag 4. snip 5. piece, strip
6. sliver, tatter 7. vestige
8. fragment, particle
shrew... 3. erd 4. tana 5. satan,
scold, Sorex, vixen 6. mammal,
migale, tartar 7. Blarina, outcast,
villain 9. scoundrel, termagant,
Xanthippe
shrewd... 3. sly 4. cagy, foxy, sage,
wily 5. acute, canny, harsh, sharp,
smart, stern 6. artful, astute, biting,
clever, crafty 7. cunning, knowing,
practic, sapient, subtile 8. shrewish

9. sagacious 10. discerning
11. penetrating, sharp–witted
13. perspicacious
shrewdness... 6. acumen 9. smartness
10. craftiness
shriek... 3. cry, yip 4. yell 5. laugh
6. holler, outcry, scream 7. screech
shrievalty... 7. sheriff (office of)
shrill... 4. keen, pipy 5. acute, clear,
sharp 6. biting, squeak 7. screech
8. piercing, strident
11. high–pitched, penetrating
shrimp... 4. pink 5. dwarf, prawn
7. artemia 8. crevette
10. crustacean
shrine... 3. box 4. case, tomb
5. altar, chest 6. chapel, temple
8. monument 9. holy place, reliquary
10. receptacle
shrine (pert to)...
ancient.. 4. naos
Buddhist.. 4. tope 5. stupa
9. Amaravati
India.. 6. dagoba (dagaba) 7. chaitya
Mecca.. 5. Kaaba (Caaba) 11. Great
Mosque
secret, of goddesses.. 9. anaktoron
shrink... 5. cower, parch, quail, rivel,
wince 6. blench, cringe, flinch,
huddle, recoil 7. dwindle, shrivel
8. contract, draw back 9. constrict
10. depreciate
shrinking... 3. coy, shy 5. timid
6. afraid 9. recoiling, sensitive
10. withdrawal 11. contraction
shrivel... 3. age, dry 5. parch, wizen
6. shrink, wither 11. deteriorate
shroud... 4. cowl, hide, mask, veil,
wrap 5. cloak, cover, sheet
6. clothe, screen 7. conceal, curtain,
foliage, protect 8. cerement
9. cerecloth 12. graveclothes
Shrove (pert to)...
cake.. 7. pancake
Sunday.. 13. Quinquagesima
tide.. 9. pre–Lenten (3 days)
Tuesday.. 9. Mardi gras 10. Pancake
Day
shrub... 4. bush 5. plant (woody)
6. frutex 8. beverage
shrub (pert to)...
Adam's needle.. 5. yucca 9. lady's
comb
Arabian tea, narcotic.. 3. kat
aromatic.. 3. tea 4. mint, sage
5. thyme 6. Aralia 7. jasmine
(jasmin) 8. lavender, rosemary
Asian.. 5. musky 8. abelmosk
cherry.. 6. Prunus 7. Cerasus
12. laurocerasus
Chinese.. 6. Kerria
climbing.. 5. grape, liana, Vitis
8. Bignonia, clematis 14. trumpet
creeper
creeping.. 5. pyxie
dogwood.. 6. aucuba, Cornus
evergreen.. 3. box, yew 4. ilex, moss,
titi 5. erica, heath, pyxie, salal, savin
6. laurel, myrtle 7. jasmine, juniper
8. camellia, oleander 9. mistletoe
flowering.. 5. lilac 6. azalea, laurel
7. spiraea, syringa 10. mignonette

fragrant .. see *aromatic* (above)
Hawaiian .. **5.** akala
Mexican .. **7.** guayule **9.** coyotillo
New Zealand .. **4.** tutu **6.** myrtle
  8. ramarama
ornamental .. **8.** hawthorn
parasitic .. **9.** mistletoe
pea .. **5.** broom
pepper .. **4.** kava **8.** kavakava
poisonous .. **4.** tutu **5.** sumac
prickly .. **5.** Rubus **6.** smilax
  8. barberry, dewberry **9.** raspberry
  10. blackberry
S America .. **5.** ceibo
tropical .. **4.** sida, titi **5.** henna
  7. lantana **8.** Oacaceae, tamarisk
  10. frangipani (frangipane)
shrunken ... **4.** lank, thin **5.** dried
  6. shrunk, wasted **8.** puckered,
  withered **9.** atrophied, shriveled
shudder ... **4.** grue **5.** abhor, dread,
  quake **6.** agrise, loathe, quiver, shiver,
  tremor **7.** frisson, tremble
shuffle ... **3.** mix **5.** scuff, shift
  6. huddle, juggle, riffle **7.** confuse,
  evasion, quibble, scuffle
  10. equivocate **12.** walk slovenly
shuffle off ... **5.** evade, shirk **6.** put
  off **7.** push off **10.** mosey along (sl)
shun ... **5.** avoid, evade, evite
  6. eschew **10.** escape from
  11. keep clear of **12.** cold shoulder
shut ... **3.** bar **4.** stop **5.** close
  7. close in, exclude **8.** prohibit
shut (pert to) ...
  in .. **3.** hem **5.** embar **6.** fenced,
  hemmed **7.** bottled, confine, impound,
  invalid, recluse **8.** confined, enclosed
  10. surrounded
  out .. **3.** ban, bar **6.** defeat
  7. exclude, lockout, occlude
  8. obstruct, preclude, prohibit
  up .. **3.** dam, end **4.** cage, pent
  5. close, mewed, pen in **6.** refute
  7. confine, enclose **8.** conclude,
  imprison **9.** terminate
shutter ... **3.** lid **4.** gate **5.** blind
  6. screen **7.** seclude **8.** jalousie
  9. diaphragm
shuttle ... **5.** train **6.** looper, weaver
  7. type bar **9.** alternate, vacillate
  10. oscillator **11.** money drawer
shy ... **3.** coy, mim **4.** wary **5.** aloof,
  dodge, throw, timid **6.** demure,
  modest, recoil, shrink **7.** bashful,
  evasive, fearful, quibble, rabbity
  8. hesitant, reserved, retiring,
  secluded, sheepish, skittish
  9. diffident, reluctant, shrinking
  10. shamefaced, unassuming
  11. distrustful, unobtrusive
Shylock (pert to) ...
  character in .. **16.** Merchant of Venice
  coin .. **5.** ducat
  daughter .. **7.** Jessica
  famed as .. **6.** usurer **11.** money
  lender **12.** extortionist
  friend .. **5.** Tubal
shyness ... **7.** coyness, reserve
  8. timidity **10.** diffidence
  11. bashfulness
Siam ... **8.** Thailand

Siamese (pert to) ...
  group .. **3.** Kui, Lao
  temple .. **3.** wat
  twins .. **9.** pygopagus (joined at spine)
  11. Chang and Eng
sib ... **4.** akin **6.** allied **7.** kinsman,
  related (by blood)
Siberia .. see also *Siberian*
  city .. **7.** Irkutsk **11.** Novosibirsk
  conqueror .. **9.** Timafeyev **11.** Genghis
  Khan
  government .. **7.** Russian
  gulf .. **2.** Ob (Arctic)
  Mongoloid .. **6.** Tartar
  mountains .. **4.** Ural **5.** Altai
  people .. **5.** Yakut **6.** Tartar (Tatar)
  9. Mongolian
  plain .. **6.** steppe, tundra
  river .. **2.** Ob, Om **4.** Lena **5.** Vitim
  6. Abakan **7.** Yenisei
  squirrel .. **7.** miniver
  storm .. **5.** buran
Siberian (pert to) ...
  antelope .. **5.** saiga
  hunters, fishers (tribe) .. **6.** Giliak
  (Gilyak)
  mammal .. **5.** sable
  squirrel fur .. **7.** calaber (calabar)
  swamp .. **5.** urman
  tent .. **4.** yurt (yurta)
  windstorm .. **5.** buran (bura)
sibilate ... **4.** hiss, lisp **8.** aspirate
sibling ... **5.** child
Sibyl (Gr) ... **6.** oracle **7.** seeress
  10. prophetess **13.** fortuneteller
Sibylline Books (3) ... **7.** oracles
  16. prophetic sayings (BC)
sic ... **4.** thus
siccity ... **7.** aridity, drought, dryness
sice .. **3.** six (dice) **8.** sixpence
Sicilian Vespers (pert to) ...
  Bull (anc) .. **8.** Phalaris
  massacre of .. **6.** French (1282)
Sicily ...
  aborigines .. **6.** Sicani
  anc name .. **9.** Trinacria
  capital .. **7.** Palermo **8.** Syracuse (anc)
  composer .. **7.** Bellini
  harbor .. **7.** Palermo
  island .. **6.** Lipari (group)
  11. Pantelleria
  river .. **4.** Acis
  secret society .. **5.** Mafia
  volcano .. **4.** Etna **7.** Vulcano
  9. Stromboli
  whirlpool .. **9.** Charybdis
sick ... **3.** ill, sad, wan **4.** pale
  5. weary **6.** sickly, unwell
  9. disgusted, nauseated
  10. indisposed
sick (pert to) ...
  be .. **3.** ail
  deathly .. **5.** amort **7.** à la mort,
  fatally **10.** terminally
  flag .. **6.** yellow **10.** quarantine
  headache .. **8.** migraine
  of .. **7.** tired of **8.** satiated
  9. disgusted
  person .. **7.** patient **9.** aegrotant
  terms .. **3.** bay **7.** hospice
  8. syndrome **9.** infirmary
  10. dispensary **13.** intensive care

worker.. 5. nurse 11. nursekeeper
sicken... 4. tire 5. weary 6. impair,
weaken 7. afflict, depress, surfeit
8. languish 10. impoverish
sickly... 4. pale, sick, weak 5. faint
6. ailing, feeble, infirm, weakly
7. languid, mawkish 8. diseased
9. unhealthy
Siddhartha, Siddhattha... 6. Buddha
side... 4. face, team, wall 6. behalf,
border, region 7. faction, lateral,
support, surface 9. declivity
side (pert to)...
board.. 5. table 6. buffet 8. dressoir,
whiskers
by side.. 8. parallel
ditch.. 6. escarp
drum.. 5. snare
hog (salted).. 6. flitch
kick.. 3. pal 7. comrade, partner
9. assistant 11. confederate
left.. 4. port 8. larboard
long.. 7. lateral, oblique, sloping
8. indirect, slanting
meat.. 5. bacon 8. salt pork
of head.. 6. temple
of triangle.. 3. leg
on the side.. 5. apart
sheltered.. 3. lee 4. alee 8. windless
sidewalk salesman.. 8. pitchman
step.. 4. duck 5. dodge, evade,
hedge 6. astral, starry 7. quibble
view.. 7. profile
ways, wise.. 7. athwart, lateral
9. laterally, obliquely
whiskers.. 9. sideburns 10. sideboards
windy.. 4. port 9. starboard
sidereal... 6. astral, starry 7. stellar
9. celestial
sidero (comb form)... 4. iron
siderography... 14. steel engraving
siderology *(science of)*... 4. iron
sides, unequal... 7. scalene
sidle... 4. cant, edge, skew, tilt
7. advance (furtive)
siècle... 3. age 7. century
siècle d'or... 9. Golden Age
siege... 7. besiege 8. assiéger
9. besetting 11. besiegement
12. wearying time 13. beleaguerment
Siegfried (pert to)...
hero of.. 5. opera (Wagner's)
slayer.. 5. Hagen
sword.. 7. Balmung
wife.. 9. Kriemhild
Sierra Nevada fog... 7. pogonip
Sierra poet... 13. Joaquin Miller
siesta... 3. nap 4. lull, rest 6. cat
nap, midday, snooze 10. forty winks
sieve... 3. lue 4. bolt, sift, sile
5. purée 6. bolter, filter, riddle,
semmet, sifter, sorter, strain
7. dilluer 8. strainer 9. segregate,
separator
sievelike... 8. cribrate
Sif (Norse), (pert to)...
goddess of.. 4. home
wife of.. 4. Thor
sift... 3. lue 4. bolt 5. sieve
6. dredge, filter, riddle, screen,
sorter, winnow 7. refiner 8. cribrate
sigh... 3. sob 5. mourn, sithe, yearn

6. bemoan, bewail, exhale, grieve,
lament 7. deplore 10. lament over
11. suspiration
sight... 3. see 4. espy, gaze, view
5. scene, sense 6. behold, descry,
vision 7. discern, display 8. aperture
10. exhibition 11. observation
sight (pert to)...
acuteness of.. 7. oxyopia
come into.. 4. loom 5. issue
disorder.. 7. anopsia 8. paropsis
imaginary.. 6. vision
offensive.. 7. eyesore
out of.. 5. range 6. absent
8. vanished 9. invisible
10. exorbitant 11. disappeared
second.. 3. ESP 7. psychic
sigil... 4. seal 5. image (magic), stamp
8. sigillum 9. signature
11. endorsement
sigmoid... 3. ess 5. curve 9. intestine
sign... 3. cue, nod 4. code, hire,
mark, neon, omen 5. token, trace
6. emblem, engage, intone, motion,
notice, signal, symbol 7. endorse,
execute, insigne, portent, presage,
symptom, vestige, warning
8. evidence, password 9. semaphore,
subscribe, watchword 10. forerunner,
indication, underwrite 11. countersign
13. advertisement, constellation
sign (pert to)...
astrological.. 5. Aries 6. Gemini,
Pisces, Taurus 8. Aquarius
9. Capricorn 11. Sagittarius
briefly.. 7. initial
by the same.. 8. likewise, moreover
11. accordingly
diacritical.. 5. tilde 7. cedilla
language.. 11. dactylology
music.. 5. presa
off.. 8. withdraw 10. Yours truly
11. discontinue
ref to.. 5. semic 7. semeion
representing a word.. 8. logogram
spiritual.. 9. sacrament
up.. 4. join 6. enlist
zodiac.. see *astrological* (above)
signal... 3. cue 4. code, fire, flag,
sign 5. alarm, flare, token
6. beacon, emblem, notify, wigwag
7. eminent, lantern, notable, warning
8. striking 9. memorable, prominent,
semaphore, watchword
10. lighthouse, remarkable
11. communicate, conspicuous
13. extraordinary
signal (pert to)...
aviator's.. 5. roger
danger, warning.. 4. bell 5. alert,
fusee
flag.. 6. ensign, wigwag
night.. 6. beacon, curlew, pharos
10. lighthouse
preceding taps.. 6. tattoo
railroad.. 5. fusee 9. semaphore
signature... 4. mark, sign, visa (vise)
5. prima, sigil, stamp 6. signum
9. autograph 11. endorsement
signed by writer... 9. onomatous (opp
of anonymous)
signet... 4. mark, seal 5. sigil, stamp

9. signature 10. impression
11. endorsement
significance... 6. import, moment, weight 7. anagoge, meaning
significant... 4. sign 5. token
6. symbol 7. ominous 8. sinister
9. important, momentous
10. expressive, indicative, meaningful, portentous, suggestive
13. consequential
signification... 6. import 7. meaning
10. indication 11. consequence
12. notification 13. comprehension, specification
signify... 4. hint, mean, sign 5. imply, utter 6. denote, import, matter, signal 7. betoken, connote, declare, specify 8. announce, evidence, foreshow, indicate, intimate, manifest
11. communicate
signum... 4. bell (tower), mark, sign
5. cross 9. signature
sika... 4. deer
sike... 4. rill 5. brook, ditch, gully
6. ravine, stream, trench
sikhara, sikhra... 5. tower (pyramidal)
silage... 4. feed 6. fodder
9. pasturage, provender
Silas (pert to)...
Bib.. 7. prophet 8. Silvanus
character.. 4. Wegg
companion of.. 4. Paul (Bib)
novel.. 11. Silas Marner
sile... 3. fry 4. beam, drip, drop, fall, flow, pass, pour, sink, skim 5. cheat, cover, glide, sieve, spawn 6. betray, filter, strain, stream 7. conceal, deceive, herring (young), subside
8. strainer
silence... 3. gag 4. hush, kill, lull, mute, rest 5. quiet, shush, still, tacet 6. defeat, muffle 7. confute, repress, secrecy 8. oblivion, preclude, restrain, suppress 9. eliminate, stillness 10. silentness 11. taciturnity
13. noiselessness, tacit omission
silent... 3. mum 4. mute, tace
5. quiet, still, tacet, tacit
8. reserved, reticent, taciturn
9. soundless 10. speechless
11. unexpressed
15. uncommunicative
silhouette... 6. shadow 7. contour, outline, picture, profile 9. delineate, hourglass
silica... 4. opal 5. silex
silicate... 4. mica 8. calamine, wellsite
silk (pert to)...
ancient.. 6. Mantua, sendal
artificial.. 5. nylon, rayon
Assam.. 4. eria
black.. 5. crape (mourning), crepe
brown.. 4. muga 6. tussah
corded.. 6. faille 7. Ottoman
embroidery thread.. 5. floss
8. arrasene
fiber.. 5. floss
gland.. 9. serictery
gland of.. 7. spiders 9. silkworms
11. insect larva 12. caterpillars
gold.. 4. tash 6. samite 7. brocade
heavy.. 4. crin

kind of.. 5. China, crepe, moiré, ninon, satin, surah, tabby, tulle
6. pongee, tobine, tussah 7. taffeta
lining.. 8. sarcenet (sarsenet)
muslin.. 16. mousseline de soie
raw.. 8. marabout
rustle of.. 6. scroop
source.. 6. cocoon
thin, glossy.. 7. alamode
thread (for velvets).. 4. tram (trame)
unspun.. 6. sleave
upholstery.. 7. tabaret
waste.. 4. noil 6. strass
watered.. 5. moiré
yarn.. 4. tram 7. schappe
yarn size.. 6. denier
silken... 5. seric, silby, sleek, suave
6. gentle, smooth, tender 7. elegant
8. delicate, lustrous, silklike
9. luxurious 10. effeminate
12. ingratiating
silkworm (pert to)...
Assam.. 3. eri 4. eria
China.. 6. pernyi 9. Ailanthus
cocoon.. 4. clew
disease.. 7. pebrine
genus (moth).. 6. Bombyx
India.. 6. tussah
Japan.. 7. yamamai
silky... 4. soft 5. quiet 6. glossy, smooth 8. delicate 9. sericeous
11. filamentary 12. ingratiating
silky fabric... 6. barège
sill... 4. base, beam, seat, sile
5. basis 6. timber 9. threshold
10. foundation
silly... 3. mad 4. daft, fond 5. anile, apish, dazed, dense, inane 6. dottle, simple 7. asinine, fatuous, foolish, shallow, trivial 9. brainless
10. indiscreet 12. simple–minded
silver... 2. Ag 4. gray 5. metal, money, plate, white 6. argent
7. bullion 8. argentum, eloquent, metallic, sterling
silver (pert to)...
alchemy.. 4. luna 6. occamy
alloy.. 6. billon
ball.. 4. pome
coin.. 6. tester
containing.. 5. lunar
German.. 6. albata
gilded.. 7. vermeil
ingots.. 5. sycee
jackal.. 9. silver fox
lace (with gold).. 5. orris 8. filigree
leaf.. 4. foil 8. hardhack
9. hydrangea, jewelweed 12. buffalo berry
oak.. 11. flannelbush
tongued.. 7. musical 8. eloquent
uncoined.. 7. bullion
silversides... 5. smelt 6. minnow
12. silver salmon
Silver State... 6. Nevada
silverware... 5. vases 6. dishes
8. flatware 9. ornaments, tableware
silvery... 7. frosted, musical
8. lustrous, metallic 9. argentine
simian... 3. ape 6. monkey 7. apelike
similar... 4. akin, like, such 5. alike
7. uniform 8. analogic 9. analogous

11. homogeneous

similarity... 7. analogy 8. likeness
11. homogeneity, resemblance
13. approximation

simile... 8. allegory, metaphor

simper... 5. smirk 10. silly smile
13. affected smile

simple... 4. easy, mere 5. naive
6. dorian, oafish 7. artless
8. innocent 9. ingenuous
10. elementary 11. open and shut
15. unsophisticated

simpleton... 3. ass, daw, oaf 4. boob,
dolt, dupe, fool, gaby, gawk, gump,
simp, zang 5. dunce, goose, idiot,
ikona, moron, Simon, yokel, zombi
6. dawkin, gander, nitwit 7. half–wit
8. Abderite 9. greenhorn
10. nincompoop 11. Simple Simon

simplicity... 6. purity 7. modesty,
naiveté 9. clearness, ignorance,
innocence, plainness, rusticity
10. homeliness, humbleness,
simpleness 11. gullibility, informality
13. ingenuousness
14. unaffectedness

simplify... 7. clarify, explain, expound
9. elucidate, interpret

simply... 5. alone, truly 6. barely,
easily, merely, purely, really, solely
7. plainly 10. informally

simulate... 3. act, ape 4. sham
5. feign 6. affect, assume 7. imitate
11. counterfeit

simulated... 4. aped, sham 5. acted
7. assumed, feigned, shammed
9. pretended 10. fictitious

simurgh, simurg (Myth)... 3. roc
12. gigantic bird

sin... 3. err 4. evil, vice 5. crime,
error, guilt, wrong 6. felony, heresy
7. offense 8. iniquity, peccancy
9. deviation 10. immorality,
wickedness 11. misdemeanor
13. transgression

Sinai (pert to)...
famed for.. 5. Moses 15. Ten
Commandments
location.. 6. Red Sea 11. Gulf of
Aqaba (Akaba)
mountain (Bib).. 5. Horeb 6. Serbal
9. Catharine, Umm Shomer

sinapis... 7. mustard

sinawa... 10. Ceylon hemp

sinay bean... 8. rice bean

since... 2. as 3. ago, for 4. ergo,
gone, past, syne 5. hence, later
7. already, because, whereas
8. inasmuch, until now 9. therefore,
thereupon 10. seeing that
11. considering 12. subsequently

sincere... 4. open, pure 5. frank
6. candid 7. correct, earnest,
genuine, intense, unmixed, upright,
zealous 9. authentic, unfeigned,
veracious 10. unaffected
11. unvarnished 13. unadulterated
15. straightforward

sincerity... 4. zeal 6. candor
7. honesty 10. heartiness
11. genuineness, sincereness

sincerity symbol... 8. amethyst

sind... 5. rinse 6. drench, quench
7. rinsing

Sind (Ind)...
capital.. 7. Karachi
ibex.. 8. wild goat
prince.. 5. ameer

Sindbad's bird... 3. roc

Sindbad the Sailor... 9. character
(Arabian Nights)

sindico... 7. trustee 8. assignee,
receiver

sine... 7. without

sinew... 4. thew 5. nerve, power
6. muscle, string, tendon

sinewy... 4. firm, wiry 5. thewy, tough
6. brawny, strong 7. fibrose, stringy
8. powerful, vigorous

sinful... 3. bad 4. evil 5. wrong
6. wicked 7. vicious 10. iniquitous
11. unrighteous

sing... 3. hum, say 4. hymn, lilt
5. carol, chant, croon, yodel
6. intone, warble 7. rejoice
8. proclaim, vocalize 9. celebrate

sing (pert to)...
exultantly.. 4. lilt 7. chortle
10. cheerfully
jovially.. 5. troll
off key.. 4. flat
or whistle.. 7. tweedle
shrilly.. 4. pipe
softly.. 5. croon
sorrowfully.. 7. despond 8. complain
Swisslike.. 5. yodel
with trills.. 6. warble 7. roulade

singe... 4. burn, sear 6. scorch
8. discolor

singer... 4. bard, bird, diva, poet
5. blues, siren, tenor, torch
6. cantor, hymner 7. caroler,
crooner, warbler, yodeler 8. minstrel,
songster, vocalist 9. chanteuse,
descanter 10. cantatrice, prima
donna 11. minnesinger

Singhalese tree... 4. poon 5. domba

singing (pert to)...
birds.. 6. Oscine
canary.. 10. white whale
fish.. 8. toadfish
group.. 5. choir 6. chorus
Memnon.. 9. Amenhotep (statue)
ref to.. 5. melic

single... 3. ace, odd, one 4. lone,
only, sole, unit 6. simple, unique
8. sporadic 9. unmarried

single (pert to)...
algebra.. 6. nomial
comb form.. 3. uni
odd.. 7. azygous
racing term.. 4. heat
tones (one of two).. 10. monotonous

singleness... 5. unity 8. celibacy
9. sincerity, unmarried

singly... 4. once, only, solo 5. alone,
apart 6. simply 8. uniquely
9. severally 12. individually,
particularly, single–handed

singular... 3. odd 4. each, rare, sole,
unit 5. queer 6. unique 7. eminent,
special, strange, unusual 8. peculiar,
separate, uncommon 9. eccentric,
fantastic, whimsical 10. individual,

remarkable, unexampled
11. exceptional 12. unparalleled
13. extraordinary, unprecedented
14. characteristic
singularity . . . 6. oddity 7. oddness,
oneness 8. peculiar 11. peculiarity
12. eccentricity 13. individuality
15. distinctiveness
Sinic . . . 7. Chinese, Sinitic
sinister . . . 4. evil, grim, left 7. adverse,
corrupt, ominous 9. dishonest,
injurious, malicious, underhand
10. disastrous, portentous
11. unfortunate
sinistral . . . 7. baneful 10. left–handed
12. illegitimate, inauspicious (opp of
dextral)
sink . . . 3. age, bog, dip, ebb, sag
4. cave, drop, fall, mire, sump
5. drain, droop, lapse, lower, quail
6. cavity, deject, engulf, go down,
recede, settle, sicken, weaken
7. decline, depress, descend,
despond 8. decrease, diminish,
submerge 10. degenerate
sinuous . . . 4. wavy 7. winding
9. deviating, intricate 10. circuitous
Sioux (pert to) . . .
division . . 5. Teton 6. Santee
famed as . . 8. warriors
tribe . . 3. Oto (Otoe) 4. Crow, Iowa
5. Omaha, Osage 6. Dakota, Plains
9. Winnebago
sip . . . 3. lap, sup 4. gulp 5. drink,
quaff, taste 6. tipple
sircar . . . 5. ruler 6. master 7. servant
8. province (Mogul) 10. government
siren . . . 5. alarm, Circe, deity, lurer,
vixen 7. charmer, enticer, foghorn,
Lorelei, mermaid 9. bewitcher,
Cleopatra, temptress
Sirenia . . . 6. dugong, mammal
7. manatee 14. Steller's sea cow
siriasis . . . 9. sunstroke
Sirius . . . 4. star 7. Dog Star 10. Canis
Major, dog of Orion (Gr Myth)
sissy . . . 5. softy 6. prissy, sister
10. effeminate, pantywaist
11. mollycoddle
sister . . . 3. kin, nun, sib 5. nurse,
soror
sisterhood . . . 4. nuns 8. sorority
Sistrurus . . . 11. rattlesnake
sit . . . 3. fit 4. isle, loll, pose, rest
5. brood, perch, press, roost, squat
6. repose 7. convene 8. incubate
site . . . 4. ruin, seat 5. place, scene,
venue 6. locale, locate 8. location,
position
site of Taj Mahal . . . 4. Agra (Ind)
sitting . . . 4. seat 6. séance, sedent
7. posture, sessile, session
10. incubation 11. convocation
situated . . . 3. lie, set 4. case, seat
5. fixed 6. clutch, placed, plight
9. ensconced, stationed
11. established
situated (pert to) . . .
at back . . 6. astern 7. postern
9. posterior
at base . . 5. basal
between folds . . 11. interplical

in middle . . 6. medial, median
on left hand . . 9. sinistrad
on right hand . . 6. dexter
situation . . . 3. job 4. case, post
5. place, situs, state 6. office, plight
7. station 8. locality, location,
position 9. condition, placement
situation (pert to) . . .
approximate . . 11. whereabouts
difficult . . 6. scrape 7. dilemma
8. quandary 9. imbroglio
11. predicament 12. circumstance
doomed . . 7. rattrap
favorable . . 7. vantage
Latin . . 5. situs
perplexing . . 6. strait
three choices . . 8. trilemma
Siva, Shiva (pert to) . . .
consort . . 3. Uma 4. Devi
dancer . . 8. Natajara
god, deity . . 8. Hinduism 9. Destroyer
title . . 8. Mahadeva
trident . . 6. trisul (trisula)
six (pert to) . . .
balls (Medici) . . 5. palle
dice number . . 4. sice
eyed . . 9. senocular
feet of earth . . 5. grave
fold . . 8. sextuple
footed . . 7. hexaped 9. hexapodal
group . . 5. hexad
lines . . 6. sestet 7. sextain
pence . . 6. bender 7. fiddler
pert to . . 6. senary
pointed figure . . 4. star
square . . 9. hexagonal
sixty, sixties . . . 5. cycle, saros
7. numeral
size . . . 3. cap 4. area, bulk, pica,
pope, pott 5. agate, grade 6. adjust
7. arrange, measure, portion
8. classify 9. magnitude
10. gargantuan 11. measurement
sizzle . . . 3. fry 4. hiss 5. speed 7. be
angry 10. effervesce
sjambok . . . 4. flog, whip
skate . . . 3. jag, ray (fish) 4. plug, skim
5. glide, horse, scull, spree
skean . . . 4. dirk 6. dagger
skedaddle . . . 4. bolt, flee, flit 6. scurry
7. run away, scamper
skein . . . 3. rap (120 yds), web
4. hank, yarn 6. thread 7. spireme
12. flight of fowl
skelder . . . 5. cheat 7. vagrant
9. panhandle
skeleton . . . 4. cage 5. bones, frame,
mummy 6. sketch 7. contour,
diagram, outline 8. thinness
9. framework
skeleton (pert to) . . .
at the feast . . 7. kill–joy 10. wet
blanket 11. crapehanger
English dialect . . 4. reme
framework . . 5. cadre
in the closet . . 4. evil 6. secret
13. mortification
key . . 6. master
marine animal . . 6. sponge
polyp . . 5. coral
skeptic, sceptic . . . 7. doubter, infidel
8. aporetic 10. Pyrrhonist, unbeliever

11. freethinker, irreligious, nullifidian
skeptical, sceptical ... 8. doubtful,
doubting 11. incredulous, unbelieving
sketch ... 3. jap, jot 4. draw, idea,
limn, plan, skit 5. draft, trace
6. aperçu, design 7. diagram,
drawing, outline 8. esquisse, treatise
9. delineate 11. delineation,
description
sketchy ... 5. rough, vague
10. unfinished
skewer ... 3. pin, rod 5. truss
6. fasten, pierce 9. brochette
skid ... 4. clog, shoe, slip, trig
5. brake, check, slide 7. travois
8. sideslip
skiff ... 4. boat, skim 5. canoe, glide,
graze 6. caique 7. rowboat
11. slight touch
skill ... 3. art 5. craft, knack 6. gifted,
talent 7. ability, address, aptness,
cunning, finesse, mastery 8. aptitude,
deftness, facility 9. adeptness,
dexterity, expertise, readiness,
smartness 10. adroitness, cleverness,
proficient 11. proficiency
skilled ... 5. adept 6. expert
7. endowed, trained 8. talented
10. conversant, proficient
skilled (pert to) ...
in government .. 9. statesman
in mechanics .. 5. sloyd
in strategy .. 7. finesse
skillful, skilful ... 3. apt 4. able, deft,
fine 6. adroit, clever, crafty, daedal,
expert 7. capable 8. artistic,
dextrous, tactical 9. daedalian,
dexterous, ingenious 10. proficient,
well–versed 12. accomplished
skim ... 4. flit, sail, scan, scud
5. glide, graze, scoon, skirr 6. slight
8. pass over
skin ... 4. bark, derm, fell, flay, hide,
pare, peel, pelt, rind, scum 5. cheat,
cutis, derma, fraud, scalp 6. fleece,
lamina, scrape 7. callous, cuticle,
defraud, swindle 8. covering,
tegument 9. epidermis
10. integument 11. decorticate
skin (pert to) ...
animal .. 4. coat, hide, pelt 7. pellage
animal's neck fold .. 6. dewlap
beaver .. 4. plew
comb form .. 4. derm 5. derma
decoration .. 6. tattoo
destitute of .. 8. apellous
disease .. 4. acne 5. hives, mange,
uredo 6. eczema, herpes, tetter
8. ringworm 9. urticaria
drying frame .. 5. herse
dryness .. 7. xerosis
fawnskin (of Dionysus) .. 6. nebris
fold .. 5. plica 6. dewlap
fruit .. 7. epicarp
gobbler's throat .. 3. tar
layer .. 5. cutis, derma
layer, outer .. 7. epicarp
opening .. 4. pore
pert to .. 6. dermal 7. dermoid
piece .. 5. blype
pigment, excess .. 8. melanism
protuberance .. 4. mole, wart

salting bin .. 5. kench
squirrel .. 4. vair
tan .. 3. taw
tanned .. 5. suede
unsheared .. 8. woolfell
skinflint ... 5. cheat, miser 9. bargainer
skink ... 4. adda 6. lizard
skinned ... 6. bested 7. euchred,
fleeced
skinned (pert to) ...
dark .. 7. melanic, swarthy
pert to .. 5. bared 7. denuded
8. stripped
slang .. 7. euchred, fleeced
thick .. 9. pachyderm 11. pachydermic
skinny ... 4. lean, thin 5. scant
6. stingy 8. skinlike 9. emaciated,
niggardly
skip ... 3. dap 4. gait, jump, leap,
omit 5. bound, caper, elide, frisk,
salto, vault 6. gambol, lackey, spring
7. abscond 8. ricochet
skipjack ... 3. fop 4. pike 5. saury
6. bonito 7. bounder, parvenu,
upstart 8. bluefish, sailboat
9. stripling (conceited) 10. butterfish
14. snapping beetle
skipper ... 5. saury 6. locust, maggot,
master, serang 8. skipjack
9. butterfly 11. grasshopper
ski race (obstacle) ... 6. slalom
skirling ... 5. trout 6. salmon
skirmish ... 4. fray 5. brush, clash,
melee 6. combat 8. conflict, flourish
9. encounter 10. velitation
skirt ... 5. dress, evade, woman
6. border, edging, fringe
9. appendage, baseboard, periphery,
petticoat 10. pass around, saddle
part
skirt (pert to) ...
armor .. 5. tasse (tace) 7. lamboys
attached to blouse .. 6. peplum
chaser .. 9. libertine 11. philanderer
dance .. 6. ballet
short .. 4. kilt
skit ... 4. joke, play 5. caper
6. parody, shower, sketch
skittish ... 3. coy, shy 5. jumpy
6. fickle, frisky, tricky 7. bashful
8. unstable, volatile 9. excitable
10. capricious 13. irresponsible
skittles ... 4. game, play 8. ninepins
9. enjoyment (not all beer and
skittles)
skoal ... 5. toast 10. salutation
11. exclamation 14. pledge of health
skulk ... 4. lurk 5. cower, dodge,
hedge, sneak 8. malinger
skull ... 4. bean, head, mind 5. brain
7. cranium, harnpan 8. brain box
skull (pert to) ...
cap .. 6. beanie 7. calotte
9. zucchetto 10. berrettino
cavity .. 5. fossa
measure .. 11. craniometer
monk's .. 6. pileus
operation .. 6. trepan
part .. 5. inion 6. bregma 7. calotte,
occiput
ref to .. 5. inial 6. cranic 7. cranial
science of .. 10. craniology

skull and crossbones... 5. death (symb) 10. danger sign
skunk... 5. zoril 6. defeat 7. fitchew, polecat, stinker 8. conepate (conepati), zorrillo 9. scoundrel
sky... 4. blue 5. ether, vault 6. caelum, canopy, heaven, welkin 7. heavens, the blue 8. empyrean 9. firmament 10. blue yonder
sky (pert to)...
  color.. 4. blue 5. azure 7. celeste 8. cerulean
  god.. 3. Anu
  lark.. 5. pipit 6. Alauda, frolic 7. titlark
  light.. 6. window 8. abatjour
  lure.. 7. horizon
  parlor.. 5. attic 6. garret
  pilot.. 8. chaplain 9. clergyman 10. missionary
  serpent.. 3. Ahi
slab... 3. mud 4. tile 5. board, dalle, plank, slime 6. lamina, ledger, pillar (stone), puddle 7. portion 8. monument 9. flagstone
slab (pert to)...
  grave.. 5. stele (stela)
  marble.. 5. dalle 6. tablet
  slablike.. 6. stelar
slack... 3. lax 4. lull, slow 5. chaff, inert, let up, loose, shirk, tardy 6. abated, remiss 7. relaxed 8. careless, dilatory, inactive, indolent, sluggish 9. reluctant, secondary 10. diminished, inadequate 11. inattentive
slacken... 5. abate, delay, relax 6. loosen, reduce, repose, retard 7. let down, relieve 8. hold back
slackening of strained relations... 7. detente (Internat)
slag... 4. lava 5. dross 6. cinder, scoria 7. residue 9. recrement 11. agglomerate
slain... 4. dead 6. fallen, killed 8. murdered 12. assassinated
slake... 4. cool, sate 5. abate, allay, slack 6. quench 7. assuage, crumble, hydrate, refresh, relieve, satisfy, slacken 8. decrease, mitigate, moderate 10. extinguish 12. disintegrate
slam... 4. bang, blow, give, shut, vole 5. abuse, score 6. impact 9. criticism, criticize
slander... 5. belie, libel 6. defame, malign, vilify 7. asperse, blacken, distort, traduce 8. derogate, disgrace, reproach 10. defamation, scandalize 12. misrepresent
slang... 4. cant 5. argot 6. jargon, patois 7. hep talk 10. vernacular
slant... 4. bend, cant, skew 5. angle, bevel, slope 6. aslant, aspect, biased, glance 7. incline, opinion 8. attitude, occasion 9. obliquely, viewpoint 10. hypotenuse 11. inclination, opportunity
slap... 3. hit 4. blow, clap, cuff, snub 5. crack, skelp, sound, twank 6. buffet, rebuff, slight, strike 8. chastise 12. chastisement

slash... 3. cut 4. gash, lash, slit 5. marsh, sever 6. attack, reduce, stripe 7. censure, scourge 8. price cut 9. criticize, reduction
slate... 4. list, rock 5. color, scold, sculp 6. ballot, enroll, record, roster, tablet, thrash 7. censure, roofing, writing 8. register, schedule, slattern 9. criticize, reprimand
slate (pert to)...
  ax.. 7. mattock
  black.. 4. gray
  blue.. 9. Swiss blue
  gray.. 7. Russian 9. red–yellow 10. sandy beige 13. oriental pearl
  roof.. 3. rag
  tool.. 3. zax 7. scantle
slater... 6. critic 7. hellier
slattern... 4. slut 5. frump, idler, mopsy 6. sloppy 7. trifler, trollop 8. careless, slovenly 9. litterbug
slaughter... 4. kill, slay 6. battue, murder, pogrom 7. butcher, carnage, killing 8. butchery, hecatomb, massacre, occision 9. bloodshed 10. butchering 11. destruction
slaughterhouse... 8. abattoir, Aceldama, butchery, matadero, shambles 9. stockyard 12. field of blood
Slav... 4. Pole, Slav, Sorb, Wend 5. Croat, Czech 6. Slovak 7. Russian, Serbian, Servian 8. Bohemian, Croatian, Moravian 9. Bulgarian
slave... 4. boor, esne, peon, serf 5. chela, helot, thane 6. drudge, lascar, minion, thrall, vassal 7. bondman, captive, chattel, enslave, odalisk, servant 8. slave ant 9. bondslave
slave (pert to)...
  block (selling).. 7. catasta
  born.. 4. neif
  comedy (stock name).. 5. Davus
  dealer.. 5. bichy, mango (obs)
  Eleusinian (Gr Relig).. 5. Baubo, lambe
  female.. 9. concubine, odalisque (odalisk)
  free.. 5. thane (thegn)
  fugitive.. 8. marooner
  Indian.. 10. Athapascan
  The Tempest.. 7. Caliban
slavery... 4. bond 7. bondage, service 8. drudgery 9. captivity, servitude, thralldom, vassalage 11. enslavement 12. enthrallment
Slave States... 5. Texas 7. Alabama, Florida, Georgia 8. Arkansas, Delaware, Kentucky, Maryland, Missouri, Virginia 9. Louisiana, Tennessee 11. Mississippi 13. North Carolina, South Carolina
slay... 4. kill 5. amuse, burke, knock, lynch, smite 6. murder, strike 7. butcher, destroy 9. slaughter 10. annihilate 11. assassinate, destroy life, exterminate
slayer... 6. killer 8. criminal, murderer, regicide, vaticide 9. matricide, patricide 10. fratricide, sororicide

sleave... 4. sley 5. floss 6. tangle
8. separate 9. floss silk
11. disentangle 13. untwisted silk
sled... 4. pung 6. sledge, sleigh,
travoy, troika 8. toboggan
sledge... 4. sled 6. hammer, sleigh,
strike 7. seven–up (game), vehicle
sleep... 3. nap, nod 4. dorm, doss,
doze, wink 5. death, sopor
6. drowse, snooze, somnus
7. slumber 10. narcolepsy,
somnipathy 11. hibernation
sleep (pert to)...
comb form.. 5. somni
deep.. 6. stupor 8. lethargy
10. narcolepsy
hypnotic.. 10. somnipathy
inducing.. 5. dwale 6. opiate, potion
8. sedative 9. soporific
10. anesthesia, belladonna
insensible.. 4. coma
midday.. 6. siesta
prolonged.. 5. sopor
upon.. 8. consider, postpone
sleeper... 3. tie 4. beam 6. rafter,
rester, timber 7. Pullman, reposer,
support 8. dormouse 9. slumberer
10. slow seller 11. sleeping car
sleeping... 4. dead 5. inert 6. asleep,
latent 7. dormant 8. dormient,
inactive 9. quiescent 10. quiescence
11. inattentive
sleeping (pert to)...
pill.. 9. soporific
place.. 3. bed, cot 4. bunk, doss
5. berth, couch 6. pallet 7. cubicle
9. dormitory
sickness.. 6. nagana, tsetse
9. lethargus
sleepwalking... 8. neurosis
12. nightwalking, somnambulism
sleepy... 4. dull 5. tired 6. drowsy
8. soporose 9. lethargic, somnolent
11. somniferous
sleeve... 3. arm 5. gigot
(leg–o'–mutton) 10. copper tube
14. British channel
sleigh... 4. pung 6. cutter
sleight of hand performer... 4. mage
8. magician 14. legerdemainist
15. prestidigitator
slender... 4. lank, lean, slim, thin
5. gaunt, lanky, leger, reedy
6. lissom, narrow, svelte 7. gracile,
tenuous, trivial, willowy 9. elongated
slender pinnacle... 3. epi
sleuth... 6. tracer 8. hawkshaw
9. detective, sleuthdog
11. sleuthhound 13. investigator
slice... 3. cut, saw 4. gash, slab
5. piece, share, shave 6. rasher,
sliver, stroke 7. portion 8. golf term,
splinter 12. cross section
slick... 4. neat, tidy 5. alert, sleek,
smart 6. clever, smooth 8. slippery,
unctuous 9. first–rate, lubricate
10. glistening 12. accomplished
slide... 3. ski 4. rule, skid, slip, slue
5. chute, clasp, glide, plane
(sloping), scoot, skate 6. elapse
7. lantern, slither 8. toboggan
9. avalanche 11. deteriorate

slight... 3. cut 4. defy, rare, snub,
thin 5. faint, frail, leger, minor, oligo
(comb form), scorn, small 6. flimsy,
ignore, little, meager 7. disdain,
fragile, neglect, nominal, scantly,
shallow, trivial 8. contempt, delicate
9. disregard, indignity 10. immaterial
11. unimportant 13. imperceptible,
unsubstantial 14. inconsiderable
slight (pert to)...
convexity.. 6. camber
sound.. 4. peep
variation.. 6. nuance 7. shading
slightest... 5. least 6. barest
slightly (pert to)...
damaged paper.. 6. retree
sour.. 8. acescent
tapering.. 6. terete
slim... 3. sly 4. lean, mean, thin
5. small, spare 6. adroit, scanty,
sparse, svelte 7. slender, tenuous
9. worthless
slime... 3. mud 4. ooze 5. filth, gleet
6. mucous
slip... 3. err, pew, sin 4. dock, fail,
pier, skid, slue 5. boner, cover,
error, fault, glide, lapse, slide, strip
6. bungle, elapse 7. blunder, cutting,
failure, faux pas, misdeed, mistake,
slither 9. youngling 10. pillowslip
12. undergarment 13. transgression
slipknot... 5. noose
slipper... 4. mule, neap, shoe
5. apron, moyle, Romeo 6. pinson,
sandal 7. scuffer 8. babouche
(baboosh), covering
slippery... 3. sly 4. eely, glib 5. slick
6. crafty, fickle, shifty, tricky, wanton
7. cunning, elusive, evasive
8. unctuous, unstable 9. deceitful,
uncertain 10. intangible, precarious,
unreliable 11. treacherous
13. untrustworthy
slit... 4. kerf 5. cleft, slash, split
6. furrow 7. severed
slither... 5. crawl, glide, sidle, slide
sliver... 3. cut 5. shred, slice, split
8. fragment, splinter
sloe... 3. haw 4. plum
sloe (pert to)...
berry.. 7. juniper
bush.. 10. blackthorn
color.. 9. blue–black
fruit (blackthorn).. 3. haw 4. sloe
gin.. 12. sloe–flavored
slogan... 3. cry 5. motto 6. phrase
9. catchword, watchword
10. shibboleth (Bib)
sloop... 5. yacht 6. cutter, schuit
(schuyt) 7. eelboat
slope... 3. dip, lie 4. bank, hade,
ramp 5. bevel, scarp, slant, talus
6. calade, decamp, escarp, glacis
7. terrace 9. declivity 10. declension
11. inclination
sloping bank... 4. brae 7. terrace
sloth... 2. ai 4. pack (bears), pazy,
unau 6. acedia, mammal 7. inertia
8. idleness, slowness 9. indolence
slothful... 4. lazy 8. inactive, indolent,
sluggish
sloth monkey... 5. lemur, loris

slough ... **3.** bog **4.** husk, mire, molt, shed, skin **5.** bayou, swamp **7.** channel, discard
sloughing ... **7.** ecdysis, molting **8.** shedding **10.** discarding
slovenly ... **5.** dowdy, messy, tacky **6.** frowzy, sloppy, untidy **8.** careless, slattern, slipshod **9.** negligent **10.** disheveled, disorderly, slatternly
slow ... **4.** dull, late, poky **5.** delay, inert, relax **6.** boring, hinder, retard, stupid **7.** slacken **8.** boresome, dilatory, inactive, moderate **9.** lingering **20.** inch by inch phlegmatic **13.** unprogressive
slow (pert to) ...
action .. **6.** dawdle **10.** deliberate
adverb .. **10.** behindhand
down .. **4.** idle **6.** retard **8.** wind down **10.** decelerate
music .. **5.** largo, lento, molto, tardo **6.** adagio **8.** andante **8.** lentando **10.** lentamento
poke .. **5.** snail **7.** dawdler
up .. **3.** lag **6.** retard **7.** decline
witted .. **4.** dull **6.** stupid
sludge ... **3.** mud **4.** gunk, mire, ooze **5.** slime **8.** sediment
slug ... **3.** hit **4.** blow, dose **5.** Arion, drink, drone, idler, Limax, space, token **6.** bullet, loiter, nugget **7.** trepang **8.** sluggard **9.** gastropod
sluggish ... **4.** logy, slow **5.** dopey, inert **6.** drowsy, stupid, supine **7.** dronish, languid **8.** dilatory, inactive, indolent, listless, stagnant **9.** stagnancy, stupidity, torpidity
sluice ... **4.** race **5.** flush **6.** drench, stream **7.** channel **9.** floodgate
slumber ... **4.** doze **5.** sleep **6.** catnap, drowse, repose, snooze, somnus **14.** arms of Morpheus
slump ... **4.** drop, fall **7.** decline, descend, dessert, sinkage **9.** fall short **10.** depreciate, depression
slur ... **4.** blur **5.** elide **6.** defame, insult, mackle, slight, stigma **7.** calumny, traduce **8.** disgrace, innuendo, reproach, skim over **9.** aspersion, disparage **10.** calumniate, stigmatize
slush ... **3.** mud **4.** mire, snow **5.** slime **14.** sentimentality
sly ... **4.** arch, foxy, wary, wily, wink **5.** cagey, catty, snaky **6.** covert, crafty, feline, shrewd, sneaky, subtle **7.** cunning, furtive **8.** craftily **9.** underhand **11.** mischievous, underhanded **15.** surreptitiously
smack ... **3.** bit, bop **4.** bang, belt, buss, glow, kiss, tang **5.** clout, taste **6.** strike, vessel, wallop **8.** chastise, sailboat
smacking ... **5.** brisk **6.** lively **7.** dashing **8.** spanking, vigorous **9.** energetic
small ... **3.** tot, wee **4.** thin, tiny, wisp **5.** dwarf, petty **6.** humble, little, meager, minute, modest, petite **7.** faintly, trivial **8.** picayune, trifling **9.** miniature, minuscule, thumbnail **10.** diminutive, undersized **11.** unimportant **13.** insignificant **14.** contemptuously, inconsiderable
small (pert to) ...
amount .. **3.** dab **4.** dram **5.** minim **6.** morsel **7.** modicum **8.** pittance
anvil .. **5.** teest
area .. **6.** areola (areole)
armadillo .. **4.** peba
arms .. **3.** bow **5.** rifle, sword **6.** pistol **7.** carbine, grenade
attractive .. **4.** cute **6.** dainty
bomb .. **6.** petard **7.** grenade
bottle .. **4.** vial **5.** phial
case, handbag .. **4.** etui
comb form .. **5.** lepto, micro
dab .. **3.** pat, wad **5.** chunk
deer .. **4.** fawn, napu
delicately .. **6.** mignon
distance .. **3.** hop **4.** step
drink .. **3.** nip **4.** pony, swig
drum .. **5.** bongo, tabor
field .. **5.** croft
fish .. **3.** ide
flag .. **6.** fanion
fruits .. **10.** low growing
fry .. **4.** fish, kids, tots **8.** children **10.** youngsters
insect .. **4.** flea **5.** midge
island .. **3.** ait **4.** isle
lake .. **4.** mere, pond
law .. **5.** petit
minded .. **4.** mean **5.** petty **6.** biased **10.** prejudiced, vindictive
neat .. **6.** dapper
number .. **3.** few **7.** paucity
opening .. **4.** pore **5.** stoma **7.** orifice
ox .. **4.** anoa
part .. **4.** iota **6.** detail **7.** snippet
particle .. **4.** atom, mote **8.** molecule
people .. **5.** elves **6.** common **7.** fairies, midgets, Pygmies
piece .. **3.** mot **4.** chip, tate **5.** speck **7.** driblet, morceau
post .. **9.** paper size
quantity .. **4.** drop, mite **5.** trace **7.** handful
rope (Naut) .. **7.** marline (marling)
Scot .. **3.** sma, wee
shield .. **3.** écu **9.** scutellum
stream .. **3.** run **4.** rill **6.** rillet
surface .. **5.** facet
talk .. **6.** babble **7.** prattle **8.** chitchat
task .. **5.** chore **6.** odd job
things .. **3.** fry
tower .. **6.** turret **7.** minaret
very .. **3.** wee **8.** picayune **11.** Lilliputian
world .. **9.** microcosm
smallpox ... **7.** variola
smaragd ... **7.** emerald
smart ... **3.** apt **4.** chic, perk, posh, trig, trim, wise **5.** acute, alert, natty, nifty, quick, sting **6.** astute, clever, shrewd, spruce, trendy **7.** dashing, painful, pungent, stylish **8.** impudent, poignant, pricking **9.** competent, ingenious **10.** precocious **11.** fashionable, intelligent
smash ... **4.** blow, mash, pulp, ruin **5.** break, crush, drink (spirits), stave, wreck **6.** defeat **7.** collide, debacle, destroy, failure, shatter, success

8. accident, beverage 9. collision, pulverize

smear... 3. dab, rub 4. daub, gaum 5. slake, stain, sully 6. anoint, bedaub, defame, defile, grease, malign, smirch, smudge 7. besmear, plaster, pollute, slander 8. besmirch

smear with...
egg white.. 5. glair 8. meringue
mud.. 5. slime
ointment.. 6. anoint

smell... 4. odor, olid, reek 5. aroma, fetor, scent, sense, sniff, stink 6. detect 7. perfume 9. fragrance, redolence 10. atmosphere

smell (pert to)...
acute.. 8. oxyrhine
loss of sense of.. 7. anosmia
offensive.. 3. bad 4. foul, olid 5. fetor 6. stench
sense of.. 6. osmics 7. osmesis 9. olfaction

smelling salts... 9. hartshorn 17. ammonium carbonate

smelt... 4. fish, fuse, melt 6. tomcod 7. scorify 10. silverside

smilax... 8. catbrier 10. greenbrier

smile... 4. grin 5. laugh, smirk, sneer 6. simper 8. greeting

smiling... 5. agrin, merry, riant 6. rident 8. gleaming, grinning

smirch... 4. blot 5. smear, stain, sully, taint 6. blotch, smutch, stigma, vilify 7. begrime, blacken, blemish, tarnish 8. discolor 10. blackening

smirk... 4. grin, leer 6. simper

smite... 4. kill, slap 6. lay low, strike 7. chasten, impress, inflict, trouble 8. chastise

smithy... 6. forger, stithy 7. farrier 8. smithery 10. blacksmith

smock... 5. kamis, shift, tunic, woman (obs) 7. chemise 9. philander 11. overgarment

smoke... 4. burn, cure, floc, fume, pipe 5. cigar, cloud, cubeb, flume, smook, vapor 6. smudge 7. incense, tobacco 9. fumigate, preserve 9. cigarette

smokestack... 6. funnel 7. chimney 8. fumiduct

smoking apparatus (Orient)... 7. tabagie 8. narghile (nargile)

smolder, smoulder... 4. burn 5. choke, smoke 6. smudge 7. smother 9. suffocate

smooth... 4. comb, ease, even, iron, lene, pave 5. bland, clear, level, plane, press, sleek, slick, suave 6. glossy, mangle, pacify, urbane 7. uniform 8. hairless, unctuous 10. facilitate, flattering 12. frictionless, ingratiating

smooth (pert to)...
breathing.. 13. spiritus lenis
comb form.. 3. lio
feathers, hair.. 5. preen
hard, transparent.. 6. glassy
phonetically.. 4. lene
tare.. 12. slender vetch
tongued.. 4. glib 5. suave 12. hypocritical

smooth and...
soft.. 5. furry, silky, soapy 7. velvety
soothing.. 5. bland
sweet.. 11. mellifluent
white.. 11. alabastrine

smother... 4. daub, kill 5. befog, choke, cover 6. deaden, hush up, muffle, stifle, welter 7. overlie, smolder 8. suppress 9. suffocate, to blanket 11. exterminate

smudge... 4. blot, smut, soil, spot 5. smear, smoke, stain 6. smutch 7. begrime, smolder

smug... 4. neat, tidy, trim 5. smart, suave 6. pilfer 7. correct 9. confident 10. complacent 13. self—satisfied

smuggler... 6. runner 9. rumrunner 13. contrabandist

smur... 4. mist 5. cloud, smurr 7. drizzle

Smyrna... 5. Izmir (present name)

Smyrna fig... 5. eleme (elemi)

Smyrna melon... 6. casaba

snail... 4. slug 5. drone, Helix, Mitra, whelk 6. Nerita, Triton 7. mollusk 9. gastropod 10. periwinkle

snake... 3. asp, ess 4. tree, worm 5. adder, cobra, coral, racer, viper 6. garter, gopher 7. hognose, rattler, reptile 8. Micrurus, moccasin 9. Heterodon 10. bushmaster, copperhead, sidewinder 11. cottonmouth, diamondback, rattlesnake 12. schaapsteker

snake (pert to)...
African.. 5. mamba
bird.. 6. darter
black.. 5. racer
cobra.. 3. nag (naga)
comb form.. 5. ophio, ophis 6. herpes
crusher.. 6. python 8. anaconda 14. boa constrictor
dance.. 4. Hopi 6. ophism
division (serpents).. 7. Ophidia 9. Serpentes
expert.. 13. herpetologist
fear of.. 13. herpetophobia
Florida.. 8. moccasin
front—fanged.. 5. cobra, mamba 6. elapid 8. Elapinne
garter.. 5. Elaps
genus.. 7. Ophidia
heraldic.. 5. bisse
horned.. 8. cerastes
India.. 5. krait 6. bongar
killer.. 8. mongoose
like.. 7. ophioid 9. colubrine
mouth.. 6. orchid
movement.. 4. coil, drag, wind 5. crawl, sneak, twist
mythical.. 6. Python (on Mt Parnassus)
nonpoisonous.. 4. king 6. garter, gopher 9. Colubrina
pert to.. 5. ophic 7. anguine 8. viperine 9. colubrine, scoundrel
poisonous.. 3. asp 5. adder, coral 7. rattler 8. moccasin 10. copperhead 11. cottonmouth 13. thanatophidia

python.. 8. anaconda
python deity.. 5. zombi (zombie)
reptilelike.. 9. herpetoid
Russell's viper.. 6. daboia, jessur
sacred.. 6. Shesha
S America.. 5. aboma
sand snake.. 4. Eryx
semihuman, race of.. 4. Naga
shaped.. 9. anguiform
skin.. 6. exuvia
spitting.. 8. ringhals
snaky... 3. sly 4. wavy 7. anguine,
sinuous, wriggly 8. spiteful, twisting,
venomous 9. snakelike 10. perfidious,
serpentine 11. treacherous
snaky sisters... 6. Erinys
17. snaky–haired Furies
snap... 3. bit 4. bite, flip 5. break,
crack, flick, quick, snarl, thump
6. energy, fasten, fillip (fingers)
7. bargain, crackle 8. easy task,
handcuff, snapshot 9. crispness,
fastening, smartness 10. gingersnap,
photograph, resilience 11. sharp
retort
snapper... 4. bean, sesi 5. error,
pargo 6. beetle, bonbon, tamure,
turtle 7. cracker, grouper 8. fastener,
rosefish 9. countfish 10. stitchwort,
stringbean, woodpecker
11. firecracker
snappy... 4. cold, fast 5. quick
6. lively, sudden 7. pungent
8. snappish 9. crackling, energetic
snare... 3. beg, gin, net, web 4. lure,
mesh, trap 5. benet, catch, noose,
steal 6. entoil, trepan 7. pitfall
9. deception
snark... 3. nag 5. snort 6. boojum
8. creature (fabled)
snarl... 4. gnar, knot 5. gnarr, growl,
scold, snare 6. tangle 7. confuse,
ensnare, grumble, quarrel
8. complain, entangle 9. confusion
10. complicate 12. complication
snatch... 4. grab, jerk, take 5. catch,
erept, grasp, gripe, pluck, seize,
steal, wrest 6. clutch, kidnap, rescue
7. seizure
sneak... 4. lead (game), lurk 5. cower,
creep, knave, slink, snoop 6. coward,
cringe, tattle 7. smuggle 11. furtive
move
sneaking... 3. sly 4. mean, poor
6. craven, hidden, paltry, secret
7. furtive 8. cowardly, stealthy
9. dastardly, niggardly, underhand
12. contemptible 13. surreptitious
sneer... 4. gibe, jeer, mock 5. fleer,
flout, laugh, scoff, scorn
sneer, expressive... 8. sardonic
snell... 4. keen 5. acute, eager, quick,
sharp, snood, swift 6. active, biting,
severe 7. caustic, pungent
8. piercing
snicker... 5. laugh, neigh, sneer
6. giggle, nicker, tittle, whinny
7. snigger 8. laughter
sniff... 4. nose 5. scent, smell, snuff
6. detect, inhale 7. sniffle 8. sibilate,
smell out 14. show of contempt
snifter... 3. nip 4. dram, good

5. drink, sniff, snort 6. snivel
9. excellent
snip... 3. bit, cut 4. clip, snap
5. notch, piece, shred 8. fragment,
particle
snipe (pert to)...
eel.. 6. thread
flock.. 4. wisp
game.. 6. godwit
hawk.. 7. harrier
verb.. 8. shoot at 10. sharpshoot
snippy... 4. curt, tart 5. brief, sharp
8. snippety, snobbish
11. fragmentary 12. supercilious
snirl... 5. gnarl, snare 6. tangle
7. wrinkle
snitch... 5. pinch, steal 6. betray,
inform, pilfer, snatch, tattle
8. informer, particle
snob... 4. prig 7. cobbler, parvenu
8. bluenose, commoner, courtier
9. sycophant
snobby, snobbish... 5. proud
6. uppish 7. haughty 8. arrogant
9. exclusive 11. overbearing
snood... 5. snell 6. fillet 7. hairnet
snook... 4. fish 5. smell 6. robalo,
search 9. barracuda
snoop... 3. pry 4. nose 5. prowl,
sneak 6. meddle 7. meddler
8. busybody 10. sneak thief
snooze... 3. nap 4. doze 5. sleep
6. cuddle, nuzzle, siesta 7. snoozle,
snuggle
snore, snoring... 4. rale 5. sleep
7. stertor 8. rhonchus, sibilate
10. sibilation, stertorous 15. hoarse
breathing
snort... 5. drink, grunt, laugh, snore
snotty... 5. dirty, nasty 6. offish,
snooty 7. high–hat 9. offensive
12. contemptible, supercilious
snow... 4. firn, neve 5. opium
8. narcotic 12. interference
snow (pert to)...
bunting.. 5. finch 9. snowflake
glacial.. 4. firn, neve
grouse, quail.. 9. ptarmigan
house.. 5. igloo
leopard.. 5. ounce
lily.. 6. violet (white)
living in.. 5. nival
mouse.. 4. vole 7. lemming
ref to.. 5. nival
ridges.. 8. sastrugi (zastrugi)
runner.. 3. ski 4. sled
shoe.. 3. pac 7. webfoot
sliding.. 9. avalanche
slope.. 8. glissade
snub... 3. cut 5. check, quell, scold
6. cut off, ignore, rebuff, rebuke,
slight 7. neglect, shorten 8. restrain
9. reprimand 10. inhalation
snuff... 5. scent, smell, sniff 6. draw
in, inhale, snoose 7. tobacco
(pulverized), umbrage 10. extinguish,
inhalation
snuff (pert to)...
a candle.. 4. snot
box.. 4. mull 9. tabatière
color.. 10. mummy brown
type.. 6. rappee 8. Maccaboy

10. Copenhagen

snug... 4. cozy, neat, safe, trim
5. close, tight 6. secure 7. compact
8. homelike, reticent 9. concealed,
secretive 10. prosperous
11. comfortable

snuggle... 6. cuddle, nestle

sny (shipbuilding)... 5. curve (of plank)

so... 2. as 3. how 4. ergo, thus, very
5. hence 6. if only 7. because
8. likewise, provided 9. therefore
11. accordingly, in order that
12. consequently

so (pert to)...
far.. 3. yet 7. thus far 8. until now
Latin.. 3. sic
so be it.. 4. Amen
to speak.. 8. as it were
12. figuratively

soak... 3. dip, sog, sop, wet 4. sock
5. souse, steep 6. drench, imbrue,
strike, tipple 7. extract, immerse
8. drunkard, macerate, marinate,
permeate, saturate 9. percolate
10. overcharge

soap... 4. sapo, suds, wash 5. bribe
6. lather 7. bribery 8. cleanser,
flattery 9. slush fund

soap (pert to)...
box.. 4. dais 5. stage 8. platform
convert to.. 8. saponify
fish.. 10. lizard fish
frame bar.. 4. sess
ingredient.. 3. lye
liniment (camphorated).. 9. opodeldoc
making.. 14. saponification
mottled.. 8. Eschwege (Eschweg)
opera.. 6. serial 9. broadcast
13. network serial
plant.. 5. amole
soft.. 8. flattery

soar... 3. fly 4. flit, rise, wing 5. float,
plane 6. ascend, aspire, be high
9. transcend

soaring... 6. flight 7. gliding, planing,
winging 8. essorant 9. skyriding
10. ballooning

sob... 3. cry 4. bawl, weep
6. boohoo, simper 7. whimper
9. shed tears

sobeit... 4. amen 8. provided

sober... 4. calm, cool, dark, sane
5. grave, quiet, staid 6. gentle,
sedate, solemn, somber, subdue,
temper 7. chasten, earnest, regular,
serious 8. composed, moderate,
sensible 9. abstinent, collected,
dignified, temperate 10. abstemious,
thoughtful 11. impassioned
13. unintoxicated

sobriety... 6. sanity 9. composure,
restraint, soberness 10. abstinence,
moderation, temperance
11. seriousness

sobriquet... 5. alias, title 6. byname
7. epithet 8. cognomen, nickname
11. appellation

sociable... 5. party 7. affable
8. familiar, friendly, informal
9. reception 10. accessible,
gregarious 13. communicative,
companionable

social... 3. tea 5. party 6. smoker
9. convivial, gathering
13. companionable

social (pert to)...
career.. 5. debut
class.. 4. clan, sept 5. caste
6. estate
ethics.. 6. morals 9. standards
10. principles
function.. 3. bee, tea 4. ball 5. party
6. soiree 7. reunion 9. reception
gathering, men.. 4. stag 6. smoker
group.. 4. sept 5. tribe 6. ethnos
8. smart set 10. upper crust
11. cafe society 13. kaffeeklatsch
insect.. 3. ant, bee
outcast.. 5. leper 6. pariah
standing.. 6. estate
system.. 6. regime

socialist... 3. Red 8. Nihilist
9. anarchist, communist
10. Bolshevist 12. collectivist

society... 5. union 7. company
8. alliance, populace 9. community
10. fellowship 11. association,
partnership 13. companionship,
confederation, participation

society (pert to)...
bud.. 3. deb
Chinese.. 4. Tong
German.. 6. Verein
high.. 5. elite 10. upper crust
Italian.. 6. maffia (mafia)
of Friends.. 7. Quakers
secret.. 5. lodge, Order

Society Islands...
capital.. 7. Papeete
chief island.. 6. Tahiti
site.. 12. South Pacific

Socrates (pert to)...
birthplace.. 6. Athens
disciple of.. 5. Plato
famed as.. 7. teacher 11. Grecian
sage
wife.. 9. Xanthippe (Xantippe)

sod... 4. soil, turf 5. divot, glebe,
sward 7. stratum 10. greensward

soda... 3. sal 8. beverage 9. saleratus,
saltpeter

sodden... 5. drunk, moist, soggy
6. soaked, stewed, stupid
7. drunken, steeped 9. saturated
11. intoxicated

sodium (pert to)...
carbonate.. 4. soda 5. borax, trona
7. sal soda, saltcat
chloride.. 3. sal, tar 4. NaCl, salt
nitrate.. 5. niter
salicylate.. 8. medicine
symbol.. 2. Na

sofa... 5. couch, divan 6. lounge,
settee 7. dos-à-dos 8. causeuse,
love seat 9. davenport, tête-à-tête
12. chesterfield

soft... 4. easy, limp, weak 5. bland,
downy, mushy, pulpy 6. dreamy,
gentle, placid, silken, supple, tender
7. clement, ductile, lenient, lightly,
quietly, squashy, velvety 8. flexible,
gullible, merciful, tranquil
9. temperate, tractable
10. effeminate, peacefully

11. comfortable, sentimental, sympathetic 13. compassionate

soft (pert to) . . .
cancer . . 11. encephaloma
coal . . 10. bituminous
food . . 3. pap
head . . 9. simpleton
job . . 4. snap 8. sinecure
mass . . 4. pulp
music . . 5. dulce, piano
palate . . 4. cion 5. uvula, velum
pedal . . 3. ban 4. curb 6. subdue 8. tone down
soap . . 7. blarney 8. blandish, flattery 9. wheedling
spoken . . 4. mild 5. suave

soften . . . 4. melt, thaw 5. allay, malax, relax 6. affect, lenify, pacify, relent, soothe, temper, weaken 7. appease, assuage, cushion, mollify, relieve 8. emoliate, enervate, enfeeble, macerate, mitigate, modulate 9. alleviate, meliorate 11. tranquilize

soften (pert to) . . .
by kneading . . 5. malax
by soaking . . 8. macerate
leather . . 5. sammy (sam)
skins . . 3. taw
temper . . 6. relent

softening . . . 7. lenient 8. emulsive 9. relenting, relieving, tempering 10. lightening, mitigating

softening of the brain . . . 8. dementia

softhearted . . . 4. kind 6. tender 8. merciful

softly . . . 3. low 5. sotto 6. easily, gently 10. delicately 13. unobtrusively

soggy . . . 3. wet 4. damp 5. heavy 6. soaked, sodden, watery 9. saturated

soil . . . 4. clay, daub, dirt, land, loam, sand, spot 5. adobe, dirty, earth, glebe, gumbo, humus, stain, sully 6. bedaub, bemire, ground, region, smirch, vilify 7. begrime, besmear, corrupt, debauch, pollute, tarnish 8. alluvium 9. bedraggle, bespatter 11. contaminate 12. fuller's earth

soil (pert to) . . .
barren . . 4. arid, gall 8. lifeless
goddess of . . 7. Demeter
kind of . . 4. clay, lair, loam, malm 5. adobe, humus
oneself . . 4. moil
poetic . . 5. glebe

sojourn . . . 4. bide, stay, stop 5. abide 6. reside 8. abidance, stop over 11. peregrinate

solace . . . 5. allay, amuse, cheer 6. soothe 7. assuage, comfort, console 9. alleviate, entertain 10. relaxation 11. consolation

solan . . . 5. goose 6. gannet

solar (pert to) . . .
deity . . 2. Ra 3. Shu (Su) 6. Helios
disk . . 4. aten
exposure . . 9. sunstroke 10. heatstroke
halo . . 6. nimbus 7. aureole 12. vesica piscis
plexus . . 10. stomach pit
system . . 6. bodies, planet

15. celestial bodies
system apparatus . . 6. orrery
year . . 5. epact

soldier . . . 3. ant 5. cadet, poilu 6. galoot 7. fighter, private, regular, trooper, veteran, warrior 8. gendarme, servitor 9. combatant, grenadier, musketeer 11. enlisted man

soldier (pert to) . . .
Algeria . . 6. Zouave
cavalryman . . 6. lancer 7. dragoon, trooper
Croatian . . 5. Croat
field worker . . 6. sapper
flask . . 7. canteen
French . . 5. poilu
Gaelic . . 4. Kern
girl . . 3. WAC (Army)
Gr Myth . . 8. Myrmidon
hireling . . 9. mercenary
Ind (Brit) . . 5. sepoy
Ind (Brit), with own horse . . 8. silladar
Moroccan . . 5. askar
of fortune . . 7. Hessian 10. adventurer
Prussian . . 5. uhlan
slang . . 6. galoot 7. chicken 8. shackman

soldiers, soldier's . . .
body of . . 5. troop 6. cohort 7. brigade, company, platoon
captured, wounded . . 6. losses
flask . . 7. canteen
Maryland (Rev War) . . 10. macaronies
overcoat . . 6. capote
quarters . . 7. billets 8. barracks
Three . . 5. tales (by Kipling)
vacation . . 4. pass 5. leave 8. furlough

sole . . . 3. one 4. base, fish, only 5. alone, slade 6. entire, lonely, single, unique 8. desolate, isolated, solitary, unshared 9. exclusive, unmarried, unmatched 10. underframe

sole (pert to) . . .
cookery . . 8. Marguéry
foot . . 4. vola 6. planta
hand (palm) . . 4. vola
pert to . . 7. plantar
plow . . 5. slade
toward the sole . . 7. plantad

solecism . . . 5. error 7. blunder 9. barbarism, deviation 11. impropriety

solemn . . . 3. sad 5. grave, pious, sober 6. august, devout, formal, gloomy, ritual, silent 7. earnest, serious, stately, sublime 8. funereal 9. dignified 10. ceremonial, devotional 11. ceremonious, reverential 12. awe-inspiring

solemnity . . . 4. pomp 7. dignity, sadness 8. ceremony 9. formality 10. importance

solicit . . . 3. ask, beg 4. lure, seek, tout 5. claim, court, crave, plead 6. accost, demand, invite, obtain 7. beseech, canvass, entreat, implore, request 8. campaign, petition 9. challenge, importune, panhandle, prosecute 10. supplicate

solicitor... 6. barker, lawyer
 8. attorney 9. canvasser
 10. petitioner
solicitude... 4. care, coda, heed
 7. anxiety, caution, concern
 9. attention 11. carefulness
 12. apprehension
 15. considerateness
solid... 4. cone, cube, firm, full, good,
 hard 5. dense, level, sound, stiff
 6. stable, strong 7. uniform
 8. complete, resolute, sensible,
 sterling 9. estimable, unanimous
 10. dependable, inflexible
 11. homogeneous, responsible,
 substantial, trustworthy
solid (pert to)...
 comb form.. 6. stereo
 geometrical.. 5. prism
 seven-faced.. 11. heptahedron
 six-faced.. 4. cube
 tapering.. 4. cone 7. pyramid
solidarity... 5. unity 10. correality
 11. nationality 12. completeness
solidity... 5. unity 6. volume
 7. density 8. firmness, hardness,
 solvency, strength 9. solidness,
 stability 11. compactness
 12. completeness 13. dependability
 14. substantiality
solidum... 4. dado 9. entire sum
soliloquy... 4. poem 9. discourse,
 monologue 16. talking to oneself
solitaire... 8. Canfield
solitary... 3. one 4. lone, only, sole
 5. alone, eremo (comb form)
 6. hermit, lonely, single 7. recluse
 8. deserted, desolate, lonesome
 10. individual 12. unfrequented
solitude... 6. desert 7. privacy, retreat
 9. aloneness, isolation, seclusion
 10. loneliness, wilderness
solo accompaniment... 9. obbligato
Solomon (pert to)...
 author of (reputed).. 8. Proverbs
 9. Canticles 12. Ecclesiastes
 15. Wisdom of Solomon
 called also.. 8. Koheleth 11. The
 Preacher
 famed as.. 4. sage 7. wise man
 12. King of Israel
 father.. 5. David
 literally.. 9. peaceable
 mother.. 9. Bathsheba
Solomon Islands site... 9. South Seas
solon... 4. sage 8. lawmaker
 9. statesman
solstice... 5. limit 13. farthest point
 (from equator)
solution... 3. key 6. answer 7. solving
 8. analysis 10. denouement,
 resolution 11. explanation
 15. disentanglement
solution (pert to)...
 alkaline.. 3. lye
 saline.. 5. brine
 strength.. 5. titer (titre)
Somalia...
 capital.. 9. Mogadishu
 people.. 6. Somali 7. Hamitic
 port.. 5. Zeila 6. Bulhar

somber, sombre... 3. sad 4. dark
 5. grave 6. solemn 7. austere
 9. depressed 10. depressing,
 foreboding, lackluster, melancholy
 11. dark-colored, dispiriting
some... 3. any, one 5. about
 6. plural, suffix 7. several
 10. indefinite, more or less
 13. approximately
somebody... 6. person 7. big name
 8. luminary 9. celebrity, personage
somersault... 4. flip, leap 8. somerset
 9. cartwheel 10. end over end
something... 6. object 8. somewhat
 9. personage 12. in some degree
something (pert to)...
 abnormal.. 5. freak 6. mutant
 11. monstrosity 12. malformation
 else.. 10. irrelevant
 extra.. 5. bonus 6. bounty
 7. premium 9. lagniappe
 found.. 5. cache, trove
 11. serendipity 13. treasure-trove
 frightening.. 7. bugbear
 heavy.. 4. onus 9. ponderant
 illogical.. 7. alogism
 imagined.. 5. story 7. figment
 inserted.. 4. gore 5. inset, wedge
 like.. 7. related, similar 8. somewhat
 similar.. 8. analogue 11. counterpart
 small.. 3. dot, jot 4. atom, iota, whit
 5. speck 6. sliver, tittle
 soothing.. 7. unction
 superfluous.. 5. luxus 6. luxury
 unexplained.. 5. poser 7. mystery
 unfinished.. 4. quab
somewhat... 4. part 6. little, partly,
 rather 12. in some degree
somnifacient... 4. drug 8. hypnotic,
 sedative 9. soporific
somniloquy... 12. sleep talking
somnolence... 8. dormancy
 10. drowsiness, sleepiness
somnus... 5. sleep
Somnus (pert to)...
 brother.. 4. Mors (Death)
 known also as.. 6. Hypnos
 son of.. 3. Nox (Night)
son, son of (pert to)...
 a gun.. 5. rogue 6. fellow, wretch
 Anak.. 5. giant
 a Scot.. 3. Mac
 God.. 11. Jesus Christ
 Heaven (China).. 7. Emperor
 in-law.. 5. gener
 in Trinity.. 6. second (person)
 Jacob.. 4. Levi
 man.. 4. male 6. mortal
 Odin.. 2. Ve
 Odysseus.. 9. Telegonus
 Priam.. 5. Paris
 reference to.. 3. ben 4. fils 5. scion
 6. filial 9. offspring 10. descendant
 Seth.. 4. Enos
 the soil.. 6. farmer 7. peasant
 youngest.. 5. cadet
sonance... 4. tune 5. sound
 7. sonancy
sonant... 5. sound, tonic, vocal
 6. voiced 8. sounding 9. intonated
song... 3. air, lay, ode 4. aria, leed,

lilt, noel, poem, tune 5. carol, chant, ditty, melos, troll, verse 6. ballad, melody, strain, trifle 7. chantey (chanty), descant 8. canticle, pittance 9. cabaletta

song (pert to)...
after.. 5. epode
Bib.. 8. canticle 11. Song of Songs 13. Song of Solomon
boat, gondolier.. 7. chantey (chanty)
choral Muse.. 11. Terpsichore
collection.. 9. anthology 10. cancionero
college.. 4. glee
depressing.. 5. blues
evening.. 6. vesper 8. evensong, serenade
French.. 7. chanson
funeral.. 5. dirge, elegy 6. lament 8. threnody 9. epicedium
gay.. 4. lilt
German.. 4. lied 9. Kunstlied
gypsy.. 10. zingaresca
Italian.. 7. canzone
lament.. 8. threnody
love.. 5. lyric 6. ballad 8. madrigal, serenade
merry.. 4. lilt
morning.. 5. matin
mountaineer.. 5. yodel
pert to.. 5. melic
praise.. 5. carol, paean (pean)
sacred.. 4. hymn 5. chant, motet, psalm 6. anthem
sailor's.. 7. chantey (chanty) 9. barcarole
short.. 7. arietta
simple.. 6. ballad
words.. 6. lyrics

songbird... 4. lark 5. mavis, robin, veery 6. canary, oriole, thrush 8. throstle 11. mockingbird
sonic recorder... 9. echograph
sonnet... 4. poem, song 5. verse
sonnet (pert to)...
first eight lines.. 5. octet
last six lines.. 6. sestet
two quatrains.. 10. Petrarchan
sonorous... 4. loud 6. tonous 7. ringing 8. resonant 9. melodious 10. impressive, resounding
sonsy, sonsie... 5. buxom, happy 6. comely 11. good–natured
sontag... 4. cape 6. jacket
soon... 3. ere 4. anon 5. early, later 6. at once 7. betimes, erelong, quickly, readily, shortly 8. promptly, speedily 9. certainly, presently 11. immediately
Sooner State... 8. Oklahoma
sooner than... 3. ere 6. before
soot... 4. smut, stup 5. black, grime, smoke 6. carbon, smudge 7. residue 9. lampblack
soothe... 3. pet 4. calm, lull 5. allay, quiet 6. pacify, please, solace 7. assuage, compose, mollify, relieve, satisfy 8. mitigate, palliate 9. alleviate 11. tranquilize
soother... 4. balm 6. luller 7. anodyne, placebo 8. lenitive, pacifier, sedative 9. flatterer

soothing... 5. balmy, sirup (syrup) 6. dulcet, gentle 7. calming 8. lenitive, sedative 9. appeasing, demulcent 13. tranquilizing
soothsayer... 4. seer 5. augur, vatis 6. mantis 7. diviner, prophet 8. Chaldean, haruspex 9. Cassandra 13. praying insect 14. prognosticator
sooty (pert to)...
brown.. 6. bister 8. teakwood
color.. 5. black
mangabey.. 6. monkey
pert to.. 9. albatross 10. fuliginous
petrel.. 7. skimmer 10. shearwater
sophistical... 8. captious 9. deceptive, sophistic
sophistication... 9. sophistry 10. corruption, experience 11. worldliness 13. ungullibility
soporific... 4. drug 6. drowsy, opiate 7. anodyne 8. hypnotic, narcotic, sedative 11. somniferous 12. sleep inducer, somnifacient
soprano (operatic)... 4. Alda, Bori, Lind, Pons 5. Calvé, Eames 6. Callas, Steber
sora... 4. rail 5. crake
sorcerer... 4. mage 5. Magus 6. wizard 7. diviner 8. conjurer, magician 11. necromancer
sorceress... 3. hex 5. Circe, lamia, Medea, witch 6. Gorgon 7. vampire 12. Witch of Endor
sorcery... 5. magic, obeah, spell 6. voodoo 8. pishogue 9. diablerie, diabolism 10. black magic, necromancy, witchcraft
sordid... 3. low 4. base, mean, vile 5. gross 6. filthy, menial 7. ignoble, servile, squalid 8. sluttish, wretched 10. despicable, slatternly 12. contemptible
sore... 4. pain, sair 5. angry, vexed, wound 6. tender 7. painful 8. abrasion, inflamed, offended 9. irritated, vexatious 11. distressing 12. inflammation
soreness... 4. ache 5. anger 8. vexation 10. bitterness, tenderness 11. painfulness 12. irritability
sorghum... 4. milo 5. durra (dari), grain, sorgo 6. imphee, shallu 8. feterita
sorority... 4. club 7. society 10. fellowship, sisterhood
sorrel... 3. oca 4. buck, herb 5. color (horse), Rumex 7. roselle
Sorrento, Italy (pert to)...
anc name.. 9. Sorrentum
famed as.. 6. resort
famed for.. 9. cathedral
site.. 11. Bay of Naples
sorrow... 3. rue, woe 4. sigh, teen, weal 5. dolor, grief, mourn 6. grieve, lament, misery, repent 7. remorse, trouble 8. calamity, distress, egrimony, mourning 9. adversity, penitence 10. affliction, contrition 11. lamentation, tribulation 12. disconsolate, wretchedness
sorrowful... 3. sad 4. blue 5. drear, sadly 6. dismal, dolent, dreary, rueful

7. doleful, grieved, tearful, unhappy
8. mournful 9. plaintive
10. afflictive, melancholy
11. distressing 12. disconsolate
sorry . . . 3. sad 4. hurt 5. vexed
6. dismal, gloomy, rueful 7. painful,
pitiful, unhappy 8. contrite, grievous,
mournful, penitent, shameful, wretched
9. afflicted, chagrined, mortified,
regretful, repentant, worthless
10. displeased, melancholy
12. disappointed
sort . . . 3. ilk, way 4. cull, kind, rank
5. blend, class, grade, group
6. assort, manner, nature, strain
7. quality, species, variety 8. classify,
separate 9. character 11. description
sortie . . . 4. raid 5. foray, onset, sally
6. attack, thrust
sottish . . . 4. dull 6. stupid 7. doltish,
drunken, foolish 8. bibulous
9. senseless
sotto (It) . . . 5. below, under
sotto voce . . . 5. aside 8. secretly
9. privately, undertone 14. under the
breath
soubrette . . . 9. lady's maid
10. intrigante 11. maidservant
soudagur . . . 8. merchant
10. shopkeeper
soul . . . 2. ba, ka 3. ego, God 4. life
5. anima 6. pneuma, spirit
7. essence 8. inspirer 9. substance
10. embodiment 15. exemplification,
personification
soul (pert to) . . .
beatified . . 5. saint
destiny of . . 8. theodicy
dwelling place . . 2. Po 6. heaven
Egypt . . 2. Ba
Hindu . . 5. atman 7. jivatma
lost . . 9. âme damnée, the damned
maligners . . 7. Harpies
music . . 14. rhythm and blues
personified . . 6. Psyche
transmigration . . 7. rebirth
13. reincarnation
sound . . . 3. bam, cry, hum 4. beep,
bong, hale, honk, rale, ring, sane, test,
tone, toot 5. drone, noise, plumb,
probe, snore, valid, whole 6. intact,
jingle, report, robust, stable, sturdy
7. feel out, perfect, resound
8. flawless, reliable, susurrus
9. undamaged 10. scrutinize
11. trustworthy
sound (pert to) . . .
addition to word end . . 8. paragoge
atonic . . 4. surd
dashing . . 5. swash 6. splash
discordant . . 6. jangle 9. cacophony
drum, beating . . 8. rataplan
explosion . . 4. boom 6. report
fixed . . 5. toned
harsh . . 3. caw 4. bray 5. creak,
twang 7. stridor 9. cacophony
insect's . . 5. chirr
loud . . 4. peal 5. blare, clang
low . . 3. hum 4. moan 5. drone
metallic . . 4. ping, ting 5. clank, clink,
twank 6. tinkle
pert to . . 5. tonal 6. sonant

10. acoustical
prosody . . 4. rime (rhyme)
reflected . . 4. echo
sharp . . 3. pop 7. rat–a–tat, tapping
shrill . . 5. reedy
sibilant . . 4. hiss
similar . . 8. assonant
small . . 4. peep 6. rustle
surf . . 4. rote 5. swish
throwing . . 8. abat–sons
trumpet . . 7. clarion
warning . . 5. alarm, siren 6. tocsin
whispering . . 8. susurrus
with rhythm . . 5. music
sounding . . . 5. depth, rawin 6. sonant
7. ringing 8. sonation
10. resounding
soundness . . . 5. truth 6. sanity
8. solidity, solvency, strength
9. integrity, rectitude, stability
10. heartiness 11. healthiness
soup . . . 3. fog 5. broth, chili, purée
6. bisque, potage, won ton
7. borscht, chowder, pottage
8. bouillon, consommé, gazpacho,
julienne 10. oyster stew
11. vichyssoise 12. mulligatawny
soupçon . . . 5. taste 7. portion
9. suspicion 10. suggestion
soup dish . . . 6. tureen
sour . . . 3. wry 4. acid, tart 5. acerb,
acrid 6. acetic, bitter, morose, off
key, rancid 7. acetose, acidify,
crabbed, pungent, tainted
8. acescent, embitter 9. acidulous
10. astringent, unpleasant
sour (pert to) . . .
apple . . 9. crab apple
aspect . . 4. dour, hard 6. sullen
berry . . 8. cranberry
bread . . 8. leavened
cherry . . 7. morello
stomach . . 4. acor
turn sour . . 5. prill 6. bleeze
source . . . 4. font, germ, mine, rise,
root, seed 5. cause, fount 6. origin,
parent, quarry 8. fountain
9. beginning 10. wellspring
12. fountainhead
source (pert to) . . .
income . . 7. revenue
insecticides . . 9. sabadilla
iodine . . 4. kelp
ipecac . . 4. evea
metal . . 3. ore 7. bonanza
opium . . 5. poppy
rubber . . 3. ule
South Africa . . . see also *South African*
capital . . 8. Cape Town, Pretoria
city . . 6. Durban 9. Germiston
12. Johannesburg
division . . 5. Natal 9. Transvaal
14. Cape of Good Hope 15. Orange
Free State
exports . . 4. gold 8. diamonds
legislature seat location . . 8. Cape
Town
people . . 5. Boers 7. British, Kaffirs
10. Hottentots 11. Afrikanders
(Dutch)
river . . 4. Vaal 6. Orange
South African (pert to) . . .

antelope .. **3.** gnu **5.** eland, oribi, peele
  6. rhebok **7.** sassaby
armadillo .. **4.** para
ass (wild) .. **6.** quagga
bird .. **4.** taha
camp .. **6.** laager
Cape ash .. **9.** essenhout
cocktail .. **9.** sundowner
cony .. **3.** das
council .. **4.** Raad
dialect .. **4.** Taal **9.** Afrikaans
diamond (blue–white) .. **5.** jager
fox .. **4.** asse **5.** caama
grass hut .. **8.** rondawel (rondavel)
grassland .. **4.** veld (veldt) **8.** bushveld
mountain, hill .. **3.** kop
snake .. **8.** eggeater
tableland .. **5.** karoo
tree (dogwood) .. **7.** assagai (assegai)
tribe .. **4.** Zulu **5.** Bantu
village .. **5.** kraal
war .. **4.** Boer
warrior .. **4.** impi
weaverbird .. **4.** taha
whip .. **7.** sjambok
South American (pert to) ...
  animal .. **2.** ai **4.** paca **5.** llama, sloth,
  tapir **6.** jaguar, tapeti **7.** agouara
  (dog) **8.** anteater **9.** armadillo
  armadillo .. **4.** apar (apara)
  10. pichiciago (burrowing)
  arrow poison .. **6.** curare (curari)
  balsam .. **4.** tolu
  bellbird .. **8.** arapunga **9.** campanero
  bird .. **4.** rara, taha **5.** agami, arara,
  chaja, macaw **6.** barbet **7.** oilbird,
  seriema, tinamou **8.** bellbird, boatbill,
  caracara, guacharo, puffbird
  blanket .. **6.** serape
  city section .. **6.** barrio
  cloth .. **4.** crea
  drink .. **5.** assai
  fiber .. **6.** yachan
  fish .. **4.** paru **7.** piranha, scalare
  8. arapaima
  Indian .. **2.** Ge (Gesan) **3.** Ona **4.** Inca
  5. Carib **6.** Tapuya (50 tribes)
  knife .. **7.** machete
  leader .. **6.** Franko **7.** Pizarro
  liberator .. **7.** Bolivar
  mammal .. **5.** llama, tapir **6.** alpaca
  8. kinkajou **10.** chinchilla
  marmoset .. **7.** tamarin
  monkey .. **3.** sai **4.** saki, titi **5.** araba
  8. orabassu **9.** barrigudo
  native .. **5.** Carib **6.** Arawak
  ostrich .. **4.** rhea
  palm .. **5.** assai **12.** chiquichiqui
  parrot .. **5.** macaw
  plains .. **6.** llanos, pampas
  plainsman .. **7.** llanero
  plant .. **6.** ipecac **11.** ipecacuanha
  poison .. **6.** curare
  river .. **3.** Apa **4.** Acre, Pará **5.** Plata
  6. Paraná
  rodent .. **5.** coypu **6.** agouti (agouty)
  8. capibara, viscacha **10.** chinchilla
  snake .. **4.** lora **5.** aboma **8.** anaconda
  10. bushmaster
  stork .. **7.** maguari
  tinamou .. **7.** tataupa
  toucan .. **7.** aracari

trumpeter .. **5.** agami
tuber .. **3.** oca
vulture .. **6.** condor
weapon .. **4.** bola
wild cat .. **4.** eyra
wind .. **7.** pampero
South Carolina ...
  capital .. **8.** Columbia
  city .. **8.** Beaufort **10.** Charleston
  11. Spartanburg
  monument .. **10.** Fort Sumter
  mountain .. **9.** Blue Ridge, Sassafras
  resort .. **11.** Myrtle Beach
  State admission .. **6.** Eighth
  State bird .. **4.** wren
  State flower .. **9.** jessamine
  State motto .. **8.** Dum Spiro, Spero
  (While I Breathe, I Hope)
  State nickname .. **8.** Palmetto
  State secession .. **5.** First (1860)
South Dakota ...
  capital .. **6.** Pierre
  city .. **5.** Huron **8.** Deadwood
  9. Rapid City **10.** Sioux Falls
  Indians .. **5.** Brule, Sioux
  mine (US largest) .. **9.** Homestake
  monument .. **10.** Crazy Horse, Mt
  Rushmore
  mountain .. **10.** Black Hills, Harney
  Peak
  river .. **5.** White **8.** Cheyenne, Missouri
  State admission .. **8.** Fortieth (or
  Thirty–ninth)
  State bird .. **8.** pheasant
  State flower .. **12.** pasqueflower
  State motto .. **21.** Under God the
  People Rule
  State nickname .. **6.** Coyote
  8. Sunshine
  topography .. **8.** Bad Lands **10.** Black
  Hills
southeast wind ... **5.** Eurus
southern ... **7.** austral
Southern (pert to) ...
  Buddhism .. **8.** Hinayana
  Cross .. **4.** Crux **12.** Stars and Bars
  Crown .. **15.** Corona Australis
  dish .. **3.** yam **4.** okra, pone **5.** gumbo
  7. catfish, hoecake **8.** chess pie, ham
  hocks **9.** cornbread **11.** hush puppies
  12. chitterlings, turnip greens
  shrub .. **8.** magnolia, oleander
  States .. **5.** Dixie **7.** Sunbelt
southernmost city ... **12.** Puerto
  Arenas (Chile)
South Pole bird ... **4.** skua **7.** penguin
South Pole constellation ... **4.** Pavo
South Sea ... **12.** Pacific Ocean
South Sea Bubble ... **6.** scheme
  (1720) **10.** stock fraud (Eng)
South Wales people ... **7.** Silures
southwest wind ... **4.** afer
south wind ... **5.** Notus
souvenir ... **5.** relic, token **6.** memory,
  trophy **7.** memento **8.** keepsake,
  memorial, reminder **11.** remembrance
  12. recollection, remembrancer
sovereign ... **5.** chief, liege, regal, ruler
  6. divine, prince, ruling **7.** empress,
  monarch, supreme **8.** princely,
  superior, suzerain **9.** effectual, gold
  piece, paramount, potentate

11. controlling, independent
sovereign (pert to)...
claim .. 11. seigniorage
coin .. 4. skiv
decree .. 5. arrêt
pardon .. 7. amnesty
petty .. 8. tetrarch
power .. 6. throne
sovereignty ... 5. realm 6. diadem,
    empery, empire 7. dynasty, scepter
    (sceptre) 8. dominion 9. supremacy
Soviet, Russian (pert to)...
committee .. 9. presidium
farm .. 7. sovkhoz (sovkhose)
government .. 9. Communism,
    Sovietism 10. Bolshevism
hero .. 5. Lenin
newspaper .. 6. Pravda 8. Izvestia
police, secret service .. 3. KGB
sow ... 3. pig 4. gilt, seed 5. plant
    7. implant, scatter 8. disperse,
    squander 9. broadcast
    10. salamander 11. disseminate
sow bug ... 6. slater
sow thistle ... 7. Sonchus
soybean ... 4. Soja 8. soya bean
soybean enzyme ... 6. urease
spa ... 3. Ems 4. Bath 5. Baden
    6. Bilina (Bilin), hot tub 7. Jacuzzi (tm)
space ... 3. gap 4. area, rank, room,
    time, void 5. blank, inane, niche,
    place, range 6. areola, areole, degree,
    extent, vacuum 7. arrange, expanse
    8. capacity, distance, interval
    9. concourse, elbow room
space (pert to)...
architectural .. 6. metope 8. pediment
blank .. 5. chasm 6. hiatus, lacuna
botany (leaves) .. 6. areola
environment .. 5. ambit 8. ambiance
larynx .. 7. glottis
occupied .. 6. volume
ref to .. 5. areal, outer 6. cosmos,
    galaxy, pulsar 7. heavens, lacunal,
    spatial 8. galactic, infinity 9. black
    hole, deep space
storage .. 4. shed 5. attic, depot
    6. cellar, garage 9. storeroom,
    warehouse
theory .. 7. plenism
time .. 8. interval
travel .. 4. NASA 7. reentry, swingby
    8. time warp
traveler .. 5. alien 6. cyborg
    8. aeronaut 9. astronaut, cosmonaut
vehicle .. 6. rocket, Skylab 7. shuttle,
    sputnik
void .. 5. chasm 7. inanity
wall .. 5. niche
spacious ... 5. ample, broad, roomy
    9. capacious, expansive, extensive
    10. commodious, far and wide,
    widespread 13. comprehensive
spadassin ... 5. bravo 7. duelist
    9. swordsman
spade ... 3. dig, loy 4. spud, stag (3-yr
    old), suit (cards) 5. slade 6. shovel
    11. playing card
spade (pert to)...
bone .. 13. shoulder blade
fish .. 5. porgy 10. paddlefish
foot .. 4. toad

grass .. 4. rush
Irish .. 5. slane
money .. 7. Chinese (early)
peat .. 5. slade
triangular .. 5. didle
spae ... 6. divine 8. foretell
Spain ... see also *Spanish*
cape .. 9. Trafalgar
capital .. 6. Madrid
city .. 4. Irun 5. Cadiz, Lorca
    6. Malaga 7. Cordoba, Granada,
    Seville 8. Valencia
city cathedral .. 9. Saragossa
islands .. 5. Ceuta 6. Canary 7. Melilla
    8. Balearic
mountain .. 8. Asturias, Pyrenees
old name .. 6. Iberia
palace .. 8. Escorial
river .. 4. Ebro, Muga 5. Tagus
span ... 3. two 4. arch, join, pair, team
    6. bridge, extend, length, period (time)
    7. breadth, measure, stretch
    8. overarch 9. encompass
spangle ... 6. aiglet, sequin 7. glitter,
    sparkle 8. ornament, zecchino
spaniel ... 5. trasy 6. cocker
    8. Brittany, springer
Spanish (pert to)...
arbor .. 6. ramada
battle .. 6. Armada (1588)
bayonet .. 5. yucca
boat .. 5. aviso 7. galleon (ship)
Christmas .. 7. Navidad
cloak .. 4. capa 5. manta 6. mantle
    7. zamarra (zamarro)
corral .. 5. atajo
dance .. 5. tango 6. bolero, gitano
    8. fandango, saraband
fabric .. 4. crea (cotton) 5. tiraz (silk)
fortress chief .. 4. caid 7. alcaide
friend .. 5. amigo
fruit .. 8. pimiento
game .. 6. pelota 7. jai alai
garment .. 6. serape 8. mantilla
gift holder .. 6. piñata
gold .. 3. oro 8. El Dorado
governor .. 10. gobernador
grass .. 5. spart 7. esparto
gruel .. 5. atole
gypsy .. 7. zincalo
holiday .. 6. fiesta
horse .. 5. genet 6. jennet 7. caballo
hotel .. 6. posada
house .. 4. casa 6. casita
jar .. 4. olla, tina 6. tinaja
knight .. 8. cavalier 9. caballero
lake .. 4. lago
language .. 6. Basque 7. Catalan,
    Spanish 8. Galician 9. Castilian
mausoleum .. 8. Escorial
musical instrument .. 6. atabel, guitar
    8. castanet
plant .. 3. aji 8. capsicum
porridge .. 5. atole
promenade .. 5. paseo
raisin .. 4. pasa
river .. 3. ria, rio
road .. 6. camino
room .. 4. sala
shawl .. 5. manta 6. serape
sheep .. 6. merino
sherry .. 5. Xeres 7. oloroso

sorcerer.. 5. brujo
street.. 5. calle
three.. 4. tres
title.. 3. don 5. señor 6. señora
   7. hidalgo 8. señorita
trail.. 6. camino
vehicle.. 7. tartana
watch.. 5. reloj
watchtower.. 7. atalaya
watchword.. 6. alerta
watercourse.. 6. arroyo
wind.. 6. solano
window.. 7. ventana
witchcraft.. 8. brujeria
year.. 3. ano
Spanish people...
chaperone.. 6. duenna
conqueror.. 7. Pizarro
dramatist.. 9. Echegaray (Nobel Prize
   1904)
explorer.. 7. Mendoza
gentleman.. 5. señor 8. cavalier
   9. caballero
God.. 4. Dios
herdsman.. 7. llanero 8. ranchero
hero.. 3. Cid
justice of the peace.. 7. entrada
king.. 6. Aragon 8. Alphonso
lady.. 4. doña 6. señora 8. señorita
letter carrier.. 6. correo
man.. 3. don 6. hombre
monk.. 5. padre
painter.. 4. Dali, Goya 9. Velasquez
peasant.. 7. paisano
people.. 5. genta
pianist.. 6. Iturbi
soldier.. 8. miquelet
soprano.. 4. Bori (Lucrezia)
spar... 3. box 4. beam, boom, gaff,
   mast, rung, yard 5. sprit, steve
   6. timber 7. dispute, quarrel,
   topmast, yardarm
spare... 4. lean, thin 5. chary, lanky
   6. afford, exempt, frugal, meager,
   scanty 7. sparing, surplus
   8. preserve 9. duplicate, parsimony
   10. economical, occasional
   11. superfluous 12. parsimonious
spare time... 7. leisure
sparing... 5. chary 6. frugal, meager,
   saving, scanty 7. scrimpy, thrifty
   8. merciful, reticent, stinting
   9. scrimping 12. parsimonious
spark... 4. beau, fire, funk 5. aizle,
   court, dandy, lover 6. incite
   7. diamond, gallant, glitter, modicum,
   sparkle 8. humorist 10. sweetheart
   11. scintillate
sparkle... 5. flash, gleam, glint, shine,
   trace 7. be smart, be witty, glisten,
   glister, glitter, radiate, reflect,
   spangle, twinkle 8. be lively
   9. coruscate 10. effervesce,
   illuminate 11. scintillate
   13. scintillation
sparkling... 4. dewy 5. crisp, witty
   6. bright, starry 7. shining
   8. cheerful, eloquent, glittery,
   gorgeous, mousseux (wine)
   9. twinkling 10. glittering, reflecting
   12. effervescent
sparoid fish... 4. scup 5. porgy

   8. sea bream 10. sheepshead
Sparta, Greece... see also *Spartan*
capital.. 7. Laconia (anc)
kingdom.. 12. Peloponnesus
river.. 7. Eurotas
spartan... 5. hardy, stoic
   10. courageous 13. uncomplaining
Spartan (pert to)...
army division.. 4. mora 6. lochus
cipher writing.. 7. scytale
class (anc).. 8. perioeci
commander.. 7. lochage
dog.. 10. bloodhound
festival.. 6. Carnea 7. Carneia
king.. 8. Leonidas, Menelaus
lawgiver.. 8. Lycurgus
magistrate.. 5. ephor
native.. 8. Laconian 9. Spartiate
serf.. 5. helot
spasmodic... 6. fitful 7. snatchy
   9. excitable, irregular 10. convulsive
   12. intermittent 13. highly wrought
spasmodic (pert to)...
disease.. 5. croup 7. tetanus
inspiration.. 8. hiccough
twitch.. 3. tic
spat... 3. row 4. slap, tiff 5. spawn
   6. gaiter, oyster, strike 7. dispute,
   legging, quarrel 10. oysterseed
spate... 4. gush 5. flood 7. freshet,
   torrent 9. overwhelm, rainstorm
   10. waterspout
spatial... 5. areal 8. sterical
   11. dimensional
spatter... 3. wet 4. soil, spot 5. spurt
   6. dabble, splash 7. sputter
   8. splutter, sprinkle
spawn... 3. ova, roe 4. eggs, germ,
   seed 7. lay eggs 8. generate
   13. numerous issue
speak... 3. say 4. chat, lisp, talk, tell
   5. orate, utter 6. reveal 7. address,
   chatter, declaim, sputter 8. converse,
   proclaim 9. discourse, pronounce
   10. articulate 11. tell in words
speak (pert to)...
affectedly.. 4. mime 5. mince
against.. 6. oppose
boastfully.. 4. brag 5. vaunt
   7. enlarge 10. exaggerate
from memory.. 6. recite
ill of.. 5. decry 8. backbite
   9. disparage
noisily.. 4. rant, rime 8. harangue
offhand.. 11. extemporize
slowly.. 5. drawl
softly.. 7. whisper
under breath.. 5. mouth 6. mumble,
   murmur, mutter 7. grumble
speaker... 5. sayer 6. lisper, orator,
   proser 8. lecturer 9. demagogue
   10. mouthpiece, prolocutor
   11. spellbinder
speaker of languages... 8. linguist,
   polyglot
speaking (pert to)...
generally.. 7. as a rule, roughly
   12. in the long run
   13. approximately
of.. 7. apropos 12. incidentally
offhand.. 13. extemporizing
privately.. 7. whisper 9. in one's ear

11. into one's ear
publicly.. 7. oratory 11. declamation
style.. 8. fluently
spear... 4. dart, pike, stab 5. catch,
lance 6. pierce, weapon 7. javelin,
missile 9. penetrate
spear (pert to)...
anc Teutons.. 6. framea (fram)
fish.. 3. gig 4. gaff
iron–tipped.. 7. assagai
shaped.. 7. hastate
three–pronged.. 7. trident
two–pronged.. 6. bident
spearfish... 6. marlin 9. quillback
special... 4. rare 5. extra 6. unique
7. notable, unusual 8. concrete,
detailed, favorite, specific, uncommon
10. individual, noteworthy, particular,
restricted 11. distinctive, exceptional
13. extraordinary
special (pert to)...
ability.. 5. forte 6. talent 7. charism
8. charisma
commodity.. 6. leader 7. feature
10. best seller
edition.. 5. extra
favor.. 9. influence, privilege
train.. 5. flier 7. express
10. cannonball
specialist (pert to)...
atomic.. 9. physicist
ear.. 6. aurist 9. otologist
eye.. 7. oculist 15. ophthalmologist
medical.. 6. doctor 7. surgeon
money.. 9. economist
specialty... 5. skill 8. aptitude,
contract 13. particularity
14. characteristic
specie... 4. cash, coin 5. money (hard)
species... 4. kind, sort, type 5. class,
genre, genus, group 7. general,
isotope, mankind, variety 8. category,
humanity 11. Homo sapiens
12. nomenclature
specific... 5. exact, virus 6. remedy
7. limited, precise, special
8. definite, detailed, explicit, peculiar
specificity... 9. haecceity
specify... 4. name 5. limit, state
6. define, detail 8. indicate 9. be
precise, designate, enumerate,
stipulate
specimen... 4. copy 5. model, piece,
taste, token 6. person, sample,
swatch 7. example, pattern
14. representative
specious... 4. fair 5. showy 7. alleged
8. illusory, pleasing 9. plausible
10. ostensible 12. hypocritical
speck... 3. bit, dot, jot, nit 4. blot,
iota, mark, mite, mote, spot, whit
5. fleck, stain 7. blemish 8. particle
10. sand darter
speckled... 6. menald 7. mottled
9. sprinkled 10. variegated
spectacle... 4. show, view 5. scene,
sight 6. wonder 7. diorama, display,
pageant 8. panorama, spyglass
10. exhibition 14. representation
spectacles... 7. glasses
spectator... 6. espier, viewer
7. watcher, witness 8. audience,

beholder, kibitzer, looker–on, observer,
onlooker 9. bystander
specter, spectre... 4. bogy (bogey,
bogie) 5. ghost, shade, spook
6. idolum, spirit, wraith 7. eidolon,
phantom 8. illusion, phantasm,
revenant 10. apparition
spectral... 5. eerie (eery) 6. ghosty,
spooky 7. ghostly, phantom
12. apparitional
speculate... 5. guess, think 6. gamble,
ponder, wonder 8. consider,
meditate, ruminate, theorize
10. deliberate, doctrinize, philosophy
11. contemplate
speculative... 5. risky 9. uncertain
10. thoughtful 11. inquisitive,
theoretical 12. experimental
13. contemplative
speculator... 7. lookout, scalper
8. explorer, observer, theorist
12. investigator
speculum... 7. diopter 9. reflector
sped... 4. hied 5. raced 6. darted,
dashed, let fly 8. galloped, hastened
10. discharged
speech... 5. spiel 6. dilogy, orison
7. address, chatter, diction, oration
8. colloquy, harangue, language
9. elocution, utterance
12. conversation
speech (pert to)...
abusive.. 6. tirade
blunder.. 8. improper, solecism
comb form.. 4. logo
conclusion.. 10. peroration
conversational.. 13. colloquialism
defective.. 10. disphrasia
difficulty.. 9. baryphony
10. baryphonia
famous.. 9. Philippic (Demosthenes)
goddess.. 3. Vac
hasty.. 7. stammer, stumble, stutter
impediment.. 4. lisp 8. betacism,
mytacism
intemperate.. 6. tirade
loss of.. 6. alalia 7. aphasia
movements.. 9. vocimotor
parts.. 4. verb 6. adverb 9. adjective
11. conjunction, preposition
12. interjection
pompous.. 12. magniloquent
provincial.. 6. patois 7. dialect
set speech (drama).. 6. rhesis
term.. 6. zeugma 9. syllepsis
understatement.. 7. litotes
vitriolic.. 6. tirade
voiceless.. 7. spirate
without.. 4. mute 6. alogia
world.. 7. Volapük 9. Esperanto
speechless... 4. dumb, mute 6. silent
7. aphasic 8. taciturn 9. voiceless
speed... 3. fly, hie, run 4. flit, race,
zoom 5. haste, hurry, spurt 6. assist,
go fast, hasten 8. celerity, dispatch,
expedite, promptly, rapidity, velocity
9. posthaste, quickness, swiftness
10. accelerate, expedition, facilitate
12. precipitance
speedily... 4. soon 5. apace 6. presto
7. betimes, quickly, rapidly, swiftly
8. promptly 13. expeditiously

speedy... 4. fast 5. apace, fleet, hasty, quick, rapid, swift 6. prompt, racing, sudden

spell... 4. bout, mean, snap, tell, turn 5. charm, magic, relay, shift 6. glamor, relate, relief, trance 7. explain, relieve, sorcery, syncope 9. take turns 11. abracadabra 12. entrancement 13. substitute for

spell (pert to)...
binder.. 6. orator 7. charmer, spieler
bound.. 10. astonished, interested 11. under a spell
brief.. 4. snap
in another alphabet.. 13. transliterate
out.. 7. explain, itemize
pretended.. 11. abracadabra
under a spell.. 9. in a trance 10. hypnotized, mesmerized
with loss of letter.. 7. syncope

spend... 3. use 4. pass 5. waste 6. employ, expend, lavish, weaken 7. consume, exhaust 8. disburse, squander 9. dissipate, sacrifice 10. distribute

spend the summer... 8. estivate (aestivate)

spendthrift... 4. daft 6. waster 7. spender, wastrel 8. prodigal 10. profligate, squanderer

Spenser, Edmund (pert to)...
character.. 3. Una
famed as.. 4. poet
famed work.. 12. Faerie Queene
poetic stanza.. 10. Spenserian

Spenser's Ireland personified...
5. Irene

spent... 4. paid 5. weary 6. effete, used up, wasted 7. worn out 8. consumed, lavished, tired out 9. exhausted 10. squandered

speos... 4. cave, tomb 6. grotto

sphenoid... 11. wedge–shaped

sphere... 3. orb 4. ball, star 5. arena, earth, field, glove, orbit, realm, scope 6. extent, planet 7. circuit, heavens 8. terrible 10. atmosphere 12. jurisdiction

sphere of...
action.. 6. domain
life.. 5. world
making.. 7. orbific

spherical (pert to)...
aberration, free from.. 9. aplanatic
geometry.. 10. magnitudes
lune.. 7. portion
magnet.. 8. terrella (terella)
nearly.. 8. obrotund
reference to.. 6. rotund 7. globose 9. orbicular 15. celestial bodies
ungula.. 5. wedge

sphericity... 9. globosity, rotundity, roundness

sphinx (pert to)...
builder (Great Sphinx).. 6. Khafre (IV Dynasty)
Great Sphinx site.. 4. Gaza (Egypt)
Greek myth.. 7. monster (sphinxlike)
reference to.. 9. enigmatic 11. inscrutable
Zool.. 8. hawk moth

spice... 4. dill, herb, mace, sage

5. chili, clove 6. cassia, nutmeg, pepper, season, stacte 7. mustard 8. marjoram, pungency 9. condiment, flavoring, fragrance, seasoning

spicy... 3. hot 4. keen, racy, sexy 5. balmy, natty, smart 6. risque 7. gingery, peppery, piquant, pungent 8. aromatic, fragrant, spirited

spider... 3. cob, pan 5. arain 6. Epeira, katipo, tripod, trivet 7. pokomoo, retiary, skillet, spinner 8. arachnid, attercop, telarian 9. tarantula 10. black widow

spider (pert to)...
comb form.. 7. arachno
crab.. 4. Maia (genus)
fly.. 4. tick
genus.. 4. Maia 6. Aranea 7. Agalena, Attidae, Pholcus 9. Drassidae
Gr Myth.. 7. Arachne (Lydian girl)
Latin.. 6. aranea
leaping.. 10. saltigrade
monkey.. 6. ateles, coaita
nest.. 5. nidus
scorpion.. 8. pedipalp
scorpion appendage.. 10. pedipalpus
study of.. 10. araneology
web (anc).. 8. attercop
weblike.. 9. arachnoid
web–spinning organ.. 9. spinneret

spieler... 5. crier 6. barker, talker 7. sharper, speaker 8. lecturer 9. solicitor 10. ballyhooer

spiffy... 4. fine, neat 5. smart 8. splendid 9. excellent

spigot... 3. peg, tap 5. spile, spout 6. dossil, faucet 7. stopper

spike... 3. cob, ear 4. brob, stab, tine, umbo 5. ament, prong, thorn 6. antler, flower, pierce, spadix 7. amentum, disable, spinule, trenail 10. adulterate 12. tenpenny nail

spikenard... 3. phu (Cretan) 4. herb, nard 8. ointment

spile... 3. pin, rod 4. plug, tube 5. spill, spout, stake 6. Aralia, spigot

spill... 4. blab, fall, shed, slop 5. flosh, waste 6. let out, splash, tumble 7. divulge, scatter 8. downpour, overflow, overture 11. tell secrets

spin... 4. birl, fish, reel, ride, turn 5. swirl, twirl, twist, whirl 6. extend, gyrate, unreel 7. prolong, revolve

spinach (wrinkled)... 5. savoy

spinal (pert to)...
column.. 9. vertebrae
cord.. 4. alba 6. myelon (marrow) 16. medulla oblongata
disease.. 8. myelitis 10. meningitis
muscle (attached).. 5. psoas

spindle... 3. pin, rod 4. axis, axle, hasp 5. pivot, xeres 6. swivel 7. mandrel

spindle–legged... 4. lean 5. lanky 14. spindle–shanked

spindling... 4. long 5. gawky, leggy 6. skinny 7. slender 11. ineffectual

spine... 3. awn 4. axis, seta 5. chine, ridge, thorn 6. spirit 7. acicula,

courage, process 8. backbone,
spiculum 9. scoliosis (curvature)
12. spinal column

spinel... 5. balas (ruby) 7. mineral
8. spinelle

spineless... 4. limp, weak 5. frail
10. weak–willed 12. invertebrate

spinet... 5. piano 7. giraffe 8. virginal
10. clavichord 11. couched harp,
harpsichord

spinnaker... 4. sail

spinner... 3. top 4. liar 6. spider,
weaver 8. narrator 8. nighthawk
10. goatsucker 11. storyteller
12. whippoorwill

spinning... 6. rotary 7. strobic
8. telarian, whirling 9. revolving

spinning device... 5. jenny 7. distaff,
spindle 8. throstle

spiracle... 4. pore, vent 7. orifice
8. aperture, blowhole

spiral... 4. coil, curl 5. helix 6. galaxy,
volute 7. helical, winding 8. circling,
helicoid 9. corkscrew

spire... 4. coil, surl 5. tower, twist,
whorl 6. ascend, finial, summit
7. steeple

spire finial... 3. épi

spirit... 3. imp, pep, vim 4. dash,
élan, fire, life, mood, pixy, soul
5. demon, devil, fairy, genie, ghost,
heart, metal, pluck, Satan, shade,
spook, verve 6. animus, breath,
energy, fervor, goblin, intent, morale,
pneuma, sprite 7. bravery, courage,
essence, extract, gremlin, specter
8. spiritus 9. animation
10. enterprise, individual 11. real
meaning 12. cheerfulness
13. consciousness

spirit, spirit of (pert to)...
avarice.. 6. Mammon
bad.. 6. afreet 7. Amaimon
(Amaymon)
Egypt.. 2. ba, ka 3. akh
English folklore.. 2. po
evil.. 4. jinn 5. Aecto, jinni (jinnel)
6. Azazel, Belial, Erinys 7. Tempter
(The) 9. Beelzebub
female.. 6. undine 7. banshee
good.. 8. Eudaemon
household.. 5. Lares 15. Lares and
Penates
infatuation.. 3. Ate
knights.. 8. errantry
malignant.. 3. Ker
mockery.. 5. Momus
people.. 5. ethos
refined.. 6. elixir
tapping (theory).. 9. typtology
the air.. 5. Ariel
the sea.. 5. siren 6. Triton
7. mermaid, Neptune 9. Davy Jones

spirited... 3. gay 4. gamy, racy
5. brisk, eager, fiery 6. lively, plucky,
spunky 7. dashing, fervent
8. eloquent, generous, vigorous
9. audacious, energetic, spiritoso,
sprightly 10. mettlesome

spiritless... 4. dead, dull, meek
5. amort, vapid 6. gloomy
8. dejected, lifeless, listless

9. depressed, heartless
10. despondent, dispirited

spirits (pert to)...
Babylonian.. 5. Igigi
dwelling.. 2. po 5. Hades 7. Elysium
low.. 5. blues, dumps, gloom
8. doldrums
of the dead.. 5. Manes (Rom)
7. lemures 9. chthonian (Gr)

spiritual... 4. holy, pure, song
5. pious 6. devout, divine, sacred
7. psychic 8. churchly, internal,
platonic, spectral 9. unworldly
10. immaterial 11. disembodied,
incorporeal 12. supernatural
14. ecclesiastical, heavenly minded

spiritual (pert to)...
affinity.. 8. soul mate
apathy.. 6. acedia
being.. 3. ens 5. angel 6. seraph
darkness.. 4. Hell 5. tamas
director.. 9. confessor
meaning of words.. 7. anagoge
meeting.. 6. séance
shrine.. 6. adytum 7. sanctum

spirt... 3. jet 4. gush 5. flare, spurt
6. squirt

spit... 3. rod 4. rain 5. eject, image,
stick 6. impale, pierce, saliva,
skewer, sputum 7. hissing, spindle,
sputter 8. likeness, sprinkle, turnspit
9. exsputory 11. expectorate

spite... 3. vex 4. hate 5. pique,
shame, venom 6. enmity, malice,
offend, thwart 7. dislike, ill will
8. disgrace, dishonor 9. animosity,
cattiness, humiliate 10. resentment
11. malevolence 12. spitefulness

spiteful... 4. mean 5. catty 7. cattish
8. annoying 9. malicious, malignant
10. irritating, vindictive

spittoon... 6. pigdan 8. crachoir,
cuspidor

splash... 3. lap, wet 4. spot 5. spray,
swash 6. blotch, flouse (floush),
ripple 7. scatter, spatter, splurge
8. cut a dash, splatter 9. dashingly
14. ostentatiously

splashboard... 4. gate (false) 5. plank
6. fender, screen 9. dashboard
10. flashboard, flushboard

splay... 3. hem 4. turn 5. adorn,
carve, slant, slope 6. clumsy,
expand, spread 7. awkward, display
9. dislocate, displayed, expansion

spleen... 3. fit 4. fire, mood, whim
5. anger, ardor, freak, gland
6. malice, temper 7. impulse 8. ill
humor 10. low spirits, melancholy,
resentment 11. impetuosity

spleen (pert to)...
amarinth.. 4. weed
excision.. 13. splenectomize
reference to.. 6. lienal 7. splenic

splendid... 4. braw, fine 5. grand,
regal, showy 6. costly, superb
7. gallant, shining, sublime
8. glorious, gorgeous 9. beautiful,
brilliant, excellent, sumptuous
10. brilliance, effulgence
11. illustrious, magnificent

splendor... 4. gite, pomp 5. éclat,

glory **6.** beauty, luster **7.** display
8. grandeur, radiance, richness
9. pageantry, showiness **10.** brilliance
12. gorgeousness, magnificence,
resplendence
splint... **4.** scob, tace **5.** brace, plate,
strip **6.** fasten, tasset **7.** confine
splinter... **4.** chip **5.** break, broom
6. shiver, sliver **7.** shatter
8. fragment **9.** matchwood
split... **3.** cut, rit **4.** chap, open, rend,
rent, rive, tear **5.** break, burst, cleft,
crack, laugh, leave (sl), riven, wedge
6. bisect, cleave, cloven, depart (sl),
divide, sunder **7.** dispart, divided,
rupture, shatter **8.** separate
9. apportion, partition **10.** separation
split (pert to)...
hairs.. **7.** quibble **12.** discriminate
13. differentiate
into two parts.. **5.** bifid **6.** cloven
pea.. **3.** dal **5.** dahll
the difference.. **5.** share **7.** average
10. compromise **12.** go fifty–fifty
up.. **5.** cleft **7.** disband, divorce
8. separate **9.** apportion, partition
spoil... **3.** mar, rot **4.** loot, prey, ruin,
sack **5.** botch, decay, harry
6. coddle, impair, injure, pamper
7. destroy, estrepe, louse up (sl),
pillage, plunder, vitiate **9.** frustrate
spoilation... **6.** rapine **7.** pillage
10. plundering, spoliation
spoiled... **3.** bad **5.** moldy, musty
6. addled, marred, molded, preyed,
wasted **7.** botched, bungled, decayed,
tainted **8.** pampered, pillaged
9. plundered **12.** deteriorated
spoiler... **6.** robber **7.** marplot
8. pillager **9.** despoiler, plunderer
spoils... **4.** loot, prey, swag **5.** booty,
perks (sl) **11.** perquisites
spoilsport... **7.** marplot **10.** wet
blanket **11.** party–pooper
spoke... **3.** bar, pin, ray, rod **4.** rung,
said **5.** check, round, spake, stake
6. radius, speech **7.** uttered
9. hindrance **10.** impediment
spoke monotonously... **6.** droned
spoken... **4.** oral **5.** parol
9. declaimed, ideophone (word)
spoliation... **6.** rapine **7.** pillage
8. ravaging **10.** spoilation
sponge... **3.** dry, wet **4.** bath, swab
5. erase, mooch **6.** absorb, animal,
efface, eraser, extort **7.** badiaga,
cleanse, sponger, zimocca
8. drunkard, parasite **9.** absorbent,
sycophant **10.** obliterate, porousness
sponge (pert to)...
Europe.. **7.** badiaga
fruit.. **5.** luffa (loofah)
Mediterranean.. **7.** zimocca
opening.. **7.** apopyle
orifice.. **7.** osculum
young.. **5.** ascon **6.** rhagon
sponger... **4.** sorn **5.** leech **6.** cadger
7. moocher **8.** parasite **9.** scrounger
10. freeloader
sponsor... **5.** angel **6.** backer, patron
7. finance **9.** financier, godparent,
guarantee, guarantor, patronize

sponsorship... **5.** aegis (egis)
7. subsidy **8.** auspices
spontaneous... **4.** free **6.** native
8. untaught **9.** automatic, voluntary
10. self–acting **11.** instinctive,
involuntary
spontoon... **4.** club, pike **7.** halberd,
pantoon **9.** espantoon, truncheon
spoof... **3.** guy **4.** fool, hoax, joke
5. trick **7.** deceive, swindle
8. nonsense **9.** deception
spook... **5.** ghost **6.** spirit, zombie
(zombi) **7.** specter **8.** frighten
9. hobgoblin **10.** apparition
spooky... **5.** eerie, weird **7.** ghostly,
haunted, uncanny **8.** spectral
spool... **4.** reel, wind **6.** bobbin
7. spindle **8.** cylinder
spoon... **4.** club **5.** labis, ladle
6. shovel **7.** fish for **8.** cochlear,
make love, runcible
spoonbill... **5.** ajaja (ayaya)
9. sandpiper
Spoon River poet... **7.** Masters (E L)
spore (pert to)...
capsule, sac.. **5.** ascus, theca
10. sporangium
cluster.. **5.** sorus
formation.. **6.** tetrad
fruit.. **7.** asocarp
sport... **3.** fun, toy **4.** game, hunt, jest,
joke, play, romp, wear **5.** dandy,
mirth **6.** banter, flaunt, frolic, gamble,
racing, skiing **7.** contest, gambler,
jesting, mockery, pastime **8.** raillery
9. amusement, bon vivant, diversion,
good loser, plaything, sportsman
10. pleasantry, recreation
13. entertainment
sport (pert to)...
art of (contests).. **10.** agonistics
cheap.. **5.** piker
of kings.. **6.** racing **7.** the turf
sportive... **3.** gay **5.** merry **7.** jocular,
playful **8.** frolicky, playsome
9. facetious **10.** frolicsome
sports... **5.** Rugby, track **6.** hockey, jai
lai, soccer, squash, tennis **7.** cricket
8. baseball, football, la crosse, softball
9. athletics, palaestra **10.** acrobatics,
gymnastics **11.** racquetball
sports attendance... **4.** gate
sports official... **5.** coach, judge
6. umpire **7.** referee **8.** linesman
10. timekeeper
sporty... **5.** rorty, showy **6.** dressy,
flashy
spot... **3.** dot **4.** blet, blot, espy, flaw,
mark, site, soil **5.** fleck, place, point,
speck, stain, taint **6.** detect, locate,
macula, macule, stigma **7.** asperse,
blemish, freckle, observe, speckle,
splotch **8.** discolor, disgrace, locality,
location, position **9.** bespatter,
limelight, recognize **11.** predicament,
small amount
spot (pert to)...
cards.. **3.** pip
fertile.. **5.** oasis
fish.. **7.** pinfish
high.. **4.** apex **5.** climax
mineral.. **5.** macle

on the spot.. 3. now 4. here
  7. imperil, present 8. promptly
payment.. 4. cash
secluded.. 6. alcove
sun.. 6. lucule 7. granule
wood.. 3. wem
spotless... 4. pure 5. clean 6. chaste
  8. innocent 9. blameless, faultless,
  unsullied 10. immaculate
  11. unblemished, untarnished
  14. irreproachable
spotted... 6. espied, marked, soiled
  7. dappled, guttate (droplike),
  mottled, stained, sullied 8. speckled
  9. blemished, sprinkled, tarnished
  11. diversified
spouse... 4. mate, wife 5. bride
  7. consort, partner 9. companion
  10. better half
spout... 3. jet, jut, lip 4. dale, gush,
  pawn, rant, spew 5. erupt, spile,
  spurt 6. pledge, recite, spigot, squirt,
  trough 7. chatter, conduit, declaim
  8. downpour, gargoyle (carved)
  9. discharge, waterfall
  10. waterspout
spouter... 5. whale 6. geyser 7. oil
  well, speaker 9. declaimer
  11. speechifier
sprat... 6. garvie 7. herring
  8. sixpence
spray... 3. jet 4. foam 5. stour, water
  6. squirt 7. atomize, flowers, gunfire
  8. perfumer, sprinkle 9. spindrift
  10. spoondrift
spread... 3. ted 4. meal 5. bruit,
  feast, flare, strew, widen 6. expand,
  extent, sprawl, unfurl 7. divulge,
  radiate, scatter 8. disperse
  9. broadcast 11. disseminate
  13. advertisement
spread (pert to)...
by defamation.. 5. libel
by report.. 6. norate
by rumor.. 6. noise
eagle.. 8. boastful, insignia
  9. patriotic 12. exaggeration
out.. 3. fan 4. open, span 5. flare
  6. deploy
over.. 5. cover, smear
thickly.. 7. slather
thin.. 3. bray
spree... 4. lark, orgy, romp 5. binge,
  revel 6. bender, frolic, shindy
  7. wassail 8. carousal
sprig... 4. trim, twig 5. scion, shoot,
  smart 6. active, spruce 8. ornament
  9. youngling
sprightly... 3. gay 4. airy, pert
  5. alive, brisk, peart 6. blithe, lively
  7. briskly, ghostly 8. vigorous
  10. enlivening, spiritedly
  11. incorporeal
spring... 3. fly, hop, spa 4. dart, font,
  jump, leap, well 5. shoot, spurt,
  vault, vigor 6. bounce, energy,
  geyser, origin, season, source
  9. saltation 10. elasticity, resilience
spring (pert to)...
back.. 6. recoil, resile 7. rebound
of the Muses.. 7. Pierian
ref to.. 6. vernal

up.. 4. grow 5. arise, occur
  6. appear, ascend 9. originate
springing into being... 9. renascent
springs... 4. spas 5. baths, fonts
  6. resort (health) 7. thermae
sprinkle... 3. deg, dot, wet 4. rain
  5. bedew, spray, strew, water
  6. bedrop, sparge, spreng 7. baptize,
  scatter 9. bespatter
sprinkler... 11. aspergillum (Eccl)
sprinkle with...
flour.. 6. dredge
grit.. 4. sand
heraldic.. 4. semé
powder.. 4. dust
water.. 3. deg
sprint... 3. run 4. dash, race
sprite... 3. elf, fay, hob, imp, nix
  4. peri 5. fairy, ghost, gnome, pixie,
  sylph 6. goblin, spirit 7. brownie
  9. hobgoblin 10. apparition
sprite (pert to)...
fiction.. 5. Ariel
Irish.. 10. leprechaun
mischievous.. 4. Puck
ref to.. 6. elfish
sprocket... 5. tooth, wheel 8. cylinder
  (toothed) 10. projection
sprout... 3. bud, son 4. cion, grow
  5. scion, shoot, spire, sprit
  6. branch, ratoon, tiller 7. burgeon,
  upstart 8. offshoot 9. germinate
  10. descendant
spruce... 4. chic, neat, posh, smug,
  tree, trig, trim 5. adorn, natty, smart
  6. dapper 7. finical, smarten
  8. titivate
spruce (pert to)...
beverage.. 4. beer
black.. 7. yew pine
fir.. 6. Norway
genus.. 5. Abies, Picea
Japanese.. 6. Alcock
type.. 7. Douglas, hemlock
white.. 8. épinette
sprue... 5. dross, waste 6. thrush
  7. disease 8. psilosis 9. asparagus
spry... 5. agile, brisk, quick, smart
  6. active, nimble 8. vigorous
  9. sprightly
spud... 5. drill, knife, spade 6. dagger,
  paddle, potato, reamer, shovel
spume... 4. foam, scum 5. froth
spunky... 4. game 5. quick 6. plucky,
  touchy 8. spirited 10. courageous,
  mettlesome 13. quick–tempered
spur... 3. egg 4. goad, move, urge
  5. drive, press, ridge, rowel, spine
  6. calcar, excite, griffe, incite, needle
  7. provoke 8. stimulus 9. instigate,
  stimulate 10. incitement
spur (pert to)...
badge.. 10. knighthood
fowl.. 5. quail 9. partridge
gamecock's.. 4. gaff 7. gablock
mountain.. 5. arête
pert to.. 7. spicate
railroad.. 5. track
wheel.. 5. rowel
spurious... 4. fake, sham 5. false
  6. pseudo 7. bastard 10. adulterate,
  apocryphal, artificial, fictitious,

fraudulent 11. counterfeit
12. illegitimate 14. supposititious
spurious (pert to)...
fruit.. 10. pseudocarp
olive.. 9. heartwood
rainbow.. 8. faint arc
wing.. 7. bastard
spurn... 4. defy 5. scorn 6. reject,
strike 7. contemn, disdain
spurt... 3. jet, jut 4. dash, gush, spew
5. burst, spout 7. outpour, upsurge
8. outbreak
spy... 3. pry, see 4. espy, note, tout
5. scout, sneak, snoop, watch
6. behold, descry, detect, search
7. examine, snooper 8. discover,
emissary, informer, perceive
10. scrutinize 11. reconnoiter
spy (pert to)...
city.. 7. Belgium
in clothing circles.. 4. keek
Man of.. 14. paleolithic man
prison.. 6. mouton
squab... 3. fat 4. fowl, sofa 5. piper,
plump 6. fat man, pigeon 7. cushion
8. nestling 9. fledgling
squabble... 5. brawl 6. bicker, jangle
7. contend, quarrel, wrangle
10. disarrange (Print)
13. collieshangie
squad... 4. team, unit 5. posse
7. company
squalid... 4. foul, mean, poor 5. dirty
6. filthy, sordid 7. unclean
8. slovenly 9. repellent, repulsive
11. squalidness 15. poverty–stricken
squall... 3. cry, row 4. blow, gale,
gust, wail, wind, yell 6. squawk,
squeal 9. commotion 11. disturbance
squalor... 4. dirt, mire 5. filth
8. slovenry 9. dirtiness 10. filthiness
11. squalidness 16. unkempt
condition
squander... 5. waste 6. lavish
7. scatter 8. disperse, misspend
9. dissipate, throw away 10. run
through
squanderer... 5. loser 7. wastrel
square... 4. even, meal 5. bribe, plaza
6. common, honest, settle 7. exactly,
obelisk, old fogy 8. absolute, cube
face, directly, equalize, quadrate
9. city block, divergent
11. unequivocal 13. parallelogram
14. unsophisticate
15. straightforward
squash... 4. mash, pepo, pulp
5. crush, gourd, press 6. cushaw,
refute, simlin, simnel, soften
7. cymling (cymbling), Hubbard,
squeeze 8. pattypan, suppress
9. crookneck 10. extinguish
11. calabazilla
squat... 3. low 5. dumpy, pudgy,
quash, stoop 6. crouch, hunker,
settle, stubby 7. sit down
8. squatter, thickset
squatter... 6. nester (illegal) 7. pioneer
9. sandpiper 11. homesteader
Squatter State... 6. Kansas
squaw... 6. coween, Indian, mahala
(mahaly)

squeal... 6. betray, inform 7. protest,
quarrel
squealer... 4. fink 6. grouse, pigeon,
plover 7. traitor 8. informer
squeamish... 4. nice 5. dizzy
6. dainty, queasy 7. prudish
8. overnice, qualmish 9. nauseated
10. fastidious, scrupulous
squeeze... 3. hug, jam, nip 4. cram,
crux 5. crowd, crush, pinch, press,
wring 6. crisis, extort 7. embrace
8. compress 9. constrict, influence
10. constraint 11. compression
squeezer, fruit... 6. juicer, reamer
squelch... 5. crush, quash, quell
6. rebuke, refute, subdue 7. repress,
silence 8. suppress 10. disconcert
squib... 4. bomb, fuse, pipe, skit, tube
6. speech, squirt 7. explode,
lampoon, writing 9. bespatter
10. pasquinade 11. firecracker
squire... 4. beau 5. court, lover
6. escort 7. gallant 8. henchman,
nobleman 9. attendant, gentleman,
landowner
squirm... 5. twist 6. wiggle, writhe
7. wriggle
squirrel (pert to)...
African.. 5. xerus
American.. 5. bunny 7. assapan
8. chipmunk 9. chickaree
American, flying.. 7. assapan
Asian.. 5. sisel 6. suslik
Austral, flying.. 9. phalanger
burrowing.. 6. gopher
cage.. 9. treadmill
color.. 4. lead
E Ind, flying.. 6. taguan
fish.. 7. serrano
fur (Her).. 4. vair
genus.. 6. Tamias 7. Sciurus
Java.. 8. jelerang
like.. 8. sciuroid
nest.. 4. dray, drey
shrew.. 4. tana 6. Tupaia
skin.. 4. vair
Spanish.. 7. ardilla
squirrellike mammal... 8. banxring,
dormouse
stab... 4. gore, pang, pink 5. knife,
knive, lunge, wound 6. attack, injury,
pierce, thrust 7. poniard, slander
8. puncture, stoccado
stability... 5. poise 7. balance
8. firmness, strength 9. constancy
10. permanence, stableness,
steadiness 11. reliability
12. immovability, immutability
13. steadfastness
stabilize... 3. set 5. poise 6. steady
7. ballast 8. regulate
stable... 3. mew (Royal) 4. barn, byre,
firm, safe 5. fixed, solid, sound, stall
6. steady, strong 7. durable, lasting,
paddock, support 8. constant, reliable
9. confirmed, permanent, steadfast
10. stationary, unwavering
11. established, trustworthy
stableman... 5. groom 7. hostler
(ostler)
staccato... 7. détaché 8. ricochet
12. disconnected

stack... 4. heap, load, pile, rick
5. mound, shock 6. pile up
7. chimney, conduit 8. quantity
stacked... 11. accumulated,
prearranged
stacked pack, cards... 8. cold deck
stadium... 5. stage 6. course, dromos
8. foot race (anc)
stadium race, start... 7. aphesis
staff... 3. rod 4. club, mace, pole
5. baton, music, stave 7. scepter,
support 8. caduceus, insignia,
pastoral 9. personnel 10. assistants,
associates
staff (pert to)...
Bacchus.. 7. thyrsus
bearer.. 5. macer
magician's.. 7. rhabdos
marshal's.. 5. baton
member, officer.. 4. aide 7. attaché
mountain climbing.. 10. alpenstock
pastoral.. 5. pedum 7. baculus,
crosier (crozier)
shepherd's.. 5. crook, pedum
sovereign's.. 7. scepter (sceptre)
stag... 4. colt, deer (red), hart
5. party, royal, spade 7. male fox,
pollard 8. gamecock, informer
stage... 4. dais, tier 5. arena, phase,
scene 6. degree 7. display, estrade,
perform, rostrum 8. platform, scaffold
9. dramatize, gradation
10. proscenium, stagecoach
stage (pert to)...
call (trumpet).. 6. sennet
direction.. 5. aside, manet 6. sennet
of disease.. 9. catabasis
of insects.. 5. imago, larva
part.. 5. stair 8. dutchman (patch)
10. proscenium
scene (side).. 8. coulisse
scenery.. 3. set
stagger... 4. reel, stot, stun, sway,
walk 5. lurch 6. excite, totter, zigzag
7. be drunk, tremble, vibrate
8. astonish, flounder, frighten,
titubate, unsettle 9. alternate,
fluctuate
staggering... 5. areel 9. startling
10. astounding 11. the staggers
12. unbelievable
Stagirite, The... 9. Aristotle
stagnant... 4. dull, foul 5. inert, stale,
still 8. inactive, sluggish, standing
10. motionless, not flowing
13. unprogressive
stagnate... 3. rot 4. dull 5. inert
8. stagnant, vegetate 10. motionless
staid... 5. grave, sober 6. demure,
sedate, solemn 7. serious, settled
8. composed, decorous, sensible
9. steadfast
stain... 3. dye 4. blot, soil, spot, tint
5. color, paint, smear, sully
6. infamy, smudge, stigma
7. blemish, corrupt, pigment, tarnish
8. discolor, disgrace, dishonor,
maculate 9. pollution 10. stigmatize
11. contaminate 13. discoloration
stained by decay... 4. doty
stained glass rod (lead)... 4. came
stair... 4. step 5. riser, stage, tread

6. degree, flight (series)
staircase (pert to)...
French.. 8. escalier
moving.. 9. escalator
outdoor.. 6. perron
post.. 5. newel
ship's.. 12. companionway
spiral.. 8. caracole
stairs to bath (Ind)... 4. ghat (ghaut)
stake... 3. bet, peg, pel, pin 4. ante,
pale, pile, post, risk, spit 5. sowel,
teest, wager 6. chance, estate,
gamble, hazard, picket, pledge
7. finance, venture
stale... 3. old 5. banal, fusty, trite,
vapid 7. insipid, spoiled
9. hackneyed, tasteless 10. flavorless
11. commonplace
stalemate... 6. corner 7. impasse
8. cul—de—sac, deadlock 10. blind
alley, standstill
stalk... 4. axis, hunt, risp, stem, walk
6. pursue, stride 7. pedicel
8. peduncle 11. reconnoiter
stalk (pert to)...
cotton, sugar cane.. 6. ratoon
dry.. 3. hay, kex 5. haulm (halm)
flower.. 7. petiole
grain, grass.. 4. culm 5. straw
6. ressum
strawberry.. 4. risp
stalkless... 7. sessile
stall... 3. cot, pew 4. crib, fail, loge,
mire, stop 5. booth, check, choir,
stick 6. hinder, manger, stable
7. disgust 9. temporize 10. dillydally
11. compartment 12. parking space
13. procrastinate
stalwart... 5. brave, stout 6. strong,
sturdy 7. valiant 8. partisan, resolute
9. corpulent 10. courageous,
unyielding
stamina... 5. pluck, vigor 7. courage
8. backbone, strength 9. endurance,
fortitude 12. staying power
stammer... 3. haw, hem 4. mant
6. falter 7. stumble, stutter
8. hesitate
stammering... 8. psellism
stamp... 3. die 4. date, dink, form,
mark, seal, sign, tool 5. brand, infix,
label 6. signet 7. engrave, impress,
imprint, postage, trading 8. tressure
(tressour) 11. endorsement
14. characteristic
stamp (pert to)...
border.. 8. tressure (tressour)
collecting.. 9. philately
collector.. 11. philatelist
madness.. 11. timbromania
paper.. 6. pelure
postage.. 6. timbre
space.. 8. spandrel
stampede... 3. run 4. rout, rush
5. panic 6. flight 7. debacle
11. wild scamper
stance... 4. pose 7. posture, station
8. position
stanch... 5. allay, check, quell
6. steady, strong 7. zealous
8. faithful 9. steadfast 10. extinguish
11. substantial

stanchion... 3. bar 4. post, prop
   5. brace, piton 6. secure 7. support, upright
stand... 4. bear, bier, halt, rack, stop, zarf 5. abide, arise, booth, easel, store, table 6. endure, tripod
   7. coaster, étagère, footing, impasse, sustain, taboret 8. attitude, foothold, pedestal, position, tolerate
   9. withstand 10. standstill
stand (pert to)...
   against.. 6. resist
   by.. 3. aid 6. defend 7. support
      9. be present
   cost of.. 5. treat
   Eccl.. 4. ambo
   for.. 6. permit, typify 9. represent, symbolize
   for candles.. 7. epergne
      10. candelabra
   in.. 6. deputy 10. substitute
   it.. 4. bear 5. brook 6. suffer
   offish.. 4. cold 5. aloof 8. reserved
      10. not cordial
   opposite.. 4. face
   three-legged.. 6. teapoy, tripod, trivot
   up to.. 5. brave 6. resist
standard... 3. par 4. flag, norm
   5. grade, model, usual 6. ensign
   7. average, classic, paragon, precept
   8. orthodox 9. customary, principle
   13. authoritative
standard (pert to)...
   battle.. 9. oriflamme (oriflamb)
   bearer.. 6. leader 7. officer
      10. politician
   chem test.. 5. titer (titre)
   ensign.. 8. gonfalon, gonfanon
   flag (Rom).. 8. vexillum
   of excellence.. 4. idea
   of intelligence.. 5. Binet
   of light.. 6. carcel
   of quantity.. 4. unit
   Ottoman Emp.. 4. alem
standardize... 9. calibrate, normalize
standing... 4. rank 5. fixed, state
   6. at rest, status 7. footing, settled, station, upright 8. duration, prestige
   9. permanent 10. durability, reputation
standing (pert to)...
   long.. 7. durable 8. duration
      11. traditional
   mode of.. 6. stance
   out.. 7. eminent, salient
   room only.. 3. SRO
   social.. 6. estate, status 8. prestige
   upright.. 11. orthostatic
stannum... 2. Sn 3. tin
stanza... 4. rann, unit 5. stave, verse
   6. octave, sestet 8. strophe, triolet (8-lined)
stanza scheme... 6. ballad 10. Gray's Elegy, Spenserian
star... 3. sun 4. hero, lead 5. actor, shine 6. étoile 7. destiny, fortune
   8. asterisk, insignia, ornament
   9. emphasize, principal
   11. hummingbird 12. heavenly body, luminous body
star (pert to)... see also *Stars*
   brightest.. 3. Cor, sun 5. Deneb
      6. Altair, Lucida, Sirius
   Bull's Eye.. 9. Aldebaran
   divination.. 9. astrology
   Dog.. 4. Sept 6. Sirius 8. Canicula
      12. Canis Majoris
   evening.. 5. Venus 6. Hesper, Vesper
      7. evestar 8. Hesperus
   feather.. 9. comatulid
   five-pointed.. 9. pentagram, pentalpha
   French.. 6. étoile
   gazer.. 4. fish 10. astronomer
   giant.. 10. Betelgeuse (Betelgeux)
   group (fixed).. 13. constellation
   guiding.. 5. Alpha, North 7. Polaris
      8. Cynosure, loadstar, lodestar, polestar
   large.. 5. Rigel
   morning.. 4. Mars 5. Venus 6. Saturn
      7. daystar, Jupiter, Mercury
      8. Phosphor
   new.. 4. Nova
   North.. 7. Polaris 8. loadstar, lodestar
   of Africa.. 15. Cullinan diamond
   of Bethlehem (Bib).. 11. guide of Magi
   of the sea.. 11. Maris Stella (Stella Maris)
   ornament.. 4. semé
   path.. 5. orbit
   ref to.. 6. astral, starry 7. sideral, stellar 8. sidereal 9. planatoid
   representation.. 6. étoile
   shooting.. 5. comet 6. Leonid, meteor
starch... 3. vim 4. sago 5. hilum, vigor 6. amidin, energy, farina, fecula
   7. cassava 8. glycogen 9. arrowroot, formality, stiffness
starchy... 5. stiff 6. formal, viscid
   7. amyloid, precise 9. unbending
stare... 4. gape, gawk, gaze, look, ogle, peer 5. glare 6. glower, goggle, wonder
starfish... 7. asteria 10. echinoderm
stark... 4. bare, mere 5. rigid, tense
   6. barren, wholly 7. violent
   8. absolute, complete, entirely
   9. downright, unadorned
   10. absolutely
starling... 4. myna, sali 6. pastor
Stars (pert to)...
   and Bars.. 15. Confederate flag
   belt, tract (luminous).. 6. Galaxy
      8. Milky Way
   circumpolar group.. 5. Draco
      6. Dragon
   four (famed).. 4. Crux 13. Southern Cross
   North Pole group.. 9. Great Bear
      10. Little Bear 11. Septentrion
   Ursa Major.. 9. Big Dipper, Great Bear
   Ursa Minor.. 10. Little Bear 12. Little Dipper
start... 4. dart, dash, jerk, rush
   5. begin, enter, sally 6. broach, origin, twitch 7. get away, startle
   8. commence 9. advantage, beginning, departure, originate
   10. inaugurate
starting point... 4. text (sermon)
   7. scratch 9. departure
startle... 5. alarm, rouse, scare, shock

6. excite, fright 8. astonish
9. electrify
starve... 3. die 4. kill 5. crave
6. famish, perish, scrimp 7. atrophy,
destroy 10. be indigent
starved... 4. thin 5. empty 6. frozen,
hungry 8. famished, ravenous
starwort... 5. aster 9. colicroot
stash... 5. cache, plant, store 7. lay
away 8. hide away
state... 3. say 4. aver, case, état,
mode, tell 5. utter 6. affirm, allege,
assert, plight, recite, remark, report
7. country, declare, expound,
express, narrate 8. announce,
propound 9. condition, enunciate,
postulate, pronounce, territory
10. government, possession
11. body politic 12. circumstance,
commonwealth
state (pert to)...
a fact.. 4. aver 5. posit 6. avouch
7. declare
agitated.. 9. disturbed, perturbed
disordered.. 9. cluttered
formally.. 8. propound 9. enunciate,
pronounce
French.. 4. état
hypnotic.. 6. trance
ideal.. 6. Utopia
office.. 8. governor 11. secretariat
on oath.. 6. depose
police.. 7. trooper
reference.. 6. statal
secret.. 7. arcanum
specifically.. 6. define 7. itemize
13. particularize
treasury.. 4. fisc 6. fiscus
ultimate.. 3. end
under foreign control..
12. protectorate
without proof.. 6. allege
stately... 5. grand, largo, lofty, regal,
royal 6. august, coldly, kingly
7. haughty, queenly, togated
8. eloquent, imperial, imposing,
majestic 9. dignified, grandiose
11. magnificent
statement... 4. bill, list 5. audit, dixit
6. dictum, remark, report, resumé
7. account, invoice, premise
8. abstract, proposal, schedule
9. affidavit, assertion, manifesto
10. accounting, expression, recitation
11. declaration 12. announcement,
presentation
statement (pert to)...
abridged.. 6. précis, resumé
7. summary 10. abridgment
11. abridgement
assumed true.. 7. premise
contradictory.. 7. paradox
defamatory.. 5. libel
detailed.. 8. schedule
dogmatic.. 6. dictum
introductory.. 5. proem 7. preface,
prelude 8. foreword, prologue
legal.. 11. declaration
mathematical.. 7. theorem
of belief.. 5. credo, creed
of introduction.. 8. prologue
precise.. 8. aphorism

self–evident.. 6. truism
sworn.. 9. affidavit
State nicknames...
Alabama.. 6. Cotton 12. Heart of
Dixie, Yellowhammer
Alaska.. (no official)
Arizona.. 11. Grand Canyon
Arkansas.. 17. Land of Opportunity
California.. 6. Golden
Colorado.. 10. Centennial
Connecticut.. 6. Nutmeg
Delaware.. 5. First
Florida.. 8. Sunshine
Georgia.. 5. Peach
Hawaii.. 5. Aloha
Idaho.. 3. Gem
Illinois.. 7. Prairie
Indiana.. 7. Hoosier
Iowa.. 7. Hawkeye
Kansas.. 9. Sunflower
Kentucky.. 9. Bluegrass
Louisiana.. 7. Pelican
Maine.. 8. Pine Tree
Maryland.. 4. Free 7. Old Line
Massachusetts.. 3. Bay 9. Old Colony
Michigan.. 9. Wolverine
Minnesota.. 6. Gopher 9. North Star
Mississippi.. 8. Magnolia
Missouri.. 6. Show Me
Montana.. 8. Treasure
Nebraska.. 4. Beef 10. Cornhusker
Nevada.. 6. Silver 9. Sagebrush
New Hampshire.. 7. Granite
New Jersey.. 6. Garden
New Mexico.. 17. Land of
Enchantment
New York.. 6. Empire
North Carolina.. 7. Tarheel 8. Old
North
North Dakota.. 5. Sioux 11. Flickertail
Ohio.. 7. Buckeye
Oklahoma.. 6. Sooner
Oregon.. 6. Beaver
Pennsylvania.. 8. Keystone
Rhode Island.. 11. Little Rhody
South Carolina.. 8. Palmetto
South Dakota.. 6. Coyote 8. Sunshine
Tennessee.. 9. Volunteer
Texas.. 8. Lone Star
Utah.. 7. Beehive
Vermont.. 13. Green Mountain
Virginia.. 11. Old Dominion
Washington.. 9. Evergreen
West Virginia.. 8. Mountain
Wisconsin.. 6. Badger
Wyoming.. 8. Equality
state of...
dissension.. 8. scission
disuse.. 9. desuetude
ecstasy.. 6. trance 7. rapture
8. paradise
hostility.. 6. feudal
mind.. 4. mood 5. humor 6. morale
8. attitude
unconsciousness.. 4. coma 5. faint
state of being...
a layman.. 9. laicality
artless.. 9. naiveté
a son.. 7. sonship
a woman.. 10. muliebrity
behindhand.. 9. in arrears
beyond natural laws.. 12. supernatural

complete.. **9**. plenitude
confined.. **10**. internment
free from error.. **9**. inerrancy
married twice, illegally.. **6**. bigamy
married twice, legally.. **6**. digamy
overfull.. **8**. plethora
passive.. **9**. stolidity
poison.. **5**. toxic **8**. toxicity
voiced.. **7**. sonancy
worse.. **8**. pejority
wrong.. **7**. errancy
static... **5**. inert, noise **6**. stable
  7. resting **8**. electric, inactive
  9. quiescent **10**. stationary
  12. atmospherics, interference
station... **4**. fire, post, rank, seat, stop
  5. berth, depot, place, radio, serai
  6. health, police **7**. calling, dignity
  8. location, position, prestige
  9. situation **11**. institution
stationary... **3**. set **5**. fixed, still
  6. stable, static, stator **8**. immobile
  9. immovable **10**. motionless,
  unchanging
stationery... **3**. pen **5**. paper **6**. pencil
  9. onionskin, papeterie **12**. writing
  paper
statue... **4**. bust **5**. image **8**. acrolith,
  figurine, monument **9**. sculpture,
  statuette
statue (pert to)...
  at Thebes.. **6**. Memnon
  gigantic.. **8**. Colossus
  Guildhall (London).. **3**. Gog **5**. Magog
  holy.. **4**. icon (ikon)
  male figure (support).. **7**. telamon
  part.. **5**. socle, trunk **6**. plinth
  primitive.. **6**. xoanon
  Pygmalion's.. **7**. Galatea
  world wonder.. **6**. Helios (Rhodes)
status... **4**. rank **5**. class, state
  7. station **8**. position, prestige,
  standing
status symbol... **11**. swivel chair
statute... **3**. act, jus, law, lex
  5. bylaw, canon, edict, title
  6. decree, rubric, treaty **8**. statutum
  9. enactment, ordinance
  10. regulation **11**. legislation
staunch, stanch... **4**. firm, true
  6. hearty **7**. devoted **8**. faithful,
  resolute **9**. steadfast **10**. dependable
  11. trustworthy
stave... **3**. bar, leg **4**. fend, pole,
  rung, slat **5**. staff, stick **6**. cudgel,
  lathee, letter, stanza **7**. baculus,
  support, ward off **8**. overcome
  11. set of verses
stave off... **4**. fend **7**. prevent
  8. postpone
staves, bundle of... **5**. shook
stay... **3**. guy, leg, rib **4**. prop, rely,
  stop, wait **5**. abide, brace, cease,
  check, pause, tarry **6**. adhere, arrest,
  linger, remain, retard, status
  7. prevent, respite **8**. postpone,
  restrain **9**. cessation, hindrance
  10. impediment **12**. postponement
stead... **4**. help, lieu **5**. place
  6. assist, behalf **7**. replace, service,
  support **9**. advantage, farmstead,
  homestead

steadfast... **4**. firm, true **5**. fixed
  6. stable **7**. durable, staunch
  8. constant, faithful, reliable
  9. unwinking **10**. unchanging,
  unswerving **11**. unalterable
steadiness... **5**. nerve **7**. balance
  9. constancy, stability **10**. uniformity
  11. reliability
steady... **4**. firm **5**. fixed, grave, sober,
  staid **6**. stable, sturdy **7**. assured,
  equable, regular, uniform **8**. constant,
  resolute **9**. incessant, steadfast
  10. invariable, unswerving
  11. unfaltering, unmitigated
  13. uninterrupted
steal... **3**. cly, cop, gyp, nim, rap, rob
  4. crib, lift, loot **5**. filch, pinch,
  poach, swipe **6**. finger, kidnap, pilfer,
  snitch **7**. purloin **8**. embezzle,
  peculate **10**. plagiarize
  11. appropriate
steal (pert to)...
  a march on.. **5**. evade **7**. precede
  10. anticipate **13**. gain advantage
  away.. **5**. creep, slink, sneak
  cattle.. **6**. rustle
  feloniously.. **6**. ratten
  game.. **5**. poach **8**. trespass
  insane desire to.. **11**. kleptomania
  nautical.. **7**. manavel
stealer... **5**. crook, thief **6**. lifter, pirate
  7. abactor, abigens, filcher, rustler
  8. pilferer **9**. embezzler, peculator,
  purloiner **10**. pickpocket, plagiarist
  11. biblioklept **12**. kleptomaniac
stealthy... **3**. sly **6**. artful, feline,
  secret **7**. catlike, cunning, furtive
  11. clandestine
steam... **4**. boil, fume, heat, mist, reek
  5. force, power, smoke, stufa, vapor
  6. energy, pother (puther) **8**. vaporize
  9. evaporate
steam (pert to)...
  boat.. **5**. liner **7**. steamer
  9. steamship **11**. side–wheeler
  jet of.. **5**. stufa **8**. suffione
  organ.. **8**. calliope
steamboat cabin (officer's)... **5**. texas
steamy... **5**. misty **7**. excited
  8. vaporous **9**. steamed up
steatite... **4**. talc **9**. soapstone
steed... **3**. nag **5**. horse **7**. charger,
  courser, Pegasus (winged)
steel... **5**. inure **6**. harden, smooth
  10. strengthen
steel (pert to)...
  armor plate.. **4**. tace **5**. tasse
  color.. **4**. gray **9**. steel blue
  12. Prussian blue
  conversion to.. **10**. acieration
  India.. **5**. wootz **10**. wootz steel
  metallurgy of.. **9**. siderurgy
  process.. **8**. Bessemer
  11. cementation
  type.. **6**. damask, Toledo
  8. Damascus
steep... **3**. ret, sop **4**. brae, buck,
  high, soak, stew, tall **5**. cleve
  (cleeve), hilly, lofty, scarp, sharp,
  sheer **6**. abrupt, clifty, escarp,
  imbrue, infuse, seethe **7**. extract,
  extreme **8**. elevated, headlong,

macerate 9. difficult, excessive,
expensive, precipice 10. exorbitant
11. precipitous 13. perpendicular
steeple... 5. spire, tower 6. flèche
7. minaret 8. pinnacle
steer... 2. ox 3. cow, ply, yaw
4. helm, luff, stot 5. guide, pilot
6. bovina, direct, govern, manage
7. bullock, control, operate
steer clear of... 4. snub 5. avert,
avoid 9. sidetrack, step aside 14. be
inhospitable
steer close to wind... 4. luff
steeve... 4. lade, pack, spar (a)
5. store, stuff 6. freeze
stein... 3. mug 4. Toby
stellar... 6. astral, starry 7. leading,
starlit 8. starlike, stellate
10. theatrical
Steller's sea cow... 6. Rytina
stem... 3. dam 4. axis, base, cion,
corm, prow, root, stop, tige
5. check, shaft, stalk, tuber
6. branch, breast, oppose, scapel,
stanch 7. lineage, petiole
8. ancestry, peduncle 9. originate
stem (pert to)...
bulblike.. 4. corm, drub
cylinder.. 5. stele
grass.. 4. culm
joint.. 4. cane, node
mushroom.. 5. stipe
plant.. 4. bine
seedling.. 7. tigella (tigelle)
9. hypocotyl
strawberry.. 4. risp
twining.. 7. tendril
underground.. 5. tuber
stemless herb (evergreen)... 5. Galax
11. acaulescent
stench... 4. odor 5. fetor, smell, stink
stenographer of Cicero... 4. Tiro
step... 3. pas, way 4. gait, pace, rung
5. dance, grise, phase, riser, stair,
stalk, strut, tread 6. degree, stride
7. advance, imprint, measure,
process 8. distance, footstep
9. footprint, gradation 10. stepladder
step (pert to)...
arrangement of troops.. 7. echelon
clumsy.. 5. stamp
dance.. 3. pas 6. chassé
mincingly.. 6. sashay
mother.. 7. noverca
stately.. 5. stalk
up.. 8. approach 9. intensify
10. accelerate
steppe... 5. plain 9. grassland
steps (outdoor flight)... 6. perron
stereotyped... 5. banal, corny, trite
6. common, old hat 9. hackneyed
11. cut and dried
sterile... 4. arid 6. barren 7. useless
8. impotent 9. fruitless 10. unfruitful
11. ineffective, ineffectual
12. unproductive
stern... 4. dour, grim, hard, rear, rump
5. harsh 6. gloomy, severe, strict,
sullen, unkind 7. austere 8. buttocks,
hind part, rigorous 9. harshness,
unfeeling 10. strictness, unyielding
11. hardhearted 14. uncompromising

sternutation... 8. sneezing
sternutative... 7. errhine
stertorous... 7. snoring 15. hoarse
breathing
stevedore... 5. lader 6. loader, stower
7. carrier 8. unloader
12. longshoreman
stew... 3. pot 4. boil, cook, food, fret,
fume, mess, olio, olla 5. anger,
imbue, steep, worry 6. bustle,
ragout, seethe, simmer 7. haricot,
swelter 8. meat dish 9. Brunswick
10. excitement, hodgepodge
11. predicament
steward... 5. agent, reeve 6. seaman,
waiter 7. dapifer, erenach, foreman,
granger, manager, servant
8. manciple 9. custodian,
major–domo, seneschal, treasurer
10. magistrate 11. chamberlain,
fiscal agent
Stewart, Stuart sovereigns (last)...
4. Anne 5. Henry
stewed fruit... 7. compote
stick... 3. bar, bat, bow, gad, gum,
rod 4. cane, dolt, glue, mast, pogo,
ship, stab, wand, wood 5. baton,
cling, fagot, paste, shaft, staff, stall,
stave, stilt 6. adhere, baffle, ballow,
cleave, cohere, mallet, pierce, puzzle,
thrust 7. defraud 8. chatwood,
revolver, transfix 9. drumstick,
persevere 10. matchstick, overcharge
13. stick–in–the–mud
stick (pert to)...
bamboo.. 6. lathee (lathi)
bundle.. 5. fagot 6. fasces
crooked.. 5. caman 7. cammock,
gambrel
insects.. 5. Emesa
mountain climbing.. 10. alpenstock
sticker... 4. burr 5. label, poser, thorn
6. poster, puzzle, weapon 7. bramble
8. adherent
sticky... 3. goo 5. gluey, humid,
moist, woody 6. clammy, slushy,
viscid 7. viscous 8. adhesive
9. difficult, glutinous, tenacious
10. saccharine
stiff... 4. dead, hard, hobo, limp, taut
5. harsh, horse, idler, rigid, stark,
tense 6. corpse, formal, proper,
severe, strict 7. awkward, cadaver,
starchy 8. resolute, rigorous, starched
9. dead–drunk, obstinate, unbending
14. uncompromising
stiff–necked... 8. stubborn
9. ankylotic, obstinate
11. strait–laced 12. contumacious
stiffness... 8. rigidity 9. formality,
toughness 10. strictness
11. starchiness
stifle... 3. gag 4. stop 5. choke
6. deaden, muffle, quench
7. repress, smother 8. strangle,
throttle 9. suffocate 10. extinguish
stigma... 4. blot, mark, scar, slur
5. brand, odium, stain, stamp, taint
6. defect 7. blemish 8. disgrace,
reproach
stigmatism... 7. blemish 10. refraction
(eye)

stigmatize ... **5.** brand **6.** defame
8. denounce
still ... **3.** but, mum, yet **4.** calm,
even, lull, moot **5.** allay, check, inert,
quiet **6.** always, hushed, pacify,
silent, soothe, subdue **7.** silence,
subdued **8.** inactive, restrain,
suppress, tranquil, until now
9. quiescent **10.** distillery,
motionless, photograph
11. continually **12.** nevertheless
15. notwithstanding
still water ... **4.** pond, pool **6.** lagoon
stilt ... **6.** crutch **7.** yeguita
(black–necked)
stilted ... **6.** formal **7.** pompous
8. elevated, inflated, on stilts
9. bombastic, inelegant
stimulant ... **3.** tea **5.** salts, tonic
6. bracer, coffee **7.** alcohol
8. caffeine, stimulus **9.** digitalis,
sassafras **10.** adrenaline, strychnine
11. epinephrine
stimulate ... **3.** jog, pep **4.** goad, stir,
urge, whet **5.** elate, impel, rouse,
sting **6.** excite, fillip (filip), incite,
spur on **7.** animate, enliven, quicken,
refresh **8.** energize, motivate
9. encourage, instigate, sensitize
10. exhilarate, invigorate
stimulating ... **4.** cool **7.** piquant
8. exciting **10.** energizing, refreshing
stimulus ... **4.** spur **5.** sting **6.** motive
7. impetus **9.** incentive, stimulant
sting ... **4.** bite, pain **5.** smart
6. offend, tingle **8.** irritate
sting of conscience ... **5.** pangs, voice
6. qualms, twinge **11.** compunction
sting organ ... **10.** nematocyst
stingy ... **4.** dree, mean, near **5.** close
6. scanty **7.** miserly, selfish
8. covetous **9.** niggardly
10. avaricious **11.** closefisted
12. parsimonious
stinkbird ... **7.** hoatzin
stint ... **4.** duty, task **5.** limit **6.** scrimp
7. confine **8.** be frugal, restrict
9. be sparing
stipend ... **3.** ann, fee, pay **5.** annat,
wages **6.** salary **7.** annates, pension,
subsidy **9.** allowance
12. compensation, remuneration
stipulate ... **5.** agree **6.** demand
7. bargain, specify **8.** contract,
indicate **9.** designate, guarantee,
postulate
stipulation ... **4.** bond **6.** clause,
demand, detail **7.** compact, proviso
8. contract, covenant **9.** agreement,
condition **11.** arrangement
13. specification
stir ... **3.** ado, mix **4.** fuss, jail, move,
poke, roil, to–do **5.** budge, churn,
rally, rouse, shake, stoke, waken
6. arouse, awaken, bestir, bustle,
excite, flurry, hubbub, pother, prison,
rustle, tumult **7.** agitate, animate,
disturb, inflame, provoke **8.** activity,
movement **9.** commotion
12. penitentiary
stir (pert to) ...
  colors (calico) .. **4.** teer

fire .. **5.** stoke
together .. **3.** mix **6.** stodge
up .. **3.** mix **4.** rile, roil **5.** anger,
awake, rouse **6.** arouse, foment,
incite
stirring ... **6.** moving **7.** rousing
8. bustling, eventful, exciting
9. animating, inspiring
11. stimulating
stirrup ... **4.** ring **5.** strap **6.** saddle
(part), stapes **7.** support **8.** footrest,
tapadera
stitch ... **3.** bit, hem, sew **4.** mend,
pain **5.** baste, piece, ridge **6.** suture,
tailor **8.** particle **9.** embroider
stitch (type) ... **3.** hem **5.** chain, coral,
cross **6.** carpet, damask, suture
7. glover's **11.** needlepoint,
over–and–over
stitchbird ... **3.** ihi **10.** honey eater
stithy ... **5.** anvil, forge **6.** smithy
8. smithery
stoa ... **7.** portico **9.** colonnade
stoat ... **6.** ermine, weasel
stob ... **4.** post, stab, stub **5.** stake
6. gibbet, pierce
stoccado, stoccata ... **4.** stab **6.** thrust
(rapier)
stock ... **4.** fund, line, race, stem
5. breed, broth, hoard, store, trunk
6. assets, cravat, pillar, strain, supply
7. capital, lineage, provide, rhizome
8. credence, original **9.** livestock,
provision, replenish **10.** progenitor
stock (pert to) ...
  book .. **6.** ledger
  breeding .. **5.** brood
  certificate .. **5.** scrip **8.** document
  flower .. **11.** gillyflower
  hawk .. **15.** peregrine falcon
  in trade .. **6.** assets, supply
    11. merchandise
  market .. **6.** Bourse **8.** Exchange
    10. Wall Street
  of goods .. **4.** line
  owl .. **8.** eagle owl
  pile .. **7.** reserve **12.** accumulation
  theater .. **5.** plays
stockade ... **3.** pen **5.** étape, pound
6. corral, kennel, laager **7.** barrier,
bulwark, parapet, rampart, redoubt
8. palisade **9.** barricade, earthwork,
enclosure
stocking ... **4.** hose, sock **6.** anklet,
argyle **7.** bandage, fortune, hosiery
8. seamless **9.** livestock
12. bluestocking **15.** Leatherstocking
(Natty Bumppo)
stocks ... **7.** pillory, shackle
10. securities
stoic, stoical ... **7.** passive, Spartan
8. enduring **9.** impassive
11. unflinching
Stoic School founder ... **4.** Zeno
stoker ... **5.** firer **6.** seaman, teaser
7. fireman, greaser **8.** trainman
stolen (pert to) ...
  goods receiver .. **5.** fence **7.** smasher,
swagman
  property .. **4.** pelf **5.** booty, spoil
stolid ... **4.** dull, slow **5.** beefy
6. stupid **7.** adamant, passive

9. impassive, inanimate
11. inexcitable, unexcitable
stoma... 4. pore 5. mouth 7. opening, orifice
stomach... 3. gut, maw 4. craw, crop, vell 5. belly, rumen, taste 6. desire, endure, gaster, paunch 7. abdomen, gizzard 8. tolerate 10. resentment
stomach (pert to)...
  ache.. 5. colic, cramp 7. gullion
    8. rumbling 11. borborygmus
  acidity.. 4. acor
  animal.. 3. maw
  bird.. 4. craw, crop
  comb form.. 6. gaster 7. gastero
  ref to.. 7. gastric, pyloric
  ruminant.. 5. rumen 6. omasum
    8. abomasum, roddikin 9. manyplies, reticulum 10. psalterium
stone... 3. gem, pit 4. kill, pelt, rock, seed 5. agate, block, geode, jewel, lapis, shale, slate, spall 6. attack, pebble 7. diamond, peridot, sharpen 8. monument, pavement 9. hailstone, sculpture, whetstone 10. gravestone, grindstone 12. philosopher's
stone (pert to)...
  abrasive.. 5. emery
  Age.. 8. Eolithic 9. Neolithic
    11. Paleolithic
  alchemy.. 6. carmot 12. philosopher's
  arch (top stone).. 8. keystone
  Bib.. 4. ezel
  broke.. 4. flat 8. strapped
  broken.. 6. rubble
  carved.. 5. cameo 8. intaglio
  chisel.. 4. celt
  cutters' disease.. 9. silicosis
    10. chalicosis
  famed.. 4. Hope, Pitt 5. Mogul, Sancy 6. Jonker, Orloff, Regent 7. Blarney, Rosetta 8. Cullinan, Kohinoor (Kohinur) 9. Excelsior 10. Great Mogul 12. Plymouth Rock, Star of Africa
  flat.. 4. flag, slab 5. slate
  fruit.. 3. pip 4. paip, seed 5. cling 7. putamen 8. endocarp
  gem.. 4. jade, opal, ruby, sard 5. agate, pearl, topaz 6. garnet, ligure, spinel 7. diamond, emerald, peridot 8. amethyst, sapphire 9. turquoise 11. alexandrite
  gem cutting.. 6. adamas
  hammer.. 5. kevel
  hard.. 7. adamant 9. chatoyant (cat's-eye)
  heap.. 5. cairn
  instrument.. 8. lapideon
  masonry.. 6. ashlar
  medical.. 4. gall 5. renal 7. biliary, otolith 8. calculus
  oil.. 4. hone
  ornamental.. 9. scagliola
  pert to:. 7. lithoid
  pillar.. 8. monolith
  pyramid.. 6. benben
  quarry.. 6. latomy
  small.. 6. pebble 8. lapillus
  special.. 3. key, lap, oil, rub 4. curb, flag, head, lime, lode, mile, tomb, whet 5. birth, flint, grave, grind

6. cobble, corner 8. stepping
  statue (part wood).. 8. acrolith
  to dress.. 3. nig
  uncut.. 4. naif
  woman turned to stone by Zeus..
    5. Niobe
stonecutter (pert to)...
  disease of.. 9. silicosis 10. chalicosis
  receptacle.. 7. sebilla
  tool.. 6. eolith
  type.. 6. jadder 7. jeweler 8. lapidary
  worker.. 5. mason
stonecutting art... 10. stereotomy
stoning, death by... 10. lapidation
stony... 4. cold, hard 5. rigid, rocky 6. rugged 7. adamant 8. lapidose, obdurate, pitiless 9. petrified 10. inflexible, relentless, unyielding 15. uncompassionate
stooge... 4. foil 5. toady 6. flunky 7. cat's-paw 8. henchman
stool... 4. seat 5. bench 6. pigeon, tripod 7. taboret 8. informer
stop... 2. ho 3. bar, dam, end 4. balk, foil, halt, kill, quit, stay, stem, whoa 5. avast, block, cease, check, choke, close, delay 6. arrest, desist, detain 7. impasse, prevent, silence 8. preclude, swear off 10. standstill 11. discontinue, obstruction, punctuation 12. lower the boom
stop (pert to)...
  close.. 8. obturate
  debate.. 7. cloture
  fermentation.. 4. stum
  gap.. 7. stopper 9. expedient, makeshift
  momentarily.. 5. pause
  nautical.. 5. avast
  organ.. 5. viola 7. gemsbok 8. dulsiana
  seams (boat).. 4. calk
  short.. 5. pause 7. respite 8. interval 12. intermission
  unintentional.. 5. stall
  watch.. 5. timer
  with clay.. 3. pug
stopper... 4. bung, cork, plug 5. spile 7. bouchon
storage (pert to)...
  bin.. 3. mow 4. loft, shed, silo 7. granary 8. elevator
  fodder (in silo).. 6. ensile
  hidden.. 5. cache
  place.. 3. bin 4. barn 5. attic, depot, étape 6. cellar, closet 7. arsenal, granary 8. cupboard, elevator, magazine 10. promptuary, repository
stork... 4. ibis 6. jabiru 7. Maguari, marabou 8. adjutant
storklike... 8. pelargic
storm... 4. blow, fume, fury, rage, rain, rave, snow, wind 5. orage 6. attack, shower, simoom (simoon), tumult 7. bluster, disturb, tempest, trouble 8. calamity, eruption, outbreak, upheaval, violence 9. agitation 11. disturbance
storm (pert to)...
  cold.. 11. northeaster
  evil storm god.. 2. Zu 9. blackbird

(symb), Hlorrithi
extreme.. 4. gale 7. cyclone,
monsoon, tempest, tornado
9. hurricane
occidental.. 6. wester
recorder (thunder).. 11. brontometer
sand.. 6. tebbad
snow.. 6. buran
stormy... 5. rainy 7. furious, riotous,
violent 8. agitated 9. inclement,
turbulent 10. tumultuous
11. tempestuous
story... 3. fib, lie 4. hoax, joke, lore,
saga, tale, tier, yarn 5. fable, floor
6. gossip, legend, serial 7. mystery,
narrate, parable, romance
8. anecdote 9. chronicle, falsehood,
tradition
story (pert to)...
absurd.. 4. hoax, yarn 6. canard
doleful.. 8. jeremiad
exclusive.. 4. beat, news 5. scoop
part.. 6. serial
short.. 5. conte 6. novella
storyteller... 4. liar 5. Aesop 6. fibber
7. relater 9. raconteur
stot... 2. ox 4. bull 5. steer
6. bounce 7. paunchy, stammer,
stumble, stutter
stout... 3. fat 4. bold 5. brave, bulky,
burly, hardy, obese, plump 6. fleshy,
rotund, stocky, strong 7. haughty,
violent 8. forcible, powerful, resolute,
thickset 9. corpulent, undaunted
10. courageous, persistent
stoutness... 7. courage 8. strength
10. corpulence, embonpoint
stove... 4. etna, kiln, oven 5. grate,
plate, range 6. heater 7. Coleman,
furnace, smelter
stove part... 4. oven, pipe 6. burner
7. firebox, griddle
stow... 4. cram, hide, mass, pack
5. crowd, lodge, store, stuff
6. steeve 7. arrange, secrete
straddle... 5. salvo 6. option
7. astride 8. bestride 9. be neutral,
go halfway
straggle... 4. rove 6. wander
7. deviate, meander
straight... 5. cards, erect, exact, rigid,
stern 6. candid, direct, honest
7. correct, exactly, unmixed
8. directly, reliable, sequence,
unbroken, vertical 9. authentic
10. horizontal, racing term
11. straightway, undeviating
13. uninterrupted 15. straightforward
straight (pert to)...
baseball.. 5. liner
course.. 7. beeline
edge.. 5. ruler
line.. 6. secant 8. enfilade
9. asymptote
Math.. 8. vinculum
out.. 6. candid 9. downright
11. unqualified 13. thoroughgoing
14. uncompromising
shooter.. 11. on the square
way.. 4. anon 8. directly 9. forthwith
11. immediately
straighten... 5. align, aline, level,

order, plumb 6. tidy up 7. rectify,
unravel 11. disentangle
straightforward... 5. frank 6. candid,
direct, honest 7. sincere 8. outright
9. outspoken 10. forthright
11. undeviating
straightway... 4. anon 8. directly
9. downright, forthwith 10. forthright
11. immediately
strain... 3. sye, tax, try, tug 4. bend,
dash, kind, mood, ooze, race, sort,
tone, vein 5. breed, shade, stock,
tense, touch 6. filter, melody,
overdo, poetry, refine, sprain, streak,
stress, strive 7. descent, fatigue,
lineage, progeny, stretch, tension,
variety 8. ancestry, endeavor, exertion
9. constrain, overheave, percolate
10. generation
strained... 4. taut 5. tense 6. forced
7. intense, labored 8. wrenched
9. stretched 10. farfetched
strainer... 4. sile 5. sieve, tamis
6. filter, screen, sifter 8. colander,
filterer 17. Hippocrates' sleeve
strait... 3. gut 4. neck, need 5. inlet
6. angust, narrow, strict 7. channel,
limited 8. rigorous 9. difficult
10. restricted, scrupulous
11. distressful, predicament
Strait... 6. Bering 7. Surigao
8. Bosporus 9. Belleisle
Strait of Gibraltar... 17. Pillars of
Hercules
Straits Settlements...
capital, Penang.. 10. Georgetown
capital, Singapore.. 9. Singapore
city.. 7. Malacca
peninsula.. 5. Malay
port.. 4. Prai
strand... 3. sea 4. bank, quay
5. beach, shore 6. maroon, thread
7. channel, current 8. filament
strange... 3. coy, new, odd, shy
4. rare, xeno (comb form) 5. alien,
eerie, novel, queer, timid 6. exotic,
quaint 7. curious, erratic, unknown,
unusual 8. peculiar, singular,
uncommon 9. eccentric, unrelated
10. extraneous, outlandish,
tramontane, unfamiliar
12. unaccustomed, unacquainted
13. extraordinary, preternatural
stranger... 3. ger 5. alien, guest
7. visitor 8. intruder 9. foreigner,
outlander
strangle... 5. choke 6. stifle
7. execute, garrote, repress, squeeze
8. suppress, throttle 9. suffocate
strap... 3. tie 4. belt, bind, hang,
jess, rein, riem, whip 5. leash, strop,
thong 6. enarme, latigo, oxreim
7. lanyard (laniard) 8. chastise
strap–shaped... 6. lorate 8. ligulate
strass... 5. glass, paste 10. silk refuse
strata... 6. layers 7. classes
10. formations
stratagem... 4. coup, ruse, trap, wile
5. trick 6. device 7. finesse
8. artifice
strategy... 7. tactics 8. artifice,
intrigue, maneuver

stratum... 3. bed 4. coat 5. layer
straw... 4. stem 5. mulch 6. fodder,
  sennit, trifle 7. remains, sabutan
straw (pert to)...
  bid.. 5. fraud 7. auction 9. worthless
  coat (Jap peasant).. 4. mino
  color.. 6. flaxen
  flower.. 11. everlasting
  hat.. 4. baku 5. milan 6. panama
  like.. 6. chaffy 11. stramineous
  vote.. 5. Roper 6. Gallup
stray... 3. err, gad, sin 4. cavy, roam,
  rove, waif 5. range 6. swerve,
  wander 7. deviate, digress
  8. aberrant, aberrate, go astray
  9. wandering 10. occasional
streak... 3. roe 4. line, seam, vein
  5. fleck, layer, stria 6. groove, strain,
  strake, stripe
streaked... 4. liny 6. banded
  7. brindle, striped 8. brindled,
  striated
stream... 3. run 4. burn, flow, rill, sike
  (syke) 5. brook, creek, river
  6. abound, course, rillet, runlet,
  runnel, throng 7. current, rivulet,
  torrent 9. streamlet 11. watercourse
stream (pert to)...
  dry.. 6. arroyo, spruit
  gold.. 6. placer
  of consciousness.. 8. thoughts
  10. psychology 11. abstraction
  of forgetfulness.. 5. Lethe
  underground.. 3. aar
street... 4. road 5. calle 6. avenue
  7. highway, roadway 8. chaussée
  9. boulevard 12. thoroughfare
street (pert to)...
  car.. 4. tram
  famed.. 4. Beal, Main, Wall 5. Canal
  6. Beacon 7. Downing 8. Broadway
  9. Peachtree 12. Threadneedle
  French.. 3. rue
  narrow.. 4. lane 5. alley
  show.. 4. peep 5. raree
  Spanish.. 5. calle
  urchin.. 4. Arab 5. gamin 7. outcast
  8. vagabond 11. guttersnipe
Street called Straight (Bib)...
  8. Damascus
strength... 3. vis 4. iron, thew
  5. brawn, force, might, nerve, power,
  rally, sinew, titer, vigor 6. energy,
  health 7. potency, stamina, sthenia,
  support 8. firmness 9. endurance,
  lustiness, stoutness, toughness,
  vehemence, willpower 10. robustness,
  stronghold
strengthen... 4. grow, prop 5. brace,
  nerve 6. deepen 7. confirm, fortify,
  nourish, toughen 8. increase,
  roborate 9. encourage, intensify,
  reinforce 10. invigorate
  11. consolidate
strengthening... 7. bracing 8. roborant
  12. invigorating, invigoration
strenuous... 6. ardent, severe
  7. zealous 8. vigorous 9. difficult,
  energetic, laborious 11. industrious
strepent... 4. loud 5. noisy
streperous... 4. loud 5. harsh
  7. noisily 9. turbulent 10. boisterous

strepor... 5. noise
stress... 5. arsis, ictus, labor
  6. accent, insist, strain, weight
  7. urgency 8. emphasis, exigency,
  pressure 9. emphasize 10. elasticity,
  exaggerate 12. exaggeration
stretcher... 3. bar, lie 6. litter, racker
  9. falsehood
stretch out... 6. be long, extend
  9. expatiate
strew... 3. ted 6. spread 7. diffuse,
  overlay, scatter 8. disperse
  10. distribute 11. disseminate
strewn... 4. semé 8. littered
  9. scattered 12. disseminated
stria... 4. line 5. ridge, strip 6. fillet,
  furrow, groove, hollow, streak, stripe
  7. channel 9. striation
stricken... 7. smitten, worn out,
  wounded 8. unnerved
  13. incapacitated
strickle... 5. rifle 7. pattern
  8. template 10. sweepboard
  13. striking board
strict... 4. hard 5. exact, harsh, rigid,
  stern 6. severe 7. ascetic, austere,
  precise 8. accurate, rigorous
  9. puritanic, stringent 10. forbidding,
  inexorable, inflexible, meticulous,
  relentless, scrupulous
  11. strait–laced, undeviating
  13. conscientious
  14. uncompromising
strict disciplinarian... 8. martinet
strict discipline... 13. regimentation
stricture... 7. binding, censure
  9. criticism, narrowing
  11. contraction 12. constriction
stride... 4. gait, pace, step, walk
  8. bestride, progress, straddle,
  velocity
strident... 6. shrill 7. grating, raucous
  11. cacophonous
strife... 3. war 4. feud 5. fight
  6. battle, combat, stasis 7. contest,
  quarrel 8. conflict, exertion, struggle
  9. logomachy 11. altercation
strike... 3. hit, pat, rap 4. bump,
  bunt, slap, swat 5. clout, labor,
  smite, whack 6. attack, revolt
  7. impinge 9. discovery
strike (pert to)...
  a balance.. 5. weigh 7. average
  8. equalize 10. compromise
  against.. 7. collide 8. illision
  and rebound.. 5. carom (carrom)
  9. carambole
  breaker.. 4. fink, scab
  dumb.. 4. stun
  heavily.. 3. lam, ram 4. bash, slam,
  slog, sock, wham 5. punch, smite
  obliquely.. 5. carom 6. glance
  out.. 3. fan 4. dele 5. elide, erase
  6. cancel, delete 9. eliminate
  to and fro.. 6. bandy
  with beak.. 4. peck
  with fist.. 5. pound, punch
  with head.. 4. butt
  with weapon.. 5. crunt
  with wonder.. 3. awe 7. astound
striking... 7. salient 8. dramatic,
  eloquent, exciting 9. arresting,

wonderful 10. noticeable, remarkable, surprising
striking effect... 5. éclat
striking part... 7. clapper
string... 3. ran, set 4. bind, cord 5. lacet, snare, twine 6. fasten, series, thread 10. succession
string (pert to)...
alphabet.. 5. knots (for blind)
of beads.. 6. rosary 8. necklace
of horses.. 6. stable
out.. 6. line up 8. lengthen 9. expatiate
pottery.. 13. Schnurkeramik (neolithic)
stringed instrument... 4. harp, lute, lyre 5. banjo, piano, recta, viola 6. fiddle, guitar, violin, zither 7. bandore, mandore, ukulele 8. mandolin, psaltery 9. mandolute 11. harpsichord
stringed instrument bridge... 5. magas
stringent... 4. ropy 5. rigid, tight 6. cogent, severe, strict 10. convincing 11. acrimonious, restrictive
stringy... 4. ropy 5. gluey, tough 6. sinewy, viscid 7. fibrous 10. threadlike 11. filamentous
strip... 4. bare, belt, live, pare, peel, skin, slat 5. cleat, shred, unrig 6. denude, divest, remove, strake 7. deprive, plunder, pull off, uncloak, uncover, undress 9. dismantle 10. dispossess, impoverish 11. decorticate
strip (pert to)...
blubber.. 6. flense
curved.. 5. stave
lead (stained glass).. 4. came
leather.. 4. welt 5. thong 6. latido 7. belting
narrow.. 4. lath, slat, tape, welt 5. reeve, stave, strap
off skin.. 4. flay
of possessions.. 4. milk 5. bleed, bunko (bunco), shear 6. fleece 7. despoil, swindle 10. dispossess
raised.. 5. ridge
tease dancer.. 8. stripper 9. ecdysiast
wood.. 5. stave 6. reglet, spline
stripe... 3. bar, pin 4. band, beat, line, mark, sort, type, wale, weal, welt, whip 5. chalk, strip, vitta 6. streak 7. chevron 8. insignia 9. striation
striped (pert to)...
alder.. 11. winterberry
antelope.. 5. bongo
gillyflower.. 9. carnation
longitudinally.. 7. vittate
stripling... 3. boy, lad 5. youth 8. juvenile 9. youngster
strive... 3. aim, try, tug 4. toil 5. labor 6. battle, buffet, strain 7. compete, contend, emulate 8. endeavor, struggle
strive (pert to)...
for.. 3. aim 4. seek
to equal.. 5. rival 6. strain 7. emulate
to overtake.. 5. ensue

with.. 3. vie 7. compete
strobile... 4. cone 8. pine cone
strockle... 6. shovel
stroke... 3. fit, pat, pet, rub 4. beat, blow, coup, flip, line, putt, shot 5. ictus, serif, spasm, trait, whisk 6. caress, fondle 7. illness, solidus
stroll... 4. roam, walk 5. range, stray 6. go slow, ramble, wander 7. meander, saunter 8. ambulate 9. promenade 11. perambulate
stroller... 5. actor, tramp 6. beggar 7. peddler, vagrant 8. wanderer 9. saunterer 12. perambulator
strolling... 7. nomadic 8. rambling 10. meandering 13. perambulation
strong... 3. fit, hot 4. able, firm, hale, hard, wiry 5. fetid, hardy, lusty, solid, sound, stout, tough 6. potent, robust, sinewy, stable, sturdy, virile 7. healthy, intense, odorous, tainted 8. accented, forceful, forcible, muscular, resonant, stalwart, vigorous 9. effective, energetic 10. outrageous, persuasive, pronounced, remarkable 11. substantial 12. concentrated
strong (pert to)...
drink.. 6. liquor 7. spirits 9. distilled
flavor.. 4. racy 5. acrid 7. pungent
hold.. 4. fort 7. citadel 8. fastness, Fort Knox, fortress, muniment, treasury
man.. 5. Atlas 6. Samson (Sampson)
muscles.. 5. brawn, thewy
music.. 4. loud 5. forte 7. saccade
willed.. 8. resolute 9. obstinate 10. determined
wind.. 7. pampero
stroygood... 7. wastrel 11. spendthrift
strubbly... 6. untidy 7. unkempt
struck... 4. smit 5. smote 7. smitten, swatted 8. shutdown (see also *strike*)
struck (pert to)...
an attitude.. 5. posed
out.. 5. deled 6. elided, erased, fanned 7. deleted
with fear.. 6. aghast 7. alarmed
with missiles.. 6. pelted
structure... 3. dam 4. dais, form, pier 5. frame, house, jetty, kiosk, stage, tower 6. bridge, make–up, pagoda 7. edifice 8. building, platform 9. formation 10. tabernacle 11. composition 12. constitution, construction
structure (pert to)...
calcareous.. 5. coral
conical.. 7. pyramid
crownlike.. 6. corona
filamentous.. 4. hair
human.. 8. physique
monumental.. 5. pylon
roof.. 6. cupola, dormer
tall.. 5. tower 7. steeple 9. campanile
tentlike.. 10. tabernacle
struggle... 3. tug, vie 4. cope, wade 5. labor 6. effort, Peniel (Bib), strife, strike, strive, tussle 7. contend, contest, scuffle, wrestle 8. endeavor, flounder, scramble 10. contention, difficulty

strumpet ... 5. belie 6. harlot
8. harridan 10. prostitute
stub ... 3. end 4. dock, tail 5. squat,
stump 6. coupon, stocky 7. remnant
8. thickset 11. counterfoil
stubble ... 5. beard, stump 6. arrish
7. bristle 8. eelgrass
stubborn ... 3. set 4. rude 5. fixed,
hardy, rough, tough 6. coarse, mulish,
sturdy 7. restive 8. perverse,
resolute, starkish, vigorous
9. obstinate, pigheaded
10. determined, headstrong, inflexible,
refractory, unyielding 11. intractable
12. recalcitrant
stuck ... 4. fast 7. baffled, cohered
8. coherent, stranded (see also *stick*)
stuck-up ... 4. vain 8. arrogant
9. conceited 10. egocentric
12. supercilious 13. self–important
stud ... 3. dot, pin 4. boss, knob
5. haras 6. enstar 7. hobnail
8. ornament, stallion 9. studhorse
student ... 4. co–ed 5. cadet, eleve,
plebe, pupil 6. tosher 7. learner,
scholar 8. disciple 9. collegian
student of ...
behavior (human) .. 12. psychologist
birds .. 13. ornithologist
birds' eggs .. 8. oologist
Eton .. 7. Etonian
law .. 8. stagiary
medical .. 6. intern (interne)
military .. 5. cadet, plebe
natural history .. 10. naturalist
navy .. 5. cadet 10. midshipman
Oxford .. 8. commoner
proverbs .. 14. paroemiologist
punishment .. 10. penologist
reptiles .. 13. herpetologist
spiders .. 13. arachnologist
students, advanced group ...
7. seminar 13. upperclassmen
studied ... 5. boned, pored 6. formal
7. learned, planned, weighed
8. designed, measured, reasoned
10. well–versed 11. intentional
12. premeditated
studio ... 4. shop 7. atelier, bottega
8. workshop 11. working room
study ... 3. con, den 4. bone, muse,
pore, scan 5. étude, grind, learn,
weigh 7. discuss 6. peruse, ponder
7. analyze, examine, pegging,
reverie, science, subject, thought
8. endeavor, learning, treatise
10. discussion, inspection
11. contemplate 13. contemplation
study of ...
animals .. 7. zoology 9. zoography
bees .. 8. apiology
birds'eggs .. 6. oology
disease .. 8. nosology
fingerprints .. 13. dactylography
handwriting .. 10. graphology
insects .. 10. entomology
man .. 12. anthropology
mountains .. 9. orology
old age .. 9. nostology 10. geriatrics
11. gerontology
population .. 10. demography,
larithmics 12. demographics

punishment .. 8. penology
sacred images .. 9. iconology
temples .. 7. naology
words .. 9. etymology
12. lexicography
stuff ... 3. goo, pad, ram, wad
4. cram, fill, stow 5. gorge, trash
6. fabric, matter, potion 7. content,
element, rubbish, satiate 8. marinate,
material, nonsense, overfill, trumpery
9. principle, substance 10. gluttonize
stuffiness ... 7. prudery 8. dullness
9. obstinacy 10. sullenness, sultriness
11. pompousness
stuffing ... 6. lining 7. padding
8. contents, dressing 9. forcemeat
stuffy ... 3. fat 4. dull, prim 5. close,
stout 6. stodgy, sullen, sultry
7. airless, pompous, prudish
8. resolute 9. bombastic, obstinate
10. old–fogyish 11. strait–laced
12. conservative 13. ill–ventilated
stulm ... 4. adit 7. passage
8. entrance
stumble ... 3. err 4. fall, trip 5. lurch
6. boggle, bungle, chance, falter,
happen 7. blunder, perplex, stagger,
stammer 8. confound, flounder
stump ... 4. butt, dare, skeg, snag,
stab, stub 5. clump, scrab 6. baffle,
trudge 7. declaim, nonplus
8. platform 9. challenge, remainder,
tortillon 11. electioneer
stun ... 4. bowl, daze 5. amaze, daunt
6. benumb, bruise, deaden
7. astound, stupefy, terrify
8. astonish, bewilder 9. overpower,
overwhelm
stunning ... 8. striking 9. beautiful
10. astounding, stupefying, terrifying
stunt ... 4. feat 5. blunt, check, cramp,
crowl, dwarf, whale (2–yr) 6. hinder
7. curtail, exploit, shorten
10. tomfoolery
stunted ... 7. blunted, checked,
dwarfed 9. curtailed, shortened
stupa ... 4. tomb 5. mound, tower
6. shrine 8. monument
stupefied ... 5. doped 6. aghast,
sotted 7. drugged, shocked, stunned
8. benumbed 9. petrified
stupefy ... 4. daze, dope, drug, numb,
pall, stun 5. besot, blunt, shock
6. bedaze, bemuse, muddle
7. astound, confuse, petrify, terrify
8. bewilder, confound 10. incrassate,
make stupid 11. flabbergast (sl)
stupid ... 4. clod, dull, dumb 5. blunt,
crass, dense, inane 6. oafish, obtuse,
simple, stolid 7. asinine, doltish,
foolish, witless 8. blockish, Boeotian,
gullible 9. brainless, senseless
11. heavywitted 13. unintelligent
stupid (pert to) ...
grossly .. 7. asinine 9. imbecilic
person .. 3. ass, oaf 4. clod, coot,
dolt, loon, lout, nerd 5. goose, klutz,
stirk 7. tomfool 11. gillygaupus
render .. 8. hebetate
stupidity ... 7. fatuity 8. dullness,
hebetude 11. foolishness
12. indifference 13. foolish remark

stupor . . . 4. coma, daze 5. sleep,
sopor 6. apathy, torpor, trance
8. lethargy, neurosis, numbness
9. lassitude 15. unconsciousness

sturdy . . . 4. firm 5. burly, hardy, lusty,
stout 6. robust, stable, steady, strong
8. resolute, stalwart, stubborn,
vigorous 10. courageous, determined,
unyielding 11. substantial

sturgeon . . . 6. beluga, caviar 7. sterlet
9. Acipenser 10. hackleback

stutter . . . 6. falter 7. stammer

sty . . . 3. pen 4. boil 5. hovel, stair,
steps, stile 6. ladder, pimple
7. pustule 8. swelling 9. enclosure

style . . . 3. air, pen, way 4. form, kind,
mode, name 5. get–up, gusto, trend,
vogue 6. gnomon, graver, phrase,
stylus 7. alamode, diction, fashion
8. elegance 9. execution
10. appearance 12. characterize,
presentation

style (pert to) . . .
architecture . . 5. Doric, Greek, Ionic,
Roman 6. Gothic, Norman 7. Italian
8. Colonial, Georgian 9. Byzantine
10. Corinthian, Romanesque
11. Renaissance
painting . . 5. genre 11. Renaissance
type . . 5. roman, runic 6. italic

styled . . . 5. named 6. called, termed,
y–clept (y–cleped) 7. phrased

stylet . . . 5. probe 6. trocar 7. poniard
8. stiletto 9. specillum

stylish . . . 3. mod 4. chic, cool, neat,
tony 5. nifty, ritzy, sharp, smart,
swank 6. chi–chi, dressy, jaunty,
modish, preppy, snazzy, trendy
7. alamode, voguish 11. fashionable

styptic . . . 4. alum 10. astringent,
tannic acid 12. constringent

Styx (pert to) . . .
ferryman . . 6. Charon

suant . . . 4. even 6. demure, smooth,
steady 7. equable, regular

suave . . . 4. oily, smug 5. bland
6. urbane 7. fulsome 8. unctuous
9. agreeable 12. ingratiating,
mealy–mouthed 13. smooth–talking

suavity . . . 7. amenity 8. civility,
courtesy, urbanity 10. gentleness

subdue . . . 3. cow 4. calm, tame
5. allay, crush, lower, quash, quell,
sober 6. disarm, muffle, reduce,
soften 7. conquer, repress, squelch
8. mitigate, overcome, suppress,
surmount, vanquish 9. overpower,
subjugate 11. subordinate

subdued . . . 4. meek, soft 7. muffled,
quelled 8. disarmed, relieved,
tempered 9. conquered, toned down
10. made gentle, subjugated 11. soft
colored, unperturbed

subject . . . 4. text, word 5. cause,
prone, theme, topic 6. matter, motive,
submit, vassal 7. citizen, servant
8. inferior 9. subjugate, substance
10. predispose 11. subordinate
12. part of speech

subjective . . . 6. mental 7. topical
8. fanciful, illusory 9. of the mind
10. nominative 11. introverted

subject of . . .
discourse . . 5. theme, topic
disease . . 4. case 7. patient
lawsuit . . 3. res 7. grounds
sentence . . 4. noun

subject to . . .
abuse . . 6. revile
analysis . . 7. titrate
argument . . 4. moot
change . . 7. mutable 8. amenable
choice . . 8. elective
control . . 7. rulable
death . . 6. mortal
depression . . 5. moody
dislike . . 8. aversion
mistakes . . 7. erratic
outbursts . . 9. irritable
tension . . 8. strained
vassalage . . 5. feoff

sublimation . . . 9. underling
12. underscoring

sublime . . . 4. high 5. grand, great,
lofty, noble, proud 6. refine
7. exalted, haughty 8. elevated,
eloquent, empyreal, majestic, splendid,
upraised, vaporize 9. beautiful,
expletive 11. magnanimous

Sublime Porte . . . 12. Ottoman Court
17. Turkish government

sublimity . . . 4. acme 5. glory
6. beauty 7. majesty 8. grandeur
9. greatness 10. excellence
11. distinction 12. magnificence

submarine . . . 3. sub 4. boat, ship
8. Nautilus, Scorpion, Thresher
11. submersible

submarine eye . . . 9. periscope

submission . . . 5. kneel 8. fatalism,
meekness, patience, yielding
9. deference, obedience, surrender
10. compliance, confession
11. resignation 13. nonresistance

submissive . . . 4. meek, tame
6. humble 7. dutiful, patient
8. obedient, resigned, uxorious (to
wife), yielding 9. compliant
11. acquiescent, conformable

submit . . . 3. bow 4. obey 5. defer,
remit, stoop, yield 6. soften, temper
7. succumb 8. moderate
9. acquiesce, postulate, surrender
10. condescend

submit to . . . 4. obey 6. endure
11. acknowledge

subordinate . . . 4. exon 5. minor
6. subdue 7. servant, subject
8. inferior, parergon 9. appendage,
assistant, dependent, secondary
10. collateral, incidental, submissive
11. subservient

subsequent . . . 5. later 7. ensuing
9. following, postnatal
10. succeeding 11. consecutive

subservient . . . 6. vassal 7. servile,
subject 9. assistant, truckling
10. obsequious, submissive
11. subordinate 12. instrumental

subside . . . 3. ebb 4. bate, fall, lull,
sink, wane 5. abate 6. settle
7. descend, relapse 8. decrease,

languish 9. gravitate 11. deteriorate
subsidiary ... 8. inferior 9. assistant,
auxiliary, extrinsic, tributary
10. collateral 11. stipendiary
12. nonessential 13. supplementary
subsist ... 2. be 4. live 5. abide, exist
6. endure, remain 7. prevail, survive
8. continue
subsist on prey ... 9. rapacious
substance ... 3. sum 4. gist, meat
5. stuff 6. import, matter, wealth
7. aliment, element, essence,
meaning, purport, summary
8. hardness, material 9. actuality,
affluence, solidness 11. consistency
substance (pert to) ...
  absorbent .. 5. fomes
  aeriform .. 3. gas 5. argon
  amorphous .. 7. ferrite
  antitoxic .. 5. serum
  aromatic .. 5. myrrh, spice 6. balsam
  basic .. 7. element
  bitter .. 5. aloes, aloin, linin
  7. amarine, emetine 8. elaterin
  brittle .. 5. glass
  cleansing, purifying .. 8. depurant
  10. abstergent, clarifiant
  corrosive .. 4. acid 7. caustic
  dissolved .. 6. solute
  dissolving .. 9. resolvent
  electrical .. 3. ion
  elemental .. 5. metal
  expanding .. 8. dilatant
  fatty .. 5. lipin, suint
  ferment .. 9. activator
  flocculent .. 4. wool
  food .. 7. protein
  fruit jellying .. 6. pectin
  gelatinous .. 4. agar
  hard .. 4. bone 5. ivory 7. adamant
  hypnotic .. 4. ural
  inflammable .. 6. tinder 7. bitumen
  inorganic .. 7. mineral
  ipecac root .. 7. emetine
  light .. 4. cork
  milk curdling .. 6. rennet
  moss (Ceylon) .. 4. agar 8. agar–agar
  neutralizing .. 6. alkali
  resinous .. 3. gum, lac 5. copal
  7. shellac
  rubberlike .. 5. gutta
  soapmaking .. 3. lye
  stabilizing .. 7. ballast
  sulphur .. 5. hepar
  tar .. 6. cresol
  unctuous .. 3. fat, oil 7. pinguid
  vegetable .. 5. resin, rosin
  wax, waxy .. 5. cerin 7. suberin
  8. paraffin
  whale (perfume) .. 9. ambergris
  wood ash .. 6. potash
substantial ... 4. firm, real, true
5. pucka (pukka), solid, stout
6. actual, bodily, hearty, stable,
strong, sturdy 7. genuine
8. abundant, tangible 9. corporeal,
essential, important 10. nourishing
12. considerable
substantiate ... 6. embody, verify
7. confirm, justify 8. underpin
9. establish 11. corroborate
substantive ... 4. firm, noun 5. sound

6. actual, entity 7. pronoun
9. essential 11. substantial
13. self–contained
substitute ... 5. proxy, vicar 6. deputy,
ersatz 7. apology, replace
8. exchange, nominate 9. alternate,
surrogate 10. understudy, viceregent
11. replacement
subterfuge ... 4. ruse 5. blind, trick
6. refuge 7. evasion, pretext
8. artifice, pretense 9. expedient
13. prevarication
subterranean ... 6. hidden, secret
8. hypogeal, plutonic 10. in the
earth 11. underground
subtile ... 3. sly 4. rare, wily 6. crafty,
subtle 7. cunning, elusive
9. beguiling
subtle ... 3. sly 4. fine, nice, rare, thin
6. artful, clever, crafty, shrewd
7. cunning, refined, subtile
8. analytic, delicate 9. beguiling,
designing, ingenious 10. mysterious
14. discriminating
subtle (pert to) ...
  emanation (invisible) .. 4. aura
  10. atmosphere
  sarcasm .. 5. irony
  variation .. 6. nuance
subtlety ... 5. guile 7. cunning, finesse,
slyness 8. delicacy, fineness
9. quodlibet 10. shrewdness
subtraction, terms ... 7. minuend
9. deduction 10. difference,
subtrahend
subversion ... 4. ruin (utter)
9. overthrow 10. corruption,
revolution 11. destruction
subvert ... 4. ruin 5. evert, upset
6. refute, uproot 7. corrupt, destroy,
pervert 8. alienate, overturn
9. overthrow, undermine
subvertive ... 8. eversive
subway ... 4. tube 5. train 6. tunnel
11. underground 18. underground
railway
succade ... 8. preserve 10. confection
succeed ... 5. ensue, occur 6. attain,
follow, thrive 7. achieve, devolve,
prosper, replace, triumph 8. come
next, flourish, supplant
10. accomplish
succeeding ... 4. next 7. ensuing,
sequent 9. following 10. subsequent,
successful 11. in the wake of
success ... 2. go 3. hit 4. luck
5. elate 7. fortune, outcome
8. accolade, smash hit 10. prosperity
11. consequence
successful ... 5. lucky 8. thriving
9. fortunate 10. prosperous,
succeeding, triumphant
11. flourishing
succession ... 3. row, run 5. music
(rhythmic) 6. series 7. dynasty,
lineage 8. sequence 9. posterity
succin ... 5. amber
succinct ... 4. curt 5. brief, hasty,
short, terse 7. compact, concise,
laconic, summary 10. compressed
11. compendious, sententious
succor, succour ... 3. aid 4. abet, help

　　6. brandy (Alpine), relief, rescue
　　7. comfort, deliver, relieve, sustain
　　8. befriend, mitigate 10. assistance
succulent... 3. uva 4. lush 5. juicy,
　　pappy, tasty 6. cactus, tender
succumb... 3. die 5. faint, yield
　　6. perish, submit 7. give way 8. get
　　tired
such (as)... 3. sic 4. like 7. certain,
　　similar 8. analogue 9. analogous
suction (as in clicks of Bantu)...
　　9. implosive
Sudan, Africa...
　　capital.. 8. Khartoum
　　desert.. 6. Libyan, Nubian
　　export.. 9. gum arabic
　　gazelle.. 4. dama
　　gum forests.. 8. Kordofan
　　lake.. 4. Chad
　　language.. 2. Ga 6. Arabic
　　people.. 4. Arab, Sere 5. Fulah
　　(Fula), Negro 6. Nubian
　　Plain.. 6. Gezira
　　river.. 8. Blue Nile 9. White Nile
　　town.. 5. Segou
sudden... 4. rash 5. hasty, swift
　　6. abrupt, prompt, speedy 7. violent
　　8. headlong 9. impetuous,
　　impromptu, impulsive
　　10. unexpected, unforeseen
　　11. precipitate, precipitous
sudden (pert to)...
　　all of a.. 5. short 6. presto
　　8. suddenly
　　and brilliant.. 8. meteoric
　　fear.. 13. consternation
　　sally.. 6. sortie
　　shock.. 4. jolt
　　stroke.. 4. coup, dash
　　thrust.. 3. jab 5. lunge
sudor... 5. sweat 8. sudation
　　9. exudation 12. perspiration
Sudra caste... 3. mal (low) 5. palli
sue... 3. beg, woo 4. plea, urge
　　5. court, plead 6. appeal, pursue
　　7. entreat, request 8. continue,
　　petition 9. prosecute, seek after
suet... 6. tallow 8. leaf lard
Suez Canal builder... 9. de Lesseps
　　(Ferdinand)
suffer... 3. let 4. bear, dree 5. admit,
　　allow 6. endure, permit, submit
　　7. undergo 8. tolerate
　　10. experience
suffer (pert to)...
　　distress.. 5. gripe, groan, smart
　　6. starve
　　from heat.. 7. swelter
　　remorse.. 3. rue
　　ruin.. 5. wreck
sufferance... 4. pain 6. misery
　　9. endurance, passivity
　　10. permission 11. forbearance
suffering, scene of... 10. Gethsemane
suffice... 2. do 5. avail, serve
　　6. answer 7. appease, content,
　　satisfy 11. sufficiency
sufficiency... 4. fill 7. ability, conceit
　　8. adequacy, capacity, validity
　　9. abundance 10. competency
　　14. self–confidence
sufficient... 3. due, fit 4. enow, full,

　　good 5. ample, valid 6. enough,
　　plenty 7. suffice 8. adequate
　　9. qualified 11. responsible
　　12. satisfactory
suffix, for or denoting...
　　abounding in.. 5. ulent
　　abundant.. 3. ose
　　act of.. 3. ure 4. ance, tion
　　advocate.. 3. ite
　　alcohol.. 2. ol
　　being.. 3. ure
　　capable of.. 3. ile
　　chemical.. 2. ac 3. ane, ene, ile, ine,
　　iol, ole, ose 4. alic, idin, itol
　　diminutive.. 2. el 3. cle, ole, ule
　　4. ette
　　disease.. 4. itis
　　doer.. 4. ator
　　enzyme.. 3. ase
　　feminine.. 3. ess
　　follower.. 3. ist, ite
　　full of.. 3. ose
　　geological age.. 4. cene
　　inflammation.. 4. itis
　　inhabitants of.. 3. ese 4. ites
　　jurisdiction.. 3. ric
　　law.. 2. ee
　　medicine.. 2. ia 3. oma 4. itis
　　profession.. 3. eer
suffocate... 5. burke, choke 6. stifle
　　7. smother 8. strangle, suppress,
　　throttle 10. asphyxiate, extinguish
　　12. deprive of air
suffrage... 4. vote 5. voice 6. assent,
　　ballot, prayer 7. witness 8. petition
　　9. franchise 10. assistance 11. right
　　to vote 12. intercession, supplication
sugar... 4. cane 5. biose, bribe,
　　candy, maple, money 6. doctor,
　　season 7. sucrose, sweeten
　　9. sugarcoat 10. endearment,
　　saccharose, sweetening
　　12. carbohydrate 13. dissaccharide
　　14. monosaccharide
sugar (pert to)...
　　and molasses.. 6. melada
　　burnt.. 7. caramel
　　chemical.. 6. acrose 7. osamine,
　　sucrose 8. fructose 10. saccharose
　　crude.. 3. gur 5. maple
　　10. massecuite, piloncillo
　　fruit, honey.. 8. levulose
　　plant.. 7. sorghum
　　raw.. 5. cassonade, muscovado
　　sand.. 5. niter
　　simple.. 6. ketose, triose 7. glucide
　　substitute.. 5. honey
　　syrup.. 7. treacle 8. molasses
　　tree.. 5. maple
　　without.. 3. sec
　　wood.. 6. xylose
sugar cane (pert to)...
　　disease.. 5. sereh
　　pulp, refuse.. 4. marc 7. bagasse
　　stalk.. 6. ratoon
sugared... 5. sweet 7. honeyed
　　9. sweetened 11. mellifluous,
　　sugarcoated
suggest... 4. hint, mean, move
　　5. imply 6. advise, allude, prompt
　　7. connote, inspire, propose
　　8. indicate, intimate 9. insinuate

suggestion... 4. clue, hint, idea, plan 5. tinge, trace 6. advice, symbol 7. soupçon 8. proposal 9. hypnotism 10. indication, intimation 11. small amount, supposition
Suidae... 5. swine
suit... 3. fit 4. plea 5. befit, cards, dress, habit, match, serve, tally 6. adjust, answer, attire, become, prayer, wooing 7. clothes, comport, conform, costume, lawsuit, retinue 8. petition, sequence 9. courtship 10. litigation 11. accommodate
suit (pert to)...
at law.. 10. litigation
for property.. 6. trover
maker.. 6. sartor, tailor
starter.. 7. relator
the occasion.. 6. timely
suitability... 7. fitness 9. propriety 10. expedience, timeliness 11. eligibility 13. qualification
suitable... 3. apt, due, fit, pat 4. meet 6. proper, timely 8. adequate, apposite, eligible, idoneous 9. accordant, agreeable, competent, congruent, congruous, consonant, expedient 10. compatible, consistent 11. appropriate 12. commensurate 13. correspondent
suitably proportioned... 13. commensurable
suite... 3. set 5. music, staff 7. retinue 8. sequence 9. apartment 10. attendance, succession 11. consequence
suitor... 5. swain, wooer 7. amoroso 10. petitioner 12. party to a suit
sulk... 3. pet 4. mope, plow, pout 6. furrow
sulky... 3. gig 4. dull, glum, plow 5. moody, pouty, surly 6. gloomy, go–cart, sullen 8. carriage 9. obstinate
sullen... 4. dour, glum, grim, sour 5. cross, gruff, harsh, moody, pouty, sulky, surly 6. crusty, gloomy, morose 7. austere, cynical, fretful, peevish, pettish 8. chumpish, churlish, petulant, spiteful 9. obstinate, saturnine
sully... 4. foul 5. dirty, smear, stain, taint 6. defile, smirch, vilify 7. blemish, corrupt, debauch, disdain, pollute 9. bespatter, denigrate 10. stigmatize 11. contaminate
sulphur (pert to)...
alchemy.. 7. chibrit
alloy.. 6. niello
butterfly.. 7. clouded 9. cloudless
color.. 6. yellow
comb form.. 5. thion
element.. 11. nonmetallic
reference to.. 7. thionic 9. brimstone
sultan (pert to)...
decree.. 5. irade
fowls.. 5. breed
home.. 5. serai
Mohammedan State.. 5. ruler 6. prince 9. sovereign
Turkish ruler.. 6. Caliph 8. Padishah

13. Grand Seignior
wife.. 7. sultana
sultana... 4. roll (dessert), wife 5. grape 8. mistress 9. gallinule
sultry... 3. hot 5. humid, lurid 6. torrid 7. dog days, sensual 10. oppressive, sweltering
sum... 3. add, tot 4. loot 5. count, gross, total, whole 6. amount, number, result 7. summary 8. addition, quantity 9. aggregate, summarize, summation 12. recapitulate
sum (pert to)...
forfeited.. 5. dédit
of money.. 6. budget
total.. 8. entirety
unexpended.. 7. savings
up.. 3. tot 5. count 8. perorate
sumac... 5. Rheus 7. dogwood 8. shadbush 9. squawbush 13. Toxicodendron 14. buckthorn brown
Sumatra...
harbor.. 6. Padang 9. Palembang
island of.. 16. Malay Archipelago
kingdom.. 5. Achin, Jambi
mountain.. 12. Bukit Barisan
raft (bamboo).. 5. rakit
river.. 4. Musi 5. Jambi, Rokan 6. Asahan
squirrel shrew.. 4. tana
wildcat.. 4. balu
sumless... 11. inestimable 12. incalculable 13. unaccountable
summary... 5. brief, short 6. digest, prompt, resume 7. epitome 8. abstract 10. compendium 11. abridgement, enumeration, reiteration 14. recapitulation
summary (pert to)...
book.. 5. blurb
concise.. 6. précis
of facts.. 7. roundup
of knowledge.. 12. encyclopedia (encyclopaedia)
of principles.. 5. creed
of speech.. 5. notes
summer... 3. été 6. season
summer (pert to)...
bird.. 7. cuckold, sparrow, tanager, wryneck
coot.. 9. gallinule
house.. 6. gazebo 9. belvedere
lilac.. 8. damewort
pert to.. 7. estival
rash.. 11. prickly heat
resort.. 4. camp
squash.. 7. cymling, scallop 9. crookneck
summit... 3. top 4. acme, apex, knap, peak 5. crest, crown, knoll, spire 6. height 7. Everest 8. pinnacle 9. fastigium 10. perfection 11. culmination, mountaintop
summon... 4. call, cite, page, sist 5. evoke 6. call up, demand, elicit, invite, muster 7. conjure, evocate 8. remember 9. conscript
sumpter... 4. mule 9. pack horse
sun... 3. orb, Sol 4. bask 6. Helios 7. Phoebus 12. heavenly body

13. celestial body
sun (pert to)...
clock.. 6. gnomon (part) 7. sundial
comb form.. 5. helio
crossing the equator.. 7. equinox
disk.. 4. aten
down.. 3. eve 8. twilight
farthest from.. 8. aphelion
fish.. 4. mola, opah 5. bream
god.. 2. Ra 4. Amen, Baal, Lier
(Llew) 6. Apollo, Helios 7. Khepera
(Chepera), Shamash, Sokaris
8. Hyperion
mock.. 9. parhelion
nearest to.. 10. perihelion
outer layer.. 6. corona
over the equator.. 7. equinox
path.. 4. halo 6. circle 8. ecliptic
pert to.. 5. solar 6. heliac
9. heliology
poetic.. 5. glory, power 6. sunset
7. daystar, sunrise 8. splendor
satellite.. 6. planet
spot.. 6. facula 7. freckle
squall.. 9. jellyfish
stroke.. 8. siriasis 9. calenture
sundang... 4. bolo 5. knife
sunder... 4. part, rend, rive 5. sever,
split 6. cleave, divide 7. divorce
8. dissever, disunite, sejugate
sundry... 6. divers 7. several, various
8. frequent, manifold, numerous
9. different 10. multiplied
12. multifarious 13. miscellaneous
sunflower... 8. marigold, rockrose
10. heliotrope
Sunflower State... 6. Kansas
sunk... 4. turf 7. baffled, concave,
lowered 8. dejected, overcome
9. depressed (see also *sink*)
sunk fence... 4. ha–ha (haw–haw)
sunny... 4. warm 5. clear, merry
6. bright, sunlit 8. cheerful
9. sparkling, vivacious
sunrise... 4. dawn
sunset... 3. eve 4. dusk 7. evening,
sundown 8. twilight
Sunset State... 6. Oregon 7. Arizona
Sunshine State... 9. New Mexico
11. South Dakota
supawn... 4. mush 12. hasty pudding
superabundance... 5. flood 6. excess,
plenty 7. surplus 8. plethora
10. exuberance 11. superfluity
superabundant... 4. rank 5. lavish
7. profuse 9. excessive, exuberant,
luxuriant, plentiful 11. overflowing
14. oversufficient
superannuate... 6. retire 9. antiquate
10. pension off 13. prove obsolete
superb... 4. rich 5. grand, noble
6. lordly 7. elegant, stately
8. majestic, splendid 9. sumptuous
11. magnificent 13. extraordinary
14. superexcellent
supercilious... 5. proud 7. haughty
8. arrogant 9. arbitrary
11. overbearing 12. contemptuous
13. hypercritical
supercilious person... 4. snob
superficial... 4. glib 6. slight, square
7. cursory, shallow, smatter, surface,

trivial 8. apparent, external
9. frivolous, insincere
superfluity... 6. excess, luxury, wealth
7. overset 8. frippery 10. redundancy
11. prodigality 14. superabundance
superfluous... 4. over 5. luxus, spare
6. excess 7. surplus, useless
8. needless, wasteful 9. redundant
10. inordinate 11. extravagant
12. nonessential 13. superabundant
14. supererogatory
superhuman... 6. divine 9. Herculean
12. supernatural 13. extraordinary
superimposed... 4. over, upon
5. above 7. covered, layered
8. overlaid 9. overlying
superintend... 4. boss 5. guide
6. direct, manage 7. oversee
8. overlook 9. look after, supervise
10. administer, have charge
superintendent... 4. boss 7. curator,
manager 8. director, overseer
9. inspector, straw boss
10. supervisor 11. chamberlain
superior... 4. over, peer 5. above,
chief, upper 6. higher, senior
7. exalted, mastery, ranking
8. goodness, priority 9. advantage,
paramount, seniority 10. ascendancy,
excellence, pre–eminent, surpassing
11. pre–eminence 12. predominancy
superlative... 4. acme, best, peak
6. utmost 7. elative, extreme,
supreme, the best 8. peerless
9. hyperbole 12. exaggeration
supernatural... 5. eerie, magic
6. divine 10. miraculous,
superhuman 13. hyperphysical,
preternatural
supernatural (pert to)...
being.. 3. God 4. atua 5. jinni
(jinnee) 7. banshee (banshie), specter
(spectre)
event.. 7. miracle
power.. 4. ngai 6. fetish 8. talisman
11. incantation
superscribe... 6. direct 7. address (a
letter), engrave 8. inscribe
supersede... 4. omit 7. replace,
succeed 8. displace, make void,
supplant
superstition... 6. notion, voodoo
8. folklore, idolatry 9. tradition
10. Aberglaube 12. old wives' tale
superstitious... 6. goetic 7. magical
10. idolatrous 11. fetishistic
(fetichistic)
supervene... 5. occur 6. accrue,
happen 7. be added 12. be
subsequent
supervise... 4. boss, read, scan
5. check 6. direct, govern, peruse,
revise 7. inspect, oversee
11. superintend
supervisor... 4. boss 7. foreman,
proctor 9. inspector, straw boss
supine... 5. inert, prone 6. abject,
drowsy 7. servile, unalert 8. careless,
inclined, indolent, listless, sluggish
9. apathetic, lethargic, recumbent
11. inattentive, indifferent,
thoughtless

supplant... 5. upset, usurp 6. remove, uproot 7. replace 8. displace, drive out 9. eradicate, extirpate, overthrow, supersede

supple... 3. sly 4. bent 5. agile, lithe 6. limber, nimble, pliant 7. fawning, lissome 8. flexible, yielding 9. compliant, resilient 10. obsequious, responsive 11. complaisant

supplement... 3. add, eke 5. add to 6. sequel 7. ripieno 8. addition, appendix, complete 9. accessory 10. complement 12. nonessential 13. reinforcement

supplementary, music... 7. ripieno

supplicate... 3. beg 4. pray 5. crave, plead 6. appeal, obtest 7. beseech, conjure, entreat, implore, solicit 8. petition 9. importune, obsecrate

supplication... 4. plea 6. litany, prayer 7. craving 8. entreaty, petition, rogative 11. obtestation 12. solicitation

supplies... 6. hoards, relays, stocks, stores 8. estovers, ordnance 9. provender

supply... 4. fund, give 5. cache, cater, hoard, relay, stock, store, yield 6. purvey, remuda 7. provide, reserve 9. provision, reservoir 10. administer, contribute

supply (pert to)...
food.. 4. feed 5. cater 9. alimental
fuel.. 5. stoke
funds.. 5. endow
horses.. 5. relay
provisions.. 6. purvey

support... 3. aid, arm, fid, guy, leg, peg, rib 4. abet, ally, back, base, buoy, limb, mast, prop 5. brace, cleat, shore, spile, stell, strut, tenon 6. backer, pillar, second, uphold 7. bolster, fulcrum, trestle 8. buttress, underlie 9. auxiliary, encourage, reinforce, stanchion 10. assistance, foundation 11. corroborate 12. substantiate 13. corroboration

support (pert to)...
anatomy.. 3. rib 5. spine
cannon.. 8. trunnion
coffin.. 4. bier
mast.. 4. bibb
resilient.. 6. spring
three–legged.. 5. easel 6. tripod, trivot
upright.. 8. baluster 9. stanchion
wedge–shaped.. 5. cleat

supporters... 6. allies, braces 7. backers, bracers, garters 10. suspenders 15. ministerialists

suppose... 3. wis 4. deem, trow 5. allow, imply, judge, opine, think 6. assume, expect, repute 7. presume 8. conclude, consider 9. apprehend, intention 10. conjecture 11. supposition

supposed... 8. putative

supposition... 2. if 6. theory 7. surmise 8. supposed 9. postulate 10. assumption, conjecture,

hypothesis 11. connotation, implication

suppress... 4. kill, stop 5. check, crush, elide, quash, quell 6. hush up, muffle, retard, stifle 7. abolish, exclude, oppress, smother 8. hold back, prohibit, restrain, withhold 9. interdict, overpower 10. extinguish

suppression... 6. hush up 7. reserve 8. hush–hush 9. overthrow, restraint 10. inhibition

supremacy... 5. power 7. control, mastery, primacy 8. dominion 9. influence 10. ascendancy, domination, first place 11. sovereignty 12. championship

supreme... 3. top 4. last 5. chief, final 6. divine, ruling 7. crucial, highest 8. foremost, greatest, peerless 9. paramount 10. preeminent

supreme being... 3. God 4. Lord 5. Allah, Deity, monad 6. Brahma, Buddha 7. Creator, Jehovah 8. autocrat

surcease... 3. end 4. rest, stop 5. defer, delay 6. desist, relief 7. respite 8. drop work, postpone 9. cessation

surd... 4. deaf, mute 7. aphonic, radical 9. voiceless

sure... 3. yes 4. fast, firm, safe, true 5. bound 6. indeed, secure, stable, steady, strong 7. assured, certain 8. positive, reliable 9. confident, steadfast, unfailing 10. guaranteed, inevitable, infallible 11. trustworthy 12. indisputable 13. incontestable 14. unquestionable

surety... 4. bail, bond, fact 6. backer, pledge, safety 7. sponsor 8. security, sureness 9. certainty 10. confidence, engagement

surf... 4. foam, rote, wave 5. bathe, spray, surge, swell 7. breaker

surface... 4. area, face, orlo, pave, plat, skin 5. facet, meros 6. facing, patina 7. outside 8. exterior 9. periphery

surface (pert to)...
artificial.. 4. rink
front (coin).. 7. obverse
gem.. 5. facet
geometric.. 6. toroid
medical.. 7. acrotic
toward.. 5. ectad
under.. 6. latent 10. internally
water.. 4. ryme

surfeit... 4. cloy, feed, glut, jade, sate 6. excess 7. replete, satiate, satisfy 9. satiation 11. overindulge, superfluity

surge... 4. eddy, flow, rush, wave 5. swarm, swell, whirl 6. billow, thrill 7. estuate 9. gurgitate 11. rise and fall

surgeon (pert to)...
ancient.. 10. chirurgeon
case (instrument).. 6. tweeze (tweese)
slang.. 8. sawbones

surgery... 7. aciurgy 8. medicine 9. operation, resection

surgery (pert to)...
chin.. **11.** mentoplasty
ears.. **9.** otoplasty
face lift.. **13.** rhytidoplasty
  14. blepharoplasty (eyelids)
fractures.. **10.** agmatology
mouth, lip.. **12.** cheiloplasty
  (chiloplasty)
nose.. **7.** nose job **11.** rhinoplasty
organ.. **10.** transplant
skin.. **12.** dermabrasion
vein.. **10.** phlebotomy
vertebra.. **11.** laminectomy
surgical (pert to)...
compress.. **4.** swab **5.** stupe
counterirritant.. **5.** seton
equpment.. **4.** X–ray **6.** splint **7.** CAT
  scan, scanner **8.** iron lung
  10. respirator, tomography, tourniquet
  11. stethoscope **12.** resuscitator
hook.. **9.** tenaculum
instrument.. **3.** saw **5.** fleam, lance,
  probe **6.** catlin, lancet, stylet, trepan,
  xyster **7.** forceps **8.** hemostat,
  keratome, speculum, tweezers
knife.. **7.** scalpel
puncture.. **8.** centesis
saw.. **6.** trepan
stitch.. **5.** seton **6.** suture
Suriname (pert to)...
capital.. **10.** Paramaribo
former name.. **11.** Dutch Guiana
mountain.. **10.** Tumuc–Humac
toad.. **4.** pipa
surly... **4.** glum, grum, rude **5.** gruff
  6. abrupt, grumpy, morose, sullen
  7. crabbed **8.** arrogant, growling
  10. ill–natured **11.** intractable
surmise... **4.** deem **5.** fancy, guess,
  judge, opine, think **7.** imagine,
  presume **8.** mistrust **9.** suspicion
  10. assumption, conclusion,
  conjecture **11.** supposition
surmount... **3.** top **4.** pass, rise
  5. climb, excel, mount **6.** subdue
  7. conquer, surpass **8.** overcome
  9. transcend
surname... **6.** eponym, family, maiden
  7. agnomen **8.** cognomen
  10. patronymic **11.** appellation
surpass... **3.** cap, top **4.** best
  5. excel, outdo **6.** better, exceed,
  outvie, outwit **7.** outrank, outride
  8. go beyond, outrange, outreach,
  outshine, outsmart, outstrip, surmount
  9. transcend
surpassing... **12.** transcendent
surplice... **3.** fee **5.** cotta, ephod
  6. collar **7.** pelisse
surplus... **4.** over, rest **5.** epact
  6. excess **7.** overage, reserve
  8. overplus **9.** remaining
  10. additional, redundancy
  11. superfluous
surprise... **3.** awe **5.** alarm, amaze,
  seize, shock **6.** wonder **7.** astound,
  capture, perplex, startle **8.** astonish,
  bewilder, confound, dumfound
  9. amazement, dumbfound,
  overwhelm, surprisal **10.** wonderment
  11. flabbergast **12.** astonishment
surprising... **7.** amazing **8.** striking

9. startling **10.** unexpected
  11. astonishing, unlooked for
  13. extraordinary
surrender... **4.** cede, give **5.** yield
  6. give up, remise, resign
  7. abandon, cession, deliver
  8. dedition, remittal **9.** extradite
  10. relinquish, submission
  11. abandonment, divestiture
  12. cancellation **14.** relinquishment
surreptitious... **3.** sly **6.** hidden,
  secret **8.** stealthy **9.** concealed,
  deceitful **10.** fraudulent
  11. clandestine
surround... **4.** gird, isle, wrap
  5. beset, hem in, inarm **6.** circle,
  encase, incase, invest **7.** besiege,
  enclave, enclose, envelop, environ
  8. encircle, inundate, overflow
  9. encompass **12.** circumscribe
  14. circumnavigate
surrounding... **5.** about, beset, midst
  7. ambient, setting **9.** hemming in,
  perioptic **10.** encircling, enveloping
  11. circumpolar **12.** circumjacent
survey... **4.** plan, poll, scan **5.** study,
  vista **6.** regard, review **7.** examine,
  inspect, oversee **8.** traverse
  9. delineate, determine **10.** scrutinize
  11. examination, reconnoiter,
  superintend **14.** reconnaissance
surveying (pert to)...
instrument.. **7.** alidade (alidad), transit
  9. stadia rod **10.** throdolite
mathematics.. **7.** geodesy
process.. **13.** triangulation
surveyor (pert to)...
helper.. **6.** rodman **7.** lineman,
  poleman
land.. **8.** measurer, overseer
  9. arpenteur
measure.. **5.** chain
mine.. **6.** dialer
survival... **5.** relic **9.** endurance,
  outliving **10.** durability
survivor... **6.** relict **8.** outliver,
  remainer, survival **11.** joint tenant
susceptibility... **5.** sense **6.** emotion,
  feeling, pliancy **11.** sensibility
  12. teachability **13.** affectibility,
  vulnerability **14.** sentimentality
susceptible... **4.** easy **6.** liable, pliant
  7. exposed, subject **8.** sensible
  9. receptive, sensitive, teachable
  10. responsive, vulnerable
  11. softhearted **13.** tenderhearted
  14. impressionable
suslik... **5.** sisel **8.** squirrel
  11. spermophile
suspect... **4.** fear **5.** doubt, fancy,
  guess **7.** imagine, presume, suppose
  8. distrust, mistrust **9.** discredit
  10. disbelieve, suspicious
suspecting... **4.** wary **8.** doubtful,
  doubting **11.** incredulous, mistrusting
suspend... **4.** hang, oust, stay, stop
  5. cease, debar, defer, expel, remit
  6. dangle, depose, recess **7.** adjourn,
  pensile **8.** intermit, postpone, set
  aside, withhold **9.** pretermit
suspended... **4.** hung **5.** inert
  6. barred, latent **7.** abeyant, pendent

8. inactive 9. pendulous
11. inoperative, interrupted

suspenders... 4. pegs 5. belts, hooks, rings 6. braces, straps 7. gallows, garters 8. galluses 9. bretelles 10. supporters 11. clothespins

suspense... 5. pause 7. anxiety 10. expectancy 11. uncertainty 12. apprehension, irresolution 14. indecisiveness

suspension... 4. stop 5. delay 7. deposal, failure, hanging, respite 8. abeyance, buoyancy 11. withholding 12. intermission, interruption

suspicious... 4. fear, hint 5. doubt, hunch, trace 7. askance, inkling, soupçon 8. distrust, jealousy, mistrust, wariness 9. mere trace, misgiving 10. diffidence, intimation, skepticism, suggestion 11. incredulity, supposition 12. apprehension

Sussex (pert to)...
breed (Eng).. 4. fowl 6. cattle
kingdom (anc).. 7. English
land measure.. 4. wist
land tract (Downs).. 5. laine
man.. 8. Piltdown (Prehist)
spaniel.. 6. gun dog

sustain... 4. bear, buoy, feed, prop 5. abide, carry 6. endure, foster, keep up, uphold 7. confirm, justify, nourish, prolong, support, undergo 8. continue, maintain, preserve 9. encourage, establish 10. strengthen 11. corroborate

sustained... 6. tenuto, upheld 9. permanent, prolonged, supported 10. unflagging

Susu... 5. tribe (Afr)

suttee... 5. widow 9. cremation, sacrifice 14. self–immolation

suture... 5. unite 6. stitch 7. pterion 12. synarthrosis

swagger... 4. brag, gait, walk 5. bluff, boast, bully, strut, swell 6. prance 7. bluster, dashing, roister, stagger, stylish 8. domineer 11. braggadocio, ostentation 16. ultrafashionable

swain... 3. boy, lad 4. beau 5. lover 6. suitor 7. admirer, gallant, peasant 8. shepherd 10. countryman

swallow... 3. sip 4. gulp 5. drink 6. absorb, englut, engulf, imbibe, ingest, recant 7. consume, engorge, retract 8. tolerate 10. bear meekly

swallow (pert to)...
chimney.. 5. swift
European.. 6. martin
hawk.. 4. kite
plover.. 10. pratincole
sea.. 4. tern
tail.. 4. coat 9. butterfly
the anchor.. 10. quit the sea

swamp... 3. bog, fen 4. mire, muck, sink, slue, sump 5. flood, marsh 6. deluge, engulf, morass, slough 7. cienaga, pocosin 8. quagmire, submerge 9. everglade, overwhelm

swamp (pert to)...
boggy.. 7. queachy 8. muskeggy
earth.. 4. muck

gas.. 6. miasma
grass.. 5. sedge
marsh.. 5. slash 8. paludine
tract.. 10. Everglades

swan... 3. cob, pen 4. Olor 5. swear 6. cygnet, cygnus 7. declare 9. trumpeter

swan (pert to)...
astronomy.. 6. Cygnus
flower.. 6. orchid
goose.. 7. Bewick's, Chinese
myth (Hind).. 5. hansa
poem.. 12. Swan of Thames (Pope) 15. Sweet Swan of Avon (Jonson)
star (brightest).. 5. Deneb
trumpeter.. 4. wild
type.. 4. mute 5. black 8. whooping 11. black–necked

swap... 4. beat 5. trade 6. barter, thrash 8. exchange 11. give–and–take

sward... 3. sod 4. lawn, turf 5. grass 10. greensward

swarm... 3. fry 5. crowd, flock, horde 6. abound, infest, throng 7. pervade 9. migration, multitude 10. congregate 11. aggregation

swarthy... 3. dun 4. dark 5. dusky 8. bistered (bistred), blackish

swashbuckler... 5. bravo 6. gascon 7. ruffian 8. Almanzor 9. blusterer, daredevil, swaggerer 10. Drawcansir

swastika (swastica)... 6. fylfot, symbol (since 1918) 9. gammadion 10. hakenkreuz

swat... 3. bat, hit 5. clout 6. strike 7. hit hard

swathe... 4. band, bind, wrap 6. enfold 7. envelop, swaddle

sway... 4. bend, bias, rock, rule, veer, wave 5. lurch, power, shake, swing, waver, wield 6. direct, empire, govern, induce, totter, waddle 7. command, control, deflect, incline 8. flounder 9. fluctuate, influence, oscillate, vacillate 10. ascendancy 11. fluctuation

swayback... 8. lordosis

swaying... 7. pensile, sagging 8. swinging, waddling 11. influential, oscillating

swear... 3. vow 4. oath 5. curse, vouch 6. adjure, pledge (sacred) 7. confirm, declare, promise 10. asseverate, deposition 11. bear witness

swear (pert to)...
at.. 5. clash (colors), curse 8. disagree
by.. 5. bet on 7. count on 8. take oath
falsely.. 7. perjure
off.. 4. stop 6. eschew, give up 7. abandon 8. renounce

sweat... 4. work 5. exude, grill, sudor 6. drudge 7. excrete, ferment 8. perspire, transude 9. exudation 10. impatience 11. nervousness

Sweden... see also *Swedish*
capital.. 9. Stockholm
city.. 7. Uppsala (Upsala)
dynasty (1st).. 8. Ynglings

gulf .. **7.** Bothnia
lake .. **6.** Vanern **7.** Vattern
mountain .. **5.** Kölen (Kjölen)
parliament .. **7.** Riksdag
peninsula .. **11.** Scandinavia
port .. **8.** Göteborg **9.** Stockholm
river .. **4.** Klar **7.** Götaalv
sea .. **6.** Baltic
university (oldest) .. **7.** Uppsula (Upsula, 1477)
Swedish (pert to) . . .
artist .. **4.** Zorn
bread .. **10.** knäckebröd
clover .. **6.** alsike
dance .. **6.** polska
explorer .. **5.** Hedin
fir .. **10.** Scotch pine
idiom .. **7.** Suecism
manual training .. **5.** sloyd (slojd)
novelist .. **8.** Lagerlöf (Pulitzer prize, 1909)
philosopher .. **10.** Swedenborg
religion (State) .. **8.** Lutheran
soprano .. **10.** Jennie Lind
  18. Swedish Nightingale
turnip .. **8.** rutabaga
sweep . . . **3.** oar **4.** scan **5.** clean, clear, cover, curve, glide, strip, surge, swish, trail **6.** course, vision **7.** contour **8.** traverse
sweeping . . . **8.** complete, thorough **9.** extensive **12.** all–embracing **13.** comprehensive
sweet . . . **5.** bonny, candy **10.** dolce douce **5.** fresh, spicy **6.** dulcet, gentle, sugary, syrupy **7.** caramel, honeyed, lovable **8.** aromatic, fragrant, luscious, pleasant, preserve **9.** agreeable, ambrosial, melodious, nectarine **10.** confection, saccharine **11.** mellifluous, mellisonant
sweet (pert to) . . .
and fair .. **5.** bonny
bread .. **4.** food **6.** thymus **8.** pancreas **9.** ris de veau
brier .. **4.** rose **9.** eglantine
drink .. **6.** nectar
meat .. **4.** cake **5.** candy **6.** comfit, éclair, pastry **7.** caramel, dessert **8.** marzipan **10.** confection
potato .. **3.** yam **6.** batata
potato, musical .. **7.** ocarina
sop .. **4.** ates, atta **6.** Annone **14.** Annona squamosa
sounding .. **11.** mellisonant
wine .. **4.** port **5.** Lunel
sweetheart . . . **2.** jo **3.** gra **4.** beau, lass **5.** flame, leman, lover, spark, swain **7.** darling **8.** dowsabel, honeybun (sl), ladylove **9.** Amaryllis, inamorata, valentine
swell . . . **3.** fob, nob **4.** grow, rise, surf, wave **5.** bulge, dandy, grand, heave, mound, surge **6.** billow, dilate, expand, growth, puff up, tiptop **7.** distend, inflate, stylish **8.** increase, protrude **9.** sumptuous **10.** aristocrat, prominence **11.** enlargement **12.** augmentation
swell (pert to) . . .
ocean .. **4.** surf **6.** billow, expand, roller

roiling .. **7.** seagate
slang .. **3.** nob **5.** dandy, grand **9.** first–rate
swelled (pert to) . . .
head .. **3.** ego **7.** conceit **9.** cockiness **14.** self–importance
out .. **4.** lump, node **5.** tumid **6.** bulged, podded, turgid **9.** grandiose
swelling . . . **4.** sore **5.** bulge, edema **6.** dropsy **9.** bombastic **10.** distention, increasing **12.** protuberance
swelter . . . **4.** fret **5.** exude, roast, sweat **8.** perspire **10.** sultry heat
swerve . . . **4.** veer **5.** dodge, sheer, shift **6.** recoil **7.** deflect, deviate **9.** deviation, turn aside
swift . . . **4.** bird, fast, racy, reel **5.** alert, fleet, hasty, quick, rapid, ready **6.** lizard, prompt, speedy, sudden, winged **8.** headlong
swift (pert to) . . .
astronomer .. **5.** Lewis (Swift)
bird .. **4.** crin **7.** chimney
boat .. **7.** flyboat **10.** Hovercraft
footed .. **5.** ariel (gazelle) **7.** Mercury
satirist .. **8.** Jonathan (Swift)
swiftness . . . **5.** haste, speed **8.** celerity, velocity **9.** quickness **10.** promptness
swimmer . . . **5.** diver **6.** bather **7.** Cloelia (Tiber Riv), Leander (Hellespont), natator
swimming . . . **5.** crawl **6.** natant **7.** vertigo **9.** dizziness, freestyle, skinny–dip **10.** sidestroke **12.** breast stroke
swimming (pert to) . . .
birds .. **9.** natatores
bladder .. **10.** air bladder (fish)
pert to .. **5.** dizzy **7.** aquatic **8.** natatory
pool .. **4.** hole, tank **10.** natatorium
sandpiper .. **9.** phalarope
swindle . . . **3.** con, gyp **4.** dupe, fake, sell **5.** bunco, cheat **6.** trepan **7.** defraud **8.** flimflam **9.** gold brick
swindler . . . **3.** gyp **5.** biter, cheat, crook, knave, rogue, shark **6.** gypper **7.** sharper **9.** defrauder
swindling . . . **6.** estafa
swine . . . **3.** hog, pig, sow, Sus **4.** boar **7.** Anthony (smallest), peccary **8.** slattern **9.** scoundrel
swine, breed of . . . **8.** Cheshire, Tamworth **9.** Berkshire, Hampshire, razorback, Yorkshire **11.** Duroc–Jersey, Poland China **12.** Chester–White
swineherd (pert to) . . .
patron saint .. **7.** Anthony
reference to .. **7.** sybotic
swinelike . . . **7.** porcine
swing . . . **4.** hang, jazz, jive, lilt, sway **5.** shake, trend, waver, wield **6.** dangle, manage, rhythm, totter **7.** suspend, trapeze, vibrate **8.** pendulum, undulate **9.** fluctuate, oscillate
swingtree . . . **11.** whippletree
swinish . . . **5.** gross **6.** carnal, filthy,

greedy 7. beastly, porcine, sensual
8. gluttony
swipe ... 4. gulp 5. draft, drink, lever,
steal, swape, swath, sweep
6. handle, pilfer, snatch 7. purloin
swipes ... 4. beer (Eng sl)
swirl ... 4. curl, eddy 5. curve, gurge,
surge, twist, whirl, whorl
swirly ... 7. knotted, tangled, twisted
Swiss (pert to) ... see also *Switzerland*
ax (ice) .. 6. piolet
bell .. 9. alpenhorn (alphorn)
cabin .. 6. chalet
composer .. 4. Raff
flower, emblem .. 9. edelweiss
herdsman .. 4. senn
hero .. 11. William Tell
language .. 6. French, German
7. Italian 8. Romansch
legislature .. 9. Bundesrat (Bundesrath),
Grosse Rat (Grossrat)
mathematician .. 5. Euler
pine .. 6. arolla
scientist .. 6. Haller (von)
surgeon .. 6. Kocher (Nobel Prize)
theologian .. 5. Vinet
warble .. 5. yodel
warbler .. 7. yodeler (yodeller)
wind .. 4. bise
wine .. 7. Dezaley
Switzerland (pert to) ...
ancient .. 8. Helvetia
canton .. 5. Aarau
capital .. 5. Berne (Bern)
city .. 5. Basel 6. Geneva, Zurich
7. Locarno, Lucerne 8. Lausanne
9. Constance
famed for .. 5. banks (Finan)
lake .. 3. Uri 6. Brienz, Geneva, Zurich
7. Lucerne 8. Maggiore
9. Constance, Neuchâtel
10. Stattersee
mountain .. 4. Alps, Jura 5. Blanc
8. Jungfrau 9. Monte Rosa (peak)
10. Matterhorn
resort .. 7. Urseren, Yverdon
river .. 3. Aar 5. Reuss, Rhine, Rhone
tunnel .. 5. Cenis 7. Gothard, Simplon
11. Loetschberg
university (oldest) .. 5. Basel
valley .. 3. Aar
swollen ... 5. pursy, tumid 6. turgid
7. bloated, bulbous, bulging,
pompous 8. enlarged, inflated, puffed
up, varicose 9. bombastic, distended,
plethoric, tumescent 11. protuberant
swoon ... 3. fit 5. faint, spell
7. ecstasy, syncope 8. languish
10. heavy sleep
swoop ... 5. seize, sweep 6. attack,
pounce 7. descend
sword (pert to) ...
ancient .. 5. estoc 6. glaive
cavalry .. 5. saber (sabre)
curved .. 7. cutlass, Ferrara
8. Claymore, scimitar
fencing .. 4. foil, epee 6. rapier
fine .. 6. Toledo 8. Damascus
handle .. 4. haft, hilt
India .. 5. kukri
like .. 7. xiphoid

Mohammedan's .. 8. scimitar
part .. 5. forte, talon 6. foible
practice .. 5. fence
scabbard tip .. 7. crampit
Scot Highlander's .. 4. dirk
seaman's .. 6. hanger
shaped .. 6. ensate 7. xiphoid
(xyphoid) 8. ensiform, gladiate
sheik's .. 4. pata
Siegfried's .. 4. Gram 7. Balmung
Sir Bevis' .. 7. Morglay
Spanish .. 5. bilbo
support .. 7. baldric
two-handed .. 7. espadon
type .. 4. epee, pata 5. blade, degen,
estoc, gully, saber 6. barong, creese,
parang, rapier 7. cutlass 9. gladiolus
swordfish ... 6. dorado, Dorado
(constellation), espada 7. espadon,
Xiphias 9. broadbill
sword of ...
Damocles .. 12. fateful thing
God .. 6. Khaled (Moslem hero)
mercy .. 7. Curtana (pointless)
Sir Bevis .. 7. Morglay (death)
St George .. 7. Askelon
the Cid .. 6. Colada
swordsman ... 6. fencer 7. duelist,
epeeist, saberer, sabreur 9. gladiator
11. Beau Sabreur
sworn statement ... 9. affidavit
sworn to secrecy ... 5. tiled
sybarite ... 7. epicure 10. voluptuary
11. luxury lover
sybil (sibil) ... 4. seer 5. witch
7. seeress 10. prophetess
13. fortuneteller
syce ... 5. groom
sycophant ... 5. toady 7. fawning,
spaniel 8. hanger–on, informer,
parasite 9. charlatan, flatterer,
toadeater 10. talebearer
sycophantic ... 7. fawning, servile,
slavish 8. obedient, toadying
10. obsequious 11. bootlicking
syllable ...
accented .. 5. arsis
by syllable .. 11. syllabation
charm .. 2. om 6. mantra
last .. 6. ultima
last, omission of .. 7. apocope
last but one .. 6. penult
last but two .. 10. antepenult
lengthening of .. 7. ectasis
ref to .. 5. affix 6. prefix, suffix
8. dactylic, syllabic
short .. 4. mora
shortening .. 7. systole
stress .. 5. ictus
table .. 9. syllabary
unaccented .. 4. lene 6. thesis
syllabled, three ... 7. triseme (3
moras) 11. trisyllabic
syllabus ... 6. aperçu, digest
8. abstract, synopsis
10. compendium, conspectus
syllogism ... 7. premise, sorites
9. deduction, reasoning
11. epicheirema (epichirema)
18. deductive reasoning
sylvan, silvan ... 5. woody 6. groved,
rustic, wooded 8. forested

10. forestlike
sylvan deity... 3. Pan 4. faun
  5. Satyr, Vidar 6. Faunus
symbol... 2. om 4. icon, palm, sign,
  type 5. badge, crest, cross, image,
  token, totem 6. emblem, ensign,
  figure, letter, number 9. character
  (graphic), prototype, trademark
  12. abbreviation
symbol (pert to)...
  authority.. 4. mace
  bondage.. 4. yoke
  ecclesiastic.. 4. ring
  England.. 4. lion
  France.. 4. lily
  mathematics.. 7. operand
  military.. 3. bar 4. star 5. eagle,
  wings 6. stripe 7. chevron, epaulet
  (epaulette) 8. caduceus
  peace.. 4. dove
  power.. 4. mace
  prayer figure (anc).. 5. orant
  royal.. 3. rod 5. crown, tiara
  6. corona 7. scepter (sceptre)
  Tammany Hall.. 5. tiger
  tribal.. 5. totem (pole)
  victory.. 4. palm
symbol for...
  arsenic.. 2. As
  calcium.. 2. Ca
  chromium.. 2. Cr
  copper.. 2. Cu
  gold.. 2. Au
  iron.. 2. Fe
  lead.. 2. Pb
  neon.. 2. Ne
  nickel.. 2. Ni
  radium.. Ra
  silver.. 2. Ag, Ar
  sodium.. 2. Na
  tin.. 2. Sn
symbolic, symbolical... 7. typical
  9. imagerial 10. figurative, relational
  11. allegorical, significant
  12. emblematical 14. representative
symbolism... 7. mystery, writing
  9. mysticism, ritualism, symbolics
  10. figuration 11. hieroglyphy
  14. representation
symmetric, symmetrical... 7. orderly,
  regular, spheral, uniform 8. balanced
  10. euphonious
symmetry... 5. order 7. balance,
  euphony, harmony 8. equality
  9. congruity 10. conformity,
  proportion 11. consistency
sympathetic... 4. kind 6. humane,
  tender 7. empathy, pitying
  8. dewy–eyed 10. responsive
  13. compassionate, understanding
sympathy... 4. pity 5. favor
  7. consent, harmony, support
  8. affinity, interest 9. agreeable,
  agreement, tolerance 11. sensitivity
  13. commiseration, understanding
sympathy, lack of... 8. dyspathy
  9. antipathy
symphony... 6. accord 7. concert,
  harmony 8. ritornel 9. orchestra
  10. consonance 11. composition
symposium... 4. book, talk 7. banquet
  8. dialogue, tippling 10. collection,

  discussion 11. compotation
symptom... 4. mark, note, omen, sign
  5. alarm, token 7. warning
  10. indication
synagogue... 6. temple 10. tabernacle
  12. congregation
synagogue (pert to)...
  founder (anc).. 4. Ezra
  platform.. 7. almemar
  singer.. 6. cantor, chazan (chazzan)
synchronize... 5. agree 6. concur
  8. coincide 9. harmonize
  12. contemporize
syncopation... 5. tempo 7. ragtime,
  syncope
syncope... 5. faint, swoon 7. elision
  8. fainting, swooning 9. haplology
  11. contraction, hyphaeresis
syndicate... 5. chain (journalistic),
  group, trust 6. cartel, school
  7. combine, council 9. committee
  10. underworld 11. association
  12. organization
synonym... 7. antonym, homonym,
  metonym 8. identity 9. heteronym
synonymous... 4. like 5. alike
  7. similar 10. equivalent,
  homonymous
synopsis... 6. digest, manual
  7. epitome, summary 8. abstract,
  syllabus 9. statement 10. abridgment
  (abridgement), compendium,
  conspectus, tabulation
synthesis... 5. logic 11. combination,
  composition 13. incorporation
  14. identification
Syracuse (pert to)...
  ancient name.. 8. Siracusa
  city of.. 6. Sicily
  famed for.. 6. battle (BC)
  founded by.. 6. Greeks
  tyrant of.. 9. Dionysius
Syria, Arab Republic... see also
  Syrian
  ancient name.. 4. Aram
  capital.. 8. Damascus
  city.. 4. Hama, Homs 6. Aleppo,
  Beirut 7. Antioch, Latakia
  8. Damascus
  language.. 6. Arabic
  organization, party.. 5. Baath
  river.. 6. Barada, Jordan 7. Orontes
  9. Euphrates
Syrian (pert to)...
  antiquarian.. 11. Syriologist
  deity.. 2. El 4. Baal 6. Mammon
  7. Resheph
  goat.. 6. Angora
  grass.. 7. Johnson
  mallow.. 4. okra
  script.. 8. Peshitta (Peshito)
  10. estrangelo 11. Syro–Chaldee
  sect.. 5. Druse
  tribe.. 7. Ansarie (Ansarieh)
  wind (hot).. 6. simoom (simoon)
syrinx... 4. tomb 6. larynx 7. Panpipe
  10. mouthpiece (anc lute)
  13. Arcadian nymph
syrup, sirup... 4. Karo, sapa 5. maple
  6. orgeat 7. dhebbus, glucose,
  sorghum, treacle 8. molasses
  9. grenadine

system... 3. ism, way 4. code, plan
5. order 6. regime, theory
8. religion, universe 9. procedure
10. hypothesis, regularity
11. arrangement, orderliness
system (pert to)...
conduct.. 4. code
eating.. 4. diet 7. dietary
geological.. 5. Trias
management.. 6. regime
manual training.. 5. sloyd
mystic.. 6. cabala
numbering.. 7. decimal
pitch (Mus).. 5. neume
religious.. 4. cult 6. cultus
solar.. 6. planet
weights.. 4. long, troy 5. cubic
6. liquid 11. avoirdupois
12. apothecaries'
systematic... 4. neat 6. formal
7. orderly, regular 9. organized,

schematic 10. methodical
systematics... 8. taxonomy
14. classification
systematize... 4. code 6. codify
7. arrange 8. classify, organize,
regiment 9. catalogue (catalog),
formulate
systematized knowledge... 7. science
systole (pert to)...
correlative.. 8. diastole
medical.. 11. contraction (heart)
14. coming and going
rhyme.. 10. shortening (syllable)
syzygy (pert to)...
astronomy.. 7. appulse
11. conjunction
Gnosticism.. 5. aeons (pair)
rhyme.. 11. coupled feet (group)
zoology.. 5. union 7. segment
szlachta... 8. nobility (Poland)
szopelka... 4. oboe (Russ)

T

T... 3. tau (Gr) 6. letter (20th)
taa... 6. pagoda
Taal... 8. language 9. Afrikaans
taar... 10. tambourine
Taaroa... 3. God
tab... 3. pan, tag 4. bill, cost, flap,
loop 5. aglet (aiglet), label, strip
6. eartab, record 7. account, latchet,
pendant (pendent) 9. afterpart,
appendage, reckoning 10. accounting
tabac... 5. brown, snuff 7. tobacco
tabard... 4. cape 5. cloak 6. chimer,
jacket, mantle
Tabard... 3. Inn (Canterbury Tales)
tabatière... 8. snuffbox
tabby... 3. cat 4. gown, silk 5. dress
6. fabric, gossip 7. old maid, taffeta
tabernacle... 4. tent 5. abode, niche
6. church, temple 7. shelter, support
8. enshrine 9. sanctuary
10. habitation
table... 4. fare, list, slab 5. board,
panel, plate, stand 6. lamina, repast,
tablet, teapoy 7. console, plateau,
weights 8. postpone, put aside,
synopsis, tabulate 9. reference
10. collection 14. multiplication
table (pert to)...
calculating.. 6. abacus
centerpiece.. 7. epergne
communion.. 5. altar 8. credence,
credenza
contents.. 5. index
cover.. 5. baize, tapis
dish.. 6. tureen
land.. 4. mesa 6. karroo (karoo),
plains 7. plateau
linen.. 6. napery
philosophy.. 13. deipnosophism

talk (versed in).. 13. deipnosophist
type.. 3. tea 4. turn 6. coffee,
gaming 7. dinette, dresser, gate–leg,
kitchen, taboret 8. captain's,
drop–leaf
tableau... 5. drama, scene 7. picture
8. schedule 14. representation
tablet... 3. pad 4. pill, slab 5. facia,
slate, stele 6. troche 7. lozenge
8. monument, notebook
taboo, tabu... 3. ban 4. deny
5. debar 6. forbid 7. embargo
8. disallow, prohibit 9. forbidden,
interdict, proscribe 11. prohibition
12. interdiction
tabulate... 4. list 6. record 7. tabular
8. classify, schedule
tabulation... 7. listing 8. calendar,
paradigm 12. registration
taccada... 9. fanflower
tacit... 6. silent 7. implied
8. unspoken, wordless 9. indicated,
noiseless 10. understood
taciturn... 6. silent 8. reserved,
reticent 9. saturnine
tack... 4. brad, gear, jibe, join, rope,
sail, trip 5. baste, lease, route
6. course, fasten, secure, staple,
tackle 7. clothes 9. fastening
10. supplement
tackle... 3. cat, rig 4. gear, tack
5. davit, seize 6. burton, collar,
garnet 7. cordage, grapple, harness,
rigging 8. football (term)
9. encounter, equipment, undertake
tacky... 5. crude, dowdy, seedy
6. shabby, sticky, untidy 8. adhesive,
slovenly
tact... 5. grace, poise, taste

7. address, finesse 8. delicacy
9. diplomacy 10. adroitness,
cleverness, discretion
11. discernment, savoir–faire
14. discrimination

tadpole . . . 4. frog, toad 8. polliwog,
porwigle 9. youngling

tag . . . 3. add, end, rag, tab 4. flap,
game, loop, name 5. aglet (aiglet),
label, sheep, strip 6. fasten, follow
7. earmark, frazzle, pendant, taglock
9. appendage 11. aiguillette
(ornamental)

Tagalog, Tagal (pert to) . . .
child, servant . . 4. anac, bata
deity . . 6. Batala
game (gambling) . . 10. panguingui
native of . . 5. Luzon 11. Philippines
peasant . . 3. tao
race . . 4. Aeta (dwarf) 7. Malayan

Tahiti . . .
arrowroot . . 3. pia
boat . . 4. pahi
capital . . 7. Papeete (of all Society
Isles)
food plant . . 4. taro
god . . 3. oro 6. Taaroa (Supreme)
old name . . 8. Otaheite
robe (coronation) . . 4. malo
woman . . 6. wahine (vahine)

Tai, Thai tribes . . . 4. Laos, Shan
7. Siamese

tail . . . 3. bun, cue, end 4. arse, back,
hair, last, rear 5. cauda, stern
6. follow, shadow 7. pendant
8. entailed, streamer 9. afterpart,
appendage, extremity

tail (pert to) . . .
aircraft's . . 9. empennage
boar's . . 6. wreath
coin . . 5. verso 7. reverse
dog's . . 5. plume, stern, twist
having a . . 7. caudate
peacock's . . 5. train
pert to . . 6. caudal 9. coccygeal
rabbit's . . 4. scut
rudimentary . . 6. coccyx
tailrace . . 5. flume 7. channel

tailing . . . 5. chaff, waste 6. refuse

tailless . . . 6. tenrec (mammal)
7. acaudal, anurous, Ranidae
8. acaudate, ecaudate

tailor . . . 3. cut, fit 4. form 6. darzee,
draper, sartor 7. fashion 8. tailleur

tailor (pert to) . . .
goose . . 4. iron 12. pressing iron
made . . 6. fitted 9. fashioned
reference to . . 9. sartorial
twist . . 10. silk thread (stout)

taint . . . 3. due, hue 5. color, imbue,
spoil, stain, sully, tinge 6. defile,
infect, poison, stigma 7. blemish,
corrupt, deprave, pollute, vitiate
8. disgrace 9. denigrate, infection
10. corruption, stigmatize
11. contaminate

tainted . . . 3. bad 6. soiled 7. stained
8. diseased 9. corrupted

taintless . . . 4. good 5. clean
6. chaste 8. flawless, innocent

Taiwan . . .
capital . . 6. Taipai

Taj Mahal (pert to) . . .
architecture . . 9. Saracenic
builder . . 9. Shah–Jahan
mausolem site . . 4. Agra
named for . . 4. wife

take . . . 2. go 3. get, win 4. deem,
doff, gain, shut 5. atone, booty, carry,
catch, seize, snare, steal, usurp
6. accept, borrow, deduce, endure,
obtain 7. capture, conduct, control,
detract, receive 8. proceeds, receipts,
subtract, tolerate 9. apprehend
11. appropriate

take (pert to) . . .
a chair . . 3. sit
a direction . . 5. steer
advantage of . . 5. abuse 6. misuse
apart . . 8. demolish 11. disassemble
as one's own . . 5. adopt 6. borrow
away . . 5. adeem, clear, reave, steal,
wrest 6. adempt, deduct, remove
7. deprive, detract, retract
8. derogate, subtract, withdraw
11. expropriate
back . . 6. recant, repeal, return
by storm . . 5. seize 6. attack
by stratagem . . 4. trap 8. outsmart
care of . . 4. mind 5. guard, nurse,
serve, watch 6. beware 7. support
10. provide for
charge of . . 8. attend to 9. look after
down . . 4. fell, raze 5. lower, write
6. humble, record 7. reprove,
swallow 8. emaciate
first . . 7. pre–empt
for granted . . 5. infer 6. assume,
expect 7. believe, presume, suppose
in . . 3. eat, see 4. hear 5. admit,
annex, learn 6. absorb, attend
7. embrace, include, involve, receive,
shorten 9. encompass
notice . . 2. NB 3. see
out . . 4. dele 5. elide 6. delete, efface
7. expunge
place of . . 8. supplant 9. supersede
the floor . . 5. speak 7. address
9. legislate
to flight . . 4. flee 7. run away,
scamper 9. skedaddle
up . . 4. fill, lift 5. adopt, begin, raise
6. absorb, assume, gather, occupy
8. engage in 9. undertake
without authority . . 5. usurp

talapoin . . . 6. monkey (guenon)
8. poonghie 12. Buddhist monk

talc . . . 6. powder, talcum 7. agalite
8. steatite 9. soapstone

tale . . . 3. lai, lay, lie 4. myth, saga,
yarn 5. conte, fable, story 6. gossip,
legend 7. romance 8. anecdote
9. discourse, falsehood, narration,
narrative 11. declaration
12. conversation

tale (pert to) . . .
adventure . . 4. gest
bearer . . 6. gossip 7. blabber, tattler
8. informer 13. scandalmonger
chivalry . . 7. romance
doleful . . 8. jeremiad
fatality . . 5. drama 7. tragedy
symbolic . . 8. allegory
traditional . . 4. saga 8. folktale

T
Z

talent ... 4. gift 5. dower, flair, forte, money (anc), skill 6. genius 7. ability, faculty 8. aptitude, artistry 9. attribute 11. disposition 14. accomplishment

talesman ... 5. juror 8. narrator

talisman ... 4. juju, mojo, tara 5. charm, karma 6. amulet, fetish, grigri (greegree), scarab 7. periapt 12. antinganting

talk ... 3. gab, gas, rap, yak, yap 4. blab, blat, chat, chin, harp, rant, rave 5. lingo, orate, parle, prate, rumor, speak, spiel, utter 6. babble, confab, confer, gabble, gossip, jargon, lesson, speech 7. address, blabber, chatter, declaim, discuss 8. causerie, chitchat, colloquy, converse, language, parlance 9. dalliance, discourse 11. communicate 12. conversation

talk (pert to) ...
about .. 5. rumor 6. gossip
affected, pretentious .. 4. cant, rant
ancient .. 5. parle
back .. 4. sass 6. retort 7. riposte 8. feedback, repartee
flattering .. 7. palaver
fluent .. 7. verbose, voluble
idiotically .. 6. drivel
long .. 9. gibberish, rigmarole
loud .. 5. blate
promoting .. 4. hype 8. ballyhoo
running .. 6. patter
silly .. 5. drool 6. drivel, footle 7. blather, prattle, twaddle
slang .. 3. gab, gas 4. sass 5. spiel
slowly .. 5. drawl
small .. 3. gab 4. chat, chin 7. prattle 8. chitchat
Spanish .. 7. palabra

talkative ... 4. glib 6. fluent 7. verbose, voluble 9. garrulous 10. loquacious 13. communicative

talker ... 6. gasser, proser, ranter 7. speaker, spieler 10. chatterbox 17. conversationalist

tall ... 4. high, long 5. lofty 6. seemly 7. procere, sky–high 8. towering, yielding 10. incredible, statuesque 11. exaggerated

tall (pert to) ...
order .. 3. falsehood 10. difficulty
person .. 10. hypermeter
structure .. 7. steeple
talk .. 4. brag 12. exaggeration 14. grandiloquence

tallest known race ... 10. Patagonian

tally ... 3. run, sum, tab 4. goal, list, mark 5. agree, check, count, match, notch, score 6. accord, reckon, record 7. account, compare, count up 8. coincide, estimate 9. reckoning 10. bottom line, correspond

Talmud ... 9. Jewish law

Talmud (pert to) ...
academy .. 8. Yeshivah (Yeshiva)
commentary .. 6. Gemara
student .. 5. bahur
text .. 7. Mishnah

talon ... 3. paw 4. claw, fang, nail 6. clutch, finger, pincer

talus ... 5. ankle 8. clubfoot

tamarisk ... 4. atle (atlee) 8. salt tree

tambo ... 3. inn 6. corral, stable, tavern 10. tambourine

tambor ... 6. puffer 8. rockfish

tambour ... 4. desk, drum, lace 5. frame 6. stitch 7. drummer 8. ornament, stockade 9. embroider

tambourine ... 4. dove, drum, taar 5. daira 7. timbrel 8. minstrel

tambourine effect (Mus) ... 7. travale

tambreet ... 8. duckbill

tamburone ... 4. drum 8. bass drum

tame ... 4. dull, meek, mild 5. inert 6. docile, gentle, humble, subdue 7. crushed, insipid, subdued 8. tone down 9. tractable 10. cultivated 11. domesticate 12. domesticated

Tamil ... 5. Hindu 8. language (oldest Dravidian) 9. Dravidian

tamis ... 5. sieve, tammy 8. strainer

Tammany (pert to) ...
Hall .. 14. Democratic Club
man .. 10. politician
officer .. 8. Wiskinky (Wiskinkie)
scandal .. 9. Tweed Ring
Society site .. 11. New York City (1789)
symbol .. 5. tiger

tamper with ... 4. plot 5. alter, bribe 6. meddle, monkey, scheme, tinker 7. falsify 9. influence, interfere

tampion, tampon ... 4. plug 6. tympan 7. stopper, turnpin 9. rhynobyon

tan ... 3. dun, taw 4. buff, ecru, tent, whip 5. beige, brown, color, tawny 6. rabbit, suntan, thrash 8. sunburn

tanager ... 4. yeni 5. lindo 7. Piranga, redbird

tanbark ... 3. oak 7. hemlock

Tancred ... 6. leader (1st crusade)

Tanganyika ... see *Tanzania*

tangible ... 4. real 7. tactile 8. palpable 9. objective, touchable 11. perceptible, substantial

tangle ... 3. mat, mop 4. kink, shag 5. ravel, snare, snarl, weave 6. entrap, medley, muddle, sleave, tousle 7. ensnare, involve 8. quandary 9. interlock 10. complicate, interweave

tank ... 3. vat 4. lake, pond, pool 5. basin 6. hot tub 7. cistern, stomach 9. reservoir 11. army vehicle, hard drinker

tanker ... 4. ship 5. oiler 8. fuel ship

tanning shrub ... 5. alder, sumac (sumach)

tantalize ... 3. vex 5. taunt, tease 6. harass, plague 7. torment

tantalum symbol ... 2. Ta

Tantalus (pert to) ...
father .. 4. Zeus
father of .. 5. Niobe 6. Pelops
genus of .. 4. ibis
king (rich) .. 6. Greece

tantamount ... 5. equal 9. identical 10. equivalent 13. corresponding

tantara ... 7. fanfare 9. tantarara 12. trumpet blare

tantrum ... 3. fit 4. rage 7. caprice 8. tirrivee (tirrivie) 10. conniption

Tanzania, Africa . . .
  capital . . 11. Dar es Salaam (Haven of
    Peace)
  famed Mt . . 11. Kilimanjaro
  famed plains . . 9. Serengeti
  famed town . . 5. Ujiji (Stanley found
    Livingstone, 1871)
  formerly . . 8. Zanzibar 10. Tanganyika
  language . . 7. Swahili
  natives . . 5. Bantu
Taoism, names . . . 6. Kwanti, Laotze
    7. Yu Hwang
tap . . . 3. dum, hit, hob, rap 4. plug,
    tamp 5. sound, spile 6. faucet,
    liquor, siphon, spigot, strike
    7. censure, petcock, reprove
tape . . . 3. gin, tie 4. band, wick
    5. strip 6. fillet, ribbon, secure
    7. bandage, measure 9. recording
taper . . . 4. ream, wick 5. point, snape,
    spire 6. candle, cierge, narrow
    7. conical 8. decrease, diminish
    9. acuminate 11. pyramidical
tapering (pert to) . . .
  blades . . 6. spires
  pert to . . 6. spired, terete 7. conical,
    pointed 8. fusiform 9. narrowing
  piece . . 4. gore 5. miter 6. gusset
  pillar . . 7. obelisk
  solid . . 4. cone
tapestry . . . 5. arras, tapis 6. Bayeux,
    dosser 7. Gobelin
tapeworm . . . 6. Taenia
tapeworm (pert to) . . .
  embryonic . . 10. oncosphere
  like . . 8. taenioid
  segment . . 8. strobila
tapioca, source . . . 5. salep 7. cassava
    (casava)
Tapirus . . . 6. tapirs
tapster . . . 7. barmaid, skinker
tar . . . 3. gob 4. brea, pave, salt
    5. black, pitch 6. cresol, maltha,
    sailor, seaman 7. mariner 8. telegram
    10. bluejacket
tarantula . . . 6. spider 7. mygalid
    10. wolf spider
tarboosh . . . 3. fez 6. red cap
tardy . . . 3. lag, lax 4. late, slow
    5. slack 6. remiss 7. belated,
    lagging, overdue 8. dilatory
    10. behindhand 11. cunctatious
tare . . . 4. weed (Bib) 5. vetch
    8. discount 9. allowance, deduction
target . . . 3. aim, tee 4. butt, goal,
    goat, mark, prey 5. sight 6. object,
    shield, tassel 8. bull's-eye, ridicule
    9. objective
tariff . . . 4. duty, list, rate 6. charge
    7. tribute 8. schedule
tariffist . . . 8. advocate
    13. protectionist
tarnish . . . 3. dim 4. dull, soil, spot
    5. cloud, stain, sully, taint 6. smirch,
    stigma, vilify 7. blemish, destroy,
    obscure 8. besmirch, discolor
    10. lose luster, stigmatize
taro . . . 3. poi 4. eddo, food, gabi
    (gabe) 5. cocco, tania (tanier)
    12. elephant's-ear
tarot . . . 14. fortunetelling (cards)
tarried . . . 6. waited 7. dallied

  8. lingered, remained
tarry . . . 3. lag 4. bide, stay, wait
    5. abide, await, dally, delay, pause,
    stall 6. dawdle, linger, loiter, retard
    7. outstay
tarsus . . . 5. ankle 7. segment
tart . . . 4. acid, sour 5. acrid, sharp
    6. pastry, severe 7. caustic, pungent,
    waspish 8. poignant, turnover
    10. astringent 11. acrimonious
tartan . . . 4. wool 5. plaid 7. pattern
    (plaid) 10. Highlander
tartar . . . 5. argol (argal), shrew, valet
    12. incrustation
Tartar, Tatar . . . 4. Turk 6. Mongol
Tartar, Tatar (pert to) . . .
  domain . . 7. Khanate
  horseman . . 7. Cossack
  lancer . . 5. uhlan
  nobleman . . 5. murza
  people of . . 6. Turkey 8. Mongolia
  title . . 4. Khan
  tribe . . 2. Hu 3. Hun 6. Mongol
tartarean . . . 5. cruel 7. hellish
    8. infernal
Tartarus (Myth) . . . 4. hell 5. Hades
    15. infernal regions (Iliad)
task . . . 3. job 4. duty, snap, test, toil
    5. chore, labor, stent, stint 6. burden,
    dargue, impost, strain 10. assignment,
    employment 11. undertaking
Tasmania (pert to) . . .
  animal (burrowing) . . 6. wombat
  discoverer . . 6. Tasman (1642)
  marsupial . . 9. phalanger
  mountain . . 6. Cradle 9. Ben Lomond
  strait . . 4. Bass
taste . . . 3. sip, sup 4. tang 5. flair,
    sapor, savor, sense, smack, style
    6. liking, palate, relish, sample
    7. soupçon 8. delicacy, elegance,
    fondness, judgment 9. gustation
    10. experience 14. discrimination
    15. aesthetic liking
taste (pert to) . . .
  bite . . 4. nosh 5. snack
  decided . . 8. fondness, penchant
  French . . 7. soupçon
  fundamental . . 4. acid, salt 5. sweet
    6. bitter
  lacking . . 4. rude 5. bland, gross, stale
    10. unpolished
  ref to . . 7. palatal 9. gustatory
  sharp . . 4. acid, tang
tasteless . . . 4. dull, flat 5. vapid
    6. vulgar, watery 7. insipid 8. lifeless
    9. savorless 10. inartistic
tasty . . . 6. savory 8. saporous, tasteful
    9. delicious, palatable, toothsome
Tatar . . . see *Tartar*
tatouay . . . 9. armadillo
tatter . . . 3. rag 4. tags, tear 5. patch,
    piece, shred 6. ribbon
tatterdemalion . . . 5. gamin
    9. ragpicker 10. ragamuffin
tattle . . . 4. blab, tell 5. prate 6. gossip
    7. chatter, divulge, prattle 8. idle
    talk, inform on
tattler . . . 6. gossip, willet 8. quidnunc,
    redshank, telltale 10. alarm clock,
    talebearer, yellowlegs
tattoo . . . 4. call (drum, bugle), pony,

scar 13. entertainment
tau... 4. ankh, crux, rood 5. cross
6. letter (Gr) 7. T–shaped
tau cross... 4. ankh 6. symbol
8. crucifix, insignia 10. St Anthony's
taunt... 4. gibe, jeer, mock, twit
5. sneer, tease 6. deride 7. provoke
8. reproach, ridicule 9. aggravate
Taurus... 4. bull 8. Pleiades
13. constellation
taut... 4. firm, snug, tidy 5. tense,
tight 6. severe, strict 7. nervous
9. distended
tautology... 8. pleonasm
10. redundancy, repetition
tavern... 3. inn, pub 5. hotel
7. barroom, cabaret, Gasthof, taberna
8. alehouse, Gasthaus, hostelry
taw... 4. game, whip 6. marble
7. tanning
tawdry... 4. loud 5. cheap, gaudy,
showy 6. garish 7. blatant
tawny, tawney... 3. tan 5. dusky,
olive, tenne 6. tanned 7. jacinth
8. brindled 9. bullfinch
tax... 4. cess, duty, geld, levy, scat
(scatt), task, toll 5. stent 6. assess,
burden, custom, excise, impose,
income, octroi, strain 7. doomage,
license, tribute 8. exaction, overtire
9. prescribe 10. assessment
tax (pert to)...
ancient.. 3. cro 4. geld 7. galanas
assessment.. 4. rate 5. ratal
7. doomage
church.. 5. tithe
commodity.. 6. octroi
French history.. 6. taille
kind.. 5. tithe 6. excise, surtax, taille
7. boscage 8. auxilium, carucage
9. surcharge
liquor.. 6. abkari (abkary)
pasturage (Shetland Isls).. 4. scat
(scatt)
tea... 5. dance, party, shrub 6. supper
8. beverage, function, sociable
9. collation, reception
tea (pert to)...
chemical content.. 6. tannin, theine
(thein) 8. caffeine
Chinese.. 5. black, hyson
Formosa.. 6. oolong
Ind Ceylon.. 5. pekoe
infusion.. 6. ptisan, tisane
Labrador.. 5. Ledum 8. gowiddie
Paraguay.. 5. yerba
receptacle.. 5. caddy 8. canister
table.. 6. teapoy (tepoy)
type.. 3. cha 4. tsia 5. Assam, black,
green, hyson, Ledum, oopak, pekoe
6. oolong 7. cambric 8. gowiddie
urn.. 3. pot 7. samovar
weak.. 7. cambric
teach... 4. show 5. coach, drill, edify,
guide, prime, train, tutor 6. direct,
impart, preach, school 7. educate,
show how 8. instruct 9. enlighten
11. demonstrate
teacher... 5. coach, guide, rabbi, tutor
6. doctor, mentor, pastor, pedant,
priest, pundit, reader, regent, rhetor,
scribe 7. edifier, starets 8. educator,

preacher 9. pedagogue, preceptor
10. instructor
teacher (pert to)...
Alexandrian.. 6. Origen
Indian.. 4. guru
Jewish.. 5. rabbi
Mohammedan.. 3. pir 4. imam
6. mullah
of the deaf.. 7. oralist
Russian.. 7. starets
teaching... 5. moral 6. docent
7. precept 8. doctrine 11. instruction
Teaching of the Twelve... 10. The
Didache
team... 3. two 4. haul, join, pain,
span, yoke 5. brood, chain, wagon
7. vehicle 8. carriage 9. yannigans
teamster... 6. carter, driver 7. carrier
Teapot Dome (pert to)...
known as.. 8. Scandals (Teapot
Dome)
leased by.. 4. Fall (Sec'y of Interior)
lease of.. 8. oil field
site.. 8. Elk Hills (Wyo)
tear... 3. rip 4. rend, rent, rive
5. revel, sever, speed, split, spree
6. cleave, hasten 7. destroy, shatter,
torment 8. lacerate, separate
10. dilacerate
tear (pert to)...
apart.. 7. disjoin 8. demolish
asunder.. 10. dilacerate
down.. 4. rase, raze
limb from limb.. 6. punish
9. dismember
to shreds.. 6. tatter
up.. 3. rip 6. damage
up the roots.. 6. arache
teardrop lace design... 5. larme
tearful... 3. sad 7. maudlin, weeping
9. lachrymal (lacrimal)
tears... 5. drops (lachrymal), grief,
rheum 6. lament 9. teardrops
tease... 3. guy, nag, rag, vex 4. twit
5. annoy, devil, taunt 6. bother,
harass, heckle, needle, pester, plague
7. provoke, torment 8. irritate
9. aggravate, tantalize
teaser... 4. gull 6. carder, curler,
sniper, stoker 7. curtain, fireman,
problem 8. pesterer, willower
9. tormentor 13. advertisement
technical... 7. skilled, trained
8. specific 11. specialized
12. professional
technocracy... 12. organization
17. rule by technicians
technology... 3. art 7. science
9. technique 10. agrotechny,
virtuosity 11. terminology
12. nomenclature 13. ethnotechnics
techy... 6. touchy, vexing 7. fretful,
peevish 9. irascible, irritable, sensitive
tedious... 3. dry 4. dull 5. bored,
prosy 6. boring, prolix 7. irksome,
noxious 11. displeasing, repetitious
13. uninteresting
tedium... 5. ennui 7. boredom
10. melancholy 11. tediousness
teeming... 4. full 6. aswarm
7. pouring, replete 8. crowding,
numerous, prolific 9. abounding

10. productive 11. overflowing

teeter ... 4. rock 5. waver 6. jiggle, seesaw 9. alternate, fluctuate, sandpiper, vacillate 12. teeter–totter

teeth ... 5. bucks, fangs 6. molars, tushes 7. canines, ivories 8. grinders, incisors

teeth (pert to) ...
all alike .. 7. isodont
cleaning .. 5. brush, floss
   10. dentrifice, toothpaste
covering .. 6. enamel
crustation .. 6. tartar
destitute of .. 5. morné (Her)
   8. edentate 10. edentulous
elephant's .. 9. scrivello 11. scrivelloes
false .. 8. choppers (sl), dentures
few .. 12. oligodontous
large .. 8. megadont 9. macrodont
pointed .. 5. fangs, tusks 6. tushes
ref to .. 4. pulp 5. molar 6. dental
   7. dentine 8. odontoid
science .. 10. odontology

teething ... 6. growth 9. dentition, odontosis 10. odontogeny

teetotaller ... 3. dry 7. non–user 9. abstainer, nephalist, Rechabite (Bib) 11. teetotalist

teg, tag ... 3. doe 5. sheep (young), woman 6. fleece (sheep's)

teguexin ... 4. teju 6. lizard

tegument ... 4. bark, coat, skin 5. cover 6. cortex 10. integument

tekke ... 3. rug 6. carpet 7. convent 9. monastery

tela ... 6. tissue 8. membrane

Telamon (Gr Myth, pert to) ...
brother .. 6. Peleus
companion .. 8. Hercules
expedition .. 8. boar hunt
   10. Argonautic
male figure .. 6. column 7. support
son .. 4. Ajax 6. Teucer

telegraph (pert to) ...
code, inventor .. 5. Morse (Samuel F)
key .. 6. tapper
service .. 5. cable 8. dispatch

telephone (pert to) ...
inventor .. 4. Bell (Alexander)
term .. 3. PBX 4. buzz, call, dial, hold, horn (sl), ring, toll 5. trunk 6. call up 7. collect, hotline 8. exchange, intercom 10. videophone 11. push–button, switchboard 12. speakerphone 14. radiotelephone

telescope ... 4. Lick 6. Yerkes 7. Palomar 8. Galilean (1609) 9. Gregorian (Scot 1663)

telescopic ... 9. farseeing

television ... 2. TV 3. box, set 4. tube 5. telly (Brit) 8. boob tube, idiot box 11. small screen

television (pert to) ...
person .. 6. anchor, viewer 7. sponsor 9. superstar 10. newscaster
program .. 4. show 6. sitcom 7. variety 8. newscast 9. docudrama, soap opera
term .. 3. air 5. audio, bleep, cable, rerun 7. channel, minicam 8. telecast 10. commercial, laugh track

tell ... 3. say 4. talk 5. count, peach,

utter 6. assail, impart, inform, recite, reckon, relate, repeat, report, reveal 7. divulge, narrate, recount 8. acquaint, disclose, rehearse 9. recognize 11. communicate

teller ... 6. banker 8. informer, narrator 9. describer, informant

telling ... 6. cogent, potent 8. forceful, striking 9. affective, narration, pertinent 11. influential, significant

telltale ... 4. blab, clue, hint 6. bearer, device, gossip 7. tattler 8. informer 9. indicator, informing 10. indication, talebearer

tellurian ... 2. Te 7. earthly 11. terrestrial 12. earth dweller

temeritous, temerarious ... 4. rash 8. heedless, reckless 10. headstrong

temerity ... 4. gall 5. cheek, nerve 8. audacity, rashness 10. effrontery 12. recklessness

temper ... 4. mood 5. humor 6. adjust, animus, anneal, attune, dander, harden, nature, season, soften 7. assuage, mollify, tantrum 8. hardness, mitigate, moderate 9. composure 10. equanimity, irritation 11. disposition, temperament

temper (pert to) ...
bad .. 5. angry, rabid 6. fuming, savage 7. furious, ranting
clay .. 6. puddle
even .. 4. calm 5. staid 6. sedate
heat of .. 6. choler
in a .. 4. huff, rage, stew 5. tizzy
metal .. 6. anneal, harden 7. toughen

temperament ... 4. mood 6. crasis, nature 8. artistic 11. disposition

temperance ... 6. virtue 8. calmness, sobriety 10. abstinence, moderation 11. self–control 13. self–restraint 14. abstemiousness

temperate ... 4. calm, cool 5. sober 8. moderate 10. abstemious, restrained 14. self–controlled

tempered ... 5. angry 6. sedate 8. annealed, disposed, moderate 9. moderated, mollified, qualified

tempest ... 4. gale, wind 5. blast, orage, storm 6. tumult 7. turmoil 9. agitation, commotion, windstorm 10. excitement 12. thunderstorm

Tempest (pert to) ...
Cuban .. 6. bayamo
in a teapot .. 10. triviality
   12. exaggeration
The (character) .. 5. Ariel (spirit) 7. Caliban, Miranda 8. Prospero

tempestuous ... 5. windy 6. stormy 7. excited, violent 9. turbulent

temple ... 4. fane, naos 5. cella, ratha, speos 6. aedile, church, pagoda 7. edifice

temple (pert to) ...
Anglo–Ind .. 5. kovil (covil)
approach .. 5. toran (torana)
Assyrian .. 8. ziggurat (anc)
Aztec temple site .. 12. Tenochtitlan
Chinese .. 6. pagoda
Hawaiian .. 5. heiau
Mexico .. 8. teocalli
Mohammedan .. 6. mosque

part.. 4. naos 5. cella 6. adytum
7. narthex, sanctum 10. penetralia
ref to.. 6. hieron
sanctuary.. 10. penetralia
Shinto.. 3. Sha 5. jinja (jinsha)
7. yashiro
Temple Bar (London)... 7. gateway
Temple Butte site... 11. Grand
Canyon
Temple of Heaven... 7. Peiping
Temple of Onias... 5. Egypt
Temple of Reason... 9. Notre Dame
Temple of the Sphinx... 5. Egypt
tempo... 4. pace, time 5. grave, largo,
speed 6. adagio, presto, rhythm
7. allegro, andante 8. moderato
11. synchronism
temporal... 4. bene, laic 5. civil
7. earthly, secular, worldly
9. ephemeral, temporary
10. transitory 11. present time
13. chronological
temporize... 5. delay 6. demand,
parley 9. negotiate 13. procrastinate
tempt... 4. lead, lure 5. decoy
6. allure, entice, induce, seduce
7. attract 8. persuade 9. seduction
10. inducement
Tempter, The... 5. Devil, Satan 7. Evil
One 10. Evil Spirit, Old Serpent
14. Prince of Devils
temptress... 5. siren 7. Delilah (Bib),
mermaid 11. enchantress
ten (pert to)...
ace.. 10. bridge game
Commandments.. 9. Decalogue
dollars.. 7. sawbuck
fold.. 6. denary 7. decuple
footed.. 7. decapod
gallon hat.. 7. Stetson 8. sombrero
geometric figure.. 7. decagon
10. decahedron
measure.. 4. acre, bath 6. decare
number.. 5. decad 7. several
physics.. 3. bel
poetic.. 9. decameter (decametre)
prefix.. 4. deca (deka)
stringed.. 9. decachord
thousand.. 6. myriad
year period.. 6. decade 9. decenniad,
decennium
tenable... 10. defensible
12. maintainable
tenacious... 5. tough 6. dogged, viscid
7. viscous 8. adhesive, cohesive,
sticking, stubborn 9. glutinous,
obstinate, retentive 10. persistent
12. pertinacious
tenant... 4. saer 5. ceile, dreng
(drengh) 6. holder, leaser, lessee,
renter, vassal 7. cottier, dweller,
villein 8. occupant 10. inhabitant
tenant's tribute... 4. cens
tend... 4. care, heed, lean, mind, wait
5. nurse, offer, serve, watch
6. attend, manage 7. incline, oversee
8. converge, minister 9. cultivate,
gravitate, look after
tendency... 4. bent, bias, tide 5. drift,
drive, trend 6. course, object
7. bearing, leaning 8. aptitude,
relation 9. direction, proneness
10. proclivity, propensity
11. disposition, inclination
tender... 3. bed, pay 4. boat, fond,
gift, give, kind, soft, sore 5. offer,
young 6. extend, gentle, humane,
waiter 7. pitiful, present, rail car
8. delicate, merciful 9. attendant,
sensitive 10. effeminate
11. softhearted, sympathetic,
warmhearted 12. affectionate
13. compassionate
tender (pert to)...
animal.. 6. cowboy, herder
farm.. 10. husbandman
feeling.. 9. sentiment
foot.. 4. dude 6. novice 8. newcomer
10. raw recruit
hearted.. 4. kind 8. merciful
horse.. 5. groom 6. ostler 7. hostler
regard.. 4. love 6. tendre
ship.. 7. pinnace
style.. 7. amoroso
tenderloin... 4. meat 7. brothel
12. city district, vice district
tenderness... 4. love, pity 8. sympathy
9. affection 10. compassion,
gentleness
tending to...
arouse.. 7. emotive
assist memory.. 8. mnemonic
check.. 10. repressive
clear of guilt.. 11. exculpatory
control.. 10. regulating
drive away.. 9. repellant
evade.. 7. elusory
lateness.. 7. tardive
separate.. 8. divisive
tear.. 10. lacerative
wear away.. 8. abrasive
tendon... 4. cord, thew 5. sinew
8. ligament 11. aponeurosis
tendril... 4. coil, curl 5. shoot, sprig
6. branch, cirrus 7. stipule
8. filament
tenet... 3. ism 4. rule 5. canon,
creed, dogma, maxim 6. belief
7. precept 8. doctrine 9. principle
tenne... 5. brown, color
Tennessee...
battle.. 11. Chattanooga 14. Above
the Clouds
capital.. 9. Nashville (Athens of the
South)
city.. 7. Memphis 8. Oak Ridge
9. Knoxville 11. Chattanooga
first State.. 8. Franklin
Mts.. 7. Lookout 10. Cumberland,
Great Smoky 13. Clingman's Dome
museum.. 9. Hermitage, Parthenon
12. Atomic Energy (Oak Ridge)
13. Ancestral Home (Pres Polk)
park.. 6. Shiloh
river.. 9. Tennessee
State admission.. 9. Sixteenth
State motto.. 16. America At Its Best
State nickname.. 9. Volunteer
tennis (pert to)...
four persons.. 7. doubles
player.. 6. netman
score.. 3. ace 4. love 5. deuce
series.. 3. set
site.. 5. court

stroke.. 3. cut, lob
term.. 3. ace, lob, net, set 5. serve
6. hazard 7. receive
two persons.. 7. singles
tenon... 3. cog 4. tusk 5. tooth
7. mortise
tenor... 4. alto (violin), copy, mode,
tone 5. drift, trend 6. course, intent,
singer 7. meaning, purport
8. tenoreno 9. male voice, procedure
10. transcript
tense... 4. rapt, taut 5. rigid, tight
6. intent 7. intense, nervous, stretch
8. strained 9. stretched
10. breathless
tense (grammar)... 4. past 6. future
7. perfect, present 9. preterite
10. pluperfect 11. past perfect,
progressive
tensile... 6. pliant 7. ductile
8. tensible
tension... 6. strain, stress 7. detente,
nervous 9. disaccord, stiffness
tent... 3. hut 4. camp, show 5. cover,
lodge 6. dossil 7. marquee
8. pavilion
tent (pert to)...
covering.. 4. tilt
Eskimo.. 5. tubik (skin)
general's.. 10. praetorium (pretorium)
India.. 4. pawl
Indian.. 5. tepee 6. teepee, wigwam
occupant.. 5. nomad 6. camper
7. tourist
Russian.. 7. kibitka
Scottish.. 6. pulpit
surgical.. 6. screen
tribe (Arab).. 5. Kedar
type.. 3. fly, pup 4. bell, wall
6. Sibley 8. pavilion
tentacle... 4. hair, palp 6. feeler
7. tendril
tentative... 7. feeling, testing
9. makeshift, temporary
10. substitute 11. making trial,
provisional 12. experimental
tenterhooks... 6. strain 8. suspense
10. uneasiness
tenth... 5. decim, tithe 6. decima
9. organ stop
tenth Muse... 6. Sappho
Tent Maker... 4. Omar
tenuity... 6. rarity 7. poverty
8. delicacy, subtlety, thinness
9. indigence, unreality
tenuous... 4. rare, thin 7. slender,
subtile 8. delicate, ethereal
13. unsubstantial
tenure... 4. term 5. lease 6. socage
7. holding 10. possession
tepee, teepee... 4. tent 6. wigwam
tepid... 4. mild, warm 8. lukewarm
tequila... 6. liquor 12. century plant
teraphim... 5. idols 6. images
teras... 7. monster
tergiversate... 3. lie 5. evade, shift
10. apostasize, equivocate
term... 3. age, end, era 4. date,
name, time, word 5. epoch, limit,
style 6. estate, period, tenure
7. premise 8. duration, semester,
terminus 12. nomenclature

term (pert to)...
connotation.. 6. intent 11. designation
death.. 4. doom, mort
for years.. 10. real estate
glacial.. 5. stoss
golf.. 4. hook 5. bogey (bogie), divot,
eagle, slice 6. birdie
grammar.. 6. phrase, syntax
11. phraseology
logic.. 4. mode 5. major, minor
of life.. 3. age 5. sands (hourglass)
Rugby.. 5. scrum
sea.. 4. ahoy 5. avast, belay
tennis.. 4. love 5. deuce, serve
termagant... 5. scold, shrew, vixen
6. Amazon, virigo 7. furious
8. scolding 9. turbulent
10. boisterous, tumultuous
11. quarrelsome
Termagant... 5. deity 14. imaginary
being
terminal... 3. end 4. goal 5. anode,
depot, final, limit 6. finish 7. limital,
station 8. desinent, terminus,
ultimate 9. end of life, extremity
10. concluding 11. desinential,
destination, termination
terminal (pert to)...
battery.. 5. anode 7. cathode
9. electrode
leaf.. 8. apiculus
ornament.. 6. finial
town (end of line).. 8. terminus
terminate... 3. end 4. halt 5. cease,
close, limit 6. expire, result 7. end
with 8. complete, conclude.
termination... 3. end 4. amen
5. close, limit 6. ending, result
7. outcome 8. terminus 9. desinence
10. completion, conclusion, expiration
termite... 3. ant (white) 4. anay (anai)
8. Isoptera (Order)
tern... 4. darr (black), gull 6. Sterna
(genus) 8. schooner (Naut)
9. threefold 10. sea swallow
ternary... 5. three, triad 6. tercet
(Poet), triple 7. ternion, trinity
9. threefold
ternate... 4. tern 9. threefold
12. trifoliolate
terpsichore... 5. dance 6. dancer
7. dancing
Terpsichore (Myth)... 13. Muse of
dancing
terra... 5. earth 10. terra firma
terrace... 4. flaw (marble), mesa, step
7. balcony, gallery, plateau, portico
8. platform (earth) 9. colonnade
terrain, terrane... 4. land 5. tract
6. region 11. environment
terrapin... 4. Emys 6. turtle
8. Chelonia, Emydinae, tortoise
9. cheloniid
terrapin, turtle (pert to)...
color.. 9. grapenuts
type.. 6. potter, slider 10. red–bellied
11. diamondback 13. yellow–bellied
War.. 14. Eighteen Twelve (1812)
terrene, terrestrial... 4. land 5. earth,
realm 6. earthy, mortal 7. earthly,
mundane, worldly
terrestrial planets... 4. Mars 5. Venus

7. Mercury

terrible... 3. bad 4. dire 5. awful
6. tragic 7. fearful, ghastly, hideous,
painful 8. dreadful, horrible, terrific
9. appalling, frightful 10. formidable,
terrifying, unpleasant

Terrible, The... 4. Ivan (Russ Czar)

terrier... 3. fox 4. bull, Skye 5. Cairn,
Irish, Welsh 6. Boston 8. Airedale,
Scottish, Sealyham 9. Kerry blue,
schnauzer 10. Bedlington, Clydesdale
13. Dandie Dinmont

terrific... 5. great 6. superb
7. extreme 8. dreadful, exciting,
terrible 9. appalling, excessive,
frightful 10. tremendous

terrify... 3. awe, cow 4. stun
5. alarm, appal, haunt, scare, shock
6. appall, freeze 7. horrify, petrify
8. affright, frighten

territory... 4. area, land 5. banat, field
6. canton, region 7. country
8. district, environs, Pashalic
(Pasha's), province 10. palatinate

terror... 3. awe 4. fear 5. alarm,
dread, panic 6. fright, horror
7. hellion, Reign of (Hist)
13. consternation

terrorism... 11. subjugation
12. intimidation

terse... 4. curt, neat 5. pithy
6. smooth 7. compact, concise,
laconic, pointed, refined 8. succinct
11. sententious 12. accomplished,
epigrammatic

Tertiary period... 6. Eocene
7. Miocene 8. Pliocene 9. Oligocene
12. Age of Mammals

tertium quid... 12. third someone
13. third somewhat

tertulia... 4. club 5. party 7. meeting

tessellated... 6. mosaic 9. checkered

tessera... 3. die 4. cube, tile 5. token
6. marble, ticket 8. password
11. certificate

test... 3. try 4. exam, feel 5. assay,
proof, prove, taste, tempt, trial
6. ordeal, sample 7. examine,
witness 8. evidence, standard
9. criterion, testimony
10. experience, experiment
11. examination, performance
12. authenticate

test (pert to)...
fineness.. 3. pyx
orally.. 7. examine
ore, value.. 5. assay
pot.. 8. crucible
severe.. 6. ordeal

testa... 7. coating 8. covering,
tegument

testament... 3. New, Old 4. will
8. covenant

testator... 7. legator, witness
9. testatrix

tester... 6. canopy, helmet, prover,
taster 7. assayer, candler, sampler

testify... 5. avow 6. affirm, depone,
depose 7. declare, profess, protest
8. indicate, manifest 11. bear
witness

testimonial... 5. token 7. tribute,

warrant 8. evidence 9. reference
10. compliment 11. certificate

testimony... 7. witness 8. evidence
10. Scriptures 11. affirmation,
attestation, declaration

testy, tetchy... 6. touchy 7. fretful,
peevish 8. petulant, snappish
9. irascible, obstinate 10. headstrong

tetched in the head... 9. pixilated

tetrad... 4. four 7. quartet (quartette),
quatern 8. foursome 10. quaternion

tetragon... 4. park 6. square
7. rhombus 9. courtyard
10. quadrangle

Tetragrammaton... 7. Jehovah
12. Supreme Being 14. four
consonants (unpronounced)

Teuton... 4. Goth 6. German

Teutonic (pert to)...
alphabet character.. 4. rune
deity.. 2. Er 3. Tiu (Tiwaz), Tyr
4. Frea, Odin, Thor 5. Aesir, Bragi,
Wodin 6. Balder, Frigga 7. Forseti
8. Heimdall
demon.. 3. alp
giantess.. 4. Norn 11. demigoddess
goddess.. 3. Eir, Hel, Ran 4. Norn,
Urth (Urthr), Wyrd
homicide (tribal).. 5. morth
land.. 4. odal
law.. 5. Salic
nymph (water).. 3. nis
race.. 5. Goths, Jutes 6. Franks,
Saxons 7. Vandals 8. Lombards
10. Norwegians 13. Scandinavians
supernatural being.. 5. troll

Teutonic goddess of...
death.. 3. Hel, Ran
healing.. 3. Eir
peace.. 7. Nerthus

Teutonic god of...
justice.. 7. Forseti (Forsete)
pantheon.. 5. Aesir (group)
peace.. 6. Balder
sea.. 5. Aegir
skill.. 3. Ull (Ullr)
sky.. 2. Er 3. Tiu (Tiwaz), Tyr
thunder.. 4. Thor 5. Donar
war.. 3. Tiu (Tiwaz), Tyr

Texas...
birthplace of Pres.. 10. Eisenhower
capital.. 6. Austin
cattle.. 8. longhorn
city.. 4. Waco 6. Dallas, El Paso
7. Abilene, Denison, Houston 9. Fort
Worth, Galveston 10. San Antonio
flags (six).. 5. Spain 6. France,
Mexico 8. Republic (of Texas)
11. Confederate 12. United States
flower.. 10. bluebonnet, yellow rose
Indian tribe.. 5. Caddo
monument (Battle).. 10. San Jacinto
police.. 7. Rangers
river.. 3. Red 5. Pecos 9. Rio Grande
shrine, mission.. 5. Alamo
State admission.. 12. Twenty–eighth
State motto.. 5. Tejas 10. Friendship
State nickname.. 8. Lone Star

text... 4. book 5. topic, verse
7. passage 8. libretto, textbook
11. letterpress

textile screw pine... 3. ara

textile shop... 7. mercery
texture... 3. web 4. wale, warp, wooz
    5. grain, weave 6. cobweb, fabric
    7. textile 9. roughness, structure
    10. smoothness
Thailand (Siam), capital... 7. Bangkok
Thames River town... 4. Eton
thana... 13. police station
thanador... 7. officer (Hind)
thanatology doctrine... 5. death
thane... 5. baron (anc) 7. servant,
    warrior 9. Scots peer
thankless... 7. ingrate 10. ungrateful
    13. unappreciated
thanks... 5. grace 6. prayer
    8. gramercy 9. gratitude
    12. appreciation 14. acknowledgment
Thanks to God... 10. Deo gratias
that (pert to)...
    is.. 2. ie 5. id est
    is to say.. 3. viz 5. to wit 6. namely
    9. videlicit
    pronoun.. 3. who 4. what
thatch (pert to)...
    grass.. 4. rope 6. slough
    hair.. 3. mop 4. crop, mane
    palm.. 5. Sabal 7. Thrinax
    roofing.. 5. reeds, straw 6. rushes
    support.. 6. wattle
thatcher... 7. hellier
thaumaturgy... 5. magic 7. sorcery
    8. wizardry 11. legerdemain
the (pert to)...
    end.. 5. omega 6. thirty
    French.. 2. la, le 3. les
    German.. 3. das, der, die
    Italian.. 2. il, la, le 4. ella
    same.. 4. idem 5. ditto
    Spanish.. 2. el, la 3. las, los
theater, theatre... 5. arena, drama,
    odeum, stage 6. lyceum 8. coliseum
    9. playhouse 12. amphitheater
theater (pert to)...
    actress.. 7. heroine, ingénue
    box.. 4. loge
    curtain.. 4. drop 6. teaser
    district.. 6. Rialto 8. Broadway
    floor (lower).. 7. parquet
    full house.. 3. SRO
    Greek.. 5. odeum (odeon)
    part.. 3. box, pit 4. loge 5. foyer,
    stage 7. balcony, gallery, parquet
    8. parterre 9. orchestra
    10. proscenium
theatrical... 5. showy, stagy
    8. affected, dramatic 10. artificial,
    histrionic 12. melodramatic
theatrical (pert to)...
    art.. 10. histrionic
    company.. 6. troupe
    machine.. 9. eccyclema
    spectacle.. 5. revue 7. pageant
    star.. 4. hero, lead 7. heroine
Theban (pert to)...
    bard.. 6. Pindar
    deity.. 4. Amen (Amon) 6. Amen–Ra
    god.. 5. Ammon (Zeus)
    king.. 5. Laius 7. Amphion, Oedipus
    8. Pentheus
    queen.. 5. Niobe 7. Jocasta
    soothsayer (blind).. 8. Tiresias
    triad.. 3. Mut 6. Amen–Ra, Khonsu

Thebes...
    capital of.. 10. Upper Egypt (anc)
    famed avenue.. 8. Sphinxes
    famed for.. 5. ruins
    location.. 4. Nile
    ruined temple.. 5. Ammon 6. Karnak
    Seven against (one of).. 6. Tydeus
theca... 3. pod 4. case, cell
    7. capsule
theft... 6. holdup, piracy 7. larceny,
    robbery 8. burglary, stealing
    10. plagiarism 12. embezzlement
theftlike... 7. piratic 9. piratical
theme... 4. text 5. essay, lemma,
    motif, thema, topic 6. matter, thesis
    7. subject 9. discourse, leitmotiv
then... 3. poi (Mus) 4. also, next,
    when 5. hence 7. besides
    8. formerly 9. therefore
    12. subsequently
thence... 4. away 5. hence 9. after
    that, elsewhere, therefore
    10. henceforth, thereafter
theogamy... 14. marriage of gods
theologian... 5. Arius (Bib) 6. Luther
    7. a divine 8. canonist
theology... 7. irenics 8. canonics,
    religion 9. depositum 10. doctrinism
theorem... 3. law 4. rule 5. axiom,
    topic 7. premise 9. principle,
    statement 11. proposition
theoretical... 5. ideal 8. academic,
    platonic 11. conjectural, impractical,
    speculative 12. hypothetical, not
    practical
theorize... 6. reason 9. postulate,
    speculate
theory... 3. ism 4. plan 6. scheme
    7. formula, opinion 8. analysis,
    doctrine 10. hypothesis
    11. speculation, supposition
    13. contemplation
theory of...
    evolution.. 9. Darwinism
    10. Lamarckism 13. Spencerianism
    knowledge.. 12. epistemology
    language.. 6. bowwow 8. ding–dong,
    pooh–pooh
    philosophy.. 13. phenomenalism
    relativity.. 8. Einstein
theosophist... 7. Mahatma
theosophy... 4. yoga 6. cabala
    7. Nirvana 8. kamarupa (Kama)
therapeutic... 7. healing 8. curative,
    remedies
therapy... 4. cure 5. faith 9. dietetics,
    medicines, treatment
    12. hydrotherapy, therapeutics
    13. psychotherapy
there... 3. yon 5. ready 6. yonder
    7. thereat, thither 11. at that place
therefore... 2. as, so 4. ergo
    5. hence, since 6. thence
    9. thereupon, to that end, wherefore
    11. accordingly 12. consequently
thermometer... 5. Hydra 7. Reaumur
    10. Centigrade, Fahrenheit
Thesaurus compiler... 5. Roget
thesis... 5. essay, theme, topic
    6. accent 7. premise 8. treatise
    9. postulate 10. assumption
    11. affirmation 12. dissertation

thespian... 3. art 5. actor 6. player, tragic 7. actress, Thespis (founder) 8. dramatic

Thessaly, Greece...
ancient name.. 9. Thessalia
famed for.. 6. horses 8. horsemen
mountain.. 4. Ossa 6. Pelion
native.. 5. Greek 10. Thessalian
town.. 7. Larissa

thew... 5. brawn, sinew 6. manner, muscle, virtue 8. strength

they go out... 6. exeunt

thick... 4. burr, dull, hazy 5. broad, bushy, close, crass, dense, gross, husky, plump, solid, squat 6. coarse, espeso, stodgy, stupid 7. crowded, grumous, muffled 8. familiar, friendly, intimate, numerous, thickset 9. luxuriant 10. indistinct 11. inspissated 12. impenetrable

thicken... 3. gel 4. clot, curd 5. cloud, flock 6. curdle, deepen, harden 7. congeal, stiffen 8. increase, solidify 9. intensify 10. incrassate, inspissate, strengthen

thicket... 4. bosk, rone 5. copse, grove, hedge, shola 6. bosket (bosquet) 7. boscage, coppice, spinney 9. brushwood, chaparral 10. underbrush

thickheaded... 4. dull 5. dense 6. stupid 7. doltish

thickness... 3. ply 5. layer 7. density 8. diameter, intimacy 10. opaqueness 11. consistency, measurement

thickset... 5. squat, stout 6. stocky, stodgy, stubby 14. closely planted

thick-skinned... 7. callous 11. hardhearted, insensitive, pachydermic 14. pachydermatous

thick soup... 5. purée

thief... 5. scamp 6. ackman, bandit, looter, pirate, rascal, robber 7. burglar, filcher, rustler, stealer 8. gangster, larcener 9. larcenist, scoundrel 10. freebooter, pickpocket, plagiarist

thieves (famed)... 5. Fagin 9. Robin Hood 10. Dick Turpin, Jesse James 11. Claude Duval 12. Jonathan Wild 13. Thief of Bagdad

thieves' Latin... 4. cant 5. slang 12. secret jargon

thigh (pert to)...
animal's.. 3. ham 4. hock 5. flank
armor plate.. 6. cuisse (cuish)
bone.. 5. femur, ilium
ref to.. 5. groin, meros (merus) 6. crural

thimble... 3. cap 4. ring 5. cover, watch

thimble (pert to)...
berry.. 9. raspberry 10. blackberry
eye.. 12. chub mackerel
flower.. 8. foxglove
rig.. 5. cheat 7. swindle 13. sleight of hand
weed.. 6. clover

thin... 4. bony, lank, lean, poor, rare, slim, weak 5. gaunt, lanky, lathy, reedy, sheer, spare, washy 6. dilute,

meager, rarefy, shrill, sleazy, slinky, sparse, watery 7. haggard, insipid, scraggy, scrawny, slender 8. araneous, rarefied 10. attenuated, diaphanous 11. transparent

thin (pert to)...
air.. 5. smoke, vapor 6. bubble
and delicate.. 8. araneous 10. diaphanous
and haggard.. 5. gaunt
and withered.. 7. wizened 9. shriveled
fabric.. 8. gossamer
out.. 5. peter
plate, bone.. 6. tegmen
plate, metal.. 4. leaf
plate, Zool.. 6. lamina 7. lamella
skinned.. 6. gentle, tender, touchy
Thin Man's dog.. 4. Asta

thine... 4. tuum

thing... 3. act, res 4. deed, fact, idea, unit 5. being, event 6. affair, entity, gadget, object 7. article, reality 8. anything, creature 9. happening, situation, something

thing (pert to)...
added.. 6. insert 8. addendum 9. insertion 10. supplement
assumed.. 7. premise 11. implication
complete.. 4. unit
cursed.. 8. anathema
done.. 5. actum
following.. 6. sequel
found.. 5. trove
hard to classify.. 11. nondescript
huge.. 7. monster
indefinite.. 7. so–and–so 10. thingumbob (thingumabob) 12. what's–its–name
nonexisting.. 9. nonentity
of little worth.. 6. stiver, trifle 7. trinket
the (thing).. 7. the rage
unique.. 4. sole

things (pert to)...
added.. 7. addenda 11. additaments
brought into being.. 9. creations
found, surprise.. 11. serendipity
intricate.. 9. involutes
little.. 16. inconsequentials
moving to and fro.. 7. wigwags
of like nature.. 8. cognates
suitable to eat.. 9. esculents
theoretical.. 7. noumena
to be done.. 6. agenda
to be learned.. 7. lessons
to follow.. 7. sequels 8. sequelae
to sharpen.. 10. whetstones
widely separated.. 8. extremes

think... 3. wis 4. deem, muse, trow 5. opine 6. reason 7. believe, imagine, reflect, suppose 8. cogitate, conceive, meditate 11. contemplate

think (pert to)...
better of.. 6. repent 10. reconsider
bring to mind.. 6. recall 7. imagine 10. conjecture
logically.. 6. reason
of.. 5. judge 6. intend, recall 8. consider, remember 9. recollect 10. call to mind
over.. 3. wis 4. mull, muse 5. brood 6. ponder 8. meditate

up.. 6. devise, scheme 7. concoct
thinker, Relig freedom...
  14. latitudinarian
thinness... 6. rarity 7. tenuity
  8. rareness 11. slenderness
third (pert to)...
  comb form.. 3. tri 4. trit
  day (Quakers).. 7. Tuesday
  estate.. 6. people
  figure.. 7. ferison
  in number.. 8. tertiary
  music.. 6. tierce
  ordinal of.. 5. three
  person.. 6. escort 7. grammar
    8. chaperon
  power.. 4. cube
  Republic.. 6. French (1871)
thirst... 6. desire, hunger 7. craving,
  dryness, longing
this... 4. near 9. the nearer
Thisbe's lover (Bab)... 7. Paramus
thisness... 9. haecceity
thistle (pert to)...
  bird.. 9. goldfinch
  color.. 6. violet (cobalt)
  emblem.. 8. Scotland
  genus.. 6. Arnica, Cosmos 7. Carlina
  star.. 7. caltrop (caltrap)
thistledown... 6. pappus
  12. thistlebeard
thither... 3. yon 5. hence 6. yonder
thong... 4. lash, riem, whip 5. knout,
  lorum, quirt, romal, strap 6. lorate
  7. amentum, lanyard (laniard)
Thor (pert to)...
  father.. 4. Odin
  German.. 5. Donar
  god of.. 7. thunder
  other name.. 9. Hlorrithi
  stepson.. 3. Ull (Ullr)
  wife.. 3. Sif
thorax... 5. chest 6. cavity 7. cuirass
  8. pectoral 11. breastplate
thorn... 4. bane 5. briar (brier), spine
  7. acantha, bramble, prickle
thorn (pert to)...
  apple.. 3. haw 6. Datura
  back.. 3. ray 4. dorn 5. skate
  10. spider crab 11. stickleback
  bill.. 11. hummingbird
  comb form.. 5. spini
  full of.. 6. briary
  letters.. 2. th 3. edh
  lizard.. 6. moloch
  pert to.. 6. spinal
  small.. 7. spinule
thornless... 5. inerm 8. inermous
thorny... 5. sharp, spiny 7. brambly,
  prickly 9. acanthoid, bristling, difficult
thorough... 4. full 8. absolute,
  complete 9. downright, intensive
  10. exhaustive 11. painstaking
thoroughfare... 4. road 6. artery,
  street 7. highway, parkway, passage,
  roadway, thruway 8. arterial,
  autobahn, highroad, pent road,
  turnpike, waterway 9. boulevard,
  concourse 10. autostrada
thoroughgoing... 4. zeal 7. extreme
  9. downright 11. painstaking
thoroughly... 3. all 9. intensive,
  out–and–out 11. intensively

  13. letter–perfect
thorp, thorpe... 4. dorp, town
  6. hamlet 7. village
those (pert to)...
  adept at table talk..
    14. deipnosophists
  brought to terms.. 11. transigents
  in office.. 3. ins
  in the stock market.. 5. bears, bulls
    7. traders 9. investors
  of a habit.. 7. addicts
  of the same goal.. 6. rivals
  outside a profession.. 5. laity
those who...
  read and write.. 9. literates
  ridicule.. 8. deriders
  verify.. 13. corroborators
  work together.. 13. collaborators
thou... 3. tha 7. pronoun 8. thousand
thought... 4. care, heed, idea, view
  5. logic 6. deemed, opined
  7. anxiety, opinion 9. attention,
  cogitated, reasoning 10. cogitation,
  meditation, reflection 11. cerebration
  12. deliberation, recollection
  13. consideration, ratiocination
thought (pert to)...
  continuous.. 10. meditation
  deep in.. 10. cogitabund
  form.. 6. ideate
  laws of.. 7. noetics
  reader.. 11. telepathist
thoughtful... 4. kind 5. moody
  7. mindful, museful, pensive,
  prudent, serious 9. attentive
  10. cogitative, meditative, reflective,
  ruminative, solicitous
  11. circumspect, considerate
  13. contemplative
thoughtless... 4. rash 6. stupid
  7. foolish 8. careless, heedless,
  reckless 9. brainless, impulsive
  11. harum–scarum, inattentive,
  thought–free 12. unreflecting
  13. inconsiderate
thousand... 3. mil 5. mille 7. chiliad
  10. ten hundred
Thousand and One Nights...
  13. Arabian Nights
thousand men, command of...
  11. chiliarchia
thousandth... 9. chiliadal
  10. millesimal
thousand years... 7. chiliad
  9. millenary 10. millennium
thrall... 4. esne, serf 5. slave
  7. bondage, bondman, captive,
  slavery 9. thralldom 10. oppression
thrash... 3. lam, tan 4. beat, cave,
  drub, flog, whip 5. flail, pound, twist
  6. defeat, punish, strike, swinge,
  thresh 7. belabor, trounce
  8. urticate, vanquish 9. pulverize,
  toss about
thrashing... 7. beating, milling
  8. drubbing, flogging, whipping
  10. punishment
thread... 4. flax, jute, line, silk, vein,
  wire, yarn 5. fiber, floss, linen, lisle,
  rayon 6. cotton, dacron, sleave
  8. arrasene, filament
thread (pert to)...

ancient.. **4.** byss
a needle.. **5.** reeve
ball.. **4.** clew (clue)
cell.. **5.** cnida
coiled.. **3.** cop
comb form.. **3.** nem **4.** nema
  5. nemat **6.** nemato
fish.. **7.** cutlass **9.** threadfin
  11. cobblerfish
herring.. **11.** gizzard shad
like.. **5.** filar **6.** filose
loose.. **4.** lint **7.** raveled
medical.. **5.** seton
metal.. **4.** wire
mystery lead.. **4.** clue
shoemaker's (obs).. **6.** lingel (lingle)
silk.. **5.** floss **9.** filoselle
tangle.. **6.** sleave
tape, braid (thread).. **5.** inkle
tester.. **9.** serimeter
weaving term.. **4.** warp, weft, woof
  5. leash
threadbare... **4.** sere, worn **5.** trite
  6. shabby
threaten... **4.** warn **5.** curse
  6. menace **7.** portend **8.** forebode
  9. comminate **10.** intimidate
  12. anathematize
threatening... **4.** dark **7.** ominous
  8. imminent, lowering, menacing
three (pert to)...
banded armadillo.. **4.** apar **5.** apara
comb form.. **3.** ter
dimensional.. **5.** bruit, cubic
  12. stereoscopic
fold.. **4.** tern **6.** ternal, treble, triple
  7. ternate
group of.. **4.** trio **5.** triad **7.** triplet
  8. triplets
hundredth anniversary..
  13. tercentennial
in one.. **6.** triune **7.** trinity **10.** The
  Godhead
legged stand.. **6.** teapoy, tripod, trivet
lined.. **9.** trilinear
masted vessel.. **5.** xebec **7.** frigate
  8. schooner
math term.. **2.** pi (3.1416)
prefix.. **3.** tri
R's.. **7.** reading, writing
  10. arithmetic
seeded.. **11.** trispermous
sided figure.. **6.** trigon **8.** triangle
spot.. **4.** trey
styled.. **10.** trystylous
toed sloth.. **2.** ai
Three Kingdoms (Chin)... **2.** Wu
  3. Shu, Wei
Three Kings of Cologne... **6.** Gaspar
  8. Melchior **9.** Balthasar **12.** Three
  Wise Men
Three Musketeers... **5.** Athos
  6. Aramis **7.** Porthos **9.** D'Artagnan
  (friend)
Three Sisters (Myth)... **5.** Fates
  6. Clotho **7.** Atropos **8.** Lachesis
Three Wise Men (Kings of Cologne)...
  6. Gaspar **8.** Melchior **9.** Balthasar
threnody... **5.** dirge **7.** requiem
  8. coronach
threshold... **3.** eve **4.** gate, sill
  5. limen **6.** portal **8.** doorsill

threw... see also *throw* **4.** cast
  5. flung, slung **6.** bunged, heaved,
  hurled, pelted, tossed **7.** pitched
thrice... **3.** ter, tri **5.** fully **6.** highly
  10. repeatedly, three times
thrift... **7.** economy **8.** prudence
  9. husbandry **10.** providence
  11. thriftiness
thriftless... **6.** lavish **8.** prodigal,
  wasteful **11.** extravagant, improvident
thrifty... **6.** frugal, saving **7.** careful,
  prudent, sparing **9.** provident
  10. economical, forehanded,
  prosperous **11.** flourishing
thrill... **4.** tirl **6.** dindle, thrush, tingle,
  tremor **7.** delight **9.** electrify
  10. excitement
thrive... **4.** grow **5.** moise (Eng)
  6. batten **7.** prosper, succeed
  8. flourish, increase
throat... **3.** maw **4.** crop, neck
  5. gular, halse, mouth, voice
  6. groove, gullet, larynx, mutter
  7. channel, glottis, jugular, orifice,
  pharynx, trachea **9.** esophagus
  10. passageway **12.** constriction
throb... **4.** ache, beat, drum, pant
  5. pulse **7.** pulsate, vibrate
  9. palpitate
throe... **4.** pang **5.** agony **7.** anguish
  8. struggle
Throgmorton Street... **13.** Stock
  Exchange (London)
throne... **3.** see **4.** apse **5.** exalt
  8. enthrone **9.** royal seat
  11. sovereignty, supreme rank
  12. Chair of State
throng... **4.** crew, host, push
  5. crowd, horde, press, swarm
  6. bustle, stress **7.** hurried
  9. confusion, multitude
throttle... **5.** choke, lever, seize
  6. throat **7.** garrote **8.** strangle,
  suppress, windpipe
through... **2.** by **3.** dia, per **4.** into,
  thru **5.** ended **7.** perpend **8.** finished
  9. because of, by means of,
  completed
throughout... **5.** about **6.** during
  8. thorough **10.** completely,
  everywhere
throw... **3.** cob, don, lob, peg, shy
  4. bear, cast, hurl, kist, pelt, toss,
  yerk **5.** chuck, fling, heave, pitch,
  sling, twist, whirl **6.** baffle, strike,
  thwart **7.** discard, project
  9. prostrate
throw (pert to)...
a scare.. **7.** terrify
away.. **7.** discard **8.** handbill,
  squander
back.. **5.** repel **6.** reject, revert
dice (term).. **4.** sise **7.** ambsace
in the towel.. **4.** cede, quit
  9. surrender
into confusion.. **7.** disturb, perturb,
  trouble **8.** stampede **10.** demoralize
into ecstasy.. **9.** enrapture
into shade.. **7.** eclipse
off.. **4.** cast, shed **6.** derail, reject
  7. abandon, discard
out.. **4.** emit, lade **5.** egest, eject,

expel 6. bounce 7. discard, project
9. eliminate
over . . 4. jilt 5. build 6. give up,
refute 7. abandon, discard
9. eliminate
overboard . . 8. jettison
water upon . . 5. douse
throwback . . . 7. setback 9. reversion
10. misfortune, regression
throwing (pert to) . . .
rope . . 5. lasso, reata, riata 6. lariat
science . . 10. ballistics
stick (anc) . . 6. womera (woomera)
thrum . . . 3. bit, hum 4. drum, tuft
5. strum 6. fringe, repeat
thrush . . . 5. brown, mavis, robin, veery
7. disease 8. shagbark, songbird
9. blackbird
thrush (pert to) . . .
American . . 5. robin, veery 12. hermit
thrush
European . . 5. ouzel (ousel) 6. missel
7. redwing 11. nightingale
golden . . 6. oriole
Hawaiian . . 4. omao
Ind . . 5. shama
Scot . . 8. throstle
thrust . . . 3. dig, jab 4. gird, poke,
push, stab 5. lunge 6. extend,
pierce 7. intrude, obtrude, riposte
8. protrude 9. interject, interpose
thrust (pert to) . . .
aside . . 5. shove 7. dismiss 8. brush
off
down . . 7. detrude
fencing term . . 5. lunge 7. allonge,
riposte 8. estocade
one's self in . . 5. enter 7. intrude
out . . 5. eject 6. extend 8. protrude
thug . . . 4. goon, yegg 6. cuttle,
gunman 7. ruffian 8. assassin
9. cutthroat, roughneck
thumb . . . 6. pollex, thenar
thumb (pert to) . . .
a ride . . 9. hitchhike
bird . . 9. goldcrest
lady's (herb) . . 9. peachwort, persicary
mark . . 4. soil 10. impression
11. fingerprint 14. identification
nail . . 5. small 8. complete
over . . 4. skim 6. browse
part . . 6. thenar
thump . . . 4. bang, beat, blow, drum,
thud, whip, yerk 5. knock, pound
6. hammer, pummel, strike, thrash
8. chastise 10. pound along
thunder . . . 4. boom, peal, roar
5. storm 9. fulminate
thunder (pert to) . . .
bolt . . 5. speed 6. Caesar 8. surprise
9. lightning 11. fulmination
fish . . 4. raad 5. loach 7. catfish
(electric)
god . . 4. Thor 6. Manito
of applause . . 5. cheer 7. ovation
peal . . 4. clap 5. crash
smitten goddess . . 6. Semele
8. Keraunia
thurible . . . 6. censer
thurifer . . . 12. censer bearer
Thursday . . . 4. Thor 8. fifth day
12. god of thunder

thus . . . 2. so 3. sic 5. hence 7. this
way 9. therefore 11. for instance
12. consequently
thwack . . . 3. rap 4. bang, blow, club
5. crush, knock, whack 6. defeat,
pommel, strike, thrash 7. belabor
thwart . . . 4. balk, foil 5. block, clash,
cross, parry, spite 6. defeat, gaffle,
oppose, outwit 7. oblique, prevent
8. obstruct, stubborn 9. frustrate,
interpose 10. across from, disappoint
thymus . . . 5. gland 10. sweetbread
(lambs, calves)
tiara . . . 5. crown 6. diadem 7. coronet
8. ornament
Tibbett opera . . . 12. Emperor Jones
(1932)
tibert . . . 3. cat
Tibet, Asia . . . see also *Tibetan*
animal . . 3. goa, sus 5. panda
capital . . 5. Lhasa
dialect . . 9. Bhutanese
kingdom . . 5. Nepal
Mts . . 8. Himalaya 9. Karakoram
religion . . 7. Lamaism
river . . 5. Hwang, Indus 7. Yangtze
11. Brahmaputra
ruler . . 9. Dalai Lama
Tibetan (pert to) . . .
beer (barley) . . 5. chang
deer . . 4. shou
food (barley) . . 6. tsamba
gazelle . . 3. goa
monk, priest . . 4. lama
ox . . 3. yak
sheep . . 3. sha 5. urial 6. bharal,
nahoor, nayaur
wild ass . . 5. kiang
wildcat . . 5. manul
tibia . . . 4. bone, shin 5. flute
6. cnemis
Tibur (anc) . . . 6. Tivoli
tiburon . . . 5. shark
Tiburtine . . . 12. Sibyl of Tibur
tick . . . 3. ked, tap 4. beat, mark, mite,
pest 5. Argas 6. acarid, Ixodes
7. instant 8. carapato, function,
ticktock 10. pajahuello (pajaroello)
ticket . . . 3. tag 4. note, pass, slip
5. check, ducat, label, token
6. ballot, billet, permit, record
7. license, voucher 8. document
11. certificate
ticket dealer . . . 7. scalper
tickle . . . 5. amuse 6. thrill, tingle
7. delight 9. titillate, vellicate
ticklish . . . 5. risky 6. fickle, queasy,
touchy 7. comical 8. unstable,
unsteady 9. uncertain 10. precarious,
unreliable
tidal (pert to) . . .
creek . . 6. estero 7. estuary
current . . 8. tiderace
flood . . 5. eagre
flow . . 3. ebb 4. bore, neap 5. surge
tidbit, titbit . . . 5. goody 6. morsel
7. saynete 8. delicacy
tide . . . 3. ebb, rip 4. high, neap, time
5. drift 6. period, stream 7. current
8. low water 9. be carried
tide (pert to) . . .
gate . . 9. floodgate

go with.. 5. drift, float 7. proceed
13. be fashionable
out with.. 3. ebb 6. recede
8. diminish, fade away
over.. 6. endure 8. surmount 11. live
through
tidings... 4. news, word 6. gospel,
report, rumors 7. message
10. evangelist 11. information
tidy... 4. neat, trig, trim 5. groom,
natty, plump 6. spruce 7. orderly
9. shipshape 10. put in order
12. antimacassar, considerable
tie... 4. bind, bond, draw, even, knot,
lash, link 5. ascot, equal, nexus,
noose, trice, truss 6. cravat, enlace,
fasten, relate, tether 7. confine,
necktie, sleeper 8. equality, fastener,
restrain, shoelace 10. allegiance,
obligation
tie (pert to)...
off.. 5. belay
ornament.. 3. pin
ready–made.. 4. teck
securely.. 7. trammel
sports.. 8. dead heat
uniting.. 4. bond 5. tache
up.. 4. bind, wrap 5. truss 6. fasten
8. restrain
tier... 3. row 5. grade, layer 6. series
Tiergarten... 4. park 16. Zoological
Garden
tiff... 3. sip 4. huff, spat 5. drink
7. dudgeon, quarrel 8. outburst
10. fit of anger
tiffin... 3. tea 5. brown, lunch
6. repast 8. luncheon
tiger... 5. bully 6. emblem, savage
9. swaggerer
tiger (pert to)...
American.. 6. jaguar
bird.. 5. finch 8. amadavat
family.. 3. cat 6. mammal 11. Felis
tigris
hunting dog.. 5. dhole
S African.. 7. leopard
Tasmania.. 9. thylacine 13. Tasmanian
wolf
wolf.. 5. hyena
young.. 3. cub
tight... 4. fast, snug, taut, trim
5. alert, close, drunk, tense
6. narrow, stingy 7. exactly, shapely
9. condensed 11. closefisted
12. close–fitting, parsimonious
tight (pert to)...
fisted.. 6. stingy 12. parsimonious
lipped.. 5. terse 9. secretive
wad.. 5. miser 10. curmudgeon
tighten... 4. frap, lace 5. brace, tense
6. fasten, tauten 7. squeeze
9. constrict
Tigris River city of ruins...
7. Nineveh (anc)
til... 4. tree 6. sesame
tilde... 4. dash, mark, sign 6. accent,
tittle 15. diacritical mark
tile... 3. red 5. slate 6. domino,
mosaic, pament (pamment), tegula
7. ceramic, pantile, tessera
8. pavement
tiler... 5. thief 6. slater 7. hellier

10. doorkeeper
till... 3. box 4. farm, plow, tray, when
5. labor, while 6. before, casket,
drawer, whilst 7. develop 9. cultivate
tillable...: 6. arable
tiller... 4. helm 5. stalk 6. farmer,
sprout 7. plowman, rancher
8. harrower 10. cultivator,
husbandman
tilt... 3. tip 4. cant, heel, list 5. joust,
pitch, slant, slope 6. careen, oliver
(hammer), seesaw, unload 7. incline
8. log house 10. tournament
11. altercation
timber... 3. log 4. beam, tree, wood
6. forest, lumber 7. support
9. underpier
timber (pert to)...
bend.. 3. sny
building.. 4. sill, stud 5. joist
6. purlin, rafter 8. stringer
convex.. 6. camber
cribs (logging).. 4. dram
cut.. 6. lumber 7. fallage
decay.. 4. doty (doaty)
end.. 5. tenon
hard, heartwood.. 7. duramen
Naut.. 3. rib 4. bitt, keel, mast, spar,
wale 8. sternson
support.. 6. corbel
upright.. 8. puncheon
wolf.. 3. lobo
timbre...: 4. tone 5. clang, crest (Her),
miter 7. coronet 9. resonance, tone
color
timbrel... 4. drum 5. tabor 7. sistrum
10. tambourine
time... 3. age, day, eon, era 4. aeon,
date, hour, term, turn, week, year
5. clock, epoch, shift, tempo
6. decade, minute, moment, period,
season, second 7. century
8. duration, occasion, schedule
9. fortnight
time (pert to)...
accurate.. 10. isochronon
equal.. 10. isochronal
Fast.. 4. Lent
geologic.. 5. azoic
granted.. 4. stay 5. delay 8. reprieve
legal.. 6. usance 11. year and a day
long ago.. 4. once, yore 8. formerly
medical.. 3. tid 8. ter in die (three
times a day)
of vigor.. 6. heyday
one.. 4. once
present.. 5. nonce 12. contemporary
prior.. 9. antedated 11. retroactive
right.. 3. tid
same.. 7. however 9. meanwhile
10. concurrent 11. synchronous
14. simultaneously
spare.. 7. leisure
waste.. 4. idle, loaf 5. dally 6. loiter
wrong.. 11. anachronism
13. anachronistic
timeless... 7. ageless, eternal, undated
8. dateless, unending, untimely
9. premature 11. everlasting
12. interminable
timely... 3. apt, pat 4. soon 5. early
6. prompt 9. opportune

10. seasonably 11. opportunity

timepiece... 4. dial 5. clock, watch
6. gnomon 8. egg glass, horologe
9. clepsydra, hourglass, metronome
10. isochronon, wristwatch
11. chronometer

times... 3. ago, eld 4. yore 5. often
10. frequently, yesterdays 11. ups
and downs

timid... 3. shy 5. eerie, henny, mousy,
pavid, scary 6. afraid, trepid
7. bashful, fearful, nervous, not bold
8. cowardly, retiring, timorous
9. diffident, shrinking 12. fainthearted
13. pusillanimous

timocracy (pert to)...
defined by.. 5. Plato
principle.. 11. love of honor
State.. 6. Sparta (anc)

Timon of Athens... 5. Cynic (The)
11. misanthrope

timorous... 5. timid 6. afraid
7. bashful, fearful 8. hesitant
9. shrinking

Timothy (pert to)...
Bib.. 7. convert 8. Epistles
grass.. 3. hay 10. herd's grass

timpani... 11. kettledrums

tin... 3. can, pan 5. money, plate
7. element, stannum 8. preserve
10. not genuine

tin (pert to)...
alloy (copper).. 6. pewter
box.. 7. trummel
coat with.. 5. terne 10. terneplate
comb form.. 6. stanni
extract.. 8. prillion
foil, plate.. 4. tain
mine.. 8. stannary
ref to.. 7. stannic
sheet.. 6. latten
symbol.. 2. Sn

tinamou... 4. yutu 7. tataupa
9. partridge

tincture... 4. dash 5. color, imbue,
myrrh, tinge, trace 6. iodine
7. extract, vestige 8. solution
9. paregoric, suspicion 10. extraction

tinder... 4. punk 5. spunk 6. amadou
9. touchwood

tine... 3. nib 5. prong, spike, tooth

tinea... 7. sycosis 8. ringworm

tinge... 3. dye 4. tint 5. color, imbue,
shade, stain, taint 6. flavor
8. coloring, tincture 10. suggestion

tingle... 4. ring 5. sting 6. dingle,
thrill 7. prickle 9. sensation,
stimulate

tinkle... 5. clink 6. dingle, tingle

tint... 3. due, hue 4. tone 5. blush,
color, tinge 6. nuance

tintinnabulum... 4. bell 6. tinkle
9. rhymester

tintype... 9. ferrotype
12. old-fashioned

tiny... 3. wee 5. small, teeny
6. atomic, infant, minute, petite
9. miniature 10. diminutive
13. infinitesimal

tip... 3. cue, end, fee, neb, top
4. apex, cant, heel, hint, lean, list,
tilt 5. crown, point, slant, spire,

upset 6. careen, inform, summit,
tiptop 7. cumshaw, incline
8. bonamano, gratuity, overturn
9. extremity, overthrow

tip (pert to)...
end.. 3. neb
French.. 9. pourboire
Italian.. 8. bonamano
near.. 6. apical
Near East.. 9. baksheesh (baksbish)
scabbard.. 5. chape 7. crampet
(crampette)
slender.. 6. arista
to one side.. 4. list, tile 5. alist
6. careen
up and over.. 4. cant

tippet... 4. cape, hood 5. amice, scarf
6. almuce 7. muffler 8. liripipe,
palatine 9. comforter

tipple... 3. bib, nip, pot, sip 4. suck
5. drink, quaff 6. fuddle, guzzle,
liquor, tumble 7. spirits 8. beverage,
overturn

tippler... 3. sot 5. souse, toper
7. drinker 9. draftsman

tipster... 4. tout 8. dopester
9. informant, predictor
10. forecaster, speculator

tipsy... 4. awry 5. drunk, shaky
6. groggy 7. fuddled, muddled
10. staggering 11. intoxicated

tiptoe... 5. alert 6. warily 7. eagerly,
quietly 8. cautious, stealthy
10. cautiously

tirade... 6. screed, speech 8. berating
9. philippic

tire... 3. fag, lag, rim 4. bore, jade
5. dress, weary 6. attire 7. exhaust,
fatigue

tired... 5. bored, jaded, spent, weary
6. aweary

tireless... 8. untiring 9. unwearied
10. unwearying 13. indefatigable

tiresome... 3. dry 4. dull, tame
6. boring, prolix 7. irksome, tedious
8. annoying 9. fatiguing, vexatious,
wearisome 10. irritating

tissue... 3. web 4. bast, tela 5. fiber,
paper 6. fabric 7. culture
8. meshwork

tissue (pert to)...
Biol.. 4. bone 5. nerve 6. muscle
8. ganglion 10. epithelium
cell.. 8. meristem
cellular.. 10. epithelium
connecting.. 6. stroma, tendon
8. ligament
decay.. 6. caries
fatty.. 3. fat 4. suet
hardening of.. 9. sclerosis
horny.. 7. keratin
layer.. 7. stratum
lymphoid.. 7. tonsils
nerve.. 8. ganglion
ref to.. 4. tela 5. telar
spinal.. 4. alba
vegetable.. 4. bast 7. endarch
8. meristem
wood.. 6. lignin, lignum

Titan... 4. Rhea, Thea 5. Coeus,
Creus, deity, Dione, giant, Theia
6. Phoebe, Tethys, Themis

7. Cronius, Iapetus, Oceanus
8. Hyperion 9. Mnemosyne
titanic... 4. huge 5. great 7. immense
8. colossal, enormous, gigantic
Titan War (Thessaly)...
11. Titanomachy
tithe... 3. tax 4. part 5. teind, tenth
11. frank pledge
titi... 6. monkey 7. sea bird
8. ironwood 9. buckwheat
Titian... 3. red 6. artist 7. red hair
9. red–haired
titillate... 5. amuse 6. thrill, tickle
7. delight 8. interest
titlark... 5. pipit
title... 3. sir 4. dame, deed, earl, lord,
name, sire, term, type 5. claim, right
6. knight, madame, squire
7. caption, epithet, esquire, heading
8. muniment 9. designate
11. appellation, designation
titled member, Stock Exchange...
6. orchid (sl)
titmouse... 3. mag, tit 4. wren
5. Parus 6. parine, tomtit 7. jacksaw
9. mumruffin
titter... 5. laugh, te–hee 6. giggle,
tee–hee 7. snicker
tittle... 3. dot, jot 4. iota, mark, whit
5. tilde 6. gossip, tattle 8. particle
tittle–tattle... 6. gossip 8. idle talk
16. scandalmongering
tittupy... 3. gay 5. shaky 6. lively
8. prancing, unsteady
titubate... 4. reel 6. totter 7. stagger,
stammer
titular... 7. nominal 9. incumbent (of a
title)
Tlingit... 6. Indian (Alaska)
TNT... 6. trotol 9. explosive
15. trinitrotoluene
to... 2. at 4. into, till, unto 5. until
6. toward 7. as far as, thither
11. preposition
to (pert to)...
to be.. 4. esse, être
to–do.. 3. ado 4. fuss, stir 6. bustle
9. commotion
to each his own.. 10. suum cuique
to which.. 7. whereto
to wit.. 3. viz 6. namely 8. scilicet
9. videlicet
toad... 4. agua, Bufo, frog, pipa
6. anuran, peeper 7. crapaud
9. amphibian, Batrachia, spadefoot
10. natterjack
toad (pert to)...
eater.. 5. toady 8. hanger–on,
parasite
fish.. 6. puffer, slimer 8. frogfish
head.. 6. plover (golden)
lily.. 9. waterlily
stabber.. 9. jackknife
tree.. 4. Hyla
toadflax... 8. flaxweed, ranstead
13. butter–and–eggs
toadstool... 5. morel 6. fungus
8. mushroom, puffball
toady... 4. ugly 8. parasite, truckler
9. repulsive, sycophant, toadeater
toast... 3. tan 4. cook, leep 5. bread,
brede, brown, parch, roast, skoal

6. pledge, sippet 7. drink to
8. cinnamon
tobacco (pert to)...
ash.. 6. dottle (dottel)
Cuban.. 4. capa 6. Vuelta (leaf)
disease.. 6. calico, mosaic 7. walloon
English.. 8. bird's–eye
epithet.. 12. Lady Nicotine
French.. 7. caporal
Greek.. 7. Knaster
hookah smoking.. 7. goracco
Indian.. 7. uppowoc
introduced by.. 7. Raleigh (Sir Walter)
Kentucky.. 6. Burley
kind.. 4. capa, shag 5. tabac
6. Burley, Vuelta 7. caporal,
henbane, Latakia, perique, Turkish
8. Virginia 9. salvadora
paste.. 7. goracco
Persian.. 6. tumbak (tumbaki)
pipe.. 7. calumet, chibouk (chibouque)
principle (active).. 8. nicotine
receptacle.. 4. pipe 7. humidor
S American.. 8. canaster
small cut.. 3. cud 4. plug, quid
6. dottle (dottel) 7. carotte
Turkish.. 7. Latakia
wrapping.. 9. broadleaf
toboggan... 4. sled 5. coast, glide
7. coaster 12. sharp decline
14. downhill course
toby... 3. dog (Punch's), jug, mug, rob
5. cigar 7. highway, pitcher
tocsin... 5. alarm 9. alarm bell
13. warning signal
toe... 3. tae, tip 5. digit 6. dactyl,
hallux 7. minimus
toehold... 7. footing 8. foothold,
purchase
toes, odd–numbered...
13. perissodactyl
together... 3. com, con, syn 4. mass,
with 5. union 10. conjointly
11. unanimously 12. coincidently,
concurrently, continuously
toggery... 3. set 4. garb, togs
5. dress 7. clothes, harness
9. trappings 12. haberdashery
tolerable... 4. so–so 8. bearable,
passable 9. endurable
10. acceptable, fairly well, sufferable
11. supportable
tolerance... 8. patience
10. indulgence, permission
tolerant... 7. lenient, patient
9. indulgent 10. forbearing,
permissive
tolerate... 4. bear, bide 5. abide,
allow, brook, stand 6. endure,
permit, suffer 9. put up with
toll... 3. due, tax 4. call, duty, peal,
ring 5. knell 6. allure, charge,
custom, entice, impost, invite, strike
7. ringing 8. exaction
10. assessment 12. compensation
Tolypeutes... 4. apar 9. armadillo
Tom, Dick and Harry... 8. everyone,
humanity 15. persons at random
tomahawk... 3. axe 4. kill 6. attack
7. hatchet
tomb... 4. cist, lair 5. crypt, grave,
speos, vault 6. shrine 7. mastaba

(mastabah), orruary, tritaph
8. catacomb, cenotaph
9. mausoleum, sepulcher
tombé... 4. drum
tomboy... 3. meg 4. romp 5. rowdy
6. hoyden (hoiden), tomrig
tomcat... 3. gib
tomcod... 8. bocaccio
tome... 4. book, opus 5. atlas
6. volume 11. papal letter,
publication
tomorrow... 5. later 6. mañana 9. the
morrow
tonant... 7. blatant 10. thundering
tone... 4. mode, mood, note, tang,
tune 5. pitch, reedy, sound, trend,
twang, vigor 6. accent, energy,
melody, nuance, timbre 7. cadence
8. modulate, monotone, tonology
9. harmonize 10. inflection,
intonation, modulation
tone (pert to)...
down.. 3. dim 6. mellow, modify,
soften 8. moderate
lacking.. 5. atony 6. atonal
quality, color.. 6. timbre
series.. 5. scale
single.. 8. monotone
succession.. 5. melos
thin.. 7. sfogato
vibrant.. 5. twang
toneless... 4. weal 5. stony 6. silent
9. colorless
tonga... 7. vehicle (2–wheeled)
Tonga... 15. Friendly Islands
tongue... 3. gab 4. meat 5. lingo,
speak 6. speech 7. clapper, lingula
8. language, lorriker, parlance
9. utterance
tongue (pert to)...
classical.. 5. Greek, Latin 6. Hebrew
fish.. 4. sole
Jesus.. 7. Aramaic
lash.. 5. scold 8. scolding
pivoted.. 4. pawl
reference to.. 7. glossal, lingual
sacred.. 4. Pali
shaped.. 9. lingulate
tied.. 4. mute 8. taciturn
wagon.. 4. neap, pole
tongueless... 4. dumb, mute
10. speechless
tonic... 6. bracer, catnip, liquor
7. bracing 8. medicine, remedial,
roborant 9. stimulant 10. refreshing
11. corroborant 12. invigorating
tonsil... 8. amygdala
tonsorialist... 6. barber
tonsured... 4. bald 5. shorn 6. shaven
7. clipped 10. baldheaded
too... 3. and 4. also, over, very
6. overly 7. besides 8. likewise
9. extremely 11. excessively
12. additionally
too (pert to)...
bad.. 4. alas
much.. 4. trop 6. excess 7. nimiety
small.. 13. unappreciable
soon.. 9. premature
tool... 3. axe, saw 4. dupe, file
5. agent 6. device, gadget, puppet
7. engrave, gimmick, utensil, utility

9. appliance 11. contrivance
tool (type)... 2. ax (axe) 3. adz (adze),
awl, bit, hob, hoe, saw, sax, tap
4. file, jack, pick, tong, vise
5. brush, burin, drill, knife, lathe,
level, plane, punch, razor, spade
6. chisel, gimlet, hammer, lifter,
peavey (peavy), pliers, reamer, shears,
slater, slicer, square, trepan, wrench
7. cleaver, mattock, mattoir, scalpel,
spatula 11. screwdriver
tools (pert to)...
category.. 5. power, speed 7. cutlery,
machine, medical 9. precision
11. labor–saving 12. straightedge
prehistoric.. 4. celt 6. eolith
9. paleolith
stone.. 6. banner
theft of.. 6. ratten
toosh... 4. gown (short), robe
9. nightgown
toot... 3. pry, spy 4. fool, gaze, peep
5. blare, drink, revel, shout, spree
6. sprout 7. whistle 8. carousal,
eminence, proclaim 9. blow a horn,
elevation
tooth... 3. cog 4. dent, fang, snag,
tine, tusk 5. ivory, molar, point,
prong, taste 6. canine, cuspid,
wisdom 7. grinder, incisor
8. bicuspid, eyetooth 10. projection
tooth, teeth (pert to)...
ache.. 8. dentagra 9. dentalgia
comb form.. 5. denti, odont
6. odonto 7. odontia
cutting of.. 8. teething 9. dentition
decay.. 6. caries, cavity
11. saprodontia
destitute of.. 8. edentate
irregularity.. 11. odontoloxia
molar.. 4. wang
ref to.. 6. dental 7. odontic
science.. 10. odontology
Scot.. 3. gam
socket.. 8. alveolus
toothlike.. 8. odontoid 9. dentiform
toothless... 8. decrepid, edentate
toothsome... 5. tasty 9. delicious,
palatable
top... 3. cap, fid, lid, tip, toy
4. acme, apex, pate, roof 5. crest,
criss, crown, excel, mensa, outdo,
ridge, scalp 6. finial, summit, vertex,
zenith 7. highest, supreme, surpass,
topmost 8. dominate, pinnacle,
teetotum 9. uppermost
topaz... 3. gem 5. color 7. mineral
11. hummingbird 13. precious stone
tope... 4. tomb, wren 5. drink, grove,
shark, stupa, tower 6. guzzle, shrine
7. dogfish
toper... 3. sot 4. tope 5. shark
6. barfly, boozer 7. guzzler, tippler,
tosspot 8. drunkard 9. alcoholic,
inebriate 12. bacchanalian
tophet, topheth... 4. hell 5. chaos
8. darkness
topi, topee... 3. cap, hat 8. antelope
topiary... 6. garden 9. gardening
topic... 4. plot, text 5. theme
6. reason, remedy 7. subject
8. argument 11. application

topical... 5. local 9. temporary
10. thematical
topknot... 5. crest, onkos 6. pigeon
8. flounder 9. headdress
topmost... 6. apical 7. highest,
supreme 8. foremost 9. uppermost
topnotcher... 3. ace 4. hero, star
6. tiptop 7. supreme 9. first–rate
11. unsurpassed
topography... 7. mapping 8. location
9. surveying 11. description
15. regional anatomy
topple... 3. tip 4. fall, tilt 5. pitch,
upset 6. totter, tumble 8. overturn
9. overthrow 10. somersault
topsail... 5. raffe (raffee)
topsy–turvy... 8. confused
10. contrarily, disordered
11. withershins
toque... 3. hat 6. monkey (bonnet)
9. headdress
tor... 4. crag, peak 5. mound
8. pinnacle
torah, tora... 3. law 7. precept
10. Law of Moses, Pentateuch,
revelation
torch... 4. lamp 5. blaze, flare, fusee
(fuzee), light 7. lighter, lucigen
8. flambeau 10. flashlight
torero... 11. bullfighter
torment... 3. rib, vex 4. bait, pain,
rack 5. agony, devil, harry, tease,
worry 6. badger, harass, harrow,
hector, pester, plague, stir up
7. afflict, anguish, bedevil, torture
8. distress, vexation 9. suffering,
tantalize 10. punishment
11. persecution
torn... 4. rent 5. riven, split 6. ripped
7. severed 8. tattered 9. alienated,
lacerated (see also *tear*)
tornado... 4. wind 7. cyclone, twister
8. blizzard, outburst 9. hurricane,
whirlwind, windstorm
12. thunderstorm
toro... 4. bull 7. cavalla, cowfish
torpedo... 3. ray 4. boat, mine
5. shoot 6. attack, gunman
7. explode 8. fire upon, firework,
numbfish 9. crampfish, detonator,
submarine
torpid... 4. dull, numb 5. inert
6. stupid 7. dormant 8. benumbed,
inactive, lifeless, listless, sluggish
9. apathetic, lethargic
torpor... 4. coma 6. acedia, apathy,
stupor 7. languor 8. dormancy,
lethargy 9. inertness 10. inactivity
12. sluggishness 13. insensibility
torque... 5. chain 6. collar 7. torsion
8. necklace, ornament
torrefy... 5. parch, roast 6. scorch
torrent... 5. flood, spate 6. stream
7. current, roaring 8. downpour,
outburst
torrential... 12. overwhelming
torrid... 3. hot 4. arid 7. burning,
parched 8. scorched, tropical
10. oppressive, passionate
tortilla cooking dish... 5. comal
tortoise... 4. emyd, Emys 6. gopher,
turtle 7. hicatee 8. Chelonia,

matamata 9. ellachick
tortuous... 6. spiral 7. devious,
sinuous, winding 8. twisting
10. circuitous, roundabout
12. labyrinthine
torture... 4. flay, pain, rack 5. agony,
twist 6. impale, punish, wrench
7. crucify, distort, torment
10. punishment
tory, Tory... 6. bandit, outlaw, Papist
8. loyalist, marauder, partisan,
Royalist 11. reactionary
12. Conservative
toss... 3. lob 4. cast, flip, hurl
5. bandy, chuck, fling, flirt, heave,
pitch, throw 6. billow, thrash
7. disturb 8. flounder, scramble
9. commotion 10. excitement
toss (pert to)...
a coin.. 4. flip
and turn.. 6. thrash 8. flounder
9. vacillate
off.. 5. drink 6. tipple 9. dispose of,
improvise
out.. 5. eject 8. trick out
together.. 8. scramble
tosspot... 3. sot 5. drunk, toper
6. flagon 8. drunkard
tossup... 6. gamble 10. even chance
11. uncertainty
tota... 6. grivet, monkey
total... 3. add, all, sum, tot 5. gross,
utter, whole 6. amount, entire
7. perfect, summary 8. absolute,
complete, entirety 9. aggregate
totally... 5. quite 6. wholly 8. entirely
10. completely
totem... 4. pole, post 6. fetish, pillar,
symbol
totem pole... 3. xat
toto... 3. all 4. baby 5. totum
totter... 4. reel, rock, sway 5. pitch,
shake, waver 6. falter, seesaw
7. stagger 8. titubate 9. fluctuate,
vacillate
toucan... 4. toco 7. aracari 8. hornbill
13. constellation (opp Southern
Cross)
touch... 3. dab, tag, tap, tig 4. abut,
feel, meet 5. taste, trait 6. adjoin,
border 7. contact 9. acuteness
touch (pert to)...
acuteness of.. 8. oxyaphia
bound.. 4. abut
closely.. 7. impinge 8. osculate
examine.. 7. palpate
light, lightly.. 3. pat 5. brush
7. attinge, lambent
off.. 4. fire 6. incite
ref to.. 7. tactile, tactual
stone.. 8. basanite 9. criterion
11. Lydian stone
wood.. 4. punk 6. amadou, tinder
touching... 6. moving 7. contact,
feeling, tangent 8. pathetic
9. affecting, attingent 10. concerning
11. interesting
touchy... 4. sore 5. cross, testy
7. peevish 8. ticklish 9. irascible,
irritable, sensitive 10. precarious
13. oversensitive
tough... 4. hard, wiry 5. hardy, rowdy,

stiff **6**. robust, sinewy, strong
7. ruffian **8**. adhesive, hardened,
leathery, stubborn **9**. difficult,
obstinate, resistant, tenacious
10. unyielding
toupee ... **3**. wig **6**. peruke **7**. periwig
9. false hair
tour ... **4**. trip **5**. shift **6**. travel
7. circuit, journey **9**. barnstorm,
excursion
tourmaline ... **3**. gem **6**. schorl
9. rubellite **10**. indicolite
tournament ... **4**. tilt **5**. games, joust,
trial **6**. battle **7**. contest, regatta,
tourney **8**. Olympics **9**. encounter
11. Turnierfest
tourniquet ... **6**. binder, garrot
7. bandage
tousle, tousel ... **4**. pull, tear
6. rumple, tussle **8**. dishevel
tout ... **3**. spy **5**. scout, watch
6. praise **7**. canvass, lookout, tipster
8. give a tip, informer, smuggler
9. predictor, solicitor
tow ... **3**. tew, tug **4**. drag, draw, haul,
pull, rope **5**. chain **6**. hawser
8. cordelle
toward ... **2**. ad, at, to **4**. near
5. anent **6**. facing **7**. forward,
towards, willing **8**. imminent
9. compliant, headed for
11. approaching
toward (pert to) ...
blood vessels .. **5**. hemad (haemad)
center .. **5**. entad **6**. inward
direction .. **7**. leeward, seaward
8. homeward, landward, windward
9. earthward **10**. heavenward
exterior .. **5**. ectad
front .. **8**. anterior
left .. **3**. haw **5**. aport **9**. sinistrad,
sinistral
mouth .. **4**. orad
right .. **7**. dextrad **9**. dextrally
stern .. **3**. aft **5**. abaft **6**. astern
towards ... **7**. ynesche
tower ... **3**. tor **4**. boom, silo, soar
5. exalt, pylon, spire, stupa **6**. belfry,
height, turret, uplift **7**. bulwark,
defense, elevate, steeple, surpass
8. domineer, fortress **9**. campanile
10. stronghold, watchtower
tower (pert to) ...
astrology .. **7**. mansion **14**. planetary
house
bell .. **9**. campanile
chess .. **6**. castle
church .. **5**. spire **6**. belfry, cupola
glacial .. **5**. serac
India .. **5**. minar **7**. sikhara
marker .. **5**. pylon
of .. **4**. Pisa **5**. Babel, Minar **6**. Eiffel,
Hunger, London **7**. silence (dakhma)
10. Kutab Minar
Oriental .. **7**. minaret
watch .. **7**. mirador
towering ... **4**. high, huge, tall
5. great, lofty **6**. Alpine **7**. eminent,
soaring **11**. overweening
towhee ... **5**. finch **7**. bunting, chewink
town ... **4**. burg, deme **6**. ciudad,
hamlet, Podunk, suburb **7**. borough,

commune, village **8**. boom town,
township **9**. ghost town
townsman ... **3**. cit **7**. citizen, oppidan
(Eton student) **8**. resident
9. selectman
toxic ... **7**. noxious **8**. poisoned,
venomous, virulent **9**. poisonous
toxicology *(science of)* ... **7**. poisons
9. antidotes
toxology ... **7**. archery
toxophilite ... **6**. archer
toy ... **3**. pet, top **4**. doll, hoop, play,
whim **5**. dally, fancy, flirt **6**. bauble,
gewgaw, hoople, rattle, trifle **7**. cat's
paw, trinket **8**. flirting **9**. plaything
10. knickknack
trace ... **4**. clew (clue), copy, find, hint,
mark, nose, seek, sign **5**. refer,
shade, tinge, track, trail **6**. deduce,
derive, detect, follow, sketch
7. glimpse, outline, thought, vestige
8. evidence, traverse **9**. delineate,
footprint **11**. investigate, small
amount
trachea ... **4**. duct **8**. windpipe
tracing ... **4**. copy **6**. record
8. ergogram **10**. cardiogram
12. reproduction
track ... **3**. rut, way **4**. path, rail, slot,
spur, wake **5**. route, spoor, trail,
tread **6**. follow, pursue **7**. nereite
(worm), vestige **8**. traverse
9. footprint, spectacle
tract ... **4**. area, plot, zone **5**. essay,
range **6**. estate, region **7**. booklet,
country, expanse, leaflet, quarter,
stretch **8**. brochure, district,
pamphlet, treatise **9**. territory
10. exposition **11**. subdivision
12. dissertation
tract (pert to) ...
arid .. **4**. dene **6**. desert
boggy, swampy .. **6**. morass
10. Everglades
grassland .. **7**. prairie
lava .. **8**. pedregal
treeless .. **5**. llano **6**. steppe **7**. prairie
tractable ... **4**. easy **6**. docile, gentle,
pliant **7**. ductile **8**. amenable, flexible
9. adaptable, compliant, malleable
10. governable **11**. conformable
trade ... **3**. buy **4**. deal, sell, swap,
wind **5**. craft **6**. barter, merger,
metier **7**. bargain, calling, dealing,
pursuit, traffic **8**. business,
commerce, exchange, practice,
purchase, vocation **10**. handicraft,
occupation, profession **11**. intercourse
trade—mark, trademark ... **5**. brand,
label
trader ... **6**. dealer, monger, sutler
8. merchant **9**. tradesman
10. shopkeeper
trading association ... **5**. hanse (hansa)
trading station (Mil) ... **2**. PX **4**. fort,
post
tradition ... **4**. lore, myth **5**. usage
6. custom, legend **7**. culture
8. folklore **10**. convention
(established) **12**. superstition
traditional ... **3**. old **9**. legendary
10. historical **12**. conventional,

long–standing 15. long–established
traditional tale... 4. saga 6. legend
traduce... 4. slur 5. abuse, belie
6. debase, defame, malign, vilify
7. asperse, pervert, slander
8. disgrace 10. calumniate
traffic... 3. buy 4. sell 5. trade
6. barter, simony (sacred)
8. business, carriage, commerce,
dealings 11. familiarity, intercourse
tragedy... 6. misery 8. calamity,
disaster 10. misfortune
tragic... 3. sad 4. dire 5. fatal
8. dramatic, pathetic 10. calamitous,
disastrous, fatal event
tragopan... 8. pheasant
trail... 3. lag 4. drag, hunt, path, slot,
spur 5. blaze, piste, route, scent,
spoor, trace, track 6. camino, follow
7. draggle 8. be behind, footpath
9. lag behind
Trail (famed)... 6. Mormon, Oregon
7. Santa Fe, Spanish 8. Chisholm, El
Camino, Heritage 10. Lewis–Clark,
Wilderness 11. Appalachian
12. Natchez Trace, Pacific Crest
trail (pert to)...
blazer.. 7. pioneer
deer.. 4. slot
mark a.. 5. blaze
marker.. 5. cairn
mountain.. 4. pass
Spanish.. 6. camino
train... 2. el 4. line, load, tail
5. breed, chain, coach, drill, flier,
focus, shape, suite 6. direct, school,
series 7. caravan, cortege, educate,
retinue 8. accustom, instruct,
railroad, rehearse 9. afterpart,
entourage, following 10. attendants,
conveyance, discipline, line of cars,
procession 11. progression,
streamliner 13. accommodation
trained mechanic... 7. artisan
trainee... 6. rookie 7. recruit, student
8. enrollee
traipse... 3. gad 5. trail, tramp
6. trudge, wander 8. gadabout
trait... 5. habit, touch 6. streak
7. feature, quality 9. lineament,
mannerism 11. peculiarity
13. individuality 14. characteristic
traitor... 3. rat 8. informer, Quisling,
turncoat 10. treasonist
13. double–crosser, Judas Iscariot
14. Benedict Arnold
traject... 3. way 4. sage 5. ferry,
route 6. course 7. passage
8. crossing
trajectory... 5. route 6. rocket
9. celestial 10. fixed orbit
tram... 3. car 4. limb 5. wagon
7. carrier, railway, tramcar, trolley,
vehicle 9. streetcar 10. conveyance
tramontane... 5. alien 8. polestar
9. foreigner, North Star
11. transalpine
tramp... 3. bum 4. hike, hobo, hoof,
step, walk 5. jaunt, nomad, tread
6. beggar, trudge, wander
7. sponger, traipse, trample, vagrant
8. vagabond 9. sundowner

10. landlouper (landloper), pedestrian
11. bindle stiff 12. foot traveler
trample... 5. crush, tread 6. bruise,
subdue 7. conquer, destroy, run over
9. press down
trance... 4. coma, doze 5. dream,
spell, swoon 6. raptus, stupor
7. amentia, ecstasy, rapture
8. hypnosis 9. catalepsy, enrapture,
hypnotize, spellbind
tranchant... 5. sharp 7. cutting
9. trenchant
tranquil... 4. calm, cool, easy, mild
5. quiet, still 6. gentle, placid,
serene 7. pacific, restful
8. composed, peaceful 9. quiescent
11. undisturbed 13. imperturbable
tranquility... 3. keg 5. peace, quiet
8. calmness, serenity 9. composure
10. quiescence 12. peacefulness
tranquilize... 4. calm, lull 5. allay,
quiet, still 6. pacify, settle, soothe
7. appease, assuage, compose
transaction... 4. deal, sale 6. action,
affair 7. bargain 8. business
9. discharge, execution
10. proceeding 11. negotiation,
performance, proposition 16. buying
and selling
transcend... 3. cap 5. excel, mount
6. ascend, exceed 7. surpass 8. go
beyond, outstrip, surmount
transcendent... 5. above 8. ethereal,
heavenly, superior 9. recondite
10. superhuman, surpassing
12. metaphysical, supernatural,
transmundane 13. extraordinary
14. transcendental 15. beyond
knowledge
transcribe... 4. copy 5. write
6. record 9. reproduce, translate
10. paraphrase
transcript... 4. copy 6. record
8. apograph 9. duplicate, imitation
12. reproduction
transfer... 4. cede, deed, pass, sale
5. grant, shift 6. assign, attorn,
change, convey, depute, remove
7. removal 8. alienate, delivery
9. transport 10. conveyance,
transcript
transfer (pert to)...
conveyance (estate).. 5. lease
6. demise
crown to successor.. 6. demise
design.. 5. decal 12. decalcomania
medical.. 10. transplant
of ownership.. 6. attorn
10. abalienate, alienation, conveyance
of property.. 8. disposal
transfigure... 5. exalt 6. change
7. glorify 8. idealize 9. irradiate,
transform, transmute
12. metamorphose
transfix... 3. pin 4. hold 5. spear
6. fasten, impale, pierce 9. hold
fixed 11. transpierce 14. hold
motionless
transform... 4. turn 5. alter
6. change, revamp 7. convert
9. transmute 10. assimilate
11. transfigure 12. metamorphose,

transmogrify 16. transubstantiate
transformation... 3. wig 6. change
8. mutation 10. conversion, false
front 13. metamorphosis,
transmutation 17. anthropomorphosis
transgress... 3. err, sin 5. cross
6. exceed, offend, thwart 7. disobey,
infract, violate 8. overstep, trespass
9. break a law
transgression... 3. sin 5. crime, fault
7. misdeed, offense 8. trespass
9. violation 10. effrontery, infraction
11. lawbreaking 12. infringement
13. nonconformity
transgressor... 6. sinner 8. offender
9. wrongdoer 10. delinquent,
malefactor
transient... 5. brief 6. lodger 7. flighty
8. fleeting, fugitive, traveler
9. ephemeral, migratory, momentary
10. evanescent, short–lived, transitory
transit... 6. travel 7. passage
9. metabasis 10. conveyance
12. transference
transition... 5. shift 7. passage
9. anabolism, evolution, metabasis
10. catabolism (katabolism),
conversion, metabolism, modulation
11. transfusion
transitory... 5. brief, fleet 8. fleeting,
temporal 9. ephemeral, temporary,
transient 10. evanescent 11. not
enduring
transitory things... 8. ephemera
translate... 4. read, rede 6. decode,
render 7. convert 8. construe,
transfer 9. interpret 10. paraphrase
translation... 4. pony, trot 7. version
9. rendition 10. paraphrase
12. transference 14. interpretation
15. transliteration
translucent... 6. limpid 8. luminous
11. transparent 14. shining through
transmit... 4. send 6. convey, render
7. devolve, forward 8. bequeath,
hand down, transfer
11. communicate
transmutation... 9. evolution
transmute... 6. change 7. convert,
resolve 9. transform 11. transfigure
12. metamorphose
16. transubstantiate
transparent... 4. open 5. clear, gauzy,
lucid, sheer 6. bright, candid, glassy,
lucent 7. crystal, pellucid, shining
8. luminous, lustrous 9. guileless
10. diaphanous 11. crystalline,
perspicuous, translucent, unconcealed
transparent thing... 4. mica, silk, veil
5. beryl, water 6. quartz, tissue
7. crystal, diamond 8. gossamer
9. isinglass
transport... 3. dak 4. boat, move, raft,
send, ship 5. bring, carry, truck
6. banish, convey, deport, vessel
7. ecstasy, freight, passion, rapture,
smuggle 8. carriage, emigrate,
entrance, palander, transfer
9. enrapture, troopship
transpose... 5. shift 6. change,
convey, invert 7. convert, reverse
8. transfer 9. rearrange, translate,

transmute 11. interchange
transposition of sounds, words...
10. metathesis, spoonerism
Transvaal (pert to)...
capital.. 8. Pretoria
city.. 12. Johannesburg
daisy.. 7. gerbera
discovery.. 4. gold, Rand (The)
famed emigration.. 9. great trek
(1836)
legislature.. 4. raad
policeman.. 4. zarp
settlers.. 5. Boers
War.. 4. Boer (1899–1902)
transverse... 6. across 7. oblique,
transom 8. diagonal 9. crosswise
10. crosspiece
trap... 3. gin, net, pat, web 4. cage,
door, lure, rock, tipe, tree, weir
5. catch, creel, mouth, snare
6. ambush, corner, device, eelpot,
enmesh, recess 7. dragnet, ensnare,
pitfall, springe 8. carriage, deadfall,
trapping, trickery 9. caparison, road
block, stratagem
trapper... 5. lurer 6. hunter, netter,
snarer 7. decoyer
trappings... 4. gear, tack 5. props
7. scenery 8. wardrobe 9. apparatus,
caparison, ornaments 10. horse cloth
13. paraphernalia
trash... 4. bosh, dirt, junk 5. waste
6. debris, refuse, rubble 7. rubbish
8. nonsense, riffraff, trumpery
10. balderdash
trashy... 5. cheap, toshy 6. paltry
7. useless 8. rubbishy 9. worthless
11. nonsensical
trauma... 5. shock, wound 6. injury
travail... 4. pain, toil 5. agony, labor
7. journey, trouble 9. suffering
11. parturition
trave... 9. crossbeam
travel... 2. go 4. fare, move, mush,
post, ride, taxi, tour, trek, wend
5. coast 6. motion 7. commute,
journey, migrate, sojourn 8. progress,
traverse 9. gallivant 11. peregrinate
travel (pert to)...
equipment.. 7. baggage 9. viaticals
expense.. 8. viaticum
group.. 7. caravan
over obstacles.. 9. roughshod
pert to.. 6. viatic
place to place.. 9. itinerate
traveler, travelers... 5. farer 6. viator
7. caravan, tourist 8. salesman,
wayfarer 9. journeyer
travels... 7. odyssey 8. journeys
14. peregrinations
traverse... 4. deny, pass 5. cross
6. refute, thwart 7. athwart, oblique,
parados 8. navigate 10. counteract
travesty... 5. drama 6. parody, satire
7. lampoon 8. disguise 9. burlesque
10. caricature 11. incongruity
tray... 6. salver, server 7. ashtray,
coaster
treacherous... 5. false, Judas, punic,
snaky 8. disloyal, plotting, unstable
9. deceitful, faithless, insidious
10. perfidious, traitorous, unreliable

11. disaffected 13. Machiavellian (Machiavelian), untrustworthy

treachery... 5. guile 6. deceit
7. perfidy, treason 8. betrayal
10. disloyalty

treacle... 4. cure 6. remedy
7. claggum, sweeten 8. molasses
10. sweetening

treacle water... 7. cordial

tread... 3. rut 4. gait, mark, pace, step, volt, walk 5. crush, stair
6. course 7. conquer, set foot, trample 8. footstep, shoe sole
9. footprint

treadle... 5. lever, pedal 7. chalaza

tread underfoot... 5. crush 6. subdue
7. oppress, run over 8. domineer
9. tyrannize

treason... 7. perfidy 8. betrayal, sedition 9. treachery

treasonable, treasonous...
10. perfidious, traitorous
11. treacherous

treasure... 4. fisc (fisk), fund, roon
5. cache, chest, hoard, prize, purse, store, trove, value 6. coffer, fiscus, riches, wealth 7. cherish 8. hold
dear 9. exchequer, thesaurus
10. appreciate, depository, repository, storehouse

treasurer... 6. bursar, purser
7. cashier, curator, officer 8. receiver
9. paymaster 11. chamberlain

Treasure State... 7. Montana

treasure–trove... 5. money (hidden)
7. bullion 9. discovery 14. buried treasure

treat... 4. dose 5. Dutch, feast
6. doctor, handle, regale, repast
7. delight, discuss, process
8. consider 9. discourse, entertain, negotiate 10. manipulate

treat (pert to)...
improperly.. 4. snub 5. flout, spite
6. insult, misuse, offend 9. humiliate
maliciously.. 5. frame, spite
of morals.. 6. ethics
royally.. 6. regale 9. with honor
silk (for rustle).. 6. scroop
snobbishly.. 7. high hat, high–hat
surgically.. 7. operate
tenderly.. 6. coddle, pamper
with contempt.. 5. flout, scorn, scout, spurn 7. contemn
with deference.. 7. respect

treatise... 5. essay, study, tract
6. thesis 7. article 9. discourse
10. discussion 12. dissertation

treatise on...
forests.. 5. silva
fruit trees.. 6. pomona
language.. 7. grammar
pines.. 7. pinetum

treatment (pert to)...
application (Med).. 5. stupe
compassionate.. 5. mercy
harsh.. 5. abuse 8. misusage, severity
ill.. 5. abuse
preparatory.. 8. training 10. ground work, processing
term.. 5. usage 8. addition (to soil), handling

treaty... 4. mise, pact 6. cartel
7. compact, entente 8. contract
9. agreement 10. convention
11. arrangement, negotiation
12. capitulation 13. understanding

treaty (pert to)...
bound nations.. 6. allies
Elm.. 12. Philadelphia (1682)
first draft.. 8. protocol
peace.. 5. truce 6. Pax Dei
9. armistice 9. pax in bella
secret.. 13. the Engagement (1647)

treble... 5. three, voice 6. latten, triple
7. soprano 9. threefold
11. high–pitched

treble clef... 3. Gee 5. G clef, staff
(G clef)

tree... 5. plant 6. corner, timber
7. gallows 9. genealogy

tree (pert to)... see also *trees*
antidote for snakebite.. 6. cedron
aromatic.. 9. sassafras
bear.. 7. raccoon
cactus.. 7. saguaro
camphor.. 5. kapur
cat.. 9. palm civet
cobra.. 6. mambra
cone–bearing.. 3. fir, yew 5. alder, cedar, larch 7. conifer
evergreen fruit.. 5. lemon 6. orange
exudation.. 3. gum, lac, sap
India.. 4. dita 10. devil's tree
lotus.. 4. sadr
mineral (formed on).. 8. dendrite
of Buddha.. 2. bo
of chastity.. 11. agnus castus
of life.. 10. arbor vitae
of strength.. 3. oak
rain.. 5. saman (zaman) 8. genisaro
resin.. 3. fir 4. pine 6. balsam
sacred (Bib).. 7. asherah
salt.. 4. atle (atlee) 8. tamarisk
snake.. 4. gimp, lora
sprout.. 5. copse, sprig 7. coppice
sugar.. 5. maple
Texas.. 5. alamo 6. poplar
tiger.. 7. leopard
toad.. 4. hyla
trunk.. 4. bole 5. caber, stock
umbrella.. 5. wahoo
victor's crown.. 6. laurel
worshiper.. 5. dryad, nymph (wood)

trees (pert to)...
grove.. 5. copse
plantation.. 6. forest 7. orchard, pinetum
poem.. 6. Kilmer (Joyce)
ref to.. 8. arboreal 9. cacuminal
science.. 7. silvics 12. silviculture
service (rowan).. 5. sorbs

trefoil... 6. clover 8. shamrock
10. black medic, clover leaf (Her)

tregetour (anc)... 7. juggler
8. magician

trek... 6. travel 7. journey, migrate
10. expedition

trellis... 5. arbor 7. lattice, pergola
8. espalier 11. latticework

tremble... 5. quake, shake 6. doddle, falter, quaver, quiver, shiver, tatter, thrill, tremor 7. shudder, tremolo, twitter, vibrate 8. be afraid 9. be excited, trepidate

trembling... 5. aspen 6. dither, trepid
7. fearful, nervous, quaking, quavery,
shaking 9. vibrating

tremendous... 3. big 4. huge
5. awful, giant, great 6. superb
8. horrible, powerful, terrific
9. frightful, momentous, monstrous
10. terrifying 13. extraordinary

tremolo... 6. quaver 10. fluttering

tremor... 5. palsy, quake, shake
6. quiver, thrill 7. tremble
9. vibration

tremulous... 5. aspen, quaky, timid
7. excited, fearful, nervous, palsied,
shaking, shivery 9. quavering,
sensitive, trembling, vibratory
11. palpitating

trench... 3. gaw 4. bury, gash, leat,
moat 5. canal, carve, ditch, drain,
fosse 6. furrow, groove, gutter
7. acequia, intrude 8. aqueduct,
encroach, entrench, infringe, trespass
10. excavation 12. entrenchment

trenchant... 4. keen 5. acute, sharp
6. biting 7. cutting 8. clear–cut,
incisive 11. penetrating

trencherman... 5. eater 7. sponger
8. gourmand 9. chowhound
11. gormandizer

trend... 4. tone, turn, vein 5. drift,
skirt, swing, tenor 6. strike
7. deviate, revolve 8. movement,
tendency 9. direction 11. inclination

trepan... 3. saw 4. lure, tool 5. snare,
trick 6. entrap 7. deceive, swindle
8. deceiver, trephine 9. stratagem,
trickster

trepang... 10. bêche–de–mer 11. sea
cucumber 14. sea caterpillar

trepid... 7. quaking 8. timorous
9. trembling

trepidation... 4. fear 5. alarm
6. dismay 7. quaking 9. agitation,
confusion 10. excitement
11. disturbance, oscillation
12. perturbation 13. consternation

trespass... 3. sin 4. tort 5. poach
6. breach, invade, trench 7. intrude,
offense 8. encroach, entrench,
infringe, overstep 10. infraction,
transgress 11. misfeasance
12. infringement 13. transgression

tress... 4. curl, hair 5. braid, plait
7. ringlet 10. lock of hair

tressure... 4. band 6. border, fillet,
ribbon 8. headdress

trestle... 5. bench 7. support, viaduct

tret... 9. allowance

triad... 5. chord, three, trine 7. trinary,
trinity 9. trivalent 12. ternary group

trial... 2. go 4. bout, case, test
5. venue 6. assize, ordeal
7. attempt, contest, empiric
8. evidence, hardship 9. prolusion,
trying out 10. experiment
11. examination, tribulation

triangle... 6. trigon 8. virginal
13. constellation

triangle (pert to)...
connection.. 5. delta

draw circle within.. 7. escribe
military.. 10. punishment
music instrument.. 10. percussion,
triquetrum (anc)
side.. 3. leg
three acute angles.. 6. oxygon
two equal sides.. 9. isosceles
unequal sides.. 7. scalene

triangular (pert to)...
decoration.. 8. pediment, triqueta
muscle.. 7. deltoid
pert to.. 10. trilateral
piece.. 4. gore 5. miter, wedge
6. gusset
sail.. 6. lateen 9. spinnaker
shaped.. 7. deltoid 8. oxygonal

tribal custom... 7. couvade (childbirth)

tribal symbol... 5. totem 9. totem
pole

tribe... 4. clan, kind, race, sept
5. class, group 6. family 7. company
11. aggregation 14. classification

tribe (pert to)...
birds.. 5. flock
head of.. 5. chief 6. sachem
9. patriarch
Israel.. 3. Dan 4. Levi 6. Reuben
migrated.. 5. Aryan
New Zealand.. 3. ati
of Ben.. 5. poets (Ben Jonson)

Tribes, Five Civilized... 5. Creek
7. Choctaw 8. Cherokee, Seminole
9. Chickasaw

Tribes, Five Nations (Iroquois)...
6. Cayuga, Mohawk, Oneida, Seneca
8. Onondaga

tribulation... 5. trial 6. ordeal, sorrow
8. distress 9. suffering

tribunal... 3. bar 4. banc, seat
5. bench, court, curia, forum
9. Areopagus (anc)

tributary... 4. fork, vein 6. branch,
feeder 8. affluent, effluent, influent
9. auxiliary 11. subordinate
12. contributary

tribute... 3. fee, pay, tax 4. cain,
duty, levy, scat 5. allow, grant
6. assign, bestow, homage, impost,
praise, rental 7. chevage (Hist),
ovation, payment, pension, respect
8. encomium 9. attribute, gratitude
10. allegiance, contribute, obligation
11. retribution

tricar... 8. tricycle 10. motorcycle (with
extra car)

trice... 5. jiffy 6. moment 7. instant
9. twinkling

trick... 3. fob, gag 4. dido, dupe,
feat, flam, gull, jest, ruse, wile
5. cheat, child, dodge, fraud, guile,
knack, prank, shift, stunt 6. deceit,
delude 7. deceive, defraud, finesse,
pretext 8. artifice, delusion, flimflam,
illusion 9. chicanery, deception,
imposture 10. subterfuge
11. contrivance, legerdemain

trickery... 5. fraud, hocus 6. deceit
7. roguery 8. artifice, cheating,
trumpery 9. chicanery, deception,
duplicity 10. hanky–panky
11. amenability, legerdemain

trickle... 4. drip, drop, flow, leak

7. distill (distil), dribble, dripple, leakage

tricks... 4. shab 5. ruses 7. roguery 10. deceptions

trickster... 3. fox 5. cheat, rogue 6. rascal 7. slicker 8. deceiver 12. Artful Dodger

tricky... 3. sly 5. snide 6. artful, clever, crafty, shrewd 7. cunning, devious 8. rascally 9. deceitful 13. Machiavellian

trident... 5. curve, spear 6. symbol 7. leister

tried... 4. true 6. proved, tested 7. devoted 8. faithful, reliable 11. trustworthy

tries... 5. tests 6. assays 8. attempts, contests

trifle... 3. ace, bit, fig, toy 4. doit, fico, fool, jest 5. dally, fable, straw 6. bauble, dabble, dawdle, doodle, fiddle, gewgaw, palter, pewter, potter, wanton 7. dessert, nothing, traneen 8. flimflam, gimcrack, make love 9. bagatelle 10. knickknack, peccadillo, triviality 11. small amount 12. treat lightly

trifler... 7. dallier, flaneur 8. palterer, putterer 10. dilettante

trifles... 4. toys 6. trivia 7. gewgaws, palters 8. minutiae, trumpery

trifling... 4. idle, mere 5. inane, petty 6. little 7. trivial 8. badinage, frippery 9. nugacious 10. immaterial 13. insignificant

trifolium... 6. clover 8. shamrock

trig... 4. chic, neat, prim, tidy, trim 5. natty, smart 6. lively, spruce 7. precise 10. methodical

trigo... 5. wheat

trigon... 4. game, harp, lyre (anc) 8. triangle

trigonometry term... 4. sine 6. cosine, secant 7. tangent 8. spherics 10. goniometry

trihoral... 11. three–hourly 15. every three hours

trill... 4. move, sing 5. shake, twirl 6. quaver, ripple, warble 7. mordent, tremolo, trickle, vibrate 8. grupetto 12. pralltriller

trillion... 5. trega (comb form) 14. million million

trim... 3. bob, cut, lop 4. chic, clip, crop, neat, perk, snod, tidy, whip 5. adorn, natty, nifty, panel, preen, prune, shear, shrag 6. border, dapper, defeat, punish, reduce 7. compact, orderly 8. decorate, ornament 9. embellish, shipshape 10. decoration

trimming... 4. gimp, lace 5. braid, jabot, ruche 6. edging, frieze, fringe, piping 7. falbala, ruching 8. furbelow, ornament 9. chicanery, garniture 10. decoration 11. accessories 13. passementerie

trinity... 5. three, triad 6. triune

Trinity (Eccl)... 7. Godhead (Father, Son, Holy Ghost) 8. Trimurti

trinket... 3. toy 4. gaud, tali (tahli) 5. bijou, jewel 6. bangle, gewgaw,

trifle 7. bibelot 8. ornament 10. knickknack

trip... 3. err, run 4. halt, skip, slip, trap 5. caper, dance, jaunt, speed 6. bungle, cruise, errand, flight, frolic, voyage 7. journey, misstep, stumble 8. obstruct 9. excursion 10. expedition

triple... 3. tri 5. trine 6. tercet, treble 9. intensify, threefold 12. three–base hit

triple crown... 5. tiara (Pope's)

triplet (one of)... 4. trin

tripletail... 4. fish, sama 9. berrugate, spadefish

tripod... 3. cat (6–legged) 5. easel, stand, three 6. trivet

Tripoli, Libya...
capital of.. 12. Tripolitania
caravan route to.. 5. Wadai 8. Lake Chad, Timbuktu
famed arch to.. 14. Marcus Aurelius
people.. 4. Arab, Turk 5. Negro 6. Berber
ruler.. 3. bey, dey

triptych... 5. volet (part) 10. altarpiece, writing pad 13. writing tablet (3–part)

trismus... 7. lockjaw, tetanus 16. gnashing the teeth

trist... see *tryst*

Tristan and Isolde... 5. opera (Wagner)

triste... 3. sad 4. full 6. dismal 10. depressing

tristful... 3. sad 10. melancholy

tristich group... 10. three lines 11. three verses (stanza)

Tristram & Iseult... 4. poem (Arnold)

trite... 5. banal, corny, petty, stale, vapid 6. betide, cliché, common, jejune 7. bromide 9. hackneyed, well–known 10. threadbare, unoriginal 11. commonplace, stereotyped 13. platitudinous

triton... 3. eft 4. newt 5. shell, snail 10. salamander

Triton (pert to)...
art figure.. 7. demigod
Gr Myth.. 10. sea demigod
symbol.. 7. trumpet

triumph... 3. win 5. exult, glory 6. defeat 8. ceremony (anc), conquest 10. exultation 11. achievement

trivia... 5. trash 7. trifles 8. trumpery

trivial... 5. banal, petty, small, trite 6. common, paltry, slight 7. nominal, piperly, shallow 8. doggerel, ordinary, trifling 9. frivolous, nugacious 11. commonplace, unimportant 13. insignificant

triviality... 3. toy 6. bauble, gewgaw, trifle 8. falderal, nugacity 9. bagatelle, frivolity 10. knickknack 14. insignificance

troche... 4. pill 6. button, rotula, tablet 7. lozenge 8. pastille (pastil) 9. cough drop 10. deer's tines

trochee... 4. foot (2–syllable) 5. meter 7. choreus

trod... see *tread*

trogger... 7. peddler, vagrant
trogon... 7. quetzal
Troilus (pert to)...
  butterfly genus.. 7. Papilio
  legendary hero of.. 7. Chaucer
  son of.. 5. Priam
Trojan (pert to)...
  astronomy.. 9. asteroids
  epic.. 5. Iliad 6. Aeneid 7. Odyssey
  expedition hero.. 4. Ajax 8. Achilles
  founder of.. 4. Troy
  hero.. 5. Paris 6. Hector
    9. Palamedes
  horse.. 6. wooden
  horse builder.. 5. Epeus
  king.. 5. Priam
  native.. 6. Dardan
  soothsayer.. 7. Helenus
  war cause.. 5. Helen (of Troy)
  war leader.. 9. Agamemnon
  warrior.. 6. Agenor
troll (Myth)... 5. dwarf, giant, gnome
troll... 4. bowl, fish, roll, sing 5. angle
  (fishing), rondo 6. allure, entice,
  propel 7. revolve, trundle 9. circulate
trolley... 4. cart, tram 5. truck
  6. barrow, sledge 7. tramcar
  8. handcart 9. streetcar
trolley, off his... 4. nuts 5. balmy,
  batty, daffy, dippy, dotty, goofy
  6. cuckoo
trollop... 5. slump 6. slouch
  8. slattern
trombone (pert to)...
  ancient.. 7. sackbut, sambuke
  instrument.. 5. brass
  mouthpiece.. 5. bocal
  popular size.. 5. tenor
troop... 4. army, band, unit 5. crowd
  7. company, march on, ressala
  8. quantity, soldiers 9. go forward
  10. armed force
troop (pert to)...
  arrangement.. 7. echelon
  encampment.. 5. étape
  formation.. 4. line
  one of.. 7. peltast 8. chasseur
  ship.. 9. transport
troops (pert to)...
  assemble.. 6. muster
  German.. 6. Panzer
  hidden.. 6. ambush
  Hungary.. 7. Hussars
  mounted.. 7. cavalry
  sally.. 6. sortie
  term for.. 4. army 5. squad 6. forces
    7. battery, militia, phalanx
    9. commandos 11. armed forces
trophy... 3. cup 4. palm 5. award,
  medal, Oscar, prize 6. reward
  7. laurels, memento 8. memorial
tropical (pert to)...
  animal.. 4. eyra 5. araba, coati, potto
    6. agouti 7. peccary
  bird.. 3. ani 4. tody 5. jalap
    6. motmot 7. jacamar
  dolphin.. 4. inia
  fish.. 4. toro 6. remora, salema
  fruit.. 3. fig 4. date 5. guava,
    mango, papaw 6. banana, papaya
  lizard.. 5. agama
  rodent.. 6. agouti

tree.. 4. coco, palm 5. balsa, seron
    6. sapota 8. tamarind
vine.. 7. cowhage, lantana
    14. trumpet creeper
trot... 3. jog, run 4. gait, pony
  5. hurry 7. routine 11. translation
trotting horse... 6. Morgan
  7. Hackney 12. Hambletonian
trottoir (rare)... 8. footpath, pavement,
  sidewalk
troubadour... 4. bard, poet
  8. jongleur, minstrel, musician
  9. trovatore
trouble... 3. ado, ail, irk 4. fuss,
  harm, stir 5. annoy, grief, worry
  6. bother, effort, grieve, harass,
  pester, plague, sorrow 7. agitate,
  anxiety, concern, disturb, perturb,
  torment 8. calamity, disorder,
  disquiet, distress, mischief
  9. adversity, annoyance, commotion
  10. affliction, difficulty, misfortune
  11. disturbance 13. inconvenience,
  interfere with
troubled... 6. queasy 7. annoyed,
  anxious 8. agitated 9. disturbed
  10. distressed
troublemaker... 8. agitator, gossiper
  13. mischief–maker
troublesome... 5. pesky 8. annoying,
  perverse 9. difficult, laborious,
  turbulent, vexatious, wearisome
  10. bothersome, burdensome,
  disturbing, oppressing 11. distressing
  12. inconvenient
trough... 3. bin 4. bosh, bowl, dale,
  tank 5. basin, chute, drain, toper
  6. coffin, gutter, manger, sluice,
  trench 7. channel, conduit
trounce... 4. beat, flog 5. scald
  6. indict, punish, thrash 7. censure,
  journey
trout... 4. char, peal 7. oquassa
  9. namaycush 11. Dolly Varden
trout (pert to)...
  genus.. 5. Salmo 6. Trutta
  lake.. 9. namaycush
  Maine.. 7. oquassa
  parasite (external).. 3. sug
  ref to.. 11. truttaceous
  type.. 3. sea 4. rock 5. brook,
    brown, river 7. oquassa, rainbow
    8. speckled 9. cutthroat
trovatore... 10. troubadour
trove... 4. find 8. treasure (buried)
  9. discovery 10. thing found
  13. treasure–trove
trow... 4. boat, hope 5. barge, think,
  trust 6. expect 7. believe, suppose
  9. catamaran
trowing... 5. creed 6. belief 7. opinion
Troy, or Ilium...
  capital of.. 5. Troad (anc)
  defender.. 6. Aeneas
  famed for.. 5. ruins
  founder (Myth).. 4. Ilus (son of Tros),
    Tros
  king.. 5. Priam 9. Agamemnon
  king's wife.. 5. Helen
  mountain.. 3. Ida
  name, present.. 9. Hissarlik
  pert to.. 5. Iliac 6. Trojan

site.. 9. Asia Minor
troy weight... 5. grain, ounce, pound
  11. pennyweight
truant... 4. idle 7. shirker, trivant,
  vagrant 8. absentee
truant, to play... 5. miche
truce... 5. pause, peace, trêve
  9. armistice, cessation 10. brief
  quiet 12. intermission
truck... 3. van 4. deal, dray, haul
  5. bogie, dance, lorry, trade
  6. barter, peddle 7. flatcar, traffic
  8. commerce, exchange, nonsense
  9. groceries
truckle... 4. fawn 5. toady 6. cringe,
  submit 7. knuckle
truculent... 4. base, mean 5. cruel
  6. fierce, savage 8. ruthless,
  scathing 9. barbarous, ferocious
  11. destructive
trudge... 4. pace, plod, slog, walk
  5. tramp 6. go slow 7. traipse
true... 2. so 4. fact, leal, pure, real
  6. gospel, honest, lawful 7. certain,
  devoted, germane, precise, sincere,
  upright 8. faithful, orthodox, reliable,
  straight, unerring 9. authentic,
  steadfast, veracious, veritable
  10. legitimate 11. trustworthy,
  unfaltering
true (pert to)...
  blue.. 5. loyal 8. faithful, orthodox
  10. man of honor
  copy.. 7. estreat
  not.. 5. false 10. figurative
  poetic.. 4. leal
  skin.. 4. derm (suff) 5. derma
  to fact.. 7. literal
  to life.. 8. lifelike 11. descriptive
truffle... 5. fungi, tuber 8. earthnut
  10. ascus fruit
truism... 5. axiom, truth 9. platitude
  11. commonplace
trull... 4. girl, lass 5. demon, fiend,
  giant, wench 7. trollop 8. strumpet
truly... 3. yea 4. amen 5. sooth
  6. indeed, justly, verily 7. exactly,
  rightly 8. properly 9. certainly
  10. accurately, positively, truthfully
trump... 3. pam 4. card, ruff (cards),
  suit 7. surpass 10. good fellow
  12. masterstroke
trumpery... 5. fraud, trash 6. deceit
  7. rubbish 8. nonsense
trumpet... 4. horn 5. blare
  6. summon 7. clarion 8. proclaim
  9. organ stop 12. elephant's cry
  14. wind instrument
trumpet (pert to)...
  blare.. 7. fanfare, tantara
  call (stage).. 6. sennet
  creeper.. 6. tecoma
  fish.. 7. bellows 10. flutemouth
  lily.. 5. calla 7. Bermuda
trumpeter... 4. bird, fish, swan
  5. agami, perch 6. pigeon 7. whiting
  8. musician 9. messenger
truncheon... 4. club 5. baton, staff
  6. cudgel 8. splinter
trunk... 3. box, log 4. body, bole,
  pool, soma, tank 5. chest, stalk,
  torso 6. coffer 7. railway 8. main

stem 9. proboscis 10. lobster pot
trunkfish... 4. toro 7. cowfish
truss... 3. tie 4. bind, gird, pack
  6. bundle, fasten 7. support
  10. strengthen
trust... 4. hope, rely, task 5. faith
  6. belief, commit, credit, dartle,
  depend, estate 7. believe, confide,
  consign, custody, entrust, loyalty
  8. credence, reliance, security
  9. assurance, syndicate
  10. confidence, dependence, give
  credit, investment 12. organization
trustee... 6. bailee 7. sindico
  9. fiduciary, treasurer 10. depository
  13. administrator
trustful... 5. liege 7. reliant 8. trusting
  9. confiding, credulous
  13. unquestioning
trustworthiness... 9. axiopisty
  12. trustability 13. dependability
trustworthy... 4. safe 5. solid
  6. honest 7. certain 8. reliable
  9. authentic 10. dependable
trusty... 7. convict 8. faithful, prisoner
  10. dependable 11. trustworthy
truth... 3. tao 4. fact, real 5. sooth
  (anc) 6. verity 7. honesty, reality
  8. fidelity, veracity 9. constancy,
  exactness, orthodoxy, sincerity
  11. correctness 14. verisimilitude
truth (pert to)...
  ancient term.. 5. sooth 6. certes
  Chinese Philos.. 3. tao
  goddess.. 4. Maat
  personified.. 3. Una 4. Maat
  ref to.. 6. verily 11. verisimilar
  14. verisimilitude
  self-evident.. 5. axiom 6. truism
truthful... 6. honest 7. veridic
  9. veracious, veridical
truthfulness... 5. truth 7. honesty
  8. accuracy, veracity
  13. veraciousness
try... 2. do 3. say 4. test 5. annoy,
  assay, ettle, prove, taste, trial
  6. purify, refine, render, sample,
  strive 7. attempt, contest, torment
  8. audition, endeavor, irritate
  9. prosecute, undertake
  10. experiment 11. demonstrate,
  investigate
trying... 7. irksome, painful, tasting
  8. annoying, sampling 10. attempting
  12. exasperating 13. experimenting
tryst... 6. invite, market 7. beguile,
  meeting 9. agreement, betrothal
  10. engagement, rendezvous
  11. appointment 12. meeting place
tsamba... 5. flour 6. barley
tsar... 4. czar, tzar 6. despot
  8. autocrat
tsetse, tsetse fly... 4. kivu
  8. Glossina, parasite
tsetse fly disease... 6. nagana
  16. sleeping sickness
T-shaped... 3. tau
tsine... 6. wild ox 7. banteng
tuatara, tuatera... 7. reptile
  (iguanalike)
tub... 3. hod, keg, kid, soe, tun, vat
  4. cask, ship, wash 5. barge, bathe,

bowie, keeve **6.** barrel, firkin, piggin;
vessel **7.** bathtub, cistern, washtub
9. container, fat person
tuba . . . **6.** liquor (palm) **7.** helicon,
trumpet (anc) **9.** bombardon
10. contrabass **11.** bass saxhorn
12. mythical tree
Tubal–cain's father . . . **6.** Lamech
Tubal's father . . . **7.** Japheth
tube . . . **3.** cop **4.** bulb, duct, hose,
pipe **5.** auget, chute, diode
6. siphon, tunnel **7.** burette, cannula,
conduit, fistula, matrass, railway,
salpinx **8.** cylinder, electron, stenosis
9. spaghetti, telescope
tuber . . . **3.** oca, yam **4.** beet, bulb,
eddo, root, taro **5.** jalap, salep
6. potato **12.** protuberance
tubular . . . **4.** pipy **5.** round **6.** tubate
8. cannular, fistular, tubiform
11. cylindrical
tuck . . . **3.** eat, nip **4.** cram, fold, poke
5. feast, pinch, pleat, press
7. shorten, tighten **9.** appendage
tucker . . . **3.** bib **4.** food, meal
5. board **6.** ration
Tuesday (pert to) . . .
French . . **5.** Mardi
Norse god . . **3.** Tyr (Tiu)
Shrove . . **9.** Mardi gras
Teutonic . . **10.** Martis dies
tufa . . . **4.** rock, toph, tuff **5.** trass
tuft . . . **4.** coma, doss, hair **5.** beard,
bunch, clump, crest **6.** button,
goatee, pompon, tassel **7.** cluster,
fetlock **8.** aigrette, feathers
tug . . . **3.** tow **4.** drag, draw, haul, pull,
toil **5.** labor **6.** drudge, effort, strain,
tussle **7.** contend, contest, wrestle
8. struggle
tulip (pert to) . . .
center (World) . . **7.** Holland
color . . **6.** auburn **9.** tulipwood
genus . . **6.** Tulipa
Mexican . . **6.** orchid
military slang . . **9.** explosive
tree . . **6.** timber **7.** majagua, waratah
type . . **6.** Darwin, parrot **7.** breeder,
cottage
tumble . . . **4.** fall, flop, trip, veer
5. pitch, spill **6.** jumble, rumple,
topple, tousle, wallow **7.** stumble
8. collapse, disorder, flounder, roll
over **9.** break down, confusing
10. handspring, somersault
11. precipitate
tumbler . . . **3.** dog **4.** cart, drum
5. glass **6.** Dunker, pigeon, vessel
7. acrobat, gymnast, tippler, tumbrel
8. lock part **13.** contortionist
tumbleweed . . . **6.** indigo **7.** bugseed,
pigweed, thistle **10.** amaranthus
tumbrel, tumbril . . . **4.** cart **5.** wagon
8. dumpcart **12.** cucking stool (Hist)
tumescent, tumid . . . **6.** turgid
7. bloated, bulging, pompous
8. inflated **9.** bombastic, disturbed,
plethoric **11.** protuberant
tumor . . . **3.** wen **4.** cyst, wart
6. cancer, goiter, growth, lipoma,
struma **7.** adenoma, sarcoma
8. ganglion, swelling **11.** excrescence

12. protuberance
tumor, eyelid . . . **9.** pladaroma
tumult . . . **3.** din, mob **4.** fray, riot
5. Babel, brawl, noise **6.** affray,
babble, bustle, émeute, hubbub,
uproar **7.** bluster, ferment, turmoil
8. disorder, outbreak, uprising
9. agitation, commotion, confusion
10. excitement, turbulence
11. disturbance
tumultuous . . . **4.** wild **5.** noisy, rough
7. lawless, riotous, violent
8. agitated, confused **9.** disturbed,
turbulent **10.** boisterous, disorderly,
hurly–burly
tumulus . . . **5.** mound, stump **6.** barrow
7. hillock
tun . . . **3.** cup (anc), jar, tub, vat
4. cask, year (Mayan, 360–day)
5. drink **6.** guzzle, vessel **7.** measure
tuna . . . **5.** tunny **8.** albacore
tune . . . **3.** air, key **4.** aria, lilt, port,
song **5.** pitch **6.** adjust, melody
7. chorale, harmony, sonance
9. harmonize **10.** adjustment,
intonation
tune (pert to) . . .
correctly . . **3.** key
down . . **6.** reduce, soften **8.** moderate
musical instrument . . **6.** string
out of . . **9.** dissonant **11.** inaccordant
12. unconforming
tungsten . . . **7.** wolfram
Tunisia . . .
cape . . **3.** Bon
capital . . **5.** Tunis
famed ruins . . **8.** Carthage
gulf . . **5.** Gabes
oasis . . **5.** Gafsa
people . . **5.** Arabs **7.** Berbers
resort island . . **6.** Djerba
river . . **8.** Medjerda
ruler . . **3.** dey **5.** pasha
seaport . . **4.** Sfax **7.** Bizorte
tunnel . . . **4.** adit, bore, cave, tube
5. drift **6.** burrow, dig out, funnel,
subway **10.** excavation, smokestack
tunny . . . **4.** tuna **8.** albacore
tup . . . **3.** ram **4.** beat, butt **5.** sheep
6. mallet **7.** cuckold
turban . . . **6.** entrée, fillet, Moslem,
mundil, squash **8.** bandanna,
seerband **9.** headdress
turbid . . . **4.** dark, dull **5.** dense,
muddy, roily **6.** cloudy, impure,
opaque **7.** clouded, muddled
8. confused, feculent, polluted
turbot . . . **5.** brill **8.** flatfish
turbulence . . . **4.** fury **6.** tumult, uproar
7. bluster, rioting, turmoil
9. agitation, commotion
10. excitement, unruliness
11. disturbance, impetuosity
14. tumultuousness
turbulent . . . **4.** loud, wild **5.** noisy,
rough **6.** stormy **7.** excited, furious
8. virulent **10.** tumultuous
turf . . . **3.** sod **4.** peat, slab **5.** divot,
glebe, grass, sward, track **10.** race
course
turgid . . . **5.** tumid **7.** bloated,
pompous, swollen **8.** inflated

9. bombastic, distended, grandiose,
redundant 12. magniloquent,
ostentatious 13. grandiloquent
Turk... 5. Tatar 6. Tartar 7. Osmanli,
Ottoman 9. Kizilbash
Turkestan people... 5. Uzbek (Uzbeg)
turkey... 4. fowl 5. poult 7. bustard,
gobbler, vulture
Turkey... see also *Turkish*
  capital.. 6. Angora (anc), Ankara
  city.. 5. Adana, Izmir (Smyrna)
  6. Edessa, Samsun 7. Scutari
  8. Istanbul (Constantinople)
  10. Adrianople
  founder.. 6. Othman
  mountain.. 6. Ararat
  peninsula.. 9. Anatolian
  river.. 5. Mesta 6. Seyhan
Turkish (pert to)...
  army corps.. 4. ordu 8. seraglio
  commander, ruler.. 3. aga (agha), bey
  4. wali 5. pasha 6. atabeg (atabek)
  court (Ottoman).. 5. Porte
  12. Sublime Porte
  dignitary.. 5. pasha
  dish (food).. 5. cabob 6. pilaff (pilau)
  drink.. 4. boza (bozah), raki 5. airan
  6. mastic 9. lion's milk
  dynasty.. 6. seljuk
  emblem.. 8. crescent
  Empire.. 7. Ottoman
  flag.. 4. alem, toug (former)
  harem girl.. 6. kadein (kadine)
  hat, cap.. 3. fez 6. calpac (calpack)
  hospice, inn.. 6. imaret
  infidel.. 6. giaour
  javelin.. 6. jereed (jerid)
  judge.. 4. cadi (kadi)
  minister of state.. 6. vizier
  money of account.. 5. asper
  mosque.. 4. jami
  music.. 8. janizary
  native.. 6. Edesan (anc)
  palace.. 5. serai
  pavilion.. 5. kiosk
  pipe (long–stemmed).. 7. chibouk
  (chibouque)
  regiment.. 4. alai
  religious war.. 5. jihad (jehad)
  rug.. 5. Melas, Tekke, Yomud, Yuruk
  6. Afghan 8. Turkoman 9. Kurdistan
  ruler.. 3. bey, dey 4. khan 6. sultan
  7. chambul
  sailing vessel.. 4. saic 6. mahone
  sailor.. 9. galiongee (galionji)
  soldier.. 5. nizan, redif 6. Arnaut
  (Arnaout) 8. Janizary
  11. bashi–bazouk
  statute.. 8. Tanzimat (1839)
  sultan.. 5. Ahmed, Selim 7. Ilderim,
  Saladin
  sultan's title.. 6. caliph (calif)
  sword.. 8. yataghan (yatagan)
  tambourine.. 5. daira
  tax (from Christians).. 6. avania
  title.. 3. aga (agha), ali 4. amir
  (ameer)
  tobacco.. 7. chibouk (chibouque),
  Latakia
  tribe.. 5. Ersar, Tatar 7. Bashkir,
  Viddhal
  Turkoman.. 11. tribal group

veil (double).. 7. yashmak (yashmac)
vest.. 6. jelick
whip, lash.. 7. kurbash
turmeric... 3. rea 4. ango, herb
5. olena 8. curcumin
turmoil... 3. ado, din 5. upset, worry
6. tumult, unrest 7. ferment,
tempest, trouble 8. disquiet
9. agitation, commotion, confusion
10. excitement, turbulence
12. perturbation
turn... 3. bow, lap 4. bend, deed,
gyre, roll, slew, slue, spin, tour,
veer, vert 5. curve, lathe, pivot,
quirk, round, shift, spell, wheel,
whirl, whorl 6. abvert, change, crisis,
gyrate, rotate, swivel, zigzag
7. deflect, deviate, reverse, revolve
8. aptitude, circuity, maneuver,
persuade, rotation, tendency
9. deviation, pirouette, reversion
11. convolution 12. metamorphose
turn (pert to)...
  about.. 9. alternate
  aside, away.. 4. slew, slue 5. avert,
  deter, repel, shunt 6. divert, swerve
  7. deflect, deviate, digress, diverge
  back.. 5. repel 6. coward, revert
  7. evolute, head off, reflect
  coat.. 7. traitor 8. apostate, deserter,
  renegade
  comb form.. 5. tropo
  down.. 4. veto 6. refuse, reject
  7. decline
  gate.. 5. stile 9. turnstile
  inside out.. 5. evert 6. invert
  7. ransack
  inward.. 8. introrse 9. introvert
  left.. 3. haw 4. port
  of duty.. 5. spell, trick
  off.. 5. shunt 7. dismiss, execute
  10. extinguish
  on axis.. 6. obvert, rotate
  one's back upon.. 4. flee, snub
  5. avoid 6. ignore, oppose, refuse,
  reject
  on pivot.. 6. swivel
  out.. 4. fare, oust 5. array, evert,
  expel, track 6. detour, output, siding
  7. dismiss 8. assemble, clearing
  9. eventuate, gathering
  10. accomplish, extinguish
  outward.. 5. evert, splay 8. extrorse
  9. extrovert
  over.. 3. pie 4. keel, tart 5. sales,
  shift, spill 6. assign, pastry
  7. capsize 8. hand over, overturn
  over a new leaf.. 6. change, reform
  over pages.. 4. leaf 5. thumb
  over to others.. 4. farm 7. farm out
  to left.. 3. haw 4. port
  to right.. 3. gee 9. starboard
  up.. 4. find, keel 5. occur 6. appear,
  arrive 7. be found
  upside down.. 4. roll 6. invert, whelve
  7. ransack 8. overturn
turned up (nose)... 9. retroussé
turning... 6. rotary 7. bending,
crooked, winding 8. rotation,
twisting, whirling 9. deviating,
deviation 10. circuitous, revolution
11. convolution, sinistrorse

turning (pert to)...
left to right.. 9. dextrorse
machine.. 5. lathe
point.. 6. crisis 8. decision, landmark
  11. climacteric 13. crucial period
right to left.. 11. sinistrorse
turnip... 4. neep, rape, root
  8. rutabaga
turnip (pert to)...
large.. 7. Russian, Swedish
  8. rutabaga
shaped.. 8. napiform
wild.. 5. navew
Turnix... 4. bird (3–toed) 5. quail
  10. Hemipodius
Turpentine State... 13. North Carolina
turpentine tree... 4. pine 6. tarata
  9. terebinth
turpid... 3. low 4. base, vile
  8. cowardly
turpitude... 6. fedity 8. baseness,
  vileness 9. decadence, depravity
  10. corruption
turquoise... 3. gem 4. blue
  7. mineral, Turkish
turret... 4. loom, soar 5. tower
  6. cupola (revolving), height
  9. structure 10. stronghold,
  watchtower
turtle (pert to)...
edible.. 8. terrapin
freshwater.. 4. emyd 8. tortoise
genus.. 4. Emys
hawklike.. 5. carat 9. hawk's–bill
large.. 5. arrau 6. jurara, mamata
largest.. 11. leatherback
ref to.. 9. chelonian
sea.. 10. thalassian
shell.. 8. carapace
snapping.. 6. cooter 8. shagtail
Tuscany...
birthplace of.. 7. Galileo (Astronomer)
capital.. 8. Florence
city.. 4. Pisa 7. Leghorn
color.. 9. colcothar
famed tower.. 4. Pisa (1174)
island.. 4. Elba (1st exile, Napoleon)
native.. 6. Tuscan
marble.. 7. Carrara
province.. 4. Pisa
river.. 4. Arno 6. Cecina 7. Ombrone
wine.. 7. chianti
tusk... 4. fang 5. ivory, tooth
  6. canine 7. incisor 9. scrivello
  (elephant's)
Tussaud, Madame's London district...
  8. Waxworks (Museum)
  10. Marylebone
tussis... 5. cough
tussle... 7. contend, contest, scuffle,
  wrestle 8. struggle
tutelage... 7. nurture 8. teaching,
  tutorage 9. oversight, tutorship
  11. instruction 12. guardianship
tutelary gods (Rom)... 5. lares
  7. penates
tutor... 5. coach, teach 6. docent,
  ground, mentor, school 7. teacher
  8. instruct 9. pedagogue (pedagog),
  preceptor
twaddle... 3. rot 6. drivel, gabble
  7. chatter, fustian, prattle

  8. claptrap, nonsense 9. absurdity,
  silly talk 10. flapdoodle 16. trash
  and nonsense
twang... 4. tang 5. strum 6. accent
  7. dialect 8. pungency
tweak... 4. jerk, pain 5. pinch
  6. snatch, twitch
tweeg... 10. hellbender, salamander
tweezers... 7. pincers 10. instrument
twelfth... 5. twait, uncia 8. duodenal
  9. duodenary
Twelfth Night character... 5. Viola
  6. Olivia, Orsino 7. Sir Toby
  8. Malvolio 12. Sir Toby Belch
Twelfthtide... 8. Epiphany
  10. Twelfth–day
twelve (pert to)...
amount.. 5. dozen
angles.. 9. dodecagon
prefix.. 5. dodec 6. dodeca
rule of.. 9. dodecarch
series.. 8. dodecade
Twelve, The... 8. Apostles
twenty (pert to)...
Anglo–Ind.. 5. carge, score
comb form.. 4. icos 5. icosa, icosi
faces.. 11. icosahedron
pert to.. 7. icosian 8. vicenary
quires.. 4. ream
symbol.. 2. XX
years.. 9. vicennial
twenty–fourth part (gold alloy)...
  5. carat (karat)
twibil (twibill)... 2. ax (axe) 6. pickax
  (pickaxe) 7. mattock 8. battle–ax
  (battle–axe)
twice... 2. bi, di 6. doubly 7. twofold
  8. two times
twig... 4. reis 5. besom, birch, bough
  6. branch, sallow, switch, twitch,
  wattle
twigs, bundle of... 5. fagot 6. barsom
  (sacred)
twilight... 3. dim 4. blue, dusk
  6. shaded 7. obscure 8. foredawn,
  gloaming 9. cocklight 10. crepuscule
Twilight of the Gods... 8. Ragnarok
twill... 3. rib 5. flute, weave 6. fabric
  9. tricotine
twilled... 3. rep 5. reedy, ridgy, sedgy,
  serge 6. corded, fluted
twin... 3. two 4. dual, mate, pair
  5. gemel, macle 6. couple, double
  7. didymus, Siamese 8. didymous,
  matching 9. duplicate, identical
  11. counterpart 12. accompanying
Twin Cities (Minn)... 6. St Paul
  11. Minneapolis
twine... 4. bend, coil, turn, wind, wrap
  5. braid, snarl, twist, weave
  6. enfold, enlace, tangle 7. embrace,
  enclasp, entwine, wreathe
  8. convolve, encircle 9. interlace
  10. intertwine, interweave
  11. intermingle
twine (pert to)...
color.. 4. dune 7. anamite
hank of.. 3. ran
left to right.. 9. dextrorse
right to left.. 11. sinistrorse
Scot.. 4. part
twinge... 4. ache, pain, pang

5. pinch, qualm 6. twitch
twin stars... 6. Castor, Pollux
twin stock... 4. bees 7. beehive (two colonies)
twirl... 4. coil, eddy, gyre, spin
 5. pitch, querl, twist, whirl 6. gyrate, writhe 7. revolve 8. flourish, rotation
 11. convolution
twist... 3. cue, ply 4. coil, curl, slew, slub, slue, spin, turn, warp, wind
 5. braid, quirk, tweak, wrest
 7. contort, deflect, distort, falsify, meander, pervert, wreathe, wriggle
 8. convolve 9. insinuate, interlace, prejudice 10. distortion
 12. eccentricity, misrepresent
twisted... 3. wry 4. awry, cued
 5. askew, kinky, torse, wrung
 6. warped 7. complex, torqued, tortile, wrested, writhed
twisted cord... 7. torsade
twister... 3. lie 7. cruller, tornado
 8. doughnut 9. dust whirl 10. sand column, somersault, waterspout
twit... 4. gibe, josh 5. blame, taunt, tease, tweet 6. banter 7. upbraid
 8. reproach, ridicule
twitch... 3. nip, tic, tug 4. hurt, jerk, yank 5. pluck, shake, tweak
 6. snatch 9. be excited, quick pull, vellicate 11. contraction
twitter... 5. chirp 6. giggle, titter
 7. chatter, tremble 9. agitation
two (pert to)...
 chambered.. 9. bicameral
 colored.. 9. dichromic
 edged.. 9. ancipital
 faced.. 5. false 6. double 9. deceitful
 11. treacherous 12. falsehearted
 fisted.. 6. virile
 fold.. 4. dual, twin 6. binary, double, duplex 8. didymous
 forked.. 6. bident 9. bifurcate
 11. dichotomous
 handed.. 7. bimanal 8. bimanous
 10. secondhand 12. ambidextrous
 headed.. 9. ancipital 11. dicephalous
 masted ship.. 4. yawl, zulu
 parts.. 3. duo 4. duad, dyad
 7. duality
 poetic.. 5. twain
 prefix.. 2. bi, di
 Scot.. 3. twa
 Spanish.. 3. dos
 spot.. 5. deuce
 time.. 7. deceive
 wheeled carriage, chariot.. 3. gig
 6. esseda 10. jinrikisha (jinriksha)
Tyche... 7. Fortuna 16. goddess of Fortune
tycoon... 6. shogun 7. magnate
 9. financier 13. industrialist
tylopod... 5. camel
tympanum... 7. eardrum 9. middle ear
 10. water wheel
tympany... 6. tympan 7. bombast
 9. inflation 10. distention
typal... 7. typical 8. symbolic
type... 2. pi 4. font, form, kind, norm, sign, sort 5. genre, genus, model, print, Roman, token 6. emblem, italic, minion, symbol 7. measure,

pattern, species 8. boldface, classify, standard 9. archetype, character
 10. transcribe 11. Baskerville
 14. characteristic, representative
type (pert to)...
 assortment.. 4. font, kern
 block of.. 4. quad 7. quadrat
 bold style.. 4. text
 bridge.. 7. bascule
 classic.. 5. Roman 6. italic 11. black letter (Gothic)
 line.. 4. slug
 measure.. 2. em, en
 mixed.. 2. pi
 mold.. 6. matrix
 perfection.. 7. paragon
 set.. 7. compose
 setter.. 8. linotype, monotype
 10. compositor
 size.. 4. norm, pica, ruby 5. agate, canon, pearl 6. minion 7. diamond
 stroke.. 5. serif
 tray.. 9. galley
typewriter (pert to)...
 bar.. 6. spacer
 cylinder.. 6. platen, spacer
 type.. 4. pica 5. elite
 type of.. 6. ticker 8. teletype
 9. stenotype
typhoon... 4. wind 5. storm
 7. cyclone
typhus fever... 10. tabardillo
typical... 4. norm 5. typal 6. normal
 7. regular 10. conforming, emblematic, figurative 11. precedental
 14. characteristic, representative
typify... 6. embody 9. prefigure, represent, symbolize
Tyr (Norse)... 3. Tiu 6. sky–god, war–god
tyrannical... 5. cruel 6. lordly
 8. despotic 9. imperious
 10. oppressive 11. domineering
tyrannize... 7. oppress 8. domineer
tyranny... 8. severity 9. despotism
tyrant... 4. czar, Ivan, Nero, tsar, tzar
 6. despot 7. monarch
Tyre... see also *Tyrian*
 capital of.. 9. Phoenicia (anc)
 famed for.. 9. purple dye
 seaport of.. 7. Lebanon
 site.. 9. peninsula 13. Mediterranean
Tyrian (pert to)...
 alphabet.. 7. Moabite
 Cynosure.. 9. Ursa Minor
 god (Teut).. 2. Er
 king.. 5. Hiram
 princess.. 4. Dido (Elissa)
tyro, tiro... 5. pupil 6. novice
 7. amateur 8. beginner, neophyte
 9. commencer, fledgling, greenhorn
 10. apprentice 11. abecedarian
Tyrol...
 capital.. 9. Innsbruck
 dialect.. 5. Ladin
 district.. 8. Trentino
 mountain.. 4. Alps 9. Dolomites
 province of.. 7. Austria
 river.. 4. Isar
tzar, tsar, czar... 4. king 5. ruler
 6. tyrant
tzigane... 5. gypsy

U

U... 6. letter (21st)
uang... 6. beetle
uberous... 7. copious 8. abundant, fruitful 9. plentiful
uberty... 6. plenty 12. fruitfulness
ubiety... 8. location, position, relation 9. whereness
ubiquity... 8. doctrine (Luther) 10. everywhere 12. omnipresence
U–boat... 3. sub 9. submarine
base.. 4. Kiel
Uca.. 11. fiddler crab
Uchean Indian... 5. Yuchi (Uchee)
udometer... 9. rain gauge
Uffizi Gallery... 8. Florence
Uganda (pert to)...
capital.. 7. Kampala
Falls.. 4. Owen 9. Murchison
lake.. 8. Victoria
lake explorer.. 7. Stanley
mountain.. 9. Ruwenzori 18. Mountains of the Moon
tribe.. 5. pygmy
ugly... 5. cross, surly 6. cranky, homely 7. crabbed, hideous, vicious 8. gruesome, uncomely, unlovely 9. frightful, loathsome, offensive, repulsive, unsightly 10. ill–favored, ill–natured, unpleasant 11. ill–tempered, quarrelsome 12. disagreeable
uhlan... 6. lancer 7. militia, soldier 10. cavalryman
uhllo... 6. wampum 8. currency (shell)
uitlander... 9. foreigner, outlander
ukase... 5. edict, order 12. proclamation
Ukraine (pert to)...
capital.. 4. Kiev 7. Kharkov
legislature.. 4. rada
official name.. 12. Ukrainian SSR
Relig.. 9. Ruthenian 13. Little Russian
scientist.. 10. Bogomolets
sea.. 5. Black
seaport.. 6. Odessa
statesman.. 7. Mazeppa
writer.. 6. Franko
ullage... 5. dregs 7. deficit, wantage 8. shortage 9. shrinkage 10. deficiency
Ulmas... 3. elm
ulna... 4. bone 5. elbow 7. cubitus
ulster... 8. overcoat
ulterior... 6. future 7. further, remoter, thither 10. additional, extraneous, subsequent, succeeding 11. undisclosed
ultima... 4. last 5. final 8. farthest 10. most remote 12. last syllable
ultimate... 3. end 4. dire, last

5. final, telus 6. future, latest, result 7. extreme, maximum 8. eventful, eventual, farthest, terminal 9. elemental 10. conclusive, end product
ultimatum... 5. offer 6. demand 13. ultimate point 14. final objective
ultimo... 3. ult 9. past month (opp of proximo)
ultra... 6. beyond 7. extreme, radical 9. excessive, extremist, fanatical 11. extravagant 14. uncompromising
ultramarine... 11. blue pigment, lapis lazuli 12. beyond the sea
ultramontane... 5. alien 6. beyond 9. foreigner 10. tramontane 13. beyond the Alps, Roman Catholic
ulu (Esk)... 5. knife
ululate... 4. hoot, howl, wail, yelp 6. bellow, lament
Ulysses (pert to)...
antagonist.. 4. Irus
dog.. 5. Argos
enchantress.. 5. Circe
father.. 7. Laertes
Greek name.. 8. Odysseus
hero.. 7. Odyssey (Homer's)
literally.. 5. hater
son.. 9. Telegonus
wife.. 8. Penelope
umber... 3. raw 5. brown, burnt 6. shadow, Turkey 8. grayling, umbrette 10. brown earth
umbilicus (pert to)...
anatomy.. 5. navel
botany.. 5. hilum
geometry.. 5. focus
paleology.. 5. stick (papyrus)
zoology.. 3. pit 10. depression
umbra... 4. fish 5. ghost, shade 6. shadow 7. phantom, vestige
umbrage... 5. doubt, pique, shade, trace 6. offend, resent 7. foliage, offense, shelter 8. disfavor 9. semblance, suspicion 10. overshadow, resentment 11. displeasure
umbrella... 4. gamp 5. cover, guard, shade 6. chatta, payong, pileus (of a jellyfish) 7. parasol, shelter 9. parachute, sea anchor 11. bumbershoot
umbrella tree... 5. bendy 7. dogwood, ginseng 8. magnolia
umbrette... 4. bird, fish 5. omber (ombre) 9. hammerkop
umpire... 5. judge 7. arbiter, referee 8. mediator 9. moderator 10. arbitrator, negotiator
Umpqua... 6. Indian 10. Athapascan

607

unable... 6. cannot 8. helpless, impotent 9. incapable 11. incompetent, inefficient, unqualified 13. incapacitated

Una boat... 7. catboat

unabridged... 8. complete 11. uncondensed

unaccented... 4. lene 6. atonic

unaccountable... 7. lawless, strange 9. fantastic 10. mysterious 12. inexplicable, unfathomable 13. irresponsible, unpredictable

unacknowledged... 9. anonymous, forgotten, unthanked 10. unrewarded

unadorned... 4. bald, bare, form 5. grace, naked, stark 7. austere 13. plain–speaking

unadulterated... 4. pure 5. naked 6. honest 7. unmixed 9. unalloyed, undiluted 11. uncorrupted

unaffected... 4. naif, real 5. naive, plain 6. simple 7. artless, genuine, natural, sincere 8. informal 9. unaltered, untouched 12. uninfluenced 13. plain–speaking

Unalaska... 5. Aleut, tribe 9. Eskimauan

unanimous... 5. solid 6. agreed, mutual, united 8. agreeing 9. of one mind 10. concordant 11. consentient 12. with one voice

unanimously... 7. una voce 12. with one voice

unapproachable... 8. reserved 10. unsociable 12. inaccessible

unapt... 4. dull, slow 5. inapt 8. backward 10. unskillful, unsuitable 13. inappropriate

unaroused... 6. latent 7. dormant 8. inactive 9. unstirred

unaspirated... 4. lene 6. smooth

unassuming... 3. shy 6. modest 7. genuine, natural 8. informal, retiring 9. diffident 11. undeceptive 14. unostentatious

unau... 5. sloth (2–toed)

unavailing... 6. futile 8. gainless

unbalanced... 6. insane, uneven, unjust 7. unequal 8. deranged, lopsided, one–sided 9. off center 10. disordered

unbecoming... 4. rude 5. inept 8. unseemly 10. indecorous, unsuitable 12. unattractive

unbelievable... 9. fantastic, untenable 10. incredible, unreliable 11. implausible, unthinkable 13. inconceivable

unbeliever... 5. pagan 6. Kaffir (Kafir) 7. atheist, doubter, heretic, infidel, skeptic 8. agnostic

unbend... 4. rest, thaw 5. frese, relax, yield 6. loosen 7. slacken 8. be pliant, unfasten 10. condescend, straighten

unbending... 5. rigid, stern, stiff 8. resolute 10. inexorable, inflexible, unyielding

unbiased... 4. fair, just 9. impartial 12. free from bias, unprejudiced

unbind... 4. free, undo 5. loose, untie 6. loosen 7. absolve, deliver, release

8. dissolve, unfasten

unbound... 4. free 5. loose 10. unconfined

unbounded... 8. infinite 9. limitless, unchecked, unlimited 10. unconfined 11. measureless 12. uncontrolled, unrestrained

unbridled... 4. free 5. loose 7. lawless, violent 10. licentious 12. uncontrolled, unrestrained

unbroken... 4. even 5. undug, whole 6. direct, entire, intact, smooth 7. untamed 8. constant, straight, unplowed 10. continuous 13. uninterrupted

uncanny... 5. eerie (eery), weird 6. spooky 7. ghostly, strange 8. careless 9. unnatural 10. mysterious

unceasing... 6. eterne 7. endless, eternal 9. continual, incessant 11. everlasting

unceremonious... 4. curt 5. blunt 6. abrupt, casual 7. offhand 8. informal 14. unconventional

uncertain... 4. hazy 5. vague 6. chancy, fickle, fitful, shifty, unsure 7. dubious 8. doubtful, unsteady, variable 9. ambiguous, irregular, undecided 10. changeable, indefinite, irresolute, precarious 11. unequivocal 12. questionable 13. indeterminate, problematical, untrustworthy

uncertainty... 5. doubt 6. wonder 7. dubiety 8. suspense 9. dubiosity 10. fickleness, skepticism 12. irresolution 14. precariousness

unchanging... 7. eternal, settled, uniform 9. immutable, unvarying 10. invariable, stationary

unchaste... 4. lewd 5. bawdy 6. impure 7. obscene 8. immodest

unchecked... 4. free 5. loose 7. rampant 9. permanent, unbridled

unchristian... 5. pagan 7. heathen, infidel, ungodly 9. barbarous, excessive 11. irreligious, uncivilized

uncivil... 4. rude 6. savage 7. ill–bred 8. impolite 9. barbarous 10. indecorous, ungracious 11. ill–mannered, uncivilized 12. discourteous 13. disrespectful

uncivilized... 4. rude, wild 5. feral 6. brutal, ferine, savage 8. barbaric 9. primitive, unrefined

uncle... 3. eme (yeme), oom

unclean... 4. foul, tref, vile 5. dirty 6. filthy, immund, impure 8. polluted, unchaste 11. unwholesome

Uncle Tom's Cabin (pert to)...
author.. 5. Stowe (Harriet Beecher)
character.. 5. Topsy 6. Legree 8. Uncle Tom 9. Little Eva
subject.. 7. slavery

unclose... 3. ope 4. open 6. reveal 7. expound 8. disclose

uncolored... 7. genuine 9. colorless 10. achromatic

uncommon... 3. odd 4. nice, rare 5. novel 6. scarce, unique 7. special, strange, unusual

8. unwonted 10. infrequent, remarkable 11. exceptional 12. unaccustomed 13. extraordinary

uncommunicative ... 6. silent 8. reserved, reticent 9. secretive 10. unsociable

uncomplaining ... 5. stoic 7. stoical

uncompromising ... 4. firm 5. rigid 6. strict 9. obstinate, unbending 10. inflexible, unyielding 12. conservative, intransigent

unconcerned ... 4. cool, free 8. careless 9. apathetic 10. insouciant 11. indifferent, not involved 13. disinterested

unconditional ... 4. free 8. absolute, explicit 10. unreserved

unconfined ... 5. loose 9. boundless, limitless, unlimited 12. unrestrained

unconscious ... 3. out 6. asleep 7. unaware 8. heedless, ignorant, mindless 9. inanimate, senseless, unfeeling 10. abstracted, insensible 11. involuntary 12. subconscious

unconstrained ... 4. easy, free 6. candid 7. natural 8. informal 11. spontaneous 12. unrestrained

uncontrolled ... 4. free, wild 5. loose 7. lawless 9. impulsive, irregular, unmanaged 10. capricious, changeable, licentious, ungoverned 11. not governed, unregulated 12. unrestrained

unconventional ... 4. easy 5. outré 6. casual 7. devious, offbeat 8. Bohemian, informal 10. unorthodox 13. unceremonious

uncorrupted ... 8. pristine

uncouth ... 3. odd 4. rude 5. crude 6. clumsy, rustic 7. awkward, boorish, strange 9. inelegant, unrefined, untrained 10. outlandish, uncultured, unpolished

uncover ... 4. bare, open 6. detect, divest, expose, remove, reveal, unveil 7. divulge, lay bare, take off, undrape 8. disclose, discover

uncovered ... 4. bald, bare, nude, open 7. exposed 8. divested, revealed, stripped, unveiled 9. décolleté 10. bareheaded 11. unprotected

unction ... 4. balm, rite 6. fervor 7. lanolin, unguent 8. flattery, function (divine), ointment 10. anointment

unctuous ... 4. oily, smug 5. bland, fatty, salvy, suave 6. fervid, greasy 7. gushing, pinguid, plastic 10. flattering, oleaginous 12. hypocritical 13. sanctimonious

uncultured ... 7. artless, boorish, uncouth 8. Bohemian 9. unlearned, unrefined 10. Philistine 11. countrified, undeveloped

undaunted ... 4. bold 5. brave 7. Spartan, untamed 8. fearless, intrepid, unafraid 9. confident, dauntless 10. courageous, undismayed 11. persevering, unconquered

undecided ... 4. moot 7. pending 8. doubtful, wavering 9. uncertain,

unsettled 10. inconstant, irresolute, unresolved 13. problematical

undependable ... 6. fickle 7. erratic 9. uncertain 13. irresponsible, untrustworthy

under ... 3. sub 4. alow 5. below, least, neath, sotto 6. nether 7. beneath 8. guidance 9. lower than 10. subjection, underneath 11. subordinate

undercover ... 6. secret 7. furtive 11. clandestine, underground 13. surreptitious

underestimate ... 8. belittle, minimize 9. set too low, underrate 10. undervalue

underfong ... 6. entrap 7. ensnare, receive, sustain 9. undertake 10. circumvent

undergo ... 4. bear, dree, pass 5. shirt 6. endure, suffer 7. sustain 9. undermine 10. experience

underhanded ... 3. sly 4. dern, mean 5. shady 6. covert, crafty, secret, sneaky 8. sneaking, unfairly 9. deceitful, dishonest 10. fraudulent 11. clandestine, short-handed 13. unobtrusively 15. surreptitiously

underling ... 6. menial, minion 7. servant 8. inferior 11. subordinate

underlying ... 5. basic 8. cardinal 11. fundamental

undermine ... 3. sap 4. ruin 5. drain, erode 6. weaken 7. subvert 8. enfeeble, excavate

understand ... 3. ken, see 4. know 5. grasp, infer, savvy, sense 6. follow, reason 7. discern, explain, realize, signify 8. conceive, perceive 9. apprehend, interpret 10. comprehend

understandable ... 5. clear, lucid 12. intelligible

understanding ... 5. amity, sense 6. accord, reason, treaty 7. compact, concept, entente, knowing 8. sympathy, Verstand 9. agreement, intellect, knowledge, tolerance, unanimity 10. acceptance, accordance, perception 11. discernment, penetration 12. intelligence 13. comprehension

understatement ... 7. litotes

understood ... 5. clear, known, lucid, tacit 7. assumed, implied, settled 8. implicit 11. traditional

undertake ... 3. try 4. dare 6. accept, assume, pledge 7. attempt, promise, reprove 8. contract, covenant, endeavor, engage in, set about 9. guarantee, underfong

undertaker ... 5. cerer 6. surety 7. manager, rebuker, sponsor 8. embalmer 9. godfather, mortician 12. entrepreneur

undertaking ... 3. act 4. task 6. cautio 7. calling, project, promise, venture 8. business 9. adventure, guarantee 10. enterprise

undertone ... 4. tone (low) 5. aside 6. murmur 12. subdued color

undertow ... 7. riptide

underworld... 3. Dis 4. hell 5. Hades,
limbo, Mafia, Orcus, Sheol
6. Erebus, Tophet 7. Abaddon,
Xibalba 8. Dis pater, gangland
9. Black Hand, chthonian, perdition,
purgatory
underwrite... 6. assure, insure
7. finance, sponsor 8. submit to
underwriter... 7. insurer 8. endorser
9. financier 10. underclerk 13. Stock
Exchange 14. Lloyd's of London
undesirable condition... 6. malady
undetermined... 5. vague 7. dubious
8. not fixed, unproved 9. uncertain,
undecided 10. irresolute
undeveloped... 5. crude 6. embryo,
latent 8. immature 10. unprepared
11. rudimentary
undignified... 6. vulgar 8. informal,
infra dig, unworthy 9. inelegant
undine... 3. nix 5. gnome, sylph
6. vessel (glass) 9. planetoid
10. salamander
undivided... 3. one 5. total, whole
6. entire, intact, joined 7. unitary
8. unbroken 9. not shared
10. continuous
undo... 4. open 5. annul, loose
6. cancel, defeat, foredo, unlash,
unwrap 7. destroy, disjoin, nullify,
release, uncover, unravel 8. unfasten
10. disconnect, invalidate
undoing... 4. ruin 6. defeat
8. downfall 9. annulment, overthrow
11. destruction, disassembly
undomesticated... 4. wild 5. feral
6. ferine
undone... 3. raw 9. neglected
10. defeasible
undue... 5. wrong 6. unjust
7. extreme 8. improper, not owing
9. excessive 10. exorbitant,
immoderate, inordinate, undeserved,
unsuitable 11. unwarranted
13. inappropriate
undulating... 4. wavy 6. waving
7. aripple, rolling 8. rippling
11. fluctuating 16. rising and falling
undulation... 4. beat, wave 5. heave,
surge, swell 6. motion, waving
7. tremolo, vibrato 8. waviness
9. pulsation 11. convolution
undying... 6. eterne 7. ageless,
endless, eternal 8. immortal,
unending 9. deathless
11. amaranthine 12. imperishable
14. indestructible
unearth... 4. find 5. dig up
6. exhume, expose 7. uncover
8. disclose, discover, disinter
12. bring to light
unearthly... 5. eerie (eery), godly,
weird 7. awesome, ghostly, strange,
uncanny 8. heavenly, terrific
9. appalling, deathlike
10. mysterious, outlandish
12. preposterous, supernatural
13. preternatural
uneasiness... 5. worry 6. unrest
7. anxiety, malaise 8. disquiet
10. impatience 11. displeasure,
disquietude, disturbance

12. apprehension
uneasy... 5. stiff 7. anxious, awkward,
inquiet, restive, worried 8. agitated,
cramping, restless 9. difficult,
impatient, perturbed 10. disquieted,
distressed 11. constrained,
troublesome
unemotional... 4. cold 5. stoic
7. stoical 10. phlegmatic
unemployed... 4. idle, lazy 6. otiose,
unused 7. not used 8. inactive,
leisured 11. not invested
unencumbered... 4. free
unending... 7. endless, eternal
8. termless, timeless 9. boundless,
perpetual 10. continuous
12. interminable
unequal... 3. odd 4. odds 5. aniso
(comb form) 6. uneven, unfair, unjust
8. variable 9. disparate, irregular
11. fluctuating, not adequate
12. asymmetrical 16. disproportionate
unequaled... 7. supreme 8. peerless
9. matchless, nonpareil, unmatched,
unrivaled 10. inimitable, surpassing,
unbeatable, unexcelled
12. unparalleled
unequivocal... 5. clear, plain 6. candid
7. sincere 8. explicit 9. downright
11. categorical, indubitable
unerring... 4. sure, true 5. exact
7. certain 8. accurate, virtuous
9. unfailing 10. infallible
unessential... 8. needless 9. extrinsic
10. irrelevant 11. superfluous,
unimportant 13. insignificant, void of
essence
unethical... 6. amoral
uneven... 3. odd 5. erose, rough
6. rugged, unfair, unjust 7. erratic,
unequal, varying 8. not level
10. ill—matched 11. fluctuating
unexamined... 7. a priori
unexampled... 8. peerless
10. unimitated 12. unparalleled
13. extraordinary, unprecedented
unexpected... 6. abrupt, sudden
7. unusual 9. inopinate
10. unforeseen 14. not anticipated
unfair... 4. foul 5. wrong 6. biased,
uneven, unjust 8. unseemly
9. dishonest, unethical 10. not
cricket, unsporting 11. inequitable,
unfavorable 12. disingenuous, not
equitable
unfaithful... 6. betray 7. infidel, traitor
8. apostate, recreant, turncoat
9. faithless 10. inaccurate
12. nonobservant 13. untrustworthy
unfamiliar... 3. new 7. strange,
unknown 8. not known
12. unaccustomed, unconversant
unfasten... 4. free, open, undo
5. unbar, unfix, unpin, untie
6. detach, loosen, unhook, unlock
7. unloose 8. unbutton 9. disengage
unfavorable... 3. bad, ill 6. averse
7. adverse, opposed 8. contrary,
untimely 9. repulsive 12. inauspicious
unfeeling... 4. dull 5. cruel, stoic,
stony 6. brutal, steely, stolid, unkind
7. callous 8. numbness, obdurate

9. apathetic, bloodless, heartless, inanimate, insensate 10. insensible 11. hardhearted 13. unsusceptible 16. unimpressionable

unfeigned... 4. real 7. genuine, natural, sincere 11. undeceptive 14. not counterfeit 15. not hypocritical

unfermented grape juice... 4. stum

unfertile... 4. arid 6. barren

unfettered... 4. free 5. broad 9. liberated, unchained 10. unshackled

unfinished... 5. crude, rough 7. sketchy 9. imperfect 10. incomplete 11. uncompleted

unfit... 5. inept 6. faulty, not fit, unable 8. disabled 9. untenable 11. handicapped, incompetent, unqualified 12. disqualified

unfledged... 4. eyas 5. green 6. callow 8. immature 11. undeveloped 12. not feathered

unflinching... 7. staunch 8. resolute, unafraid 9. steadfast 10. unwavering, unyielding 12. not shrinking

unfold... 3. ope 4. open 6. evolve, expand, flower, reveal, spread, unfurl 7. develop, display, divulge, evolute, explain, release 8. disclose

unfortunate... 3. ill 4. poor 6. wretch 7. hapless, unlucky 8. luckless, untimely 10. calamitous 12. inauspicious, unsuccessful

unfounded... 4. idle, vain 8. baseless 9. untenable 10. chimerical 11. unsupported, unwarranted

unfriendly... 3. icy 4. cool 7. asocial, hostile, not kind, opposed 8. inimical, unsocial 10. unsociable 12. inhospitable

unfruitful... 6. barren, wasted 7. sterile, useless 9. fruitless, infertile 12. unproductive, unprofitable 13. not productive

unfurl... 4. open 6. expand, spread, unfold, unroll

ungainly... 5. gawky, lanky 6. clumsy, gauche 7. awkward, uncouth 8. bungling 10. cumbersome, ungraceful

ungenteel... 6. vulgar 7. ill–bred 8. plebeian 9. inelegant 10. unmannerly

ungentle... 4. rude 5. harsh, rough 7. ill–bred 12. discourteous

ungodly... 6. sinful, wicked 7. impious 9. atheistic 11. unbelieving

ungovernable... 4. wild 6. unruly 9. unbridled 10. disorderly, licentious, rebellious, refractory 12. incorrigible, obstreperous, recalcitrant 13. irrepressible 14. uncontrollable

unguent... 4. balm 5. salve 6. cerate, chrism, pomade 7. unction 8. ointment 9. lubricant, unguentum

ungula... 4. claw, hoof, nail 6. unguis

ungulate... 3. pig 4. deer 5. horse, swine, tapir 6. hoofed 8. elephant, Ungulata 10. rhinoceros 15. hoofed quadruped

unhallowed... 6. unholy, wicked 10. desecrated

unhappy... 3. sad 6. dismal, woeful 8. dejected, ill–fated, wretched 9. miserable, sorrowful 10. calamitous, displeased 11. melancholic, unfortunate 12. discontented, unsuccessful

unhealthy... 3. ill 4. sick 6. sickly, unsafe 11. unwholesome

unhesitating... 4. sure 5. ready 8. implicit, resolute 10. undoubting

unholy... 6. wicked 7. impious, profane 8. shocking 10. scandalous, unhallowed

unicorn... 4. reem (Bib), unie 7. monster 8. narwhale 9. monoceros, spike team 10. pursuivant (Her), rhinoceros (one–horned)

uniform... 4. even 5. equal 6. livery, outfit, simple, smooth 7. equable, orderly, regular 8. constant, equiform 9. unvarying 10. consistent, invariable, unchanging 11. symmetrical

uniformity... 5. order 8. equality, evenness, sameness, symmetry 10. compliance, conformity, smoothness 11. consistency, homogeneity 13. invariability

unify... 5. merge, unite 7. combine, make one 8. coalesce 9. integrate 11. consolidate

unimaginative... 4. dull 7. literal, prosaic 10. unfanciful

unimpaired... 4. free 6. entire, intact 8. unmarred 9. undamaged, unspoiled

unimpressed... 6. unawed 7. unmoved 9. unstirred 10. unaffected, uninspired

uninformed... 8. ignorant, nescient 9. unknowing 10. unapprized 13. unenlightened, unintelligent

uninhabited... 5. empty 6. vacant 8. deserted, desolate, forsaken 9. abandoned, unpeopled 10. unoccupied, untenanted

uninspired... 4. dull 6. stodgy 9. uninhaled

unintelligent... 4. dumb 5. brute 6. stupid, unwise 7. foolish 8. ignorant 9. senseless

unintentional... 7. unmeant 9. unwitting 10. accidental, unintended 11. inadvertent, involuntary, unmeditated 14. unpremeditated

uninterested... 5. bored 9. apathetic, impartial, incurious 11. unconcerned 13. disinterested

uninteresting... 3. dry 4. arid, drab, dull 6. boring, prolix, stupid 7. humdrum, insipid, prosaic, tedious 8. tiresome 9. colorless 10. unexciting

union... 3. one 4. bond 5. joint, unity 6. accord, fusion, league, merger 7. amalgam, entente, liaison, oneness 8. alliance, junction, marriage 9. coalition 10. federation

11. affiliation, association,
combination, concurrence,
confederacy, conjunction
13. juxtaposition
Union (pert to)...
ensign, British.. 12. three crosses (St
Andrew, St George, St Patrick)
General.. 7. Sherman (Civil War)
of States.. 6. Empire 12. United
States
of workers.. 5. artel, guild
Union of So Africa...
capital.. 8. Cape Town (Legis),
Pretoria (Admin)
city.. 6. Durban 9. Germiston
12. Johannesburg
famed Park.. 6. Kruger
**Union of Soviet Socialist
Republics**... see also *Russia*
anc citadel.. 7. Kremlin
capital.. 6. Moscow
city.. 9. Leningrad
Republics (number).. 7. fifteen
resort.. 5. Yalta 6. Crimea
river.. 2. Ob 3. Don 4. Lena, Neva,
Ural 5. Volga 7. Dnieper
sea.. 4. Aral, Azov 5. Black, White
6. Baltic 7. Caspian
strait.. 6. Bering
unique... 3. odd, one 4. rare, sole
5. alone, novel 6. single 7. notable,
special, unusual 8. original, peculiar,
peerless, singular 9. matchless
12. single–valued 13. extraordinary
unison... 6. union 6. accord, assent
7. concord, harmony 9. agreement,
unanimity 10. concordant,
consonance
unit... 3. ace, ane, one 4. item, word
5. digit, group 6. entity 7. measure
8. syllable
unit (pert to)...
astronomy.. 6. parsec
biology.. 5. idant
electrical.. 3. amp, mho, ohm, rel
4. volt, watt 5. farad, henry, joule
6. ampere, proton 7. coulomb
energy.. 3. erg, rad 5. ergon 6. kilerg
7. quantum
fluidity.. 3. rhe
force.. 4. dyne 5. tonal 7. kinetic
heat.. 5. therm (therme) 7. calorie
(calory)
induction.. 5. henry
light.. 3. lux, pyr, rad 5. lumen
6. Hefner
linear.. 3. ell 4. foot, inch, mile, yard
7. furlong
magnetic.. 5. gauss, weber
7. maxwell, oersted
matter.. 5. monad
measure.. 3. are, rod 4. pint
5. maund, meter, stere
military.. 7. brigade, platoon
8. regiment
power.. 2. HP 3. bel 5. dynam,
horse
pressure.. 5. barad, barie
reluctance.. 3. rel
resistance.. 3. ohm
speed.. 4. velo

telegraphic.. 4. baud
thermal.. 7. calorie (calory)
velocity.. 4. velo
volume.. 3. ton 4. cord, peck, pint
5. ounce, pound 6. barrel, bushel,
gallon 8. hogshead
weight.. 3. ton 5. carat (karat),
ounce, pound
wire.. 3. mil
work.. 3. erg 5. ergon, joule 6. kilerg
yarn.. 6. denier
unite... 3. fay, tie, wed 4. ally, bind,
fuse, join, knit, link, meld, weld
5. annex, graft, marry, merge
6. adhere, cement, concur, mingle,
solder 7. combine, connect
8. coalesce, condense, converge,
federate, side with 9. affiliate,
associate 10. amalgamate, federalize
11. consolidate, incorporate
unite (pert to)...
by freezing.. 8. regelate
by interweaving.. 5. plash 6. pleach,
splice
by joints.. 10. articulate
closely.. 11. concentrate
in concordance.. 9. harmonize
timbers.. 6. rabbet
united... 3. one, wed 4. knit, tied
5. added 6. allied, banded, joined,
linked, merged, welded 7. cohered,
grafted, rallied, spliced 8. cemented,
clannish 9. concerted, corporate
10. concurrent, corporated
United Provinces... 11. (The)
Netherlands 13. Dutch Republic
United States... 9. Etats–Unis
United States... see also *American*
artist.. 4. Pyle, Wood 5. Flagg,
Moses (Grandma), Peale, Ryder,
Sloan 6. Eakins, Stuart
author.. 3. Ade, Poe 4. Pyle, Ward
5. Alger, Barth, Beach, Davis, Field,
Harte, James, Lewis, Stowe
6. Alcott, Bryant, Cooper, Ferber,
Hersey, Holmes, Irving, London,
Lowell, O'Henry, Porter 7. Clemens,
Dreiser, Emerson, Stewart, Thoreau,
Whitman 8. Faulkner, Sinclair,
Whittier 9. Hawthorne, Hemingway
10. Longfellow, Tarkington
canal.. 4. Erie 6. Panama
capital.. see separate States
composer.. 4. Kern 5. Foote, Nevin
6. Berlin, Foster 7. Rodgers
8. Gershwin 9. Bernstein
emblem.. 5. eagle
explorer.. 4. Byrd, Long, Pike
5. Boone, Clark, Lewis, Logan, Perry
Falls.. 7. Niagara 8. Yosemite
9. Multnomah
Indian.. see under *Indian (Am)*
inventor.. 3. Hoe 4. Bell, Howe
5. Fiske, Fitch, Morse 6. Edison,
Fulton 7. Whitney
mountain.. 4. Hood 6. Elbert, Helena,
Shasta 7. Rainier, Whitney
8. Katahdin, McKinley
naturalist.. 4. Muir 5. Beebe, Seton
7. Thoreau
ornithologist.. 7. Audubon

philosopher.. **5.** James
pirate.. **4.** Kidd
poet.. **3.** Poe **4.** Nash **5.** Benét,
Field, Moore, Wylie **6.** Bryant,
Holmes, Kilmer, Lanier, Lowell, Millay
7. Whitman **8.** Whittier
10. Longfellow

unity... **3.** one **5.** union **6.** accord
7. concord, harmony, oneness
8. alliance **9.** agreement
10. singleness, uniformity
11. conjunction, unification
12. completeness

universal... **3.** all **5.** local, total, usual,
whole **6.** cosmic, entire, public
7. general **8.** catholic **9.** prevalent,
unlimited, well–known **11.** widely
known

universal (pert to)...
knowledge.. **9.** pantology
language.. **2.** Ro **3.** Ido **9.** Esperanto
language, written.. **10.** pasigraphy
remedy.. **7.** panacea
solvent.. **8.** alkahest
successor, heir.. **5.** heres (haeres)

universe... **4.** olam **5.** world
6. cosmos, system **9.** macrocosm
10. Great World

universe, controlling principle...
5. logos

unkempt... **5.** messy, rough **6.** frowsy,
shaggy, untidy **7.** ruffled, squalid,
tousled, uncouth **9.** unrefined
10. disarrayed, disheveled, unpolished

unkind... **3.** ill **5.** cruel, harsh, stern
6. brutal, severe **8.** ungenial
9. inclement **10.** ungracious,
ungrateful **13.** unsympathetic
15. uncompassionate

unknowable... **6.** mystic **8.** mystical,
noumenon **9.** enigmatic
13. indiscernible **14.** unintelligible
15. absolute reality (Kant), ultimate
reality (Spencer)

unknowable object... **3.** God **7.** the
soul **8.** noumenon

unknown... **7.** inconnu, strange
8. stranger **9.** anonymous, hereafter,
incognito, unheard of **10.** unfamiliar,
unrenowned **12.** incalculable

unlawful... **7.** bastard, illegal, illicit,
lawless **9.** irregular **10.** contraband
11. unwarranted **12.** illegitimate,
unauthorized

unlearned... **4.** lewd **5.** gross
8. ignorant, untaught **10.** illiterate,
uneducated **11.** instinctive

unleashed... **4.** free **5.** loose **6.** untied
8. released **10.** unfettered,
unshackled, untethered

unleavened... **7.** azymous

unleavened bread... **4.** azym **5.** azyme
7. matzoth

unless... **4.** nisi, save **6.** except
7. without **9.** except for, excepting
10. except that

unlettered... **8.** ignorant **10.** illiterate,
uneducated

unlike... **6.** sundry, uneven **7.** dislike,
diverse **9.** different, irregular
10. dissimilar, improbable
11. unpromising **12.** disagreeable

13. heterogeneous

unlikelihood... **11.** small chance
13. improbability

unlikeness... **8.** contrast
13. dissimilarity

unlimited... **4.** vast **9.** boundless,
unbounded, universal **10.** unconfined
11. illimitable **12.** immeasurable,
unrestricted **13.** indeterminate

unload... **3.** rid **4.** dump, sell
5. empty **7.** discard, lighten
9. disburden, discharge, liquidate

unlucky... **3.** bad, fey, ill **7.** infaust
8. ill–fated, untimely **9.** ill–omened
11. unfortunate **12.** inauspicious, not
favorable

unmannerly... **4.** rude **7.** boorish,
uncivil **8.** impolite **10.** mannerless
12. discourteous

unmelodious... **9.** dissonant
11. cacophonous

unmerciful... **5.** cruel **6.** unkind
7. extreme, inhuman **8.** pitiless,
ruthless **9.** heartless, merciless
10. relentless

unmistakable... **4.** open **5.** clear, plain
6. patent **7.** certain, evident, obvious
8. apparent, distinct, manifest
11. unqualified

unmitigated... **4.** mere **5.** sheer
6. arrant **8.** clear–cut, thorough
9. downright **11.** not softened,
unqualified

unmoved... **4.** calm, dead, firm
5. inert **6.** serene **8.** obdurate,
unshaken **9.** apathetic

unnatural... **5.** eerie (eery) **7.** labored,
strange, uncanny **8.** abnormal,
affected **9.** eccentric, irregular
10. artificial, factitious

unnecessary... **4.** fuss **7.** useless
8. needless **11.** not required,
superfluous, uncalled–for
12. nonessential

unobtrusive... **6.** modest **8.** retiring
11. clandestine

unoccupied... **4.** idle, void **5.** empty
7. not busy **8.** deserted
10. unemployed, untenanted
11. empty–headed, uninhabited

unorthodox... **9.** heretical
10. fallacious, left–handed
14. unconventional

unostentatious... **5.** quiet **6.** lenten,
modest **10.** restrained

unparalleled... **5.** alone **6.** unique
8. peerless **9.** matchless, unequaled,
unmatched **10.** inimitable
13. extraordinary

unpleasant... **8.** unsavory **9.** offensive
10. not amiable, ungracious
11. displeasing, distasteful
12. disagreeable

unpolished... **5.** bruit, crude, rough
6. coarse, rugged **7.** uncouth
8. agrestic, unpolite **9.** inelegant
10. agrestical **11.** countrified

unprecedented... **3.** new **5.** novel
10. unexampled, unimitated
13. extraordinary

unprejudiced... **4.** fair **7.** neutral
8. unbiased **9.** impartial

10. impersonal 13. dispassionate
unprepared... 3. raw 5. unfit
6. unwary 7. unready 9. premature, unskilled
unprepossessing... 4. grim, ugly
9. grim–faced 10. ill–looking
unpretentious... 6. humble, modest, simple 7. natural 10. unaffected
11. in good taste
unprincipled... 7. corrupt 9. dishonest
10. fraudulent, perfidious
12. dishonorable, unscrupulous
unprofessional... 3. lay 6. laical
7. amateur 9. unskilled
10. amateurish 14. unbusinesslike
unprofitable... 6. barren 7. useless
8. gainless 9. fruitless 10. unfruitful
unpropitious... 7. adverse, ominous, opposed 8. untimely 10. disastrous
12. inauspicious
unqualified... 5. unfit 6. unable
7. genuine, plenary 8. absolute, complete, unfitted 9. incapable
10. ineligible 11. incompetent
12. not qualified 13. unconditional
unquestionable... 7. certain, decided, evident 8. positive 10. undeniable
11. indubitable, irrefutable
12. indisputable 13. unimpeachable
unravel... 4. undo 5. feaze, solve
6. unfold, unlace 8. separate
9. disengage 10. disinvolve
11. disentangle
unreal... 5. false, ideal 7. fancied
8. fanciful, illusory, spurious
9. fantastic, imaginary, visionary
10. artificial, fictitious 11. imaginative
13. unsubstantial
unreasonable... 3. mad 6. absurd, unwise 9. excessive, fanatical, illogical, senseless 10. capricious, exorbitant, immoderate, irrational
11. extravagant, impractical
13. unjustifiable
unrecognizable... 3. dim 5. vague
7. blurred, obscure, unclear
9. undefined 10. indistinct
14. unintelligible
unrecognized... 6. unsung 7. unknown
13. unappreciated
unrefined... 3. raw 4. loud, rude
5. crass, crude, gross, rough
6. coarse, common, earthy, vulgar
7. uncouth 9. inelegant
11. countrified 12. uncultivated
unrefuted... 4. true 6. proved
8. undenied 10. unanswered
unrelaxed... 4. taut 5. rigid, tense
7. nervous
unrelenting... 4. grim, hard, iron
5. stern 6. severe, strict 8. rigorous
9. merciless 10. inexorable, relentless, unyielding
unreliable... 6. fickle, unsafe
9. uncertain 10. capricious, changeable 12. undependable
13. irresponsible, untrustworthy
14. tergiversature
unremitting... 4. busy 8. constant
9. continual, incessant, perpetual
10. continuous, persistent
11. persevering

unrequited... 6. unpaid 9. forgotten, unthanked 10. ungrateful, unrewarded
unreserved, unreservedly... 4. free, open 6. frank 6. openly 7. frankly
8. candidly, outright, thorough
9. outspoken 12. unrestricted
unrest... 6. bustle 8. disquiet
9. commotion 12. restlessness
unrestrained... 3. lax 4. free, wild
5. loose 6. candid, wanton
7. lawless, riotous 9. unbridled, unlimited 10. capricious
unrestricted... 4. free, open
9. unlimited 11. extravagant
12. undiminished 13. communicative
unruffled... 4. calm, cool 5. still
6. placid, poised, sedate, serene, smooth 9. quiescent, unexcited
10. unaffected 11. undisturbed
unruly... 7. lawless 9. fractious, obstinate, turbulent 10. disorderly, licentious, refractory 11. disobedient
12. recalcitrant, ungovernable, unmanageable
unsafe... 7. dubious, exposed, unsound
8. insecure, perilous 9. dangerous
10. unreliable 12. undependable
unsatisfactory... 8. inferior
10. inadequate, unbearable
11. intolerable 12. insufficient, ungratiating 13. disheartening, unsupportable
unsavory... 7. insipid 9. offensive, tasteless 10. unpleasant
11. unpalatable 12. disagreeable
unscrupulous... 7. devious
9. dishonest 12. unparticular, unprincipled 13. untrustworthy
16. indiscriminating
unseasonable... 8. untimely
9. premature 11. inopportune
unseemly... 5. inapt, wrong 6. vulgar
8. improper, indecent 9. inelegant
10. indecorous, solecistic, unbecoming 11. undignified
13. ungrammatical
unseen... 6. hidden 8. unheeded, viewless 9. invisible, unnoticed
12. undiscovered
unsettled... 4. moot 6. fickle, queasy
8. confused, deranged, restless, unplaced, unproved, unstable
9. ambiguous, disturbed, irregular, uncertain, unquieted 10. irresolute, unoccupied, up in the air
11. unpopulated
unshorn... 5. hairy, whole 6. shaggy
unshorn sheep (2nd year)... 3. tag, teg
unsightly... 4. ugly 8. uncomely, unlovely 9. inelegant, not comely
12. unattractive
unskilled... 5. green 6. puisne
8. ignorant, malapert
unskillful... 5. inept 7. artless, awkward 9. maladroit
12. unproficient 13. inexperienced
unsophisticated... 4. naif, pure, soft
5. green, naive 6. simple 7. artless, genuine 8. gullible, innocent
9. ingenuous 11. uncorrupted
unsound... 4. weak 5. crazy, dotty,

risky, shaky 6. addled, fickle
8. impaired, insecure 9. defective,
imperfect
unspoken... 5. tacit 6. silent
7. implied 9. ineffable, unuttered
unstable... 4. weak 6. fickle, fitful,
labile, scanty 7. astatic, erratic,
flighty, plastic 8. insecure, not solid,
ticklish, unsteady 9. ephemeral,
irregular, unsettled 10. inconstant,
precarious, unreliable 11. fluctuating,
vacillating
unsteady... 5. dizzy, shaky 6. groggy,
wobbly 7. quavery, rickety, unsound
8. titubate, unstable, wavering
9. irregular, uncertain 10. capricious,
changeable, flickering, inconstant,
precarious 11. fluctuating,
ill-balanced, lightheaded, vacillating
unsubstantial... 4. airy, rare, slim
5. filmy, light 6. aerial, flimsy,
papery 8. illusory 9. illogical,
visionary 10. immaterial, intangible,
unreliable
unsuitable... 5. inept, undue, unfit
8. untimely 10. unbecoming
11. inexpedient 13. inappropriate
14. unsatisfactory
unsullied... 4. pure 5. clean 6. chaste
8. innocent, spotless, virginal
10. immaculate
unsure... 4. weak 5. timid 6. infirm
8. doubtful 10. precarious
11. vacillating
unsweetened... 3. dry, sec 4. sour,
tart 10. unpleasant
unsympathetic... 6. unkind 7. hostile
8. pitiless 9. heartless 10. intolerant
11. hardhearted 12. unresponsive
untamed... 4. wild 6. feral 6. savage
9. unsubdued 11. uncivilized
untangle... 4. free 5. loose, solve
6. sleave 9. extricate 11. disentangle
untenable... 10. incredible
11. implausible 12. unbelievable,
unreasonable 13. inconceivable
unthinking... 4. rash 7. puerile
8. careless, heedless 9. impetuous,
impulsive 11. injudicious, instinctive,
involuntary, thoughtless
13. inconsiderate
untidy... 5. dowdy, messy 6. frowzy,
shabby 8. careless, frumpish,
slipshod, slovenly, unsuited, untimely
10. disheveled
untie... 4. free 5. loose 6. loosen,
unbind, unknot, unlash 8. unfasten
9. disengage
until now... 8. hitherto
untiring... 8. sedulous, tireless
9. unwearied 10. unflagging
13. indefatigable
untold... 4. vast 8. infinite
9. boundless, countless
10. uninformed, unrevealed
11. innumerable, unexpressed
12. immeasurable, incalculable,
undetermined
untouched... 3. new 4. pure 6. intact,
unused 8. pristine, virginal
10. impenitent, unaffected
untoward... 6. unruly 7. unlucky

8. perverse, stubborn, unseemly
10. indecorous, ungraceful
11. unfavorable, unfortunate
12. unpropitious
untrained... 4. soft, wild 5. green
8. indocile 9. unskilled, untutored
10. amateurish 11. unpracticed
14. unaccomplished
untrammeled... 4. free 5. loose 8. not
bound 9. unimpeded, unlimited
10. unfettered, unhampered,
unhindered
untransferable... 11. inalienable
untried... 3. new 5. fresh, green
8. unproved 9. unhandled
13. inexperienced
untrue... 5. false, wrong 8. disloyal
9. dishonest, erroneous, incorrect,
not honest 10. fallacious, unfaithful
untrustworthy... 6. tricky, unsafe
8. slippery 9. deceitful, dishonest,
uncertain 10. perfidious
untruth... 3. lie 5. error, fable
7. falsity 9. falsehood, treachery
10. disloyalty 11. fabrication
13. faithlessness
unusual... 3. odd 4. rare 5. novel,
queer 6. exotic, quaint, unique
7. strange 8. terrific, uncommon
9. anomalous 10. infrequent,
remarkable 11. exceptional
13. extraordinary
unutterable... 6. sacred, secret
9. ineffable, wonderful
11. unspeakable 13. inexpressible
unvarnished... 5. plain 6. simple
7. genuine 9. unadorned, unglossed
11. undeceptive 13. unembellished
unvarying... 7. uniform 8. constant
9. permanent 10. monotonous
unwarranted... 4. idle, vain 5. undue
7. illegal 8. baseless 9. excessive,
unfounded, untenable 10. exorbitant,
unentitled 11. unjustified
unwary... 4. rash 7. unaware
8. heedless, off guard 9. unguarded
10. unwatchful
unwavering... 4. firm, sure 5. solid
8. constant 9. steadfast
10. unweakened 11. not yielding,
persevering
unwelcome... 8. non grata, unwanted
9. intrusive, uninvited
unwholesome... 4. evil, sick 6. impure
7. corrupt, immoral, noisome,
noxious 9. unhealthy 12. insalubrious
unwieldy... 5. bulky 6. clumsy
7. awkward, restive 8. ungainly
9. ponderous 10. cumbersome
12. unmanageable 13. insubordinate
unwilling... 5. loath (loth) 6. averse
9. reluctant 11. disinclined,
involuntary
unwilling to prosecute... 7. nol-pros
13. nolle prosequi
unwise... 7. foolish 9. impolitic,
imprudent, senseless 10. irrational
11. inexpedient, injudicious
unwonted... 4. rare 6. unused
7. unusual 8. uncommon 9. not
wonted 10. infrequent
12. unaccustomed

unworldly... 5. eerie (eery), godly, naive, weird 8. heavenly 9. spiritual, unearthly 10. immaterial 12. supernatural

unyielding... 3. set 4. firm, hard, iron 5. rigid, stern, stiff 6. strict 7. adamant 8. obdurate, stubborn 9. immovable, obstinate 10. adamantine, determined, inexorable, inflexible 14. uncompromising

up (pert to)...
and coming.. 7. go–ahead 8. hustling
and down.. 6. seesaw, uneven 8. vertical 10. undulating 13. perpendicular
in arms.. 6. at odds 8. prepared 9. resistant
ref to.. 10. at the plate (game)
to.. 4. able, till, unto 5. until 9. cognizant, competent
to date.. 3. new 6. modern 7. stylish 11. fashionable

upas tree, arrow poison... 6. antiar

upbraid... 4. twit 5. blame, chide, scold, score 6. rebuke 7. reprove 8. admonish, reproach 9. reprimand 10. put to shame

upheaval... 5. storm 6. revolt 9. agitation, cataclysm, elevation 10. convulsion

upheld... 5. aided 6. backed 7. abetted 8. defended 9. supported, sustained 10. encouraged, maintained

uphill... 6. upward 7. upgrade 9. ascending, difficult, laborious 10. slantingly

uphold... 3. aid 4. abet, back, buoy 5. favor, raise 6. defend 7. confirm, support, sustain 8. maintain, preserve 9. encourage 11. corroborate, countenance, lend support

upkeep... 4. cost 6. repair 7. support 11. maintenance

upland... 4. wold 5. weald 6. coteau, inland 7. country, plateau 8. highland

uplands... 7. country 9. highlands 10. the country

uplift... 5. elate, erect, raise 7. elevate, ennoble, glorify, improve 8. upheaval 9. elevation 11. inspiration

upon... 2. on 3. sur 4. atop, onto 5. about, above 7. against 9. by means of 10. after which

upon (pert to)...
law.. 3. sur
prefix.. 3. epi, sur
that.. 7. whereat 9. whereupon
which.. 7. whereat

upper... 6. higher 8. superior

upper (pert to)...
bed.. 4. bunk
crust.. 7. society 11. aristocracy 13. highest circle
end.. 3. tip 4. apex, head
hand.. 7. mastery 8. dominion 9. advantage, influence 10. preference
House of Congress.. 6. Senate
shoe part.. 4. vamp

uppermost... 3. top 6. upmost

7. highest, supreme, topmost 8. farthest, foremost 9. outermost

uppish... 5. drunk, proud 6. uppity 7. haughty, peevish, stuck–up 8. arrogant, assuming, snobbish 9. high–flown

upright... 4. good, just, true 5. erect, moral, piano 6. honest, square 7. endwise, sincere 8. vertical, virtuous 9. equitable, honorable, righteous 13. perpendicular

upright (pert to)...
chair part.. 4. slat
comb form.. 5. ortho
posture.. 8. orthotic 11. orthostatic
slab.. 5. stela
timber.. 4. jamb, stud

uprising... 4. riot 6. ascent, mutiny, revolt 7. sloping 9. acclivity, ascending, rebellion 12. insurrection

uproar... 3. din 4. riot, rout 5. noise 6. bedlam, bustle, clamor, fracas, hubbub, outcry, tumult 7. turmoil 8. outbreak 9. commotion, confusion 10. donnybrook, hurly–burly, tintamarre, turbulence 11. pandemonium 12. insurrection

upset... 3. irk 4. rile, ruin, stir 6. defeat, refute, topple 7. agitate, capsize, confuse, disturb, fluster, startle, subvert, unnerve 8. distress, overturn, startled, unnerved 9. embarrass, overthrow 10. discompose, disconcert, distressed, frustrated, overturned, refutation, revolution 11. frustration, overwrought

upshot... 3. end 5. fruit, issue 6. result, sequel 7. outcome 10. conclusion 11. consequence, eventuality, termination 12. consummation

upside down... 8. confused, disorder 9. confusion 10. resupinate, topsy–turvy

upsilon (Gr)... 5. hyoid, vowel 7. Y–shaped

upstart... 4. snob 7. bounder, parvenu 13. social climber

up–to–date... 6. modern 7. alamode, topical 8. informed 11. fashionable

upward... 2. up 3. ano (comb form) 4. over 5. above, aloft 6. onward 7. skyward 8. upstream 9. ascending

upward movement of vessels... 5. scend

uraeus (Egypt Relig)... 3. asp 6. symbol 8. symbolic

Ural... 5. river 9. mountains

Urania (pert to)...
blue.. 12. independence
epithet of.. 9. Aphrodite
genus of.. 5. moths
Gr Myth.. 4. Muse (Astron)

uranology (*study of*)... 7. heavens 15. celestial bodies

Uranus (pert to)...
astronomy.. 6. planet
daughter.. 4. Rhea
father of.. 9. The Titans (12)
personification of.. 6. heaven
satellite.. 5. Ariel 6. Oberon

7. Titania, Umbriel
son.. 6. Cronus
urare, urari... 6. curare
urban... 5. civic 6. ghetto, polite,
uptown 7. oppidan, refined
8. downtown, polished 9. courteous,
municipal 12. metropolitan
13. sophisticated
urbane... 5. civil, suave 6. polish,
polite 7. affable 8. gracious
9. courteous 11. deferential
urbanity... 7. amenity 8. civility,
courtesy 9. deference
urchin... 3. boy, elf, imp, tad 4. arab,
brat 5. gamin 6. elfish 8. hedgehog
9. dandiprat, sea urchin, youngster
urge... 3. dun, egg, hie, ply, yen
4. abet, coax, goad, prod, push,
spur 5. drive, egg on, impel, press
6. advise, compel, dehort, desire,
exhort, fillip, hasten, incite, induce
7. animate, entreat, solicit
8. persuade 9. constrain, importune,
influence, instigate 10. inducement
urgent... 3. hot 5. grave 7. clamant,
exigent, instant 8. critical, pressing
9. impelling, important, insistent,
necessary 11. importunate
urial... 3. sha 5. sheep 6. oorial
Uriel... 9. archangel 10. flame of God
(Bib)
Urim and Thummim (Bib)...
11. instruments 12. interpreters
(Mormon)
urn... 3. jar 4. ewer, urna (anc), vase
5. grave, steen 6. vessel 7. pitcher,
samovar, vaselet 10. jardiniere
urn–shaped... 8. urceolus 9. urceolate
Ursa... 4. bear 9. Ursa Major (Great
Bear), Ursa Minor (Little Bear)
ursal... 7. fur seal
ursuk... 11. bearded seal
Ursula... 5. Saint 7. she–bear
9. butterfly 15. British princess
(legend)
urubu... 7. vulture
Uruguay...
capital.. 10. Montevideo
city.. 4. Melo 5. Minar 9. Maldonado
estuary.. 5. Plata 12. Rio de la Plata
lake.. 5. Merim
river.. 7. Uruguay
settler.. 5. Cabot (Sebastian, 1527)
university.. 10. Montevideo (1849)
windstorm.. 7. pampero
urus... 2. ox 3. tur 7. aurochs
usable... 3. fit 9. practical
10. functional 11. serviceable,
utilitarian
usage... 3. use 4. wont 5. habit, ritus
6. custom, method 7. utility
8. behavior, practice 9. treatment
10. convention
use... 3. try 5. apply, avail, exert,
spend, treat, wield 6. employ,
expend, occupy 7. consume, exploit,
utilize 8. function 10. manipulate
11. consumption, utilization
use (pert to)...
abusive language.. 4. rail
divining rod.. 5. dowse
frugally.. 5. stint

pert to words.. 7. neology, verbose
8. enallage, pleonasm 9. verbosity
poetry.. 4. vail
refrain from.. 7. boycott
subterfuge.. 7. chicane
up.. 3. eat 7. consume, deplete,
exhaust, fatigue
useful... 4. good 5. utile 7. helpful
9. practical 10. beneficial,
commodious 11. serviceable,
subservient 12. advantageous,
instrumental
usefulness... 5. avail, value 6. profit
7. utility 13. conduciveness
useless... 4. idle, null, vain 6. futile,
otiose 7. of no use 8. bootless,
hopeless 9. fruitless, worthless
10. fifth wheel 11. ineffectual,
superfluous 12. unprofitable
13. unserviceable 14. good for
nothing
uselessness... 8. futility 9. inutility
10. inefficacy
usher... 4. lead, page 5. guide
6. escort 7. chobdar, teacher
9. attendant, harbinger, precursor
10. doorkeeper, forerunner,
inaugurate
usquebaugh... 6. whisky 7. cordial
ustion... 7. burning 13. cauterization
ustulate... 8. scorched 10. discolored
usual... 7. average, typical, usitate
8. everyday, frequent 11. status in
quo
usuer... 5. shark 6. loaner 7. Shylock
11. moneylender
usurp... 4. take 5. seize 6. assume
8. arrogate 11. appropriate
Utah...
capital.. 12. Salt Lake City
city.. 5. Logan, Ogden, Provo
7. Bingham
dam.. 10. Glen Canyon 12. Flaming
Gorge
lake.. 6. Powell 9. Great Salt
mountain.. 5. Uinta 7. Wasatch
9. King's Peak
name desired.. 7. Deseret
natural wonder.. 4. Zion 5. Bryce
13. Rainbow Bridge
settled by.. 7. Mormons 12. Brigham
Young 15. Latter–day Saints
State admission.. 10. Forty–fifth
State motto.. 8. Industry
State nickname.. 7. Beehive
utensil... 3. mop, pan, pot 4. tool
5. broom, brush 6. device, ramrod
7. skillet, sweeper 9. apparatus,
appliance, implement 10. instrument
utilitarian... 5. plain 6. useful
8. economic 9. practical
10. functional 12. matter–of–fact
utility... 3. use 4. tool 5. avail
6. profit 7. benefit, service
9. appliance, happiness, implement
10. usefulness
utmost... 4. best, last 5. final
7. extreme, maximum, supreme
8. farthest, greatest 9. uttermost
11. most distant
Utopia... 4. Eden 6. heaven, island
(imaginary) 7. Erewhon 8. paradise

9. fairyland, Shangri–La
10. millennium
utopian... 5. ideal 6. Edenic
8. Quixotic, romantic 9. visionary
10. chimerical, idealistic, millennial
utter... 3. say 4. emit, pass, tell, vent
5. issue, sheer, speak, total, voice
6. assert, entire, mumble, reveal
7. deliver, divulge, express, extreme,
publish, unusual 8. abnormal,
absolute, complete, disclose,
disperse, intonate 9. downright,
enunciate, out–and–out, pronounce
10. peremptory 11. unqualified
13. unconditional
utter (pert to)...
harshly.. 3. rap 4. bray
heedlessly.. 4. blat
in devotion.. 4. pray
in slow tone.. 5. drawl
musically.. 6. warble
publicly.. 4. tell 5. voice 7. enounce
softly.. 6. murmur 7. whisper
want.. 9. indigency 11. destitution

with effort.. 5. heave
with impulse.. 9. ejaculate
without voice.. 4. surd 7. spirate
utterance (pert to)...
dogmatic.. 6. dictum
gushing.. 8. effusion
rhythmic.. 7. cadence
voice.. 8. phonesis, speaking
9. phonation 12. articulation
wise.. 6. oracle
utterer of pithy remarks... 8. aphorist
utterly... 5. fully, stark 7. totally
8. entirely 10. absolutely, completely
17. straightforwardly
uttermost... 5. final 6. utmost
7. extreme
utu... 6. reward 12. compensation,
satisfaction
uva... 5. fruit, grape
uvate... 8. conserve (grape)
uvea... 4. iris
uxor... 4. wife
uxoricide... 10. wife murder
Uz (Bib)... 8. Job's home
Uzziel... 5. angel (Paradise Lost)

V

V... 5. notch 6. letter (22nd), symbol
14. five–dollar bill
vaagmer... 8. dealfish (mare of the
sea)
Vac (Hind)... 7. goddess (of speech)
vacant... 4. free, idle, void 5. blank,
empty, inane 6. barren, devoid
7. leisure, vacuous 8. unfilled
10. disengaged, untenanted
11. thoughtless 12. unencumbered
14. expressionless
vacate... 4. free, quit, void 5. annul,
empty, leave 6. depart 7. abandon
8. abdicate, abrogate, evacuate,
withdraw
vacation... 4. rest 5. leave 6. outing,
recess, repeal 7. nonterm, respite
8. furlough, justitum 10. recreation
12. intermission 14. leave of
absence
vacation place... 3. spa 4. lake, park
5. beach 6. forest, resort
9. mountains
vaccination... 11. inoculation
vaccine (pert to)...
discoverer.. 4. Salk 6. Jenner
protection for.. 5. virus 6. cowpox
term.. 5. lymph, serum, virus
vacillate... 4. sway 5. waver 6. dacker
(daiker), seesaw, teeter, totter
7. flutter, stagger 8. hesitate,
titubate 9. fluctuate, oscillate
13. procrastinate
vacillation... 5. doubt 8. wavering
9. faltering, hesitancy 10. fickleness,

indecision, titubation 11. oscillation,
uncertainty 12. irresolution
14. changeableness
15. procrastination
vacuate... 5. empty 8. evacuate
vacuous... 4. dull, void 5. blank,
empty 6. stupid 8. unfilled
9. senseless 11. empty–headed,
thoughtless 13. unintelligent
vacuum... 3. gap 4. void 9. emptiness
11. rarefaction
vagabond... 3. bum, vag 4. hobo
5. lorel, scamp, tramp 6. beggar,
picaro, rascal, rodney 7. vagrant,
wastrel 8. Bohemian, brodyaga,
wanderer 10. ne'er–do–well
vagary... 4. whim 5. caper, fancy,
jaunt, prank, trick 6. notion, ramble
7. caprice, whimsey (whimsy)
9. excursion, wandering
10. digression 13. manifestation
vagrant... 3. bum 4. hobo 5. rogue,
tramp 6. roving, truant 7. nomadic,
prowler, wayward 8. brodyaga,
vagabond, wanderer 9. desultory,
deviative, itinerant 10. capricious
vague... 3. dim 4. dark, hazy 5. loose,
misty 6. dreamy 7. obscure,
shadowy, unfixed 8. confused,
formless, nebulous, not clear
9. ambiguous, unsettled, wandering
10. indefinite, indistinct, intangible
13. indeterminate
vail... 3. tip 4. doff (a hat), dole
5. avail, bribe, yield 6. humble,

submit 7. descend 8. gratuity
  10. beneficial 12. advantageous
vain... 4. idle 5. empty, proud
  6. devoid, futile, otiose, snooty
  7. foolish, trivial, useless 8. arrogant,
  boastful, nugatory 9. conceited,
  fruitless, worthless 10. unavailing,
  unrewarded 11. empty–headed,
  overweening, unimportant
  12. vainglorious
vain boasting... 11. fanfaronade
vainglorious... 4. vain 7. heroics
  8. boastful 9. gasconade
vair... 3. fur
vajra (Buddh)... 7. diamond, trident
  (Indra's) 10. adamantine
  11. thunderbolt
valance... 5. drape 6. border, pelmet,
  ruffle 7. curtain, drapery, hanging
vale... 4. dale, dell, glen 5. earth,
  glade, world 6. valley
valediction... 5. adieu 7. address
  8. farewell 11. valedictory
valedictory... 7. address, oration
  10. apopemptic 11. leave–taking,
  valediction
Valentine (pert to)...
  romance.. 5. Orson 8. love song
  Saint.. 6. martyr (Rom) 7. holiday
    8. feast day
  State.. 7. Arizona (adm 2/14/1912)
  sweetheart.. 11. one's beloved
valerian... 4. drug 5. plant 7. panacea
valet... 3. man 7. Crispin
  9. attendant, cameriere, chamberer
  10. manservant 11. body servant
  14. valet de chambre
valetudinarian... 6. infirm, shut–in,
  sickly, weakly 7. invalid
  11. languishing
Valhalla (Valhall)... 8. Pantheon
  (Bavaria) 10. hall of Odin (Norse
  Myth)
valiant... 4. bold, fine 5. brave
  6. heroic, strong, sturdy 7. doughty
  8. intrepid, stalwart, vigorous,
  virtuous 9. steadfast 10. chivalrous,
  courageous 11. meritorious
  12. stouthearted
valid... 4. good, just, true 5. legal,
  sound 6. cogent, lawful, proved
  7. binding, weighty 9. authentic,
  effective 10. sufficient 11. efficacious
  12. well–grounded
validate... 6. affirm, attest 7. confirm
  8. legalize 12. substantiate
validity... 5. force 7. cogency
  9. authority, soundness
  14. substantiality
Valjean (pert to)...
  discoverer.. 6. Javert
  friend.. 6. Marius
  hero of.. 13. Les Miserables (Victor
    Hugo)
  protégé.. 7. Cosette
valley... 4. dale, dell, dene, glen, vale,
  wady 5. glade, gully 6. coulee,
  dingle, ravine, trough 10. depression
valley (pert to)...
  anatomy.. 9. vallecula
  circular.. 6. rincon
  deep.. 6. canyon

  geology.. 5. atrio
  India.. 5. dhoon
  Jerusalem (near).. 6. Hinnom
    7. Gehenna, Rephaim
  moon.. 5. rille
  open.. 6. canada
  where David killed Goliath.. 4. Elah
    (Bib)
valonia oak... 6. camata (fruit)
  9. evergreen
valor... 5. merit, worth 6. virtue
  7. bravery, courage, heroism,
  prowess 8. boldness, chivalry
  9. gallantry 11. distinction
  12. fearlessness
valuable... 4. dear 5. asset 6. prized,
  useful, worthy 8. precious
  9. estimable, treasured
  10. worthwhile
value... 3. par, use 4. rate 5. price,
  prize, worth 6. assess, esteem,
  parity, status 7. apprize (apprise),
  cherish, compute, meaning, respect,
  utility 8. appraise, estimate, evaluate
  9. valuation 10. estimation,
  excellence, importance
value (pert to)...
  equal.. 6. parity
  least possible.. 5. plack
  nominal.. 3. par
  reduction.. 12. depreciation
valueless... 4. baff 9. worthless
  10. threepenny 14. good–for–nothing
valve... 3. tap 4. cock, door, gate
  6. faucet, piston, spigot 7. petcock
vamoose... 2. go 4. blow, scat
  5. leave, scram 6. beat it, decamp
  7. skiddoo 9. skedaddle
vamp... 4. hose, sock 5. flirt, patch,
  upper 6. recoct, repair, seduce
  7. beguile, bewitch, concoct, touch
  up 9. improvise, temptress, transform
vampire... 3. bat 5. fiend, ghost,
  lamia, witch 6. Alukah 9. bewitcher,
  sorceress, temptress 11. bloodsucker,
  extortioner 12. extortionist
van... 4. lead, wing 5. front, wagon
  6. shovel, summit, winnow 7. vehicle
  9. forefront 10. baggage car
  12. advance guard
vandal... 3. Hun 7. wrecker
  9. destroyer, mutilator, plunderer
  10. iconoclast
vandalize... 3. mar 5. wreck 6. deface
Vandyke... 5. beard, brown 6. artist,
  collar 7. picture
vane... 4. cock 11. weathercock,
  weathervane
vanish... 3. die 4. fade, flee, melt,
  pass 6. perish 8. evanesce 9. cease
  to be, disappear
vanity... 5. pride 6. egoism
  7. conceit, egotism, falsity 8. futility
  9. arrogance, emptiness, vainglory
  10. hollowness 11. fatuousness,
  self–conceit 12. boastfulness
  13. dressing table
vanity case... 4. etui 6. make–up
  7. compact 9. cosmetics
vanquish... 3. win 4. beat, best, rout
  5. expel 6. defeat, subdue
  7. conquer 8. confound, overcome,

suppress, surmount 9. overthrow
vantage... 4. gain 9. advantage
10. perquisite 11. opportunity,
superiority
vapid... 3. dry 4. dead, dull, flat
5. inane, stale 7. insipid, prosaic
8. lifeless 9. pointless, tasteless
10. spiritless, unanimated
11. indifferent 13. uninteresting
vapor... 3. air, fog, gas 4. fume, haze,
mist 5. brume, cloud, fancy, humor,
smoke, steam 6. breath, bubble
7. halitus 8. humidity, illusion,
phantasm 9. evaporate 10. exhalation
vaporous... 4. vain 5. foggy, misty
6. cloudy, steamy 7. gaseous
8. ethereal, fanciful, fleeting
13. unsubstantial
variable... 6. fickle, fitful, mobile
7. protean, unequal 8. shifting,
unstable, unsteady 10. capricious,
changeable, inconstant
variance... 3. out 7. dissent
9. deviation, disaccord
10. contention, difference
11. discrepancy 12. disagreement
varied... 5. mixed 6. daedal, motley
7. changed, dappled, diverse,
mottled, piebald, several, various
8. speckled 9. different
10. variegated 11. diversified
variegated... 5. pinto 6. daedal,
motley, varied 7. dappled, diverse,
mottled, painted 9. different
11. diversified, many-colored
variegation... 7. variety 9. diversity
10. multicolor
variety... 4. kind, mode, sort 5. class
6. change 7. species 9. diversity,
variation 10. assortment, difference
13. entertainment
variola... 6. cowpox 8. smallpox
various... 4. many 6. divers, sundry
7. diverse, several 8. manifold,
variable 9. different, many-sided,
uncertain 10. changeable, inconstant,
variegated 11. diversified
varnish... 4. spar 5. adorn, gloss,
japan, paint 7. distort, falsify, furbish,
lacquer, pretext 8. coat over
9. embellish
Varuna (pert to)...
art consorts.. 5. Jumna 6. Ganges
deity.. 6. cosmic (supreme)
god.. 3. sea
Vedic equiv.. 13. Avestan Ormazd
Vedic Relig.. 5. Aditi (fem deity)
vary... 5. alter, range, shift 6. change,
differ, modify 7. deviate, dissent,
diverge 8. disagree 9. alternate,
diversify, fluctuate, vacillate, variegate
13. differentiate
vas... 4. duct 6. pledge, surety, vessel
vascular (pert to)... 5. hemic (haemic)
6. vessel (blood, lymph) 7. tubular
9. vesicular 10. hot-blooded
vase... 3. jar, urn 4. bowl 5. ascus
6. vessel 8. ornament
10. cassolette, jardiniere
vase (pert to)...
covered.. 7. potiche
Etruscan.. 7. canopic

Greek.. 5. askos, diota 6. deinos
(dinos) 7. amphora
Roman.. 8. murrhine
vassal... 3. man 4. esne, serf
5. helot, liege, slave 6. varlet
7. bondman, servant, servile, subject
9. dependent, feudatory
11. subordinate, subservient
12. feudal tenant
vassalage... 5. valor 6. fealty
7. courage, enfeoff, prowess, slavery
8. dominion 9. servitude
10. subjection
vast... 4. huge 5. broad, great, large
6. cosmic, mighty, untold
7. immense, mammoth 8. colossal,
enormous, gigantic, spacious
9. cyclopean, extensive
11. far-reaching
vast (pert to)...
expanse.. 5. ocean 6. desert, empire,
region
numbers.. 6. myriad
period.. 3. eon, era 5. cycle
space.. 5. waste 9. boundless,
immensity, limitless
vastness... 6. extent 7. expanse
9. greatness, magnitude
vat... 3. bac, pit, tub, tun 4. cask,
gyle, kier, tank 6. barrel, vessel
7. caldron (cauldron), chessel,
cistern, measure, salt pit 8. chessart
Vatican (pert to)...
chapel.. 7. Sistine
church.. 8. St Peter's
city.. 10. Papal State (Rome)
palace of.. 4. Pope
statuary group.. 7. Laocoon
vaticination... 8. prophecy
10. prediction 11. prophesying
vault... 3. sky 4. arch, dome, leap,
over, tomb 5. bound, crypt, enbow,
groin 6. canopy (of heaven), coffer,
curvet, grotto, welkin 10. depository
11. testudinate
vaunt... 4. brag 5. boast
Vauxhall... 6. resort 13. London
Quarter (Thames) 14. Lambeth
Gardens
Veda (pert to)...
hymns.. 8. Sama-Veda
language.. 13. Vedic Sanskrit
literature.. 6. sacred (most anc)
oldest.. 7. Rig-Veda
prose, poetry (popular)..
11. Atharva-Veda
ritualistic.. 9. Yajur-Veda
Vedic (pert to)...
cosmic order.. 4. Rita
dialect.. 4. Pali
god.. 4. Agni 5. Dyaus 6. Aditya,
Varuna 7. Savitar
goddess.. 5. Aditi
hymn.. 6. mantra
language.. 4. Pali 8. Sanskrit
sky serpent.. 3. Ahi
text, treatise.. 6. shakha (sakha)
9. Upanishad
veer... 3. shy, yaw 4. slue, sway, turn
5. alter, shift, sidle 6. careen,
change, swerve 7. deviate, digress
9. fluctuate

veery... **6.** thrush **13.** Wilson's thrush
vegetable... **3.** pea, yam **4.** bean, beet, corn, leek, okra **5.** onion **6.** carrot, celery, lentil, potato, radish, squash, tomato, turnip **7.** cabbage, lettuce, parsnip, rhubarb, shallot, spinach (spinage) **8.** broccoli, eggplant, rutabaga, scallion **9.** artichoke **11.** cauliflower
vegetable (pert to)...
and meat dish.. **4.** stew **6.** ragout
caterpillar.. **5.** aweto
dealer.. **8.** huckster **11.** greengrocer **12.** costermonger
green.. **5.** sabzi
herb.. **7.** salsify
leafy, salad.. **5.** chard **6.** endive **7.** lettuce, romaine, spinach
oil.. **7.** soybean **8.** macassar
poison.. **5.** abrin
stew.. **11.** ratatouille
sugar yielding.. **4.** beet
vegetate... **4.** grow, rest **5.** exist
vegetation, goddess of... **5.** Ceres
vehemence... **3.** ire **4.** fire, fury, rage, zeal **5.** anger, ardor **8.** violence **9.** eloquence **11.** impetuosity
vehement... **3.** hot **5.** angry, eager, fiery **6.** ardent, fervid, heated **7.** animose, furious, intense, violent, zealous **8.** forceful, vigorous **9.** impetuous **10.** passionate
vehicle... **3.** ark, bus, cab, car, van, wag **4.** auto, cart, dray, hack, jeep, limo (sl), semi, shay, sled, tank **5.** buggy, coach, lorry, moped, sulky, tonga, truck, wagon **6.** go–cart, hansom, hot rod, jalopy, landau, sleigh, travoy, troika, wheels (sl) **7.** caleche, caravan, chariot, clunker (sl), kibitka, minibus, omnibus, phaeton, scooter **8.** brougham, carriage, dragster **9.** buckboard, dune buggy, limousine **10.** automobile, conveyance, jinrikisha (jinriksha), motorcycle **11.** convertible
vehicle for oil colors... **6.** megilp (meguilp)
veil... **3.** dim **4.** caul, film, mask **5.** cloak, cover, orale, shade, velum, volet **6.** fannel, masque, screen, shroud, soften **7.** conceal, curtain, garment, pretext, secrecy **8.** disguise **9.** incognito **11.** superimpose
veiled... **5.** vague **6.** masked, shaded, velate **7.** covered **8.** shrouded **9.** curtained
veiling... **5.** tulle, voile **7.** curtain **8.** covering **10.** obvelation
vein... **3.** rib **4.** dash, hilo, lode, mood, tang, vena, wave **5.** cista, shade, smack, spice, tinge, touch **6.** cavity, streak **7.** bonanza, channel, crevice, fissure, mineral, stratum
vein (pert to)...
arrangement.. **9.** neuration
inflammation.. **9.** phlebitis
leaf.. **3.** rib
ref to.. **5.** veiny **6.** veinal, venous **7.** marbled **8.** venulose
small.. **6.** venule **7.** veinlet
stone.. **6.** gangue, matrix **9.** lodestuff

without a.. **7.** avenous
velar... **7.** palatal, throaty **8.** gutteral
veld, veldt... **6.** meadow **8.** bushveld **9.** grassland, grassveld
velleity... **4.** hope **6.** desire **8.** volition **9.** faint hope **10.** slight wish
vellicate... **3.** nip **5.** pinch **6.** tickle, twitch **9.** titillate
vellum... **9.** parchment **10.** manuscript (on parchment)
velocity... **4.** pace **5.** speed **8.** celerity, rapidity **9.** quickness, swiftness **10.** speediness
velocity measure... **4.** velo
velum... **6.** palate (soft) **8.** membrane
velvet (pert to)...
breast.. **9.** merganser
cotton.. **9.** velveteen
fabric.. **5.** panne **6.** velure
Japanese.. **6.** birodo
knife.. **6.** trevet
leaf.. **6.** mallow **7.** mullein
return.. **4.** gain **6.** profit
texture.. **4.** soft **5.** nappy **6.** smooth
venal... **5.** hired **6.** venous **7.** corrupt, salable (saleable), vedible **8.** hireling, vendible **9.** mercenary **11.** corruptible
vend... **4.** hawk, sell **5.** trade **6.** market, peddle **8.** dispense **13.** publish abroad
vender, vendor... **6.** seller **7.** alienor
vendetta... **4.** feud **8.** bad blood
vendue... **4.** sale **7.** auction
venerable... **3.** old **4.** aged, hoar, sage **5.** hoary, olden, title **6.** august, sacred **7.** ancient, antique, classic, elderly, revered **9.** dignified **11.** reverential
venerate... **4.** love **5.** adore **6.** revere **7.** worship
veneration... **3.** awe **4.** fear **5.** dulia, piety **6.** esteem, latria **7.** respect, worship **8.** devotion **9.** adoration, reverence
Venetian (pert to)...
barge.. **9.** bucentaur
beach, resort.. **4.** Lido
boat.. **4.** topo (toppo) **7.** gondola
bridge (famed).. **6.** Rialto
magistrate.. **4.** doge **7.** podesta
medal (New Year's).. **5.** osela (osella)
painter.. **6.** Titian **7.** Bellini (family), Vecchio **10.** Tintoretto
school of.. **8.** painting
song.. **9.** barcarole
window (Arch).. **9.** Palladian
Venezuela...
anc name.. **12.** Little Venice
capital.. **7.** Caracas
city.. **8.** LaGuaira, Valencia **9.** Maracaibo **6.** Ciudad, Guyana **13.** Cuidad Bolivar
copper center.. **4.** Aroa
Falls (world's tallest).. **5.** Angel (found 1937)
hero, liberator.. **7.** Bolivar
lake.. **9.** Maracaibo, Tacarigua
Mt.. **5.** Andes **6.** Concha, Parima, Sierra **9.** Pacaraima
plains.. **6.** llanos

river.. 6. Caroni 7. Orinoco
sea.. 9. Caribbean
snake.. 4. lora
vengeance... 4. harm 7. revenge
  8. reprisal, requital 10. avengement,
  punishment 11. retaliation, retribution
Vengeance, goddess of (Gr)... 3. Ara,
Ate 7. Nemesis
Vengeance, god of (Gr)... 6. Erinys
  7. Alastor
veni, vidi, vici... 19. I came, I saw, I
  conquered (Caesar)
venial... 7. trivial 9. excusable,
  tolerable 10. pardonable
  13. insignificant
Venice... see also *Venetian*
  beach.. 4. Lido
  bridge.. 6. Rialto
  canal.. 5. Grand 8. Merceria, San
  Marco
  capital of.. 7. Venetia (province)
  color.. 4. blue
  island.. 6. Rialto
  landmark.. 9. Campanile 12. Doges'
  Palaces 13. Bridge of Sighs
  of the North.. 9. Stockholm
  river.. 6. Brenta
venison... 8. pemmican (pemican)
vennel... 4. lane 5. alley, sewer
  6. gutter
venom... 4. gall 5. spite, virus
  6. malice, poison 9. animosity,
  malignity, virulence
venomous... 5. toxic 6. deadly
  7. baneful, noxious 8. spiteful,
  virulent 9. envenomed, malicious,
  malignant, poisonous, rancorous
vent... 3. say 4. exit, hole, slit
  5. eject, utter 6. egress, escape,
  outlet 7. air hole, fissure, opening,
  publish, release, ventage, volcano
  8. aperture, let loose
  10. escapement
venta... 3. inn
ventilate... 3. air, fan 5. utter
  6. aerate 7. discuss, publish, refresh
  9. oxygenate
ventose... 5. windy 9. flatulent
  12. cupping glass
ventral... 7. sternal 9. abdominal
venture... 3. hap, try 4. dare, risk,
  wage 5. brave, guess, stake 6. be
  bold, chance, danger, gamble, hazard
  7. attempt, presume 8. run a risk
  9. adventure, haphazard, speculate
  10. enterprise, investment
  11. speculation, undertaking
venturesome... 4. bold, rash 5. brave,
  risky 6. daring, heroic 8. fearless,
  reckless 9. dangerous, foolhardy,
  venturous 11. adventurous,
  temerarious 12. enterprising
venturous... 4. bold, rash 5. hardy,
  risky 6. daring 8. fearless
  9. dangerous, hazardous
  11. temerarious, venturesome
venue... 4. bout, site 5. match, onset
  6. thrust 7. arrival, assault
  9. encounter
Venus (pert to)...
  astronomy.. 6. planet
  church.. 11. Verticordia

  goddess.. 7. Victrix 9. Aphrodite
  goddess of (Rom).. 6. Beauty
  son.. 5. Cupid
  sweetheart.. 6. Adonis
  zoology.. 7. mollusk
Venus statue (marble)...
  Florence.. 8. de Medici
  Louvre.. 7. of Arles 8. Genetrix
  Melos.. 6. de Milo
  Naples.. 7. of Capua
  Rome.. 8. Borghese 12. of the
  Capitol
veracity... 5. truth 7. honesty
  8. accuracy, trueness 11. correctness
  12. truthfulness
veranda, verandah... 4. pyal, stoa
  5. lanai, porch, stoep 6. loggia,
  piazza 7. gallery, portico
verb (Gram)... 5. rhema 6. action
verbal... 4. oral 5. wordy 7. literal,
  verbose 8. verbatim 9. talkative,
  vocabular
verbal noun... 6. gerund
verbatim... 6. orally 7. literal
  8. verbally 11. word for word
verbiage... 4. talk 7. chatter, diction,
  fustian, wording 8. claptrap
  9. prolixity, verbosity, wordiness
  10. redundancy
verbose... 5. wordy 6. prolix 7. diffuse
  9. redundant
verbosity... 10. redundancy
verboten... 5. taboo (tabu)
  9. forbidden 10. prohibited
verdant... 3. raw 5. color, green
  6. unripe 9. evergreen
  13. inexperienced 15. unsophisticated
verdelho... 4. wine (white)
verdict... 4. word 7. finding, opinion
  8. decision, judgment
  13. consideration
verdigris... 4. drug 5. green 6. aerugo
  7. deposit (on copper)
verecund... 6. modest 7. bashful
verge... 3. lip, rim, top 4. edge, tend,
  wand 5. brink, limit, marge, range,
  scope 6. border, emblem, extend,
  margin 7. incline 9. extremity
  10. contiguous 13. circumference
Vergil (pert to)...
  birthplace.. 6. Mantua (It)
  called.. 10. Roman Homer
  famed as.. 4. poet
  friend.. 8. Maecenas
  name (last).. 4. Maro
  poem.. 6. Aeneid 8. Eclogues,
  Georgics
  poetic form.. 4. epic 15. heroic
  hexameter (Aeneid)
verification... 4. oath, test
  8. averment 9. collation
  12. confirmation 13. ascertainment
verify... 3. back, test 5. check, prove
  6. affirm, attest, second 7. confirm,
  support 8. maintain 12. authenticate,
  substantiate
verily... 3. yea 4. amen 5. truly
  6. certes, indeed, in fact, really
  9. certainly 10. positively
  11. confidently
verisimilitude... 5. truth 10. likelihood
  11. probability, verisimilar

veritable... 4. real, true 6. actual,
gospel, honest 7. genuine
9. authentic
verity... 4. fact 5. truth 7. honesty,
reality 8. veracity
vermilion... 3. dye, red 7. pigment,
vermeil 8. cinnabar
vermin... 4. lice, mice, rats 5. filth,
fleas, flies, moths, worms
7. bedbugs, beetles, insects, spiders,
weasels, weevils 8. riffraff, termites
9. parasites 10. centipedes,
mosquitoes 11. cockroaches
Vermont...
capital.. 10. Montpelier
city.. 5. Barre 7. Rutland
10. Burlington 11. Brattleboro
first town.. 10. Fort Dummer
hero.. 10. Ethan Allen
historic group.. 17. Green Mountain
Boys
lake.. 9. Champlain
mountain.. 5. Green 7. Taconic
9. Mansfield
museum.. 9. Shelburne
10. Bennington
product.. 6. marble 10. maple sugar
river.. 5. Otter 11. Connecticut
State admission.. 10. Fourteenth
State motto.. 15. Freedom and Unity
State nickname.. 13. Green Mountain
vernacular... 5. lingo, local
6. common, jargon, native, patois,
vulgar 7. dialect 10. colloquial,
indigenous
vernal... 4. mild, warm 5. fresh
10. springlike
verse... 4. epic, poem, rime 5. canto,
lyric, rhyme, stave, stich 6. poetry,
rondel, sonnet, stanza 7. measure,
strophe, triolet, trochee 8. limerick
verse (pert to)...
art.. 10. orthometry
book of.. 5. poesy 9. anthology
devotion.. 8. antiphon
form.. 7. virelay 10. villanelle
Homeric.. 4. epic 6. epopee
Irish.. 4. rann
pause.. 6. cesura 9. diaeresis
(dieresis)
romantic.. 7. sestina
satiric.. 6. iambic
scripture.. 4. text
stress.. 5. ictus
term.. 5. ictic, meter 6. accent,
poetic, rhythm, scheme 7. cadence
8. eye rhyme, scansion
10. synaeresis (syneresis)
12. alliteration
trivial.. 6. jingle 8. doggerel, limerick
verse (pert to feet)...
eight.. 9. octameter
four.. 10. tetrameter
one.. 9. monometer
three.. 7. tripody
two.. 7. dimeter
versed... 5. adept 7. erudite, learned,
skilled 8. familiar 9. practiced
10. acquainted, conversant, proficient
versification... 7. prosody
10. orthometry
versifier... 4. bard, muse, poet

5. rimer 6. rhymer 7. poetess
8. ballader, eulogist 9. poetaster,
rhymester
version... 7. edition 9. rendition
10. paraphrase 11. translation
version, Bible... 5. Douay, Greek,
Latin 6. Coptic, Geneva, Gothic, Italic
(Itala) 7. Aramaic, Bishops', Luther's,
Revised, Targums, Vulgate
8. Cranmer's, Georgian, Matthew's,
Peshitta, Slavonic 9. Apocrypha, King
James, Serampore 10. Pentateuch,
Septuagint 11. Alexandrian
vers libra... 9. free verse
verso (opp of recto)... 7. reverse
9. back cover 12. left–hand side
versus... 3. con 7. against 8. contrast,
opposite 11. alternative
vertebra, vertebrae... 4. axis
8. backbone 12. spinal column
vertebrate... 6. linked 8. well–knit
9. backboned
vertebrates (pert to)...
division.. 6. somite 10. Vertebráta
feathered.. 5. birds
group.. 4. Aves 7. Amniota
vertex... 3. top 4. apex 6. summit
11. culmination
vertical... 5. apeak, erect, plumb,
sheer 6. height 7. upright
10. upstanding 13. perpendicular
vertical panel... 5. stile
verticil... 5. whorl 6. circle
vertigo... 5. dinus 6. megrim
9. confusion, dizziness, giddiness
11. disturbance 12. bewilderment
verve... 3. pep 4. dash, élan 5. vigor
6. energy, fervor, spirit 8. vivacity
9. animation 10. liveliness
vervet... 6. monkey
very... 3. eri (comb form) 4. much,
real, très, true 5. truly, utter
6. actual, in fact, really 7. exactly,
genuine 8. absolute, especial,
peculiar, truthful 9. extremely,
precisely, veracious, veritable
10. legitimate 11. exceedingly
Very light... 5. flare 6. signal (Very
system)
vesica... 7. bladder
vesicate... 7. blister
vesicle... 3. sac 4. cyst 5. bulla
6. bubble, cavity, vessel 7. bladder,
blemish, blister
Vespa... 4. wasp 6. hornet
vespers... 6. prayer 7. service
8. ceremony, evensong
vessel... 3. ark, can, cup, jar, jug,
mug, pod, pot, tub, urn, vas, vat
4. boat, bowl, dhow, drum, duct,
ewer, junk, olla, olpe, proa, said,
seed, ship, tank, vase, yawl 5. bocal,
craft, crock, cupel, glass, gourd,
jorum, ketch, stein 6. aftaba, aludel,
ampule, barrel, bottle, bucket, caster,
cutter, dipper, firkin, goblet, kettle,
picard, retort, trader, trough
7. catboat, cistern, coracle, cruiser,
frigate, pitcher, psykter, steamer,
tankard, utensil 8. aiguière, ciborium,
decanter, demijohn, hogshead,
schooner 9. alcarraza, catamaran,

privateer, washbasin 10. receptacle
11. earthenware
vessel (pert to)...
anc.. 3. nef 5. yanky 6. bireme
7. caravel, galleon, trireme
Arab.. 4. dhow
baptismal.. 4. font 7. piscina
chemist.. 4. etna 6. aludel, beaker,
retort
Columbus.. 7. caravel
cooking.. 9. autoclave
druggist.. 4. vial 5. phial 8. gallipot
Dutch.. 4. koff 5. yanky 6. galiot
(galliot)
Eccl.. 3. ama, pyx 4. wine 5. amula
7. stamnos
Hebrides.. 7. birlinn (birling)
heraldry.. 7. lymphad
India.. 6. shibar
Mediterranean.. 5. xebec 6. settee
(setee), tartan 7. polacre
merchant.. 6. argosy 7. baggala
Nile houseboat.. 8. dahabeah
oil–burning.. 7. cresset
part.. 4. deck, keel, prow, skeg
5. brail 8. steerage
sacred.. 3. ama
Scottish.. 6. pourie
Thames (fishing).. 6. bawley
Venice.. 9. bucentaur
war.. 3. sub 5. Maine 6. corvet
7. carrier, cruiser, felucca, flattop,
Monitor 9. submarine
11. dreadnaught 12. Old Ironsides
vessel (sailing)... 3. hoy 4. bark, brig,
koff, proa, saic, ship, yawl 5. ketch,
sloop, smack, xebec
vest.. 4. robe 5. endow, gilet
6. invest, jerkin, linder, weskit
7. furnish, garment 9. waistcoat
vesta... 5. match
Vesta (Rom)... 7. goddess (Hearth)
8. asteroid
vestal... 4. pure 6. chaste 8. virginal
vestige... 4. mark, sign 5. relic, shred,
tinge, trace, track 7. remains
8. footstep 9. vestigium
vestiture... 4. garb 5. dress
8. clothing, covering
vestment... 3. alb 4. cope, garb,
gown, hood, robe 5. amice, cotta,
dress, ephod, miter, orale, tunic
6. saccos, tippet 7. cassock,
garment, maniple 8. chasuble,
crucifix, dalmatic, scapular, surplice
10. habiliment, omophorion
vestry... 4. room 5. group (Eccl)
8. sacristy, wardrobe 10. repository
Vesuvius (pert to)...
Great Eruption (79 AD).. 6. buried
city.. 7. Pompeii 11. Herculaneum
mountain.. 8. volcanic
site.. 6. Naples
veteran... 4. long 7. old hand, soldier
8. seasoned 9. practiced
11. experienced
veterinarian... 7. farrier, surgeon
veto... 6. forbid 8. negative, prohibit
10. disapprove 12. interdiction
vex... 3. irk 4. cark, fret, fuss, gall,
miff, rile, roil 5. anger, annoy, harry,
spite, tease, worry 6. bother, harass,

nettle, plague, pother, ruffle
7. agitate, chagrin, despite, dispute,
disturb, pervert, provoke, torment
8. disquiet, irritate 9. displease
vexation... 7. anxiety, chagrin, fatigue,
trouble 8. disquiet, irritate
9. annoyance, weariness
10. affliction, foreboding, harassment,
irritation 11. disturbance
13. mortification
vexatious... 5. pesky 6. thorny
7. irksome 8. annoying 9. disturbed,
pestilent, provoking, worrisome
10. afflictive 11. troublesome
vexillum... 3. web 4. flag 5. cross
6. banner, colors, ensign 7. labarum,
pennant 8. standard 10. Jolly Roger
via... 2. by 3. way 4. away, road
6. begone 7. by way of, passage,
through
viaduct... 4. span 6. bridge 7. trestle
vial... 5. cruet, phial 6. bottle, caster,
castor, vessel 7. ampoule (ampul),
ampulla 9. container
viameter... 7. measure 8. odometer
12. perambulator
viander... 4. host 6. vendor
viands... 4. cate, fare, food 7. viandry
8. victuals 10. provisions
viaticum... 5. money 8. supplies
9. allowance, last rites 10. provisions
14. Extreme Unction
viator... 8. traveler, wayfarer
vibrant... 5. alive 7. pulsing, travale
8. resonant, sonorous, vigorous
9. energetic, thrilling, vibrating
10. resounding
vibrate... 4. beat, rock, tirl, whir
5. pulse, quake, swing, throb, waver
6. dindle, quaver, quiver, shimmy,
shiver, thrill 7. agitate, resound,
tremble 8. brandish, flichter, resonate
9. fluctuate, oscillate
vibration... 6. quiver, thrill, tremor
7. flutter, pulsing 9. resonance,
throbbing 11. oscillation
vibration, music... 5. trill 7. sonance,
tremolo, vibrato
vibration measure... 9. tonometer
vicar... 5. proxy 6. curate, deputy,
priest 9. churchman, clergyman
10. substitute, vicegerent
vice... 3. sin 4. evil 5. crime, fault,
taint 6. defect 7. blemish, stopper
8. iniquity 9. depravity, in place of,
instead of 10. corruption, substitute,
succeeding, wickedness, wrongdoing
11. viciousness
viceroy... 5. nabob 6. satrap
8. governor 9. butterfly
vicinity... 6. region 9. proximity
11. propinquity 12. neighborhood
vicious... 3. bad, ill 4. evil, foul, lewd,
mean, ugly, vile 6. faulty, impure,
wicked 7. corrupt, immoral, noxious
8. depraved, spiteful 9. dangerous,
malicious, nefarious, obstinate,
perverted 10. iniquitous, profligate
11. ill–tempered
vicissitude... 6. change 8. mutation,
shifting 9. variation 10. revolution
11. fluctuation

victim... 4. dupe, gull, prey 5. cully 6. sucker 7. patient 8. sufferer
victor... 6. captor, master, winner 8. unbeaten 9. conqueror 10. vanquisher
victor fish... 3. aku 6. bonito
Victoria, victoria... 4. plum 5. cross (Maltese) 7. goddess 8. asteroid, carriage 10. automobile
Victorian... 3. era 4. prim 6. stuffy 7. antique, archaic, prudish 10. antiquated 11. puritanical, strait-laced
victorious... 7. winning 8. unbeaten 9. defeating 10. conquering, triumphant
victory... 7. mastery, success, triumph 8. conquest 9. supremacy
victory (pert to)...
at too great cost.. 7. Pyrrhic
Day.. 9. Armistice
goddess.. 4. Nike
hymn.. 9. epinicion (epinikion)
memorial.. 6. trophy
symbol.. 4. palm
Victrola dog (symbol)... 6. Nipper
victuals... 4. food, grub 6. viands 8. supplies 11. nourishment
videlicet... 3. viz 5. to wit 6. namely 8. scilicet
vie... 3. bet 4. cope, life 5. bandy, stake, wager 6. endure, oppose, strive 7. compare, compete, contend, contest, emulate 8. struggle 9. challenge
Vienna...
artist.. 4. Lieb, Pilz 6. Makart, Zauner 7. Kisling
boulevard (famed).. 11. Ringstrasse
capital of.. 7. Austria
Ger name.. 4. Wien
musician.. 5. Gluck, Haydn 6. Czerny, Mozart 7. Strauss 8. Schubert, Schumann 9. Beethoven
palace.. 10. Schönbrunn
park.. 6. Prater
river.. 6. Danube
Vietnam road... 14. Ho Chi Minh Trail
view... 3. aim, end, eye, ken, see 4. look, scan 5. scene, vista 6. aperçu, aspect, object, regard, survey 7. examine, glimpse, opinion, outlook, picture 8. attitude, judgment, panorama, prospect 9. intention 10. appearance, perception, scrutinize 11. contemplate, expectation 13. contemplation
vigil... 3. eve 4. wake 5. guard, watch 6. patrol 7. watchman 9. keep guard 11. wakefulness 13. sleeplessness
vigilant... 4. agog, wary 5. alert, awake, aware 6. awatch 7. wakeful 8. cautious, open-eyed, watchful 9. attentive, observant, sleepless 11. circumspect
vigilantes... 5. posse 9. committee (vigilance)
vigor, vigour... 3. pep, vim, vir 4. life, zeal 5. force, power, verve 6. energy, health 7. potency,

stamina, sthenia 8. strength, validity, virility 9. animation, fraîcheur, vehemence 10. liveliness
vigorous... 4. able, hale, racy, spry 5. eager, frank, fresh, hardy, lusty, tough 6. potent, robust, strong 7. healthy, zealous 8. athletic, forceful, spirited, vehement 9. effective, energetic, sprightly, strenuous 11. efficacious, flourishing
Viking... 4. Eric 5. rover 6. pirate 8. Norseman, Northman, sea rover 9. plunderer 12. Scandinavian
vile... 3. bad 4. base, evil, foul, mean 5. cheap, lowly, nasty 6. coarse, filthy, impure, odious, sinful, sordid, wicked 7. corrupt, debased, ignoble, obscene, unclean, vicious 8. depraved, infamous 9. degrading, loathsome, nefarious, repulsive 10. abominable, disgusting 12. contaminated
vilify... 5. abuse, curse, libel 6. debase, defame, malign, revile 7. asperse, cheapen, degrade, slander, traduce 8. belittle, disgrace, reproach, vilipend 9. blaspheme, disparage 10. calumniate, stigmatize
vilipend... 6. slight 7. despise 8. belittle 9. disparage 10. depreciate, slanderous 12. calumniatory
villa... 5. aldea, dacha 9. residence, villaette 10. villanette
village... 3. mir 4. dorp, stad 5. thorp (thorpe), tract 6. aldeia, castle, hamlet, pueblo
Village Blacksmith author... 10. Longfellow
villain... 4. boor, lout, ogre, serf 5. demon, heavy, knave, rogue 6. rascal 7. caitiff 9. miscreant, scoundrel
villainous... 3. bad, low 4. base, evil, mean, vile 6. vulgar, wicked 7. boorish, knavish 8. criminal, rascally, terrible, wretched 9. dastardly 10. detestable, iniquitous 11. scoundrelly 13. objectionable
villous... 5. nappy 6. napped, shaggy
vim... 3. pep, zip 4. dash, élan, fire, gimp, kick 5. drive, force, verve, vigor 6. energy, esprit, spirit 8. strength
vinaigre... 7. vinegar
vindicate... 4. free 5. claim, clear 6. acquit, assert, avenge, defend, excuse, uphold 7. absolve, justify, support, sustain 8. maintain 9. exculpate, exonerate
vindication... 7. defense
vindictive... 7. hostile 8. punitive, spiteful, vengeful 10. revengeful 11. retaliatory, retributive
vine... 3. hop, ivy 4. bine, odal 5. betel, grape, liana (liane), Vitis 7. cupseed, trailer 8. clematis, wisteria 9. grapevine 10. chilicothe 11. honeysuckle 12. morning glory
vinegar... 4. acid, sour 6. acetum, alegar 8. vinaigre
vinegar (pert to)...

acid.. 6. acetic
comb form.. 5. aceto
dregs.. 6. mother
eel.. 4. worm
ester.. 7. acetate
fly.. 5. fruit
preserve in.. 6. pickle 8. marinate
salt.. 7. acetate
spice.. 8. tarragon
tree.. 13. staghorn sumac
Vinegar Joe (Army)... 9. Stillwell (Gen)
vinegarroon... 8. scorpion, vinagron
vinegary... 4. sour, tart 7. acetose,
  crabbed, pungent 9. unamiable
vineyard... 3. cru 7. Priapus (god of)
  10. plantation
vinology (science of)... 5. vines
  10. grapevines
vinous... 4. winy 5. color
vintner... 8. merchant (wine)
viol... 3. gue 4. rope 5. rebec, ruana
  6. vielle 7. quinton, sarinda 9. organ
  stop
viola... 5. gamba 7. sarangi 9. organ
  stop 11. tenor violin
violate... 5. abuse, break, wrong
  6. defile, invade, ravage, ravish
  7. debauch, outrage, pollute, profane
  8. deflower, dishonor, mistreat
  9. desecrate 10. transgress
violation... 7. offense 10. infraction
  11. anacoluthon, disturbance,
  profanation 12. infringement,
  interruption 13. nonobservance,
  transgression
violence... 5. anger, force 6. unjust
  7. assault, cruelty, outrage
  8. coercion 9. vehemence
  10. roughhouse 11. profanation
  12. infringement
violent... 4. loud 5. acute, great,
  rabid, sharp, vivid 6. fierce, savage,
  stormy 7. extreme, furious, intense
  8. coercive, vehement 9. turbulent
  10. passionate 11. tempestuous
violent (pert to)...
Norse folklore.. 8. warriors
  9. beserkers
outbreak.. 4. riot 6. tumult, uproar
  8. eruption
pain:. 4. pang 5. throe 6. fierce
violet (pert to)...
color.. 5. mauve 6. purple
  7. blue–red
dye.. 6. archil (orchil)
emblem of.. 7. gravity 8. chastity
genus.. 9. Violaceae
perfume.. 5. irone 6. ionone
  9. orrisroot
tip.. 9. butterfly
violin (pert to)...
ancient.. 5. rebab, rebec, rocta
  12. viola de gamba
bar.. 4. fret
bass.. 11. violoncello
bow.. 5. arcus
city (famed).. 7. Cremona (It)
make.. 5. Amati 7. Cremona
  10. Guarnerius 12. Stradivarius
maker.. 5. Amati 9. Guarnieri
  10. Stradivari
reference to.. 4. pins 5. belly

Scot.. 6. fiddle
small.. 3. kit
tenor.. 4. alto
violinist (famed)... 5. Elman, Stern
  7. Heifitz, Menuhin
violinist, first... 13. concertmaster
viper... 3. asp 5. adder, Echis, snake
  6. kupper 7. serpent 8. cerastes,
  ophidian 9. scoundrel
  10. bushmaster
vir... 5. vigor
virage... 5. scold, shrew, vixen, woman
  7. beldame, rullion 9. termagant
Virgil... see Vergil
virgin... 3. new 4. maid, pure
  6. chaste, maiden, vestal 8. spinster
  9. undefiled, unsullied, untouched
  13. unadulterated
virginal... 3. new 5. piano (spinet)
  6. chaste, ritual 7. natural
  8. maidenly 9. unmarried, unsullied
Virginia...
bay.. 10. Chesapeake
capital.. 8. Richmond
city.. 7. Norfolk, Roanoke
  9. Arlington, Lexington, Lynchburg
  11. Newport News 12. Hampton
  Roads
famed sites.. 8. Mt Vernon
  10. Monticello 12. Williamsburg
  13. Stratford Hall
first white child born.. 12. Virginia
  Dare
historic town.. 8. Yorktown
  9. Jamestown 10. Appomattox
Indian sachem.. 8. Powhatan
mountain.. 9. Blue Ridge
  11. Alleghenies
resort.. 13. Virginia Beach
river.. 4. York 5. James 7. Potomac,
  Rapidan 12. Rappahannock
settlement (first).. 9. Jamestown
State admission.. 5. Tenth
State motto.. 17. Sic Semper
  Tyrannis 19. Thus Always to Tyrants
State nickname.. 11. Old Dominion
Virgin Islands, British...
capital.. 8. Road Town
crop.. 9. sugar cane
group.. 7. Leeward
number islands.. 6. thirty
Virgin Islands, United States...
capital.. 8. St Thomas 15. Charlotte
  Amalia (former)
discoverer.. 8. Columbus (1493)
largest.. 6. St John 7. St Croix 8. St
  Thomas
virginity... 8. celibacy, chastity
  10. maidenhood 12. spinsterhood
Virgin Mary... 5. Pietà (image) 7. Our
  Lady 11. Maris Stella, Mother of
  God 12. Star of the Sea 13. Mother
  of Jesus
viridity... 5. youth 7. verdure
  9. freshness, greenness 10. grass
  color
virile... 4. male 5. manly 8. forceful,
  powerful, vigorous 9. masculine,
  masterful
virose... 5. fetid 8. virulent
  9. poisonous 10. malodorous
virtu... 5. curio 7. antique 8. artistry

12. love of curios 15. artistic quality, study of fine arts

virtual... 9. essential, potential 10. energizing 12. constructive

virtually... 7. morally 11. potentially, practically

virtue... 5. valor, value, worth 6. energy, purity 7. potency, probity 8. chastity, efficacy, goodness, morality 9. godliness, innocence, integrity, rectitude 11. uprightness 13. righteousness

virtue, logic... 8. aretaics

virtues, cardinal... 4. hope 5. faith 7. charity

virtuoso... 6. expert 7. scholar 11. connoisseur, philosopher

virtuous... 4. good, pure 5. brave, godly, moral 6. chaste, honest, potent 7. upright, valiant 8. valorous 9. righteous 11. efficacious

virulent... 5. acrid, rabid 6. deadly, potent 7. noxious 8. venomous 9. animosity, malignant, poisonous 10. infectious, resentment 11. acrimonious

visa, visé... 7. endorse 9. signature 11. certificate, endorsement (passport)

visage... 4. face, look 5. image 11. countenance 14. visible surface

vis-à-vis... 4. seat, sofa 8. carriage, opposite 9. encounter 10. face to face

viscera... 4. guts 6. bowels, vitals 7. insides 8. entrails 10. intestines 11. inside parts

visceral... 7. enteric 10. intestinal, splanchnic

viscid... 4. ropy, waxy 5. slimy 6. sticky 7. viscous 8. adhering, adhesive 9. glutinous

viscosity... 8. tenacity 10. stickiness

viscous... 4. ropy, sizy 5. gluey, gummy, tarry 6. mucous, sticky, viscid 7. stringy 9. glutinous 10. stickiness

vise... 3. jaw 4. tool 5. clamp, winch 6. device 7. squeeze

Vishnu (pert to)...
consort.. 3. Sri 7. Lakshim
deity (supreme).. 6. bhakti 9. preserver
eighth.. 7. Krishna
epithet.. 8. bhagavat
seventh.. 4. Rama
tenth, last incarnation.. 5. Kalki
vehicle.. 6. Garuda

visible... 4. open, seen 5. clear 6. extant, in view 7. evident, in sight, obvious 8. apparent, manifest 10. noticeable 11. discernible, perceivable, perceptible

Visigoth king... 6. Alaric

vision... 3. eye 5. dream, fancy, image, sight 6. glance, mirage 7. glimpse, imagine, specter 8. eyesight 10. apparition

vision (pert to)...
comb form.. 4. opto
daylight.. 8. photopia
defect.. 6. anopia, myopia

double.. 8. diplopia
illusory.. 5. image
lacking.. 8. purblind
measure.. 9. optometer
night.. 8. scotopia
science of.. 9. optometry
term.. 5. optic 6. ocular 9. binocular, monocular

visionary... 4. aery, airy, seer, wild 5. ideal 6. dreamy, unreal 7. dreamer, Laputan, utopian 8. delusive, idealist, quixotic, romantic 9. fantastic, imaginary 10. chimerical, rhapsodist 11. imaginative, impractical

visit... 3. see, vis 4. call, chat, go to, slum 5. haunt 6. attend, call on 10. inspection, visitation 12. conversation

visitor... 5. guest 6. caller 7. company 8. visitant

visne... 5. venue 8. neighbor, vicinage

vison... 4. mink

visor, vizor... 4. mask 6. vizard 8. disguise 10. camouflage

vista... 4. view 5. scene, visto 7. outlook 8. corridor, panorama, prospect

visual... 5. optic 6. ocular 11. perceptible

visualize... 7. imagine, picture 8. envisage, envision 9. objectify

vital... 4. live 5. basic 6. living, mortal, viable 7. animate, exigent, needful, organic 8. inherent, vigorous 9. essential, important, necessary, requisite 10. imperative 11. fundamental 13. indispensable

vital (pert to)...
air.. 6. oxygen
force.. 6. energy, spirit 7. neurism 8. bathmism, phrenism 9. theosophy
impulse.. 6. libido 8. instinct
organs.. 6. vitals 7. viscera
records.. 10. demography, statistics
strength.. 7. stamina

vitality... 3. sap, vim 4. life 5. vigor 8. strength 9. animation, lustiness 10. liveliness

vitals... 7. insides, viscera 9. internals 11. vital organs (heart, liver, lungs, brain)

vitamin... 6. biotin, niacin 7. carotin, thiamin 10. riboflavin 11. lactoflavin 12. ascorbic acid

vitellus... 4. yolk 7. egg yolk

vitiate... 5. spoil, taint 6. debase, impair, poison, weaken 7. corrupt, deprave, pervert, pollute 10. adulterate, demoralize, invalidate 11. contaminate

vitiated... 5. pical 6. wicked 7. corrupt, debased, spoiled 9. defective 11. ineffective, invalidated

vitiosity... 4. vice 6. defect 9. depravity 11. viciousness

vitium... 5. fault 6. defect

vitric... 9. glasslike

vitrics... 9. glassware, glasswork

vitrify... 5. glaze 13. make into glass

vitriolic... 4. acid 5. sharp 6. biting,

bitter 7. caustic 8. scathing, virulent
11. acrimonious
vituperate... 5. abuse, curse, scold
6. berate, revile 7. censure
vituperative... 7. abusive, railing
8. reviling, scolding 10. scurrilous
11. maledictory, opprobrious
vivacious... 3. gay 4. airy 5. merry
6. active, lively 8. animated,
gamesome, spirited, sportive
9. energetic 12. lighthearted
vivacity... 4. dash, élan, fire, keen,
zeal, zest 5. ardor, verve, vigor
6. energy, gaiety (gayety)
9. animation 10. liveliness
Viverra... 6. civets 9. civet cats
vivers... 4. food 8. victuals
vix... 8. scarcely
vixen... 3. cat, fox 5. scold, shrew,
witch 6. virago 9. termagant
12. female animal
viz... 5. to wit 6. namely 9. videlicet
vizard... 4. mask 5. guise, visor
8. disguise
vlei (vley)... 5. creek, marsh, swamp
voar... 6. spring (of the year)
vocabulary... 5. words 6. jargon
7. diction, lexicon 8. glossary,
wordbook 10. dictionary
vocabulist... 6. writer
13. lexicographer
vocal (pert to)...
chink.. 7. glottis
composition.. 4. aria, song 5. motet
7. cantata
expression.. 4. oral 9. utterance
flourish.. 7. roulade
handicap.. 4. lisp 7. stutter
sound.. 5. vowel 6. sonant
statue.. 6. Memnon
vocalist... 4. alto 5. basso, tenor
6. artist, cantor, singer 7. caroler,
crooner, soprano, yodeler 8. songster
10. coloratura, prima donna,
songstress
vocalization... 11. melismatics
vocalize... 4. sing 5. sound, utter
6. phrase
vocation... 4. call 5. trade 6. career
7. calling 8. business
10. employment, occupation,
profession
vociferous... 4. loud 5. noisy
7. blatant 8. brawling, strident
9. clamorous, turbulent
11. loudmouthed 12. obstreperous
vogue... 3. ton 4. mode 5. style
6. custom 7. fashion 8. practice
10. popularity
voice... 3. say, vox 4. alto, bass,
tone, vote, wish 5. rumor, tenor,
utter 7. divulge, opinion, soprano
8. announce, falsetto 9. utterance
10. expression 12. articulation
voice (pert to)...
box.. 6. larynx
Greek.. 9. phthongos
handicap.. 4. lisp 7. stammer, stutter
loss of.. 7. anaudia, aphonia
loud.. 12. megalophonic
phonetics.. 9. affricate

quality.. 6. timbre (timber)
quiet.. 5. sotto
raise.. 6. insist 10. supplicate
raise against.. 5. decry 6. accuse,
object
singing, above natural.. 8. falsetto
singing, natural.. 7. dipetto
stress.. 5. arsis
with one.. 9. unanimous
12. concurrently
voiced... 6. sonant, spoken 7. sounded
9. phthongal 11. articulated
voiceless... 4. dumb, mute, surd
6. atonic, silent 7. spirate 9. not
voiced 12. not expressed
void... 4. idle, lack, null, want
5. abyss, annul, egest, empty
6. devoid, hollow, vacant, vacuum
7. abolish, nothing, nullify, useless
8. evacuate 9. destitute, emptiness
10. unoccupied 11. ineffectual,
nonexistent
void of...
interest.. 6. jejune 7. insipid
sense.. 5. inane, silly
space.. 5. blank 6. vacuum
volaille... 4. fowl 7. poultry
volant... 5. agile, light, quick 6. flying,
nimble 7. current 8. volatile, volitant
volatile... 4. airy 5. light 6. fickle,
flying, lively, volant 7. alcohol,
ammonia, buoyant, flighty, gaseous
8. fleeting, vaporous 9. ephemeral,
mercurial 10. capricious, changeable,
transitory 11. vaporizable
12. lighthearted
volatile (pert to)...
alkali.. 7. ammonia
flux.. 5. smear
liquid.. 5. ether 7. alcohol
oil.. 7. essence, perfume
volcanic (pert to)...
glass.. 6. pumice 7. perlite
8. obsidian
matter.. 2. aa 4. lava, slag, tufa
5. trass 6. pumice 8. lapillus,
pahoehoe
mud.. 5. salse
orifice of gas issue.. 8. fumarole
ref to.. 9. excitable, explosive
11. hot–tempered
rock.. 5. trass 6. dacite 8. tephrite
saucer.. 6. crater
volcano (pert to)...
Africa.. 11. Kilimanjaro
Alaska.. 6. Katmai 8. Wrangell
Chile.. 6. Lascar
Ecuador.. 8. Cotopaxi
goddess.. 4. Pele (Hawaii)
Guatemala.. 5. Fuego 7. Atitlan
Hawaii.. 8. Mauna Loa
Iceland.. 5. Askja, Hekla
Italy.. 4. Etna 8. Vesuvius
9. Stromboli
Japan.. 4. Fuji 9. Asamayama
Java.. 4. Gede
Mexico.. 12. Popocatepetl
Philippines.. 3. Apo (Mindanao)
Sumatra.. 6. Merapi
United States (mainland).. 6. Lassen,
Shasta 7. Rainier
West Indies.. 5. Pelée

vole... 6. craber, rodent 8. water rat
  10. field mouse 11. meadow mouse
volée... 6. flight, volley
volery (volary)... 6. aviary 8. bird
  cage
volition... 4. will 6. choice
  11. voluntarily 13. determination
volley... 4. fire 5. blast, salvo, shots
Voltaire... 11. philosopher (of Ferney)
voluble... 4. glib 6. fluent 8. rotating,
  unstable 9. garrulous, revolving,
  talkative 10. loquacious
volume... 4. book, bulk, mass, size,
  tome 6. amount 7. compass
  8. capacity, fullness (fulness)
  9. aggregate, Decameron
  10. crassitude 14. fullness of tone
voluntary... 4. free 7. prelude, willing
  8. elective, intended, purposed
  9. volunteer, willingly 10. deliberate,
  volitional 11. intentional, spontaneous
  13. not accidental
volunteer... 5. offer 6. enlist 7. proffer
  9. be willing, voluntary 11. be of
  service
Volunteer State... 9. Tennessee
volute... 4. turn 5. whorl 6. cilery
  (cillery) 8. rolled up 10. scroll–like
voodoo... 5. magic, obeah 6. fetish
  8. sorcerer
voracious... 6. greedy, hungry
  8. edacious, esurient, ravening,
  ravenous 9. devouring, rapacious
  10. gluttonous, immoderate,
  unsatiable
voracity... 5. greed 7. edacity
  8. gluttony, rapacity 9. esurience
vorago... 4. gulf 5. abyss
vortex... 4. apex, eddy 5. whirl
  7. tornado 8. flatworm 9. whirlpool,
  whirlwind 10. waterspout
votary... 6. zealot 7. devotee
  8. adherent, aesthete, follower
  9. supporter 10. enthusiast
vote... 3. vow 5. elect, straw
  6. ballot, choice, ticket 7. declare
  8. suffrage 9. designate
  10. plebescite, referendum
vote (pert to)...
  group.. 4. bloc
  in.. 5. elect
  of assent.. 6. placet
  plump.. 14. straight ticket
  receptacle.. 6. situla
voter... 6. poller 7. elector 8. balloter
  11. constituent
voters... 10. electorate
votive... 7. devoted 11. consecrated
vouch... 4. back 6. affirm, attest,
  depose 7. confirm, declare, promise,
  sponsor, support 8. accredit
  9. assertion 11. attestation, bear
  witness
vouchsafe... 4. give 5. deign
  6. accept, assure, bestow, permit
  7. concede 8. guarantee
  10. condescend
voussoir... 8. keystone
vow... 3. vum 4. oath 5. swear,
  vouch 6. behest, devote, pledge
  7. declare, promise 8. dedicate

9. assertion 10. consecrate,
  obligation 11. asservation
  12. supplication
vowel (pert to)...
  change of.. 6. umlaut
  contradiction.. 6. crasis 7. digraph
  9. diphthong
  loss of.. 7. aphesis
  mark.. 6. macron
  point (Heb).. 4. sere (tsere)
  separate syllables.. 9. diaeresis
  (dieresis)
  short.. 5. breve
  two, contracted.. 6. crasis
  two, group.. 6. digram 7. digraph
  9. diphthong (dipthong)
  unaspirated.. 4. lene
vowels, none... 6. syzygy
vowels in sequence... 8. caesious
vox (pert to)...
  clandestina.. 7. whisper
  Dei.. 10. Voice of God
  Latin for.. 5. voice
  populi.. 16. voice of the people
voyage... 4. trip 6. cruise, travel
  7. journey, passage, passing (sea)
  9. excursion 10. expedition,
  pilgrimage 11. undertaking
Vulcan (pert to)...
  consort.. 4. Maia
  epithet.. 8. Mulciber
  feast of.. 10. Vulcanalia
  god of.. 4. fire
  Greek.. 10. Hephaestus
  work site.. 4. Etna
vulcanite... 7. ebonite
vulcanize... 9. rubberize
vulgar... 3. low 4. lewd 5. crude,
  gross 6. coarse, common, garish,
  public, ribald 7. boorish, general,
  obscene, profane 8. indecent,
  ordinary, plebeian 9. inelegant,
  offensive, unrefined 10. boisterous, in
  bad taste, rowdydowdy
vulgarian... 4. snob 9. pretender
Vulgate... 10. Scriptures
vulnerable... 6. liable 7. exposed
  8. beatable 9. pregnable, subject to
  10. expugnable 11. conquerable,
  defenseless, susceptible
vulpine... 4. foxy 6. artful, crafty,
  tricky 7. cunning, foxlike 9. alopecoid
  10. vulpecular
vult... 4. mien 6. aspect
  10. expression 11. countenance
vulture (pert to)...
  African.. 8. aasvogel
  American.. 4. aura 5. urubu
  6. condor 13. turkey buzzard
  European.. 7. griffin 11. lammergeier
  (lammergeir)
  king.. 4. papa
  large.. 6. condor 11. lammergeier
  Mexican.. 8. zopilote
  raven.. 9. Corvultur
  Spanish.. 9. gallinazo
  term.. 5. harpy 9. raptorial 10. bird
  of prey, predacious
vulturous... 6. lupine 7. wolfish
  8. ravenous 9. rapacious
vying... 7. emulous 8. rivaling
  9. competing 11. competitive

W

W... 6. letter (23rd) 7. double U
WAAC... 24. Women's Auxiliary Army
Corps
waag... 6. grivet, monkey
waapa... 5. canoe
wabber... 4. cony 5. daman
wabble... see *wobble*
wabby... 4. loon (red–throated)
wabe, wabi... 5. shrub 8. huisache
wachna... 7. codfish
wad... 3. pad, ram 4. cram, lump,
mass, plug, roll, tuft 5. money, stuff,
track 6. bundle, pledge, wealth
7. stopper 8. bankroll
wadding... 4. wads 6. lining
7. padding 8. compress, stopping,
stuffing
waddle... 4. sway 5. mince 6. toddle,
wabble, wamble, wobble 10. clumsy
gait
waddy, waddie... 3. peg 4. beat, club
5. stick 6. attack, cowboy
wade... 4. ford, pass 5. study
6. attack, drudge, paddle, plodge
8. struggle
wader... 4. coot, ibis, rail 5. crane,
heron, snipe, stork 6. jaçana
9. sandpiper, shore bird
11. Grallatores
wadi, wady... 5. oasis, river 6. ravine,
valley 7. channel 11. watercourse
waeg... 9. kittiwake
wafer... 4. cake, disk, ring, seal, snap
5. bread 7. biscuit, cracker 10. altar
bread
waff... 3. wag 4. flap, wave 5. ghost
7. lowborn, vagrant 8. inferior
9. worthless 12. disreputable
waft... 4. gust, puff, wave 5. carry,
float, whiff 6. beckon, convey,
convoy, signal 7. glimpse, pennant
9. beckoning, transport
wag... 3. wit 4. card, wave 5. joker,
rogue, shake 6. signal, waddle,
wiggle 7. farceur, vibrate
8. humorist, jokester 9. oscillate
wagang... 5. death 9. departure
11. leave–taking
wage, wages... 3. bet, fee, pay, utu
4. hire, levy, pawn, risk 5. fight,
incur, stake, yield 6. employ, engage,
pledge, reward, salary 7. attempt,
contend, hire out, stipend, venture
9. emolument 10. recompense
12. compensation, remuneration
wage insurance... 7. chômage
wager... 3. bet, bid, vie 4. risk
5. sport, stake 6. gamble, hazard,
parlay, pledge 7. venture
waggish... 5. droll, merry 7. jesting,

jocular, parlous, roguish
8. humorous, sportive 9. facetious
10. frolicsome 11. mischievous
Wagnerian opera... 6. Rienzi
8. Parsifal 9. Lohengrin
10. Tannhauser
15. Gotterdammerung
wagon... 3. car, van 4. cart, dray,
tram, wain 5. araba, coach, lorry,
tonga 6. telega 7. caisson, chariot,
vehicle 8. carryall, schooner (prairie)
12. perambulator
wagon (pert to)...
canvas–covered.. 15. prairie schooner
lit.. 7. Pullman 11. sleeping car
load.. 6. fother
maker.. 10. wagonsmith, wainwright
on the (wagon).. 8. sworn off, teetotal
part.. 4. neap 5. blade, thill
police.. 3. van 10. Black Maria
sideless.. 6. rolley
wah... 5. panda
wahine... 4. wife 5. woman
8. mistress 10. sweetheart
wahoo... 4. bark, fish, peto 5. shrub
7. rock elm 8. nonsense, tommyrot
9. buckthorn, guarapucu
12. umbrella tree
waif... 4. Arab, flag 5. gamin, stray
7. vagrant, wastrel 8. castaway,
homeless, wanderer 9. lost sheep
wail... 3. cry, sob 4. howl, moan,
weep 5. mourn 6. bemoan, grieve,
lament 7. deplore, screech, ululate
11. lamentation 14. mournful outcry
wainscot... 4. base, ceil, line 5. panel
6. lining 8. paneling (panelling)
9. partition
waist... 4. wasp 5. shirt 6. basque,
blouse, bodice, dickey, middle, taille
7. corsage, garment 9. garibaldi
12. undergarment
waistcoat... 4. vest 5. benjy 6. jacket,
jerkin, weskit
wait... 4. bide, rest, stay, stop
5. dally, defer, delay, hover, serve,
tarry, watch 6. attend, expect, linger,
remain 7. observe 8. hesitate,
postpone 11. expectation
12. watchfulness
waiter... 4. tray 6. garçon, salver,
server 7. messboy, messman,
servant, steward 8. servitor
9. attendant
wait on... 4. help 5. await, cater,
serve 6. escort 7. toady to
9. accompany
waive... 5. defer, forgo (forego)
6. desert, give up, reject, vacate
7. abandon, cast off, forsake

8. postpone 9. disregard
10. condescend, relinquish
waka ... 5. canoe
Wakashan Indian ... 6. Nootka
8. Kwakiutl
wake ... 4. call, stir 5. rouse, track,
vigil, waken, watch 6. arouse,
awaken, excite, revive 10. death
watch
wakeful ... 5. alert 8. restless, vigilant,
watchful 9. sleepless, wide–awake
Wake Island ... 6. Ottori (Jap name)
wake–robin ... 4. Arum 8. Trillium
9. Anthurium 10. cuckoopint
12. philodendron
wale ... 3. rib 4. welt 5. ridge, wheal
6. stripe
Wales ... see also *Welsh*
anc .. 7. Cambria
city .. 7. Rhondda, Swansea
8. Hereford, Pembroke 9. Carnarvon
congress of literati .. 10. eisteddfod
deity .. 4. Bran
emblem (floral) .. 4. leek
language .. 7. Cymraeg
mountain .. 7. Snowdon
native .. 5. Cymry (Kymry)
patron saint .. 5. David
port .. 7. Cardiff
river .. 3. Dee, Wye 6. Severn
sea .. 5. Irish
walk ... 3. mog, pad 4. foot, gait,
hike, hoof, pace, path, plod, ramp,
step 5. allee, amble, scuff, strut,
tramp, tread 6. ramble, sphere,
stride, stroll, toddle, travel, trudge
7. conduct, shuffle, traipse
8. ambulate, behavior, frescade,
province, sidewalk 9. esplanade,
promenade, wandering
10. passageway 11. base on balls,
perambulate 13. peregrination
walk (pert to) ...
a beat .. 6. patrol
about .. 11. perambulate
clumsily .. 5. mince 6. lumber, totter
health .. 14. constitutional
lime–bordered .. 9. tilicetum
proudly .. 5. strut 6. prance
public .. 4. mall 6. arcade 7. alameda
9. esplanade, promenade
wearily .. 4. limp, plod 5. tramp
6. hobble, trudge
with speed .. 10. heel and toe
walking (pert to) ...
about .. 7. passant (Her)
11. peripatetic
bearlike .. 11. plantigrade
meter .. 9. pedometer
papers .. 7. deposal, the sack
8. mittimus, pink slip 9. discharge,
dismissal 10. retirement
wall ... 4. dado, dike, ha–ha, mure,
pier 5. fence, levee, panel, redan
6. escarp, hinder, immure, paries,
podium, septum, shut in 7. barrier,
defense, enclose, fortify, parapet,
rampart 8. espalier, palisade, restrain,
stockade 9. barricade, enclosure,
encompass, partition, precipice,
revetment 13. fortification
wall (pert to) ...

bracket .. 6. corbel, sconce
creeper .. 4. bird
go to the (wall) .. 4. fail 10. go
bankrupt
lining .. 8. wainscot
lizard .. 4. newt 5. gecko
masonry .. 9. revetment
pert to .. 5. mural 8. parietal
recess .. 5. niche 6. alcove
Street .. 9. Manhattan 11. money
market, stock market
up .. 6. immure
wallaby ... 8. kangaroo, Macropus,
wallaroo 10. paddymelon
wallah, walla ... 5. agent 6. master,
person 7. servant
waller ... 4. wels 9. saltmaker,
sheatfish
wallet ... 3. bag 4. pack, poke, sack
5. purse 8. billfold, knapsack
10. pocketbook 12. porte–monnaie
walleye ... 9. exotropia 10. strabismus
wallow ... 4. fade, sail 5. surge
6. grovel, welter, wither 7. debauch,
founder, insipid 8. flounder,
kommetje, nauseous 9. tasteless
walnut ... 6. bannut
walrus ... 3. pod (group) 5. morse
6. mammal, sea cat 8. pinniped
9. rosmarine (fable) 10. pinnipedia
Waltonian ... 6. angler 16. disciple of
Walton (Izaak)
wamble ... 5. twist 6. quiver, ramble,
rumble, totter, writhe 7. revolve,
stagger, wriggle
wame ... 4. room, womb 5. belly
7. stomach
wampum ... 4. peag 5. beads, money,
uhllo 6. shells 7. jewelry, roanoke
8. ornament 10. wampumpeag
wan ... 3. dim, sad 4. ashy, dark, pale,
sick 5. ashen, black, dusky, faint,
lurid 6. dismal, gloomy, pallid, sickly
7. ghastly, languid 9. deathlike,
sorrowful 10. lusterless
11. lead–colored
wand ... 3. rod 4. mace, pole
5. baton, osier, staff, stick (magic)
6. switch, wattle 7. pointer, rhabdos
(magic), scepter (sceptre)
8. caduceus 9. horsewhip
wander ... 3. err, gad 4. moon, rave,
roam, rove 5. drift, prowl, range,
stray 6. cruise, depart, ramble, stroll,
travel 7. digress, meander, saunter,
traipse 8. divagate, traverse
9. circulate, itinerate, scamander
11. peregrinate
wanderer ... 4. Arab, waif 5. gypsy,
nomad, rover 6. ranger, roamer,
truant 7. migrant, pilgrim, vagrant
9. butterfly, itinerant, straggler
10. covenanter 12. peregrinator
wandering ... 5. vague 6. astray,
errant, roving, vagary 8. aberrant,
delirium, straying 9. delirious,
deviating, deviation, itinerant
10. circuitous, discursive, journeying
11. noctivigant, perambulant
13. peregrination
wandering (pert to) ...
bird .. 9. albatross

long .. 7. odyssey
minstrel .. 4. bard 10. troubadour
stars .. 12. seven planets
tattler .. 9. shore bird
votary .. 6. palmer
wanderoo ... 6. langur, monkey
7. macaque
wand–shaped ... 7. virgate
wane ... 3. age, ebb 4. fail, sink, want
5. abate, peter 6. defect, lessen,
recede, repine 7. decline, grow dim,
subside 8. decrease, diminish
10. defervesce 13. deterioration
wanga ... 5. charm, spell 6. voodoo
7. philter, sorcery
wangle ... 4. fake, plot 6. adjust,
juggle, obtain, totter, wiggle
7. finagle (finaigue), wriggle
8. contrive, maneuver (manoeuvre)
9. extricate 10. manipulate
want ... 4. lack, miss, need, wish
5. crave 6. dearth, desire, hunger,
penury 7. absence, craving, lacking,
poverty 8. scarcity, shortage
9. deficient, indigence, privation
10. inadequacy 11. destitution,
requirement
want (of) ...
appetite .. 6. asitia
desire .. 11. inappetence
lacking .. 4. sans 5. out of 7. empty
of, scant of, short of 8. bereft of
10. deprived of
power .. 5. atony
sense (good) .. 5. folly
wanting ... 4. void 5. minus, needy
6. absent, bereft, devoid 7. lacking,
missing, short of, without
9. deficient, destitute, imperfect
wanting (pert to) ...
be found .. 9. fall short 10. be inferior
confidence .. 11. distrustful
in energy .. 6. atonic
in firmness .. 7. flaccid
in intelligence .. 12. feebleminded
wanton ... 3. gay 4. lewd 5. merry
6. frisky, harlot, unruly 7. immoral,
lustful, wayward 8. flagrant, insolent,
sportive, unchaste 9. dissolute,
merciless 10. capricious, frolicsome,
licentious 11. extravagant
13. undisciplined
wapiti ... 3. elk 4. deer, stag
war ... 5. fight 6. attack, battle
8. conflict
war (pert to) ...
agreement .. 6. cartel
cause of .. 10. casus belli
club .. 4. mace
fleet .. 6. armada
gas .. 8. adamsite
German .. 5. krieg 10. blitzkrieg
god .. 3. Ira, Tyr 4. Ares
goddess .. 5. Bella 6. Ishtar
hating .. 13. misopolemical
hawk .. 5. jingo 7. bailiff
horse .. 5. steed 7. charger
8. partisan 10. campaigner, politician
of words .. 9. logomachy
religious .. 5. jihad (jehad)
vessel, ship .. 3. sub 7. cruiser, frigate
8. corvette (corvet) 9. destroyer,

submarine 11. dreadnought
(dreadnaught)
war bird ... 7. aviator, tanager (scarlet)
warble ... 4. sing 5. carol, trill, yodel
6. quaver 7. twitter, vibrate
warbler ... 4. wren 6. singer
8. blackcap, grosbeak, redstart,
songster 9. beccafico 10. bluethroat
11. whitethroat
ward ... 4. jail, part, rule 5. watch
6. govern, prison 7. custody, keeping
8. district, garrison, guardian,
watchman 9. dependent
10. stronghold 12. guardianship
ward (pert to) ...
division .. 4. army, jail 6. forest
8. hospital
French .. 14. arrondissement
heeler .. 8. henchman 10. politician
off .. 4. fend 5. fence, parry, repel,
stave 7. expiate, forfend, prevent
warden ... 5. guard, nazir 6. dizdar
(disdar), jailer, keeper, ranger, sexton
7. alcaide (alcaid), turnkey
8. director, guardian, official,
watchman 9. concierge, custodian
10. gatekeeper
warder ... 6. warden 7. turnkey
wardrobe ... 4. room 6. closet
7. almirah, apparel, cabinet, clothes
8. costumes 12. clothespress
ware ... 4. sage, wary, wise 5. aware,
china, goods, spend 6. shrewd
7. careful, heedful, pottery, prudent,
seaweed 8. cautious, vigilant
9. cognizant, commodity, conscious,
porcelain 11. commodities,
earthenware, merchandise
warehouse ... 4. silo 5. depot, étape
6. fonduk (fondouk), godown
7. storage 8. entrepôt
warfare ... 7. contest 8. conflict,
struggle 11. hostilities 12. armed
contest
wariness ... 7. stealth 8. distrust
9. chariness, suspicion
warlock ... 6. wizard 7. monster (Myth)
8. conjuror, magician, sorcerer
warm ... 3. red 4. heat, keen, mild
5. angry, calid, eager, humid,
muggy, tepid, toast 6. ardent, excite,
genial, hearty, heated, torrid
7. clement, cordial, fervent
8. friendly, generous 10. responsive
11. sympathetic 12. affectionate,
enthusiastic 13. near discovery, near
the object (see also *hot*)
warm (pert to) ...
bath .. 5. therm
growing .. 9. calescent
hearted .. 4. kind 6. hearty, kindly,
tender 7. cordial 8. friendly,
generous 11. sympathetic
12. affectionate
pert to .. 7. thermal
praise .. 8. encomium
room .. 10. tepidarium
springs (Rom) .. 7. thermae
warmblooded ... 6. ardent 9. irascible
13. homoiothermic, quick–tempered
14. haematothermal (hematothermal)
warmed over ... 5. stale, trite

8. rehashed, reheated 9. rechauffé, twice–told

warmth ... 4. élan, glow, heat, zeal 5. ardor 7. ardency, thermal 8. fervency 9. animation, eloquency, geniality, vehemence 10. enthusiasm, excitement 11. calefaction, earnestness

warn ... 4. flag 5. alarm, alert 6. advise, exhort, inform, notify, remind, signal 7. apprise (apprize), caution, counsel, previse 8. admonish, forebode, threaten 9. reprehend

warning ... 4. bell, omen 5. alarm, alert, radar, siren 6. alarum, beacon, beware, caveat, signal, threat, tocsin 7. blinker, sematic, summons 10. admonition, admonitive 12. caveat emptor

warp ... 4. bend, bias, hurl, sway, turn, woof 5. fling, throw, twist, weave 6. buckle, swerve 7. contort, deflect, distort, pervert 7. fabricate 10. aberration, distortion 12. misinterpret

warp (pert to) ...
cross threads .. 4. woof
threads .. 5. lease 6. stamen
yarn .. 3. abb

warragal, warrigal ... 5. dingo, horse, myall

warrant ... 4. earn, writ 5. order 6. attest, ensure, permit, secure 7. defense, justify, precept, promise, voucher 8. document, guaranty, sanction, security 9. authorize, guarantee, safeguard 10. credential, instrument, protection 11. acknowledge, certificate 13. authorization

warranty ... 4. writ 5. proof 7. promise, warrant 8. guaranty, sanction, security 13. authorization

warrior ... 4. hero, impi 5. brave 6. Amazon 7. fighter, martial, soldier 10. halberdier

warrior (pert to) ...
Bib .. 4. Ehud
female .. 6. Amazon
Indian .. 6. sannup
Roman .. 9. gladiator
Trojan .. 6. Agenor, Hector
Zulu .. 4. impi 7. Kaffirs

Warsaw (pert to) ...
capital .. 6. Poland
river .. 7. Vistula
suburb .. 5. Praga

wary ... 3. shy 5. alert, canny, chary, leery 6. careful, guarded, prudent 8. cautious, discreet, watchful 10. economical 11. circumspect

wash ... 3. lap, pan 4. lave 5. bathe, clean, elute, flush, leach, marsh, paint, purge, rinse, slosh, swash 6. debris, drench, dry bed (river), purify, splash 7. cleanse, immerse, launder, overlay, shampoo 8. ablution 9. lixiviate

wash (pert to) ...
basin .. 4. bowl 6. lavabo
bear .. 7. raccoon

dish .. 11. pied wagtail
for gold .. 3. pan
one's hands of .. 6. give up, refuse 10. relinquish
out .. 4. fade 5. elute, flunk 7. failure, freshet
sale (finance) .. 10. fictitious

washing ... 7. coating 8. ablution 9. drenching

Washington, DC (famed sites) ... 7. Capitol (Bldg), The Mall 8. Pentagon, Treasury 10. Blair House, White House 11. Mount Vernon 12. Ford's Theater (Lincoln Museum), Supreme Court 14. cherry blossoms 15. Iwo Jima Monument, Lincoln Memorial 16. National Archives, Naval Observatory 17. Jefferson Memorial, Library of Congress 18. Walter Reed Hospital, Washington Monument 19. Unknown Soldier's Tomb 22. Smithsonian Institution 25. Arlington National Cemetery

Washington (State of) ...
capital .. 7. Olympia
city .. 6. Tacoma, Yakima 7. Everett, Seattle, Spokane 10. Bellingham, Walla Walla
dam .. 10. Bonneville 11. Grand Coulee
discoverer .. 4. Gray 9. Vancouver
explorer .. 5. Clark, Lewis 6. Wilkes 7. Fremont
Falls .. 10. Snoqualmie
Fort .. 5. Lewis
lake .. 5. Union 6. Chelan 8. Crescent
mountain .. 7. Rainier 8. Cascades, Olympics
river .. 5. Snake, White 7. Spokane 8. Columbia
Sound .. 5. Puget 7. Rosario
State admission .. 11. Forty–second
State motto .. 4. Al–Ki (By and By)
State nickname .. 9. Evergreen
wind (SW) .. 7. chinook

wasp ... 5. Sphex, vespa, whamp 6. dauber, hornet, Tiphia, vespid 8. Vespidae 12. Hymenopteron, yellow jacket

waspish ... 4. mean 5. cross, testy 6. cranky 7. bearish, peevish, slender 8. choleric, churlish, petulant, snappish, spiteful 9. fractious, irascible, irritable 12. cantankerous

wasp's nest ... 8. vespiary

wassail ... 4. lark, orgy, romp 5. toast 6. frolic, shindy 7. carouse 8. beverage, carousal 9. festivity 10. salutation 11. celebration 12. drinking bout

waste ... 3. eat 4. idle, junk, loss, rind, ross, sack, slag, vain, wear, wild 5. chaff, chips, dross, havoc, spill, trash 6. barren, desert, expend, lavish, ravage, refuse 7. atrophy, exhaust, fritter, rubbish 8. clinkers, demolish, desolate, squander 9. dissipate 10. desolation, diminution 11. destruction, devastation, dissipation, prodigality, uninhabited 12. uncultivated,

unproductive 13. unserviceable
waste (pert to)...
allowance.. 4. tret
away.. 3. age 6. shrink, sicken
  7. decline 8. marasmus
  11. deteriorate
lay waste.. 4. sack 6. ravage
  7. destroy 8. decimate
matter.. 3. ort 4. slag 5. dross
  7. clinker
mine.. 3. gob
silk.. 4. knob, noil 6. frison
time.. 4. idle, lazy 5. dally 6. daddle,
  footle, loiter 10. dillydally
wasted... 7. haggard 8. phthisic
wasteful... 6. lavish 10. thriftless
  11. extravagant, improvident
wasteland... 5. heath, marsh, swamp
  6. desert, morass 8. badlands
  10. barren land, everglades
wasting... 5. aging 6. awaste
  8. marasmic 10. enfeebling
  11. consumption, devastating
  13. deteriorating
wastrel... 4. waif 5. idler 8. vagabond
  10. profligate 11. spendthrift
watch... 3. eye, spy 4. espy, heed,
  mark, mind, tend, time, wake
  (funeral) 5. guard, vigil 6. ambush,
  patrol, police, sentry 7. bivouac,
  lookout, observe 8. horologe, sentinel
  9. ambuscade, timepiece, vigilance
  11. chronometer, observation,
  wakefulness
watch (pert to)...
chain.. 3. fob 6. Albert
face.. 5. bezel
maker.. 10. horologist
military.. 5. perdu (perdue) 6. sentry
  7. vedette
stop.. 5. timer
tower.. 6. beacon 7. atalaya, mirador
  10. lighthouse
word.. 6. signal 10. shibboleth (Bib)
  11. countersign
works.. 10. escapement
watchful... 3. Ira (Heb) 4. wary
  5. alert, aware 7. careful, heedful
  8. cautious, open—eyed, vigilant
  9. observant, regardful
  11. circumspect
watchman... 5. guard 6. sentry,
  warder 8. sentinel, watchdog
  10. gatekeeper
watchword... 4. hint, word 6. signal
  8. party cry 10. intimation,
  shibboleth (Bib) 11. countersign
watchworks... 10. escapement
water... 3. eau, ice, wet 4. aqua, rain
  5. fluid, flume, spray 6. dilute,
  lagoon, liquid 7. moisten
  8. beverage, calendar, irrigate,
  sprinkle 10. adulterate
water (pert to)...
baptismal.. 5. laver
bath.. 7. balneum
bird.. 4. coot, loon 5. diver, ouzel
  6. dipper 7. pintail, swimmer
  9. merganser
bottle.. 4. olla 6. carafe
buffalo.. 2. ox 7. carabao
channel.. 5. canal, flume 6. strait

8. tailrace
chart.. 10. hydrograph
color (art).. 9. aquarelle
comb form.. 5. hydro 6. hydato
congealed.. 3. ice 4. snow 5. glacé
  6. icicle
course.. 4. clow 5. bayou, gorge,
  gully 6. nullah, ravine, sluice
  9. watergate
cow.. 6. sea cow 7. buffalo, manatee
cure.. 10. hydropathy
  12. hydrotherapy
deer.. 10. chevrotain
destitute of.. 9. anhydrous
divination by.. 10. hydromancy
eagle.. 6. osprey
element.. 6. oxygen 8. hydrogen
elephant.. 12. hippopotamus
exhibition.. 8. aquacade
fowl.. 7. pelican
gauge (rain).. 8. udometer
goddess.. 4. Nina 7. Anahita, Anaitis
hare.. 11. swamp rabbit
heater.. 4. etna
history.. 10. hydrognosy
hog.. 8. capybara
hole.. 5. oasis 6. tinaja 7. alberca
jug.. 4. lota (lotah), olla 5. banga
  6. hydria, kalpis
lava.. 12. hellgrammite
lily.. 5. lotus 6. Nuphar 7. Nelumbo
  8. Nymphaea, Victoria
  11. spatterdock
measure.. 10. hydrometer
meter.. 7. Venturi
mineral.. 5. Vichy 6. Shasta
  7. Seltzer
monster.. 6. nicker (fabled)
nymph.. 5. naiad 6. undine
  7. Oceanid
of oblivion.. 5. Lethe 12. river of
  Hades
opossum.. 5. yapok (yapock)
pert to.. 7. aqueous 8. hydatoid
plug.. 3. tap 4. cock, cork 6. faucet,
  spigot 7. hydrant
pocket.. 6. tinaja
rat.. 4. vole 8. vagabond
reddish (with iron).. 6. riddam
reservoir (underground).. 6. cenote
rough.. 4. eddy 5. ocean 6. rapids
  7. riptide 8. undertow
sapphire.. 6. iolite 10. saphir d'eau
scorpion.. 4. Nepa 7. Ranatra
search for.. 5. dowse
sheet of.. 5. nappe
spirit.. 3. Nix 5. Ariel, Nixie 6. kelpie,
  nicker, sprite
spout.. 5. spate 8. gargoyle
sprite.. 3. Nix 5. Nixie
stratum.. 7. aquifer
study, science of.. 9. hydrology
  11. hydrography
surface.. 4. ryme
swelling.. 5. edema
turkey.. 9. snakebird
vessel.. 3. jug 4. ewer, lota (lotah),
  pail 5. cruse, flask 6. bottle, bucket,
  tinaja 7. pitcher, stamnos
  8. decanter
wheel.. 5. noria 6. sakieh (sakiyeh)
  7. turbine 8. tympanum

without .. **9.** anhydrous
watery ... **8.** ichorous
Watling Street (London) ... **6.** Galaxy
　8. Milky Way **9.** Roman road
wattle ... **3.** rod **4.** beat, flog, plat,
　wand **5.** fence, twist, weave, withe
　6. barbel, dewlap, hurdle, lappet
　8. caruncle **9.** boobyalla, loose flap
　10. intertwine, interweave **11.** skin
　process **12.** native willow
wattlebird ... **4.** crow **10.** honey eater
　11. brush turkey
Wattle Day ... **7.** holiday
wave ... **3.** ola, sea, wag **4.** flap, tide
　5. crest, eagre, flood, ridge, surge,
　swell, tilde **6.** beckon, billow,
　comber, flaunt, hairdo, marcel, ripple,
　roller, signal **7.** breaker, decuman,
　flutter, tsunami, vibrate **8.** brandish,
　coiffure, flourish, greeting, undulate
　9. fluctuate, vibration **10.** undulation
waver ... **4.** reel, sway, veer **5.** demur,
　quake **6.** falter, quiver, totter
　7. flicker, flutter, stagger, tremble,
　vibrate **8.** hesitate **9.** fluctuate,
　oscillate, vacillate **12.** be indecisive
wavering ... **6.** fickle **8.** doubtful,
　unsteady **9.** desultory **10.** irresolute
wavy ... **4.** onde, undé (undee)
　5. curly, snaky **6.** repand, undate
　7. billowy, rolling, sinuous
　8. undulant **9.** undulated
　10. undulatory
wax ... **4.** cere, grow **6.** candle, cerate,
　polish **7.** beeswax, cerumen
　8. increase, paraffin **9.** lubricant,
　lubricate **12.** zietrisikite (mineral)
wax (pert to) ...
beeswax cells .. **9.** honeycomb
beeswax substitute .. **7.** ceresin
candle .. **6.** cierge
chemical .. **9.** adipocere
Chinese .. **8.** pela
molded in .. **7.** fictile **9.** ceroplast
ref to .. **5.** ceral
substance .. **5.** cerin
way ... **3.** via **4.** lane, mode, path,
　plan, ramp, road **5.** alley, habit,
　means, Milky, route, track **6.** avenue,
　course, manner, method, street
　7. highway, passage **8.** causeway,
　distance, sidewalk **9.** banquette,
　direction, procedure
way (pert to) ...
astronomy .. **6.** Galaxy **8.** Milky Way
give .. **5.** break, yield **6.** weaken
　7. despair **10.** depreciate
god of .. **6.** Hermes
in .. **7.** ingress **8.** entrance
in a way .. **8.** as it were, somewhat
　13. theoretically
inclined .. **4.** ramp
out .. **4.** exit **6.** egress, escape
roundabout .. **6.** detour
waylay ... **3.** rob **5.** await, seize
　6. ambush, lay for **8.** surprise
　9. ambuscade
wayward ... **6.** unruly **7.** erratic, willful
　8. perverse, stubborn, untoward
　10. capricious, headstrong, refractory
　11. disobedient, intractable
weak ... **3.** dim, lax, wan **4.** pale,

puny, thin, worn **5.** faint, frail, washy
　6. dotish, feeble, infirm, sickly,
　simple, unwise, watery **7.** flaccid,
　foolish, fragile, insipid **8.** cowardly,
　decrepit, fatigued, impotent, wavering
　9. enfeebled, exhausted, nerveless,
　powerless **10.** effeminate
　11. debilitated, ineffective
　12. unconvincing
weak (pert to) ...
fish .. **7.** totuava **9.** gray trout
　10. squeteague
hearted .. **6.** afraid **7.** fearful
　12. fainthearted
kneed .. **8.** cowardly, yielding
　10. irresolute
sister .. **6.** coward **8.** weakling
　11. mollycoddle
weaken ... **3.** sap **4.** tire **5.** break
　6. dilute, impair, lessen, reduce
　7. cripple, disable, exhaust, unnerve
　8. enervate **9.** undermine
　10. debilitate
weakness ... **4.** flaw **5.** atony, fault
　6. defect, foible, liking **7.** failing,
　fatigue, frailty **8.** asthenia, debility
　9. cowardice, impotence, infirmity
　10. feebleness, infirmness
　11. decrepitude **12.** imperfection
　13. powerlessness
weal ... **4.** mark, wale, welt **5.** ridge,
　wheal **6.** riches, wealth **7.** welfare
　9. happiness, well–being
　10. commonweal
wealth ... **4.** good, weal **5.** money
　6. assets, mammon, riches
　7. capital, fortune, welfare
　8. opulence, property, treasure
　9. abundance, affluence, well–being
　10. prosperity **11.** possessions
wealth (pert to) ...
god of .. **6.** Plutus
person of .. **6.** monied **7.** magnate,
　opulent **9.** plutocrat
pursuit of .. **10.** plutomania
study of .. **9.** economics, plutology
worship of .. **10.** plutolatry
wealthy ... **4.** rich **5.** ample
　8. abundant, affluent
wealthy (pert to) ...
English slang .. **4.** oofy
man .. **5.** nabob **10.** capitalist
rule by .. **10.** plutocracy
wean ... **6.** detach **8.** alienate, estrange
　9. reconcile
weapon ... **3.** arm, gat, gun **4.** bola,
　bolo, celt, club, dart, epee, snee
　5. arrow, knife, lance, rifle, saber
　(sabre), spear, sword **6.** dagger,
　musket, pistol, poleax (poleaxe),
　rapier **7.** bayonet, bazooka, carbine,
　gisarme, halberd, machete, trident
　8. battle–ax (battle–axe), catapult,
　crossbow, revolver, stiletto, tomahawk
　9. derringer, Excalibur
　11. blunderbuss
wear ... **3.** use **4.** bear, fray, fret, show
　5. chafe, weary **7.** fatigue
　12. disintegrate
wear (pert to) ...
away .. **3.** eat, end **5.** erode
　6. abrade **7.** corrode, decline

down.. **4.** tire **8.** persuade
9. influence
out.. **4.** tire **5.** waste **7.** fatigue
weariness... **5.** ennui **6.** tedium
7. boredom, fatigue **9.** lassitude
wearisome... **4.** hard **6.** boring,
dismal, dreary, tiring **7.** irksome,
tedious **8.** tiresome, toilsome
9. fatiguing, laborious, vexatious
10. monotonous
weary... **3.** fag, irk, sad **4.** bore, jade,
pall, tire, weak **5.** bored, spent, tired
6. plague **7.** fatigue, languid
9. forjesket
weasel... **4.** stot, vare **5.** ratel, stoat
6. ermine, ferret
weasellike... **4.** mink **5.** otter, tayra
9. musteline, musteloid
weather (pert to)...
cock.. **4.** vane
glass.. **9.** barometer, baroscope
man.. **13.** meteorologist
map.. **6.** isobar
weave... **3.** mat **4.** knit, lace, reel,
spin, sway **5.** plait, unite **6.** devise,
wattle **7.** canelle, entwine, fashion
8. contrive **9.** fabricate, interlace,
interwind **10.** intertwine, intertwist
11. push one's way
weaver bird... **4.** baya, maya, taha
5. Munia
weaving (pert to)...
art of.. **4.** loom
fabric (rich).. **3.** web **7.** brocade,
webbing
French.. **5.** lisse **8.** Jacquard
material.. **5.** reeds, twigs **6.** raffia
term.. **4.** beam, dent, loom, sley
7. shuttle
together.. **7.** plexure
weazen (wizen)... **6.** shrink, wither
7. shrivel
web... **3.** net, ply **4.** caul, tela, trap,
veil, warp **5.** snare **6.** tissue
7. network, texture **8.** filament,
gossamer, membrane, vexillum
12. entanglement
web (pert to)...
footed.. **7.** palmate
like.. **4.** lacy **5.** telar **7.** spidery
spinning.. **6.** telary **7.** retiary
term.. **5.** telar
toed.. **11.** totipalmate
winged.. **3.** bat
work.. **4.** maze, mesh **6.** tangle
11. Gordian knot
wed... **4.** join, mate **5.** marry, mated,
unite **6.** joined **7.** espouse, pledged,
spliced **13.** give in wedlock
wedding... **8.** ceremony, espousal,
marriage, nuptials
wedding (anniversary)...
1st.. **5.** paper
2nd.. **5.** straw
3rd.. **5.** candy
4th.. **7.** leather
5th.. **6.** wooden
7th.. **6.** floral
10th.. **3.** tin
12th.. **5.** linen
13th.. **4.** lace
15th.. **7.** crystal

20th.. **5.** china
25th.. **6.** silver
30th.. **5.** pearl
35th.. **5.** coral
40th.. **7.** emerald
45th.. **4.** ruby
50th.. **6.** golden
75th.. **7.** diamond
wedding (pert to)...
flower.. **13.** orange blossom
proclamation.. **5.** banns (bans)
snow.. **4.** rice
term.. **7.** marital, wedlock
8. marriage, nuptials **9.** matrimony
11. espousement
wedge... **3.** jam **4.** club, shoe
5. cleat, ingot, split **6.** sector,
wedgie **7.** niblick **8.** triangle, voussoir
9. machinery
wedge–shaped... **7.** cuneate
9. cuneiform (cuniform)
Wednesday... **5.** Woden (wise god)
9. fourth day, Woden's Day
wee... **3.** bit **4.** dock, fine, tiny
5. small, teeny **6.** little, minute
10. diminutive, teeny–weeny
weed... **3.** bur (burr), hoe, rag **4.** loco,
milk, sida, tare **5.** cigar, flesh, vetch
6. darnel, excise, Jimson, knawel,
spurge, tumble **7.** allseed, mallows,
mustard, ragweed, tobacco
8. plantain, purslane, toadflax
9. cultivate, dandelion
11. undergrowth
weeds... **8.** garments (mourning)
week... **8.** hebdomad **9.** seven days
week (pert to)...
day.. **6.** ferial
Eccl.. **4.** Holy **7.** Passion
of Sundays.. **5.** seven **8.** hebdomad
of years.. **5.** seven
past.. **10.** yesterweek
weekly... **5.** aweek **10.** hebdomadal,
periodical **11.** publication
weeks, two... **9.** fortnight
weel... **4.** pool, trap **6.** basket **8.** fish
trap
ween... **5.** think **6.** expect **7.** believe,
imagine, suppose **8.** conceive
weep... **3.** cry, orp, sob **4.** drip, rain,
wail **5.** exude, mourn **7.** blubber,
lapwing **9.** percolate, shed tears
weeping... **6.** crying **7.** sobbing
9. festering
weeping (pert to)...
monkey.. **8.** capuchin
queen.. **5.** Niobe
tree.. **5.** cedar **6.** spruce, willow
Weeping Philosopher (anc)...
10. Heraclitus
weevil (pert to)...
cotton.. **4.** boll
malt.. **4.** boud
snout.. **8.** curculio
type (other).. **3.** pea **4.** palm, pine,
rice, seed **5.** flour
weigh... **4.** tare, test **5.** hoist, poise,
scale **6.** ponder, regard **7.** balance,
be heavy, compare, measure
8. consider, encumber, estimate,
ruminate **9.** apportion, press hard
weigh down... **4.** lade, load

6. burden, hamper 7. ballast,
depress, oppress 11. overbalance
weight... 4. load, mass 5. force,
power 6. burden, import, moment
7. gravity, tonnage 8. encumber,
pressure 9. authority, heaviness,
influence 10. importance
11. consequence 12. significance
weight (pert to)...
allowance.. 4. tare, tret 7. scalage
comb form.. 4. baro
gem.. 5. carat (karat)
light.. 6. suttle
system.. 3. net 4. troy 6. metric
10. apothecary 11. avoirdupois
total.. 5. gross
weighty... 3. fat 5. bulky, heavy, hefty,
large, obese 6. solemn 7. massive,
onerous, serious 8. forcible, powerful
9. corpulent, important, momentous,
ponderous 10. burdensome,
cumbersome, impressive, oppressive
11. influential 13. authoritative
weir... 3. dam, net 4. bank 5. fence,
levee, seine 7. barrier, milldam
9. floodgate
weird... 3. odd 4. omen, wild 5. eerie
(eery), queer, scary 6. creepy, spooky
7. awesome, curious, ghostly,
macabre, strange, uncanny 8. eldritch
9. deathlike, frightful 10. mysterious,
prediction
Weird Sisters (Scot)... 5. Fates
welcome... 4. hail 5. adopt, greet
7. acclaim, accueil 8. grateful,
greeting, pleasing 9. agreeable,
bienvenue, desirable 10. acceptable,
salutation
weld... 5. unite 11. consolidate
welfare... 4. good, weal 5. Salus
(goddess) 9. good cheer
10. prosperity 14. material plenty
welkin... 3. air, sky 6. heaven
10. atmosphere
well... 3. fit, gay, pit 4. gush, hale,
pool 5. aweel, fount, fully 6. easily,
gusher, hearty, justly, kindly, source
7. cistern, closely 8. artesian,
expertly, fountain, friendly 10. full
degree, intimately 11. excellently
12. satisfactory
well (pert to)...
being.. 4. weal 7. comfort 8. eucrasia
9. happiness
Bib.. 4. Esek
born.. 5. noble 7. eugenic
bred.. 6. polite 7. genteel, refined
8. cultured, wellborn 9. pedigreed
10. cultivated 11. gentlemanly
12. thoroughbred
comb form.. 4. mene
defined.. 8. distinct 11. distinctive
groomed.. 4. neat 5. sleek 6. soigné
(soignée)
grounded.. 5. valid 7. logical
9. plausible 11. established,
substantial 12. well–informed
gushing.. 8. artesian
heeled.. 4. rich 5. armed
7. moneyed, wealthy, well–off
8. well–to–do
known.. 6. famous 7. eminent

12. acknowledged
land drain.. 4. sump
lining.. 5. steen
off.. 5. lucky 10. prosperous
oil.. 6. gusher
pole.. 5. sweep
prefix.. 2. eu
timed.. 6. timely 9. opportune
versed.. 7. erudite
watered.. 9. irrigated, irriguous
welsh (welch)... 5. cheat 6. not pay,
renege 7. swindle 10. shirk out of
Welsh (pert to)... see also *Wales*
boat.. 7. coracle
congress of literati.. 10. eisteddfod
fine, for murder.. 7. galanas
god, underworld.. 4. Bran
instrument (reed).. 7. pibcorn
man.. 5. Taffy 8. Cambrian
onion.. 5. cibal
population.. 6. Cymric
rabbit.. 7. ramekin (ramequin), rarebit
romance collection.. 10. Mabinogion
(Mabinogi)
welt... 4. mark, wale 5. ridge
6. stripe, thrash
welter... 4. reel, roll, sail, toss
6. grovel, tumble, wallow 7. stagger
8. flounder, overturn 9. confusion
wen... 4. cyst, rune 5. tumor
7. blemish 11. excrescence
12. protuberance
wench... 4. doxy, gill, girl 5. child,
squaw, trull, woman 6. damsel,
maiden 7. consort, servant
8. strumpet 11. maidservant
wend... 2. go 4. fare, pass 6. depart,
direct, travel 7. circuit, proceed
8. progress
went (pert to)... see also *go*
astray.. 6. failed 10. miscarried
away.. 4. left 8. departed
before.. 3. led 8. preceded
9. anteceded
swiftly.. 3. ran 4. sped 6. darted
7. scooted, scudded 8. decamped
wenzel... 4. jack (card game) 5. knave
werewolf... 6. jaguar 8. uturuncu,
werefolk 11. lycanthrope
wergild... 3. cro 4. eric 7. galanas
9. Brehon Law
Wesleyan... 9. Methodist 14. Wesley
follower
West African (pert to)...
baboon.. 5. drill 8. mandrill
city.. 5. Accra, Dakar
gazelle.. 4. kudu, mohr (mhorr), oryx
lemur.. 5. potto 8. kinkajou
monkey.. 4. mona 6. guenon
native.. 7. Ashanti (Ashantee)
pepper.. 5. cubeb
tree.. 5. iroko, odoom
tribe.. 5. Igara
West End, London... 7. Mayfair
9. Belgravia 11. fashionable
12. aristocratic
Western... 9. Hesperian 10. Occidental
Westernmost US... 9. Aleutians
11. Attu Islands 12. Cape Wrangell
West Indies...
bird.. 4. tody 6. mucaro
boat.. 7. drogher (droger)

chief.. 7. cacique
clingfish.. 6. testar
crop.. 5. sugar 7. bananas
ebony.. 9. cocuswood
fish.. 4. cero, paru, sesi 6. testar
flea.. 6. chigoe
fruit.. 5. papaw (pawpaw)
islands.. 4. Cuba 5. Haiti 6. Cayman,
   Virgin 7. Antigua, Bahamas, Leeward
   8. Antilles, Windward
liquor.. 5. mobby (mobbie), tafia
   (taffia)
lizard.. 6. arbalo
magic.. 5. obeah
music.. 7. calypso
owl.. 6. mucaro
resident.. 9. Antillean
rodent.. 6. agouti (agouty)
snuff.. 8. Maccaboy
tea.. 8. goatweed
tortoise.. 7. hicatee
tree.. 4. ausu 5. ebony, papaw
   6. bonduc 8. bayberry 9. sapodilla,
   satinwood
volcano.. 5. Pelée
wood.. 9. cocuswood, sapodilla
   10. granadilla
Westminster clock (London)... 6. Big
Ben
West Pointer... 5. cadet, plebe
   8. yearling
West Point motto... 16. Duty, Honor,
   Country
West Virginia...
capital.. 10. Charleston
city.. 5. Logan 8. Wheeling
   11. Parkersburg
crop.. 4. coal
mountain.. 10. Spruce Knob
   11. Alleghenies
park (famed).. 12. Harpers Ferry
river.. 4. Ohio 7. Kanawha
   11. Monongahela
Springs (resort).. 8. Berkeley
   12. White Sulphur
State admission.. 11. Thirty–fifth
State motto.. 19. Montani Semper
   Liberi 22. Mountaineers Always Free
State nickname.. 8. Mountain
West wind... 8. Favonius, Zephyrus
wet... 4. asop, damp, dank, dewy, rain
   5. foggy, humid, leach, misty, moist,
   mushy, rainy, soggy, soppy
   6. dampen, drench, soaked, sodden,
   watery 7. moisten 8. sprinkle
wet blanket... 7. kill–joy 8. deadhead
   10. discourage, spoilsport
whale... 3. orc 4. cete, lash, whip
   5. whack 6. beluga, blower, thrash
   7. grampus, ripsack 8. hardhead
   9. zeuglodon 13. sulphur–bottom
whale (pert to)...
Arctic.. 7. narwhal
bird.. 4. gull 6. petrel 9. phalarope
blubber pot.. 6. try–pot
blue.. 9. Sibbaldus
bone.. 6. baleen
carcass.. 5. kreng
constellation.. 5. Cetus
fat.. 7. blubber
food.. 4. brit
gray.. 7. ripsack 8. hardhead

killer.. 4. orca
killer of.. 8. ceticide
legendary.. 9. Mysticeti
monster.. 4. Cete
mustache (legend).. 9. Mysticeti
Order.. 7. Cetacea
ref to.. 5. cetic, sperm 6. baleen
   7. blubber 8. cetacean
school of.. 3. gam, pod
secretion (perfume).. 9. ambergris
small.. 7. grampus
sperm type.. 8. cachalot
study of.. 8. cetology
toothed.. 10. odontocete, zeuglodont
type.. 3. orc 4. blue, orca 5. right,
   sperm 6. killer 7. dolphin, rorqual
   8. cachalot, humpback, porpoise
   9. whalebone
wax.. 10. spermaceti
whalebone.. 6. baleen 10. stiffening
young.. 4. calf 9. shorthead
wharf... 4. dock, pier, quay 5. jetty
   6. staith 7. landing
wharf (pert to)...
fish.. 6. cunner
master.. 10. wharfinger
worker.. 9. stevedore
whatnot... 5. thing 6. object
   (nondescript) 7. étagère
   10. miscellany
what's what... 4. fact 5. truth
   7. reality 10. what's right
what wonders has God wrought
   (Arabic exclamation)... 9. mashallah
whaup... 6. curlew, outcry
   9. scoundrel
wheal... 4. wale, weal, welt 5. whelk
   6. stripe 7. pustule
wheat (pert to)...
beard.. 3. awn
beverage.. 6. zythem
bird.. 4. lark 8. wheatear 9. chaffinch
chaff.. 4. bran
duck.. 7. widgeon 8. baldpate
Europe.. 5. emmer, spelt (speltz)
flour.. 4. atta 5. Hovis
hard.. 5. durum
India.. 4. suji 8. semolina
storage bin.. 4. silo 8. elevator
wheedle... 4. coax, gain 5. tease
   6. banter, cajole, entice 7. blarney,
   flatter 8. blandish, inveigle, persuade
   9. influence
wheel... 3. cam, cog 4. bike, disc,
   helm, ride, roll, rota 5. drive, pivot,
   rotor, rowel, whirl 6. caster, roller,
   rotate 7. bicycle, revolve, rotator,
   torture, vehicle 8. tricycle 10. water
   wheel
wheel (pert to)...
gem–grinding.. 5. skive
hub.. 4. nave
man.. 5. pilot 7. cyclist 8. helmsman,
   pedalist 9. bicyclist
monkey.. 3. gin
part.. 3. rim 5. felly (felloe), spoke
   6. hubcap
pulley.. 6. sheave
shaped.. 8. circular, rotiform
spoke.. 6. radius
spur.. 5. rowel
stopper.. 4. grig 5. sprag

swiveled .. **6.** caster
toothed .. **3.** cog **4.** gear **6.** pinion
turbine .. **5.** rotor
type .. **3.** cog, fly, pin **4.** cart, mill, spur **5.** wagon **6.** Ferris, paddle **7.** balance, potter's **9.** of fortune
water .. **5.** noria **6.** sakieh (sakiyeh)
wheels, logging ... **7.** katydid
wheen ... **3.** few **5.** group **7.** several **8.** division, quantity
wheerikins ... **10.** posteriors
wheetle ... **5.** chirp **7.** whistle
wheeze ... **3.** gag **4.** joke **5.** hoose (hooze) **6.** cliché, saying **7.** breathe **8.** sibilate **9.** witticism **10.** sibilation
whelk ... **4.** acne **5.** snail **6.** papule, pimple **7.** pustule
whelp ... **3.** boy, cub, pup **5.** child, puppy, tiger, youth **9.** give birth, youngling
when ... **2.** as **3.** tho **5.** until **6.** though **7.** how soon, whereas **8.** although, whenever **10.** how long ago **11.** at which time
where ... **4.** here, spot **5.** place, there **7.** whither **10.** inasmuch as **11.** at what place, whereabouts
whereas ... **5.** since
whereby ... **7.** perquod
whereness ... **6.** ubiety
whereupon ... **4.** when **7.** on which **9.** upon which **10.** after which
wherewithal ... **5.** means, money **9.** resources
whet ... **4.** hone **5.** grind, point, rouse **6.** excite **7.** quicken, sharpen **9.** intensify, stimulate
whether ... **2.** if **6.** either
whey ... **4.** curd **5.** serum
whiff ... **4.** blow, fish, gust, odor, puff, waft **6.** breath, exhale, stanch **7.** puff out **8.** blow away **10.** inhalation
while ... **2.** as **3.** yet **4.** time **5.** until **7.** beguile, interim, whereas **11.** space of time
whilom ... **4.** erst, once **5.** of old **6.** former **8.** sometime **9.** erstwhile
whim ... **3.** fad, pun, toy **4.** idea **5.** fancy, freak **6.** megrim, notion, vagary **7.** boutade, caprice, whimsey (whimsy), widgeon **8.** migraine
whimper ... **3.** cry, sob **4.** mewl, moan, pule, weep **5.** whine **7.** sniffle
whimsey, whimsy ... **3.** wit **4.** whim **5.** craze, fancy, freak **7.** caprice
whimsical ... **3.** fad, odd **4.** dish **5.** droll, queer, witty **7.** amusing **8.** fanciful, freakish, notional **9.** crotchety, eccentric, fantastic, grotesque **10.** capricious
whine ... **4.** moan, pule, wail **6.** snivel **7.** screech, ululate, whimper **8.** complain **12.** moaning sound
whinny ... **4.** bray **5.** neigh, whine
whip ... **3.** cat, tan **4.** beat, crop, flag, flog, goad, lace, lash, wale **5.** birch, froth, quirt, seize, spank, strap **6.** defeat, incite, punish, strike, swinge, thrash **7.** agitate, chabouk (chabuk), conquer, scourge **8.** emulsify, lambaste **9.** bullwhack

10. discipline **11.** congressman
whip (pert to) ...
hand .. **8.** dominion **9.** advantage, influence
mark .. **4.** wale, weal, welt
political .. **5.** party **11.** floor leader
riding .. **4.** crop **5.** quirt
Russian .. **4.** plet (plete) **5.** knout
sewing .. **8.** overcast
socket .. **5.** snead
whir ... **3.** fly **4.** burr, buzz, whiz **5.** hurry, swirl, whizz **6.** hurtle **7.** revolve, vibrate **9.** commotion
whirl ... **4.** eddy, reel, spin, tirl, turn **5.** twirl **6.** circle, gyrate, rotate **7.** revelry, revolve **9.** commotion, pirouette, turn about **10.** excitement
whirlpool ... **4.** eddy **6.** gurges (Her), vortex **7.** sea puss (sea purse) **9.** maelstrom
whirlwind ... **2.** oe (Faroes) **7.** cyclone, tornado, twister, typhoon **9.** hurricane, maelstrom **10.** willy–willy
whisk ... **4.** tuft, whip, wist **5.** froth, sweep, swish **6.** convey **7.** agitate
whiskers ... **4.** chin **5.** beard **8.** vibrissa **9.** sideburns
whisky, whiskey ... **3.** rye **4.** corn **6.** poteen, redeye **9.** moonshine **10.** usquebaugh
whisky (pert to) ...
base .. **3.** rye **5.** wheat **6.** barley
drink .. **4.** soda, sour **5.** punch, smash **7.** stinger
Insurrection .. **12.** Pennsylvania (1794)
Ring .. **10.** Conspiracy (1875)
term .. **6.** lively **7.** flighty
whisper ... **3.** tip **4.** blow, buzz **5.** rumor **6.** breeze, murmur **7.** divulge **14.** vox clandestina
whist, game ... **9.** Cavendish **10.** Yarborough
whistle ... **4.** hiss, pipe, sing, toot **5.** alarm **6.** rustle, warble, wheeze **12.** interference
whistle (pert to) ...
duck .. **9.** goldeneye
fish .. **8.** rockling
pig .. **9.** woodchuck
stop .. **12.** one–horse town
tree (for boys' whistles) .. **5.** maple **6.** willow
Whistler painting ... **15.** Little White Girl, Whistler's Mother
whistling (pert to) ...
coot .. **6.** scoter
dick .. **6.** thrush
duck .. **6.** scoter **9.** goldeneye
hawk .. **5.** eagle
snipe .. **8.** woodcock
sound .. **7.** stridor
teal .. **6.** scoter **8.** tree duck
whit ... **3.** bit, jot **4.** atom, iota **5.** bodle, speck **8.** particle
white ... **3.** wan **4.** milk, pale, snow **5.** ashen, chalk, color, happy, ivory, snowy **6.** albino, chalky, chaste, honest, pallid **7.** ivorine, silvery **8.** innocent, platinum **9.** alabaster, albescent, Caucasian, favorable, fortunate, honorable

11. snow–covered
white (pert to)...
admiral.. 9. butterfly
ant.. 4. anay (anai) 7. termite
belly.. 6. pigeon 7. widgeon
   14. prairie chicken
cat.. 7. catfish
cell.. 9. leucocyte
chub.. 10. spawneater
cloud.. 6. cirrus 7. tendril
coal.. 10. water power
crow.. 7. vulture
curlew.. 4. ibis
devil.. 7. nailrod
elephant.. 6. burden 8. Oriental
ensign.. 12. British naval
fish.. 5. cisco 6. atinga, beluga
   8. menhaden 9. Coregonus
   10. white whale
grouse.. 9. ptarmigan
growing (hoary).. 9. canescent
head.. 6. pigeon 9. blue goose
   10. surf scoter
heat.. 5. anger 13. incandescence
livered.. 6. feeble 8. cowardly
   13. pusillanimous
matter (nerve).. 4. alba
merganser.. 4. smew
miller.. 11. clothes moth
monk.. 10. Cistercian
mule.. 3. gin 6. whisky (illicit)
   9. moonshine
oak.. 5. roble
of egg.. 5. glair
partridge.. 9. ptarmigan
plague.. 7. disease 8. phthisis
   11. consumption 12. tuberculosis
plantain.. 8. pussytoe
poplar.. 5. aspen
pot.. 7. pudding
pudding.. 7. sausage 9. whitehass
pyrite.. 9. marcasite
shark.. 8. man–eater
throat.. 6. muffet (Eng) 7. warbler
whale.. 6. beluga
White (pert to)...
Chapel (Jewish).. 13. London Quarter
Holland.. 6. turkey
Horse.. 6. emblem (Saxons) 7. carving
House designer.. 5. Hoban
Relig.. 6. Friars 7. Fathers, Sisters
   8. Brethren
Rose (Eng).. 6. emblem (House of
   York)
Sands (N Mex).. 13. proving ground
Squadron.. 4. Navy (US Navy 1883)
Tower.. 13. Tower of London
whiten... 6. blanch, bleach 8. etiolate
   9. whitewash
whitewash... 5. paint 6. defeat,
   whiten 7. conceal 9. disinfect,
   exculpate, gloss over
whither... 5. where 7. whereto 11. to
   what place, whereabouts
whiting... 4. fish 5. chalk 6. tomcod
   10. butterfish
whitish... 4. pale 5. white
   9. albescent
whitlow... 4. herb, sore 5. felon
   6. agnail, fetlow 8. hangnail
   9. saxifrage 10. paronychia
   12. inflammation

Whitsunday... 9. Pentacost
Whittington, Dick... 9. Lord Mayor
(London)
whittle... 3. cut, hew 4. gash, hack,
   pare, trim 5. knife 6. reduce
   7. blanket
whiz, whizz... 3. hum 4. buzz, hiss,
   pirr, whir, zizz 5. whirr 6. corker,
   rotate 8. sibilate 10. speed along
   12. clever person
who... 3. wer, wha 5. which
   6. person 7. one that, pronoun
whole... 3. all, sum 4. pure, sole, unit
   5. gross, total, uncut, unity
   6. entire, intact, mostly, system
   7. healthy, perfect 8. absolute,
   complete, entirety, totality
   9. aggregate, generally, unanimous,
   undivided
whole (pert to)...
comb form.. 4. toti, toto
footed.. 5. frank 8. intimate
   9. ingenuous 10. flat–footed
hearted.. 7. devoted, earnest, sincere
   8. complete 10. unreserved
   11. unmitigated
hog.. 8. whole way 12. all or nothing
note.. 9. semibreve
number.. 7. integer
skinned.. 6. unhurt 9. unscathed
souled.. 5. noble 7. devoted, sincere,
   zealous 11. noble–minded
   12. wholehearted
wholesome... 4. sane 5. sound
   6. hearty, robust 7. healthy
   8. salutary, vigorous 9. favorable,
   healthful 10. beneficial, propitious,
   salubrious
wholly... 3. all 4. toto (comb form)
   5. fully, quite 6. solely 7. totally
   8. entirely, entirety 9. perfectly
   10. altogether, completely, thoroughly
   11. exclusively
whoop... 4. call, hoot, urge, yell
   5. cheer, shout 6. halloo, hoopee
   10. enthusiasm
whooping cough... 9. pertussis
whoop it up... 7. be noisy 8. energize
   9. make merry 12. create gaiety
whop... 4. bang, beat, bump, fall,
   flop, whip 5. knock 6. strike, stroke
whopper... 3. lie (monstrous) 5. story
(false)
whorl... 4. curl 5. helix, spire
   8. flywheel, verticil, volution (shell)
   11. fingerprint
wicked... 3. bad, ill 4. evil, vile
   6. guilty, sinful, unjust 7. heinous,
   hellish, profane, roguish, ungodly,
   vicious 8. criminal, depraved, devilish,
   diabolic, flagrant 9. abandoned,
   atrocious, malicious, nefarious,
   perverted 10. diabolical, flagitious,
   iniquitous, villainous 11. irreligious,
   mischievous, unrighteous
wickedness... 3. sin 4. evil 6. Belial
(Bib) 7. badness 8. baseness, iniquity
   10. sinfulness 13. maliciousness
wicked one... 5. Demon, Satan 7. Evil
One 8. The Devil
wicker (pert to)...
basket.. 5. cesta 6. hamper, kipsey

7. pannier
cradle.. 8. bassinet
material.. 5. twigs 6. osiers, willow,
   withes
ware.. 8. basketry, plaiting
wicket... 4. arch, door, gate, hoop
   6. grille, window 7. grating, guichet,
   lattice 8. loophole 12. grated
   window, ticket window
wickiup, wikiup... 3. hut 7. shelter
Widal's, Widal reaction... 16. typhoid
   fever test
widbin... 7. dogwood 8. woodbine
   11. honeysuckle
widdy... 4. rope (twig) 5. noose,
   widow, withy 6. halter 7. gallows
   11. gallows bird
wide... 5. ample, broad, large, loose,
   roomy 6. opened 7. liberal
   8. expanded, spacious 9. capacious,
   distended 13. comprehensive
wide–awake... 3. hat 4. keen, tern
   (sooty) 5. alert 7. knowing
   8. watchful
widemouthed... 4. loud 5. noisy
   6. greedy 7. barking 9. devouring
widen... 4. ream 6. dilate, expand,
   extend, spread 7. amplify, broaden,
   enlarge
widespread... 4. rife 5. broad
   7. diffuse, general 8. not local,
   sweeping 9. dispersed, extensive,
   prevalent, scattered, universal
   13. comprehensive
widgeon... 4. duck, smee 5. goose
   6. Mareca, zuisin 7. poacher
   8. baldpate 9. simpleton
widow... 6. relict 7. bereave, dowager,
   viduate
widow (pert to)...
bird.. 5. finch, Vidua 6. whidah
cremated.. 6. suttee
fish.. 5. viuva
monkey.. 4. titi
suicide.. 6. suttee
widower... 6. relict
widow's (pert to)...
lock.. 8. hairline 10. widow's peak
mite.. 4. coin 6. lepton
portion.. 5. dower
right.. 5. terce
weeds.. 8. mourning 9. black veil,
   widowhood
width... 5. girth 7. breadth
   8. diameter, latitude, wideness
wield... 3. ply, use 4. cope, deal, rule
   5. power, swing 6. direct, employ,
   handle, manage 7. control
   8. brandish 10. manipulate
wife... 4. frau, mate, rani, uxor
   5. bride, mujer 6. matron, spouse
   7. consort 8. gudewife (guidwife),
   helpmate, helpmeet 10. better half
   12. married woman
wife (pert to)...
French.. 5. femme
killing.. 9. uxoricide
of a rajah.. 4. Rani (Ranee)
one.. 8. monogamy
pert to.. 7. uxorial
slave's.. 9. broadwife
wig... 4. tête 5. jasey 6. peruke,

toupee 7. censure, periwig 8. seal
   hood 9. dignitary
wight... 3. man 4. loud 5. brave,
   fairy, swift, witch 6. active, nimble
   7. valiant 8. creature, powerful
   11. living being
wigwag... 6. signal 8. to and fro
   11. oscillation
wigwam... 4. tent 5. hogan, tepee
   6. teepee
wild... 3. mad 5. feral, myall, waste,
   weird 6. ferine, savage, stormy,
   unruly 7. bestial, howling, riotous
   8. aberrant, desolate, dramatic,
   frenetic, reckless, untilled, wildwood
   9. barbarian, barbarous, ferocious,
   imprudent, primitive, unbridled,
   uncertain 10. boisterous, chimerical,
   irrational, profligate, tumultuous,
   unexplored, wilderness
   11. harum–scarum, uncivilized,
   uninhabited 12. obstreperous,
   uncontrolled, uncultivated
   14. uncontrollable
wild (pert to)...
alder.. 8. goutweed
animal.. 3. gnu 4. bear, deer, lion,
   lynx 5. kiang, moose, tiger
   6. dragon, onager 7. polecat
   8. antelope 10. wildebeest
banana.. 5. papaw (pawpaw)
beasts.. 4. ziim
buffalo.. 4. arna 5. arnee
carrot.. 8. hilltrot
cat.. 4. balm, eyra 6. ocelot
   7. panther
coffee.. 9. feverroot
crocus.. 12. pasqueflower
fancy.. 6. vagary
fowl.. 4. duck 5. goose, quail
   8. pheasant 9. partridge
garlic.. 4. moly
goat.. 3. tur 4. tahr 7. markhor
   (markhoor)
gourd.. 7. pumpkin 11. calabazilla
growing.. 8. agrarian
hog.. 4. boar 9. razorback
   10. babiroussa
hop.. 6. bryony
horse.. 6. tarpan
ibex.. 5. Capra
Irishman (shrub).. 10. tumatakuru
jalap.. 8. mayapple
mustard.. 8. charlock
ox.. 3. yak 4. anoa
pieplant.. 7. rhubarb
pineapple.. 7. pinguin
plum.. 4. sloe 5. islay
sheep.. 3. sha 5. urial (oorial)
   6. argali
sweet potato.. 7. manroot
West show.. 5. rodeo
wildebeest... 3. gnu
wilderness... 5. waste, wilds 6. forest
   8. wildwood 9. confusion
   12. complication
wile... 3. art, toy 4. lure, ruse
   5. fraud, guile, trick 6. deceit
   7. cunning 8. artifice, trickery
   9. stratagem
will... 4. wish 6. behest, choice,
   decree, demise, desire 7. bequest,

command 8. volition 9. intention,
testament 10. resolution
11. disposition, inclination
13. determination
will (pert to)...
appendix.. 7. codicil
convey.. 6. demise 7. bequest
having made.. 7. testate
maker of.. 8. testator
power.. 7. purpose 10. resolution
13. determination 14. strength of
mind
proof of.. 7. probate
to live (Buddh).. 5. tanha
willful, wilful... 3. mad 4. rash
5. heady 7. wayward 8. perverse,
stubborn 9. impetuous, obstinate,
voluntary 11. intentional
14. self–determined
willing... 4. free 5. prone, ready
6. minded 8. desirous, disposed,
unforced 9. agreeable, voluntary
10. consenting, deliberate, ready to
act, volitional 11. intentional
12. well–disposed
willingly... 4. fain, lief 6. freely, gladly
7. happily, readily 10. cheerfully
12. with pleasure
willow... 3. iva 4. Itea 5. osier, salix
6. sallow, teaser
willow (pert to)...
basket.. 7. prickle
genus.. 5. Salix
green.. 6. reseda
lark.. 12. sedge warbler
pattern.. 7. Nanking 11. earthenware
twig.. 5. withe 6. sallow
wren.. 10. chiffchaff
willowy... 5. lithe 6. pliant, supple,
svelte 7. slender 8. flexible, graceful
15. tall and graceful
Will Rogers' plane... 9. Winnie May
wilsome... 4. wild 6. astray, dreary
7. violent, willful (wilful) 8. desolate
10. bewildered
wilt... 3. sag 4. flag, tire 5. droop,
quail 6. sicken, wither 8. languish
11. deteriorate, lose courage, make
flaccid
Wilton... 3. rug 6. carpet
wily... 3. sly 4. foxy 5. canny, smart
6. artful, astute, crafty, shrews,
subtle 7. cunning 9. cautelous
wimble... 3. awl 4. bore 5. auger,
brace, scoop, twist 6. gimlet, pierce
9. sprightly, whimsical
wimick... 3. cry 7. whimper
wimple... 4. fold, veil 7. meander
8. covering (head)
win... 3. get 4. earn, gain 5. to get
6. attain, defeat, obtain, secure
7. achieve, acquire, succeed, triumph
8. be victor, endeavor, vanquish
9. captivate 10. accomplish
win (pert to)...
all tricks (game).. 4. slam
by guile.. 8. inveigle
one's spurs.. 10. knighthood
over.. 7. convert 8. convince
persuade.. 10. conciliate
wince... 4. reel 5. start 6. cringe,
flinch, recoil, shrink 8. draw back,

windlass 10. shrink from
wind... 2. oe 3. air 4. bora, coil,
gale, gust, talk, turn, wrap 5. blast,
buran, crank, trade 6. boreal, breath,
breeze, simoom, zephyr 7. chinook,
conceit, cyclone, deviate, etesian,
meander, monsoon, sinuate, sirocco,
tempest, tornado, typhoon
8. convolve, williwaw 9. hurricane,
idle words, windstorm 10. instrument
wind (pert to)...
action on land.. 8. eolation
around.. 6. master 8. dominate
9. influence 13. lead by the nose
cloud.. 4. scud
comb form.. 5. anemo
fall.. 7. godsend 8. buckshee, gratuity
flower.. 7. anemone
gauge.. 4. vane 10. anemometer
god.. 4. Adad 6. Aeolus
god of north wind.. 6. Boreas
god of SE wind.. 5. Eurus
instrument.. 3. sax 4. fife, horn
5. flute, organ 6. cornet 7. bassoon,
hautboy, helicon, ocarina 8. clarinet
9. harmonica, saxophone
in the (wind).. 5. drunk 7. sailing
8. imminent 9. happening
into a ball.. 11. agglomerate
personified.. 6. Caurus 7. Caecias
8. Favonius, Zephyrus
ref to.. 7. Aeolian (Eolian)
rose.. 5. poppy
science.. 9. anemology
storm.. 4. gale 7. cyclone, typhoon
9. hurricane
up.. 3. end 7. prepare 8. complete,
conclude
yarn.. 6. windle
wind (type)...
Adriatic (cold).. 4. bora
cold.. 4. bise, bora, puna 7. mistral
8. williwaw
desert.. 6. simoom 7. sirocco
dry.. 9. harmattan
East.. 8. levanter
Egypt.. 7. khamsin (kamsin)
equator.. 5. trade
fierce.. 4. gale 6. buster, squall
7. monsoon 8. blizzard 9. hurricane
gentle.. 4. aura 6. zephyr
Malta (cold).. 7. gregale
Mediterranean.. 6. solano 7. etesian
8. levanter
North.. 6. Boreas
Northwest.. 6. Caurus 7. etesian
Oriental.. 7. monsoon
Peru.. 4. puna
S America.. 4. puna 7. pampero
South.. 6. Auster
Southeast.. 5. Eurus
Southwest.. 7. chinook
Spain.. 6. solano
West (personified).. 8. Favonius
whirl.. 2. oe
windiness... 7. conceit
12. boastfulness
winding... 5. curve, snaky 6. spiral
7. sinuous, twining 8. rambling,
tortuous 9. deviative, meandrous
10. circuitous
windjammer... 6. bugler, talker, vessel

(sailing) 8. bandsman 9. trumpeter
windlass... 4. reel 5. winch 6. windle
7. capstan, machine (hoisting)
windle... 4. reel 5. winch 6. basket
7. measure, redwing
window (pert to)...
arrangement.. 8. fanlight
12. fenestration
bay.. 5. oriel
dormer, roof.. 5. gable 7. lucarne
8. skylight
frame.. 4. sash
Latin.. 8. fenestra
leading.. 4. came
nautical.. 8. porthole
oval.. 5. oxeye
part.. 4. pane, sash, sill 5. glass
7. shutter
recess.. 6. exedra 9. embrasure
ship's.. 4. port 8. porthole
ticket.. 6. wicket 7. guichet
type.. 4. port 5. gable, oriel
7. eucarne 8. casement, skylight
windpipe... 6. gullet, throat
7. trachea, weasand
windrow... 5. swath (swathe) 6. furrow
Winds, Father of (Gr)... 8. Astraeus
windward... 5. aloof 8. aweather
9. weatherly
Windy City... 7. Chicago
wine (pert to)...
and honey.. 5. clary, mulse
7. oenomel
Baden.. 8. Ruländer
bag.. 8. wineskin
bibber.. 3. sot 5. toper 7. tippler
8. drunkard
Bordeaux.. 6. claret
bottle.. 6. magnum 8. decanter
cask.. 3. tun
cellar.. 6. bodega
comb form.. 4. oeno
cruet.. 7. burette
cup.. 3. ama 6. goblet 7. chalice
divination by.. 9. oenomancy
dry.. 3. sec
film.. 8. beeswing
French.. 6. Masden, Pontac (Pontacq)
8. muscatel 9. Hermitage
10. Montrachet 12. Saint–Emilion,
Saint–Estèphe
glass.. 6. rummer (Rom)
grower.. 8. vigneron
hater of.. 11. oenophobist
Italian.. 7. Orvieto 8. muscatel
kind.. 4. port 5. Medoc, Rhine, tinta,
Tokay 6. canary, claret, Malaga,
sherry 7. Chablis, Madeira
8. Burgundy, muscatel, sauterne,
vermouth 9. champagne
lover of.. 11. oenophilist
maker.. 6. abkari (abkary)
making.. 10. oenopoetic
merchant.. 5. abkar
miracle scene.. 4. Cana (Bib)
palm.. 5. taree
Persian.. 6. Shiraz
pitcher.. 4. olpe 8. oenochoe
reference to.. 5. vinic
residue.. 4. marc
sherry.. 5. Xeres 7. Catawba, Moselle,
oloroso

shop.. 3. bar 6. bistro, bodega
Spain.. 6. Malaga
sparkling.. 8. mousseux
study of.. 8. oenology
sweet.. 5. lunel
taster.. 10. oenologist
Tuscan.. 7. Chianti
white.. 6. Malaga 8. Riesling,
sauterne, verdelho 12. Marcobrunner
year.. 7. vintage
wing... 3. ala, arm, fly 6. convey,
flight, member, pinion 7. faction
8. addition, dispatch
wing (pert to)...
anterior.. 7. elytron
comb form.. 7. pterygo
false.. 5. alula
fish.. 8. sea robin
footed.. 8. aliped
Greek.. 6. pteryx
quill.. 7. remiges
shaped.. 7. aliform
tip.. 7. aileron
winglike.. 4. alar 7. pteroid
9. pterygoid
winged... 4. aile (Her), fast 5. alate,
lofty, rapid, swift 7. pennate, sublime
9. aliferous, aligerous
winged (pert to)...
boots (of Hermes).. 7. talaria
child.. 6. cherub
fruit.. 6. samara
monster.. 5. harpy
Winged Horse (Gr Myth)... 7. Pegasus
Winged Victory... 4. Nike
wingless... 7. apteral, Apteryx, exalate
8. dealated (dealate)
wink... 3. nap, nod 4. hint 5. blink,
flash 6. glance, signal, twitch
7. flicker, instant, nictate, twinkle
9. nictation, nictitate, twinkling
10. palpebrate, periwinkle
winker... 3. eye 7. blinker, eyelash
8. blinkard
winking... 13. blepharospasm
winks, forty... 3. nap 6. catnap
10. light sleep
winner... 3. ace 6. earner, reaper,
victor 7. sleeper 8. bangster
9. conqueror 11. breadwinner
winning... 7. gaining, lovable, victory,
winsome 8. alluring, charming
10. attractive, successful, victorious
11. acquisition, captivating
winninish, winnonish... 6. salmon
(landlocked) 10. ouananiche
winnock... 6. window
winnow... 3. fan 4. sift, stir 6. assort,
select, thresh 8. disperse, separate
9. eliminate
winsome... 3. gay 5. bonny, merry
7. lovable, winning 8. alluring,
charming, cheerful, pleasant
10. attractive 11. captivating
12. lighthearted
winter... 4. bise, snow 5. hiems
6. old age, season 8. coldness
winter (pert to)...
beer.. 6. Schenk
berry.. 4. Ilex 5. holly
bloom.. 6. azalea 10. witch hazel
bonnet.. 4. gull

duck.. 7. pintail 8. old squaw
fever.. 9. pneumonia
god.. 5. Hiems
lettuce.. 6. endive
mew.. 4. gull
pert to.. 6. brumal, hiemal
quarters.. 10. hibernacle
    12. hibernaculum
sleep.. 11. hibernation
teal.. 9. greenwing
Winter Palace (Leningrad)...
    6. museum
wipe... 3. dry, mop, rub 5. cheat,
    clean, erase 6. cancel, remove
    7. abolish, defraud 10. obliterate
    11. exterminate
wire... 4. coil, cord, line, whip
    5. cable, snare 6. thread 7. fencing,
    lametta (gold), netting, reticle
    8. telegram, wirework 9. cablegram,
    telegraph 10. pickpocket 14. knitting
    needle
wirepuller... 10. influencer, machinator,
    politician, strategist
wiry... 4. lean 5. hardy, stiff, tough
    6. sinewy, strong 7. stringy
    8. enduring, muscular
wis... 5. think 7. imagine, suppose
Wisconsin...
capital.. 7. Madison
city.. 6. Racine 7. Kenosha, Oshkosh
    8. Green Bay 9. Fond du Lac,
    Milwaukee
famed as.. 17. America's Dairyland
first white man.. 7. Nicolet (Jean)
lake.. 8. Michigan, Superior
    9. Winnebago
river.. 7. St Croix 11. Mississippi
State admission.. 9. Thirtieth
State motto.. 7. Forward
State nickname.. 6. Badger
wisdom... 5. logos 8. judgment,
    learning, sagacity, sapience
    9. erudition, knowledge
    10. discretion, profundity
wisdom god... 4. Nebo (Nabu)
    6. Ganesa (Ganesha)
wisdom goddess... 6. Athena
    7. Minerva (Gr)
wise... 3. hep 4. sage, sane, wary
    5. aware 6. shrewd, subtle, versed
    7. erudite, knowing, learned, politic,
    sapient 8. discreet, informed,
    profound 9. cognizant, expedient,
    judicious, provident 10. omniscient
    11. circumspect, enlightened,
    philosophic 13. sophisticated
wise (pert to)...
councilor.. 6. mentor, nestor
man.. 4. sage 5. solon, witan
    6. nestor, wizard 7. Solomon
saying.. 4. rede 5. adage
Wise Men (three)... 6. Gaspar
    8. Melchior 9. Balthasar
Wise Men of Greece... 5. Seven
Wise Men of the East... 19. Three
    Kings of Cologne
wish... 4. care, hope, will, wuss
    5. yearn 6. aspire, desire, invoke
    7. longing, request 8. optative,
    petition 10. aspiration
    11. imprecation

wishbone... 7. furcula 8. furculum
    10. fourchette 12. merry thought
wisp... 4. floc 5. brush, flock, shred
    6. bundle 7. handful 8. fragment
wistful... 7. longing, pensive
    8. desirous, yearning 9. nostalgic
    10. melancholy
wit... 3. pun, wag 5. humor, sense
    6. acumen, esprit, satire, wisdom
    7. punster 8. comedian, humorist,
    repartee 9. alertness 11. philosopher,
    savoir-faire 12. intelligence
    13. understanding
wit (to)... 3. viz 5. truly 6. indeed,
    namely, that is 8. scilicet 9. videlicet
witch... 3. hag, hex 4. baba 5. Circe,
    crone, lamia, shrew, vixen
    6. cummer, Hecate (Hekate), Lilith
    (Lilis), wizard 7. warlock 8. old
    woman 9. grimalkin, sorceress
    11. witch doctor 12. ugly old
    woman
witchcraft... 5. charm, magic, wanga
    7. cunning, hexerei, sorcery
    8. brujeria 9. sortilege, voodooism
    10. bewitchery, black magic
    11. enchantment 12. invultuation
witch doctor... 3. hex 6. shaman
    9. voodooist, wangateur
witchery... 5. charm, spell 7. sorcery
    8. wizardry 10. allurement,
    necromancy 11. enchantment,
    fascination
with (pref)... 2. co 3. com, con, cum,
    mit, syn 4. avec
with... 5. among 7. jointly 8. together
    9. alongside, including 10. hand in
    hand 11. association
    12. concurrently 13. co-operatively
withal... 5. still 9. thereupon 10. for
    all that
withdraw... 6. absent, deduct, recall,
    recant, recede, remove, repeal, retire,
    secede 7. abandon, detract, disavow,
    forsake, refrain, regress, retract,
    retreat, subside 8. alienate, evacuate,
    renounce 9. disengage 10. relinquish
withdrawal... 6. repeal 7. regress,
    retiral, retreat 8. escapism
    9. departure, recession, seclusion
    10. detachment, extraction,
    retraction, separation
    11. abandonment, recantation,
    resignation
withdrawn... 7. ingrown 8. detached,
    secluded
withe... 4. band, rope 5. snare
    6. halter, wattle, willow
wither... 3. age, die, dry 4. fade,
    sear, sere, wilt 5. decay, droop, dry
    up, wizen 6. blight, shrink 7. shrivel,
    wrinkle 8. languish 11. deteriorate
withered... 4. sere 8. shrunken
    9. shriveled
withering... 7. caustic 9. shrinking
    10. marcescent 12. contemptuous
    13. deteriorating
withhold... 4. curb, deny 5. check
    6. detain, refuse, retain 7. abstain,
    prevent, refrain, repress, reserve
    8. hold back, postpone, restrain
within... 6. at home, during, inside

7. indoors 8. inside of, inwardly
9. inner side

without... 4. sans, sine 5. minus
6. beyond, except, lack of, unless
7. lacking, not with 9. absence of,
outwardly 10. externally, out–of–doors

without (pert to)... see also *absence of*
action.. 8. deedless
animation.. 5. amort
appointment (of day).. 7. sine die
beginning, or end.. 7. eternal
cause.. 10. unprovoked
connections.. 7. tieless
delay.. 9. summarily
doubt.. 9. sine dubio
ethics.. 6. amoral
exception.. 11. universally
feet.. 4. apod 6. apodal
foliage.. 8. aphylous
friends.. 4. lorn 7. forlorn 8. forsaken
knowledge.. 8. ignorant
mate.. 3. odd
prefix.. 4. ecto
rule.. 8. anarchic
substance.. 5. inane
support.. 7. legless 9. dependent
teeth.. 8. edentate 9. toothless
this.. 7. sine hoc
warning.. 12. out of the blue
wings.. 7. apteral

withstand... 4. bear, bide, defy, last
5. abide 6. endure, oppose, resist
8. confront 10. contradict

witless... 3. mad 5. crazy, dazed
6. stupid 7. foolish, unaware
8. heedless 9. brainless, unknowing
10. indiscreet 13. unintelligent

witness... 3. eye, see 4. know
5. swear, teste, vouch 6. attend,
attest, beheld, behold, testor
7. observe, testify 8. beholder,
deponent, evidence, observer,
onlooker 9. informant, spectator,
subscribe, testimony 11. attestation

witticism... 3. mot, pun 4. jest, joke,
quip 5. droll, sally, slent 8. repartee
9. wisecrack 10. pleasantry
11. gauloiserie, witty saying

wittingly... 8. by design 9. knowingly
13. intentionally

witty... 4. wise 5. comic, droll, sharp
6. clever, facete, jocose, jocund
7. amusing, comical, jocular, knowing
8. humorous 9. facetious, whimsical

wivern, wyvern (Her)... 6. dragon
(2–legged)

wizard... 4. mage, sage 6. expert,
genius, Merlin, pellar, shaman
7. magical, prodigy 8. conjurer,
magician, sorcerer 10. Wizard of Oz
11. necromancer, thaumaturge, witch
doctor 13. thaumaturgist

Wizard of the North... 14. Sir Walter
Scott

wizen... 3. age, dry 4. thin 6. gullet,
shrink, weazen, wither 7. shrivel
8. windpipe 11. deteriorate

wlo (obs)... 3. hem 6. fringe

woad... 3. dye 4. herb 5. tinge
8. dyestuff 10. pastel blue

wobble, wabble... 4. walk 5. shake,

waver 7. stagger, tremble
8. hobbling 9. fluctuate, oscillate,
vacillate

Woden, Wodan (Myth)... 3. god
(chief) 4. Odin 9. Wednesday (named
for Woden)

woe... 4. bale, bane 5. grief
6. misery, sorrow 7. anguish, trouble
8. anathema, calamity 10. affliction,
melancholy, misfortune

woebegone... 3. sad 6. woeful
7. unhappy 8. dejected, desolate
10. dispirited, melancholy

woeful... 3. sad 6. paltry 7. direful,
pitiful 8. grievous, mournful, wretched
9. afflicted, miserable, sorrowful,
woebegone 10. deplorable
12. disconsolate

wold... 3. lea 4. wood 5. downs,
plain, weald 6. forest, meadow
7. low hill

wolf... 4. lobo 5. lupus 6. coyote,
mammal 7. Isegrim 8. werewolf
9. libertine 11. philanderer

wolf fish... 6. blenny

wolfhound... 6. borzoi

wolflike... 6. lupine, thooid

wolverine... 4. Gulo 11. Michigander,
Michiganite

Wolverine State... 8. Michigan

woman... 4. dame, girl, lady, rani, wife
5. adult, begum, gemme, madam,
squaw 6. female 7. distaff
8. feminine, paramour, senorita
9. weaker sex, womankind
10. sweetheart

woman (pert to)...
adviser.. 6. Egeria (Rom Myth)
apartment of.. 3. oda (harem)
8. thalamus
beautiful.. 4. doll 5. filly, pin–up,
siren, sylph, Venus 7. charmer,
Zenobia 8. Musidora
bewitching.. 4. peri 5. siren, vixen
7. charmer
celibate.. 7. agapeta
chaser.. 9. libertine 11. philanderer
club (of women).. 7. sorosis
8. sorority
comb form.. 3. gyn
dignified, elderly.. 7. dowager
dowdy.. 5. frump 6. untidy 8. slattern
gossipy.. 3. cat 15. flibbertigibbet
graceful.. 5. sylph 7. slender
gypsy.. 5. romni
hater.. 10. misogynist
hatred of.. 8. misogyny
kept.. 8. mistress 9. concubine
12. demimondaine
killer.. 8. femicide
learned.. 12. bluestocking
loose.. 4. drab 5. whore 6. harlot
7. trollop 10. prostitute
12. streetwalker
lover of.. 11. philogynist
modest (affectedly).. 5. prude
mythical (ugly).. 6. Gorgon
noisy.. 9. termagant
of rank.. 4. dame
old.. 5. crone, frump 6. granny
7. carline, dowager 8. grandame
9. cailleach

ruler.. 9. matriarch
scolding.. 5. shrew 6. virago
socialite.. 3. deb 6. subdeb
  9. debutante 13. fashion leader
stately.. 4. lady 6. matron
suffragist.. 8. feminist
vixenish.. 5. shrew 6. virago
  8. harridan
weeping.. 5. Niobe
will maker.. 9. testatrix
young, unmarried.. 4. lass 6. damsel
  8. spinster 10. demoiselle
womanhood... 4. Emer 10. femininity
woman's property (free)...
  10. parapherna
wonder... 3. awe 6. marvel, rarity
  7. miracle, prodigy 8. surprise
  9. amazement 10. admiration,
  wonderment 12. astonishment
wonderful... 6. superb, unique
  7. amazing, corking, mirific, strange
  8. wondrous 9. admirable,
  marvelous, mirifical 10. remarkable,
  surprising 11. astonishing
  13. extraordinary
wont... 3. use 5. habit, usage
  6. custom
woo... 3. sue 6. invite 7. beseech,
  entreat, solicit
wood... 4. tree 5. xylon 6. lignum,
  lumber, timber 8. firewood
wood (pert to)...
aromatic.. 5. aloes, cedar 8. agalloch
ash.. 6. potash
black.. 5. ebony
block.. 3. nog 4. dook
boring (of insects).. 8. xylotomy
bundles.. 6. fagots
carving.. 10. xyloglyphy
clearing.. 5. glade
color.. 7. biscuit
comb form.. 4. hylo, xylo 5. ligni,
  ligno, xylon
core.. 3. ame
curved strip.. 5. stave
dealer.. 10. xylopolist
deity.. 3. Pan 4. faun 5. Diana, Satyr
  7. Silenus 8. Silvanus
eating.. 11. xylophagous
goddess.. 5. Diana
growing on.. 6. fungus
  11. xylophilous
growth.. 7. boscage, coppice, thicket
hard.. 3. ash, elm 4. rate, teak
  5. ebony, maple 6. walnut
  8. mahogany
inlay.. 9. marquetry
nymph.. 4. moth 5. dryad
overlay.. 6. veneer
resembling.. 6. xyloid
stork.. 4. ibis
strip.. 4. lath, slat 5. sprag, stave
  6. batten
touch.. 4. punk 5. spunk (sponk)
  9. touchwood
tough, elastic.. 3. ash
tract.. 5. grove 6. forest
woodchuck... 6. marmot 9. ground
  hog
Woodchuck Day... 9. Candlemas
woodcock... 5. pewee 6. peewee,
  shrups 10. woodpecker

wooden (pert to)...
container.. 3. box 4. case 6. barrel
horse.. 6. Trojan
Indian.. 15. cigar–store brave
joint.. 5. tenon
made of.. 5. treen
pert to.. 4. dull 6. clumsy, stolid,
  stupid 8. lifeless 14. expressionless
pin.. 3. fid, nog, peg 5. dowel, spile
pole.. 4. palo
shoe.. 5. sabot 6. patten
stand.. 5. criss
tub.. 3. soe
woodpecker... 4. chab 5. Picus
  6. yaffle, yukkel (yuckle) 7. flicker,
  wryneck 8. hickwall 9. sapsucker
  10. carpintero, pickerwood
  11. woodknacker
woods (pert to)...
inhabiting.. 7. nemoral
lover of.. 11. nemophilist
pert to.. 6. sylvan (silvan)
  10. sylvestral
sacred (grove).. 10. Nemorensis
woodwind... 4. oboe 5. flute
  7. bassoon, piccolo 8. clarinet
  9. saxophone
woody... 6. sylvan, xyloid 8. ligneous
woof... 3. abb 4. weft 6. fabric
  7. filling, texture
wool... 3. fur 4. down, hair 5. cloth,
  llama, sheep 6. fleece 8. barragan
  (barragon)
wool (pert to)...
card.. 3. tum 4. comb 5. tease
clean.. 7. garnett
cloth.. 5. serge, tweed, yerga
  6. angora, duffel, kersey, satara,
  tartan, tricot, vicuña 7. doeskin,
  flannel, ratteen 8. cashmere
  10. broadcloth
comb form.. 4. lani
dead sheep's.. 8. mortling
dryer.. 5. fugal
fat.. 7. lanolin (lanoline)
fatty substance.. 5. suint
garment.. 6. alpaca, linder
implement.. 6. carder, shears, teaser
  7. distaff, spindle
inferior, dirty.. 7. cleamer
kind.. 6. alpaca, angora, merino
  8. picklock
leg.. 4. gare
reclaimed.. 5. mungo 6. shoddy
reference to.. 5. wooly 6. lanate,
  lanose 10. flocculent
spun.. 4. yarn
tuft.. 8. floccule 9. flocculus
undyed, natural.. 5. beige
waste.. 3. fud 4. noil
yarn.. 3. abb 7. eis wool
wooly (woolly)... 5. downy, fuzzy
  6. fleecy, lanate 7. blurred
  8. confused, floccose, peronate
word... 4. news, oath 5. adage,
  maxim, parol 6. avowal, remark,
  report 7. command, dispute,
  message, promise, tidings, vocable
  8. acrostic, password 9. discourse,
  statement 11. declaration, information
  13. communication
word, words (pert to)...

action .. **4.** verb
battle of .. **9.** logomachy
blindness .. **6.** alexia
book .. **6.** Gradus **7.** lexicon, speller
　8. glossary **9.** thesaurus
　10. dictionary
contraction .. **9.** haplology
deletion at end .. **7.** apocope
derivation .. **6.** etymon **9.** etymology
distinguishing (Bib) .. **10.** shibboleth
divine .. **5.** Logos
excessive interest .. **10.** verbomania
figurative use .. **5.** trope
figure of speech .. **7.** metonym,
　paronym
first on walls (Bib) .. **21.** mene, mene,
　tekel, upharsin
for word .. **8.** verbatim **9.** literally
hard to pronounce .. **10.** jawbreaker
inventor of .. **6.** coiner **9.** neologist
last syllable .. **6.** ultima
last syllable but one .. **6.** penult
last syllable omitted .. **7.** apocope
law .. **7.** by parol **11.** word of mouth
letter .. **8.** logogram **9.** logogriph
　11. grammalogue
longest in dictionary ..
　28. antidisestablishmentarianism
loss from middle .. **7.** syncope
magical .. **6.** presto, sesame
meaning .. **9.** semantics
misuse .. **11.** catachresis, heterophemy,
　malapropism
mysterious (Bib) .. **5.** selah
new .. **9.** neologism
new usage .. **7.** neology
of different name for same thing ..
　9. heteronym
of honor .. **6.** parole **7.** promise
of opposite meaning .. **7.** antonym
of same derivation .. **7.** paronym
of same meaning .. **7.** synonym
of same sound .. **7.** homonym
of imitation .. **6.** echoic **9.** onomatope
　12. onomatopoeia
popular .. **5.** cliché **8.** buzzword
pretentious use .. **10.** lexiphanic
puzzle .. **5.** rebus **7.** anagram
　8. acrostic **9.** crossword
repetition .. **5.** ploce
root .. **6.** etymon
same back to front .. **10.** palindrome
science .. **10.** lexicology
scrambled .. **7.** anagram
song hits .. **6.** lyrics
substitution .. **5.** trope **7.** metonym
theory .. **6.** bowwow **8.** pooh–pooh
The Word (Bib) .. **5.** Logos
with loss of vowel at beginning ..
　7. aphasia
without vowels .. **6.** rhythm, syzygy
with vowels (all) .. **7.** eulogia, miaoued,
　sequoia **12.** ambidextrous
with vowels in sequence .. **8.** caesious
wordiness ... **8.** pleonasm, verbiage
　9. prolixity, verbacity **10.** redundance
wording ... **8.** phrasing **10.** expression
wordless ... **5.** tacit **6.** silent
wordy ... **6.** prolix **7.** verbose
　9. garrulous **10.** long–winded
　12. long–drawn–out
work ... **3.** gig, job, mix **4.** book, deed,

duty, make, opus, plan, task, to–do,
toil **5.** chore, ergon, labor, solve,
trade **6.** action, Arbeit, create, effect,
effort **7.** ferment, operate, perform,
product, travail **8.** business, drudgery,
endeavor, function, industry, struggle
　10. accomplish, employment,
engagement, management,
occupation, profession
　11. achievement, performance,
undertaking
work (pert to) ...
agreement .. **4.** code, pact **8.** contract
bag .. **7.** tote bag **8.** reticule
carelessly .. **5.** scamp
clothes .. **8.** overalls **9.** blue jeans,
　coveralls, dungarees
comb form .. **3.** erg **4.** ergo
divine .. **7.** miracle, theurgy **9.** occult
　art
hard .. **3.** peg, tew **4.** char, moil, plug,
　toil **5.** labor, sweat **6.** drudge
　7. travail **9.** lucubrate **18.** burn the
　midnight oil
hate of .. **10.** ergophobia
helper .. **3.** aid (aide) **9.** assistant,
　paralegal, paramedic
horse .. **4.** mule **5.** burro
hours .. **9.** flexitime (flextime)
household .. **4.** char **5.** chare
incomplete art .. **7.** ébauche
inlay .. **6.** mosaic, niello
lover of .. **9.** ergophile
measure of .. **9.** ergometer
of excellence .. **4.** opus **7.** classic
out .. **5.** solve **7.** arrange, develop
　9. calculate
over .. **6.** recast, rehash, revamp
　9. brainwash, influence
shift .. **5.** swing **9.** graveyard,
　moonlight
slowly .. **6.** potter, putter **7.** ca'canny
study of .. **8.** ergology
together .. **4.** team **9.** cooperate
　11. collaborate
unit of .. **3.** erg **5.** ergon, joule
up .. **4.** plan **5.** rouse **6.** excite, incite
　7. advance, agitate, develop
　10. manipulate
workable ... **6.** pliant **7.** operant
　8. feasible, operable, solvable
　9. practical **11.** practicable
worker ... **3.** CPA **5.** diver, mason,
　miner **6.** barman, cooper, slater,
　smithy, tanner, warper, wright
　7. analyst, cobbler, glazier, plumber,
　riveter, sandhog, servant, spinner
　8. honeybee, mechanic, strapper
　9. carpenter, clinician, machinist,
　stevedore **10.** accountant
　11. breadwinner
worker (pert to) ...
fellow .. **5.** buddy **8.** confrere
group .. **4.** crew, gang, team **5.** corps,
　staff **9.** personnel
hard .. **6.** beaver, drudge, fagger
　10. workaholic
head .. **4.** boss **7.** foreman
　8. employer, overseer
　14. superintendent
indifferent .. **4.** scab **11.** scissorbill
migrant .. **4.** hobo **6.** boomer

7. floater, wetback

workhouse ... 6. prison 9. almshouse, poorhouse

workman ... 4. peon 6. coolie, earner 7. artisan, laborer 8. operator, opificer 9. artificer, craftsman, performer

workshop ... 3. lab 4. mill 5. plant 6. studio 7. atelier, factory 10. laboratory 11. ergasterion

world ... 5. globe, realm 6. cosmos, domain 7. kingdom, society 8. creation, humanity, universe 9. multitude, the public

world (pert to) ...
external .. 6. nonego
great .. 9. macrocosm
lower .. 5. Hades, Orcus
miniature .. 9. microcosm
of fairies .. 6. faerie (faery)
precreation .. 10. premundane 11. antemundane
reference to .. 7. mundane 11. terrestrial

worldly ... 7. earthly, mundane, secular, terrene 11. terrestrial 13. materialistic, sophisticated

world's oldest city, still inhabited ... 8. Damascus

world's speech ... 7. Volapuk 9. universal

worm ... 3. ess 4. coil, grub, wind 5. borer, tinea 6. blight, insect, maggot, vermin, wretch 8. helminth 9. trematode, vermicule 10. Nemertinea (Nemertina)

worm (pert to) ...
Africa .. 3. loa 6. Guinea
aquatic, marine .. 7. eunicid, lugworm 8. flatworm 9. planarian 13. platyhelminth
arrow .. 7. sagitta
bait .. 9. angleworm, earthworm
bloodsucking .. 5. leech
caddie .. 5. cadew
cotton .. 8. bollworm 10. boll weevil
edible .. 6. palolo
eye–infecting .. 3. loa
genus .. 6. Virmes 7. Ascaris, Filaria 8. Annelida 10. Nemertinea (Nemertina)
grublike .. 5. larva
killer .. 9. vermicide
larva .. 4. army, slug 5. cadew 6. caddis, looper 8. wireworm 11. caterpillar
luminous .. 8. glowworm
marine .. 7. eunicid
measuring .. 6. looper 8. inchworm
parasitic .. 7. Ascaris, Filaria 8. trichina, woodworm 9. trematode 10. Guinea worm 12. enthelmintha
ref to .. 8. anneloid 9. nemertean, nemertine, nemertoid, trematoid
ring .. 5. tinea 7. annelid
round .. 7. ascarid, Ascaris
segmented .. 8. Annelida
ship .. 5. borer 6. teredo
silk .. 4. eria
soft .. 4. grub
study of .. 10. vermeology 13. helminthology

tape .. 6. taenia
track .. 7. nereite 11. helminthite
wire .. 4. lava 9. millepede

worm (type) ... 3. cut, dew, lug, pin 4. army, boll, eria, flat, glow, inch, ring, ship, silk, slug, tape, wire, wood 5. angle, earth, larva, leech, round, tinea 6. marine 9. measuring, parasitic

wormlike ... 7. vermian 11. helminthoid

wormy ... 6. earthy, humble, rotten 8. crawling 9. groveling

worn ... 3. old 4. sere, used 5. stale, trite 7. abraded, haggard 8. attrited, tattered, weakened 9. exhausted, hackneyed 10. secondhand 11. commonplace

worn–out ... 4. used 5. jaded, passé, seedy, spent, trite 6. shabby, used up 7. haggard 8. consumed, fatigued, impaired, tired out 9. enfeebled, exhausted 10. threadbare

worried ... 5. cared, fazed 6. stewed 7. annoyed, anxious, fearful, fretted 8. troubled 9. perturbed

worry ... 3. nag, rux, vex 4. care, cark, faze, fret, stew 5. annoy, brood, harry 6. bother, harass, pester, plague, pother 7. anxiety, bedevil, concern, perturb, torment, trouble 8. distress 9. annoyance 10. harassment, uneasiness

worship ... 5. adore, honor, serve 6. bhakti, homage, revere 7. idolize, liturgy, respect 8. blessing, devotion, idolatry, venerate 9. adoration, deference, reverence 10. veneration

worship (pert to) ...
form of .. 6. preces, ritual 7. liturgy
house of .. 6. chapel, church, mosque, shrine 9. cathedral, synagogue 10. tabernacle
object of .. 4. icon, idol 5. totem 6. fetish
place of .. 5. altar
system of .. 4. cult 6. cultus, fetish, ritual 8. doctrine

worshiper ... 6. adorer, bhakti, votary 8. disciple, idolater 10. ignicolist 12. iconomachist

worshipful ... 6. devout 7. notable 8. esteemed 9. honorable, venerable 13. distinguished

worship of ...
a god .. 7. theolatry
angels .. 5. dulia
genii .. 10. geniolatry
god .. 6. latria (RCCh)
idols .. 8. idolatry
images .. 10. iconolatry
nature .. 11. physiolatry
one god .. 9. monolatry
snakes .. 10. ophiolatry
soul .. 7. animism
sun .. 10. heliolatry
the mob .. 9. mobolatry

worst ... 3. bad 4. beat, evil 6. defeat, wicked 7. harmful 8. inferior 10. calamitous, pernicious, unpleasant 12. disagreeable

worsted ... 4. yarn 6. crewel

7. genappe

worth . . . 5. merit, price, value
6. desert, repute, riches, stiver,
wealth 8. eminence, meriting,
property 9. deserving 10. excellence,
importance, usefulness

worthless . . . 3. bad, ort 4. base, evil,
mean, raca (Bib), vile 6. futile,
nought (naught), paltry 7. fustian,
useless 8. nugatory, rubbishy,
unworthy 9. valueless
11. undeserving
14. good–for–nothing

worthwhile . . . 6. useful 7. gainful
9. expedient, well–spent
10. invaluable, profitable

worthy . . . 3. fit 7. merited 8. eligible,
valuable 9. celebrity, competent,
deserving, estimable, excellent,
honorable, qualified, reputable
11. meritorious

worthy of . . . 8. credible, meriting
9. deserving 10. entitled to

wound . . . 3. cut 4. gore, harm, hurt,
pain, rist, scar, sore, stab 5. sting
6. breach, damage, grieve, injury,
lesion, offend, trauma 8. distress
9. detriment

wound (pert to) . . .
discharge . . 5. ichor 6. sanies
dressing . . 7. bandage, pledget
mark . . 4. scab, scar, welt 7. blister

woven . . . 4. spun 10. fabricated

wow . . . 4. howl, rave, wail 5. whine

wrack . . . 4. kelp, rack, ruin 5. tease,
trash, weeds, wreck 6. refuse
7. seaweed 8. eelgrass, wreckage
9. shipwreck 11. destruction

wraith . . . 4. food 5. ghost, spook
8. illusion 10. apparition
12. Doppelgänger, doubleganger

wrangle . . . 4. herd, spar 5. argue,
brawl 6. bicker, debate 7. contend,
dispute, quarrel 8. haggling
9. altercate, bickering 11. altercation,
controversy 12. disagreement

wrangler . . . 6. cowboy 7. debater,
student (Cambridge, Eng)
8. herdsman, opponent
9. combatant, disputant
10. antagonist

wrangling . . . 11. belligerent,
contentious

wrap . . . 3. rug 4. cape, cere, furl, roll,
wind 5. cloak, gange 6. afghan,
encowl, enfold, swathe 7. blanket,
conceal, package 8. covering,
enshroud, enswathe, envelope
9. encompass

wrapped up . . . 7. bound up, selfish
8. absorbed, included, involved
9. dependent, devoted to, engrossed
11. inseparable

wrapper . . . 4. gown 5. cerer 6. fardel,
kimono, tillot 7. garment, pelisse
8. envelope, peignoir

wrapping . . . 6. charta 7. wrapper
8. cerement, covering 9. parchment

wrasse . . . 4. fish 6. ballan, cunner,
Labrus 7. seawife 11. peacock fish

wrath . . . 3. ire 4. fury, grim, rage
5. anger 6. choler 7. passion

8. violence 10. turbulence
11. indignation 12. exasperation

wrathful . . . 3. mad 5. angry, irate
6. ireful, raging 7. angered
8. incensed 9. indignant, malignant
10. passionate

wreak . . . 4. do to 6. avenge 7. gratify,
indulge, inflict 13. bring down upon

wreath . . . 3. lei 4. band, orle
5. crown, torse (Her), whorl
6. anadem, circle, corona, laurel,
trophy 7. coronet, festoon, garland,
Iresine 8. encircle

wreathe . . . 4. coil, wind 5. crown,
twine, twist 7. entwine 8. decorate,
encircle 9. interlace 10. twist about

wreck . . . 4. raze, ruin, undo 5. crash,
smash 6. jalopy 7. destroy, disable
8. accident, demolish, derelict
9. shipwreck 10. broken form
11. disassemble, The Hesperus

wreckage . . . 5. ruins 6. jetsam
7. flotsam 8. driftage

wrench . . . 4. jerk, pipe, pull, tear
5. twist, wrest 6. sprain, twinge
7. distort 8. crescent, distress

wrench, type of . . . 3. box, pin
5. wramp 6. monkey 7. spanner
8. carriage, Stillson 9. alligator

wrest . . . 4. rend, turn 5. exact, force,
seize, twist, wring 6. elicit, extort,
wrench 7. distort, extract, pervert,
wrestle 8. misapply

wrestle . . . 3. tug 6. squirm, tussle
7. contend, grapple, scuffle, wriggle
8. struggle 9. throw down 10. twist
about 11. come to grips

wrestling school . . . 9. palaestra
(palestra)

wretch . . . 3. dog 5. miser, ronin
6. outlaw, pariah 7. caitiff, cullion,
outcast 8. derelict, sufferer
9. miscreant 10. base person
11. offscouring, rapscallion
14. good–for–nothing 16. pitiable
creature

wretched . . . 3. sad 4. base, mean
6. dismal, paltry, woeful 7. baleful,
forlorn, squalid, unhappy, very bad
8. grievous 9. execrable, miserable
10. despicable, distressed
12. contemptible, disreputable

wretchedness . . . 6. misery 8. distress,
meanness, poorness 10. paltriness
11. unhappiness 13. penuriousness

wriggle . . . 5. twist 6. squirm, writhe
7. meander

wriggle out of . . . 4. turn, wind
5. dodge, snake, twist 6. squirm,
writhe 8. slip away 10. crawl out of
11. squirm out of 13. find a
loophole

wring . . . 5. twist, wrest 6. extort,
wrench 7. extract, torture, wrestle
8. compress, convolve 9. cause pain
10. contortion, extraction

wrinkle . . . 3. fad 4. fold, idea, ruga,
seam 5. crimp, knack, ridge, rivel
6. crease, furrow, pucker, rimple,
ripple, rumple 7. crinkle, novelty
8. contract 9. corrugate
11. corrugation 12. clever notion

wrinkled... 4. aged 5. savoy
  6. rugate, rugose, rugous 7. creased
  8. crinkled, crumpled, furrowed,
  puckered, rugulose 9. shriveled
  10. contracted, corrugated
wrinkles... 5. rugae
wrist... 5. joint 6. carpal, carpus
  8. os magnum 9. capitatum
writ... 5. breve, tales 6. capias, elegit,
  venire 7. process 8. detainer,
  document, mittimus, replevin,
  subpoena 10. certiorari, instrument
  11. fieri facias
writ (pert to)...
  common law.. 11. fieri facias
  court.. 7. summons 8. subpoena
  execution.. 6. elegit
  jury.. 5. tales 6. venire
  law.. 4. capo, pone 5. breve, error
  6. capias, elegit 7. mandate,
  process, warrant 8. citation
  10. certiorari
write... 3. pen 5. draft, trace
  6. decree, depict, draw up, enroll,
  indite, record, scrive 7. compose,
  scriven 8. inscribe, scribble
  11. communicate
write (pert to)...
  carelessly.. 6. scrawl 8. scrabble,
  scribble
  in large hand.. 7. engross
  off.. 4. drop 6. cancel, deduct, repeal
  out.. 6. record 8. spill out 12. put in
  writing
  poetry.. 7. versify
  up.. 6. record, report 7. article
  9. publicize 11. press report
writer... 4. hack, poet 6. author,
  penman, penner, scribe 7. elegist,
  glosser, hymnist 8. annalist,
  composer, lyricist, novelist, parodist,
  scriptor 9. annotator, columnist,
  scrivener 10. chronicler, journalist
  13. correspondent
writer's afterthoughts... 7. addenda
writhe... 4. bend, coil, curl, wind
  5. twist, wring 6. squirm 7. contort,
  distort, wriggle
writing... 4. book, poem 6. script
  7. article, epistle 8. covenant,
  document, makimono 10. expression,
  penmanship, profession
  11. chirography, composition,
  handwriting, inscription, publication
writing (pert to)...
  alternate.. 13. boustrophedon
  ancient characters.. 9. cuneiform
  ancient manuscript.. 6. uncial
  cipher.. 12. cryptography
  instrument.. 3. pen 5. quill 6. stylus
  italic.. 7. cursive
  mania for.. 11. graphomania
  material.. 3. pad 5. paper, slate
  6. tablet 9. parchment 10. stationery
  omission of a letter.. 8. lipogram
  10. lipography
  pert to.. 7. scribal
  record.. 3. log 5. album, diary
  script.. 5. ronde
  scroll.. 8. makimono
  scroll hanging.. 8. kakemono
  secret.. 4. code 10. cryptogram

  12. cryptography
  unrhymed.. 5. prose
writings, sacred... 5. Bible, Koran
  6. Psalms, Talmud 9. Testament
  (Old, New) 10. Scriptures
written (pert to)...
  agreement.. 6. cartel
  characters.. 6. script
  it is.. 8. it must be 10. in the
  books, in the cards 12. the die is
  cast
  law.. 10. legislated
  law, unwritten.. 6. common
  memo.. 5. scrip
wrong... 3. bad, off, out, sin 4. awry,
  evil, harm, side, tort, vice 5. amiss,
  cheat, crime, false, malum, unfit
  6. faulty, injure, injury, seduce,
  sinful, unjust, wicked 7. defraud,
  immoral, misdeed, offense
  8. improper, iniquity, mistaken
  9. erroneous, incorrect, injustice,
  violation 10. inaccurate, iniquitous
  11. impropriety, inexpedient,
  malfeasance, misfeasance
  12. illegitimate
wrong (pert to)...
  go (wrong).. 3. err 4. fail 5. lapse
  8. go astray, go to ruin 9. backslide
  10. misbelieve 11. go to the dogs
  in the.. 6. guilty 7. at fault, in error
  8. mistaken 9. violation
  law.. 4. tort 5. crime, malum
  name.. 8. misnomer
  nor right (neither).. 7. neutral
  11. adiaphorous
  prefix.. 3. mis
  side of.. 5. shady
  way.. 5. amiss 6. astray 10. out of
  place
wrongdoer... 6. sinner 8. criminal,
  evildoer, violator 10. malefactor,
  trespasser 12. transgressor
wroth... 3. mad 5. angry, irate
  7. violent 8. incensed, wrathful
  9. turbulent, wrought up
  11. exasperated
wrought... 4. made 6. formed,
  shaped, worked 9. decorated,
  fashioned, processed 10. elaborated,
  ornamented 11. embroidered
  12. manufactured
wrought up... 4. agog 5. angry, eager
  7. excited 9. disturbed, stirred up
wry... 4. awry 5. biased, swerve,
  turned 6. crooked, twisted
  9. contorted
wryneck... 4. Jynx, weet 5. loxia
  9. snakebird 11. torticollis
Württemberg, Germany...
  capital.. 9. Stuttgart
  city.. 3. Ulm 9. Esslingen, Heilbronn,
  Hohenheim
  lake.. 9. Constance
  river.. 6. Danube, Neckar
Wyandot... 6. Indian (Iroquois)
Wyandotte... 4. cave, city, fowl
Wycliff (Wyclif), John (pert to)...
  birthplace.. 9. Yorkshire (Eng)
  disciple.. 4. Huss
  remains cast into.. 10. Swift River
  translator of.. 5. Bible

Wyoming ...
capital .. **8.** Cheyenne
city .. **4.** Cody **6.** Casper **7.** Big Horn,
  Laramie **8.** Cheyenne, Sheridan
historic site .. **11.** Fort Laramie
  17. Buffalo Bill Center
mountain .. **6.** Tetons **7.** Rockies
  11. Gannett Peak
park .. **10.** Grand Teton

  11. Yellowstone
river .. **4.** Wind **6.** Platte **7.** Big Horn
river source .. **8.** Colorado, Columbia,
  Missouri
State admission .. **11.** Forty–fourth
State bird .. **10.** meadowlark
State flower .. **16.** Indian paintbrush
State motto .. **11.** Equal Rights
Woman Suffrage .. **10.** First State

X

X ... **3.** ten **5.** error **6.** letter (24th),
  symbol **7.** unknown
xanthic ... **6.** cyanic, yellow
Xanthippe, wife of ... **8.** Socrates
xanthoma ... **9.** xanthosis **11.** skin
  disease **13.** yellow patches
xanthos ... **6.** yellow
Xanthus (pert to) ...
ancient site .. **7.** marbles (Xanthian)
placed now .. **13.** British Museum
xebec ... **6.** vessel **7.** corsair
xen, xeno (comb form) ... **7.** foreign
  8. stranger
xenium ... **4.** gift **7.** present (official)
Xenocrates (Gr) ... **11.** philosopher
xenogamy ... **18.** cross–fertilization
xenophobic ... **9.** strangers (afraid of)
  12. chauvinistic
Xenophon's historic tale ...
  8. Anabasis
xenophthalmia ... **11.** foreign body
  (eye) **14.** conjunctivitis
Xenopus ... **5.** toads
Xenorhynchus ... **6.** storks
Xenurus ... **7.** tatouay **10.** armadillos
Xeres ... **5.** jerez **6.** sherry
xerophagy ... **4.** Fast (Lenten)
xerotes ... **7.** dryness (body)
Xerox (tm) ... **4.** copy **9.** duplicate,
  replicate, reproduce
Xerus ... **9.** squirrels
Xerxes (pert to) ...

crossing of .. **10.** Hellespont
destroyer of .. **6.** Athens (BC)
king of .. **6.** Persia
xibalba ... **10.** underworld
Xinca ... **6.** Indian, Jincan
Xipe, Xipe–totec ... **11.** god of sowing
Xiphias ... **5.** comet (sword–shaped)
  6. Dorado (constellation) **9.** swordfish
xiphoid ... **4.** bone **8.** ensiform
  9. swordlike **12.** xiphisternum
Xiphopagus ... **7.** monster (twinlike)
Xiphosura ... **8.** king crab
Xiuhtocutli ... **7.** fire god (Aztec)
Xmas ... **9.** Christmas
X ray (pert to) ...
measure .. **3.** rad **11.** quantimeter
named .. **12.** Roentgen rays
type .. **7.** CAT scan **8.** tomogram
  9. myelogram **11.** arteriogram
xyloglyphy ... **11.** wood carving (art)
xylography ... **13.** wood engraving
xyloid ... **5.** woody **8.** ligneous,
  woodlike
xylomancy, divination by ... **4.** wood
  10. wood pieces
xylophone ... **5.** saron **7.** gambang,
  marimba **8.** gamelang (gamelan),
  gigelira, sticcado
xyrid ... **4.** iris **5.** Xyris
xystus, xyst (Gr) ... **16.** portico
  colonnade

Y

Y ... **4.** tube **5.** curve, track **6.** letter
  (25th), prefix, suffix
yabber ... **4.** talk **6.** jabber
yabby, yabbie ... **8.** crayfish
yaboa ... **10.** night heron
yabu, yaboo ... **4.** pony
yacht ... **4.** boat, race, sail, ship

yaffle ... **6.** armful **7.** handful
  10. woodpecker
yahoo ... **4.** lout, rube **5.** brute
Yahoo (pert to) ...
represented by .. **10.** Houyhnhnms
  (horses of reason)
tale .. **16.** Gulliver's Travels

yakalo, yakattalo... 8. creature
  10. crossbreed (yak, cattle)
yakka... 4. work 5. labor
yaksha... 4. ogre 5. demon, dryad,
  fairy, gnome, jinni 6. Kubera (Chief),
  spirit 7. tree–god 13. guardian angel
Yale (pert to)...
  college.. 8. New Haven
  color.. 4. blue 7. Rameses
  founded at.. 8. Saybrook
  founder.. 9. Elihu Yale
  graduate.. 9. Yalensian
Yalta Conference... 6. Crimea (1945)
yam (pert to)...
  Fiji.. 6. uviyam 8. white yam
  Hawaiian.. 3. hoi
  reference to.. 5. tuber 6. igname
  Scot.. 6. potato
  tropical.. 8. cush–cush
  US.. 11. sweet potato
yamstchik... 7. postboy 8. coachman
  9. postilion
yang... 4. good, male 6. bright (opp
  of yin)
yang–kin... 8. dulcimer
yank... 4. jerk, pull 6. Yankee
Yankee... 12. New Englander
Yannigans... 9. scrub team (baseball)
Yao... 6. Indian 9. aborigine
yap... 3. cur, dog, gab 4. bark, talk,
  yell, yelp 6. jabber 7. bumpkin,
  hoodlum 8. easy mark 9. greenhorn
yapok, yapock... 6. monkey
  7. opossum
yapp... 11. bookbinding
yapster... 3. dog
Yaqui... 6. Indian
yard... 3. rae (sail) 4. lawn, spar,
  wand 5. garth, stick, verge
  6. campus 7. confine, enclose,
  measure 9. courtyard, curtilage,
  enclosure, yardstick 10. playground
yarn... 3. abb, cop 4. hank, joke, tale
  5. fiber, skein, story 6. caddis,
  crewel, spinel, thread 7. genappe
  9. falsehood
yarn (pert to)...
  clew.. 4. ball
  holder.. 3. cop
  measure.. 4. hank, hasp 5. skein
  7. spangle
  size.. 6. denier
  winder.. 10. yarnwindle
yashiro... 3. sha 6. temple (Shinto)
yashmak... 4. veil (double)
yati... 7. ascetic, devotee
yaw... 4. sail, tack 5. steer, tumor
  7. deviate 9. deviation
yawl... 4. boat, howl, wail, yell, yowl
  5. ketch 9. jolly boat
yawn... 3. gap 4. gape 5. chasm,
  mouth 7. opening, stretch 8. open
  wide, oscitate 12. seek greedily
yaws... 9. frambesia
yawweed... 5. shrub 7. rhubarb
  12. wild mulberry
Yazoo (pert to)...
  Fraud.. 9. land grant (1795)
  Indian.. 11. Mississippi
  river.. 11. Mississippi
yclept, ycleped... 5. named 6. called,
  styled

year (pert to)...
  after year.. 10. constantly, repeatedly
    11. over and over
  book.. 7. almanac
  division of.. 6. season 8. semester
    9. trimester
  Latin.. 5. annus
  of mourning.. 11. annus luctus
  of our Lord.. 10. Anno Domini
    11. annus Domini, year of grace
  of thirteen months (384 days)..
    10. embolismic
  of travel.. 10. sabbatical, Wanderjahr
    14. leave of absence
  old (Zool).. 10. annotinous
  pert to.. 5. epact
  quarter.. 5. raith
  record.. 5. annal 8. calendar
yearly (pert to)...
  church income.. 7. annates
  payment.. 4. cens
  recurring.. 6. annual 7. etesian
    8. annually
yearn for... 3. yen 4. ache, hope,
  itch, long, pine, sigh, wish 6. desire,
  hanker
yearning... 3. yen 4. wish 5. eager
  7. anxious, longing 9. hankering,
  nostalgia 10. tenderness
  11. languishing 12. homesickness
years (pert to)...
  adolescent.. 4. teen
  ago.. 4. ages 9. long since 10. days
    of yore, yesteryear
  eight.. 9. octennial
  fifteen.. 9. indiction
  five.. 6. pentad 7. lustrum
  hundred.. 9. centenary 10. centennial
  ten.. 6. decade 9. decennary
  thousand.. 7. chiliad 10. millennium
  two.. 8. biennial, biennium
yeast... 4. barm, foam, koji 5. froth
  6. leaven 7. anamite, ferment
  9. agitation
yeasty... 5. foamy, light, spumy
  6. frothy 8. restless 9. frivolous,
  leavening
yegg... 5. thief, tramp 6. robber
  7. burglar, yeggman 8. criminal
  10. safeblower 11. safebreaker,
  safecracker
yell... 3. cry 4. howl, roar, wail, yowl
  5. cheer, shout 6. outcry, scream,
  shriek
yelling... 7. bawling 8. shouting,
  strident 9. clamorous 11. full of yells
yellow... 3. dun, sil 4. buff, cuir,
  deer, ecru, flax, gull, mean, nude,
  yolk 5. amber, beige, color, cream,
  grège, jaune, lemon, maize, ocher
  (ochre), straw, taupe, topaz, twine
  6. bisque, butter, canary, Cassel,
  chrome, citron, creamy, flaxen,
  golden, mimosa, sallow, Seasan
  7. anamite, annatto, aureate, egg
  yolk, envious, etiolin, jealous, jonquil,
  saffron, sulphur, xanthic, xanthin
  8. cowardly, ocherous, primrose,
  recreant 9. champagne, dandelion,
  flavicant, goldenrod, jaundiced,
  lutescent, sunflower 10. flavescent,
  melancholy 11. treacherous

yellow (pert to)...
  brown.. 3. dun 5. straw 6. manila
  coloring.. 7. xanthic 8. xanthine
  comb form.. 5. luteo
  dyestuff.. 5. morin 7. annatto
   8. luteolin
  golden.. 2. or (Her) 4. gild, gilt
  green.. 5. olive 8. tarragon
   10. chartreuse, serpentine
  herb.. 3. iva
  jacket.. 4. wasp
  medical.. 7. icterus 8. jaundice
   11. xanthoderma
  mustard.. 8. charlock
  ocher, ochre.. 3. sil
  pert to.. 7. xanthic
  pigment.. 7. etiolin 8. orpiment
  race.. 9. Mongolian
  red.. 4. roan 5. aloma, sandy
   6. bisque, dorado, orange
   7. annatto, nacarat
  sensational.. 5. press 7. journal
yellow fever mosquito... 12. Aëdes
  aegypti
yellowhammer... 4. yite 5. ammer,
  finch, skite 6. gladdy 7. flicker
  10. woodpecker 13. yellow bunting
Yellowhammer State... 7. Alabama
yellow jacket... 4. wasp 8. eucalypt
Yellowstone Park geyser... 11. Old
  Faithful
yelp... 3. cry, yip 4. bark, yell
  5. shout 6. outcry, shriek, squeal
  7. ululate 8. complain 9. criticize
yelper... 8. redshank 10. yellowlegs
  11. hunting call
yeme... 4. heed 5. guard 6. govern,
  regard
Yemen (pert to)...
  archeology site.. 4. Sana 5. Marib
  Bib kingdom.. 5. Sheba (Saba)
  capital.. 4. Sana
  citadel.. 5. Damar
  division of.. 6. Arabia
  plateau.. 7. El Jebel
  port.. 5. Mocha 7. Hodeida, Loheiya
  ruler.. 4. Imam
  sea.. 3. Red
yemochik... see *yamstchik*
yen... 4. coin, urge 5. yearn 6. desire,
  hanker 7. longing
yeoman... 4. exon 5. clerk 6. butler,
  seaman 8. retainer 9. assistant,
  attendant 10. freeholder
  11. subordinate 12. petty officer
yep... 3. yes 4. bold 5. alert, smart
  6. active 8. vigorous
yerba... 4. herb, maté 5. plant
  11. Paraguay tea
yes...
  English.. 3. aye, yea, yep 5. uh–huh
   6. assent 11. affirmation
  French.. 3. oui
  German.. 2. ja
  Italian, Spanish.. 2. si
  Russian.. 2. da
yesterday... 6. yester 7. the past
  10. days gone by, heretofore,
  yesteryear 11. bygone times
yet... 3. but 5. still 6. algate
  7. besides, however 10. eventually

  11. nonetheless 15. notwithstanding
yew... 5. green, Taxus 7. conifer,
  hemlock 9. evergreen
Yiddish... 6. Jewish
  12. Judaeo–German (Judeo–German)
yield... 3. bow, net 4. bear, bend,
  cede, crop, give, lose, obey, vail
  5. admit, allow, defer, grant, stoop,
  waive 6. accede, afford, comply, give
  up, relent, render, reward, soften,
  submit 7. concede, consent,
  produce, provide, requite, revenue,
  succumb 9. acquiesce, surrender
  10. capitulate, relinquish
  11. acknowledge
yielding... 4. meek, soft 6. pliant,
  supple 7. bearing 8. flexible
  9. compliant, deference, producing,
  tractable 10. compliance,
  manageable, submissive
Yigdal... 4. poem (Jew Relig)
yill–caup... 6. ale cup
yin... 4. dark, evil (opp of yang)
Ymir, Ymer (pert to)...
  blood of.. 3. sea
  bones of.. 9. mountains
  brains of.. 6. clouds
  flesh of.. 5. earth
  killed by.. 2. Ve 4. Odin, Vili
  Norse Myth.. 3. God 13. rime–cold
  giant (body–shaped world)
yodel, yodle... 4. call, sing (falsetto)
  5. carol, shout 6. warble
yoga (pert to)...
  follower of.. 4. yogi (yogin) 5. fakir
   7. ascetic 9. occultist
  objective.. 16. mental discipline
  stages.. 5. jnana, karma 6. bhakti
  trance.. 6. dhyana 7. dharana,
  samadhi
yoke... 3. two 4. join, link, pair, span,
  team 5. frame, marry 6. cangue,
  couple, inspan 7. bondage, enclave,
  harness, oppress, pillory, shackle,
  slavery 9. associate, servitude
yoked... 6. united 7. coupled
  9. conjugate
yokel... 3. oaf 4. boor, clod, hick,
  lout, rube 6. rustic 7. bumpkin,
  hayseed, plowboy 8. Abderite (anc),
  gullible 9. simpleton 10. countryman,
  slow–witted
yokemate... 4. mate 6. fellow, spouse
  7. partner 9. companion
yolked (egg)... 6. yellow 8. lecithal,
  vitellus
Yom Kippur (Jew)... 7. fast day
  14. Day of Atonement
Yom Teruah (Jew)... 15. Feast of
  Trumpets
Yom Tob, or Tov (Jew)... 8. festival
yon, yonder... 4. away 6. beyond
  7. distant, thither 11. at a distance
yore... 5. of old, olden 6. before 9. in
  old time, long since
young... 3. fry, new 4. tyro 5. brood,
  fresh, green 6. litter, novice, tender
  7. pliable 8. childish, immature,
  juvenile, youthful 9. offspring,
  succulent 13. inexperienced
young (pert to)...
  bear, fox.. 3. cub

birds .. **5.** brood
calf (motherless) .. **5.** dogie
hare .. **7.** leveret
herring .. **4.** brit
horse .. **4.** colt, foal
oyster .. **4.** spat
pigeon .. **5.** piper
youngling ... **5.** youth **6.** novice
  8. beginner, neophyte
youngster ... **3.** boy, kid, lad, pup, tad
  4. baby, lass, tike **5.** child, youth
  6. filius, shaver, urchin **7.** Aladdin
  (Arab Nights) **8.** teenager **9.** fledgling,
  stripling
younker ... **5.** child, youth **6.** knight
  7. gallant **8.** nobleman **9.** stripling
youth goddess ... **4.** Hebe
yo–yo ... **3.** top, toy
Ypres, Belgium ...
famed for .. **7.** Battles (WWI)
lace .. **12.** Valenciennes
province of .. **8.** Flanders
ruins rebuilt .. **9.** Cloth Hall **15.** Gothic
  Cathedral (St Martin)
ypsiliform, shape of ... **7.** letter T (Gr)
yu (Chin) ... **4.** jade
Yucatan, Cent America ...
anc domain of .. **5.** Mayas
capital .. **6.** Mérida
city .. **5.** Sisal
peninsula of .. **6.** Mexico
yucca (pert to) ...
called .. **11.** Adam's needle
family .. **9.** Liliaceae
native of .. **7.** America
species .. **9.** bear grass

State flower of .. **9.** New Mexico
Yugoslavia ...
capital .. **8.** Belgrade
city .. **5.** Senta **7.** Skoplje
former leader .. **4.** Tito (Communist)
lead works (among world's largest) ..
  6. Trepca
natives .. **5.** Serbs **6.** Croats
  8. Slovenes
river .. **5.** Drava, Drina **6.** Danube
sea .. **8.** Adriatic
seaport .. **6.** Rijeka
yukkel ... **7.** flicker **10.** woodpecker
Yukon ...
famed for .. **4.** gold (mining)
ocean .. **6.** Arctic
river .. **5.** Lewes, Yukon
territory of .. **6.** Canada
town .. **10.** Whitehorse
Yule ... **4.** Noel **8.** Nativity (Feast of
  the), yuletide **9.** Christmas
  13. Christmastide
Yule (pert to) ...
plant .. **5.** holly **9.** mistletoe
good cheer .. **11.** wassail bowl
Yuma (Ariz) ... **4.** city **9.** Talkepaia
  (Indian)
yun ... **9.** Laos tribe (tattooed)
Yunca ... **6.** Indian (Peru)
Yurma ... **6.** Indian (Brazil)
Yurok ... **6.** Indian (Calif)
yurt, yurta ... **4.** tent (Siberia)
Yuruk ... **10.** Turkish rug
yutu ... **7.** tinamou
Yuzen birodo ... **6.** velvet (designed)

Z

Z ... **3.** end, zed, zee **5.** omega
  6. izzard, letter (26th)
zac ... **4.** ibex
zacate ... **7.** herbage **9.** rice grass
Zacchaeus, Zaccheus ... **4.** pure
  8. innocent, publican (Bib)
Zachariah, Zacharias (Bib) ...
father .. **9.** Barachias
father of .. **14.** John the Baptist
literally .. **21.** Jehovah hath
  remembered
Zadkiel (Jew) ... **5.** angel (of planet
  Jupiter)
zaftig ... **5.** buxom **7.** shapely
Zagreus ... **3.** god **8.** Dionysus
  (identified with)
Zaire, Africa ...
capital .. **8.** Kinshasa
formerly .. **12.** Belgian Congo
river .. **5.** Kasai, Zaire (Congo)
zaman, zamang ... **8.** rain tree
Zambia, Africa ...
capital .. **6.** Lusaka
formerly .. **16.** Northern Rhodesia

wealth .. **6.** copper (3rd largest)
Zamenhof, inventor of ...
  9. Esperanto
zampogna ... **7.** bagpipe, panpipe
zanja ... **5.** canal, gully **6.** arroyo
zany ... **3.** wag, wit **4.** dolt, fool
  5. clown, crazy, goofy, kooky, nutty
  6. madcap, sawney **7.** acrobat,
  bonkers, buffoon, idiotic **8.** clownish
  9. simpleton **10.** lieutenant,
  mountebank **11.** merry–andrew
Zanzibar, Africa ... see *Tanzania*
zap ... **4.** slay, stun **5.** smite **6.** strike
zapatero ... **7.** boxwood, cobbler,
  dogwood
zarf ... **9.** cup holder (Levant)
zati ... **6.** monkey (bonnet)
zeal ... **5.** ardor, piety **6.** desire, fervor
  7. passion **8.** devotion **9.** eagerness
  10. enthusiasm, fanaticism
zealot ... **4.** sect **5.** bigot, freak (sl)
  6. votary **7.** devotee, faddist, fanatic,
  pietist **8.** partisan **10.** enthusiast
zealous ... **5.** eager, pious **6.** ardent,

fervid **7.** devoted, fervent
9. phrenetic **11.** industrious
zebra (pert to)...
ally.. **6.** quagga
Burchell's.. **4.** dauw (nonstriped legs)
hybrid.. **8.** zebrinny
insect.. **9.** butterfly
ref to.. **7.** zebrine, zebroid
zebrawood... **5.** shrub **7.** araroba
10. marblewood
zebu... **2.** ox **5.** zebus (group)
6. cattle **12.** Brahmany bull (sacred)
zecchino... **6.** sequin (chequeen)
Zechariah (Bib)... **7.** prophet **12.** King
of Israel
zed... **7.** letter Z (Brit)
zeekoe... **12.** hippopotamus
zeism... **8.** pellagra **11.** morbid state
zemi... **4.** holy (Peru) **5.** huaca (huaco)
6. fetish, sacred, spirit (magic)
Zemzem... **10.** sacred well (Mecca)
Zen... **12.** Buddhist sect
zenana... **5.** harem, serai **7.** mission
8. seraglio
Zenda, Prisoner of... **9.** Ruritania
Zend–Avesta... **10.** sacred text
(Zoroastrian)
zenith... **3.** top **4.** acme, apex, blue,
peak **6.** apogee, climax, summit,
vertex **11.** culmination **14.** greatest
height (opp of nadir)
Zeno... **5.** Stoic **11.** philosopher (Gr)
zenography, study of... **7.** Jupiter
(planet)
zenu... **5.** sheep
zephyr... **5.** shawl **6.** breath, breeze
zero... **3.** nil **4.** hour **5.** zilch
6. cipher, nought (naught) **7.** nothing,
nullity **11.** temperature
zest... **4.** tang **5.** gusto, savor
6. flavor, relish **8.** membrane (fruit),
piquancy **9.** eagerness
10. enthusiasm
Zeus (pert to)...
attendant.. **4.** Nike
consort.. **6.** Europa
brother of.. **5.** Hades **8.** Poseidon
deity.. **7.** supreme **12.** father of gods
father.. **6.** Cronus
games in his honor.. **6.** Nemean
8. Olympian
messenger.. **4.** Iris **6.** Hermes
mother.. **4.** Rhea
oracle.. **6.** Dodona
Roman.. **7.** Jupiter
sister.. **4.** Hera
son.. **4.** Ares **5.** Argus **6.** Apollo,
Hermes **7.** Perseus **8.** Dionysus,
Hercules, Tantalus
temple (Athens).. **8.** Olympium
ziara, ziarat... **4.** tomb (Moslem saint)
6. shrine
zibet, zibeth... **5.** civet
ziganka... **5.** dance (rustic)
zigeuner... **5.** gypsy **7.** czigany,
Zincalo, zingaro
ziggurat... **11.** temple tower
12. Tower of Babel (Bib)
zigzag... **5.** turns **6.** angles **7.** stagger
8. flexuous, wavering **9.** alternate
zillion... **4.** many **9.** countless

Zimbabwe...
capital.. **6.** Harare
Falls.. **8.** Victoria
Falls discoverer.. **11.** Livingstone
(1855)
formerly.. **8.** Rhodesia
tribe.. **5.** Bantu
zinc (pert to)...
alloy.. **5.** bidri **7.** paktong
alloy with copper.. **6.** oroide
crude.. **7.** tutenag (tutenague)
slabs.. **6.** solder **7.** spelter
symbol.. **2.** Zn
zing... **3.** pep, vim, zip **5.** vigor
6. energy, spirit, thrill **10.** enthusiasm
zingaresca (gypsy)... **4.** song **5.** dance
zingaro... **5.** gypsy
Zion (pert to)... **4.** hill (Jerusalem)
10. Israelites **12.** chosen people
zip... **4.** zing **5.** close, speed
6. energy **8.** pungency **10.** sibilation
zizith... **7.** fringes (Bib), tassels
zoanthropy... **9.** monomania
15. changed to animal (belief)
zobo... **6.** hybrid **10.** zebu and yak
zodiac... **4.** belt, zone **5.** stars
7. circuit
zodiac signs (twelve)... **3.** Leo
5. Aries, Libra, Virgo **6.** Cancer,
Gemini, Pisces, Taurus **7.** Scorpio
8. Aquarius **9.** Capricorn
11. Capricornus, Sagittarius
zoetic... **5.** vital **6.** living **7.** organic
zombi, zombie... **5.** corpse **6.** voodoo
zone... **4.** area, band, belt, isle, path
5. Canal, clime, girth, tract **6.** assise,
circle, course, Frigid, region, Torrid
7. stratum **8.** cincture, latitude
9. Temperate
zoo... **9.** menagerie **10.** collection
12. animal garden
zoo, zo (comb form)... **6.** animal
zoologist... **9.** biologist, scientist
zoology, science of... **7.** animals
zoology branches... **8.** taxonomy
9. bionomics, phylogeny
10. embryology, entomology
11. herpetology, ornithology
zoom... **4.** lens, rise **5.** climb
zoopathology, science of...
8. diseases (animal) **11.** zoonosology
zoophilist... **11.** animal lover
zoophobia... **13.** fear of animals
zoophyte... **5.** coral **6.** sponge
10. sea anemone
zootomy... **13.** animal anatomy
16. animal dissection
zootrophy... **13.** animal rearing
zoril, zorillo... **5.** skunk **7.** polecat
Zoroaster, Zarathustra... **7.** Persian
8. reformer (Relig)
Zoroastrianism (pert to)...
adherence to.. **5.** Parse (Parsee)
doctrine.. **7.** dualism **11.** good and
evil
evil spirit.. **4.** deva **7.** Ahriman
fire worshiper.. **6.** Gheber
founder.. **9.** Zoroaster
literature.. **6.** Avesta
lord of creation.. **6.** Ormazd
religion of.. **6.** Persia (anc)

zoster... 4. zona 6. girdle 8. shingles
(Med) 12. herpes zoster
Zouave... 4. Zu–Zu 8. chasseur
11. infantryman
Zu (Bab Myth)... 8. storm god (evil)
9. blackbird (symbol)
Zuider Zee (pert to)...
gulf.. 8. North Sea
Netherlands.. 4. dike 7. highway
present name.. 9. Ijsel Lake, Ijselmeer
zuisin... 7. widgeon
Zulu (pert to)...
army.. 4. impi 7. Kaffirs
boy.. 6. umfaan
conference.. 6. indaba
marauders.. 4. Viti
people.. 6. Santus 7. Kaffirs
spear.. 7. assagai (assegai)

Zululand capital... 6. Eshowe
Zuñi (pert to)...
famed for.. 19. Seven Cities of Cibola
(Myth)
Indian.. 4. Hopi 6. Ashivi
kingdom of Cibola.. 16. gold–paved
streets (Myth)
zwieback... 4. rusk 7. biscuit (toasted)
Zwinger... 6. palace (Dresden)
zygal... 7. H–shaped
zygodactyl (zygodactyle)...
8. yoke–toed 10. paired toes
zygon... 5. bench 6. thwart 9. brain
part
zygous... 5. yoked 6. paired
zymology *(science of)*...
12. fermentation
zymosis... 12. fermentation
zythum... 4. beer (anc Egypt)